Manual

OF

CULTIVATED PLANTS

Most commonly grown in the continental United States and Canada

Manual
OF
CULTIVATED PLANTS

Most commonly grown in the continental United States and Canada

BY
L.H. BAILEY
AND THE STAFF OF THE BAILEY HORTORIUM AT CORNELL UNIVERSITY

Revised Edition
Completely Restudied

GYAN

Published by

Gyan Publishing House
5, Ansari Road
Daryaganj, New Delhi-110002
Phone: 011-47034999, 9811692060
E-mail: books@gyanbooks.com

Distribution Network
gyanbooks.com
India, USA, Canada, UK, Australia, France

ISBN : 978-81-212-2818-3 (HB)
First Published, 1949

2nd Impression 2021

Printed at: Gyan Press, Delhi.

Manual of Cultivated Plants
Author: L.H. Bailey

Manual
OF CULTIVATED PLANTS

Most commonly grown in the continental United States and Canada

By L. H. BAILEY

AND THE STAFF OF THE BAILEY HORTORIUM
AT CORNELL UNIVERSITY

Revised Edition
Completely Restudied

THE MACMILLAN COMPANY · NEW YORK

1949

EXPLANATION

The purpose of this Revised Manual of Cultivated Plants, as of the original work, is to provide a ready means for the identification of the species in the usual domestic flora of the continental United States and Canada.

It is manifestly impossible to describe within the limits of a single volume all the plants that may be in cultivation in the territory. Many species are known only in botanic gardens, experiment stations, test-grounds, or in the collections of specialists and fanciers. To attempt to include these species would make a work of unmanageable size, and the subject would necessarily be greatly complicated for the general student; moreover, the species in these institutions and collections are usually well known to those who grow them. Any number of native plants are also likely to be transferred to grounds and many of them are offered by dealers; one never knows what species these may be; to include them all would introduce into the book a good part of the native flora and duplicate the field of the regular manuals of American plants. Most of these native species are not cultivated plants in the sense in which the term is understood in this book, even though they may be planted in grounds: they have not become familiar citizens of gardens, nor have they given rise to varieties and races under cultivation; that is, they are not domesticated.

Persons desiring to go further in the subject must consult special monographs. The Standard Cyclopedia of Horticulture is also available, in which 20,602 species are accounted for, although the Cyclopedia does not include all plants cultivated in North America. They may also consult Hortus Second (1941), which is a continuing development of the Standard Cyclopedia; this volume contains regular accounts of 31,905 plants, species and main varieties, besides great numbers of synonyms. The original edition of this Manual (1924) contained 3,665 species (in black-face type) and 1,246 genera in 170 natural families, of which 167 are regularly numbered, aside from many Latin-named varieties and incidental references to other plants. The present Revised Manual includes 194 natural families, 1,523 genera, and 5,347 species in black-face type, and many incidental references to species.

The user of this book must understand that it deals only with species. To include horticultural varieties, even those bearing Latin names, would greatly increase the bulk and complexity of the volume. The identification of these varieties constitutes quite another problem, and one that is essentially yet new. The varieties must be worked out in monographic treatments for the use of specialists and of professionals who have charge of test-grounds, parks, landscape-gardens, and investigational work. To describe the main varieties of cultivated plants, even those customarily meriting Latin names, requires long and painstaking study, collections for the most part not in existence, historical perspective, a special application of nomenclature, and an appreciation of systematic values yet little developed.

Although the purpose of this book is to describe the species most commonly cultivated, there are three classes of rather marked exceptions: (1) Many plants not offered by dealers nor appearing in printed lists are in cultivation in old premises and private gardens, and are likely to be exchanged from hand to hand; these plants have established themselves in the affections of growers and they should be recorded, even though not common or perhaps in the process of passing out in a commercial epoch. (2) Species of rather recent introduction that promise to be acquisitions but which are not yet well known; it is impossible to forecast which ones are likely to become fairly common or established. (3) Certain species of great historic interest in Europe and other countries that should be known as a matter of general knowledge but which may be little cultivated in North America; an example is *Lupinus albus,* lupine of the ancients and still grown in parts of Europe for human food, forage, and green-manuring, but rarely seen in this country; in this category are many food-plants likely at any time to awaken interest here, and also such things as are frequently grown in "economic collections"; these subjects are always interesting to students in the educational institutions. While some of the species in these three categories may not be common, they may nevertheless be significant to man or to the development of horticulture and agriculture, and therefore are in place in the book.

The limits of the book are necessarily indefinite and subject to personal judgment. What species may be omitted without loss and what should be added will develop with the use of the book; the results may be recorded in a subsequent edition.

The plants entered in this volume represent all parts of the world. They bring the names now current among the specialists of different countries. The application of the International Rules of Nomenclature naturally follows.

In the study of the flora of a region, the habitat and range afford clues to the species; but with cultivated plants such aids are usually not available, as even the part of the world from which a given subject comes may be wholly unknown to the collector; one must approach the subject in a different attitude and rely on diagnoses alone. In this Revised Manual, the tendency is to conceive genera and species rather broadly. It is easy to go to such a degree of refinement that the subdivision ceases to have utility.

The author is under great and continuing obligation to the many helpers in the preparation of this Revised Manual, inasmuch as his contribution aside from a few groups has been advisory and in editorial supervision. My first indebtedness is to my daughter, Ethel Zoe Bailey, who collaborated in the original edition and has been my critical and faithful side-companion in the subsequent years. Next I name Dr. G. H. M. Lawrence, also of the Bailey Hortorium staff, taxonomist, grower and lover of cultivated plants. Extended contributions were made by two former members of the Hortorium staff, Dr. Philip A. Munz and Miss Mary L. Hall. The family Crassulaceæ is contributed by Dr. Robert T. Clausen and the genus Juniperus by Dr. John F. Cornman. Many American botanists have been consulted on special problems, and valuable aid has been given by W. T. Stearn of the Royal Horticultural Society, London. Illustrations are by Florence Mekeel (Mrs. Harry Lambeth) and Marion E. Ruff, except Fig. 89 which is by Miss E. M. Abbe.

L. H. BAILEY

Ithaca, N. Y.
January 1, 1948

ABBREVIATIONS

ann. .... annual
bien. .... biennial
caps. .... capsule
cent. .... central
cult. .... cultivated, cultivation
diam. .... diameter
E. .... East
fl. .... flower
fld. .... flowered
fls. .... flowers
fr. .... fruit
frs. .... fruits
ft. .... foot, feet
hort. .... horticulture, horticultural
in. .... inch, inches
infl. .... inflorescence
intro. .... introduced
isl. .... island
isls. .... islands
lf. .... leaf
lft. .... leaflet
lfts. .... leaflets
lvd. .... leaved
lvs. .... leaves
mts. .... mountains
N. .... North
nat. .... naturalized
per. .... perennial
S. .... South
segm., segms. .... segment, segments
st., sts. .... stem, stems
subtrop. .... subtropical
temp. .... temperate
trop. .... tropical
var. .... variety (of a species)
vars. .... varieties
W. .... West

THE NAMES

Horticulturists often wonder about the reasons for changes in names of plants. These changes are mostly the result of the current effort to harmonize botanical systematic literatures that have grown up independently through the years. This effort took definite shape at the International Botanical Congress at Vienna in 1905, modified by subsequent Congresses at intervals of five years when international conditions permitted. The changes arise largely from application of the law of priority whereby the first authoritative name must hold, modified by new and more accurate studies on structure and relationships of plants. Some years yet will be required to discover and to eliminate the disagreements. An example is the royal palm of the farther West Indies and now widely planted. This tree was first nomenclatorially described by Jacquin in 1763 as *Areca oleracea* (oleraceous, the great terminal bud being edible). Sprengel in 1825 thought the plant to belong to the genus Euterpe and transferred the name as *Euterpe oleracea.* Von Martius, the great palm authority, decided it was not a Euterpe, and in 1837 referred it to Willdenow's genus Oreodoxa as *O. oleracea.* The generic name Oreodoxa means "glory of the mountains" whereas the royal palm is a low-country plant with different characters, and we now know that Willdenow had a Euterpe in hand when he founded the genus. Euterpe dates from 1788, and Oreodoxa from 1807; Oreodoxa therefore becomes a synonym of Euterpe, leaving the royal palm without a tenable binomial. In 1900 O. F. Cook established the genus Roystonea to take over the royals, and the Trinidad palm becomes *Roystonea oleracea.*

It is not necessary to an understanding of a plant that the species-name be translated into English; yet the student is interested to know what the word means; and the following list is inserted to supply this knowledge for characteristic Latin or Latinized descriptive adjectives applied to the species of plants. These words are likely to be used in differing meanings in different genera and as applied by different authors; in many cases, they do not follow the usages of classical Latin; therefore a list of this kind cannot be exact or give all the meanings in which the words may be applied as specific names. The name may be even inapplicable, yet it must stand if it has priority and meets the other conditions of accepted nomenclatorial practice. Thus, *Duranta repens* is not repent or creeping, the name having been applied under a misapprehension; yet the name *repens* holds as against the better known *D. Plumieri.* In a cultivated species, the plant may have varied so as to contradict the original name, yet the name must hold; examples are frequent in plants with color-races, as in *Nymphæa alba,* named for its white flowers, which sometimes vary to red: we therefore have the anomaly *N. alba* var. *rubra.*

In some cases, different names are employed for the same signification. Thus, the fact that a plant hails from China may be expressed in one case as *Brassica chinensis,* in others as *Rhododendron sinense, Rosa cathayensis, Begonia cathayana, Crinum asiaticum* var. *sinicum.* The name must hold as originally written and published, for that author had the right to adopt the word of his preference. If the author desires to bestow a name to suggest red-leaved, he has access to the Latin derivation *rubrifolius* or to the Greek derivation *erythrophyllus.*

It should be said that a geographical specific name may not indicate the natural range of a species. A plant may have been discovered in Japan and named *japonica* (or *nipponica*) and may subsequently be found to be native also in China and other countries; but the first name holds, even though, as in a few examples, it was applied erroneously. Linnæus supposed the rose-of-Sharon to be native to Syria and named it *Hibiscus syriacus,* but it is probably native only in eastern Asia.

Personal specific names and those likely to occur but once are explained in the text where they are found. Species-names derived from persons may be in the genitive or in the form of an adjective; as *Pandanus Veitchii,* Veitch's pandanus, *Calathea Veitchiana,* Veitchian calathea. If named for a woman, the termination is feminine, as *Lilium Sargentiæ,* if written in the genitive. The International Rules of Botanical Nomenclature prescribe that in making new specific names the masculine genitive terminates in a single *i* following a vowel (*Lemoinei*) and the letter *r,* but in a double *i* following a consonant (*Giraldii*).

Substantive names in apposition hold their own termination, and the word in such cases is here printed with a capital letter to show its non-conformity and to add character to the treatment, if it is a proper name or an old generic name, as *Achillea Millefolium, Zea Mays, Salvia Horminum, Nicotiana Tabacum.* Such words are usually old generic names or prominent vernacular substantives, and they record some historical connection of the plant. The capitalizing of the apposites is not only essential to truth but to the dignity and significance of language; present practice of decapitalizing all specific names, as an editorial expedient, is only a concession to supposed convenience and inactive memory and has no potency in an historical treatment.

In botanical practice, the species-name is made to agree with its genus in gender: thus the Latin adjective *albus* (white) takes the regular masculine termination in *Lupinus albus,* because Lupinus is masculine; the feminine termination in *Rosa alba;* the neuter in *Sedum album;* in Quercus it is feminine (*Q. alba*), because most trees have been treated linguistically in Latin as feminine whatever the termination of the name. Thus *niger* (black) retains the masculine form in

Helleborus niger, becomes feminine in *Betula nigra*, neuter in *Solanum nigrum*.

abietì-nus: abies-like.
abrotanifò-lius: abrotanus-leaved.
absím-ilis: unlike.
absinthoì-des: absinthe-like.
abyssín-icus: Abyssinian.
acanthò-des: acanthus-like.
acaù-lis: stemless, acaulescent.
acéph-alus: headless.
acerifò-lius: maple-leaved.
aciculà-ris: needle-like.
ác-idus: acid, sour.
aconitifò-lius: aconite-leaved.
à-cris, à-cer: acrid, sharp.
acrostichoì-des: acrostichum-like.
aculeà-tus: prickly.
acuminà-tus: acuminate, long-pointed, tapering.
acutifò-lius: acutely leaved, sharp-leaved.
acutíl-obus: acutely lobed.
adenóph-orus: gland-bearing.
adenophȳl-lus: glandular-leaved.
adiantifò-lius: adiantum-leaved.
adiantifór-mis: resembling adiantum.
adprés-sus: pressed against.
adstrín-gens: constricted.
adsúr-gens: ascending.
adún-cus: hooked.
ád-venus: newly arrived, adventive.
æquitríl-obus: equally three-lobed.
æstivà-lis: pertaining to summer.
æstì-vus: summer.
æthióp-icus: Ethiopian, African.
æthnén-sis: native of Etna, Sicily.
affì-nis: related (to another species).
à-fra: African.
africà-nus: African.
agavoì-des: agave-like.
ageratifò-lius: ageratum-leaved.
aggregà-tus: aggregate, clustered.
ailanthifò-lius: ailanthus-leaved.
aizoì-des: aizoon-like.
ajanén-sis: native of Ajan in Asia.
alabamén-sis: native of Alabama.
alà-tus: winged.
albertià-nus: of Alberta.
ál-bidus: white.
albiflò-rus: white-flowered.
ál-bulus: whitish.
ál-bus: white.
alcicór-nis: elk-horned.
alép-picus: of Aleppo (Syria).
alexandrì-nus: of Alexandria (Egypt).
alleghenién-sis: native of the Allegheny Mountains.
allià-ceus: of the alliums, garlic-like, usually connoting odor.
alliariæfò-lius: alliaria-leaved.
ál-mus: bountiful.
alnifò-lius: alder-leaved.
aloifò-lius: aloe-leaved.
alopecurioì-des: alopecurus-like.
alpés-tris: nearly alpine.
alpíc-ola: inhabitant of high mountains.
alpì-nus: alpine; growing on mountains above the tree line.
alternifò-lius: alternate-leaved.
altifò-lius: tall-leaved.
ált-ilis: fat, large.
altís-simus: very tall, tallest.
ál-tus: tall.
alúm-nus: well-nourished, flourishing.
amáb-ilis: lovely.
amaranthoì-des: amaranth-like.
amarantíc-olor: amaranth-colored.
amà-rus: bitter.
amazṓn-icus: of the River Amazon region.
ambíg-uus: ambiguous, doubtful.
amblȳ-odon: blunt-toothed.
ambrosioì-des: ambrosia-like.
amelloì-des: amellus-like.
americà-nus: American.
amethȳs-tinus: amethystine, violet-colored.
amœ̀-nus: charming, pleasing.
amplexicaù-lis: stem-clasping.
amplexifò-lius: leaf-clasping.
amplís-simus: most or very ample.
amurén-sis: of the Amur River region (northeastern Asia).
anagyroì-des: anagyris-like.
ananás-sa: resembling the pineapple, Ananas.
án-ceps: two-edged, two-headed.
andelyén-sis: native of Les Andelys, France.
anethifò-lius: anethum-leaved.
anethoì-des: anethum-like.
án-glicus: English, of England.
angulà-ris, angulà-tus: angular, angled.
angustifò-lius: narrow-leaved.
angús-tior: narrower.
anisà-tum: anise-scented.
anisodò-rus: anise-odor.
annulà-ris: annular, ringed.
án-nuus: annual.
anóm-alus: anomalous, out of the ordinary or usual.
anopét-alus: erect-petaled.
antárc-ticus: of the Antarctic regions.
anthemoì-des: anthemis-like.
anthyllidifò-lius: anthyllis-leaved.
antioquién-sis: native of Antioquia, Colombia.
antiquò-rum: of the ancients.
antirrhiniflò-rus: antirrhinum-flowered.
antirrhinoì-des: antirrhinum-like, snapdragon-like.
apennì-nus: pertaining to the Apennines (Italy).
apét-alus: without petals.
aphȳl-lus: leafless.
apiculà-tus: apiculate, tipped with a point.
apiifò-lius: apium-leaved.
áp-odus: footless.
aquât-icus, aquât-ilis: aquatic.
aquilegifò-lius: aquilegia-leaved.
aquilì-nus: aquiline, eagle-like.
aráb-icus: Arabian.
arachnoì-des: spider-like, cobwebby.
araucà-nus: from Chile.
arborés-cens: becoming tree-like, or nearly the size of a tree.
arbò-reus: tree-like, pertaining to a tree.
arbús-culus: like a small tree.
arbutifò-lius: arbutus-leaved.
árc-ticus: arctic, of the Arctic regions.
ár-dens: glowing, fiery.
arenà-rius: of sand or sandy places.
areolà-tus: pitted.
argentà-tus: silvery, silvered.
argenteo-guttà-tus: silver-spotted.

THE NAMES

argén-teus: silvery.
argillà-ceus: of clay, growing in clay, clay-colored.
argù-tus: sharp-toothed.
argyphý́l-lus: silver-leaved.
argyræ̀-us: silvery.
argyroneù-rus: with silver-colored nerves or veins.
arietì-nus: like a ram's head.
aristà-tus: aristate, bearded.
arizón-icus: of Arizona.
armà-tus: armed (as with thorns).
armenì-acus: Armenian.
armè-nus: Armenian.
armillà-ris: with a bracelet, arm-ring or collar.
aromát-icus: aromatic.
artemisioì-des: artemisia-like.
articulà-tus: articulated, jointed.
arundinà-ceus: reed-like.
arvén-sis: pertaining to cultivated fields.
arvernén-sis: native of Auvergne, France.
ascalón-icus: of Ascalon (Syria).
ascén-dens: ascending.
asclepiadè-us: asclepias-like.
asiát-icus: Asian.
asparagoì-des: asparagus-like.
ás-per: rough, as with hairs or points.
asperà-tus: rough.
asplenifò-lius: asplenium-leaved.
asplenioì-des: asplenium-like.
assám-icus: of Assam.
assím-ilis: similar or like.
assurgentiflò-rus: flowers ascending.
asteroì-des: aster-like.
astilboì-des: astilbe-like.
atalantioì-des: atalanta-like.
atlánt-icus: Atlantic, growing in Atlantic regions.
atriplicifò-lius: atriplex-leaved.
atrocærù-leus: dark cerulean or blue.
atrococcín-eus: dark scarlet.
atropuníc-eus: dark reddish-purple.
atropurpù-reus: dark purple.
atrór-ubens: dark red.
atrosanguín-eus: dark blood-red.
atróv-irens: dark green.
attenuà-tus: attenuated, produced to a point.
aubretioì-des: aubretia-like.
augús-tus: august, notable, majestic.
aurantì-acus: orange-colored.
aurantifò-lius: golden-leaved.
aù-reus, aurà-tus: golden.
auríc-omus: golden-haired.
auriculà-tus: eared.
austrà-lis: southern.
austrì-acus: Austrian.
autumnà-lis: autumnal, of autumn.
à-vium: of the birds.
axillà-ris: axillary, borne in the axils, pertaining to the axils.
azór-icus: of the Azores.
azù-reus: azure, sky-blue.

babylón-icus: Babylonian.
baccà-tus: berried.
baicalén-sis: native of Baikol, central Asia.
balcà-nus: Balkan.
baldén-sis: native of Baldo Mountains, northern Italy.
baleár-icus: of the Balearic Islands.
balsà-meus: balsamic.
balsamíf-era: balsam-bearing.
balsaminæflò-rus: balsam-flowered.
bambusoì-des: bamboo-like.
barbadén-sis: native of Barbados.
bár-barus: foreign.
barbà-tus: barbed, bearded.
barbinér-vis: nerves bearded.
barbinò-de: bearded at nodes.
basà-lis: basal, sessile.
basilà-ris: pertaining to the base or bottom.
bél-gicus: Belgian.
bellidifò-lius: beautiful-leaved.
bellidifór-mis: resembling bellis.
bellidioì-des: bellis-like.
bellobà-tus: beautiful bramble.
bél-lus: handsome.
benedíc-tus: blessed.
benghalén-sis: of Bengal (eastern India).
bermudià-nus: Bermudan.
berolinén-sis: of Berlin.
betà-ceus: of the beet, beet-like.
betonicifò-lius: betonica-leaved.
betulifò-lius: birch-leaved.
bicapsulà-ris: having two capsules.
bíc-olor: two-colored.
bicór-nis: two-horned.
bién-nis: biennial.
bíf-idus: twice cut.
biflò-rus: two-flowered.
bì-frons: two-fronded.
bifurcà-tus: twice-forked.
bignonioì-des: bignonia-like.
bíj-ugus: yoked, two together.
bíl-obus: two-lobed.
bipartì-tus: two-parted.
bipinnatíf-idus: twice pinnately cut.
biserrà-tus: twice-toothed.
bistór-tus: twice twisted; also an old substantive, the bistort, one of the Polygonums.
blán-dus: agreeable, charming, pleasant.
blephariglót-tis: fringed-tongued.
blepharophý́l-lus: fringed leaved.
bolivià-nus, bolivién-sis: of Bolivia.
bonarién-sis: of Buenos Aires.
borbonià-nus: of Bourbonne (France).
boreà-lis: northern.
bostonién-sis: of Boston.
botryoì-des: cluster-like, grape-like.
botryóph-orus: bearing clusters.
bò-trys: cluster, as of grapes; sometimes used as equivalent to raceme.
botrý-tis: racemose.
brachyán-drus: short-stamened.
brachýc-alyx: with short calyx.
brachyphý́l-lus: short-leaved.
bracteà-tus: bracteate, bearing bracts.
brasilién-sis: of Brazil.
brevicaù-lis: short-stemmed.
brevifò-lius: short-leaved.
breviligulà-tus: short-liguled.
brevipedunculà-tus: short-peduncled.
brév-ipes: short-footed or -stalked.
breviscà-pus: short-scaped.
brigantì-acus: of Brigantium or Bregenz, frontier town of Austria.
brizæfór-mis: briza-formed.
bronchià-lis: bronchial.
bruniifò-lius: brunia-leaved.
buccinatò-rius: known, trumpeted forth.
buchár-icus: of Buchara (Bokhara), Asia.
bulbíf-era: bulb-bearing.
bulbispér-mus: with bulb-shaped seeds.

bulbò-sus: bulbous.
bulgár-icus: Bulgarian.
bullà-tus: blistered, puckered.
bupleuroì-des: bupleurum-like.
burmán-icus: of Burma.
buxifò-lius: buxus- or box-leaved.

cachemirià-nus, cachemír-icus: same as *cashmerianus.*
cærulés-cens: becoming dark blue.
cærù-leus: cerulean, sky-blue, dark blue.
cæ̀-sius: bluish-gray.
cæspitò-sus: cespitose, tufted.
cáf-fer, cáf-fra: Kafir (in South Africa).
calán-thus: beautiful-flowered.
calathì-nus: basket-like.
calcarà-tus: spurred.
calendulà-ceus: calendula-like, with reference to color of flowers.
califór-nicus: of California.
callián-themus: beautiful-flowered.
callistegioì-des: callistegia-like.
callò-sus: thick-skinned, with calluses.
calocár-pus: beautiful fruit.
calýc-inus, calycò-sus: calyx-like.
calyculà-tus: calyx-like.
cambodgén-sis: of Cambridge, England.
campanulà-ria: bell-flowered.
campanulà-tus: campanulate, bell-shaped.
campés-tris: of the fields or plains.
campylacán-thus: with crooked spines.
camtschát-icus: of Kamtschatka.
canadén-sis: Canadian.
canaliculà-tus: channelled, grooved.
canarién-sis: of the Canary Islands.
cán-dicans: white, hoary, particularly white-hairy or white-woolly.
candidís-simus: very white-hairy or hoary.
cán-didus: pure white, white-hairy, shining.
canés-cens: gray-pubescent.
canì-nus: canine, pertaining to a dog.
cannáb-inus: like cannabis or hemp.
cantáb-ricus: Cantabrian, of Cantabria (norht of Spain).
cantonién-sis: of Canton (in southern China).
cà-nus: ash-colored, hoary.
capén-sis: of the Cape (of Good Hope)
capillà-ris, capillà-tus: hair-like.
capità-tus: capitate, headed.
capitulà-tus: having little heads.
cappadóc-icum: Cappadocian (Asia Minor).
capreolà-tus: winding, twining.
capsulà-ris: having capsules.
caracasà-nus: of Caracas, Venezuela.
cardinà-lis: cardinal-red.
cardiopét-alus: petals heart-shaped.
carduà-ceus: thistle-like.
caribæ̀-us: of the Caribbean.
carinà-tus: keeled.
carinthì-acus: from Carinthia, Austria.
carmín-eus: carmine.
cár-neus: flesh-colored.
carníc-olor: flesh-colored.
carnò-sus: fleshy.
carolinià-nus, carolì-nus: Carolinian, pertaining to North or South Carolina, or indefinitely to the Carolinas.
carpáth-icus, carpát-icus: of the Carpathian region (Europe).
carpinifò-lius: carpinus-leaved.
carthusianò-rum: of the Carthusian monks.
cartilagín-eus: like cartilage.
caryotíd-eus: caryota-like.
cashmerià-nus: of Cashmere (Asia).
cassinoì-des: cassine-like.
catawbién-sis: from the Catawba, North Carolina.
cathár-ticus: cathartic.
cathayén-sis: of Cathay (China).
caucás-icus: belonging to the Caucasus (mountain region between the Black and Caspian Seas).
caudà-tus: caudate, tailed.
caulés-cens: having a stem.
cauliflò-rus: stem-flowering.
cautleoì-des: resembling cautlea.
cà-vus: hollow.
cayennén-sis: of Cayenne (French Guiana).
centifò-lius: hundred-leaved.
centranthifò-lius: centranthus-leaved.
cephalón-icus: of Cephalonia (one of the Ionian islands).
cerasíf-era: cerasus- or cherry-bearing.
cerasifór-mis: cherry-formed.
cerastioì-des: cerastium-like.
cereà-le: pertaining to Ceres or agriculture.
cerif-era: wax-bearing.
cér-nuus: drooping, nodding.
chalcedón-icus: of Chalcedon (on the Bosphorus).
chalepén-sis, halepén-sis: of Aleppo, in southwestern Asia.
chamædryoì-des: chamædrys-like.
Chamæ̀-drys, chamædrifò-lius: ante-Linnæan name, meaning dwarf oak, in allusion to shape of leaves of certain plants to which it was applied.
cheilanthifò-lius: cheilanthus-leaved.
cheilán-thus: lip-flowered.
chermesì-nus: red.
chilén-sis, chiloén-sis: belonging to Chile.
chinén-sis: Chinese.
chionán-thus: snow-flower.
chlorán-thus: green-flowered.
chloropét-alus: green-petaled.
chrysán-drus, chrysán-thus: golden-flowered.
chrysóg-raphes: marked with gold.
chrysomál-lus: with golden wool.
chrysophœníc-eus: golden-red.
chrysophýl-lus: golden-leaved.
chrysót-oxum: golden-arched.
chusà-nus: of Chusan, an island off the coast of China.
cicutà-rius: of or like cicuta.
cigarettíf-era: bearing cigarettes.
cilià-ris, cilià-tus: ciliate, fringed.
cilíc-icus: of Cilicia (in southeastern Asia Minor).
ciliò-sus: ciliate, fringed.
cinerariæfò-lius: cineraria-leaved.
cinè-reus: ash-colored.
cinnabarì-nus: cinnabar-red.
cinnamò-meus: cinnamon-brown.
circinà-tus, circinà-lis: circinate, coiled.
cirrhò-sus: tendrilled.
citrà-tus: citrus-like.
citrì-nus: citrus-leaved.
citriodò-rus: lemon-scented.
citrulloì-des: like citrullus.
cladóc-alyx: club-calyx.
clár-us: clear.
clavà-tus: club-shaped.
clematíd-eus: like clematis.
clethroì-des: clethra-like.

coarctà-tus: crowded together.
coccíg-era: berry-bearing.
coccín-eus: scarlet.
cochlearifò-lius: cochlearia-leaved.
cochleà-ris: spoon-like.
cœlés-tinus: sky-blue.
cœlés-tis: celestial, sky-blue.
cól-chicus: of Colchis (eastern Black Sea region).
collì-nus: pertaining to a hill.
columbià-nus: Columbian (western North American).
columellà-ris: pertaining to a small pillar or pedestal.
columnà-ris: columnar.
columníf-era: bearing a column.
cò-mans: furnished as with hair, or hair-like.
commù-nis: growing in common or community, gregarious; sometimes taken in the sense of "common."
commutà-tus: changed or changing.
comorén-sis: of the Comoro Islands, between Africa and Madagascar.
comò-sus: with long hair.
compác-tus: compact, dense.
compléx-us: encircled, embraced.
compós-itus: compound.
comprés-sus: compressed, flattened.
conchæfò-lius: shell-leaved.
concín-nus: neat, well made, elegant.
cón-color: colored similarly.
confér-tus: crowded.
confù-sus: confused, uncertain.
congés-tus: congested, brought together.
conglomerà-tus: crowded together.
cón-icus: conical.
conspér-sus: scattered.
conspíc-uus: conspicuous, marked, visible.
contór-tus: contorted, twisted.
conyzoì-des: conyza-like.
copallì-nus: like copal or resin.
coræén-sis: of Korea.
coràl-linus: coral-red.
cordà-tus: heart-shaped.
cordifò-lius: cordate-leaved, heart-leaved.
cordifór-mis: heart-form.
corniculà-tus: horned.
corníg-era: horn-bearing.
cornù-tus: horned.
corollà-tus: corollate, corolla-like.
coronà-rius: used for or belonging to garlands.
coronà-tus: crowned.
coronopifò-lius: coronopus-leaved.
cór-sicus: Corsican.
cortusoì-des: cortusa-like.
corymbò-sus: corymbose.
corynóc-alyx: club-like calyx.
costà-tus: costate, ribbed.
cò-us: from the island Cos, near Turkey.
cracò-vius: of Cracow, Poland.
crassifò-lius: thick-leaved.
crás-sipes: thick-footed or -stalked.
crè-brus: close, frequent, repeated.
crenatiflò-rus: crenate-flowered.
crenà-tus: crenate, scalloped.
crenulà-tus: crenulate, somewhat scalloped.
crét-icus: of Crete (island in eastern Mediterranean).
crinì-tus: provided with long hair.
crispifò-lius: leaves crisped or curled.
crís-pus: crisped, curled.
Crista-gál-li: cockscomb.
cristà-tus: cristate, crested.
crò-ceus: saffron-colored, yellow.
crocosmæflò-rus: crocosma-flowered.
crucià-tus: cruciate, cross-like.
cruén-tus: bloody.
Crus-gál-li: cockspur.
crustà-tus: encrusted.
crystál-linus: crystalline.
cucullà-tus: hooded.
cucumerifò-lius: cucumber-leaved.
cultò-rum: of the cultivators or gardeners.
cultrifór-mis: shaped like broad knife-blade.
cuneà-tus: wedge-shaped.
cuneifò-lius: wedge-leaved.
cupreà-tus: coppery.
cupressoì-des: cypress-like.
cù-preus: copper-like or -colored.
curvifò-lius: leaves curved.
cuspidà-tus: cuspidate, with a cusp or sharp stiff point.
cuspidifò-lius: leaves cuspidate.
cyanán-thus: blue-flowered.
cyà-neus: blue.
cyanophýl-lus: blue-leaved.
cyclamín-eus: cyclamen-like.
cylín-dricus: cylindrical.
cymbifór-mis: boat-shaped.
cynán-chicus, cynanchoì-des: cynanchum-like.

dactylíf-era: finger-bearing.
dahù-ricus, daù-ricus, davù-ricus: of Dahuria or Dauria (in Trans-Baikal Siberia, near the frontier of China).
dalecárl-icus: of the province of Dalecarlia or Dalarne, Sweden.
dalmát-icus: Dalmatian.
damascè-nus: of Damascus.
daphnoì-des: daphne-like.
dasycár-pus: with thick-hairy fruits.
dasyphýl-lus: with thick-hairy leaves.
dasystè-mon: with thick-hairy stamens.
dasystý-lus: with thick-hairy styles.
dealbà-tus: whitened, white-washed.
déb-ilis: weak, frail.
decapét-alus: ten-petaled.
decíd-uus: deciduous.
decíp-iens: deceptive.
decorà-tus: decorative.
decò-rus: elegant, comely, becoming.
decúm-bens: decumbent.
decúr-rens: decurrent, running down the stem.
decussà-tus: decussate, opposite.
defléx-us: bent abruptly downward.
deliciò-sus: delicious.
delphinifò-lius: delphinium-leaved.
deltoì-des: triangular.
demér-sus: under water.
demís-sus: low, weak.
dendroíd-eus: tree-like.
densà-tus: dense.
densiflò-rus: densely flowered.
dén-sus: dense.
dentà-tus: toothed.
denticulà-tus: denticulate, slightly toothed.
denudà-tus: denuded, naked.
deprés-sus: depressed.
deús-tus: burned.
dichót-omus: forked in pairs.
dicóc-cus: with two berries.
díd-ymus: in pairs (as of stamens).
diffù-sus: diffuse, spreading.

digità-tus: digitate, hand-like.
dilatà-tus: dilated, expanded, as a filament much broadened.
dilèc-tus: valuable, precious.
dioì-cus: diœcious.
dioscoreifò-lius: dioscorea-leaved.
diphýl-lus: two-leaved.
diplostephioì-des: like diplostephium.
dipsà-ceus: of the teasel or dipsacus.
dipterocár-pus: two-winged carpel or fruit.
dís-color: of two or of different colors.
disjúnc-tus: separated, not grown together.
dissèc-tus: dissected, deeply cut.
dissitiflò-rus: remotely or loosely flowered.
distà-chyus: two-spiked.
dís-tichus: two-ranked, with leaves or flowers in ranks on opposite sides of stem.
diúr-nus: of the day, as day-flowering.
divaricà-tus: divaricate, spreading, widely divergent.
divér-gens: wide-spreading.
diversiflò-rus: diversely flowered, variable-flowered.
diversifò-lius: variable-leaved.
dolabrà-tus, dolobrà-tus: mattock-shaped or hatchet-shaped.
dolomít-icus: from the Dolomites in the Alps.
domés-ticus: domestic, domesticated.
drabifò-lius: draba-leaved.
drepanophýl-lus: leaves sickle-shaped.
drupà-ceus: drupe-like.
dúl-cis: sweet.
durác-inus: hard-berried.
dù-rior: harder.
duriús-culus: somewhat hard or rough.
dù-rus: hard.

ebúr-neus: ivory-white.
ecalcarà-tus: without spurs.
echinà-tus: prickly, bristly.
echioì-des: echium-like.
editò-rum: of the editors.
edù-lis: edible.
effù-sus: very loose-spreading.
elás-ticus: elastic.
elà-tior; elà-tius: taller.
elà-tus: tall.
él-egans: elegant.
elegantís-simus: most elegant, very elegant.
elegán-tulus: elegant.
ellíp-ticus: elliptic.
elongà-tus: elongated, lengthened.
emarginà-tus: with a shallow notch at apex.
emò-di: from Emodus in the Himalayas.
empetrifór-mis: empetrum-shaped.
ensà-tus: sword-shaped.
ensifò-lius: sword-leaved.
ensifór-mis: sword-formed or -shaped.
epithymoì-des: thyme-like.
equisetifò-lius: equisetum-leaved.
equisetifór-mis: equisetum-like.
eréc-tus: erect, upright.
ericifò-lius: erica-leaved.
ericoì-des: erica-like, heath-like.
erinà-ceus: hedge-hog.
eriocár-pus: woolly-fruited.
eriós-pathus: woolly-spathed.
eriostè-mon: stamens woolly.
erò-sus: erose, jagged, as if gnawed.
errǿm-enus: strong, robust.
erubés-cens: blushing.
erythrocár-pus: red-fruited.
erythrò-pus: red-footed or -stalked.
erythrosép-alus: red-sepaled.
erythrosò-rus: red sori.
esculén-tus: esculent, edible.
etrús-cus: Etruscan (in Italy).
euchlò-rus: beautiful green.
eugenioì-des: eugenia-like.
europǽ-us: European.
evér-tus: expelled, turned out.
exalbés-cens: allied to albescens.
exaltà-tus: exalted, very tall.
excél-sior: taller.
excél-sus: tall.
excì-sus: cut away.
exiliflò-rus: few- or meager-flowered.
exím-ius: distinguished, out of the ordinary, excelling.
exót-icus: exotic, from another country.
expán-sus: expanded.
expatrià-tus: without a country.

falcà-tus: falcate, sickle-shaped or scythe-shaped.
falcifò-lius: falcate-leaved.
fál-lax: deceptive.
farinò-sus: mealy, powdery.
fasciculà-tus: fascicled.
fastigià-tus: fastigiate, branches erect and close together.
fastuò-sus: proud.
fát-uus: foolish, simple; may be used in the sense of insipid.
fenestrà-lis: with window-like openings.
fenestrellà-tus: with small window-like openings.
fè-rox: ferocious, very thorny.
ferrugín-eus: rusty, of the color of iron-rust.
fér-tilis: fertile, fruitful.
ferulæfò-lius: ferula-leaved.
ficifò-lius: fig-leaved.
ficoì-des: ficus- or fig-like.
filamentò-sus: filamentous, composed of threads or bearing threads.
filicifò-lius: fern-leaved.
filicoì-des: fern-like.
filíf-era: bearing filaments or threads.
filifór-mis: thread-like.
filipendulì-nus: like filipendula.
fimbrià-tus: fringed.
fír-mus: firm, strong.
fissurà-tus: fissured, cleft.
fistulò-sus: fistular, hollow-cylindrical.
flabellà-tus: flabellate, with fan-like parts.
flác-cidus: flaccid, soft.
fladnizén-sis: of Fladnitz, a town in Steiermark, Austria.
flagellà-ris: whip-like.
flagellifór-mis: whip-formed.
flám-meus: flame-colored.
flavés-cens: yellowish, becoming yellow or yellowish.
flaviflò-rus: yellow-flowered.
flavirà-meus: yellow-branched.
flavís-simus: deep yellow, very yellow.
flavovì-rens: yellow-green.
flà-vus: yellow.
fléx-ilis: flexible, pliant, limber.
flexuò-sus: flexuose, tortuous, zigzag.
floccò-sus: woolly.
florentì-nus: Florentine.
flore-plè-no: with full or double flowers.
floribún-dus: free-flowering, blooming profusely.

floridà-nus: of Florida.
flór-idus: flowering, full of flowers.
-florus: in descriptive botany used to indicate flower, as **albiflò-rus**, white-flowered, **multiflò-rus**, many-flowered. The name Flora, in Latin the goddess of the flowering of plants, is used to designate either the plants of a region taken together, as "the flora of Canada," or a treatise describing the plants.
fluminén-sis: of a river.
fœm-ina: feminine.
fœtidís-simus: very fetid.
fœ́t-idus: fetid, bad-smelling.
—foliolatus, refers to leaflets, as **trifoliolà-tus**, with three leaflets.
foliolò-sus: having leaflets.
foliò-sus: leafy, full of leaves.
—folius: folium is Latin for leaf; **rotundifò-lius**, round-leaved; **unifolià-tus**, one-leaved.
forficà-tus: shear-shaped.
formosà-nus: of Formosa.
formosís-simus: most or very beautiful.
formò-sus: beautiful, handsome.
foveolà-tus: pitted, with small depressions.
fragarioì-des: strawberry-like.
fragíf-era: bearing strawberries.
fragifór-mis: strawberry-form.
frág-ilis: fragile, brittle.
frà-grans: fragrant, odorous.
fragrantís-simus: very fragrant.
franciscà-nus: of San Francisco.
fríg-idus: cold, of cold regions.
frondò-sus: leafy.
frumentà-ceus: pertaining to grain (or corn).
frutés-cens: shrubby, bushy.
frù-tex: a shrub or bush.
frù-ticans: shrubby, shrub-like.
fruticò-sus: shrubby, bushy.
fuchsioì-des: fuchsia-like.
fúl-gens: shining, glistening.
fúlg-idus: fulgid, shining.
fúl-vus: fulvous, tawny, orange-gray-yellow.
fumariæfò-lius: fumaria-leaved.
fù-nebris: funereal.
fungò-sus: fungous, pertaining to a fungus, spongy.
fúr-cans, furcà-tus: furcate, forked.
fuscà-tus: dark brown.
fús-cus: fuscous, brown, dusty.
fusifór-mis: spindle-shaped.

galacifò-lius: galax-leaved.
galegifò-lius: galega-leaved.
gál-licus: of Gaul or France; also pertaining to a cock or rooster.
gandavén-sis: belonging to Ghent, Belgium.
gangét-icus: of the Ganges.
gargán-icus: belonging to Gargano (Italy).
gemmíf-era: bud-bearing.
generà-lis: general, prevailing.
genevén-sis: belonging to Geneva (Switzerland).
genistifò-lius: genista-leaved.
gentianoì-des: gentian-like.
geomét-rizans: symmetrical, equal.
geóph-ilus: growing on the ground.
germán-icus: German.
gibbiflò-rus: gibbous-flowered.
gibbò-sus: swollen on one side.
gíb-bus: gibbous, swollen on one side.
gibraltár-icus: of Gibraltar.
gigantè-us: gigantic, very large.
gigán-thes: giant-flowered.
glabél-lus: smoothish.
glà-ber: glabrous, smooth.
glabér-rimus: very smooth, smoothest.
glabrà-tus: somewhat glabrous.
glabrés-cens: smoothish.
glacià-lis: icy, frozen.
gladià-tus: sword-like.
glandulíf-era: gland-bearing.
glandulò-sus: glandular, full of glands, very glandular.
glaucés-cens: glaucescent, becoming glaucous.
glaucophý́l-lus: glaucous-leaved.
glaucóp-sis: glaucous-like.
glaù-cus: glaucous, with a bloom.
globò-sus: globose, spherical, nearly or quite globular.
glomerà-tus: glomerate, clustered.
gloriò-sus: glorious, superb.
glutinò-sus: glutinous, gluey, sticky.
gracíl-ior: more graceful.
gracíl-ipes: slender-footed.
grác-ilis: graceful, slender.
gracíl-limus: graceful, very slender.
græ̀-cizans: becoming widespread.
græ̀-cus: of Greece, Greek.
gramín-eus: grassy, grass-like.
graminifò-lius: grass-leaved.
granadén-sis: of Granada, Spain.
grandicór-nis: large-horned.
grandidentà-tus: large-toothed.
grandiflò-rus: large-flowered.
grandifò-lius: large-leaved.
grán-dis: large, big.
granít-icus: granite-loving.
granulà-tus: granulate, covered with minute grains.
gratianopolità-nus: from Gratianopolis or Grenoble, France.
gratís-simus: very pleasing or agreeable.
gravè-olens: heavy-scented.
grís-eus: gray.
grœnlán-dicus: of Greenland.
grós-sus: thick, large.
guadalupén-sis: from the island of Guadalupe, off the coast of Lower California.
guatemalén-sis: of Guatemala.
guineén-sis: of Guinea, coast of western Africa.
guttà-tus: spotted or speckled.
gymnán-therus: naked-flowered.
gymnocár-pus: naked-fruited.

hæmán-thus: blood-red-flowered.
halepén-sis, chalepén-sis: of Aleppo, ancient region east of the Mediterranean.
halimifò-lius: halimium-leaved.
halóph-ilus: salt-loving.
hamatocán-thus: with blood-red spines.
hastæfò-lius: hastate- or spear-leaved.
hastà-tus: hastate, spear-shaped.
hebecár-pus: pubescent-fruited.
hederà-ceus: of the ivy (Hedera).
helianthoì-des: helianthus-like.
helodóx-a: marsh beauty.
hemisphǽr-icus: hemispherical.
hepaticifò-lius: hepatica-leaved.
heptalò-bus: seven-lobed.
heracleifò-lius: heracleum-leaved.
herbà-ceus: herbaceous, not woody.
hespè-rius: of the West.
heterocár-pus: various-fruited.

heterophýl-lus: various-leaved, with leaves of more than one shape.
hexagonóp-terus: six-angled-winged.
hexagò-nus: six-angled.
hexán-drus: with six stamens.
hexapét-alus: six-petaled.
hexaphýl-lus: six-leaved.
hibér-nicus: of Ireland.
hieroglýph-icus: marked as if with signs.
himalà-icus: Himalayan.
hippophaeoì-des: like hippophae.
hircì-nus: with goat odor.
hirsutís-simus: very hairy.
hirsù-tus: hirsute, hairy.
hirtél-lus: somewhat hairy.
hír-tus: hairy.
hispán-icus: Spanish, of Spain.
hispíd-ulus: somewhat bristly.
hís-pidus: hispid, bristly.
hollán-dicus: of Holland.
holophýl-lus: entire-leaved.
homól-epis: homologous scales.
hondoén-sis: of Hondo, the largest island of Japan.
horizontà-lis: horizontal.
hór-ridus: prickly, horridly armed.
hortén-sis, hortò-rum, hortuà-lis, hortulà-nus, hortulò-rum: belonging to a hortus or garden, or to gardens.
humilifò-lius: hop-leaved.
hù-milis: low-growing, dwarf.
hupehén-sis: from Hupei, a province of China.
hyacínth-inus: hyacinth-like.
hýb-ridus: hybrid, mixed, mongrel.
hydrangeoì-des: hydrangea-like.
hyemà-lis, hiemà-lis: of winter.
hymenosép-alus: sepals membranous.
hypericifò-lius: hypericum-leaved.
hypnoì-des: moss-like.
hypochondrì-acus: melancholy, hypochondriac.
hypogǽ-us: underground, subterranean.
hypoleù-cus: whitish, pale.
hyssopifò-lius: hyssop-leaved.

ibér-icus, iberíd-eus: of Iberia (the Spanish peninsula).
iberidifò-lius: iberis-leaved.
idǽ-us: of Mt. Ida (Asia Minor).
íg-neus: fiery.
ilicifò-lius: ilex-leaved, holly-leaved.
illecebrò-sus: of the shade.
illinoén-sis: of Illinois.
illús-tris: bright, brilliant, lustrous.
ilvén-sis: of Elba.
ím-bricans: imbricating.
imbricà-rius, imbricà-tus: imbricated, overlapping, shingled.
impéd-itus: impeded, hindered.
imperià-lis: imperial, kingly.
incà-nus: hoary.
incarnà-tus: flesh-colored.
incisifò-lius: cut-leaved.
incì-sus: incised, cut.
incomparáb-ilis: incomparable, excelling.
indentà-tus: indented, dented.
ín-dicus: Indian, of India or the East Indies.
indivì-sus: undivided.
indurà-tus: hard, hardened.
inér-mis: unarmed, without thorns or spines.
infectò-rius: used for dying, pertaining to dyes.
inflà-tus: inflated, swollen up.
infundibulifór-mis: funnelform, trumpet-shaped.
ín-gens: enormous.
innominà-tus: unknown, nameless.
inodò-rus: without odor, scentless.
ín-quinans: polluting, discoloring.
insér-tus: inserted.
insíg-nis: remarkable, distinguished, marked.
insitít-ius: grafted.
insulà-ris: insular, belonging to an island.
ín-teger: entire.
integér-rimus: very entire.
integrifò-lius: entire-leaved.
intermè-dius: intermediate.
intricà-tus: intricate, entangled.
involucrà-tus: involucred, with an involucre.
ioén-sis: of Iowa.
ionán-thus: violet-flowered.
iridifò-lius: iris-leaved.
iridioì-des: iris-like.
irrorà-tus: bedewed.
isophýl-lus: equal-leaved.
istrì-acus: of Istria (southern Europe).
itál-icus: Italian.
ixioì-des: ixia-like.
ixocár-pus: sticky- or glutinous-fruited.

japón-icus: Japanese.
jasminoì-des: jasmine-like.
javán-icus: Javan, of Java.
jezoén-sis: from Jezo or Yezo, Hokkaido, northernmost island of Japan.
jubà-tus: crested, with a mane.
jún-ceus: juncus-like, rush-like.
juncifò-lius: rush-leaved.
juniperifò-lius: juniper-leaved.
juniperì-nus: juniper-like.

kamtschát-icus, camtchát-icus, and other spellings: of Kamtschatka.
kansuén-sis: from Kansu, province of China.
kewén-sis: belonging to Kew (Royal Botanic Gardens, Kew, England).
kiusià-nus: from Kiushiu, southernmost of the main Japanese islands.
koreà-nus, koraién-sis: of Korea.

labià-tus: labiate, lipped.
lác-erus: torn.
lacinià-tus: laciniate, torn.
laciniò-sus: much laciniate.
lác-teus: milk-white.
lactiflò-rus: flowers milk-colored.
lacús-tris: pertaining to lakes.
ladaníf-era: ladanum-bearing.
lætiflò-rus: bright- or pleasing-flowered.
lǽ-tus: bright, vivid.
lævigà-tus: smooth.
lǽ-vis: smooth.
lagenà-rius: of a bottle or flask.
lanà-tus: woolly.
lanceolà-tus: lanceolate.
lancifò-lius: lance-leaved.
langleyén-sis: of Veitch's Langley Nursery, England.
lanicaù-lis: woolly-stemmed.
lantoscà-nus: of Lantosca or Lantosque, in the Maritime Alps.
lanuginò-sus: woolly, downy.
lapíd-eus: hard and stony.
lappón-icus: of Lapland.
laricifò-lius: larch-leaved.

laríc-inus: larch-like.
lasián-drus: pubescent-stamened.
lasián-thus: woolly-flowered.
lasiocár-pus: rough- or woolly-fruited.
lateríit-ius: brick-red.
latifò-lius: broad-leaved.
latíl-obus: broad-lobed.
latispì-nus: broad-spined.
latisquà-mus: broad-scaled.
latiús-culus: somewhat broad.
laudà-tus: lauded, worthy.
laurifò-lius: laurel-leaved.
laurì-nus: laurel-like.
laxiflò-rus: loose-flowered.
láx-us: lax, open, loose.
leián-thus: smooth-flowered.
leióg-ynus: smooth pistil.
lén-tus: pliant, tenacious, tough.
lepidophýl-lus: scaly-leaved.
leptocaû-lis: thin-stemmed.
leptóc-ladus: thin-stemmed or -branched.
leptól-epis: thin-scaled.
leptophýl-lus: thin-leaved.
lép-topus: thin- or slender-stalked or -footed.
leptosép-alus: thin-sepaled.
leucán-thus: white-flowered.
leucocár-pus: white-fruited.
leuconeù-rus: white-nerved.
leucophýl-lus: white-leaved.
leucós-tachys: white-spiked.
libán-i, libanót-icus: of Lebanon.
lignò-sus: woody.
ligulà-ris, ligulà-tus: ligulate, strap-shaped.
ligulís-tylis: with ligular style.
ligusticifò-lius: ligusticum-leaved.
ligustrì-nus: privet-like.
lilifò-lius: lily-leaved.
liliiflò-rus: lily-flowered.
linariifò-lius: linaria-leaved.
linearifò-lius: linear-leaved.
lineà-ris: linear.
lineà-tus: lined, with lines or stripes.
lingulà-tus, linguifór-mis: tongue-shaped.
liniflò-rus: flax-flowered.
linifò-lius: flax-leaved.
litorà-lis, littorà-lis: of the seashore.
lobà-tus: lobed.
longés-tylus: long-styled.
longiflò-rus: long-flowered.
longifò-lius: long-leaved.
longipét-alus: long-petaled.
longipinnà-tus: long-pinnate.
longiscà-pus: long-scaped.
longís-simus: longest, very long.
longistipà-tus: long-stiped or -stemmed.
longís-tylus: long-styled.
lón-gus: long.
lophán-thus: crest-flowered.
lorifò-lius: strap-leaved.
louisià-nus: of Louisiana.
lù-cidus: lucid, bright, shining, clear.
lunà-tus: lunate, moon-shaped, moon-like, crescent-shaped.
lupulì-nus: lupulus-like, hop-like.
lù-ridus: lurid, wan, sallow, pale yellow.
lusitán-icus: of Portugal.
lutè-olus: yellowish.
lutés-cens: yellowish, becoming yellow.
lù-teus: yellow.
lycopodioì-des: lycopodium-like, club-moss-like.
lyrà-tus: lyrate, pinnatifid with large terminal lobe.
macedón-icus: Macedonian.
macracanthoì-des: like macracanthus (large spines).
macradè-nus: with large glands.
macrán-thus: large-flowered.
macrocár-pus: large-fruited.
macrocéph-alus: large-headed.
macromè-ris: with large parts.
macropét-alus: large-petaled.
macrophýl-lus: large-leaved.
macróp-odus: large-stemmed.
macrorhì-zus: large-rooted.
macrosì-phon: large-beaked.
macrostà-chyus: large-spiked.
macrós-temmus: large-stemmed.
macrós-tylus: large-styled.
macrothýr-sus: with large thyrse.
maculà-tus: spotted.
madagascarién-sis: of Madagascar.
maderén-sis: of Madeira.
mæsì-acus: of Mœsia, ancient name of Bulgaria and Serbia.
magellán-icus, magellén-sis: Strait of Magellan region.
magníf-icus: magnificent, eminent, distinguished.
magnifoliò-sus: large-leaved.
majà-lis: of May, Maytime.
malacoì-des: soft, mucilaginous.
malifór-mis: apple-formed.
malvà-ceus: malva-like, mallow-like.
malvæflò-rus: mallow-flowered.
mammillà-ris: with breasts or nipples.
mandshúr-icus, mandschúr-icus, and other spellings: of Manchuria (northeastern Asia).
manicà-tus: manicate, long-sleeved, covered densely as with thick hairs so that the covering can be removed as such.
manipurà-nus: of Manipur, India.
margaritíf-era: pearl-bearing.
margarì-tus, margarità-ceus: pearly, of pearls.
marginà-lis: marginal.
marginà-tus: margined.
marià-nus: of Maryland.
marilánd-icus, marylánd-icus: of the Maryland region.
marít-imus: maritime, of the sea.
marmorà-tus: marbled, mottled.
maroccà-nus: of Morocco.
más, más-culus: male.
matronà-lis: pertaining to matrons.
mauritán-icus: of Mauritania (northern Africa).
máx-imus: largest.
mediopíc-tus: pictured or striped at the center.
mediterrà-neus: of the Mediterranean region.
mè-dius: medium, intermediate.
megalophýl-lus: large-leaved.
melanchól-icus: melancholy, hanging or drooping.
melanocár-pus: black-fruited.
melanót-richus: black-haired.
melanóx-ylon: black-wooded.
melanthè-rus: black-anthered.
meleà-gris: like a guinea-fowl, speckled.
melocactifór-mis: resembling melocactus.
mentorén-sis: native of Mentor (Ohio).
meridionà-lis: southern.
metál-licus: metallic (color or luster).
mexicà-nus: Mexican.
mì-cans: glittering, sparkling, mica-like.
michiganén-sis: native of Michigan.
micrán-thus: small-flowered.
microcár-pus: small-fruited.

micród-asys: small, thick, shaggy.
micról-epis: small-scaled.
micromà-lus: small apple or fruit.
micropét-alus: small-petaled.
microphýl-lus: small-leaved.
mikanioì-des: mikania-like.
milià-ceus: pertaining to millet.
minià-tus: cinnabar-red.
mì-nor, mì-nus: smaller.
minù-tus: minute, very small.
miráb-ilis: marvellous, extraordinary.
mì-rus: wonderful, unusual.
missourién-sis: native of Missouri.
mi-tis: mild, gentle.
mitrifór-mis: mitre- or turban-form.
modés-tus: modest.
mœsì-acus: of the Balkan region (the ancient Mœsians).
mól-lis: soft, soft-hairy.
mollis-simus: very soft-hairy.
moluccà-nus: of the Moluccas (East Indies).
monadél-phus: in one group or bundle.
monán-drus: one-stamened.
monghól-icus, mongól-icus: of Mongolia.
monocóc-cus: one-fruited or -berried.
monóg-ynus: of one pistil.
monospér-mus: one-seeded.
monspelién-sis, monspessulà-nus: of Montpellier, France.
monstrò-sus: monstrous, abnormal.
montà-nus: pertaining to mountains or mountainous regions.
montevidén-sis: of Montevideo (Uruguay).
montíc-olus: inhabiting mountains.
morifò-lius: morus-leaved, mulberry-leaved.
mosà-icus: parti-colored, as of a mosaic.
moschà-tus: musky, musk-scented.
moupinén-sis: of Mupin, China.
mucronà-tus: mucronate, tipped with a short sharp point or mucro.
mucronulà-tus: with a small mucro or point.
multicaù-lis: many-stemmed.
multicà-vus: with many hollows.
múl-ticeps: many-headed.
multíc-olor: many-colored.
multiflò-rus: many-flowered.
múl-tiplex: many-folded.
multiradià-tus: many-radiate, with numerous rays.
multiscapoíd-eus: like multiscapus (many-scaped).
multisèc-tus: much cut.
munì-tus: armed, fortified.
murà-lis: of walls, growing on walls.
muricà-tus: muricate, roughed by means of hard points.
musà-icus: musa-like.
muscíp-ula: fly-catcher.
muscív-orus: fly-eating.
muscò-sus: mossy.
mutáb-ilis: changeable, changing color.
myriophýl-lus: myriad-leaved.
myriostíg-mus: with myriad stigmas.
myrtifò-lius: myrtle-leaved.

nairobén-sis: of Nairobe, Africa.
nanél-lus: very small or dwarf.
nà-nus: dwarf.
napaulén-sis: of Nepal, Himalayas.
narbonén-sis: of Narbonne (ancient region or province of southern France).
narcissiflò-rus: narcissus-flowered.
narinò-sus: broad-nosed.
natalén-sis: of Natal, South Africa.
nà-tans: floating, swimming.
neapolità-nus: Neapolitan, of Naples.
nebulò-sus: nebulous, clouded, indefinite, obscure; making a cloud (of bloom or sprays).
negléc-tus: neglected, overlooked.
nelumbifò-lius: nelumbo-leaved.
nemorà-lis, nemorò-sus: of groves or woods.
neodioì-cus: new or segregate from dioicus.
nepalén-sis: of Nepal (Himalayan region).
neriifò-lius: nerium-leaved, oleander-leaved.
nervò-sus: nerved.
nevadén-sis: from the state of Nevada or from Sierra Nevada Mountains, Spain.
nidifór-mis: nest-formed.
nì-ger: black.
nigrés-cens: blackish, becoming black.
níg-ricans: swarthy, blackish.
nigrofrúc-tus: black-fruited.
nippón-icus: of Nippon (Japan).
nì-tens, nít-idus: shining.
nivà-lis: snowy, pertaining to snow.
nív-eus: snowy.
nivò-sus: snowy, full of snow.
nób-ilis: noble, famous, renowned.
noctúr-nus: of the night, night-blooming
nodiflò-rus: with flowers at nodes.
nodò-sus: with nodes, jointed.
nodulò-sus: with small nodes.
nonpíc-tus: not painted.
nonpinnà-tus: not pinnate (in comparison with those that are pinnate).
nonscríp-tus: underscribed.
nootkatén-sis, nutkatén-sis: of Nootka (Nootka Sound is by Vancouver Island).
novæ-án-gliæ: of New England.
noveboracén-sis: of New York.
novi-bél-gi: of New Belgium (one-time name for New York).
nucíf-era: nut-bearing.
nudicaù-lis: naked-stemmed.
nudiflò-rus: naked-flowered.
nù-dus: nude, naked.
numíd-icus: of Numidia (ancient country of northern Africa).
nummularifò-lius: money-leaved.
nummulà-rius: money-like.
nutáb-ilis: resembling nutans.
nù-tans: nodding.
nymphoì-des: nymphea-like.

obcón-icus: inversely conical.
obcordà-tus: inversely cordate.
obè-sus: obese, fat.
oblà-tus: oblate.
oblongifò-lius: oblong-leaved.
oblón-gus: oblong.
obovà-tus: inverted ovate, obovate.
obtusà-tus: obtuse, blunt.
obtusifò-lius: obtuse-leaved.
obtù-sior: more obtuse.
obtù-sus: obtuse, blunt, rounded.
occidentà-lis: occidental, western.
ocellà-tus: with small eyes.
ochnà-ceus: ochna-like.
ochroleù-cus: yellowish-white.
octán-drus: with eight anthers.
octopét-alus: eight-petaled.
oculà-tus: eyed.

ocymoi-des: ocimum-like.
odessà-nus: of Odessa (Black Sea region).
odoratís-simus: most fragrant.
odorà-tus, odoríf-era, odò-rus: odorous, fragrant.
officinà-lis: officinal, medicinal, recognized in the pharmacopea.
officinà-rum: of the apothecaries.
oleíf-era: oil-bearing.
olerà-ceus: oleraceous, vegetable-garden herb used in cooking.
olitò-rius: pertaining to vegetable-gardens or -gardeners.
olým-picus: of Olympus or Mt. Olympus (in Greece).
opà-cus: opaque, shaded, not transparent.
operculà-tus: with a lid.
ophiocár-pus: snake-fruit.
ophioglossoì-des: ophioglossum-like.
ophiuroì-des: ophiurus-like.
oppositifò-lius: opposite-leaved.
opulifò-lius: opulus-leaved.
orbiculà-ris, orbiculà-tus: round or circular, disk-shaped.
orchioì-des, orchiò-des: orchid-like.
oregà-nus, oregonén-sis, oregò-nus: of Oregon.
orgyà-lis: length of the arms extended, about 6 feet.
orientà-lis: oriental, eastern.
origanifò-lius: origanum-leaved.
origanoì-des: origanum-like.
ornà-tus: ornate, adorned.
ornithorhýn-chus: shaped like a bird's beak.
oroboì-des: orobus-like.
orthosép-alus: straight-sepaled.
ovalifò-lius: oval-leaved.
ovà-lis: oval.
ovà-tus: ovate.
ovì-nus: pertaining to sheep.
oxyacanthoì-des: like oxyacanthus (sharp-spined).
oxysép-alus: sharp-sepaled.

pabulà-rius: of fodder or pasturage.
pachyphlœ-us: thick-barked.
pachyphýl-lus: thick-leaved.
pacíf-icus: of the Pacific, of regions bordering the Pacific Ocean.
pæoniflò-rus: peony-flowered.
palæstì-nus: of Palestine.
pallés-cens: becoming pale.
pál-lidus: pale.
palmà-ris, palmà-tus: palmate.
palmatíf-idus: palmately cut.
palmifò-lius: palm-leaved.
palús-tris: marsh-loving.
pandurà-tus: fiddle-shaped.
paniculà-tus: paniculate.
pannò-sus: ragged, tattered.
papilionà-ceus: butterfly-like.
papyríf-era: paper-bearing.
paradì-si, paradisì-acus: of parks or gardens.
paradóx-us: unusual.
paraguarién-sis, paraguayén-sis: native of Paraguay.
parcifrôn-difer: bearing parcifronds.
pardalì-nus: leopard-like, spotted.
parnás-sii: of Parnassus in Greece.
parviflò-rus: small-flowered.
parvifò-lius: small-leaved.
pás-cuus: of pastures.
patavì-nus: of Padua.
pà-tens: spreading.
pát-ulus: spreading.
pauciflò-rus: few-flowered.
paucifò-lius: few-leaved.
pavonì-nus: peacock-like.
pectinà-tus: pectinate, comb-like, pinnatifid, with very narrow close divisions or parts.
pedatíf-idus: pedately cut.
pedà-tus: footed, bird-footed; palmately divided with side divisions again cleft.
pedunculà-ris, pedunculà-tus: peduncled.
pedunculò-sus: with many peduncles.
pekinén-sis: of Peking, China.
peltà-tus: peltate, shield-shaped.
peltóph-orus: shield-bearing.
penduliflò-rus: pendulous-flowered.
pén-dulus: pendulous, hanging.
pennà-tus: feathered, as the veins or lobes standing off at right angles from a midrib; pinnate.
pennsylván-icus, pensylván-icus: of Pennsylvania.
pentán-drus: of five stamens.
pentapét-alus: five-petaled.
pentaphýl-lus: five-leaved.
peregrì-nus: exotic, foreign, from a strange country.
perén-nis: perennial.
perfolià-tus: perfoliate, with leaf surrounding the stem.
perforà-tus: perforated, with holes.
perpusíl-lus: exceptionally small.
pér-sicus: of Persia; also the peach.
perulà-tus: wallet-like or pocket-like.
peruvià-nus: Peruvian.
pervír-idis: deep green.
petiolà-ris, petiolà-tus: petioled, with a leaf-stalk.
petræ-us: rock-loving.
philadél-phicus: of the Philadelphia region.
philippinén-sis: of the Philippines.
phillyræoì-des: phillyrea-like.
phlogiflò-rus: flame-flowered, phlox-flowered.
phlogifò-lius: phlox-leaved.
phœníc-eus: purple-red.
phœnicolà-sius: purple-haired.
phyllanthoì-des: phyllanthus-like.
phyllomanì-acus: running wildly to leaves.
picturà-tus: painted-leaved, pictured, variegated.
píc-tus: painted.
pileà-tus: with a cap.
pilíf-era: bearing soft hairs.
pilosél-lus: finely tomentose.
pilò-sus: pilose, shaggy, with soft hairs.
pimpinellifò-lius: pimpinella-leaved.
pinetò-rum: of pine forests.
pinnatíf-idus: pinnately cut.
pinnà-tus: pinnate.
piperás-cens: resembling piper.
piperì-ta: peppermint-scented.
pisíf-era: pisum-bearing, pea-bearing.
planifò-lius: flat-leaved.
planisíl-iquus: with flat siliques or fruits.
plantagín-eus: plantain-like.
plà-nus: plane, flat.
platanoì-des: platanus-like, plane-tree-like.
platycén-tra: broad-centered.
platýc-eras: broad-horned.
platýc-ladus: broad-branched.
platyneù-rus: broad-nerved.
platypét-alus: broad-petaled.
platyphýl-los, platyphýl-lus: broad-leaved.

pleiospér-mus: thick-seeded.
pleniflò-rus: double-flowered.
plenís-simus: very full or double.
plicà-tus: plicate, plaited, folded lengthwise.
plumà-rius: plumed.
plumbaginoì-des: plumbago-like.
plumò-sus: feathery.
pluriflò-rus: many-flowered.
pluríj-ugus: many-yoked.
pluvià-lis: reporting rain.
podalyriæfò-lius: podalyria-leaved.
poét-icus: pertaining to poets.
polifò-lius: polium-leaved, white-leaved.
polì-tus: polished.
polón-icus: Polish.
polyacán-thus: many-spined.
polyán-drus: with many stamens.
polyán-thus: many-flowered.
polycár-pus: many-fruited.
polýg-amus: polygamous, sexes mixed.
polymór-phus: of many forms, variable.
polyneù-rus: many-nerved.
polyphýl-lus: many-leaved.
polypodioì-des: polypodium-like.
polyrrhì-zus: many-rooted.
polystà-chyus: many-spiked.
pomeridià-nus: afternoon.
pomíf-era: pome-bearing.
pompò-nius: of a tuft or topknot; pompons are small-headed button-like races, as in chrysanthemum and dahlia.
ponderò-sus: ponderous, heavy.
pón-ticus: of Pontus (in Asia Minor).
populifò-lius: poplar-leaved.
popúl-neus: pertaining to poplars.
porrifò-lius: porrum- or leek-leaved.
portoricén-sis: of Puerto Rico.
portulà-ceus: portulaca-like.
poukhanén-sis: of Pouk Han, Korea.
præ-cox: precocious, premature, very early.
præmór-sus: bitten at the end.
præ-stans: distinguished, excelling.
pratén-sis: of meadows.
pravís-simus: very crooked.
primulifò-lius: primrose-leaved.
primúl-inus, primuloì-des: primrose-like.
prín-ceps: princely, first.
prismát-icus: prismatic, prism-shaped.
procè-rus: tall.
procúm-bens: procumbent.
procúr-rens: extending.
prolíf-era: producing offshoots.
prolíf-icus: prolific, fruitful.
prolongà-tus: prolonged, elongated.
prostrà-tus: prostrate, lying flat.
pruinà-tus, pruinò-sus: with a hoary bloom.
prunifò-lius: plum-leaved.
psilostè-mon: slender- or naked-stamened.
psittác-inus: parrot-like.
psycò-des: fragrant.
ptarmicoì-des: ptarmica-like.
pterán-thus: with winged flowers.
pteridoì-des: like pteris.
pù-bens: downy.
pubér-ulus: somewhat pubescent.
pubés-cens: pubescent, downy.
pudì-cus: bashful, retiring, shrinking.
pugionifór-mis: dagger-formed.
pulchél-lus: pretty, beautiful.
púl-cher: handsome, beautiful.
pulchér-rimus: very handsome.
púl-lus: dark colored, dusky.
pulpò-sus: fleshy.
pulverulén-tus: powdered, dust-covered.
pulvinà-tus: cushion-like.
pù-milus: dwarf.
punctà-tus: punctate, dotted.
punctilób-ulus: dotted-lobed.
pún-gens: piercing, sharp-pointed.
puníc-eus: reddish-purple, crimson.
púr-gans: purging.
purpurás-cens: purplish, becoming purple.
purpurà-tus: purple.
purpù-reus: purple.
pycnacán-thus: densely spined.
pycnán-thus: densely flowered.
pycnostà-chyus: thick-spiked.
pygmæ-us: pigmy.
pyramidà-lis: pyramidal.
pyrenà-icus: of the Pyrenees.
pyrifò-lius: pear-leaved.
pyrifór-mis: pear-shaped.

quadrangulà-ris, quadrangulà-tus: four-angled.
quadriaurì-tus: four-eared.
quadríc-olor: of four colors.
quadríf-idus: four-cut.
quercifò-lius: oak-leaved.
quinà-tus: in fives.
quinquefò-lius: five-leaved.
quinquelocula-ris: five-celled.

racemiflò-rus: raceme-flowered.
racemò-sus: racemose, flowers in racemes.
radià-tus: radiate, rayed.
radì-cans: rooting.
radiiflò-rus: with radiating flowers.
rád-ula: rough, like a scraper.
ramosís-simus: much-branched.
ramò-sus: branched.
rapà-ceus: pertaining to turnips.
rariflò-rus: scattered-flowered.
reclinà-tus: reclined, bent back.
réc-tus: straight, upright.
recurvà-tus, recúr-vus: recurved.
redivì-vus: restored, brought to life.
refléx-us: reflexed, bent back.
refrác-tus: broken, broken in pieces.
regà-lis: regal, royal.
Regì-na: queen.
rè-gius: regal, royal, kingly.
religiò-sus: used for religious purposes, venerated, sacred.
renifór-mis: kidney-shaped.
repán-dens: repand.
rè-pens: repent, creeping.
rép-tans: creeping.
resinò-sus: full of resin.
reticulà-tus: reticulate, netted, net-veined.
retór-tus: twisted back.
retrofrác-tus: broken or bent backwards.
retù-sus: retuse, notched slightly at a rounded apex.
revolù-tus: revolute, rolled backwards.
Réx: king.
rhamnoì-des: rhamnus-like.
rhizophýl-lus: root-leaved, leaves rooting.
rhodán-thus: rose-flowered.
rhodopæ-us, rhodopén-sis: of the Rhodope Mountains in the Balkans.
rhombifò-lius: leaves rhombic.
rhomboidà-lis: of rhombic outline.

rhomboíd-eus: rhomboidal.
rhytidophýl-lus: wrinkled-leaved.
ricinifò-lius: ricinus-leaved.
rì-gens: rigid, stiff.
rigén-sis: of Riga, a Baltic port.
ríg-idus: rigid, stiff.
rín-gens: gaping.
ripà-rius: of river banks.
rivà-lis: pertaining to brooks.
rivulà-ris: brook-loving.
robús-tus: robust, stout.
romà-nus: Roman.
roribác-cus: dewberry.
rosæflò-rus: rose-flowered.
rosæfò-lius: rose-leaved.
rò-seus: rose, rosy.
rostrà-tus: rostrate, beaked.
rotundifò-lius: round-leaved.
rubellì-nus, rubél-lus: reddish.
rù-bens: red, ruddy.
rù-ber: red.
rubés-cens: becoming red.
rubiginò-sus: rusty.
rubríc-alyx: calyx red.
rubrifò-lius: red-leaved.
rù-dis: wild, not tilled.
rudiús-culus: wild, wildish.
rúf-idus: brownish or reddish.
rù-fus: red, reddish.
rugò-sus: rugose, wrinkled.
rugulò-sus: somewhat rugose.
rupés-tris: rock-loving.
rupíc-ola: growing on cliffs or ledges.
ruscifò-lius: ruscus-leaved.
rusticà-nus: rustic, pertaining to the country.
ruthén-icus: Ruthenian (Russian).

saccharà-tus: containing sugar, sweet.
saccharì-nus: saccharine.
sác-charum: of sugar.
sachalinén-sis: of Saghalin Island (northern Japan).
sacrò-rum: sacred, of sacred places.
sagittà-lis, sagittà-tus: of the arrow, sagittate, arrow-like.
sagittifò-lius: arrow-leaved.
salicariæfò-lius, salicifò-lius: willow-leaved.
salíci-nus, sál-icis, salíg-nus: willow-like, of the willow.
salsoloì-des: like salsola.
salsuginò-sus: salt-marsh-loving.
salvifò-lius: salvia-leaved.
sánc-tus: holy.
sanguín-eus: bloody, blood-red.
sáp-idus: savory, pleasing to taste.
sapién-tum: of the wise men or authors.
saponà-rius: soapy.
sardén-sis: of Sardes or Sardis, Asia Minor.
sarmentò-sus: sarmentose, bearing runners.
sarnién-sis: of Sarnia or the island of Guernsey.
satì-vus: cultivated.
satureioì-des: like satureia.
savannà-rum: of the savannas.
saxát-ilis: found among rocks.
scà-ber: scabrous, rough, not smooth.
scabér-rimus: very rough or scabrid.
scabiosæfò-lius: scabiosa-leaved.
scán-dens: scandent, climbing.
scariò-sus: scarious, thin and not green.
scép-trum: of a scepter.
schistò-sus: schistose, slaty as to tint.
schizopét-alus: with cut petals.
scilloì-des: squill-like.
scopà-rius: broom or broom-like.
scopulì-nus: rock-like.
scopulò-rum: of the rocks.
scorpioì-des: scorpion-like.
scutà-tus: buckler-shaped, like a small shield.
sebíf-era: tallow-bearing.
secundiflò-rus: secund-flowered.
secún-dus, secundà-tus: secund, side-flowering.
sedifò-lius: sedum-leaved.
sedifór-mis: sedum-formed.
ség-etum: of cornfields.
semidecán-drus: half ten-stamened, with about 5 stamens.
semipersís-tens: partly or semi-persistent.
semperflò-rens: ever flowering.
sempér-virens: ever green.
sempervivoì-des: sempervivum-like.
senanén-sis: of Senan, China.
senés-cens: becoming old or gray.
senì-lis: senile, old, white-haired.
sensíb-ilis: sensitive.
sè-pium: of hedges or fences.
septém-fidus: seven-cut.
septentrionà-lis: northern.
seríc-eus: silky.
sericóf-era, sericíf-era: silk-bearing.
serís-simus: very late.
serót-inus: late, late-flowering or late-ripening.
serpentì-nus: of snakes, serpentine, looping or waving.
serpyllifò-lius: thyme-leaved, serpyllum-leaved.
serrà-tus: serrate, saw-toothed.
serrulà-tus: serrulate, somewhat serrate.
sesquipedà-lis: one foot and a half long or high.
sessilifò-lius: sessile-leaved, without petiole.
sés-silis: sessile, stalkless.
setíf-era, setíg-era: bristly, bristle-bearing.
setispì-nus: bristle-spined.
setò-sus: setose, full of bristles.
sexangulà-ris: six-angled.
sià-meus: of Siam.
sibír-icus: of Siberia.
síc-ulus: of Sicily.
signà-tus: marked, designated, attested.
sikkimén-sis: of Sikkim, Himalayas.
silenoì-des: like silene.
sím-ilis: similar, like.
sím-plex: simple, unbranched.
simplicifò-lius: simple-leaved.
simplicís-simus: simplest.
sím-ulans: similar to, resembling.
sinén-sis: Chinese, of China.
sín-icus: Chinese.
sinuà-tus: sinuate, wavy-margined.
siphilít-icus: syphilitic.
sitchén-sis: of Sitka, Alaska.
smarág-dinus: of emerald.
sobolíf-era: bearing creeping rooting stems or shoots.
solanì-nus: solanum-like.
soldanelloì-des: like soldanella.
solidifò-lius: entire-leaved.
somníf-era: sleep-bearing or -producing.
sorbifò-lius: sorbus-leaved.
sór-didus: dirty.
spathulà-tus: spatulate, spoon-shaped.
spathulifò-lius: spatulate-leaved.
spatiò-sus: spacious, wide.
speciò-sus: showy, good-looking.

spectáb-ilis: spectacular, worth seeing, remarkable, showy.
speculà-tus: shining, as if with mirrors.
sphærocéph-alus: spherical-headed.
sphæroíd-eus: sphere-like.
spicà-tus: spicate, with spikes.
spicíg-era: spike-bearing.
spiculifò-lius: spicule-leaved.
spinosís-simus: most or very spiny.
spinò-sus: full of spines.
spinulò-sus: somewhat or weakly spiny.
spirà-lis: spiral.
splén-dens, splén-didus: splendid.
spù-rius: spurious, false, bastard.
squà-lens, squál-idus: squalid, filthy.
squamà-tus: squamate, with squamæ or small scale-like leaves or bracts.
squamíg-era: scale-bearing.
squamò-sus: squamate, full of scales.
squarrò-sus: squarrose; as ordinarily used, with parts spreading or even recurved at ends.
stamín-eus: bearing prominent stamens.
stáns: standing, erect, upright.
stellà-tus: stellate, starry; often said of hairs that have radiating branches from base or of separate hairs similarly aggregated.
stellíp-ilus: with stellate hairs.
stellulà-tus: somewhat stellate.
stenopét-alus: narrow-petaled.
stenophýl-lus: narrow-leaved.
stenostà-chyus: narrow-spiked.
stér-ilis: sterile, infertile.
stipulà-tus: having stipules.
stœchadifò-lius: stœchas-leaved (Lavandula Stœchas).
stoloníf-era: bearing stolons or runners that take root.
stramineofrúc-tus: with straw-colored fruit.
strià-tus: striated, striped.
stríc-tus: strict, upright, erect.
strigò-sus: strigose, hispid.
strumò-sus: strumous, having cushion-like swellings.
stylò-sus: with style or styles prominent.
suavè-olens: sweet-scented.
suà-vis: sweet, agreeable.
subacaù-lis: somewhat stemmed.
subcarnò-sus: rather fleshy.
subcaulés-cens: somewhat stemmed.
subcaulialà-tus: somewhat wing-stemmed.
subcordà-tus: somewhat cordate.
subdivaricà-tus: slightly divaricate.
subhirtél-lus: somewhat hairy.
subsés-silis: nearly sessile.
subspicà-tus: nearly spicate.
subtomentò-sus: somewhat tomentose.
subulà-tus: subulate, awl-shaped.
succulén-tus: succulent, fleshy.
sudanén-sis: of the Sudan.
suéc-icus: of Sweden.
suffruticò-sus: somewhat shrubby.
sulphù-reus: sulfur-colored.
supér-bus: superb, proud.
supì-nus: prostrate.
susià-nus: of Susa, an ancient city of Iran.
suspén-sus: suspended, hung.
sylvát-icus: sylvan, forest-loving (also written *silvaticus*).
sylvés-tris, sylvés-ter: of woods or forests, growing wild.
syrì-acus: Syrian.
syringán-thus: syringa-flowered.

tabulæfór-mis: table-formed.
tamariscifò-lius: tamarisk-leaved.
tanacetifò-lius: tansy-leaved.
tangù-ticus: geographical name for the region of Tibet.
tardiflò-rus: late-flowered.
tár-dus: late.
tartà-reus: with a loose or rough crumbling surface.
tatár-icus: of Tartary (old name for Central Asia).
taù-ricus: Taurian, Crimean.
taxifò-lius: yew-leaved.
téch-nicus: technical, special.
tectò-rum: of roofs or houses.
temulén-tus: drunken.
tè-nax: tenacious, strong.
tenél-lus, tè-ner: slender, tender, soft.
tenuifò-lius: slender-leaved.
tenù-ior: more slender.
tén-uis: slender, thin.
tenuiséc-tus: finely cut.
terebinthifò-lius: terebinthus-leaved.
terebínth-inus: of turpentine.
tè-res: terete, circular in cross-section.
tereticór-nis: with terete or cylindrical horns.
terminà-lis: terminal, at the end of a stem or branch.
ternifò-lius: leaves in threes.
tessellà-tus: tessellate, laid off in squares or in dice-like pattern.
testá-ceus: light brown, brick-colored.
tetragonól-obus: with four-angled pod.
tetragò-nus: four-angled.
tetrán-drus: four-anthered.
tetrapét-alus: four-petaled.
texà-nus, texén-sis: of Texas, Texan.
téx-tilis: textile, woven.
thalictroì-des: thalictrum-like.
thapsifór-mis: similar to thapsus (Verbascum).
thelypteroì-des: thelypterum-like.
thibét-icus: of Tibet.
thuringì-acus: of Thuringia, Germany.
thuyoì-des, thyoì-des: like thuja (thuya) or arborvitæ.
thymifò-lius: thyme-leaved.
thyrsiflò-rus: thyrse-flowered.
thyrsoíd-eus: thyrse-like.
tibét-icus: of Tibet.
tigrì-nus: tiger-striped.
tilià-ceus: tilia-like (like linden or basswood).
tiliæfò-lius: tilia-leaved.
tinctò-rius: belonging to dyers, of dyes.
tingità-nus: of Tangiers.
tità-nus: very large.
tithymaloì-des: like tithymalus (Euphorbia).
tomentò-sus: tomentose, densely woolly.
toringoì-des: like toringo (Malus).
tortuò-sus: much twisted.
torulò-sus: somewhat torose or contracted at intervals.
trachysán-thus: rough-flowered.
tremuloì-des: like tremulus, the trembling poplar.
trém-ulus: quivering, trembling.
triacanthóph-orus: bearing three spines.
triacán-thos, triacán-thus: three-spined.
trián-drus: with three anthers or stamens.
triangulà-ris: triangular, three-cornered.
trichóc-alyx: calyx hairy.

trichocár-pus: hairy-fruited.
trichomanifò-lius: trichomanes-leaved.
trichosán-thus: hairy-flowered.
trichót-omus: three-branched or -forked.
tricóc-cus: three-seeded, three-berried.
tríc-olor: three-colored.
tricór-nis: three-horned.
tricuspidà-tus, tricús-pis: having three points.
trifascià-tus: three-banded.
tríf-idus: three-cleft.
triflò-rus: three-flowered.
trifolià-tus: three-leaved.
trifurcà-tus: three-forked.
triglochidià-tus: with three barbed bristles.
trilobà-tus, tríl-obus: three-lobed.
trimés-tris: of three months, as lasting that period or maturing within it.
trinervà-tus, trinér-vius: three-nerved.
tripartì-tus: three-parted.
tripét-alus: three-petaled.
triphýl-lus: three-leaved.
triplinér-vius: triple-nerved.
tríp-terus: three-winged.
trís-tis: sad, bitter, dull.
trivià-lis: common, ordinary, very frequent, found everywhere.
truncà-tus: truncate, cut off square.
tuberculà-tus: having tubercles.
tuberò-sus: tuberous.
tubiflò-rus: trumpet-flowered.
tunicà-tus: tunicate.
tuolumnén-sis: of the Tuolumne River in California.
túr-gidus: turgid, inflated, full.
typhì-nus: pertaining to fever.

uliginò-sus: of wet or marshy places.
ulmifò-lius: elm-leaved.
ulmoì-des: elm-like.
umbellà-tus: with umbels.
umbraculíf-era: umbrella-bearing.
umbrò-sus: shaded, shade-loving.
uncinà-tus: hooked at the point.
undà-tus: waved.
undulà-tus: undulated, wavy.
unguiculà-ris: clawed, narrowed to a petiole-like base.
uniflò-rus: one-flowered.
unilaterà-lis: one-seeded.
unioloì-des: uniola-like.
ù-rens: burning, stinging.
ursì-nus: pertaining to bears, northern (under the Great Bear).
urticifò-lius: nettle-leaved.
usitatís-simus: most commonly used.
usneoì-des: usnea-like.
ù-tilis: useful.
utilís-simus: most useful.

vaccinifò-lius: vaccinium-leaved.
và-gans: wandering, vagrant.
vaginà-lis: sheathed.
valdivià-nus, valdivién-sis: Valdivian, of province or region of Valdivia (Chile).
vál-idus: strong.
variáb-ilis: variable, of many forms.
varicò-sus: varicose, veins or filaments dilated.
variegà-tus: variegated.
variifò-lius: variable-leaved.
và-rius: various, diverse, changeable.
vég-etus: vigorous.
vè-lox: rapidly growing.
velù-tinus: velvety.
venenà-tus: poisonous.
venò-sus: veiny.
ventricò-sus: ventricose, swelling or inflated on one side or unevenly.
venús-tus: handsome, charming.
vè-ris: the true or genuine or standard.
vér-nus, vernà-lis: of spring, vernal.
verrucò-sus: verrucose, warted.
verruculò-sus: very warty or verrucose.
versíc-olor: variously colored, as of one color passing into another, or changing in color.
verticillà-tus: verticillate, whorled, arranged in a circle about the stem.
vè-rus: the true or genuine or standard.
vés-cus: weak, thin, feeble.
vespertì-nus: of the evening, western.
vestì-tus: covered, clothed as with hairs or pubescence.
vexillà-rius: of the standard petal (as of pea-like flowers), with a standard.
viatò-ris: of the roadways.
viciæfò-lius, viciifò-lius: vetch-leaved.
villós-ulus: finely villous.
villò-sus: villous, soft-hairy.
viminà-lis: of osiers, of basket willows.
vincæflò-rus: vinca-flowered.
viníc-olor: wine-color.
viníf-era: wine-bearing.
violà-ceus: violet.
vì-rens: green.
virés-cens: becoming green.
virgà-tus. twiggy.
virginà-lis: virgin.
virginià-nus, virginién-sis: of Virginia.
viridiflò-rus: green-flowered.
vír-idis: green.
viridís-simus: greenest, very green.
vís-cidus: viscid sticky.
viscò-sus: viscid.
vità-ceus: vitis-like.
vitellì-nus: dull yellow approaching red.
vitifò-lius: grape-leaved.
vittà-tus: striped.
vivíp-arus: freely producing asexual propagating parts, as bulblets in the inflorescence.
volù-bilis: twining.
vomitò-rius: emetic.
vulcán-icus: of Vulcan or of a volcano, vulcanic.
vulgà-ris: vulgar, common, usual.
vulpì-nus: of the fox.

xanthì-nus: yellow.
xanthocár-pus: yellow-fruited.
xanthorrhì-zus: yellow-rooted.

yedoén-sis: of Yedo or Yeddo (Japan).
yuccæfò-lius: yucca-leaved.
yunnanén-sis: of Province of Yunnan, China.

zanzibarién-sis: native of Zanzibar.
zebrì-nus: zebra-striped.
zeylán-icus: Ceylonian, of Ceylon; Cingalese.
zinniæflò-rus: zinnia-flowered.
zizanioì-des: zizania-like.
zonà-lis, zonà-tus: zonal, zoned, banded.

GLOSSARY

Abortive. Defective; barren; not developed.

Abrupt. Changing suddenly rather than gradually, as a leaf that is narrowed quickly to a point, not tapering; also pinnate leaf that has no terminal leaflet.

Acaulescent. Stemless, or apparently stemless; sometimes the stem is subterranean or protrudes only slightly; descriptive rather than morphological term.

Acephalous. Headless.

Achene (akene). A dry indehiscent one-seeded pericarp.

Acicular. Needle-shaped.

Acorn. The fruit of the oak (Quercus) and comprised of a nut and its cup or cupule.

Actinomorphic. Regular, symmetrical.

Acuminate. Said of an acute apex whose sides are somewhat concave and that tapers to a protracted point.

Acute. Sharp ending in a point, the sides of the tapered apex essentially straight or slightly convex.

Adherent. A condition existing when two dissimilar organs or parts touch each other conivently but not grown or fused together.

Adnate. Grown to, organically united with another part; as stamens with the corolla-tube or an anther in its whole length with the filament.

Adventitious buds. Buds appearing on occasion, rather than resident in regular places and order, as those arising about wounds.

Æstivation. The arrangement of floral envelopes in the bud (æstivus, summer, when flowers mostly appear Vernation is leaf-arrangement in the bud).

Aggregate fruit. One formed by the coherence of pistils that were distinct in the flower, as blackberry.

Albumen. Starchy or other nutritive material accompanying the embryo; commonly used in the sense of endosperm, for the material surrounding the embryo.

Alternate. Any arrangement of leaves or other parts not opposite or whorled; placed singly at different heights on the axis or stem.

Ament. Catkin.

Amphitropous. Said of an ovule whose stalk (funiculus) is curved about it so that the ovule tip and stalk base are near to each other.

Anastomosing. Netted; interveined; said of leaves marked by cross-veins forming a network; sometimes the vein branches meeting only at the margin.

Anatropous. Said of an ovule that is reversed, one whose opening (micropyle) is close to the point of funiculus attachment.

Ander. Male; occurs in combinations, as monandrous, having one stamen.

Annual. Of one season's duration from seed to maturity and death.

Anterior. Front; on the front side; away from the axis; toward the subtending bract.

Anther. The pollen-bearing part of the stamen, borne at the top of the filament or sometimes sessile.

Antheridium. In Cryptogams the organ corresponding to an anther or male organs in flowering plants.

Antheriferous. Anther-bearing.

Anthesis. Flowering; strictly, the time of expansion of a flower, but often used to designate the flowering period; the act of flowering.

Apetalous. No petals; petals missing.

Apocarpous. Carpels separate, not united; frequently applied to a gynœcium of separate pistils; see *Syncarpous.*

Appendage. An attached subsidiary or secondary part, as a projecting part or a hanging part or supplement.

Appressed. Closely and flatly pressed against; adpressed.

Arachnoid. Cobwebby by soft and slender entangled hairs; also spider-like.

Archegonium. In higher Cryptogams the organ corresponding to a pistil or female organs in flowering plants.

Areole. The open spaces formed by anastomosing veins; a small pit or raised spot, often bearing a tuft of hairs, glochids or spines.

Aril. An appendage or an outer covering of a seed, growing out from the hilum or funiculus; sometimes it appears as a pulpy covering.

Aristate. Bearing a stiff bristle-like awn or seta; tapered to a very narrow much-elongated apex.

Armature. Any covering or occurrence of spines, barbs, hooks or prickles on any part of the plant.

Armed. Provided with any kind of strong and sharp defence, as of thorns, spines, prickles, barbs.

Articulate. Jointed; provided with nodes or joints, or places where separation may naturally take place.

Ascending. Rising up; produced somewhat obliquely or indirectly upward.

Asexual. Sexless; without sex.

Assurgent. Ascending, rising.

Attenuate. Showing a long gradual taper, applied to bases or apices of parts.

Auricle. An ear-shaped part or appendage, as the projections at the base of some leaves and petals.

Awl-shaped. Narrow and sharp-pointed; gradually tapering from base to a slender orstiff point.

Awn. A bristle-like part or appendage.

Axil. Upper angle that a petiole or peduncle makes with the stem that bears it.

Axile. Belonging to the axis; see *Placentation.*

Axillary. In an axil.

Axis. The main or central line of development of any plant or organ; the main stem.

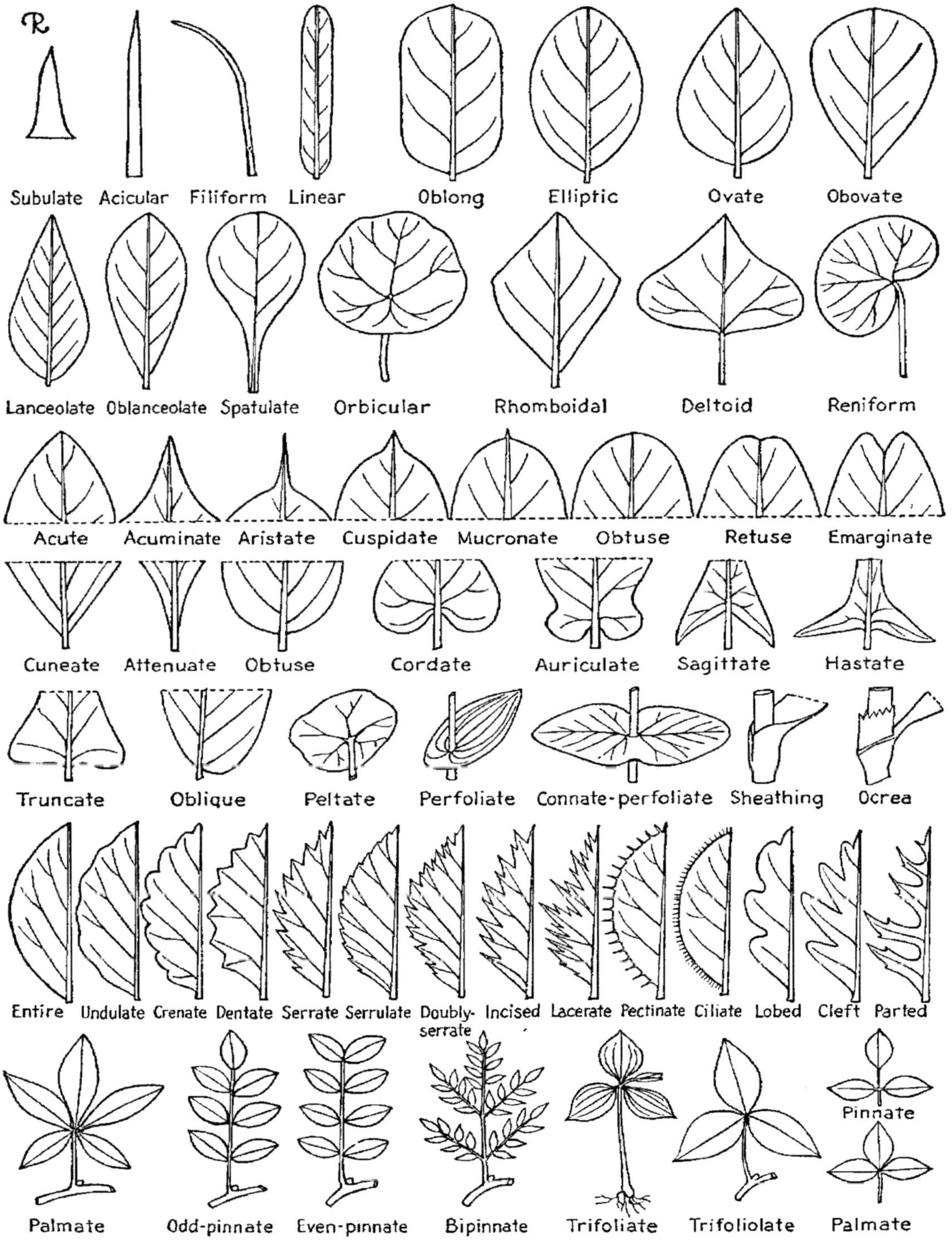

Fig. 1. Terms of vegetative structures.

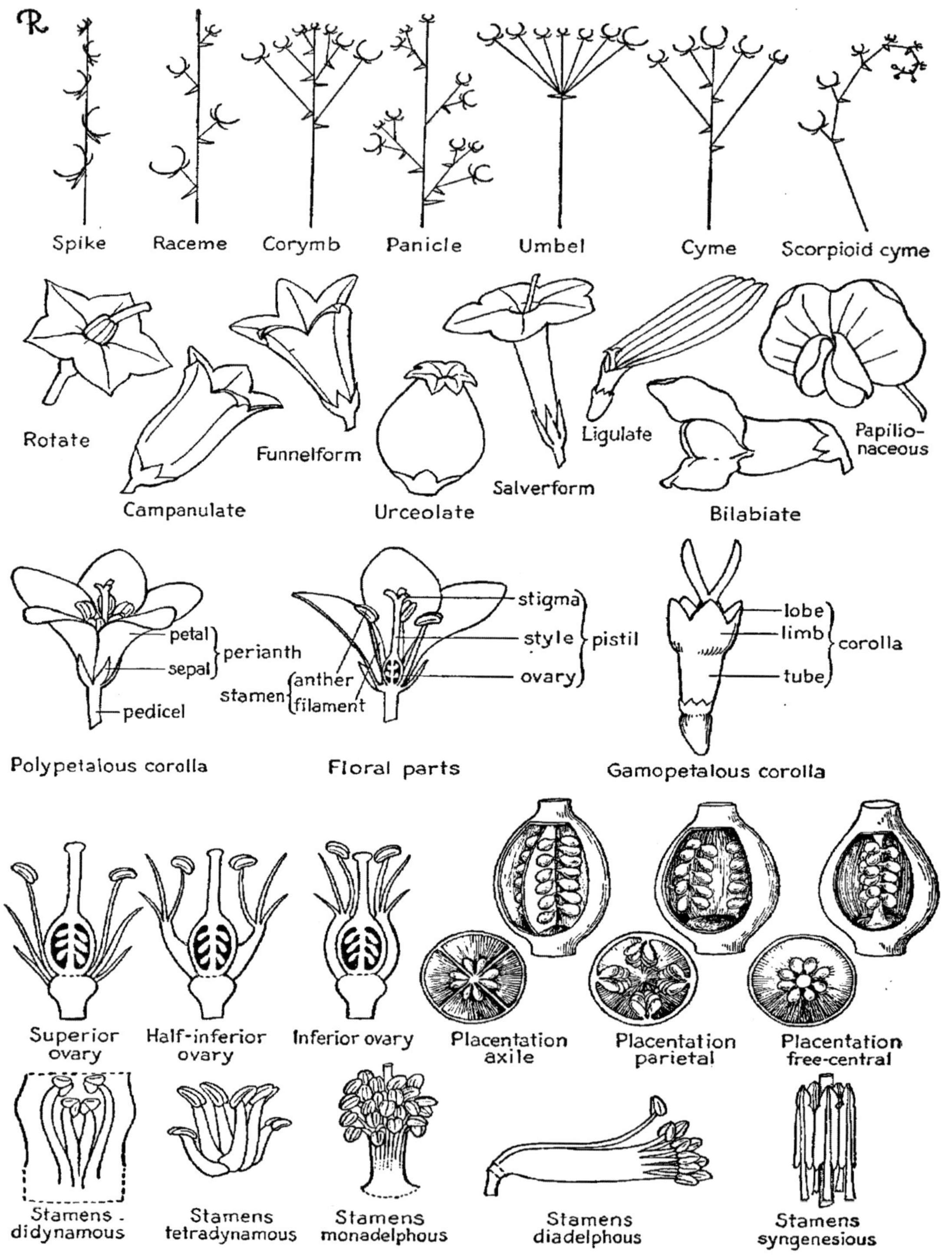

Fig. 2. Terms of reproductive structures.

Baccate. Berry-like; pulpy or fleshy.
Barbed. Bristles or awns provided with terminal or lateral spine-like hooks that are bent backwards sharply.
Basifixed. Attached or fixed by the base, as an ovule or anther that is affixed to its support by its bottom rather than by its side.
Beak. A long prominent and substantial point; applied particularly to prolongations of fruits and pistils.
Beard. A long awn or bristle-like hair.
Berry. Pulpy indehiscent few- or many-seeded fruit; technically, the pulpy fruit resulting from a single pistil, containing one or more seeds but no true stone, as the tomato.
Biennial. Of two seasons' duration from seed to maturity and death.
Bifid. Two-cleft, as in apices of some petals or leaves.
Bifurcate. Forked, as some Y-shaped hairs.
Bilabiate. Two-lipped, often applied to a corolla or calyx; each lip may or may not be lobed or toothed.
Bladdery. Inflated; empty, and the walls thin like the bladder of an animal.
Blade. The expanded part of a leaf or petal.
Bole. A strong unbranched caudex; the trunk.
Bract. A much-reduced leaf, particularly the small or scale-like leaves in a flower-cluster or associated with the flowers.
Bractlet. Bract borne on a secondary axis, as on the pedicel or even on the petiole.
Bristly. Bearing stiff strong hairs or bristles.
Bulb. A thickened part in a resting state and made up of scales or plates on a much-shortened axis.
Bulbel. Bulbs arising around the mother bulb.
Bulblet. Little bulbs produced in the leaf-axils, inflorescence or other unusual areas.
Bullate. The surface blistered or puckered, as the leaf of a Savoy cabbage.
Bush. A low and thick shrub, without distinct trunk.

Caducous. Falling off early, or prematurely, as the sepals in some plants.
Calcarate. Spurred.
Callus. A hard prominence or protuberance; in a cutting or on a severed or injured part, the roll of new covering tissue.
Calyculate. Calyx-like; bearing a part resembling a calyx; particularly, furnished with bracts against or underneath the calyx resembling a supplementary or outer calyx.
Calyptra. A hood or lid; particularly the hood or cap of the capsule of a moss or lid in fruit of Eucalyptus.
Calyx. The outer circle of floral envelopes, comprised of the sepals; the latter may be distinct or connate in a single structure.
Calyx-tube. The tube of a gamosepalous calyx; sometimes employed for hypanthium, which see.
Campanulate. Bell-shaped.
Canescent. Gray-pubescent and hoary, or becoming so.
Cap. A convex removable covering of a part, as of a capsule; in the grape, the cohering petals fall off as a cap.
Capillary. Hair-like; very slender.
Capitate. Headed; in heads; formed like a head; aggregated into a very dense or compact cluster.
Capsular. Pertaining to a capsule; formed like a capsule.
Capsule. Compound pod; a dry fruit of more than one carpel, usually opening at maturity by one or more lines of dehiscence.
Carinate. Keeled; provided with a projecting central longitudinal line or ridge on the lower or under surface.
Carpel. One of the foliar units of a compound pistil or ovary; a simple pistil has one carpel. See *Pistil.*
Carpophore. The stalk of a sporocarp; a prolongation of the receptacle that projects between the carpels of a pistil and serves as an axis to them. See *Gynophore.*
Catkin. A scaly-bracted usually flexuous spike or spike-like raceme with diclinous flowers; ament; prominent in willows and poplars.
Caudate. Bearing a tail-like appendage, as in spadices of some aroids.
Caudex. Stem.
Caulescent. More or less stemmed or stem-bearing; having an evident stem above ground.
Cauline. Pertaining or belonging to the stem.
Centralium. A central lengthwise cavity, as found in seeds of some palms.
Cernuous. Drooping.
Cespitose, cæspitose. Matted; growing in tufts; in little dense clumps; said of low plants that make tufts or turf of their basal growth.
Chaff. A small, thin, dry and membranous scale or bract; in particular, the bracts in the flower-heads of composites.
Chalaza. The basal part of an ovule where it is attached to the funiculus.
Chartaceous. Of papery or tissue-like texture and not usually green in color.
Ciliate. Fringed with hairs; bearing hairs on the margin.
Cinereous. Ash-colored; light gray.
Circinate. Rolled coilwise from top downward, as in unopened fern fronds.
Circumscissile. Opening or dehiscing by a line around the fruit or anther, the valve usually coming off as a lid.
Cladophyll. A flattened foliaceous stem having the form and function of a leaf, but arising in the axil of a minute bract-like, often caducous, true leaf. Example, Ruscus and Asparagus.
Clasping. Leaf partly or wholly surrounding stem.
Clavate. Club-shaped; said of a long body thickened toward the top.
Claw. The long narrow petiole-like base of the petals or sepals in some flowers.
Cleft. Divided to or about the middle into divisions, as a palmately or pinnately cleft leaf.
Cleistogamous flowers. Small closed self-fertilized flowers, as in some violets and in many other plants; they are mostly on or under the ground.
Clone. A group of individuals resulting from vegetative multiplication; any plant propagated vegetatively, and therefore presumably a duplicate of its parent. Originally spelled "clon" but changed to clone by its coiner (H. J. Webber) for reasons of philology and euphony; proposed in application to horticultural varieties.
Coccus. A berry (plural *cocci*); in particular, one of the parts of a lobed fruit with one-seeded cells.
Coherent. Two or more similar parts or organs touching one another more or less adhesively but the tissues not fused; see also *Connate.*

Columella. The carpophores of the mericarpous fruits of Umbelliferæ.

Column. Body formed of union of stamens, style and stigmas in orchids, or of stamens, as in mallows.

Coma. The leafy crown or head, as of many palm trees.

Commissure. The place of joining or meeting; as the face by which one carpel joins another.

Comose. Bearing a tuft or tufts of hair.

Composite. Compound; said of an apparently simple or homogeneous organ or structure made up of several really distinct parts.

Compound. Of two or more similar parts in one organ.

Compound leaf. A leaf of two or more leaflets; in some cases (Citrus) the lateral leaflets may have been lost and only the terminal leaflet remains. *Ternately compound* when the leaflets are in 3's; *palmately compound* when three or more leaflets arise from a common point to be palmate (if only three are present they may be sessile); *pinnately compound* when arranged along a common rachis or if only three are present at least the terminal leaflet is stalked; *odd-pinnate* if a terminal leaflet is present and the total number of leaflets for the leaf is an odd number; *even-pinnate* if no terminal leaflet is present and the total is an even number.

Compound pistil. A pistil comprised of two or more carpels. The number of cells or locules within the ovary may or may not indicate the number of carpels. An ovary having more than one complete cell or locule is always compound, but many one-celled ovaries are compound also. A pistil having a one-celled ovary, but more than one placenta or more than one style or more than one stigma, or any combination of these duplicities, may be presumed to be compound insofar as taxonomic considerations are concerned.

Compressed. Flattened, especially flattened laterally.

Conduplicate. Two parts folded together lengthwise.

Cone. A dense and usually elongated collection of flowers or fruits that are borne beneath scales, the whole with scales and axis forming a detachable homogeneous fruit-like body; some cones are of short duration, as the staminate cones of pines, and others become dry and woody durable parts.

Connate. United or joined; in particular, like or similar structures joined as one body or organ.

Connective. The filament or tissue connecting the two cells of an anther, particularly when the cells are separated.

Connivent. Coming together or converging, but not organically connected; coherent.

Convolute. Said of floral envelopes in the bud when one edge overlaps the next part or petal or sepal or lobe while the other edge or margin is overlapped by a preceding part; rolled up.

Cordate. Heart-shaped; with a sinus and rounded lobes at the base and ovate in general outline.

Coriaceous. Of leathery texture, as a leaf of Buxus.

Corm. A solid bulb-like part, usually subterranean, as the "bulb" of crocus and gladiolus.

Cormel. A corm arising from a mother-corm.

Corniculate. Bearing or terminating in a small horn-like protuberance or process.

Corolla. Inner circle or whorl of floral envelopes; if the parts are separate, they are petals and the corolla is said to be polypetalous; if not separate, they are teeth, lobes, divisions or are undifferentiated, and the corolla is said to be gamopetalous or sympetalous.

Corona. Crown, coronet; any appendage or extrusion that stands between the corolla and stamens, or on the corolla, as the cup of a daffodil, or that is the outgrowth of the staminal part or circle, as in the milkweeds.

Corymb. Short and broad, more or less flat-topped indeterminate flower-cluster; outer flowers opening first.

Costapalmate. Said of a palmate palm leaf whose petiole continues through the blade as a distinct midrib, as in the palmetto.

Cotyledon. Seed-leaf; the primary leaf or leaves in the embryo; in some plants the cotyledon always remains in the seed-coats and in others (as bean) it emerges on germination.

Creeper. A trailing shoot that takes root mostly throughout its length; sometimes applied to a tight-clinging vine.

Cremocarp. A dry dehiscent two-seeded fruit of the umbellifer family, each half a mericarp borne on a hair-like carpophore.

Crenate. Shallowly round-toothed or obtusely toothed, scalloped.

Crested. With elevated and irregular or toothed ridge.

Crown. Corona; also that part of the stem at the surface of the ground; also a part of a rhizome with a large bud, suitable for use in propagation.

Crownshaft. A trunk-like extension of the bole formed by the long broad overlapping petiole-bases of some palms.

Culm. The stem of grasses and bamboos, usually hollow except at the swollen nodes.

Cultigen. Plant or group known only in cultivation; presumably originating under domestication; contrast with indigen.

Cultivar. A variety or race that has originated and persisted under cultivation, not necessarily referable to a botanical species.

Cuneate. Wedge-shaped; triangular, with the narrow end at point of attachment, as the bases of leaves or petals.

Cupule. Cup-like structure at base of some fruits (as in some palms) formed by the dry and enlarging floral envelopes.

Cuspidate. With an apex somewhat abruptly and sharply concavely constricted into an elongated sharp-pointed tip.

Cyathium. A type of inflorescence characteristic of Euphorbias; the unisexual flowers condensed and congested with a bracteate envelope from which they emerge at anthesis.

Cymba. A woody durable boat-like spathe or spathe-valve that incloses the inflorescence, opens and persists, as in many palms; see *Manubrium.*

Cymbiform. Boat-shaped.

Cyme. A broad more or less flat-topped determinate flower-cluster; with central flowers opening first.

Cymule. Diminutive of cyme, usually few-flowered.

GLOSSARY OF TERMS

Deciduous. Falling, as the leaves of non-evergreen trees.
Decompound. More than once compound.
Decumbent. Reclining or lying on the ground, but with the end ascending.
Decurrent. Running down the stem, as the leaf of mullein.
Decussate. Opposite leaves in four rows up and down the stem; alternating in pairs at right angles.
Deflexed. Reflexed.
Dehiscence. The method or process of opening of a seed-pod or anther: *loculicidally* dehiscent when the split opens into a cavity or locule, *septicidally* dehiscent when at point of union of septum or partition to the side wall, *circumscissally* when the top valve comes off as a lid, *poricidally* when by means of pores whose valves are often flap-like. The term is commonly applied to anthers or seed-pods.
Deliquescent. The primary axis or stem much-branched above, as in an elm or banyan tree.
Deltoid. Triangular; delta-like.
Dendron. In Greek compounds, signifying a tree.
Dentate. With sharp spreading rather coarse indentations or teeth that are perpendicular to the margin.
Denticulate. Minutely or finely dentate.
Depressed. More or less flattened endwise or from above; pressed down.
Determinate. Said of an inflorescence when the terminal (or central) flower opens first and axis prolongation is thereby arrested.
Diadelphous. In two sets as applied to stamens when the andrœcium is comprised of two bundles or clusters. In many legumes represented by nine stamens in one bundle and one solitary stamen in the second.
Diandrous. Having two stamens, as in Veronica.
Dichotomous. Forked in pairs.
Diclinous. Unisexual.
Didynamous. With four stamens in two pairs of different length.
Diffuse. Loosely branching or spreading; of open growth.
Digitate. Hand-like; compound with the members arising from one point, as the leaflets of horse-chestnut; see *Palmate.*
Dimorphic. Occurring in two forms, as in ferns with sterile foliaceous fronds and fertile fronds (or segments) not leaf-like.
Diœcious. Staminate and pistillate flowers on different plants; a term properly applied to plants, not to flowers.
Discoid. Having only disk-flowers, as in some Compositæ; or the stigma disk-shaped.
Disk. A more or less fleshy or elevated development of the receptacle about the pistil; receptacle in the head of Compositæ; a flattened extremity, as on tendrils of Virginia creeper.
Disk-flowers. The tubular flowers in the center of heads of most Compositæ, as distinguished from the ray-flowers.
Dissected. Divided into many slender segments.
Distichous. Two-ranked, with leaves, leaflets or flowers on opposite sides of a stem and in the same plane.
Distinct. Separate; not united with parts in the same series; compare *Free.*
Diurnal. Opening only during hours of daylight.
Divaricate. Spreading very far apart; extremely divergent.
Divergent. Spreading broadly.
Divided. Separated to the base.
Dorsal. Back; relating to the back or outer surface of a part or organ.
Dorsifixed. Attached by the back; often but not necessarily versatile.
Double. Said of flowers that have more than the usual or normal number of floral envelopes, particularly of petals; full.
Double-serrate. Coarse serrations bearing minute teeth on their margins.
Downy. Covered with very short and weak soft hairs.
Drupe. A fleshy one-seeded indehiscent fruit with seed inclosed in a stony endocarp; stone-fruit.
Drupelet. One drupe in a fruit made up of aggregate drupes, as in the raspberry.

E- or *Ex-*. In Latin-formed words, usually denoting, as a prefix, that parts are missing, as exstipulate, without stipules, estriate, without stripes.
Echinate. With stout bluntish prickles.
Elliptic. A flat part or body that is oval and narrowed to rounded ends and widest at or about the middle.
Elongate. Lengthened; stretched out.
Emarginate. With a shallow notch at the apex.
Embryo. The plantlet in the seed.
Endosperm. The starch- and oil-containing tissue of many seeds; often referred to as the albumen.
Ensiform. Sword-shaped.
Entire. Margin continuous; not in any way indented; whole.
Ephemeral. Persisting for one day only, as flowers of spiderwort.
Epi-. A Greek prefix signifying on or upon.
Epigynous. Borne on the ovary; used of floral parts when ovary is inferior and flower not perigynous.
Epiphyte. Air-plant; a plant growing on another or on some other elevated support.
Equitant. Overlapping in two ranks, as the leaves of Iris.
Erose. Said of a margin when appearing eroded or gnawed; of a jaggedness too small to be fringed or too irregular to be toothed.
Even-pinnate. See *Compound leaf.*
Evergreen. Remaining green in its dormant season; sometimes applied to plants that are green throughout the year.
Excurrent. Extending beyond the margin or tip, as a midrib developing into a mucro or awn.
Exfoliate. To peel off in shreds, thin layers or plates, as bark from a tree trunk.
Exserted. Sticking out; projecting beyond, as stamens from a perianth; not included.
Exstipulate. Without stipules.
Extrorse. Looking or facing outward; said of anther dehiscence and best determined by a cross-section of an undehisced anther.
Eye. The marked center of a flower; a bud on a tuber, as on a potato; a single-bud cutting.

Falcate. Sickle-shaped.
Falls. Outer whorl or series of perianth parts of an iridaceous flower, often broader than those of inner series and, in some Iris, drooping or flexuous.

Farinaceous. Containing starch, or starch-like materials.
Fasciated. Much flattened; an abnormal or teratological widening and flattening of the stem.
Fascicle. A condensed or close cluster, as of flowers, or of most pine leaves.
Fastigiate. Branches erect and more or less appressed, as in Lombardy poplar.
Feminine. Pistillate (in higher plants).
Fenestrate. Perforated with openings or with translucent areas.
Fertile. Said of pollen-bearing stamens and seed-bearing fruits.
Fetid. Having a disagreeable odor.
Filament. Thread, particularly the stalk of the anther.
Filiform. Thread-like; long and very slender.
Fimbriate. Fringed.
Flabellate. Fan-like.
Flaccid. Limp, floppy.
Flexuous. Having a more or less zigzag or wavy form; said of stems of various kinds.
Floccose. A surface covered with tufts of soft woolly hairs that usually rub off readily.
Florets. Individual flowers of composites and grasses; also other very small flowers that make up a very dense form of inflorescence.
Floricane. The flowering and fruiting stem, especially of a bramble or Rubus.
Floriferous. Flower-bearing.
Flower. An axis bearing one or more pistils or one or more stamens or both: when only the former, it is a *pistillate flower*, when only the latter a *staminate flower*, when both are present it is a *perfect flower* (i.e. bisexual or hermaphroditic). When this perfect flower is surrounded by a perianth represented by two floral envelopes (the inner envelope comprising the corolla, the outer the calyx), it is a *complete flower*.
Foliaceous. Leaf-like; said particularly of sepals and calyx-lobes and of bracts that in texture, size or color look like small or large leaves.
Follicle. Dry dehiscent fruit opening only on the front suture and the product of a simple pistil.
Free. Not joined to other organs; as petals free from the stamens or calyx or the veinlets (as in ferns) not united. Sometimes, however, the word is used in the sense of *distinct*.
Free-central. See *Placentation*.
Frond. Leaf of fern; sometimes used in the sense of foliage.
Fruit. The ripened ovary with the adnate parts; the seed-bearing organ.
Fruticose. Shrubby or shrub-like in the sense of being woody.
Fugacious. Falling or withering away very early.
Funiculus. The stalk by which an ovule is attached to the ovary wall or placenta.
Funnelform. With tube gradually widening upward and passing insensibly into the limb, as in many flowers of Convolvulus; infundibuliform.
Furcate. Forked.
Furrowed. With longitudinal channels or grooves.
Fusiform. Spindle-shaped; narrowed both ways from a swollen middle, as dahlia roots.

Galea. A helmet, as one sepal in an aconite flower.
Gamopetalous. Corolla of one piece; petals united, at least at base, the corolla removable as a single structure; sympetalous.
Geniculate. Bent, like a knee.
Gibbous. Swollen on one side, usually basally, as in a snapdragon corolla.
Glabrate. Nearly glabrous, or becoming glabrous with maturity or age.
Glabrous. Not hairy; often incorrectly used in the sense of *smooth* (which see).
Gland. Properly a secreting part or prominence or appendage, but often used in the sense of gland-like.
Glandular. Having or bearing secreting organs, or glands.
Glandular-pubescent. With glands and hairs intermixed.
Glandular-punctate. See *Punctate*.
Glaucescent. Slightly glaucous.
Glaucous. Covered with a "bloom" or a whitish substance that rubs off.
Glochid. A minute barbed spine or bristle, often in tufts as in many cacti.
Glomerate. In dense or compact cluster or clusters.
Glume. A small chaff-like bract; in particular, one of the two empty bracts at the base of a grass spikelet.
Glutinous. Sticky.
Granular, granulose. Covered with very small grains; minutely or finely mealy.
Gymnos. In Greek compounds, signifying naked or not covered; as gymnosperms, with naked seeds (not in a pericarp).
Gynœcium. The female element of a flower; a collective term employed for the several pistils of a single flower when referred to as a unit; when only one pistil is present the two terms (pistil and gynœcium) are synonymous.
Gynophore. Stipe of an ovary prolonged within the calyx.

Hastate. Of the shape of an arrow-head but the basal lobes pointed or narrow and standing nearly or quite at right angles; halberd-shaped.
Hastula. Terminal part of petiole on upper surface of leaf-blade of a palmate-leaved palm, sometimes called a ligule.
Head. A short dense spike; capitulum.
Heart-shaped. Cordate; ovate in general outline but with two rounded basal lobes; has reference particularly to the shape of the base of a leaf or other expanded part.
Hemi-. In Greek compounds, signifying half.
Herb. Plant naturally dying to the ground; without persistent stem above ground; lacking definite woody firm structure.
Herbaceous. Not woody; dying down each year; said also of soft branches before they become woody.
Herbage. Vegetative parts of plant.
Hermaphroditic. Bisexual.
Hetero-. In Greek composition, signifying various, or of more than one kind or form; as heterophyllous, with more than one kind or form of leaf.
Heterogamous. With two or more kinds or forms of flowers.
Hilum. In the seed, the scar or mark indicating the point of attachment.
Hippocrepiform. Horseshoe-shaped.
Hirsute. With rather rough or coarse hairs.
Hirtellous. Softly or minutely hirsute or hairy.
Hispid. Provided with stiff or bristly hairs.
Hispidulous. Somewhat or minutely hispid.

GLOSSARY OF TERMS

Hoary. Covered with a close white or whitish pubescence.
Homo-. In Greek compounds, signifying alike or very similar.
Hyaline. Translucent when viewed in transmitted light.
Hybrid. A plant resulting from a cross between two or more parents that are more or less unlike.
Hypanthium. The cup-like "receptacle" derived usually from the fusion of floral envelopes and androecium and on which are seemingly borne calyx, corolla and stamens (as in fuchsia or plum); once believed to have been formed solely by the enlargement of the torus; literally "beneath the flower"; the fruit-like body (as the rose-hip) formed by enlargement of the cup-like structure and bearing the achenes (the true fruits) on its upper and inner surface; sometimes termed the calyx-tube.
Hypocotyl. The axis of an embryo below the cotyledons which on seed germination develops into the radicle.
Hypocrateriform. See *Salverform.*
Hypogynous. Borne on the torus, or under the ovary; said of the stamens or petals.

Imbricated. Overlapping, as shingles on a roof.
Imparipinnate. Unequally pinnate; odd-pinnate; with a single terminal leaflet.
Incised. Cut; slashed irregularly, more or less deeply and sharply; an intermediate condition between toothed and lobed.
Included. Not protruded, as stamens not projecting from the corolla; not exserted.
Incumbent. Said of cotyledons that, within the seed, lie face to face with the back of one against the hypocotyl; anthers are incumbent when turned inward.
Indehiscent. Not regularly opening, as a seed-pod or anther.
Indeterminate. Said of those kinds of inflorescence whose terminal flowers open last, hence the growth or elongation of the main axis is not arrested by the opening of the first flowers.
Indigen. Indigenous inhabitant; a native.
Indumentum. Hairy or pubescent with rather heavy covering.
Induplicate. Rolled or folded inwards.
Indusium. The epithelial excrescence that, when present, covers or contains the sporangia of a fern when the latter are in sori.
Inferior. Beneath, lower, below; as an inferior ovary, one that is below the calyx-leaves.
Inflated. Blown up; bladdery.
Inflorescence. Mode of flower-bearing; technically less correct but much more common in the sense of a flower-cluster.
Infra-. In combinations, signifying below.
Infrafoliar. Below the leaves.
Infundibular. Funnel-shaped.
Inserted. Attached; as a stamen growing on the corolla.
Integument. The covering of an organ; the outer envelope of an ovule.
Inter-. In composition, signifying between, particularly between closely related parts or organs.
Interfoliar. Among the leaves.
Internode. The part of an axis between two nodes.
Interrupted. Not continuous; in particular, the interposition of small leaflets or segments between others.
Introrse. Turned or faced inward or toward the axis, as an anther whose line of dehiscence faces toward the center of flower.
Inverted. Turned over; end-for-end; top-side down.
Involucel. A secondary involucre; small involucre about the parts of a cluster.
Involucre. One or more whorls of small leaves or bracts (phyllaries) standing close underneath a flower or flower-cluster.
Involute. Said of a flat body (as a leaf) rolled inward or toward the upper side. See *Revolute.*
Irregular flower. Some parts different from otner parts in same series.

Jointed. With nodes, or points of real or apparent articulation.
Jugum. A pair, as of leaflets.

Keeled. Ridged like the bottom of a boat; also the two front united petals of a papilionaceous flower.

Labellum. Lip, particularly the lip of orchids.
Labiate. Lipped; a member of the Labiatæ.
Lacerate. Torn; irregularly cleft or cut.
Laciniate. Slashed into narrow pointed lobes.
Lacuna. A cavity, hole, or gap.
Lageniform. Gourd-shaped.
Lamina. A blade or expanded portion.
Lanate. Woolly, with long intertwined curly hairs.
Lanceolate. Lance-shaped; much longer than broad; widening above the base and tapering to the apex.
Lanuginose. Woolly or cottony; downy, the hairs somewhat shorter than in lanate.
Lanulose. Very short-woolly.
Lateral. On or at the side.
Latex. Milky sap.
Lax. Loose, the opposite of congested.
Leaflet. One part of a compound leaf; secondary leaf.
Leaf-stalk. The stem of a leaf; petiole; footstalk.
Legume. Simple fruit dehiscing on both sutures, and the product of a simple uni-carpellate ovary.
Lemma. In grasses, the flowering glume, the lower of the two bracts immediately inclosing the flower.
Lenticular. Lens-shaped.
Lepidote. Surfaced with small scurfy scales.
Ligulate. Strap-shaped, as a leaf.
Ligule. A strap-shaped organ or body; particularly, a strap-shaped corolla, as in the ray-flowers of composites; also a projection from the top of the sheath in grasses and similar plants.
Limb. The expanded flat part of an organ; in particular, the expanding part of a gamopetalous corolla.
Linear. Long and narrow, the sides parallel or nearly so, as blades of most grasses.
Lineate. Lined; bearing thin parallel lines.
Lingulate. Tongue-shaped.
Lip. One of the parts in an unequally divided corolla or calyx; these parts are usually two, the upper lip and the lower lip, although one lip is sometimes wanting; the upper lip of orchids is by a twist of the stipe made to appear as the lower; a labium.

GLOSSARY OF TERMS

Lobe. Any part or segment of an organ; specifically a part of petal or calyx or leaf that represents a division to about the middle.
Lobule. A small lobe.
Locule. Compartment or cell of an ovary, anther or fruit.
Loculicidal. Dehiscence on the back, between the partitions into the cavity.
Lorate. Strap-shaped; often also flexuous or limp or with apex not acuminate or acute.
Lyrate. Pinnatifid, but with an enlarged terminal lobe and smaller lower lobes.

Macrospore. The larger of the two kinds of spores, as in Selaginella and related plants; a megaspore.
Manubrium. The long thin more or less cylindrical base of certain cymbas or palm-spathes.
Marcescent. Withering, but the remains persisting.
Masculine. Staminate (in higher plants).
Membranous, membranaceous. Of parchment-like texture.
Mericarp. See *Schizocarp.*
-merous. In composition, referring to the numbers of parts; as flowers 5-merous, in which the parts of each kind or series are five or in fives.
Microsporangium. The microspore-containing case; an anther-sac.
Microspore. The smaller of the two kinds of spores in such pteridophytes as Selaginella; sometimes applied to pollen-grains.
Midrib. The main rib of a leaf or leaf-like part, a continuation of the petiole.
Monadelphous. Stamens united in one group by their filaments as in many Leguminosæ and mallows.
Moniliform. Constricted laterally and appearing bead-like.
Monœcious. Staminate and pistillate flowers on the same plant, as in corn. See *Diœcious.*
Monogynous. With one pistil.
Mucro. A short and sharp abrupt spur or spiny tip.
Mucronate. Terminated abruptly by a distinct and obvious mucro.
Mucronulate. Diminutive of mucronate.
Multiple fruit. One formed from several flowers into a single structure having a common axis, as in mulberry.
Muricate. Rough, due to presence of many minute spiculate excrescences on the epidermis.
Muriform. With brick-like markings, pits or reticulations, as on some seed-coats and achenes.

Naked flower. With no floral envelopes (perianth).
Navicular. Boat-shaped, as in glumes of most grasses.
Nectary. A nectar-secreting gland, often appearing as a protuberance, scale or pit.
Neutral flower. A sterile flower comprised of a perianth less any essential organs.
Nocturnal. Said of flowers that open at night and close during the day.
Node. A joint where a leaf is borne or may be borne; also incorrectly the space between two joints, which is properly an internode.
Novirame. A flowering or fruiting shoot arising from a primocane, sometimes encountered in blackberries.
Nut. An indehiscent one-celled and one-seeded hard and bony fruit, even if resulting from a compound ovary.
Nutlet. A small or diminutive nut; nucule.

Ob-. A Latin syllable, usually signifying inversion; as *obconical*, inversely conical, cone attached at the small point; *oblanceolate*, inversely lanceolate, with the broadest part of a lanceolate body above the middle; *obovate*, inverted ovate; *obovoid*, an ovoid body attached at the smaller end.
Obcordate. An apex, deeply lobed, the opposite of cordate.
Oblique. Slanting; unequal-sided.
Oblong. Longer than broad, and with the sides nearly or quite parallel most of their length.
Obsolete. Not evident or apparent; rudimentary.
Obtuse. Blunt, rounded.
Ocrea. A nodal sheath formed by fusion of two stipules.
Odd-pinnate. See *Compound leaf.*
Oligo-. In Greek compounds, signifying few, as *oligandrous*, with few stamens.
Operculate. With a cap or lid.
Opposite. Two at a node, on opposing sides of an axis.
Orbiculate. Circular or disk-shaped, as leaf of lotus or nasturtium.
Ortho-. In Greek compounds, signifying straight, as *orthotropous* (ovule or seed), an erect straight seed with the micropyle at the apex and hilum at the base.
Ovary. Ovule-bearing part of a pistil; one borne above the point of attachment of perianth and stamens, or surrounded by an hypanthium that is not adnate to it, is a *superior ovary;* when below attachment of these floral envelopes and adnate to them it is an *inferior ovary;* when intermediate it is a *half-inferior ovary;* when inferior the perianth and stamens are *hypogynous.*
Ovate. With an outline like that of hen's egg cut in two lengthwise, the broader end below the middle.
Ovoid. A solid that is oval (less correctly ovate) in flat outline.
Ovule. The body which, after fertilization, becomes the seed; the egg-containing unit of the ovary.

Palate. In personate corollas, a rounded projection or prominence of the lower lip, closing the throat or very nearly so.
Palea, palet. In the grass flower, the upper of the two inclosing bracts, the lower one being the lemma.
Palman. Undivided part of a palmate leaf between the petiole and segments of the blade, of particular pertinence to leaves of fan-palms.
Palmate. Lobed or divided or ribbed in a palm-like or hand-like fashion; digitate, although this word is usually restricted to leaves compound rather than to merely ribbed or lobed.
Palmatifid. Cut about half way down in a palmate form.
Pandurate. Fiddle-shaped.
Panicle. An indeterminate branching raceme; flower-cluster in which the branches are racemose, the flower being pedicellate
Papilionaceous corolla. Butterfly-like; pea-like flower, with a standard, wings and keel.

Papillate. Bearing minute pimple-like protuberances (papillæ).

Pappus. Peculiar modified calyx-limb of composites, borne on the ovary (persisting in fruit), being plumose, bristle-like, scales, or otherwise.

Parcifrond. A long leafy usually sterile shoot of a floricane, arising from below the ordinary floral branches.

Parietal. Borne on the side walls of an ovary (or capsule), or on invaginations of the wall that form incomplete partitions or false septæ within the ovary.

Parted. Cut or cleft not quite to the base.

Pectinate. Comb-like or pinnatifid with very close narrow divisions or parts; also used to describe spine conditions in cacti when small lateral spines radiate as comb-teeth from areole.

Pedate. Said of palmately lobed or divided leaf of which the two side lobes are again two-cleft.

Pedicel. Stem of one flower in a cluster.

Peduncle. Stem of a flower-cluster or of a solitary flower when that flower is the remaining member of an inflorescence.

Pellucid. Clear, transparent; that can nearly be seen through in transmitted light.

Peltate. Attached to its stalk inside the margin; peltate leaves are usually shield-shaped.

Penninerved. Nerves arising along the length of a central midrib.

Perennate. Lasting the whole year through; to renew itself by lateral shoots from the base.

Perennial. Of three or more seasons' duration.

Perianth. The two floral envelopes considered together; commonly used for flowers in which there is no clear distinction between calyx and corolla, as the lilies, the individual parts then sometimes called *tepals*.

Pericarp. The wall of a ripened ovary; sometimes used to designate a fruit.

Perigynous. Borne around the ovary and not beneath it, as when calyx, corolla and stamens arise from the edge of a cup-shaped hypanthium; such cases are said to exhibit perigyny.

Persistent. Remaining attached; not falling off.

Personate. Said of a two-lipped corolla the throat of which is closed by a palate, as in toadflax.

Perulate. Scale-bearing, as most buds.

Petal. One unit of the inner floral envelope or corolla of a polypetalous flower, usually colored and more or less showy.

Petaloid. Petal-like; of color and shape resembling a petal.

Petiole. Leaf-stalk.

Petiolule. Stalk of a leaflet.

Phylloclade. A branch, more or less flattened, functioning as a leaf, as in Christmas cactus.

Phyllodium. Leaf-like petiole and no blade, as in some acacias and other plants.

Phyllotaxy. The arrangement of leaves or floral parts on their axis; generally expressed numerically by a fraction, the numerator representing the number of revolutions of a spiral made in passing from one leaf past each successive leaf to reach the leaf directly above the initial leaf and the denominator representing the number of leaves passed in the spiral thus made.

Pilose. Shaggy with soft hairs.

Pinna. A primary division or leaflet of a pinnate leaf.

Pinnate. Feather-formed; with the leaflets of a compound leaf placed on either side of the rachis.

Pinnatifid. Cleft or parted in a pinnate (rather than palmate) way.

Pinnatisect. Cut down to the midrib in a pinnate way.

Pinnule. A secondary pinna or leaflet in a pinnately decompound leaf.

Pistil. The unit of the gynœcium, comprised of ovary, style and stigma: it may consist of one or more carpels; when with one carpel and a single placenta it is a *simple pistil*, when with two or more carpels it is a *compound pistil*. See *Carpel* and *Ovary*.

Pistillate. Having pistils and no functional stamens; female.

Pitted. Having little depressions or cavities.

Placenta. Part or place in the ovary where ovules are attached, a location only, not a structure.

Placentation. The arrangement of ovules within the ovary. Several types are recognized: *parietal placentation*, which see: *axile placentation*, the ovules borne in the center of the ovary on the axis formed by the union and fusion of the septæ (partitions) and usually in vertical rows; in two-celled ovaries they are borne in the center and on the cross-partition or on a proliferation of it often filling the loculi; *free central placentation*, the ovules borne on a central column with no septæ present; *basal placentation*, the ovules few or reduced to one and borne at the base of the ovary, the solitary ovule often filling the cavity; *lamellate placentation*, the ovules completely sunken in spongy ovarian and receptacular tissues with only the discoid stigmas exserted, or borne on plate-like lamellæ within the ovary, as in Nuphar.

Plicate. Folded, as in a fan, or approaching this condition.

Plumose. Plumy; feather-like; with fine hairs, as the pappus of some composites.

Pod. A dehiscent dry pericarp; a rather general uncritical term.

Pollen. Spores or grains borne by the anther, containing the male element.

Pollinium. A coherent mass of pollen, as in orchids and milkweeds.

Polygamo-diœcious. Said of a species that is functionally diœcious but having a few flowers of opposing sex or a few bisexual flowers on all plants at flowering time.

Polygamous. Bearing unisexual and hermaphrodite flowers on the same plant.

Polypetalous. With a corolla of separate petals.

Pome. Fruit of apple, pear, quince, and similar things.

Poricidal. See *Dehiscence*.

Porrect. Said of cactus spines when the central spines of an areole stand perpendicular to the surface

Posterior. At or toward the back; opposite the front; toward the axis; away from the subtending bract.

Præmorse. Appearing as if the end had been chewed or bitten off, very coarsely erose.

Prickle. A small and weak spine-like body borne irregularly on the bark or epidermis.

Primocane. The first season's shoot or cane of a biennial woody stem, as in many brambles.

Procumbent. Trailing or lying flat, but not rooting.

Proliferous. Bearing offshoots or redundant parts; bearing other similar structures on itself.

Prostrate. A general term for lying flat on the ground.

Protandrous. Said of a flower whose anthers mature and release their pollen before the stigma of the same flower is receptive.

Protogenous. A flower whose stigma is receptive to pollen before pollen is shed from anthers of the same flower.

Prothallus. The gametophyte stage or generation of pteridophytes, a cellular and usually flattened thallus-like structure on the ground, bearing the sexual organs, as the antheridia and archegonia

Pruinose. Having a bloom on the surface.

Pseud-, Pseudo-. In combinations means false, not genuine, not the true or the typical.

Pseudobulb. The thickened or bulb-form stems of certain orchids, the part being solid and borne above ground.

Pseudo-terminal bud. Seemingly the terminal bud of a twig, but actually the uppermost lateral bud with its subtending leaf-scar on one side and the scar of the terminal bud often visible on opposite side

Puberulent. Minutely pubescent.

Pubescent. Covered with short soft hairs; downy.

Pulvinate Cushion-shaped.

Pulvinus. A minute gland or swollen petiole (petiolule) base responsive to vibrations, as in leaves of sensitive-plant (Mimosa).

Punctate. With translucent or colored dots or depressions or pits.

Pungent. Ending in a stiff sharp point or tip; also acrid (to the taste).

Pustular. Blistery, usually minutely so.

Pyrene, pyrena. Nutlet particularly the nutlet in a drupe.

Pyriform. Pear-formed or -shaped.

Pyxis. A capsule dehiscing circumscissally, the top coming off as a lid.

Raceme. A simple elongated indeterminate inflorescence with pedicelled or stalked flowers.

Racemose. Having flowers in racemes.

Rachilla, rhachilla A diminutive or secondary axis, or rachis; in particular, in the grasses and sedges the axis that bears the florets

Rachis. Axis bearing flowers or leaflets; petiole of a fern frond (plural *rachides* or *rachises*).

Radiate. Standing on and spreading from a common center; also, with ray-flowers, as in the Compositæ.

Radical. Belonging or pertaining to the root.

Radicle The embryonic root of a germinating seed

Ramiform. Branching.

Raphides. Needle-like crystals of calcium oxalate.

Ray. Outer modified florets of some composites, with an extended or strap-like part to the corolla; also the branches of an umbel or umbel-like cluster.

Receptacle. Torus; the more or less enlarged or elongated end of the stem or flower-axis on which some or all of the flower-parts are borne; sometimes the receptacle is greatly expanded, as in the Compositæ.

Reclinate, reclining. Bent down or falling back from the perpendicular.

Recurved. Bent or curved downward or backward.

Reflexed Abruptly recurved or bent downward or backward.

Regular flower. With the parts in each series or set alike; as stamens all like each other, petals all like each other.

Reniform. Kidney-shaped.

Repand. Weakly sinuate.

Replum. Partition between the two loculi of cruciferous fruits.

Retrorse. Bent or turned over back or downward.

Retuse. Notched slightly at a usually obtuse apex.

Revolute. Rolled backward, margin rolled toward lower side. See *Involute.*

Rhizome. Underground stem; rootstock; distinguished from a root by presence of nodes, buds or scale-like leaves.

Rhomboidal. Shaped like a rhomboid.

Rib. In a leaf or similar organ, the primary vein; also any prominent vein or nerve.

Rootstock. Subterranean stem; rhizome.

Rosette. An arrangement of leaves radiating from a crown or center and usually at or close to the earth, as in dandelion.

Rostellum. A small beak.

Rostrate. Having a beak or beak-like projection.

Rotate. Wheel-shaped; with short or obsolete tube and a flat and circular limb.

Rotund. Nearly circular; orbicular inclining to be oblong.

Rugose. Wrinkled, usually covered with wrinkles.

Ruminate. Mottled in appearance, applied to a surface or tissue showing dark and light zones of irregular outline.

Runner. A slender trailing shoot taking root at the nodes.

Saccate. Bag-shaped, pouchy.

Sagittate. Like an arrow-head in form; triangular with the basal lobes pointing downward or concavely toward the stalk.

Salverform. With a slender tube and an abruptly expanded flat limb, as that of the phlox; hypocrateriform.

Samara. Indehiscent winged fruit, as of the maple and ash.

Sarmentose. Producing long flexuous runners or stolons.

Scabrous. Rough; feeling roughish or gritty to the touch.

Scale. A name given to many kinds of small mostly dry and appressed leaves or bracts; a vestige.

Scandent. Climbing without aid of tendrils.

Scape. Leafless peduncle arising from the ground; it may bear scales or bracts but no foliage-leaves and may be one- or many-flowered.

Scapose. Bearing its flowers on a scape.

Scarious. Leaf-like parts or bracts that are not green, but thin, dry, and membranaceous, often more or less translucent.

Schizocarp. A dry dehiscent fruit that splits into two halves, each half a mericarp, as in members of most umbellifers.

Scorpioid. Said of a circinnately coiled determinate inflorescence in which the flowers are two-ranked and borne alternately at the right and the left

Scutate. Like a small shield.

Secund. One-sided; said of inflorescences when the flowers appear as if borne from only one side.

Seed. The ripened ovule; the essential part is the embryo, and this is contained within integuments.

Segment. One of the parts of a leaf, petal, calyx, or perianth that is divided but not truly compound.

Sepal. One of the separate leaves of a calyx, usually green and foliaceous.

Septate. Partitioned; divided by partitions.

Septicidal. Dehiscence along or in the partitions, not directly into the locule.

Septum. A partition.

Sericeous. Silky.

Serrate. Said of a margin when saw-toothed with the teeth pointing forward.

Serrulate. Minutely serrate.

Sessile. Not stalked; sitting.

Seta. A bristle.

Setiform. Bristle-shaped.

Setose. Covered with bristles.

Sheath. Any long or more or less tubular structure surrounding an organ or part.

Shrub. A woody plant that remains low and produces shoots or trunks from the base.

Sigmoid. Said of a leaflet or segment that is curved sidewise in opposing directions; S-shaped.

Silicle. The short fruit of certain Cruciferæ, usually not more than twice as long as wide.

Silique. The long fruit of certain Cruciferæ.

Silky. A condition produced by a covering of soft appressed fine hairs; sericeous.

Silvery. With a whitish metallic more or less shining luster.

Simple. Said of a leaf when not compounded into leaflets, of an inflorescence when not branched.

Sinus. The space or recess between two lobes or divisions of a leaf or other expanded organ.

Smooth. Said of surfaces that have no hairiness, roughness or pubescence, particularly of those not rough or scabrous. See *Glabrous.*

Solitary. Borne singly or alone.

Sorus. A heap or cluster. The fruit-dots or -clusters of fruiting bodies of ferns (plural *sori*) usually located on the dorsal side of the frond.

Spadix. A thick or fleshy spike of certain plants, as the Araceæ, surrounded or subtended by a spathe.

Spathe. The bract or leaf surrounding or subtending a flower-cluster or a spadix; it is sometimes colored and flower-like, as in the calla. See *Cymba.*

Spathe-valves. One or more herbaceous or scarious bracts that subtend an inflorescence or flower and generally enveloping the subtended unit when in bud.

Spatulate. Spoon-shaped.

Spicate. With spikes or spike-like structures.

Spike. A usually unbranched, elongated, simple, indeterminate inflorescence whose flowers are sessile; the flowers may be congested or remote; a seemingly simple inflorescence whose "flowers" may actually be composite heads (Liatris).

Spikelet. A secondary spike; one part of a compound inflorescence which of itself is spicate; the floral unit, or ultimate cluster, of a grass inflorescence comprised of flowers and their subtending bracts.

Spine. A strong and sharp-pointed woody body mostly arising from the wood of the stem.

Spinescent. More or less spiny.

Sporangium. A spore-case; a sac or body bearing spores.

Spore. A simple reproductive body, usually composed of a single detached cell, and containing no embryo; used particularly in the pteridophytes and lower orders.

Sporocarp. A receptacle containing sporangia or spores.

Sporophyll. A spore-bearing leaf.

Spreading. Standing outward or horizontally.

Spur. A tubular or sac-like projection from a blossom, as of a petal or sepal; it usually contains a nectar-secreting gland.

Squamate. With small scale-like leaves or bracts; scaly.

Squamose. Covered with small scales, more coarsely so than when lepidote.

Stachys-. In Greek compounds, signifying a spike.

Stalk. The stem of any organ, as the petiole, peduncle, pedicel, filament, stipe.

Stalked bud. One whose outer scales are attached above the base of the bud axis.

Stamen. The unit of the andrœcium and typically comprised of anther and filament, sometimes reduced to only an anther; the pollen-bearing organ of a seed-plant.

Staminate. Having stamens and no pistils; male.

Staminode, staminodium. A sterile stamen, or a structure resembling such and borne in the staminal part of the flower; in some flowers (as in canna) staminodia are petal-like and showy.

Standard. The upper and broad more or less erect petal of a papilionaceous flower; the narrow usually erect or ascending inner series of perianth of an iris flower as opposed to the broader often drooping falls.

Stellate. Star-like; stellate hairs have radiating branches or when falsely stellate are separate hairs aggregated into star-like clusters; hairs once or twice forked are often treated as stellate.

Stem. The main axis of a plant; leaf-bearing and flower bearing as distinguished from the root-bearing axis.

Stigma. The part of the pistil that receives the pollen.

Stigmatic. Pertaining to the stigma.

Stipe. The stalk of a pistil or other small organ; also the petiole of a fern leaf.

Stipel. Stipule of a leaflet.

Stipule. A basal appendage of a petiole; the three parts of a complete leaf are blade, petiole, stipules (usually two).

Stolon. A shoot that bends to the ground and takes root; more commonly, a horizontal stem at or below surface of the ground that gives rise to a new plant at its tip.

Striate. With fine longitudinal lines, channels or ridges.

Strict. Straight and upright, little if any branched, often rigid.

Strobile. Cone.

Style. More or less elongated part of the pistil between the ovary and the stigma.

Stylopodium. A disk-like enlargement at the base of the style, as in some umbellifers.

Sub-. As a prefix, usually signifying somewhat, slightly or rather.

Subtend. To stand below and close to, as a bract underneath a flower, particularly when the bract is prominent or persistent. The flower is in the axil of the bract.
Subulate. Awl shaped, tapering from base to apex.
Succulent. Juicy; fleshy; soft and thickened in texture.
Suffruticose. Pertaining to a low and somewhat woody plant; diminutively shrubby or fruticose; woody at base with herbaceous shoots produced perennially.
Sulcate. Grooved or furrowed lengthwise.
Superior. Said of an ovary that is free from the calyx or perianth; see *Ovary*.
Supine. Lying flat and with face upwards.
Suprafoliar. Above the leaves.
Suture. A line or mark of splitting open; a groove marking a natural division or union; the groove lengthwise a plum or similar fruit.
Syconium. The fruit of a fig.
Symmetrical. Said of a regular flower that has the same number of parts in each series or circle as five stamens, five petals.
Sympetalous. The petals united, at least at the base: see *Corolla*.
Sympodial inflorescence. A determinate inflorescence that simulates an indeterminate inflorescence, as if a scorpioid cyme were straight rather than circinnate.
Synandrium. An andrœcium coherent by the anthers as in some aroids; when anthers are connate they are termed syngenesious.
Syncarpous. Having carpels united; sometimes used when separate pistils within one flower are partially united. See *Apocarpous*.
Syngenesious. Stamens connate by their anthers to form a cylinder about the style, as in all of the Compositæ.

Tailed. Said of anthers having caudal appendages.
Tapering. Gradually becoming smaller or diminishing in diameter or width toward one end; not abrupt.
Tendril. A rotating or twisting thread-like process or extension by which a plant grasps an object and clings to it for support; morphologically it may be stem or leaf.
Tepal. A segment of those perianths not clearly differentiated into typical corolla and calyx, as in tulip or onion.
Terete. Circular in transverse section; imperfectly cylindrical because the object may taper both ways.
Terminal. At the tip or distal end.
Ternate. In threes.
Testa. Outer coat of a seed.
Tetradynamous. An andrœcium of six stamens, four longer than the other two, as in Cruciferæ.
Thallus. A flat leaf-like organ; in some cryptogams, the entire cellular plant body without differentiation as to stem and foliage.
Throat. The opening or orifice into a gamopetalous corolla, or perianth; the place where the limb joins the tube.
Thyrse, thyrsus. Compact and more or less compound panicle; more correctly a panicle-like cluster with main axis indeterminate and other parts determinate, as in most lilacs.
Tomentose. With tomentum; densely woolly or pubescent; with matted soft wool-like hairiness.
Tomentulose. Somewhat or delicately tomentose.
Torulose. Twisted or knobby; irregularly swollen at close intervals.
Torus. Receptacle.
Tree. A woody plant that produces one main trunk and a more or less distinct and elevated head.
Tri-. Three or three times.
Trichoma. A hair or bristle.
Trifoliate. Three-leaved, as in Trillium.
Trifoliolate. Having a leaf or leaves of three leaflets, as most clovers.
Triquetrous. Three-angled in cross-section.
Triternate. Three times three; the leaflets or segments of a twice ternate leaf again in three parts.
Truncate. Appearing as if cut off at the end; the base or apex nearly or quite straight across.
Tuber. A short congested part; usually defined as subterranean (as of a rootstock), although this is not essential.
Tubercle. A small tuber, or rounded protruding body.
Tumid. Swollen, inflated.
Tunic. A loose membranous outer skin not the epidermis; the loose membrane about a corm or bulb.
Tunicated. Provided with a tunic as defined above; having concentric or enwrapping coats or layers, as bulb of onion.
Turbinate. Inversely conical; top-shaped.
Turgid. Swollen from fullness.
Turion. A young shoot or sucker as an emerging stem of asparagus.
Twig. A young woody stem; more precisely the shoot of a woody plant representing the growth of the current season and terminated basally by circumferential terminal bud-scar.

Umbel. An indeterminate often flat-topped inflorescence whose pedicels and peduncles (rays) arise from a common point, resembling the stays of an umbrella; umbels are characteristic of the Umbelliferæ and are usually compound, each primary ray terminated by a secondary umbel (*umbellet*).
Umbellate. Umbelled; with umbels; pertaining to umbels.
Umbo. A conical projection arising from the surface.
Uncinate. Hooked obtusely at the tip.
Undulate. Wavy (up and down, not in and out), as some leaf or petal margins.
Unguiculate. Narrowed into a petiole-like base; clawed.
Unijugate. A compound leaf comprised of one pair of leaflets.
Unisexual. Of one sex; staminate only or pistillate only.
Urceolate. Urn-shaped.
Utricle. A small bladder; a bladdery one-seeded usually indehiscent fruit.

Vaginate. Sheathed.
Valvate. Opening by valves or pertaining to valves; meeting by the edges without overlapping, as leaves or petals in the bud.
Valve. A separable part of a pod; the units or pieces into which a capsule splits or divides in dehiscing.
Vasiform. Of elongated funnel-shape.

Velutinous. Clothed with a velvety indumentum comprised of erect straight moderately firm hairs.

Venation. Veining; arrangement or disposition of veins.

Ventral. Front; relating to the anterior or inner face or part of an organ; opposite the back or dorsal part.

Ventricose. A one-sided swelling or inflation, more pronounced than when gibbous.

Vernation. The disposition or arrangement of leaves in the bud.

Verrucose. Having a wart-like or nodular surface.

Versatile. Hung or attached near the middle and usually moving freely, as an anther attached crosswise on apex of filament and capable of turning.

Verticil. A whorl.

Verticillate. Arranged in whorls, or seemingly so.

Verticillate inflorescence. One with the flowers in whorls about the axis, the whorls remote from one another (as in many salvias) or congested into head-like structures (catnip). Such whorls are false whorls since they are actually sessile cymes arranged opposite one another in the axils of opposite bracts or leaves.

Vesicle. A small bladdery sac or cavity filled with air or fluid.

Vesture. Anything on or arising from a surface causing it to be other than glabrous.

Vexillum. The broad upper petal of a papilionaceous corolla; the standard or banner.

Villous. Provided with long and soft, not matted, hairs; shaggy.

Virgate. Wand-like; long, straight and slender.

Viscid. Sticky, or with appreciable viscosity.

Voluble. Twining.

Whorl. Three or more leaves or flowers at one node, in a circle.

Wing. A thin dry or membranaceous expansion or flat extension or appendage of an organ; also the lateral petals of a papilionaceous flower.

Woolly. Provided with long, soft and more or less matted hairs; like wool; lanate.

Zygomorphic. Irregular; said of corollas when divisible into equal halves in one plane only, usually along an anterior-posterior line: see *Actinomorphic*.

AUTHORITIES FOR THE BINOMIALS

When the student finds "*Asparagus officinalis, L.*," he is to understand that the authority for the same is Linnæus (L.)—the person who first put the two words together to designate this particular kind of plant, with proper authority. When he finds "*Iris halophila*, Pall.," he knows that Pallas made the name; the citation of the author identifies the species, gives a clue to its place of publication and its history, and distinguishes it from the plant called *I. halophila* by Ker or by any other author. The authority is not part of the plant name, but it becomes so closely associated with the binomial as to be cited whenever botanical and historical accuracy is necessary. In common popular writing and speech it is seldom necessary, or even in good taste, to cite the authority.

To save space and to give the presentation a simpler aspect, most names of authors are abbreviated when used in connection with the binomial. The present list explains what the abbreviations mean, and also provides certain information about the authors.

Sometimes the species is transferred to another genus from the one in which it was first described. The species-name follows it wherever it goes. The name of the original author, in such cases, is sometimes cited in parentheses and the author of the accepted combination follows it, as *Ipomœa purpurea* (L.) Roth, which means that Linnæus first employed the name but in another connection (under Convolvulus) and that Roth transferred it to Ipomœa, where it now rests. This method of double citation is not employed in this book inasmuch as it is cumbersome in a popular treatment and in most cases not significant; the authorities here cited are those responsible for the current binomial, genus and species together. The synonyms provide the history, in this book.

The following list will be useful also in identifying the authors of genera; thus "Chrysalidocarpus, Wendl.," means that Hermann Wendland founded the genus.

ABBOTT. George Abbott, contemporaneous, American palm specialist.

ADANS. Michel Adanson, 1727-1806. France.

AGARDH. Jacob Georg Agardh, 1813–1901. Sweden.

AHRENDT. Leslie Walter Allan Ahrendt, 1903–. Great Britain.

AIRY-SHAW. Herbert Kenneth Airy-Shaw, 1902–. Royal Botanic Gardens, Kew, England.

AIT. William Aiton, 1731–1793. England.

AIT. f. William Townsend Aiton, the son, 1766–1849. England.

AITCH. James Edward Tierney Aitchison, 1836–1898, collector in Asia. Great Britain.

ALEF. Friedrich Alefeld, 1820–1872. Germany.

ALL. Carlo Allioni, 1725–1804. Italy.

ALLAN. Henry Howard Allan, 1882–. New Zealand.

ALSTON. Arthur Hugh Garfit Alston, 1902–. British Museum, London, England.

AMBROSI. Francesco Ambrosi, 1821–1897. Italy.

AMES. Oakes Ames, 1874–, orchid specialist. Harvard University.

L. M. AMES. Lawrence M. Ames, 1900–. United States.

E. ANDERS. Edgar Anderson, 1897–. Missouri Botanical Garden, St. Louis.

T. ANDERS. Thomas Anderson, 1832–1870, director of Botanic Garden in Calcutta.

AUTHORITIES FOR THE BINOMIALS

Andersen. Johannes C. Andersen, 1873–. New Zealand.

Anderss. Nils Johan Andersson, 1821–1880. Sweden.

Andr. Henry C. Andrews, died 1830, botanical artist and engraver, conducted the Botanists' Repository from 1799–1811.

André. Edouard André, 1840–1911, first editor of L'Illustration Horticole, later editor-in-chief of Revue Horticole. France.

Ant. Franz Antoine, 1815–1886. Austria.

Applegate. Elmer Ivan Applegate, 1876–. California.

Arcang. Giovanni Arcangeli, 1840–1921. Italy.

Arends. H. A. Arends, contemporaneous German nurseryman.

Armstr. John B. Armstrong, superintendent of public gardens, Christchurch, New Zealand, wrote about 1880.

Arn. George Arnold Walker Arnott, 1799–1868. Scotland.

Arnold. Johann Franz Xaver Arnold, published 1785. Austria.

Arthur. Joseph Charles Arthur, 1850–1942. Indiana.

Aschers. Paul Friedrich August Ascherson, 1834–1913, professor of botany, Berlin.

Ashe. William Willard Ashe, 1872–1932. Washington, D. C.

Aubl. Jean Baptiste Christophe Fusée Aublet, 1720–1778. France.

Audubon. John James Audubon, 1785–1851, American ornithologist.

Auth. Authors; referring to usage by various or many writers.

Avé-Lall. Jules Léopold Edouard Avé-Lallemant, 1803–1867. Germany.

Bab. Charles Cardale Babington, 1808–1895. Great Britain.

Backeberg. Curt Backeberg, 1894–, cactus specialist. Germany.

Backer. Cornelius Adries Backer, 1874–. Holland.

Backh. James Backhouse, 1825–1890, British nurseryman.

Bailey. L. H. Bailey, 1858–.

Baill. Henri Ernest Baillon, 1827–1895, author of the natural history of plants in French.

Baker. John Gilbert Baker, 1834–1920, Keeper of the Herbarium of the Royal Botanic Gardens, Kew, England.

Bal. Benedict Balansa, 1825–1891. France.

Balbis. Giovanni Battista Balbis, 1765–1831. Italy.

Balf. John Hutton Balfour, 1808–1884. Great Britain.

Balf. f. Isaac Baily Balfour, 1853–1922. Great Britain.

Ball. John Ball, 1818–1889. Great Britain.

Banks. Sir Joseph Banks, 1743–1820. Great Britain.

Barbier. Barbier & fils, French nurserymen about 1900.

Barb.-Rodr. João Barbosa-Rodrigues, 1842–1909. Brazil.

Barn. François Marius Barnéoud, born 1821. France.

Barnhart. John Hendley Barnhart, 1871–. Southampton, New York.

Baroni. Eugenio Baroni, 1865–. Italy.

Barry. Patrick Barry, 1816–1890, nurseryman. Rochester, New York.

Bartling. Friedrich Gottlieb Bartling, 1798–1875. Germany.

Barton. Benjamin Smith Barton, 1766–1815. Pennsylvania.

Bartram. William Bartram, 1739–1823. Pennsylvania.

Batalin. Alexander Batalin, 1847–1898. Russia.

Batem. James Bateman, 1811–1897, writer on orchids. England.

Batsch. August Johann Georg Karl Batsch, 1761–1802. Germany.

Batt. Jules Aimé Battandier, 1848–1922. Algiers.

Baumann. Charles & Constantin Auguste Napoleon Baumann, 1804–1884, French nurserymen.

Baumg. Johann Christian Gottlob Baumgarten, 1765–1843. Germany.

Bayer. Johann Nepomuk Bayer, 1802–1870. Austria.

Beal. William James Beal, 1833–1924. Michigan.

Bean. William Jackson Bean, 1863–1947. Royal Botanic Gardens, Kew, England.

Beauv. Ambroise Marie François Joseph Palisot de Beauvois, 1755–1820. France.

Beauverd. Gustave Beauverd, 1867–1942. Switzerland.

Becc. Odoardo Beccari, 1843–1920, Italian botanist and world authority on palms.

Beck. Lewis Caleb Beck, 1798–1853. New York.

G. Beck. Guenther Beck von Mannagetta, 1856–1931. Austria.

Becker. Johannes Becker, 1769–1833. Germany.

Beckmann. Johan Beckmann, 1739–1811. Germany and Sweden.

Beer. Joseph Georg Beer, 1803–1873, writer on orchids and bromeliads. Austria.

Beissn. Ludwig Beissner, 1853–1927. Germany.

Bell. Carlo Antonio Ludovico Bellardi, 1741–1826, Italian botanist and physician.

Benedict. Ralph Curtiss Benedict, 1883–. Brooklyn Botanic Garden.

Benson. Lyman Benson, 1909–. Pomona College, Claremont, California.

Benth. George Bentham, 1800–1884. England.

Bercht. Friedrich, Graf von Berchtold, 1781–1876. Austria.

Berckmans. Prosper Jules Alphonse Berckmans, 1830–1910, American nurseryman.

Berg. Otto Karl Berg, 1815–1866. Germany.

Berger. Alwin Berger, 1871–1931. Germany.

Bergg. Sven Berggren, 1837–1917. Sweden.

Bergius. Peter Jonas Bergius, 1730–1790. Sweden.

Bergmans. Johannes Baptista Bergmans, 1892–, Dutch horticulturist and author.

Berl. Jean Louis Berlandier, 1805–1851. France.

Bernh. Johann Jacob Bernhardi, 1774–1850. Germany.

Bert. Antonio Bertoloni, 1775–1869, Italian botanist and physician.

Bertero. Carlo Guiseppe Bertero, 1789–1831. Italy.

Berth. Sabin Berthelot, 1794–1880, author, with Webb, of Flore des Iles Canaries.

Berthault. Pierre Berthault, contemporaneous. France.

BERTIN. Pierre Bertin, 1800–1891, French nurseryman.
BESS. Wilibald Swibert Joseph Gottlieb Besser, 1784–1842. Russia.
BETCKE. Ernst Friedrich Betcke, died 1865. Mecklenburg, Germany.
BICKN. Eugene Pintard Bicknell, 1859–1925. New York and Massachusetts.
BIEB. Friedrich August Marschall von Bieberstein, 1768–1826. Germany, later Russia.
BIGEL. Jacob Bigelow, 1787–1879. Massachusetts.
BINN. Simon Binnendijk, 1821–1883. Holland and Java.
BITTER. Georg Bitter, 1873–1927. Germany.
BLAKE. Sidney Fay Blake, 1892—. United States Department of Agriculture.
BLANCH. William Henry Blanchard, 1850–1922. Vermont.
BLANCO. Manuel Blanco, 1780–1845. Philippines.
BLUME. Karl Ludwig Blume, 1796–1862, writer on Javan plants. Holland.
BOEHMER. Georg Rudolph Boehmer, 1723–1803. Germany.
BOEHMER. Louis B. Boehmer & Co., died 1896, nurserymen in Japan.
BOENN. Clemens Maria Friedrich Boenninghausen, 1785–1864. Germany.
BOERL. Jacob Gijsbert Boerlage, 1849–1900. Holland.
BOIS. Désiré Georges Jean Marie Bois, 1856–1946. France.
BOISS. Edmond Boissier, 1810–1886, author of Flora Orientalis. Switzerland.
BOJER. Wenjel Bojer, 1797–1856, author of Hortus Mauritianus. Austria.
BOLANDER. Henry Nicholas Bolander, 1831–1897, early California botanist, German-born.
L. BOLUS. Louisa Bolus, 1877–. South Africa.
BOMHARD. Miriam Lucille Bomhard, 1898–. United States Forest Service.
BONAF. Matthieu Bonafous, 1793–1852, French horticulturist.
BONG. Heinrich Gustav Bongard, 1786–1839. Russia.
BONPL. Aimé Jacques Alexandre Bonpland, 1773–1858. France and South America.
BOOTT. Francis Boott, 1792–1863. United States and England.
BORB. Vincze tól Borbás, 1844–1905. Hungary.
BOREAU. Alexandre Boreau, 1803–1875. France.
BORG. John Borg, 1873–. Italy.
BORNM. Joseph Friedrich Nicolaus Bornmueller, 1862–. Germany.
BORT. Katherine Stephens Bort, born 1870, United States Department of Agriculture (retired 1923).
BORY. Jean Baptiste Geneviève Marcelin Bory de St. Vincent, 1778–1846. France.
BOUCHÉ. Carl David Bouché, 1809–1881. Germany.
BOULENGER. George Albert Boulenger, 1858–1937. Belgium.
BOWERS. Clement Gray Bowers, 1893–, geneticist. Maine, New York.
BOWLES. Edward Augustus Bowles, 1865–. Royal Horticultural Society, England.
A. BR. Alexander Braun, 1805–1877. Germany.
F. E. BR. F. E. Brown.
N. E. BR. Nicholas Edward Brown, 1849–1934. Royal Botanic Gardens, Kew, England.
P. BR. Patrick Browne, 1720–1790. Great Britain.
R. BR. Robert Brown, 1773–1858. Great Britain.
S. BR. Stewardson Brown, 1867–1921. Academy of Natural Sciences, Philadelphia.
BRACK. William D. Brackenridge, 1810–1893, botanist on Wilkes Expedition.
BRAND. August Brand, 1863–1931. Germany.
BRANDEGEE. Townsend S. Brandegee, 1843–1925. California.
BR.-BLANQ. Josias Braun-Blanquet, 1884–. France.
BREWER. William H. Brewer, 1828–1910, collector in California.
BRIOT. Charles Briot, 1804–1888, French nurseryman.
BRIQ. John Isaac Briquet, 1870–1931. Switzerland.
BRITT. Nathaniel Lord Britton, 1859–1934, Director, New York Botanical Garden.
BRITTEN. James Britten, 1846–1924. England.
BRONGN. Adolphe Théodore Brongniart, 1801–1876. France.
BROT. Felix de Avellar Brotero, 1744–1828. Portugal.
BROUSS. Pierre Marie August Broussonet, 1761–1807. France.
BRUEGG. Christian Georg Bruegger, 1833–1899. Switzerland.
BRUMH. Philipp Brumhard, 1879–, author monograph of Erodium. Breslau, Germany.
BSP. N. L. Britton, E. A. Sterns, J. Poggenburg, authors of a catalogue of plants growing within 100 miles of New York City, 1888.
BUBANI. Pietro Bubani, 1806–1888. Italy.
BUCHENAU. Franz Georg Buchenau, 1831–1906. Germany.
BUCH.-HAM. Francis Buchanan, later Lord Hamilton, 1762–1829, British botanist, wrote on Indian plants.
BUCHHOLZ. John Theodore Buchholz, 1888–. University of Illinois.
BUC'HOZ. Pierre Joseph Buc'hoz, 1731–1807. France.
BUCKL. Samuel Botsford Buckley, 1809–1884. United States.
BULL. William Bull, 1828–1902, plant merchant. England.
BUNGE. Alexander von Bunge, 1803–1890, Russian physician and botanist.
BUR. Edouard Bureau, 1830–1918. France.
BURB. Frederick William Burbidge, 1847–1905. Great Britain.
BURCK. William Burck, 1848–1910. Holland and Java.
BURGSD. Friedrich August Ludwig von Burgsdorf, 1747–1802. Germany.
BURKART. Arturo Burkart, contemporaneous. Argentina.
BURKWOOD. Albert Burkwood, 1890–, and Arthur Burkwood, 1888–, British nurserymen.
BURM. Johannes Burman, 1706–1779. Holland.
BURM. f. Nicolaus Laurens Burman, the son, 1734–1793. Holland.
BURV. Frédéric Burvenich, 1857–1917, Belgian horticulturist.
BUSE. L. H. Buse, 1819–1888. Holland.
BUSH. Benjamin Franklin Bush, 1858–1937. Missouri.
BUTTERS. Frederic King Butters, 1878–1945. University of Minnesota.

CAMBESS. Jacques Cambessèdes, 1799–1863. Montpellier, France.
CARIOT. Abbé Antoine Cariot, wrote 1820–1833. France.
CARR. Elie Abel Carrière, 1816–1896, editor of Revue Horticole. France.
CARUEL. Teodoro Caruel, 1830–1898. Italy.
CASP. Johann Xavier Robert Caspary, 1818–1887. University of Konigsberg, Germany.
CASS. Comte de Alexandre Henri Gabriel Cassini, 1781–1832. France.
CAV. Antonio José Cavanilles, 1745–1804. University of Madrid, Spain.
CERV. Vicente Cervantes, 1755–1829. Mexico.
CHABAUD. S. B. Chabaud, 1833–1915. France.
CHAIX. Dominique Chaix, 1731–1800. France.
CHAM. Adalbert von Chamisso, 1781–1838, poet and naturalist. Germany.
CHAMP. Lieut.-Col. John George Champion, 1815–1854. Scotland.
CHANDLER. Harley Pierce Chandler, 1875–1918. California.
CHAPM. Alvan Wentworth Chapman, 1809–1899, author of Flora of the Southern United States. Florida.
CHASE. Agnes Chase, 1869–, specialist on grasses. United States National Herbarium.
CHAUB. Louis Anastase Chaubard, 1785–1854. France.
CHEVAL. Auguste J. B. Chevalier, 1873–. France.
CHITTENDEN. Frederick James Chittenden, 1873–, British horticulturist.
CHODAT. Robert Hippolyte Chodat, 1865–1934. Switzerland.
CHOISY. Jacques Denys Choisy, 1799–1859. Switzerland.
C. CHR. Carl Christensen, 1872–1942. Denmark.
CHRIST. Hermann Christ, 1833–1933. Switzerland.
CHRISTM. Gottlieb Friedrich Christmann, born 1752. Germany.
CLARKE. Charles Baron Clarke, 1832–1906. Great Britain.
CLAUSEN. Robert Theodore Clausen, 1911–. Cornell University.
CLAYTON. John Clayton, 1686–1773. Virginia.
CLOS. Dominique Clos, 1821–1908, professor of botany and director of the gardens in Toulouse.
CLUTE. Willard Nelson Clute, 1869–. Indianapolis.
COCKAYNE. Leonard C. Cockayne, 1855–1934. New Zealand.
COCKERELL. Theodore Dru Alison Cockerell, 1866–1948. Colorado.
COE. Howard Sheldon Coe, 1888–1918. United States Department of Agriculture.
E. F. COE. Ernest F. Coe, contemporaneous American horticulturist.
COEM. Abbé Henri Eugène Lucien Coemans, 1825–1871. Ghent, Belgium.
COGN. Célestin Alfred Cogniaux, 1841–1916. France.
COLL. Sir Henry Collett, 1836–1901. Great Britain.
COLLA. Luigi (Aloysius) Colla, 1766–1848. Italy.
COMES. Orazio Comes, 1848–1923. Italy.
COMM. Philibert Commerson, 1727–1773. France and Mauritius.
CONARD. Henry Shoemaker Conard, 1874–. Grinnell, Iowa.
CONSOLE. Michelangelo Console, 1812–1897. Palermo, Italy.
O. F. COOK. Orator Fuller Cook, 1867–. United States Department of Agriculture.
COPELAND. Edwin Bingham Copeland. 1873–. Berkeley, California.
CORNER. Edred John Henry Corner, 1906–. England and Singapore.
CORNMAN. John F. Cornman, 1913–. Cornell University.
CORRELL. Donovan Stewart Correll, 1908–. Botanical Museum, Harvard University.
CORREVON. J. Henry Correvon, 1855–1939, Swiss horticulturist.
CORY. Victor Louis Cory, 1880–. Southern Methodist University, Dallas, Texas.
COSS. Ernest Saint-Charles Cosson, 1819–1889. France.
COSTE. Abbé Hippolyte Jacques Coste, 1858–1924. France.
COULT. John Merle Coulter, 1851–1928. United States.
COURT. Richard Joseph Courtois, 1806–1835. Belgium.
COV. Frederick Vernon Coville, 1867–1937. Washington, D. C.
COWELL. John Francis Cowell, 1852–1915. United States.
CRAIB. William Grant Craib, 1882–1933. Great Britain.
CRANTZ. Heinrich Johann Nepomuk von Crantz, 1722–1797. Austria.
CRÉP. François Crépin, 1830–1903. Belgium.
CRIVELLI. Giuseppe Gabriel Balsamo-Crivelli, 1800–1874. Italy.
CROIZAT. Leon Camille Marius Croizat, 1894–. Caracas, Venezuela.
CRONQUIST. Arthur Cronquist, 1919–. Georgia.
CROOM. Hardy Bryan Croom, 1797–1837. United States.
CROUCHER. George Croucher, 1833–1905, gardener to Mr. Peacock of Hammersmith, England.
CROVETTO. Raul Martinez Crovotto, 1921–. Argentina.
CUNN. Allan Cunningham, 1791–1839, British collector in Australia.
R. CUNN. Richard Cunningham, 1793–1835. Great Britain.
CURT. William Curtis, 1746–1799, founder of Botanical Magazine. England.
M. A. CURT. Moses Ashley Curtis, 1808–1872. United States.
CYR. Domenico Cyrillo, 1739–1799. Italy.

DAHLST. Gustav Adolph Hugo Dahlstedt, 1856–1934. Sweden.
DALL. Alexis Dallière, 1823–1901. Belgium.
DANIELS. Francis Potter Daniels, 1869–. Milledgeville, Georgia.
DARNELL. Anthony William Darnell, 1880–, botanical artist. England.
DAUVESSE. Dauvesse, French nurseryman about 1880.
DAVIDSON. Anstruther Davidson, 1860–1932. California.
DAVIS. Kary Cadmus Davis, 1867–1936, agricultural educator. Tennessee.
DC. Augustin Pyramus de Candolle, 1778–1841, projector of the Prodromus and head of a distinguished family. Switzerland.
A. DC. Alphonse de Candolle, the son, 1806–1893.

C. DC. Casimir de Candolle, the grandson, 1836–1918.
Deane. Walter Deane, 1848–1930. Boston, Massachusetts.
Debx. Jean Odon Debaux, 1826–1910. France.
De Chambray. Georges de Chambray, 1783–1849. France.
Decne. Joseph Decaisne, 1809–1882. France.
DeFrance. Jesse Allison DeFrance, 1899–. Kingston, Rhode Island.
Degen. Arpad von Degen, 1866–1934. Hungary.
Dehnhardt. Friedrich Dehnhardt, published 1829–1841. Naples, Italy.
De Jonghe. Jean de Jonghe, 1804–1876. Belgium.
Delar. François Delaroche, 1780–1813. France.
Delavay. Abbé Jean Marie Delavay, 1834–1895, French missionary and botanist.
De Not. G. de Notaris, 1805–1877. Italy.
Desf. Réné Louiche Desfontaines, 1750–1833. France.
Desp. Narcisse Henri François Desportes, 1776–1856. France.
Desr. Louis Auguste Joseph Desrousseaux, 1753–1838, contributor to Lamarck's Encyclopédie Methodique.
Desv. Augustin Nicaise Desvaux, 1784–1856. France.
DeVries. Hugo DeVries, 1848–1935. Holland.
De Vriese. W. H. de Vriese, 1806–1862. Holland.
Dickson. Edward Dalzell Dickson, died 1900, physician to British Embassy at Constantinople.
Dieck. Georg Dieck, 1847–1925, German horticulturist.
Diels. Friedrich Ludwig Emil Diels, 1874–1945. Germany.
Dietr. Friedrich Gottlieb Dietrich, 1768–1850. Germany.
A. Dietr. Albert Dietrich, 1795–1856. Germany.
Dill. Johann Jacob Dillenius, 1687–1747, professor of botany in Oxford.
Dinter. Moritz Kurt Dinter, 1868–1945. student of succulent plants. Germany.
Dipp. Ludwig Dippel, 1827–1914. Germany.
Dode. Louis Albert Dode, 1875–. France.
Doerfler. Ignaz Doerfler, 1866–. Austria.
D'Ombrain. Henry Honywood D'Ombrain, 1818–1905, British horticulturist.
Domin. Karel Domin, 1882–. Czechoslovakia.
Don. George Don, 1798–1856. England.
D. Don. David Don, brother of George, 1799–1841. Scotland.
Donn. James Donn. 1758–1813, author of Hortus Cantabrigiensis. England.
Dougl. David Douglas. 1799–1834, collector in northwestern America Scotland.
Dreer. Henry A. Dreer, 1818–1873, seedsman. Philadelphia.
Drescher. Aubrey A. Drescher, 1910–. United States.
Druce. George Claridge Druce, 1850–1932. Oxford. England.
Drude. Carl Georg Oscar Drude, 1852–1933. Germany.
Drumm. James Drummond, 1784?–1863. West Australia
Drummond. James Ramsay Drummond, 1851–1921. England.
Dry. James Dryander, 1748–1810. Sweden.
Duby. Jean Etienne Duby, 1798–1885. Switzerland.
Duchartre. Pierre Etienne Simon Duchartre, 1811–1894. France.
Duchesne. Antoine Nicolas Duchesne, 1747–1827. France.
Dufr. Pierre Dufresne, 1786–1836. Geneva, Switzerland.
Duham. Henri Louis Duhamel du Monceau, 1700–1781. France.
Dulac. Abbé Joseph Dulac, published 1867. France.
Dum. Barthélemy Charles Dumortier, 1797–1887. Belgium.
Dum.-Cours. Georges Louis Marie Dumont de Courset. 1746–1824. France.
Dunal. Michel Felix Dunal, 1789–1856. France.
Dunn. Stephen Troyte Dunn. 1868–1938. Great Britain.
Dur. Michel Charles Durieu de Maissonneuve, 1796–1878, director of the Jardin des Plantes in Bordeaux.
Th. Dur. Theophile Alexis Durand, 1855–1912. Belgium.
Durand. Elias Magloire Durand, 1794–1873. United States.
Durande. Jean François Durande, 1730–1794. France.
Durazz. Antonio Durazzini, about 1772. Italy.
DuRoi. Johann Philipp DuRoi, 1741–1785. Germany.
D'Urv. J. S. C. Dumont D'Urville, 1790–1842. France.
Duthie. John Ferminger Duthie, 1845–1922. England.
Duval. Ch. J. Duval, 1751–1828. France.
Dyer. Sir William Turner Thiselton-Dyer, 1843–1929. England.
Dykes. William Rickatson Dykes, 1877–1925, English specialist on Iris and Tulipa.

E. A. Eames. Edward Ashley Eames, 1872–. United States.
Eastw. Alice Eastwood, 1859–. California.
A. Eaton. Amos Eaton, 1776–1842. United States.
D. C. Eaton. Daniel Cady Eaton, 1834–1895, professor at Yale and writer on ferns.
Eberm. Carl Heinrich Ebermaier, 1802–1870. Germany.
Ecklon. Christian Friedrich Ecklon, 1795–1868, apothecary and botanical collector.
Edgew. Michael Pakenham Edgeworth, 1812–1881, in Bengal Civil Service.
Edwards. Alexander Edwards, 1904–, Director of Parks. Salford, Lancashire, England.
Ehrh. Friedrich Ehrhart, 1742–1795. Germany.
B. Ehrh. Balthasar Ehrhart, 1700–1756. Germany.
Ehrenb. Christian Gottfried Ehrenberg, 1795–1876. Berlin, Germany.
Ell. Stephen Elliott. 1771–1830. South Carolina.
Elliot. George Francis Scott Elliot, 1862–1934. Great Britain.
Ellis. John Ellis, 1710–1776. Great Britain.
Ellwanger George Ellwanger, 1816–1906, nurseryman. Rochester, New York.
Elwes. Henry John Elwes, 1846–1922. England.
Endl. Stephan Ladislaus Endlicher, 1804–1849, professor at Vienna.
Engelm. George Engelmann, 1809–1884. Missouri.
Engler. Heinrich Gustav Adolph Engler, 1844–1930. Germany.

ERICKSON. Ralph Orlando Erickson, 1914–. University of Pennsylvania.
ESCH. Johann Friedrich Eschscholtz, 1793–1831. Russia.
EVANS. Walter Harrison Evans, 1863–1941. United States Department of Agriculture.
EVERETT. Thomas Henry Everett, 1903–. New York Botanical Garden.
EYSTER. William Henry Eyster, 1889–, geneticist. Bucknell University, Lewisburg, Pennsylvania.

FABR. Philipp Konrad Fabricius, 1714–1774. Germany.
FACCH. Francesco Facchini, 1788–1852. Italy.
FARRER. Reginald John Farrer, 1880–1920, British horticultural writer.
FARRINGTON. Edward Irving Farrington, 1876–, editor and author. Boston, Massachusetts.
FARWELL. Oliver Atkins Farwell, 1867–1942. Michigan.
FASSETT. Norman Carter Fassett, 1900–. University of Wisconsin.
FEDDE. Friedrich Karl Georg Fedde, 1873–1942. Germany.
B. FEDTSCH. Boris Aleksyevitch Fedtschenko, 1873–. Russia.
O. FEDTSCH. Olga Alexandrovna Fedtschenko, 1845–1921, mother of Boris, Russian traveller in Asia.
FÉE. Antoine Laurent Apollinaire Fée, 1789–1874. France.
FEER. Heinrich Feer, published on Campanulaceæ in 1890. Geneva, Switzerland.
FENZL. Eduard Fenzl, 1808–1879. Austria.
FERN. Merritt Lyndon Fernald, 1873–. Gray Herbarium.
FERRISS. James Henry Ferriss, 1849–1926. Illinois.
FIORI. Adriano Fiori, 1865–. Italy.
FISCH. Friedrich Ernst Ludwig von Fischer, 1782–1854. Russia.
FITZG. Robert D. Fitzgerald, 1830–1892. Great Britain.
FITZHERBERT. S. Wyndham Fitzherbert, died 1916, British horticulturist.
FLOTO. Ernst Vilhelm Floto, 1902–, assistant curator botanical garden, Copenhagen, Denmark.
FLUEGGE. Johann Fluegge, 1775–1816. Germany.
FOCKE. Wilhelm Olbers Focke, 1834–1922. Germany.
FOMIN. Alexander Vasiljevic Fomin, 1869–1935. Russia.
FORBES. James Forbes, 1773–1861. Great Britain.
FORM. Eduard Formánek, 1845–1900, professor in Brunn, Austria.
FORREST. George Forrest, 1873–1932. Great Britain.
FORSK. Pehr Forskal, 1736–1768, Swedish collector in Egypt and Arabia.
FORST. Johann Reinhold Forster, 1729–1798. Germany. Also Georg Forster, son, 1754–1794.
FORT. Robert Fortune, 1812–1880. Great Britain.
FOSBERG. Francis Raymond Fosberg, 1908–. Honolulu, Hawaii.
M. FOSTER. Sir Michael Foster, 1836–1907. England.
R. FOSTER. Robert C. Foster, 1904–. Gray Herbarium.
FOUC. Julien Foucaud, 1847–1904. France.
FOUG. Auguste Denis Fougeroux, 1732–1789. France.
FOURNIER. Eugène Fournier, 1834–1884, medical botanist. France.
FOURR. Jules Pierre Fourreau, 1844–1871. France.
FRAHM. G. Frahm, German nurseryman about 1898.
FRANCESCHI. Francesco Franceschi (Emanuele Orazio Fenzi), 1843–1924. Italy and California.
FRANCH. Adrien Franchet, 1834–1900. Jardin des Plantes, Paris.
FRASER. John Fraser, 1750–1811, English botanist who collected in America.
FREEM. George F. Freeman, 1876–1930. United States.
FREM. John Charles Fremont, 1813–1890, explorer in western United States.
FREYER. C. F. Freyer, 1802–1866. Austria.
FREYN. Joseph Freyn, 1845–1903. Austria.
FRIES. Elias Magnus Fries, 1794–1878. Sweden.
TH. FRIES. Theodor Magnus Fries, 1832–1913. Sweden.
FRITSCH. Karl Fritsch, 1864–1934. Austria.
FRIV. Emmerich Frivaldszky von Frivald. 1799–1870. Hungary.
FROEBEL. Karl Otto Froebel, 1844–1906, Swiss nurseryman.
FROEL. Joseph Aloys Froelich, 1766–1841. Germany.
FROST. John Frost, 1803–1840. England.
FRUWIRTH. Karl Fruwirth, 1862–1930, Austrian horticulturist.

GAERTN. Joseph Gaertner, 1732–1791. Germany.
GAGNEP. François Gagnepain, 1866–. France.
GALEOTTI. Henri Guillaume Galeotti, 1814–1858, director botanical gardens, Brussels.
GAMS. Helmut Gams, 1893–. Innsbruck, Austria.
GARDNER. George Gardner. 1812–1849. Ceylon.
GARKE. Friedrich August Garke, 1819–1904. Germany.
GASPAR. Gulielmo Gasparrini, 1804–1866. Italy.
GATES. Reginald Ruggles Gates, 1882–. Woods Hole, Massachusetts
GATT. August Gattinger, 1825–1903. Tennessee.
GAUD. Charles Gaudichaud-Beaupré, 1789–1854. France.
GAUDIN. Jean François Gottlieb Philippe Gaudin, 1766–1833. Switzerland.
GAWL. See Ker.
J. GAY. Jacques E. Gay, 1786–1864. France.
GEORGI. Johann Gottlieb Georgi, 1729–1802. Russia.
GIBBS. Vicary Gibbs, 1853–1932. Great Britain.
GILG. Ernst Gilg, 1867–1933. Germany.
GILIB. Jean Emmanuel Gilibert, 1741–1814. France.
GILL. John Gillies, 1747–1836, traveller in South America. Scotland.
GIRARD. Frédéric de Girard, author of a work with Saint Hilaire. France.
GLAZEBR. Thomas Kirkland Glazebrook, 1780–1855. Great Britain.
GLEDITSCH. Johann Gottlieb Gleditsch, 1714–1786, director botanic garden at Berlin.
GLOX. Benjamin Peter Gloxin, botanist and physician who wrote in 1785.
GMEL. Samuel Gottlich Gmelin, 1743–1774. Russia.

AUTHORITIES FOR THE BINOMIALS

GODEFROY. Alexandre Godefroy-Lebeuf, 1852–1903, French botanical collector in Cochin-China.
GODR. Dominique Alexandre Godron, 1807–1880. France.
GOEBEL. Karl Christian Goebel, 1794–1851, professor of botany at Dorpat, Russia.
GOESCHKE. Franz Goeschke, 1844–1912, German pomologist.
GOEZE. Edmond Goeze, 1838–1929. Coimbra, Portugal.
GOLDRING. W. Goldring, 1854–1919, British horticulturist.
GOMEZ. Bernardino Antonio Gomez, 1769–1823. Portugal.
GOODDING. Leslie Newton Goodding, 1880–. Beard, California.
GORD. George Gordon, 1806–1879. Great Britain.
GOUAN. Antoine Gouan, 1733–1821. France.
GOWER. William Hugh Gower, 1835–1894 British horticulturist.
GRAEBN. Karl Otto Robert Peter Paul Graebner. 1871–1933. Germany.
R. GRAH. Robert Graham 1786–1845. Scotland
GRANT. Adele Lewis Grant. 1881–. University of Southern California, Los Angeles.
GRAY. Asa Gray, 1810–1888. Harvard University.
S. F. GRAY. Samuel Frederick Gray, 1780–1836. Great Britain.
M. L. GREEN. Mary Letitia Green (Mrs. T. A Sprague), 1886–. England.
GREENE. Edward Lee Greene, 1842–1915. United States.
GREENMAN. Jesse More Greenman, 1867–. Missouri Botanical Garden, St. Louis.
GREN. Jean Charles Marie Grenier, 1808–1875. France.
GREY Charles Hervey Grey 1875–, author Hardy Bulbs. Great Britain.
GRIFF. William Griffith, 1810–1845. Great Britain.
GRIGNAN. G. T. Grignan French horticulturist about 1900.
GRISEB. August Heinrich Rudolph Grisebach, 1814–1879, author Flora of the British West Indian Islands. Germany.
GROENL. Johannes Groenland, 1824–1891, Dutch nurseryman.
GRONOV. Jan Fredrik Gronovius, 1690–1762. Holland.
GROSSER. Wilhelm Grosser, 1869–. Germany
GUERKE. Robert Louis August Max Guerke, 1854–1911, cactus specialist Germany.
GUILL. André Guillaumin. 1885–. France.
GUSS. Giovanni Gussone, 1787–1866 Naples, Italy.

HAAGE. Ferdinand Haage, 1859–1930. Germany.
HAAGE JR Friedr. Ad Haage Jr.
HACK. Eduard Hackel, 1850–1926, agrostologist Austria.
HACQ. Balthasar Hacquet 1740–1815. Austria
HAENKE. Thaddeus Haenke, 1761–1817, traveller in Philippines and South America Bohemia
HAINES. Henry Hazelfoot Haines 1867–. England and India.
HALACSY. Eug. von Halacsy, 1842–1913 medical botanist. Austria.
A. D. HALL. Sir A. Daniel Hall, 1864–, authority on tulips. Great Britain.
H. M. HALL. Harvey Monroe Hall, 1874–1932. California.
HALLER. Albrecht von Haller, 1708–1777, Swiss naturalist, doctor and author.
HALLER f. Albert von Haller, the son, 1758–1823.
HAMET. Raymond Hamet, contemporaneous. France.
HANCE. Henry Fletcher Hance, 1827–1886. Great Britain.
HAND.-MAZZ. Heinrich von Handel-Mazzetti, 1862–1940. Austria.
HANKS. Lenda Tracy Hanks, 1879–1944. California.
HANNIBAL. L. S. Hannibal, contemporaneous. Concord, California.
HANSEN. Carl Hansen, 1848–1903. Denmark.
N. E. HANSEN. Niels Ebbesen Hansen, 1866–. South Dakota.
HANST. Johannes Hanstein, 1822–1880. Germany.
HARA. Hiroshi Hara, 1908–. Tokyo University, Japan.
HARBISON. T. G. Harbison, 1862–1936. United States.
HARDW. Thomas Hardwicke, 1757–1835. Great Britain.
HARMS. Hermann August Theodor Harms, 1870–1942. Germany.
F. HARPER. Francis Harper, 1886–. John Bartram Association, Swarthmore, Pennsylvania.
HARTIG. Theodor Hartig, 1805–1880. Germany.
HARTM. Carl Johan Hartman, 1790–1849. Sweden.
HARTW. Karl Theodor Hartweg, 1812–1871, collector in Mexico for Horticultural Society of London. Germany.
HARTWIG. August Karl Julius Hartwig, 1823–1913, German horticulturist.
HARVEY. William Henry Harvey, 1811–1866. Great Britain.
HASSK. Justus Karl Hasskarl, 1811–1894. Germany.
HAUMAN. Lucien Hauman, 1880–. Brussels, Belgium, formerly Argentina.
HAUSSK. Heinrich Carl Haussknecht, 1838–1903. Germany.
HAW Adrian Hardy Haworth, 1768–1833. England.
HAYATA. Bunzo Hayata, 1874–1934. Japan.
HAYEK. August Hayek, 1871–1928. Austria.
HAYNE. Friedrich Gottlob Hayne, 1763–1832. Germany.
HBK Friedrich Alexander von Humboldt, 1769–1859. Germany Aimé Bonpland, France. Carl Sigismund Kunth, Germany. Authors of a great work on plants of the New World.
HEDR. Ulysses Prentiss Hedrick, 1870–, pomologist. Geneva. New York.
HEDWIG f. Romanus Adolf Hedwig, 1772–1806 Germany
HEESE Emil Heese 1862–1914, collector of cacti in West Indies and Mexico.
HEGETSCHW. Johann Jacob Hegetschweiler, 1789–1839, author Flora der Schweiz.
HEGI. Gustav Hegi, 1876–1932 Switzerland.
HEISTER. Lorenz Heister, 1683–1758. Germany.
HELDR. Theodor von Heldreich, 1822–1902. Greece.
HELLER Amos Arthur Heller, 1867–1944. California
HEMSL. W. Botting Hemsley, 1843–1924. Kew, England.
L. F HENDERSON. Louis Fourniquet Henderson, 1853–1942. botanist and collector in northwestern America.

AUTHORITIES FOR THE BINOMIALS

HENRY Augustine Henry, 1857–1930, collector of Chinese plants and dendrologist. Ireland.

L. HENRY. Louis Henry, 1853–1903, French horticulturist.

HERB. William Herbert, 1778–1847. England.

HERBICH. Franz Herbich, 1791–1865. Poland.

HERD Ferdinand Gottofred Theobald Maximilian von Herder, 1828–1896. Russia.

HÉRINCQ. François H. Hérincq, 1820–1891. France.

HERRM. Johann Herrmann, 1738–1800. France.

HERTER. Wilhelm Gustav Herter, 1884–. Uruguay.

HESSE. Hermann Albrecht Hesse, 1852–1937, German nurseryman.

HEUFF. Johann Heuffel, 1800–1857. Hungary.

HIBB. James Shirley Hibberd, 1825–1890, writer on ivy. Great Britain.

HICKEL. Robert Hickel, 1861–1935. France.

HIERN. William Philip Hiern, 1839–1925. England.

HIERON. Georg Hieronymus, 1846–1921. Germany.

HILDMANN. H. Hildmann about 1891.

HILL. John Hill, 1716–1775. Great Britain.

A. F. HILL. Albert Frederick Hill, 1889–. Harvard University.

D. HILL. Hills Nurseries, Dundee, Illinois.

HITCHC. Albert Spear Hitchcock, 1865–1935. Washington, D. C

HOCHST. Christian Friedrich Hochstetter, 1787–1860. Germany.

HOESS. Franz Hoess, 1756–1840. Austria.

HOFFM. Georg Franz Hoffmann 1761–1826. Germany.

O HOFFM. Karl August Otto Hoffmann, 1853–1909. Germany.

HOFFMGG Johann Centurius von Hoffmannsegg, 1766–1849. Germany

HOHEN Rudolph Friedrich Hohenacker, 1798–1874. Switzerland.

HOLM. Theodor Holmskiold. 1732–1794. Denmark.

HOLMES. Edward Morell Holmes. 1843–1930. Great Britain

HONCKENY. Gerhard August Honckeny, 1724–1805 Germany.

HOOG. Hoog Brothers, contemporaneous Dutch horticulturists and plant-breeders.

HOOK. William Jackson Hooker, 1785–1865. England.

HOOK f. Joseph Dalton Hooker, the son, 1817–1911. England.

HOOPES. Josiah Hoopes, 1832–1904, American horticulturist.

HOOVER. Robert Francis Hoover, 1913–. Modesto, California.

HOPFFER. Carl Hopffer, born 1810.

HOPPE D. H. Hoppe, 1760–1846. Germany.

HORAN. Pavel Fedorovich Horaninow, 1796–1866. Russia.

HORNEM. Jens Wilken Hornemann, 1770–1841. Denmark.

HORNIBR. Murray Hornibrook, 1874–, specialist in cultivated conifers. Great Britain.

HORT. Hortorum, literally *of the gardens*. Placed after names current among horticulturists, but not necessarily of all horticulturists. Often used with less exactness than names of authors; frequently indicates garden or unknown origin. Many of these plants have never been sufficiently described.

HOST. Nicolaus Thomas Host, 1761–1834, botanist and physician. Austria.

HOTTES. Alfred Hottes, 1891–, horticulturist. La Jolla, California.

HOUGHTON. Arthur Duvernoix Houghton, 1870–1938. California.

HOUSE. Homer Doliver House, 1878–. Albany, New York.

HOUTT. Martinus Houttuyn, 1720–1798. Holland.

HOWELL. Thomas Howell, 1842–1912. Oregon.

HUBBARD. Frederic Tracy Hubbard, 1875–. Harvard University.

HUDS. William Hudson, 1730–1793. Great Britain.

HUEG Baron Karl von Huegel, 1794–1870, world traveller. Austria.

HUET Augustin Louis Pierre Huet, 1814–1888. France.

HUGHES. Dorothy K. Hughes (Mrs. Wilson Popenoe), 1899–1932. Washington, D. C.

HULL. John H. Hull, 1761–1843. Great Britain.

HUMB. Friedrich Alexander von Humboldt, 1769–1859. Germany.

HUTCHINS. J. Hutchinson, 1884–. Great Britain.

J. B. HUTCHINS J. B. Hutchinson, contemporaneous. England.

HUTER. Rupert Huter, 1859–1934. Austria.

HUTH. Ernst Huth, 1854–1897.

IRISH. Henry Clay Irish, 1868–, horticulturist. St Louis. Missouri.

IRMSCH. Edgar Irmscher, 1887–. Hamburg, Germany.

JACK. William Jack, 1795–1822, physician. Scotland and Malaya.

A B. JACKSON. Albert Bruce Jackson 1876–1947. England.

A. K. JACKSON. Arthur Keith Jackson, 1914–, formerly at Kew. England.

DAYDON JACKSON. Benjamin Daydon Jackson, 1846–1927 botanical bibliographer. England.

JACQ. Nicolaus Joseph Jacquin 1727–1817. Austria.

JACQUEM Victor Jacquemont, 1801–1832. France and India.

JACQUES Henri Antoine Jacques, 1782–1866, French horticulturist.

JAEG Hermann Jaeger, 1815–1890, German horticulturist

JAMES. Edwin James, 1797–1861, collector in the Rocky Mountains.

JANCZ. Edward Janczewski von Glinka, 1846–1920. Poland.

JANKA. Victor Janka von Bules, 1837–1890. Austria.

JEFFREY John Jeffrey, died about 1853, collector in western North America. Scotland.

JENKINS. Edmund Howard Jenkins, 1856–1921, British horticulturist.

JEPSON. Willis Linn Jepson, 1867–1946. California.

JOHNSTON. Ivan Murray Johnston, 1898–. Arnold Arboretum.

JONES. Marcus Eugene Jones, 1852–1934. California.

G. N. JONES. George Neville Jones, 1904–. University of Illinois.

JORDAN Alexis Jordan, 1814–1897. France.

JUEHLKE. Ferdinand Juehlke, 1815–1893, German horticulturist.

JUSL. Abraham D. Juslenius, pupil of Linnæus.
JUSS. Antoine Laurent Jussieu, 1748–1836, the first to introduce the natural families of plants. France.

KALM. Peter Kalm, 1717–1779. Sweden.
KANEHIRA. Ryozo Kanehira, 1882–. Tokyo, Japan, formerly Formosa.
KANITZ. Agost Kanitz, 1843–1896. Hungary.
KAREL. Grigorij Silych Karelin, 1801–1872. Russia.
KARST. Gustav Karl Wilhelm Hermann Karsten, 1817–1908. Germany.
KARW. Baron von Karwinski of Munich, 1780–1855, traveller in Mexico and Brazil.
KAULF. Georg Friedrich Kaulfuss, 1786–1830, described the ferns collected by Chamisso, professor at Halle.
KAY. Alfred and Elizabeth Kay. Florida.
KELLER. Johann Christopher Keller, 1737–1796, German botanical artist.
KELLERER. Johann Kellerer published in 1890. Sofia.
KELLERM. Maude Kellerman (Mrs. Walter T. Swingle), 1888–. Washington, D. C.
KELLOGG. Albert Kellogg, 1813–1887. California.
KENG. Yi Li Keng, 1898–. China.
KENNEDY. P. B. Kennedy, 1874–1930. Nevada and California.
KER (KER-GAWL.). John Bellenden Ker, 1765–1842, botanist, wit, and man of fashion. First known as John Gawler. In 1793 was compelled to leave army because of sympathy with French Revolution. His name was changed in 1804 to John Ker Bellenden, but he was known to his friends as Bellenden Ker. First editor of Edwards' Botanical Register.
KERCHOVE. Comte Oswald de Kerchove de Denterghem, 1844–1906, Belgian horticulturist.
KERNER. Anton Josef Kerner von Marilaun, 1831–1898. Austria.
KING. Sir George King, 1840–1909. Calcutta and Scotland.
KIRCHN. Georg Kirchner, 1837–1885. Germany.
KIT. Paul Kitaibel, 1757–1817. Hungary.
KITAGAWA. Masao Kitagawa, 1909–. Tokyo, Japan.
KLATT. Friedrich Wilhelm Klatt, 1825–1897. Hamburg, Germany.
KLOTZSCH. Johann Friedrich Klotzsch, 1805–1860, monographer of Begoniaceæ, curator of herbarium at Berlin.
KNIGHT. Joseph Knight, 1781–1855, British nurseryman.
O. W. KNIGHT. Ora Willis Knight, 1874–1913. Maine.
KNOWLES. George Beauchamp Knowles, died 1852, editor Floral Cabinet, Birmingham, England.
KNUTH. Reinhard Gustav Paul Knuth, 1874–. Berlin, Germany.
KNUTH. Count Frederik Marcus Knuth, 1904–, writer on cacti.
KOBUSKI. Clarence Emmeren Kobuski, 1900–. Arnold Arboretum.
KOCH. Karl Heinrich Emil Koch, 1809–1879. Germany.
W. KOCH. Wilhelm Daniel Joseph Koch, 1771–1849. Erlangen, Germany.
KOEHNE. Emil Koehne, 1848–1918, author Deutsche Dendrologie.
KOENIG. Johann Gerhard Koenig, 1728–1757. India.
KOERN. Friedrich Koernicke, 1828–1908. Russia.
KOIDZ. Gen'ichi Koidzumi, 1883–. Yonezawa, Japan.
KOM. Vlademir Leontyevitch Komarov, 1869–1946. Russia.
KORSH. Sergyei Ivanovitch Korshinsky, 1861–1900. Russia.
KORT. Antoine Kort. Belgium.
KORTE. Franz Körte.
KOSANIN. Nedelyko Kosanin, 1874–1934. Jugoslavia and Austria.
KOSTEL. Vincenz Franz Kosteletzky, 1801–1887. Czechoslovakia.
KOTSCHY. Theodor Kotschy, 1812–1866, collector in Europe, Asia and north Africa. Austria.
KRÄNZL. Friedrich Wilhelm Ludwig Kränzlin, born 1847, orchidologist. Germany.
KUHN. Maximilian Friedrich Adalbert Kuhn, 1842–1894. Berlin, Germany.
KUNTH. Carl Sigismund Kunth, 1788–1850. Germany.
KUNTZE. Otto Kuntze, 1843–1907. Germany.
KUNZE. Gustav Kunze, 1793–1851, author of work on ferns, published at Leipzig.
KUPPER. W. Kupper, writer on cacti 1929. Germany.
KURTZ. Fritz (Federico) Kurtz, 1854–1920, cactologist. Austria, Argentina.
KURZ. Sulpiz Kurz, 1833?–1878, curator Royal Herbarium, Calcutta.
KUSN. Nikolai Ivanovitch Kusnezov, 1864–1932. Russia.

L. Carolus Linnæus (Carl von Linné), 1707–1778, the "Father of Botany" and author of binomial nomenclature. Sweden.
L. f. Carl von Linné, the son, 1741–1783. Sweden.
LAB. J. Labouret, French cactologist, published 1853–1858.
LABILL. Jacques Julien Houtton de La Billardière, 1755–1834. France.
LAG. Mariano Lagasca y Segura, 1776–1839. Spain.
LAKELA. Olga Lakela, 1890–. Duluth, Minnesota.
LAM. Jean Baptiste Antoine Pierre Monnet Lamarck, 1744–1829. France.
LAMB. Aylmer Bourke Lambert, 1761–1842. Great Britain.
LAMOTTE. Martial Lamotte, 1820–1883. France.
TH. LANG. Thomas Lang, about 1853. Great Britain.
LANGE. Johan Martin Christian Lange, 1818–1898. Denmark.
LANGSD. Georg Heinrich von Langsdorff, 1774–1852. Germany.
LAPEYR. Philippe Picot, Baron de Lapeyrouse, 1744–1818, writer on flora of Pyrenees.
LAUCHE. Wilhelm Lauche, 1827–1882, German horticulturist.
LAV. Alphonse Lavallée, 1835–1884. France.
LAWRENCE. George Hill Mathewson Lawrence, 1910–.
LAWS. Marmaduke Alexander Lawson, 1840–1896. Great Britain.
LAWSON. Lawson & Son: Peter, died 1820; Charles, 1794–1873. Great Britain.
LAXM. Erich Laxmann, 1737–1796. Russia.
LEBAS. E. Lebas, French nurseryman from 1866–1888.

LECOQ. Henri Lecoq, 1802–1871. France.

LEDEB. Carl Friedrich von Ledebour, 1785–1851. Russia.

LEE. Henry Atherton Lee, 1894–. United States.

LEHM. Johann Georg Christian Lehmann, 1792–1860, professor at Hamburg.

LEICHT. Max Leichtlin, 1831–1910, German horticulturist.

LEJ. Alexander Louis Simon Lejeune, 1779–1858. Belgium.

LEM. Charles Lemaire, 1800–1871, works on cacti and botany of cultivated plants. Belgium.

LEMAN. Dominique Sebastian Leman, 1781–1829. Italy and France.

LEMM. John Gill Lemmon, 1832–1908. California.

LEMOINE. Victor Lemoine, 1823–1911; Emile Lemoine, 1862–. French nurserymen.

LEONARD. Emery Clarence Leonard, 1892–. United States National Herbarium.

LEPECH. Iwan Lepechin, 1737–1802. Russia.

LERESCHE. Louis Leresche, 1808–1885. Switzerland.

LESS. Christian Friedrich Lessing, 1810–1862. Germany.

LEST. Themistocle Lestiboudois, 1797–1876. France.

LEVIER. Emile Levier, 1839–1911. Italy.

LÉVL. Auguste Abel Hector Léveillé, 1863–1918. France.

LEX. Juan Lexarza, 1785–1824. Mexico.

LEYSS. Fr. W. von Leysser, 1731–1815. Germany.

L'HER. Charles Louis L'Heritier de Brutelle, 1746–1800. France.

LIBOSCH. Joseph L. Liboschitz, 1783–1824. Germany and Austria.

LIEBLEIN. Franz Kaspar Lieblein, 1744–1810. Germany.

LIEBM. Fr. M. Liebmann, 1813–1856. Denmark.

LIND. J. Linden, 1817–1898, for many years director of L'Illustration Horticole, Belgium.

L. LIND. Lucien Linden, associated with J. Linden for some years on L'Illustration Horticole.

LINDAU. G. Lindau, 1866–1923. Germany.

LINDL. John Lindley, 1799–1865. England.

LINDSAY. Robert Lindsay, 1846–1913, curator Royal Botanic Garden, Edinburgh, Scotland.

LINGELSHEIM. Alexander Lingelsheim, 1874–1937. Germany.

LINK. Johann Heinrich Friedrich Link, 1767–1851. Germany.

LITVINOV. Dmitri Ivanovitch Litvinov, 1854–1929. Russia.

LLAVE. Pablo de la Llave, 1773–1833. Mexico.

LODD. Conrad Loddiges, 1732–1826 and George, his son, 1784–1846, nurserymen near London, conducted Loddiges' Botanical Cabinet from 1817–1834.

LOES. Ludwig Eduard Theodor Loesener, 1865–. Germany.

LOISEL. Jean Louis Auguste Loiseleur-Deslongchamps, 1774–1849. France.

LÖNNR. Krut Johan Loennroth, 1826–1885. Sweden.

LOUD. John Claudius Loudon, 1783–1843, English horticulturist and writer.

LOUR. Juan Loureiro, 1715–1796, missionary and botanist in China. Portugal.

LOW. Hugh Low, 1794–1863, & Company, British nurserymen.

LOWE. Rev. Richard Thomas Lowe, 1802–1874. England.

MACB. J. Francis Macbride, 1892–. University of California.

MACDANIELS. Lawrence Howland MacDaniels, 1888–. Cornell University.

MACF. James Macfadyen, 1800–1850. Scotland and Jamaica.

MACKAY. James Townsend Mackay, 1775?–1862, founder and curator Trinity College botanic garden, Dublin, Ireland.

MACKENZIE. Kenneth Kent Mackenzie, 1877–1934. New York.

MACM. Conway MacMillan, 1867–1929. United States.

MACOUN. John Macoun, 1832–1920. Ontario, Canada.

MAEKAWA. Fumio Maekawa, 1908–. Tokyo University, Japan.

MAIRE. René Charles Joseph Ernest Maire, 1878–. Algiers.

MAKINO. Tomitaro Makino, 1863–. Japan.

MALINVAUD. Luis Jules Ernst Malinvaud, 1836–1913. France.

MANETTI. Giuseppe Manetti, 1831–1858. Italy.

MANGELSDORF, Paul Christoph Mangelsdorf, 1899–. Harvard University.

MANNING. Jacob W. Manning, 1826–1904, American nurseryman.

MANSFIELD. Rudolph Mansfield, 1901–. Germany.

MARCH. Elie Marchal, 1839–1923. Belgium.

MARLOTH. Rudolf Marloth, 1855–1931. Germany and South Africa.

MARQUAND. Cecil Victor Boley Marquand, 1897–. Great Britain.

MARSH. Humphrey Marshall, 1722–1801. Pennsylvania.

MARSHALL. W. Taylor Marshall, cactus specialist. California.

MARSILI. Giovanni Marsili, 1727–1795. Italy.

MART. Karl Friedrich Philipp von Martius, 1794–1868, professor at Munich, monographer of palms, founder of the great Flora Brasiliensis.

MARTENS. Martin Martens, 1797–1863. Belgium.

MARTINEZ. Maximino Martinez, 1888–. Mexico.

MASF. Ramon Masferrer y Arquimbau, 1850–1884. Spain and Philippines.

MASSART. J. Massart, 1865–1925, world traveller. Belgium.

MASSON. Francis Masson, 1741 1805, traveller in America and Africa. Scotland.

MAST. Maxwell Tylden Masters, 1833–1907, editor of Gardeners' Chronicle.

W. MAST. W. Masters, 1796–1874. Great Britain.

MATHEWS. J. W. Mathews. Bolus Herbarium, South Africa.

MATON. William George Maton, 1774–1835. England.

MATSUM. Jinzo Matsumura, 1855–1928. Japan.

MATTUSCHKA. Heinrich Gottfried von Mattuschka, 1734–1779. Germany.

MAUND. Benjamin Maund, 1790–1863, British horticulturist.

MAXIM. Carl Johann Maximowicz, 1827–1891. Russia.

MAXON. William Ralph Maxon, 1877–1948. United States National Herbarium.

MAXWELL. T. C. Maxwell, 1822–1908, nurseryman. Geneva, New York.

MAYR. Heinrich Mayr, 1856–1911. Germany.

MAZZ. Giovanni Mazzucato, 1787–1814. Italy.

MCCLELLAND. John McClelland, 1805–1883. Great Britain.

MEDIC Friedrich Casimir Medicus, 1736–1808, director of the garden at Mannheim, wrote on North American plants in 1792.
MEEHAN. Thomas Meehan, 1826–1901, American nurseryman.
MEISN., MEISSN. Carl Friedrich Meisner or Meissner, 1800–1874. Switzerland.
MERR. Elmer Drew Merrill, 1876–. Arnold Arboretum.
MERT. F. K. MERTENS, 1764–1831. Germany.
METT. Georg Heinrich Mettenius, 1823–1866, professor at Leipzig.
METZ. Johan Metzger, 1789–1852, director botanic garden, Heidelberg.
MEY. Carl Anton Meyer, 1795–1855. Russia.
B. MEY. Bernhard Meyer, 1767–1836, florist in Wetterau.
E. MEY. Ernst Heinrich Friedrich Meyer, 1791–1858. Germany.
G. F. W. MEY. Georg Friedrich Wilhelm Meyer, 1782–1856. Germany.
MEYEN. Franz Julius Ferdinand Meyen, 1804–1840. Germany.
MEZ. Karl Christian Mez, 1864–1944, monographer of the bromeliads. Königsberg, Germany.
MICH. Pier Antonio Micheli, 1679–1737. Florence, Italy.
MICHX André Michaux, 1746–1802. France, but for ten years a resident of North America.
MICHX f François André Michaux, the son, 1770–1855. France.
MIERS. John Miers, 1789–1879. Great Britain.
MIKAN. Johann Christian Mikan, 1769–1844, traveller in Brazil. Czechoslovakia.
MILL. Philip Miller, 1691–1771, author of a celebrated dictionary of gardening which had many editions. Chelsea, England.
MILLAN. Roberto Millan, 1892–. Argentina.
W. MILLER. Wilhelm or William Tyler Miller, 1869–1938. California.
MILLSP. Charles Frederic Millspaugh, 1854–1923. Chicago, Illinois.
MILNE-REDHEAD. Edgar Wolston Bertram Handsley Milne-Redhead, 1906–. Kew, England.
MIQ. Friedrich Anton Wilhelm Miquel, 1811–1871. Utrecht, Holland.
MIRBEL. Charles François Brisseau de Mirbel, 1776–1854. France.
MITCH. John Mitchell, 1676–1768. England and Virginia.
MITF. Algernon Bertram Freeman-Mitford, Lord Redesdale, 1837–1916, author of The Bamboo Garden.
MOC. Joseph Marian Mociño, 1757–1820. Spain.
MOENCH. Konrad Moench, 1744–1805. Germany.
MOLDENKE. Harold N. Moldenke, 1909–. New York Botanical Garden.
MOLINA. Juan Ignacio Molina, 1737–1829. Spain.
MOORE. Thomas Moore, 1821–1887, curator of Chelsea Botanic Garden, author of Index Filicum.
J. W. MOORE. John William Moore, 1901–. University of Minnesota.
S. MOORE. Spencer LeMarchant Moore, 1851–1931. England.
MOQ. Alfred Moquin-Tandon, 1804–1863. France.
MOR. Alexander Moritzi, 1806–1850. Switzerland.
MORD. DE LAUN. Jean Claude Michel Mordant de Launay, 1750–1816. France.
MORELET. Piere Marie Arthur Morelet, 1809–1892. France, Algiers.
MORETTI. Giuseppe Moretti, 1782–1853. Italy.
MORIC. Moise Etienne Moricand, 1780–1854. Switzerland.
MORIS. J. Moris.
G. MORIS. Giuseppe Giacinto Moris, 1796–1869. Italy.
MORR. Charles Jacques Edouard Morren, 1833–1886. Ghent, Belgium.
MORRIS. Frank Morris.
MORTON. Conrad Vernon Morton, 1905–. United States National Herbarium.
MOTT. Seraphin Mottet, 1861–1930, French horticulturist.
MOUILLEF. Pierre Mouillefert, 1845–1903. France.
CH. DES MOULINS. Charles des Moulins, 1797–1875. France.
MUEHLENPFORDT. F. Muehlenpfordt, cactologist.
MUELL. ARG. Jean Mueller of Aargau, 1828–1896. Switzerland.
F. MUELL. Ferdinand von Mueller, 1825–1896, royal botanist of Australia, author of works on economic plants.
O. F. MUELL. Otto Frederik Mueller, 1730–1784. Denmark and Germany.
P. J. MUELL. Philipp Jakob Mueller, 1832–1889. France.
MUENCHH. Otto von Muenchhausen, 1716–1774. Germany.
MUHL. Henry Ludwig Muhlenberg, 1756–1817. Pennsylvania.
MULERTT. Hugo Mulertt, horticulturist. Cincinnati, Ohio.
MUNRO. William Munro, 1816–1880. Great Britain.
MUNSON. Thomas Volney Munson, 1843–1913. Texas.
MUNZ. Philip Alexander Munz, 1892–. Anaheim, California.
MURBECK. Svante Murbeck, 1859–1946. Sweden.
MURITH. Laurent Joseph Murith, 1742–1816. France.
MURR. Johann Andreas Murray, 1740–1791. Germany.
A. MURR. Andrew Murray, 1812–1878. Great Britain.
MUTEL. Auguste Mutel, 1795–1847. France.
MUTIS. José Celestino Mutis, 1732–1808. Colombia.

NAKAI. Takenoshi Nakai, 1882–. Japan.
NANNF. Johan Axel Nannfeldt, 1904–. Uppsala, Sweden.
NASH. George Valentine Nash, 1864–1919. New York.
NAUD. Charles Naudin, 1815–1899, frequent contributor to Revue Horticole. France.
NECK. Noel Joseph de Necker, 1729–1793. France.
NÉE. Luis Née, Spanish botanist of the eighteenth century.
NEES. Christian Gottfried Nees von Esenbeck, 1776–1858. Prussia.
NEILR. August Neilreich, 1803–1871. Austria.
NELSON. John Gudgeon Nelson (Senilis), 1818–1882. Great Britain.
A. NELS. Aven Nelson, 1859–. University of Wyoming.

AUTHORITIES FOR THE BINOMIALS

NEUBERT. Wilhelm Neubert, 1808–1905, German horticulturist.

NEWM. Edward Newman, 1801–1876, fern specialist. England.

NICHOLS. George Nicholson, 1847–1908, curator at Kew, author of The Illustrated Dictionary of Gardening.

NIEDZ. Franz Niedenzu, 1857–1937. Germany.

NIEUWL. Julius Aloysius Nieuwland, 1878–. Notre Dame University, Indiana.

NOIS. Louis Claude Noisette, 1772–1849. France.

NOOT. Bertha Hoola vanNooten, published 1866. Belgium.

NORL. Tycho Norlindh, 1906–. Lund, Sweden.

J. B. S. NORTON. John Bitting Smith Norton, 1872–. University of Maryland.

NUTT. Thomas Nuttall, 1786–1859. Massachusetts.

NYM. Carl Fredrick Nyman, 1820–1893. Sweden.

OAKES. William Oakes, 1799–1848. Vermont and Massachusetts.

O'BRIEN. James O'Brien, 1842–1930, writer on orchids. Great Britain.

OEDER. Georg Christian Oeder, 1728–1791. Germany.

OHLEND. J. H. Ohlendorff, German nurseryman at Hamburg from 1819–1840.

OHWI. Jisaburo Ohwi, 1905–. Tokyo Science Museum, Japan.

OLIV. Daniel Oliver, 1830–1917. Royal Botanic Gardens, Kew, England.

ONNO. Max Onno, 1903–. Vienna, Austria.

OPIZ. Philipp Maximilian Opiz, 1787–1858. Czechoslovakia.

ORBIGNY. M. Alcide d'Orbigny, 1802–1857, collector in South America. France.

ORCUTT. C. R. Orcutt, 1864–1929. California.

ORT. Casimir Gomez Ortega, 1740–1818. Spain.

OSBECK. Pehr Osbeck, 1723–1805. Sweden.

OSBORN. Arthur Osborn, 1878–. Great Britain.

OTTO. Friedrich Otto, 1782–1856. Germany.

OUDEM. Cornelius Antoon Jan Abraham Oudemans, 1825–1906. Holland.

PAINE. John Alsop Paine, 1840–1912. United States.

PALIBIN. Ivan Vladimirovitch Palibin, 1872–. Russia.

PALL. Peter Simon Pallas, 1741–1811, professor and explorer in Russia.

PAMPAN. Renato Pampanini, 1875–, writer on Chinese plants. Florence, Italy.

PANC. Josef Pancic, 1814–1888. Jugoslavia.

PANT. Josef Pantocsek, 1846–1916. Austria.

PAR. Rev. Charles Samuel Pollock Parish, 1822–1897, who collected in Burma.

PARDÉ. Leon Gabriel Charles Pardé, 1865–1944. France.

PARISH. S. B. Parish, 1838–1928. California.

PARKINSON. Sydney C. Parkinson, 1745–1771, British explorer.

PARL. Filippo Parlatore, 1816–1877. Italy.

PARRY. Charles Christopher Parry, 1823–1890, American botanical explorer.

PARSONS. Samuel B. Parsons, 1819–1906, American nurseryman.

PASQ. Giuseppe Antonio Pasquale, 1820–1893. Naples, Italy.

C. PAU. Carlos Pau y Español, 1857–1937. Spain.

PAUL. William Paul, 1822–1905, English nurseryman and rosarian, published on ivy in 1867.

PAV. José Antonio Pavon, died 1844. Spain.

PAX. Ferdinand Pax, 1858–1942. Germany.

PAXT. Joseph Paxton, 1802–1865. England.

PAYSON. Edwin Blake Payson, 1893–1927. Northwestern United States.

PECK. Morton Eaton Peck, 1871–. Willamette University, Salem, Oregon.

PENHALL. David Pearce Penhallow, 1854–1910. Canada.

PENNELL. Francis Whittier Pennell, 1886–. Academy of Sciences, Philadelphia.

PENNY. J. Compton Penny, Tasmanian forester.

PERKINS. Janet Russell Perkins, 1853–1933. United States.

PERP. Candida Leni Perpenti, 1764–1846. Italy.

PERR. George Samuel Perrottet, 1793–1870. Switzerland.

PERRIER. E. Perrier de la Bathie, 1825–1916. France.

PERRY. Thomas A. Perry, British nurseryman.

L. M. PERRY. Lily M. Perry, 1895–. Arnold Arboretum.

PERS. Christian Hendrik Persoon, 1755–1837. Germany.

PETERM. Wilhelm Ludwig Petermann, 1806–1855. Germany.

PETERS. Otto Georg Petersen, 1847–1937. Copenhagen, Denmark.

PETROV. Sava Petrovich or Petrovic, 1839–1889. Jugoslavia.

PFEIFFER. Ludwig Pfeiffer, 1805–1877. Germany.

PFITZ. Ernst Hugo Heinrich Pfitzer, 1846–1906. Germany.

PHIL. Rudolph Amandus Philippi, 1808–1904. Santiago, Chile.

PIERRE. Jean Baptiste Louis Pierre, 1833–1905. France and Cochin-China.

PILGER. Robert Knud Friedrich Pilger, 1876–. Germany.

PIPER. Charles Vancouver Piper, 1867–1926. United States Department of Agriculture.

PLANCH. Jules Emile Planchon, 1833–1900, professor at Montpellier, France.

PLENCK. Joseph Jakob von Plenck, 1738–1807. Austria.

v. POELLNITZ. Karl von Poellnitz, 1896–1945. Germany.

POEPPIG. Eduard Friedrich Poeppig, 1798–1868. Germany.

POHL. Johann Baptist Emanuel Pohl, 1782–1834. Austria.

POIR. Jean Louis Marie Poiret, 1755–1834. France.

POIT. Antoine Poiteau, 1766–1854, French horticulturist.

POLL. Johann Adam Pollich, 1740–1780. Germany.

POLLARD. Charles Louis Pollard, 1872–. Arlington, Vermont.

PORTENS. Fr. Edler von Portenschlag-Ledermayer, 1772–1822. Austria.

PORTER. Thomas Conrad Porter, 1822–1901. United States.

POSELGER. Heinrich Poselger, died 1883. Germany.

POURR. Pierre André Pourret, 1754–1818. France.

PRAEGER. Lloyd Praeger, 1865–. Dublin, Ireland.

PRAIN. Sir David Prain, 1857–1944. Great Britain.

AUTHORITIES FOR THE BINOMIALS

PRANTL. K. A. E. Prantl, 1849–1893. Germany.

PRESL. Karel Boriwog Presl, 1794–1852. Czechoslovakia.

PRÉV. Honoré Albert Prévost, 1822–1883, French horticulturist.

PRINCE. Arthur Reginald Prince, 1900–. Nova Scotia Agricultural College, Truro.

PRITZ. Ernst Pritzel, 1875–. Germany.

PUISSANT. Abbé Pierre A. Puissant, 1831–1911, Belgian botanist who was head of a Catholic seminary in Troy, New York, from 1864–1886.

PURDY. Carl Purdy, 1861–1945, California plantsman.

PURKYNE. Emanuel Purkyne, 1831–1882. Austria.

PURPUS. Joseph Anton Purpus, 1860–1933. Germany.

PURSH. Frederick T. Pursh, 1774–1820. Germany, but for twelve years in the United States and died in Montreal, Quebec.

PUSCHK. Apollis Apollosowitsch Mussin-Puschkin, died 1808. Russia.

PUTZ. J. A. Putzeys, 1809–1882. Belgium.

RABENH. Ludwig Rabenhorst, 1806–1881, German cryptogamic botanist.

RADDE. Gustav Johannes Radde, 1831–1903, traveller in Siberia.

RADDI. Giuseppe Raddi, 1770–1829, student of Brazilian flora. Italy.

RADLK. Ludwig Adolph Timotheus Radlkofer, 1829–1927. Germany.

RAEUSCH. Ernest Adolf Raeuschel, about 1772. Germany.

RAF. Constantino Samuel Rafinesque-Schmaltz, 1784–1842, professor of natural history, Transylvania University, Lexington, Kentucky.

RAFFILL. C. P. Raffill, gardener. Royal Botanic Gardens, Kew, England.

RAMAT. Abbé Thomas Albin Joseph d'Audibert de Ramatuelle, 1750–1794. France.

RAMOND. Louis François Elisabeth Ramond de Carbonnières, 1753–1827. France.

REDOUTÉ. Pierre Joseph Redouté, 1761–1840. France.

REEVES. Robert Gatlin Reeves, 1898–. College Station, Texas.

REGEL. Eduard von Regel, 1815–1892, founder of Gartenflora. Germany and Russia.

REHD. Alfred Rehder, 1863–. Arnold Arboretum.

REHNELT. F. Rehnelt, 1861–. Germany.

REICHARD. Johann Jakob Reichard, 1743–1782. Germany.

REICHB. Heinrich Gottlieb Ludwig Reichenbach, 1793–1879. Germany.

REICHB. f. Heinrich Gustav Reichenbach, the son, 1823–1889, authority on orchids. Germany.

RENDLE. Alfred Barton Rendle, 1865–1938. Great Britain.

REQ. Esprit Requien, 1788–1851. Corsica.

RETZ. Andres Johan Retzius, 1742–1821. Sweden.

REUSS. Gustav Reuss, died 1861. Czechoslovakia.

REUT. Georges François Reuter, 1805–1872. Switzerland.

REYN. Alfred Reynier, 1845–1932. France.

RICCOBONO. V. Riccobono.

RICH. Louis Claude Marie Richard, 1754–1821. France.

A. RICH. Achille Richard, 1794–1852. France.

RICHARDSON. Sir John Richardson, 1787–1865, botanist on two polar expeditions. Great Britain.

RICKER. Percy Leroy Ricker, 1878–. United States Department of Agriculture.

RICKETT. Harold William Rickett, 1896–. New York Botanical Garden.

RIDDELL. John Leonard Riddell, 1807–1865. Ohio.

RILEY. Laurence Athelstan Molesworth Riley, 1888–1928. Kew, England.

RISSO. J. Antoine Risso, 1777–1845. France.

RIV. Marie Auguste Rivière, 1821–1877; Charles Marie Rivière, 1845–. French nurserymen.

RIVERS. Thomas Rivers, 1798–1877, nurseryman. Great Britain.

ROB. Benjamin Lincoln Robinson, 1864–1935, former director Gray Herbarium.

W. ROB. William Robinson, 1839–1935, British horticulturist.

ROCHEL. A. Rochel, 1770–1847. Hungary.

RODIN. L. Rodin, contemporaneous. Russia.

RODRIGUEZ. José Demetrio Rodriguez, 1780–1846. Director botanic garden, Madrid, Spain.

ROEM. Johann Jacob Roemer, 1763–1819. Switzerland.

ROEM. Max J. Roemer, about 1840. Germany.

ROEZL. Benito Roezl, 1824–1885, Czechoslovakian collector in South America, Mexico, California.

ROHRB. Paul Rohrbach, 1847–1871. Germany.

ROLFE. Robert Allen Rolfe, 1855–1921. Great Britain.

RONN. Karl Ronniger, 1871–. Vienna, Austria.

ROSCOE. William Roscoe, 1753–1831. England.

ROSE. Joseph Nelson Rose, 1862–1928. United States National Herbarium.

ROSENDAHL. Carl Otto Rosendahl, 1875–. University of Minnesota.

ROTA. Lorenzo Rota, 1819–1855. Bergamo, Italy.

ROTH. Albrecht Wilhelm Roth, 1757–1834. Germany.

ROTTLER. Johann Peter Rottler, 1749–1836, Danish missionary in India.

ROUY. Georges Rouy, 1851–1924. France.

ROWLEE. Willard Winfield Rowlee, 1861–1923. Cornell University.

ROXB. William Roxburgh, 1759–1815. India.

ROYLE. John Forbes Royle, 1799–1858. Great Britain.

RUDGE. Edward Rudge, 1763–1846. England.

RUDOLPH. Karl Asmund Rudolph, 1771–1832. Germany.

RUEMPL. Theodor Ruempler, 1817–1891, German horticulturist.

RUIZ. Hipolito Ruiz Lopez, 1764–1815, author with Pavon of a flora of Peru and Chile. Spain.

RUPR. Franz Josef Ruprecht, 1814–1870, Czechoslovakian botanist and long curator at Leningrad Academy of Science.

RUSBY. Henry Hurd Rusby, 1855–1940. New York.

RUSSELL. Paul George Russell, 1889–. United States Department of Agriculture.

RUYS. Jan Daniel Ruys, 1897–1931. Utrecht, Holland.

RYDB. Per Axel Rydberg, 1860–1931. New York Botanical Garden.

AUTHORITIES FOR THE BINOMIALS

SABINE. Joseph Sabine, 1770–1837. Great Britain.

SAFFORD. William Edwin Safford, 1859–1926. United States Department of Agriculture.

SAGOT. Paul Sagot, 1821–1888. France.

SAKATA. Sakata & Company, Japanese nurserymen.

SALISB. Richard Anthony Salisbury, 1761–1829. England.

SALM-DYCK. Joseph, Prince and High Count Salm-Reifferscheidt-Dyck, 1773–1861. Germany.

SALZM. Philipp Salzmann, 1781–1853, French botanist and plant explorer.

SANDER. Henry Frederick Conrad Sander, 1847–1920, British nurseryman.

SANTI. Giorgio Santi, 1746–1822. Italy.

SARG. Charles Sprague Sargent, 1841–1927, first director of the Arnold Arboretum.

SART. Giovanni Battista Sartorelli, 1780–1853. Italy.

SAV. Ludovic Savatier, 1830–1891. France.

SAVI. Gaetano Savi, 1769–1844. Pisa, Italy.

SCHAUER. Johan Konrad Schauer, 1813–1848. Germany.

SCH. BIP. Karl Heinrich Schultz Bipontius, 1805–1867. Germany.

SCHEELE. Georg Heinrich Adolph Scheele, 1808–1864. Germany.

SCHEIDWEILER. Michael J. Scheidweiler, 1799–1861. Germany.

SCHELLE. Ernst Schelle, 1893–1929. Germany.

SCHENK. Joseph August von Schenk, 1815–1891. Germany.

SCHERB. Johannes Scherbius, 1769–1813. Germany.

SCHERY. Robert Walter Schery, 1917–. Missouri Botanical Garden.

SCHIFFN. Victor Felix Schiffner, 1862–. University of Prague.

SCHINDL. Anton Karl Schindler, 1879–. Germany.

SCHINZ. Hans Schinz, 1858–1941. Switzerland.

SCHK. Christian Schkuhr, 1741–1811. Germany.

SCHLECHT. Diedrich Franz Leonhard von Schlechtendahl, 1794–1866. Halle, Germany.

SCHLECHTER. Rudolf Schlechter, 1872–1925. Germany.

SCHLEICH. Johann Christoph Schleicher, 1768–1834. Switzerland.

FR. SCHMIDT. Friedrich Schmidt, 1832–1908. Russia.

F. W. SCHMIDT. Franz Wilibald Schmidt, 1763–1796. Czechoslovakia.

J. SCHMIDT. Johann Anton Schmidt, 1823–1905. Germany.

SCHNEEVOGT. G. Voorhelm Schneevogt, wrote in 1793. Holland.

SCHNEID. Camillo Schneider, 1876–. Germany.

SCHNITTSP. Georg Friedrich Schnittspahn, director botanic garden in Darmstadt in 1855.

SCHNIZL. A. Schnizlein, 1814–1868. Germany.

SCHOTT. Heinrich Wilhelm Schott, 1794–1865. Austria.

SCHOUSB. Peder Kofod Anker Schousboe, 1766–1832. Denmark.

SCHRAD. Heinrich Adolph Schrader, 1767–1836. Germany.

SCHRANK. Franz von Paula von Schrank, 1747–1835. Germany.

SCHREBER. Johann Christian Daniel von Schreber, 1739–1810. Germany.

SCHULT. Joseph August Schultes, 1773–1831 Germany.

SCHULZE. Arnold E. Schulze, 1914–. New York.

SCHUM. Karl Moritz Schumann, 1851–1904. Berlin, Germany.

SCHUMACHER. Heinrich Christian Friedrich Schumacher, 1757–1830. Denmark.

SCHUR. Philipp Johann Ferdinand Schur, 1799–1878. Austria.

SCHW. Lewis David de Schweinitz, 1780–1834. Pennsylvania.

SCHWANT. G. Schwantes. Kiel, Germany.

SCHWARZ. Otto Schwarz, 1880–. Germany.

SCHWEICKERDT. Herold Georg Wilhelm Johannes Schweickerdt, 1903–. Kew, England.

SCHWEIGG. August Friedrich Schweigger, 1783–1821. Germany.

SCHWENCKE. Martin Wilhelm Schwencke, 1707–1785. Holland.

SCHWERIN. Graf Fritz von Schwerin, 1856–1934. Germany.

SCOP. Giovanni Antonio Scopoli, 1723–1788. Italy.

SCRIBN. Frank Lamson-Scribner, 1851–1938. United States Department of Agriculture.

SEALY. J. R. Sealy, contemporaneous. Royal Botanic Gardens, Kew, England.

SEEM. Berthold Carl Seemann, 1825–1871. Germany.

SELLO. Friedrich Sello, later spelled Sellow, 1789–1831, German traveller in South America.

SENDT. Otto Sendtner, 1814–1859. Germany.

SÉNÉCL. Adrien Sénéclauze, French horticulturist about 1840–1867.

SER. Nicolas Charles Seringe, 1776–1858. France.

SERVETTAZ. Camille Servettaz, about 1909. Switzerland.

SESSÉ. Martino Sessé, died 1809. Mexico.

T. B. SHEPHERD. Theodosia B. Shepherd. United States

SHERFF. Earl Edward Sherff, 1886–. Chicago Teachers College.

SHIBATA. Keita Shibata, 1877–. Tokyo, Japan.

SHIRAS. Homi Shirasawa, 1868–. Japan.

SIBTH. John Sibthorp, 1758–1796. Great Britain.

SIEB. Philipp Franz von Siebold, 1796–1866. Holland.

SIEBER. Franz Wilhelm Sieber, 1785–1844. Austria.

SILOW. R. A. Silow, contemporaneous. England.

SILVA TAROUCA. See Tarouca.

SIM. Thomas Robertson Sim, 1856–1938. South Africa.

SIMONK. Lajos tól Simonkai, 1851–1910. Hungary.

SIMON-LOUIS. Simon-Louis, Léon Louis, 1834–1913, French nurserymen.

SIMS. John Sims, 1792–1838, for many years editor of Curtis' Botanical Magazine. England.

SKAN. Sidney Alfred Skan, 1870–1940. Kew, England.

SKEELS. Homer C. Skeels, 1873–1934. United States Department of Agriculture.

SLAVIN. Arthur Daniel Slavin, 1903–, horticulturist. Rochester, New York.

SMALL. John Kunkel Small, 1869–1938. New York Botanical Garden.

SMITH. Sir James Edward Smith, 1759–1828, first president of the Linnean Society. England.

J. SMITH. John Smith, 1798–1888. Great Britain.

L. B. SMITH. Lyman Bradford Smith, 1904–. United States National Herbarium.
R. SMITH. Richard Smith & Company, British nurserymen about 1875.
R. B. SMITH. R. B. Smith, Camla Gardens, East Grinstead, England.
TH. SMITH. Thomas Smith, British nurseryman about 1911.
W. G. SMITH. Worthington George Smith, 1835–1917, editor The Floral Magazine.
W. W. SMITH. Sir William Wright Smith, 1875–. Director Royal Botanic Garden, Edinburgh, Scotland.
SOLAND. Daniel Carl Solander, 1733–1782. England.
SOLMS. Herman, Graf zu Solms Laubach, 1842–1915. Germany.
SOMM. Stefano Sommier, 1848–1922. Italy.
SOND. Otto Wilhelm Sonder, 1812–1881. Germany.
SONGEON. André Songeon, 1826–1905. France.
SONN. Pierre Sonnerat, 1749–1814. France.
SOWERBY. James DeCarl Sowerby, 1787–1871, secretary Royal Botanical Society, England.
SPACH. Edouard Spach, 1801–1879. Strassburg.
SPAE. Dieudonné Spae, 1819–1858, Belgian horticulturist.
SPAETH. Franz Ludwig Spaeth, 1839–1913; Hellmut Ludwig Spaeth, 1885–. German nurserymen.
SPEGAZZINI. Carlos Spegazzini, 1858–1926. Argentina.
SPENNER. Fridolin Karl Leopold Spenner, 1798–1841. Germany.
SPRAGUE. Thomas Archibald Sprague, 1877–. Royal Botanic Gardens, Kew, England.
SPRENG. Kurt Sprengel, 1766–1833. Germany.
SPRENGER. Karl Sprenger, 1847–1918, Italian nurseryman.
SPRING. Anton Fr. Spring, 1814–1872. Belgium.
ST. AMANS. Jean Florimond Boudon de Saint Amans, 1748–1831. France.
STANDL. Paul Carpenter Standley, 1884–. Chicago Natural History Museum.
STAPF. Otto Stapf, 1857–1933. Royal Botanic Gardens, Kew, England.
STEARN. W. T. Stearn, 1911–. Royal Horticultural Society, London, England.
STEFF. Boris Stefanoff, 1894–. University of Sofia.
STEPH. Friedrich Stephan, 1757–1814. Russia.
STERNB. Caspar, Graf von Sternberg, 1761–1838. Germany.
STEUD. Ernst Gottlieb Steudel, 1783–1856. Germany.
STEVEN. Christian von Steven, 1781–1863. Russia.
STEVENS. S. G. Stevens, contemporaneous. England.
S. R. STEWART. Sara R. Stewart (Mrs. George Metcalf Hinckley), 1913–. Hanover, Pennsylvania.
ST. HIL. Auguste de Saint Hilaire, 1779–1853. France.
ST. JOHN. Harold St. John, 1892–. University of Hawaii.
ST. LAGER. Jean Baptiste Saint Lager, 1825–1912. France.
STOKES. Jonathan Stokes, 1755–1831. Great Britain.
STOY. Nickolaai A. Stoyanoff, contemporaneous. University of Sofia.
STROBL. P. Gabriel Strobl, 1846–1925.
STURT. Edward Lewis Sturtevant, 1842–1898, agricultural writer. Massachusetts and New York.
SUDW. George Bishop Sudworth, 1864–1927, dendrologist, United States Forest Service.
SUKS. William Nikolaus Suksdorf, 1850–1932. United States.
SÜNDERM. F. Sündermann, 1864–, German nurseryman.
SURINGAR. Jan Valckenier Suringar, 1865–1932. Holland.
SUTER. Johann Rudolf Suter, 1766–1827. Bern, Switzerland.
SW. Olof Swartz, 1760–1818. Sweden.
SWEET. Robert Sweet, 1783–1835, British horticulturist and botanist.
SWINGLE. Walter Tennyson Swingle, 1871–. United States Department of Agriculture.
SYME. J. T. I. Boswell-Syme, 1822–1888. England.
SZYSZ. Ignaz Szyszylowicz, 1857–1910. Poland.

TAKEDA. Hisayoshi Takeda, 1883–. Tokyo, Japan.
TANAKA. Yoshio (or Ushio) Tanaka, 1838–1916. Japan.
TANFANI. Enrico Tanfani, 1848–1892. Italy.
TAROUCA. Graf Ernst Silva Tarouca, 1860–1936. Austria.
TAUB. Paul Hermann Wilhelm Taubert, 1862–1897. Germany.
TAUSCH. Ignaz Friedrich Tausch, 1793–1848. Austria.
N. TAYLOR. Norman Taylor, 1883–, horticulturist. New York.
TEMPLE. F. L. Temple & Beard, American nurserymen about 1890.
TEN. Michele Tenore, 1780–1861. Italy.
TEYS. J. E. Teysmann, 1808–1882. Holland and Java.
THELL. Albert Thellung, 1881–1928. Switzerland.
THIEL. Hugo Thiel, 1834–1918. Bonn, Germany.
THOMAS. David Thomas, 1776–1859. United States.
THOMS. Thomas Thomson, 1817–1878. Great Britain and India.
THONN. Peter Thonning, 1775–1848. Denmark.
THORY. Claude Antoine Thory, 1759–1827. France.
THOUARS. Louis Marie Aubert DuPetit Thouars, 1758–1831. France.
THOUIN. André Thouin, 1747–1824. France.
THUILL. Jean Louis Thuillier, 1757–1822. France.
THUNB. Carl Peter Thunberg, 1743–1822, author Flora Japonica and Flora Capensis. Sweden.
THURBER. George Thurber, 1821–1890. United States.
THURSTON. Edgar Thurston, 1855–1935. Great Britain.
THWAITES. George Henry Kendrik Thwaites, 1811–1882. Ceylon.
TIDESTR. Ivar Tidestrom, 1865–. Washington, D. C.
TINEO. Vincenzo Tineo, 1791–1856. Italy.
TISCH. A. Tischer, contemporaneous. Baden, Germany.
TOD. Agostino Todaro, 1818–1892. Italy.
TOPF. Alfred Topf, German horticulturist in the 1850's.

TORR. John Torrey, 1796–1873. New York.
TRACY. Samuel Mills Tracy, 1847–1920. United States Department of Agriculture.
TRATT. Leopold Trattinick, 1764–1849. Austria.
TRAUTV. Ernst Rudolph von Trautvetter, 1809–1889. Russia.
TREL. William Trelease, 1857–1945. Illinois.
TREV. Conte Victore Trevisan, 1818–1897. Italy.
TREW. Christoph Jacob Trew, 1695–1769. Germany.
TRIANA. José Triana, 1828–1890. Bogota, Colombia.
TRIN. Carl Bernhard Trinius, 1778–1844. Russia.
TUBEUF. Karl, Freiherr von Tubeuf, 1862–1941. Germany.
TURCZ. Nikolai Stepanovich Turczaninow, 1796–1864. Russia.
TURPIN. Pierre Jean François Turpin, 1775–1840. France.
TURRA. Antonio Turra, 1730–1796. Italy.
TURRILL. W. B. Turrill, 1890–. Royal Botanic Gardens, Kew, England.
TUSSAC. F. Richard, Chevalier de Tussac, 1751–1837. France.

ULB. Eberhard Ulbrich, 1879–. Berlin, Germany.
UNDERW. Lucien M. Underwood, 1853–1907, specialist on ferns. United States.
UNGER. Franz Joseph Andreas Nicolaus Unger, 1800–1870. Austria.
URBAN. Ignatius Urban, 1848–1931, writer on Brazilian and West Indian plants. Germany.
URUM. Ivan Kiroff Urumoff, 1856–1937. Bulgaria.

VAHL. Martin Vahl, 1749–1804. Denmark.
VAIL. Anna Murray Vail, published about 1896. United States.
VAILL. S. Vaillant, 1669–1722. France.
VANDAS. Karl Vandas, 1861–1923. Czechoslovakia.
VANESELTINE. Glen Parker VanEseltine, 1888–1938. New York.
VANHOUTTE. Louis VanHoutte, 1810–1876, Belgian horticulturist, founder and publisher of Flore des Serres.
VANIOT. Eugène Vaniot, nineteenth-century French botanist.
VAN MELLE. Peter Jacobus van Melle, 1891– nurseryman. Poughkeepsie, New York.
VANSTEENIS. Cornelis G. G. J. VanSteenis, 1901–. Buitenzorg, Java.
VASEY. George R. Vasey, 1822–1893. United States Department of Agriculture.
VATKE. Georg Carl Wilhelm Vatke, 1849–1889. Germany.
VAUPEL. Friedrich Johann Vaupel, 1876–1927, writer on cacti. Germany.
VAUV. Léopold Eugene Vauvel, 1848–1915, French horticulturist.
VEITCH. John Gould Veitch, 1839–1870, and successors, horticulturists at Chelsea, England.
VELEN. Josef Velenovsky, 1858–. Czechoslovakia.
VELL. José Marianno Vellozo de Conceiçao, 1742–1811, Catholic priest. Brazil.
VENT. Etienne Pierre Ventenat, 1757–1808. France.
VEST. L. Chr. von Vest, 1776–1840. Austria.
VIC. Carlos Vicioso, contemporaneous. Spain.
VICTORIN. Fr. Marie-Victorin, 1885–1944. University of Montreal.
VIERHAPPER. Fritz Vierhapper, 1876–1902. Austria.
VIG. René Viguier, 1880–1931. France.
VIGNET. A. von Vignet, about 1795. Austria.
VILL. Dominique Villars, 1745–1814. France.
F. VILL. Celestine Fernandez-Villar, 1838–1907. Spain and Philippines.
VILM. Several generations of the family of Vilmorin, Paris, seedsmen and authors of many books and memoirs on botany and horticulture; Pierre Philippe André Levéque de Vilmorin, 1746–1804; Pierre Vilmorin, 1816–1860; Henry L. de Vilmorin, died 1899; Maurice Levéque de Vilmorin, 1849–1919; Philippe de Vilmorin, 1872–1917.
VINES. Sydney Howard Vines, 1849–1934. England.
VIS. Roberto de Visiani, 1800–1878. Italy.
VITM. Fulgenzio Vitman, 1728–1806. Italy.
VIV. Domenico Viviani, 1772–1840. Italy.
VOG. Julius Rudolph Theodor Vogel, 1812–1841, German botanist who collected at Fernando Po.
VOIGT. Johann Otto Voigt, 1798–1843. Calcutta, India.
VOS. C. de Vos, about 1880, Dutch horticulturist.
VOSS. Andreas Voss, 1857–1924. Germany.

WAHL. Goran Wahlenberg, 1780–1851. Sweden.
WAHLB. Pehr Frederick Wahlberg, 1800–1877. Sweden.
WALDST. Franz de Paul Adam, Graf von Waldstein, 1759–1823. Austria.
WALL. Nathaniel Wallich, 1786–1854, wrote on plants of India and Asia. Denmark.
WALLACE. P. Wallace & Company, nurserymen, Colchester, England; R. W. Wallace.
WALLIS. Gustav Wallis, 1830–1878. Germany and South America.
WALLR. Carl Friedrich Wilhelm Wallroth, 1792–1857. Germany.
WALP. Wilhelm Gerhard Walpers, 1816–1853. Germany.
WALT. Thomas Walter, 1740?–1789. South Carolina.
E. WALTHER. Eric Walther, 1892–. Golden Gate Park, San Francisco, California.
WANGERIN. Walter Wangerin, 1884–1938. Germany.
WANGH. Friedrich Adam Julius von Wangenheim, 1747–1800. Germany.
WARB. Otto Warburg, 1859–1938. Germany.
WARD. Francis Kingdon Ward, 1885–. Great Britain.
WARDER. John Aston Warder, 1812–1883, physician and horticulturist. Cincinnati, Ohio.
WATS. Sereno Watson, 1826–1892. Harvard University.
H. C. WATS. Hewett Cottrell Watson, 1804–1881. England.
W. WATS. William Watson, 1858–1925, horticulturist. Royal Botanic Gardens, Kew, England.
WATT. George Watt, 1851–1930. India.
WAUGH. Frank Albert Waugh, 1869–1943, horticulturist. Massachusetts.
WAWRA. Heinrich Ritter von Fernsee Wawra, 1831–1887. Austria.
WEATHERBY. Charles Alfred Weatherby, 1875–. Gray Herbarium.

WEBB. Philip Barker Webb, 1793–1854. Great Britain.
WEBER. Georg Heinrich Weber, 1752–1828. Germany.
WEDD. Hugh Algernon Weddell, 1819–1877, collector in South America.
WEHRHAHN. Heinrich Rudolf Wehrhahn, 1887–1940, director Wurttemberg horticultural school gardens, Hohenheim, Germany.
WEICK. Adolphe Weick, horticulturist in Strassburg in 1863.
WELW. Friedrich Martin Josef Welwitsch, 1806–1872. Austria.
WENDEROTH. Georg Wilhelm Franz Wenderoth, 1774–1861. Germany.
WENDL. Hermann Wendland, 1823–1903, director royal botanic garden at Herrenhausen, writer on palms.
WENZ. Theodor Wenzig, 1824–1892. Germany.
WERD. Erich Werdermann, contemporaneous, writer on cacti. Germany.
WERN. Ludwig Friedrich Franz von Werneck, about 1791. Germany.
WESM. Alfred Wesmael, 1821–1905. Belgium.
WEST. Richard Weston, 1733–1806. Great Britain.
WESTC. Frederic Westcott, died 1861, editor Floral Cabinet. Birmingham, England.
WETTST. Richard von Wettstein, 1862–1931. Austria.
WHEELER. Louis Cutter Wheeler, 1910–. University of Pennsylvania.
WHEELOCK. William Efner Wheelock, 1852–1926. New York.
WHERRY. Edgar Theodore Wherry, 1885–. University of Pennsylvania.
C. T. WHITE. Cyril Tenison White, 1890–. Brisbane, Queensland, Australia.
WIBEL. August Wilhelm Eberhard Christoph Wibel, 1775–1814. Germany.
WIEGAND. Karl McKay Wiegand, 1873–1942. Cornell University.
WIGHT. Robert Wight, 1796–1872, writer on Indian plants. Great Britain.
W. F. WIGHT. William Franklin Wight, 1874–. Bonsall, California.
WILLD. Karl Ludwig Willdenow, 1765–1812. Germany.
WILLIAMS. Frederic N. Williams, 1862–1923, writer on Caryophyllaceæ. England.
B. S. WILLIAMS. Benjamin Samuel Williams, 1824–1890, British nurseryman.
L. O. WILLIAMS. Louis Otho Williams, 1908– Harvard University.
WILLK. Heinrich Moritz Willkomm, 1821–1895. Germany.
WILLM. Ellen Ann Willmott, 1860–1934. Warley Place, England.
WILMOTT. Alfred James Wilmott, 1888–. British Museum, London.
WILS. Ernest Henry Wilson, 1876–1930. Arnold Arboretum.
P. WILS. Percy Wilson, 1879–1944. New York Botanical Garden.
WIMM. Christian Friedrich Heinrich Wimmer, 1803–1868. Germany.
WINK. Hubert Winkler, 1875–1941; Hans Winkler, 1877–. Germany.
WITH. William Withering, 1741–1799. Great Britain.
WITTE. Heinrich Witte, 1825–1917, Dutch horticulturist.
WITTM. Max Carl Ludwig Wittmack, 1839–1929, editor of Gartenflora, Germany.
WOOD. Alphonso Wood, 1810–1881. United States.
WOODS. Joseph Woods, 1776–1864. England.
WOODSON. Robert E. Woodson, Jr., 1904–. Missouri Botanical Garden, St. Louis.
WOOT. Elmer Otis Wooton, 1865–. Arlington, Virginia.
WORMSK. Morten Wormskjold, 1783–1845. Denmark.
WOYNAR. Heinrich Woynar, 1865–1917. Austria.
C. H. WRIGHT. Charles Henry Wright, 1864–. England.
J. WRIGHT. John Wright, 1811–1846. United States.
WULFEN. Franz Xaver von Wulfen, 1728–1805. Austria.

YOUNG. Maurice Young, British nurseryman about 1872.

ZABEL. Hermann Zabel, 1832–1912, writer on woody plants. Germany.
ZENARI. Silvia Zenari, 1896–. Italy.
ZENKER. Jonathan Carl Zenker, 1799–1837. Germany.
ZOLL. Heinrich Zollinger, 1818?–1859. Switzerland and Java.
ZUCC. Joseph Gerhard Zuccarini, 1797–1848, professor at Munich.

THE VEGETABLE COMMUNITY

The community of organisms known broadly as Plants is divided into four great groups or subcommunities; botanists call them Divisions.

I. THALLOPHYTA. The THALLOPHYTES.

Usually not chlorophyll-bearing, destitute of vascular tissue, with little or no woody structure, seldom exhibiting well-marked alternation of generations; the plant body is thalloid—without differentiation of stems and leaves; there is no archegonium and no antheridium at least not as known in the Pteridophyta; propagation is by spores and division.—The lowest in organization of the four great Subcommunities, including the bacteria, the diatoms, desmids and multicellular algæ, myxomycetes, lichens, fungi. Many of the plants are microscopic and detached, often motile; others, as some of the great seaweeds, are of large bulk and attached to rocks or the sea-bed. Most of them lack the green color of ordinary vegetation, and many of them are colorless. Most of the "diseases" of plants are reactions to the attacks of parasitic fungi. The Thallophytes are of many families and genera, and of thousands of species, on all parts of the globe. The genus Agaricus provides the edible mushroom of commerce. Its cultivation is recommended only to specialists and it is not included in this Manual.

II. BRYOPHYTA. MOSSES and LIVERWORTS.

Small green plants, simple in structure, sometimes with merely a thalloid body and in other groups with stem and differentiated leaves, but without true roots and vascular system. The alternation of generations is well marked, and the gametophyte is the dominant one. They are without flowers in the popular sense, and for the most part are not showy plants; none is cultivated, or included in this Manual. There are numerous families, genera, and species widely distributed on the earth, particularly in moist places.

III. PTERIDOPHYTA. FERNS and FERN ALLIES.

Green plants with vascular tissue, true roots, and usually with clear differentiation of leaf (frond) and stem: alternation of generations distinct, the sporophyte or asexual generation constituting "the plant" as known to cultivators and others: gametophyte a small thallus-like body (prothallus), usually flat on the ground, bearing the eggs in a structure known as an archegonium and the sperm-cells in an antheridium; from the fertilization of the egg arises the sporophyte, which in turn produces asexual spores, the prothallus usually disappearing; from the asexual organs of the sporophyte arises the prothallus or gametophyte of the succeeding generation; the male cells or bodies are often motile; propagation by means of spores, without embryo.—This Subcommunity comprises the higher cryptogams, the more familiar of the so-called "flowerless plants." It comprises some 6,000 widely distributed species, largely tropical. Many of them are choice and popular subjects in cultivation.

This Subcommunity is divided into five main classes: 1, *Filicales*, the ferns; 2, *Equisetales*, the equisetums or scouring-rushes, not represented in this book; 3, *Lycopodiales*, the club-mosses and selaginellas; 4, *Psilotales*, comprising the single tropical genus Psilotum sometimes grown as a curiosity but not accounted for in this book; 5, *Isoetales*, the quillworts, widespread aquatics not much grown and not represented in this book.

Formerly it was the custom to comprise all the ferns in one group known as Filices. Now most authorities separate them into about 10 families, with a very recent treatment recognizing 19 families in the Filicales alone. The recognized genera by conservative standards are about 160, although the most recent revision of Filicales accepts 309 genera as the valid number. Characters to be observed in a fern prior to attempting identification are: the nature of the veining between the midrib of the segment and the margin, the veinlets "free" (not joined with others) or anastomosing (when they run together, joining other veinlets, sometimes forming a clear reticulation); the nature of the fronds, whether dimorphic or monomorphic; whether sporangia are clustered in sori or scattered over the surface; the sori may or may not be enveloped by a thin indusium and are of varying shapes from round to linear and variously disposed on the frond. These and other characters are of prime importance in comprehending the relationships and identities of ferns.

IV. Spermatophyta. The Spermatophytes, or Seed-Plants.

Plants producing seeds, which contain an embryo or dormant plant that becomes active under favorable conditions and "germinates"; the male generative cells or bodies are usually not motile, and fertilization is effected by means of a tube that results from the "germination" of a pollen-grain and penetrates to the macrosporangium or ovule; plants green (with minor exceptions), containing chlorophyll.—The Spermatophyta are the highest in organization of the Vegetable Community, constituting the greater part of the vegetation of the earth, represented in many families and probably 130,000 or more known species. These are the "flowering plants" or phenogams as distinguished from all the lower orders formerly called "flowerless plants" or cryptogams, but these distinctions cannot be defended on morphological grounds. Usually the Spermatophytes bear distinct flowers, but it is only by the broadest definition that the reproductive parts of the Gymnosperms can be called flowers.

This Subcommunity divides itself as follows:

Subdivision I. *Gymnospermæ:* ovules naked, not inclosed in an ovary.
Subdivision II. *Angiospermæ:* ovules within an ovary.
- **Class I.** *Monocotyledonæ*: seed-leaf or cotyledon 1, vascular bundles scattered through a large pith.
- **Class II.** *Dicotyledonæ:* seed-leaves or cotyledons 2 or more.
  - **Subclass I.** *Polypetalæ* (*Choripetalæ*)*:* petals (or sepals) distinct or separate when present.
  - **Subclass II.** *Gamopetalæ* (*Sympetalæ*)*:* petals (or sepals) united.

Each Subclass is in turn divided into relatively large groups called Orders. These are given Latin names taken usually from that of an included family and bear the suffix *-ales*, as Rosales. Orders in turn are comprised of families, as for example the Rose family, and the Latin names of families usually bear the suffix *-aceæ* (Rosaceæ). There are nearly 300 families of Spermatophyta of which about 50 belong in the Monocotyledonæ. Of the total families 194 are accounted for in this Manual.

KEY TO THE FAMILIES AS REPRESENTED IN THIS MANUAL

Plants without seeds or fls., reproducing by spores borne in sporangia..... Division I. PTERIDOPHYTA
Plants with seeds usually produced from cones or by fls............... Division II. SPERMATOPHYTA

Division I. PTERIDOPHYTA. FERNS and FERN ALLIES.

Plants with distinct alternation of generations, the leafy plant (sporophyte) reproducing by non-sexual spores which are formed in sporangia. These are produced on the under side of the lvs., in the upper axil of the lvs., on the margins, or on special branches. Spores developing into prothallia (gametophyte) which bear antheridia (containing swimming sperms) and archegonia (containing eggs). The fertilized egg forms the new sporophyte.

A. Plants free-floating aquatics.
  B. Lvs. 2–20 in. long, 1–4-pinnate .... 7. PARKERIACEÆ
  BB. Lvs. to 1 in. long, the sterile parts entire .... 8. SALVINIACEÆ
AA. Plants not free-floating aquatics.
  B. Lvs. minute, less than ¼ in. long, very numerous; those of certain special terminal branches aggregated into green cone-like clusters and each with a single sporangium in the axil .... 9. SELAGINELLACEÆ
  BB. Lvs. larger, not forming cone-like bodies: plants fern-like.
    C. Fertile fronds or portions of fronds conspicuously unlike the sterile.
      D. Species of slender twining or climbing ferns with palmate or pinnate pinnæ: annulus of sporangium apical, cap-like .... 3. SCHIZÆACEÆ
      DD. Species not twining or climbing.
        E. Rootstock almost none, the usually solitary frond seeming to arise from a cluster of fleshy roots: sporangia large, globular, borne in a stalked spike or panicle above the base of the green blade which appears lateral .... 1. OPHIOGLOSSACEÆ
        EE. Rootstock well developed or the st. forming a trunk above ground.
          F. The fertile fronds or segms. green and lf.-like .... 6. POLYPODIACEÆ
          FF The fertile fronds or segms. brown and not green and lf.-like.
            G. Sporangia naked, large, globose, opening by a longitudinal slit .... 2. OSMUNDACEÆ
            GG. Sporangia minute, inclosed in round bodies formed by the inrolled segms., and opening transversely .... 6. POLYPODIACEÆ
    CC. Fertile fronds or portions of fronds essentially like the sterile.
      D. Species small to large, but not tree-ferns: annulus of sporangium vertical, not a complete ring .... 6. POLYPODIACEÆ
      DD. Species of tree-ferns: annulus oblique, a complete ring.
        E. Sori on back of segms. or in forks of fertile veins .... 4. CYATHEACEÆ
        EE. Sori at ends of veins or on lf.-margins .... 5. DICKSONIACEÆ

Division II. SPERMATOPHYTA. SEED-PLANTS.

Plants without distinct alternation of generations, the sexual generation (gametophyte) much reduced and parasitic upon the asexual generation (sporophyte). The egg-cell fertilized in most cases by means of the pollen-tube and developing into an embryo which becomes dormant in the seed.

Seeds not inclosed in ripened pistils, but naked and usually borne on the surface of a scale; the imbricated or crowded scales usually forming a cone or strobilus: plants without typical fls. .... Subdivision I. GYMNOSPERMÆ
Seeds inclosed in ripened pistils: plants with typical fls. .... Subdivision II. ANGIOSPERMÆ

Subdivision I. GYMNOSPERMÆ. CONE-BEARING PLANTS.

Trees or shrubs, mostly evergreen, usually with needle-like or scale-like lvs.: ovules and seeds borne naked on the surface of a scale or on a modified lf.: stamens in catkin-like clusters: ovuliferous scales or carpels commonly in cones; ovules becoming dry or drupe-like seeds.

A. Foliage pinnate, persistent: plants palm-like .... 10. CYCADACEÆ
AA. Foliage simple: plants not palm-like.
  B. Seeds 1, rarely 2, drupe-like or berry-like; embryo with 2 cotyledons.
    C. Lvs. fan-shaped, usually bilobed, deciduous .... 11. GINKGOACEÆ
    CC. Lvs. needle-shaped or linear, persistent.
      D. Anthers 2-celled: lf. mostly 1½–4 in. long .... 13. PODOCARPACEÆ
      DD. Anthers 3–9-celled.
        E. Lf. ½–1¼ in. long, either with pale green to tawny bands beneath or with 2 glaucous lines narrower than the 3 green ones: branchlets alternate or subopposite .... 12. TAXACEÆ

EE. Lf. 1–3 in. long, with 2 glaucous lines beneath broader than the 3 green lines: branchlets opposite.............................14. CEPHALOTAXACEÆ
BB. Seeds several or many, in a more or less woody dry cone or (in Juniperus) in a berry-like cone formed by the union of several scales; embryo with 2 to several cotyledons.
C. Lvs. alternate, ovate-lanceolate, ⅓in. or more in width at base: each cone-scale with 1 ovule.............................15. ARAUCARIACEÆ
CC. Lvs. alternate, opposite or whorled, needle-shaped, linear or scale-like, usually narrower at base: each cone-scale with 2 or more ovules.
D. Species with opposite or whorled usually scale-like lvs.: cotyledons usually 2.
E. Length of all lvs. less than 1 in.............................18. CUPRESSACEÆ
EE. Length of some lvs. 3–6 in.............................17. TAXODIACEÆ (Sciadopitys)
DD. Species with alternate or fascicled usually linear or needle-like lvs.: cotyledons commonly more than 2.
E. Cone-scales in axils of distinct bracts; scales flattened, with 2 seeds..16. PINACEÆ
EE. Cone-scales without bracts; scales often peltate, with 2–9 seeds.....17. TAXODIACEÆ

Subdivision II. ANGIOSPERMÆ. FLOWERING PLANTS.

Herbs, shrubs or trees: ovules and seeds borne in an ovary (base of pistil) which ripens into a dry or fleshy fruit: plants with true fls. bearing various combinations of sepals, petals, stamens and pistils.

Floral parts usually in 3's: lvs. mostly parallel-veined: cotyledon usually 1: st. commonly with scattered vascular bundles and, even when woody, not forming ann. rings.............................Class I. MONOCOTYLEDONÆ
Floral parts usually in 4's or 5's: lvs. mostly net-veined: cotyledons usually 2: st. commonly with the vascular bundles in a ring and, if woody, having ann. rings.............................Class II. DICOTYLEDONÆ

Class I. MONOCOTYLEDONÆ.

Mostly per. herbs, sometimes ann., or shrubs or trees: sts. not forming ann. rings even when increasing in thickness: lvs. usually parallel-veined: fls. commonly on the plan of 3.

A. Foliage of the palm type, i.e. large stiff palmate or pinnate lvs.
B. Ovary 3-celled and 3-ovuled: fr. 1-seeded by abortion.............................27. PALMACEÆ
BB. Ovary 1-celled (but of 2 or 4 carpels), many-ovuled: fr. a syncarp.........28. CYCLANTHACEÆ
AA. Foliage not palm-like (lvs. not large, stiff, palmate or pinnate).
B. Perianth none or rudimentary and the parts of bristles or scales, not petaloid.
C. Fls. in the axils of dry or chaffy usually imbricated bracts (glumes or scales).
D. Sts. mostly hollow, closed at the nodes: lvs. 2-ranked, with split sheaths.............................25. GRAMINEÆ
DD. Sts. solid: lvs. 3-ranked, with closed sheaths.............................26. CYPERACEÆ
CC. Fls. not in the axils of dry or chaffy bracts (glumes or scales).
D. Parts of perianth represented by bristles: plants monœcious, with staminate fls. above and pistillate fls. below, in long terminal spikes, called "cat-tails".............................19. TYPHACEÆ
DD. Parts of perianth lacking, or of 4–8 scales.
E. Plants diœcious, woody, with long stiff sword-like lvs. which are spine-margined in ours.............................20. PANDANACEÆ
EE. Plants monœcious or with perfect fls., mostly herbaceous and with broad lvs.............................29. ARACEÆ
BB. Perianth present, usually of 2 series, at least the inner petaloid, not of bristles or scales.
C. Pistils several, not united, each representing 1 carpel: plants of wet places.
D. Parts of perianth usually 2, rarely 1 or 3, petaloid.............................21. APONOGETONACEÆ
DD. Parts of perianth 6, in 2 series, the inner petaloid.
E. Ovules few: fr. indehiscent: fls. (ours) white.............................22. ALISMACEÆ
EE. Ovules many: fr. dehiscent: fls. (ours) pink or yellow.............................23. BUTOMACEÆ
CC. Pistils 1, of united carpels, as evidenced by placentæ, stigma-lobes, style-branches: plants usually not of wet places.
D. Ovary, and fr., superior.
E. Outer segms. of perianth calyx-like and different from the inner corolla-like segms.
F. Lvs. few, not overlapping or sheathing.............................33. LILIACEÆ
FF. Lvs. many, overlapping or sheathing.
G. Ovules many in each cell: plants terrestrial or epiphytic: lvs. often spiny-toothed: sap not viscid.............................30. BROMELIACEÆ
GG. Ovules few to 1 in each cell: plants terrestrial: lvs. not spiny-toothed: sap viscid.............................31. COMMELINACEÆ
EE. Outer and inner segms. of perianth essentially alike, at least all petaloid.
F. Infl. a scapose umbel subtended by more or less membranous spathe-like bracts.............................35. AMARYLLIDACEÆ
FF. Infl. not an umbel, or if subumbellate not with spathe-like bracts.

G. Fls. irregular: aquatic plants..............................32. PONTEDERIACEÆ

GG. Fls. regular (except sometimes in Camassia where 1 segm. may curve downward): not aquatic.

H. Plants not or only slightly xerophytic: lvs. not fibrous: style usually divided: fls. variously arranged..........33. LILIACEÆ

HH. Plants usually very xerophytic and woody: lvs. mostly fibrous, sword-like, in dense basal or apical tufts: style simple: fls. commonly in large panicles................34. AGAVACEÆ

DD. Ovary, and fr., partly or wholly inferior.

E. Fertile stamens 1 (or 2), the others often becoming petaloid staminodia and more conspicuous than the perianth.

F. Stamen or stamens grown together with the pistil to form a gynandrium or column: ovary twisted....................42. ORCHIDACEÆ

FF. Stamen and pistil not so grown together: ovary not twisted.

G. Anthers 2-celled: sepals united into a sometimes spathaceous tube..39. ZINGIBERACEÆ

GG. Anthers 1-celled: sepals free or at most connivent.

H. Ovules many in each cell: fls. large, mostly more than 2 in. long..40. CANNACEÆ

HH. Ovules 1 in each cell: fls. small, less than 1 in. long.........41. MARANTACEÆ

EE. Fertile stamens 3 or more; no petaloid staminodia.

F. Habit aquatic, submerged or floating: ovules spread all over the inner surface of ovary: fls. mostly unisexual................24. HYDROCHARITACEÆ

FF. Habit terrestrial or epiphytic: ovules confined to placentæ: fls. usually bisexual.

G. Segms. of perianth in 2 series, the outer differing from the inner in size, shape or color.

H. Petals dissimilar, or only 1: plants mostly large, almost tree-like..38. MUSACEÆ

HH. Petals essentially alike, 3 in number: plants usually not very large.

I. Stamens 3: bracts usually green or membranous.......37. IRIDACEÆ

II. Stamens 6.

J. Lvs. many, overlapping: fls. more than 1, usually with brightly colored bracts..........................30. BROMELIACEÆ

JJ. Lvs. 2–3: fl. 1, with single membranous bract.........35. AMARYLLIDACEÆ

GG. Segms. of perianth not in 2 distinct series, but all petaloid.

H. Plants herbaceous vines with small inconspicuous unisexual fls..36. DIOSCOREACEÆ

HH. Plants not vine-like: fls. bisexual.

I. Stamens 3..37. IRIDACEÆ

II. Stamens 6.

J. Ovary only partially inferior: small scapose herbs with linear lvs..33. LILIACEÆ

JJ. Ovary wholly inferior.

K. Fls. 1 or usually several in a scapose umbel, commonly subtended by 1 or more spathe-like bracts. 35. AMARYLLIDACEÆ

KK. Fls. not so arranged and subtended.

L. Anthers versatile: fls. many, in large panicles or long open racemose spikes..................34. AGAVACEÆ

LL. Anthers basifixed: fls. few, in dense heads or spikes..35. AMARYLLIDACEÆ

Class II. DICOTYLEDONÆ.

Herbs, shrubs or trees: sts. increasing in thickness by a cambium which in woody plants forms ann. rings: lvs. not parallel-veined: fls. usually on the plan of 4 or 5.

A. Corolla lacking or not apparent: calyx present or absent, sometimes simulating a corolla and sometimes in more than 1 whorl. (For AA, see page 63.)

B. Species (trees) with jointed rush-like branchlets resembling pine-needles: lvs. whorled and reduced to minute scales.......................43. CASUARINACEÆ

BB. Species otherwise, woody or herbaceous, with ordinary foliage.

C. Arrangement of fls., at least the staminate, in catkins.

D. Fls. of both sexes in catkins, without calyx; ovary superior.

E. Fr. with many comose seeds: plants diœcious: fls. subtended by a minute gland or a fimbriate bract....................46. SALICACEÆ

EE. Fr. 1-seeded, without coma: fls. not so subtended (bract, if present, not fimbriate).

F. Pistillate fl. solitary in axil of scale; catkins upright: plants diœcious or monœcious..............................47. MYRICACEÆ

FF. Pistillate fls. 2–3 in axil of scale; catkins usually pendulous: plants monœcious....................................49. CORYLACEÆ

DD. Fls. of usually only one sex in catkins, those of at least one sex having a calyx (or perianth).

E. Ovary superior, becoming fleshy in fr......................52. MORACEÆ

EE. Ovary inferior, eventually becoming a dry fr. (the husk sometimes fleshy until mature).

F. Lvs. pinnate..48. JUGLANDACEÆ

FF. Lvs. simple..50. FAGACEÆ

CC. Arrangement of fls. not in catkins.

D. Pistils more than 1, often numerous.

E. Calyx absent.
F. Lvs. opposite, palmately veined.......................... 69. CERCIDIPHYLLACEÆ
FF. Lvs. alternate, pinnately veined.
G. Plants herbaceous: fls. in dense spikes.................. 44. SAURURACEÆ
GG. Plants woody: fls. in axillary clusters.................. 68. EUPTELEACEÆ
EE. Calyx present.
F. Fr. a berry 3 in. or more long: twining shrubs with digitate lvs.. 71. LARDIZABALACEÆ
FF. Fr. not so.
G. Fls. hypogynous, no hypanthium developed.
H. Plant an herb or woody vine...................... 70. RANUNCULACEÆ
HH. Plant a tree or shrub, not vine-like.
I. Stamens united into a tube: sepals connate at base.. 124. STERCULIACEÆ
II. Stamens separate: sepals separate.
J. Length of fls. 1 in. or more: fr. not fleshy.......... 74. MAGNOLIACEÆ
JJ. Length of fls. less than 1 in.: fr. a berry.......... 60. PHYTOLACCACEÆ
GG. Fls. perigynous, the stamens inserted on a hypanthium or "calyx-tube."
H. Lvs. opposite: plants woody...................... 76. CALYCANTHACEÆ
HH. Lvs. alternate: plants mostly herbaceous............ 95. ROSACEÆ
DD. Pistils 1, simple or compound (comprised of 1 or more carpels).
E. Calyx absent.
F. Habit of plant submerged aquatic, with whorled lvs........ 67. CERATOPHYLLACEÆ
FF. Habit of plant not as above.
G. Ovary inferior, 6–10-celled: fls. in globose heads..........146. NYSSACEÆ (Davidia)
GG. Ovary superior, 1–3-celled.
H. Plant a deciduous tree, diœcious: fr. a winged 1-seeded nutlet 1 in. long or more...................... 93. EUCOMMIACEÆ
HH. Plant herbaceous or woody, not diœcious: fr. not a winged nutlet.
I. Fls. in dense spikes or racemes, bisexual or unisexual; stamens 1–10; ovary 1-celled: sap not milky.
J. Ovule 1, basal: lvs. mostly fleshy: plants not hardy N.. 45. PIPERACEÆ
JJ. Ovules 3–8, on 3–4 parietal placentæ: lvs. thin: plants hardy N.......................... 44. SAURURACEÆ
II. Fls. in cyathia, the naked pistillate fl. surrounded by several staminate fls. each consisting of 1 stamen on a jointed pedicel, the whole cluster surrounded by an involucre; ovary usually 3-celled and 3–6-ovuled: sap milky..................................106. EUPHORBIACEÆ
EE. Calyx present.
F. Fls., at least the pistillate, in small globular heads or dense spikes or inside a hollow receptacle: plants woody.
G. Fr. dry.
H. Nodes sheathed by stipules: fr. a nutlet.............. 94. PLATANACEÆ
HH. Nodes not so sheathed.
I. Lvs. palmately lobed: fr. a caps.................. 92. HAMAMELIDACEÆ (Liquidambar)
II. Lvs. pinnate, or simple phyllodia: fr. a legume...... 96. LEGUMINOSÆ (Acacia)
GG. Fr. fleshy.
H. Ovary inferior: fr. a drupe..........................146. NYSSACEÆ (Davidia)
HH. Ovary superior: frs. aggregated into a syncarp, or inside a hollow receptacle........................... 52. MORACEÆ
FF. Fls. not in globular heads, or if so the plant not woody.
G. Ovary wholly or partly inferior.
H. Foliage and young shoots scurfy with peltate or stellate scales: shrubs..........................142. ELÆAGNACEÆ
HH. Foliage and shoots not scurfy.
I. Plants aquatic, with whorled feathery lvs...........151. HALORAGACEÆ (Myriophyllum)
II. Plants terrestrial.
J. Habit climbing, vines.
K. Color of fls. white: stamens 15–20: fr. a winged achene................................ 60. PHYTOLACCACEÆ (Agdestis)
KK. Color of fls. yellow-green, sometimes with purple stripes: stamens 6 or 12: fr. a caps........... 55. ARISTOLOCHIACEÆ
JJ. Habit not climbing.
K. Plant an herb.
L. Lvs. cauline: plant a prostrate ann. grown for food................................ 61. AIZOACEÆ (Tetragonia)
LL. Lvs. basal.
M. Blades of lvs. large, 2–6 ft. across: fls. in very large spikes or panicles............151. HALORAGACEÆ (Gunnera)
MM. Blades of lvs. smaller, 2–8 in. across: fls. solitary............................ 55. ARISTOLOCHIACEÆ
KK. Plant woody.
L. Lvs. opposite: shrubs with terminal cymose fl.-clusters........................... 90. SAXIFRAGACEÆ (Hydrangea)

LL. Lvs. alternate.
M. Style 1: mostly trees, evergreen, with entire lvs.
N. Fls. solitary or in umbels or heads; stamens 10: fr. a drupe................147. COMBRETACEÆ (Terminalia)
NN. Fls. in loose spikes; stamens many: fr. a woody caps........................148. MYRTACEÆ (Eucalyptus)
MM. Styles mostly 2: shrubs, mostly deciduous, with lvs. lobed or dentate.
N. Fr. a berry: fls. axillary, solitary or in racemes.......................... 90. SAXIFRAGACEÆ (Ribes)
NN. Fr. a caps.: fls. terminal, in spikes or heads............................ 92. HAMAMELIDACEÆ (Fothergilla)

GG. Ovary superior.
H. Plants trees or shrubs.
I. Lvs. opposite or whorled.
J. Arrangement of lvs. whorled, in 3's or 4's.......... 54. PROTEACEÆ (Macadamia)
JJ. Arrangement of lvs. opposite, in 2's.
K. Fls. in large dense terminal cymes or globose clusters: lvs. 3–8 in. long, very broad......... 90. SAXIFRAGACEÆ (Hydrangea)
KK. Fls. solitary or in small mostly axillary clusters: lvs. often smaller.
L. Fr. a samara: lvs. usually lobed or compound.
M. Samara 1-celled, single: lvs. pinnate.......166. OLEACEÆ (Fraxinus)
MM. Samara 2-celled, double: lvs. usually palmately lobed........................114. ACERACEÆ
LL. Fr. not a samara: lvs. entire and simple.
M. Cells of ovary 3, with 2 ovules in each cell: calyx greenish........................107. BUXACEÆ (Buxus)
MM. Cells of ovary 1–2, with 1 ovule in each cell.
N. Lf. strongly 3-nerved from base: fls. yellow to yellow-white................ 79. LAURACEÆ (Cinnamomum)
NN. Lf. 1-nerved from base.
O. Fls. rose or lilac, in axillary clusters of 3–7 or in heads..................141. THYMELÆACEÆ
OO. Fls. scarlet or yellow, solitary in axils..143. LYTHRACEÆ (Cuphea)
II. Lvs. alternate.
J. Blades of lvs. compound.
K. Lf. odd-pinnate, with 3–11 lfts.: fr. dry.
L. Lfts. 3–11: fls. brownish-green; stamens 5.....110. ANACARDIACEÆ (Pistacia)
LL. Lfts. 3: fls. white-tomentose; stamens 10......106. EUPHORBIACEÆ (Hevea)
KK. Lf. even-pinnate, with 4–8 lfts.
L. Fr. juicy: lfts. sharply acute...............116. SAPINDACEÆ (Litchi)
LL. Fr. a leathery indehiscent legume: lfts. obtuse. 96. LEGUMINOSÆ (Ceratonia)
JJ. Blades of lvs. simple, but often lobed.
K. Anthers opening by pores: plants aromatic..... 79. LAURACEÆ
KK. Anthers opening by slits.
L. Ovules several in each cell of ovary.
M. Cells of ovary 1.
N. Stamens many: trees or shrubs........134. FLACOURTIACEÆ
NN. Stamens 4–5: woody climbers.......... 58. AMARANTHACEÆ (Deeringia)
MM. Cells of ovary usually 2–8.
N. Stamens united into a column: fr. dry..124. STERCULIACEÆ
NN. Stamens separate: fr. fleshy...........134. FLACOURTIACEÆ (Dovyalis)
LL. Ovules 1–2 in each cell of ovary.
M. Cells of ovary 2 to many.
N. Stamens as many as and alternating with the sepals........................119. RHAMNACEÆ
NN. Stamens opposite the sepals or more numerous.
O. Ovary of 5–16 cells: fr. a berry....... 60. PHYTOLACCACEÆ
OO. Ovary of 2–4 cells.
P. The ovules bent upward and inward, so that the raphe is toward the axis of the ovary: sap often milky: fr. a caps. or berry.......106. EUPHORBIACEÆ
PP. The ovules bent downward, so that the raphe is turned away from the axis of the ovary: sap not milky: fr. drupe-like.................107. BUXACEÆ

MM. Cells of ovary 1.
N. Styles or stigmas 2–4.
O. Fls. bisexual.
P. Species of trees: fr. a nutlet surrounded by a broad membranous wing........................ 51. ULMACEÆ (Ulmus)
PP. Species of low shrubs or woody vines: fr. an achene sometimes surrounded by a berry-like body.. 56. POLYGONACEÆ
OO. Fls. unisexual.
P. Fr. a drupe, nut or samara, not inclosed in bracts................ 51. ULMACEÆ
PP. Fr. an achene, inclosed by 2 persistent bracts.................. 57. CHENOPODIACEÆ (Atriplex)
NN. Styles or stigmas 1.
O. Calyx with long cylindrical tube, often swollen at base.................. 54. PROTEACEÆ
OO. Calyx not tubular, or if so quite short.
P. Habit climbing, species of woody vines: fls. surrounded by involucres of gaudy bracts........... 59. NYCTAGINACEÆ (Bougainvillea)
PP. Habit not climbing: fls. not so bracted.
Q. Lf. 3-nerved from base: trees with fleshy frs................ 78. MYRISTICACEÆ
QQ. Lf. 1-nerved from base: trees or shrubs usually with dry frs.
R. The calyx green, 4–5-parted: fls. in axillary panicles, unisexual: plant monœcious.... 53. URTICACEÆ (Boehmeria)
RR. The calyx petaloid, 4-lobed: fls. solitary or in racemes or heads, bisexual, or if unisexual the plant diœcious.
S. Stamens 4................ 54. PROTEACEÆ
SS. Stamens 8 or 10...........141. THYMELÆACEÆ (Daphne)

HH. Plants herbaceous, sometimes slightly woody at base.
I. Foliage modified for catching insects—"pitcher-plants"..................................... 87. NEPENTHACEÆ
II. Foliage not so modified.
J. Cells of ovary 2 or more.
K. Lvs. palmately 5–11-lobed, 1–3 ft. long: fr. a spiny caps..............................106. EUPHORBIACEÆ (Ricinus)
KK. Lvs. obovate, toothed, 3-nerved, 1–3 in. long: fr. a smooth caps...........................107. BUXACEÆ (Pachysandra)
JJ. Cells of ovary 1.
K. Styles or stigmas 1.
L. Lvs. opposite.
M. Calyx showy and petaloid: fl. or fls. surrounded by greenish involucre.......... 59. NYCTAGINACEÆ
MM. Calyx not showy: fls. not involucrate...... 53. URTICACEÆ (Pilea)
LL. Lvs. alternate.
M. Fls. solitary in axils: lvs. simple, entire, less than ½ in. long...................... 53. URTICACEÆ (Helxine)
MM. Fls. clustered: lvs. more than 1 in. long.
N. Lf. lobed to pinnate: fr. an achene inclosed in a hypanthium............. 95. ROSACEÆ
NN. Lf. entire: fr. a berry................. 60. PHYTOLACCACEÆ (Rivina)
KK. Styles or stigmas 2–5.
L. Stipules forming a sheath or ocrea about the st.................................... 56. POLYGONACEÆ
LL. Stipules not forming such a sheath.
M. Involucre surrounding the fls............ 56. POLYGONACEÆ
MM. Involucre not present.
N. Sepals 2: lvs. large, 7-lobed, heart-shaped, alternate........................ 80. PAPAVERACEÆ (Macleaya)
NN. Sepals, at least in staminate fls., mostly 4–5, rarely 2: lvs. not lobed, or if so opposite.
O. Fr. an achene inclosed in the tight calyx or a persistent bract: plants aromatic, diœcious................ 52. MORACEÆ
OO. Fr. a utricle, or if achene-like the plants not diœcious.

P. Lvs. alternate.
Q. Fls. subtended by scarious bracts. 58. AMARANTHACEÆ
QQ. Fls. not so subtended.......... 57. CHENOPODIACEÆ
PP. Lvs. opposite.
Q. Blades of lvs. 1–4 in. long....... 58. AMARANTHACEÆ
QQ. Blades of lvs. less than ⅓ in. long.................... 64. ILLECEBRACEÆ
AA. Corolla present, usually the calyx also, forming 2 differentiated series or the calyx petaloid and subtended by calyx-like bracts.
B. Petals separate or nearly so, normally falling away individually when shed (only 1 in Amorpha). (For BB, see page 68.)
C. Ovary superior. (For CC, see page 67.)
D. Stamens numerous, more than twice as many as the petals.
E. Habit aquatic, the lvs. submerged, floating, or standing above the water.. 66. NYMPHÆACEÆ
EE. Habit terrestrial.
F. Pistil more than 1, distinct or nearly so.
G. Filaments of stamens united into a tube...............122. MALVACEÆ
GG. Filaments not so united.
H. Insertion of stamens on hypanthium or calyx-tube.
I. Sepals and petals in 2 distinct series of 5 each: lvs. alternate.................................. 95. ROSACEÆ
II. Sepals and petals intergrading, spirally arranged: lvs. opposite................................ 76. CALYCANTHACEÆ
HH. Insertion of stamens on the receptacle, hypanthium not developed.
I. Plants herbaceous (1 species of Pæonia shrubby)..... 70. RANUNCULACEÆ
II. Plants woody.
J. Sepals and petals valvate: fls. not showy: fr. fleshy.. 77. ANNONACEÆ
JJ. Sepals and petals imbricate: fls. showy: fr. dry.
K. Pistils in 1 whorl about a short axis............ 75. ILLICIACEÆ
KK. Pistils in several spirals on an elongated axis, the gynœcium strobiliform.................. 74. MAGNOLIACEÆ
FF. Pistil 1, of 1 to several carpels.
G. Foliage modified and insect-catching.
H. Blades of lvs. modified as pitchers.................. 86. SARRACENIACEÆ
HH. Blades of lvs. flat, clothed with gland-bearing hairs or with stiff marginal hairs...................... 88. DROSERACEÆ
GG. Foliage not so modified.
H. Number of sepals 2 or 3.
I. Fr. a drupe: trees.
J. Lf. pinnate-veined, punctate with pellucid dots.... 128. GUTTIFERÆ (Mammea)
JJ. Lf. palmate-veined, not pellucid-punctate......... 106. EUPHORBIACEÆ (Aleurites)
II. Fr. dry: herbs or shrubs.
J. Ripened fr. a lenticular or angled achene: sts. climbing or if not often sheathed by the stipules or ocrea or fls. in an involucre.................. 56. POLYGONACEÆ
JJ. Ripened fr. a follicle or caps.: sts. and fls. not as above.
K. Sepals petaloid and white: fr. a follicle.......... 70. RANUNCULACEÆ (Cimicifuga)
KK. Sepals not petaloid: fr. a caps.
L. Juice milky or colored: lvs. not fleshy: sepals usually caducous........................ 80. PAPAVERACEÆ
LL. Juice not milky or colored: lvs. mostly fleshy: sepals usually not caducous.............. 62. PORTULACACEÆ
HH. Number of sepals 4, 5 or more.
I. Insertion of stamens on the hypanthium or calyxtube.
J. Lvs. mostly opposite: sepals and petals usually 6... 143. LYTHRACEÆ (Lagerstrœmia)
JJ. Lvs. alternate: sepals and petals usually 4 or 5.
K. Ripened ovary a follicle, caps. or drupe: lvs. simple or compound....................... 95. ROSACEÆ
KK. Ripened ovary a legume: lvs. pinnately decompound, or reduced to phyllodia............. 96. LEGUMINOSÆ
II. Insertion of stamens on the receptacle.
J. Sap milky..106. EUPHORBIACEÆ
JJ. Sap not milky.
K. Lvs. opposite.
L. Species of tropical trees with large edible frs. .. 128. GUTTIFERÆ (Garcinia)
LL. Species of herbs and shrubs, usually with capsules.
M. Blades of lvs. punctate with pellucid dots: stamens usually in 3 or 5 bundles........129. HYPERICACEÆ
MM. Blades of lvs. not so punctate: stamens separate...........................131. CISTACEÆ
KK. Lvs. alternate.
L. Stamen-filaments connate at base or united into tube (monadelphous).

M. Anthers 2-celled........................124. STERCULIACEÆ
MM. Anthers 1-celled.
N. Carpels of pistil 5 to many: herbs or shrubs (except Lagunaria)..................122. MALVACEÆ
NN. Carpels of pistil 2–5: tropical trees......123. BOMBACACEÆ
LL. Stamen-filaments separate or sometimes in fascicles (not monadelphous).
M. Ovary elevated on a stipe: sepals and petals 4.................................. 82. CAPPARIDACEÆ (Capparis)
MM. Ovary sessile or nearly so.
N. Species of herbs.
O. Fls. regular; ovary closed at top...... 70. RANUNCULACEÆ
OO. Fls. irregular; ovary open at top before seeds are ripe............... 84. RESEDACEÆ
NN. Species of woody plants.
O. Plants woody climbers: fr. a berry.... 125. ACTINIDIACEÆ
OO. Plants trees or erect shrubs.
P. Fr. a spiny caps.: lvs. palmate-veined.
Q. Fls. pink or rose, in terminal panicles......................132. BIXACEÆ
QQ. Fls. white, in cymose umbels.... 121. TILIACEÆ (Sparmannia)
PP. Fr. not spiny: lvs. mostly pinnate-veined.
Q. Lf. punctate with pellucid dots...101. RUTACEÆ
QQ. Lf. not punctate.
R. The ovary deeply 3–10-lobed, becoming a group of sessile black drupes on a red receptacle......................126. OCHNACEÆ
RR. The ovary not so lobed: fr. a nut, caps. or berry.
S. Sepals (and usually petals) valvate: fls. small, in cymes or panicles.......121. TILIACEÆ
SS. Sepals (and usually petals) imbricate: fls. usually large and showy, solitary or few in clusters........127. THEACEÆ
DD. Stamens few, not more than twice as many as the petals.
E. Pistil more than 1, nearly or quite separate.
F. Species aquatic, with dissected submerged and narrow floating lvs.. 66. NYMPHÆACEÆ (Cabomba)
FF. Species terrestrial.
G. Insertion of stamens on the hypanthium or calyx-tube, perigynous.
H. Plant fleshy, a "succulent"........................ 89. CRASSULACEÆ
HH. Plant not fleshy.
I. Stipules usually present: pistils as many as sepals (fewer in Neillia)............................ 95. ROSACEÆ
II. Stipules usually lacking: pistils mostly fewer than sepals.. 90. SAXIFRAGACEÆ
GG. Insertion of stamens on the receptacle, hypogynous.
H. Sepals petaloid: petals 2-lobed: pistils becoming 1-seeded follicles.............................. 70. RANUNCULACEÆ (Xanthorhiza)
HH. Sepals, petals and pistils not all in same combination as above.
I. Lf. punctate with pellucid dots...................101. RUTACEÆ
II. Lf. not so.
J. Plants fleshy, mostly herbaceous: lvs. commonly simple.. 89. CRASSULACEÆ
JJ. Plants not fleshy.
K. Blades of lvs. simple.
L. Lvs. opposite............................104. MALPIGHIACEÆ
LL. Lvs. alternate.
M. Fls. unisexual, minute, inconspicuous, the plants diœcious...................... 73. MENISPERMACEÆ
MM. Fls. showy, bisexual, or infrequently unisexual and the plants then monœcious... 90. SAXIFRAGACEÆ
KK. Blades of lvs. pinnate: lvs. alternate.
L. Subject a low herb with white or pinkish fls.... 109. LIMNANTHACEÆ
LL. Subject a tree with greenish fls..............102. SIMARUBACEÆ
EE. Pistil 1, made up of 1 or more united carpels.
F. Styles 2–5.
G. Foliage modified and catching insects by long gland-tipped sensitive hairs.................................. 88. DROSERACEÆ
GG. Foliage not so.
H. Arrangement of lvs. opposite.
I. Sepals 2: lvs. fleshy.............................. 62. PORTULACACEÆ
II. Sepals 5: lvs. not fleshy.

J. Caps. not lobed: mostly herbaceous .... 65. CARYOPHYLLACEÆ
JJ. Caps. 2–3-lobed: shrubs or trees .... 113. STAPHYLEACEÆ
HH. Arrangement of lvs. alternate or basal.
I. Sepals 2–3, if more than 2 the lvs. fleshy.
J. Plants climbing .... 63. BASELLACEÆ
JJ. Plants not climbing.
K. Species woody: lvs. stiffly needle-like, to ¼ in. long: ovary 5–9-celled: fls. unisexual .... 108. EMPETRACEÆ
KK. Species herbaceous or suffrutescent: lvs. succulent, foliaceous, ½–6 in. long: ovary 1-celled· fls. bisexual .... 62. PORTULACACEÆ
II. Sepals 5, rarely 4.
J. Species of climbers, usually with a corona (outgrowth between corolla and fertile stamens) ..... 136. PASSIFLORACEÆ
JJ. Species not climbing, nor with corona.
K. Calyx scarious, usually colored: stamens 5, opposite the petals: ovary 1-celled, 1-ovuled, forming a dry dehiscent or indehiscent fr. ...... 161. PLUMBAGINACEÆ
KK. Calyx and stamens not as above.
L. Lvs. small, sessile, scale-like: ovary 1-celled and becoming a caps. .... 130. TAMARICACEÆ
LL. Lvs. of normal development.
M. Blades of lvs. simple.
N. Cells of ovary 3–10: plants herbaceous, or if shrubby with showy yellow fls. ...... 100. LINACEÆ
NN. Cells of ovary 1: plants woody, with small inconspicuous fls. .... 110. ANACARDIACEÆ
MM. Blades of lvs. compound.
N. Filaments of the 10 stamens connate at base: ovules 2 or more in each cell: lvs. digitately compound, or if pinnate the plant with fr. 2–5 in. long .... 98. OXALIDACEÆ
NN. Filaments of the usually fewer stamens separate: ovule 1 in each cell: lvs. pinnate: fr. usually smaller .... 110. ANACARDIACEÆ
FF. Styles 1.
G. Lvs. opposite or whorled: ovary with 2–5 cells.
H. Shape of corolla irregular.
I. Plant a tree or large shrub with palmately compound lvs. .... 115. HIPPOCASTANACEÆ
II. Plant an herb or low shrub with simple sometimes dissected lvs.
J. Cells of ovary 5.
K. Number of stamens 10, separate: carpels separating individually from central column when ripe, 1-seeded .... 97. GERANIACEÆ
KK. Number of stamens 5, united: fr. an elastically dehiscent caps. expelling the seeds .... 118. BALSAMINACEÆ
JJ. Cells of ovary 2: anthers 8–10 opening by terminal pores, separate .... 105. POLYGALACEÆ
HH. Shape of corolla regular or nearly so.
I. Species herbaceous or semi-shrubby.
J. Stamens 4 long and 2 short, or 2 long and 2 short: sepals and petals 4 .... 83. CRUCIFERÆ
JJ. Stamens not as above.
K. Blades of lvs. with 3–9 veins running lengthwise .. 149. MELASTOMACEÆ
KK. Blades of lvs. not so veined.
L. Sepals distinct: carpels separating from central column individually when ripe: stipules usually evident .... 97. GERANIACEÆ
LL. Sepals more or less connate: carpels not as above: stipules reduced or lacking.
M. Caps. 2-celled, completely inclosed by calyx: plants 2–4 ft. high .... 143. LYTHRACEÆ (Lythrum)
MM. Caps. 4–5-celled, not so inclosed: plants not more than 1 ft. high .... 156. PYROLACEÆ
II. Species well-developed shrubs or trees.
J. Fr. a samara.
K. Plant a climber: samaras 1–3 .... 104. MALPIGHIACEÆ (Stigmaphyllon)
KK. Plant not climbing.
L. Samaras double: lvs. usually palmately lobed, rarely pinnate .... 114. ACERACEÆ
LL. Samaras single: lvs. often pinnate .... 166. OLEACEÆ
JJ. Fr. not a samara.
K. Lf. with translucent oil-glands (lacking in Phellodendron, trees with odd-pinnate lvs. and aromatic when bruised) .... 101. RUTACEÆ
KK. Lf. not so.
L. The fr. inflated, bladdery: lvs. compound ..... 113. STAPHYLEACEÆ
LL. The fr. not inflated: lvs. simple.
M. Filaments united at base .... 104. MALPIGHIACEÆ
MM. Filaments separate.

N. Anthers opening by pores: prostrate shrub....157. ERICACEÆ (Leiophyllum)
NN. Anthers opening by slits.
O. Stamens opposite the petals....119. RHAMNACEÆ
OO. Stamens alternate with the petals, or more numerous.
P. Number of stamens normally 8. style long....143. LYTHRACEÆ (Lawsonia)
PP. Number of stamens normally 2 or 4: style short.
Q. Seeds with fleshy aril: fr. a caps.: stamens 4, sometimes 5....112. CELASTRACEÆ
QQ. Seeds without aril: fr. a drupe: stamens normally 2....166. OLEACEÆ
GG. Lvs. alternate or basal.
H. Cells of ovary 2–5.
I. Foliage punctate with translucent dots....101. RUTACEÆ
II. Foliage not so punctate.
J. Pistil of 5, sometimes fewer, carpels adnate to central style-bearing column, lobed at base, each 1-seeded carpel pulling away from base upward when ripe.... 97. GERANIACEÆ
JJ. Pistil not so constructed.
K. Sepals 4: petals 4: stamens 4 long and 2 short, or 2 long and 2 short.... 83. CRUCIFERÆ
KK. Sepals, petals and stamens not in above combination.
L. Hypanthium (calyx-tube) well-developed, with sepals, petals and stamens borne on its margin.... 90. SAXIFRAGACEÆ
LL. Hypanthium not conspicuously developed.
M. Shape of corolla irregular.
N. Fls. pea-like, the showy part of 2 inner sepals and 3 petals....105. POLYGALACEÆ
NN. Fls. not pea-like.
O. Plants herbaceous.
P. Lf. biternately compound: caps. inflated, papery....116. SAPINDACEÆ (Cardiospermum)
PP. Lf. simple, sometimes lobed or dissected.
Q. Veining of lvs. palmate: fr. of 3 corky 1-seeded carpels.... 99. TROPÆOLACEÆ
QQ. Veining of lvs. pinnate: fr. a caps.118. BALSAMINACEÆ
OO. Plants woody: lvs. pinnately compound.
P. Stamens 4: fls. in racemes....117. MELIANTHACEÆ
PP. Stamens 7–10: fls. in panicles or cymes....116. SAPINDACEÆ
MM. Shape of corolla regular.
N. Stamen-filaments united.
O. Lf. compound.
P. Blades of lvs. pinnate....103. MELIACEÆ
PP. Blades of lvs. digitate....123. BOMBACACEÆ (Ceiba)
OO. Lf. simple.
P. Stamens 2–5....124. STERCULIACEÆ
PP. Stamens 10....165. STYRACACEÆ
NN. Stamen-filaments not united.
O. Lf. palmately veined or compound, or with 3 prominent veins from base.
P. Species of tendril-bearing vines: fr. a berry....120. VITACEÆ
PP. Species not so.
Q. And a tree with cymose panicles..106. EUPHORBIACEÆ (Aleurites)
QQ. And an herb.
R. Fls. in spike-like racemes....158. DIAPENSIACEÆ (Galax)
RR. Fls. solitary or in small cymes. 121. TILIACEÆ (Corchorus)
OO. Lf. pinnately veined or compound.
P. Blades of lvs. compound: plants woody.
Q. Stamens 8–10: ovules 1–few in each cell of ovary....116. SAPINDACEÆ
QQ. Stamens 4–6: ovules 8–12 in each cell....103. MELIACEÆ (Cedrela)
PP. Blades of lvs. simple.
Q. Fertile stamens 10.
R. Fls. bright scarlet; anthers opening by slits: trees....117. MELIANTHACEÆ (Greyia)

RR. Fls. white or pinkish; anthers opening by terminal pores.
S. Plants large deciduous shrubs or small trees..... 155. CLETHRACEÆ
SS. Plants low evergreen shrubs. 157. ERICACEÆ
QQ. Fertile stamens 4–6.
R. Ovules many in each ovary-cell: plants evergreen.
S. Anthers opening lengthwise. 91. PITTOSPORACEÆ
SS. Anthers opening by terminal pores............... 157. ERICACEÆ (Ledum)
RR. Ovules 1–2 in each cell: plants deciduous or evergreen.
S. Stamens opposite to the petals: fr. a caps. or a drupe................. 119. RHAMNACEÆ
SS. Stamens alternate with the petals.
T. Fr. a caps.; seeds with scarlet or orange aril: disk conspicuous and with stamens inserted on it................ 112. CELASTRACEÆ
TT. Fr. a drupe; seeds lacking aril: disk absent...... 111. AQUIFOLIACEÆ
HH. Cells of ovary 1 (sometimes partially divided by false partitions growing in from the wall).
I. Plants floating herbs with roundish lvs............ 168. GENTIANACEÆ (Nymphoides)
II. Plants terrestrial.
J. Number of petals 1: plant a shrub with odd-pinnate lvs.............................. 96. LEGUMINOSÆ (Amorpha)
JJ. Number of petals more than 1.
K. Shape of corolla irregular.
L. Petals 4 in 2 series (2 larger and 2 smaller): sepals 2............................ 81. FUMARIACEÆ
LL. Petals 4–7, not as above.
M. Fr. a 3–6-lobed caps. opening at apex toward maturity and exposing the seeds... 84. RESEDACEÆ
MM. Fr. not so.
N. Ovary with 1 placenta and ripening into a legume, typically but not always dehiscent by 1 or both sutures into 2 valves.......................... 96. LEGUMINOSÆ
NN. Ovary with 3 (2–5) placentæ, the fr. a caps. dehiscing by 3 valves.
O. Caps. 1–1½ ft. long: plant a tree..... 85. MORINGACEÆ
OO. Caps. small: plant an herb.......... 133. VIOLACEÆ
KK. Shape of corolla regular.
L. Calyx scarious, usually colored, spreading, 10-ribbed................................ 161. PLUMBAGINACEÆ
LL. Calyx not so.
M. Species climbing by tendrils: fls. usually with a corona between the petals and fertile stamens.......................... 136. PASSIFLORACEÆ
MM. Species not climbing by tendrils.
N. Fr. (including receptacle) fleshy and over 2 in. long: tropical trees......... 110. ANACARDIACEÆ
NN. Fr. dry, if fleshy smaller than above.
O. Lf. small, sessile, scale-like: fls. small.. 130. TAMARICACEÆ
OO. Lf. larger and more normal.
P. Sepals and petals usually imbricated in 2 or more series: anthers usually opening by hinged valves. 72. BERBERIDACEÆ
PP. Sepals and petals in single series: anthers opening lengthwise.
Q. The sepals 4: petals 4.
R. Stamens 6: fr. dry.
S. Pod on long stipe: stamens equal.................. 82. CAPPARIDACEÆ (Cleome)
SS. Pod sessile: stamens of 2 lengths................ 83. CRUCIFERÆ
RR. Stamens 8: fr. fleshy......... 135. STACHYURACEÆ
QQ. The sepals 5: petals 5.
R. Fls. in compact heads or spikes: fr. a legume............. 96. LEGUMINOSÆ
RR. Fls. in racemes or corymbs: fr. an achene or follicle..... 95. ROSACEÆ
CC. Ovary inferior or partly so.
D. Stamens numerous, more than twice as many as the petals.

E. Styles more than 1, sometimes partly united.
F. Plants aquatic, with floating or emergent lvs. and fls......... 66. NYMPHÆACEÆ
FF. Plants terrestrial.
G. Fls. imperfect; petals 2–5; styles 2–5.....................139. BEGONIACEÆ
GG. Fls. perfect; petals 4 or 5 to many.
H. Petals many: herbs or subshrubs.................... 61. AIZOACEÆ
HH. Petals normally 4 or 5: well-developed shrubs or trees.
I. Lvs. alternate: petals 5: fr. a pome................ 95. ROSACEÆ
II. Lvs. opposite: petals usually 4: fr. a caps............ 90. SAXIFRAGACEÆ (Philadelphus)

EE. Styles 1.
F. Sepals and petals indefinite in number and not sharply differentiated from each other: plants spiny, usually succulent..140. CACTACEÆ
FF. Sepals and petals 3–7 (except in "double fls.") and in distinct series.
G. Species of ann. herbs (ours) with barbed or stinging hairs..138. LOASACEÆ
GG. Species of trees or shrubs lacking such hairs.
H. Fr. large (5–8 in. diam.), woody, dehiscing by a lid: lvs. 8–24 in. long...................................145. LECYTHIDACEÆ
HH. Fr. smaller, not dehiscing by a lid: lvs. smaller.
I. Seeds surrounded by juicy pulp, packed in superposed ovary-cells: lvs. not aromatic..............144. PUNICACEÆ
II. Seeds dry (any pulpy tissue is of ovary-wall); cells of ovary not superposed: lvs. often aromatic.......148. MYRTACEÆ
DD. Stamens few, not more than twice as many as the petals.
E. Styles more than 1.
F. Plants submerged aquatics: styles 4........................151. HALORAGACEÆ (Myriophyllum)

FF. Plants not submerged aquatics.
G. Sepals 2: plants fleshy: seeds many.................... 62. PORTULACACEÆ (Portulaca)

GG. Sepals more than 2 or obscure.
H. Seeds many in each cell of ovary.................... 90. SAXIFRAGACEÆ
HH. Seeds 1–2 in each cell of ovary.
I. Fr. splitting into 2 indehiscent carpels: aromatic herbs: fls. with 2 styles.........................153. UMBELLIFERÆ
II. Fr. not splitting into indehiscent carpels: mostly woody.
J. Pubescence stellate: fr. a woody caps.: styles 2..... 92. HAMAMELIDACEÆ
JJ. Pubescence not stellate, or if so plants vine-like: fr. fleshy: styles 1–10.
K. Number of stamens 4–5: lvs. usually compound, not stipulate: fr. a berry or drupe-like.......152. ARALIACEÆ
KK. Number of stamens usually 10, if fewer plants with well-developed thorns: lvs. simple, stipulate: fr. a pome.......................... 95. ROSACEÆ
EE. Styles 1.
F. The stamens of same number as petals and opposite them..119. RHAMNACEÆ
FF. The stamens alternate with the petals if of same number, sometimes of different number.
G. Species tendril-bearing vines, monœcious................191. CUCURBITACEÆ
GG. Species not tendril-bearing vines: fls. usually perfect.
H. Ovules more than 1 in each cell of ovary.
I. Lvs. with 3–9 longitudinal veins and peculiar cross-veining, so as to be broken up into many squarish cells...149. MELASTOMACEÆ
II. Lvs. not so veined.
J. Sepals and petals 5: stamens 10.................147. COMBRETACEÆ (Quisqualis)

JJ. Sepals and petals 4 or 2: stamens 2, 4 or 8..........150. ONAGRACEÆ
HH. Ovules 1 in each cell of ovary, or reduced to 1 in each ovary.
I. Sepals and petals 4 or 2.
J. Fr. dry, nut-like: plants herbaceous..............150. ONAGRACEÆ
JJ. Fr. a drupe: plants mostly woody...............154. CORNACEÆ
II. Sepals and petals 5: fr. a drupe: trees...............146. NYSSACEÆ
BB. Petals united, the corolla usually falling away as a whole when shed.
C. Ovary inferior or partly so.
D. Species of tendril-bearing vines..............................191. CUCURBITACEÆ
DD. Species not bearing tendrils.
E. Anthers united in a tube about the style.
F. Fls. in a close head subtended by an involucre simulating a calyx; corolla regular or irregular......................194. COMPOSITÆ
FF. Fls. not in involucrate heads.
G. Shape of corolla regular.............................192. CAMPANULACEÆ
GG. Shape of corolla irregular, often bilabiate...............193. LOBELIACEÆ
EE. Anthers separate.
F. All stamens free from corolla or essentially so.
G. Stamens as many as corolla-lobes: herbs with dehiscent capsules..192. CAMPANULACEÆ
GG. Stamens twice as many as corolla-lobes: woody.

H. Fr. a berry: anthers opening by terminal pores.........157. ERICACEÆ
HH. Fr. a dry longitudinally winged drupe: anthers opening by longitudinal slits.........................165. STYRACACEÆ (Halesia)
FF. All stamens inserted on the corolla, either at the throat or well in the tube.
G. Ovaries 2 and distinct above, each 1-celled...............169. APOCYNACEÆ
GG. Ovaries 1.
H. Stamens fewer than corolla-lobes.
I. Number of stamens 2 or 4 (5): ovules many..........183. GESNERIACEÆ
II. Number of stamens 1–3: ovules 1 or 0.
J. Fls. in cymose or capitate clusters, but not involucrate; ovary 1- or 3-celled....................189. VALERIANACEÆ
JJ. Fls. in heads or spikes with involucral bracts: ovary 1-celled...190. DIPSACEÆ
HH. Stamens at least as many as corolla-lobes.
I. Number of stamens 15 or more: lvs. alternate........164. SYMPLOCACEÆ
II. Number of stamens 4–6: lvs. opposite or whorled.
J. Lvs. opposite and markedly stipulate, or whorled and destitute of stipules.....................187. RUBIACEÆ
JJ. Lvs. opposite or perfoliate, rarely stipulate and when so stipules minute.....................188. CAPRIFOLIACEÆ
CC. Ovary or ovaries superior.
D. Pistils more than 1, nearly or quite separate at maturity.
E. Number of pistils 4, 5 or more: juice not milky: plant succulent. 89. CRASSULACEÆ
EE. Number of pistils 2: juicy milky.
F. Filaments of stamens distinct except sometimes at summit: style 1...169. APOCYNACEÆ
FF. Filaments united: styles united by the stigmas.............170. ASCLEPIADACEÆ
DD. Pistils 1.
E. Number of stamens more than corolla-lobes.
F. Cells of ovary 1.
G. Ripened fr. usually a lenticular or angled achene: sts. often sheathed at the nodes by the stipules or ocrea, if not sheathed the fls. in involucres or the st. climbing... 56. POLYGONACEÆ
GG. Ripened fr. not an achene.
H. Fr. a legume, normally dehiscent on both sutures: fls. regular and stamens many, or fls. papilionaceous and stamens 9 plus 1............................ 96. LEGUMINOSÆ
HH. Fr. not a legume.
I. Species trees with frs. large, fleshy and with 5 placentæ: lvs. large, palmately lobed.................137. CARICACEÆ
II. Species shrubs with deeply 4-lobed fr.: lvs. small, entire...101. RUTACEÆ (Correa)
FF. Cells of ovary 2 to many.
G. Styles more than 1.
H. Filaments more or less united: fr. dry or fleshy.........127. THEACEÆ
HH. Filaments separate: fr. a berry.....................163. EBENACEÆ
GG. Styles 1.
H. Stamens borne on the corolla: ovary 3–5-celled at base, 1-celled at apex......................................165. STYRACACEÆ
HH. Stamens not borne on the corolla.
I. Caps. 3-celled: corolla very deeply divided.........155. CLETHRACEÆ
II. Caps. 5-celled: corolla usually definitely gamopetalous...157. ERICACEÆ
EE. Number of stamens as many as the corolla-lobes or fewer.
F. Habit climbing by means of tendrils.
G. Fr. a berry: fls. inconspicuous, regular..................120. VITACEÆ
GG. Fr. a caps.: fls. showy, irregular........................180. BIGNONIACEÆ
FF. Habit not climbing by means of tendrils.
G. Stamens as many as the corolla-lobes and opposite them.
H. Styles 5: ovary 1-celled with 1 ovule: fr. dry...........161. PLUMBAGINACEÆ
HH. Styles 1.
I. Species herbaceous: fr. dry. ovary 1-celled with many ovules...160. PRIMULACEÆ
II. Species woody: fr. fleshy.
J. Cells of ovary 2 to many, with 1 ovule in each cell: corolla-lobes often with small appendages at base. 162. SAPOTACEÆ
JJ. Cells of ovary 1, with few to many ovules: corolla without appendages.........................159. MYRSINACEÆ
GG. Stamens as many as and alternate with the corolla-lobes, or fewer.
H. Cells of ovary 1, sometimes partly or seemingly several-celled by incomplete partitions.
I. Ovules 1: fr. a ribbed achene: herbs with opposite lvs.. 59. NYCTAGINACEÆ (Mirabilis)
II. Ovules more than 1.
J. Shape of corolla usually irregular: fertile stamens 4 or 2.
K. Fr. a woody caps. with long recurved beak......182. MARTYNIACEÆ
KK. Fr. not so.
L. Species of trees with hard-rinded frs. 1 or more ft. long..............................180. BIGNONIACEÆ
LL. Species of herbs or shrubs with small capsules..183. GESNERIACEÆ

JJ. Shape of corolla regular: fertile stamens 5.
K. Lvs. opposite.
L. Plants herbaceous.
M. Calyx with reflexed or spreading appendage in each sinus........................173. Hydrophyllaceæ (Nemophila)
MM. Calyx lacking reflexed or spreading appendage in each sinus.................168. Gentianaceæ
LL. Plants shrubs, often climbing...............169. Apocynaceæ (Allamanda)
KK. Lvs. mostly alternate or basal.
L. Foliage along st. or if basal then palmately 5–7-lobed..............................173. Hydrophyllaceæ
LL. Foliage in basal rosettes.
M. Lf. simple, coarsely dentate..............183. Gesneriaceæ (Ramonda)
MM. Lf. compound, 3-foliolate................168. Gentianaceæ (Menyanthes)

HH. Cells of ovary 2 or more.
I. Fr. of 4 (rarely 1 or 2 or more) 1-seeded nutlets or drupelets, or a more or less lobed drupe with bony seeds (if fr. is fleshy corolla is irregular).
J. Fertile stamens 5: corolla regular: lvs. alternate.
K. Filaments inserted in the corolla-tube: fls. usually in scorpioid cymes...................174. Boraginaceæ
KK. Filaments inserted at base of corolla-tube: fls. solitary...................................177. Nolanaceæ
JJ. Fertile stamens 4 or 2: corolla usually irregular: infl. not scorpioid: lvs. opposite or whorled.
K. Ovary entire: style terminal.................175. Verbenaceæ
KK. Ovary 4-lobed: style arising from between the ovary-lobes.............................176. Labiatæ
II. Fr. a caps. or fleshy, not of nutlets (if fr. is fleshy corolla is usually regular).
J. Fertile stamens fewer than the corolla-lobes.
K. Foliage punctate with translucent dots........186. Myoporaceæ
KK. Foliage not punctate with translucent dots.
L. Fls. in involucrate heads: lvs. alternate: fr. small, indehiscent......................184. Globulariaceæ
LL. Fls. not in involucrate heads: fr. a caps.
M. Caps. about 1 in. long, grooved, setose, short-beaked; seeds pale, flat-obovoid: plant an herb: fls. rose to white...........181. Pedaliaceæ
MM. Caps., habit, color and seeds not all as above.
N. Lvs. mostly alternate, occasionally opposite in upper sts.: placentation axile.
O. Ovules 1–2 in each locule: vines with compound lvs. and yellow fls....... 166. Oleaceæ (Jasminum)
OO. Ovules more numerous.
P. Lobes of corolla valvate or plicate in bud: crushed plant usually with rank odor................178. Solanaceæ
PP. Lobes of corolla imbricate in bud: crushed plant not usually with rank odor.....................179. Scrophulariaceæ
NN. Lvs. mostly opposite or whorled or basal.
O. Placentation parietal: plants woody (except Incarvillea with caps. dehiscing more deeply on ventral suture): seeds winged or compressed.. 180. Bignoniaceæ
OO. Placentation axile: plants often herbaceous: seeds not winged.
P. Corolla regular: shrubs...........166. Oleaceæ
PP. Corolla irregular (if regular the plant herbaceous): mostly herbs.
Q. Anthers usually free from each other: ovules many in each cell: plants largely temperate, hence hardy................179. Scrophulariaceæ
QQ. Anthers connivent or connate, at least in pairs: ovules few to many: plants mostly tropical, hence tender................185. Acanthaceæ
JJ. Fertile stamens of same number as corolla-lobes.
K. Lvs. opposite or whorled (alternate in a purple-fld. species of Buddleia).
L. Stipules present, sometimes represented by a line joining opposite lvs..................167. Loganiaceæ
LL. Stipules absent.
M. Sap milky: fr. a berry: plant a large shrub..169. Apocynaceæ (Acokanthera)

MM. Sap not milky: fr. dry: plants frequently herbaceous.
N. Lf. 3–5-nerved from base: corolla-lobes contorted in bud....................168. GENTIANACEÆ (Exacum)
NN. Lf. 1-nerved from base: corolla-lobes convolute or imbricate in bud.
O. Stigmas 3: herbs or mostly so........172. POLEMONIACEÆ
OO. Stigmas 1: prostrate evergreen shrubs.157. ERICACEÆ (Loiseleuria)

KK. Lvs. alternate or basal.
L. The ovary 3–10-celled.
M. Plant a large climber with lvs. 3–12 in. across and rose-purple fls. 2–3 in. long.... 171. CONVOLVULACEÆ (Argyreia)
MM. Plant not as above.
N. Fls. minute, greenish-white, usually imperfect..........................111. AQUIFOLIACEÆ (Ilex)
NN. Fls. showy, not greenish-white, perfect.
O. Style 3-cleft: ovary 3-celled.
P. Species of tufted evergreen somewhat woody per. herbs: lvs. simple: fls. few................158. DIAPENSIACEÆ
PP. Species of different habit than above, or if of same with lvs. lobed or divided: fls. usually more numerous.....................172. POLEMONIACEÆ
OO. Style 1 with capitate stigma: ovary 5–10-celled: shrubs or trees........157. ERICACEÆ (Rhododendron)
LL. The ovary 1–2-celled, sometimes also with false partitions.
M. Calyx of 5 separate sepals, or the sepals united only at the base: styles 2, or 1 and then usually partly divided.
N. Plants mostly twining or trailing: infl. not coiled; corolla plaited in bud.....171. CONVOLVULACEÆ
NN. Plants erect or diffuse: infl. cymose, often scorpioid; corolla not plaited in bud... 173. HYDROPHYLLACEÆ
MM. Calyx mostly 4–5-lobed or -toothed: style 1, entire.
N. Stamens not bearded except sometimes in a ring near the base: corolla plicate or valvate in the bud: fr. a berry or caps.: fls. solitary or in cymose clusters. 178. SOLANACEÆ
NN. Stamens all or the 3 posterior bearded: corolla imbricate in bud: fr. a caps.: fls. in terminal spikes or racemes......179. SCROPHULARIACEÆ (Verbascum)

PTERIDOPHYTA

1. OPHIOGLOSSACEÆ. ADDERS-TONGUE FAMILY

A family of 3 genera and 52 species of usually small herbaceous ferns, widely distributed.—Rootstocks short and fleshy with numerous fibrous usually fleshy roots and 1 or few lvs. or fronds: fronds erect, with a sessile or stalked sterile blade and, in the fertile lvs., a stalked spore-bearing spike or panicle, these two parts borne on a short to elongate common stalk: sporangia naked, opening by a transverse or oblique slit, the spores uniform (homosporous).

BOTRYCHIUM, Sw. An almost cosmopolitan genus of about 25 species of rather fleshy plants.—Rootstocks erect, rather small: fronds 1–3, common stalk wholly or partly underground, erect; sterile blade sessile to long-stalked, one to four times pinnately or ternately divided or compound; fertile part a stalked spike or 1–5-pinnate panicle, erect: sporangia large, round, distinct, nearly or quite sessile, borne in 2 rows on the ultimate divisions; spores sulfur-yellow. (Botrych-ium: Greek, referring to the grape-like arrangement of the sporangia.)

B. virginianum, Sw. (*Osmunda virginiana*, L.). RATTLESNAKE-FERN. Plants ½–3 ft. high, the common stalk making up one-half to two-thirds of this height: sterile blade broadly triangular, spreading, sessile, 2–16 in. broad, nearly as long, ternate, the primary divisions short-stalked, 1–2-pinnate, ultimate segms. mostly oblong; fertile part long-stalked, the panicles 2–3-pinnate. Lab. to B. C. south to Fla. and Mex., Eu., Asia.

2. OSMUNDACEÆ. OSMUNDA FAMILY

Three genera of large ferns in both Old and New Worlds, with about 17 species.—Rootstocks creeping to erect: fronds (lvs.) erect or spreading; stipes winged at the base; blades 1–3-pinnate or -pinnatifid, with free mostly forked veins extending to the margins; fertile segms. (in ours) much contracted and forming separate panicles on a foliage lf., or occupying a whole lf.: sporangia naked, large, globose, mostly stalked, with no annulus or a short broad transverse one, opening into 2 valves by a longitudinal slit.

OSMUNDA, L. Nine species of N. and S. Amer. and Asia.—Rather coarse but attractive ferns, deep-rooted, with large crowns of 2-pinnate or -pinnatifid fronds; fertile segms. ultimately red or brown: spores green. (Osmun-da: from *Osmunder*, a name of a Saxon god.)

A. Sterile fronds 2-pinnate; fertile pinnæ above the sterile but on the same frond... 1. *O. regalis*
AA. Sterile fronds 1-pinnate, then pinnatifid: fertile pinnæ on separate fronds or in middle of a green frond.
B. Sterile and fertile pinnæ on wholly different fronds........................2. *O. cinnamomea*
BB. Sterile pinnæ below and above the fertile but on same frond................3. *O. Claytoniana*

1. **O. regalis,** L. ROYAL-FERN. FLOWERING-FERN. Smooth, pale green, 1–6 ft.: stipes long, glabrous; blades 2-pinnate, ovate in outline, the pinnules separated, oblong-

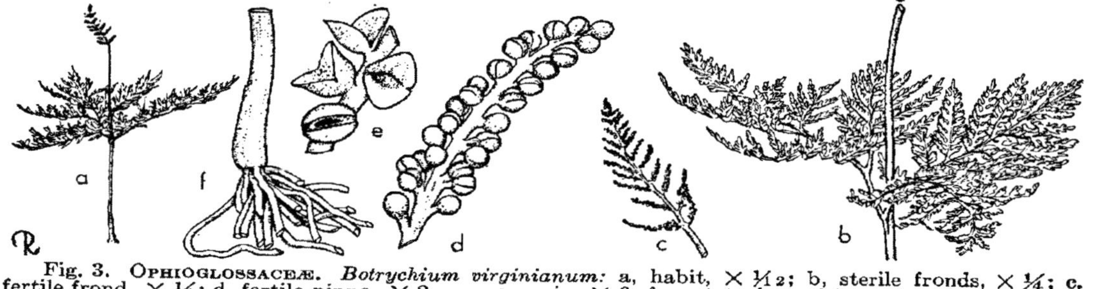

Fig. 3. OPHIOGLOSSACEÆ. *Botrychium virginianum:* a, habit, × 1/12; b, sterile fronds, × ¼; c, fertile frond, × ¼; d, fertile pinna, × 2; e, sporangia, × 6; f, rootstock, × ½.

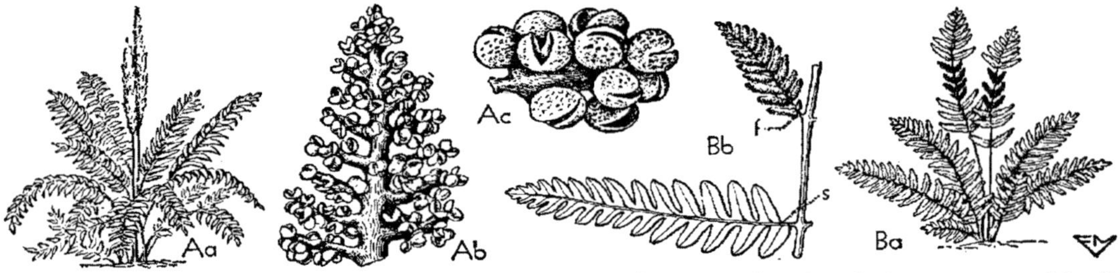

Fig. 4. Osmundaceæ. A, *Osmunda cinnamomea:* Aa, habit, much reduced; Ab, segments of fertile frond, × 3; Ac, sporangia, × 10. B, *Osmunda Claytoniana:* Ba, habit, much reduced; Bb, portion of frond with sterile (s) and fertile (f) segments, × ½.

elliptic, 1–3 in. long, serrulate, sessile or short-stalked; fertile pinnæ, if present, in the terminal portion of the frond forming a 3-pinnate panicle, brownish in maturity, commonly 4–8 in. long, the rachis with many black hairs. Eu., Afr. Var. **spectabilis,** Gray (*O. spectabilis,* Willd.), fruiting panicle almost without hairs; Newf. to Sask. south to Fla. and La., S. Amer.

2. **O. cinnamomea,** L. Cinnamon-Fern. Sterile fronds (stipe and blade) 2–5 ft. long, the stipes 6–15 in. long, rusty-tomentose when young; blades lanceolate to oblong-lanceolate, 1-pinnate, the pinnæ numerous, narrowly lanceolate, pinnatifid into oblong or ovate obtuse segms.; fertile fronds in the center, 1–3 ft. high, 2-pinnate, contracted, covered with cinnamon-brown sporangia. Newf. to Minn., Fla. and New Mex., Mex. to S. Amer., Asia.

3. **O. Claytoniana,** L. Interrupted-Fern. Fronds clustered, arching, 2–5 ft. long, some of them spore-bearing near the middle; stipes 1–2 ft. long; blades lanceolate, 1-pinnate then pinnatifid, the pinnæ oblong-lanceolate with obtuse oblong segms.; about 3–5 pairs of middle pinnæ sometimes fertile, entirely pinnate, with cylindric clusters of crowded sporangia. (Bears the name of J. Clayton, page 41.) Newf. to Minn., Ga. and Ark., Asia.

3. SCHIZÆACEÆ. SCHIZEA-FERN FAMILY

A small family of ferns of wide distribution, mostly trop., those of the genus Lygodium climbing and some of them cult. under glass for ornament; there are 4 commonly recognized genera and more than 100 species.—Fronds with simple pinnate or dichotomous and palmate-lobed blades: sori in rows on specialized segms. which may be spike-like, the sporangia ovoid, sessile, naked or indusiate, provided with a transverse apical annulus and opening vertically by a longitudinal slit. The small localized curly-grass fern, *Schizæa pusilla,* Pursh, occurs in the coastal region, Newf. to N. J.; the sterile fronds are grass-like, the fertile have a terminal close pinnate fertile portion.

LYGODIUM, Sw. Climbing-Fern. Twenty to 30 species, mainly trop.—Fronds radical, long and slender, the rachis twining and simulating a st.; the "lvs." are secondary pinnæ, which are palmately or pinnately compound or decompound; the stalk or petiole of the pinnæ branches near its base, bearing a pinnule on either fork,

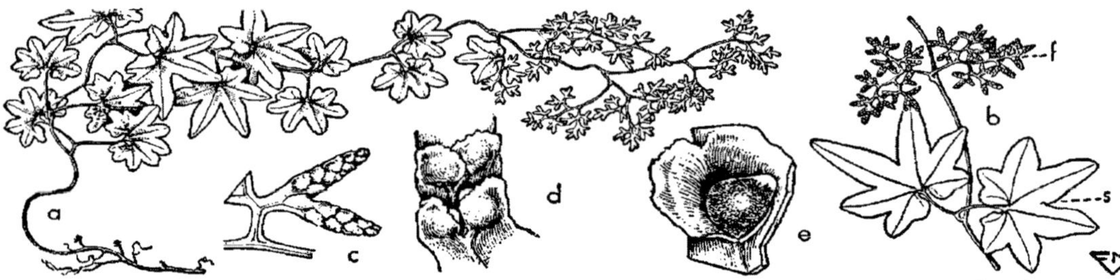

Fig. 5. Schizæaceæ. *Lygodium palmatum:* a, plant, × ¼; b, section of frond showing sterile (s) and fertile (f) pinnæ, × ½; c, fertile segments, × 2; d, sporangia covered by indusia, × 5; e, sporangium with indusium cut and opened back, × 10.

or sometimes the fork is so near the rachis that the petiolule practically disappears and is unobserved: sporangia single under scale-like imbricated indusia, borne on narrowed divisions of the pinnules, which sometimes lose their foliar character and become wholly specialized fruiting panicles, and which in other species become strongly toothed or pinnate from the contraction of the margins. (Lygo-dium: Greek *flexible.*)

A. Sterile pinnules palmately lobed, or forked.
  B. Segms. usually 2½–8 in. long, at least four times as long as wide..............1. *L. circinatum*
  BB. Segms. usually ½–1½ in. long, usually less than three times as long as wide.......2. *L. palmatum*
AA. Sterile pinnules pinnate or pinnately lobed.
  B. Segms. not pinnate and usually not lobed.
    C. All segms. long-lanceolate, usually several in. long........................3. *L. volubile*
    CC. All segms. usually ovate to long-ovate.......................................4. *L. scandens*
  BB. Segms. prominently pinnate or lobed..5. *L. japonicum*

1. **L. circinatum,** Sw. (*Ophioglossum circinatum,* Burm. *L. dichotomum,* Sw.). Robust, tall, with long-persistent foliage: common stalk or petiolule nearly obsolete; secondary petiolule 1–2 in.; pinnules large, bright green, palmately divided nearly to the base, the segms. 4–12 in. long and entire: sporangia in short marginal spikes on very narrow segms. Trop. Asia, Malaya.

2. **L. palmatum,** Sw. (*Gisopteris palmata,* Bernh.). HARTFORD-FERN. Fronds 1–5 ft. long; foliage lfts. round to reniform in outline, 1–3 in. broad, palmately lobed half to one-third the way to the cordate base and into 4–8 spreading unequal lobes, the outer of these small, the main ones elliptic to lanceolate, rounded-obtuse; fertile lfts. usually the upper ones, 3–4-pinnate, 1–3 in. long, the divisions linear or nearly so, somewhat revolute and covered beneath with the scale-like indusia of which the free edge is uneven. N. H. to Ohio, Fla., Tenn.

3. **L. volubile,** Sw. Common petiolule obsolete; secondary 1–2 in. long; pinnules pinnate, with alternate minutely serrate long-lanceolate segms. 4–12 in. long that are jointed to the short stalks: sporangia in rows of short marginal spikes, the fertile segms. not much contracted. Trop. Amer.

4. **L. scandens,** Sw. (*Ophioglossum scandens,* L.). Slender, somewhat bushy, the foliage bluish-green: common petiolule evident but short; secondary about 1 in.; pinnules pinnate, the segms. 1–2 in. long, ovate to ovate-lanceolate, standing at right angles, truncate or cordate at base and sometimes obscurely lobed, jointed on the very short stalks: sporangia in short spikes around the margin of short broad segms. E. Asia.

5. **L. japonicum,** Sw. (*Ophioglossum japonicum,* Thunb.). Slender elegant plant with much-divided soft pale green foliage: common petiolule short; secondary 1 in. or less; pinnules pinnate, the alternate or opposite short-stalked non-jointed segms. pinnatifid or even pinnate or some of them only deeply lobed at base, margins variously dentate: sporangia in short spikes on the margins of broad segms. E. Indies, E. Asia, Australia.—Foliage on young or undeveloped plants much smaller with finer divisions.

4. CYATHEACEÆ. TREE-FERN FAMILY

Trop. and subtrop. ferns from warm regions of both sides of the world, with distinct trunks or sts.; genera 5, species about 425; grown under glass or in the open in warmer parts of the U. S.—Fronds pinnately compound, with sori on backs of segms. or in the forks of the fertile veins: indusium globular to beaker-shaped or scale-like or lacking; annulus oblique, continuous, stomium scarcely differentiated.

A. Fruit-dot or sorus provided with an indusium which at first covers it..............1. CYATHEA
AA. Fruit-dot naked...2. ALSOPHILA

1. **CYATHEA,** Smith. Tall tree-ferns, the trunk sometimes more than 50 ft. in height; species more than 100, trop. and subtrop., both eastern and western hemispheres.—Fronds very large and attractive, in the cult. species 2–3-pinnate, the stipes frequently somewhat prickly: sori on the back of the segm. rather than at its margin, on an elevated receptacle; indusium covering the young sorus but soon splitting at the top and remaining as a cup or fringe around the fruit-dot. (Cyath-ea: Greek *cup,* referring to the indusia.)

C. dealbata, Sw. (*Polypodium dealbatum,* Forst.). Stout fern, the trunk in nativity becoming 30 ft. and more tall and 18 in. diam.: fronds spreading horizontally, 5–12 ft. long, 2–4 ft. broad. 2–3-pinnate, yellowish-green above and powdery-white beneath making a striking foliage; young plants green, the white appearing irregularly; stipes slender, scaly at base; rachides woolly-scaly when young; pinnæ 10–18 in. long; pinnules 2–4 in. long, long-lanceolate, bearing many nearly entire segms., the brown sori conspicuous on the colored lower surface. New Zeal., Lord Howe Isls.

2. **ALSOPHILA,** R. Br. Tree-ferns as known in cult., but in some species the trunk is very short or even almost wanting, sometimes prostrate; species more than 100, mostly trop., in Amer. and the eastern hemisphere.—Fronds large, 2–3-pinnate in the cult. kinds; stipes smooth, scaly or even spiny: sori on the back of the segm., more or less elevated, naked (without indusium), in this respect differing from Cyathea. (Alsoph-ila: Greek *grove-loving*.)

A. australis, R. Br. Trunk straight, 20 ft. or more, not very thick, with a spreading head of 2–3-pinnate fronds 5–12 ft. long, light green above and somewhat bluish beneath: stipes and rachis rough and more or less chaffy, the stipe 12–18 in. long; pinnæ about 18 in. long and 6–10 in. broad; pinnules 3–6 in. long and about 1 in. broad at base, long-pointed, the curved segms. serrate and bearing the naked sori between margin and rib. Australia.

5. DICKSONIACEÆ. DICKSONIA FAMILY

Trop. and subtrop. ferns, in many parts of the globe; genera about 3, species perhaps 30; a few are rather common in choice glasshouse collections.—Usually with a distinct caudex or trunk which often attains many ft. in height and is provided with hairs but not scales: fronds very large, pinnately divided, usually leathery, in a crown: sori marginal or terminal on the veins of the under surface; indusium 2-valved, beaker-like; annulus of sporangium oblique, a continuous ring and with a somewhat differentiated stomium with thin-walled cells.

A. Outer valve of indusium apparently formed of the incurved little modified segm.-tooth. 1. DICKSONIA
AA. Outer indusium valve free from the normal frond margin........................2. CIBOTIUM

1. **DICKSONIA,** L'Her. Handsome tree-ferns, the trunk in some species very short but usually rising several ft. (or in nature 30 ft. and more); species a dozen or more, mostly in the southern hemisphere, trop. and subtrop.—Trunk usually more fibrous in structure than many other tree-ferns: fronds large, 2–3-pinnate, the stipes smooth or sometimes slightly prickly, pinnæ ovate to long-lanceolate: sori at the margin at the tip of a veinlet and borne on an elevated receptacle, covered by 2-valved indusia of which the upper valve is continuous with the segm.-tooth. (Dickso-nia: James Dickson, 1738–1822, English seedsman and cryptogamic botanist.)—The native *D. punctilobula* is now placed in the genus Dennstaedtia, one of the Polypodiaceæ.

D. antarctica, Labill. One of the common tree-ferns in cult., making a stout trunk, in its native country 20–50 ft., the head symmetrical and attractive: fronds very large (often 6 ft. long), rhomboid or deltoid, 3-pinnate; stipes short, tan-colored, smooth or light brown-hairy; pinnules distinct, numerous, 20–30 pairs, alternate and close together, sessile, long-lanceolate-acute, 1–2 in. long, with many acute serrulate segms., some of which bear the 2–6 sori incurved on the under margin. Australia.

2. **CIBOTIUM,** Kaulf. Stout tree-ferns but sometimes grown only as young plants; about 8 species in Cent. Amer., Mex., and Polynesia.—Trunks in some species very woolly: fronds mostly 3-pinnate, the pinnules usually with linear or

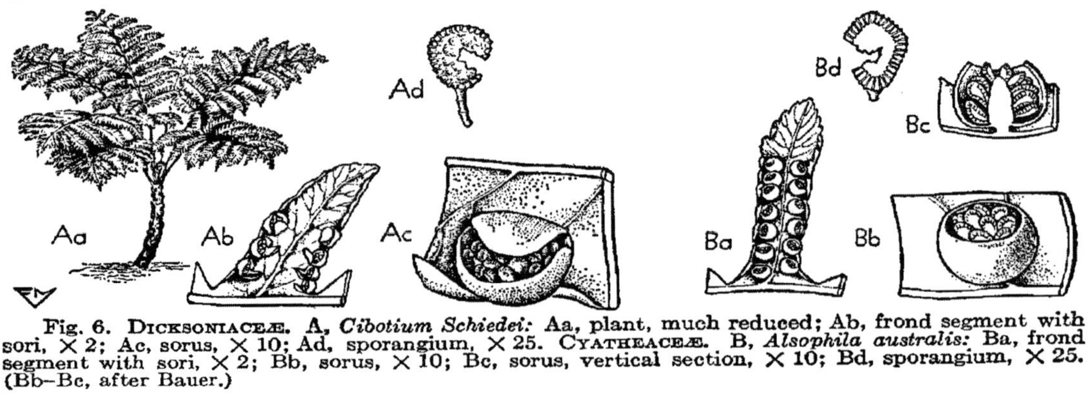

Fig. 6. DICKSONIACEÆ. A, *Cibotium Schiedei:* Aa, plant, much reduced; Ab, frond segment with sori, × 2; Ac, sorus, × 10; Ad, sporangium, × 25. CYATHEACEÆ. B, *Alsophila australis:* Ba, frond segment with sori, × 2; Bb, sorus, × 10; Bc, sorus, vertical section, × 10; Bd, sporangium, × 25. (Bb–Bc, after Bauer.)

lanceolate segms.: sori at tips of veinlets, the indusia 2-valved of which the outer valve is distinct from the margin of the segm. (Cibo-tium: Greek *a little seed-vessel.*)

C. Schiedei, Schlecht. & Cham. Handsome and popular tree-fern, trunk to 15 ft.: fronds very large, 5–10 ft., oblong-triangular in outline, gracefully drooping, 3-pinnate; stipes short and stout, brown, hairy; pinnules many, 25 or more pairs, opposite or sub-opposite, separated, very short-stalked, long and narrow, pointed, 4–8 in. long, glaucous-gray beneath, with many obtusely serrate segms. of which the margin is not incurved to form part of the indusium, sori mostly 3–7 to a segm. (Bears the name of Christian J. W. Schiede, German botanist who travelled in Mex.; died 1836.) Mex., Guatemala.

6. POLYPODIACEÆ. COMMON-FERN FAMILY

Mostly low plants lacking a distinct caudex or trunk, of widely differing habits and structure, with mostly creeping rhizomes, numbering three-fourths of all ferns, distributed all over the world, perhaps 6,000 species, many of them familiar glass-house subjects.—Fronds coiled in vernation, usually once or more pinnate but sometimes simple and entire: sporangia associated in sori or fruit-dots of many sizes and shapes, borne on the backs or at the margins of the fronds, in most genera covered with an indusium and long-stalked, provided with an incomplete vertical ring (annulus) and opening transversely.—Many of the species are remarkably variable, and run into forms that may not be recognized as belonging to the parent species.

A. Fertile fronds very different from sterile fronds.
  B. Segms. of fertile fronds rolled together into bead-like or pod-like bodies.
    C. Sterile fronds 2-pinnatifid, borne in a circle about the fertile ones .... 29. PTERETIS
    CC. Sterile fronds 1-pinnatifid, scattered .... 30. ONOCLEA
  BB. Segms. of fertile fronds not bead-like or pod-like.
    C. Sori not in marginal lines.
      D. Indusium absent; sporangia in large patches toward the ends of the antler-like fertile fronds .... 5. PLATYCERIUM
      DD. Indusium present.
        E. Sori one pair, forming continuous line parallel to midrib .... 14. BLECHNUM
        EE. Sori 8–12 pairs, at an angle to the midrib .... 18. ASPLENIUM
    CC. Sori in continuous marginal lines along each side of segm. and covered by conspicuous indusium, or of chain-like links.
      D. The fertile segms. with sori in chain-like links .... 15. WOODWARDIA
      DD. The fertile segms. with sori contiguous.
        E. Sterile fronds 2–8 in. long; fertile fronds definitely taller .... 12. CRYPTOGRAMMA
        EE. Sterile fronds 12–18 in. long; fertile fronds about as high .... 13. ONYCHIUM
AA. Fertile fronds essentially like sterile fronds or all fertile.
  B. Indusium none, not evident even in very young sori.
    C. Blade of frond entire, or forked at apex, but not pinnatifid.
      D. Hairs on under side of blade stellate; blade acuminate at apex .... 3. PYRROSIA
      DD. Hairs on under side of blade simple; blade blunt at apex .... 4. ELAPHOGLOSSUM
    CC. Blade of frond pinnatifid to pinnate.
      D. Sori linear, more or less confluent: under side of blade covered with white or yellow powder .... 6. PITYROGRAMMA
      DD. Sori rounded: lf.-blade not powdery.
        E. Fronds 1-pinnatifid.
          F. Veins free: plant about 1 ft. or less tall, hardy .... 1. POLYPODIUM
          FF. Veins reticulated: plant 2–3 ft. tall, tender .... 2. PHLEBODIUM
        EE. Fronds 2–3-pinnate.
          F. The blades about as broad as long .... 23. DRYOPTERIS
          FF. The blades less than half as broad as long .... 27. WOODSIA
  BB. Indusium present.
    C. Sori under the edge of the reflexed lf.-margin, which forms the indusium.
      D. Fertile segms. with sori separate and distinct, not confluent in a continuous marginal line .... 7 ADIANTUM
      DD. Fertile segms. with sori forming a continuous marginal line.
        E. Segms. brown-tomentose beneath and with vein-ends distinctly enlarged .... 8. CHEILANTHES
        EE. Segms. not brown-tomentose nor with vein-ends much enlarged.
          F. Sporangia at or near the tips of the free veins: pinnæ not more than 2 in. long .... 11. PELLÆA
          FF. Sporangia borne on a vein-like receptacle connecting the ends of the veins: pinnæ mostly 6 in. or more long.
            G. Indusia only 1, the reflexed margin itself: blades not both ternate and 1–3 ft. long .... 9. PTERIS
            GG. Indusia 2, an outer and a smaller inner one almost concealed by the sporangia: blade ternate, 1–3 ft. long .... 10. PTERIDIUM
    CC. Sori on the back of the segms., or if marginal not under the reflexed lf.-margin.
      D. Shape of sori linear or oblong, twice or more as long as broad.
        E. Segms. with the sori parallel to and near the midvein.
          F. Fronds 1-pinnatifid or 1-pinnate: sori continuous .... 14. BLECHNUM
          FF. Fronds pinnate, then pinnatifid: sori in chain-like rows .... 15. WOODWARDIA

EE. Segms. with sori oblique to and away from the midvein.
F. Veins copiously anastomosing: sori irregularly arranged: fronds rooting at tips.......................................17. CAMPTOSORUS
FF. Veins free: sori uniformly oblique: fronds not rooting at tips.
G. Blade of frond simple and entire (except in some hort. forms): sori in pairs so that the indusium seems double, one from each edge.......................................16. PHYLLITIS
GG. Blade of frond usually pinnatifid to pinnate: sori solitary.
H. Plants evergreen: stipes often dark: indusia straight.........18. ASPLENIUM
HH. Plants with deciduous fronds: stipes pale: indusia usually curved.......................................19. ATHYRIUM
DD. Shape of sori round or reniform, less than twice as long as broad.
E. Indusium spread over the sorus, covering it, attached at or near the middle and opening all around.
F. Veins anastomosing.......................................20. CYRTOMIUM
FF. Veins free.
G. The indusium round, peltate, attached by a central stalk.......21. POLYSTICHUM
GG. The indusium cordate or reniform, attached by the sinus........23. DRYOPTERIS
EE. Indusium attached under the sorus, opening at the top or side or appearing as if cup-shaped.
F. Fronds 1-pinnate (more divided in hort. forms), the pinnæ jointed to the rachis: indusia round or reniform, attached only at base.22. NEPHROLEPIS
FF. Fronds 2–4-pinnate or -pinnatifid, the pinnæ not jointed: indusia commonly attached at base and sides.
G. Stipes jointed to the rootstocks: indusia tubular..............24. DAVALLIA
GG. Stipes not jointed to the rootstocks: indusia cup-shaped to broader than long.
H. The indusium scale-like, at end of segm. and releasing the spores through slit-like opening at apical end.............25. SPHENOMERIS
HH. The indusium not scale-like nor concealing sporangia.
I. Indusia cup-shaped: lvs. 3–4-pinnatifid.................26. DENNSTAEDTIA
II. Indusia hood-like or opening into narrow lobes: lvs. 2–3-pinnatifid.
J. Attachment of indusium wholly inferior, the indusium with stellate or spreading divisions.................27. WOODSIA
JJ. Attachment of indusium by the base at one side, the indusium hood-shaped and pushed back by the ripening sporangia.......................................28. CYSTOPTERIS

1. **POLYPODIUM,** L. POLYPODY. As now interpreted a genus mostly of the northern hemisphere comprised of about 75 species, most numerous in the American tropics; mostly epiphytes.—Rhizome branched and creeping, to which the stipes are jointed, a scar remaining after detachment: fronds pinnatifid to pinnately compound, veins forked or branching and free or anastomosing: sporangia in naked circular sori on the back of the frond and terminally disposed. (Polypo-dium: Greek *many feet,* alluding to the branching rhizome.)—Formerly a very large and unnatural genus, recently divided into many smaller genera having more natural affinities; the plant long known as *P. aureum* is now placed in the genus Phlebodium.

P. vulgare, L. COMMON POLYPODY. WALL-FERN. Low, forming mats, commonly 6–15 in. tall, the stipe about one-third the length of the oblong smooth green blade which is deeply pinnatifid; segms. narrow-oblong, often curved, obtuse or semi-acute: sori numerous and large, in a row on either side the midrib. On rocks, banks and trees, Eurasia and W. N. Amer.—There are many forms, dissected, crested and plumed, and these are sometimes in cult. in collections of hardy ferns. The hort. vars. belong probably to the true *P. vulgare* rather than to **P. virginianum,** L., of E. N. Amer., inasmuch as it is the more variable species. *P. vulgare* is the larger species; lowest pinnæ commonly shorter than the middle ones (usually equalling or exceeding them in *P. virginianum*), midribs curving rather than straight, sori usually median rather than nearly marginal; rhizome sweet, not so in *P. virginianum.*

2. **PHLEBODIUM,** R. Br. A small genus, perhaps only a single polymorphic species, common throughout the American tropics, nat. in parts of Old World tropics and long cult. in the open far S. and in conservatories N.—A large epiphyte with stout brown-scaly creeping rhizome, differing from Polypodium in the reticulated anastomosing veins forming narrow areolæ (small spaces between vein branches) along the midvein of the segms. that extend from one vein to the next without included veinlets, and adjoined by a series of areolæ, each with 2 included veinlets that meet at their apex. (Phlebo-dium: Greek *vein,* referring to the many branched veins.)

P. aureum, Smith (*Polypodium aureum,* L. *P. glaucum,* Hort. *Chrysopteris glauca,* Fée). HARES-FOOT-FERN. Stout coarse fern with thick densely coarsely brown-scaly rhizomes on the surface of the pot or tree (often epiphytic) from which arise a few fronds 2–4 ft. tall: stipes very long; blades broadly oblong in outline, 1 ft. and more broad, green or densely glaucous-blue, deeply pinnatifid with obtuse sutures, often completely pinnate on the lower half; pinnæ or lobes 6–12 in. long and 1–2 in. wide, with parallel sides, acuminate, the margins wavy: sori large and prominent: veins not free or nearly so. Trop. Amer.—Widely variable, especially in cult.; the very glaucous forms, often originating from spores of the green-lvd., are mostly known as *P. glaucum* and *glaucophyllum*, Hort. There are crested and laciniate forms, one of which (a spore sport) is known as *Polypodium Mandaianum* (intro. by W. A. Manda, N. J.).

3. **PYRROSIA,** Mirbel (*Cyclophorus*, Desv.). As now defined, the genus comprises some 100 species, mostly in E. Asia, E. Indies, S. Afr., to New Zeal. and Australia; often included in Polypodium.—Rhizome scaly or hairy, creeping, slender or stout: fronds normally simple and entire, tomentose on the back with stellate hairs, leathery in texture and with a fine scarcely evident network of veins: sori circular, without indusia, often so close together as to cover the back of the frond. (Pyrro-sia: Greek *fire-color*, in allusion to the color of the fruiting structures.)

P. Lingua, Farwell (*Acrostichum Lingua*, Thunb. *Niphobolus Lingua*, Spreng. *Polypodium Lingua*, Sw. *Cyclophorus Lingua*, Desv.). Tongue-Fern. Japanese-Fern. Fronds many, erect, from a slender rhizome, 6–15 in. long of which the stout stipe comprises from one-fourth to more than one-half; blades entire, lanceolate to oblong- or ovate-lanceolate, more or less acuminate, rusty beneath: sori contiguous, more or less rowed. (Lingua: Latin *the tongue;* used here as a substantive in apposition.) China, Japan, and southward. Var. **corymbifera,** Bailey (*Cyclophorus Lingua* var. *corymbiferum*, Benedict), Crested-Fern, has the fronds forked at the apex; a hort. state. There is also a variegated kind.

Fig. 7. Polypodiaceæ. A, *Nephrolepis exaltata:* Aa, pinna with sori, × 1; Ab, sorus, × 15; Ac, sporangium, × 25. B, Blechnum: pinna, × 1. C, *Asplenium bulbiferum:* Ca, pinna, × ½; Cb, sorus, × 5. D, *Pellæa viridis:* Da, pinna, × ½; Db, contiguous sori, × 2. E, *Platycerium bifurcatum:* habit showing fertile portion (f) of frond, × ⅙. F, *Phyllitis Scolopendrium:* Fa, distal end of frond with sori, × ½; Fb, sorus with double indusium, × 3. G, *Polystichum setiferum:* Ga, portion of rachis with fertile pinna, × ½; Gb, sorus, × 10. H, Adiantum: frond with sori. I, Davallia: Ia, pinna with sori, × 2; Ib, sorus, × 10; Ic, sporangium, × 25.

4. **ELAPHOGLOSSUM,** Schott. Simple-fronded ferns of the tropics of both hemispheres, 250–300 in number, very few cult. and only one at all common.—Fronds erect from creeping rhizomes, usually firm or thick in texture: sporangia covering the under surface of the fertile frond, which may be narrower and smaller than the sterile: veins either free or anastomosing (netted), commonly the former. (Elaphoglos-sum: Greek *deer tongue.*)

E. **crinitum,** Christ (*Acrostichum crinitum,* L. *Chrysodium crinitum,* Mett. *Hymenodium crinitum,* Fée). ELEPHANT-EAR-FERN. Fronds thick, 1–2 ft. long, one-fourth or one-third of which is the conspicuous shaggy-hairy stout stipe; blades entire, oblong to paddle-shaped, 6–8 in. broad at maturity, blunt or very short-acute, base rounded or subcordate, with scattered long hairs below and on the edge and sometimes on the upper surface: sporangia making a felt-like covering on the lower surface of the fertile blades. W. Indies, Mex., Cent. Amer.

5. **PLATYCERIUM,** Desv. (*Alcicornium,* Gaud.). STAGHORN-FERN. A dozen or more striking epiphytic ferns, trop. Afr. and Asia to temp. Australia, some frequent in public conservatories and fine collections.—Fronds of two kinds—usually flat rounded shield-shaped or dish-shaped parchment-like entire sterile lvs. (like a great thallus) that lie close to the support on which they grow, and erect or spreading mostly antler-forked fertile lvs.: sori naked, united to form great dense patches on the under side of the frond, mostly at or toward the end of the antlers. (Platycerium: Greek *broad-horn.*)—In some species the sterile fronds are also forked, as in *P. grande,* J. Smith, from Malaysia and trop. Australia, with the fertile fronds in pairs and the plant glabrous or nearly so, *P. Wallichii,* Hook., of Malaya, with the plant yellow-woolly or pubescent and fertile fronds in pairs, and *P. Willinckii,* Moore, Java, with fertile fronds in 3's, all the parts being narrow; these species are not common in cult.

A. Segms. and sinuses of fertile fronds very broad, the tips short and wide-spreading . . . 1. *P. Stemaria*
AA. Segms. and sinuses narrow, the tips more nearly erect.
B. Fertile fronds erect or ascending, segms. 1–2 in. wide and sharply acute . . . . 2. *P. Hillii*
BB. Fertile fronds pendent, segms. ½–1 in. wide and somewhat blunt . . . . 3. *P. bifurcatum*

1. **P. Stemaria,** Desv. (*Acrostichum Stemaria,* Beauv. *P. æthiopicum,* Hook.). TRIANGLE STAGHORN-FERN. Sterile fronds rounded and convex, somewhat lobed; fertile fronds pendent or declined, twice forked, to 3 ft. long, white-tomentose beneath, the tips short and divaricate: fructification a V-shaped patch under the sinus and extending part way on the forks. (Stemaria, Stemmaria: Latin *garlands.*) W. trop. Afr.

2. **P. Hillii,** Moore. Plant deep green, more or less stellate-pubescent beneath when young: sterile fronds rounded, convex; fertile fronds erect or strongly ascending, repeatedly forked, to 1½ or more ft. long: fructification on the ultimate segms. above the sinus and not extending to the tips. (Named for W. Hill, from whom Veitch & Sons received the plant.) Australia.

3. **P. bifurcatum,** C. Chr. (*Acrostichum bifurcatum,* Cav. *P. alcicorne,* Desv.). COMMON STAGHORN-FERN. Plant grayish-green, more or less cottony- or silky-pubescent: sterile fronds rounded and convex, the margin undulate and sometimes lobed; fertile fronds clustered, pendent, 2–3 ft. long, forked into narrow segms.: fructification on the ends of the forking segms., usually beginning beneath the terminal sinus and extending to the tips. Australia. Var. **majus,** Weatherby, is a larger and greener plant from Polynesia, with thick leathery more erect fronds.

6. **PITYROGRAMMA,** Link. GOLD- and SILVER-FERNS. Probably 15 species, as now defined, trop., mostly American, one common in greenhouses.—Fronds 1–3-pinnate, tufted, with copious white or yellow powder on the under side: sori linear, nearly confluent along the veins on the back of the frond; no indusia. (Pityrogramma: Greek *bran-line,* alluding to the powder.)

A. Expanded portion of frond 3–6 in. long; stipe barely ½5 in. thick . . . . 1. *P. triangularis*
AA. Expanded portion of frond 1–3 ft. long; stipe usually ⅛ in. or more thick.
B. Fronds 1-pinnate, the pinnæ dentately pinnatifid . . . . 2. *P. tartarea*
BB. Fronds 2–3-pinnate . . . . 3. *P. calomelanos*

1. **P. triangularis,** Maxon (*Gymnogramma triangulare,* Kaulf.). GOLD-FERN. Fronds erect, 6–16 in. long; stipes dark brown, polished, about twice as long as blades, slender; blades deltoid-pentagonal, 3–6 in. long, almost as broad, pinnate or 2-pinnate as to the large spreading basal pinnæ, the ultimate segms. with broad rounded teeth, coriaceous, subglabrous above, yellowish beneath. B. C. to Lower Calif. Var. **viscosa,** Weatherby

(*Gymnogramma triangularis* var. *viscosa*, D. C. Eaton), has reddish-brown stipes and white powder beneath the blades; S. Calif.

2. **P. tartarea,** Maxon (*Gymnogramma tartarea*, Desv. *Ceropteris tartarea*, Link). Fronds broad-lanceolate to oblong-lanceolate to deltoid-lanceolate in outline, 6 in.–2 ft. long, powdery-white beneath, pinnate and the pinnæ (which are 2–6 in. long and not long-pointed, entire or nearly so) pinnatifid; stipes shining; segms. close together, obtuse or sometimes a minute point on a rounded end. Trop. Amer.—One of the silver-ferns, but less common in cult. than no. 3; a gold var. is recorded.

3. **P. calomelanos,** Link (*Gymnogramma calomelanos*, Kaulf. *Ceropteris calomelanos*, Underw.). SILVER-FERN. Attractive and popular greenhouse fern: fronds long-lanceolate to narrowly ovate-lanceolate in outline, 1–3 ft. long, powdery-white beneath, the long (3–12 in.) and mostly long-acuminate pinnæ again pinnate; stipes handsome shining black; segms. or pinnules acute or short-acute for the most part, sometimes pinnatifid at the base. (Calomelanos: Greek *beautiful black*.) Trop. Amer. Var. **aureo-flava,** Weatherby (*Gymnogramma chrysophyllum*, Kaulf. *Ceropteris chrysophylla*, Link), GOLD-FERN, has gold-colored powder.

7. **ADIANTUM,** L. MAIDENHAIR-FERN. Small thin-lvd. delicate ferns making broad dense pot specimens with many slender wiry usually shining stipes; species 100–200, mostly of shaded habitats, largely of trop. Amer., a few in temp. N. Amer.—Sori at or near the ends of free-forking veins on the edge of the frond and covered by specialized reflexed tips of the margin which form an indusium, often at the bottom of a sinus: fronds pinnately or pedately compound or decompound, the pinnules broad, variously oblong, cuneate, rhomboid or trapeziform: rhizomes horizontal, forming a mat. (Adian-tum: Greek *unwetted*, alluding to the shedding of the rain by the character of foliage and growth. Vernacular name from the graceful locks or tresses.)

A. Fronds forked at the top of the stipe, blade usually not longer than wide...... 1. *A. pedatum*
AA. Fronds pinnate, blade usually longer than wide.
B. Sori oblong or sausage-shaped, little or not curved.
C. Blades mostly 1–2-pinnate, the segms. usually small, most of them about ½ in. across and often less..2. *A. Capillus-Veneris*
CC. Blades mostly 4–5-pinnate, the segms. usually larger, the main ones ¾ in. or more across..3. *A. tenerum*
BB. Sori circular, reniform or horseshoe-shaped.
C. Fertile segms. each bearing 2–6 sori: foliage thin......................4. *A. cuneatum*
CC. Fertile segms. each bearing 6–12 sori: foliage firm.....................5. *A. decorum*

1. **A. pedatum,** L. AMERICAN MAIDENHAIR. Rootstocks slender, often elongate: fronds forked into strongly divergent branches; stipes purplish, polished, 8–20 in. high; blades rounded to reniform in outline, mostly 8–18 in. broad, the several pinnæ pointing forward, horizontal, 4–16 in. long, pinnate into rather numerous oblong pinnules commonly ½–1 in. long with upper margin toothed to lobed: sori oblong to linear, on ends of segm.-lobes. Que. to Minn., Ga. and La. Var. **aleuticum,** Rupr., has the main branches slightly divergent, pinnæ strongly ascending; Newf. to Vt., W. N. Amer.

2. **A. Capillus-Veneris,** L. VENUSHAIR. TRUE or BLACK MAIDENHAIR. Slender erect-spreading fern, 12–18 in. high, with slender chaffy-hairy rhizomes and thin brown-black stipes: blades ovate to oblong-ovate, often curved, mostly 6–12 in. long, 2–3-pinnate except toward the top; pinnules lively green, stalked, cuneate-rhomboid, notched, ¼–1 in. across, the 1–5 prominent indusia transverse and straight or somewhat curved. (Capillus-Veneris: Latin *hair of Venus*.) Variable in nature and in cult.; temp. and trop. Amer., warmer parts of the Old World.—Frequent in greenhouses. Several Latin-named forms are referable to this species and its derivatives. Var. **daphnites,** Moore, has simpler fronds with very broad semi-cristate pinnules.

3. **A. tenerum,** Sw. BRITTLE MAIDENHAIR. Strong erect plant, 1½–3 ft. and more, with stout glossy black-brown stipes: blades very broad, usually more or less deltoid, about as broad as long, 3-pinnate; pinnules dull green, stalked, usually falling with age, rhombic to cuneate-ovate or cuneate-orbicular, mostly ¾ in. and more across, notched or almost cut, bearing 5–10 prominent broad usually nearly straight indusia. Trop. Amer.—In cult. under several names, but apparently not common. The hort. names *A. acutum*, *A. Bausei*, *A. Lathomii*, *A. magnificum*, *A. scutum*, and *A. rhodophyllum* and *A. Victoriæ*, Moore, are considered to represent forms or derivatives of this species. Known in cult. chiefly in var. **farleyense,** Nichols. (*A. farleyense*, Moore), fronds large and striking (sometimes 2–3 ft. long and 2 ft. broad), with curving drooping light green sometimes rose-tinted graceful spray; pinnules overlapping, 2 in., more or less across, cuneate-reniform, deeply cut or almost fringed, the fertile ones narrower; named and described in 1866 from specimens received from Farley Hill gardens, Barbados; one of the handsomest greenhouse ferns, in different forms.

4. **A. cuneatum,** Langsd. & Fisch. The prevailing greenhouse fern in N. Amer., in many forms: low slender species, producing many graceful fronds with thin brown-black stipes: blades ovate-oblong or narrowly deltoid-oblong, often one-sided, 4–12 in. long, 2–3-pinnate, dull green; pinnules cuneate-rhomboid, numerous, stalked, ¼–½in. across, lobed, bearing 3–5 small orbicular-reniform indusia. Brazil.—A cult. form with white-striped pinnules is var. **variegatum,** a crested form is var. **grandiceps,** Moore. Var. **Croweanum,** Benedict (*A. Croweanum,* Hort. Crowe), is a large very vigorous hardy form, the fronds keeping well when cut and useful for florist's work; bears the name of Peter Crowe, Utica, N. Y.; intro. about 1904. Var. **gracilimum,** Schneid. (*A. gracillimum,* Moore), has very finely divided fronds, the pinnules 1/32–3/16 in. across. To *A. cuneatum* or its derivatives are to be referred the names *A. fragrantissimum,* Hends., *A. mundulum,* Moore, *A. versailiense,* Schneid., and many others. *A. Wrightii,* Hort., is probably a form of *A. cuneatum.*

5. **A. decorum,** Moore. Erect rather stiff fern with narrow fronds on stout dull brown-black stipes: blades oblong to ovate-oblong, 5–10 in. long and half or more as broad, dull green, rather thick; pinnules rhomboid or cuneate-rhomboid, short-stalked, notched, with very few large reniform indusia. Peru.—The cult. plant is mostly known as **A. Weigandii,** Moore, which differs, according to Moore, in the larger and less cuneate or cuneate-trapezoid pinnules; bears the name of Mr. Weigand, Astoria, Long Island, N. Y.; described by Moore in 1883. To *A. decorum* are probably to be referred *A. Wagneri,* Mett., and *A. elegans,* Moore; perhaps the species itself is to be combined with *A. tinctum,* Moore, which is an older name.

8. **CHEILANTHES,** Sw. About 125 species of small rock-loving greenhouse or semi-hardy ferns, widely distributed in temp. and trop. regions.—Often hairy or woolly: fronds uniform, the blades 1–4-pinnate, or 1-pinnate and variously pinnatifid, the segms. often minute, even bead-like: sori borne at the enlarged tips of the veins; indusia formed by the revolute margin of the segms. either as separate areas or an almost continuous one. (Cheilan-thes: Greek *lip-flower,* referring to the indusium.)

C. gracillima, D. C. Eaton. LACE-FERN. Rootstocks tufted, short, densely paleaceous: fronds many, 4–12 in. high, the stipes about half the total length, dark brown, soon nearly naked; blades narrow, 2-pinnate, the segms. mostly oblong, brownish-tomentose beneath, somewhat scaly above, margins subentire, recurved, nearly hiding the many sporangia. B. C. to Mont. and Calif.

9. **PTERIS,** L. BRAKE. Plants of medium or large size on many parts of the globe, of 150 or more species, a few among the commonest greenhouse and window-garden ferns.—Fronds 1- or more-pinnate: sori on a narrow receptacle connected in a marginal line under a simple indusium formed of the revolute edge of the frond, mostly connecting the ends of free veins. (Pter-is [ter-is]: Greek *wing,* applied to ferns because of their feathery or wing-like character.)—The five species of Pteris here described comprise the usual ones in cult.; they have free (not meshed or reticulating) veins. While the first three species are distinct in their native condition, it is not always easy to distinguish them in some of the cultivars.

A. Fronds small, rarely to 2 ft. long, 1-pinnate, but the lower pairs of pinnæ forked or divided.
  B. Upper pairs of pinnæ strongly decurrent, i. e., the rachis conspicuously winged in two or more spaces. . . . . 1. *P. serrulata*
  BB. Upper pinnæ little or not at all decurrent (in some hort. forms the terminal pinna divided nearly to midrib).
    C. Sterile fronds unlike the fertile. . . . . 2. *P. ensiformis*
    CC. Sterile fronds much like the fertile except pinnæ broader and perhaps shorter . 3. *P. cretica*
AA. Fronds large, usually 2–4 ft. long, bipinnate.
  B. Ultimate divisions of the frond serrate. . . . . 4. *P. tremula*
  BB. Ultimate divisions entire. . . . . 5. *P. quadriaurita*

1. **P. serrulata,** L. f. (*P. multifida,* Poir.). Slender: fronds 8–24 in. long including the slender pale stipe which is 6–8 in. long, the blade oblong or ovate-oblong in outline, 6–10 in. broad, with 4–8 pinnæ which are opposite or nearly so; pinnæ very narrow, the fertile ones usually less than ¼in. wide (broader forms in cult.) and very long, the lower ones 2–3-forked; rachis prominently winged toward the top, the wing narrowing below; sterile fronds much like the fertile but the parts mostly broader and the margins sharp-serrate, as usually, also, are the long slender tips of the fertile fronds. China, Japan, also escaped from cult. in S. U. S.—Many cristate and other forms, represented by such hort. names as vars. *angustata, corymbifera, cristata, nana, variegata, voluta;* perhaps *P. Ouvardii,* Hort., is of this species rather than the following.

2. **P. ensiformis,** Burm. (*P. crenata,* Sw.). Very slender: fertile fronds erect, long and

narrow, overtopping the sterile ones, rising 12–20 in. with long naked stipes, the divisions ¼in. or less broad and usually almost linear, the lower ones 5–7-parted; sterile fronds shorter, small and narrow, the divisions short and broad and obtuse, the terminal parts sometimes fertile (sterile segms. ½–¾in. long and nearly or quite half as broad). E. Asia, Malaysia, Australia. Var. **Victoriæ,** Baker, has divisions of foliage banded and cross-barred with white.

3. **P. cretica,** L. A stouter plant than no. 1, with all frond-divisions normally broader, more than ¼in. wide (narrower forms in cult.); rachis mostly not winged at top, except in some hort. forms and then not much below the first pair of pinnæ, although the forking and cresting of the terminal pinna may give the appearance of a long-winged rachis. Tropics and subtropics in many parts of the world. Var. **albo-lineata,** Hook., a very common fern, has divisions prominently whitened along the center.—Cristate, multifid, enlarged, and other forms are known as vars. (or as if species) *Alexandræ, Childsii, cristata, magnifica, Mayii, nobilis, Rivertoniana, Wilsonii, Wimsettii.*

4. **P. tremula,** R. Br. Strong bright green large decorative fern with finely cut soft foliage: stipes smooth, brown, shining; blades 1–3 ft. or more long and 6–24 in. broad, 2–3-pinnate in the lower part, the narrow segms. finely serrate. New Zeal., Australia.—Modified and variegated forms are in cult.

5. **P. quadriaurita,** Retz. Strong rather coarse fern, with heavy foliage: stipes 1–2 ft. long, usually chaffy, at least when young; blades 1–2 ft. long, 2–3-pinnate below, the long-oblong mostly curved stiffish segms. entire and strongly veined, nearly or quite ¼in. broad. Tropics around the world.—Most familiar in var. **argyræa,** Hook., the pinnæ whitish-banded lengthwise. There is also a form (var. *tricolor*, Lind.) with bands whitish and reddish.

10. **PTERIDIUM,** Scop. As most recently treated a single world-wide species.—Coarse ferns with slender woody freely branched rootstocks: fronds stout, borne singly; stipes with basal felt-like covering; blades large, deltoid to elongate, 3–4-pinnate, the ultimate segms. entire, toothed or lobed: sori linear, marginal, continuous, the indusium double, the outer one prominent formed by the reflexed membranous lf.-margin, the inner obscure, delicate, nearly concealed by the sporangia. (Pterid-ium: diminutive of the Greek word *pteris*, an ancient name of ferns.)

P. aquilinum, Kuhn (*Pteris aquilina*, L.). BRACKEN. BRAKE. Fronds dull green; stipes erect, stout, 8–30 in. high, straw-colored with dark base; blades somewhat triangular with nearly equal pinnæ, tripinnate below, densely pubescent beneath, 1–3 ft. long; segms. ovate to oblong, obtuse, margined all around with the ciliate indusium. Eurasia. Var. **pubescens,** Underw. (var. *lanuginosum*, Fern.), has linear-oblong segms. strongly pubescent beneath; W. N. Amer., Mich., Ont., E. Que. Var. **latiusculum,** Underw. (*Pteris latiuscula*, Desv. *Pteridium latiusculum*, Hieron.), has segms. thinly pubescent along veins beneath and the indusium not ciliate; E. N. Amer. and E. Asia.

11. **PELLÆA,** Link. CLIFF-BRAKE. Sixty to 70 species of wide distribution, the plants mostly small and with tufted hard shining stipes, growing mostly on or among rocks.—Fronds pinnate or 2–3-pinnate, the fertile ones usually with narrower pinnæ or segms.: sori at or near the tips of free veins, circular or oblong, usually becoming confluent to form a marginal line covered by the reflexed edge of the frond. (Pellæ-a: Greek *dusky*, alluding to the dark-colored stipes.)

A. Blades of fronds 1-pinnate..1. *P. rotundifolia*
AA. Blades of fronds 2–3-pinnate, at least basally.
B. Fronds about as wide as long, often triangular........................2. *P. densa*
BB. Fronds two to five times as long as wide, ovate to linear.
C. Lvs. 2-pinnate, the segms. linear-oblong to linear....................3. *P. atropurpurea*
CC. Lvs. 3-pinnate, the segms. lanceolate to ovate........................4. *P. viridis*

1. **P. rotundifolia,** Hook. (*Allosurus rotundifolius*, Kunze). Fronds 6–12 in. long, narrow, 1-pinnate, the stipe and rachis brown-hairy and chaffy; pinnæ 20–40, alternate, orbicular to broad-oblong, ¼–½in. long, the terminal one ovate to hastate-ovate, all very short-stalked, entire, slightly toothed or coarsely angled. New Zeal.

2. **P. densa,** Hook. (*Onychium densum*, Brack. *Cryptogramma densa*, Diels. *Cheilanthes siliquosa*, Maxon). Rootstocks cespitosely branched: fronds crowded, 3–12 in. long; stipes 2–8 in. long, flexuous, dark red-brown; blades broadly ovate to deltoid, 3-pinnate below, glabrous, the pinnæ few, close, oblique; segms. narrowly linear, mostly ¼–½in. long, mucronate, margins sharply revolute, forming a continuous erosely toothed indusium. Que., Ont., Mont. to B. C. and Calif.

3. **P. atropurpurea,** Link (*Pteris atropurpurea*, L.). Rootstocks with short crowded branches, densely red-scaly: fronds loosely tufted, 3–12 in. long; stipes dark purple, polished, 1–8 in. long; blades 1–2-pinnate, coriaceous, broadly lanceolate; segms. oblong

center: fronds long-oblong to spatulate-ovate, 2–4 ft. long, 2–8 in. broad, attenuate below and with no distinct stipe, the margins entire, undulate, or sometimes with 1 or 2 sinuses as if accidentally lobed: sori linear, along veins in pinnate fashion. (Nidus: Latin *nest;* Nidus-Avis, *bird's nest.*) Asia, Polynesia.

2. **A. Belangeri,** Kunze (*Darea Belangeri,* Bory). Fronds evergreen, long and narrow, dark green, 12–18 in. long, 2–4 in. wide, pinnate, often with little bulblets at the axils; pinnæ deeply pinnatifid into linear-obtuse segms. about ¼in. long: sorus single on the segm., occupying half or more the length of it. (Bears the name of Charles Belanger, French botanical traveller of the last century.) Malaya.

3. **A. bulbiferum,** Forst. MOTHER SPLEENWORT. Fronds 1½–4 ft. long, 6–12 in. broad, 2–4-pinnate, with stipes chaffy or at length smooth, arching or bending with the weight of the numerous little plants borne on the upper surface; pinnæ 3–6 in. long, 1–1½ in. broad; segms. deltoid- or rhomboid-ovate to oblong in outline, lobed or divided, the lobes narrow and obtuse: sori short, oblong, often at maturity as wide as the lobe. New Zeal., Australia, Malaysia. Var. **laxum,** Hook. f., is smaller, with narrower pinnæ and more finely divided foliage.

4. **A. platyneuron,** Oakes (*Acrostichum platyneuron,* L.). EBONY SPLEENWORT. Rootstocks short, erect or ascending: fronds tufted, the fertile 8–20 in. tall; stipes purplish-brown, shining, 1–3 in. long; blades linear-oblanceolate in outline, firm, pinnate; pinnæ ⅓–1 in. long, sessile, spreading, oblong, finely serrate to incised: sori 8–12 pairs, nearer the midvein than the margin, elliptic: sterile fronds short, spreading. Me. to Ga., Tex., Colo.

5. **A. Trichomanes,** L. MAIDENHAIR SPLEENWORT. Much like no. 4 but fronds not differentiated into fertile and sterile; pinnæ roundish-oblong or oval, ⅛–¼in. long: sori 2–6 pairs. (Bears the name of a genus of filmy ferns.) N. Amer., Eu., Asia.

19. **ATHYRIUM,** Roth. Nearly or quite 100 pinnate or pinnatifid ferns, of medium size, largely trop. and subtrop. in eastern and western hemispheres, one of which has given many forms in garden cult.; formerly included in Asplenium.—The special generic character lies in the sori, which are oblong or narrow-oblong, usually curved and sometimes more or less horseshoe-shaped, mostly crossing a vein. (Athyrium: Greek *without shield,* the indusium only on the side.)

A. Pinnules entire or bluntly toothed: sori rather long, some of them double and placed back to back....................1. *A. thelypteroides*
AA. Pinnules coarsely toothed or cut: sori short, oblong, sometimes curved across the vein.
B. Rootstock erect: fronds forming a crown with the new growth in the center: largest indusia more than half as broad as long....................2. *A. Filix-femina*
BB. Rootstock horizontal or oblique: fronds loosely clustered, the new growth in front of the old: largest indusia less than half as broad as long....................3. *A. angustum*

1. **A. thelypteroides,** Desv. (*Asplenium thelypteroides,* Michx. *Asplenium acrostichoides,* Sw. *Athyrium acrostichoides,* Diels). Fronds 2–3 ft. long, deeply bipinnatifid, segms. broadly oblong or somewhat ovate, ⅛–⅜in. long, cut squarely off or broadly rounded at apex, the sides subparallel, entire or only slightly toothed; sori 3–6 pairs on a segm., oblong, nearly or quite straight, some of them double. N. S. to Ga. and Mo., E. Asia.

2. **A. Filix-femina,** Roth (*Polypodium Filix-femina,* L. *Asplenium Filix-femina,* Bernh.). LADY-FERN. Tall soft-foliaged bright green fern with erect rhizomes: stipes shaggy but becoming smooth and shining, 1 ft. or less long; blades 1–3 ft. long, broad-lanceolate or ovate-oblong in outline, tapering about equally both ways from the center, 2-pinnate; pinnæ alternate, bearing 15–20 or more pairs of deeply pinnatifid and toothed acute segms. ¼–1 in. long: sori strongly curved, fringed with relatively long non-glandular cilia; spores yellow, somewhat warty. Moist woods, W. N. Amer., also Eu., Afr., Asia.—Many odd kinds of lady-fern have received names, but the plant is little cult. from hort. sources in N. Amer.; the variations run into the hundreds. Such vars. as *crispum, grandiceps, laciniatum, latifolium, multifidum, plumosum,* may be expected in collections. Var. **Craigii,** Moore, is a dwarf crested fern with red stipes. Var. **Victoriæ,** Moore, is a remarkable form with pinnæ forked to the base, these forks extending forward and backward giving the frond a criss-cross effect, the tips being forked and crested; for Queen Victoria, "queen of the lady-ferns." The lady-ferns of E. N. Amer. are now mostly classified under no. 3.

3. **A. angustum,** Presl (*Aspidium angustum,* Willd. *Asplenium Michauxii,* Spreng. *Athyrium Filix-femina* var. *Michauxii,* Farwell). Close to no. 2: rootstocks horizontal or oblique: fronds loosely clustered, the new growth in front of the old; blades commonly less reduced below: indusia mostly toothed or short-ciliate; spores yellow, nearly smooth. Que. to Man., Pa. and Ohio.—**A. asplenioides,** Desv., is much like *A. angustum,* with young indusia glandular-ciliate, spores blackish; Mass. to Ind. and Gulf states.

20. **CYRTOMIUM,** Presl. A segregate from Polystichum, differing in the anastomosing veins; distinguished also from Dryopteris by this character and by the centrally attached indusium; species 4 or 5, Asia, Afr., Pacific isls.—Fronds pinnate, firm: sori large, sown over the large pinnæ. (Cyrto-mium: Greek *a bow.*)—By some authorities placed in the genus Phanerophlebia.

A. Margins of pinnæ entire or obscurely undulate (except in certain hort. forms).
B. Pinnæ ovate....................1. *C. falcatum*
BB. Pinnæ lanceolate or oblong-lanceolate....................2. *C. Fortunei*
AA. Margins distinctly serrate....................3. *C. caryotideum*

1. **C. falcatum,** Presl (*Polypodium falcatum,* L. f. *Aspidium falcatum,* Sw. *Polystichum falcatum,* Diels). HOUSE HOLLY-FERN. Stiff erect fern, with stout very shaggy stipes: fronds dark heavy green, 1–2½ ft. long, 4–8 in. broad, long-oblong in outline, pinnate, glossy above; pinnæ alternate, short-stalked, usually 3–4 in. long, ovate to falcate-ovate, long-acuminate, the margin entire or obscurely wavy: sori circular, large, abundantly scattered over the lower surface. Widespread in Japan, China and adjacent continental regions, S. Afr., Polynesia.—Forms with incised pinnæ are known as *C. Butterfieldii,* Hort., and *C. Rochefordianum,* Hort. There are also condensed and dwarf forms, as var. **compactum,** Hort.

2. **C. Fortunei,** J. Smith (*Aspidium falcatum* var. *Fortunei,* Nichols.). Fronds not glossy above; pinnæ smaller and much narrower, usually 1–3 in. long and ¾–1 in. or less broad, the base truncate or truncate auricled. (Named for Robert Fortune, page 43.) Japan.

3. **C. caryotideum,** Presl (*Aspidium caryotideum,* Wall. *A. falcatum* var. *caryotideum,* Nichols.). Drooping in habit, light green: pinnæ mostly larger than in no. 1, distinctly serrate-dentate. Japan, India.

21. **POLYSTICHUM,** Roth. HOLLY-FERN. Probably 100 species as now defined, mostly woods ferns in temp. regions, widely distributed on the globe; few are well known to cultivators.—Fronds pinnatifid to 4-pinnate, mostly of rough texture, from mostly shaggy rhizomes; ultimate divisions usually spinulose or sharp-serrate, the segms. likely to be auriculate; veins free: sori orbicular, covered by superior indusia attached by the center. (Polys-tichum: Greek *many rows,* from the sori in the originally described species.)—Many of these ferns are familiarly known under the name Aspidium.

A. Fronds 1-pinnate, the pinnæ entire, toothed or rarely 1-pinnatifid.
B. Lower pinnæ reduced to mere triangular lobes....................1. *P. Lonchitis*
BB. Lower pinnæ not or only scarcely smaller than upper ones.
C. Pinnæ, at least upper ones, usually bluntly acute or rounded; lateral veins indistinct or forking into 4's....................2. *P. acrostichoides*
CC. Pinnæ acuminate; lateral veins usually distinct, forking into 3's....................3. *P. munitum*
AA. Fronds 2–4-pinnate, at least basally.
B. Lower part of frond more than 2-pinnate, lower pinnæ much the largest.
C. Segms. with teeth aristate or the segms. terminally so; stipes coarsely brown-scaly.
D. Ultimate pinnæ finely toothed, glabrous....................4. *P. aristatum*
DD. Ultimate pinnæ coarsely toothed or pinnatifid, remotely brown fibrillose-scaly beneath....................8. *P. setiferum*
CC. Segms. or teeth not aristate; stipes not scaly or only finely so....................5. *P. adiantiforme*
BB. Lower part of frond only 2-pinnate, ultimate pinnæ sometimes pinnatifid basally.
C. Pinnules broadly oblong, apex rounded but spine-tipped....................6. *P. Braunii*
CC. Pinnules mostly lanceolate, apex acute and tapering.
D. Scales of stipe black to purplish-brown, usually confined to basal half of stipe....................7. *P. tsus-simense*
DD. Scales of stipe cinnamon-brown, usually present throughout scape and most of rachis....................8. *P. setiferum*

1. **P. Lonchitis,** Roth (*Polypodium Lonchitis,* L. *Aspidium Lonchitis,* Sw.). MOUNTAIN HOLLY-FERN. Rootstocks large, woody, erect or ascending: fronds several, leathery, persistent, rigidly ascending, 6–24 in. long, 1–3 in. wide; stipes 1–6 in. long, straw-colored, with large rusty-brown scales; blades 1-pinnate, the rachis stout, paleaceous; pinnæ many, close, falcate, oblong-lanceolate, 1–1½ in. long, spiny-toothed, with strongly auricled base, the lowest greatly reduced: sori large, contiguous, usually in 2 rows; indusia entire. (Lonchitis: a genus of trop. ferns.) N. S. to Alaska, Mich., Calif., Eu., Asia.

2. **P. acrostichoides,** Schott (*Nephrodium acrostichoides,* Michx. *Aspidium acrostichoides,* Sw. *Dryopteris acrostichoides,* Kuntze). CHRISTMAS-FERN. DAGGER-FERN. Rootstocks stout: fronds persistent, 10–30 in. long, 1–3 in. wide; stipes stout, rusty, chaffy; blades 1-pinnate, the pinnæ lanceolate, half-hastate, more or less falcate, with somewhat appressed bristly teeth; fertile pinnæ largely terminal, reduced, with many mostly con-

tiguous sori which may cover almost whole lower surface; indusia glabrous, entire. N. S. to Tex.

3. **P. munitum,** Presl (*Aspidium munitum,* Kaulf.). Western Sword-Fern. Giant Holly-Fern. Rootstocks stout, ascending: fronds leathery, persistent, 1–4 ft. long, 2–10 in. wide; stipes stout, 2–20 in. long, brown-scaly; blades 1-pinnate, linear-lanceolate, the pinnæ many, subfalcate, linear, sharp-toothed or cut, auriculate at base: sori large, in 2 or sometimes several crowded rows; indusia papillose-toothed to ciliate. Alaska to Mont. and Calif. Var. **imbricans,** Maxon, fronds half as long, with crowded obliquely imbricated pinnæ; B. C. to Calif.

4. **P. aristatum,** Presl (*Polypodium aristatum,* Forst. *Aspidium aristatum,* Sw. *Lastrea aristata,* Moore). Broad-fronded fern, with shaggy or chaffy stipes 10–18 in. long, deltoid-ovate in outline, the blades 1–2 ft. long and half as broad; upper pinnæ 1-pinnate, lower deltoid and 2–3-pinnate, at least at the base; pinnules rhombic-ovate, sessile or very short-stalked, pinnatifid, the segms. or lobes aristate: sori many, not large. Asia to Australia.—A var. has the pinnæ banded along the midrib with whitish-green.

5. **P. adiantiforme,** J. Smith (*Polypodium adiantiforme,* Forst. *Polystichum capense,* J. Smith. *P. coriaceum,* Schott). Tall spreading plant with stout stipes scaly below but usually becoming smooth: blades nearly deltoid, 1–3 ft. long, coriaceous, the upper pinnæ 1-pinnate, the lower 2–3-pinnate; pinnules oblong, about ¾–1 in. long, blunt or short-acute, rather coarsely dentate: sori prominent, midway between rib and margin. Tropics, eastern and western hemispheres.

6. **P. Braunii,** Fée (*Aspidium Braunii,* Spenner). Shield-Fern. Rootstocks short, stout, ascending to suberect: fronds fairly persistent, 10–28 in. long, mostly 4–6 in. wide; stipes 2–6 in. long, copiously brown-scaly; blades 2-pinnate, rather thin, the veins distinctly seen in dried specimens, the rachis with more thread-like scales than broad ones; pinnules oblong-ovate with appressed-bristly teeth, and covered with hair-like scales: sori small, not confluent, nearer the midrib than the margin; indusia glabrous, entire. (A. Braun, page 40.) Eu. Var. **Purshii,** Fern., blades rather thick, the veins obscure in dried specimens, rachis with more broad scales than thread-like ones; Newf. to Pa. and Wis.

7. **P. tsus-simense,** J. Smith (*Aspidium tsus-simense,* Hook.). Small thin-lvd. plant often grown in fern-baskets: fronds 10–24 in. long including the slender very shaggy stipe, 2-pinnate, long-lanceolate in outline, acuminate; pinnæ alternate, the upper pinnatifid, the lower pinnate, the pinnules small, pointed, and the teeth short-spinulose and straight: sori large, brown, midway between rib and margin. (Tsus-sima, an island of Japan.) Japan.

8. **P. setiferum,** Woynar (*Polypodium setiferum,* Forsk. *Polystichum aculeatum,* Auth.). Stout dark-colored fern with thick very shaggy stipes and rachis, the fronds 3–6 in. broad and 1–2 ft. long: pinnæ numerous and close together, alternate, sessile, squarrose, straight or somewhat curved, pinnatifid and the pinnæ again pinnatifid, the segms. and teeth all terminated by slender curved cusps or aristæ: sori usually closely placed and covering the under surface. Practically throughout the world except in arctic regions and N. Amer.—Immensely variable and comprising very many synonyms when conceived in the broad sense, including *P. angulare,* Presl. A proliferous form is frequent in greenhouses. The species is often planted in the open. It has been shown that the name *P. aculeatum,* Roth, should be applied to the fern that has been called *P. lobatum,* Huds.

22. **NEPHROLEPIS,** Schott. Sword-Fern. A dozen or more trop. and subtrop. plants, the world around, terrestrial and epiphytic, comprising the most popular living-house and conservatory ferns.—Fronds long and narrow, pinnatifid or pinnate, the numerous pinnæ jointed to the rachis and often falling; veins forking, free: sori on the upper forks of the veins, the circular or kidney-shaped indusia attached only at the base. (Nephrol-epis: Greek *kidney scale.*)—Some of the species are in an active state of mutation, giving rise to many odd forms, particularly *N. exaltata.*

A. Rootstocks with small tubers: veins of frond-segms. mostly 1-forked.
  B. Pinnæ orbicular or nearly so, about ¼in. long .... 1. *N. Duffii*
  BB. Pinnæ lanceolate, about 1 in. long .... 2. *N. cordifolia*
AA. Rootstocks lacking tubers.
  B. Pinnæ about ½in. long; veins of segms. mostly 1-forked .... 3. *N. pectinata*
  BB. Pinnæ 1½–7 in. long; veins of segms. mostly 2-forked.
    C. Sori solitary on special narrow segms. of fertile fronds: fronds drooping, usually 12–15 in. wide .... 4. *N. acuminata*
    CC. Sori along margins of normal frond-segms.: fronds various.
      D. The pinnæ remote, more than their own width apart, leathery .... 5. *N. biserrata*
      DD. The pinnæ closer than above, herbaceous .... 6. *N. exaltata*

1. **N. Duffii,** Moore (*N. cordifolia* var. *Duffii,* Goebel). Graceful slender plant of tufted habit: fronds 1–2 ft. long, arching, ½in. wide more or less, usually furcate or crested at the top, stipes and rachis chaffy-hairy; pinnæ numerous, alternate, sessile, nearly or

quite orbicular, about ¼in. across longest way, indistinctly wavy-toothed. (Duffii: Mr. Duff, of the Sidney Botanic Garden, New S. Wales.)—A sterile fern supposed to have come from New Zeal. or the South Sea Isls., widespread in cult. in American tropics; probably a mutant from *N. cordifolia.*

2. **N. cordifolia,** Presl (*Polypodium cordifolium,* L. *N. tuberosa,* Presl. *N. cordata,* Hort.). Erect or nearly so, tufted, with numerous bright green fronds and shaggy stipes, the rhizome tuberiferous: fronds 1–2 ft. long, about 2 or 2½ in. wide, with many pairs of pinnæ close together or overlapping; pinnæ 1–1¼ in. long, long-oblong to lanceolate, very blunt, auricled on upper side at base, rather sharply toothed (at least the sterile ones), the veins mostly 1-forked: sori many, midway between midvein and margin, the indusia reniform. Tropics and subtropics, around the world.—Planted in full sunshine in S. Calif.

3. **N. pectinata,** Schott (*Aspidium pectinatum,* Willd. *N. cordifolia* var. *pectinata,* Nichols.). Small and slender compact species with grayish-green spreading or pendulous foliage: fronds 12–18 in. long, about 1 in. wide, with slender nearly or quite naked stipes; pinnæ many, alternate, close together and often overlapping, about ½in. long, oblong, rounded at apex, auricled on base above, obtusely toothed or small-notched: sori midway between midvein and margin, the indusia broad-reniform. Trop. Amer.

4. **N. acuminata,** Kuhn (*Ophioglossum acuminatum,* Houtt. *N. davallioides,* Kunze). Large plant with arching or drooping fronds, and producing many runners: stipes grooved, scaly at the base, rachis hairy; fronds 2–3 ft. long and 8–12 in. and more broad; pinnæ alternate, far apart, long-linear-lanceolate, acuminate, base auricled or truncate above, coarsely obtusely dentate, the upper ones much narrower and with projecting teeth on which the reniform indusia are borne. Malaysia.

5. **N. biserrata,** Schott (*Aspidium biserratum,* Sw. *N. acuta,* Presl). Stout fern with arching or drooping habit, thick foliage, the stipes and rachis more or less scurfy-hairy: fronds 2–4½ ft. long, 4 or 6–12 in. broad, the pinnæ distant or well separated; pinnæ 2–6 in. long, long-oblong-lanceolate, short-pointed, the base rounded below and more or less short-auricled on the upper side, the margins obscurely crenate to crenate-serrate: sori nearer the margin than the midrib, the indusia orbicular. Tropics around the world.—A forked form, var. **furcans,** Hort., is common in cult. and is likely to be named as no. 4.

6. **N. exaltata,** Schott (*Polypodium exaltatum,* L.). Strong erect stiff fern, with the tops of the narrow fronds spreading: stipes channelled, shaggy or smooth, upper rachis mostly hairy but sometimes smooth; fronds 2–5 ft. long, 3–5 or 6 in. broad, the pinnæ close together; pinnæ oblong-lanceolate or the sterile ovate-lanceolate, 1½–3 in. long, acute, the veins mostly 2-forked, base truncate and auricled on upper side, entire or obscurely crenulate: sori about midway, the indusia reniform. Tropics and adjacent regions (as S. Fla.) of both hemispheres.—In recent time, this species has given rise to great numbers of sports or mutants, some with much-divided delicate fronds, even 4- and 5-pinnate. Crested forms are among them. The extreme mutants bear little resemblance to Nephrolepis, and they are likely to bear few sori. However, simpler fronds are likely to arise in the midst of the modified ones, and from these the student is able to make identification as to species. *N. exaltata* seems now to be rare in cult., its place being taken by the spreading drooping variously modified mutants.

Var. **bostoniensis,** Davenport. Boston-Fern. Strong free grower with widely spreading or drooping foliage less stiff and rigid than in *N. exaltata* itself: fronds large, broad; pinnæ 3–4 in. long and often ¾in. wide, entire or crenulate, more or less undulate.—Intro. 1895. From this mutant, or its derivatives, have arisen most of the other forms, as vars. *elegantissima, magnifica, muscosa, robusta, Scholzelii, Scottii, superbissima, Whitmanii.*

23. **DRYOPTERIS,** Adans. (*Nephrodium,* Rich. *Lastrea,* Bory). As the genus is now mostly understood it comprises several hundred mostly woods ferns in trop. and temp. regions, chiefly the former, on many parts of the globe, very few common in cult.; native species known under Aspidium are included in this genus.—Fronds 1- or more-pinnate, usually erect: sori borne on veins, sometimes naked, but mostly with circular, cordate or kidney-shaped indusia attached at the sinus. (Dryop-teris: Greek *oak fern.*)

A. Fronds 2–3-pinnate, or at least basally so.
B. Indusia wanting .... 1. *D. disjuncta*
BB. Indusia present, usually horseshoe-shaped.
C. Blades 3-pinnate or 2-pinnate-pinnatifid .... 2. *D. spinulosa*
CC. Blades 2-pinnate, at least in the lowest pinnæ.
D. Sori marginal on the pinnules .... 3. *D. marginalis*
DD. Sori on the midrib or between it and the margin.
E. Pinnæ broadest at the middle, pinnules entire to bluntly serrate .... 4. *D. Goldiana*
EE. Pinnæ broadest at the base.
F. Basal scales of rachis linear-lanceolate, with attenuate apices .... 5. *D. Filix-mas*
FF. Basal scales of rachis oblong-ovate, with blunt apices.

G. Frond distinctly narrowed toward base, lower pinnæ becoming progressively shorter.......... 6. *D. cristata*
GG. Frond not becoming narrowed toward base.
H. The pinnæ serrate, falcate.......... 6. *D. cristata* var.
HH. The pinnæ spinulose-dentate, straight.......... 2. *D. spinulosa*
AA. Fronds 1-pinnate or 2-pinnatifid.
B. Indusium wanting.
C. Blades usually broader than long, puberulent to scaly beneath, rachis winged between lowest pair of pinnæ.......... 7. *D. hexagonoptera*
CC. Blades longer than broad, pubescent beneath, rachis not winged between lowest pair of pinnæ.......... 8. *D. Phegopteris*
BB. Indusium present.
C. Pinnules toothed or incised; veins, at least the lowest, more than 1-forked.
D. Sori marginal.......... 3. *D. marginalis*
DD. Sori not marginal.
E. Pinnæ broadest at the middle; pinnules obscurely serrate, oblong-linear.......... 4. *D. Goldiana*
EE. Pinnæ broadest at the base; pinnules coarsely spinulose-serrate, short-oblong.......... 6. *D. cristata*
CC. Pinnules entire or repand; veins simple or 1-forked.
D. Pinnæ divided three-fourths way or more toward midvein; stipes quite glabrous.
E. The sori submarginal: lowermost pinnæ notably smaller than middle ones.......... 9. *D. noveboracensis*
EE. The sori about half way from margin to midvein: lowermost pinnæ somewhat smaller than middle ones..........10. *D. Thelypteris*
DD. Pinnæ divided about half way toward the midvein; stipes pubescent.... 11. *D. dentata*

1. **D. disjuncta,** Morton (*Polypodium disjunctum*, Rupr. *Dryopteris Linnæana*, C. Chr. *Polypodium Dryopteris*, L. *Phegopteris Dryopteris*, Fée). OAK-FERN. Rhizomes cord-like, wide-creeping: fronds erect, distant, 8–24 in. long; stipes slender, straw-colored, from a chaffy dark base; blades deltoid, 3–10 in. long and broad, subternate, 2–3-pinnate, the ultimate segms. oblong, rounded-obtuse, entire to serrate-crenate: sori naked, small, submarginal. N. N. Amer., Eu., Asia.

2. **D. spinulosa,** Kuntze (*Polypodium spinulosum*, O. F. Muell. *Thelypteris spinulosa*, Nieuwl.). SPINULOSE WOOD-FERN. Rootstocks stout, creeping, chaffy: fronds 1½–3 ft. high, erect or spreading; stipes rather coarse, pale brown, with similarly colored scales; blades narrow-ovate to oblong, bipinnate or bipinnate-pinnatifid, the segms. sharply toothed or incised, glabrous: sori submarginal, terminal on veinlets; indusium glabrous. Lab. to Mont., Va., Iowa, Eurasia. Var. **dilatata,** Underw. (*Polypodium dilatatum*, Hoffm.), lvs. 3-pinnate; Eu. Var. **intermedia,** Underw. (*Polypodium intermedium*, Muhl.), lvs. bipinnate-pinnatifid, more or less glandular beneath; indusia with marginal glands; Newf. to Wis., N. C., Tenn.

3. **D. marginalis,** Gray (*Polypodium marginale*, L.). MARGINAL SHIELD-FERN. Rootstocks stout, woody, ascending: fronds 1–2½ ft. long, coriaceous; stipes stout, chaffy and with a dense mass of scales at base; blades ovate-oblong in outline, pinnate-pinnatifid or 2-pinnate, 10–20 in. long; pinnules oblong, broadly obtuse, entire or wavy-margined or lowest obtusely toothed: sori near the margin, distant, rather small; indusium glabrous. N. S. to Ga. and Kans.

4. **D. Goldiana,** Gray (*Aspidium Goldianum*, Hook.). GOLDIE'S-FERN. Rootstocks stout, woody, horizontal and ascending: fronds 2–4 ft. long; stipes about as long as blade; blades broadly ovate to ovate-oblong, 2-pinnate; pinnæ 6–11 in. long, oblong-lanceolate, broadest in the middle; pinnules oblong-lanceolate, slightly scythe-shaped, serrate with appressed teeth: sori near the midvein, rather large; indusium glabrous. (Named for J. Goldie, Scotch visitor to N. Amer. in 1817.) N. B. to N. C. and Tenn.

5. **D. Filix-mas,** Schott (*Polypodium Filix-mas*, L. *Aspidium Filix-mas*, Sw. *Nephrodium Filix-mas*, Rich. *Lastrea Filix-mas*, Presl). MALE-FERN. Stout woods fern with chaffy rhizome and stipes, the foliage growing in a crown: fronds 2–4 ft. high, firm and nearly persistent, 2-pinnate, oblong-lanceolate in outline, 6–12 in. broad, pointed; pinnæ ¾–1 in. broad, long-tapering, with sessile oblong obtuse serrate pinnules: sori large, brown, near the midvein, contiguous and occupying most of the lower two-thirds of the pinnule. Many parts of the world, in the U. S. very northern except in the western mts.—Little grown in N. Amer., although it runs into very many crested, crisped, forked, dwarf, and other forms.

6. **D. cristata,** Gray (*Polypodium cristatum*, L. *Aspidium cristatum*, Sw.). Rootstocks stout, creeping: fronds 1–3 ft. long; stipes one-third to one-half the length of the whole frond, straw-colored above the base, with brownish scales; blades narrowly lanceolate, stiffly upright, mostly 3–5 in. wide, 2-pinnatifid; pinnæ triangular-oblong, 2–3 in. long, often horizontal, with their planes set at right angles to the direction of the rachis; lobes of pinnæ oblong, 6–10 pairs, finely toothed: sori half way between midvein and margin; indusium glabrous. Newf. to Va. and Ark., Eu., Asia. Var. **Clintoniana,** Underw. (*Aspidium cristatum* var. *Clintonianum*, D. C. Eaton), blades broadly lanceolate, 6–8 in. wide, pinnæ in same plane as rachis; N. H. to Wis. and N. C.

7. **D. hexagonoptera,** C. Chr. (*Polypodium hexagonopterum*, Michx. *Phegopteris hexagonoptera*, Fée). Broad Beech-Fern. Rootstocks horizontal, often elongate, slender: fronds 1–2½ ft. long, the stipes comprising half or more of that length; blades triangular, 8–14 in. long and at least as wide, slightly pubescent and often glandular beneath, 2-pinnatifid, the primary divisions (pinnæ) lanceolate, acuminate, the secondary lance-oblong, entire to round-toothed: sori near the margin, small, naked. Que. to Fla. and Tex.

8. **D. Phegopteris,** C. Chr. (*Polypodium Phegopteris*, L. *Phegopteris polypodioides*, Fée). Narrow or Long Beech-Fern. Rootstocks horizontal, slender: fronds 8 in.–2 ft. long, of which one-half to three-fourths is the slender stipe; blades triangular, long-acuminate, 1-pinnate into deeply pinnatifid subentire pubescent segms.: sori almost on the margin, small, naked. N. N. Amer., Eu., Asia.

9. **D. noveboracensis,** Gray (*Polypodium noveboracense*, L. *Aspidium noveboracense*, Sw.). New-York-Fern. Rootstocks slender, wide-creeping: fronds erect, 1–2 ft. long, the stipes 4–7 in. long, rather slender; blades lanceolate or elliptic-lanceolate, tapering both ways from near the middle, acuminate, 1-pinnate; pinnæ 1–2½ in. long, lanceolate, somewhat pilose, deeply pinnatifid into oblong segms.: sori submarginal, not confluent; indusium minute, delicate, glandular. Newf. to Ga. and Ark.

10. **D. Thelypteris,** Gray (*Acrostichum Thelypteris*, L. *Aspidium Thelypteris*, Sw. *Thelypteris palustris*, Schott). Marsh-Fern. Rootstocks rather slender, widely creeping: fronds erect, 1–4 ft. long; stipes rather slender, purplish at base, subglabrous, equalling or longer than the blade; blades lanceolate or elliptic-lanceolate, glabrous, 1-pinnate; pinnæ 1–3 in. long, pinnatifid into oblong segms.: sori about medial, many; indusium small, glandular-toothed. Eurasia. Var. **pubescens,** Prince, with pubescent blades and ciliate not glandular indusium, is the E. American marsh-fern, also in E. Asia.

11. **D. dentata,** C. Chr. (*Polypodium dentatum*, Forsk. *D. mollis*, Hieron. *Aspidium molle*, Sw. *Nephrodium molle*, R. Br.). A common greenhouse fern, under various names, as *Dryopteris parasitica*, *Aspidium violescens*, as well as those above: fronds 1–3 ft. long, pinnate, blades 6–12 in. broad, surfaces as well as the long stipe and the rachis hairy; pinnæ long and narrow, ½–¾in. broad, acuminate, cut one-half of the depth into closely placed obtuse entire lobes, lower pinnæ shorter and more distant; veins running together: sori small and many, covering most of the segms. Tropics of both hemispheres.—There are crested and other forms.

24. **DAVALLIA,** Smith. Terrestrial and epiphytic ferns of mostly small size and finely divided foliage but diverse habit; 60–70 species in warm and trop. parts of the Old World.—Rhizome creeping, mostly densely chaffy, the stipes not jointed to it: fronds 1–3-pinnate, usually ovate or deltoid in outline: sori at or near the margins, the indusia tubular or semi-cylindric and opening toward the margin, attached by both base and side; the indusium usually occupies nearly or quite the width of the lobe on which it is borne, but the apex of the lobe may project beyond it forming one or two horns. (Daval-lia: Edmund Davall, 1763–1798, Swiss botanist.)—The abundant slender tortuous rhizomes of the commonly cult. species spread on the surface of the ground or cling over the side of the pot or block.

A. Ultimate lobes or divisions linear, usually less than 1/16 in. broad, not sharp-toothed: no horns beyond the indusium . . . . 1. *D. fejeensis*
AA. Ultimate lobes broader, 1/16 in. or more: one or more horns usually present.
  B. Lobes usually sharp-toothed at apex.
    C. Fronds deciduous, the blades usually less than 1 ft. long . . . . 2. *D. bullata*
    CC. Fronds not deciduous, blades usually more than 1 ft. long at maturity . . . . 3. *D. dissecta*
  BB. Lobes not sharp-toothed at apex; blades of frond 12–18 in. long . . . . 4. *D. canariensis*

1. **D. fejeensis,** Hook. Handsome evergreen fern with very finely divided foliage: rhizomes thick, nearly straight: fronds erect but drooping with age, with angled stipes smooth except at base; blades deltoid, 12–18 in. long, 4-pinnatifid, the many ultimate lobes linear and somewhat broadened at the summit where the sori are borne, producing no horns beyond the indusia. (Fejeensis: Fiji Isls., whence it comes.)—It runs into several forms in cult.

2. **D. bullata,** Wall. Squirrels-foot-Fern. Small fern with deciduous fronds from creeping forking rhizomes, grown in fern-balls and otherwise: blades 6–12 in. long and half or more as broad, ovate, 4-pinnatifid but the sharp-toothed divisions not very narrow: sori usually near one margin of the lobe, a horn commonly projecting beyond it. Malaysia, India, Japan.

3. **D. dissecta,** J. Smith. Finely divided delicate but strong plant, with extensively creeping rhizomes: blades 12–18 in. long when full grown, nearly as broad, deltoid, 4-pinnatifid, the ultimate lobes mostly rather broader than in no. 2: sori central, occupying nearly or quite the width of the lobe, the teeth or horns often or commonly 2. Java.—Often grown as *D. elegans* and *D. affinis*, which are properly synonyms of other species.

4. **D. canariensis,** Smith (*Trichomanes canariensis,* L.). Strong-growing decorative fern: rhizomes crooked: blades 12–18 in. long and 8–12 in. broad, broad-deltoid in outline, 4-pinnatifid; lobes very many, usually obtuse and not sharp-toothed or horned at the apex: sori occupying the width of the lobe. Canary Isls., as also on adjacent isls. and mainlands.

25. **SPHENOMERIS,** Maxon. A segregate from Odontosoria (a genus not known to be cult.) and differing from the related genus Davallia in the scale-like indusium which opens at the top, the ultimate segms. of the decompound fronds mostly short-cuneate; species 18, mostly trop., eastern and western hemispheres. (Sphenom-eris: Greek for *wedge* and *part*, referring to the wedge-shaped segms.)

S. chusana, Copeland (*Adiantum chusanum,* L. *Trichomanes chinensis,* L. *Odontosoria chinensis,* J. Smith. *O. tenuifolia,* J. Smith. *Davallia tenuifolia,* Sw. *D. chinensis,* Smith. *Stenoloma tenuifolium,* Fée). Small graceful fern with prostrate chaffy-hairy rhizomes: blades 18 in. or less long and about half as wide, broad-ovate to ovate-oblong in outline, 3–4-pinnatifid; ultimate lobes cuneate, about ⅛in. long, more or less truncate: sori 1 or 2 at the apex of a lobe, usually 1, mostly broader than long. Trop. and E. Asia, Polynesia.

26. **DENNSTAEDTIA,** Bernh. CUP-FERN. Large or medium-sized ferns, 50–60 species mostly within the tropics, one native in N. N. Amer. and sometimes transferred to grounds.—Rhizomes hairy, erect or creeping: fronds 1–3-pinnate, veins free: sori at or very near the margin; indusium inferior, cup-like, attached at both base and side, open at top, joined on the outer side to the margin or a reflexed tooth. (Dennstaed-tia: August Wilhelm Dennstaedt, early German botanist.)

A. Fronds 3-pinnate, then pinnatifid, to 7 ft. long........1. *D. cicutaria*
AA. Fronds 2-pinnate, then pinnatifid, to 3 ft. long........2. *D. punctilobula*

1. **D. cicutaria,** Moore (*Dicksonia cicutaria,* Sw. *Sitolobium cicutarium,* J. Smith). Rhizomes creeping: fronds large, 3–8 ft. high, with stout brown often hairy stipes; blades 3-pinnate, 2–3 ft. across at base, the pinnæ pinnatifid into oblong nearly or quite obtuse strongly toothed segms.: sori cup-shaped or urn-shaped, in a sinus. Trop. Amer.

2. **D. punctilobula,** Moore (*Nephrodium punctilobulum,* Michx. *Dicksonia punctilobula,* Gray). HAY-SCENTED-FERN. Rhizomes very slender, creeping: fronds clustered, 1–3 ft. long, 5–9 in. wide; stipes slender, pale brown, smooth; blades 2-pinnate, then pinnatifid, the segms. thin and delicate, numerous, finely toothed, minutely pubescent beneath: sori minute, each on or at the base of a recurved toothlet; indusium pouch-like. N. S. to Ga. and Ark.

27. **WOODSIA,** R. Br. About 35 species of small ferns of rocky places, native in temp. and cold countries.—Rootstocks tufted: fronds numerous, 1–2-pinnate: sori round, separate, borne on the back of simply forked free veins; indusia thin, attached under the sporangia, roundish and early cleft into lacerate divisions, or deeply stellate, the narrow divisions mostly hidden by the sporangia. (Wood-sia: in honor of Joseph Woods, 1776–1864, English architect and botanist.)

A. Fronds with rusty bristle-like chaff especially on lower surface: indusium of slender hairs curled over the sporangia........1. *W. ilvensis*
AA. Fronds glandular or white-hairy beneath.
B. Indusium of a few broad segms., at first covering the sorus: pinnules minutely glandular-puberulent beneath........2. *W. obtusa*
BB. Indusium of very narrow segms., entirely hidden by the sorus: pinnules with fine white hairs beneath........3. *W. scopulina*

1. **W. ilvensis,** R. Br. (*Acrostichum ilvensis,* L.). RUSTY WOODSIA. Fronds tufted, 3–15 in. long; stipes straw-colored or purplish, jointed near the base, 1–6 in. long, with rusty bristle-like chaff; blades lanceolate in outline, rusty-chaffy beneath, 2–9 in. long, ½–1½ in. wide, pinnate; pinnæ crowded, oblong, obtuse, pinnatifid into oblong crowded obscurely crenate segms.: sori near the margins, confluent in age; indusia minute, largely concealed, the filiform segms. inflexed over the sporangia. Arctic Amer. to N. C., Minn., Eu., Asia.

2. **W. obtusa,** Torr. (*Polypodium obtusum,* Spreng.). COMMON WOODSIA. BLUNT-LOBED WOODSIA. Fronds clustered, 4–15 in. long; stipes straw-colored or purplish, not jointed, often scaly, 1–5 in. long; blades broadly lanceolate or elliptical in outline, 3–10 in. long, 1½–4 in. wide, 1–2-pinnate at least below, glandular-puberulent beneath; pinnæ rather remote, ovate to oblong, pinnate or pinnatifid, the segms. obtuse, crenate-dentate: sori nearer the margin than midvein; indusia splitting into several broad jagged lobes. Me. to Alaska, Fla. and Tex.

3. **W. scopulina,** D. C. Eaton. Rocky Mountain Woodsia. Fronds numerous, 3–16 in. long; stipes 1–6 in. long, straw-colored, brownish at the chaffy base; blades linear to oblong-lanceolate in outline, 2–10 in. long, ½–2½ in. wide, 1–2-pinnate, glandular-puberulent and with flat whitish hairs beneath; pinnæ with 5–9 pairs of toothed oblong segms.: sori near the margin, somewhat confluent; indusia deeply cleft, mostly concealed, the very narrow lobes spreading. Que. to Alaska, N. C., Colo., Calif.

28. **CYSTOPTERIS,** Bernh. Bladder-Fern. About 10 species of small delicate ferns of shaded rocky or alluvial places, chiefly temp. and boreal.—Rootstocks slender, creeping: fronds erect to recurved-spreading, 1–4-pinnate, the fertile commonly less leafy and longer-stiped than the sterile: sori rounded, separate; indusia hood-like, membranous, attached at inner side of the broad base, early thrust back and concealed. (Cystop-teris: Greek, *bladder-fern*, from the inflated indusium.)

A. Fronds lanceolate, tapering to apex, often bearing bulbels; pinnules mostly oblong....1. *C. bulbifera*
AA. Fronds ovate-oblong, acute, not bulbel-bearing; pinnules ovate....2. *C. fragilis*

1. **C. bulbifera,** Bernh. (*Polypodium bulbiferum*, L.). Berry Bladder-Fern. Fronds lanceolate, elongate, attenuate, 1–2½ ft. long, mostly 2–4 in. wide, decumbent to pendent; stipes slender, mostly purplish, 2–7 in. long, naked; blades 2-pinnate, commonly bearing bulbels underneath, the pinnules toothed to pinnatifid: sori small. Newf. to Ga. and Ariz.

2. **C. fragilis,** Bernh. (*Polypodium fragile*, L.). Brittle-Fern. Fronds few or several, 6–20 in. long; stipes about as long as the blades, straw-colored; blades 3–12 in. long, nearly or quite 2-pinnate, the pinnules toothed to incised, without bulbels: sori small. Greenland to Alaska and New England, Mo., New Mex., Calif., Eu., Asia.

29. **PTERETIS,** Raf. Ostrich-Fern. Three species of large ferns of N. Amer., Eu. and Asia.—Sterile fronds deeply 2-pinnatifid and borne in a circle surrounding the fertile fronds which have segms. contracted into pod-like bodies around the sori and arranged in a pinnate panicle. (Ptere-tis: derived from *pteris*, the Greek name for fern.)

A. Scales of lower stipe brownish: pinnæ obliquely ascending....1. *P. nodulosa*
AA. Scales of lower stipe blackish: pinnæ horizontal....2. *P. Struthiopteris*

1. **P. nodulosa,** Nieuwl. (*Onoclea nodulosa*, Michx. *Matteucia nodulosa*, Fern.). Rootstocks stout, giving off slender stolons: sterile fronds 2–10 ft. long, the stipes dark and scaly at base, the blades broadly lanceolate in outline, narrowed toward base, rather firm in texture, with many linear-lanceolate pinnatifid pinnæ commonly 2–7 in. long; fertile fronds 1–2 ft. long, becoming brown, persistent, with pod-like or somewhat necklace-shaped pinnæ commonly 1 in. or so long. N. S. to Va. and Iowa.

2. **P. Struthiopteris,** Nieuwl. (*Osmunda Struthiopteris*, L. *Onoclea Struthiopteris*, Hoffm. *Matteucia Struthiopteris*, Tod. *Struthiopteris germanica*, Willd.). Much like no. 1 but not exceeding 5 ft. in height, the stipes with blackish scales; sterile fronds broadly oblong to oblong-lanceolate, of thinner texture and with horizontal pinnæ. (Struthiopteris: an old generic name.) Eu.

30. **ONOCLEA,** L. One coarse and not very attractive fern with creeping rhizomes and two kinds of fronds; native in north temp. regions.—Sterile fronds scattered, long-stiped, deltoid-ovate, pinnatifid into few undulate, toothed or lobed segms.; fertile fronds erect, bipinnate, the segms. rolled up into bead-like bodies. (Onocle-a: Greek *closed vessels*, alluding to the closely rolled fertile pinnules.)

O. sensibilis, L. Sensitive-Fern. Sterile fronds 1–4½ ft. high, the segms. 2–6 in. long and lanceolate; fertile fronds 1–2½ ft. high, the pinnæ ½–1½ in. long, becoming dark brown: sori roundish; indusia delicate, hood-shaped. Newf. to Gulf states.

7. PARKERIACEÆ. FLOATING-FERN FAMILY

Aquatic succulent plants, floating or rooting in mud; few species in one genus, distributed in warmer regions of the world.—Lvs. borne in rosettes and of two kinds; the sterile floating or emergent, 1–3-pinnatifid; fertile more erect, 2–4-pinnate and with very narrow segms. having revolute margins which more or less cover the 1 or 2 longitudinal lines of subsessile rounded sporangia.—The name Ceratopteridaceæ, sometimes applied to this family, is antedated by nearly a century by Parkeriaceæ.

CERATOPTERIS, Brongn. FLOATING-FERN, WATER-FERN. Characters of the family. (Ceratopteris: Greek *horned-fern.*)

A. Blade of mature sterile frond oblong, considerably longer than broad; stipes slender .... 1. *C. thalictroides*
AA. Blade of sterile frond broadly deltoid or pentagonal, scarcely longer than broad; stipes bulbous near the middle .... 2. *C. pteridoides*

1. **C. thalictroides,** Brongn. (*Acrostichum thalictroides,* L.). Sterile fronds narrowly deltoid, the stipes slender, 2–10 in. long; laminæ 2–10 in. long, 1–2-pinnatifid into lanceolate or oblong segms., not floating; fertile fronds taller, 2–4-pinnate, with ultimate segms. linear. Old World tropics.

2. **C. pteridoides,** Hieron. (*Parkeria pteridoides,* Hook.). Sterile fronds to 10 in. long, broadly deltoid, the stipes short, inflated at middle; laminæ 2½–8 in. long, 1–3-pinnatifid into deltoid segms., floating; fertile fronds to 16 in. long, completely divided into linear segms. Fla. to S. Amer.

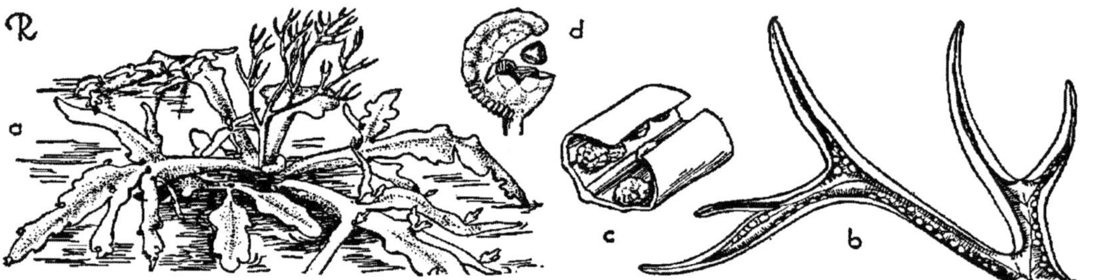

Fig. 8. PARKERIACEÆ. *Ceratopteris thalictroides:* a, habit with sterile and fertile fronds, × ⅙; b, fertile frond segment, × 1; c, section of fertile frond showing sporangia, × 4; d, sporangium, × 12. (c and d after Bauer.)

8. SALVINIACEÆ. SALVINIA FAMILY

A score or less of small free-floating plants in 2 genera, widely spread on the globe, frequently grown in aquaria and greenhouse tanks.—Spore-bearing bodies soft and delicate, borne on a peduncle beneath the lvs. or fronds: spores of two kinds, the macrospores producing an archegonium-bearing prothallus and the microspores an antheridium-bearing prothallus or gametophyte: fronds appearing to be 2-ranked, as they float flat or nearly so, or else imbricated.

A. Lvs. $\frac{3}{16}$in. long or longer: sts. 1–2 in. long .... 1. SALVINIA
AA. Lvs. $\frac{1}{16}$in. long or less: sts. usually less than 1 in. long .... 2. AZOLLA

1. **SALVINIA,** Adans. SALVINIA. Ten species in trop. Amer. and Afr.—Lvs. arranged on the rhizome in whorls of 3, the 2 lateral floating, round to oblong ½–¾in. long, the lower dissected into several filiform root-like hairy segms.; floating lvs. with papillose projections and stiff hairs on upper surface; no true roots or root-hairs present: fruiting bodies (sporocarps) in clusters on the segms. of the submerged lvs.; peduncle of sporocarps very short, the bodies globose or nearly so, the sori contained within them. (Salvin-ia: Antonio Maria Salvini, 1633–1729, professor in Florence, Italy.)

Fig. 9. SALVINIACEÆ. A, *Salvinia rotundifolia:* Aa, habit, × ½; Ab, single plant with sporocarp and submerged pinnatisect leaves, × 1; Ac, sporocarp, × 5; Ad, sporocarps, vertical section with megasporangia (left) and microsporangia (right), × 10. B, *Azolla filiculoides:* Ba, habit, × 1; Bb, sterile branch, × 2; Bc, leaf, × 8. (Ab–Ad after Schinzlein.)

S. rotundifolia, Willd. (*S. auriculata*, Aubl. *S. natans*, Hort. not All. *S. brasiliensis*, Hort.). Lvs. circular or nearly so (distinctly oblong in the true *S. natans*), often heart-shaped at base, short-stalked, about 3/8in. across, forming masses on the water. Trop. Amer.—Frequent in greenhouses where it is grown as a floating aquatic.

2. **AZOLLA,** Lam. Mosquito-Fern. Delicate moss-like free-floating aquatics, blue-green in color often becoming reddish in full sunlight; 6 species, widely distributed.—Rhizomes fragile, covered by crowded minute imbricated lvs., producing simple unbranched roots and lvs., the latter alternate, 1/16in. long or less, arranged on upper side in 2 ranks, each lf. divided into a smaller aërial lobe and a larger submerged lobe with exposed surfaces usually papillate: sporocarps situated on the first lf. of a lateral branch and covered by the hood-like upper lobe; microsporangia numerous, megasporangium solitary, each type in individual sporocarps. (Azol-la: Greek *to destroy by drying.*)

A. caroliniana, Willd. Plants small, to 1/2in. long, rhizomes dichotomously branched: lvs. nearly orbicular, about 1/48 in. long, divaricate, nearly smooth, not densely imbricated. E. U. S., W. Indies.—Plants forming dense mats over surface of water, reproducing readily vegetatively. A related species, *A. filiculoides*, Lam., produces a rhizome to 2 in. long covered with densely imbricated papillose lvs. about 1/24 in. long.

9. SELAGINELLACEÆ. SELAGINELLA FAMILY

Moss-like branching terrestrial plants, usually per., creeping or erect or climbing, mostly trop., of a single genus.

SELAGINELLA, Beauv. More than 500 species, a few grown in glasshouses for the decorative habit and herbage sometimes under the name Lycopodium.—Plants mostly rooting from the sts.: lvs. scale-like, all alike and imbricated, or in most species of two kinds or sizes and 4-ranked, one kind (usually the larger) on either side of the st. (technically known as lvs. of the lower plane) and the other kind on the upper or under surface of the st. or both (upper plane): fructification in terminal leafy or bracted mostly 4-ranked sessile spikes, comprising two kinds of spores in spore-cases, microspores usually in the upper axils and macrospores in the lower axils, but sometimes the two opposite each other along the spike. (Selaginel-la: diminutive of *selago*, ancient name of a lycopodium.)

A. Plant prized in dry state, the sts. curling up in a ball when dry, expanding when put in water.......... 1. *S. lepidophylla*
AA. Plant prized in its growing state.
 B. Main sts. creeping and rooting.
  C. Sts. mostly 2–3 in. long: longer lvs. scarcely 1/16 in. long.......... 2. *S. apoda*
  CC. Sts. mostly 3–20 in. long: longer lvs. almost 1/8 in. long.
   D. Lvs. of branches separated by their own width, sharply acute and with faint midrib.......... 3. *S. Kraussiana*
   DD. Lvs. of branches almost touching, blunt, with evident midrib.......... 4. *S. uncinata*
 BB. Main sts. erect, ascending, or climbing.
  C. Principal sts. climbing, the branches resembling decompound fronds.......... 5. *S. Willdenovii*
  CC. Principal sts. erect or ascending.
   D. Sts. leafy to the base, branching low.
    E. Roots confined to base of st.......... 6. *S. pallescens*
    EE. Roots produced from lower half of st.......... 7. *S. Martensii*

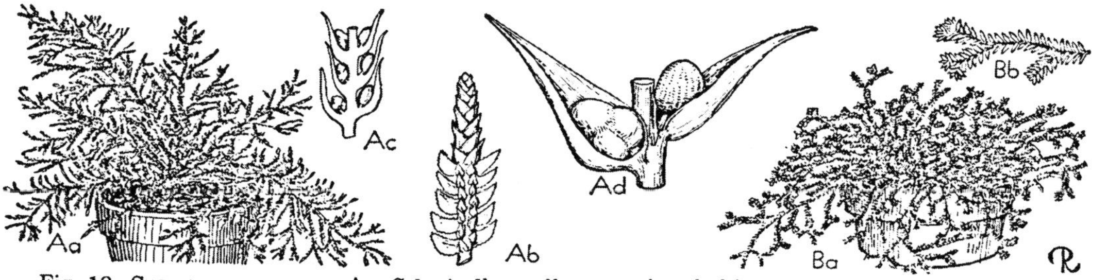

Fig. 10. Selaginellaceæ. A, *Selaginella pallescens:* Aa, habit, × 1/10; Ab, branch tip, × 2; Ac, fertile branch, vertical section, × 3; Ad, same, showing megasporangium (left) and microsporangium (right), × 10. B, *Selaginella Kraussiana:* Ba, habit, × 1/10; Bb, branch tip, × 1.

DD. Sts. naked or nearly so below with lvs. scale-like and appressed, branching above so that lower st. is stipe-like.
E. Color of sts. crimson........ 8. *S. umbrosa*
EE. Color of sts. greenish, straw-colored, or sometimes pinkish.
F. Tips of lvs. on main sts. scarcely if at all below the base of the next lvs. above, or if so the base cordate.
G. Lvs. on main sts. cordate at base; lvs. on branches about 1/12 in. long........ 9. *S. caulescens*
GG. Lvs. on main sts. rounded at base; lvs. on branches about 1/25 in. long........ 10. *S. amœna*
FF. Tips of lvs. on main sts. definitely below the base of the next lvs. above, bases not cordate.
G. Lvs. on branches about 1/16 in. long, blunt: sts. straw-colored to whitish........ 11. *S. Braunii*
GG. Lvs. on branches about 1/8 in. long, acute: sts. pinkish to brownish. 12. *S. Vogelii*

1. **S. lepidophylla,** Spring. Resurrection Plant. Sts. densely tufted, stiff, 2–4 in. long, 1/4–1/2in. and more broad, the growth flattened but rolling up and curling when dry into a ball which expands when wet and discloses the green upper surfaces: lvs. firm, closely imbricated, ovate and obtuse, scarious-margined, lighter beneath: spikes erect and prominent, with sharp-pointed bracts and sporophylls. Tex. and S.—Probably not cult., but often sold as a curiosity and sometimes kept alive; even when dead it will "resurrect" or expand several times when placed in water. **S. pilifera,** Braun, of Tex. and Mex., is distinguished by the cuspidate lvs.

2. **S. apoda,** Fern. (*Lycopodium apodum,* L. *S. apus,* Spring). Basket Selaginella. Plant moss-like; sts. mostly 1–3 or 4 in. long, pinnately branched, creeping; lvs. pale green, those of lower plane ovate, acutish, scarcely 1/16 in. long, with serrulate margins and distinct midribs, those of upper plane half as large, tapering: spikes 1/4–1/2in. long, obscurely 4-angled, half erect. Moist places, Me. to Ont., Fla. and Tex.—Sometimes grown in rockwork and greenhouses for its soft mat-like herbage.

3. **S. Kraussiana,** Braun (*S. japonica,* Miq. not Macnab). Soft moss-like bright green creeping plant, freely rooting, the growing tips usually not projecting beyond the foliage and the plant therefore with tufted or furcate ends, the st. jointed or articulated where the branches arise, the main st. between the branches with closely separated foliage: lvs. of lower plane slightly separated on the short branchlets, about 1/8in. long, oblong or lance-oblong and acute, cordate or rounded at base, margins minutely ciliate, midrib not conspicuous; lvs. of upper plane much shorter, long-acute: spikes short, with 4-ranked cuspidate keeled scales. (Named for Herr Krauss, a collector in S. Afr.) Azores to Cape Colony.—The commonest species in cult., grown as a pot-cover and spreading under benches and in open places in the greenhouse. Known erroneously as *S. denticulata* (and *Lycopodium denticulatum*), a species apparently not in cult. Var. **Brownii,** Hort. (*S. Brownii,* Hort.), is a dwarf compact form, scarcely running. There is also a variegated form.

4. **S. uncinata,** Spring (*S. cæsia,* Hort. *Lycopodium cæsium,* Hort.). Soft delicate creeping very leafy plant with a blue-green cast, the sts. 1–2 ft. long and producing many long roots, not jointed where the branches start, the main st. projecting beyond the branches and between the branches bearing large separated lvs. 1/8in. long: lvs. of the lower plane placed close together and spreading, making short flat branches or sprays 1/4in. wide, cordate-ovate and acute, not ciliate, the midrib prominent; lvs. of upper plane much smaller, imbricated, cuspidate. China.

5. **S. Willdenovii,** Baker (*S. lævigata,* Spring not Baker. *S. cæsia arborea,* Hort.). Climbing to 20 ft. or more, but young plants erect, producing many decompound fronds at intervals, the foliage usually with a blue-green cast, sending down long roots freely; main sts. more or less angled, light straw-colored, bearing few oval obtuse lvs., widely spaced: lvs. of lower plane crowded and overlapping, oblong, obtuse, 1/8–1/16 in. long, with strong midrib; lvs. of upper plane much shorter, oblong-ovate, acute: spikes 1 in. or less long, 4-sided, with sharp-pointed keeled scales. (K. L. Willdenow, page 54.) Old World tropics.

6. **S. pallescens,** Spring (*Lycopodium pallescens,* Presl. *S. Emmeliana,* Van Geert. *S. cuspidata* var. *Emiliana,* Nichols.). A bright green erect-spreading very ornamental plant; sts. 6–12 in. high, rather closely covered with ovate-cuspidate ciliate lvs., more or less bipinnate-branching nearly or quite to the base and rooting only at or near the base: lvs. on lower plane on the branches falcate-ovate and cuspidate, ciliolate, less than 1/16 in. long; lvs. on upper plane about half as large, ovate and long-cuspidate, ciliolate: spikes 1/4–1/2in. long, 4-sided, with very sharp imbricated ciliate scales. Trop. Amer.—Probably the commonest species grown for pot specimens. Hort. forms with yellowish foliage and with whitish markings are known.

7. **S. Martensii,** Spring. A soft profuse grower, making heavy frond-like foliage that breaks easily at the surface of the ground; sts. 6–12 in. long, ascending, throwing down roots freely from the lower half, leafy nearly or quite to the base: lvs. of lower plane oblong, 3/8in. long, obtuse or muticous, ciliolate, the midrib prominent, those on the main st. separated or contiguous and on the branchlets close together; lvs. of the upper plane

much smaller, ovate or oval, aristate, imbricated: spikes ¼–½in. long, 4-sided, the scales ovate-acute, keeled. (Georg von Martens was a German botanist of last century, who wrote also on Mex. plants.) Mex. Var. **variegata,** Hort., has albinous branchlets and markings.

8. S. **umbrosa,** Hieron. (*S. erythropus,* Spring). Plant erect, 10–12 in. high, with deltoid outline of frond, densely foliaged; sts. branchless in lower third or half, crimson, the naked part terete and bearing small crimson acute lvs. which are separated but contiguous: lvs. of lower plane close together and more or less overlapping, falcate-oblong or -ovate, short-acute: lvs. of upper plane smaller, ovate, short-pointed, overlapping: spikes ⅓–½in. long, 4-sided, the scales cuspidate and keeled. W. Indies, Cent. Amer., S. Amer.

9. S. **caulescens,** Spring. Tall erect bright green plant 12–24 in. high, with elongated frond-like character; sts. stiff, terete, lower half or third branchless and bearing small narrow appressed separated lvs. with slender sharp points and cordate base: lvs. of lower plane falcate-oblong, acute, close together, about 1/12 in. long; lvs. of upper plane much smaller, ovate, appressed and overlapping, very acute: spikes numerous, giving a fruiting frond an appearance of many narrow hard branchlets, about ½in. long, 4-sided, with ovate sharply acute keeled scales. Malaya, China, Japan. Var. **japonica,** Baker (*S. japonica,* Macnab not Miq.), is less decompound, and lvs. of lower plane broadly ovate, lvs. of naked sts. somewhat spreading and broad.

10. S. **amœna,** Bull. Confused with no. 9, but lvs. of main sts. not cordate at base and those of branches about 1/25 in. long. Trop. Amer.—Much material cult. as *S. pulcherrima* belongs here.

11. S. **Braunii,** Baker (*S. pubescens,* A. Br. not Spring). Slender erect species, 10–18 in., with small fine foliage, open narrow growth, and whitish or straw-colored sts. that bear few scattered oblong, obtuse or acutish lvs., more or less pubescent at least toward the top, the lower half or third destitute of branches: lvs. of lower plane short, oval, obtuse, close but not overlapping, somewhat revolute, about 1/16 in. long; lvs. of upper plane about one-half as large, oblong-ovate, acute: spikes short, 4-sided, the scales cuspidate and not concealing the sporangia. (For A. Braun, page 40.) W. China.

12. S. **Vogelii,** Spring (*S. africana,* A. Br.). Stout plant with broad green or bronzed fronds, 1–2 ft.; sts. stiff and terete, brown, branchless on lower half or two-thirds, bearing remote almost setaceous ascending lvs. below and oblong-acute lvs. above: lvs. of lower plane oblong-lanceolate, close together but not overlapping, short-acute, more or less revolute, about ⅛in. long; lvs. of upper plane very small, ovate, long-cuspidate: spikes ½in. or less long, the scales ovate, long-pointed, keeled. (Named for Vogel, page 53.) Afr.

SPERMATOPHYTA

10. CYCADACEÆ. CYCAS FAMILY

A family of 9 genera and about 85 species, distributed in trop. and subtrop. regions, several genera having representatives in cult. for greenhouse use and out-of-doors far S.—Plants of palm-like habit, more or less woody, with thick columnar mostly unbranched or tuber-like st.: lvs. alternate, pinnate or bipinnate, circinate when unfolding like those of the fern: stamens and carpels borne in cones or in temporarily terminal clusters like a crown in the center of the rosette of lvs.; scales of the staminate cone bearing very many scattered anthers on the under side: carpels open, not forming a closed ovary, either lf.-like, pinnatifid and bearing marginal ovules, or peltate with 2 or more suspended ovules, the latter very large, often 1 in. long, with 1 integument, becoming drupe-like.—A family isolated among the Gymnosperms, and in geologic ages represented by a much larger number. Species of Dion and Encephalartos are sometimes grown in the larger conservatories.

CYCAS, L. Among the most striking ornamentals of trop. and subtrop. gardens, also common in cult. under glass; species about 16, mostly in trop. Asia, Australia, and Polynesia; often spoken of as "palms" although having nothing in common with palms except the general habit and stout mostly unbranched caudex.—Diœcious plants with columnar st. covered by the persisting bases of the old lvs.: lvs. pinnately divided into segms. having only the single mid-nerve: staminate infl. cone-like, erect, terminal, composed of modified scale-like lvs. which bear on the under surface globose pollen-sacs corresponding to microsporangia; pistillate infl. consisting of a tuft of spreading carpellary lvs., the margins with coarse notches in which are borne the naked ovules. (Cy-cas: from the Greek name for a palm tree.)

A. Margins of pinnæ flat . . . . 1. *C. circinalis*
AA. Margins of pinnæ revolute . . . . 2. *C. revoluta*

1. **C. circinalis,** L. Palm-like with cylindric trunk 10–12 ft. or more: lvs. 5–8 ft. long, with short spines near base of petiole; pinnæ alternate, 10–12 in. long, linear-lanceolate, acuminate, with flat margins: staminate infl. a woolly cone often 2 ft. long and 5 in. diam., scales tapering into a long hooked spine; pistillate infl. a tuft of spreading, buff-colored, woolly, pinnately notched carpophylls about 6–12 in. long, spinose-toothed along the margin and bearing the naked ovules in the notches: fr. about the size of a walnut, with a thin fleshy covering. Trop. Afr. to Guam.

2. **C. revoluta,** Thunb. SAGO-PALM. Palm-like, 6–10 ft. high, the trunk simple or branched: lvs. recurved, 2–7 ft. long; pinnæ numerous, curved downward, narrow, stiff, acute, terminating in a spine-like tip, dark shining green, the margin revolute: staminate infl. cylindric, usually 18–20 in. long; pistillate infl. a semi-globose head; carpophylls broadly ovate, densely clothed with a brownish felt-like wool, pectinate: fr. ovate, compressed, red, about 1½ in. long. Java.—The commonest cycad in cult.

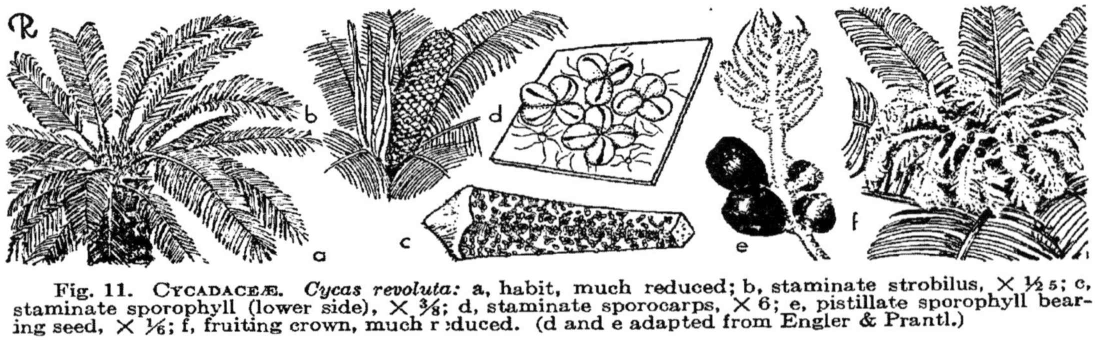

Fig. 11. CYCADACEÆ. *Cycas revoluta:* a, habit, much reduced; b, staminate strobilus, × ½5; c, staminate sporophyll (lower side), × ⅜; d, staminate sporocarps, × 6; e, pistillate sporophyll bearing seed, × ⅙; f, fruiting crown, much reduced. (d and e adapted from Engler & Prantl.)

11. GINKGOACEÆ. GINKGO FAMILY

One deciduous broad-lvd. resinous tree of E. China (but not known natively wild), planted as a street or ornamental subject; remainder of a geological group.—Lvs. alternate or in clusters of 3–5 on spurs, fan-shaped, parallel-veined: diœcious; staminate fls. catkin-like, the anthers borne in pedicelled pairs on a slender axis, fertilization occurring by motile sperm-cells; pistillate fls. usually long-pedicelled and bearing 2 ovules: fr. drupe-like, having a fleshy outer and bony inner coat.

GINKGO, L. One species, technical characters as for family. (Gink-go: Chinese name.)

G. biloba, L. (*Salisburia adiantifolia,* Smith). GINKGO. MAIDENHAIR-TREE. Glabrous sparsely branched tree to 120 ft. high: lvs. 2–4 in. across, on long slender petioles, more or less incised or divided at broad summit, striated with numerous parallel veins: fr. obovoid or ellipsoid, about 1 in. long, yellowish, with ill-smelling pulp surrounding the thin-shelled 2-angled creamy-white nut which contains an edible sweet kernel.—There are forms with variegated and deeply incised lvs., and with pendulous branches.

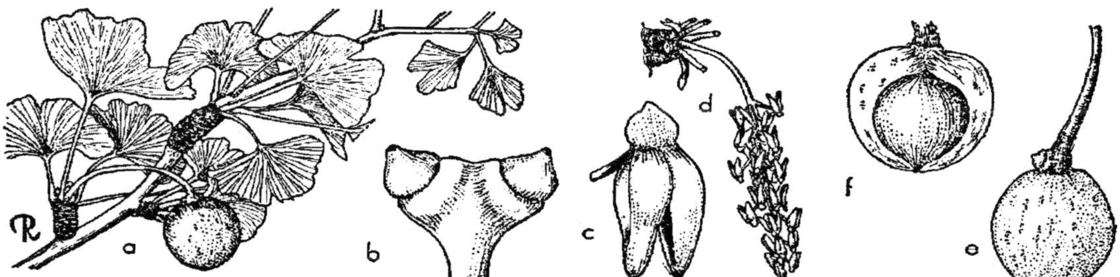

Fig. 12. GINKGOACEÆ. *Ginkgo biloba:* a, fruiting branch, × ¼; b, pistillate strobilus, × 4; c, anther, × 8; d, staminate inflorescence, × 1; e, seed, × ½; f, seed, vertical section, × ½.

12. TAXACEÆ. YEW FAMILY

Evergreen shrubs or trees of 3 genera and about 15 species, in both hemispheres, furnishing ornamental subjects for landscape planting.—Bark with resin-tubes: lvs. alternate or rarely opposite, often 2-ranked, usually needle- or scale-like: plants diœcious or rarely monœcious; staminate fls. solitary or in small spikes in axils of lvs.; pistillate fls. of imbricated scales and 1 terminal ovule: fr. berry- or drupe-like, consisting of a bony-coated seed surrounded by the fleshy often highly colored aril.

A. Aril surrounding seed open at apex, scarlet: staminate fls. globular: albumen of seed uniform.......1. TAXUS
AA. Aril completely surrounding seed, green or purplish: staminate fls. oblong: albumen of seed ruminate.......2. TORREYA

1. **TAXUS,** L. YEW. Eight species distributed throughout the northern hemisphere, or sometimes considered 1 variable species; planted as lawn specimens and the low forms for ground-cover.—Bark scaly, reddish-brown; branchlets irregularly alternate; winter-buds with imbricate scales: lvs. linear, usually 2-ranked, pale green or yellowish beneath, without resin-ducts: fls. small, solitary, axillary, in early spring; staminate fls. in globose stalked heads, the scales opening at flowering to expose 4–8 stamens with 3–8 anther-cells; pistillate fls. of a single terminal ovule with several bracts at base: fr. a bony seed surrounded except at apex by a fleshy cup-shaped scarlet disk; albumen uniform. (Tax-us: ancient Latin name.)

A. Lvs. gradually acuminate: scales of winter-buds not keeled.......1. *T. baccata*
AA. Lvs. abruptly pointed: scales of winter-buds keeled.
B. Arrangement of lvs. irregularly 2-ranked, ascending and forming a V-shaped trough.......2. *T. cuspidata*
BB Arrangement of lvs. flatly 2-ranked.
C. Plant a low straggling shrub. fr. broader than high.......3. *T. canadensis*
CC. Plant a tree: fr. ovoid.......4. *T. brevifolia*

1. **T. baccata,** L. ENGLISH YEW. Tree to 60 ft., with a short thick trunk and spreading branches which form a broad low head; mature branchlets greenish; scales of winter-buds obtuse, not keeled: lvs. ¾–1¼ in. long and 1/12 in. or less across, gradually acumi-

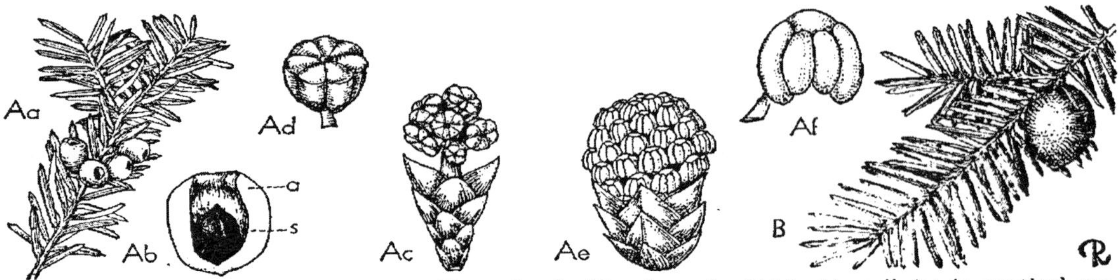

Fig. 13. TAXACEÆ. *A, Taxus cuspidata:* Aa, fruiting branch, × ¼; Ab, aril (a) in vertical section to show seed (s), × 1; Ac, pistillate strobilus, × 4; Ad, pistillate flower, × 8; Ae, staminate strobilus, × 8; Af, stamen, × 16. B, Torreya: branch with seed, × ¼. (Ac–Ae after Hooker.)

nate, midrib prominent, dark green and glossy above and pale beneath: fr. ⅓–½in. across, the aril almost globose, longer than the brown broadly ellipsoid slightly 2-angled seed, Sept.–Oct. Eu., N. Afr., W. Asia.—Runs into numerous named forms, some of them being: var. **adpressa,** Carr. (*T. brevifolia,* Hort.), shrub or low tree with lvs. to ½in. long; var. **aurea,** Carr., lvs. yellow; var. **Dovastonii,** Lawson, branches horizontal and branchlets pendulous (named for John Dovaston, who raised it in 1777, near Shrewsbury, England); var. **elegantissima,** Beissn., compact, young lvs. striped pale yellow; var. **erecta,** Loud., upright and bushy; var. **repandens,** Parsons, nearly prostrate, lvs. bluish-green; var. **stricta,** Lawson (var. *fastigiata,* Loud. var. *hibernica,* Loud.), IRISH YEW, columnar, lvs. very dark green; var. **Washingtonii,** Beissn., wide-spreading, lvs. golden-yellow.

2. **T. cuspidata,** Sieb. & Zucc. (*T. cuspidata* var. *capitata,* Hort.). JAPANESE YEW. Tree to 50 ft., with spreading or upright branches; mature branchlets reddish-brown; scales of winter-buds acute, keeled: lvs. ¾–1 in. long and 1/12–⅛ in. across, abruptly mucronate, contracted into distinct petiole, dull green above with prominent midrib and with 2 broad yellow bands beneath, the 2 ranks often upright and forming a V-shaped trough: seed about ¼in. long, ovoid, compressed, slightly 3–4-angled, Oct.–Nov. Japan, Korea, Manchuria. Var. **nana,** Rehd., shrub 6–8 ft. or more high.—A V-shaped form with low center and spreading upright branches is known as **expansa.** A popular hybrid between *T. cuspidata* and *T. baccata* is **T. media,** Rehd., mature branchlets olive-green, scales of winter-buds obtuse. Forms of this hybrid are: var. **Brownii,** Hort., erect, conical, to 8 ft., lvs. short and dense; var. **Hatfieldii,** Rehd., conical, with ascending branches and wide-spreading lvs. (named for T. D. Hatfield of Wellesley, Mass.); var. **Hicksii,** Rehd., columnar with ascending branches (raised at Hicks Nurseries, Westbury, L. I.).

3. **T. canadensis,** Marsh. GROUND-HEMLOCK. Straggling shrub with green or reddish-brown ascending branches 3–6 ft. high; scales of winter-buds acute and keeled: lvs. ½–1 in. long and 1/12 in. across, abruptly pointed, dark green above with prominent midrib and with pale green bands beneath, flatly 2-ranked, reddish in winter: fr. broader than high, July–Aug. Newf. to Va. and Iowa. Var. **stricta,** Hort., is dwarf with stiff upright branches.—A hybrid between *T. canadensis* and *T. cuspidata* is **T. Hunnewelliana,** Rehd., resembling the latter parent but of more slender habit and reddish tint in winter (named for Hunnewell estate, Wellesley, Mass.).

4. **T. brevifolia,** Nutt. WESTERN YEW. Tree to 45 or rarely 80 ft., with horizontal somewhat drooping branches; mature branchlets yellowish-green or light brown; scales of winter-buds acute and keeled: lvs. ½–¾in. long and 1/12 in. across, abruptly short-pointed, midrib somewhat prominent above, with broad pale bands beneath, flatly 2-ranked: fr. ovoid, seed 2–4-angled, Aug.–Oct. B. C. to Calif. and Mont.

2. **TORREYA,** Arn. (*Tumion,* Raf.). Six evergreen trees native in N. Amer. and E. Asia, two sometimes planted.—Bark fissured; branches whorled, the branchlets subopposite; winter-buds with few decussate deciduous scales: lvs. linear or linear-lanceolate, 2-ranked, spiny-pointed, with 2 narrow glaucous bands beneath, midrib not distinct above, with resin-duct in middle: staminate fls. ovoid or oblong, of 6–8 whorls of stamens surrounded by bud-scales at base; pistillate fls. of solitary ovule surrounded at base by fleshy aril and several scales: fr. ovoid, drupe-like, a bony seed surrounded by thin fleshy aril; albumen ruminate. (Torre-ya: for John Torrey, 1796–1873, American botanist.)

A. Lvs. lanceolate, ¾–1¼ in. long .... 1. *T. nucifera*
AA. Lvs. linear, 1½–3½ in. long .... 2. *T. californica*

1. **T. nucifera,** Sieb. & Zucc. (*Taxus nucifera,* L.). Tree to 80 ft. but shrubby in cult., with grayish-brown bark: lvs. lanceolate, ¾–1¼ in. long and ⅛–⅙in. wide, rigid and

spiny-pointed, glossy dark green above: fr. obovoid-oblong, about 1 in. long, green tinged with purple. Japan.

2. **T. californica,** Torr. CALIFORNIA-NUTMEG. Tree to 70 ft. or more, with slightly pendulous branches and grayish-brown bark tinged with orange: lvs. linear, 1–3½ in. long, ⅛in. or less wide, acuminate, dark green above: fr. oblong-oval or oval, 1–1½ in. long, green streaked with purple. Calif.

13. PODOCARPACEÆ. PODOCARPUS FAMILY

Evergreen trees or shrubs of 7 genera and more than 100 species, in warm regions mostly of the southern hemisphere, a few grown for ornament in S. U. S.—Lvs. alternate or sometimes opposite, needle- or scale-like to linear and broad-oblong: plants diœcious or rarely monœcious; staminate fls. terminal or axillary, with or without scales at base, the anthers 2-celled; pistillate fls. axillary or terminal on leafy shoots, of 1 or more carpels and 1 ovule: fr. sometimes cone-like but usually drupe-like, consisting of a seed surrounded by a fleshy aril.

PODOCARPUS, L'Her. About 60 species of evergreen trees or shrubs of wide distribution.—Lvs. linear to elliptic, entire, sessile or short-petioled, rarely scale-like: fls. axillary, solitary or in fascicles at the ends of short branchlets; staminate fls. catkin-like, consisting of spirally disposed 2-celled anthers; pistillate fls. of a scale inclosing the ovule with several bracts at its base: fr. drupe-like, the seed borne on a fleshy receptacle. (Podocar-pus: Greek *foot* and *fruit.*)

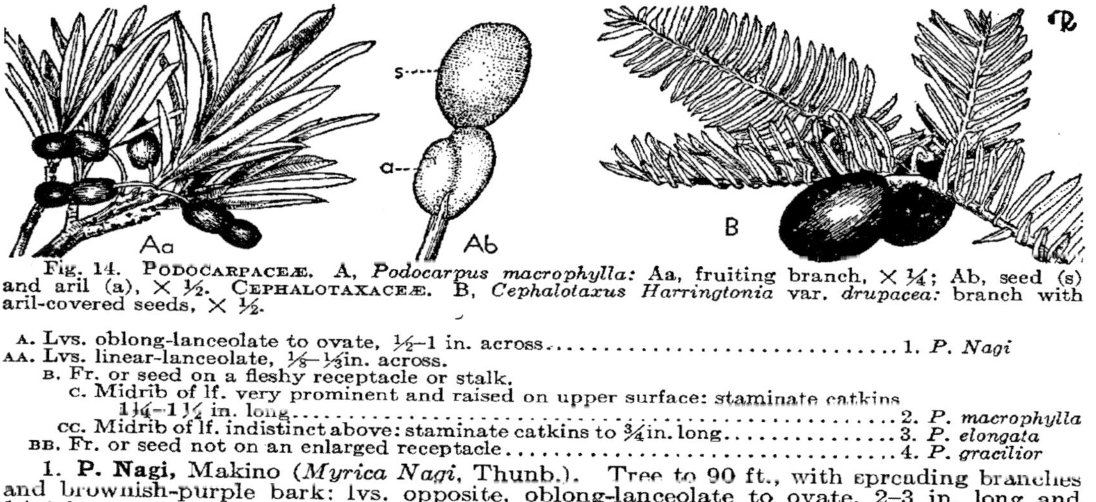

Fig. 14. PODOCARPACEÆ. A, *Podocarpus macrophylla:* Aa, fruiting branch, × ¼; Ab, seed (s) and aril (a), × ½. CEPHALOTAXACEÆ. B, *Cephalotaxus Harringtonia* var. *drupacea:* branch with aril-covered seeds, × ½.

A. Lvs. oblong-lanceolate to ovate, ½–1 in. across . . . . 1. *P. Nagi*
AA. Lvs. linear-lanceolate, ⅛–⅓in. across.
B. Fr. or seed on a fleshy receptacle or stalk.
C. Midrib of lf. very prominent and raised on upper surface: staminate catkins 1¼–1½ in. long . . . . 2. *P. macrophylla*
CC. Midrib of lf. indistinct above: staminate catkins to ¾in. long . . . . 3. *P. elongata*
BB. Fr. or seed not on an enlarged receptacle . . . . 4. *P. gracilior*

1. **P. Nagi,** Makino (*Myrica Nagi,* Thunb.). Tree to 90 ft., with spreading branches and brownish-purple bark: lvs. opposite, oblong-lanceolate to ovate, 2–3 in. long and ½–1 in. across, narrowed to short petiole, many-nerved, bright green and shining above, paler beneath: staminate catkins about 1 in. long: fr. dark purple and bloomy, about ½in. across, the peduncle only slightly thickened. (Nagi: native Japanese name.) Japan.

2. **P. macrophylla,** D. Don (*Taxus macrophylla,* Thunb. *P. longifolia,* Hort.). Tree to 50 ft., with pendent branchlets and gray shallowly fissured bark: lvs. narrowly lanceolate, 3–4 in. long and ⅓in. across, acute or obtusish, narrowed into short petiole, lustrous above and with distinct midrib, paler beneath: staminate catkins 1¼–1½ in. long: fr. ovoid, ⅓–½in. long, greenish or purplish, the fleshy receptacle purplish. Japan. Var. **Maki,** Endl. (*P. japonica,* Sieb.), has lvs. to 3 in. long and ¼in. wide and more upright than the type (Maki is a Japanese name).

3. **P. elongata,** L'Her. (*Taxus elongata,* Ait.). Tree becoming 70 ft. high, with very leafy branches: lvs. linear-lanceolate, 1–2 in. long and 1/12–⅛ in. across, tapering at each end, very acute, midrib indistinct above: staminate catkins to ¾in. long: fr. globose, ¼–⅓in. across, the fleshy receptacle red. S. Afr.

4. **P. gracilior,** Pilger. Tree to 60 ft. or more, with long slender branches: lvs. linear-lanceolate, 2–4 in. long and ⅙–¼in. across, long-acuminate, stiff, midrib indistinct above: staminate fls. 1–3 in axils, ½–1 in. long: fr. globose, ½–¾in. long, hard, the peduncle not thickened. Trop. Afr.—Some of the material grown as *P. elongata* belongs here.

14. CEPHALOTAXACEÆ. PLUM-YEW FAMILY

Evergreen shrubs or trees of 6 genera from Japan to the Himalayas, formerly included in Taxaceæ.—Branchlets opposite: lvs. linear, spirally arranged: plants diœcious or rarely monœcious; staminate fls. in short-stalked globose axillary heads or in short spikes, of 4–12 stamens with short filaments and 3 anther-cells; pistillate fls. in axils of scales at base of branchlets, short-stalked, with several pairs of 2-ovuled carpels: fr. drupe-like, only 1 or 2 seeds developing.

CEPHALOTAXUS, Sieb. & Zucc. Plum-Yew. Five evergreen trees or shrubs native in Asia.—Winter-buds with persistent imbricated scales: lvs. linear, pointed, arranged in 2 rows, with 2 broad glaucous bands beneath and midrib prominent above: staminate clusters 1–8-fld., of 4–6 stamens inclosed in a bract; pistillate fls. with several bracts, each bearing 2 naked ovules: fr. drupe-like, the seed inclosed in a fleshy envelope. (Cephalotax-us: Greek for *head,* and *taxus,* the fls. in heads or clusters.)

A. Lvs. abruptly pointed, 1–2 in. long....1. *C. Harringtonia*
AA. Lvs. gradually tapering into point, 2–3 in. long....2. *C. Fortunii*

1. **C. Harringtonia,** Koch (*Taxus Harringtonia,* Knight. *C. pedunculata,* Sieb. & Zucc. *C. drupacea* var. *pedunculata,* Miq. *C. drupacea* var. *Harringtonia,* Pilger). Shrub or small tree to 30 ft., with gray fissured bark: lvs. in semi-erect ranks, to 2 in. long, abruptly pointed, dark green above: staminate fls. in branched heads on stalks ½–¾in. long: fr. commonly obovate, about 1 in. long, green or purplish. (Named for Earl Harrington of Elvaston Castle near Derby, England, who first grew the plant.) Known only in cult. Var. **drupacea,** Koidz. (*C. drupacea,* Sieb. & Zucc.), Japanese Plum-Yew, is the native form in Japan, with lvs. about 1 in. long and staminate heads on stalks ¼in. long.

2. **C. Fortunii,** Hook. Chinese Plum-Yew. Tree to 30 ft., with reddish-brown bark peeling off in flakes and branches often pendulous at ends: lvs. spreading nearly horizontally, 2–3 in. long, gradually tapering into sharp point, dark green and shining above: fr. oval, about 1¼ in. long, purplish. (For Robt. Fortune, page 43.) China.

15. ARAUCARIACEÆ. ARAUCARIA FAMILY

Evergreen resinous trees of 2 genera and about 30 species in the southern hemisphere, grown in greenhouses in the juvenile stages or out-of-doors in S. U. S.—Branches whorled: lvs. awl-shaped to broad-ovate, compressed: plants diœcious or rarely monœcious; staminate fls. large and cone-like, axillary or terminal on short branches, with numerous stamens and many-celled anthers; pistillate fls. in terminal heads becoming a large woody deciduous cone; scales with 1 seed, without distinct bracts.

A. Seeds united with cone-scales: lvs. scale-like or flattened, under ½in. across, pungent-pointed....1. Araucaria
AA. Seeds not united with cone-scales: lvs. broad and flattened, ½in. or more across, not pungent-pointed....2. Agathis

1. **ARAUCARIA,** Juss. Tall evergreen trees of about 12 species in S. Amer., Australia, and Pacific isls., grown out-of-doors in subtrop. regions and in their juvenile stage as pot-plants N.—Branches regularly whorled: lvs. spirally arranged, scale-like and stiff and usually closely imbricated or subulate or flattened, pungent-pointed: staminate catkins cylindrical, of numerous spirally crowded and imbricated anthers; pistillate fls. in ovoid or globose heads, of many spirally arranged scales each with a single ovule: cones large and woody, the numerous scales 2-edged or 2-winged, shattering at maturity; seeds wingless, adnate to scale. (Arauca-ria: from *Arauco,* a province in S. Chile.)

A. Lvs. ¾–2 in. long: cone-scales not winged.
B. Base of lvs. contracted: lvs. spreading....1. *A. Bidwillii*
BB. Base of lvs. broad: lvs. imbricated....2. *A. araucana*
AA. Lvs. ½in. or less long: cone-scales winged.
B. Adult lvs. with obscure midrib, ½in. long....3. *A. excelsa*
BB. Adult lvs. with prominent midrib, ¼in. long....4. *A. columnaris*

1. **A. Bidwillii,** Hook. Bunya-Bunya. Tree to 150 ft., with trunk free of branches for about half its height: juvenile lvs. lanceolate, ¾–2 in. long, very sharp-pointed, contracted at base, spreading in two rows, thick and shining; adult lvs. spirally imbricated,

Fig. 15. ARAUCARIACEÆ. A, *Araucaria excelsa:* Aa, branch with juvenile foliage, × ¼; Ab, cone-scale, lower side, with seed, × ½; Ac, cone, × ¼. B, *Araucaria Bidwillii:* juvenile branch, × ½. (Ab redrawn from Engler.)

ovate, to ½in. long, woody: staminate catkins 3–5 in. long and ⅓–½in. diam.: fruiting cones globose-ovoid, 7–9 in. long and 6–8 in. diam.; scales terminating in an acute edge. (Named for J. C. Bidwill, 1815–1853, botanical explorer.) Australia.

2. **A. araucana,** Koch (*Pinus araucana,* Molina. *A. imbricata,* Pav.). MONKEY-PUZZLE. Pyramidal tree to 100 ft., with spreading upward-curved branches: lvs. ovate-lanceolate, 1–2 in. long, stiff and sharp-pointed, broad at base, imbricated and persisting for many years, bright green on both sides: staminate catkins 3–5 in. long: fruiting cones globose-ovoid, 5–8 in. diam.; scales with lanceolate acuminate appendage. Chile.

3. **A. excelsa,** R. Br. NORFOLK-ISLAND-PINE. Pyramidal tree to 200 ft.: juvenile lvs. subulate, ⅓–½in. long, curved and sharp-pointed; adult lvs. densely imbricated, lanceolate to ovate-triangular, with obscure midrib: staminate catkins 1½–2 in. long: fruiting cones subglobose, 3–6 in. diam.; scales terminating in an incurved spine. Norfolk Isl.

4. **A. columnaris,** Hook. (*Cupressus columnaris,* Forst. *A. Cookii,* R. Br.). NEW-CALEDONIAN-PINE. Columnar tree to 200 ft., narrower than *A. excelsa:* juvenile lvs. subulate, to ½in. long; adult lvs. imbricated, lanceolate-ovate to triangular, to ¼in. long, obtuse, with prominent midrib: staminate catkins 1½–3½ in. long and ½–¾in. diam.: fruiting cones ovoid, 4–5 in. long. New Caledonia, New Hebrides.—Much of the material grown as *A. excelsa* belongs here.

2. **AGATHIS,** Salisb. DAMMAR-PINE. Evergreen trees from Philippines to Australia and New Zeal., adapted only to S. U. S.; perhaps 20 species.—Lvs. opposite or alternate, somewhat 2-ranked, flat and broad, leathery: staminate catkins cylindrical, axillary: cones ovoid or globose, the numerous scales broadly obovate; seeds winged on one side, not united with scales. (Ag-athis: from Greek referring to shape of cone.)

A. robusta, F. Muell. QUEENSLAND KAURI. Tree to 160 ft. in nature: juvenile lvs. mostly opposite, oblong-elliptic to ovate, 2–4 in. long; adult lvs. narrow-elliptic: staminate catkins sessile, 2–4 in. long and ¼–⅓in. diam.: fruiting cones ovoid or nearly globose, 4–5 in. long. Australia.

16. PINACEÆ. PINE FAMILY

Resinous trees furnishing valuable timber and ornamental subjects; as now defined containing 9 genera and over 200 species, widely distributed.—Lvs. spirally arranged, solitary or fascicled, linear, needle-like, mostly persistent, sometimes deciduous: plants usually monœcious; fls. borne in cones and surrounded at base by persistent bud-scales; staminate cones with many stamens having 2 pollen-sacs; ovules 2 on inner surface of a scale: fr. a woody cone with dry usually winged seeds.

A. Lvs. in fascicles or clusters, solitary only on shoots.
  B. Fascicles of 2–5 or rarely 8 lvs., with persistent or deciduous sheaths at base......1. PINUS
  BB. Fascicles of many lvs., 10 or more, without basal sheaths.
    C. Foliage persistent..........2. CEDRUS
    CC. Foliage deciduous.
      D. Staminate fls. solitary: cone-scales persistent..........3. LARIX
      DD. Staminate fls. clustered: cone-scales deciduous..........4. PSEUDOLARIX
AA. Lvs. solitary.
  B. Cones upright; scales deciduous..........5. ABIES
  BB. Cones reflexed or pendulous; scales persistent.
    C. Branchlets roughened by persistent lf.-bases: bracts of cone-scales not exserted.
      D. Lf. sessile, usually 4-sided, when flattened stomatiferous only above........6. PICEA
      DD. Lf. short-petioled, flattened, stomatiferous below or on both sides.....7. TSUGA
    CC. Branchlets not roughened: bracts conspicuously exserted..........8. PSEUDOTSUGA

1. **PINUS,** L. PINE. Evergreen trees, of about 80 species in the northern hemisphere.—Winter-buds covered with imbricate scales: lvs. of two kinds, the primary ones scale-like and deciduous, bearing in their axils the secondary linear lvs. in fascicles of 2–5 (rarely reduced to 1), surrounded at base by sheaths of bud-scales: staminate fls. axillary, clustered at base of young shoots, catkin-like, yellow, orange, or scarlet, composed of numerous spirally arranged 2-celled anthers with connective enlarged and scale-like at apex; pistillate fls. lateral or subterminal, greenish or purplish, of numerous spirally arranged scales in the axils of small bracts, each bearing 2 ovules inside: cones subglobose to cylindric, with woody imbricated persistent scales; the exposed part of the scale is called the apophysis, the umbo or elevation being either dorsal or terminal. (Pi-nus: classical Latin name.)

A. Fascicles containing 5 lvs.
B. Lvs. 8–13 in. long, with persistent sheaths.......39. *P. Torreyana*
BB. Lvs. less than 8 in. long, with deciduous sheaths.
C. Cones with dorsal umbo armed with slender spine.......11. *P. aristata*
CC. Cones with terminal unarmed umbo.
D. Seeds wingless.
E. A shrub with prostrate branches.......2. *P. pumila*
EE. A tree.
F. Lf. entire and smooth on edges.......4. *P. flexilis*
FF. Lf. serrulate and rough on edges.
G. Length of cone 4–6 in., scales with recurved apex.......3. *P. koraiensis*
GG. Length of cone 2–3½ in., scales rounded at apex.
H. Branchlets densely tomentose: cones indehiscent.......1. *P. Cembra*
HH. Branchlets glabrous or only slightly pubescent: cones dehiscent. 5. *P. parviflora*
DD. Seeds winged.
E. Shape of cone ovoid; wing shorter than seed.......5. *P. parviflora*
EE. Shape of cone cylindric; wing much longer than seed.
F. Length of cone 10–20 in.: branchlets pubescent.......6. *P. Lambertiana*
FF. Length of cone 3–10 in.: branchlets glabrous or soon becoming so.
G. Scales of cone convex, thickened toward apex.
H. Lf. stiff and straight, 3–4 in. long.......7. *P. Peuce*
HH. Lf. slender and drooping, 5–8 in. long.......8. *P. Griffithii*
GG. Scales of cone flat and thin.
H. Lf. soft and flexible: cones usually less than 5 in. long.......9. *P. Strobus*
HH. Lf. stiff: cones usually 6–10 in. long.......10. *P. monticola*
AA. Fascicles containing 2–3 lvs.
B. Sheaths at base of lf. deciduous.
C. Lvs. 1–2 in. long, entire.......12. *P. cembroides*
CC. Lvs. 2–4 in. long, serrulate.......13. *P. Bungeana*
BB. Sheaths at base of lf. persistent.
C. Number of lvs. in fascicle 3.
D. Scales of cone unarmed.
E. Lvs. 8–12 in. long.......14. *P. canariensis*
EE. Lvs. 6 in. or less long.
F. Cones 2½ in. or less long.
G. And persistent: lvs. stiff.......22. *P. tabulæformis*
GG. And deciduous: lvs. flexible.......27. *P. echinata*
FF. Cones 3–4½ in. long.......29. *P. halepensis*
DD. Scales of cone armed with prickles or spines, or with spur-like projections.
E. Length of lvs. less than 6 in.
F. Cones symmetrical, 1½–3 in. long.
G. Lvs. usually 2 in a fascicle, flexible: cones deciduous.......27. *P. echinata*
GG. Lvs. always 3 in a fascicle, stiff: cones persistent.......32. *P. rigida*
FF. Cones lopsided, 3–6 in. long.
G. Prickles of cone minute: lvs. sometimes 2.......37. *P. radiata*
GG. Prickles stout: lvs. always 3.......36. *P. attenuata*
EE. Length of lvs. more than 6 in.
F. Cone-scales with stout spur-like projections; wing of seed thick.
G. Wing about one-half as long as seed: lvs. slender and usually drooping, gray-green.......38. *P. Sabiniana*
GG. Wing twice as long as seed: lvs. stout, not drooping, dark green...40. *P. Coulteri*
FF. Cone-scales without spur-like projections, the prickles slender; wing of seed thin and membranous.
G. Cones short-stalked.......28. *P. caribæa*
GG. Cones sessile or nearly so.
H. Winter-buds with white-fringed scales.......25. *P. palustris*
HH. Winter-buds brown.
I. The cones 6–12 in. long.......24. *P. Jeffreyi*
II. The cones 2–6 in. long.
J. Foliage yellowish-green: cones subterminal.......23. *P. ponderosa*
JJ. Foliage bluish-green: cones lateral.......26. *P. Taeda*
CC. Number of lvs. in fascicle 2.
D. Lvs. short, not exceeding 3 in.
E. Scales of cone with unarmed umbo.
F. Cones long-persistent: lvs. seldom exceeding 1 in., basal sheath ⅛in..33. *P. Banksiana*

FF. Cones deciduous at maturity: lvs. usually 2–3 in. long, the basal sheath ⅛–½in. long.
G. Foliage bluish-green: cones short-stalked: a tree .... 21. *P. sylvestris*
GG. Foliage dark green: cones nearly sessile: usually a shrub .... 20. *P. Mugo*
EE. Scales of cone armed with prickles or spines.
F. Twigs glaucous: cones symmetrical .... 31. *P. virginiana*
FF. Twigs not glaucous: cones often lopsided.
G. Cones persistent and often remaining closed for years, the prickles prominent: lf.-sheath ¼in. or less long .... 34. *P. contorta*
GG. Cones deciduous, the prickles usually small: lf.-sheath ½in. or more long .... 20. *P. Mugo*
DD. Lvs. prevailingly more than 3 in. long.
E. Wing much shorter than seed, deciduous .... 15. *P. Pinea*
EE. Wing twice or more as long as seed.
F. Scales of cone without prickles.
G. Cones tenaciously persistent.
H. Length of cone 2½ in. or less .... 22. *P. tabulæformis*
HH. Length of cone 3–4½ in. .... 29. *P. halepensis*
GG. Cones deciduous.
H. Twigs glaucous.
I. Basal lf.-sheath ½in. long, with 2 long points .... 19. *P. densiflora*
II. Basal lf.-sheath ¼in. or less long .... 27. *P. echinata*
HH. Twigs not glaucous.
I. Winter-buds resinous, brown: lvs. flexible, 5–7 in. long ...... 17. *P. resinosa*
II. Winter-buds not resinous, grayish-white, with fimbriate scales: lvs. stiff, 3–4½ in. long .... 18. *P. Thunbergii*
FF. Scales of cone armed with prickles.
G. Basal lf.-sheath ending in 2 long points or filaments.
H. Twigs glaucous .... 19. *P. densiflora*
HH. Twigs not glaucous .... 18. *P. Thunbergii*
GG. Basal lf.-sheath not ending in long points.
H. Cones lopsided, one side not fully developing.
I. Prickles minute, the cone short-stalked and 3–6 in. long: lvs. usually 3 .... 37. *P. radiata*
II. Prickles stout, the cone sessile and 2–3½ in. long: lvs. always 2 .... 35. *P. muricata*
HH. Cones symmetrical.
I. The cone persistent and often remaining closed for years ..... 30. *P. Pinaster*
II. The cone deciduous and dehiscent at maturity.
J. Lf. 8–12 in. long .... 28. *P. caribæa*
JJ. Lf. 3–7 in. long.
K. Twigs glaucous: lvs. flexible: cones dull brown .... 27. *P. echinata*
KK. Twigs not glaucous: lvs. stiff: cones yellow-brown and glossy .... 16. *P. nigra*

1. **P. Cembra,** L. SWISS STONE PINE. Tree to 100 ft. or more, of pyramidal habit when young; bark of old trunks reddish-gray and divided into thin scaly flakes; branchlets brownish-tomentose: lvs. in fascicles of 5, straight, 2–5 in. long, serrulate, dark green on back, bluish-white inside, the sheaths deciduous: cones ovoid, 2–3½ in. long, short-stalked, light brown, indehiscent and deciduous at maturity; cone-scales with terminal umbo, rounded at apex; seeds wingless, ½in. long. (Cembra: native Italian name.) Alps of Cent. Eu. to Mongolia.

2. **P. pumila,** Regel (*P. Cembra* var. *pumila*, Pall.). DWARF STONE PINE. Shrub to 10 ft. with prostrate branches: lvs. in fascicles of 5, 1½–3 in. long, obscurely serrulate, the sheaths deciduous: cones ovoid, 1¼–1¾ in. long, very short-stalked, indehiscent; cone-scales few, with reflexed apex; seeds wingless, about ¼in. long. N. E. Siberia to Japan.

3. **P. koraiensis,** Sieb. & Zucc. KOREAN PINE. Pyramidal tree 75–100 ft. high; bark gray or gray-brown, scaly; branchlets brownish-pubescent: lvs. in fascicles of 5, straight, 2½–5 in. long, serrulate, dark green and glossy on back, bluish-white inside, the sheaths deciduous: cones conic-oblong, 4–6 in. long, yellowish-brown, short-stalked, indehiscent; cone-scales with recurved obtuse apex; seeds brown, wingless, about ½in. long. Japan, Korea.

4. **P. flexilis,** James (*Apinus flexilis*, Rydb.). LIMBER PINE. Tree 50–80 ft. high; bark gray and smooth when young, becoming dark brown and deeply fissured; branchlets soon glabrous: lvs. in fascicles of 5, slightly curved and stiff, 1–3 in. long, entire, dark green, the sheaths deciduous: cones ovoid to nearly cylindric, 3–10 in. long, light brown, short-stalked, dehiscent; cone-scales with terminal obtuse dark umbo, often reflexed; seeds dark brown mottled with black, wingless, ⅓–½in. long. Alta. to New Mex. and Calif.

5. **P. parviflora,** Sieb. & Zucc. JAPANESE WHITE PINE. Pyramidal tree to 80 ft. or more; bark fissured in age, red-brown; branchlets slightly pubescent to glabrous: lvs. in fascicles of 5, slender, curved, 1–3 in. long, serrulate, bluish-green, whitish inside, the sheaths deciduous: cones ovoid, 2–3 in. long and about 1 in. broad, reddish-brown, nearly sessile, dehiscent; scales few and leathery, rounded; seeds dark brown, with short wing falling off when ripe, ½in. or less long. Japan. Var. **glauca,** Beissn., has more glaucous foliage.

6. **P. Lambertiana,** Dougl. Sugar Pine. Very large tree attaining 200 ft. and more; bark fissured in age, with purple-brown scales; branches pubescent, brown: lvs. in fascicles of 5, stiff and sharp-pointed, 3–4 in. long, serrulate, dark green with white lines on back, the sheaths deciduous: cones cylindric, becoming pendulous, 10–20 in. long, light brown and shining, on stalks 2–3 in. long, dehiscent; scales with terminal umbo, rounded at apex; seeds dark brown, ½in. long with wing 1 in. long. (Named for A. B. Lambert, page 46.) Ore. to Lower Calif.

7. **P. Peuce,** Griseb. Macedonian Pine. Narrow-pyramidal tree 50 ft. and more high; bark grayish-brown, becoming fissured; branchlets greenish, glabrous: lvs. in fascicles of 5, straight and stiff, 3–4 in. long, serrulate, bluish-green, the sheaths deciduous: cones cylindric, 3–6 in. long and 1½–2 in. broad, brown, dehiscent; scales abruptly convex and thickened at apex; seed about ⅓in. long with wing about twice as long. Balkan Mts.

8. **P. Griffithii,** McClelland (*P. excelsa,* Wall. not Lam. *P. nepalensis,* DeChambray not Forbes). Himalayan Pine. Tree to 150 ft., with grayish-brown bark which is fissured into small plates; branchlets glabrous and glaucous: lvs. in fascicles of 5, 5–8 in. long, slender and drooping, minutely serrulate, grayish- or bluish-green, the sheaths deciduous: cones cylindric, 6–10 in. long, light brown, on stalks 1–2 in. long, dehiscent; scales prominently convex with terminal umbo; seeds brown, ⅓in. long, with wing ¾–1 in. long. (Named for Wm. Griffith, page 44.) Himalayas.

9. **P. Strobus,** L. (*Strobus Strobus,* Small). White Pine. Tree to 150 ft., with horizontal branches in regular whorls and deeply fissured bark; branchlets greenish, glabrous or slightly puberulous when young: lvs. in fascicles of 5, soft and slender, 2–5 in. long, minutely serrulate, soft bluish-green, the sheaths deciduous: cones cylindric, slender and often curved, 3–8 in. long, on stalks ½–1 in. long, dehiscent; scales thin and flat, with terminal umbo; seeds brown mottled with black, ¼in. long, with wing about 1 in. long. Newf. to Ga. and Iowa. Var. **nana,** Carr., is dwarf with short lvs.

10. **P. monticola,** Dougl. (*Strobus monticola,* Rydb.). Western or Mountain White Pine. Resembling *P. Strobus* but of narrower and denser habit, stiffer lvs. and larger cones to 10 in. long. B. C. to Mont. and Calif.

11. **P. aristata,** Engelm. Hickory or Bristle-cone Pine. Usually a bushy tree but sometimes to 50 ft. high; bark reddish-brown, ridged; branchlets light orange, soon glabrous: lvs. in fascicles of 5, 1–1½ in. long, entire, dark green and resinous, whitish inside, the sheaths deciduous: cones ovoid, 2–3½ in. long, purplish-brown, nearly sessile; scales with dorsal umbo armed with slender curved spine ¼in. long; seeds light brown mottled with black, winged, about ⅓in. long. Colo. to Ariz. and Calif.

12. **P. cembroides,** Zucc. Mexican Stone Pine. Piñon or Pinyon. Small tree to 25 ft., with spreading branches; bark with reddish-brown scales; branchlets dark orange, becoming glabrous: lvs. in fascicles of 2 or 3, slender and curved, 1–2 in. long, entire, dark green, the sheaths deciduous: cones nearly globose, 1–2 in. across, shining brown, dehiscent; scales few, with broad dorsal umbo; seeds dark brown, ½–¾in. long, with very narrow wing. Ariz. to Mex. and Lower Calif. Var. **edulis,** Voss (*P. edulis,* Engelm. *Caryopitys edulis,* Small), Nut-Pine, is a larger tree with stiff lvs. usually in 2's; Wyo. to Tex. and N. Mex.

13. **P. Bungeana,** Zucc. Lacebark Pine. Tree to 80 or 100 ft. but often shrubby in cult., with long slender branches; bark flaky, becoming chalky-white; branchlets grayish-green, glabrous: lvs. in fascicles of 3, stiff and sharp-pointed, 2–4 in. long, serrulate, light green, the sheaths deciduous: cones conic-ovoid, 2–3 in. long, light yellowish-brown, nearly sessile; scales with triangular recurved spine-like umbo; seeds dark brown, ⅓–½in. long, with short wing. (Named for Alexander von Bunge, page 40.) N. W. China.

14. **P. canariensis,** C. Smith. Canary Pine. Tree to 80 ft., the st. and branches usually with scattered short leafy branchlets; bark reddish, slightly fissured; branchlets yellowish, pruinose when young; winter-buds with reflexed white-fringed scales: lvs. in fascicles of 3, slender and drooping, 8–12 in. long, minutely serrulate, light green and lustrous, the persistent sheaths about ¾in. long: cones cylindric-ovoid, 4–9 in. long, brown and glossy, short-stalked; scales broad-pyramidal with dorsal obtuse umbo; seeds ½in. long, with long wing adnate to the nut. Canary Isls.

15. **P. Pinea,** L. Italian Stone Pine. Tree to 80 ft., with a flat-topped umbrella-like unsymmetrical head; bark reddish-gray, deeply fissured; branchlets pale brown, glabrous; winter-buds with reflexed scales: lvs. in fascicles of 2, rather stiff and sharp-pointed, 4–8 in. long, serrulate, bright green, the persistent sheaths about ⅓in. long: cones ovoid or nearly globular, 4–6 in. long, chestnut-brown and shining, maturing the third year and persistent, short-stalked; scales with flat obtuse dorsal umbo; seeds brown, ½–¾in. long, with a deciduous wing less than ¼in. long. (Pinea: Latin for pine cone.) Medit. region.

16. **P. nigra,** Arnold (*P. Laricio,* Poir. *P. austriaca,* Hoess. *P. nigra* var. *austriaca,* Aschers. & Graebn. *P. nigricans,* Host.). Austrian Pine. Tree to 100 ft., with bark deeply fissured into scaly plates; branchlets light brown, glabrous: lvs. in fascicles of 2, stiff, 3–7 in. long, minutely serrulate, dark green, with persistent sheaths about ½in. long:

Fig. 16. Pinaceæ. A, *Larix leptolepis:* coning branch, × ½. B, *Pseudotsuga taxifolia:* coning branch, × ½. C, *Picea pungens:* coning branch, × ½. D, *Abies homolepis:* coning branch, × ½. E, *Pinus Strobus:* Ea, coning branch, × ½; Eb, fascicle of leaves, × ½; Ec, base of fascicle showing bracts, × 2; Ed, staminate strobilus, × 3; Ee, staminate sporophyll bearing pollen-sacs, × 10; Ef, pistillate strobilus, × 3; Eg, pistillate sporophyll, distal edge, × 10; Eh, same, lower side showing two naked ovules, × 20. (Ed–Eh redrawn from Sargent.)

cones ovate, 2–3½ in. long, sessile, yellowish-brown and glossy, dehiscent, deciduous; scales conspicuously keeled, with flattened dorsal umbo usually with a short prickle; seeds gray, ¼in. long, with long wing. Eu., W. Asia.

17. **P. resinosa,** Ait. RED PINE. Tree to 100 ft. or more, with spreading or pendulous branches; bark red-brown, shallowly fissured; branchlets orange, glabrous: lvs. in fascicles of 2, slender and flexible, sharp-pointed, 5–7 in. long, serrulate, dark green and shining, the persistent sheaths ½–¾in. long: cones conic-ovoid, 1½–2½ in. long, light brown, deciduous, dehiscent; scales keeled, with a small dark unarmed dorsal umbo; seeds brown and mottled, ⅛in. long with wing ¾in. long. N. S. to Pa. and Minn.

18. **P. Thunbergii,** Parl. JAPANESE BLACK PINE. Tree to 100 ft. or more, with broad pyramidal head and blackish-gray bark fissured into irregular plates; branchlets orange-yellow, glabrous; winter-buds grayish-white, with fimbriate scales: lvs. in fascicles of 2, stiff and sharp-pointed, minutely serrulate, 3–4½ in. long, bright green, the persistent sheaths to ½in. long and ending in 2 long filaments: cones conic-ovate, 2–3 in. long, brown, short-stalked, dehiscent; scales flattened, with small dorsal usually prickly umbo; seeds grayish-brown, ¼in. long, with wing about ¾in. long. (For Carl Peter Thunberg, page 52.) Japan.

19. **P. densiflora,** Sieb. & Zucc. JAPANESE RED PINE. Tree to 100 ft., with scaly orange-red bark, the young branchlets orange-yellow and bloomy: lvs. in fascicles of 2, slender and bright green, 3–5 in. long, minutely serrulate, the persistent sheaths about ½in. long and ending in 2 long points: cones conical, about 2 in. long, short-stalked, tawny-yellow, deciduous, dehiscent; scales thin, with small dorsal umbo sometimes with a prickle; seeds grayish-yellow, about ¼in. long, with wing ½–¾in. long. Japan. Var. **umbraculifera,** Mayr, TANYOSHO or JAPANESE UMBRELLA PINE, is a dwarf form with umbrella-like head.

20. **P. Mugo,** Turra (*P. montana,* Mill.). SWISS MOUNTAIN PINE. Low prostrate shrub or pyramidal tree to 40 ft. high; bark gray and scaly; branchlets dark brown, glabrous: lvs. in fascicles of 2, stiff and twisted, 1–3 in. long, bright green, the persistent sheaths about ½in. long: cones ovoid, ¾–2½ in. long, nearly sessile, tawny-yellow to dark brown, dehiscent, deciduous; scales with dorsal light gray prickle-like umbo. (Mugo: vernacular Swiss or Italian name.) Mts. of Cent. and S. Eu. Var. **Mughus,** Zenari (*P. montana* var. *Mughus,* Willk.), is a shrubby prostrate form and var. **rostrata,** Hoopes (*P. montana* var. *rostrata,* Ant. *P. uncinata,* Ramond), a tree to 80 ft. tall. Var. **Pumilio,** Zenari (*P. montana* var. *prostrata,* Tubeuf. *P. Pumilio,* Haenke), usually a prostrate shrub.

21. **P. sylvestris,** L. SCOTS PINE. Tree to 100 ft. or more, with smooth bright red bark which becomes fissured at base; branchlets grayish-yellow: lvs. in fascicles of 2, rigid and twisted, 1½–3 in. long, minutely serrulate, bluish- or grayish-green, the persistent sheaths about ⅛in. long: cones conical, 1–2½ in. long, grayish- or reddish-brown, short-stalked, deciduous; scales with dorsal obtuse gray umbo; seeds ⅛in. long, with long membranaceous wing. Eu., Asia. Var. **rigensis,** Loud., has a straight st. and very red bark. Var. **Watereri,** Beissn., is a dense columnar form with steel-blue foliage.

22. **P. tabulæformis,** Carr. (*P. sinensis,* Mayr not Lamb.). CHINESE PINE. Tree to 70 ft.; bark of trunk dark gray and fissured, red on limbs; branchlets orange- or grayish-yellow, glaucous when young: lvs. in fascicles of 2 or 3, stiff and sharp-pointed, 4–6 in. long, serrulate, bluish-green, the persistent sheaths about ¼in. long: cones ovoid, 1½–2½ in. long, yellow changing to brown, nearly sessile, persistent; scales keeled, with dorsal obtuse or mucronate umbo; seeds brown and mottled, ¼in. long with wing ¾in. long. China.

23. **P. ponderosa,** Dougl. WESTERN YELLOW PINE. Massive tree 100–150 ft. high, usually with narrow spire-like head; bark on old trees separating into cinnamon-red plates; branchlets orange-brown: lvs. in fascicles of 3, forming tufts at ends of branches, stiff and sharp-pointed, 5–11 in. long, yellowish-green, minutely serrulate, the persistent sheaths nearly 1 in. long: cones ovoid, 3–6 in. long, nearly sessile, reddish-brown, deciduous; scales thin, with dorsal umbo armed with a stout often hook-like prickle; seeds mottled purple, ¼in. long with wing 1 in. or more long. B. C. to Nev. and Lower Calif.

24. **P. Jeffreyi,** A. Murr. (*P. ponderosa* var. *Jeffreyi,* Vasey). JEFFREY or BLACK PINE. Similar to *P. ponderosa* but with denser darker bluish-green more persistent foliage, stronger sweet odor, glaucous branchlets, and cones 6–12 in. long, the slender prickles mostly deflexed and less evident to the touch. (John Jeffrey, page 45.) S. Ore. to Lower Calif.

25. **P. palustris,** Mill. (*P. australis,* Michx.). LONGLEAF PINE. Tree to 100 ft. or more, with ascending branches forming an open head; bark light orange-brown, separating into large papery scales; branchlets orange-brown; winter-buds with fringed whitish scales: lvs. in fascicles of 3, forming tufts at ends of branches, 8–18 in. long, serrulate, dark green, the persistent sheaths ¾–1 in. long: cones cylindric, 6–10 in. long, nearly sessile, dull brown; scales thin, with dorsal umbo having a short reflexed prickle; seeds about ½in. long with wing 1–1½ in. long. Va. to Fla. and Miss.

26. **P. Taeda,** L. LOBLOLLY PINE. Tree to 100 ft. and more, with ascending branches and round-topped head; bark bright red-brown, fissured into broad scaly ridges; branchlets yellowish-brown, often glaucous: lvs. in fascicles of 3, stiff and sharp-pointed, 5–10 in. long, minutely serrulate, bright green, the persistent sheaths to 1 in. long: cones ovoid-oblong, 2–5 in. long, sessile, pale reddish-brown; scales with dorsal umbo having a triangular reflexed spine; seeds dark brown and mottled, ¼in. long with wing about 1 in. long. N. J. to Fla. and Tex.

27. **P. echinata,** Mill. (*P. mitis*, Michx.). SHORTLEAF PINE. Tree 75–120 ft. high, with broad-ovoid head; bark reddish, divided into irregular plates; branchlets red-brown, glaucous when young: lvs. in fascicles of 2 or sometimes 3, slender and flexible, 3–5 in. long, serrulate, dark bluish-green, the persistent sheaths about ¼in. long: cones conic-ovoid, 1½–2½ in. long, sessile or very short-stalked, dull brown, deciduous; scales thin, with dorsal umbo armed with a short prickle which is soon deciduous; seeds mottled, about ¼in. long with wing ½in. long. N. Y. to Fla. and Tex.

28. **P. caribæa,** Morelet. SLASH PINE. Tree to 100 ft. and more, with horizontal branches high on the trunk; bark reddish, shedding in thin scales; branchlets orange-brown, glaucous when young: lvs. in fascicles of 2 or 3, crowded, 8–12 in. long, serrulate, dark green and glossy, the persistent sheaths ½–¾in. long: cones conic-oblong, 3–6½ in. long, short-stalked, dark brown and glossy; scales with small dorsal umbo having a minute recurved prickle; seeds less than ¼in. long with wing 1 in. long. Ga. to Fla. and Miss., W. Indies, Cent. Amer.

29. **P. halepensis,** Mill. ALEPPO PINE. Tree to 60 ft., with short branches and yellowish or brownish branchlets; bark gray and smooth becoming fissured: lvs. in fascicles of 2 or sometimes 3, slender, 2½–6 in. long, minutely serrulate, light green, the persistent sheaths ⅓in. long: cones conic-ovoid, spreading or deflexed, 3–4½ in. long, short-stalked, yellowish- or reddish-brown and glossy, persistent for several years, with unarmed scales and dorsal obtuse umbo; seeds ¼in. long with wing to 1 in. long. Medit. region.

30. **P. Pinaster,** Ait. CLUSTER PINE. Tree to 100 ft., with pyramidal head and deeply fissured brown bark; branchlets bright reddish-brown: lvs. in fascicles of 2, stiff and usually twisted, 5–9 in. long, minutely serrulate, glossy green, the persistent sheaths 1 in. or more long: cones conic-ovoid, clustered, 4–7 in. long, short-stalked, light brown and glossy, persistent, with prominent dorsal prickly umbo; seeds ⅓in. long with wing 1–1½ in. long. (Pinaster: Latin for a wild pine.) Medit. region.

31. **P. virginiana,** Mill. SCRUB PINE. Usually a small tree with straggly top but sometimes to 100 ft.; bark thin and scaly; branchlets glaucous: lvs. in fascicles of 2, stiff and twisted, 1½–3 in. long, minutely serrulate, the persistent sheaths ¼in. or less long: cones conic-ovoid, 1½–2½ in. long, nearly sessile, reddish-brown and glossy, dehiscent and persistent; scales with prominent dorsal umbo armed with sharp prickle; seeds pale brown and mottled, about ¼in. long with wing ½in. long. N. Y. to Ga. and Ala.

32. **P. rigida,** Mill. PITCH PINE. Irregular tree to 80 ft., with horizontal branches; bark red-brown, deeply fissured and scaly; branchlets light brown: lvs. in fascicles of 3, stiff and spreading, 3–5 in. long, minutely serrulate, dark green, the persistent sheaths to ½in. long: cones conic-ovoid, 2–3 in. long, nearly sessile, light brown and glossy, dehiscent and persistent; scales with prominent dorsal umbo armed with a sharp recurved prickle; seeds dark brown, ¼in. long with wing ¾in. long. N. B. to Ga. and Ky.

33. **P. Banksiana,** Lamb. JACK PINE. Low tree or sometimes to 70 ft. high, with a broad open head; bark reddish-brown, deeply ridged and scaly; branchlets yellowish- or purplish-brown: lvs. in fascicles of 2, stiff and twisted, ¾–1½ in. long, minutely serrulate, the persistent sheaths about ⅛in. long: cones conic-ovoid, usually curved and oblique, 1½–2 in. long, yellowish-brown and glossy, persistent and indehiscent; scales with small dorsal unarmed umbo; seeds black and mottled, about ⅛in. long with wing ½in. long. (Named for Sir Joseph Banks, page 39.) N. S. to N. Y. and Minn.

34. **P. contorta,** Loud. SHORE PINE. Scrubby tree 20–30 ft. high; bark reddish-brown, deeply fissured and scaly; branchlets orange to brown: lvs. in fascicles of 2, stiff and twisted, 1–2 in. long, nearly entire, dark green, the persistent sheaths ¼in. or less long: cones conic-ovoid, very oblique at base, 1–2 in. long, sessile, yellowish-brown and glossy, persistent and often remaining closed for years; scales with dark dorsal umbo armed with a slender incurved spine; seeds ⅙in. long with wing to ½in. long. Alaska to Calif. Var. **latifolia,** Wats. (*P. contorta* var. *Murrayana*, Engelm. *P. Murrayana*, Balf.), LODGEPOLE PINE, is a taller tree with longer lighter green lvs. and less oblique cones; Rocky Mts.

35. **P. muricata,** D. Don. BISHOP PINE. Tree to 50 or more ft., with round-topped head; bark dark brown, deeply furrowed and scaly; branchlets orange-brown: lvs. in fascicles of 2, stiff and tufted at ends of branches, 4–6 in. long, minutely serrulate, dark green, the persistent basal sheaths to ½in. long: cones conic-ovoid, oblique, 2–3½ in. long, sessile, chestnut-brown and glossy, persistent and remaining closed for years; scales with prominent dorsal umbo armed with a stout spine; seeds black, ¼in. long with wing to 1 in. long. Calif. and Lower Calif.

36. **P. attenuata,** Lemm. (*P. tuberculata,* Gord. not Don). KNOB-CONE PINE. Usually a small tree to 30 ft. but sometimes to 100 ft.; bark dark brown, shallowly fissured and scaly; branchlets orange-brown: lvs. in fascicles of 3, slender and stiff, 3–7 in. long, nearly entire, yellowish-green, the persistent sheaths to ½in. long: cones narrow-ovoid, oblique, 3–6 in. long, short-stalked, persistent and remaining closed for years; scales on outer side of cone enlarged into conical knobs armed with thick incurved spine; seeds ¼in. long with wing to 1½ in. long. Ore. to Calif.

37. **P. radiata,** D. Don (*P. insignis,* Dougl.). MONTEREY PINE. Tree to 100 ft., with thick deeply furrowed red-brown bark and yellowish-brown branchlets: lvs. in fascicles of 2 or 3, slender, 4–6 in. long, minutely serrulate, grass-green, the persistent sheaths to ½in. long: cones ovoid, oblique, 3–6 in. long, short-stalked, clustered and deflexed, persistent and often remaining closed on the branches for many years; scales thickened at top, the dorsal umbo with minute prickle; seeds black, ¼in. long with wing 1 in. long. S. Calif.

38. **P. Sabiniana,** Dougl. DIGGER PINE. Tree 50–80 ft. high, dividing into several trunks; bark brown, irregularly furrowed and scaly; branchlets glaucous: lvs. in fascicles of 3, slender and usually drooping, 8–12 in. long, minutely serrulate, gray-green, the persistent sheaths to 1 in. long: cones ovoid, deflexed, 6–10 in. long, long-stalked, persistent and dehiscent; scales with stout recurved projections, the umbo ending in a sharp point; seeds dark brown, about ¾in. long with wing about ⅓in. long. (Named for Joseph Sabine, page 50.) Calif.

39. **P. Torreyana,** Parry. TORREY or SOLEDAD PINE. Tree 40 ft. or more high, with branched trunk; bark red-brown, irregularly fissured and scaly; branchlets glaucous and glabrous: lvs. in fascicles of 5, stiff, 8–13 in. long, minutely toothed toward tip, dark green, the persistent sheaths about ¾in. long: cones broad-ovoid, 4–6 in. long, long-stalked, chocolate-brown and glossy, persistent and dehiscent; scales thickened into a knob at tip and armed with minute prickle; seeds ¾–1 in. long with deciduous wing about half as long. (Named for John Torrey, page 52.) S. Calif.

40. **P. Coulteri,** D. Don. COULTER or BIG-CONE PINE. Tree to 80 ft., of loose habit; bark blackish-brown, deeply fissured and scaly; branchlets glaucous: lvs. in fascicles of 3, very stout, 6–12 in. long, margins serrulate, dark bluish-green, the persistent sheaths to 1½ in. long: cones long-ovoid, 10–12 in. long, short-stalked, yellowish-brown, persistent and dehiscent; scales elongated, with spiny-tipped curved umbo; seeds dark brown, ½in. long with wing 1 in. or more long. (Named for Thomas Coulter, 1793–1843, Irish botanist.) Calif., Lower Calif.

2. **CEDRUS,** Loud. CEDAR. Four large evergreen trees from N. Afr. and Asia; sometimes regarded as forms of one species.—Monœcious or diœcious: bark dark gray, at first smooth but thick and fissured on old trees: lvs. alternate and single on young shoots but fascicled on spurs on older shoots, quadrangular and stiff: staminate fls. upright, cylindric, about 2 in. long, terminal on spurs; pistillate fls. ovoid, purplish, about ½in. long, consisting of numerous 2-ovuled scales subtended by small bracts: cones erect, ovoid to ovoid-oblong, with broad closely imbricated scales which usually fall apart at maturity; seeds with large membranaceous wings. (Ced-rus: from *kedrus,* the ancient Greek name.)

A. Leading shoot upright or spreading, the branchlets rarely pendulous: cones flat and often concave at apex.
 B. Lvs. usually 1–1¼ in. long: branchlets glabrous or only slightly pubescent: cones 3–4 in. long. . . . . 1. *C. libani*
 BB. Lvs. usually less than 1 in. long: branchlets densely pubescent: cones 2–3 in. long . . . 2. *C. atlantica*
AA. Leading shoot and branchlets pendulous: cones rounded at apex. . . . . 3. *C. Deodara*

1. **C. libani,** Loud. (*Pinus Cedrus,* L. *C. libanotica,* Link. *C. libanitica,* Pilger). CEDAR OF LEBANON (whence the name *libani*). Tree to 120 ft., with wide-spreading horizontal branches, the leading shoot nodding near tip; branchlets glabrous or slightly pubescent: lvs. 1–1¼ in. long, broader than thick in cross-section: cones brown, 3–4 in. long and about 2 in. across. Asia Minor.

2. **C. atlantica,** Manetti. ATLAS CEDAR. Pyramidal tree to 120 ft., the leading shoot upright; branchlets densely short-pubescent: lvs. less than 1 in. long, usually higher than broad, pale or bluish-green: cones light brown, 2–3 in. long and about 1¾ in. across. Atlas Mts. of Algeria. Var. **glauca,** Carr., has glaucous foliage.

3. **C. Deodara,** Loud. (*Pinus Deodara,* Roxb.). DEODAR CEDAR. Tree to 150 ft. and more, with the leading shoot and branchlets pendulous; branchlets densely pubescent: lvs. 1–2 in. long, as thick as broad, dark bluish-green: cones reddish-brown, 3½–5 in. long and 2–3½ in. across. (Deodara: native name.) Himalayas.

3. **LARIX,** Mill. LARCH. Deciduous resinous monœcious trees of about 10 species in the colder regions of the northern hemisphere.—Branches irregularly whorled

and spreading; bark thick, furrowed nd scaly: lvs. linear, spirally arranged on the leading shoots but in crowded clusters on short spurs: fls. solitary and terminal, the staminate yellow, globose to oblong, composed of numerous short-stalked spirally arranged anthers; pistillate fls. oblong, consisting of several or many scales borne in the axil of a much longer bract, each scale with 2 naked ovules at base: cones ovoid-oblong to subglobose, short-stalked, of woody persistent scales; seeds with large thin wings. (La-rix: ancient Latin name.)

A. Lvs. with 2 white bands beneath: cone-scales reflexed at apex....................1. *L. leptolepis*
AA. Lvs. without conspicuous white bands beneath: cone-scales straight or slightly incurved at apex.
  B. Scales of cone glabrous outside and shining.
    C. Cones ½–¾in. long, of 12–15 scales: branchlets glabrous....................2. *L. laricina*
    CC. Cones ¾–1 in. long, of 20 or more scales: branchlets usually pubescent..........3. *L. Gmelinii*
  BB. Scales of cone pubescent outside.
    C. Length of lvs. ¾–1½ in.: scales of cone 40–50, not incurved at apex, the bracts slightly projecting....................4. *L. decidua*
    CC. Length of lvs. to 2 in. and more: scales of cone about 30, slightly incurved at apex, the bracts concealed....................5. *L. sibirica*

1. **L. leptolepis,** Gord. (*L. Kaempferi,* Sarg. not Carr. *Abies leptolepis,* Sieb. & Zucc.). Japanese Larch. Tree to 90 ft., with short horizontal branches and gray bark peeling off in narrow strips, the glabrous branchlets yellowish- or reddish-brown: lvs. ½–1½ in. long and 1/12 in. or less wide, soft, bluish-green, with 2 white bands beneath: cones ovoid-oblong, ½–1½ in. long, with ovate rounded emarginate scales reflexed at tip, bracts concealed. Japan.

2. **L. laricina,** Koch (*Pinus laricina,* DuRoi. *L. americana,* Michx.). Tamarack. Hackmatack. American Larch. Tree to 60 ft., with short horizontal branches forming a narrow head and reddish-brown bark, the glabrous branchlets reddish-yellow and usually glaucous: lvs. 1–1½ in. long, light bluish-green: cones ovoid, ½–¾in. long, of 12–15 nearly orbicular entire glabrous scales, shining, bracts concealed. Alaska to B. C., Lab. to Pa. and Minn.

3. **L. Gmelinii,** Litvinov (*Abies Gmelinii,* Rupr. *L. dahurica,* Turcz.). Dahurian Larch. Tree to 90 ft., with wide-spreading branches and brown bark, the reddish branchlets usually pubescent: lvs. about 1¼ in. long, bright green: cones ovoid, ¾–1 in. long, of 20 or more orbicular glabrous scales rounded or emarginate at apex, shining, bracts concealed. (Named for S. G. Gmelin, page 43.) E. Siberia.

4. **L. decidua,** Mill. (*L. europæa,* DC. *L. Larix,* Karst.). European Larch. Tree to 100 ft. or more, with dark grayish-brown bark and slender glabrous yellowish branchlets: lvs. triangular, ¾–1½ in. long, soft, bright green: cones ovoid, ¾–1½ in. long, with 40–50 rounded orbicular straight scales pubescent on back, bracts with point slightly projecting. N. and Cent. Eu.

5. **L. sibirica,** Ledeb. (*L. decidua* var. *sibirica,* Regel). Siberian Larch. Differs from *L. decidua* in the slender lvs. to 2 in. long, scales of cone about 30 and slightly incurved at apex, and shorter bracts. N. E. Russia to Siberia.

4. **PSEUDOLARIX,** Gord. Golden-Larch. One deciduous resinous tree native in E. China, differing from Larix in the staminate fls. being clustered and pendulous, and in the deciduous cone-scales. (Pseudola-rix: *false larix.*)

P. amabilis, Rehd. (*Larix amabilis,* Nelson. *P. Kaempferi,* Gord. *P. Fortunei,* Mayr). Tree to 130 ft., with horizontally spreading branches and reddish-brown bark: lvs. linear, 1½–2 in. long and 1/12–⅛in. wide, bluish-green beneath, turning bright yellow in autumn: cones ovate, 2½–3 in. long and 1½–2 in. across, reddish-brown, with triangular emarginate deciduous woody scales.

5. **ABIES,** Mill. Fir. Evergreen trees of pyramidal habit, of about 40 species in the northern hemisphere.—Branches whorled and spreading; bark smooth and thin on young trees, often thick and furrowed when old: lvs. linear to linear-lanceolate, entire, sessile, flattened and usually grooved above, keeled beneath and with 2 white or pale stomatic bands, rarely 4-sided, with 2 resin-canals, spirally arranged but often appearing 2-ranked by a twist at their base: fls. axillary, in early spring from buds formed the previous season on branchlets of the year, surrounded at base by involucres of enlarged bud-scales; staminate fls. pendent on branches above middle of tree, with yellow or scarlet anthers; pistillate fls. erect on topmost branches, with numerous 2-ovuled imbricated scales: cones erect, ovoid or oblong-cylindric, scales deciduous, longer or shorter than their bracts, narrowed at base into long stipe; seeds with large thin wing. (A-bies: ancient Latin name.)

A. Lvs. with stomata on both sides, grayish-green or glaucous.
  B. Arrangement of lvs. radial (standing in all directions or planes); lf. ½–¾in. long.......... 1. *A. Pinsapo*
  BB. Arrangement of lvs. not radial; lf. 1–2½ in. long.
    C. Cones 5½ in. and more long.
      D. Bracts of cone much exserted and reflexed: lvs. flat, grooved above..... 2. *A. procera*
      DD. Bracts of cone hidden: lvs. 4-sided.......... 3. *A. magnifica*
    CC. Cones 2–5 in. long.
      D. Branchlets nearly glabrous: lvs. 1½–2½ in. long, with marginal resin-ducts.......... 4. *A. concolor*
      DD. Branchlets reddish-pubescent: lvs. 1–1½ in. long, with internal resin-ducts.......... 5. *A. lasiocarpa*
AA. Lvs. with stomata only on lower surface, green and shining above.
  B. Apex of lf. entire, acute and sharp-pointed.
    C. Bracts of cone exserted and reflexed: stomatic bands on under side of lf. white and conspicuous.......... 6. *A. cephalonica*
    CC. Bracts of cone hidden: stomatic bands on under side of lf. inconspicuous.. 7. *A. holophylla*
  BB. Apex of lf. rounded or emarginate.
    C. Under surface of lf. without conspicuous white bands.......... 8. *A. firma*
    CC. Under surface of lf. with 2 conspicuous white or glaucous bands.
      D. Bracts of cone exserted and reflexed.
        E. Cones 1½–2½ in. long.
          F. Branchlets brown: resin-ducts marginal.......... 9. *A. Veitchii*
          FF. Branchlets grayish: resin-ducts internal.
            G. Lines of stomata 8–12 in each band: bracts much-exserted..... 10. *A. Fraseri*
            GG. Lines of stomata 4–8 in each band: bracts only slightly exserted.......... 11. *A. balsamea*
        EE. Cones 4–6 in. long.
          F. Arrangement of lvs. pectinate (lvs. 2-ranked or nearly so and wide-spreading).......... 12. *A alba*
          FF. Arrangement of lvs. not pectinate (more or less imbricate or overlapping).......... 13. *A. Nordmanniana*
      DD. Bracts of cone hidden.
        E. Twigs with dense rusty pubescence.......... 14. *A. Mariesii*
        EE. Twigs with scattered grayish pubescence or glabrous.
          F. Cones purple when young: resin-ducts of lf. internal.
            G. Branchlets deeply grooved.......... 15. *A. homolepis*
            GG. Branchlets not grooved.......... 11. *A. balsamea*
          FF. Cones brown or green: resin-ducts of lf. marginal.
            G. Lf. ½–¾in. long: branchlets glabrous and shining.......... 16. *A. numidica*
            GG. Lf. 1–2½ in. long: branchlets slightly pubescent.
              H. Arrangement of lvs. pectinate, forming flat sprays.......... 17. *A. grandis*
              HH. Arrangement of lvs. not pectinate, V-shaped.......... 18. *A. cilicica*

1. **A. Pinsapo,** Boiss. SPANISH FIR. Tree to 80 ft., with glaucous brownish branchlets; bark smooth, becoming fissured; winter-buds resinous: lvs. ½–¾in. long, acute or obtuse, thick and rigid and radially spreading at nearly right angles, dark green and stomatiferous above, with grayish bands beneath; resin-ducts internal: cones cylindric, 4–5 in. long, purplish-brown; bracts hidden. (Pinsapo: native Spanish name.) Spain. Var. **glauca,** Beissn., has glaucous foliage.

2. **A. procera,** Rehd. (*Pinus nobilis,* Dougl. *A. nobilis,* Lindl. not Dietr.). NOBLE FIR. Tree 150–250 ft. tall, with deeply fissured reddish-brown bark; branchlets with fine reddish pubescence; winter-buds resinous: lvs. 1–1½ in. long, obtuse, entire or emarginate at apex, pectinate on lower branches, erect and crowded on upper branches, bluish-green, stomatiferous and grooved above, paler beneath; resin-ducts marginal: cones oblong-cylindric, 5½–10 in. long, green becoming purplish-brown; bracts exserted and reflexed and nearly concealing the scales. Wash. to N. Calif. Var. **glauca,** Bailey (forma *glauca,* Rehd.), has glaucous foliage.

3. **A. magnifica,** Murr. (*A. nobilis* var. *magnifica,* Kellogg). RED FIR. Tree to 200 ft.; branchlets soon glabrous and gray; winter-buds resinous: lvs. 1–1¾ in. long, obtuse and entire at apex, pectinate below, erect on upper branches, bluish-green, 4-sided and stomatiferous on all sides; resin-ducts marginal: cones oblong-cylindric, 5½–9 in. long, purplish when young; bracts hidden. Ore. to Calif.

4. **A. concolor,** Hoopes (*Picea concolor,* Gord.). COLORADO or WHITE FIR. Tree to 120 ft., with gray bark and yellowish-green nearly glabrous branchlets; winter-buds resinous: lvs. 1½–2½ in. long, acute or rounded at apex, irregularly arranged, bluish-green and stomatiferous above, with pale bands beneath; resin-ducts marginal: cones cylindric, 3–5 in. long, greenish or purplish becoming brown; bracts hidden. Colo. to N. Mex. and Lower Calif.

5. **A. lasiocarpa,** Nutt. (*Pinus lasiocarpa,* Hook.). ALPINE FIR. Tree to 100 ft. or more, with silvery-gray smooth bark becoming fissured; branchlets reddish-pubescent; winter-buds resinous: lvs. 1–1½ in. long, rounded or emarginate at apex, much crowded and becoming erect, bluish-green, stomatiferous on both sides, with paler bands beneath; resin-ducts internal: cones oblong-cylindric, 2–4 in. long, dark purple; bracts hidden. Alaska to New Mex. Var. **arizonica,** Lemm. (*A. arizonica,* Merriam), CORK FIR, differs in having thick corky whitish bark.

6. **A. cephalonica,** Loud. Greek Fir. Tree to 100 ft., with grayish-brown bark and lustrous red-brown glabrous branchlets; winter-buds reddish, resinous: lvs. ½–1 in. long, stiff, acuminate into a sharp point, radially spreading and slightly directed forward, shining deep green above with 2 white bands beneath; resin-ducts marginal: cones cylindric, 5–7 in. long, brownish; bracts exserted and reflexed. Greece.

7. **A. holophylla,** Maxim. Needle Fir. Tree to 100 ft.; branchlets yellowish-gray, slightly grooved, glabrous; winter-buds slightly resinous: lvs. 1–1¾ in. long, entire at apex and spiny-pointed when young, spreading at nearly right angles or pectinate below, shining bright green above, with inconspicuous stomatic bands beneath; resin-ducts internal: cones cylindric, 5–6 in. long, green becoming light brown; bracts hidden. Manchuria, Korea.

8. **A. firma,** Sieb. & Zucc. Momi Fir. Tree to 150 ft., with dark gray bark and brownish slightly grooved branchlets which are pubescent in the grooves; winter-buds only slightly resinous: lvs. to 1½ in. long, the apex bifid and pungent-pointed or on older plants obtuse and emarginate, pectinate, shining dark green above with grayish inconspicuous bands beneath; resin-ducts marginal and internal: cones cylindric, 4–5 in. long, yellowish-green before maturity; bracts exserted, not reflexed. Japan.

9. **A. Veitchii,** Lindl. Tree to 80 ft., with grayish bark and brown densely pubescent branchlets; winter-buds purplish, very resinous: lvs. ½–1 in. long, truncate and notched at apex, crowded and directed forward and more or less upward, shining dark green above and with 2 broad silvery-white bands beneath; resin-ducts marginal: cones cylindric, 1¾–2½ in. long, at first bluish-purple; bracts slightly exserted and reflexed. Cent. Japan, where it was discovered by John Gould Veitch in 1860.

10. **A. Fraseri,** Poir. (*Pinus Fraseri*, Pursh). Southern Balsam Fir. Tree to 75 ft., with reddish bark; branchlets yellowish-gray, densely reddish-pubescent; winter-buds very resinous: lvs. ½–1 in. long, rounded and bifid at apex, spreading upward and forward, pectinate below, shining dark green above and with broad white bands beneath; resin-ducts internal: cones ovoid, 1½–2 in. long, purple before maturity; bracts exserted and reflexed. (Named for its collector, John Fraser, page 43.) Mts., W. Va. to N. C. and Tenn.

11. **A. balsamea,** Mill. (*Pinus balsamea*, L.). Balsam Fir. Tree to 75 ft., with grayish-brown bark; branchlets gray, short-pubescent; winter-buds very resinous: lvs. ½–1 in. long, rounded at apex and slightly bifid, pectinate or spreading, shining dark green above, with narrow grayish-white bands beneath; resin-ducts internal: cones oblong, 2–2½ in. long, violet-purple before maturity; bracts hidden or slightly exserted. Lab. to W. Va. and Minn.

12. **A. alba,** Mill. (*A. pectinata*, DC. *A. Picea*, Lindl.). Silver Fir. Tree to 150 ft., with grayish bark and gray slightly pubescent branchlets; winter-buds not resinous: lvs. ½–1¼ in. long, rounded and notched at apex, pectinate, shining dark green above with 2 white bands beneath; resin-ducts marginal: cones cylindric, 4–5½ in. long, green becoming reddish-brown; bracts exserted and reflexed. Mts. of Cent. and S. Eu.

13. **A. Nordmanniana,** Spach (*Pinus Nordmanniana*, Steven). Tree to 150 ft. or more, with grayish-brown bark and gray slightly pubescent branchlets; winter-buds not resinous: lvs. ¾–1½ in. long, rounded and notched at apex, directed forward and densely covering the branchlets, shining dark green above with whitish bands beneath; resin-ducts marginal: cones cylindric, 5–6 in. long, reddish brown; bracts exserted and reflexed. (Named for Alexander Nordmann, Finnish botanist, who discovered it in 1837.) Caucasus, Asia Minor, Greece.

14. **A. Mariesii,** Mast. Tree to 80 ft., with pale gray bark; branchlets densely rusty-pubescent; winter-buds resinous: lvs. ⅓–¾in. long, rounded or notched at apex, crowded, shining above, with white bands beneath; resin-ducts marginal: cones ovoid, 1¾–3½ in. long, dark purple before maturity; bracts hidden. (Named for its collector, Chas. Maries.) Japan.

15. **A. homolepis,** Sieb. & Zucc. (*A. brachyphylla*, Maxim.). Nikko Fir. Tree to 120 ft., with grayish glabrous deeply grooved branchlets; winter-buds resinous: lvs. about 1 in. long, rounded and slightly bifid at apex, spreading outward and upward, shining dark green above with 2 white bands beneath; resin-ducts internal: cones cylindric, about 4 in. long, narrowed at ends, purple becoming brown; bracts hidden. Japan.

16. **A. numidica,** DeLannoy. Algerian Fir. Tree to 60 ft., with gray bark and glabrous shining branchlets; winter-buds not or slightly resinous: lvs. ½–¾in. long, rounded or emarginate at apex, much crowded and spreading outward and upward, dark green above with 2 white bands beneath; resin-ducts marginal: cones cylindric, 5–7 in. long, brown; bracts hidden. N. Afr.

17. **A. grandis,** Lindl. Giant Fir. Gigantic tree to 300 ft., with brownish bark; branchlets minutely pubescent to glabrous; winter-buds resinous: lvs. 1¼–2¼ in. long, rounded and bifid at apex, pectinate to form flat sprays, shining dark green above with white bands below; resin-ducts marginal: cones cylindric, 2–4 in. long, bright green; bracts hidden. Vancouver Isl. to Calif. and Mont.

18. **A. cilicica,** Carr. (*Pinus cilicica,* Ant. & Kotschy). CILICIAN FIR. Tree to 100 ft., with ashy-gray bark and gray slightly pubescent branchlets; winter-buds not resinous: lvs. about 1 in. long, rounded or notched at apex, spreading upward and forward leaving a V-shaped depression, shining dark green above with 2 narrow white bands beneath; resin-ducts marginal: cones cylindric, 6–8 in. long, reddish-brown; bracts hidden. Asia Minor, Syria.

6. **PICEA,** A. Dietr. SPRUCE. Nearly 40 species of evergreen pyramidal trees, native in cold and temp. regions of the northern hemisphere.—Branches usually whorled, the branchlets roughened by the persistent lf.-bases; bark thin and scaly: lvs. linear, spirally arranged, usually 4-angled with rows of stomata on all sides, or sometimes compressed and with stomata on only the upper or ventral side, sessile and jointed at base to a stalk-like woody projection: fls. terminal or axillary, catkin-like; staminate fls. yellow or red, consisting of numerous spirally arranged anthers with connective enlarged at apex and scale-like; pistillate fls. greenish or purple, of spirally arranged 2-ovuled scales each subtended by a small bract: cones ovoid or oblong, cylindric, pendulous or spreading, the scales persistent; seeds with large thin wing. (Pi-cea, Pic-ea: ancient Latin name.)

A. Lvs. flattened, with white bands above but without stomata below.
  B. Branchlets pubescent .... 1. *P. Omorika*
  BB. Branchlets glabrous.
    C. Lf. with a sharp horny point, to 1 in. long .... 2. *P. sitchensis*
    CC. Lf. with short not horny point, to ¾in. long .... 3. *P. jezoensis*
AA. Lvs. quadrangular, with stomatic lines on all four sides.
  B. Length of lvs. 1–2 in. .... 4. *P. Smithiana*
  BB. Length of lvs. 1 in. or usually less.
    C. Cones less than 2 in. long.
      D. Branchlets glabrous .... 5. *P. glauca*
      DD. Branchlets pubescent.
        E. Stomatic bands equal on both sides of lf.: winter-buds without persistent scales at base .... 17. *P. Engelmannii*
        EE. Stomatic bands broader on upper surface of lf.: winter-buds with persistent blackish scales at base.
          F. Foliage shining: cones oblong, soon deciduous, green when young .... 6. *P. rubens*
          FF. Foliage dull or bluish-green: cones ovoid, persistent for several years, purple when young .... 7. *P. mariana*
    CC. Cones prevailingly more than 2 in. long.
      D. Lf. broader than high in cross-section, with only half as many stomata beneath as on upper surface.
        E. Tip of lf. sharply acuminate; lf. ½–¾in. long .... 8. *P. bicolor*
        EE. Tip of lf. obtuse or acute; lf. ¼–½in. long.
          F. Branchlets glabrous or glandular-pubescent .... 9. *P. Koyamai*
          FF. Branchlets pubescent but not glandular .... 10. *P. Glehnii*
      DD. Lf. as high or higher than broad, equally stomatiferous on all four sides.
        E. Tip of lf. obtuse .... 11. *P. orientalis*
        EE. Tip of lf. acute.
          F. Scales of cone with entire apex.
            G. Branchlets yellowish, pubescent or glabrous .... 12. *P. asperata*
            GG. Branchlets brown, pubescent .... 13. *P. obovata*
          FF. Scales of cone with denticulate or emarginate apex.
            G. Branchlets glabrous.
              H. Pistillate fls. bright purple: lvs. pointing forward .... 14. *P. Abies*
              HH. Pistillate fls. green: lvs. radially spreading at nearly right angles.
                I. Winter-buds dark brown: lvs. dark green .... 15. *P. polita*
                II. Winter-buds light yellowish-brown: lvs. bluish-green .... 16. *P. pungens*
            GG. Branchlets pubescent.
              H. Size of cone 4–7 in. long .... 14. *P. Abies*
              HH. Size of cone 2–3 in. long.
                I. Color of lvs. deep green: branchlets brown .... 13. *P. obovata*
                II. Color of lvs. usually bluish-green: branchlets yellowish .... 17. *P. Engelmannii*

1. **P. Omorika,** Purkyne (*Pinus Omorika,* Panc.). SERBIAN SPRUCE. Tree to 100 ft., with narrow pyramidal head and short pendent brown pubescent branchlets; bark brown; winter-buds dark brown, not resinous: lvs. flattened, ⅓–½in. long, ridged on both sides, with whitish bands above but without stomata and shining below, obtuse and mucronulate: fls. purple: cones ovoid-oblong, 1½–2½ in. long, brown and glossy; margin of scales finely denticulate. (Omorika: vernacular name.) S. E. Eu.

2. **P. sitchensis,** Carr. (*Pinus sitchensis,* Bong.). SITKA SPRUCE. Tree to 100 or 200 ft.; bark red-brown; branchlets glabrous, light brownish-yellow; winter-buds light brown, resinous: lvs. flattened, ½–1 in. long, slightly keeled and with white stomatic bands above, rounded and shining beneath without stomata, spiny-pointed: staminate fls. dark red: cones cylindric-oblong, 2–4 in. long, yellow to red-brown; margin of scales denticulate above the middle. Alaska to Calif.

3. **P. jezoensis,** Carr. (*Abies jezoensis,* Sieb. & Zucc. *P. ajanensis,* Fisch.). YEDDO SPRUCE. Tree to 150 ft.; bark gray; branchlets glabrous and shining, yellowish; winter-buds shining, resinous: lvs. flattened, ½–¾in. long, slightly keeled, with white bands above, shining below and without stomata, acute: fls. carmine: cones cylindric-oblong, 1½–3½ in. long, light brown; margins of scales denticulate. N. E. Asia and Japan. Var. **hondoensis,** Rehd. (*P. hondoensis,* Mayr), has shorter more obtuse lvs. dull green below; Japan.

4. **P. Smithiana,** Boiss. (*Pinus Smithiana,* Wall. *Picea Morinda,* Link). HIMALAYAN SPRUCE. Tree to 150 ft., with wide-spreading branches and slender pendulous gray glabrous and lustrous branchlets; bark brownish-gray; winter-buds reddish-brown, resinous: lvs. radially disposed and pointing forward, usually higher than broad, 1–2 in. long, acute, dark green: pistillate fls. purple: cones cylindric, dark brown and glossy, 5–7 in. long; scales with entire margin. (For Sir James Edward Smith, page 51.) Himalayas.

5. **P glauca,** Voss (*Pinus glauca,* Moench. *Picea canadensis,* BSP. *P. alba,* Link). WHITE SPRUCE. Tree to 70 ft. or more, with ascending branches and usually pendent grayish or pale brown glabrous branchlets; bark grayish; winter-buds obtuse, not resinous, with loosely imbricated scales bifid at apex: lvs. quadrangular, ⅓–¾in. long, acute, bluish-green: cones oblong-cylindric, 1½–2 in. long, pale brown and lustrous; scales with entire margin. Lab. to Alaska, south to Mont. and N. Y. Var. **albertiana,** Sarg. (*P. albertiana,* S. Br.), ALBERTA SPRUCE, tree to 150 ft., of narrow pyramidal habit, the branchlets with more prominent lf.-stalks; winter-buds with entire scales; cones shorter, the scales stiffer; Alaska to Mont. Var. **densata,** Bailey, BLACK HILLS SPRUCE, tree of compact habit, slow-growing, foliage bright or bluish-green; S. D.

6. **P. rubens,** Sarg. (*P. rubra,* Link not Dietr. *P. australis,* Small). RED SPRUCE. Tree to 100 ft., with narrow-pyramidal head; bark red-brown; branchlets brown, pubescent: lvs. quadrangular, to ½in. long, acute and mucronate, shining, with more stomatic lines above than below: cones oblong, 1½–2 in. long, green becoming reddish-brown, soon deciduous; scales stiff, the margins entire or slightly denticulate. N. S. to mts. of N. C.

7. **P. mariana,** BSP. (*Abies mariana,* Mill. *P. nigra,* Link). BLACK SPRUCE. Usually 20–30 ft. high but sometimes to 100 ft., branches often pendulous; bark gray-brown; branchlets brown, pubescent: lvs. quadrangular, ¼–¾in. long, dull or bluish-green, with broader stomatic bands above than below: cones ovoid, ½–1½ in. long, purple becoming grayish-brown, persistent for several years; scales stiff, the margins denticulate. Alaska to Lab., south to Wis. and Va.

8. **P. bicolor,** Mayr (*Abies bicolor,* Maxim. *P. Alcockiana,* Carr.). ALCOCK SPRUCE. Tree to 150 ft., with stiff branches and yellowish-brown pubescent or glabrous shining branchlets; winter-buds brown, slightly resinous: lvs. quadrangular, slightly flattened, ½–¾in. long, sharply acuminate, dark green, with about twice as many stomatic bands above as below: cones oblong, 3–4 in. long, purple becoming brown; scales finely denticulate. Japan.

9. **P. Koyamai,** Shiras. Narrow-pyramidal tree to 60 ft., with grayish-brown bark; branchlets reddish-brown becoming grayish, glandular-pubescent or nearly glabrous; winter-buds brown, resinous: lvs. quadrangular, slightly flattened, ⅓–½in. long, acute or obtuse, with about twice as many stomatic bands above as below: cones cylindric-oblong, 2–4 in. long, green becoming pale brown; scales denticulate. (Koyamai: Japanese name.) Japan, Korea.

10. **P. Glehnii,** Mast. (*Abies Glehnii,* Fr. Schmidt). SAGHALIN SPRUCE. Narrow-pyramidal tree to 120 ft., with red-brown bark; branchlets reddish-brown, densely pubescent; winter-buds brown, resinous: lvs. quadrangular, slightly flattened, ¼–½in. long, obtuse or acute, dark green, with more stomata above than below: cones cylindric-oblong, 2–3 in. long, shining brown, usually violet before maturity; scales entire, somewhat erose. (Named for Glehn, who collected it in 1861.) Saghalin, Japan.

11. **P. orientalis,** Carr. (*Pinus orientalis,* L.). ORIENTAL SPRUCE. Tree to 100 ft. or more, with brown bark and somewhat pendulous brown pubescent branchlets; winter-buds brown, not resinous: lvs. crowded and more or less appressed to the branches, quadrangular, ¼–⅜in. long, obtuse, thick, dark green and shining: fls. carmine: cones cylindric-ovoid, 2½–3½ in. long, violet turning brown; scales entire at margins. Caucasus, Asia Minor.

12. **P. asperata,** Mast. Tree to 75 ft. or more; bark grayish-brown; branchlets yellowish, pubescent or glabrous; winter-buds yellowish-brown, resinous: lvs. quadrangular, ½–¾in. long, acute, dark green: cones cylindric-oblong, 3–4 in. long, gray changing to brown; scales entire at margins. W. China.

13. **P. obovata,** Ledeb. (*P. Abies* var. *obovata,* Voss). SIBERIAN SPRUCE. Tree to 100 ft. or more; branchlets brown, pubescent; winter-buds not resinous: lvs. quadrangular, ½–¾in. long, acute, deep green: cones cylindric-ovoid, 2½–3 in. long, purple turning brown; scales with entire margins or sometimes emarginate. N. Eu., N. Asia.

14. **P. Abies,** Karst. (*P. excelsa,* Link. *Pinus Abies,* L.). NORWAY SPRUCE. Tree to 150 ft., with spreading branches and usually pendulous brown glabrous or pubescent

branchlets; bark reddish-brown; winter-buds reddish or light brown, not resinous: lvs. quadrangular, ½–¾in. long, spirally crowded around the branchlets, those on upper side pointing forward, acute, dark green and usually shining: pistillate fls. bright purple: cones cylindric-oblong, 4–7 in. long, light brown; scales with erose-denticulate margin. Cent. and N. Eu.—Some of the hort. vars. are: **aurea,** Nash, lvs. golden-yellow; **Clanbrasiliana,** Th. Fries, compact bush 7 ft. high with very short lvs.; **compacta,** Nash, nearly globose dense form; **conica,** Th. Fries, dense conical form with ascending branches; **Ellwangeriana,** Rehd., broad pyramidal form; **finedonensis,** Nash, lvs. pale yellow becoming bronzy, then green; **Gregoryana,** Nash, dwarf bush 2–3 ft. high, with crowded pale branchlets; **Maxwellii,** Nash, dense dwarf form to 2 ft. with short clustered branchlets; **Merkii,** Rehd., low form with thin grass-green lvs.; **nana,** Nash, dwarf with short orange-yellow branchlets; **nidiformis,** Bailey, low form with very dense head, having a nest-like mass of branchlets; **pendula,** Nash, branches pendulous; **procumbens,** Rehd., prostrate, with horizontal bright yellow branchlets; **pumila,** Nash, dense dwarf form; **pygmæa,** Rehd., dense small conical form; **pyramidalis gracilis,** Slavin, dwarf nearly globose form with bright green foliage; **Remontii,** Rehd., dense pyramidal form with crowded yellow branchlets.

15. **P. polita,** Carr. (*Abies polita*, Sieb. & Zucc.). Tigertail Spruce. Pyramidal tree to 90 ft., of stiff habit; bark gray; branchlets yellowish-brown, glabrous; winter-buds dark brown, not resinous, the scales persisting as blackish sheath at base of branchlets: lvs. quadrangular, ½–¾in. long, radially spreading, higher than broad, spiny-tipped, shining dark green: pistillate fls. green: cones oblong, 4–5 in. long, brown and glossy; scales with irregularly denticulate margins. Japan.

16. **P. pungens,** Engelm. (*P. Parryana*, Sarg.). Colorado Spruce. Pyramidal tree to 150 ft., with stiff horizontal branches and yellowish-brown glabrous branchlets; winter-buds light yellowish-brown, not resinous, with conspicuous long-pointed scales at base: lvs. quadrangular, ¾–1 in. long, radially spreading, rigid and spiny-tipped, bluish-green to silvery-white: cones cylindric-oblong, 2½–4 in. long, light brown and glossy; scales flexuose on margins, erose at apex. Wyo. to New Mex. Var. **glauca,** Regel, foliage bluish-green. Var. **Kosteriana,** Henry, has bluish-white foliage and pendulous branches; originated in Koster nurseries in Holland. Var. **Moerheimii,** Rujis, is a compact form with blue foliage.

17. **P. Engelmannii,** Engelm. (*Abies Engelmannii*, Parry). Tree to 150 ft., with slender spreading branches and brownish-yellow pubescent branchlets; winter-buds brownish-yellow: lvs. quadrangular, more or less directed forward, ½–1 in. long, acute, bluish-green to steel-blue, with strong odor when bruised: fls. purple: cones cylindric-oblong, 1½–3 in. long, light brown and shining; margins of scales erose-denticulate. (Named for Geo. Engelmann, page 42.) B. C. to New Mex.

7. **TSUGA,** Carr. Hemlock. Evergreen trees of 10 species in temp. N. Amer., Japan, China, and E. Himalayas.—Branches slender and horizontal, roughened by persistent lf.-bases; bark cinnamon-red, furrowed; winter-buds minute, not resinous: lvs. linear, flat or angular, short-petioled, usually 2-ranked, having only 1 resin-duct in middle of lf.: fls. solitary; staminate of numerous anthers with connectives produced into gland-like tips; pistillate fls. terminal, the 2-ovuled scales about as long as bracts: cones ovate or oblong, pendulous, with thin entire scales much longer than bracts; seeds winged. (Tsu-ga: Japanese name.)

A. Lvs. spirally arranged around the branches, rounded above, with whitish stomatiferous lines on both sides: cones 2–3 in. long . . . . . 1. *T. Mertensiana*
AA. Lvs. 2-ranked, flat, with whitish bands below: cones ½–1½ in. long.
  B. Branchlets glabrous . . . . . 2. *T. Sieboldii*
  BB. Branchlets pubescent.
    C. Scales of cone nearly as wide as long, glabrous outside.
      D. Tip of lf. emarginate; lf.-margins entire . . . . . 3. *T. diversifolia*
      DD. Tip of lf. rounded and entire; lf.-margins denticulate toward apex . . . . . 4. *T. canadensis*
    CC. Scales of cone longer than broad, finely pubescent outside.
      D. Margins of lf. entire; stomatic bands conspicuous . . . . . 5. *T. caroliniana*
      DD. Margins of lf. with small teeth; stomatic bands inconspicuous . . . . . 6. *T. heterophylla*

1. **T. Mertensiana,** Carr. (*Pinus Mertensiana*, Bong. *T. Pattoniana*, Sénécl.). Mountain Hemlock. Tree to 100 ft. or more, with slender pendent branches and reddish-brown pubescent branchlets: lvs. spirally arranged around the branches, rounded above, ½–1 in. long, blunt-pointed, narrowed toward base, blue-green and with stomatic lines on both sides: cones sessile, cylindric-oblong, 2–3 in. long; scales thin, nearly as broad as long, finely pubescent outside. (Named for Karl Heinrich Mertens, 1795–1830, physician and naturalist.) Alaska to Calif. and Mont.

2. **T. Sieboldii,** Carr. Tree to 100 ft., with slender spreading branches and pale yellowish-brown glabrous and glossy branchlets: lvs. usually broadest at the emarginate apex, ¼–¾in. long, shining dark green and grooved above, with narrow white bands beneath: cones ovoid, 1–1¼ in. long, stalked: scales orbicular, glossy. (Named for Philipp Franz von Siebold, page 51.) Japan.

3. **T. diversifolia,** Mast. (*Abies diversifolia,* Maxim.). JAPANESE HEMLOCK. Tree to 80 ft., with reddish-brown pubescent branchlets: lvs. broadest at middle or toward base, ⅓–½in. long, emarginate at apex, shining dark green above, with narrow white bands below: cones ovoid, ½–¾in. long, short-stalked; scales orbicular-ovate, shining. Japan.

4. **T. canadensis,** Carr. (*Pinus canadensis,* L.). COMMON or CANADA HEMLOCK. Tree to 100 ft., with horizontal or pendulous branches and yellowish-brown pubescent branchlets: lvs. ¼–⅝in. long, obtuse or acutish, the margins finely denticulate, shining dark green and obscurely grooved above, with 2 narrow whitish bands beneath: cones ovoid, ½–¾in. long, on slender stalks; scales nearly orbicular, glabrous. N. S. to Ala. Var. **pendula,** Beissn. (var. *Sargentiana,* Kent. var. *Sargentii pendula,* Bean), SARGENT'S WEEPING HEMLOCK, low form with pendulous branches.—There are many named hort. vars.

5. **T. caroliniana,** Engelm. CAROLINA HEMLOCK. Tree to 70 ft., with handsome pyramidal head and often pendulous branches; branchlets reddish-brown, pubescent: lvs. ⅓–¾in. long, obtuse or only slightly emarginate at apex, dark green and glossy above, with white bands beneath: cones oblong, 1–1½ in. long, short-stalked; scales oblong, finely pubescent outside, wide-spreading at maturity. Mts., S. W. Va. to N. Ga.

6. **T. heterophylla,** Sarg. (*Abies heterophylla,* Raf. *T. Mertensiana,* Auth. not Carr.). WESTERN HEMLOCK. Tree to 200 ft., with usually pendulous branches; branchlets yellow-brown, pubescent: lvs. ¼–¾in. long, rounded at apex, dark shining green above, the stomatic bands beneath not well defined: cones oblong-oval, ¾–1 in. long; sessile; scales obovate, longer than broad, finely pubescent outside. Alaska to Ida. and Calif.

8. **PSEUDOTSUGA,** Carr. Five evergreen trees native in W. N. Amer., Japan, and China.—Branches irregularly whorled, the nearly smooth branchlets marked with oval scars where the lvs. have fallen; winter-buds acute, not resinous: lvs. linear, flattened, more or less 2-ranked, grooved above, with white bands beneath on each side of the prominent midrib: fls. solitary, the staminate axillary, with numerous anthers, their connectives ending in short spurs; pistillate fls. terminal, of spirally arranged ovate scales shorter than bracts: cones ovate-oblong, pendulous, the scales persistent; bracts longer than scales, with midrib produced into rigid awn and pointed lobe on each side; seeds winged. (Pseudotsu-ga: *false tsuga.*)

P. taxifolia, Britt. (*Abies taxifolia,* Poir. *Pinus taxifolia,* Lamb. not Salisb. *Abies mucronata,* Raf. *Pseudotsuga Douglasii,* Carr. *P. mucronata,* Sudw.). DOUGLAS FIR. Tree to 200 ft. or more, with dark red-brown bark and horizontal branches with pendulous branchlets: lvs. ¾–1¼ in. long, obtuse: staminate catkins orange, pistillate reddish: cones 2–4 in. long, the bracts much-exserted. B. C. to N. Mex. and Colo. Var. **glauca,** Schneid. (*P. Douglasii* var. *glauca,* Mayr), is the Rocky Mt. form, with shorter bluish-green lvs. and cones 2 in. long.

17. TAXODIACEÆ. TAXODIUM FAMILY

About 8 genera and 15 species of resinous trees of wide distribution, often included in Pinaceæ.—Evergreen or sometimes deciduous, monœcious: lvs. spirally arranged, needle- or scale-like: staminate fls. terminal or axillary, of spirally ar-

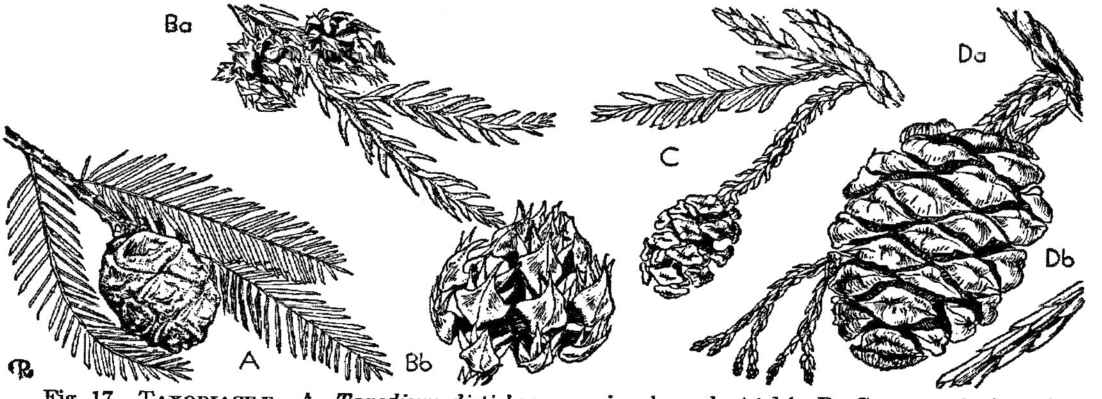

Fig. 17. TAXODIACEÆ. A, *Taxodium distichum:* coning branch, × ½. B, *Cryptomeria japonica:* Ba, coning branch, × ½; Bb, cone, × 1. C, *Sequoia sempervirens:* coning branch, × ½. D, *Sequoiadendron giganteum:* Da, coning branch, × ½; Db, portion of leafy twig, × 1.

ranged stamens having several pollen-sacs; pistillate fls. in terminal cones, of many scales bearing 2–9 ovules: cones woody, with thickened wide-spreading scales without distinct bracts; seeds with small wing-like borders.

A. Linear lvs., when present, scattered, 2½ in. or less long.
  B. Cone-scales peltate, standing like shields on the cone.
    C. Staminate fls. in drooping panicles: scales of cone with 2 seeds: foliage deciduous.......1. TAXODIUM
    CC. Staminate fls. solitary: scales of cone with 2–9 seeds: foliage persistent.
      D. Lvs. of two kinds, the linear ones spreading in 2 ranks.......2. SEQUOIA
      DD. Lvs. all scale-like, appressed.......3. SEQUOIADENDRON
  BB. Cone-scales flattened and imbricated.
    C. Lvs. keeled on both sides.......4. CRYPTOMERIA
    CC. Lvs. flat.......5. CUNNINGHAMIA
AA. Linear lvs. in whorls, 3–6 in. long.......6. SCIADOPITYS

1. **TAXODIUM,** Rich. Trees, of 3 species in E. N. Amer. and Mex.—Bark furrowed and scaly; branchlets deciduous: lvs. alternate, subulate or flat: staminate fls. catkin-like, in terminal drooping panicles, consisting of spirally arranged anthers; pistillate fls. solitary or in pairs at ends of branchlets of previous year, of imbricated scales bearing 2 erect ovules inside at base: cones globose, short-stalked, of woody peltate scales enlarged at apex into an irregularly 4-sided often mucronate disk; seeds winged. (Taxo-dium: from resemblance of lvs. to taxus.)

A. Lvs. linear, spreading in 2 ranks.......1. *T. distichum*
AA. Lvs. subulate, appressed.......2. *T. ascendens*

1. **T. distichum,** Rich. (*Cupressus disticha,* L.). BALD CYPRESS. Deciduous tree to 150 ft., with trunk attaining 12 ft. diam. and light cinnamon-brown bark, forming knees or projections from the roots when growing in swampy land; branches spreading, becoming slightly pendulous: lvs. linear-lanceolate, 2-ranked, ½–¾in. long, acute, thin and light green: staminate panicles 4–5 in. long, purplish: cones rugose, about 1 in. diam., without mucros. Del. to Fla. and La.

2. **T. ascendens,** Brongn. (*T. distichum* var. *imbricarium,* Croom). POND CYPRESS. Differs from *T. distichum* in smaller stature, upright branchlets, and subulate appressed lvs. less than ½in. long. Va. to Fla. and Ala.

2. **SEQUOIA,** Endl. One evergreen tree native in W. N. Amer., attaining great size.—Bark red, thick and fibrous; winter-buds with imbricated scales: lvs. alternate, linear, subulate or scale-like, of two kinds: fls. small, solitary; staminate terminal in axils of upper lvs., of numerous spirally arranged stamens; pistillate fls. terminal, composed of 15–20 spirally arranged scales each with 3–7 erect ovules at base: cones woody, pendulous, persistent, the scales widened into a thickened disk which is depressed in center; wings narrower than seed. (Sequo-ia: named for Sequoyah, about 1770–1843, a Cherokee half-breed of Ga.)

S. sempervirens, Endl. (*Taxodium sempervirens,* Lamb.). REDWOOD. Tree to 340 ft., with trunk 10–25 ft. diam., clothed with branches to base or in mature specimens clear of branches for 100 ft., buttressed at base; bark 6–12 in. thick: lvs. of lateral shoots linear, ½–1 in. long, usually with rigid points, spreading in 2 ranks, dark green and shining above, glaucous below: cones oval, ¾–1 in. long and ½in. across, maturing the first autumn. N. and Cent. Coast Ranges of S. Ore. to Cent. Calif.

3. **SEQUOIADENDRON,** Buchholz. One California evergreen tree, separated from Sequoia by the lvs. all scale-like and appressed, naked winter-buds, cones maturing the second year, of 25–40 scales, wings broader than seed. (Sequoiaden-dron: *sequoia* and *tree.*)

S. giganteum, Buchholz (*Wellingtonia gigantea,* Lindl. *Sequoia gigantea,* Decne. *S. Washingtonia,* Sudw. *S. Wellingtonia,* Seem.). GIANT SEQUOIA. CALIFORNIA BIG-TREE. Tree to 300 ft. or more, with a trunk 10–30 ft. or more diam., in age usually free of branches for considerable distance, much enlarged and buttressed at base; bark 1–2 ft. thick; branches pendulous, cord-like: lvs. scale-like, ⅛–½in. long, sharp-pointed, adherent to and densely clothing the st.: cones ovoid, 2–3½ in. long and 1½–2 in. broad, maturing the second summer, dark reddish-brown. Western slopes of Sierra Nevada, Calif.

4. **CRYPTOMERIA,** D. Don. One evergreen pyramidal tree with a straight slender trunk, native in Japan and China.—Branches whorled and spreading; bark reddish-brown: lvs. spirally arranged, linear-subulate, acute, decurrent at base,

slightly curved: staminate fls. axillary, in short terminal racemes, yellow, of numerous spirally arranged anthers; pistillate fls. terminal and solitary, each scale with 4–5 erect ovules: cones globose, with 20–30 thick wedge-shaped scales with pointed processes at apex and the adnate bracts with recurved points; seeds narrowly winged. (Cryptome-ria: Greek for *hidden* and *part;* meaning obscure.)

C. japonica, D. Don (*Cupressus japonica,* L. f.). To 125 ft.: lvs. ½–1 in. long, bluntly keeled on the dorsal and sharply keeled on the ventral side, bluish-green: cones reddish-brown, ¾–1 in. across.—Runs into many vars., the commonest in cult. being var. **Lobbii,** Carr. (named for Wm. Lobb, collector for Veitch), of more compact habit and more appressed dark green lvs.; var. **elegans,** Mast., a low form with pendulous branchlets and longer lvs. which turn bronzy-red in autumn; var. **nana,** Carr., dwarf and procumbent densely branched form.

5. **CUNNINGHAMIA,** R. Br. China-Fir. Two evergreen trees from China and Formosa.—Branches whorled and spreading: lvs. rigid, densely spirally arranged and 2-rowed in direction, flattened: fls. in small terminal clusters; staminate fls. oblong, of numerous spirally crowded stamens; pistillate fls. globose, the scales with 3 pendulous ovules: cones roundish-ovate, with leathery serrate and pointed scales; seeds narrowly winged. (Cunningham-ia: for James Cunningham, who discovered the tree in 1702.)

C. lanceolata, Hook. (*Pinus lanceolata,* Lamb. *C. sinensis,* R. Br.). Tree to 80 ft.: lvs. linear-lanceolate, 1½–2½ in. long, sharp-pointed, with a broad decurrent base, finely serrate, with 2 broad whitish bands beneath: cones 1–2 in. long. China.

6. **SCIADOPITYS,** Sieb. & Zucc. One Japanese evergreen tree of narrow pyramidal habit and dense growth.—Lvs. of two kinds, one small, scale-like and scattered but crowded at the ends of the branchlets and bearing in their axils whorls of linear flat lvs. furrowed on each side: staminate fls. in dense clusters at ends of shoots, composed of spirally arranged anthers; pistillate fls. solitary at ends of shoots, of numerous spirally arranged scales bearing 7–9 ovules and subtended by a small bract: cones oblong-ovate, woody, bracts adnate to the thick orbicular scales; seeds with narrow wing. (Sciadop-itys: Greek for *umbrella* and *pine.*)

S. verticillata, Sieb. & Zucc. (*Taxus verticillata,* Thunb.). Umbrella-Pine. To 120 ft.; bark gray to grayish-brown, separating in thin shreds; scale-like lvs. ⅙in. long, dark brown; conspicuous lvs. 3–6 in. long and ⅛in. wide, obtuse and emarginate, dark green and glossy above, with 2 white bands beneath: cones 3–5 in. long. Cent. Japan.

18. CUPRESSACEÆ. CYPRESS FAMILY

Resinous trees or shrubs, furnishing ornamental subjects and valuable timber; about 15 genera and 125 species of wide distribution. Monœcious or diœcious: lvs. opposite or whorled, usually scale-like and decurrent, rarely linear: fls. small, terminal or axillary; stamens with short filaments and several pollen-sacs: cones woody or leathery or sometimes berry-like, with 1 to many erect ovules at base of scales.

A. Fr. a woody dehiscent cone.
 B. Scales of cone peltate.
  C. Seeds many under each scale: branchlets usually cylindrical or 4-winged.....1. Cupressus
  CC. Seeds 2 under each scale: branchlets flattened........................2. Chamæcyparis
 BB. Scales of cone flattened and imbricate.
  C. Seeds 3–5 under each cone-scale..3. Thujopsis
  CC. Seeds 2 under each scale.
   D. Number of cone-scales 4 or 6...4. Libocedrus
   DD. Number of cone-scales 8–12 (sometimes 6)..............................5. Thuja
AA. Fr. berry-like and indehiscent..6. Juniperus

1. **CUPRESSUS,** L. Cypress. Evergreen trees or rarely shrubs, of more than 20 species in Pacific N. Amer. and Mex., S. E. Eu. to China, planted in warm regions. —Bark separating into long rather persistent shred-like plates or exfoliating annually in thin curling non-fibrous plates; branchlets cylindrical or 4-winged, rarely compressed: lvs. small and scale-like, appressed, minutely denticulate, the juvenile lvs. needle-shaped and spreading: fls. minute, terminal, solitary, the sexes on separate branches; staminate fls. oblong, of 6–12 decussate stamens, yellow; pistillate

fls. subglobose, the scales with numerous erect ovules: cones nearly globular, ripening the second year, with peltate scales and winged seeds. (Cupres-sus: classical name.)—Of the native species in cult., *C. macrocarpa* has been largely destroyed in recent years by a canker-producing fungus and is being replaced by more immune species.

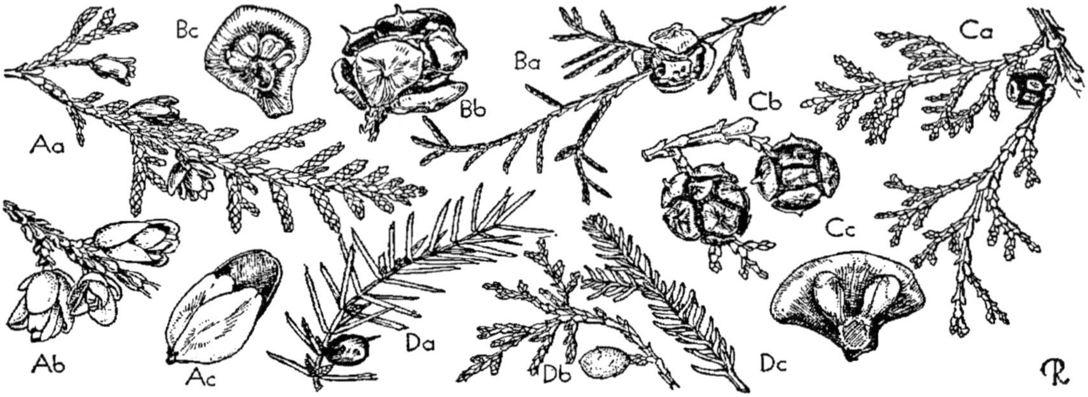

Fig. 18. Cupressaceæ. A, *Thuja occidentalis:* Aa, coning branch, × ½; Ab, cones, × 1; Ac, two-seeded cone-scale, × 2. B, *Cupressus macrocarpa:* Ba, coning branch, × ½; Bb, cone, × 1; Bc, four-seeded cone-scale, × 2. C, *Chamæcyparis pisifera:* Ca, coning branch, × ½; Cb, cones, × 1; Cc, two-seeded cone-scale, × 2. Da, *Juniperus rigida*, coning branch, × ½; Db, *Juniperus virginiana*, coning branch, × ½; Dc, *Juniperus communis*, juvenile foliage, × ½.

A. Lvs. with conspicuous usually resinous pit on the back.
  B. Branchlets compressed, forming flat sprays; bark of trunk rough and fibrous, not exfoliating .... 1. *C. Macnabiana*
  BB. Branchlets not thus compressed.
    C. Bark of mature trunk rough, fissured, gray-brown, not exfoliating .... 2. *C. arizonica*
    CC. Bark of mature trunk smooth, mahogany-brown, exfoliating annually .... 3. *C. glabra*
AA. Lvs. with obscure or closed pit on the back.
  B. Trees with pendulous branchlets.
    C. Branchlets much flattened: cones ⅓–½in. across: lvs. light green .... 4. *C. funebris*
    CC. Branchlets slightly or scarcely flattened: cones ½–¾in. across.
      D. Cones glaucous before maturity: lvs. acute, glaucous-green .... 5. *C. lusitanica*
      DD. Cones not glaucous: lvs. obtusish, bright or bluish-green .... 6. *C. Duclouxiana*
  BB. Trees with erect or stiff branchlets.
    C. Trunks with a cherry-red or mahogany-brown smooth exfoliating bark.
      D. Foliage bright to dull green but not glaucous: staminate cones with 10–14 scales .... 7. *C. Forbesii*
      DD. Foliage blue-green or sometimes glaucous: staminate cones with 14–18 scales .... 8. *C. guadalupensis*
    CC. Trunks with fibrous non-exfoliating bark and not cherry-red nor mahogany-brown.
      D. Branchlets rather stout and harsh, about 1/16in. thick: central scales of staminate cones with 6–10 pollen-sacs; pistillate cones mainly longer than broad .... 9. *C. macrocarpa*
      DD. Branchlets thinner, not harsh: pollen-sacs 4–6; pistillate cones nearly spherical.
        E. Pistillate cones ⅘–1⅕ in. across, with 8–14 scales: lvs. obtuse, dark green .... 10. *C. sempervirens*
        EE. Pistillate cones ½–¾in. across, with 6–10 scales: lvs. acutish, light green .... 11. *C. Goveniana*

1. **C. Macnabiana**, Murr. Shrub or small tree to 20 ft. or more, with thin dark reddish-brown bark and dense pyramidal head: lvs. obtuse, thickened at apex, conspicuously resinous-glandular on back, dark green or glaucous: cones ½–¾in. across, dark red-brown, often glaucous, with usually 6 scales with prominent conical and curved bosses on back. (Bears the name of James McNab, 1810–1878, English gardener.) Calif., S. Ore.—There is a kind with golden-tipped branchlets.

2. **C. arizonica**, Greene (*C. arizonica* var. *bonita*, Lemm.). Rough-barked Arizona Cypress. A small or larger tree to 70 ft., the bark brownish-gray and persistent except in saplings, rough; crown narrow-pyramidal or broad and flat: lvs. acute, usually conspicuously glandular on back, very glaucous when young: cones ¾–1 in. across; scales 6–8, with stout pointed often curved bosses; seeds rarely glaucous. Ariz. to New Mex. and N. Mex.—Rare in cult. and much material so grown is *C. glabra*.

3. **C. glabra**, Sudw. Smooth Arizona Cypress. Tree 20–50 ft., the bark smooth,

cherry-red, exfoliating annually; crown dense or openly branched: lvs. acute, keeled, glandular on back, grayish: cones to 1⅓ in. across; scales 6–10; seeds usually glaucous. Ariz.—Usually grown as *C. arizonica*.

4. **C. funebris,** Endl. MOURNING CYPRESS. Tree to 60 ft., with smooth brown bark and wide-spreading pendulous branches and flattened branchlets in the same plane: lvs. appressed or spreading at apex, acute, light green, not glandular: cones ⅓–½in. across, with 8 scales with a short-pointed boss. China.

5. **C. lusitanica,** Mill. PORTUGUESE CYPRESS. Tree to 50 ft., with reddish-brown bark and irregularly ramified, slightly compressed, pendulous branchlets: lvs. appressed, slightly free at tips, acute, glaucous: cones about ½in. across, covered with glaucous bloom, with 6–8 scales with elongated, pointed and usually hooked boss. Mex. Var. **Benthamii,** Carr., has the branchlets pinnately and regularly ramified in one plane (named for Geo. Bentham, page 39). Var. **Knightiana,** Rehd. (*C. Knightiana*, Knight & Perry), is more regularly branched and has glaucous foliage.

6. **C. Duclouxiana,** Hickel (*C. torulosa*, Rehd. & Wils. not D. Don). Pyramidal tree to 150 ft., with brown bark, short horizontal branches ramified in one plane and slender drooping branchlets: lvs. appressed or slightly spreading at apex, obtusish, bright or bluish-green: cones ½–¾in. across, with 8–10 scales with short obtuse inconspicuous boss. (Named for François Ducloux, 1864–, French missionary and collector.) Himalayas.

7. **C. Forbesii,** Jepson. TECATE CYPRESS. Slender tree to 30 ft., with stiff spreading branches; bark cinnamon-brown, exfoliating: lvs. bright to dull green, obscurely or not pitted: cones globose, ⅔–1 in. across; scales 6–10, brownish, with subconical or appressed bosses. (Named for C. N. Forbes, former student of Univ. of Calif.) S. Calif.

8. **C. guadalupensis,** Wats. GUADALUPE CYPRESS. A wide-spreading tree to 40 ft. or more, with grayish-brown bark which exfoliates in cherry fashion and exposes more reddish layers beneath: lvs. acutish, glaucous, obscurely glandular on backs: cones 1–1½ in. across, subglobose; scales 8–10, very thick, strongly bossed. Guadalupe Isl., Mex.

9. **C. macrocarpa,** Hartw. (*C. Lambertiana*, Gord.). MONTEREY CYPRESS. Tree to 70 ft., with dark reddish-brown ridged bark and horizontal branches: lvs. closely appressed, swollen toward the tip, obtuse, not glandular, dark green: cones 1–1½ in. across, with 8–12 scales with short ridge-like obtuse boss on back. Peninsula of Monterey, Calif. Var. **Crippsii,** Gord., is a juvenile form with spreading sharp-pointed lvs. and rigid short silvery-tipped branchlets.

10. **C. sempervirens,** L. ITALIAN CYPRESS. Tree to 80 ft., with thin gray bark and erect or ascending branches: lvs. scale-like, closely appressed, obtuse, glandular on back, dark green: cones 1–1½ in. across, with 8–14 scales with short boss on back. S. Eu., W. Asia. Var. **horizontalis,** Gord. (*C. horizontalis*, Mill.), has branches horizontally spreading. Var. **stricta,** Ait. (var. *fastigiata*, Hansen), has erect branches forming a columnar head.

11. **C. Goveniana,** Gord. GOWEN CYPRESS. Shrub or small tree a few ft. high; bark fibrous, persistent: lvs. not pitted, or with closed pits, acutish, light to yellowish-green: cones subglobose or oval, ½–¾in. across; scales 6–8, with short thin-edged upwardly appressed bosses; seeds dark. (Named for James Robt. Gowen, secretary of the Royal Hort. Soc. 1845–1850.) Monterey, Calif.—Confused with *C. pygmæa*, Sarg., a taller tree of more irregular outline and darker foliage.

2. **CHAMÆCYPARIS,** Spach. FALSE-CYPRESS. Six species of evergreen trees native in N. Amer. and E. Asia.—Bark scaly or fissured; branchlets flattened: lvs. scale-like, opposite in pairs, densely clothing the branchlets, in juvenile state needle-shaped: fls. minute, terminal, the two sexes on separate branches; staminate oblong, yellow or red, of numerous decussate stamens; pistillate fls. globose, the scales with 2, rarely 5, erect ovules: cones erect, globose, maturing the first year, with 6–12 peltate scales; seeds winged. (Chamæcyp-aris: Greek for *dwarf* or *on the ground* and *cypress*.)

A. Lateral lvs. much larger than facial ones.
  B. Lvs. obtuse, not glandular: staminate fls. yellow. . . . . 1. *C. obtusa*
  BB. Lvs. acutish, with conspicuous gland on back: staminate fls. red. . . . . 2. *C. Lawsoniana*
AA. Lateral lvs. about same size as facial ones.
  B. Lvs. with a conspicuous gland on back. . . . . 3. *C. thyoides*
  BB. Lvs. without conspicuous glands.
    C. Branchlets terete or slightly flattened: lvs. dark green, without white markings below. . . . . 4. *C. nootkatensis*
    CC. Branchlets flattened: lvs. with glaucous or white markings below. . . . . 5. *C. pisifera*

1. **C. obtusa,** Sieb. & Zucc. (*Retinispora obtusa*, Sieb. & Zucc. *Cupressus obtusa*, Koch). HINOKI CYPRESS. Tree to 120 ft., with reddish-brown bark and horizontal branches with flattened frond-like pendulous branchlets: lvs. closely appressed, the lateral much longer than the facial, not glandular, obtuse, bright shining green above with whitish lines beneath: cones nearly ½in. diam., brown. Japan.—Runs into many vars. varying in color

and habit, a few of which are: **aurea,** Beissn., lvs. golden-yellow when young; **compacta,** Hartwig & Ruempl., broad-conical dwarf form; **Crippsii,** Rehd., lvs. pale yellow; **filicoides,** Hartwig & Ruempl., branches short, densely frond-like; **gracilis,** Rehd., pyramidal form with dark green foliage; **lycopodioides,** Carr., low form with spreading rigid branches and thick nearly terete branchlets; **magnifica,** Beissn., vigorous form with shining bright green lvs.; **nana,** Carr., low spreading form; **Sanderi,** Bailey (forma *Sanderi*, Rehd. var. *ericoides*, Boehmer. *Juniperus* and *Retinispora Sanderi*, Sander), a juvenile form of low subglobose habit with bluish-gray linear lvs.; **tetragona,** Hornibr., dwarf, branches somewhat 4-angled.

2. C. **Lawsoniana,** Parl. (*Cupressus Lawsoniana*, Murr.). Lawson Cypress. Tree to 200 ft., with reddish-brown bark and horizontally spreading usually pendulous branches with flattened frond-like branchlets: lvs. closely appressed, the lateral much longer than the facial lvs., acute or acutish, with conspicuous gland on back, bright green marked below with indistinct white streaks: staminate fls. bright red: cones about ⅓in. diam., red-brown and often glaucous. (Named for Chas. Lawson, page 46.) S. W. Ore. to N. W. Calif.—There are numerous garden vars., a few being: **Allumii,** Beissn., Scarab Cypress, columnar very glaucous form; **erecta,** Sudw., dense columnar bright green form; **pendula,** Beissn., branchlets drooping; **Stewartii,** Hort., young shoots with deep yellow foliage; **Wisselii,** Hort., columnar form with glaucous foliage.

3. C. **thyoides,** BSP. (*C. sphæroidea*, Spach. *Cupressus thyoides*, L.). White-Cedar. Tree to 80 ft., with reddish-brown bark and flattened slender spreading branchlets: lvs. closely imbricated or spreading at apex on leading shoots, acute, keeled, with conspicuous gland on back, glaucous or light green: cones ¼in. diam., bluish-purple with glaucous bloom. Swamps, Me. to Fla. and Miss. Var. **andelyensis,** Schneid. (*C. leptoclada*, Hochst.), upright form with loosely appressed lanceolate lvs.

4. C. **nootkatensis,** Spach (*Cupressus nootkatensis*, Lamb. *Thujopsis borealis*, Hort.). Nootka Cypress. Tree to 120 ft., with brownish-gray bark and terete or slightly flattened pendulous branchlets: lvs. densely imbricate or spreading at apex on leading shoot, acute, mostly without glands, dark green: cones nearly ½in. diam., dark red-brown with glaucous bloom. Alaska to Ore.; first described from specimens collected at Nootka Sound. Var. **glauca,** Beissn., has very glaucous foliage.

5. C. **pisifera,** Sieb. & Zucc. (*Cupressus pisifera*, Koch. *Retinispora pisifera*, Sieb. & Zucc.). Sawara Cypress. Tree to 150 ft., with red-brown bark and flattened somewhat pendulous branchlets: lvs. slightly spreading, with mucronate tips, obscurely glandular, dark green and shining above and with glaucous or white lines below: cones ¼–⅓in. diam., brown. Japan.—Runs into many vars., those most commonly cult. being: **aurea,** Carr., foliage golden-yellow; **filifera,** Hartwig & Ruempl. (*Retinispora filifera*, Gord.), with slender thread-like gracefully pendulous branches; **plumosa,** Otto (*Retinispora plumosa*, Veitch), of dense conical habit, the almost erect branches with slender leathery branchlets, and light green foliage or tipped with yellow in the form *lutescens*; **squarrosa,** Beissn. & Hochst. (*Retinispora squarrosa*, Sieb. & Zucc.), of densely branched habit, with spreading feathery branchlets and spreading lvs. glaucous above and silvery below.

3. **THUJOPSIS,** Sieb. & Zucc. One evergreen tree of dense broad pyramidal habit, native in Cent. Japan.—Branchlets much broadened and frond-like, arranged in horizontal planes: lvs. opposite in pairs: staminate fls. with 6–10 decussate pairs of stamens: cones subglobose, with 6–10 woody, flattened, imbricated scales bearing 3–5 winged seeds. (Thujop-sis: *like thuja.*)

T. **dolobrata,** Sieb. & Zucc. (*Thuja dolobrata*, L. f.). Hiba Arbor-Vitæ. Tree to 50 ft. high, with branchlets to ¼in. broad: lvs. green and glossy above with broad white band below, to ¼in. long, the lateral ones spreading, ovate-lanceolate and curved, the upper and under ones appressed, obovate-oblong: cones ½–⅗in. long, the scales with prominent often curved umbo below apex.

4. **LIBOCEDRUS,** Endl. Incense-Cedar. Eight species of evergreen resinous trees native in W. N. Amer., S. Amer., New Zeal., New Caledonia, New Guinea, Formosa, and S. W. China.—Bark scaly; branches erect or spreading, with flattened frond-like branchlets: lvs. opposite in pairs, scale-like, with decurrent bases: fls. solitary, terminal, the sexes on different branchlets; staminate with 12–16 decussate stamens: cones oblong, with 4 or rarely 6 woody flat scales, the middle pair bearing 2 long-winged seeds. (Liboced-rus: Greek *tear*, and *cedrus.*)

A. Lvs. green on both sides .... 1. *L. decurrens*
AA. Lvs. with white band beneath .... 2. *L. chilensis*

1. L. **decurrens,** Torr. (*Thuja gigantea*, Carr.). Tree 100–200 ft. high, with bright cinnamon-red bark, erect spreading branches and much flattened branchlets: lvs. with long decurrent base, adnate to the branchlets except at the acuminate tips, dark lustrous

green on both sides, the inner pair glandular on back: cones light reddish-brown, ¾–1 in. long, with 3 pairs of scales, the upper connate. Ore. to Nev. and Lower Calif.

2. **L. chilensis,** Endl. Tree to 60 ft. high: lvs. in 4 ranks, the lateral pair much larger, boat-shaped, keeled, acute and spreading at apex, with white band beneath: cones ½in. long, with 2 pairs of scales. Chile.

5. **THUJA, L.** Arbor-Vitæ. Aromatic resinous evergreen trees of 6 species in N. Amer. and E. Asia.—Bark thin and scaly; branchlets flattened, frond-like: lvs. scale-like, opposite in pairs, appressed, usually glandular on back, the juvenile lvs. needle-shaped: fls. minute, solitary, terminal, the two sexes commonly on different branchlets; staminate fls. yellow, of 6–12 decussate stamens; pistillate fls. with 8–12 scales in opposite pairs, with 2 ovules at base inside: cones ovoid-oblong, erect, the scales with thickened ridge or umbo at apex; seeds thin and winged or thick and wingless. (Thu-ja: classical name.)

A. Branchlets in vertical planes: cone-scales thick; seeds wingless.................1. *T. orientalis*
AA. Branchlets in horizontal planes. cone-scales thin; seeds winged.
B. Lvs. yellowish-green beneath, with conspicuous gland on back...............2. *T. occidentalis*
BB. Lvs. with triangular white markings beneath, not or inconspicuously glandular.
C. Apex of lvs. acute: fertile cone-scales usually 6..........................3. *T. plicata*
CC. Apex of lvs. obtuse: fertile cone-scales usually 4........................4. *T. Standishii*

1. **T. orientalis,** L. (*Biota orientalis*, Endl.). Oriental Arbor-Vitæ. Shrub or small tree to 25 ft., with thin reddish-brown bark and spreading and ascending branches: lvs. of main axes with free spreading apex, of lateral branchlets closely appressed, acute, bright green, with small gland on back: cones ½–1 in. long, with usually 6 woody scales, the upper pair sterile; seeds thick and wingless. N. China, Korea.—There are many garden vars., as: **aurea,** Dauvesse, golden-yellow in spring; **Bakeri,** Hort., foliage pale green; **beverleyensis,** Rehd., of pyramidal habit, foliage golden-yellow; **bonita,** Hort., cone-shaped form with lvs. tipped golden-yellow; **conspicua,** Berckmans, compact form, golden-yellow suffused with green; **elegantissima,** Vos, compact, bright yellow in spring; **excelsa,** Hort., dwarf pyramidal form with bright green foliage; **Sieboldii,** Laws. (var. *compacta*, Beissn. var. *nana*, Carr.), low globose form with bright green foliage; **stricta,** Loud. (*Biota orientalis* var. *pyramidalis*, Endl.), dense pyramidal bright green form; **texana glauca,** Hort., pyramidal blue-green form.

2. **T. occidentalis,** L. American Arbor-Vitæ. Tree to 60 ft., with light red-brown bark and horizontal branches ascending at end: lvs. acute or apiculate, usually conspicuously glandular, bright green above and yellowish-green beneath: cones about ½in. long, brownish-yellow, with 8–10 scales, 4 of which are fertile; seeds winged. N. S. to N. C. west to Ill.—Runs into numerous cult. vars.: **aurea,** Nelson, broad bushy form with deep yellow foliage; **Boothii,** Hort., low and compact with rather large lvs.; **Columbia,** Parsons, lvs. variegated with silver; **compacta,** Carr., dense pyramidal slow-growing form; **conica,** Hort., cone-shaped form; **Douglasii aurea,** Hort., foliage bronzy-yellow; **Douglasii pyramidalis,** Spaeth, dense pyramidal form with crowded frond-like branchlets; **Ellwangeriana,** Beissn., low pyramidal form with both scale-like and linear lvs.; **ericoides,** Hoopes, dwarf or bushy form with needle-like lvs.; **globosa,** Gord. (var. Tom Thumb), dwarf globose bright green form; **Hoveyi,** Hoopes, dwarf globose-ovoid form with light green lvs.; **lutea,** Kent (var. *elegantissima*, Hort.), pyramidal form with bright yellow foliage; **Mastersii,** Bailey (var. *plicata*, Mast.), pyramidal form with much-flattened branchlets; **nigra,** Hort., compact dark green form; **Ohlendorfii,** Beissn., bushy, with scale-like and linear lvs.; **pumila,** Beissn. (Little Gem), dwarf and dense, dark green; **recurva nana,** Hort., dwarf, with recurved branchlets; **Reidii,** Hort., dwarf broad form; **Riversii,** Beissn., of compact pyramidal habit, foliage yellowish-green; **robusta,** Carr. (var. *Wareana*, Nelson. var. *sibirica*, Hoopes), pyramidal bright green form; **Rosenthalii,** Ohlend., columnar, foliage shining dark green; **spiralis,** Hort., branchlets appearing as if spirally arranged; **umbraculifera,** Beissn., dwarf, with umbrella-like top; **Vervæneana,** Gord., branchlets bronzy in winter; **Woodwardii,** Spaeth, dense globose dark green form.

3. **T. plicata,** Donn (*T. gigantea*, Nutt. *T. Lobbii*, Hort.). Giant Arbor-Vitæ. Tree to 200 ft., with cinnamon-red bark, trunk much buttressed at base, and horizontal branches often pendulous at ends: lvs. of vigorous shoots widely spaced, ending in long points parallel to axis, of lateral branchlets acute and scarcely glandular, glossy bright green above with whitish triangular spots beneath: cones about ½in. long, with 10–12 scales of which 6 are usually fertile; seeds winged. Alaska to N. Calif. and Mont. Var. **atrovirens,** Sudw., foliage dark green.

4. **T. Standishii,** Carr. (*T. japonica*, Maxim. *Thujopsis Standishii*, Gord.). Japanese Arbor-Vitæ. Tree to 50 ft., with reddish-brown bark and spreading or ascending branches with rather thick compressed branchlets: lvs. of the main axes with rigid free points, of the lateral branchlets obtuse, bright green above with triangular white marks below, glandless: cones ⅓–½in. long, with 10–12 scales of which 4 are fertile; seeds winged. (Intro. by Fortune to the nursery of Mr. Standish in England, about 1861.) Japan.

6. **JUNIPERUS,** L. JUNIPER. Evergreen trees or shrubs of about 60 species, almost exclusively in the northern hemisphere.—Bark of most kinds thin and shredding: lvs. opposite or in whorls of 3, needle-like and spreading or scale-like and closely imbricated: diœcious or rarely monœcious; fls. minute, axillary or terminal; staminate fls. usually solitary, yellow at maturity, consisting of numerous anthers united into an ovoid or oblong catkin; pistillate fls. ovoid, greenish, minute, of several whorls of bracts, some or all bearing 1 or 2 erect ovules: fr. a succulent or fibrous berry-like or drupe-like cone formed by the union of the enlarged fl.-scales. (Junip-erus: classical name.)

A. Foliage needle-shaped and jointed to the twig, in whorls of 3: winter-buds distinct: staminate fls. axillary. (OXYCEDRUS.)
  B. Upper lf.-surface bearing 2 white bands.......... 1. *J. macrocarpa*
  BB. Upper lf.-surface bearing a single white band.
    C. Lvs. concave above, rounded or slightly keeled below.......... 2. *J. communis*
    CC. Lvs. narrowly grooved above, conspicuously keeled below.
      D. Plant a tree or large shrub, branchlets commonly pendulous: lvs. straight, spreading, rigid, ½–1 in. long: fr. ¼–⅓in. across.......... 3. *J. rigida*
      DD. Plant a low shrub to 3 ft. high: lvs. crowded and curving forward, ¼in. or less long: fr. ⅓–½in. across.......... 4. *J. conferta*

AA. Foliage scale-like or, if needle-shaped, then decurrent on the twig, opposite or in whorls of 3; distinct winter-buds lacking: staminate fls. terminal. (SABINA.)
  B. Plants erect, trees or tree-shaped shrubs at least as tall as wide.
    C. Lvs. all needle-shaped.
      D. All or most of the lvs. opposite.......... 8. *J. virginiana*
      DD. All or most of the lvs. in whorls of 3.
        E. Lf. with a conspicuous green midrib above: plants hardy and commonly cult. in the N.......... 10. *J. chinensis*
        EE. Lf. completely whitened above, the midrib not green: plants of S. W. U. S., probably enduring in the N. for a few years at most.
          F. Backs of lvs. or many of them with an extruded resin droplet.......... 5. *J. Deppeana* var. *pachyphlæa*
          FF. Backs of all or nearly all lvs. without an extruded resin droplet.......... 6. *J. californica*
    CC. Lvs., at least some of them, scale-like.
      D. Margins of scale-lvs. minutely denticulate.
        E. Scale-lvs. mostly opposite, many with an extruded resin droplet on the back: bark of trunk red-brown, broken into conspicuous rectangular plates.......... 5. *J. Deppeana* var. *pachyphlæa*
        EE. Scale-lvs. mostly in whorls of 3, without an extruded resin droplet on the back: bark ash-gray, separating in loose scales.......... 6. *J. californica*
      DD. Margins of scale-lvs. entire.
        E. Scale-lvs. obtuse; needle-shaped lvs. all or mostly in whorls of 3: fr. brown or purplish-brown beneath the bloom, ¼in. or more across at maturity.......... 10. *J. chinensis*
        EE. Scale-lvs. acute; needle-shaped lvs. mostly opposite, in whorls of 3 on vigorous twigs only: fr. blue-black at maturity, less than ¼in. across.
          F. Needle-shaped lvs. about 1/12 in. long: fr. ¼–½in. long, 4–9-seeded.......... 7. *J. excelsa*
          FF. Needle-shaped lvs. ⅙–¼in. long: fr. ⅛–¼in. long, 1–3-seeded.
            G. Mature scale-lvs. overlapping the ones directly above; dorsal gland shorter than the distance from the gland to the lf.-tip.......... 8. *J. virginiana*
            GG. Mature scale-lvs. rarely overlapping and then only slightly; dorsal gland equalling or exceeding the distance from the gland to the lf.-tip.......... 9. *J. scopulorum*
  BB. Plants shrubby, usually broader than high, not tree-like in outline.
    C. Crushed lvs. with strong disagreeable odor.......... 11. *J. Sabina*
    CC. Crushed lvs. without disagreeable "Sabina" odor.
      D. Lvs. all needle-shaped and all or mostly all in 3's.
        E. Branches irregularly ascending, forming an irregular and picturesque shrub: lvs. intensely glaucous.......... 13. *J. squamata* var. *Meyeri*
        EE. Branches spreading, the lower ones prostrate; plants much wider than high.
          F. Twigs conspicuously glaucous: lvs. with 2 conspicuous decurrent white lines running downward from their bases: seeds 2–6: in common cult.......... 10. *J. chinensis* var. *procumbens*
          FF. Twigs green or slightly glaucous: decurrent white lines lacking or weakly developed: seed solitary: rare in cult.......... 13. *J. squamata*
      DD. Lvs. scale-like, or scale-like and needle-like, or if all needle-like then most or many of them opposite.
        E. Branches of mature plants all long, slender and prostrate for much of their length, forming low wide-spreading ground-covers, never building up into mound-like shrubs.
          F. Scale-lvs. obtuse; needle-lvs. conspicuously both opposite and in whorls of 3.......... 10. *J. chinensis* var. *Sargentii*

FF. Scale-lvs. acute to apiculate; needle-lvs. mostly opposite, in whorls of 3 on vigorous twigs only........................12. *J. horizontalis*

EE. Branches variously arranged, building up into mound-like or spreading shrubs, at most with only the lowest branches resting on the soil.

F. The lvs. all needle-shaped.

G. Winter color rosy-violet; depressed shrub to about 18 in. high; summer color gray-green..............................12. *J. horizontalis* var. *plumosa*

GG. Winter color differing little from summer color, not rosy-violet; habit various.

H. Arrangement of lvs. in whorls of 3 on many twigs..........10. *J. chinensis* var. *Sargentii*

HH. Arrangement of lvs. almost all opposite.

I. Odor of crushed lvs. moderate "Sabina": plants rarely to 3 ft. high; branches arching gracefully outward, the twigs often disposed in 2 rows to form a V-shaped trough..11. *J. Sabina* var. *tamariscifolia*

II. Odor of crushed lvs. not "Sabina": plants to 6 ft. high; branches stout and stiff, spreading irregularly or ascending; twigs on some vigorous branchlets or branch-tips usually disposed in 3 definite planes............. 8. *J. virginiana* var. *tripartita*

FF. The lvs. scale-like, or some of them so.

G. Lower branches stout, spreading horizontally above the ground but not resting upon it; twigs of scale-lvs. cord-like and little-branched..............................10. *J. chinensis* var. *Parsonsii* & *alba*

GG. Lower branches ascending or arching outward well above the ground; plants commonly widest at or above the middle.

H. Twigs cord-like, in irregular mop-like clusters; plants taller than wide, soon more than 5 ft. high, the branches ascending or irregularly disposed..................10. *J. chinensis* var. *torulosa*

HH. Twigs not cord-like; plants low, wider than tall, usually about 4 ft. high.

I. Outline globose or depressed-globose, compact.

J. Scale-lvs. acute.. 8. *J. virginiana* var. *globosa*

JJ. Scale-lvs. obtuse.......................................10. *J. chinensis* var. *globosa*

II. Outline irregular; branches spreading or arching outward, forming shrubs much wider than high.

J. Height commonly to 4 ft.; branches slightly arching, graceful...10. *J. chinensis* var. *Pfitzeriana*

JJ. Height rarely to 3 ft.; branches stouter and stiffer, the plant outline lower and less graceful.......... 8. *J. virginiana* var. *Kosteri*

1. **J. macrocarpa,** Sibth. & Smith. PLUM JUNIPER. Shrub or small tree to 15 ft.: lvs. all needle-like, in whorls of 3, not decurrent, spreading, with 2 white bands above: fr. usually dark brown and glaucous, ½in. across, 3-seeded. Medit. region.—Occasionally grown in mild climates.

2. **J. communis,** L. COMMON JUNIPER. Typically a tree to 20 ft. and more, in some vars. a shrub: lvs. all needle-like, in whorls of 3 and not decurrent, spreading, with a single broad white band above, bluntly keeled below: fr. dark blue and glaucous, mostly ½–⅓in. across, 3-seeded. Eu., Asia, N. Amer.—The kinds most common in cult. are: var. **hispanica,** Endl. (var. *hibernica*, Gord. var. *stricta*, Carr. var. *Ashfordii*, Hottes), IRISH JUNIPER, very narrow columnar form with erect twigs and deep green lvs.; var. **suecica,** Ait. (*J. suecica*, Mill.), SWEDISH JUNIPER, similar to the preceding but a broader column with nodding twigs; var. **cracovia,** Carr., POLISH JUNIPER, similar to the above vars. but becoming almost pyramidal with age, the lvs. yellow-green and less glossy; var. **oblongo-pendula** Sudw. (*J. communis oblonga pendula*, Loud.), loosely columnar with drooping twigs; var. **depressa,** Pursh (*J. canadensis*, Burgsd.), broad spreading shrub with branches ascending to about 4 ft.; var. **aureo-spica,** Rehd., like the preceding but with new growth golden-yellow; var. **saxatilis,** Pall. (var. *montana*, Ait. *J. nana*, Willd. *J. alpina*, S. F. Gray), branches prostrate or nearly so, lvs. commonly incurved.

3. **J. rigida,** Sieb. & Zucc. NEEDLE JUNIPER. Shrub or most commonly an erect tree to 35 ft.: lvs. all needle-like and in whorls of 3, not decurrent, very sharp, deeply and narrowly grooved above with a single narrow white band: fr. ¼–⅓in. across, glaucous, eventually brownish-black and somewhat glossy, 3-seeded. Japan, Korea, N. China.

4. **J. conferta,** Parl. (*J. litoralis*, Maxim.). SHORE JUNIPER. Low mat-forming shrub to 2 ft.: lvs. all needle-like, not decurrent, in whorls of 3, ⅓–½in. long, with a single white line above: fr. spherical, ⅓–½in. across, purplish-brown to black, 3-seeded. Japan, Saghalin.

5. **J. Deppeana,** Steud. Small tree to 30 ft., bark thick, red-brown, broken into conspicuous rectangular plates: lvs. of two kinds, the adult scale-like and denticulate on the margins: fr. about ½in. across, light brown with fibrous flesh, seeds mostly 3–4. (For F. Deppe, who collected in Mex. in 1828.) Mex.—Known in American gardens only through its var. **pachyphlœa,** Martinez (*J. pachyphlœa,* Torr.), ALLIGATOR JUNIPER, differing in minor details from *J. Deppeana,* occasionally seen in cult. and then as a short-lived pyramidal small tree with lvs. all needle-like and decurrent, intensely blue-white, spreading, about ¼in. long, commonly each with an extruded resin droplet on the back; Ariz., N. Mex., Tex.

6. **J. californica,** Carr. Shrub or shrubby tree to 30 ft.: needle-shaped lvs. often intensely glaucous; twigs of adult lvs. stout, the lvs. yellow-green, backs thickened and often conspicuously pitted, margins denticulate: fr. reddish-brown, fibrous, to ½in. across, seeds mostly 1–2. Desert slopes of Calif. and Lower Calif. and occasionally cult. in adjacent regions.

7. **J. excelsa,** Bieb. GREEK JUNIPER. Pyramidal tree to 60 ft.; twigs slender, about 1/32in. thick: lvs. of two kinds, the juvenile ones mostly opposite, to 1/12in. long, the scale-lvs. appressed and slightly shorter: fr. resinous, blue-black when ripe, ¼–½in. across, seeds 4–9. Greece, Asia Minor.—Both *J. excelsa* and its intensely glaucous var. *stricta,* Gord., are scarcely known in American cult., the plant grown as var. *stricta* in gardens being the much coarser and hardier *J. chinensis* var. *pyramidalis.*

8. **J. virginiana,** L. RED-CEDAR. Tree to 100 ft.: lvs. of two kinds, the juvenile needle-shaped, opposite, ⅛–¼in. long, the adult scale-like, opposite, acute, appressed, about 1/12in. long: fr. blue-black, glaucous, ⅛–¼in. long, 1–3-seeded. N. Amer. east of the Rocky Mts.—Of the many forms in cult. the commonest tree-like kinds are: var. **glauca,** Carr., with glaucous lvs.; var. **Burkii,** Bailey, dense narrow column, three and a half times as high as wide, lvs. intensely blue-white; var. **pendula,** Lawson, with branchlets pendulous; var. **Hillii,** Cornman (*J. virginiana pyramidiformis Hillii,* D. Hill), dense narrow pyramid, lvs. mostly needle-like, gray-green, becoming plum-colored in winter sun; var. **elegantissima,** Hochst., some twig-tips bright yellow; var. **Canærtii,** Rehd. (*J. virginiana Canærtii,* Sénécl.), compact pyramidal small tree, lvs. rich green, fr. usually abundant and showy; var. **Schottii,** Gord. (*J. virginiana Schottii,* R. Smith), similar to the preceding but slower growing, lvs. bright yellow-green. Shrubby kinds are: var. **globosa,** Rehd. (*J. virginiana globosa,* Beissn.), compact globose shrub to about 3 ft.; var. **Kosteri,** Beissn., low spreading shrub rarely to 3 ft., similar in aspect to *J. chinensis* var. *Pfitzeriana* but lower-growing, more wide-spreading, with stiffer branches and less graceful aspect; var. **tripartita,** Sénécl., dense spreading shrub to 5 ft. and twice or more as wide, branches stout, spreading irregularly, lvs. mostly needle-like, light green, glaucous above.

9. **J. scopulorum,** Sarg. ROCKY MOUNTAIN JUNIPER. Tree to 35 ft.: lvs. of two kinds, the juvenile needle-shaped and sharp, ⅙–¼in. long, the adult scale-like, opposite, acute, about 1/12in. long, appressed: fr. dark purplish-brown or blue-black, glaucous, about ¼in. across, often bilobed, commonly 2-seeded. Rocky Mts. of W. N. Amer.—Scarcely distinguishable from its eastern counterpart, *J. virginiana.* Known in cult. largely through numerous named but undescribed seedling variants. The best known of these is var. **Hillii,** D. Hill, one of the many erect intensely glaucous forms.

10. **J. chinensis,** L. (*J. sphærica,* Hort. *J. chinensis* var. *fœmina,* Gord.). CHINESE JUNIPER. Tree to 60 ft. or sometimes shrubby: lvs. of two kinds, the juvenile needle-shaped, decurrent, to ½in. long, mostly in 3's, the adult scale-like, opposite, obtuse and appressed: fr. brownish-violet, bloomy, ¼–⅓in. across, 2–5-seeded. China.—Many clones and habit forms are cult. Tree-like kinds with definite trunk, erect terminals and main branch-tips, usually with both kinds of lvs. are: var. **columnaris,** Hottes, narrowly columnar, three times as high as wide, with mostly needle-like lvs.; var. **mascula,** Rehd. (*J. chinensis mascula,* Carr. *J. chinensis mas,* Gord. *J. Fortunei,* Hort.), somewhat broader, rarely twice as high as wide, often conspicuously staminate; var. **Keteleeri,** Cornman (*J. chinensis Keteleeri,* Beissn. *J. virginiana Keteleeri,* Rehd.), conspicuously broad-pyramidal tree, fr. large, ½in. across, globular, glaucous, blue-black. Tree-like kinds with terminals and main branch-tips slanting, nodding or pendulous are: var. **oblonga,** Bailey (*J. chinensis oblonga,* Slavin. *J. chinensis sylvestris,* Hort.), with lvs. mostly needle-like, spreading, yellow-green, scale-like on the nodding twig-tips only; var. **arbuscula,** Cornman (*J. media* var. *arbuscula,* van Melle. *J. chinensis Smithii,* Slavin not Loud. *J. virginiana Smithii,* Hort.), bushy dense pyramid with short trunk and numerous erect main branches, lvs. mostly scale-like, fr. bilobed at apex; var. **torulosa,** Eastw., tree-like and irregular, twigs cord-like, aggregated in mop-like clusters, bright rich green. Conical small trees without a main trunk are: var. **pyramidalis,** Rehd. (*J. japonica pyramidalis,* Carr.), dense prickly plant, lvs. all needle-like and glaucous, the "Spiny Greek" juniper of American gardens; var. **densa,** Cornman, similar but less regular because the upper twigs bear scale-like lvs.; the variegated counterpart var. **variegata,** Gord. (*J. chinensis albo-variegata,* Fort. *J. sinensis variegata,* Maxwell), with tips of some twigs creamy-white. Several of the taller-growing shrubby kinds are: var. **Pfitzeriana,** Mast. (*J. chinensis Pfitzeriana,* Spaeth), broad-spreading shrub usually to 5 ft., branches long,

spreading almost horizontally, nodding, much planted and very adaptable; var. **globosa,** Hornibr., globose or depressed-globose, to 5 ft. wide and nearly as high. The best-known mat-forming or mound-like kinds are: var. **Parsonsii,** Hornibr., primary branches stout, spreading horizontally above the ground but not resting upon it, twigs of scale-like lvs. cord-like and little-branched; the variegated counterpart is var. **alba,** Rehd., with some twig-tips creamy-white; var. **Sargentii,** Henry, SARGENT JUNIPER, low, spreading, to about 2 ft. high, forming a broad mat with procumbent sts., needle-like lvs. opposite on many conspicuous twigs, scale-lvs. often conspicuous; Saghalin, N. Japan; var. **procumbens,** Endl. (*J. procumbens*, Miq.), wide-spreading mound-like shrub to 2½ ft., lvs. all needle-shaped, bluish, in whorls of 3, each with 2 white blotches decurrent from the lf. bases. The names *J. chinensis* var. *japonica* and *J. japonica* have been applied to numerous low-growing clones. The proper application of these names is undeterminable.

11. **J. Sabina,** L. (*J. Sabina* var. *cupressifo`ia*, Ait.). SAVIN. Spreading vase-shaped shrub eventually to 6 ft. or more, in erect variants tree-like, to 25 ft.: lvs. of two kinds, the juvenile needle-shaped, opposite, acute and spreading, the adult scale-like, appressed, rich green, obtuse to acutish, of bitter taste and disagreeable odor when crushed: fr. dark brownish-purple, glaucous, about ¼in. across, pendulous on recurved pedicels, commonly 2-seeded. Mts. of Cent. and S. Eu., Asia Minor and Caucasus.—Commonly planted is var. **tamariscifolia,** Ait., broad mound-like shrub rarely 3 ft. high, branches arching horizontally, twigs often forming a V-shaped spray, lvs. needle-like, gray-green, somewhat spreading, with definite but milder odor than *J. Sabina*. Less common are: var. **variegata,** Laws., with scattered twig-tips creamy-white to yellow; var. **fastigiata,** Rehd. (*J. Sabina fastigiata*, Beissn.), a narrowly columnar dark green tree.

12. **J. horizontalis,** Moench (*J. prostrata*, Pers.). CREEPING JUNIPER. Procumbent shrub with long trailing branches: lvs. of two kinds, the juvenile needle-like, the adult scale-like, acute to apiculate, mostly opposite, green or somewhat bluish: fr. blue-black, somewhat glaucous, about ⅓in. across, on mostly recurved pedicels, seeds 1–6. N. S. to N. Y., Ill. to N. D. and Mont., Alta. and B. C.—The more common of the variants are: var. **Douglasii,** Rehd. (var. *glauca*, Hornibr.), WAUKEGAN JUNIPER, with steel-blue lvs.; var. **plumosa,** Rehd. (*J. communis depressa plumosa*, Hort.), ANDORRA JUNIPER, depressed shrub to 2 ft., branches spreading horizontally, lvs. all needle-like, gray-green, becoming rosy-violet in winter sun.

13. **J. squamata,** Lamb. Decumbent wide-spreading shrub to about 2 ft.: lvs. all needle-like, in whorls of 3, decurrent, ⅛–¼in. long, spreading or loosely appressed, usually slightly incurved: fr. reddish-brown, becoming purplish-black, ½–⅜in. long, 1-seeded. Himalayas, W. China.—Almost unknown in American gardens. More common is var. **Meyeri,** Rehd., irregular shrub with erect or ascending branches to 10 ft., lvs. intensely glaucous, becoming blue-green the second year, often fruiting abundantly.

19. TYPHACEÆ. CAT-TAIL FAMILY

A single genus of about 18 species, widespread throughout the world except south of the equator in Afr., comprising the Cat-tail Family, so named because of the dense spike-like infl. having a brown velvety appearance at time of fr. maturity; members of the family are known in classical literature as reeds and as reed mace.—Per. monœcious marsh plants, growing in wet heavy soil and often in a ft. or so of water, with creeping rootstocks and long-linear erect mostly basal lvs.: fls. unisexual, having a perianth comprised of short bristles, arranged in a dense terminal spike, the staminate fls. confined to the upper end of the spike and pistillate fls. on lower half; staminate fls. of 2–5 stamens, the filaments free or variously connate subtended by silky hairs not much exceeding anthers; pistillate fls. monocarpellate, ovary 1-celled with

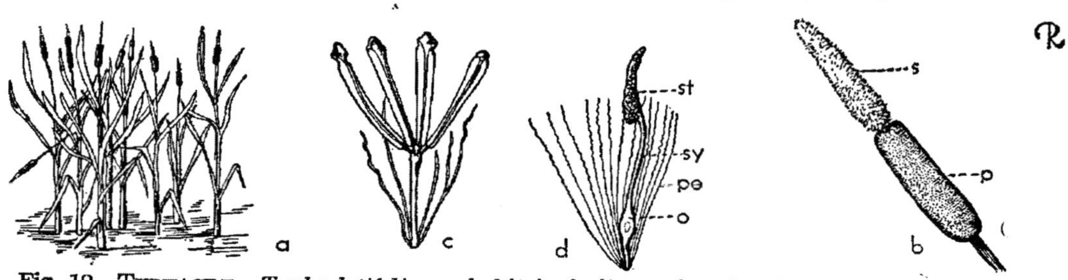

Fig. 19. TYPHACEÆ. *Typha latifolia:* a, habit in fruit, much reduced; b, spike of staminate (s) and pistillate (p) flowers, × ⅛; c, staminate flower, × 5; d, pistillate flower with perianth (pe), ovary (o), style (sy) and stigma (st), × 10.

1 suspended ovule, subtended by many long brown hairy bristles arranged in 1–3 whorls representing a perianth, style elongate and slender terminated by a narrow or ligulate stigma; sterile fls. with club-shaped-tipped and non-functional ovaries among the pistillate fls.: fr. a nutlet, dehiscing at maturity; seed with mealy endosperm.—Grown as an ornamental in aquatic gardens or shallow pools and also employed in wild-life conservation and limnological projects. The lvs. are harvested, dried, and woven into matting and chair bottoms. The dried fruiting spikes are used in floral arrangements.

TYPHA, L. Generic characters as for the family. (Ty-pha: ancient name.)

A. Staminate and pistillate parts of spike contiguous: sts. stout: lower lvs. ½–1 in. wide........1. *T. latifolia*
AA. Staminate and pistillate parts of spike separated by an interval of ¼–2 in. of exposed axis: sts. slender: lower lvs. ⅙–⅓in. wide........2. *T. angus ifolia*

1. **T. latifolia,** L. COMMON CAT-TAIL. Stout coarse leafy reeds to 6 ft. high or more: lvs. to 4 ft. long and mostly ½–1 in. wide, tapering to acute apex: spikes dark brown, the staminate and pistillate ones contiguous, each 4–12 in. long; pistillate fls. with spatulate to rhomboid stigmas; staminate fls. with pollen-grains in 4's. Marshes throughout all but northern extremities of N. Amer., Eu., Asia.

2. **T. angustifolia,** L. Similar to *T. latifolia* but with more slender sts., usually lower in height: lower lvs. rarely more than ½in. wide: spikes light brown, the staminate usually separated from pistillate but on same axis, each 4–8 in. long and more slender; pistillate fls. with linear to linear-oblong stigmas; staminate fls. with pollen-grains solitary. Eu., N. Amer., S. Amer.

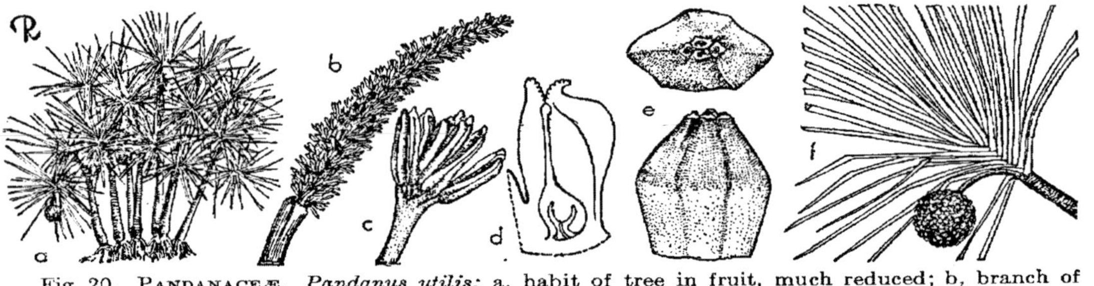

Fig. 20. PANDANACEÆ. *Pandanus utilis:* a, habit of tree in fruit, much reduced; b, branch of staminate inflorescence, × ½; c, staminate flower, × 3; d, pistillate flower, vertical section, enlarged; e, drupe, side and top views, × ½; f, fruiting branch, much reduced. (d redrawn from Engler.)

20. PANDANACEÆ. SCREW-PINE FAMILY

Three genera and about 400 species comprise the Screw-pine Family, so called because of the spiral masses of pineapple-like lvs. on the summits of the branches; they are natives in tropics of the Old World, mostly in Malaya and the Pacific isls.—Plants diœcious, more or less arboreous, sometimes climbing, mostly producing stilt-like roots above ground: lvs. long, stiff and sword-like (sometimes almost grass-like), often spine-margined: staminate and pistillate organs separate, scattered over the floral axis and not in definite orthodox fls. (parts diœcious by abortion), in axillary or terminal heads and spikes (panicles in one non-hort. genus), the leafy spadix-bracts mostly conspicuous or colored, caducous; fertile parts usually closely aggregated; perianth mostly wanting; stamens few to many, with free or connate filaments, rarely represented in fertile fls. by staminodes; ovary 1- to many-celled, with ovules solitary or several: fr. a syncarpium or aggregate, formed of the union or the close crowding of the carpels, ball-like or cone-like, often large and heavy.

PANDANUS, L. SCREW-PINE. Species probably 250; a very few are cult. for ornament after the manner of palms; they rarely fruit except in warm and trop. countries.—Shrubs or trees, the trunk sometimes prostrate but usually stiffly erect, simple or forked, with long persistent hard lvs.: fls. naked; stamens numerous on the spike; pistils densely crowded in a head or oblong spike: fr. a hard composite mass, with many detachable parts angled and straight-sided by pressure, the top conical or shouldered and more or less 6-angled. (Panda-nus: Latinized from a Malayan name.)—Cult. forms are likely to be sterile and the botanical position therefore undeterminable.

A. Lvs. very narrow and slender, ½in. or less broad.......................1. *P. pygmæus*
AA. Lvs. broad, 2 in. or more.
B. Foliage uniformly green throughout.......................2. *P. utilis*
BB. Foliage variegated.
C. Lf. margined white.......................3. *P. Veitchii*
CC. Lf. with several yellow lengthwise bands.......................4. *P. Sanderi*

1. **P. pygmæus,** Thouars. Small plant, the trunk reaching only 1–2 ft.: lvs. very narrow, 1–2 ft. long and about ⅓in broad, very long slender pointed, with small very sharp ascending spines on margin and rib beneath: fertile infl. terminal, short and surrounded by the foliage. Madagascar.—This is apparently the name of the plant grown as *P. graminifolius*.

2. **P. utilis,** Bory. Stout branching tree to 50 and 60 ft. and more, making many brace-roots: lvs. glaucous, erect, 1–3 ft. long, 3 in. broad, with many very sharp ascending reddish spines on margins and rib beneath: syncarp solitary, pendulous, long-peduncled, 6–8 in. diam., comprising about 100 fibrous carpels 3–8-celled and upward of 1 in. long with the lower part prism-shaped and the upper part convex-pyramidal, each one containing a hard several-seeded nut. Madagascar.—Widely cult. for ornament, and lvs. also used for making baskets and domestic articles; fr. provides a starchy food, palatable when cooked.

3. **P. Veitchii,** Dall. Much grown as a pot plant: lvs. 2–3 ft. and more long, long-pointed, spine-margined throughout, 2–3 in. broad when grown (narrower in young specimens), somewhat recurved, with bands of silvery-white on or near the margins. Polynesia.—Botanical position yet in doubt; intro. in. 1868 by Messrs. Veitch, nurserymen of London.

4. **P. Sanderi,** Mast. Of denser more tufted habit than no. 3: lvs. with golden-yellow bands from midrib to margin. Timor, E. Indies.—Botanical position in doubt; exhibited as a novelty in 1898 at Ghent by Messrs. Sander.

21. APONOGETONACEÆ. APONOGETON FAMILY

Aquatic per. herbs with tuberous rhizomes and floating or submerged lvs., grown in ponds and aquaria, of a single genus.

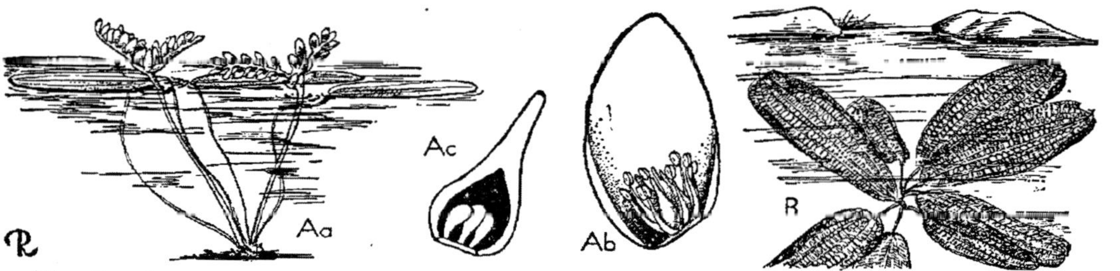

Fig. 21. APONOGETONACEÆ. A, *Aponogeton distachyus:* Aa, habit, leaves floating, × ⅛, Ab, flower habit, × 3; Ac, pistil, vertical section, × 6. B, *Aponogeton fenestralis:* habit, leaves submerged, × ⅛. (Ab and Ac after Hutchinson.)

APONOGETON, L. f. About 25 species, native in Afr., trop. Asia, and Australia.—Lvs. long-petioled, rarely sessile, oblong or linear-lanceolate, with many parallel and transverse veins, sometimes the tissue wanting between: infl. a simple or 2–4-forked non-bracted spike; fls. bisexual or plant rarely diœcious; perianth-parts usually 2, less frequently 1 or 3, obovate or oblong, sometimes petaloid and bract-like, persistent or deciduous; stamens 6 or more in 2 whorls, rarely in 3–4 whorls, hypogynous, anthers 2-celled, extrorse: gynœcium comprised usually of 3–4 free 1-celled pistils, ovules 2–8, basal. (Aponoge-ton: Greek, referring to the habitat in the water.)

A. Lvs. solid, with no openwork.......................1. *A. distachyus*
AA. Lvs. skeletonized, lattice-like.......................2. *A. fenestralis*

1. **A. distachyus,** L. f. CAPE POND-WEED. WATER-HAWTHORN. Smooth, glabrous: lf.-blades floating, long-petioled, linear-oblong, base obtuse or slightly rounded: infl. 2-

spiked; bracts usually 1 but in terminal fls. commonly 2, white, conspicuous, very fragrant; anthers purplish. Cape of Good Hope. Var. **Lagrangei,** André, with violet bracts and lvs. violet beneath, is sometimes cult.

2. **A. fenestralis,** Hook. f. (*Ouvirandra fenestralis,* Poir.). LACE-LEAF. LATTICE-LEAF. Lvs. submerged, reduced to a network of veins; several strong veins parallel with midrib, with numerous cross-veins; blade broad-oblong, apex truncate or retuse but with a minute point at the middle, green: infl. usually 2-spiked, borne on a peduncle a ft. or more long; perianth-parts 2, white. Madagascar.—Grown in aquaria for its foliage.

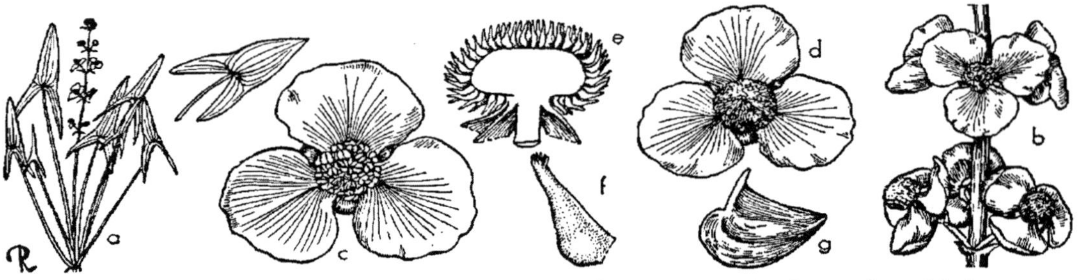

Fig. 22. ALISMACEÆ. *Sagittaria sagittifolia:* a, flowering plant, × 1/20; b, portion of inflorescence, × 1/2; c, staminate flower, × 1; d, pistillate flower, × 1; e, same, vertical section, less perianth, × 3; f, pistil, × 12; g, fruit, × 5.

22. ALISMACEÆ. WATER-PLANTAIN FAMILY

Marsh or aquatic per. herbs, of about 12 genera and 50 species, distributed over the warm and temp. zones, little planted.—Lvs. mostly basal, sheathing, very variable: monœcious or rarely diœcious: fls. borne in bracted whorls, pedunculate, on scapose sts., bisexual or imperfectly so; perianth of 3 persistent sepals and 3 white deciduous petals; stamens 6 or more, rarely 3, hypogynous or essentially so; pistils 6 or more, rarely 3; ovary 1-celled, 1- rarely 2- or more-ovuled, becoming an indehiscent achene in fr.

SAGITTARIA, L. ARROWHEAD. DUCK-POTATO. About 30 species, a few of which are grown in ponds and aquaria.—Stoloniferous, with milky juice: lvs. erect, infrequently floating or submerged, sagittate, lanceolate, ovate or hastate: fls. pedicelled, borne in whorls of 3, racemose or paniculate; pistils numerous. (Sagitta-ria: from Latin *sagitta,* arrow, referring to the shape of the lvs.)—Some species produce edible tubers.

A. Lf.-blades linear to linear-oblong or narrowly elliptic........................1. *S. graminea*
AA. Lf.-blades sagittate to somewhat hastate.
B. Sepals enlarged and erect after flowering........................2. *S. montevidensis*
BB. Sepals withering after flowering........................3. *S. sagittifolia*

1. **S. graminea,** Michx. Plants varying in height from 4 in. to 2 ft.: lvs. usually differentiated into long petiole and linear to narrow-elliptic blade, but when growing in deep water all lvs. may be submerged and ribbon-like without distinction between petiole and blade, such plants usually sterile: fls. white, about 1/3in. across; stamens with filaments oblong, abruptly dilated and pubescent: achene very short-beaked. E. U. S.—Plants grown as *S. sinensis* probably belong here. *S. subulata,* Buchenau (*Alisma subulata, L.*), native to Atlantic coastal areas, may be cult.; it has linear lvs. and very short, erect, and not recurved, beak.

2. **S. montevidensis,** Cham. & Schlecht. GIANT ARROWHEAD. To 6 ft. and more, glabrous, smooth: lf.-blades to 2 ft. long, sagittate, with long, sharply diverging acute basal lobes: petals white with brownish-purple blotch at base; sepals erect and enlarged after flowering: achenes appressed. Brazil to Argentina, Peru; run wild in Calif., Ala. and N. C.—Tender to frost.

3. **S. sagittifolia,** L. OLD-WORLD ARROWHEAD. From 3–4 ft. tall, glabrous, smooth: lf.-blades broad and sagittate, variable: sepals withering after flowering, spreading or reflexed; petals clawed, white, base purple spotted: beak of achene short, erect. Widely distributed through Eu. and Asia. Var. **flore-pleno,** Hort. (*S. japonica,* Hort.), has double fls.—The native *S. latifolia,* Willd., may occasionally be transferred from the wild; it differs from *S. sagittifolia* in the beak being almost four times the length of the body of the achene.

23. BUTOMACEÆ. BUTOMUS FAMILY

Marsh or aquatic per. herbs, of 4 genera and about 10 species, in temp. and trop. regions of Old World and trop. Amer.—Closely allied to the Alismaceæ, but differs in having numerous ovules and frs. dehiscent on the ventral suture: fls. solitary or in umbels, bisexual, conspicuous.

A. Plants not having milky juice: embryo straight........................1. BUTOMUS
AA. Plants with milky juice: embryo shoe-shaped.
B. Pistils numerous; stigma sessile........................2. LIMNOCHARIS
BB. Pistils 3–6; stigma borne on end of long style........................3. HYDROCLEYS

1. **BUTOMUS,** L. FLOWERING-RUSH. One species distributed in Eu., Asia, N. India, and nat. on shores of St. Lawrence River and adjoining waters.—Lvs. long-linear, 3-cornered, becoming acuminate: perianth-segms. 6, all colored, persistent; stamens 9, all fertile; pistils 6; seeds numerous, small, embryo straight. (Butomus: from Greek for *ox* and *cut*, referring to the sharp lvs., which cut the mouths of cattle.)

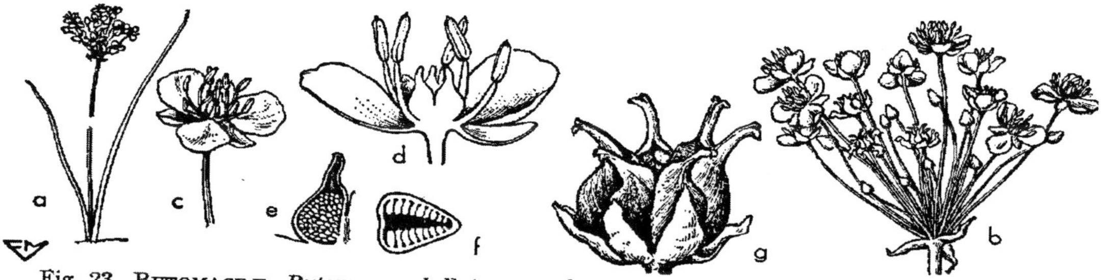

Fig. 23. BUTOMACEÆ. *Butomus umbellatus:* a, plant (many leaves omitted), × 1/16; b, inflorescence, × 1/4; c, flower, × 1/2; d, flower, vertical section, × 1; e, pistil, vertical section, × 2; f, pistil, cross-section, × 3; g, follicles, × 2.

B. umbellatus, L. Lvs. 2–3 ft long, ribbon-like, erect: fls. in a bracted umbel terminating an erect scape to nearly 4 ft high, rose-pink, showy.—Grown along edges of ponds and reported to be of value in wild-life conservation projects.

2. **LIMNOCHARIS,** Humb. & Bonpl. Two species in trop. Amer.—Lvs. emersed, lanceolate or ovate, petiolate: fls. bisexual; sepals 3, persistent; petals 3, fugacious, thin; stamens numerous, outer ones sterile; pistils 15–20; style lacking, stigma sessile, extrorse. (Limnoch-aris: Greek, referring to the marsh habitat.)

L. flava, Buchenau (*L. Plumieri,* Rich. *L. emarginata,* Humb. & Bonpl.). Erect-growing, standing 1–2 ft. or more out of water: lvs. large, blunt, velvety green: fls. 2–12 in an umbel, scapose: sepals green; petals yellow. W. Indies, Peru to Cent. Brazil.

3. **HYDROCLEYS,** Rich. Three species in Brazil, one grown in ponds and aquaria.—Fls. bisexual, with 3 persistent sepals and 3 fugacious petals; stamens many, outer sterile; pistils 3 or 6, rarely 4 or 8, connate at base, ovaries gradually attenuate into the styles. (Hydro-cleys: Greek for *water* and *key.*)

H. nymphoides, Buchenau (*Limnocharis Humboldtii,* Rich.). WATER-POPPY. Sts. prostrate, rooting at the nodes: lvs. mostly floating, broad-ovate, cordate at base, long-petioled, glabrous above, sparsely hairy beneath: lvs. and fls. arising from bracted nodes: fls. about 2 in. across, yellow; fertile stamens violet or purple; pistils usually 6. Spread in trop. S. Amer. to Buenos Aires.

24. HYDROCHARITACEÆ. FROGS-BIT FAMILY

Aquatic herbs submerged or rarely floating, of 14 genera and about 40 species widely distributed over the world, little known horticulturally.—Lvs. various, crowded at base of st., sessile, linear to lanceolate, or fascicled, petiolate, expanded and floating: fls. regular, unisexual or rarely bisexual (plants diœcious when fls. unisexual), arising from a bracted spathe; perianth in 2 series, the 3 outer parts calyx-like, 3 inner petaloid; stamens 3–12, distinct or monadelphous; ovary inferior, 1-celled with 3 parietal placentæ, or rarely 3-celled with axillary placentæ.

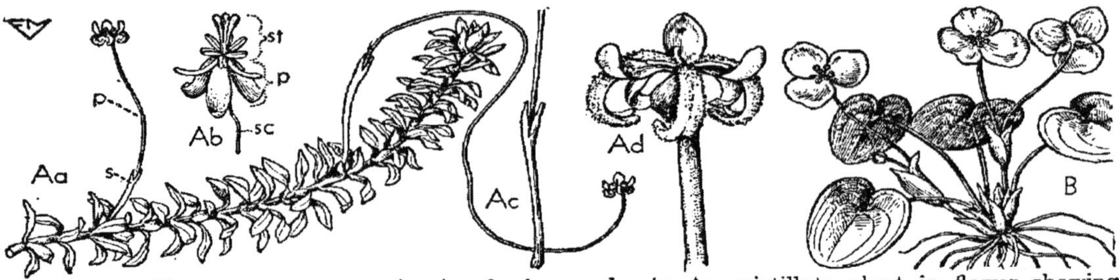

Fig. 24. Hydrocharitaceæ. A, *Anacharis canadensis:* Aa, pistillate plant in flower showing spathe (s), perianth-tube (p), × 1; Ab, staminate flower showing stamens (st), perianth (p) and scape (sc), × 2; Ac, spathe of staminate flower; Ad, pistillate flower, × 4. B, *Hydrocharis Morsus-ranæ:* flowering plant, × ¼. (Ab after Marie-Victorin.)

A. Plants floating on surface .... 1. Hydrocharis
AA. Plants submerged, the crown not floating.
B. Lvs. linear, ribbon-like, all from basal crown .... 2. Vallisneria
BB. Lvs. ovate-lanceolate, cauline on elongated st .... 3. Anacharis

1. **HYDROCHARIS,** L. Two species, one of which is grown in aquaria.—Lvs. long-stalked, roundish, with heart-shaped base: sts. having thin runners which form winter-buds in the fall: petals white; styles 6, 2-parted. (Hydroch-aris: Greek for *water* and *grace.*)

H. Morsus-ranæ, L. Frogs-Bit. A delicate floating plant, with thick glabrous lvs. 2 in. across, and fine silky roots: peduncles of staminate plant bearing 2–4 fls. on long pedicels. (Morsus-ranæ: Latin *morsus*, bite, and *rana*, frog.) Eu. and E. Asia.

2. **VALLISNERIA,** L. Wild Celery. Tape-Grass. Eel-Grass. About 6 species of aquatic diœcious perennials, submerged beneath surface of water or only with distal ends of elongate ribbon-like lvs. floating.—Staminate fls. nearly sessile, at base of plant, breaking from pedicels while in bud and floating to surface at anthesis, perianth 3-parted, stamens 1–3, usually 2; pistillate fls. on a very long flexuous or spiral leafless scape, perianth 3-lobed and with 3 small petals, subtended by a tubular 2-cleft spathe, perianth-tube adnate to ovary, stigmas 3. (Vallisne-ria: named for Antonio Vallisneri, 1661–1730, Italian naturalist.)

V. spiralis, L. Lvs. from 6 in.–6 ft. long and to ⅓in. wide: staminate fls. on slender filiform scape ⅝–2¾ in. long, spathe ovoid, to ⅜in. long. Medit. region.—Plants grown extensively in aquaria as oxygenators and for decoration. The plants known in the trade as the "Italian type" are not hardy. The hardy native E. N. American species, *V. americana*, Michx., is very similar, differing in the staminate fls. subsessile or on a short thickened club-shaped scape not over ¾in. long and usually less; grown as a source of food for aquatic wild-life.

3. **ANACHARIS,** Rich. Waterweed. About a dozen species of diœcious or hermaphrodite submerged per. aquatics, one of which is grown extensively in aquaria and garden pools.—Sts. succulent, flexuous, to 2 ft. long or more, densely lvd.: lvs. small, whorled, with short internodes: fls. unisexual in known cult. species, the pistillate arising from a 2-lipped tubular spathe sessile in lf.-axils and borne on an elongated slender tube; perianth 3–6-parted, with segms. all petaloid or outer 3 much reduced; ovary adnate to spathe at base of tube, styles 3 with entire or 2-cleft stigmas; stamens 3–12, commonly 9; staminate fls. borne on filament-like scapes on surface of water or sessile and then separating from plant and floating on surface at anthesis: fr. indehiscent, ripening under water, seeds numerous. (Anach-aris: from Latin and Greek Anas-charis, *duck-loving*, as it is sought by aquatic fowl for food.)

A. canadensis, Planch. (*Elodea canadensis*, Michx.). Elodea. Ditch-Moss. Lvs. obtuse, about ½in. long and ⅛in. wide, strongly imbricated at apices of st., fls. white, to ⅛in. across; staminate fls. on long slender scapes; pistillate fls. with slender perianth-tube to 4 in. long. N. E. U. S.—The plant often sold by aquarists is likely to be **A. densa,** Victorin (*Elodea densa*, Planch. *E. canadensis* var. *gigantea*, Hort.), a more tender plant having larger lvs. and fls., longer internodes and fls. about ¾in across, several being inclosed by a broad loose spathe not constricted at base; S. Brazil to Argentina; nat. in S. Calif. and in isolated areas along Atlantic coast as far north as Mass.

25. GRAMINEÆ. GRASS FAMILY

One of the most important to man of the families of plants, the products comprising human foods in rice, wheat, oats, barley, rye, maize, bamboo, sugar-cane, and others; forage and fodder for live-stock; materials used in construction and the arts, as the bamboos; sand-binding plants, as the beach-grasses; many species grown for ornament; and they contribute much to the landscape of the earth. The recognized genera are about 400 and the species now known about 4,500, represented in all parts of the world. The grasses are probably the most cosmopolitan of the higher plants. The animal husbandry of the world, as now developed, could not subsist without the grazing grasses and the cereal grains. The fls. are highly specialized and minute, but they are not difficult to understand by careful study. The species are ann. and per. herbs, and the bamboos are mostly woody and some of them are climbers. Grasses of one kind or another grow in all kinds of soils and situations.—Fls. known as *florets* (flt.) 1 or more borne in a *spikelet;* the spikelets are assembled into spikes (timothy), heads (wheat), tassels (maize), or panicles (blue-grass). The spikelet typically has a short axis, *rachlila,* on which the fls. are borne in the axils of 2-ranked imbricate *bracts.* The 2 lowest bracts of the spikelet are empty and called *glumes.* The flt. itself is comprised of (1) the essential organs, (2) usually 2 very small scales or *lodicules* at the base of the essential organs, (3) subtending and partially enveloping the lodicules and essential organs is a bract called the *palea,* while opposite and slightly below it is (4) a second bract known as the *lemma;* below all of these, on the rachilla, are the glumes. The parts of a typical grass flt. are shown in Fig. 25. The fls. are perfect or imperfect (plant monœcious or diœcious); stamens commonly 3, but sometimes 1, 2, or 6, with 2-celled usually versatile anthers; pistil 1, with usually 2 plumose stigmas, the ovary superior, 1-celled, 1-ovuled: fr. a ripened ovary, 1-seeded, mostly forming a hard grain known as *caryopsis,* which (as in oats and rye) is often permanently enveloped in the indurated lemma and palea: culms (sts.) jointed, mostly hollow, tall and slender or sometimes prostrate: lvs. 2-ranked (third over the first), at the base sheathing the culm, the sheath usually open on the side opposite the blade and provided at the junction with the blade with a hyaline or hairy projection known as a *ligule.*—Other grasses than those here described are likely to be in cult. for special purposes, and some of the other native species are used and more or less sown for forage, but are as yet not integral parts of the domesticated flora.

A. Plants woody, at least at base, bamboos, per., not branching or forking: lvs. usually jointed to the sheath and, in most genera, finally separating from it, sometimes distinctly petioled: fls. (seldom produced in cult. in the U. S.) mostly in 2–8-fld. spikelets which are panicled, racemed, or in clusters at the nodes; glumes 2; lower lemmas often empty; stamens 3 or 6; styles 2 or 3: fr. a thin-walled caryopsis, nut or berry.
  B. Culms very large and tall, solid (at least in dry climates): plant mostly of great size (in ours), not spiny: fr. a small nut or berry, the seed free....... 1. DENDROCALAMUS
  BB. Culms large or slender, usually hollow: plant mostly relatively small or medium, sometimes bearing spines: fr. thin-walled, the seed adnate to the wall.
    C. The culms more or less flattened on one side of the node above the base of the plant: style long, stigmas 3.
      D. Lvs. lanceolate to linear-lanceolate: culms straight or arched, 10–80 ft. high.. 2. PHYLLOSTACHYS
      DD. Lvs. ovate-lanceolate to ovate-oblong: culms strongly zigzag, 3–6 ft. high.. 3. SHIBATÆA
    CC. The culms terete: style short with 3 stigmas, or styles 2.
      D. Branches mostly solitary at a node, rarely 2.
        E. Lf.-sheaths with scabrous rigid bristles .... 4. SASA
        EE. Lf.-sheaths without bristles, or if present smooth and flexuous. 5. PSEUDOSASA
      DD. Branches several at a node.
        E. Lf.-sheaths early-deciduous, or falling with the lvs................ 6. SINARUNDINARIA
        EE. Lf.-sheaths persistent.
          F. Bristles of lf.-sheath smooth: nodes with 2 or more buds each..... 7. PLEIOBLASTUS
          FF. Bristles of lf.-sheath stiff, scabrous: nodes with 1 bud each.
            G. Stamens 6: fls. with 3–4 lower glumes (lemmas) empty......... 8. BAMBUSA
            GG. Stamens 3: fls. with 1 or 2 lower glumes empty............. 9. ARUNDINARIA
AA. Plants herbaceous (a few ann. grasses may be ligneous at base but are not bamboo-like).
  B. Grown for cereals, forage, or sugar production.

Fig. 25. GRAMINEÆ. A, typical grass floret: essential parts, × 4. B, culm showing sheath and base of blade, × ½. C, leaf-base with ligule, × ½. D, *Phleum pratense:* Da, inflorescence, × 1; Db, spikelet, × 8. E, *Lagurus ovatus:* Ea, inflorescence, × 1; Eb, spikelet, × 8. F, *Uniola latifolia:* portion of inflorescence, × 1. G, *Zea Mays*, × 1/10. H, *Avena sativa:* Ha, spikelet, × 4; Hb, floret, × 8. I, *Triticum æstivum:* Ia, spikelet, × 4; Ib, floret, × 8. J, *Dactylis glomerata:* Ja, inflorescence, × 1; Jb, spikelet, × 4. K, *Briza maxima:* inflorescence, × 1. (c culm, f floret, l lemma, lg ligule, lo lodicule, l.s. leaf-sheath, o ovary, p palea, s stigma, st stamen).

C. Grasses producing sugar; sugar-cane, strong ann. or per. erect grasses.
D. Spikelets in pairs, both perfect: robust per. 8–20 ft. high, culms to 2 in. thick...10. SACCHARUM
DD. Spikelets in pairs, one fertile, one sterile: ann. or per. 2–12 ft. high, culms ½–1 in. thick..11. SORGHUM
CC. Grasses of the cereal and ann. forage kind: rice, wheat, emmer, spelt, barley, rye, oats, maize, sorghum, milo, kafir, millets: plants not closely allied botanically, but a marked cultural group, annuals grown regularly in fields and harvested for the grain, straw, and stalks.
D. The corn crops (maize, kafir) and their kin: fls. staminate or pistillate, in the kafir tribe perfect and staminate.
E. Plant not monœcious, although some of the flts. are sterile: 3 spikelets together or sometimes only 2, the central lower one with a perfect and fertile flt. and the 2 lateral and upper ones staminate: sorghum, kafir, etc...11. SORGHUM
EE. Plant monœcious, the staminate and pistillate flts. in different spikelets or even in different inflorescences: the cult. cereal kinds are coarse erect annuals.
F. Staminate flts. terminating the infl., the pistillate at the base and inclosed in a bead-like body..12. COIX
FF. Staminate flts. in a terminal panicle or tassel; pistillate in axillary sheathed spikes or ears.
G. Ears large and separate, remaining intact..................13. ZEA
GG. Ears small, clustered at the nodes, breaking at maturity into little pieces..14. EUCHLÆNA
DD. The small grains and their kin: spikelets with imperfect flts. at the bottom or top.
E. Infl. digitate or umbellate, radiating spikes at top of culm..........15. ELEUSINE
EE. Infl. paniculate or spicate.
F. Spikelets 1-fld.: rice..16. ORYZA
FF. Spikelets 2- to many-fld.
G. Imperfect flts. above the fertile ones in the spikelet.
H. Infl. paniculate; spikelets pedicelled.
I. Length of spikelets 1 in. or more, nodding in an open panicle: flts. all alike...17. AVENA
II. Length of spikelets ¼ in., erect in narrow panicle: lower flt. staminate...18. ARRHENATHERUM
HH. Infl. spicate; spikelets sessile on opposite sides of a zigzag jointed channelled axis.
I. Arrangement of spikelets in clusters of 2–3 at each joint of the axis...19. HORDEUM
II. Arrangement of spikelets solitary at each joint of the axis.
J. Glumes very narrow, 1-nerved: rye..................20. SECALE
JJ. Glumes broad, 3-nerved: wheat, spelt................21. TRITICUM
GG. Imperfect flts. (when present) at base of spikelet.
H. Glumes 2 in the spikelet...18. ARRHENATHERUM
HH. Glumes 3 in the spikelet.
I. Prominent bristles accompanying or subtending the spikelets, forming an involucre.
J. Bristles falling with maturity and with the spikelets.....22. PENNISETUM
JJ. Bristles persisting on the rachis after the spikelets fall...23. SETARIA
II. Prominent bristles not subtending the spikelets.
J. Awns wanting on the lemmas.......................24. PANICUM
JJ. Awns or sharp point present on the sterile lemma.......25. ECHINOCHLOA
BB. Grown in pastures, meadows or lawns: grasses of the sod-forming kind or grown for ornament or for use in dry bouquets.
C. Grasses forming sod: the "agricultural grasses," small perennials for the most part, of many botanical affinities, comprising such kinds as redtop, rye-grass, june-grass, orchard-grass, bermuda-grass, timothy, fescue, bent, carpet-grass.
D. Infl. digitate or umbellate, the few slender branches radiating from a common point at the top of the culm.
E. Spikelets of 3 perfect flts. each...................................15. ELEUSINE
EE. Spikelets of only 1 perfect flt., imperfect flts. may or may not be present.
F. Flts. all perfect...26. CYNODON
FF. Flts., or one of them, imperfect.
G. Upper flts. imperfect, lower one perfect...................27. CHLORIS
GG. Upper flts. perfect, lower ones sterile or neutral, and if the latter then represented only by an empty glume..............28. AXONOPUS
DD. Infl. spicate, a panicle, or a raceme.
E. Spikelets in a raceme or panicle, usually open-branching.
F. Perfect flt. 1 in the spikelet and no sterile lemmas...............29. AGROSTIS
FF. Perfect flts. 2 or more in the spikelet.
G. Glumes and lemmas awned; flts. subtended by an abundance of silky hairs and (in ours) rose-colored..........................47. TRICHOLÆNA
GG. Glumes or lemmas awned or awnless; flts. not silky-hairy.
H. Awn arising from the back of the lemma.........................18. ARRHENATHERUM
HH. Awn wanting, or arising from the tip of lemma.
I. Arrangement of spikelets in 1-sided glomerules, these in a panicle that contracts in fr.............................30. DACTYLIS
II. Arrangement of spikelets otherwise.

J. Infl. a single main axis with small secund racemes.......50. PASPALUM
JJ. Infl. a compoundedly branched panicle.
K. Lemmas bifid at apex: stigmas separated by a stylopodium....................................31. BROMUS
KK. Lemmas usually entire: no stylopodium between stigmas.
L. Tip of lemma acute or awned..................32. FESTUCA
LL. Tip of lemma obtuse or essentially so, lemma usually cobwebby at base...................33. POA
EE. Spikelets in a spicate infl. (a single spike or spike-like cluster with no long-stalked lateral branches).
F. Rachis of spike thickened and spikelets sunken therein: lawn-grasses of warm climates.
G. Glume hard and chaffy, not winged; primary axis of infl. nearly ¼in. thick....................................34. STENOTAPHRUM
GG. Glume membranous, the first glume winged at apex; primary axis of infl. less than ⅛in. thick.........................35. EREMOCHLOA
FF. Rachis slender, spikelets not sunken.
G. The spikelets of two kinds, perfect and sterile, in pairs, in dense 1-sided panicle..36. CYNOSURUS
GG. The spikelets alike.
H. First glume wanting; spikelets sessile on opposite sides of rachis.
I. Flts. 1 in the spikelet: plants to 10 in. high, mat-forming...37. ZOISIA
II. Flts. several in the spikelet, edgewise to rachis: plants mostly 1–2 ft. high, not mat-forming................38. LOLIUM
HH. First glume present; spikelets short-pedicelled in spike-like panicles.
I. Plants pleasingly strong-scented (vanilla-like odor): panicle not dense.......................................39. ANTHOXANTHUM
II. Plants not scented: panicle dense and spike-like.
J. Glumes falling with the spikelet, the pedicel articulated..40. ALOPECURUS
JJ. Glumes persistent, no articulation.................41. PHLEUM
CC. Grasses of the ornamental kind: a division well known to cultivators but not constituting a botanical class or group; some are small ann. grasses grown for pot and table ornament, especially for dried bouquets; others are stout perennials planted in borders, lawns, or pools.
D. Plant monœcious (diœcious kinds accounted for below).
E. Staminate infl. terminal on the culm in a tassel, the pistillate on separate ears...13. ZEA
EE. Staminate infl. terminating in a cluster that is pistillate at the base.
F. Height 4–12 ft., aquatic: pistillate spikelets pendent on long slender pedicels...42. ZIZANIA
FF. Height 1–3 ft., not aquatic: pistillate spikelets erect on stout pedicels and inclosed in a bead-like body......................12. COIX
DD. Plant not monœcious, some or all the flts. in each spikelet being perfect, or the plants diœcious in nos. 60 and 61.
E. Infl. digitate or umbellate, radiating spikes at the top of culm.......15. ELEUSINE
EE. Infl. paniculate, racemose, or spicate, not digitate.
F. Spikelets with 1 perfect terminal flt., the lower flts., if any, neutral or staminate.
G. Lemma and palea very thin and hyaline, usually translucent; glumes firm.
H. The spikelets all alike, perfect.
I. Axis continuous in racemes; panicle fan-shaped or V-shaped...43. MISCANTHUS
II. Axis of raceme separating into parts or joints; panicle plume-like but not strikingly V-shaped................44. ERIANTHUS
HH. The spikelets not all alike.
I. Racemes, or infl. branches, whorled in a long narrow panicle; no sheathing bract present...................45. VETIVERIA
II. Racemes in pairs from a large sheathing bract, panicled....46. CYMBOPOGON
GG. Lemma and palea not hyaline and translucent, mostly thickened and hardened.
H. Bristles subtending the spikelet..........................22. PENNISETUM
HH. Bristles not subtending the spikelet.
I. Glumes and lemmas awned.
J. Infl. paniculate.......................................47. TRICHOLÆNA
JJ. Infl. a single main axis with small secund racemes.....48. OPLISMENUS
II. Glumes and lemmas awnless.
J. First and second glumes about equal.................49. PHALARIS
JJ. First glume minute or absent.
K. The spikelets in loose panicles..................24. PANICUM
KK. The spikelets in spike-like 1-sided racemes..........50. PASPALUM
FF. Spikelets with 1, several, or many flts., the upper flts., if any, neutral or staminate.
G. The infl. spicate, the spikelets in spikes or spike-like heads.
H. Spikes secund, or 1-sided...................................27. CHLORIS
HH. Spikes not secund.
I. Shape of infl. ovoid, short and woolly.................51. LAGURUS
II. Shape of infl. long, not short or ovoid.
J. Spike cylindrical, usually uniformly so.

K. Length of infl. 5–15 in. and about ½in. diam.: plant stoloniferous: lvs. strongly involute: beach-grass... 52. AMMOPHILA
KK. Length of infl. usually 1½–3 in., stiffly erect and fine-textured: lvs. not involute.
L. Color of spikes green or tinged purplish, about ¼in. diam.: plant per., culms erect, 3–5 ft. high...... 41. PHLEUM
LL. Color of spikes tawny-yellow, ½–¾in. diam., fluffy: plant ann., culms ascending, 6–30 in. high. 53. POLYPOGON
JJ. Spike flattened or rowed, not smoothly and uniformly cylindrical.
K. Number of spikelets 1 at each node of rachis....... 38. LOLIUM
KK. Number of spikelets 2 or more at each node.
L. Flts. solitary in each spikelet; spikelets 3 at a node, at least in most of spike.................... 19. HORDEUM
LL. Flts. 2–6 in each spikelet; spikelets 2 at a node throughout most of spike.................... 54. ELYMUS
GG. The infl. paniculate or racemose.
H. Spikelet of 1 perfect flt.
I. Perfect flt. with 2 sterile lemmas beneath............... 39. ANTHOXANTHUM
II. Perfect flt. without sterile lemmas.
J. Awns long and stout, bent or twisted................ 55. STIPA
JJ. Awns none, or short and straight, or weak............ 29. AGROSTIS
HH. Spikelet of 2 or more perfect flts.
I. Lemmas awned from the back or from between the teeth.
J. Plant velvety-pubescent........................... 56. HOLCUS
JJ. Plant not velvety-pubescent.
K. The spikelets large, 2–6-fld....................... 17. AVENA
KK. The spikelets small and delicate, 2-fld.............. 57. AIRA
II. Lemmas awnless or awned from a tip that is entire.
J. Of great size, reed-like, usually in clumps, 4 ft. high or more.
K. Species perfect-fld., not diœcious: lvs. usually 1¼ in. wide or wider.
L. Rachilla hairy.............................. 58. NEYRAUDIA
LL. Rachilla naked.............................. 59. ARUNDO
KK. Species diœcious: lvs. ¾in. wide or less.
L. Lvs. crowded at base of culms................. 60. CORTADERIA
LL. Lvs. distributed along the culms................ 61. GYNERIUM
JJ. Of small size (1 to 3½ ft. tall), like ordinary grasses.
K. Fertile spikelets 1-fld. and long-awned; sterile spikelets with obtuse glumes........................ 62. LAMARCKIA
KK. Fertile spikelets with glumes and awns not different from sterile ones.
L. The spikelets much flattened, sessile, on a common rachis.. 63. DESMAZERIA
LL. The spikelets little or not flattened, or if so not sessile on a single rachis.
M. Lemmas thick coriaceous, smooth and glossy, margin scarious........................ 64. UNIOLA
MM. Lemmas thin, membranous, or if thickish then the margin not scarious.
N. Nerves of lemmas 3.
O. Spikelets nearly terete, in a narrow elongated panicle, bluish.................. 65. MOLINIA
OO. Spikelets somewhat flattened, in open or short panicle, mostly green........... 66. ERAGROSTIS
NN. Nerves of lemmas 5 or more.
O. Spikelets in 1-sided heads or fascicles...... 30. DACTYLIS
OO. Spikelets not secund.
P. Breadth of spikelets about as great as length: lemma cordate at base........ 67. BRIZA
PP. Breadth of spikelet much less than length: lemma cuneate at base.
Q. Lemma obtuse or nearly so......... 33. POA
QQ. Lemma acute or awned.
R. Tip of lemma bifid: stigmas separated by a stylopodium......... 31. BROMUS
RR. Tip of lemma usually entire: no stylopodium between stigmas.... 32. FESTUCA

1. **DENDROCALAMUS,** Nees. A dozen to a score of species in S. Asia and Malaya, shrubby or tree-like, one of which is sometimes planted far S. and in the American tropics.—Flts. mostly bisexual, in globular clusters in long panicles; spikelets 2- to many-fld., 2 to many of the lower glumes empty; stamens 6: fr. small with thick hard wall and free seed. (Dendrocal-amus: Greek *tree-reed.*)

D. strictus, Nees. MALE BAMBOO. Making great clumps, 40–50 ft. tall; culms 1–3 in. diam., nearly or quite solid (said to be hollow in moist climates), glaucous-green when young but becoming yellowish; branches long and slender: lvs. 1 ft. or less long, about 1 in. wide, with prominent midrib and strong nerves on either side: panicles large, with dense heads 1–1½ in. diam., the spikelets usually hairy. India, Java.

2. **PHYLLOSTACHYS,** Sieb. & Zucc. Probably 30 known species, in farther Asia, several of which are useful hort. plants in this country.—Flts. bisexual, in 1–4-fld. spikelets mostly on fascicled branchlets, the rachilla articulate and breaking between the flts.; lower 2 or 3 glumes empty; palea narrow, 2-keeled, lightly many-nerved; stamens 3; styles 3: lvs. mostly short and distinctly petioled, the venation mostly tessellate, the sheaths deciduous leaving the old culm bare: culms woody, the inner faces of the internodes above the base of the plant, flattened. (Phyllos-tachys: Greek *leaf-spike.*)—This genus provides much of the bamboo of domestic commerce and most of the pulp paper of the Orient.

A. Culms and sts. becoming black....................1. *P. nigra*
AA. Culms and sts. green, yellow or yellowish.
B. Plants with culms openly spaced, not clump-forming....................2. *P. viridi-glaucescens*
BB. Plants with culms in compact clumps.
C. Internodes at base of st. very short....................3. *P. aurea*
CC. Internodes well developed.
D. St.-sheaths yellowish-green or lightly spotted purple: rhizome buds terete....................4. *P. sulphurea*
DD. St.-sheaths conspicuously spotted or blotched purple: rhizome buds obtusely angled....................5. *P. bambusoides*

1. **P. nigra,** Munro (*Bambusa nigra,* Lodd.). BLACK BAMBOO. Hardy plant 10–20 ft., culms and sts. green but becoming black the second year (bearing brownish-black spots in var. **punctata,** Hort., a more robust and hardier form); joints prominent, nearly black on the upper rim and white-edged on the lower: lvs. thin, 2–6 in. long, nearly 1 in. broad or less, long-pointed, finely serrate on one edge, closely tessellate. China, Japan.

2. **P. viridi-glaucescens,** Riv. (*Bambusa viridi-glaucescens,* Carr.). Tall hardy plant to 60 ft., with arched sts. that are at first green but become dull yellow with age and st.-sheaths striped with purple: lvs. 3–4 in. long, ½in. or somewhat more wide, bright green above and whitened beneath, minutely sharp-serrate on one edge, finely tessellate; ligule of sheath with fringed auricles. China, Japan.

3. **P. aurea,** Riv. (*Bambusa aurea,* Carr.). YELLOW BAMBOO. Diffuse, 10–15 ft. high, sts. yellow, often brilliant, internodes at base of plant very short: lvs. 2–5 or 6 in. long, ½–¾in. broad, narrowed to a long acuminate point, minutely serrulate on one edge, finely tessellate, light green and mostly glaucous beneath, dark green above; sheaths with few small purplish spots, with 1 tuft of cilia-like bristles each side of petiole. China, Japan.

4. **P. sulphurea,** Riv. (*Bambusa sulphurea,* Carr.). To 30 ft., culms and branches of clear sulfur-yellow, but frequently with 1 or 2 narrow green stripes on the rounded portion of each internode; plants clump-forming, the rhizome buds terete: lvs. 2–3 clustered at twig tips, lanceolate-oblong, 2–4 in. long, green and often variegated; sheaths yellowish-green, sparsely blotched or spotted purple. China, Japan. Var. **viridis,** Young (*P. mitis,* Riv. not Bean), has culms and branches green, taller with non-variegated lvs.; perhaps more commonly cult.

5. **P. bambusoides,** Sieb. & Zucc. (*P. Quilioi,* Riv. *P. reticulata,* Koch in part). Plants 15–75 ft. high, culms bright green, st.-sheaths streaked or blotched purple: lvs. 3–6 in. long, lanceolate, bright green above, glaucous beneath. China. Var. **Castilloni,** Makino, is smaller, with sts. and culms yellow striped green and smaller often variegated lvs.; Japan.

3. **SHIBATÆA,** Makino. Low shrubs, represented by 2 species.—Sts. strongly zigzag, to 5 ft. high, the internodes nearly solid; branches 3–5 at a node, short: lvs. short-petioled, terminal; sheaths bristleless: spikelets 1–2-fld.; flts. with 3 stamens, stigmas 3 on a long style. (Shibatæ-a: named for Keita Shibata, Japanese botanist.)

S. Kumasasa, Makino (*S. Kumasaca,* Nakai. *Phyllostachys Kumasaca,* Munro. *P. ruscifolia,* Nichols. *Bambusa ruscifolia,* Sieb. *B. Kumasasa,* Steud.). Very dwarf, 1–3 ft., culm nearly solid, zigzag, green; sheaths purple, fringed; branches in 3's and 4's, 1–2 in. long, the foliage therefore all borne close to the main culm: lvs. 2–3 in. long, ¾–1 in. wide, narrowing into acute ends, tessellated or minutely cross-veined. (Kumasasa: the Japanese name, *kumazasa,* for certain bamboos.) Japan.

4. **SASA,** Makino & Shibata. About 20 species of low shrubs in E. Asia.—Culms terete, unspotted, having 1 or rarely 2 branches at each node: lvs. crowded with short internodes at ends of twigs; culm-sheaths persistent: spikelets 2–9-fld., in lax panicles; flts. with 6 stamens, stigmas 3 on short style. (Sas-a: Japanese name for small bamboos.)

A. St.-sheaths with margins involute: lvs. with 15–18 pairs of veins....................1. *S. tessellata*
AA. St.-sheaths convolute: lvs. with 5–13 pairs of veins.
B. Lvs. about 2 in. wide; apex of lf.-sheaths bearing brown bristles....................2. *S. Veitchii*
BB. Lvs. about 3 in. wide; apex of lf.-sheaths without bristles....................3. *S. senanensis*

1. **S. tessellata,** Makino & Shibata (*Bambusa tessellata*, Munro. *B. Ragamowskii*, Pfitz.). Dwarf, 3–4 ft., hardy: lvs. very large, 12–18 in. long and 1½–4 in. broad, smooth and shining above and whitened beneath, beautifully tessellate, sharply serrate, the midrib prominent and showing a tomentose line on one side. China, Japan.

2. **S. Veitchii,** Rehd. (*Arundinaria Veitchii*, N. E. Br. *Bambusa Veitchii*, Carr.). Dwarf, 3 ft. or less; culms purple, white-waxy below the nodes: lvs. 5–8 in. long and about 2 in. broad, bright green above, pale and minutely pubescent beneath, the margins serrate. (Named for John Gould Veitch, page 53.) Japan.

3. **S. senanensis,** Rehd. (*Bambusa senanensis*, Franch. & Sav.). Plants to 7 ft.; culms hollow, waxy below the nodes: lvs. 6–15 in. long, about 3 in. wide, serrulate, bright green above, glaucous beneath. Japan. Var. **nebulosa,** Rehd. (*Bambusa palmata*, Burb. *Arundinaria palmata*, Bean. *A. paniculata* var. *nebulosa*, Makino), of somewhat lower stature, sts. tinged purple.

5. **PSEUDOSASA,** Makino. An eastern Asiatic genus of 3 species.—Sts. terete, fistulose, to 20 ft. high; st.-sheaths hispid and persistent; branches 1 at a node: spikelets of 2–8 fls., the latter with 3 or rarely 4 stamens, stigmas 3 on a short style. (Pseudosas-a: Greek, *false sasa*.)

P. japonica Makino (*Arundinaria japonica*, Sieb. & Zucc. *Bambusa Metake*, Sieb.). Hardy, commonly planted, 5–10 ft.; culms somewhat covered with waxy bloom; bud a simple flattish scale; branches borne singly in the axils: lvs. 4–10 in. long, 1–2 in. broad, smooth and shining above, whitened and minutely pubescent beneath; sheaths large and conspicuous. Japan.

6. **SINARUNDINARIA,** Nakai. Three Chinese and Himalayan moderately tall species of terete-stemmed bamboos.—St.-sheaths deciduous, appendaged; several branches at a node: lf.-sheaths early deciduous or falling with the lvs., having smooth flexuous bristles: flts. with 3 stamens, stigmas 3 on short style. (Sinarundina-ria: Latin *Chinese arundinaria*.)

S. nitida, Nakai (*Arundinaria nitida*, Mitf.). Hardy, to 15 ft.; culms size of a lead-pencil, arching, black-purple: lvs. 2–3 in. long and ½in. broad, shining green above and pale beneath; sheaths purple, ligules not hairy or ciliate. China.—Reported to require shade and considerable moisture.

7. **PLEIOBLASTUS,** Nakai. About 30 species of E. Asia.—Shrubs producing erect or arching sts. from creeping or cespitose rhizomes; nodes with 3–7 branches each, the st.-sheaths persistent: lf.-sheaths producing flexuous smooth bristles at apex: flts. on jointed rachis in spikelet, stamens 3, style with 3 stigmas. (Pleioblastus: Greek *pleios*, more, and *blastos*, bud, there being several buds at each node.)

A. Lvs. soft-pubescent beneath.
  B. Foliage pubescent on both sides, striped with white........................1. *P. variegatus*
  BB. Foliage nearly glabrous above, green or striped with yellow................2. *P. viridi-striatus*
AA. Lvs. glabrous or only slightly puberulent.
  B. Plants 1–3 ft. high: lvs. slightly hairy..............................3. *P. distichus*
  BB. Plants 10–30 ft. high: lvs. glabrous..............................4. *P. Simonii*

1. **P. variegatus,** Makino (*Bambusa variegata*, Miq. *B. Fortunei*, VanHoutte. *Arundinaria Fortunei*, Riv.). Dwarf, 1–3 ft., with vigorous rhizomes, the internodes of the culms usually only 1 in. long: lvs. 4–5 in. long, ¾in. or less broad, striped with white. Japan.

2. **P. viridi-striatus,** Makino (*Bambusa viridi-striata*, André. *Arundinaria auricoma*, Mitf. *A. Fortunei* var. *aurea*, Hort.). Plant 2–3 ft., strict; internodes 3–5 in.: lvs. 4–6 in. long, 1 in. wide, brightly striped yellow, strongly pubescent beneath, serrate particularly on one margin, rounded at base and very short-petioled, the hairy sheaths purplish. Japan.

3. **P. distichus,** Nakai (*Bambusa disticha*, Mitf. *B. nana*, Hort. not Mitf.). Dwarf, rising 2–3 ft.; culms slender, zigzag, green or tinged purple, the branches borne singly: lvs. 2–2½ in. long, ½in. or less broad, tessellate, serrate on both edges, the sheaths overlapping, the spreading blades rather close together and parallel, giving the plant a striking appearance. Japan.

4. **P. Simonii,** Nakai (*Arundinaria Simonii*, Riv. *Bambusa Simonii*, Carr. *B. Narihira*, Hort.). Hardy, to 20 ft.; culms with conspicuous waxy bloom; bud complex and scaly; branches in dense somewhat verticillate clusters in the axils: lvs. 6–12 in. long, ½in. or less broad, tapering to a very long point, the midrib glaucous on one side toward the apex but green on the other side. (Named for Simon Brothers, nurserymen at Metz, in Alsace.) Himalayas to Japan. Var. **variegatus,** Nakai (*Arundinaria variegata*, Hook. f.), has lvs. striped with white.

8. **BAMBUSA,** Schreber. Perhaps 100 tenable species, mostly in the tropics of the Old World; a number are intro. to cult. in this country; erect or scandent woody plants, sometimes bearing spines.—Flts. bisexual or imperfect, in 2- to many-fld. spikes combined in glomerules on the branches of panicles, the rachilla jointed below the flts.; 3–4 lower glumes empty; stamens 6; ovary hirsute at top, with elongated divided or undivided style: fr. a thin-walled caryopsis with adherent seed: lvs. short-petioled, the blade articulated with the sheath. (Bambu-sa: from the aboriginal name in Malaya or adjacent regions.)

A. Plant spine-bearing...1. *B. Bambos*
AA. Plant not spiny..2. *B. vulgaris*

1. **B. Bambos,** Druce (*Arundo Bambos,* L. *Bambusa arundinacea,* Willd.). A giant bamboo with stout rootstocks, the dense clumps reaching 100 ft. in height; culms green and shining when young and zigzag, becoming straight and golden-yellow, the graceful curving branches bearing spines: lvs. 4–8 in. long, ½in. or more broad, nearly glabrous: plant monocarpous—perishing after producing a crop of seeds, but the crop may be long delayed: panicle of great size. India.

2. **B. vulgaris,** Schrad. Feathery Bamboo. Tender plant, withstanding little frost, 50–80 ft. high; culms stout, becoming 4 in. or more in diam., bright green, arching with age, the branches many and striate, not spine-bearing: lvs. 6–10 in. long, ¾–1¼ in. broad, rough on the margins and near them and also on the lower surface, striate and not tessellate: panicle large and leafy, with large clusters of spikelets at the nodes. Java, but widely cult. Var. **aureo-variegata,** Hort., the Golden Bamboo, has golden-yellow culms with pencilings of green.

9. **ARUNDINARIA,** Michx. As now constituted, about 6 species in Amer. and Asia, mostly trop. but two American species native as far north as Va., Md., and Mo. —Fls. mainly bisexual, in 2- to many-fld. flattened often large spikelets disposed in racemes or panicles, the rachilla more or less articulated below the flts.; 1 or 2 lower glumes empty, the fertile scales longer, many-nerved; paleæ scarcely shorter than the lemmas; stamens 3; ovary usually hirsute at top, with 2–3-divided style and rather long plumose stigmas: fr. an oval or narrowly oblong thin-walled caryopsis with adnate seed: lvs. flat, short-petioled, articulated with the sheath which is persistent: plant usually not arboreous, the culms (canes) simple or branched. (Arundina-ria: Latin *arundo*, reed.)

A. falcata, Nees (*Bambusa falcata,* Hort.). Culms very slender, ann., 10–20 ft., but not exceeding ½in. diam., with a bluish-white waxy coating when young but becoming yellow-green: lf.-blades 3–6 in long, about ½in. wide, oblong-lanceolate, striate, glabrous; sheaths downy, ciliate at the top: racemes falcate, fascicled at the nodes. Himalayas.

10. **SACCHARUM,** L. A dozen species of tall grasses, mostly of the Old World tropics, one the principal source of cane-sugar.—Infl. a large terminal panicle; spikelets in pairs at the articulating joints of the rachis, each 1-fld. and perfect or the upper one rarely pistillate, one spikelet sessile and one pedicelled, a tuft of long soft hairs subtending each spikelet; stamens 3; styles long and plumose: fr. free. (Sac-charum: from an old Greek word for sugar.)

S. officinarum, L. Sugar-Cane. Stout coarse strong per. 6–15 ft. tall, yielding sugar from the solid jointed maize-like canes: lvs. stiff and 1 to several ft. long, 1–2 in. broad, glabrous and smooth on both surfaces but sharp-serrate on the margins, midrib broad, long-attenuate-pointed; sheaths long, more or less overlapping, hairy at the throat, ligule prominent: panicle terminal 1–2 ft. long, open and fluffy; rachillæ and pedicels disarticulating, liberating the immense number of little spikelets with their white downy tufts. Probably a cultigen, the original species not having been discovered; supposed to be native in farther Asia or E. Indies.—The plant is propagated by pieces of the culm. It does not bloom in the U. S., but flowers freely in the tropics and some kinds produce seeds with which experiments in breeding have been made.

11. **SORGHUM,** Moench. Ann. and per. warm-country stout grasses of perhaps several species, native to the Old World and sometimes nat. in the New World; grown for grain, syrup, forage and broom production.—Spikelets in pairs, 1 sessile and fertile, the other pedicellate and sterile although staminate; infl. a terminal or close panicle, the rachis and pedicels hairy, staminate spikelets soon falling; stigmas exserted laterally; stamens 3. (Sorgh-um: from *sorgho*, the Italian name for the

plant.)—The forms are many and their botanical origin is unknown. The generic name has been a subject of study and controversy; as now accepted, Sorghum has been segregated as a genus from Holcus, the latter represented in cult. by *H. lanatus.*

A. Rhizomes creeping; plant per.: spikelets deciduous at maturity.................. 1. *S. halepense*
AA. Rhizomes not creeping; plant. ann.: spikelets persistent at maturity (except in some vars.).. 2. *S. vulgare*

1. **S. halepense,** Pers. (*Holcus halepensis,* L. *Andropogon halepensis,* Brot.). JOHNSON-GRASS. MEANS-GRASS. ALEPPO-GRASS. Persistent per. where not killed by frost, making strong creeping large-sheathed rootstocks; culms 3–6 ft. high, glabrous, very leafy: lvs. with long sheath and short scarious ciliate ligule, the blades smooth or scabrous on the edges, many-nerved, the midrib conspicuous: panicle loose and spreading, to 2 ft. long, branches 2 or 3 at a node and more or less drooping; terminal spikelets in 3's, the lateral mostly in 2's, muticous or short-awned; fertile spikelet in the middle or at the base of the sterile, elliptic to broad-lanceolate, pubescent or smooth; staminate spikelets narrower, soon falling and leaving the slender hairy pedicels. Probably Mediterranean, but now widely scattered and nat.—A hay and pasture grass in mild countries, but also a very noxious weed. Intro. into the U. S. by Wm. Johnson of Ala. and Gov. Means of S. C.

2. **S. vulgare,** Pers. (*Holcus Sorghum,* L. *Andropogon Sorghum,* Brot. *Andropogon Sorghum* subsp. *sativus* var. *vulgaris,* Hack.). SORGHUM. Strong erect ann. looking like Indian corn when not in bloom, although the foliage is usually narrower; culms 4–12 ft. or more, prominently jointed and sheathed, sometimes producing brace-roots and frequently sprouting from the stumps after harvest, the pith in some kinds juicy and in others dry: panicles terminal, of many kinds; spikelets large and broad, hairy, the lemmas awned or awnless. Afr. probably, but exact nativity unknown.—A related species is **S. virgatum,** Stapf (*Holcus virgatus,* Bailey. *Andropogon Sorghum* var. *virgatus,* Hack.). TUNIS-GRASS. Panicle very slender, narrow, open, 6–24 in. long; spikelets narrowly lanceolate, green, finely awned. Afr.—Of the great range of vars. of *S. vulgare,* some grown in other parts of the world and known in N. Amer. mostly in an experimental way, only a few need be treated here.

A. *Sweet sorghums, with sweet juicy pith, grown for the making of syrup from the stalks and also for fodder: panicle open or compact.*

Var. **saccharatum,** Boerl. (*Holcus saccharatus,* L. *H. Sorghum* var. *saccharatus,* Bailey. *Sorghum saccharatum,* Pers. *Andropogon Sorghum* var. *saccharatus,* Alef.). SORGHO. SWEET or SUGAR SORGHUM. A heterogeneous series in descriptive botanical characters but constituting a cultural group, grown for the sweet juice from which syrup is made; herbage used as fodder: panicle dense or loose, mostly erect but sometimes recurved (peduncle goose-necked), ovate to cylindrical in outline; spikelets ovate to obovate, awned or awnless: culms 5–12 ft.—Sometimes erroneously called sugar-cane.

B. *Sorghums grown for the long stiff rays of the panicle.*

Var. **technicum,** Jav. (*Andropogon Sorghum* var. *technicus,* Koern. & Wern. *Holcus Sorghum* var. *technicus,* Bailey). BROOM-CORN. Panicle or "brush" long and loose, in the large kinds 18–30 in. long and the plant 10–15 ft. high, in the dwarf kinds 12–24 in. long and the plant 4–6 ft.; rays of the panicle naked below, stiff, arising from nearly a common point or part but branching toward the end; spikelets usually awned.

C. *Sorghums grown for forage.*

Var. **sudanense,** Hitchc. (*Andropogon Sorghum* var. *sudanensis,* Piper. *Holcus Sorghum* var. *sudanensis,* Hitchc. *H. sudanensis,* Bailey. *Sorghum sudanense,* Stapf). SUDAN-GRASS. Ann., very like no. 1, the spikelets usually prominently awned: culm rather slender, 6–10 ft.: lvs. many, ½in. or less wide: panicle ovate or pyramidal, 6–12 in. long and half as broad, the slender ascending branches whorled; spikelets oblong or elliptic, mostly brownish. Afr.

D. *Grain sorghums, grown for the kernels in the infl., sometimes for fodder.*
a. *Mature panicle with short branches but more or less open or loose: grains mostly small.*

Var. **Drummondii,** Hitchc. (*Andropogon Drummondii,* Nees. *Holcus Sorghum* var. *Drummondii,* Hitchc. *Andropogon Sorghum* var. *Drummondii,* Hack. *Sorghum Drummondii,* Nees). CHICKEN-CORN. Ann., more or less spontaneous in cult. ground in La. and Miss.; culms few or solitary, 6 ft., the lvs. pale and flat: panicle pyramidal-oblong, erect and rather dense, 12–16 in. long, the branches ascending; lower glume of fertile spikelet elliptic, constricted at base; grain oval, orange-colored, not exposed. (Named for Wm. Drummond, who collected specimens at New Orleans in 1832.) Guinea.

Var. **Roxburghii,** Haines (*Andropogon Sorghum* var. *Roxburghii,* Hack. *Holcus Sorghum* var. *Roxburghii,* Bailey. *Sorghum Roxburghii,* Stapf). SHALLU. Ann.; culms stout and tall, often somewhat waxy: panicle oblong or ovoid-oblong, erect, mostly contracted and dense or becoming loose at maturity, the slender branches verticillate; spikelet ovate and acute, tawny; glumes equal, lower 10–13-nerved, upper 7–9-nerved: grain elliptic, often exposed. (Bears the name of Wm. Roxburgh, page 50.) Afr., India.

aa. *Mature panicles compact, often dense, the spikelets clustered: grains large.*

Var. **Durra,** Hubbard & Rehd. (*Holcus Durra,* Forsk. *H. Sorghum* var. *Durra,* Bailey. *Sorghum Durra,* Stapf). DURRA. Medium to stout ann. with dry or not sweet pith: panicle compact, ovate or broad-elliptic, erect or inclined but mostly recurved (goosenecked); spikelets very broad, rhombic-ovate when in bloom, awned or awnless, hairy; lower glume with greenish usually strongly nerved tip: grain nearly globose to lenticular, with a rounded top, included. Nile region.—Yellow milo and Jerusalem corn are forms of durra.

Var. **caffrorum,** Hubbard & Rehd. (*Holcus caffrorum,* Thunb. *H. Sorghum* var. *caffrorum,* Bailey. *Sorghum caffrorum,* Beauv.). KAFIR. Mostly stouter and taller, the pith dry or subacid: panicle oblong or cylindric, dense, erect; spikelets elliptic-ovate, loosely hairy, short-acute but not awned; glumes about half as long as the broad or obovate subglobose grain. (Caffrorum: of the Kafirs.) S. Afr.—Red, White and Blackhull kafirs are leading vars.

Var. **caudatus,** Bailey (*Andropogon Sorghum* subsp. *sativus* var. *caudatus,* Hack. *Sorghum caudatum,* Stapf. *Holcus Sorghum* var. *caudatus,* Bailey). FETERITA. Tall, slender or stout, 6–14 ft.: panicle oblong, often very narrow, very dense, erect, the branches somewhat flexuose, at maturity sometimes spreading open; spikelets elliptic-oblong with rather straight sides, muticous, hairy or glabrous, acute or rarely with short awns: grain broad-elliptic or orbicular, more or less compressed, white, yellow, or red. Cent. Afr.

12. **COIX,** L. Three or 4 tall branching leafy species in the E. Indies and Asia, one well known as a curiosity and for its yield of beads.—Monœcious, the staminate spikelets terminating the infl.: fl.-clusters terminal on axillary simple peduncles; pistillate spikelets (1 fertile, 1 or 2 sterile) borne inside a hollow globular or ovoid body representing a lf.-sheath and which at maturity becomes a very hard dense structure that is used as a bead; staminate spikelets several, in pairs on the axis that projects from the bead, falling at maturity. (Co-ix: old Greek name.)

C. Lacryma-Jobi, L. Ann., 2–6 ft., loose-growing, prominently jointed, smooth: lvs. large, sword-shaped, long-pointed, with prominent midrib and a short basal sheath: peduncles 1 to several from upper sheaths, 1–3 in. long, bearing a single bead about ¼in. across and ⅓in. long which becomes shining white or lead-color or violet at maturity: fr. with the fl.-chaff filling the bead, a smooth plump kernel. (Lacryma-Jobi: *tears of Job,* a fanciful allusion to the large tear-like bead-sheaths.) E. Asia and Malaya.—Several vars. are known in the Orient. Long and widely grown for the beads, which are used in rosaries and other articles; also for ornament and curiosity in the fl.-garden; also forms of it as cereal foods in parts of Asia, as the Adlay of the Philippines; used medicinally; run wild in trop. countries.

13. **ZEA,** L. Coarse annuals of many forms, but considered to represent a single species or at least a single origin; the nativity and origin of the plant are unknown. —Zea differs from Euchlæna in the many-rowed ear with its continuous rachis or cob and the very different flat grains, the rows supposed to represent pistillate spikes; potentially each node may bear an ear, or even more than one, but usually only one to three ears are produced to a stalk and but one at a node; sometimes staminate flts. are produced at the tip of the ear, and pistillate flts. (bearing rounded grains) may be borne in the tassel or staminate infl. (Ze-a: old Greek name.)

Z. Mays, L. MAIZE. INDIAN CORN. Plant low or tall, 3–12 ft. and more, strict, suckering at the base but otherwise usually unbranched, with brace-roots springing from the lower joints: lvs. 1 at every joint or node, long sword-shaped or linear-lanceolate, acuminate-pointed, curving, with prominent rib: staminate spikelets 2 at each node in the panicle or tassel, one sessile or nearly so and one pedicelled, each spikelet 2-fld. with empty ciliate glumes, thin paleæ and lemmas, the stamens 3; pistillate spikelets in 8–24 rows on the rachis, the floral envelopes consisting of 2 glumes, 2 paleæ, 2 lemmas, and left as chaff on the cob (except in pod corn), the style from the single pistil very long and constituting the "silk": fr. a flattened grain with convex or indented top and more or less pointed base. (Mays: a name used by the American aborigines.) Var. **tunicata,** St. Hil. (*Z. tunicata,* Sturt.), POD CORN, floral parts enlarging so that each kernel is inclosed in a husk; supposed by some to be near the original form. Var. **japonica,** Koern. (*Z. japonica* and *Z. japonica vittata,* Hort.), is grown for its ornamental foliage, which is longitudinally striped with yellow and nearly white and sometimes with pink. Var. **gracillima,** Koern. (*Z. gracillima* and *Z. minima,* Hort.), a very dwarf narrow-lvd. green form grown for ornament. Var. **everta,** Bailey (*Z. everta,* Sturt.), POP CORN, kernel small, usually much pointed at base and sometimes at apex, containing much hard endosperm that explodes or pops when heated, turning the kernel inside out; ear and plant small. Var. **indurata,** Bailey (*Z. indurata,* Sturt.), FLINT CORN, YANKEE CORN, kernel hard and smooth on top, due to the thick corneous wall; ears usually long and slender, mostly brown-yellow at maturity; plant of medium size, often strongly suckering. Var. **indentata,** Bailey (*Z. indentata,* Sturt.), DENT CORN, kernel falling in or becoming indented at the top; ears usually relatively short, thick and heavy, yellow or white; the main corn of the U. S.; plant usually tall. Var. **rugosa,** Bonaf. (*Z. saccharata,* Sturt. *Z. Mays* var. *saccharata,* Bailey), SWEET or SUGAR CORN, kernel much wrinkled, the horny endosperm more or less translucent, sweet; plant small or intermediate in size.

14. **EUCHLÆNA,** Schrad. Probably 2 or 3 species, native in Mex. and Cent. Amer., one of which is cult.—Maize-like monœcious broad-lvd. prominently jointed plants: staminate spikelets 2-fld., collected in a terminal panicle; pistillate spikelets with 1 flt. (a rudimentary flt. below), single, on opposite sides of a thickened zigzag jointed rachis, sunken in its cavities, the hardened first glume closing the cavity; these spikes, each wrapped in a little husk, clustered 2 or 4 together in the lf.-sheaths, the long styles protruding from the mouth of the sheath; spikes disarticulating at maturity into trapezoid joints, each permanently inclosing the grain. (Euchlæ-na: Greek *well covered,* probably alluding to the fruiting spikes.)

E. mexicana, Schrad. (*Reana luxurians,* Dur. *Zea mexicana,* Reeves & Mangelsdorf). TEOSINTE. Coarse ann. to 10 ft. and more, branching from the base, very leafy, smooth, the culm between the dark-colored fruiting nodes flattened on one side: lvs. sword-shaped or narrower, long-pointed, midrib prominent, the expanded sheath very strongly veined: grain about ¼in. long, shining, with a pupa-like marking on the face. Mex.—Planted far S. for forage.

15. **ELEUSINE,** Gaertn. A half dozen Old World ann. and per. grasses, one of which is cult.—Mostly not tall plants, tufted: infl. of several radiating or erect one-sided spikes, forming a kind of terminal umbel, or one of the spikes beneath the others; spikelets several-fld., sessile and imbricated, in 2 rows; glumes shorter than the flt., unequal, keeled; lemmas ribbed and keeled. (Eleusi-ne: Greek name of the town where Ceres was worshiped.)—*E. indica,* Gaertn., is a common weed.

E. coracana, Gaertn. (*Cynosurus coracanus,* L. *E. Coracan,* Aschers. & Graebn.). AFRICAN MILLET. Coarse ann., 1–4 ft., grown in parts of the Old World for its grain and sometimes in N. Amer. for ornament; culms stout, glabrous, much ensheathed: lvs. many, about ¼in. broad, soft, glabrous but somewhat scabrous, hairy in throat of sheath: spikes 5 or more, short and thick, 1–1½ in. and perhaps more long and more than ¼in. broad, upright, the lower one an inch or so remote; floral parts tapering, acute or muticous but not awned: fr. small, nearly globular, free, with a loose membranaceous pericarp. (Coracana is a rendering of a S. Indian vernacular name.) Probably Asia and Afr.—The plant is known as RAGI in China and India, where it is cult. extensively for its grain and is a staple food.

16. **ORYZA,** L. A half dozen paludose grasses of the E. Indies, one of vast importance as a grain-food.—Spikelets strongly flattened sideways, paniculate, perfect, 1-fld. with 2 small glumes; stamens usually 6: fr. with a linear hilum. (Ory-za: adaptation of the Arabic name *eruz.*)

O. sativa, L. RICE. Handsome erect-growing grass of wet habitats (but there are races adapted to uplands), 3–4 ft., stooling; culms angled, smooth, nearly all inclosed in the glabrous strongly nerved lf.-sheaths: lf.-blades long, flat, ½in. broad, more or less scabrous: panicle terminal, narrow, curved or nodding to one side, 6–12 in. long, with many long ascending branches; spikelets in bloom ¼–⅓in. long, very flat and very strongly ribbed, oblong, pubescent, awned or awnless; palea with 2 nerves near margin: fr. free inside the husk, oblong, flattened on the sides, with a very long hilum, straw-colored or yellow, becoming white when polished; there are red vars. and about a dozen vernacular-named vars. are cult. Escaped in some regions.

17. **AVENA,** L. About 50 grasses, mostly ann. species, of the cooler temp. regions, oats being one of them.—Plants of diverse habit but agreeing in a loose paniculate infl., 2–6-fld. spikelets with beards beneath the flts., many-nerved glumes large and membranaceous and nearly equal, lemmas hard, 2-toothed at apex, and usually bearing a long twisted awn from the back (but the awn sometimes lacking or modified in cult. kinds); flts. often disarticulating and falling intact: fr. free or tightly inclosed in the unrolled lemma and palea. (Ave-na: the classical Latin name of the oat.)

A. Flts. disarticulating and easily shedding from the large glumes; lemmas hairy; awn developed.
  B. Glumes nearly 2 in. long; awns 2–3 in. . . . . 1. *A. sterilis*
  BB. Glumes about 1 in. long; awns about 1–1½ in.
    C. Lemma-teeth awned . . . . 2. *A. barbata*
    CC. Lemma-teeth acute . . . . 3. *A. fatua*
AA. Flts. not readily disarticulating, remaining in the glumes; lemmas glabrous or nearly so; awn short or wanting.
  B. Grain permanently inclosed in the lemma or hull . . . . 4. *A. sativa*
  BB. Grain separating from the hull . . . . 5. *A. nuda*

1. **A. sterilis,** L. Animated Oat. Ann., 2–3 ft., with panicles 6–12 in. long: spikelets long, the glumes nearly or quite 2 in. long; awns 2 in. or more long, with a prominent twisting lower part; lemmas densely hairy. Medit. region and eastward.—Grown as a curiosity, the mature flts. twisting and moving when planted or placed on the ground, due to hygroscopic action of the awns. *A. fa ua* is sometimes grown under this name.

2. **A. barbata,** Brot. Slender Wild Oat. Ann., 2–3½ ft., with slender panicle 6–12 in. long, the spikelets slender and narrow, 2- to several-fld., the glumes about 1 in. long; lemma lightly hairy, 7-nerved, awn-toothed; awn from back of lemma 1–1½ in. long, bent. S. Eu.; nat. on the Pacific coast and forms part of the wild-oat hay.

3. **A. fatua,** L. Wild Oat. Ann., 2–3 or 4 ft. high, tufted: panicle 6–12 in. or more long, stout, with drooping 2-fld. broad spikelets, the glumes 1 in. or less long; lemma 9-nerved, the marginal nerves faint, with stiff usually brownish hairs, the teeth acute but not awned; awn from the back 1–1½ in. long, bent. Eu., Asia.—Intro., and on the Pacific coast established and constituting part of the wild-oat hay.

4. **A. sativa,** L. Oat. Erect tufted ann., 2–3 or 4 ft., with culms smooth, or scabrous beneath the panicle: lvs. ¼–½in. broad, mostly short or medium in length (blade 6–12 in.), flat, more or less scabrous, the sheaths long and loose, ligule short and jagged: panicle terminal, 6–12 in. long, open and spreading on all sides or variously condensed, or (in the Side Oats) the branches hanging from one side; spikelets usually 2-fld., ¾–1 in. long, slender-pedicelled; glumes strongly several-nerved; lemmas glabrous or with few hairs at the base, teeth acute, the dorsal awn absent, or one to a flt. and short (usually not exceeding ½–¾in.) and straight: fr. about ¼–⅓in. long, narrow, with nearly parallel sides, hairy, grooved lengthwise on the face, tightly inclosed in the inrolled lemma which also covers the palea on the front, these envelopes constituting the hull or chaff. Cultigen; supposed to be derived from *A. fatua* for the most part, and some races (known mostly in other countries) from *A. sterilis* and *A. barbata;* the species is therefore not a homogeneous group. —The oat sometimes is spontaneous but does not long persist. The winter oat is any hardy race that may be planted in autumn, maturing the following year.

5. **A. nuda,** L. Naked Oat. Spikelets usually more than 2-fld.: fr. free, escaping from the lemma as a naked grain. Probably a cultigen.

18. **ARRHENATHERUM,** Beauv. Species 6, per., in the Medit. region, much like Avena but the lower flt. in the spikelet staminate, the upper one perfect, an awn from one or both flts. (Arrhenathe-rum: Greek *masculine awn*, from the awned male flt.)

A. elatius, Mert. & Koch (*A. avenaceum*, Beauv. *Avena elatior*, L.). Tall Oat-Grass. Tufted, erect, 2–4 ft.; culms very slender, glabrous or sometimes slightly pubescent at the nodes, sheaths glabrous: lvs. ¼in. or less wide, slightly scabrous, soft: panicle 6–15 in. long, narrow, mostly interrupted, light green or purplish with a luster; spikelets 2-fld., the lower staminate and with an awn about ½in. long, the upper perfect and sometimes with a shorter awn. Eu.—Sometimes sown as a meadow-grass; also nat. Var. **bulbosum,** Spenner (*A. bulbosum*, Presl. *A. elatius* var. *tuberosum*, Thiel. *Avena bulbosa*, Willd.), bears a cluster or string of tubers at the surface of the ground; a striped-lvd. form of it is in cult. for ornament.

19. **HORDEUM,** L. About 16–20 species in temp. regions, ann. and per., widely distributed; one an important grain and forage plant.—Spikelets 1-fld., 3 together in a "breast" at each node of the jointed rachis, alternating, one or all of the spikelets fertile, the lateral ones sometimes sterile and reduced to awns; when all are fertile and distinct, the head or spike is 6-rowed; when all are fertile and the outside spikes on the opposite sides overlap (as is usual), the spike is 4-rowed; when the central spikelet only is fertile, the spike is 2-rowed; glumes very narrow, like an involucre subtending the 3 spikelets; lemmas awned: fr. inclosed. (Hor-deum: ancient Latin name for barley.)

A. Plant bien. or per.: spike nodding: cult. for ornament . . . . 1. *H. jubatum*
AA Plant ann.: spike erect: cult. for grain and forage . . . . 2. *H. vulgare*

1. **H. jubatum,** L. Squirrel-tail-Grass. Bien. or per.; culms 12–30 in. high, simple and erect (base sometimes inclined), slender: lvs. short: spike 2–4 in. long, gracefully curving and nodding, silvery-green or brown, with many very slender awns 1–3 in. long. N. Amer., Eurasia.—A weed and often troublesome, but sometimes planted for ornament.

2. **H. vulgare,** L. (*H. sativum*, Pers.). Barley. Erect stout ann., 1½–3 ft.; culms simple, glabrous or scabrous beneath the spike: lvs. ¼–¾in. broad, rather short, long-tapering to the point; sheaths loose, glabrous, ligules short and thin: spike terminal, 3–4 in. long, densely fld., erect (vars. with nodding spikes), with many stout very long erect rough beards that far overtop the spike, the rachis not disarticulating; glumes narrow, short-awned; lemma longer, with a very flat awn 3–6 in. long: fr. elliptic, about ⅜in. long, short-pointed, furrowed the length of the face, smooth, more or less tightly inclosed in the lemma and palea but sometimes (as in the hulless barley) quite free. Var. **trifurcatum,** Alef. (*H. cœleste* var. *trifurcatum*, Schlecht.), is a teratological beardless state in which the awns are represented by short furcate branches.—Barley is a cultigen, probably derived from *H. spontanum*, Koch, and perhaps *H. ischnatherum*, Schulz, wild plants of the Orient. The two-rowed barley, *H. distichon*, L., and the six-rowed, *H. hexastichon*, L., may be variants of a polymorphous species, known as *H. vulgare*, or represent different phyla in the evolution of the cult. group.

20. **SECALE,** L. Three Eurasian grasses, one cult. for grain and forage.—Differs from Triticum in the subulate 1-nerved glumes: spikelets 2-fld., alternating on a long zigzag rachis; lemmas keeled and long-awned: fr. elongated, inclosed in the lemma. (Seca-le: old Latin name of some grain.)

S. cereale, L. Rye. Tall hardy tufted ann., 3–5 ft., with blue-green cast; culms slender but erect, overtopping the foliage, glabrous except pubescent near the spike, glaucous: lvs. many, rather soft, ½in. or less broad, smooth or slightly scabrous, long-pointed; sheaths long and loose, the ligule short and jagged: spike terminal, 3–6 in. long, curved, much awned, narrow but closely fld., the spikelets with 2 fertile flts. and perhaps a third one rudimentary; lemmas long and narrow, tapering into awns, the keels prominently set with stiff points or teeth: fr. oblong, about ⅓in. long, light brown, narrowly grooved on the face, short-pointed, glabrous. Cultigen; supposed to have developed from *S. montanum*, Guss., a per. in the mts. of Eu. and Asia.

21. **TRITICUM,** L. Ann. and bien. grasses, as now recognized represented by about 15 species, of the Medit. region and W. Asia; source of bread-grain.—Erect plants with flts. in terminal spikes: spikelets 1 at each node or joint of the rachis (which is either articulating or continuous), placed flatwise, alternating, 2–5-fld.; lower 1 or 2 flts. perfect, the upper staminate or neutral; glumes ovate, 3- to many-nerved, often with an awn from glume and lemma: fr. free or remaining in the hull. (Trit-icum: Latin name for wheat.)

A. Flts. in spikelets 2, 1 perfect, 1 sterile; palea dividing lengthwise when mature and incompletely enveloping the grain. . . . . 1. *T. monococcum*
AA. Flts. in spikelets more than 2, 2 or more flts. being fertile; palea remaining entire at maturity.
B. Culms with spikes disarticulate at maturity; usual methods of threshing ineffective.
C. Spikelets closely and densely imbricated in the spike; inner surface of each spikelet flattened or straight longitudinally. . . . . 2. *T. dicoccum*
CC. Spikelets not closely imbricated, but more open along the rachis; inner surface of each spikelet arched or convex longitudinally. . . . . 3. *T. Spelta*
BB. Culms with spikes not disarticulate at maturity; the free-grained readily threshed wheats.
C. Glumes membranaceous or herbaceous (as in oats), as long or longer than lemmas. . . . . 4. *T. polonicum*
CC. Glumes coriaceous, shorter or not longer than lemmas.
D. Spikelets with glumes having an indistinct keel that often disappears toward base of glume. . . . . 5. *T. æstivum*
DD. Spikelets with glumes distinctly and sharply keeled to the base.
E. Length of glumes about equalling lemmas: grain comparatively long and sharp-pointed, very hard. . . . . 6. *T. durum*
EE. Length of glumes about two-thirds the lemmas: grain short and thick, obtusely pointed or rounded, not very hard. . . . . 7. *T. turgidum*

1. **T. monococcum,** L. (*T. æstivum* var. *monococcum*, Bailey). Einkhorn. Spikelets 1-seeded, the second flt. not fertile; spike slender, long-awned and laterally compressed, resembling a small-headed bearded wheat with much flattened spikelets; palea splitting into two parts at maturity; glumes with lateral tooth pointed: kernels remaining in the spikelets after threshing, pale red, slender, much compressed with almost no crease. Greece, Asia Minor.

2. **T. dicoccum,** Schrank (*T. æstivum* var. *dicoccum*, Bailey). Emmer. Autumn- or

spring-maturing ann. with culms often pithy within and lvs. usually pubescent: spikes very dense, usually bearded, laterally compressed, on very brittle rachis; spikelets with inner face flattened and essentially straight longitudinally, usually 2-fld.; glumes tapering toward apex, with an acute tooth, prominently keeled: grains remaining within glumes after threshing, red, long and slender, acute at each end.—Sometimes, and incorrectly, called "Speltz."

3. **T. Spelta,** L. (*T. æstivum* var. *Spelta*, Bailey). Spelt. Spikes slender, somewhat 4-sided, bearded or beardless, lax, on slender brittle rachis; spikelets well separated, 2-kernelled, arched longitudinally on inner side; glumes firm, pubescent, with 1 obtuse tooth but otherwise truncate, obscurely keeled: grain inclosed by glumes after threshing, pale red, long, laterally compressed, apex acute, shallow narrow crease present.—Much material grown as "Speltz" is properly *T. dicoccum.*

4. **T. polonicum,** L. (*T. æstivum* var. *polonicum*, Bailey). Polish Wheat. A spring wheat, having tall sts. and pithy peduncle: spikes lax, large, awned; glumes lanceolate, about 1 in. long, equalling or exceeding the spikelet and membranous in texture: grain nearly ½in. long, narrow, hard, resembling a grain of rye, of inferior milling and nutritional value.—Grown only occasionally in W. U. S.

5. **T. æstivum,** L. (*T. sativum*, Lam. *T. vulgare*, Vill.). Common Wheat. Ann., sown early in the year as spring wheat, or certain races in autumn as winter wheat and maturing the following season, tillering at the base; culms erect, simple, 2–4 ft., glabrous or at the nodes somewhat pubescent: lvs. flat, about ½in. wide and 8–15 in. long, taper-pointed, the long loose sheath glabrous or slightly pubescent, ligule short, thin and jagged: spikes stout and erect, 1–4 in. long, cylindrical, or in the Club Wheats short and thicker toward the top, "bearded" (awned) or "smooth," the rachis not breaking up; spikelets or "breasts" erect and appressed; glumes shorter than the spikelet, broader on the outer side and with a shoulder or projecting tooth on the upper angle, the keel awned or muticous, indistinct and not extending to base; lemmas somewhat 3-toothed, the central tooth often an awn: fr. a free oblong grooved naked grain nearly or quite ¼in. long, pubescent at the top.—One of the most important food plants of man, over 175 hort. vars. of this species being cult. in U. S. with perhaps as many more in Eu. Nativity unknown and a cultigen, having been originally described and subsequently known only as a domesticated subject. Its origin is undetermined. The species with articulated rachis (*T. monococcum, T. dicoccum, T. Spelta, T. spontaneum* and others) are presumably nearest the aboriginal condition. It is probable that *T. ægilopoides*, Bal., *T. dicoccoides*, Koern., and related wild grasses of the E. Medit. region and eastward are approximate originals.

6. **T. durum,** Desf. Durum Wheat. A spring wheat, tall with pithy peduncle in upper part of culm: spikes compact, laterally compressed; glumes sharply keeled to base; lemmas usually bearded, the awns long and coarse: grain white or red, long, pointed with short apical tuft, exceedingly hard.—About 10 hort. vars. cult. in north-central U. S.; flour used primarily for macaroni and spaghetti products.

7. **T. turgidum,** L. English Wheat. Poulard Wheat. Mediterranean Wheat. Tall winter or spring wheat with broad lvs.; culms thick, solid or less often pithy: spikes long and occasionally compounded or branched; spikelets closely imbricated; glumes shorter than lemmas and sharply keeled; awns brittle, longer than the spike and attached directly to the convex glume: grain thick, humped, very starchy.—The var. Alaska is grown in U. S. to a limited extent and primarily as a source of stock feed.

22. **PENNISETUM,** Rich. Per. and ann. grasses, widely spread in trop. regions, about 50 species; one cult. in U. S. for grain and forage and others for ornament.—Infl. spicate in the cult. kinds (spicate panicle); perfect flt. 1, terminal in the spikelet, with staminate flt. beneath; spikelets subtended by involucral bristles that are not united at the base and fall at maturity. (Pennise-tum: Latin *penna, seta,* feather, bristle.)

A. Involucral bristles little, if at all, exceeding the spikelet and therefore not prominent on the spike: ann., 6–9 ft. high........1. *P. glaucum*
AA. Involucral bristles much exceeding the spikelet and therefore prominent on the spike: ornamental perennials often grown as border grasses: the Fountain-Grasses.
B. Bristles, or some of them, plumose toward the base.
C. Spikes 2–4 in. long........2. *P. villosum*
CC. Spikes 6–10 in. long........3. *P. Ruppelii*
BB. Bristles naked, not plumose, although sometimes finely serrate.
C. Spikes 2 or more on each culm........4. *P. latifolium*
CC. Spikes solitary, 1 on a culm, terminal.
D. Length of spike 2–5 in........5. *P. alopecuroides*
DD. Length of spike 8–12 in........6. *P. macrostachyum*

1. **P. glaucum,** R. Br. (*Panicum glaucum*, L. *Pennisetum americanum*, Auth. *P. typhoideum*, Rich.). Pearl Millet. Indian and African Millet. Stout and erect,

6–9 to 10 ft., with the aspect of maize, the culm with prominent nodes: lvs. long and narrow, 2–3 ft., scabrous on nerves and margin, the sheaths long and loose, ligule short and densely ciliate: spike single and terminal, long and dense as on cat-tail, 12–20 in. long, straight, about 1 in. thick at base and guarded by a lf.-like spreading bract, somewhat tapering or pointed at apex, the axis villous; spikelets mostly 2 together, subtended by unequal somewhat plumose bristles: fr. outgrowing the floral envelopes and bursting them, obovoid, ⅛in. long, bluish or whitish. Nativity unknown; by some thought to be a cultigen, probably of hybrid origin.—Grown for forage and in warm countries for the grain which is used for human food; there are many forms and the botany of them is yet confused.

2. **P. villosum,** R. Br. (*P. longistylum,* Hort. not Hochst.). Per.; culms 1–2 ft., pubescent beneath the spike: spike 1, 2–4 in. long, broad, with showy feathery bristles. Abyssinia.

3. **P. Ruppelii,** Steud. (*P. Ruppelianum,* Hort.). Per., much planted in borders for varied color effects and in masses; culms 3–4 ft. high, gracefully curving, scabrous beneath the spike: lvs. long and narrow, numerous, sheaths long, ciliate at the ligule: spike 1, mostly curved or nodding, 6–10 in. long; bristles prominent, 1 in. or more long, the slender points scabrous. (Ruppelii: Edouard Ruppel, 1794–1884, German botanist.) Abyssinia.—Usually grown with rose-colored, purple, and copper-colored spikes, the foliage also being colored. *P. atrosanguineum* and *P. cupreum,* Hort., belong here.

4. **P. latifolium,** Spreng. (*Gymnothrix latifolia,* Schult.). Per.; culms 3–4 ft., ciliate at the nodes: lvs. about 1 in. broad, tapering to very long point, prominently many-veined, slightly scabrous, with a long sheath, ciliate at the short ligule: spikes several, green, nodding, 2–3 in. long, with long serrulate or pubescent bristles. Argentina.

5. **P. alopecuroides,** Spreng. (*P. japonicum,* Hort. *Panicum alopecuroides,* L.). Per., hardy in northern states, 2–4 ft. tall; culms slender, pubescent below the spike which stands above the foliage: lvs. long and narrow, bright green: spike 1, 2–5 in. or even 6 in. long, silvery in color, the large anthers purplish; bristles long and prominent, scabrous. China.

6. **P. macrostachyum,** Trin. (*Gymnothrix macrostachys,* Brongn.). Per., 4–5 ft.: lvs. broad and flat: spike 1, 8–12 in. long. E. Indies.—A form with purplish foliage is var. **atropurpureum,** Hort.

23. **SETARIA,** Beauv. (*Chætochloa,* Scribn.). About 60 ann. or sometimes per. grasses in warm countries but some of them extensively spread as weeds; one polymorphous species grown for fodder and grain.—Infl. spicate (spike-like panicle), terminating the culm; distinguished from Pennisetum largely by the persistent bristles which remain on the rachis after the spikelets have fallen. (Seta-ria: Latin *seta,* a bristle.)

A. Head or panicle thick and heavy: millet.................................1. *S. italica*
AA. Head or panicle long, slender and open: ornamental grass...................2. *S. palmifolia*

1. **S. italica,** Beauv. (*Panicum italicum,* L. *Chætochloa italica,* Scribn.). FOXTAIL MILLET. Strong-growing ann. 3–5 ft. high, branching somewhat from the crown but the smooth prominently jointed culms mostly simple: lvs. many, ¾–1 in. broad, flat, long-pointed, scabrous, many-nerved, sheaths long and ciliate at the throat: spikes terminal, thick, 1–12 in. long, ½–2 in. diam., erect, curved or nodding, continuous or lobed, the bristles long or short and green, brown or purplish: fr. $1/16$in. long, ovoid, plano-convex, smooth, yellow, brown, red, or nearly black. Cultigen, perhaps derived from *S. viridis,* Beauv., which is now a widespread weed.—Foxtail millet is cult. in many forms, in this country for hay and forage but in some other countries as a cereal grain. Var. **stramineo-fructa,** Bailey, comprises forms with yellow fr. and very large spikes (which are often lobed), bristles variously colored, known as GERMAN MILLET and GOLDEN WONDER MILLET. Var. **rubrofructa,** Bailey, has reddish or orange fr. and purple bristles, comprising SIBERIAN and TURKESTAN MILLET. Var. **nigrofructa,** Bailey, with purplish or nearly black fr., small dense heads 3 in. or less long, and dark brown bristles in HUNGARIAN-GRASS.

2. **S. palmifolia,** Stapf (*Panicum palmifolium,* Willd. *P. plicatum,* Auth. not Lam. *Chætochloa palmifolia,* Hitchc. & Chase). PALM-GRASS. Slender per. with flexuose culms rising 4–6 ft.: lvs. broad in the middle (to 1½ in.) and tapering both ways, running to a very fine point, 1–2 ft. long, strongly plicate-ribbed, sparsely hairy; sheaths more or less hairy, strongly ciliate on upper margins: panicle narrow and open, often interrupted, 8–12 in. long, comprised of many short rather loosely-fld. racemes; spikelets short-pedicelled, some of the upper ones often subtended by a single bristle, ovate, with strong green nerves, the empty glume broad, scarious-margined and obtuse. E. Indies.—Common in greenhouses, grown for its foliage, becoming spontaneous along the walks; also in the open S. There is a striped-lvd. form.

24. **PANICUM,** L. A great genus, probably 400 species, widely spread over the globe, very few of which are cult. subjects.—Ann. or per. grasses, mostly of small stature, with panicled or rarely racemose infl.: spikelets bearing 1 fertile flt., and beneath it 2 empty glumes and a neutral or staminate lemma; glumes unequal, the lower one often small or minute; lemma and palea of the fertile flt. more or less hardened, without evident nerves, the grain free within these tightly closed envelopes; bristles none subtending the spikelets. (Pan-icum: old Latin name, once applied to another plant.)

A. Plants ann.
  B. Infl. of several more or less spike-like racemes....................1. *P. texanum*
  BB. Infl. a more or less diffuse panicle....................2. *P. miliaceum*
AA. Plants per.
  B. Spikelets short-pedicelled along one side of the rachis, forming spike-like racemes: nodes bearded....................3. *P. purpurascens*
  BB. Spikelets in open or sometimes contracted or congested panicles, not 1-sided.
    C. Rhizomes short, stout: fr. transversely rugose....................4. *P. maximum*
    CC. Rhizomes creeping, scaly: fr. not transversely rugose....................5. *P. virgatum*

1. **P. texanum,** Buckl. COLORADO-GRASS. TEXAS MILLET. Ann., variable in height to 6 ft., culms erect or ascending: lvs. to 8 in. long and ½in. wide: infl. to 8 in. long, branches appressed and loosely fld.; spikelets pilose, fusiform, nearly ¼in. long. Native in the Colorado Valley and Tex.; nat. in S. E. U. S., and sometimes planted for forage.

2. **P. miliaceum,** L. BROOM-CORN MILLET. HOG MILLET. Ann., 3–4 ft. or more, culms slender, glabrous or hairy, mostly simple: lvs. soft, narrow, long-pointed, sparsely hairy; sheaths loosely hairy, bearded at the throat: panicle drooping, with long more or less naked branches (whence the name Broom-Corn Millet), bearing the ovate-pointed strongly nerved spikelets on slender pedicels: fr. nearly globular, more than 1/16in. across, straw-colored or white, smooth and shining. Probably E. Indies.—Cult. from earliest times, the millet of history; grown for the food grain and for forage. In N. Amer. not much grown, and as a forage plant, under the name of French Millet, Proso Millet.

3. **P. purpurascens,** Raddi (*P. barbinode,* Trin.). PARA-GRASS. Per., decumbent at base and stoloniferous, spreading by the extensive rooting of the joints, the smooth culms rising 2–10 ft.: lvs. 6–18 in. long, flat, long-pointed, scabrous on edges; sheaths glabrous or hairy, ciliate at the throat: panicle open, more or less 1-sided, 6–15 in. long, of ascending closely fld. racemes; spikelets ovoid-pointed, strongly nerved, the lower glume pointed: nodes bearded. Brazil.—Grown in tropics and warm regions for hay and forage.

4. **P. maximum,** Jacq. GUINEA-GRASS. Per., culms mostly erect, 4–8 or 10 ft. high, in large bunches: lvs. 1–2 ft. long and nearly 1½ in. wide: panicle to 20 in. long and a third as wide, with stiff branches in whorls; spikelets small, the grain transversely rugose. Afr.; nat. in S. Fla. and S. Tex.—Sometimes grown along the Gulf Coast for forage.

5. **P. virgatum,** L. SWITCH-GRASS. Per. with scaly abundant creeping rhizomes, culms erect to 7 ft. but usually only 3–5 ft.: lvs. 4–20 in. long: panicle open, often diffuse, to 2 ft. long. U. S., Mex.—Sometimes grown for ornament.

25. **ECHINOCHLOA,** Beauv. About a dozen annuals and perennials, of warm countries, some of them weeds and one or two cult. for forage and for the grain.—Infl. comprised of short or long racemes arranged in a heavy terminal panicle: lvs. ample, broad or narrow, with compressed sheaths: spikelets with 1 perfect flt., with empty lemmas or a staminate flt. beneath, the sterile lemma and sometimes the second glume either awned or cusp-pointed: fr. pointed. (Echinoch-loa: Greek *hedgehog grass.*)

E. Crus-galli, Beauv. (*Panicum Crus-galli,* L.). BARNYARD-GRASS. Ann. to 4 ft., culms erect or decumbent, stout: lvs. to 15 in. long or more and ½in. wide: panicles erect and rather stiff, nodding when heavy with grain, often tinged purple, to 8 in. long; spikelets conspicuously hispid, awns ½–1¼ in. long. U. S. Not known to be cult. except in var. **frumentacea,** Wight (*Panicum frumentaceum,* Roxb. *E. frumentacea,* Link. *E. Crus-galli* var. *edulis,* Hitchc.), JAPANESE BARNYARD MILLET, BILLION-DOLLAR-GRASS, differing primarily in its purplish more appressed and thicker infl. and awnless spikelets more turgid; native probably in Asia and Afr.—Grown in N. Amer. for forage, in Asia also for the grain. *E. colonum,* Link, is grown in parts of the Old World for fodder and sometimes the grain for human food, now a weed in N. Amer.

26. **CYNODON,** Rich. (*Capriola,* Adans.). Six small per. grasses of the Old World and Australia, one used for lawns and pastures in the S.—Creeping and stoloniferous: lvs. short and flat: infl. of several slender digitate spikes with articulated rachillæ; spikelets 1-fld., flattened, awnless, sessile in 2 rows on one side of the rachis;

glumes narrow and acute, the lemmas broad and ciliate on the keel: fr. free. (Cynodon: *dog tooth,* probably in allusion to the tooth-like sheaths on the stolons.)

C. Dactylon, Pers. (*Panicum Dactylon,* L.). BERMUDA-GRASS. BAHAMA-GRASS. Culms rising 3–16 in. from the extensively creeping base, glabrous, terminated by 3–5 slender radiating 1-sided spikes ½–2 in. long: lvs. mostly near base of culm and on the runners, short, the ligule hairy: spikelets small, pointed, sessile, appressed, imbricated; lemma exceeding the sharp glumes. (Dac-tylon: refers to the dactyls or fingers of the infl.) Eu., Asia, now widely spread over the globe.—A lawn and pasture grass in warm countries; also an invading weed and roadside cover.

27. **CHLORIS,** Sw. Species about 40, ann. and per., mostly in trop. and subtrop. regions around the world, sometimes grown for forage and ornament.—Erect leafy grasses, with perfect spikelets sessile in 2 rows on one side of a slender rachis, the spikes few to several, aggregate and spreading at the summit of the culm; glumes keeled, unequal; lower flt. perfect, its lemma short-awned; upper 1–2 flts. rudimentary, the lemmas often reduced to 1–3 awns. (Chlo-ris: Greek.)

C. Gayana, Kunth. RHODES-GRASS. Strong per. producing running branches that root at the nodes; culms slender but erect, 3–4 ft. and more, flattened, glabrous or near the umbel scabrous, the brown nodes constricted: lvs. many, conduplicate when dry, scabrous: infl. a terminal spreading umbel, well above the foliage, of 6–15 narrow spikes 3 in. and more long; spikelets deciduous, leaving the sharp-pointed glumes. (Named after Jacques E. Gay, page 43.) S. Afr.—Grown to some extent far S. for forage.

28. **AXONOPUS,** Beauv. Stoloniferous or tufted perennials, rarely annuals, represented by about 60 species, mostly in trop. Amer., one of which is grown as a pasture and lawn grass far S.—Infl. comprised of slender spike-like racemes, digitate, or racemose along the axis; spikelets sessile, alternate, solitary in 2 rows on one side of a 3-angled rachis; flts. with first glume wanting and the sterile lemma without a palea. (Axon-opus: Greek, *axis foot.*)

A. affinis, Chase. CARPET-GRASS. Per., culms ascending, 2–20 in. high, flattened: lvs. rather short, about ⅛in. wide, flat with abruptly sharp apex: spikes in pairs or digitate, 1–4 in. long, slender; spikelets about 1⁄10 in. long, sparsely appressed-silky. S. E. U. S.—A predominant pasture grass on alluvial or heavy soils of the S., also employed for lawns where it is established by the sowing of pieces of stolons. A related species, *A. furcatus,* Hitchc. (*Paspalum furcatum,* Fluegge), has much larger glabrous spikelets and is reported cult. as a pasture grass in n.-cent. Fla. True *A. compressus,* Beauv. (*Milium compressum,* Sw. *Anastrophus compressus,* Schlecht.), long considered to be the plant now known as *A. affinis,* is a broader-lvd. more stoloniferous species whose natural distribution is limited to La. and Fla. and in W. Indies and Cent. Amer.; cult. for forage purposes in Australia and to a lesser extent in S. E. U. S.

29. **AGROSTIS,** L. BENT-GRASS. Ann. and per. narrow-lvd. paniculate grasses of about 100 widely distributed species, most abundant in temp. regions; two or three have much agricultural value.—Spikelets small, 1-fld., in open graceful panicles that usually have capillary branchlets; glumes acute, nearly equal, mostly longer than the obtuse awnless or dorsally awned lemma, the palea less than the lemma or even wanting; styles short; stamens mostly 3: fr. free, but inclosed in the lemma. (Agros-tis: Greek *field,* the place of growth; in Latin *couch-grass;* from its use in this large genus of grasses is derived the name of grass science, *agrostology,* and grass student, *agrostologist.*)

A. Plants ann.
- B. Spikelets awnless or essentially so. . . . . 1. *A. nebulosa*
- BB. Spikelets prominently awned. . . . . 2. *A. retrofracta*

AA. Plants per.
- B. Panicle branches without spikelets along basal portion, the latter usually on distal half of the branch: ligule about 1⁄12 in. long on culm-lvs. . . . . 3. *A. tenuis*
- BB. Panicle branches, or some of them, with spikelets near base and close to primary axis: ligule to ¼in. long on culm-lvs.
  - C. Infl. a contracted panicle, the branches appressed: plants producing long stolons. 4. *A. palustris*
  - CC. Infl. an open panicle, the branches ascending: no long stolons produced.
    - D. Awn of lemma distinct, originating from middle, exserted slightly from spikelet and bent. . . . . 5. *A. canina*
    - DD. Awn of lemma much reduced in size or absent.
      - E. Culms erect: rhizomes present. . . . . 6. *A. alba*
      - EE. Culms decumbent: rhizomes absent. . . . . 7. *A. stolonifera*

1. **A. nebulosa,** Boiss. & Reut. (*A. capillaris,* Hort. not L.). Cloud-Grass. A dainty ann. grass 1 ft. high, with few very narrow short lvs. overtopped by a diffuse very delicate open panicle 4–6 in. long, with verticillate fine branches: spikelets very small, long-pedicelled, shining, sometimes slightly awned; palea present. Spain.—Grown for dry bouquets.

2. **A. retrofracta,** Willd. (*A. laxiflora,* Hort.). Ann. slender grass 1–2 ft., with very open large wide-spreading panicles much overtopping the narrow lvs., glabrous: spikelets borne at the ends of long capillary branches, each with a slender awn exceeding the acute glumes which are much longer than the flts. New Zeal., Australia, Hawaii, and intro. into U. S.

3. **A. tenuis,** Sibth. (*A. vulgaris,* With. *A. capillaris,* Huds. not L.). Colonial Bent. Rhode Island Bent. Slender erect per. usually 8–16 in. tall, with short stolons but no creeping rhizomes: lvs. 2–4 in. long, very narrow: panicle open, 2–4 in. long, slenderly branched; spikelets not dense, generally restricted to the distal half of the branches. Probably of European origin but nat. in N. E. U. S. and B. C. to N. Calif.—Much prized as a lawn grass in the cooler more humid parts of U. S. where numerous strains have been segregated, creeping sorts being known as Astoria and Oregon Bent, and non-creeping forms as Rhode Island, Colonial, New Zealand and Prince Edward Island Bents.

4. **A. palustris,** Huds. (*A. maritima,* Lam. *A. alba,* Auth. not L.). Creeping Bent. Per., producing long stolons; culms erect from an inclined or decumbent base, 1½–3½ ft. high, slender: lvs. short, flat and firm, ⅛–¼in. broad, taper-pointed, the scarious ligule about ¼in. long: panicle 3–12 in. long, at first spreading but becoming narrower, green or reddish; lemma 3-nerved, nearly as long as the glumes, seldom short-awned, the palea one-half or more as long. Eu.; extensively nat. in marsh lands, N. E. U. S. and Canada, N. W. U. S. and B. C.—Cult. clones known as Metropolitan and Washington Bents are propagated by stolons; other races as Cocoos and Coos Bay Bents are propagated by seeds; all are grown for lawn or golf-turf purposes.

5. **A. canina,** L. Velvet Bent. Brown Bent. Slender delicate grass, with culms 12–18 or 24 in. high, and erect fine glabrous culms weak or reclining at base: lvs. short and very narrow, the lower ones almost setaceous and more or less inrolled: panicle with very slender hair-like branches, becoming contracted or narrowed at maturity; glumes one-fourth longer than lemmas, the latter with a bent awn borne below the middle; palea none or minute. Eu. and perhaps N. E. U. S.—Cult. for golf course putting greens.

6. **A. alba,** L. Redtop. Fiorin. Erect robust per. 2–4 ft. high, with vigorous creeping rhizomes: panicle to 10 in. long, pyramidal-oblong, reddish when in fl.; spikelets small, lemmas awnless or rarely awned. Eurasia; escaped and nat. in U. S.—A common pasture and lawn grass to which the name *A. palustris* has erroneously been applied. It intergrades with *A. stolonifera* and is not always readily separated.

7. **A. stolonifera,** L. Culms decumbent, 8–20 in. high, often rooting at nodes and forming a spreading base when in wet soil: panicle 2–6 in. long, greenish to purplish, lemmas awnless or rarely awned. N. N. Amer., N. Eu.—Probably not much cult. and material so listed referable to other species; var. *major,* Hort., is probably *A. alba* and the hort. vars. *compacta* and *maritima* may be referred to *A. palustris.*

30. **DACTYLIS,** L. A single species of the temp. parts of the Old World, grown widely as a hay and forage grass, and extensively nat. in N. Amer.—Spikelets 2–5-fld., in compact 1-sided bunches or glomerules, these collected in an open divaricately branched panicle that contracts after flowering; glumes hispid on the keel, unequal, sharp-pointed; lemma nerved, short-awned, exceeding the palea; stigmas plumose, on distinct styles; stamens 3: fr. free, inclosed in lemma and palea. (Dac-tylis: Greek name referring to dactyls or fingers, originally applied to some other grass.)

D. glomerata, L. Orchard-Grass. Cocks-foot. Stout per., 2–4 ft., forming tussocks; culms glabrous, angled, simple: lvs. many, flat, ¼–⅓in. wide, scabrous; sheaths long, ligule thin and prominent: panicle 3–8 in. long, the branches few and in anthesis wide-spreading or even declined. Var. **variegata,** Hort., sometimes planted for ornament, has lvs. silvery-striped.

31. **BROMUS,** L. Brome-Grass. Rather coarse ann., bien., and per. grasses, with heavy often awned spikelets, some of the kinds grown for forage and others for ornament; species about 100, mostly in the north temp. zone.—Spikelets several- to many-fld., mostly oblong, commonly diverging or drooping on the slender branches of the open panicle; glumes sharp-pointed, unequal, shorter than the several-nerved lemmas which are mostly 2-toothed and often awned from just beneath the teeth; palea shorter than lemma; stigmas plumose, a distinct stylopodium arising from apex of ovary; stamens mostly 3: fr. long and furrowed, adnate to the palea. (Bro-mus: Greek *food,* applied to the oat.)—There are many weedy species in the genus. *B.*

secalinus, L., is the common chess or cheat, formerly supposed by many farmers to come from wheat.

A. Plant per.: lower glume 1-nerved...1. *B. inermis*
AA. Plant ann., or sometimes bien.: lower glume 3–5-nerved.
B. Panicle narrow, erect: plants grown for forage.......................................2. *B. catharticus*
BB. Panicle with branches nodding: plants grown for ornament.........................3. *B. brizæformis*

1. **B. inermis,** Leyss. AWNLESS or HUNGARIAN BROME. Per. with creeping rootstocks, grown for pastures and meadows, and somewhat escaped, 1–4 ft. high, the culms leafy and glabrous: lvs. flat, ¼–⅓in. wide, usually somewhat scabrous, length 4–12 in., long-pointed; sheaths closed nearly to the top, ligule short and truncate: panicle 3–6 in. long, the slender branches whorled and ascending, usually several at a node; spikelets 6–10-fld., 1 in. long more or less, narrow, purplish, awnless or the few awns very short and not spreading; lower glume 1-nerved, second glume 3-nerved. Eu.

2. **B. catharticus,** Vahl (*B. unioloides*, HBK. *B. Schraderi*, Kunth). RESCUE-GRASS. SCHRADERS BROME. Erect ann. (or bien.), grown S. for forage; culms 2–3 ft., glabrous: lvs. 3–12 in. long, ⅓in. or less broad, scabrous; sheaths glabrous or pubescent, ligule short: panicle 10 in. or less long, rather narrow, erect, the branches mostly ascending; spikelets 5–10-fld., much flattened, pale green, awnless; lower glume 3–5-nerved, the upper 5–9-nerved. S. Amer.

3. **B. brizæformis,** Fisch. & Mey. QUAKE-GRASS. Ann., grown for the handsome panicle of large drooping briza-like spikelets, 1–2 ft., erect, glabrous: lvs. 4–8 in. long, ¼in. or less broad, pubescent; sheaths pubescent, ligule short and truncate: panicle 2–8 in. long, the branches mostly nodding; spikelets few, ovate-oblong and shapely, ½–1 in. long, several- to many-fld., awnless, the lemmas inflated; lower glume 3–5-nerved, the second or upper larger and 5–9-nerved. Eu. and Asia; somewhat established in N. Amer.

32. **FESTUCA,** L. FESCUE. Ann. and per. mostly small grasses, about 100 species widely distributed but most frequent in temp. regions; a very few are agricultural and lawn grasses.—Spikelets 2- or more-fld., in mostly narrow panicles: lvs. usually narrow and stiffish: glumes narrow and acute, unequal, the lower usually 1-nerved and the other 3-nerved; lemma 5-nerved, mostly acute or awned; stigmas plumose on a very short style; stamens 1–3: fr. free or adherent. (Festu-ca: old Latin name for a grass.)

A. Lvs. flat: tall...1. *F. elatior*
AA. Lvs. folded or rolled (at least in drying) and therefore very narrow: culms short or medium.
B. Plant with stolons, not tufted; culms decumbent at base: lvs. smooth, the sheath closed to top...2. *F. rubra*
BB. Plant not stoloniferous, densely tufted; culms erect: lvs. often scabrous, the sheath open from top to middle or below...3. *F. ovina*

1. **F. elatior,** L. (*F. pratensis*, Huds.). TALL FESCUE. MEADOW FESCUE. Upright strong per., sometimes producing short rootstocks; culms glabrous, many-grooved, 2–5 ft., the internodes usually conspicuous above the sheaths: lvs. 1 ft. or so long, ⅓in. or less wide, flat, glabrous, somewhat scabrous, the ligule very small: panicle 3–8 in. long, erect or flexuose, usually rather simple, the branches erect or spreading; spikelets about ½in. long, narrow, green, 5–9-fld., awnless but lemmas sharp. Eu., and widely nat. in N. Amer.—A prominent meadow- and pasture-grass.

2. **F. rubra,** L. RED FESCUE. Per., with short rootstocks; culms few to many, usually reddish at the base, 6–24 or 36 in. high, the lvs. and sheaths smooth: lvs. infolding and narrow, more or less puberulent, shorter than the culms: panicle 2–5 in. long, dark green, reddish or glaucous, at first open but becoming contracted, the branches erect or ascending; spikelets 3–8- or 10-fld.; lemmas indistinctly nerved, with an awn half or less as long. North temp. zone; sometimes grown in meadows. Var. **heterophylla,** Mutel (*F. heterophylla*, Lam.), has flat culm lvs. and involute basal lvs. in dense tufts; 2–3 ft. Var. **commutata,** Gaud. (*F. rubra* var. *fallax*, Hack.), CHEWINGS FESCUE, is a form producing a closer firmer sod, and with erect culms and is grown for turf especially in locations of partial shade, and not as wiry in texture as var. *heterophylla* nor as cespitose.

3. **F. ovina,** L. (*F. vulgaris*, Hort.). SHEEPS FESCUE. Low tufted grass with many sts. and fine lvs., not producing stolons; culms smooth and erect, much overtopping the foliage, 6–18 or 24 in. high: lvs. strongly involute and almost capillary, those on the culm few and short: panicle 2–6 in. long, often 1-sided, green, narrow but open at first and then becoming contracted; spikelets 3–6-fld.; lemmas nerveless or nearly so, short-awned. North temp. zone.—Used in dry pastures and often found in poor lawns. The species is widely variable. Var. **duriuscula,** Koch (*F. duriuscula*, L.), HARD FESCUE, has stiff lvs. which are broader than thick. Var. **glauca,** Koch (*F. glauca*, Lam.), BLUE FESCUE, has silvery-glaucous foliage, and is sometimes grown for ornament. Var. **capillata,** Alef. (*F. tenuifolia*, Hort.), has very narrow lvs. and awnless spikelets.

33. **POA,** L. More than 100 species in temp. and cold regions, a few of which are agricultural and lawn grasses; annuals and perennials, of small stature.—Spikelets 2–6-fld., in panicles, the flts. bisexual or rarely unisexual, uppermost flt. imperfect or undeveloped; glumes keeled, 1–3-nerved; lemmas 5-nerved, awnless, a tuft of cobwebby hairs often at the base, midnerve usually pubescent; palea 2-toothed, shorter than the lemma, keeled or nerved; stigmas plumose; stamens 3: fr. free or adherent. (Po-a: Greek *grass* or *fodder.*)

A. Plant not tufted, the culms few or scattered: panicle small and close. . . . . 1. *P. compressa*
AA. Plant tufted: panicle open, mostly large.
B. Rhizomes creeping. . . . . 2. *P. pratensis*
BB. Rhizomes not creeping.
C. Lemmas glabrous or keel slightly pubescent. . . . . .3. *P. trivialis*
CC. Lemmas pubescent on both keel and marginal nerves.
D. Ligule very short, minute: glumes about as long as first lemma . . . . .4. *P. nemoralis*
DD. Ligule prominent, especially of culm-lvs.: glumes shorter than first lemma. . . . 5. *P. palustris*

1. **P. compressa,** L. CANADA BLUE-GRASS. WIRE-GRASS. Low bluish-green per., with long creeping rootstocks, not tufted; culms decumbent or geniculate at base, 1–2 ft., flattened, stiff: culm-lvs. short and narrow, glabrous: panicle narrow and small, contracted, 1–3 in. long, erect, the branches very short and in pairs; spikelets 3–9-fld., crowded, often brownish; glumes acute, 3-nerved; lemmas faintly 3-nerved. Eu., Asia.—Extensively nat., and used as a pasture-grass; it becomes a persistent weed in tilled hard lands.

2. **P. pratensis,** L. KENTUCKY BLUE-GRASS. JUNE-GRASS. Tufted per. with slender creeping rhizomes; culms erect, 1–3 ft., nearly or quite terete: lvs. flat, long and narrow, soft, the sheaths compressed, ligule short: panicle pyramidal, 3–8 in. long, the branches fascicled and slender; spikelets 3–5-fld., pedicelled, green; glumes acute, rough-keeled; lemmas 5-nerved, the intermediate nerves prominent and glabrous, the others pubescent below. North temp. zone.—A favorite pasture- and lawn-grass; early flowering.

3 **P. trivialis,** L. ROUGH-STALKED MEADOW-GRASS. Per., without creeping rhizomes; culms slender, erect from decumbent base, often lax, 1–3 ft. high; culm-sheaths scabrous and culm-lvs. with ligule ⅛–¼in. long: panicle to 6 in. long; flts. with lemma glabrous except for slightly pubescent keel. Eu.; nat. and sometimes sown as a pasture plant.

4. **P. nemoralis,** L. WOOD MEADOW-GRASS. Tufted per., culms 1–3 ft. tall: lvs. with very short ligule: panicle short, to 4 in. long, branches spreading; flts. with lemmas pubescent on marginal nerves and keel; glumes narrow and sharply acuminate. Eu.; nat. N. E. U. S. and Ore.—Used in lawn seed mixtures because of adaptability to shaded habitats.

5. **P. palustris,** L. (*P. serotina*, Ehrh. *P. triflora*, Gilib.). FOWL MEADOW-GRASS. Tufted open-growing per., without rootstocks; culms 1–4 or 5 ft., smooth and glabrous: lvs. narrow, flat, sheaths glabrous, ligule medium: panicle loose and open, many-fld., 6–12 in. long, the fascicled branches very slender; spikelets small and numerous, 2–5-fld.; glumes acute, rough on the keel; lemmas obtuse, with obscure middle nerves. North temp. zone.—A meadow-grass.

34. **STENOTAPHRUM,** Trin. Three creeping per. grasses of wide distribution in warm and trop. countries, one used for lawn-making.—Low; culms compressed: infl. a straight or curved thickened spike in which the spikelets are sunken; spikelets 1-fld., with a staminate or empty flt. beneath, pointed, with a short hyaline glume or scale showing at the base. (Stenotaph-rum: Greek *narrow trench*, alluding to the pits holding the spikelets.)

S. secundatum, Kuntze (*Ischæmum secundatum*, Walt. *S. americanum*, Sw.). ST.-AUGUSTINE-GRASS. SHORE-GRASS. Small but stocky stoloniferous grass, rooting at the joints, the leafy culms rising 3–12 in. and bearing distichous branches at the nodes: lvs. short and flat, usually only 2–4 in. long, obtuse, the flat sheaths prominent: spikes stiff, terminal and from lateral branches, 2–5 in. long, with the spikelets sunken on one side; rachis breaking up at maturity. S. C. to Tex. and trop. Amer.—Popular far S. for lawns.

35. **EREMOCHLOA,** Buse. An Asiatic and E. Indian genus of per. grasses of about a dozen species, one grown in far S. for turf.—Creeping plants: lvs. more or less equitant and stiffish: spikelets 1-fld., flat, secund, awnless, solitary, sessile; glumes nearly flat, membranous, with pectinate margins. (Eremoch-loa: Greek for *solitary* and *grass.*)

E. ophiuroides, Hack. (*Ischæmum ophiuroides*, Munro). CENTIPEDE-GRASS. LAZY-MANS-GRASS. Low per., stolons stout, with short internodes, leafy and rooting at the nodes, forming a dense turf; culms decumbent or ascending, to 4 in. high: infl. a smooth spike-like terminal raceme, axillary on slender peduncles to 2 in. long; rachis flattened;

spikelets sessile, first glume winged at apex. S. Asia.—Cult. in Fla. and Tex. as a coarse stemmy lawn-grass, the flowering culms so short as to require little trimming of the turf, hence the name Lazy-Mans-Grass.

36. **CYNOSURUS,** L. Half dozen or fewer perennials and annuals of the Old World, one an agricultural grass of minor importance.—Small grasses, tufted: clusters of spikelets sessile and continuous, forming a spike-like infl., each cluster consisting of a sterile and a perfect spikelet; lower (outer) spikelet in the cluster comprised of sterile lemmas, the upper (inner) one of fertile flts.; style short; stamens 3. (Cynosu-rus: Greek *dog's tail.*)

C. cristatus, L. Crested Dogs-tail. Low per., sometimes sown in meadow-grass mixtures; culms slender, glabrous, 1–2½ ft.: lvs. numerous from the crown, soft, smooth, narrow and flat, shorter than the culms, the culm-lvs. mostly few and short, the long sheaths and hyaline ligule prominent: spike terminal, 1–3 to 4 in. long, more or less distichous, the clusters of spikelets at first separated; sterile outer spikelet in the cluster larger with narrow awn-pointed empty alternating lemmas ciliate on the margins, giving the spike a crested appearance. Eu., adventive in N. Amer.

37. **ZOISIA,** Willd. About a dozen species of E. Asiatic per. grasses having creeping rhizomes, cult. in S. for turf.—Lvs. short and stiffly pointed: infl. a spike-like raceme; spikelets 1-fld., appressed against the rachis, disarticulating below the glume; first glume wanting and second enveloping the thin lemma. (Zois-ia: named for Karl von Zois, 1756–1800?, Austrian botanist.)—The spelling Zoisia is conserved by the International Rules over Zoysia.

A. Lf.-blades involute, capillary and thread-like . . . . 1. *Z. tenuifolia*
AA. Lf.-blades flat.
B. Lvs. 5–9 in. long, about ⅛in. wide . . . . 2. *Z. japonica*
BB. Lvs. 2–3 in. long, about ⅟₁₆in. wide . . . . 3. *Z. Matrella*

1. **Z. tenuifolia,** Willd. Mascarene-Grass. Korean Velvet-Grass. Creeping per.: lvs. thread-like and capillary, acute, 1–2 in. long, strongly involute: fls. in narrow compressed spikelets.—Intro. to S. Fla. and Calif. where it forms a very dense fine-textured almost wiry turf, tolerating drought conditions when well established.

2. **Z. japonica,** Steud. Korean or Japanese Lawn-Grass. Creeping per. with rhizomes underground: lvs. flat, obtuse, usually 5–9 in. long and about ⅛in. wide or more: spikelets about ⅛in. long, pale purplish-brown, in spike-like raceme usually 1 in. long.—One of the first species of this genus to be cult. in U. S. and reputedly more hardy than others; its coarse foliage detracts from its turf value.

3. **Z. Matrella,** Merr. (*Agrostis Matrella,* L.). Manila-Grass. Fine-textured per. forming a dense close turf that is shade-tolerant, drought-resistant and durable: lvs. flat, to 4 in. long, filiform, erect or ascending: spikelets slightly smaller than in *Z. japonica* and generally greenish, the infl. to 1½ in. long.—Best suited as a turf grass in the S., fairly hardy N. but remains dormant with poor color until early summer; known also by the trade name of Flawn; propagated vegetatively.

38. **LOLIUM,** L. Rye-Grass. Species probably 6, of temp. Eurasia, ann. and per.; two are agricultural grasses.—Small, with flat lvs.: culms ascending or erect, simple; spikes terminal, interrupted; spikelets many-fld., flat, with the edge toward the culm, alternate, the rachis of the spike more or less zigzag; glume next the rachis small, the opposite one developed and 5–7-nerved; lemmas convex and with converging nerves, sometimes produced into awns. (Lo-lium: Latin name for one of the species.)

A. Spikelets not bearing awns . . . . 1. *L. perenne*
AA. Spikelets with awns . . . . 2. *L. multiflorum*

1. **L. perenne,** L. Perennial or English Rye-Grass. A pasture- and meadow-grass, and sometimes in lawns; tufted per., erect, glabrous, culms 1–2½ ft. high: lvs. abundant from the base, relatively few on the culms, narrow, flat, the sheaths glabrous and ligule very short: spike 4–12 in. long, straight or curved; spikelets 5–10-fld., with awnless lemmas; outer glume half or more the length of the spikelet. Var. **cristatum,** Pers., has the infl. seemingly cristate by the spikelets crowded and spreading horizontally. One non-crested strain, used in lawn mixtures, is known as Pacey's English rye-grass.

2. **L. multiflorum,** Lam. (*L. italicum,* A. Br.). Italian Rye-Grass. Per., but mostly shorter-lived than no. 1: spikelets larger, with more flts., the lemmas conspicuously awned.—Both species have run wild in N. Amer., as also to a less extent has the Darnel, **L. temulentum,** L., in which the outer glume is longer than the spikelet and which produces a narcotic poison.

39. **ANTHOXANTHUM,** L. Less than a half dozen ann. and per. aromatic species in Eurasia and N. Afr., two sparingly known as agricultural grasses.—Infl. spike-like at the top of the slender culm; spikelets 1-fld. with 2 lobed sterile slender-awned lemmas beneath, longer than the fertile flt.; lemma of the fertile flt. truncate and awnless; palea faintly 2-nerved; styles long and stigma plumose; stamens 2. (Anthoxan-thum: Greek *yellow flower*.)

A. odoratum, L. Sweet Vernal-Grass. Early-flowering per. making small clumps; culms very slender, erect, naked above, glabrous and shining, 1–2 ft.: lvs. short, flat and soft, sparsely hairy: spicate panicle terminal, 1–3 in. long and ½in. broad in anthesis, bronzy-green, often somewhat interrupted; sterile lemmas unequally awned, exceeding the fertile lemma. Eurasia.—Because of the very fragrant herbage (vanilla-like) the plant is often included in meadow-grass mixtures; however, it imparts a bitter flavor to hay and is unpalatable to cattle; common as an intro. plant.

40. **ALOPECURUS,** L. Species about 30 of the north temp. zone, largely of cold climates, ann. and per., one an agricultural grass.—Infl. spike-like; spikelets densely crowded, 1-fld., shedding from the axis; glumes equal and awnless, joined at the base, ciliate-keeled; lemma 5-nerved, obtuse, awned from below the middle; palea wanting; stigmas hairy; stamens 3. (Alopecu-rus: Greek *fox tail.*)

A. pratensis, L. Meadow Foxtail. Per. grass of meadow mixtures, distinguished from timothy by the mostly lower stature, shorter heads, and the many fine awns; culms simple and erect from creeping base, 1–3 ft., glabrous: lvs. short, the blades 1–6 in. long, flat, more or less scabrous, the sheaths somewhat swollen: spikes 1–3 in., erect, well above the foliage; lemmas bearing a slender soft somewhat bent awn. Eu.; also nat. in N. Amer.

41. **PHLEUM,** L. About 10 mostly per. grasses in the temp. zone, one of great agricultural prominence in E. N. Amer.—Infl. dense and spike-like, terminating the culm, composed of a great number of compressed 1-fld. spikelets; glumes 2, keeled and usually prominently ciliate, awn-pointed, exceeding the thin 5-nerved lemma; styles long; stamens 3, exserted in anthesis: fr. free, but inclosed in the lemma and palea. (Phle-um: old Greek name for some other plant.)

P. pratense, L. Timothy. Herds-Grass. Per., strong-growing; culms 2–5 ft., simple, smooth, erect or ascending from a somewhat thickened bulb-like base: lvs. many from both crown and culm, flat, variable in width and length but ¼in. broad in large plants and 1 ft. long; sheath long and striate, smooth, ligule thin: spike cylindrical, ¾–8 in. long, obtuse, continuous or interrupted below; glumes so placed that the appressed awn-points seem to be on the outer edges of one truncate scale, the spreading hairs conspicuous under a lens; anthers long-exserted. Eu.; extensively nat. in N. Amer., a leading meadow-grass.

42. **ZIZANIA,** L. Wild Rice. About 3 species of ann. and per. fresh-water aquatic grasses.—Lvs. flat: panicles large and open, terminal, the lower branches spreading and bearing early deciduous pendulous staminate spikelets, the upper branches less spreading to erect and bearing late deciduous appressed pistillate spikelets; spikelets unisexual, 1-fld.; glumes indistinct or absent; stamens 6: grain narrowly cylindrical, to ¾in. long, purplish-black. (Ziza-nia: Greek from *zizanion*, meaning a weed growing amongst grain.)

Z. aquatica, L. Ann. robust erect coarse grass to 10 ft. high, culms hollow: lvs. ½–1½ in. wide and 1–4 ft. long, scaberulous: panicle to 2 ft. long, the lateral branches to 8 in. long. N. Amer.—Now planted extensively as a food and shelter plant for aquatic wild life, especially in game preserves, metropolitan watersheds, and wild-life sanctuaries; grain used as food by the aborigines and the plant known by some as Indian wild rice and Squaw rice; seed of wild rice intended for germination must be stored at near freezing temperatures and kept submerged under water or in wet moss if viability is to be retained until time to plant.

43. **MISCANTHUS,** Anderss. (*Eulalia,* Trin.). Half dozen or more Asian tall perennials, one common as a lawn and border subject.—Spikelets 2 at the nodes of the rachis, 1-fld., one sessile or nearly so and one pedicelled, mostly awned, subtended by silky hairs; axis of panicle short: plants making very large heavy clumps with much foliage: differs from Erianthus in the rachis not disarticulating and in the short panicles. (Miscan-thus: Greek *stem-flower,* probably indicating the pedicelled spikelets.)

M. sinensis, Anderss. (*M. polydactylos,* Voss. *Eulalia japonica,* Trin.). EULALIA. Strong hardy clumpy grass producing much herbage; culms 4–10 ft. high, glabrous, mostly inclosed in the many long glabrous finely striate sheaths which are not hairy at the throat: lf.-blades long, ½–1 in. wide, long-pointed, margins more or less scabrous, midrib whitish and prominent: panicle open-spreading, 6–24 in. long, the main axis not continuing to the apex, the very slender long flexuous branches spreading or drooping, the spreading silky tufts conspicuous but not making a woolly cluster. China, Japan; sparingly spontaneous at places in N. Amer. Var. **variegatus,** Beal, has lvs. striped lengthwise with white or yellowish. Var. **zebrinus,** Beal, ZEBRA-GRASS, has lvs. banded at intervals with whitish or yellowish. Var. **gracillimus,** Hitchc. (*Eulalia gracillima,* Hort. *E. japonica* var. *gracillima,* Grier), has lvs. very narrow, usually ¼in. or less wide and strongly canaliculate. Var. **gracillimus-univittatus,** Hort. (*Eulalia gracillima* var. *univittata,* Hort.), is reported to have the dark green very narrow lvs. striped longitudinally with white.

44. **ERIANTHUS,** Michx. About a score of tall stout per. grasses in temp. and trop. regions on both sides of the globe, one grown for ornament.—Spikelets 2 at the nodes of the jointed disarticulating rachis, one sessile, one pedicelled, perfect, mostly 1-fld., with a tuft of silky hairs at the base of each; glumes nearly equal, the first or lower somewhat double-keeled and the upper keeled toward the apex; one lemma sterile and awnless, the other with a straight or twisted awn; stamens 3; axis of panicle elongated: lvs. long and flat. (Erian-thus: Greek *wool-flower,* from the silky hairs.)

E. ravennæ, Beauv. (*Saccharum ravennæ,* L.). PLUME-GRASS. RAVENNA-GRASS, from the specific name, referring to Ravenna, Italy. Strong per. to 12 ft., hardy as far north as N. Y. City; culms stiff, glabrous: lvs. about ½in. wide, long and long-pointed, more or less scabrous on the nerves, midrib prominent and lighter colored, the sheaths very long, many-striate, scabrid, with long hairs at the throat: panicle plume-like, 1–2 ft. long, narrow, soft-silky shiny from the great quantity of tufts subtending the spikelets, giving the plant a pampas-grass effect and for which it is grown. S. Eu.

45. **VETIVERIA,** Thouars. Two species, per., with long narrow panicles.—Spikelets in pairs, narrow, acute, mostly appressed, ours awnless or sharp-pointed, one sessile and perfect, one pedicelled and staminate, the perfect spikelet bearing short sharp spines and somewhat flattened laterally; stigmas plumose; stamens 3. (Vetive-ria: Latinization of the English common name of one species.)

V. zizanioides, Nash (*Phalaris zizanioides,* L. *Anatherum zizanioides,* Hitchc. & Chase). VETIVER. KHUS-KHUS. Culms erect, 4–7 or 8 ft. tall, glabrous; sheaths glabrous: lf.-blades stiffish, long and narrow, ⅓in. or less wide, glabrous but rough on edges: panicle 6–12 in. long, very narrow, the ascending or strict branches 1–2 in. long and whorled. Trop. and subtrop. Asia, E. Indies.—Cult. far S. and in tropics for the very aromatic roots, which are employed in perfumery and medicine and for domestic use; also grown as a division plant, to which its numerous tall stiff culms adapt it; escaped in La.

46. **CYMBOPOGON,** Spreng. About 40 species, usually per., mostly native in the Old World tropics, some of them yielding fragrant oils.—Spikelets in pairs, some of the lower ones in each spike staminate, borne on a common peduncle which is supported by a sheathing spathe or bract: racemes often hairy: awns present or often absent in cult. kinds, otherwise much like Andropogon and Anatherum. (Cymbopo-gon: Greek *boat* and *beard.*)—This genus comprises most of the oil-grasses of India, which are sometimes grown in Amer., the perfumery and drug product being obtained from herbage and roots.

A. Joints of raceme hairy all over, the hairs covering or concealing the sessile spikelets....... 1. *C. Schœnanthus*

AA. Joints hairy or bearded only on the sides, the hairs not concealing the sessile spikelets.

B. Sessile spikelets concave on back, linear to lance-linear....... 2. *C. citratus*

BB. Sessile spikelets flat on back, lanceolate or broader....... 3. *C. Nardus*

1. **C. Schœnanthus,** Spreng. (*Andropogon Schœnanthus,* L.). CAMEL-HAY. Prized in former time for its yield of oil, but the product apparently now coming from other grasses: per., 2 ft., with fragrant herbage: basal sheaths tight, clasping, lf.-blades long, edges rough, sheaths persistent and expanded below: panicle narrow, comprised of dense fascicles, the joints villous all over; spikelet with very short straight awn; first or outer glume of sessile spikelet double-keeled. (Schœnanthus: Greek, an old substantive, *rush flower.*) N. Afr., S. Asia.

2. **C. citratus,** Stapf (*Andropogon citratus,* DC.). Lemon-Grass. Per.: panicle large, usually very compound, loose, the branches slender and the ultimate branches somewhat nodding, the joints of the racemes bearded or villous along the sides; spathe-bracts long and narrow; sessile spikelets awnless, linear to linear-lanceolate, concave on the lower part of the back. Known only in cult.

3. **C. Nardus,** Rendle (*Andropogon Nardus,* L.). Citronella-Grass. Per.: panicle large and mostly compound; spikelets awnless, the sessile ones lanceolate or ovate-lanceolate or obovate-lanceolate, flat on the back. (Nar-dus: Latin form, through Greek, of nard, Asian name of the aromatic oil.) Known only in cult.

47. **TRICHOLÆNA,** Schrad. Per. and ann. grasses in the eastern hemisphere about 15 species, one an ornamental and also a forage plant far S.—Spikelets panicled, villous, on short very slender pedicels; lower glume much shorter than spikelet; upper glume and a sterile lemma equal, silky-hairy; fertile lemma inclosing the palea but the margins not inrolled, shorter than the spikelet; stamens 3. (Tricholæ-na: Greek *hair mantle,* referring to the villous spikelets.)

T. repens, Hitchc. (*Saccharum repens,* Willd. *T. rosea,* Nees. *T. violacea,* Hort.). Natal-Grass. Wine-Grass. Ruby-Grass. Handsome per. but cult. as an ann.; culms slender, erect, 2–4 ft., glabrous: lvs. rather short, the blades on the culm 4–8 in. and ¼in. or less broad, fine pointed, glabrous or lightly hairy, sheaths sparsely hairy at least at throat: panicle open and graceful, pink to red-brown, glossy and attractive, 3–10 in. long, the pointed silky spikelets shedding. S. Afr.—Grown in Fla. for forage, and sometimes planted for ornament; also extensively nat.

48. **OPLISMENUS,** Beauv. About 15 perennials and some annuals in the tropics and subtropics of both hemispheres, mostly weak with ascending base, one grown for ornament.—Spikelets solitary or paired, nearly sessile, in two rows on a slender rachis, the racemes alternate and rather distant on the axis; glumes approximately equal, 2-lobed or slightly notched at apex with an awn between the lobes; sterile lemma exceeding glumes, sharp-pointed or short-awned; fertile lemma convex, acute, clasping the palea; styles long, the stigmas plumose; stamens 3. (Oplismenus: Greek *awned.*)

O. compositus, Beauv. (*Panicum compositum,* L. *O. hirtellus,* Hort. not Beauv.). Weak slender per., more or less trailing, rooting at the lower joints; culms 1–3 ft. or more long, many-jointed, glabrous or slightly hairy: lvs. short, flat and broad, to 4 in. long and ⅓–1 in. wide, acuminate, glabrous or somewhat velvety beneath, the base mostly clasping at the top of the ciliate sheath: floral axis 3–4 in. long, bearing separated awned racemes ½–1 in. long. Afr., trop. Amer.—Used for edgings, baskets, and underbench cover in greenhouses; the usual form, var. **vittatus,** Hort., has lvs. striped with white and pink. The New World species *O. hirtellus,* Beauv. (*Panicum hirtellum,* L.), is reported to have a variegated form known in the trade as *Panicum variegatum,* Hort. and may not be different from var. *vittatus.* Often known as Basket-grass.

49. **PHALARIS,** L. About a score of ann. and per. upright grasses in temp. Eu. and N. Amer., two frequently planted.—Spikelets flattened laterally, with 1 perfect flt. and 1 or 2 very small sterile lemmas beneath, the rachilla disarticulating above the glumes which are equal and boat-shaped; fertile lemma hard, shorter than the glumes; stigmas plumose; stamens 3: panicle close or semi-open, or spike-like. (Phal-aris: ancient Greek name.)

a. Plant ann.: infl. spike-like; glumes winged .... 1. *P. canariensis*
aa. Plant per.: infl. narrow-paniculate; glumes not winged...................... 2. *P. arundinacea*

1. **P. canariensis,** L. Canary-Grass. Ann., erect, 1–2 ft., the slender culms glabrous or somewhat scabrous: lvs. short, 3–6 in., long-pointed, several-nerved, lightly scabrous, upper sheaths inflated: spikes ovoid, peduncled; outer glumes widely winged on one side (keel) and therefore very broad, very short-pointed or muticous, white or yellowish with green stripes, the margins entire: "seeds" (fr. in integuments) lance-oblong, about ⅜in. long, straw-colored and shining, compressed but convex on both sides, strongly few-nerved. Eu.—Grown for bird-seed, and also run wild. *P. minor,* Retz., of Eu., is to be looked for: it differs in the cylindric-oblong spike, the less winged and narrower sharp-pointed glumes that are notched or erose toward the apex.

2. **P. arundinacea,** L. Reed Canary-Grass. Tall rather coarse per., 2–6 ft., native in N. Amer. and Eu. and sometimes transferred to grounds; known in cult. mostly in var. **picta,** L., Ribbon-Grass (var. *variegata,* Hort.), with lvs. striped with white and yellowish, probably all intro.: lvs. flat, 6–12 in. long, ½–¾in. wide, mostly lightly scabrous, the

ligule papery and prominent: panicle 4–8 in. long, loose in anthesis but becoming spike-like, the spikelets sharp-pointed but awnless.

50. **PASPALUM,** L. About 200 species of mostly per. grasses distributed in the warmer parts of both hemispheres, some cult. for forage purposes and one with creeping stolons, *P. distichum*, L., in soil-erosion control and as a binder for drainage ditches and roadside banks.—Culms mostly erect: infl. consisting of 1 or more spike-like racemes that are single or paired at the summit of the culms or arranged racemosely along the main axis; spikelets small, subsessile, solitary or in pairs, first glume usually wanting, the sterile lemma about as long as second glume. (Paspalum: Greek for a kind of millet.)

P. dilatatum, Poir. Dallis-Grass. Per. to 4 ft., culms erect or ascending from decumbent base: lvs. flat, to 18 in. long and ½in. wide, margins often finely undulate: infl. a panicle with several to many racemes, each usually 2–4 in. long and spreading; spikelets ovate, scarcely ⅛in. long, sparsely silky. N. Amer.—Cult. in the S. for forage and pasture. *P. racemosum*, Lam., an ann. S. American species, is cult. for ornament to some extent.

51. **LAGURUS,** L. One ann. grass of the Medit. region, grown for ornament, and also sparingly run loose in Calif.—Spikelets 1-fld., combined into an ovoid or oblong head; rachilla extending as a bristle beyond the palea, disarticulating above the glumes, hairy beneath the flt.; glumes villous, 1-nerved, awn-pointed, exceeding the lemma which bears a slender exserted awn; stigma plumose; stamens 3. (Lagurus: Latin *hare's tail.*)

L. ovatus, L. Hares-tail-Grass. Erect, 1–2 ft., bearing a soft-woolly head 1–2 in. long, with slender awns projecting ½in.: sheaths and lf.-blades soft-hairy.—Grown in pots and for dry bouquets.

52. **AMMOPHILA,** Host. Beach-Grass. A small genus of about 3 erect coarse per. grasses producing scaly creeping rhizomes and long tough lvs., cult. in connection with soil-conservation projects for cover on arid saline sand dunes, sometimes under the name of Marram-grass.—Infl. a straw-colored dense spike-like panicle; spikelets 1-fld., compressed, the rachis disarticulating above the about equal glumes as a short bristle, lemma slightly shorter than glumes. (Ammoph-ila: Greek *sand-loving*, referring to the habitat.)

A. arenaria, Link (*Arundo arenaria*, L.). European Beach-Grass. Coarse per. 3–6 ft. high; rhizomes deep-penetrating and extensive: lvs. to 2 ft. long, quickly becoming involute and tapering to slender point, ligule ½–1 in. long: panicle to 10 in. long, dense; spikelets about ½in. long; glumes glabrous but scabrous on the keel; lemmas scabrous. Coasts of Eu.—The closely related American species, *A. breviligulata*, Fern., differs in the ligule ⅛in. long or less; it has been reported to be in cult. for similar uses.

53. **POLYPOGON,** Desf. About 10 species of temp. region small ann. or per. grasses, primarily of the Old World, some intro. to N. Amer. and one grown for ornament in bedding and in dried bouquets.—Infl. a dense spike-like panicle; spikelets 1-fld., the pedicel disarticulating slightly below the glumes; glumes with straight slender awn, equal, entire or 2-lobed; lemmas much shorter than glumes, usually with awn shorter than that of glumes. (Polypo-gon: Greek *many hairs*, referring to the spikelet awns.)

P. monspeliensis, Desf. (*Alopecurus monspeliensis*, L.). Rabbit-foot-Grass. Ann. to 1½ ft.: lvs. flat, with ligule about ¼in. long: panicle usually 3–6 in. long, becoming tawny-yellow; awns to ⅓in. long, glumes hispidulous. Eu.; nat. N. Amer. south to Argentina.

54. **ELYMUS,** L. Wild Rye. Tall erect per. grasses, represented by about 45 species in temp. northern hemisphere, half of which are in W. U. S., a few grown for forage purposes and for ornament.—Lf.-blades flat or convolute: infl. a slender long terminal spike; spikelets dense or distant, 2–6-fld., usually sessile in pairs at each node; rachilla disarticulating above the glumes; glumes equal, mostly stiff, acute to aristate and often situated in front of the spikelet; lemmas usually awned from the tip. (El-ymus: Greek for a kind of grain.)

A. Spikelets awned: plant without rhizomes..1. *E. glaucus*
AA. Spikelets awnless: plant with rhizomes..2. *E. arenarius*

1. **E. glaucus,** Buckl. Blue Wild Rye. Tufted leafy per. to 4 ft.: lvs. flat, lax, to ½in. wide, scabrous: spike usually densely fld., 4–8 in. long or more, erect or nodding; glumes to ½in. long; lemma awns sometimes to 1 in. long, erect or spreading. N. Amer.—Widely advertised as an ornamental, but material so offered may not be this species. Valued as a forage crop in wooded areas in N. W. U. S.

2. **E. arenarius,** L. Sea Lyme-Grass. Coarse stout per. to 8 ft., with vigorous-growing rhizomes: lvs. to 3 ft. long, stiffish, smooth: spike dense, terminal, 6–12 in. long; spikelets about 1 in. long, awnless. Eu.—Of increasing importance as a soil binder when grown on coastal sand dunes; it is intermixed with plants of *Ammophila arenaria* when employed for this purpose.

55. **STIPA,** L. Spear-Grass. One hundred or more per. grasses in temp. and trop. regions, a few sometimes grown for ornament.—Infl. paniculate; spikelets 1-fld., separating above the glumes, which are thin or papery and acute to awned; lemma terete, convolute, concealing the 2-nerved palea, ending in a conspicuous awn which is usually twisted or bent; styles short and distinct; stamens usually 3: lvs. mostly convolute. (Sti-pa: Greek *tow*, alluding to plumose awns.)—The awns often manifest odd hygroscopic action when the frs. are planted. *S. tenacissima*, L., of Spain and N. Afr., is Esparto-grass, one of the sources of esparto paper and cordage.

A. Awns not plumose..1. *S. elegantissima*
AA. Awns plumose..2. *S. pennata*

1. **S. elegantissima,** Labill. Culms erect from a horizontal rhizome, 2–3 ft.: panicle loose and open, 6–8 in. long, the branchlets and pedicels (but not the bent awns) plumose; spikelets ¼–⅓in. long; awn 1¼ in. Australia.

2. **S. pennata,** L. Feather-Grass. Tufted, 2–3 ft.: panicle close and narrow; glumes ½in. or more long, with awn twice or more as long; awn of lemma often 1 ft. long, smooth and twisted below, very plumose and feathery above, making a handsome effect. Eurasia.

56. **HOLCUS,** L. (*Notholcus*, Nash. *Ginannia*, Bubani not Scop. nor Dietr.). Rather small per. and ann. grasses, about 8 species, one sometimes grown for ornament.—Infl. paniculate; spikelets 2-fld., first perfect and awnless, second staminate and short-awned on back of lemma, pedicel disarticulating; glumes about equal, exceeding the 2 flts.; stigmas plumose; stamens 3: fr. free. (Hol-cus: Latin for a kind of grain.)—The Sorghums were formerly included in the genus Holcus, but now they are considered as belonging to the genus Sorghum, Moench.

H. lanatus, L. (*Notholcus lanatus*, Nash). Velvet-Grass. Per., 2–3 ft., with sheaths and short flat lvs. velvety-pubescent: panicle 2–4 in. long, at length contracted or close, pale or purplish in color, soft to the touch; glumes ciliate on keel; fertile lemmas glabrous and shining, nearly or quite obtuse, the upper one bearing a minute hooked awn below the 2-toothed apex. Eu.; nat. in N. Amer.—A kind with variegated foliage is sometimes cult.

57. **AIRA,** L. (*Aspris*, Adans.). About 9 small species of the Medit. region, a few nat. in N. Amer.; sometimes grown for ornament.—Spikelets 2-fld. (thereby differing from Agrostis, with which they are likely to be confused), in loose or contracted panicles, the rachilla disarticulating above the glumes which are about equal and acute; lemmas rounded, produced into 2 slender teeth, with short tuft of hairs, usually awned from below the middle; stigmas plumose; stamens 3. (Ai-ra: old Greek name for a weed.)—The name Aira, as first used by Linnæus, included species now assigned to three different genera and the generic name Aspris was long applied to those now properly reinstated under the Linnæan generic name Aira.

A. capillaris, Host (*Aspris capillaris*, Hitchc.). A small delicate ann., sometimes grown in pots for its profuse tops and perhaps for dry bouquets, 12–18 in. high, diffuse, with short capillary lvs. and spreading panicles with hair-like branchlets: spikelets light and small, the lower flt. bearing a short awn and the upper awnless. Eu.; nat. in N. Amer. Var. **pulchella,** Bailey (*A. pulchella*, Link. *Aspris capillaris* var. *pulchella*, Bailey. *Agrostis pulchella*, Hort.), has both flts. awned.

58. **NEYRAUDIA,** Hook. f. Very large reed-like Old World grasses of few species, grown for ornament in S. Fla. and S. Calif.—Lvs. flat, to 3 ft. long: infl. a large de-

compound nodding panicle; spikelets laterally compressed; rachilla pubescent below the lemmas, disarticulating between the second glume and the lemmas; glumes membranous, lanceolate; lemmas membranous, often recurved, ending in a slender tip with 2 setaceous points and a scabrous interposed awn, 3-nerved; flts. perfect, stigmas feathery, stamens 3: grain terete, cylindrical. (Neyrau-dia: an anagram of Reynaudia.)

N. madagascariensis, Hook. f. (*Arundo madagascariensis*, Kunth). Tender per. to 8 ft. or more, coarse in texture and habit; culms leafy to the panicle, solid: lvs. variable, from filiform and convolute to 1 in. broad and flat, smooth: panicle 1–3 ft. long, large and plume-like, tan-colored; spikelets to ¼in. long, 4–8-fld., glumes glossy; first lemma sometimes empty. Trop. Afr., Madagascar, Kashmir to Burma.—A related species, *N. Reynaudiana*, Keng (*Arundo Reynaudiana*, Kunth), with darker brown panicle and lemma awns recurved, is grown in S. Fla.; native S. Asia.

59. **ARUNDO,** L. A half dozen giant per. reeds, from the tropics and subtropics of the Old World, one frequently planted for its bold habit and showy terminal panicles.—Spikelets 2- to several-fld., the upper flts. smaller, disarticulating above the glumes, the rachilla glabrous; glumes more or less equal, narrow and 3-nerved, about the length of the spikelet; lemmas 3-nerved, densely long-hairy, the mid-nerve running into a straight awn; stigmas plumose; stamens 3. (Arun-do, Do-nax: ancient Latin names, from the Greek for *reed.*)

A. Donax, L. Giant Reed. Culms very strong, somewhat woody, 6–20 ft. tall, from horizontal knotty rootstocks: lf.-blades 1–2 ft. long, flat, 1–3 in. broad, glabrous except on edges, regularly distichously spaced along the culm, auriculate at base, the throat of the sheath with a hairy tuft: panicle erect, 1–2 ft. long, rather narrow with many slender ascending branches; spikelets numerous and crowded, ½in. long, pointed, in anthesis displaying the copious hairs. Medit. region, and escaped far S. and in the tropics.—Seldom blooms in the northern parts. Var. **versicolor,** Kunth (*A. Donax* var. *variegata*, Vilm.), has lvs. striped with white or yellowish; auricles often dark brown.

60. **CORTADERIA,** Stapf. Five species of large per. grasses in S. Amer., forming large clumps, one commonly planted in Calif. and elsewhere.—Plants diœcious: spikelets 3–7-fld., with glabrous rachilla which disarticulates above the very narrow thin 1-nerved glumes; lemmas acuminate, 3-nerved and awnless, in the staminate flts. glabrous or nearly so, in the pistillate very hairy toward the base; palea much shorter than the lemmas, 2-keeled; stamens 3, reduced to staminodes in the pistillate flts.; stigmas slender, plumose: fr. narrow-oblong, free. (Cortade-ria: *cutting*, referring to the lf.-margins.)

C. Selloana, Aschers. & Graebn. (*Arundo Selloana*, Schult. *C. argentea*, Stapf. *Gynerium argenteum*, Nees). Pampas-Grass. Per. in leafy clumps, with culms 4–10 or 20 ft. high overtopping the foliage: lvs. long and narrow, rough-margined, with tufted hairs at the throat of the sheath: pistillate panicles white or pink, 1–3 ft. long, silky hairy, plumy and fluffy; staminate panicles with naked spikelets; spikelets 2–3-fld., with slender-awned lemmas. (Named for Fr. Sello, page 51.) Argentina.—**C. rudiuscula,** Stapf (*C. Quila*, Stapf), more tender, with lavender-colored plumes and bien. culms from a per. root, is sometimes cult.; Chile.

61. **GYNERIUM,** Humb. & Bonpl. Perhaps 3 species of trop. American diœcious grasses, coarse, leafy-culmed and tall-growing, one cult. for ornament in far S.—Panicle plume-like, tan-colored; spikelets several-fld., the staminate with short glumes and glabrous lemmas, the pistillate with long-attenuate glumes and shorter long-silky lemmas. (Gyne-rium: Greek *female wool*, referring to the woolly pistillate spikelets.)

G. sagittatum, Beauv. (*Saccharum sagittatum*, Aubl.). Uva-Grass. One of the tallest cult. herbaceous grasses, culms growing to 30 ft. or more, the lf.-sheaths persisting after lvs. have fallen: lvs. to 8 ft. long and 2½ in. wide, finely and sharply serrulate: panicle cream-colored to pale tan, very densely fld., large, becoming 3 ft. long or more in vigorous specimens, the primary axis erect and lateral branches arching or drooping.

62. **LAMARCKIA,** Moench (*Achyrodes*, Boehmer). One species, an ann. of S. Eu. and nat. in Calif., cult. for ornament.—Spikelets in raceme-like fascicles which are aggregated into a secund panicle, terminal one in each fascicle fertile and the

others sterile; fertile spikelet of 1 perfect long-awned flt. and a sterile short-awned lemma; glumes 1-nerved, acuminate or short-awned; sterile spikelets with acuminate glumes and blunt lemmas. (Lamarck-ia: J. B. Lamarck, 1744–1829, French naturalist and philosopher.)

L. aurea, Moench (*Cynosurus aureus,* L. *Chrysurus cynosuroides,* Pers.). GOLDEN-TOP. Tufted branching soft-lvd. grass about 1 ft. high· lvs. many, flat, glabrous, with inflated sheaths, ligule papery, long and prominent: panicle rather dense, 1–3 in. long, glossy, golden-yellow sometimes shading to violet; fascicles squarrose or drooping, with tuft of hairs at base.

63. **DESMAZERIA,** Dum. (*Brizopyrum,* Link). Four species in Eu. and Afr., ann. and per., one sometimes grown for ornament.—Spikelets many-fld., flattened, borne separately on a simple axis; lemmas firm, keeled, 3- or 5-nerved, awnless; styles short, stigma plumose; stamens 3. (Desmaze-ria: J. B. Desmazieres, a French botanist.)

D. sicula, Dum. (*Cynosurus siculus,* Jacq. *Brizopyrum siculum,* Link). Ann., about 1 ft. high, with aspect of a Lolium, branching, decumbent or geniculate at base: lvs. 3–6 in. long, narrow, thin, glabrous, the papery ligule prominent: flat awnless spikelets about ½in. long, about 12 of them alternate and sessile in a distichous spike. Medit. region.

64. **UNIOLA,** L. Nine or 10 N. American erect per. grasses, of which one is sometimes grown for its handsome panicles.—Spikelets 3- to many-fld., flat and 2-edged, the rachilla disarticulating between the flts.; 1–4 lower glumes empty; other flts. perfect or the upper ones staminate; glumes keeled, acute, nerved; lemmas compressed, acute, many-nerved; stigmas plumose; stamens 1–3. (Uni-ola: ancient Latin name, diminutive of *unio,* unity; application not evident.)

U. latifolia, L. Handsome woodland grass, native from Pa. south and west, sometimes planted in borders; culms slender, erect, 2–5 ft.: lvs. 5–9 in. long, ½–1 in. wide, flat, thin, glabrous except on the rough margins, the base often ciliate: panicle 4–10 in. long, opening, drooping, with attractive flat green spikelets ½–1½ in. long hanging on thread-like pedicels.—**U. paniculata,** L., SEA OATS, differs in having creeping rhizomes and is reported cult. for controlling sand-dune erosion along southern seacoast.

65. **MOLINIA,** Schrank. About 5 species of Eurasian tufted per. grasses, one sparingly planted for ornament.—Spikelets 2–4-fld., separated along a long axis, rachilla disarticulating above the glumes and extending beyond upper flt. and bearing a rudiment; glumes more or less unequal, 1-nerved, acute, the first lemma somewhat exceeding them; lemmas thin, obtuse or acute, 3-nerved. (Moli-nia: J. Molina, Chilean botanist.)

M. cærulea, Moench (*Aira cærulea,* L.). Culms erect, simple, 2–5 ft. or more, stiff, glabrous: lvs. rather stiff, 6–12 in. long, narrow, nearly or quite glabrous: panicle 6–18 in. long, with a few erect branches, bearing separated acute awnless green or purplish spikelets. Eu., where it is prized for forage; sparingly adventive in N. Amer.—Sometimes planted for edgings in a form with striped lvs.

66. **ERAGROSTIS,** Host. Species more than 100, in temp. and trop. regions, ann. and per. mostly small grasses of little economic importance, a very few grown sparingly for ornament.—Spikelets 2- to many-fld., small, usually somewhat flattened, in diffuse or contracted panicles; rachilla disarticulating above the glumes or sometimes continuous, lemmas deciduous, palea persistent; glumes more or less unequal, shorter than first lemma, acute, 1–3-nerved; lemmas acute, 3-nerved; stigmas plumose; stamens 2 or 3. (Eragros-tis: Greek combination, probably signifying *love-grass.*)

A. Spikelets mostly about 5-fld.: plant fragrant. . . . . 1. *E. abyssinica*
AA. Spikelets mostly about 10-fld.: not fragrant. . . . . 2. *E. suaveolens*

1. **E. abyssinica,** Link (*Poa abyssinica,* Jacq.). TEFF. Ann., 2–3 ft., branching and spreading, the culms slender and glabrous: lvs. long and narrow: panicle very loose and open, 10–15 in. long, with long capillary virgate and drooping alternate branches; spikelets mostly about 5-fld. but sometimes 7–9-fld., small, usually not exceeding ¼in. long, the lemmas acuminate and roughish on the nerves and tip. Afr.—Sometimes grown for ornament; in N. E. Afr. the seeds are used in bread-making.

2. **E. suaveolens,** Becker. Ann., 1–3 ft., with rather soft short lvs., the diffuse panicle

comprising half or more the height of the plant: spikelets 7–11-fld., mostly more than ¼in. long, oblong, the lemmas short-acute and not acuminate. W. Asia.—Grown for bouquets, sometimes under the names *E. amabilis*, *Poa amabilis*, *E. maxima*.

67. **BRIZA,** L. Quaking-Grass. Species perhaps 20, Old World and S. Amer., ann. and per., of small stature, grown for the ornamental open panicles.—Spikelets several-fld., perfect, the uppermost small, large and heavy, flattened, more or less tumid, often hanging on capillary pedicels; rachilla disarticulating between the flts.; glumes nearly equal, broad, papery, with rough margins; lemmas papery, cordate, several-nerved, margins rough; stigmas plumose; stamens 3. (Bri-za: old Greek name for a grain.)

A. Spikelets very large, ½in. or more long at maturity.......... 1. *B. maxima*
AA. Spikelets small, ¼in. or less long.
B. Glumes shorter than lowest flts.......... 2. *B. media*
BB. Glumes exceeding lowest flts.......... 3. *B. minor*

1. **B. maxima,** L. Ann., 1–2 ft.: lvs. soft, blades 4–6 in. long, about ¼in. broad, glabrous, ligule prominent and obtuse: spikelets ovate, mostly ½in. or more long at maturity, pale or bronzy, hanging on slender pedicels, handsome. Eu.

2. **B. media,** L. Per., 12–20 in., with narrow lvs.: ligule very short, obtuse or truncate: panicle 3–10 in. long, with slender branches, not much compound; spikelets broad-ovate, about as broad as long, usually purplish; glumes slightly shorter than lowest flt.; lemmas round-oval, not gibbous. Eu.

3. **B. minor,** L. (*B. gracilis*, Hort.). Ann., 6–20 in., with rather broad lvs.: ligule long, lanceolate-acute: panicle broad and compound; spikelets triangular, the well-developed ones usually somewhat longer than broad, green; glumes slightly exceeding the lowest flts.; lemmas round-cordate, gibbous. Eu.

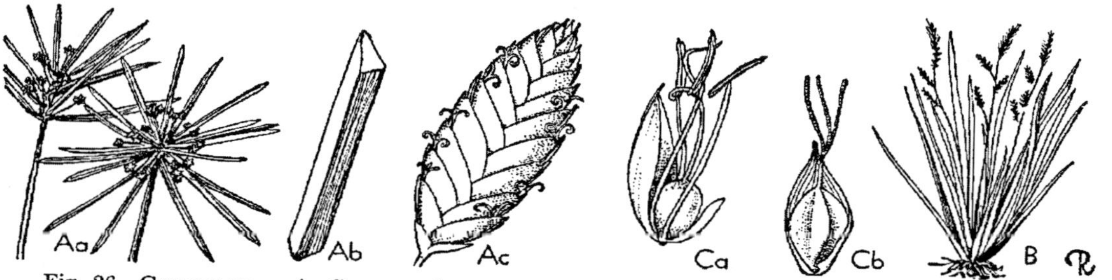

Fig. 26. Cyperaceæ. A, *Cyperus alternifolius:* Aa, habit flowering axis, side and top view, × ⅕; Ab, stem section, × ½; Ac, inflorescence, × 4. B, *Carex Morrowii:* habit, × ⅛. C, *Carex plantaginea:* Ca, flower, × 10; Cb, fruit, × 10. (C after Mackenzie.)

26. CYPERACEÆ. SEDGE FAMILY

Many sedgy commonly per. plants around the globe, distinguished from grasses by the mostly 3-angled and solid culms, 3-ranked lvs., closed rather than open or split lf.-sheaths, and very different fls. which are commonly aggregated into spikes or heads and not usually in open panicles; the genera and species are many, but very few kinds are in cult. and these mostly for ornament in foliage.—Fls. small and green, inconspicuous, bisexual or unisexual, borne in spikelets and covered by subtending bracts; perianth none, or represented by scales or bristles; stamens 2 or 3; ovary 1-celled, naked or contained in a closed sac, the styles 2 or 3 and the achene lenticular or trigonous.

A. Pistil not inclosed, surrounded by scales or bristles.
B. Spikelets flattened, the scales being 2-ranked and keeled: infl. an umbel.......... 1. Cyperus
BB. Spikelets globular or cylindrical, the scales imbricated on all sides.......... 2. Scirpus
AA. Pistil in a closed sac or perigynium.......... 3. Carex

1. **CYPERUS,** L. Galingale. About 600 widely distributed species, bearing the spikes mostly in umbel-like clusters subtended by involucre-like lvs.; two are well known in conservatories.—Fls. bisexual, in flattened spikelets under 2-ranked keeled scales; stamens 1–3; pistil 1, the style 2–3-cleft, and the achene lenticular or trigonous; perianth none. (Cype-rus: ancient Greek name for these plants.)

A. Rays of umbel very many, long-filiform: plant 5 ft. and more tall............1. *C. Papyrus*
AA. Rays of umbel few to many, short: plant 4 ft. or less tall.
B. Spikelets linear, ⅜–1 in. long, sessile, spreading from the rachis............2. *C. esculentus*
BB. Spikelets globose to oblong.
C. Culm-lvs. reduced to sheaths............3. *C. alternifolius*
CC. Culm-lvs. well developed............4. *C. adenophorus*

1. **C. Papyrus,** L. (*Papyrus antiquorum,* Willd.). Papyrus. Plant cespitose; culms strong and erect, 5–8 ft. and more, smooth, obtusely 3-angled, the lvs. reduced to short-pointed sheaths near the thick spongy base: umbel terminal, large, comprising 50–100 and more drooping filiform rays 10–20 in. long and much exceeding the few small involucral lvs.; involucels of several long slender lvs or bracts; spikelets linear, sessile, squarrose, pale chestnut, the rachis winged. S. Eu., Syria, Afr.—The paper plant (Papyrus) of the Egyptians, often grown in aquaria and ponds for its striking effect.

2. **C. esculentus,** L. Chufa. Rather stout leafy plant to 3 ft. high, bearing oblong underground edible tubers (chufas): umbel large, terminal, with long broad involucral lvs., some of the rays much longer than others; spikelets numerous, linear, 1 in. or less long, sessile and squarrose on the rachis forming a short straw-colored spike: achene oblong, obtuse, 3-angled. N. Amer., Eu., Asia, and sometimes a weed.

3. **C. alternifolius,** L. Umbrella-Plant. Cespitose, from tough matted roots, 2–4 ft.; culms stout, erect, angled and striate, clothed below with leafless brown sheaths: umbel terminal in an involucre of many long firm spreading lvs. that give the plant its umbrella effect, the primary rays 1–2 in. long, secondary rays few or none; spikelets oblong to short-oblong (about ⅓in. or less), flattened, 6–12-fld. on either side, mostly sessile in bunches at the end of the primary rays. Afr., nat in W. Indies and S. Amer.—A common pot and porch plant. Var. **variegatus,** Hort., has white-lined culm and lvs. Var. **gracilis,** Hort., is a foot or so high with more erect involucral lvs. which are 1–3 in. long.

4. **C. adenophorus,** Schrad. Culms about 2 ft. high, angled, leafy below: umbels terminal, diffuse, bearing many globular or ovoid to lanceolate small spikelets on slender secondary and tertiary rays (spikelets all stalked), the involucral lvs. many and ascending: achene obovate, 3-angled. Brazil.—Sometimes grown in pots, not very common.

2. **SCIRPUS,** L. Bulrush. Species about 150 in many parts of the world, the plants various, sometimes hair-like and without lf.-bearing culms and sometimes tall, stout and leafy; one little species is prevalent in greenhouses and a stouter one is sometimes grown about ponds.—Fls. bisexual, in heads or in spikelets that are variously umbelled; perianth sometimes absent but usually represented by 1–6 or 8 bristles; stamens 2 or 3; pistil 1, with a 2–3-cleft style: achene lenticular or trigonous. (Scir-pus: the classical Latin name.)

A. Plant of many filiform culms and single terminal head or spike............1. *S. cernuus*
AA. Plant of fewer stiff tall culms, and clustered spikes............2. *S. Tabernæmontani*

1. **S. cernuus,** Vahl (*S. gracilis,* Koch. *Isolepis gracilis,* Hort.). Small tufted plant with numerous filiform culms 6–12 in. long, erect at first but becoming weak or drooping: lf.-blades short or none from the basal sheaths: spikelet small and terminal, usually ¼in. or less long (in the wild in Eu. reported sometimes 1 in. long), ovoid to oblong-lanceolate, subtended by a bract usually less than its own length; scales obtuse, thin; styles 3. Eu., and elsewhere.—Frequent in pots and as edging in greenhouses.

2. **S. Tabernæmontani,** Gmel. Culms stiff and erect, terete, glaucous, 2 ft. or more high, with 1 or 2 long lf.-pointed sheaths at base: spikelets ovoid, in a small terminal more or less drooping cyme subtended by a bract usually shorter than the developed cluster; scales fringed, mucronate; styles 2, the achene lenticular or compressed and short-oblong, convex on one side. (Tabernæmontani: Latinized name of a German pre-Linnæan botanist, J. T. Tabernæmontanus.) Eu., shores and ponds. Cult. in var. **zebrinus,** Nichols. (*Juncus zebrinus,* Hort.), marked on the culm by alternate broad bands of green and white.—The American representative of *S. Tabernæmontani* is *S. validus,* Vahl, native on the margins of ponds.

3. **CAREX,** L. Sedge. Probably 800–900 known species of grassy plants, per., mostly outside the tropics, of the widest distribution, usually of wet lands but many of them of uplands; very few are cult., although many of them bear ornamental spikes.—Fls. always unisexual, mostly separated on the same plant (monœcious) but sometimes diœcious, the staminate fls. in a separate terminal spike or at the base of a spike bearing pistils (spike androgynous); perianth none; stamens 3, under a scale; pistil 1, inclosed in a sac or perigynium which is subtended by a scale; spikes erect or drooping, in the axils of lvs. or bracts, mostly at or near the top of the culm. (Ca-rex: classical Latin name.)—The native *C. plantaginea,* Lam., may also be cult.

A. Lvs. flat, about ⅛in. wide, often striped .... 1. *C. Morrowii*
AA. Lvs. filiform .... 2. *C. comans*

1. **C. Morrowii,** Boott (*C. japonica,* Hort.). Tufted, evergreen, the bright green flat lvs. long-pointed, in the cult. form usually white-striped; culms nearly as long as the lvs., 12 in. or so, bearing a long-stalked terminal spike and 3 or 4 stalked pistillate spikes from sheaths: perigynium long-beaked, strongly few-ribbed, 2-toothed, about the length of the sharp-pointed scale; styles 3. Japan, where it was first collected by Dr. James Morrow, attached to Commodore Perry's Expedition to the China Sea and Japan.—A good pot and border-plant; sometimes seen in greenhouses.

2. **C. comans,** Bergg. (*C. Vilmorinii,* Mott.). Densely tufted pale green or reddish plant with many very narrow (filiform) lvs., used for grass-like edgings; culms shorter or longer than the lvs., slender, 12–18 in. long: terminal spikelet (or 2 of them) staminate, slender, sessile or short-stalked; lateral spikes 3–5, 1 in. or less long, scattered, short-stalked, pistillate: perigynium broad, rather short-beaked, more or less ribbed on the back, 2-toothed, equalling or exceeding the awned scale; styles 3. New Zeal.

27. PALMACEÆ. PALM FAMILY

Woody plants of characteristic appearance yet of widely variable form, most of them trees of diverse dimensions, some of them erect shrubs, others climbers, all with woody rather than herbaceous sts. usually not branched, and stiff persistent lvs. mostly forming a crown at top of plant; genera upward of 140, and species several thousand, many of which are yet imperfectly understood; inhabitants of tropics around the world, extending into warm-temp. regions. Many kinds are planted in the warmer parts of the U. S., but the botany of some of them is obscure. In the juvenile stage, several species are common in conservatories and are much used for decoration; as these plants are not seen in fl. and fr. and the trunk may not develop, the observer may have difficulty in determining them.—Fls. small or minute, mostly greenish and individually inconspicuous, unisexual or bisexual, usually many in conspicuous simple or much-branched spadices among the lvs. or below them or sometimes above them, a spathe commonly present and covering the bud and often becoming woody; perianth usually of 6 parts or lobes, representing 3 sepals and 3 petals; stamens mostly 6, but sometimes more; pistil 1 and 3-celled, or sometimes the 3 carpels separate, ovule 1 in each cell or carpel: fr. mostly 1-seeded by abortion of the other 2 ovules, a berry, drupe, or nut, in many sizes and forms: lvs. usually very large, palmate or pinnate, rarely entire or nearly so at maturity, plicate, entire in the bud, mostly on long petioles which are commonly imbricated at the base: vernation (unfolding of lvs. from the bud) of two main types—induplicate when the faces or upper surfaces of the plaits are folded together and reduplicate when the backs of the plaits lie against each other: growth of the caudex is from a single terminal bud, but a few of the species branch as they grow although these are not included in the present treatment. In the tropics palms provide much material for building and for household supplies, as well as food, oil and waxes. Three species yielding important commercial products are planted or known in the U. S., *Cocos nucifera, Phœnix dactylifera, Elæis guineensis.*

Fl.-bearing in palms is mostly *interfoliar,* in clusters among the lvs.; *infrafoliar,* in clusters below the lvs. and free from the foliage, sometimes (as in Roystonea) at the base of a *crownshaft* or trunk-like extension of the bole formed by long broad overlapping petiole-bases; sometimes *suprafoliar,* or above the coma or lf.-head.

A. Species of fan-lvd. or palmate palms, the lf.-blade nearly circular and cut or divided toward the petiole and not directly to a continuing midrib.
  B. Divisions of lf.-blade (in ours) few and extending practically to its base, not long-acuminate at apex: trunks slender and cane-like in a cluster. 1. RHAPIS
  BB. Divisions of blade many and extending to less than base, points long-acute, and lf. very fan-like in form: trunk (if any) single and stout.
    C. Fr. with a podium or a conspicuous hollow obtuse protrusion into base of plain albumen sometimes filled with brown testa or fiber, ⅜in. or more thick, lopsided, exterior soft and pulpy at fresh maturity: petiole either dentate or entire .... 2. ERYTHEA
    CC. Fr. without evident podium, smaller, not fleshy at fresh maturity, and usually not prominently lopsided.
      D. Petiole armed along the two edges, at least toward base, with fine teeth, saw-tooth prongs on slender spines (teeth sometimes nearly or quite disappearing on mature lvs. of old plants).

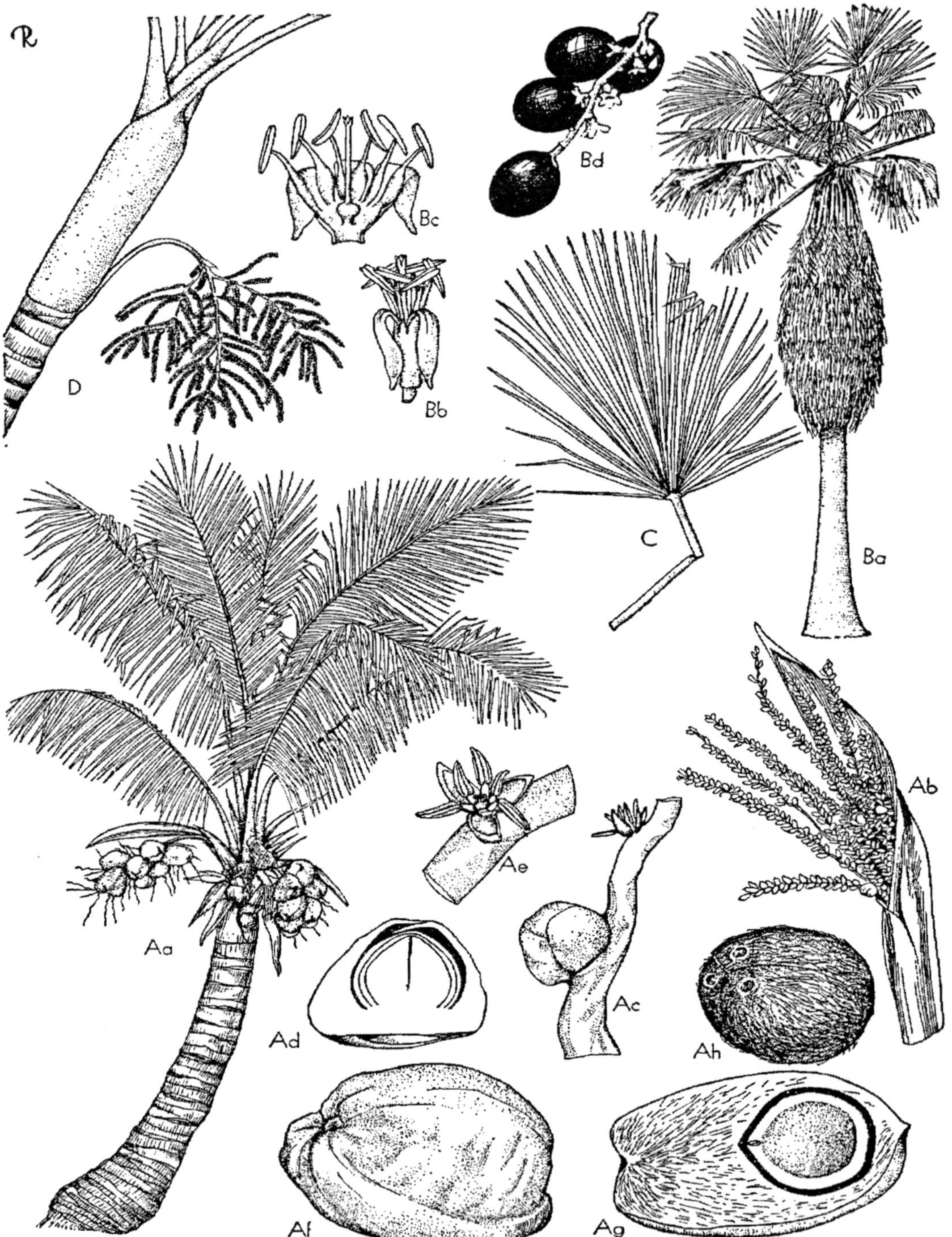

Fig. 27. PALMACEÆ. A, *Cocos nucifera:* Aa, tree in fruit, much reduced; Ab, flowering inflorescence and spathes, × 1/10; Ac, section of rachilla with pistillate and staminate flower, × 1/2; Ad, pistillate flower, vertical section, × 1; Ae, staminate flower, × 1; Af, fruit, × 1/8; Ag, same, longitudinal section, × 1/8; Ah, nut, × 1/6. B, *Washingtonia filifera:* Ba, tree, much reduced; Bb, flower, × 2; Bc, same, perianth expanded, × 2; Bd, fruit, × 1. C, *Thrinax microcarpa:* leaf, much reduced. D, *Chrysalidocarpus lutescens:* trunk apex showing flowering inflorescence, crownshaft and leaf-petioles, much reduced. In Ae, one stamen is removed.

E. Teeth small and fine, hardly prickly or spinose, the petiole narrow and slender, serrate whole length.
F. Plant low in dense clumps without trunks above ground...... 3. SERENOA
FF. Plant tree-like with evident trunks.......................... 4. TRACHYCARPUS
EE. Teeth on petioles of the saw-tooth or prong-like kind, most pronounced toward base of stalk unless in no. 5.
F. Marginal teeth on mature petioles becoming long and straight and slender, usually occupying whole length of stalk: low clumpy palm.. 5. CHAMÆROPS
FF. Marginal teeth of the saw-tooth kind, mostly toward base.
G. Trunk massive and columnar, dead lvs. hanging and persisting as a covering shag: embryo at or near base of fr......... 6. WASHINGTONIA
GG. Trunk more or less slender, or not massive and columnar, shag not covering the bole unless perhaps at top: embryo on side or back of fr.. 7. LIVISTONA
DD. Petiole smooth on the two edges, nude, with no teeth or prongs or spines.
E. Lf.-blade costapalmate, the petiole continuing through the blade as a midrib, and blade with strong downward twist............ 8. SABAL
EE. Lf.-blade not costapalmate, flat or not with downward curve at middle.
F. Fr. small and pea-like, not tapering to a pedicel-like attachment at base, borne in loose branched spadices or branches; albumen with intruding parts: slender small trees.
G. Albumen in mature seed divided by a central lengthwise cavity or centralium, remainder not separated into parts even though thin lines may project part way from walls, therefore practically homogeneous: fr. often white when ripe: lvs. mostly green.. 9. THRINAX
GG. Albumen divided into separable parts, without centralium, therefore ruminate: fr. black or brown-black at maturity: lvs. mostly silvery...10. COCCOTHRINAX
FF. Fr. about ⅗in. thick, cylindric and whitish, with a pedicel-like attachment at base, borne in ball-like clusters hanging conspicuously between the lvs., albumen plain: large columnar tree...11. PRITCHARDIA
AA. Species of feather-lvd. palms, the divisions (or the ribs and veins) lateral from a continuing rachis or midrib, in pinnate fashion.
B. Lower pinnæ represented by stiff long spines: plant diœcious: spadices interfoliar: fr. cylindric with long grooved seed, the pulp usually edible. . 12. PHŒNIX
BB. Lower pinnæ not developed into spines.
C. Pinnæ or segms. short, broadening and jagged toward the top..........13. CARYOTA
CC. Pinnæ long and narrow, either taper-pointed and perhaps in some cases bifid at apex or slenderly erose.
D. Infl. strongly infrafoliar, at base of crownshaft (in Howea, no. 25, the spadices may seem to be infrafoliar by the dropping of the lvs., but there is no crownshaft).
E. Albumen plain or homogeneous, consisting of a white hard seed content.
F. Apex of pinnæ broad or obliquely truncate and jagged: small or medium-sized palms in clumps....................................14. ACTINOPHLŒUS
FF. Apex of pinnæ long-tapering, narrow and acute.
G. Palm small or medium-sized, mostly bushy or in clumps: spathes like large bracts at nodes of spadix: fr. elongate, less than ¼in. thick...15. CHRYSALIDOCARPUS
GG. Palm tall and columnar, trunks solitary, tumid at some part: spathe a long woody more or less cylindric cymba: fr. semi-globular, ⅝in. or less thick...........................16. ROYSTONEA
EE. Albumen ruminate or else divided by strong intrusions from the walls.
F. Fr. large, 1¼ in. or more long.
G. Cupule of fr. not cup-shaped or particularly large, flaring.....17. ARECA
GG. Cupule deeply cup-shaped or cylindric, closely involved in the nut one-fourth or more its length..........................18. ADONIDIA
FF. Fr. small, 1 in. or much less long.
G. Apex of pinnæ narrow and long-attenuate: spathe very narrow, mostly 28–32 in. long; strands of spadix mostly long and hanging when in fl. and fr.........................19. ARCHONTOPHŒNIX
GG. Apex of pinnæ præmorse, broad and erose as if cut off: spathe 12–20 in. long; strands of spadix bushy and spreading, not hanging in fr...20. PTYCHOSPERMA
DD. Infl. interfoliar (sometimes apparently infrafoliar in Howea by shedding of the lvs.): trunk commonly not columnar.
E. Fr. very large, 8 in. and more in diam., with edible and liquid content: coconut...21. COCOS
EE. Fr. a small nut or drupe, not exceeding 2¼in. thick, often much less, not directly edible.
F. Petiole margined with spine-like teeth.
G. Fls. densely placed on long fingers in a close hand-like cluster at base of petioles compactly in the center of the crown: spathe fibrous...22. ELÆIS
GG. Fls. in open panicle-like projecting clusters: spathe shield-like, woody...23. BUTIA

FF. Petiole not margined with thongs or spiny teeth: albumen plain.
G. Plant diœcious, therefore the pistillate rachillæ bearing no lateral scars of staminate fls., and the staminate rachillæ no central scars of pistillate fls.: small palm grown in pots for house, porch and table decoration . . . . 24. COLLINIA
GG. Plant with hermaphrodite fls. or else monœcious, 3 scars determining position of 2 staminates and 1 pistillate even after fls. have fallen.
H. Spathe paper-like, inclosing or subtending long slender simple spadix that arises direct from trunk or is a branch from a wrist-like base; fls. sunken in pits: fr. pecan-like, tapering to apex, 1-celled . . . . 25. HOWEA
HH. Spathe a woody cymba that incloses a compound paniculate usually hanging spadix; fls. not sunken: fr. ovoid with more or less fleshy exterior, suddenly narrowed to apex, 1-seeded by abortion with remnant of sterile cell.
I. Seed regular in shape; sterile cell in fr. a membranous vestige . . . . 26. SYAGRUS
II. Seed very irregular in shape, curved; sterile cell a cavity in the bony wall of fr . . . . 27. ARECASTRUM

1. **RHAPIS,** L. f. LADY PALMS. Nine or 10 species of small palms with many reed-like sts., E. Asia, one a common tub-plant in greenhouses.—Mostly diœcious, fls. in short branching bracteate clusters among the foliage; calyx and corolla 3-toothed; stamens 6, represented by 6 staminodia in the fertile fls.: carpels 3 and distinct, making 1–3 small 1-seeded berries: sts. encased in network sheath: lvs. slender-petioled, palmately parted nearly or quite to the base, strongly parallel-ribbed, remaining broad at the end: vernation induplicate. (Rha-pis: Greek *needle;* application not obvious.)

R. excelsa, Henry (*R. flabelliformis,* Ait.). Cespitose, making a dense mass of foliage a few ft. high: petiole flattened, more or less rough on the edges, fibrillose at base; blade 5–10-parted nearly to the base, the segms. spreading, reticulate between the strong veins, finely serrate, the apex short-toothed. China, Japan.

2. **ERYTHEA,** Wats. (*Glaucothea,* O. F. Cook). HESPER PALMS. Half dozen sturdy hermaphrodite fan-palms of northwestern Mex., five of which are planted in S. Calif.—Fls. very small, sessile, superficial on the rachis, with 3 valvate corolla-lobes and 3 shorter calyx-lobes; stamens 6, little if at all exserted; pistil single, 3-lobed or of nearly separate carpels: fr. globose to ovoid, exterior more or less soft and pulpy, 1–1½ in. thick; seed very hard, albumen plain but entered at the bottom by an empty or fibrous cavity or podium that extends nearly or quite to the center; embryo lateral: palman occupying about half the blade, segms. long-acute, usually not distinctly hanging; hastula mostly brief and irregular, sometimes triangular; petiole armed or nude. (Erythe-a: one of the Hesperides, daughters of the West.)

A. Lvs. conspicuously glaucous or blue on one or both surfaces; petiole prominently prickly.
B. Spines or teeth on petiole reaching ⅜in. or more in length. infl. long, curved and much surpassing the lvs.: fr. not soft or fleshy.
C. Thyrses or separate fl.-clusters 2 ft. or more long, composed of many slender hanging strands: fr. oblong or ovoid, narrowed somewhat to apex . . . . 1. *E. armata*
CC. Thyrses 18 in. or less long, with spreading not hanging strands: fr. globose, rounded at apex . . . . 2. *E. clara*
BB. Spines short and commonly slender, about ¼in. long: infl. equalling the lvs. or sometimes surpassing them: fr. with a soft or fleshy exterior.
C. Infl. conspicuous in or beyond the foliage: fr. globular to obscurely pyriform, unicolored . . . . 3. *E. elegans*
CC. Infl. short and usually inconspicuous among the lvs.: fr. oblong-globular, shiny, with spots and stripes . . . . 4. *E. Brandegeei*
AA. Lvs. green on both surfaces; petiole spineless or with only very small teeth ⅛in. or less long . . . . 5. *E. edulis*

1. **E. armata,** Wats. (*E. Roezlii,* Lind.). BIG BLUE HESPER PALM. Heavy tree reaching 30–36 ft. high but bearing when trunk is still short: foliage glaucous-blue, with waxy covering; lvs. large and stiff, 3–6 ft. across, cut one-half or more their depth into many strongly veined segms.; petiole 3 ft. or more long, armed with bent or curved spine-like teeth about ⅓in. long: fls. not clustered and subtended by narrow acute bracts, very numerous in ample hanging thyrses on long arms or spadices beyond the coma and 12–15 ft. long: fr. short-ovoid and mostly narrowed to apex, about ¾in. long, paper-like on outside with stripes and spots. N. Lower Calif.

2. **E. clara,** Bailey (*E. Roezlii,* Bailey not Lind.). SHORT-ARM BLUE HESPER PALM. More slender tree than *E. armata,* foliage usually blue but variable in this respect, or-

dinarily not waxy: arms or spadices one-half as long, 6–9 ft. and not prominently outarching: fr. nearly globose with rounded apex, the exterior drying hard and wrinkled. N. Sonora, probably Lower Calif., Mex.

3. **E. elegans,** Franceschi. FRANCESCHI PALM. Dwarf palm in cult., trunk 3–6 ft. high as usually seen: foliage thinly glaucous on both surfaces, not waxy unless on under surface; lf. nearly or quite 3 ft. broad, the long and pointed segms. mostly on same plane as palman and not hanging; petiole 3 ft. or less long, slender with small not prominent spines about ⅛ in. long: arm or spadix slender, little if at all exceeding lvs., clusters very open: fr. pyriform to globular-oblong, about ¾ in. long. Sonora, Mex.

4. **E. Brandegeei,** Purpus. SAN JOSÉ HESPER PALM. Slender, the hardwooded trunk 28–36 ft. tall: lvs. dull green above and waxy-glaucous underneath, 3 ft. or more broad, cut to middle or somewhat below into narrow long-pointed segms. usually overbent at end; petiole slender, 3 ft. or more long and 1¾ in. or less broad, bordered with tooth-like spines ⅛ in. or less long: arm or spadix commonly a little shorter or not exceeding the lvs.: fr. oblong-globular, ¾ in. more or less long, lined with shades of brown. (Named for T. S. Brandegee, co-discoverer of the species, page 40.) Region of San José, S. Lower Calif. Var. **spiralis,** Jones, is a form in cult. with spiral arrangement of petiole-bases on trunk.

5. **E. edulis,** Wats. GUADALUPE PALM. Stout, 30–36 ft. tall: lvs. green on both surfaces, 3–6 ft. across, segms. cut to one-third or one-half the blade and usually not hanging; petiole about as long as blade, margins nude or with many very short not spinose teeth: arm or spadix shorter than lvs. or perhaps somewhat surpassing them in fr. with many hanging strands: fr. globose or short-oblong, 1⅓ in. or more thick, black, with a thick much wrinkled pulpy exterior when dry. Guadalupe Isl., Mex.

3. **SERENOA,** Hook. f. SAW PALMETTO. One low species in S. E. U. S., sometimes transplanted or left as a background plantation when new homes are built.—Trunk or rhizome commonly subterranean and the plant apparently acaulescent but sometimes rising 3–20 ft. or more: lvs. palmate, hastula not prominent: fls. hermaphrodite, calyx and corolla 3-lobed or petals nearly separate, stamens 6: fr. drupe-like, the more or less succulent exterior soon drying, oblong to nearly globular, 1-seeded. (Sereno-a: Sereno Watson, 1826–1892, American botanist.)

S. repens, Small (*S. serrulata,* Nichols. *Corypha repens,* Bartram). Growing in dense continuous stands on the Coastal Plain, S. C. to Fla. and Miss.: lvs. divided nearly or quite to base, green to heavily glaucous, the saw-toothed petiole not continuing through the blade: infl. a branching cluster usually not exceeding foliage: fr. variable in size or shape, 1 in. or less long and perhaps two-thirds as thick, the grooved seed contained in an inner shell.

4. **TRACHYCARPUS,** Wendl. Few species of small or medium fan-palms of Asia, the trunks single or cespitose, planted on the colder limits of palm climates.—Fls. small, becoming yellow, unisexual or bisexual, in branching short spadices among the foliage, the spathes many and prominent; calyx and corolla 3-parted; stamens 6; ovaries 3, joined at the base: fr. globose, oblong or somewhat reniform, the stigma terminal: lvs. many-plicate, with long bifid segms.; petiole convex both sides or plano-convex, mostly serrate along the margins, at the base involved in fibers: vernation induplicate: trunk spineless. (Trachycar-pus: Greek *rough fruit.*)

A. Trunk single.
  B. Lf.-segms. rather thin, declined or hanging on mature lvs. .... 1. *T. Fortunei*
  BB. Lf.-segms. stiff or even rigid, straightly outstanding. .... 2. *T. Wagnerianus*
AA. Trunks few or several together from one base. .... 3. *T. cæspitosus*

1. **T. Fortunei,** Wendl. (*T. excelsus,* Wendl. *Chamærops excelsa,* Mart. not Thunb. *C. Fortunei,* Hook.). WINDMILL PALM. Slender tree with single trunk to 30 ft. or so tall, bole covered with black hair-like fiber: lvs. nearly orbicular, 3 ft. more or less across, petiole with small points or serratures, segms. narrow and flexible and usually drooping on mature blades: fl.-clusters ½–¾ in. long, branched: fr. 3-carpelled and deeply angled, each part about as large as pea. (For Robt. Fortune, page 43.) E. Asia.—Hardy from N. C. south and on Pacific Coast, Ore. south.

2. **T. Wagnerianus,** Becc. (*T. nepalensis,* Hort.). Mostly a lower tree than *T. Fortunei:* segms. stiff and outstanding, not drooping. Origin not known.—Planted from Ga. south and in Calif.

3. **T. cæspitosus,** Becc. Trunks several or few from each stand or base, making a clump to 15 ft. tall, boles with much fiber and often old lvs.: blade usually less than 3 ft. broad, segms. stiff and outstanding, petiole sharply serrate: fr. much as in *T. Fortunei* but minutely hairy. Probably E. Asia.—Planted in southeastern states and Calif.

5. **CHAMÆROPS,** L. Two small fan-palms in the Medit. region, one frequently used as a hardy planted palm and often seen in greenhouses.—Diœcious or polygamo-diœcious, fls. in short erect densely-fld. spadices among the lvs., spathes 2–4, the lower ones split; calyx 3-parted; petals 3, free; stamens 6–9; ovaries 3 or rarely more, the stigma nearly sessile: fr. ovoid or nearly globular, becoming reddish or yellowish, small: lvs. deeply cut, with narrow spreading segms., petiole slender and usually spiny: plant commonly branching near the base, producing several clustered trunks: vernation induplicate. (Chamæ-rops: Greek *dwarf bush.*)

C. humilis, L. European Fan-Palm. Main trunk usually 1–3 ft., branching and suckering from the bottom, but plant in the open reaching 15–30 ft.: lvs. glaucous above and beneath, cut one-third to two-thirds into narrow spreading not drooping segms. which are entire or bifid at apex; petiole slender, long, usually with straight spines along the margins.—There are variations under several hort. names.

6. **WASHINGTONIA,** Wendl. (*Neowashingtonia,* Sudw.). Washington Palms. Two stout and mostly massive palms of S. Calif. and adjacent Ariz. and Mex., by some authors included in Pritchardia, extensively planted in Calif. and also eastward on the Gulf region.—Fls. bisexual, white, in long paniculate spadices among the foliage, the spathes long and thin; perianth toothed; stamens 6; ovary 3-lobed: fr. a small ellipsoid black drupe with stigma basal: lvs. large and plicate, cut nearly to the middle, often bearing copious filaments, petiole armed: vernation induplicate: trunk becoming smooth and ringed below, but upward bearing an immense shaggy mane of remains of lvs. (Washingto-nia: George Washington.)

A. The gray-green Washington palm in respect to foliage: trunk heavy and columnar, usually without expanded base: blade lacking a brownish patch underneath about hastula; lf. very filiferous .... 1. *W. filifera*
AA. The bright-lvd. Washington palm: trunk slender, not thick and columnar, with expanded or swollen base: blade bearing a tomentose tawny patch about hastula underneath; lf. little if at all filiferous at mature stage of tree .... 2. *W. robusta*

1. **W. filifera,** Wendl. Heavy-trunked tree to 45 ft. and more tall, the bole barrel-like and little or not at all swollen at base; head open from long petioles: shag of dead lvs. broad and dense and tapering at its base when it does not extend to base of bole; petiole green or light colored, not heavily armed; lf. bearing many filaments on the segms., ends of segms. declined or hanging. S. Calif., W. Ariz., Lower Calif.—Much planted about the world.

2. **W. robusta,** Wendl. (*W. sonoræ,* Wats. *W. gracilis,* Parish). More slender and taller tree than no. 1, with brilliantly shining foliage; trunk commonly swollen at base; head close because of short petioles: shag of dead lvs. narrow and ragged; petiole red-brown and heavily armed; lf. practically or wholly without filaments except when tree is very young, ends of segms. mostly not declined. Mex. in Sonora and Lower Calif.—Commonly planted.

7. **LIVISTONA,** R. Br. Fountain Palms. A dozen or more species, comprising the most common fan-palms of greenhouses and decorative use; native in E. Asia and Malaya to Australia.—Fls. bisexual, small and greenish, borne in elongated branching spadices among the lvs., mostly drooping in fr., the spathes many and sheathing the peduncle; calyx and corolla 3-lobed nearly or quite to the base; stamens 6; ovary 3-celled, the style short: fr. globose to oblong-ellipsoidal, small, smooth, the seed erect: lvs. strongly plicate, with many long bifid segms.; petiole plano- or concavo-convex, spiny the whole length on the edges or only toward the base, becoming spineless in old plants: vernation induplicate: trunk short or tall, becoming ringed, bearing toward the top more or less dead lf.-sheaths and brown articulated fiber, in greenhouses usually not evident. (Livisto-na: in honor of P. Murray of Livistone near Edinburgh.)—*L. chinensis* is common in cult. in palm regions of U. S., *L. rotundifolia* infrequent; two or three others may be found in special places.

A. Lvs. (at least on bearing trees) with hanging segms .... 1. *L. chinensis*
AA. Lvs. with rigid or horizontal segms., or at most in some cases only declined .... 2. *L. rotundifolia*

1. **L. chinensis,** R. Br. Chinese Fan- or Fountain Palm. The common tub fan-palm for decoration, producing a short caudex bearing the bases of the removed petioles and the fibrous tissue, but in nature making a ringed trunk 50 ft. high: lvs. 3–5 ft. across, broader than long, cut to about the middle, the long bifid segms. bending sharply downward with age; petiole plano-convex, spiny on the lower part in the young plants common

in cult. in U. S.: fr. ellipsoid-oblong, ¾–1 in. long, black, olive-like. China.—In cult. it often erroneously bears the name *Latania borbonica.* Mature trees in the open produce a graceful fountain-like effect with the slender pendent lf.-lobes.

2. **L. rotundifolia,** Mart. (*L. altissima,* Zoll.). Slender tall palm to 50 ft.: lvs. large, circular in outline, 3–5 ft. across, with 60–90 long-acuminate bifid segms.; petiole of adult plant spiny at the base but elsewhere unarmed: spadix 3–5 ft. long, of 3 main parts that are free from their bases and arising from one flattened spathe: fr. ½in. or less diam., spherical, dark violet drying black. Java.

8. **SABAL,** Adans. PALMETTO PALMS. Upwards of two dozen species in U. S. to Trinidad, Panama and Colombia.—Usually plants with stiff long trunks but in one species mostly acaulescent, usually with broad costapalmate lvs. (petiole continued more or less through the lf., the blade curving downward toward the end), petiole two-edged and unarmed, hastula well developed on upper face: fls. hermaphrodite, in lengthened clusters on a long arm among the lvs.; calyx cup-shaped and lobed, petals 3 and usually separate, stamens 6 and conspicuously exserted: fr. a small nearly globular berry without conspicuously soft exterior; seed 1, albumen homogeneous. (Sa-bal: name unexplained.)

A. Lf. scarcely costapalmate, practically flat, blade mostly split into two parts, hastula under 2½ in. long and obtuse: infl. erect and overtopping lvs.: plant usually nearly or quite acaulescent. (EUSABAL.) .... 1. *S. minor*
AA. Lf. costapalmate, blade downward-bent, hastula long and acute: infl. horizontal or becoming so: trees. (INODES.)
B. Palman (undivided basal part of blade) one-fourth to one-third or more length of blade in mature bearing trees.
C. Fr. small, ½in. or less thick, nearly or quite globular .... 2. *S. Palmetto*
CC. Fr. large, up to ¾in. thick or even more, usually not globular.
D. Infl. shorter than lvs. or even of petioles .... 3. *S. umbraculifera*
DD. Infl. equalling or usually much exceeding the lvs. .... 4. *S. texana*
BB. Palman very small or none, the lf. with an open divided look due to deep segmentation.
C. Fr. tapering to prominent base: filaments none in lf.-sinuses .... 5. *S. peregrina*
CC. Fr. not tapering to base, globular: filaments prominent in sinuses .... 6. *S. viatoris*

1. **S. minor,** Pers. (*S. glabra,* Sarg. *S. louisiana,* Bomhard). BUSH PALMETTO. Unarmed low palm mostly without bole above ground but sometimes with real emergent trunk 6–9 ft. or more tall: lvs. green or lightly bluish, 2–4 ft. broad, nearly flat and only indifferently if at all costapalmate, segms. 1–2 in. broad at base, filaments in sinuses few or none, segms. not hanging, hastula short and blunt: fr. black, commonly shining, globular to oblate, ⅓–½in. thick. River-bottoms and flat lands, N. C. to Fla., Ala. and E. Tex.—A good hardy palm for low plantings in rear and about borders. Not to be confused with saw palmetto, *Serenoa repens,* of sandy lands, which has very slender petioles with sharp fine teeth on margins.

2. **S. Palmetto,** Lodd. COMMON PALMETTO. Familiar tree, trunk even at bearing age 3–90 ft. tall, bole straight or curved: lvs. strongly costapalmate, blade 3–6 ft. long, segms. hanging or declined, many fibers in sinuses, hastula 4–5 in. long and narrowly acuminate: infl. more or less horizontal, exceeding the lvs.: fr. black or nearly so, globular usually with short tapering base, ¼–½in. thick. In lowlands and on dunes, coastal parts of N. and S. C., Fla. and westward to St. Andrews Bay in Fla.—Often an effective tree in plantings.

3. **S. umbraculifera,** Mart. (*S. Blackburnia,* Glazebr.). HISPANIOLAN PALMETTO. Massive columnar tree to 60 ft. or more tall, commonly bearing a heavy shag under the head: lvs. very large, strongly costapalmate, blade perhaps 6 ft. long, segms. stiff but hanging on mature trees, filaments mostly few, seldom conspicuous, hastula 7–8 in. long and narrowly pointed: infl. shorter than lvs.: fr. large, to nearly 1 in. thick, globular-pyriform. Haiti and Santo Domingo.—Widely planted; most stately of palmettoes.

4. **S. texana,** Becc. (*Inodes texana* and *I. exul,* O. F. Cook). TEXAN PALMETTO. Stout tree 40–60 ft. tall, with dense round green head that usually sheds its shag before maturity: lvs. costapalmate, blade 3 ft. and more long and deeply cut, moderately filiferous, segms. little if at all hanging: infl. commonly exceeding the lvs. and hanging: fr. normally flat on bottom, to ¾in. across, curved on top. Extreme S. Tex., adjacent Mex.—More or less planted.

5. **S. peregrina,** Bailey. Erect to 25 ft. but not strict or rigid, with a thick head of long-hanging segms.: lvs. light green, blade 3–6 ft. broad, palman very short, filaments none, hastula about 3 in. long, broad, not very acute: infl. shorter than lvs., commonly very floriferous and fruitful: fr. shining black, ⅓–½in. thick, globular but more or less tapering at base. Nativity not determined.—Planted at Key West, in W. Indies and S. Amer.

6. **S. viatoris,** Bailey. Strict erect tree, 12 ft. and more tall, with a thin open small head and trunk covered with crisscross of lf.-bases: lvs. light green, thin in texture, sinuses bending over and perhaps hanging, filaments abundant in sinuses, hastula narrow, long-acuminate, 2½–3 in. long: fr. shining, black or dark brown, globular, ⅓in. thick. Origin unknown.—Planted in S. Calif.

9. **THRINAX,** L. f. (*Simpsonia,* O. F. Cook). PEABERRY PALMS. About 10 small or slender unarmed graceful fan-palms, native in S. Fla. and W. Indies, a few sometimes planted for ornament.—Lvs. flat, segmented one-half or more the length of the blade, filaments usually none, petiole slender, not serrate or toothed, hastula short and broad with a point or rounded rim projecting over blade: fls. very small, hermaphrodite, borne on interfoliar branching spadices that may equal or exceed the lvs.; calyx a toothed cup without blades, petals none, stamens 6: fr. small, globose, about size of a pea, blackish or brown or even white at maturity, albumen divided through the center by a cavity or centralium, with partial intrusion from the exterior wall. (Thri-nax: Greek *fan,* from fancied application in the lvs.)

A. Fls. and frs. pedicellate..1. *T. parviflora*
AA. Fls. and frs. sessile.
B. Plant a tree: lvs. usually silvery underneath........................2. *T. microcarpa*
BB. Plant very dwarf, bush-like: lvs. green..............................3. *T. Morrisii*

1. **T. parviflora,** Sw. (*T. floridana,* Sarg. *T. Wendlandiana,* Becc.). Slender erect tree 25–30 ft. tall, bole enlarged at base and perhaps 4 in. thick at middle; head small, condensed in age: lvs. light green, 3 ft. or more across, hastula broad but pointed in middle: infl. horizontal, 3 ft. or more long, bearing separate alternate clusters: fr. globular, ¼in. or less thick, distinctly stalked. Fla. Keys, Bahamas, Cuba, Haiti, Jamaica.

2. **T. microcarpa,** Sarg. (*T. keyensis,* Sarg.). Stout stocky tree usually less than 25 ft. tall, commonly only 10–12 ft., base of bole with masses of root-like covering; head open because of long petioles: lvs. segmented nearly to base, tips more or less drooping, hastula with very brief point or none: fr. usually white at first maturity, globular, about ⅛in. across, sessile. Upper Fla. Keys to Puerto Rico.

3. **T. Morrisii,** Wendl. Dwarf palm, fruiting when 3–6 ft. tall: lvs. to 3 ft. broad, shining green, segms. not long-attenuate, hastula rounded and sometimes notched at apex: spadices shorter than lvs.: fr. small, about ⅛in. thick, dark brown, sessile. (Bears the name of Daniel Morris, of the Royal Gardens at Kew, England, who called attention to it in 1891.) Anguilla and Anegada Isls. in W. Indies.—Frequently planted.

10. **COCCOTHRINAX,** Sarg. SEAMBERRY PALMS. Few species of small slender palms in Fla. and W. Indies.—Genus separated in 1899 from Thrinax chiefly because of the divided or ruminate seamy albumen in the black fr.: lvs. usually silvery at least underneath. (Coccothri-nax: *berry thrinax.*)

C. argentata, Bailey (*C. argentea,* Auth. not Sarg. *C. jucunda,* Sarg. *C. Garberi,* Sarg. *Palma argentata,* Jacq.). Bright-lvd. small tree 15–20 ft. tall but bearing when much lower, suckering at base: lvs. deeply divided, silvery underneath and shiny above, segms. commonly about ¾in. broad, usually many of the parts hanging: fr. ⅜in. or less thick, brown, globular, short-stalked. S. Fla., Bahamas.—The Hispaniolan *C. argentea,* Sarg., probably not planted in U. S., is a larger tree, lvs. dull green on upper face, segms. broader and not drooping, fr. sessile.

11. **PRITCHARDIA,** Seem. & Wendl. (*Eupritchardia,* Kuntze. *Styloma,* O. F. Cook). About a half dozen species in the Pacific isls., of comely erect spineless fan-palms, of which one is frequently planted far S. and is sometimes seen under glass.—Fls. bisexual, in branching mostly short clusters among the lvs. but which are very long-peduncled in some species, hanging in fr., the spathe prominent but bract-like; calyx and corolla each shallowly 3-lobed, the tube persistent; stamens 6; ovary 3-angled or 3-lobed, style long and sulcate and terminal on the ovary: fr. a small globular or ellipsoid hard berry supported on the hardened perianth-tube, 1-seeded, the prominent but short style terminal: lvs. large, not deeply cut, many-plicate, often bearing a few thread-like filaments: vernation induplicate: trunk mostly smooth and ringed, often somewhat shaggy toward the top. (Pritchar-dia: W. T. Pritchard, British consul and author in Polynesian subjects.)—Conserved as against the earlier paleobotanical genus Pritchardia.

P. pacifica, Seem. & Wendl. (*Eupritchardia pacifica,* Kuntze). Bole straight, to 30 ft.:

lvs. nearly circular, 3–5 ft. across, prominently plicate, tomentose when young, divided about one-third their depth into attenuate bifid segms. and bearing a few filaments; petiole thin, concave above, more or less fibrillose: fr. globular, ⅜–½in. diam., with a tapered base, borne in heavy ball-like clusters. Samoa, Fiji.

12. **PHŒNIX, L.** Ten or a dozen species of feather-palms native in the trop. and subtrop. parts of Afr. and Asia; one is the date palm and others are grown in the open for ornament.—Plant diœcious: fls. in branching spadices borne among the foliage; calyx 3-lobed; petals 3 and usually distinct; stamens mostly 6, represented in fertile fls. by scales or a rim; ovaries 3, distinct, sometimes represented in the sterile fls. by minute pistillodes: fr. cylindrical, with 1 long grooved seed: lvs. long-pinnate, the lower pinnæ sometimes reduced to spines: vernation induplicate: trunk single or several, erect or reclined, usually clothed with old lf.-bases. (Phœ-nix: Greek, an early name for the date palm whether from Phœnicia or the fabled bird of Egypt is not clear.)

A. Staminate fls. oblong or ovate, apex obtuse: lvs. not white-floccose on ribs and folds underneath.
B. Plant a tree, with conspicuous trunk or trunks.
C. Tree soboliferous, sprouting from base, trunks therefore several unless the offshoots are removed for propagation or otherwise: fr. cylindric, with thick sweet flesh, fruiting perianth spread out flat; seed usually compressed and acute. . . . . 1. *P. dactylifera*
CC. Tree with solitary trunk: fruiting perianth cup-shaped; seed more or less terete.
D. Pinnæ prevailingly more than 2-ranked; lvs. stiff or almost rigid.
E. Lvs. glaucous or gray-green: fr. oliviform or oblong-elliptic. . . . . 2. *P. sylvestris*
EE. Lvs. bright green: fr. globose or nearly so. . . . . 3. *P. canariensis*
DD. Pinnæ 2-ranked; lvs. flaccid or soft. . . . . 4. *P. rupicola*
BB. Plant very low, trunks several and 3–6 ft. tall: lvs. more or less glaucous. . . . . 5. *P. Loureiri*
AA. Staminate fls. very narrow, lanceolate, acuminate: lvs. white-floccose on ribs underneath. . . . . 6. *P. reclinata*

1. **P. dactylifera,** L. DATE PALM. Strong palm to 100 ft. and more, producing offsets which are often removed in cult., the trunk usually not perfectly erect and straight: lvs. very long, stiff, arching upward, more or less glaucous; pinnæ strongly keeled, the intermediate nerves fine, sharp and stiff-pointed, the lower ones represented by long and stiff spines, 4-ranked or the upper ones 2-ranked: fr. cylindric, 1–2 in. long, borne profusely on the long hanging strands of the spadix, with edible flesh; seed flattened, acute at apex. Long domesticated; exact origin undetermined but probably native to W. Asia and N. Afr.—Grown for fr. in Calif. and Ariz. Sometimes a tree is apparently bisexual.

2. **P. sylvestris,** Roxb. WILD DATE. Fast-growing tree with stout solitary trunk to 50 ft.: lvs. glaucous or grayish-green, pinnæ fascicled and usually in more than two planes, very many in number, rigid, petiole spines ⅕–⅖in. long: fr. olive-shaped, ¾in. or more long, the thin flesh very astringent. India.—Widely planted for ornament, and the sap yields sugar.

3. **P. canariensis,** Chabaud. Stout stocky tree to 60 ft. with single trunk and dense great head of light green foliage, bole covered with old petiole-bases: pinnæ very many in different planes, the lowest ones represented by long strong spines: fr. globose to somewhat ellipsoid, about ¾in. long, yellow, somewhat pulpy; seed ⅗–¾in. long, terete, obtuse at ends. Canary Isls.—Hardy in Calif. and Fla. where it is much planted along avenues, boundary markers, and as single trees on private properties.

4. **P. rupicola,** T. Anders. Graceful slender palm to 25 ft., trunk solitary: lvs. green, soft or limp in appearance, pinnæ in single plane, alternate or subopposite, not fascicled, lower ones represented by weak spines on petiole, not long-attenuate to apex: fr. oblong, about ¾in. long, shining yellow. India.—Good subject in warm regions and in tubs or pots.

5. **P. Loureiri,** Kunth (*P. Roebelenii*, O'Brien. *P. humilis* var. *Loureiri*, Becc.). Low palm with several trunks 6 ft. or less tall: lvs. many, shiny green and somewhat glaucous, rather soft in texture, pinnæ opposite to more or less fascicled, petiolar spines slender and weak: fr. oblong, about ½in. long. (J. Loureiro, page 47.) Burma, Cochin-China.—Good pot-plant.

6. **P. reclinata,** Jacq. (*P. spinosa*, Thonn. *P. natalensis*, Hort.). Trunks mostly several, tree to 25 ft. but a single bole when suckers are removed often much taller: lvs. green, white-floccose underneath toward base particularly when young, pinnæ opposite, alternate or somewhat fascicled, rigid in texture, not very long, with sharp stiffish apex: fr. ovoid-ellipsoidal, about ¾in. long, brown or reddish. Afr. from tropics to Natal.

13. **CARYOTA,** L. FISH-TAIL PALMS. Ten to 12 palms producing tall trunks or several soboles (suckers), with bipinnate lvs. bearing fan-shaped or deltate segms.; trop. Asia to Australia.—Mostly monœcious: fls. in separate interfoliar spadices

with long hanging branches, spathes few or several; perianth somewhat unlike in the sterile and fertile fls., the 6 parts separate or at base somewhat connate, the petals in the sterile fls. much elongated; stamens many to very numerous; ovary 3-celled, with erect ovules: fr. globose or short-oblong, ½in. or somewhat more diam., becoming purplish: lvs. horizontal, with drooping graceful spray: vernation reduplicate: trunks spineless, erect: monocarpic. (Caryo-ta: Greek name first applied to the cult. date.)

A. Segms. (ultimate pinnæ) light green, thin, not stoutly ribbed, with a short point or acumen....................1. *C. mitis*
AA. Segms. dark green, stiff, stoutly ribbed, with a long point or cauda....................2. *C. urens*

1. **C. mitis,** Lour. (*C. sobolifera,* Wall.). Low tree to 25 ft., finally suckering freely: lvs. 4–9 ft. long, light green; segms. rather thin and flexible, with many rather light ribs, the terminal ones variously irregularly lobed at the apex, the lateral nearly truncate to truncate-oblique, the toothed edge usually not covering more than half the length of the blade and the outer margin produced into a short point: spathe and spadix scurfy (as are petioles and lf.-sheaths), the spadix much smaller than in no. 2; staminate fls. about ¼in. long, the stamens 15–25: fr. ½in. diam., bluish-black, the seed globose. Trop. Asia and Malaya.—Frequent in greenhouses.

2. **C. urens,** L. Wine Palm. Much taller, to 75 ft. and more, ringed, not soboliferous: lvs. large and stout, 12–20 ft. long, dark green; segms. thick and stiff, strongly ribbed and fish-tail-like, terminal ones jagged or irregularly lobed at top, lateral ones long-oblique so that the coarsely toothed edge usually covers more than half the length and the outer margin commonly produced into a long part like an index finger: spathe and spadix not scurfy, the spadix to 10 or 12 ft. long, hanging; staminate fls. ½in. or more long, one on either side in fertile fl., the stamens 40 or more: fr. to ¾in. diam., reddish. Trop. Asia and Malaya.

14. **ACTINOPHLŒUS,** Becc. Cluster Palms. Perhaps a dozen species in New Guinea and other Pacific isls., one of which is grown in S. Fla. and probably also as a tub-plant under glass.—Very slender, unarmed, monœcious, the pinnæ with broad obtuse truncate or jagged apex, sheath of petiole bearing 2 projections from the apex: infl. infrafoliar, simple or branched, 6 ft. or less long; fls. unisexual, staminate with many stamens: fr. cartridge-shaped, ⅘in. or less long, deeply 5-sulcate, red at maturity; albumen homogeneous but 5-angled. (Actinophlœ-us: Greek *ray* and *bark,* application not obvious.)

A. Macarthuri, Becc. (*Kentia Macarthuri,* Wendl. *Ptychosperma Macarthuri,* Nichols.). Sts. or trunks many, 20–25 ft. tall: lvs. 9 ft. or less long, pinnæ 20–30 subopposite pairs with soft flexible habit: fr. ⅗in. or less long aside from the cupule in which it sits, abruptly pointed, carmine-red when ripe. (Dedicated more than sixty-five years ago to Sir W. Macarthur of New S. Wales.) New Guinea.

15. **CHRYSALIDOCARPUS,** Wendl. One feather-palm from Madagascar (in a small genus) frequent as a florists' pot subject and much planted in the American tropics.—Plant monœcious: fls. in short spadices below the foliage, the sterile with recurving branches; sepals and petals 6; stamens 6, the short broad anthers dorsifixed; ovary 1, with short style and broad stigma: fr. somewhat turbinate, violet or nearly black: lvs. smooth and slender, with many narrow pinnæ, the petiole and rachis grooved above: vernation reduplicate: trunk spineless. (Chrysalidocar-pus: Greek *golden fruit.*)

C. lutescens, Wendl. (*Areca lutescens,* Bory). Madagascar Palm. Branching at crown and above, making clump of smooth erect-spreading bamboo-like ringed caudices, 10–25 ft. tall: lvs. gracefully spreading, light green and with yellow smooth petiole and rachis, the pinnæ somewhat arching, ½–¾in. wide, the very long slender points short-bifid, usually with one prominent vein midway the midrib and margin: crownshaft prominent above the short fr.-clusters, even though sometimes hidden by abundant foliage: fr. about ⅗in. long and one-third as thick, attenuate to apex, albumen plain.

16. **ROYSTONEA,** O. F. Cook (*Oreodoxa,* Mart. not Willd.). Tall striking unarmed feather-palms with columnar single bole, a few species in the American tropics, planted far S.—Plant monœcious: fls. borne in heavy branching spadices beneath the crown of foliage at base of prominent crownshaft: parts of perianth 6; stamens 6–12; staminodia in fertile fls. 6, scale-like; ovary 1, 3-celled, the stigmas

sessile; pistillodes in sterile fls. spherical or ovoid: fr. small, ½in. or less long, bluish, nearly globular or oblong, albumen homogeneous: lvs. very large, gracefully spreading-curving, the petiole concavo-convex: vernation reduplicate. (Roysto-nea: General Roy Stone, 1836–1905, American engineer known for his work in Puerto Rico.)

A. Trunk swollen near base then nearly or quite straight or columnar and cylindrical, very tall and massive: lvs. flat crosswise, the pinnæ in a single row or plane on either side: fr. oblong, trusses below the flat-based crown of lvs. . . . . 1. *R. oleracea*
AA. Trunk irregularly swollen or tumid and commonly much above the base, medium or tall: lvs. recurved crosswise, pinnæ in two tiers or planes on either side: fr. globular or briefly globular-oblong, often covered in the hanging foliage.
B. Pinnæ strongly several-nerved lengthwise: fr.-clusters short and thick; fr. more or less tapered to apex, short-oblong: trunk medium height, thickened mostly at about the middle: dry lands. . . . . 2. *R. regia*
BB. Pinnæ not at all or indifferently nerved lengthwise: fr.-clusters mostly long and loose; fr. rounded at apex, nearly globular: trunk becoming very tall and commonly thickened or shouldered near the top: native in wetlands. . . . . 3. *R. elata*

1. **R. oleracea,** O. F. Cook (*Oreodoxa oleracea,* Mart.). CABBAGE PALM. PALMISTE. Magnificent columnar tree with cylindrical trunk from an enlarged base, to 120 ft., bearing a horizontally spreading crown, conspicuous erect lightning-rod unfolding bud in the top, and erect-spreading branching panicles far below the mass of foliage: lvs. with a single row or tier of pinnæ on either side the rachis: stamens protruding in the bud: fr. oblong, ½–⅝in. long, about half as wide, straight or slightly concave on one side. Farther W. Indies.—A much-planted and characteristic tree in trop. Amer.

2. **R. regia,** O. F. Cook (*Oreodoxa regia,* HBK.). CUBAN ROYAL PALM. Erect but bole not always straight, 40–60 ft. tall in fields but attaining greater heights, thickened mostly at about the middle: pinnæ in two rows or ranks either side the rachis and standing in different planes, 1 in. and more broad, strongly several-nerved lengthwise particularly on the under side: trusses of fr. mostly about as broad as long, more or less tapered to end. Cuba, in fields, on plains, in valleys and mountains in several forms or vars.—The abundant fr. is much used for pig feed; perhaps planted in Fla.

3. **R. elata,** F. Harper (*Palma elata,* Bartram. *R. floridana,* O. F. Cook). FLORIDIAN ROYAL PALM. Tree likely to be taller than *R. regia,* mostly straight, thickened usually toward the upper part with shoulder at the top: pinnæ commonly lacking prominent longitudinal nerves or ribs: trusses usually long and open; fr. nearly globular and ½in. long. S. Fla., now confined to wet places and low isls. in and about the Everglades, but once reported as far north as Lake and Volusia counties.—Now much planted for ornament and interest in lower Fla.

17. **ARECA,** L. A number of tall slender unarmed monœcious pinnate Asian and Australian palms, one sometimes seen in S. Fla. and moist American tropics.—Trunk usually ringed, solitary in our species, clustered in others, crownshaft prominent beneath the crown: petiole with broad clasping base; pinnæ mostly narrow and long-acuminate, sometimes joined at base: infl. much-branched, staminate fls. at ends with 3–6 stamens, pistillate fls. few at base: fr. oblong or ovoid, exterior usually fleshy, 1-seeded, base inclosed in perianth-cup; albumen deeply ruminate. (Are-ca: native name.)

A. Cathecu, L. (commonly misspelled *Catechu*). ARECA-NUT. BETEL-NUT. Very tall and slender, sometimes 75 ft. and more, trunk solitary: pinnæ many, upper ones confluent, blade 3 ft. or more across, green, glabrous: infl. conspicuously infrafoliar; stamens 6; stigmas 3, short: fr. ovoid or globular-ovoid, to 2 in. long, orange or scarlet, exterior soft. India or Malaya.—Nativity in doubt but much planted for the nut which is chewed by natives; planted in S. Fla. and American tropics as an ornamental tree.

18. **ADONIDIA,** Becc. One showy pinnate monœcious unarmed palm native on Coron and Palawan of the Philippines, now planted in S. Fla.—Trunk single, solitary, stocky, strongly ringed, crownshaft long and prominent at the base of which the stout branchy spadices are borne: pinnæ regularly placed along the midrib, attenuate to apex, bearing a prominent nerve or ridge on either margin as well as at the center: fr. large and handsome. (Adonid-ia: from Adonis, mythical youth of beauty.)

A. Merrillii, Becc. MANILA PALM. MERRILL PALM. Stoutly erect to 25 ft., tapering toward top: lvs. to 6 ft. long, short-petioled, with about 50 pairs of bright green glabrous pinnæ: spadix short-peduncled, glaucous; buds of staminate fls. ⅜in. or more long: fr. ovoid-pointed, 1¼ in. long or more, bright red, in compact showy clusters, pointed and beaked at apex; albumen ruminate. (Dedicated to E. D. Merrill, page 48.)

19. **ARCHONTOPHŒNIX,** Wendl. & Drude (*Loroma*, O. F. Cook). KING PALMS. A few species of monœcious feather-palms in Australia, planted in the open in U. S.—Trunks single, annular, spineless: lvs. terminal, forming a large crown, often light colored beneath, the segms. or pinnæ entire or somewhat split at the end, the intermediate longitudinal veins very pronounced, the keel for the most part not strongly ridged: infl. standing on the trunk far below the lvs. at base of crownshaft, with many pendulous branches, the spathes 2; fls. sessile, the staminate with sometimes 8 segms. and the pistillate with 3 or more and sometimes bearing 6 staminodia, the petals valvate; stamens 9–24, the filaments usually connate at or near the base: fr. small, globose or elliptic-globose, the nut in a shell that discloses a mace-like structure beneath; seed with broken or ruminate albumen. (Archontophœ-nix: Greek *majestic phœnix* or *palm.*)

A. Pinnæ broad, 3–4 in., green underneath and somewhat chaffy, lacking prominent secondary ribs: fls. lilac: seed bearing coarse and loose fibers..........1. *A. Cunninghamiana*
AA. Pinnæ narrow, 1–2 in., not chaff-bearing underneath, with prominent secondary ribs: fls. white or cream: seed covered with slender and tight fibers.....2. *A. Alexandræ*

1. **A. Cunninghamiana,** Wendl. & Drude (*Ptychosperma Cunninghamiana*, Wendl. *Loroma amethystina*, O. F. Cook). PICCABEEN BANGALOW PALM. Tall straight tree with solitary ringed trunk to 60 ft. or more: pinnæ green underneath, lvs. overcurving and hanging: spadix a short-peduncled cluster of long hanging branches bearing lilac or lavender fls., the staminate about ⅙in. long before anthesis, stamens 12–16, fls. slightly fragrant, cluster becoming more or less spreading at age: fr. about ⅜in. long, ovoid and short-pointed, seed fibers exposed by decay of the exocarp strong and loose. (Named for Allan Cunningham, page 41.) Queensland, New S. Wales.

2. **A. Alexandræ,** Wendl. & Drude (*Ptychosperma Alexandræ*, F. Muell.). ALEXANDRA PALM. NORTHERN BANGALOW PALM. Taller and probably more slender than *A. Cunninghamiana*, to 90 ft., trunk enlarged toward base: lvs. hanging, whitish or ashy underneath, the side ribs heavy: fls. whitish or cream-colored, in spreading clusters or spadices, staminate ¼–⅓in. long before anthesis: fr. about ½in. or less long, the exposed fibers slender and not loose. (Dedicated to Princess Alexandra of Denmark, later Queen Dowager of Great Britain.) Queensland.—A more tropical palm than *A. Cunninghamiana*. Var. **Beatricæ,** C. T. White, STEP PALM, has a stout bole with strong or deep rings like steps, lf.-crown with ascending base and lvs. not strongly hanging; N. Queensland.

20. **PTYCHOSPERMA,** Labill. (*Seaforthia*, R. Br.). SEAFORTHIA PALM. Erect pinnate small trees; a dozen or more species in Australia and Pacific isls.—Trunk solitary, often ringed, unarmed, with diffuse branching spadices beneath the rather short crownshaft: pinnæ oblique or truncate at apex and erose or jagged: fls. spiralled on the somewhat fleshy rachillæ; stamens 20–30: fr. drupe-like, nearly ¾in. long, ovoid or ellipsoid, with short point or beak, with large calyx cupule; seed grooved lengthwise, albumen ruminate. (Ptychosper-ma: *folded seed.*)

P. elegans, Blume (*Seaforthia elegans*, R. Br.). Bole to 20 ft. tall and prominently ringed, 3–4 in. thick, swollen at base; head or crown loose and small, petiole short: lvs. bright green, with 20 or more pairs of pinnæ: spadix bushy with many angled branches: fr. short-oblong, bright red, with soft thin flesh that soon dries hard.—Sometimes erroneously known in cult. as *Hydriastele Wendlandiana*.

21. **COCOS,** L. COCONUT. One ubiquitous and probably the best known palm, abundant on trop. strands and low plains, nativity not determined but probably Asian or Polynesian.—Monœcious tree, unarmed, bole solitary but seldom straight and the palm variously leaning: lvs. pinnate, very long, apices long-acuminate: staminate fls. on the upper part of the interfoliar branching spadices with 6 stamens, pistillates on lower parts with 3-celled ovary but fr. 1-seeded by abortion: nut very large, often weighing several pounds when fresh, 3-sided at least when dried, the thick fibrous husk yielding coir, the hard interior shell with 3 "eyes" or pores, endosperm exteriorly solidified into an edible white homogeneous albumen or meat from which, when dry, copra or an oil-cake is produced, the interior supplied with a drinkable whitish liquid or milk. (Co-cos: Portuguese *monkey*, in reference to the face of the stripped nut.)—At one time the genus Cocos was held to include many species of palms but is now rightly restricted to a single species; separated genera include Arecastrum, Butia and Syagrus.

C. nucifera, L. Tree to 100 ft., the trunk commonly inclined or curved; head or crown large and heavy, with many drooping lvs. 15–20 ft. long; petiole based in net-like brown fiber: nuts 10–20 in a bunch, 9 in. and more long and 8 in. or more thick, the base retuse, apex not pointed.—It runs into many cult. vars.

22. **ELÆIS,** Jacq. OIL PALM. One monœcious species with many botanical vars., native in trop. Afr. where it yields great produce in its nuts and seeds for the extraction of oil; another species was ascribed to trop. Amer., but this is now separated in the genus Corozo.—Erect, of medium stature, with dense head of pinnate lvs. in the axils of which are borne dense sessile separate heads of staminate and of pistillate fls.: stamens 6, the filaments joined into a tube; sepals very narrow, aggregated in dense fingers 8 in. or more long; pistillate fls. larger than the staminate, containing an ovoid or nearly cylindrical 3-celled ovary in broad sepals and petals, subtended by a long horn-like bract that becomes stiff in the head: fr. 1- or 2-loculed, not retaining the perianth-cup, the integuments forming a loose husk that may remain on the plant. (Elæ-is: Greek *oil.*)

E. guineensis, Jacq. Stout tree to 30 ft., bole 12 in. and more thick and retaining remains of old lvs. which may be 10–15 ft. long; petiole spiny on margin: heads of fr. 8 in. and more thick, carrying many erect horns; fr. irregular, ovoid-oblong to obovoid, pointed, about 1¾ in. long, shell of seed hard and bony, with 1 or 2 locules and 2–4 apical pores.—Planted for ornament and interest in western hemisphere, for oil in eastern.

23. **BUTIA,** Becc. About a half dozen monœcious pinnate palms of S. Amer., a number of species planted for ornament in Fla. and Calif.—Of low height, the solitary trunks sometimes very short and holding remains of lvs. which are long-pinnate with glaucous or bluish tint, pinnæ 25–50 pairs, narrow and attenuate to apex and variously bilobed, petiole with marginal prongs or spines: infl. interfoliar, the inner spathe or cymba woody, persistent, often more than 3 ft. long; spadix a long axis with simple slender lateral branches or rachillæ bearing staminate fls. on upper part and pistillates toward base; stamens 6; pistillate fls. with single pistil and 3 stigmas: fr. a more or less soft drupe, broad-conic, bluntly pointed, cupule at base, about 1 in. long and nearly or quite as broad; albumen homogeneous. (Bu-tia: corruption of native name.)

A. Cymba (spathe) glabrous on outside.
B. Cupule of fr. short, of very broad more or less rounded parts . . . . 1. *B. capitata*
BB. Cupule long, one-third to one-half length of drupe, narrow and long-pointed . . . . . . 2. *B. Yatay*
AA. Cymba brown-woolly outside . . . . 3. *B. eriospatha*

1. **B. capitata,** Becc. (*Cocos capitata,* Mart.). Bole stout, 10–15 ft. tall but often lower in the fruiting stage: lvs. 3–6 ft. or more long, overarching, making a heavy head or crown of glaucous shade; petiole bearing spines to 1½ in. long: spadix perhaps 3 ft. long, densely fld., the spathe more than 3 ft. long and 2–3 in. broad: fr. ovoid with conic apex, yellow, pulpy, about 1 in. long and nearly as thick, the cupule commonly not more than one-fourth length of drupe; nutlet globular-oblong, abruptly narrowed to apex. E. Brazil.—Frequently planted in suitable parts of U. S. Var. **odorata,** Becc. (*Cocos odorata,* Barb.-Rodr.), has very broad-conic fr. about ⅘in. long and width often greater than that, nut nearly globular; S. Brazil; variable. Var. **pulposa,** Becc. (*Cocos pulposa,* Barb.-Rodr.), bears very large and pulpy fr. about 1¼ in. long and 1½ in. thick, nutlet nearly globular; S. Brazil. Var. **virescens,** Becc., bears brilliant green foliage; fr. depressed, about ⅘in. high and of greater thickness, whitish with rose color at base, succulent and fragrant; nut about ½in. diam. either way. Var. **Nehrlingiana,** Bailey (*B. Nehrlingiana,* Abbott. *Cocos Nehrlingii,* Kay), large tree with violet-red fls. of both sexes, and bright red oblong-conic small frs.; lvs. glaucous-green; named for Henry Nehrling, 1853–1929, Florida plantsman. Var. **strictior,** Bailey, tree erect and very strict in growth; lvs. all upright and none of them hanging.

2. **B. Yatay,** Becc. (*Cocos Yatay,* Mart.). Stout palm to 25 ft.: lvs. to 9 ft. long, the outer ones curving or hanging, more or less glaucous: fr. very large, distinctly taper-pointed, 1⅓ in. or more in length, ⅘in. broad, yellow to orange tinted red, cupule with acuminate outer parts that extend one-third or more length of drupe. (Yatay: vernacular name.) Argentina.

3. **B. eriospatha,** Becc. (*Cocos eriospatha,* Mart.). Tree to 15–20 ft., foliage gracefully overarching, glaucous-green: main spathe often more than 3 ft. long, prominently brown-woolly, eventually vanishing by weather: fr. about ⅘in. long, yellow, cupule very small and often inconspicuous. S. Brazil.

24. **COLLINIA,** Liebm. (*Neanthe,* O. F. Cook). Low pinnate unarmed slender diœcious Mexican and Guatemalan palms of few species, one suitable for growing in pots, enduring indifferent conditions.—More or less soboliferous or sometimes the trunk solitary: pinnæ green and thin, nearly or quite opposite, long-attenuate to an entire point: infl. of long stalk that may overtop the lvs., paniculate; fls. small, unisexual on different plants, corolla of both sexes campanulate-tubular and of staminate fls. united at base and with filaments and pistillode, in these floral structures differing from Chamædorea: fr. very small, globular. (Collin-ia: name not explained.)

C. elegans, Liebm. (*Chamædorea elegans,* Mart. *Neanthe bella,* O. F. Cook). PARLOR PALM. Slender, flexuose in habit but trunk erect to 3–6 ft.: lvs. with a dozen or more pairs of very narrow pinnæ broadest (⅜–⅝in.) at middle, with prominent side veins: peduncle 3 ft. or less long, bearing scarious sheaths with short terminal point, the slender open panicle terminal; fls. pale yellow. Mex.

25. **HOWEA,** Becc. (*Denea,* O. F. Cook). Two erect monœcious feather-palms, extensively grown for florists' use and decoration usually under the name of Kentia; from Lord Howe's Isl., S. Pacific, whence the name Howe-a.—Fls. sunken in simple large spadices among the foliage; perianth of 3 broad sepals and 3 broad petals; stamens 30–40, clustered, sessile or nearly so; ovary 1, with 3 stigmas: fr. ovoid or olive-shaped, smooth, like a large pecan, containing 1 large seed: lvs. erect-spreading, smooth, of many graceful pinnæ with long-pointed bifid hanging ends: vernation reduplicate.

A. Pinnæ arching away from the rachis: fr. turgid, suddenly narrowed to beak, about 1¼ in. long. . . . . 1. *H. Belmoreana*
AA. Pinnæ standing away from the rachis nearly horizontally: fr. long-attenuate to apex, not beaked, to 2 in. long. . . . . 2. *H. Forsteriana*

1. **H. Belmoreana,** Becc. (*Kentia Belmoreana,* F. Muell.). Smooth-trunked tree to 35 ft.: lvs. 5–8 ft. long, gracefully curving; pinnæ long and narrow, strongly rising and arching from the rachis, then pendent. (Dedicated to De Belmore, Governor of New S. Wales.)

2. **H. Forsteriana,** Becc. (*Kentia Forsteriana,* F. Muell.). As a pot-plant less compact than no. 1, less leafy: pinnæ mostly fewer, spreading nearly horizontally from the rachis for the first third or half their length and then pendent, giving the lf. a flat appearance. (Bears the name of Wm. Forster, Senator, New S. Wales.)

26. **SYAGRUS,** Mart. Monœcious pinnate trees, about 40 species in S. Amer.—One of the Cocos segregates, unarmed unless on edges of petiole, some of the species nearly acaulescent: cymba or major spathe large and long, grooved on outside, interfoliar: fr. small, oblong-ovoid or globose, sitting in a prominent cupule, ordinarily bearing a short beak; seed longitudinally 3-striped, albumen homogeneous, sterile locule an inconspicuous membranous vestige. (Syag-rus: *wild pig,* name employed by Pliny for a palm.)

S. Weddelliana, Becc. (*Cocos Weddelliana,* Wendl.). Low tree, 3–6 ft. tall, bole covered with dark network: lvs. 3 ft. long or more, green and not glaucous, ascending and attractively curving, more or less scurfy, the very narrow pinnæ placed singly: fr. globose-oblong, about ⅜in. long, abruptly contracted to short point, cupule small and not cup-like. (Named for H. A. Weddell, page 53.) S. Brazil.—Known in cult. in the N. in the juvenile seedling stage, with graceful drooping foliage, pinnæ very narrow and only 4–6 in. long.

27. **ARECASTRUM,** Becc. QUEEN PALM. Cocos segregate; pinnate-lvd. single-trunk monœcious palms, one species and several botanical vars., native in Brazil, now much planted as an avenue and lawn tree.—Bole erect, soon becoming naked, prominently ringed; head or coma wide-spreading, of gracefully curving long lvs., pinnæ narrow and many, narrow-pointed, petiole with shaggy margins but not armed: infl. interfoliar, the long woody cymba deeply sulcate on the outside, spadix long-peduncled and lengthened, hanging in fr.; staminate fls. angular and long-pointed, stamens 6: fr. drupe-like but dry or soon becoming so, about 1 in. long, 1-seeded by abortion, sterile locule a narrow vestige in bony wall of the seed, albumen homogeneous. (Arecas-trum: *areca-like.*)

A. Romanzoffianum, Becc. (*Cocos Romanzoffiana,* Cham. *C. plumosa,* Hook., under which name it is known in cult.). Erect tree with slender trunk to 40 ft. or more, soon shedding the dead lvs.: petiole much expanded at base and set in a mass of fibers; blade 6–12 ft. long, bearing many narrow long-pointed glabrous green pinnæ 3 ft. or so long: spathes arising in lower lf.-axils, main cymba 3 ft. or more long: fr. yellow at maturity, ovoid to oblong, short-beaked, variable in size and form; nutlet very broad, not attenuate at either end. (Named for N. P. Romanzoff, 1754?–1826, of Russia.) Cent. Brazil to Argentina. Var. **australe,** Becc. (*Cocos australis,* Mart., but *Cocos australis* of hort. is *Butia capitata. C. Datil,* Griseb. & Drude), differs in its narrow fr. with more or less attenuate seeds, at maturity usually 1 in. long and ½in. thick. Var. **botryophorum,** Becc. (*Cocos botryophora,* Mart.), strong and robust tree with very large head and big fr. which is to 1½ in. long and ⅘in. or more broad.

28. CYCLANTHACEÆ. CYCLANTHUS FAMILY

Stemless or sometimes caulescent monœcious plants, in some cases climbing, with the foliage of palms and the infl. of aroids; a few cult. for ornament, frequent in greenhouses; all trop. American.—Fls. unisexual, in a dense simple spadix subtended by several bract-like spathes, the staminate and pistillate closely associated; perianth none or small; stamens mostly numerous, sometimes represented in the fertile fls. by long staminodia; carpels 2 or 4, spirally placed or sunken in the spadix, constituting a single ovary 1-celled and many-ovuled usually on 2–4 placentæ: fr. made up of the cohering carpels: lvs. fan-like, long-petioled, sometimes with holes in the blade.

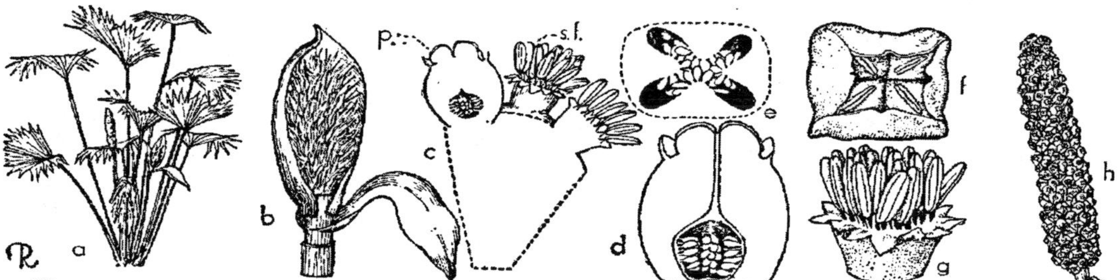

Fig. 28. CYCLANTHACEÆ. *Carludovica palmata:* a, habit, much reduced; b, inflorescence, × ⅙; c, segment of flowering spadix, × 2 (p.f. pistillate flower, s.f. staminate flower); d, pistillate flower, vertical section, × 5; e, ovary, cross-section, × 10; f, pistillate flower, top view, × 4; g, staminate flower, × 5; h, fruiting spadix, × ⅙. (b redrawn from Martius.)

CARLUDOVICA, Ruiz & Pav. Thirty to 40 species, shrubby or herbaceous, the st. erect, decumbent or climbing: lvs. 2–5-parted: staminate fls. in 4's surrounding a pistillate fl. which is sunken in the spadix; staminodia 4, long: fr. an aggregate of 4-sided many-seeded berries. (Carludov-ica: Carlos IV and Ludovia, his queen, of Spain.)

A. Lvs. 2-parted or -lobed........1. *C. atrovirens*
AA. Lvs. 3- or more-parted........2. *C. palmata*

1. **C. atrovirens,** Wendl. Lvs. on long slender smooth angled petioles from the crown (as seen in greenhouses), very dark green and lighter beneath; blade with many strong parallel veins, split much below the middle into 2 lobes 2–3 in. wide terminating in a plicate or a lacerate apex: spadix short and small, hidden in the foliage. N. S. Amer.

2. **C. palmata,** Ruiz & Pav. St. very short or not evident: lvs. fan-shaped, standing 3–6 ft. high on slender channelled petioles; blades about 4-lobed nearly to the base and the lobes again divided into long more or less bifid segms. like a palm, the lower part often with hole, the margins drooping: fr. a cob-like long-peduncled body about 6 in. long. Peru.—Probably the main source of fiber for panama hats.

29. ARACEÆ. ARUM FAMILY

The aroids are upward of 100 genera and perhaps 1,500 species around the world, being specially developed in trop. countries; they are mostly of wet, damp, or shady places; many are cult. for ornament and interest, and a few yield important food products in their underground parts; many contain acrid principles.—Herbs, but sts. sometimes becoming hard and woody and tree-like in form, erect, prostrate, or tall-climbing by means of roots, sometimes epiphytic, a few floating, mostly more

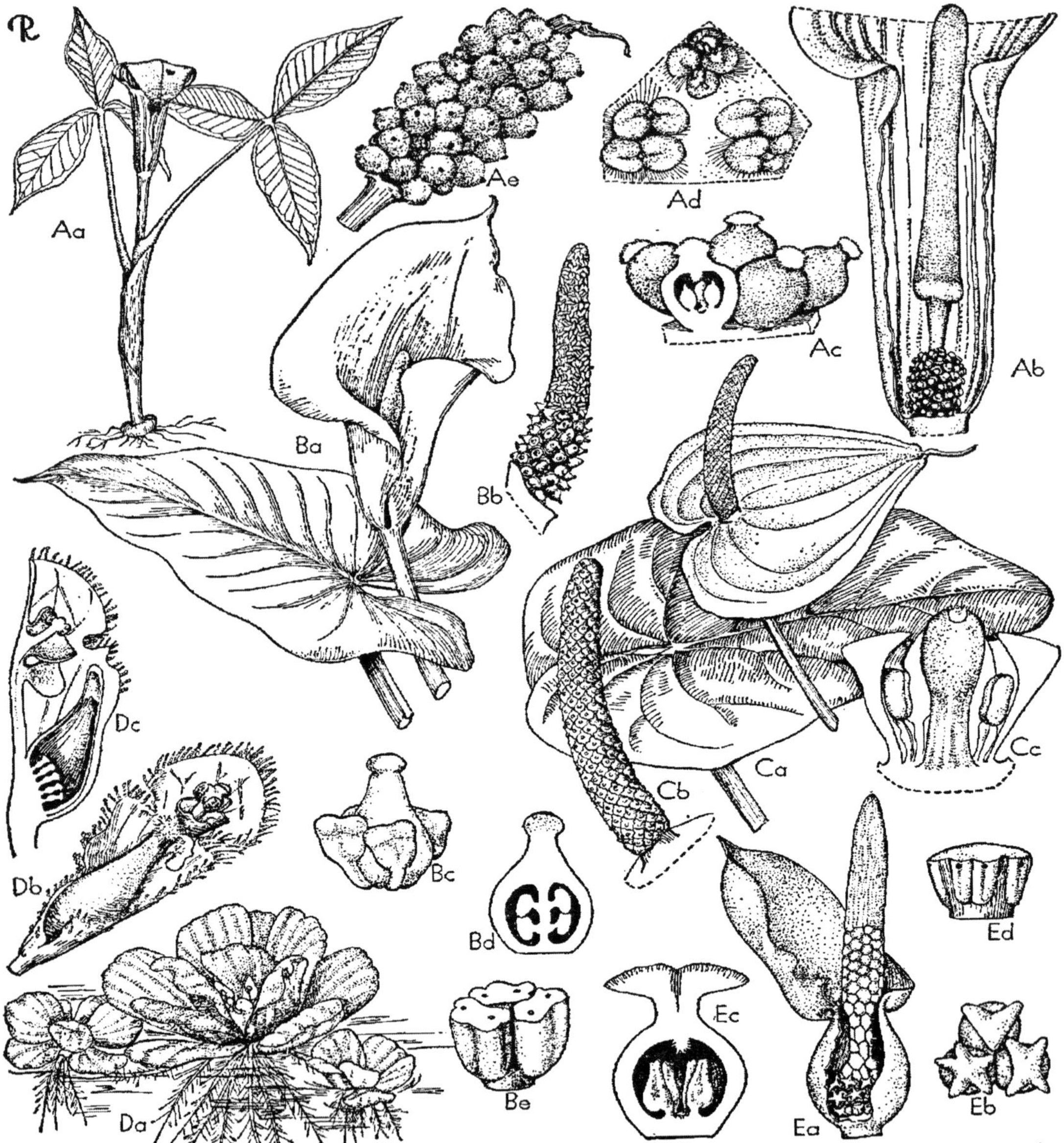

Fig. 29. ARACEÆ. A, *Arisæma atrorubens:* Aa, plant in flower, × 1/6; Ab, spathe base showing spadix with pistillate flowers, × 1; Ac, fertile section of spadix with pistillate flowers, × 5; Ad, fertile section of spadix with staminate flowers, × 5; Ae, fruit-cluster, × ½. B, *Zantedeschia æthiopica:* Ba, leaf-blade and inflorescence, × 1/8; Bb, spadix, × ¼; Bc, pistillate flower with staminodia, × 8; Bd, same, vertical section, × 8; Be, staminate flower, × 8. C, *Anthurium Andræanum:* Ca, leaf-blade and inflorescence, × ¼; Cb, spadix, × ½; Cc, flower, one perianth-segment and stamen removed, × 8. D, *Pistia Stratiotes:* Da, habit, × ½; Db, inflorescence, × 3; Dc, same, vertical section, × 3. E, *Alocasia Lowii:* Ea, inflorescence, spathe sectioned to show spadix, × ½; Eb, cluster of pistillate flowers, top view, × 3; Ec, pistillate flower, vertical section, × 6; Ed, staminate flower, × 4. (Ea–Ed adapted and redrawn from Engler.)

or less fleshy, juice sometimes milky: lvs. very various, from sword-shaped and parallel-veined to broad-hastate and netted-veined, the margins entire or lobed, some species with prominent holes in the blade, sometimes compound: the infl. is the most characteristic feature, being a densely-fld. simple spadix subtended or surrounded by a bract (the spathe) which is often showy and constitutes "the flower" of gardeners, as in the cult. calla, the staminate fls. at the top and pistillate fls. beneath; fls. bisexual or unisexual, regular, the perianth lacking or represented by 4–8 scale-like parts, never showy; stamens 1 to many, sessile or with very short filaments, often united, sometimes represented by staminodia; ovary usually 1, with 1 to several carpels, and ovules 1 or more in each cell: fr. usually baccate, densely packed on the spadix.

A. Plants free-floating aquatics .... 1. PISTIA
AA. Plants not free-floating, terrestrial, or bog plants.
B. Lvs. parallel-veined (large secondary veins may arise from midrib, but their veinlets not netted; if no midrib present, see below under BB).
C. Sts. subterranean; lvs. arising from basal crown.
D. Lf. long and grass-like, no petiole present .... 2. ACORUS
DD. Lf. differentiated into blade and petiole.
E. Spathes green; staminodia of pistillate fl. connate about the gynœcium .... 3. PELTANDRA
EE. Spathes white, yellow or pink; staminodia of pistillate fls. free and separate .... 4. ZANTEDESCHIA
CC. Sts. above ground and obvious.
D. Habit climbing .... 5. PHILODENDRON
DD. Habit erect.
E. Lf. with 3–10 pairs of lateral veins: pistillate fls. without staminodia. 6. AGLAONEMA
EE. Lf. with 9–20 pairs of lateral veins: pistillate fls. separated by interspersed staminodia.
F. Stamens united; ovary 2–3-celled; spathe persistent .... 7. DIEFFENBACHIA
FF. Stamens free; ovary 1-celled; spathe falling at maturity .... 8. SCHISMATOGLOTTIS
BB. Lvs. netted-veined (i.e., the ultimate branches netted, midrib may be absent).
C. Without milky sap.
D. Foliage pinnately cut or perforated .... 9. MONSTERA
DD. Foliage not as above.
E. Sts. elongated, plants clambering or vine-like .... 10. SCINDAPSUS
EE. Sts. short, consisting of a basal crown.
F. Spathe flat, usually not recurved or waxy, mostly white or greenish: lf.-blades obtuse or tapering basally, not lobed: stigma 3–4-lobed .... 11. SPATHIPHYLLUM
FF. Spathes recurved, reflexed, or widely spreading, usually in shades of white, salmon-pink to dark red, infrequently green: lf.-bases variously lobed or cuneate: stigma obscurely 2-lobed .... 12. ANTHURIUM
CC. With milky sap.
D. Lf. compound or deeply many-lobed.
E. Spathe incurved closely about spadix or forming a hood over it..... 13. ARISÆMA
EE. Spathe strongly recurved marginally and not hood-forming.
F. Staminate and pistillate fls. contiguous with no neutral organs between them and not restricted to distinct regions of the fertile portion of the spadix .... 14. HYDROSME
FF. Staminate fls. all borne above the pistillate fls.; neutral organs often between areas occupied by the two sexes.
G. Spadix with staminate fls. remote from the pistillate fls., rudimentary fls. perhaps separating the sexes; appendage of spadix hairy .... 15. HELICODICEROS
GG. Spadix with staminate fls. contiguous to and immediately above the pistillate fls .... 16. DRACUNCULUS
DD. Lf. simple or only sagittately or hastately lobed.
E. Base of lf. tapering to petiole; blades not arrow-shaped.
F. Spathe early deciduous, not showy; spadix bright yellow on white scape .... 17. ORONTIUM
FF. Spathe persistent, white and showy; spadix dull white .... 18. CALLA
EE. Base of lf. sagittate or hastate; blades arrow-shaped.
F. Spadix terminating in a long sterile part or appendage (not fl.-bearing) .... 19. ARUM
FF. Spadix not appendaged, or not manifestly so, fl.-bearing to top (except infrequently in Alocasia).
G. Ovules anatropous, attached to broad nearly central placenta.
H. Style none: lvs. (ours) peltate .... 20. CALADIUM
HH. Style evident and disk-shaped: lvs. not peltate .... 21. XANTHOSOMA
GG. Ovules orthotropous, attached at base of ovary or to the 3–5 parietal placentæ.
H. The ovules numerous, parietal: lvs. always peltate .... 22. COLOCASIA
HH. The ovules few, basal: lvs. peltate when young but frequently not or obscurely so when mature .... 23. ALOCASIA

1. **PISTIA,** L. One free-floating clumpy little monœcious plant (sometimes rooting in mud) with not at all the look of an aroid, used in aquaria and warm water-gardens.—Lvs. simple and entire, oblong to cuneate with very rounded ends, many-ribbed, lively green but velvety-scurfy: spathes small, sessile or nearly so in the axils, lf.-like, white, the spadix adnate to it and shorter; fls. unisexual, naked; stamens 2; ovary 1-celled with many ovules: fr. baccate. (Pis-tia: probably from the Greek *pistos*, in reference to the aquatic habit.)

P. Stratiotes, L. Water-Lettuce. Stoloniferous, with long hanging roots; rosette-like tufts 2–10 in. across. (Stratiotes: an ancient name, applied here by ante-Linnæan writers.)—In many parts of the world in warm and trop. regions, native Fla. to Tex.; runs into several lf.-forms.

2. **ACORUS,** L. Two paludose species in the northern hemisphere, planted in bog-gardens.—Rhizome creeping: lvs. grass-like or sword-shaped, long and slender without distinction of petiole and finely parallel-veined: peduncle or scape keeled, bearing 1 apparently lateral naked greenish spadix but the spathe lf.-like and continuing the direction; fls. bisexual, with perianth of 6 concave or hooded segms.; stamens 6, with flattened anthers; ovary 2–4-celled with 2 to several ovules in each: fr. baccate, closely set on the spadix. (Ac-orus: the ancient name.)

A. Plant about 1 ft., grass-lvd.: spathe not much prolonged. . . . . 1. *A. gramineus*
AA. Plant 2 ft. and more, sword-lvd.: spathe prolonged like a lf. . . . . 2. *A. Calamus*

1. **A. gramineus,** Soland. Small tufted plant with narrow long-pointed grass-like lvs., about 1 ft. high, planted in water-gardens, particularly the striped-lvd. var.: spadix slender, 1–2 in. long, lengthening in fr., the spathe narrow and usually not prominent, 3–6 or 8 in. long. Cent. and E. Asia. Var. **variegatus,** Hort., has lvs. longitudinally striped cream-colored.

2. **A. Calamus,** L. Sweet Flag. Rootstocks stout and aromatic, yielding the drug calamus: lvs. 2–6 ft., ⅓–¾in. broad (with narrower-lvd. forms), cult. mostly in the striped-lvd. var.: spadix hard and dense, 2–4 in. long, the spathe produced to the length of the lvs. (Calamus is an ancient name for reed.) Around northern hemisphere. Var. **variegatus,** Hort., has lvs. with longitudinal yellow stripes.

3. **PELTANDRA,** Raf. Arrow-Arum. An E. N. American genus of 2 stemless easily colonized herbs, one sometimes grown for its decorative foliage in the bog-garden or at margins of informal pools.—Monœcious perennials with thickened cord-like fibrous roots, clump-forming, the glossy sagittate to hastate lvs. long-petioled: fls. unisexual and naked; staminate on upper part of elongated spadix, comprised of 6–10 sessile anthers imbedded in the spadix, opening by terminal pores; pistillate fls. confined to lower part of spadix and closely adjoining the staminate, naked, each pistil surrounded by 4–5 white fleshy scale-like staminodia, ovary 1-celled containing 1–5 amphitropous ovules, style short and thick, erect, terminated by a small stigma: fr. a 1–3-seeded green or red leathery berry forming large globose clusters at maturity: spadix partially enveloped by green elongated spathe, convolute or expanded above. (Peltan-dra: Greek, referring to the shield-shaped anthers.)

P. virginica, Kunth (*Arum virginicum,* L.). Green Arrow-Arum. Lvs. bright green, 4–30 in. long, narrowly sagittate-hastate, acuminate or acute, basal lobes long and nearly or quite acute: spathe 4–8 in. long, green, closely enveloping the spadix for its entire length; spadix shorter than spathe, only the basal fourth or less being covered with pistillate fls., staminate fls. on the remainder. N. E. U. S. to Fla., Mich. and La.

4. **ZANTEDESCHIA,** Spreng. (*Calla* of cultivators. *Richardia,* Kunth). Per. rhizomatous herbs of S. Afr., with showy spathes, one in common cult. and others frequently grown; 8 species are recognized.—Lvs. all basal, long-petioled, the blade hastate to cordate-ovate to lanceolate, sometimes spotted: peduncles equalling or exceeding the lvs. and appearing with them; spathe white or yellow, open and corolla-like, with pointed usually recurved tip, blade not deciduous; spadix pistillate on lower part, staminate on upper part, not appendaged at top; fls. naked; stamens 2–3, free; ovary 1- or more-celled, ovules usually 4 in each cell, sometimes bearing staminodia: fr. baccate, included in the tube of the spathe. (Zantedesch-ia: Fran-

cesco Zantedeschia, who wrote on Italian plants in 1825.)—Here belong the callas of florists. Of the true Calla there is but a single species, *C. palustris*, which see page 187. For Black Calla see *Arum palæstinum.*

A. Lvs. lanceolate....................1. *Z. Rehmannii*
AA. Lvs. sagittate or deeply cordate.
  B. Lf.-blade uniformly green: spathe large and white....................2. *Z. æthiopica*
  BB. Lf.-blade spotted: spathe milk-white or yellow.
    C. Spathe crimson at the base....................3. *Z. albo-maculata*
    CC. Spathe without blotch at base....................4. *Z. Elliottiana*

1. **Z. Rehmannii,** Engler. RED OR PINK CALLA. Dwarf: lvs. lanceolate to long-lanceolate, taper-pointed, gradually narrowing to petiole, white- or translucent-dotted: spathe 3–4 in. long, trumpet-shaped with cuspidate tip, rose-color or red, sometimes almost white. S. Afr. (Natal; discovered by Mr. Rehmann.)

2. **Z. æthiopica,** Spreng. CALLA of gardeners. Robust plant standing 2½ ft. and more high, with smooth shining green cordate-ovate or sagittate-ovate lvs. with slender cusp at apex, and fragrant fls.: spathe white or creamy-white, 5–10 in. long, with an open broad and flaring limb and a long recurved cusp; spadix prominent but much shorter than spathe. S. Afr. (Cape, Natal).—Variable; double and triple spathes sometimes occur. Var. **minor,** Engler, is smaller, 12–18 in. high, with spathes 3–4 in. long.

3. **Z. albo-maculata,** Baill. SPOTTED CALLA. Petiole short and blade much longer than broad (12–18 in. long), with spreading triangular lobes at base, at apex long-acute and cuspidate, prominently white-spotted: spathe 4–5 in. long, trumpet-shaped, yellow or milk-white, with crimson or purplish spot in throat; spadix included. S. Afr. (cent. Cape region).

4. **Z. Elliottiana,** Engler. GOLDEN CALLA. Petiole long, 2 ft. or more; blade ovate to orbicular-ovate, cordate, abruptly narrowed to a cuspidate apex, with white or translucent spots: spathe 4–6 in. long, rich yellow, not blotched; spadix included. S. Afr. (Cape, Natal, Transvaal).—First exhibited 1890 before Royal Hort. Society, London, by Capt. Elliott of Farnborough Park.

5. **PHILODENDRON,** Schott. Tree-climbers (rarely erect) of the American tropics, more than 200 recognized species, a few grown under glass for ornament.—Mostly with hard woody sts., branching, the internodes often elongated: lvs. thick, ovate to oblong, more or less cordate or sagittate, entire, lobed, or pinnately parted, the petiole sheathing: peduncles commonly short, single or fascicled, axillary or terminal, the spathe thick and persistent, variously colored and often fragrant, the limb boat-shaped; spadix not exceeding the spathe, densely fld., becoming succulent in fr.; fls. unisexual and naked, plant monœcious; stamens 2–6 united into one body; ovary 2- to several-celled. (Philoden-dron: Greek *tree-loving.*)—Of some of the plants named Philodendron in cult. the fls. are unknown and their botanical position is doubtful. *P. pertusum*, Kunth & Bouché, is *Monstera deliciosa.*

A. Petiole densely pubescent or hairy....................1. *P. verrucosum*
AA. Petiole glabrous or only papillate.
  B. Lf. red, at least when young....................2. *P. Devansayeanum*
  BB. Lf. green.
    C. Blade of lf. 20–30 in. long....................3. *P. giganteum*
    CC. Blade of lf. 4–15 in. long....................4. *P. cordatum*

1. **P. verrucosum,** Math. (*P. Carderi* and *P. Lindenii,* Hort.). St. gray-green, angular, swollen at nodes: petiole red, bearing long bristles and hairs; lf.-blade usually 6–10 in. long, ovate-cordate with a deep close sinus, acute at apex, glabrous, polished green and often with paler lines and sunken nerves, beneath bright green with salmon-violet lines: spathe purplish. Costa Rica to S. Amer.

2. **P. Devansayeanum,** Lind. St. short and stout: petiole terete, green, or when young purplish, perhaps with rough points; blade 1½–2 ft. long, broadly ovate-cordate or almost orbicular, long-acuminate, deep red at least when young: spathe margined red. (Dedicated to M. de la Devansaye, president Société Hort. d'Angers et du Maine et Loire, France.) Peru.

3. **P. giganteum,** Schott. Very large, tall-climbing, with hanging roots: petiole often 3 ft. and more long; blade cordate-ovate, 2–3 ft. long, entire, with sinus open near the blade, apex acute: spathe 6–10 in. long, the tube purplish outside, limb pale green becoming yellowish. W. Indies.

4. **P. cordatum,** Kunth (*Arum cordatum,* Vell.). Climbing: lvs. 4–15 in. long, glabrous, green, cordate-oblong, the basal lobes to 4 in. long and nearly oblong: infl. on peduncle to 1¼ in. long, spathe to 3 in. long and exceeding spadix. S. Brazil.

6. **AGLAONEMA,** Schott. Upwards of 40 small herbs of India and Malaysia, a number grown in hothouses for the white-marked foliage and a few suitable as house plants.—Sts. erect or sometimes decumbent and clambering, short or long, with basal shoots: petiole equalling or shorter than blade, sheathing; blade oblong or oblong-lanceolate to ovate-lanceolate, with thick midrib and few lateral nerves: peduncles in clusters from the lower sheaths, shorter than the petioles; spathe small, straight, green or yellowish, open above, finally withering; spadix equalling or less than the spathe; fls. unisexual and naked; stamens 2, free; ovary 1- or 2-celled, ovules 1 in each cell: frs. few, baccate, yellow or red, not included in spathe and therefore conspicuous in little clusters on slender stalks. (Aglaone-ma: Greek *bright thread,* perhaps referring to stamens.)

A. Lvs. with 5–10 pairs of lateral veins: st. very short, not over 2 in. long, sometimes branched at base.......................................1. *A. costatum*
AA. Lvs. with 3–5 pairs of veins: st. evident, from 6–30 in. long.
B. Petiole one-half as long as lf.-blade or less, latter 2¾–5 in. long..............2. *A. pictum*
BB. Petiole two-thirds to three-quarters as long as lf.-blade, latter 4–12 in. long.
C. Lf. oblong, spotted white or very pale green..........................3. *A. commutatum*
CC. Lf. ovate-acuminate, not spotted......................................4. *A. modestum*

1. **A. costatum,** N. E. Br. St. short, branching at base, making a low spreading plant: lvs. thickish, ovate or oblong-ovate, rounded or mostly somewhat cordate at base, acute at apex, 4–5 or more in. long, the main lateral nerves 7 (or 5)–10 on either side and strongly arching: spathe ¾–1¼ in. long, ½in. diam., whitish-green; spadix stipitate, 1 in. long, protruding, milk-white. Malaya. Var. **maculatum,** Engler, has lvs. spotted white. Var. **lineatum,** Engler, has lvs. with midrib and often the main lateral veins whitish, while plants having dark green lvs. spotted with pale green are var. **Foxii,** Engler.

2. **A. pictum,** Kunth. St. 2–3 ft., mostly erect: lvs. oblong-elliptic, obtuse or acute at base, apex acuminate and cuspidate, to 6 in. long, main lateral nerves 4–5 on either side, curving upward toward the margin, often variously white-clouded or spotted: spathe about 1 in. long and half or less broad, acuminate. Malaya.—Plants having lvs. blotched yellowish and yellowish-green are probably var. **tricolor,** N. E. Br.

3. **A. commutatum,** Schott. Erect, with sts. to 20 in. high, often branched: lvs. usually 4–7 in. long, oblong, acuminate, the base obtuse and often oblique, petiole slightly shorter than blade, green with cinereous blotches along portions of the 4–5 pairs of lateral veins: infl. on peduncle 1¾–3 in. long, spathe about 2 in. long, greenish-white, spadix stipitate and about 1¼ in. long: berries red to purple. Malaya.

4. **A. modestum,** Schott. Chinese Evergreen. Erect, with sts. 12–20 ft. high, lower internodes to ¾in. long: lvs. 6–10 in. long, uniformly dark green, ovate, acuminate, base obtuse, petiole about two-thirds as long as lf.-blade: infl. on axillary peduncle 1½–2½ in. long, spathe 2½–3 in. long, spadix stipitate, to 2 in. long. Philippine Isls.—Distributed extensively in recent years as a house plant capable of growing in water without soil and with a minimum of light; individuals so grown are known to remain alive and in good vigor for many months. Sometimes treated as *A. simplex,* Blume, a Malayan species differing markedly in characters of spathe and spadix.

7. **DIEFFENBACHIA,** Schott. Trop. American woody-stemmed plants grown under glass for the spotted or variegated foliage, 25–30 species.—Caudex thick, erect or at base creeping, leafy toward the top: lvs. with long clasping or sheathing petiole and oblong to ovate entire blade, mostly broad and conspicuous midrib and curving-ascending side-veins: peduncles from the sheaths, shorter than petioles; spathe oblong, persistent, the lower part convolute and including the pistillate fls., throat open, blade narrow, trough-shaped or partially open, straight or recurved; spadix erect, nearly as long as spathe; ovary 2–3-celled, with similarly lobed stigma. (Dieffenbach-ia: J. F. Dieffenbach, 1794–1847, German physician and botanist.)—Many named kinds are known to fanciers, nearly all referable to 2 species.

A. Petiole broadly grooved or channelled..1. *D. picta*
AA. Petiole little or not at all channelled or not broadly so........................2. *D. Seguine*

1. **D. picta,** Schott. St. 3–4 ft. long, more or less prostrate at base, 1 in. or less thick: petioles of lower lvs. long, broadly canaliculate, with obtuse margins; blade oblong to oblong-elliptic or oblong-lanceolate, the base rounded or acute, narrowed to apex and acuminate-cuspidate, dull green and shining both sides, with many white or yellowish irregular marks and blotches, the primary lateral nerves 15–20 on either side and ascending: spathe narrowly long-cuspidate. S. Amer.—As now understood, this species apparently produces the greater number of the white-spotted vars. Both species are widely variable.

2. **D. Seguine,** Schott. St. ascending, 3–6 ft.: petioles not channelled (or very little so), green or white-striped and -dotted; blade oblong or ovate-oblong, rounded or somewhat cordate or even acutish at base, short-cuspidate at apex, green above and light green beneath, sometimes spotted, midrib broad and thick, the primary lateral nerves imbedded above and very prominent beneath and about 9–15 on either side: spathe short- or long-cuspidate. W. Indies and S. Amer.—The "dumb cane" of the W. Indies, those who chew it said to lose the power of speech.

8. **SCHISMATOGLOTTIS,** Zoll. & Mor. Seventy to 80 species in the Malayan region, one of which is frequent in glasshouses for its white-marked foliage.—Resembling Dieffenbachia, but technically differing in floral characters, the stamens being free, ovary 1-celled, blade of spathe articulated and falling entire: caudex or rhizome mostly evident: lvs. oblong to ovate-cordate, sometimes hastate, in the cult. plants usually marbled, spotted, or striped (often with translucent areas), the sheathing petiole longer than the blade: peduncles solitary or fascicled, shorter than petioles: spathe with convolute tube which incloses the oblong green or yellowish fr. (Schismatoglot-tis: Greek *falling tongue,* referring to the deciduous spathe-limb.)

S. picta, Schott. The common species and the one to which most of the hort. names are probably to be referred, native in the E. Indies: st. above ground: petioles 8–12 in. long, pale green; blade thin, pale green above, marked on either side the midrib by white dots and patches, cordate, ovate or oblong-ovate, acuminate, 6–8 in. long: spathe 1½–2½ in. long, green, greenish-yellow, short-cuspidate.—Another species, **S. concinna,** Schott, from Borneo, is frequently cult.; lvs. with obtuse to nearly truncate bases, blades often variously variegated.

9. **MONSTERA,** Adans. Climbing plants of trop. Amer., of nearly or quite 30 species, one common in greenhouses for its great lvs. full of holes.—Differs technically from Scindapsus in having 2 ovules in each cell: stout branching, more or less woody plants, with large usually distichous thick lvs. which are entire, sometimes pinnatifid, often conspicuously perforated, petiole long and sheathing: spathes on axillary peduncles, lanceolate, ovate or oblong-ovate, short-pointed or apiculate, boat-shaped, becoming deciduous; spadix thick and densely-fld., sessile, shorter than the spathe; fls. bisexual, naked: frs. cohering into a cone-like body. (Monste-ra: name unexplained.)

M. deliciosa, Liebm. (*Pothos pertusa,* Hort. not Roxb.). Ceriman. Tall straggling strong climber with hanging cord-like roots: lvs. 2–3 ft. long and broad, thick, pinnately cut and much perforated with oblong or elliptic spaces: spathe white, about 1 ft. long, the main part open with revolute margins; spadix 8–10 in. long, ripening into a large fr. that is eaten in the tropics. Mex., Cent. Amer.

10. **SCINDAPSUS,** Schott. Ivy-Arum. Frequently grown in the warmhouse for the maculate foliage; the number of species in the genus is about 20, in Malaysia.—Climbing by rootlets, more or less woody, usually large: petioles broad and sheathing, abruptly bent; lf.-blades oblong-lanceolate to ovate-lanceolate or ovate, acuminate: peduncles short; spathe boat-shaped, expanded, deciduous; spadix about equalling spathe, densely fld.; fls. bisexual, naked; stamens 4, more or less coherent; ovary 1-celled and 1-ovuled, the style none. (Scindap-sus: old Greek name of some kind of vine.)

A. Lvs. glaucous, unequal-sided .... 1. *S. pictus*
AA. Lvs. not glaucous, sides nearly equal .... 2. *S. aureus*

1. **S. pictus,** Hassk. Very tall climber with angular st., branching: lvs. thick, glaucous, obliquely ovate-oblong or broader, rounded or slightly cordate at base, narrowed and cuspidate at apex, one side narrower than other, spotted above with dark green: spathe white, ovate-oblong, prominently pointed. E. Indies. Var. **argyræus,** Engler, is the form mostly in cult., the lvs. silvery-spotted.

2. **S. aureus,** Engler. Frequent in warmhouses under the name *Pothos aureus;* of Pothos proper, a genus of the Old-World tropics, no species appear to be in general cult. in this country: tall climber usually with pendulous branches, st. sulcate between the nodes: lvs. not very thick, ovate to ovate-oblong, more or less cordate at base, short-pointed, margins sometimes lobed on mature plants, smooth and shining, not glaucous, blotched with pale yellow: apparently does not bloom in cult. Solomon Isls. Var. **Wil-**

coxii, Hort. (*Pothos aureus* var. *Wilcoxii,* Hort.), has the variegations ending abruptly and not blending into the adjoining green zone; petioles and portions of the stem often ivory-white in color.

11. **SPATHIPHYLLUM,** Schott. Nearly or quite 30 species, mostly in the American tropics, a few frequently grown as warmhouse foliage plants.—Acaulescent or short-stemmed: petioles equalling or exceeding blade, the latter oblong or nearly lanceolate and sharp-acuminate, tapering or rounded at base, midrib strong, side veins many and ascending or nearly right angled to rib: peduncles equalling or exceeding lvs.: spathe oblong or lanceolate, ascending or wide-spreading, acuminate, persistent, white or greenish, exceeding the free erect spadix; fls. bisexual and fertile, with perianth of free or connate segms.; stamens as many as segms.; ovary mostly 3-celled with few to several ovules in each; stigma 3–4-lobed: fr. baccate. (Spathiphyl-lum: Greek *leaf-spathe,* referring to the character of the spathe.)

A. Lf.-blade rounded at base.......1. *S. floribundum*
AA. Lf.-blade tapering at base.......2. *S. Patinii*

1. **S. floribundum,** N. E. Br. Petioles 4–6 in. long; blades oblong-elliptic or oblong-lanceolate, about 6 in. long and 1–1½ in. broad, rounded at base, acuminate at apex, unequal-sided, rich green above and paler beneath: spathe oblong-lanceolate, long-cuspidate, about 3 in. long, spreading, white on both sides; spadix yellowish or nearly white, shorter than spathe. Colombia.

2. **S. Patinii,** N. E. Br. (*S. candidum,* N. E. Br.). Petioles 8–12 in. long, equalling or exceeding the blades which are oblong-lanceolate, narrowed at both ends, very acute at apex, green: spathe oblong-lanceolate, acuminate, spreading or recurved, about 3 in. long, white- or greenish-nerved; spadix slender, usually less than spathe. (Intro. to the Williams Nursery, England, by the collector, M. Patin.) Colombia.

12. **ANTHURIUM,** Schott. Trop. American aroids of about 500 species, some grown under glass for the foliage and showy infl.; many of the hort. names represent hybrids and variants.—Plants of various habit, the st. woody or herbaceous, erect, ascending, creeping or climbing by roots: lvs. entire, lobed or deeply parted or digitate, thick and usually stiffish, mostly ovate with cordate, sagittate, or hastate base, green or variously colored, the petiole long or short and geniculate or kneed near the top: peduncle usually long; spathe ovate, elliptic, or lanceolate, green, yellowish, or purple, widely spreading or reflexed and sometimes twisted, the spadix mostly standing alone, sometimes coiled, without sterile end or appendix; fls. bisexual, with perianth of 4 narrow segms.; stamens 4; ovary 2-celled, with 1 or 2 ovules in each; stigma somewhat 2-lobed: fr. baccate. (Anthu-rium: Greek *tail-flower.*)

A. Lvs. plain green: infl. the showy part.
  B. Spadix straight or lightly curved.......1. *A. Andræanum*
  BB. Spadix coiled.......2. *A. Scherzerianum*
AA. Lvs. conspicuously marked with white or dark colors.
  B. Markings green or essentially so.......3. *A. Veitchii*
  BB. Markings white or silvery-white.
    C. Blade of lf. oblong-lanceolate, three times as long as wide or more.......4. *A. Warocqueanum*
    CC. Blade of lf. ovate, not more than twice as long as wide.
      D. Petiole 4-angled and somewhat winged at top.......5. *A. magnificum*
      DD. Petiole terete or nearly so, not winged.......6. *A. crystallinum*

1. **A. Andræanum,** Lind. St. short and erect, the plant low: petioles slender and longer than blades, the latter broad, oblong- to oblong-ovate-cordate, prominently pointed, with a deep narrow sinus and slightly peltate, 10–12 in. long, green: spathe cordate-ovate, thick, 4–6 in. and more long, strongly nerved, horizontal or spreading, brilliant orange-red (but varying to pink, rose-color, and even white); spadix 3–5 in. long, yellowish with white band below. (Collected in Colombia in 1876 by Ed. André.) Colombia.—Common and variable in cult.

2. **A. Scherzerianum,** Schott. St. very short: petioles equalling or exceeding blades, slender, sulcate above; blades narrow, long-lanceolate or long-elliptic, 4–8 in. or more long and 1–2 in. broad, long-pointed, green, with a strong vein parallel with each margin: spathe on a long and slender peduncle, broadly ovate to ovate-oblong, deep intense red (forms running to rose, salmon, white, spotted, and other colors), 2–4 in. long, lightly parallel-veined; spadix curled or coiled, yellow. (Discovered in Guatemala by M. Scherzer.) Cent. Amer.—Forms numerous.

3. **A. Veitchii,** Mast. Robust species, the st. 1–3 ft.: petioles slender, more or less angled; blades large, 2–3 or 4 ft., and narrow, long-oblong, hanging, obtuse or short-acute, the base deeply cordate with close sinus, stiff, rich metallic-green with very prominent veins (specially beneath) arching from the midrib: peduncle 1–2 ft. long; spathe greenish or white-green, oblong- or ovate-lanceolate, horizontal, long-pointed, mostly 3–5 in. long; spadix nearly equalling or somewhat exceeding spathe, straw-color. (Intro. by Messrs. Veitch, nurserymen, England.) Colombia.

4. **A. Warocqueanum,** Moore. Very strong, of striking character: petioles terete; blades large, 2–4 ft. and narrow, oblong-lanceolate and long-acuminate, deeply and closely cordate, rich velvety-green and rib and main veins nearly white, the 2 main lateral veins running parallel to margins: peduncle about 1 ft. long; spathe very narrow, linear-lanceolate, green, reflexed, 3–4 in. long; spadix about equalling spathe. (Dedicated to M. Warocqué, eminent Belgian amateur.) Colombia.

5. **A. magnificum,** Lind. Petioles 4-angled and somewhat winged at top; blades not narrow, cordate-ovate, 1–2 ft. long, the sinus broad, apex short-acuminate, upper surface olive-green with prominent white nerves that more or less join toward the margins: peduncle long, the spathe lanceolate to oblong, 4–8 in. long, green or reddish, becoming recurved; spadix equalling or exceeding spathe, dull violet. Colombia.

6. **A. crystallinum,** Lind. & André. Stout species on the order of no. 5, but petiole terete; sinus shallow and narrow (basal lobes often overlapping), upper surface deep velvety-green, veins very prominent and broadly banded and conspicuously interlocked: peduncle about 2 ft. long; spathe very narrow, linear-oblong and sharp-pointed, 4–6 in. long, horizontal or reflexed, green; spadix slender, equalling or exceeding spathe. Colombia, perhaps Peru.

13. **ARISÆMA,** Mart. About 60 species of diœcious or monœcious per. herbs, mostly native in trop. and temp. Asia, a few in N. Amer.—Corms tuber-like, producing 1–3 slender-petioled divided lvs. or lfts. whorled, appearing with the fls.: infl. borne on a slender scape; spathe convolute and in many kinds forming a hood incurved over the spadix, contracted or open at the throat and often acuminate or tailed; spadix included or exserted, terminated by a sterile appendage that is often long and filiform; fls. unisexual, without perianth, borne at base of spadix; staminate fls. of 2–5 almost sessile 2–4-celled anthers, sessile or stipitate; pistillate fls. with an ovoid 1-celled ovary, stigma peltate or capitate, containing 1 to many orthotropous ovules: fr. a 1-to many-seeded berry, usually bright red, borne in clusters and showy when ripe. (Arisæ-ma: Greek, referring to the red-blotched lvs. of some species.)

A. Spathe convolute, spadix long-exserted: lvs. of 5 or more segms. . . . . 1. *A. Dracontium*
AA. Spathe hooded, spadix included: lvs. of 3 lfts.
  B. Lvs. glaucous beneath, the lower side of lateral lfts. rounded to nearly subtruncate: fruiting heads 1¼–2½ in. long. . . . . 2. *A. atrorubens*
  BB. Lvs. not glaucous, lateral lfts. oblique but tapering acutely basally: fruiting heads ½–1½ in. long.
    C. Hoods deeply corrugated on inner face, ridges white and green to purple zones: fruiting heads 1–1½ in. long . . . . 3. *A. Stewardsonii*
    CC. Hoods uniformly green to purplish within: fruiting heads ½–¾ in. long. . . . . 4. *A. triphyllum*

1. **A. Dracontium,** Schott (*Arum Dracontium,* L. *Muricanda Dracontium,* Small). GREEN DRAGON. DRAGON-ROOT. Corms several and clustered: lf. usually solitary, to 4 ft. long, divided pedately into 5–17 lobes or segms., much exceeding the infl., lobes oblong to oblanceolate, to 10 in. long and rarely to 4 in. wide: scape 3–8 in. long; spathe green or whitish, 2–3 in. long, narrowly involute but not forming hood; spadix with caudate terminal appendage much exceeding spathe and drooping, fls. all of one sex or both sexes present: fr. reddish-orange, in large ovoid heads. Me. to Minn. south to Fla. and Tex.

2. **A. atrorubens,** Blume (*Arum atrorubens,* Ait. *Arisæma triphyllum,* Auth. not Torr.). JACK-IN-THE-PULPIT. INDIAN TURNIP. Corms solitary, to nearly 2 in. across: lvs. 1 or 2–3 ft. long, glaucous beneath, terminal lft. cuneate, lateral lfts. with distinctly rounded to subtruncate base on lower side: scape usually 4–12 in. long; spathe involute and forming an incurved hood over spadix, the hood uniformly purple or bronze within with pale longitudinal stripes; spadix to 3 in. long, club-shaped, often purplish, the fls. confined to basal portion: fr. red, clustered in heads 1¼–2½ in. long. N. B. to Man. south to D. C. and Tex.—This is the plant more commonly known as *A. triphyllum* and until recently considered conspecific with it.

3. **A. Stewardsonii,** Britt. Differs from *A. atrorubens* in foliage not glaucous but distinctly lustrous green beneath, in the lateral lfts. oblique and their lower side obtusely cuneate but not broadly rounded nor subtruncate: spathe tube and hood deeply and sharply corrugated within with white ridges and green or purple bands between them: fruiting heads 1–1½ in. long. (Named in honor of Stewardson Brown, page 40.) N. S. to Minn. south to N. J. and Pa.

4. **A. triphyllum,** Torr. (*Arum triphyllum*, L. *A. pusillum*, Nash). Similar to *A. Stewardsonii* but with hood of spathe uniformly green to purplish within and not corrugated or with white stripes, although latter may be present in the tube: fruiting heads ½–¾in. long. S. Mass. to S. N. Y. south to Ky. and Fla.

14. **HYDROSME,** Schott. About 13 species of coarse foul-smelling herbs from trop. regions of Afr. and Asia, one cult. as an oddity and for bizzare effects.—Closely allied to Amorphophallus and differing technically in seed integument united to the funiculus and the very short-stalked ovule: lf. pedately compound, appearing after infl., the latter having an ovate spathe broadly enveloping the spadix; fls. unisexual, at base of spadix; staminate numerous, of 3–4 stamens; pistillate few, with a club-shaped 2–4-celled ovary, ovules solitary in each cell, basal, the style elongated with a 2–4-lobed stigma. (Hydros-me: Latin referring probably to its native wet or aquatic habitat.)

H. Rivieri, Engler (*Amorphophallus Rivieri*, Dur.). Devils-Tongue. Leopard-Palm. Tuber-producing plant to 4 ft. high: lf. palmately decompound, to 4 ft. across, borne subpeltately on an erect petiole, mottled brown and white: infl. on a stout dark reddish-purple peduncle or scape 3–4 ft. high, mottled with light red; spathe to 1 ft. long, convolute basally about lower portion of spadix and flaring outward with revolute wavy margins, varying in color from greenish with white to rose-pink blotches to rose-red blotched whitish-green; spadix stout, usually 1–2 ft. long, dark red, producing a strong carrion odor. (Named for Aug. Rivière, page 50.) Indo-China.—A tender plant not hardy N. but may be grown outdoors if tubers are lifted in autumn and stored in cool dry place until early spring.

15. **HELICODICEROS,** Schott. A monotypic genus native in Corsica and Sardinia.—Closely allied to Arum and differing in the compoundly lobed lvs. and technical characters of the ovary and andrœcium. (Helicodic-eros: Greek meaning *spirally 2-horned*, probably referring to the 2 lateral lfts. of each lf.)

H. muscivorus, Engler (*Arum muscivorum*, L. f. *A. crinitum*, Ait.). Twist-Arum. Tuberous stemless per. 1½–2 ft. high, infl. and foliage appearing together: lvs. basal, palmate with lateral lobes 3-parted, often contorted and erect: scape stout, arising from ground, about 9–15 in. high; spathe to 1 ft. long, bright green outside with olive-colored square-ended spots and blotches, involute and forming a tube for one-third its length that is bent at right angles near its mouth, mostly livid-purple inside becoming paler towards apex of the calla-like limb and covered with purple hairs over the inner surface that are bristle-like within the tube; spadix shorter than spathe, tapering toward apex, olive-green but the long sterile appendage purple-hairy: infl. producing a fetid carrion-like odor, attracting many insects within spathe-tube.—May be grown outdoors as far north as Philadelphia if tubers are planted deep and mulched heavily.

16. **DRACUNCULUS,** Schott. Two species in the Medit. region.—Differs from Arum in the compound lvs. and ovules attached in 1 (not 2) series at the sides of the carpels, and from Helicodiceros in the fls. of each sex being in close proximity to each other at the base of the appendaged spadix. (Dracun-culus: Latin, *little dragon.*)

D. vulgaris, Schott (*Arum Dracunculus*, L.). Tuberous-stemmed per. with 3–9 pedately-lobed lvs. appearing with or before the infl.: lvs. of 9–15 lanceolate-oblong segms. arising from a falcate or sickle-shaped base, green with livid reddish-purple streaks or spots on a green petiole: peduncle or scape stout, mostly 2–6 in. long; spathe 16–20 in. long, constricted into a short tube basally, the limb wavy-margined, flaring to somewhat recurved, apex long-acuminate to subcaudate, tube green outside streaked purple, limb reddish-purple and more darkly so approaching margins; spadix erect, tapering apically, purple, nearly as long as spathe and often somewhat contorted; infl. emitting an unpleasant carrion-like odor, but of less pungency than in Helicodiceros.—Grown from tubers, hardy almost to Philadelphia if mulched heavily in winter.

17. **ORONTIUM,** L. Golden-Club. A single species, a hardy deep-rooted aquatic native to E. U. S.—Lvs. appearing in early spring with infl. and remaining throughout growing season: fls. mostly bisexual, surrounded by a scale-like 4–6-parted perianth and covering entire golden-yellow spadix; ovary 1-celled and 1-ovuled; spathe early deciduous and not showy; infl. borne on an elongated white peduncle. (Oront-ium: ancient name of a water plant of the Syrian river Orontes.)

O. aquaticum, L. Lvs. velvety-green above and silvery beneath, ascending or floating depending on depth of water, blade to 1 ft. long, oblong-elliptic, without midrib, parallel-veined, petiole 4–20 in. long: showy when in bloom because of its pure white slender scapes and bright yellow spadices; scapes 6–24 in. long, spadix 2–4 in. long. S. Mass. to Fla. and La.—Suited for naturalizing in shallow ponds or swamp margins or grown in tubs in pools; difficult of eradication when established.

18. **CALLA,** L. WATER-ARUM. One species, a bog plant native in N. Amer.—Non-tuberous but with acrid rootstocks: lvs. broadly ovate, petioled: infl. arising from crown on an elongated scape, the spathe small but longer than spadix; spadix with fls. perfect or the uppermost staminate, no perianth present, stamens usually 5–7 on linear filaments and with divaricate anther-sacs; ovary 1-celled with 6–9 anatropous ovules: fr. a depressed obconical berry. (Cal-la: ancient name of unknown meaning.)—The calla of florists, or calla-lily, is a Zantedeschia.

C. palustris, L. Lvs. with long-sheathed cylindrical petioles to 8 in. long, blades ovate to suborbicular, to 8 in. long and 4 in. wide, often cordate at base, apex abruptly acute or cuspidate: scapes as long as petioles and with basal sheath; spathe white, elliptic to ovate-lanceolate, acuminate, mostly 1½–2½ in. long, spreading and open, rather fleshy; spadix about half as long as spathe, stout, densely covered with fls.: red berries forming a dense head when mature. N. S. to Minn. south to N. J. and Iowa.—Suited for naturalizing in muddy soil of pond margins or in tubs in shallow pool.

19. **ARUM,** L. A dozen species now recognized, some very variable, in Eurasia, a few occasionally grown for curiosity, often under the name Calla.—Low simple herbs with underground rounded or depressed tubers, hastate or sagittate stalked lvs., and scape bearing a terminal "flower" which is a spathe (that withers rather than falls after anthesis) and a spadix of minute crowded naked fls., the spathe being the showy part, the spathe-tube constricted at the top and inclosing the lower fruitful part of the spadix which is terminated by a long sterile cylindrical appendage: fls. unisexual, the fertile at base, the staminate above with pistillodes (unfruitful pistils) below them and staminodes above them; ovules affixed on the side walls of the cell: fr. a fleshy berry. (A-rum: the ancient name.)—Many plants once referred to Arum are now named in other genera.

A. Lvs. cordate at base when mature: plants autumn-flowering....................1. *A. pictum*
AA. Lvs. hastate or sagittate at base when mature; plants spring- or early summer-flowering.
  B. Spathe black-purple inside....................2. *A. palæstinum*
  BB. Spathe green or yellowish.
    C. Spadix violet-purple or yellow, suffused or flecked violet-purple; spathe greenish-yellow flecked purple....................3. *A. maculatum*
    CC. Spadix yellow; spathe whitish-green sparsely flecked purple....................4. *A. italicum*

1. **A. pictum,** L. (*A. corsicum*, Loisel.). Hardy tuberous per.: lvs. appearing in spring, light green, blades and petioles each about 10 in. long, former oblong ovate, deeply cordate at base: spathe a bright violet limb with tube green and swollen at base; spadix purplish-black, exceeding the spathe; peduncle to 4 in. long: berries red, 1–5-seeded. Medit. region.

2. **A. palæstinum,** Boiss. (*A. sanctum*, Dammann). BLACK CALLA. Lvs. cordate-hastate, 6–8 in. long: scape shorter than petioles; spathe about equalling lvs., the tube short and green; blade oblong-lanceolate, greenish outside and black-purple within; spadix not equalling spathe, upper part dark purple. Syria, Palestine.

3. **A. maculatum,** L. CUCKOO-PINT. About 1 ft. high: lvs. appearing in spring, hastate or sagittate, with deflexed lobes, often spotted black: spathe 6–10 in. long, constricted in middle, edges inflexed, edged and more or less spotted purple; spadix usually purple. Eu., N. Afr.—Variable.

4. **A. italicum,** Mill. Large and stouter than no. 3, blooming later: lvs. earlier, triangular-hastate with spreading lobes: spathe folded or falling down in front at anthesis closing the opening; spadix yellow. W. Eu., N. Afr.

20. **CALADIUM,** Vent. A dozen to a score of trop. American plants, two in common cult. under glass and in the open far S. for the thin colored lvs. of very many patterns, known as the "fancy-leaved caladiums."—From Alocasia and Colocasia the genus differs in the ovary, in which the many ovules are borne in the middle, on a central placenta: style none: lvs. peltate in the usual cult. kinds but not so

throughout the genus: spathe with boat-shaped limb; spadix somewhat shorter than spathe: berry white. (Cala-dium: name probably of E. Indian origin, published in 1800.)

A. Lf. broad, ovate to round-ovate in general outline............................1. *C. bicolor*
AA. Lf. narrow, lance-ovate to oblong-ovate............................2. *C. picturatum*

1. **C. bicolor,** Vent. The commoner species, in endless vars. under a multitude of names: petiole elongated, glaucous or pruinose toward top, otherwise green; blade variously colored above, somewhat glaucous beneath, sagittate-ovate, ovate-triangular to round-ovate, the basal lobes joined one-fifth to one-third their length and separated by a narrow sinus: spathe with tube green outside and whitish-green inside, the throat usually purplish, the blade cuspidate and white at apex. W. Indies to Brazil and Andes.—The spotted, blotched, and variegated thin almost translucent lvs. are well known, the marks being white, grayish, purple, rose, and others.

2. **C. picturatum,** Koch. Petiole green, more or less variegated; blade variously colored above, pale or not glaucous beneath, sagittate-lanceolate, the basal lobes one-sixth to one-fourth their length and separated by a broad triangular sinus: spathe with tube green outside and purplish inside, the blade white throughout, more or less apiculate. Brazil and Peru.—Runs into fewer forms than no. 1.

21. **XANTHOSOMA,** Schott. The New World analogue of Colocasia and Alocasia, with about 40 species, grown for ornament and esculent underground tubers.—Closely allied to Caladium, but differing technically in the shield-like style that projects out beyond the ovary: strong herbs, sometimes with woody stock, thick more or less tuberous rhizomes: lvs. thick, long-petioled, not peltate, the blade sagittate or hastate and the main nerve at the lower side of either basal lobe more or less marginal as it joins the petiole, sometimes 3-lobed or even pedatisect: spathe with an ovoid or oblong convolute tube, and a narrow boat-shaped or trough-shaped blade exceeding the spadix; anthers 4–6, united into an angular column. (Xanthosoma: Greek *yellow body*, referring to the yellow stigmoid disk.)—This genus yields the native taro-like tubers of the American tropics, known as Tanier, Yautia, Malanga, and others, the product apparently of the first three below, and perhaps of other species.

A. Lvs. and petioles uniformly light green, not pruinose or glaucous..............1. *X. sagittifolium*
AA. Lvs. or petioles pruinose or glaucous, of different shades of green, or colored.
B. Lf. in shades of green............................2. *X. atrovirens*
BB. Lf. marked with purple or white.
C. Nerves and rib violet or purplish............................3. *X. violaceum*
CC. Nerves and rib white............................4. *X. Lindenii*

1. **X. sagittifolium,** Schott. Eventually producing a caudex or trunk 3–4 ft. high: lvs. plain green with very long green petiole; blade 1½–3 ft. long and nearly as broad, sagittate-ovate, abruptly sharp-pointed, the main part twice longer than the rounded basal lobes, the bottom nerves nearly marginal at the petiole: scape or peduncle longer than the greenish-white spathe; spadix much shorter than spathe, the fertile (pistillate) part nearly as long as the sterile (staminate) part. W. Indies, S. Amer.—Much like a Colocasia, but the lvs. not peltate.

2. **X. atrovirens,** Koch. Plant without above-ground trunk: lvs. dark rich green above and gray-green beneath, pruinose or glaucous, on long dark green sometimes lined petiole, the rib and nerves paler; blade as large as in no. 1 or even larger, sagittate-ovate, the main part somewhat oblong and short-cuspidate and twice or more exceeding the obtuse ovate or somewhat rhomboid basal lobes: blade of spathe dull green; spadix stipitate, with pistillate part one-third length of the reddish staminate part, the sterile part pale rose-color. S. Amer.

3. **X. violaceum,** Schott. Plant without trunk above ground: lvs. pruinose (at least when young), green, paler beneath, rib and nerves and usually the margin violet or purplish, on long purplish petiole; blade oblong-sagittate-ovate, abruptly sharp-pointed, the main part three to four times longer than the somewhat triangular obtuse basal lobes, the bottom nerves at margin near the petiole: spathe whitish-yellow inside; spadix with pistillate part four times shorter than staminate part, the sterile part violet. W. Indies and S. Amer.

4. **X. Lindenii,** Engler (*Phyllotænium Lindenii*, André). Plant with strong stock: lvs. pale green with rib and main side nerves white, making an ornamental subject, the petiole pale green; blade hastate-oblong and acute, the main part about twice as long as the obtuse usually conspicuously spreading basal lobes: spathe white. Colombia.—A glasshouse plant; early grown by Messrs. Linden, Belgian horticulturists.

22. **COLOCASIA,** Schott (*Leucocasia*, Schott). ELEPHANTS-EAR. Seven or 8 recognized species in trop. Asia and Polynesia, large coarse herbs grown for the ornament of their large lvs. and stately habit, and also for edible tubers.—From Alocasia the genus differs technically in the ovary characters, the ovules being many and borne on the walls (on the parietal placentæ): lvs. always peltate, mostly thick in texture: tuber-bearing: as in related genera, the pollen-bearing staminate part of the spadix is separated from the pistillate part by a section of staminodes. (Colocasia: an old Greek name, associated with the colcas or culcas, of the Arabs and used in Egypt.)

A. Grown mostly for ornament: appendage of spadix as long as the two staminate parts (polliniferous and staminode parts)........1. *C. antiquorum*
AA. Grown mostly for food: appendage much shorter than polliniferous staminate part..2. *C. esculenta*

1. **C. antiquorum,** Schott (*Arum Colocasia*, L. *C. esculenta* var. *antiquorum*, Hubbard & Rehd.). Growing to great size, a few ft. high under favorable conditions, with short thick stock and lf.-blades hanging nearly to the ground: petioles long and stout; blades green, oblong-ovate, cordate but the sinus not reaching to the petiole, main part apiculate at apex, the basal lobes rounded and with the basal midribs well inside the margin: peduncle or scape usually solitary, much shorter than petioles; limb of spathe wide open, pale yellow, 6–15 in. long, the spadix with a long terminal appendage. E. Indies.—Yields the Egyptian taro or culcas, inferior to the taro of Amer. and the Pacific. There are several color forms: var. **illustris,** Engler (*Alocasia illustris*, Bull. *C. esculenta* var. *illustris*, A. F. Hill), petioles purplish, blades large, oblong-ovate, with black-green spots between main veins; var. **Fontanesii,** Schott (*C. Fontanesii*, Schott. *C. esculenta* var. *Fontanesii*, A. F. Hill), petioles purplish, blades dull green with violet margins and nerves; var. **euchlora,** Schott (*C. euchlora*, Koch & Sello. *C. esculenta* var. *euchlora*, A. F. Hill), petioles purplish, blade dark green with violet margins.

2. **C. esculenta,** Schott (*Arum esculentum*, L. *C. antiquorum* var. *esculenta*, Schott. *Caladium esculentum*, Vent.). TARO. EDDO. DASHEEN. Similar, but yielding large spherical underground tubers abundantly, which are important articles of food; the blanched shoots from the tubers may be utilized as a winter vegetable: limb of spathe trough-shaped or inrolling, the spadix with a very short appendage. Probably native in Pacific isls.

23. **ALOCASIA,** Neck. Sixty to 70 species of trop. Asia and isls., grown as specimen plants for the large foliage, mostly under glass; the foliage is often handsomely colored and variegated, the substance of the lvs. usually thick and stiffish.—Strong or small plants with a thick short stock: lvs. with long sheathing petioles, the blade sagittate-cordate, often shallowly peltate (always peltate in young state): spathe usually glaucous, convolute, the blade oblong and mostly boat-shaped, the tube ovoid or oblong and much shorter than blade; spadix shorter than spathe, sometimes produced into a short sterile appendage; fls. unisexual and naked; stamens joined to form a 6-angled body; sterile staminate fls. or staminodes beneath the others; ovary 3–4-celled, with few ovules affixed at base of cell: fr. mostly a reddish berry. (Alocasia, variant of Colocasia.)—Many named kinds are in choice hothouse collections, some of them hybrids.

A. Lvs. with deeply notch-lobed margins........1. *A. Sanderiana*
AA. Lvs. entire or only undulate.
  B. Blades green.
    C. Lf.-blades 15–30 in. long, petioles banded dark green and white........2. *A. zebrina*
    CC. Lf.-blades 36–42 in. long, petioles striated dark brown to black........3. *A. macrorhiza*
  BB. Blades not uniformly green but variously colored.
    C. Lf. variegated with colors other than white or silvery-green to -white.
      D. Lvs. peltate........4. *A. cuprea*
      DD. Lvs. not peltate........5. *A. indica* var. *metallica*
    CC. Lf. variegated or veined white to silvery-green.
      D. Blades 15–18 in. long........6. *A. Lowii*
      DD. Blades 2–4 ft. long.
        E. Lf. with veins and midrib silvery-white........7. *A. Korthalsii*
        EE. Lf. with blade blotched and mottled silvery-white.
          F. Petioles about 3 ft. long........3. *A. macrorhiza*
          FF. Petioles 1½–2 ft. long........5. *A. indica* var. *variegata*

1. **A. Sanderiana,** Bull. Small or medium-sized handsome plant: blades sagittate-ovate, peltate, 6–16 in. long, main part narrow-triangular and cuspidate-acuminate, basal lobes narrow-triangular and obtuse, margins deeply sinuate-lobed, upper surface dark metallic-green with white nerves and usually white margins, under surface tinged purple;

petioles striped brownish: spathe greenish and spadix greenish-white. (Bears the name of Messrs. Sander & Co., nurserymen of Belgium and England.) Mindanao, Philippines.

2. **A. zebrina,** Koch & Veitch. St. short or none: blades green, 15–30 in. long, broadly ovate or triangular-ovate, not peltate, with deep sinus at base, main part oblong-triangular and short-acuminate, basal lobes oblong-ovate and obtuse; petioles equalling or exceeding lvs., banded with dark green and white: spathe long-peduncled, greenish; spadix white. Luzon, Philippines.

3. **A. macrorhiza,** Schott. St. tall; large stout plant of striking appearance, 6–15 ft. and more: blades 3 ft. long, broad-sagittate and pointed, somewhat undulate, main part triangular-ovate and acute, the basal lobes much shorter, the midrib broad and conspicuous, green in the type but blotched and mottled white in the variegated form: spathe with glaucous-green yellowish blade. India, Malaya.

4. **A. cuprea,** Koch (*A. metallica,* Hook. f.). Rhizome tuberous: blades 1½ ft. long and 1 ft. broad, ovate, peltate, dark metallic green with darker midrib and veins, under side purple, main part oblong-ovate and acuminate, basal lobes ovate; petioles to 2 ft., green: spathe with purple tube and blade green to purple. Malaya.

5. **A. indica,** Schott, var. **metallica,** Schott (*A. plumbea,* VanHoutte). Stout coarse plant, with st. to 6 ft.: blades 2–4 ft. long, deep reddish-purple with lead-green sheen, triangular-sagittate with slightly undulate margins, deeply cordate, not peltate, the main part triangular-acute, basal lobes ovate and nearly acute, the petioles long and stout: spathe stalked, blade yellowish or purplish inside. Malaya.—*A. indica* itself (India and Malaya) is green-lvd. Var. **variegata,** Engler, has lvs. mottled and lined with grayish-white.

6. **A. Lowii,** Hook. f. Rhizome elongated and tuberous: blades long-sagittate, 1½ ft. long and 6 in. broad, main part long-triangular and acuminate, basal lobes oblong-triangular and obtuse, above olive-green with silvery-white side nerves and whitish margins, beneath purple; petioles long, rose-color: spathe whitish-green. (Early grown by Messrs. Hugh Low & Son, nurserymen, England.) Malaya.

7. **A. Korthalsii,** Schott (*A. Thibautiana,* Mast.). St. short: blades 2 ft. long and 18–20 in. broad, cordate-ovate, sharp-acuminate, the basal lobes short and obtuse, peltate, olive-green with broad silvery rib and veins, deep purple beneath; petioles long, greenish: spathe pale green. (Peter W. Korthals was a German botanist of the 19th century who travelled in Malaya.) Malaya.

30. BROMELIACEÆ. BROMELIA OR PINEAPPLE FAMILY

About 59 genera and above 1,300 species of herbs and subshrubs, usually with persistent stiff equitant or rosette lvs. and mostly epiphytic, natives in trop. Amer. with minor extensions into extra-trop. regions; a few are in frequent cult. for ornament, and the pineapple for food.—Plants sometimes scurfy, largely monocarpic (fruiting but once and then dying, although suckers may arise from the base): lvs. various, but in representative groups elongated and stiff, with entire or spinulose margins, sheathing or overlapping at base: fls. regular or (in Pitcairnia) irregular

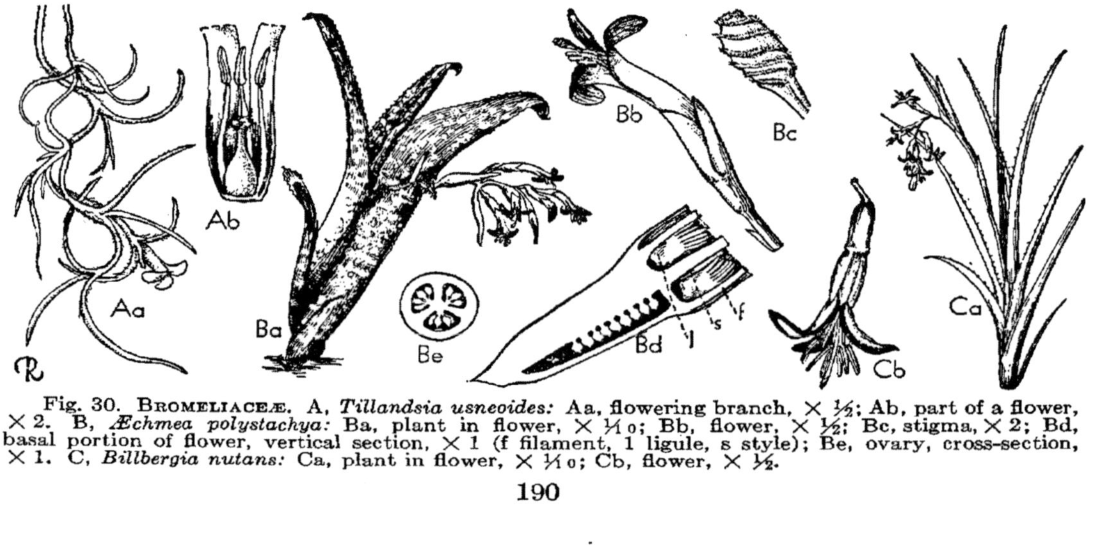

Fig. 30. BROMELIACEÆ. A, *Tillandsia usneoides:* Aa, flowering branch, × ½; Ab, part of a flower, × 2. B, *Æchmea polystachya:* Ba, plant in flower, × 1/10; Bb, flower, × ½; Bc, stigma, × 2; Bd, basal portion of flower, vertical section, × 1 (f filament, l ligule, s style); Be, ovary, cross-section, × 1. C, *Billbergia nutans:* Ca, plant in flower, × 1/10; Cb, flower, × ½.

and commonly bisexual, in dense spikes or heads provided with large often colored and showy imbricated bracts, in other species in branching panicles; perianth small, of 6 parts in 2 series, representing calyx and corolla, each series sometimes united into a tube, the segms. erect and spreading, inner ones clawed; inner segms. or petals sometimes with ligules or scales at base; stamens 6, attached in base of perianth, anthers dorsifixed or basifixed; ovary inferior, superior or semi-superior, 3-celled, the ovules many; stigmas 3 or style 3-parted: fr. a berry or caps. to which the remains of the perianth is more or less adherent.—Recent introductions of other genera and species than those here treated are cult. by fanciers and specialists, and choice hothouse collections may contain bromeliads not described here.

A. Ovary superior or nearly so, at least not strictly inferior: fr. a dehiscent caps.
  B. Lf.-margins or petioles (ours) spinose.
    C. Pistil with ovary semi-superior: fls. zygomorphic. . . . . 1. PITCAIRNIA
    CC. Pistil with ovary completely superior: fls. regular.
      D. Style filiform: fr. a loculicidal caps. . . . . 2. PUYA
      DD. Style very short or not apparent: fr. a septicidal caps. . . . . 3. DYCKIA
  BB. Lf.-margins or petioles not spinose.
    C. Petals connate basally or closely connivent. . . . . 4. GUZMANIA
    CC. Petals free.
      D. Scales absent from petals. . . . . 5. TILLANDSIA
      DD. Scales present on inner side of petals, often basally so . . . . 6. VRIESIA
AA. Ovary inferior: fr. a berry.
  B. Infl. close among the lvs. or surrounded by an involucre-like rosette of reduced often colored lvs.
    C. Petals free to base or slightly connate; scales present. 7. CANISTRUM
    CC. Petals connate by their margins or adnate to the more or less connate filaments, at least basally so; scales mostly absent.
      D. The infl. mostly few-fld.; sepals united into a tube . . . . 8. CRYPTANTHUS
      DD. The infl. mostly many-fld.; sepals mostly free and not united into a tube.
        E. Fls. in simple racemose infl. . . . . 9. AREGELIA
        EE. Fls. in compound usually paniculate infl. that may be reduced and almost head-like . . . . 10. NIDULARIUM
  BB. Infl. on a prominent scape or st., not closely surrounded by the basal rosette or involucre of reduced lvs. (but not necessarily exceeding the lvs.).
    C. Pistils fusing to form a compound fr.: infl. and fr. bearing a crown of sterile foliaceous bracts at apex. . . . . 11. ANANAS
    CC. Pistils always separate, even in fr.: infl. and fr. usually without a crown of foliaceous bracts.
      D. The infl. simple, or if compound each pollen-grain with a longitudinal membranous groove . . . . 12. BILLBERGIA
      DD. The infl. compound, at least basally so: pollen-grains dotted by pores. . . . . 13. ÆCHMEA

1. **PITCAIRNIA,** L'Her. About 185 species of terrestrial, rarely epiphytic, herbs, grown under glass for the showy infl. or in the open in nearly frost-free areas.—Mostly stemless: lvs. in whorls or imbricated and many-ranked along a st., linear to lanceolate and sometimes with a distinct petiole, often heavily farinose beneath, margins entire or spinose: infl. simple or compound, usually exceeding the foliage; fls. perfect, mostly slightly zygomorphic, pedicelled to subsessile; sepals free; petals free, with or without scale-like appendages on inner side; stamens shorter than petals or slightly exserted; ovary half inferior or semi-superior when viewed in vertical section; style mostly with 3 linear lobes and equalling petals: caps. mostly septicidal; seeds caudate at both ends or rarely winged. (Pitcair-nia: Archibald Pitcairn, 1652–1713, professor of medicine in Scotland and Holland.)

P. corallina, Lind. & André. Stemless: lvs. 2–3 ft. long and 2–3 in. wide, plicate, scurfy blade spineless on a stout spiny petiole 1 ft. long: infl. a heavy and strongly arching or pendulous raceme 12–18 in. long, peduncle and pedicels bright red; fls. about 3 in. long; sepals 1 in. long, vivid scarlet-red; petals coral-red; stamens scarcely exserted on white filaments; style with stigmas twisted before anthesis. Colombia.

2. **PUYA,** Molina. Stout stiff xerophytic terrestrial monocarpic herbs of S. Amer., 40–50 species, very few grown under glass or in the open in nearly frost-free regions.—Mostly with trunk or st.: lvs. in dense rosettes, usually spiny at tip and on margins, glabrous, or scaly on back: fls. bisexual, often very showy, blue, purple or yellow, in a spike or raceme; segms. all free and usually nearly or quite equal; petals scaleless; ovary completely superior, style slender, 3 stigmas becoming twisted: caps. ellipsoid or nearly globose, fleshy, loculicidally dehiscent into 6 valves or parts; seeds suborbicular, surrounded by a wing. (Pu-ya: Chilean name.)

A. Fls. greenish-yellow: infl. 3 ft. long or more, with apical half of branches sterile........1. *P. chilensis*
AA. Fls. blue: infl. mostly 1½–2 ft. long, with branches fertile to tip or nearly so..........2. *P. cærulea*

1. **P. chilensis,** Molina (*Pitcairnia chilensis*, Lodd. *Pourretia chilensis*, Hort.). Strong plant, growing 4–6 ft. high or more: lvs. 2–4 ft. long, very narrow, glaucous, ascending or recurved, the margins strongly armed: fls. greenish-yellow, 2 in. long, sessile or nearly so, in a tall branching bracted densely racemose infl. with terminal half of lateral branches sterile. Chile.

2. **P. cærulea,** Lindl. (*Pourretia cærulea*, Miers. *Pitcairnia cærulea*, Benth.). Robust plant to 6 ft. high or more: lvs. about 2 ft. long, narrowly ensiform, heavily white-glaucous, spiny-margined: fls. blue, sepals violet-blue, about 2 in. long, essentially sterile, subtended by bracts about one-half as long as sepals, in a much-branched infl. whose fls. are fertile almost to the branch tips. Chile.

3. **DYCKIA,** Schult. f. Stemless very stiff and semi-succulent-lvd. terrestrial xerophytes, grown occasionally under glass or in the open far S. for foliage effects and for the not too-showy fls.; about 70 species in S. Amer.—Foliage resembling the genus Aloe; lvs. many in dense rosettes, lanceolate, spine-tipped, often fleshy, margins usually spinulose, farinose-mealy beneath: infl. long-scaped, much exceeding the lvs., spicate to paniculate and usually erect; fls. mostly small, in shades of yellow, orange or red; sepals commonly free, much shorter than petals; petals imbricated, adnate basally to filaments and producing a tube; stamens about as long as petals; ovary wholly superior, with a very short 3-parted twisted style: fr. a septicidal caps., the seeds winged. (Dyck-ia: Prince Salm-Dyck, 1771–1861, German botanist and author of work on succulent plants.)

A. Petals and filaments adnate to form a distinct tube almost to apex; fls. sessile or without distinct pedicel....................1. *D. rariflora*
AA. Petals and filaments adnate and forming a tube at base of perianth only; fls. with short but distinct pedicel....................2. *D. brevifolia*

1. **D. rariflora,** Schult. f. Lvs. 6–8 in. long, becoming flat and dark green above and rounded and glaucous beneath, margins distantly spinose: infl. a spike about 2 ft. high, erect and somewhat woolly; fls. 10–15, orange; sepals ½in. long, imbricate, deep yellow, about twice as long as subtending bract; petals about 1 in. long, orange-yellow; stamens slightly longer than style. Brazil.

2. **D. brevifolia,** Baker (*D. sulphurea*, Koch). Lvs. 4–6 in. long, rigid and thick, inner ones erect and outer recurved, marginal spines minute and about ¼in. apart: scape 8–15 in. long, infl. of 30–40 yellow fls. subtended by lanceolate bracts to ¾in. long; fls. with yellow sepals to ⅓in. long, petals to nearly ¾in. long and recurved; stamens about as long as style but much shorter than perianth. Brazil.

4. **GUZMANIA,** Ruiz & Pav. Probably 65–75 species in trop. Amer., monocarpic, terrestrial or epiphytic, one not uncommon in glasshouses.—Much like the non-spinose stiff-lvd. tillandsias, differing in the inner perianth-segms., and usually also the outer ones, connate or connivent into a tube, and from Vriesia in having all segms. without ligules inside: ovary superior: acaulescent or rarely caulescent herbs, with scurfy lvs. in dense rosettes, the scape short and borne amongst the foliage: fls. yellow or white, in a spicate or cone-like infl.: fr. a septicidal caps.; seeds with basal brownish coma. (Guzma-nia: A. Guzmann, Spanish naturalist.)

A. Outer segms. exceeding the inner....................1. *G. musaica*
AA. Outer segms. shorter than inner....................2. *G. lingulata*

1. **G. musaica,** Mez (*Tillandsia musaica*, Lind. *Billbergia musaica*, Regel. *Vriesia musaica*, Cogn. & March. *Caraguata musaica*, André. *Massangea musaica*, Morr.). Terrestrial or rarely epiphytic, stemless: lvs. 12–20 in. long, 2–3 in. broad, rounded at end, strongly decurved, prominently marked with transverse wavy lines that are dark green on the upper surface and purple on the back: infl. 3–4 in. long, short-peduncled, bracts golden-yellow striped rose; fls. 2 in. or less long, yellowish; sepals corolla-like and exceeding the petals. Colombia.

2. **G. lingulata,** Mez (*Tillandsia lingulata*, L. *Caraguata lingulata*, Lindl.). Stout-stemmed epiphyte: lvs. many, lanceolate or sword-shaped, 1–1½ ft. long, about 1 in. broad, remotely toothed: scape bearing a drooping terminal dense head or spike with showy red to scarlet bracts; fls. about as long as the bracts, tube yellowish and limb purplish, sepals small and not corolla-like. Trop. Amer.

5. **TILLANDSIA,** L. Species nearly 400, widely spread in trop. and subtrop. Amer., epiphytic or sometimes terrestrial, a few choice glasshouse subjects.—Herbs,

caulescent or acaulescent, of diverse habit: lvs. basal, or a few smaller ones on the scape, crowded or in rosettes, dilated and sometimes distended at base, margins entire: scape simple or branched (rarely almost wanting), bearing few or many fls., the bracts often colored but usually not broad or strongly distichous; fls. blue, purple, red, orange, or white, the segms. free, without ligules or scales at base inside; ovary superior: caps. oblong or prismatic, septicidal; seeds long-stipitate, with pappus-like appendage. (Tilland-sia: Elias Tillands, 1640–1693, Sweden, made catalogue of the plants of Abo, Finland, in 1673.)

A. Stamens longer than inner segms. 1. *T. fasciculata*
AA. Stamens shorter than inner segms. or not exceeding them.
  B. Lvs. 6–12 in. or more long: fls. showy . . . . 2. *T. Lindeniana*
  BB. Lvs. 1–2 in. long: fls. inconspicuous . . . . 3. *T. usneoides*

1. **T. fasciculata,** Sw. Tall and strong, with rosettes of grayish-green linear-lanceolate lvs. 1–1½ ft. long and expanded at base, more or less scurfy: scape exceeding foliage, branched, the parts of the panicle with distichous keeled acute greenish red-tinged bracts; fls. erect, subsessile; sepals more or less connate; petals to 2½ in. long, white to purple; stamens and style exserted. W. Indies, Cent. Amer.—A very variable species.

2. **T. Lindeniana,** Regel (*T. Lindenii,* Morr. *Vriesia Lindenii,* Lem. *Phytarhiza Lindenii,* Morr.). Epiphyte, acaulescent: lvs. rosulate, about 1 ft. long, ½–¾in. broad, dilated at base, recurving: spike large, with carmine bracts; fls. bluish-purple, large, much projecting beyond the bracts. (J. Linden, page 47.) Ecuador, Peru.

3. **T. usneoides,** L. (*Renealmia usneoides,* L. *Dendropogon usneoides,* Raf.). SPANISH-MOSS. Pendent-growing rootless plant, suspended from branches of trees in branching strands to 25 ft. long; sts. less than 1⁄16 in. diam., branching sympodially with internodes to 2½ in. long: lvs. seemingly axile in fascicled clusters of 2–3, mostly 1–2 in. long, distichous, very densely covered with gray to brownish lepidote scurfy scales: infl. reduced to a single short-bracted subsessile fl. having short connate sepals slightly exceeded by the pale green to blue petals; stamens deeply included: caps. cylindrical, to 1 in. long. S. E. U. S. to Chile and Argentina.

6. **VRIESIA,** Lindl. About 100 species, mostly epiphytic, monocarpic, with very showy large-bracted spikes.—Lvs. in dense rosettes, rather broad, scurfy or becoming glabrous above, not spinose, sometimes spotted, barred or striped: fls. bisexual, in mostly flattened spikes with highly colored large bracts; segms. free, usually equal, with a ligule or scale at base of petals inside and in this character differing from Tillandsia, yellow, greenish, white or rose-color, covered and sometimes concealed by the bracts; ovary superior or semi-superior: caps. septicidally dehiscent from base; seeds with a coma-like crown of hairs. (Vrie-sia: Dr. W. H. de Vriese, 1806–1862, botanist of Amsterdam.)

A. Stamens shorter than petals . . . . 1. *V. hieroglyphica*
AA. Stamens longer than petals.
  B. Infl. branched . . . . 2. *V. Saundersii*
  BB. Infl. simple.
    C. Lvs. transversely banded . . . . 3. *V. splendens*
    CC. Lvs. not banded . . . . 4. *V. carinata*

1. **V. hieroglyphica,** Morr. (*Tillandsia hieroglyphica,* Bull. *Massangea hieroglyphica,* Carr.). Lvs. many, in stout robust rosettes, lorate, usually 1–1½ ft. long and to 2½ in. wide, recurved, abruptly and coarsely cuspidate, irregularly transversely banded with alternate zones of yellowish to dark green and brown-purple: infl. a branched panicle, the yellowish fls. subtended by broadly elliptic bracts; stamens shorter than petals. Brazil.

2. **V. Saundersii,** Morr. (*Tillandsia Saundersii,* Koch. *Encholirion Saundersii,* André). Plant about 1½ ft. high: lvs. many, linear, grayish and somewhat white-dotted above, spotted red-brown beneath: infl. loosely paniculate, the bracts ovate-elliptic; fls. nearly erect, yellow, cylindrical. (Named for Wilson Saunders, who grew the plant in England.) Brazil.

3. **V. splendens,** Lem. (*Tillandsia splendens,* Brongn. *V. speciosa,* Hook.). Stout plant to 3 ft. tall: lvs. 1 ft. or more long and 2–3 in. broad, stiff, concave above, arching, transversely irregularly banded with dark brown (whence the garden names *V.* or *Tillandsia zebrina* and *picta*): st. or scape equalling or exceeding foliage, spotted, with spike of densely imbricated bright red bracts; fls. yellowish-white, exserted from bracts. Guiana.

4. **V. carinata,** Wawra (*Tillandsia carinata,* Baker. *V. brachystachys,* Regel). Lvs. mostly 5–7 in. long, sheathing basally, apex mucronate to long-acuminate, somewhat glaucous but not spotted: fls. pale yellow, exserted; bracts divaricate, scarlet basally and yellowish-green apically, acuminate, shorter than fls. Brazil.

7. **CANISTRUM,** Morr. About 10 Brazilian species, epiphytic or terrestrial, monocarpic, sometimes grown under glass.—Lvs. in a dense rosette, expanded and vaginate at base, linear or sword-shaped above, spinulose on margin, more or less scurfy: scape either short or tall, the simple spike or head dense and subtended by a separate whorl of broad colored bracts; fls. usually green, sometimes yellow or blue; segms. mostly free to base but sometimes connate and the outer ones (sepals) awned, the inner ones (petals) with 2 ligules which are cut or nearly plumose or in some cases represented by calluses; ovary inferior, style filiform and about equalling stamens; stigma 3-parted: fr. a many-seeded more or less succulent berry. (Canis-trum: Greek for *basket*, probably alluding to the cup-like whorl of bracts.)

A. Petals free to base........................1. *C. aurantiacum*
AA. Petals connate........................2. *C. amazonicum*

1. **C. aurantiacum,** Morr. (*Æchmea aurantiaca*, Baker). Vigorous: lvs. many in a rosette, spreading and curving from near the bottom, 1–2 ft. long and about 2 in. broad, expanded at base, uniform green or at first spotted dark green, with small marginal teeth: scape erect, hidden in the greenish cup of lvs. and bracts, the innermost of which are bright red; fls. in dense head, orange-yellow, about 2 in. long.

2. **C. amazonicum,** Mez (*Nidularium amazonicum*, Lind. & André. *Karatas amazonica*, Baker). Stemless and stoloniferous: lvs. many in the rosette, lanceolate, 12–18 in. long and 2–3 in. broad, brownish but not spotted or banded, the teeth very small: scape short, bearing a dense head that has lanceolate short bracts; fls. greenish-white, tube of corolla as long as calyx.

8. **CRYPTANTHUS,** Klotzsch. About a dozen epiphytes of S. Amer., one or two in common cult. under glass for the foliage.—Stemless, stoloniferous, much depressed or flattened herbs, with densely rosulate spreading stiff lvs. finely or rather coarsely prickly on the margins: fls. white, in a head nested in the foliage; sepals connate into a tube, not mucronate or awned; petals longer, little united at base, wide-spreading in anthesis, without ligules; stamens inserted on corolla, filaments slender; ovary inferior, with many ovules in each cell; style filiform, stigmas very narrow: fr. berry-like but dry, the seeds very small. (Cryptan-thus: Greek *hidden flower*.)

A. Lvs. cross-banded........................1. *C. zonatus*
AA. Lvs. plain, not banded........................2. *C. acaulis*

1. **C. zonatus,** Beer (*Tillandsia zonata*, Hort.). Lvs. several to many, 5–9 in. long, 1–1½ in. broad, crinkly, transversely banded above with whitish and green or brown, white-scurfy beneath, margins thickly set with spinulose small teeth, apex short-acute: fls. in a small central sessile head or cluster; calyx ½in. long; petals oblanceolate, about 1 in. long. Brazil.

2. **C. acaulis,** Beer (*C. undulatus*, Otto & Dietr. *Tillandsia acaulis*, Lindl.). Lvs. several to many, 3–6 in. long and 1–1½ in. broad, prominently undulate, plain green above and white-scurfy beneath, margins finely spinulose-dentate: fls. in a close short cluster; calyx 1½ in. long; petals clawed, about 1 in. long. Brazil.

9. **AREGELIA,** Kuntze (*Regelia*, Lind. not Schauer). About 30 species of mostly acaulescent stiffly rosulate epiphytes, native in Guiana and Brazil, a few grown under glass for the foliage.—Fls. in a condensed racemose cyathium nested in axils of innermost lvs. of the rosette; sepals mostly connate basally; petals united into a tube with no scales within, the lobes spreading; ovary inferior, style shorter than stamens, stigmatic lobes twisted: fr. a many-seeded berry. (Arege-lia: named for von Regel, see page 50.)

A. Lvs. conspicuously barred on the back........................1. *A. spectabilis*
AA. Lvs. not barred........................2. *A. princeps*

1. **A. spectabilis,** Mez (*Nidularium spectabilis*, Moore. *Karatas spectabilis*, Ant.). Lvs. 20–30, mostly 14–18 in. long, lorate, recurved, bright green above, gray-green and glaucous beneath with conspicuous dark transverse bands, tip rose- to blood-red, apex obtuse with a mucro about ⅛in. long, margins remotely and finely spinose: fls. numerous in much condensed infl. about 2 in. across; calyx blood-red, as long as corolla-tube; corolla with pale obtusely 3-angled tube, lobes violet-blue and spreading; anthers sessile in mouth of tube. Brazil.

2. **A. princeps,** Mez (*Nidularium princeps*, Morr. *N. spectabilis*, Hort. not Moore.

Karatas princeps, Baker). Lvs. 10–15 in. long and about 1½ in. wide, usually 15–20 in number, oblong-elliptic, glaucous, margins spinose: fls. with white tube and violet-purple limb, about 1½ in. long, numerous, surrounded by 8–10 bright red ovate much shorter bract-like lvs. Brazil.

10. **NIDULARIUM,** Lem. Twenty to 30 Brazilian monocarpic epiphytes, sometimes cult. for the foliage and showy bracts.—Lvs. mostly large, in a dense rosette, the base dilated but otherwise sword-shaped, strap-shaped or linear, prickly on margin: scape very short, the composite infl. sessile in a crater-like or nest-like rosette of lvs. which, variously modified, form a kind of involucre: fls. red, purplish or white; sepals free; petals connate at base forming a tube, without ligules; ovary inferior, style filiform and about equalling anthers, stigma 3-parted: fr. a many-seeded berry. (Nidula-rium: Latin *nidus*, nest, from the habit.)

N. fulgens, Lem. (*N. pictum*, Hort.). Stemless: lvs. many in a dense rosette, strap-shaped, spreading, 1 ft. or less long, 1½–2 in. broad, green with usually darker spots, scurfy on back, sharply toothed, cuspidate or obtuse at tip: fls. many in a close cluster among the brilliant scarlet inner short lvs., the ovary white, long tube of corolla white and limb violet.

11. **ANANAS,** L. One monocarpic polymorphic species (or several segregates), native in trop. Amer., widely cult. in warm and trop. countries for the edible head of fr., and some forms for ornament.—Terrestrial, with rosettes of long and strong spiny-serrate lvs., and mostly elongated leafy st. bearing a very dense head at top, the head crowned with a tuft of lvs.: fls. sessile, violet or reddish, bisexual, the segms. free but connivent and tube-like, petals provided with 2 ligules at the base, the calyx very short; ovary inferior, style filiform, 3-branched: fr. a syncarpium, formed of the coalescence of thickened rachis, spiny-toothed bracts, abortive ovaries and adhering parts into one large globose, ovoid or elongated fleshy body known as a "pineapple"; in the wild the coalescence is less complete, and regular fls. may be produced. (Anan-as: modified from aboriginal S. American name.)

A. comosus, Merr. (*Bromelia comosa*, L. *A. sativus*, Schult. f.). PINEAPPLE. St. single, erect, 2–4 ft. high, bearing the pineapple, suckers arising from the base: lvs. long and sword-shaped, with saw-toothed edges.—The species runs into many forms; some of them have striped or margined lvs. (as var. *variegatus* and that known as *A. Porteanus*, Koch) and are grown for ornament. In the cult. pineapple, the edible part is mostly the greatly thickened pulpy rachis or st.; in this the frs. (berries) are imbedded. These frs., spirally arranged, form the exterior; below each fr. is the enlarged jagged-edged bract with its point extended over the fr. and sometimes split by the expansion. The fls. are sterile; but the sharp point of the berry is comprised of the 6 modified segms., one series of 3 inside the other; the cavity underneath the segms. contains the dried remains of the functionless stamens and style. Many vernacular-named vars. of the commercial pineapple occur, among the more common being Cayenne, Red Spanish, and Abakka or Golden.

12. **BILLBERGIA,** Thunb. Monocarpic mostly epiphytic plants, usually larger than æchmeas and tillandsias; 50–60 species.—Stemless: lvs. rosulate or fasciculate, usually scurfy at least beneath, in most species with spinulose margins: infl. a prominent spike or spicate panicle that usually exceeds the lvs., erect or drooping, sometimes slender, bracts often prominent and colored; fls. showy, blue, seldom red or greenish-yellow; segms. free to base, sepals obtuse or rarely only mucronate; petals free to base, ligules 2 at base of each and cut or fimbriate; stamens exserted at anthesis; ovary inferior, style equalling or exceeding stamens, stigma 3-parted: fr. a berry, many-seeded. (Billber-gia: J. G. Billberg, 1772–1844, Swedish botanist.)

A. Petals curling or twisting spirally after fl. expands.
  B. Lvs. banded transversely on lower side: fls. green to yellow-green. . . . . 1. *B. zebrina*
  BB. Lvs. not banded: fls. red. . . . . 2. *B. pyramidalis*
AA. Petals not spiralled.
  B. Infl. erect or nearly so. . . . . 3. *B. Liboniana*
  BB. Infl. manifestly nodding.
    C. Lvs. linear: fls. few. . . . . 4. *B. nutans*
    CC. Lvs. 1½ in. and more wide: fls. many. . . . . 5. *B. Morelii*

1. **B. zebrina,** Lindl. (*Bromelia zebrina*, Herb.). St. short or none: lvs. few in a rosette, connivent or close together in lower part, strap-shaped, 2–3 ft. long and 2–3 in. broad,

hard and stiff, edges prickly, with white spots and transverse bands: scape cernuous, shorter than lvs., with long pink or salmon bracts toward the top, rachis of spike and ovaries white-scurfy; fls. green or yellow-green, petals 2 in. long. Brazil.

2. **B. pyramidalis,** Lindl. (*Bromelia pyramidalis*, Sims. *Billbergia thyrsoidea*, Mart.). Stemless: lvs. 6–15, broadly lorate to lanceolate, with expanded base, mostly 12–15 in. long, green above and uniformly glaucous-green beneath, erect to slightly recurved, margins short-spinose at least along distal half and rarely completely entire, apex obtuse and abruptly mucronate to narrowly acute: infl. spicate, erect, not much exceeding foliage; fls. subtended by conspicuous rose-colored sterile lanceolate to elliptic-lanceolate bracts that are 2–3 in. long; calyx very scurfy, dark rose-red, about one-third as long as corolla, sepals obtuse to acute; corolla 1¾ in. long, rose-colored, petals twisting spirally at anthesis. Brazil.

3. **B. Liboniana,** de Jonghe. Rather small: lvs. few in a rosette, connivent below, sword-shaped, to 2½ ft. long and 1–1½ in. wide, firm but not hard, not banded, upper surface green and concave, the lower side white-scurfy and convex, margins minutely spinulose-toothed: scape 1 ft. long, slender, with small and inconspicuous bracts throughout, the fls. 6–10 in an erect or nearly erect simple spike; sepals 1 in. long, bright red to orange-yellow; petals twice as long and green with blue tips. (Intro. to Eu. about 1850 by M. Libon.) Brazil.

4. **B. nutans,** Wendl. Stemless slender plant with many rosulate linear lvs. about ½in. wide and 12–18 in. long, not stiff, the teeth very small and remote: scape 1 ft. long, slender, curving over at the end, with narrow rose-pink to bright red bracts; fls. 4–12, on slender pedicels; calyx ½in. long, salmon-pink, edged purplish-blue toward apex; petals 1½ in. long, pale yellowish-green margined deep bluish-purple, lobes reflexed; stamens much-exserted. Brazil.—One of the most commonly cult. species.

5. **B. Morelii,** Brongn. Lvs. several in a rosette, sword-shaped, 2 ft. or less long and 1½–2 in. wide, connivent below, stiff, finely spinose on margins, not banded: scape 1 ft. long, with long red very showy bract-like lvs. near and in the loose drooping ovate scurfy spike; fls. 10–15, to 2 in. long, reddish in sepals, the petals blue-limbed. (Named for M. Morel, Paris, who first flowered it in cult.) Brazil.

13. **ÆCHMEA,** Ruiz & Pav. Large and very variable genus, of more than 140 species, mostly S. American, monocarpic, usually epiphytic; a few sometimes grown under glass for ornament.—Stemless: scape usually conspicuous, only rarely short and in the nest of foliage: lvs. in a rosette, dilated at base, mostly scurfy, linear to sword-shaped but sometimes broader, acute or rounded at apex, margins variously spinose: fls. mostly yellow or in shades of red, often blue-tipped, sessile or less commonly pedicillate, the bracts sometimes colored and forming the conspicuous part; sepals free or connate, mostly sharp or long-awned; petals free to base, with 2 ligules at base of each; ovary inferior, style shorter than stamens, stigma with 3 narrow lobes: fr. a berry or berry-like, many-seeded. (Æchme-a: from Greek word, referring to the pointed sepals.)

A. Infl. simple, spicate or capitate throughout.
  B. Sepals united above the ovary .... 1. *Æ. recurvata*
  BB. Sepals free or nearly so .... 2. *Æ. Mariæ-Reginæ*
AA. Infl. openly paniculate, at least at base.
  B. Bracts of fls. prominent and distichous, somewhat exceeding calyx .... 3. *Æ. polystachya*
  BB. Bracts minute or none.
    C. Apex of infl. simple and long-spicate .... 4. *Æ. fulgens*
    CC. Apex of infl. composite .... 5. *Æ. miniata*

1. **Æ. recurvata,** L. B. Smith (*Macrochordium recurvatum*, Klotzsch). Lvs. 9–12, very hard in texture, lorate, falcately incurved, to 15 in. long and 1¾ in. broad, dull green above, gray-green beneath with faint broad bands of darker green, apex deltoid-cuspidate, margins closely and finely spinose: infl. 9–12 in. high, bearing 30–50 fls. in a dense capitate thyrsoid panicle; fls. subtended by rose-red lanceolate-acuminate entire bracts, about ½in. long; petals connivent, light blue, about twice as long as the dry rose-tipped greenish sepals; stamens shorter than corolla. Brazil.—Some material grown as *Æ. Ortgiesii* belongs here; Baker's species has narrowly linear lvs. to ¾in. broad and red fls. and straw-colored bracts.

2. **Æ. Mariæ-Reginæ,** Wendl. Strong plant with many strap-shaped prickly margined lvs. 2–3 ft. long and 2–3 in. broad, plain green, scurfy: infl. a dense spike 1 ft. long, with minute red bracts, the stiff scape or peduncle 1 ft. high; sepals and ovary ½in. long, mucronate; petals exceeding sepals, violet at tip, the spike brilliant with long reflexed crimson bract-lvs. (Flor de Santa Maria, the "flower of St. Mary.") Costa Rica.

3. **Æ. polystachya,** Mez (*Æ. brasiliensis*, Regel. *Æ. Glaziovii*, Baker. *Tillandsia polystachya*, Vell. not L.). Lvs. several to many, linear-lanceolate above expanded base,

1½–2 ft. long, 1–1½ in. broad, spinulose on margins, spine-pointed at apex: fls. many in flattened spikes in an erect panicle, the showy distichous fl.-bracts nearly orbicular and many-veined; fls. violet, the petals exceeding the sepals, ligules obscurely crenate. Brazil.

4. **Æ. fulgens,** Brongn. Lvs. many, densely rosulate, dilated at base, 12–16 in. long and 2–3 in. broad, with small distant teeth: infl. equalling or exceeding lvs., branched below and simple spicate above; petals about ½in. long, red and blue-tipped, the sepals about half as long and blue-violet, ligules serrate, the fl.-bracts minute or none. Brazil. Var. **discolor,** Brongn. (*Æ. discolor*, Hook.), has lvs. brownish-red or violet-red beneath and usually faintly striped.

5. **Æ. miniata,** Baker. Lvs. with close-set teeth: infl. much exceeding lvs., many-fld., branched throughout and red; petals blue, ovary red, ligules crenate-dentate, bracts minute or none. Brazil. Var. **discolor,** Baker, has lvs. suffused purple or violet-brown on back.—Likely to be cult. as *Æ. fulgens*.

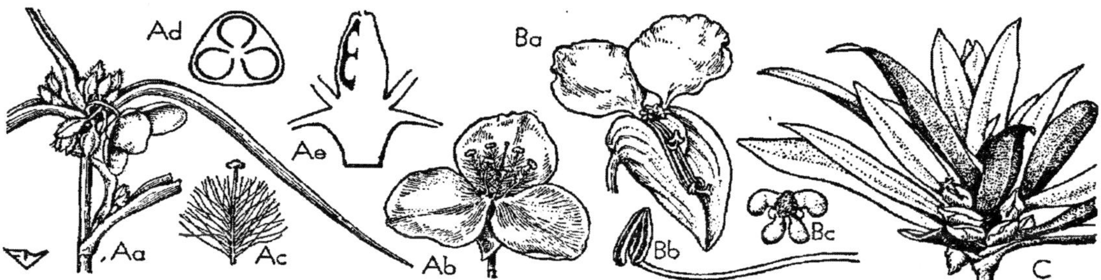

Fig. 31. COMMELINACEÆ. A, *Tradescantia virginiana:* Aa, inflorescence, × ¼; Ab, flower, × ½; Ac, stamen, × 1; Ad, ovary, cross-section, × 5; Ae, ovary, vertical section, × 3. B, *Commelina cœlestis:* Ba, flower, × 1; Bb, fertile stamen, × 4; Bc, staminodium, × 4. C, *Rhœo discolor:* flowering plant, × ⅛.

31. COMMELINACEÆ. SPIDERWORT FAMILY

Ann. or per. herbs, of 34 genera and about 500 species, widely distributed in trop. and subtrop. regions.—Sts. knotty and leafy: lvs. alternate, entire, ovate-lanceolate or linear, vaginate or amplexicaul: fls. bisexual, usually almost regular; sepals 3 or parts slightly connate, green; petals 3, free or united into a tube, alternating with sepals, colored, withering; stamens usually 6, in 2 whorls, sometimes 3, often some reduced to staminodia, filaments often hairy; style 1, stigma simple or obscurely 2–3-lobed; ovary superior, 2–3-celled, with few or many ovules: fr. a caps.

A. Fertile stamens 2–3, sterile 0–4 .... 1. COMMELINA
AA. Fertile stamens 6, rarely 5.
 B. Petals grown into tube .... 2. ZEBRINA
 BB. Petals free or nearly so.
  C. Sts. erect.
   D. Infl. largely terminal.
    E. Ovules 3 or more in each cell of ovary: infl. racemose-paniculate .... 3. DICHORISANDRA
    EE. Ovules 2 in each cell of ovary: infl. umbellate .... 4. TRADESCANTIA
   DD. Infl. axillary .... 5. RHŒO
  CC. Sts. prostrate .... 4. TRADESCANTIA

1. COMMELINA, L. DAY-FLOWER. About 180 species, two grown out-of-doors or in pots; some of the native species may also be intro. as ground-cover.—Peduncles solitary or clustered, subtended below by a large foliaceous spathe-like bract; fls. irregular; sepals 3, colored, sometimes connate, persistent; petals 3, free, the 2 inner ones often long-clawed, blue or yellow, rarely white, withering; stamens 6, only 3 being fertile, filaments glabrous; ovary sessile, 2–3-celled, dorsal cell 1-ovuled, ventral cells 1–2-ovuled: fr. usually a 3-celled caps. (Commeli-na: after Kaspar (1667–1731) and Johann (1629–1698) Commelin, Dutch botanists.)

A. Plant erect .... 1. *C. cœlestis*
AA. Plant diffuse, branching .... 2. *C. tuberosa*

1. **C. cœlestis,** Willd. Roots fibrous or tuberous; plant erect: lvs. oblong-lanceolate, 3–6 in. long, minutely scabrous or glabrous: spathes pubescent, round or cordate at base, wavy-margined: upper racemes 4–10-fld., lower 1–2-fld., hairy; 2 inner sepals slightly connate; petals deep blue, almost ½in. long. Mex. Var. **alba,** Hort., fls. white. Var. **variegata,** Hort., fls. blue and white.

2. **C. tuberosa,** L. Roots tuberous; plant diffuse and branching: lvs. narrow-lanceo-

late, margins often hairy: spathes hairy or almost glabrous, cordate-ovate and lanceolate: racemes 6–10-fld.; 2 inner sepals slightly connate; petals blue, ¼–⅜in. long. Mex.

2. **ZEBRINA,** Schnizl. Three to 4 species in Mex., New Mex., and Tex.—Decumbent or pendulous herbs, sparingly hairy: lvs. ovate or oblong, base vaginate: fls. clustered, almost sessile, between 2 conduplicate bracts; sepals and petals united into a tube, the limb ovate or lanceolate, blue-purple; stamens 6, equal, inserted at throat of tubular corolla; ovary 3-celled with 2 ovules in each cell. (Zebri-na: referring to the striped lvs.)

Z. pendula, Schnizl. (*Tradescantia zebrina*, Hort. *T. tricolor*, Hort., in part. *Commelina zebrina*, Hort.). WANDERING JEW (in part). Decumbent, branched: lvs. ovate-oblong, 1–3 in. long, acute to acuminate or somewhat obtuse, pubescent or glabrous beneath, striped white and green above, purple below; sheaths hairy at top and bottom: infl. between 2 sessile lvs., one much smaller than other; calyx-tube whitish; corolla-tube white, segms. red-purple, ⅓in. long; style filiform, stigma capitate, 3-lobed. Mex. Var. **quadricolor,** Bailey (forma *quadricolor*, Voss. *Tradescantia quadricolor* and *T. multicolor*, Hort.), has lvs. with metallic-green undertone, striped with green, red, and white.

3. **DICHORISANDRA,** Mikan. Nearly 30 species in trop. Amer., two grown in greenhouses or out-of-doors in the S.—Per. with erect or partially scandent sts.: lvs. sheathing at nodes: infl. racemose-paniculate, racemes solitary; pedicels subtended by bract; sepals 3, free, unequal, green or colored, persistent; petals 3, free, with short claws, blue or purple; stamens 6 or 5, equal, filaments short, naked; ovary sessile, 3-celled with 4–5, rarely 2–3, ovules in each cell: fr. an ovate 3-angled caps. (Dichorisan-dra: Greek, referring either to the 2 series of stamens or the 2-valved anthers.)

A. Lvs. not variegated........1. *D. thyrsiflora*
AA. Lvs. variegated........2. *D. mosaica*

1. **D. thyrsiflora,** Mikan. From 3–4 ft. high: lvs. 6–12 in. long, lanceolate, narrowed into distinct petiole, glabrous, shining green; sheaths glabrous or minutely pubescent: fls. in dense racemes shorter than lvs., dark or light blue to dark purple; sepals glabrous, about ⅜in. long; anthers bright yellow. Brazil.

2. **D. mosaica,** Lind. Lvs. 6–8 in. long, broadly elliptic, rounded at base, sessile, glabrous, striped longitudinally above and along transverse veins with green and white: racemes short, densely thyrsoid; sepals corolla-like, white; petals blue. Peru. Var. **gigantea,** Hort., is a large-fld. form. Var. **undata,** W. Miller (*D. undata*, Koch & Lind.), has foliage without mosaic, the variegation being only longitudinal.

4. **TRADESCANTIA,** L. SPIDERWORT. More than 30 species, one a common greenhouse and basket plant and another, *T. virginiana*, a hardy border subject.—Lvs. various: peduncles solitary, fascicled, or rarely paniculate; fls. in umbels, rarely solitary; umbels sessile or pedunculate; sepals 3, free, green or colored, persistent; petals 3, free, somewhat orbicular, blue, red-purple, or white; stamens 6, free, hypogynous, all fertile, filaments naked or hairy; ovary sessile, 3-celled with 2 ovules in each cell. (Tradescant-ia: for John Tradescant, gardener to Charles I, who died about 1638.)

A. Plant prostrate........1. *T. fluminensis*
AA. Plant erect.
B. Sepals glabrous to villous but not glandular........2. *T. virginiana*
BB. Sepals with some hairs gland-tipped........3. *T. bracteata*

1. **T. fluminensis,** Vell. (*T. tricolor*, Hort., in part). WANDERING JEW (in part). Sts. prostrate, rooting at nodes: lvs. oblong or ovate-oblong, 1–3 in. long, acute, glabrous; sheaths hairy at top: umbels many-fld., subtended by 2 broad-lanceolate bracts much exceeding the pedicels; petals white, ¼in. long; filaments hairy. Brazil, Uruguay, Paraguay.—Common under benches in greenhouses.

2. **T. virginiana,** L. (*T. brevicaulis*, Raf.). COMMON SPIDERWORT. Erect, glabrous or slightly hairy, 1–3 ft. high: lvs. linear, to 15 in. long: umbels terminal, many-fld., subtended by linear-lanceolate bracts, 2–8 in. long; pedicels and sepals often villous; petals violet-purple, ½–1 in. long; filaments hairy. N. Y. to S. D., Va. and Ark., and escaped farther north.—Various forms are in the trade: white (var. **alba,** Hort.); red (vars. **coccinea, rosea, rubra,** Hort.); blue (var. **cærulea,** Hort.); double-fld. (var. **major,** Hort.). Many are of hybrid origin, an improved form being J. C. Wegelin.

3. **T. bracteata,** Small. Erect, glabrous or minutely puberulent above, ½–1½ ft.

high: lvs. linear-lanceolate, 6–12 in. long: umbels few- to many-fld., terminal, subtended by foliaceous bracts 4–12 in. long; pedicels and sepals with gland-tipped and non-glandular hairs; petals usually rose, sometimes blue, ¾in. long; filaments hairy. Minn. and Wis. to Kans. and Mo.

5. **RHŒO,** Hance. One species from Mex. and W. Indies, cult. in greenhouses.—Lvs. densely imbricated, narrow-lanceolate, base vaginate: peduncles axillary, sometimes divided; fls. many in a dense umbel, inclosed by 2 boat-shaped bracts; sepals 3, ovate-lanceolate, withering; petals 3, ovate, withering; stamens 6, hypogynous, fertile, filaments hairy; ovary sessile, 3-celled with 1 ovule in each cell. (Rhœ-o: name obscure.)

R. discolor, Hance (*Tradescantia discolor*, L'Her.). Short-stemmed low herb: lvs. purplish underneath, 6–12 in. long, 1–3 in. wide: fls. white, about ¼in. long. Var. **vittata,** Hook. (*Tradescantia variegata*, Hort.), is the common form in cult., with lvs. purple beneath and above striped longitudinally with pale yellow.

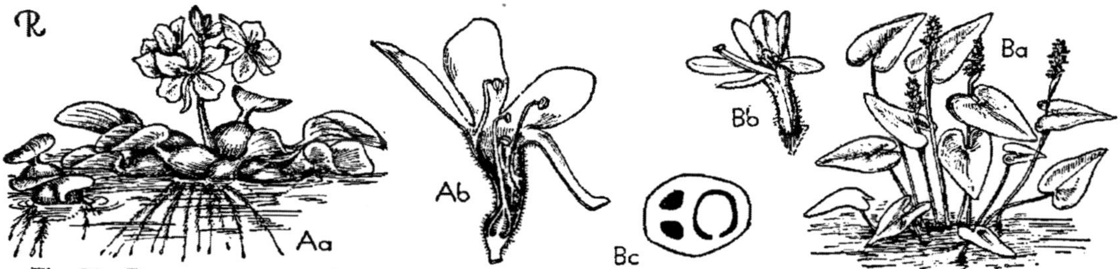

Fig. 32. Pontederiaceæ. A, *Eichhornia crassipes:* Aa, plant in flower, × 1/12; Ab, flower, vertical section, × ½. B, *Pontederia cordata:* Ba, plant in flower, × 1/15; Bb, flower, × 1; Bc, ovary, cross-section, × 10.

32. PONTEDERIACEÆ. PICKEREL-WEED FAMILY

Aquatic herbs, erect or floating, of 6 genera and about 20 species in the swamps of the warmer parts of the earth, except Eu., one common in ponds and tanks.—Lvs. fluitant and long-petioled or blade floating or sometimes emersed, variously dilated or rarely narrow, those on flowering branches short-petioled, sometimes submerged lvs. reduced to form of petioles: infl. usually spike-like, without bracts; fls. bisexual, more or less irregular; perianth of 6 parts, in 2 series, free from ovary, persistent; stamens 3 or 6, on tube or base of perianth; ovary superior, 3-celled with axillary placentæ or 1-celled with 3 parietal placentæ, style 1, stigma entire or 3-parted: fr. a caps. or achene.

A. Fls. 1½–2 in. long: plants floating........1. Eichhornia
AA. Fls. ⅓in. long: plants not floating........2. Pontederia

1. **EICHHORNIA,** Kunth (*Piaropus*, Raf.). About 6 species in S. Amer., one reaching trop. Afr.—Plant floating, rooting at nodes: floating or emersed lvs. obovate, cordate or rarely lanceolate: fls. spicate or rarely paniculate; perianth funnel-shaped with long or short tube; stamens 6, unequally inserted on tube, some of them exserted; ovary sessile, 3-celled, with numerous ovules; style filiform. (Eichhor-nia: J. A. F. Eichhorn, 1779–1856, Prussian statesman.)

A. Petioles inflated........1. *E. crassipes*
AA. Petioles not inflated........2. *E. azurea*

1. **E. crassipes,** Solms. Water-Hyacinth. Floating or rooting in mud: lvs. erect, ½–5 in. broad, ovate to orbicular, glabrous, slightly scarious above; petioles much inflated at base: scape simple, with conspicuous sheath near middle; spikes many-fld.; perianth about 2 in. long, 6-lobed, violet, upper lobe larger with patch of blue having yellow spot in center. Trop. and subtrop. Amer.; nat. in Fla. where it obstructs navigation by choking the rivers and streams. Var. **major,** Hort., has rosy-lilac fls.

2. **E. azurea,** Kunth. Lvs. variable in size and shape, usually very broad-ovate to orbicular, glabrous; petioles not inflated: scapes gradually dilated into a hooded spathe; fls. scattered or crowded in pairs along a hairy rachis, lavender-blue with rich purple center; inner segms. toothed. Brazil.

2. **PONTEDERIA, L.** Three species in the New World.—Stout aquatic or bog plants, with thick creeping rootstocks producing erect long-petioled lvs. and a 1-lvd. st. bearing a spike of ephemeral blue fls.: spike subtended by thin spathe; perianth funnelform, 2-lipped, the 3 upper divisions united to form the 3-lobed upper lip, the 3 lower spreading and more separate; stamens 6, unequally inserted; ovary 3-celled, 2 cells empty, the third 1-ovuled: fr. a 1-seeded utricle. (Pontederia: in honor of G. Pontedera, 1688–1757, Italian botanist.)

P. cordata, L. Pickerel-Weed. St. 1–4 ft. tall: **lvs.** ovate with cordate base, 4–10 in. long, obtuse: perianth ⅓in. long, bright blue, the middle lobe of upper lip with 2 basal yellow spots. N. S. to Minn., Fla. and Tex.

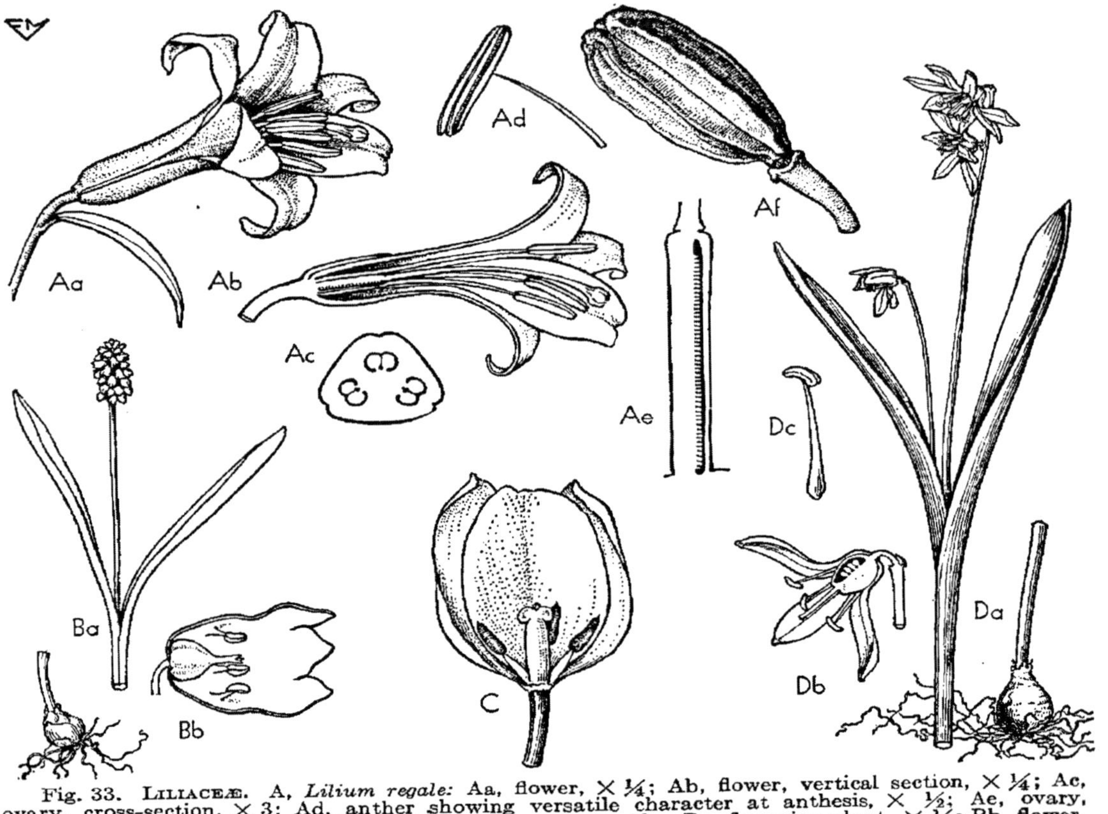

Fig. 33. Liliaceæ. A, *Lilium regale:* Aa, flower, × ¼; Ab, flower, vertical section, × ¼; Ac, ovary, cross-section, × 3; Ad, anther showing versatile character at anthesis, × ½; Ae, ovary, vertical section, × 1; Af, capsule, × ½. B, *Muscari botryoides:* Ba, flowering plant, × ¼; Bb, flower, perianth in vertical section, × 3. C, *Tulipa Gesneriana:* flower, some perianth-segments and 3 stamens removed. D, *Scilla bifolia:* Da, flowering plant, × ½; Db, flower, vertical section, × 1; Dc, stamen, × 2

33. **LILIACEÆ.** LILY FAMILY

A large family of wide distribution over the earth, most abundant in temp. and subtrop. regions, comprising some of the choicest ornamental plants. Species perhaps 2,000 in more than 175 genera, per. (rarely ann.), dying down after flowering to a bulb, bulb-like organ, or to a crown of fleshy rootstocks; certain species climbing; a number yield medicine, and some have poisonous properties. A large part of the florists' "bulbs" are of this family.—Fls. mostly showy and with colored parts, sometimes small and greenish but then usually many in racemes, spikes or panicles, the perianth typically of 6 distinct parts or gamophyllous and 6-lobed, rarely 4-merous or 3-merous, commonly all the parts petal-like; ovary single and usually distinctly superior, mostly 3-celled, with axile placentation, maturing into a dehiscent caps. or a berry, mostly many-seeded; stamens chiefly 6 but sometimes 3, 1 before each part or lobe of the perianth, hypogynous or sometimes attached on the perianth, the anthers 2-celled: fls. not in spathe; perianth-segms. sometimes differentiated to represent calyx and corolla. The prevailing corolla-like 6-merous hypogynous fls. (superior ovary) are characteristic of the Liliaceæ, although in Aletris and Ophiopogon the ovary is wholly or partly inferior.

A. Plant not bulbous, producing a rootstock or thickened often tuberous more or less branching underground parts.
B. Lvs. conspicuously fleshy, often prickly: plant a succulent.
C. Fls. white with green or rosy stripes, less than 1 in. long....17. HAWORTHIA
CC. Fls. red and yellow or purple, 1 in. or more long.
D. Perianth-tube cylindrical or bell-shaped, straight....16. ALOE
DD. Perianth-tube basally enlarged, somewhat curved above....18. GASTERIA
BB. Lvs. not fleshy nor prickly: plant not a succulent.
C. Sts. not equally leafy at time of flowering, lvs. all basal or the basal ones much larger than the cauline.
D. Fls. without subtending bracts, although the st. may have bracts lower down.
E. Infl. racemose; fls. ⅛–¼in. long.
F. Color of fls. rose-lilac; fls. perfect.... 1. HELONIAS
FF. Color of fls. white; fls. imperfect.... 2. CHAMÆLIRIUM
EE. Infl. umbellate or fls. solitary; fls. mostly ½–6 in. long.
F. Perianth-segms. distinct.
G. With slender rootstocks: fr. a berry....26. CLINTONIA
GG. With tunicated corms: fr. a caps....35. ERYTHRONIUM
FF. Perianth-segms. united forming long basal tube....50. COLCHICUM
DD. Fls. with subtending bracts.
E. Anthers extrorse (splitting on the side facing outward): lvs. 2–2½ ft. long, linear, dry.... 3. XEROPHYLLUM
EE. Anthers introrse (splitting on the surface facing inward) or opening to the side.
F. Lower part of perianth adnate to ovary.
G. Foliage much shorter than scape: fr. a caps.... 4. ALETRIS
GG. Foliage equalling or exceeding scape: fr. berry-like....11. OPHIOPOGON
FF. Lower part of perianth free from ovary.
G. Perianth-segms. not much united at base.
H. Foliage much shorter than scape.
I. Fl. bell-shaped or funnelform.
J. Anthers erect (although dorsifixed); filaments very slender.... 5. EREMURUS
JJ. Anthers versatile; filaments basally dilated.... 8. ASPHODELINE
II. Fl. rotate.
J. Lf. narrowly linear, to ¼in. wide: caps. not sharply angled.... 6. ANTHERICUM
JJ. Lf. ⅜–⅝in. wide: caps. sharply angled.... 7. CHLOROPHYTUM
HH. Foliage about as long as or exceeding scape.
I. Fl. 1½–2 in. long.... 9. PARADISEA
II. Fl. scarcely ¼in. long....10. LIRIOPE
GG. Perianth-segms. definitely united at least in lower part.
H. Tube of perianth cylindrical, not much expanded above.
I. Fl. red and yellow....12. KNIPHOFIA
II. Fl. white....15. LEUCOCRINUM
HH. Tube of perianth widely expanded above.
I. Lf. not narrowed into a petiole-like base: fls. large and lily-like....14. HEMEROCALLIS
II. Lf. narrowed into petiole-like base.
J. Fl. 1½–5 in. long, blue or white, on stout bracted scape...13. HOSTA
JJ. Fl. smaller.
K. Length of lvs. 4–8 in.: fls. small, white, cup-shaped, in racemes....19. CONVALLARIA
KK. Length of lvs. 1–2½ ft.
L. The fls. solitary at surface of ground, 4-merous....20. ASPIDISTRA
LL. The fls. in thick short spikes, 3-merous....21. ROHDEA
CC. Sts. almost equally leafy throughout at flowering time, lower lvs. not conspicuously larger than others.
D. Green foliage represented by lf.-like branches either expanded and lf.-like or needle-like (cladodes), borne in axils of small dry scales (true lvs.).
E. Fls. from axils of the little scales; anthers 6....33. ASPARAGUS
EE. Fls. borne on midrib of expanded cladode (or "leaf"); anthers 3....34. RUSCUS
DD. Green foliage of the ordinary kind, of true lvs. not borne in axils of scales.
E. Species diœcious, the fls. in umbels: fr. a berry....53. SMILAX
EE. Species monœcious or with perfect fls.
F. Cauline lvs. whorled.
G. St.-lvs. in 1 involucre-like whorl of 3....51. TRILLIUM
GG. St.-lvs. in 2 whorls of 5–9 and 3–5....52. MEDEOLA
FF. Cauline lvs. not whorled.

G. Style 1, entire or obscurely lobed at summit: fr. a berry.
  H. Perianth-segms. united into a cylindrical tube, the lobes short .... 23. POLYGONATUM
  HH. Perianth-segms. distinct.
    I. Fls. 4-parted .... 24. MAIANTHEMUM
    II. Fls. 6-parted.
      J. Arrangement of fls. in 1's or 2's in the lf.-axils .... 22. STREPTOPUS
      JJ. Arrangement of fls. racemose or paniculate .... 25. SMILACINA
GG. Styles 3, distinct or united to about the middle.
  H. Fls. 2–3 in. long: plant often climbing .... 28. GLORIOSA
  HH. Fls. smaller: plant not climbing.
    I. The styles united to near the middle .... 27. UVULARIA
    II. The styles distinct.
      J. Perianth-segms. about 1 in. long; fls. few to several in the lf.-axils .... 29. TRICYRTIS
      JJ. Perianth-segms. about ⅓in. long; fls. in large terminal panicles .... 32. VERATRUM

AA. Plant bulbous, producing 1 or more scaly bulbs underground at base of st.
  B. St. climbing, leafless; st. and infl. much-branched .... 49. BOWIEA
  BB. St. not climbing, plants with lvs.
    C. Species with leafy sts. often branched toward the top.
      D. Styles 2–3, distinct to base.
        E. Perianth-segms. lacking basal glands .... 30. STENANTHIUM
        EE. Perianth-segms. with basal glands .... 31. ZIGADENUS
      DD. Style 1, more or less lobed at top.
        E. Anthers attached to filament at middle of the back, versatile.
          F. Perianth-segms. separate .... 39. LILIUM
          FF. Perianth-segms. united into basal tube .... 48. GALTONIA
        EE. Anthers attached at base, erect.
          F. Outer perianth-segms. essentially like the inner ones, not sepal-like.
            G. Fls. nodding or pendulous; perianth-segms. with nectariferous pits or grooves.
              H. Number of lvs. 2 or few: plants from tunicated corms .... 35. ERYTHRONIUM
              HH. Number of lvs. several to many: plants from scaly bulbs, the scales sometimes appearing as bulblets .... 36. FRITILLARIA
            GG. Fls. erect; perianth-segms. without nectariferous pits or grooves .. 37. TULIPA
          FF. Outer perianth-segms. smaller and sepal-like .... 38. CALOCHORTUS
    CC. Species with scapes rather than leafy sts.
      D. Scapes very short, not appearing above the ground .... 50. COLCHICUM
      DD. Scapes evident, usually prominent above ground.
        E. Perianth-segms. distinct or essentially so.
          F. Anthers basifixed.
            G. Fls. nodding or pendulous; perianth-segms. with nectariferous grooves .... 35. ERYTHRONIUM
            GG. Fls. erect; perianth-segms. without nectariferous grooves .... 37. TULIPA
          FF. Anthers dorsifixed.
            G. Filaments flattened; perianth-segms. not prominently nerved .... 42. ORNITHOGALUM
            GG. Filaments filiform (sometimes flattened at base).
              H. Fls. blue or purple to white.
                I. Nerves of perianth-segms. 1 .... 40. SCILLA
                II. Nerves of segms. 3 to many .... 41. CAMASSIA
              HH. Fls. red or yellow .... 43. LACHENALIA
        EE. Perianth-segms. plainly united at lower portion.
          F. Fls. 1–1½ in. long.
            G. Length of lvs. not over 1 ft.: fls. with yellow and red.
              H. Ovules many to a locule; fls. 3–12 or more in lax racemes ...... 43. LACHENALIA
              HH. Ovules 2–3 to a locule; fls. many, in dense racemes .... 45. VELTHEIMIA
            GG. Length of lvs. 2–3 ft.: fls. white .... 48. GALTONIA
          FF. Fls. ⅛–1 in. long (or more in Hyacinthus).
            G. Perianth urn-shaped or cylindrical, not expanded at throat, lobes very short .... 47. MUSCARI
            GG. Perianth funnelform to bell-shaped, open at top.
              H. Tube of perianth much shorter than lobes; perianth open-campanulate or rotate, not swollen at base .... 44. CHIONODOXA
              HH. Tube of perianth almost equal to or longer than lobes; perianth funnelform to campanulate, swollen at base .... 46. HYACINTHUS

1. HELONIAS, L. SWAMP-PINK. One species of E. U. S.—A glabrous per. bog herb with stout rootstock and fibrous roots: scape erect, hollow, bracted below the fls.: lvs. basal, persistent: fls. perfect, rose-lilac, racemose; segms. 6, spreading, spatulate, persistent; stamens 6, hypogynous, with filiform filaments, exserted; styles 3, stigmatic along the inner side, deciduous: caps. 3-lobed, obovoid, with many linear seeds which are white-appendaged at both ends. (Helo-nias: Greek name referring to swamps.)

H. bullata, L. Sts. 1–2 ft. high, stout, with lanceolate bracts: lvs. several to many, thin, oblanceolate, 6–15 in. long, ½–2 in. wide, acute: raceme dense, cylindrical, 1–3 in. long in fl., longer in fr.; pedicels spreading, ⅛–¼in. long; segms. ¼in. long. S. N. Y. to Va.

2. **CHAMÆLIRIUM,** Willd. Fairywand. Blazing-Star. Monotypic genus of E. N. Amer.—A glabrous diœcious herb with tuberous rootstock; sts. erect, with lanceolate lvs.; basal lvs. spatulate to elliptical: fls. small, white, in a long spike-like bractless raceme; segms. 6, linear-spatulate, 1-nerved; staminate fls. with 6 stamens, the filaments filiform; pistillate fls. with 3-celled oblong ovary, 3 short styles and usually 6 staminodia: caps. oblong, slightly 3-lobed; seeds 6–12 in each locule, broadly winged at each end. (Chamælir-ium: Greek *ground* or *low lily.*)

C. luteum, Willd. (*Veratrum luteum,* L.). Staminate plant 1½–2 ft. tall, pistillate to 4 ft.: basal lvs. obtuse, 2–8 in. long, petioled; cauline lvs. lanceolate to linear, acutish, sessile or nearly so, 1–4 in. long: staminate raceme 3–9 in. long, slender, more or less nodding, the pistillate erect; pedicels to ⅛in.; segms. to about ⅛in. long. Ont. and Mich. to Fla. and Ark.

3. **XEROPHYLLUM,** Michx. Turkey-Beard. American genus of 2 or 3 species.—Tall per. herbs with short woody rootstocks; sts. stout, simple, leafy: lvs. linear, dry, rough-margined, many, somewhat reduced up the st.: fls. many, white, in a dense terminal raceme; segms. persistent, oblong or ovate, 5–7-nerved, spreading; stamens 6, filaments subulate; styles 3: caps. ovoid, 3-grooved; seeds 5, oblong, scarcely appendaged. (Xerophyl-lum: Greek, referring to the xerophytic lvs.)

X. tenax, Nutt. (*Helonias tenax,* Pursh). Sts. 1–5 ft. high: basal lvs. 20–30 in. long, ⅛–¼in. wide, pale green: raceme becoming 1–2 ft. long, the lower bracts leafy; pedicels to ¼in.; segms ⅓in. long; stamens longer. B. C. to Wyo. and Calif.

4. **ALETRIS,** L. Star-Grass. Colic-Root. Several species of E. N. Amer. and E. Asia.—Per. scapose herbs with fibrous roots: lvs. basal, spreading, lanceolate: fls. small, white or yellow, bracted, perfect, roughened without, in a terminal spike-like raceme; perianth oblong or campanulate, 6-lobed, the lower part adnate to the ovary; stamens 6, inserted at the bases of the lobes, included, filaments short; style 3-cleft above, stigmas minutely 2-lobed: caps. ovoid, inclosed by the persistent perianth; seeds many, oblong, ribbed. (Al-etris: Greek, a female slave who grinds corn, referring to the rough mealy fls.)

A. farinosa, L. Sts. 1½–3 ft. tall: basal lvs. pale yellowish-green, 2–6 in. long, ¼–1 in wide: raceme 4–12 in. long, bracts linear, acute; pedicels very short; perianth tubular-oblong, white or with yellowish lobes, ¼–⅓in. long. Me. to Ont., Minn., Fla., La.

5. **EREMURUS,** Bieb. Desert-Candle. Some 25 perennials in Asia, known by their towering racemose spikes of white, rose-colored or yellow bloom; a few species sometimes grown as border and specimen plants.—Root of strong parts and fleshy fibers: lvs. radical in a tuft or rosette, long and narrow, much shorter than the high naked scape: fls. bell-shaped or broader, the segms. distinct or lightly connate at base, 1- to several-nerved; stamens 6, hypogynous, often exceeding the segms., filaments very slender, anthers dorsifixed; ovary sessile, 3-celled, style slender: caps. loculicidal, few- to many-seeded. (Eremu-rus: Greek, probably referring to the solitary spike.)

A. Fls. pink to salmon.
  B. Scape 2–4 ft.: fls. pink with brown keels.......... 1. *E. robustus*
  BB. Scape 6 ft.: fls. salmon-pink within, purplish without.......... 2. *E. Warei*
AA. Fls. white to yellow or orange.
  B. Color of fls. white or creamy; anthers yellow.
    C. Fl. 1½ in. across: lvs. apically tomentose.......... 1. *E. robustus*
    CC. Fl. 1 in. across: lf.-margins lightly ciliate.......... 3. *E. himalaicus*
  BB. Color of fls. bright yellow to orange; anthers reddish.......... 4. *E. stenophyllus* var. *Bungei*

1. **E. robustus,** Regel. Lvs. in dense basal rosette, strap-shaped, 2 ft. or so long, 1–2 in. broad, glabrous, with narrow cartilaginous border: scape 2–4 ft. and more, strict, unbranched; raceme 2–3 ft. long and 4–5 in. through, erect, with spreading jointed pedicels longer than the fls. and subtended by much shorter narrow-linear dry bracts; fls. about 1½ in. across when open, bright pink with brown keels on the oblong segms. which are about the length of the stamens; anthers yellow. Cent. Asia. Var. **Elwesii,** Leicht. (*E. Elwesii,* Mich. *E. Elwesianus,* Hort.), lvs. to 3½ ft., light green, apically tomentose; for H. J. Elwes, page 42; habitat unknown; a white-fld. form is offered as *E. Elwesianus* var. *albus.*

2. **E. Warei,** Reuthe. Lvs. linear, glaucous: scape 6 ft. high; raceme 2 ft.; fls. salmon-pink within, purplish without. (Named for Messrs. Ware of Feltham, England.) A natural hybrid, probably between no. 4 and *E. Olgæ*, Regel.

3. **E. himalaicus,** Baker. Lvs. several, broadly ligulate, bright green, 12–18 in. long, ½–2¼ in. wide, lightly ciliate on margins: scape 3 or more ft. high; bracts linear, ⅛in. long; raceme to 2 ft. long, 4 in. through; pedicels about 1 in. long; fls. white with brown keels, about 1 in. across, segms. oblong, equalling the stamens; anthers yellow. Himalayas.

4. **E. stenophyllus** var. **Bungei,** O. Fedtsch. (*Eremurus Bungei*, Baker). Lvs. erect, linear, glabrous, minutely ciliate on margins, 1 ft. long, ¼–½in. wide: scape 2 ft. or more high; bracts subulate; raceme dense, 4–6 in. long, 2 in. through; pedicels ascending-arcuate, to 1 in. long; fls. bright yellow to orange, scarcely 1 in. across; segms. oblong, much shorter than filaments; anthers golden-red. S. W. Asia.—Differs from *E. stenophyllus*, Baker, in its wider lvs. and saucer-shaped rather than campanulate fls. A hybrid with *E. himalaicus* is **E. Tubergenii,** Hort., with yellow fls. on scapes 8–10 ft. high.

6. **ANTHERICUM,** L. About 50 species as the genus is now usually limited, but with about twice that number if related groups are included; mostly in Afr., but 1 in Eu. and a few in Amer.: planted in borders and vases.—Rhizome short or none, the roots more or less fleshy or tuberous: lvs. radical, linear, mostly shorter than the slender leafless scapes: fls. rather small, white, slender-pedicelled, in a terminal usually open raceme; perianth rotate, the segms. distinct and 3–5-nerved; stamens 6, hypogynous or essentially so, filaments slender, anthers dorsifixed; ovary sessile, 3-celled, mostly many-ovuled, style filiform: caps. loculicidal, 3-celled but not sharply angled; seeds 3-angled. (Anther-icum: Greek *flower hedge.*)

A. Infl. simple: caps. pointed .... 1. *A. Liliago*
AA. Infl. branched: caps. rounded .... 2. *A. ramosum*

1. **A. Liliago,** L. St.-Bernard-Lily. Lvs. many, narrow-linear, 6–12 in. long, ⅛–¼in. wide, shorter than the slender naked glaucous scapes: fls. several to many in a loose raceme, white, ½–¾in. long and 1½ in. across, erect or spreading, on short pedicels subtended by lanceolate long-pointed bracts; segms. oblong, 3-nerved on back; ovary green. (Liliago: ante-Linnæan substantive name.) Eu.

2. **A. ramosum,** L. Lvs. narrow-linear, 8–12 in. long, ¼in. wide: st. about 2 ft. high, bright green, branched, with lax few-fld. racemes; pedicels filiform, up to 1 in. long; fls. about 1 in. across; segms. lanceolate, obtuse, ½in. long, 3-nerved; ovary yellow. Eu.

7. **CHLOROPHYTUM,** Ker. More than 50 species in the tropics of both hemispheres, grown mostly for foliage, but the fls. more or less ornamental; useful in vases.—Differs from Anthericum in bearing an acutely 3-angled caps., seeds flattened or disk-like, filaments often flattened upward, lvs. mostly broader and often petioled. (Chloroph-ytum: Greek *green plant.*)

C. capense, Kuntze (*Asphodelus capensis*, L. *C. elatum*, R. Br. *Anthericum elatum*, Ait.). Rhizome horizontal or oblique, with many thick roots: lvs. many, radical, relatively short and broad (12 in. or less long, ⅜–⅝in. broad but becoming longer and broader), long-pointed, narrowed into petiole-like base: scape exceeding the foliage, sometimes transformed into stolons and often bearing leafy clusters or offsets; fls. whitish, in a long open raceme, ¾in. across, rotate with narrow separate segms. S. Afr.—Known in cult. mostly in the striped-lvd. forms, sometimes under such names as *Anthericum vittatum* and *A. picturatum.*

8. **ASPHODELINE,** Reichb. Jacobs-Rod. About 18 species in the Medit. region.—Rhizome with fascicled often fleshy roots: st. erect, mostly simple, forming a leafy scape: fls. often yellow and 3 stamens sometimes abortive. (Asphodeli-ne: one of the asphodels.)

A. lutea, Reichb. (*Asphodelus luteus*, L.). Asphodel. Radical lvs. many, very narrow, channelled: scape 2–4 ft., erect, with many linear very long-pointed lvs., bearing a dense prominently bracted raceme 1–1½ ft. long; fls. yellow, fragrant, 1 in. long, with very long narrow wide-spreading segms. Medit.—This is the asphodel of the ancients.

9. **PARADISEA,** Mazz. One per. herb in Cent. and S. W. Eu., sometimes planted for its showy white fls.—Rhizome very short, the roots fascicled and fleshy: lvs. radical, narrow, about the length of the leafless but long-bracted scapes: fls. funnel-shaped, the 6 segms. distinct and narrow at base, 3-nerved; stamens 6, hypogynous,

nearly equalling perianth, anthers versatile; ovary sessile, 3-celled, style slender and equalling the perianth, lightly 3-lobed: caps. many-seeded, loculicidal. (Paradisea: Greek *paradise*, a garden or garden of the future world.)

P. Liliastrum, Bert. (*Anthericum Liliastrum,* L.). ST.-BRUNO-LILY. Scapes 1–2 ft., slender: lvs. linear: fls. few to several in an open raceme, 1½–2 in. long, tapering from top to base, the segms. not spreading or reflexed, bracts usually exceeding the pedicels. (Liliastrum: lily-like.) Eu. Var. **major,** Hort., is taller and with larger fls.

10. **LIRIOPE,** Lour. LILY-TURF. Small grass-lvd. tufted or matted herbs used largely as pot-plants; 3 or 4 species in E. Asia.—Rhizome short and thick, plant often stoloniferous: fls. small, whitish, blue or violet, in a raceme or spike terminating the scape; pedicels subtended by scarious mostly obtuse bracts, jointed close to the tubeless perianth which is obtuse or shouldered at base; stamens 6, hypogynous, filaments about as long as blunt anthers; ovary superior, 3-celled, style stout, stigma 3-toothed: fr. a caps., usually with 1 or 2 fleshy seeds. (Liri-ope: the nymph Liriope.)

A. Lvs. to ¼ in. wide, grass-like: fls. light lilac to almost white, in open spikes.......... 1. *L. spicata*
AA. Lvs. ⅜–1 in. wide, stiffer: fls. lilac-purple, in dense spikes.......................... 2. *L. Muscari*

1. **L. spicata,** Lour. Root-system shallow, mostly horizontal with many slender jointed rootstocks just under surface and slender tuber-bearing roots: lvs. flexuose, mostly longer than scapes, these 4–12 in. long, with 5–9 whorls of 2–4 fls.; pedicels to ⅛in.; fls. ⅙–¼in. across: fr. globose, ¼in. diam. China, Japan.—Plants cult. as *L. graminifolia,* Baker, belong here, that species having longer pedicels and smaller fls.

2. **L. Muscari,** Bailey (*Ophiopogon Muscari,* Decne.). Root-system of straight upright stock or clump of stocks and matted descending roots with few tubers: lvs. stiffer, darker green, not or scarcely exceeding scapes, these 10–28 in. high, dense, mostly with 10 or more whorls of 4–7 fls.; pedicels to about ⅛in.; fls. ¼–⅓in. across: fr. globose, to ⅓in. diam. China, Japan. Var. **exiliflora,** Bailey, a slender form with lax spikes. Var. **variegata,** Bailey, lvs. yellow-striped; here belongs most material grown as *Ophiopogon Jaburan* var. *variegatus.*

11. **OPHIOPOGON,** Ker. LILY-TURF. Habit and looks of Liriope, and similarly used; species about 20, Himalayas and Japan.—Differs from Liriope in technical characters as inferior ovary, the perianth arising nearly or quite from its top; filaments very short, less than the anthers; ovules 2 in each cell of ovary. (Ophiopogon: Greek *snake's beard,* probably in allusion to the spike of fls.)—A *nomen conservandum* and therefore to be used instead of the older Mondo.

A. Plant low and grassy: lvs. ⅛in. or less broad................................ 1. *O. japonicus*
AA. Plant 1–3 ft.: lvs. ¼in. and more broad.................................... 2. *O. Jaburan*

1. **O. japonicus,** Ker (*Convallaria japonica,* Thunb. *Mondo japonicum,* Farwell). Tufted little stoloniferous per. with somewhat tuberous-thickened roots, used for sod-like edgings: lvs. many, rather rigid, ⅛in. or less broad, 6–15 in. long, more or less curved: scape less than the lvs., bearing few to several violet or bluish-tinged drooping fls. about $^3/_{16}$in. long. Japan, Korea.—There is a var. with striped lvs.

2. **O. Jaburan,** Lodd. (*Slateria Jaburan,* Sieb. *Mondo Jaburan,* Bailey). More ornamental in foliage and bloom: lvs. nearly or quite flat, ¼ to more than ½in. broad, to 3 ft. long, obtuse or abruptly pointed, many-nerved: scape nearly as long as lvs., prominently bracted, the raceme 3–6 in. long; fls. white to lilac, in clusters in the raceme, ¼ to nearly ½in. long. (Jaburan: an oriental vernacular name.) Japan.—There are vars. with striped lvs.

12. **KNIPHOFIA,** Moench (*Tritoma,* Ker). Probably 60–70 species in trop. and S. Afr., stout herbs with clumps of long radical lvs. and tall scapes of red and yellow drooping fls. in a terminal poker-like spike or dense raceme.—Plants with short stout mostly upright rootstock, and long cord-like roots; mostly acaulescent and lvs. all radical but in some species with a short caudex: fls. cylindrical or funnel-form with long tube much surpassing the small lobes, on short pedicels articulated near top; stamens 6, hypogynous, equalling or exceeding perianth, outer 3 shorter, anthers versatile; ovary sessile, 3-celled, style long, stigma very small: caps. loculicidal. (Knipho-fia: J. J. Kniphof, 1704–1765, professor at Erfurt, Germany.)—Garden forms are supposed to represent various hybrid origins.

A. Perianth 1–2 in. long; stamens scarcely or not exserted.............................. 1. *K. Uvaria*
AA. Perianth less than 1 in. long; stamens well exserted.

B. Lvs. 1–2 in. wide, 2–3 ft. long....2. *K. foliosa*
BB. Lvs. less than 1 in. wide, 1–2 ft. long.
C. Fls. ¾in. long; segms. rounded, spreading....3. *K. rufa*
CC. Fls. ½in. long; segms. acutish, erect....4. *K. Tuckii*

1. **K. Uvaria,** Hook. (*K. alooides*, Moench). POKER-PLANT. TORCH-FLOWER. Lvs. many, 2–3 ft., in radical clump, long-pointed, 1 in. or less broad: scape 1½–4 ft. high, bearing many drooping imbricated fls. in late summer and autumn in a dense spike-like raceme 6–10 in. long, upper ones normally scarlet and lower ones yellow; bracts lanceolate, acute, membranous; perianth 1–2 in. long, segms. semi-orbicular, stamens barely exserted, style protruding. (Uvaria: Latin *uva*, a bunch of grapes.) S. Afr.—Grown in several colors and sizes, under the names *K. Pfitzeri*, *K. grandiflora* and others.

2. **K. foliosa,** Hochst. (*K. Quartiniana*, A. Rich.). Lvs. densely tufted, 2–3 ft. long, 2 in. or less broad, acuminate, sharply keeled, about length of the stout scape: fls. 1 in. or less long, in elongated racemes, slender-cylindrical, on very short bracted pedicels, the short small segms. somewhat spreading, short-acute; stamens much-exserted. Trop. and S. Afr.—*K. pyramidalis* of the trade is the same or similar. Plants grown as *K. Saundersii* may be either this or *K. Uvaria*.

3. **K. rufa,** Baker. Lvs. few, linear, acuminate, acutely keeled, 12–16 in. long, ½in. wide, slightly shorter than the stout naked scape: bracts ovate-lanceolate, acute, white with brown keel, ⅓in. long; raceme 4–6 in. long; fls. pendulous, cylindrical, primrose-yellow, upper with red flush, ¾in. long; lobes small, round, spreading; stamens and style longer than perianth. S. Afr.

4. **K. Tuckii,** Baker. Lvs. densely tufted, 2 ft. long, ¾in. wide, acutely keeled: scape 30–40 in. high; bracts oblong-lanceolate, ⅓in. long; raceme dense, to 6 in. long; fls. slender-funnelform, sulfur-yellow when mature, crimson-tipped in bud, ½in. long; lobes subacute, erect; stamens slightly exserted. (Named for W. Tuck, who collected it in 1892.) S. Afr.

13. **HOSTA,** Tratt. (*Funkia*, Spreng.). PLANTAIN-LILY. Tufted plants with broad several-ribbed radical lvs. and scapes of white or blue ascending horizontal or drooping fls., commonly planted both for the ornamental clumps of foliage and the bloom; species about 40 in China and Japan.—Root-part of many strong cord-like members: scapes simple, sometimes with lf.-like bracts below the infl., longer or shorter than the lvs.: fls. with a tube, often very long, which is much expanded at the throat, the lobes 6 and nearly erect or spreading; stamens 6, hypogynous or attached to the tube, curved, mostly equalling the perianth or somewhat exserted; ovary sessile, 3-celled, style filiform, stigma small usually protruding: caps. elongated, loculicidal. (Ho-sta: commemorates N. T. Host, 1761–1834, Austrian botanist and physician.)

A. Fls. 4–5 in. long, scented, tilted upwards, white; filaments adnate to tube....1. *H. plantaginea*
AA. Fls. 1½–2½ in. long, not scented, soon declined, usually lilac or bluish; filaments free.
B. Tube of perianth abruptly widely expanding into bell-shaped part of fl. which is usually deep or purple-blue....2. *H. ventricosa*
BB. Tube of perianth expanding gradually; fls. lilac to almost white.
C. Lvs. glaucous, at least underneath, broadly ovate-cordate, not twice as long as broad.
D. Scape normally shorter than lvs....3. *H. glauca*
DD. Scape prominently exceeding lvs....4. *H. Fortunei*
CC. Lvs. not glaucous, usually not cordate.
D. Color of lf. uniform green, not striped white.
E. Blade of lf. broad, elliptic to broadly ovate....5. *H. erramena*
EE. Blade of lf. narrow, to nearly lanceolate, two or more times longer than broad....6. *H. lancifolia*
DD. Color of lf. green with prominent longitudinal lines or bands of white.
E. Tip of lf. sharp or acute, margins wavy....7. *H. undulata*
EE. Tip of lf. blunt....8. *H. decorata*

1. **H. plantaginea,** Aschers. (*Hemerocallis plantaginea*, Lam. *Funkia grandiflora*, Sieb. & Zucc. *F. subcordata*, Spreng. *Niobe plantaginea*, Nash). FRAGRANT PLANTAIN-LILY. Strong plant blooming in late summer and autumn: scapes 1½–2½ ft., overtopping the foliage, often with a green lf.-like bract toward the top: lvs. not glaucous, large, long-petioled; blade ovate to cordate-ovate, 6–10 in. long, 4–6 in. broad, with many strong side ribs: fls. white, fragrant, ascending, pedicelled often from 2 scarious bracts (1 bract very large and smaller one inside); perianth 4–5 in. long, the lobes much shorter than the long slender tube: caps. narrow, 2–3 in. long, sharp-pointed. Japan, China.

2. **H. ventricosa,** Stearn (*Bryocles ventricosa*, Salisb. *H. cærulea*, Tratt. *Funkia ovata*, Spreng. *F. cærulea*, Sweet. *Niobe cærulea*, Nash). BLUE PLANTAIN-LILY. Commonly planted, blooming in summer: scape overpassing the clump of foliage, 1½–2½ ft., usually leafy-bracted below the infl., lower bracts in raceme 1 in. or less long: lvs. broadly

ovate, sometimes subcordate at base but usually abruptly narrowed to winged petiole that equals or exceeds blade, the latter 4–9 in. long and 3–5 in. broad, margin often wavy, nerves 6–9 on either side: fls. 1½–2 in. long, usually deep blue but sometimes pale, tube less than half length of perianth and suddenly widened into bell-shaped part: caps. 1–1½ in. long. Japan, China, Siberia.

3. **H. glauca,** Stearn (*Funkia glauca,* Sieb. *H. Sieboldiana,* Engler. *Hemerocallis Sieboldtiana,* Lodd. *Funkia Sieboldiana,* Hook. *Niobe Sieboldiana,* Nash). SHORT-CLUSTER PLANTAIN-LILY. Strong clumps of heavy very glaucous foliage that overtops the scapes, and therefore usually hides the fls., blooming in late spring and early summer: scapes without bracts or lvs. below the infl., lower bracts of raceme 1½–3 in. long: lvs. large, the blade cordate-ovate, 10–15 in. long and 6–10 in. wide, short-pointed, petiole equalling or exceeding the blades, nerves about 12 either side of midrib: fls. many, faint lilac, most of them pendulous (except at top), pedicelled from single scarious bracts; perianth 2–2½ in. long, tube very slender at base but expanded upward, lobes about ¾in. long: caps. narrow, declined, 1–1½ in. long, not prominently pointed. Japan.

4. **H. Fortunei,** Bailey (*Funkia Fortunei,* Baker. *Niobe Fortunei,* Nash). TALL-CLUSTER PLANTAIN-LILY. Season of no. 3 but less massive and the raceme much surpassing the foliage: scape without several bracts or lvs. below the infl.; lower bracts of raceme about 1 in. long: lvs. smaller, the blades 4–5 in. long and 2½–3½ in. broad, cordate-ovate, pale green and glaucous, the petiole 3½ in. or less long and shorter than the blade, the nerves 10–12 on either side the midrib: fls. about 1½ in. long, pale purple or nearly white, gradually widening from base, lobes about half length of tube. (For Robt. Fortune, page 43.) Japan.—This species runs into large forms, var. **gigantea,** Bailey (*H. montana,* Maekawa), and those with lvs. broadly and irregularly margined white, var. **marginato-alba,** Bailey (*H. crispula,* Maekawa).

5. **H. erromena,** Stearn (*H. undulata* var. *erromena,* Maekawa). MIDSUMMER PLANTAIN-LILY. Robust, making large clumps with pale lilac fls. standing above the foliage, to 3 ft. high: lf.-blade 7–8 in. long and 4–5 in. broad, elliptic to broadly ovate, curved prominent ribs 5–9 on either side, cuneate or rounded but not cordate at base, uniformly green: fls. pale lilac, about 2 in. long, horizontal or becoming inclined, bracts mostly longer than the pedicels, raceme long with 15–30 fls. Nativity undetermined.

6. **H. lancifolia,** Engler (*Hemerocallis lancifolia,* Thunb. *Funkia lancifolia,* Spreng. *F. lanceolata,* Sieb. *Hosta japonica,* Voss. *Niobe japonica,* Nash). NARROW-LEAVED PLANTAIN-LILY. Summer: scape 1½–2 ft., bearing a few small lvs., surpassing the foliage: lvs. many, petioles much exceeding blade, the latter lanceolate to ovate-lanceolate, tapering both ways and sharp-pointed, 4–6 in. long and 1½–2 in. broad, with 3–5 nerves either side midrib: fls. 1½–2 in. long, lilac or pale lavender, gradually widening, tube less than half length of perianth. Japan. Var. **albo-marginata,** Stearn, lvs. margined white. Var. **tardiflora,** Bailey (*Niobe japonica* var. *tardiflora,* Nash. *H. sparsa,* Nakai), blooms in autumn.

7. **H. undulata,** Bailey (*H. lancifolia* var. *undulata,* Bailey. *Funkia undulata,* Otto & Dietr. *Niobe undulata,* Nash). WAVY-LEAVED PLANTAIN-LILY. Late spring, usually following nos. 3 and 4: scape very tall, often 3 ft. and more, usually bearing prominent small long-petioled lvs., much surpassing the foliage: lvs. many, with margined petioles usually longer than blades, the latter 6–8 in. long and 5 in. or less broad, broadly ovate, abruptly narrowed to petiole, at first splashed white, nerves 6–10 either side midrib, margins undulate: fls. many, about 2 in. long, pale lavender, gradually widening and funnelform, lobes half length of tube. Japan.—Listed foliage forms include such names as *media picta* and *variegata,* which may not be distinct from the typical form.

8. **H. decorata,** Bailey. BLUNT PLANTAIN-LILY. Compact rather small plant with spike somewhat exceeding the lvs. and perhaps 2 ft. high: lf.-blade oval, 3–8 in. long, obtuse or blunt at apex (or only very briefly acute), broad and unequal at base, margined with prominent white band: fls. dark lilac, 2 in. or more long, the short bracts very broad, racemes with few to many blooms. Origin unknown, probably Japanese.

14. **HEMEROCALLIS,** L. DAY-LILY. Perhaps 15 species, Cent. Eu. to China and Japan, much prized in open planting for the large lily-like yellow, orange, and reddish fls.—Root of many strong fleshy and tuberous parts: scapes tall, usually much exceeding the many radical or basal narrow keeled lvs., branching above so that the infl. is sometimes semi-paniculate: perianth funnelform to bell-shaped with tube widely expanding upward and wide-flaring border, lobes often recurved; stamens 6, inserted in the throat, filaments slender, anthers more or less versatile; ovary oblong, sessile or nearly so, 3-celled, style long and slender, stigma small: caps. (when produced) loculicidal, with rather few seeds. (Hemerocal-lis: Greek *beautiful for a day,* the fls. short-lived.)

A. Fls. yellow.
  B. Scapes to 2 ft. high: inner perianth-lobes with membranaceous margins, the veins more or less joined.
    C. Lvs. ½in. or more wide: scape unbranched, the 2–4 fls. sessile or nearly so, with bracts broad and overlapping.
      D. Segms. narrow-oblong and tapering to apex, not much recurved: lvs. mostly surpassing scapes....1. *H. Dumortieri*
      DD. Segms. broad-spatulate, not long-tapering, becoming strongly recurved: lvs. usually shorter than scapes....2. *H. Middendorffii*
    CC. Lvs. about ¼in. wide: scape branched at top; fls. 2–6....3. *H. minor*
  BB. Scapes 3–4 ft. high: inner perianth-lobes not membranaceous on margins and veins not running together.
    C. Lobes three to four times as long as wide; fls. diurnal.
      D. Roots fleshy and enlarged: flowering in late spring....4. *H. flava*
      DD. Roots cylindrical and scarcely enlarged: flowering in midsummer....5. *H. Thunbergii*
    CC. Lobes five to eight times as long as wide; fls. opening toward night....6. *H. citrina*
AA. Fls. orange to reddish.
  B. Blossoms fragrant; lobes nearly erect....7. *H. aurantiaca*
  BB. Blossoms inodorous; lobes wide-spreading....8. *H. fulva*

1. **H. Dumortieri,** Morr. NARROW DWARF DAY-LILY. Lvs. 12–18 in. long, ¾in. or less broad, equalling or exceeding scape: fls. 2–3, yellow, fragrant, 2½ in. or less long, the tube very short (¼in. or less), pedicels ¼–½in. long with broad lanceolate bracts of equal length; outer lobes less than ½in. broad, inner ones ½in. broad and membranaceous margins and veins running together. (In honor of B. C. Dumortier, page 42.) Siberia, Japan.

2. **H. Middendorffii,** Trautv. & Mey. BROAD DWARF DAY-LILY. Lvs. 12–18 in. long, ¾–1 in. broad, not equalling the scape: fls. 2–4, yellow, fragrant, 3–4 in. long, cylindrical tube ½in. long, pedicels very short and large deltoid bracts 1 in. long; outer lobes ½–¾in. broad, the inner ones mostly broader and obtuse with membranaceous margins and veins running together. (Name commemorates Dr. A. Th. von Middendorff, 1815–1894, Russian botanist.) E. Siberia.

3. **H. minor,** Mill. DWARF YELLOW DAY-LILY. Narrow-lvd. species; lvs. 12–20 in. long, ¼in. or less wide, usually lower than the scape: fls. 3–6, yellow, fragrant, 4 in. or less long, the cylindrical tube ½–1 in. long, pedicels short or long (to 2 in.), with small lanceolate bracts; outer lobes less than ½in. broad, inner broader with membranaceous margins and veins running together. E. Siberia to Japan.—Resembling this species are garden plants listed as **H. gracilis,** Hort., early-flowering, 2 ft. tall, lvs. narrow, fls. yellow or light orange.

4. **H. flava,** L. COMMON YELLOW DAY-LILY. Early-flowering, in middle and late spring: lvs. 1–2 ft. long, ½–¾in. broad, not equalling scape: fls. 5–9, yellow, fragrant, 3–4 in. long, cylindrical tube ½–1 in. and more long; pedicels 1–2 in. long with small lanceolate bracts; lobes about ¾in. or less broad, veins not anastomosing or running together. E. Siberia to Japan. Var. **major,** Hort., taller and later to bloom, fls. paler; probably hybrid.

5. **H. Thunbergii,** Baker. LATE YELLOW DAY-LILY. Late-blooming, in summer: lvs. to 2 ft., equalling scape, linear: fls. 8–10, lemon-yellow, about 3 in. long, the cylindrical tube nearly 1 in. long; outer lobes ½in. wide, inner to ⅞in.; upper part of scape thickened and flattened. (For Carl Peter Thunberg, page 52.) Japan.—**H. luteola,** Hort., is possibly a hybrid of *H. Thunbergii* and *H. aurantiaca* var. *major:* to 3 ft., lvs. to 30 in., fls. golden-yellow, to 5 in. across and with broad lobes. Var. **major,** Hort., has lvs. wider, fls. larger.

6. **H. citrina,** Baroni. LONG YELLOW DAY-LILY. Midsummer: lvs. to 40 in. long and over 1 in. broad: scape stiffly erect, about 4 ft. tall; fls. many, lemon-yellow, fragrant, not opening broadly in sunlight, usually nocturnal, to 6 in. long, the tube to 1½ in. long, lobes ⅜–⅝in. wide. China.—Listed as a hybrid with *H. Thunbergii* is **H. ochroleuca,** Spreng.: lvs. somewhat erect, dark green, fls. sulfur-yellow, fragrant, opening in evening.

7. **H. aurantiaca,** Baker. GOLDEN SUMMER DAY-LILY. Lvs. 6–8 to a scape and as long, 2–3 ft., 1 in. or more broad, sharply keeled: fls. 6–8, bright orange, fragrant, 3–4 in. long, cylindrical tube about ¾in. long, outer lobes oblong-lanceolate and 1 in. broad, the inner narrow, fl. not opening widely as in other species. Japan.—The cult. plant is var. **major,** Baker, fls. larger, wide open, 6 in. across.

8. **H. fulva,** L. COMMON ORANGE DAY-LILY. Summer-blooming, common in yards and also run wild: lvs. 2 ft. or more long and 1 in. broad more or less, not equalling the scape: fls. 6–10 or 12, orange-red or fulvous-red, not fragrant, 3–5 in. long, slender tube 1 in. or less long, pedicels short with small lanceolate bracts; outer lobes ½–¾in. broad, inner ones 1 in. broad with somewhat undulate margins and veins much run together. France to Japan, probably early intro. into Eu. Var. **Kwanso,** Regel, has double fls. of longer duration. Var. **maculata,** Baroni, fls. marked and banded inside with red-purple and larger in size.—Of uncertain affinity is **H. Goldenii,** Hort., 3 ft. tall, fls. deep golden-orange.

15. **LEUCOCRINUM,** Nutt. SAND- or STAR-LILY. One species of W. U. S.—Acaulescent spring herb from deep-seated short rhizome, with fleshy roots and narrowly linear lvs. surrounded at base by scarious bracts: fls. white, in central sessile umbels, salverform with long slender tube and linear-lanceolate lobes; stamens 6, filaments filiform, inserted below throat, anthers linear, basifixed; ovary superior, sessile, ovate-oblong, 3-celled, style persistent, filiform, slightly 3-lobed: caps. loculicidal, the ovules several in each locule. (Leucoc-rinum: Greek *white lily.*)

L. montanum, Nutt. Lvs. 4–8 in. long, to ¼in. wide, flat and thick, the base underground: fls. 4–8, fragrant; pedicels ½–1½ in. long; perianth-tube 2–3 in. long; lobes 1 in. long; stamens about ⅓in. long: caps. about ⅓in. long. Ore. to Calif., Dak., New Mex.

16. **ALOE,** L. ALOE. Species perhaps 200 in the Old World, largely in trop. and S. Afr., plants often with stiff basal rosettes of succulent lvs. from which arise the flowering sts. or scapes, but sometimes with elongated leafy sts.—Per.; caudex (when present) simple or branched: lvs. mostly sharp-pointed and hard-toothed or spiny on the edges: fls. in racemes or umbels, often much elevated above the lvs. and showy, mostly bright red and yellow, on solitary pedicels with scariose bracts; perianth tubular and straight or curved, cylindrical or nearly so, the segms. distinct or connate at base and the tips more or less spreading; stamens 6, hypogynous, sometimes exserted, filaments slender, anthers dorsifixed; pistil 1, with sessile many-ovuled 3-loculed ovary, filiform style and capitate stigma: caps. 3-angled, loculicidal. (Al-oe: from old Arabic name.)—Many aloes are to be expected in choice collections of succulents, and several species are planted out from greenhouses. The so-called American aloe is Agave.

A. Marginal teeth on lvs. lacking … 1. *A. striata*
AA. Marginal teeth present on lvs.
  B. Fls. yellow or yellow-green.
    C. St. well developed: lvs. 4–6 in. wide: fls. 1½ in. long … 2. *A. ferox*
    CC. St. scarcely developed: lvs. 3 in. wide: fls. 1 in. long … 3. *A. barbadensis*
  BB. Fls. red or purple.
    C. Foliage conspicuously blotched or banded: plants almost stemless.
      D. Lvs. 6–10 in. long, 1½–2½ in. wide … 4. *A. saponaria*
      DD. Lvs. 3–5 in. long, 1¼–1½ in. wide … 5. *A. variegata*
    CC. Foliage not conspicuously blotched or banded.
      D. Plants nearly or quite stemless.
        E. Lvs. long-acuminate and curving inward at tips, spiny-tuberculate above and beneath or beneath only … 6. *A. humilis*
        EE. Lvs. acute, ascending, with few spiny tubercles mostly on upper surface. 7. *A. brevifolia*
      DD. Plants with well-developed sts.
        E. Lvs. about 24 in. long: sts. erect, to 15 ft … 8. *A. arborescens*
        EE. Lvs. 3–6 in. long: sts. weak, even prostrate, lower.
          F. Backs of lvs. not prickly, width ¾in.: segms. of fls. green … 9. *A. ciliaris*
          FF. Backs of lvs. more or less prickly, width 2–3 in.: segms. of fls. red.
            G. Length of fls. 2 in.; pedicels three times the subtending bracts … 10. *A. mitriformis*
            GG. Length of fls. 1½ in.; pedicels twice the bracts … 11. *A. nobilis*

1. **A. striata,** Haw. (*A. albo-cincta,* Haw.). CORAL ALOE. St. to 2 ft., nearly simple: lvs. 10–20, upcurved-spreading, oblong-triangular, short-acuminate, 15–20 in. long, 4–6 in. wide, pale or reddish, striate, with entire white margin: infl. 2–3 ft. high, divaricately branched, the individual racemes 1–3 in. long; pedicels spreading-erect; fls. 1¼ in. long, coral-red, segms. pale-tipped, erect, ⅓in. long; stamens scarcely exserted. S. Afr.

2. **A. ferox,** Mill. Trunk robust, 3–10 ft.: lvs. about 50, curved, lanceolate, glaucous, becoming reddish, 18–30 in. long, 4–6 in. wide, more or less prickly on both surfaces, with purplish margin and red-brown teeth: infl. 4 ft. high, with several branches, racemes 10–13 in. long; fls. 1½ in. long, greenish-yellow, the segms. erect, longer than tube, smoky-tipped; stamens exserted. S. Afr.

3. **A. barbadensis,** Mill. (*A. perfoliata* var. *vera,* L. *A. vera,* Auth. not Mill.). BARBADOS ALOE. Nearly or quite acaulescent, the rosette arising from the ground or st. to 1½ ft., propagating by stolons: lvs. 1–2 ft. long, erect, numerous, thick and full of juice, glaucous-green, narrow-lanceolate and long-acuminate, smooth except for the spiny teeth on margins: infl. 3–4½ ft., simple or few-branched, racemes to 18 in. long; fls. yellow, about 1 in. long, cernuous, the segms. somewhat recurved, about as long as tube; stamens equalling perianth, style usually exserted. Medit. region.

4. **A. saponaria,** Haw. (*A. perfoliata* var. *saponaria,* Ait. *A. umbellata,* Salm-Dyck). Almost acaulescent: lvs. 12–20, ascending or spreading, lance-oblong, acuminate, 6–10 in. long, 1½–2½ in. wide, with irregular transverse rows of whitish spots and large mar-

ginal brown teeth: infl. 1½–2½ ft. high, simple or branched, racemes 2–3 in. long; pedicels arcuate-erect; fls. 1½–1¾ in. long, red, the segms. greenish, ⅛in. long; stamens equalling perianth. S. Afr.

5. **A. variegata,** L. St. to 9 in. high, densely leafy: lvs. lance-deltoid, in 3 close oblique ranks, 3–5 in. long, 1¼–1½ in. wide, acute, serrulate, conspicuously transversely banded: infl. about 1 ft. high, simple, racemes 10–30-fld.; fls. spreading-arcuate, 1¼–1½ in. long, red, segms. green-nerved, shorter than tube; stamens slightly exserted. S. Afr.

6. **A. humilis,** Haw. (*A. perfoliata* var. *humilis*, L.). Tufted: lvs. 20–30, suberect, incurved, triangular-lanceolate, long-acuminate, 4 in. long, ¾in. wide, white-prickly at least on back, white-toothed on margin: infl. 1½–2 ft. high, simple, racemes 4–6 in. long; pedicels erect; fls. deflexed, 1½ in. long, red, segms. tipped green, distinct nearly to base; stamens included. S. Afr.—**A. spinosissima,** Hort., a hybrid of *A. humilis* var. *echinata*, Baker, and *A. arborescens* var. *pachythyrsa*, Berger, has lvs. to 1 ft. long, fls. purple, stamens short-exserted.

7. **A. brevifolia,** Mill. Proliferous and forming round clumps: lvs. 30–40, ascending, deltoid, glaucous, 3 in. long, 1–1½ in. wide, acute, white-toothed on margins and with few prickles on upper surface: infl. 1½ ft. tall, simple, racemes 6–8 in. long; pedicels erect; fls. pale red, spreading-deflexed, 1½ in. long, segms. tipped green, distinct nearly to base; stamens slightly exserted. S. Afr.

8. **A. arborescens,** Mill. (*A. arborea*, Medic.). Trunk simple, becoming 10–15 ft. high: lvs. many, dense, the lower withering and deflexed, upper spreading, linear-lanceolate, 2 ft. long, 2 in. wide, long-acuminate, white-prickly on the wavy margins: infl. elongate, simple or few-branched, racemes dense, many-fld.; fls. 1½ in. long, red, segms. distinct to base; stamens barely exserted. S. Afr.—A number of vars. occur.

9. **A. ciliaris,** Haw. St. elongate, weak and decumbent or climbing, branched: lvs. thin and wavy, linear-lanceolate, long-acuminate, 4–6 in. long, ¾in. wide, white-toothed on margins, sheathing at base: infl. 6–8 in. high; pedicels spreading; fls. bright red, 1⅛ in. long, segms. greenish, much shorter than tube; stamens scarcely exserted. S. Afr.—Rather frequent in greenhouses and in Calif.

10. **A. mitriformis,** Mill. St. 3–4 ft., procumbent, branched at base: lvs. upcurved, ovate, acute, 4–6 in. long, 2–3 in. wide, concave above, somewhat prickly toward tip beneath, prickly-margined: infl. 1 ft. or more high, few-branched, racemes dense, 6 in. long; pedicels erect-spreading, about 2 in. long; fls. deflexed to nodding, bright red, 2 in. long, segms. paler, recurved, distinct almost to base; stamens slightly exserted. S. Afr.—Variable.

11. **A. nobilis,** Haw. Similar to *A. mitriformis*, the lvs. less concave above, pedicels 1–1½ in. long, fls. 1½ in. long. S. Afr.

17. **HAWORTHIA,** Duval. Perhaps 70 species in S. Afr., plants cespitose or with short sts. and succulent lvs.—Per., the lvs. usually small and crowded: fls. white with green or rosy stripes, in simple racemes or panicles, tubular with somewhat irregular recurving limb and included stamens and style; segms. of perianth 6, oblong, nearly equal; stamens 6, shorter than perianth, anthers dorsifixed; ovary sessile, 3-angled and -loculed, style short, ovules many in each locule: caps. oblong or rounded, loculicidal. (Hawor-thia: A. Haworth, page 44.)

A. St. 6–8 in. high: lvs. tuberculate.......................................1. *H. coarctata*
AA. St. scarcely elongate, plant cespitose.
  B. Lvs. tuberculate, to 3 in. long, toothed on margins: infl. branched...........2. *H. margaritifera*
  BB. Lvs. not tuberculate, 1–1½ in. long, entire: infl. simple....................3. *H. cymbiformis*

1. **H. coarctata,** Haw. (*Aloe coarctata*, Roem. & Schult.). St. 6–8 in. high: lvs. densely spiral, ascending, with incurved tips, lance-deltoid, long-acuminate, 1½–2½ in. long, ½in. wide, plano-convex, with small white knobs on the back: infl. 1 ft. high, simple, about 30-fld.; pedicels ⅛in. long; fls. white with green striation, ¾in. long, segms. with red lines. S. Afr.

2. **H. margaritifera,** Haw. (*Aloe pumila* var. *margaritifera*, L.). Acaulescent: lvs. 3 in. long, 1–1¼ in. wide, fleshy, plano-convex, short-acuminate, white-tuberculate on both surfaces, more so on margins: infl. branched above, 24–28 in. tall, the racemes 4–6 in. long; fls. suberect, ⅝in. long, with green lines, segms. linear and obtuse. S. Afr.—Variable.

3. **H. cymbiformis,** Haw. (*Aloe cymbiformis*, Haw.). Acaulescent, cespitose: lvs. very fleshy, water-pellucid, 1–1½ in. long, ¾in. wide, obovate, entire, the tip often abruptly deciduous leaving a scar, about 7-nerved and with cross-veins: peduncle simple, about 1 ft. high; pedicels to ¼in.; fls. red-keeled, ¾in. long, segms. recurved. S. Afr.

18. **GASTERIA,** Duval. Perhaps 50 species of S. Afr., mostly acaulescent and small succulents.—Lvs. usually elongated, crowded in rosettes or on short sts.,

mostly 2-ranked, plane or somewhat carinate, spotted or tuberculate: infl. elevated, racemose or loosely paniculate; rachis and pedicels reddish; fls. pendulous, with red or rosy usually ventricose curved tube and short equal suberect greenish segms.; stamens 6, hypogynous, not exserted; ovary sessile, 3-loculed, 3-angled, ovules many, style filiform: caps. obtusely angled, loculicidally dehiscent. (Gaste-ria: Greek *gaster*, belly, referring to the usually swollen base of the fls.)

G. verrucosa, Haw. (*Aloe verrucosa*, Mill.). Cespitose: lvs. arranged in 2 vertical ranks, lanceolate, somewhat concavely 3-sided, cuspidate at apex, 4–9 in. long, to 1 in. wide, dull gray, rough with white crowded tubercles: infl. 2 ft. high, mostly simple; pedicels ½in. long; fls. 1 in. long, slightly curved, segms. short, slightly spreading. S. Afr.—A number of vars. occur.

19. **CONVALLARIA,** L. Lily-of-the-Valley. Low scapose plants, everywhere prized for the fragrant dainty fls. in spring; native Eu. to E. Asia, N. Amer., apparently 2 species.—Rootstocks (pips) more or less erect from long horizontal deep slender branches: lvs. 2, which with the single scape arise from basal scarious sheaths: fls. few to many, drooping in a secund small-bracted raceme; perianth teacup-shaped, gamophyllous, with 6 short recurved lobes; stamens 6, attached on base of perianth, shorter than the straight style; ovary sessile, 3-celled: fr. a globular few-seeded red berry. (Convalla-ria: Latin *Lilium convallium*, "lily of the valley.")

C. majalis, L. Lvs. oblong-oval, one above the other, 4–8 in. long, 1–3 in. wide: fls. white, ⅜in. across or larger in cult. races, the raceme usually about equalling the lvs. and with bracts lanceolate, ¼–⅓in. long. Eurasia.—*C. montana*, Raf., is probably not in cult.; raceme shorter than lvs.; lvs. 6–12 in. long, 2–5 in. wide; bracts sublinear, ⅓–¾in. long; mts., Va. to S. C.

20. **ASPIDISTRA,** Ker. Half dozen or less species of acaulescent plants with strong radical foliage, from Himalayas, China, Japan, one commonly grown as a pot and window-garden subject.—Rhizome strong: fls. borne singly at surface of ground beneath the foliage and therefore not often observed, dull brown or brown-purple to greenish, subtended by scarious bracts; perianth bell-shaped, the tube short, the segms. usually spreading; stamens 8, attached at middle of tube, anthers dorsifixed; ovary sessile and free, 4-celled, stigma expanded and peltate: fr. an indehiscent 1-seeded berry. (Aspidis-tra: Greek *small round shield*, describing the stigma.)

A. elatior, Blume (*A. lurida*, Hort. not Ker). Lvs. many from matted tough rootstocks, persistent, stiff, 1–2½ ft. high, petioled, the blade strongly veined, 3–4 in. broad, wide-oblong-elliptic: fls. about 1 in. across, purple-brown, in spring. China. Var. **variegata,** Hort., lvs. striped green and white.—Sometimes called "cast-iron plant" from ability to withstand hard usage.

21. **ROHDEA,** Roth. Perhaps 2 species in China and Japan, with the look of an aroid, grown for the decorative foliage, particularly by Chinese and Japanese.—Rhizome short and thick: scape much shorter than foliage: lvs. many, radical, erect, lorate, veiny: fls. packed in a thick short spike or head terminating the scape; perianth globose-campanulate, with 6 short segms.; stamens 6, anthers sessile; stigma peltate, nearly or quite sessile on a 3-celled ovary: fr. an indehiscent red-fleshed large berry, usually 1-seeded. (Roh-dea: Dr. Michael Rohde, 1782–1812, physician and botanist of Bremen.)

R. japonica, Roth & Kunth. Lvs. flat or somewhat conduplicate, 2–3 in. broad, 1–2 ft. long, coriaceous, narrowed at base into petiole-like part: fls. deep cream-colored.—The Omoto or Mannensei of the Japanese, and national fl. of the Manchus. There are very many fancier's vars., with variegated and striped lvs. of different sizes, and plants of different stature. Sometimes cult. in Calif. and elsewhere.

22. **STREPTOPUS,** Michx. Twisted-Stalk. Seven species in Eu., Asia and N. Amer., low per. herbs from horizontal rootstocks.—St. leafy, simple to several times forking: lvs. alternate, elliptic to ovate, thin, many-nerved, more or less tapering at tip, sessile to clasping at base: fls. 1 or 2 together on slender supra-axillary peduncles; perianth campanulate or rotate, of 6 separate segms., the outer usually a

little broader than the inner; stamens 6, hypogynous, filaments short, flat, anthers fixed near base, apiculate to aristate at tip; ovary 3-celled, with numerous ovules, style slender, entire or cleft at apex: fr. a berry. (Strep-topus: Greek *twisted stalk*, because of bent or twisted peduncles.)

A. Lvs. clasping: segms. of fls. with spreading or recurved tips.................. 1. *S. amplexifolius*
AA. Lvs. sessile but not clasping: segms. of fls. with scarcely spreading tips........ 2. *S. roseus*

1. **S. amplexifolius**, DC. (*Uvularia amplexifolia*, L. *Tortipes amplexifolius*, Small). St. 1½–3 ft. high, glabrous, with glabrous nodes: lvs. 2–5 in. long, 1–2 in. wide, cordate-clasping at base, acuminate at apex, glaucous beneath: fls. greenish-white, ⅓–½in. long; segms. lanceolate, acuminate; stigma barely 3-lobed.—The typical European plant has pedicels $\frac{5}{16}$–$\frac{11}{16}$in. long, and lvs. beyond the uppermost fl. usually 3–5, while the several American vars. have pedicels to ⅜in. and usually only 1–3 lvs. beyond the uppermost fl.

2. **S. roseus**, Michx. St. 1–2½ ft. high, pubescent, with fringed nodes: lvs. 2–4½ in. long, sessile, acuminate at apex, green and sparingly pubescent beneath: fls. rose or purple, ⅓–½in. long; stigmas 3-parted at tip. A variable species from E. N. Amer. to Alaska.

23. **POLYGONATUM,** Adans. SOLOMONS-SEAL. About 30 species of the north temp. zone, with thick horizontal jointed and scarred rootstocks.—Sts. simple, arching or erect, leafy above: lvs. ovate to lanceolate, alternate to opposite or whorled, sessile: fls. greenish, drooping, axillary, solitary or in umbels; pedicels jointed at base of fl.; perianth cylindrical, the lobes 6, short, deltoid to lanceolate; stamens 6, included, the filaments adnate to perianth-tube for half their length or more; ovary superior, 3-loculed, style slender, stigma capitate or slightly 3-lobed, ovules 2–6 to a locule: fr. a berry. (Polygon-atum: Greek *many-knee*, referring to the jointed rootstock.)

A. Lowest lf. a papery bract, deciduous, leaving a ring-like scar on the st.; lvs. pubescent on veins beneath.. 1. *P. pubescens*
AA. Lowest lf. persistent, green; lvs. glabrous.
B. Major nerves of lvs. usually 1–5, only the midrib being prominent toward lf.-tip: peduncles mostly 1–2-fld.. 2. *P. biflorum*
BB. Major nerves of lvs. 7–11 or more, prominent into upper part of lf.: peduncles mostly with 2–5 or more fls.
C. St. 2–6 ft. high, the upper leafy part longer than lower naked part: fls. scarcely constricted in middle... 3. *P. commutatum*
CC. St. mostly 1–2 ft. high, the upper leafy part equalling lower naked part: fls. evidently constricted in middle... 4. *P. multiflorum*

1. **P. pubescens**, Pursh (*Convallaria pubescens*, Willd. *P. biflorum* of many authors). St. slender, 1–2 or even 3 ft. tall, the upper leafy portion shorter than lower naked portion: lvs. alternate, elliptic-lanceolate to elliptic or oval, 1½–6 in. long, ½–2½ in. wide, glaucous and pubescent beneath, with 3–9 prominent nerves; bract-like lowest lf. some distance beneath the others, deciduous, leaving a ring-like scar: peduncles usually 1- or 2- (sometimes 3–5-) fld.; fls. about ½in. long: berry dark blue. N. S. to Ga. and Man.

2. **P. biflorum**, Ell. (*Convallaria biflora*, Walt.). St. to 4 ft. high, usually less, the upper leafy part shorter than lower naked part: lvs. alternate, elliptic-lanceolate, 1½–4½ in. long, ⅜–1¼ in. wide, glabrous and glaucous beneath, usually with 1–5 nerves, only the middle prominent toward lf.-tip; lowest lf. not a papery bract: peduncles 1- or 2- (rarely 3-) fld.; fls. ½–¾in. long. Conn. to Fla. and Miss. Valley.

3. **P. commutatum**, A. Dietr. (*Convallaria commutata*, Schult. *P. giganteum*, A. Dietr.). St. 2–6 ft. high, the upper leafy part longer than lower naked part: lvs. alternate, ovate-lanceolate to oval, 2½–7 in. long, ⅝–4 in. broad, glaucous and glabrous beneath, with 7–19 major nerves prominent the full length of lf.: peduncles 1–15-fld.; fls. ⅝–1 in. long. N. H. to Ga., Man. and Nuevo Leon, Mex.

4. **P. multiflorum**, All. (*Convallaria multiflora*, L.). St. 1–2, sometimes 3 ft. high, the upper leafy part about as long as the lower naked part: lvs. alternate, elliptic to ovate, 2–6 in. long, 1–2½ in. wide, glaucous and glabrous beneath, with about 7–9 principal nerves: peduncles 2–5- (11-) fld.; fls. ½–⅔in. long, constricted in middle. Eu., Asia.

24. **MAIANTHEMUM,** Weber (*Unifolium*, Haller). FALSE LILY-OF-THE-VALLEY. Three or 4 species of the north temp. zone; low per. herbs with creeping rhizomes and slender roots.—St. erect, simple, few-lvd.: lvs. sessile or petioled, cordate-ovate: fls. small, white, in a terminal raceme; perianth of 4 separate spreading segms.; stamens 4, inserted at base of segms., filaments filiform; ovary sessile, globose, 2-loculed, with 2 ovules in each cavity, style equalling ovary, stigma 2-lobed: fr. a 1–2-seeded berry. (Maian-themum: Greek *May* and *flower*.)

M. canadense, Desf. St. slender, 2–7 in. high: lvs. ovate to lance-ovate, usually 2, 1–3 in. long: raceme 1–2 in. long; perianth-segms. 1/16 in. long, oblong, obtuse: berry brownish-red, speckled. Newf. to N. C. and S. D.

25. **SMILACINA,** Desf. (*Vagnera,* Adans.). False Solomons-Seal. About 25 species native in N. Amer. and Asia; herbaceous with creeping rootstocks and simple sts. scaly below and leafy above.—Lvs. alternate, sessile or nearly so, ovate or lanceolate: fls. small, spreading, usually white, in a terminal panicle or raceme, the perianth of 6 separate spreading equal segms.; stamens 6, inserted at base of segms., filaments slender, anthers minute; ovary subglobose, superior, 3-loculed, ovules 2 in each cavity, style columnar, stigma capitate or trifid: fr. a berry. (Smilaci-na: diminutive of Smilax.)

A. Fls. numerous, panicled...1. *S. racemosa*
AA. Fls. few to several, racemose...2. *S. stellata*

1. **S. racemosa,** Desf. (*Convallaria racemosa,* L.) Rootstock fleshy, rather thick; st. 1–3 ft. high, more or less pubescent above: lvs. several, oblong-lanceolate to oval, 3–10 in. long, 1½–4 in. wide, acuminate, pubescent beneath: peduncle less than half the panicle, the latter ovoid to pyramidal, 3–10 in. long; fls. ⅛in. broad: berry red with small purple spots. Que. to Va., Tenn., Ariz., B. C. Var. **cylindrata,** Fern., st. to 2½ ft.; lvs. to 7 in. long and 2½ in. wide; peduncle one-half to longer than the cylindrical panicle; N. H. to Ga., Ariz. and Ont.

2. **S. stellata,** Desf. (*Convallaria stellata,* L.). Rootstock slender: lvs. linear-lanceolate to oblong, 2–6 (8) in. long, ½–1½ in. wide, puberulent, obtuse to acuminate: fls. several in a simple sessile or short-peduncled raceme, about ⅓in. broad: berry green with blue stripes or dark blue. Newf. to B. C., Va., Calif.

26. **CLINTONIA,** Raf. About 6 species of N. Amer. and E. Asia; scapose herbs with slender rootstocks.—Lvs. few, largely basal, broad, petioled, sheathing: fls. bractless, terminal, solitary or umbellate; segms. 6, ascending, distinct, subequal; stamens 6, inserted at bases of segms., filaments filiform, anthers oblong, dorsifixed; ovary 2–3-celled, with 2 to several ovules in each locule, style stout or slender, stigma obscurely 2–3-lobed: fr. a berry. (Clinto-nia: in honor of DeWitt Clinton, 1769–1828, once governor of N. Y.)

A. Fls. 1 or 2, white...1. *C. uniflora*
AA. Fls. 3–16, not white.
B. Color of fls. crimson-purple, fl. erect...2. *C. Andrewsiana*
BB. Color of fls. greenish-yellow, fl. nodding...3. *C. borealis*

1. **C. uniflora,** Kunth (*Smilacina borealis* var. *uniflora,* Schult.). Queen-Cup. Lvs. 2–3, rarely 4–5, oblanceolate to obovate, acute, 3–6 in. long, 1–2½ in. wide, more or less pubescent: peduncle slender, shorter than lvs., pubescent, naked or with 1–2 bracts; fls. erect, white; segms. ¾–1 in. long, ¼in. wide, spreading; filaments pubescent, anthers ⅛in. long: berry blue, ⅓–½in. thick. Alaska to Mont. and Calif.

2. **C. Andrewsiana,** Torr. Lvs. mostly 5 or 6, oval to oblanceolate, acute, sparsely villous-pubescent on margins, 6–8 in. long, 3–5 in. wide: peduncle stout, 10–20 in. high, with 1–3 bracts; infl. villous-pubescent, of a terminal umbel and often 1 or 2 smaller lateral ones; pedicels unequal; fls. deep rose-purple, segms. ⅓–⅔in. long; filaments pubescent, anthers 1/16in. long: berry metallic-blue, to ⅜in. long. (Named for Dr. T. L. Andrews, who collected in Calif. in the middle of the 19th century.) Calif.

3. **C. borealis,** Raf. (*Dracæna borealis,* Ait.). Lvs. 2–5, ovate or obovate, short-acuminate or cuspidate, ciliate, 4–7 in. long, 1½–3½ in. wide: peduncle 6–15 in. high, glabrous to pubescent above; umbel with 3–6 drooping greenish-yellow fls.; segms. ¾in. long, narrowly lanceolate, obtusish; filaments pubescent near base, anthers to ⅛in.: berry blue, ⅓in. diam. Newf. to Ont. and N. C.

27. **UVULARIA,** L. Bellwort. Five species of E. N. Amer., with slender sparsely branched rootstocks.—St. forked, sheathed below, leafy above: lvs. alternate, sessile or perfoliate: fls. fairly large, slender-campanulate, usually solitary at ends of branches; segms. 6, distinct, nectariferous at base; filaments short, filiform, shorter than the linear anthers; ovary 3-lobed, 3-celled, ovules several in each cell, styles united to about the middle, stigmatic along upper inner surface: fr. a caps., 3-angled or 3-winged, loculicidal. (Uvula-ria: Latin *uvula,* a palate, because of the hanging fls.)

A. Lvs. perfoliate, 2–5 in. long.
 B. Stamens sharp-pointed: lvs. glabrous.......................................1. *U. perfoliata*
 BB. Stamens blunt: lvs. pubescent beneath, at least when young.....................2. *U. grandiflora*
AA. Lvs. sessile, 1½–3 in. long..3. *U. sessilifolia*

1. **U. perfoliata,** L. St. 6–20 in. high: lvs. ovate to oblong or lance-ovate, perfoliate, rounded at base, acute at apex, lengthening after anthesis: fls. pale yellow, ⅚–1⅛ in. long; segms. narrow-oblong, more or less papillose within; stamens two-thirds the length of the segms., anthers sharp-pointed: caps. truncate, obovoid, obtusely 3-angled. Que. to Ont., Fla. and Miss.

2. **U. grandiflora,** Smith. Much like the preceding, but lvs. pubescent beneath: fls. lemon-yellow, 1–1½ in. long; segms. linear-lanceolate, smooth; stamens one-half to two-thirds the segms.; anthers blunt-tipped. Que. to Minn., Ga. and Iowa.

3. **U. sessilifolia,** L. (*Oakesiella sessilifolia,* Small). Glabrous, to 1 ft. high: lvs. oblong-elliptic, eventually 1½–3 in. long, marginally roughened: fls. ⅔–1¼ in. long, greenish-yellow; segms. oblong-linear, acute, smooth; stamens less than half the length of segms.: caps. sharply 3-angled, acute at each end. N. B. to Minn., Ga. and Ark.

28. **GLORIOSA,** L. GLORY or CLIMBING-LILY. Six tuberous-rooted species in trop. Afr. and Asia, most of them climbing by tendril-like prolongations of the lvs.; fls. showy.—Sts. long and weak: lvs. opposite, verticillate or alternate: fls. solitary in upper axils, lily-like, red or yellow; segms. narrow and separate, often crisped, erect, wide-spreading or reflexed; stamens 6, hypogynous or on the very base of perianth, the filaments long and slender, anthers versatile; pistil 1, with sessile 3-celled ovary and filiform 3-parted style which is bent at right angles near the base, stigmas filiform: caps. loculicidal. (Glorio-sa: Latin *gloriosus,* full of glory.)

A. Perianth-segms. one-sixth as wide as long, much crisped........................1. *G. superba*
AA. Perianth-segms. one-fourth as wide as long, scarcely crisped, perhaps undulate...2. *G. Rothschildiana*

1. **G. superba,** L. Climbing 5 ft. or more: lvs. long-lanceolate to narrowly ovate-lanceolate, 4–5 in. long, ½–1 in. wide: perianth-segms. linear to narrow-lanceolate, 2–3 in. long, much crisped as if twisted, yellow changing to red (a yellow-fld. form in cult.), horizontal to reflexed. Trop. Afr. and Asia.

2. **G. Rothschildiana,** O'Brien. Tall climbing: lvs. broad-lanceolate to broadly ovate-lanceolate, 5–7 in. long, 1½–2 in. wide: fls. deflexed by crook in the slender pedicel; segms. oblong-lanceolate to ovate-lanceolate, 2–3 in. and more long, plane or undulate on the margins, whitish and yellow at the base, crimson and more or less margined above (citron-yellow form in cult.), strongly reflexed. (Walter Rothschild, who cultivated it in England from tubers received from Uganda.) Trop. Afr.

29. **TRICYRTIS,** Wall. About 9 species of erect herbs with short or obsolete rhizomes, of E. Asia, one frequently planted in the open for its spotted axillary fls.—St. leafy, mostly simple: lvs. alternate, broad, nearly sessile or clasping: fls. terminal or axillary, rather large but not lily-like, spotted inside; perianth bell-shaped, of 6 distinct segms. of which the 3 outer are saccate at base; stamens 6, hypogynous, the flattened filaments connate; pistil 1, ovary 3-celled, styles 3 and each 2-parted: caps. septicidal, many-seeded. (Tricyr-tis: Latin *three convexities,* referring to nectar-sacs on outer segms.)

T. hirta, Hook. (*Compsoa hirta,* Kuntze). TOAD-LILY. Strict, 1–3 ft., soft-hairy all over: lvs. ovate, clasping, strongly several-nerved, 4–6 in. long: fls. few to several in axils of lvs. and bracts, erect, pedicelled, trumpet-shaped, about 1 in. long, whitish with many purple or blackish spots inside. Japan.

30. **STENANTHIUM,** Kunth. Erect glabrous bulbous herbs; 5 species, 4 of N. Amer. and 1 Asiatic.—Lvs. many, basal and cauline, linear: st. slender, fairly tall: infl. paniculate or racemose; fls. perfect, campanulate or rotate; segms. linear-lanceolate, almost distinct, acuminate, persistent, adnate to base of ovary, glandless; stamens 6, shorter than segms., inserted at their base, anthers small, confluently 1-celled; ovary almost superior, ovoid, 3-loculed, styles 3, linear: caps. septicidal, with about 4 winged seeds in each cell. (Stenan-thium: narrow perianth-segms.)

S. robustum, Wats. FEATHER-FLEECE. St. stout, 3–5 ft. tall: lvs. 12–15 in. long, ⅓–¾ in. wide: panicle dense, 1–2¼ ft. long; fls. greenish or white, broad-campanulate, ½–¾ in. broad: caps. ovoid-oblong, ⅙–¼ in. long, with short recurved-spreading beaks. Pa. to S. C. and Mo.

31. **ZIGADENUS,** Michx. About 18 species of erect glabrous per. herbs from N. Amer. and N. Asia.—With bulbs or rootstocks and leafy sts.: lvs. linear: fls. greenish or yellowish-white, in terminal panicles or racemes, perfect or unisexual; perianth withering-persistent, free or adnate to lower part of ovary; segms. lanceolate or ovate, with 1 or 2 glands just above the narrowed base; stamens 6, free from and about equal to segms., anthers small, reniform; ovary 3-celled, styles 2: caps. 3-lobed, the cells dehiscent to the base; seeds many. (Zigad-enus: Greek *yoke* and *gland,* referring to the paired glands of some species.)—Zygadenus is a later spelling.

Z. elegans, Pursh (*Anticlea elegans,* Rydb.). Bulb with membranous coats; plant glaucous, 1–3 ft. high: lvs. keeled, the lower ½–1 ft. long, ⅙–½in. wide, upper much shorter: infl. open, simple or branched, 6–12 in. long; segms. almost ½in. long, ovate, obtuse, each with a large obcordate basal gland; ovary partly inferior: caps. almost 1 in. long. Alaska to Sask., New Mex. and Ariz.

32. **VERATRUM,** L. False Hellebore. Stout per. herbs with short thick rootstocks; 12–14 species of the north temp. zone.—St. stout, pubescent, leafy: lvs. broad, clasping, strongly veined and plaited: fls. greenish-white or purple, widely expanded, fairly large, perfect, imperfect or both on same plant, on short stout pedicels, in large terminal panicles; segms. 6, oblong-ovate, obtuse, glandless or nearly so; stamens 6, opposite the segms. and free from them, almost as long, filaments filiform, anthers cordate at base, the sacs confluent; ovary superior, 3-celled, conical, styles 3, persistent: caps. septicidal, 3-lobed, 3-celled, each cell several-seeded. (Vera-trum: ancient name of hellebore.)

V. viride, Ait. St. 2–8 ft. high: lvs. acute, the lower boadly oval or elliptic, 6–18 in. long, 3–12 in. wide, sessile or short-petioled, the upper narrower and smaller: panicle 8–24 in. long; fls. yellowish-green; segms. oblong or oblanceolate, acute, ⅓in. long, woolly-pubescent, ciliate-serrulate: caps. to 1 in. long. N. B. to Ga., Ore. and Alaska.

33. **ASPARAGUS,** L. About 150 species, from Siberia to S. Afr., one everywhere grown for food and a few others common as ornamental plants.—Erect or climbing, branching, sometimes more or less woody, the roots cord-like, rhizomatous or tuberous: lvs. reduced to mere dry scales, the foliage represented by green lf.-like branchlets or cladodes which are sometimes needle-like and sometimes expanded: fls. small, usually greenish, few or many, in racemes or umbels, or sometimes 1 and axillary, pedicels jointed; perianth bell-shaped, of 6 separate more or less connivent segms.; stamens 6, attached on base of perianth, anthers versatile; pistil 1, with sessile 3-celled 2- or few-seeded ovary and mostly 3-lobed stigma: fr. a berry. (Asparagus: the ancient Greek name.)

A. Cladodes solitary, many-nerved, ovate........1. *A. asparagoides*
AA. Cladodes in fascicles of 3–20, linear.
  B. Plant erect, grown for food, diœcious........2. *A. officinalis*
  BB. Plant climbing or drooping, grown for ornament (erect in no. 9), not diœcious.
    C. The cladodes flat.
      D. Length of cladodes not over ½in.: fls. 1 or 2 in the axils........3. *A. scandens*
      DD. Length of principal cladodes 1–3 in.: fls. in racemes.
        E. Arrangement of cladodes in horizontal plane on twigs forming frond-like branches........4. *A. drepanophyllus*
        EE. Arrangement of cladodes simple, separate, not in one plane.
          F. And almost straight, about 1 in. long........5. *A. Sprengeri*
          FF. And curved, 2–3 in. long........6. *A. falcatus*
    CC. The cladodes needle-like.
      D. Base of lf.-scale a spur or sharp spine: sts. climbing or weak.
        E. Root tuberous: cladodes in 3's........7. *A. crispus*
        EE. Root not tuberous: cladodes several to many in each fascicle........8. *A. plumosus*
      DD. Base of lf.-scale appressed, bract-like: st. erect, stiff........9. *A. virgatus*

1. **A. asparagoides,** Wight (*Medeola asparagoides,* L. *A. medeoloides,* Thunb. *Myrsiphyllum asparagoides,* Willd.). Smilax of florists. Tall much-branched glabrous vine with a cluster of tuberous roots: cladodes ("lvs.") ovate, sharp-pointed, about 1 in. long, stiffish, shining, strongly many-veined: fls. 1 or 2 to a scale or true lf., greenish-white, about ⅜in. long, on very slender pedicels of nearly or quite equal length: berry dark purple, about ¼in. diam., with 1–3 seeds; seeds globular, black. S. Afr. Var. **myrtifolius,** Hort., Baby Smilax, is a lighter and more graceful form with smaller lvs.—Smilax of botanists is a very different plant, represented by the greenbriers (see page 237).

2. **A. officinalis,** L., var. **altilis,** L. COMMON OR GARDEN ASPARAGUS. Abundantly grown for the edible spring shoots, and also more or less run wild: roots of many cord-like fleshy parts; st. 3–10 ft., erect and much-branched, glabrous and slightly glaucous, the strong spring shoots bearing prominent appressed scale-like lvs.: cladodes ("lvs.") thread-like, ½in. or less long, 1 to several in the axil: diœcious: fls. 1–4 in axils of cladodes, bell-shaped, the sterile yellowish-green and nearly ¼in. long and with undeveloped pistil, the fertile smaller and less conspicuous with 3 protruding stigmas: berry hanging, red, ⅜in. or less diam.; seeds several, ⅛in. or less diam., rounded on back, black. Coasts and sandy areas, Great Britain to Cent. Asia, the native form with prostrate base and short branches.

3. **A. scandens,** Thunb. Slender, climbing, branching: cladodes flat, in 3's, ½in. or less long, linear and curved, prominently costate: fls. greenish-white, solitary or in 2's, about ⅛in. long, pendulous on a slender pedicel ¼–½in. long: berry scarlet, 1-seeded, globose, ⅙in. diam. S. Afr. Var. **deflexus,** Baker, is smaller with deflexed and zigzag branches, cladodes ¼in. or less long and firmer in texture, fls. smaller.

4. **A. drepanophyllus,** Welw. (*A. Duchesnei*, Lind.). Roots tuberous, very long; sts. very tall (20–30 ft.), woody, climbing, without main branches: cladodes in fascicles of 2–5 (sometimes single), the central one 1–3 in. long and others shorter, flat, linear-falcate, arranged in one plane on shoots 1 in. to 2 ft. long making a fern-like frond or cladophyll, the scales spiniferous: fls. greenish, in close erect racemes, pedicels deflexed: berry 3-lobed, scarlet, ½in. diam., usually 1-seeded. Cent. Afr.

5. **A. Sprengeri,** Regel. Commonly cult.: roots with white short tubers; sts. drooping or scrambling, 3–6 ft. long, glabrous, much-branched: cladodes about 1 in. long (more or less), flat, linear, straight or only slightly curved, 3–8 together, scales on main sts. spiniferous: fls. pinkish, fragrant, in loose racemes 1–3 in. long: berry somewhat 3-lobed, bright red, ½in. or less diam., 1–3-seeded. (Bears name of Karl Sprenger, page 52.) S. Afr. Var. **compactus,** Hort., is seldom over 18 in. long, and var. **variegatus,** Hort., has variegated lvs.

6. **A. falcatus,** L. Spreading woody vine 20–40 ft. long, much-branched above: cladodes 3–5, or more at ends of twigs, falcate, lance-linear, crisped on margins, 2–3 in. long; lf.-scales with stout basal spines: fls. sweet-scented, white, in loose racemes 2–3 in. long: berry dull brown. Trop. Asia. and Afr.

7. **A. crispus,** Lam. (*A. decumbens*, Jacq.). Roots with clustered short tubers; st. very slender and weak, not woody, climbing or drooping, branched, 3–6 ft.: cladodes 2 or 3, reflexed and 3-angled, or somewhat flattened, ⅜in. or less long: fls. axillary, solitary or in 2's, white and fragrant, on pedicels about ¼in. long: berry white or pink, ⅓–½in. diam., with several small black seeds. S. Afr.

8. **A. plumosus,** Baker. ASPARAGUS-FERN. Commonly cult. by florists to be cut in strands for decoration: roots with long slightly fleshy not tuberous parts; st. tall climbing, woody, glabrous; branches and cladodes very many, close together, in flat horizontal frond-like decorative sprays that are more or less triangular in outline: cladodes many in a fascicle, filiform and bright green, mostly ¼in. or less long; main lf.-scales spiniferous: fls. whitish, 1–3 or 4 on short pedicels, about ⅛in. long: berry purple-black, globose, ¼in. diam., 1–3-seeded. S. Afr.—Runs into several forms: var. **nanus,** Nichols., DWARF ASPARAGUS-FERN, common in cult., plant not making tall vine, cladodes very many and short; var. **compactus,** Hort., dwarf; var. **robustus,** Hort., a strong grower, cladodes shorter than in *A. plumosus* and the fronds longer and more irregular; var. **comorensis,** Hort., a very robust form with very regular broad-triangular delicate fronds.

9. **A. virgatus,** Baker (*A. elongatus*, Hort.). Roots fibrous, crown with long semi-woody rhizomes; sts. erect, 3–6 ft. high, bushy, with many stiff branches above: cladodes in 3's, not very abundant, stiff, ¼–¾in. long, angled; lf.-scales white, with a basal appressed bract-like part similar to the upper part: fls. greenish-white, solitary at nodes on drooping pedicels, no cladodes in axils with fls.: berry dull orange-red. S. Afr.

34. **RUSCUS,** L. Erect low herbs, 3–5 species from the Madeira Isls. to the Caucasus, one frequently planted in warmer parts of the U. S.—Lvs. represented by minute scales subtending expanded flat stiff strongly nerved persistent lf.-like cladodes: plants diœcious, the fls. solitary or fascicled, small, greenish, attached on the midrib on the upper or lower surface of the cladodes; perianth of 6 distinct segms.; stamens 3, filaments connate forming a short tube with the anthers at its summit; pistil 1, with sessile 1-celled 2-ovuled ovary, stigma capitate: fr. a globose pulpy 1-seeded berry. (Rus-cus: old Latin name.)

R. aculeatus, L. BUTCHERS BROOM. Evergreen, 2–3 ft., stiff, with crowded lf.-like ovate spine-pointed cladodes ¾–1½ in. long, in shape much like those of florists' smilax: berry red or yellow, ½in. or less diam.—Dried sprays are often dyed for use in decoration.

35. **ERYTHRONIUM,** L. FAWN-LILY. ADDERS-TONGUE. TROUT-LILY. Low herbs from deep-seated corms; 15 species of N. Amer. and 1 in Eurasia.—St. simple, with 2, sometimes more, broad or narrow unequal lvs. which appear almost basal: fls. large, more or less nodding, bractless, solitary to several; perianth-segms. 6, separate, deciduous, with a nectar-bearing groove; stamens 6, hypogynous, anthers linear-oblong, basifixed; ovary 3-celled with several to many ovules in each cell, style narrow or thickened above, 3-lobed to entire: fr. a loculicidal caps. (Erythronium: Greek word for *red*, being applicable to the European species.)

A. St. branching at the lvs. so that the fls. seem umbellate: stigma-lobes long, filiform.......... 1. *E. multiscapoideum*
AA. St. branching above lvs., if at all, so that fls. seem racemose.
B. Stigma 3-lobed, the lobes finally recurved.
C. Fls. bright yellow: lvs. not mottled.......... 2. *E. grandiflorum*
CC. Fls. cream or whitish or bluish: lvs. mottled.
D. Filaments filiform.......... 3. *E. californicum*
DD. Filaments dilated downward.
E. Inner perianth-segms. sacculate or auriculate-appendaged at base: caps. 1–1½ in. long.
F. Perianth-segms. white or creamy: caps. obtuse or retuse at apex.......... 4. *E. oregonum*
FF. Perianth-segms. rose-pink: caps. acutish at apex.......... 5. *E. revolutum*
EE. Inner perianth-segms. not sacculate or auricled: caps. ½–¾in. long: fls. white, blue or purple.......... 6. *E. albidum*
BB. Stigma entire or obscurely 3-notched, the style clavate.
C. Perianth pale purple with darker base.......... 7. *E. Hendersonii*
CC. Perianth yellowish to white, rarely with purplish tinge.
D. Fls. white to cream, with lemon-yellow base.......... 8. *E. citrinum*
DD. Fls. yellow.
E. Lvs. mottled, 3–8 in. long: perianth-segms. with reddish dots near base.......... 9. *E. americanum*
EE. Lvs. not mottled, 8–12 in. long: perianth-segms. greenish-yellow near base.......... 10. *E. tuolumnense*

1. E. **multiscapoideum,** A. Nels. & Kennedy (*Fritillaria multiscapoidea*, Kellogg. *E. Hartwegii*, Wats.). Plant to 6 in. high; corms small, producing new ones on ends of long filiform offshoots: lvs. oblong-lanceolate, mottled, 5–7 in. long, 1–2 in. wide: fls. suberect, solitary, or 2–3 in an umbel-like cluster from between the lvs.; segms. white to cream with pale greenish-yellow base, lanceolate, 1–1½ in. long; filaments filiform, ⅓in. long, anthers white, ⅓in. long; stigma with 3 recurved lobes: caps. oblong-ovoid, ⅓in. long. Calif.

2. E. **grandiflorum,** Pursh (*E. giganteum*, Lindl. not Auth.). Plant 1–2 ft. high; corms arising in succession from short rhizomes: lvs. oblong-elliptic, obtuse, 4–8 in. long, not mottled: fls. 1 or 2–6 in a raceme, nodding; segms. golden-yellow with lighter base, lanceolate, ¾–1¾ in. long, strongly recurved; filaments about half as long as segms., anthers dark red, ¼in. long; stigma with 3 recurved lobes: caps. lance-oblong, 1 in. long. B. C. to Ore., Mont., Utah. Var. **chrysandrum,** Applegate (*E. parviflorum*, Goodding), anthers yellow; Wyo., Colo., Utah. Var. **pallidum,** St. John, anthers white; B. C. to Calif. and Mont.

3. E. **californicum,** Purdy. Plant to 1 ft.: lvs. strongly mottled, 4–6 in. long, oblong-lanceolate to -ovate: fls. 1–4; segms. creamy-white, usually marked by an irregular transverse band of deeper color, broadly lanceolate, 1–1½ in. long; filaments not dilated at base, ⅓in. long, anthers cream, ⅙in. long; stigma-lobes erect or spreading: caps. obovoid, 1–1½ in. long. Calif. Var. **bicolor,** Purdy, fls. white and chrome-yellow.

4. E. **oregonum,** Applegate (*E. giganteum*, Hort.). Plant to 1 ft.: lvs. mottled, lanceolate or lance-oblong, 4–6 in. long: fls. 1–5, nodding; segms. cream-white, marked with orange at base and sometimes with band of greenish-brown, lanceolate, acuminate, 1–2 in. long; filaments ⅓in. long, dilated at base, anthers cream-yellow; stigma-lobes recurved: caps. narrow-obovoid, 1¼ in. long. B. C. to Ore.

5. E. **revolutum,** Smith. Plant to 1 ft.: lvs. mottled, oblong-lanceolate, subobtuse, 3–4 in. long, on narrowly winged petioles half as long: fls. 1–4, suberect; segms. pinkish-white within, rose-pink without, yellowish near base, linear-lanceolate, acuminate to blunt, 1½–2 in. long; filaments basally dilated, ⅓in. long, anthers yellow, 3/16in. long; stigma-lobes recurved: caps. oblong, 1–1½ in. long. B. C. to Calif. Var. **Johnsonii,** Purdy (*E. Johnsonii*, Bolander), lvs. mottled in dark brown, fls. dark rose; collected by A. J. Johnson.

6. E. **albidum,** Nutt. To 1 ft.: lvs. mottled or green, lanceolate, acute, 4–6 in. long: fls. solitary; segms. white, pink or purplish, oblong, acute, 1½ in. long; filaments one-third as long, basally dilated, anthers cream-white; stigma-lobes linear, recurved: caps. obovoid or oblong, ½–¾in. long. Ont. to Ga. and Tex.

7. E. **Hendersonii,** Wats. To 1 ft.: lvs. mottled, oblong-lanceolate, acutish, 4–8 in. long, with petiole 1–1½ in. long: fls. 1–4, nodding; segms. light to dark lavender, with

dark purple base surrounded by a whitish or yellowish tinge, lanceolate, acuminate, 1–1½ in. long, strongly recurved; filaments narrow, ½in. long, anthers brownish; stigma almost entire: caps. obovoid to ellipsoid, 1½ in. long. (L. F. Henderson, page 44.) Ore.

8. **E. citrinum,** Wats. To 1 ft.: lvs. mottled, broadly lanceolate, acutish, 3–6 in. long, very short-petioled: fls. often several; segms. white to creamy-white with light yellow base, lanceolate, recurved, 1¼ in. long; filaments slender, ½in. long, anthers cream-color; stigma obscurely lobed: caps. long-obovoid. Ore. and Calif.

9. **E. americanum,** Ker. To 1 ft.: lvs. usually mottled, oblong or spatulate, 3–8 in. long, acutish, short-petioled: fls. solitary, nodding; segms. yellow, with some pinkish or other tinge, with reddish basal dots, narrow-oblong, recurved, 1–2 in. long; filaments dilated, one-half length of segms., anthers brown or yellow: caps. obovoid, ½–¾in. long. N. S. to Fla. and Ark.

10. **E. tuolumnense,** Applegate. To 1 ft.: lvs. not mottled, yellow-green, lanceolate to broadly oblanceolate, 8–12 in. long, long-petioled: fls. 1 to several; segms. golden-yellow with pale greenish-yellow base, lanceolate, 1¼ in. long; filaments slender, unequal, young anthers yellow, ⅓in. long; stigma almost entire: caps. obovoid, retuse. Calif.

36. **FRITILLARIA,** L. FRITILLARY. About 100 species of bulbous simple-stemmed herbs of the north temp. zone.—Bulbs with thick fleshy scales; sts. erect: lvs. alternate or whorled, mostly rather narrow and sessile: fls. in racemes or umbels or solitary, leafy-bracted, nodding, often dull colored, campanulate or funnelform; segms. 6, uniform, distinct, oblong-oblanceolate, concave, with basal nectary, often blotched or tinged; stamens 6, inserted on the base of the segms., filaments slender, anthers oblong, basifixed; ovary 3-celled, style slender, sulcate or trifid, deciduous, stigmas linear or shorter: caps. membranous, ovoid or oblong, loculicidal, with 2 rows of flat seeds in each cell. (Fritilla-ria: Latin *fritillus*, checker-board or dice-box, referring to markings on perianth of some species.)

A. Fls. underneath a crown of lvs. . . . . 1. *F. imperialis*
AA. Fls. at summit of sts.
  B. Style entire or shortly 3-lobed; perianth-segms. not mottled; nectaries obscure.
    C. Fl. yellow, ½–¾in. long . . . . 2. *F. pudica*
    CC. Fl. pinkish-purple, 1–1½ in. long . . . . 3. *F. pluriflora*
  BB. Style trifid with linear stigmas; perianth-segms. mottled; nectaries prominent.
    C. Lvs. alternate . . . . 4. *F. Meleagris*
    CC. Lvs. whorled.
      D. Fl. almost tubiform, scarlet checkered with yellow, becoming purple in age . . . 5. *F. recurva*
      DD. Fl. campanulate, brownish-purple mottled with greenish-yellow . . . . 6. *F. lanceolata*

1. **F. imperialis,** L. (*Imperialis coronata*, Dum.-Cours.). CROWN IMPERIAL. Striking, stout and erect, spotted purple on st. above, 2–4 ft., with strong odor, from large bulb: lvs. many, scattered, ascending, lanceolate, often more than 1 in. wide, glabrous: fls. several hanging on curved pedicels under a crown or whorl of lvs. that stands well above the other foliage, purplish, brick-red or yellow-red, with large nectar-drops in bottom; segms. 1½–2 in. long, oblong to oblanceolate, veiny; 3-parted style eventually protruding. Himalayas and Iran.

2. **F. pudica,** Spreng. (*Lilium pudicum*, Pursh). Bulbs of small thick scales: st. 3–15 in. high: lvs. alternate, few, linear to lanceolate, 2½–8 in. long: fls. 1–3, yellow to orange, sometimes brown-veined outside, becoming brick-red with age, campanulate; segms. ½–¾in. long; stamens almost as long as segms.; style about as long, with knobbed stigma: caps. oblong-obovoid, ⅔in. long. B. C. to Calif., Mont. and New Mex.

3. **F. pluriflora,** Torr. Bulbs of few large fleshy scales: st. 8–16 in. high: lvs. clustered on lower part of st., alternate, elliptical to obovate-oblong, 2½–5 in. long: fls. 2–8, campanulate, pinkish-purple; segms. 1–1½ in. long, obovate; stamens half as long as segms.; style with 3-lobed stigma: caps. obtusely angled, truncate at apex, as broad as long. Calif.

4. **F. Meleagris,** L. SNAKES-HEAD. CHECKERED-LILY. St. erect, 12–18 in., glabrous: lvs. few, alternate, linear to oblong-lanceolate, with semi-clasping base, 4–6 in. long: fls. normally 1 but sometimes 2 or 3 in cult., hanging, short open-bell-shaped, 2–3 in. across, checkered and veined with purplish or maroon on a paler ground; segms. oblong, obtuse, nearly 2 in. long. England and continental Eu. to S. W. Asia. Var. **alba,** Hort., has pure white fls.

5. **F. recurva,** Benth. Bulbs of thick scales with many rice-grain bulblets: st. 12–30 in. tall: lvs. 8–10, mostly in two whorls above middle of st., linear to lance-linear, 2–4 in. long: fls. 1–6, tubiform-campanulate, scarlet checkered with yellow, becoming purple in age; segms. oblanceolate, recurved at tips, ¾–1½ in. long; nectary oval, depressed, yellow with red spots; stamens slightly shorter than segms.; style cleft one-quarter to one-fifth its length: caps. almost ½in. long. S. Ore., Calif. Var. **coccinea,** Greene, segms. usually not recurved; Calif.

6. **F. lanceolata,** Pursh. Bulbs of a few scales and rice-grain bulblets: st. ½–4 ft.: lvs. in several whorls on upper st., usually 3–5 in a whorl, ovate-lanceolate, 1½–5 in. long: fls 1 to several, bowl-shaped, brownish-purple mottled with greenish-yellow, sometimes almost solidly purple; segms. 1–1½ in. long, ovate to oblong; nectary yellowish-green with minute purple dots; stamens half as long as segms.; style cleft to middle: caps. ¾–1 in. long. B. C. to Ida. and Calif.

37. **TULIPA,** L. Tulip. Low spring-blooming plants of much beauty; species 150 or more in the Medit. region and across Asia to Japan; the commonest garden tulips are considered to be referable to two species (nos. 10 and 14), but other species are sometimes grown as "botanical tulips."—Bulbs tunicated, mostly tapering upward; st. simple (in some species branched), scape-like but lf.-bearing, to 30 in. high, glabrous and glaucous or sometimes pilose or scabrous: lvs. largely radical, in the garden forms broad and thick and more or less glaucous: fls. mostly erect, bell-shaped to saucer-shaped; segms. of perianth 6, distinct, without nectaries; stamens 6, hypogynous, included, anthers basifixed, introrse; style wanting in the garden forms, stigma usually 3-lobed: fr. a loculicidal caps. with many seeds. (Tu-lipa: from oriental word for turban.)—Fls. in solid colors are "selfs" or "breeders"; those with mixed colors are said to be "broken"; when the under color is white and markings lilac or purple, they are "bybloems"; when under color is yellow and markings red to brown, they are "bizarres."

A. Filaments of stamens hairy at base: buds often nodding.
B. Fls. yellow to orange within; anthers yellow to orange.
C. St. colored: fls. star-like when mature.
D. Segms. of perianth 2 in. long, the outer mostly greenish, sometimes reddish without. . . . . 1. *T. australis*
DD. Segms. of perianth 1¼ in. long, the outer much colored with red without. 2. *T. Celsiana*
CC. St. green: fls. bell-shaped when mature. . . . . 3. *T. sylvestris*
BB. Fls. red or white within, at least on upper half of segms.
C. Segms. incurved, coppery to red within; anthers purple-black. . . . . 4. *T. Hageri*
CC. Segms. spreading, white within (at least in upper half).
D. Length of segms. ¾ in.; anthers with purple tips. . . . . 5. *T. biflora*
DD. Length of segms. to 2 in.; anthers yellow. . . . . 6. *T. tarda*
AA. Filaments of stamens lacking hairs: buds erect.
B. Fls. soft green, bell-shaped, about 2½ in. long. . . . . 13. *T. viridiflora*
BB. Fls. not green.
C. Segms. eight to ten times as long as wide, with long-acuminate tips. . . . . 11. *T. acuminata*
CC. Segms. much less than eight times as long as wide, not so tipped.
D. Size of fls. large, the segms. mostly 3–4 in. long, red with a usually dark blotch edged yellow; anthers dark.
E. Lvs. marked with broken purple or brown stripes. . . . . 20. *T. Greigii*
EE. Lvs. not so marked.
F. Sts. 12–20 in. high: inner segms. with median yellow stripe. . . . . 16. *T. præcox*
FF. Sts. 6–10 in. high: inner segms. not so striped.
G. Inner surface of fl. dull scarlet of a brownish shade: lvs. not glaucous: inner surface of tunic felt-like. . . . . 15. *T. Oculus-solis*
GG. Inner surface of fl. brilliant glossy scarlet: lvs. glaucous: inner surface of tunic more or less silky.
H. Perianth-segms. acuminate or with terminal mucro. . . . . 17. *T. Eichleri*
HH. Perianth-segms. rounded at apex. . . . . 18. *T. Fosteriana*
DD. Size of fls. smaller, the segms. 1½–2 in. long, or if larger the segms. usually lacking a conspicuous dark blotch.
E. St. pubescent and somewhat scabrous: segms. usually red with yellow margins and streaks; anthers yellow. . . . . 14. *T. suaveolens*
EE. St. mostly glabrous and smooth.
F. Fl. star-like and yellow to white within.
G. Anthers dark purple or red; fls. blotched basally. . . . . 8. *T. Clusiana*
GG. Anthers yellow; flowers not blotched within.
H. The fls. pale yellow. . . . . 7. *T. stellata*
HH. The fls. bright clear yellow. . . . . 8. *T. Clusiana* var. *chrysantha*
FF. Fls. more or less cup- or bell-shaped, sometimes opening wider.
G. Inner segms. sharp-pointed: st. 3–6 in. high. . . . . 9. *T. linifolia*
GG. Inner segms. rounded at apex (sometimes with a mucro).
H. Length of inner segms. about two and one-half times the width; segms. red, pink, white or yellow, with a yellow blotch; anthers yellow. . . . . 19. *T. Kaufmanniana*
HH. Length of inner segms. not more than twice the width.
I. Perianth brick-red; filaments vermilion, anthers purple. . . . 21. *T. præstans*
II. Perianth red to yellow or white; filaments white or purple, anthers purple or yellow.
J. Stamens with filaments blue-black above and pale yellow anthers: fl. yellowish becoming white. . . . . 12. *T. Marjolettii*
JJ. Stamens with filaments and anthers purple or yellow: fl. color variable. . . . . 10. *T. Gesneriana*

1. **T. australis,** Link. Tunic tough, reddish-brown, usually short-haired within: lvs. 3–5, linear, parallel-sided and folded in the middle, mostly 6–8 in. long, ¾in. wide: st. glabrous, pigmented, usually solitary, about 6 in. high; bud green, nodding; fls. erect, urn-shaped before opening, later star-shaped; segms. pointed, 2 in. long, uniform clear yellow within, greenish to reddish without; filaments half as long as segms., short-hairy at base, anthers yellow: midseason. Medit. region.

2. **T. Celsiana,** DC. (*T. persica*, Hort. not Willd.). Near to the above but tunic hairless within, more reddish: segms. 1¼ in. long, more red on backs; flowering about two weeks later. (Named for C. Cels, who grew the plant in Holland.) W. Medit. region.—The so-called *T. persica* is sometimes referred to *T. patens*, Agardh, but that species has white fls. with a yellow base, the backs of the outer segms. stained with violet.

3. **T. sylvestris,** L. (*T. florentina*, Hort. *T. florentina odorata*, Hort.). Tunic bright yellow tinged with red, with few straight hairs within at base, almost a tuft at apex: lvs. 2–3, very glaucous, little channelled, 5–8 in. long, ¾in. wide: st. to 1 ft., glabrous, not pigmented, often with 2 fls.; bud green, usually nodding; fls. slender-campanulate; segms. clear yellow to orange within, with some green or red without, 2 in. long, ¾in. wide, inner segms. fringed near base; filaments yellow or orange, one-third as long as segms., hairy at base, anthers yellow or orange: midseason to late. Eu.

4. **T. Hageri,** Heldr. Tunic tough, brown, often abundantly hairy within toward apex: lvs. 4–5, strap-shaped, 6–8 in. long, channelled, dark green with red edges: st. rather longer than lvs., glabrous, brown; bud erect, green; fls. usually 1, sometimes 2–4, cup-shaped; segms. 2 in. long, 1 in. wide, incurved, coppery to scarlet within, with more or less of a basal blotch, the outer green and buff on back, the inner copper-colored with green median rib, hairy on edges near base; stamens half as long as segms., hairy at base, purple-black: early. (Named for Friedrich Hager of Hanover, who accompanied Heldreich.) E. Medit. region.

5. **T. biflora,** Pall. Tunic yellow-brown, silky-haired within at apex: lvs. 3–4, strap-shaped, bronze-green, a little folded, 4–5 in. long, ⅔in. wide: st. about 5 in. high, with 1–5 fls.; bud erect, green; fls. star-like; segms. ¾in. long, lanceolate, white within, with yellow basal blotch, backs of outer segms. stained with green and red, of inner with green median line; stamens one-third as long as segms., filaments basally pilose, pale yellow, anthers yellow with purple tips: early. S. Russia.

6. **T. tarda,** Stapf (*T. dasystemon*, Hort. not Regel). Tunic thin, yellow, with few hairs at base and apex: lvs. up to 7, lanceolate to linear, glabrous, at first folded, later flat, 5–9 in. long, ¾in. wide: st. glabrous or nearly so, 2–3 in. high, 2–7-fld.; bud erect; fls. opening to a flat star; segms. to almost 2 in. long, elliptic-lanceolate, acute to acuminate, within yellow at base white toward tips, on backs the outer tinged green and slightly red, the inner with 2 purple lines and a green median one; filaments yellow, basally hairy, scarcely ½in. long, anthers yellow: midseason. Turkestan.—*T. dasystemon*, Regel, with which this has been confused, has 2 lvs. and pale yellow segms. dirty-violet without.

7. **T. stellata,** Hook. (*T. Clusiana* var. *stellata*, Regel). A species of uncertain taxonomic status and probably only varietally distinct from *T. Clusiana*, not known to be cult., but the name occasionally encountered in trade lists: fls. uniformly pale yellow over a ground color of white, not blotched, Kashmir to Afghanistan.—See under no. 8 for var. *chrysantha*.

8. **T. Clusiana,** DC. LADY TULIP. Tunic brown and leathery, woolly within near apex: lvs. 2–5, somewhat glaucous, sometimes red on edges, sharply folded, the lower 8–10 in. long, ⅜in. wide: st. glabrous, to 1 ft. high; bud solitary, green, erect; fls. at first campanulate, later almost a flat star; segms. 1½–2 in. long, ⅝in. wide, acute, white within with basal carmine blotch, backs of outer segms. red with white margin; stamens less than half as long as segms., purple: midseason. (Named for Clusius, or Charles de l'Escluse, 1526–1609, professor of botany at Leiden.) Iran; nat. in S. Eu. Var. **chrysantha,** Sealy (*T. stellata* var. *chrysantha*, A. D. Hall. *T. chrysantha*, Auth. not Boiss.), differs in fls. bright clear yellow within, blotchless, stamens yellow and not purplish. India.—Easily cult., long-persisting when in well-drained soil in sunny location. *T. chrysantha*, Boiss. (*T. montana* var. *chrysantha*, Dykes), has segms. twice as wide and pale lemon-yellow.

9. **T. linifolia,** Regel. Tunic leathery, light brown, with tuft of yellowish wool at apex: lvs. several, linear, 3–5 in. long, somewhat glaucous and edged with red: st. green, 3–6 in. high; bud green; fls. solitary, at first cylindrical, later opening widely; outer segms. rhomboidal, 2 in. long, ⅘in. wide, subacuminate, inner shorter and obovate, all brilliant scarlet with deep purple basal blotch; stamens short, black: midseason. Bokhara.

10. **T. Gesneriana,** L. COMMON GARDEN or LATE TULIP. Tunic thin, papery, with a few appressed hairs near base and summit: lvs. 3–5, glaucous, lanceolate to almost ovate, about 6 in. long and 1 in. or more wide, fringed with few short hairs near tips: st. usually 1-fld., glabrous, 8–15 in. high; fls. campanulate, opening widely, scarlet with obscure black-purple center, varying to yellow or white; outer segms. 2–3 in. long, about 1 in. wide, elliptic to lanceolate, acute, the inner shorter, broader, obovate, obtusish; stamens one-third as long as segms., often deep purple: midseason and late. (Named for C. Gesner,

1516–1565, botanist:) Asia. Var. **Dracontia,** Baker, PARROT or DRAGON TULIP, segms. deeply cut and crisped. Var. **Darwinia,** Bailey, DARWIN TULIP, tall, late-flowering, large-lvd.; fls. self-colored, deep rich reds, crimsons and purple, cup-shaped; the Rembrandt tulips are of the Darwin class but with parti-colored fls.

11. **T. acuminata,** Vahl (*T. cornuta,* Redouté. *T. stenopetala,* Mord. de Laun.). TURKISH TULIP. Doubtfully distinct botanically from no. 10: fls. yellow or pink, obconical in bud; segms. oblong-linear, crisped, long-acuminate, spirally twisted, splotched with red lines, 4–5 in. long; filaments white or yellow, anthers reddish-yellow: midseason. Probably of garden origin.

12. **T. Marjolettii,** Perrier & Songeon. Also doubtfully distinct botanically from no. 10: fls. campanulate, yellowish becoming white, purple tinted outside; outer segms. elliptic, subacute, over 1½ in. long, the inner obovate, very obtuse, mucronulate, flushed blue near the base externally; stamens one-third as long as segms., filaments blue-black above, anthers pale yellow: midseason. (Named for J. M. Marjollet, 1823–1894.) Savoy.

13. **T. viridiflora,** Hort. Somewhat like the Parrot tulip: lvs. large, ovate-lanceolate, 6–10 in. long, 2–3 in. wide: st. to 2 ft. tall; fls. cup-shaped, light soft green with yellowish or whitish edges; segms. abruptly acute or cuspidate, 2½ in. long; stamens one-third the length of segms.: midseason to late. Of garden origin.

14. **T. suaveolens,** Roth. DUC VAN THOL TULIP. Tunic brown, papery, with few appressed hairs near base and apex: lvs. 3 or 4, long-lanceolate, glaucous, more or less pubescent on upper surface, about as long as st.: st. 3–6 in. high, pubescent and scabrous at least above; bud erect; fls. 1, fragrant, chalice-shaped; segms. 2 in. long, to ¾in. broad. oblong, acute, bright red with yellow margins; stamens yellow: very early. S. Russia to Iraq.

15. **T. Oculus-solis,** St. Amans. Tunic brown, papery, thick-felty within: lvs. usually 4, channelled, oblong, acute, 4–5 in. long, 2 in. wide, or the lowest to 10 in. long: st. glabrous, to 8 in. long; bud erect, green; fls. 1, campanulate, dull scarlet within, flushed yellow without, the outer segms. 3 in. long, 1 in. wide, with an inner basal black blotch bordered yellow, inner segms. a little smaller with similar blotch; stamens less than half as long as segms., filaments glabrous, black, anthers black: early. (Oculus-solis: Latin *eye of the sun.*) S. Eu.

16. **T. præcox,** Ten. Tunic thick, brown, densely brown-woolly within: lvs. 3–5, glaucous, the lowest oblong-ovate, up to 12 in. long and 3 in. wide, the upper oblong-lanceolate: st. 12–20 in. high, slightly tomentose, pigmented; bud erect, green; fls. wide-campanulate, deep red with central black blotches bordered yellow; outer segms. elliptical, 3½ in. long and 1½ in. wide, dull orange or green without, inner segms. shorter, less pointed and with median yellow stripe; stamens one-third as long as segms., deep olive to black: early. S. Eu. to Asia.

17. **T. Eichleri,** Regel. Tunic dark brown, stiff-hairy within: lvs. 4–5, broadly strap-shaped, the lowest up to 8 in. long and 2½ in. wide, upper reduced: st. slightly pubescent, 6–8 in. high; bud 1, green, erect; fls. campanulate, brilliant scarlet within, with basal third of each segm. having a black blotch with yellow margin; segms. with tuft of white hairs at tips and slightly pubescent on backs; outer segms. 4 in. long, 2 in. wide, acuminate or mucronate, light buff on backs, the inner obovate; stamens about two-fifths as long as segms., deep violet: early. (Named for the collector, Wilhelm Eichler.) S. W. Asia.

18. **T. Fosteriana,** Hoog. Tunic papery, purple-brown, silky-hairy within: lvs. 3–4. usually glaucous, occasionally pubescent, ciliate, the 2 lower broadly ovate, channelled, blunt, up to 8 in. long, 4 in. wide, upper smaller and flat: st. glaucous, 8–10 in. long; bud 1, erect, green; fls. at first cup-shaped, later flat, brilliant scarlet with basal black blotches margined with yellow; segms. about 4 in. long, elliptical or obovate, with minute tuft of hairs at each apex; stamens one-third as long as segms., black (sometimes the basal blotch and anthers are yellow): early. (Named for Sir Michael Foster, 1836–1907, English physician.) Cent. Asia.

19. **T. Kaufmanniana,** Regel. WATER-LILY TULIP. Tunic papery, brown, scattered-hairy within: lvs. 2–5, broad-oblong, the lowest 10 in. long, 3 in. wide: st. slightly pubescent, 6–8 in. high; fls. at first chalice-shaped, opening to a flat star, varying from pink or scarlet through white and yellow; segms. narrow-elliptical to obovate, 2–3 in. long, to 1 in. wide, with basal yellow blotch covering lower half; stamens one-third as long as segms., yellow: early. (Named for Gen. von Kaufmann, Governor-General of province where discovered.) Turkestan.—Markings and colors very variable.

20. **T. Greigii,** Regel. Tunic brown, papery, with some long silky hairs within: lvs. 3–4, broadly lanceolate, channelled, subacute, glaucous, with some linear striping in purple-brown, 4–8 in. long, to 3 in. wide: st. 8–16 in. high, slightly downy: fls. chalice-shaped, brilliant scarlet with bright yellow base within which is a rounded dark blotch on each segm.; outer segms. rhomboidal, abruptly pointed, 3 in. long, 1½ in. wide, the inner a little larger, obovate, all minutely tufted with apical hairs; stamens one-fourth as long as segms., black: early. (Named for S. A. Greig, 1827–1887?, Russian horticulturist.) Turkestan.

21. **T. præstans,** Hoog. Tunic thick, leathery, with few silky hairs· lvs 3–6, narrowly lanceolate, long-acuminate, glaucous, sharply channelled along middle: st. 8–12 in. high, with 1–4 fls.; fls. cup-shaped, bright brick-red; segms. elliptic, subobtuse, apiculate, 2–2½ in. long, 1 in. wide, without basal blotches; stamens one-third as long as segms., filaments vermilion, anthers purple: early. Cent. Asia.

38. **CALOCHORTUS,** Pursh. Globe-Tulip. Mariposa- or Butterfly-Lily. About 60 cormous plants of W. N. Amer., some of which are more or less planted.—Plant producing tunicated corms; st. more or less branched, slender or flexuose, a few in. to 6 ft. tall: lvs. linear to lanceolate: fls. showy, yellow, white, bluish or lilac, often spotted or marked in center, terminal singly or fascicularly, broadly campanulate, wide open to globose, erect or nodding; segms. 6, the 3 inner ones or petals showy and bearing gland or spot at base, the outer ones smaller and sepal-like; stamens 6, the anthers basifixed, introrse; ovary superior, 3-loculed, many-ovuled, stigmas sessile, recurved: fr. a 3-angled or 3-winged mostly septicidal caps. with many flattened seeds. (Calochor-tus: from Greek words for *beautiful* and *grass*.)

A. Fls. nodding; perianth-parts incurved.
B. Color of fls. white, or with reddish-purple tinge .... 1. *C. albus*
BB. Color of fls. yellow .... 2. *C. amabilis*
AA. Fls. erect; perianth open.
B. Color of fls. yellow; gland round or lunate.
C. Gland at base of petal round, deep, surrounded by a membrane; petals 1⅜–1¾ in. long, and with transverse band of clavate hairs .... 3. *C. clavatus*
CC. Gland lunate, not deep nor surrounded by a membrane; petals 1–1⅜ in. long, sparsely invested with slender hairs .... 4. *C. luteus*
BB. Color of fls. white to lavender or purplish, if yellow with glands quadrate or shaped like an inverted V.
C. Petals ½–¾ in. long, hairy on whole upper surface .... 5. *C. cæruleus*
CC. Petals 1–2 in. long, not hairy on whole upper surface.
D. Caps. winged: petals long-ciliate, whitish to lavender and with central red-purplish blotch .... 6. *C. nitidus*
DD. Caps. not winged: petals not ciliate.
E. Gland depressed, surrounded by a membrane; petals purple, with median longitudinal green stripe and sometimes with transverse purple band above the gland .... 7. *C. macrocarpus*
EE. Gland not depressed or surrounded by a membrane; various colors.
F. The gland quadrate; petals variable in color, white to yellow, purple or dark red and with median dark red blotch, often a second paler blotch above the first .... 8. *C. venustus*
FF. The gland not quadrate; petals usually pencilled with purple or red at base, median dark blotch bordered yellow.
G. Shape of gland an inverted V; petals white to yellowish or lavender .... 9. *C. superbus*
GG. Shape of gland doubly lunate; petals white to purplish .... 10. *C. Vesta*

1. **C. albus,** Dougl. Fairy Lantern. St. stout, branching, glaucous, ½–2 ft. tall: basal lf. 1–2 ft. long, ½–2 in. wide, cauline lvs. 2–6, reduced up the st.: fls. several, white to rose, subglobose, nodding on slender pedicels; sepals ovate to lanceolate, acuminate, glabrous, one-half to two-thirds as long as petals; petals almost orbicular, long-hairy above gland, ciliate, about 1 in. long; gland depressed, lunate, with 4–5 transverse fringed membranes; anthers oblong, ⅙in. long: caps. oblong, nodding, 3-winged, ¾–1½ in. long. Calif.

2. **C. amabilis,** Purdy. Golden Fairy Lantern. St. stout, 4–12 in. high: basal lf. 1–2 ft. long, ¼–1 in. wide, cauline lvs. 2–4, reduced: fls. deep yellow, often tinged brown, globose to somewhat campanulate, nodding on slender pedicels; sepals not shorter than petals, ovate to lanceolate, acute to acuminate, glabrous; petals lance-ovate, obtuse, fringed, scarcely hairy on surface; gland depressed, lunate, covered with dense fringe from upper margin; anthers oblong, ⅙in. long: caps. oblong, 3-winged, nodding. Calif.

3. **C. clavatus,** Wats. (*Mariposa clavata,* Hoover). St. stout, 1–5 ft. high: lvs. deeply channelled, broadly linear, up to 12 in. long: fls. 1–6, subumbellate, erect, cup-shaped, lemon-yellow, sometimes with reddish markings; sepals lance-ovate, 1–1½ in. long, glabrous; petals broadly fan-shaped, 1½–2 in. long, with transverse band of club-shaped hairs; gland circular, depressed, surrounded by a fringed membrane; anthers red-brown, oblong, ½in. long: caps. lanceolate, 3-angled, 2–3 in. long. Calif.

4. **C. luteus,** Dougl. (*C. venustus* var. *citrinus,* Auth. not Baker. *Mariposa lutea,* Hoover). St. rather slender, ½–2 ft. high: basal lvs. 1–2, narrowly linear, 4–8 in. long, cauline 1–2, reduced: fls. 1–4, subumbellate, erect, campanulate, deep yellow; sepals oblong-lanceolate, acuminate, glabrous, equalling petals; petals fan-shaped, 1–1½ in. long, slightly hairy near gland, usually pencilled brown below and often with median brown blotch; anthers oblong, pale yellow, ⅓in. long: caps. lanceolate, 3-angled, 1½–2 in. long. Calif.

5. **C. cæruleus,** Wats. (*Cyclobothrya cærulea,* Kellogg. *Calochortus Maweanus,* Leicht.). St. 3–6 in. high, usually simple, slender: basal lf. 4–8 in. long, the others bract-like: fls. erect, 1–5 or more, subumbellate, bluish; sepals slightly shorter than petals, oblong-lanceolate, acuminate, glabrous; petals almost round, ½–¾in. long, bearded over most of upper surface; gland transverse, arched upward, bordered below with a fringed membrane and above with series of short thick papillose processes; anthers oblong, acute, ⅙in. long: caps. elliptic, nodding, winged, 1 in. long. Calif.—Material cult. as *C. Maweanus* may possibly be *C. Tolmei,* Hook. & Arn., with branched sts. and less conspicuously fringed petals.

6. **C. nitidus,** Dougl. St. 1–1½ ft. tall, with single cauline lf. about the middle: basal lf. 4–12 in. long, ¼–1 in. wide, bracts 2 or more: fls. erect, 1–5, subumbellate, creamy-white to lavender; sepals ovate to lanceolate, usually shorter than petals; petals fan-shaped, to 1½ in. long, with few long hairs about the gland and median red-purple blotch; gland triangular-lunate, with narrow fringed membrane below and often with a narrow crenate one above; anthers oblong, obtuse, ⅛in. long: caps. elliptic-oblong, 3-winged, almost 1 in. long, erect. Wash. to Ore. and Mont.

7. **C. macrocarpus,** Dougl. (*Mariposa macrocarpa,* Hoover). St. stout, glaucous, 1–2 ft. tall, usually simple: lvs. linear, several, recurved, 2–4 in. long: fls. 1–3, subumbellate, erect, open-campanulate, purple; sepals lanceolate, long-acuminate, usually exceeding petals; petals obovate, short-acuminate, 1½–2 in. long, with slender hairs above the gland, with median longitudinal green stripe and sometimes a transverse dark purple band; gland triangular-oblong, surrounded by a fringed membrane; anthers lanceolate, obtuse, almost ½in. long: caps. linear-lanceolate, angled, erect, nearly 2 in. long. B. C. to Mont. and N. Calif.

8. **C. venustus,** Dougl. (*Mariposa venusta,* Hoover). St. erect, usually branched, 1–2½ ft. high, mostly with 1–4 bulblets at base: basal lvs. linear, 1 or 2, 4–8 in. long, glaucous, cauline 1 or 2, reduced: fls. 1–3, subumbellate, erect, campanulate, white to yellow, purple or dark red; sepals narrow-lanceolate, equalling petals, attenuate, with tips curled back; petals broadly cuneate-obovate, 1–1½ in. long, sparingly slender-hairy near the gland, with median dark red blotch and often a second paler blotch above the first; gland quadrate in outline, densely covered with short hair-like processes, not bordered by a membrane; anthers usually lilac, narrow, about ⅓in. long: caps. linear, 3-angled, erect, 2–2½ in. long. Calif.

9. **C. superbus,** Purdy (*C. venustus* var. *citrinus,* Baker. *C. venustus* var. *oculatus,* Hort. *C. venustus* var. *superbus,* Bailey. *Mariposa superba,* Hoover). Near to the preceding: fls. white to yellowish or lavender; sepals usually shorter than petals; petals pencilled with purple below and marked with a median reddish-brown or purple blotch surrounded by a bright yellow zone; gland linear, like an inverted V; anthers cream-color, ¼–⅓in. long: caps. lanceolate-linear, 2 in. long. Calif.

10. **C. Vesta,** Wallace (*C. venustus* var. *Vesta,* Purdy. *C. luteus* var. *Vestæ,* Jepson). Near to *C. superbus* but larger: fls. white to purplish; sepals usually shorter than petals; petals pencilled with red or purple below and marked with a larger median reddish-brown blotch surrounded by a pale yellow zone; gland transverse, doubly lunate. (Named for Mrs. Carl [Vesta] Purdy.) Calif.

39. **LILIUM,** L. LILY. Attractive plants of the north temp. zone, probably less than 100 species; several species are common in gardens, and others appear in choice collections.—Per. erect leafy-stemmed herbs, with underground scaly bulbs: fls. pendulous, inclined, horizontal or erect, solitary or clustered, with 6 separate segms. which are scarcely differentiated as between sepal-like and petal-like organs, each bearing a nectar-groove or -furrow at base; stamens 6, hypogynous or slightly adherent to perianth, mostly shorter than the segms., the anthers versatile, filaments very slender; pistil 1, with long style and 3-lobed stigma: fr. a 3-celled loculicidal many-seeded caps. (Lil-ium: the Latin name; the Greek word is *lirion,* used in the naming of some of the subdivisions of the genus.)

A. Fls. erect, open bowl-shaped, the segms. usually clawed and wide-spreading but scarcely reflexed; style quite straight. (PSEUDOLIRIUM.)
  B. Style short, not longer than ovary; perianth-segms. 1–2 in. long. . . . . 1. *L. concolor*
  BB. Style two to three times as long as ovary; segms. mostly 2–4 in. long.
    C. Lvs. whorled: sts. glabrous . . . . 2. *L. philadelphicum*
    CC. Lvs. scattered: sts. pubescent at least above.
      D. Perianth-segms. mostly less than 3 in. long.
        E. Pedicels erect, straight; segms. ¼–1 in. wide . . . . 3. *L. dauricum*
        EE. Pedicels curved outward, mostly divaricate; segms. 1–1½ in. wide . . . . 4. *L. bulbiferum*
      DD. Perianth-segms. 3–4 in. long, 1–1½ in. wide . . . . 5. *L. maculatum*
AA. Fls. horizontal to nodding, segms. not usually clawed.

B. Lvs. heart-shaped, broad, long-petioled: fls. funnel-shaped. (CARDIOCRINUM.) .... 6. *L. giganteum*
BB. Lvs. not heart-shaped.
C. Perianth-segms. curved or spreading only in their distal third; stamens not divergent. (LEUCOLIRION.)
D. The lvs. mostly whorled.
E. Color of fls. mostly white, becoming rose-purple.
F. Segms. 3–4 in. long .... 7. *L. Washingtonianum*
FF. Segms. 1½–2 in. long .... 8. *L. rubescens*
EE. Color of fls. red.
F. Shape of lvs. obovate to oblanceolate, 1½–2 in. long: fls. red-purple with darker spots .... 9. *L. Bolanderi*
FF. Shape of lvs. lanceolate, 2–4 in. long: fls. red, spotted gold .... 10. *L. Grayi*
DD. The lvs. scattered, not whorled.
E. Color of fls. essentially white, often flushed purplish or tinged with green especially on outside.
F. Tube of perianth slender, widening but little from base to middle.
G. Fl. usually pure white: lvs. ⅜–⅝in. wide .... 11. *L. longiflorum*
GG. Fl. white tinged green or purple without.
H. Segms. tinged green without, 7–10 in. long: lvs. ⅛in. wide .... 12. *L. philippinense*
HH. Segms. tinged purple without, 5–6 in. long: lvs. ⅛–⅜in. wide .... 13. *L. formosanum*
FF. Tube of perianth widening from base upward.
G. Length of segms. 2–3 in.: fls. white .... 14. *L. candidum*
GG. Length of segms. 4–7 in.
H. Fl. white with green blotch in throat .... 15. *L. leucanthum* var. *centifolium*
HH. Fl. white with some purple without or within.
I. Lf.-axils with bulblets; lvs. 3–5-nerved .... 16. *L. Sargentiæ*
II. Lf.-axils without bulblets.
J. Lf. 1-nerved, to ¼in. wide .... 17. *L. regale*
JJ. Lf. 5–7-nerved, ¾in. wide .... 18. *L. Brownii*
EE. Color of fls. rose or yellow.
F. Fl. yellow, at least within.
G. Segms. 2–4 in. long .... 19. *L. Parryi*
GG. Segms. 7–12 in. long .... 20. *L. myriophyllum*
FF. Fl. rose-pink.
G. Segms. 5–6 in. long .... 21. *L. japonicum*
GG. Segms. 2–3 in. long .... 22. *L. rubellum*
CC. Perianth-segms. strongly recurved or spreading from the middle or below; stamens divergent.
D. Infl. of horizontal fls., inner segms. broadest below their middle, white with yellow median band. (ARCHELIRION.) .... 23. *L. auratum*
DD. Infl. of pendulous fls., inner segms. broadest about the middle. (MARTAGON.)
E. Arrangement of lvs. mostly in whorls.
F. Color of fls. white to rose or purple.
G. Width of lvs. 1–1½ in.; whorls with 6–9 lvs.: bulb yellow .... 24. *L. Martagon*
GG. Width of lvs. ½–¾in.; whorls with 8–12 lvs.: bulb white .... 25. *L. Kelloggii*
FF. Color of fls. yellow to orange-red.
G. Segms. of perianth 1–1½ in. long.
H. Width of lvs. ½–1½ in.: fls. orange-yellow .... 26. *L. Hansonii*
HH. Width of lvs. ¼–⅓in.: fls. orange-red .... 27. *L. Roezlii*
GG. Segms. 2–4 in. long.
H. Anthers to about ¼in. long at mid-anthesis.
I. Bulb-scales not jointed: anthers yellow .... 28. *L. columbianum*
II. Bulb-scales jointed: anthers brownish-red .... 29. *L. occidentale*
HH. Anthers mostly ½–¾in. long at mid-anthesis.
I. Lf. finely roughened on the margins and veins of under surface: perianth-segms. lacking a prominent green basal blotch.
J. Whorls of 4–10 lvs.: anthers usually yellow .... 30. *L. canadense*
JJ. Whorls of 9–20 lvs.: anthers red to orange.
K. Bulb-scales jointed: perianth-segms. 2–3 in. long, ½–¾in. wide: lvs. lanceolate .... 31. *L. pardalinum*
KK. Bulb-scales not jointed: perianth-segms. 3–4 in. long, ½–1 in. wide: lvs. oblanceolate .... 32. *L. Humboldtii*
II. Lf. perfectly smooth: perianth-segms. with prominent green basal blotch.
J. Shape of lf. lanceolate, ½–¾in. wide .... 33. *L. superbum*
JJ. Shape of lf. oblanceolate, 1–1½ in. wide .... 34. *L. Michauxii*
EE. Arrangement of lvs. scattered, not in whorls.
F. Color of fls. white to rose or lilac.
G. Segms. to 2 in. long, lilac spotted purple .... 35. *L. cernuum*
GG. Segms. 3–4 in. long, white suffused rose, spotted red .... 36. *L. speciosum*
FF. Color of fls. scarlet to orange or yellow.
G. Segms. of perianth 1–2 in. long.
H. St. with stiff hispid hairs .... 37. *L. amabile*
HH. St. glabrous or slightly soft-pubescent, but not hispid.

I. Nerves of lf. 1: style about twice as long as ovary...... 38. *L. pumilum*
II. Nerves of lf. 3–7.
J. Margins of lvs. not glandular-ciliate: style shorter than ovary.................................... 39. *L. callosum*
JJ. Margins of lvs. glandular-ciliate: style equalling or longer than ovary.
K. Veins underneath lvs. with gland-like hairs, lf. mostly 2–3 in. long: fls. usually not spotted..... 40. *L. chalcedonicum*
KK. Veins underneath lvs. bare, lf. mostly 3–5 in. long: fls. spotted.
L. Blades of lvs. 3-nerved, canaliculate and keeled: fls. scarlet.................................. 41. *L. pomponium*
LL. Blades of lvs. 5–7-nerved, not canaliculate or keeled: fls. yellow........................ 42. *L. pyrenaicum*
GG. Segms. of perianth mostly 2½–4 in. long.
H. Blades of lvs. many-nerved, ½–1¼ in. wide.
I. Fl. orange with brown spots; segms. 2½–3 in. long..... 43. *L. Henryi*
II. Fl. yellow with purple tinge or spots; segms. 3–4 in. long.. 44. *L. monadelphum*
HH. Blades of lvs. 1–7-nerved, 1/16–¾ in. wide.
I. Upper axils with bulblets: lvs. with 5–7 nerves........ 45. *L. tigrinum*
II. Upper axils lacking bulblets: lvs. mostly with 1–3 nerves.
J. Lf. 1-nerved, 1/12–⅙in. wide..................... 46. *L. Davidii*
JJ. Lf. 1–3- (rarely 7-) nerved, ¼–½in. wide.
K. Fl. yellow to apricot.
L. Perianth not spotted, sometimes lightly dotted red.. 47. *L. testaceum*
LL. Perianth spotted purple.................... 48. *L. Leichtlinii*
KK. Fl. red to orange-red.
L. St. puberulent, faintly spotted.
M. Plant not stem-rooting: fls. vermilion-scarlet, seldom dotted...................... 40. *L. chalcedonicum*
MM. Plant stem-rooting: fls. salmon-red, spotted purple............................... 48. *L. Leichtlinii* var. *Maximowiczii*
LL. St. glabrous or nearly so, much spotted......... 49. *L. Willmottiæ*

1. **L. concolor,** Salisb. STAR LILY. Bulbs ovoid, white, scarcely 1 in. diam., with firmly imbricated scales: plant stem-rooting; st. pubescent, 1–3 ft. high, more or less tinged with purple: lvs. scattered, narrowly lanceolate, acute, mostly 1–2 in. long, ⅛–¼in. wide, 3–5-nerved: fls. 1 to several, erect, star-shaped, vermilion, unspotted; pedicels 1–2 in. long; segms. lanceolate, 1–2 in. long, ¼–½in. wide; stamens and style colored like segms.; ovary to ⅜in. long, style slightly shorter: caps. ½–¾ in. long, obtusely angled. China. Var. **pulchellum,** Baker (*L. pulchellum*, Fisch. *L. Buschianum*, Lodd.), st. glabrous and green; fls. vermilion to orange, usually spotted; E. Asia.

2. **L. philadelphicum,** L. ORANGECUP LILY. WOOD LILY. Bulbs white, to 1 in. diam., with narrow jointed scales: plant not stem-rooting; st. glabrous, green, 1½–3 ft.: lvs. more or less definitely whorled, lanceolate, acute, 1–4 in. long, ¼–½in. wide, 3–5-nerved: fls. 1–5, erect, widely cup-shaped, orange-red spotted with purple; segms. lanceolate, 1½–2½ in. long; filaments yellow, anthers red; ovary ½–1 in. long, style 1½ in. or longer: caps. 1¼–2 in. high, obovoid. Me. to N. C. and Mo.

3. **L. dauricum,** Ker (*L. davuricum*, Auth.). CANDLESTICK LILY. Bulbs white, 1–1½ in. diam., with loosely imbricated jointed scales: plant stem-rooting; st. green, red-spotted, 1–3 ft. high, floccose-hairy: lvs. scattered, lanceolate, 2–4 in. long, ¼–½in. wide, 3–5-nerved: fls. 2–6, erect, widely opened, bright red, yellow at base, more or less spotted with purplish-black; pedicels erect, 1–2 in. long; segms. obovate or narrower, mostly 2–2½ in. long, ¼–1 in. wide; filaments green, anthers orange-red; style green, twice as long as ovary: caps. oblong-obovoid, about 2 in. long. N. E. Asia. (The correct botanical name is *L. pensylvanicum*, Ker, 1805, which was changed by its author to *L. dauricum* four years later, and which is not used in the official lily list.)—Many types occur. Var. **venustum,** Wils. (*L. venustum*, Kunth), fls. clear apricot and unspotted; Japan; an improved form of this var. is *L. Batemanniæ*, Hort. Var. **Wallacei,** Wils. (*L. Wallacei*, Wallace), very stoloniferous, fls. orange-brown with maroon spots; Japan; intro. to England by Wallace and Co.

4. **L. bulbiferum,** L. Bulbs white, globose, 2–3 in. diam., with broad scales: plant stem-rooting; st. 1½–4 ft. high, green, floccose at nodes and toward apex: lvs. lanceolate, scattered, acute, 1½–2½ in. long, ¼–⅝in. wide, 3–5-nerved, the upper commonly bulbiferous: fls. 1–3, widely opened, bright red, black-spotted; pedicels to 1 in. long, curved outward; segms. oblong-oblanceolate, about 2 in. long, 1–1⅓ in. wide; filaments yellow to orange, anthers brownish; ovary not more than half as long as style: caps. obovoid, 1½ in. long. Cent. Alps. Var. **croceum,** Pers. (*L. croceum*, Chaix. *L. aurantiacum*, West.), st. 3–6 ft. with none or very few bulbels in upper axils; fls. 1–20, orange, usually with red-purple spots, segms. 2–3 in. long; Pyrenees to Austria.—**L. hollandicum,** Bergmans (*L. umbellatum*, Hort. not Pursh), is probably *L. bulbiferum* × *L. maculatum*, or forms.

Var. **erectum,** Hort., fls. bright red suffused with orange. Var. **grandiflorum,** Hort., orange shading to red at tips. Var. **incomparabile,** Hort., rich crimson.

5. **L. maculatum,** Thunb. (*L. elegans,* Thunb. *L. Thunbergianum,* Schult. f. *L. dauricum* subsp. *Thunbergianum,* Wils.). Bulbs white, 1–1⅔ in. diam., with firmly imbricated lance-ovate scales: plant stem-rooting; st. 1½–2 ft. tall, sparsely floccose to glabrous: lvs. scattered, 2–4 in. long, ½–1 in. wide, 5–7-nerved: fls. 1 to several, open, erect, reddish-orange, scarcely to much spotted; pedicels 1–4 in. long; segms. 3–4 in. long, 1–1½ in. wide, oblong-spatulate; anthers orange: caps. about 2 in. long. Japan. Var. **atrosanguineum,** Bailey (forma *atrosanguineum,* Nakai. *L. Thunbergianum* var. *atrosanguineum,* Sieb. *L. elegans* var. *atrosanguineum,* Baker & Dyer), fls. rich dark crimson with black spots.

6. **L. giganteum,** Wall. (*Cardiocrinum giganteum,* Makino). Bulbs dark, blackish-green, 4–7 in. high, with loose scales: plant not stem-rooting; st. hollow, 6–12 ft. tall, 2 in. thick at base, green-purple: basal lvs. in a rosette, cordate-ovate, 12–18 in. long, on petioles about as long; cauline lvs. scattered, gradually reduced upward and becoming truncate at base: fls. 10 or more, funnel-shaped, nodding to horizontal, white with green tinge without, red-purple within; pedicels scarcely 1 in. long; segms. oblong, 5–6 in. long; filaments green, anthers yellow: caps. 2–3 in. long. Himalayas.

7. **L. Washingtonianum,** Kellogg. Washington Lily. Bulbs 6–8 in. long, oblique, somewhat stoloniferous, with imbricated lanceolate scales: plant not stem-rooting; st. 2–5 ft. high: lvs. in 5–6 whorls of 6–12, lanceolate, acute, 2–5 in. long, ½–1½ in. wide: fls. 2–20, racemose, fragrant, horizontal, funnel-shaped, white becoming purplish, sometimes dotted; pedicels ascending, 2–3 in. long; segms. 3–4 in. long, lanceolate, subobtuse, the upper third recurved; anthers golden: caps. 1 in. long. (Named for Martha Washington.) Ore., Calif. Var. **purpurascens,** Stearn (var. *purpureum,* Purdy not Baker), fls. wine-colored.

8. **L. rubescens,** Wats. Chaparral Lily. Bulbs 2 in. diam., oblique, with thick lanceolate scales: plant not stem-rooting; st. 2–5 ft. high: lvs. oblanceolate, 1½–3½ in. long, ½–1 in. wide, acute, the upper in 3–7 whorls: fls. 3–8, ascending, pale lilac or nearly white, becoming rose-purple, dotted with brown, funnelform; pedicels suberect, 1–2 in. long; segms. lanceolate, 1½–2 in. long, almost ½in. broad, acutish; anthers golden-red: caps. 1 in. long, slightly winged. Ore. to Calif.

9. **L. Bolanderi,** Wats. (*L. Howellii,* Johnston). Thimble Lily. Bulbs 1½ in. diam., with lanceolate appressed scales: plant not stem-rooting; st. 1–2½ ft. high: lvs. obovate or broadly lanceolate, acutish, 1½–2 in. long, mostly whorled: fls. 2–3 to many, more or less racemose, somewhat nodding to horizontal, campanulate, reddish-purple spotted with dark purple; pedicels slender, suberect, 1–1½ in. long; segms. elliptic, 1–1½ in. long, somewhat spreading above; anthers brown-purple. (Named for H. N. Bolander, page 40.) Ore. and adjacent Calif.

10. **L. Grayi,** Wats. Bulbs stoloniferous, with thick ovate scales: plant not stem-rooting; st. 2–3 ft., slender: lvs. oblong-lanceolate, acute, 2–4 in. long, mostly in whorls of 3–8: fls. 1–6, spreading or somewhat nodding, campanulate, red, spotted with gold in the throat, 2–3 in. long; pedicels slender, 2–5 in. long; segms. oblong-ovate; anthers red-purple: caps. obovoid, 1½ in. long. (Named for Asa Gray, page 44.) Mts., Va., N. C., Tenn.

11. **L. longiflorum,** Thunb. White Trumpet Lily. The most popular lily for greenhouse growing and frequently planted in the open: bulbs subglobose, white, 1–2 in. high, with closely imbricated scales: plant stem-rooting; st. 1½–3 ft., smooth, green and unspotted, reddish toward base: lvs. many, scattered, long narrow-lanceolate, acuminate, 4–7 in. long, smooth, finely nerved: fls. few to several, horizontal or somewhat inclined or declined, clear waxy-white, green-tinged toward base, long-tubular, 4–7 in. long, the upper part flaring like a trumpet and 4–5 in. across, very fragrant; segms. oblanceolate, obtuse, 1–1½ in. broad toward top; style long and slender, curving upward. Japan. Var. **eximium,** Baker (*L. eximium,* Court. *L. Harrisii,* Carr.), is a large vigorous-growing race, known as Easter Lily and Bermuda Lily, formerly much grown under glass. Var. **insulare,** Hort. (var. *formosum,* Hort.), fls. borne horizontally on erect pedicels, with reflexed segms. The form known as Erabu is more floriferous. Var. **takesima,** Duchartre (var. *giganteum,* Hort.), st. purple-brown, fls. purple-flushed before opening.

12. **L. philippinense,** Baker. Bulbs white tinged rose-purple, stoloniferous, subglobose, 1½ in. diam., with lanceolate scales: st. slender, tinged purple-brown, 1–1½ ft. high: lvs. scattered, sparse, linear, 4–6 in. long, about ⅛in. wide, 3-nerved: fls. 1, 2 or more, horizontal, narrow funnel-shaped, white with green tinge without and purplish on base of keels, 7–10 in. long; pedicels 1–2 in. long; segms. oblanceolate, 1–2 in. wide; anthers yellow. Philippine Isls.

13. **L. formosanum,** Wallace (*L. longiflorum* var. *formosanum,* Baker. *L. philippinense* var. *formosanum,* Wils.). Bulbs whitish, stoloniferous, 1 in. or more thick, with lanceolate scales: st. 1–6 ft. tall, more or less purple-brown: lvs. scattered, linear-lanceolate, 3–8 in. long, ⅛–⅜in. wide: fls. 1 to several, horizontal, narrowly funnel-shaped, white within, flushed wine-purple without, 5–6 in. long; pedicels 2–6 in. long; segms. oblanceolate or spatulate, about 1 in. wide; anthers yellow: caps. cylindric, 3 in. long. Formosa.

14. **L. candidum,** L. Madonna Lily. The commonest hardy outdoor white lily, also forced, early-blooming: bulbs white or yellowish, ovoid, 2–3 in. diam., with many flat scales: plant not stem-rooting; st. 2–4 ft., smooth, green: radical lvs. appearing in autumn and persisting over winter, long-oblanceolate, 8–10 in. long, strongly 3-nerved, shining; st.-lvs. many, scattered, the lower ones oblanceolate, the upper becoming short narrow-lanceolate to nearly linear and long-pointed: fls. several to many in a rather close erect raceme, horizontal or somewhat declined, 2–3 in. long, bell-shaped or broad-funnel-shaped with short tube, clear waxy-white, the obovate segms. somewhat recurved; anthers yellow; style very long. S. Eu. to S. W. Asia.—There are double-fld. and lf.-margined vars.

15. **L. leucanthum** var. **centifolium,** Stearn (*L. centifolium,* Stapf). Bulbs yellow-brown, globose, flattened, 3 in. diam., with thick firmly overlapping scales: plant stem-rooting; st. gray, purple-mottled, 4–8 ft. high: lvs. many, almost linear, 5–10 in. long, ¼–½in. wide: fls. 4–8, funnel-shaped, 4–7 in. long, white within with green blotch in throat, occasionally flushed purplish without; pedicels to 4 in., spreading to ascending; segms. apically recurved, ¾in. wide; anthers reddish. W. China.—*L. leucanthum,* Baker, has lanceolate lvs. and lacks the green blotch in the throat.

16. **L. Sargentiæ,** Wils. (*L. leucanthum* var. *Sargentiæ,* Stapf). Showy and desirable summer-blooming species: bulbs wine-red, ovoid, 2–6 in. high, with thick imbricate scales: plant stem-rooting; st. 4–8 ft., smooth, purplish, with bulblets in upper lf.-axils: lvs. very many, scattered, lanceolate, 4–8 in. long, ¼–¾in. wide, 3–5-nerved: fls. mostly few, sometimes several, funnel-shaped, 5–6 in. long and opening nearly as wide, waxy-white inside with tinge of yellow at throat, reddish-purple outside, fragrant; outer segms. ½–¾in. wide, inner 1½–2 in. wide, the apices spreading; anthers orange-brown; stigma purple. (Named in compliment to Mrs. Charles Sprague Sargent.) W. China.

17. **L. regale,** Wils. (*L. myriophyllum,* Hort. not Franch.). Regal Lily. Hardy graceful very showy summer-blooming lily: bulbs red, 4 in. or more thick: plant stem-rooting; st. 4–6 ft., slender, smooth, purplish with dark spot at lf.-attachment: lvs. very many, linear, 2–5 in. long, ⅛–¼in. wide, long-pointed, 1-nerved, without bulblets: fls. few to several, nearly horizontal, 4–6 in. long, the segms. opening widely and somewhat recurved, fragrant, white inside but yellowish deep in the tube, outside light lilac and purple, the ribs strongly colored; anthers yellow. W. China.—**L. imperiale,** Wils. (*L. princeps,* Wils.), is a hybrid of *L. regale* and *L. Sargentiæ:* lvs. 1–5-nerved: fls. open funnel-shaped, 6 in. long, color of *L. regale;* anthers orange-brown.

18. **L. Brownii,** F. E. Br. Vigorous very showy summer-bloomer: bulbs whitish, about 2 in. thick, with spreading scales: plant stem-rooting; st. 2–4 ft., smooth, more or less tinged and spotted brown: lvs. many, scattered, lanceolate to elliptic-lanceolate, narrowed both ways, strongly pointed, 4–12 in. long, ⅗–¾in. wide, prominently about 5-nerved: fls. 1, 3 or 4, nearly horizontal, 6–8 or 9 in. long, tubular part comprising about one-third the length, fragrant, body color creamy-white with brown backs outside; segms. oblanceolate, obtuse, flaring or somewhat recurved at top; anthers brown; style very long. (Made known to commerce by Messrs. Brown, Windsor, England.) China.

19. **L. Parryi,** Wats. Bulbs white, oblong, stoloniferous, 1 in. thick, with many jointed scales: plant not stem-rooting; st. slender, 2–5 ft. high: lvs. scattered, lanceolate, 4–6 in. long, ¼–½in. wide: fls. 1 to few, horizontal, funnelform, lemon-yellow with small purplish dots, fragrant; pedicels erect, about 4 in. long; segms. 2–4 in. long, about ½in. wide, the upper third spreading or recurved; anthers brownish: caps. 2 in. long. (Named for C. C. Parry, page 49.) Calif., Ariz.

20. **L. myriophyllum,** Franch. (*L. myriophyllum* var. *superbum,* Wils. *L. sulphureum,* Baker). Bulbs red-purple, large, globose, with fleshy appressed scales: st. 6–10 ft. high, green throughout: lvs. many, linear, the lower 3–5 in. long, ¼–1 in. wide, 3–7-nerved, the upper with axillary bulblets: fls. 1–5, horizontal or declined, funnel-shaped, 7–8 or even 12 in. long, sulfur-yellow with claret-red flush outside; pedicels ascending or horizontal; segms. lanceolate-oblong, 1–2 in. broad, the upper third recurved; anthers red-brown; stigma conical. Burma, Yunnan.—For *L. myriophyllum,* Hort., see no. 17.

21. **L. japonicum,** Thunb. (*L. Krameri,* Hook. f. *L. Makinoi,* Koidz.). Handsome species, rather difficult to maintain: bulbs small, white, with closely overlapping scales: plant stem-rooting; st. 2–3 ft., smooth, more or less purple tinged and dotted: lvs. scattered, narrow-lanceolate, 2–6 in. long, ¼–½in. wide: fls. 1 or 2 or sometimes more, broadly funnel-shaped, 5–6 or 7 in. long and nearly as wide, fragrant, rose-pink inside and out, varying in intensity and sometimes blush-white; segms. oblanceolate, 1–1½ in. wide; anthers red. Japan.

22. **L. rubellum,** Baker. Much like the above, of better constitution: low (1–2 ft.): lvs. few, 2–4 in. long, 1–1½ in. wide, lance-ovate: fls. smaller, funnel-shaped, 2–3 in. long; segms. oblanceolate, slightly recurved at tips; anthers yellow or orange. Japan.

23. **L. auratum,** Lindl. Goldband Lily. Summer- and autumn-blooming: bulbs greenish-yellow, 2–4 in. diam., with thick incurved scales: plant stem-rooting; st. purple-green, glabrous, 3–6 ft. high: lvs. narrowly lanceolate, scattered, 4–6 in. long, ½–1½ in. wide, 5-nerved: fls. horizontal, 10–30, racemose, powerfully scented, with short tubular

throat and wide-open trumpet, white spotted with carmine and sometimes yellow; pedicels 2–4 in. long; segms. broadly oblong, undulate, strongly recurved, 4–7 in. long, 1–2 in. wide, each with median yellow band; stamens arcuate, with chocolate-red pollen: caps. 2–3 in. long. Japan. Var. **pictum,** Wallace, fls. heavily spotted with crimson and yellow band tipped with crimson. Var. **platyphyllum,** Baker, lvs. 1½–2½ in. wide, segms. broad and the spots concentrated in the throat.

24. **L. Martagon,** L. MARTAGON OR TURKS-CAP LILY. An old hardy garden species, early summer: bulbs yellow, ovoid, 1 in. or more high, with many imbricated scales: plant not stem-rooting; st. 3–6 ft., glabrous or toward the top puberulous, sometimes spotted purple: lvs. in whorls of 6–9, scattered above and seldom throughout, oblanceolate or spatulate, 2–3 in. long, 1–1½ in. wide, sessile, finely veined: fls. several to many, hanging on divaricate pedicels in a long panicle-like terminal raceme, 2–3 in. across and 1½–2 in. long, rose, dull purple or purplish-red with many purplish-black spots, with disagreeable odor; segms. lanceolate, pubescent on back, papillose on margins at base, reflexed to the pedicel; anthers red. (Martagon is a special form of turban.) S. Eu. to Japan.—There are several cult. vars., one (var. **album,** Hort.) with white fls. and yellow anthers, another double.

25. **L. Kelloggii,** Purdy. Midsummer: bulbs white, ovoid, to 2 in. high, with many tightly appressed scales: plant not stem-rooting; st. slender, 2½–4 ft. tall: lvs. in 4–8 whorls of up to 12, lanceolate to oblanceolate, 2–4 in. long, ½–¾in. wide: fls. up to 20, nodding, fragrant, mauve-pink with median yellow band and dark purple dots in lower part, 1½–2¼ in. long, the oblanceolate segms. recurved from the base, ⅜in. wide; anthers pinkish-yellow: caps. cylindrical, 1½–2 in. long. (Named for Dr. Albert Kellogg, page 46.) N. W. Calif.

26. **L. Hansonii,** Leicht. JAPANESE TURKS-CAP LILY. Spring and early summer: bulbs white tinged rose, ovoid to rounded, 2 or more in. high, with closely imbricated scales: plant stem-rooting; st. 3–4 ft., slender, glabrous: lvs. in whorls of 8–12, oblanceolate, 4–7 in. long, mostly 1–1½ in. wide, the whorls few and other lvs. scattered: fls. few to several in lax raceme, somewhat fragrant, drooping, 1–2½ in. across, bright orange-yellow spotted purplish-brown; segms. 1–1½ in. long, thick, waxy in texture, lanceolate, revolute; anthers orange-red. (Bears the name of an American amateur of lilies.) Korea.

27. **L. Roezlii,** Regel. Bulbs small, on unbranched rhizomes, with 3–4-jointed scales: plant not stem-rooting; st. 2–3½ ft. tall: lvs. mostly whorled, linear-lanceolate, 2½–3½ in. long, ¼–⅓in. wide: fls. nodding, orange-red with black-purple spots; segms. about ⅜in. wide, 1½ in. long; anthers red. (Named for B. Roezl, page 50.) S. Ore., N. Calif.

28. **L. columbianum,** Hanson. Midsummer: bulbs small, ovoid, 2 in. diam., with whitish lanceolate appressed non-jointed scales: plant not stem-rooting; st. 2–4 ft. high, slender, green: lvs. in whorls of 5–9, oblanceolate, 2–4 in. long, ½–1 in. wide: fls. 3 to many, nodding, red to yellow, spotted purple, 1½–2½ in. long; segms. lance-ovate, ⅓–½in. wide, recurved; anthers to ¼in. long, yellow. B. C. to Calif.

29. **L. occidentale,** Purdy. Midsummer: bulbs short-rhizomatous, with 1–2-jointed scales: plant not stem-rooting; st. slender, 2–6 ft. high, dark green: lvs. in whorls of 5–12, lanceolate, acute, 2–4 in. long, ¼–1 in. wide: fls. few to 15, nodding, red or orange, usually spotted purple, 1½–2 in. long; segms. lanceolate, recurved; anthers ⅛in. long, brownish-red. S. Ore., N. Calif.

30. **L. canadense,** L. MEADOW LILY. Early summer: bulbs white, subglobose, stoloniferous, with many thick white scales: plant not stem-rooting; st. 2–5 ft. tall, reddish-green: lvs. lanceolate, in whorls of 4–10, acuminate, 2–6 in. long, one-tenth to one-fifth as broad, finely roughened on margins and veins of lower surface: fls. 1–16, nodding, orange-yellow with dark spots; segms. lanceolate, spreading-recurved, acute, 2–3 in. long, ½–¾in. wide; anthers yellow: caps. 1½–2 in. long, oblong. Que. and N. S. to Va. Var. **flavum,** Pursh (forma *flavum,* Victorin), fls. yellow. Var. **coccineum,** Pursh (forma *rubrum,* Britt.), fls. suffused with red. Var. **editorum,** Fern., lvs. one-fifth to one-half as broad as long, fls. red, the inner segms. to ½in. broad; Pa. to Ala., Ky.—*L. michiganense,* Farwell, Ont. to Mo., differs from *L. canadense* by more strongly recurved reddish segms. 3–3½ in. long.

31. **L. pardalinum,** Kellogg. LEOPARD LILY. Frequent in cult., midsummer, with bulb-bearing branching rootstock, forming mats: bulbs white, with jointed scales: plant not stem-rooting; st. 3–6 ft., glabrous, green: lvs. in whorls of 9–15, or fewer above, sometimes scattered, linear-lanceolate to oblanceolate, 4–7 in. long, ¼–1 in. wide, finely roughened on veins of lower surface and on margins: fls. few to many, usually whorled below and racemose above, hanging on long spreading pedicels, 2–4 in. diam.; segms. lanceolate, 2–3 in. long, ½–¾in. wide, yellow at base and orange-scarlet above, purple-spotted toward base, reflexed to the pedicel; anthers red, ½in. long. Coast Ranges and Sierra Nevadas in Calif. Var. **giganteum,** Hort., SUNSET LILY, supposed hybrid of *L. pardalinum* and *L. Humboldtii,* st. to 8 ft., fls. crimson and golden, thickly spotted with purple-black.—Shuksan is a hybrid of *L. pardalinum* and *L. Humboldtii.*

32. **L. Humboldtii,** Roezl & Leicht. Stately species, midsummer: **bulbs** purplish, lopsided, 2–6 in. high: plant not stem-rooting; st. 3–6 ft., purplish, very stout, glabrous or slightly pubescent: lvs. in whorls of 10–20, oblanceolate, 3–5 in. long, ½–1 in. wide, finely roughened beneath and on margins: fls. few to many, large, 4–5 in. across, orange-yellow to orange-red spotted purple-brown or maroon, pendulous; segms. oblong-lanceolate, recurved but not reflexed to pedicel, 3–4 in. long, ½–1 in. wide; anthers red, ½in. long. (Discovered in 1869, the centenary of the birth of Alexander von Humboldt.) Calif. Var. **ocellatum,** Elwes (*L. Bloomerianum ocellatum,* Kellogg. *L. Humboldtii* var. *magnificum,* Purdy), taller and having more numerous fls. with larger spots.

33. **L. superbum,** L. American Turks-cap Lily. Midsummer: bulbs globose, white, stoloniferous, 1–2 in. diam., with thick imbricated scales: plant not stem-rooting; st. 3–8 ft. high, green-purple: lvs. in whorls of 3–8, lanceolate, 2–6 in. long, mostly ½–¾in. wide: fls. many, nodding, orange to yellow or red, purple-spotted; segms. lanceolate, acuminate, strongly recurved from below the middle, 2½–4 in. long, ⅜–⅝in. wide; anthers orange-red, ½–¾in. long. N. B. to Minn., Va. and Mo.

34. **L. Michauxii,** Poir. (*L. carolinianum,* Michx. not Catesby). Toward late summer: bulbs white, 1–2 in. diam., globose, stoloniferous: plant not stem-rooting; st. 1½–3 ft. high: lvs. whorled, oblanceolate or wider, 1–3 in. long, 1–1½ in. broad: fls. few, nodding, orange-red, purple-spotted; segms. lanceolate, 3–4 in. long, about 1 in. wide, with green basal blotch; anthers orange-red, ½–¾in. long. (Named for André Michaux, page 48.) Va. to Fla. and La.

35. **L. cernuum,** Kom. Early summer: bulbs ovoid, white, 1–1½ in. diam., with smooth flat scales: plant stem-rooting; st. green or spotted with purple-brown, 1–2 ft. high: lvs. scattered and nearly in middle of st., narrowly linear, 2–7 in. long, to ⅛in. wide: fls. 1–6, nodding, lilac with wine-purple dots; segms. oblong-lanceolate, obtuse, much recurved, 1½–2 in. long; anthers lilac, ½in. long: caps. obovoid, ½–¾in. long. Korea, Manchuria.

36. **L. speciosum,** Thunb. Hardy showy and adaptable lily, summer and autumn: bulbs globose, white to brown, 3–4 in. high, with thick incurved scales: plant stem-rooting; st. usually 2–3 ft., small, often purplish: lvs. scattered and not crowded, oblong-lanceolate, 4–6 in. long, 1–2 in. wide, many-nerved, rather abruptly contracted into an appressed petiole, acuminate: fls. several on long divaricate bracted pedicels, declined or drooping, fragrant, 3–5 or 6 in. diam., white overlaid with rose-pink and bearing rose-purple elevated spots; segms. broad-lanceolate, 3–4 in. long, 1–2 in. wide, bearded, reflexed from near the base; anthers cinnamon-brown, about 1 in. long; style long, equalling the stamens. Japan.—Variable, with many named vars. as: var. **Melpomene,** Hort., deeper colored fls. with white-edged segms.; var. **magnificum,** Hort., large in all its parts and early-blooming; var. **album,** Hort., fls. nearly white; var. **rubrum,** Hort., fls. carmine-pink.

37. **L. amabile,** Palibin. Early summer: bulbs ovoid, white, 1–1½ in. diam., with many closely imbricated scales: plant stem-rooting; st. dull green, 1–3 ft. high, hispid with short decurved stiff hairs: lvs. scattered, many, lanceolate, 2–3½ in. long, ¼–½in. wide, hispid, obscurely 3- or more-nerved: fls. 2–6, brick-red spotted with black, nodding; segms. lanceolate or inner lance-ovate, about 2 in. long, sharply recurved; filaments pinkish, anthers chocolate-brown. Korea.

38. **L. pumilum,** DC. (*L. tenuifolium,* Fisch.). Coral Lily. Graceful bright-fld lily with grass-like foliage, early blooming: bulbs small, white, with few tightly packed scales: plant not stem-rooting; st. slender, 1–2 ft., glabrous to puberulous, green or suffused with purple: lvs. many, scattered, very narrow-linear or almost capillary, 2–4 in. long, 1/12–⅛in. wide, 1-nerved: fls. few to several on slender remote pedicels, drooping, 1¼–2 in. across, brilliant scarlet seldom slightly dotted; segms. oblong-lanceolate, 1–1½ in. long, ¼–⅜in. broad, reflexed to the pedicel; anthers red; style about twice as long as ovary. Siberia, China.

39. **L. callosum,** Sieb. & Zucc. Early summer: bulbs white, subglobose, 1 in. high, with few scales free at apex: plant not stem-rooting; st. slender, green, 1–2 ft. high: lvs. scattered, many, linear, 1–4 in. long, 1/12–⅛in. wide, not glandular-ciliate, 3–5-nerved: fls. 2–9, nodding, dull or orange-red, obscurely dotted at base; segms. oblanceolate, sharply reflexed, 1¼–1½ in. long, ¼–⅓in. wide; anthers orange-red; style shorter than ovary. Siberia to China, Japan.

40. **L. chalcedonicum,** L. Scarlet Turks-cap Lily. Old hardy garden species, summer-blooming: bulbs yellowish, ovoid, 3 in. diam., with broadly lanceolate scales: plant not stem-rooting; st. 3–4 ft., slightly pubescent, tinted purple: lvs. very many, scattered, lower ones oblanceolate, central and upper ones linear, 1½–4 in. long, ¼–½in. wide, 3–7-veined, silver-margined, glandular-ciliate: fls. few or several, pendulous, odor not agreeable, 2–3 in. diam., vermilion-scarlet seldom slightly dotted; segms. oblanceolate, 2½ in. long, ½in. or less broad, thick and waxy, papillose at base, reflexed to pedicel; anthers scarlet; style equalling or exceeding ovary. Greece and adjacent isls., but named for Chalcedon farther east.

41. **L. pomponium,** L. MINOR TURKS-CAP LILY. Small graceful species, early summer: bulbs globose-ovoid, yellowish on exposure, 2 in. diam.: plant not stem-rooting; st. 1½–3 ft., stout, furrowed: lvs. very many, scattered, narrow-linear, 3–4 in. long, 1/12–1/6 in. wide, ciliate, 3-nerved: fls. few to several, pendulous, 2 in. or less across, brilliant scarlet dotted purplish-black, with offensive odor; segms. oblanceolate, 1½–2 in. long, ⅓ in. or less broad, reflexed to the pedicel forming a little ball or pompon; anthers scarlet. S. France, N. Italy.—*L. rubrum,* Lam. & DC., is a synonym of *L. pomponium* but plants so offered in the trade may be one of the vars. of *L. canadense* or *L. auratum.*

42. **L. pyrenaicum,** Gouan. YELLOW TURKS-CAP LILY. Early summer: bulbs globose, 2½ in. diam., pale heliotrope on exposure, with many lance-ovate scales: plant not stem-rooting; st. green, sometimes with purple, 1–3 ft. high, glabrous: lvs. many, lance-linear, glandular-ciliate, 3–5 in. long, ¼–⅜ in. wide, 5–7-nerved: fls. 3–12, nodding, sulfur-yellow, spotted purple; segms. oblong, 1½–2 in. long, much recurved; anthers brick-red. Pyrenees.

43. **L. Henryi,** Baker. Hardy good lily, summer-blooming: bulbs mahogany, subglobose, 3–7 in. diam., with thick acuminate scales: plant stem-rooting; st. 4 ft. or more, smooth, purple-spotted: lvs. many, crowded, scattered, elliptic-lanceolate to ovate-lanceolate, narrowed to a short petiole-like base, many-nerved, 2–5 or 6 in. long, ¾–1¼ in. broad, the upper ones passing into broad-ovate short pointed bracts about 1 in. long: fls. several to many, on long wide-spreading bracted pedicels, more or less nodding, not fragrant, orange-yellow; segms. brown-spotted, papillose and greenish toward base, narrow and separate and much spreading or recurved, 2½–3 in. long, ½–¾ in. wide; anthers orange; style long and straight, about the length of stamens. (Named for Augustine Henry, page 45.) China.

44. **L. monadelphum,** Bieb. CAUCASIAN LILY. Stately spring and early summer lily: bulbs large, globose, yellowish, with many lanceolate scales: plant not stem-rooting; st. 3–6 ft., stout, somewhat pubescent: lvs. many, scattered, linear-lanceolate, lanceolate to oblanceolate, 4–5 in. long, ½ in. wide, 10–12-veined: fls. usually several to many in tall terminal panicle-like raceme, 3–5 in. across, golden-yellow sometimes tinged purple, spots slight or absent, odor not pleasant; segms. waxy, oblanceolate, reflexed, 3–4 in. long; filaments sometimes coherent or monadelphous at base; anthers greenish or orange. Caucasus and Iran.

45. **L. tigrinum,** Ker. TIGER LILY. Old lily common about yards and sometimes escaped: bulbs white, broadly ovoid, 2–3 in. diam., with thick broad scales: plant stem-rooting; st. 2–6 ft. high, dark brown, with cobwebby covering: lvs. many, crowded, narrowly lanceolate, 4–6 in. long, ½–¾ in. wide, 5–7-nerved, with dark axillary bulblets: fls. few to many, nodding, open and spreading, without a tube, orange-red or brick-red, freely spotted black; segms. lanceolate, sharply reflexed, 3–4 in. long, ½–1 in. wide; anthers purple; style 2 in. long, stigma purple. China, Korea, Japan. Var. **Fortunei,** Hort., st. densely floccose; Dagelet Isl. Var. **splendens,** Hort., fls. large, salmon-pink, numerous, with sharply pointed segms.

46. **L. Davidii,** Duchartre (*L. Thayeræ,* Wils.). Midsummer: bulbs small, white, ovoid, with acute ovate scales: plant stem-rooting; st. with some brown-purple, scaberulous, floccose above, 2–6 ft. tall: lvs. many, crowded, linear, 1-nerved, 4–5 in. long, 1/12–1/6 in. wide: fls. 2–20, nodding, scarlet or orange-red, spotted black; segms. reflexed, lance-oblong, 3 in. long, ½–¾ in. broad, apically villous; anthers scarlet; stigma orange-brown. (Named for Abbé David, 1826–1900, who discovered it in 1869.) W. China.

47. **L. testaceum,** Lindl. NANKEEN LILY. Hardy graceful lily, early summer: bulbs large, globose, white, with closely overlapping ovate scales: plant not stem-rooting; st. 4–6 or 7 ft., brown-tinted, lightly pubescent: lvs. many, scattered, linear, 3–4 in. long, ¼–⅓ in. wide, 3–5-nerved: fls. few to several, umbellate or racemose, nodding, fragrant, 2–3 in. and more across, apricot or nankeen-yellow often flushed pink and rarely slightly dotted red; segms. reflexed to the pedicel, lightly papillose at base, 3 in. long; anthers red. Japan; probably a hybrid of *L. candidum* and *L. chalcedonicum.*

48. **L. Leichtlinii,** Hook. f. Summer-blooming: bulbs globose, stoloniferous, 4 in. thick, with thick overlapping scales: plant stem-rooting; st. 2–4 ft., erect, indistinctly puberulent, shaded dark brown: lvs. many, scattered, linear, 3–6 in. long, ⅓ in. wide, 3-nerved: fls. few, sometimes several, nodding, 3–4 in. across, lemon-yellow spotted dark purple; segms. lanceolate, purplish outside, reflexed to the pedicels, 2½–3 in. long, ½–¾ in. wide; anthers reddish-brown. (Named for Max Leichtlin, page 47.) Japan. Var. **Maximowiczii,** Baker (*L. Maximowiczii,* Regel. *L. pseudo-tigrinum,* Carr.), lvs. frequently 5–7-nerved, fls. salmon-red spotted purple; named for Maximowicz, page 47; China, Japan.

49. **L. Willmottiæ,** Wils. (*L. warleyense,* Hort. *L. Davidii* var. *Willmottiæ,* Raffill). Midsummer: bulbs white, stoloniferous, small, with firmly imbricated scales: strong, 3–4 ft., glabrous or essentially so, spotted red-purple: lvs. many, spirally scattered, 1–3-nerved, 4–5 in. long, mostly less than ¼ in. broad, linear or nearly so, lighter colored beneath: fls. 3–25 or more on horizontal or declined pedicels 4 in. long with a narrow bract near the middle, orange-red and dark spotted, pendulous, 2½–3 in. across, not fragrant; segms. oblong-lanceolate to narrowly ovate-lanceolate, 2–3 in. long, about ¾ in. broad

at middle, papillose near base and the nectary prominent, reflexed to the st.; anthers orange. (Grown at Warley Place, exhibited by Miss Ellen Willmott, page 54.) China.

40. **SCILLA,** L. Squill. Species 90 or more, in temp. regions in Old World; several are planted for ornament, mostly for early spring bloom.—Low plants with tunicate bulb and radical mostly very narrow lvs. in nearly all the species appearing with the fls., and simple leafless scape: fls. commonly small, bracted, few, several to many in terminal racemes, blue, purple, to white, the perianth campanulate or wide open; segms. 6, 1-nerved, distinct or lightly connate at base, not long persisting; stamens 6, attached in the perianth, anthers dorsifixed, filaments very slender or sometimes somewhat dilated at base; pistil 1, with 3-celled nearly or quite sessile ovary, capitate stigma, and various style: caps. 3-lobed or -angled, loculicidal, with mostly few seeds in each cell. (Scil-la: ancient Greek and Latin name.)

A. Shape of fls. campanulate to tubular.
  B. Segms. strongly recurved; pedicels not over ½in. long........................1. *S. nonscripta*
  BB. Segms. flaring but not recurved; lower pedicels to 1½ in. long................2. *S. hispanica*
AA. Shape of fls. saucer-shaped or open-rotate.
  B. Fls. 50 or more in a dense short spicate raceme...............................3. *S. peruviana*
  BB. Fls. 1–15 (to 30 in *S. italica*).
    C. Pedicels without or with very minute bracts at base and two to five times as long as fls.: lvs. 2, sometimes 3...............................4. *S. bifolia*
    CC. Pedicels with evident bracts: lvs. 2–7.
      D. Bracts small, deltoid; pedicels one-fourth to twice as long as fls.
        E. Number of fls. usually 4–8...............................5. *S. amœna*
        EE. Number of fls. 1–3...............................6. *S. sibirica*
      DD. Bracts prominent, long-pointed; pedicels one to four times as long as fls.
        E. Lvs. exceeding scape: segms. glabrous...............................7. *S. verna*
        EE. Lvs. shorter than scape: segms. apically puberulous...............................8. *S. italica*

1. **S. nonscripta,** Hoffmgg. & Link (*S. nutans*, Smith. *Endymion nutans*, Dum. *S. festalis*, Salisb.). English Bluebell. Scape 1, about 1 ft. high, exceeding the several to many strap-shaped lvs.: fls. blue, sometimes white, 6–12 or more, nodding in a terminal raceme, bracts 2, about as long as pedicel; perianth cylindrical or tubular when the fls. open but perhaps attaining a bell-form as they spread with age, the segms. revolute at tip, to about ½in. long; stamens united half way up perianth. Great Britain and continent.—There are hort. color forms in lilac, pink, and others.

2. **S. hispanica,** Mill. (*S. campanulata*, Ait.). Spanish Bluebell. Scape 1, 10–20 in., about the length of the several or many strap-shaped blunt or short-acute lvs.: fls. blue to rose-purple, usually a dozen or more, ascending or nodding in an open raceme, bracts 2, about as long as pedicel; perianth campanulate to open-campanulate, the parts beginning to flare or spread below the middle and often at or near the base, the segms. flaring or curved but not revolute; all or alternate stamens attached to perianth nearly half way up. Spain, Portugal.—Color forms in white, flesh-color, and rose. Nos. 1 and 2 are apparently mixed in gardens, bulbs of both being planted together; the narrow fls. of no. 1 are characteristic, but as they begin to pass with age may assume somewhat the broad form of no. 2.

3. **S. peruviana,** L. Bulb large: scape 4–12 in.: lvs. many, 12 in. or less long, linear-lanceolate, ciliate on margins: fls. purple to reddish or whitish, ½in. or less long, 50 or more in a short and compact spicate somewhat lengthening raceme; perianth rotate, the oblong segms. green-striped on back, over ½in. long; anthers short. Medit. region; the specific name perpetuates an old misnomer.

4. **S. bifolia,** L. Small plant, very early: scape 1, 3–6 in. high, almost the length of the mostly 2 (sometimes 3) linear or lance-linear lvs.: fls. 3–12, blue varying to reddish or nearly white, mostly nodding in an open raceme, the lower ones on long slender pedicels; perianth rotate or stellate, ½in. or less across; anthers blue. Eu., S. W. Asia.—There are forms with white, rose, and red fls. in cult.

5. **S. amœna,** L. Star-Hyacinth. Early: scapes several, 4–6 in. high, about equalling the long-lanceolate lvs. which are ¾in. or less broad: fls. several, mostly 4–6, blue to whitish, horizontal or spreading or ascending (scarcely cernuous), ¾in. or less across; perianth rotate. Germany, N. Italy, and E.

6. **S. sibirica,** Haw. Early: scapes 1–6 and 3–6 in. high, usually somewhat overtopping the long-lanceolate lvs. which are ¾in. or less broad and blunt or short-acute: fls. about 3, horizontal or cernuous, deep blue, about ½in. across, in a short-pedicelled open raceme; perianth rotate, the segms. obtuse, oblong, ½in. long. Russia, S. W. Asia.—There are garden color races.

7. **S. verna,** Huds. Small and delicate, early: scape 1 or 2, 6 in. or less: lvs. 4–6, narrow-linear, to ⅛in. wide, exceeding the scape: fls. several, blue, erect, fragrant, in short corymb-like racemes; bracts mostly equalling or exceeding the pedicels; lower pedicels about 1 in. long; segms. lanceolate, ¼in. long. W. Eu.

8. **S. italica,** L. Scape 6–18 in. high: lvs. 4–6, linear, to ½in. wide, strongly keeled, not as long as scape: fls. 6–30, lilac-blue, star-like, fragrant, in dense racemes; bracts in pairs, linear, sheathing the pedicels; lower pedicels ½in. long; segms. narrowly elliptic, apically puberulous, ¼in. long. S. Eu.

41. **CAMASSIA,** Lindl. (*Quamasia*, Raf.). CAMASS. Bulbous scapose plants of temp. N. Amer., 5 or 6 species, all but one western; bulbs eaten by Indians; sometimes planted for the showy fls.—Lvs. linear or lance-linear, radical or basal: fls. in terminal racemes, blue to purple to almost white, pedicels in axil of conspicuous bract; perianth open to rotate, of 6 narrow distinct nerved segms., one of which may curve downward and differ from the others; stamens 6, inserted on base of segms., the filaments very slender, anthers versatile; ovary superior, triloculed, style filiform, stigma shortly trifid: caps. 3-lobed, loculicidal, with several black seeds in each cell. (Camas-sia: Latinized from *camass* or *quamash,* the Indian name.)

A. Segms. ¼–½in. long: caps. subglobose........1. *C. scilloides*
AA. Segms. ½–1½ in. long: caps. oblong or ovoid.
B. Number of fls. in bloom at once usually many; withered segms. persistent: caps. closely appressed to axis of raceme........2. *C. Quamash*
BB. Number of fls. in bloom at once only 1–3; withered segms. soon deciduous: caps. not appressed to axis of raceme........3. *C. Leichtlinii*

1. **C. scilloides,** Cory (*Cyanotris scilloides,* Raf. *Camassia esculenta,* Rob.). Bulbs black or brown, about 1 in. diam.: lvs. 8–24 in. long, ¼–¾in. broad: scape 10–24 in. high, usually 15–35-fld.; pedicels spreading-erect, ¼–1¼ in. long; fls. regular, violet to blue or white; segms. ¼–½in. long, 3–5-nerved; anthers yellow: caps. subglobose, ¼–½in. diam. W. Pa. to Ga., Minn., Tex.

2. **C. Quamash,** Greene (*Phalangium Quamash,* Pursh. *C. esculenta,* Lindl. not Rob.). Bulbs, lvs. and scape as in no. 1: fruiting pedicels usually incurving-erect, ¼–¾in. long; fls. regular or irregular (1 segm. curving downward), both kinds in the same raceme, blue-violet, blue or white; segms. ½–1¼ in. long, 3–9-nerved; anthers yellow to purple: caps. ovoid, ⅓–1 in. long. (Quamash: Indian name.) B. C. to Calif., Mont., Utah.—Variable, with many named variants.

3. **C. Leichtlinii,** Wats. (*Chlorogalum Leichtlinii,* Baker). To 4 ft. tall: fls. 4–60 or more, regular; pedicels ½–2 in. long, spreading-erect; segms. blue-violet to cream-white, 1–1½ in. long, 5–9-nerved: caps. oblong or ovoid, ½–1 in. long. (Named for Max Leichtlin, page 47.) B. C. to Calif.

42. **ORNITHOGALUM,** L. Bulbous scapose plants of probably 100 or more species, some of them planted in the open and in pots for the bloom; Old World, where the bulbs of some species are used as food.—Bulbs tunicate, often large: scape short or tall, simple: lvs. radical, strap-shaped to linear, few to several from each bulb, sometimes fleshy: fls. several to many in terminal bracted racemes or corymbs, sometimes umbel-form, white, yellow, reddish, perianth persistent; segms. distinct; stamens 6, hypogynous, the filaments usually dilated, anthers dorsifixed and versatile; pistil 1, with sessile 3-celled ovary, style short or stout-columnar, with more or less 3-lobed stigma: caps. 3-lobed, loculicidal; seeds few, black or dark colored. (Ornithog-alum: Greek *bird's milk,* probably alluding to egg-like color of fls. of some species.)

A. Perianth-segms. conspicuously keeled green outside.
B. Fls. corymbose or somewhat umbellate: lvs. to 1 ft. long........1. *O. umbellatum*
BB. Fls. long-racemose: lvs. to 2 ft. long........2. *O. caudatum*
AA. Perianth-segms. self-colored, not green on back.
B. Pistil large and prominent, nearly black........3. *O. arabicum*
BB. Pistil not conspicuous, greenish.
C. Segms. less than 1 in. long.
D. Fls. white to pale yellow........4. *O. thyrsoides*
DD. Fls. deep yellow to orange........5. *O. miniatum*
CC. Segms. 1 in. or more long, vermilion........6. *O. splendens*

1. **O. umbellatum,** L. STAR-OF-BETHLEHEM. Tufted from ovoid bulbs: scape 1 ft. or less high, about equalling the linear lvs.: fls. few to several on long spreading pedicels subtended by pointed relatively short scarious bract, opening in sunshine, 1 in. and more across when open; segms. narrowly oblong-lanceolate, acute, wide-spreading, white inside, green and white-margined outside, much exceeding the stamens; filaments expanded. Medit. region; frequent in yards and also run wild.

2. **O. caudatum,** Ait. Bulbs very large, ovoid: scape stout, 2–3 ft.: lvs. few, nearly or quite as long as scape, fleshy, strap-shaped, long-taper-pointed (caudate), many-veined,

1½ in. broad or nearly so toward base: fls. 50 or more in a long raceme, about 1 in. across; bracts narrow, about equalling the older pedicels; segms. oblong, nearly or quite obtuse, ½in. long, about the length of the stamens, white with prominent green center; filaments expanded below. S. Afr.

3. O. **arabicum,** L. Bulbs large, ovoid to nearly globular: scape 1½–2 ft., strong: lvs. several, nearly or quite as long as scape, glaucous-green, narrowly strap-shaped and long-pointed, ¾–1 in. broad: fls. several, large and fragrant, showy, white inside and out but with black center due to the large pistil, on slender pedicels (lower ones 2½–3 in. long) which exceed the large long-pointed scarious bracts; segms. oblong, about 1 in. long, short-acute, twice or more longer than stamens; filaments somewhat expanded below. Medit. region.

4. O. **thyrsoides,** Jacq. Bulbs large, globose: scape 1½ ft. or less, rather stout: lvs. few, lanceolate, the largest ones 1–2 in. broad, about length of scape, margin finely ciliate: fls. several to many in a dense raceme, white with brownish-green claws; segms. lanceolate, pointed, spreading, ½–¾in. long, twice or more exceeding stamens; filaments somewhat expanded below, anthers brownish-yellow. S. Afr.

5. O. **miniatum,** Jacq. (*O. aureum*, Curt. *O. thyrsoides* var. *aureum*, Ait.). Bulbs small, green: scape brownish-green, 6–12 in. high: lvs. 6–9 in. long, less conspicuously ciliate: fls. 8–12, orange-yellow, subumbellate; segms. broadly-oblong, obtuse, more or less concave, ⅝in. long; filaments expanded below, anthers bright yellow. S. Afr.

6. O. **splendens,** L. Bolus. Bulbs large, globose: scape stout, 1 ft. high: lvs. 4, ensiform, glaucous, 4 in. long: fls. about 12, racemose, vermilion, with satin sheen; segms. 1 in. or more long, ovate or obovate; filaments orange, the alternate ones widened below, anthers pale yellow. S. Afr.

43. **LACHENALIA,** Jacq. CAPE-COWSLIP. Upwards of 50 species of small bulbous scapose plants in S. Afr., two or three frequently grown mostly in pots.—Bulbs tunicate: lvs. 1, 2, or several, often spotted: fls. mostly in reds and yellows, small to medium in size, borne in a terminal raceme or spike on single-bracted pedicels, in the following species pendulous; perianth often gamophyllous, campanulate or cylindric; segms. 6, the 3 outer ones often shorter, spreading or nearly erect; stamens 6, attached on the tube, filaments very slender, anthers versatile; pistil 1, with 3-celled ovary, slender style and capitate stigma: caps. more or less 3-angled, loculicidal. (Lachena-lia: named for Werner de Lachenal, 1736–1800, professor of botany at Basel.)

A. Outer segms. much shorter than inner, calyx-like....................1. *L. tricolor*
AA. Outer segms. about length of inner....................2. *L. pendula*

1. L. **tricolor,** Thunb. Scape 1 ft. or less: lvs. usually 2 to each scape, lance-lorate, nearly or quite 1 in. broad, equalling or exceeding infl., often spotted purple or dark green: fls. 3–12 or more, about 1 in. long, pendulous on short pedicels, yellow, red at tip and sometimes at base, the short outer segms. tipped green and about half the length of the inner. Var. **Nelsonii,** Baker (*L. Nelsonii*, Hort.), has bright yellow fls. with all segms. tinged faintly green.

2. L. **pendula,** Ait. More robust: lvs. often 2 in. broad: fls. drooping or cernuous, to 1½ in. long; outer segms. nearly as long as inner, narrow, yellow with red above; inner segms. bright red-purple at top. Var. **superba,** Hort., is an improved form.

44. **CHIONODOXA,** Boiss. GLORY-OF-THE-SNOW. Five or 6 little bulbous scapose alpine and subalpine plants from Crete and Asia Minor, one commonly cult.—Bulbs tunicate: scape short, rising little above the ground: lvs. 2 or 3 to each scape and at length equalling or exceeding it: fls. blue (red and white color forms), few, in a short open raceme with prominent pedicels, ascending, horizontal or cernuous; perianth gamophyllous, open-campanulate or rotate, the tube very short; stamens 6, attached on throat, filaments expanded, anthers versatile; pistil 1, with 3-celled many-ovuled ovary, short or wanting style and capitate stigma: caps. 3-angled or -winged, loculicidal. (Chionodox-a: Greek *glory of the snow*.)

A. Segms. over ½in. long, subacute; ovary blue-violet....................1. *C. Luciliæ*
AA. Segms. ⅓in. long, obtuse; ovary olive-green....................2. *C. sardensis*

1. C. **Luciliæ,** Boiss. Variable in cult., blooming in earliest spring: scape 3–6 in., usually lengthening in fr.: lvs. from linear and grass-like to oblanceolate, at first shorter than infl.: fls. less than a dozen, usually 4–6, lower ones cernuous on slender pedicels, bright blue with white center, 1 in. or less across; segms. over ½in. long: fr. broad as long, strongly 3-sided, freely produced. (Named for Lucile Boissier, 1822–1849.) Asia

Minor. Var. **alba,** Hort., fls. white. Var. **gigantea,** Hort., large in all parts. Var. **grandiflora,** Hort., fls. large, blue-violet with white throat. Var. **Tmolusii,** Hort., late-blooming, dark blue with white.

2. **C. sardensis,** Drude. Fls. 2–6, sky-blue, usually with a small white disk at the throat; segms. ⅓in. long. Mts. near Smyrna.

45. **VELTHEIMIA,** Gleditsch. Bulbous scapose plants flowering in spring or summer; 5 species from S. Afr.—Bulbs tunicate: lvs. basal: fls. tubular, drooping, in dense terminal racemes; perianth gamophyllous, persistent; segms. 6, short, tooth-like; stamens 6, adnate to the perianth to beyond its middle; pistil 1, ovary sessile, trilocular, style slender, stigma capitate: caps. large, membranous, triquetrous, loculicidal; seeds 2–3 in each locule, obconical, black. (Velthei-mia: for the botanist Count von Veltheim, 1741–1801.)

V. viridifolia, Jacq. Bulbs 3 in. diam.: lvs. oblong, to 1 ft. long and 3 in. wide: st stout, mottled purple, 1¼ ft. high: fls. many, yellow or tinged red, 1½ in. long, with obtuse straight short lobes.

46. **HYACINTHUS,** L. Hyacinth. Species probably exceeding 30, Medit. region, trop. and S. Afr., bulbous scapose plants, of which one is everywhere cult.—Bulbs tunicate, often large: lvs. radical, narrow: fls. in terminal racemes, erect or pendulous, red, blue, white, yellowish, the pedicels subtended by narrow scariose bracts; perianth funnelform to bell-shaped, gamophyllous, the 6 segms. spreading or reflexed, tube sometimes gibbous at or near the base; stamens 6, short, attached on tube or throat of perianth, anthers versatile; pistil 1, with sessile 3-celled ovary and capitate stigma, style erect, filiform: caps. usually 3-angled or -lobed, loculicidal. (Hyacin-thus: an early Greek name.)

A. Lvs. 8–12 in. long: fls. 1 in. long....................1. *H. orientalis*
AA. Lvs. 4–6 in long: fls. ½in. long....................2. *H. azureus*

1. **H. orientalis,** L. Common Hyacinth. Bulbs large, nearly globular: scape 6–18 in. tall, hollow: lvs. several, thick, strap-shaped, obtuse, many-nerved, 1 in. and more wide, at length equalling or exceeding the scape: fls. in many colors and sometimes double, about 1 in. long, declined or drooping, tube swollen at base, the long lobes wide-spreading or reflexed; pedicel shorter than fl., with very small bract: early spring. Greece to Syria and Asia Minor. Var. **albulus,** Baker, Roman Hyacinth of florists, smaller, very early; fls. fewer in more open raceme, white to light blue, tube slender and little; S. France.

2. **H. azureus,** Baker (*Muscari azureum,* Fenzl). Scape 4–8 in. tall: lvs. 4–6 in. long, strongly channelled, to ½in. wide: raceme dense, 20–40-fld., 1 in. long; fls. blue, tubular, scarcely ½in. long, more or less nodding; segms. broadly ovate, spreading, obtuse: early spring. Asia Minor.—*H. ciliatus,* Cyr., has ciliate lvs. and scapes 9–18 in. tall; S. Eu. to Kurdistan.

47. **MUSCARI,** Mill. Grape-Hyacinth. Small plants, 40–50 species of Medit. region and S. W. Asia, several planted.—Lvs. few, from a tunicate bulb, narrow, more or less fleshy: fls. small, racemose or spicate at top of scape, sometimes paniculate, nodding or pendulous, mostly blue, the bracts of the short pedicels small and scariose; perianth gamophyllous, mostly urn-shaped, sometimes globose or oblong, the 6 segms. or teeth recurved or reflexed; stamens 6, attached on the perianth in two rows, anthers versatile; pistil 1, with 3-celled sessile ovary and short filiform style, stigma 3-lobed: caps. 3-angled, loculicidal. (Musca-ri: Latin, alluding to musky odor of some species.)

A. Lvs. ⅛–⅜in. broad: fertile fls. not over ¼in. long.
B. Teeth of fls. recurved; fertile fls. about ⅛in. long....................1. *M. botryoides*
BB. Teeth of fls. erect; fertile fls. 3/16–¼in. long....................2. *M. armeniacum*
AA. Lvs. ⅜–1 in. broad: fertile fls., if present, ¼–⅜in. long....................3. *M. comosum*

1. **M. botryoides,** Mill. Bulbs ovoid or oblong: scape 4–12 in. high, slender: lvs. linear, about equalling the scape, to ¼in. broad, blunt or short-acute: fls. more or less than a dozen, aggregated at top of scape or sometimes open-racemed, subglobose, blue (but running to white in var. **album,** Hort.), about ⅛in. long, somewhat restricted at apex, uppermost fls. sterile; segms. very short, recurved: spring. S. Eu.; common in yards and also nat.

2. **M. armeniacum,** Leicht. Scape 4–9 in. high: lvs. exceeding scape, ¼–⅜in. broad: fertile fls. many, deep violet, ¼in. long, oblong, the teeth erect, white; sterile fls. at tip of raceme, crowded, pale blue: spring. S. W. Asia.—The form "Heavenly Blue" belongs here.

3. **M. comosum,** Mill. Scape spotted brown, 12–18 in. high: lvs. 3–4, 12–18 in. long, ⅜–1 in. broad: fls. many in a lax raceme, the fertile ones greenish-brown, ¼–5⁄16 in. long, cylindrical, with recurved teeth; sterile fls. smaller, purple-blue: spring. W. Eu., N. Afr.—The forms commonly cult. are: var. **monstrosum,** Hort., raceme branched, fls. all sterile, converted into tufts of narrow violet-blue segms.; var. **plumosum,** Hort. (*M. plumosum,* Hort.), more branched, segms. longer, intertwined, reddish-purple.

48. **GALTONIA,** Decne. Three stout bulbous scapose plants from S. Afr., one in common cult.—Bulbs tunicated: lvs. few or several, large, somewhat fleshy: fls. in a long open raceme, white or tinged green, on large-bracted pedicels; perianth gamophyllous, the tube relatively short, segms. oblong and prominent; stamens 6, attached below the throat, filaments slender, anthers versatile; pistil 1, with sessile 3-celled many-ovuled ovary, cylindrical style and capitate stigma: caps. more or less 3-sided, loculicidal. (Galto-nia: Sir Francis Galton, 1822–1911, anthropologist.)

G. candicans, Decne. (*Hyacinthus candicans,* Baker). Summer-Hyacinth. Showy summer- and autumn-blooming plant: bulbs large, globose: scape 2–4 ft., strict and stout: lvs. 2–3 ft. long, strap-like, 1–2 in. broad: fls. 20–30, white, fragrant, cernuous at least toward top, 1–1½ in. long, narrow-campanulate; segms. exceeding tube; pedicels becoming 1–2½ in. long, equalling or exceeding great bract: caps. ascending, 1–1½ in. long.

49. **BOWIEA,** Harvey (*Schizobasopsis,* Macb.). One species, a twining leafless bulbous plant from S. Afr., grown as a curiosity in greenhouses.—Bulbs large, globose: st. with many forked branches below and branching fl.-stalks which are green and perform the function of lvs.: fls. small, green to whitish, on long pedicels, 6-cleft to base, the segms. persistent, ultimately reflexed; stamens 6, the filaments dilated at base; ovary superior, 3-loculed, style short, stigma capitate: caps. loculicidal, with several elongate seeds in each locule. (Bowie-a: named for J. Bowie, 1789–1869, collector for Kew.)—The name Bowiea is a *nomen conservandum.*

B. volubilis, Harvey. Bulb 4–7 in. thick: st. 5–6 ft. high: perianth-segms. ⅛in. long.

50. **COLCHICUM,** L. Sixty and more species of small cormous plants, mostly autumn-blooming, one frequently planted and others in choice collections; northern hemisphere in Old World.—Scape very short, underground, so that the fls. are stemless: lvs. appearing with fls. or long after them, strap-shaped or linear: fls. crocus-like, purple or white (rarely yellow), long-tubular, segms. 6; stamens 6, inserted in the perianth, the anthers versatile; pistil with 3-celled ovary and 3 long slender styles separate to base: caps. 3-grooved, septicidal. (Col-chicum: from Colchis, ancient name of a country on the Black Sea.)

A. Plants blooming in autumn or late summer: lvs. in spring.
  B. Fls. 1–4 in number, 3–4 in. across....................1. *C. autumnale*
  BB. Fls. 4–20 in number, 5–6 in. across.
    C. Tube four to five times as long as segms.: tunics of corms thickened.........2. *C. speciosum*
    CC. Tube three times as long as segms.: tunics of corms membranous.........3. *C. Bornmuelleri*
AA. Plants blooming in spring: lvs. just after the fls....................4. *C. vernum*

1. **C. autumnale,** L. Autumn-Crocus. Corm tunicate: lvs. few, appearing usually in spring, lanceolate, 12 in. or less long and 2 in. or less wide: fls. 1–4 or 6, 3–4 in. across when expanded, appearing in autumn, with slender tube several inches long that elevates the purple oblong obtuse veined segms. above the ground; segms. 1–2½ in. long; stamens less than half as long as segms., anthers yellow: caps. arising with foliage in spring. England, Eu., N. Afr. Var. **album,** Hort., fls. white. Var. **majus,** Hort., more robust.

2. **C. speciosum,** Steven. Corm large, long-necked, with thickened tunics: lvs. 4–6, broadly oblong, 10–30 in. long, mostly 3–4 in. wide, obtuse: fls. 4–20, purple, pale pink, rarely white, yellow-spotted at base within, 5–6 in. across; tube stout, four to five times as long as segms. which are broadly elliptic, 1½–3 in. long; stamens slightly more than half as long as segms., anthers yellow: autumn. S. W. Asia. Var. **giganteum,** Hort. (*C. giganteum,* Hort.), pink-fld. form.

3. **C. Bornmuelleri,** Freyn. Near to no. 2 but differing in corm with membranous tunics and a longer tapering spur, earlier flowering: lvs. large: fls. with greenish-white tube three times as long as the segms., these first white, later colored as in *C. speciosum;* anthers bicolored; styles longer. (Named for J. F. Bornmueller, page 40.) Syria, Iran.

4. **C. vernum,** Ker (*Bulbocodium vernum,* L.). Corm about 1 in. diam. with brownish-black tunics: lvs. 3, lanceolate, obtuse, channelled: fls. usually solitary, dark rose-lilac, the segms. free to the base, very long-clawed, the blades narrow-oblong, about 1½ in. long, ⅛–3⁄16 in. wide; style 1, 3-lobed: spring. Eu., Asia.

51. **TRILLIUM,** L. Wake-Robin. A genus of perhaps 30 species from N. Amer. and Asia.—Erect unbranched herbs with short rootstocks scarred by the fracture of the old sheaths: sts. with scarious sheaths at base: lvs. in whorl of 3 near apex of st. and subtending the sessile or peduncled solitary bractless perfect fl.: outer 3 perianth-segms. or sepals usually green, persistent, the inner 3 or petals white, pink, purplish or yellow, deciduous or withering; stamens 6, hypogynous, with short filaments and linear mostly introrse anthers; ovary sessile, 3-celled, with several to many ovules, style trifid, often to the base: fr. a globose or ovoid berry. (Tril-lium: Latin, alluding to the 3-parted fls. and the 3 lvs.)

A. Fls. sessile.
B. Lvs. sessile: petals not clawed.
C. Anthers ⅛–⅝in. long.
D. Petals purple or green; stamens half as long as petals................ 1. *T. sessile*
DD. Petals yellow; stamens not more than one-third the length of petals... 2. *T. luteum*
CC. Anthers ⅝–1 in. long; petals maroon to greenish-yellow or white.......... 3. *T. chloropetalum*
BB. Lvs. petioled: petals clawed................................ 4. *T. recurvatum*
AA. Fls. peduncled.
B. Lvs. sessile or nearly so: ovary winged or angled.
C. Petals ascending at base, spreading above.
D. Fl. usually raised above the lvs.; filaments and anthers slender....... 5. *T. grandiflorum*
DD. Fl. below lvs. on cernuous or declined peduncles; stamens stout.
E. Style present; stamens long and curved; petals recurved........... 6. *T. nervosum*
EE. Style absent; stamens short and straight; petals spreading......... 7. *T. cernuum*
CC. Petals spreading from the base.
D. Color of fls. brown or greenish-purple; anthers purple................ 8. *T. erectum*
DD. Color of fls. white, soon becoming rose; anthers yellow............... 9. *T. ovatum*
BB. Lvs. petioled: ovary not strongly winged or angled.
C. Length of lvs. 1–2 in.: fls. ½–1 in. long.
D. Peduncle ½–1 in. long; stamens about one-third as long as petals.....10. *T. nivale*
DD. Peduncle 1–2 in. long; stamens about half the length of petals........11. *T. rivale*
CC. Length of lvs. 3–8 in.: fls. mostly 1–2 in. long......................12. *T. undulatum*

1. **T. sessile,** L. Rootstock short, stout: sts. 4–12 in. tall, dark green, fairly stout: lvs. sessile, ovate to suborbicular, often mottled, mostly acute, 1½–6 in. long: fl. sessile, erect; sepals lanceolate, somewhat spreading, ½–1½ in. long, green with some purple streaking near base; petals broadly lanceolate, purple or green, erect, not clawed, slightly surpassing sepals; stamens about half as long, the anthers purplish, ¼–½in. long; style trifid to base: berry globose, 6-angled. Pa. to Fla. and Miss.

2. **T. luteum,** Harbison (*T. sessile* var. *luteum,* Muhl.). Sts. 4–24 in. high: lvs. sessile broadly ovate to orbicular, mottled, acuminate: fl. sessile; sepals 1–1½ in. long, lanceolate, blunt; petals erect, 1½–2¼ in. long, not clawed, yellow; stamens ⅜–⅝in. long, yellow. N. C., Tenn.

3. **T. chloropetalum,** Howell (*T. sessile* var. *chloropetalum,* Torr. *T. sessile* var. *californicum,* Wats.). Sts. 1–2 ft. high: lvs. round-ovate, sessile, 3–6 in. long, almost as wide, obtuse to almost acuminate, usually mottled: fl. sessile; sepals oblong-lanceolate, 1–2 in. long; petals not clawed, ascending, obovate to narrow-lanceolate, 1½–3½ in. long, deep maroon to greenish-yellow or white; anthers ⅝–1 in. long. Wash. to Calif.

4. **T. recurvatum,** Beck. Rootstock short, horizontal: sts. 6–18 in. tall: lvs. ovate to oblong, acute, 2–4 in. long, narrowed into petioles ¼in. to more than 1 in. long: fl. sessile, erect; sepals narrow-lanceolate, acute, purplish-green, ½–1¼ in. long, reflexed between the petioles; petals purple-maroon, clawed, lanceolate to oblong or spatulate, erect, 1–1¼ in. long; filaments ⅛in. long, anthers ⅓–½in. long, purple, incurved: berry winged above. Ohio to Minn., Miss., Ark.

5. **T. grandiflorum,** Salisb. (*T. rhomboideum* var. *grandiflorum,* Michx.). Rootstock short, stout: sts. stout, 8–18 in. long: lvs. broadly rhombic-ovate or rhombic-oval, 2½–6 in. long, short-acuminate, the cuneate base sessile: peduncle nearly erect, 1½–3 in. long; sepals lanceolate, spreading, green, 1–2 in. long; petals erect-spreading, obovate, white fading to rose-pink, 1½–3 in. long; stamens one-third the petals, anthers yellow: berry globose, somewhat 6-lobed. Que. to N. C. and Mo.

6. **T. nervosum,** Ell. (*T. stylosum,* Nutt. *T. Catesbæi,* Auth. not Ell.). Rootstock short, horizontal: sts. 8–20 in. tall: lvs. elliptic to narrow-ovate, acute at each end, 1½–3 in. long, subsessile, occasionally mottled: peduncle spreading or deflexed, 1–2 in. long; sepals lanceolate, green, curled or reflexed, ¾–1½ in. long; petals pink to rose, oblong-lanceolate, recurved, abruptly pointed, 1–2 in. long; stamens about half as long as petals, anthers yellow, recurved; style present. N. C. to Ala.

7. **T. cernuum,** L. Rootstock very short: sts. 8–20 in. tall: lvs. broadly rhombic-ovate, subsessile, short-acuminate, 2–3 in. long: peduncle recurved beneath the lvs., ½–2 in. long; sepals lanceolate, acuminate, green, ½–1 in. long; petals white or pink, ovate- or oblong-lanceolate, ⅝–1 in. long, spreading, somewhat recurved; stamens straight, about half the length of petals; style absent. Newf. to Ga. and Mo.

8. **T. erectum,** L. Rootstock slender, short: sts. stout, 8–16 in. high: lvs. broadly rhombic, sessile, acuminate at apex, narrowed at base, 3–7 in. long: peduncle suberect, 1–4 in. long; sepals green, lanceolate, acuminate, ½–1½ in. long; petals broadly lanceolate to ovate, purple, spreading, equalling or slightly exceeding sepals; stamens less than one-third as long as petals, anthers purple; style short, spreading or recurved. N. S. to N. C. and Tenn. Var. **album,** Pursh, petals white; S. E. U. S.

9. **T. ovatum,** Pursh. Rootstock short, thick: sts. 12–20 in. high: lvs. rhombic-ovate, 2–6 in. long, short-acuminate at apex, abruptly narrowed to the more or less sessile base: peduncle erect, 1–3 in. long; sepals lanceolate to broadly oblong-lanceolate, green, 1–2 in. long, spreading; petals white, turning rose, ascending, lanceolate, equalling or slightly longer than sepals; stamens almost half the petals, anthers yellow: berry broadly ovoid, somewhat winged. B. C. to Mont. and Calif.

10. **T. nivale,** Riddell. Rootstock short, thick: sts. 2–6 in. high: lvs. oblong-ovate, 1–2 in. long, obtuse, rounded or narrowed to petiole, ⅛–½in. long: peduncle erect to recurved, ½–1 in. long; sepals spreading, green, lance-oblong, ½–1 in. long; petals white, aging rose-pink, ascending, oblong or oval, slightly longer than sepals; stamens about one-third the length of the petals, anthers yellow; style trifid to base: berry globose, 3-lobed. Ohio to Minn., Ky., Iowa.

11. **T. rivale,** Wats. Rootstock short, slender: sts. 4–8 in. high: lvs. ovate-lanceolate, acute to acuminate, 1–2 in. long, rounded or subcordate at base, with petioles ¼–1 in. long: peduncle slender, erect or eventually nodding, 1–2 in. long; sepals green, lance-elliptic, spreading, ½–¾in. long; petals white or marked with rose-carmine, ascending, ovate-cordate, acute, ½–1 in. long; stamens about half as long as petals: berry globose, scarcely angled. Ore., Calif.

12. **T. undulatum,** Willd. (*T. erythrocarpum,* Michx.). Rootstock stout, short: sts. 8–24 in. high: lvs. ovate, 3–8 in. long, acuminate, obtuse or rounded at base with petiole ¼–¾in. long: peduncle erect or somewhat inclined, 1–2½ in. long; sepals lanceolate, acuminate, green often with purple tinge, ¾–1¼ in. long; petals ovate, acute or acuminate, white with purple veins or striped, spreading, crisped along margins, ¾–2 in. long; stamens scarcely one-third as long as petals: berry ovoid, bluntly 3-angled. N. S. to Ga. and Mo.

52. **MEDEOLA,** L. Indian Cucumber-Root. A monotypic genus of E. N. Amer.—Rootstock thick, tuber-like: sts. slender, erect, simple, with loose deciduous wool: lvs. in two whorls, the lower with 5–9 oblong-lanceolate to obovate lvs., the upper with 3–5 ovate or oval lvs. which subtend the sessile umbel of small greenish-yellow declined fls.: perianth-segms. equal, oblong, recurved; stamens 6, hypogynous, filaments slender, anthers oblong, extrorse; ovary 3-celled, with several ovules in each cell, styles 3, recurved: berry globose. (Mede-ola: from Medea, a sorceress, because of the supposed healing properties.)

M. virginiana, L. Sts. 1–2½ ft. tall: lvs. of lower whorl 2½–5 in. long, of upper 1–2 in. long: fls. 2–9, segms. ¼–½in. long. N. S. to Ont., Minn., Fla., Tenn.

53. **SMILAX,** L. Greenbrier. Shrubby or herbaceous climbing or straggling plants; about 200 species of general distribution.—Mostly diœcious: shoots arising from a rootstock: lower lvs. reduced to scales, upper simple or slightly lobed, 3–7-(or more) nerved, deciduous to persistent, usually with paired tendrils on the base of the petiole: fls. small, in axillary peduncled umbels, greenish or yellowish, regular, the perianth-segms. distinct, deciduous; stamens 6, anthers 1-celled by confluence: fr. a berry with 1–6 seeds. (Smi-lax: ancient Greek name of obscure meaning.)

A. St. herbaceous, not prickly .... 1. *S. herbacea*
AA. St. woody, armed with scattered prickles.................................... 2. *S. rotundifolia*

1. **S. herbacea,** L. Carrion-Flower. Sts. 3–16 ft. high: lvs. ovate or rounded, 7–9-nerved, 1½–5 in. long, obtuse or heart-shaped at base, petioles ½–2½ in. long: peduncle 2–8 in. long, 20–40-fld.: berries bluish-black, glaucous, seeds 2–6. E. U. S.

2. **S. rotundifolia,** L. Horse-Brier. Bull-Brier. Sts. woody, with scattered stout prickles: lvs. ovate to rounded, slightly heart-shaped, 5-nerved, 2–6 in. long, petioles ¼–½in. long: peduncle flattened, ¼–1 in. long, 6–25-fld.: berries black, 1–3-seeded. E. U. S.

34. AGAVACEÆ. AGAVE FAMILY

A family of about 19 genera and 500 species, usually put partly in Liliaceæ and partly in Amaryllidaceæ, characterized for the most part by their xerophytic adaptations, the lvs. fibrous, linear, closely set near base or apex of sts., fls. mostly in very

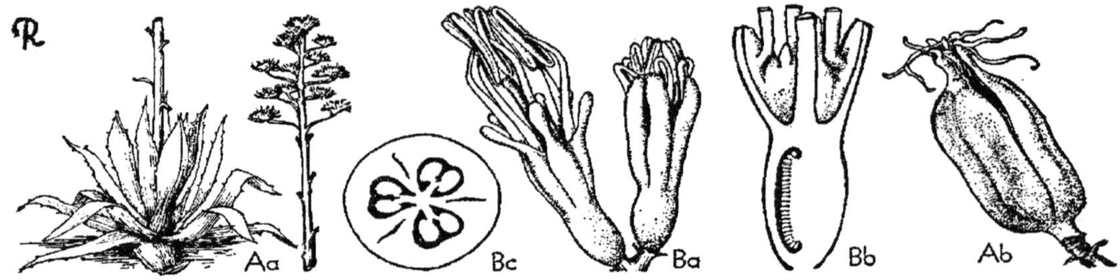

Fig. 34. Agavaceæ. A, *Agave americana:* Aa, rosette and flowering scape, much reduced; Ab, capsule, × ½. B, Agave species: Ba, flower and bud, × ½; Bb, flower, vertical section (basal portion), × 1; Bc, ovary, cross-section, × 2.

large panicles; mostly of warm regions, including many important fiber-producing plants.—Rootstock a rhizome; st. short or well-developed: lvs. usually crowded on or near base of st., narrow, often thick or fleshy, entire or prickly on the margin: fls. bisexual or unisexual, regular or somewhat irregular, racemose or paniculate, the branches subtended by bracts; perianth-tube short to long; segms. subequal to unequal; stamens 6, on the tube or segm.-bases, filaments filiform to thickened, free, anthers linear, usually dorsifixed; ovary superior or inferior, 3-celled, style slender, ovules many to 1 in each cell: fr. a berry or loculicidal caps.

A. Ovary inferior.
  B. Fls. regular; infl. paniculate in ours..1. Agave
  BB. Fls. irregular; infl. racemose..2. Polianthes
AA. Ovary superior.
  B. Lvs. equitant: anthers with a pit on the back into which the filament intrudes..3. Phormium
  BB. Lvs. not equitant: anthers not so pitted.
    C. Foliage erect: plant stemless..4. Sansevieria
    CC. Foliage divergent to spreading.
      D. Perianth-segms. 1–4 in. long, generally not grown together.
        E. Fls. in a simple raceme..5. Hesperaloe
        EE. Fls. in a compound infl..6. Yucca
      DD. Perianth-segms. ¼–1 in. long, united at the base.
        E. Ovules solitary: rhizome not creeping..7. Dracæna
        EE. Ovules many: rhizome creeping..8. Cordyline

1. **AGAVE,** L. Three hundred or more species of striking plants, in the arid and semi-arid trop. parts of the western hemisphere, with great stiff heavy persistent lvs. mostly in basal rosettes and towering panicles or spikes of relatively small fls.; planted for formal and architectural effects.—St. short or none: plants of differing habit, some blooming from year to year, others at intervals, and still others once, at which time they die: lvs. fleshy, mostly with spiny edges, and spine-tipped: perianth more or less funnelform, with short tube, the 6 segms. narrow and nearly equal; stamens inserted at throat or in the tube, the filiform filaments usually long-exserted, the anthers versatile; ovules many and superposed in each cell; style awl-shaped; stigma capitate but 3-lobed: caps. oblong, loculicidally 3-valved; seeds numerous, thin and flat, b ack. (Aga-ve: from the Greek word for *admirable.*)—Many species of Agave are grown in collections of succulents, and a number are planted in warm dry regions for lawn and foundation effects. They bloom only seldom and are therefore difficult of determination except by specialists. Only one species is a common and general plant in cult. In Mex., where agaves are many, several species have great economic importance, yielding the liquors *pulque* and *mescal,* the fiber *sisal,* or *henequen,* and other products. The genus Furcræa yields a few cult. species, much like Agave, but the fls. white and rotate rather than funnelform and greenish-yellow, the stamens swollen at base rather than filiform. The species are trop. American.

A. Lvs. plane, not prickly-toothed on margins..1. *A. Victoriæ-Reginæ*
AA. Lvs. prickly-toothed on margins.
  B. Width of lvs. 6–8 in., length 3–6 ft..2. *A. americana*
  BB. Width of lvs. 2½–4 in., length 1–3 ft..3. *A. decipiens*

1. **A. Victoriæ-Reginæ,** Moore. Rosette trunkless, simple, subspherical, 1½–2⅓ ft. broad: lvs. many, dark green with gray margin, stiff, leathery-fleshy, 4–6 in. long, 2 in.

wide at middle, blunt, the terminal spine less than 1 in. long: infl. to 12 ft.; fls. greenish, 1¼ in. long, segms. lance-linear, blunt; filaments over 2 in. long: caps. about 1 in. long. (Named for Queen Victoria.) Mex.

2. **A. americana,** L. CENTURY PLANT, so called from the erroneous notion that it blooms only when 100 years old. Lvs. borne next the ground in a massive rosette, 3–6 ft. long and 6–8 in. broad, thick and heavy, gray, smooth, upcurved, prickly on the edges: fls. in a bracted scape or stalk 20–40 ft. tall, about 2½ in. across with segms. yellowish-green, borne erect on many horizontal branches; the infl. is produced at the maturity of the plant, at 10 years or more, whereupon the plant dies but usually leaves suckers about the base. Trop. Amer., and established also in parts of Eu. Var. **marginata,** Trel., lf.-margins white or yellow. Var. **variegata,** Hort., lvs. dark green and yellow, twisted.—Much grown as a tub-plant for placing on porches and lawns in summer, particularly in the kinds with yellow- or white-margined or striped lvs.

3. **A. decipiens,** Baker. St. 3–8 ft. high, with offsets: lvs. 1–3 ft. long, thickened at base, 2½–4 in. broad near middle, convex beneath, green, leathery-fleshy, with brownish marginal recurved spiny teeth, gradually attenuate to terminal spine ½in. long: infl. 15–20 ft. high; fls. greenish-yellow, 3 in. long; filaments 1½ in. long. S. Fla.

2. **POLIANTHES,** L. About a dozen Mexican herbs, one in common cult. for its fragrant fls. in summer.—Rootstock a tuber: lvs. grass-like, basal and cauline, those on the st. reduced or bract-like: fls. white, somewhat lily-shaped, in a long raceme or spike terminating the erect st.; tube slender; segms. short and nearly or quite equal; stamens inserted in tube, included; ovules many in each cell, one above the other; style slender; stigmas 3: caps. bearing the persistent perianth on top, the seeds flat. (Polian-thes: probably from Greek words meaning *white* or *shining flowers*.)

P. tuberosa, L. TUBEROSE. Tuber bulb-shaped (whence the name *tuber-ose*) and the plant commonly classed among the "bulbs": st. 2–3½ ft. tall, strict and simple, bearing successively smaller long-pointed clasping lvs.: fls. 2½ in. or less long, in pairs in an open spike, waxy-white and very fragrant; tube 1–1½ in. long, bent near base, expanding widely where it meets the oblong obtuse segms.: some forms are double. Unrecognized wild.

3. **PHORMIUM,** Forst. Two species of New Zeal. and Norfolk Isls., one grown in warm temp. regions as a striking lawn plant, for its many long lvs. (which produce a strong fiber).—Rhizome fleshy, short and branched: lvs. many, radical, long-sword-shaped, equitant, very tough: scape tall, usually exceeding the foliage, bearing the bloom on alternate bracted branches: fls. dull red or yellow, 1–2 in. long, on jointed pedicels; perianth tubular and curved, the 6 segms. connate at base, 3 inner ones longer; stamens 6, inserted at base of segms., exserted; ovary sessile, 3-celled, style declinate, stigma capitate: fr. a loculicidal caps. (Phor-mium: Greek *basket*, alluding to the uses of the fiber.)

P. tenax, Forst. NEW ZEALAND FLAX. Lvs. 3–9 ft. long in its native country and 2–5 in. broad, slit at apex when mature, keeled, very tough, margins and midrib bordered with red or orange line: scape to 15 ft., with numerous fls.: caps. 2–4 in. long. Var. **variegatum,** Hort., has lvs. striped with creamy-yellow and white.

4. **SANSEVIERIA,** Thunb. BOWSTRING-HEMP. Stiff-lvd. plants used for pot and porch decoration, the lvs. being barred, striped or variegated (in cult. forms); species more than 50, in Afr. and Asia.—Rhizome prominent, horizontal, bearing the (in ours) erect mostly rigid flat or concave or terete lvs. with large bracts at their bases: scape about as long as lvs., slender, bracted: fls. racemose or spicate or fascicled, whitish or yellowish, on jointed pedicels; perianth tubular, with 6 narrow spreading somewhat unequal lobes, tube usually swollen at the base; stamens 6, attached on the throat, usually curved and exserted, anthers versatile; ovary free, 3-celled, with solitary ovules, stigma capitate and usually exserted: fr. a 1–3-seeded berry. (Sansevie-ria: Raimond de Sangro, Prince of Sanseviero, born at Naples, Italy, 1710.)—What species of Sansevieria may be in cult. in N. Amer. is difficult to say; they have not been carefully collected. The lvs. yield strong fiber.

A. Lvs. nearly or quite flat at middle, to 3½ in. broad....................1. *S. thyrsiflora*
AA. Lvs. concave at middle, ¾in. broad....................2. *S. zeylanica*

1. **S. thyrsiflora,** Thunb. (*S. guineensis*, Willd. *Cordyline guineensis*, Britt.). Lvs. few (2–4) in a cluster, 1–1½ ft. long, to 3½ in. broad, lanceolate, acute or obtuse, flat or nearly so, but tapering into a channelled petiole, with close pale green transverse bands on both surfaces but which become faint with age, yellow-margined: fls. 2–6 together in a spike-like raceme, greenish-white, fragrant, the tube about ¾in. long, the linear revolute segms. of similar length. S. Afr.—Several species are cult. as *S. guineensis*.

2. **S. zeylanica,** Willd. Lvs. 5–11 in a cluster, 1½–2½ ft. long, ¾in. or less broad, linear-semiterete, channelled down the face and very rounded on the back, dark green and transversely banded with somewhat lighter green and with darker green longitudinal lines on back. Ceylon.—The plants grown under this name probably do not belong to this species. That known as *S. zeylanica* var. *Laurentii* is probably **S. trifasciata,** Prain, var. **Laurentii,** N. E. Br., having linear-lanceolate or narrow long-lanceolate lvs. longitudinally striped golden-yellow, channelled at least below; Belgian Congo, intro. by Emile Laurent.

5. **HESPERALOE,** Engelm. A genus of 2 or 3 species from Tex. and N. Mex.—Very short-stemmed plants with crowded thick linear deeply channelled lvs. having filiferous margins: infl. loosely few-branched; fls. narrowly cylindric or oblong, the segms. oblong, succulent, with recurved tips; filaments slender; ovary superior, style long, slender, stigma small, capitate: caps. loculicidal. (Hesperal-oe: Latin *western aloe*.)

H. parviflora, Coult. (*Yucca parviflora*, Torr. *Aloe yuccæfolia*, Gray). Usually cespitosely suckering: lvs. 3–4 ft. long, about 1 in. wide: infl. 3–4 ft. high; fls. rose, 1–1¼ in. long, nodding. Tex.

6. **YUCCA,** L. About 30 bayonet-lvd. showy-fld. species, of the tablelands of Mex. and northward, also somewhat in W. Indies and E. U. S.; all are striking plants, but few are commonly planted.—Stemless or rising to stature of small trees: lvs. stiff and long-pointed, often toothed or fibrillose on margins, mostly in rosettes at surface of ground or ends of trunk or branches: fls. cup-shaped or saucer-shaped, usually of waxy texture, white, cream, or violet, opening and fragrant at night, commonly hanging, borne mostly in erect panicles that usually overtop the lvs.; segms. 6, distinct or connate at base; stamens 6, hypogynous; ovary sessile, 3-celled, style thick and 3-lobed at top: fr. a caps. or somewhat fleshy. (Yuc-ca: modification of an aboriginal name, applied to another plant.) *Y. brevifolia*, Engelm., is the wild Joshua-Tree of far western deserts.

A. Plant stemless or nearly so, the lvs. in dense basal rosette.
 B. Margins of lvs. serrulate, not filiferous: style slender........ 1. *Y. Whipplei*
 BB. Margins of lvs. not serrulate, usually filiferous: style stout.
  C. Lvs. ¼–½in. wide: infl. simple........ 2. *Y. glauca*
  CC. Lvs. wider: infl. branched.
   D. Perianth 1–2 in. long; infl. long-peduncled.
    E. Foliage firm: petals gradually acuminate; filaments pruinose-pilose........ 3. *Y. Smalliana*
    EE. Foliage thin, pliable: petals abruptly short-acuminate; filaments ciliate.. 4. *Y. flaccida*
   DD. Perianth 2–4 in. long; infl. scarcely peduncled........ 5. *Y. baccata*
AA. Plant caulescent, the lvs. not in basal rosette.
 B. Ovary stipitate: fr. coreless, 3–3½ in. long: lvs. sharply rough-edged........ 6. *Y. aloifolia*
 BB. Ovary mostly sessile: fr. with central core and 2–2½ in. long: lvs. not rough-edged........ 7. *Y. gloriosa*

1. **Y. Whipplei,** Torr. (*Hesperoyucca Whipplei*, Baker). OUR LORDS CANDLE. Simple to cespitose, acaulescent: lvs. in dense basal rosette, 8–20 in. long, mostly ½in. wide, grayish-green, more or less serrulate: infl. 5–16 ft. tall, compactly branched; fls. pendent, creamy-white sometimes purplish, 1–1½ in. long; style short, slender: caps. dry, 1½ in. long. (Named for Lt. A. W. Whipple, 1818–1863, leader of a western expedition.) Calif., Ariz.

2. **Y. glauca,** Nutt. SOAP WEED. Subacaulescent or short-branched: lvs. rigid, 8–16 in. long, ¼–½in. wide, finely filiferous on margins: infl. 3–6 ft. high, compact, rather simple; fls. greenish-white, to 2 in. long, segms. ovate: caps. oblong, 2–3 in. long. Plains east of Rocky Mts.

3. **Y. Smalliana,** Fern. (*Y. filamentosa*, Auth. not L.). ADAMS-NEEDLE. Acaulescent or nearly so: lvs. many, firm, in a basal rosette, 1–2½ ft. long, to 1 in. wide, gradually narrowed toward both ends, attenuate to a slender apical spine, with fairly coarse curly marginal fibers: scape stout, strict, bracteate, 3–12 ft. high, with a long panicle with spreading or ascending branches; fls. many, hanging, nearly white, the segms. 1–2 in. long, gradually acuminate; filaments pruinose-pilose; style to ¼in. long: caps. 1½—2½ in. long, with rounded angles. (Named for John K. Small, page 51.) N. C. to Fla. and Miss., but hardy and cult. in the N.—There is a variegated form.

4. **Y. flaccida,** Haw. Similar to *Y. Smalliana* but with thinner more pliable lvs. and finer marginal threads: petals longer, abruptly short-acuminate; filaments flatter, coarsely ciliate; style longer. Mts., N. C. to Ala.—Some material cult. as *Y. filamentosa* belongs here.

5. **Y. baccata,** Torr. Simple, occasionally clumped, usually acaulescent: lvs. 2–3 ft. long, 1–2 in. wide, dark blue- or yellow-green, fibrous on margins, spine-tipped: infl. 2–2½ ft. long, heavy, fleshy, mostly glabrous, with about 15 branches; fls. 2–4 in. long, campanulate, pendent, the segms. united at base for ¼–½in., lanceolate; filaments sturdy, 1½–2½ in. long: caps. 6–7 in. long, 2–2½ in. thick, fleshy, pendent. Colo. to Tex. and Calif.

6. **Y. aloifolia,** L. SPANISH BAYONET. Common in gardens and division lines in warm temp. regions: trunk 2–3 ft. and the plant often much taller and sometimes 25 ft., simple or branched, the main trunk often inclining: lvs. 1½–2½ ft. long, to 2½ in. wide, stiff and bayonet-like, very sharp-pointed: fls. many, hanging, white often purple-tipped, 3–4 in. across at full anthesis: fr. fleshy, black-purple, 3–4 in. long; summer. N. C. south and along the Gulf to La.; also W. Indies and Mex., probably nat.—There are forms with striped and colored lvs.

7. **Y. gloriosa,** L. SPANISH DAGGER. Trunk short or rising to 6 or 8 ft.: lvs. 2–2½ ft. long, 2 in. wide, often with a few threads when old and a few deciduous teeth when young, tip short, stiff and red: fls. many, hanging, greenish-white to reddish, 3–4 in. across at full anthesis: caps. 6-ridged, not dehiscent, 2–2½ in. long; summer and autumn. Along coast N. C. to Fla., and planted S.—There are forms with striped lvs., and smaller stature.

7. **DRACÆNA,** L. DRACENA. Some 50 species of woody-stemmed plants in trop. regions, mostly in the eastern hemisphere, a few grown under glass and bedded out for the ornamental foliage.—Sometimes tree-like, but mostly shrubby with single or few sts.: lvs. various, either long and sword-shaped or broad and more or less distinctly petioled, often marked with stripes, bands or dots, in mature plants usually crowded at summit of trunk or branches: fls. many, mostly in little clusters or fascicles arranged in panicles, small and not showy, greenish, whitish, yellowish; perianth funnelform or narrowly bell-shaped, with long or short tube, the 6 segms. nearly or quite alike and spreading or reflexed; stamens 6, inserted on tube or throat, filaments various, anthers versatile; ovary nearly or quite sessile, 3-celled, style slender, stigma capitate or somewhat lobed: fr. a globose berry, with 1–3 seeds. (Dracæ-na: Greek *female dragon;* the juice when thickened supposed to resemble dragon's blood.)

A. Lvs. only twice or less than thrice as long as broad, 3–8 or 9 in. long.
  B. Blade marked with light dots....................1. *D. Godseffiana*
  BB. Blade crosswise banded....................2. *D. Goldieana*
AA. Lvs. elongated, usually 10–12 in. and more.
  B. Blade white-margined; petiole part distinct and long....................3. *D. Sanderiana*
  BB. Blade not white-margined; no distinct petiole part.
    C. Width of lvs. 1–1¾ in.; lvs. glaucous....................4. *D. Draco*
    CC. Width of lvs. 2–4 in.; lvs. green.
      D. Lf. 2½–4 in. wide, 1½–3 ft. long: fl. ½in. long, yellow....................5. *D. fragrans*
      DD. Lf. 2 in. wide, 1½ ft. long: fl. longer, red without, white within....................6. *D. deremensis*

1. **D. Godseffiana,** Sander. St. slender, much-branched: lvs. 2–3 at a node, short-petioled, oblong to oblong-ovate, 4–5 in. long and 1½–2½ in. broad, abruptly narrowed to point, marked with many irregular white spots: fls. in a short open raceme with minute bracts, greenish-yellow, very slender, about ¾in. long; stamens about the length of perianth. (Bears the name of Mr. Godseff, with the Messrs. Sander.) Upper Guinea.

2. **D. Goldieana,** Bull. St. short and woody: lvs. crowded, rather long-petioled, ovate, 4–9 in. long and 3–5 in. broad, abruptly short-pointed, banded transversely with bright green and gray: fls. in dense globose heads with oblong-cuspidate bracts, white, 1 in. long; stamens somewhat shorter than tube. (Rev. Hugh Goldie, missionary in China, who sent the plant out.) Upper Guinea.

3. **D. Sanderiana,** Sander. St. tall and erect, nearly or quite simple: lvs. long-lanceolate, petiole 3 or 4 in., blade 5–9 in. long and ¾–1¼ in. broad, gradually very long-pointed, either margin with broad longitudinal band of white and often other stripes farther in. (Bears the name of Messrs. Sander, plantsmen, St. Albans, England, and Bruges, Belgium.) Cameroons.

4. **D. Draco,** L. DRAGON-TREE. Arborescent, to 60 ft. high, branched: lvs. many, crowded, erect or recurved, 1½–2 ft. long, 1¼–1¾ in. broad, glaucous, scarcely narrowed at base, long-attenuate at apex: pedicels ¼–½in. long; bracts minute; perianth ⅛in. long, greenish: berries orange. Canary Isls.

5. **D. fragrans,** Ker. Tree-like, to 20 ft. and more, sometimes branched: lvs. crowded,

long-oblong-lanceolate, 1–3 ft. long and 2¼–4 in. broad, narrowed below sometimes abruptly and sometimes gradually, rather gradually narrowed into sharp point, green or variously striped and colored, erect, spreading or recurved: fls. fragrant, clustered on branches of an open panicle 1 ft. or more long with small white dry bracts; perianth yellowish, about ½in. long, with narrow segms. about as long as the tube. Upper Guinea.—A common decorative plant, with lvs. of different sizes, directions, and color markings; the markings are mostly longitudinal stripes of yellow and greenish-white. Such hort. names as *D. Victoria, D. Lindenii, D. Massangeana*, belong here.

6. **D. deremensis,** Engler. Apparently not so tall as no. 5; lvs. 1½–2 ft. long and 2 in. broad, narrowed both ways, the point long and sharp: fls. in a large panicle on evident pedicels, dark red outside and white inside, with unpleasant odor; perianth above ½in. long, one-half of which is tube. Trop. Afr.—Grown usually as var. *Warneckii.*

8. **CORDYLINE,** Comm. (*Taetsia*, Medic.). Very like Dracæna, under which name the plants are known in cult.; they differ in technical characters, as many rather than single ovules in each cell, and solitary pedicels with 3 involucre-like bracts at base; species 10 or 12, in trop. parts of both hemispheres. (Cordyli-ne: Greek *club*, alluding to the thickened roots.)

A. Lvs. with distinct petioles .... 1. *C. terminalis*
AA. Lvs. without petioles.
B. Blade about 1 in. broad .... 2. *C. stricta*
BB. Blade 1½–2½ in. broad .... 3. *C. australis*

1. **C. terminalis,** Kunth. Stout, 3–10 ft., simple or somewhat branched: lvs. crowded or close together at end of st., lance-elliptic to lance-ovate to long-oblong, 1–2½ ft. long and 2–5 in. broad, many-veined, narrowed to channelled clasping petiole, rather abruptly narrowed at apex to aristate point, green or variously colored: fls. alternate on the branches of an open panicle 1 ft. long, yellowish, white, lilac or reddish; perianth nearly or quite ½in. long, the mostly erect segms. about as long as the tube. E. Himalayas to China and E. Indies.—The prevailing dracena of cult., in many forms and colors of foliage. Some of the forms have gracefully arched lvs.; others have very narrow or very broad lvs. The color forms run to metallic hues, suffused tints of rose, purple, white, yellowish, bronze-green, sometimes spotted; striped forms also are common. The plant and its forms are known under such names as *Dracæna terminalis, Dracæna* and *Cordyline cannæfolia, Baptistii, metallica, nigro-rubra, norwoodiensis, Robinsoniana, Youngii.* Cultural forms arise readily and are likely to be given Latin-form names.

2. **C. stricta,** Endl. (*C. congesta*, Endl.). Slender plant, 6–12 ft.: lvs. 1–2 ft. long, ¾–1¼ in. broad, sword-shaped and sessile, not glaucous, margins obscurely denticulate acuminate: fls. in terminal or lateral erect or cernuous panicles on very short pedicels subtended by bracts; perianth lilac, ¼–⅓in. long, tube campanulate, inner segms. distinctly longer than the others. Subtrop. Australia.

3. **C. australis,** Hook. f. (*Dracæna australis*, Forst.). Tree-like, 15–40 ft., branching at maturity, trunk becoming 1–5 ft. diam. in its native country: lvs. densely rosulate at ends of branches, 1½–3 ft. long and 1½–2½ in. broad, sword-shaped, contracted just above base but not petiolate, acute or acuminate, flat, green beneath, lateral veins fine: fls. in large terminal erect or drooping much-branched panicles, white, fragrant, ¼–⅓in. diam., on very short pedicels; segms. of equal length. New Zeal.—Vars. with striped and colored lvs. are in cult., under various names. This plant is apparently sometimes cult. as *indivisa*, but the true *C. indivisa*, Kunth, has very stiff and thick broader lvs. which are 2–6 ft. long, glaucous beneath, lateral veins heavy and conspicuous, red or yellow; it is also native in New Zeal.

35. AMARYLLIDACEÆ. AMARYLLIS FAMILY

Upwards of 90 genera and 1,200 species in temp. and warm regions of the world, largely in S. Afr., S. Amer., and Medit. regions; many are showy garden plants.—Closely allied to Liliaceæ, from which it is technically distinguished by the mostly inferior ovary and the arrangement of fls. in a scapose umbel subtended by more or less spathaceous bracts, and to Iridaceæ from which it differs in prevailingly 6 stamens and the absence of iris-like fls.; many of the cult. kinds have lily-like fls. and may be known as lilies: per. herbs, either caulescent or acaulescent, bulbous, cormous, rhizomatous or fibrous-rooted: lvs. radical or cauline, alternate, mostly narrow, entire: fls. usually bisexual, the perianth of 6 parts or lobes, subtended by a spathe-like bract or bracts, at least the 3 inner parts simulating a corolla; stamens usually 6, inserted in the throat or on base of segms., the anthers introrse; style long; stigma usually 3-lobed or -fid; ovary inferior (below the perianth) or superior,

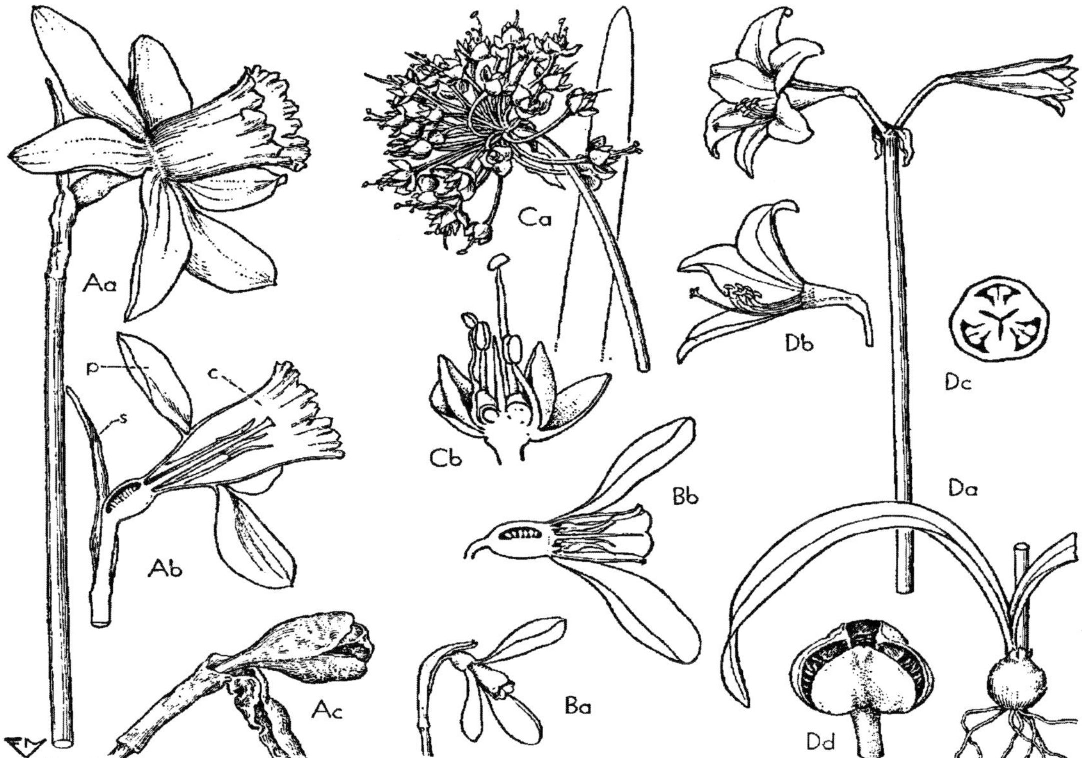

Fig. 35. AMARYLLIDACEÆ. A, *Narcissus Pseudo-Narcissus:* Aa, flower, × ½; Ab, flower, vertical section showing corona (c), perianth-segment (p), and spathe (s), × ½; Ac, capsule, × ½. B, *Galanthus nivalis:* Ba, flower, × ½; Bb, flower, vertical section, × 1. C, *Allium cernuum:* Ca, inflorescence and leaf-tip, × ½; Cb, flower, vertical section, × 2. D, *Amaryllis vittata:* Da, plant in flower, × ⅙; Db, flower, perianth partially removed, × ⅙; Dc, ovary, cross-section, × 1; Dd, capsule, × ⅓.

3-celled, each cell with many or sometimes only few ovules which are superposed (one above the other) or collateral, placentation typically axile: fr. a caps. or sometimes baccate, mostly loculicidal.—For the most part, the amaryllids are grown as pot specimens or are planted out for summer; marked exceptions are the narcissi, galanthus, allium and leucojum, and in the S. the crinums and others are planted in yards. Many of them are seen mostly in summer window-gardens and on porches and in conservatories, as vallota, sprekelia, amaryllis, brunsvigia, clivia. Some of the groups are much hybridized; cult. kinds are usually poorly represented in herbaria; therefore the species are often confused.

A. Ovary superior.
  B. Perfect stamens 6, anthers versatile.
    C. Infl. 6–12 in. across: rootstock a coarsely fibrous rhizome: large tender scapose herbs.......... 1. AGAPANTHUS
    CC. Infl. mostly smaller than above: rootstock a corm or a bulb.
      D. Perianth-segms. free or united only below the middle.......... 2. ALLIUM
      DD. Perianth-segms. united to above the middle.
        E. Stamens united into a tube.......... 4. BESSERA
        EE. Stamens free from one another.
          F. Spathe-valves 2: fls. solitary.......... 3. IPHEION
          FF. Spathe-valves of 3 or more bract-like parts subtending an umbel: fls. rarely solitary.
            G. The stamens shortly exserted: perianth-segms. over 1 in. long.......... 5. MILLA
            GG. The stamens included within perianth-tube: perianth-segms. usually not over 1 in. long.......... 6. TRITELEIA
  BB. Perfect stamens 3, anthers basifixed.
    C. Involucre of 2 linear bracts: rootstock a bulb.......... 9. LEUCOCORYNE
    CC. Involucre of 1; or of 3 or more bracts: rootstock a corm.
      D. Lvs. keeled beneath: stigma obscurely 3-lobed or seemingly not lobed.......... 7. DICHELOSTEMMA
      DD. Lvs. rounded beneath: stigma with 3 spreading and recurving lobes.......... 8. BRODIÆA

AA. Ovary inferior.
B. Plants with fleshy fibrous roots, or a tuberous rhizome or corm with membranous or fibrous sheaths.
C. Rhizome with thick fleshy roots: st. leafy, the lvs. more or less twisted.
D. Sts. and infl. usually erect: perianth-segms. of similar size............32. ALSTRŒMERIA
DD. Sts. twining: infl. drooping; outer perianth-segms. shorter than inner.....33. BOMAREA
CC. Rhizome tuberous or corm-like: st. scapose, the lvs. basal and plane.
D. Fr. a membranous caps.: lvs. to ⅓in. wide..........................34. HYPOXIS
DD. Fr. fleshy, indehiscent, ending in a long beak: lvs. 2–6 in. wide.......35. CURCULIGO
BB. Plants with bulbs: fls. mostly lily-like, on leafless scapes or directly from the bulb.
C. Corona absent, no scales or teeth between the filaments.
D. Scape leafy in lower part; umbel subcompound......................24. IXIOLIRION
DD. Scape leafless except at the base.
E. Ovules few, 2–6 in each cell: fr. a berry (caps. in Lycoris and Crinum).
F. Lvs. persistent: perianth 2–3 in. long..........................22. CLIVIA
FF. Lvs. not persistent.
G. Perianth 1 in. long: fr. a berry..............................23. HÆMANTHUS
GG. Perianth 1½ in. and more long: fr. a caps.
H. Tube of perianth equalling or exceeding segms..............15. CRINUM
HH. Tube of perianth short, much less than segms..............30. LYCORIS
EE. Ovules numerous: fr. a caps.
F. Perianth-tube absent or very short; stamens epigynous or inserted near the base of the segms.
G. Perianth regular; fls. 1 to few.
H. Segms. of perianth subequal................................10. LEUCOJUM
HH. Segms. of perianth unequal................................11. GALANTHUS
GG. Perianth declinate or irregular.
H. Fls. solitary, bilabiate....................................29. SPREKELIA
HH. Fls. umbellate.
I. The scape solid.
J. Filaments free and not swollen at the base..............12. BRUNSVIGIA
JJ. Filaments swollen at base and continued beyond the point of insertion down to the ovary..................13. NERINE
II. The scape hollow: segms. broad...........................28. AMARYLLIS
FF. Perianth-tube present; stamens inserted on perianth-tube.
G. Fls. several together.
H. Anthers subbasifixed.......................................14. CHLIDANTHUS
HH. Anthers medianly dorsifixed, versatile.
I. Fl. subsessile or very short-pedicelled; seeds subglobose; scape not hollow.......................................15. CRINUM
II. Fl. on pedicels 1 or more in long: seeds flat: scape hollow.
J. Segms. of perianth much shorter than tube; fls. more or less curved...16. CYRTANTHUS
JJ. Segms. of perianth nearly as long as tube; fls. straight.... 17. VALLOTA
GG. Fls. 1 or 2.
H. Segms. of perianth narrow, lanceolate: seeds round........21. STERNBERGIA
HH. Segms. of perianth broad, elliptic to obovate: seeds flat.
I. Anthers basally dorsifixed, filaments very short..........20. COOPERIA
II. Anthers medianly dorsifixed, filaments well-developed.
J. Perianth erect; stamens of two lengths..................18. ZEPHYRANTHES
JJ. Perianth oblique to declinate; stamens of four lengths....19. HABRANTHUS
CC. Corona present, formed by expanded filaments or of teeth, scales or an annulus or tube.
D. Crown or corona a cup formed of expanded filaments.
E. Segms. of perianth not much longer than wide: lvs. broad.........27. EUCHARIS
EE. Segms. of perianth lanceolate: lvs. narrow.
F. Ovules numerous, one above the other; free part of filaments ¼in. long...25. PANCRATIUM
FF. Ovules 2 in each cell, side by side; free part of filaments ½–2 in. long...26. HYMENOCALLIS
DD. Crown or corona not as above.
E. Perianth having a corona which is annular or tubular and separate from the filaments...31. NARCISSUS
EE. Perianth having a corona of separate often inconspicuous scales between the filaments.
F. Fls. solitary, bilabiate...29. SPREKELIA
FF. Fls. umbellate.
G. Ovules numerous in each locule; perianth 4–5 in. long.........28. AMARYLLIS
GG. Ovules 2–3 in each locule; perianth 1½–3 in. long..............30. LYCORIS

1. **AGAPANTHUS,** L'Her. (*Abumon,* Adans.). One variable species, or several segregates, in S. Afr., common as a pot-plant.—Scapose: lvs. many, long and narrow, radical: fls. many in terminal umbel, the cluster issuing from a 2-bracted caducous spathe; perianth gamophyllous, funnel-shaped, the segms. oblong and about the length of the tube or exceeding it; stamens 6, inserted on throat, filaments filiform; ovary 3-celled, sessile, superior: caps. loculicidal. (Agapan-thus: Greek *love flower.*)

A. africanus, Hoffmgg. (*Crinum africanum,* L. *A. umbellatus,* L'Her. *Tulbaghia africana,* Kuntze). AFRICAN-LILY. Root of many strong cord-like parts: scape strong, erect, 2–3 ft.: lvs. linear-lanceolate to lorate, basal: fls. 10–50 or more in a strongly rayed umbel, bright blue, 1–2 in. long, the narrow segms. prominent and spreading; anthers at first yellow, becoming dark: summer.—Runs into many forms, varying in stature, in number and size of fls., in size and breadth of lvs., in season of bloom. There are white-fld. and striped-lvd. vars. **A. Mooreanus,** Hort., plant smaller, fls. deeper blue, anthers persistently yellow.

2. **ALLIUM,** L. ONION. A large genus, probably 500 species, in the northern hemisphere, many native in N. Amer., with strong characteristic odor; a very few grown for ornament and others as vegetable-garden subjects.—Scapose plants with mostly only radical or subbasal lvs. (which, as well as the scape, are often fistulose or hollow), with tunicate bulbs: fls. small, few to many in a terminal umbel, emerging from a scarious 1-, 2- or 3-lvd. cap or spathe, white, greenish, yellow, pink or purple, with 6 withering segms. that are distinct or connate at base; stamens 6, usually attached to base of perianth; pistil with 3-celled superior ovary, slender style and entire or 3-parted stigma: fr. a small loculicidal caps. (Al-lium: Latin name for garlic.)

A. Lvs. cylindrical and usually hollow (fistulose).
B. Scapes inflated.
C. The lvs. large, not numerous.
D. Bulb little thicker than the neck .... 1. *A. fistulosum*
DD. Bulb large and rounded .... 2. *A. Cepa*
CC. The lvs. slender, awl-like, many .... 3. *A. ascalonicum*
BB. Scapes not inflated.
C. Bracts of spathe broad, shorter than umbel.
D. Filaments much shorter than perianth-segms.
E. Segms. rose-purple, ¼–⅔in. long, longer than pedicels .... 4. *A. Schœnoprasum*
EE. Segms. white with purplish nerve, ⅜in. long, much shorter than pedicels .... 17. *A. ramosum*
DD. Filaments as long as or longer than segms.; segms. to 3/16in. long .... 5. *A. sphærocephalum*
CC. Bracts of spathe lanceolate, two to five times as long as umbel.
D. Fls. red-purple: caps. almost round .... 6. *A. pulchellum*
DD. Fls. yellow: caps. ovoid .... 7. *A. flavum*
AA. Lvs. plane or flat or keeled, not hollow.
B. Bulb consisting of 6–10 small bulblets or cloves inclosed in a common membrane: fls. often displaced by bulbels .... 12. *A. sativum*
BB. Bulb not so constituted: fls. usually not displaced by bulbels.
C. Plants with broad lvs. (½–1½ in. wide).
D. Filaments all simple; fls. not pink.
E. Fls. bright yellow .... 8. *A. Moly*
EE. Fls. white to greenish-white.
F. Foliage green at time of flowering: perianth-segms. ½in. long .... 9. *A. neapolitanum*
FF. Foliage withering before flowering: segms. to ¼in. long .... 10. *A. tricoccum*
DD. Filaments having inner ones 3-branched at base, the middle branch anther-bearing; fls. pinkish .... 11. *A. Porrum*
CC. Plants with narrow lvs. (1/16–⅓in. wide).
D. Fls. bright blue.
E. Scapes 1½–2 ft. high: lvs. ⅛in. wide .... 13. *A. cæruleum*
EE. Scapes ½–1 ft. high: lvs. 1/16in. wide .... 14. *A. cyaneum*
DD. Fls. not blue.
E. Coat of bulb of thread-like fibers.
F. Perianth-segms. ⅙–¼in. long; stamens almost as long.
G. Scapes mostly 4–10 in. high: bulbs usually solitary .... 15. *A. textile*
GG. Scapes 1–1½ ft. high; bulbs clustered on a rhizome .... 16. *A. tuberosum*
FF. Perianth-segms. almost ½in. long; stamens half as long .... 17. *A. ramosum*
EE. Coat of bulb membranous.
F. Bulbs oblong, clustered on a rhizome: stamens exserted.
G. Filaments much expanded toward their base; umbel erect in fl. .... 18. *A. senescens*
GG. Filaments nearly filiform; umbel nodding in fl. .... 19. *A. cernuum*
FF. Bulbs ovoid or round, mostly solitary.
G. Inner perianth-segms. minutely serrulate; stamens included.
H. Width of lvs. ¼–⅓in., longer than the flattened 2-edged scape .... 20. *A. falcifolium*
HH. Width of lvs. 1/16–⅛in., shorter than the terete scape .... 21. *A. acuminatum*
GG. Inner perianth-segms. entire.
H. Bracts of spathe 1 in. long; perianth-segms. ½in. long; stamens included .... 22. *A. unifolium*
HH. Bracts ½in. long; perianth-segms. ¼in. long; stamens exserted .... 23. *A. stellatum*

1. **A. fistulosum,** L. WELSH ONION. SPRING ONION. Stout, more or less tufted, glaucous, very leafy: scape short and thick, hollow, 12–20 in., swollen in middle, arising from bulbous base little thicker than st. or crown: lvs. fistulose, about equalling scape: fls.

white or whitish, in dense terminal umbel, less than ½in. long and equalling or exceeding the pedicels during anthesis; segms. acuminate; stamens long-exserted, alternate filaments broadened at base. Asia.—Lvs. used for seasoning.

2. **A. Cepa, L.** ONION. Various in habit, relatively large in bloom, potentially bien., usually not forming clumps or tufts: bulbs large: scape 2–4 ft., hollow, swollen below middle, much taller than lvs.: first-year lvs. radical and basal, hollow, thickest below middle, glaucous: fls. many, lilac or nearly white, in large umbel subtended by 2 or 3 reflexed bracts, the pedicels 1 in. or less long; segms. narrow-lanceolate, acute; stamens exserted, 3 inner filaments expanded at base and lobed or toothed on either side. (Cepa: Latin for onion.) W. Asia. Var. **aggregatum,** Don (var. *solaninum,* Alef. var. *multiplicans,* Bailey), POTATO and MULTIPLIER ONION, propagating by natural division or separation of the bulb; scape (infrequently produced) short and few-fld. Var. **viviparum,** Metz. (var. *bulbelliferum,* Bailey), TOP ONION, underground bulb small and undeveloped; bulbels borne in fl.-cluster (which is often proliferous) and used for propagation.

3. **A. ascalonicum,** L. SHALLOT. From *A. Cepa* differs in small stature, slender awl-like lvs., and small ovate-oblong or somewhat conical gray more or less angular bulbs that break up into distinct parts or bulblets that cohere at base: fls. (usually not produced) white or violet, in globose heads, scarcely exceeding pedicels; segms. oblong-lanceolate, acute. Probably a cultigen, perhaps derived from *A. Cepa;* supposed to be Asian, and it is named for Ascalon, of the E. Medit. region.—Little known in cult.; forms of *A. Cepa* are commonly called shallot in the market.

4. **A. Schœnoprasum,** L. CHIVES. Per., forming firm tufts or sods, with tough roots: scape 6–24 in. tall, bulbous-thickened at base: lvs. grass-like, hollow, equalling or surpassing the scape: fls. many in a head, rose-purple; pedicels usually one-third to one-half as long as segms.; segms. long-acuminate, ¼–⅔in. long; filaments one-third to one-half as long. (The specific name is a Greek substantive compound meaning rush- or reed-leek.) Eu., Asia. Var. **sibiricum,** Hartm. (*A. sibiricum,* L.), lvs. shorter than scapes; segms. pale, ½–⅝in. long; Siberia. Var. **laurentianum,** Fern., segms. intensely colored, ⅓–½in. long; N. N. Amer.

5. **A. sphærocephalum,** L. Outer bulb-coats brown, coriaceous: scape 1–3 ft. tall, clothed one-third the way with lf.-sheaths: lvs. 3–5, semi-cylindric, to ⅛in. wide, much shorter than scape: spathe of 2 bracts half as long as many-fld. umbel; pedicels unequal, once or twice longer than perianth; segms. rose or purple, oblong, ⅙in. long; filaments slightly longer, connate and somewhat ciliate at base, the inner trifid; style exserted. S. Eu., W. Asia, N. Afr.

6. **A. pulchellum,** Don. Outer bulb-coats papery, grayish or brownish: scape 1–1½ ft. tall, clothed half way with lf.-sheaths: lvs. 3–4, semi-cylindric, 1/25in. wide, usually somewhat shorter than scape: spathe of 2 narrow bracts two to four times as long as many-fld. umbel; pedicels unequal, two to ten times the perianth; segms. red-purple, ⅙in. long, elliptic-oblong, obtuse; filaments once and a half to twice as long; style exserted. S. E. Eu., W. Asia.

7. **A. flavum,** L. Bulb-coats membranous, brownish: scape terete, slender, bluish, to 2 ft. tall, leafy to middle: lvs. subcylindrical, bluish, solid, to 1/16in. thick, as long as scape: spathe of 2 long lanceolate bracts much exceeding the many-fld. umbel; pedicels unequal, loose, curving, two to three times the perianth; segms. soft yellow, ⅕in. long, oblong, rounded-obtuse; filaments once and a half to twice as long. S. Eu., W. Asia.

8. **A. Moly,** L. Bulbs clustered, with membranous coats: scape terete, 1–1½ ft. high, leafy below: lvs. 1–2, flat, almost as long as scape, ½–1¼ in. wide, acuminate: spathe of 2 bracts about half as long as many-fld. umbel; pedicels spreading, two to three times the perianth; segms. bright yellow, spreading, oblong, shining, subacuminate, ½in. long; filaments about half as long. (Moly: ancient name for a plant with marvellous medicinal powers.) S. W. Eu.

9. **A. neapolitanum,** Cyr. (*A. Hermettii,* Hort.). Bulbs solitary, with membranous grayish or brownish coats: scape 3-angled especially above, to 1 ft. high, leafy at base: lvs. 1–3, minutely toothed on edge, ½–1 in. wide, shorter than scape: spathe 1-bracted, much shorter than several-fld. umbel; pedicels two to three times the perianth; segms. white, spreading, oblong, rounded at apex, almost ½in. long; filaments much shorter. S. Eu.—Not hardy N.

10. **A. tricoccum,** Ait. Bulbs clustered, fibrous-coated, on a short rootstock: scape 4–15 in. high: lvs. 2–3, basal, appearing in spring and withering before flowering time, 6–12 in. long, 1–2 in. wide: spathe 2-bracted, about as long as many-fld. umbel; pedicels stiff, two to three times the perianth; segms. whitish, oblong, ⅙–¼in. long; filaments about as long, dilated toward base. N. B. to Minn. and N. C.

11. **A. Porrum,** L. LEEK. Plant stout and tall, bien.: bulbs simple, the first year little broader than the thick neck: scape pithy and not hollow, 2–3 ft., leafy on lower third: lvs. equitant, keeled, the halves flat, 2–3 ft. long and 2 in. or less broad: fls. pinkish, ⅙in. long, very many in a large dense terminal umbel subtended by single long-pointed spathe; anthers exserted, filaments of 3 stamens with slender branch on either side over-

topping anthers. (Porrum: Latin word for leek.) Cultigen; probably derived from *A. Ampeloprasum*, L., of Eu. and W. Asia, which has two bulbs within a common many-layered tunic and with the st. arising between these bulbs.

12. **A. sativum,** L. Garlic. Bulbs with several parts or cloves, all inclosed in a silky white or pink general envelope or skin: scape to 2 ft. high, terete, exceeding lvs.: lvs. several from base or crown, flat, 1 in. or less wide, long-pointed: spathe with point 3–4 in. long; umbels small and dense, with long scarious bracts; fls. often displaced by bulbels, usually sterile, pinkish, about 1/6in. long, exceeded by the slender pedicels, with equal lance-acute segms., anthers and style exserted, ovary oblong-ovoid and emarginate at apex. Eu.; sometimes escaped.

13. **A. cæruleum,** Pall. (*A. azureum*, Ledeb.). Bulbs with gray papery envelopes: scape wiry, 1–3 ft. high, leafy on lower third: lvs. 2–4, triquetrous, to 1/6in. wide, shorter than scape: spathe 2-bracted, acuminate, one-half to two-thirds the length of the dense many-fld. umbel; pedicels equal, two to five times the perianth; segms. sky-blue with darker nerves, spreading, subobtuse, 1/6in. long, oblong-lanceolate; filaments about as long as segms., simple and undivided. Cent. Asia.

14. **A. cyaneum,** Regel. Bulbs clustered, dark-coated, cylindrical: scape 4–12 in. high, slender, leafy on lower third: lvs. 1–4, shorter than scape, to 1/16in. wide: spathe 1-bracted, ovate, to 1/3in. long, umbel 5–18-fld., more or less nodding; pedicels once or twice the purplish-blue perianth; segms. 1/6in. long, obtuse, elliptic-oblong; filaments somewhat longer, the inner usually toothed on each side. China.

15. **A. textile,** A. Nels. & Macb. (*A. reticulatum*, Nutt.). Bulbs with fibrous outer coats: scape 4–10 in. high, slender, terete: lvs. commonly 2, almost or quite equal to scape, to 1/6in. wide: spathe usually of 2 broad bracts, about half as long as the many-fld. umbel; pedicels two to three times the perianth; segms. white to pink with greenish or reddish midrib, ovate-lanceolate, 1/6–1/4in. long; filaments almost as long. Sask. to Ariz.

16. **A. tuberosum,** Rottler (*A. odorum* of many auth.). Bulbs 1–3 together, attached to a horizontal rhizome, brownish: scape 1–1½ ft. tall, leafy at base: lvs. 2–3, flat, to 1/4in. wide, somewhat shorter than scape: spathe 1-bracted, shorter than the many-fld. umbel; pedicels equal, two to three times the perianth; segms. white with brownish or greenish nerve, spreading, narrow-ovate, 1/6–1/4in. long; filaments four-fifths as long, white: caps. with valves broadest above the middle and exposed by reflexed withered segms. E. Asia.

17. **A. ramosum,** L. (*A. odorum*, L.). Habit of *A. tuberosum* but earlier flowering: lvs. slightly fistulose: perianth somewhat campanulate, the segms. white with a purplish nerve, 3/8in. long, lance-oblong; filaments half as long, reddish: caps. with valves broadest below the middle, clasped by the withered perianth-segms. Siberia.

18. **A. senescens,** L. Bulbs 2–3 together, on a horizontal rhizome and with dark membranes: scape 1–2 ft.: lvs. basal, 5–8, flat, obtuse, usually shorter than scape, to 1/4in. wide: spathe 1-bracted, about half as long as many-fld. umbel; pedicels equal, two to three times the perianth; segms. rose to purplish, 1/4in. long, oblong-lanceolate to ovate; filaments somewhat longer, connate at base, simple, the inner dilated. Eurasia.—Very variable. The European strain (*A. montanum*, F. W. Schmidt. *A. fallax*, Roem. & Schult.), has narrow lvs. to 1/6in. wide. Much material cult. as *A. tibeticum* is referable to *A. senescens*, the true *A. tibeticum*, Rendle, being a small blue-fld. plant.

19. **A. cernuum,** Roth. Bulbs clustered on short rootstock, with membranous coats: scape slender, 1–2 ft. high: lvs. several, basal, flattish, to 1/6in. wide, shorter than scape: spathe of 2 broad often deciduous bracts half as long as many-fld. nodding umbel; pedicels four to five times the perianth; segms. white to rose, ovate-oblong, to 1/4in. long; filaments much-exserted, filiform. N. Y. to B. C., S. C. and New Mex.

20. **A. falcifolium,** Hook. & Arn. Bulbs with reddish-brown outer membranous coats: scape 1–2 in. high, flattened and 2-edged: lvs. 2, flat, longer than scape, to 1/3in. wide: spathe of 2 acuminate bracts to 2/3in. long; fls. 10–30; pedicels about as long as perianth; segms. deep rose, 1/2in. long, narrow-lanceolate, attenuate and spreading above; filaments about half as long; ovary 3-crested. Ore. to N. Calif.

21. **A. acuminatum,** Hook. Bulbs with gray outer membranous coats: scape 4–12 in. high: lvs. 2–3, basal, shorter than scape, to 1/8in. wide: spathe of 2 bracts about 1 in. long; umbel 7–25-fld.; pedicels once or twice the perianth; segms. deep rose-purple, 1/2in. long, the outer ones lanceolate, acuminate, with recurved tips; filaments two-thirds as long; ovary scarcely crested. B. C. to Calif. and Utah.

22. **A. unifolium,** Kellogg. Bulbs from lateral bulblet produced on stout rhizome: scape 1–1½ ft.: lvs. 2–4, basal, shorter than scape, to 1/3in. wide: spathe of 2 bracts, about 1 in. long; fls. many, the pedicels once and a half to twice the perianth; segms. bright rose, 1/2in. long, lance-oblong, acutish; filaments two-thirds as long, widened and connate at base. Calif.

23. **A. stellatum,** Ker. Bulbs 1 to several together, with outer coats membranous: scape slender, 8–18 in. tall: lvs. basal, nearly flat, to 1/12in. wide, shorter than scape: spathe of 2 bracts, much shorter than many-fld. umbel; pedicels slender, equal, three times the perianth; segms. rose, oblong-ovate, to 1/4in. long; filaments somewhat exserted, slightly widened at base; ovary crested. Minn. to Ill. and Kans.

3. **IPHEION,** Raf. (*Beauverdia,* Herter). About 10 species, native to Uruguay, Argentina and Chile.—Scapose, bulbose, per., with onion- or garlic-like odor when bruised; bulbs with membranous tunic: lvs. basal, linear, not keeled: scape 1-fld., spathe split into 2 valves united basally; fl. erect, funnelform, perianth-segms. more or less equal, basally connate into a tube; stamens 6, inserted on perianth-tube, shorter than perianth-segms., anthers versatile; ovary superior, 3-celled, each cell several-ovuled; style filiform, erect, stigma obscurely 3-lobed. (Iph-eion: Greek, of obscure origin and allegedly an old name for Asphodelus.)

I. uniflorum, Raf. (*Triteleia uniflora,* Lindl. *Milla uniflora,* R. Grah. *Brodiæa uniflora,* Engler. *Leucocoryne uniflora,* Greene. *Beauverdia uniflora,* Herter). Spring Star-Flower. Spring-blooming plant with onion-like odor, from small deep-seated bulbs: lvs. nearly flat, slightly glaucous, broad-linear: scape 6–8 in. high, bracted about midway by 2-valved dry spathe; fl. 1 1/4–1 1/2 in. across, salver-shaped, white with bluish tinge, the oblong segms. with darker blue and the under sides ribbed bluish-brown. Argentina.

4. **BESSERA,** Schult. About 3 species in Mex.—Scapose: lvs. few, basal, narrowly linear: fls. in a terminal umbel, campanulate, nodding; filaments connate for half their length, pubescent in free part, anthers oblong, dorsifixed, exserted; ovary superior, trilocular; style filiform. (Bes-sera: after Dr. Besser, professor of botany at Brody.)

B. elegans, Schult. Coral-Drops. Scape about 2 ft. high: lvs. 2–3, about as long as scape; umbels 10–12-fld.; pedicels slender, about 2 in. long; fls. bright red, about 3/4in. long, the perianth-segms. oblanceolate, acute, concave, green-keeled, divergent; staminal tube whitish, 1/3in. long, anthers grayish-blue; style and filaments red.

5. **MILLA,** Cav. Mexican Star. Low bulbous plant from Mex., a monotypic genus.—Lvs. several, slender, terete, tubular, glaucous: scape slender, erect, with many small linear scarious bracts at base of a terminal umbel; perianth slender, funnelform with 6 spreading segms.; stamens 6, at mouth of perianth-tube, approximate about the pistil; ovary superior: caps. elongate, trilocular, with numerous seeds. (Mil-la: J. Milla, court gardener in Madrid.)

M. biflora, Cav. Scape 6–18 in. high; pedicels suberect, 2–6 in. long; umbels 1–6-fld.; fls. white, fragrant, the perianth-tube 1/2in. long, the perianth-segms. oblong-lanceolate, fleshy, over 1 in. long, with external green keel; anthers lemon-yellow, 1/4in. long.

6. **TRITELEIA,** Dougl. (*Hesperoscordum,* Lindl. *Calliprora,* Lindl. *Seubertia,* Kunth). About 14 species native to S. W. Ore. and N. Calif.—Cormous, scapose, per.: lvs. 1 or 2 from each reticulately-fibrous-coated corm, narrowly linear, keeled below with 2 channels above: scape slender; infl. an umbel subtended by several distinct acuminate bracts, pedicels jointed to fl.-bases; fls. with perianth-segms. connate into a tube; fertile stamens 6, anthers versatile; ovary superior, 3-celled, stipitate; style slender, short, stigma of 3 small lobes: fr. a loculicidal caps. (Triteleia: Greek, alluding to the ternary arrangement of fl. parts.)

A. Perianth-segms. rotate-spreading, the tube narrow; fls. yellow .... 1. *T. ixioides*
AA. Perianth-segms. little or not at all spreading; fls. not yellow.
  B. Tube of perianth open-campanulate, stamens all attached at same level on tube; fls. white .... 2. *T. hyacinthina*
  BB. Tube of perianth funnelform or tubular, stamens attached alternately at two levels in tube; fls. typically blue.
    C. Perianth-tube tubular, obtuse and rounded at base; filaments dilated .... 3. *T. grandiflora*
    CC. Perianth-tube funnelform, acute or attenuate at base; filaments slender .... 4. *T. laxa*

1. **T. ixioides,** Greene (*Ornithogalum ixioides,* Ait. f. *Milla ixioides,* Baker. *Brodiæa ixioides,* Wats. not Hook. *Calliprora ixioides,* Greene). Pretty Face. Scape 1/2–1 1/2 ft. high: lvs. 2, exceeding the scape: umbels open, mostly 10–35-fld., rays 3/4–1 1/2 in. long; perianth yellow with dark purple band on outside of each midvein, 1/2–3/4in. long, with turbinate tube and lance-ovate segms.; filaments winged, tooth-forked at tip above anther. Calif. Var. **splendens,** Hort., is said to be more vigorous and colorful.

2. **T. hyacinthina,** Greene (*Hesperoscordum hyacinthinum,* Lindl. *Milla hyacinthina,* Baker. *Brodiæa hyacinthina,* Baker. *B. lactea,* Wats. *B. dissimulata,* Peck). WILD-HYACINTH. Scape 1–1⅔ ft. high: lvs. equalling or shorter than scapes: umbels 10–40-fld.; pedicels 1–2 in. long; perianth open-campanulate, about ½in. long, cleft below the middle, white or lilac with green midveins, the segms. obtuse, oblong-ovate; filaments short, broad-triangular, slightly united. B. C. to Calif.

3. **T. grandiflora,** Lindl. (*Milla grandiflora,* Baker. *Brodiæa grandiflora,* Macb. not Smith. *B. Douglasii,* Wats.). Scape 1–2 ft. high: lvs. almost as long, ¼–⅓in. wide: umbels 6–20-fld.; pedicels ½–1½ in. long; perianth usually bright blue, ½–1 in. long, the segms. equalling the tube, oblong-ovate, spreading; filaments of upper row of stamens about 1/12in. long, slender but dilated toward base, other row shorter. B. C. to Ore., Mont., Wyo., Utah.

4. **T. laxa,** Benth. (*Milla laxa,* Baker. *Brodiæa laxa,* Wats.). GRASS-NUT. TRIPLET-LILY. Scape ½–2¼ ft. high: lvs. about two-thirds as long as scape, ¼–¾in. wide: umbels 8–40-fld.; pedicels ½–3 in. long; fls. tending to be horizontal, blue or rarely white, ⅔–2 in. long, the perianth-segms. oblong-ovate, slightly shorter than perianth-tube, the latter attenuate at base and with 6 narrow membranous appendages from base of filaments; filaments filiform, ⅛–¼in. long. Ore. to Calif.

7. **DICHELOSTEMMA,** Kunth. About 6 species of low cormous plants of W. Amer.—Per. herbs with scape and lvs. arising from fibrous-coated corm: lvs. 2–5, long-linear, flat, keeled beneath, grooved above: scape slender, bearing an umbel subtended by an involucre of several often colored bracts; fl. jointed to pedicel, subtended by single bract, perianth-tube as long as segms. or longer, inflated or campanulate; fertile stamens 3, basifixed, inserted on inner perianth-segms., with 3 staminodia inserted on outer segms.; ovary superior; style slender, enlarged apically and there narrowly 3-winged, stigmas 3 terminating style-wings. (Dichelos-temma: Greek, alluding to a bifid corona here represented by the appendage-like staminodia at base of perianth-segms.)

A. Pedicels flexuous or recurved when in fl.; perianth with bright red or yellow tube and green segms.; style about ¾in. long.......1. *D. Ida-maia*
AA. Pedicels ascending; perianth purple; style ¼in. or less long.......2. *D. pulchellum*

1. **D. Ida-maia,** Greene (*Brevoortia Ida-maia,* Wood. *Brodiæa Ida-maia,* Greene. *B. coccinea,* Wats.). FIRE-CRACKER FLOWER. Scape slender, 1–3 ft. high: lvs. to ⅓in. wide, shorter than scape: umbels 5–20-fld.; pedicels ½–1½ in. long; fls. mostly nodding, 1–1⅓ in. long; perianth-tube scarlet, about 1 in. long; segms. green, ovate, erect or reflexed, about ¼in. long; staminodia 3, whitish, stamens 3. (Brought to the attention of Alphonso Wood by a stage driver, Mr. Burke, who had called the plant for his little daughter, Ida May, and the name thought appropriate as the plant blooms in the ides of May.) Ore., Calif.

2. **D. pulchellum,** Heller (*Hookera pulchella,* Salisb. *Brodiæa pulchella,* Greene. *B. capitata,* Benth. *Dipterostemum pulchellum,* Rydb. *Dichelostemma capitata,* Wood). Scape ½–2 ft. high: lvs. shorter, ¼–½in. wide: umbels subcapitate, 4–20-fld.; pedicels to ½in. long; perianth violet-purple, rarely whitish, broadly funnelform, ½–¾in. long, the segms. about as long as tube, oblong-ovate, obtuse; stamens 6, the inner anthers subsessile and on filaments with a broad membrane-like wing extended beyond the anthers as 2 lanceolate appendages. Ore. to Lower Calif.

8. **BRODIÆA,** Smith (*Hookera,* Salisb., the oldest but rejected generic name). A small genus of per. cormous herbs, about 10 species indigenous to W. N. Amer.; formerly embracing many species here treated as belonging to other genera.—Corms fibrous-coated: lvs. few, basal, linear, rounded and not keeled beneath, flat or concave above: scape very slender, rigid, umbel subtended by several small scarious bracts forming an involucre; fls. on jointed pedicels; perianth-segms. widely spreading, connate basally into a tube, the 3 outer segms. commonly narrower than inner; fertile stamens 3, anthers erect, appressed to style, sagittate; staminodia 3, usually present; style stout, stigmas 3, of spreading or recurving lobes: caps. loculicidal. (Brodiæ-a: James Brodie, 1744–1824, Scotch botanist.)

A. Perianth-tube one-half as long as segms.; staminodia not exceeding stamens........1. *B. coronaria*
AA. Perianth-tube scarcely one-third as long as segms.; staminodia usually exceeding stamens.......2. *B. californica*

1. **B. coronaria,** Engler (*Hookera coronaria,* Salisb. *B. grandiflora,* Smith). HARVEST BRODIÆA. Scape ½–1½ ft. high: lvs. about as long, 1/12in. wide: umbels 3–11-fld.; pedicels ½–3 in. long; perianth violet to lilac, 1–1⅔ in. long, the tube campanulate at an-

thesis and half as long as the spreading lance-oblong segms.; staminodia white, involute, erect, not longer than stamens, approximate in center about the style; stamens 3, with anthers ⅓in. long and sagittate at base. B. C. to Lower Calif.—Material cult. as this species may be **B. elegans,** Hoover (*B. coronaria,* Auth. not Engler), which differs in perianth-tube funnelform at anthesis and staminodia flat and shorter than stamens.

2. **B. californica,** Lindl. Scape ½–1½ ft. high, often scabrous: lvs. ⅛in. wide: umbels 2–12-fld.; pedicels 1–3 in. long; perianth lilac to violet-purple, 1–1⅔ in. long, the narrow-funnelform tube scarcely one-third the oblong spreading segms.; staminodia white, slightly involute; stamens 3, anthers ⅓in. long, oblong. Calif.

9. **LEUCOCORYNE,** Lindl. A small genus of about 10 species native to Chile.—Bulbous, scapose: lvs. basal, narrowly linear: bracts 2, linear-lanceolate; umbels few-fld.; perianth-tube cylindrical, slightly constricted above the ovary, the segms. oblong-ovate or narrower, spreading; stamens 3, inserted at base of perianth-tube, the filaments very short, anthers dorsifixed; staminodia 3, narrower and shorter than stamens; ovary superior, trilobed, style short-columnar. (Leucocor-yne: *white* and *club*, referring to the staminodia.)

L. ixioides, Lindl. Lvs. many, 1 ft. long: st. 12–18 in. long: umbels 3–10-fld.; pedicels 1–1½ in. long; fls. fragrant, lavender-lilac, the tube ½in. long, the segms. almost ¾in. long. Var. **odorata,** Lindl., fls. deep lilac, very sweet.

10. **LEUCOJUM,** L. SNOWFLAKE. Nine or 10 species of small hardy bulbous plants grown in the open for spring, and some of them for autumn, bloom; Eu. and Medit. region.—Bulbs small: scape hollow: lvs. few to several, linear and strap-shaped, appearing with the fls. in the vernal species and after them in the autumnal species: fls. 1 or several in a small umbel, white tinged green or red, from a single spathe-valve, cernuous or declined; perianth without tube, segms. all alike; stamens inserted on inferior ovary or hypanthium, filaments short, anthers erect and basifixed; ovules many, one above another; stigma small and capitate: caps. 3-valved loculicidally; seeds nearly globose. (Leuco-jum: old Greek name, etymologically *white violet.*)

A. Pedicel about as long as ovary and much shorter than spathe: fls. usually 1, in early spring....1. *L. vernum*
AA. Pedicel slender, equalling or exceeding spathe: fls. usually more than 1.
  B. Perianth white, tipped green: middle to late spring....2. *L. æstivum*
  BB. Perianth white, tinged red: autumn....3. *L. autumnale*

1. **L. vernum,** L. Lvs. short, becoming 6–9 in. long, ½in. or less broad, obtuse: scape 12 in. or less, usually bearing 1 declined or cernuous short-pedicelled fl.: segms. ¾in. long and ⅓–½in. broad, making a rather heavy fl., white tipped green: very early spring. Cent. Eu.

2. **L. æstivum,** L. Lvs. 12–18 in. long and ½in. broad, narrowed above but short-obtuse at apex: scape about 12 in., bearing 2–8 fls. on long drooping pedicels; segms. ¾in. or less long, ¼–⅓in. broad, making a rather light fl., white tipped green: mid to late spring. Cent. and S. Eu.

3. **L. autumnale,** L. Lvs. filiform, mostly appearing after the fls.: scape very slender, 9 in. or less, bearing 1–3 fls. on long cernuous pedicels; segms. ½in. or less long, 5–7-nerved, white tinged red: autumn. Medit. region.

11. **GALANTHUS,** L. SNOWDROP. Very like Leucojum, but scape solid, lvs. only 2 or 3, fl. 1, segms. in two series, the 3 inner ones shorter, connivent and erect; 8–10 little hardy plants, grown for very early spring bloom (one unusual species autumnal); Eu. and W. Asia. (Galan-thus: Greek *milk flower.*)

A. Inner segms. green only at sinuses....1. *G. nivalis*
AA. Inner segms. green on lower half as well as in sinuses....2. *G. Elwesii*

1. **G. nivalis,** L. The common snowdrop, blooming in earliest spring, in several forms: lvs. linear and glaucous, about ¼in. wide and becoming 8–9 in. long: fl. 1, declined or nodding on a slender pedicel, the scape usually less than 1 ft. high; outer segms. white, ½–1 in. long, veiny, obtuse or nearly so; inner segms. half as long, emarginate, white with green at the sinuses. Cent. and S. Eu. to Caucasus.

2. **G. Elwesii,** Hook. f. GIANT SNOWDROP. Plant and fls. larger: inner segms. green at sinuses and also on the lower half: several forms. (Named for H. J. Elwes, 1846–1922, England, who collected it near Smyrna.) Asia Minor.

12. **BRUNSVIGIA,** Heister. About a dozen species in S. Afr.—Bulbous: lvs. appearing after the fls., strap-shaped: perianth funnel-shaped, with short tube and nearly equal oblong acute ascending segms.; stamens declinate, inserted at throat, not exserted; ovary inferior, oblong, with many superposed ovules in each of the 3 cells; style slender and declinate, with capitate stigma: caps. globose, irregularly bursting, maturing few globose seeds. (Brunsvig-ia: after the Duke of Brunswick.)

B. rosea, Hannibal (*Amaryllis rosea,* Lam. *A. Belladonna,* Auth. not L. *Callicore rosea,* Link). BELLADONNA-LILY. CAPE BELLADONNA. Fls. summer and autumn, rose-red, fragrant, 3–3½ in. long, lily-like, several in an umbel on a solid compressed peduncle or scape 1–2 ft. or more high; segms. connivent below, ½in. or more broad at widest.—Kinds are cult. with fls. purple, white fading to blush, white-striped, and otherwise. Hybrids of *B. rosea* and *Crinum Moorei,* called **Amarcrinum Howardii,** Hort., in this country and *Crinodonna Corsii,* Hort., in Eu. are described as having fls. soft pink, open funnelform with recurved segms. and declinate style, borne in very large clusters on sts. to 4 ft. long; evergreen; they are also called Brunscrinum hybrids.

13. **NERINE,** Herb. (*Imhofia,* Heister). Fifteen recognized species in S. Afr., some frequently grown for autumn bloom.—Bulbous: lvs. strap-shaped, produced with the fls. or after them: fls. in shades of red, on solid scape; perianth funnelform, erect or somewhat declined, tube practically none; segms. all alike, falcate, usually crisped; stamens on base of segms., usually exserted, 3 shorter than the others; ovary inferior, globose, with few superposed ovules in each cell, stigma obscurely 3-lobed: caps. loculicidal, 3-valved; seeds globose. (Neri-ne: a nereid.)

A. Stamens and style almost straight.
B. Lvs. green and straight....1. *N. sarniensis*
BB. Lvs. glaucous and laterally curved....2. *N. curvifolia*
AA. Stamens and style declinate.
B. Lvs. about 1 in. wide, to 15 in. long: perianth-segms. 2½–3 in. long....3. *N. Bowdenii*
BB. Lvs. about ⅛in. wide, 6–8 in. long: perianth-segms. 1 in. long....4. *N. filifolia*

1. **N. sarniensis,** Herb. (*Amaryllis sarniensis,* L.). GUERNSEY-LILY, from place of its early cult., recorded in the name *sarniensis.* Lvs. linear, after fls., ¾in. or less broad: scape somewhat flattened, 12–18 in. long; fls. many in a close umbel, on pedicels 1–2 in. long; perianth about 1½ in. long, crimson; segms. oblanceolate, ½in. or less broad, falcate, slightly crisped; filaments bright red, exceeding segms.—There are color forms and other variants.

2. **N. curvifolia** var. **Fothergillii,** Baker (*N. Fothergillii,* Roem.). Lvs. ligulate, glaucous, laterally curved, to 1 ft. long: scape about 1½ ft.; umbel many-fld.; pedicels 1–2 in. long; fls. scarlet, erect or ascending, the segms. linear-oblanceolate, over 1 in. long, recurved; filaments and style red, exceeding segms., anthers greenish-yellow.—*N. curvifolia,* Herb. (*Amaryllis curvifolia,* Jacq.), is occasionally cult. and differs in less robust habit and few-fld. umbel of bright paler red fls.

3. **N. Bowdenii,** W. Wats. Lvs. up to 15 in. long, 1 in. wide, obtuse: scape longer than lvs., hollow, fairly stout; umbel 8–12-fld.; pedicels about 2 in. long; fls. horizontal, bright rose-pink, segms. to 3 in. long, spreading, crisped, reflexed at tip; stamens and style declinate, longer than segms.; filaments pink. (Named for Mr. Cornish Bowden, who discovered the plant in 1903.)

4. **N. filifolia,** Baker. Lvs. many, linear, 6–8 in. long: scape slender, 1 ft. high; umbel 8–12-fld.; pedicels to 1½ in. long; fls. rose-pink, the segms. linear-oblanceolate, crisped, 1 in. long; filaments declinate, pink, anthers red-brown.

14. **CHLIDANTHUS,** Herb. Two species of trop. Amer.—Lvs. basal, 6, linear, acute, suberect: scape solid, with terminal umbel of few bright yellow fragrant fls. which are sessile or on short pedicels; perianth-tube long, flushed green, the segms. lanceolate; stamens 6, inserted at throat of the tube, filaments short, subulate, anthers erect; ovary inferior, trilocular, style exserted. (Chlidan-thus: Greek *delicate* and *flower.*)

C. fragrans, Herb. Lvs. glaucous, 4–8 in. long: scape to 2 ft. high; perianth-tube to 3 in. long, the segms. spreading; ovary dark. Chile.

15. **CRINUM,** L. Perhaps 80–100 species in the warm temp. and trop. parts of both eastern and western hemispheres; most of them are striking plants of much beauty; many are planted in warm countries by collectors, but those in general cult. are few; sometimes called "crinum lilies"; mostly spring and summer bloomers.

—Bulbous, the neck of the bulb often columnar like a caudex: lvs. often persistent and broad and thick, strap-shaped or sword-shaped, not narrowed to petiole: fls. white or whitish, but striped, tinged or overlaid with red, few or many in an umbel subtended by 2 large broad spathe-valves, the pedicels short or none, scape solid; perianth large, funnelform or salverform, with a long cylindrical straight or curved tube equalling or exceeding the equal or nearly equal segms.; stamens inserted at throat, filaments long and usually declinate; ovary inferior, globose, oblong or oval, with few (sometimes only 2) ovules in each cell; style long and slender; stigma small, capitate: caps. bursting irregularly; seeds large and green. (Cri-num: Greek name for a lily.)

A. Perianth funnelform, the upper part of the naturally curved tube much broadened and passing gradually into the limb; segms. usually as much as 1 in. broad; stamens and style close together and commonly declinate; fls. curving outwards or even drooping. (CODOCRINUM.)
  B. Fls. distinctly pedicelled 1 in. or more in the umbel (exceptions perhaps in no. 1).
    C. Lvs. long and comparatively narrow (usually less than 3 in. broad), scabrous or denticulate on the margins.......... 1. *C. bulbispermum*
    CC. Lvs. broad (3–4 in.), smooth on margins.......... 2. *C. Moorei*
  BB. Fls. sessile or essentially so in the umbel.
    C. Lvs. narrow (2 in. or less broad).
      D. Margins of lvs. denticulate and much crisped.......... 3. *C. Sanderianum*
      DD. Margins of lvs. merely scabrous.......... 4. *C. scabrum*
    CC. Lvs. very broad (3–4 in. or more).
      D. Margins of lvs. only slightly scabrous; blade mostly less than 4 in. broad. 5. *C. zeylanicum*
      DD. Margins of lvs. denticulate; blade 4 in. or more broad.......... 6. *C. Kirkii*
AA. Perianth salverform, the tube long and slender and standing nearly or quite erect and not markedly expanded at summit; segms. usually linear or narrow-lanceolate; stamens spreading, not contiguous to style; fls. erect or strongly ascending, the tube usually straight. (STENASTER incl. Platyaster.)
  B. Tube of perianth 7–8 in. long.......... 7. *C. Kunthianum*
  BB. Tube of perianth 3–5 or sometimes 6 in. long.
    C. Fls. white; segms. linear or nearly so (not exceeding ½in. broad).
      D. Lvs. 2 in. or less broad: fls. 3–6 in the umbel.......... 8. *C. americanum*
      DD. Lvs. 3–5 in. broad: fls. 20–50.......... 9. *C. asiaticum*
    CC. Fls. purplish-red at least outside.
      D. Segms. about half as long as tube, reflexing.......... 10. *C. erubescens*
      DD. Segms. about as long as tube, spreading.
        E. Width of segms. mostly less than ½in.: bulb small.......... 11. *C. amabile*
        EE. Width of segms. usually above ½in.: bulb massive, 6 in. diam.......... 12. *C. augustum*

1. **C. bulbispermum,** Milne-Redhead & Schweickerdt (*Amaryllis bulbisperma,* Burm. *C. longifolium,* Thunb. *C. capense,* Auth. not Herb.). Hardy in middle states or northward; bulbs flask-shaped, with gradual neck: lvs. several to many, strap-shaped, firm and glaucous, 2–3 ft. long and 2–3 in. broad, rough-edged, long-tapering and acute: fls. on scape 1–2 ft. long, pink with deeper red outside (a white var.), 8–12 or more on pedicels 1–2 in. long, spathe-valves 3 in. long; tube curved, cylindrical, 3–4 in. long; segms. about equalling tube, oblong, acute, 1 in. or less broad; stamens nearly equalling segms. S. Afr.—Apparently the commonest outdoor crinum, blooming over a long season. **C. Powellii,** Hort., is an old hybrid between *C. bulbispermum* and *C. Moorei,* probably not in cult. or not recognizable here: lvs. sword-shaped, green, smooth on edge: fls. dark rose-color, about 8 on a flattened glaucous scape, pedicels about 1 in. long; tube curved, about 3 in. long; segms. oblong-lanceolate and acute, 4 in. long, 1 in. broad; stamens much shorter than segms.

2. **C. Moorei,** Hook. f. Bulbs very large, 6–8 in. diam., with stem-like neck 10–12 in. or more long: lvs. long, thin and wavy, bright green, strap-shaped, 2–3 ft. long and 3–4 in. broad, not ciliate or rough on margin, the veins distinct and prominent, briefly contracted to a point: fls. rosy or pinkish-red (a white var.), very fragrant, 4–10 on a green scape, pedicels 1½–3 in. long, spathe-valves large and thin; tube curved, 3–4 in. long; segms. length of tube, oblong and scarcely acute, 1–1½ in. broad; stamens declinate, much shorter than segms., the filaments pink. (Named after Dr. David Moore, 1807–1879, Glasnevin, Ireland.) S. Afr.—An attractive plant for pot cult. in the N., with a long season of bloom.

3. **C. Sanderianum,** Baker. Bulbs small, 2 in. diam. with neck of equal length: lvs. thin, 2 ft. or less long, 1½ in. or less broad, the edge denticulate and crisped: fls. white, keeled bright red, sessile, the spathe-valves 3–4 in. long; tube curved, 5–6 in. long; segms. 3–4 in. long, oblong-lanceolate and acute, less than 1 in. broad. (Named after Sander & Co., page 51.) W. trop. Afr.

4. **C. scabrum,** Herb. Bulbs large: lvs. several to many, strap-shaped, 2–3 ft. long and 2 in. or less broad, closely veined, firm in texture, the edge rough to the feel but not denticulate or crispate: fls. white but with crimson keels and stripes, amaryllis-like, sessile or nearly so, the broad spathe-valves 2–3 in. long; tube curved, 3–5 in. long and greenish; segms. about 3 in. long, oblong, acute; stamens not exceeding segms. Trop. Afr.

5. **C. zeylanicum,** L. (*Amaryllis zeylanica,* L.). Bulbs large, 5–6 in. diam. with short neck: lvs. several, strap-shaped, thin, 2–3 ft. long, 3–4 in. broad, slightly rough on edge: fls. white with red stripes, very fragrant, 10 or more in an umbel on tall purple scapes, pedicels very short, spathe-valves reddish, 3–4 in. long; tube curved, 3–6 in. long; segms. 3–4 in. long, oblong-lanceolate, acute, 1 in. broad; stamens declinate, shorter than segms. Trop. Asia and Afr.

6. **C. Kirkii,** Baker. Bulbs large, 6–8 in. diam. with neck 5–6 in. long: lvs. strap-shaped, 3–4 ft. long and 4 in. or more broad, very acute, with denticulate margins: scapes sometimes more than 1, 12–18 in. long; fls. a dozen or more to the umbel, white with bright red broad keels, pedicels none or very short, spathe-valves 3–4 in. long, broad and reddish-brown; tube greenish, 4 in. long; segms. about the same length, more than 1 in. broad, oblong and acute; stamens shorter than segms. Zanzibar, whence the original bulb was sent to Kew by Sir John Kirk, the plant blooming in Sept. 1879.

7. **C. Kunthianum,** Roem. Bulbs medium size, 3 in. diam., neck short: lvs. about 20, strap-shaped, 2–3 in. broad and somewhat undulate, the margins entire: fls. 4 or 5, white (a var. purplish outside), salverform, sessile or nearly so, spathe-valves 3 in. long and lanceolate; tube slender, 7–8 in. long; segms. lanceolate, less than 3 in. long. (Bears the name of Carl S. Kunth, page 46; collaborator with Humboldt.) Colombia and Cent. Amer.

8. **C. americanum,** L. Southern Swamp Crinum or Lily. Bulbs 2–4 in. diam., the neck short: lvs. narrowly strap-shaped, 2 in. or less broad, sparingly denticulate: fls. white, fragrant, salverform, 2–6 to the umbel, sessile or nearly so, spathe-valves 2–3 in. long and broad-lanceolate; tube very slender and 4–5 in. long; segms. much shorter and ½in. or less broad; stamens spreading and prominent. Glades and swamps, Ga., Fla. to Tex.

9. **C. asiaticum,** L. A large variable species of trop. Asia, hardy along the Gulf Coast, forming clumps of tropical-looking foliage and flowering continuously for a long season: bulbs long and columnar, 1 ft. or so long, 4–5 in. thick: lvs. many and closely placed, 3 ft. or more long and 3–5 in. broad, gradually tapering to a sharp point, light bluish-green: fls. pure white, very fragrant, salverform, borne a little above foliage, 20 or more on 2-edged stout scape, pedicels 1 in. or less long, spathe-valves 3–4 in. long; tube erect, 3–4 in. long; segms. linear, about 3 in. long, ½in. or less broad, strongly curving or hanging; stamens 2 in. long, red: seeds large and fleshy. Var. **sinicum,** Baker, St.-Johns-Lily, is a big form with broader undulate lvs., stouter scape, tube and segms. longer.

10. **C. erubescens,** Ait. Bulbs 3–4 in. diam., the neck short: lvs. many, strap-shaped, 2–3 ft. long, 2–3 in. broad, thin and close-veined, margin slightly rough: fls. rather few, usually 4–6 but sometimes 10–12, white inside and purplish-red outside with a light pink rib, fragrant, salverform, on a scape 2–3 ft. long, the pedicels very short or none, the green spathe-valves 3 in. long; tube straight and erect, 5–6 in. long; segms. lanceolate, becoming reflexed, half as long as tube; filaments bright red, not exserted. Trop. Amer.

11. **C. amabile,** Donn. Bulbs small, the neck 1 ft. or more long: lvs. many and large, strap-shaped, 3–4 ft. long and 3–4 in. broad, green, gradually tapering, smooth on margin: fls. bright red on tube and center of segms., otherwise white or blush, exceedingly fragrant, salverform, 20 or more on a stout flattened scape 2–3 ft. long, pedicels 1 in. or less long, spathe-valves 4–5 in. long, red; tube straight, cylindrical, 3–4 in. long; segms. 4–5 in. long, ½in. or less broad; stamens slender and prominent but shorter than the curved segms. Sumatra.

12. **C. augustum,** Roxb. (*C. amabile* var. *augustum,* Ker). Doubtfully specifically distinct from *C. amabile:* bulbs larger, often 6 in. diam. with a thick column-like neck: lvs. less tapering: fls. brighter colored and with a less powerful perfume, the segms. narrow-lanceolate and ½–¾in. broad: as grown in the open in frostless countries regarded as a larger plant than no. 11. Mauritius and Seychelles.

16. **CYRTANTHUS,** Ait. About 30 species, mostly S. African.—Rootstock a tunicated bulb: lvs. several, basal, linear or lorate, contemporary with or after the infl.: scape hollow, bearing terminal umbel of several pedicelled drooping waxy tubular fls.; perianth-segms. much shorter than tube; stamens inserted below the throat of the tube, filaments slender, anthers versatile, oblong; ovary inferior, tri-loculed, style filiform with 3-lobed stigma, ovules numerous: fr. an oblong 3-valved caps.; seeds many, black, flattened and winged. (Cyrtan-thus: Greek *curved* and *flower.*)

A. Umbel 2–4-fld.; fls. yellow....1. *C. ochroleucus*
AA. Umbel 4–10-fld.; fls. white....2. *C. Mackenii*

1. **C. ochroleucus,** Burch. (*Monella ochroleuca,* Herb. *C. lutescens,* Herb.). Lvs. apparently after the fls., to 1 ft. long and ⅛in. wide: scape to 15 in. tall, slender; pedicels scarcely 1 in. long; fls. 2–4, suberect, 1⅔–2 in. long, light yellow, the perianth-segms. oblong, to ½in. long, spreading. S. Afr.

2. **C. Mackenii,** Hook. f. Lvs. contemporary with the fls., 8–12 in. long, ¼–⅓in. wide: scape taller, glaucous; pedicels to about 1 in. long; fls. 4–10, suberect, white or with yellowish throat, 2 in. long, the perianth-segms. ovate-oblong, ¼in. long. (Named for M. John MacKen, 1823–1872, botanist in S. Afr.) S. Afr.

17. **VALLOTA,** Herb. One species in S. Afr., grown for summer bloom.—Bulbous: lvs. several to many, appearing with the fls., strap-shaped, 1–2 ft. long and 1 in. or more broad: fls. few or several in an umbel, scarlet, the spathe-valves 2–3 in. long; perianth erect, funnelform, with prominent tube and equal segms. connected at base by callus; stamens inserted in top of tube; ovary inferior, oblong, each cell with many ovules, style slender, stigma capitate and faintly 3-notched: caps. loculicidally 3-valved, the compressed seeds with wing at base. (Vallo-ta: A. Vallot, 1594–1671, French botanist.)

V. speciosa, Th. Dur. & Schinz (*Crinum speciosum,* L. f. *Vallota purpurea,* Herb. *Amaryllis purpurea,* Ait.). SCARBOROUGH-LILY. Lvs. dying in autumn: scape hollow, 2–3 ft. high, equalling or exceeding the lvs.; pedicels 1–2 in. long: fls. 2½–3 in. across.—There are color forms, one with white fls., others with fls. 4–5 in. across, marked with white blotches or eye.

18. **ZEPHYRANTHES,** Herb. (*Atomosco,* Greene). ZEPHYR-LILY. More than 50 species in the warmer parts of western hemisphere, low plants with grassy lvs., planted in borders and sometimes in pots and window-gardens; bloom in spring, summer, autumn.—Bulbous: lvs. few to several, usually appearing with the blossoms: fls. 1 to each scape (which is hollow), white, yellow, pink, or red, from a simple tubular spathe 2-notched at apex; perianth erect, funnelform, with short or long tube that often has minute scales near throat, the segms. about equal; stamens erect or slightly declinate, inserted at throat or in tube, 3 longer alternating with 3 shorter; ovules many in each cell of inferior ovary, style filiform and declinate, stigma 3-parted or -notched: caps. nearly globose, loculicidally 3-valved; seeds black, more or less flattened. (Zephyran-thes: Greek *wind flower.*)

A. Fls. white to rose.
B. Stigma deeply 3-parted or -branched.
C. Color of fls. white or with purplish tinge.............1. *Z. Atamasco*
CC. Color of fls. rose-red.............2. *Z. grandiflora*
BB. Stigma obscurely 3-lobed or -notched.............3. *Z. candida*
AA. Fls. light yellow.............4. *Z. Ajax*

1. **Z. Atamasco,** Herb. (*Amaryllis Atamasco,* L.). ATAMASCO-LILY (*Atamasco,* an Indian word or name). Spring-flowering: bulbs about 1 in. diam.: lvs. appearing with the fls., narrow-linear, 1 ft. more or less long: fl. pure white varying to purple-tinged, on a pedicel shorter than the 2-cleft spathe; perianth 2–3 in. high, with tube longer than segms.; stamens shorter than limb of perianth; style prominent, trifid. Pa. to Ala. and Fla.

2. **Z. grandiflora,** Lindl. (*Z. carinata,* Herb. *Z. rosea,* Hort. not Lindl.). Spring and summer: bulbs 1 in. diam.: lvs. with the fls., linear, 12 in. or less long: fl. rose-red or pink, on a pedicel shorter or longer than the colored spathe; perianth 2¼–3 in. long, the tube prominent, the segms. obovate, obtuse or nearly so, veiny, ½–¾in. broad; stamens half or more length of limb; style prominent and strongly trifid. Cuba, Jamaica, Mex. and S.

3. **Z. candida,** Herb. (*Amaryllis candida,* Lindl.). Summer and autumn: bulbs 1 in. diam., with prominent neck: lvs. with the fls. and remaining through winter in mild climates, linear, 1 ft. more or less long: fl. white, often tinged rose outside, on pedicel included in spathe; perianth 2 in. long, without tube; segms. obtuse or short-acute, ½in. or less broad; stamens much shorter than segms.; style somewhat exceeding stamens, stigma slightly 3-notched. La Plata region, S. Amer.—The trade name *Z. alba* possibly applies here.

4. **Z. Ajax,** Sprenger. Lvs. to 8 in.: scape 6–8 in.; fls. light yellow, 1½ in. across. (Ajax: mythological name.) A hybrid between *Z. citrina,* Baker and *Z. candida.*

19. **HABRANTHUS,** Herb. Perhaps 18–20 species of temp. S. Amer.—Like Zephyranthes and often included in it: fls. oblique to declinate; stamens fasciculate, unequal, of four different lengths. (Habran-thus: Greek *graceful flower.*)

H. robustus, Herb. (*Zephyranthes robusta,* Baker). Summer: bulbs 1–1½ in. diam.: lvs. after the fls., linear, glaucous: sts. 6–9 in. high: fl. rose-red, on pedicel 1½–2 in. long, tube short, greenish; perianth-limb suberect, obovate, 2½–3 in. long; stamens half the limb; stigma trifid. Argentina.

20. **COOPERIA,** Herb. RAIN- or PRAIRIE-LILY. About 4 species of S U. S. and Mex., very similar to Zephyranthes.—Bulbous night-blooming herbs with basal grass-like lvs. and fragrant white salverform fls. solitary at end of scapes, the perianth with a long tube; stamens very short, inserted at throat of the tube; ovary inferior. (Coope-ria: Joseph Cooper, English gardener.)

A. Bulb-neck less than 1½ in. long: perianth-tube 3–5 in. long....................1. *C. Drummondii*
AA. Bulb-neck over 2 in. long: perianth-tube 1½–2 in. long....................2. *C. pedunculata*

1. **C. Drummondii,** Herb. Bulbs subglobose, 1 in. thick: lvs. linear, erect, 12 in. long, produced with the fls. in summer: st. 4–12 in. high: fl. 1, white tinged with red outside, the perianth-segms. oblong, spreading, about 1 in. long; style as long as tube, stigma trifid. (Named for Thomas Drummond, Scotch botanist who collected in N. Amer., died 1835.) Tex., New Mex., Mex.

2. **C. pedunculata,** Herb. Bulbs flattened-globose: lvs. ¼in. wide, about 12 in. long: st. 5–8 in. high: fls. white tinged red externally, the perianth-segms. oblong, obtuse, 1–1½ in. long. Tex., Mex.

21. **STERNBERGIA,** Waldst. & Kit. Four species of low bulbous herbs from S. E. Eu. and S. W. Asia.—Bulbs with many tunics and long neck: lvs. narrow, basal: st. short: spathe single, more or less tubular, membranous; fl. solitary, erect, funnelform, golden-yellow; perianth-segms. ascending, oblong or lanceolate; stamens inserted at throat of tube, filaments filiform, anthers versatile; ovary inferior, style filiform, stigma capitate or trilobed. (Sternber-gia: named for Count Caspar Sternberg, 1761–1838, botanist and writer.)

S. lutea, Roem. & Schult. (*Amaryllis lutea,* L.). Lvs. produced with the fls., 5–6, 6–12 in. long, ¾in. wide: st. 6–9 in. long: fl. about 1¾ in. long, in autumn, the tube very short, segms. 1¼–1½ in. long, ½in. broad. Medit. region.

22. **CLIVIA,** Lindl. KAFIR-LILY. Species 3, one frequent in greenhouses for spring and summer bloom.—Plants with fleshy roots and bulb-like parts formed of the expanded lf.-bases: lvs. many, persistent, distichous: fls. several or many, in a close but not compact umbel, red-yellow or scarlet, not fragrant, subtended by several imbricated green spathe-valves; perianth funnelform, the tube short, 3 outer segms. narrower than others; stamens inserted in throat, about equalling segms.; ovary globose, inferior, with 5 or 6 ovules in each cell, style 3-lobed: fr. a red berry, with large globose seeds. (Cli-via: a Duchess of Northumberland, of the Clive family.)

C. miniata, Regel (*Imantophyllum miniatum,* Hook.). Strong plant, spreading and filling a large pot or tub: lvs. thick and glossy, broadly strap-shaped, 1–2 in. broad: fls. 10–20 and more, erect, scarlet with yellow inside, pedicels 1–2 in. long; perianth 2–3 in. long; inner segms. broadly obovate and obtuse, a little exceeding the stamens; style somewhat protruded. S. Afr.

23. **HÆMANTHUS,** L. BLOOD-LILY. Probably more than 60 species, in Afr., one or two sometimes grown in pots for summer and autumn bloom.—Bulbous, with broad mostly obtuse lvs. more or less narrowed at base: scape solid, somewhat flattened: fls. many in a dense head subtended by a whorl of spathes, red or white; perianth straight, erect or spreading, with tube shorter than the narrow (linear or lanceolate) equal segms.; stamens inserted at throat, often longer than perianth and sometimes strongly exserted; ovary globose, inferior, each cell with solitary or paired ovules, stigma minutely 3-lobed: fr. berry-like, indehiscent; seed or seeds globose. (Hæman-thus: *blood flower,* from Greek words.)

H. coccineus, L. Bulbs large: lvs. 2, thick and fleshy, appearing early in season, to 2 ft. long and 6 or 8 in. broad: scape shorter than lvs.: head or umbel 2–3 in. diam., with several large obtuse bright red bracts or spathe-valves; fls. red, about 1 in. long, very thin in texture, segms. linear; stamens much-exserted. S. Afr.—Other species are now and then grown, as **H. Katharinæ,** Baker (named after Mrs. Katharine Saunders), which has 3–5 thin lvs. appearing at the same time as the fls. and not exceeding or not equalling the head of bright red fls.; spathe-valves lanceolate-pointed, soon falling.

24. **IXIOLIRION,** Herb. About 3 species of Asiatic bulbous plants.—Lvs. linear, almost basal: st. slender, erect, bearing a racemose umbel of fairly large blue trumpet-shaped fls.: perianth-segms. free to the inferior ovary, oblanceolate, tubular in basal

half, spreading-recurved above; stamens inserted near the base, anthers oblong, basifixed; style filiform, stigma trifid: fr. a caps. (Ixiolir-ion: Greek *ixia-like lily.*)

I. tataricum, Herb. (*Amaryllis tatarica,* Pall. *I. montanum,* Herb. *I. Pallasii,* F. Muell.). SIBERIAN-LILY. Bulbs ovoid, 1 in. thick, with neck 3 in. long: basal lvs. 3–8, persistent, linear: fls. 2–8, lilac to blue, on unequal pedicels; segms. 1½ in. long; filaments, style and stigma violet, anthers white. Asia.

25. **PANCRATIUM,** L. Species 14 or more in subtemp. and trop. regions of Old World, little cult. in N. Amer.—Bulbous: lvs. linear or strap-shaped: fls. white, few or many in an umbel on a solid scape, the outer spathe-valves 2 and lanceolate; perianth with a cylindrical tube broadening at the top, the segms. narrow, equal and spreading; stamens inserted at throat, the filaments united in a cup at base but free above, anthers versatile; ovary inferior, ovules many in each cell, one above another, stigma capitate but somewhat 3-lobed but not divided or branched: caps. loculicidal, 3-valved. (Pancra-tium: Greek *all-powerful,* from supposed medicinal virtues.)

P. maritimum, L. Bulbs globose, tapering into neck: lvs. persistent, linear, glaucous, 2–2½ ft. long: fls. very fragrant, 5–10 in an umbel, the scape compressed; tube 2–3 in. long; segms. linear, 1½ in. long; staminal cup conspicuous, with short teeth, the free part of filaments only ¼in. long. Medit. region.

26. **HYMENOCALLIS,** Salisb. SPIDER-LILY. The American representatives of Pancratium, about 40 species, differing technically in having usually 2 ovules side by side in bottom of each cell (rarely 4–6): lvs. sometimes broad and narrowed into distinct petiole. (Hymenocal-lis: Greek *beautiful membrane,* alluding to the staminal cup.)—Several kinds are grown for the pure white (rarely red-tinged) fragrant fls.: there is one Peruvian yellow-fld. species, apparently not in general cult. One species occurs in trop. Afr., but may have been intro. Native species occur from the Carolinas south in low places and sandy soil.

A. Free filaments 1½–2 in. long; perianth-segms. linear.......... 1. *H. americana*
AA. Free filaments ½in. long; perianth-segms. lanceolate.......... 2. *H. calathina*

1. **H. americana,** Roem. (*H. littoralis,* Salisb. *Pancratium americanum,* Mill.). Lvs. several to many, sword-shaped, 1½–2½ ft. long, 1–2½ in. broad, bright green, tapering to apex, finely many-veined: fls. white, sessile, 3–8 on a flattened scape 1–2½ ft. high, the outer spathe-valves 2–3 in. long and very broad at base; tube variable in length, 4 in. or more; segms. linear, usually shorter than tube; staminal cup bell-shaped or broadly funnelform, about 1 in. long, dentate, the free filaments 1½–2 in. long, anthers linear, ½–¾in. long; style equalling or exceeding stamens. Trop. Amer.—Frequent in yards far S.

2. **H. calathina,** Nichols. (*Pancratium calathinum,* Ker. *Ismene calathina,* Herb.). Bulbs with a long hyaline-sheathed neck: lvs. several, strap-shaped, thin, 1½–2 ft. long and 1–2 in. broad, short-pointed or nearly obtuse: fls. white, large, sessile, 2–4 in the umbel, the outer spathe-valves lanceolate or ovate-lanceolate; tube 2½–4 in. long, expanding at top; segms. lanceolate, nearly or quite as long as the tube; cup funnel-shaped, striped green, 2 in. long and rather broader, with spreading rounded fringed lobes, the free filaments ½in. long. Andes, Peru, Bolivia.—Sometimes called Basket-Flower.

27. **EUCHARIS,** Planch. Six or 8 species of Colombia, one common in greenhouses and as a pot-plant.—Bulbous: lvs. with expanded blade, narrowed into petiole: fls. pure white, showy and large, few in an umbel on a mostly terete scape; outer spathe-valves 2 and ovate-lanceolate, inner several to many and linear; perianth with spreading equal segms., and a cylindrical somewhat curved tube that is expanded at top; stamens inserted at throat, shorter than segms., the filaments broadened or appendaged to form a cup; ovules mostly many in each cell of inferior ovary, stigma 3-lobed: caps. 3-lobed, becoming dehiscent. (Eu-charis: Greek *very graceful,* well applied to these pleasing plants.)

E. grandiflora, Planch. (*E. amazonica,* Lind.). AMAZON-LILY (although from the Andes of Colombia). Bulbs 2 in. diam., tapering to neck: lvs. few to each st., thin, the blade oblong or oval, 4–6 in. broad and twice or more as long, acuminate, petiole slender and equalling or exceeding the blade: scape 1–2 ft., bearing 3–6 fragrant fls. on short pedicels; perianth wide open, the segms. 1–1½ in. broad and little longer, making a fl. about 2½–3 in. across; tube slender, 2 in. long above the prominent globose ovary; staminal cup protruded and prominent.

28. **AMARYLLIS,** L. Perhaps 70 species, from trop. Amer., usually grown for spring and summer bloom or late winter under glass.—Bulbous: lvs. linear or strap-shaped, sometimes with the fls. and sometimes succeeding them: fls. large and lily-like (in cult. species), red or whitish and sometimes white-striped, few or several in an umbel on a hollow scape; perianth funnel-shaped, horizontal or declinate, tube short in the cult. kinds, usually with minute scales in the throat, segms. equal or the inner ones narrower; stamens inserted in throat, somewhat declinate; ovary inferior, ovules many, superposed, stigma capitate or 3-parted: caps. globose, loculicidally 3-valved, seeds usually flattened. (Amaryl-lis: classical name, applied to a woman by early writers.)—Most of the cult. kinds are probably hybrids.

A. Stigma 3-branched....................1. *A. vittata*
AA. Stigma capitate, not branched or parted but sometimes obscurely 3-notched.
 B. Tube of perianth ½in. or less long....................2. *A. Reginæ*
 BB. Tube of perianth more than ½in. long.
  C. Segms. tessellated or cross-barred....................3. *A. reticulata*
  CC. Segms. not tessellate or checkered....................4. *A. Belladonna*

1. **A. vittata,** Ait. (*Hippeastrum vittatum,* Herb.). Bulbs large, globose: lvs. several, long, green, appearing with or after the fls.: fls. few and large, 4–6 in. long and nearly as broad, red-and-white striped; tube about 1 in. long with obscure little crown at throat; segms. long-obovate, exceeding the stamens; style equalling or exceeding perianth. Peruvian Andes.—The common commercial hybrid amaryllises are of this type or group. **A. Johnsonii,** Hort., an old hybrid between this and the next species, is still occasionally cult. as a pot-plant; it is deep uniform red.

2. **A. Reginæ,** L. (*Hippeastrum Reginæ,* Herb.). Bulbs large, globose: lvs. developing after the fls., large and broad, much narrowed at base: fls. few and large, 4–5 in. long, bright red not striped, but throat with large whitish star but without crown; tube ½in. or less long; segms. obovate and acute, exceeding stamens; stigma capitate in form but obscurely 3-lobed or -notched. Mex. and W. Indies to S. Amer.

3. **A. reticulata,** L'Her. (*Hippeastrum reticulatum,* Herb.). Bulbs medium, nearly globose: lvs. few, thin, appearing with fls., oblanceolate, 2 in. broad toward top: fls. few, horizontal or declined, about 4 in. long; tube 1 in. or more long and slender below, without crown; segms. obovate, narrowed to base, rose-pink, beautifully cross-barred with darker rose; stamens shorter than perianth; stigma capitate but obscurely 3-lobed or -notched. Brazil. Var. **striatifolia,** Herb., has broad lvs. with prominent white rib.

4. **A. Belladonna,** L. (*A. equestris,* Ait. *Hippeastrum equestre,* Herb. *H. puniceum,* Urban). Bulbs medium, globose, producing runners or stolons: lvs. few, fully developed after fls., strap-shaped: fls. few, 4–5 in. long; tube 1 in. or more long and greenish and with obscure little crown in throat; segms. red or salmon-red and lighter colored toward base, the inner ones narrower; stamens shorter than perianth; stigma capitate but obscurely 3-lobed or -notched. Mex. and W. Indies to S. Amer.

29. **SPREKELIA,** Heister. One species in Mex., often cult.—Bulbous: lvs. narrow, with the bloom: fl. 1, terminating the scape; perianth without tube but 3 lower segms. rolled together forming a horizontal cylinder from which the narrow segms. depend, the other 3 segms. erect or nearly so; stamens in the cylinder, attached to base of segms., exserted, with large hanging versatile anthers; ovary inferior, top-shaped, 6-angled, each cell with many superposed ovules, style 3-parted: caps. 3-valved; seeds disk-like, narrowly winged. (Spreke-lia: J. H. von Sprekelsen, who sent the plant to Linnæus and wrote on plants; died 1764.)

S. formosissima, Herb. (*Amaryllis formosissima,* L.). JACOBEAN-LILY. ST.-JAMES-LILY. AZTEC-LILY. Spring bloomer with several lvs. nearly equalling or exceeding the hollow scape: fls. bright crimson, from an erect colored 2-toothed spathe, the perianth 3–4 in. long; upper segms. sometimes 1 in. broad, others narrower.

30. **LYCORIS,** Herb. About a half dozen species from China and Japan, frequently planted for summer and autumn bloom and to some extent under glass.—Bulbous: scape solid: lvs. usually after or before the fls., strap-shaped or narrower: fls. yellow or red, few, several or many in an umbel terminating the scape; perianth funnel-shaped, somewhat irregular, the cylindrical tube short but expanded at top, throat bearing scales, the segms. clawed, nearly equal; stamens inserted near throat, declinate; style long, with a very small capitate stigma; ovules few in each cell of inferior ovary: fr. a caps. (Lyco-ris: a name in Greek mythology.)

A. Fls. yellow or orange........ 1. *L. aurea*
AA. Fls. red or lilac (rarely varying to white).
B. Stamens much-exserted........ 2. *L. radiata*
BB. Stamens about as long as segms........ 3. *L. squamigera*

1. **L. aurea,** Herb. (*Amaryllis aurea*, L'Her.). Fls. yellow, in summer, not fragrant, following the glaucous sword-shaped lvs.; perianth 3 in. long, tube ¾in. or less, with scales in the throat, segms. more or less crisped or wavy, ½in. or less broad; stamens and style mostly exceeding perianth. China.

2. **L. radiata,** Herb. (*Amaryllis radiata*, L'Her.). Fls. bright red (a white form), not fragrant, in autumn, linear and glaucous lvs. appearing later; perianth about 1½ in. long, tube very short, segms. crisped, wide-spreading and recurved; stamens twice exceeding the segms.; style protruded. China, Japan.

3. **L. squamigera,** Maxim. (*Amaryllis Hallii*, Hort.). Fls. rose-lilac or pink, in summer, fragrant, following the strap-shaped lvs.; perianth 3 in. long, the tube ½in. or more long and with scales in throat, the segms. obtuse and crisped and ½in. or more broad; stamens nearly or about as long as segms.; style exserted. Japan.

31. **NARCISSUS,** L. Probably 25 or 30 original species, in Cent. Eu. and Medit. region to China and Japan, mostly European; handsome and hardy bulbous plants, familiar for spring bloom and for forcing; the autumn-fld. species are not popularly cult.—Lvs. linear and flat or narrow and rush-like, appearing with the fls., more or less equalling the unbranched scape, which is 2 ft. or less high (usually 10–18 in.): fls. yellow or white, mostly declined or nodding but sometimes upward-looking, 1 or several issuing from a 1-valved thin tubular spathe; perianth salverform, with a rather short cylindrical or funnelform tube, the segms. equal or very nearly so and ascending or reflexed; crown (corona) long and tubular like a corolla, medium length, or reduced to a shallow ring-like cup; stamens inserted in tube, the filaments mostly included in the crown, the anthers erect and basifixed; ovary inferior, ovules many, one above another; stigma 3-lobed: caps. dehiscing loculicidally. (Narcis-sus: a classical Latin name, from the Greek; perhaps, as the etymology suggests, in allusion to narcotic qualities; probably not connected with the youth Narcissus in mythology.)—The hort. narcissi are much hybridized and modified, with many Latin names, and the fanciers' groups cannot be clearly followed or defined botanically.

A. Lvs. terete or semi-terete and narrowly channelled on the face, green.
B. Crown small, much less than half as long as segms........ 9. *N. Jonquilla*
BB. Crown at least half as long as segms.
C. Length of crown equal to or exceeding segms........ 1. *N. Bulbocodium*
CC. Length of crown about half the segms.
D. Segms. oblong, obovate or ovate, spreading.
E. Lf. channelled on the face........ 6. *N. odorus*
EE. Lf. terete........ 7. *N. juncifolius*
DD. Segms. lanceolate, reflexed straight backwards........ 4. *N. triandrus*
AA. Lvs. flat or essentially so, mostly glaucous.
B. Crown half as long to longer than segms.
C. Segms. reflexed from base, not much longer than crown........ 3. *N. cyclamineus*
CC. Segms. spreading.
D. Corona equalling or exceeding segms........ 2. *N. Pseudo-Narcissus*
DD. Corona about half as long as segms........ 5. *N. incomparabilis*
BB. Crown much less than half as long as segms.
C. Fls. 1–2 on a scape; crown crisped.
D. Corona not red-edged; fls. usually 2........ 10. *N. biflorus*
DD. Corona red-edged; fls. usually 1........ 11. *N. poeticus*
CC. Fls. 4 or more; crown not crisped........ 8. *N. Tazetta*

1. **N. Bulbocodium,** L. Hoop-Petticoat Daffodil. Small, early flowering: lvs. slender, subterete, channelled, usually exceeding the scape, 4–15 in. long: fl. 1, horizontal or ascending, usually standing 8 in. or less above the ground, bright yellow throughout; perianth 1–1½ in. long; crown large and thin, megaphone-shaped, ½–1 in. long, crenulate or entire, exceeding the very narrow segms. and about as long as the perianth-tube. S. France to Morocco. Var. **citrinus,** Baker, perianth 1½–2 in. long, lemon-yellow, style not exserted. Var. **conspicuus,** Baker, perianth large, style exserted.

2. **N. Pseudo-Narcissus,** L. Daffodil. Trumpet Narcissus. Strong stout plant: lvs. flat, ⅓–¾in. broad, glaucous, obtuse or only short-acute, 10–15 in. and about as long as scape: fl. 1, horizontal or ascending, not stalked beyond the spathe, 2–2½ in. long, the segms. and crown usually different shades of yellow; tube broad, about ½in. long; crown 1½–2 in. long with erect more or less frilled edge, about as long as oblong or ovate segms. Sweden to England, Spain and Romania.—The prevailing narcissus in cult. for forcing and the open. It runs into many forms, some of them double. The color sorts run to

white-fld. kinds and to the Bicolors (var. *bicolor*, Willk. & Lange, or *N. bicolor*, L., segms. white, corona yellow); in the wild the corona is lemon-yellow, and the segms. pale sulfur-yellow. To this group belong the Ajax narcissi. There are forms with cernuous fls., with twisted segms., of large and small stature (*N. minimus*, Hort., a small early form).

3. **N. cyclamineus,** DC. (*Ajax cyclamineus*, Haw.). Lvs. narrowly linear, keeled: st. slender, 8 in. tall: fl. nodding, tube obconic, ½in. long; segms. reflexed from base, lance-linear, lemon-yellow, over 1 in. long: corona almost as long, bright yellow, almost cylindric, under ½in. diam. Portugal.

4. **N. triandrus,** L. (*Ganymedes albus*, Haw.). Angels-Tears. Small: lvs. and scape very slender, subterete, channelled, 6–15 in. high: fls. 1–6, drooping or horizontal, pure white throughout, about 1 in. long; tube ½–¾in. long; crown cup-like, entire, half as long as the lanceolate reflexed segms. Spain and Portugal.—Little grown.

5. **N. incomparabilis,** Mill. Strong species: lvs. narrow but flat, ¼–⅜in. broad, glaucous, obtuse, nearly or quite equalling scape: fl. 1, horizontal or ascending, yellow, inodorous, the pedicel little if at all protruded from spathe; tube rather thick, ¾in. long; crown about ½in. long and somewhat broader, plicate, about one-half length of the ovate or oblong mostly acute overlapping segms. Spain and S. France to Tyrol.—Popular and variable in cult. The segms. are sometimes white; usually the yellows of segms. and crown are different. There are double forms. **N. Barrii,** Hort., represents a series of medium-crowned kinds, intermediate between *N. incomparabilis* and *N. poeticus:* fl. 1, horizontal or ascending, yellow; crown crenulate, about one-third length of oblong spreading segms. **N. Leedsii,** Hort., in several forms, is intermediate between *N. Pseudo-Narcissus* and *N. poeticus:* fl. 1, horizontal or declined; crown yellow, crenate, nearly or quite half as long as oblong spreading whitish segms.

6. **N. odorus,** L. (*N. calathinus*, L. *N. Campernellii*, Hort.). Campernelle Jonquil. Lvs. and scape subterete, channelled on the face, of about equal length: fls. 2–4 (sometimes 1), bright yellow throughout, fragrant, on pedicels little or not projecting from long-pointed spathe; tube not slender, ¾in. long; crown about ½in. long and somewhat broader, crenate-lobed, about half the length of the obovate or oblong spreading segms. France and Spain eastward.—Sometimes grown as jonquil.

7. **N. juncifolius,** Lag. Small and slender: lvs. and scape very slender, terete and rush-like, the lvs. usually 6 in. or less long and scape somewhat longer: fls. 1–4, horizontal or ascending, bright yellow or the crown perhaps darker; tube ½in. long; crown cup-shaped and crenulate, about half the length of the ovate spreading segms. S. France, Spain, Portugal.—Little grown.

8. **N. Tazetta,** L. (*N. canaliculatus*, Guss.). Polyanthus Narcissus. Strong species: lvs. long and flat, to 18 in., ⅜–¾in. broad, somewhat glaucous, obtuse, about the length of flattened scape: fls. few to several, usually 4–8, horizontal or declined, segms. white and crown light yellow, fragrant, rather small (1–1½ in. across), pedicels projecting from the large spathe and sometimes very long; tube slender, ¾–1 in. long; crown cup-shaped and very short, much less than the obovate overlapping spreading or reflexed segms. (Tazetta: old S. European name, probably connected with Italian tarza, *a cup.*) Canary Isls. to Japan.—A popular plant, widely variable. The Paper-White narcissus (var. **papyraceus,** Hort.), much used under glass for midwinter bloom, is a clear white-fld. sort. Var. **orientalis,** Hort. (*N. orientalis*, L.), is a robust form with long erect or curving pedicels (sometimes 4 in. long), segms. sulfur-yellow, crown prominent and one-third length of segms., dark yellow; often grown in water and sometimes known as "Chinese sacred-lily." Var. **polyanthos,** Baker, lvs. bright green; fls. 12–20, segms. ovate, white, corona pale yellow; France. The Poetaz narcissi (*N. Poetaz*, Hort.), are hybrids of *N. poeticus* var. *ornatus* crossed by *N. Tazetta*, originating in Holland in 1885; now popular; they are like large-fld. Tazetta, with more open better-formed perianth and pleasanter fragrance.

9. **N. Jonquilla,** L. Jonquil. Slender and graceful: lvs. and scape 10–18 in. high, slender, subterete: fls. 2–6, horizontal or somewhat declined, some of the pedicels longer than the spathe, yellow throughout, fragrant; tube slender, nearly or quite 1 in. long; crown ⅛in. or less long, crenate, much shorter than the obovate spreading segms. (Jonquilla: old name of the plant, connected with Latin Juncus, *a rush.*) S. Eu. and Algeria.—Common in old gardens.

10. **N. biflorus,** Curt. Primrose Peerless Narcissus. Strong plant: lvs. ½in. or so broad, faintly glaucous, about length of scape: fls. commonly 2 (sometimes 1 or 3), milky-white with pale yellow cup, the pedicels shorter than spathe; tube about 1 in. long, fairly thick; crown very short, ¼in. across, the crisped edge not red or different colored, several times shorter than obovate obtuse apiculate overlapping segms. France to Tyrol.—Little grown.

11. **N. poeticus,** L. Poets Narcissus. Pheasants-Eye. Strong plant: lvs. flat, glaucous, ¼–⅜in. broad, obtuse: fl. 1 (rarely 2), horizontal or ascending, clear white, very fragrant, the pedicels little or not at all projecting from spathe; tube about 1 in. long, rather thick; corona a very shallow cup with a crisped red edge, several times shorter than the broad obovate apiculate overlapping segms. France to Greece. Var. **radiiflorus,** Burb.

(*N. radiiflorus*, Salisb.), has narrower-based segms. not overlapping; also narrower and more erect crown and narrower lvs. Var. **ornatus**, Hort., is early-flowering, with broad and rounded overlapping segms. Var. **recurvus**, Voss, lvs. and segms. much recurved.

32. **ALSTRŒMERIA,** L. About 60 species, in S. Amer., grown in pots and also in the open for summer bloom.—Sts. mostly slender, leafy, often weak and even inclined to climb, from a root of thickened fibers not bulbous or rhizomatous: lvs. narrow, often twisted at base, more numerous on the sterile shoots: fls. showy, more or less lily-like, usually not over 2 in. long, red, yellow or purple and frequently spotted, in a terminal simple or compound umbel; perianth without tube, the limb somewhat irregular, the 2 series of segms. being slightly dissimilar and the lower segm. of the inner row mostly different from the other two; stamens inserted on base of segms., declined, often unequal, anthers relatively small and basifixed; ovary inferior, ovules many in each cell, one above the other, style slender and stigma 3-parted: caps. loculicidal, 3-valved. (Alstrœme-ria: Claus Alstrœmer, friend of Linnæus, who wrote somewhat on botany.)

A. Fls. yellow or orange, with brown spots....................1. *A. aurantiaca*
AA. Fls. red to purple or white.
  B. Outer segms. lilac with green tips, or white....................2. *A. Pelegrina*
  BB. Outer segms. reddish.
    C. Umbel about 5-fld., simple....................3. *A. psittacina*
    CC. Umbel 9–50-fld., compound.
      D. Lvs. lanceolate: fls. 9–12....................4. *A. hæmantha*
      DD. Lvs. obovate or spatulate: fls. 15–50....................5. *A. Ligtu*

1. **A. aurantiaca,** D. Don. Erect and slender, 2–4 ft. high: lvs. many, lanceolate, 3–4 in. long including the narrow petiole-like base, several-nerved, scattered on st. but whorled under umbel: fls. 10–30, in an umbel with branching rays or pedicels, orange with long brown spots on inner segms., about 1½ in. long above the ovary; outer segms. spatulate, inner ones narrower. Chile. Var. **lutea,** Hort., fls. clear yellow.—Hardy in northern states.

2. **A. Pelegrina,** L. St. stout, 9–24 in. long: lvs. lanceolate, ascending, 2–3 in. long: umbels branched; fls. lilac, the segms. 1½–2 in. long, the outer green toward tips, cordate, inner oblong-spatulate, freely spotted with maroon. Chile. Var. **alba,** Hort., fls. white and not spotted.

3. **A. psittacina,** Lehm. (*A. pulchella*, Hort. not L. f.). St. 20–30 in. long: lvs. lanceolate to oblong, 3 in. long: umbel simple, 5-fld.; fls. dark red, the segms. about 2 in. long, green-tipped, with brown-purple spots within, upper segm. obovate. Brazil.

4. **A. hæmantha,** Ruiz & Pav. (*A. Ligtu*, Hort.). St. 30 in. or more high: lvs. lanceolate, thin, ciliate, glaucous beneath, 3 in. long, dying at time of flowering: umbel compound, commonly 9–12-fld.; outer segms. about 2 in. long, oblong, acute, pink to bright red with green tips; inner oblanceolate, reddish-yellow with red-purple spots; stamens much shorter than segms. Chile.

5. **A. Ligtu,** L. (*A. chilensis*, Hort.). St. stout, 3–5 ft. tall: lvs. scattered, spatulate or obovate, ciliate, somewhat glaucous: fls. 15–50 to an umbel; segms. rose or red to orange, 2 in. long, the 2 uppermost marked with deep purple. Chile.

33. **BOMAREA,** Mirbel (*Collania*, Herb.). About 90 species of tender per. usually twining herbs of American tropics from Mex. to Chile.—Closely allied to Alstrœmeria, differing primarily in outer 3 perianth-segms. shorter than inner, sts. usually twining, infl. commonly umbellate, pendulous or the fls. drooping, and rootstock often tuberous. (Boma-rea: French botanist, J. C. W. de Bomare, 1731–1807.)

B. Caldasii, Aschers. & Graebn. (*Alstrœmeria Caldasii*, HBK. *B. Caldasiana*, Herb.). Sts. twining to 4 ft.: lvs. 3–6 in. long, oblong, acute, spreading, glaucous, puberulent beneath, petioled: infl. a 6–30-fld. simple umbel subtended by many lanceolate bracts, pedicels 1–2 in. long, pilose; fls. with reddish-brown outer segms. about 1 in. long and bright yellow inner segms. about 1½ in. long. (Named for Francisco José de Caldas, 1771–1816, Spanish botanist in S. Amer.) Guatemala to Bolivia.—An allied and more showy species from Ecuador, known in the trade as *B. patacocensis*, is **B. racemosa,** Killip, with scarlet fls. to 3 in. long in a many-fld. very short raceme.

34. **HYPOXIS, L.** STAR-GRASS. Small herbs, of about 50 species.—Rootstocks corm-like or tuberous: lvs. 3–20, sessile, plane, basal: sts. shorter than lvs., usually pilose: fls. rather small, on few-fld. scapes; tube short; outer segms. lanceolate, inner oblong; anthers basifixed; ovary inferior, 3-celled, style short, stigmas 3, erect: caps. membranous, indehiscent. (Hypox-is: old Greek name, of no application here.)

H. hirsuta, Cov. (*Ornithogalum hirsutum,* L. *H. erecta,* L.). Corm less than 1 in. thick: lvs. 4–24 in. long, to ⅓in. wide, hairy: sts. to 1 ft. high, 2–7-fld.: perianth-segms. ¼–⅔in. long, yellow. N. H. and Man. to Fla. and Tex.

35. **CURCULIGO,** Gaertn. A dozen species in tropics of both hemispheres, one or two grown as foliage plants in greenhouses and conservatories.—Stemless, with short more or less tuberous rhizome: lvs. from the crown, long, plicate, firm, sometimes split or divided longitudinally into 2 lobes: fls. small and inconspicuous, in dense heads or spikes near the ground and mostly concealed by the foliage; perianth with 6 nearly or quite equal spreading segms. on a long beak-like projection of the ovary; stamens inserted on base of segms., filaments short, anthers attached at or near the base; ovary inferior, ovules 2 to many in each cell, style short and columnar, bearing 3 stigmas: fr. more or less fleshy, indehiscent. (Curcu-ligo: Latin *curculio,* a weevil, from the beaked ovary.)

C. capitulata, Kuntze (*Leucojum capitulatum,* Lour. *C. recurvata,* Dry.). Lvs. 1–3 ft. long and 2–6 in. broad, entire, plaited, the blade recurving, petiole long and channelled: scapes mostly shorter than petioles, often scarcely rising above the crown, brown-hairy, recurved or bent downward at the end; fls. yellow, about ¾in. across. Trop. Asia, Australia. — **C. latifolia,** Dry., has a very short-stalked erect rather than recurved infl.: lvs. 1–2 ft. long, 1–5 in. broad, curving, graceful and decorative; Asia.

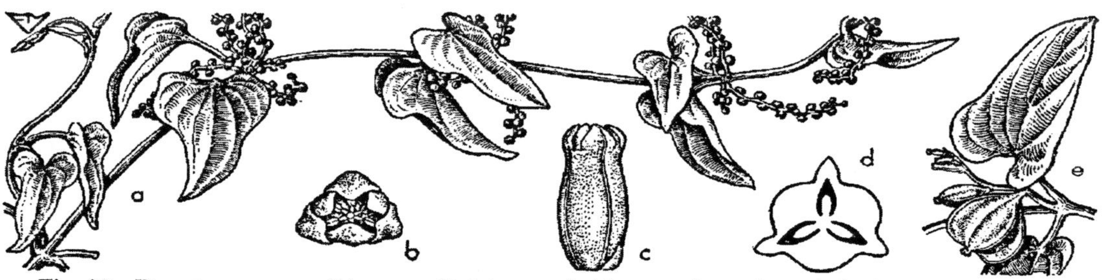

Fig. 36. Dioscoreaceæ. *Dioscorea Batatas:* a, habit, staminate branch in bud, × ½; b, staminate flower, × 5; c, pistillate flower, × 5; d, ovary, cross-section, × 20; e, fruit, × ½. (b–d redrawn from LeMaout and Decaisne.)

36. DIOSCOREACEÆ. YAM FAMILY

Ten genera and more than 600 species, most of them in the genus Dioscorea, widely spread in temp. and trop. regions around the world, constitute this family; several of the species are cult. for their large edible subterranean and aërial tubers, yielding important staple food materials in warm countries; a few are grown for ornament.—Vines, prevailingly herbaceous, most of them twining, a few merely procumbent: lvs. alternate or opposite, broad and petiolate, entire or digitate, with a middle vein and strong side veins from the base of the blade, netted-veined, the lvs. therefore among the exceptions in the monocotyledons: fls. small, in spikes or racemes, diclinous, the plants monœcious or diœcious, but in one tribe bisexual; perianth regular, of 6 parts in 2 series but not clearly differentiated into calyx and corolla, in fertile fls. adherent to the ovary; stamens 6 or sometimes 3; ovary 3-celled or with 3 placentæ, 1 or 2 of the compartments sometimes abortive; styles 3, distinct: fr. a 3-winged or strongly 3-angled caps. or flattened when only 1 cell develops, or sometimes baccate.—Aside from Dioscorea, the genus **Rajania,** with a half dozen species in the W. Indies, yields species with large tubers; **R. pleioneura,** Griseb., is probably best known; it bears large cockscombed aërial tubers and cordate-ovate 9-nerved cuspidate lvs.: fr. with broad wing. The genus differs in having a flat fr., only 1 carpel developing.

DIOSCOREA, L. Yam. Distributed in both eastern and western hemispheres, numerous in the tropics and subtropics; in the N. U. S. one species (*D. villosa,* L.) is native, and this has several segregates.—Fr. a 3-celled caps. with 2 winged seeds in each cell: fls. diclinous. (Dioscore-a: dedicated to Dioscorides, Greek physician and naturalist, A. D., 1st or 2nd century.)—Aside from the following species grown for the edible tubers, certain others have been cult. under glass for ornamental foliage, but it is doubtful whether they are known in this country; other species of yams are also grown in the tropics for food. The word yam is also applied to the sweet potato.

A. St. terete or somewhat angled, wingless: lvs. entire.
  B. Lvs. mainly opposite.
    C. Base of lf. deeply cordate, not angled or lobed: no aërial tubers................1. *D. cayenensis*
    CC. Base of lf. angle-lobed, more or less halberd-shaped: bearing small seed-like aërial tubers................2. *D. Batatas*
  BB. Lvs. mainly alternate.
    C. Axillary tubers present: lvs. glabrous................3. *D. bulbifera*
    CC. Axillary tubers absent: lvs. pubescent beneath................4. *D. villosa*
AA. St. sharply angled or winged.
  B. Lvs. deeply lobed................5. *D. trifida*
  BB. Lvs. entire................6. *D. alata*

1. **D. cayenensis,** Lam. YELLOW OR ATTOTO YAM. St. terete or angular, glabrous, usually prickly toward base, without tubers in axils: lvs. usually opposite, ovate to oblong-ovate, deeply cordate at base, abruptly short-pointed, entire, 7–9-nerved, 3–5 in. long: racemes 2 or more in the axil, simple, the anthers 6. W. Afr.; nat. W. Indies to Brazil.

2. **D. Batatas,** Decne. CHINESE YAM; when grown for ornament in the N. (the root being hardy) the plant is known as CINNAMON-VINE. Tubers long and deep in the ground (sometimes 2–3 ft. long), therefore difficult to dig: st. more or less angled, sometimes twisted, glabrous, bearing small rounded bulblet-like tubers in the axils: lvs. opposite, ovate or deltoid in outline, cuspidate at apex, usually strongly broadened and angled at base, 7–9-nerved, 1½–3 in. long: fls. sessile in 1 or 2 simple raceme-like spikes from the axils, cinnamon-scented. (Batatas: *potato;* see *Ipomœa Batatas.*) China.

3. **D. bulbifera,** L. AIR POTATO. Root tubers small or none: tall strong glabrous vine, st. terete, bearing in the axils large angular tubers often 1 ft. long and weighing several pounds: lvs. alternate, cordate-ovate, cuspidate, 7–9-nerved, 3–6 in. long, petiole longer than blade, margin entire: fls. in numerous slender panicled drooping axillary spikes 3–4 in. long. Trop. Asia, Malaya, and Philippines.—Grown sometimes for the aërial tubers.

4. **D. villosa,** L. Rootstock slender, elongate, rarely forked, with few more slender lateral branches; st. glabrous, subterete: lvs. usually alternate but lower sometimes in 2's or 4's, broadly ovate with heart-shaped base, more or less pubescent beneath, 2–6 in. long, 9–13-nerved, petioles often longer than the blades: fls. greenish-yellow, the staminate in drooping panicles 3–6 in. long, the pistillate in drooping spicate racemes: caps. membranous, ½–1 in. long, strongly 3-winged. R. I. to Minn., Fla. and Tex.

5. **D. trifida,** L. f. CUSH-CUSH. YAMPEE. Tubers rather small, but of superior quality: st. glabrous, sharply angled or narrowly winged, often twisted, not tuber-bearing: lvs. large, very broad in outline, truncate or nearly so at base, 4–10 in. long, 3–5-lobed to the middle or lower, strongly 7–9-nerved, the middle lobe 3-nerved, the lateral lobes sometimes partially lobed at base: staminate fls. in slender and simple racemes, the pistillate in spikes. S. Amer.; cult. and spontaneous in W. Indies.

6. **D. alata,** L. Root tubers very large, reaching 6–8 ft. in length: st. climbing, 4-winged or sharply 4-angled, often with small axillary bulb-like tubers: lvs. opposite, cordate-ovate to cordate-oblong, with deep basal sinus, sharply acuminate, 4–8 in. long, 7–9-nerved: staminate fls. in narrow axillary panicles 8–12 in. long, green; pistillate fls. in simple spikes: caps. leathery, elliptic, 3-winged. India to Malaya; cult. for the subterranean tubers, and run wild.

37. IRIDACEÆ. IRIS FAMILY

About 90 genera and 1,200 species comprise the Iris family, which is represented in temp. and trop. regions around the world; many of the choicest hort. plants are included, as irises, gladioli, freesias, and crocuses; all are per., usually with rhizomes, corms, or bulbs.—Herbs, at least the cult. species, mostly low plants with simple or branching sts. (in Crocus the st. not rising above the ground), mostly basal and equitant parallel-veined linear or sword-shaped lvs.: fls. showy, bisexual, issuing from a spathe of usually 2 or more herbaceous or scarious bracts; perianth of 6 parts in 2 series, the outer 3 often calyx-like, all generally connate into a tube that is adnate to the ovary; stamens 3, with extrorse anthers, opposite the outer perianth-segms.; pistil 1, with inferior mostly 3-celled ovary, single style and 3 stigmas which are sometimes expanded and petal-like or divided, placentation typically axile: fr. a loculicidal few- to many-seeded caps.

Fig. 37. IRIDACEÆ. A, *Gladiolus tristis:* Aa, inflorescence, × ¼; Ab, flower, × ¼; Ac, same vertical section, × ¼. B, *Crocus susianus:* plant with flower, vertical section, × ½. C, *Freesia refracta:* Ca, inflorescence, × ½; Cb, flower, vertical section, × ½; Cc, ovary, cross-section, × 5. D, *Iris Xiphium:* inflorescence, × ½. E, *Iris germanica:* flower, × ¼ (b beard, f fall, p.t. perianth-tube, sp spathe, std standard, stg stigma-branch.) F, *Iris sibirica:* capsule, × ½.

A. Fls. sessile on a corm, or the peduncle wholly subterranean; no aërial fl.-st. or scape evident but fls. with very long perianth-tube........................ 1. CROCUS
AA. Fls. not as above, plant with a definite fl.-st. or scape.
B. Perianth-tube none or very short.
C. Roots from a bulb or corm.
D. Filaments free.. 2. IRIS
DD. Filaments connate into a tube, at least basally so.
E. Style-branches deeply 3-parted.................................. 3. TIGRIDIA
EE. Style-branches shortly 2-fid with crests that overtop the anthers..... 4. MORÆA

cc. Roots from a rhizome.
  D. Style-branches deeply divided.
    E. Branches of style winged and more or less petaloid................ 2. IRIS
    EE. Branches of style not winged or petaloid........................ 5. NEOMARICA
  DD. Style-branches undivided.
    E. Infl. umbellate, not coarsely branched (but fls. may be in several peduncled or sessile spathes); fls. mostly ¾ in. or less across.......... 6. SISYRINCHIUM
    EE. Infl. coarsely and dichotomously branched (each branch several-fld.); fls. 1½ in. or more across, not in umbels..................... 7. BELAMCANDA
BB. Perianth with a distinct tube.
  C. Fl. regular, the perianth-tube straight or essentially so; stamens equidistant one from the other.
    D. Roots from a rhizome, or fibrous, conspicuously thickened and fleshy.
      E. Style-branches petaloid and divided............................ 2 IRIS
      EE. Style-branches not petaloid, undivided, clavate................ 8. SCHIZOSTYLIS
    DD. Roots from a bulb or corm.
      E. Style-branches undivided.
        F. Branches of style linear.. 9. IXIA
        FF. Branches of style cuneate or clavate.
          G. Anthers spirally twisted; fls. few............................10. STREPTANTHERA
          GG. Anthers not spirally twisted; fls. many......................11. DIERAMA
      EE. Style-branches 2-fid
        F. Number of fls. usually more than 1 to a spathe, stalked, the style-branches petaloid.. 2. IRIS
        FF. Number of fls. never more than 1 to a spathe, sessile or nearly so; style-branches not petaloid.
          G. Tube of perianth slender throughout; filaments very short......12. LAPEIROUSIA
          GG. Tube of perianth much enlarging and dilated above the base.
            H. Spathes oblong to lanceolate, long: fls. borne on erect rachises.13. WATSONIA
            HH. Spathes ovate, short: fls. secund, or on a sidewise rachis......14. FREESIA
  CC. Fl. irregular or the perianth-limb oblique and tube more or less curved; stamens usually more or less together on one side.
    D. Lvs. plicate in bud, hairy..15. BABIANA
    DD. Lvs. not plicate in bud, glabrous.
      E. Spathe-valves fimbriate or lacerate at apex........................16. SPARAXIS
      EE. Spathe-valves not fimbriate (may be divided).
        F. Perianth-tube constricted near or below middle into a narrowly cylindrical or filiform basal part.................................17. CHASMANTHE
        FF. Perianth-tube tapering gradually from base to throat.
          G. Tube of perianth curved; fls. large, often 3–6 in. across..........18. GLADIOLUS
          GG. Tube of perianth straight; fls. usually less than 2 in. across.
            H. The perianth-tube very slenderly cylindrical, longer than lobes: spathe-valve green...19. ACIDANTHERA
            HH. The perianth-tube dilated apically or funnelform, usually shorter than lobes: spathe-valve brown.
              I. Caps. oblong to ovoid: spathe-valves (or the outer one) emarginate...20. TRITONIA
              II. Caps. globose, inflated: spathe-valves entire or 2-fid.......21. CROCOSMIA

1. **CROCUS**, L. Well-known earliest spring "bulbs," also several autumn-blooming kinds, opening in sunshine, from the Medit. region and S. W. Asia; probably 75 species; many species have been grown by fanciers, but the common crocuses are not more than 8 or 10.—Corm globose or depressed, tunicated: st. none above ground, the fls. produced at the surface among the linear grass-like lvs., or preceding them, which lengthen after blooming, or after the lvs. in the case of autumn-blooming kinds: spathes of two kinds, not always present, basal spathe between lvs. and scape, and proper spathes (2) from base of ovary covering the young bud, the inner ligulate one absent in some species: fls. white, yellow, lilac to deep purple, with a long slender tube that raises the expanded part above ground; segms. 6, nearly or quite equal; stamens 3, included, inserted in throat of tube; ovary 3-celled, many-ovuled; style long, the 3 stigmas generally one of three types, wedge-shaped, lacerate, or of linear forked branches: caps. small, mostly oblong, loculicidal, ripening at or beneath the surface. (Cro-cus: Greek name of the saffron, *Crocus sativus.*)

A. Plants blooming in autumn.
  B. Style-branches wedge-shaped, entire or only toothed (if fimbriate see BB).
    C. Fls. with style-branches blood-red, much exceeding stamens, usually drooping.. 1. *C. sativus*
    CC. Fls. with style-branches deep yellow to orange, about equalling stamens, usually erect or only arching................................ 2. *C. Salzmannii*
  BB. Style-branches irregularly forked, branched, or apically fimbriated.
    C. Fls. rose-pink to lilac with orange-spotted throat.
      D. Anthers orange; style-branches very slender, apically forked......... 2. *C. Salzmannii*
      DD. Anthers creamy-white; style-branches stout, apically fimbriate...... 3. *C. Kotschyanus*
    CC. Fls. lilac veined blue, not spotted in throat........................ 4. *C. speciosus*

AA. Plants blooming in spring.
  B. Fls. yellow, at least on the inside.
    C. Style-branches pale yellow, shorter than stamens; perianth cup-shaped, segms. suborbicular, obtuse, uniformly colored.................... 5. *C. mæsiacus*
    CC. Style-branches orange-red, exceeding stamens; perianth star-like, segms. ovate, acute, outer ones flushed or striped brown without............ 6. *C. susianus*
  BB. Fls. purple, lilac or white.
    C. Segms. of perianth bicolored without, the outer ones stramineous (or veined purplish) and inner ones rose-purple........................ 7. *C. Imperati*
    CC. Segms. of perianth unicolored without or differing only in presence or absence of stripes or venation.
      D. Throat of perianth yellow or orange within.
        E. Perianth-throat bearded: basal spathe absent.................. 8. *C. biflorus*
        EE. Perianth-throat beardless: basal spathe present................. 9. *C. Sieberi*
      DD. Throat of perianth not yellow or orange within.
        E. Lvs. tapering at each end: perianth-segms. obtuse, usually striped.. 10. *C. vernus*
        EE. Lvs. linear, not tapering at ends: perianth-segms. acute, not striped.11. *C. Tomasinianus*

1. **C. sativus,** L. Saffron Crocus. Autumn flowering: corms about 1¼ in. across, globose: lvs. numerous, narrowly linear, usually 1–1½ ft. long after blooming, ciliate, gray-green: proper spathe 2-valved: fls. lilac, reddish-purple or white, throat of same color and pubescent, fragrant; perianth-segms. 1½–2 in. long, obtuse; anthers yellow, exceeding filaments; style-branches blood-red, cuneate and toothed, drooping or lying on the perianth, much exceeding the stamens: caps. not produced. Not now known in the wild, believed to have originated in Asia Minor.—The prominent style-branches yield saffron, a yellow dye of decreasing commercial importance, used in coloring medicinal preparations and food-stuffs; not to be confused with Safflower (*Carthamus tinctorius*).

2. **C. Salzmannii,** J. Gay. Autumn flowering: corms to 2 in. across, depressed-globose, tunics of parallel fibers: lvs. 5–6, narrowly linear: proper spathe 1-valved: fls. pale lilac with yellowish throat; perianth-segms. nearly 2 in. long, broadly oblong, subobtuse; stamens orange, anthers exceeding filaments; style-branches orange, forked, slender, about equalling or scarcely exceeding the stamens. (Named for Philipp Salzmann, page 51.) Spain, Tangiers.

3. **C. Kotschyanus,** Koch (*C. zonatus*, J. Gay). Autumn flowering: corms to 3 in. across, flattened, with 2–3 irregular protuberances, tunics membranous: lvs. appearing after the fls., linear, 1–1½ ft. long and to nearly ¼in. wide, glabrous: fls. rose-purple to lilac with ring of orange spots in throat; perianth-segms. to 2 in. long, oblong, subobtuse, veined deep purple basally within; anthers pale cream-colored, exceeding the pale yellow filaments; style-branches basically cuneate but markedly fimbriate apically, yellow, forked, exceeding the stamens. (Named for its discoverer, Theodor Kotschy, page 46.) Lebanon, Cilicia.—The name *C. zonatus*, although more widely established in the literature, was given the plant several years after it had been validly named *C. Kotschyanus*.

4. **C. speciosus,** Bieb. Autumn flowering: corms depressed-globose, to 1¼ in. diam., tunics membranous, not extending to base of corm: lvs. 4–5, about 1 ft. long in spring: proper spathe 2-valved, very long: fls. bluish-lilac, finely veined dark blue within and dotted dark blue without; perianth-segms. to 2 in. long, broadly oblong, acute or obtuse; anthers deep yellow, the white filaments one-half as long; style-branches scarlet, much-branched but tips often cuneate, exceeding the stamens. S. E. Eu. to Asia Minor and Iran. Var. **Aitchisonii,** Hort., has fls. larger, to 3½ in. long, pale lavender veined blue, and is later flowering.

5. **C. mæsiacus,** Ker (*C. aureus*, Sibth. & Smith). Spring flowering: corms depressed-globose, about 1 in. diam., tunics of matted fibers: lvs. narrowly linear, exceeding the fls., usually about 5 in number: proper spathe usually 2-valved: fls. bright yellow, cup-shaped; perianth-segms. 1¼–1½ in. long, suborbicular to ovate-triangular, subobtuse to rounded; anthers pale yellow, hastate at base, filaments yellow, slightly shorter than anthers; style-branches pale yellow, fimbriate with narrowly cuneate tips. Greece, Serbia to W. Asia Minor.—Long cult. and sometimes known as "Dutch crocus" although not from Holland. The plant is frequently given in literature as *C. aureus*, a name antedated by *C. mæsiacus*, the latter the original spelling for Moesia, classical name of Serbia.

6. **C. susianus,** Ker. Cloth-of-Gold Crocus. Spring flowering: corms to ¾in. diam., ovoid, tunics of netted fibers: lvs. 5–6, narrowly linear: proper spathe 2-valved: fls. bright yellow within, star-like; perianth-segms. ovate, acute, outer ones usually flushed or striped chocolate-brown outside; filaments shorter than the orange anthers; style-branches orange-red, broadly cuneate, spreading, exceeding the stamens. Caucasus south to Crimea.

7. **C. Imperati,** Ten. Spring flowering: corms large, with fibered tunics: lvs. 4–6, as long as fls., narrowly linear: proper spathe usually 2-valved, but 1-valved in some variants: fls. bright lilac within, almost saucer-shaped when fully opened and to 3½ in. across; outer perianth-segms. oblong, acute, buff-colored outside and finely veined purple, inner ones ovate, obtuse, pale rose-purple in color; filaments orange, shorter than the yellow anthers; style-branches only 3, simple, fimbriate apically, bright scarlet. (Named for Ferrante Imperate, an Italian botanist of the late 16th century.) Italy.

8. **C. biflorus,** Mill. Spring flowering: corms small, globose, tunics thick-membranous, not covering lower third: lvs. 4–6, overtopping fls., narrowly linear: proper spathe 2-valved, basal spathe absent: fls. large, white with purple venation and feathering especially on the outer perianth-segms., the throat hairy, flushed yellow; stamens orange; style-branches simple, cuneate, orange-red. Italy to S. W. Asia.—One variant was formerly called "Scotch crocus" although not from Scotland.

9. **C. Sieberi,** J. Gay. Spring flowering: corms less than 1 in. diam., globose, tunics of stout netted fibers: lvs. 4–6, broadly linear, about equalling fls.: proper spathe 2-valved, basal spathe present: fls. clear lilac with orange-yellow throat; perianth-segms. 1–1½ in. long, oblong, obtuse or bluntly acute; stamens orange; style-branches cuneate, nearly entire, orange-red. (Named for Fr. W. Sieber, page 51.) Greece, Crete.

10. **C. vernus,** Wulfen (*C. officinalis* var. *vernus*, L.). Spring flowering: corms about 1 in. diam., globose, tunics of netted fibers: lvs. broadly linear, about as long as fls., tapering at ends: proper spathe 1-valved: fls. lilac or white, often striped purple, throat pubescent; perianth-segms. 1–1½ in. long, obtuse; white filaments shorter than lemon-yellow anthers; style-branches entire or fringed, orange-scarlet. S. and Cent. Eu.—One of the commonest garden crocuses. By some authors *C. vernus* is not considered distinct from *C. albiflorus*, Kit., and when combined the latter name, being the older, must be used.

11. **C. Tomasinianus,** Herb. (*C. vernus* var. *Tommasinianus*, Baker). Spring flowering: corms about ¾in. diam., globose, tunics of finely netted fibers: lvs. narrowly linear, not tapering at ends: proper spathe 1-valved: fls. lilac, star-shaped, throat hairy; perianth-segms. to nearly 2 in. long, narrowly oblong, acute; anthers pale orange, somewhat longer than white filaments; style-branches shorter than stamens, cuneate, entire, bright orange. (Named for M. Van Tomasini, 1794–1879, botanist of Trieste.) Bosnia, Dalmatia.

2. **IRIS,** L. IRIS. FLEUR-DE-LIS. Probably upward of 150 species, in the north temp. zone; several species are well known garden plants and many others are prized by fanciers; mostly spring and early summer bloomers; perennials.—Plants with rhizomes or bulbs: st. erect, simple or branched, bearing 1 to several fls. at its top, the fls. mostly of short duration, one following another: lvs. mostly radical and basal but usually a few on the st., linear to sword-shaped, flat, equitant or flexuously grass-like, many-nerved lengthwise: fls. showy, in many colors, borne in "heads," a term used to denote the issue from each spathe or pair of bracts, one fl. following another, but sometimes only 1 fl. is borne and in some kinds the infl. is clearly racemose or paniculate; each of the bracts is known as a spathe-valve; segms. of fl. generally united into a long or short tube; 3 outer segms. hanging or reflexed, known as "falls," in many species bearded on part of upper surface, narrowed toward the base to a "haft"; 3 inner usually erect and often arched, known as "standards" and narrowed to a "claw" (in fanciers' descriptions the standards are described, according to their position, as flat, arching, domed or over-arched, conic, cupped, floppy, tips appressed); 3 style-branches expanded, colored and petal-like, outwardly spreading and covering the 3 stamens, bifid or crested at the tip beyond the stigmatic part beneath; ovary 3-celled, many-ovuled, sessile or pedicelled within the spathe: caps. oblong, 3- or 6-angled, many-seeded. (I-ris: Greek *the rainbow.*)—Numbers of irises are grown by fanciers and specialists, many being cultural forms and hybrids. The commonest species and the main groups are included in this treatment. The lilac and purple irises of yards are known as "blue flags."

A. Rootstock a bulb.
  B. Inner perianth-segms. (standards) small, often minute, spreading or deflexed: bulb with fleshy roots remaining attached during dormant period. (JUNO.)
    C. St. very short or none: fls. with lateral wings on haft of falls. . . . . 1. *I. persica*
    CC. St. 3–15 in. long, sometimes obscured by crowded lvs.: fls. in axils of st.-lvs., the narrow haft of falls not winged.
      D. Lvs. with conspicuous horny edge: fls. white with broad yellow blade of falls. . . . . 2. *I. bucharica*
      DD. Lvs. without horny edge: fls. golden-yellow to white. . . . . 3. *I. orchioides*
  BB. Inner perianth-segms. large, erect; stamens free from style-branches: bulb with fleshy roots not persisting during dormant period. (XIPHIUM.)
    C. St. very short or none: lvs. acutely quadrangular. . . . . 4. *I. reticulata*
    CC. St. 1 ft. or more long: lvs. not quadrangular.
      D. Perianth-tube 1–2 in. long. . . . . 5. *I. tingitana*
      DD. Perianth-tube very short or none.
        E. Falls with fiddle-shaped haft, separated from blade by a somewhat constricted neck. . . . . 6. *I. Xiphium*
        EE. Falls with a wedge-shaped haft, not separated from blade by a constricted neck. . . . . 7. *I. xiphioides*

AA. Rootstock a short thick or a slender rhizome.
B. Outer perianth-segms. (falls) with fringed petal-like crest on the claw and lower part of blade. (EVANSIA.)
C. Spathes with 1 valve only: fls. on very slender wiry pedicels 1–2 in. long.... 8. *I. gracilipes*
CC. Spathes with 2 valves: pedicels not as above.
D. St. very short or none, exceeded by the lvs.: plants dwarf.
E. Perianth-tube very slender, exceeding the spathe-valves; blade of falls obovate........ 9. *I. cristata*
EE. Perianth-tube expanded above, not exceeding spathe-valves; blade of falls cuneate........10. *I. lacustris*
DD. St. evident, equalling or exceeding lvs.: plants large.
E. Spathe about as long as pedicel or only slightly exceeding it: lvs. persisting through winter........11. *I. japonica*
EE. Spathe much exceeding the pedicel: lvs. produced in spring, not winter-persisting........12. *I. tectorum*
BB. Outer perianth-segms. not bearded at all or with beard an aggregation of thick multicellular hairs.
C. Falls bearded with multicellular hairs.
D. Beard very widely scattered over the haft of the fall: fls. solitary: lvs. about ¾in. wide and 6–9 in. long. (ONCOCYCLUS.)........13. *I. susiana*
DD. Beard linear to oblong, confined to a definite and usually narrow line: sts. usually 2- to many-fld. (1-fld. in no. 16).
E. The falls and standards both bearded: rhizome spreading by stolons: seeds with a large cream-colored circular collar-like aril. (REGELIA.).14. *I. Hoogiana*
EE. The falls only bearded: rhizome not usually stoloniferous: seeds usually without cream-colored aril. (POGONIRIS.)
F. Plants dwarf, sts. less than 1 ft. high and sometimes wanting.
G. Perianth-tube to ¼in. long or none: rhizome slender, stoloniferous: sts. 1–4 in. high........15. *I. flavissima*
GG. Perianth-tube ½in. long or more.
H. St. obsolete or very short........16. *I. pumila*
HH. St. 1–10 in. long.
I. Spathes with both valves acutely keeled........17. *I. Reichenbachii*
II. Spathes with only 1 valve partially keeled, or neither keeled .18. *I. Chamæiris*
FF. Plants with prominent sts., mostly 1 ft. high or more.
G. Fl.-sts. about equalling the lvs.
H. Spathe-valves wholly green or partially flushed purple when fls. first open, at least not scarious........19. *I. variegata*
HH. Spathe-valves partially scarious when fls. first open........21. *I. Kochii*
GG. Fl.-sts. exceeding and overtopping the lvs.
H. Spathe-valves wholly silvery-scarious in bud and at flowering: fls. mostly pale purple to lilac........22. *I. pallida*
HH. Spathe-valves green or only partly scarious.
I. Fls. bright lemon-yellow with beard deep yellow........23. *I. flavescens*
II. Fls. not wholly yellow throughout........20. *I. germanica*
CC. Falls without a beard or crest, sometimes pubescent.
D. Sts. branching regularly and forming a raceme: seeds conspicuously winged. (PARDANTHOPSIS.)........24. *I. dichotoma*
DD. Sts. not forking more than once, nor infl. a true raceme: seeds not conspicuously winged. (APOGON.)
E. Lvs. ensiform and generally much more than ½in. wide (if lvs. ensiform and less than ½in. wide, see under EE.)
F. Plants dwarf, not over 8 in. high: fls. deep violet........25. *I. verna*
FF. Plants large, over 1 ft. high.
G. Cauline lvs. several and long.
H. Fls. yellow, or brick red to reddish-brown.
I. Color of fls. deep yellow........31. *I. Pseudacorus*
II. Color of fls. brick-red to reddish-brown........32. *I. fulva*
HH. Fls. in shades of blue, lilac, purple or white.
I. Standards minute, setose: seeds with conspicuous raphe down one side........28. *I. setosa*
II. Standards at least half as long as falls, not setose: seeds with an inconspicuous raphe or none.
J. St. flattened with an acutely keeled flange down each edge.39. *I. graminea*
JJ. St. terete or essentially so.
K. Fl.-pedicel to 1 in. long or scarcely apparent: falls 3–5 in. long: seeds covered by a thickened corky husk . . .33. *I. hexagona*
KK. Fl.-pedicel 1½ in. long or more: falls 1¾–3 in. long: seeds various.
L. Outer spathe-valves frequently foliaceous: seeds with dull corky covering: standards oblanceolate to spatulate, longer and broader in proportion to falls........26. *I. virginica*
LL. Outer spathe-valves rarely foliaceous: seeds glossy: standards lanceolate, short and narrow in proportion to falls........27. *I. versicolor*
GG. Cauline lvs. 1–4, much reduced.
H. St. hollow.
I. Standards erect........48. *I. sanguinea*
II. Standards divergent or ascending........51. *I. Delavayi*
HH. St. solid.

I. Fls. inconspicuous, not at all showy, mostly dull brownish-purple: seeds scarlet, showy, persistent in ripened caps...60. *I. fœtidissima*
II. Fls. showy: seeds not scarlet-red nor persistent in caps.
J. Ovary 3-angled, but no intermediate vertical ribs present: stigma-branches not toothed beneath the crests.
K. Standards ¾in. long or less........................28. *I. setosa*
KK. Standards 2 in. long or more.
L. Lf. with raised midrib: standards shorter than falls..29. *I. Kaempferi*
LL. Lf. smooth: standards as long as falls...............30. *I. lævigata*
JJ. Ovary with 2 vertical ridges at each of its 3 angles: stigma-branches with a sharp projecting point beneath each of its 2 crests.
K. Blade of fall very small, extending horizontally: sts. shorter than lvs...38. *I. halophila*
KK. Blade of fall large and drooping: sts. longer than lvs.
L. Fall with blade long-oblong, margin wavy; fls. rich golden-yellow..35. *I. crocea*
LL. Fall with blade ovate or rounded, margin not wavy; fls. not as above but may be pale yellow.
M. Fls. blue-purple: seed-coats firm to the seed......34. *I. spuria*
MM. Fls. white to pale yellow: seed-coats very loose.
N. Color of fls. uniformly pale yellow.............36. *I. Monnieri*
NN. Color of fls. white with blade of falls blotched golden-yellow..37. *I. orientalis*
EE. Lvs. linear, generally less than ½in. wide.
F. Foliage flushed or tinged pink, red, or purple at base and becoming reddish-brown on dying: sts. solid.
G. St. usually branched.
H. Spathes scarious (sometimes herbaceous basally or along keel): perianth-tube spreading immediately above ovary.........40. *I. tenuis*
HH. Spathes wholly herbaceous: perianth-tube linear for some distance above ovary..41. *I. Douglasiana*
GG. St. simple.
H. Species with sts. almost completely covered with short inflated bract-like lvs.
I. Perianth-tube narrowly cylindrical above ovary; stigmas truncately flattened..42. *I. Purdyi*
II. Perianth-tube becoming funnelform immediately above ovary; stigmas tongue-shaped.......................43. *I. bracteata*
HH. Species with sts. having few lvs. that do not at all cover sts.: plants usually 5–15 in. high.
I. Spathe-valves distant one from the other (alternate): perianth-tube ⅓in. long or less...............................44. *I. tenax*
II. Spathe-valves opposite: perianth-tube usually ½–3¼ in. long.
J. Perianth-tube ½–1¼ in. long: spathe-valves ovate......45. *I. innominata*
JJ. Perianth-tube 2–3½ in. long: spathe-valves linear-lanceolate...46. *I. chrysophylla*
FF. Foliage green to base or becoming whitish basally, or if reddish-pink the sts. hollow, becoming yellowish-brown on dying.
G. St. hollow (walls may be thick with small channel, or thin with large channel).
H. Standards erect or nearly so.
I. Lf. glossy above and dull beneath: fls. yellow.............49. *I. Forrestii*
II. Lf. dull green on both sides: fls. usually violet-purple or white.
J. Fls. raised well above foliage; pedicels of unequal length: caps. short, scarcely twice as long as wide; seeds thin and flat..47. *I. sibirica*
JJ. Fls. overtopped by foliage; pedicels subequal: caps. about three times as long as wide; seeds thick, subcubical.....48. *I. sanguinea*
HH. Standards divergent, midway between erect and horizontal.
I. Lf. glossy green above, dull beneath.......................50. *I. Bulleyana*
II. Lf. dull green or glaucescent on both sides.
J. Height of sts. 3–4½ ft., much exceeding the lvs...........51. *I. Delavayi*
JJ. Height of sts. 1–2 ft., about as long as the lvs.
K. Fl.-pedicels ¼–2 in. long; fls. deep reddish-purple, veined golden-yellow..........................52. *I. chrysographes*
KK. Fl.-pedicels 1½–5 in. long; fls. yellow...............53. *I. Wilsonii*
GG. St. solid.
H. Perianth-tube 4–9 in. long; backs of style-branches as if dusted with gold (due to presence of minute raised glandular processes)..54. *I. unguicularis*
HH. Perianth-tube less than 1½ in. long; style-branches not as above.
I. Spathe-valves entirely scarious........................55. *I. prismatica*
II. Spathe-valves green and herbaceous.
J. Tube of perianth ½–1 in. long: plants 5–10 in. high......56. *I. ruthenica*
JJ. Tube of perianth mostly less than ½in. long: plants usually 1–3 ft. high.

K. Cauline lvs. exceeding the st. (1 ft. or more long): sts. flattened, keeled acutely down each edge .... 39. *I. graminea*
KK. Cauline lvs. much reduced or shorter than st.: sts. terete or essentially so.
L. Ovary long-cylindrical, with 6 equidistant vertical ribs .... 57. *I. ensata*
LL. Ovary cylindrical, 3-angled.
M. Basal lvs. shorter than sts.................... 58. *I. missouriensis*
MM. Basal lvs. longer than sts...................... 59. *I. longipetala*

1. **I. persica,** L. PERSIAN IRIS. Grown in pots and also lifted and carried over winter: bulb 1 in. or less diam., the fleshy roots persisting when dormant: st. none or very short: head 1 and mostly 1-fld., valves colorless veined green and 2–3 in. long: lvs. few in a basal tuft, linear, recurved, only 2 or 3 in. long at flowering time but elongating to 6 in.: fls. pale lilac, tube 2–3 in. long; falls 2–2½ in. long, with orbicular emarginate blade ½in. broad, purple-blotched at top, orange-keeled, purple-lined and spotted; haft auricled at top; standards about ¾in. long, white shaded pale blue, spreading: caps. 1½–2 in. long, tapering at each end, trigonal. Asia Minor, Iran.—Long cult., with several color variations.

2. **I. bucharica,** M. Foster. Half hardy: bulb subglobose, to 2 in. diam., fleshy roots persisting when dormant: st. 12–18 in. high, jointed, bearing 5–7 axillary fls.: lvs. 8–12 in. long and 2–2½ in. wide, mostly cauline, strongly recurved and canaliculate, glossy above, glaucous beneath, margin narrowly white-horny: valves 3 in. long, pale green, scariously margined apically; fls. about 2½ in. long, white with broad yellow blade to falls; tube 1½–2 in. long; standards broadly lanceolate, small, white, depressed; falls over 2 in. long, haft lorate, white, blade orbicular, 1 in. across, golden-yellow with wavy golden crest sometimes veined purple or sometimes white with yellow tip: caps. 2½ in. long, cylindrical, hexagonal. Bokhara.

3. **I. orchioides,** Carr. ORCHID IRIS. Sometimes grown in pots: bulb 1–1½ in. diam.: st. jointed, 12–15 in., leafy, bearing 3–6 solitary fls. in axils; spathes 2 in. long, 1-fld., valves pale green: lvs. few, lanceolate, 6–12 in. long at flowering time, glossy above, glaucous beneath, recurved: fls. yellow with purple blotch on either side crest on the haft; tube 1½–2 in. long; blade of falls ½in. broad and obovate; standards less than 1 in. long, oblanceolate and pointed, horizontal or deflexed: caps. 2–2½ in. long, tapering at each end, hexagonal. Turkestan.—Two or three color vars. are known.

4. **I. reticulata,** Bieb. Early-flowering iris, sometimes grown in pots, in several color forms: bulb 1 in. diam., coat netted, cream-colored: st. very short; spathes 1-fld., valves 3–6 in. long, inclosing the tube of fl.: lvs. 8–10 in. high at flowering time but becoming 1½ ft. and more long, 4-angled and with horny edges, narrow, usually 2–4 together from a single bulb: fls. deep violet-purple in cult. material, probably red-purple in native state, violet-scented; tube slender and 2–3 in. long, elongating materially during anthesis; falls with ovate blade ⅓in. broad and shorter than haft, pale at throat and bearing yellow crest; standards only ¼in. broad: caps. 1½–2 in. long, cylindrical, tapering at each end. Caucasus.

5. **I. tingitana,** Boiss. & Reut. TANGERIAN IRIS. Tender, sometimes grown in pots: bulb about 1 in. across, ovoid, tapering apically to a point: st. 1½–2 ft. high or more, enveloped by clasping lvs., normally 2-fld.; spathes 4–6 in. long, bright green, keeled, margin membranous: lvs. 12–18 in. long, glaucous-green above, silvery-gray beneath, rather rigid, usually 6–7 to a bulb and sheathing basally: fls. purplish-blue with yellow patch on falls, about 3 in. across; tube 1½–2 in. long, enveloped by spathes; falls with purple haft and blade orbicular, pale blue veined purple and blotched yellow; standards 3–4 in. long, linear-lanceolate, to ¾in. wide, purplish-blue, erect, margin wavy: caps. long and narrow triangular, concavely grooved longitudinally. Morocco.

6. **I. Xiphium,** L. SPANISH IRIS. One of the oldest cult. irises: bulb 1 in. or so diam., ovate, tunics membranous: st. 1½–2 ft., 1-headed; spathes 1- or 2-fld., outer valves 4–5 in. long, green, pedicels long: lvs. 1 ft. long or shorter above, linear and deeply furrowed, glaucous: fls. violet-purple, tube none; falls with orbicular blade 1 in. broad and much shorter than fiddle-form haft, streaked or patched yellow to orange; standards oblong, as long as falls, ½–¾in. broad: caps. 2–3 in. long, trigonal, each face deeply concave; seeds tight in the caps. (Xiphium: from Greek for *sword*, ancient name of a plant with sword-shaped lvs.) Spain and adjacent regions, N. Afr.—There are numerous vars. and vernacularly named color strains. Var. **præcox,** Hort. (*I. filifolia*, Hort. not Boiss.), has a very short perianth-tube, is earlier flowering and of more vigorous growth; a cultivar of probable hybrid origin with *I. tingitana* probably involved in its parentage. The DUTCH IRISES of the trade are comprised of two strains, one (van Tubergen strain) with large yellow blotch on falls, perhaps of *I. filifolia* and *I. Xiphium* parentage, and the other (deGraaff strain) with narrow yellow stripe on falls, of vars. of *I. Xiphium*. The WEDGWOOD IRISES represent crosses between *I. Xiphium* and *I. tingitana*.

7. **I. xiphioides,** Ehrh. ENGLISH IRIS. Later blooming than no. 6: bulb ovate, tunics dark brown: st. 1½–2 ft., 1-headed, of 2–3 fls., pedicels much shorter than the keeled ventricose spathe: lvs. 12–18 in. long, deeply channelled: fls. dark violet-purple; tube

¼–½in. long; falls somewhat larger, usually yellow in center, narrowed to a longer cuneate haft; standards oblong or obovate, shorter than falls, ½–1 in. broad: caps. 3–4 in. long, tapering at ends; seeds loose within at maturity. Pyrenees.—Several color vars. are listed.

8. **I. gracilipes,** Gray. Graceful dwarf delicate-appearing iris: rhizomatous: st. 9–12 in. high, slender, usually branching twice: lvs. about 1 ft. long but shorter at flowering time, ensiform, to ⅓in. wide, somewhat ribbed, uniformly green: spathes of a single lanceolate valve, membranous, scarious: fls. lilac to mauve-pink, the tube 1½–2½ in. long, linear, the pedicels slender, wiry, mostly 1–2 in. long; falls obovate, cuneate, about 1 in. long, deeply emarginate, the wavy linear petaloid crest orange on the blade and becoming yellowish-white on haft; standards slightly shorter than falls, oblanceolate, emarginate, uniformly lilac-pink; crests on falls nearly ⅜in. long, much fringed: caps. less than ½in. long, ovoid, locules strongly convex; seeds pyriform, reddish-brown with conspicuous cream-colored raphe. Japan.—Prefers cool moist location in partial shade, intolerant of transplanting and should be moved only near the start of growing season; not reliably hardy.

9. **I. cristata,** Soland. Rhizome slender, greenish, spreading by means of stolons that form new rhizomes distally: st. usually less than 1 in. long, the st.-lvs. few, much reduced: lvs. 4–5, about 6 in. long at flowering time, becoming 1 ft. long later, ensiform, about ½in. wide, somewhat lax, pale to yellowish-green: spathes 2½–3 in. long, 1–2-fld., sharply keeled, green, acuminate: fls. pale lilac; crest white, tipped orange along the haft and lilac along the blade, and margined deep lilac-purple on blade; falls with obovate blade and cuneate haft, deeply emarginate to obtuse, about 1½ in. long; standards lilac-purple, unguiculate, about 1 in. long: caps. ½in. long, ovoid, trigonous, sharply angled, dehiscing within spathe while still green; seeds globose, brown, with gelatinous aril coiled around them. S. E. and Cent. U. S.—White-fld. forms are known in cult. as var. **alba,** Dykes.

10. **I. lacustris,** Nutt. (*I. cristata* var. *lacustris,* Dykes). Similar to no. 9 but differing in its more slender rhizome, fls. about one-half as large, the perianth-tube usually less than ¾in. long and infundibular from the base, the falls cuneate and not obovate and standards cuneate rather than obovate-oblanceolate, and the caps. more ovoid and not sharply triangular in cross-section. Ont. to Wis. and Ohio.—This and *I. cristata* do not readily survive transplanting except early during the growing season or new growths moved immediately after flowering.

11. **I. japonica,** Thunb. Rhizome slender, greenish, stolons 6 in. long or more, forming patches: st. 1–1½ ft. high, with many fls. in a long loose raceme; outer spathe-valve green and ¾in. long and about equalling the pedicel, spathes 3–5-fld.: lvs. about as long as st., ½–1 in. (sometimes to 2 in.) wide, dark green, glossy above, glaucous beneath, persisting through winter: fls. thin and delicate, 2 in. across, short-lived, lilac or bluish; falls 1½ in. long, obovate-cuneate, with crisped edges and yellow lower part and haft, bearing a central fimbriated orange silky-white-haired crest; standards nearly equal in length to falls, spreading, apex serrate, broadly emarginate: caps. ellipsoidal, to ⅞in. long; seeds pyriform, with cream-colored aril. Japan, N. China.—Adapted to warmer parts of the U. S., requiring a dry rest period of several weeks prior to flowering.

12. **I. tectorum,** Maxim. (*I. chinensis,* Bunge. *I. fimbriata,* Klatt). An Evansia iris similar to no. 11 in characteristics and requirements: differs in spathes 1½–2 in. long, much exceeding the pedicel, lvs. produced in spring and not persisting through the winter, fls. bright lilac, falls orbicular, crests of falls finely serrate, white and lilac, and caps. more than 1½ in. long, oblong, 6-ribbed. China, Japan. Var. **alba,** Dykes, has pure white fls.

13. **I. susiana,** L. Mourning Iris. An Oncocyclus iris, cult. in E. Eu. for many centuries: rhizome stout, reddish: st. about 1 ft. high, with 2–3 reduced lvs.: lvs. 6–9 in. or more long and ¾–1 in. wide, yellowish-green, the outermost of each tuft falcate: spathes 1-fld., valves 3–4½ in. long, green sometimes flushed purple: fls. grayish heavily veined and dotted dark purplish-black, tube 1–1½ in. long, distally purplish; falls about 3 in. long, drooping, haft cuneate with a diffused beard of brownish-black hairs, blade ovate, pale gray with purplish-black patch; standards paler, orbicular with short sparsely black-hairy haft: caps. 2–4 in. long, ellipsoid, tapering at ends; seeds reddish-brown, with conspicuous cream-colored aril. (Name from Susiani, the Turkish word for iris.) Probably Lebanon.

14. **I. Hoogiana,** Dykes. A member of the Regelia section: rhizome slender, reddish, stoloniferous: st. 18–30 in. high, producing one head of 2–3 fls.: lvs. 15–18 in. long, about ¾in. wide, green, slightly glaucous, often reddish at base: spathes 3–3½ in. long, sharply keeled, green but membranous in upper third: fls. uniformly pale lavender varying to blue-purple with orange beard, tube about 1 in. long, striped dark purple; falls about 3 in. long, the blade not distinct from haft, beard bright orange-yellow on both haft and blade ending acutely; standards broadly oblanceolate, bearded on haft: caps. narrowly cylindrical, tapering apically; seeds brown, wrinkled, pyriform, with large cream-colored aril. (Named in honor of Hoog Bros., page 45.) Turkestan.—Rhizome may be lifted in autumn, stored in cool dry place and replanted early in spring.

15. **I. flavissima,** Pall. (*I. arenaria*, Waldst. & Kit.). Rhizome slender, much-branched, stoloniferous: st. 2–4 in. high, bearing single 2–3-fld. head: lvs. 3–4 in. long at flowering time, linear-ensiform, to ¼in. wide, in basal tufts of 3–4, rather blunt: spathes 1–1¾ in. long, somewhat scarious, the outer acuminate and inner more blunt: fls. clear bright yellow, tube ¼in. or less long; falls about 1½ in. long, blade oblong, haft cuneate and faintly veined brown-purple, beard orange; standards slightly shorter, oblong-unguiculate: caps. cylindrical, angled, about 1½ in. long, tapered apically, the withered twisted perianth often persisting; seeds brown, pyriform, with creamy-white flat collar-forming aril. Hungary and S. Siberia.

16. **I. pumila,** L. (*I. cærulea*, Spach. *I. violacea*, Sweet). Plant making a dense rapidly spreading clump: st. very short or none, bearing 1 fl.: lvs. linear to broad-linear, about ¼in. wide, 2–5 in. long: fls. not fragrant, with very slender green tube about 2 in. long, the segms. somewhat shorter and yellow or lilac; falls ¾in. broad, recurved, densely bearded, standards of similar length. Cent. Eu. to Asia Minor.—Fls. typically dark reddish-purple with bluish to yellow beard. Var. **flaviflora,** Fuss, has primrose-yellow fls. Other color forms occur, including pale blue, dull purple and bright red-purple, under varietal names *atroviolacea, aurea, cærulea, cyanea, excelsa, lutea*. See note under no. 18.

17. **I. Reichenbachii,** Heuff. (*I. serbica*, Panc. *I. athoa*, M. Foster. *I. balkana*, Janka). Rhizome compact, stout: st. 3–12 in. long, 1-headed, mostly with reduced lvs.: lvs. 3–9 in. long at flowering time and ½–¾in. wide, ensiform, glaucescent, becoming somewhat falcate: spathes 1½–2 in. long, 1–2-fld., valves green, trough-shaped, acutely keeled, usually only abruptly acute or rounded: fls. either clear yellow (*I. serbica*) or brownish-purple (*I. balkana*) or reddish-purple (*I. athoa*), tube 1–1½ in. long, funnelform; falls obovate-cuneate, drooping, about 3¼ in. long, beard bluish in purple-fld. forms and orange in yellow-fld. ones; standards somewhat longer than falls, oblong-elliptic, emarginate, erect and inarching: caps. long-ellipsoidal with 6 shallow grooves. (For Reichenbach, page 50.) Balkans.—Forms with fls. yellow weakly veined purple are cult.

18. **I. Chamæiris,** Bert. Very similar to no. 17, differing primarily in the spathe-valves not keeled or the inner one only very slightly keeled: fls. variable in color but the beard usually of a contrasting color: caps. oblong to ovoid and trigonal. S. E. France to N. W. Italy.—Much material grown as *I. pumila* may properly belong here but in *I. pumila* the fl.-st. is absent or less than ¼in. long and the perianth-tube much longer. Hybrids of the two species are in cult.

19. **I. variegata,** L. St. 1–1½ ft. tall, with 1–4 2-fld. heads, about equalling the sword-shaped slightly glaucous lvs. which are 1 in. wide: spathe-valves 1–1½ in. long, inflated, light green, sometimes very narrowly membranous at margin: fls. yellow-brown, the yellow-green tube cylindrical, 1 in. or less long; falls oblong, less than 1 in. broad, veined brown on a yellow ground, brown toward the tip and yellow on the cuneate haft, beard yellow; standards oblong, erect, bright yellow, claw veined brown: caps. 1 in. long and half as wide, 6-ribbed; seeds small, gray-brown. S. E. Eu.—**I. squalens,** L., is now believed to be a hybrid between this species and *I. pallida* and has characteristics of and intermediate between the parents. *I. variegata* is now considered to be a probable ancestor of much of the *I. germanica* group.

20. **I. germanica,** L. German Iris. This species yields many garden forms, varying in stature and color, some of them the result of hybridization; one of the sources of orris-root: rhizome stout: st. 2–3 ft., bearing 2-fld. terminal head and 2 usually 1-fld. stalked branches: spathe-valves oblong-lanceolate, tinged purple, green on lower part at flowering time: lvs. 1–1½ ft., sword-shaped, 1–1½ in. wide, shorter than st.: fls. lilac and lilac-purple (varying to white), not fragrant, the cylindrical tube greenish and about 1 in. long; falls obovate, dark violet-purple, 1–1½ in. broad, reflexed, the beard yellow; standards obovate, size of falls, usually lighter colored: caps. 1½–2 in. long, trigonal, tapering to apex. Cent. and S. Eu.—Not all the plants known as German iris are *I. germanica:* some of them are nos. 19, 21, 22 and 23. Var. **florentina,** Dykes (*I. florentina*, Ker. not L. nor Redouté), has heads sessile or nearly so, spathe-valves nearly or partly scarious, and fls. white, the falls tinged lavender, with yellow beard; runs to pure white forms and to those with blue tints; the binomial *I. florentina*, L., is of questionable application and seems to be a synonym of *I. spuria*, L.; so far as known no valid binomial exists for the plant here treated as var. *florentina* and it may be of hybrid origin independent of that of *I. germanica*; **I. atroviolacea,** Lange, known only from cult., may not be distinct and is said to differ in the spathe-valves wholly scarious and brownish in color; a tall-growing plant with dark violet-purple fls. **I. neglecta,** Hornem., known only in cult.; standards lighter colored than fls., the latter blue to bright lilac, the haft striped lilac on white ground. Still other species are probably involved in the parentage of cult. forms.

21. **I. Kochii,** Kerner (*I. germanica* var. *Kochii*, Grey). Very similar to *I. germanica*, perhaps only a variant of it, and by some thought to be its prototype although the place of nativity of this species is itself in doubt: from *I. germanica* it differs in its lower stature (20–24 in. high) and st. about equalling the lvs., and in the veining on the falls not obvious beyond the ends of the style-branches: fls. reported to be rich red-purple without any white showing between the heavy brownish veins at the end of the haft; spathe-valves partially

scarious at time of flowering: caps. oblong, obtusely trigonal. (Named for W. D. J. Koch, page 46.) N. Italy.—Considered to be of hybrid origin of probably considerable antiquity.

22. **I. pallida,** Lam. (*I. Cengialtii,* Ambrosi). Differs from *I. germanica* in shorter spathe-valves that are wholly silvery-white scarious, fl.-heads of greater number, fls. fragrant and later in season: fl.-st. 36 in. or more high, overtopping the lvs., the lateral branches very short, fls. violet (varying to white), beard yellow. S. Eu. to W. Asia. Var. **dalmatica,** Hort., has very glaucous lvs. to 2¼ in. wide, st. shorter, stouter, and fls. lavender-blue with falls more spreading than drooping: perhaps not a true var. and reported to be of hybrid origin with *I. pallida* one of its parents.

23. **I. flavescens,** DC. St. 2–3 ft., bearing 3 or 4 heads, the spathes 2–3-fld.: lvs. 12–15 in. long and 1 in. wide, sword-shaped, glaucous: fls. yellow, not fragrant, tube cylindrical and less than 1 in. long; falls 1 in. and more broad, obovate, reflexed, beard deeper yellow than limb; standards somewhat broader, pale yellow: not known to have produced caps. or set seed.—The status and identity of this plant is not clear and by some authorities it is considered to be only a cultigen of uncertain origin and closely related to plants of the *I. germanica* complex; its claim to standing as a species has been challenged as has been also its reputed nativity in Bosnia, and there is much evidence that it may be a garden hybrid of long standing.

24. **I. dichotoma,** Pall. The only species of the Pardanthopsis section (so named for its resemblance in habit to Belamcanda, once known as Pardanthus): rhizome slender: st. 2–3½ ft. high, much-branched, the slender branches often in pairs and bracted at each fork, terminating in racemes: lvs. 8–14 in. long, equitant in basal fan-shaped clusters about the st., blue-green with distinct white edge: spathes less than ½in. long, 3–5-fld., entirely scarious, valves obtuse: fls. beardless, white with few brownish-purple spots or reddish-purple with white blotches on blade of falls, tube scarcely apparent; falls about ¾in. long, with cuneate haft rising suberectly and the nearly square blade extending horizontally, beardless; standards oblanceolate, shorter than falls, similarly colored; style-crests long, narrow, deeply divided: caps. 1–1½ in. long, oblong, trigonal with a deeply concave vertical channel on each side; seeds dark brown, with pale wings at each end. Siberia, Manchuria, Mongolia.—Floriferous short-lived hardy iris blossoming well into midsummer; easily propagated from seed; unfertilized fls. break off below the ovary when touched, perianth twisting on withering.

25. **I. verna,** L. Rhizome slender, torulose, stoloniferous: stemless or essentially so: lvs. 4–9 in. long, mostly 3–5 in a tuft, ensiform, outer ones of tuft streaked reddish-purple, others pale glaucous green: spathes a series of 4–6 imbricated bracts ½–2 in. long, the short outer ones green and longer inner ones tan-colored: fls. lilac-blue to reddish-violet with yellow mid-section on each segm., tube 1–2½ in. long; falls about 1¾ in. long, drooping, the blade obovate, beardless; standards smaller, spatulate, erect and inarching: caps. about ½in. long, ovoid, beaked; seeds pyriform, with distinct white aril. S. E. U. S.—Small-lvd. plants in the trade have been confused with the bearded *I. pumila.*

26. **I. virginica,** L. (*I. georgiana,* Britt.). Rhizome stout: st. 1–3½ ft. high, coarse, stout, upper cauline lvs. often exceeding the infl.: lvs. ¾–3 ft. long, linear-ensiform, green: spathes unequal, 1½–5 in. long, green or partly membranous, outer ones often foliaceous: fls. blue to violet, on pedicels 1½–2¾ in. long, tube to ¾in. long, funnelform; falls 3 in. long, obovate-cuneate, the haft yellowish-green expanding into a bright yellow beardless blotch in the lavender-blue blade; standards 2–2½ in. long, obovate-spatulate, colored as falls: caps. 1½–2¾ in. long, globose to subglobose, trigonal, valves strongly reflexed at maturity; seeds D-shaped or round, with dull corky covering. S. E. U. S. Var. **Shrevei,** E. Anders. (*I. Shrevei,* Small), has caps. at least twice as long as wide; Mississippi Valley, especially in its northern branches; collected by Ralph Shreve.

27. **I. versicolor,** L. Very similar to *I. virginica* and by some authorities formerly not considered distinct but recent detailed studies show it to differ in the spathes 1½–2 in. long, not or infrequently foliaceous; standards lanceolate, short and narrow in proportion to the falls whereas in *I. virginica* they are longer and broader than the falls and oblanceolate to spatulate in outline: seeds with thin glossy hard covering, D-shaped, and valves of caps. not or only slightly reflexed. N. E. N. Amer.—It has been postulated that this species represents a fertile hybrid of great antiquity between *I. virginica* and *I. setosa.*

28. **I. setosa,** Pall. Rhizome short, thick: st. 1½–2 ft. high, usually exceeding the lvs. and bearing 1–2 cauline lvs.: lvs. 8–18 in. long, in fans of 3–6, ensiform, distally glaucous: spathes 1–2 in. long, 2-fld., green or flushed purple, ovate-lanceolate: fls. blue- to reddish-purple, veined darker, falls weakly blotched white at base of blade, tube about ¼in. long; falls to 2 in. long, orbicular-cuneate, haft yellowish-white veined purple, beardless; standards less than ¾in. long, mostly lanceolate, setose: caps. about 1 in. long, short-cylindric to ovoid, trigonal, sides grooved; seeds pale brown, very glossy. E. and N. Asia to Alaska. Var. **canadensis,** M. Foster (*I. Hookeri,* Penny. *I. canadensis,* Wherry), dwarfer, lvs. fewer, smaller, with often undulate margins, the one cauline lf. reduced to a bract, a larger white blotch on blades of falls and smaller standards; Lab. to N. Maine.—White-fld. forms and those with transversely-banded lvs. have been described.

29. **I. Kaempferi,** Sieb. (*I. lævigata* var. *Kaempferi,* Maxim.). JAPANESE IRIS. Showy hardy iris, much cult. in many forms, blooming just after the other beardless kinds: rhizome stout, short-creeping: st. 1½–2½ ft. high, reduced cauline lvs. 1–2, usually with 1 lateral branch, heads mostly 2-fld.: lvs. 2–2½ ft. long, ensiform, with distinct raised midrib along entire length: spathes 2–3 in. long, narrow, green with very narrow membranous margin: fls. 3½–6 in. across, flat and open in appearance, reddish-purple or shades of yellow to white, tube ½–¾in. long; falls nearly horizontal, lopping, with narrowly oblong haft about 1 in. long, yellow in center, and oval to obovate beardless blade 2–3½ in. long typically an intense red-purple or wine-color; standards two-thirds as long as falls and of same color, narrowly oblanceolate: caps. to 1 in. long, short-ellipsoid, obtusely beaked, trigonal with concave sides; seeds flat circular disks. (Named for Engelb. Kaempfer, 1631–1716, a Swedish consular official who studied and collected plants of Japan while stationed there in the late 17th century.) Manchuria, Korea, Japan.—The commonest Japanese iris and long considered synonymous with *I. lævigata* but from which it differs genetically as well as morphologically. Not a true bog or marsh plant. From this, and perhaps influenced by no. 30, have come many cultivars that may represent mutations, hybrids in which perhaps other species are involved, and segregations of extreme conditions. Many hundred named vars. are known in Japan; double-fld. forms whose standards resemble falls or whose styles are petaloid are frequent in cult.

30. **I. lævigata,** Fisch. JAPANESE IRIS. Very similar in general appearance to *I. Kaempferi,* differing in the lvs. without a midrib, fls. typically almost clear blue to white, ovate standards 2½ in. long and equalling the falls, and the caps. about 2 in. long, oblong, obtusely trigonal with blunt ends, the fawn-colored seeds thick and semi-circular. Manchuria, Korea, China.—The typical form is not commonly cult.; most material identified with this species probably represents cultivars of mixed parentage. A true bog plant that will thrive where it is wet the year around.

31. **I. Pseudacorus,** L. Robust, forming large strong clumps: st. 2–3 ft., branched, leafy below, terete, bearing several clusters of fls.: spathes 2–3-fld., the valves large and lf.-like and exceeding pedicels: fls. bright yellow, the tube about ½in. long; falls with orbicular blade 1½ in. or less broad, haft with a bright spot; standards narrow, ¼–¾in. long, erect: caps. 1½–2½ in. long, oblong, apex short, beaked; seeds flattened, pale brown, D-shaped to circular. (Pseudacorus: *false acorus,* known as Acorus in pre-Linnæan days.) Eu., N. Afr., Syria, in several forms; also nat. in N. Amer. Var. **gigantea,** Hort., is reported to be a large-fld. form, and var. **mandschurica,** Hort., has pale yellow fls. There is a var. with striped lvs.

32. **I. fulva,** Ker. One of the showiest species native in the lower Mississippi Valley: rhizome about ½in. diam., much-branched: st. about 2 ft. high, overtopping the lvs.: lvs. 2–3½ ft. long, linear-ensiform, arching or reflexed, inconspicuously ribbed: spathes very unequal in length, the outer ones green and inner somewhat scarious: fls. coppery-red, tube about 1 in. long; falls broadly obovate-oblanceolate, to 3¼ in. long, drooping; standards oblanceolate-spatulate, about 1½ in. long, emarginate: caps. ellipsoidal, to 2 in. long, hexagonal, green at maturity; seeds flattened, with corky spongy covering. S.-Cent. U. S.—Hybrids between this species and *I. foliosa* are known as **I. fulvala,** Dykes, and have larger fls. that are reddish-purple or wine-purple. **I. vinicolor,** Small, is probably only a rufus-wine-colored form and not a distinct species or hybrid, a view supported also by cytological evidence. The plant known as **I. chrysophœnicia,** Small, is considered a hybrid between *I. fulva* and *I. hexagona* var. *giganticærulea,* and has fls. in shades of violet-purple to red-purple, with orange-yellow haft; La.

33. **I. hexagona,** Walt. Half-hardy: rhizome stout, much-spreading and branched: st. 1–3 ft. high, cauline lvs. 3–4 and large: lvs. 2–3 ft. long, ensiform, erect, yellowish- to glaucous-green: spathes 6–8 in. long, outer one green, inner shorter with scarious margins to wholly scarious: fls. lavender-purple, large, the tube about 1¼ in. long; falls 3½–4 in. long, the haft oblong and greenish, blade obovate-orbicular with yellow to whitish patch or streak basally; standards about two-thirds as long, oblanceolate to spatulate, similarly colored, erect: caps. ovoid, 1½–2½ in. long, hexagonal, abruptly beaked with rounded base; seeds light brown, corky covered. Swamps of S. E. U. S. Var. **savannarum,** R. Foster (*I. savannarum,* Small), differs primarily in falls 4 in. long, oblanceolate with nearly elliptical blade and standards 3 in. long and narrowly oblanceolate; Fla.—**I. brevicaulis,** Raf. (*I. foliosa,* Mackenzie & Bush), is very similar and differs primarily in st. 6–12 in. long or decumbent; Ohio to La.; its var. **boonensis,** Daniels, has pure white fls.

34. **I. spuria,** L. Rhizome slender, old non-fibrous lf.-bases persisting: st. stout, 1–2 ft., sparingly branched, 3–4 reduced lvs. covering the internodes, with 1–3 heads: spathes 2- or 3-fld., valves narrow and green and longer than pedicels: lvs. shorter than st., broad-linear, about ½in. broad, 1 ft. long, somewhat glaucous: fls. lilac to bluish-purple, beardless, pedicel about 1 in. long, tube ½in. or less long, ovary with 2 ridges extending down each of its 3 angles; falls with orbicular blade ½in. broad and half as long as haft; standards somewhat shorter and ½in. or less broad; anthers purple, edged yellow: caps. 1–2 in. long, oblong, beaked, doubly ridged at each trigonous angle; seeds smooth, brown, enveloped by a dark papery covering. Eu. and Algeria to Iran, in many forms.—Several

habit forms of this species complex are cult.: one a slender unbranched plant with a single 2-fld. head; a second has in addition 1 or 2 lateral heads set far apart on st. with internodes not covered by sheathing lvs.; and a third differs from the second in its dwarf habit and short internodes covered by lf.-bases: fls. of all types are similar.

35. **I. crocea,** Jacquem. (*I. aurea,* Lindl. not Raf. nor Link. *I. spuria* var. *aurea,* Dykes). Rhizome slender, hard and compact: st. 2½–3½ ft., stout and terete, bearing several reduced lvs., 1 terminal head and about 2 sessile lateral heads: spathes 2–3-fld., pedicels long, spathe-valves 3–4 in. long and green: lvs. sword-shaped, little if at all glaucous, 1 in. or so broad, to 2 ft. long: fls. bright yellow, with slender tube about ½in. long; falls to 3½ in. long, with wavy-margined oblong blade 1 in. broad and as long as haft; standards shorter and much narrower: caps. much as in no. 34. W. Himalayas.

36. **I. Monnieri,** DC. (*I. spuria* var. *Monnieri,* Dykes). Similar to *I. spuria* and perhaps only a variant, differing in fls. lemon-yellow and anthers pale yellow; differs from *I. crocea* in paler fl. color and blades of falls orbicular with no wavy or crisped margin. (Named for M. Lemonnier of Versailles, in whose garden the plant was found by Redouté prior to 1808.) Cultigen not known from the wild, reports of its nativity in Crete believed to have been based on misidentified plants of *I. Pseudacorus.*

37. **I. orientalis,** Mill. (*I. ochroleuca,* L. *I. spuria* var. *ochroleuca,* Dykes). Tall-growing, to 3½ ft. high, differing from *I. spuria* in fls. white or very pale yellow with showy deep yellow blotch on blade of fall, the latter widely and deeply emarginate. W. Asia Min. Var. **gigantea,** Hort., is reported to be a larger more vigorous form.—Recent authors have reestablished the validity of Miller's older name *I. orientalis* (1768) as applying to the plant sometimes treated as *I. ochroleuca,* L. (1771).

38. **I. halophila,** Pall. (*I. Gueldenstaedtiana,* Lepech. *I. desertorum,* Ker. *I. spuria* var. *halophila,* Dykes). Vigorous short-stemmed very floriferous iris, perhaps not distinct from *I. spuria,* from which it differs primarily in much smaller fls. whose falls are reduced with the very small ovate-orbicular blade extending horizontally and scarcely drooping; fls. self fertilize readily and seed is abundantly produced; usually fls. white with yellow veins or dull yellow shaded with gray-purple. Cent. Asia.—Much alleged species material ascribed in the trade to other binomials belongs here, especially that distributed as seed.

39. **I. graminea,** L. Densely foliaceous iris with fragrant leafy-stemmed fls. suitable for cutting: rhizome slender, mat-forming: st. 8–12 in. high, flattened, with distinct flanges, st.-lvs. 1–2, usually overtopping the fls., heads 1–2-fld.: lvs. 1¼–3 ft. long and ¼–1 in. wide, linear to ensiform, glossy above and dull or glaucescent beneath: spathes green, variable in length (2–10 in.) on the same plant: fls. yellowish-white, densely veined blue-purple on blade and red-purple on haft, small, of plum-like fragrance; falls 1½–2 in. long, haft ovate and horizontal, blade orbicular and somewhat drooping; standards 1–1½ in. long, broadly lanceolate, erect: caps. 1–2 in. long, ovoid to short-oblong, beaked, roundly trigonal with 2 vertical ribs on each locule. Cent. and S. Eu. to Caucasus.—Purple to reddish-mauve forms are known.

40. **I. tenuis,** Wats. Rather low slender deeply-forked stemmed iris: rhizome scarcely ⅛in. diam., creeping: st. about 1 ft. long, slender, branched below middle, with 1–2 cauline lvs.: lvs. linear-ensiform, about 1 ft. long and ½in. wide, equitant at base, margins scarious: spathes ¾–1¼ in. long, unequal, scarious but sometimes herbaceous basally or along keel, 1–fld.: fls. white veined purple, small, beardless, tube about ⅛in. long; falls about 1 in. long, oblong-spatulate, haft yellowish, becoming horizontal, oblanceolate blade somewhat drooping; standards ¾in. long, oblanceolate-spatulate, bluish-white, erect: caps. ovoid, to ¾in. long, obtuse; seeds light brown with whitish raphe and funicle. Ore.—Numbers 40–46 belong to the California subsection of the section Apogon: beardless, having in common the characteristics of narrow prominently nerved lvs. flushed pink, red or purple at base, fls. usually with a well-developed perianth-tube, and very slender few-rooted rhizomes; not adaptable to cult. if requiring transplanting of plants once established.

41. **I. Douglasiana,** Herb. Densely foliaged: rhizome about ⅜in. diam.: st. simple or branched, exceeded by the lvs. and with 1–2 short cauline lvs.: lvs. 1–1½ ft. long, light to dark green, usually flexuous in upper third: spathes to 3 in. long, green or flushed purplish basally, lanceolate-acuminate: fls. usually 3 in head, deep purple, mauve or flesh-colored, sometimes white, veined darker, tube about 1 in. long, ovary sharply trigonal, tapering at ends; falls oblanceolate, about 2 in. long; standards mostly 1¾ in. long, oblanceolate: caps. 1½–2 in. long, acutely trigonal, tapering at ends; seeds spherical. (For David Douglas, page 42.) S. Ore. to Calif.

42. **I. Purdyi,** Eastw. Similar to *I. Douglasiana,* differing in foliage less dense, lvs. dark glossy green on one side and glaucous on the other, cauline almost completely covering the simple fl.-sts., fls. usually yellowish, the undulate stigma-tip truncate not acute as in other related species, seeds D-shaped: from *I. bracteata* it differs also in perianth-tube narrowly cylindrical. (Named for Carl Purdy, page 50.) Calif.

43. **I. bracteata,** Wats. Large and handsome iris: rhizome slender, sheathed by old lf.-bases: st. 6–12 in. long, simple, sheathed by 3–6 bract-like lvs.: spathes nearly 3 in. long, herbaceous with scarious margins, acuminate: lvs. to 20 in. long, linear, few, rigid, glossy on one side, glaucous on other: fls. bright yellow veined brownish-purple, tube less than ½in. long, funnelform; falls oblanceolate, about 1½ in. long; standards 2 in. long, veinless, narrowly oblanceolate: caps. about 1 in. long, subterete, abruptly tapered at ends; seeds angular, flattened. Ore.

44. **I. tenax,** Dougl. Graceful densely foliaged clump-forming iris: rhizome slender: st. 6–12 in. long, slender, simple, with 1–3 linear lvs. to 6 in. long: basal lvs. 1–1½ ft. long and to nearly ¼in. wide, laxly overtopping sts., pale green: spathes 2–3 in. long, outer as much as 1 in. below the inner, herbaceous with scarious margins, lanceolate, 1–2-fld.: fls. variable in color from dark purple blotched white through shades of blue, lavender, pink, apricot, cream-colored and pure white, tube about ⅓in. long or less, funnelform; falls obovate-cuneate, to 2¼ in. long, usually with central yellowish ridge and emarginate; standards to 2 in. long, lanceolate to oblanceolate: caps. to 1½ in. long, oblong, prominently 6-ribbed; seeds D-shaped, thickened. Wash. to N. Calif. Var. **Gormanii,** R. Foster (*I. Gormanii*, Piper), has falls white to deep yellow, more broadly obovate and both falls and standards usually entire margined; named for M. W. Gorman, who first collected it in 1922; N. Ore.—The stout fibrous lvs. have been employed by the Indians in making fish-nets and crude ropes.

45. **I. innominata,** L. F. Henderson. Dwarf slender-rhizomed iris: st. 4–10 in. high, simple, bearing 3–4 short cauline lvs. basally: lvs. to 15 in. long and ⅙in. wide, striate but not prominently nerved, dark green on one side, pale and glaucous on the other: spathes nearly 1¾ in. long, mostly ovate and obtuse, herbaceous with scarious margins: fls. variable in color from clear yellow to orange with lavender- and purple-fld. variants, tube ½–1¼ in. long, linear; falls nearly 2 in. long, broadly oblanceolate, usually veined purple; standards slightly shorter, narrower, weakly veined: caps. 1 in. long, oblong-ovoid; seeds sharply angled. Ore.—A closely related species occasionally cult is **I. macrosiphon,** Torr. (*I. californica*, Leicht.); differs from *I. innominata* in perianth-tube ⅓in. long or less and linear-lanceolate acuminate spathes; from *I. chrysophylla* differs in short non-linear style-crests; Calif.

46. **I. chrysophylla,** Howell. Low-growing: rhizome slender: st. simple, to 1 ft. high and often much shorter, cauline lvs. 1–3, linear, reduced: lvs. 10–18 in. long and ¼in. wide, linear, light green: spathes about 2–2½ in. long, acuminate, mostly 2-fld., outer shorter than inner: fls. pale yellow to white, veined, flushed or edged pink or dull reddish-purple, tube 1–3 in. long, linear; falls about 2 in. long, oblanceolate; standards shorter: caps. about 1¼ in. long, oblong, beaked. Ore., Calif.

47. **I. sibirica,** L. Widespread and variable species, with short rhizome, compact, growing in tufts: st. 1½–3 ft., surpassing the foliage, terete and hollow, simple or forked, bearing 1 terminal and 1 lateral head: spathes 2- or 5-fld., valves brown-scarious, 1–1½ in. long: lvs. ⅙in. or less broad, linear, the sheaths splitting into slender fibers: fls. lilac, not large, tube none or to ½in. long, peduncles of varying length in fls. of same plant; falls with orbicular blade ¾–1 in. across, beardless; standards erect, ½in. or less across: caps. short-oblong, trigonal with strongly convex sides, apex not beaked; seeds large, D-shaped, thin. Eu.—For var. Snow Queen see no. 48.

48. **I. sanguinea,** Donn (*I. orientalis*, Thunb. acc. Dykes, not Thunb. nor Mill. *I. sibirica* var. *orientalis*, Maxim.). Similar to *I. sibirica*, differing in foliage overtopping fl. sts., peduncles of nearly uniform length, spathes never scarious, caps. nearly three times as long as wide, trigonal with flattened sides, and seeds small, thick and subcubical: in many plants the lvs. are sometimes slightly more than ½in. wide. Manchuria, Korea, Japan. Var. **alba,** Hort., fls. white. The plant known as var. Snow Queen belongs here and not to *I. sibirica;* it is less vigorous and floriferous than var. *alba*.—This plant has long been known as *I. orientalis* and is yet so listed, but the name is a later homonym of *I. orientalis*, Mill. and cannot be used here. *I. orientalis*, Thunb., is properly *I. extremorientalis*, Koidz.

49. **I. Forrestii,** Dykes. St. 12–18 in. high, simple or 1-branched, hollow, mostly 1-headed, cauline lvs. 2–3 and reduced: lvs. mostly 8–15 in. long, linear-ensiform, glossy above and dull beneath: spathes 2–3 in. long, acuminate, keeled, herbaceous often with scarious tip: fls. clear yellow or lightly veined purple, tube less than ½in. long, broad; falls about 2½ in. long, ovate-oblong, often drooping, beardless; standards nearly erect, oblanceolate, shorter than falls: caps. nearly twice as long as wide, long-beaked, trigonal; seeds thin and flat. (Named for George Forrest, page 43.) W. China.

50. **I. Bulleyana,** Dykes. St. 15–18 in. high, simple, hollow, with single 1–2-fld. head, 2–3 cauline lvs. present: lvs. 1½–2 ft. long, to ½in. wide, linear-ensiform, glossy above and glaucous beneath: spathes 3–4 in. long, narrowly acuminate, scarious at tip: fls. blue-purple flecked cream-colored, segms. paler toward margins, tube ½in. long; falls obovate-oblong, about 2 in. long, beardless; standards oblanceolate, divergently ascending: caps. 1¼–1¾ in. long, tapering at ends, distinctly flanged at angles, with raised rib on each face; seeds disk-like, thick, small. (Named for A. K. Bulley, British botanist and horticulturist.) Origin uncertain, possibly a garden hybrid.

51. **I. Delavayi,** Mich. Very tall-growing showy iris: rhizome creeping, not densely tufted: st. 3–4½ ft. high, hollow, bearing a terminal and usually 2 lateral heads of 2 fls. each, cauline lf. usually 1, reduced: lvs. 2–2½ ft. long and ⅓in. wide, glaucescent on both sides, linear-acuminate: spathes 3–4 in. long, scarious at tip, outer longer than inner: fls. red- to blue-purple, irregularly blotched white, tube ½in. long; falls with orbicular to ovate blade 1–1¼ in. across, beardless; standards divergent, midway between erect and horizontal, small, emarginate: caps. 1¾–2½ in. long, narrowly oblong, acutely trigonal, tapering abruptly at ends; seeds flat round disks. (Named for Abbé Delavay, page 42.) S. W. China.—Does best in moist soil.

52. **I. chrysographes,** Dykes. Rhizome slender, not mat-forming: st. 15–18 in. high, hollow but thick-walled, usually simple, cauline lvs. 1–2, much reduced: lvs. 15–20 in. long and to ½in. wide, linear-ensiform, flexuous distally, glaucescent: spathes 3–4 in. long, green, subopposite: fls. vivid violet-purple veined golden-yellow, tube about ½in. long, ribbed, pedicels ¼–2 in. long; falls to 3½ in. long, oblong-spatulate, drooping, beardless; standards to 2½ in. long, narrowly oblanceolate, veinless, ascending at angle of about 45 degrees: caps. 1½–2½ in. long, otherwise as in no. 50; seeds pyriform, flattened. W. China.

53. **I. Wilsonii,** C. H. Wright. Similar to *I. chrysographes*, differing in fls. yellow veined red or purple-brown, pedicels of unequal length varying from 1½–4 in. in fl. and all 4–6 in. long in fr., caps. short-ovoid, raised on pedicels far above spathe-remnants. (Named for E. H. Wilson, page 54.) W. China.

54. **I. unguicularis,** Poir. (*I. stylosa*, Desf.). Blooming very early: rhizome stout: st. very short or practically none, solid, fls. borne among foliage: spathes 1–3-fld., outer valve long and green: lvs. 1–2 ft., ½in. or less wide, linear: fls. bright lilac (to white), fragrant, with very long tube (4–9 in.) and long narrow ovary; falls obovate, 1 in. broad, keeled, yellow, at throat streaked lilac on lighter ground, beardless; standards long-unguiculate, ¾in. broad; style-branches as if dusted with gold on back due to presence of minute glandular processes: caps. near base of lvs., trigonal with seed outlines apparent from without. Algeria.

55. **I. prismatica,** Pursh. Rhizome very slender, stoloniferous: st. 1–2 ft. high, slender, wiry, solid, simple or 1-branched: lvs. 1–2 ft. long and ⅛–½in. wide, glaucous: spathes 1–2 in. long, lanceolate, somewhat membranous: fls. bluish-purple veined darker, tube ⅛in. long; falls to 2 in. long, ovate blade blotched whitish basally, beardless; standards to 1¾ in. long, lanceolate, pale blue-purple: caps. trigonal, flanged edges at each angle; seeds subcubical, smooth, brown. Swampy regions, Atlantic coast of N. Amer.

56. **I. ruthenica,** Ker. Rhizome slender, much-branched: st. 1–8 in. long, simple, cauline lf. 1, subtended by 2 foliaceous bracts: lvs. to 8 in. long, ⅛–¼in. wide, becoming 1–1½ ft. long after flowering, glossy above and glaucescent beneath: spathes 1–1½ in. long, green often edged pink, inflated: fls. with bluish-purple shading and darker veining over a nearly white ground, tube ½–1 in. long; falls about 2 in. long, ovate-cuneate, the beardless blades nearly horizontal with tips upcurving; standards somewhat shorter, suberect: caps. nearly spherical, opening widely at maturity; seeds globose, conspicuous when fresh by presence of soft white aril that shrivels and disappears. Transylvania to Korea.—Readily grown from seed but because of its slender few-rooted rhizomes does not respond well when transplanted. An unrelated species of this section but of similar size, habit and appearance is **I. minuta,** Franch. & Sav.; differs from *I. ruthenica* in fls. yellowish suffused with brown, haft of falls with raised edge on either side of midrib, lvs. 4 in. long and ¼–½in. wide at flowering, becoming 12–15 in. long at fr. maturity; place of nativity indefinite, perhaps Japan where it has long been cult.

57. **I. ensata,** Thunb. Rhizome stout, making tough clump: st. 6–16 in. high, 1-headed: spathes 3–4 in. long, green and leafy, 1–3-fld.: lvs. linear, about equalling the sts., ⅛in. or less broad, somewhat glaucous, strongly nerved, basal sheaths splitting into slender fibers: fls. lilac, not showy, tube practically wanting, ovary long-cylindrical, eight to ten times as long as broad or more, with 6 equidistant vertical ribs; falls narrowly oblanceolate with fiddle-shaped haft, ¾in. or less broad, veined dark blue, yellowish toward haft; standards oblanceolate, erect, about ¼in. wide, darker than falls: caps. 2–3 in. long, narrowly oblong, on pedicel often to 4 in. long, abruptly beaked, equally 6-ribbed; seeds globose, dark brown. Caucasus to Japan. Var. **pabularia,** Naud. (*I. pabularia*, Naud.), KRISHUM, large foliaceous robust plant 2–3 ft. high; Cent. Asia; intro. to N. Amer. for forage but little known; reported to endure dry conditions.

58. **I. missouriensis,** Nutt. Rhizome stout (to 1¼ in. diam.), with fleshy roots: st. 1½–2 ft. high, simple or branched, usually overtopping lvs., slender: lvs. to 1½ ft. long and less than ½in. wide, erect, light glaucous green: spathes 1½–3 in. long, scarious except herbaceous basally and along keel: fls. lilac-purple, blotched yellowish-white basally, tube less than ½in. long; falls about 2½ in. long, obovate-spatulate; standards slightly shorter, oblanceolate to spatulate, emarginate, veinless: caps. 1¼–2 in. long, oblong, trigonal, ends tapering; seeds subglobose to pyriform, dark brown. U. S., mostly at high altitudes.—A highly variable species of somewhat moist habitats.

59. **I. longipetala,** Herb. Similar to *I. missouriensis*, differing in larger size, lvs. longer than sts., spathe-valves foliaceous and green, and foliage remaining green until new lvs. are produced. Coast of Calif.

60. **I. fœtidissima,** L. SCARLET-SEEDED IRIS. Inconspicuously-fld. iris, foliage emitting a disagreeable odor when crushed, grown for showy frs. whose seeds remain attached after maturity: rhizome slender, slow-growing: st. 2 ft. high, branched, with cauline lvs. 2–3, clasping, reduced: lvs. 1–1½ ft. long, to 1 in. wide, thick, dark glossy green, usually persisting through the winter: spathes about 3 in. long, lanceolate, herbaceous, rigid: fls. typically pale grayish-purple veined dark purple, not showy, tube about ½in. long; falls 1½–2 in. long, with obovate-orbicular blade ¾in. across, beardless; standards oblanceolate: caps. 1½–2 in. long, roundly trigonal, beaked, obscurely 6-ribbed; seeds scarlet-red, globose, persisting in caps. after dehiscence. W. and S. Eu., N. Afr.—Forms with variegated lvs. and yellow fls. are known. The dehisced capsules with their showy persistent seeds are sometimes used in dried bouquets.

3. **TIGRIDIA,** Juss. TIGER-FLOWER. About a dozen bulbous or cormous plants, Mex. to Chile, one sometimes planted: fls. wide open, fugitive, without tube, yellow, orange or purplish, oddly spotted.—Sts. terete, simple or forked, 2½ ft. or less tall, with a few narrow-plicate lvs., and bearing 1 or more fls. from each of the 1- or 2-valved lf.-like spathes: fls. erect; segms. 6 in 2 rows, the rows usually much unlike, with the inner ones smaller, connivent into a broad cup from which the blades stand nearly or quite horizontally; stamens 3, the filaments united into a long slender tube that includes the style and projects from the fl.; ovary 3-celled, style long and 3-parted at end, each part again parted: caps. loculicidal. (Tigrid-ia: Latin *tigris*, tiger; applied here to markings of the fl.)

T. Pavonia, Ker. Corm 1½ in. diam.: sts. erect, branched or unbranched, 1½–2½ ft., bearing several rather rigid lvs., the spathe-valves 3–5 in. long: fls. red and spotted, produced in succession, 3–6 in. across, very showy, with cup-like center, the staminal column prominent; outer segms. spreading, obovate and obtuse, the claw purple or yellow; inner segms. half the length of outer, blade ovate-acute. Mex., Guatemala.—Very variable in color under cult., and several named vars. are known; it runs to lilac, yellow, and pure white. In colder temp. regions the corms should be lifted in autumn, dried and treated as for gladiolus. Plants from seed usually flower the second season.

4. **MORÆA,** Mill. Much like Iris, being the representative of that genus in the southern hemisphere.—Differs in species mostly cormous, perianth not possessed of a tube above the ovary, filaments more or less connate basally into a tube: outer segms. cuneate, with reflexing limb; inner segms. either similar and smaller or in some kinds reduced to small tricuspidate parts. (Moræ-a: J. Moræus, Swedish physician, father-in-law of Linnæus.)

A. Rootstock a stout creeping rhizome.
  B. Fls. white, bearded .... 1. *M. iridioides*
  BB. Fls. yellow, not bearded .... 2. *M. bicolor*
AA. Rootstock a corm.
  B. Fls. in lax corymb of 5–20 branches: plants 2–3½ ft. high .... 3. *M. polystachya*
  BB. Fls. on simple or 2–3-branched sts.: plants 1–2 ft. high.
    C. Inner perianth-segms. with 3 large cusps .... 4. *M. tricuspis*
    CC. Inner perianth-segms. with a large central cusp and 2 lateral lobes .... 5. *M. glaucopis*

1. **M. iridioides,** L. St. 1–2½ ft. or more from a short stout creeping rhizome: lvs. 1–1½ ft. long, linear, rigid, in fan-shaped distichous rosettes: fls. 3–4 to a spathe, white with yellow bearded midsection on hafts of outer segms., the lanceolate lilac style-crests deeply bifid and marked bluish, perianth about 1½ in. long: caps. 1–1½ in. long, ellipsoidal. S. Afr. Var. **prolongata,** Leicht., has pure white fls.

2. **M. bicolor,** Spae (*Iris bicolor*, Lindl.). Similar in habit to *M. iridioides*, differing in lvs. slightly longer, fls. lemon-yellow, not bearded, about 2 in. across. S. Afr.

3. **M. polystachya,** Ker (*Iris polystachya*, Thunb.). Rootstock a corm to 1 in. diam., ovoid, black, tunic coarsely fibrous: st. 2–3½ ft. high, erect, stout: fls. 3–6 to a spathe, usually 1–1½ in. long, bright lilac, fugacious, in a lax corymb of 5–20 clusters, outer segms. oblong-spatulate with bright yellow spot at base of blade: caps. ½in. long, clavate-oblong. S. Afr.

4. **M. tricuspis,** Ker (*Iris tricuspis*, Jacq.). Corm small, globose, with fibrous tunic: basal lf. linear, firm and glabrous: st. 1–2 ft. long, simple or with 2–4 erect short branches: fls. white suffused lilac, usually ¾–1 in. long, outer segms. with blue blotch at base of obovate blade, inner segms. with long claw and 3 filiform cusps: caps. ½in. long, clavate. S. Afr.

5. **M. glaucopis,** Baker (*Vieusseuxia glaucopis,* DC.). Corm ½in. diam., with coarse reticulate tunic: basal lf. narrowly linear: st. 1½–2 ft. high, simple or with 1–3 short erect branches: fls. to 2 in. long, white obscurely veined dark blue, outer segms. with blue-black basal blotch, orbicular, inner segms. very small, with large central cusp and 2 small lateral lobes: caps. clavate, about ¾in. long. S. Afr.

5. **NEOMARICA,** Sprague (*Marica,* Ker not Schreber). About 14 species of rhizomatous trop. American and west African plants closely resembling Iris in foliage and fls. and distinguished by the wingless and non-petaloid style-branches; fls. lasting usually only a day; one species is grown widely as a house plant and is readily propagated by division. (Neomar-ica: Latin, probably *new nymph,* Marica being a nymph and legendary mother of the Latins, here perhaps alluding to the fugacious fls.)—Widely known as Marica, but this name as originally used by Schreber becomes a synonym of the closely allied genus Cipura.

N. gracilis, Sprague (*Marica gracilis,* Herb.). Lvs. 6–8 in flabellate rosettes, mostly 1–1½ ft. long and to 1 in. wide, ensiform, somewhat lax apically: st. somewhat flattened, to 1½ ft. long or more, lf.-like: fls. about 2 in. across, outer segms. obovate, white with basal cross marks of yellow and brown, horizontal or slightly reflexed; inner segms. oblanceolate, blue, reflexed, small; usually several fls. to a spathe, each remaining open for only a day. Mex. to Brazil.

6. **SISYRINCHIUM,** L. Blue-eyed-Grass. Satin-Flower. About 70 species of hardy or half-hardy New World grassy-foliaged, rhizomatous or fibrous-rooted herbs producing mostly bluish-purple or yellowish starry fls. in summer.—Sts. simply or few-branched, usually compressed or occasionally terete: lvs. linear-lanceolate and flat, or terete: fls. small, in lax umbellate clusters from a usually 2-valved spathe, the perianth regular, rotate or campanulate, the 6 segms. nearly equal and tube none or very short but segms. connate at base; stamens 3, inserted at base of segms., filaments separate, somewhat connate basally or connate to top; ovary 3-celled, style filiform or the undivided branches thickened and channelled above: caps. loculicidal, ovoid to short-cylindrical. (Sisyrin-chium: old Greek name first applied to some other plant.)—By some authorities the genus has been considered to have over 250 species.

A. Sts. terete or slightly compressed, not winged or lf.-like........................ 1. *S. Douglasii*
AA. Sts. flattened and compressed, angled or winged.
  B. Fls. yellow or cream-colored.
    C. Lvs. to ⅝in. wide: sts. longitudinally striated by flanges: fls. spotted or streaked brown within.................................... 2. *S. striatum*
    CC. Lvs. narrower, to ⅜in. wide: sts. not flanged: fls. not streaked or spotted brown.
      D. Filaments connate to below middle: perianth-tube not swollen, glabrous without: fls. bright yellow.................................... 3. *S. californicum*
      DD. Filaments connate to above the middle: perianth-tube swollen, hairy without: fls. pale cream-colored.................................... 4. *S. iridifolium*
  BB. Fls. blue-violet, purple, reddish or white; filaments connate to top or nearly so.
    C. St. simple, producing usually only a single spathe........................ 5. *S. montanum*
    CC. St. branched, producing 2 to many spathes and each on distinct peduncles.
      D. Basal lvs. about ¼in. wide, equalling or exceeding the coarse stout sts.... 6. *S. Bermudiana*
      DD. Basal lvs. half as wide or narrower than above, often much shorter than sts., the sts. slender.
        E. Plants with basal lvs. about half as long as sts.: spathes very unequal in length.................................... 7. *S. bellum*
        EE. Plants with basal lvs. more than half as long as sts. and usually nearly equalling them: spathes about equal in length.................. 8. *S. angustifolium*

1. **S. Douglasii,** Dietr. (*Olsynium Douglasii,* Bickn. *S. grandiflorum,* Dougl. not Cav.). Sts. 6–12 in. high, simple, somewhat compressed to nearly terete: cauline lvs. 1–2, much reduced and less than one-fourth st. length, stiffly erect: spathe-valves very unequal, the outer long and foliaceous: fls. 1–2, reddish-purple, segms. about ⅝in. long, oblong; filaments connate only at base; style-branches filiform. (Named for David Douglas, page 42.) B. C. to N. Calif.

2. **S. striatum,** Smith. Sts. 15–24 in. high, strongly compressed and narrowly winged, simple or branched: cauline lvs. 1–2, to 1 ft. long and ⅝in. wide: spathe-valves membranous, outer strongly scarious, subequal: fls. several, in numerous sessile spathes that are clustered close together on st., greenish-yellow veined brown, segms. about ⅝in. long, obovate with truncate-mucronate apex; filaments connate only at base; style-branches thickened, channelled above. Chile.

3. **S. californicum,** Dry. (*Marica californica,* Ker. *Hydrastylus californica,* Salisb.). Sts. 6–24 in. high, broadly winged, simple, leafless: lvs. mostly half as long as st., to ¼in. wide, glaucescent: spathe-valves subequal: fls. bright yellow veined black, 2–3 in the solitary spathe, segms. ½–¾in. long, elliptic, pedicels mostly longer than spathes; filaments connate only at base; style-branches filiform. Ore., Calif.

4. **S. iridifolium,** Kunth (*S. chilense,* Hort.). Sts. to 1 ft. high, flattened and winged, branched: lvs. shorter than sts., equitant, to ⅜in. wide: spathes several-fld., the valves subequal: fls. white to cream-colored, about ¾in. across, tube inflated and hairy without; filaments connate to above the middle forming an urceolate tube. Chile.

5. **S. montanum,** Greene (*S. angustifolium,* Auth. in part, not Mill.). Sts. 6–20 in. high or more, usually simple, flattened, winged, pale green to glaucous: lvs. half as long as sts. or longer, to ⅙in. wide, pale or whitish-green: spathes with outer valve nearly twice as long as inner: fls. deep violet-blue, about ½in. across; filaments connate to top or nearly so. Newf. to B. C. south to N. Y. and Utah. Var. **crebrum,** Fern., has sts. and foliage deep green sometimes suffused purple; Greenland to Ont. and Va.

6. **S. Bermudiana,** L. Tender: sts. 1–2 ft. high, stout, branched, flattened and winged, somewhat falcate: lvs. as long as sts. or longer, cauline ones shorter, to ¼in. wide: outer spathe-valves about twice as long as inner, margins narrow white-scarious: fls. deep blue with yellow throat, lobes veined blue-black; filaments connate to top or nearly so. (Bermudiana: early substantive name.) Bermuda.

7. **S. bellum,** Wats. (*S. angustifolium* var. *bellum,* Hort.). Sts. 4–20 in. high, branched, flattened, narrowly winged: lvs. about half as long as sts., to ⅙in. wide: outer spathe-valve longer than inner: fls. violet-blue, segms. about ½in. long, truncate-mucronate; filaments connate to top or nearly so. Calif.

8. **S. angustifolium,** Mill. (*S. graminoides,* Bickn. *S. gramineum,* Lam. *S. anceps,* Cav.). Sts. 10–18 in. high, branched, flattened, broadly winged: lvs. equalling or shorter than st., to ¼in. wide, often lax: spathe-valves usually subequal but occasionally the outer much longer: fls. violet-blue with yellow throat, mostly ½–¾in. across, segms. oblong-spatulate, mucronate; filaments connate to top or nearly so. E. U. S.

7. **BELAMCANDA,** Adans. (*Gemmingia,* Fabr. *Pardanthus,* Ker). Two species in China and Japan, one frequently planted and somewhat nat. in N. Amer.—Strong-growing branching perennials with rhizome, distichous iris-like lvs., and fls. in a dichotomous or laxly corymbose infl.: fls. on pedicels exceeding the spathes; segms. 6, united at base into very short tube above the large ovary, twisting as they fade, the 3 inner ones somewhat shorter; stamens 3, attached at base of segms., anthers basifixed; ovary 3-celled, club-shaped to obovoid, style 3-branched: caps. loculicidal, many-seeded. (Belamcan-da: made from native E. Asian name.)

B. chinensis, DC. (*Ixia chinensis,* L. *B. punctata,* Moench). BLACKBERRY-LILY, from the cluster of large shining round black seeds that remain when the caps. splits. St. 2–3 or 4 ft.: lvs. equitant, sword-shaped, 1 in. wide, many-nerved: fls. 1½–2 in. across, orange with red spots, fugitive, segms. obtuse at apex and narrowed at base: caps. about 1 in. long.—The second species, **B. flabellata,** Grey, less frequently cult., has lvs. closely imbricated for three-quarters their length in flabellate tufts, and yellow unspotted fls. usually appearing later in the autumn.

8. **SCHIZOSTYLIS,** Backh. & Harvey. Two species of rhizomatous herbs of S. Afr., with grass-like foliage, the crimson or lavender fls. in lax distichous spikes.—Sts. terete, slender: fls. 2–8 in unbranched equilateral spikes, the spathe-valves green, lanceolate; perianth regular, tube cylindrical, straight, the oblong lobes forming a campanulate limb; stamens 3, inserted on throat of tube, filaments free, filiform, anthers linear, basifixed; ovary 3-celled, clavate; style as long as tube with 3 spreading subulate or filiform branches: caps. obovoid-oblong, obtuse, loculicidal; seeds small and angular. (Schizos-tylis: Greek *cut style.*)

S. coccinea, Backh. & Harvey. CRIMSON FLAG. Rootstock fleshy with fibrous roots: sts. 1–2 ft. high, with 2–3 erect sheathing reduced lvs.: basal lvs. usually 2–3, to 1½ ft. long and ⅓in. wide, somewhat falcate, midrib distinct: spathe-valves 1–1¼ in. long, lanceolate: fls. 4–8, to 2½ in. long, deep crimson to scarlet, tube to 1¼ in. long, erect; stamens ⅔in. long, anthers bright yellow, equalling filaments in length; style-branches ¾in. long: caps. ½in. long, sessile.—A color form with clear pink fls. is cult. and is not to be confused with the second species of the genus, **S. pauciflora,** Klatt, that is less frequently cult. and differs from typical *S. coccinea* in rootstocks slender, lvs. to 12 in. long and ¼in. wide, spathe-valves shorter; perianth purplish-pink with tube slightly longer than limb.

9. **IXIA,** L. (*Hyalis,* Salisb.) Cormous plants from S. Afr., probably 25 species, with grass-like foliage and spikes or panicled racemes of showy rather small fls. in lilac, yellow, white, and other colors.—Sts. simple or branched in the infl., slender, mostly exceeding the linear distichous nerved lvs.: fls. open, tube long, short or almost none, 1–2 in. across, segms. about equal and oblong; stamens 3, inserted at throat, filaments short; ovary 3-celled, many-ovuled, style exceeding tube, the 3 filiform branches short and curved: caps. small, loculicidal. (Ix-ia: Greek *bird lime,* perhaps referring to the juice of the species.)—Handsome plants for pots, frames, and spring bloom, usually not grown under specific names.

A. Perianth-tube funnelform; filaments as long as anthers or longer....................1. *I. scariosa*
AA. Perianth-tube cylindrical; filaments much shorter than anthers.
B. Fls. green with black throat....................2. *I. viridiflora*
BB. Fls. white or yellow, often with black throat....................3. *I. maculata*

1. **I. scariosa,** Thunb. (*I. incarnata,* Jacq.). Corm to ¾in. diam., tunic of matted fibers: basal lvs. 2–3, to 5 in. long, ensiform: sts. 8–12 in. long, very slender, branched: fls. 3–6 in lax spike, reddish-purple to lilac, about 1 in. long, perianth-tube ¼–½in. long, funnelform, segms. obtuse; filaments as long as anthers or longer.—By some authors *I. incarnata* is kept distinct and reported to differ in having one basal lf. falcate and the others nearly erect.

2. **I. viridiflora,** Lam. (*I. maculata* var. *viridis,* Jacq.). Corm depressed-globose, to ½in. diam., tunic fibrous: lvs. to 15 in. long, narrowly linear, strongly ribbed: sts. to 20 in., slender, simple: fls. many in lax erect spike, green with black throat, to 1½ in. long, perianth-tube about ⅓in. long, cylindrical, segms. oblong-lanceolate, outer obtuse and inner acute; filaments 1/12in. long, much shorter than anthers.

3. **I. maculata,** L. Corm tunicated, about 1 in. diam.: sts. 1–2 ft., mostly simple or nearly so: lvs. 6–12 in. long, ¼in. or less broad: fls. many, in a dense erect spike, yellow with very dark spot in throat, the oblong obtuse segms. about 1 in. long, tube very thin and slender and exceeding spathe; outer spathe-valve 3-toothed or -angled, inner 2-toothed; anthers much exceeding the filaments.—Runs into color vars., with segms. red or purple outside, segms. white but throat nearly black or yellow with brown throat.

10. **STREPTANTHERA,** Sweet. Two species of S. African cormous herbs, having short lvs. in fan-shaped basal rosettes and ixia-like fls.—Corms small with fibrous tunics: sts. forked basally, somewhat longer than lvs., terete: lvs. lanceolate, firm: fls. few, in spikes, perianth regular, rotate, with short funnelform tube, the lobes obovate, obtuse, equal; stamens 3, inserted on throat of tube, filaments flattened, valvate, short, bearing linear erect and twisted anthers; ovary 3-celled; style filiform with the 3 branches clavate and spreading, undivided: caps. loculicidal, nearly globose, small; seeds subglobose, usually crowded in caps. (Streptanthe-ra: Greek *twisted anthers.*)

S. cuprea, Sweet. Corm ovoid, to nearly ¾in. across, producing rather fleshy roots: lvs. 4–7 in. long, lanceolate, abruptly acute to obtuse, narrowed basally: sts. about as long as lvs., 2–5-fld., the spathes to ¾in. long, toothed apically: fls. bright copper-orange, about 1½ in. across, rotate or slightly campanulate, throat dark purple becoming yellow within tube and giving an "eye" appearance to fl.; stamens about ½in. long, the reddish-yellow filaments connivent and anthers bright yellow. Var. **nonpicta,** L. Bolus, has larger bright red fls.

11. **DIERAMA,** Koch. About a half dozen species (25 or more as interpreted by one authority) of S. African cormous summer-bloomers with funnelform fls. on very slender sts.—Corms 1 in. or more across, mostly globose, with fibrous tunics: sts. slender, terete, the infl. in slender pendulous panicled spikes: spathe-valves long-pointed, membranous: lvs. linear, distichous, stiff: fls. many, tube short and cylindrical with longer oblong, ascending and subequal lobes with perianth essentially regular; stamens 3, inserted at throat, anthers linear on short filaments; ovary 3-celled, oblong, ovules many and crowded; style exceeding perianth-tube, the 3 branches very short, club- or wedge-shaped and spreading: caps. small, loculicidal, 3-valved. (Diera-ma: Greek *funnel,* alluding to shape of fls.)

D. pulcherrima, Baker (*Sparaxis pulcherrima,* Hook f.). Sts. 4–6 ft. high: lvs. 1½–2 ft. long and ½in. wide, about 6 in basal rosette, very rigid, strongly nerved, acuminate: fls. typically bright blood-red-purple, the tube about ½in. long and lobes to 1½ in.; anthers longer than filaments; style-branches about 1/12in. long.—A white-fld. form is cult.

12. **LAPEIROUSIA,** Pourr. (incl. *Anomatheca,* Ker). About 50 species in trop. and S. Afr., one or two occasional in gardens.—Cormous small plants on the order of Ixia and Freesia, with distichous flat or linear or even subterete lvs., and rather small fls. in summer, mostly red or blue: spathe-valves bract-like, small or large: perianth tubular, long or short, the tube slender throughout or only slightly enlarged under the spreading essentially equal segms.; stamens inserted in throat, the filaments short, anthers basifixed; ovules many, style slender, each of the 3 branches bifid: caps. small, 3-valved, loculicidal. (Lapeirou-sia: Jean François Galoup de Lapeyrouse, French naval officer of the 18th century; usually written Lapeyrousia, but not so spelled by the founder of the genus.)

L. cruenta, Baker (*Anomatheca cruenta,* Lindl.). Lvs. several, from the base, thin and flat, 6–12 in. long and 1/4–5/8in. broad, about equalling the slender simple scape: fls. few in a secund open spike or raceme, red; tube 1–1½ in. long, very slender, two to three times exceeding the green spathe-valves. S. Afr.

13. **WATSONIA,** Mill. (*Meriana,* Trew). Erect simple-stemmed or branching herbs of S. Afr., with spikes of showy fls., probably 20–30 species.—Gladiolus-like, but differing in the divided style-branches, perianth regular or essentially so, and the tube much more evident and curved; segms. spreading, oblong, nearly or quite equal and alike: fls. large and showy, in terminal and lateral open or spike-like racemes, red varying to white: spathe-valves rigid and entire, usually not lf.-like. (Watso-nia: Sir William Watson, 1715–1787, English botanist, member of the Royal Society.)

A. Perianth-lobes as long as tube; fls. rose-red, of papery texture.................... 1. *W. rosea*
AA. Perianth-lobes half as long as tube; fls. vivid apricot-red, of waxy texture.......... 2. *W. Beatricis*

1. **W. rosea,** Ker (*Neuberia rosea,* Ecklon). Lvs. rigid, usually 2–3 ft. long and 1–2 in. wide, ensiform: sts. 4–6 ft. high, mostly much-branched in infl.: fls. bright rose-red, of papery texture, to 2½ in. long, tube as long as lobes, broadly funnelform in upper part; anthers brown-purple; style-branches overtopping stamens. Var. **Ardernei,** Mathews & L. Bolus (*W. iridifolia* var. *O'Brienii,* N. E. Br.), has pure white fls. (first collected from the wild by H. M. Arderne of Cape Province).

2. **W. Beatricis,** Mathews & L. Bolus. Lvs. 3, to 30 in. long, broadly ensiform: sts. to 3½ ft. high, usually simple or 2–3-branched, cauline lvs. 6–8: fls. bright apricot-red, of waxy texture, abundant, about 3 in. long, tube narrowly funnelform, twice as long as lobes; anthers white becoming violet on pink filaments, style-branches about 1/3in. long. (Named for Miss Beatrice Hops, who first collected it in Cape Province.)

14. **FREESIA,** Klatt (*Nymanina,* Kuntze). One or more species, or 1 variable species of 10 or 12 segregates, in S. Afr., much grown under glass by florists.—Small plants, with bulb-like tunicated corms: sts. slender, branched, with few small lvs., producing a few very fragrant upright fls. in loose raceme-like spikes bent sidewise, and seemingly secund, the spathe-valves ½in. or less long and scarious: lvs. linear, ½in. or less broad: fls. narrow-funnelform, 1–2 in. long, the tube very slender for some distance beyond spathe and then rather abruptly expanding; limb half or less as long as the expanded part of the tube, irregular, central upper segm. being broad and obtuse; 3 stamens inserted below throat, about equalling tube; ovary 3-celled, style slender, style-branches short and bifid: caps. small, loculicidal. (Freesia: named for a Dr. Fr. H. T. Freese, 1795–(?) 1876, a native of Kiel, a student of Ecklon's and of South African plants.)

A. Segms. yellow or white .... 1. *F. refracta*
AA. Segms. bordered rose-purple.. 2. *F. Armstrongii*

1. **F. refracta,** Klatt. Corm ovoid or conical, with heavy tunics: sts. weak, 1–1½ ft. high, about the length of the lowest lvs., bearing a few shorter lvs.: fls. on a horizontal or sidewise rachis, greenish-yellow to bright yellow, tube abruptly narrowed below the middle, the segms. distinctly unequal; spathe-valves narrow, not covering the ovary. Var. **odorata,** Baker, has bright yellow fls. with abruptly narrowed tube, the segms. less unequal, spathe-valves broader and covering the ovary. Var. **alba,** Baker, has large pure white fls. with tube gradually narrowed and segms. nearly equal. Var. **Leichtlinii,** W. Miller (*F. Leichtlinii,* Klatt), has large pale yellow fls. and an abruptly narrowed perianth-tube. Var. **xanthospila,** Voss (*F. xanthospila,* Klatt), is like var. *alba* in color but has abruptly narrowed tube.

2. **F. Armstrongii,** W. Wats. A strong grower with much-branched sts. to 20 in. high: tube of fl. white with orange at base; segms. strongly margined with rose-purple. (Bears the name of W. Armstrong of S. Afr., who sent corms to England in 1898.)—It is from this species that the red, lilac and mauve colors of races of garden hybrids have been derived.

15. **BABIANA,** Ker. Nearly or quite 30 cormous species of low stature, all but 1 in S. Afr., one sometimes planted for the handsome spicate fls. in spring.—Sts. simple, or branched in the infl., slender: lvs. several on the st., plicate and strongly ribbed, mostly hairy, sometimes narrowed to petiole: fls. prevailingly lilac but running to yellow, pink and reds, 1 to a small spathe; perianth with slender tube broadening at top, the 6 oblong or oblanceolate segms. nearly equal; 3 stamens inserted near throat, mostly shorter than segms.; ovary 3-celled, many-ovuled; style-branches short and simple, usually flattened at tip: caps. loculicidal. (Babia-na: Dutch for *baboon*, which is said to eat the bulbs or corms.)

B. stricta, Ker. Corm ½in., long-necked, covered with fibers: sts. 6–12 in., bearing 1–3 spikes and hairy ribbed spathe-valves ¾in. or less long: lvs. shorter than st., sword-shaped, hairy: fls. red or lilac (color forms), funnel-shaped tube equalling or exceeding spathe; segms. obtuse, ¾–1 in. long; stamens about half as long as segms. S. Afr.

16. **SPARAXIS,** Ker. WAND-FLOWER. Much like Babiana and Tritonia, without hairy plicate lvs. as in the former, and with lacerate (cut-lobed) spathe-valves which the other two do not have, the valves wrapped about ovary and short upwardly funnel-shaped perianth-tube; style exceeding tube, the 3 very slender curved branches entire: a series of forms in S. Afr. that may be covered as one variable species or treated as four or five species. (Sparax-is: Greek, denoting the torn spathe-valves.)

S. tricolor, Ker (*Ixia tricolor*, Curt.). Corm about ¾in. diam., with white tunics: sts. 6–18 in. long, simple or forked, with 2 or 3 small lvs. toward base: radical lvs. lanceolate to linear, 6–12 in. long: fls. few, from spathes ½in. long, with yellow throat and dark blotch at base of each segm., otherwise the segms. dark purple, tawny or yellow tinted brown-purple, or sometimes white with purple on upper part outside.

17. **CHASMANTHE,** N. E. Br. As now constituted, a genus of 9 species of cormous summer-bloomers from S. and S. W. Afr.—Sts. usually simple, sometimes 1–2-branched, bearing fls. in a spike, the spathe-valves shorter than the tube and entire: perianth-tube curved, constricted near or below the middle, lower part filiform and more cylindrical above; lobes unequal, upper one spatulate, slightly hooded and much longer than the other 5 lobes, the latter not unequal among themselves and spreading; stamens 3, under upper lobe of fl. and about as long as it, inserted near or below middle of tube; ovary 3-celled, many-ovuled; style with simple branches flattened at tip: caps. angular and winged or thinly compressed, not angular and wingless. (Chasman-the: Greek *gaping flower*, alluding to the gaping mouth of the perianth.)

C. æthiopica, N. E. Br. (*Antholyza æthiopica*, **L.**). Corm large and globose with thin brown tunics: sts. 3–4 ft., usually branched above, spathe-valves greenish, ½–¾in. long: basal lvs. in rosette, sword-shaped, 1–1½ ft. long and 1 in. broad: fls. red-yellow, 1½–2½ in. long, the slender tube part ½in. or less long, the cylindrical curved part 1 in. long; upper segms. long and slender, 1–1¼ in., continuing the curve of the tube, the other 5 much smaller, ½in. or less long, spreading; stamens and style equalling or exceeding upper segms. S. Afr.—Until relatively recently treated as belonging to Antholyza, L., a much misinterpreted genus now considered to be represented by only a single species, *A. ringens*, L., not known to be cult. in U. S. and distinguished from related genera by st. bearing 1 dense sessile lateral spike near its base and whose axis projects beyond as a naked st. bearing sterile bracts. Other species of Antholyza are now assigned to various newly established genera of which only Chasmanthe is much cult. in N. Amer.

18. **GLADIOLUS,** L. Probably about 250 species in the Medit. region and trop. and S. Afr., the Cape being especially rich; certain of the species have given rise to the many vars. grown in the open for summer bloom and also for forcing under glass.—Corm tunicated: sts. 2–4 ft., erect, mostly simple, more or less leafy, with large usually herbaceous spathes (bracts) each yielding 1 sessile fl.: lvs. mostly sword-shaped, 1–2 in. broad, many-nerved, sometimes linear or terete: fls. 2–8 in.

across, commonly showy, red, purple, yellow, white, and other colors, with dilating funnel-shaped tube, curved upward in most species; segms. usually oblong, obtuse or acute, the 3 upper prominently larger than the 3 lower; 3 stamens inserted below throat; ovary 3-celled, many-ovuled; style slender, with short simple branches expanded at tip: caps. oblong to obovoid, loculicidal, ¾–1¼ in. long, shorter than the very acute lanceolate outer spathe-valve but sometimes nearly or quite equalling the inner one; seeds mostly flattened or winged. (Gladi-olus: Latin *small sword,* used here originally because of the sword-like lvs.)—The garden gladioli do not represent any one species. They have been derived by variation and hybridization from several species. It is, therefore, impossible to give them clear botanical names. The beginning of the modern cult. gladioli was the introduction of *G. gandavensis* (from Gand or Ghent, Belgium) in 1841, itself a hybrid (reportedly *G. psittacinus* × *G. cardinalis*), although *G. Colvillei,* another hybrid, was of earlier origin and is apparently yet represented in cult. Of the species of Gladiolus, *G. primulinus* is probably most nearly preserved in garden stock; it is of relatively recent introduction, although now much represented in hybrids, one group of them known by its name. A hybrid with marked characters may be intro. under a Latin name, but by subsequent hybridizations it becomes blended in other hybrids and its original character is modified or lost. Probably none of the old named hybrids is now in cult. in its original form.

Several fl. forms and color marks are characteristic of present garden gladioli, represented by such historic names and groups as here described; but with the continuing breeding, it is impossible to refer all the named vars. to definite groups. Vars. with ruffled fls. are produced. The cultivars are many, and other groups than the following are recognized by fanciers. Except for the first two, the kinds treated below represent, for the most part, progenitors of hort. races and are of hybrid origin.

A. Color of fls. prevailingly clear light yellow (may be veined purple in throat).
  B. Lvs. flat: spike 4–6-fld. .... 1. *G. primulinus*
  BB. Lvs. terete: spike mostly 3-fld. .... 2. *G. tristis*
AA. Color of fls. not characteristically clear yellow.
  B. Fls. hooded (upper segms. more or less arching over).
    C. Blooms red and reddish-yellow, not purple, streaked .... 3. *G. gandavensis*
    CC. Blooms running into purple, blotched .... 4. *G. Lemoinei*
  BB. Fls. wide open, spreading, not hooded.
    C. Size of fls. very large; segms. broad .... 5. *G. nanceianus*
    CC. Size of fls. small; segms. narrow, long-acute .... 6. *G. Colvillei*

1. **G. primulinus,** Baker. Lvs. flat, linear-ensiform, about 1 ft. long: fls. clear primrose-yellow throughout; tube 1 in. or more long, much curved above; 3 upper segms. ovate or obovate-acute, hooded, 3 lower segms. deflexed and much smaller. Trop. Afr.—Subsequently considered by Baker as a color form of *G. Quartinianus,* Rich. It has entered into the recent hort. gladioli, with its hooded fls. of characteristic yellow.

2. **G. tristis,** L. Lvs. terete, 3 in number, sometimes spirally twisted and occasionally so prominently ribbed as to seem weakly winged: fls. yellowish-white, flushed or veined purple in throat, not hooded, segms. acute, spreading or recurved at tips, margins sometimes undulate; anthers yellow. S. Afr. Var. **concolor,** Baker (*G. concolor,* Salisb.), has clear grayish-yellow fls. devoid of purple coloration in throat.

3. **G. gandavensis,** Van Houtte. Late- or summer-flowering, with long spikes: fls. red and reddish-yellow, variously streaked and lined; segms. obtuse or short-acute, the upper ones horizontal or somewhat hooded. Hybrid, supposed to be between *G. psittacinus,* Hook., and *G. cardinalis,* Curt., S. African species, perhaps then or subsequently with infusion of *G. oppositiflorus,* Herb., also S. Afr.—The basic race on which modern gladioli apparently rest.

4. **G. Lemoinei,** Hort. Known by the purple blotches on the lower segms.; colors tinted white to bright yellow, red and purple; perianth somewhat bell-shaped, the upper ones either projected forward horizontally or strongly hooded; segms. broad and heavy. Cross of *G. gandavensis* and *G. purpureo-auratus,* Hook. f., the latter from S. Afr., at the nurseries of Victor Lemoine, Nancy, France, in 1875.

5. **G. nanceianus,** Hort. Characterized by very large open wide-spreading fls., not hooded or bell-shaped, upper segm. long and upright, 2 side segms. widely flaring and measuring 4–8 in. from tip to tip; color brilliant shades of red and purple, more or less blotched. Cross of *G. Lemoinei* and *G. Saundersii,* Hook. f., the latter from S. Afr., at the Lemoine establishment at Nancy, made in 1883.—Of similar parentage as no. 4 is **G.**

Childsii, Hort. (*G. Leichtlinii,* Hort.), a race with large wide-open fls. and very broad segms.; it had much influence on the development of gladioli in N. Amer., but is now little separated as a race. As originally known, *G. Childsii* had highly colored fls. in shades of red with variegated and spotted throats, but lighter colors later developed; plants of great vigor and size. It originated with Leichtlin, Germany, first blooming in 1877.

6. **G. Colvillei,** Sweet. Early-flowering, with short spikes: fls. open or flaring, not distinctly hooded, segms. oblong-acute and spreading, scarlet with long yellow blotches at base of lower segms., running into white. Raised in 1823 at Colville's nursery, Chelsea, England, the progeny of *G. concolor,* Salisb. × *G. cardinalis,* Curt., both from S. Afr.—This race is used for growing under glass. It is a marked race, with relatively small fls. and narrow spreading sharp segms.

19. **ACIDANTHERA,** Hochst. About 18 species in trop. and S. Afr., one sometimes grown for summer bloom.—Cormous, with linear lvs. and fls. in a loose spike, on a somewhat leafy erect usually simple st., the spathe-valves long and green: fls. whitish, pink, yellowish, to purple, usually with a long cylindrical tube only slightly dilated upwards; segms. nearly or about equal, spreading, oblong; 3 stamens in throat, filaments slender, the connective of the anthers sometimes produced as a cusp; ovary 3-celled, many-ovuled; style long, the 3 branches short and simple and flattened at end: caps. oblong, loculicidal. (Acidanthe-ra: Greek *cusp* and *anther.*)

A. bicolor, Hochst. Corm 1 in. diam., with brown tunics: sts. simple, 1–1½ ft. long, bearing 1 or 2 small lvs., and very loose few-fld. spike, the outer spathe-valve 2–3 in. long: fls. creamy-white, blotched chocolate-brown within, the slender tube 4–5 in. long; segms. 1½ in. long, acute; stamens nearly as long as segms. Trop. Afr.

20. **TRITONIA,** Ker (*Montbretia,* DC.). S. African plants of perhaps 40–50 species, a few grown for the showy summer bloom.—Corm with reticulated tunics: sts. branched and with many sheathing linear or sword-shaped lvs. toward base, the spathe-valves not lacerate but apiculate at tip: fls. pink, yellow, tawny, red, white, or otherwise, in panicled spikes; perianth with narrow short or long tube that dilates at top; segms. oblong or obovate and nearly equal, in some species with a callus or process on the 3 lower ones; 3 stamens inserted at base of funnel; ovary 3-celled, many-ovuled, the style-branches short and simple: caps. loculicidal, 3-lobed; seeds (by abortion) 1–2 in each locule. (Trito-nia: *weather-cock,* alluding to variable direction of stamens in different species.)

T. crocata, Ker. Corms about 1 in. diam.: lvs. 4–8 in. long and to ½in. wide, 4–6 in number: sts. 1–1½ ft. high, terminated by lax secund spike: fls. bright fulvous-yellow, about 1¼ in. long, perianth-tube less than half as long as the broadly cuneate to obovate lobes. Var. **miniata,** Baker (*Ixia miniata,* Jacq.), has bright red fls.

21. **CROCOSMIA,** Planch. About 5 species in trop. and S. Afr.—Distinguished from Tritonia by spathe-valves notched or cut, thin and membranous; tube of perianth little dilated upward: caps. longer than broad, not lobed and scarcely grooved; seeds 4 or more in each locule. (Crocos-mia: Greek *saffron smell,* when the dried fls. are placed in water.)

A. Perianth-tube twice as long as lobes. . . . . 1. *C. Pottsii*
AA. Perianth-tube shorter than the spreading lobes.
  B. Fls. orange-yellow. . . . . 2. *C. aurea*
  BB. Fls. crimson to orange-crimson. . . . . 3. *C. crocosmæflora*

1. **C. Pottsii,** N. E. Br. (*Tritonia Pottsii,* Baker). Corms stoloniferous: lvs. 12–18 in. long and to ¾in. wide, 4–6 in number: sts. 2½–4 ft. high, terminated by lax distichously branched infl.: fls. orange-yellow tinged reddish, about 1¼ in. long; perianth-tube broadly funnelform, twice as long as oblong lobes; anthers half as long as filaments. (Intro. by Mr. G. H. Potts of Lasswade near Edinburgh.)

2. **C. aurea,** Planch. Coppertip. Sts. 2–4 ft., branched, with only few small lvs., spathe-valves brownish, acute, about ¼in. long: radical or basal lvs. shorter than st., linear or sword-shaped: fls. bright orange-yellow; tube ¾–1 in. long, exceeded by the oblong-lanceolate wide-spreading segms.; stamens and style equalling segms.

3. **C. crocosmæflora,** N. E. Br. (*Tritonia crocosmæflora,* Lemoine). The common montbretia of gardens, hybrid of *C. Pottsii* and *C. aurea,* blooming first in 1880 in France: sts. slender, branching, 3–4 ft., equalling or exceeding the broad-linear or sword-shaped lvs. which are ¼–1 in. broad: fls. orange-crimson, 1½–2 in. across, variable in size and shape as well as in length of stamens and style; tube curved, shorter than the oblong usually

spreading segms. or sometimes much longer than the nearly erect small segms.; the segms. are sometimes darker colored or barred below middle.—Apparently the forms exhibit one or the other parent.

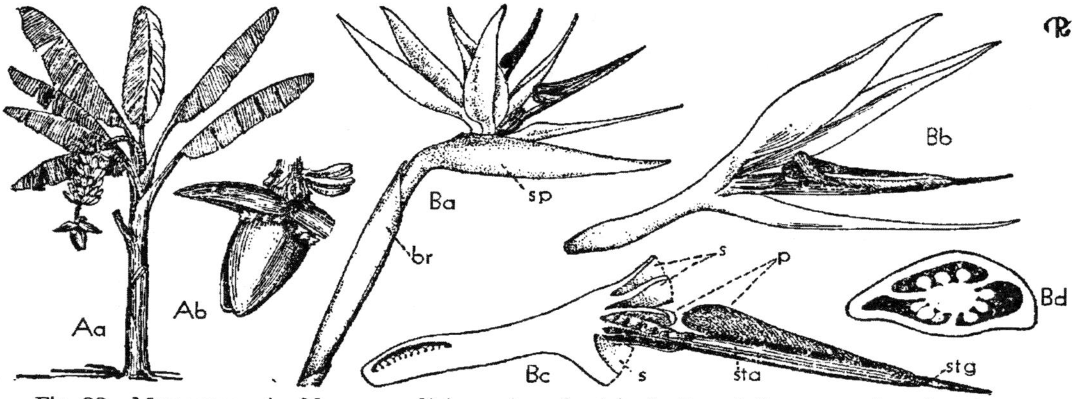

Fig. 38. MUSACEÆ. A, *Musa paradisiaca:* Aa, plant in fruit and flower, much reduced; Ab, inflorescence, × 1/20. B, *Strelitzia Reginæ:* Ba, inflorescence, × 1/6 (br bract, p petal, s sepal, sp spathe, sta stamen, stg stigma); Bb, single flower, × 3/8; Bc, same, vertical section (sepals partially removed), × 1/2; Bd, ovary, cross-section, × 2.

38. MUSACEÆ. BANANA FAMILY

A half dozen genera and perhaps 100 species of the tropics of both hemispheres, a few striking ornamental plants, two producing the bananas of commerce and one yielding important fiber.—Stout usually per. herbs, or partially woody, often of gigantic stature, the st. sheathed by the petioles or lf.-bases: lvs. mostly large, entire, pinnately-nerved, the blade sword-shaped to lanceolate or oblong: infl. spicate or paniculate, subtended by spathes, heavily and often peculiarly bracted, the fls. mostly sessile or nearly so and each one either small-bracted or bractless; fls. bisexual or plants monœcious, borne in axils of large bracts, the perianth clearly differentiated as calyx and corolla, the sepals mostly 3 and united or not; petals 3 or less, distinct or somewhat united; stamens 6, 1 a sterile staminode and the others anther-bearing, all free; ovary inferior, 3-celled, the ovules single or mostly many; style simple, but stigma often 3- or 6-lobed: fr. either baccate or capsular, indehiscent, dehiscent, or separating into 3 carpels.

A. Lvs. and bracts spirally arranged: calyx tubular, soon split down one side: fr. not dehiscent. . . . . 1. MUSA
AA. Lvs. and bracts distichous: calyx not tubular: fr. dehiscent.
B. Petals not united: plant tree-like: fr. a caps. . . . . 2. RAVENALA
BB. Petals more or less united: plant usually not tree-like.
C. The 2 lateral petals united to form an organ in which lie the stamens and style: fr. a loculicidal many-seeded caps. . . . . 3. STRELITZIA
CC. The petals forming a short tube: fr. splitting into 3 1-seeded parts. . . . . 4. HELICONIA

1. **MUSA**, L. Fifty or more robust and rapidly-growing species in the tropics of the eastern hemisphere, comprising ornamental subjects and plants yielding food and fiber, some stoloniferous and forming large clumps.—Rhizomatous or bulb-form at base: sts. 1 or several, each blooming once, stout, short or tall, sometimes of great height: lvs. spirally arranged and the great bases successively sheathing forming the trunk, the blade long, large and heavy, with age splitting transversely in the wind: infl. terminal, emerging from the leafy sheaths, in the form of a long drooping or erect spike bearing flat clusters of fls. underneath broad colored bracts; fls. unisexual by abortion, the upper clusters on the rachis functioning as males, the lower fertile and giving rise to the "hands" of fr.; calyx tubular but soon splitting down one side to base; corolla represented by a single opposed petal, entire or toothed; stamens usually 6, 1 a staminode: fr. a long berry-like indehiscent body with few or many seeds, in the cult. bananas seedless. (Mu-sa: Antonio Musa, physician to

Octavius Augustus, first emperor of Rome, 63–14 B. C.)—**M. textilis,** Née, the Abacá or Manila Hemp, extensively grown in the Philippines (where it is endemic) and now in Cent. Amer., for the fiber in the sheathing lf.-bases, is a plant reaching 20 ft., with oblong often spotted lvs. glaucous beneath, and a short drooping spike; outer calyx-lobes with short horn-like hooks: fr. not edible, 2–3 in. long, 3-angled and curved, seedy. The Fe'i banana, commonly cult. for food throughout most of the Pacific isls. and represented by a score or more of clones, is **M. Troglodytarum,** L. (*M. Fehi,* Bertero), and clones of its var. **acutæbracteata,** MacDaniels, are encountered most frequently.

A. Grown for the edible fr., stoloniferous, spreading in clumps.
B. Plant dwarf, usually not exceeding a man's height: petiole 6 in. or less long...... 1. *M. nana*
BB. Plant tall: petiole 1 ft. or longer........ 2. *M. paradisiaca*
AA. Grown for ornament, not stoloniferous: fr. not edible........ 3. *M. Ensete*

1. **M. nana,** Lour. (*M. Cavendishii,* Lamb.). DWARF BANANA. Dwarf and compact, trunk usually not over 6 ft., stoloniferous, 5–6 in. thick: lvs. spreading, 2–4 ft. long and 1–2 ft. broad, somewhat glaucous, more or less spotted and colored when young: spike drooping, short, with red-brown bracts 3–6 in. long and very broad; calyx yellowish-white, 1–1¼ in. long, the free petal half as long: frs. very many in a bunch or spike (often 200 or more), 4–5 in. long, 6-angled, somewhat curved, fragrant, seedless. S. China.—Not to be confused with small-fruited forms of the tall or common banana. Hardier than the tall banana; much grown in Bermuda, and planted in S. U. S.

2. **M. paradisiaca,** L. (*M. sapientum* var. *paradisiaca,* Baker). PLANTAIN. Plant tall, 10–30 ft., stoloniferous, the st. thick and heavy: lvs. erect or ascending, 5–9 ft. long, 1½–2 ft. broad, bright green: spike drooping, 2–5 ft. long, bracts red or violet, 6–12 in. or more long, lanceolate, oblong-lanceolate or ovate-lanceolate, the male fls. and their bracts nearly or quite persistent; calyx yellowish-white, mostly 1½–2 in. long, the free petal usually more than half as long: frs. usually less than 100 in a bunch or spike, 8–14 in. long, hard and mostly strongly angled, yellowish-green, edible when cooked, seedless. (Paradisiaca: of paradise; *i. e.,* of gardens.) Native in India, but widely cult. in tropics.

Var. **sapientum,** Kuntze (*M. sapientum,* L.). BANANA. Male fls. and bracts deciduous: fr. yellow at maturity, sweet and edible without cooking, seedless. (Sapientum: of men or mankind; literally, *of the wise men.*) Races have red frs. (*rubra*), small thin-skinned "lady-finger" frs. (*Champa*), and many others. Some kinds are practically inedible and are seed-bearing. If a banana is cut across, the 3 carpels or cells may be made out, and dark-colored rudiments of seeds are usually visible. A crude fiber is produced in the lf.-sheaths.

3. **M. Ensete,** Gmel. (*Ensete edule,* Horan.). ABYSSINIAN BANANA. Stout plant, growing to a single st. or trunk 20–40 ft. high, swollen at base: lvs. very large, 10–20 ft. long and 2–3 ft. broad, oblong and acute-cuspidate: spike globose, erect, densely covered with dark reddish-brown bracts 8–12 in. long; fls. many to a bract, in 2 series, whitish, 1½–2 in. long, with 3-lobed calyx and corolla: fr. dry, 2–3 in. long, inedible, with a few very large black seeds ¾–1 in. long, and having a sunken area on one side. (Ensete: from the native name.) Abyssinia.—Largest known species.

2. **RAVENALA,** Adans. Two species, one in Madagascar, the other in Guiana and Brazil, the former planted in warm countries for its striking appearance.—Trunk palm-like: lvs. immense, musa-like, in 2 ranks toward top of st., giving the plant a narrow fan-like aspect, the long petioles little sheathing: infl. in the axils, much shorter than the lvs., the bracts stiff and boat-like, one above the other in heavy distichous spikes; fls. bisexual, whitish, several from each bract, of elongated stiff free parts; sepals 3, equal, 6–8 in. long; petals 3, the lateral ones like the sepals, the other shorter; stamens 6 in the Madagascar species, 5 in the American, 4 or 5 in. long: fr. a 3-celled woody caps. with many seeds. (Ravena-la: the name in Madagascar.)

R. madagascariensis, Sonn. TRAVELERS-TREE, so-called because the cup-like lf.-bases hold water which travellers are said to drink. Trunk rising 30 ft. and even more, making a striking and unmistakable object. Madagascar.

3. **STRELITZIA,** Banks. BIRD-OF-PARADISE FLOWER. About 5 S. African plants, two grown under glass and in the open far S. for the odd and showy infl. and the banana-like lvs.—Per., the trunk sometimes more or less woody, often wanting: lvs. distichous, the long petiole channelled: fls. several in a rigid boat-like spathe-bract on a long or short peduncle, bisexual and very irregular; sepals 3, yellow or

white, narrow-lanceolate and long-pointed, much projecting; petals 3, 1 small the other 2 conniving to form an arrow-shaped organ (the "tongue") in the groove of which the stamens and style lie; stamens 5, perfect; ovary 3-celled, style 3-branched, ovules many: caps. 3-angled, loculicidal. (Strelit-zia Reginæ: dedicated to Queen Charlotte Sophia, of the house of Mecklenburg-Strelitz, wife of George III.)

A. Outer parts of fl. (sepals) yellow; tongue blue.......................................1. *S. Reginæ*
AA. Outer parts white.
  B. Tongue white: spathe purple.......................................2. *S. augusta*
  BB. Tongue blue: spathe reddish-brown.......................................3. *S. Nicolai*

1. **S. Reginæ,** Banks. Trunkless: lf.-blades oblong-lanceolate, 10–18 in. long, acute at apex, rounded or cuneate at base, 4–6 in. broad, the petiole very long: scape nearly or quite as long as lvs., with sheaths, the upper floral one oblique, 6–8 in. long, from which the long-pointed fl.-parts stand erect; sepals 3–4 in. long, yellow; tongue of similar length, auricled on either side, dark blue, the stamens not exserted, the 3 style-branches projecting.—The commonest species in cult.

2. **S. augusta,** Thunb. Plant larger, with trunk a few in. to 18 ft. high: lf.-blades 2–4 ft. long and 1–2 ft. broad, banana-like, the petiole deeply wing-channelled: scape short; spathe purplish, 10–15 in. long, the projecting fl.-parts white, the sepals 5–8 in. long; tongue about 3 in. long.

3. **S. Nicolai,** Regel & Koern. Resembling *S. augusta* but larger and more tree-like, up to 25 ft. tall: spathe reddish-brown; sepals white, about 7 in. long; tongue blue, about 4 in. long. (Named for Grandduke Nicolai Nicolajewitsch, patron of gardening in Russia.)

4. **HELICONIA,** L. (*Bihai*, Adans. *Bihaia*, Kuntze). Thirty to 40 species in the American tropics, sometimes planted for the large banana-like foliage and showy fl.-bracts.—The genus differs from the other cult. genera of the family in the acaulescent or slender-stemmed character (many long-stalked lvs. rising from the ground), and the usually blue caps. that breaks up into berry-like parts or frs.: fls. bisexual, few to several crowded in conduplicate or boat-shaped bracts on peduncles or scapes; sepals 3, free or somewhat united with corolla, the latter short-tubular and with 2 lateral lobes small and the third mostly wanting; perfect stamens 5; ovary inferior, with solitary ovules in each of the 3 cells, the style slender, stigma capitate or shallowly 3-lobed. (Helico-nia: bears the name of Mt. Helicon, seat of the Muses; application fanciful.)

A. Lvs. plain green.......................................1. *H. caribæa*
AA. Lvs. striped yellow.......................................2. *H. aureo-striata*

1. **H. caribæa,** Lam. (*H. Bihai*, Auth. not L.). WILD PLANTAIN. BALISIER. Striking plant with many lvs. standing 10–15 ft. high, transversely ribbed, the petioles very long: bracts scarlet and showy, sometimes green or yellow, 4–12 in. long, distichous and alternate on the scape (which is about the length of the petioles), broad-clasping at base: fls. included in the bracts. W. Indies, Cent. and S. Amer.; nat. in oriental tropics.—*H. Bihai*, L., with which this species has been confused, has the bracts variegated.

2. **H. aureo-striata,** Bull. Perhaps a derivative of *H. caribæa:* at least nativity unknown. Lvs. more or less feathered or splashed along midrib with bright yellow and striped transversely following veins with same.

39. ZINGIBERACEÆ. GINGER FAMILY

About 40 genera and 400 or more trop. species, mostly in the Old World, a few grown for the ornamental foliage and habit; ginger and other spices and condiments are derived from certain species.—Nearly all per. rhizomatous herbs, with short mostly simple sts., the petiolate or sessile sheathing entire lvs. linear, lanceolate or oblong and mostly acuminate, with ligule at summit of petiole, radical and cauline: fls. bisexual, irregular, commonly in bracted spikes, heads or panicles, one or more under each bract; perianth of 6 parts, in a calyx series and corolla series; calyx tubular or somewhat spathe-like, generally 3-toothed; corolla tubular, unequally 3-lobed; fertile stamen 1, the 2 anther-cells sometimes separated by a connective; staminodia 1 and petal-like (lip), and sometimes more, in which case the lateral ones may be filiform or petal-like; ovary inferior, 1-celled, sometimes 2–3-celled, many-ovuled; style and stigma 1, the style held by the anther: fr. a loculicidal often tardily dehiscent caps. or fleshy and indehiscent.—Aside from the following genera, species of Costus (with petal-like filament and infl. cone-like) may be planted far S.

A. Lateral staminodes not petal-like, none, or small and toothed, or sometimes narrow and adnate to the lip.
B. Filament of fertile anther short or nearly wanting and not petal-like: infl. cone-like.
C. The 2 anther-cells parallel, and the connective commonly produced into a long appendage........ 1. ZINGIBER
CC. The 2 anther-cells divergent above or pointing in different directions, the connective mostly expanded, crested or 2-lobed........ 2. AMOMUM
BB. Filament elongated: infl. not cone-like........ 3. ALPINIA
AA. Lateral staminodes large and petal-like.
B. Connective between 2 anther-cells appendaged at base; filament of fertile stamen short and broad.
C. Filament of fertile stamen not united with lateral staminodes: caps. elongate.... 4. ROSCOEA
CC. Filament of fertile stamen united with lateral staminodes: caps. spherical..... 5. CURCUMA
BB. Connective not appendaged at base; filament of fertile stamen long and slender .... 6. HEDYCHIUM

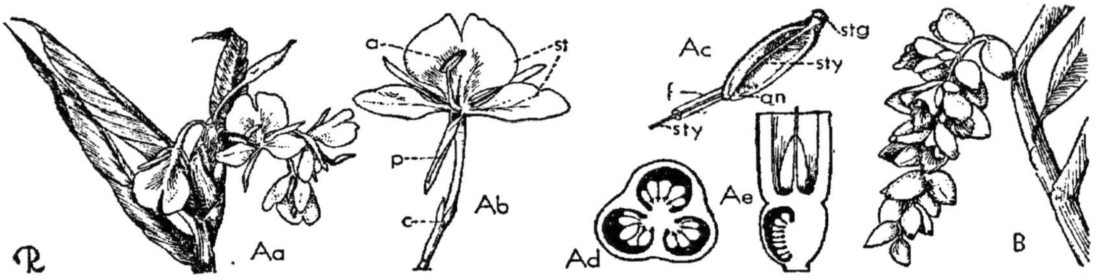

Fig. 39. ZINGIBERACEÆ. A, *Hedychium coronarium:* Aa, flowering stem, × 1/6; Ab, flower habit (c calyx, p petal, st staminodia, a stamen, style and stigma), × 1/4; Ac, anther and stigma (f filament, sty style, an anther-cell, stg stigma), × 1; Ad, ovary, cross-section, × 3; Ae, ovary, vertical section, × 2. B, *Alpinia speciosa:* inflorescence, × 1/6.

1. **ZINGIBER,** Adans. GINGER. Fifty to 60 species are recognized, in tropics of farther Asia to New Guinea.—Rootstocks tuberous, aromatic: sts. leafy: lvs. sheathing at base, oblong-lanceolate: infl. spicate, usually radical, but sometimes arising from the sides or apex of the st., the bracts persistent and commonly with 1 fl. underneath; calyx cylindrical and shortly 3-lobed; corolla cylindrical, the tube enlarged at summit, the lobes lanceolate; lip deflexed, entire, emarginate or shortly 3-lobed, the lateral staminodes (if present) very small and adnate to it; filament of anther short, the anther-cells joined by a long-spurred connective equalling or exceeding themselves, the spurs standing above the lip: caps. oblong or globose, 3-valved or rupturing irregularly. (Zin-giber: classical name, coming from the Sanskrit.)—The zingibers are little grown for ornament, although various species may be found in choice collections.

Z. officinale, Roscoe. COMMON GINGER, grown in trop. countries. St. 3 ft. or more high: lvs. lanceolate to linear-lanceolate, sessile, narrowing to base, 6–12 in. long and 3/4in. broad: spike 2–3 in. long and 1 in. thick, dense, on a bracted peduncle shorter than foliage, the ovate green often yellow-margined bracts 1 in. long: corolla yellow-green, the segms. about 3/4in. long, exceeding the purple yellow-spotted lip. Probably native in Pacific isls., but widely cult. for the irregular rhizome that provides much of the ginger of commerce.—**Z. Zerumbet,** Smith, is also cult. for its rhizome: the lvs. are broader and usually puberulent beneath, lip yellow.

2. **AMOMUM,** L. Nearly 100 species in farther Asia, one or two grown for habit and fragrant foliage.—From Zingiber the genus differs in the connective between the anther-cells not long-spurred although sometimes crested or 2-lobed or variously broadened, the cells diverging from each other at the top, the lip not 3-lobed: plants with leafy sts. and mostly densely-fld. spikes directly from the creeping rhizome and therefore beneath the foliage. (Amo-mum: from the Greek, referring to poison antidote, for which some of the plants may have been used.)

A. Cardamon, L. Plant 4–8 ft. tall, the st. less: lvs. sessile, glabrous, linear-lanceolate, 6–10 in. long, narrowed to a caudate apex: scape 2–4 in. long, with ovate-acute scales; calyx 3-lobed, the tube about equalling the silky ovary; corolla yellow, the narrow tube about 3/4in. long; lip nearly 3/4in. long, obovate. E. Indies.—Not to be confused with

Elettaria Cardamomum, Maton, which provides the true cardamons (seeds) used as spice, seasoning and in medicine, although inferior seeds of *A. Cardamon* may be substituted; the Elettaria is a larger plant with large lvs. pubescent beneath, and few-fld. loose spikes or panicles, connective without appendages.

3. **ALPINIA,** L. About 140–150 species in trop. Asia and Polynesia, a few grown in warm countries for ornament.—From Zingiber and Amomum it differs in bearing the spike or panicle terminating a tall leafy st.: calyx tubular and shallowly 3-toothed, corolla with cylindrical tube commonly not exceeding the calyx and the segms. narrow; lip spreading, often broad and showy; anther-cells diverging at apex, the connective usually not prominent: fr. mostly indehiscent, dry or fleshy. (Alpin-ia: Prosper Alpinus was an Italian botanist, 1553–1617.)

A. Lvs. green..1. *A. speciosa*
AA. Lvs. striped with white..2. *A. Sanderæ*

1. **A. speciosa,** Schum. (*A. nutans*, Roscoe. *Renealmia nutans*, Andr. *Languas speciosa*, Small). Shell-Flower. A striking plant from E. Asia, often seen in warm regions: sts. 6–12 ft. high, leafy, the lvs. oblong-lanceolate or elliptic-lanceolate, glabrous and shining, blades 1–2 ft. long and 2–5 in. broad, with long parallel veins: fls. fragrant, in a terminal spike-like at length nodding raceme with hairy rachis, orchid-like because of the crinkled yellow lip with red and brown variegations; calyx about 1 in. long; corolla white tinged purplish.

2. **A. Sanderæ,** Hort. Lvs. 6–8 in. long, ¾–1 in. wide, striped and marked with clear white: plant sterile. Botanical position uncertain.

4. **ROSCOEA,** Smith. About 15 species in Himalayas and China, half-hardy, occasionally grown.—Per. herbs with thick fleshy roots: lvs. parallel-veined, lanceolate or oblong: fls. few, in terminal spikes at ends of leafy sts.; calyx more or less tubular, split down one side; corolla-tube long, slender, the upper lobe broad, cucullate, erect, the lateral lobes spreading, narrower; lateral staminodia oblanceolate, petaloid, erect, the lip large, cuneate, deflexed, 2-cleft or emarginate; filament of fertile stamen short, anther narrow, connective with 2 basal spurs; stigma spherical or circular: caps. elongate. (Rosco-ea: named after Wm. Roscoe, 1753–1831, English botanist.)

R. cautleoides, Gagnep. Height 9–12 in.: lvs. usually sessile, to 6 in. long and 1 in. wide, with long tapering apex: fls. 4–7, pale yellow, sometimes purplish, 2–3 in. long. China.

5. **CURCUMA,** L. Forty to 50 species in trop. Asia and Afr., mostly the former, and to Australia; strong herbs sometimes raised for foliage and habit and the showy bracts.—From the Zingiber tribe it is separated by the large petal-like lateral staminodia: rhizome tuber-bearing: st. none or very short: lvs. mostly large, lanceolate or oblong or only rarely linear: spikes dense, compound, terminated by a tuft of large colored bracts; fls. 2 or more to each bract, bearing 2 prominent lateral staminodes; calyx with short cylindrical minutely-toothed tube; corolla funnelform, with broad segms.; lip rounded, deflexed at tip; anther-cells close together, the connective spurred at base: caps. globular, 3-valved. (Cur-cuma: from a native name.)

A. Lvs. rounded at base..1. *C. petiolata*
AA. Lvs. narrowed at base..2. *C. longa*

1. **C. petiolata,** Roxb. Rhizome small: lvs. with petiole 6–12 in. long, the blade 6–10 in. and 3–6 in. broad, prominently rounded at base, strongly veined and curved: scape not exceeding radical petioles, 4–6 in. long and 2 in. diam., with green bracts except those of the tuft at top which are purple and showy; fls. yellowish-white, nearly as long as bracts, the corolla-tube 1 in. long, lip nearly orbicular. E. Asia.

2. **C. longa,** L. Rhizome large, yielding turmeric (condiment and dye): lvs. oblong or elliptic, narrowed at base, 12–18 in. long and 4–8 in. broad, the petiole equalling the blade: spike 4–7 in. long and 2 in. diam., the peduncle inclosed in petiole-sheath, bracts green except pale pink tuft: fls. pale yellow, equalling the bracts. Farther India; much cult. by E. Indians.

6. **HEDYCHIUM,** Koenig. Ginger-Lily. Some 40 species in E. Asia and Malaysia, one in Madagascar, two cult. in warm countries and also planted about ponds in N.—Belongs with Curcuma in the tribe having well-developed petal-like lateral staminodes, but differs in having very slender connective not spurred or

crested and without crown of bracts on the spike: rootstock strong, more or less tuberous: st. long and bearing oblong or lanceolate distichous lvs.: fls. in a terminal spike or thyrse, sometimes few, the bracts ovate or oblong and large; calyx cylindrical, 3-toothed or -lobed; corolla slender-tubed with linear spreading segms. little longer than calyx; lip large, 2–3-lobed or -toothed; anther-cells near together: caps. globose, 3-valved. (Hedych-ium: Greek combination, *sweet snow*, from the color and fragrance of some species.)

A. Fls. white..1. *H. coronarium*
AA. Fls. yellow..2. *H. Gardnerianum*

1. **H. coronarium**, Koenig. GARLAND-FLOWER. Strong free grower, 3–6 ft.: lvs. sessile, oblong-lanceolate or lanceolate, 8–24 in. long and 2–5 in. broad, acuminate, finely pubescent or thinly hairy beneath: spike 6–12 in. long, imbricated with broad pointed green finally brown bracts, terminating the leafy sts.; fls. white and fragrant, the showy parts long-exserted, the corolla-tube 3 in. long, in summer and autumn. India and Malay Isls. and nat. elsewhere.—Sometimes called Butterfly-Lily.

2. **H. Gardnerianum**, Wall. Plant 3–6 ft. high: lvs. 8–18 in. long, 4–6 in. wide, acuminate, thin-hairy beneath: spike to 18 in. long: fls. light yellow, with long-exserted red filament; corolla-tube 2 in. long, lobes 1½ in. long. (Named for Edward Gardner, English colonel who served in Nepal in 1817.) India.

40. CANNACEÆ. CANNA FAMILY

One genus, represented in the warm parts of both hemispheres, some of the species or derivatives much used for summer planting for subtrop. and floral effects.—Per. erect strong branched or unbranched herbs with stately habit, branching and sometimes tuberiferous rootstocks, bearing large alternate broad entire lvs. with sheathing petioles: fls. mostly red or yellow, very showy in the improved cult. kinds, in a terminal spike, raceme or narrow panicle, very irregular; sepals 3, small and usually green, looking like bracts; petals 3, sepal-like, mostly narrow and pointed, green or colored, exceeding the sepals and alternate with them, one of them usually smaller than the others; floral parts more or less united at base into a tube; stamens represented by staminodia and comprising the showy part of the fl., 5 in number in the common cult. kinds (less in certain others), 3 (or 2) much enlarged and broadened and forming the main "petals," one mostly narrower and reflexed and forming the "lip," another still narrower and more or less coiled and bearing 1 fertile anther-cell on its side; style single and long, flat or club-shaped, prominent in the center of the fl.; ovary inferior, 3-celled, many-ovuled: fr. a 3-valved and mostly 3-angled papillose, warty, or somewhat bristly caps., bearing the persistent calyx.

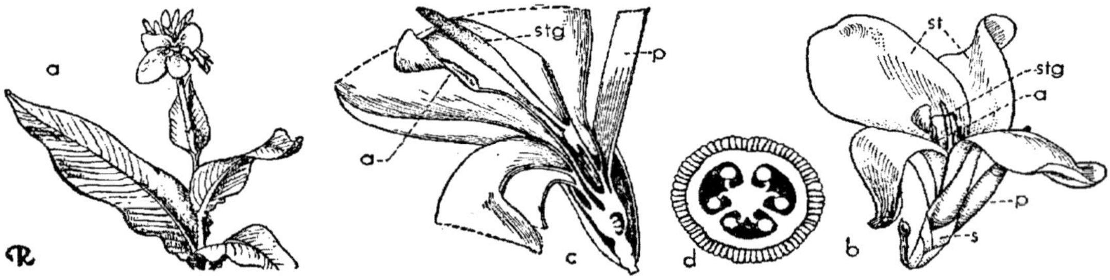

Fig. 40. CANNACEÆ. *Canna generalis:* a, flowering plant, much reduced; b, flower (s sepal, p petal, a anther, stg stigma, st staminodia), × ¼; c, flower, vertical section, × ½; d, ovary, cross-section, × 4.

CANNA, L. Upwards of 50 species, mostly in the western hemisphere, some of them nat. outside their native regions. (Can-na: Latin name of a reed or cane.)—The large garden cannas of the present day are the results of hybridization and breeding and are not referable to botanical species, although the marks of one or another species may be prominent in them. One of the earliest of the modern cult. cannas (1863) was an offshoot of *C. iridiflora*, probably a cross with *C. Warscewiczii*, known as *C. Ehemannii* (or *Ehmannii*) and as *C. iridiflora hybrida*. Several species have probably gone into subsequent crosses, the main ones of which are described herewith. At first cannas were grown for stature and foliage, but subsequently were bred for fls. and compact habit. The bronze or purple color of herbage appears to have come with *C. Warscewiczii*. The Ehemannii cannas crossed with probably *C. glauca* and others produced the Crozy or French cannas, whence have descended many of the cannas (*C. generalis*) of gardens.

A. Fls. hanging, very long-tubed .... 1. *C. iridiflora*
AA. Fls. erect or essentially so, the tube various.
B. Petals becoming reflexed; tube long, prominent.
C. Showy parts of fl. ("petals") yellow; tube 2 or more in. long .... 2. *C. flaccida*
CC. Showy parts in various colors; tube shorter: cultigen .... 3. *C. orchiodes*
BB. Petals remaining erect or strongly ascending; tube very short or none.
C. Plant glaucous throughout (less evident in no. 5).
D. Lvs. lanceolate: fls. yellow, not large; upper staminodia mostly less than ¾in. broad .... 4. *C. glauca*
DD. Lvs. broader: fls. various, the upper staminodia usually 1 in. or more broad: cultigen .... 5. *C. generalis*
CC. Plant not glaucous (except perhaps in infl.): lvs. oblong to elliptic: fls. typically red (running to orange).—The small-fld. cannas.
D. St. green, also lvs. on both surfaces .... 6. *C. indica*
DD. St. purple or bronze, as also lvs. either above or beneath or both.
E. Pedicel of second fl. in pair bractless; upper staminodia usually 2 .... 7. *C. Warscewiczii*
EE. Pedicel of second fl. 2-bracted; upper staminodia 3 .... 8. *C. edulis*

1. **C. iridiflora,** Ruiz & Pav. Tall, to 8 or 10 ft., st. and foliage green: lvs. very large, 3–4 ft. by 1–1½ ft. broad in full-grown specimens, widely spreading: panicle of several drooping branches, with large branch-bracts; fls. large and pendulous, rose-color; tube of corolla slender, 2½ in. long, the lobes of equal length; upper staminodia 3, equalling or exceeding corolla-lobes, 1 in. or less broad. Peru.—Probably not in general cult., but a prominent parent in garden hybrids.

2. **C. flaccida,** Salisb. St. and foliage green, plant 4–5 ft.: lvs. oblong-lanceolate, 10–24 in. long and 4–5 in. broad: raceme loose and few-fld., simple, with very small bracts, erect; fls. yellow, showy, soft or flaccid in texture; sepals 1 in. long, the corolla-tube about twice as long, the petals nearly as long as tube and strongly reflexed: upper staminodia 3, rounded, 2–3 in. long, the lip orbicular. Swamps near the coast, S. C. to Fla.—It has contributed an important element to the orchid-fld. or Italia group of garden cannas.

3. **C. orchiodes,** Bailey. The orchid-fld. cannas, represented in Italia and other vars., derivatives from *C. flaccida* with other stocks: fls. very large, usually 5 or 6 in. across, bright yellow to deep red, striped and splashed, not clear white or pink; floral parts (staminodes) broad and soft, with flowing outlines, the lip funnelform at base; tube 1 in. or more long, much exceeding calyx; petals reflexed after about the first day.

4. **C. glauca,** L. St. and foliage green and glaucous, the plant 5–6 ft.: lvs. narrow-lanceolate, 4 in. or less broad, very acute at apex, tapering to base, white hyaline-edged: raceme rather loose, erect, simple or forked, little exceeding the foliage, fl.-bracts orbicular; fls. clear unspotted yellow, narrow and erect, the green sepals ½in. long; petals 1½–2 in. long, the tube about ¾in. long; upper staminodia 3, entire, 2½–3 in. long and ¾in. or less broad; lip narrow, emarginate. Mex. and W. Indies to S. Amer.; also more or less spontaneous about grounds in trop. Amer.—It runs into red-tinged and spotted fls.

5. **C. generalis,** Bailey. The common flowering cannas, in many named vars.: fls. medium to large, in many colors; floral parts usually well separated in outline, narrow to broad, most of them erect or strongly upright; tube ½in. or so long, little if any exceeding calyx; petals narrow, remaining erect or ascending. Cultigen.

6. **C. indica,** L. INDIAN SHOT. St. and foliage green and glabrous, plant slender, 3 or 4 ft. tall: lvs. oblong, about twice as long as broad: raceme nearly or quite simple, loose, fl.-bracts nearly orbicular, most of the fls. 2 together, fls. narrow and erect, small; petals about 1¼ in. long, connate at base; upper staminodia 3, bright red, oblanceolate and entire, about 2 in. long; lip entire, orange spotted red. Trop. Amer.; supposed by Linnæus to be native in Asia and Afr. as well as in Amer.; considerably nat. far S. in U. S. and in tropics.—One of the old-fashioned garden cannas, grown mostly for its foliage effects.

7. **C. Warscewiczii,** Dietr. St. and foliage purplish or brown-purple, plant 3–5 ft.: lvs. oblong, acute at apex, about twice as long as broad or sometimes a little more: raceme scarcely overtopping foliage, simple, not loose, the fls., or at least the lower ones, 2 together and the upper one without bracts, the fl.-bracts ovate-pointed, brown-purple, conspicuously glaucous; beneath the infl. is usually a spathe-like glaucous bract 4–6 in. long; fls. scarlet and more or less blue-tinged, erect and narrow, not large; petals about 2 in. long, oblanceolate, the tube short; upper staminodia 2 or 3, entire or nearly so, 2–3 in. long and ½in. broad; lip oblanceolate, emarginate. (Warscewiczii: J. von Warscewicz, 1812–1866, a Pole, collector for Van Houtte of Belgium.) Costa Rica to S. Amer.—More or less spontaneous in the S., and probably often confused with *C. indica*.

8. **C. edulis,** Ker. Rootstock bearing edible tubers: st. purple, very strong, to 8 or 10 ft., or more: lvs. mostly suffused purple beneath but usually green above, oblong, 1–2 ft. long, acute, usually more than twice longer than broad: raceme loose, simple or forked, with large sheath at base, fls. mostly 2 together and the upper one with 2 small bractlets, fl.-bracts oblong or nearly orbicular; fls. bright (staminodia varying to orange) red, erect and rather narrow; petals 2 in. or less long, tube very short; upper staminodia 3, oblanceolate, 2½ in. long and ½in. or less broad, entire or emarginate. W. Indies, S. Amer.—Cult. for food under the name of *Tous-les-mois;* grown also for foliage effects.

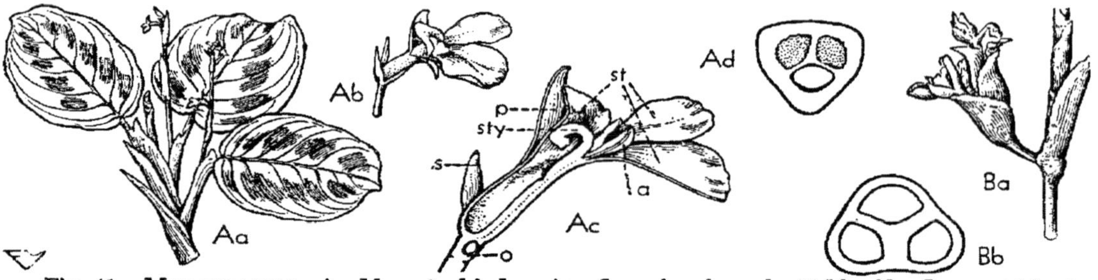

Fig. 41. Marantaceæ. A, *Maranta bicolor:* Aa, flowering branch, × 1/6; Ab, flower, × 1; Ac, flower, vertical section (o ovary, s sepal, p petal, st staminodia, a anther, sty style), × 2; Ad, ovary, cross-section, × 15. B, *Calathea Lietzei:* Ba, inflorescence, × ½; Bb, ovary, cross-section, × 15.

41. MARANTACEÆ. MARANTA or ARROWROOT FAMILY

Nearly 30 genera and something like 260 species in tropics of both hemispheres, largely American, one grown in warm countries for its starchy rhizomes and many others under glass and planted out for the interesting and showy foliage.—Per. rhizomatous or tuberiferous herbs, stemless or caulescent: lvs. broad or narrow, pinnately nerved and narrowed to petiole, more or less distichous: fls. usually not showy, bisexual, very irregular, mostly in spike-like or head-like clusters, 1, 2, or more together, the infl. surrounded by spathe-like bracts; perianth parts 6, the 3 inner clearly differentiated as corolla; sepals free, equal or nearly so; petals usually joined into a long or short tube, the outer one commonly large and more or less hooded and colored or white; stamens mostly 6, of which 1 is fertile (bearing a 1-celled anther) and the others represented by petal-like irregular staminodia in 2 series; ovary inferior, 3-celled but 1 or 2 cells often abortive, ovule 1 in each cell; style slender and stigma simple: fr. capsular or baccate.—Many species and forms are grown under glass for the broad colored, barred, metallic or lustrous foliage; they may not bloom, and they are commonly named in Maranta but most of them are Calatheas.

A. Ovary with 1 developed cell and 1 ovule: infl. branched.
  B. Outer staminodia 2 .... 1. Maranta
  BB. Outer staminodium 1 .... 2. Thalia
AA. Ovary with 3 cells, each with 1 ovule: infl. mostly capitate or cone-like .... 3. Calathea

1. **MARANTA,** L. About 25 species, all of trop. Amer.—Low or tall herbs, caulescent or stemless, erect or prostrate: lvs. radical and cauline, the petioles sheathing at least at base: fls. in panicles or more or less branched infl.; upper conspicuous staminodia 2, exceeding petals; ovary 1-celled by abortion. (Maran-ta: B. Maranta was a Venetian physician and botanist; died 1754.)

A. Plant tall, with erect branching leafy sts .... 1. *M. arundinacea*
AA. Plant low, stemless or nearly so, and lvs. practically radical.
  B. Blade of lf. with dark blotches midway .... 2. *M. bicolor*
  BB. Blade white-striped along veins .... 3. *M. leuconeura*

1. **M. arundinacea,** L. Arrowroot. Grown in tropics for the starchy rhizome which is a source of tapioca: sts. slender and much branching or forking, 2–6 ft.: lvs. ovate-oblong to ovate-lanceolate, acute, 6–12 in. long, 1½–4 in. wide, prominently petioled: fls. scattered, small, white; upper staminode broad and emarginate, much exceeding the lip and corolla. S. Amer. and native probably elsewhere in trop. Amer. Var. **variegata,** Hort., lvs. yellow-variegated; cult. by gardeners, often under name of *Phrynium variegatum.*

2. **M. bicolor,** Ker. Low compact plant 10–15 in. high, bearing tubers at base: lvs. oblong, oval to elliptic and ovate, 3–5 or 6 in. long, rounded or cordate at base, margins more or less undulate, light purple beneath, glaucous-green above and with large brownish spots either side the midrib and a central lighter strip: fls. small, white with violet spots and striped. Brazil, Guiana.—Some of the stock cult. as *Calathea roseo-picta* belongs here.

3. **M. leuconeura,** Morr. Dwarf, very short-stemmed, about 1 ft. high, not tuberiferous: lvs. oblong to broad-elliptic, obtuse or very short acuminate, light green above and becoming white along the midrib and main veins, more or less spotted toward margins, beneath glaucous or purple: fls. small, white with more or less purple stripes. Brazil. Var. **Massangeana,** Schum., lvs. smaller, purple beneath, fls. smaller with deep violet upper staminode. Var. **Kerchoveana,** Morr., lvs. larger, glaucous or red-spotted beneath, fls. large.

2. **THALIA,** L. About 7 species of tall subtrop. or trop. American aquatic or marsh herbs.—Lvs. basal, long-petioled, canna-like: fls. purplish or violet to blue, rather numerous, in panicles at end of stout scapes; bracts in 2 ranks, broad at apex, one above and one beneath each pair of fls.; sepals 3, free, minute; petals 3, nearly or quite distinct; outer staminodium 1, exceeding petals; anthers 1-celled; ovary 1-celled, 1-ovuled, stigma 2-lipped: fr. indehiscent. (Tha-lia: named after Johann Thalius, German naturalist of the 16th century.)

T. dealbata, Fraser. Plant covered with white powder: lvs. oblong-ovate to lance-elliptic, 8–20 in. long, acute to acuminate at apex, rounded or cordate at base, on petioles 1–2 ft. long: scape 3–10 ft. high; panicle with erect or ascending spikes; bracts broad at apex, the longer about ½in. long; fls. purple, petals ⅓in. long, larger staminodium ⅝in. long. S. C. to Fla., Tex., Mo.

3. **CALATHEA,** G. F. W. Mey. One hundred and more species, of trop. Amer. and Afr., mostly the former; popular foliage plants under glass.—Differs from Maranta in technical characters, as ovary fully 3-celled, upper staminode 1 and usually large, infl. mostly capitate or cone-like with spiral arrangement of bracts and borne among the lvs. (Calathe-a: Greek *basket,* probably bestowed in allusion to the basket-like setting of the fls.)—Favorite pot- and tub-plants; the lvs. are rich in metallic hues, and many of them attractively barred, striped and blotched. They are cult. under many Latin names, some of which have no botanical standing. All the following are known also as Marantas. *C. Allouia,* Lindl., is cult. in American tropics for the edible underground tubers.

A. Plant very small, not more than 5–9 in. high.
B. Lvs. oblong-lanceolate, 2–4 in. long.............................. 1. *C. micans*
BB. Lvs. ovate to orbicular, 4–9 in. long.
C. Lf. feathered or marked brown or red above.......................... 2. *C. roseo-picta*
CC. Lf. feathered or marked silvery-white above......................... 8. *C. illustris*
AA. Plant medium to large, mostly much more than 1 ft. high.
B. Mature lf. plain green above, not colored.
C. Lower surface of lf. purple-red... 3. *C. ornata*
CC. Lower surface of lf. green...10. *C. insignis*
BB. Mature lf. colored above, or shaded and metallic green, variously marked.
C. Upper surface of lf. striped from midrib toward margin, along or between the side veins.
D. Under surface green.. 4. *C. vittata*
DD. Under surface violet, purplish or purple-red.
E. Lf. large, 1–2 ft. long.
F. Striping of lvs. in shades of green.................................... 5. *C. zebrina*
FF. Striping of lvs. pink or white.. 3. *C. ornata*
EE. Lf. small, 9 in. or less long... 6. *C. Lietzei*
CC. Upper surface of lf. not striped, but variously feathered along the midrib or marbled or blotched.
D. Lf. continuously circled or zoned above, with a color strip extending around the blade or either side of midrib.
E. Zone olive-green, pattern repeated on under surface.............. 7. *C. Lindeniana*
EE. Zone silvery-white, not repeated beneath.
F. Midrib feathered, whitish either side; blade ovate................ 8. *C. illustris*
FF. Midrib marbled, whitish either side; blade elliptic............... 9. *C. Vandenheckei*
DD. Lf. not zoned as above.
E. Blade of lf. green beneath..11. *C. medio-picta*
EE. Blade of lf. reddish beneath.
F. Lvs. olive-green or cream-colored above with blotches of dark green from midrib outward.............................12. *C. Makoyana*
FF. Lvs. dark glossy green above feathered along midrib with pale green band containing brownish blotches.........................13. *C. Veitchiana*

1. **C. micans,** Koern. Very small plant: lvs. 2–3 or sometimes 4 in. long, about 1½ in. or less broad, oblong-lanceolate, acute or acuminate, green and shining above and somewhat feathered with white, paler green beneath: spike about ½in. long; staminode violet. Brazil.

2. **C. roseo-picta,** Regel. Small, 6–8 in. high: lvs. 4–8 or 9 in. long, nearly orbicular, dark green above with red rib and one or two zones of bright red near the margin, under side purple: spike about 3 in. long. Brazil.—See *Maranta bicolor*.

3. **C. ornata,** Koern. Strong vigorous plant, 1½–3 ft. high: lvs. elliptic, more or less cordate at base, acute, 1–2 or 3 ft. long, the adult blades rich green above and dull purple-red beneath, the petiole becoming 2 ft. or more long with age: spike about 3 in. long, ovoid; staminode 2-lobed, yellowish. Guiana, Colombia, Ecuador.—The young foliage is usually striped pink between the veins, and the intermediate foliage striped white; names have been applied to the juvenile forms. *C. imperialis* and *C. Sanderiana*, Hort., are apparently variants of this species.

4. **C. vittata,** Koern. Plant mostly dwarf, but sometimes 3 ft. tall: lvs. elliptic-lanceolate, 6–12 in. long, mostly 2½–3½ in. wide, acute, light green above, but transversely striped with white from bottom to top, under side green shaded yellowish-green: spike ovoid, on a short peduncle; staminode broadly obovate. Probably Colombia.

5. **C. zebrina,** Lindl. Zebra Plant. Of compact and good habit, 1–3 ft. high, common under glass: lvs. elliptic, obtuse or very short-acute, 1–2 ft. long and nearly or quite half as broad, upper side velvety green and with alternating bars of pale yellow-green and olive-green extending outward from the midrib, under side purplish-red in the adult: spike nearly globular or ovoid; staminode pale lilac. Brazil.

6. **C. Lietzei,** Morr. Dwarf in habit, 1–2 ft. high: lvs. elliptic and acute, 9 in. or less long, velvety green above and striped along principal veins with dark olive-green, feathered between veins with yellowish-green splashes, under side purplish-red: spike flattened, 2–3 in. long; staminode oblong, white. (Bears the name of M. Lietze, correspondent in Brazil of the firm of Jacob Makoy of Belgium.) Brazil.

7. **C. Lindeniana,** Wallis (often written *C. Lindenii*). Plant 3 ft. or so high: lvs. elliptic-oblong, 1 ft. or less long, short-acuminate, deep green above with olive-green zone either side of rib and a darker green zone between that and margin, under side with purplish zone repeating the pattern of upper zone: spike ellipsoid, about 4 in. long; staminode yellow. (Linden, page 47.) Brazil.

8. **C. illustris,** Nichols. Dwarf and compact plant, usually 6–9 in. high, and by some writers regarded as offshoot of *C. roseo-picta:* lvs. ovate and acute, blade 4–6 in. long and 2–5 in. broad, upper side dark shining olive-green with metallic luster, midrib feathered with silvery-white and a zone of white circling the blade, under side dull red: spike nearly globular; fl. white blotched purple. Ecuador.

9. **C. Vandenheckei,** Regel. Compact in habit, 1–2½ ft. high: lvs. elliptic or elliptic-ovate, 9 in. or less long, acute, upper side dark green marbled silvery-white along rib and an irregular line or band of same (often very broad and almost filling blade) circling the lf., under side purplish-red: spike cone-like, 3–5 in. long; fls. white, more or less brown-striped. (Name bestowed in honor of M. Van den Hecke, president Royal Agricultural and Botanical Society of Ghent.) Probably Brazil.

10. **C. insignis,** Peter. Plant coarse, 3–7 ft. tall, glabrous: lf.-blades elliptic or oval, thin, abruptly pointed, 1–1½ ft. long, 8–10 in. wide, green above and beneath, long-petioled: spikes elongate, 4–6 in. long, compressed, the broad soft bracts 2-ranked, pale bronze-green; perianth yellow. Mex. to Ecuador.

11. **C. medio-picta,** Regel. Plant 20 in. or more high: lvs. oblong to oval-lanceolate, 6–8 in. long, tapering both ways, acuminate at apex, dark green above with midrib feathered white from bottom to top, under side pale green: spike nearly globular or ellipsoid, about 2 in. long; staminode obovate-oblong, obtuse, purplish. Brazil.

12. **C. Makoyana,** Nichols. Showy plant, 2–4 ft. high: lvs. broad-oblong, obtuse or very short-pointed, upper side olive-green or cream-colored with oval, oblong or pear-shaped blotches of dark green extending outward from midrib, under side red but repeating the pattern. (Early cult. by Jacob Makoy & Co., Liege, Belgium.) Brazil.

13. **C. Veitchiana,** Hook. f. Strong-growing spreading plant 1–4 ft. high: lvs. ovate to elliptic-ovate, the blade 8–12 in. long and about half as broad, very short-acute, upper side dark glossy green feathered on either side rib with very irregular band of pale green in which band are set large brownish frayed blotches, under side reddish and repeating the pattern: spike top-shaped, 2–3½ in. long; fls. white, with violet blotch on staminode. (Named in 1865 for the father of James Veitch, noted horticulturist of England.) Peru.

42. ORCHIDACEÆ. ORCHID FAMILY

A vast range of herbaceous plants, circling the world in temp. and trop. climates except in desert regions, terrestrial and epiphytic, many grown by florists, amateurs, and fanciers for the odd and showy bloom; the recognized species are more than

Fig. 42. ORCHIDACEÆ. A, *Paphiopedilum insigne:* Aa, plant in flower, × 1/8; Ab, column, side view, × 1; Ac, same, from below, × 1; Ad, flower, vertical section, × 1/2. B, *Cattleya Lueddemanniana:* Ba, plant in flower, × 1/6; Bb, flower, vertical section, × 1/2; Bc, column from beneath, × 1/2; Bd, ovary, cross-section, × 2. C, *Dendrobium nobile:* Ca, flower, × 1/2; Cb, column, × 2. D, *Phalænopsis amabilis:* Da, flowers, × 1/4; Db, flower, vertical section, × 1/2; Dc, column, vertical section, × 1 1/2; Dd, pollinia, × 3. (c column, f foot, l labellum, l.p. lateral petal, o ovary, ps pseudobulb, s stamen, se sepal, st stigma.)

15,000, in several hundred genera. The distinctive mark of the orchids is the gynandrium or column, an organ formed by the union of style, stigma and stamens; within the column is a canal leading from the stigmatic surface to the ovary; the gynandrium may bear 1 fertile stamen represented by an anther terminal on the column, or (as in the Cypripedium tribe) of 2 lateral stamens situated midway along the column, and there may be staminodes inasmuch as the stamens are morphologically or basically derived from 6; the pollen is mostly in masses (pollinia) that are removed by insects in the act of pollination, the number of pollinia varying in most cases from 2–8 and they may be borne on simple or forked stalks or be sessile; the style often ends in a beak or projection lying between the anther-cells or standing at the base of the anther, and is known as a rostellum. Orchid flowers are explained in Fig. 42, page 295.—The orchids are perennials, with tuberous, bulbous, or mostly thickened roots, erect, prostrate, or climbing, most of them green, but a few leafless, decolored and saprophytic: sts. sometimes with thickened internodes known as pseudobulbs; some of them have a monopodial growth, the st. elongating indefinitely from the terminal bud; other kinds are sympodial, each shoot coming to a stop and the growth continued by axillary shoots: lvs. various, linear, oblong, oval, or orbicular, more or less thick and fleshy, simple and entire, parallel-veined, alternate or scattered; lf.-buds conduplicate (lvs. folded together lengthwise within the bud) or convolute (lvs. rolled in bud, edges overlapping): fl.-st. basal or arising from axils on a leafy st., simple or branched: fls. usually bisexual, very irregular, often grotesque, highly specialized, showy in the cult. kinds but very small and inconspicuous in many of the species, subtended by a bract; 3 outer segms. (sepals) similar, usually narrow and not showy; 3 inner segms. (petals) with 2 similar lateral ones, and the third forming a lip which is sometimes saccate and often spurred; in some genera the middle lobe of the lip is divided into 2 distinct parts, an epichil (terminal segm.) and a hypochil (basal segm.), these may comprise a single rigid structure or the epichil may be movably jointed to the hypochil; ovary inferior, mostly elongated and twisted, 3-celled or 1-celled by abortion, placentation axile or parietal in one genus: fr. a caps., mostly dehiscent, with very many minute seeds.—The native terrestrial orchids of the U. S. and Canada are sometimes used in bog- and rock-gardening. The larger part of the orchids of cult. are mainly trop. species, many of them epiphytes, together with numbers of hybrids; these species are in great numbers, and only the most usual kinds encountered in the florist trade and conservatories can be entered here, with sufficient entries to illustrate some of the leading genera.

A. Species of hardy orchids, frost-resistant and generally surviving freezing weather; plants grown in the open and not under glass or lath shelter.
  B. Green lvs. lacking at flowering time, rarely with a withered basal lf. persisting.
    C. Sts. bulbous or cormous .... 21. APLECTRUM
    CC. Sts. not bulbous or cormous .... 8. SPIRANTHES
  BB. Green lvs. present at flowering time.
    C. Sts. with pseudobulbs.
      D. Infl. on lateral sts.: pollinia 2 .... 28. CYMBIDIUM
      DD. Infl. terminal at summit of st.: pollinia 4–8.
        E. Plant epiphytic .... 14. EPIDENDRUM
        EE. Plant terrestrial.
          F. Fls. purple, about 1 in. across: lvs. 3–5 .... 10. BLETILLA
          FF. Fls. greenish-yellow to whitish, less than ¾in. across: lvs. 2 .... 12. LIPARIS
    CC. Sts. without pseudobulbs.
      D. Spur of fl. conspicuous.
        E. Lvs. all cauline .... 4. HABENARIA
        EE. Lvs. all basal, usually only 2.
          F. Fls. with pinkish hoods and white or spotted lips: lf.-blades usually large and fleshy .... 3. ORCHIS
          FF. Fls. greenish-yellow or -white: lf.-blades not fleshy .... 4. HABENARIA
      DD. Spur of fl. lacking.
        E. Plants 1-lvd. (small cauline bracts may exist).
          F. Lf. ovate to orbicular .... 13. CALYPSO
          FF. Lf. linear to lanceolate-ovate.
            G. Fls. 1–2, subtended by a large foliaceous bract almost as long as the fl.: lf. lanceolate-ovate .... 5. POGONIA
            GG. Fls. usually 3–12, rarely solitary, not subtended by a large green bract: lf. linear .... 19. CALOPOGON
        EE. Plants with more than 1 lf.
          F. Fls. solitary or spicate, at least not in racemes, inflated and slipper-shaped .... 1. CYPRIPEDIUM
          FF. Fls. in racemes, the lip not inflated or slipper-shaped.
            G. Lvs. all near the base of st. and usually conspicuously veined white or very pale green: fls. about ⅛in. long .... 9. GOODYERA
            GG. Lvs. cauline and basal or only cauline, not conspicuously white-veined: fls. usually larger.

H. Color of fls. white: lvs. linear, mostly less than ½in. wide, the lower ones petioled .... 8. SPIRANTHES
HH. Color of fls. greenish, suffused madder-purple: median st.-lvs. ovate, often more than 1 in. wide, sessile .... 7. EPIPACTIS
AA. Species of tender orchids, not frost-hardy; plants grown under glass or in lath houses.
B. Fertile stamens 2, with a broad shield-shaped staminodium between and above them; lip inflated and slipper-like .... 2. PAPHIOPEDILUM
BB. Fertile stamen 1, terminal on column with no staminodium; lip not slipper-like, but perhaps inflated or sac-like.
C. Infl. terminal, at apex of st.
D. Lf.-buds convolute, the edges overlapping.
E. Lvs. confluent with, and not jointed to, st. or petiole: plant a vine .... 6. VANILLA
EE. Lvs. with blades distinctly jointed to petiole.
F. Pollinia 8: st. slender, with pseudobulbs .... 10. BLETILLA
FF. Pollinia 4: st. a short pseudobulb .... 11. CŒLOGYNE
DD. Lf.-buds conduplicate (folded together lengthwise).
E. Lvs. usually not jointed .... 12. LIPARIS
EE. Lvs. jointed at junction with st. or pseudobulb.
F. Nerves of lvs. several .... 18. SOBRALIA
FF. Nerves of lvs. 1.
G. Lip adnate to column, at least basally so .... 14. EPIDENDRUM
GG. Lip free from column.
H. Pollinia 4 .... 15. CATTLEYA
HH. Pollinia 8.
I. Stigma situated in a pit on the front or apparent "lower side" of column; anther inclined .... 16. LÆLIA
II. Stigma extending upwards on 2 extensions of the column-apex; anther erect .... 17. SOPHRONITIS
CC. Infl. on lateral branches or else on special separate shoots apart from the primary sts. or pseudobulbs.
D. Lvs. convolute in bud.
E. St. slender or gradually swollen, not a short distinct pseudobulb.
F. Lip free, the lateral lobes enveloping the column .... 20. PHAIUS
FF. Lip basally adnate to column, the limb spreading .... 22. CALANTHE
EE. St. a short distinct pseudobulb.
F. Lip continuous with the column-foot and not jointed to it.
G. Sepals and petals erect or incurved; lip with terminal lobe (epichil) movably attached to basal segm. (hypochil) .... 24. PERISTERIA
GG. Sepals and petals spreading or reflexed; epichil not movable from hypochil .... 25. STANHOPEA
FF. Lip jointed to the column-foot.
G. Callus-ridges of lip transverse, horseshoe-shaped .... 26. ZYGOPETALUM
GG. Callus-ridges extending lengthwise of lip .... 23. LYCASTE
DD. Lvs. conduplicate in bud.
E. St. increasing in length from year to year.
F. Lip movably jointed to column .... 32. RENANTHERA
FF. Lip immovably united to column.
G. Fls. spurless .... 33. PHALÆNOPSIS
GG. Fls. spurred or saccate.
H. Column without a foot .... 34. VANDA
HH. Column with a foot, the lateral sepals attached to it .... 35. AERIDES
EE. St. terminating its growth in one year.
F. Lip movably jointed to foot of column.
G. Lvs. not lorate: pollinia unappendaged, or with either caudicles or stipes but not both .... 27. DENDROBIUM
GG. Lvs. lorate: pollinia with broad caudicles and stipes .... 28. CYMBIDIUM
FF. Lip immovably united basally to foot of column.
G. Base of lip parallel to column and not spreading from it .... 29. ODONTOGLOSSUM
GG. Base of lip spreading from the base of the column.
H. The lip entire, flat, broad .... 30. MILTONIA
HH. The lip mostly 3-lobed, with wart-like callosities or a cushion at the base .... 31. ONCIDIUM

1. **CYPRIPEDIUM,** L. LADY-SLIPPER. MOCCASIN-FLOWER. Showy hardy terrestrial orchids, of about 30 species, frequently planted in moist shaded borders, bog margins, and rock-gardens.—Sts. very short and 2-lvd. or elongated and with many cauline lvs., the latter commonly many-nerved and not leathery: fls. terminal, 1 to few, the withered remains persisting on the ovary; lateral sepals free or united; petals spreading and narrower; lip saccate and slipper-like, margins inrolled; ovary 1-celled with 3 parietal placentæ; column short, bearing 2 stamens (1 on either side) and a dorsal gland-like staminode (sterile stamen) above and distal to them; stigma situated ventrally, spreading from a constricted base, somewhat 3-lobed. (Cypripedium: Greek for Venus slipper.)—The foliage of some cult. kinds may cause an urtication and dermatitis when contacted by sensitive individuals. The tender cypripediums of conservatory and greenhouse cult. properly belong to the related genera Paphiopedilum and Phragmipedium.

A. Lvs. 2, opposite: plant stemless: lip split in front........................1. *C. acaule*
AA. Lvs. several, alternate: plant caulescent: lip not split.
B. Lateral sepals free; lip white veined reddish-purple........................2. *C. arietinum*
BB. Lateral sepals united nearly or to the apex, situated beneath the lip; lip variously colored.
C. Lip yellow..3. *C. Calceolus*
CC. Lip white or greenish, sometimes veined or suffused pink to purple.
D. Sepals and petals shorter than lip, sepals obtuse to cuspidate.
E. Fls. 1–3; sepals and petals white to very pale rose-colored..............4. *C. Reginæ*
EE. Fls. 3–9; sepals and petals yellow suffused brown..................5. *C. californicum*
DD. Sepals and petals equalling lip or longer, sepals acute to acuminate.
E. Plants 1–2½ ft. high: sepals and petals brownish-purple; staminode oblong-ovate..6. *C. montanum*
EE. Plants ½–1 ft. high: sepals and petals greenish with purple spots; staminode lanceolate..7. *C. candidum*

1. **C. acaule,** Ait. (*C. humile,* Salisb. *Fissipes acaulis,* Small). Pink Lady-Slipper. Lvs. usually only 2, ovate to oblong-elliptic, mostly 6–9 in. long, basal, opposite, occasionally a third lf. near base of scape, thick: fls. solitary, fragrant, with showy rose-pink lip to 2½ in. long split in front; sepals and petals greenish-purple; staminode triangular, acuminate: scape 4–12 in. high. N. E. N. Amer.; grows in sandy well-drained soil in shaded areas.—A white-fld. form is known.

2. **C. arietinum,** R. Br. Rams-head Lady-Slipper. Lvs. 3–4, cauline, elliptic to lanceolate, usually 2–5 in. long: sts. 8–12 in. high: fls. solitary; lip scarcely ¾ in. long, white with reddish-purple veins, prolonged at apex into an elongated distorted blunt spur; sepals and petals greenish-brown, exceeding the lip, the former all separate. Que., Ont. to N. Y. and Minn.; requires damp shaded cool situations.

3. **C. Calceolus,** L. Yellow Lady-Slipper. Lvs. several, ovate to ovate-lanceolate, 2–8 in. long, acuminate, many-nerved, plicate, sheathing at base: sts. 4–28 in. high, mostly glandular-pubescent throughout, strongly so at nodes: fls. 1–2, on long slender peduncles, fragrant; lip dull cream-colored to citron-yellow, about 1¾ in. long, dotted brown within; sepals and petals usually crimson-purple, lateral sepals united nearly to apex. Cent. and N. Eu. to Siberia.—Not much grown in N. Amer. Var. **pubescens,** Correll (*C. pubescens,* Willd. *C. parviflorum,* Salisb. *C. hirsutum,* Mill. sensu Auth. *C. luteum,* Ait. *C. parviflorum* var. *pubescens,* O. W. Knight. *C. planipetalum,* Morris & E. A. Eames), differs from the species in fls. with lip ⅝–2½ in. long, dull cream to golden-yellow, commonly veined or spotted magenta-purple, the shorter-stalked staminode, and sepals and petals often shading to greenish-yellow: a polymorphic entity varying in degree of fragrance, shape of staminodia and shape and coloration of fls.; E. U. S.; seemingly adapted to wide range of soil types and exposures.

4. **C. Reginæ,** Walt. (*C. spectabile,* Salisb.). Showy Lady-Slipper. Stout sts. 1–3 ft. high, leafy to apex, hairy: lvs. ovate-elliptic, 3–10 in. long, acute, minutely pubescent on nerves beneath, ciliate: fls. 1–3; lip much inflated, 1–2 in. long, white variegated with crimson and white stripes; sepals and petals white, sometimes suffused pale rose-pink, shorter than lip, former ovate-orbicular, obtuse, lateral ones united, petals narrower; staminode ovate-cordate. N. E. U. S.; plant of cold boggy swamps or in cool damp shaded woods.—By some authors the older name of *C. hirsutum,* Mill., has been applied to this plant, but it has also been applied to other species of the genus and its identity and proper application is in dispute since no specimen of Miller's plant is known to be extant.

5. **C. californicum,** Gray. Sts. 1–2½ ft. high, glandular-hairy, leafy: lvs. 3–5 in. long, ovate-lanceolate, acute to acuminate, upper ones becoming lanceolate, short-glandular-pilose on nerves: fls. 3–9, sometimes to 12, solitary on slender peduncles in lf.-axils or foliaceous bracts; lip about ¾ in. long, white to rose-pink, brown-spotted; sepals and petals yellow suffused with brown, shorter than lip, lateral sepals united to tip; staminode subsessile, rounded and arching. S. Ore., Calif., in damp soils in open woods.

6. **C. montanum,** Dougl. Similar to *C. Calceolus* and perhaps only a white-fld. variant of it, differing primarily in the lip being white, tinged or veined purple, and the staminode oblong-ovate and deeply grooved above. Sask. to B. C. south to Wyo. and Calif.

7. **C. candidum,** Muhl. White Lady-Slipper. Sts. 6–12 in. high, leafy: lvs. 3–4, oblong-lanceolate to elliptic, mostly 3–5 in. long, acute to acuminate, minutely glandular-hairy on nerves, ciliate: fls. solitary, terminal on elongated slender pedicels; lip about ¾ in. long, white, striped purple within; sepals and petals longer than lip, greenish often spotted purple, lateral sepals connate, petals wavy and twisted; staminode lanceolate. N. Y. to Minn. south to N. J. and Mo., in open bogs and meadows.

2. **PAPHIOPEDILUM,** Pfitz. (*Cordula,* Raf.). The glasshouse lady-slippers, commonly known as Cypripediums, but that genus is now restricted to species of the north temp. and boreal regions; the species of Paphiopedilum are about 50 in the tropics of farther Asia and to New Guinea, differing from Cypripedium in the conduplicate rather than convolute or rolled lf.-buds and in the perianth deciduous

rather than withering on ovary.—Terrestrial or epiphytic herbs, with many basal oblong, elliptic or strap-shaped thick lvs., and 1 to several showy saccate fls. on long peduncles: sepals 3, imbricate in bud, the dorsal erect and showy, the 2 lateral united; petals spreading or long and pendulous; lip inflated, with the edges of the orifice not or rarely inflexed; ovary 1-celled: fr. a 3-valved dehiscent caps. (Paphiopedilum: from Paphos, city of Cyprus sacred to Venus, and Latin for *sandal.*)—Some of the greenhouse lady-slippers are of the genus Phragmipedium, of the American tropics, which differs in having a 3-celled ovary and valvate æstivation. Hybrids and variants in Paphiopedilum are numerous, many of them bearing regular binomials mostly under the genus Phragmipedium (which should now be restricted to plants of the western tropics). The name Paphiopedilum has been conserved over the older Cordula.

A. Lvs. netted-veined or reticulated (tessellate).
  B. Petals with wart-like protuberances on upper and lower margins .... 1. *P. Lawrenceanum*
  BB. Petals with warts on upper margin only.
    C. Lower sepal elliptic-ovate, obtuse; lobes of lip with small warts .... 2. *P. barbatum*
    CC. Lower sepal narrowly ovate, acute; lobes of lip with large warts .... 3. *P. callosum*
AA. Lvs. not netted or reticulated.
  B. Staminode lunate (quarter-moon-shaped)............................ 4. *P. Fairieanum*
  BB. Staminode other than lunate.
    C. Petals strongly undulate on margins; staminode margin revolute .... 5. *P. Spicerianum*
    CC. Petals flat or only slightly undulate on margins; staminode margin flat.
      D. Ovary white-villous.............................. 6. *P. villosum*
      DD. Ovary purple-pubescent.
        E. Staminode glabrous.............................. 7. *P. Charlesworthii*
        EE. Staminode pilose above.............................. 8. *P. insigne*

1. **P. Lawrenceanum,** Pfitz. (*Cordula Lawrenceana,* Rolfe. *Cypripedium Lawrenceanum,* Reichb. f.). Lvs. tessellated, 8–10 in. long and 2–2½ in. broad, shorter than pubescent scape: fls. 1 or 2, 4–5 in. across, June–Sept.; dorsal sepal white with alternately longer and shorter purple veins, nearly orbicular; petals ligulate and ciliate, green with purple tips and 5–10 warts on each margin; lip dull purple, brownish above and green beneath. (Dedicated to Sir John Trevor Lawrence, 1831–1913, English orchidist.) Borneo.

2. **P. barbatum,** Pfitz. (*Cordula barbata,* Rolfe. *Cypripedium barbatum,* Lindl.). Lvs. tessellated, 6 in. or less long, shorter than pubescent scape: fls. 1 or 2, 2½–3 in. across, Feb.–June; dorsal sepal white and more or less purplish and with green at the base, veins prominent and purple, nearly orbicular, but pointed and folded at the middle; petals somewhat deflexed, oblong-linear and ciliate, apex purple, with small blackish warts on upper margin; lip helmet-shaped, brown-purple, lobes infolded and deeply spotted. Malaya.

3. **P. callosum,** Pfitz. (*Cypripedium callosum,* Reichb. f.). Lvs. 4–5, tessellated, to 10 in. long, marbled: scape 1–2 ft. high, 1- or infrequently 2-fld.; fls. 3–4 in. across, Mar.–July; dorsal sepal white with base greenish, striped or suffused dark crimson; petals dark green tinged rose-purple apically, margins ciliate and warted; lip brownish-purple. Thailand, Indo-China. Var. **Sanderæ,** Hort., has dorsal sepal white with green stripes and dots, pale green petals margined white and a waxy pale green lip.

4. **P. Fairieanum,** Pfitz. (*Cypripedium Fairieanum,* Lindl.). Plant dwarf, scape 5–7 in. high: lvs. linear-oblong, to 6 in. long and ½–1 in. wide, bright green: fls. about 2¼ in. across, July–Sept.; dorsal sepal broadly elliptic, white, yellowish-green at base, veined purple, margins wavy; petals falcate, white with violet stripes, margins wavy; lip green, coarsely veined purplish-red; staminode lunate. Assam.

5. **P. Spicerianum,** Pfitz. (*Cypripedium Spicerianum,* Reichb. f.). Lvs. not netted or tessellated, 1 ft. or less long and 2 in. broad, broadly linear-lanceolate, pale beneath, about equalling the glabrous scape: fls. 1, about 3 in. across; dorsal sepal white with a crimson band down the center and green speckled basal blotch, the margins strongly reflexed; petals deflexed and somewhat falcate, oblong, undulate, pilose at base, green-brown; lip violet with green claw; staminode nearly orbicular, its margins revolute. India, Assam; received by Mr. Spicer, England.

6. **P. villosum,** Pfitz. (*Cypripedium villosum,* Lindl.). Lvs. 10–18 in. long and to 1¾ in. wide, lorate: scape 1-fld., 6–15 in. high: fls. about 6 in. across, waxy, Nov.–May; dorsal sepal broadly elliptic, rounded, olive-brown becoming greenish distally, narrowly margined white; petals yellowish-brown distally and paler towards base; lip brownish-yellow with brighter veins; staminode margins flat; ovary white-villous. Burma.

7. **P. Charlesworthii,** Pfitz. (*Cypripedium Charlesworthii,* Rolfe). Plant dwarf: lvs. 6–10 in. long, broadly linear, uniformly green: scape 4–8 in. high, 1-fld.: fls. about 2½ in. across, Sept.–Nov.; dorsal sepal very broadly orbicular, quite flat, suffused and veined rose-red; petals extending horizontally, oblong, greenish to yellowish-brown, waxy; lip small, helmet-shaped, yellowish-brown, waxy; staminode white. (Intro. by British firm of Charlesworth, Shuttleworth & Co. in 1893.) Burma.

8. **P. insigne,** Pfitz. (*Cypripedium insigne*, Wall.). Lvs. not netted, very narrow, only ¾in. broad and 1 ft. or so long, mostly longer than the densely pubescent scape: fls. 1 or rarely 2, 4–5 in. across, smooth and glossy, Nov. – Jan.; upper part of dorsal sepal white and lower part green with brown spots and stripes, broad-oval, margins somewhat revolute; petals nearly linear, spreading, undulate, yellow-green with purple veins; lip yellow-green shaded brown; staminodia obcordate. India.—Very variable, running into numerous color forms and with many hybrids. Var. **Sanderæ,** Hort., has lvs. and scape pale green; dorsal sepal primrose-yellow with very small reddish-brown dots, upper part white; petals yellow; lip waxy-yellow.

3. **ORCHIS,** L. About 60 species of north temp. hardy terrestrial orchids, adapted for the bog-garden or moist ground in the border.—With bien. fleshy tubers or a per. rootstock producing numerous fleshy roots: lvs. solitary or few, usually basal: st. scape-like: infl. a short open spike or loose raceme, fls. usually rose-pink, subtended by long foliaceous bracts; sepals and petals nearly equal, sepals free or connate; lip 3-lobed or entire, turned downward, adnate to base of column, spurred below; column short, scarcely exceeding base of lip; anther-cells almost parallel and contiguous, pollinia 2, borne on slender caudicles that are attached to the glands or viscid disks of stigma, 3 glands situated in a small pouch (bursicule) located just above the orifice of the spur; stigma a concave surface between the anther-sacs, the rostellum a knobbed projection beneath the anther: caps. erect, oblong, beakless. (Or-chis: ancient Greek name.)

O. spectabilis, L. (*Galeorchis spectabilis*, Rydb.). Showy Orchis. Lvs. 2, basal, 3–6 in. long, oblong-obovate, thick and glossy; scape 3–8-fld., 2–8 in. high, 4–5-angled: bracts lanceolate, sheathing the ovaries and exceeding the fls., foliaceous: fls. mostly magenta-pink, about 1–2 in. long; lip ovate, much paler than sepals and petals or sometimes pure white, entire, spur about ⅝in. long: caps. 1–2 in. long, strongly angled. N. B. to Minn. south to Ga. and Neb.

4. **HABENARIA,** Willd. A large genus of about 500 species of glabrous herbs, of which only the hardy sorts are cult. in N. Amer.; distributed more or less throughout the north temp. regions, in the Canary Isls., 1 from S. Afr. and a few from the warmer regions of S. Amer.—Sts. generally leafy, arising from tuberous, fibrous or rhizomatous rootstocks, usually per. but sometimes only bien.: infl. a spike or more commonly a raceme; fls. usually small; sepals mostly similar, spreading; petals erect, connivent with the dorsal sepal; lip 3-lobed, entire, toothed or laterally fringed and if lobed the divisions cuneate and variously toothed or fringed, lip produced below into a spur longer or shorter than lip itself; column short, scarcely or not at all extending beyond base of lip; anther 1, terminal on column, pollinia 2, in separate somewhat divergent anther-sacs, attached by caudicles to glands or viscid disks that are separate, exposed and naked; stigma-beak sometimes with 2–3 appendages. (Habena-ria: Greek, possessing a strap or rein in allusion to the lip or spur of some species.)

A. Lip not fringed; fls. white, fragrant.......... 1. *H. dilatata*
AA. Lip fringed or toothed.
  B. Body of lip oblong to lanceolate, not parted or lobed, fringed along sides and tip.
    C. Fls. orange-yellow, fringe about ⅙in. long.......... 2. *H. ciliaris*
    CC. Fls. white, fringe less than 1/12in. long.......... 3. *H. blephariglottis*
  BB. Body of lip 3-parted or lobed, the divisions fringed or toothed.
    C. Fls. greenish, petals entire, lip deeply parted.......... 4. *H. lacera*
    CC. Fls. rose-pink to purple, petals usually minutely denticulate.......... 5. *H. psycodes*

1. **H. dilatata,** Hook. (*Orchis dilatata*, Pursh. *Platanthera dilatata*, Lindl. *Limnorchis dilatata*, Rydb.). Tall White Bog Orchis. Rootstocks thick, fleshy: sts. leafy, to 3½ ft. high: lvs. 3–8 in. long, lanceolate, acute or obtuse: raceme 3–12 in. long, bracts acute, the lower longer and upper shorter than ovary; fls. white, somewhat fragrant, about ½in. across, July–Aug.; sepals ovate; lip lanceolate, entire or obtusely 3-lobed and rhomboidal at base, spur incurved and longer than lip; stigma narrow, its beak between bases of anther-sacs. Bogs and wet woods areas, N. U. S.

2. **H. ciliaris,** R. Br. (*Orchis ciliaris*, L. *Platanthera ciliaris*, Lindl. *Blephariglottis ciliaris*, Rydb.). Yellow Fringed Orchis. Sts. 15–24 in. high: lvs. 4–8 in. long, lanceolate: raceme 3–6 in. long, densely many-fld., sometimes 3 in. broad; fls. orange-yellow, nearly ¾in. long plus a very slender spur 1–1½ in. long, July–Aug.; sepals broadly ovate

to orbicular, ⅛in. long; petals much smaller, narrowly oblong, toothed at apex; lip oblong, about ½in. long, fringed more than half way to center, lower fringe segms. often branched. E. U. S., in acid soils of bogs and sphagnum meadows.

3. **H. blephariglottis,** Hook. (*Orchis blephariglottis*, Willd. *Platanthera blephariglottis*, Lindl. *Blephariglottis blephariglottis*, Rydb.). WHITE FRINGED ORCHIS. Rootstocks tuberous or fleshy: sts. 1–2 ft. high: lvs. and infl. as in *H. ciliaris:* fls. pure white, July–Aug., about ½in. long plus a ¾in. long spur; dorsal sepal elliptic, lateral ones orbicular; petals linear-oblong, toothed to fringed apically; lip scarcely ½in. long, narrowly ovate-lanceolate, shortly fringed. N. E. U. S.

4. **H. lacera,** Lodd. (*Orchis lacera*, Michx. *Platanthera lacera*, D. Don. *Blephariglottis lacera*, Farwell). RAGGED or GREEN FRINGED ORCHIS. Sts. 1–2 ft. high, slender: lvs. 5–8 in. long, lanceolate: raceme 2–6 in. long, rather open; fls. greenish-yellow, July–Aug., about ½in. long plus a ⅝in. long spur; sepals ¼in. long, ovate, obtuse; petals linear, entire; lip deeply 3-parted, the segms. deeply fringed. N. E. U. S.

5. **H. psycodes,** Spreng. (*Orchis psycodes*, L. *Platanthera psycodes*, Lindl. in part. *Blephariglottis psycodes*, Rydb.). SMALL PURPLE FRINGED ORCHIS. Sts. 1–3 ft. high: lvs. ovate, lanceolate or elliptic, to 9 in. long and 2¾ in. wide: raceme 2–6 in. long and to 1½ in. broad; fls. deep lilac-purple, rarely white, fragrant, July–Aug.; sepals about ⅛in. long, ovate, obtuse; petals oblong-lanceolate to spatulate, upper margin denticulate; lip about ½in. long and as wide, 3-parted, spreading, the divisions fringed to less than one-third their depth. N. E. U. S. Var. **grandiflora,** Gray (*Orchis grandiflora*, Bigel. *O. fimbriata*, Dry. *H. fimbriata*, R. Br. *Platanthera fimbriata* var. *grandiflora*, Hook.), differs primarily in its greater stature, fls. lilac-pink, in racemes 3–12 in. long and 1½–3 in. broad, June–Aug.

5. **POGONIA,** Juss. Two species of N. American hardy low-growing terrestrial orchids, grown in moist well-drained soil of the border or in bog-gardens.—Rootstocks slender, fibrous-rooted: cauline lvs. few, alternate: fls. usually solitary, terminal; sepals and petals equal, free, erect or ascending; lip 3-lobed or entire, blade broad, papillose-crested; column elongated, somewhat clavate; anther 1, terminal, pollinia 2, in separate parallel anther-sacs, borne on a distinct fleshy and thickened stalk, powdery-granular without caudicles or glands; stigma a flattened disk situated below the anther. (Pogo-nia: Greek *bearded*, from the lip of some of the original species.)

P. ophioglossoides, Ker (*Arethusa ophioglossoides*, L.). Plants 4–21 in. high, slender: lf. solitary, cauline, ovate to lanceolate-ovate, to 3¼ in. long: fl. solitary (rarely 2), rose-pink, fragrant, subtended by a foliaceous bract, declined or nodding; sepals about ¾in. long, elliptic-ovate; petals similar but more broadly ovate, lip spatulate, inclosing the column basally but not adnate to it, fringed, crest yellow to white. E. U. S.

6. **VANILLA,** Juss. About 50 root-climbing branching herbs, in tropics around the world, one yielding the natural vanilla of commerce.—Lvs. various, thick or papery, present or absent: fls. large but not usually showy, in mostly short axillary racemes or spikes, with ovate bracts; sepals nearly or quite alike, free and spreading, and petals similar to them; lip with claw attached to the footless column, the blade broad and concave and enveloping the long wingless column: caps. usually long and fleshy, bean-like in shape, little or not at all dehiscing. (Vanil-la: the Spanish name for the fr.—*little sheath* or *pod*—recorded by Linnæus as *Epidendrum Vanilla*.)

V. fragrans, Ames (*Myrobroma fragrans*, Salisb., *V. planifolia*, Andr.). COMMON VANILLA. St. leafy and somewhat fleshy, tall-climbing: lvs. thick, oblong, acute or acuminate, 6–9 in. long, 2 in. or more broad, parallel nerves obscure, but becoming prominent when dried: fls. many in the raceme, greenish-yellow, about 2 in. long; sepals and petals narrowly oblanceolate; lip narrow, trumpet-shaped, shorter than other parts, with small crenulate lobes: caps. 3-angled, usually 6–9 in. long. Mex. and Cent. Amer.—Planted in warm and trop. countries for the pod, which yields vanilla extract. Other species yield similar products. The striped-lvd. vanilla sometimes grown under glass for ornament is var. **variegata,** Hort.

7. **EPIPACTIS,** Rich. As now interpreted, a genus of about 10 species of north temp. hardy plants having simple sts. from a creeping rootstock; adapted to partly shaded areas as along stream banks and springs.—Lvs. lanceolate to ovate, clasping: infl. a terminal few-fld. bracted raceme; fls. with sepals and petals separate, similar; lip sessile, free from column, broad and constricted near the middle with a petaloid dilated limb above and concave below, spur absent; column erect, short; anther 1,

terminal and in back of the broad truncate stigma, pollinia 2, attached to stigma-beak, granulose: caps. oblong, without a beak. (Epipac-tis: Greek name for hellebore and alluding to a milk-curdling property once ascribed to some kinds.)

E. gigantea, Dougl. (*Serapias gigantea*, A. Eaton. *Amesia gigantea*, A. Nels. & Macb.). GIANT HELLEBORINE. Sts. simple, 1–3 ft. high, sparsely pubescent: lvs. ovate to lanceolate, 2–8 in. long: infl. a sparse raceme; fls. 3–15, about 1½ in. across, greenish or purplish, pedicelled, somewhat pendulous, June–Aug.; sepals oblong-lanceolate, to ⅝in. long, the laterals horizontal; petals orange-purple with purple veins; lip ovate to lanceolate, tubercled from base, the lobes short and erect: caps. ¾–1¼ in. long, reflexed. Mont. to B. C. south to Mex. and Calif.

8. **SPIRANTHES,** Rich. (*Gyrostachys*, Pers. *Ibidium*, Salisb.). LADIES-TRESSES. Erect hardy or subtrop. per. terrestrial orchids, suited to shaded locations in moist soil of border or wild-garden; variously interpreted as 40–80 species of wide distribution in Asia, Eu. and the New World.—Roots fleshy-fibrous or tuberous, often clustered: sts. slender, simple, leafy below or at the base: fls. small, spurless, in more or less spirally twisted racemes; sepals free or coherent or the dorsal sepal forming a galea by adnation to oblong petals; lip sessile or clawed, entire, toothed or lobed, erect, partially enveloping the column and often adnate to it, the limb usually spreading and crisped or recurved with minute basal callosities; column short, arched below, attached obliquely to top of ovary bearing an ovate stigma on the front and a single erect anther on the back; anther lidless, of 2 pollinia each in an anther-cell, each pollinium 2-cleft and split into 2 wafer-like plates united by elastic filaments, coherent to a narrow viscid gland set in the thin tapering beak that terminates the column: caps. erect, ovoid to oblong. (Spiran-thes: Greek, alluding to the spiral character of the twisted infl.)

S. cernua, Rich. (*Ophrys cernua*, L. *G. cernua*, Kuntze. *I. cernuum*, House). NODDING LADIES-TRESSES. Sts. 8–22 in. high or more: lvs. basal and cauline; basal 3–14 in. long, linear to oblanceolate with sheathing petioles; cauline 2–6, acuminate, bract-like, mostly appressed to the st.: infl. 1½–5 in. long and about ¾in. broad, fls. subtended by bracts that exceed the ovary and in 2–3 spiral to vertical rows, white, fragrant, spreading or more commonly nodding, about ½in. long, Aug.–Oct.; lip oblong to ovate with hairy callosities. E. U. S.

9. **GOODYERA,** R. Br. (*Epipactis*, Boehmer not Rich. *Peramium*, Salisb.). RATTLESNAKE-PLANTAIN. About 25 species of terrestrial orchids of the north temp. zone, trop. Asia, New Caledonia and the Mascarene Isls., grown in terraria and nat. in the wild-garden.—Rootstock somewhat fleshy, creeping, the roots thickened and fibrous: lvs. all basal, dark green or with conspicuous white reticulations throughout: fls. whitish, glandular-hairy, in bracted spike-like racemes; lateral sepals free, dorsal adnate to petals forming a galea; lip saccate or concave, sessile, entire, somewhat ovate with reflexed apex; column short, the anther borne on the back and attached by a short stalk; pollinia 2, granulose, in separate sacs, attached to small glandular disk that is coherent to top of stigma. (Goodye-ra: after John Goodyear, 1592–1664, British botanist and assistant to Johnson in his edition of Gerard's Herbal.)

A. Infl. loosely-fld., one-sided; lip of fl. with recurved margins....................1. *G. repens*
AA. Infl. dense, not one-sided; lip margins not recurved....................2. *G. pubescens*

1. **G. repens,** R. Br. (*Satyrium repens*, L. *P. repens*, Salisb. *E. repens*, Crantz). LESSER RATTLESNAKE-PLANTAIN. Scape 4–12 in. high: lvs. to about 1¾ in. long, ovate, dark green, self-colored or with indistinct greenish-white veins: infl. one-sided; fls. white or greenish-white, to ¼in. long, July–Aug.; galea ovate, concave, the tip short-spreading or slightly recurved; lip saccate or inflated with short-recurved tip. N. Eu., N. Asia, Japan, N. N. Amer. Var. **ophioides,** Fern., has distinctly white-veined lvs. and is the more common American representative; Newf. to N. C. west to Alaska and Minn.

2. **G. pubescens,** R. Br. (*Neottia pubescens*, Willd. *P. pubescens*, Salisb. *E. pubescens*, A. Eaton). DOWNY RATTLESNAKE-PLANTAIN. Scape 6–16 or rarely to 24 in. high, densely glandular-hairy, with 5–10 lanceolate foliaceous scales or bracts: lvs. ovate, to 3 in. long, dark green with white reticulations: infl. 2–4 in. long, densely many-fld., not one-sided; fls. greenish-white, nearly ⅓in. long, July–Sept.; lateral sepals and galea ovate, tip of latter not usually recurved; lip globose, inflated, the margins not recurved; stigma with 2 short teeth. E. U. S.

10. **BLETILLA,** Reichb. f. Asiatic terrestrial orchids, of 2 species, having pseudobulbs and a leafy st. bearing a racemose terminal infl.; grown in the open garden in near frost-free areas or those not subject to extended periods of hard freezing, or in the cooler conservatory with stove plants.—Lf.-buds convolute, the lvs. with blades jointed to petiole: sepals and petals nearly alike, somewhat spreading; lip strongly 3-lobed with the lateral lobes partially enveloping the column, central lobe oblong; column small, briefly winged; stamen 1, distal, pollinia 8, minute, in pairs with distinct caudicles. (Bletil-la: diminutive of Bletia, a terrestrial orchidaceous genus named for Louis Blet, an 18th-century Spanish botanist.)

B. striata, Reichb. f. (*Limodorum striatum*, Thunb. *Bletia hyacinthina*, R. Br. *Bletilla hyacinthina*, Reichb. f.). Pseudobulbs tuber-like, to ¾in. across: sts. 8–12 or rarely to 20 in. high, with 3–6 plaited lvs., stiffly erect, stout: fls. amethyst-purple, to 1½ in. long, on short pedicels, June; middle lobe of lip denticulate. China, Japan. Var. **alba,** Hort., is offered as a white-fld. form.—Best suited for half-shaded location in moist soil where it forms large clumps. The second species from Yunnan, China, **B. chinensis,** Schlecht. (*Arethusa chinensis*, Rolfe), is reported to have smaller fls. that are rose-purple with darker purple apices to sepals, petals and lip.

11. **CŒLOGYNE,** Lindl. More than 100 species of epiphytic orchids of the eastern hemisphere, mostly of the Indo-Malayan region; many are grown by fanciers, but only one is generally known.—Pseudobulbs tufted on the rhizome or borne at intervals on the st.: lvs. persistent, the blades jointed to the petiole, usually 2 to each pseudobulb, lf.-buds convolute: fls. in terminal racemes, often many, medium or large, with similar spreading or reflexed sepals and petals; lip 3-lobed and sessile at base of column, the side lobes erect, the front one spreading or recurved and keeled; column winged on both sides and inclosed by side lobes of lip; anther 1, pollinia 4. (Cœlog-yne: Greek, referring to the *hollow* or *depressed stigma.*)

C. cristata, Lindl. Handsome plant bearing many drooping racemes of white fls. with orange-yellow throat, Jan.–Mar.; sepals and petals lance-oblong, acute, undulate; lip oval, 3-lobed, the side lobes slightly incurved, the front lobe denticulate; fl. about 2½ in. long. Trop. Himalayas.—Grown in several forms.

12. **LIPARIS,** Rich. Twayblade. About 75–100 species of low-growing terrestrial orchids, widely distributed in trop. and temp. regions of both hemispheres; one of the native species grown in naturalized areas or in shaded part of the border.—Plants with small solid usually subterranean pseudobulb rarely exceeding ¾in. across: lvs. few: fls. small, in terminal racemes; sepals and petals nearly equal, oblong-linear to filiform, spreading; lip entire, quite flat; column very short, curved, thickened basally and winged distally; anther 1, terminal, operculate, pollinia 4 with 2 in each sac, slightly united in pairs, stalkless and glandless. (Lip-aris: Greek for *fat* or *glossy*, alluding to the smooth sometimes waxy lvs.)

L. liliifolia, Rich. (*Ophrys liliifolia*, L. *Leptorchis liliifolia*, Kuntze). Plants 4–10 in. high: lvs. 2, elliptic to ovate, mostly 2–7 in. long, usually obtuse, glossy, keeled beneath: scapes 5–10-striate, the infl. 5–15-fld., to 6 in. long; fls. mauve- to madder-purple, showy, June–July; sepals alike, oblong-lanceolate, petals filiform and purple; lip obovate-cuneate, mauve-purple tinged green, somewhat translucent; column scarcely ⅙in. long, with 2 gland-like tubercles on inner face at base, dilated apically: caps. ½in. long, subclavate. E. U. S.

13. **CALYPSO,** Salisb. A monotypic genus of temp. Old and New World distribution, suited for outdoor use in the shaded parts of the border or wild-garden.—Scapose terrestrial perennials: rootstock cormous, with coralloid roots: lf. 1, basal: scape 1-fld., bearing 2–3 scale-like bracts; fl. terminal, bracted, showy; sepals and petals alike, subequal in size; lip saccate, inflated, large, 2-parted below, with 3 longitudinal rows of yellowish translucent hairs in front and a translucent apron-like appendage formed by the overlapping of the lip, the sac of the lip bearing 2 conspicuous horns basally; column dilated or winged, petaloid, operculate, the single anther just below the apex; pollinia 2, each 2-parted, without caudicles, sessile on a thickened square gland; stigma at base of column. (Calyp-so: Greek after the goddess Calypso.)

C. bulbosa, Oakes (*Cypripedium bulbosum,* L. *Cytherea bulbosa,* House). Corm about ½in. diam. or less: scape 3–9 in. high: basal lf. ovate-orbicular, about 2 in. or more long, petioled, often subcordate: fl. variegated, purple, pink and yellow, May–July; petals and sepals magenta-crimson, rarely white, about ½in. long, with 3 purple stripes; lip spotted madder-purple with sac whitish and marked irregularly with purple and bearing a patch of yellow woolly hairs: caps. scarcely ½in. long, many-nerved. Cool bogs, N. Amer., Eu., Asia.

14. **EPIDENDRUM,** L. Species probably 500, native from S. C. and Fla. through the American tropics, about 50 in cult.—Epiphytic: sts. branching or sometimes represented by pseudobulbs: lvs. sometimes grass-like but mostly short and fleshy, the buds conduplicate: infl. terminal, spicate, racemose or sometimes paniculate; fls. variously colored, short-pedicelled; dorsal sepal usually broader or longer than the lateral ones; petals as broad as sepals or narrower, similar to them; lip with a distinct claw which is more or less adnate to the column, the limb expanded and usually deeply lobed; pollinia 4 with 2 in each anther-sac. (Epiden-drum: *on trees,* alluding to the habit.)

A. Sts. with pseudobulbs .... 1. *E. vitellinum*
AA. Sts. without pseudobulbs .... 2. *E. radicans*

1. **E. vitellinum,** Lindl. Plant bearing pseudobulbs 1½–2 in. long: lvs. 6–9 in. long, linear-lanceolate, glaucous-green: fls. 10–15, cinnabar-red, 1½ in. across. Oct.–Dec.; lip and column orange-yellow; sepals and petals broad-lanceolate, acute, the lip narrower and shorter. Mex., Guatemala.—Cult. in the form var. **majus,** Veitch, with shorter and thicker pseudobulbs, larger and more brilliantly colored fls.

2. **E. radicans,** Pav. Sts. 3–6 ft. long, without pseudobulbs, cylindric, leafy, 2–3-lvd., scandent with many white aërial roots: lvs. to 4 in. long: fls. bright orange-scarlet, lip sometimes orange-yellow, usually 1–1¾ in. across, in dense many-fld. racemes at summit of a long peduncle, Nov.–Aug.; lip with front lobe cleft, the edges of it and of lateral lobes raggedly toothed. Cent. Amer.—A much cult. hort. hybrid of which this is one parent is **E. Obrienianum,** Rolfe (*E. evectum* × *E. radicans*).

15. **CATTLEYA,** Lindl. The most popular and showy of florist's orchids, all trop. American, about 40–50 species (or fewer if *C. labiata* is defined inclusively).—Epiphytes: sts. slender or club-shaped, often distinctly pseudobulbous: lvs. thick and stiff, with sunken midrib, 1–3 or in pairs at top of st., the buds conduplicate: fls. single or several, borne mostly at the apex of the st. or pseudobulb but sometimes on a leafy st. from the base of the pseudobulb, large and of brilliant colors; sepals and petals similar, or the petals much broader, the sepals free, spreading or rarely connivent; lip convolute or apparently tubular inclosing the column but free from it, 3-lobed, the middle lobe spreading and prominent; pollinia 4, in 2 pairs, each furnished with a tail. (Catt-leya: William Cattley, of Barnet, England, was an ardent collector and grower of rare plants; died 1832.)

A. Pseudobulbs with 2–3 lvs.
  B. Lip emarginate: autumn bloomer .... 1. *C. Bowringiana*
  BB. Lip not emarginate, acute: spring bloomer .... 2. *C. Skinneri*
AA. Pseudobulbs 1-lvd.
  B. Lip narrower than lateral petals.
    C. Blade of lip about as long as tube, its margin much crisped.
      D. Throat of tube with golden eye or spot on either side .... 3. *C. labiata*
      DD. Throat without eye.
        E. Margin of blade (of lip) prominent, different in color from center.
          F. Petals longer than sepals and lip .... 4. *C. Percivalliana*
          FF. Petals about as long as sepals and lip .... 5. *C. Gaskelliana*
        EE. Margin not evident, or wanting .... 6. *C. Warneri*
    CC. Blade much shorter than tube, its margin little crisped .... 7. *C. Trianæi*
  BB. Lip about as broad as petals, or broader.
    C. Blade with white border .... 8. *C. Mossiæ*
    CC. Blade without white border.
      D. Throat with yellow or white eye or spot on either side.
        E. Tube same color as petals .... 9. *C. Lueddemanniana*
        EE. Tube and limb of one color .... 10. *C. Warscewiczii*
      DD. Throat without eye .... 11. *C. Mendelii*

1. **C. Bowringiana,** Veitch. Sts. or pseudobulbs club-shaped, about 1 ft. or more long, the 2 lvs. oblong or elliptic-oblong, 6–8 in. long: fls. 5–13, about 3–4½ in. across, rose-purple, Oct.–Dec.; sepals oblong, acute, somewhat undulate; petals oval-oblong, obtuse, undulate; lip rose becoming lilac within, shorter than lateral sepals, front lobe emarginate, throat bearing a large white spot bordered chestnut-brown, basal lobes convolute over

column. (Dedicated to J. C. Bowring, 1821?–1893, England, ardent amateur of orchids.) British Honduras.

2. **C. Skinneri,** Lindl. Sts. or pseudobulbs 5–10 in. tall, club-shaped and much attenuate below, the 2 oval-oblong lvs. 6–8 in. long: fls. 5–10, about 4–5 in. across, bright rose-purple, Jan.–Aug.; sepals elliptic-lanceolate, acutish; petals oval-oblong, broader than sepals; lip with throat yellowish-white bordered purple, the front lobe open and short-acute, the side lobes convolute over column. (Discovered by G. Ure Skinner in Guatemala in 1836.) Guatemala to Costa Rica.

3. **C. labiata,** Lindl. AUTUMN CATTLEYA. Well-known plant, intro. to cult. in 1818: sts. or pseudobulbs club-shaped, somewhat flattened, covered with greenish thin sheath when young, becoming furrowed, 4–8 in. long, bearing 1 oblong obtuse thick durable lf.: fls. 2–5, about 6 in. across, rose-lilac, Oct.–Mar., the peduncle arising from a double sheath; sepals lanceolate; petals much broader than sepals, ovate, undulate; lip ovate-oblong, obscurely 3-lobed, the front lobe large and emarginate, crisped on margin, magenta-purple bordered rosy-lilac, throat yellow with orange spot on either side, lateral lobes small, entire and convolute. W. Indies to Brazil.—Several forms are cult.

4. **C. Percivalliana,** O'Brien (*C. labiata* var. *Percivalliana,* Reichb. f.). CHRISTMAS CATTLEYA. Fls. smaller, 4–5 in. across, rosy-lilac suffused with amethyst-purple, Jan.–Mar., the petals usually deeper colored than sepals, the latter linear-lanceolate; lip rather small, shorter than petals and the tube of same color as petals, tinged yellow, the front lobe purple-crimson shaded maroon and the undulate border lilac, throat without eye-spots, yellow to orange and streaked purple. (For R. P. Percival, England.) Venezuela.

5. **C. Gaskelliana,** Sander (*C. labiata* var. *Gaskelliana,* N. E. Br.). SUMMER CATTLEYA. Pseudobulbs 1-lvd.: lvs. about 1 ft. long, oblong: fls. 6–7 in. across, 2–3 together, amethyst-purple suffused white but sometimes darker in color, May–Sept.; sepals and petals purple-violet suffused with white, sepals lanceolate, petals oval and undulate, equalling sepals in length; lip about as long as sepals and petals, the tube of same color as petals, front lobe emarginate and crisped, purple-violet with paler border, throat tawny-yellow or orange and striped but without eye. (Named for Holbrook Gaskell, orchid cultivator near Liverpool.) Venezuela, Brazil.

6. **C. Warneri,** Moore (*C. labiata* var. *Warneri,* Veitch). Lf. solitary, oblong, to 7 in. long: fls. large and open, 6–8 in. across, 3–5 together, rose-colored shaded mauve or amethyst-purple, May–July; sepals lanceolate; petals oval; lip shorter than lateral sepals, tube the color of petals, the front lobe strongly crisped and emarginate, rich veined purple, the throat orange-yellow or tawny striped pale lilac or white, without eye-spots. (Bloomed in England in 1860 in collection of Robert Warner.) Brazil.

7. **C. Trianæi,** Lind. & Reichb. f. (*C. labiata* var. *Trianæi,* Duchartre). WINTER CATTLEYA. Lf. solitary, oblong, to 8 in. long: fls. about 7 in. across, 2–3 together, variable in color or tint but commonly delicate rose more or less shaded amethyst-purple, Dec.–Mar.; sepals oblong-lanceolate; petals much broader, oval-rhomboid, obtuse, crisped; lip very narrow and little spreading, the relatively long tube rose-color, the front lobe shorter than tube and not much crisped, throat yellow often streaked. (For Dr. Triana, page 53.) Colombia. Var. **Schroederiana,** Hort., EASTER CATTLEYA, fls. fragrant, uniform delicate blush suffused with white, petals much crisped, disk yellow, Mar.–May; dedicated to Baroness Schroeder; hort. forms of this are *alba, cærulea, citrina.*

8. **C. Mossiæ,** Hook. (*C. labiata* var. *Mossiæ,* Lindl.). SPRING CATTLEYA. Lvs. usually 1, oblong, to 8 in. long: fls. 5–8 in. or more across, 3–5 together, rosy-lilac (varying to white), Mar.–Aug., the sepals and petals of equal length; sepals lanceolate; petals oval-elliptic, crisped especially on upper margin; lip large, equalling lateral petals in breadth, tube colored like the petals, the front limb large and much crisped, emarginate, center purple and variegated violet with white margin, throat yellow veined purplish. (First bloomed in England in the collection of Mrs. Moss, near Liverpool.) Venezuela.—Many named vars. are cult.

9. **C. Lueddemanniana,** Reichb. f. (*C. labiata* var. *Lueddemanniana,* Reichb. f.). Lf. solitary, oblong to elliptic-oblong, to 10 in. long: fls. 5–6 in. across, 2–5 together, delicate purplish-rose suffused white (running to white var.), July–Sept.; sepals oblong, acute; petals elliptic, somewhat undulate, nearly three times as broad as sepals; lip broad, the tube same color as petals, front lobe crisped and emarginate and amethyst-purple, the throat with 2 yellow or white blotches between which are radiating lines of amethyst-purple. (Bloomed middle of last century in the collection of M. Pescatore near Paris, Lueddemann, gardener.) Venezuela, Brazil.

10. **C. Warscewiczii,** Reichb. f. (*C. labiata* var. *Warscewiczii,* Reichb. f.). ST.-JOHNS CATTLEYA. Lf. solitary, oblong, to 10 in. long: fls. 7–9 in. across, 3–5 together, rose-mauve, May–Aug.; sepals violet-rose, lanceolate, acute; petals oval, obtuse, undulate; lip somewhat fiddle-shaped, entirely bright to deep crimson-purple except 2 yellow spots in throat with lines of same color, the front lobe large, crisped with deep notch at end. Colombia; first collected about 1848 or 1849 by J. von Warscewicz. Var. **gigas,** Hort. (var. *Sanderiana,* Hort.), fls. very large, sepals and petals dark rose with deep purple-magenta lip. Var. **alba,** Hort., fls. pure white.

11. **C. Mendelii,** Backh. (*C. labiata* var. *Mendelii,* Reichb. f.). VIRGINS CATTLEYA. Lf. solitary, oblong, to 10 in. long: fls. 7–8 in. across, 2–3 together, white or tinted mauve, Apr.–Sept.; sepals oblong-lanceolate; petals obliquely oval, obtuse, notched and crisped; tube of lip white or colored like petals, front lobe broad and spreading and much crisped and indented, rich crimson-purple, throat yellow without eye but reddish-streaked. (Named in compliment to Sam Mendel, near Manchester, England.) Colombia.

16. **LÆLIA,** Lindl. About 30 species in trop. Amer., differing from Cattleya in the presence of 8 pollinia: other features more or less distinguish the genus from Cattleya although not constant, as short ovoid or pyriform pseudobulbs and long slender peduncles often with fls. clustered at the end. (Læ-lia: probably an historic personal name.)—Lælia and Cattleya hybridize freely, the crosses constituting the group Læliocattleya, Rolfe. Many species forms are named in this group. The plants are irregular in their pollinia.

A. Pseudobulbs short, scattered on the rhizome, rounded, pyriform or ovate.........1. *L. anceps*
AA. Pseudobulbs long, forming sts., long-oblong, club-shaped or spindle-shaped.
  B. Fls. purple, rose or white, with no yellow except in throat.....................2. *L. purpurata*
  BB. Fls. predominantly yellow.
    C. Sepals and petals tawny-yellow; lip whitish veined purple....................3. *L. grandis*
    CC. Sepals and petals yellow-green or tinged purplish; lip cream-colored...........4. *L. Digbyana*

1. **L. anceps,** Lindl. Pseudobulbs to 4¾ in. long, ovate-oblong and compressed, scattered on the rhizome: lvs. solitary or only 2, 6–8 or 9 in. long, oblong-lanceolate, stiff: scape or peduncle from top of pseudobulb, 1½–3 ft. long, jointed and bracted, bearing 2–5 (seldom 1) showy pale rose-purple fls. about 4 in. across, Nov.–Jan.; sepals lance-acuminate; petals ovate-acuminate, broader than sepals; lip 3-lobed, the 2 lateral lobes folded over column and yellowish inside, front lobe oblong and sharply short-pointed, more or less reflexed, deep purple with white on the disk and a yellow keel. Mex.—Many vars. in cult.

2. **L. purpurata,** Lindl. & Paxt. Robust: sts. or pseudobulbs 6–24 in. tall, long-elliptic, sheathed when young, furrowed when old, bearing 1 oblong dark green leathery lf. 1 ft. or so long: fls. 3–7 or more, 7–8 in. across, white suffused light rose or amethyst-purple, May–July; sepals linear-oblong; petals ovate, much broader, undulate; lip very large, bell-shaped or rhomboidal when flattened out, somewhat 3-lobed, the front lobe rounded and crisped, spreading, rich purple with darker veins, yellow in the throat. Brazil.

3. **L. grandis,** Lindl. & Paxt. Sts. or pseudobulbs to 1 ft. high, compressed, slender below, bearing 1 oblong-lanceolate stiff lf. 8–10 in. long: fls. 3–5, medium size, 4–7 in. across, May–July, sepals and petals tawny-yellow and lip whitish with purple veins; sepals lanceolate or elliptic-lanceolate, undulate and twisted; petals ovate; lip 3-lobed, the front lobe large and crenate-toothed. Brazil. Var. **tenebrosa,** Gower, with larger fls., has sepals and petals citron-yellow and less undulate, lip with a broad band of white.

4. **L. Digbyana,** Benth. (*Brassavola Digbyana,* Lindl.). Sts. or pseudobulbs club-shaped, compressed, with 1 linear or elliptic fleshy stiff glaucous lf. 5–8 in. long: fl. 1 to a peduncle, large, 4–6 in. across, fragrant, yellow-green, rose, and white, May–July; sepals and petals oblong and spreading, pale yellow-green or the petals sometimes tinged purplish; lip very large, entirely inclosing the column, fringed, cream-colored. (Bloomed in England in 1847 by St. Vincent Digby, Dorsetshire.) Honduras.

17. **SOPHRONITIS,** Lindl. About a half dozen Brazilian orchids, one well known under glass.—Small epiphytes, differing from Cattleya, among other things, by the 8 pollinia and from Lælia by the erect anther and projecting points of stigma rather than a stigmatic depression: pseudobulbs small and clustered on the rhizome each with a single stiff lf.: fl. usually 1, borne from top of pseudobulbs, bright colored; sepals and petals spreading, nearly equal; lip with broad middle lobe and small erect side lobes, the base of the lip leading to a cavity in wall of ovary. (Sophroni-tis: Greek *modest,* alluding to the pretty fls.)

S. coccinea, Reichb. f. (*S. grandiflora,* Lindl.). Pseudobulbs about 1 in. long, clustered: lvs. elliptic, 2–3 in. long: fl. 1, about 1½–2 in. across, sometimes more, brilliant scarlet with base and sides of lip orange-yellow streaked scarlet, in winter; lip narrow, with folded lobes. Organ Mts. of Brazil.

18. **SOBRALIA,** Ruiz & Pav. About 30 orchids of trop. Amer., with reed-like leafy sts. and showy fls. with tubular lip.—Terrestrial: lvs. broad, strongly-veined, more or less plicate, the nerves several, sheathing and jointed at base, folded in the bud: fls. solitary or few in short terminal racemes, the parts all spreading; lip large

and prominent, convolute around the column and with a large flat or expanding often undulate or fringed limb; pollinia 8. (Sobra-lia: F. M. Sobral was an 18th century Spanish botanist.)

S. macrantha, Lindl. Sts. tall and slender, to 6–7 ft., lf.-bearing to top: lvs. broad-lanceolate, taper-pointed, 6–10 in. long: fls. several, short-lived, 5–6 in. across, pink-purple, the large expanded undulate limb of lip deep purple, May–July; tube of lip long, whitish with yellow and ridges in the throat. Mex. and Guatemala.

19. **CALOPOGON,** R. Br. (*Limodorum*, L. in part). Terrestrial hardy orchids, grown in the bog-garden in open exposures; 4 species in N. Amer.—Scapose, arising from underground corms: lf. solitary: infl. a loose spike-like raceme; fls. several; sepals and petals similar, separate, spreading; lip linear-oblong basally, dilated at apex, bearded above with clavate hairs reduced to papillæ at the apex; column free, elongated, winged toward apex; anther 1, terminal, operculate, pollinia 4 with 2 in each anther-sac, granulose: caps. usually oblong and nearly erect. (Calopo-gon: Greek *beautiful beard,* with reference to the bearded lip.)

C. pulchellus, R. Br. (*Limodorum pulchellum,* Salisb. *C. tuberosus,* BSP. *L. tuberosum,* Rydb. not L.). Grass-Pink Orchid. Scapes 6–19 in. high: lf. linear, to 10 in. long: fls. 2–11 in bracted raceme, about 1½ in. across, magenta-crimson, rarely white, June–Aug.; lateral sepals ovate-lanceolate, falcate, acute, about ¾in. long, dorsal sepal narrower; petals lanceolate, obtuse, constricted near middle; lip broadly triangular at apex, bearded with golden-yellow hairs, appearing as if hinged at base. E. N. Amer.

20. **PHAIUS,** Lour. Species about a score, in trop. Asia and Pacific isls., one frequent under glass.—Large plants, terrestrial or epiphytic, with clustered sts. terminating in racemes, usually pseudobulbous at base: lvs. convolute in bud: scape tall, leafless but sheathed, bearing several to many yellow to brown, sometimes white or rose, fls.; sepals and petals similar, spreading or partially so, free; lip 3-lobed, free from the wingless column but the lateral lobes inclosing it, swollen or spurred behind; pollinia 8, each on own caudicle. (Pha-ius: *dark* or *swarthy,* Greek, from color of fls. of the original species.)

P. grandifolius, Lour. Long in cult.: pseudobulbs roundish or ovate, thick, sheathed: lvs. 4–6, oblong-lanceolate, 2–3 ft. and more long, dark green, plaited, acute: scape 3–4 ft. high, bearing a 12–18-fld. raceme; fls. 3–4 in. across, yellow-brown inside and silvery-white outside with yellow-brown bordered purple lip; sepals and petals oblong-lanceolate, acute, nerved; lip broadly obovate, convolute most of its length, with a yellow streaked purple disk. China, Indo-China, Himalayas, Australia.

21. **APLECTRUM,** Torr. Terrestrial orchids, of perhaps 3 species in N. Amer., adapted to moist shaded locations outdoors.—Corm somewhat gelatinous within, about 1 in. across, producing a single lf. in autumn which persists through the winter and from which originates the raceme early the following summer; after flowering a new corm is produced: scapes partially enveloped by sheathing bract-like fibrous scales; fls. bracted, in terminal racemes; sepals and petals similar, narrow; lip free, clawed, 3-lobed and 3-ridged or -crested, spurless; column compressed, free, the single anther borne somewhat below its apex; pollinia 4, lenticular, situated obliquely. (Aplec-trum: Greek *without a spur.*)

A. hyemale, Torr. (*Cymbidium hyemale,* Muhl. *A. spicatum,* BSP. not *Arethusa spicata,* Walt.). Putty-Root. Adam-and-Eve. Lf. 4–7 in. long, elliptic to ovate, many-nerved, plaited, petioled: scape 12–24 in. high, glabrous, bearing 2–3 sheathing scales: raceme 2–4 in. long, loosely 4–16-fld.; fls. yellowish-brown mixed with purple, pedicelled, about 1 in. long, May–June; sepals and petals oblong, the latter slightly the shorter; lip white marked with magenta, shortly 3-lobed, undulate, about ⅓in. long; column to ¼in. long, somewhat curved, the petals arching over it: caps. oblong-ellipsoidal, about ¾in. long, slightly beaked. Vt. to Sask. south to N. C. and Kans.

22. **CALANTHE,** R. Br. About a half hundred species in tropics of eastern and western hemispheres, mostly the former; one commonly cult.—Terrestrial or epiphytic, of sympodial growth, sometimes pseudobulbous, with few plicate rather large petiolate lvs.: scapes erect or nodding, simple, loosely or densely many-fld.;

fls. white, rose-colored or yellow; sepals nearly equal, free, mostly widely spreading; petals similar to sepals or narrower; lip with claw that is adnate to column forming a tube or a broad turbinate cavity, mostly spurred at base, the blade spreading and 3-lobed, the middle lobe usually emarginate or 2-lobed; column short and erect, footless; pollinia 8, 4 in each cell, each on own caudicle. (Calan-the: Greek *beautiful flower.*)

C. vestita, Lindl. A beautiful and popular plant with broad-lanceolate lvs. 1½–2 ft. long appearing after the bloom from angled grayish pseudobulbs 3–5 in. long: fls. 2–3 in. across, in 6–12-fld. very hairy bracted racemes, milk-white with yellow blotch on lip, Nov.–Dec.; sepals oval-oblong and apiculate; petals obovate-oblong, obtuse; lip flat and 4-lobed, large, with slender spur. Burma, Malaya.—There are many forms. **C. Veitchii,** Lindl., is a hybrid with rose-colored fls., the lip with white spot; *C. vestita* is one of the parents.

23. **LYCASTE,** Lindl. One popular cult. orchid, and about 30 others, all native in trop. Amer.—Epiphytic and terrestrial, with ovate or oblong-ovate pseudobulbs bearing 1 to several plicate lvs. at summit and sheathing lvs. from base, lvs. convolute in bud: peduncle 1–2- or 3-fld., rising from base of pseudobulb; sepals nearly equal, spreading, lateral ones united with foot of column; petals smaller, standing forward, the tips often recurved; lip jointed to foot of column, 3-lobed, the side lobes erect, middle lobe ascending or reflexed and with a tongue-like callus lengthwise on disk; pollinia 4, borne on a long slender stalk. (Lycas-te: name in Greek mythology.)

L. Skinneri, Lindl. (*Maxillaria Skinneri,* Lindl.). Pseudobulbs 3–5 in. high, oblong-ovate, 1–3-lvd.: lvs. oblong-lanceolate, 9–18 in. or more long, much exceeding the single-fld. scape: fl. waxy, rose-and-white (a white var.), 5–6 in. across, Jan.–May, Nov.; sepals ovate-oblong, white tinged rose; petals similar in shape but much shorter, more deeply colored; lip ovate, 3-lobed, mostly deep crimson-purple or -carmine and variously spotted with paler shades or white, the middle lobe recurved and with a fleshy tongue-shaped callus. (Collected by G. Ure Skinner in Guatemala and sent to England in 1841.) Mex., Honduras, Guatemala.

24. **PERISTERIA,** Hook. Terrestrial or epiphytic pseudobulbous warmhouse orchids producing laterally spike-like racemes of small waxy fls.; about 5 species of Cent. and S. Amer.—Plant of sympodial growth: pseudobulbs subglobose: lvs. large, plicate, convolute in bud, unfolding successively: fls. somewhat globose or cup-shaped; sepals and petals similar, broad and concave from within; lip with claw adnate to column by its broad lateral wing-like lobes, the terminal lobe movably jointed to the basal structure; anther 1, of 2 pollinia, sessile or very short-stalked. (Periste-ria: Greek *dove-like,* alluding to the form of the column and wings.)

P. elata, Hook. Dove-Flower. Holy-Ghost-Flower. Pseudobulbs 4–5 in. high, ovoid, bearing 3–5 lanceolate-elliptic strongly veined lvs. 2–3½ ft. high: infl. 3–5 ft. high, the raceme itself about 15–18 in. long, open and many-fld.; fls. waxy-white with purple-spotted lip, about 2 in. across, fragrant, Aug.–Oct.; sepals broadly ovate to orbicular, petals more delicate; lip broadly obovate, truncate. Costa Rica, Panama, Colombia.—Requires situation with high humidity prior to and during blossoming period followed by a more arid rest period.

25. **STANHOPEA,** Frost. Probably 50 species, in trop. Amer., a few more or less frequent in cult.—Epiphytic, with many ovoid pseudobulbs clustered on the short rhizome and sheathed with scales: plant of sympodial growth: lvs. 1 to each pseudobulb, petioled, plaited, usually large, convolute in bud: scape simple, deflexed or pendulous, bearing 2–3 or sometimes more large and fragrant pedicillate mostly white, yellow, tawny or reddish purple-spotted fls.; sepals and petals spreading or reflexed, thin, soon fading; dorsal sepal of medium size, the lateral sepals mostly larger and the petals mostly smaller; lip attached to the winged column and continuous with it, remarkably formed, in 3 parts:—lower part (hypochil) boat-shaped or saccate, often with 2 horns on upper margin; middle part (mesochil) fleshy with 2 lateral horns; terminal part (epichil) usually fleshy and keeled; pollinia 2. (Stanho-pea: named in compliment to Earl Stanhope.)

A. Sepals broadly ovate, obtuse..1. *S. tigrina*
AA. Sepals oblong to narrowly elliptic, acute.
B. Petals and sepals deep golden-yellow; hypochil sessile........................2. *S. Wardii*
BB. Petals and sepals pale yellow; hypochil stalked..............................3. *S. oculata*

1. **S. tigrina,** Batem. Fls. 3–4 to a scape, 6–7 in. across, waxy and fragrant, red-yellow-and-white, in summer; sepals broadly ovate, concave, obtuse, red with yellow spots and mottles; petals oblong-lanceolate or linear-oblong, margins revolute, red and yellow; lip broad-oval, the hypochil orange-yellow blotched maroon-purple, the mesochil white spotted purple, the epochil 3-toothed and white spotted purple. Mex.

2. **S. Wardii,** Lodd. Fls. 5–7 to a scape, yellow to orange with red or red-purple spots; sepals oblong and acute; petals much narrower, acute, revolute; hypochil variously orange-yellow and purple-spotted, the cavity dark velvety-purple; mesochil yellow or white; epichil pale yellow spotted red. Mex. to Venezuela; first sent from the latter country to Loddiges by Mr. Ward, 1828.

3. **S. oculata,** Lindl. (*Ceratochilus oculatus*, Lodd.). Pseudobulbs 2–3 in. high: lvs. ovate to elliptic-lanceolate, 12–21 in. long: scape 4–9-fld., to 14 in. long; fls. about 5 in. across, very fragrant, Apr.–Oct.; sepals and petals reflexed, oblong to narrowly elliptic, acute, pale yellow to ivory-white with numerous small reddish-purple maculate spots; lip with boat-shaped orange-yellow to white stalked hypochil having 1 or sometimes 2 large oculate purple-black or -red spots on each side, the horns white, sharp-pointed. Mex. to Honduras.

26. **ZYGOPETALUM,** Hook. Probably a dozen species as the genus is now limited, in trop. Amer., one frequent under glass.—Mostly epiphytic and usually pseudobulbous: lvs. many, distichous, sheathing, rather thin, plicate or very veiny, convolute in bud: fls. mostly showy, solitary or in racemes, vari-colored; sepals and petals much alike and usually united at base, the lateral sepals jointed to foot of column; lip 3-lobed, jointed to the column-foot, the side lobes small, the middle lobe broad and flat, spreading or at apex recurved, with a prominent transverse crest or horseshoe-shaped callus on disk; pollinia 4. (Zygopet-alum: Greek *yoked* or *joined petals.*)

Z. Mackayi, Hook. (*Eulophia Mackayana*, Lindl.). Pseudobulbs ovoid, 2–3 in. long, with 2–3 linear-lanceolate lvs. 12–20 in. long: scape 18–30 in. long, bearing 5–8 separated fls. 3 in. across up and down, yellow-green and white, spotted and marked purplish-brown, Nov.–June; sepals and petals oblong, acute, united at base, blotched purplish or yellow-green; lip large, rounded or fan-shaped, emarginate, white with streaks and spots of blue-purple. (Intro. into Botanic Gardens at Dublin by Mr. Mackay.) Brazil. Var. **crinitum,** Hook. (*Z. crinitum*, Lodd.), has the petals as long as sepals, dorsal sepal and lip densely velvety or long-hairy, and the lip about 2 in. across and white with purplish lines radiating from crest to margin.

27. **DENDROBIUM,** Sw. Orchids of the eastern tropics, mostly of the Malayan region, of 600 species and many hybrids, popular among collectors.—Epiphytic: st. system various; parts sometimes short and pseudobulbous, but mostly elongated and articulated, tufted or springing at intervals from the rhizome, often thickened at or near the base, sometimes leafless at flowering time, terminating its growth in one season: lvs. various, conduplicate in bud, usually short and fleshy, deciduous or persistent, not strap-shaped or plicate: fl.-st. or scape arising from near the apex of the slender st. or from top of pseudobulb: fls. showy in the cult. species, in terminal or lateral long or short racemes, sometimes only 1 or 2, of many forms and colors; sepals of nearly equal length, the 2 lateral adnate to foot of column and forming a sac-like or spur-like body; petals much like dorsal sepal, either broader or narrower; lip movably jointed to base of column, 3-lobed or entire; pollinia 4, each separate and free, unappendaged. (Dendro-bium: Greek compound, *tree* and *life*, from the epiphytic habit.)

A. Lf.-sheaths black-hairy when young: fls. white with yellow spot on lip.......... 1. *D. formosum*
AA. Lf.-sheaths not so: fls. usually colored.
B. Fls. 3 to usually many in a raceme.
C. Color of lip or its blotches rose-purple or red.
D. Perianth-segms., except lip, tinged or suffused pale yellow............ 2. *D. pulchellum*
DD. Perianth-segms. not suffused or tinged yellow...................... 3. *D. Phalænopsis*
CC. Color of lip yellow.
D. Lip deeply fringed, the divisions ciliate........................... 4. *D. chrysotoxum*
DD. Lip not fringed or only shallowly so.............................. 5. *D. densiflorum*

BB. Fls. in pairs, rarely solitary or in 3's.
C. Pseudobulbs with nodes much thickened, the internodes gradually thickened toward apex........ 6. *D. Findleyanum*
CC. Pseudobulbs with nodes not thickened or only slightly so.
D. Sepals and petals yellow........ 7. *D. heterocarpum*
DD. Sepals and petals not yellow.
E. Width of fls. 2–2½ in........ 8. *D. Bensoniæ*
EE. Width of fls. 2½–4 in.
F. Throat deep purple........ 9. *D. nobile*
FF. Throat yellow with 2 purple spots........ 10. *D. Wardianum*

1. **D. formosum,** Roxb. Sts. 12–18 in. high, cylindric, about as thick as little finger, leafy, bearing blackish hairs when young: lvs. ovate-oblong, about 5 in. long, clasping: fls. in racemes or fascicles of 2–5 in upper axils, white with yellow mark on lip, 3–4 in. across, Jan.–May; sepals oblong-elliptic, about half as broad as petals; lip ovate-oblong, retuse, the front margin jagged. Burma, Himalayas. Var. **giganteum,** VanHoutte, has fls. 4–5 in. across.

2. **D. pulchellum,** Roxb. (*D. Dalhousieanum*, Wall.). Sts. 2–4 ft. long, cylindric, size of little finger, spotted purple when young: fls. often 6–10 or more in a pendulous raceme, 4–5 in. across, pale yellow tinted and veined rose with large purple blotch on either side lip near base, May–June; sepals ovate-lanceolate, much narrower than petals, 2 lateral ones falcate; lip oval and concave, obscurely 3-lobed, hairy on front. India.

3. **D. Phalænopsis,** Fitzg. Sts. 1–2 ft., about as thick as little finger, leafy above: peduncle terminal or nearly so and slender, bearing 4–18 fls., white, rose, and purple, 2½–3½ in. across, May–Nov.; sepals lanceolate, acute, white flushed rose; petals rhomboid, mauve, veined; lip 3-lobed, the lateral lobes curved over column and maroon-purple, the front lobe oblong, maroon-purple at base and lighter above. (Named for its resemblance to Phalænopsis.) Australia and Isls. Var. **Schroederianum,** Reichb. f., has white sepals and petals and a deep violet or white lip.

4. **D. chrysotoxum,** Lindl. Sts. to 18 in. high, clavate to fusiform: lvs. 3–8 at apex, oblong, to 6 in.: racemes pendulous, loosely 8- or more-fld., 6–9 in. long; fls. golden yellow except the reddish-streaked disk on lip, about 2 in. across, Mar.–July; sepals oblong-elliptic, the obovate-oblong petals about twice as wide; lip orbicular, fimbriate, pubescent on upper surface. Burma, Indo-China, China.

5. **D. densiflorum,** Wall. Sts. to 20 in. high, clavate, 4-angled, with 3–5 leathery elliptic lvs. about 6 in. long near apex: infl. a pendulous raceme, many-fld., about 9 in. long; fls. pale or golden yellow, about 2 in. across, Mar.–May; sepals acute, oblong-ovate, nearly transparent, narrower than the denticulate nearly orbicular petals; lip suborbicular, orange-yellow, pubescent on upper surface. Himalayas, Burma, Indo-China.—A closely related entity, and perhaps only a variant, is **D. thyrsiflorum,** Reichb. f. (*D. densiflorum* var. *albo-luteum*, Hook.), differing primarily in sts. nearly terete (not angular) and sepals and petals white; Burma.

6. **D. Findleyanum,** Par. & Reichb. f. Sts. to 2 ft. high, internodes clavate and gradually thickened towards apex: lvs. about 3 in. long, lanceolate, acute, pseudobulbs leafless at flowering time: fls. 2–3 in. across, usually in pairs, sometimes solitary, Feb.–May; sepals and petals white suffused or tinged rose and becoming lilac, petals much broader than sepals; lip deep yellow with throat fading to white near edges, broadly ovate with short spur, sparsely papillose. (James Findlay received plant from Burma in 1817.) Burma.

7. **D. heterocarpum,** Wall. (*D. aureum*, Lindl.). Sts. to about 30 in. high, stout, somewhat clavate: lvs. to over 7 in. long, lanceolate, acute: fls. in 2's or 3's, fragrant, mostly 2½–3 in. across, appearing throughout the year; sepals and petals cream-colored, sepals oblong-lanceolate and slightly narrower than the oblong-ovate petals; lip yellow, streaked with reddish-purple, disk velvety, terminal lobe ovate, acuminate, recurved. Himalayas to Java and Philippines.

8. **D. Bensoniæ,** Reichb. f. (*D. signatum*, Reichb. f.). Sts. to about 3 ft. high, slender: lvs. about 5 in. long, lanceolate, absent at flowering time: fls. white, solitary, paired or in 3's, usually 2–2½ in. across, May–June; sepals oblong, obtuse, much narrower than petals; lip white with yellow disk bearing 2 maroon spots, terminal lobe orbicular, denticulate, downy on upper surface. (Named for the wife of Col. Robt. Benson, British Army officer, 1822–1894, long stationed in Burma and India.) Siam, Burma.

9. **D. nobile,** Lindl. One of the best-known species in many color vars.: sts. tufted, 1–2 ft., nearly cylindric, nodose: lvs. ovate-lanceolate, 3–4 in. long, persistent two years: fls. in 2's or 3's, about 2–4 in. across, waxy-white with amethyst-purple tips or over-color and maroon-purple disk bordered yellowish-white and purple spot at tip of lip (the color and markings variable), Jan.–June; sepals oblong, obtuse; petals broader, oval and undulate; lip with nearly orbicular blade, downy on both surfaces. India and eastward.

10. **D. Wardianum,** Warner. Sts. 2–3 ft., pendulous, cylindric, as thick as little finger or less: fls. in 2's and 3's, about 3–4 in. across, white tipped amethyst-purple with yellow throat in lip and a maroon spot on either side, Feb.–May; sepals oblong, about half as wide as oval petals; lip nearly orbicular. (Dedicated to Dr. N. B. Ward, 1791–1868, cultivator, England.) India.

28. **CYMBIDIUM,** Sw. Probably 50 species of the Old World tropics and warm regions, mostly of farther Asia and Malaya.—Mostly epiphytic, usually with pseudobulbs: lvs. long for the most part, narrow, persistent: infl. on a loosely sheathed peduncle, nearly erect or drooping, the fls. few to many and usually large and showy; sepals and petals similar and nearly equal, spreading or erect, free; lip sessile at base of column and jointed to it, usually 3-lobed, the side lobes erect and front lobe recurved, concave at base, the disk or throat with 2 prominent ridges; column long, erect, footless; pollinia 2. (Cymbid-ium: Greek *boat*, from shape of the lip.)

A. Fls. white with yellow ridge on lip........1. *C. eburneum*
AA. Fls. not white.
B. Sepals and petals uniformly green or sometimes spotted, not veined purple-red.. 2. *C. grandiflorum*
BB. Sepals and petals veined with red, brown or purple.
C. Central lobe of lip yellow spotted purple........3. *C. insigne*
CC. Central lobe of lip purple-maroon with yellow margin........4. *C. Lowianum*

1. **C. eburneum,** Lindl. Sts. tufted: lvs. to 2 ft. long and ¾in. wide, linear, bifid or acute: raceme 1–3-fld., to 8 in. long; fls. 4–5 in. across, ivory-white sometimes tinged rose, fragrant, Mar.–June; sepals and petals oblong-lanceolate, about 2½ in. long; lip 3-lobed, with a golden-yellow ridge extending along the center and with 3–4 short-hairy keels. Himalayas, Indo-China.

2. **C. grandiflorum,** Griff. (*C. Hookerianum,* Reichb. f.). Sts. thickened, short, usually 6–8-lvd.: lvs. linear to ligulate, about 2 ft. long, acute: peduncle 2–4 ft. long, erect basally, arching above, usually 6–12-fld.; fls. to 5 in. across, Sept.–Dec.; sepals and petals oblong, olive-green; lip 3-lobed, bright yellow with purple-brown dots; column white speckled brown. Himalayas, China.

3. **C. insigne,** Rolfe (*C. Sanderi,* Hort.). Lvs. oblong-linear, acute, to 3½ in. long and ¾in. wide: infl. 10–15-fld., to 5 ft. high; fls. about 3½ in. across, rosy-white, Feb.–Mar.; sepals and petals pale rose, elliptic, about 2 in. long; lip 3-lobed, pale rose spotted with purple-red and with 2 yellow thickened lines, middle lobe short, obtuse to emarginate, disk yellow. Indo-China.

4. **C. Lowianum,** Reichb. f. Pseudobulbs oblong, compressed, 4–6 in. long: lvs. very narrow, acute, 2–3 ft. long, recurved: fls. usually 20 or more in strong arching racemes, 3–4 in. across, yellowish and brown, Feb.–July; sepals and petals oblong-lanceolate, acute, greenish-yellow with brownish or reddish veins; side lobes of lip roundish-oblong, light buff-yellow; front lobe slightly undulate, reflexed, pubescent, purple-maroon with yellow margin. (Received in England in 1877 by Messrs. Low, nurserymen.) Burma.—**C. Gottianum,** Sander, is a hybrid; fls. white, sepals with greenish tinge, lip blotched ruby-purple.

29. **ODONTOGLOSSUM,** HBK. About 100 species in the warm and higher parts of the American trop. region, yielding favorites for glasshouse cult.—Epiphytic: rhizomes short, bearing short broad 1–3-lvd. pseudobulbs: fls. odd and showy, few or many in slender racemes or panicles from the base of the pseudobulbs; sepals and petals mostly similar or the latter sometimes broader, spreading, free or very nearly so; lip with large spreading variously shaped middle lobe that bears a fleshy crest near the base and small often erect lateral lobes, the base parallel to the club-shaped often elongate column and sometimes adnate to it; pollinia 2, pear-shaped or ovoid. (Odontoglos-sum: Greek *tooth-tongue,* because of the crests or teeth on lip.)

A. Fls. dark purple........1. *O. Edwardii*
AA. Fls. yellow or white, variously spotted brown, crimson or purple.
B. Lip yellow, banded or spotted reddish-brown........2. *O. grande*
BB. Lip white, variously spotted or blotched.
C. Infl. 2–3 ft. long, exceeding lvs........3. *O. crispum*
CC. Infl. usually much shorter than above, not exceeding lvs.
D. Lip reniform........4. *O. pendulum*
DD. Lip oblong........5. *O. pulchellum*

1. **O. Edwardii,** Reichb. f. Pseudobulbs 2-lvd., ovate, to 4 in. high: lvs. lorate, to 2 ft. long and 1½ in. wide: infl. a suberect many-fld. panicle to 4 ft. high; fls. mauve to dark purple, about 1 in. across, Jan.–Apr.; sepals and petals lanceolate-spatulate, scarcely ¾in. long, ciliate; lip tongue-shaped, somewhat shorter than sepals, obscurely lobed, with a prominent yellow lobulate callus on disk at lip base. (Named for its collector, Mr. Edward Klaboch.) Ecuador.

2. **O. grande,** Lindl. Baby Orchid. Pseudobulbs ovoid and compressed, 3–4 in. long, light green, bearing 2–3 oval-oblong or broad-lanceolate lvs. to 14 in. long: fls. few on erect stout peduncles that exceed the lvs., very large, 5–6 in. across, yellow barred cinnamon-brown, Oct.–Mar.; lip pale yellow or whitish; sepals lanceolate, lateral ones

keeled; petals broader, somewhat undulate but entire; lip nearly orbicular, usually spotted brown near edges; column with small auricles, downy. Guatemala.

3. **O. crispum,** Lindl. Showy, floriferous and very variable: pseudobulbs ovate, compressed, about 3 in. long, bearing at top 2 linear-lanceolate pointed lvs. about 1 ft. long: fls. many in panicle 2 ft. or more long, 2–3½ in. across, white variously spotted crimson or brown, sometimes tinged rose or even yellow, Mar.–May; sepals ovate to ovate-lanceolate, often undulate; petals ovate to rhomboid, toothed and crisped; lip longer than broad, fringed and undulate, bright yellow in throat; column with jagged wings. Colombia.

4. **O. pendulum,** Batem. (*O. citrosmum,* Lindl.). Pseudobulbs ovoid or nearly globular, compressed, 4–6 in. long, bearing 1 or 2 oblong obtuse lvs. 1 ft. or less long: fls. a dozen more or less, large, 3 in. across, white to rose with violet or deep rose lip, May–June; sepals and petals similar, oval, entire; lip with a reniform clawed emarginate blade; column with 1 dorsal and 2 lateral wings. Mex., Guatemala.

5. **O. pulchellum,** Batem. Pseudobulbs oblong, compressed, 2–3 in. high, 2-lvd.: lvs. linear, about 1 ft. long, acute: scape 6–10-fld., weak, to 15 in. long; fls. 1–1½ in. across, fragrant, white, Dec.–May; sepals ovate, acute, petals obovate, acute, often undulate; lip with base yellow dotted with red, terminal lobe oblong, somewhat quadrate, apex recurved, lateral lobes triangular; column with 3 fimbriate wings, very short. Colombia.

30. **MILTONIA,** Lindl. Twenty or more S. American species of great beauty.—Closely allied to Odontoglossum, from which it is separated by its short narrow-winged or wingless column to the base of which the sessile unlobed lip is adnate and from which the lip spreads at nearly or quite a right angle; from Oncidium it is distinguished by the unswollen column, and the sessile practically entire crestless lip: epiphytic: pseudobulbs short, bearing 1 or 2 lvs. at top and others at base: fls. 1, several or many, on a peduncle arising from base of pseudobulbs; sepals nearly equal and spreading, free or somewhat united; petals similar, sometimes broader; lip large, without distinct claw, expanded and not lobed but sometimes bifid. (Miltonia: dedicated to Viscount Milton, 1786–1857, patron of hort. and natural science.)

A. Pseudobulbs spaced apart from each other on the rhizome: lvs. few, yellow-green. 1. *M. candida*
AA. Pseudobulbs crowded together: lvs. many, dark or gray-green.
  B. Infl. longer than lvs.; fls. rose .... 2. *M. vexillaria*
  BB. Infl. shorter than lvs.; fls. white or marked with red or yellow.
    C. Fls. about 4 in. across; lip sagittate at base .... 3. *M. Roezlii*
    CC. Fls. 1½–2½ in. across; lip constricted in middle, not sagittate .... 4. *M. Phalænopsis*

1. **M. candida,** Lindl. Pseudobulbs ovate-oblong, 2-lvd. with few basal lvs.: lvs. linear-lanceolate, acute, to 18 in. long: infl. erect, usually 2–8-fld., to 20 in. high; fls. about 3–3½ in. across, July–Oct.; sepals and petals chestnut-brown, tipped and spotted bright yellow, spreading, oblong, acute, somewhat undulate; lip white with 2 purple-brown spots at base, broadly obovate, convolute, crenate on margin; column short. Brazil.

2. **M. vexillaria,** Nichols. (*Odontoglossum vexillarium,* Benth.). Habit and size of *M. Roezlii,* with broader lvs., longer infl. and fls. somewhat larger, Apr.–June; sepals and petals obovate and not acute or only apiculate; lip deeply bifid, light or dark rose, the parts sometimes white-margined, more or less streaked yellow and red. Colombia, Ecuador.

3. **M. Roezlii,** Nichols. (*Odontoglossum Roezlii,* Reichb. f.). Pseudobulbs ovate-oblong, about 2 in. long, each bearing 1 linear pale green lf. 1 ft. or less long: fls. 2–3 on scapes about half as long as lvs., 3–4 in. across and opening flat, white with purple blotch or band at base of each petal and orange-yellow or brownish at base of lip (a pure white var.), blooming usually twice a year, in spring and winter; sepals and petals ovate-oblong and acute; lip large, obcordate, bearing a small horn-like spur on each side near base; column wingless. Colombia; first collected in 1873 by Benito Roezl.

4. **M. Phalænopsis,** Nichols. (*Odontoglossum Phalænopsis,* Lindl. & Reichb. f.). Pseudobulbs ovoid, 1–2-lvd., clustered and clump-forming: lvs. grass-like, to 9 in. long: infl. loosely 2–5-fld., shorter than lvs.; fls. 1½–2½ in. across, flat, white, the large 2-lobed lip streaked and variegated crimson, Apr.–Aug.; sepals 1 in. long, oblong, acute, petals wider and obtuse; lip constricted in middle and expanded above into 2 rounded lobes. (Named for its resemblance to Phalænopsis.) Colombia.

31. **ONCIDIUM,** Sw. Orchids of the western hemisphere, more than 300 species, many grown by fanciers, one or two generally known.—Epiphytic plants characterized technically by the short winged column that is tumid or swollen below the top, and 3-lobed lip that is crested, cushioned or tuberculate at base: pseudobulbs usually present, 1–2-lvd.: lvs. plane, terete or angled: sepals nearly or quite equal,

spreading or reflexed, the 2 lateral sometimes partially united; petals similar to dorsal sepal or larger; lip various, but never with its base parallel to the column as in Odontoglossum, spreading nearly at right angles to the column. (Oncid-ium: from the Greek for *swelling* or *tubercle*, alluding to the crest of lip.)

A. Lateral sepals more or less united at base.
  B. Petals clawed with a broad obovate blade nearly as large as lip.......... 1. *O. Marshallianum*
  BB. Petals very small, not nearly as large as lip.
    C. Lip with bifid blade.......... 2. *O. flexuosum*
    CC. Lip with quadrifid blade.......... 3. *O. varicosum*
AA. Lateral sepals free and separate.
  B. Segms. with dorsal sepal and petals elongate, linear, erect, with an obsolete blade; lateral sepals with distinct blade.......... 4. *O. Papilio*
  BB. Segms. all having distinct blades, none of them linear or subterete.
    C. Lip with large reniform middle lobe, lateral lobes small or none; fls. yellow.......... 5. *O. tigrinum*
    CC. Lip with middle lobe other than reniform, lateral lobes large; fls. rose..... 6. *O. ornithorhynchum*

1. **O. Marshallianum,** Reichb. f. Pseudobulbs ovoid, 2–3-lvd., to 4 in. high: lvs. narrowly oblong-lanceolate, about 1 ft. long, acute: infl. a lax many-fld. panicle, to about 5 ft. high; fls. to 2½ in. across, Apr.–June; sepals greenish-yellow barred with brown, ovate-elliptic, nearly 1 in. long, concave; petals golden-yellow with brown spots, larger than sepals, fiddle-shaped and clawed, wavy, 2-lobed; lip yellow with red basal spots, middle lobe large, spreading and bifid, lateral lobes small and ear-like; column-wings short and quadrate. (Flowered by W. Marshall, Enfield, England.) Brazil. Var. **sulphureum,** Hort., has clear yellow fls.

2. **O. flexuosum,** Lodd. Pseudobulbs ovoid, about 2 in. long, flattened, 1–2-lvd.: lvs. linear-oblong, to 9½ in. long, acute: infl. paniculate, many-fld., to 3 ft. high; fls. ¾–1¼ in. across, Oct.–Mar., June–Aug.; sepals and petals small, yellow with chestnut-brown bars, recurved, lateral sepals basally connate; lip yellow with few reddish spots, middle lobe kidney-shaped and bifid, lateral lobes small. Brazil, Paraguay. Var. **unicolor,** Hort., has unspotted clear yellow fls.

3. **O. varicosum,** Lindl. GOLDEN BUTTERFLY ORCHID. Pseudobulbs 2–4 in. long, ovoid and angled: lvs. stiff and very narrow, almost linear, 6–9 in. long: infl. nodding, branched, 3–5 ft. long, bearing many green-and-yellow fls. about 1 in. across, Oct.–Dec.; sepals and petals small, green with brownish blotches; lip very large and comprising most of the bloom, bright yellow, with a toothed crest and sometimes a red-brown blotch, the middle lobe quadrifid. Brazil. Var. **Rogersii,** Reichb. f., has much larger blade 2 in. or more across and more spreading, rich yellow with red bars; exhibited in 1868 by Dr. Rogers before Royal Hort. Soc.

4. **O. Papilio,** Lindl. BUTTERFLY ORCHID. Pseudobulbs to 2 in. high, ovoid, mostly 1-lvd.: lvs. lorate, to 9 in. long and 2¾ in. wide, mottled with purplish-brown: infl. to 4 ft. long, peduncle 2–3 ft. long, flattened, jointed, producing fls. several years in succession; fls. 1 to several, successive, to about 4 in. across, blooming all year; dorsal sepal and petals linear, erect, with an obsolete blade, reddish-brown sparingly marked with yellow; lateral sepals chestnut-brown with yellow markings, oblong, wavy, curved downward; lip pandurate, usually flat, yellow with broad brown marginal band, the middle lobe rounded, somewhat reniform, emarginate; column with toothed wings. Trinidad, Venezuela, Brazil, Peru.

5. **O. tigrinum,** Llave & Lex. Pseudobulbs suborbicular, 2½–3 in. high, 2–3-lvd., compressed: lvs. oblong-lanceolate, to 12 in. long, thickened, acute: infl. usually loosely paniculate, to about 1 ft. high, erect, stout; fls. to nearly 3 in. across, Oct.–Feb.; sepals and petals greenish-yellow, blotched with red-brown, lanceolate, undulate, distinctly bladed and clawed; lip with large reniform middle lobe borne on a long claw, the lateral lobes small and oblong. Mex. Var. **splendidum,** Hook. f. (*O. splendidum*, A. Rich.), has slightly shorter 1–2-lvd. pseudobulbs, claw of lip broader than the species and with smaller lateral lobes, Dec.–Feb.; Guatemala.

6. **O. ornithorhynchum,** HBK. DOVE ORCHID. Pseudobulbs ovoid, 1½–2 in. long, 2-lvd., compressed: lvs. linear, to 10 in. long: infl. a slender drooping many-fld. panicle to 1½ ft. long; fls. about ¾in. across, rose-lilac, Aug.–Dec.; sepals linear-oblong, wavy, about ½in. long; petals ovate-oblong; lip pandurate, with lateral lobes smaller than the larger dilated emarginate middle lobe which bears a warty yellow crest. Mex. to Salvador.

32. **RENANTHERA,** Lour. Perhaps a score of species in the Malay Archipelago and Cochin-China, one fairly well known in cult.—Epiphytic leafy-stemmed diffuse or climbing plants without pseudobulbs, and distichous spreading stiff or fleshy lvs., conduplicate in bud: fls. in long drooping racemes or panicles, showy in the cult. kinds, mostly red; sepals and petals spreading, the parts similar or the lateral sepals sometimes larger and differently colored; lip small and movably jointed to the

column, with or without spur, often with small erect lateral lobes; pollinia 2. (Renan-the-ra: *reniform anther* or pollinia of the original species.)

R. Imschootiana, Rolfe. Dwarf: sts. about 1 ft. long: lvs. linear-oblong, 2–4 in. long and 1 in. broad: fls. red and yellow, about 2 in. across, in a panicle with bright red branches, May–June; dorsal sepal linear-oblong, obtuse, dull yellow; lateral sepals twice longer, oval and clawed, cinnabar-red above and ochre-yellow beneath; petals narrow-spatulate, a little shorter than dorsal sepal, yellow spotted blood-red; lip very small, 3-lobed; column scarlet. (Dedicated to A. Van Imschoot, Ghent.) India (Assam).

33. **PHALÆNOPSIS,** Blume. About 50 species of trop. Asia, Philippines, and Malaya, yielding some of the best hothouse orchids.—Epiphytic, with leafy sts. and no pseudobulbs: lvs. few, oblong, thick and leathery, often mottled: fls. mostly white or whitish with over-colors of rose or purple, attractive in form and color, in drooping panicles; sepals wide-spreading, nearly equal, the lateral ones more or less adnate to base of column; petals equalling or much exceeding sepals; lip united immovably with base of column, various in shape, spurless, sometimes with marked or odd appendages at apex; column straight or slightly curved, with short foot; pollinia 2. (Phalænop-sis: Greek *moth-like.*)

A. Appendages at front of lip tendril-like .... 1. *P. amabilis*
AA. Appendages short and horn-like.
  B. Fls. white, with red and yellow spots .... 2. *P. Stuartiana*
  BB. Fls. rose-purple .... 3. *P. Schilleriana*

1. **P. amabilis,** Blume. One of the favorite orchids: lvs. pale green, broadly obovate-oblong, 6 in. to 1 ft. or more long: fls. in an ascending or arched panicle, 3–5 in. across, flat white with stains of deep yellow and few purple spots on lip and column, mostly in autumn; dorsal sepal elliptic-oblong; lateral sepals lance-oblong; petals broad, more or less rhomboid, contracted at base; lip 3-lobed, the lateral ones rounded and incurved, the middle or front one very narrow and with 2 yellow tendril-like appendages. Philippines and Malay Archipelago. Var. **Aphrodite,** Ames (*P. Aphrodite,* Reichb. f.), has a broader trowel-shaped middle lobe of lip, fls. mostly smaller, the lip streaked and spotted yellow and red; lvs. deeper glossy green, purplish beneath. The form known more commonly as **P. Sanderiana,** Reichb. f. (*P. Aphrodite* var. *Sanderiana* Rolfe. *P. amabilis* subvar. *Sanderiana,* Ames), has fls. suffused with rose, the lip variegated with brown-purple and yellow; Dec.–Mar. (*Aphrodite* is the Greek name of Venus, applied here because of the beauty of the fls.; and *Sanderiana* bears the name of Messrs. Sander, nurserymen of Belgium and England.)

2. **P. Stuartiana,** Reichb. f. Lvs. elliptic-oblong, obtuse, about 1 ft. long and 4 in. wide, mottled when young: fls. in a branched drooping panicle, 2½ in. across, white or nearly so, Jan.–Feb., May; sepals elliptic, obtuse, the lateral ones speckled purple and yellowish on basal half; petals angled, rounded, white with few purple dots at base; lip 3-lobed, yellow or orange at base, spotted crimson, middle lobe orbicular with 2 anchor-like appendages at apex. (Bears the name of Stuart Low, nurseryman, England.) Philippines.

3. **P. Schilleriana,** Reichb. f. Lvs. oblong, to 20 in. long and 4½ in. wide, mottled gray above and purple beneath: fls. in a drooping flat panicle often 3 ft. long and broad, the fls. 2½–3 in. across, rose-purple, spring and early summer; dorsal sepal obovate and acute; lateral sepals ovate; petals large, rhomboid; lip often paler than other parts or white, sometimes spotted red-brown and with 2 incurved appendages. (Bloomed in 1860 in the collection of Consul Schiller, Hamburg, Germany.) Philippines.

34. **VANDA,** R. Br. Species about 25, India and eastward, Malaya to New Guinea, yielding a few popular glasshouse plants.—Epiphytic, with short or long sometimes climbing leafy sts., not pseudobulbous: lvs. distichous, spreading, stiff or somewhat fleshy, often emarginate at apex, flat, keeled or terete, conduplicate in bud: fls. in simple axillary racemes, short-pedicelled, often showy, in several colors; sepals and petals similar, narrowed at base, spreading; lip immovably united to base of footless column, short-spurred or saccate, lateral lobes small, middle lobe spreading and various in form with fleshy disk and usually ridged; pollinia 4, with stalks broadened, at least apically. (Van-da: Sanscrit name.)

A. Fls. blue .... 1. *V. cærulea*
AA. Fls. in shades of rose-red or yellow.
  B. Sts. short, to 6 in. long: lvs. deeply channelled .... 2. *V. Kimballiana*
  BB. Sts. 3 ft. long or more.
    C. Lvs. terete: infl. few-fld .... 3. *V. teres*
    CC. Lvs. not terete: infl. 7- to many-fld .... 4. *V. tricolor*

1. **V. cærulea,** Griff. Beautiful species, with sts. 1–3 ft. tall: lvs. leathery, linear, 5–10 in. long and 1 in. or less broad, toothed at tip: fls. pale blue, 3–4 in. across, several to many in a raceme 1–2 ft. long, July–Jan.; sepals and petals oval or obovate, much narrowed at base, faintly tessellated; lip dark blue, less than one-third length of sepals, oblong, 3-lobed, the side lobes with incurved point and middle lobe with 2 thickened ridges. Himalayas, Burma.—Many named vars. are cult.

2. **V. Kimballiana,** Reichb. f. Sts. 6 in. high: lvs. subcylindric, channelled above, to 12 in. long, acute: raceme 4–12-fld., to about 15 in. long, drooping; fls. 2–3 in. across, Aug.–Nov.; petals and dorsal sepal obovate-spatulate, the lateral sepals much larger, oblong-falcate, all pure white; lip smaller than lateral sepals, lateral lobes small, yellow spotted with red, middle lobe orbicular, notched, rose- to violet-purple veined darker, margin erosely toothed, spur 1 in. long. (Named for William Smith Kimball, 1837–1895, American orchid specialist.) Burma, China.

3. **V. teres,** Lindl. (*Dendrobium teres,* Roxb.). Sts. several ft. long, climbing: lvs. to 8 in. long, terete, obtuse: raceme to 12 in. long, mostly 3–6-fld., erect; fls. to 4 in. across, May–Aug.; sepals and petals pale rose-purple, sepals suborbicular, petals slightly larger and somewhat darker colored; lip with lateral lobes broad, incurved, tawny-yellow banded with red spots, the middle lobe flabellately reniform, exceeding the sepals, yellow basally and rose-purple near apex. Himalayas, Burma.

4. **V. tricolor,** Lindl. Sts. tall and branched: lvs. strap-shaped, about 1 ft. long and 1¼–1½ in. broad, unequally 2-lobed at apex: fls. yellow with red-brown spots on sepals and petals and purple lip, 2–3 in. across, fragrant, several on ascending or spreading raceme; sepals and petals similar in shape and color but petals narrower, obovate-oblong to obovate-orbicular, clawed, thick, undulate; lip about as long as sepals with small rounded side lobes and lyrate notched middle lobe. Java. Var. **suavis,** Reichb. f. (*V. suavis,* Lindl.), fls. more numerous; sepals and petals white with fewer spots red-purple; middle lobe of lip deep purple in lower half; Mar.–May.

35. **AËRIDES,** Lour. About 30 species, India to Japan and Malay Archipelago, one well known under glass.—Epiphytic, with leafy sheathed sts. and no pseudobulbs: lvs. distichous, stiff and somewhat fleshy: fls. in simple or compound lateral clusters, medium or rather large, mostly white with rose or purple spots or overtints; sepals spreading, 2 lateral about equal and attached to foot of column, dorsal broader; petals much like the dorsal sepal; lip attached to foot of column, with a hollow spur usually upturned, 3-lobed, the lateral lobes erect, the middle one spreading; pollinia 2. (Aëri-des: Greek signifying "children of the air," i.e. *air-plant.*)

A. odoratum, Lour. Sts. erect or ascending, with many strap-shaped horizontal or arching lvs. 6–8 in. long standing off from either side: axillary racemes equalling or exceeding lvs., with many fragrant white fls. more or less tinged and spotted, about 1 in. long, July–Sept.; sepals oval-oblong, the dorsal narrower and petals still narrower, all with purple spot at obtuse apex; lip funnel-shaped, sometimes purple-tinged or spotted, middle lobe linear-oblong with a purple line in center. India to Cochin-China.—**A. falcatum,** Lindl. & Paxt. (*A. expansum,* Reichb. f.), has infl. longer than lvs., white sepals and petals spotted purple, and an amethyst-red lip; May–June; Burma.

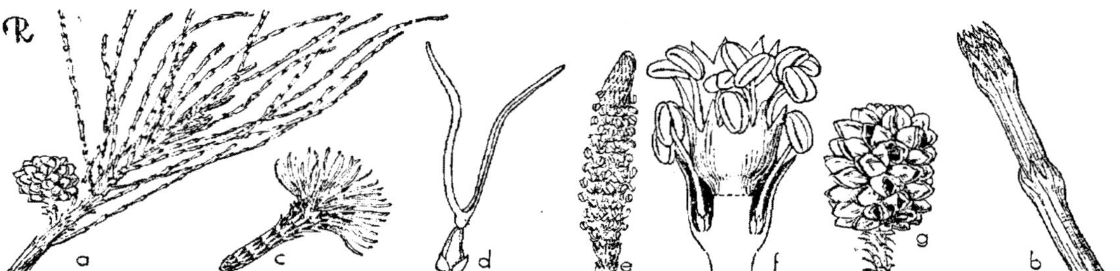

Fig. 43. CASUARINACEÆ. *Casuarina equisetifolia:* a, fruiting branch, × ½; b, twig tip, × 3; c, pistillate inflorescence, enlarged; d, pistillate flower, × 15; e, staminate inflorescence, × 1; f, staminate flower, partly excised, × 10; g, fruit, × 1.

43. CASUARINACEÆ. CASUARINA FAMILY

About 25 species of Australia and the Pacific isls., a few commonly planted in our southern regions and in Calif.—Branchlets very slender and equisetum-like, usually jointed, striate, more or less deciduous, the lvs. represented by whorls of minute scales, foliage lvs. wanting: monœcious or diœcious; staminate fls. in slender spikes terminating the green or gray branchlets (which are sometimes taken for rush-like lvs.), and sometimes lateral, consisting of 1 stamen attended by 2 scales and with 1 or 2 perianth scales, the anthers large and conspicuous; pistillate fls. in short dense heads in the axils along the axis, without perianth, consisting of 1 pistil with 1-celled 2-ovuled ovary, the head or spike becoming a dry cone-like or ball-like body: fr. a thin winged nutlet, held between 2 hard persistent bractlets that open at maturity like the valves of a caps.

CASUARINA, L. Beefwood. She-Oak. Australian-Pine. The only genus, with characters of the family. (Casuari-na: probably *casuarius-like,* from the resemblance of the branches to feathers of the cassowary.)—The casuarinas are called oaks in Australia from a fancied resemblance in the wood. The species in cult. in N. Amer. are not well understood or distinguished.

A. Internodes less than ½in. long: bractlet-valves (of fruiting cone) not keeled on back........1. *C. equisetifolia*
AA. Internodes more than ½in. long: bractlet-valves keeled on back........2. *C. stricta*

1. **C. equisetifolia,** L. Horsetail-Tree. Narrow very tall tree 50–70 ft. and more, with rush-like scant branch-foliage moving widely in the wind, the branches drooping, producing hard wood, growing well in sand and by the sea: branches grayish-green, wire-like, with internodes about ¼in. long, the short-acute or fine-pointed teeth about 7 in each whorl, suggesting twigs of equisetum (whence the name *equisetifolia*): male spikes about ¾in. long, with imbricating lf.-whorls: cones very short-stalked, globular, about ½in. diam., the broad-ovate obtuse bractlet-valves pubescent outside. N. Australia and Queensland and elsewhere; widely nat.—Known also as South-Sea Ironwood, Mile-Tree (from the height); much planted in the semi-trop. parts and farther south; nat. in Fla.

2. **C. stricta,** Dry. (*C. quadrivalvis,* Labill.). Small tree or tall shrub with pendulous branches: branchlets with internodes ½in. or more long, the whorls bearing mostly 10–12 lf.-scales: male spikes often 2 in. and more long, the lf.-whorls scarcely overlapping at maturity: cones globular or ovoid, often 1 in. and more diam., the bractlet-valves smooth and prominently keeled. Widespread in Australia and Tasmania.

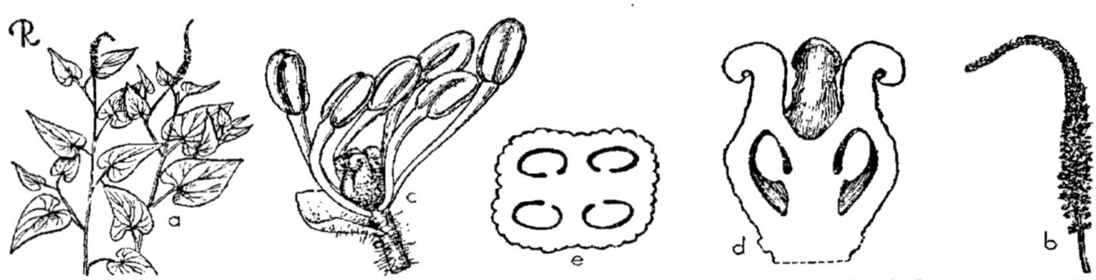

Fig. 44. Saururaceæ. *Saururus cernuus:* a, flowering stems, × 1/10; b, inflorescence, × ¼; c, flower, × 5; d, pistil, vertical section, × 18; e, ovary, cross-section, × 18.

44. SAURURACEÆ. LIZARDS-TAIL FAMILY

A small family of per. herbs represented by 3 genera and 4 species, of which only one genus is cult. for use at pool margins and in the wild- or bog-garden.—Sts. erect: lvs. alternate, broad and cauline, mostly ovate: fls. perfect, without true perianth, bracteate, in dense slender peduncled spikes; stamens 6–8 or occasionally fewer by abortion, hypogynous, filaments distinct the 2 anther-cells of each stamen dehiscing vertically; gynœcium superior, of 3–4 distinct 1-celled 1-carpelled pistils or the simple pistils incompletely united in a single compound pistil, carpels 1–2-ovuled, ovules orthotropous, placentation basically parietal or axile when ovary is compound; styles as many as pistils or 3–4 in compound pistil, basally connate or coherent, stigmas as many as styles, recurving: fr. and indehiscent caps. or berry-like.

SAURURUS, L. Lizards-Tail. Two species of marshes or bogs.—Rootstocks slender: sts. with swollen nodes sheathed by petioles: lvs. heart-shaped, palmately-veined, stipules adnate to petiole: spikes 1–2, opposite upper lvs., on distinct erect peduncles; fls. small, on minute bracted pedicels; pistils usually 4, united at base: fr. rugose, depressed-globose, separating into 3–4 indehiscent cocci. (Sauru-rus: Greek for *lizards-tail*, in allusion to the slender rat-tail-like infl.)

S. cernuus, L. Sts. 1½–3 ft. high or more, sparingly branched: lvs. 3–6 in. long, ovate-acuminate, thin, pubescent soon becoming glabrous, petioles shorter than blades: spikes white, fragrant, usually 4–6 in. long on somewhat shorter peduncles, apex drooping in fl., June–Aug.: fr. about ⅛in. diam. R. I. to Fla. west to Minn. and Tex.

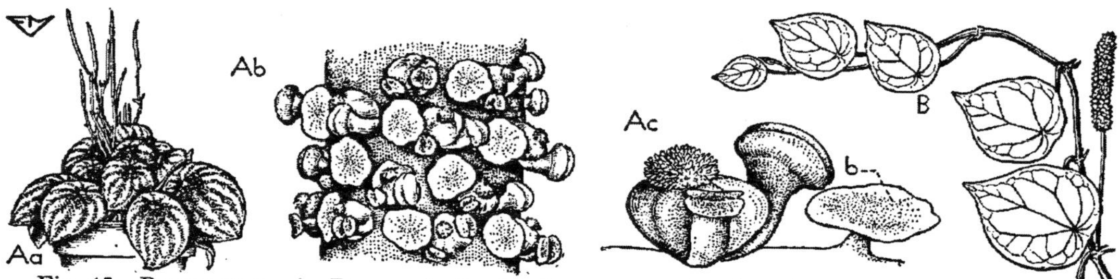

Fig. 45. PIPERACEÆ. A, *Peperomia Sandersii* var. *argyreia:* Aa, plant in flower, × ⅙; Ab, section of inflorescence, × 10; Ac, flower and bract (b), × 25. B, *Piper nigrum:* branch with fruit, × ⅙

45. PIPERACEÆ. PEPPER FAMILY

Herbs, shrubs, and even trees, sometimes climbers, in tropics and subtropics around the world, a very few cult. for ornament and for the commercial products; genera 9 to a dozen, and 1,000–1,400 species.—Plants often jointed at the nodes, sometimes succulent: lvs. mostly broad, sometimes very large, entire, frequently pellucid-dotted, commonly alternate but rarely opposite or whorled: fls. very small, in dense spikes or rarely in racemes, naked (without perianth) but each one with a subtending bractlet, bisexual or unisexual, regular; stamens 1–10; ovary 1-celled and 1-ovuled, the stigmas usually 1–4: fr. a dry or fleshy small indehiscent berry.

A. Anther-cells prominently 2 (sometimes apparently 4): mostly woody climbers or shrubs, or tree-like. . . . . 1. PIPER
AA. Anther-cells confluent into 1 (sometimes apparently 2): low herbs . . . . 2. PEPEROMIA

1. **PIPER,** L. PEPPER. Species 600–700 on both sides of the world.—Sometimes tall herbs, but mostly woody climbers, shrubs, and small trees: lvs. alternate: fls. mostly unisexual (plant monœcious or diœcious), borne beneath decurrent bracts in slender catkin-like spikes; stamens mostly 1–4, the anthers of 2 distinct cells (the cells sometimes appearing as if again partitioned); stigmas 2–4, mostly 3. (Pi-per: the ancient name.)—The genus abounds in aromatic properties. The pepper of kitchen-gardens is Capsicum of the Solanaceæ. *P. excelsum,* Forst., sometimes grown under glass for a form with yellow-blotched lvs., is more properly **Macropiper excelsum,** Miq.: glabrous aromatic erect shrub or small tree from the South Seas and New Zeal.: lvs. 2–4 in. broad, cordate-orbicular to ovate, 7–9-nerved from the base; staminate spikes 2–3 in. long, the pistillate shorter.

A. Lvs. green, not spotted.
B. Fr. sessile: lvs. broad-ovate to nearly orbicular. . . . . 1. *P. nigrum*
BB. Fr. pedicelled: lvs. elliptic-ovate or narrower. . . . . 2. *P. Cubeba*
AA. Lvs. spotted and mottled. . . . . 3. *P. ornatum*

1. **P. nigrum,** L. PEPPER of commerce, sometimes grown with economic plants: strong somewhat woody glabrous climber with terete st. emitting roots: lvs. broad-ovate or -ovate-oblong to nearly orbicular, rounded or more or less cordate at base and oblique, 5–9-nerved: fls. bisexual or at base of slender but dense spike unisexual: fr. small, sessile, globose, yellowish-red, ⅕–¼ in. diam. Oriental tropics, but widely distributed in warm countries.—The dried berries yield the black pepper of commerce; when the pericarp is removed, the product is white pepper.

2. **P. Cubeba,** L. f. (*Cubeba officinalis,* Raf.). CUBEB (E. Indian name), sometimes grown with economic plants, the berries being used in medicine: climbing when given support or more or less tree-like: lvs. glabrous, elliptic-ovate, oval, or narrower, short-acuminate, obliquely cordate, varying somewhat on plants of the two sexes: fr. nearly globose, with remains of stigma at top, brownish, ⅕–¼ in. diam. E. Indies.

3. **P. ornatum,** N. E. Br. Glabrous climber, rooting at the nodes: lvs. slender-petioled, blade peltate, ovate-orbicular and with a short not acute point, 7-nerved, 2½–5 in. long, the upper surface pink-spotted when young and whitish-spotted when old. Celebes.

2. **PEPEROMIA,** Ruiz & Pav. Probably more than 500 species in many parts of the world, a few pot-grown for foliage.—Mostly low herbs, not climbing, ann. or per. by tubers or creeping rootstock, more or less succulent: lvs. alternate, opposite or whorled, often color-marked and pellucid-dotted: fls. bisexual, very small, in dense but small and slender spikes; stamens 2, the anther-cells confluent to form a single anther (but by false partition sometimes appearing 2-celled); stigma 1, capitate or tufted: fr. a small thin-coated berry. (Pepero-mia: *pepper-like.*)

A. Plant without evident st., erect....................1. *P. Sandersii*
AA. Plant with branching st.
  B. Length of lvs. less than ⅓in....................2. *P. rotundifolia*
  BB. Length of lvs. ¾–6 in.
    C. Lvs. opposite or whorled, less than 2 in. long....................3. *P. blanda*
    CC. Lvs. alternate, 2–6 in. long.
      D. Blades of lvs. typically obovate-spatulate, mostly 4–6 in. long....................4. *P. obtusifolia*
      DD. Blades of lvs. typically suborbicular to obovate, mostly 2–4 in. long....................5. *P. floridana*

1. **P. Sandersii,** C. DC. (*P. arifolia,* Hort. not Miq. *P. maculosa,* Hort. not Dietr.). Stemless or essentially so: lvs. broad-ovate or round-ovate, 3–5 in. long, peltate but often splitting with deep sinus at base at maturity, somewhat fleshy, smooth, with broad lighter colored areas (in the var. **argyreia,** Bailey) between the 5–9 main veins, the long petioles dark red: peduncles branched, about equalling the lvs., bearing slender terminal spikes 1–3 or 4 in. long. (Named for Wilson Sanders.) Brazil.

2. **P. rotundifolia,** Dahlst. (*Piper rotundifolium,* L. *Peperomia nummularifolia,* HBK. *P. prostrata,* B. S. Williams). Low plant, 4–6 in. high from creeping sts., hairy: lvs. alternate, many and crowded, oblong to nearly or quite orbicular, ¼–⅓in. long, very short-petioled: spikes ½–1 in. long, terminal. Trop. Amer.

3. **P. blanda,** HBK. Sts. long and weak, hairy: lvs. opposite or in 3's, obovate, pubescent, ciliate on margins, narrowed to very short petiole, ¾–1½ in. long, obtuse or very short-acute: spikes filiform, 2–4 in. long, from the upper whorls and on the summits of divaricate branches. Venezuela to Bolivia.

4. **P. obtusifolia,** A. Dietr. (*Piper obtusifolium,* L. *Rhynchophorum obtusifolium,* Small). Sts. decumbent, rooting at nodes, to 1 ft. long: lvs. alternate, elliptic to obovate, blade 3–6 in. long, rounded or notched at apex, somewhat glossy above: spikes to 5 in. long, slender. Trop. Amer.

5. **P. floridana,** Small (*Rhynchophorum floridanum,* Small). Sts. decumbent, often matted: lvs. alternate, ovate to suborbicular, often broadest above the middle, 1¾–4 in. long, obtuse to emarginate: spikes 2–4 in. long, slender, on short peduncle. S. Fla. Var. **aurea,** Trel., has lvs. strongly margined yellow.

46. SALICACEÆ. WILLOW FAMILY

Willows and poplars; 3 or more genera, of over 300 species mostly in temp. climates, most abundant in the northern hemisphere; trees and shrubs, only the more hort. ones included here.—Rapid-growing soft-wooded plants with alternate simple stipulate lvs., petioles often gland-bearing: diœcious; fls. in catkins, mostly in early spring in advance of the lvs.; perianth lacking, the 1 or more stamens and single pistil borne in the axils of bracts, and a disk at base of fl.; placentæ 2–4, parietal; stigmas mostly 2, often 2-lobed: fr. a 2–4-valved 1-celled small caps., bearing many seeds with long down or hairs.—The species in each genus hybridize extensively.

A. Stamens 1–2 (rarely 3–12): scales in catkins entire: disk gland-like: willows....................1. SALIX
AA. Stamens many: scales in catkins laciniate: disk cup-shaped: poplars....................2. POPULUS

1. **SALIX,** L. WILLOW. OSIER. Shrubs and trees, or in arctic and alpine regions certain species prostrate and almost herbaceous, of about 300 species.—Plants with lithe branches and winter-buds covered with a single scale: stamens in caducous catkins, 1–2 (rarely 3–12) to a fl., distinct or united, borne under entire more or less hairy scales and accompanied by 1 or 2 small stalked glands; pistil in separate catkins, 1 under an entire also more or less hairy scale and with a small gland at base, the stigmas short: caps. 2-valved, the seeds with hair or down. (Sa-lix: classical name of willow.)—There are many hybrids in the collections of parks and nurseries, but these need not be considered here.

A. Catkins appearing with or after the lvs. on short lateral more or less leafy shoots.
  B. Tree of erect or spreading growth.
    C. Length of lvs. less than three times the breadth: stamens 5–12.......... 1. *S. pentandra*
    CC. Length of lvs. more than three times the breadth: stamens 2 or 1.
      D. Petiole never exceeding 3/10 in. long, glandless: catkins up to 3/5 in. long... 2. *S. Matsudana*
      DD. Petiole 1/5–1 in. long, sometimes glandular: catkins 1–2½ in. long.
        E. Lvs. glabrous when mature, bluish-green beneath: ovary stalked...... 3. *S. fragilis*
        EE. Lvs. silky (glabrous in some vars.), glaucous beneath: ovary subsessile.............. 4. *S. alba*
  BB. Tree with long pendulous growth: "weeping willows."
    C. Lvs. all less than 4 in. long, more or less silky beneath; stipules lanceolate... 4. *S. alba* var. *tristis*
    CC. Lvs. mostly over 4 in. long, glabrous to silky.
      D. Petioles up to 1/5 in. long; lvs. less than 3/5 in. wide; stipules ovate-lanceolate, rare.............. 5. *S. babylonica*
      DD. Petioles more than 1/5 in. long; lvs. more than 3/5 in. wide.
        E. Veins divergent from midrib at more than 45 degrees; stipules semicordate.............. 6. *S. elegantissima*
        EE. Veins divergent from midrib at 45 degrees or less; stipules ovate..... 7. *S. blanda*
AA. Catkins appearing in advance of lvs., mostly lateral on the winter branches: "pussy willows."
  B. Branches with bloom (glaucous).............. 8. *S. irrorata*
  BB. Branches without bloom (not glaucous).
    C. Length of lvs. less than four times the breadth.
      D. Lvs. glabrous when mature.............. 9. *S. discolor*
      DD. Lvs. felty-tomentose beneath.............. 10. *S. caprea*
    CC. Length of lvs. more than four times the breadth.
      D. Lvs. pubescent beneath.
        E. Shape of lf. lanceolate to narrow-lanceolate; pubescence dense, short and appressed.............. 11. *S. viminalis*
        EE. Shape of lf. linear; pubescence villous.............. 12. *S. Elæagnos*
      DD. Lvs. glabrous, often subopposite.............. 13. *S. purpurea*

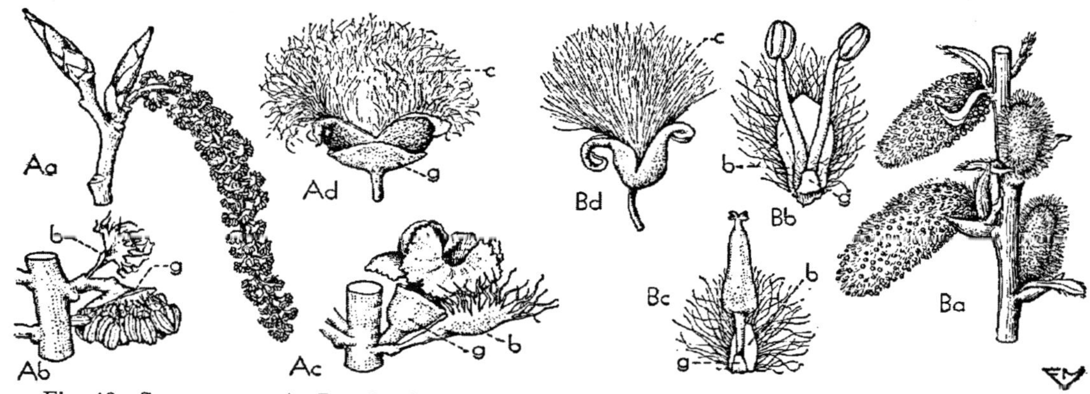

Fig. 46. SALICACEÆ. A, *Populus balsamifera:* Aa, twig with staminate catkin, × ½; Ab, staminate catkin axis with flower, × 2; Ac, pistillate flower, × 4; Ad, capsule, × 2. B, *Salix fragilis:* Ba, staminate catkins × 1 (catkins on left of twig at anthesis, others less mature); Bb, staminate flower, × 6; Bc, pistillate flower, × 6; Bd, capsule, × 2. (b bract, c seed coma, g gland.)

1. **S. pentandra,** L. (*S. laurifolia,* Wesm.). LAUREL-LEAVED WILLOW. BAY WILLOW. Attractive clean-looking tree to 60 ft., with shining brown twigs: lvs. ovate to elliptic-lanceolate, 2–5 in. long and 1–2 in. broad, acuminate, finely and evenly serrate, glabrous, shining above and lighter beneath, short-petioled, usually gland-bearing at top of petiole and on lower margin; stipules broad but soon caducous: catkins 1–2½ in. long, appearing after the early lvs., on prominently leafy shoots: caps. glabrous. Eurasia.—Planted for windbreaks and screens.

2. **S. Matsudana,** Koidz. Tree to 40 ft., with yellow-green twigs: lvs. narrow-lanceolate, 2–4 in. long, long-acuminate, serrate, glaucescent beneath; stipules lanceolate, sometimes wanting: catkins to 3/5 in. long, on leafy stalks, appearing with the lvs. N. E. Asia. Var. **tortuosa,** Hort. (forma *tortuosa,* Rehd.), has branches, twigs and midribs contorted.

3. **S. fragilis,** L. BRITTLE WILLOW. CRACK WILLOW. Tree 50–90 ft., rapid-growing, with brown or gray twigs, the branchlets breaking and falling freely: lvs. lanceolate or narrower, 3–7 in. long, long-acuminate, prominently glandular-serrate, glabrous when mature, green both sides but paler beneath, short-petioled, usually with 2 glands at base of blade; stipules semi-cordate, soon caducous and sometimes wanting: catkins 1–2½ in. long, slender, appearing with the lvs. on leafy stalks: caps. glabrous, usually not fertile. Eurasia.—Planted for hedges and shade, and also spontaneous.

4. **S. alba,** L. WHITE WILLOW. Tree to 75 ft., branches somewhat pendent at ends, yellowish-brown, pubescent when young: lvs. lanceolate, 2–4 in. long, acuminate, serrate, ashy-gray and silky throughout the season: catkins to 2 in. long, on leafy stalks, appearing with the lvs. Eu., N. Afr., Cent. Asia. Var. **chermesina,** Hartig (*S. vitellina britzensis,* Spaeth), branches bright red, mature lvs. almost glabrous. Var. **tristis,** Gaudin (*S. alba* var. *vitellina pendula,* Rehd. *S. chrysocoma,* Dode), branches pendulous, yellow; lvs. more or less silky beneath when mature. Var. **vitellina,** Stokes (*S. vitellina,* L.), YELLOW WILLOW, branches yellow, lvs. almost glabrous when mature; Eu.

5. **S. babylonica,** L. WEEPING WILLOW. Broad-headed large tree with long flexile hanging greenish to brown branches: lvs. narrow-lanceolate, 3–6 in. long, sometimes falcate, very long-acuminate, finely serrate, more or less silky at first but soon becoming glabrous, pale and somewhat glaucescent beneath, short-petioled, glands minute or none; stipules rarely developed: catkins very slender, appearing with the lvs., pistillate to 1 in. long, staminate to 1½ in.: caps. small and glabrous. China; supposed by Linnæus to be of the Babylonian region.—Commonly planted.

6. **S. elegantissima,** Koch (*S. Sieboldii,* Koch). THURLOW WEEPING WILLOW. Branches long and pendulous, twigs brown, shining: lvs. lanceolate, 3–6 in. long, long-acuminate, finely toothed, bluish-green beneath, glaucous except for midrib above: catkins to 2 in. long, on leafy stalks, appearing with the lvs. Origin unknown; perhaps *S. babylonica* × *S. fragilis.*

7. **S. blanda,** Anderss. (*S. babylonica* var. *dolorosa,* Rowlee. *S. Petzoldii pendula,* Hort.). WISCONSIN WEEPING WILLOW. NIOBE WILLOW. Tree with pendulous branches, green to brown: lvs. lanceolate, 3–6 in. long, long-acuminate, finely toothed, bluish-green and glabrous beneath: catkins about 1 in. long. Hybrid between *S. babylonica* and *S. fragilis.*

8. **S. irrorata,** Anderss. Shrub to 12 ft., young branchlets purple, glabrous, bloomy: lvs. oblong-lanceolate, to 4 in. long, entire or somewhat toothed, glabrous, glaucous beneath: catkins subsessile, to 1 in. long, before the lvs. W. Tex. to Colo. and Ariz.

9. **S. discolor,** Muhl. (*S. conifera,* Wangh.). PUSSY WILLOW. Shrub or tree to 20 ft., branches pubescent when young: lvs. oblong, 1½–4 in. long, irregularly wavy-toothed to entire, glaucous beneath, glabrous when mature; stipules semi-cordate, deciduous: catkins in advance of lvs., staminate to 1½ in. long, pistillate to 3 in. in fr., ovary pubescent, beaked. N. S. to Man., Va. and Mo.

10. **S. caprea,** L. GOAT WILLOW. SALLOW. Small tree or tree-like, with brown twigs tomentose or pubescent when young: lvs. variable, broadly ovate to oval to oblong-orbicular, 2–4 in. long, mostly rounded at base, rugose, obscurely irregularly toothed or jagged, felty-tomentose beneath, with stout pubescent glandless petioles; stipules prominent but soon caducous: catkins appearing well before the lvs., subsessile, staminate to 1½ in. long, very showy, pistillate to 4 in. long in fr.: caps. long, pubescent. (Caprea is a Latin name for a kind of goat.) Eurasia. Var. **pendula,** Th. Lang, KILMARNOCK WILLOW (grafted on other stock), has crooked drooping branches.

11. **S. viminalis,** L. OSIER WILLOW. BASKET WILLOW. COMMON OSIER. Large shrub or small tree to 30 ft., with long slender straight greenish or brown branches: lvs. lanceolate to narrow-lanceolate (sometimes small and linear on fr.-bearing shoots), 3–7 in. long, long-pointed, entire, scarcely revolute, silvery-white beneath with fine silky pubescence, dark green and glabrous above, short-petioled; stipules small and narrow and soon falling: catkins sessile, 1–3 in. long: caps. pubescent. Eurasia.—Grown for use in basketry.

12. **S. Elæagnos,** Scop. (*S. incana,* Schrank. *S. rosmarinifolia,* Hort. not L.). Shrub or small tree to 45 ft., with long and slender branches: lvs. close together, linear and rather stiff, 2–3½ in. long, narrowed into very short petiole, revolute, white-tomentose beneath; stipules wanting: catkins slender, 1–1½ in. long appearing just in advance of lvs., staminate practically sessile, pistillate more or less short-stalked and with leafy bracts at base: caps. glabrous. Eu., Asia Minor.—Common in cult.

13. **S. purpurea,** L. PURPLE OSIER. Shrub to 10 ft., with many long erect branches: lvs. oblanceolate, 1–3 in. long, glabrous, paler and somewhat glaucous beneath, finely serrulate, sometimes nearly opposite, nearly or quite sessile; stipules wanting: catkins nearly sessile, slender and recurved, scales purple: caps. tomentose. Eu., N. Afr. to Cent. Asia and Japan; run wild somewhat in N. Amer. Var. **nana,** Hort., is a dwarf form with lvs. mostly less than 1½ in. long.—Planted for ornament and sometimes used in basketry.

2. **POPULUS,** L. POPLAR. ASPEN. COTTONWOOD (from the floating seeds). Small or large trees, of 30–40 species, many planted on roadsides and in public places for immediate effects and for windbreaks; native in the northern hemisphere, mostly in extra-trop. regions.—Wood soft and white: winter-buds with several or many scales: lvs. mostly broad, the petiole often much flattened sidewise: stamens in caducous catkins mostly 8–30 or more, under laciniate scales; pistils in separate catkins and also subtended by laciniate scales, the 2–4 stigmas often long; all fls.

provided with a cup-like disk: caps. 2–4-valved, the seeds provided with copious down. (Pop-ulus: the classical name.)

A. Mature lvs. cottony-pubescent beneath, often lobed: twigs and buds downy-pubescent. . . . . 1. *P. alba*
AA. Mature lvs. glabrous or pubescent on veins, not lobed: twigs and buds glabrous to pubescent.
B. Petioles compressed; mature lvs. greenish beneath.
C. Shape of lvs. ovate to orbicular, obtuse, acute, or abruptly short-acuminate: stamens 6–12.
D. Buds and young growth glabrous or practically so: lf.-blades 1–3 in. long.
E. Lvs. with rounded irregular notches. . . . . 2. *P. tremula*
EE. Lvs. finely and regularly toothed. . . . . 3. *P. tremuloides*
DD. Buds and young growth gray-pubescent: lf.-blades 3–4 in. long, with large irregular teeth. . . . . 4. *P. grandidentata*
CC. Shape of lvs. triangular to ovate-triangular, with gradually tapering long-acuminate apex: stamens 15–60.
D. Lvs. cuneate to truncate, usually without distinct glands at base, edge sparingly ciliate.
E. Base of lf. mostly cuneate, fine teeth only slightly if at all incurved. . . . . 5. *P. nigra*
EE. Base of lf. mostly truncate, prominent teeth with incurved callous points. . . . . 6. *P. canadensis*
DD. Lvs. truncate to subcordate, with glands present at base, edge densely ciliate.
E. Buds glabrous: lvs. longer than broad. . . . . 7. *P. deltoides*
EE. Buds pubescent: lvs. often broader than long. . . . . 8. *P. Sargentii*
BB. Petioles terete; lvs. whitish beneath.
C. Tips of lvs. acuminate, not twisted.
D. Young branches and petioles pubescent: lvs. subcordate. . . . . 10. *P. candicans*
DD. Young branches and petioles glabrous: lvs. cuneate to rounded.
E. Lvs. broadest below middle; petioles more than 1 in. long. . . . . 9. *P. balsamifera*
EE. Lvs. broadest at or above middle; petioles less than 1 in. long. . . . . 11. *P. Simonii*
CC. Tips of lvs. obtuse to short-acuminate, twisted. . . . . 12. *P. Maximowiczii*

1. **P. alba,** L. WHITE POPLAR. ABELE. Large broad-headed much-branched suckering tree to 100 ft., with bark white on young trunks and branches but becoming rough and dark colored on the older parts: lf.-buds downy-pubescent: lvs. broad-ovate to orbicular, 2–5 in. long, irregularly angular-toothed or sinuate, often obscurely palmately 3–5-lobed, somewhat cordate at base, cottony-white beneath, those on the young shoots prominently palmately 5-lobed: catkins about 2 in. long or the staminate somewhat longer, appearing much before the lvs.; stamens 6–10; stigmas 2 and bifid, the linear parts standing cross-like, yellow. Eu.; spontaneous about old yards and plantations. Var. **nivea,** Ait. (*P. nivea,* Willd. *P. alba argentea,* Hort. *P. alba acerifolia,* Hort. *P. alba arembergica,* Hort.), lvs. lobed, densely white-tomentose beneath. Var. **pyramidalis,** Bunge (*P. alba Bolleana,* Lauche. *P. Bolleana,* Lauche), a narrow-topped fastigiate tree with strongly lobed lvs.; Turkestan.

2. **P. tremula,** L. EUROPEAN ASPEN. Small suckering open-headed tree: buds not sticky or only very slightly so: lvs. mostly small, 1–3 in. long, rather thin, orbicular, rhomboidal or round-oval, with rounded angular irregular notches, glabrous and green on both sides, but sometimes whitened beneath when young, with very compressed petioles; lvs. on young shoots often ovate with rather small nearly regular teeth: catkins 3½–4 in. long; stamens commonly 6–8; stigmas 2, bifid. Eu., N. Afr., W. Asia, Siberia.—There are purple-lvd. and pendulous forms.

3. **P. tremuloides,** Michx. (*P. græca,* Loud.). QUAKING ASPEN. AMERICAN ASPEN. Small tree but sometimes reaching 100 ft.: buds slightly sticky: lvs. ovate to orbicular, 1–3 in. long, abruptly short-acuminate, truncate at base, finely toothed, becoming glabrous on both sides: catkins 3–4 in. long, slender. Lab. to Alaska, Pa., Mo. and Mex.

4. **P. grandidentata,** Michx. LARGE-TOOTHED ASPEN. Straight tree sometimes to 75 ft.: buds pubescent: lvs. ovate, 3–4 in. long, acute at apex, cuneate to truncate at base, with large irregular sinuate teeth, tomentose when young, becoming glabrous: catkins 1½–2 in. long. N. S. to Minn., Tenn. and N.C.

5. **P. nigra,** L. BLACK POPLAR. Round-headed or somewhat pyramidal non-suckering tree of medium to large size, with gray bark: buds glabrous, more or less viscid but not resinous or balsamic: lvs. triangular to ovate-triangular, or somewhat triangular-rhomboid, the blade mostly somewhat longer than broad, to 4 in. long and 3 in. broad, either gradually or abruptly acuminate, margins with small coarse teeth that are little or not at all incurved, petiole glandless or nearly so, both surfaces glabrous (at least at maturity) and green: staminate catkins 2–3 in. long, pistillate shorter and ascending in fl., to 6 in. long in fr.; stamens 20–30; stigmas 2, bifid. Eurasia. Var. **betulifolia,** Torr. (*P. betulifolia,* Pursh), has young growth and petioles pubescent; Eu. Var. **italica,** DuRoi (*P. italica,* Moench. *P. fastigiata,* Poir.), LOMBARDY POPLAR, staminate tree with very narrow tall erect growth and suckering habit; lvs. very broad, the blade mostly as broad as long.—The black poplar is a variable species, and many named forms are associated with it, some of them probably hybrids; some are very hardy and adaptable to colder prairie regions.

6. **P. canadensis,** Moench (*P. deltoides* × *P. nigra*). Planted as a street tree under the name CAROLINA POPLAR. Strong-growing upright tree with more or less ascending branches, the trunk or bole continuing through the top, little or not at all suckering, staminate only: lvs. mostly triangular-ovate, broadest at or below the middle, long-acuminate, truncate or slightly cuneate and lacking distinct glands at base, with prominent teeth or serratures terminating in an incurved callus, the margins usually with few short slight hairs: catkins 3–5 in. long, rather slender, pendent, from long pointed buds with large scales; stamens 15–25. Var. Eugenei, Schelle (*P. Eugenei*, Simon-Louis), EUGENE POPLAR, is of more pyramidal growth and may be involved in street plantings; it originated in the nursery of Simon-Louis near Metz, France, in 1832.

7. **P. deltoides,** Marsh. (*P. balsamifera* var. *virginiana*, Sarg. *P. monilifera*, Ait. *P. deltoidea* var. *monilifera*, Henry. *P. canadensis*, Michx. f. not Moench). COTTONWOOD. NORTHERN COTTONWOOD. Large broad-headed tree to 100 ft.: buds sticky, glabrous: lvs. triangular to broad-ovate, 3–5 in. long, about as broad as long, acuminate, truncate to somewhat cordate at base, coarsely crenate-dentate with teeth curved, ciliate, green and glabrous, with 2 or 3 glands at base of blade near petiole: catkins 3–4 in. long, becoming 8 in. long in fr.; stamens 40–60. Que. to Fla., Tex. and N. D. Var. **missouriensis,** Henry (*P. angulata* var. *missouriensis*, Henry. *P. angulata*, Michx. f. not Ait. *P. deltoidea* var. *angulata*, Sarg. *P. balsamifera*, L. not Muenchh. and Auth.), SOUTHERN COTTONWOOD, lvs. usually longer than broad, 4–6 in. long, more finely toothed; Vt. to Mo. and Fla.

8. **P. Sargentii,** Dode. GREAT PLAINS COTTONWOOD. Similar to *P. deltoides:* branches light yellow: buds usually pubescent: lvs. commonly broader than long, 3–4 in. wide, more coarsely toothed. (Named for C. S. Sargent, page 51.) Sask. to New Mex. and Tex.

9. **P. balsamifera,** L. (*P. Tacamahacca*, Mill.). TACAMAHAC (Indian name). BALSAM POPLAR. Large narrow-topped tree 75–100 ft. tall at maturity and 6–7 ft. diam. at stump, the branchlets and sticky varnished winter-buds usually glabrous: lvs. thick and firm, erect or strongly ascending, ovate to ovate-lanceolate, 3–5 in. long, gradually acuminate, obtuse or rounded (sometimes slightly cordate) at base, finely and obscurely serrate, prominently whitened beneath but glabrous, petioles glabrous: catkins drooping, peduncled, 2–3 in. long, the pistillate lengthening in fr. to 6 in.; stamens 12–20: caps. glabrous. Lab. to Alaska, N. Y., Mich. and Ore.

10. **P. candicans,** Ait. (*P. balsamifera* var. *candicans*, Gray). BALM-OF-GILEAD. More spreading tree than no. 9, not so large, with open irregular top, the large resinous buds very aromatic, the young twigs variously hairy mostly sparsely so, and heavy dark rich foliage whitish beneath: lvs. broad-ovate-deltoid, 4–6 in. long, cordate, more or less hairy at least on the veins beneath, the petioles thinly hairy to densely hairy and pubescent: catkins to 6 in. long in fr. Origin unknown, but thought to be native in N. Amer.—Frequently planted and apparently sometimes spontaneous.

11. **P. Simonii,** Carr. (*P. Przewalskii*, Maxim.). Tree to 40 ft., with somewhat narrow habit, branches glabrous: buds slender, pointed: lvs. rhombic-ovate, 1½–5 in. long, acuminate, cuneate to rounded at base, fine-toothed, glabrous, somewhat whitish beneath: catkins 1–2 in. long, to 6 in. long in fr.; stamens 8. (Sent to the museum of M. E. Simon, France, about 1861.) N. China.

12. **P. Maximowiczii,** Henry. JAPAN POPLAR. Tree to 100 ft., with spreading branches, twigs pubescent: buds pointed: lvs. leathery, elliptic to suborbicular, 2½–5 in. long, short-acuminate with twisted apex, subcordate at base, toothed, whitish beneath and pubescent on veins: catkins 2–4 in. long, to 10 in. in fr.; stamens 30–40. (Named for Maximowicz, page 47.) N. E. Asia, Japan.

47. MYRICACEÆ. SWEET GALE FAMILY

Deciduous or evergreen monœcious or diœcious trees and shrubs, of 2 genera and about 50 species in temp. and subtrop. regions, planted for ornament, and some species for edible frs.—Lvs. alternate, entire to pinnatifid, usually aromatic, resinous-dotted: fls. unisexual, each subtended by 1 (staminate) or more (pistillate) bracts, but lacking perianth; catkins linear to globular; stamens 2–16, sometimes united at base, anthers 2-celled; ovary 1-celled with 1 erect basal ovule, with short style and 2 slender stigmas: fr. a 1-seeded round or ovoid drupe or nut usually with waxy coat.

A. Lvs. entire to serrate, without stipules.......................................1. MYRICA
AA. Lvs. pinnatifid, with stipules.......................................2. COMPTONIA

1. **MYRICA,** L. (*Morella*, Lour. *Cerothamnus*, Tidestr.). About 50 species of deciduous or evergreen shrubs or small trees: lvs. alternate, short-petioled: stamens 2–8 (16): fr. gray to purple usually with a waxy or resinous covering. (Myri-ca: ancient Greek, possibly the name for tamarisk.)

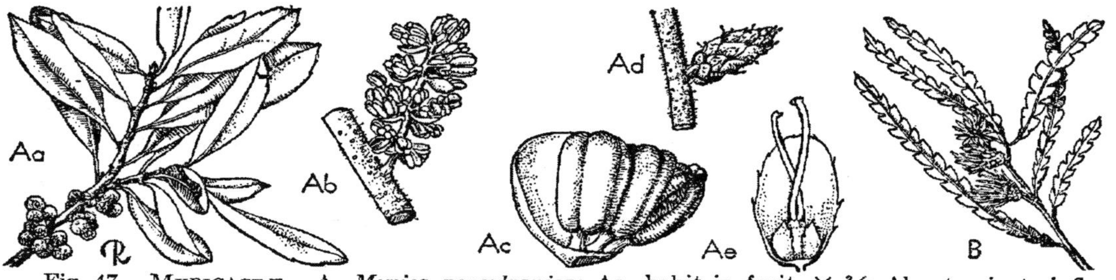

Fig. 47. Myricaceæ. A, *Myrica pensylvanica:* Aa, habit in fruit, × 3/8; Ab, staminate inflorescence, × 2; Ac, staminate flower, × 8; Ad, pistillate inflorescence, × 2; Ae, pistillate flower, × 8. B, *Comptonia peregrina* var. *asplenifolia*, with young fruit, × 3/8.

A. Fr. compressed, inclosed in bracts, in dense short catkins....................1. *M. Gale*
AA. Fr. round, with waxy coat, bractless.
B. Lvs. pubescent above, obovate to oblong, subacute....................2. *M. pensylvanica*
BB. Lvs. glabrous above except sometimes for midrib, lanceolate to oblong-lanceolate, acute....................3. *M. cerifera*

1. **M. Gale,** L. (*Gale palustris*, Cheval.). Sweet Gale. Deciduous shrub to 5 ft., branchlets usually puberulous: lvs. oblanceolate, 1–2½ in. long, obtuse, serrate toward apex, more or less glandular-pubescent on both surfaces: fr. yellowish, compressed, inclosed in 2 wing-like bracts, in dense catkins ¼–½in. long. N. Amer. south to Va., Eu., Asia.

2. **M. pensylvanica,** Loisel. (*M. caroliniensis*, Auth. not Mill. *M. cerifera* var. *latifolia*, Ait.). Bayberry. Deciduous shrub to 10 ft., branchlets usually glandular-pubescent: lvs. obovate to oblong, 1½–4 in. long, subacute, with few blunt teeth near apex, pubescent and gland-dotted on both surfaces: fr. bluish-white. Newf. to N. Y. and Md.

3. **M. cerifera,** L. (*M. caroliniensis*, Mill.). Wax-Myrtle. Evergreen shrub or small tree to 35 ft., branchlets somewhat glandular-pubescent: lvs. lanceolate to oblong-lanceolate, 1–3 in. long, acute, entire to serrulate in upper half, gland-dotted, puberulous beneath: fr. grayish-white. N. J. to Fla. and Tex.

2. **COMPTONIA,** L'Her. One species, a deciduous shrub.—Lvs. alternate, pinnatifid, short-petioled: stamens (3)–4: fr. a glabrous ovoid nutlet, subtended by bracts, in clusters. (Compton-ia: Henry Compton, bishop of Oxford, 1632–1713.)

C. peregrina, Coult. (*Liquidambar peregrina*, L. *Myrica asplenifolia*, Auth. in part. *C. asplenifolia*, Ait.). Sweet-Fern. Shrub to 5 ft., branchlets pubescent: stipules semi-cordate; lvs. linear-oblong, 2–5 in. long, deeply pinnatifid, the lobes broader than long, pubescent: fr. to ¼in. long, brown, shining. N. S. to N. C., Md. Var. **asplenifolia,** Fern. (*Myrica asplenifolia*, L.), is less pubescent, with smaller lvs. and catkins, and confined to coastal plain pinelands.

48. JUGLANDACEÆ. WALNUT FAMILY

Six genera and about 40 species of deciduous trees native in the north temp. zone, in Amer. extending along the Andes to Bolivia, planted for ornament and the edible nuts.—Lvs. alternate, pinnately compound, exstipulate: plant monœcious; staminate fls. in drooping catkins with 3 to many stamens with an irregular perianth adnate to the bract or rarely perianth lacking; pistillate fls. solitary or several together, bracted and usually 2-bracteolate, with usually 4-lobed calyx adnate to the inferior ovary which is incompletely 2–4-celled but only 1-ovuled, stigmas 2–4-branched: fr. usually a drupe with dehiscent or indehiscent fibrous exocarp or husk, containing a large 2–4-lobed orthotropous seed.

A. Husk of fr. indehiscent: catkins of staminate fls. simple....................1. Juglans
AA. Husk of fr. splitting into 4 valves: catkins of staminate fls. branched....................2. Carya

1. **JUGLANS,** L. Walnut. About 15 arborescent species, grown for their edible nuts and for ornament, native in N. and S. Amer., S. E. Eu. and Asia.—Branches with lamellate pith: lvs. odd-pinnate, of aromatic fragrance when bruised: staminate fls. in catkins on twigs of previous year, with 3–6-lobed calyx and 8–40 stamens in 2 or more series; pistillate fls. in few-fld. spikes at the end of shoots of the season, with 4-lobed calyx, 4 small petals adnate to the ovary at the sinuses, 2 short styles

with club-shaped fimbriate stigmas: drupe large, with a thick indehiscent husk; nut irregularly furrowed, 2–4-celled at base, indehiscent or finally separating into 2 valves. (Jug-lans: ancient Latin name from *Jovis glans*, nut of Jupiter.)

A. Lfts. nearly entire, usually 7–9 .... 1. *J. regia*
AA. Lfts. serrate, 11–23.
 B. Fr. pubescent but not sticky; nut 4-celled at base .... 2. *J. nigra*
 BB. Fr. sticky-pubescent; nut 2-celled at base.
  C. Nut prominently ridged; frs. 2–5 .... 3. *J. cinerea*
  CC. Nut nearly smooth; frs. in long racemes .... 4. *J. cordiformis*

1. **J. regia,** L. PERSIAN WALNUT. ENGLISH WALNUT of common speech, although not from England. Round-headed tree to 100 ft., with silvery-gray bark: lfts. usually 7–9 (5–13), oblong or oblong-ovate, acute or acuminate, almost glabrous, nearly entire, 2–5 in. long: frs. 1–3 together, green, almost globular, glabrous; nut reticulate and rather thin-shelled, 4-celled at base. S. E. Eu., Himalayas, China.—Planted in mild climates but races of it successful in N. Y. There are many vars., having pendulous branches, simple or 3-foliolate lvs., narrowly pinnately-cut lfts., elongated nuts.

2. **J. nigra,** L. BLACK WALNUT. Round-headed tree to 150 ft., with brown furrowed bark; twigs pubescent: lfts. 15–23, ovate-oblong to oblong-lanceolate, acuminate, irregularly serrate, glabrous above at maturity, pubescent beneath, 2–5 in. long: frs. round, to 2 in. across, pubescent; nut ovoid or sometimes depressed, thick-shelled, deeply ridged. Mass. to Minn., Fla. and Tex.

3. **J. cinerea,** L. BUTTERNUT. WHITE WALNUT. Tree occasionally to 100 ft., with gray bark; twigs, petioles and rachis pubescent and glandular: lfts. 11–19, oblong-lanceolate, acuminate, irregularly serrate, glandular-pubescent, 2–5 in. long: frs. 2–5 together, ovoid-oblong, 2–3 in. long, sticky-pubescent; nut ovoid-oblong, thick-shelled, with 4 more and 4 less prominent irregular ridges and broken ridges between. N. B. to Ga. and Ark.

4. **J. cordiformis,** Maxim. HEARTNUT. Broad-headed tree to 60 ft.: lfts. 11–17, oval to oval-oblong, short-acuminate, serrate, becoming glabrous above, pubescent and usually glandular beneath, 3–6 in. long: frs. in long racemes, sometimes 20, globose to ovate-oblong, covered with viscid hairs; nut heart-shaped or ovoid, much flattened, sharply 2-edged, rather thin-shelled. Japan. Var. **ailanthifolia,** Rehd. (*J. Sieboldiana*, Maxim. not Goeppert. *J. ailanthifolia*, Carr. *J. ailanthifolia* var. *cordiformis*, Rehd.), JAPANESE WALNUT, differs in the rugose thick-shelled nut, subglobose or ovoid, with thick wing-like sutures.—Hardy in northern states and Ont.

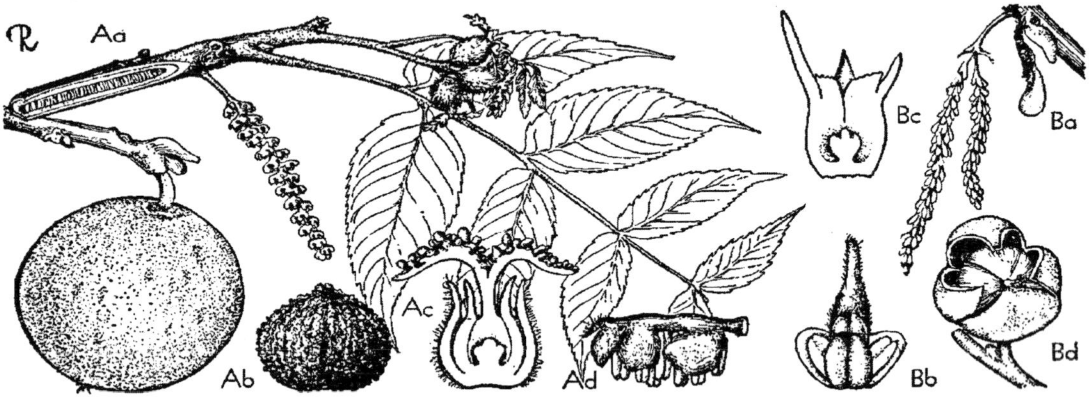

Fig. 48. JUGLANDACEÆ. A, *Juglans nigra:* Aa, flowering branch, stem sectioned to show chambered pith, × ½; Ab, fruit and seed, × ½; Ac, pistillate flower, vertical section, × 2; Ad, staminate flower, × 2. B, Carya: Ba, staminate catkins, × ½; Bb, staminate flower, × 4; Bc, pistillate flower, vertical section, × 2; Bd, fruit (dehiscing), × ½.

2. **CARYA,** Nutt. (*Hicoria*, Raf.). Deciduous trees with hard strong wood and smooth gray bark becoming rough or scaly on old specimens; of about 20 species in N. Amer. south to Mex. and 2 species in Asia.—Branches with solid pith: lvs. odd-pinnate: staminate fls. in slender pendulous 3-branched catkins, solitary or fascicled in axils of lvs., with 2–3-lobed calyx and 3–10 stamens in 2 or 3 series; pistillate fls. in terminal 2–10-fld. spikes, apetalous, with 1-celled ovary inclosed by 4-lobed involucre: fr. globular to oblong, with thick husk separating into 4 valves; nut bony, smooth or angled, incompletely 2–4-celled. (Ca-rya: Greek name for the walnut.)

A. Bud-scales 4–6, valvate in pairs: lfts. often sickle-shaped: nuts thin-shelled.
B. Winter-buds yellow-brown: lfts. 11–17: fr. oblong, to 3½ in. long............1. *C. illinoensis*
BB. Winter-buds bright yellow: lfts. 5–9: fr. round, to 1½ in. long............2. *C. cordiformis*
AA. Bud-scales more than 6, overlapping: lfts. not sickle-shaped: nuts thick-shelled.
B. Bark not shaggy; young growth rather densely tomentose............3. *C. tomentosa*
BB. Bark shaggy; young growth pubescent.
C. Lfts. usually 7, about equal in size............4. *C. laciniosa*
CC. Lfts. usually 5, the lowest pair much smaller............5. *C. ovata*

1. **C. illinoensis**, Koch (*Juglans illinoinensis*, Wangh. *C. olivæformis*, Nutt. *Hicoria Pecan*, Britt. *C. Pecan*, Engler & Graebn. not Nutt.). PECAN. To 170 ft., bark deeply furrowed; winter-buds yellow, scales 4–6, valvate: lfts. 11–17, short-stalked, oblong-lanceolate, acuminate, 4–7 in. long, serrate, usually glabrous at maturity: frs. 3–10 in terminal spikes, 1½–3½ in. long; nut oblong, smooth, brown, thin-shelled, pointed, 2-celled at base, kernel sweet. Iowa and Ind. south to Tex. and Mex.

2. **C. cordiformis**, Koch (*Juglans cordiformis*, Wangh. *Hicoria cordiformis*, Britt. *H. minima*, Britt. *C. amara*, Nutt.). BITTERNUT. SWAMP HICKORY. Tree to 90 ft., with light gray rarely scaly bark, twigs becoming glabrous; winter-buds bright yellow: lfts. 5–9, ovate-lanceolate, acuminate, serrate, 3–6 in. long, pubescent when young, later glabrous except for veins beneath: fr. almost round, with 4 wings from the apex to the middle, to 1½ in. long; nut almost smooth, thin-shelled, gray. Que. to Minn., Fla. and La.

3. **C. tomentosa**, Nutt. (*Juglans tomentosa*, Poir. *Hicoria alba*, Britt. *C. alba*, Koch not Nutt.). MOCKERNUT. BIG-BUD HICKORY. WHITE-HEART HICKORY. Tree sometimes to 100 ft.; branchlets tomentose, practically glabrous by autumn: lfts. 7–9, oblong to oblong-lanceolate, acuminate, serrate, 3–7 in. long, subsessile, pubescent beneath: fr. round to obovoid, to 2 in. long; nut almost round to ellipsoid, angled, light brown. Mass. to Neb., Fla. and Tex.

4. **C. laciniosa**, Loud. (*Juglans laciniosa*, Michx. f. *Hicoria laciniosa*, Sarg. *H. acuminata*, Dipp. *C. sulcata*, Nutt.). BIG or BOTTOM SHELLBARK HICKORY. KING-NUT. Tree to 120 ft., with shaggy bark; branchlets pubescent when young: lfts. 7 (5–9), oblong-lanceolate, acuminate, serrate, 4–8 in. long, pubescent beneath: fr. round to ellipsoid, to 3 in. long, 4-winged above middle; nut almost round, slightly 4-angled, yellow to reddish. N. Y. to Tenn. and Okla.

5. **C. ovata**, Koch (*Juglans ovata*, Mill. *Hicoria ovata*, Britt. *C. alba*, Nutt.). SHAGBARK HICKORY. LITTLE SHELLBARK HICKORY. Tree to 120 ft., with gray shaggy bark; branchlets soon glabrous: lfts. 5 (7), elliptic, acuminate, serrate, 3–6 in. long, pubescent below: fr. subglobose, to 2½ in. long; nut ellipsoid, slightly angled, white. Que. to Minn., Fla. and Tex.

49. CORYLACEÆ. HAZELNUT FAMILY

Deciduous trees and shrubs, of 6 genera and over 100 species, mostly in the northern hemisphere, some planted for ornament and others for the edible nuts.—Lvs. alternate, simple, straight-veined, petioled; stipules fugacious: plants monœcious; staminate fls. in long pendulous catkins, 1–6 together in the axils of the bracts, with 2–4-parted calyx or none and 2–20 stamens; pistillate fls. in short lateral or capitate catkins, with or without a calyx adnate to the 2-celled ovary, each cell containing 1 ovule, style 2-parted: fr. a small indehiscent 1-celled 1-seeded nut or samara.—This family has been almost universally known as Betulaceæ, but recent studies show that Betulaceæ of Braun in 1864 is antedated by nearly a half century by Corylaceæ of Mirbel.

A. Staminate fls. 3–6 together in the axils of each bract, with calyx: nut without an involucre; scales of pistillate fls. forming a strobile.
B. Winter-buds sessile, with 3 or more imbricate scales: pistillate catkins solitary, with deciduous scales: stamens 2, bifid............1. BETULA
BB. Winter-buds stalked, with 2 valvate scales: pistillate catkins racemose, the scales forming a woody cone: stamens 4, not bifid............2. ALNUS
AA. Staminate fls. solitary in the axil of each bract, without calyx: nut more or less inclosed by involucre.
B. Pistillate fls. few, included in a small scaly bud: nut large, in a lf.-like involucre......3. CORYLUS
BB. Pistillate fls. numerous, spicate: nut subtended or surrounded by a large bract.
C. Involucre flat, 3-lobed: staminate catkins appearing in the spring............4. CARPINUS
CC. Involucre tubular or sac-like: staminate catkins naked during winter............5. OSTRYA

1. **BETULA**, L. BIRCH. About 40 species of smooth-barked trees or shrubs native in N. Amer., Eu. and Asia.—Winter-buds covered by imbricate scales: lvs. serrate or crenate: staminate catkins formed in autumn and remaining naked during the winter, fls. 3 together in the axil of each scale, having a minute 4-toothed calyx and 2 stamens with 2-cleft filaments; pistillate catkins solitary at ends of branchlets,

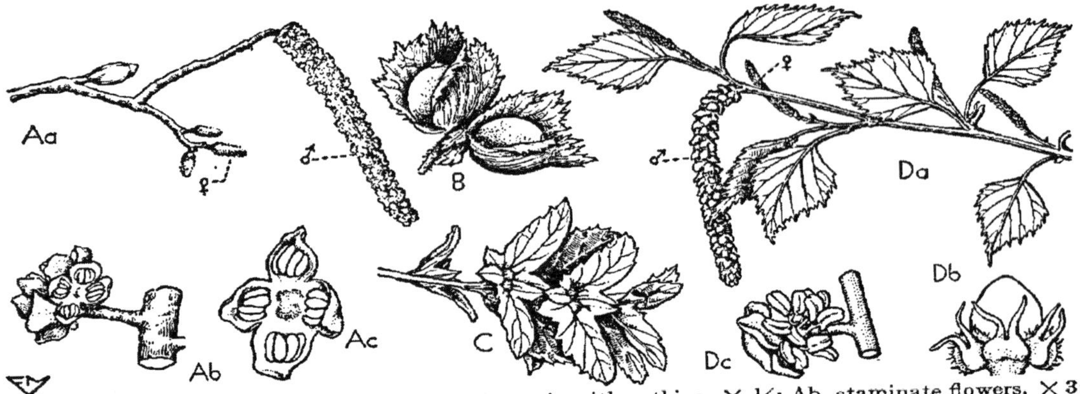

Fig. 49. CORYLACEÆ. A, *Alnus rugosa:* Aa, twig with catkins, × ½; Ab, staminate flowers, × 3; Ac, single staminate flower, × 5. B, *Corylus Avellana:* fruit, × ½. C, *Carpinus caroliniana:* fruiting branch, × ½. D, *Betula pendula:* Da, twig with catkins, × ½; Db, pistillate flowers, × 10; Dc, staminate flowers, × 3.

oblong or cylindrical, fls. without calyx, having 3 ovaries in axil of every scale which consists of 3 connate bracts: nut small with membranaceous wings, deciduous at maturity together with scales of the strobile or cone. (Bet-ula: ancient Latin name.)

A. Lvs. with 7 or more pairs of veins: strobiles subsessile or short-stalked; wings of nutlet not broader than its body: bark yellow to brown.
B. Lvs. cuneate at base, whitish beneath.......................... 1. *B. nigra*
BB. Lvs. rounded to subcordate at base, green beneath.
C. Bark dark, close: twigs, bud-scales, and bracts of strobiles glabrous.......... 2. *B. lenta*
CC. Bark yellowish, peeling: twigs, bud-scales, and bracts of strobiles pubescent... 3. *B. lutea*
AA. Lvs. with 3–7 pairs of veins: strobiles slender-stalked; wings of nutlet broader than its body: bark white.
B. Lvs. triangular-ovate, long-acuminate: twigs predominantly glandular......... 4. *B. populifolia*
BB. Lvs. rhombic-ovate to ovate, acuminate: twigs almost glandless.
C. Lf. rhombic-ovate, glabrous.......................... 5. *B. pendula*
CC. Lf. ovate, usually pubescent on veins beneath.......................... 6. *B. papyrifera*

1. **B. nigra,** L. (*B. rubra,* Michx.). RIVER or RED BIRCH. Tree occasionally to 100 ft., with reddish-brown bark, peeling into papery layers: lvs. rhombic-ovate, 1–3 in. long, acute, cuneate at base, doubly serrate, tomentose at first, becoming glabrous above and with pubescence on veins beneath: strobile on a short stalk, cylindric, 1–1½ in. long; wings of nutlet one-half to nearly as broad as nutlet. Mass. to Fla., Minn. and Kans.

2. **B. lenta,** L. (*B. carpinifolia,* Ehrh.). CHERRY, SWEET, or BLACK BIRCH. Tree to 75 ft., with dark reddish-brown bark, not peeling but broken into plates: lvs. oblong-ovate, 2½–5 in. long, acuminate, subcordate at base, doubly serrate, long-pubescent on veins beneath: strobiles subsessile, ovoid-oblong, to 1½ in. long; wings of nutlet about as broad as its body. Me. to Ala. and Ohio.

3. **B. lutea,** Michx. (*B. excelsa,* Pursh not Ait.). YELLOW, GRAY, or SILVER BIRCH. Tree to 100 ft., with yellow-gray peeling bark: lvs. ovate, 3–5 in. long, acuminate, rounded to subcordate at base, doubly serrate, pubescent: strobiles sometimes short-stalked, ovoid-oblong, to 1½ in. long; wings of nutlet slightly narrower than its body. Newf. to Man., Ga. and Tenn.

4. **B. populifolia,** Marsh. (*B. alba* var. *populifolia,* Spach). GRAY or WHITE BIRCH. Tree to 30 ft., with white chalky bark peeling slightly on the trunk· lvs triangular-ovate, 2–3 in. long, long-acuminate, truncate at base, doubly serrate, glabrous, glandular: strobiles stalked, slender, cylindric, ½–1 in. long; wings broader than nutlet. N. S. and Ont. to Del., Va. and Ind.

5. **B. pendula,** Roth (*B. alba,* L. in part. *B. verrucosa,* Ehrh.). EUROPEAN WHITE BIRCH. Tree to 60 ft., with slender usually pendulous branches and white bark readily peeling off in layers: lvs. rhombic-ovate, acuminate, cuneate or truncate at base, doubly serrate, to 2½ in. long, glutinous when young but glabrous and shining at maturity; petioles slender, about 1 in. long: strobiles on slender peduncles, usually pendulous, cylindric, about 1 in. long; wings of nutlet one and a half to two and a half times as broad as its body. Eu. to Asia Minor. The common vars. include: var. **dalecarlica,** Rehd. (forma *dalecarlica,* Schneid. *B. alba* var. *dalecarlica,* L. *B. laciniata,* Wahlb.), lvs. deeply lobed, branches pendulous on old trees; var. **fastigiata,** Koch (*B. alba fastigiata,* Carr. *B. pendula* var. *pyramidalis,* Dipp.), branches upright forming a narrow head; var. **purpurea,** Rehd. (forma *purpurea,* Schneid. *B. vulgaris purpurea,* André. *B. alba atropurpurea,* Jaeg. & Beissn.), lvs. purple; var. **Youngii,** Rehd. (forma *Youngii,* Schneid. *B. alba pendula*

Youngii, Moore. *B. pendula* forma *elegans*, Wink.), branches very slender, strongly pendulous, head irregular and picturesque.

6. **B. papyrifera,** Marsh. (*B. papyracea*, Ait. *B. latifolia*, Tausch). CANOE OR PAPER BIRCH. Tree to 100 ft., with white bark peeling into papery layers: lvs. ovate, 1½–4 in. long, acuminate, cuneate to rounded at base, doubly serrate, more or less pubescent on veins beneath: strobiles stalked, cylindric, 1–2 in. long; wings broader than nutlet. Lab. to B. C. to Wash., Neb. and Pa.

2. **ALNUS,** B. Ehrh. ALDER. About 30 species of trees or shrubs with scaly bark, native in the northern hemisphere and the Andes of S. Amer.—Winter-buds (in ours) stalked, with 2 or 3 scales: lvs. serrate: staminate catkins appearing the preceding season, erect and naked during winter, fls. 3–6 together in the axil of each bract, having 4-parted calyx and usually 4 undivided stamens; pistillate catkins erect, clustered, developing into woody ovoid strobiles (cones) with persistent 5-lobed scales, fls. 2 in the axil of each bract, without calyx; nut very small, compressed, with or without wings. (Al-nus: ancient Latin name.)

A. Lvs. distinctly gray, velvety-pilose: bark grayish. . . . . 1. *A. incana*
AA. Lvs. green to glaucescent beneath, when hairy not velvety: bark brown to blackish.
B. Margin of lvs. finely and evenly serrate. . . . . 2. *A. serrulata*
BB. Margin of lvs. coarsely serrate or doubly serrate.
C. Lf. orbicular to obovate, apex rounded or emarginate: tree. . . . . 3. *A. glutinosa*
CC. Lf. ovate to broadly elliptic, acute: shrub. . . . . 4. *A. rugosa*

1. **A. incana,** Moench not American Auth. (*Betula Alnus* var. *incana*, L.). EUROPEAN ALDER. Tree to 85 ft. or a large shrub; bark becoming gray; twigs velvety-pilose: lvs. ovate-elliptic, 1½–4 in. long, acute to acuminate, base usually broadly cuneate, margin doubly serrate, persistently gray in color, soft-velvety-pilose, cross-veins slender and delicate beneath: pistillate catkins 3–6, bracts with terminal lobes depressed and slightly recurving. Siberia to W. Eu.

2. **A. serrulata,** Willd. (*Betula serrulata*, Ait. *A. rugosa*, American Auth. not Spreng.). SMOOTH OR HAZEL ALDER. Shrub or shrubby tree to 25 ft.; bark blackish, sparsely speckled with small orange to grayish lenticels: lvs. elliptic to obovate, broadest above the middle, 2–4 in. long, acute or obtuse, cuneate or sometimes rounded at base, finely and evenly serrate, usually pubescent beneath, cross-veins weak and slender: catkins 4–10, the upper sessile, the lower short-peduncled. N. S. to Okla., Fla. and La.

3. **A. glutinosa,** Gaertn. (*Betula Alnus* var. *glutinosa*, L. *A. vulgaris*, Hill. *A. rotundifolia*, Mill. *A. communis*, Desf.). BLACK ALDER. Tree to 80 ft.: lvs. orbicular or obovate, 2–4 in. long, rounded or emarginate at apex, usually doubly serrate, occasionally coarsely serrate, downy in the axils of the veins beneath, glutinous when unfolding: fls. opening before lvs.; catkins peduncled, pistillate axillary. Eu., N. Afr., Asia; locally nat. in N. Amer.—There are several vars. in which the lvs. are pinnately lobed or incised.

4. **A. rugosa,** Spreng. (*Betula Alnus rugosa*, DuRoi. *A. incana*, American Auth. not Moench). SPECKLED ALDER. Shrub to 20 ft., not tree-like; bark dark brown or blackish, abundantly speckled with large white lenticels to ¼in. long; twigs glabrous to sparsely pilose, often sticky-viscid: lvs. ovate to round-elliptic, broadest below or near the middle, coarsely undulate to doubly serrate, mostly 2–4 in. long, green and glabrous to pilose beneath, often pubescent above, cross-veins coarse and prominent beneath: pistillate catkins 4–10, bracts with lobes suberect or arching and prolonged. E. N. Amer. Var. **americana,** Fern. (*A. incana* var. *americana*, Regel), differs in lvs. glaucous or whitened beneath.—This shrubby plant has long been treated as conspecific with the Eurasian tree, the two passing under the name *A. incana;* now that the two are considered distinct the name *incana* remains with the European alder and the American speckled alder must be known as *A. rugosa;* the shrub long called *A. rugosa* is now *A. serrulata.*

3. **CORYLUS,** L. HAZELNUT. FILBERT. Shrubs or small trees grown for ornament or for the edible nuts, of about 15 species in N. Amer., Eu. and Asia.—Lvs. ovate to oblong, serrate: fls. appearing before the lvs.; staminate fls. solitary in the axil of each bract, formed the previous year and remaining naked during the winter, without calyx, having 4–8 bifid stamens; pistillate fls. included in a small scaly bud with only the red styles protruding: fr. usually in clusters at the end of short branches, the large ovoid or oblong nut included in a leafy involucre which is nearly distinct or united into a tubular beak. (Cor-ylus: ancient Greek name.)

A. Involucre of 2 bracts, sometimes connate at base.
B. Length of involucre rarely exceeding nut. . . . . 1. *C. Avellana*
BB. Length of involucre twice exceeding nut. . . . . 2. *C. americana*
AA. Involucre tubular.
B. Tubular involucre slightly narrowed. . . . . 3. *C. maxima*
BB. Tubular involucre abruptly narrowed above the nut. . . . . 4. *C. cornuta*

1. **C. Avellana,** L. COMMON or EUROPEAN FILBERT. Shrub to 15 ft., branchlets glandular-pubescent: lvs. roundish-oval or obovate, 2–4 in. long, acuminate, slightly cordate, doubly toothed or slightly lobed, becoming glabrous, pubescent on veins beneath: fr. in clusters of 1–4; involucre of 2 bracts irregularly divided into lanceolate or triangular lobes, shorter than the roundish-ovoid nut. (Avellana: from Avellino, a city in Italy.) Eu.—Many vars. are cult. for their fr.; there are hort. forms having pendulous branches, lvs. purple or yellow or laciniately incised, one of which is var. **fusco-rubra,** Goeschke (var. *atropurpurea,* Kirchn. var. *purpurea,* Bean), lvs. purple or brownish-red. **C. Colurna, L.,** TURKISH HAZELNUT, of S. E. Eu., is a tree to 80 ft., with nut in deeply divided campanulate involucre.

2. **C. americana,** Marsh. (*C. calyculata,* Dipp.). AMERICAN HAZELNUT. Shrub to 10 ft., branchlets glandular-pubescent: lvs. ovate to oval, 2½–5 in. long, acuminate, rounded to subcordate at base, doubly serrate, slightly pubescent above, finely pubescent beneath: frs. 2 (1)–6; involucre of 2 bracts connate at base, irregularly lobed, twice as long as the roundish nut. N. E. N. Amer. to Sask. and Fla.

3. **C. maxima,** Mill. (*C. tubulosa,* Willd.). FILBERT. Shrub or tree to 30 ft., branchlets glandular-pubescent: lvs. as in *C. Avellana* but 2–6 in. long: frs. 1–3; tubular involucre irregularly lobed and twice as long as the ovoid-oblong nut. S. E. Eu., W. Asia.

4. **C. cornuta,** Marsh. (*C. rostrata,* Ait.). BEAKED HAZELNUT. Shrub to 10 ft., branchlets pubescent, glandless: lvs. ovate to ovate-oblong, 1½–4 in. long, acuminate, subcordate at base, sharply doubly serrate, almost glabrous above, soft-pubescent beneath: tubular involucre much narrowed above the nut and projecting to 1½ in. beyond the ovoid nut. Que. to Sask., Mo. and Ga.

4. **CARPINUS,** L. HORNBEAM. About 26 species of trees with smooth gray bark, native in Asia, Eu., N. and Cent. Amer., a few grown for ornament.—Winter-buds conspicuous, acute with many imbricate scales: staminate catkins inclosed in bud during the winter, sessile near the ends of short lateral branches of the preceding year, fls. solitary in the axils of bracts, without calyx, having 3–13 stamens with 2-forked filaments; pistillate catkins terminal on leafy branches of the year, each bract bearing 2 fls., the bracts and bractlets developing into a large leafy more or less 3-lobed bract, embracing the small ovoid acute nut at their base. (Carpi-nus: ancient Latin name.)

A. Fruiting bracts to 1 in. long: buds pubescent.............................1. *C. caroliniana*
AA. Fruiting bracts over 1 in. long: buds almost glabrous.......................2. *C. Betulus*

1. **C. caroliniana,** Walt. AMERICAN HORNBEAM. Tree sometimes to 40 ft., with furrowed trunk, bark ashy-gray: lvs. oblong to narrowly oblong-ovate, 1–3 in. long, acute, serrations short, pubescent on veins beneath: fr.-cluster 1½–4 in. long; bracts ovate to ovate-lanceolate, 3-lobed, the middle lobe longest, to 1 in. long, obtuse to subacute at tip, with few blunt teeth. Fla. to Tex. to S. Ill. and Va.—The plant common in cult. is var. **virginiana,** Fern. (*C. americana,* Michx. *C. Betulus virginiana,* Marsh.), BLUE BEECH, distinguished by its blue-gray bark; lvs. ovate-oblong, 2½–5 in. long, acuminate, doubly serrate; bracts acute with 1–5 pointed teeth; N. S. to Ont., N. C. and Ark.

2. **C. Betulus,** L. EUROPEAN HORNBEAM. Tree to 70 ft.: lvs. ovate or ovate-oblong, acute or acuminate, cordate or rounded at base, sharply and doubly serrate, 2–5 in. long: fr.-cluster to 5 in. long; bracts 1½–2 in. long, 3-lobed, usually 3-nerved at base, middle lobe much longer, oblong-lanceolate, the margins almost entire or remotely denticulate. Eu. to W. Asia.—There are garden vars. with incised or lobed lvs., lvs. purplish when young, and of more upright habit.

5. **OSTRYA,** Scop. HOP-HORNBEAM. Seven species of deciduous trees, native in N. and Cent. Amer., Eu. and Asia.—Buds acute with many imbricate scales: lvs. doubly serrate: staminate catkins naked during winter, pendulous, fls. without calyx, stamens 3–14 with filaments 2-forked near apex; pistillate catkins erect, each bract (deciduous) bearing 2 fls., each fl. subtended by a bract and 2 bractlets which unite forming a persistent tubular involucre, becoming bladder-like in fr. (Os-trya: ancient Greek name.)

O. virginiana, Koch (*Carpinus virginiana,* Mill. *O. virginica,* Willd. *O. italica* subsp. *virginiana,* Wink.). AMERICAN HOP-HORNBEAM. IRONWOOD. Tree to 60 ft., with brown bark, branchlets pubescent the first season: lvs. ovate to oblong-ovate, 2–5 in. long, acuminate, rounded to subcordate at base, sharply and doubly serrate, somewhat pubescent above and below, petioles mostly less than ⅕ in. long and often glandular: fr.-cluster to 2 in. long; nutlets fusiform. Ont. to Minn., Fla. and Tex.—The European *O. carpinifolia,* Scop., differs in lvs. not subcordate at base, glandless petioles ⅕ in. long or longer, and nutlets ovoid.

50. FAGACEÆ. BEECH FAMILY

Trees or shrubs, mostly natives of the subtrop. and temp. regions of the northern hemisphere, one genus in the antarctic, of 6 genera and over 600 species; some are important timber trees, and many are planted for shade and ornament.—Lvs. alternate, simple, cleft or entire, stipules deciduous: monœcious; fls. apetalous; staminate in catkins or capitate, with 4–7-lobed perianth and 4–20 stamens; pistillate fls. solitary or slightly clustered, with 4–8-lobed perianth adnate to the 3–7-celled ovary, ovules basal, 1–2 in each cell, but only 1 in the ovary ripening, styles 3–7: fr. a 1-seeded nut, inclosed in a cup or bur of partly or wholly united bracts.

A. Staminate fls. in small pendulous heads: nut sharply 3-angled.......................1. FAGUS
AA. Staminate fls. in slender catkins: nut rounded or plano-convex.
B. Involucre forming cup in fr. subtending acorns, 1-fld.......................2. QUERCUS
BB. Involucre forming prickly hard bur inclosing nuts, 1–7-fld.......................3. CASTANEA

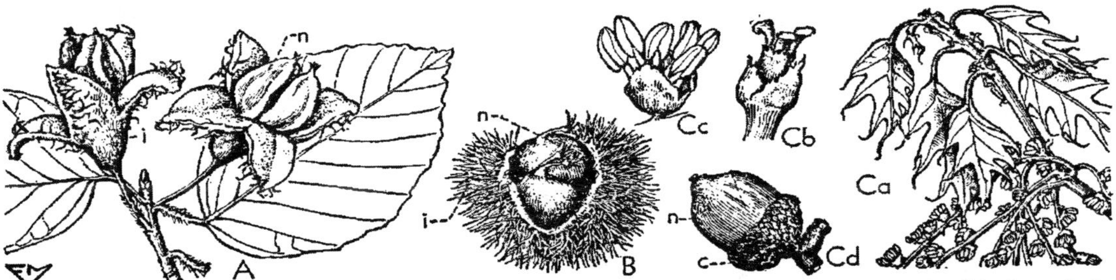

Fig. 50. FAGACEÆ. A, *Fagus sylvatica:* fruiting branch, × ½. B, *Castanea mollissima:* fruit, × ½. C, *Quercus borealis:* Ca, twig with staminate catkins, × ½; Cb, pistillate flower, × 3; Cc, staminate flower, × 3; Cd, acorn, × ½. (c cup, i involucre, n nut.)

1. FAGUS, L. BEECH. Ornamental deciduous trees with smooth light gray bark, of about 10 species native in the cooler regions of the northern hemisphere.—Lvs. dentate, straight-veined: fls. appearing with the lvs.; staminate fls. in slender-peduncled pendulous heads, yellowish-green, subtended by deciduous scale-like bracts, with 5–7-lobed bell-shaped calyx and 8–16 stamens; pistillate fls. usually in pairs in an axillary peduncled involucre, with 6-lobed calyx adnate to 3-celled ovary, styles 3: nut brown, ovoid, sharply 3-angled, 1 or 2 in a prickly involucre which dehisces into 4 valves. (Fa-gus: ancient Latin name.)

A. Lvs. with 9–14 pairs of veins, margin serrate.......................1. *F. grandifolia*
AA. Lvs. with 5–9 pairs of veins, margin denticulate.......................2. *F. sylvatica*

1. **F. grandifolia,** Ehrh. (*F. ferruginea,* Ait. *F. americana,* Sweet). AMERICAN BEECH. Tree to 100 ft., sometimes 120 ft.; winter-buds reddish-brown, shining: lvs. ovate-oblong, 2–5 in. long, acuminate, cuneate to rounded at base, serrate, silky when young, becoming glabrous except on veins, bluish-green above, turning yellow in autumn: involucre about ¾in. long, with prickles sometimes recurved. N. B. and Ont. to Fla. and Tex.

2. **F. sylvatica,** L. EUROPEAN BEECH. Tree to 80 ft., sometimes 100 ft.; winter-buds brownish, dull: lvs. ovate or elliptic, 2–4 in. long, acute, cuneate to rounded at base, remotely denticulate, silky and ciliate when young, becoming glabrous except on veins, dark green above, turning reddish-brown in autumn: involucre about 1 in. long, with usually upright prickles. Cent. and S. Eu. to Crimea. Numerous vars. are cult., some of which are: var. **asplenifolia,** Sweet (forma *comptoniæfolia,* Kirchn. *F. sylvatica salicifolia,* Hort.), lvs. narrow, often linear, deeply lobed or toothed; var. **heterophylla,** Loud. *F. sylvatica laciniata,* Vignet. *F. sylvatica incisa,* Hort.), FERNLEAF or CUTLEAF BEECH, lvs. lanceolate to narrow-elliptic, deeply serrate to lobed, sometimes linear and almost entire; var. **atropunicea,** West. (var. *purpurea,* Ait. var. *cuprea,* Loud. var. *Riversii,* Rehd. *F. sylvatica atropurpurea,* Kirchn. *F. sylvatica sanguinea,* Kuntze. *F. sylvatica nigra,* Hort.), PURPLE or COPPER BEECH, lvs. purple; var. **pendula,** Loud., WEEPING BEECH, branches drooping, the larger limbs usually horizontal.

2. QUERCUS, L. OAK. Noble deciduous or evergreen trees, rarely shrubs, of over 300 species native in temp. regions of the northern hemisphere and in the mts. of the tropics.—Lvs. short-petioled, serrate, lobed or pinnatifid, rarely entire: fls. appearing with or before lvs.; staminate fls. in slender pendulous catkins, with usually

6-parted calyx and 4–12 stamens; pistillate fls. in 1-to many-fld. spikes in axils of young lvs., with 6-lobed calyx adnate to the 3- or rarely 4–5-celled ovary surrounded by an involucre of imbricated bracts which becomes the cup of the fr., styles as many as cells of ovary: fr. a 1-seeded subglobose to oblong nut (acorn), surrounded at base or almost inclosed by cup-like involucre. (Quer-cus: ancient Latin name.)

A. Tree evergreen, foliage lasting more than one season.
B. Bark corky: lvs. with 5–7 pairs of veins .... 12. *Q. Suber*
BB. Bark scaly: lvs. with 7–10 pairs of veins.
C. Lvs. acute, with undulate margins .... 11. *Q. Ilex*
CC. Lvs. obtuse, with revolute margins .... 13. *Q. virginiana*
AA. Tree deciduous, foliage lasting only one season.
B. Lvs. entire.
C. Shape of lvs. broadly obovate, often obscurely 3-lobed at apex .... 4. *Q. nigra*
CC. Shape of lvs. lanceolate to oblong.
D. Mature lvs. pubescent beneath .... 2. *Q. imbricaria*
DD. Mature lvs. practically glabrous beneath.
E. Lf. mostly lanceolate, revolute in bud, deciduous in autumn .... 1. *Q. Phellos*
EE. Lf. elliptic to oblong-obovate, flat in bud, deciduous in late winter .... 3. *Q. hemisphærica*
BB. Lvs. lobed or toothed.
C. Lobes bristle-tipped.
D. Twigs pubescent at least the first year: lvs. pubescent beneath.
E. Lf. densely tomentose beneath, glabrescent above .... 5. *Q. falcata*
EE. Lf. with scattered pubescence usually on both surfaces but more beneath .... 6. *Q. velutina*
DD. Twigs glabrescent the first season: mature lvs. pubescent only in axils of veins beneath.
E. Lf. lobed not more than half way to midrib .... 8. *Q. borealis*
EE. Lf. lobed more than half way to midrib.
F. Acorn-cup saucer-shaped: axillary tufts of hair beneath lvs. conspicuous .... 7. *Q. palustris*
FF. Acorn-cup hemispherical: axillary tufts of hair beneath lvs. small .... 9. *Q. coccinea*
CC. Lobes or teeth not bristle-tipped, but sometimes mucronate.
D. Axillary buds with long slender persistent scales .... 10. *Q. Cerris*
DD. Axillary buds without persistent scales.
E. Foliage glabrous to slightly pubescent.
F. Lf. lobed more than half way to midrib .... 16. *Q. alba*
FF. Lf. lobed less than half way to midrib.
G. Petioles usually less than ¼in. long: fr. on peduncles 1–3 in. long .... 14. *Q. Robur*
GG. Petioles ½–1½ in. long: fr. subsessile or on peduncles much shorter than petioles .... 15. *Q. petræa*
EE. Foliage pubescent to tomentose.
F. Lf. sinuate-dentate or shallowly lobed.
G. Veins of lf. mostly less than 12 pairs: acorns on peduncles longer than petioles .... 20. *Q. bicolor*
GG. Veins of lf. more than 12 pairs: acorns on peduncles shorter than petioles .... 21. *Q. Prinus*
FF. Lf. lyrate-lobed more than half way to midrib.
G. Petioles and twigs glabrous .... 18. *Q. lyrata*
GG. Petioles and twigs pubescent.
H. Pubescence of lf. yellowish: acorn-cup without a fringe around top .... 17. *Q. stellata*
HH. Pubescence of lf. grayish-white: acorn-cup with scales forming a fringe around top .... 19. *Q. macrocarpa*

1. **Q. Phellos,** L. WILLOW OAK. Deciduous tree to 80 (100) ft., with round-topped head, branchlets glabrous: lvs. linear-oblong to lanceolate, 2–4 in. long, acute at both ends, entire, undulate, pubescent below becoming glabrous, light green and shining above, turning yellow in autumn: acorn hemispherical, about ½in. high, enveloped at base by saucer-shaped cup. (Phellos: Greek for *cork.*) N. Y. to Fla., Mo. and Tex.

2. **Q. imbricaria,** Michx. SHINGLE OAK. Deciduous tree to 60 (100) ft., with round-topped head, branchlets pubescent: lvs. oblong or oblong-lanceolate, 3–6½ in. long, acute to rounded at both ends, entire, undulate, pubescent below, dark green and shining above, turning reddish-brown in autumn: acorn subglobose, about ½in. high, inclosed one-third to one-half by bowl-shaped cup. Pa. to Ga., Neb. and Ark.

3. **Q. hemisphærica,** Willd. (*Q. laurifolia,* Auth. not Michx.). LAUREL OAK. Deciduous or half-evergreen tree to 60 (100) ft., with dense round-topped head, branchlets glabrous: lvs. elliptic to oblong-obovate, 2–5 in. long, acute to rounded at ends, entire or sometimes slightly lobed, soon glabrous, dark green and shining above: acorn subglobose, about ½in. high, with thin flat cup. Va. to Fla. and E. Tex.—**Q. laurifolia,** Michx. (*Q. rhombica,* Sarg. *Q. obtusa,* Ashe), has larger thinner readily deciduous lvs., acorn about ¾in. high, and a deeply saucer-shaped to turbinate cup; S. N. J. to Fla. and E. Tex.

4. **Q. nigra,** L. (*Q. aquatica,* Walt. *Q. uliginosa,* Wangh.). WATER OAK. Tardily deciduous tree to 80 ft., with rounded top: lvs. obovate, with 3 lobes at apex or sometimes entire to pinnately lobed, 2–6 in. long, soon glabrous except for axils of veins beneath, bluish-green above: acorn globose-ovoid, about ½in. high, one-third to one-quarter inclosed by saucer-shaped cup. Del. to Fla., Ky. and Tex.

5. **Q. falcata,** Michx. (*Q. rubra,* L. not DuRoi. *Q. digitata,* Sudw. *Q. triloba,* Michx. *Q. cuneata,* Auth. not Wangh.). SPANISH OAK. Deciduous tree to 80 (100) ft., with open rounded top: lvs. obovate to elliptic-oblong, 3–8 in. long, usually cuneate at base, commonly deeply 3–7-lobed, the acute lobes sometimes sickle-shaped, entire or toothed, dark green and practically glabrous above, densely pubescent beneath: acorn subglobose, about ½in. high, not more than one-third inclosed by saucer-shaped cup. N. J. to Fla., Mo. and Tex.

6. **Q. velutina,** Lam. (*Q. tinctoria,* Bartram). BLACK OAK. Deciduous tree to 80 (120) ft., with open narrow head, young growth tomentose: lvs. ovate to oblong, 4–10 in. long, mostly cuneate at base, pinnately lobed about half way to the midrib with 7–9 broad toothed slightly wavy lobes, with scattered pubescence on both surfaces becoming more or less glabrescent above, shining dark green above, turning brownish in autumn: acorn ovoid, ½–¾in. long, about half inclosed by cup with loose scales around edge forming a fringe. Me. to Fla., Minn. and Tex.

7. **Q. palustris,** Muenchh. PIN OAK. Deciduous tree to 80 (120) ft., with somewhat pendulous branches: lvs. elliptic to oblong, 3–5 in. long, cuneate at base, pinnately lobed almost to the midrib with 5–7 oblong dentate lobes, becoming glabrous except in axils of veins beneath, bright green, turning scarlet in autumn: acorn subglobose, about ½in. diam., inclosed about one-third by saucer-shaped cup. Mass. to Del., Wis. and Ark.

8. **Q. borealis,** Michx. f. (*Q. ambigua,* Michx. f. not HBK. *Q. rubra* var. *ambigua,* Fern.). RED OAK. Deciduous tree to 80 ft., with round broad head: lvs. elliptic-oblong, 4–9 in. long, mostly cuneate at base, pinnately lobed about half way to midrib, with 7–11 triangular to oblong lobes, irregularly dentate, glabrous except for axils of veins beneath, dull green, turning dark red in autumn: acorn ovoid, about 1 in. high, one-third inclosed by turbinate cup. N. S. to Pa., Minn. and Iowa. Var. **maxima,** Ashe (*Q. rubra maxima,* Marsh. *Q. rubra,* DuRoi not L.), is a somewhat taller tree, with acorns slightly over 1 in. long and inclosed only at the base by a flat cup; N. S. to Fla., Minn. and Tex.

9. **Q. coccinea,** Muenchh. SCARLET OAK. Deciduous tree to 80 ft., with round open head: lvs. oblong or elliptic, 3–6 in. long, usually truncate at base, deeply pinnatifid into 7 (9) dentate lobes, glabrous except for axillary tufts of hair beneath, bright green turning brilliant scarlet in autumn: acorn ovoid, ½–¾in. long, inclosed about half by hemispherical cup. Me. to Fla., Minn. and Mo.

10. **Q. Cerris,** L. TURKEY OAK. Deciduous tree to 120 ft., with broad pyramidal head; winter-buds surrounded and exceeded by slender subulate scales: lvs. oblong or obovate-oblong, 2½–5 in. long, usually rounded at base, deeply and unequally pinnatifid, with 3–9 pairs of entire or few-toothed lobes, dark green and somewhat rough above, grayish-pubescent or finally glabrous beneath, turning brown in autumn: fr. short-stalked, ripening the second year; acorn oblong-ovoid, to 1 in. or more long, inclosed about half by large mossy cup having spreading and recurved scales. (Cerris: probably from the Latin for *fringe,* referring to the mossy cup.) S. Eu., W. Asia.

11. **Q. Ilex,** L. HOLLY or HOLM OAK. Evergreen tree to 60 ft., with large round-topped head, bark smooth: lvs. very variable, leathery, 1–3 in. long, ovate to lanceolate, acute, cuneate to rounded at base, serrate or entire, dark green above, yellowish or whitish tomentose or rarely glabrescent beneath: fr. 1–3 together, ripening the first year, short-peduncled; acorn ovoid, 1–1½ in. long, inclosed about half by the cup having thin appressed or rarely slightly spreading scales. S. Eu.

12. **Q. Suber,** L. CORK OAK. Very similar to *Q. Ilex* but differing in its deeply furrowed spongy and elastic bark and usually dentate lvs. (Suber: ancient name of the cork oak tree.) S. Eu., N. Afr.

13. **Q. virginiana,** Mill. (*Q. virens,* Ait.). LIVE OAK. Evergreen tree to 60 ft., with very spreading head and almost horizontal branches: lvs. obovate to elliptic or oblong, 1½–5 in. long, usually obtuse, cuneate at base, revolute margins mostly entire, shining green above, tomentose beneath: fr. 1–5 clustered on peduncles ½–3 in. long; acorn ovoid, about 1 in. long, one-quarter inclosed by tomentose turbinate cup. Va. to Fla. and Mex.

14. **Q. Robur,** L. (*Q. pedunculata,* Ehrh.). ENGLISH OAK. Deciduous tree to 80 (150) ft., with broad round-topped head, young branches glabrous: lvs. short-petioled, oblong-obovate, 2–5 in. long, rounded to subcordate at base, with 3–7 rounded lobes on each side, quite glabrous: fr. on slender peduncles 1–3 in. long; acorn ovoid or oblong, about 1 in. long, inclosed about one-third by cup having imbricated appressed scales. (Robur: ancient name of an oak.) Eu., N. Afr., W. Asia. Var. **fastigiata,** A. DC. (*Q. fastigiata,* Lam. *Q. pyramidalis,* Gmel.), has a columnar head.

15. **Q. petræa,** Lieblein (*Q. Robur* var. *petræa,* Mattuschka. *Q. Robur,* Mill. not L. *Q. sessiliflora,* Salisb. *Q. sessilis,* Ehrh.). DURMAST OAK. Deciduous tree to 120 ft., with less spreading limbs and head less broad than in *Q. Robur,* young branches sometimes pubescent: lvs. on petioles sometimes 1 in. long, obovate to oblong, with 5–9 rounded lobes on each side, glabrous or sometimes slightly pubescent beneath, to 5 in. long: fr. almost sessile, somewhat larger than in *Q. Robur.* Eu., W. Asia.—Runs into a pendulous form and also vars. with variously lobed and colored lvs.

16. **Q. alba,** L. WHITE OAK. Deciduous tree to 100 (150) ft., with broad open head: lvs. obovate to oblong, 4–9 in. long, cuneate at base, with 5–9 rounded obtuse usually entire lobes, glabrescent beneath, bright green, turning reddish-purple in autumn: acorn ovoid-oblong, ¾–1 in. long, inclosed one-quarter by hemispherical cup with thickened basal scales. Me. to Fla., Minn. and Tex.

17. **Q. stellata,** Wangh. (*Q. obtusiloba*, Michx. *Q. minor*, Sarg.). POST OAK. Deciduous tree to 60 (100) ft., with round head, branchlets tomentose: lvs. obovate, 4–8 in. long, usually cuneate at base, lyrate-pinnatifid with 2–3 obtuse lobes on each side, scattered stellate hairs above, yellowish-pubescent beneath: fr. sessile; acorn ovoid, ½–1 in. long, one-third to one-half inclosed by hemispherical cup. Mass. to Fla., Neb. and Tex.

18. **Q. lyrata,** Walt. OVERCUP OAK. Deciduous tree to 100 ft., with round head and short somewhat pendulous branches: lvs. obovate-oblong, 4–7 in. long, cuneate at base, lyrate-pinnatifid with 3–4 obtuse lobes on each side, glabrous above, usually white-tomentose beneath, sometimes green and pubescent: acorn subglobose, up to 1 in. long, usually nearly completely inclosed by cup. N. J. to Fla., Ill. and Tex.

19. **Q. macrocarpa,** Michx. BUR or MOSSY-CUP OAK. Deciduous tree to 80 (170) ft., with broad head, branchlets pubescent becoming glabrous, sometimes with corky wings: lvs. obovate to oblong-obovate, 4–10 in. long, usually cuneate at base, lyrate-pinnatifid, the terminal lobe largest and crenate to doubly lobed, green and shining above, whitish-tomentose beneath: acorn broadly ovoid to ellipsoid, 1–1½ in. long, about half inclosed by cup with upper scales prolonged into filiform tips forming a fringe. N. S. to Pa., Man. and Tex.

20. **Q. bicolor,** Willd. (*Q. platanoides*, Sudw.). SWAMP WHITE OAK. Deciduous tree to 70 (100) ft., with narrow round head and lower branches pendulous: lvs. oblong-obovate, 4–6 in. long, cuneate at base, with 5–10 pairs of coarse obtuse teeth or lobes, whitish-tomentose beneath, dark green above, turning yellow to reddish in autumn: fr. on peduncles 1–3 in. long; acorn oblong-ovoid, about 1 in. high, inclosed about one-third by cup. Que. to Ga., Mich. and Ark.

21. **Q. Prinus,** L. (*Q. Michauxii*, Nutt. *Q. Prinus palustris*, Michx.). BASKET OAK. Deciduous tree to 100 ft., with compact round head: lvs. obovate to oblong, 4–7 in. long, acute to acuminate, cuneate to rounded at base, regularly crenate toothed, with 5–14 pairs of obtuse to mucronate teeth, gray-tomentose beneath, bright green above, turning crimson in autumn: acorn oblong-ovoid, 1–1½ in. long, inclosed one-third to one-half by cup with a stiff fringe around edge. Del. to Fla., Ind. and Tex.

3. **CASTANEA,** Mill. CHESTNUT. Deciduous trees or shrubs with furrowed bark, grown for their edible nuts or for ornament, of about 10 species native in temp. regions of the northern hemisphere.—Branchlets without terminal bud; winter-buds with 3–4 scales: lvs. elliptic-oblong to lanceolate, serrate, straight-veined: staminate fls. in long erect cylindrical axillary catkins, with 6-parted calyx and 10–20 stamens; pistillate fls. usually 3 together in a prickly involucre, borne at the bases of the upper catkins, with 6-parted calyx adnate to 6-celled ovary and 6–9 linear styles: fr. a large brown nut, 1–7 together in a prickly 2–4-valved involucre or bur; nut rounded or plano-convex, marked at base with conspicuous pale oval thickened scar. (Casta-nea: classical name of the chestnut tree.)—In the trade, the nuts of Bertholletia, Brazil-nut, a very different tree of S. Amer., are often known as castaneas.

A. Lvs. glabrous (except when unfolding in the bud) . . . . 1. *C. dentata*
AA. Lvs. pubescent beneath, sometimes becoming more or less glabrous.
  B. Nuts usually solitary: plant shrubby . . . . 2. *C. pumila*
  BB. Nuts 2–3: trees, sometimes shrubby in no. 5.
    C. Young twigs with dense short pubescence and often long hair also: teeth of lvs. subtriangular, flattened almost to apex . . . . 3. *C. mollissima*
    CC. Young twigs soon practically glabrous: teeth of lvs. needle-like for some distance below apex.
      D. Lf. 4–9 in. long, with rounded sinuses between teeth . . . . 4. *C. sativa*
      DD. Lf. 3–5 in. long, teeth without sinuses . . . . 5. *C. crenata*

1. **C. dentata,** Borkh. (*Fagus Castanea dentata*, Marsh. *C. americana*, Raf.). AMERICAN CHESTNUT. Tree to 100 ft., branchlets soon glabrous: lvs. oblong-lanceolate, 5–10 in. long, acuminate, cuneate at base, coarsely serrate, glandular and slightly pubescent at first, soon glabrous: bur 2–2½ in. across; nut ½–1 in. across, usually 2–3 together. Me. to Mich., Ala., and Miss., now reduced by blight.

2. **C. pumila,** Mill. (*Fagus pumila*, L.). CHINQUAPIN. Shrub or small tree to 50 ft., branchlets tomentose: lvs. elliptic-oblong, 2½–6 in. long, acute to short-acuminate, rounded or cuneate at base, serrate or teeth reduced to bristles, dark green and glabrous above, remaining whitish-tomentose beneath: bur 1–1½ in. across; nut ovoid, solitary, rarely 2, ½–¾in. long. Pa. to Fla. and Tex.

3. **C. mollissima,** Blume. CHINESE CHESTNUT. Tree to 60 ft., branchlets with short pubescence and often with long coarse hairs: lvs. oblong-lanceolate, 3–7 in. long, acuminate, rounded at base, coarsely serrate, tomentose beneath, glabrous above except for veins: bur with pubescent spines; nut about 1 in. across, usually 2–3 together. China, Korea.

4. **C. sativa,** Mill. (*C. vesca*, Gaertn.). SPANISH or EURASIAN CHESTNUT. Tree to 100 ft., buds large: lvs. oblong-lanceolate, 4–9 in. long, acute to acuminate, narrowed or rounded at base, coarsely serrate with spreading teeth and marked rounded sinuses between, tomentose beneath when young, becoming more or less glabrous, dark green above, light green beneath: bur very large, with long branching spines; nut over 1 in. wide. S. Eu. and N. Afr., W. Asia.—There are garden vars. with variegated and laciniately cut lvs.

5. **C. crenata,** Sieb. & Zucc. (*C. japonica*, Blume). JAPANESE CHESTNUT. Very similar to the above, but a small precocious tree to 30 ft. or a shrub, buds small: lvs. oblong-lanceolate, 3–5 in. long, acuminate, subcordate or truncate at base, finely serrate, often teeth reduced to long bristle-like point, tomentose and often glandular beneath when young: bur with short widely branching spines: nut over 1 in. wide. Japan.

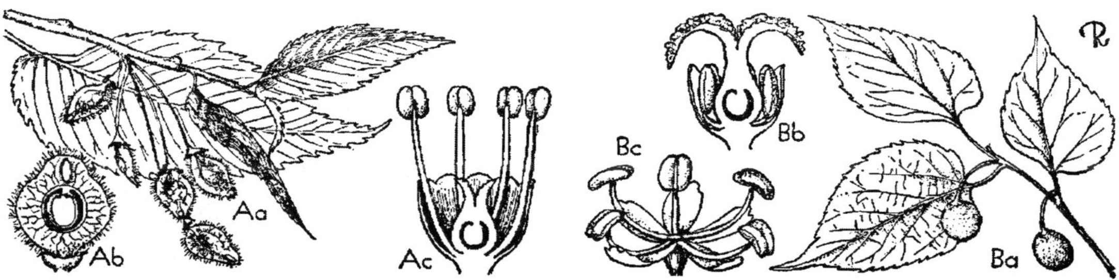

Fig. 51. ULMACEÆ. A, *Ulmus americana:* Aa, fruiting branch, × ½; Ab, fruit, vertical section, × 1; Ac, flower, vertical section, × 4. B, *Celtis occidentalis:* Ba, fruiting branch, × ½; Bb, flower, vertical section, × 4; Bc, staminate flower, × 6.

51. ULMACEÆ. ELM FAMILY

About 15 genera and more than 150 species of deciduous trees and shrubs with watery juice, widely distributed in trop. and temp. regions, yielding important street and shade trees.—Buds scaly: lvs. alternate, simple, serrate, pinnately veined, petioled, stipules usually fugacious: fls. bisexual or unisexual, small, clustered or the pistillate solitary, apetalous; calyx 3–9-parted; stamens as many as calyx-lobes and opposite them, rarely twice as many, filaments straight; ovary superior, usually 1-celled, 1-ovuled, styles 2: fr. a samara, nut or drupe.

A. Lvs. with 7 or more pairs of parallel pinnate veins: parts of perianth connate.
  B. Fr. a samara: lvs. usually doubly serrate. . . . . 1. ULMUS
  BB. Fr. a drupe: lvs. simply serrate. . . . . 2. ZELKOVA
AA. Lvs. 3-veined at the base: parts of perianth distinct. . . . . 3. CELTIS

1. **ULMUS,** L. ELM. About 18 species native in the northern hemisphere, well-known forest and street trees.—Buds with numerous imbricated scales: lvs. 2-ranked, usually unequal at base: fls. bisexual or rarely unisexual, in axillary clusters or racemes, on twigs of preceding season; calyx campanulate, 4–9-lobed; ovary sessile or stalked: fr. a flat ovate or roundish samara, with a broad, rarely narrow, membranaceous wing all around. (Ul-mus: ancient Latin name of the elm.)

A. Lvs. usually simply serrate, subequal at base.
  B. Branchlets soon glabrous: fls. before lvs.: samara ½in. long . . . . 1. *U. pumila*
  BB. Branchlets pubescent: fls. in late summer: samara ⅓in. long. . . . . 2. *U. parvifolia*
AA. Lvs. doubly serrate, unequal at base.
  B. Fls. pendulous: samara with ciliate margins.
    C. Samara glabrous: fls. fascicled: branchlets without corky wings . . . . 3. *U. americana*
    CC. Samara tomentose: fls. in racemes: branchlets with corky wings.
      D. Veins of lf. 16–20 pairs: samara ¾in. long, with small notch. . . . . 4. *U. Thomasii*
      DD. Veins of lf. 8–12 pairs: samara ⅓in. long, with incurved beaks. . . . . 5. *U. alata*
  BB. Fls. upright, fascicled: samara with glabrous margins.
    C. Bud-scales rusty-tomentose: samara tomentose in center: branchlets scabrous. 6. *U. fulva*
    CC. Bud-scales pale pubescent to glabrous: samara glabrous: branchlets smooth, glabrous or pubescent.
      D. Seed in center of samara: lvs. with 16–20 pairs of veins . . . . 7. *U. glabra*
      DD. Seed toward tip of samara, sometimes touching notch: lvs. with 8–18 pairs of veins.

E. Lf. with scattered pubescence, very rough above: branchlets pubescent the second year.......... 8. *U. procera*
EE. Lf. sometimes glabrous or with pubescence usually only in the axils of veins, commonly smooth above: branchlets often glabrous the second year.
F. Length of lvs. 2–3½ in.; petioles ¼–½in. long.......... 9. *U. carpinifolia*
FF. Length of lvs. 3–5 in.; petioles ¼–⅓in. long..........10. *U. hollandica*

1. **U. pumila,** L. (*U. campestris* var. *pumila*, Maxim.). SIBERIAN or DWARF ELM. Tree to 75 ft. or sometimes shrubby; branchlets soon glabrous: lvs. elliptic to oblong-lanceolate, ¾–2½ in. long, short-acuminate, subequal at base, almost simply serrate, smooth above, glabrous to somewhat pubescent in axils of veins beneath: samara suborbicular, about ½in. long, notched half way to nutlet. E. Siberia to Turkestan.

2. **U. parvifolia,** Jacq. (*U. chinensis*, Pers.). CHINESE ELM. Small tree to 45 (75) ft., with broad open head, partially evergreen in mild climates; branchlets pubescent: lvs. elliptic to ovate, ¾–2½ in. long, acute, rounded and slightly unequal at base, simply serrate or nearly so, smooth above, glabrous to slightly pubescent in axils of veins beneath: fls. in late summer: samara elliptic-ovate, about ⅜in. long, with a notch at apex. China, Japan.

3. **U. americana,** L. AMERICAN ELM, sometimes called WHITE or WATER ELM. Tall wide-spreading tree to 120 ft., much planted for avenues; bark gray and flaky; branchlets pubescent when young: lvs. ovate-oblong, 3–6 in. long, abruptly acuminate, unequal at base, doubly serrate, almost glabrous and rough above, pubescent or almost glabrous beneath: fls. long-pedicelled, in drooping many-fld. clusters; stamens 7–8, with bright red anthers, exserted; samara about ½in. long, reticulate-veined, glabrous, the margins densely ciliate, wings deeply notched. Newf. to Fla. west to base of Rocky Mts.—Varies much in form, sometimes being "feathery," having the limbs and main trunk clothed with short somewhat pendent branchlets, or often with slender pendulous branches. The "Moline elm" is of narrow pyramidal habit.

4. **U. Thomasii,** Sarg. (*U. racemosa*, Thomas not Borkh.). ROCK or CORK ELM. Tree to 100 ft., with narrow round head; branchlets pubescent usually the first year, developing irregular corky wings: lvs. elliptic to oblong-obovate, 2–5 in. long, short-acuminate, unequal at base, doubly serrate, glabrous or practically so above, pubescent beneath: fls. in racemes to 2 in. long; stamens 5–8, exserted: samara about ¾in. long, with a small notch at apex, pubescent, margins ciliate. (Named for D. Thomas, page 52.) Que. to Tenn. and Neb.

5. **U. alata,** Michx. WAHOO or WINGED ELM. Tree to 50 (100) ft., with an oblong round-topped head; branchlets more or less pubescent, developing 2 opposite corky wings: lvs. ovate-oblong, ½–3 in. long, acutish, doubly serrate, almost glabrous above, pubescent beneath: fls. in short racemes: samara about ⅓in. long, with narrow wings and incurved beaks, villous. Va. to Fla., Ill. and Tex.

6. **U. fulva,** Michx. (*U. rubra*, Michx. f. *U. Heyderi*, Spaeth). SLIPPERY or RED ELM. Tree to 60 ft., with broad open head; branchlets scabrous; bud-scales brown-tomentose: lvs. obovate-oblong, 4–8 in. long, acuminate, very unequal at base, doubly serrate, very rough above, pubescent beneath: fls. in dense clusters; stamens 5–9, exserted: samara ½–¾in. long, slightly notched, wings broad and almost glabrous, tomentose in center. Que. to Fla., Dak. and Tex.

7. **U. glabra,** Huds. (*U. scabra*, Mill. *U. montana*, With. *U. campestris*, L. in part). SCOTCH ELM. WYCH ELM. Tree to 120 ft., with round-topped head, without suckers; bark remaining smooth for many years; branches never with corky wings, young branchlets pubescent: lvs. very short-petioled, broadly obovate, 3–6 in. long, abruptly acuminate, sharply and doubly serrate, usually rough above and pubescent beneath: fls. short-pedicelled, clustered, not pendulous: samara to 1 in. long, with small notch, seed in the center. Eu. to W. Asia. Var. **camperdownii,** Rehd. (*U. montana* var. *pendula camperdownii*, Henry), CAMPERDOWN ELM, has pendulous branches, forming a round head.—There are other vars. varying in habit of growth and color of lvs. or bark.

8. **U. procera,** Salisb. (*U. campestris*, Mill.). ENGLISH ELM. Tree to 130 ft., with upright habit and oval head, usually suckering abundantly; bark deeply fissured; young branchlets pubescent: lvs. short-petioled, 2–3 in. long, broadly oval or ovate, short-acuminate, very unequal at base, coarsely and doubly serrate, dark green and scabrous above, pubescent beneath: fls. in clusters, short-stalked: samara ¾–1 in. long, with short closed notch at apex, seed touching base of notch. England, W. and S. Eu.—There are forms with variegated, colored or small lvs.

9. **U. carpinifolia,** Gleditsch (*U. foliacea*, Gilib. *U. nitens*, Moench. *U. glabra*, Mill. not Huds. *U. campestris*, L. in part). SMOOTH-LEAVED ELM. Tree to 100 ft., with straight trunk, wide-spreading branches and usually pendulous branchlets, suckering; bark deeply fissured, gray; young branchlets glabrous or nearly so: lvs. with petiole ¼–½in. long, oval or obovate, 2–3½ in. long, acuminate, doubly serrate, lustrous and smooth above, with white axillary tufts beneath: fls. short-pedicelled, in dense clusters: samara obovate, cuneate at base, broad and rounded at apex, the seed near apex and nearly touching the

closed notch. Eu., N. Afr., W. Asia. Var. **Dampieri,** Rehd. (*U. campestris Dampieri,* Wesm.), a fastigiate tree with narrow pyramidal head; lvs. deeply doubly serrate, almost lobulate. Var. **Koopmannii,** Bailey (forma *Koopmannii,* Rehd. *U. Koopmannii,* Lauche), has a dense ovoid head, small lvs., and branches often corky. Var. **sarniensis,** Bailey (forma *sarniensis,* Rehd. *U. campestris sarniensis,* Lodd. *U. campestris Wheatleyi,* Simon-Louis), GUERNSEY or JERSEY ELM, has narrow pyramidal head and broadly obovate lvs. Var. **umbraculifera,** Rehd. (*U. campestris* var. *umbraculifera,* Trautv.), GLOBE ELM, has dense globose head, slightly pubescent branchlets, lvs. rather small and often rough above. Var. **Wredei,** Bailey (forma *Wredei,* Rehd. *U. Dampieri* var. *Wredei,* Juehlke), similar to var. *Dampieri* but with yellow lvs.

10. **U. hollandica,** Mill. (*U. glabra* × *U. carpinifolia. U. Dippeliana,* Schneid. *U. major,* Smith. *U. hollandica* var. *major,* Rehd. *U. campestris* var. *major,* Planch.). DUTCH ELM. Tree to 100 ft. or more, with short trunk and wide-spreading branches, suckering; bark deeply fissured; young branchlets glabrous or with few scattered hairs: lvs. with petiole ¼–⅓in. long, broadly oval, 3–5 in. long, acuminate, lustrous and nearly smooth above, slightly pubescent beneath, with 12–14 pairs of veins: fls. short-pedicelled: samara oval-obovate, ¾–1 in. long, with seed near apex and touching base of the notch. Origin unknown. Var. **belgica,** Rehd. (*U. belgica,* Burgsd.), BELGIAN ELM, tall tree with unbranched st., good for street planting; lvs. mostly obovate, with 14–18 pairs of veins, slightly rough above. Var. **pendula,** Rehd. (*U. pendula,* W. Mast. not Willd.), DOWNTON ELM, branchlets somewhat pubescent, pendulous; lvs. elliptic, with 14–18 pairs of veins. Var. **vegeta,** Rehd. (*U. vegeta,* Lindl. *U. glabra* var. *vegeta,* Loud. *U. Huntingdonii,* Hort.). HUNTINGDON ELM, erect vigorous tree, with usually forked st., branchlets more or less pubescent; lvs. elliptic, with 14–18 pairs of veins.—Many other vars. and garden forms are known.

2. **ZELKOVA.** Spach. About 5 species native in the Caucasus and E. Asia, one hardy N. and grown as an avenue or specimen tree.—Lvs. short-petioled, serrate: polygamous, fls. borne on the young growth; staminate fls. clustered in axils of the lower lvs., calyx campanulate, 4–5-lobed, stamens 4–5; pistillate or bisexual fls. solitary or few in axils of the upper lvs.: fr. a 1-seeded drupe, usually broader than high, oblique, with eccentric style. (Zelko-va: from the vernacular name in the Caucasus.)

Z. serrata, Makino (*Corchorus serrata,* Thunb. *Z. acuminata,* Planch. *Z. Keakii,* Mayr). Tree to 100 ft., with broad round-topped head; branches slender, not spiny: lvs. ovate to oblong-ovate, 1–4 in. long, acuminate, rounded or slightly cordate at base, sharply and coarsely serrate, somewhat rough above, more or less pubescent beneath: fr. not winged. Japan.

3. **CELTIS,** L. HACKBERRY. About 70 species of trees and shrubs of the northern hemisphere and tropics.—Deciduous or sometimes evergreen; bark usually smooth, gray: lvs. 3-nerved at base, entire or serrate: polygamous or functionally monœcious; fls. appearing with the lvs., borne on the young growth, staminate in clusters toward the base, bisexual fls. solitary in axils of lvs. above; calyx 4–5-lobed; stamens 4–5: fr. an ovoid or globose drupe with thin pulp and a thick outer coat; stone bony, with surface sometimes sculptured; embryo with cotyledons broad and folded. (Cel-tis: Greek name of a tree with sweet fr.)

A. Lvs. usually entire, oblong-lanceolate .... 1. *C. lævigata*
AA. Lvs. serrate, ovate to ovate-oblong.
  B. Petioles ¼–½in. long: stone pitted .... 2. *C. occidentalis*
  BB. Petioles ¼in. or less long: stone smooth .... 3. *C. sinensis*

1. **C. lævigata,** Willd. (*C. mississippiensis,* DC.). SUGARBERRY. MISSISSIPPI HACKBERRY. Tree to 100 ft., with broad head and branches more or less pendulous: lvs. oblong-lanceolate, 2–4 in. long, long-acuminate, cuneate to rounded at base, entire or sometimes serrate, glabrous or sometimes slightly pubescent beneath: fr. about ¼in. across, orange-red turning dark purple, on stalks slightly longer than petioles; stone pitted. Ill. to Tex. and Fla.

2. **C. occidentalis,** L. Tree to 120 ft., with round head and branches sometimes pendulous: lvs. ovate or ovate-oblong, 2–5 in. long, acuminate, oblique and rounded at base, serrate, usually smooth above, glabrous except for veins beneath: fr. about ⅓in. across, orange-red turning dark purple, on stalks longer than petioles. Que to Ala. and Kans.

3. **C. sinensis,** Pers. Tree to 60 ft.: lvs. ovate to oblong-ovate, 2–4 in. long, acute to acuminate, cuneate and somewhat oblique at base, crenate-serrate, slightly rough above, somewhat pubescent beneath: fr. dark orange, on stalks about as long as petioles. China; Korea, Japan.

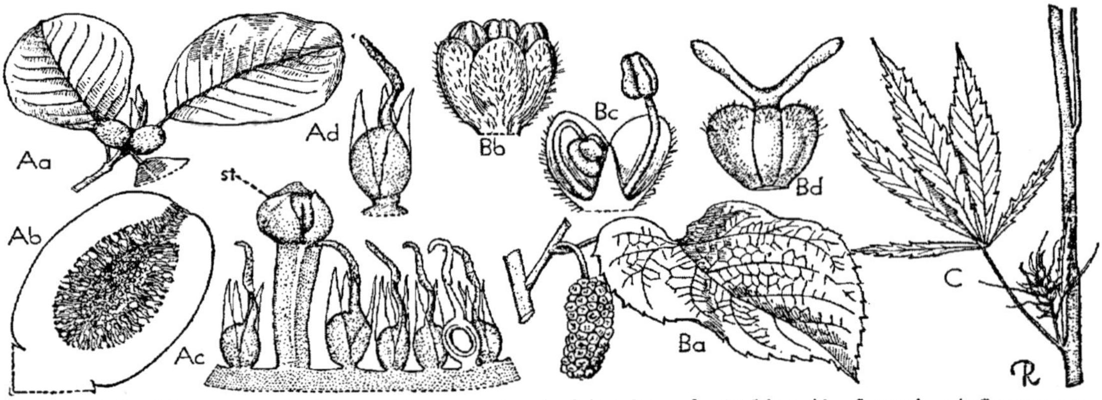

Fig. 52. MORACEÆ. A, *Ficus altissima:* Aa, fruiting branch, × 1/10; Ab, flowering inflorescence, vertical section, × 1; Ac, section of "receptacle" bearing pistillate and staminate flowers, × 5; Ad, pistillate flower, × 6. B, *Morus alba:* Ba, fruit and leaf, × 1/2; Bb, staminate flower, × 6; Bc, same, vertical section, × 6; Bd, pistillate flower, × 12. C, *Cannabis sativa:* pistillate inflorescence and leaf, × 1/4. (Bb–Bd redrawn from Sargent.)

52. MORACEÆ. MULBERRY FAMILY

As now delimited, the Mulberry Family comprises about 55 genera and 900–1,000 species of herbs, shrubs, and trees, sometimes vines, mostly tropical, yielding various subjects for hort.—Plants often with milky juice: lvs. mostly alternate and usually simple: fls. small and inconspicuous, regular, mostly imperfect and plants monœcious or diœcious, usually aggregated into heads or spikes or the staminate racemose, the pistillate sometimes (Ficus) on the inside of a hollow receptacle or (as in Dorstenia, not treated here) on a much-flattened expanded receptacle; perianth single, without clear distinction of sepals and petals, in 1–6, mostly 4, imbricated parts which are of the same number as the stamens and opposite them; ovary 1–2-celled and 1–2-ovuled, superior or inferior, stigmas 1–2: fr. various, sometimes a separate achene as in hemp, sometimes achenes or drupes imbedded in or enveloped by the thickening fleshy perianth and thereby forming a syncarp as in mulberry, or achenes contained inside a fleshy body or syconium as in the fig.

A. Species woody, arborescent, with milky juice: fr. not a separate achene.
  B. Fls. external, in a dense spike or head.
    C. Sterile and fertile fls. in separate similar short small catkin-like spikes: lvs. dentate or often lobed . . . . 1. MORUS
    CC. Sterile fls. in spikes or racemes; fertile fls. in dense globular heads, or forming great syncarps.
      D. Plants diœcious; sterile fls. in loose spikes or racemes.
        E. Lvs. toothed, often lobed: fr. small . . . . 2. BROUSSONETIA
        EE. Lvs. entire: fr. 4–5 in. long . . . . 3. MACLURA
      DD. Plants monœcious; sterile fls. in large dense thick oblong or club-shaped spikes . . . . 4. ARTOCARPUS
  BB. Fls. inside a closed receptacle that often arises from an axil-like branch: lvs. usually thick, entire or lobed . . . . 5. FICUS
AA. Species herbaceous, with watery juice: fr. an achene. (Sometimes separated as family Cannabinaceæ.)
  B. Plant an erect herb: lvs. digitate . . . . 6. CANNABIS
  BB. Plant a twining vine: lvs. lobed . . . . 7. HUMULUS

1. **MORUS, L.** MULBERRY. Trees cult. for the edible fr. and the lvs. for silk-worm forage; the genus has about 12 species, although they are so variable that ten times that many have been described; temp. and warm temp. regions, eastern and western hemispheres.—Plants without spines, with milky juice, alternate simple but variously lobed lvs. that are 3- or 5-nerved from base: monœcious or diœcious; fls. in small hanging cylindrical catkin-like spikes, the staminate soon falling, the pistillate ripening into a blackberry-like juicy snycarp; perianth 4-parted; stamens 4, incurved in the bud; ovary small, sessile, style 2-parted, becoming a drupelet inclosed in the enlarging succulent perianth. (Mo-rus: the classical name.)

A. Lvs. glabrous or pubescent only on veins beneath.
  B. Upper surface of lvs. glossy and smooth, 2–6 in. long........................1. *M. alba*
  BB. Upper surface of lvs. dull and somewhat rough, sometimes over 12 in. long........2. *M. multicaulis*
AA. Lvs. pubescent beneath.
  B. Base of lf. deeply cordate..3. *M. nigra*
  BB. Base of lf. truncate to subcordate..4. *M. rubra*

1. **M. alba,** L. WHITE MULBERRY. Wide-spreading round-headed tree to 50 ft., trunk attaining 2 ft. diam., branches gray or grayish-yellow: lvs. thin, light green, rather small (blade 2–6 in. long), broad-ovate to orbicular-ovate, rarely oblong-ovate, apex acute or short-acuminate, base semi-truncate to subcordate and mostly oblique, shining above, glabrous or with slight pubescence particularly on veins and in axils beneath, margins coarsely scallop-toothed, often oddly and irregularly lobed: fr. variable, 1–2 in. long in improved forms but often much smaller, whitish to dark violet or purple, sweet. China; escaped in N. Amer. Var. **tatarica,** Loud. (*M. tatarica,* L.), RUSSIAN MULBERRY, is a smaller bushy tree, very hardy, lvs. small and commonly much lobed, frs. about ½in. long. Var. **pendula,** Dipp., has drooping branches and lobed lvs.; it is grafted on upright stocks.

2. **M. multicaulis,** Perr. (*M. alba* var. *multicaulis,* Loud.). Very large shrub with many trunks or sometimes a tree, with gray or brown twigs: lvs. very large (blade often 1 ft. and more long on strong shoots), dull green, mostly long-pointed, ovate, semi-truncate or shallowly cordate at base, rough above and more or less pubescent on veins beneath, margins with many scalloped or somewhat acute teeth, seldom lobed: fr. black, sweet. China.—Used for silkworm forage, and long ago intro. into this country for that purpose and still to be found in old places; the original Downing mulberry, grown for fr., was probably of this species.

3. **M. nigra,** L. BLACK MULBERRY. Rather small spreading tree to 30 ft., with dark heavy foliage and more or less pubescent young growth, twigs dark colored: lvs. 2–8 in. long, rather thick, dull green and not glossy, cordate-ovate with a deep and nearly or quite symmetrical basal sinus, abruptly short-pointed, rough above, more or less pubescent beneath, margins with coarse angled or pointed teeth, sometimes lobed: fr. to 1 in. long, purple to black. Asia.—Provides the fr.-bearing vars. of S. Eu. and also planted in S. U. S. and Calif.; hardy only in protected places in N. Y. and New England.

4. **M. rubra,** L. RED or AMERICAN MULBERRY. Tree to 60 ft., with broad round top: lvs. ovate to oblong-ovate, 3–5 (8) in. long, acuminate, truncate to subcordate at base, sharply serrate, sometimes lobed, more or less rough above, pubescent beneath: fr. to 1¼ in. long, becoming dark purple. Mass. to Fla., Mich. and Tex.

2. **BROUSSONETIA,** L'Her. PAPER-MULBERRY (bark used for paper-making in the Far East). About 2 species of deciduous unarmed trees or large shrubs in E. Asia, one planted for ornament and also more or less run wild, N. Y. and southward.—Juice milky: lvs. petioled, serrate or dentate, often lobed: diœcious; fls. small, the staminate in nodding cylindrical spikes, pistillate in dense globular short-stalked small heads; stamens 4, the perianth 4-parted; pistillate fls. with a tubular toothed perianth, ovary stalked, style filiform: fr. a collection of orange-red drupelets standing in the persistent perianths and bracts, forming a small globular syncarp. (Broussone-tia: P. M. A. Broussonet, 1761–1807, a French naturalist.)

B. papyrifera, L'Her. (*Morus papyrifera,* L. *Papyrius papyrifera,* Kuntze). Tree to 40 or 50 ft., with grayish pubescent twigs: lvs. sometimes opposite, mostly ovate or oblong-ovate, 3–8 in. long, often deeply lobed with obtuse sinuses, the lobe sometimes on only one side, margins serrate, apex prominently pointed, rough above and grayish-tomentose beneath, petiole 1–4 in. long: pistillate spikes with long projecting styles, ripening into a globular tomentose syncarp about ¾in. diam. China, Japan.—Variable.

3. **MACLURA,** Nutt. OSAGE-ORANGE. One species native in the Ark.–Tex. region, much used for hedges.—Deciduous tree 50–60 ft. high, with glabrous twigs, axillary spines, and entire long-pointed oblong-lanceolate glabrous slender-petioled lvs.: diœcious; fls. very small, the staminate in short racemes with 4-parted perianth and 4 inflexed stamens; pistillate in a small dense globular head with 4-parted perianth inclosing the ovoid sessile ovary, styles filiform and exserted: fr. a syncarp, formed of the enlarged fleshy perianths in which the drupelets are embedded. (Maclu-ra: William Maclure, 1763–1840, American geologist.)

M. pomifera, Schneid. (*Toxylon pomiferum,* Raf. *M. aurantiaca,* Nutt.). Known in cult. as a small tree to 30 ft., or persisting as a large shrub: lvs. 2–5 in. long: syncarp as large as an orange (4–5 in.), yellow: wood orange, bark containing tannin.—There is a spineless form.

4. **ARTOCARPUS,** Forst. About 50 milky-juiced trees of Asiatic tropics and Polynesia, two planted in our extreme southern borders and in trop. regions for the edible fr.—Lvs. alternate, large and stiff, entire or lobed or compound: monœcious; fls. small and very numerous, on a fleshy rachis; staminate fls. on oblong or club-shaped stiff spikes, 2 or more in. long, perianth 2–4-lobed and stamen 1; pistillate fls. in a dense globose or oblong usually large head, the perianth tubular and immersed in the fleshy rachis, contracted and toothed at top, inclosing the ovary, style mostly exserted and stigma entire or 2–3-lobed: fr. a syncarp, containing the large seeds (or seedless by abortion) imbedded in the flesh, echinate or prickly (in ours) from the hardened projecting apices of the perianths and carpels. (Artocar-pus: Greek *breadfruit.*)

A. Lvs. deeply lobed, over 1 ft. long . . . . 1. *A. altilis*
AA. Lvs. usually entire, 4–8 in. long . . . . 2. *A. heterophyllus*

1. **A. altilis,** Fosberg (*Sitodium altile,* Parkinson. *A. communis,* Forst. *A. incisa,* L. f.). BREADFRUIT. Striking broad tree to 50 ft. and more, with heavy profuse foliage: lvs. 1½–2 ft. and more long, thick and leathery, stout-petioled, ovate in general outline, narrowing and entire at base, pinnately several-lobed with narrow sinuses and acute lobes, more or less pubescent beneath and on the veins above, the large stipules deciduous: staminate spikes 6–12 in. or more long, club-shaped, yellow, drooping or downward-curving; pistillate spikes globular to oblong, ripening into echinate syncarps 4–8 in. diam. Polynesia, now widely dispersed in trop. countries where it is grown for edible frs.—The frs. are commonly seedless or nearly so, but a seed-bearing race is grown under the name breadnut, the seeds being eaten; the pericarp is about 1 in. long, with a rounded back and flattened or with 2 flat faces, immersed in the pulp of the syncarp. The breadfruit is eaten cooked, more as a vegetable than dessert fr.

2. **A. heterophyllus,** Lam. (*A. integrifolius,* Auth. not L. f.). JAKFRUIT or JACKFRUIT. Tree 30–50 ft. or more: lvs. stiff, elliptic or obovate, 4–8 in. long, very short-blunt-pointed, entire or 3-lobed on young shoots, glabrous: staminate spikes cylindric or clavate, 3–4 in. long, terminal or axillary; pistillate spikes cylindric or oblong, arising from the trunk and main branches and maturing into great syncarps 1–2 ft. long and weighing 20–40 lbs. India, but now widely dispersed, the fr. eaten by natives and coolies.

5. **FICUS,** L. FIG. Woody plants, trees, erect shrubs, and climbers, in great variety in trop. and subtrop. countries, nearly 2,000 species; one grown for its fr. and many others for shade and ornament; some of the species are at first epiphytal and become self-supporting when they have strangled the host.—The genus is distinguished by fr. a syconium, the minute fls. being on the inside of a closed pyriform, ovoid, or globose receptacle or branch that arises from the axil of a present or former lf. or is supernumerary, the receptacle ripening into a more or less fleshy body (fr.) with the many achenes, succulent pedicels, and inter-floral scales, on the inner walls; staminate perianth 2–6-parted, with 1 or more erect stamens; pistillate perianth sometimes wanting; receptacles unisexual or bisexual, usually the latter; pollination performed by special insects. (Fi-cus: ancient Latin name of the fig.)—Two are indigenous in S. Fla., **F. aurea,** Nutt., and **F. populnea,** Willd., var. **brevifolia,** Warb. (*F. brevifolia,* Nutt.). The former has frs. sessile or nearly so, the latter long-stalked; both are epiphytal trees, sometimes planted. Aside from the common fig and the species grown by florists as pot and tub specimens, the tree-like kinds described here are planted only in S. Fla., S. Calif., and similar climates, and southward in the tropics. The species are not well understood. Those planted in this country are either evergreen or deciduous: lvs. mostly alternate.

A. Plant climbing or trailing, often rooting on walls.
  B. Lvs. equal at base, about 2 in. long . . . . 1. *F. radicans*
  BB. Lvs. unequal at base, up to 1 in. long.
    C. Shape of lvs. ovate (elliptic on fruiting branches) . . . . 2. *F. pumila*
    CC. Shape of lvs. oblong-rhomboidal . . . . 3. *F. falcata*
AA. Plant erect or essentially so: trees or shrubs.
  B. Lvs. usually lobed.
    C. Lf. 4–8 in. long, usually with 3–5 palmate lobes . . . . 4. *F. carica*
    CC. Lf. 2–6 in. long, irregularly pinnately lobed . . . . 5. *F. quercifolia*
  BB. Lvs. entire to sinuate-dentate (sometimes lobed in *F. ulmifolia*).
    C. Foliage fiddle-shaped, or with a long tail at apex.
      D. Lf. fiddle-shaped, 10–15 in. long . . . . 6. *F. lyrata*
      DD. Lf. with a long tail at tip . . . . 7. *F. religiosa*
    CC. Foliage not unusual in shape.

D. Margin of lf. irregularly undulate to lobed.
E. Lf. variegated, almost smooth .... 8. *F. Parcellii*
EE. Lf. green, very rough .... 9. *F. ulmifolia*
DD. Margin of lf. entire but sometimes crinkled.
E. Main lateral veins 10 or more (fewer on small lvs.).
F. Young growth and lf. beneath rusty-pubescent .... 10. *F. rubiginosa*
FF. Young growth and foliage glabrous.
G. Lf. 2–5 in. long, stipular sheath not rosy .... 11. *F. benjamina*
GG. Lf. 5–12 in. long, stipular sheath rosy.
H. Lateral nerves of lvs. with lowermost pair more oblique than the others .... 12. *F. macrophylla*
HH. Lateral nerves of lvs. all nearly parallel .... 13. *F. elastica*
EE. Main lateral veins less than 10 (except on large lvs. of 20 and 21).
F. Frs. (receptacles) in clusters on leafless branchlets or tubercles .... 14. *F. racemosa*
FF. Frs. axillary or from lf.-scars, mostly 1–2, sessile or peduncled.
G. Petiole 1 in. long or less.
H. Lf. mostly less than 2 in. long, with dark glands beneath .... 15. *F. diversifolia*
HH. Lf. 2–7 in. long, without glands.
I. Width of lf. not over 1½ in. .... 16. *F. retusa*
II. Width of lf. 2–3 in. .... 17. *F. indica*
GG. Petiole 1¼–4 in. long.
H. Young parts glabrous: lvs. 3–7 in. long .... 18. *F. Lacor*
HH. Young parts more or less pubescent: lvs. 4–15 in. long.
I. Under surface of lf. minutely soft-pubescent .... 19. *F. bengalensis*
II. Under surface of lf. glabrous.
J. Lf. with lowest pair of lateral nerves broadly oblique and others parallel .... 20. *F. altissima*
JJ. Lf. with all lateral nerves parallel .... 21. *F. Nekbudu*

1. **F. radicans,** Desf. A hort. plant of unknown origin, of trailing habit and useful for vases and hanging-baskets, particularly the var. with foliage variegated creamy-white; young growth closely pubescent: lvs. oblong-lanceolate, acuminate, about 2 in. long, base rounded or slightly notched, margins entire, glabrous except perhaps along the veins, petiole about ¼in. long, stipules awl-like and nearly or quite as long as petiole.

2. **F. pumila,** L. CREEPING FIG. Polymorphous, young parts lightly hairy: in greenhouses it is common in the creeping stage, rooting flat to walls, under the name *F. repens*, with cordate-ovate veiny lvs. 1 in. or less long, the base oblique, petiole almost none: in the fruiting stage the branches are stiff and erect, bearing much larger thick longer-petioled lvs. that are 2–4 in. long, elliptic to oblong-elliptic, slightly or not at all cordate, nearly or quite obtuse at apex, margins entire: fr. large, pyriform or obovoid, short-peduncled, axillary, 2 in. long. Japan, China, Australia; common in the open in the southern parts of the U. S. and S. Var. **minima,** Bailey, is a very small slender form of the creeping stage, lvs. thinner, about ½in. long.

3. **F. falcata,** Miq. Creeping rooting plant with slender brown lightly hairy sts.: lvs. thick, oblong and more or less angled or rhomboidal, ½–1 in. long, not tapering at base, the midrib near one side, very obtuse, much lighter colored beneath, very short-petioled and with small very sharp stipules: fr. single or in fascicles, ovoid to pyriform, about ½in. long, brown to orange. Malaya.

4. **F. carica,** L. COMMON FIG. Small soft-wooded much-branched deciduous tree to 30 ft.: lvs. thick, long-petioled, strongly palmately ribbed, the blade broad-ovate to nearly orbicular in outline, 4–8 in. long, usually deeply 3–5-lobed, rough above and pubescent beneath: fr. single, axillary and subterminal, pear-shaped, variable in size and in many vars. (Carica: named for Caria in Asia Minor.) Medit. region.

5. **F. quercifolia,** Roxb. Shrub or somewhat prostrate, young growths pubescent: lvs. elliptic or ovate in outline, 2–6 in. long, lobed and notched on the sides but margins entire, short-pointed, narrowed or somewhat rounded at base, petiole 1 in. more or less, green, rough beneath and perhaps above: fr. ½in. or less diam., single or in pairs in axils, peduncled, globular or ovoid, rough. Burma and southeastward.—Grown under glass for its decorative foliage.

6. **F. lyrata,** Warb. (*F. pandurata,* Sander). Tree to 40 ft., but grown under glass as a pot and tub subject, growths nearly or quite glabrous: lvs. very large, blade 10–15 in. long, thick, fiddle-shaped with the large end rounded, nearly truncate or even sunken, but mostly with a short point in the center, with few strong pinnate ribs, margins somewhat wavy but entire, petiole short and stout and base cordate, dull green above and lighter beneath, glabrous: fr. in pairs at axils, sessile, globular or nearly so, about 2 in. diam., pitted with white dots. Trop. Afr.

7. **F. religiosa,** L. PEEPUL. BO-TREE. Large tree, usually epiphytal, glabrous: lvs. singular in having a terminal narrow projection or tail sometimes more than half the length of the remainder of the blade which is round-ovate with a truncate or subcordate base, margins entire, petiole long and slender: fr. in axillary pairs, sessile, glabrous, nearly globular, ½in. diam., dark purple. India, where it is a sacred tree.

8. **F. Parcellii,** Veitch. Shrub, with pubescent young growths: lvs. thin, oblong-oval or -ovate, 4–8 in. long, acuminate, short-petioled, obliquely subcordate at base, thinly hairy

particularly beneath, green above and strongly marked with cream-white mosaic, lighter beneath, margins sinuate: fr. axillary, globular, short-peduncled, pubescent, often 3-colored. (Bears the name of Mr. Parcell, collector for an Australian firm.) Pacific isls.—Often grown under glass.

9. **F. ulmifolia,** Lam. Tall shrub with rough and hispid twigs: lvs. variable, oblong or elliptic, very rough on both surfaces, abruptly mostly long-pointed, narrow or rounded at base, short-petioled, undulate or dentate or sometimes deeply lobed, blade 5–8 in. long: fr. solitary or twin, axillary, peduncled, ovoid or ellipsoid, about ½in. long, orange-red or purplish. Philippines.

10. **F. rubiginosa,** Vent. (*F. australis*, Willd.). Spreading tree, throwing down roots that form trunks, the young parts rusty-pubescent: lvs. oval or elliptic, 3–4 (6) in. long, with short obtuse apex, rounded at base, margins entire, glabrous above and rusty-pubescent beneath, primary nerves 10–12 on either side with secondary ones between, petiole 1 in. or less long: fr. mostly in pairs, axillary, peduncled, globular, about ½in. diam., usually warty. Australia.

11. **F. benjamina,** L. Very large broad-headed tree with drooping branches, glabrous, the young trees with a light somewhat poplar-like aspect: lvs. small, 2–5 in. long, shining and moderately thick, oval to ovate-elliptic and ovate-lanceolate, rather abruptly narrowed into a short not sharp point, rounded or somewhat narrowed at base, finely many-nerved, margins entire, crinkled, petiole 1 in. or less long: fr. in sessile axillary pairs, globular or ovoid, ⅓in. diam., becoming dark red, or in var. **comosa,** Kurz, ¾in. diam. and yellow. (The name benjamina probably refers to the supposed relation of the tree to the source of a resin or benzoin early procured from the East.) India.

12. **F. macrophylla,** Desf. Moreton Bay Fig (from the inlet of that name in Queensland). Very large tree in its native place in N. New S. Wales and Queensland, glabrous: lvs. thick, oval, elliptic to oblong, to 10 in. long, obtuse, or only short-pointed, rounded or somewhat narrowed at base, margins entire, main lateral nerves 12—20 but secondary ones numerous, petiole 1–3 in. long, stipules often to 4 in. long and showy: fr. 3–4 together on a peduncle, globular or pyriform, nearly or quite 1 in. diam.—Planted in S. Calif.

13. **F. elastica,** Roxb. Rubber-Plant of greenhouses and living-rooms. A large forest tree in India and Malaya, often epiphytal part of its life, grown in its juvenile state as a pot- or tub-plant; source also of Assam or India rubber; glabrous throughout: lvs. very thick, deep glossy green (a variegated or yellowed form), with very many fine parallel side-nerves, 5–12 in. long, oblong or elliptic with a rather short sharp point, rounded or somewhat narrowed at base, petiole stout and 1–2 in. long, stipules about one-half as long as lvs.: fr. in pairs in old axils, sessile, oblong, yellowish, about ½in. long.

14. **F. racemosa,** L. (*F. glomerata*, Roxb.). Cluster Fig. Tree, making dense shade, young growths glabrous or nearly so: lvs. ovate to oblong, 4–6 or 7 in. long, strongly marked with 4–8 lateral nerves, short-acute, base rounded, margin entire, mostly glabrous above and either pubescent or glabrous beneath, petiole 1–2 in. long: fr. several or many on short scaly leafless branchlets, about 2 in. diam., top-shaped to nearly globular, reddish, with a delicate sweet flavor. India.

15. **F. diversifolia,** Blume (*F. lutescens*, Desf.). Mistletoe Fig (bears resemblance to mistletoe in foliage and is sometimes epiphytal). Shrub or small tree, but grown as a pot-plant, glabrous, young parts with caducous scales: lvs. various on same shoot, some of them perhaps elliptic but most of them broadly obovate with wide rounded top, 2 in. or less long, entire, tapering into a very short petiole, with small dark glands beneath in the axils of veins: fr. single or twin in the axils, peduncled, nearly globose to pyriform, ¼–⅓in. diam., yellow. Malaya.

16. **F. retusa,** L. (*F. nitida*, Thunb.). Large evergreen, producing few aërial roots, glabrous: lvs. broad-ovate to rhomboid-elliptic, apiculate, narrowed at base, 2–4 in. long, petiole ½in. or less long: fr. about ⅓in. diam., sessile in pairs at axils, purplish. India.

17. **F. indica,** L. Large wide-spreading leafy tree, shoots glabrous: lvs. thick, small, 3–6 or 7 in. long, oblong or elliptic, cuspidate, base narrowed and with 2 prominent nerves, main nerves 4–6 on either side, glabrous, finely pimpled at least above, petiole ½in. long but sometimes to 1 in.: fr. in pairs, sessile, about ⅓in. diam., mostly globose, smooth, yellowish-red. Burma, Malaya.—Often called "Evergreen" in the W. Indies.

18. **F. Lacor,** Buch.-Ham. (*F. infectoria*, Roxb. *F. lucescens*, Blume). Deciduous, glabrous: lvs. thin, ovate or oblong-ovate, 3–7 in. long, acuminate, base rounded, margins entire but slightly crinkled, petiole 1½–2 in. and slender: fr. in pairs in axils, sessile, globose, ½in. diam., whitish tinged red and dotted. (Lacor: vernacular name.) India.

19. **F. bengalensis, L.** Banyan. Large evergreen tree reaching 100 ft. and extending laterally indefinitely by sending down trunks from the branches, young growths pubescent: lvs. ovate to orbicular-ovate and elliptic, 4–8 in. long, obtuse, rounded to truncate at base, margins entire, more or less minutely soft-pubescent on both surfaces, petiole long or short: fr. in axillary pairs, sessile, about ½in. diam., globose, slightly pubescent, red. India.

20. **F. altissima,** Blume. Large spreading tree, with young parts lightly pubescent, aërial roots many: lvs. thick, oval or ovate-elliptic, 4–6 (8) in. long, with a short obtusely cuspidate apex, base rounded but not cordate, margins entire, glabrous both surfaces, petiole 2 in. or less long: fr. in axillary pairs, sessile, when young inclosed in pubescent bracts, about ¾in. diam. when mature and yellow to orange. India to China and the Philippines.

21. **F. Nekbudu,** Warb. (*F. utilis*, Sim). Great forest tree, yielding cloth for the natives in trop. Afr., where it is native; young growth closely pubescent: lvs. standing nearly horizontal, thick, 6–15 in. long, elliptic or somewhat obovate, rounded or with slight obtuse elevation at apex, rounded or slightly subcordate at base, glabrous both sides, with about 5 or 6 strong distant side veins, margins entire, petiole 2–4 in. long: fr. sessile, mostly in pairs in the axils, nearly globular, about ½in. diam., pubescent. (Nekbudu is apparently an African vernacular name.)—Grown somewhat under glass for decoration.

6. **CANNABIS,** L. Strong-smelling stout erect ann. herbs, in temp. parts of Asia, regarded as a single species, widely grown for fiber.—Diœcious, rarely monœcious; fls. regular, the staminate in long-panicled racemes, the pistillate in short leafy axillary glomerules or spikes; stamens 5, drooping, sepals free; pistillate fl. in the axil of a small inclosing bract, the inconspicuous calyx closely adherent to the long ovary, stigmas 2, caducous: fr. a somewhat compressed seed-like achene, held in the persistent bract. (Can-nabis: the ancient Greek and Latin name.)

C. sativa, L. (*C. gigantea*, Hort., a robust form). HEMP. MARIJUANA. Leafy rough-puberulent herb, branched or nearly simple, 3–12 (16) ft.: lvs. alternate, thin, long-petioled, the blade digitate with 3–7 (11) long lanceolate or linear-lanceolate large-toothed long-acuminate lfts.—To be grown under government permit.

7. **HUMULUS,** L. HOP. Three species of rough-stemmed twining annuals and perennials in north temp. zone, grown for ornament, and also for the hops.—Lvs. opposite: diœcious; staminate fls. in panicled tassel-like racemes, with 5-parted calyx and 5 erect stamens; pistillate fls. 2 together under large imbricating persistent bracts in a spike that at maturity may form a cone-like body or "hop," each fl. with an entire calyx that embraces the ovary and 2 caducous stigmas: fr. an achene in the enlarged tight calyx. (Hu-mulus: late Latin name of uncertain derivation.)

A. Lvs. deeply 5–7-lobed: pistillate catkins (hops) not greatly enlarging in fr., the bracts narrow and acuminate: grown for ornament........................1. *H. scandens*
AA. Lvs. mostly 3-lobed: pistillate catkins much enlarging, becoming cone-like, the scales broad and obtuse or only short-acute: grown mostly for the hops.
B. Terminal lobe of main lvs. usually not more than one and a half times as long as broad........................2. *H. Lupulus*
BB. Terminal lobe of main lvs. usually at least twice as long as broad........................3. *H. americanus*

1. **H. scandens,** Merr. (*Antidesma scandens*, Lour. *H. japonicus*, Sieb. & Zucc.). JAPANESE HOP. Grown as an ann. from Japan and China, also more or less spontaneous in this country: rapid-growing tall twiner: lvs. 5–7-lobed mostly much beyond the middle, coarsely serrate, petiole mostly equalling or exceeding the blade, very rough above, less rough and often pubescent beneath: staminate fls. small, in long narrow open panicles (6–10 in. long) with long-peduncled parts: fruiting spikes nearly globular, few-fld., not much enlarging at maturity, the scales narrow and long-acuminate and not covering the achenes, ciliate on margins and not resinous-dotted, remaining nearly or quite green. Var. **variegatus,** Hort., has lvs. irregularly variegated with white.

2. **H. Lupulus,** L. EUROPEAN HOP. Per.: lvs. mostly 3-, sometimes 5- or even 7-lobed, to the middle or a little more, or often less deeply, the points abrupt and short or often obtuse, terminal lobe broad (not more than one and a half times as long as broad), those in the infl. often not lobed, margins coarsely serrate or dentate, very rough above but little rough beneath and with rather sparse glands beneath, petiole usually not exceeding and often not equalling the blade: staminate fls. in less diffuse panicles than in *H. scandens* and with shorter-peduncled parts, the anthers with usually less than 10 glands, the perianth with few or no glands: fruiting spikes oblong, 1–2 in. long at maturity, the thin light colored scales then large and nearly or quite obtuse and covering the achene, finely resinous-dotted and little or not at all ciliate. (Lupulus: diminutive of *lupus*, wolf; the plant was called *lupus salictarius* by Pliny, the "willow wolf," because it clings tenaciously to willows and osiers.) Eu., Asia; escaped in N. Amer. Var. **aureus,** Hort., has yellow lvs.—The common hop of hop-yards; also sometimes grown for ornament and screens.

3. **H. americanus,** Nutt. AMERICAN HOP. Lobes of lvs. 3, sometimes 5–11, attenuate at apex and more finely serrate, the terminal lobe narrow (at least twice as long as broad), stipules often reflexed, glands on under surface more numerous: secondary parts of staminate panicle more open, the pedicels usually curved at right angles beneath the fl., the

glands on anthers commonly more than 10, the perianth conspicuously glandular: hop with a stronger odor, the scales probably more acuminate. N. S. to Fla. and Ariz.—Apparently yielding hop-yard vars. as the "Oregon Cluster."

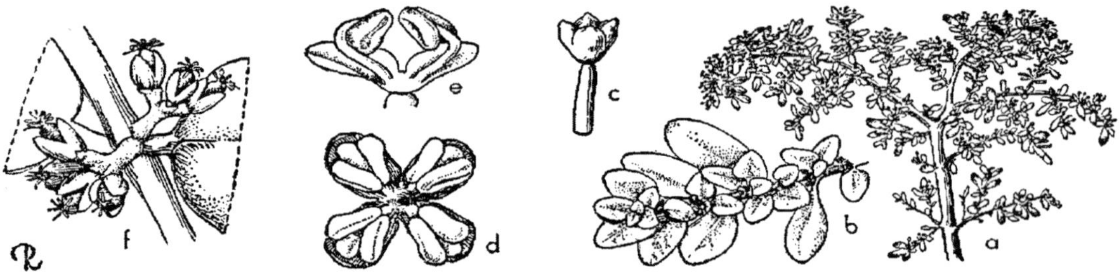

Fig. 53. URTICACEÆ. *Pilea microphylla:* a, flowering branch, × ½; b, same, × 3; c, staminate flower-bud, × 5; d, staminate flower, face view, × 15; e, same, vertical section, × 15; f, pistillate flowers, × 5.

53. URTICACEÆ. NETTLE FAMILY

Upwards of 40 genera and about 500 species are recognized in many parts of the world, chiefly trop.; a very few are grown for ornament and fiber.—Herbs, shrubs, and trees, some of them annuals and a few climbers, often bearing stinging hairs: lvs. alternate or opposite, simple: fls. bisexual or unisexual (the latter in ours), small and mostly inconspicuous, variously disposed in cymes, small clusters or rarely on a fleshy receptacle; staminate fl. mostly with a 4–5-parted calyx, the lobes sometimes bearing appendages, the stamens usually of same number as lobes; pistillate fls. with tubular or 3–5-parted calyx, the ovary solitary, 1-celled and 1-ovuled, stigma single but various: fr. a small achene, more or less invested by the enlarging dry or succulent calyx.

A. Plant 3–6 ft. high: lvs. 3–6 in. long....................1. BŒHMERIA
AA. Plant not over 15 in. high: lvs. not exceeding 2 in. long.
  B. Fls. in cymes: lvs. opposite, ¼–2 in. long....................2. PILEA
  BB. Fls. solitary: lvs. alternate, mostly less than ¼ in. long....................3. HELXINE

1. **BŒHMERIA,** Jacq. More than 50 species of herbs, shrubs and trees, mostly native in warm regions; one is an important fiber plant.—Lvs. opposite or alternate: diœcious or monœcious, the fls. in globose or elongated clusters or spikes; staminate fls. with 3–5-parted calyx and as many stamens; pistillate fls. with tubular 2–4-toothed calyx, usually contracted at top, persistent and inclosing the achene as a dry envelope; style long and slender, hairy or papillose on one side. (Bœhme-ria: Georg Rudolph Böhmer, 1723–1803, German botanist.)

B. nivea, Gaud. (*Urtica nivea,* L.). RAMIE. CHINESE SILK-PLANT. An important fiber plant in trop. and subtrop. countries, native in China, Japan, and Malayan Isls., sometimes grown in the warmer parts of this country; also ornamental because of the felt-white under surfaces of the broad-ovate abruptly acuminate coarsely toothed long-petioled alternate lvs. 3–6 in. long; erect-branched shrub or herb, 3–6 ft. or more: fls. small, in axillary panicles usually shorter than the petioles; monœcious, the staminate fls. in lower part of infl.

2. **PILEA,** Lindl. (*Adicea,* Raf.). About 200 ann. and per. herbs and subshrubs in many countries, mostly in warm regions, a very few grown for ornament.—Lvs. opposite, usually petiolate, stipules connate: plants diœcious or monœcious; fls. unisexual, in small axillary cymes or sometimes paniculate; staminate fls. 4- (2–3-) parted, stamens of same number as segms.; pistillate calyx 3-parted with unequal segms. and a scale-like staminode before each, stigma sessile, brush-like: fr. an achene somewhat invested in persistent calyx-segms. (Pi-lea: from *pileus,* the Roman felt cap, because of the calyx-covering of achene.)

A. Lvs. entire, 1-nerved from base, glabrous....................1. *P. microphylla*
AA. Lvs. crenate, 3-nerved from base, pubescent.
  B. St. creeping: lvs. orbicular, less than 1 in. long....................2. *P. nummularifolia*
  BB. St. erect: lvs. ovate to obovate, to 2 in. long....................3. *P. involucrata*

1. **P. microphylla,** Liebm. (*Parietaria microphylla,* L. *Pilea callitrichoides,* Kunth. *P. muscosa,* Lindl. *P. serpyllifolia,* Hort. not Wedd.). ARTILLERY PLANT. Grown in greenhouses and in the open far S. as a border plant, its fine close foliage and habit being ornamental; the staminate fls. open forcibly in a sunny place, with an artillery-like discharge of pollen: plant much-branching, 2–15 in. high, the sts. succulent and glabrous, small plants sometimes almost prostrate, ann. or bien.: lvs. of two sizes, the larger with blade about ¼in. long and petiole shorter than lf., the opposite one usually much smaller, oblong to spatulate, entire; smaller lvs. commonly much less than half the size and clustered in the axils: monœcious or diœcious; fls. minute on short-stalked clusters shorter than the lvs. S. Fla., trop. Amer.—Variable in stature, thickness and size of lvs.

2. **P. nummularifolia,** Wedd. (*Urtica nummularifolia,* Sw.). CREEPING CHARLEY. Creeping rooting per. covering mounds in trop. and subtrop. regions and sometimes grown in hanging-baskets and vases, hairy: lvs. nearly orbicular, ¾in. or less across, rounded at base, petioled, crenate, hairy: usually diœcious; fl.-clusters axillary, very small. W. Indies, Panama to Peru.

3. **P. involucrata,** Urban (*Urtica involucrata,* Sims). PANAMIGO. Sts. erect, repent only at base, hirsute: lvs. ovate to obovate, ⅓–2 in. long, rounded at apex, usually rounded at base, crenate, pubescent on both surfaces, purplish beneath: fls. in many-fld. cymes. Panama and W. Indies to Colombia and Venezuela.

3. **HELXINE,** Req. One species in Corsica and Sardinia, making a matted moss-like covering and used on rock-work and sometimes on greenhouse benches.—Lvs. alternate: monœcious; fls. minute, solitary in axils; staminate fls. with 4-parted calyx and 4 stamens, with a 3-lvd. involucre; pistillate calyx tubular, 4-lobed, contracted at mouth, with 1-lvd. 3-lobed involucre: achene ovoid, included in the enlarged involucre. (Helxi-ne: from the Greek name of the pellitory, a related plant.)

H. Soleirolii, Req. BABYS-TEARS. Delicate little creeping sparsely-hairy plant with very many sts.: lvs. mostly less than ¼in. across, of different sizes, unequal-sided, nearly orbicular, very short-petioled. (Capt. Soleirol, born 1791, collector in Corsica.)

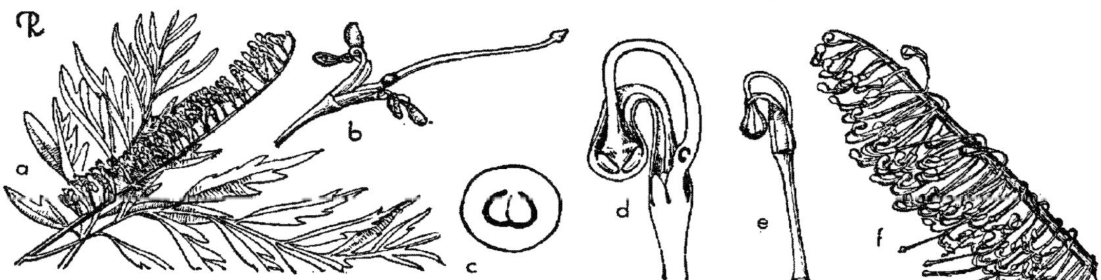

Fig. 54. PROTEACEÆ. *Grevillea robusta:* a, inflorescence and leaf, × ¼; b, flower, × 1; c, ovary, cross-section, × 10; d, flower (before anthesis), vertical section, × 2; e, same, habit, × 1; f, inflorescence, × ½.

54. PROTEACEÆ. PROTEA FAMILY

Trees or shrubs, rarely per. herbs, of 50 or more genera and about 1,000 species, native in Australia, S. Afr., trop. E. Asia and trop. S. Amer., yielding ornamental plants and one recommended for edible nuts.—Lvs. alternate or scattered, rarely opposite or verticillate, usually coriaceous, entire, toothed or variously divided, exstipulate: fls. solitary or in pairs in the axils of persistent or deciduous bracts, borne in racemes, spikes, umbels or heads, bisexual or rarely unisexual; perianth inferior, of one series (apetalous), composed of 4 sepals valvate in the bud, with tube cylindrical or dilated toward base and globular ovoid limb; stamens 4, opposite perianth-segms. and usually inserted on them; ovary 1-celled, sessile or stipitate, sometimes with hypogynous scales or annular or cupular disk at base; ovules 1 to many, pendulous or parietal; style terminal, undivided, with small terminal or lateral stigma: fr. a nut, drupe, caps. or follicle; seeds often compressed and winged.

A. Lvs. verticillate, in 3's or 4's..1. MACADAMIA
AA. Lvs. alternate or scattered.
  B. Fls. solitary in the axils of bracts; plant diœcious........................2. LEUCADENDRON
  BB. Fls. in pairs in axils of bracts which may be deciduous, bisexual.
    C. Seed with long terminal wing: fls. (in ours) in heads, clusters or very short racemes..3. HAKEA
    CC. Seed without long terminal wing: fls. (in ours) in racemes 1–6 in. long........4. GREVILLEA

1. **MACADAMIA,** F. Muell. A half dozen or more trees or tall shrubs native in Australia, one species cult. in warm countries for its nuts.—Lvs. verticillate, entire or serrate: fls. small, bisexual, pedicellate in pairs, in terminal or axillary racemes; bracts small, caducous; perianth regular or nearly so; stamens inserted a little below perianth-limb, filaments short; ovary sessile, with long straight style ovoid or clavate at end and small terminal stigma; ovules 2; hypogynous glands 4, distinct or united into cup or ring around the ovary: fr. a globular follicle containing a single thick-shelled indehiscent "nut." (Macada-mia: after John Macadam, M.D., 1827–1865, Sec. Philosophical Institute, Victoria, Australia.)

M. ternifolia, F. Muell. QUEENSLAND NUT. Upright tree to 50 ft., with very dense foliage, glabrous or young branches and infl. minutely pubescent: lvs. in whorls of 3 or 4, short-petioled, glabrous and shining, oblong or lanceolate, entire or remotely serrate with fine or prickly teeth, from few in. to 1 ft. or more long: racemes often as long as lvs.; fls. ivory-white, about ¼in. across: fr. with 2-valved leathery exocarp. Queensland, New S. Wales.

2. **LEUCADENDRON,** R. Br. Trees or shrubs native in S. Afr., of about 70 species, one grown in warm countries for its silvery foliage.—Lvs. scattered, narrow or even needle-like, entire, with hardened apex, glabrous or silvery-tomentose: diœcious; fls. regular, solitary in axils of bracts; staminate fls. numerous, in terminal sessile heads, sometimes involucrate, the perianth-segms. separated to middle or beyond, the anthers sessile at base of perianth-limb; pistillate fls. subtended by woody bracts and aggregated into cone-like heads, with linear staminodia, slender terminal style and solitary ovule: fr. a broad nut. (Leucaden-dron: Greek for *white tree*.)

L. argenteum, R. Br. SILVER-TREE. Evergreen tree to 30 ft., with densely pubescent leafy branches: lvs. alternate, sessile, lanceolate, 3–6 in. long, densely pubescent on both surfaces with silvery silky hairs: involucres spreading, longer than the globular showy head of fls.: nut oblong-obovoid, with persistent calyx and style. S. Afr.

3. **HAKEA,** Schrad. About 100 species of evergreen shrubs or low trees native in Australia, many planted for ornament in warm countries.—Lvs. alternate, of diversified shape: fls. bisexual, irregular or rarely regular, in pairs in the axils of deciduous bracts, crowded in close axillary racemes or globose clusters; perianth-tube slender, usually recurved beneath the limb, which is mostly globose, the 4 lobes cohering long after the tube has opened; anthers sessile at the base of the concave perianth-lobes; ovary stipitate, 2-ovuled; style long or short, dilated at end: fr. a hard woody caps. opening in 2 valves; seeds 2, compressed, with long terminal wings which are sometimes continued down the sides. (Ha-kea: after Baron von Hake, 1745–1818, German friend of botany.)

A. Lvs. flat, ¼in. or more wide.
  B. Fls. white: lvs. obscurely pinnately-veined. . . . . 1. *H. saligna*
  BB. Fls. crimson: lvs. parallel-veined. . . . . 2. *H. laurina*
AA. Lvs. terete, needle-like.
  B. Lf. pinnately parted. . . . . 3. *H. suaveolens*
  BB. Lf. entire. . . . . 4. *H. gibbosa*

1. **H. saligna,** Knight. A pale or grayish shrub to 8 ft., glabrous except the young shoots: lvs. entire, short-petioled, oblong or lanceolate, 3–6 in. long, ¼in. or more wide, obtuse but usually with callus tip, obscurely pinnately-veined: fls. white, in small dense sessile cluster: caps. about 1 in. long, rough or covered with tubercles, with short incurved beak. Queensland, New S. Wales.

2. **H. laurina,** R. Br. (*H. eucalyptoides*, Meissn.). SEA URCHIN. Tall tree-like shrub attaining 30 ft.: lvs. entire, lanceolate or narrowly elliptic, 3–6 in. long, ½–1 in. wide, tapering to a very short petiole, with 3–7 prominent nearly parallel veins, glabrous, pale gray-green: fls. crimson, in dense globular sessile clusters, the globular rachis densely villous; styles golden-yellow, projecting nearly 1 in.: caps. ovoid, about 1¼ in. long, short-beaked, nearly smooth. W. Australia.

3. **H. suaveolens,** R. Br. (*H. pectinata*, Colla). Dense rounded shrub to 10 ft. or more: lvs. 2–4 in. long, terete, spiny-tipped, usually branched into 2–15 rigid terete lobes of unequal length: fls. white, fragrant, in dense short racemes; pedicels and perianth glabrous: caps. ovoid, about 1 in. long, glabrous but corrugated, with small incurved beak. W. Australia.

4. **H. gibbosa,** Cav. Spreading shrub to 10 ft., twigs and young branches hirsute: lvs. terete, entire, rigid, with spiny tips, 1–3 in. long: fls. white, in sessile clusters; pedicels densely pubescent but corolla glabrous: fr. ovoid, oblique, about 1½ in. long, nearly 1 in. broad, abruptly narrowed to short oblique beak. New S. Wales.

4. **GREVILLEA,** R. Br. Trees or shrubs, of perhaps 200 species mostly native in Australia, several grown out-of-doors in warm countries and *G. robusta* also as a pot-plant farther N.—Very closely allied to Hakea from which it is not distinct in any one organ, but differs in the seed being bordered all around by a membranaceous wing or narrowly winged at the end or outer margin only or wingless, and the infl. being prevailingly terminal and often showy. (Grevil-lea: after Charles F. Greville, once vice-president of the Royal Society of England, and a patron of botany in the early part of the 19th century.)

A. Length of lvs. 6–12 in.
  B. Lvs. 2-pinnatifid..1. *G. robusta*
  BB. Lvs. pinnate or deeply pinnatifid........................2. *G. Banksii*
AA. Length of lvs. 1–2 in.
  B. Lvs. with numerous filiform divisions....................3. *G. Thelemanniana*
  BB. Lvs. entire..4. *G. obtusifolia*

1. **G. robusta,** Cunn. SILK-OAK. A robust tree sometimes attaining 150 ft., but known in the N. only as a greenhouse plant 2–5 ft. high; young branches hoary or rusty-tomentose: lvs. 2-pinnatifid, the secondary lobes entire or again lobed, lanceolate, the margins recurved, silky beneath: fls. orange, in secund racemes 3–4 in. long which are solitary or several together on short leafless branches of the old wood; ovary glabrous, stipitate; style long: fr. broad, very oblique, about ¾ in. long. Queensland, New S. Wales.—There is a var. with silvery foliage and deep bright red fls., and others of compact and pyramidal habit.

2. **G. Banksii,** R. Br. Tall shrub or slender tree to 20 ft., the branches and infl. rusty-tomentose: lvs. pinnate or deeply pinnatifid, the segms. 3–13 and broad-linear or lanceolate, silky beneath, margins revolute: fls. red, in dense erect secund racemes 2–4 in. long which are solitary or 2 or 3 together on a terminal leafless peduncle; ovary sessile, densely villous; style very long: fr. obliquely ovate, villous, 1 in. or less long. (After Sir Joseph Banks, page 39.) Queensland.

3. **G. Thelemanniana,** Hueg. Spreading shrub to 5 ft.: lvs. pale or glaucous, heath-like, 1–2 in. long, divided into numerous terete slender linear pinnæ, the lower pinnæ usually again divided: fls. pink with green tips, in terminal dense secund racemes 1½ in. or less long; style about twice as long as perianth; ovary glabrous, on a long stipe: fr. smooth, about ½ in. long. (Named for C. Thelemann, 1811–1889, a German.) S. and W. Australia.

4. **G. obtusifolia,** Meissn. Spreading or procumbent shrub: lvs. oblong-linear or linear-spatulate, ¾–1¼ in. long, obtuse, tapering to a short petiole, margins entire and revolute, glabrous above, rusty-pubescent beneath: fls. in loose secund more or less recurved subsessile racemes 1–1½ in. long; ovary glabrous, stipitate, with long style: fr. about ½ in. long, nearly smooth. W. Australia.

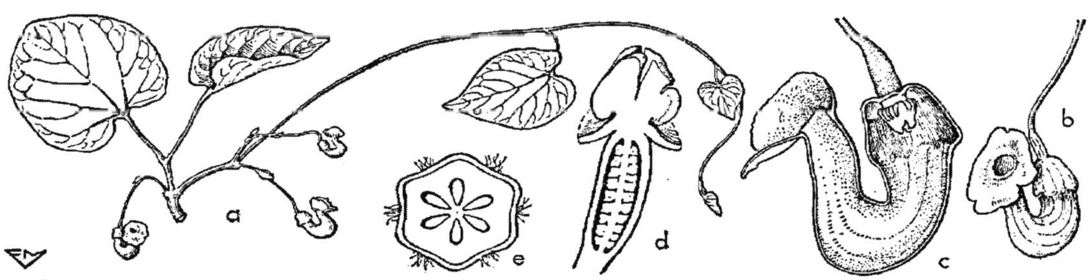

Fig. 55. ARISTOLOCHIACEÆ. *Aristolochia durior:* a, flowering branch, × ⅙; b, flower, × ½; c, flower, perianth excised, × 1; d, same, in vertical section, perianth removed, × 2; e, ovary, cross-section, × 6.

55. ARISTOLOCHIACEÆ. BIRTHWORT FAMILY

Herbs or woody plants, the latter usually climbing, of 5 genera and about 200 species, distributed in warm regions, most numerous in S. Amer.—Lvs. alternate, petiolate, often cordate, entire or 3–5-lobed: fls. medium or large, rarely small, lurid greenish-yellow, purple or variegated, often carrion-scented, bisexual, epigynous; perianth (calyx) simple, usually 3-lobed, petaloid, very diverse; petals 0 in ours;

stamens 6–36, free and inserted on the ovary or united with the style; ovary inferior, rarely superior, 4–6-celled (rarely 5), ovules many, placentation axile; styles united into column, stigmas 4–6: fr. a caps.

A. Plant a woody climber (in ours): perianth irregular........................1. ARISTOLOCHIA
AA. Plant an acaulescent herb: perianth regular........................2. ASARUM

1. **ARISTOLOCHIA, L.** BIRTHWORT. About 180 species, two rather commonly grown in greenhouses and one, *A. durior*, as a porch vine.—Herbs with per. rhizomes, woody climbers, rarely arborescent: fls. irregular and of many forms, axillary, solitary, fascicled or in short racemes; perianth tubular, variously bent; stamens usually 6, placed in a row about the style and united with it; ovary inferior, 6-celled (rarely 5 or 4). (Aristolo-chia: Greek, referring to medicinal qualities.)

A. Limb of perianth 6 in. or more across, with long tails........................1. *A. grandiflora*
AA. Limb of perianth 3 in. or less across.
B. Perianth-limb about 3 in. across, entire........................2. *A. elegans*
BB. Perianth-limb 1 in. or less across, 3-lobed.
C. Fls. glabrous outside........................3. *A. durior*
CC. Fls. pubescent outside........................4. *A. tomentosa*

1. **A. grandiflora,** Sw. (*A. gigas*, Lindl.). PELICAN-FLOWER. Climbing shrub, becoming glabrous: lvs. cordate-acuminate, 3–5 in. diam.: peduncles solitary, bracteate, exceeding the petiole; tube of perianth inflated, contracted in middle, yellowish-green; limb greatly expanded, several in. across, cordate-ovate, wavy margined, with long slender tail, blotched and veined with purple. Jamaica. Var. **Sturtevantii,** W. Wats., is the commonest form in cult., having very large fls. and a tail sometimes 3 ft. long; it was brought prominently to notice by E. D. Sturtevant, Bordentown, N. J., later of Calif.

2. **A. elegans,** Mast. CALICO-FLOWER. Slender glabrous climber; flowering branches pendulous, filiform: lvs. long-petioled, broadly reniform-cordate, 2–3 in. long, basal lobes rounded, tip rounded or obtuse; stipules falcately reniform or almost orbicular: fls. solitary, long-pedicelled, borne on young shoots; perianth-tube 1½ in. long, rather inflated, pale yellow-green, limb nearly circular, shallow, cordate at base, 3 in. diam., on outside white with red-purple veining, inside rich purple-brown. Brazil.

3. **A. durior,** Hill (*A. macrophylla*, Lam. *A. Sipho*, L'Her.). DUTCHMANS-PIPE. PIPE-VINE. Woody climber to 30 ft., nearly glabrous: lvs. 6–15 in. broad when mature, broadly reniform or rounded, becoming glabrous: peduncles solitary or 2–3 together in the axils, with large clasping bract: fls. U-shaped, inflated above the ovary, greenish-yellow, with 3-lobed spreading flat brown-purple limb about 1 in. across: caps. oblong-cylindric, 2–3 in. long, strongly parallel-nerved. Pa. to Ga., Minn. and Kans.

4. **A. tomentosa,** Sims. Woody climber to 30 ft., sts. woolly: lvs. orbicular-ovate, 3–6 in. long, usually rounded at apex, base open-cordate, pubescent on both surfaces: fls. U-shaped, greenish-yellow, pubescent outside, with a narrow purple mouth and a 3-lobed reflexed yellow limb about ¾in. across: caps. about 1 in. long. N. C. to Fla., Ill. and Mo.

2. **ASARUM, L.** WILD GINGER. About 12 species, native in north temp. regions. —Per. acaulescent herbs, with slender aromatic branched rootstalks: lvs. long-petioled, heart- or kidney-shaped, entire or crenulate: fls. solitary, borne near the ground, purplish or brown; calyx campanulate or hemispheric, with 3 regular lobes; corolla wanting or rudimentary; stamens 12, inserted on the ovary, filaments short, projecting beyond anthers; ovary partly or wholly inferior, 6-celled: caps. subglobose or hemispheric. (As-arum: ancient name, meaning not clear.)

A. Plant more or less pubescent: calyx-lobes longer than broad.
B. Calyx-lobes without a long-attenuate tip: plant deciduous........................1. *A. canadense*
BB. Calyx-lobes with long-attenuate tip to 3 in. long: plant evergreen........................2. *A. caudatum*
AA. Plant glabrous: calyx-lobes broader than long........................3. *A. Shuttleworthii*

1. **A. canadense,** L. WILD GINGER. CANADA SNAKEROOT. Deciduous: petioles 6–12 in. long, pubescent; lvs. usually 2 to a plant, reniform, 2–7 in. across, rounded to acute at apex, with a deep open sinus at base, not mottled, pubescent on both surfaces: fls. on slender peduncles, 1 in. or more across at the expanded mouth, purplish-brown, pubescent outside; ovary inferior: caps. ½–¾in. across. N. B. to N. C. and Mo.

2. **A. caudatum,** Lindl. Evergreen: petioles to 7 in. long, usually pubescent; lvs. 2 at a node, cordate or reniform, 2–6 in. across, acute to obtuse at apex, more or less cupped, usually somewhat pubescent on both surfaces: fls. short-stalked, calyx-lobes oblong or triangular and long-attenuate to 3 in. long, brownish-purple, usually pubescent outside; ovary inferior. B. C. to Calif.

3. **A. Shuttleworthii,** Britten (*Hexastylis Shuttleworthii*, Small). Evergreen: petioles 3–8 in. long, glabrous; lvs. 1 at a node, cordate to suborbicular-reniform, 2–3 in. across,

acutish, with a more or less open sinus, usually mottled, glabrous: fls. short-stalked, 1–2 in. long, mottled violet within, glabrous, calyx-lobes broad and often with incurved tips; ovary more or less free. (Named for Robert Shuttleworth, 19th century writer.) Va. to Ga. and Ala.

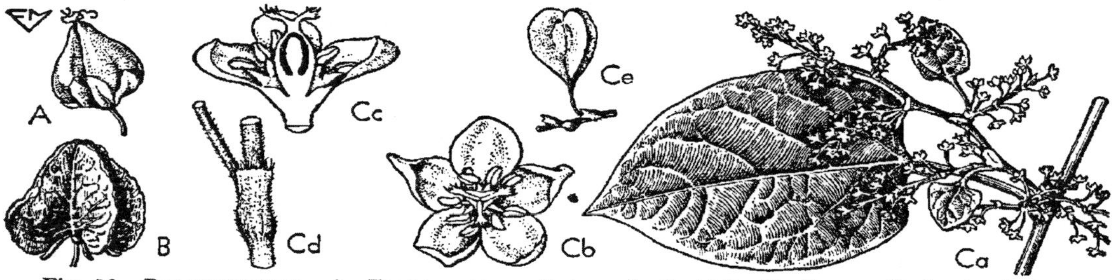

Fig. 56. POLYGONACEÆ. A, *Fagopyrum sagittatum:* fruit, × 2. B, *Rumex Patientia:* fruit, × 2. C, *Polygonum cuspidatum:* Ca, portion of inflorescence, × ½; Cb, flower, face view, × 5; Cc, flower, vertical section, × 5; Cd, stem, node and ocrea, × ½; Ce, fruit, × 1.

56. POLYGONACEÆ. BUCKWHEAT or KNOTWEED FAMILY

Herbs, shrubs, and trees, erect or climbing, of 30–40 genera and probably 800 species, widely distributed in both cold and warm countries; several species are grown for ornament and a few for food products.—Sts. jointed: lvs. simple, alternate, opposite or whorled, stipules commonly forming a sheath or ocrea: fls. small, unisexual or bisexual, mostly the latter, plants sometimes monœcious or diœcious; infl. spicate, racemose, paniculate, or otherwise, often becoming showy by the mass of little fls.; perianth of 1 or 2 series, more or less persistent, petals absent, the parts 2–6-cleft or parted, or sometimes distinct and sometimes developing wings, protuberances or spines; stamens 2–9, rarely more, mostly separate and opposite the perianth parts; pistil solitary and superior, mostly 1-celled but of 2–4 carpels, ovule 1, basal; style 2–4-cleft: fr. usually a lenticular or angled achene, sometimes inclosed in the enlarging perianth which forms a berry-like body.

A. Plants climbing.
  B. Lvs. orbicular, ¼–¾in. long.......... 8. MUEHLENBECKIA
  BB. Lvs. triangular or cordate-ovate to oblong-ovate, 1–3 in. long.
    C. Climbing by tendrils.......... 7. ANTIGONON
    CC. Climbing without tendrils.......... 1. POLYGONUM
AA. Plants not climbing.
  B. Sts. flattened, ½in. or more across.......... 9. HOMALOCLADIUM
  BB. Sts. round, not flattened.
    C. Plant a shrub or small tree.......... 10. COCCOLOBA
    CC. Plant not tree-like.
      D. Lvs. not over ¼in. long, glabrous.......... 8. MUEHLENBECKIA
      DD. Lvs. over ½in. long, or if shorter tomentose.
        E. Sheaths lacking at the nodes of st. and branches.
          F. Involucre 1–3 fld., with teeth spine-tipped.......... 5. CHORIZANTHE
          FF. Involucre many-fld., teeth without spines.......... 6. ERIOGONUM
        EE. Sheaths surrounding st. at the nodes, sometimes deciduous on old parts.
          F. Perianth-parts 5 (rarely 4), erect in fr. and equal, not much enlarging.
            G. Achene little if at all exceeding perianth: mostly perennials cult. for ornament.......... 1. POLYGONUM
            GG. Achene much exceeding perianth: annuals cult. for food grain.. 2. FAGOPYRUM
          FF. Perianth-parts 6 or more, inner ones erect and winged in fr. or the wings from the achene, outer ones reflexed and often smaller.
            G. Herbs stout and large with abundant broad basal lvs.: stamens usually 9.......... 3. RHEUM
            GG. Herbs weedy with many prominent st.-lvs.: stamens usually 6.. 4. RUMEX

1. POLYGONUM, L. KNOTWEED. Species about 200 if the genus is accepted broadly, widely spread over the earth from frigid to warm climates, several grown for ornament and interest.—Ann. and per. herbs (some common weeds, as the smartweeds), a few more or less woody, erect or climbers, sometimes aquatic and with floating lvs.; sts. usually manifestly jointed: lvs. various, almost linear, lanceolate, to broad-ovate and hastate, simple and entire, sheaths or ocreæ usually well developed: fls. small but often showy because of the numbers and the bright colors of perianth, on short jointed pedicels mostly in racemes, spikes or heads; perianth mostly 5-parted, often pink or red, the parts erect and all alike in fr.; stamens 3–9, usually 5, exserted or included; style 2–3-parted, the stigmas capitate: achene small, lenticular or triangular, nearly or quite covered by the persisting perianth; embryo on one side of albumen. (Polyg-onum: Greek *many-kneed*, from the jointed sts.)

A. Plant tall-twining.
  B. Fls. small, greenish-white or very pale in color; infl. mostly erect . . . . 1. *P. Aubertii*
  BB. Fls. larger, ¼in. or more across, bright rose; infl. mostly drooping . . . . 2. *P. baldschuanicum*
AA. Plant erect or spreading.
  B. Fls. in axillary clusters, greenish or whitish: grown primarily for the heavy foliage.
    C. Lvs. rounded to truncate at base . . . . 3. *P. cuspidatum*
    CC. Lvs. shallow-cordate at base . . . . 4. *P. sachalinense*
  BB. Fls. in conspicuous terminal peduncled spikes, pink, red or clear white: grown primarily for the bloom.
    C. Length of lvs. less than 1 in. . . . . 5. *P. vaccinifolium*
    CC. Length of lvs. 2–10 in.
      D. Lvs. mostly radical: plant to 18 in. high . . . . 6. *P. affine*
      DD. Lvs. cauline: plant 2–6 ft. high.
        E. Shape of lvs. broad-ovate: hairy ann. . . . . 7. *P. orientale*
        EE. Shape of lvs. ovate-lanceolate: nearly glabrous per. . . . . 8. *P. alpinum*

1. **P. Aubertii,** L. Henry. CHINA FLEECE-VINE. SILVER LACE-VINE. Tall vigorous hardy per. vine, twining, glabrous, 20 ft. or more: lvs. bronzy-red when young, ovate to oblong-ovate, slender-petioled, blade 1½–2½ in. long, thin, varying from pointed to nearly obtuse, at base mostly shallowly cordate, more or less shining, entire but more or less crinkled: fls. small, less than ¼in. across at full expansion, greenish-white or sometimes slightly pinkish, in long slender erect racemes that are branched or combined into a very open panicle, fragrant, 3 outer sepals winged: fr. not setting freely, whitish with brown bands. (Georges Aubert, 1871–, French missionary in Tibet.) W. China, Tibet.

2. **P. baldschuanicum,** Regel. Differs in its larger fls., which are ¼in. or more across and rose-colored, borne in denser drooping panicles and larger frs. which are usually borne in profusion. (Bears the geographical name Baldschuan.) Bokhara.

3. **P. cuspidatum,** Sieb. & Zucc. (*P. Sieboldii*, de Vriese. *P. Zuccarinii*, Small). JAPANESE KNOTWEED. MEXICAN-BAMBOO. Persistent stout per. 4–8 ft. high, forming large clumps, with long underground rhizomes; sts. simple or little branched, glabrous: lvs. short-oval to orbicular-ovate, 3–6 in. long, abruptly pointed, with an abrupt or truncate base, petiole about 1 in. long; sheaths short, deciduous: fls. small and greenish-white, pedicelled, numerous in slender axillary panicled racemes that usually do not equal or exceed the lvs., late summer and autumn; stamens 8: achene 3-sided in a broadly winged calyx. Japan; escaped in N. Amer. Var. **compactum,** Bailey (*P. compactum*, Hook. f. *P. Sieboldii* var. *compactum*, Bailey), is a closer-growing form about 2 ft. tall.—A related species is **P. Reynoutria,** Makino, hardy per. 4–6 in. high, grown as ground-cover; panicled racemes of pink fls. from deep red buds; Japan.

4. **P. sachalinense,** Fr. Schmidt. SACALINE. Larger than *P. cuspidatum*, very robust and spreading rapidly, 8–12 ft.: lvs. very large, the blades sometimes 1 ft. and more long, oval-oblong, shallowly cordate at base, not manifestly acuminate-pointed: fls. greenish, in rather short and close axillary clusters in autumn; stamens 8: achenes 3-sided. Saghalin Isl.—Recommended sometimes as a forage plant.

5. **P. vaccinifolium,** Wall. Woody per. to 1 ft., with trailing rooting branches, glabrous: lvs. elliptic, ½–¾in. long, acute at both ends, entire, glabrous, slightly glaucous beneath; sheaths laciniate, ⅓in. long: fls. rose-red, ⅓in. across, in dense upright spikes 1½–3 in. long. Himalayas.

6. **P. affine,** D. Don (*P. Brunonis*, Wall.). Tufted glabrous per. from long strong rootstocks, 12–18 in. high; sts. simple or forked: lvs. mostly radical, oblanceolate, 2–4½ in. long, tapering to petiole, obtuse or only short-acute, finely serrate; sheaths brown, long-produced opposite the lvs., lower ones split and frayed: fls. bright rose-red, in erect dense obtuse spikes 2–3 in. long, in autumn; stamens 8: achene 3-sided. High Himalayas.

7. **P. orientale,** L. PRINCES-FEATHER. Vigorous much-branched hairy ann. 4–6 ft. (but dwarfer races, 18–30 in. high, are in cult.): lvs. large, blade 4–10 in. long on lower parts, broad-ovate or somewhat narrower above, sometimes subcordate, acuminate-pointed; sheaths prominent, ciliate, sometimes with a spreading or reflexed border: fls. attractive, bright pink or rose-pink, in many dense long-peduncled cylindrical spikes 1–3½ in. long, more or less curved or nodding, in autumn; stamens usually 7, somewhat exserted. Asia, Australia; sometimes spontaneous.

8. **P. alpinum,** All. Stout branching per. to 2–3 ft. or more, with glabrous sts. and short ciliate sheaths: lvs. lanceolate to ovate-lanceolate, 3–6 in. long, very long-acuminate, thinly hairy beneath and ciliate on margins: fls. numerous, snow-white, in many panicled racemes, in summer; sepals blunt; stigmas 3. Alps and Asia.—Has been cult. as *P. sericeum* (not *P. sericeum*, Pall.).

2. **FAGOPYRUM,** Gaertn. BUCKWHEAT. About a half dozen ann. or per. soft-stemmed herbs of Eu. and Asia.—Distinguished technically from Polygonum by the achene prominently projecting beyond the persisting old perianth, and the embryo contained within the albumen: quick-growing usually glabrous plants with alternate deltoid or hastate more or less angle-lobed lvs., and small white fls. in racemes or rather dense corymbs; stamens 8, included or only slightly exserted; styles 3, stigmas capitate: fr. a triangular-pointed achene. (Fagopy-rum: Greek *beech wheat,* from the likeness of the achene to a small beech-nut; *buckwheat* is of similar significance: German *buche,* beech.)—The genus is sometimes limited to the 2 following ann. species.

A. Racemes slender and open, from axils along the st., not aggregated at summit: fr. with obtuse often corrugated angles..1. *F. tataricum*
AA. Racemes short and dense, mostly aggregated into dense clusters: fr. with sharp continuous angles..2. *F. esculentum*

1. **F. tataricum,** Gaertn. INDIA-WHEAT. Slender plant, 1½–2 ft.: st.-lvs. rather small, blade 1–2 in. long and breadth often greater than length, broadly halberd-shaped with wide-spreading basal lobes mostly acute, petiole very slender: racemes remote in the axils, loosely fld., not aggregated; fls. small, greenish or yellowish: fr. ⅙in. long, with rounded or obtuse often wavy or corrugated angles, and a sulcus or groove between, oblong-pointed rather than triangular in form, gray. India.—Sometimes grown for the grain, and also escaped; known also as Tartarian, Iceland, Kangra, Rye buckwheat, and as Duck-wheat.

2. **F. esculentum,** Moench (*F. sagittatum,* Gilib.). COMMON BUCKWHEAT. A stouter plant than no. 1: lvs. mostly larger, 1–3 in. long, and stronger-petioled, triangular-ovate, manifestly pointed, the basal lobes mostly acute: fls. much larger, white and fragrant, with honey-bearing glands, in short and dense racemes or clusters mostly at or near the summit of the plant: fr. larger, ¼–⅓in. long, with sharp continuous angles and flat or not grooved sides, distinctly triangular, mostly bright brown. Probably Cent. or N. Asia.—Much cult. and sometimes spontaneous; the Silver Hull, Japanese, and other buckwheats belong here.

3. **RHEUM,** L. Stout per. herbs of Asia, probably 25 species, with clumps of large radical lvs. and erect towering fl.-sts., one grown in the vegetable-garden and others sometimes for ornament.—Lvs. broad and large, entire or divided; sheaths long and prominent: fls. bisexual, greenish or whitish, small but numerous, pedicelled, in panicled fascicles or racemes, the perianth not much enlarging in fr. and the outer parts reflexed; perianth 6-parted and open or spreading; stamens mostly 9, sometimes as few as 6; styles 3: achene becoming strongly winged. (Rhe-um: from *rha,* the old Greek word for rhubarb.)

A. Radical lvs. entire..1. *R. Rhaponticum*
AA. Radical lvs. deeply lobed..2. *R. palmatum*

1. **R. Rhaponticum,** L. GARDEN RHUBARB (sometimes called Pie-Plant and Wine-Plant). Grown for the thick edible petioles of radical lvs., cooked and eaten in spring: roots large, fleshy: lvs. mostly radical, cordate-ovate and entire but crinkled, the blade 12–18 in. or more long: fl.-sts. 4–6 ft., strict but more or less branching, hollow; fls. greenish-white, on slender jointed pedicels: fr. cordate-ovate, ¼–½in. long, winged. Siberia.—The specific name *Rhaponticum* (the Pontic Rha or rhubarb) is used tentatively; the common rhubarb is very likely a race of hybrids or variants.

2. **R. palmatum,** L. Grown for the bold effect of its foliage: radical lvs. broadly cordate or nearly orbicular, deeply palmately lobed, the lobes entire, dentate or pinnatifid: fl.-sts. 5–6 ft., the panicle leafy and branches pubescent, pedicels short. N. E. Asia. Var. **tanguticum,** Regel, has longer lvs. that are not so deeply lobed. The form known as *atrosanguineum* has a dark red panicle.

4. **RUMEX,** L. DOCK. SORREL. Weedy herbs, mostly per., a few grown for greens; species 125 or more, of wide distribution in temp. regions.—Sts. mostly leafy, in some species the lvs. radical, usually erect, more or less branched: lvs. various, sometimes hastate, mostly entire, in some species crinkled; sheaths usually breaking up and falling away early: fls. bisexual or unisexual (plants sometimes diœcious), on jointed pedicels, green, the perianth deeply 6-parted, the 3 outer parts remaining small and becoming reflexed, the 3 inner enlarging and winged and in some species 1 or all of them (called "valves") bearing a tubercle or grain at the center or base. (Ru-mex: the Latin name.)

A. Lvs., some or all, hastate, sour: fls. unisexual: sorrels.
  B. Plants 2–3 ft. high: lvs. usually much longer than broad..................1. *R. Acetosa*
  BB. Plants 4–20 in. high: lvs. usually about as broad as long..................2. *R. scutatus*
AA. Lvs. not hastate, and usually not sour: fls. mostly bisexual.
  B. Valves bearing tubercles: plants 3–6 ft. high..................3. *R. Patientia*
  BB. Valves without tubercles: plants 1½–3 ft. high..................4. *R. hymenosepalus*

1. **R. Acetosa,** L. GARDEN SORREL. Lvs. thin, light green, long-petioled, becoming subsessile high on the st., mostly oblong or oblong-oval in outline, to 7 in. long, obtuse or short-acute at apex, spear-lobed at base, margins entire and more or less crinkled: panicle erect and crowded, standing 2–3 ft. above ground: valves rounded, about ⅙in. long, very veiny, nearly or quite entire, cordate with a callosity or swelling below. (Acetosa is a pre-Linnæan generic or substantive name, from the acetose character of the plants.) Eu. and Asia; sparingly nat. in N. Amer.—Grown somewhat for the radical lvs. used as spring greens, Large Belleville being one cultivar.

2. **R. scutatus,** L. FRENCH SORREL. A low glaucous plant 4–20 in. high, with many branching prostrate or ascending sts., sometimes grown for greens: lvs. somewhat fleshy, petioled, cordate-ovate, obtuse, those of the st. hastate, sometimes more or less lobed: valves thin, cordate, without callosities. Eu., Asia.

3. **R. Patientia,** L. SPINACH-DOCK. HERB PATIENCE. Very stout, 3–6 ft., with a deep strong tap-root: lvs. long-elliptic-ovate, 1 ft. or more long and long-petioled, the upper st.-lvs. long-lanceolate, crinkled, and short-stalked or nearly sessile: infl. sometimes 2 ft. long, very heavy, dense in fr.: valves cordate, about ¼in. across, very veiny, entire or wavy-margined, one of them with a small tubercle or swelling near base. Eu., W. Asia; nat. in N. Amer.—Grown for early greens.

4. **R. hymenosepalus,** Torr. CANAIGRE. WILD RHUBARB. St. erect, 1½–3 ft., nearly simple, from a fascicle of spindle-shaped tubers (which produce tannin for which the plant is sometimes cult.): lvs. oblong to oblong-lanceolate, sometimes 1 ft. long, narrowed either way, crinkled, short-petioled; sheaths prominent: panicle 6–12 in. long; fls. bisexual, large: valves large, ½in. or more across at maturity, veiny and entire, rose-colored, without tubercles. Okla. to Calif.

5. **CHORIZANTHE,** R. Br. About 50 species of ann. or per. herbs, native in S. W. U. S., Mex. and Chile.—Sts. usually dichotomously branched: lvs. in basal rosettes, st.-lvs. commonly reduced: fls. in cymes, usually completely included in the 1-(3-)fld. involucre; involucre with 3–6 ribs and spiny teeth; perianth 6-lobed; stamens 9 (3 or 6), commonly included, mostly adnate to the base of the perianth; styles 3: achene 3-angled. (Chorizan-the: Greek for *divide* and *flower*, referring to the calyx.)

C. Palmeri, Wats. Erect ann. 4–8 in. tall, branching about the middle, short-tomentose: lvs. mostly basal, oblanceolate, 1–1½ in. long, petiolate, pubescent; cauline bracts foliar and whorled: fls. in dense bracteate cymes; involucre about ¼in. long. (Named for Dr. Edward Palmer, collector in California about the middle of last century.) Calif.—Sometimes planted for ornament.

6. **ERIOGONUM,** Michx. About 150 species of ann. or per. herbs, or sometimes shrubby, native for the most part in W. U. S.—Lvs. entire, exstipulate, alternate, opposite or whorled: involucre with 4–8 lobes or teeth, not spine-tipped, with several to many fls.; fls. perfect, on pedicels usually exserted from the involucre; calyx petaloid, 6-parted; stamens 9; styles 3: achene triangular. (Eriog-onum: Greek for *woolly joint.*)

A. Flowering st. umbellate at summit: lvs. ½–1 in. long..................1. *E. umbellatum*
AA. Flowering st. with one head: lvs. less than ½in. long..................2. *E. ovalifolium*

1. **E. umbellatum,** Torr. Per. to 1 ft.: lvs. basal, obovate to oval, ½–1 in. long, narrowing to petiole of about the same length, green and becoming glabrous above, white-tomentose beneath: bracteate umbel simple, with 5–10 (2–15) rays to 2 in. long; involucre tomentose, with 20–30 fls.; calyx yellow, glabrous. Wash. and Mont. to Calif.

2. **E. ovalifolium,** Nutt. Per., forming a low dense mat: lvs. obovate to oval, to ⅜in. long, petiolate, grayish-tomentose: flowering st. leafless, 1–5 in. high, tomentose, each st. bearing 1 head formed from several many-fld. involucres; calyx yellow, with pink or green veins, glabrous. B. C. to Calif. east to the Great Basin.

7. **ANTIGONON,** Endl. Three or 4 tendril-climbing vines of Mex. and Cent. Amer., one widely planted for ornament in warm and trop. countries.—St. slender: lvs. alternate, cordate to hastate, entire, petioled: fls. in racemes that terminate in a tendril; perianth of 5 parts, the 2 or 3 outer ones cordate or ovate and the inner ones

oblong, all parts colored and showy; stamens 8; styles 3: achene large, 3-angled, at least above, loosely covered in the enlarging papery perianth-parts. (Antig-onon: Greek, perhaps referring to jointed character of fl.-sts.)

A. leptopus, Hook. & Arn. CORAL-VINE. CORALLITA. ROSA-DE-MONTANA. PINK-VINE. CONFEDERATE-VINE. Attractive robust vine with slender racemes from the axils of cordate-ovate or hastate-ovate or triangular very veiny acutish to acuminate lvs. 1–3 in. long, the lower lvs. much larger: fls. bright pink, enlarging to 1½ in. long: achene conical, sharply 3-angled above, about ⅜in. long, much exceeded by the veiny persistent enlarged perianth. Mex.—Frequently white-fld.; the name White Corallita is sometimes applied improperly to Porana. Grown in southern states and Calif. and in tropics under several names.

8. **MUEHLENBECKIA,** Meissn. (conserved over the older name *Calacinum,* Raf.). More or less woody, erect or climbing, including species of widely different looks and habit, grown for ornament; species about 15, in southern temp. zone.—Lvs. alternate, with short sheathing stipules, or sometimes wanting: fls. unisexual, the plants polygamous or diœcious, small and not showy, fascicled in the axils or in short spikes or racemes; perianth deeply 5-parted, the outer parts becoming succulent; stamens commonly 8; style 1 or the parts not long, stigma 3-lobed: achene ovoid, 3-angled, inclosed in fleshy perianth, forming a berry-like body. (Muehlen-beck-ia: H. G. Muehlenbeck, a physician in Alsace, 1798–1845.)

A. Plant a tall climber: lvs. ¼–¾in. long........................1. *M. complexa*
AA. Plant small and bushy: lvs. ⅒–¼in. long........................2. *M. axillaris*

1. **M. complexa,** Meissn. (*Polygonum complexum,* Cunn. *Calacinum complexum,* Macb.). WIRE-PLANT. MAIDENHAIR-VINE. A tall climber on chimneys and elsewhere in Calif., and also grown in greenhouses and hanging-baskets, on the ground forming dense masses: diœcious: sts. slender and wiry, reddish, much-branched, more or less hairy or pubescent on the young parts: lvs. ¼–½ or ¾in. across, nearly or quite orbicular in outline, often contracted in the middle or fiddle-shaped, or even obscurely lobed, petiolate: fls. few in axillary and terminal spikes: fruiting perianth ¼–⅓in. diam., usually succulent, waxy-white, forming a cup or urn about the black achene. New Zeal.—Reported to be root-hardy without protection north to Philadelphia, Pa., and St. Louis, Mo.

2. **M. axillaris,** Walp. (*Polygonum axillare,* Hook. f. *Calacinum axillare,* Macb. *M. nana,* Thurston). A small plant with many slender branches forming sprawling or prostrate matted clumps about 1 ft. across, or sometimes straggling: lvs. oblong to orbicular, ⅒–¼ in. long, obtuse, petiolate: fls. 1 or 2 in axils, or rarely the staminate fls. in short terminal spikes: fruiting perianth usually succulent and white. New Zeal.

9. **HOMALOCLADIUM,** Bailey. A monotypic genus of distinct habit.—Branches flat, jointed, striate, glabrous: lvs. on young or sterile shoots; sheaths soon becoming vestigial: fls. bisexual, 1–7, in sessile clusters at the joints; perianth deeply 4–5-parted; styles 3: fr. berry-like, achene triangular and smooth. (Homalocla-dium: from Greek for *like* and *leaf-like branches.*)

H. platycladum, Bailey (*Polygonum platycladum,* F. Muell. *Muehlenbeckia platyclados,* Meissn. *Calacinum platycladum,* Macb.). RIBBON-BUSH. CENTIPEDE-PLANT. Erect shrub 2–4 ft., to 12 ft. in the tropics, with flat thin ribbon-like branches ½in. or more broad: lvs. lanceolate, ½–2½ in. long, often lobed at base: fr. a deep red or purplish berry-like body formed of the perianth. Solomon Isls.—Grown as a curiosity.

10. **COCCOLOBA,** L. (*Coccolobis,* P. Br.). More than 125 species of evergreen shrubs and trees in the American tropics and subtropics.—Lvs. alternate, variable in size and shape, entire; sheaths mostly small: fls. greenish, in racemes or spikes in axils of minute bracts, bisexual or sometimes unisexual by abortion; perianth 5-parted, tube enlarging and becoming succulent, inclosing the achene; stamens 8; styles 3: achene 3-angled, contained within the fleshy berry-like body. (Coccolo-ba: Greek, referring probably to the lobed perianth persisting on the fr.)

C. Uvifera, L. (*Polygonum Uvifera,* L.) SEA-GRAPE. Shrub or small tree to 15 ft. or more: lvs. orbicular, 1½–8 in. across, obtuse or retuse, cordate at base, leathery, glossy, with red veins; sheaths funnelform, about ⅜in. long: fls. white, in dense racemes 4–10 in. long or more: frs. resembling bunches of grapes, each about ¾in. across, purple. S. Fla. and W. Indies to Mex. and S. Amer.—Planted in tropics and subtropics for its attractive foliage which becomes bronzy-red before falling.

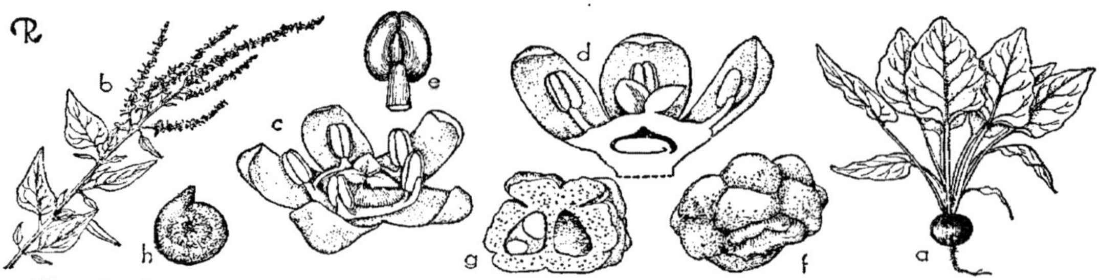

Fig. 57. CHENOPODIACEÆ. *Beta vulgaris:* a, garden beet foliage and root, reduced; b, flowering stem, × ½₀; c, flower, × 10; d, same, vertical section, × 10; e, anther, dorsal side, × 20; f, fruit, × 3; g, same, vertical section, × 3; h, seed, × 3. (c–e after LeMaout and Decaisne.)

57. CHENOPODIACEÆ. GOOSEFOOT FAMILY

About 102 genera and some 1,400 species of wide distribution, ann. and per. herbs, some of them succulent and inhabitants of sea-shores and saline places, a few shrubby, all with small inconspicuous fls.; many are world-wide weeds; several species are grown for ornament and others yield garden vegetables.—Mostly unattractive often mealy or scurfy plants: lvs. usually alternate and without stipules, simple: fls. greenish, bisexual or unisexual, plants sometimes diœcious; calyx persistent, 2–5-lobed or -parted, or reduced to 1 sepal, in the pistillate fls. sometimes wanting; petals none; stamens as many as calyx-lobes and opposite them, or frequently fewer; pistil of a single 1-celled and 1-ovuled ovary superior or nearly so, styles 1–3; disk sometimes present: fr. a utricle or achene, more or less inclosed in the enlarging calyx; in some cases 2 or more fls. in the dense cluster grow together and form a multiple fr.

A. Fls. usually bisexual; perianths all alike on the same plant.
B. Lvs. (in ours) broad, mostly variously angled, toothed, or deeply lobed.
C. Calyx merely more or less enlarging in fr., but not changing in character: fls. without bracts, mostly in panicled spikes........1. CHENOPODIUM
CC. Calyx becomng hard and woody in fr., several often growing together: fls. bracted........2. BETA
BB. Lvs. linear or even narrower and entire, crowded........3. KOCHIA
AA. Fls. unisexual, the plant monœcious or diœcious; perianths (or bracts) of two kinds.
B. Stigmas 2: fr. between 2 large flat bracts........4. ATRIPLEX
BB. Stigmas 4 or 5: fr. inclosed in a carpel-like body formed of the bracts........5. SPINACIA

1. CHENOPODIUM, L. GOOSEFOOT. PIGWEED. Weedy ann. and per. herbs, or rarely subshrubs, of about 250 species, usually mealy and often with strong odor: lvs. alternate, mostly angled and toothed, sometimes almost dissected: fls. bractless, sessile, mostly bisexual, perianth usually 5-parted; stamens 5 or less; style usually absent, the stigmas 2–5 and very slender: fr. a utricle, inclosed in the mostly dry and little modified persistent calyx. (Chenopo-dium: Greek *goose-foot,* from the shape of the lvs. of some species.)—The common pigweed or lambs-quarters (*C. album,* L.) is sometimes collected and cooked for greens.

A. Plant glandular-pubescent, strong-smelling.
B. Calyx glandular: plant aromatic........1. *C. Botrys*
BB. Calyx glabrous: plant ill-smelling........2. *C. ambrosioides*
AA. Plant mealy, at least on the young parts, not glandular-pubescent.
B. Margins of lf. strongly toothed: ann........3. *C. amaranticolor*
BB. Margins of lf. entire or essentially so: per........4. *C. Bonus-Henricus*

1. **C. Botrys,** L. (*Ambrosia mexicana,* Hort.). FEATHER-GERANIUM. JERUSALEM-OAK. Much-branched glandular-pubescent ann. 1–2 ft. or more high, grown for its strong aromatic odor and long profuse fine panicles and knots: lvs. oval or oblong, ½–2 in. long, sinuate-toothed or pinnatifid: fls. very numerous, small, in little cymes arranged in elongate terminal panicles. (Botrys is the name used by old herbalists; as Greek it implies a cluster, as of grapes.) Eurasia, Afr.; also nat.

2. **C. ambrosioides,** L. AMERICAN WORMSEED. MEXICAN TEA. Ann. or per. to 3½ ft., much-branched from the base, glandular-pubescent, strong-smelling: lvs. oblong-ovate, 2–3½ in. long, coarsely repand-dentate, the upper small ones subentire, tapering to petiole: fls. in heads arranged in more or less interrupted spikes, the spikes compound on old plants. Trop. Amer.; widely nat.

3. **C. amaranticolor,** Coste & Reyn. Robust much-branched ann. to 8 ft., the young parts mealy but the plant otherwise glabrous, grown for the ornament of its bright violet-red top foliage (used also for greens) and red-striped st.: lvs. triangular-ovate to rhomboidal, 2–5 in. long, semi-truncate or tapering to petiole, irregularly strongly toothed and notched: fls. in axillary and terminal panicled spikes. Origin not known; perhaps a cultigen; escaped in some places.

4. **C. Bonus-Henricus,** L. GOOD KING HENRY (an old herbalist name, Latinized in the specific name). MERCURY. Per. with deep dock-like root, the plant sometimes grown as a pot-herb, glabrous or nearly so; st. 1–2½ ft. high, several from a root, with weak side branches: lvs. spinach-like, triangular-hastate, 2–4½ in. long, slender-stalked, obtuse or only short-pointed, margins entire or obscurely sinuate: fls. in short panicled spikes, axillary and terminal. Eu.; sometimes escaped.

2. **BETA,** L. BEET. About 12 species in Eu., N. Afr., and Asia, one widely cult.—Ann., bien., per., herbaceous, with alternate entire or sinuate mostly basal lvs., nearly or quite glabrous: fls. greenish, sessile in long paniculate more or less open spikes, usually 2 or 3 together with minute bracts beneath the incurving 5-parted calyx; stamens 5; ovary sunk in a disk or hypanthium, the stigmas usually 3: fr. mostly aggregate, formed of the cohesion of 2 or more fls. grown together at their bases and forming a very irregular dry body (the "seed" of commerce); each seed is inclosed in a hard shell formed of the enlarging disk and calyx, the calyx forming thickened protuberances. (Be-ta: Latin name of the beet.)

B. vulgaris, L. BEET. BEET-ROOT of the English. SUGAR-BEETS and MANGELS are common forms. Bien., sometimes ann., grown for the thickened root in different sizes, forms, and colors, young lvs. also eaten as greens, glabrous; st. produced the second year from the top of the tuber, 2–4 ft.: lvs. ovate to oblong-ovate, passing into linear bracts in the infl.: fls. very many, in a tall open panicle. Cultigen; presumably derivative from *B. maritima*, L. (*B. vulgaris* var. *perennis*, L.), of the coasts of Eu. Var. **Cicla,** L., LEAF-BEET, is without fleshy root and the lvs. are much developed; in some races the foliage is highly colored and the plants are grown for ornament; in others, as Swiss Chard, the midrib is much enlarged, and plants are grown as pot-herbs; Cicla is a geographical name, connected with Sicily.

3. **KOCHIA,** Roth. Ann. and per. herbs, sometimes shrubby, about 80 species mostly in the Old World, 4 in W. Amer., one grown for ornament.—Lvs. very narrow or even terete, entire: fls. bisexual or sometimes pistillate, sessile, single or in small clusters in the axils; calyx with 5 incurved lobes which in fr. develops horizontal wings; stamens 5, exserted; stigmas mostly 2: fr. a utricle, in which the seed is free from the pericarp. (Ko-chia: W. D. J. Koch, 1771–1849, German botanist, was Director of the Botanic Garden at Erlangen and author of a flora of Germany and Switzerland.)

K. scoparia, Schrad. (*Chenopodium scoparia*, L.) SUMMER-CYPRESS. BELVEDERE. Erect much-branched lightly hairy or glabrous ann. to 5 ft., sometimes grown for its pyramidal habit and interesting herbage: lvs. alternate, linear-acute, usually ciliate, the larger ones to 2 in. or more long, narrowed to short petiole, the many smaller ones very narrow and without evident petiole and much exceeding the little fl.-clusters. Eu., Asia, and escaped in N. Amer. Var. **culta,** Farwell (var. *trichophila*, Bailey. forma *trichophila*, Schinz & Thell. *Bassia scoparia* var. *culta*, Voss. *K. trichophylla*, Voss. *K. Childsii*, Hort.), the common form in cult., has a denser more ovoid or globular habit, very narrow lvs. mostly with long hairs particularly toward the base, and purple-red autumn color; planted for its formal effect.

4. **ATRIPLEX,** L. SALTBUSH. Ann. and per. herbs and shrubs, widely distributed, one grown as a pot-herb; species many, of which more than 100 are in N. Amer. north of the Isthmus.—Usually scurfy or canescent, often the whole plant gray, monœcious or diœcious: lvs. various, alternate or opposite, stalked or sessile: fls. usually in small clusters in the axils or terminal, rarely solitary; staminate fls. with 3–5-parted calyx and no bracts, the stamens as many as the segms.; pistillate fls. usually without calyx and with 2 bracts, the bracts enlarging and covering the fr.; stigmas 2 and very slender: fr. a utricle, with the seed usually free. (At-riplex: Latin name of the orach.)

A. Plant an ann. herb: lvs. green, 1½–5 in. long .... 1. *A. hortensis*
AA. Plant a shrub: lvs. gray-scurfy, not over 2 in. long.................................. 2. *A. Breweri*

1. **A. hortensis,** L. ORACH. Tall somewhat branched nearly or quite glabrous ann. to 7 ft., with chenopodium-like lvs., grown for greens: monœcious: lower lvs. opposite and upper alternate, triangular-ovate to hastate, 1½–5 (8) in. long, long-petioled, margins angled or dentate or sometimes nearly continuous, apex obtuse or short-acute: fls. with very short pedicels which elongate in fr., in axillary and terminal more or less panicled racemes, most of the pistillate ones naked and with 2 large bracts and others with a 3–5-lobed green calyx without large bracts: fr. a utricle mostly covered between the 2 large (about ⅓in. long) oval or ovate flat bracts. Asia; sometimes escaped.—There is a form with red foliage.

2. **A. Breweri,** Wats. Erect much-branched shrub 3–8 ft. high, planted for hedges: lvs. ovate to rhombic-ovate, ½–2 in. long, mostly cuneate at base, entire to dentate, gray-scurfy: diœcious or monœcious; fls. in paniculate spikes, fruiting bracts broadly orbicular, about ⅓in. long, convex. (Named for Wm. H. Brewer, page 40.) Calif.

5. **SPINACIA,** L. SPINACH. Three or 4 species of ann. diœcious erect herbs of S. W. Asia, one widely cult.—Lvs. alternate, usually triangular-ovate to hastate: fls. unisexual (only rarely bisexual), the pistillate usually axillary and the staminate in terminal spikes or panicles; staminate calyx 4–5-parted, stamens of equal number with lobes and exserted; pistillate fl. subtended by 2 perianth-like bracts that grow together and inclose the utricle in the tube; stigmas 4 or 5, exserted. (Spina-cia: Latin *spina*, from the spiny fr.)

S. oleracea, L. PRICKLY-SEEDED SPINACH or SPINAGE. Smooth and glabrous, producing in cool weather a crown of large lvs. used as a pot-herb: radical lvs. narrow-oblong or ovate-oblong, in the usual vars. broad-ovate to almost orbicular with projecting lobes at base on either side and sometimes extra lobes on the side; st.-lvs. smaller, becoming lanceolate in the infl.: st. simple or somewhat branched, 6 in.–2 ft. high, glabrous: staminate fls. mostly in leafless spikes or panicles; pistillate fls. clustered in the axils: fr. a utricle inclosed in a 2–4-spined caps.-like body ("seed" of commerce) formed of the calyx-like bracts. Var. **inermis,** Peterm., ROUND-SEEDED SPINACH, differs in having the "seed" without spines.

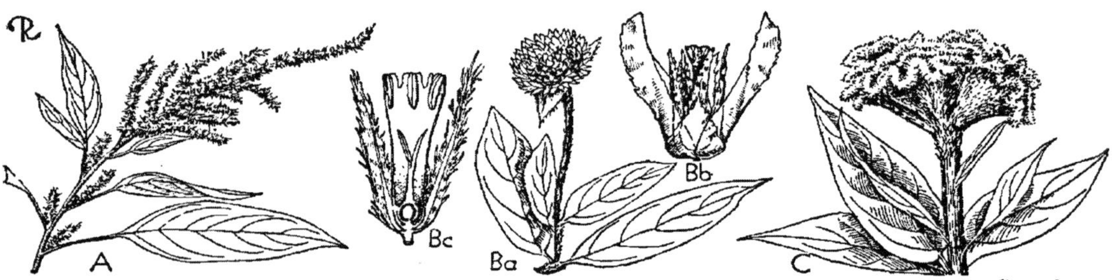

Fig. 58. AMARANTHACEÆ. A, *Amaranthus caudatus*, flowering branch, reduced. B, *Gomphrena globosa:* Ba, flowering branch, × ½; Bb, flower with involucre, × 2; Bc, flower, vertical section, × 3. C, *Celosia argentea* var. *cristata:* flowering branch, × ⅙.

58. AMARANTHACEÆ. AMARANTH FAMILY

Mostly weedy plants, a few grown for ornament and also for food as pot-herbs; genera about 40 and species 450–500 of wide distribution, but most abundant in warm countries.—Herbaceous, a few woody: lvs. opposite or alternate, usually simple, sometimes fleshy: fls. small and inconspicuous but the infl. often showy because of the mass and the colored perianths and subtending scales, unisexual or bisexual, plants sometimes monœcious and diœcious; perianth 2–5-parted or cleft, or the segms. sometimes distinct, the parts in one series and petals therefore lacking, parts nearly or quite equal; stamens 1–5, usually opposite the perianth-parts, sometimes united into a tube; ovary superior, 1-celled, ovule 1 (rarely more) and basal, style none or 1 or more: fr. various, commonly a circumscissile utricle but sometimes berry-like or an achene, usually surrounded by a persistent perianth: family marked by the scarious imbricated fl.-scales, usually 3 to each fl., and the glomerate, spicate, racemose, or paniculate dry infl.

A. Lvs. alternate.
  B. Plant an ann. herb: fr. dry, utricular.
    C. Fr. with 1 seed: filaments of stamens free .... 1. AMARANTHUS
    CC. Fr. with 2 or more seeds: filaments united at base .... 2. CELOSIA
  BB. Plant a woody climber: fr. a berry .... 3. DEERINGIA

AA. Lvs. opposite.
B. Fls. in large showy heads on long peduncles: lvs. green....................4. GOMPHRENA
BB. Fls. in panicles or small sessile heads: grown mostly for the variegated foliage.
C. Infl. of little clusters or spikes forming a diffuse open panicle..............5. IRESINE
CC. Infl. of small dense sessile axillary heads..............................6. ALTERNANTHERA

1. **AMARANTHUS,** L. AMARANTH. Ann. herbs, mostly of coarse appearance, about 50 species of wide distribution, some of them among the plants known as pigweeds; some of the weedy ones are more or less gathered when young for greens and others are grown for that purpose in other countries; others are cult. for ornament.—Fls. usually not bisexual, in chaffy dense spikes and panicles, each fl. subtended mostly by 3 bracts; perianth glabrous, of 2–5 parts distinct or nearly so; stamens commonly 5, sometimes 2 or 3, separate, anthers 2-celled; stigmas 2 or 3: fr. a 1-seeded utricle, the persistent styles forming beaks. (Amaran-thus, sometimes spelled Amarant-us: Greek *unfading*, in allusion to the unwithering bracts.)

A. Fl.-clusters small and closely glomerate in the axils even toward base of plant, as well as also in more or less elongated spikes at top of plant..............1. *A. tricolor*
AA. Fl.-clusters all elongate and at or near top of plant, forming a terminal panicle.
B. Panicle clumpy or narrow with broad blunt spikes: utricle usually exceeding the sepals..2. *A. hybridus* var.
BB. Panicle large and broad with acute narrow spikes: utricle usually not longer than sepals..3. *A. caudatus*

1. **A. tricolor,** L. (*A. melancholicus*, L. *A. gangeticus*, L.). Diffuse and branching, 1–4 ft., st. usually glabrous: lvs. ovate or oval, 2½–6 (8) in. long and mostly 2–4 in. wide, abruptly tapering to long petiole, short-pointed or obtuse, green and not thick or stiffish and comprising races with blotched and colored lvs. in shades of red and green, grown for ornament under such names as Josephs-Coat (*A. bicolor*, *A. coleifolius*): glomerules small and sessile in nearly or quite all the axils often even to the ground, those in the uppermost axils becoming 1 or 2 in. long and spike-like but usually interrupted, those terminating branches and st. longer: scales long-pointed, mostly prominent. Tropics, probably Asian. Var. **angustior,** Bailey (*A. salicifolius*, Hort. not Veitch), has narrow lf.-blades, mostly ¾–1½ in. wide, lanceolate to lance-ovate, the petioles thereby appearing prominent. Var. **splendens,** Bailey (*A. splendens*, Hort.), has bright red foliage toward the top of the plant, and veins of lf. and small sts. red.—Sometimes grown as a pot-herb, particularly in oriental countries.

2. **A. hybridus,** L., var. **hypochondriacus,** Rob. (*A. hypochondriacus*, L.) PRINCES-FEATHER. Tall glabrous plant to 5 ft.: lvs. 1–6 in. long, ½–3 in. wide, on slender petioles ½–3½ in. long: infl. narrow, stiff and clumpy, with erect rather stiff panicle of short lateral mostly blunt spreading spikes and a strong terminal one: scales or bracts long-awned-twice the sepals. Tropics; frequently cult. and sometimes escaped. Panicles usually red but some vars. are greenish and of different shades of red. *A. hybridus* itself is a prevalent weed, often assuming red tints.

3. **A. caudatus,** L. (*A. paniculatus*, L. *A. cruentus*, L.). LOVE-LIES-BLEEDING. TASSEL-FLOWER. Stout branching profuse plant, 3–8 ft.: lvs. ovate to ovate-oblong to ovate-lanceolate, 2–10 in. long, ½–4 in. wide, attenuate at base into petioles 1–6 in. long: panicle of numerous or few spikes, the lateral ones 1–10 in. long, crowded or not, spreading or drooping, the terminal spike usually one to several times the lateral, drooping or erect: bracts lanceolate to ovate, mostly one to one and a half times the sepals, carinate, often red; sepals about ¹⁄₁₆ in. long, usually red or purplish, sometimes yellow or green; seeds black to yellowish-white. Tropics; commonly cult. and sometimes spontaneous.—Variable. Garden plants known as *A. abyssinicus*, *atropurpureus*, *Dussii*, *elegantissimus*, *Margaritæ*, *monstrosus*, *sanguineus*, *superbus*, belong here.

2. **CELOSIA,** L. Probably about 60 species, in warm countries of eastern and western hemispheres, the cult. kinds ann.—Differs technically from Amaranthus in the 2 or more ovules: lvs. alternate, entire or rarely lobed: st. and branches terminated by dense chaffy spikes which in cult. forms are enlarged and highly colored, the st. often much fasciated and forming a cockscomb: fls. bisexual, the perianth 5-parted; stamens 5, filaments united at base: fr. a utricle, mostly dehiscent, included in persistent perianth or exserted, 2- or more-seeded. (Celo-sia: Greek *kelos*, burned, from the color and character of infl.)

C. argentea, L. A weed in trop. countries, probably of Asian origin: erect, glabrous, 2–3 ft.: lvs. 2 in. and more long, linear-lanceolate to lance-ovate: spikes terminal, dense, conical to long-oblong, 1 to several in. long, silvery-white.—Some of the cult. forms are very like the wild plant, with long narrow silvery-white spikes; but most of the domesticated improved races may be referred to var. **cristata,** Kuntze (*C. cristata*, L.), COCKSCOMB: mostly lower: infl. modified through a wide range of forms between which grades of intermediates occur, necessitating careful attention to seed-breeding: some forms are heavy-headed short plants with widely fasciated convoluted combs; others are cristate or feathered; others are open-growing plants with plumy slender spikes and panicles; the colors range from white to yellow, purple, and shades of red; there are also kinds with variegated lvs.: grotesque forms are not uncommon. Latin-form names have been given to the cult. races as *C. Thompsonii, Childsii, plumosa, floribunda, pyramidalis, spicata;* a series of hybrids is known as "Gilbertia."

3. **DEERINGIA,** R. Br. Herbs and subshrubs sometimes climbing, of about 8 species, Madagascar, Australia, and the Pacific isls.—Lvs. alternate, petiolate, not lobed, usually ovate: fls. bisexual or unisexual (plants sometimes diœcious), small and not showy, in axillary and terminal spikes and racemes that are sometimes assembled in panicles; perianth of 5 segms.; stamens 4 or 5, filaments connate at base into a cup or ring; stigmas 2–4: fr. more or less baccate, with few or many seeds. (Deering-ia: Geo. C. Deering, 1695–1749, physician and botanist in England.)

D. amaranthoides, Merr. (*Achyranthes amaranthoides,* Lam. *D. celosioides,* R. Br. *D. baccata,* Moq.). Glabrous woody climber from Australia, somewhat grown in Calif., 10–15 ft.: lvs. ovate to ovate-lanceolate, 2–4 in. long, acuminate, entire: fls. greenish-white, in axillary and terminal clusters, sometimes in simple racemes but oftener in little racemed clusters which are more or less collected in panicles: fr. a red nearly globular berry about ¼in. or less in diam., giving the plant an ornamental appearance. There is a var. with variegated foliage.

4. **GOMPHRENA,** L. One common garden ann. grown as an "everlasting"; 90 or more species, the larger number in the New World tropics.—Ann. and per. hairy herbs, erect or prostrate: lvs. opposite, not lobed: fls. bisexual, mostly in dense chaffy usually peduncled heads which are sometimes provided with involucre-like bracts at base; perianth sessile under the bracts, 5-parted, the parts equal or unequal; filaments united into long 5-parted tube, the lobes emarginate or bifid: fr. a 1-seeded mostly indehiscent utricle. (Gomphre-na: from an ancient name for an amaranth.)

G. globosa, L. Globe-Amaranth. Rather stiff erect branching plant 12–36 in. high, with a clover-like aspect due to the globular or short-oblong dense long-peduncled heads which are white, yellowish, violet, or red in different garden races, and closely subtended by 2 broad leafy bracts: lvs. oblong to elliptic or somewhat obovate, 2–4 in. long, hairy, margins entire and ciliate. Probably American tropics.

5. **IRESINE,** P. Br. Blood-Leaf. Herbs and subshrubs, mostly erect, a few cult. for the colored foliage; native in many trop. and temp. regions, about 70 species. —Lvs. opposite, usually ovate, simple, petioled: fls. bisexual or unisexual, white or straw-colored, very small, in axillary and terminal mostly small spikes that are aggregated into panicles; bracts usually 3 to each fl.; perianth 5-parted, in the fertile fls. usually woolly; stamens prevailingly 5, filaments united at base; stigmas 2 or 3: fr. a 1-seeded indehiscent utricle. (Iresi-ne: Greek allusion to the woolly fls. and seeds.)—The two following are much used as bedding plants, rarely blooming, being propagated by cuttings; probably per.

A. Lvs. nearly orbicular, notched at apex. . . . . 1. *I. Herbstii*
AA. Lvs. lance-ovate, pointed. . . . . 2. *I. Lindenii*

1. **I. Herbstii,** Hook. f. (*Achyranthes Verschaffeltii,* Lem.). Lvs. broadly ovate to nearly orbicular, 1–2 in. long, most of them deeply notched at apex, purplish-red with lighter midrib and arched side veins, or green or bronzy with yellowish veins: fls. very small, whitish, numerous in long-peduncled axillary and in terminal compound panicles 2–4 in. long: plant reaches 6 ft. high in tropics, with lvs. 5 in. across. (Named for Mr. Herbst, propagator at the Royal Botanic Gardens, Kew, England.) S. Amer.

2. **I. Lindenii,** VanHoutte (*Achyranthes* and *Iresine acuminata,* Hort.). St. and lvs. usually deep red in cult. stock, but sometimes green: lvs. lance-ovate or somewhat broader, 1–2½ in. long, acuminate, with prominent thin veins. (Named for J. Linden, page 47.) Ecuador.

6. **ALTERNANTHERA,** Forsk. About 170 species, mostly of the New World tropics, the cult. kinds herbaceous or treated as such, used for carpet-bedding.—Lvs. opposite, narrow, petiolate or tapering at base: fls. bisexual, small, in dense small usually sessile glomerules mostly in the axils; perianth 5-parted, the parts in

two unlike series; filaments united into a short or long tube that bears 5 anthers and 5 sterile points or staminodia: fr. a 1-seeded indehiscent utricle. (Alternanthe-ra: referring to the sterile staminodes alternate with the stamens.)—The following species are probably Brazilian; they are sometimes placed in the genus Achyranthes or the genus Telanthera; the kinds in cult. are not clearly understood botanically. The plants are usually kept down to a few in. high; little whitish fl.-clusters may appear late in the season; propagated by cuttings.

A. Petiole longer than blade or at least half as long; blade palmately nerved at base, pinnate at tip .... 1. *A. Bettzickiana*
AA. Petiole less than half as long as blade; blade pinnately veined.
  B. Lvs. broadest at or below the middle .... 2. *A. amœna*
  BB. Lvs. broadest above the middle .... 3. *A. versicolor*

1. **A. Bettzickiana,** Nichols. (*Telanthera Bettzickiana*, Regel). Erect ann. or per. to 16 in.: lvs. rhombic to narrow-spatulate, ½–1½ in. long, gradually tapering into long petiole, acute or even somewhat mucronate at apex, blotched and colored in many shades, white-yellow to red. (Named in compliment to Hofgartner Bettzick.)—Apparently the common species in cult.

2. **A. amœna,** Voss (*A. sessilis* var. *amœna*, Lem. *Telanthera amœna*, Regel). Very dwarf plant with lanceolate or somewhat oblong-lanceolate or elliptic short-petioled long-acute lvs. mostly veined and blotched red and orange.

3. **A. versicolor,** Regel (*Telanthera versicolor*, Regel. *T. ficoidea* var. *versicolor*, Lem.). Somewhat bushy, to about 1 ft.: lvs. broad- or round-spatulate, main part of blade nearly as broad as long, obtuse, abruptly narrowed into short petiole, copper- or blood-red.

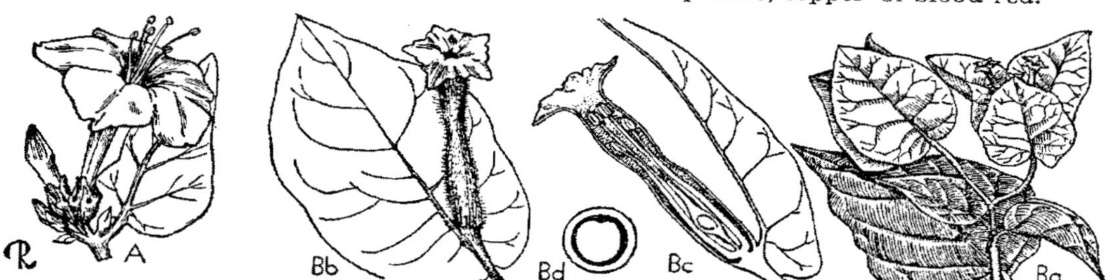

Fig. 59. NYCTAGINACEÆ. A, *Mirabilis Jalapa:* flowering branch tip, × ½. B, *Bougainvillea spectabilis:* Ba, flowering branch, × ¼; Bb, flower and subtending bract, × 1; Bc, same, vertical section, × 1; Bd, ovary, cross-section, × 3.

59. NYCTAGINACEÆ. FOUR-O'CLOCK FAMILY

About 30 genera and 300 species of herbs, shrubs, and trees, of wide geographical distribution in warm regions but most abundant in Amer.; a few grown for ornament.—Lvs. simple, opposite or alternate, entire, exstipulate: infl. various; fls. regular, bisexual or rarely unisexual, usually subtended by an involucre of separate or united bracts; petals 0; calyx inferior, often petaloid, campanulate, tubular or salverform, persistent after flowering and enveloping the fr., often woody or leathery; stamens 1 to many, hypogynous, free or united at base; style 1; ovary 1-celled, 1-ovuled, sessile or stipitate: fr. a ribbed, grooved, or winged achene.

A. Lvs. alternate: fls. inclosed by showy colored bracts: woody .... 1. BOUGAINVILLEA
AA. Lvs. opposite: involucral bracts not colored, small: herbs.
  B. Bracts united, calyx-like: fls. 1 to an involucre (in ours) .... 2. MIRABILIS
  BB. Bracts 5–15, distinct: fls. in peduncled heads .... 3. ABRONIA

1. **BOUGAINVILLEA,** Comm. (originally spelled *Buginvillæa* but present spelling conserved). Characteristic porch and arbor vines in warm countries and sometimes grown in greenhouses in the N.; about 13 species of shrubs from S. Amer.—Lvs. alternate, petioled, ovate or elliptic-lanceolate: fls. small and inconspicuous, usually inclosed by large showy purple, red, orange to white bracts, commonly 3 together, the pedicels adnate to the midvein of the bracts; tube of perianth usually green, limb 5–6-lobed, rose or yellow; stamens 5–10, included, on unequal filaments; ovary stipitate, style lateral: achene 5-ribbed. (Bougainvil-lea; after de Bougainville, 1729–1811, French navigator.)

A. Perianth-tube more or less puberulent: lvs. and sts. subglabrous................1. *B. glabra*
AA. Perianth-tube densely pubescent: lvs. and sts. pubescent......................2. *B. spectabilis*

1. **B. glabra,** Chois. Glabrous or only slightly pubescent, with a woody trunk attaining 1 ft. or more in diam. and often growing over buildings in the tropics and warm countries; sts. with stout usually straight spines: lvs. oblong-lanceolate or ovate-oblong to broadly ovate, 2–4 in. long, acuminate, tapering or wedge-shaped at base: fls. mostly scattered on long leafy wand-like branches with elliptic or elliptic-lanceolate bracts 1 in. or more long, subequal to fls. when mature, magenta or purple to lighter colored. Brazil. Var. **Sanderiana,** Hort., blooms readily when small and is suitable for pot cult. as well as planting out. Var. **variegata,** Hort., has white-variegated lvs.—Material cult. as "Crimson Lake" and much of that as *B. brasiliensis* belongs here.

2. **B. spectabilis,** Willd. (*B. brasiliensis,* Raeusch.). Very similar to *B. glabra* but differing in being densely tomentose, the spines more predominantly recurved at the tip, the fls. more or less glomerate at the ends of the branches with long outer ray-like peduncles, the bracts in shades of red, elliptic-ovate, exceeding the fls. when mature. Brazil. Var. **lateritia,** Lem., is a race with brick-red bracts.—Named variants are in cult., characterized by white, cream- and salmon-colored bracts.

2. **MIRABILIS,** L. Per. herbs, grown as annuals in fl.-gardens, of about 60 species in the warmer parts of Amer.—Roots often thickened and tuberous; sts. often swollen at the nodes: lvs. opposite, petioled or the upper sessile: fls. 1 or many in a 5-lobed calyx-like involucre; calyx variously colored, tube elongated, constricted above ovary, limb spreading, 5-lobed, deciduous; stamens 3–5 (6), as long as the perianth or sometimes exserted, on unequal filaments which are united at base; style filiform with capitate stigma: fr. leathery, ribbed. (Mirab-ilis: Latin for *wonderful.*)

M. Jalapa, L. Four-O'Clock. Marvel-of-Peru. Quick-growing herb with erect much-branched sts. from 1–3 ft. high, glabrous or slightly pubescent: lvs. deep green, ovate, 2–6 in. long, acuminate, truncate or cordate at base, with petioles almost half as long as blades: fls. about 1 in. across, blooming in late summer and autumn, opening late in the afternoon, white, red, yellow, or striped; involucre containing only 1 fl.; calyx trumpet-shaped, the tube 1–2 in. long. (Jalapa: the tuberous roots were once supposed to be the source of jalap.) Trop. Amer.; spontaneous in the S.—There are dwarf and compact vars. and kinds with variegated foliage.

3. **ABRONIA,** Juss. Sand-Verbena. About 33 species of ann. and per. herbs, native mostly in W. N. Amer., grown in borders, rockeries, and baskets.—Erect or prostrate, usually glandular-pubescent: lvs. opposite, petioled, unequal, rather thick: fls. few to many in a peduncled head which is subtended by 5 or more distinct bracts, red, yellow or white, fragrant; calyx corolla-like, with elongated tube constricted above ovary, and 5-lobed limb; stamens 3–5, unequal, inserted on tube of perianth, included: fr. leathery, 1–5-ribbed or -winged. (Abro-nia: from Greek for *delicate.*)

A. umbellata, Lam. Prostrate per. with sts. 1–3 ft. long: lvs. thin, ovate to narrowly oblong, 1–3 in. long, obtuse, on slender petioles longer than the blades: heads 10–15-fld., on peduncles 2–6 in. long, with small narrowly lanceolate bracts; calyx rose-purple or rarely white: fr. attenuate at each end, usually with 2–5 thin wings much narrowed below and truncate or tapering above. Sea-coast, B. C. to Calif.

60. PHYTOLACCACEÆ. POKEWEED FAMILY

Herbs, shrubs, or trees mostly native in trop. and subtrop. Amer. and S. Afr., of about 17 genera and 110 species; little known in general cult.—Lvs. alternate, entire, usually exstipulate: fls. mostly in axillary or terminal racemes, bisexual or unisexual, regular; calyx 4–5-parted, persistent; petals usually 0; stamens as many as the calyx-segms. and alternate with them, or more numerous, hypogynous, distinct or united at base; ovary usually superior with 1 to many distinct or united pistils, ovary 1-celled, ovules solitary, styles as many as pistils, short or none, the stigmas linear or filiform: fr. a berry, caps., or samara.

A. Plant an upright herb or tree: ovary superior: fr. a berry.
B. Ovary of 5–16 distinct or united pistils: stamens 6–33......................1. Phytolacca
BB. Ovary of 1 pistil: stamens 4......................2. Rivina
AA. Plant a vine: ovary inferior: fr. an achene......................3. Agdestis

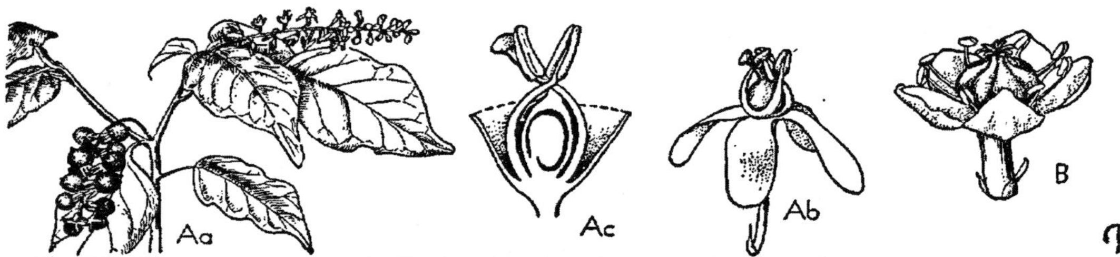

Fig. 60. PHYTOLACCACEÆ. A, *Rivina humilis:* Aa, flowering and fruiting branch, × ½; Ab, flower, × 4; Ac, flower, vertical section, perianth removed, × 8. B, Phytolacca: flower habit, × 5 (after Schnizlein).

1. **PHYTOLACCA,** L. POKEWEED. POKEBERRY. About 35 species of herbs, shrubs, or trees, of trop. or subtrop. regions, mostly Amer. but a few in Afr. and Asia.—Glabrous or nearly so: lvs. petioled or rarely sessile, ovate, elliptic or lanceolate: fls. small, in erect or nodding terminal racemes which by further growth of the st. may come opposite the lvs.; pedicels bracted at base; stamens 6–33, in two series; ovary subglobose, of 5–16 free or united pistils: fr. a fleshy berry. (Phytolacca: from Greek for *plant* and French *lac*, lake (a color), referring to the crimson juice of the berries.)

A. Fls. bisexual: a tall herb...1. *P. americana*
AA. Fls. unisexual: an evergreen tree...2. *P. dioica*

1. **P. americana,** L. (*P. decandra,* L.). POKE. SCOKE. Strong-smelling herb 4–12 ft. high: lvs. oblong- or ovate-lanceolate, 4–12 in. long, acute or acuminate: fls. bisexual, white, about ¼in. across, in peduncled racemes 2–8 in. long which are nodding in fr.: berry dark purple, about ½in. across. Me. to Fla. and Tex.

2. **P. dioica,** L. (*Pircunia dioica,* Moq.). Evergreen diœcious tree of very rapid growth, to 60 ft. and more and attaining great thickness of trunk and spread of top: lvs. slender-petioled, elliptic or ovate, 4 in. or more long, mostly broadly acute at apex, the midnerve prominent: fls. unisexual, white, in suberect or pendulous racemes scarcely surpassing the lvs.; staminate fls. with 20–30 stamens much longer than calyx; pistillate fls. with about 10 staminodia and 7–10-carpelled ovary: berry with pistils united at base and free at apex. S. Amer.—Grown in S. Calif. and Fla.

2. **RIVINA,** L. Erect herbs native of trop. and subtrop. Amer., but intro. into Asia, Australia, and African isls.; one species is commonly grown for its red berries under glass and out-of-doors as a summer ann.—Shrubby at base: lvs. slender-petioled, ovate, acuminate, rounded or subcordate at base: racemes many-fld., erect or flexuous; pedicels with minute bracts at base; fls. bisexual, small; calyx 4-parted; stamens 4, shorter than calyx; ovary ovoid, of 1 pistil, style shorter than ovary, slightly curved: berry red, pea-shaped. (Rivi-na: for A. Q. Rivinus, 1652–1723, professor of botany at Leipzig.)

R. humilis, L. ROUGE-PLANT. From 1–3 ft. high, with spreading branches, pubescent when young: lvs. 2–4 in. long: racemes about as long as lvs.; calyx white or rosy: berry about ⅛in. diam. Ark. to Fla. and Tex., W. Indies, Cent. and S. Amer.

3. **AGDESTIS,** Moc. & Sessé. One vine native in Mex. and Guatemala, grown out-of-doors in S. U. S. and somewhat established.—Roots large, gray and turnip-like: lvs. cordate-ovate, long-petioled: fls. white, fragrant, bisexual, in terminal and lateral panicles; sepals 4 or rarely 5, persistent and becoming papery; stamens 15–20; ovary inferior, of 4 pistils, style short: fr. a 4–5-winged achene, 1-celled and 1-seeded. (Agdes-tis: mythical name.)

A. clematidea, Moc. & Sessé. Sts. much-branched, climbing to 50 ft.: lvs. 1–4 in. across, obtuse: fls. star-shaped, to ½in. across, in many-fld. panicles 4–6 in. long: achene with wings, about ½in. diam.

61. AIZOACEÆ. CARPET-WEED FAMILY

Erect or prostrate herbs or subshrubs, often fleshy and inhabitants of deserts and sea-shores; as formerly constituted genera above 20 and species probably 500 and more, but the genus Mesembryanthemum is now divided into more than 100 genera and numberless new species; of wide distribution, mostly in warm countries.—Habit various, the plant sometimes reduced to a small succulent body without foliage lvs., in other cases much-branched and with well-developed lvs. which may be opposite, whorled, or alternate, but mostly opposite and without stipules: fls. bisexual, regular, petals often lacking, the perianth then of one set of 4 or 5 parts which are united or distinct; stamens as many as the perianth-parts and alternate with them, or in some genera numerous and many of them perhaps represented by showy staminodia or staminoid petals and causing the fl. to look like one of the Compositæ; ovary mostly superior, but in ours wholly or partly inferior, 2- or more-celled, with as many stigmas; ovules solitary to many, basal, apical or axile: fr. a caps. or nut-like body, mostly many-seeded; embryo curved or ring-like.

A. Petals lacking.......... 1. TETRAGONIA
AA. Petals present.
  B. Sts. lacking or very short, thick and unbranched, bearing 1 to few pairs of lvs.
    C. Lvs. united into a solid body with only a fissure on top.......... 2. LITHOPS
    CC. Lvs. distinct, at least in the growing state.
      D. Margins of lvs. strongly toothed.......... 3. FAUCARIA
      DD. Margins of lvs. not toothed.
        E. Stigmas and cells of caps. 5.......... 4. RHOMBOPHYLLUM
        EE. Stigmas and cells of caps. 7–20.
          F. Fls. sessile or very short-stalked.
            G. Foliage spotted, as broad as long.......... 5. PLEIOSPILOS
            GG. Foliage not spotted, tongue-shaped, twice as long as broad.......... 6. GLOTTIPHYLLUM
          FF. Fls. long-stalked.
            G. Foliage in resting stage surrounded by cup-like sheaths: fls. yellow.......... 7. CHEIRIDOPSIS
            GG. Foliage never surrounded by sheaths: fls. (in ours) purple.......... 8. CEPHALOPHYLLUM
  BB. Sts. branching and leafy.
    C. Stigmas and cells of ovary 8–20.
      D. Fr. indehiscent and fleshy: lvs. 3-angled.......... 9. CARPOBROTUS
      DD. Fr. a dehiscent caps.: lvs. flat.......... 10. CARPANTHEA
    CC. Stigmas and cells of ovary 4–6, usually 5.
      D. Lvs. petioled or conspicuously narrowed at base, ovate and flat.
        E. Herbage covered with large glistening vescicles.......... 11. CRYOPHYTUM
        EE. Herbage only minutely papillose.......... 12. APTENIA
      DD. Lvs. sessile, not much narrowed at base, linear to obovate.
        E. Plant a low ann.......... 13. DOROTHEANTHUS
        EE. Plant a per., often woody, 1 ft. or more high.
          F. Fls. (in ours) 1½–2 in. and more across.
            G. Herbage densely papillose.......... 14. DROSANTHEMUM
            GG. Herbage smooth although sometimes punctate.......... 15. LAMPRANTHUS
          FF. Fls. ½–¾ in. across.
            G. Lvs. smooth and not toothed, in ours 1½–2 in. long.......... 16. ASTRIDIA
            GG. Lvs. papillose or toothed, in ours ½ in. long.
              H. Lf. with toothed edges, not hispid.......... 17. OSCULARIA
              HH. Lf. not toothed, hispid.......... 18. DELOSPERMA

Fig. 61. AIZOACEÆ. A, *Faucaria tigrina:* Aa, plant in flower, × ⅜; Ab, flower fully open, top view, × ⅜; Ac, flower, vertical section, × ¾. B, *Carpobrotus edulis:* flowering branch, × ¼. C, *Cryophytum crystallinum:* Ca, flowering branch, × ¼; Cb, flower, vertical section, × ½; Cc, ovary, cross-section, × 1. (All redrawn: A from Flowering Plants South Africa; B from Botanical Magazine; C from Reichenbach, Icones.)

1. **TETRAGONIA**, L. About 50 species of herbs and subshrubs, erect, trailing or partially scandent, in E. Asia, and the southern hemisphere on both sides of the world; one is a hort. subject.—Lvs. alternate, more or less fleshy: fls. small, axillary, solitary or few together, petals wanting, perianth 3–5-lobed and adnate to ovary

and often extended above it; stamens 1 or more, inserted on perianth-tube; ovary 2–8-celled, ovules solitary in each cell: fr. indehiscent, obconic or globose, often horned at top. (Tetrago-nia: *four-angled,* in allusion to the fr.)

T. expansa, Murr. NEW-ZEALAND-SPINACH. Vigorous spreading prostrate ann., often covering several ft., thick and somewhat succulent, papillose, glabrous: lvs. deltoid to deltoid-ovate, 2–5 in. long, obtuse or nearly so, abruptly narrowed into short petiole: fls. 1 or 2 in the axils, nearly sessile, yellowish-green, not conspicuous: fr. somewhat top-shaped, angled, ⅓in. long, dry and hard, crowned with horns. Japan, Australia, New Zeal., extra-trop. S. Amer.; cult. as a pot-herb and sometimes escaped.

2. **LITHOPS,** N. E. Br. STONEFACE. Per. very succulent plants, often forming clumps, of 50 or more species in S. Afr.—Stemless: lvs. in pairs united into a solid stone-like body with only a fissure on top from which arises the sessile usually solitary yellow or white fl.; petals many, free to base; stamens many, united into an erect column; stigmas 4–7, filiform; ovary inferior, 4–7-celled: caps. small, the valves with winged keel. (Lith-ops: from Greek for *stone* and *face.*)

L. pseudotruncatella, N. E. Br. (*Mesembryanthemum pseudotruncatellum,* Berger). Tufted: growths conical, about 1 in. high, depressed and roundish on top and 1–1¼ in. across, brownish-gray with brown lines and dots, glabrous: fls. golden-yellow, 1½–2 in. across. Var. **Mundtii,** Tisch. (*L. Mundtii,* Tisch.), is somewhat larger, the yellow or orange petals tipped with red; named for Farmer Mundt in S. Afr.

3. **FAUCARIA,** Schwant. Tufted succulents, of perhaps 30 species native in S. Afr.—Stemless or when older with very short st.: lvs. 4–6 to a growth, united at base, thick, spreading, half-cylindrical in cross-section, 3-angled and keeled at tip, strongly toothed: fls. large, nearly sessile, without bracts; stigmas 5–6, filiform: caps. long, 5-celled but appearing 10-celled, the valves winged. (Fauca-ria: name unexplained.)

F. tigrina, Schwant. (*Mesembryanthemum tigrinum,* Haw.). Lvs. crowded, rhombic-ovoid, 1½–2 in. long and ½–1 in. wide, glaucous-green spotted with white, margins with 9–10 strong recurved teeth: fls. 1–2, golden-yellow, 1–2 in. across.

4. **RHOMBOPHYLLUM,** Schwant. Small shrubby or tufted succulents, of about 3 species in S. Afr.—Sts. very short or none: lvs. crowded, somewhat united at base, rhombic, half-cylindrical, keeled at tip, spotted with white: fls. 1–3, long-stalked, yellow, with bracts; stigmas 5, filiform: caps. 5-celled. (Rhombophyl-lum: referring to the rhombic lvs.)

R. rhomboideum, Schwant. (*Mesembryanthemum rhomboideum,* Salm-Dyck. *Bergeranthus rhomboideus,* Schwant.). Stemless: lvs. 8–10 forming thick rosettes, pairs somewhat unequal, 1–2 in. long and ½–¾in. wide, glabrous, dark green spotted with white, the angles rarely with 1–2 small teeth: fls. golden-yellow, reddish outside, 1 in. or more across, on stalks 1 in. long.

5. **PLEIOSPILOS,** N. E. Br. As now defined a genus of about 30 species of stemless succulent perennials, native in S. Afr.—Lvs. usually of 1–2 pairs united at base, equal, very thick, conspicuously punctate: fls. solitary or few between the lvs., sessile or short-stalked, with bracts; stigmas 9–14, filiform: caps. 9–14-celled, the valves winged toward top. (Pleiospi-los: from Greek meaning *full of spots.*)

A. Fls. sessile .... 1. *P. Bolusii*
AA. Fls. short-stalked .... 2. *P. Nelii*

1. **P. Bolusii,** N. E. Br. (*Mesembryanthemum Bolusii,* Hook. f.). Lvs. usually 2, spreading, broad-ovate, the flat faces 1–2 in. long and broad, 1–2 in. thick at top, gray-green or brownish thickly spotted with green, glabrous but surface uneven: fls. sessile, golden-yellow, 2–3 in. across. (Named for Harry Bolus, 1834–1911, British botanist in S. Afr.)

2. **P. Nelii,** Schwant. Similar to *P. Bolusii* but more compact, the lf. surface even and fls. short-stalked. (Named for Gert Cornelius Nel, professor of botany at Stellenbosch, S. Afr.)

6. **GLOTTIPHYLLUM,** N. E. Br. Nearly 50 species of low succulent perennials, native in S. Afr.—Stemless or nearly so: lvs. crowded, 4 or more to a growth, tongue-shaped to nearly cylindrical, two to three times as long as broad, thick and soft, usually not spotted: fls. solitary, sessile or short-stalked, yellow, without bracts;

stigmas 7–11, plumose: caps. 7–11-celled, the valves with awn-like points and wingless keels. (Glottiphyl-lum: from Greek for *tongue* and *leaf*.)

G. linguiforme, N. E. Br. (*Mesembryanthemum linguiforme*, L.). Lvs. in two ranks, 2–3 in. long and 1–1½ in. wide, ⅓in. thick, spreading and somewhat curved, upper edge acute and slightly cartilaginous, shining green and smooth: fls. sessile, golden-yellow, 2–3 in. across.

7. **CHEIRIDOPSIS,** N. E. Br. A large S. African group of 100 or more species, per. very succulent cespitose plants.—Lvs. in 1–3 pairs of different forms, in the resting stage surrounded by cup-like sheaths, green or whitish, usually spotted: fls. solitary and terminal, stalked, with bracts; stigmas 8–19, somewhat plumose: caps. 8–19-celled, the valves usually wingless. (Cheiridop-sis: *sleeve-like*, referring to the cup-like sheaths.)

C. cigarettifera, N. E. Br. (*Mesembryanthemum cigarettiferum*, Berger). Plant in resting stage a tuft of cup-like sheaths ⅓in. long inclosing a pair of erect lvs. ½in. long; free lvs. slightly united at base, to 1½ in. long, ⅓in. wide and ⅙in. thick, glaucous and dotted, keel at apex minutely toothed, second pair of lvs. united into oblong-ovoid body 2-lobed at top: fls. bright yellow, 1–1½ in. across, on pedicels ½–1½ in. long.

8. **CEPHALOPHYLLUM,** N. E. Br. Low succulents, of perhaps 50 species in S. Afr.—Stemless or with short main st., sometimes with stolon-like branches and lvs. in rosettes: lvs. 3-angled or nearly cylindrical, punctate, spreading or ascending: fls. solitary and terminal, long-stalked, without bracts; stigmas 10–20: caps. 10–20-celled. (Cephalophyl-lum: Greek *head* and *leaf*, referring to the crowded lvs.)

C. Alstonii, Marloth. Lvs. pale glaucous, to 4½ in. long and ⅓in. across: fls. ruby-purple with violet anthers, 2–3 in. across. (Collected in S. Afr. by Capt. E. Alston.)

9. **CARPOBROTUS,** N. E. Br. Woody perennials with decumbent sts., of wide distribution in S. Afr., New Zeal., Australia, Chile and Calif., about 20 species.—Lvs. opposite and united at base, 3-angled and very fleshy, scimitar-shaped: fls. large, solitary, peduncled; stigmas 10–16, plumose: fr. fleshy and indehiscent, edible. (Carpobro-tus: in reference to the edible fr.)

A. Lvs. serrate on keel: fls. commonly yellow..1. *C. edulis*
AA. Lvs. not serrate: fls. rose-purple..2. *C. chilensis*

1. **C. edulis,** L. Bolus (*Mesembryanthemum edule*, L.). Hottentot-Fig. Sts. woody and angular, 3 ft. or more long, covering banks: lvs. 3–4 in. long and ½in. thick, the keel finely serrate: fls. yellow varying to rose-purple, 2½–4 in. across, on peduncles 1 in. long: fr. large. S. Afr.; somewhat escaped in Calif.

2. **C. chilensis,** N. E. Br. (*Mesembryanthemum chilense*, Molina. *M. æquilaterale*, Auth. not Haw.). Sea-Fig. Similar to *C. edulis* but smaller: lvs. 1–2 in. long, straighter and not serrate: fls. 1–2 in. across, rose-purple. Chile, coasts of Ore. and Calif. and used for a sand-cover.

10. **CARPANTHEA,** N. E. Br. One succulent ann. from S. Afr.—Sts. prostrate, with opposite flat lvs. united at base: fls. 1–3, terminal, stalked; stigmas 12–20: caps. 12–20-celled, the keels ending in awns, wingless. (Carpan-thea: name unexplained.)

C. pomeridiana, N. E. Br. (*Mesembryanthemum pomeridianum*, L.). Diffuse or branches ascending to 1 ft.: lvs. spatulate or spatulate-lanceolate, 2–4 in. long and ½–1 in. wide, tapering into a grooved petiole, smooth, ciliate: fls. golden-yellow, 1½–3 in. across, on hairy peduncles 1½–4 in. long.

11. **CRYOPHYTUM,** N. E. Br. Succulents native in S. Afr., Medit. region, S. W. Asia and Calif., probably 50 species.—Ann., bien. or per.: lvs. scattered or opposite, or alternate on flowering branches, flat or somewhat terete: fls. solitary or in cymes; stigmas 5 or rarely 4, filiform: caps. 5-celled, the valves with winged keels. (Cryoph-ytum: Greek *ice* and *plant*.)

C. crystallinum, N. E. Br. (*Mesembryanthemum crystallinum*, L.). Ice-Plant. Ann. and bien., sts. 1–2 ft. long, spreading on the ground, with large glistening vescicles: lvs. flat, fleshy, spatulate or broad-ovate, to 6 in. long and 3 in. wide, undulate, narrowed into a short clasping base, the lower lvs. petioled and subcordate: fls. whitish to light rose, about 1 in. across, almost sessile in the axils. Greece and Canary Isls., S. Afr., S. and Lower Calif. —Grown as a window-plant, garden ann., and reported in the vegetable-garden for greens.

12. **APTENIA,** N. E. Br. One S. African succulent, somewhat escaped in Calif.—Per. with leafy prostrate branches: lvs. flat, petioled: fls. solitary in the axils, pedicelled; stigmas 4: caps. 4-celled, the valves wingless. (Apte-nia: from Greek for *wingless*.)

A. cordifolia, Schwant. (*Mesembryanthemum cordifolium,* L. f.). DEW-PLANT. Diffusely branching, glabrous, minutely papillose, little or scarcely fleshy, sts. to 2 ft. long: lvs. cordate-ovate and petiolate, 1 in. or less long: fls. purple, about ½in. across, on pedicels ½in. long. Var. **variegata,** Hort., has variegated lvs.—Grown in window-boxes and conservatories.

13. **DOROTHEANTHUS,** Schwant. Low annuals, of about 4 species in S. Afr.—Lvs. linear or spatulate, with crystalline papillæ: fls. solitary, pedicelled, without bracts; stigmas 5: caps. 5-celled, valves with small wings. (Dorothean-thus: named for Mrs. Dorothea Schwantes of Kiel, Germany.)

A. Lvs. linear....................1. *D. gramineus*
AA. Lvs. obovate....................2. *D. bellidiformis*

1. **D. gramineus,** Schwant. (*Mesembryanthemum gramineum,* Haw. *M. lineare,* Thunb. *M. pyropæum,* Haw. *M. tricolor,* Willd.). Main st. very short, the branches arising from near the base, tuberculose or papillose, making densely-fld. clumps 6–8 in. across but not so high: lvs. somewhat joined at base, rather fleshy, linear, canaliculate, 2–3 in. long, sometimes broader near apex: fls. on peduncles 1–4 in. long that are radical or terminate the branches, 1–1½ in. diam., varying from light pink with red center to self-colored white, pink and red.

2. **D. bellidiformis,** N. E. Br. (*Mesembryanthemum bellidiformis,* Burm. *M. criniflorum,* L. f. *D. criniflorus,* Schwant.). Similar to *D. gramineus* but with obovate lvs. to 3 in. long and ¼in. wide: fls. pink, red or white with pink stamens.

14. **DROSANTHEMUM,** Schwant. Succulent perennials woody at base, nearly 100 species named from S. Afr.—Sts. branching and spreading or diffuse, rough with small pustules: lvs. compressed, 3-angled or terete, with glistening papillæ: fls. 1–3, usually pedicelled, white or rose; stigmas 4–6: caps. 4–6-celled, the valves with winged keels. (Drosan-themum: flowers resembling drosera.)

D. speciosum, Schwant. (*Mesembryanthemum speciosum,* Haw.). Shrubby, to 2 ft. high: lvs. semi-terete, ½in. long and ¼in. wide, spreading or curved upward: fls. solitary and terminal, orange-red with green base, 2 in. and more across, on pedicels 2–4 in. long.

15. **LAMPRANTHUS,** N. E. Br. Per. branching herbs, as now defined over 100 species in S. Afr.—Shrubby: lvs. slightly united at base, very narrow: fls. solitary or sometimes 3, large and showy, in many colors; stigmas usually 5, subulate or plumose, often inconspicuous: caps. 5-celled, the valves with keels winged. (Lampranthus: Greek for *glossy* and *flower*.)

A. Color of fls. yellow or orange.
  B. Lvs. 2 in. long: fls. 2–2½ in. across....................1. *L. aureus*
  BB. Lvs. 1 in. long: fls. 1½ in. across....................2. *L. aurantiacus*
AA. Color of fls. rose, red, purple or white.
  B. Fls. scarlet....................3. *L. coccineus*
  BB. Fls. rose, purplish or white.
    C. Sts. prostrate: lvs. 2–3 in. long....................4. *L. spectabilis*
    CC. Sts. erect or spreading: lvs. 1–1½ in. long....................5. *L. multiradiatus*

1. **L. aureus,** N. E. Br. (*Mesembryanthemum aureum,* L.). Erect, shrubby, 1–2 ft. high: lvs. 3-angled, 1½–2 in. long and ⅛in. wide, with small reddish tip, glaucous and smooth, punctate: fls. mostly solitary on pedicels 2 in. long, golden-yellow, 2–2½ in. across.

2. **L. aurantiacus,** Schwant. (*Mesembryanthemum aurantiacum,* DC.). Similar to *L. aureus,* but lvs. 1 in. or less long and orange fls. 1½ in. across.

3. **L. coccineus,** N. E. Br. (*Mesembryanthemum coccineum,* Haw.). Shrubby, with erect sts. 2–3 ft. high: lvs. 3-angled, ½–1 in. long and 1⁄12in. wide, grayish-green and punctate: fls. solitary or in 3's, on pedicels 2–4 in. long which have 2 lf.-like bracts near the middle, scarlet, 1½ in. across.

4. **L. spectabilis,** N. E. Br. (*Mesembryanthemum spectabile,* Haw.). Sts. prostrate and woody, the flowering sts. ascending: lvs. crowded, 3-angled, incurved, 2–3 in. long and ¼in. wide, with short reddish tip, glaucous and punctate: fls. solitary or in 3's, on bracted pedicels 3–6 in. long, purple varying to white, 2–3 in. across.

5. **L. multiradiatus,** N. E. Br. (*Mesembryanthemum multiradiatum,* Jacq.). Branches spreading, 1–2 ft. high, somewhat woody: lvs. 3-angled, about 1 in. long, glaucous and

punctate: fls. solitary or few, on bracted peduncles 2–4 in. long, pale rose, about 1½ in. across.—Closely related and perhaps indistinguishable species are *L. blandus*, Schwant. (*Mesembryanthemum blandum*, Haw.), with pale rose fls. 2 in. across, and *L. roseus*, Schwant. (*Mesembryanthemum roseum*, Willd.), with deep rose fls.

16. **ASTRIDIA,** Dinter & Schwant. Succulent branching shrubs of 2 species in S. Afr.—Lvs. 3-cornered, slightly united at base: fls. solitary or few, terminal, short-stalked; stigmas 5–6, filiform, long: caps. 5–6-celled, the valves winged; seeds usually hairy. (Astrid-ia: named for Mrs. Astrid Schwantes of Kiel, Germany.)

A. maxima, Schwant. (*Mesembryanthemum maximum*, Haw.). Shrub to 1 ft. and more: lvs. crowded, half-moon-shaped, 3-angled but strongly flattened, 1½–2 in. long, glaucous and punctate: fls. rose, to ¾ in. across.

17. **OSCULARIA,** Schwant. Small shrubby perennials of 2 species in S. Afr.—Branches spreading or erect: lvs. somewhat united at base, 3-angled, grayish-green, toothed on the edges: fls. 1–3, terminal, small, short-stalked, with bracts; stigmas 5: caps. 5-celled, the valves with small wings. (Oscula-ria: name unexplained.)

O. deltoides, Schwant. (*Mesembryanthemum deltoides*, Mill.). Much-branched, erect, the branches reddish: lvs. incurved, about ½ in. long and ⅓ in. wide, with few reddish teeth on all three edges: fls. in 3's, rose, ½ in. across, on pedicels 1–1½ in. long.

18. **DELOSPERMA,** N. E. Br. Per. herbs or subshrubs, of probably 100 species in Afr.—Much-branched: lvs. 3-angled, sessile, soft: fls. solitary or in cymes, short-stalked; stigmas 5: caps. 5-celled, the cells open, without cell-wings and exposing the seeds. (Delosper-ma: Greek for *exposed seed.*)

D. echinatum, Schwant. (*Mesembryanthemum echinatum*, Ait.). Sts. erect or spreading, to 1 ft., covered with white papillæ: lvs. thick, about ½ in. long and ¼ in. wide, with large hispid papillæ: fls. solitary, white or yellowish, about ½ in. across, on short papillose pedicels.

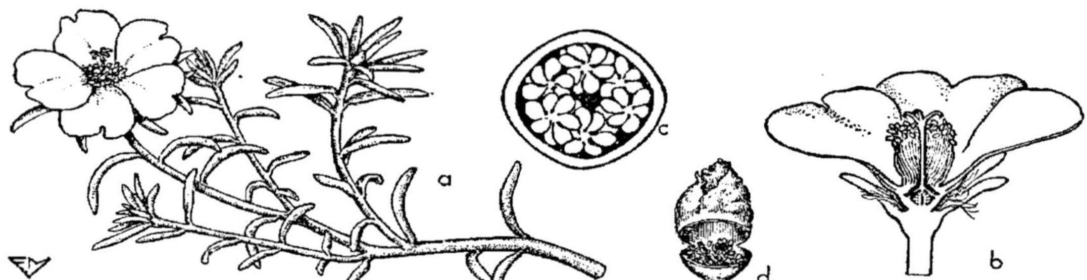

Fig. 62. PORTULACACEÆ. *Portulaca grandiflora:* a, flowering branch, × ½; b, flower, vertical section, × 1; c, ovary, cross-section, × 4; d, capsule, × 1.

62. PORTULACACEÆ. PURSLANE FAMILY

Mostly more or less fleshy herbs and small subshrubs, the larger part native of the Americas in tropics and subtropics and beyond, but some widely native in the Old World; grown for ornament and a few as pot-herbs; genera about 20 and species 220.—Plants prostrate or erect, mostly glabrous: lvs. alternate or opposite, sometimes connate, entire: fls. bisexual, regular or irregular; sepals usually 2; petals 4–5 or seldom more, sometimes connate at base, often emarginate, mostly fugacious; stamens few or many, in most genera hypogynous; pistil 1, ovary 1-celled, with free-central or basal placenta, ovules 1 to many; style 2–3-parted: fr. commonly a dehiscent caps. circumscissile or 2–3-valved; seeds mostly many, with curved or ring-like embryo.

A. Plant a shrub or tree: fr. indehiscent, 3-winged.............................1. PORTULACARIA
AA. Plant herbaceous: fr. dehiscent.
  B. Caps. circumscissile.
    C. Ovary partly inferior, adnate to calyx: caps. not splitting in upper part......2. PORTULACA
    CC. Ovary superior, free: caps. with upper part splitting to apex................3. LEWISIA
  BB. Caps. dehiscing from apex into 2–3 valves.
    C. Seeds many: st.-lvs. alternate.

D. Lvs. (in ours) terete..4. TALINUM
DD. Lvs. flat..5. CALANDRINIA
CC. Seeds 1–6: st.-lvs. (in ours) opposite.
D. Root from a corm or tuber: petals distinct..6. CLAYTONIA
DD. Root fibrous: petals united at base..7. MONTIA

1. **PORTULACARIA,** Jacq. Two S. African fleshy shrubs or small trees, grown under glass or in the open in Calif.—Glabrous: lvs. opposite, obovate, deciduous: fls. small, rose-colored, in clusters; sepals 2, persistent; petals 5, persistent; stamens 4–7; ovary superior, 3-angled, with sessile stigma: fr. indehiscent, 3-winged, 1-seeded. (Portulaca-ria: *resembling portulaca.*)

P. afra, Jacq. Small tree to 12 ft., the branches articulate: lvs. flat, roundish, to ½in. long: fls. about 1⁄12in. long, short-pedicelled.

2. **PORTULACA,** L. PURSLANE. Trailing fleshy mostly ann. herbs, of over 100 species, widely distributed in warm regions.—Lvs. usually alternate or scattered, flat or terete, the upper ones forming an involucre to the inconspicuous or showy fls. which open in sunshine; sepals 2, forming a tube at base and adnate with ovary; petals mostly 6, inserted on calyx, as also are the 7 or more stamens; style 3–9-parted: fr. a little dry pod, circumscissile near the middle, 1-celled, containing many seeds. (Portula-ca: an old Latin name.)

A. Lvs. broad and flat, although thick: plant glabrous..1. *P. oleracea* var.
AA. Lvs. terete: plant more or less pilose.
B. Plant with long thin hairs but not prominently woolly..2. *P. grandiflora*
BB. Plant looking white-woolly from the abundant tufts of hairs at nodes and with the fls..3. *P. pilosa* var.

1. **P. oleracea, L.,** var. **sativa,** DC. KITCHEN-GARDEN PURSLANE. Erect, 12–20 in., finally spreading, branches thick and soft, wholly glabrous: lvs. obovate or spatulate, very obtuse, 1–1½ in. long, tapered to a very short petiole or petiole-like base: fls. ½in. or more across, bright light yellow, strongly clustered at top of st.; petals erect-spreading, retuse; stamens usually 11 or more; stigmas 5 or 6, large and long. Grown somewhat as a pot-herb; probably a cultigen. Var. **giganthes,** Bailey, plant prostrate and widely spreading: fls. very double, bright yellow, 1 in. or more across, well set off against the prominent lf.-bracts: cultigen; a showy plant, to be expected in southern gardens.

2. **P. grandiflora,** Hook. ROSE-MOSS. Prostrate or ascending, with loose hairs at the joints and among the fls.: lvs. scattered, terete, 1 in. or less long, mostly long and prominent beneath the fls.: fls. 1 in. and more across, in bright colors, rose, red, yellow, striped, white, soon withering; sepals broad, short-acute; petals obovate, more or less notched at the end. Brazil and S.—A popular fl.-garden ann., and sometimes escaped.

3. **P. pilosa,** L., var. **hortualis,** Bailey. SHAGGY GARDEN PURSLANE. Small plant, spreading or ascending, with a woolly or white-shaggy look due to the copious tufts of hairs at the joints and beneath the fls.: lvs. terete, about ½in. long: fls. red-purple, ¾in. across, showy; petals broadly obovate, obtuse but more or less emarginate; sepals oblong, nearly or quite acute. Cultigen.—A fl.-garden ann., probably occurring south within our borders. *P. pilosa* itself, native from N. C. and Kans. south to the tropics, has much smaller and not showy fls.

3. **LEWISIA,** Pursh. Fleshy per. herbs of nearly 20 species in W. N. Amer., planted in rock-gardens.—Roots thick and starchy: lvs. mostly basal: fls. solitary or in panicles, white, pink or red; sepals 2–6, persistent; petals 4–18; stamens 5 or more; ovary superior, with 3–8 styles united at base: caps. circumscissile near base and dehiscing toward apex, seeds 6 to many. (Lewis-ia: named for Meriwether Lewis, 1774–1809, of the Lewis and Clark Expedition.)

A. Fls. in panicles or umbels, on scapes much longer than basal lvs.
B. St.-lvs. similar to basal lvs.: stamens many..1. *L. oppositifolia*
BB. St.-lvs. bract-like: stamens 4–8.
C. Lvs. broad-spatulate: fls. ½in. or more long..2. *L. Cotyledon*
CC. Lvs. linear-spatulate or oblanceolate: fls. less than ½in. long.
D. Branches of infl. ascending: lvs. flat..3. *L. columbiana*
DD. Branches of infl. spreading: lvs. nearly terete..4. *L. Leana*
AA. Fls. 1–3, on scapes shorter than or little exceeding basal lvs.
B. Floral bracts similar to and subtending sepals..5. *L. brachycalyx*
BB. Floral bracts not similar to sepals and remote from them.
C. Sepals 4–8..6. *L. rediviva*
CC. Sepals 2.
D. Lvs. obovate: fls. 1 in. long..7. *L. Tweedyi*
DD. Lvs. linear: fls. less than ½in. long..8. *L. pygmæa*

1. **L. oppositifolia,** Rob. (*Calandrinia oppositifolia,* Wats.). Sts. 4–10 in. high: lvs. both basal and cauline, linear-spatulate, 2–4 in. long, deciduous: fls. in 2–6-fld. umbels, white or pinkish, about ½in. long; sepals 2, irregularly fimbriate; stamens many. Ore., Calif.

2. **L. Cotyledon,** Rob. (*Calandrinia Cotyledon,* Wats. *L. Finchæ,* Purdy). Lvs. all basal, many and very fleshy, broad-spatulate, 1¼–4 in. long, persistent: fls. many, in panicles on scapes 4–12 in. high, white veined with pink, about ½in. long; sepals 2, with gland-tipped teeth; stamens 5–8. Ore., Calif. Var. **Howellii,** Jepson (*L. Howellii,* Wats. *Oreobroma Heckneri,* Morton. *L. Heckneri,* R. B. Smith), lvs. narrower with crisped or fimbriate margins.

3. **L. columbiana,** Rob. (*Calandrinia columbiana,* Howell). Basal lvs. flat, fleshy, linear-spatulate, 1–3 in. long, persistent, st.-lvs. few and bract-like: fls. several to many, in panicles 6–12 in. high, the branches ascending, white or pink veined with red, ⅓in. long; sepals 2, irregularly toothed and glandular; stamens 5–6. Mts., B. C. to Calif. Var. **rosea,** Hort., has rose-colored fls.

4. **L. Leana,** Rob. (*Calandrinia Leana,* Porter). Similar to *L. columbiana* but lvs. nearly terete, ½–2 in. long, infl. with numerous spreading branches, fls. magenta or white veined with red. (Named for its discoverer, L. W. Lee.) Ore., Calif.

5. **L. brachycalyx,** Engelm. Lvs. in rosettes, spatulate or oblanceolate, 2–3 in. long, deciduous: fls. solitary on scapes 1–2 in. high, white, ½–¾in. long; sepals 2, entire, subtended by floral bracts which resemble sepals; stamens 12–15. Utah to Ariz. and Calif.

6. **L. rediviva,** Pursh. Bitter-Root. Lvs. basal, very fleshy and nearly terete, 1–2 in. long, deciduous: fls. solitary on jointed scapes ½–1½ in. high, rose or white, about 1 in. long; sepals 4–8, rose or white, becoming scarious; stamens many. B. C. to Calif. and Ariz.

7. **L. Tweedyi,** Rob. (*Calandrinia Tweedyi,* Gray). Lvs. basal, obovate, 3–6 in. long, persistent: fls. 1–3 on scapes equalling or somewhat longer than lvs., yellowish or white, about 1 in. long; sepals 2, obtuse, scarious; stamens about 15. (Named for its collector, Frank Tweedy.) Wash.

8. **L. pygmæa,** Rob (*Talinum pygmæum,* Gray). Lvs. basal, linear, 1–2 in. long: fls. 1–3, on scapes 2 in. high, white or rose, ¼–⅓in. long; sepals 2, erose with glandular teeth; stamens 5–8. Mts., Wash. to Calif. and New Mex.

4. **TALINUM,** Adans. Fame-Flower. Glabrous fleshy herbs of over 50 species in warm parts of both hemispheres.—Lvs. alternate or basal, flat or terete: fls. in cymes or solitary; sepals 2, usually deciduous; petals 5, ephemeral; stamens 10–30; ovary sessile or stalked, with 3-parted style: caps. dehiscent into 3 valves, many-seeded. (Tali-num: aboriginal name.)

T. calycinum, Engelm. Per. 6–10 in. high, with thick root: lvs. clustered at base of st., terete, 1½–2 in. long: fls. in terminal cymes with ascending branches, pink, about ½in. long; sepals broad-ovate, persistent. Mo. to Mex.

5. **CALANDRINIA,** HBK. Rock-Purslane. Herbs grown in the fl.-garden; species more than 150, mostly on the western side of N. and S. Amer.—More or less fleshy, ann. and per.: lvs. alternate or basal, flat: fls. red or rose-colored, in bracted racemes of short duration; petals 3–7, usually 5; sepals 2, persistent; stamens 3–14; ovary superior, with short style and 3-parted stigma: caps. dehiscing by 3 valves, seeds many. (Calandri-nia: J. L. Calandrini, 1703–1758, of Geneva, Switzerland, who wrote an important thesis in 1734.)

A. Lvs. oval, 4–8 in. long...1. *C. grandiflora*
AA. Lvs. linear or oblanceolate, less than 3 in. long.
B. Fls. racemose or scattered along the branches......................2. *C. ciliata* var. *Menziesii*
BB. Fls. many in terminal umbel-like cluster..........................3. *C. umbellata*

1. **C. grandiflora,** Lindl. Per. 1–3 ft. high, but grown as an ann.: lvs. oval, 4–8 in. long, acute, narrowed into a broad petiole: fls. light purple or rose-red, 1–1½ in. across. Chile.

2. **C. ciliata,** DC., var. **Menziesii,** Macb. (*Talinum Menziesii,* Hook. *C. caulescens* var. *Menziesii,* Gray. *C. speciosa,* Lindl.). Red Maids. Ann. branching from the base, 8–12 in. high: lvs. narrow-spatulate to linear, to 3 in. long, acute, narrowed at base: fls. crimson or rose-red to purplish, rather large, the petals ¼–⅓in. long and retuse at apex; sepals ciliate on margins. B. C. to Mex. and Ariz.

3. **C. umbellata,** DC. (*Talinum umbellatum,* Ruiz & Pav.). Per. with ascending sts. 6–8 in. high, but grown as an ann.: lvs. mostly radical, linear, 1–2 in. long, acute, pilose: fls. many in terminal clusters, bright crimson-magenta, about ½in. long. Chile.

6. **CLAYTONIA,** L. Spring Beauty. Per. spring-blooming herbs attractive in the rock-garden; about 20 American species.—Roots from a corm or tuber: lvs.

rather fleshy, mostly basal, those of st. 2 and opposite: fls. in terminal racemes, white or rose; sepals 2, persistent; petals 5, distinct; stamens 5; ovary superior, the style 3-lobed: caps. dehiscent by 3 valves, with 1–6 seeds. (Clayto-nia: named for John Clayton, about 1686–1773, American botanist.)

C. virginica, L. Corm globose, ½–1 in. thick: sts. ascending or erect, 6–12 in. high: lvs. linear-lanceolate, 2–8 in. long and ⅙–½in. wide, acute, narrowed to petiole: fls. white or pink with darker veins, ½–¾in. across, in loose racemes. N. S. to Va. and Kans.

7. **MONTIA**, L. Glabrous ann. and per. herbs of small size, about 40 species mostly in Amer.—Lvs. opposite in the following species but in certain others alternate, more or less fleshy: fls. minute, in loose racemes, white or pinkish, usually nodding; sepals 2, persistent; petals 3–5, more or less connate at base; stamens 2–5; style 3-parted: fr. a 3-valved caps. with 1–3 seeds. (Mon-tia: Guiseppe Monti, 1682–1760, professor of botany at Bologna.)

M. perfoliata, Howell (*Claytonia perfoliata*, Donn. *Limnia perfoliata*, Haw.). Winter-Purslane. Short-lived ann., mostly a winter plant in warm countries, sometimes grown as a salad and pot-herb: lvs. all radical except 2 that are connate into a broad disk beneath the fls., rhomboid-ovate to spatulate-obovate, with very long petioles: scapes 3–12 in. high bearing the small white short-pedicelled fls. at the summit. B. C. to Mex.; intro. into other regions and countries.

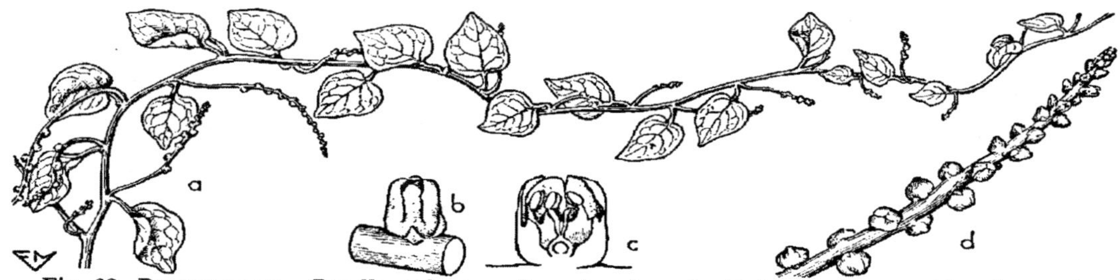

Fig. 63. Basellaceæ. *Basella rubra:* a, flowering branch, × ⅛; b, flower, side view, × 2; c, flower, vertical section, × 3; d, inflorescence, × ½.

63. BASELLACEÆ. BASELLA FAMILY

Climbing per. fleshy herbs, of 5 genera and about 20 species, native mostly in trop. Amer., a few cult. for food and ornament.—Rootstocks tuberous: lvs. alternate, usually petioled, broad, entire, mostly fleshy, glabrous: fls. bisexual, regular, racemose, small, with 2 bracts; sepals 2, sometimes adnate to the base of the corolla; petals 5, separate or somewhat united, persistent, remaining closed; stamens 5, opposite the petals; ovary superior, 1-celled, 1-ovuled; styles usually 3, with entire or cleft stigmas: fr. indehiscent and fleshy, inclosed by the persistent corolla.

A. Fls. sessile..1. Basella
AA. Fls. pedicelled..2. Boussingaultia

1. **BASELLA**, L. Malabar-Nightshade. Fleshy ann. or bien. herbs grown in the tropics and warm countries as pot-herbs, of 4 variable species distributed throughout the tropics, probably Asian.—Twining glabrous vines: fls. small, sessile, in clusters on elongated thickened peduncles in an open branching infl.; sepals somewhat carinate but not winged in fr.; filaments erect in bud. (Basel-la: native Malabar name.)

A. Lvs. as broad as long, cordate or subcordate at base: fls. reddish....................1. *B. rubra*
AA. Lvs. narrower, prevailingly longer than broad, rounded or tapering at base: fls. whitish...2. *B. alba*

1. **B. rubra**, L. A rampant-growing vine with green or purplish sts.: lvs. 2–6 or more in. wide, about as broad as long, ovate to suborbicular, cordate at base, obtuse or somewhat emarginate: fls. on short spikes, in small clusters, reddish: fr. ovoid or globose, about ¼in. diam.

2. **B. alba**, L. Very similar but with narrower lvs. ovate to ovate-lanceolate, prevailingly longer than broad, rounded or tapering at base, acute or slightly obtuse, somewhat undulate, and whitish fls. in longer-peduncled spikes arranged in very loose clusters.

2. **BOUSSINGAULTIA,** HBK. Per. herbaceous vines, of 14 species in trop. Amer., one of which is grown over arbors and porches.—Sts. much-branched: fls. small, pedicelled, in axillary and terminal spike-like racemes; sepals nearly flat, not winged; filaments bent over in bud. (Boussingaul-tia: after J. B. Boussingault, 1802–1887, French agricultural chemist.)

B. gracilis, Miers, var. **pseudo-baselloides,** Bailey (*B. baselloides*, Auth. not HBK., Hook. or Hemsl. *B. gracilis* forma *pseudo-baselloides*, Hauman). MADEIRA-VINE. MIGNONETTE-VINE. A rapidly-growing twining vine attaining 10–20 ft. in a season, producing little tubercles in the axils of the lvs. by means of which the plant is propagated as it is not known to produce fr.; root tuberous and hardy in the N.: lvs. ovate, 1–3 in. long, subcordate at base, short-petioled: racemes slender, sometimes 1 ft. long, many-fld.; fls. white, becoming black with age, fragrant, blooming in late summer or autumn. Trop. Amer.

64. ILLECEBRACEÆ. KNOTWORT FAMILY

About 19 genera and 100 species of ann. and per. herbs widely distributed in both hemispheres.—Lvs. mostly opposite, entire, stipulate: fls. small, greenish or whitish, in cymes; calyx persistent, 4–5-parted, sepals distinct or united; petals none or minute; stamens 4–5 (1–10), borne on the calyx; styles 2, often united; ovary superior, 1-celled, with 1 ovule: fr. a utricle, inclosed in the calyx-tube; embryo curved.

Fig. 64. ILLECEBRACEÆ. *Herniaria glabra:* a, flowering branches, × 2; b, sterile branch, × 2; c, flower, face view, × 20; d, same, vertical section, × 30 (adapted from Hegi).

HERNIARIA, L. RUPTURE-WORT. Trailing herbs; about 20 species in Eu., W. Asia, N. Afr. and the Canaries, and 1 species in S. Afr., growing in sandy places usually near the sea.—Prostrate, much-branched, glabrous or hirsute: lvs. small, sessile, with very small scarious stipules: fls. green, crowded in axillary fascicles; sepals 5; petals 0; stamens 5. (Hernia-ria: from Greek *hernia*, referring to its supposed cure of rupture.)

H. glabra, L. Nodose per. 4–6 in. high, sts. spreading along the ground several in.: lvs. oblong or rarely orbicular, less than ¼in. long, glabrous except a few hairs at edges, usually bronzy-red in winter: fls. sessile, in axillary clusters on the lateral branches, making a leafy spike. Eu., Asia.—Grown for carpet-bedding, rock-gardens, and covering graves.

65. CARYOPHYLLACEÆ. PINK FAMILY

About 55 genera and more than 1,300 species of herbs, rarely suffruticose, widely distributed over the earth, most abundant in temp. and cold regions; the family contributes many annuals and perennials to the fl.-garden, and the carnation is also extensively grown under glass; there are no "foliage plants" amongst them.—Sts. usually swollen at the joints: lvs. opposite, entire, often united at base: fls. regular, usually bisexual; sepals 4–5, persistent, free or united; petals 4–5 or rarely wanting; stamens 8–10 or seldom fewer, hypogynous or perigynous; styles 2–5, free or sometimes united; ovary superior, 1-celled, rarely 2–5-celled, with free-central placentæ, ovules many: fr. a caps., rarely a berry, opening by valves or indehiscent; seeds albuminous; embryo strongly curved or coiled.

A. Sepals distinct, or nearly so.
  B. Stipules present; lvs. much fascicled in the axils, appearing whorled .... 1. SPERGULA
  BB. Stipules lacking; lvs. opposite (rarely in whorls of 4).
    C. Petals entire or rarely emarginate.

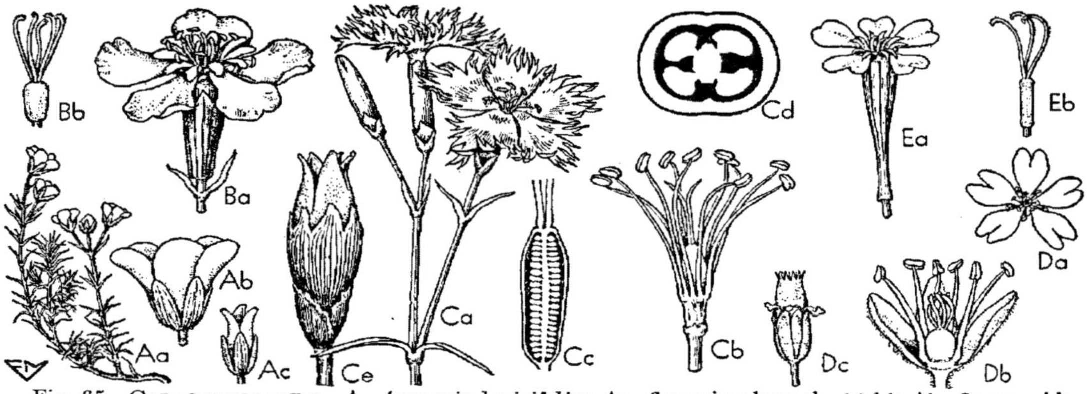

Fig. 65. CARYOPHYLLACEÆ. A, *Arenaria laricifolia:* Aa, flowering branch, × ¼; Ab, flower, side view, × 1; Ac, capsule, × 1. B, *Lychnis Viscaria:* Ba, flower, × 1; Bb, pistil, × 1. C, *Dianthus plumarius:* Ca, flowering branch, × ½; Cb, flower, less perianth, × 1; Cc, ovary, vertical section, × 2; Cd, ovary, cross-section, × 5; Ce, capsule, × 1. D, *Cerastium tomentosum:* Da, flower, face view, × ½; Db, same, side view, less corolla, × 2; Dc, capsule, × 1. E, *Silene Armeria:* Ea, flower, × 1; Eb, pistil, × 1½.

D. Styles as many as sepals, 4 or 5 .... 2. SAGINA
DD. Styles fewer than sepals, usually 3 .... 3. ARENARIA
CC. Petals 2-cleft.
D. Styles usually 3: caps. dehiscent beyond the middle .... 4. STELLARIA
DD. Styles usually 5: caps. dehiscent at apex by teeth .... 5. CERASTIUM
AA. Sepals united into a tube or cup for one-half or more their length.
B. Base of calyx with scaly bracts or small lvs.
C. Calyx conspicuously scarious between its 5 (in ours) green nerves .... 6. TUNICA
CC. Calyx not scarious, many-veined (striate) .... 7. DIANTHUS
BB. Base of calyx naked.
C. Styles 5, rarely 4.
D. Lvs. 1–4 in. or more long, if shorter then fls. many, in dense heads .... 8. LYCHNIS
DD. Lvs. ⅙–¾in. long: fls. few, not in heads .... 9. PETROCOPTIS
CC. Styles 2–3.
D. Number of styles 3 .... 10. SILENE
DD. Number of styles 2.
E. Calyx scarious between its 5 green nerves: caps. deeply 4-valved .... 11. GYPSOPHILA
EE. Calyx not scarious, obscurely nerved: caps. with 4 apical teeth .... 12. SAPONARIA

1. **SPERGULA,** L. About 5 species of ann. herbs native in temp. regions of the world; one, the spurry, cult. for forage on poor sandy soils and as a green-manure crop.—Lvs. subulate, with small scarious stipules, much fascicled in the axils: fls. white, in terminal cymes, pedicelled; sepals 5; petals 5, entire; stamens 10 or 5, alternate with sepals: caps. many-seeded, 5-valved, the valves opposite the sepals. (Sper-gula: Latin *to scatter*.)

S. sativa, Boenn. SPURRY. Dull green, viscid, 6–24 in. tall: lvs. linear, 1–2 in. long, clustered at nodes in two opposite sets of 6–8 together, appearing as if verticillate: fls. small, numerous: seeds margined, with obscure dots but not papillate. Eu.; sparingly adventive in E. U. S.—*S. arvensis*, L., differs in being bright green, not viscid, and seeds with whitish papillæ.

2. **SAGINA,** L. PEARLWORT. Ann. or per. small tufted herbs; 20–30 species in temp. regions of the northern hemisphere, south in the mts. to Chile.—Lvs. awl-shaped or linear: fls. small, white, on long axillary pedicels, seldom in cymes; sepals 4 or 5; petals 4 or 5 or wanting, sometimes emarginate; stamens 4–5 or 8–10; styles 4 or 5 and alternate with the sepals: caps. dehiscent to the base by 4 or 5 valves opposite the sepals. (Sagi-na: ancient name of spurry.)

A. Fls. 5-merous; petals subequal to sepals .... 1. *S. subulata*
AA. Fls. 4-merous; petals one-half as long as sepals .... 2. *S. procumbens*

1. **S. subulata,** Presl (*Spergula subulata*, Sw. *Spergula pilifera*, Hort. not DC.). Low-growing densely tufted evergreen per. forming a mossy mat: lvs. awl-shaped, mostly less than ¼in. long, with a bristle-tip as long as width of lf., usually somewhat pubescent: fls. 1–3, on slender pedicels to 1¼ in. long; petals subequal to the sepals: caps. scarcely longer than calyx. Eu.—Much of the material cult. as *Arenaria verna* var. *cæspitosa* and *A. cæspitosa* belongs here or the following species.

2. **S. procumbens,** L. Similar in habit to *S. subulata:* lvs. linear, ¼–½in. or more long, with a short bristle-tip, usually glabrous: fl. solitary, on slender pedicels; petals about half as long as sepals: caps. slightly longer than calyx. Eu.; widely nat.

3. **ARENARIA,** L. Sandwort. About 250 species of low-growing ann. or per. herbs native in temp. regions of the world; the cult. species are mostly per., used for mats and borders.—Lvs. opposite, narrow, entire, sessile: fls. usually white, in terminal cymes or heads, rarely axillary and solitary; sepals 5; petals 5, usually entire, rarely lacking; stamens 10; styles 3 (2–5): caps. with as many or twice as many valves or teeth as the styles. (Arena-ria: Latin for *sand,* referring to the habitat of many species.)—The genus as described here includes Alsine and Minuartia of various authors.

A. Length of lvs., at least the basal or lower st.-lvs., 2–10 in. . . . . 1. *A. Biebersteinii*
AA. Length of all lvs. less than 1 in.
  B. Lvs. ovate to elliptic, to ⅛in. long: all fls. solitary . . . . 2. *A. balearica*
  BB. Lvs. linear-filiform to narrowly ovate, ⅛–¾in. long: fls. usually not solitary.
    C. Fls. rose, rarely white: caps. twice as long as calyx. . . . . 3. *A. purpurascens*
    CC. Fls. white: caps. one to one and a half times as long as calyx.
      D. Shape of lvs. linear-lanceolate to narrowly ovate.
        E. Margins of lvs. ciliate only near base; lvs. ¼–½in. long, with prickly-acute tip. . . . . 4. *A. grandiflora*
        EE. Margins of lvs. minutely ciliate from base to tip; lvs. ½–¾in. long, obtusely acute. . . . . 5. *A. montana*
      DD. Shape of lvs. linear-filiform to subulate.
        E. Sepals 1-nerved: caps. one and a half times as long as calyx. . . . . 4. *A. grandiflora*
        EE. Sepals distinctly 3-nerved, at least at base: caps. usually only slightly longer than calyx.
          F. Diam. of fls. ½–¾in.; sepals obtuse. . . . . 6. *A. laricifolia*
          FF. Diam. of fls. ¼–⅓in.; sepals acute or acuminate.
            G. St.-lvs. mostly ½–¾in. long, spreading. . . . . 7. *A. stricta*
            GG. St.-lvs. ¼–⅓in. long, not spreading. . . . . 8. *A. verna*

1. **A. Biebersteinii,** Schlecht. (*Alsine Preslii,* Reuss. *Arenaria Preslii,* Nym. *Arenaria graminifolia,* Schrad. not Arduini). Tufted per. 8–15 (20) in. high, with basal sterile shoots and many upright unbranched sparingly leafy fl.-sts.: lvs. linear-filiform, 2–10 in. long, margins usually rough-serrulate-ciliate: fls. white, about ¼in. across, in loose cymes; sepals ovate, usually obtuse, with 1 distinct midrib, margins membranous, one-third to one-half as long as petals: caps. about twice as long as calyx, dehiscent by 6 short recurved teeth. (Named for von Bieberstein, page 40.) Cent. Eu.—Most of the material in the trade as *A. tmolea* belongs here; *A. tmolea,* Boiss., has ovate-oblong lvs. about ⅓in. long.

2. **A. balearica,** L. Creeping per. to 3 in., forming a dense mat: lvs. ovate to elliptic, to ⅛in. long, thick, glossy, usually somewhat coarsely pubescent: fls. white, to ¼in. across, solitary, on long thread-like purplish peduncles; sepals erect, purplish, pubescent, about half as long as petals. Sardinia, Corsica.

3. **A. purpurascens,** Ramond. Tufted per. to about 4 in., with bare grayish decumbent sts., bearing leafy branches at the tips: lvs. ovate-lanceolate to oblong-linear, ⅛–¼ (½) in. long, acute, margins usually slightly rolled but lacking cilia: fls. rose or sometimes white, 1–3 to a st., on pubescent pedicels; sepals glabrous, one-half to three-fourths as long as petals: caps. glabrous, about twice as long as calyx. Pyrenees.

4. **A. grandiflora, L.** Per. 1–6 (10) in. high, with a woody branching rootstock; sts. slender, decumbent or upright, with thin white hairs: lvs. linear-lanceolate, ¼–½in. long, tip prickly, with distinct midrib and 2 marginal veins, margins ciliate in lower half: fls. white, to ⅔in. diam., 1–3 to a st.; sepals pubescent, with 1 conspicuous midrib, tip prickly; petals to twice as long as calyx: caps. about one and a half times as long as calyx, dehiscent by 6 apical teeth. Cent. and S. Eu.—Some of the material cult. as *A. pinifolia* belongs here.

5. **A. montana,** L. Per. 2–4 (10) in. high, with weak decumbent sts. to 1 ft. long, usually finely pubescent throughout: lvs. linear-lanceolate to narrowly ovate, ½–¾in. long, subacute, midrib distinct, margins slightly thickened and ciliate: fls. white, to about 1 in. across, 1 to few to a st.; sepals with single midrib, one-third to one-half as long as petals: caps. subequal to calyx. S. W. Eu.

6. **A. laricifolia,** L. Tufted per. to 8 in., with erect or decumbent somewhat leafy flowering sts., glabrous below, pubescent above, lacking glands: lvs. narrow-linear, to ¾in. long, acute, 1-nerved, often somewhat recurved and sickle-shaped: fls. white, ½–¾ (1) in. across, in few-fld. cymes; sepals 3-nerved, pubescent, one-half to two-thirds as long as petals: caps. with 3 teeth, equal to or longer than calyx. Alps.—Part of the material cult. as *A. pinifolia* and *A. grandiflora* belongs here.

7. **A. stricta,** Michx. Tufted per. 6–12 (16) in. high, glabrous, with many slender usually simple (below the cymes) erect or ascending sts.: lvs. linear-filiform, ¼–¾in. long, 1-nerved, margins revolute on young lvs., stiff, spreading, with numerous lvs. in

axillary fascicles: fls. white, about ⅓in. across, in loose many-fld. cymes; sepals distinctly 3-ribbed, about half as long as petals: caps. slightly exceeding calyx. N. H. to S. C., Minn. and Mo.

8. **A. verna,** L. Tufted per. 2–6 in. high, with many basal sterile shoots and upright or ascending slender usually branched sparingly leafy flowering sts.: lvs. linear-subulate, to about ⅓in. long, 3-nerved, erect: fls. white, about ¼in. across, in 2- to many-fld. cymes; sepals ovate-lanceolate, acuminate, 3-nerved, with a membranous margin, subequal to the petals: caps. with obtuse teeth, slightly longer than calyx. Arctic and subarctic in both hemispheres. Var. **aurea,** Hort., has yellow-green foliage. Var. **cæspitosa,** Ser. (*A. cæspitosa,* Ehrh.), is a more compact low-growing glabrescent form; sts. few-fld., more leafy; much of the material cult. as *A. verna* var. *cæspitosa* and *A. cæspitosa* is to be referred to *Sagina subulata* or *S. procumbens,* both of which have almost veinless obtuse sepals and styles as many as sepals. Var. **pubescens,** Fern. (*A. hirta* var. *pubescens,* Cham. & Schlecht.), has calyces and pedicels glandular-pubescent.

4. **STELLARIA,** L. More than 100 species of herbs scattered all over the world but chiefly in temp. regions, the following grown in borders and for ground-cover.—Usually diffuse, tufted: fls. white, in terminal leafy or naked cymes, rarely axillary or solitary; sepals 5, rarely 4; petals as many as sepals, usually 2-cleft, or sometimes lacking; stamens 10 or fewer; styles 3, rarely 4 or 5 and then alternate with sepals: caps. globose, ovoid or oblong, many-seeded, dehiscent beyond the middle by twice as many valves as there are styles. (Stella-ria: Latin *star,* referring to the shape of the fls.)

S. Holostea, L. EASTER BELLS. Erect per. from a creeping rootstock, 6 in.–2 ft. high, with simple or somewhat branched sts., glabrous or somewhat downy: lvs. sessile, lanceolate, 1–3 in. long, ciliate on midvein and margins: fls. ½–¾in. across, blooming in May and June; sepals one-half to two-thirds length of petals; petals bifid about half their length. (Holostea: old Greek name of a plant.) Eu., N. Asia; sparingly adventive in E. U. S.

5. **CERASTIUM,** L. MOUSE-EAR CHICKWEED. Ann. or per. herbs, a few species grown for edgings and in rock-gardens; species variable, probably about 50 but by some authors described as 100, of world-wide distribution, most abundant in temp. zones.—Usually pubescent or hirsute: fls. white, in terminal dichotomous cymes; sepals 5, rarely 4; petals as many, usually emarginate or 2-cleft, rarely wanting; stamens 10 or fewer; styles 5, rarely 4 or 3, opposite the sepals: caps. cylindric, many-seeded, dehiscing at apex by twice as many teeth as there are styles. (Cerastium: Greek for *horn,* alluding to the shape of the pod.)

A. Pubescence of clearly twisted hairs.
  B. Lvs. ½–¾in. long, about ⅛in. wide.................................1. *C. tomentosum*
  BB. Lvs. 1–1½ in. long, about ⅙in. wide.................................2. *C. Biebersteinii*
AA. Pubescence of straight hairs.
  B. Lvs. mostly linear; fascicles of sterile lvs. present in lower lf.-axils..............3. *C. arvense*
  BB. Lvs. mostly ovate-lanceolate; fascicles of sterile lvs. lacking..................4. *C. alpinum*

1. **C. tomentosum,** L. (*C. Columnæ,* Ten.). SNOW IN SUMMER. Diffuse per. with creeping sts., 6–12 in. high, grayish-tomentose: lvs. linear-lanceolate, ½–¾in. long, about ⅛in. wide: fls. ½–¾in. across, blooming in early summer, in 7–15-fld. cymes; pedicels two to three times longer than calyx: caps. longer than calyx. Eu.

2. **C. Biebersteinii,** DC. Very similar to *C. tomentosum* but with larger lvs. averaging 1–1½ in. long and about ⅙in. wide, and the larger fls. and fr. (Named after F. A. M. von Bieberstein, page 40.) Mts. of Asia Minor.

3. **C. arvense,** L. STARRY GRASSWORT. Densely tufted per. 4–12 in. high, with erect or ascending sts.: lvs. linear or narrowly lanceolate, ½–1½ in. long, about ⅙in. wide: fls. numerous, blooming Apr.–May; petals bifid about one-fourth their length, about twice as long as calyx: caps. one-third or more longer than calyx. Widespread in N. Amer., also Eu. and Asia.

4. **C. alpinum,** L. Per. forming a more or less dense mat, with weak flowering sts. to 12 in. long, usually silky-hairy and sometimes glandular: lvs. ovate-lanceolate to oblong, ¼–¾in. long, ⅛–¼in. wide: fls. 1–6, on pedicels about four times as long as calyx; petals about twice as long as calyx, shallowly bifid: caps. to twice as long as calyx. Arctic and alpine regions of northern hemisphere.—The material cult. is mostly var. **lanatum,** Hegetschw. (*C. lanatum,* Lam.), with long white-woolly tomentose pubescence, not glandular.

6. **TUNICA,** Scop. About 30 species of ann. or per. slender wiry-stemmed herbs, native in the Medit. region, one grown in fl.-gardens.—Lvs. narrow: fls. in cymose

panicles or heads, similar to Dianthus but smaller; calyx top-shaped or prismatic, obtusely 5-toothed, 5–15-nerved, conspicuously scarious between the green nerves, with scaly bracts at base or rarely naked; petals 5, long-clawed, limb emarginate or 2-cleft; stamens 10; styles 2: caps. ovoid or oblong, dehiscent by 4 valves. (Tu-nica: from Latin for *tunic* or coat, referring to the imbricated calyx.)

T. Saxifraga, Scop. (*Dianthus Saxifragus,* L.). TUNIC-FLOWER. COAT-FLOWER. Per. to 10 in., tufted, spreading, downy or glabrous: lvs. narrow-linear, mostly ¼–½in. long, acute, margins rough: fls. pink or pale purple, about ⅓in. across, summer-blooming; bracts acute, scarious-margined: caps. slightly longer than calyx. Eu.; adventive in E. U. S.—Has much the appearance of a saxifrage, whence the name. Two color vars. are: **alba,** white, and **rosea,** rose-pink; there are also double-fld. vars.

7. **DIANTHUS,** L. PINK. Ann. or mostly per. herbs in cult., widely grown in gardens for their showy fls. and the carnation also under glass; probably about 300 species in the Medit. region, some extending through Siberia to arctic Amer. and to Japan and the Himalayas, a few through Abyssinia to the Cape.—Lvs. narrow, usually grass-like: fls. terminal, solitary or cymose-paniculate; calyx 5-toothed, cylindrical, with many fine nerves, subtended by 2 or more bracts; petals 5, long-clawed, entire, toothed or fringed; stamens 10; styles 2: caps. cylindric or oblong, dehiscent by 4 (5) teeth or valves at apex. (Dian-thus: from Greek for *flower of Jove.*)—Nine hort. classes of pinks may be distinguished: (1) the Carnation (*D. Caryophyllus*), in N. Amer. known as a glasshouse plant, although the outdoor border kinds are somewhat grown; (2) Rainbow pinks (*D. chinensis*), short-lived per. but grown as ann. or bien.; (3) Cottage and Hortulan pinks (*D. plumarius* and derivatives), very fragrant, low tufted per., the "pink" of literature; (4) Cheddar pinks (*D. gratianopolitanus*), hardy small per.; (5) Maiden pinks (*D. deltoides*), making broad mats with many small fls., sometimes used for per. borders and for colonizing; (6) Sweet Williams (*D. barbatus* and *D. latifolius*), with small fls. in bracteate heads; (7) Clusterheads (*D. carthusianorum* and related kinds), with dense heads of small fls. on long stiff sts.; (8) general garden pinks of many species, with open growth and fls. mostly single or in loose clusters; (9) rock-garden pinks, species of low tufted growth.

A. Fls. in heads or dense clusters surrounded by involucre-like bracts.
  B. Lvs. flat and broad, main ones ⅜–½in. or more wide.
    C. Clusters compact, cymose, terminating the main st. .... 1. *D. barbatus*
    CC. Clusters several or many, smaller, sts. much forked .... 2. *D. latifolius*
  BB. Lvs. narrow, grass-like, not over ¼in. wide.
    C. Color of fls. yellow .... 3. *D. Knappii*
    CC. Color of fls. rose, lilac, red, varying to whitish.
      D. Plant viscid-pubescent .... 4. *D. viscidus*
      DD. Plant glabrous or only scabrous, not viscid.
        E. Outer involucral bracts usually much shorter than calyx, the setiferous tips ⅛–3/16 in. long .... 5. *D. carthusianorum*
        EE. Outer involucral bracts equalling or longer than calyx, the setiferous tips over ½in. long .... 6. *D. cruentus*
AA. Fls. solitary, or if somewhat aggregate then loose and each fl. on its own pedicel; involucre-like bracts usually not evident.
  B. Petals entire to dentate, the clefts not over one-fourth the depth of the limb.
    C. Plant low, usually cespitose, fl.-sts. rarely over 6 in. high.
      D. The petals glabrous.
        E. Diam. of fls. ½–¾in.; calyx ½–⅝in. long .... 7. *D. sylvestris* var.
        EE. Diam. of fls. not over ½in.; calyx ⅜in. long .... 8. *D. subacaulis*
      DD. The petals barbulate.
        E. Bracts (at least the outer ones) more than half as long as calyx.
          F. Length of lvs. ½in. or less .... 9. *D. brevicaulis*
          FF. Length of lvs. ½–3 in.
            G. Lvs. acute, not tapering toward base .... 10. *D. neglectus*
            GG. Lvs. obtuse, tapering toward base.
              H. Limb of petal subequal to calyx: fl.-sts. much surpassing basal lvs. .... 11. *D. alpinus*
              HH. Limb of petal about half as long as calyx: fl.-sts. subequal to basal lvs. .... 12. *D. glacialis*
        EE. Bracts one-third to half as long as calyx.
          F. Number of bracts usually 2.
            G. Fl.-sts. unbranched, leafless .... 13. *D. microlepis*
            GG. Fl.-sts. usually branched, bearing lvs. .... 18. *D. deltoides* var.
          FF. Number of bracts 4.

G. Lvs. narrowly linear, sharp-pointed, erect................14. *D. graniticus*
GG. Lvs. broad and flaccid......................................15. *D. gratianopolitanus*
CC. Plant taller, with fl.-sts. 8–30 in. high.
D. The petals glabrous.
E. Bracts often exceeding calyx..................................16. *D. Sundermannii*
EE. Bracts about one-fourth as long as calyx.
F. Foliage glaucous: fls. 1–4 in. across, fragrant................17. *D. Caryophyllus*
FF. Foliage green: fls. 1 in. or less across, odorless .... 7. *D. sylvestris*
DD. The petals barbulate.
E. Bracts usually 2: plants forming thin mats by means of stolons... 18. *D. deltoides*
EE. Bracts 4 or rarely 6.
F. Species with fl.-sts. erect, leafy to summit: lvs. usually broad and flat: fls. few to many to a st.
G. Duration ann. or per., basal lvs. gone by flowering time....19. *D. chinensis*
GG. Duration distinctly per., basal lvs. present at flowering time..20. *D. Seguieri*
FF. Species cespitose, lvs. mostly basal: fls. 1–4 to a st.
G. Lvs. usually less than 1 in. long..........................14. *D. graniticus*
GG. Lvs. 1–3 in. long.
H. Bracts long-acuminate, outer ones often as long as calyx.10. *D. neglectus*
HH. Bracts abruptly short-pointed, about one-third as long as calyx...15. *D. gratianopolitanus*
BB. Petals fimbriate, the clefts one-third or more the depth of the limb.
C. Plant not cespitose (basal lvs., if present, usually gone before flowering time).
D. Fl. 1 in. or less across, usually solitary..........................21. *D. orientalis*
DD. Fl. 1½–4 in. across, 2–15 to a st.
E. The petals irregularly cut about half their depth, fls. odorless..... 19. *D. chinensis* var.
EE. The petals cut narrowly to the claw, fls. very fragrant..........22. *D. superbus*
CC. Plant cespitose.
D. The petals glabrous; fls. white, sometimes tinged or spotted rose.
E. Fringe about one-third depth of petals..........................23. *D. fragrans*
EE. Fringe nearly to claw of petals..................................24. *D. Noeanus*
DD. The petals barbulate; fls. rose, pink, or white.
E. Foliage glaucous.
F. Lvs. 1-nerved, side veins indistinct..........................25. *D. plumarius*
FF. Lvs. 3–5-nerved..26. *D. Sternbergii*
EE. Foliage green.
F. Bracts short-acute...27. *D. arenarius*
FF. Bracts long-acuminate.
G. Lvs. less than 1½ in. long: fls. fragrant...................28. *D. spiculifolius*
GG. Lvs. 2–3 in. long: fls. odorless ....29. *D. hyssopifolius*

1. **D. barbatus,** L. Sweet William. Glabrous, 9–30 in. high, sts. 4-angled, simple or branched only above: lvs. broad and flat, lanceolate to ovate-lanceolate or narrowly elliptic, 1½–3 in. long, margins ciliate, indistinctly 5-nerved, green: fls. usually red spotted with white, odorless, short-pedicelled, several to many in a round-topped dense cyme which is subtended by narrow pointed spreading lf.-like bracts; petals contiguous, toothed and bearded; calyx striate, teeth acuminate; bracts 4, long-pointed, equalling calyx. Russia to China, south to the Pyrenees; escaped in E. U. S.—Runs into many other colors as dark scarlet (*atrococcineus*), pink, rose, purple, and white; there are also double-fld. kinds. There are several hybrids between this and other related species.

2. **D. latifolius,** Willd. Button Pink. Glabrous, 6–18 in. high, sts. 4-angled and branched: lvs. oblong-lanceolate to oblanceolate, 2–4 in. long, tapering both ways, margins ciliate: fls. usually red or red-purple, 1 in. or less across, 2–4 together at ends of branchlets, clusters subtended by usually narrow awl-pointed lf.-like bracts; petals shallowly dentate; calyx striate, teeth acute; bracts about 6, slender-pointed, of various lengths. Habitat unknown, possibly of garden origin; an intermediate between *D. barbatus* and *D. chinensis* or *D. plumarius* and accounted a hybrid. Var. **atrococcineus,** Hort., has dark scarlet fls.

3. **D. Knappii,** Aschers. & Kanitz. Hardly cespitose, lightly glaucous, with many erect terete sts. 8–20 in. tall, unbranched except near top: lvs. to 2½ in. long, flat, long-tapering to a sharp point: fls. pale yellow with brownish mark in center, 8–10 in dense terminal heads; petals crenate-dentate and usually barbulate; calyx striate, teeth acuminate; bracts 4, very long-pointed, one-half or more length of calyx, below them a floral lf. that may be as long as head. (Named for J. A. H. Knapp.) Hungary, Jugoslavia.

4. **D. viscidus,** Bory & Chaub. Cespitose, viscid-pubescent, with many simple ascending sts. to about 1 ft. high: lvs. soft, flat, to about 1 in. long at base of plant, shorter and somewhat recurved above, 1–3-nerved underneath when dry: fls. purplish and spotted, usually 3–6 in loose head-like cymes; petals barbulate and dentate; calyx striate, with acuminate teeth; bracts 4, very long-pointed, half or more length of calyx. Balkans, Greece. Var. **Grisebachii,** Boiss. (*D. Grisebachii,* Boiss.), somewhat shorter, glandular-pubescent, fls. 1–3; Macedonia; material cult. as *D. pyridicola* may belong here.

5. **D. carthusianorum,** L. Cespitose, usually glabrous, 3–24 in. high, sts. 4-angled and simple: lvs. linear and pointed, 2–4 in. long, erect, green, rarely glaucous: fls. short-peduncled or sessile, odorless, in shades of red, in a dense 2-to many-fld. head which is subtended by narrow or awl-like lvs. sometimes longer than head; petals irregularly toothed, barbulate, often contiguous; calyx striate, teeth long-acuminate; bracts 4, broad and mu-

cronate, shorter than calyx, yellowish or straw-colored. Denmark to Portugal and Egypt. Var. **atrorubens,** Ser. (*D. atrorubens,* All.), tall, involucral-bracts with attenuate tips, petals dark red; some of the material cult. as *D. cruentus* may belong here. Var. **giganteus,** Hort. (*D. giganteus,* Hort. not D'Urv.), large stout race with heads 1½ in. across, fls. bright pink.

6. **D. cruentus,** Griseb. Cespitose, usually glabrous and glaucous, with 4-angled sts. to about 2 ft. high: lvs. narrow, to about 6 in. long, acute, usually 5-nerved: fls. red, in dense few- to many-fld. heads; petals dentate, usually glabrous; calyx reddish, striate, teeth acuminate; bracts broad, with abruptly aristate tip, half as long as or subequal to calyx. S. E. Eu.—Some of the material cult. under this name may be *D. carthusianorum* var. *atrorubens.*

7. **D. sylvestris,** Wulfen. Wood Pink. Cespitose, with erect angled sts. much surpassing basal foliage: lower lvs. 1–4 in. long, very narrow and long-pointed, glabrous, margins usually serrulate, mostly 3-nerved beneath when dry; st.-lvs. in successively smaller pairs, erect or spreading: fls. rose, 1 in. or less across, odorless, 1–2 (3) to a st.; petals contiguous, not barbulate, margins usually serrate; calyx ¾–1 in. long, subcylindric, finely striate, teeth rather short; bracts usually 4, short and broad, abruptly short-acuminate, about one-fourth length of calyx. Spain to E. Eu. Var. **subacaulis,** Koch (*D. frigidus,* Kit. *D. sylvestris* var. *frigidus,* Williams), dwarf, 3–5 in. high; fls. ½–¾in. across, calyx ½–⅝in. long; high mts. of S. Eu.

8. **D. subacaulis,** Vill. Densely cespitose, with a much-branched caudex or root bearing short clustered lvs. above which the 1- or 2-fld. angled sts. project 1–2 (4) in.: basal lvs. 1 in. long, narrow, acute, recurved, 3-nerved beneath when dry: fls. rose, ½in. or less across; petals non-contiguous, dentate or entire, lighter colored beneath; calyx about ⅜in. long, purplish, striate, teeth acute or obtusish; bracts 4, pointed, about one-third as long as calyx. France, Spain.

9. **D. brevicaulis,** Fenzl. Tufted, somewhat glaucous, 1–3 (5) in. high, with numerous sts., usually with 1 pair of lvs. close to the solitary fl.: lvs. ¼–½in. long, obtusish, distinctly serrulate, somewhat curved: fls. purple, about ½in. across; petals irregularly toothed; calyx about ½in. long, striate, purple at least at tip, teeth acute; bracts 4, purple or red, long-pointed and spreading, one-half or more length of calyx. Cilicia, Asia Minor.

10. **D. neglectus,** Loisel. (*D. glacialis* var. *neglectus,* Williams). Tufted, glabrous, somewhat glaucous, with 1-fld. sts. 1–6 (12) in. tall: lvs. narrow, mostly 1–2 in. long, acutish: fls. brilliant crimson-pink with lighter eye, to 1 in. across; petals conspicuously toothed; calyx about ½in. long, striate, purplish, teeth sharp-pointed; bracts 4, unequal, long-acuminate. W. Alps and Tyrol.—**D. Roysii,** Hort., is sometimes listed as *D. neglectus* var. *Roysii;* it is of hybrid origin and similar in habit to *D. neglectus.*

11. **D. alpinus, L.** Loosely cespitose, glabrous, with 1-fld. sts. 1–4 (6) in. high, bearing 2–3 pairs of lvs. which are sometimes longer than the internodes: basal lvs. 1/10–⅕in. wide, about 1 in. long, obtuse, with a prominent midrib: fls. crimson-pink or sometimes white, about 1 in. across; petals broad, contiguous, finely dentate, with dark purple spots at base, forming a ring that often fades with age; calyx dull purple, glabrous, striate, with acute puberulent teeth; bracts 4 (2–6), longer than half the calyx. E. Alps.

12. **D. glacialis,** Haenke. Glabrous, green, tufted, with sts. 2–3 (4) in. high, unbranched, 1–2-fld.: lvs. linear, sometimes slightly wider above the middle, to about 2 in. long, obtuse, sometimes overtopping fls.: fls. not fragrant, about ¾in. across but not quite flat at expansion; petals magenta or pink, yellowish underneath, whitish at center, contiguous, serrulate; calyx ½–⅔in. long, rose-crimson, striate; bracts 2–4, lanceolate with long awns, subequal to calyx. Alps and Carpathians.

13. **D. microlepis,** Boiss. Gray- or blue-green, tufted, with sts. 1–2 (4) in. high, unbranched, leafless or with 1–3 pairs of membranous bracts: lvs. ½–⅔in. long, keeled, 1-nerved, obtuse: fls. rose-lilac to white, solitary, ½–¾ in. across; petals irregularly dentate; calyx ⅓–½in. long, strongly nerved, with short acute teeth; bracts 2, obtuse, one-third to half as long as calyx and more or less separated from it. Mts. of Bulgaria.—**D. Freynii,** Vandas, is closely related to this species but can be separated by its cauline lvs. (1 or 2 pairs) which are similar to the basal lvs., and bracts with long points subequal to calyx, fls. pink; collected by Rev. J. Freyn; material cult. as *D. Freynii* may not be the true species but a hybrid. Material cult. as *D. arvernensis* probably should be referred here; **D. arvernensis,** Rouy & Fouc., is described as a natural hybrid of *D. hyssopifolius* and *D. sylvaticus;* it is 12–14 in. high, with st.-lvs. shorter than the internodes; fls. about 1 in. across, 3 together in terminal clusters, limb cut about one-third into narrow teeth.

14. **D. graniticus,** Jordan. Cespitose, sts. subterete, 4–8 (16) in. high, more or less scabrous-pubescent below, glabrous above: lvs. narrowly linear, usually less than 1 in. long, acuminate, glabrous, 3-nerved, st.-lvs. spreading: fls. reddish-purple, 1 to few at top of st.; petals dentate, somewhat barbulate; calyx about ½in. long, subcylindric, striate, purplish, teeth lanceolate, pointed; bracts 4, outer pair narrower than inner, one-third to half as long as calyx. France.—*D. deltoides* is sometimes cult. under this name.

15. **D. gratianopolitanus,** Vill. (*D. cæsius*, Smith). CHEDDAR PINK. Glabrous, glaucous, cespitose, with 1–2-fld. angled sts. 2–6 (12) in. high, simple or branched above: lvs. (except the uppermost short-pointed cauline pairs) rather flaccid and broad, 2 in. or less long, 3-nerved beneath, margins often serrulate: fls. rose-pink, fragrant, about 1 in. across; petals contiguous, sharp-dentate, more or less barbulate; calyx ½–¾in. long, subcylindric, purplish, striate, teeth acutish; bracts 4, broad, abruptly pointed, about one-third as long as calyx. England to S. Eu.

16. **D. Sundermannii,** Bornm. Sts. mostly 6–12 in. high, ascending: lvs. linear, about 2–3 in. long, tapering at both ends, 3–5-nerved, margins usually finely ciliate: fls. white, fragrant, ½in. or more across, 1 to few to a st.; limbs of petals about ⅓in. broad, overlapping, usually entire; calyx about ¾in. long, striate, teeth almost ¼in. long; bracts usually 4, long-attenuate, outer pair usually longer than inner and often exceeding calyx. (First grown in gardens of Sündermann, Lindau, Germany.) Greece.

17. **D. Caryophyllus,** L. CARNATION. CLOVE PINK. PICOTEE. GRENADINE. Glabrous and glaucous, tufted, 1–3 ft. high; sts. branched, hard or almost woody below, with conspicuous nodes: lvs. thick, linear, mostly 3–6 in. long, obtuse, stiff at the ends, keeled, 3–5-nerved: fls. 1 in. or more across (to 4 in. in hort. vars.), 2–5 or more to a st., showy, very fragrant, long-pedicelled, rose, purple, or white; petals contiguous, irregularly dentate, not bearded; calyx subcylindric, 1 in. or more long, striate, with erect sharp-pointed teeth; bracts 4, very broad, acute, about one-fourth length of calyx. (Caryophyllus—whence clove pink—is an ante-Linnæan substantive.) S. Eu. to India.—The carnation has been modified by cult. so that the fls. are very variable in size, form and color; numberless garden vars. are offered and it also hybridizes with related species. The American forcing type has very long sts. and is a continuous bloomer.

18. **D. deltoides,** L. MAIDEN PINK. Low invading minutely scabrous-puberulent per. forming loose mats: fl.-sts. 8–12 in. or more high, with narrow acute lvs. usually much shorter than the internodes; sterile shoots 2–5 in. long, somewhat repent, with broad obtuse lvs. ½–¾in. long, 3-nerved, ciliate: fls. about ¾in. across, solitary, terminating the st. or its forked branches; petals sharp-toothed, bearded, light or dark rose to purple or white, usually spotted, often with a V-shaped pattern in the throat (whence the name *deltoides*); calyx about ¾in. long, terete, usually purplish, striate, teeth erect and sharp; bracts 2 (4), abruptly long-pointed, appressed, striate, about half as long as calyx. Great Britain to Japan; nat. in U. S.—In the trade under many names including *D. caucasicus, graniticus, Grisebachii, procumbens, Sternbergii, strictus*. Two varietal garden names are *alba* and *erecta*. Var. **serpyllifolius,** Borb., flatly mat-forming, usually 1–2 in. tall; lvs. of sterile shoots mostly less than ½in. long; Pyrenees, Balkans, Greece; this or similar forms are in cult. under various names, as *D. Grisebachii, Prichardii, pyrenæus, Richardii, supinus*.

19. **D. chinensis,** L. (*D. sinensis*, Hort.). RAINBOW PINK. Bien. or short-lived per., or sometimes classed an ann. in hort vars., erect, green, 6–30 in. high, nearly or quite unbranched except at top, glabrous or closely pubescent: basal lvs. usually gone by flowering time; st.-lvs. 1–3 in. long, exceeding internodes, very narrow to ¼in. broad, acute, margins usually ciliate: fls. rose-lilac with purplish eye, inodorous, ½–1 in. across, few to 15 to a st., loosely fascicled; petals contiguous, toothed; calyx about ¾in. long, striate, teeth short-acuminate and slightly purplish; bracts 4–6, abruptly awned, about half as long as calyx. E. Asia. Var. **Heddewigii,** Regel, DENTATE RAINBOW PINK, fls. flat, 2–3 in. or more across, petals typically 5, dentate or jagged on edges, in many colors and patterns; there are double-fld. races; named for Carl Heddewig, florist and horticulturist of Petrograd; material cult. as *D. diadematus* is a somewhat compact strain with white-margined intensely colored petals; *D. nobilis* is a strain with fls. in shades of red-purple to rose; material cult. as *D. dentosus* is mostly referable here. Var. **laciniatus,** Regel, FRINGED RAINBOW PINK, fls. flat or the petals recurved, 2–4 in. across, single or double, petals irregularly cut or lacerated half or more their length, in the same range of colors as var. *Heddewigii*; plants cult. as *D. laciniatus splendens* comprise a strain with red fls. having a white eye and narrow white border. A recent strain, known as **D. heddensis,** Hort., has the long sts. of *D. chinensis* and the large open fls. of var. *Heddewigii*.

20. **D. Seguieri,** Vill. (*D. chinensis* var. *asper*, Rohrb.). The European extension of *D. chinensis* and perhaps a distinct species: more slender lower plant, mostly 8–12 in. high, distinctly per., usually retaining basal lvs.; petals with sharp or narrow teeth; calyx bracts and floral lvs. often longer and more spreading: fls. sometimes aggregated into rather dense clusters, occasionally slightly fragrant. (Dedicated to Jean François Séguier, auth. of a flora of Verona.) Himalayas to N. Spain.—Part of the material cult. as *D. caucasicus* and *D. montanus* belongs here.

21. **D. orientalis,** Adam (*D. fimbriatus*, Bieb.). Glabrous, woody at base, rootstock dividing into many branches to 12 or 16 in. high; sts. erect, simple, usually 1-fld.: lvs. linear-subulate, ½–1½ in. long: fls. rose or pink, about ¾in. across; petals glabrous or barbulate, fringed about half their depth; calyx ¾–1 in. long, usually reddish, teeth narrowly acuminate; bracts 4–8 (rarely more), about one-third as long as calyx. Portugal to Tibet.—Much of the material in cult. as *D. fimbriatus* is *D. chinensis* or *D. plumarius*.

22. **D. superbus,** L. Stout erect green plant with large-jointed subterete glabrous forking sts. to 2 ft. tall: basal lvs. few or none at flowering time, 2½ in. or less long, to ⅜in. or more wide, 3–5-nerved, margins finely serrate, not prominently long-pointed; st.-lvs. mostly shorter and more narrowly tapering to point: fls. showy and very fragrant, rose to white, often 2 in. or more across, 2–12 together in a dichotomous cluster; petals barbulate, narrowly and deeply cut even to the claw; calyx ¾–1¼ in. long, tapering toward apex, striate, teeth to ¼in. long, acute; bracts 4, broad, abruptly mucronate, appressed, about one-third as long as calyx. Norway to Spain and Japan. Var. **speciosus,** Reichb. (*D. speciosus,* Reichb.), has fewer larger usually redder fls., calyx purple; Eu.

23. **D. fragrans,** Adam. Glabrous, cespitose, with 1–2-fld. sts. to 1 ft. or more high, terete on the lower part, angled above: lvs. 1–2 in. long, acuminate, 3–5-nerved beneath, margins usually serrulate; lvs. on fl.-sts. usually 4–5 pairs: fls. white or sometimes tinged or spotted with rose, very fragrant, 1 in. or less across; petals glabrous, fringed about one-third depth of limb; calyx about 1 in. long, subcylindric, striate, teeth long and narrow; bracts about 6, one-fourth to half as long as calyx, appressed. N. Afr., Caucasus, S. Russia.

24. **D. Noeanus,** Boiss. Densely cespitose, with angled 2–5-fld. sts. 6–10 in. high: lvs. linear-lanceolate, 1 in. or less long, 3–5-nerved, stiffish, very long needle-pointed, the st.-lvs. erect: fls. white, fragrant, ¾in. across; petals narrowly fringed nearly depth of limb, not barbulate; calyx 1 in. or more long, narrow, finely striate, teeth sharply long-pointed; bracts 6, lowest pair more or less separate. (Named for its collector, Wilhelm Noe, died 1856.) Serbia to the Euphrates.—Sometimes cult. as *D. tymphresteus* and as *Acanthophyllum spinosum.*

25. **D. plumarius,** L. Cottage Pink. Glabrous, glaucous, cespitose, with 1–2-fld. sts. 6–12 in. high, or to twice that stature in cult.: basal lvs. 1–4 in. long, narrow, linear, acute, keeled, midrib prominent, the intermediate nerve on either side faint, margins finely serrulate: fls. rose or pink, with a striate or darker center, very fragrant, 1–1½ in. across in the wild; petals bearded, prominently clawed, the limb fringed to about one-third its depth into narrow divisions; calyx to 1 in. long, narrow, striate, usually purplish, teeth broad and short but mucronate; bracts 4, broad, abruptly short-acuminate, appressed, one-fourth to one-third as long as calyx. Austria to Russia and Siberia. Var. **semperflorens,** Hort. (*D. semperflorens,* Hort.), is a hardy race of more continuous bloomers with stout tall often forked sts.; petals fringed or dentate, often not barbed; material cult. as *D. Winteri* probably belongs here.—This group frequently shows characteristics of *D. Caryophyllus* as if of mixed parentage. **D. Allwoodii,** Hort., is recorded as a hybrid between *D. Caryophyllus* and *D. plumarius;* the plants are stocky, 9–16 in. high, usually well branched; lvs. firm, somewhat glaucous; fls. fragrant; *D. Allwoodii* var. *alpinus* is said to be a dwarf strain developed by further hybridization.

26. **D. Sternbergii,** Sieber. Glaucous, cespitose, with 1–4-fld. angled sts. to 10 in. high: lvs. to 2 in. long, long-pointed and divergent, rather soft, 3–5-nerved beneath when dry, the pairs of st.-lvs. 2–4 and shorter: fls. rose, somewhat spotted, fragrant, about 1 in. across; petals well separated, narrowly fringed to the middle, barbulate; calyx ¾in. or more long, thickest at base, reddish, finely striate, teeth sharp; bracts 4, abruptly long-pointed, one-third to half as long as calyx. (Named for Count von Sternberg, page 52.) Mts., Portugal to Italy and Switzerland.—Material cult. under this name is sometimes *D. Noeanus* or *D. sylvestris* var. *subacaulis.*

27. **D. arenarius,** L. Glabrous, cespitose, with erect angled sts. to 8 or 9 in. high: lvs. 1–2 in. long, long-linear, narrow, keeled, narrowly sharp-pointed, cauline lvs. usually short and in 3 or 4 pairs: fls. white with grayish or spotted center, somewhat fragrant, about 1½ in. across, solitary, or several to a st. on long forks petals barbulate, cut into narrow fringes more than half the depth of limb; calyx narrow, about 1 in. long, tapering to top, many-striate, teeth acute; bracts 4, broad, short-acute, appressed, about one-fourth length of calyx. Eu. to Siberia.

28. **D. spiculifolius,** Schur. Cespitose, with angled 1- (2–3-) fld. sts. 5–7 in. or more high: lvs. flat, usually not exceeding 1½ in. long, acute, 3-nerved, margins finely ciliate, st.-lvs. spreading: fls. rose or pink to whitish, fragrant, 1 in. or more across; petals deeply fringed and somewhat barbulate; calyx about 1 in. long, broadest at base, purplish, striate, teeth sharp-pointed; bracts 4, rather abruptly acuminate, about one-fourth length of calyx. S. W. Russia and Romania.

29. **D. hyssopifolius,** L. (*D. monspessulanus,* L.). Loosely cespitose, making short horizontal stocks that give rise to small tufts of lvs. from which the sts. arise; sts. 1-to several-fld., erect, subterete, 4–18 in. high: lvs. linear, 2–3 in. long, flat, acuminate, 3–5-nerved, margins somewhat serrulate: fls. bright rose, odorless, to 1½ in. or more across; petals well separated, fringed below middle, barbulate; calyx about 1 in. long, usually purplish, finely striate, teeth narrow and sharp-pointed; bracts 4, long-pointed, about half length of calyx. S. Eu. to Caucasus.—There are several color vars.

8. LYCHNIS, L. About 35 species of ann. and per. herbs of the north temp. and arctic zones, grown in fl.-gardens.—Mostly erect-growing: calyx 5-toothed, 10-nerved, ovoid, tubular or inflated, naked at base; petals 5, narrow-clawed, the blade entire, 2-cleft or laciniate, usually crowned; stamens 10; styles 5, rarely 4, alternate with petals; ovary many-ovuled: caps. dehiscent at apex with 5 or 10 teeth. (Lychnis: from Greek for *lamp*, referring to the flame-colored fls. of some species.)—Very closely allied to Silene and by some authors also separated into several genera.

A. Plant white-woolly throughout.
B. Fls. few to a st. .... 1. *L. Coronaria*
BB. Fls. in dense clusters .... 2. *L. Flos-Jovis*
AA. Plant not white-woolly, but sometimes hairy or glandular-pubescent.
B. Fls. in dense terminal heads.
C. Lvs. linear-lanceolate, mostly basal .... 3. *L. alpina*
CC. Lvs. ovate to oblong, cauline.
D. Petals 2-cleft; fls. about 1 in. broad .... 4. *L. chalcedonica*
DD. Petals 4-cleft; fls. larger .... 5. *L. fulgens*
BB. Fls. in loose panicles, or 2–3 together.
C. Lvs. linear to lanceolate, at least nine times as long as broad.
D. Petals deeply 4-parted .... 6. *L. Flos-cuculi*
DD. Petals entire to notched.
E. Pedicels longer than calyx: ann. .... 7. *L. Cœli-rosa*
EE. Pedicels shorter than calyx: per. .... 8. *L. Viscaria*
CC. Lvs. ovate-lanceolate to ovate, not over six times as long as broad.
D. Petals 2-cleft.
E. Fl. white, opening at evening .... 9. *L. alba*
EE. Fl. usually red, opening in the morning .... 10. *L. dioica*
DD. Petals several-toothed.
E. Species practically glabrous .... 11. *L. coronata*
EE. Species somewhat pubescent .... 12. *L. Haageana*

1. **L. Coronaria**, Desr. (*Agrostemma Coronaria*, L.). MULLEIN-PINK. DUSTY MILLER. ROSE CAMPION. Densely white-woolly bien. or per. 1–3 ft. high: lvs. oval or oblong to ovate, 1–4 in. long, lower ones narrowed into petiole, upper sessile: fls. few to a st., long-peduncled, 1 in. or more across, crimson; calyx somewhat campanulate, with filiform twisted teeth; petals emarginate, with appendages at throat. (Coronaria: Latin for *garland;* but in this case an old substantive used here in apposition.) S. Eu.; escaped in N. Amer.—Some of the listed color vars. are **alba,** white, and **atrosanguinea,** bright carmine-red turning blood-red. There are also double-fld. forms, and a hybrid with *L. Flos-Jovis*, **L. Walkeri,** Hort., which has carmine-red fls. on slightly shorter pedicels, and usually with more fls. to a st.

2. **L. Flos-Jovis**, Desr. (*Agrostemma Flos-Jovis*, L.). FLOWER-OF-JOVE (as the Latin name implies). White-tomentose per. 1–1½ ft. high: lvs. oval-lanceolate, somewhat clasping, both rosulate and cauline: fls. pink or red to purple, about 1 in. across, in dense umbel-like clusters, pedicels shorter than calyx; petals 2-lobed. Mts. of S. Eu.

3. **L. alpina**, L. (*Viscaria alpina*, Don). ARCTIC CAMPION. Glabrous tufted per. 1 ft. or less high: lvs. linear-lanceolate, forming dense rosette, st.-lvs. few: fls. small, in dense terminal glomerules, on short pedicels, pink; calyx campanulate with short rounded teeth; petals 2-lobed, appendages minute. Arctic and alpine regions in Eu., Asia, N. Amer.

4. **L. chalcedonica**, L. MALTESE CROSS. Per. to 3 ft., with simple or slightly branched sts., usually loose-hairy: lvs. ovate or the upper lanceolate, 2–4 in. long, rounded or cordate at base, usually clasping: fls. in dense terminal heads, scarlet, about 1 in. across; calyx oblong, enlarging in fr.; petals 2-cleft. Russia and Siberia; adventive in E. U. S. Var. **alba,** Hort., has white fls.

5. **L. fulgens**, Fisch. Erect-stemmed hairy per. 1–2 ft. high: lvs. ovate to ovate-oblong, hairy, tapering below: fls. to 2 in. across, few, in dense terminal clusters, bright scarlet; calyx oblong or ovate, woolly; petals divided into 2 broad slightly toothed lobes, on the outer side of which are 2 very narrow lobes. Siberia.

6. **L. Flos-cuculi**, L. (*Agrostemma Flos-cuculi*, Don). RAGGED ROBIN. CUCKOO-FLOWER (indicated in the name). Slender profusely blooming per. to 2 ft., pubescent below, viscid above: lvs. narrowly lanceolate to oblanceolate, to 4 in. long, the upper ones small and sessile: fls. in loose panicles, red or pink; calyx short-oblong; petals cut into 4 linear segms. Eu., N. Asia; nat. in E. U. S.—There are double-fld. and white vars.

7. **L. Cœli-rosa**, Desr. (*Agrostemma Cœli-rosa*, L.). ROSE-OF-HEAVEN (indicated in the specific name). Glabrous floriferous ann. 1–1½ ft. high: lvs. linear, long-acuminate and very sharp-pointed: fls. on long slender pedicels, almost 1 in. across, rose-red; calyx club-shaped with filiform teeth; petals slightly notched, with linear bifid scale at throat. Medit. region.—There is a white-fld. var. and one with deeply toothed petals.

8. **L. Viscaria**, L. (*Viscaria viscosa*, Aschers.). GERMAN CATCHFLY. Per. blooming in May and June, 6–20 in. high, glabrous but with viscid patches beneath fl.-clusters: lvs. long-linear, to 5 in. long, the lower ones tapering toward base: fls. red or purple, ½–1 in. across, in opposite short-stalked clusters forming an interrupted glomerate panicle; calyx somewhat swollen above middle; petals slightly notched. Eu., N. Asia. Var. **splendens,** Hort., has rose-pink fls.—A strain of hybrids under the name of *L. Forrestii* is closely related to this species.

9. **L. alba,** Mill. (*L. vespertina,* Sibth.). EVENING OR WHITE CAMPION. Freely-branching bien. or per. to 2 ft., viscid-pubescent: lvs. ovate-lanceolate or oblong, 1–3 in. long, the lower tapering into a margined petiole: often diœcious; fls. few in loose panicles, usually white and fragrant, opening in the evening; calyx enlarging in fr.; petals 2-cleft, about 1 in. across, crowned: teeth of caps. erect. Eu.; adventive in E. U. S.

10. **L. dioica,** L. RED OR MORNING CAMPION. Similar to *L. alba,* but differing in the usually red odorless fls. opening in the morning, shorter calyx and teeth of caps. recurved. Eu., Asia; adventive in E. U. S.—There are double-fld. sorts.

11. **L. coronata,** Thunb. (*L. grandiflora,* Jacq.). Erect nearly glabrous bien. or per. to 1½ ft.: lvs. oval-elliptic, 2–4 in. long, acute, sessile or nearly so: fls. scattered or in an open panicle, 2 in. or more across, brick-red, salmon or cinnabar; petals laciniately-toothed. China, Japan. Var. **Sieboldii,** Bailey (*L. Sieboldii,* VanHoutte), has large pure white fls.—Runs into many other forms.

12. **L. Haageana,** Lem. (*L. fulgens* × *L. coronata* var. *Sieboldii*). Somewhat hairy per. to 1 ft., intermediate in characters between the parents: fls. in 2's or 3's, about 2 in. across; petals with 2 large dentate lobes and 2 short side teeth, orange-red, scarlet, or crimson; calyx hairy.—There are several cultivars and also a hybrid with *L. chalcedonica,* **L. Arkwrightii,** Hort., with fls. in shades of scarlet.

9. **PETROCOPTIS,** A. Br. Four species of perennials native in the Pyrenees and the mts. of N. Spain.—Allied to Lychnis and sometimes considered a section of it, but differing in the parts being imbricated rather than convolute in the bud, and seeds with a tomentose beard at the hilum: low-growing, lvs. tufted or in rosettes, petals uncut and crowned. (Petrocop-tis: Greek, meaning *to break the rock.*)

P. Lagascæ, Willk. (*Lychnis Lagascæ,* Hook. f.). Forming low tufts with flowering sts. to 4 in. high, glabrous and glaucous: lvs. spatulate to linear, to about ¾in. long, the upper ones ovate, acute, sessile: fls. light rose with white center, ½–⅔in. across, on long pedicels. (Named for M. Lagasca, page 46.) N. Spain.

10. **SILENE,** L. CATCHFLY. CAMPION. Over 400 species of ann. and per. herbs of wide distribution over the earth, some grown in fl.- and rock-gardens.—Of erect, tufted, decumbent or diffusely climbing habit: fls. solitary or in cymes, white, red, or pink; calyx 5-toothed or -cleft, ovoid, campanulate, cylindrical, often inflated, 10- to many-nerved, naked at base; petals 5, with narrow claw, usually crowned with a scale at the base of the blade; stamens 10; styles usually 3; ovary many-ovuled: pod dehiscent by 6, rarely 3, teeth at apex. (Sile-ne: from Greek for *saliva,* referring to the stickiness of st. and calyx of some species.)

A. Calyx with 20 nerves.
B. Fls. ½–¾in. across, in open cymose panicles.......... 1. *S. Cucubalus*
BB. Fls. ¾–1 in. across, 1–4 to a st.......... 2. *S. maritima*
AA. Calyx with 10 nerves.
B. Species ann. or bien.
C. Plant pubescent, to 10 in. high: petals 2-parted.......... 3. *S. pendula*
CC. Plant glabrous, 1–2 ft. high.
D. Fls. in dense terminal heads subtended by ovate st.-lvs.; petals entire.......... 4. *S. compacta*
DD. Fls. in dense terminal compound cymes subtended by lanceolate bracts; petals emarginate.......... 5. *S. Armeria*
BB. Species per.
C. Length of lvs. ¼–1 (1½) in.
D. Plant acaulescent, not over 2 in. high.......... 6. *S. acaulis*
DD. Plant caulescent, 3–8 (12) in. high.
E. Calyx-tube 1 in. long.......... 7. *S. Schafta*
EE. Calyx-tube less than ½in. long.
F. Petals 2-parted.......... 8. *S. Saxifraga*
FF. Petals with 4 teeth or lobes.......... 9. *S. alpestris*
CC. Length of lvs. 1–5 (6) in.
D. Lvs., at least some of them, in whorls of 4.......... 10. *S. stellata*
DD. Lvs. all opposite.
E. Fls. in dense head-like cymes or globose heads.......... 11. *S. Asterias*
EE. Fls. solitary or in loose open cymose panicles.
F. Color of fls. crimson.
G. Lf. mostly two to three times as long as broad: fls. erect after anthesis.......... 12. *S. californica*
GG. Lf. mostly four to five times as long as broad: fls. tending to become recurved after anthesis.......... 13. *S. virginica*
FF. Color of fls. pink or rose to white.
G. Petals 4-lobed.......... 14. *S. Hookeri*
GG. Petals emarginate.......... 15. *S. caroliniana*

1. **S. Cucubalus,** Wibel (*S. inflata,* Smith. *S. venosa,* Aschers. *S. latifolia,* Britten & Rendle not Poir.). BLADDER CAMPION. Per. 4–18 (24) in. high, branching from base,

usually glabrous and glaucous: lvs. ovate to lanceolate or spatulate, ¾–2½ in. long, lower lvs. tapering to short petiole, upper ones sessile: polygamo-diœcious; fls. white, ½–¾in. across, in open cymose panicles; calyx inflated, 20-nerved, greenish-white to reddish, inclosing caps.; petals 2-cleft and usually without a crown. Eu., Asia; widely nat. in E.U.S.

2. **S. maritima**, With. Diffuse per. 8–12 (16) in. high, glaucous: lvs. lanceolate to ovate, ⅜–2 in. long, acute, glabrous: fls. 1–4 to a st., white, ¾–1 in. across; calyx campanulate, glabrous, much inflated after anthesis, 20-nerved; petals 2-cleft with 2 small scales at base. Eu. Var. **plena**, Hort., grows 4–10 in. high, and has much larger and extremely double fls. which last longer. Var. **rosea**, Niven, to about 6 in., with rose-colored fls.

3. **S. pendula**, L. Pubescent ann. to 10 in., with sts. decumbent at base, branched above: lvs. ovate-lanceolate to elliptic-oblong, to about 2 in. long: fls. in loose racemes, becoming pendulous, about ¾in. across, flesh-colored, on peduncles shorter than calyx; calyx hirsute, 10-nerved, somewhat inflated after anthesis; petals 2-parted, crowned. Medit. region.—There are numerous color vars. and also with double fls.

4. **S. compacta**, Fisch. (*S. orientalis*, Hort.). Glabrous and glaucous bien. 1–2 ft. high, simple or slightly branched above: upper lvs. broadly ovate, clasping, 1–2 in. long, lower lvs. oblong-lanceolate, to 3½ in. long: fls. pink, subsessile, in a dense terminal head 1–3½ in. across, the upper lvs. involucrate; calyx club-shaped, 10-nerved, about ⅘in. long; petals entire, crowned with 10 linear scales or rays. E. Eu., Asia Minor.

5. **S. Armeria**, L. Sweet William Catchfly. Erect branching ann. 1–2 ft. high, glabrous or minutely puberulent, glaucous, viscid above: lvs. ovate-lanceolate to oblong, 1–3 (5) in. long, subcordate and clasping at base: fls. in terminal peduncled compound cymes, pink or rose, short-pedicelled; calyx club-shaped, 10-nerved, about ⅔in. long; petals emarginate, crowned with narrow scales. S. Eu.; adventive in E. U. S.—There is a white-fld. var.

6. **S. acaulis**, L. Cushion Pink. Moss Campion. Almost stemless per. to 2 in., forming a moss-like mat of compact rosettes: lvs. linear-subulate, to about ⅝in. long, sessile, clustered on the branched rootstock, glabrous with minutely prickly-ciliate margins: fls. reddish-purple, sometimes white, about ½in. across, solitary; calyx campanulate, 10-nerved, glabrous; petals entire or notched, with small appendages: caps. cylindric to oval. Mts. of northern hemisphere.

7. **S. Schafta**, Gmel. Moss Campion. Pubescent per. 3–6 in. high; sts. simple or slightly branched, decumbent, arising laterally from the rosettes of oblanceolate to spatulate lvs. ¼–1¼ in. long: peduncles axillary or terminal, 1–2-fld.; fls. rose or purple; calyx somewhat hirsute, reddish, long-cylindrical, not inflated, 10-nerved; petals notched, with 2 scales at base. (Schafta: probably a geographical name.) Caucasus.

8. **S. Saxifraga**, L. Densely tufted almost shrubby per. 3–8 (12) in. high, with many ascending subglabrous sts., viscid above: lvs. linear to linear-lanceolate, ¼–1 in. long, acute, sessile, subglabrous, margins ciliate: fls. white, yellow-green to reddish on the outside, often solitary or 2–3 to a st., on very long pedicels; calyx tubular-clavate, glabrous, with 10 puberulent nerves; petals 2-parted, crowned: caps. ovoid-oblong. Eu., Asia Minor.

9. **S. alpestris**, Jacq. Alpine Catchfly. Compact per. to 8 (12) in. high, with simple or branching sts., more or less viscid above: lvs. lanceolate-linear to obovate-lanceolate, ½–1½ in. long, rather obtuse: fls. white, about ½in. across, shining, paniculate; calyx hirsute, short, campanulately club-shaped, 10-nerved, not inflated; petals 4-lobed, with 2 teeth at base. Mts. of E. Eu.

10. **S. stellata**, Ait. f. (*Cucubalus stellatus*, L.). Starry Campion. Erect usually branching per. 2–3½ ft. high, with fine rough pubescence throughout: lvs. ovate-lanceolate, 2–4 in. long, acuminate, sessile in whorls of 4 (lowest and upper often opposite): fls. white, nodding, in loose open cymose panicles 4–20 in. long; calyx campanulate, strongly inflated; petals to ¾in. long, laciniate, without a crown: caps. subglobose, about equalling calyx. Mass. to Minn., Ga. and Tex.

11. **S. Asterias**, Griseb. Glabrous per. to 3 ft., with unbranched sticky sts.: basal lvs. lanceolate-spatulate, 3–5 in. long, obtuse, attenuate at base; st.-lvs. ovate-lanceolate to oblong, shorter, acute, connate: fls. purple, subsessile, in dense head-like cymes; calyx reddish, subcylindric, ½–¾in. long; petals entire: caps. oblong. Balkans. Var. **grandiflora**, Hort., has crimson-scarlet fls. in heads.

12. **S. californica**, Durand. California Indian Pink. Per. 6–12 in. or more high, glandular-pubescent; sts. several, more or less decumbent: lvs. oblanceolate to elliptic, 1–3½ in. long, acuminate: fls. crimson, ¾–1¼ in. across, 1 to few to a st.; calyx cylindric, becoming distended in fr. and inclosing the caps.; petals deeply 4-cleft, lobes entire to toothed, crowned. Calif., Ore.

13. **S. virginica**, L. Fire Pink. Per. 8–24 in. high, sticky-pubescent, with 1 to several usually simple sts.: lower lvs. oblanceolate to spatulate, 2–5 in. long, mostly acute, narrowed to a winged ciliate-margined petiole; upper lvs. becoming oblong to lanceolate, sessile: fls. crimson, about 1 in. across, somewhat nodding, in loose cymes; calyx tubular-campanulate, to 1 in. long; petals linear, with 2 (4) lobes, crowned. N. Y. to Ont., Minn., Ark. and Ga.

14. **S. Hookeri,** Nutt. Per. 3–10 in. high, grayish-tomentose throughout, sts. usually several from the base, erect or decumbent: lvs. elliptic-lanceolate to spatulate, 1–3 in. long, tapering to a winged petiole: fls. pink to rose or white, in few-fld. terminal or axillary cymes or solitary; calyx cylindric-funnelform, to ¾in. long; petals 4-lobed, crowned, spreading, forming a wheel-shaped corolla 1¼–1½ (2) in. across: caps. globose-ovoid, stipitate. (Named for J. D. Hooker, page 45.) N. Calif. and Ore.

15. **S. caroliniana,** Walt. Wild Pink. Per. 3–8 in. high, with a basal rosette and few to several flowering sts., erect or decumbent, pubescent with glands above: basal lvs. mostly oblong-spatulate, usually obtuse, 1–5 in. long, tapering to a petiole, pubescent with ciliate margins; st.-lvs. linear-oblong, ½–2 in. long, subsessile: fls. light to deep pink, ½–1 in. across, in terminal cymes; calyx tubular, glandular-pubescent, enlarging in fr.; petals cuneate, emarginate, crowned, the claw slightly exceeding calyx: caps. elliptic. N. C. to Ga. Var. **pensylvanica,** Fern. (*S. pensylvanica*, Michx. *S. caroliniana* subsp. *pensylvanica*, Clausen), to 12 in., with sts. glandular-pubescent especially above; basal lvs. usually oblanceolate, acute or obtuse, to 6 in. long, glabrous on both surfaces, margins ciliate; st.-lvs. lanceolate to ovate or elliptic, to 3 in. long; N. H. to N. C., Ohio and Tenn. Var. **Wherryi,** Fern. (*S. Wherryi*, Small. *S. caroliniana* subsp. *Wherryi*, Clausen), to 13 in., with pubescent sts., glands lacking; basal lvs. usually elliptic-lanceolate or oblanceolate, mostly acute, to 3 in. long, glabrous on both surfaces, margins ciliate; st.-lvs. lanceolate, to 3½ in. long; calyx broadly tubular, pubescent but lacking glands, usually not exceeded by claws of petals; named for E. T. Wherry, page 54; Ohio to Ala. and Mo.

11. **GYPSOPHILA,** L. Ann. and per. herbs, grown in rock-gardens, borders, and as trimming for bouquets; about 140 species in Eu., Asia and N. Afr.—Branching or diffuse, glaucous, with scant foliage when in bloom: fls. small and numerous, loosely or densely (head-like) cymose-paniculate, white or rosy; calyx 5-toothed, conspicuously scarious between its green nerves, bractless, 5-nerved; petals 5, entire or emarginate, lacking crowns, sometimes with narrow claws; stamens 10; styles 2 (3); ovary with many ovules: caps. globose or ovoid, dehiscent by 4 (6) valves extending to or below the middle. (Gypsoph-ila: from Greek for *gypsum-loving*, referring to preference for calcareous soils.)

A. Plant 24–36 in. or more high.
  B. Fls. in loose open paniculate cymes.
    C. Lower lvs. four to eight or more times as long as broad.
      D. Lvs. usually 1-nerved, mostly less than ½in. wide.................... 1. *G. paniculata*
      DD. Lvs. 3- (5-) nerved, ½–1 in. or more wide.................... 2. *G. acutifolia*
    CC. Lower lvs. about twice as long as broad.................... 3. *G. pacifica*
  BB. Fls. in dense head-like cymes.................... 4. *G. Oldhamiana*
AA. Plant 3–12 (18) in. high.
  B. Duration per., sts. prostrate (at least at base) and sometimes tufted.
    C. Lvs. pubescent on both surfaces.................... 5. *G. cerastioides*
    CC. Lvs. glabrous.................... 6. *G. repens*
  BB. Duration ann., sts. usually erect.
    C. Lvs. lanceolate.................... 7. *G. elegans*
    CC. Lvs. narrowly linear.................... 8. *G. muralis*

1. **G. paniculata,** L. Babys-Breath (also erroneously applied to *Galium Mollugo*). Tall-growing diffusely branched glaucous per. to 3 ft. or more: lvs. linear-lanceolate, acute, the largest to 4 in. long, becoming smaller on the branches, usually 1-nerved: fls. white, about 1/16in. across, in many-branched many-fld. (to 1,000 fls.) panicles; pedicels usually glabrous, two to three times as long as calyx. Eu., N. Asia; escaped sparingly in N. Amer. Var. **compacta,** Hort., is a dwarf garden form.—Double-fld. races are var. *flore-pleno*, *G. Ehrlei*, *G.* "Bristol Fairy" (fls. to ¼in. or more across).

2. **G. acutifolia,** Fisch. Very similar to *G. paniculata*, differing in being less glaucous, the lvs. broader, 3- (5-) nerved, the pedicels glandular-pubescent, and calyx longer; fls. white or rosy. Caucasus.

3. **G. pacifica,** Kom. (*G. perfoliata* var. *latifolia*, Maxim.). Smooth glabrous per. to 3 or 4 ft.: lvs. ovate-oblong, acute or obtuse, sessile, somewhat fleshy: fls. pink to pale purple, to ¼in. or more across, in much-branched open panicles; petals about twice as long as campanulate calyx. Siberia.

4. **G. Oldhamiana,** Miq. Glabrous per. with erect sts. to 2½ ft., branched only above: cauline lvs. oblong-lanceolate, to 2½ in. long, acute, 3- (5-) nerved, longer than internodes, becoming linear and shorter than internodes toward top: fls. pink, ⅛in. or more across, in dense cymes; petals subtruncate, about twice as long as calyx. (Named for R. Oldham, collector in the Orient, died 1864.) Korea.

5. **G. cerastioides,** D. Don. Mouse-ear Gypsophila. Downy creeping per. (cerastium-like, as the name implies) to about 4 in.: lvs. to ½in. long, pubescent on both surfaces, radical ones spatulate and long-petioled, cauline obovate, subsessile: fls. ¼–½in. across, white with pink veins, in short few-fld. cymes; calyx very narrowly membranous between the nerves. Himalayas.

6. **G. repens,** L. Somewhat fleshy glabrous per. 3–10 in. or more high, with trailing or prostrate sts., not or slightly glaucous: lvs. linear, mostly less than 1 in. long, acutish, blue-green: fls. about ⅓in. across, in few-fld. panicles, white to reddish; petals about twice longer than sepals. Alps, Pyrenees, mts. of Austria. Var. **rosea,** Hort., usually less than 6 in. high, fls. rosy-pink; material in the trade as *G. fratensis* is very close to this var.—**G. Bodgeri,** Hort., is a hybrid between var. *rosea* and a double-fld. *G. paniculata,* raised by Bodger, Calif.; to 1 ft. or more, sts. prostrate at base; fls. white to pink, double, in many-fld. loose panicles.

7. **G. elegans,** Bieb. Ann. 1–1½ ft. high, with upright forking sts., glabrous: lvs. lanceolate, sometimes to 3 in. long, acute, somewhat fleshy: fls. white or rosy, to ½in. or more across, long-pedicelled, in loose open panicles; petals emarginate, two or three times as long as calyx. Caucasus.

8. **G. muralis,** L. Very diffusely branched ann. 6–12 in. high: lvs. narrowly linear, to 1 in. long, attenuate at each end: fls. on pedicels much longer than calyx, in very loose cymes; petals crenate, rosy, about twice as long as calyx. Eu.; adventive in E. U. S.

12. **SAPONARIA,** L. Soapwort. Ann. and per. herbs, of about 40 species, native in Eu., Asia, and N. Afr., a few grown in rockeries and borders.—Habit erect or diffuse: lvs. usually broad and flat: fls. in dichotomous cymes; calyx ovoid- or oblong-tubular, obscurely nerved, 5-toothed, naked; petals 5, with narrow claws as long as calyx, the blade entire or emarginate; stamens 10; styles 2; ovary with many ovules: caps. ovoid or oblong, dehiscent by 4 teeth at apex. (Sapona-ria: Latin *soap,* the juice of some kinds forming a lather with water.)

A. Petals not appendaged: ann. .... 1. *S. Vaccaria*
AA. Petals with an appendage at top of claw: per.
  B. Lvs. 2–5 in. long: plant to 3 ft. high .... 2. *S. officinalis*
  BB. Lvs. mostly less than 1 in. long: plant less than 1 ft. high.
    C. Plant densely tufted: fls. in head-like cymes .... 3. *S. cæspitosa*
    CC. Plant half-trailing: fls. in loose cymes .... 4. *S. ocymoides*

1. **S. Vaccaria,** L. (*Vaccaria vulgaris,* Host). Cow-Herb. Glabrous ann. to 3 ft., branching above: lvs. ovate-lanceolate, ½–4 in. long, connate at base, 1-nerved: fls. deep pink, long-peduncled, in loose corymbose cymes; calyx 5-angled, much inflated and wing-angled in fr., glabrous; petals without appendage, crenulate. Eu., Asia; widely nat. in N. Amer. Var. **rosea,** Hort., has pale pink fls.

2. **S. officinalis,** L. Bouncing Bet. Stout sparingly branched per. to 3 ft., glabrous or with scattered pubescence, leafy: lvs. ovate-lanceolate, 2–3 (5) in. long, strongly 3-nerved, acute or short-acuminate: fls. short-peduncled, in dense terminal corymbs with many small floral lvs., pink or whitish, 1–1½ in. across; calyx terete; petals with appendage at top of claw, notched at apex. Eu., W. Asia; nat. widely in N. Amer.—Many double-fld. forms are advertised, one as var. *caucasica,* Hort.

3. **S. cæspitosa,** DC. Densely tufted per. with a much-branched woody st. bearing usually simple ascending few-lvd. reddish fl.-sts. 2–6 in. high: lvs. linear-lanceolate, to about ⅔in. long, keeled beneath, with a scarious somewhat ciliate margin: fls. rose, subsessile, in few-fld. head-like cymes; calyx oblong-tubular, with short teeth, pubescent, 15-nerved; petals entire, crowned, the spreading limb half as long as calyx: caps. oblong. Pyrenees.

4. **S. ocymoides,** L. Trailing much-branched per. to 9 in., pubescent: lvs. ovate-lanceolate to elliptic, mostly less than 1 in. long, acute or obtuse, attenuate at base or subsessile, pubescent, margins ciliate: fls. in loose broad cymes, bright pink; calyx cylindrical, villous, purplish; petals entire, with appendage at top of claw. Cent. and S. Eu. Var. **alba,** Hort., has white fls. Var. **splendens,** Hort., has larger deeper rose fls.

66. NYMPHÆACEÆ. WATER-LILY FAMILY

Aquatic herbs, mainly with floating foliage, 8 genera and about 80 species in many parts of the world, many highly ornamental.—Per., often with large horizontal rootstocks: lvs. various, mostly large and simple and rising directly from the rootstock, or from floating sts. (as in Cabomba) and then usually small and perhaps dissected: fls. usually bisexual, large or small, floating or upstanding high above the water, regular; sepals commonly 4, sometimes more but not numerous; petals few in Cabomba and Brasenia, but otherwise many or even indefinite and commonly showing transition to stamens which are then also numerous; pistils 2 or 3 to many, free or connate or immersed in a spongy receptacle with lamellate placentation: fr. formed of the separate pistils or usually (as in the true water-lilies) of many connate pistils indicated by the rayed marks of stigmas or (as in the Nelumbos) of several pistils immersed in a greatly enlarged spongy receptacle and open by large holes at the tops.

A. Lvs. simple, entire to dentate.
 B. Sinus of lf. deep, reaching almost or entirely to the petiole.
  C. Veins mostly radiating from the petiole: petals and stamens attached on sides of ovary.......... 1. NYMPHÆA
  CC. Veins pinnate from the midrib: petals and stamens attached below ovary.......... 2. NUPHAR
 BB. Sinus lacking, lvs. centrally peltate.
  C. Plants very prickly: lvs. 3–6 ft. across, floating.......... 3. VICTORIA
  CC. Plants not prickly: lvs. smaller.
   D. Lf. orbicular, 1–3 ft. across, usually standing above the water.......... 4. NELUMBO
   DD. Lf. elliptic, 2–5 in. long, floating.......... 5. BRASENIA
AA. Lvs. mostly dissected into thread-like divisions.......... 6. CABOMBA

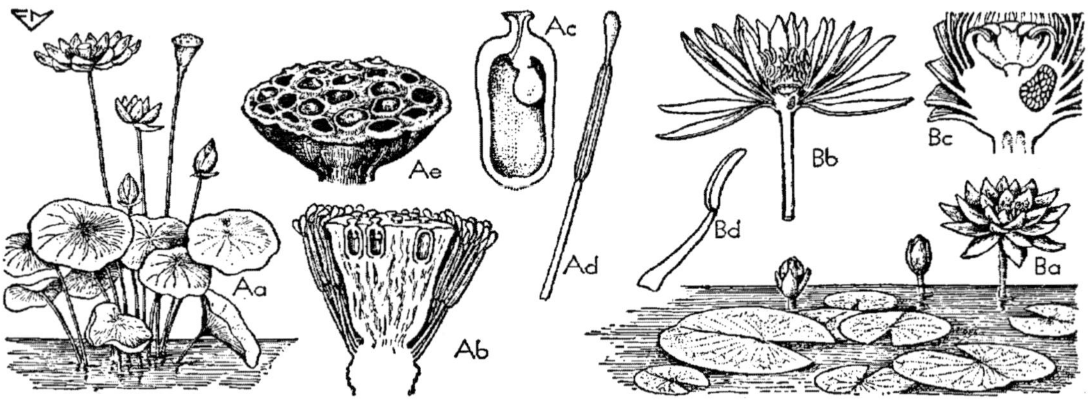

Fig. 66. NYMPHÆACEÆ. A, *Nelumbo nucifera:* Aa, flowering plant, much reduced; Ab, flower, vertical section, less perianth, × ½; Ac, pistil, vertical section, × 2; Ad, stamen, × 1; Ae, pod, × ⅓. B, *Nymphæa odorata:* Ba, flowering plant, much reduced; Bb, flower, vertical section, × ¼; Bc, same, less perianth, × 1; Bd, stamen, × 1.

1. **NYMPHÆA,** L. (*Castalia,* Salisb.). NYMPHEA. WATER-LILY. Widely distributed in temp. and trop. regions, about 40 species and numerous hort. hybrids.—Rootstocks horizontal or erect, sometimes tuberous: lvs. usually floating, orbicular or oval, often cordate, sometimes peltate near the margin but not centrally, entire, sinuate or toothed, often colored beneath: fls. usually showy, often large, floating or standing near the surface but the fr. under water, in many colors, some kinds blooming by day and others at night; sepals 4; petals and stamens many, not soon caducous, attached on the sides and near the summit of the ovary: fr. a single compound body of many pistils with a depressed saucer-like center and radiating style-processes. (Nymphæ-a: Nymphæ, the water-nymphs.)—The hort. nympheas are largely hybrids and some of the named kinds cannot be definitely placed botanically; but the main species of importance to the cultivator are included here. The Marliac vars. (*N. Marliacea,* Hort.) are of various origins, but probably issue mostly from *N. alba* and var. *rubra,* although some of them apparently have *N. mexicana* and other influence; raised by M. Latour-Marliac, France.

A. Distance from bottom of sinus to petiole ¼–2 in.; lf.-margins usually sinuate to dentate (nearly entire in *N. cærulea*).
 B. Fls. opening in the evening; sepals prominently veined: lvs. more or less pubescent beneath.
  C. Color of fls. white: lvs. green above.......... 1. *N. Lotus*
  CC. Color of fls. red: lvs. bronzy above becoming greenish.......... 2. *N. rubra*
 BB. Fls. opening in the morning; sepals obscurely veined: lvs. glabrous.
  C. Diam. of lvs. 5–6 in.......... 3. *N. stellata*
  CC. Diam. of lvs. 12–18 in.
   D. Lvs. entire, or slightly wavy at base, blotched with purple beneath: fls. closing at noon.......... 4. *N. cærulea*
   DD. Lvs. distinctly often deeply sinuate, usually green beneath: fls. closing 4–6 P.M.
    E. Color of fls. white: lobes of lf. rounded.......... 5. *N. flavovirens*
    EE. Color of fls. blue: lobes of lf. usually acuminate.......... 6. *N. capensis*
AA. Distance from bottom of sinus to petiole less than ¼ in.; lf.-margins entire to wavy.

B. Diam. of lvs. 1½–3 in.: fls. 1–2 in. across. . . . . 7. *N. tetragona*
BB. Diam. of lvs. 3–16 in.: fls. 2–9 in. across.
C. Fls. yellow. . . . . 8. *N. mexicana*
CC. Fls. white, pink or rose-colored.
D. Lvs. crowded on rhizome: petals 12–24; fls. closing in late afternoon. . . . . . . 9. *N. alba*
DD. Lvs. scattered loosely on rhizome: petals usually more than 24; fls. closing about noon.
E. Under side of lvs. red to purple. . . . . 10. *N. odorata*
EE. Under side of lvs. green. . . . . 11. *N. tuberosa*

1. **N. Lotus,** L. WHITE LOTUS of Egypt. Lvs. orbicular, 12–20 in. across, sharply toothed, basal lobes not projecting, dark green on top, brownish and puberulent beneath: fls. 5–10 in. across, white with outer petals pinkish, opening evening till nearly next noon; petals 19 or 20, broad and concave; sepals green, with 10–16 creamy-white veins; stamens 96 or more, yellow, the filaments longer than anthers. Egypt. Var. **dentata,** Schumacher & Thonn., fls. pure white, 8–10 in. across, open till past noon; petals narrower, ovate, becoming horizontal; filaments shorter than anthers: lvs. glabrous, or somewhat puberulent beneath: Cent. Afr.

2. **N. rubra,** Roxb. Lvs. orbicular or nearly so, 12–18 in. across, sharply dentate, basal lobes not projected, bronzy reddish-brown but becoming greenish, pubescent beneath: fls. 6–10 in. across, deep purplish-red, opening three or four nights till nearly noon; petals 12–20, narrow-oval, blunt; sepals purplish-red and prominently 7-nerved, never fully expanding; stamens about 55, cinnabar-red or brownish. India.—There are many hort. derivatives, as *N. Arnoldiana, Bissetii, columbiana, Deaniana, devoniensis, indica* vars., *kewensis, Omarana, rubicunda, Sturtevantii.*

3. **N. stellata,** Willd. BLUE LOTUS of India. Lvs. elliptic-orbicular, rather broadly peltate, 5–6 in. across, irregularly repand-dentate, the basal lobes scarcely lengthened, blue-violet beneath: fls. 3–7 in. across, pale blue, whitish at base (pink and white races are known but apparently not in cult.), opening three days in forenoon and early afternoon; petals 11–14; stamens 33–54. India to S. E. Asia.

4. **N. cærulea,** Sav. BLUE LOTUS of Egypt. Not showy, blooming freely: lvs. oval, narrowly peltate, 12–16 in. across, entire or slightly sinuate at base, under surface green with purple blotches: fls. 3–6 in. across, light blue with dull white in center, opening three days in forenoon; petals 14–20, lanceolate-acute; stamens 50 or more. N. and Cent. Afr.—*N. pennsylvania,* Conard, a good blue, is a hybrid between this species and *N. capensis* var. *zanzibariensis.*

5. **N. flavovirens,** Lehm. (*N. gracilis,* Hort. not Zucc.). Lvs. nearly orbicular, narrowly peltate, 15–17 in. across, nearly entire or deeply and irregularly sinuate, basal angles rounded, green underneath: fls. 6–8 in. across, white, opening morning till late afternoon; petals 16–20, acuminate; sepals green outside, white inside; stamens about 60, deep yellow. Mex.

6. **N. capensis,** Thunb. CAPE BLUE WATER-LILY. Lvs. orbicular-ovate, 12–16 in. across, rather narrowly peltate, strongly sinuate-dentate, basal lobes produced and acuminate: fls. 6–8 in. across, sky-blue, whitish in bottom, opening four days in forenoon to late afternoon; petals 20–30, narrow-elliptic; sepals whitish within; stamens about 150. S. Afr. Var. **zanzibariensis,** Casp. (*N. zanzibariensis,* Casp.), variable and inconstant from seeds: lvs. tending to orbicular (as well as orbicular-ovate), the basal angles scarcely pointed, closely sinuate-dentate, often smaller: fls. often larger (to 12 in. across), deeper blue, opening and closing three to five days somewhat later; sepals purple-blue within and on margins; stamens often or usually more numerous: Zanzibar.

7. **N. tetragona,** Georgi. PYGMY WATER-LILY. Unbranched rootstock erect and short: lvs. ovate, 2–4 in. long, 1½–3 in. across, entire, green above (blotched with red-brown when young), dull reddish beneath: fls. white, 1–2 (3) in. across, open three or four afternoons; petals 8–17; stamens about 40. Siberia, Japan, N. Ida. to Ont.—Hardy; much used in hybridization, contributing to the Marliacea, Laydekeri, and other hybrids; see note on page 382.

8. **N. mexicana,** Zucc. YELLOW WATER-LILY. Spreading by runners, the rootstock erect and tuber-like; some of the lvs. stand above the water when crowded; floating lvs. ovate, 4–8 in. across, obscurely and finely sinuate, dark green and blotched brown above, crimson-brown with blackish dots beneath: fls. 4 (2–5) in. across, standing 4–5 in. above the water, bright yellow, open before midday to late afternoon; petals about 23, passing gradually into the 50 yellow stamens. Mex.—Hardy N. under cult.

9. **N. alba,** L. EUROPEAN WHITE WATER-LILY. Strong robust species with lvs. crowded on the horizontal branching black rhizome: lvs. roundish, 4–12 in. across, entire, red when young: fls. white, 4–5 in. across, open nearly all day; petals broad, ovate, somewhat concave. Eu. and N. Afr. Var. **rubra,** Lönnr., fls. rosy-red, with anthers and stigma yellow: Sweden.—Material cult. as *N. Gladstoniana* is closely related and probably a hybrid. *N. alba* var. *rubra* has apparently contributed largely to cultural hybrids: *N. Robinsonii, Andreana, aurora, chrysantha, Laydekeri, formosa, gloriosa,* and others, represent crosses with *N. odorata, N. mexicana, N. tetragona.*

10. **N. odorata,** Ait. FRAGRANT WATER-LILY. Rootstock continuous, little branching, not tuber-bearing: lvs. orbicular or oblong-orbicular and entire, 3–10 in. across, with sinus less than half depth of blade, rather thick, dull green above and mostly purplish beneath: fls. white, 3–5 in. across, very fragrant, opening three days in the forenoon; petals 23–32, ovate or narrower; sepals tinged brown; stamens 55 to more than 100, yellow. Common in E. U. S.; in the wild it is represented at Cape Cod by a pink-fld. var. (var. *rosea,* Pursh) and in the S. and American tropics by a larger white-fld. var. (var. *gigantea,* Tricker).—Numbers of hybrids and derivatives have been produced, as *N. caroliniana, Luciana, speciosa, superba.*

11. **N. tuberosa,** Paine. TUBEROUS WATER-LILY. Horizontal rootstock bearing detachable short tuber-like branches: lvs. roundish, 5–16 in. across, green on both sides (purplish when young), entire, lobes short-acuminate: fls. 4–9 in. across, pure white, opening three to four days till shortly after noon, with faint or no fragrance; petals broad and concave; sepals green. N. and Cent. U. S. Var. **Richardsonii,** Conard, has more numerous petals.—The species has entered into garden hybrids.

2. **NUPHAR,** Smith (*Nymphozanthus,* Rich.). COW-LILY. SPATTERDOCK. YELLOW POND-LILY. About 25 species, widely distributed in the northern hemisphere.—Per. aquatic herbs, with stout creeping rootstocks: floating or erect lvs. orbicular to lanceolate, entire, with a deep sinus; submerged lvs. usually present, thin and delicate: fls. yellow to purplish, solitary, usually standing above the water; sepals 5–12, conspicuous, yellow at least inside; petals and stamens similar, numerous, inserted on a receptacle below the ovary; pistil with several cells, the stigma disk-like with 5 to many rays: fr. ovoid to columnar, usually ripening above the water. (Nuphar: the Arabic name.)

N. advena, Ait. f. (*Nymphæa advena,* Ait.). COMMON SPATTERDOCK. Lvs. erect, usually above the water surface, blades ovate to oblong, 6–12 in. long, green, glabrous: fls. subglobose, 1–1½ in. across (3 in. across when flattened); sepals usually 6, ovate to suborbicular, about 1¼ in. long, the 3 outer ones green outside, lighter within, and the 3 inner yellow tipped with green; petals about 20, ⅓in. long and ⅛in. wide, yellow tinged red; stamens usually more than 200, yellowish becoming dull red. Vt. to Neb., Tex. and Fla.

3. **VICTORIA,** Lindl. Probably 3 species in S. Amer., known for the great size of the floating lvs. and for the large fragrant fls.—Per., with erect rhizome: peduncles, petioles, under side of lvs., calyces and ovaries very prickly: lvs. floating, circular, with great bars and cross-ribs showing beneath, the margins turned up straight 3–8 in.: fls. 6–18 in. across when open, floating, opening on two successive days late in the afternoon and remaining till the following morning, changing from white to pink or red, fragrant; petals 50 or more, oblong or narrower, obtuse; sepals 4; stamens 150 or more; inside the stamens a deep cup is formed by about 25 paracarpels; true pistils 30–40; stigma in the bottom of the fl., 2–2½ in. broad: fr. a large more or less berry-like prickly body crowned by the remains of the torus-tube. (Victo-ria: dedicated to Queen Victoria.)

A. Sepals prickly nearly or quite to tips: lvs. scarcely pubescent beneath, but prickly. . . 1. *V. amazonica*
AA. Sepals prickly only at base: lvs. densely villous beneath. . . . . 2. *V. Cruziana*

1. **V. amazonica,** Sowerby (*Euryale amazonica,* Poeppig. *V. regia,* Lindl. *V. regia* var. *Randii,* Sturt.). ROYAL WATER-LILY. Lvs. 3–6 ft. across, only sparingly pubescent beneath, larger lvs. turned up 5–6 in. at the edges, deep red beneath: fls. turning crimson the second day; sepals prickly nearly or quite to tips, spines about ¼in. or less long; ovaries with prickles about ⅖in. long: seed elliptic-globose, nearly ⅓in. long, with indistinct raphe. Amazon, British Guiana.

2. **V. Cruziana,** Orbigny (*V. Trickeri,* Hort.). SANTA CRUZ WATER-LILY. Lvs. densely villous beneath, the upturned margins green and 6–8 in. high: fls. turning deep red-pink second day; sepals prickly only at base; ovary with longer prickles, ½in. and more: seed nearly globose, about ⅓in. long, with prominent raphe. (Bears the name of General Santa Cruz.) Paraguay.—Apparently the kind now in cult. in N. Amer., although it may be called *V. regia.*

4. **NELUMBO,** Adans. (*Nelumbium,* Juss.). Species probably 3.—Stout large perennials from creeping rootstocks: lvs. peltate, suborbicular, concave, mostly standing above the water on high stout petioles: fls. large, single, on peduncles usually overtopping the lvs.; sepals 4 or 5; petals and stamens many, caducous, anthers

narrow, with a broad prolonged connective; pistils many (9–17 or more), immersed in the large nearly flat-topped spongy receptacle, each opening on top by a large hole: fr. size of small hazelnut. (Nelum-bo: name in Ceylon.)

A. Fls. pink to red or white: petioles and peduncles rather rough..................1. *N. nucifera*
AA. Fls. pale yellow: petioles and peduncles almost glabrous.......................2. *N. pentapetala*

1. **N. nucifera,** Gaertn. (*Nelumbium Nelumbo*, Druce. *Nymphæa Nelumbo*, L. *Nelumbium speciosum*, Willd.). East Indian Lotus. Rootstock bearing small scale-like lvs., many ft. long and an article of food in some countries: most of the lvs. high (3–6 ft.) above the water, the blade orbicular and centrally peltate, entire, 1–3 ft. across, glaucous: fls. 4–10 in. across, fragrant, pink or rose, with variants to white and dark red, sometimes striped; also double-fld. forms as well as dwarf races. S. Asia to Australia.; sometimes nat. —One of the most striking plants in cult., in many named vars. The Egyptian lotus is *Nymphæa Lotus*.

2. **N. pentapetala,** Fern. (*Nymphæa pentapetala*, Walt. *Nelumbium luteum*, Willd.). American Lotus. Water Chinkapin. Lvs. standing well out of the water or sometimes floating, orbicular, 1–2 (3) ft. across, centrally peltate, entire, strongly nerved, bluish-green; petioles and peduncles 3–7 ft. high: fls. pale yellow, 4–10 in. across. Ont. to Fla., Minn. and Tex.

5. **BRASENIA,** Schreber. One aquatic herb native in N. Amer., Asia, Afr. and Australia.—Creeping rootstocks bearing slender branching sts. with petioled peltate alternate entire floating lvs., the submerged parts coated with thick transparent jelly: fls. small, purple, axillary; sepals and petals similar, 3–4, persistent; stamens 12–18 or more; pistils 4–18 (20), free: fr. leathery, indehiscent, 1–2-seeded. (Brasenia: name unexplained.)

B. Schreberi, Gmel. (*B. peltata*, Pursh. *B. purpurea*, Casp.). Water-Shield. Sts. slender, several ft. long, trailing: lf.-blades oval to elliptic, 2–5 in. long, bright green above, often purplish beneath: fls. purple, ½–¾in. across: fr. about ⅓in. long, beaked. (Named for J. C. D. von Schreber, page 51.)

6. **CABOMBA,** Aubl. Fanwort. Water-Shield. About 4 species native in trop. and temp. Amer.—Delicate mucilaginous branching herbs: lvs. petioled, peltate, the floating lvs. entire and often alternate, the submerged lvs. palmately and finely dissected, opposite or whorled: fls. small, white to yellow, axillary, solitary; sepals 3, petaloid; petals 3, auricled near base; stamens 3–6; pistils 3 (2–4), free: fr. leathery, indehiscent, (1-) 3-seeded. (Cabom-ba: the Guiana name.)

C. caroliniana, Gray (*C. aquatica*, DC. not Aubl. *C. viridifolia*, Hort.). Washington Plant. Fish-Grass. Sts. 3–6 ft. long: floating lvs. linear-oblong, about ¾in. long, entire; submerged lvs. 1–2 in. across, repeatedly divided into filiform segms.: fls. about ½in. across, white with 2 yellow spots at base of each petal: fr. flask-shaped. N. J. to Mich., Fla. and Tex.

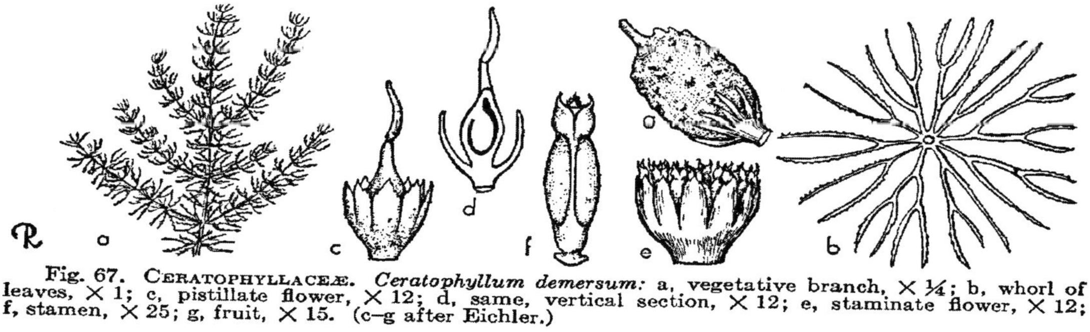

Fig. 67. Ceratophyllaceæ. *Ceratophyllum demersum:* a, vegetative branch, × ¼; b, whorl of leaves, × 1; c, pistillate flower, × 12; d, same, vertical section, × 12; e, staminate flower, × 12; f, stamen, × 25; g, fruit, × 15. (c–g after Eichler.)

67. CERATOPHYLLACEÆ. HORNWORT FAMILY

One genus of submerged green aquatic herbs, widely distributed throughout the world.—Rootless, the lower end of the branched st. usually buried in mud and colorless: lvs. whorled, forked into thread-like often stiff and brittle serrate to serrulate divisions: plants monœcious, the staminate and pistillate inflorescences usually on separate nodes; fls. sessile, bracteate, perianth lacking; stamens distinct, 8–18, the anthers subsessile on the convex receptacle which is surrounded by 10–12 forked involucral bracts; pistils usually solitary, with 10–20 bristle-tipped bracts; ovary 1-celled, 1-ovuled; style persistent: fr. an achene with spines.

CERATOPHYLLUM, L. HORNWORT. COONTAIL. Several species, two of which are native in the U. S.—Lvs. often crowded by the shortening of the internodes, spinulose serrulate. (Ceratophyl-lum: Greek *horn leaf.*)

C. demersum, L. Sts. 2–8 ft. long: lvs. to 1 in. long, two or three times forked: fr. oval, nearly ¼in. long, smooth, marginless, the persistent style subtended by a short basal spine or tubercle on each side. N. Amer. Var. **echinatum,** Gray, has a narrowly winged and toothed margin and the sides roughened and pimpled.

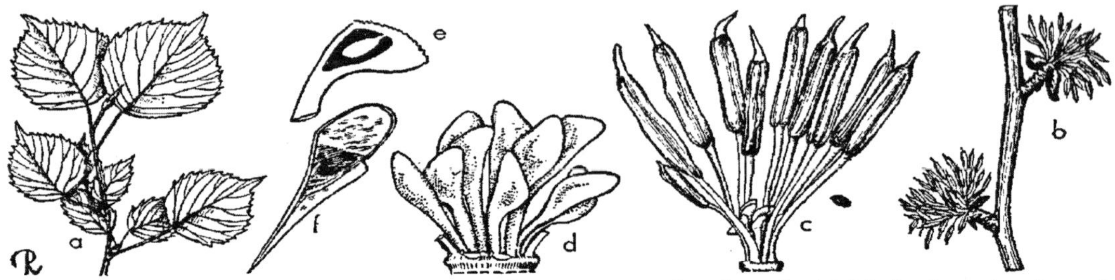

Fig. 68. EUPTELEACEÆ. *Euptelea polyandra:* a, vegetative branch, × ⅙; b, flowering branch, × ½; c, flower, × 3; d, gynœcium, × 9; e, ovary, vertical section, × 10; f, fruit, × 2.

68. EUPTELEACEÆ. EUPTELEA FAMILY

A monogeneric family of hardy deciduous trees or shrubs, sometimes grown for ornament.—Twigs with imbricately-scaled buds, terminal bud absent: lvs. exstipulate, alternate, petioled, pinnately veined, glabrous, acuminate, serrate: fls. perfect, without perianth, in axillary fascicles of 6–12, appearing before or with the lvs.; stamens numerous, in a single whorl, borne on torus margin, anthers oblong-linear, basifixed on filiform filaments; pistils 8–18, free, in a single whorl, stipitate, monocarpellate, 1-celled, ovules mostly 1–3, placentation parietal: fr. a small stipitate samara, usually in clusters, seeds 1–3.—Until recently most authors have retained this in the Trochodendraceæ, a family which now also is considered to be monogeneric and differs, apart from fundamental details of floral and vascular anatomy, in the lvs. persistent, pistils sessile and basally imbedded in receptacle and the fr. a follicle.

EUPTELEA, Sieb. & Zucc. Three species of woody plants having the characteristics of the family; one is sometimes cult. as a novelty. (Eupte-lea: Greek *handsome elm,* in allusion to its elm-like frs.)

E. polyandra, Sieb. & Zucc. Shrub or slender tree to 45 ft., bark gray and becoming rough: lvs. ovate to deltoid-ovate, to 6 in. long, broadly cuneate to truncate, irregularly serrate, the largest teeth to ⅝in. long, glabrous: stamens 8–18, about ½in. long; pistils less than 1/12in. long: fr. to ⅓in. long and half as wide. Japan.—Another species, **E. pleiosperma,** Hook. f. & Thoms., of China, is also cult. and differs in the lf.-margins with largest teeth to ⅙in. long and lf. more narrowly cuneate at base.

69. CERCIDIPHYLLACEÆ. KATSURA-TREE FAMILY

One monotypic genus native in E. Asia.—Deciduous tree with short spurs on the branches: lvs. usually opposite on the shoots, solitary on the spurs, slender-petioled, orbicular to broad-ovate, cordate or subcordate at base, obtuse, palmately nerved, crenate-serrate: plant diœcious, the fls. solitary, appearing before or with the lvs., 4-bracteate, lacking perianth; staminate fls. subsessile, stamens 15–20, filaments slender, anthers 2-celled, basifixed, dehiscing lengthwise; pistillate fls. pedicelled, of 3–5 pistils ending in long purplish styles; ovary 1-celled, many-ovuled, placentation parietal: fr. a dehiscent pod with many winged seeds.

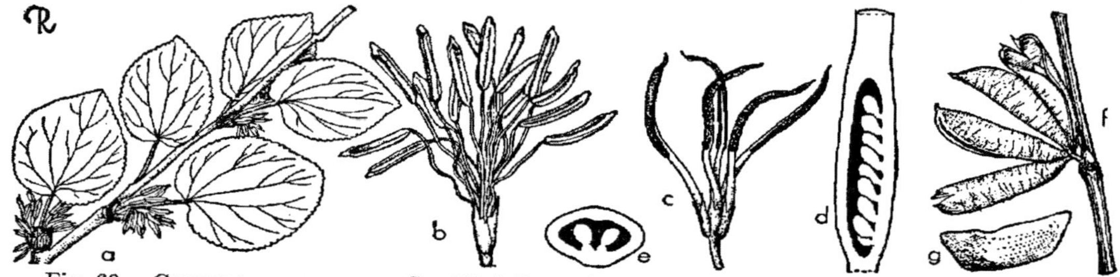

Fig. 69. CERCIDIPHYLLACEÆ. *Cercidiphyllum japonicum:* a, branch with staminate flowers, × ½; b, staminate flower, × 2; c, pistillate flowers, × 1; d, ovary, vertical section, × 10; e, ovary, cross-section, × 10; f, follicles, × 1; g, seed, × 5.

CERCIDIPHYLLUM, Sieb. & Zucc. Characters of the family. (Cercidiphyllum, *cercis* and *phyllon*, leaf; the lvs. resemble those of Cercis.)

C. japonicum, Sieb. & Zucc. KATSURA-TREE. Bushy tree of pyramidal habit 20–30 (100) ft. high, usually with several trunks: lvs. 2–4 in. long, glabrous, dark blue-green above, glaucescent beneath, purplish when young, turning bright yellow or partly scarlet in autumn: pod about ¾in. long. Japan.

70. RANUNCULACEÆ. CROWFOOT FAMILY

Mainly herbs, sometimes little shrubs and woody climbers, mostly in the temp. and arctic regions of the northern hemisphere, many of them favorite fl.-garden subjects; genera probably 35 or more, and species perhaps 1,500.—Typically defined as plants with all the floral parts present, regular, free and distinct; to this definition, however, there are many exceptions: in some cases the petals are lacking and the sepals are petaloid; in others the petals and sepals are spurred, making specialized nectaries; in still others (as Nigella) the pistils are more or less united. In general, the sepals are 3–15; petals, if present, of similar number; stamens usually many, hypogynous; pistils few or many; ovary superior, 1-celled, ovules 1 to many, placentation basal or parietal: fr. an achene or follicle, sometimes a berry or caps.: lvs. alternate or opposite, petiole with dilated base, blade simple or compound.—By many authors the pistils are referred to as carpels and perianth-parts as tepals.

A. Pistils 1-ovuled (if fr. a berry or follicle see under AA): fr. an achene.
B. Fls. not subtended by involucres.
C. Lvs. alternate: sepals imbricate (overlapping) in the bud.
D. Petals and sepals present, the petals the more showy.
E. The petals bearing a nectar-pit or -scale at base: lvs. not usually finely dissected........ 1. RANUNCULUS
EE. The petals without such nectary: lvs. finely dissected........ 2. ADONIS
DD. Petals lacking; fls. small and numerous........ 3. THALICTRUM
CC. Lvs. opposite: sepals valvate (edge to edge) in bud, petal-like........ 4. CLEMATIS
BB. Fls. with subtending involucre which sometimes simulates a calyx.
C. Cauline lvs. sepal-like, entire, close beneath the fls.; radical lvs. with 3 entire lobes........ 5. HEPATICA
CC. Cauline lvs. whorled, distant from the fls.
D. Achenes not ribbed: lower lvs. palmately lobed, incised, parted or divided.. 6. ANEMONE
DD. Achenes ribbed: lvs. ternately decompound........ 7. ANEMONELLA
AA. Pistils several-ovuled (1 or 2 in Hydrastis and Xanthorhiza): fr. a follicle or berry.
B. Fls. irregular.
C. Upper sepal spurred; petals 4, the upper pair spurred and included in the spurred sepal........ 8. DELPHINIUM
CC. Upper sepal hooded; petals 2, clawed, inclosed in the hooded sepal........ 9. ACONITUM
BB. Fls. regular.
C. Petals usually produced backward into long spurs........10. AQUILEGIA
CC. Petals not spurred.
D. Fl. with subtending involucre.
E. Plant with scape-like st. bearing single yellow fl........11. ERANTHIS
EE. Plant branching: fls. white or blue........12. NIGELLA
DD. Fl. without involucre.
E. Lvs. palmately nerved or compound.
F. Lf. simple: petals absent.
G. Pistils ripening into a head of red berries: fls. solitary........13. HYDRASTIS
GG. Pistils becoming dry follicles: fls. cymose........14. CALTHA
FF. Lf. compound or parted: petals present, nectariferous, shorter than sepals: fr. not berry-like.
G. Petals flat, pitted above the base........15. TROLLIUS
GG. Petals tubular........16. HELLEBORUS

EE. Lvs. pinnately or ternately compound, or simple.
F. Fls. solitary, usually ¾–4 in. across.
G. Sepals persistent, not petal-like; petals broad, large and showy .... 17. PÆONIA
GG. Sepals caducous, petal-like; petals small.
H. Pistils united into a caps.: petals bifid .... 12. NIGELLA
HH. Pistils free: petals entire .... 18. COPTIS
FF. Fls. racemose, smaller than above.
G. Plant a shrub: fls. brownish-purple .... 19. XANTHORHIZA
GG. Plant an herb: fls. white.
H. Infl. a short open raceme: fr. a berry .... 20. ACTÆA
HH. Infl. an elongated dense raceme or panicle: fr. a follicle .... 21. CIMICIFUGA

1. **RANUNCULUS,** L. BUTTERCUP. CROWFOOT. A wide range of herbs, perhaps 250 species, widely dispersed in temp. and cold countries, some of them weedy and a few grown for the ornamental bloom.—Ann. and per., with alternate entire or compound lvs., plant erect, creeping, or aquatic and floating, root sometimes tuberous: fls. solitary on the ends of st. or many branches or sometimes more or less corymbed or panicled, rarely sessile, mostly yellow; sepals and petals usually 5, sometimes fewer, petals sometimes more numerous; petals with a nectary at base; stamens mostly many, short; pistils 5 to many, ovary 1-ovuled ripening into small hard achenes clustered on the torus to form a little head. (Ranun-culus: Latin word for a *little frog,* alluding to the habitat—in ponds and wet places—of many of the species.)

A. Lvs. grass-like, elongate, simple .... 1. *R. gramineus*
AA. Lvs. not grass-like.
B. Fls. large, 1½–2½ in. broad, few .... 2. *R. asiaticus*
BB. Fls. smaller, numerous.
C. Plant creeping, rooting at the nodes .... 3. *R. repens*
CC. Plant not creeping.
D. Height of plant 3–6 in.
E. Upper sts. and lvs. appressed-hairy: lvs. 3–5-lobed, the lobes again divided .... 4. *R. montanus*
EE. Upper sts. and lvs. glabrous: lvs. entire to broadly 3-lobed .... 5. *R. glaberrimus*
DD. Height of plant 1–4 ft.
E. Species hairy about petioles, sepals, etc.: fls. yellow .... 6. *R. acris*
EE. Species glabrous throughout: fls. usually white .... 7. *R. aconitifolius*

1. **R. gramineus,** L. (*R. graminifolius,* Hort.). Per. ½–1 ft. high, from short thick fibrous-coated rootstock and fleshy roots; sts. 1–2, glabrous, 1- to few-fld.: lvs. mostly basal, lance-linear, 2–6 in. long: fls. yellow, ¾–1 in. wide; sepals glabrous: achenes in ovoid head. S. Eu., N. Afr.

2. **R. asiaticus,** L. TURBAN and PERSIAN BUTTERCUPS. Erect from irregular tubers (which are classed with bulbs in the market), 6–18 in., simple or only sparingly branched, hairy: lvs. ternately compound, lfts. with narrow divisions that are dentate at apex and more or less obtuse: fls. few (1–4 to a st.) on long peduncles, mostly very double in cult. kinds and 1–1½ in. across, bright yellow; petals obovate, rounded. S. E. Eu., S. W. Asia. Var. **superbissimus,** Hort., is taller, with larger fls.

3. **R. repens,** L., var. **pleniflorus,** Fern. DOUBLE-FLOWERED CREEPING BUTTERCUP. Vigorous plant, sparsely hairy, the runners extending several ft. in a season and rooting at the joints; fl.-sts. ascending, much-branching, 1–2 ft.; roots of thick fibers but not tuberous: radical and lower lvs. very long-petioled, nearly orbicular in outline, ternately compound, the lower lfts. making a cordate or subcordate base to the lf., margins coarsely crenate-dentate: fls. bright yellow, full double, about ¾in. across, peduncled, freely produced in spring.—Frequent in yards and sometimes escaped; grown as "double buttercup," *R. repens flore-pleno, R. speciosus,* and sometimes as *R. acris flore-pleno;* origin apparently obscure and perhaps not a form of true *R. repens.*

4. **R. montanus,** Willd. Rootstock short-creeping; plant 2–6 in. high, soft-pubescent: radical lvs. few, rounded in outline, blades ½–1 in. broad, 3–5-parted, then lobed with narrow blunt segms., subglabrous to hairy, petioles usually longer than blades: sts. 1 to few, subscapose, or with 1 or 2 reduced lvs.: fls. yellow, ½–1 in. wide, petals with small scale and pore at base: beak of achene strongly hooked. Eu.

5. **R. glaberrimus,** Hook. Glabrous per.; sts. reclining, 1½–7 in. long: basal lvs. rounded, blades about 1 in. long, thick, entire or with 3 blunt lobes: peduncles 2–5 in.; sepals tinged with lavender; petals bright yellow, ¼–⅝in. long: achenes many in a globose head about ½in. diam. B. C. to Colo. and Calif.

6. **R. acris,** L. A common and widespread variable weed of grass lands, but sometimes cult. in a double-fld. yellow race: root of copious long fibers: erect but diffuse, much-branched, many-fld., hairy, 2–3 ft.: lvs. ternately divided nearly to base, the divisions not stalked and again 3-cleft into mostly lanceolate or almost linear toothed segms.: double fls. about ½–¾in. across; sepals and fl.-buds hairy: achenes not manifestly nerved. Eu.

7. **R. aconitifolius,** L. Taller plant, branching above; sts. nearly or quite glabrous, from tuberous roots: lvs. deeply 3–5-parted, the divisions ovate to lance-ovate and again lobed or notched into broad segms., the divisions on the upper lvs. very acuminate: fls. several to many, 1 in. across, more or less double in the garden kinds, normally white but with yellow double races; sepals and fl.-buds glabrous or only sparsely hairy: achenes veined. Eu.

Fig. 70. RANUNCULACEÆ. A, *Trollius europæus:* Aa, flowering branch, × ½; Ab, basal leaf-blade, × ½; Ac, flower, vertical section, × ½; Ad, pistil, vertical section, × 3; Ae, petal, × 2. B, *Thalictrum rugosum:* Ba, portion of inflorescence, × ½; Bb, node with cauline leaf, × ½; Bc, staminate flower, × 2. C, *Delphinium elatum:* Ca, flower, × 1; Cb, flower, vertical section, × 1. D, *Aconitum Carmichaelii* var. *Wilsonii:* Da, flower, side view, × ½; Db, flower, vertical section, × ½. E, *Aquilegia flabellata:* flowering branch, × ½. F, Nigella: flower and leaf, × 1. G, *Helleborus niger:* Ga, flower, face view, × ½; Gb, flower, vertical section, × ½. (p petal, pi pistil, s sepal.)

2. **ADONIS,** L. PHEASANTS-EYE. About a score of species in Eu. and Asia.—Ann. and per., erect: lvs. alternate, dissected: fls. yellow or of the red series, solitary and terminal; sepals 5–8; petals 5–16, flat, deciduous, without nectaries; stamens many; pistils many, ovary 1-ovuled: fr. an achene, several or many of them aggregated in a globular or elongated head. (Ado-nis: a name in mythology.)

A. Plant per.: pistils hairy, with hooked beak.
 B. Lvs. many, sessile, 1–2 in. long: sts. mostly 6–18 in. tall. . . . . 1. *A. vernalis*
 BB. Lvs. few, petioled, 3–6 in. long: sts. 3–6 in. tall. . . . . 2. *A. amurensis*
AA. Plant ann.: pistils glabrous, with straight or incurved beak.
 B. Petals little longer than sepals: sts. much-branched . . . . 3. *A. annua*
 BB. Petals much longer than sepals: sts. little branched.
  C. Fls. 1½–2 in. across: achenes very rough, without tooth on inner face and narrowed into straight beak of equal length to body of achene. . . . . 4. *A. aleppica*
  CC. Fls. 1–1½ in. across: achenes less rough, with a tooth on inner face and with shorter incurved beak . . . . 5. *A. æstivalis*

1. **A. vernalis,** L. SPRING ADONIS. Per. 4–18 in. high, sts. simple or sparingly branched with ascending branches, very leafy: lvs. dissected into filiform segms.: fls. solitary and terminal, yellow, opening wide, 2–3 in. across, in early spring; petals 10 or more, lightly toothed: achenes hairy, in dense oblong head. Cent. and S. E. Eu.—White-fld. and double-fld. races are cult.

2. **A. amurensis,** Regel & Radde. Per. from fascicled fleshy roots; sts. glabrous, few, low: lvs. few, remote, with petioles almost as long as triangular blades, dissected into confluent segms.: fls. appearing before lvs., orange to yellow, 1½–2 in. across: achenes pubescent, in dense globose head. Manchuria, Japan.—Double-fld. forms are cult.

3. **A. annua,** L. (*A. autumnalis*, L.). AUTUMN ADONIS. Ann. 8–24 in. high, much-branched: fls. deep red with darker center, not opening wide, about ¾in. across, summer to early autumn; petals 6–8, concave, not much exceeding calyx: achenes glabrous. Cent. Eu. to W. Asia.

4. **A. aleppica,** Boiss. Ann. about 1 ft. high, glabrous, simple or little branched: lvs. numerous, 1–2½ in. long, subsessile to petioled, blades dissected into linear segms.: fls. terminal, few, 1½–2 in. broad, red; petals oblong-obovate: pistils in a cylindrical spike, the achenes ¼in. long, with deeply and irregularly pitted obovoid body and slender smooth erect beak. Syria.

5. **A. æstivalis,** L. SUMMER ADONIS. Ann. 12–18 in. high, sparingly branched and mostly toward the top: fls. crimson, opening wide, 1–1½ in. across, June–July; petals flat, obtuse, twice as long as sepals: achenes glabrous, beaked. Cent. Eu. Var. **citrina,** Hoffm., fls. lemon-yellow.

3. **THALICTRUM,** L. MEADOW-RUE. Erect and mostly tall per. herbs chiefly of the north temp. zone, 80–90 species, a very few cult. for ornament.—Lvs. ternately compound and decompound, the angled or notched ultimate segms. graceful and ornamental: fls. bisexual or unisexual, small and separately inconspicuous but borne in profuse panicles or racemes that have a tassel-like appearance and often showy from the colored stamens; some species diœcious; petals lacking; sepals 4 or 5, usually falling early, sometimes neutrally colored and petal-like; stamens many; pistils few, 1-ovuled, maturing into a little cluster of sessile or stalked achenes, which are sometimes inflated or winged. (Thalic-trum: old Greek name.)

A. Plants low, usually not more than ½ft. tall.
 B. Sepals greenish: lvs. basal: filaments not dilated. . . . . 1. *T. alpinum*
 BB. Sepals pink to purple: lvs. cauline and basal: filaments dilated. . . . . 2. *T. kiusianum*
AA. Plants taller, 1–6 ft. tall.
 B. Frs. 2–3-winged, strongly angled, stipitate and hanging: sepals white to rose or lilac.
  C. Wings of fr. 3.
   D. Plant diœcious; sepals about as long as stamens; filaments about one-third as wide as long. . . . . 3. *T. Delavayi*
   DD. Plant monœcious; sepals much shorter than stamens; filaments much more slender. . . . . 4. *T. aquilegifolium*
  CC. Wings of fr. 2: sepals about as long as stamens. . . . . 5. *T. dipterocarpum*
 BB. Frs. 6–8-ribbed or -winged, quite or almost sessile: sepals white to green or yellow.
  C. Fls. white; filaments dilated upward: pistils almost ¼in. long in maturity. . . . . 6. *T. polygamum*
  CC. Fls. green to yellowish; filaments not so dilated: pistils ⅛in. long.
   D. Herb diœcious, 1–2 ft. high. . . . . 7. *T. dioicum*
   DD. Herb with perfect fls.
    E. Lfts. mostly distinctly less than ½in. long: sts. mostly 1–2 ft. high: rhizome short. . . . . 8. *T. minus*
    EE. Lfts. ½–1½ in. long: sts. 2–5 ft.
     F. Plant glaucous: lfts. obovate: achenes attenuate at apex. . . . . 9. *T. rugosum*
     FF. Plant green: lfts. mostly ovate: achenes rounded at apex. . . . . 10. *T. flavum*

1. **T. alpinum,** L. Sts. scape-like, 2–6 (12) in. high, leafless or nearly so, subglabrous: lvs. biternate, basal, mostly ½–2 in. long, the lfts. rounded or obovate, 3–5-toothed at the tips and with revolute margins: fls. perfect, in a simple raceme: achenes sessile. Boreal Amer., Eu., Asia.

2. **T. kiusianum,** Nakai. Stoloniferous, 2–5 in. high, glabrous: basal lvs. 1–2-ternate. 1–2 in. long, the lfts. broad-ovate, 3–5-toothed, purplish above; st.-lvs. reduced: sepals pink to purple, shorter than the numerous dilated stamens. Japan.

3. **T. Delavayi,** Franch. Two to 3 ft. tall, glabrous, diœcious: lower lvs. 2–3-pinnate, the lfts. long-petioluled, 3–5-lobed, cuneate at base, rounded at apex; st.-lvs. much reduced: fls. unisexual, pendulous; sepals pink or lilac: achenes 10–12, stipitate, 3-winged. (For Abbé Delavay, page 42.) China.

4. **T. aquilegifolium,** L. Graceful plant with hollow sts., 2–3 ft., glabrous, mostly glaucous, imperfectly diœcious: segms. of decompound lvs. suborbicular to short-oblong, entire on lower sides and base (the base subcordate, truncate or oblique), bluntly few-notched at the broad apex: infl. of many slender-rayed little umbels, May–June; staminate fls. with many lilac-purple or pink erect stamens with very long somewhat inflated filaments, highly ornamental; pistillate fls. less showy, with few or several stipitate pistils that in fr. become large hanging 3-winged somewhat inflated achenes. Eu., Asia. Vars. **album** and **purpureum,** Hort., are common in the trade, with white and rose-purple stamens respectively.

5. **T. dipterocarpum,** Franch. Plant 2–7 ft.: lvs. decompound, the segms. oblong to round, mostly 3-toothed at apex: polygamous; fls. nodding; sepals large, rose to lilac, about as long as stamens; filaments ivory, not inflated: achenes 2-winged, 3-nerved on each side. W. China. Var. **album,** Hort., has white sepals.

6. **T. polygamum,** Muhl. (*T. Cornutii,* Torr. & Gray). Stout, 4–8 ft. high: lvs. decompound, the segms. oblong to orbicular, 3-lobed: polygamous; panicle compound, 1 or more ft. long; sepals usually white; filaments broadened: achenes 6–8-winged, short-stalked. Lab. to Ohio and Fla.

7. **T. dioicum,** L. Glabrous, 1–2 ft. high, diœcious: lvs. decompound, the segms. orbicular, 5–9-lobed: stamens not dilated, longer than the greenish sepals: achenes ovoid, sessile, strongly ribbed. Lab. to Mo. and Ala.

8. **T. minus,** L. (*T. majus,* Smith. *T. adiantifolium,* Hort.). St. usually not hollow, 1–1½ ft. high, striate, leafless but sheathed at the base: lvs. 2–3-pinnate; segms. 3-cleft and glaucous, numerous and small, roundish or broadly wedge-shaped, stipules with spreading auricles: fls. bisexual, mostly drooping in panicles, with ascending branches, greenish-yellow, the anthers apiculate: achenes fusiform, 8-ribbed. Eu.—An exceedingly variable species.

9. **T. rugosum,** Ait. (*T. glaucum,* Desf.). Plant 3–6 ft. high, glaucous, exstipulate: lvs. 2–3-pinnate, the segms. obovate, glaucous beneath, 3-lobed, and toothed: fls. bisexual, crowded in umbel-like clusters in panicles, yellow, sepals shorter than the filiform stamens: achenes sessile, deeply furrowed, sharply beaked. S. Eu.

10. **T. flavum,** L. Plant 2–5 ft. high, usually green: lvs. stipuled, 2–3-pinnate, the segms. usually ovate, coarsely 3-toothed at the tips: fls. bisexual, sepals pale yellow, shorter than the filiform stamens: achenes sessile, striate, apex obtuse. Eu.

4. **CLEMATIS,** L. CLEMATIS. VIRGINS-BOWER. Defined broadly, the genus has over 200 species in many regions, mostly temp.; many have been intro. to cult., and are known in botanic gardens and choice collections, but relatively few are common.—Woody vines climbing by clasping petioles and sometimes erect per. herbs: lvs. opposite, entire or pinnately compound: fls. small or large, solitary or variously paniculate, sometimes showy individually and in other species only in the mass; sepals mostly 4 or 5, valvate in the bud; petals none, or in one section represented by staminoid bodies; stamens many; pistils many, ovary 1-ovuled, forming 1-seeded mostly tailed achenes in a head. (Clem-atis: an old Greek name for a climbing plant.)—The large-fld. kinds of gardens are mostly hybrids and other cultivars.

A. Plants herbaceous or essentially so (dying to ground in winter), erect or at least not climbing.
  B. Lvs. simple and broad, entire or toothed.
    C. Fls. purple or blue.
      D. Lf. thin, mostly acute: styles of achenes plumose.................... 1. *C. integrifolia*
      DD. Lf. coriaceous, obtuse: styles naked above.................... 2. *C. Fremontii*
    CC. Fls. yellow; styles plumose.................... 3. *C. ochroleuca*
  BB. Lvs. lobed to pinnate.
    C. Lf. ternate, the lfts. 4–6 in. long.................... 4. *C. heracleifolia*
    CC. Lf. pinnate to pinnatifid, the lfts. smaller.
      D. Sepals erect, purplish: lvs. decompound.................... 5. *C. hirsutissima*
      DD. Sepals spreading, white: lvs. pinnate.................... 6. *C. recta*

AA. Plant manifestly woody, climbing.
B. Sepals erect (except at the flaring tips), forming a tubular or urn-shaped fl.
C. Lvs. glaucous: fls. red.. 7. *C. texensis*
CC. Lvs. not glaucous: fls. purple to white.
D. Margins of sepals wide, undulate or crisped: achene-tails pubescent...... 8. *C. crispa*
DD. Margins of sepals lacking or narrow: achene-tails plumose........... 9. *C. Viorna*
BB. Sepals spreading, the fls. usually wide open.
C. Fls. large, 1½ or more in. across, solitary or in 3's or sometimes in axillary panicles.
D. Lfts. or lvs. entire or essentially so.
E. Fruiting style glabrous at least in upper half.
F. Width of fls. 1–2 in.: lvs. bipinnate.......................... 10. *C. Viticella*
FF. Width of fls. 3–6 in.: lvs. pinnate or upper simple................ 11. *C. Jackmanii*
EE. Fruiting style plumose or pubescent to tip.
F. Pedicels shorter than sepals: lvs. simple or ternate, woolly beneath.. 12. *C. lanuginosa*
FF. Pedicels longer than sepals: lvs. ternate or pinnate, glabrous or somewhat pubescent beneath.
G. Fl.-stalk with 2 bracts: style silky in fr...................... 13. *C. florida*
GG. Fl.-stalk without bracts: style plumose in fr.
H. Number of sepals 6–8; filaments glabrous, narrow.
I. The sepals not clawed, overlapping...................... 14. *C. Lawsoniana*
II. The sepals clawed, not overlapping...................... 15. *C. patens*
HH. Number of sepals 4; filaments pubescent, broad............ 16. *C. columbiana*
DD. Lfts. serrate or dentate or lobed.
E. Outside of sepals silky, white................................ 17. *C. lasiantha*
EE. Outside of sepals glabrous or pubescent especially toward margins.
F. Color of fls. yellow; filaments pubescent.
G. Inside of sepals pubescent: lfts. lobed or coarsely toothed...... 18. *C. orientalis*
GG. Inside of sepals glabrous: lfts. serrate......................... 19. *C. tangutica*
FF. Color of fls. white to pink; filaments glabrous..................20. *C. montana*
CC. Fls. small, rarely more than 1 in. across, usually many.
D. Fl. unisexual: lfts. usually serrate.
E. Lfts. 3, mostly 1½–4 in. long..................................21. *C. virginiana*
EE. Lfts. 5–7, mostly 1–2 in. long.................................22. *C. ligusticifolia*
DD. Fl. bisexual.
E. Lvs. pinnate, the lfts. mostly 1–3½ in. long.
F. Lfts. largely entire: anthers four to five times as long as wide........23. *C. dioscoreifolia*
FF. Lfts. often serrate: anthers two to three times as long as wide....... 24. *C. Vitalba*
EE. Lvs. usually bipinnate, the lfts. ½–1½ in. long.................. 25. *C. Flammula*

1. **C. integrifolia**, L. Herbaceous or subshrubby, erect, 1½–3 ft. tall; sts. slender, diffuse, finely pubescent: lvs. sessile, 2–4 in., simple and entire, ovate, usually acute, thin, with 1 or 2 strong veins on each side of midrib: fls. solitary, terminal, nodding, urn-shaped, 1–1½ in. long, dull blue to purple; sepals 4, tomentose near margins; styles 1–1½ in. long, plumose in fr. Eu., Asia. Var. **cærulea**, Hort., is 1½–2 ft. high with porcelain-blue fls.

2. **C. Fremontii**, Wats. Plant coarser, ½–1½ ft. tall: lvs. very coriaceous, reticulate-veiny, ovate, obtuse: fruiting styles ½–⅔in. long, glabrous above. (J. C. Fremont, page 43.) Neb., Kans. Var. **Riehlii**, Erickson, plant 1–2½ ft. tall, lvs. elliptical; Mo.

3. **C. ochroleuca**, Ait. Plant 1–2 ft. tall and with coriaceous veiny ovate lvs.: fls. yellow, ⅔–1 in. long: achene-styles 1–2 in. long, plumose. Staten Isl. to Ga.

4. **C. heracleifolia**, DC. (*C. tubulosa*, Turcz.). Herbaceous or somewhat woody at base, stout and erect, sts. many-striate and glabrous: lvs. ternate, the 3 lfts. stalked, large, broad-ovate, rounded at base, 3–6 in. long, with large mucronate-pointed teeth: polygamous; fls. tubular, many in axillary and terminal clusters, light blue, ¾–1 in. long; sepals 4, reflexing: fruiting stigmas club-shaped and recurved. China. Var. **Davidiana**, Hemsl. (*C. Davidiana*, Decne.), apparently the more usual form in cult.; di cious; lfts. cuneate at base; fls. bright blue, fragrant, 6–15 together in heads and also few or single in the axils.

5. **C. hirsutissima**, Pursh (*C. Douglasii*, Hook.). Plant ½–2 ft. tall: lvs. pinnate, with 7–13 bi-multifid lfts., their divisions being lanceolate to linear, pubescent when young: fls. solitary, terminal, 1–1½ in. long; sepals hirsute without, purple: fruiting styles plumose, about 2½ in. long. Mont. to Wash., Ariz. and New Mex. Var. **Scottii**, Erickson (*C. Scottii*, Porter), lfts. simple or lobed, lanceolate, petioluled; S. D. to New Mex.

6. **C. recta**, L. (*C. erecta*, L.). Herbaceous and erect or ascending, or perhaps slightly woody at base, 2–3 ft., glabrous: lvs. pinnate; lfts. 5–9, petiolulate, narrowly ovate-pointed, entire: fls. many in a large terminal compound panicle-like infl., white, fragrant, ¾–1 in. across, summer: there is a double-fld. var. S. Eu. Var. **mandshurica**, Maxim. (*C. mandshurica*, Rupr.), sts. longer, more slender, usually decumbent; lfts. often subcordate at base, obtuse; fls. pure white, in both terminal and axillary panicles; E. Asia. Var. **grandiflora**, Hort., has white fls. to 2 in. across in large clusters.

7. **C. texensis**, Buckl. (*C. coccinea*, Engelm. *Viorna coccinea*, Small). SCARLET CLEMATIS. Suffruticose climber to 6 ft. and more, glabrous: lvs. pinnate, somewhat glaucous; lfts. broad-ovate, ¾–1½ in. and more long, rather thick, mostly subcordate at base, obtuse or very short-pointed at apex and usually apiculate: fls. solitary on long peduncle with a pair of broad simple bracts near base, nodding, urn-shaped or pitcher-shaped, ¾–1 in. long, glabrous outside, scarlet, in summer: fruiting styles 1–2 in. long, plumose. Tex.—

Hardy N. Several hybrids have been produced between this species and *C. crispa* and others.

8. **C. crispa,** L. (*Viorna crispa,* Small). Shrubby climber, with very thin pinnate lvs., lfts. 3–5 or more, often divided into 3's, the parts mostly ovate in outline: fls. solitary, nodding, 1 in. long more or less, urn-shaped with open flaring top with recurved crisped sepals, purple to whitish: fruiting styles silky, not plumose. Va. to Fla. and Tex.—*C. cylindrica*, Sims, is a hybrid with *C. integrifolia.*

9. **C. Viorna,** L. VIORNA. Climbing 10 ft. and more: lvs. thin, not glaucous; lfts. ovate-lanceolate and long-pointed, 2–4 in. long, subcordate: fls. solitary, the long peduncle usually with a pair of narrow bracts, nodding, purplish; sepals very thick, finely or thinly pubescent outside: fruiting styles 1 in. long, plumose. (Viorna: name adopted by Linnæus without explanation.) Pa. to Miss. and Mo.

10. **C. Viticella,** L. Strong climber; sts. glabrous: lvs. bipinnate, with 5–7 pinnæ, the lowermost of these usually of 3 nearly or quite entire lfts.: fls. solitary or in 3's, blue, purple or rose-purple, 1½–2 in. diam.; sepals 4, obovate, pointed, reflexed; stamens yellow: fruiting styles short and glabrous. (*Viticella:* diminutive of Vitis, the vine.) S. Eu., S. W. Asia.—Many hybrids issue from this species, known mostly by the sepals being reflexed or recurved at tip. *C. eriostemon*, Decne. (*C. Hendersonii*, Hort.), blue, is *C. Viticella* × *C. integrifolia.*

11. **C. Jackmanii,** Moore. Hybrid, or name applied to a series of hybrids, constituting a well known large-fld. cultural race, issuing from *C. lanuginosa* and forms of *C. Viticella,* with lvs. pinnate, the upper often simple: fls. large and flat, 5–6 in. across, usually in 3's and forming terminal panicles, velvety purple with 3 ribs on the back and 3 corresponding furrows down the front center of each of the 4–6 very broad sepals; stamens pale green: styles glabrous above. Produced at the nursery of G. Jackman & Son, Woking, England; first bloom appeared in 1862.

12. **C. lanuginosa,** Lindl. Rather low or short climber: lvs. simple or with 3 lfts., each cordate-acuminate, woolly beneath: fls. in summer, erect on stout pedicels that are shorter than the sepals, woolly in the bud, 6 in. across when expanded, lavender or blue-gray; sepals 5 or 6, ovate, thick; stamens pale reddish-brown: fruiting styles plumose. E. China. —The largest fld. of the wild species and the chief parent of the large-fld. garden clematises.

13. **C. florida,** Thunb. Slender but tall climbing: lvs. various, mostly ternate or biternate: lfts. small, ovate-lanceolate, acuminate or pointed: fls. flat, 2–4 in. across, creamy-white with green bands beneath; sepals 5–6, broad-ovate, sharp-pointed; stamens purplish: fruiting styles silky. Japan. Var. **Fortunei,** Moore (*C. Fortunei,* Hort.), has double creamy-white fls. becoming pink; named for Robt. Fortune, page 43.

14. **C. Lawsoniana,** Moore & Jackman. Hybrid between *C. lanuginosa* and *C. florida* var. *Fortunei,* with fls. 6 in. across and flat, rose-purple with 2 or more darker parallel veins or ribs and also darker side veins, the very broad sepals 6–8: styles hairy throughout. Intro. in England about 1872 by P. Lawson & Son, nurserymen. Var. **Henryi,** Rehd. (*C. Henryi,* Anderson-Henry not Oliv.), has large flat creamy-white fls.; strong plant, much like *C. lanuginosa.*

15. **C. patens,** Morr. & Decne. (*C. cærulea,* Lindl.). Woody climber: lvs. ternate or pinnate; lfts. ovate to ovate-lanceolate, 1½–4 in. long: fls. in spring, on pedicels longer than sepals, borne on old (last year's) wood, delicate lilac; sepals about 8, narrow, spreading; stamens purple: styles plumose. China, cult. in Japan.—One parent of many garden kinds.

16. **C. columbiana,** Torr. & Gray (*Atragene columbiana,* Nutt.). Half-woody climber with slender sts.: lvs. ternate; lfts. ovate, cordate at base, 1–1½ in. long, acute or short-acuminate, entire or coarsely toothed: fls. solitary, purple or blue; sepals acuminate, 1½–2 in. long: styles plumose, 1½–2 in. long. B. C. to Colo.

17. **C. lasiantha,** Nutt. PIPESTEM CLEMATIS. Tomentulose climber: lvs. ternate, silky-pubescent at least beneath; lfts. elliptic, broad-ovate to orbicular, 1–2 in. long, coarsely toothed and more or less lobed: polygamous; fls. 1–3 on axillary peduncles from last year's wood, 1½–2½ in. across, white, fragrant, the sepals broad-oblong to oval and silky-pubescent outside: fr. pubescent with feathery tails 1 in. or more long. Calif., and planted in that region.

18. **C. orientalis,** Lam. (*C. graveolens,* Lindl.). Rapidly growing nearly or quite glabrous climber: lvs. pinnate, with 3 or 4 pairs of lfts., thin, glaucous and more or less glossy; lfts. ovate to long-oblong, 1–3 in. long, stalked, 3-parted or -lobed, the divisions strongly dentate to entire: fls. solitary, or few in cymes, nearly or quite erect, yellow-veined and tinted greenish. scented, 1½ in. or somewhat more across, the 4 spreading or recurved sepals more or less lightly pubescent both sides: styles plumose in fr. Iran, Himalayas.—Cult. in Calif. and probably in the S.

19. **C. tangutica,** Korsh. (*C. orientalis* var. *tangutica,* Maxim.). GOLDEN CLEMATIS. Near to *C. orientalis* but lfts. more lanceolate, serrate with spreading teeth, sometimes deeply 2–3-lobed: sepals glabrous on both sides, 1¼–2 in. long, acuminate: fruiting styles 2½–3 in. long. Mongolia to N. W. China. Var. **obtusiuscula,** Rehd. & Wils., lfts. smaller; sepals obtusish to short-acuminate, 1–1¼ in. long; N. W. China.

20. **C. montana,** Buch.-Ham. Tall climber to 15 and 20 ft.: lvs. ternate; lfts. oblong-acuminate, cut-toothed: fls. several in the axils appearing successively, anemone-like, about 2 in. across, open, fragrant, white becoming pink; stamens yellow and conspicuous: fruiting styles long and plumose, the achene glabrous. Himalayas. Var. **rubens,** Wils., has purplish lvs. and rose or pink fls. Var. **undulata,** Hort., is a hybrid between *C. montana* and *C. gracilifolia,* with large bluish-white fls.

21. **C. virginiana,** L. Strong mostly diœcious climber, covering bushes and fences in its native places and also planted: lvs. ternate; lfts. ovate to narrow-ovate, acuminate, sharp-toothed, subcordate or rounded at base, 2–5 in. long, stalked, villous beneath when young: fls. many in leafy cymose panicles, white, about ¾–1 in. across, summer to autumn; sepals oblong to narrow-ovate, spreading: fr. in prominent heads with long profuse plumose styles. N. S. to Ga. and Kans.

22. **C. ligusticifolia,** Nutt. Lvs. pinnately 5–7-foliolate, coarsely toothed, thickish in texture: otherwise similar to *C. virginiana.* B. C. and N. D. to New Mex. and Calif.

23. **C. dioscoreifolia,** Lévl. & Vaniot, var. **robusta,** Rehd. (*C. Flammula robusta,* Carr. *C. paniculata,* Thunb. not Gmel.). Vigorous nearly glabrous climber, planted for its hardiness, good profuse foliage and profusion of fragrant white fls. in autumn: lvs. odd-pinnate, the pairs 1 or 2; lfts. mostly small, 1–2½ in. long but sometimes longer, short-ovate to ovate to broad-ovate, obtuse or short-acute, apiculate, tapering, rounded or even subcordate at base, sometimes lobed but margins entire, terminal one very long-stalked: fls. paniculate, 1– sometimes 1½ in. across; sepals 4: fruiting style rather long, plumose. Japan.

24. **C. Vitalba,** L. TRAVELERS-JOY. OLD-MANS-BEARD of England. Very vigorous climber; sts. striate, glabrous: lvs. odd-pinnate, of 2–3 pairs; lfts. ovate to narrow-ovate, acuminate, cordate to rounded at base, stalked, 2–3 in. long, entire or usually toothed: fls. many in axillary panicles, greenish-white and fragrant, ¾–1 in. across, summer to autumn: fruiting styles long and plumose, the heads dense. (Vitalba: *Vitis alba,* white vine.) Eu., N. Afr., S. W. Asia.

25. **C. Flammula,** L. Slender but vigorous; sts. glabrous: lvs. mostly 2-pinnate, dark green, stiffish and semi-persistent, the pairs 2–5; lfts., at least those at middle and base of lf., ternate, the segms. ½–1½ in. long, stalked, ovate to nearly oval, short-acute or obtuse, apiculate: fls. many in axillary and terminal panicles, ½–¾in. across, pure white, fragrant; sepals 4, linear-oblong: fruiting styles long and plumose. (Flammula: Latin *a little flame,* an ante-Linnæan application to this plant.) Medit. region to Iran.

5. **HEPATICA,** Mill. LIVERLEAF. A genus of several species in woods of the north temp. zone.—Per. low scapose herbs with petioled thick 3-lobed persistent basal lvs. and white to purple solitary fls. on slender scapes, each fl. apetalous, with a calyx-like involucre of 3 small sessile bracts; sepals petal-like: pistils several to many, ovary 1-ovuled: achenes short-beaked, pubescent. (Hepat-ica: name from the fancied resemblance of the lvs. to the liver.)

A. Involucral bracts and lobes of lvs. obtuse.......................................1. *H. americana*
AA. Involucral bracts and lobes of lvs. acute.......................................2. *H. acutiloba*

1. **H. americana,** Ker (*H. triloba* var. *americana,* DC. *H. triloba* of Amer. authors. *Anemone Hepatica,* L.). Scapes 4–6 in. high, hairy: lobes of lvs. ovate, obtuse: fls. 6–12, blue, purplish or almost white, ½–¾in. across: achenes hairy. N. S. to Fla., Minn., Mo. —*H. nobilis* of Eu., also under the name *H. triloba,* is less hairy and with fls. 1 in. or broader.

2. **H. acutiloba,** DC. Scapes 4–9 in. high: lobes of lvs. and of involucral bracts acute. Que. to Ga., Minn., Mo.

6. **ANEMONE,** L. ANEMONY. WINDFLOWER. Spring-, summer- and autumn-flowering perennials, some of them very early; species about 100 if the genus is defined broadly, mostly of the north temp. zone, some in high mts.; a few are grown for the handsome fls.—Plants very short or 2–3 ft. or more high: lvs. mostly radical, lobed, divided or dissected, sometimes compound; st.-lvs. 2 or 3 together forming a kind of involucre to the fl. although sometimes remote from it: fls. mostly showy although lacking petals, the colored parts being few or many petaloid sepals; stamens many, shorter than the sepals; pistils many, ovary 1-ovuled, ripening into 1-seeded often tailed or appendaged achenes. (Anemo-ne: ancient Greek name.)

A. Styles in fr. elongated and plumose: fls. solitary.
B. Involucral or upper lvs. twice ternate, short-petioled.......................1. *A. alpina*
BB. Involucral lvs. cleft into linear lobes and sessile.
C. Foliage lvs. palmately 3–7-parted.......................2. *A. patens*
CC. Foliage lvs. mostly pinnate.

D. Lvs. once-pinnate, the pinnæ in turn 3–4-parted.
E. Foliage persistent, yellow-haired: fls. whitish within, violet without... 3. *A. vernalis*
EE. Foliage deciduous, white-haired: fls. violet........................ 4. *A. Halleri*
DD. Lvs. two or three times pinnate.
E. Fls. erect: fruiting styles 1½–2 in. long........................... 5. *A. Pulsatilla*
EE. Fls. nodding: fruiting styles about 1¼ in. long..................... 6. *A. montana*
AA. Styles not elongated nor plumose in fr.
B. Sts. usually 1-fld. and with 1 involucre.
C. Achenes woolly; fruiting head usually somewhat elongate.
D. St. from a tuber: lvs. of involucre usually sessile.
E. Involucral lvs. divided into narrow or linear parts: fls. red, blue, white. 7. *A. coronaria*
EE. Involucral lvs. little or not at all laciniate.
F. Fls. lilac or rose-lilac; segms. 12–19.............................. 8. *A. hortensis*
FF. Fls. scarlet to pink and purple; segms. mostly 8–10................. 9. *A. pavonina*
DD. St. from a crown or woody tap-root or horizontal rootstock: lvs. of involucre usually petioled.
E. Lvs. simply ternate (or 5-palmate), the segms. broadly cuneate.
F. Width of lvs. ¾–1½ in.: fls. ¾ in. wide............................10. *A. parviflora*
FF. Width of lvs. 1½–4 in.: fls. 1½–2½ in. wide.......................11. *A. sylvestris*
EE. Lvs. 2–4-ternate, the segms. linear or flabelliform.
F. Lf.-blades practically glabrous: fls. white suffused with pink.......12. *A. baldensis*
FF. Lf.-blades with some long hairs: fls. white suffused with blue.......13. *A. Drummondii*
CC. Achenes pubescent or nearly glabrous; fruiting head subglobose.
D. St. from a tuber.
E. Sepals glabrous on backs; peduncle recurved after anthesis..........14. *A. blanda*
EE. Sepals hairy on backs, at least near base; peduncle erect............15. *A. apennina*
DD. St. from a horizontal rootstock.
E. Veins of sepals strongly anastomosing below the free tips; fls. 1–1½ in. across..16. *A. nemorosa*
EE. Veins of sepals mostly not anastomosing; fls. mostly less than 1 in. across..17. *A. quinquefolia*
BB. Sts. 2–5- (mostly 3-) fld., usually with secondary involucres (except in *A. narcissiflora*).
C. Achenes glabrous.
D. Fls. subumbellate; styles less than 1/16 in. long......................18. *A. narcissiflora*
DD. Fls. cymose; styles more than ⅛ in. long in fr.......................19. *A. rivularis*
CC. Achenes hairy.
D. Styles stout, almost deltoid, persistent; fruiting head more or less elongate.
E. Divisions of lvs. wedge-lanceolate: sepals rather obtuse..............20. *A. cylindrica*
EE. Divisions of lvs. ovate-lanceolate: sepals usually acute ....21. *A. virginiana*
DD. Styles slender, deciduous; fruiting head subglobose.
E. Fruiting styles ⅛ in. or more long; achenes sparsely hairy: fls. 1–1½ in. across..22. *A. canadensis*
EE. Fruiting styles much shorter; achenes densely hairy.
F. Fls. 2–3 in. across: plant 2–5 ft. high: ultimate divisions of lvs. broad..23. *A. hupehensis*
FF. Fls. ½–1 in. across: plant 1–1½ ft. high: ultimate divisions of lvs. linear..24. *A. multifida*

1. **A. alpina,** L. (*Pulsatilla alpina,* Schrank. *A. acutipetala,* Hort.). Per., sts. simple, soft-hairy, 4–12 (16) in. high from thick strong rootstock: lvs. large, basal, long-petioled, ternate, then twice pinnate; involucre of 3 much divided lvs. well below the fl.: fls. cream-colored inside, purple outside, 2–3 in. across: achenes in fr. with plumose tails about 2 in. long. Eu.

2. **A. patens,** L. (*Pulsatilla patens,* Mill.). Soft-hairy, 3–6 in. high in fl., taller in fr.: lvs. basal, palmately 3-cleft, then divided into narrowly lanceolate lobes; involucre divided into many linear lobes: fls. 2–3 in. across, usually violet: fruiting styles hairy, 2 in. long. Eu., N. Asia. Var. **Wolfgangiana,** Koch (var. *Nuttalliana,* Gray. *A. Wolfgangiana,* Bess. *Pulsatilla hirsutissima,* Britt.), PASQUE-FLOWER, lf.-segms. linear; Ill. to B. C., Siberia; doubtfully distinct.

3. **A. vernalis,** L. (*Pulsatilla vernalis,* Mill.). Plant with soft bronzy hairs, 2–6 in. tall in fl., somewhat taller in fr.: basal lvs. pinnate, 1–2 in. long, the pinnæ deeply palmately cut into segms. ⅛–¼ in. wide; involucral segms. linear: sepals 6, white within, violet to purple without, about 1 in. long, spreading in age: fruiting styles 1½ in. long. Eu.

4. **A. Halleri,** All. (*Pulsatilla Halleri,* Willd.). Somewhat taller, the hair whiter: lf.-segms. linear, 1/16 in. wide: sepals purple, 1¼–1½ in. long. (Named for Albrecht von Haller, page 44.) Eu.

5. **A. Pulsatilla, L.** (*Pulsatilla vulgaris,* Mill.). PASQUE-FLOWER. Soft-hairy, ½–1¼ ft. in fr.: basal lvs. 4–6 in. long, thrice pinnate into linear segms., appearing after the fls.; involucral lobes linear: fls. erect; sepals usually 6, blue to reddish-purple, spreading late, 1¼–2 in. long: fruiting styles 1½–2 in. long. Eu.—Color vars. are **alba** and **rubra,** Hort.

6. **A. montana,** Hoppe (*Pulsatilla nigricans,* Baumg.). Near to the preceding, but with fls. nodding and fruiting styles mostly less than 1¼ in. long. Eu.

7. **A. coronaria, L.** POPPY ANEMONY. Root irregularly tuberous; main st. a very short crown or caudex at surface of ground, from which rises the nearly glabrous peduncle or

scape 6–18 in. high: basal lvs. ternately compound or twice compound, with narrow-cuneate segms.; involucral lvs. close to the fl. or 1–3 in. removed, cut into many narrow divisions, spreading: fls. solitary and terminal, 1½–2½ in. across, poppy-like, in many shades in red and blue, also white; stamens blue. Medit. region.—The leading florists' anemone for pots; there are many named races, as The Bride, St. Brigid, var. *chrysanthemiflora;* some of them are double-fld. Nos. 7, 8, 9 are tuberous-rooted anemones sold with bulbs for florists' and gardeners' use, with large very showy fls.; usually bloomed in spring.

8. **A. hortensis,** L. BROAD-LEAVED ANEMONY. Lvs. 1-ternate, sometimes only ternately lobed, the parts broad, teeth sharp-pointed; involucre mostly remote from the fl., the lvs. erect or even appressed and little or not at all divided: fls. with numerous (12–19, often 15) narrowly elliptic segms. ¼in. wide or less, lilac to rose-lilac throughout. S. France to Albania.—Not commonly cult.

9. **A. pavonina,** Lam. emend. Stearn. Similar to and often confused with or grown as *A. hortensis*, from which it differs in fls. of 7–12 (frequently 8–9) broader segms., scarlet to pink and purple, with or without a yellowish basal zone. Greece to N. W. Asia Minor.—The typical element has single scarlet fls. Var. **purpureo-violacea,** Halacsy (*A. purpureo-violacea*, Boiss.), has purplish single fls. Other vars. have scarlet double fls. or scarlet single fls. with yellow eyes. **A. fulgens,** J. Gay, SCARLET ANEMONY, is considered to be a hybrid of *A. hortensis* and *A. pavonina* and is a scarlet-fld. plant with fls. usually having 10–15 segms. narrower than in the latter parent and without the yellow basal zone; it does not reproduce true from seed; occurs in S. France as a garden escape.

10. **A. parviflora,** Michx. Rootstock slender; sts. simple, 1-fld., 4–12 in. high, sparingly hairy: basal lvs. 3-parted into broadly cuneate divisions; involucre sessile: sepals 5–6, oval, ⅓–½in. long, white or purplish-tinged without: fruiting head short-ovoid; achenes densely hairy. N. Asia, N. N. Amer.

11. **A. sylvestris,** L. SNOWDROP ANEMONY. Rootstock short; peduncle or scape 8–18 in., hairy, simple or sometimes forked at involucre: basal lvs. ternately cleft or divided, more or less hairy beneath and on the petioles; involucral lvs. long-petioled, very remote from fl., ternately parted: fls. solitary or 2, pure white, 1½–2½ in. across, inclined or nodding, fragrant, spring; sepals 5–8, blunt, emarginate and perhaps erose. Eu., S. W. Asia.

12. **A. baldensis,** L. Rootstock elongate, slender; sts. 2–6 in. tall, pubescent: lvs. small, glabrescent, two to four times ternate, the segms. incised; involucre remote from fl., short-petioled: sepals 5–8, white suffused with pink, ½–¾in. long. Alps.

13. **A. Drummondii,** Wats. Rootstock woody; sts. 4–12 in. high, soft-villous: lvs. 1–2 in. broad, villous, three to four times ternate; involucre remote, short-petioled: sepals 6–10, oval, about ½in. long, white, often suffused blue outside. (For Thomas Drummond, page 255.) Rocky Mts. to B. C. and Calif.

14. **A. blanda,** Schott & Kotschy. SAPPHIRE ANEMONY. Sts. 2–8 in. tall, from a tuberous rootstock, villous: lvs. 1 to few, long-petioled, twice ternate, the segms. ovate, obtusish, incised; involucral lvs. petioled, ternate: fls. 1, sky-blue, the sepals 9–14, narrowly oblong, glabrous, ⅜–⅝in. long: fruiting head recurved. Greece and Asia Minor.—Various color forms occur.

15. **A. apennina,** L. Much like the preceding but lf.-segms. more acute; sepals somewhat hairy without; fruiting head erect. Mts. of S. Eu.

16. **A. nemorosa,** L. EUROPEAN WOOD ANEMONY. Rootstock woody, slender; sts. simple, 3–9 in. high, slightly pubescent: lvs. 1–2, long-petioled, palmately separated into 3–5 petioluled incised segms.; involucral lvs. similar, short-petioled: fls. white, rose or purple; sepals 5–9, oval, glabrous, ½–¾in. long. Eu., Siberia.—With various colors and double-fld. forms.

17. **A. quinquefolia,** L. (*A. nemorosa* var. *quinquefolia*, Pursh). AMERICAN WOOD ANEMONY. Sts. more slender than in *A. nemorosa*: fls. smaller, the sepals mostly less than ½in. long, less reticulate-veined. Que. to Man., Iowa and Ga.

18. **A. narcissiflora,** L. (*A. umbellata*, Lam.). Rootstock fibrous, short: lvs. several, long-petioled, 3–5-parted, the divisions deeply cut into narrow segms.; sts. 1–1½ ft., hairy, with sessile involucre and usually 2–6 whitish or cream-colored fls. 1–1½ in. diam.; sepals oval. Mts. of Eu.—The western American *A. zephyra* does not seem distinct from this species.

19. **A. rivularis,** Buch.-Ham. Root crown woody; sts. coarse, 2–3 ft. tall, branched above: basal lvs. several, 4–6 in. wide, long-petioled, 5–7-lobed, each division wide, cuneate, and further divided and serrate; primary involucre sessile, with secondary ones above: fls. several, cymose, 1½–2 in. wide; sepals 5, white with purplish-blue outside. Mts. of India, Ceylon, W. China.

20. **A. cylindrica,** Gray. CANDLE ANEMONY. Silky-hairy, 1½–2 ft. tall, branched at involucre: basal lvs. several, long-petioled, 3–5-parted, the divisions cuneate and coarsely toothed; involucral lvs. similar to basal: fls. greenish-white, several, ¾in. wide: fruiting head cylindric. Woods, N. B. to N. J., Kans., New Mex., B. C.

21. **A. virginiana,** L. Plant hairy, 2–3 ft. high, stout, branching at involucre: basal lvs. 3-parted, the divisions broadly cuneate-oblong, divided into serrate lobes; primary and secondary involucres similar to basal: fls. greenish or white, 1–1½ in. across, the sepals usually 5: achenes in oblong head. Woods, N. S. to S. C. and Kans.

22. **A. canadensis,** L. (*A. pensylvanica,* L. *A. dichotoma,* Michx.). MEADOW ANEMONY. Stout, 1–2 ft. high, somewhat hairy, branching at involucre: basal lvs. petioled, 5–7-parted, the divisions broad, oblong, cleft and toothed; primary and secondary involucres sessile: fls. white, 1½–2 in. broad, the sepals 5, obtuse: achenes in a globose head, flat, suborbicular, pubescent. Low places, Que. to Md., Colo., Assiniboia.

23. **A. hupehensis,** Lemoine .(*A. japonica* var. *hupehensis,* Lemoine). JAPANESE ANEMONY. Per. to 3 ft. but commonly 1–2 ft. high, branched: basal lvs. long-petioled, 3-parted, lfts. shallowly 3–5-lobed, serrate, acuminate, the central narrowly ovate, laterals asymmetrical, all sparingly pilose above and below: fls. 2½–3 in. across, rose-pink, silky on back, sepals 5–6, almost orbicular. Cent. and W. China. Var. **japonica,** Bowles & Stearn (*Atragene japonica,* Thunb. *Anemone japonica,* Sieb. & Zucc. not Houtt. *A. vitifolia* var. *japonica,* Lévl. & Vaniot. *A. hybrida* var. *japonica,* Ohwi. *A. nipponica,* Merr.), a semi-double variant to 2 or at most 3 ft., having usually more than 20 rather narrow sepals; Japan, S. China.—Taller sorts grown as *A. japonica* and having 6–20 sepals should be treated as named garden hybrids or clones of **A. hybrida,** Paxt. (*A. elegans,* Decne.).

24. **A. multifida,** Poir. (*A. globosa,* Nutt. *A. magellanica,* Hort.). Rootstock stout; sts. 4–18 in. high, soft-villous: basal lvs. long-petioled, two to three times ternately cleft into linear or narrow divisions, villous; involucral lvs. similar, short-petioled: fls. 1–3; sepals oval, ¼–½in. long, yellowish to pinkish to bluish-purple: achenes densely villous, in subglobose head. Alaska to Sask., Colo., Calif., Que., Chile.

7. **ANEMONELLA,** Spach. RUE-ANEMONE. One species, N. American.—Low glabrous per.; roots clustered, tuberous-thickened; st. slender: lvs. radical, compound; involucre compound, at the base of an umbel of fls.: sepals 5–10, showy; petals none; stamens all anther-bearing; pistils several, 1-ovuled, free: achenes 4–15, ovoid, 8–10-ribbed. (Anemonel-la: *little anemone.*)

A. thalictroides, Spach (*Anemone thalictroides,* L. *Syndesmon thalictroides,* Hoffmgg.). St. 4–12 in. high: lvs. 2–3-ternate, with rounded somewhat 3-lobed petiolulate lfts.: fls. white to pink, to 1 in. across, spring. Woods from N. H. to Minn., Kans., Fla.—Rose and double-fld. forms are in the trade.

8. **DELPHINIUM,** L. LARKSPUR. Per. and ann. erect branching herbs, upwards of 250 species in the north temp. zone, some of them showy and popular fl.-garden subjects.—Lvs. palmately lobed or divided: fls. in showy racemes or spikes which are often paniculate, prevailingly blue but also in other colors, very irregular; sepals 5 and colored, the posterior one prolonged into a spur into which are projected the spurs of the upper pair of petals, the other or lateral pairs of petals (if present) small and short-clawed; stamens many; pistils 1–5, sessile, ovary many-ovuled, maturing into dehiscent follicles. (Delphin-ium: Latin *delphin,* dolphin, from the shape of the fl.)—In common cult. four groups may be clearly recognized: ann. rockets; ann. branching or forking; per. rockets or candle kinds; per. forking or bouquet larkspurs. In the per. kinds, particularly in the candle group, botanical names have been singularly misapplied. The per. garden larkspurs are mainly cultivars.

A. Plant ann.: lvs. finely divided into nearly or quite linear parts: seeds scaly.
B. Petals united into 1 body or part: follicle normally solitary.
C. Fls. in long simple racemes, the main st. forming the axis of the plant with any side branches obviously secondary.......... 1. *D. Ajacis*
CC. Fls. fewer on ends of forking branches so that plant has a diffuse look.
D. Follicles glabrous: fls. 1 in. or more across.......... 2. *D. Consolida*
DD. Follicles pubescent: fls. ¾in. or less across.......... 3. *D. divaricatum*
BB. Petals free, making 4 bodies or parts: follicles usually 3.......... 4. *D. cardiopetalum*
AA. Plant per.: lf.-segms. usually ¼in. or more wide.
B. Fls. (sepals with spurs) yellow.......... 5. *D. Zalil*
BB. Fls. not yellow.
C. Color of fls. (sepals with spurs) red.
D. Fl. scarlet; limb of lower petal entire or merely emarginate: sts. 3–6 ft. tall, not scapose.......... 6. *D. cardinale*
DD. Fl. orange- or dull red; lower petal bifid: sts. mostly about 1½ ft. tall, subscapose.......... 7. *D. nudicaule*
CC. Color of fls. blue or purple to white.
D. Lvs. geranium-like, lobed to near middle then toothed.......... 8. *D. cashmerianum*
DD. Lvs. divided to near base, then again lobed.

E. Height of plant mostly less than 1½ ft.
F. Sepals nearly equal.
G. Width of lvs. 1½–2½ in.: follicles straight; seeds wing-margined........ 9. *D. Menziesii*
GG. Width of lvs. 2–4 in.: follicles arcuate when ripe; seeds indistinctly angled........ 10. *D. tricorne*
FF. Sepals markedly unequal, the 2 lower larger, the single upper smallest........ 11. *D. bicolor*
EE. Height of plant mostly 1½–5 ft.
F. Infl. a long spike-like raceme standing well above basal foliage and continuing the main central axis of the plant........ 12. *D. elatum*
FF. Infl. a short or open raceme, not spike-like or candle-like on a central axis.
G. Lf. finely cut, segms. mostly not more than ¼in. wide.
H. Spur straight or nearly so; infl. axially racemose........ 13. *D. grandiflorum*
HH. Spur hooked or much curved; infl. corymbose........ 14. *D. tatsienense*
GG. Lf. more coarsely divided, segms. ½in. or wider........ 15. *D. cheilanthum*

1. **D. Ajacis**, L. emend. J. Gay (*D. Gayanum*, Wilmott). ROCKET LARKSPUR, so called because of the narrow spike-like erect racemes. The common ann. fl.-garden larkspur in many statures and colors; st. usually 1–2 ft. tall, but sometimes 3–4½ ft., mostly puberulent at least above, the branches rather few and strongly ascending: basal and lower st.-lvs. long-petioled, the blade divided to the petiole into 3 sections and these multifid into linear segms., the upper lvs. sessile and similarly multifid giving a crowded or bunched appearance at the nodes: pedicels ascending, 1½ in. or less long, subtended by a subulate bract and with a pair of similar but smaller bracts midway: fls. 1–1½ in. across at expansion, the parts broad and nearly or quite obtuse, blue or violet varying to rose, pink, and white, often double, the upwardly-curving spur about as long as the remainder of the fl.: pistil 1, or sometimes multiple in doubling forms, maturing into a pubescent follicle ½–1 in. long abruptly beaked by the style; seeds transversely thin-ridged. S. Eu.; somewhat nat. in N. Amer.—The application of the name **D. Ajacis, L.**, has been interpreted variously and, subject to clarification by future legislation, it is here retained as conventionally applied. Some authors treat it as the correct name of *D. orientale*, J. Gay, a view not adopted here.

2. **D. Consolida**, L. FORKING LARKSPUR. Small puberulous or nearly glabrous ann. 8–18 in. tall, forking and diffuse with simpler and more upright lvs. than *D. Gayanum* and without the bunched appearance at the nodes: fls. few or scattered, terminal on the branches, 1 in. or more in expansion, mostly blue or violet, the parts narrow and acute: follicles 1, glabrous, about ½in. long. (Consolida: ante-Linnæan substantive name, referring to the consolidated petals.) Eu.; in grainfields, and sometimes adventive in N. Amer.—There are cult. forms listed, but they probably belong to *D. Ajacis*.

3. **D. divaricatum**, Ledeb. Diffuse much-branching ann., 1½–2 ft., appressed-puberulent, sparsely leafy: lvs. multifid into short linear segms.: fls. purplish, on the ends of slender peduncles or branches, ¾in. across at expansion, the parts short-acute, spur straight and nearly horizontal and twice as long as petals: follicles 1, erect or cernuous, pubescent; seeds shaggy, like cones. S. W. Asia.—Sometimes grown in the fl.-garden.

4. **D. cardiopetalum**, DC. (*D. halteratum*, Sibth. & Smith, var. *cardiopetalum*, Huth). Erect pubescent ann., 10–20 in., with ascending branches: lvs. with linear segms.: fls. blue, in short racemes, expanding ½–¾in. across; petals heart-shaped, the upward-projecting spur exceeding the remainder of the fl.: follicles 3, nearly or quite glabrous, ⅜in. long, tipped with slender style-beak; seeds with transverse ridges. S. France, and cult.

5. **D. Zalil**, Aitch. & Hemsl. Simple or little-branched per., producing tubers, becoming glabrous or nearly so, 1–2 ft., the bright yellow fls. in loose racemes: lvs. palmatifid, the segms. linear and stiffish: spur straight, equalling the broad-oval obtuse sepals which are glabrous on the outside and less than ½in. long; lower petal bifid and lightly hairy: follicles 3, ribbed, glabrous. Iran.—The yellow fls. are used as a dye; zalil is the native name.

6. **D. cardinale**, Hook. SCARLET LARKSPUR. Stout large leafy species, 3–6 ft., puberulent: lvs. 3–9 in. across, divided into linear acute segms.: fls. bright scarlet, ¾–1 in. across at expansion, in long open erect racemes; sepals ½in. long, exceeded by the large curved spur; petals mostly yellow, 2-lobed or emarginate: follicles 3 or 5, glabrous. Calif.

7. **D. nudicaule**, Torr. & Gray. RED LARKSPUR. Lower than no. 6, st. few-lvd. or nearly naked: lvs. rather thick, 3–5-parted into divisions ¼in. or more wide and mostly obtuse: fls. few in a loose raceme, the sepals and spur red; sepals ⅓–½in. long, half or somewhat more the length of the spur; petals more or less yellow, notched or cleft: follicles usually 3, glabrous. Calif., Ore.

8. **D. cashmerianum**, Royle. Low per., usually less than 1½ ft.: lvs. mostly radical and long-petioled, almost round, 2–4 in. wide, usually 5–7-lobed about to the middle, then cut-toothed: infl. corymb-like, of 10–12 or fewer fls.; pedicels pubescent; fls. 1½ in. long, azure-blue, pubescent; sepals broad, obtuse, not expanding widely, spur broad, somewhat curved, much shorter than sepals; upper petals black-purple, others greenish: follicles 3, hairy. Himalayas.

9. **D. Menziesii,** DC. Low per., mostly less than 1½ ft.: lvs. pentagonal to orbicular, 1½–2½ in. wide, the ultimate lobes about ⅛in. wide: racemes short-oblong, 5–10-fld.; sepals ovate-oblong, ⅓–½in. long, deep blue, spur about ½in. long; lower petals round, dark blue, upper pale, rhomboid: follicles 3, pubescent. (Named for Archibald Menzies, 1754–1842, physician and early collector in N. Amer.) B. C. to Wash.

10. **D. tricorne,** Michx. Low per., mostly less than 1½ ft.: lvs. orbicular to pentagonal, 2–4 in. wide, with 3 primary divisions, deeply palmatifid into narrow glabrous lobes: racemes spicate, many-fld.; sepals ovate-oblong, ½in. long, light blue, spur often longer; lower petals ovate, bifid, with spreading white hairs, the upper petals clavate with a distinct lower ear, whitish: follicles 3, ½–⅔in. long, glabrous. Pa. to N. C., Ill., Okla.

11. **D. bicolor,** Nutt. Low per., up to 1¼ ft., pubescent at least above: lvs. few, reniform to rounded, 1–1½ in. wide, dissected into narrow segms.: raceme short-pyramidal; fls. spectrum-violet; 2 lower sepals ½–1 in. long, single upper one much reduced, spur somewhat longer; lower petals almost round, violet, floccose, the upper white with purple pencilling: follicles 3, ⅔in. long, villous. B. C. to Alta., N. D. and E. Wash.

12. **D. elatum,** L. Candle Larkspur. Spicate per. to 6 ft.: lvs. large, palmately 5–7-parted about to base, or upper 3-parted, the ultimate lobes mostly more than ¼in. wide: infl. dense, erect and spiciform, terminating the main axis; fls. blue, small in the wild plant, 1–1¼ in. long; sepals blunt, ½in. long; petals dark or dull purple, the 2 lower notched and yellowish-bearded: follicles 3, glabrous, ½–¾in. long. Siberia.—This species is an old garden plant and, with *D. cheilanthum* and others, has been the basis of great departures in garden vars. and strains, such as *D. cashmerianum*, Hort. not Royle, *D. hybridum*, Hort. not L. or Steph.

13. **D. grandiflorum,** L. (*D. chinense*, Fisch.). Bouquet Larkspur. Rather slender usually much-branched and diffused per., 1–3½ ft. (but which may bloom the first year from seed); st. and foliage finely pubescent: basal and main st.-lvs. petiolate, base of petiole not expanded or clasping, uppermost lvs. nearly or quite sessile; blades palmatifid into many linear segms. mostly ¼in. and less broad: peduncles spreading or arched away from axis, 2–3 in. long or the upper ones shorter, bearing a solitary blue or violet fl. (white vars.) wide-expanding 1–1½ in., the sprays therefore diffuse and not racemose or consolidated; sepals ½– about 1 in. long, broad and nearly or quite obtuse, usually somewhat exceeded by the straight or slightly curved spur; upper petals yellowish or color of sepals, the lower ones color of sepals and bearded: follicles 3, ½–1 in. long, pubescent. Siberia, China.—The larkspurs grown as *D. chinense* or var. *chinense* are low races, 1–about 2 ft., blooming freely first year from seed, with large fls.

14. **D. tatsienense,** Franch. Much like *D. grandiflorum* but the fl. arrangement more diffuse: fls. violet-blue, 1¼ in. long; sepals broad, obtuse, ½in. long, with a spot near end; spur ¾–1 in. long; upper petals dull yellow, lower ones blue and yellow-bearded: follicles 3, pubescent, ½in. or more long. W. China.

15. **D. cheilanthum,** Fisch. Garland Larkspur. Racemose open-fld. tall per.: lvs. palmate, 5-parted to base, the main divisions ½in. or less wide: infl. of 2–6-fld. racemes; fls. deep blue to whitish, 1½–2 in. across in cult. forms; sepals blunt, spur about as long as sepals; upper petals pale yellow or blue, lower large, rounded: follicles 3, to 1 in. long. E. Asia. Var. **formosum,** Huth (*D. formosum*, Hort. not Boiss. & Huet. *D. Belladonna*, Hort. *D. Bellamosum*, Hort. *D. cœlestinum*, Hort.), fls. 1½–2 in. across, rich blue, petals yellowish, spur over 1 in. long; the usual cult. form. Var. **Moerheimii,** Hort., is a white form.

9. **ACONITUM,** L. Aconite. Monkshood. Wolfsbane. Showy herbaceous summer- and autumn-flowering perennials (sometimes essentially bien.) with hooded fls., in temp. and cooler parts of north temp. zone; the species are many or numerous, according to the opinion of the monographers, as they are variable, probably more than 100; the aconites contain powerful poisons, and drugs are derived from the roots and lvs. of certain species.—Roots tuberous or thickened; sts. erect, trailing, or semi-scandent, mostly somewhat branched: lvs. palmately veined, lobed or cleft: fls. irregular, mostly blue or purple, sometimes white or yellow, racemose or paniculate; sepals 5, petaloid, the upper one large and hood-like or helmet-shaped; petals 2–5, small, the 2 upper ones spur-like and contained under the hood, the others (if present) minute; stamens many; pistils 3–5, sessile, ovary many-seeded, ripening into several- or many-seeded follicles. (Aconi-tum: ancient classical name.)

a. Fls. yellow or yellowish-white.
  b. Sepals persistent around the young fr.: lf.-segms. linear .... 1. *A. Anthora*
  bb. Sepals deciduous, the growing fr. naked: lf.-segms. wider .... 2. *A. Vulparia*
aa. Fls. blue or purple, rarely white.
  b. Sts. twining or at least slender and flexuous above, with the slender branches in the infl. deflexed-spreading or flexuous to twining.
    c. Pedicels with spreading hairs: lf.-blades not divided to base.

D. Lvs. mostly 5-cleft: lower pedicels often longer than fls.; helmet taller than long (lower margin).......................................3. *A. columbianum*
DD. Lvs. mostly 3-cleft: lower pedicels usually shorter than fls.; helmet scarcely taller than long.......................................4. *A. uncinatum*
CC. Pedicels crisp-pubescent to almost glabrous: lf.-blades divided to base......5. *A. Henryi*
BB. Sts. stiffly erect, simple or with few ascending or suberect stiff branches in the infl.
C. Lf.-blades not divided to base.
D. Pedicels crisp-pubescent: main lvs. coriaceous, dark green, 3-parted: fls. in late autumn.......................................6. *A. Carmichaelii*
DD. Pedicels with spreading hairs: main lvs. thin, light green, mostly 5-parted: fls. in summer.......................................3. *A. columbianum*
CC. Lf.-blades divided to base.
D. Pedicels pubescent, with spreading or appressed hairs.................7. *A. Napellus*
DD. Pedicels glabrous.
E. Segms. of lf. linear, ⅛in. wide, or if lanceolate and ¼in. wide then the fls. mostly deep blue and not more than 1¼ in. high and the helmet not gaping: infl. dense and not branched: plant fertile.............7. *A. Napellus*
EE. Segms. of lf. lanceolate, ¼in. wide: fls. mostly white with purple margins, 1½ in. high, helmet gaping: infl. branched: plant sterile.......8. *A. bicolor*

1. **A. Anthora,** L. Root of bulb-like elongated tubers; st. erect and strict, 1–2 ft., pubescent at least above: lvs. divided to base into many linear rather stiff segms.: fls. in spicate racemes, pale yellow, summer; helmet high and rounded, tapering below, produced into a short beak or visor: follicles 5, pubescent. (Anthora: an ante-Linnæan name.) S. Eu.

2. **A. Vulparia,** Reichb. (*A. Lycoctonum*, Auth. not L.). St. slender and mostly simple, pubescent or glabrate, 3–6 ft. high, the root bulb-like: lvs. orbicular-reniform in general outline, parted nearly to base into 3–9 broad lobes which are again lobed and toothed: fls. yellow or whitish-yellow, in terminal erect spike-like racemes, summer or autumn, standing up and down or somewhat spreading, the upright helmet narrow-conical but constricted below the rounded summit, the sepals little if at all spreading: follicles 3. Eu.

3. **A. columbianum,** Nutt. St. often rather coarse, 1–5 ft. high, the root tuberous: lvs. rounded-pentagonal in outline, 2–5 in. wide, 5–7-cleft to near base, the lobes rhombic-ovate to -lanceolate and lobed or toothed: fls. purplish to blue, in pubescent racemes or panicles, in summer; helmet rounded-conic, ⅔–1 in. high, usually plainly beaked: follicles mostly 3. B. C. to Dak., New Mex., Calif.

4. **A. uncinatum,** L. St. 2–5 ft., erect but weak and tending to climb: st.-lvs. 2–3 in. wide, mostly 3-lobed, the lateral lobes in turn frequently 2-lobed, all lance-ovate, coarsely toothed: fls. blue, in open panicles, in summer; helmet erect, about ⅔in. high, equally broad: follicles 3. Pa. to Ga. and Ind.

5. **A. Henryi,** Pritz. (*A. autumnale*, Lindl. not Reichb. *A. californicum*, Hort. *A. Napellus* var. *Sparksii*, Hort.). St. 3–7 ft. high, erect at base, sinuous to climbing above, with slender spreading flexuous branches in the open infl.: lvs. deep green, rather coarse, 2–7 in. wide, 3–5-cleft almost or quite to base, the lobes cuneate, usually 3-lobed or pinnately so and coarsely few-toothed: fls. deep bluish-purple, in late summer; helmet ⅔–1 in. high, convex-rounded on top, almost straight in front: follicles 3–5, more or less pubescent. (Named for Augustine Henry, page 45.) China.—Some garden plants under the name *A. Napellus* belong here and others as *A. autumnale* may be *A. Carmichaelii* var. *Wilsonii*.

6. **A. Carmichaelii,** Debx. (*A. Fischeri*, Forbes & Hemsl.). Sturdy, erect, mostly 2–4 ft. tall, densely leafy: lvs. coriaceous, dark green, 2–5 in. wide, 3-cleft to near base, the lateral divisions soon 2-lobed, all 5 usually lobed and coarsely toothed: fls. deep purple-blue, in dense racemose panicles 4–8 in. long, in autumn; helmet broad and rounded, ¾–1¼ in. high: follicles 3–5. Cent. China. Var. **Wilsonii,** Munz (*A. Wilsonii*, Stapf. *A. Fischeri* var. *Wilsonii*, Davis), to 6 or 8 ft. tall, infl. more open, 10–18 in. long.—Some plants in the trade under *A. autumnale* belong here.

7. **A. Napellus,** L. Erect and strict, 2–4 ft., usually with some pubescence at least above, nearly or quite simple, leafy: lvs. 2–5 in. wide, divided to the base and again divided or lobed into narrow linear to lanceolate segms.: fls. mostly blue or violet, in erect close spike-like terminal racemes, in summer; helmet hemispheric above, almost 1 in. high and about as broad, more or less beaked in front; filaments glabrous or pilose: follicles mostly 3. (Napellus: *little turnip*, from the shape of the tuberous root; a pre-Linnæan name.) Eu.—Poisonous and source of the drug aconite. Very variable in all respects.

8. **A. bicolor,** Schult. (*A. Stoerkianum*, Reichb. *A. Napellus* var. *bicolor*, Ser. *A. intermedium*, DC. and var. *versicolor*, Ser.). About 3 ft. tall, glabrous: lvs. 2–4 in. wide, 5–7-cleft, the primary segms. cuneate at base, often 3-lobed near middle then with few lanceolate lobes or teeth ⅛–¼in. wide: infl. pyramidal, compact, fls. usually white and purple, 1½ in. high, in summer; helmet strongly arched forward, short-beaked; filaments pilose: pistils 3–5, not fertile. Eu.—Supposedly a hybrid between some form of *A. Napellus* and *A. variegatum*. Some plants in the trade as *A. Napellus* belong here.

10. AQUILEGIA, L. COLUMBINE. Attractive herbaceous perennials of the north temp. zone, variable, 65–70 species, many of them cult., together with hybrid races that cannot be referred directly to an original species.—Mostly prominently branching, erect: lvs. 2–3-ternately compound: fls. terminating the branches, showy, hanging or erect, in spring and early summer, characterized by usually having long hollow nectariferous backward-projecting spurs of the 5 petals which have a short broad lip (the lamina) projected to the front; sepals 5, regular, colored like the petals, mostly much shorter than the petal-spurs; stamens numerous, the inner ones represented by staminodia; pistils usually 5, free, sessile, ovary many-ovuled, maturing into dehiscent separate erect follicles. (Aquile-gia: origin of the word open to doubt.) —The doubling of aquilegia fls. under cult. may be the multiplication of petals or of sepals. The petals are perhaps specialized staminodia rather than true perianth. The "long-spurred hybrids," now popular in gardens, are derivatives probably of *A. cærulea*, *A. chrysantha*, and others.

A. Spurs lacking or saccate, less than 1/8in. long.
  B. Fls. almost erect; staminodia acutish .... 1. *A. ecalcarata*
  BB. Fls. nodding, staminodia blunt .... 6. *A. vulgaris* var. *stellata*
AA. Spurs longer.
  B. The spurs strongly hooked.
    C. Fls. yellow .... 14. *A. flavescens*
    CC. Fls. not yellow.
      D. Pistils essentially glabrous.
        E. Sts. nearly or quite leafless except for leafy bracts near the summit: pedicels glabrous .... 3. *A. sibirica*
        EE. Sts. with 1–3 well-developed lvs. as well as upper bracts: pedicels glandular-pubescent .... 2. *A. flabellata*
      DD. Pistils pubescent over their general surface.
        E. Spur shorter than lamina; laminæ 3/5–1 in. long .... 5. *A. glandulosa*
        EE. Spur not shorter than lamina.
          F. Sepals 1/4–1/2in. wide, mostly 3/5–1 1/5 in. long; laminæ 2/5–1/2in. long.
            G. Lvs. mostly glabrous beneath: staminodia acute .... 8. *A. oxysepala*
            GG. Lvs. pilose beneath: staminodia blunt .... 6. *A. vulgaris*
          FF. Sepals 3/5–1 in. wide, 1–2 in. long; laminæ 1/2–4/5in. long.
            G. Color of sepals claret to purplish: lfts. pilose beneath, the ultimate lobes 1/8–1/4in. wide .... 7. *A. olympica*
            GG. Color of sepals blue: lfts. subglabrous, the ultimate lobes 3/5–1 in. wide .... 12. *A. alpina*
  BB. The spurs straight or slightly curved.
    C. Fls. yellow or red and yellow, and nodding.
      D. Stamens shorter than laminæ; fls. yellow: lvs. subglabrous .... 13. *A. Buergeriana*
      DD. Stamens exceeding laminæ.
        E. Sepals horizontally spreading or reflexed, longer than spurs.
          F. Laminæ 1/3–2/5in. long; fls. mostly yellow .... 14. *A. flavescens*
          FF. Laminæ to 1/4in. long; fls. red and yellow .... 15. *A. formosa*
        EE. Sepals erect to divergent, shorter than spurs.
          F. Lvs. mostly biternate: sepals 2/5–4/5in. long, red; spurs 2/5–1 in. long .. 16. *A. canadensis*
          FF. Lvs. mostly triternate: sepals 2/3–1 1/8 in. long, greenish; spurs 1 1/2–2 in. long .... 17. *A. Skinneri*
    CC. Fls. not both yellow or red and yellow, and not nodding.
      D. Length of spurs less than 1 in.
        E. Fl. distinctly bicolored, the laminæ much lighter in color than the sepals.
          F. Laminæ and spurs subequal; laminæ 1/4–1/3in. long, whitish; sepals blue .... 11. *A. discolor*
          FF. Laminæ distinctly shorter than spurs; laminæ 2/5–3/5in. long, yellowish; sepals purple .... 13. *A. Buergeriana*
        EE. Fl. concolored, the laminæ and sepals essentially of the same color.
          F. Follicles glabrous: lfts. crowded, 1/5–2/5in. wide .... 4. *A. Jonesii*
          FF. Follicles pubescent: lfts. expanded.
            G. Sepals 4/5–1 2/5 in. long; spurs about as long as laminæ.
              H. Lfts. glabrous beneath: follicles 2/3in. long .... 10. *A. pyrenaica*
              HH. Lfts. pilose beneath: follicles 1/2in. long .... 9. *A. Bertolonii*
            GG. Sepals 1 1/5–2 in. long; spurs longer than laminæ .... 12. *A. alpina*
      DD. Length of spurs 1–6 in.
        E. Stamens not or scarcely exserted; sepals mostly blunt; fls. blue and white to white or ochroleucous .... 18. *A. cærulea*
        EE. Stamens plainly exserted; sepals sharp-pointed.
          F. Laminæ 2/5–3/5in. long; spurs 1 3/5–2 1/2 in. long .... 19. *A. chrysantha*
          FF. Laminæ 3/5–1 in. long; spurs 3 1/2–6 in. long .... 20. *A. longissima*

1. **A. ecalcarata,** Maxim. (*Semiaquilegia ecalcarata*, Sprague & Hutchins.). Plant 1/2–2 ft. high, soft-pubescent: lvs. biternate to triternate, the basal petioles 2–5 in. long, lfts. up to 1 in.: fls. wine-color to rich purple, rarely almost white, erect or somewhat nodding; sepals elliptic-oblong, 1/2–2/3in. long; petals mostly spurless, slightly shorter than sepals; stamens half the petals: follicles scarcely 1/2in. long. W. China.

2. **A. flabellata,** Sieb. & Zucc. (*A. akitensis*, Huth). Plant 1–1½ ft., with few fls.: lfts. nearly sessile: fls. nodding, about 2 in. across, bright lilac or pale purple, sometimes white, summer; sepals about 1 in. long, obtuse, twice as long as the often white limb of the petals; spurs shorter than laminæ, slender toward the end and much incurved; stamens not exserted: follicles glabrous. Japan. Var. **nana,** Hort., is a dwarf white-fld. form.

3. **A. sibirica,** Lam. Plant 1–2 ft., bearing many fls.; st. pubescent or sometimes nearly smooth: lvs. biternate; terminal lfts. large, 1 in. or more broad, with rather shallow and rounded lobes; lower st.-lvs. biternate and petiolate: fls. somewhat nodding, 2–3 in. across, lilac-blue, summer; sepals oblong, 1 in. or more long, spreading or a little reflexed; laminæ half as long as sepals, often white; spurs rather stout, ¼–½in. long, much incurved or even coiled; stamens not exserted: follicles glabrous, 1 in. long. E. Siberia.

4. **A. Jonesii,** Parry. Plant 1–4 in. high, scape-like: lvs. in basal tuft, crowded, glaucous, pubescent: fls. erect; sepals blue or purple, ½–⅔in. long; laminæ blue, ⅓in. long; spurs blue, ⅓–½in. long; stamens not exserted: follicles glabrous, ½–¾in. long. (Named for Capt. W. A. Jones, who led an expedition into N. W. Wyo. in 1873.) Mont., Wyo.

5. **A. glandulosa,** Fisch. (*A. jucunda*, Fisch. & Avé-Lall.). Plant ½–1½ ft., pubescent and glandular, at least above, with few large fls.: lvs. biternate; lf.-segms. narrow; st.-lvs. few and mostly bract-like: fls. nodding, 2–3 in. across, lilac-blue, spring and early summer; sepals ovate-acute, 1–2 in. long and half as broad; laminæ lilac-blue (as are the sepals) but usually tipped and bordered creamy-white, very broad, half as long as sepals; spurs very short, ½in. or less, stout and much incurved; stamens not exserted: follicles densely hairy, about 1 in. long and bearing short falcate styles. Siberia.—**A. Stuartii,** Balf. f., is a hybrid of this species and *A. olympica*, with similar larger fls.

6. **A. vulgaris,** L. Plant stout, finely pubescent or the st. sparsely short-hairy, 1–2½ ft., many-fld.: lower st. and basal lvs. biternate, ultimate lfts. or segms. broad-cuneate, the lobes shallow and more or less rounded: fls. nodding (in double-fld. kinds perhaps nearly or quite erect), 2 in. or less across, blue, purple, or white, summer; sepals spreading, ovate, acute, about 1 in. long and half as broad, exceeding laminæ; spurs about ¾in. long, about equalling laminæ, stout, knobbed and much incurved; stamens not exserted, staminodia blunt: follicles densely pubescent, 1 in. long. Eu.; nat. in E. U. S.—Common in cult. with many colors and forms: var. **nivea,** Reichb. (var. *alba*, Hort.), fls. white; var. **plena,** Hort. (var. *flore-pleno*, Hort.), fls. double; var. **stellata,** Schur, spurless. A large-fld. spurless plant is *A. clematiquila*, Hort.

7. **A. olympica,** Boiss. (*A. vulgaris* var. *olympica*, Baker. *A. caucasica*, Ledeb. *A. Witmanniana*, Hort.). Much like the preceding, but with sepals 1–2 in. long, ½–¾in. wide, claret to lilac; laminæ lilac to white, ½–¾in. long; staminodia acute. Caucasus.

8. **A. oxysepala,** Trautv.& Mey. St. 1½–3 ft. high, glandular-pubescent above: basal lvs. biternate, the petioles 6–10 in. long; lfts. coriaceous, quite glabrous, 1–3 in. long: fls. nodding; sepals divergent, about 1 in. long, claret-red to violet; laminæ yellowish, ½in. long; spurs hooked; stamens not exserted, staminodia acute: follicles 1 in. long, pubescent. E. Siberia and Manchuria. Var. **Yabeana,** Munz (*A. Yabeana*, Kitagawa), sepals slightly shorter, sepals and laminæ purplish, follicles shorter; E. China.

9. **A. Bertolonii,** Schott (*A. Reuteri*, Boiss.). Plant 4–12 in. high, 1–3-fld.: lvs. biternate, petioles 1–4 in. long; lfts. up to ¾in. long, pilose beneath: fls. nodding, violet-blue; sepals spreading, ⅔–1⅓ in. long; laminæ ½in. long; spurs straight to curved, ½in. long; stamens not exserted, staminodia acute: follicles pubescent, ½in. long. (Named for A. Bertoloni, page 39.) S. Eu.

10. **A. pyrenaica,** DC. Habit of the preceding: lvs. glabrous beneath: fls. bright lilac-blue: follicles ⅔in. long. Pyrenees.

11. **A. discolor,** Levier & Leresche. Like the two preceding in size: lvs. glabrous: fls. suberect at anthesis; sepals ½–⅔in. long, blue; laminæ whitish, ¼–⅓in. long; spurs the same; stamens slightly exserted. Spain.

12. **A. alpina,** L. Plant ½–2 ft. high, pubescent above, 1–3-fld.: lfts. to 1 in. long, subglabrous, with the ultimate lobes linear-oblong: fls. bright blue; sepals 1–2 in. long, ⅔–1 in. wide; laminæ ⅔in. long; spurs straight to curved, ¾–1 in. long; stamens not exserted, staminodia sharp-pointed: follicles 1 in. long. Alps.

13. **A. Buergeriana,** Sieb. & Zucc. Plant 1½–3 ft. tall, branched, glandular-puberulent above: basal lvs. biternate, the petioles to 6 in.; lfts. ½–2 in. long, mostly glabrous, with rounded-oblong lobes: fls. nodding; sepals purple, ⅔–1 in. long; laminæ yellowish, about ½in. long; spurs about ⅔in., slightly curved; stamens included: follicles about 1 in. long, pubescent. Japan.—A yellow-fld. type (forma *flavescens*, Makino) occurs.

14. **A. flavescens,** Wats. Plant ½–2 ft. tall: basal lvs. biternate, the lfts. ½–1½ in. long: fls. yellow, nodding; sepals spreading to reflexed, ½–¾in. long; laminæ ⅓in. long; spurs ¼–⅔in. long; stamens well-exserted: follicles glandular-puberulent, ⅔–1 in. long. Rocky Mts.

15. **A. formosa,** Fisch. (*A. arctica*, Loud.). Plant 18 in. – 3 ft. high, mostly glabrous below but pubescent and viscid at top: basal lvs. biternate, upper ones 3-cleft or simple,

more or less pubescent: fls. nodding, 1½–2 in. across, red and yellow; sepals ovate-lanceolate, acute, widely spreading or reflexed, about 1 in. long, red; laminæ rounded or truncate, yellow, ⅙in. long; spurs stout and straight, a little shorter than sepals, red; stamens long-exserted: follicles pubescent, about 1 in. long. Utah and Calif. to Alaska. Var. **truncata,** Baker (*A. truncata,* Fisch. & Mey. *A. californica,* Lindl.), differs in having a very short or almost obsolete lamina; Calif. Var. **hybrida,** Hort., supposed hybrid between forms of *A. formosa* and *A. chrysantha;* fls. large, with scarlet sepals, yellow laminæ and long slender spreading spurs.

16. **A. canadensis,** L. Plant 1–2½ ft. high, glabrous or pubescent, very floriferous: basal lvs. biternate, glaucous; lfts. crowded: fls. nodding, 1–1½ in. across, red and yellow; sepals lance-ovate, usually acute or acuminate, somewhat spreading, ½–¾in. long, red; laminæ shorter than sepals, rounded and more or less truncate, yellow; spurs straight, about ¾in. long, red, the tips often connivent; stamens exserted: follicles glandular-pubescent, nearly 1 in. long, with spreading tips. N. S. to Ga. and Tenn.—Source of hybrids with blue-fld. species under cult. Var. **nana,** Hort., is a dwarf race.

17. **A. Skinneri,** Hook. Plant large, mostly 2–3 ft. tall, glandular-pubescent above, many-fld.: basal lvs. triternate; lfts. small, with rounded lobes, more or less pubescent beneath: fls. nodding, 1½ in. across, yellowish and red; sepals lanceolate-acuminate, ¾–1 in. long, somewhat spreading, greenish-yellow; laminæ much shorter than sepals, truncate or rounded, yellowish, spurs straight, 1½–2 in. long, pale red; stamens much-exserted: follicles pubescent, 1 in. long. (G. Ure Skinner, collector in Guatemala.) Mts. of Mex.

18. **A. cærulea,** James. Plant 1½–3 ft., mostly glabrous below but somewhat viscid-pubescent above: basal lvs. biternate, glabrous, glaucous beneath, those on the st. rather few: fls. commonly erect, large, 2 in. or more across, blue and white; sepals ovate-oblong, spreading, 1¼–1½ in. long, deep to light blue; laminæ shorter than sepals, ovate-spatulate, rounded, white; spurs straight or spreading, 1–2 in. long: follicles 1 in. long. Rocky Mts. Var. **ochroleuca,** Hook., sepals 1–1½ in. long, whitish. Var. **pinetorum,** Payson, lvs. triternate.—This species hybridized with *A. chrysantha* and others is the source of many long-spurred hybrids of cult. Spurless double races are cult. **A. Helenæ,** Hort., hybrid with *A. flabellata.* **A. clematiflora** is a spurless sport from Mrs. Scott Elliott hybrids.

19. **A. chrysantha,** Gray. Plant large, 3–4 ft., much-branched, somewhat pubescent: basal lvs. usually triternate; lfts. often densely pubescent beneath: fls. erect, 1½–3 in. across, clear yellow; sepals narrow and acuminate, 1–1½ in. long, much exceeding the laminæ which are rounded at apex; spurs very slender, 2–2½ in. long: follicles pubescent. Rocky Mt. region and Tex. Var. **alba,** Hort., fls. white. Var. **Jaeschkanii,** Hort., is a dwarf or small plant with large fls. bearing red spurs and sepals and yellow laminæ; perhaps a hybrid.

20. **A. longissima,** Gray. Plant 2–3½ ft. tall, glandular-pubescent above: lvs. triternate, glaucous, with petioles 1 ft. long: fls. many, erect, pale yellow; sepals spreading, lanceolate, acuminate, 1–1¼ in. long; laminæ spreading, ⅔–1 in. long; spurs filiform, pendent, 4–6 in. long; stamens exserted: follicles 1 in. long, glandular-pubescent. W. Tex. and N. Mex.

11. **ERANTHIS,** Salisb. Winter Aconite. About a half dozen species of little European and Asian herbs with tuberous per. rootstocks, one listed among florists' bulbs.—Lvs. mostly basal, palmately dissected; cauline lf. 1, just beneath the fl. and forming an involucre: fls. solitary, yellow, the showy part being the 5–8 sepals; petals represented by scale-like nectaries; stamens many; pistils few to many, stipitate, ovary many-ovuled, maturing into a cluster of dehiscent follicles. (Eran-this: Greek *flower of spring.*)

E. hyemalis, Salisb. (*Helleborus hyemalis,* L.). Glabrous; st. or scape erect and simple, 2–8 in.: basal lvs. orbicular, long-petioled, cut nearly to the base into cuneate lobes which are again lobed into linear or oblong segms.; involucral lf. similar, the lobes unequally divided and not to base: fls. 1–1½ in. across, wide-opening, equalled or exceeded by the calyx-like involucre; sepals ¼–5⁄16in. wide; anthers oblong: follicles about ½in. long, shaped like a bean pod. Eu.; somewhat nat. Var. **cilicica,** Huth (*E. cilicica,* Schott & Kotschy), involucre divided equally and almost to base; sepals almost ½in. wide; anthers ovate; Asia Minor.—Blooms early spring, or earlier in mild winters and climates.

12. **NIGELLA,** L. Fennel-Flower. Erect ann. herbs of the Medit. region and W. Asia, about a dozen species, a few cult., mostly in the fl.-garden.—Lvs. alternate, pinnately multifid into linear or filiform parts: fls. white, blue, or yellow, often showy, sometimes closely subtended by a leafy involucre; sepals 5 and petal-like, showy; petals 5, clawed, bifid, the blade small; pistils 5, sometimes less or more, united at base to form a compound ovary which is exceptional in the family: caps. dehiscing at top, many-seeded. (Nigel-la: Latin *little black,* alluding to the seeds.)

A. Fls. closely subtended and surrounded by a multifid involucre..................1. *N. damascena*
AA. Fls. not so subtended..................2. *N. hispanica*

1. **N. damascena,** L. LOVE-IN-A-MIST. Glabrous, erect, 12–20 in., much-branching: fls. solitary at ends of branches, white or light blue, 1–1½ in. across, surrounded by a profuse very finely cut involucre (whence the English name); anthers apiculate: fr. united to the top making a globular-oblong somewhat inflated caps., with long erect styles. S. Eu.—A common fl.-garden ann., and sometimes escaped; there are dwarf and double-fld. kinds.

2. **N. hispanica,** L. Glabrous, erect or diffuse, 12–20 in., branching: fls. solitary or 2 together, deep blue with red stamens, 1¼–2½ in. across, without involucre or sometimes an uppermost spreading lf. near the fl. but not enveloping it: pistils not joined at summit, the beaks and styles wide-spreading, the caps. narrow and ribbed. Spain and N. Afr.—Fl.-garden ann., less frequent than no. 1.

13. **HYDRASTIS,** Ellis. ORANGE-ROOT. GOLDENSEAL. A genus of 2 species.—Erect per. herbs sending up in the early spring, from a yellow rootstock, a single radical lf. and simple hairy st. with 2 lvs. near the summit and a greenish-white fl.: sepals 3; petals 0; stamens many; pistils 12 or more in a head, ovary 2-ovuled, the pistil becoming fleshy and berry-like in fr. (Hydras-tis: Greek *water-acting,* from supposed drastic properties.)

H. canadensis, L. Sts. about 1 ft. high: lvs. rounded, 5–9-lobed, doubly serrate, becoming 8 in. across: fls. ⅓in. across: berry-like fr. crimson. Rich woods, Conn. to Minn., Kans. and Ga.

14. **CALTHA, L.** MARSH-MARIGOLD. Succulent per. herbs, of about 15 species inhabiting swamps and wet meadows of arctic and north temp. regions.—Lvs. large, simple, cordate or reniform: fls. showy, yellow, white or pink; sepals petaloid, 5–9; petals 0; stamens many with short filaments; pistils several to many, sessile, becoming many-seeded follicles. (Cal-tha: Latin name for the marigold.)

A. Fls. usually yellow, 1–2 in. broad: lf.-blades almost round in outline, deeply cordate..1. *C. palustris*
AA. Fls. whitish, 1 in. broad: lf.-blades oblong, shallowly cordate..................2. *C. leptosepala*

1. **C. palustris,** L. Sts. hollow, to 2 ft. high: lvs. cordate, 2–7 in. wide: fls. several, bright yellow, 1–2 in. broad, the sepals broadly oval, usually 5, Apr.–June. Newf. to S. C., Sask. and Neb.—Cowslip of Americans; collected for "greens."

2. **C. leptosepala,** DC. Sts. 1–2-fld., 4–12 in. tall: lvs. broadly oblong, the blades ½–2 in. wide: sepals 6–12, oblong, white. Mt. bogs, Alaska to Ore., Alta., New Mex.

15. **TROLLIUS,** L. Low per. herbs, sometimes grown for the showy fls., of about a dozen species in the north temp. zone, in moist and marshy places.—Erect or ascending from thickened fibrous roots: lvs. basal and cauline, palmately lobed or divided and usually sharp-toothed: fls. terminal and mostly solitary, large, yellow, nearly white or purplish; sepals 5–15, petaloid, providing the showy part; petals 5 to many, small and staminoid, with a nectar pit at base; stamens many; pistils 5 to many, sessile, ovary many-ovuled, forming a cluster of dehiscent follicles. (Trollius: Germanic *trol,* round, from the shape of fls. of some species.)—The names are likely to be confused in cult.

A. Petals about as long as stamens, or shorter.
  B. Sepals 10–15, incurving..................1. *T. europæus*
  BB. Sepals 5–8, spreading.
    C. Sts. almost leafless, scape-like, 3–8 in. tall..................2. *T. pumilus*
    CC. Sts. rather leafy, 10–30 in. tall.
      D. The petals shorter than stamens; fls. white to cream..................3. *T. laxus*
      DD. The petals equalling stamens; fls. yellow.
        E. Styles hooked in fr.: lower lvs. palmate, the segms. incised-dentate.....4. *T. caucasicus*
        EE. Styles not hooked: lower lvs. with very broad not much dissected segms.5. *T. yunnanensis*
AA. Petals much exceeding stamens.
  B. Sepals 5..................6. *T. Ledebouri*
  BB. Sepals 10–15.
    C. The petals not prominent nor protruding..................7. *T. asiaticus*
    CC. The petals long and conspicuous..................8. *T. chinensis*

1. **T. europæus,** L. GLOBE-FLOWER. Simple or considerably branched, 1–2 ft., several sts. from the root: radical lvs. petiolate, the cauline sessile, 5-parted or -divided into broad or cuneate parts, variously toothed: fls. lemon-yellow, May–July, sometimes in 2's, globular, 1–2 in. across; sepals 10–15, very broad, obtuse; petals narrow-spatulate, about equalling stamens but sometimes a little longer or a little shorter. Mts. and uplands of Eu.

2. **T. pumilus,** D. Don. Sts. glabrous, simple, 3–8 in. tall: lvs. near the base, petiolate, ½–2 in. wide, palmately 5–7-lobed, the lobes laciniate: fls. yellow, 1 in. across, the sepals 5–7, spreading, broadly elliptic; petals and stamens subequal, shorter than sepals. Himalayas.

3. **T. laxus,** Salisb. (*T. americanus,* Muhl. *T. albiflorus,* Rydb.). Sts. rather slender, weak, 8–20 in. high: basal lvs. long-obovate, 5–7-palmately parted, 2–4 in. wide; st.-lvs. short-petioled: fls. cream to almost white, 1–1½ in. broad; sepals 5–7, ovate to obovate; petals much shorter than stamens. Swamps, N. H. to B. C., Del. and Utah.

4. **T. caucasicus,** Steven. Sts. up to 3 ft. high: basal lvs. palmately dissected, the segms. incised-dentate: fls. yellow, with 5–8 elliptical sepals; petals and stamens subequal, shorter than sepals. S. W. Asia.—Much garden material referred to this species apparently belongs to **T. hybridus,** Hort., a name including a series of large plants with large fls. more or less spherical and arising from crosses between European and Asiatic species.

5. **T. yunnanensis,** Ulb. (*T. pumilus* var. *yunnanensis,* Franch.). Plants 15–24 in. high: basal lvs. 4–5 in. broad, palmately 5-lobed into segms. 1½–2 in. wide, these somewhat shallowly divided: fls. 2½–3 in. broad, about 3 on each st.; sepals 6–8, bright yellow; petals about as long as stamens. W. China.

6. **T. Ledebouri,** Reichb. f. Stout, 2 ft.: lvs. divided to base, the divisions lobed and toothed: fls. yellow, about 2½ in. wide; sepals 5, spreading, ovate; petals 10–12, narrow-linear, exceeding the stamens. (Named for von Ledebour, page 47.) Siberia.

7. **T. asiaticus,** L. (*T. giganteus,* Hort.). Rather tall: radical lvs. bronze-green, finely cleft and lobed: fls. orange, in spring; sepals 10, spreading; petals 10, longer than stamens. Siberia.

8. **T. chinensis,** Bunge (*T. sinensis,* Hort.). Sts. often branching above: radical lvs. deficient or obsolete; lower st.-lvs. reniform and upper ones orbicular-reniform, very large (sometimes 5 in. long and 6–7 in. across), 5-parted with broadly oblanceolate segms.: sepals 12 or 13, spreading, the inner ones usually narrower and somewhat longer than the outer, all obtuse and sometimes with angled margins; petals 20, linear, more than 1 in. long, exserted and surpassing the stamens; May. N. China.

16. **HELLEBORUS,** L. HELLEBORE. Fifteen or more species are recognized by some authors, but others consider them fewer; per. herbs of Eu. and W. Asia, one commonly grown for ornament.—Erect low plants, with roots of thick fibers; st. with sheaths at base, naked above or bearing a few small sessile lvs. or large bracts: basal lvs. palmately divided or compound, long-petiolate: fls. large, solitary, few or several; sepals 5, petaloid and showy, usually becoming dry and persistent, white, greenish, red, purple, or yellowish; petals small and tubular, inconspicuous, usually shorter than the many stamens; pistils 3–10, sessile, maturing into leathery or papery dehiscent several-seeded follicles. (Helleb-orus: the classical name of one of the species.)—White hellebore is Veratrum, of the Liliaceæ.

A. Sts. simple, with few small involucral bracts below infl.: fls. usually solitary, white to pale purple. . . . . 1. *H. niger*
AA. Sts. branched, without involucral bracts: fls. 2–6, green to dark purple. . . . . 2. *H. orientalis*

1. **H. niger,** L. CHRISTMAS-ROSE, so-called because it may bloom in midwinter in mild regions, or even under the snow if the ground is not too cold, but in cold climates very early in spring. St. or stock not rising above the ground; scape-like flowering st. 6–18 in., simple or forked, bearing small lvs. or clasping bracts: basal lvs. often overtopping the fls., deeply divided into 7 or more oblong or narrowly obovate dentate glabrous lfts., thick and evergreen: fls. 1½–2½ in. across, white or purplish; petals green, shorter than stamens. Eu.; somewhat nat. Var. **altifolius,** Hayne (var. *major,* Hort.), petiole up to 1 ft. long; fls. 3–5 in. across, several.

2. **H. orientalis,** Lam. (*H. Kochii,* Schiffn.). Fl.-sts. branched, leafless: basal lvs. palmate with 5–11 elliptic-oblong acute sharply serrate segms., pubescent beneath: fls. 2–6, green to dark purple: pistils free at base. Asia Minor.

17. **PÆONIA,** L. PEONY. Some 30 or more strong per. herbs and subshrubs, in the northern hemisphere, largely Asian, yielding ornamental subjects of high value.—Erect from tuberous or thickened underground parts: lvs. basal and cauline, large, alternate, ternate or pinnately compound or dissected: fls. large and mostly showy, usually terminal and solitary but sometimes clustered, red, purple, white or yellow; sepals 5 and persistent; petals 5–10, becoming more numerous in cult. kinds; stamens many; pistils 2–5, free, on a fleshy disk or base, becoming large dehiscent follicles; seeds large and mostly fleshy. (Pæo-nia: ancient name, said to commemorate

a physician Pæon.)—Most of the species have been intro. into cult., but very few enter into the hort. kinds. The shrubby or "tree" peonies are *P. suffruticosa;* the common herbaceous kinds are mostly forms of *P. lactiflora.*

A. Plant shrubby: disk enlarging in fr., becoming ¾in. or more across............1. *P. suffruticosa*
AA. Plant herbaceous: disk little or not at all enlarging.
 B. Fls. nodding, brownish-red............2. *P. Brownii*
 BB. Fls. erect.
  C. Lvs. dissected into very narrow parts.
   D. Lfts. wholly glabrous above, segms. not narrowed at apex............3. *P. tenuifolia*
   DD. Lfts. hairy along veins above, segms. narrowed and pointed............4. *P. anomala*
  CC. Lvs. not dissected into narrow parts.
   D. Carpels white-tomentose: lf.-segms. obtuse or short-acute............5. *P. officinalis*
   DD. Carpels glabrous or nearly so (not tomentose): lf.-segms. acuminate......6. *P. lactiflora*

1. **P. suffruticosa,** Haw. (*P. Moutan,* Sims. *P. arborea,* Donn). Tree Peony. Little shrub 3–5 ft. and sometimes higher, much-branched: lvs. biternate, lfts. stalked; ultimate lfts. or segms. ovate to broad-oval, 3–5-lobed, whitish beneath, margins thick or somewhat revolute: fls. large, red, rose-red to white, mostly solitary; petals 8 or more, obovate, erose or crenate: follicles wide-spreading, densely hairy-pubescent. China. Var. **Humei,** Bailey, fls. semi-double, whitish or blush with darker center.—Long in cult., producing double-fld. and many other vars.

2. **P. Brownii,** Dougl. Western Peony. Somewhat glaucous, sts. several, 8–16 in. long: lvs. mostly basal, ternately or biternately divided into obovate rounded to obtuse divisions: peduncle 1–2 in. long; sepals orbicular, concave, ½in. long; petals slightly longer, brownish-red, thick and leathery; disk of fleshy lobes at base of carpels: follicles usually 5, 1–1½ in. long. W. U. S.

3. **P. tenuifolia,** L. Roots large, fascicled, producing creeping stolons; sts. simple and 1-fld., glabrous, very leafy, 12–20 in.: lvs. ternate, cut into many narrow-linear not attenuate lobes, glabrous: fls. dark crimson or purple; petals 8–10, elliptic-cuneate, 1½ in. or less long; stigmas red and spiral: follicles 3–4, erect-spreading, villous. S. E. Eu., Caucasus.—Sometimes seen in cult.; ornamental in foliage.

4. **P. anomala,** L. Root tuberous, without stolons; sts. usually simple and 1-fld., glabrous, 2–3 ft.: lvs. biternate, divided into many lanceolate or linear-lanceolate long-acute segms., glabrous beneath but sparsely hairy along nerves above: fls. very large, bright crimson; outer sepals often extended into lobed leafy ends; petals obovate to oblong: follicles 3–5, glabrous. N. Eu., Asia.—Best known in var. **intermedia,** O. & B. Fedtsch. (*P. intermedia,* Mey.), with showy magenta fls., crimson stigmas and red-pubescent follicles.

5. **P. officinalis,** L. Sts. stout, nearly or quite simple and 1-fld., 2–3 ft.: lvs. biternate or the lower ones more divided, somewhat pubescent and pale beneath but glabrous and dark above; ultimate lfts. more or less lobed, with oblong-lanceolate obtuse or short-acute segms. 1 in. or more wide: fls. dark crimson but running to whitish or yellowish; outer sepals lf.-like; petals about 8, obovate, 1½–2 in. wide; stamens yellow; stigmas crimson: follicles 2–3, erect or spreading, white-tomentose. S. Eu., W. Asia.—Infrequently cult. although it has given rise to double-fld. and other forms, many with Latin names such as *alba, rosea* and *rubra.*

6. **P. lactiflora,** Pall. (*P. albiflora,* Pall. *P. edulis,* Salisb. *P. fragrans,* Redouté. *P. edulis* var. *sinensis,* Sims). Root of fusiform tubers; sts. simple and 1-fld. or branched at top and 2–5-fld., glabrous, 2–3½ ft.: lvs. biternate or the upper ones simpler; ultimate lfts. not lobed and oblong to lanceolate to elliptic, long-acute, usually veined red: peduncle long, often bracted; fls. large, white or pink but now much modified; outer sepals lf.-like; petals 8 or more, large and broad; stamens golden-yellow: follicles 3–5, usually glabrous. Siberia, China.—The chief source of the contemporaneous herbaceous peonies, in many cultivars, listed under numerous binomials as *Delachei, festiva, festiva maxima, gigantea, grandiflora, umbellata rosea.* This species has long been known by the name *P. albiflora.*

18. **COPTIS,** Salisb. Goldthread. Low per. herbs forming a genus of about 10 species of the cooler parts of the north temp. zone.—Rootstock slender: lvs. basal, compound or divided: fls. small, white, on scapes; sepals 5–7, petal-like, deciduous; petals 5–7, club-shaped; stamens many; pistils 3–7, on slender stalks, several-ovuled, becoming divergent follicles. (Cop-tis: name from a Greek word, *to cut,* alluding to the divided lvs.)

C. grœnlandica, Fern. (*Anemone grœnlandica,* Oeder). Rootstocks of long yellow fibers: lvs. shining, persistent, the lfts. 3, broadly obovate, 3-toothed, petiolulate: scapes to 6 in., the fls. ½in. broad, the petals broader than long. Boggy places, N. E. U. S.—Confused with *C. trifolia,* Salisb. (*Anemone trifolia,* L.), with sessile lfts. and narrower petals.

19. **XANTHORHIZA,** Marsh. One species, a little shrub in E. N. Amer.—Lvs. pinnate or 2-pinnate: fls. small, in slender drooping simple or branched racemes;

sepals 5, petaloid and deciduous; petals usually 5, smaller than sepals, 2-lobed; stamens 5–10; pistils 5 or more, sessile, 2-ovuled but maturing into 1-seeded dehiscent follicles, the short style becoming dorsal. (Xanthorhi-za: from Greek words, *yellow root.*)

X. simplicissima, Marsh. (*Zanthorhiza apiifolia,* L'Her.). SHRUB YELLOW-ROOT from the color of root (wood of st. also yellow). Suckering; sts. 1–2 ft. high: lfts. about 5, sharply lobed and toothed, often again divided: racemes at base of lf.-crown, with brown-purple star-shaped fls. ¼in. or less across.

20. **ACTÆA,** L. BANEBERRY. COHOSH. A genus of erect per. herbs with about a half dozen species of rich woods in the north temp. zone.—Lvs. large, 2–3-ternately compound: fls. small, white, in terminal racemes; sepals 4–5, petaloid, caducous; petals 4–10, small, flat, spatulate, on slender claws; stamens many; pistil 1, with a broad sessile 2-lobed stigma, ovary 1-celled, placentæ 2 and parietal, ovules several to numerous: fr. a berry with seeds smooth, lenticular and in 2 horizontal rows. (Actæ-a: Greek name for the elder.)

A. Pedicels slender; berries usually red .... 1. *A. rubra*
AA. Pedicels thickened in fr.; berries usually white .... 2. *A. alba*

1. **A. rubra,** Willd. (*A. spicata* var. *rubra,* Ait.). One to 2 ft. high: lvs. mostly petioled, pinnate, the lfts. ovate or terminal obovate, toothed to cleft, usually scattered-pubescent beneath: raceme ovoid; pedicels slender, about ½in. long: berries ovoid-ellipsoid, red. Lab. to N. J., S. D. and Neb.—A white-fruited form occurs.

2. **A. alba,** Mill. (*A. pachypoda,* Ell. *A. spicata* var. *alba,* L.). Lfts. more incised and sharply toothed, almost glabrous beneath: raceme ellipsoid; pedicels thickened in fr.: berries globular-ovoid, white. N. S. to Ga., Minn., Mo.—A red-fruited form occurs.

21. **CIMICIFUGA,** L. BUGBANE. A dozen or more tall upright per. herbs, sometimes planted for ornament, native in north temp. zone.—Lvs. large, ternately decompound: fls. small, white, many in long racemes; sepals 2–5, petaloid, caducous; petals 1–8 or none, small, clawed, 2-lobed; stamens many; pistils 1–8, sessile or stipitate, many-ovuled, maturing into dehiscent follicles. (Cimicif-uga: Latin *bugbane.*)

A. Pistils sessile.
B. Lfts. cordate: pistils 5 .... 1. *C. dahurica*
BB. Lfts. not at all cordate: pistils 1–2 .... 2. *C. racemosa*
AA. Pistils stalked.
B. Number of pistils 3–8: pedicels evidently bracted .... 3. *C. americana*
BB. Number of pistils 2–3: pedicels very inconspicuously bracted .... 4. *C. simplex*

1. **C. dahurica,** Huth (*Actinospora dahurica,* Turcz.). Plant 3–5 ft. high: lvs. mostly twice ternate; lfts. (especially the terminal one) cordate, irregularly and rather coarsely incised-toothed, mostly 2–4½ in. long: fls. creamy-white, autumn; pedicels bracted; pistils 5, sessile, glabrous. Asia.

2. **C. racemosa,** Nutt. (*Actæa racemosa,* L.). BLACK SNAKEROOT. Sts. 3–8 ft. high: lvs. ternate, then pinnate and then sometimes again divided; lfts. ovate or oblong, incisely toothed, mostly 1½–3 in. long: fls. white, June–Aug.; pedicels bracted; pistils 1–2, sessile, the stigma broad and flat. Woods, Me. and Ont. to Wis., Ga., Mo.

3. **C. americana,** Michx. Sts. slender, 3–5 ft. high: lvs. much as in the preceding, the lfts. 1–3 in. long: pedicels bracted; pistils 3–8, stipitate, the stigma minute; Aug.–Sept. N. Y. to Pa. in mts. to Ga. and Tenn.

4. **C. simplex,** Wormsk. (*C. racemosa* var. *simplex,* Regel). Plant 2–3 ft.: lvs. much as in the preceding: pedicels with very minute or almost no bracts; pistils 2–3, stipitate, the stigma minute; autumn. Kamtschatka.

71. LARDIZABALACEÆ. LARDIZABALA FAMILY

Mostly climbing woody plants, of 8 genera and about 20 species native in the Himalayas, China, Japan, and Chile, a few planted for ornament.—Lvs. compound, palmate, or sometimes pinnate: fls. bisexual or unisexual, with rudiments of the other sex organs present, regular, borne in racemes or solitary; sepals 6, petaloid, in 2 whorls, sometimes 3; petals 0; stamens 6, free or united, hypogynous, usually with nectaries between sepals and stamens; pistils 3 or more, divergent, ovary 1-celled, ovules 1 to many, parietal: fr. a berry, sometimes dehiscent.

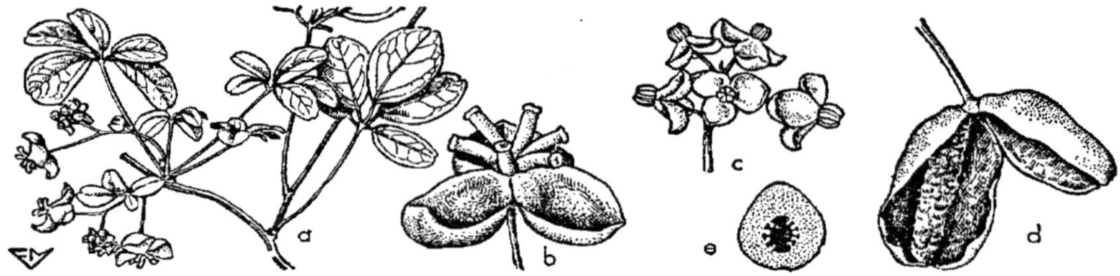

Fig. 71. Lardizabalaceæ. *Akebia quinata:* a, flowering branch, × ¼; b, pistillate flower, × 1; c, staminate flower, × 1; d, fruit, × ¼; e, ovary, cross-section, × 6.

AKEBIA, Decne. Two species of attractive glabrous twining shrubs from China and Japan.—Lvs. digitately 3–5-foliolate: monœcious; fls. in axillary racemes; sepals 3; stamens 6, free; pistils 3–12 with sessile stigma, ovary 1-celled, placentæ 2 and parietal, ovules numerous: fr. a large oblong berry with numerous seeds imbedded in a pulp, opening along the inner suture. (Ake-bia: the Japanese name.)

A. Lfts. 5, entire........1. *A. quinata*
AA. Lfts. 3, entire to crenate........2. *A. trifoliata*

1. **A. quinata,** Decne. (*Rajania quinata,* Thunb.). Climbing to 30 ft. and more; young branchlets purplish: lfts. 5, oval or oblong-obovate, to 3 in. long, entire, emarginate, very dark green: fls. fragrant, the pistillate purplish-brown, 1 in. across, the staminate rosy-purple, ½in. across: berry 3–5 in. long, purple-violet with glaucous bloom, dehiscing by carpellary lines after maturity, showy, seeds black. China, Japan.—Grown as a porch and arbor vine, affording good shade; fr. production best assured by hand cross-pollination of fls.

2. **A. trifoliata,** Koidz. (*Clematis trifoliata,* Thunb. *A. lobata,* Decne.). Similar to *A. quinata* but with 3 broad-ovate sometimes coarsely crenate lfts. China, Japan.

72. BERBERIDACEÆ. BARBERRY FAMILY

Herbs or shrubs, many of them ornamental, of 10 or more genera and about 200 species, native in temp. regions of the northern hemisphere, but Berberis distributed from Cent. Asia to the mts. of trop. India and along the Andes to Straits of Magellan. —Lvs. alternate, simple or compound: fls. solitary or racemed, bisexual, regular, hypogynous; sepals and petals usually imbricated in 2 or more series, the petals often changed to nectaries; stamens as many as petals and opposite them, rarely twice as many; anthers usually opening by 2 valves hinged at top; ovary superior, 1-celled, with few to many ovules, basal or parietal; style short or none: fr. a berry or caps.

A. Plant a shrub.
 B. Branches spiny: lvs. simple........1. Berberis
 BB. Branches unarmed: lvs. pinnate (rarely simple).
  C. Lvs. simple to 3-foliolate: plant not producing fls........2. Mahoberberis
  CC. Lvs. pinnate.
   D. Lfts. serrate: fls. yellow: fr. blue or black........3. Mahonia
   DD. Lfts. entire: fls. white: fr. red........4. Nandina

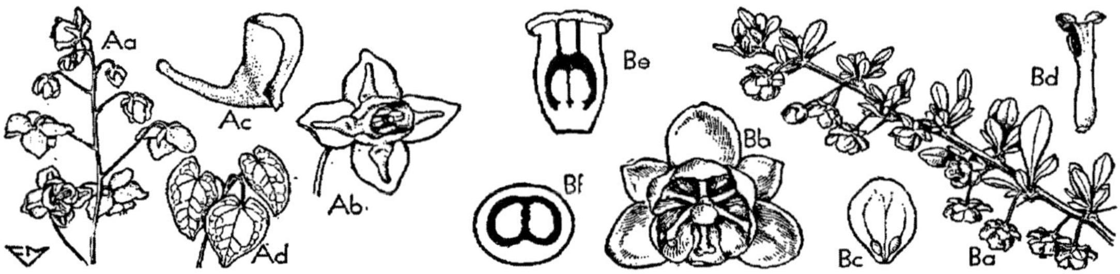

Fig. 72. Berberidaceæ. A, *Epimedium versicolor:* Aa, inflorescence branch, × ½; Ab, flower, × 1; Ac, petal, × 2; Ad, leaf, × ⅓. B, *Berberis Thunbergii:* Ba, flowering branch, × ½; Bb, flower, × 2; Bc, petal, × 2; Bd, stamen, × 4; Be, pistil, vertical section, × 5; Bf, ovary, cross-section, × 8.

AA. Plant an herb.
B. Lvs. palmately veined or lobed: petals flat.
C. Petals 6–9; anthers without valves: fr. a berry........5. PODOPHYLLUM
CC. Petals 8; anthers with valves: fr. a caps........6. JEFFERSONIA
BB. Lvs. 1–3-pinnate: petals nectary-like.
C. Petals and stamens 4........7. EPIMEDIUM
CC. Petals and stamens 6.
D. Foliage basal: seeds ⅛in. thick........8. VANCOUVERIA
DD. Foliage not basal: seeds ⅓in. thick........9. CAULOPHYLLUM

1. BERBERIS, L. BARBERRY. Deciduous and evergreen shrubs cult. for their ornamental foliage which assumes brilliant colors in autumn, and the attractive fls. and fr.; nearly 175 species native in N. and S. Amer., Asia, Eu., N. Afr.—Wood and inner bark yellow; branches armed with spines which are morphologically lvs.: foliar or expanded lvs. simple: fls. yellow, in drooping racemes, fascicled or solitary; sepals 6, subtended by 2–3 bractlets; petals 6, usually with 2 glands near base; stamens 6, irritable: fr. a 1- to several-seeded berry. (Ber-beris: Arabic name.)

A. Plant evergreen or half-evergreen: fr. blue to black (dull red in *B. mentorensis*).
B. Lvs. entire.
C. Shape of lf. elliptic to obovate: fls. 1–2........1. *B. buxifolia*
CC. Shape of lf. narrow-oblong: fls. 2–6........2. *B. stenophylla*
BB. Lvs. dentate.
C. Fls. in racemes.
D. Racemes longer than lvs., 6–20-fld.: lvs. ¾–1 in. long........3. *B. Darwinii*
DD. Racemes shorter than lvs., 4–10-fld.: lvs. 1–2 in. long........4. *B. ilicifolia*
CC. Fls. in fascicles or solitary.
D. Under surface of lvs. glaucous or white.
E. Branchlets warty to slightly warty: fls. 1 to few, yellow.
F. The branchlets densely warty: lvs. elliptic to ovate-lanceolate, ½–1 in. long........5. *B. verruculosa*
FF. The branchlets slightly warty: lvs. narrow-oblong, ¾–1¾ in. long........6. *B. Chenaultii*
EE. Branchlets glabrous to subglabrous.
F. Number of fls. 8–25, yellow: lvs. elliptic-oblong: spines stout........7. *B. pruinosa*
FF. Number of fls. 2–5, whitish: lvs. lanceolate: spines slender........8. *B. triacanthophora*
DD. Under surface of lvs. green.
E. Foliage coriaceous.
F. Lf. slightly reticulate beneath: fls. 2–6: fr. black, slightly bloomy, with sessile stigma........9. *B. Sargentiana*
FF. Lf. with veinlets invisible: fls. about 15: fr. black, bloomy, style distinct........10. *B. Julianæ*
EE. Foliage thinly coriaceous.
F. Length of lvs. about 1 in.: fls. 1 to few: fr. dull red........11. *B. mentorensis*
FF. Length of lvs. 1½–3½ in.: fls. 3–12: fr. blue-black.
G. Lf. elliptic: pedicel ½–1 in. long: fr. almost black, slightly bloomy, with sessile stigma........12. *B. manipurana*
GG. Lf. narrow-lanceolate: pedicel ¼–¾in. long: fr. blue-black, bloomy, with nearly sessile stigma........13. *B. Gagnepainii*
AA. Plant with deciduous foliage: fr. red to purple.
B. Fls. solitary or fascicled.
C. Spines simple: fls. 1–3 (4–10 in one var.)........14. *B. Thunbergii*
CC. Spines 3-parted: fls. 3 to many.
D. Lvs. ¼–1 in. long, glaucous beneath: fls. in short-stalked umbels or dense clusters........15. *B. Wilsoniæ*
DD. Lvs. 1–2 in. long, green beneath: fls. in umbel-like racemes........16. *B. Sieboldii*
BB. Fls. in racemes or panicles.
C. Twigs puberulous: lvs. to 1 in. long: fls. in panicles........17. *B. aggregata*
CC. Twigs glabrous to glaucous: lvs. mostly over 1 in. long: fls. in racemes.
D. Lvs. ½–1½ in. long, entire: spines simple........18. *B. Vernæ*
DD. Lvs. 1–3 in. long, toothed: spines simple to 3-parted.
E. Raceme 3–6-fld., umbel-like........16. *B. Sieboldii*
EE. Raceme many-fld., 1–4 in. long.
F. Branchlets reddish: spines usually simple........19. *B. koreana*
FF. Branchlets grayish: spines usually 3-parted.
G. Lf. elliptic to obovate-oblong, 1–3 in. long: racemes 2½–4 in. long........20. *B. amurensis*
GG. Lf. oblong-spatulate or obovate, 1–2 in. long: racemes to 2 in. long........21. *B. vulgaris*

1. **B. buxifolia,** Poir. (*B. dulcis,* Sweet). MAGELLAN BARBERRY. Evergreen, to 10 ft., branchlets slender, grooved, puberulous, with 3-parted to simple spines: lvs. entire, obovate to elliptic, ½–1 in. long: fls. 1–2, orange-yellow, ⅓in. across: fr. dark purple, subglobose. Chile. Var. **nana,** Mouillef., dwarf compact form.

2. **B. stenophylla,** Lindl. (*B. Darwinii* × *B. empetrifolia*). From 3–9 ft., with slender arching branches armed with 3-parted spines: lvs. narrow-oblong, revolute at margins, spiny-pointed, ½–1 in. long, coriaceous: fls. golden-yellow, 2–6 in peduncled nodding umbels: fr. black. Garden origin.

3. **B. Darwinii,** Hook. From 3–10 ft.; branches brown, pubescent when young, with 3–7-parted spines: lvs. obovate, cuneate, ¾–1 in. long, spiny-toothed and usually 3-pointed at apex, coriaceous, glossy dark green above, light green below: fls. in pendulous racemes longer than lvs., 6–20-fld., orange-yellow; style as long as ovary: fr. dark purple. (After Charles Darwin, 1809–1882, naturalist.) Chile to Patagonia.

4. **B. ilicifolia,** Forst. HOLLY BARBERRY. Evergreen, to 8 ft., with grooved glabrous to puberulous branchlets: lvs. obovate, 1–2 in. long, spiny-toothed near apex: fls. orange-yellow, in short dense racemes. S. Chile.—The plant cult. as *B. ilicifolia* is usually *Mahoberberis Neubertii* var. *latifolia.*

5. **B. verruculosa,** Hemsl. & Wils. Spreading evergreen shrub to 5 ft., with densely warty branches and slender 3-parted spines: lvs. elliptic or ovate-lanceolate, ½–1 in. long, remotely spiny-toothed, glaucous beneath: fls. solitary or in small fascicles, golden-yellow, ½in. across: fr. black with purplish bloom, ⅓in. long. W. China.

6. **B. Chenaultii,** Chenault (*B. verruculosa* × *B. Gagnepainii*). Branches slightly warty; spines slender, 3-parted: lvs. narrow-oblong, ¾–1¾ in. long, glossy above, glaucous beneath, spiny-toothed: fls. 1–3, ½in. across. (Named for Leon Chenault, 1833–1930, French nurseryman.) Garden origin.

7. **B. pruinosa,** Franch. Evergreen, to 10 ft., with 3-parted stout spines and subglabrous twigs: lvs. coriaceous, elliptic-oblong, 1–2 in. long, spiny-toothed, glossy dark green above, white beneath: fls. 8–25, yellow, ¼in. across: fr. bluish-black, pruinose. China.

8. **B. triacanthophora,** Fedde. Shrub to 5 ft., with spreading slender glabrous branches and slender 3-parted spines up to 1 in. long: lvs. lanceolate, 1–2 in. long, spiny-toothed, bright green above, glaucous beneath: fls. whitish, 2–5, subglobose, fascicled: fr. blue-black. China.

9. **B. Sargentiana,** Schneid. To 6 ft.; branches grayish-brown, armed with 3-parted spines: lvs. elliptic-oblong to oblong-lanceolate, to 4 in. long, densely spiny-serrate, coriaceous, dark green above, light green and slightly reticulate below: fls. 2–6, fascicled, pale yellow, ½in. across: fr. globose-ovoid, black at maturity, with sessile stigma. (After C. S. Sargent, page 51.) China.

10. **B. Julianæ,** Schneid. WINTERGREEN BARBERRY. To 6 ft., with glabrous branchlets and 3-parted spines: lvs. ovate to lanceolate, 1–3 in. long, acute, spiny-toothed: fls. in fascicles of about 15, yellow, about ¼in. across: fr. black, bloomy, about ⅓in. wide, with short style; seed usually 1. (Named for Mrs. C. K. Schneider.) China.

11. **B. mentorensis,** L. M. Ames (*B. Julianæ* × *B. Thunbergii*). To 3 ft.; branchlets grooved, glabrous, spines 1- or 3-parted: lvs. subcoriaceous, elliptic-ovate, about 1 in. long, sparingly spinulose-toothed: fls. 1 to few, yellowish: fr. dull dark red. Garden origin.

12. **B. manipurana,** Ahrendt (*B. Knightii*, Hort. not Koch. *B. xanthoxylon*, Schneid. in part). Shrub up to 10 ft.; branchlets glabrous, yellowish-brown, with 3-parted spines: lvs. elliptic, spinulose-toothed, 2–3 in. long, green beneath: fls. 6–12, fascicled, ½in. across, petals emarginate: fr. oblong, almost black, with sessile stigma. Assam.

13. **B. Gagnepainii,** Schneid. To 6 ft., with glabrous branchlets and 3-parted spines: lvs. narrow-lanceolate in cult. forms, 1½–3½ in. long, spiny-toothed with revolute margins, indistinctly veined beneath: fls. in fascicles of 3–8, bright yellow, ½in. across: fr. bluish-black, bloomy, ¼in. across; stigma nearly sessile; seeds 4. (Bears the name of François Gagnepain, page 43.) China.

14. **B. Thunbergii,** DC. (*B. sinensis*, Koch not Desf. *B. japonica*, Hort.). JAPANESE BARBERRY. Low dense deciduous shrub 2–8 ft. high; branches glabrous, deeply grooved, brown, with simple spines: lvs. obovate or spatulate, entire, ½–1½ in. long, glaucescent beneath: fls. 1–3, borne profusely on the whole length of sts., pale yellow: fr. elliptic or nearly globose, bright red, persistent until following spring. (For Carl Peter Thunberg, page 52.) Japan. Var. **atropurpurea,** Chenault, lvs. deep purple to bronzy-red. Var. **erecta,** Hort., branches strictly upright forming a dense column. Var. **minor,** Rehd. (var. *Dawsonii*, Bean), low dense form, ½–1½ ft. high, lvs. about ½in. long. Var. **pluriflora,** Koehne, infl. subumbellate, 4–10-fld.

15. **B. Wilsoniæ,** Hemsl. & Wils. Deciduous or half-evergreen, from 3–6 ft., with spreading reddish-brown puberulous branches armed with 3-parted slender spines: lvs. oblanceolate or narrowly obovate, entire, ¼–1 in. long, rounded or acutish at apex, pale green and dull above, glaucous beneath: fls. in short-stalked umbels or dense clusters, golden-yellow: fr. globose, salmon-red. (Named for Mrs. E. H. Wilson, wife of the former vice-director of the Arnold Arboretum.) W. China. Var. **subcaulialata,** Schneid. (*B. subcaulialata*, Schneid. *B. Coryi*, Veitch), branchlets glabrous, strongly angled; lvs. obovate, occasionally toothed near apex, whitish beneath; China.

16. **B. Sieboldii,** Miq. Up to 5 ft.; branchlets slender, angled, red-brown, glabrous, with 3-parted spines: lvs. oblong-obovate, 1–3 in. long, ciliate-toothed, green beneath: fls. pale yellow, ¼in. across, in 3–6-fld. umbel-like racemes: fr. subglobose, bright red, lustrous. (Philipp Franz von Siebold, page 51.) Japan.

17. **B. aggregata,** Schneid. (*B. Geraldii,* Veitch). SALMON BARBERRY. Deciduous, to 10 ft.; branchlets strongly angled, puberulous, with slender 3-parted spines: lvs. oblanceolate to obovate, to 1 in. long, mostly with few spinulose teeth, reticulate and pale beneath: fls. pale yellow, ¼in. across, panicle sessile, dense, to 1½ in. long: fr. subglobose, red, bloomy, with distinct style. W. China. Var. **Prattii,** Schneid. (*B. Prattii,* Schneid. *B. brevipaniculata,* Bean not Schneid.), lvs. to 1½ in. long, obovate, often entire; panicles subsessile or peduncled, 1½–4 in. long; bears the name of the collector, A. E. Pratt.

18. **B. Vernæ,** Schneid. Shrub to about 6 ft., with glabrous grooved branchlets and simple spines: lvs. spatulate or oblanceolate, ½–1½ in. long, obtuse, entire: fls. in densely-fld. racemes, yellow, about ⅛in. across: fr. red, about ⅛in. across. (Bears the name of Miss Verna Berger.) W. China.

19. **B. koreana,** Palibin. Up to 6 ft.; branchlets grooved, at first reddish, bloomy, with mostly simple spines: lvs. obovate, 1–3 in. long, spinulose-serrulate, paler and reticulate beneath: fls. several to many, ¼in. across, racemes up to 2 in. long: fr. subglobose, bright red. Korea.

20. **B. amurensis,** Rupr. Up to 10 ft.; branchlets grooved, grayish with usually 3-parted spines: lvs. elliptic to obovate-oblong, 1–3 in. long, densely setose-serrulate: fls. 10–25, about ¼in. across, racemes 2½–4 in. long: fr. ellipsoid, red. N. E. Asia.

21. **B. vulgaris,** L. COMMON BARBERRY. Glabrous shrub to 8 ft.; branches grooved, gray, upright or arching: lvs. oblong-spatulate or obovate, 1–2 in. long, bristly-dentate, grayish-green beneath, many on young shoots reduced to 3-parted spines: racemes pendulous, terminating lateral branches, many-fld.; fls. bright yellow: fr. oblong-ovoid, scarlet to purple, acid. Eu. to E. Asia; nat. in E. N. Amer.—Host of wheat rust. Running into forms with white or yellow fr., berries seedless or less acid, lvs. purple or variegated with white or with yellow margin; of these the commonest is var. **atropurpurea,** Hort. (forma *atropurpurea,* Regel. var. *purpurea,* Bertin not DC.), lvs. deep purple.

2. **MAHOBERBERIS,** Schneid. Unarmed half-evergreen shrub; a hybrid between *Mahonia Aquifolium* and *Berberis vulgaris.*—Like Mahonia in the unarmed branches, solitary (not fascicled) lvs. which are simple to pinnate; like Berberis in having lvs. usually simple, thinner and serrulate on the older branches, more coriaceous and sinuately spiny on the shoots; not known to bloom.

M. Neubertii, Schneid. (*Berberis Neubertii,* Baumann). Shrub up to 6 ft. high: lvs. to 3 in. long, toothed or spiny, cuneate at base. (Bears the name of W. Neubert, page 49.) Var. **latifolia,** Schneid. (*Berberis latifolia,* Hort. *B. ilicifolia,* Hort. not Forst.), lvs. of the shoots broader, subtruncate at base.

3. **MAHONIA,** Nutt. (*Odostemon,* Raf.). Evergreen shrubs, of about 50 species native in N. and Cent. Amer. and E. and S. E. Asia; grown for the handsome foliage and yellow fls.—A segregate from Berberis, differing in having unarmed branches, pinnate lvs., the many-fld. infl. springing from axils of bud-scales, and the 9 sepals. (Maho-nia: after Bernard M'Mahon, 1775–1816, American horticulturist.)

A. Bud-scales glumaceous, persistent, ½–1½ in. long .... 1. *M. nervosa*
AA. Bud-scales deciduous, not over ¼in. long.
B. Plant less than 1 ft. high: lvs. minutely papillose beneath .... 2. *M. repens*
BB. Plant more than 1 ft. high: lvs. smooth beneath.
C. Lfts. 5–9, with 10 or more teeth on each side .... 3. *M. Aquifolium*
CC. Lfts. 9–15, mostly with 1–6 teeth on each side .... 4. *M. Bealei*

1. **M. nervosa,** Nutt. (*Berberis nervosa,* Pursh). OREGON-GRAPE. Sts. simple, 8–24 in. high; scales of the terminal bud conspicuous, lanceolate, persistent: lvs. in a terminal tuft; petioles to 5 in. long; lfts. 9–19, ovate to ovate-lanceolate, 1–3 in. long, with 6–10 spinulose teeth on each side: racemes 4–8 in. long: berries glaucous, blue. B. C. to Calif.

2. **M. repens,** Don (*Berberis repens,* Lindl.). Stoloniferous, to 1 ft.: lfts. 3–7, ovate, 1–3 in. long, dull blue-green above, gray-green and with epidermal of lower surface papillose, teeth 6–14 on each side, small and bristle-tipped: racemes to 3 in., densely fld.: fr. black, bloomy. Alta. to B. C., New Mex. and Calif.

3. **M. Aquifolium,** Nutt. (*Berberis Aquifolium,* Pursh). HOLLY MAHONIA or BARBERRY. To 3 ft. or more: lfts. 5–9, ovate-lanceolate, 1–3 in. long, glossy dark green above, light green beneath, the teeth small and spinulose: racemes fascicled, 2–3 in. long: fr. blue, glaucous. B. C. to Ida. and Ore.

4. **M. Bealei,** Carr. (*Berberis Bealei,* Fort.). To 12 ft.: lfts. 9–15, ovate to quadrangular, to 5 in. long, yellowish-green above, glaucescent beneath, with mostly 1–4 teeth on upper edge and 3–6 on lower: racemes 3–6 in. long, upright, densely fld., with acute bracts ⅛in. long: fr. ⅜in. long, blue-black. (Named for Thomas Chay Beale, consul from Portugal to Shanghai before 1860.) China.—Cult. material passing as *M. japonica* is *M. Bealei; M. japonica,* DC. (*Ilex japonica,* Thunb.), has less rigid somewhat narrower lfts. yellowish-green beneath: racemes spreading, 4–8 in., lax-fld., acuminate bracts ¼in. long; Japan.

4. **NANDINA,** Thunb. A small erect evergreen shrub grown for its bright red berries; 1 species in China and Japan.—Lvs. 2- or 3-pinnately compound, the ultimate lfts. 1–5, entire: fls. small, in terminal panicles; sepals and petals many, the sepals gradually changing into petals which are larger and whiter than the somewhat leathery sepals; stamens 6, free; ovules 2. (Nandi-na: Japanese name.)

N. domestica, Thunb. To about 8 ft., the young growth often tinged with red: lfts. 1–2 in. long, turning red in winter: fls. white, the dry floral envelopes shelling and exposing the stamens: berries about ¼in. across.

5. **PODOPHYLLUM,** L. About 4 species of per. herbs with horizontal rootstocks, native in E. N. Amer. and Asia.—Lvs. large, peltate, palmately lobed: fls. white, sometimes pink to purple or brown; sepals 6, petaloid, shed early; petals 6–9, longer than sepals; stamens as many or twice as many as petals; pistil 1 (seldom several) with sessile stigma: fr. a fleshy berry. (Podophyl-lum: Greek *foot-leaf.*)

P. peltatum, L. May-Apple. Mandrake. Erect, to 1½ ft.: lvs. to 1 ft. across, 5–9-lobed, the lobes oblong and usually 2-cleft and dentate at apex; fl.-sts. with usually 2 similar lvs.: fls. white, solitary, nodding, borne on the fork between the 2 lvs., 2 in. across; stamens twice as many as petals: fr. ovoid, yellowish, 1–2 in. long, edible. Que. to Fla. and Tex.—Fr. pulp edible and used in preserves and beverages; lvs. and roots poisonous.

6. **JEFFERSONIA,** B. S. Barton. Two species of per. glabrous herbs native in E. N. Amer. and Asia.—Lvs. basal, palmately veined or lobed: fls. white or blue, solitary on slender scapes; sepals 4, shed early; petals and stamens 8; pistil 1, stigma 2-lobed: caps. leathery, pyriform, half circumscissile near summit. (Jefferso-nia: after Thomas Jefferson, 1743–1826.)

J. diphylla, Pers. (*Podophyllum diphyllum,* L. *J. binata,* Barton). Twinleaf. Erect, to 18 in. in fr., 6–8 in. high when in fl.: lvs. 3–6 in. long, 2–5 in. wide, parted into 2 half-ovate lfts.; petioles as long as the scape: fl. white, 1 in. broad: caps. about 1 in. long, short-stipitate. Ont. to Wis. south to Tenn.

7. **EPIMEDIUM,** L. Per. almost woody herbs with creeping underground sts., grown in the border or rock-garden; of about 23 species in temp. regions of the northern hemisphere.—Lvs. 1–3-pinnate; lfts. denticulate: racemes simple or slightly branched, terminal or opposite the lvs.; sepals 8 in 2 whorls, the inner usually petaloid, often colored; petals 4, in the form of nectaries, spurred or hooded; stamens 4, free: caps. opening by valve on back; seeds few. (Epime-dium: Greek, a name from Dioscorides, retained by Linnæus, of obscure meaning.)

A. Flowering st. leafless .... 1. *E. pinnatum*
AA. Flowering st. with a lf.
  B. Infl. seemingly lateral, shorter than the st.-lf. .... 2. *E. alpinum*
  BB. Infl. evidently terminal, equalling or exceeding the st.-lf.
    C. Fls. large, 1–2 in. across .... 3. *E. grandiflorum*
    CC. Fls. smaller, up to 1 in. across.
      D. Petals spurless or nearly so; stamens much shorter than petals .... 4. *E. Youngianum*
      DD. Petals with a slender spur; stamens nearly as long as or longer than petals.
        E. Inner sepals narrow-ovate, boat-shaped, crimson: infl. usually compound .... 5. *E. rubrum*
        EE. Inner sepals broad-ovate, flat, yellow, coppery or rose: infl. simple .... 6. *E. versicolor*

1. **E. pinnatum,** Fisch. To 1 ft.: lvs. all basal, usually 2-ternate; lfts. 9, ovate, acute, spinose-serrate, cordate at base, up to 3 in. long: fls. yellow, ⅔in. across, with reddish petals; stamens protruding. Iran, Caucasus.—Cult. material is var. **colchicum,** Boiss. (var. *elegans,* Mill.), lfts. 3–6; Transcaucasus.

2. **E. alpinum,** L. To 1 ft.: lvs. basal and cauline, usually 2-ternate, the st.-lf. commonly exceeding the compound infl.; lfts. ovate, acute or acuminate: fls. dull red with yellow slipper-like petals. S. Eu.—Cult. material bearing this name is mostly *E. rubrum.*

3. **E. grandiflorum,** Morr. (*E. macranthum,* Morr. & Decne.). To about 1 ft.: lvs. basal and cauline, 2–3-ternate; lfts. ovate, acute to acuminate, spinose-serrate, cordate: fls. 1–2 in. across, outer sepals red, inner pale violet; petals white with long subulate spurs. Japan, Korea, Manchuria. Var. **violaceum,** Stearn (*E. violaceum,* Morr.), petals light violet.

4. **E. Youngianum,** Fisch. & Mey. (*E. diphyllum* × *E. grandiflorum*). To about 1 ft.: lvs. basal and cauline, usually 9-foliolate; lfts. ovate, acuminate: fls. 3–8, white with a greenish tinge. (Named for a Mr. Young, who sent the plant to the botanic garden in Edinburgh in 1838.) Of garden origin. Var. **roseum,** Stearn (*E. macranthum* forma *roseum,*

Vilm. *E. lilacinum* of present-day cult.), lfts. blunt or acute, 2–7; fls. rose-lilac. Var. **niveum,** Stearn (*E. niveum,* Vilm. *E. macranthum* var. *niveum,* Mill. *E. Musschianum* as now used in the trade), lfts. 2–9; fls. white.

5. **E. rubrum,** Morr. (*E. alpinum* × *E. grandiflorum. E. coccineum,* Silva Tarouca). Lvs. basal and cauline, usually biternate; lfts. ovate, acuminate, spinose-serrate, more or less cordate: infl. compound, 10–23-fld.; fls. nearly 1 in. across; inner sepals bright crimson; petals slipper-like, pale yellow or white tinged with red, the spurs slightly upcurved. Of garden origin.

6. **E. versicolor,** Morr. (*E. grandiflorum* × *E. pinnatum* var. *colchicum*). Lvs. basal and cauline, usually biternate; lfts. ovate, commonly 9, conspicuously mottled or red when young, later green: fls. ⅘in. across; inner sepals old rose; petals yellow with red-tinged spurs. Of garden origin. Var. **sulphureum,** Stearn (*E. macranthum* var. *sulphureum,* Morr. *E. pinnatum* var. *sulphureum,* Bergmans), st.-lf. usually with 9 lfts., not red-mottled; inner sepals pale yellow; petals brighter yellow. Var. **neo-sulphureum,** Stearn, lfts. of st.-lf. usually 3; fls. yellow; spur of petal short.

8. **VANCOUVERIA,** Morr. & Decne. Three species of per. herbs in W. N. Amer.—Rhizome horizontal: lvs. usually biternate, basal, fl.-st. usually leafless: fls. pendulous, white or yellow; outer sepals 6–9, soon falling; inner sepals 6, petaloid; petals 6, usually forming a pouch shorter than the inner sepals; stamens 6: caps. splitting to base. (Vancouve-ria: after Capt. George Vancouver, 1757–1798, English explorer.)

V. hexandra, Morr. & Decne. (*Epimedium hexandrum,* Hook.). To 1½ ft., not evergreen: lfts. ovate, ½–1½ in. long: scape well exceeding foliage; panicle loose, 6–45-fld.; fls. white, ½in. long, with reflexed sepals and petals. Wash. to N. Calif.

9. **CAULOPHYLLUM,** Michx. Two species of per. herbs with thickened rootstocks, 1 in E. N. Amer. and 1 in Asia.—Lvs. ternately compound: fls. in terminal panicles; sepals, petals and stamens 6; pistil 1, with short style and unilateral stigma: pericarp bursts soon after flowering leaving 2 naked seeds which become blue with fleshy integument. (Caulophyl-lum: Greek *stem-leaf.*)

C. thalictroides, Michx. (*Leontice thalictroides,* L.). Blue Cohosh. Papoose Root. Sts. to 3 ft., with a large triternate almost sessile lf. near the summit and a smaller usually biternate lf. near the base of the panicle; lfts. oval to obovate, 3–5-lobed, 1–4 in. long: fls. yellow-green, to ½in. across; petals forming hoods and smaller than the sepals: seeds ⅓in. thick, blue-black. N. B. to Man., S. C. and Miss.

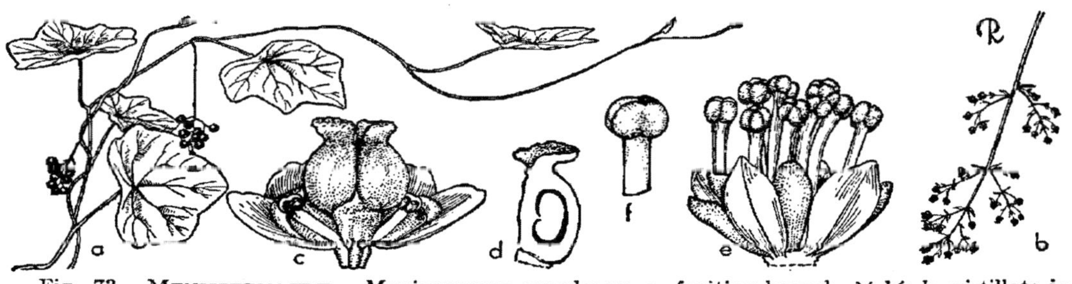

Fig. 73. Menispermaceæ. *Menispermum canadense:* a, fruiting branch, × ⅙; b, pistillate inflorescence, × ½; c, pistillate flower, × 6; d, pistil, vertical section, × 8; e, staminate flower, × 6; f, anther, × 12.

73. MENISPERMACEÆ. MOONSEED FAMILY

Woody diœcious twining vines, rarely erect trees or shrubs, mostly of trop. distribution and sometimes grown for ornament over arbors or walls.—Lvs. alternate, exstipulate, usually simple, sometimes palmately lobed or trifoliolate: fls. unisexual, mostly in cymose or paniculate infl., with calyx and usually with corolla; corolla commonly regular and of 6 free petals; staminate fls. with sepals in 2–4 whorls, larger than petals, stamens 6, 3 or indefinite, free or variously united; pistillate fls. with usually 3–6 free pistils, staminodia present or absent, ovary 1-celled with 1 of the 2 ovules soon aborting, stigma entire or lobed: fr. a drupe or drupaceous.

A. Stamens 9–24, free: lvs. with 5 or more palmate veins........................1. Menispermum
AA. Stamens 6, incompletely monadelphous: lvs. pinnately veined or with 3 palmate veins........................2. Cocculus

1. **MENISPERMUM,** L. Moonseed. Two species of twining diœcious vines with alternate long-petioled lvs., peltate near margin and often palmately lobed, usually 5–7-nerved: fls. unisexual, inconspicuous, small, panicled or cymose; sepals 4–8, in two series; petals 6–8, shorter than sepals; stamens 9–24, with filaments several times longer than the 4-celled anthers, or only 6 with no functional anthers in pistillate fls.; pistils 2–4, each with an enlarged flattened stigma, accompanied by sterile stamens: fr. a globose to ovoid drupe, the stone spiral-form with crest on sides and back. (Menisper-mum: Greek *moonseed,* in allusion to the shape of the stone within the fr.)

M. canadense, L. Common Moonseed. Suffrutescent vine to 15 ft.: herbage finely pubescent when young; lvs. orbicular-ovate, 4–8 in. across, shallowly peltate, entire or shallowly 5–7-palmately lobed, acute or obtuse, base truncate or obtuse: fls. greenish-white, many in loose axillary panicles to 1½ in. across, on slender peduncles 1–3 in. long, fls. minute; stamens about ⅙in. long and several times longer than sepals: fr. to ⅓in. across, bluish-black. Que. to Ga., Man. and Ark.—The other species, *M. dauricum,* DC., of E. Asia, is sometimes cult.; it has smaller glabrous lvs., deeply peltate.

2. **COCCULUS,** DC. About 11 species of climbing or erect diœcious shrubs.—Lvs. pinnately veined or with 3 main veins, entire or lobed, deciduous or persistent: fls. unisexual, in panicles or racemes; sepals and petals 6; stamens 6–9, anthers 4-celled or 4-lobed, staminodes 6 when present; pistils 3–6, free, cylindrical style terminated by lateral stigma: drupe subglobose, stone flattened, transversely ribbed on back and sides. (Coc-culus: Greek *small berry.*)

A. Plant a twining vine: lvs. ovate, often 3-lobed.................................. 1. *C. carolinus*
AA. Plant an erect shrub: lvs. lanceolate, simple.................................. 2. *C. laurifolius*

1. **C. carolinus,** DC. (*Menispermum carolinum,* L.). Carolina Moonseed. Trailing or twining vine to 15 ft.: lvs. deciduous, broadly ovate, 2–4 in. long, entire or lobed, cordate or obtuse at base, acute, densely pubescent to glabrous beneath, essentially glabrous above: fls. greenish-white, about 1/12in. across, in elongated terminal and axillary racemes: drupe red, ¼in. across. Va. to Fla., Kans. and Tex.

2. **C. laurifolius,** DC. (*Menispermum laurifolium,* Roxb.). Erect shrub to 15 ft., glabrous: lvs. persistent, oblong-lanceolate to narrowly elliptic, 2–5 in. long, acute to acuminate, cuneate at base, strongly 3-nerved, finely undulate, glossy: fls. in stout racemes: fr. about ⅛in. across. Himalayas.—Attractive shrub suitable for cult. in subtrop. regions.

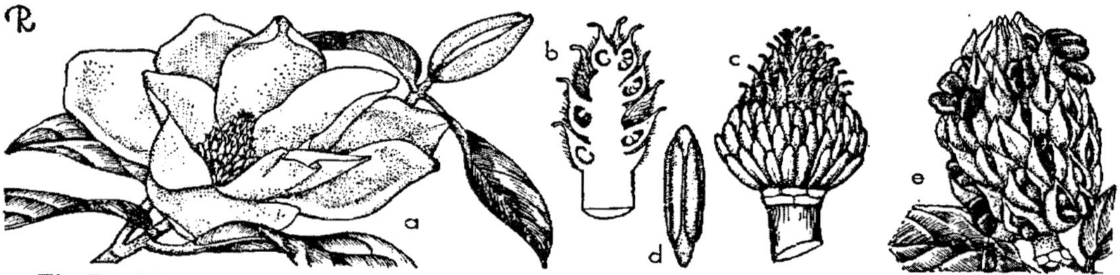

Fig. 74. Magnoliaceæ. *Magnolia grandiflora:* a, flowering branch, × ¼; b, gynœcium, vertical section, × ½; c, flower, less perianth, × ½; d, stamen, × ½; e, fruit, × ¼. (Redrawn from Sargent.)

74. MAGNOLIACEÆ. MAGNOLIA FAMILY

Ten genera of woody plants, 80 or more species, in trop., subtrop., and temp. parts of N. Amer. and Asia, including highly ornamental flowering trees and shrubs.—Lvs. alternate, mostly entire, usually pinnate-veined; stipules large (when present) and inclosing the budding lf., leaving characteristic scars: fls. commonly with all parts present, free and mostly distinct, the envelopes imbricated and deciduous and usually in whorls of 3, the petals 6 to many; stamens commonly numerous, with adnate anthers; pistils typically many and imbricated on an elongated receptacle, ovules 1 or 2 or sometimes more: fr. a follicle or samara, often all of them aggregated into a cone-like body.—Schisandra, a genus of twining diœcious or monœcious shrubs, is now placed in a family by itself (Schisandraceæ), and is not treated here.

A. Lvs. entire, acute or acuminate: ripe carpel a follicle.
  B. Pistil-bearing receptacle sessile within the fl. .... 1. MAGNOLIA
  BB. Pistil-bearing receptacle stalked within the fl. .... 2. MICHELIA
AA. Lvs. lobed, truncate at tip: ripe carpel a samara .... 3. LIRIODENDRON

1. **MAGNOLIA,** L. About 35 species of trees and tall shrubs in E. N. Amer., S. Mex., and Asia, some of them well-known ornamentals.—Evergreen or deciduous: lvs. mostly entire: fls. commonly showy, white, yellow, rose, or purple, appearing with or before the lvs., terminal; sepals 3 and petals 6–12; anthers falling early; pistils many, ovate, aggregated on a sessile receptacle or gynophore, more or less coherent into a cone-like somewhat fleshy brownish or scarlet body, each follicle dehiscent and 2-seeded (or by abortion 1-seeded), the seeds for a time suspended on thread-like cords. (Magno-lia: bears the name of Pierre Magnol, 1638–1715, botanist of Montpellier.)

A. Fls. appearing in advance of the lvs. or with the earliest foliage.
  B. Sepals petaloid.
    C. Petals and sepals usually 12 or more, four times as long as broad .... 1. *M. stellata*
    CC. Petals and sepals 9, twice as long as broad .... 2. *M. denudata*
  BB. Sepals differentiated from the petals.
    C. Color of fls. white.
      D. Lvs. broader below the middle; lf.-buds glabrous .... 3. *M. salicifolia*
      DD. Lvs. broader above the middle; lf.-buds pubescent .... 4. *M. Kobus*
    CC. Color of fls. purple to pink, sometimes white.
      D. Petals three times or more as long as sepals, purple outside .... 5. *M. liliflora*
      DD. Petals about twice as long as sepals, lighter colored to white outside .... 6. *M. Soulangeana*
AA. Fls. appearing after the lvs. or with the full-grown foliage.
  B. Color of fls. greenish-yellow, not showy .... 7. *M. acuminata*
  BB. Color of fls. white, showy.
    C. Lvs. cordate at base.
      D. Branchlets pubescent: lvs. 1–3 ft. long .... 8. *M. macrophylla*
      DD. Branchlets glabrous: lvs. 8–20 in. long .... 9. *M. Fraseri*
    CC. Lvs. narrowed at base, rarely subcordate.
      D. Foliage deciduous to semi-persistent.
        E. Length of lvs. 8–24 in.: fls. 6–10 in. across.
          F. Lf. cuneate at base, with usually more than 25 veins on each side of the midrib .... 10. *M. tripetala*
          FF. Lf. abruptly contracted at base, with usually less than 25 veins on each side of the midrib .... 11. *M. obovata*
        EE. Length of lvs. 3–6 in.: fls. 2–4 in. across.
          F. Young branches pubescent: sepals pink .... 12. *M. Sieboldii*
          FF. Young branches glabrous: sepals white .... 13. *M. virginiana*
      DD. Foliage persistent, rusty-tomentose beneath .... 14. *M. grandiflora*

1. **M. stellata,** Maxim. (*Buergeria stellata,* Sieb. & Zucc. *M. Halleana,* Hort.). STARRY MAGNOLIA. Glabrous shrub or small tree, blooming in advance of lvs. from furry buds: lvs. oblong-obovate to elliptic, 2–5 in. long, obtuse or short-pointed, narrowed to short petiole, dull green above and pubescent on veins beneath when young: fls. 3 in. across, white or with faint streaks of pink, fragrant; sepals and petals alike, usually 12 or more, 1½–2 in. long, oblong or oblanceolate: fr. an interrupted cone, with few pea-like scarlet seeds usually only 1 in a follicle. Japan. Var. **rosea,** Veitch, petals suffused pink outside.

2. **M. denudata,** Desr. (*M. conspicua,* Salisb. *M. Yulan,* Desf. *M. precia,* Loisel.). Tree, becoming 50 ft. high, with large fls. in advance of lvs. from hairy-furry buds: lvs. usually obovate, the apex broad-rounded or even retuse with a short stout point, 4–7 in. long and 3–4 in. broad, pubescent beneath when young: fls. about 5–6 in. across and cup-shaped but broader if fully opened, white (a purplish var.), fragrant; petals and sepals 9, similar, obovate or obovate-oblong, obtuse, concave, thick: fr. 3–4 in. long. China.

3. **M. salicifolia,** Maxim. (*Buergeria salicifolia,* Sieb. & Zucc.). Tree to 30 ft.; lf.-buds glabrous; fls. before lvs., from densely pubescent buds: lvs. elliptic to oblong-lanceolate, 3–5 in. long, acuminate, slightly appressed-pubescent beneath: fls. about 5 in. across, white, sometimes purplish at base outside, fragrant; petals 6, narrowly oblong-obovate; sepals lanceolate, about half as long as petals, greenish-white: fr. rose, to 3 in. long. Japan.

4. **M. Kobus,** DC. (*M. Thurberi,* Hort.). Tree to 30 ft., often shrubby in cult., producing white fls. in advance of foliage; lf.-buds pubescent, fl.-buds densely so: lvs. broad-obovate, 3–6 in. long, abruptly pointed, tapering below, pubescent below when young: fls. 4–5 in. across, white; petals 6, thin and spreading; sepals 3, narrow, about ½in. long: fr. 4–5 in. long, dark brown. (Kobus: Japanese name.) Japan.

5. **M. liliflora,** Desr. (*M. obovata,* Willd. not Thunb. *M. purpurea,* Curt. *M. discolor,* Vent. *M. denudata,* Schneid. not Desr.). Large often tree-like shrub to 10 ft., blooming in advance of foliage: lvs. obovate or obovate-oblong to nearly oval, acute or short-acuminate, tapering at base, 3–6 or 7 in. long, slightly pubescent above, finely pubescent on veins beneath: fls. lily-shaped, purple outside but whitish within, 3–4 in. long, slightly fragrant; sepals 3, about one-third or less length of the 6 oblong-obovate petals: fr. broad-

oblong, brownish. China. Var. **nigra**, Rehd. (*M. Soulangeana* var. *nigra*, Nichols.), has larger fls. about 5 in. long, dark purple outside, light purple inside; intro. from Japan.

6. **M. Soulangeana**, Soul. (*M. conspicua* var. *Soulangeana*, Lindl.). Hybrid of *M. denudata* and *M. liliflora*, intermediate between the parents, and the most popular of the precocious-blooming magnolias, being hardy and floriferous in the N.: large shrub or little tree, with broad-ovate to obovate to broad-oblong abruptly short-pointed lvs.: fls. open-bell-shaped, 4–6 in. across, purplish or rose-colored outside and white within, little if at all fragrant; sepals usually colored and half as long as petals but sometimes small and greenish; petals few, oblong-ovate to obovate. (Bears the name of the Chevalier Soulange-Bodin, who raised the hybrid in his garden in France.)—There are many races, often sold under separate specific names: var. **alba**, Rehd. (var. *alba superba*, Hort.), fls. white; var. **Alexandrina**, Rehd., very early, fls. white inside and deep purple outside toward base; var. **Lennei**, Rehd. (*M. Lennei*, Topf), more shrubby, fls. deep crimson to rosy-purple outside, white inside; var. **Norbertiana**, Rehd., late, fls. white and light purple, foliage showy; var. **rubra**, Hort. (forma *rubra*, Rehd. var. *rustica*, Rehd. *M. rustica rubra*, Nichols.), fls. rose-red; var. **speciosa**, Rehd., fls. white within, striped purple outside, later than the species and a little smaller and more durable.

7. **M. acuminata**, L. Cucumber-Tree. Large commanding tree reaching nearly 100 ft., with gray-brown deeply furrowed bark and usually glabrous branchlets: lvs. oblong-ovate to broad-oval to nearly obovate, 6–10 in. long, short-acuminate, obtuse or somewhat rounded at base: fls. with the lvs., glaucous-green or greenish-yellow, 2–3 in. high, not showy, acute sepals reflexing; petals 6, ovate or obovate: fr. ("cucumber") 3–4 in. long, oblong or cylindric, becoming pink or red. Forest tree, N. Y. to Ga. to Ill. and Ark., and often planted.

8. **M. macrophylla**, Michx. Large-leaved Cucumber-Tree. Spreading shrub or tree to 50 ft., with pubescent branchlets: lvs. very large, 1–3 ft. long, oblong-obovate, obtuse, auriculate-cordate at base, canescent beneath: fls. cup-shaped, 10–12 in. across, white, fragrant, appearing with the lvs.; sepals narrower than the 6 ovate petals: fr. 2½–3 in. long, ovoid or nearly globular, rose-color at maturity. Ky. to Fla., Ark. and La.

9. **M. Fraseri**, Walt. (*M. auriculata*, Lam.). Ear-leaved Umbrella-Tree. Tree to 45 ft., with branches and buds glabrous: lvs. 8–20 in. long, spatulate-obovate, auriculate at base, glabrous: fls. 8–10 in. across, white, fragrant; petals 6–9, with narrow claw; sepals 3, shed early, shorter than petals: fr. 3–5 in. long, ovoid to oblong, rose-colored. (Named for John Fraser, page 43.) Va. to Ga. and Ala.

10. **M. tripetala**, L. (*M. Umbrella*, Lam.). Umbrella-Tree. Medium-sized branching tree to 40 ft.: lvs. crowded at the ends of branches, oblong-obovate or somewhat narrower, 1–2 ft. long, short-acute, narrowed to short petiole, pubescent beneath when young: fls. white, 6–10 in. across, cup-shaped, with unpleasant odor, appearing when lvs. are well grown; sepals light green, reflexing; petals 6 or 9, oblong-obovate; filaments purple: fr. oval-oblong or ovoid, 3–4 in. long, rose-colored at maturity. Pa. to Ala., Ark. and Miss.

11. **M. obovata**, Thunb. not Willd. (*M. hypoleuca*, Sieb. & Zucc.). Great tree to 100 ft., with purplish branchlets: lvs. obovate to obovate-oblong, 8–16 in. long, nearly or quite obtuse, glaucous and pubescent beneath at least while young: fls. white, 6–7 in. across, appearing with the foliage, cup-shaped, fragrant; petals 6–9; filaments and pistils crimson: fr. oblong-cylindric, 6–8 in., scarlet. Japan.

12. **M. Sieboldii**, Koch (*M. Oyama*, Kort. *M. parviflora*, Sieb. & Zucc. not Blume). Small tree to 30 ft., with young branches and buds appressed-pubescent: lvs. elliptic to obovate, 3–6 in. long, obtusely pointed, pubescent beneath at first: fls. white, 3–4 in. across, cup-shaped, fragrant; petals usually 6; sepals somewhat shorter than petals, reflexed, pink; filaments and pistils crimson: fr. ovoid, 1½ in. long, crimson. Japan, Korea.

13. **M. virginiana**, L. (*M. glauca*, L.). Sweet Bay. Large shrub or tree to 60 ft., evergreen S. but deciduous N.: lvs. oblong or elliptic, 3–6 in. long, obtuse or nearly so, prominently glaucous-gray beneath: fls. white, globose, fragrant, 2–3 in. across, opening for a long time after lvs. appear; sepals obtuse, somewhat shorter than the 9–12 broad-obovate petals: fr. ellipsoidal, 1–2 in. long, red. Mass. to Fla. and Tex., near the coast.

14. **M. grandiflora**, L. Bull Bay. Great evergreen tree to 100 ft. and even more, with stiff lvs. shining green above and rusty-tomentose beneath, bearing large wax-like fragrant white fls. with the lvs. issuing from great silky-hairy conical buds: lvs. oval-oblong to obovate, tapering both ways, 4–8 in. long, sometimes becoming glabrate beneath: fls. 7–8 in. across, with petaloid sepals; petals 6–12, obovate; filaments purple; carpellary cone prominent: fr. cylindric, 3–4 in. long, heavy. Near the coast, N. C. to Fla. and Tex.—A well-known tree, commonly planted S., sometimes in named vars.

2. **MICHELIA, L.** About a dozen Asian trees and shrubs, differing technically from Magnolia in the mostly axillary infl., the pistil-bearing receptacle or gynophore distinctly stalked in the fl.; ovules usually more than 2 in each ovary. (Miche-lia: Peter A. Michel was a Florentine botanist, 1679–1737.)

M. fuscata, Blume (*Magnolia fuscata,* Andr.). BANANA-SHRUB. Large evergreen bush, 10–15 ft., much-branched but compact, the branchlets prominently brown-hairy: lvs. 2–4 in. long, elliptic to broad-oval or oval-oblong, rather bluntly pointed, becoming nearly or quite glabrous beneath, glossy above: fls. erect, 1–1½ in. across, brownish-yellow edged carmine or maroon, with pronounced banana fragrance, produced in spring and early summer; sepals and petals narrow-oblong; gynophore equalling or exceeding the linear anthers. China.—Useful shrub in southern states.

3. **LIRIODENDRON,** L. Two species of deciduous trees in N. Amer. and China.—Lvs. alternate, broadly truncate at apex, usually with 1 or 2 lobes on each side: fls. solitary, terminal, bell-shaped; sepals 3, petaloid, spreading; petals 6, upright; stamens and pistils numerous: fr. cone-like, brown. (Lirioden-dron: Greek *lily-tree.*)

L. Tulipifera, L. TULIP-TREE. WHITEWOOD. Tree to 200 ft., with spreading branches and unbranched trunk, glabrous: lvs. 3–5 in. long and almost as broad, with 1 apical and 1–4 basal lobes on each side, or sometimes entire: fls. greenish-yellow, orange within, about 2 in. long; stamens somewhat shorter than petals: fr. to 3 in. long. Mass. to Wis., Fla. and Miss.

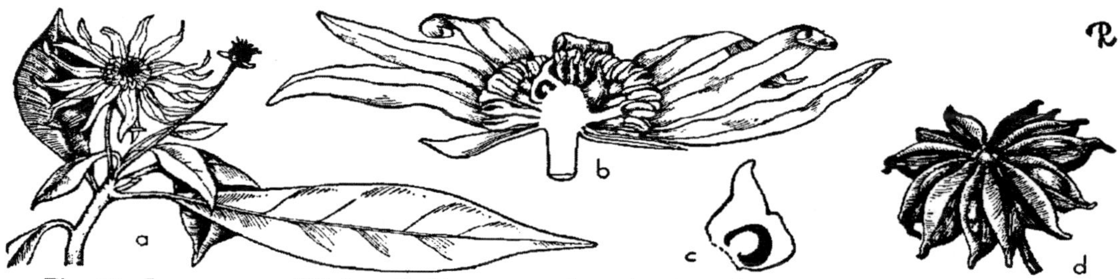

Fig. 75. ILLICIACEÆ. *Illicium floridanum:* a, flowering branch, much reduced; b, flower, vertical section, × 1; c, pistil, × 2; d, fruits, × 1.

75. ILLICIACEÆ. ILLICIUM FAMILY

A small family of a single genus, Illicium, of temp. and subtrop. regions of S. E. Asia and S. E. N. Amer.—Technical characters as given below for the genus. The family has long been united with Magnoliaceæ from which it is readily separated by the pistils arranged in a single whorl around the very short central axis.

ILLICIUM, L. About 40 species of shrubs and small trees of which 5 are indigenous to S. E. N. Amer.; one widely planted in tropics and subtropics.—Lvs. aromatic, persistent, alternate or pseudo-verticillate near twig tips, glabrous, with short petiole, entire: fls. bisexual, solitary or in 3's in the axils, small, inclined or nodding, yellow or purplish; perianth-segms. 7–33, not differentiated into calyx and corolla but inner ones often becoming progressively larger than the outer, latter often bract-like; stamens 4–50; pistils usually 7–15, free, 1-ovuled, in a single whorl within the fl., becoming dry and woody tardily dehiscent follicles, sometimes collectively termed a follicetum; style 1, conduplicate, stigmatic along most its length. (Illic-ium: the Latin word for *allurement* or *that which entices,* from the agreeable odor.)

I. anisatum, L. (*I. religiosum,* Sieb. & Zucc.). Small tree: lvs. alternate, elliptic, about 3 in. long, somewhat acuminate but obtuse: fls. greenish-yellow, mostly solitary, on short bracted peduncles, not fragrant; petals many, narrow, spreading. Japan, Korea. —Grown in southeastern states. **I. floridanum,** Ellis, sometimes cult., is distinguished by longer naked peduncles and reddish-purple fls.; Fla. to La.

76. CALYCANTHACEÆ. CALYCANTHUS FAMILY

Two genera and about 6 species of shrubs with aromatic bark, native in N. Amer. and E. Asia.—Lvs. opposite, entire, short-petioled, exstipulate: fls. solitary, on lateral leafy branches, bisexual, regular; sepals and petals similar, imbricated in many series; stamens many, inserted on the receptacle, the filaments short; pistils

Fig. 76. CALYCANTHACEÆ. *Calycanthus floridus:* a, flowering branch, × ¼; b, flower, × 1; c, flower, vertical section, × 1 (p pistil, s stamen); d, pistil, vertical section, × 5.

numerous, distinct, inserted on the inner face of the hollow receptacle, each 1-celled and 1–2-ovuled; style filiform: fr. consisting of many 1-seeded achenes completely inclosed by the ovoid or pyriform receptacle.

A. Stamens many: fls. brownish-purple. . . . . 1. CALYCANTHUS
AA. Stamens 5 or 6: fls. yellow. . . . . 2. CHIMONANTHUS

1. **CALYCANTHUS,** L. (*Butneria,* Duham.). SWEET-SCENTED SHRUB. SWEET-SHRUB. Four species of deciduous shrubs in N. Amer., often grown for ornament and the sweet fragrance of the fls.—Winter-buds small, naked: fls. large, terminal on leafy branches; sepals and petals brownish-purple; stamens many. (Calycan-thus: from Greek for *calyx* and *flower,* referring to the colored calyx.)

A. Lvs. densely pubescent beneath. . . . . 1. *C. floridus*
AA. Lvs. glabrous or nearly so beneath. . . . . 2. *C. occidentalis*

1. **C. floridus,** L. CAROLINA ALLSPICE. To 10 ft., with branchlets and petioles pubescent: lvs. ovate or elliptic, to 5 in. long, acute or obtuse, dark green above, pale or grayish-green and densely pubescent beneath: fls. about 2 in. across, fragrant, dark reddish-brown: fr. obovoid or oblong, about 2½ in. long, contracted at mouth. Va. to Fla.

2. **C. occidentalis,** Hook. & Arn. (*C. macrophyllus,* Hort.). Tall erect shrub to 10 ft.: lvs. ovate to oblong-lanceolate, 3–7 in. long, acute, green and sometimes slightly pubescent beneath: fls. 3 in. across, slightly fragrant, light brown: fr. campanulate, 1½–2 in. long, not markedly contracted at mouth. Calif.

2. **CHIMONANTHUS,** Lindl. (*Meratia,* Loisel.). Two species of evergreen or deciduous shrubs in China and Japan, one grown for ornament.—Often united with Calycanthus but differing in its scaly winter-buds, the yellow fls. appearing long before the lvs. on scaly branchlets axillary on branches of the previous year, and the 5 or 6 stamens. (Chimonan-thus: Greek *winter flower.*)

C. præcox, Link (*C. fragrans,* Lindl. *Calycanthus præcox,* L. *Meratia præcox,* Rehd. & Wils.). Deciduous shrub to 10 ft.: lvs. elliptic-ovate to oblong-lanceolate, 3–6 in. long, acuminate, bright green and lustrous above, glabrous beneath: fls. ¾–1½ in. across, fragrant, yellow, the inner sepals striped purplish-brown. Var. **grandiflorus,** Makino (*C. fragrans* var. *grandiflorus,* Lindl.), has larger brighter colored fls.

77. ANNONACEÆ. CUSTARD-APPLE FAMILY

Probably 600 species of shrubs and trees, in 40–50 genera, in the tropics of Old and New World, with extensions into temp. regions, some grown for edible fr., for ornament, and for perfume.—Lvs. alternate, simple, entire: fls. mostly bisexual, regular but of odd form or appearance, often in tones of brown and tawny-yellow, for the most part not showy; sepals and petals often much alike; sepals 3 or calyx 3-lobed; petals usually 6, mostly valvate; stamens many, with long adnate anthers disposed spirally; pistils usually many and separate, ovules 1 to several, in some genera pistils on an elongated receptacle and becoming an aggregate fleshy syncarp in which the seeds (frs.) are imbedded, but fr. in other genera dry or capsular.

A. Fr. a fleshy syncarp or "apple" formed by the fusion of pistils and receptacle. . . . . 1. ANNONA
AA. Fr. a cluster of distinct pistils.
  B. Plant a tree.
    C. Fls. purplish: fr. 2 in. or more long. . . . . 2. ASIMINA
    CC. Fls. greenish to yellowish: fr. 1 in. long. . . . . 3. CANANGA
  BB. Plant climbing. . . . . 4. ARTABOTRYS

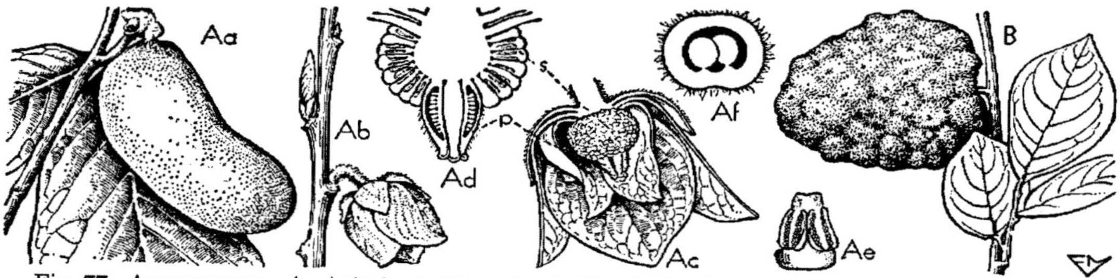

Fig. 77. ANNONACEÆ. A, *Asimina triloba:* Aa, fruit, × ¼; Ab, flowering branch, × ½; Ac, flower, perianth excised, × 1; Ad, same, vertical section, less perianth, × 2; Ae, stamen, × 5; Af, ovary, cross-section, × 10. B, *Annona Cherimola:* fruit, × ⅙. (p pistil, s stamens.)

1. **ANNONA,** L. CUSTARD-APPLE. More than 50 shrubs and trees, mostly in trop. Amer., some of which yield important edible frs.—Lvs. firm or coriaceous, without stipules, deciduous or persistent: fls. super-axillary, often opposite the lvs., solitary or in clusters; calyx usually tubular and 3-parted; petals 6 in 2 series, the inner series sometimes represented by scales or even wanting; stamens many, crowded, with fleshy filaments bearing pollen-sacs; pistils many, 1-ovuled, crowded: syncarp large and fleshy, formed by fusion of pistils and receptacle. (Anno-na: Latinized from native name.)—In the American tropics several species of Annona are known for their edible frs. and they are often planted; within the region of the U. S. they are of less importance although grown more or less by amateurs and experimentally. One species, *A. glabra*, L., the Pond-Apple, of no value for fr., is native in S. Fla. and southward.

A. Fr. spiny and holding together: inner petals nearly as large as outer ones..........1. *A. muricata*
AA. Fr. without spiny processes: inner petals minute and scale-like.
B. Lvs. velvety-pubescent beneath..........2. *A. Cherimola*
BB. Lvs. not velvety beneath.
C. The fr. of loosely cohering pistils that separate and fall apart..........3. *A. squamosa*
CC. The fr. with solid exterior, pistils marked by depressions..........4. *A. reticulata*

1. **A. muricata,** L. SOURSOP. GUANABANA. Small branching tree, evergreen: lvs. thick, obovate-oblong to elliptic, 2–5 in. long, short-acute, shining above and becoming glabrous beneath: fls. about 1½ in. or more across; exterior petals thick and valvate, interior ones thinner and somewhat smaller and imbricate: fr. 6–8 in. or more long, ovoid, more or less depressed or heart-shaped at base, dark green, with very many soft spines pointing toward apex, with slightly acid white juicy pulp. Trop. Amer.; now widespread and frequently planted.—Used in making a drink, in flavoring, and for jelly and conserves.

2. **A. Cherimola,** Mill. CHERIMOYA. Small erect or somewhat spreading tree to 25 ft., with grayish-pubescent branchlets: lvs. deciduous, ovate to ovate-lanceolate, 4–10 in. long, obtuse or nearly so, dull above, velvety-pubescent beneath: fls. solitary or 2 or 3 together, nodding on short peduncles, long and narrow, about 1 in. long, brown- or yellowish-tomentose outside; outer petals narrow, inner ones very small and scale-like: fr. of many kinds in the cult. races, from nearly globular to ovoid to conical, 3–5 in. long, sometimes nearly smooth and with finger-print depressions, sometimes with tubercles marking the pistils, the pulp white, somewhat acid, delicious, the seeds readily separated from it. (Cherimola is an adaptation of its aboriginal name.) Andes of Peru and adjacent regions but widely spread in cult., subtrop.

3. **A. squamosa,** L. SUGAR-APPLE. SWEETSOP. Small branching tree to 20 ft.: lvs. more or less distichous, deciduous, lanceolate to oblong-lanceolate, 3–6 in. long, short-acute, dull above, lightly hairy when young but becoming glabrous: fls. 2–4 together or sometimes solitary, narrow, about ¾–1 in. long, erect, greenish-yellow; exterior petals narrow, thick, interior ones minute: fr. globular, cordate-ovoid or conical, 2–3 in. diam. (size of orange), yellowish-green, glaucous, comprised of loosely cohering rounded pistils that readily fall apart, the pulp custard-like and very sweet. Trop. Amer., widely dispersed in cult.—Fr. used in sherbets and for jellies and preserves.

4. **A. reticulata,** L. COMMON CUSTARD-APPLE. BULLOCKS-HEART. Small branching tree to 25 ft., with gray-pubescent growth becoming glabrate: lvs. mostly close together, deciduous or semi-deciduous, lanceolate to oblong-lanceolate, 4–8 in. long, long-acuminate, glabrous or nearly so: fls. several on nodding peduncles, narrow, about 1 in. long; exterior petals fleshy, yellowish, the interior ones very small and scale-like: fr. heart-shaped or nearly globular, 3–5 in. diam., smooth, the pistils shown by rhomboid areas, parts not separating; pulp tallow-like, adhering to seeds. Trop. Amer., now widespread.—Although much planted, the fr. is inferior to cherimoya and sugar-apple.

2. **ASIMINA,** Adans. Eight species of shrubs or trees in N. Amer., with more or less edible frs.—Deciduous or evergreen: lvs. alternate, usually large: fls. axillary, solitary or few, nodding, short-stalked; sepals 3, deciduous; petals larger, 6, the inner smaller and usually erect; pistils 3–15: fr. of 1 to few oval to oblong berries with large compressed seeds. (Asim-ina: Assiminier, French-Indian name.)

A. triloba, Dunal (*Annona triloba,* L.). PAPAW. Small tree to 40 ft., dark-pubescent on young growth: lvs. oblong-obovate, 6–12 in. long, short-petioled: fls. about 2 in. across, dark purple; sepals ovate; outer petals nearly round, spreading, inner smaller, erect: fr. 3–7 in. long, 1–2 in. thick, yellow at first, finally brown. Ont. and Mich. to Fla. and Tex.—Commercial vars. are being developed for their edible frs.

3. **CANANGA,** Hook. f. & Thoms. (*Canangium,* Baill.). Two or 3 trees in Malaya, prized for the fragrant extracts.—Fls. rather large, in axillary fascicles; sepals 3, ovate and valvate; petals 6 in 2 series, long and flat and nearly equal; stamens many, crowded, the anthers with connectives prolonged into a point; pistils many in 2 series, maturing into several oblong stalked fleshy many-seeded frs. (Canan-ga: from a native name.)

C. odorata, Hook. f. & Thoms. YLANG-YLANG, fls. the source of the famous perfume of the Pacific isls.; sometimes planted in S. Fla. Tree of medium to rather large size with somewhat drooping branches: lvs. oblong-ovate, 6–8 in. long, long-acuminate with sharp point, glossy above, slightly pubescent beneath: fls. many, very fragrant, greenish to yellowish, narrow, hanging; sepals ovate, pubescent; petals lanceolate, acute, 2 in. long more or less: fr. nearly 1 in. long, greenish, oblong-cylindric. S. India, Java, and the Philippines.

4. **ARTABOTRYS,** R. Br. TAIL-GRAPE. About 40 evergreen woody trop. climbers or semi-scandent shrubs, with very fragrant fls.—Climbing by means of thickened peduncles that hook or grip the support: lvs. glabrous: fls. remarkable for a constriction in the corolla above the stamens, beyond which the 6 petals (in 2 series) are free and either spreading or somewhat incurved; stamens packed together; pistils several, rarely many, 2-ovuled: fr. of separate olive-like pistils clustered on the hardened receptacle. (Artab-otrys: Greek combination, *hanging grapes,* from the suspended frs.)

A. odoratissimus, R. Br. CLIMBING YLANG-YLANG. Strong climber or scrambler, the young growth becoming glabrous: lvs. oblong to broad-lanceolate, 3–6 in. long, acuminate but with a blunt point, glossy above: fls. 1 or 2 on the hooked peduncle, greenish or yellowish, very fragrant; petals becoming 1½ to about 2 in. long, constricted near base: fr. of a few clustered yellow smooth fragrant pointed drupe-like pistils about 1¼ in. long. India to China and the Philippines.—Sometimes planted in S. Fla.

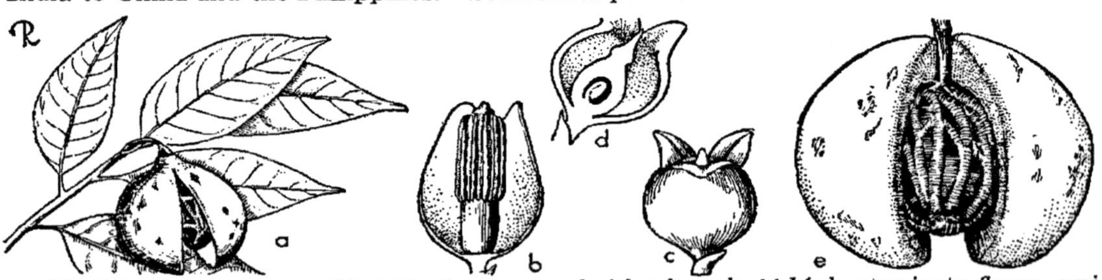

Fig. 78. MYRISTICACEÆ. *Myristica fragrans:* a, fruiting branch, × ¼; b, staminate flower, perianth removed to show andrœcium, × 2; c, pistillate flower, × 1; d, same, vertical section, × 1; e, fruit showing aril (mace) about seed, × ½.

78. MYRISTICACEÆ. NUTMEG FAMILY

Eight genera and more than 100 species of evergreen diœcious trees, widely distributed in the tropics, the following species yielding the well-known nutmeg and mace.—Lvs. alternate, entire, exstipulate: fls. small, regular, in axillary fascicles or umbels; calyx 3-lobed; corolla none; stamens 2–30, monadelphous; ovary 1, sessile and superior, free, 1-celled, 1-ovuled; style short or none: fr. fleshy, dehiscing into 2, rarely 4, valves; seed with a fleshy laciniate aril.

MYRISTICA, L. Nutmeg. About 80 species in farther India, Australia and Pacific isls.—Characters mainly of the family: lvs. usually white or glaucous beneath, the 3 nerves not parallel and often sunken above: filaments united into a column, the anthers elongated and connate. (Myris-tica: from Greek, alluding to aromatic qualities of these plants.)

M. fragrans, Houtt. Tall glabrous tree: lvs. elliptic- or oblong-lanceolate, 2–5 in. long, petioled, pale yellow-brown: fr. pyriform to nearly globular, 1½–2 in. long, hanging, reddish or yellowish, splitting into 2 valves disclosing the scarlet aril or mace surrounding the nutmeg which is inclosed in a hard shell. Molucca.—Planted widely in tropics, and sometimes seen in economic collections under glass.

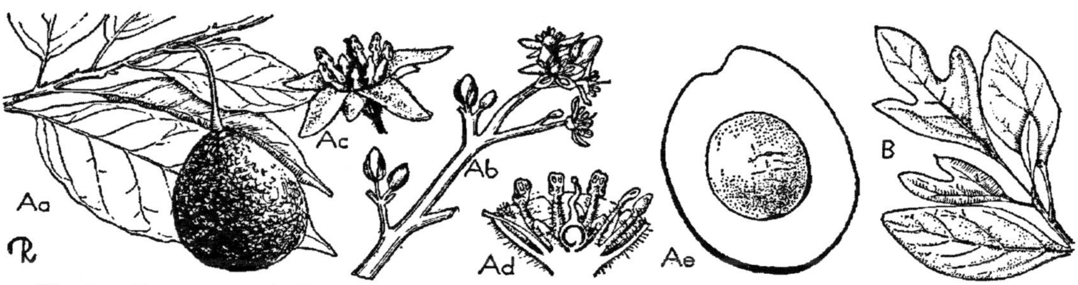

Fig. 79. Lauraceæ. A, *Persea americana:* Aa, fruiting branch, × ⅙; Ab, twig with flowers, × ½; Ac, flower, × 1; Ad, same, vertical section, × 2; Ae, fruit, vertical section, × ¼. B, *Sassafras albidum:* foliage, × ¼.

79. LAURACEÆ. LAUREL FAMILY

About 40 genera and 1,000 species of aromatic trees and shrubs, of wide distribution in trop. and a smaller number in temp. regions; a few genera are cult. for ornament, and the avocado, cinnamon, and camphor are articles of commerce.—Lvs. alternate, rarely opposite, simple, usually leathery and persistent, sometimes membranaceous and deciduous, punctate, exstipulate: fls. yellow or greenish, regular, bisexual or unisexual, the infl. various; calyx usually 6-parted, the segms. in 2 whorls; petals 0; stamens in 3–4 whorls of 3 each, some often reduced to staminodia, perigynous or epigynous; anthers 2–4-celled, opening by uplifting valves; ovary usually superior and free, rarely inferior, 1-celled, 1-ovuled; style filiform or short: fr. a berry or drupe, indehiscent.

A. Lvs. feather-veined (see also *Cinnamomum Camphora*).
  B. Foliage persistent.
    C. Perfect stamens 12 or more: lvs. 1–3½ in. long .... 1. Laurus
    CC. Perfect stamens 9: lvs. 2½–16 in. long.
      D. Fls. in few-fld. cymes: odor of crushed lvs. mild: calyx persistent below fr.. 2. Persea
      DD. Fls. in umbels: odor of crushed lvs. pungent: calyx deciduous .... 3. Umbellularia
  BB. Foliage deciduous.
    C. Plant a shrub: lvs. entire, pale but not glaucous beneath .... 4. Lindera
    CC. Plant a tree: lvs. sometimes lobed, always glaucous beneath .... 5. Sassafras
AA. Lvs. with 3–5 main longitudinal veins.
  B. The lvs. alternate, sometimes lobed: anthers all introrse .... 5. Sassafras
  BB. The lvs. mostly opposite, entire: inner anthers extrorse .... 6. Cinnamomum

1. LAURUS, L. Laurel. Sweet Bay. Two species of trees, one native in the Medit. region, the other in the Canary Isls. and Madeira; one widely grown as a tub-plant.—Fls. small, bisexual or unisexual, in small axillary umbels which in bud are inclosed in a globose involucre; calyx 4-parted; perfect stamens usually 12 or more, staminodia often present, usually 4 in fertile fls.; ovary scarcely sunk in the receptacle, the style short: fr. a small berry. (Lau-rus: ancient name.)

L. nobilis, L. Evergreen tree to 40 ft., but cult. as a tub-plant and sheared into various forms, glabrous: lvs. stiff, dull green, lanceolate or oblong-lanceolate, 1–3½ in. long, short-petioled: fls. yellowish, inconspicuous, blooming in early spring: berries dark purple, ½–¾ in. long. Medit. region.—There are forms with curled, variegated and willow-shaped lvs. This is the laurel of history. Other plants known as laurel are *Kalmia latifolia, Umbellularia californica,* and several species of Prunus, as *P. Laurocerasus, P. lusitanica,* and *P. caroliniana.*

2. **PERSEA,** Gaertn. Trees and shrubs, of about 50 species, native in N. and S. Amer., a few from S. E. Asia, and 1 from the Canary Isls., including the avocado which is widely grown in the tropics for its edible frs.—Lvs. leathery, feather-veined: fls. bisexual, small, in cymes or small panicles; calyx persistent, deeply 6-parted; stamens usually 12, in 4 series, the inner reduced to gland-like staminodia, anthers 4-celled; ovary sessile, tapering into slender style: fr. globose or oblong, baccate. (Per-sea: ancient name.)

A. Frs. large and fleshy, 2–8 in. long.
B. Perianth puberulous within; ovary pilose............................1. *P. americana*
BB. Perianth essentially glabrous within; ovary glabrous............................2. *P. leiogyna*
AA. Frs. small and scarcely fleshy, about ¾in. long............................3. *P. indica*

1. **P. americana,** Mill. (*P. gratissima*, Gaertn.). AVOCADO. Large broad-topped tree to 60 ft.: lvs. petioled, oblong- or elliptic-lanceolate to oval, 3–16 in. long, acute or truncate at base, usually somewhat glaucous below: fls. small, greenish, shortly pedicellate, in broad compact panicles at the ends of the young branchlets; calyx gray-tomentulose on both sides; perfect stamens 9, with 2 oval flattened orange-colored glands at the base of each: fr. large and fleshy, from 2–8 in. long, commonly pyriform, ovate or spherical, yellow-green to maroon and purple in color, the skin thick and sometimes woody. Trop. Amer.—Formerly called "alligator-pear." Cult. in the warmest parts of the U. S. as West Indian and Guatemalan avocado. Var. **drymifolia,** Blake (*P. drymifolia*, Schlecht. & Cham.), MEXICAN AVOCADO of cult., lvs. mostly elliptic and acute at each end, anise-scented when crushed; fr. thin-skinned.

2. **P. leiogyna,** Blake. TRAPP AVOCADO. Differs from *P. americana* in perianth glabrous within and sparsely pilose without, pistil and staminodes glabrous. Probably trop. Amer.

3. **P. indica,** Spreng. Handsome small tree sometimes planted for ornament in southern regions: lvs. petioled, elliptic- or lanceolate-oblong, 3–8 in. long, attenuate-acute, glabrous: fls. small, white, in panicles 3–6 in. long, the peduncles compressed and the branches 3–5-fld.: fr. ovoid, about ¾in. long, scarcely fleshy, very dark blue. Canary Isls., Madeira, Azores.

3. **UMBELLULARIA,** Nutt. Evergreen pungently aromatic tree; 1 species of Ore. and Calif. sometimes grown as an ornamental shade tree.—Lvs. alternate, entire, coriaceous, involute in bud: fls. bisexual, several in peduncled umbels which are clustered in the terminal axils; calyx 6-parted, deciduous; petals 0; stamens 9, those of third whorl with 2 orange glands at base: fr. a drupe. (Umbellula-ria: from Latin *umbellula*, a small umbel.)

U. californica, Nutt. (*Tetranthera californica*, Hook. & Arn.). CALIFORNIA BAY or CALIFORNIA-LAUREL. Tree 50–80 ft. high: lvs. 2½–5 in. long, obtusely acuminate, lanceolate to ovate-oblong, shining: fl.-clusters 1½–2 in. across, yellowish-green: fr. purplish to yellow-green, 1 in. long.

4. **LINDERA,** Thunb. Deciduous or evergreen aromatic trees and shrubs; about 60 species in Asia and N. Amer.—Diœcious or polygamous: fls. small, in axillary clusters, with involucre of 4 deciduous scales; sepals mostly 6; stamens 9, anthers 2-valved; pistillate fls. with 9–15 staminodia and a globose ovary: fr. a subglobose drupe. (Linde-ra: for J. Linder, 1676–1723, Swedish physician.)

L. Benzoin, Blume (*Laurus Benzoin*, L. *Benzoin æstivale*, Nees). SPICE-BUSH. Deciduous glabrous shrub 4–18 ft. high: lvs. entire, alternate, elliptic to obovate, 2–5 in. long, acute or short-acuminate, short-petioled: fls. small, yellowish, in dense subsessile clusters: fr. about ⅓in. long, scarlet. Me. to Ont., Fla. and Tex.

5. **SASSAFRAS,** Nees. Three species of aromatic deciduous trees in N. Amer., China and Formosa, the American one grown as an ornamental.—Lvs. alternate, entire or 3-lobed: diœcious; fls. unisexual or apparently bisexual, in several-fld. racemes before the lvs.; calyx 6-parted; staminate fls. with 9 stamens in 3 whorls, those of inner whorl with 2 stalked glands at base, anthers 4-celled; pistillate fls. with an ovoid ovary, slender style: fr. an ovoid drupe. (Sas-safras: Spanish *salsafras* or Saxifraga, supposed to have similar medicinal properties.)

S. albidum, Nees (*Laurus albida*, Nutt. *S. variifolium*, Kuntze. *S. Sassafras*, Karst. *S. officinale*, Nees & Eberm. *S. officinale* var. *albidum*, Blake). SASSAFRAS. Tree occasionally up to 125 ft. high, with yellowish-green soon glabrous twigs: lf.-blades ovate to elliptic, 3–5 in. long, entire or 3-lobed, soon glabrous; petioles up to 1 in. long: fr. ½in. thick, dark blue. Me. to Mich. south to Fla. and Tex.

6. **CINNAMOMUM,** Blume. More than 50 species of evergreen trees and shrubs native in Asia and Australia, a few grown for ornament far S. and for their aromatic and medicinal products.—Lvs. opposite or sometimes alternate, mostly strongly 3-nerved from the base: fls. small, usually bisexual or sometimes unisexual and then the staminate fls. smaller than pistillate, borne in axillary and subterminal panicles; calyx-tube short, the 6 segms. almost equal; perfect stamens 9 or less, in 3 unlike series, the fourth series of staminodes, anthers 4-celled; ovary sessile, tapering into style: fr. a berry, in the cup-like perianth the segms. of which are deciduous or persistent. (Cinnamo-mum: ancient Greek name.)

A. Buds inclosed by large imbricated scales.......1. *C. Camphora*
AA. Buds naked or with very small scales.
  B. Lvs. opposite.
    C. Lf. caudate- or long-acuminate.......2. *C. Cassia*
    CC. Lf. obtuse or subacute.......3. *C. zeylanicum*
  BB. Lvs., at least the upper, alternate.......4. *C. japonicum*

1. **C. Camphora,** Nees & Eberm. (*Laurus Camphora*, L. *Camphora officinarum*, Nees). CAMPHOR-TREE. Stout dense-topped tree to 40 ft., with enlarged base, twigs and bruised lvs. having marked camphor odor; buds inclosed by orbicular imbricated scales: lvs. alternate, long-petioled, ovate-elliptic, acuminate, 2–5 in. long, pinkish on the young growths, smooth and shining above, whitish or glaucous beneath: fls. yellow, in axillary panicles shorter than the lvs.; perianth-lobes deciduous in age: fr. about ⅜in. diam. China, Japan.

2. **C. Cassia,** Nees & Eberm. (*Laurus Cassia*, Nees). CASSIA-BARK-TREE. Handsome tree with aromatic bark sometimes used as a substitute for cinnamon, young branches somewhat 4-angled: lvs. oblong to nearly lanceolate, stiff, 3–6 in. long, caudate- or long-acuminate, slender-petioled: fls. small, in axillary or terminal silky-tomentose panicles 3–6 in. long; perianth-lobes persistent in fr.: fr. size of a small pea. China.

3. **C. zeylanicum,** Blume (*Laurus Cinnamomum*, L.). CINNAMON-TREE. Tree to 20 or 30 ft., the bark yielding the cinnamon of commerce: lvs. ovate or ovate-lanceolate, very stiff, 4–7 in. long, obtuse or somewhat acute: fls. yellow-white, in loose somewhat silky panicles which often exceed the lvs.: fr. ⅜in. long, dry, pointed. India, Malaya, and widely cult. in tropics.

4. **C. japonicum,** Sieb. (*C. pedunculatum*, Nees). Glabrous tree: lvs. at least the upper alternate, long-petioled, oblong-lanceolate, acuminate, 2–5 in. long: fls. in axillary or subterminal corymbs which almost equal the lvs.: fr. globose-ovoid, about ¼in. long. Japan, Korea, Formosa.

80. PAPAVERACEÆ. POPPY FAMILY

About 25 genera and 200 species of herbs, rarely shrubs, of wide distribution but most abundant in the north temp. zone, many of them choice fl.-garden subjects.—Juice usually milky and often colored: lvs. alternate, rarely the upper ones opposite or verticillate, entire or lobed or divided, exstipulate: fls. solitary or in clusters, bisexual, regular; sepals 2 or seldom 3, caducous; petals 4–6, rarely more or wanting, deciduous, imbricated, often wrinkled; stamens numerous, in whorls, hypogynous, free, with filiform filaments; pistil 1 with superior 1-celled 2- to many-carpelled ovary or pistils 6 or more and each with superior 1-celled 1-carpelled ovary, in either case ovules many, with parietal placentæ as many as stigmas which are simple or divided, style short or none: fr. a caps. dehiscent by valves or apical pores or when pistils several or more of as many follicles.

A. Stigma prominently expanded and disk-like, extending over openings of caps.....1. PAPAVER
AA. Stigma not expanded and disk-like.
  B. Foliage spiny.......2. ARGEMONE
  BB. Foliage not spiny (in cult. kinds).
    C. Lvs. multifid into linear segms.
      D. Sepals united, forming a conical cap which is pushed off as the fl. opens....3. ESCHSCHOLZIA
      DD. Sepals separate, falling as fl. opens.......4. HUNNEMANNIA
    CC. Lvs. not multifid into linear segms.
      D. Fr. of several distinct linear follicles, finally breaking transversely between the seeds.......5. PLATYSTEMON
      DD. Fr. a caps.
        E. Petals 0.......6. MACLEAYA
        EE. Petals present, although deciduous.
          F. Fls. normally white.
            G. Plant scarcely 1 ft. high: fls. 1–2 in. across.......7. SANGUINARIA
            GG. Plant 3–8 ft. high: fls. 5–6 in. across.......8. ROMNEYA
          FF. Fls. yellow or blue to purple or red.
            G. Plant a shrub.......9. DENDROMECON
            GG. Plant an herb.

H. Caps. dehiscing by short teeth or valves near summit: stigmas 4 or more, sessile .... 10. MECONOPSIS
HH. Caps. dehiscing by valves to the base: stigmas 2, or if 4 on a distinct style.
I. Style elongate: caps. ovoid .... 11. STYLOPHORUM
II. Style lacking or nearly so: caps. linear.
J. Diam. of fls. about 2 in.: caps. 6–12 in. long .... 12. GLAUCIUM
JJ. Diam. of fls. less than 1 in.: caps. 1–2 in. long .... 13. CHELIDONIUM

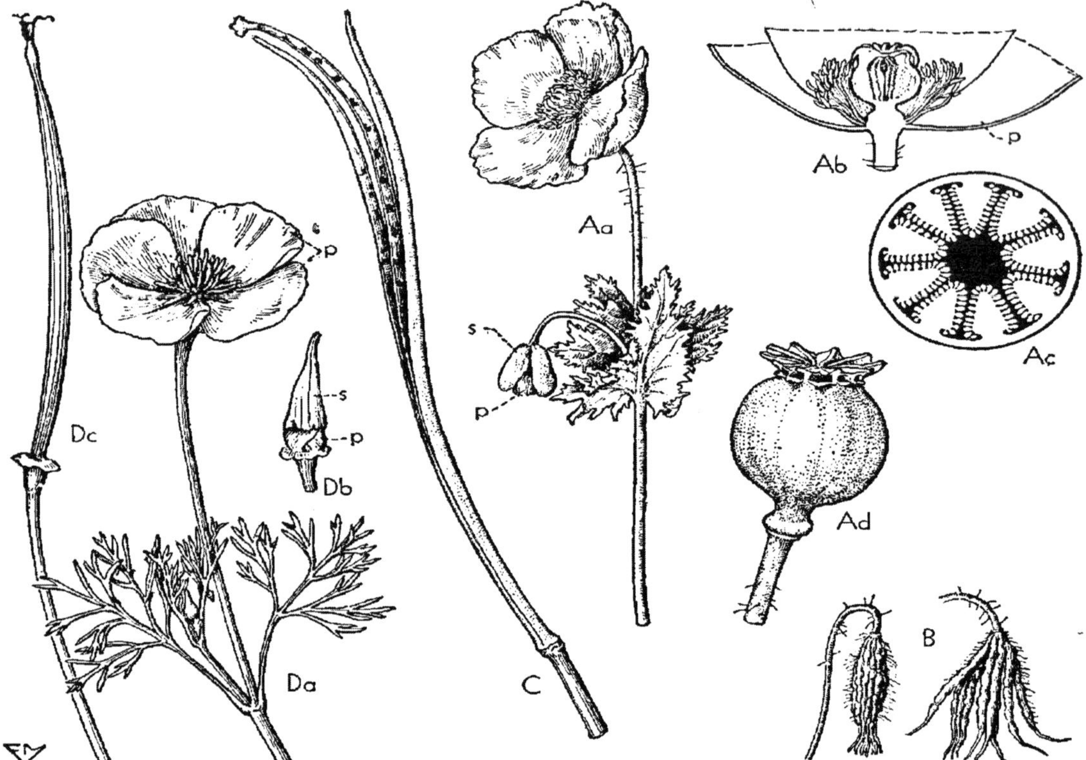

Fig. 80. PAPAVERACEÆ. A, *Papaver somniferum:* Aa, flowering branch, × ¼; Ab, flower, vertical section, × ½; Ac, ovary, cross-section, × 2; Ad, capsule, × ½. B, *Platystemon californicus:* fruits, × 1. C, *Glaucium flavum:* capsule, × ½. D, *Eschscholzia californica:* Da, flowering branch, × ½; Db, bud, × ½; Dc, capsule, × ½. (s sepal, p petal.)

1. **PAPAVER,** L. POPPY. Probably about 50 species, although many more have been described, mostly in the Old World, but a few native in W. N. Amer.; poppies are amongst the best-known garden fls.—Ann., bien., or per. herbs, rarely subshrubs, hispid or glaucous, with milky juice: lvs. lobed or dissected: fls. showy, solitary on long peduncles, the buds nodding; sepals 2, rarely 3; petals usually 4; stamens many: caps. globose, ovoid or oblong, dehiscent under the top by transverse pores between the placentæ which project into center of caps., the stigmas united into a radiate persistent disk. (Papa-ver: old Latin name for the poppy.)

A. Fls. on leafless scapes: lvs. all basal.
B. Lvs. 1-pinnate, the blades 1½–3 in. long: scapes 1–2 ft. high .... 1. *P. nudicaule*
BB. Lvs. 2–3-pinnate, the blades mostly not over 1 in. long: scapes usually ½–1 ft. high .... 2. *P. alpinum*
AA. Fls. on branching more or less leafy sts.
B. St.-lvs. with broad clasping base.
C. Lvs. pinnately lobed .... 3. *P. glaucum*
CC. Lvs. coarsely dentate, more or less lobed.
D. Petioles of basal lvs. 1–2 in. long: caps. globose .... 4. *P. somniferum*
DD. Petioles of basal lvs. 4–6 in. long: caps. club-shaped .... 5. *P. pilosum*
BB. St.-lvs. not clasping, the base narrowed.
C. Peduncle with coarse appressed hairs.
D. The fls. without bracts.

E. Caps. club-shaped: petals about 1 in. long.........................6. *P. atlanticum*
EE. Caps. subglobose: petals 2–3 in. long..............................7. *P. orientale*
DD. The fls. subtended by large leafy bracts............................8. *P. bracteatum*
CC. Peduncle with weak spreading hairs...................................9. *P. Rhœas*

1. **P. nudicaule,** L. ICELAND POPPY. Cespitose nearly stemless per., more or less hirsute, somewhat glaucous: lvs. all radical and petioled, pinnately lobed or cleft, the segms. oblong and entire or lobed: scapes erect, slender, much exceeding the lvs., usually 1–2 ft. high: fls. fragrant, 1–3 in. across; petals obovate, sinuate, the 2 inner ones smaller, white with a yellow base or yellow with a greenish base, but often orange or reddish in cult.: caps. oblong or obovate-globose, usually densely hispid, about ⅔in. long. Arctic regions in eastern and western hemispheres.—There are double-fld. kinds and many named color forms. **P. amurense,** Hort., is a form from E. Siberia with primary lf.-blades somewhat divided and orange fls.

2. **P. alpinum,** L. ALPINE POPPY. Cespitose nearly stemless per.: lvs. mostly radical, glaucous, glabrous, petioled, sometimes pilose, 2–3-pinnately parted into short narrow lobes: peduncles 5–12 in. high, usually appressed-hairy, sometimes with single small lf.: fls. 1–1½ in. across; petals round-obovate, white or with yellow base to pink or orange: caps. oblong to obovate, ½–⅔in. long. Alps.—**P. thibeticum,** Hort., is similar in dissected lvs. but with blades 2½–4 in. long, scapes 1–2 ft. high, fls. yellow or orange; Tibet.

3. **P. glaucum,** Boiss. & Haussk. TULIP POPPY. Glaucous ann. branching at the base, to about 2 ft. high, glabrous except a few short appressed bristles on peduncles: st.-lvs. clasping and cordate at base, radical lvs. narrowed into petiole, pinnately lobed or parted, the lobes triangular and usually dentate: fls. 3–4 in. across; petals scarlet, spotted at base, the 2 inner shorter, forming a loose cup: caps. about ¾in. long. Syria to Iran.

4. **P. somniferum,** L. OPIUM POPPY. Glaucous ann. glabrous or rarely slightly hairy, 2–4 ft. high: lower lvs. narrowed into short petiole, upper clasping, cordate, unequally and coarsely dentate or more or less lobed, 4–10 in. long, oblong: fls. 3–4 in. across; petals orbicular, entire, undulate or cut, from white through pink and red to purple, but not yellow or blue: caps. 1–2 in. long. Greece, Orient; sparingly run wild in N. Amer.—Many double-fld. sorts are advertised, some with fringed petals, also many color cultivars. The species is widely grown for its caps. from the milky juice of which opium is derived.

5. **P. pilosum,** Sibth. & Smith (*P. olympicum,* Sibth. & Smith). OLYMPIC POPPY. Per., sts. several, erect, branched, leafy, many-fld., with spreading or appressed hairs, 1½–3 ft. tall: lvs. appressed-hairy, oblong to ovate-oblong, irregularly crenate-serrate to somewhat lobed: peduncles about 6 in. long; petals bright red or orange, rounded, 1½ in. long: caps. oblong-clavate, about ½in. long; stigmas 6–7. Asia Minor.

6. **P. atlanticum,** Ball. Cespitose per. 6–24 in. high, sts. erect to ascending, appressed-hairy, branched near base, scapiform: lvs. with stiff appressed hairs, oblong-oblanceolate, coarsely and irregularly crenate-serrate, basal 6–10 in. long, petioled, cauline reduced and subsessile: peduncles up to 16 or 18 in.; sepals hairy; petals obovate, orange to reddish, 1¼–1½ in. long: caps. clavate, glabrous, almost 1 in. long. Morocco.—Cult. material seen under *P. rupifragum,* Boiss. & Reut. (a species characterized by almost glabrous lvs. and sepals) belongs to *P. atlanticum.*

7. **P. orientale,** L. ORIENTAL POPPY. Robust stiff-hairy per. 3–4 ft. high: lvs. to 1 ft. long and regularly pinnatifid, the segms. oblong-lanceolate and sharply lobed or toothed: peduncles with coarse appressed white hairs; fls. 4–6 in. and more across; petals sometimes 6, obovate, narrowed below, scarlet with black spot at base; stigmas 11–15: caps. about 1 in. long. Medit. region to Iran.—Runs into many variations, some without the dark spot, some with bracts, others double-fld., and many color vars. due to hybridizing with *P. bracteatum.*

8. **P. bracteatum,** Lindl. Similar to *P. orientale* but differing in having lvs. concave not flat, 2 large leafy bracts at the base of the fls., the blood-red petals not spotted or the claw dark violet, stigmas 16–18, the teeth of the disk spreading not reflexed. Medit. region to Iran.

9. **P. Rhœas,** L. CORN POPPY. Slender branching ann. 1–3 ft. high, with spreading shaggy hairs or rarely glabrescent: lvs. short, more or less clustered at base of peduncles, irregularly pinnatifid and divided, rarely nearly entire, the segms. lanceolate and serrate: fls. 2 in. or more across; petals orbicular, entire or sometimes crenate and incised, cinnabar-red, deep purple to scarlet, rarely white, white or reddish margined, sometimes dark-spotted: caps. less than 1 in. long. (Rhœas: classical name for the corn poppy.) Eu. and Asia; run wild in N. Amer.—Very variable, and known to gardeners mostly in the cultivars. The most popular race in gardens is the Shirley poppy, in many kinds.

2. **ARGEMONE,** L. PRICKLY-POPPY. Prickly herbs grown as annuals for their showy fls., of about 10 species in N., Cent. and S. Amer.—Robust and branching, glaucescent, with yellow juice: lvs. pinnatifid, the segms. sinuate-dentate with spiny teeth: fls. large; sepals 2 or 3, with horn-like appendage; petals 4–6; stamens many;

carpels 4–6 with many-ovuled placentæ, the style very short or none and 3–6-radiate stigma: caps. oblong, prickly, opening at top by 3–6 valves. (Argemo-ne: classical name for another plant.)

A. Sts. densely spiny.. 1. *A. platyceras*
AA. Sts. practically spineless.. 2. *A. grandiflora*

1. **A. platyceras,** Link & Otto. Whole plant very spiny, 1–4 ft. high: fls. 2 in. or more across, white or rarely purple, subtended by 2–3 leafy bracts: caps. 1–2 in. long, completely covered with rigid spines. N. and S. Amer.—Variable; a var. with rose fls. is advertised.

2. **A. grandiflora,** Sweet. Sts. glabrous or only slightly spiny, 1–3 ft. high: lvs. white-veined, only weakly spiny: fls. 3–6 near together, 2 or more in. across, white: caps. about 1 in. long, with a few spines. S. W. Mex.

3. **ESCHSCHOLZIA,** Cham. Ann. or per. herbs widely grown for their showy fls.; probably about a dozen species in W. N. Amer., or by some authors separated into more than 100 species.—Glabrous and glaucous, with watery juice: lvs. multifid: fls. large, solitary on long peduncles; receptacle prominently hollowed and surrounding base of pistil; sepals coherent into a narrow pointed hood which is pushed off over the bud as the petals expand; petals 4, inserted on the receptacle together with the numerous stamens which have short filaments and linear anthers; style very short, stigma 4–6-lobed, spreading: caps. very long and slender, dehiscent by 2 valves from base to tip, after separating from receptacle. (Eschschol-zia: after J. F. Eschscholtz, 1793–1831, member of Kotzebue's scientific expedition.)

E. californica, Cham. California-Poppy. Per. but cult. as an ann., 1–2 ft. high, erect or diffuse: lvs. ternately dissected into linear or oblong segms., long-petioled: fls. 2–3 in. across, opening in sunshine, pale yellow to orange, deep orange at base of petals; rim of receptacle expanded: caps. 3–4 in. long, strongly ribbed. Calif., Ore.—Many named variants, such as var. **aurantiaca,** Hort., bright rich orange, fls. 2½–3 in. across.

4. **HUNNEMANNIA,** Sweet. Mexican Tulip-Poppy. Per. herb grown for its showy yellow fls., but usually treated as an ann.; only 1 species in xerophytic regions of Mex.—Closely related to Eschscholzia but differing in the 2 separate sepals, the receptacle scarcely dilated, and the orange-colored stamens. (Hunneman-nia: John Hunneman, English botanist, died 1839.)

H. fumariæfolia, Sweet. Golden-Cup. Two ft. high: lvs. glaucous, ternately dissected into linear obtuse segms.: fls. 2–3 in. across, yellow: caps. about 4 in. long.

5. **PLATYSTEMON,** Benth. Low ann. herb, of 1 species in Calif., or by some authors divided into 60 species, sometimes grown in fl.-gardens.—Branching at base, erect or decumbent, hirsute or glaucescent, with colorless juice: lvs. narrow, entire, lower alternate, upper opposite or verticillate: fls. solitary, on erect elongated peduncles; sepals 3; petals 6 or sometimes more, deciduous or rarely persistent; stamens numerous, unequal, the filaments petal-like; pistils 6–20 or more, distinct, with linear stigmas: fr. of 6–20 linear torulose follicles, distinct at maturity, finally breaking transversely between the seeds. (Platyste-mon: from Greek for *broad* and *stamen*, referring to the flattened filaments.)

P. californicus, Benth. Cream-Cups. From 6 in.–1 ft. high: lvs. linear-oblong, sessile or clasping: fls. about 1 in. across, light yellow or cream-colored. Calif. to Utah.

6. **MACLEAYA,** R. Br. Two species of per. herbs native in China and Japan, grown in the hardy border.—Erect, glaucescent, with saffron juice: lvs. petioled, lobed, cordate at base, white-glaucous beneath: fls. in elongated terminal panicles; sepals 2, cream-colored; petals 0; stamens many, with filiform filaments not exceeding the anthers; style very short, the 2 stigmas at first connate with style, at length diverging: caps. ovoid, short-stalked, 2-valved, dehiscent to base, 1- to several-ovuled. (Maclea-ya: after Alex. Macleay, 1767–1848, Colonial secretary of New S. Wales.)

M. cordata, R. Br. (*Bocconia cordata*, Willd. *B. japonica*, Hort.). Plume-Poppy. Tree Celandine. Five to 8 ft. high: lvs. usually very large, long-petioled, heart-shaped, about 7-lobed, the lobes sinuate or dentate, glabrous or pubescent beneath: panicles sometimes 1 ft. long, on erect branches. China, Japan.

7. **SANGUINARIA,** L. One species of E. N. Amer.—Per. herb with thick rootstock, orange-red juice: lvs. basal, palmately lobed: scapes normally 1-fld.; sepals 2; petals 8–12; stamens about 24; stigma 2-grooved; style short: caps. ellipsoid, dehiscent to the base, the valves persistent. (Sanguina-ria: because of the reddish juice.)

S. canadensis, L. Bloodroot. Glabrous, glaucous: scape 5–8 in. tall, finally overtopped by the solitary lf. which is reniform to cordate and becomes 6–12 in. wide, 4–7 in. long, on a petiole 6–14 in. high: fls. 1–2 in. across, white, sometimes pale purple or pink. N. S. to Fla. and Neb. Var. **multiplex,** Wils., has double fls.

8. **ROMNEYA,** Harvey. Erect per. herbs or subshrubs with colorless juice, native in S. Calif. and Mex., planted for the showy fls.—Glabrous and glaucous; sts. branching: lvs. petioled, pinnatifid: fls. large, white, solitary at the ends of the branches; sepals 3, with a broad membranaceous dorsal wing; petals 6, in 2 series; stamens many; stigmas numerous, connate at base into ring: caps. ovate, narrowed at top, densely covered with stiff yellowish bristles, dehiscing to the middle by 7–12 valves. (Rom-neya: after T. Romney Robinson, astronomer and discoverer of the plant about 1845.)

A. Sepals glabrous, beaked: peduncles mostly glabrous. . . . . 1. *R. Coulteri*
AA. Sepals appressed-setose, beakless: peduncles setose below the fls. . . . . 2. *R. trichocalyx*

1. **R. Coulteri,** Harvey. Matilija-Poppy. Much-branched above, 3–8 ft. high: lvs. 2–4 in. long, lobes lanceolate, the terminal one 3-cleft, sparingly dentate, the margins sometimes slightly ciliate: fls. fragrant, about 6 in. across; calyx glabrous, somewhat beaked: caps. with spreading hairs. (Named after Thos. Coulter, page 110.) S. Calif.

2. **R. trichocalyx,** Eastw. Much like the preceding but sts. more slender: lvs. dissected into narrower lobes: peduncles setose at summit; sepals setose and beakless; petals less crinkled; fls. with disagreeable odor. S. Calif.

9. **DENDROMECON,** Benth. One polymorphous species, or by some authors divided into 20 species; a shrub native in Calif., grown for its bright yellow fls.—Glabrous, branching, the juice not milky: lvs. rigid, entire: fls. solitary, terminal on the short branches; sepals 2; petals 4; stamens many, with short filaments; stigmas 2, sessile: caps. linear-curved, grooved, 2–4 in. long, dehiscing to the base by 2 valves the margins of which bear the placentæ. (Dendrome-con: from Greek for *tree* and *poppy*.)

D. rigida, Benth. Bush-Poppy. Rigid leafy shrub from 2–10 ft. high, with whitish bark: lvs. glaucescent, lanceolate to ovate-lanceolate, acute, mucronate, coriaceous, reticulately veined: fls. 1–2 in. across, golden-yellow. Calif., dry parts of coast ranges and Sierras.

10. **MECONOPSIS,** Vig. Ann. and per. herbs, suitable for borders and rock-gardens; about 30 species in northern extra-trop. regions, mostly in Asia.—Juice yellow: lvs. entire, lobed or dissected, the radical petioled, the st.-lvs. short-stalked or sessile: fls. solitary or in cymose racemes or panicles, yellow, reddish, or blue; sepals 2; petals 4 or sometimes 5–9; stamens many; stigmas forming a globular mass on the 4- to many-carpelled ovary: caps. oblong, club-shaped or rarely cylindrical, with 4 or more intruding placentæ, dehiscing by short teeth or valves near the summit. (Meconop-sis: Greek for *poppy-like*.)—Some of the recently discovered Asiatic species are likely to appear in the trade.

A. Fls. yellow, erect. . . . . 1. *M. cambrica*
AA. Fls. blue to red, pendulous.
B. Basal lvs. in a dense rosette; lvs. pinnately cut: fls. as many as 17 to a st. . . . . 2. *M. napaulensis*
BB. Basal lvs. not in dense rosette; lvs. toothed, sometimes lobed: fls. about 6 to a st. . . . . 3. *M. betonicifolia*

1. **M. cambrica,** Vig. Welsh-Poppy. Erect branching per., forming large tufts with thick roots, 1–1½ ft. high, sparsely hairy or glabrescent: lvs. glaucous beneath, pinnate, the segms. ovate or lanceolate and dentate or lobed: fls. 2–3 in. across, pale yellow, on long peduncles which exceed the lvs. (Cambrica: Cambrian or Welsh.) E. Eu.—There is a double-fld. var.

2. **M. napaulensis,** DC. (*M. Wallichii,* Hook.). Satin-Poppy. Branching per. up to 8 ft. high, more or less stiff-hairy and puberulent: basal lvs. pinnate, up to 21 in. long, cauline

shorter and entire to pinnately lobed: petals red to purple or blue, 4, obovate to rounded, 1¼–1¾ in. long: caps. oblong, appressed-bristly. Cent. Asia.

3. **M. betonicifolia,** Franch. (*Cathcartia betonicifolia,* Prain). Branching per. up to 5 ft. high, glabrous or with scattered reddish hairs: lvs. oblong, coarsely crenate-toothed, the lower petioled, with reddish bristles especially on margins: petals blue, 1–2 in. long: caps. oblong, glabrous. Yunnan.—The form in cult. is var. **Baileyi,** Edwards (*M. Baileyi,* Prain), with ovary covered with yellowish bristles; Tibet (named for Col. F. M. Bailey, who visited Tibet in 1911).

11. **STYLOPHORUM,** Nutt. A genus of about 3 species, native in E. N. Amer. and E. Asia.—Herbs, with stout rootstocks, yellow sap, pinnatifid lvs.: fls. clustered or solitary; buds nodding; sepals 2; petals 4; stamens many; stigma 2–4-lobed, radiate; style distinct: caps. linear or ovoid, dehiscing to the base. (Styloph-orum: from Greek *style-bearing.*)

S. diphyllum, Nutt. (*Chelidonium diphyllum,* Michx.). CELANDINE-POPPY. Glaucous, sparingly pubescent, 12–18 in. high: lvs. basal and cauline, 4–10 in. long, the divisions obovate: fls. 2–4, 1–1½ in. across, yellow; sepals hairy. Pa. to Tenn., Wis. and Mo.

12. **GLAUCIUM,** Mill. HORNED-POPPY. SEA-POPPY. A dozen or perhaps more species of chiefly bien. and per. herbs, native in the Medit. region, one often grown for borders or edgings.—Glaucous, with saffron-colored juice: lvs. lobed or dissected: fls. large, solitary, on long peduncles, yellow or red; sepals 2; petals 4; stamens many; stigma almost sessile, 2-lobed: caps. very long and linear, 2-celled by a spongy false partition, dehiscent to the base. (Glauc-ium: from Greek, referring to the glaucous foliage.)

G. flavum, Crantz (*G. luteum,* Scop.). Stout, branching, 2–3 ft. high: lower lvs. pinnatifid and petioled, the upper clasping and sinuately lobed and toothed: fls. golden-yellow or orange, about 2 in. across: caps. 6–12 in. long. Eu.; nat. in E. N. Amer.—There is a form with parti-colored fls. (var. *tricolor*).

13. **CHELIDONIUM,** L. CELANDINE. A monotypic genus native in temp. Eu. and Asia, comprising a bien. or per. herb, often seen in old gardens, sometimes double-fld.—Erect, loosely-branching, with acrid saffron-colored juice: lvs. deeply pinnatifid, the segms. ovate or obovate, crenate or lobed, sometimes 2-pinnatifid: fls. in a small peduncled umbel; sepals 2; petals 4; stamens many; ovary of 2 carpels, the style very short with 2-lobed stigma: caps. linear, dehiscing from base upward. (Chelido-nium: Greek for *swallow;* the fls. bloom about the time the swallow comes.)

C. majus, L. From 2–4 ft. high: lvs. glaucous beneath: fls. yellow, ½–⅔in. across: caps. 1–2 in. long. Eu.; nat. in E. N. Amer. as a weed about yards.

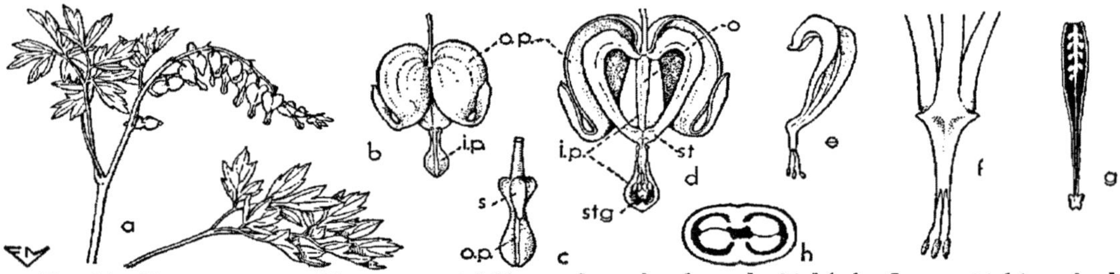

Fig. 81. FUMARIACEÆ. *Dicentra spectabilis:* a, flowering branch, × ⅛; b, flower, × ½; c, bud, side view, × 1; d, flower, outer petal removed, × ¾; e, three connate stamens, × ¾; f, same, distal end, × 2; g, pistil, vertical section, × 1; h, ovary, cross-section, × 8. (i.p. inner petal, o.p. outer petal, o ovary, s sepal, st stamens, stg stigma.)

81. FUMARIACEÆ. FUMITORY FAMILY

Five genera and about 170 species of herbaceous plants, mostly natives of the north temp. zone.—The family is closely allied to the Papaveraceæ with which it is often united, but differs in its watery juice, the irregular fls. with 2 small scale-like sepals, 4 petals in 2 series, one or both of the outer ones spurred or gibbous, the 2 inner smaller, crested and united over the stigma; stamens 6, in 2 series, the filaments often united; ovary 1-celled, ovules 1 to many on usually 2 parietal placentæ: fr. 1-seeded and indehiscent or a 2-valved several-seeded caps.

A. Fls. 2-spurred or with 2 basal gibbosities.
  B. Plant vine-like: petals permanently united....................1. ADLUMIA
  BB. Plant not climbing: petals only slightly united....................2. DICENTRA
AA. Fls. 1-spurred with a spur-like nectary....................3. CORYDALIS

1. **ADLUMIA,** Raf. One climbing bien., native in E. N. Amer., a vine ornamental in both foliage and fl.—Lvs. 3–4-pinnate, the lfts. delicate and cut-lobed: fls. in axillary drooping panicles; petals permanently united into a narrow cordate-ovate spongy corolla which is persistent and incloses the fr.; stamens monadelphous below, diadelphous above, adherent to corolla; stigma 2-crested: caps. oblong, slightly dehiscent by 2 valves, the seeds not crested. (Adlu-mia: Major John Adlum, 1759–1836, was an American grape experimenter.)

A. fungosa, Greene (*A. cirrhosa,* Raf.). CLIMBING FUMITORY. MOUNTAIN FRINGE. ALLEGHENY-VINE. Delicate vine climbing by the slender petioles: fls. about ½in. long, white or purplish. Ont. to Mich. south to N. C.

2. **DICENTRA,** Bernh. (*Bikukulla,* Adans.). Per. herbs of about 15 species in N. Amer. and Asia, a few grown in the border for their attractive fls. and foliage.—Habit erect, diffuse, or sometimes climbing, often stemless, with rhizome horizontal and branching or more or less bulbous: lvs. ternately compound or dissected: fls. in racemes; pedicels 2-bracted; petals slightly united into a heart-shaped or 2-spurred corolla; style slender, the stigma 2–4-crested or sometimes 2–4-horned: caps. oblong or linear, dehiscent to the base by 2 valves, the seeds crested. (Dicen-tra: from Greek for *two-spurred.*)

A. Racemes simple.
  B. Fls. rosy-red: rootstocks not bearing tubers....................1. *D. spectabilis*
  BB. Fls. white to yellow, tinged with pink or purple: rootstocks tuber-bearing.
    C. Spurs long, divergent....................2. *D. Cucullaria*
    CC. Spurs short, rounded....................3. *D. canadensis*
AA. Racemes compound.
  B. Corolla separating to much below middle; crests of inner petals projecting........4. *D. eximia*
  BB. Corolla not separating to middle; crests of inner petals not projecting.
    C. Outer petals rose-purple: lvs. green above, glaucous beneath....................5. *D. formosa*
    CC. Outer petals white to yellow: lvs. densely glaucous on both sides....................6. *D. oregana*

1. **D. spectabilis,** Lem. (*Dielytra spectabilis,* Don). BLEEDING-HEART. From 1–2 ft. high, the sts. leafy: lvs. broadest in the group, the segms. obovate or cuneate: fls. in simple secund racemes, rosy-red, 1 in. or more long; corolla heart-shaped, with 2 short obtuse spurs; inner petals white, protruding. Japan.—There is a white-fld. var.

2. **D. Cucullaria,** Bernh. (*Fumaria Cucullaria,* L.) DUTCHMANS-BREECHES. From 5–15 in. high, from a bulbous base: lvs. basal, ternately compound, the segms. linear to oblanceolate: raceme secund, with 4–10 fls.; fls. white or tinged with pink at base, yellow at tip, with 2 widely divergent spurs longer than the pedicel. N. S. to Mo. and N. C.

3. **D. canadensis,** Walp. SQUIRREL-CORN. From 5–12 in. high, rootstock with many small tubers: lvs. as in the preceding but glaucous beneath: raceme with 4–8 fls.; fls. greenish-white, tinged with purple, with short rounded spurs. N. S. to Minn., Mo. and Ky.

4. **D. eximia,** Torr. From 1–2 ft. high, stemless, from a branching scaly rootstock, glabrous and somewhat glaucous: lvs. decompound, the segms. broadly oblong: scape slender, about equalling lvs.; fls. in compound racemes, rose or pink, less than 1 in. long; corolla tapering from cordate base into a narrow neck, separating to much below the middle, the inner petals with projecting crests. N. Y. to Ga.—There is a var. with more finely cut foliage.

5. **D. formosa,** Walp. (*Fumaria formosa,* Andr.) WESTERN BLEEDING-HEART. Very similar to the above but the rose-purple corolla with a very short neck, the petals united to above the middle, and the crests of the inner petals scarcely surpassing the spreading tips of the outer petals. B. C. to Cent. Calif.

6. **D. oregana,** Eastw. (*D. glauca,* Hort.). Very similar to *D. formosa* but the lvs. densely glaucous: fls. broader toward base; outer petals white at base, yellow at tips; inner petals rose-tipped. Siskiyou Mts., Ore. to W. Calif.

3. **CORYDALIS,** DC. (*Capnoides,* Adans.). Ann. or mostly per. herbs of about 100 species of the north temp. zone and S. Afr., a few used in gardens for the fls. and foliage.—Erect or sometimes prostrate or climbing, the per. ones with rhizome

or tubers: lvs. basal and cauline, pinnately decompound: fls. in racemes; sepals 2, deciduous or lacking; petals 4, one of the outer pair spurred at base; style slender; stigmas 2, several-rayed: caps. elongate, 2-valved; seeds appendaged. (Coryd-alis: Greek name for the crested lark.)

A. Plants tuberous, 2–3-lvd.: fls. purplish.
  B. St. not bracted near base; floral bracts entire .... 1. *C. cava*
  BB. St. plainly bracted near base; floral bracts lobed .... 2. *C. solida*
AA. Plants not tuberous, many-lvd.: fls. yellowish except in no. 5.
  B. St. mostly less than 1 ft. high: style deciduous.
    C. Lower petioles not winged: fls. golden: seeds shining .... 3. *C. lutea*
    CC. Lower petioles winged: fls. yellowish-white: seeds dull .... 4. *C. ochroleuca*
  BB. St. 1–3 ft. high: style persistent.
    C. Fls. pink to purplish with yellow tips and spur: caps. not tortuous .... 5. *C. sempervirens*
    CC. Fls. yellow: caps. tortuous .... 6. *C. ophiocarpa*

1. **C. cava,** Schweigg. & Körte (*Fumaria bulbosa* var. *cava*, L. *C. bulbosa*, Pers.). Per. from 6–14 in. high, glabrous, the sts. from a tuber having a deep depression on the lower side: lvs. 2–3, green, petioled, 3–6 in. wide, twice-ternate, the segms. wedge-shaped or oblong, more or less lobed: fls. purplish, almost 1 in. long, the subtending bracts ovate, entire. Cent. Eu. Var. **albiflora,** Bailey (*C. albiflora*, Kit.), fls. white.

2. **C. solida,** Sw. (*Fumaria bulbosa* var. *solida*, L. *F. solida*, Mill. *C. bulbosa*, DC. *C. Halleri*, Willd.) Like the preceding, but with solid tuber, conspicuous bract on st. below the lvs.; bracts of infl. lobed. Var. **australis,** Hausmann, fls. larger, earlier.

3. **C. lutea,** DC. (*Fumaria lutea*, L.). Per. from 6–15 in. high, from a vertical rootstock, many-stemmed: lvs. pale green, 1–4 in. wide, long-petioled, 2–3-pinnate, the segms. subelliptic, entire or lobed: fls. golden-yellow, ¾in. long, spur short and gibbous; bracts linear-lanceolate, up to ⅛in. long: fruiting pedicels ¼–¾in.; pod about ½in. long, seeds glossy. S. Eu.

4. **C. ochroleuca,** Koch (*C. capnoides*, DC. not L.). Like the preceding but with winged petioles, yellowish-white fls.; bracts lance-ovate, toothed: pod longer than pedicels, seeds dull. S. Eu.

5. **C. sempervirens,** Pers. (*Fumaria sempervirens*, L. *C. glauca*, Pursh). ROMAN WORMWOOD. Ann. or bien. 1–2 ft. high, freely branched, glaucous: lvs. 1–2½ in. wide, short-petioled, the upper subsessile, 2-pinnate, the segms. obovate or cuneate, entire or lobed: fls. numerous, panicled, ½–¾in. long, pink to purplish with yellow tips and spur: caps. linear, 1–2 in. long. N. S. to Ga. and Alaska.

6. **C. ophiocarpa,** Hook. f. & Thoms. Per. 2–3 ft. high, sts. slender, branched: lvs. glaucous beneath, blades 4–8 in. long, basal ones long-petioled, cauline shorter, all 2-pinnate, the segms. oblong-elliptic, ¼–2 in. long, entire or lobed: fls. yellow, many, to ½in. long, in racemes opposite the lvs., spur short, constricted at base; bracts subulate, entire: caps. tortuous, ½–1 in. long, much exceeding pedicel and with persistent style. Himalayas. —Plants cult. as *C. cheilanthifolia*, Hemsl. (a Chinese species with basal lvs., smaller and more sharply cut lf.-segms., simple st. not much longer than lvs.) are mostly *C. ophiocarpa*.

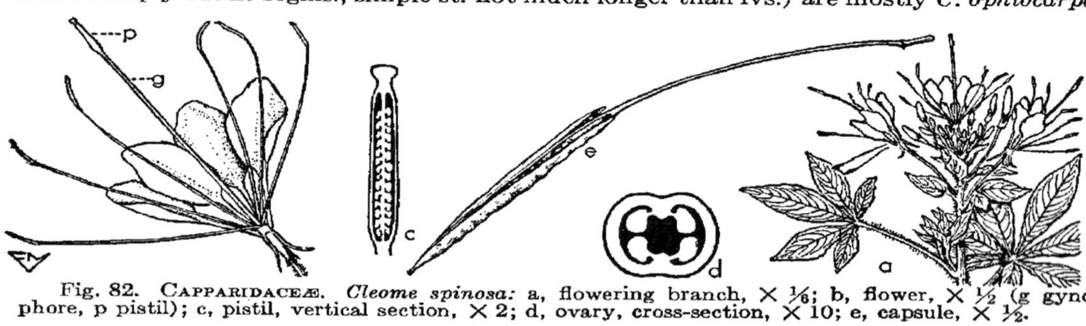

Fig. 82. CAPPARIDACEÆ. *Cleome spinosa:* a, flowering branch, × ⅙; b, flower, × ½ (g gynophore, p pistil); c, pistil, vertical section, × 2; d, ovary, cross-section, × 10; e, capsule, × ½.

82. CAPPARIDACEÆ. CAPER FAMILY

About 35 genera and 450 species of herbs and shrubs, mostly of trop. and subtrop. distribution, a few sometimes grown as ornamentals and one furnishing the capers of commerce.—Sap watery: lvs. alternate, rarely opposite, simple or palmately compound, margins mostly entire: fls. usually bisexual, more or less irregular, in axillary or terminal racemes or solitary; sepals 4–8, free or united; petals 4–8, rarely 0, sessile or clawed; disk ring- or scale-like or sometimes tubular at base of petals; stamens 6 to many, not tetradynamous, inserted on the receptacle; ovary sessile or stipitate, usually 1-celled with 2 parietal placentæ, many-ovuled: fr. a caps. or berry, rarely a drupe, usually (and in ours) on an elongating stipe or gynophore beyond the corolla.

A. Plant a shrub: fr. a berry..1. CAPPARIS
AA. Plant an herb: fr. a caps..2. CLEOME

1. **CAPPARIS,** L. Shrubs or trees of wide distribution in warm regions, of about 150 species; the fl.-buds of *C. spinosa,* when pickled, are the well-known capers.—Lvs. simple, petioled, usually with spiny or bristle-like stipules: fls. white, often bracted; sepals 4; petals 4; stamens many, the filaments filiform and free; ovary long-stalked, the stigma sessile: berry many-seeded, globose or cylindrical, rarely dehiscent. (Cap-paris: ancient classical name of the caper.)

C. spinosa, L. CAPER-BUSH. A straggling spiny shrub 3 ft. or more high: lvs. roundish or ovate, 1–2 in. long, the petiole short with 2 reflexed spines at base: fls. axillary, solitary on thick peduncles, white; petals about 1 in. long, exceeded by the numerous stamens; gynophore about twice as long as corolla. Medit. region. Var. **rupestris,** Boiss., has straight subulate spines which are soon deciduous.

2. **CLEOME,** L. About 75 species of herbs or subshrubs, mostly in the tropics, particularly of Amer. and Afr., sometimes grown for their odd fls.—Lvs. simple or 3–7-foliolate, the lfts. entire or serrulate: fls. solitary or racemose; sepals 4; petals 4, nearly equal, cruciate, entire; stamens 6, rarely 4; ovary stalked, with a gland at base, style very short or none: caps. linear to oblong, many-seeded. (Cleo-me: derivation uncertain.)

A. Plant spiny: fls. rose-purple to white..1. *C. spinosa*
AA. Plant not spiny: fls. orange-yellow..2. *C. lutea*

1. **C. spinosa,** L. (*C. pungens,* Willd. *C. gigantea,* Hort. not L.). GIANT SPIDER-FLOWER. A clammy-pubescent strong-scented ann. 3–4 ft. high: lvs. 5–7-foliolate, the lfts. oblong-lanceolate, lower lvs. long-petioled, the floral lvs. or bracts simple, petioles with stipular spines at base: fls. numerous, rose-purple or white, long-pedicelled; petals about 1 in. long, long-clawed; stamens 2–3 in. long, blue or purple: caps. linear, erect, on stipe 2–6 in. long. Trop. Amer.; adventive from N. Y. to La.—Material grown as *Gynandropsis speciosa* may sometimes belong here; the genus Gynandropsis is distinguished from Cleome by the stamens borne on a stalk (androphore) raising them above point of perianth attachment and the pistil likewise borne on a stalk (gynophore) elevating it above point of staminal attachment.

2. **C. lutea,** Hook. Ann. to 5 ft.: lvs. glabrous, 5–7-foliolate (the upper 3); lfts. ½–2 in. long: fls. bright orange-yellow, racemes elongating in fr.; petals ¼in. long; stamens ½in. long, yellow: caps. recurved, stipe ½in. long. Neb. and New Mex. to Wash. and Calif.

83. CRUCIFERÆ. MUSTARD FAMILY. CRUCIFERS

A well-marked family characterized in general by 4 petals standing opposite each other in a square cross (whence *Cruciferæ,* "cross-bearing"), 6 stamens of which 2 are short, and a special kind of pod or silique; mostly herbs, yielding many fl.-garden plants and important kitchen-garden vegetables and field crops, oil and table mustard; genera upwards of 300, and species perhaps 3,000, in many parts of the world, largely in temp. and subarctic regions.—Lvs. exstipulate, alternate (except sometimes opposite in Lunaria, Æthionema, and few others), usually simple although often deeply pinnatifid, frequently variable in a genus: fls. small but showy because of their numbers, bisexual, regular; sepals 4, mostly soon deciduous; petals 4 (seldom wanting), usually clawed and with a spreading limb; stamens typically 6 and tetradynamous (4 long and 2 short); pistil 1; ovary superior, of 2 carpels, 1–2-celled, placentation parietal, ripening into a thin-partitioned pod; when the pod is longer than broad it is called a *silique,* when as broad as long a *silicle;* the pod is usually dehiscent by 2 valves or sides, but sometimes indehiscent and breaking crosswise into 1-seeded bodies; seeds small, often globular, filled with the embryo, the cotyledons in characteristic positions (seen by cutting crosswise the seeds or better by soaking the seeds until they swell),—*accumbent* when the edges stand against the radicle o ⊖, *incumbent* when they are backed up to the radicle o ⦶, *conduplicate* when they fold on either side the radicle o >>.—Although Cruciferæ is a "natural"

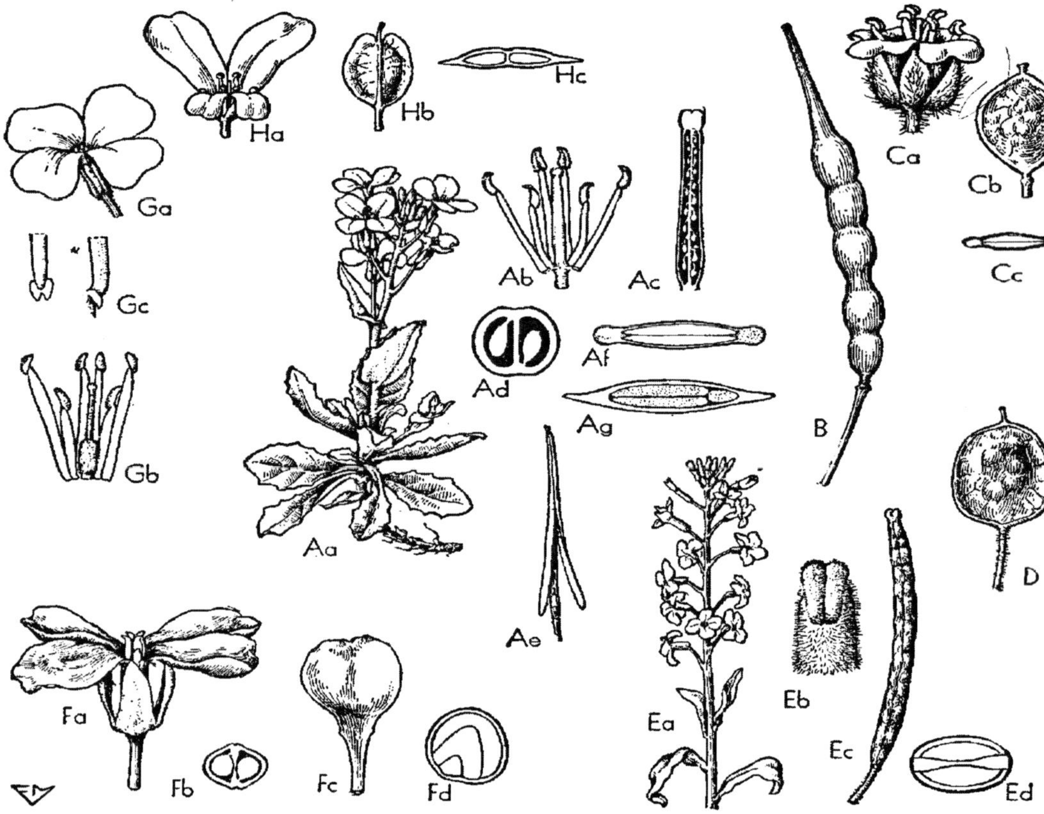

Fig. 83. CRUCIFERÆ. A, *Arabis caucasica:* Aa, plant in flower, × ½; Ab, flower, less perianth, × 2; Ac, pistil, vertical section, × 4; Ad, ovary, cross-section, × 15; Ae, silique, × ½; Af, silique, cross-section (less seeds), × 10; Ag, seed, cross-section, cotyledons accumbent, × 16. B, *Raphanus sativus:* fruit, × ½. C, *Alyssum saxatile:* Ca, flower, × 2; Cb, silicle, × 4; Cc, same, cross-section (less seeds), × 4. D, *Lunaria annua:* silicle, × ⅜. E, *Matthiola incana:* Ea, flowering branch, × ⅛; Eb, stigma, × 5; Ec, silicle, × ½; Ed, same, cross-section (less seeds), × 2. F, *Brassica kaber:* Fa, flower, × 1; Fb, ovary, cross-section, × 4; Fc, petal, × 1; Fd, seed, cross-section, cotyledons conduplicate, × 5. G, *Aubrieta deltoidea:* Ga, flower, × 1; Gb, same, less perianth, stamens expanded, × 2; Gc, base of filament with gland (face and side view), × 4. H, *Iberis sempervirens:* Ha, flower, × 1½; Hb, silicle, × 1; Hc, same, cross-section (less seeds), × 2.

family, the genera are largely artificial or arbitrary and the delimiting of them is often difficult.

A. Lvs. (ours) oblong, long-petioled, 15–24 in. long, entire to fimbriate, not lobed, glabrous, in basal rosettes .... 20. ARMORACIA
AA. Lvs. not characterized as above.
  B. Fr. divided into an upper and lower valve (the stylar distal end usually partitioned from the pod proper and forming the upper valve); cotyledons almost always conduplicate.
    C. Pod a much elongated linear silique, not conspicuously torulose or if so not sharply 2-celled in cross-section.
      D. Stigma distinct, more or less 2-lobed: pod with seeds in 1 row .... 1. BRASSICA
      DD. Stigma small, not lobed or scarcely distinguishable from style, style narrowly conical and tapering: pod with seeds in 2 rows .... 2. ERUCA
    CC. Pod a short silique, strongly torulose or with prominent transverse constrictions, usually 2-celled in cross-section.
      D. Silique of 2 joints or less, the terminal 1-seeded .... 4. CRAMBE
      DD. Silique of several joints, the terminal 2-seeded .... 3. RAPHANUS
  BB. Fr. with stylar end not partitioned off into a separate valve above; cotyledons never conduplicate.
    C. Pods usually less than ½5in. wide, or if wider strongly constricted laterally; cotyledons transversely biplicate: fls. (ours) blue with yellow center .... 5. HELIOPHILA
    CC. Pods not as above; cotyledons not biplicate: fls. not as above or if so the fr. a short broad silicle.

D. Petals fringed or laciniate.. 6. SCHIZOPETALON
DD. Petals (ours) not fringed.
E. Valves of pod compressed at right angles to septum, the latter very short.
F. Fls. small, mostly less than ⅛in. long: fr. usually less than ⅛in. wide.. 7. LEPIDIUM
FF. Fls. and fr. larger than above; fls. showy.
G. Length of petals unequal, 2 much longer.................... 9. IBERIS
GG. Length of petals approximately equal.
H. Plants with hairs forked or stellate or predominately so.......12. HUTCHINSIA
HH. Plants glabrous or with simple hairs only.
I. Silicle with valves winged or broadly margined: lvs. sessile or very short-petioled..............................10. ÆTHIONEMA
II. Silicle with valves neither winged nor broadly margined: lvs. long-petioled.
J. Petioles and pod pedicels eight to twelve times longer than lf.-blades or pods respectively: plants 2–4 in. high......11. IONOPSIDIUM
JJ. Petioles and pod pedicels four times as long as lf.-blades or pods respectively or less: plants 6 in. high or more.... 13. COCHLEARIA
EE. Valves of pod parallel to septum or hard and globose or inflated.
F. The pod hard and nut-like, indehiscent.
G. Shape of fr. orbicular to obovate: fls. white or rose............16. PELTARIA
GG. Shape of fr. oblong, often narrowly so: fls. yellow............ 8. ISATIS
FF. The pod not as above, usually dehiscent, inflated or much compressed.
G. Pod a silicle, rarely more than three times as long as wide; cotyledons accumbent.
H. Plant glabrous, or only with straight simple hairs.
I. Calyx open with definite sinus between sepals: pod ⅝in. long or less..16. PELTARIA
II. Calyx with sepal margins overlapping or touching: pod mostly more than ¾in. long.
J. Anthers and stigmas blunt: sepals often purplish-colored apically: pod long-stalked beyond calyx..............14. LUNARIA
JJ. Anthers and stigmas acute or sharp-pointed: sepals not purplish: pod subsessile in calyx..................15. RICOTIA
HH. Plant stellate-hairy or with some of the hairs branched or forked.
I. Filaments of the 2 shorter stamens winged basally or toothed above..26. AUBRIETA
II. Filaments neither toothed nor winged.
J. Shape of pod narrowly elliptic to oblong-linear, usually many-seeded.......................................19. DRABA
JJ. Shape of pod orbicular, obovate or broadly elliptic, usually few-seeded.
K. Fls. white to purple; short stamens with 2 nectary glands on each side at base, 1 gland much longer than other: plants 3–6 in. tall, ann......................18. LOBULARIA
KK. Fls. pale to deep yellow, rarely white or pinkish; short stamens with single basal nectary gland on each side: plants mostly 6–24 in. tall, mostly per................ 17. ALYSSUM
GG. Pod a silique, usually four times as long as wide or longer; cotyledons accumbent or incumbent.
H. Sepals overlapping, calyx seemingly tubular: anthers often acute.
I. Lf. palmately divided or cleft..........................22. DENTARIA
II. Lf. simple or pinnatifid.
J. Stigmas erect, connate into a cone or free and somewhat spreading.
K. Stigma-lobes distinct, slightly spreading and with a swollen gibbosity or horned projection from the back (dorsal) side: cotyledons accumbent...............27. MATTHIOLA
KK. Stigma-lobes usually erect and fused, the back (dorsal) side flat: cotyledons incumbent.
L. Lobes of stigmas blunt, erect and parallel, standing face to face..................................29. HESPERIS
LL. Lobes of stigmas connate to form a tapering cone or beak...28. MALCOLMIA
JJ. Stigmas capitate or only shortly 2-lobed.
K. Plants mostly 3–5 in. high: fls. pale lilac to purple; short filaments toothed..........................26. AUBRIETA
KK. Plants 6–20 in. high or more: fls. yellow to orange and brown (lilac in one species of Erysimum); filaments entire.
L. Pods compressed; seeds more or less in 2 rows: nectary glands absent.................................30. CHEIRANTHUS
LL. Pods terete, quadrangular or only slightly compressed; seeds in 1 row: nectary glands present at base of filaments...............................31. ERYSIMUM
HH. Sepals not overlapping, spreading nor with prominently open sinuses.

I. Fls. bright yellow: basal lvs. lyrate......................23. BARBAREA
II. Fls. white to purple, rarely very pale yellow or pale orange.
J. Valves of pods nerveless.............................21. CARDAMINE
JJ. Valves of pods nerved, at least with a median nerve.
K. Sides of pod convex..............................25. NASTURTIUM
KK. Sides of pod more or less flattened.
L. Plant glabrous...............................24. ARABIS
LL. Plant hairy, or bearing hairs.
M. The valves of pod soon falling: petals white to purple..................................24. ARABIS
MM. The valves of pod not soon falling: petals dark yellow and orange-brown....................30. CHEIRANTHUS

1. BRASSICA, L. COLES. MUSTARDS. Per., bien. and ann. herbs, about 100 species, native in north temp. parts of eastern hemisphere, many widely spread as weeds and others affording important food materials.—Sts. in cult. species erect, branched, glabrous or with scattered simple hairs, sometimes very glaucous: lower and basal lvs. mostly more or less lyrate: fls. yellow or ochroleucous, rarely white, in long simple racemes or at least the clusters elongating in anthesis or in fr.; sepals erect or spreading, saccate or plane; petals long-clawed; stigma capitate, sometimes obscurely bidentate: fr. a long stalked or nearly sessile pod or silique, often slender, nearly terete or angled, tipped with an indehiscent and usually seedless beak; seeds globular, brown-black or yellowish, in a single row, cotyledons conduplicate. (Brassica: the classical name for cabbage.)—The exact nativity of most of the cult. species is unknown. They are mostly bland plants, but some of them yield the table mustard of commerce from the seeds, and from the seeds of certain kinds colza oil is abstracted. Many species yield pot-herb material in the large tender radical lvs., mostly in spring, but in the semi-coles the lvs. may be picked in summer if seeds are sown in spring or in mild climates seeds may be sown in autumn for spring use.

A. The coles: plant thick-lvd., glaucous-blue or blue-green or glaucous-red (sometimes hort. vars. with "glazed" foliage), the herbage wholly free of hairs and spicules at maturity unless in some cases on radical lvs., even though sometimes slightly pubescent: fls. large, nearly ½–1 in. long, cream-yellow, light yellow to ochroleucous, and white; sepals mostly erect: seed-coats featureless. (BRASSICA proper.)
B. Seeds large, mostly 1/12–⅛in. long, rounded, not tapering to either end nor cornered, raphal creases not prominent (or only in smaller and not fully developed samples). The true coles.
C. Infl. elongated and open at anthesis, 4–10 in. long; fls. mostly ¾in. or more long: young radical lvs. glabrous.
D. Lvs. large and usually thick, entire or only somewhat lobed (not fimbriate), those on fl.-sts. sessile or clasping: main st. not globular-tuberous.. 1. *B. oleracea*
DD. Lvs. relatively small (blades mostly 8–10 in. long), those on flowering sts. with slender petioles: st. globular-tuberous above ground........ 2. *B. caulorapa*
CC. Infl. short in anthesis, with fls. clustered at top, the blooming part not more than 2 in. long: young radical lvs. with scattered hairs.
D. Root slender and not tuberous, dividing into stout horizontal branches: pedicels strongly ascending: beak of pod slender: prevailing st.-lvs. oblong-lanceolate, toothed or notched.............................. 3. *B. Napus*
DD. Root a large conic or elongated tuber, main root fairly straight even when run wild, and side roots fine and short: pedicels stout and wide-spreading: beak usually not much exceeding ⅜in. long: prevailing lower st.-lvs. with large terminal part and smaller lobes at base..... 4. *B. Napobrassica*
BB. Seeds small, mostly less than 1/12in. long or broad at maturity, commonly angled or cornered, raphal lines and creases usually prominent (exception in nos. 14, 15). The semi-coles, thin-lvd. and green-lvd. plants intermediate between the true thick-lvd. glaucous coles and the mustards.
C. Root consistently tuberous and fleshy, bien.: fl.-st. stout and strict, commonly not branching near base.. 5. *B. Rapa*
CC. Root not tuberous (unless sometimes indifferently so in no. 9) or thick-fleshy: plant mostly ann. but sometimes bien.: sts. usually diffusely branching.
D. Fls. very large at full bloom, expanding to ¾in. or more across, the blooming cluster elongated and open: pod 2¼–2¾ in. long at full maturity, beak very long.
E. Radical and cauline lvs. deeply lobed and cut or fimbriate, often curled, thick and glaucous, the lobes or large teeth often prong-like. 6. *B. fimbriata*
EE. Radical and cauline lvs. not lobed or cut, although sometimes obscurely dentate or crenate, thin and very green.................. 7. *B. perviridis*
DD. Fls. small or medium, usually less than ¾in. across and often only ½in., the blooming cluster short and mostly compact although perhaps elongated somewhat in fr.: pod 1½–2 in. or less long at maturity.

E. Cluster of radical lvs. not developing into a clump or close rosette; st.-lvs. cordate-clasping: plant ann., thinly glaucous, root not enlarged and usually branching or forking........................ 8. *B. campestris*

EE. Cluster of radical lvs. much developed, usually large and prominent (at least in the cult. plant) and providing an article of food; st.-lvs. various: plant ann., bien., perhaps sometimes per. in mild climates, green or essentially so.

F. Main sts. or axes conspicuously several from a single crown, clustered: plant nearly or quite green: cauline lvs. broad-based and auriculate, radical lvs. lyrate: root thick or woody but hardly tuberous, bien.. 9. *B. septiceps*

FF. Main sts. only 1 or 2 from crown, or at least not clustered: plant green: lvs. various: root not thickened, ann. or bien.

G. Lvs. evidently lobed, with separate distinct small lobes on petiole-like base.. 10. *B. Ruvo*

GG. Lvs. mostly not lobed, margins not regularly notched or angled, usually nearly or quite entire except perhaps along a margined petiole.

H. St.-lvs. prominently clasping or auriculate.

I. Radical and lowermost lvs. tapering to broad flat winged toothed petiole.................................. 11. *B. pekinensis*

II. Radical and lower st.-lvs. not wing-petioled.

J. Beak of pod very short, ⅕–¼in. or less long.

K. Cauline lvs. almost orbicular, sessile and clasping...... 12. *B. narinosa*

KK. Cauline lvs. oval or longer, long-petioled, not clasping.. 13. *B. carinata*

JJ. Beak of pod of ordinary length: st.-lvs. long and narrow.. 14. *B. chinensis*

HH. St.-lvs. not clasping, more or less tapering to base .... 15. *B. parachinensis*

AA. The mustards: plant thin-lvd., green or only thinly glaucous, more or less pilose or spiculose: fls. small, mostly less than ⅜in. broad, light to medium yellow: seeds various in size and shape, the coat conspicuously foveate or pitted under a strong lens, raphal line or the hilum usually prominent: annuals, the root not tuberous, grown for "greens" and the condimental seeds. (SINAPIS.)

B. Surface of pod glabrous or at most only finely pubescent or with a very few caducous spicules: seed small, not much exceeding 1/25 in. thick, dark brown to black: lobes of lf. and teeth usually acute.

C. Pod short, the body mostly not exceeding 1½ in. long, more or less appressed to rachis, or nearly parallel to it, at maturity.

D. Beak of pod conspicuously flat at maturity, often seedful, centrally ribbed, prominent, pedicel of pod very short and thick .... 16. *B. kaber*

DD. Beak slender and not prominent, not flattened or seed-bearing or noticeably ribbed, body of pod usually about ½in. long, pedicel of pod very thin.. 17. *B. nigra*

CC. Pod long, usually 2 in. or more, widely spreading or divaricate at maturity; beak not flat or seedful.. 18. *B. juncea*

BB. Surface of pod bristly-hairy, pedicels divaricate; seed large, often exceeding 1/12in. thick, light yellow: lobes of lf. and teeth usually blunt.............. 19. *B. hirta*

1. **B. oleracea,** L. Stout very glaucous glabrous per., perhaps sometimes bien., st. 1–3 ft. long, often decumbent: radical and lower lvs. thick, fleshy, obovate or oblong, 6–20 in. long; st.-lvs. narrow, some of them clasping: fls. in long racemes, opening for some distance along the axis, often 1 in. long, whitish-yellow; calyx narrow and erect, the sepals more or less saccate: pod 2–4 in. long, with a long conical beak. Coasts of W. Eu.—Following are the main culture-races, mostly bien., probably all of them originating as cultigens:

Var. **fruticosa,** Metz. BRANCHING BUSH KALE. THOUSAND-HEADED KALE. Plant stocky, woody, persisting three years or more, the main trunk stout and 3–5 ft. high, branched or bearing many lateral rosettes or "heads": lvs. mostly removed singly as food for humans and livestock; much like the wild *B. oleracea.*

Var. **acephala,** DC. COMMON KALE. TREE KALE. A name of somewhat indefinite application, perhaps to be discarded as a systematic category when the cult. races have received greater study. It comprises the borecoles (*boerenkool,* peasant cole or kraut) with main st. or trunk not very stocky and not usefully durable after about two years, st. usually unbranched, lvs. separate or in only loose rosettes and not making solid heads, foliage thick and glaucous sometimes purplish and not fimbriate or deeply cut; sometimes the main st. is thickened and edible, as in the Marrow kales. The tall simple-stemmed Cow cabbages of Eu. belong here. Georgia collards probably belong here, but more than one kind may be grown under this name; some of it may be var. *fruticosa,* and sometimes it is young plants of *B. Napobrassica.* The Curled kales are *B. fimbriata.*

Var. **Tronchuda,** Bailey. PORTUGUESE OR TRONCHUDA KALE OR CABBAGE. Low stocky compact plant, main st. perhaps 1 ft. high but fls. rising above the foliage: lvs. very broad, thick and cabbage-like, obtuse or rounded, with wide fleshy edible petiole and ribs something like chard, forming a single loose rosette. Much grown among the Portuguese in Bermuda and shipped to U. S.; it has been offered by American seedsmen.

Var. **gemmifera,** Zenker. BRUSSELS SPROUTS. St. simple and erect, 2–3 ft., bearing little edible heads or "sprouts" about 1 in. diam. in the axils: lvs. short and broad, about as broad as long, often with ear-like lobes at base.

Var. **capitata,** L. CABBAGE. Low and stout, with short stock, bearing a dense terminal head: lvs. large, often 1 ft. across, oblong-obovate to nearly circular, little if at all lobed at base. In the Savoy cabbage the lvs. are blistered and puckered. There is a purple-lvd. race, as well as vars. with green (not glaucous) "glazed" foliage.

Var. **botrytis,** L. (*B. cauliflora,* Gars. *B. botrytis,* Mill.). CAULIFLOWER. BROCCOLI. Low, with stout short stock, bearing a dense terminal teratological head, overtopped by lvs., comprised of the transformed and consolidated mass of short thick decolored peduncles and pedicels and undeveloped fls. and bracts: lvs. long-oblong or elliptic, strongly ascending.

Var. **italica,** Plenck. ASPARAGUS OR SPROUTING BROCCOLI. Differs from var. *botrytis* in not producing a solid head, but grown for the thickened fl.-shoots that arise from the lf.-axils and also in the crown, making a more or less open and variously aborted panicle.

2. **B. caulorapa,** Pasq. (*B. oleracea* var. *caulo-rapa,* DC.). KOHLRABI. Low and stout bien., with short stock that enlarges just above the ground into a shapely edible tuber 2–4 in. or more diam., bearing lvs. on the top; plant glaucous and glabrous throughout: lvs. thin, relatively small, 8–10 in. long, of which one-third to one-half is slender marginless petiole, the blades oval to round-oval or oval-oblong with irregularly dentate margins and mostly with 1 or 2 lobes at base: fls. as in *B. oleracea:* beak of pod usually very short. (Caulorapa: that is, stem-turnip.)

3. **B. Napus,** L. RAPE. COLZA. Ann., but when sown late blooms following spring withstanding the winter in the northern states and Canada where it is grown for forage; glaucous throughout, mostly with a hard and branching root; st. 2–3½ ft., much-branching, often purple toward base: lvs. of young plant (seedling) and of unfolding crown bearing few scattered setose hairs, otherwise plant glabrous; basal lvs. 4–12 or more in. long and half or less as wide, lyrate-pinnatifid, the lobes decreasing in size to petiole, terminal lobe very large and obtuse; lower st.-lvs. several-lobed and contracted into narrow part like a winged petiole; upper st.-lvs. oblong-lanceolate, sharply dentate, broad at base and clasping: infl. an elongating raceme, the fls. in anthesis mostly more or less aggregated at the end and not prominently overtopping the buds; fls. light yellow, ¼–¾in. across, on slender strongly ascending pedicels; sepals not saccate: pod 2–4 in. long, with slender beak. (Napus is a classical name for a kind of turnip.) Known only as a cultigen, and sometimes escaped.—Underground part curved or crooked for 2 or 3 in. and then dividing into stout horizontal branches.

4. **B. Napobrassica,** Mill. (*B. oleracea* var. *Napobrassica,* L.). RUTABAGA. Glaucous bien., producing a large solid hard-fleshed underground tuber bearing roots on its lower half or third and usually gradually tapering downward, flesh mostly yellow but sometimes white, produced above into a lf.-bearing neck or crown, often withstanding northern winters and flowering freely in spring: lvs. of seedlings and unfolding crown usually with scattered setose hairs; lvs. like those of *B. Napus* except that those on the st. are prevailingly like the basal ones only smaller: fruiting pedicels stout and strongly divaricate: pod mostly shorter than in *B. Napus* with a very short beak. Var. **solidifolia,** Bailey, is a race with unlobed radical lvs.; infrequent.—Underground part in spontaneous plants mostly straight or nearly so, the roots lateral, weak and small and often many.

5. **B. Rapa,** L. TURNIP. Green-lvd. bien., with an underground mostly flat or globular soft-fleshed tuber producing roots only on the slender tap-root beneath it, usually white-fleshed, and not produced into an extended neck or crown above, the root usually not withstanding winters in the northern states: radical lvs. soft, prickly with few strong setose hairs, lyrate-pinnatifid, long and narrow, 12–20 in. long; st.-lvs. sometimes glaucous, with a clasping base: fls. small, ⅜in. or less long, bright yellow, those in anthesis close together and commonly overtopping the unopened buds: pod on divaricate-ascending pedicels, about 1½–2½ in. long, with slender beak. (Rapa is an old Latin name for turnip.) Cultigen. Var. **lorifolia,** Bailey, has unlobed mostly shorter radical lvs., the "strap-leaved" turnips; infrequent.

6. **B. fimbriata,** DC. (*B. oleracea* var. *fimbriata,* Mill.). CURLED KITCHEN KALE. DWARF SIBERIAN and SCOTCH KALE. Hardy bien., with thick deeply cut and curled glaucous or bluish-green foliage or tinted brownish or purplish, stock or st. short and hard the first year but reaching 24–36 in. the second year in bloom: lvs. the first autumn 12–16 in. long of which about one-third is bare plain petiole, blade oblong in outline, lyrate-pinnatifid, lobes overlapping giving a crinkled look, glabrous at maturity: fl.-cluster 3–6 in. or perhaps more long, somewhat lengthening in fr.; fls. ¾in. or less long, sulfur-yellow: pod 2–3 in. long, continued into a prominent beak, wide-spreading on short pedicels; seeds small, less than 1⁄12in. long, brown-black, somewhat cornered, radical mark prominent. Eurasia.—Grown for the first-year foliage, available autumn to spring, the much-curled forms also ornamental.

7. **B. perviridis,** Bailey (*B. Rapa* var. *perviridis,* Bailey.). TENDERGREEN. SPINACH MUSTARD. Plant ann., perhaps bien. in mild climates if sown late in season, with long fragile lvs. very green above and lighter colored or thinly glaucous underneath: blade of radical lvs. oblong to obovate, obtuse, sinuate-dentate to entire, tapered into a long

winged narrow petiole, 1–2 ft. long; st.-lvs. sessile and sometimes auriculate, blade oblong to broad-ovate to narrow-lanceolate: infl. a raceme 2–3 ft. long and the plant at that period 5–6 ft. tall; fls. bright yellow, ½in. or more across: pod 2–3 in. long, with slender tapering beak, ascending on slender pedicels; seeds small, usually less than 1/12in. long, smooth, not cornered, raphal scar not deep. Probably E. Asia.—Plant of recent introduction, probably within the last twenty years; grown in N. Amer. for its edible foliage, but the thick crown-tuber 1–3 in. diam. is pickled in oriental countries.

8. **B. campestris,** L. Field Mustard. Slender erect ann. 1–3 ft. high and perhaps sometimes more, with hard slender (not tuberous) usually branched root, more or less lightly glaucous, glabrous, without a developed clump of root-lvs., sometimes growing to a single st. in grain fields but usually branching: basal and lower st.-lvs. lyrate-pinnatifid, 3–6 in. long, the terminal part large and ovate to oblong; middle and upper lvs. oblong, obtuse or short-acute, not petioled and prominently cordate-amplexicaul: fls. small, bright yellow, slender-pedicelled; sepals exceeding claws of petals, somewhat spreading: pod slender, 1–2 in. long, on divaricate or somewhat ascending pedicels, the beak to ½in. long, conical at base. Eu. or Eurasia, a widespread weed.—Strains are cult. in some countries for the oil-bearing seeds, but not known in U. S. as a cult. plant, inserted here to clarify related species; prevailingly, at least in the E., a slender rather small plant.

9. **B. septiceps,** Bailey (*B. Rapa* var. *septiceps,* Bailey). Seven-top Turnip. Stout bien., surviving the winter even sometimes as far north as Cent. N.Y., adventive in middle latitudes of U. S. and commonly not recognized under a Latin name; sts. 1–12 or several from crown of a thick woody base, leafy all the way up: lvs. abundant, used (with young shoots) for "greens," more or less spiculose when young, thinly glaucous, much divided and lyrate, 6–12 in. long, rounded at end and crenate-dentate, petiole-like base clasping, those in infl. long-lanceolate, sessile and auriculate: fls. small, less than ¾in. across, light yellow, in short umbelliform clusters terminating the branches: pod 1½–2 in. or somewhat more long, slender-beaked, ascending on short divaricating pedicels; seeds small, 1/25–1/16in. long, featureless, raphal line not prominent. Probably Eu.—As a salad crop it is usually sown in late summer and early autumn. Has been grown as "Italian kale."

10. **B. Ruvo,** Bailey. Ruvo Kale. Quick-growing ann. or bien. with straight hard slender tap-root, and not thick or succulent nor glaucous glabrous foliage, used as a pot-herb: lvs. bright or shining green, lyrate-pinnatifid, 18 in. long and 8 in. wide at the large expanded apex, lobes on the petiole many, base clasping, margins wavy or obscurely dentate, upper cauline lvs. very narrow or lanceolate and sessile-auriculate: infl. short and not greatly exceeding lower foliage, usually of several or many erect branches; fls. light yellow, small, about ⅜in. across, in close unbelliform clusters that elongate in fr.: pod 2½ in. or less long, thick, beak short but slender, ascending or upwardly curved on short stout divaricate pedicels; seeds very small, not much exceeding 1/25in. thick, not cornered, featureless, raphal line inconspicuous. Probably Eu.—Living over winter when sown in autumn. It has been grown as Italian turnip broccoli and *Rapa Ruvo.*

11. **B. pekinensis,** Rupr. (*Sinapis pekinensis,* Lour. *B. Pe-Tsai,* Bailey). Pe-Tsai. Green soft-lvd. ann., grown mostly as a late autumn and winter vegetable, glabrous except sometimes sparsely setose-hairy on midribs beneath: basal lvs. many and large, 1–2 ft. long and less than half as broad, obovate-oblong to broad-obovate, thin and veiny, margins undulate but only indistinctly dentate, the midrib broad and light colored and extending downward as a broad jagged-winged base of the blade; st.-lvs. either clasping or petiolate or both on same plant: fls. light yellow, mostly less than ⅜in. long, commonly crowded at end of raceme and overtopping unopened buds: pod rather short and stout, 1¼–2½ in. long, spreading or ascending, the beak short and stout. Probably farther Asia.—Now considerably grown as "Chinese" or "celery cabbage," forming more or less compact elongated heads the inside of which is blanched. In China grown to solid heads of different shapes.

12. **B. narinosa,** Bailey. Broad-beaked Mustard. Bien. but grown as an ann., relatively thick-lvd., grown for greens but infrequently seen in N. Amer., glabrous or the radical lvs. sometimes sparingly setose; st. short, erect, 12–20 in. high, branched above: basal lvs. orbicular-ovate to obovate, usually puckered, the blade 4–8 in. long, entire or nearly so, the white petiole broad; st.-lvs. smaller, amplexicaul, orbicular or very broad, few on the flowering branches: fls. yellow, on short pedicels, sepals not saccate: pod short and very thick and more or less inflated, 1–1½ in. long and sometimes nearly ½in. diam., the beak short, broad and thick. Probably Asia.

13. **B. carinata,** A. Br. Abyssinian Mustard. Erect ann. 3–4 ft. tall at full height, with many upright strict branches, foliage green or light glaucous, glabrous or bearing few hairs on the ribs, main sts. more or less glaucous and sometimes purplish: lvs. slender-petioled, comprised mostly of an oval or oblong part 3–5 in. long, more or less sinuate, small lobes often at base or on the petiole: fls. light yellow, about ⅝in. across, on short pedicels in lengthening racemes: pod mostly less than 2 in. long, stout and broad, with carinate angles, seed elevations prominent at maturity, the beak only 1/12–⅙in. long and thin; seeds about 1/12in. thick, somewhat cornered, featureless, raphal line prominent. Attributed to Abyssinia.—Cult. as a pot-herb, lvs. being taken as the plant grows.

14. **B. chinensis,** L. PAK-CHOI. Dull green ann. or bien., more or less glaucous when in bloom, glabrous throughout: basal lvs. firm and shining, spreading and not forming a compact head, 10–20 in. long, obovate or very broad-obovate, entire or only obscurely crenate or sinuate-dentate, narrowed gradually into a distinct narrow-margined but not jagged petiole; st.-lvs. auriculate-clasping: fls. pale yellow, about ⅜in. long, aggregated at top of raceme and overtopping the unopened buds: pod 1¼–2½ in. long, slender, beak slender; seeds little more than 1/25in. thick, featureless, raphal line indistinct. Probably farther Asia.—Infrequently grown as pot-herb unless among the Chinese.

15. **B. parachinensis,** Bailey. MOCK PAK-CHOI. Ann. and bien., tap-rooted, with glabrous somewhat glaucous foliage, the basal lvs. making an ascending clump 10–16 in. high, the strongly ribbed nearly or quite entire oval or oblong blades flaring outward, the thickish white wingless petioles ½in. or less broad, petiolar lobes usually wanting, the white ribs and veins prominent on under side of blade: fls. cream-colored or very light yellowish, small, less than ⅜in. across, terminating branches of infl. in umbelliform clusters that elongate in fr., the floral lvs. not clasping unless at base of petiole: pod rather slender, about 2 in. long, with slender brief beak, ascending on short divaricate pedicels; seeds small, about 1/25in. or little more thick, featureless, not angled, raphal line faint. Probably E. Asia.—Relatively small plant, 2–3 ft. high when in pod, apparently little grown in N. Amer. unless by Chinese. Basal lvs. more orbicular than in *B. chinensis* and petiole not margined, st.-lvs. not decidedly clasping.

16. **B. kaber,** Wheeler (*Sinapis kaber,* DC. *S. arvensis,* L. *B. arvensis,* Rabenh.). CHARLOCK. The prevailing mustard weed of oat fields and common in waste places: erect, branching, 2–3 ft. or more, the st. hispid or glabrate: lower lvs. mostly imperfectly lyrate, often large; main st.-lvs. ovate to oblong-ovate, obtuse or short-acute, angled, notched or indistinctly lobed, sometimes pinnatifid, usually setose-hairy beneath: fls. yellow, calyx not saccate: pod 1–1½ in. long, stiff and tardily dehiscing, pedicel short and stout, sometimes bearing a few translucent caducous hairs, more or less constricted between the seeds, beak 2-edged, often containing a single seed, shorter than the body; seeds small but variable, brown to very dark brown, hilum prominent. (Kaber: vernacular name.) Eu.—Not cult., although once grown as "California rape," but the seed is said to have been used in times of shortage in the manufacture of mustard. It is a variable plant; the var. *pinnatifida,* Wheeler, is included in the above diagnosis.

17. **B. nigra,** Koch (*Sinapis nigra,* L. *S. cernua,* Thunb.). BLACK MUSTARD. Much-branched green ann., st. usually more or less hispid-hairy but sometimes glabrous, in some cases slightly glaucous, 3–10 ft. and even more tall: lvs. various, often hispid, radical ones not greatly developed, pinnatifid or lobed, terminal lobe very large, margins dentate or notched, long-petioled as also are the st.-lvs.: fls. small, about ¼in. long, bright yellow, in twig-like racemes, usually not overtopping central unopened buds: pod short, less than 1 in. long, 4-sided, abruptly contracted into a thin beak, on short pedicels and closely appressed to the rachis; seeds very small, usually less than 1/25in. diam., angled, minutely pitted. Eurasia; now a widespread weed.—Principal source of table mustard (from the seeds), some kinds used abroad for greens.

18. **B. juncea,** Coss. (*Sinapis juncea,* L. *B. rugosa,* Hort.). LEAF MUSTARD. Widely variable ann., mostly green but st. sometimes thinly glaucous, glabrous except frequently setose-hispid on young lvs. and sts., erect and much-branched, 2–4 ft., seedful: basal lvs. large in the cult. plant and used for greens, oval to broad-oblong to obovate, 6–12 in. long and one-third to one-half as broad, obtuse, prevailingly lyrate-lobed or -divided, margins notched or scalloped: fls. bright yellow, ⅜in. or less long, scattered in the raceme or more typically aggregate at end and overtopping the unopened buds: pod 1½–2½ in. long, strongly ascending or erect, beak short and stout. Asia; much cult. for spring greens as Chinese mustard and under other names; also spontaneous in forms with less developed basal lvs. Var. **crispifolia,** Bailey (*B. japonica,* Hort. not Thunb.), has lvs. cut, curled, and crisped, represented in Southern Curled mustard, Ostrich Plume, and others. Var. **foliosa,** Bailey, BROAD-LEAVED MUSTARD, makes great stools of long-standing large sinuately margined lvs. Var. **longidens,** Bailey, bears oblong lvs. with narrow long forward-pointing more or less acute lobes. Var. **multisecta,** Bailey, has lvs. divided into linear filiform shred-like lobes, not crispate.—A related plant in the American tropics is *B. integrifolia,* Rupr., differing in main lvs. not lobed but the margins evenly dentate-serrate or doubly serrate.

19. **B. hirta,** Moench (*B. alba,* Rabenh. *Sinapis alba,* L.). WHITE MUSTARD. Stout ann., mostly sparsely hairy, branching above, 2–4 ft. tall: lvs. oval or ovate or obovate in outline, divided deeply or even quite to the midrib into 1–3 pairs of notched or angled lobes, st.-lvs. long-petioled: fls. yellow, about ½in. long, aggregated at apex of raceme and overtopping the unopened buds, showy and more or less fragrant: pod ¾–1½ in. long, squarrose, lower part setose and seed-bearing with constrictions between the seeds, equalled or exceeded by the flat mostly scythe-curved beak; seeds commonly light yellow, large. Eurasia.—Cult. for mustard from the seeds and for the lvs. as greens; also spontaneous. Raised under such mustard names as White London, Dutch Yellow, English Yellow, Caucasian Yellow, California Yellow.

2. **ERUCA,** Adans. A few species of erect ann. or per. herbs of Eu. and W. Asia, one sometimes grown for salad.—Lvs. strongly dentate or pinnatifid: fls. large, whitish, yellow, purplish, in elongating terminal bractless racemes, the style prominent, stigma undivided: fr. oblong to linear-oblong, turgid with strongly keeled valves; seeds globose, not winged, in 2 rows, cotyledons conduplicate. (Eru-ca: ancient name for some cruciferous plant.)

E. sativa, Mill. (*Brassica Eruca*, L.). ROCKET-SALAD. ROQUETTE. Ann., erect, much-branching, 1–2½ ft., with scattered simple hairs: lvs. irregularly pinnately lobed, the margins angled and notched, lower lvs. long-petioled, upper sessile: fls. ¾–1 in. long, on short pedicels, whitish or cream-yellow with darker veins: fr. about 1 in. long, erect and appressed, with a prominent flat beak. S. Eu.; sparingly adventive.—Infrequently grown in N. Amer. for spring and autumn piquant salad from the young lvs.

3. **RAPHANUS,** L. Species 8 or 10, ann., bien., per., Eu. to E. Asia, one much grown for food.—Glabrous or with scattered hairs, much-branched: lvs. mostly lyrate-lobed or -pinnatifid: fls. mostly showy, white, pink, purplish, yellowish, slender-pedicelled, in open branched bractless racemes; lateral sepals somewhat saccate; stamens free and unappendaged; style slender with slightly lobed stigma: fr. a long terete spongy indehiscent silique more or less constricted between the seeds, with a long beak; seeds globose or nearly so, wingless, cotyledons conduplicate. (Raph-anus: classical name.)

R. sativus, L. RADISH. Ann. and bien.; root thick and fleshy, in many sizes, shapes and colors, much prized as a vegetable to be eaten raw; st. 2–3 ft., more or less glaucous: lvs. stalked, glabrous or with sharp hairs, lyrate-divided, the terminal segm. very large, the lateral pinnæ mostly 1–3 pairs: fls. white to lilac, mostly dark-veined: fr. 1–3 in. long, spongy and containing 1–6 seeds, with extended beak. Cultigen; perhaps a derivative from *R. Raphanistrum*, L., now a widely distributed weed.

Var. **longipinnatus,** Bailey. Large and stout plant, with radical lvs. very long and narrow, sometimes 2 ft. long, with 8–12 pairs of pinnæ: usually a winter radish, with long, hard, and durable roots. The Chinese radishes, somewhat grown in N. Amer., are mostly of this var. or race: so also is the daikon of the Japanese, to which the following names apply: *R. Taquetii*, Lévl., *R. raphanistroides*, Nakai, and *R. sativus* forma *raphanistroides*, Makino. Other lf.-races are recognized but they are probably not grown in this country.

4. **CRAMBE,** L. Ann. and per. mostly fleshy glaucous herbs; about 20 species native mostly from Canary Isls. to W. Asia, one known in vegetable-gardens and another somewhat planted for the bold stature and showy bloom.—Glabrous or somewhat setose: lvs. large, pinnately lobed or pinnatisect: fls. white, in long corymbosed racemes, rather large; sepals all alike; filaments free, the longer ones usually toothed; stigma sessile: fr. a globular hard indehiscent 1-seeded body but borne on another slender undeveloped part or joint that looks like a stipe beyond the calyx; seeds large and globose, hanging in the pod, cotyledons conduplicate. (Cram-be: the Greek name.)

A. Plants glabrous: pod ¼–⅜in. across....................1. *C. maritima*
AA. Plant more or less hirsute, especially on the petioles: pod about ⅛in. across..........2. *C. cordifolia*

1. **C. maritima,** L. SEA-KALE. Fleshy big-lvd. per., grown for the succulent spring shoots which are blanched: lvs. more or less cabbage-like, ovate-oblong in outline but variously shallowly lobed and notched, sometimes 2 ft. and more long: fls. showy, about ½in. across, on sts. to 3 ft. tall: fr. (or "seed") a globular or globular-oblong pod ¼–⅜in. diam. Seacoasts and cliffs of W. Eu.

2. **C. cordifolia,** Steven. Tall per. 4–7 ft. high, stately in bloom: lvs. large and heavy, to 2 ft. and more across, the lower ones ovate in outline, cordate at base, dentate, lobed; st.-lvs. not distinctly cordate: fls. many, about ⅛in. across, white, the leafless panicle overtopping the cluster of root-lvs. and several ft. across. Caucasus.—Grown for ornament.

5. **HELIOPHILA,** L. About 100 species of annuals or suffruticose perennials, native in S. Afr.—Lvs. often small, sometimes pinnately parted: fls. in loose bractless racemes, white, yellow, rose or bluish; sepals erect, the outer pointed and sometimes horned, the inner obtuse; filaments linear, broadened at base, the outer ones sometimes toothed; ovary usually sessile, style distinct, stigma subglobose: fr. a compressed or subterete dehiscent silique, usually constricted between the seeds

giving a necklace appearance (moniliform); seeds in 1 row, often winged, cotyledons biplicate. (Helioph-ila: Greek *sun* and *to love.*)

A. Pod erect, linear with straight margins........................1. *H. linearifolia*
AA. Pod pendulous, moniliform........................2. *H. leptophylla*

1. **H. linearifolia,** Burch. Sts. erect or decumbent, 1–3 ft. high, woody at base, subglabrous: lvs. linear, about 1 in. long, acute, entire: fls. 10–16 in racemes, the petals blue with yellow claws: pod 1½–2 in. long, about ⅛in. wide, the valves 3-nerved.

2. **H. leptophylla,** Schlechter. Sts. ascending, 1–1½ ft. high, glabrous, somewhat branched at base: lvs. filiform, ¾–2 in. long, erect, blue-green: fls. in many-fld. lax racemes, blue with a yellow center, the petals obovate, obtuse, about ⅓in. long; sepals about half as long as petals, with a narrow membranous margin: pod moniliform, pendulous, beaked.

6. **SCHIZOPETALON,** Sims. About 8 annuals from Chile, one an attractive little fl.-garden subject.—Erect, somewhat branched, low, with sinuate, toothed or pinnatifid lvs., the pubescence of branching hairs: fls. white or purple, in terminal bracted racemes; petals long-clawed, with unequally cut or pinnatifid limb (whence the generic name, Schizopet-alon, *cut-petals*): fr. narrow-linear, more or less flattened and torulose; seeds in 1 row, not winged or margined, cotyledons incumbent.

S. Walkeri, Sims. St. weak, ascending, to 9 in. or more high: lvs. long-oblong, the lower ones to 5 in. long, sinuate-pinnatifid, attenuate at base, scabrous on both surfaces: fls. forming a loose raceme, white, fragrant, closing in forenoon and opening again toward night, ½in. or more across; petals ovate, pinnatifid, giving the bloom a feathery effect. (Seeds long ago received in England from Chile by John Walker, who grew it.)

7. **LEPIDIUM,** L. Pepper-Grass. Species about 130, widely distributed, one grown for salad and garnishing.—Annuals, perennials, and subshrubs, erect or spreading, glabrous or pubescent with simple hairs, not showy or attractive: lvs. various, simple or pinnate: fls. small and inconspicuous, in elongating bractless racemes, the petals white or nearly so but sometimes wanting; stamens often only 2–4: fr. an orbicular, oblong, or obovate silicle, with septum or partition across the short diam., valves boat-shaped; seeds 1 or rarely 2 in each compartment, not winged, the cotyledons mostly incumbent. (Lepid-ium: Greek *little scale,* from the pods.)

L. sativum, L. Garden Cress. Ann. 1–2 ft., erect, glabrous and glaucous: basal lvs. (for which the plant is grown) pinnatifid and the segms. toothed, or in the common curled vars. more finely divided and crispate; st.-lvs. becoming successively simple, linear and entire in the upper infl.: fls. very small, in elongating racemes, but the oblong-oval winged retuse frs. conspicuous. W. Asia; somewhat escaped.

8. **ISATIS,** L. Woad. Some 30 species of annuals, biennials, and perennials of the Medit. region, one or two somewhat known in cult.—Erect branching herbs, glabrous or pubescent or even tomentose: lvs. mostly undivided, those on the st. usually auriculate-clasping: fls. small, yellow, in open often panicled bractless racemes; stamens free, without teeth or appendages: fr. samara-like, 1-celled, indehiscent, flat, pendulous, either narrow or more or less expanded and winged; seeds 1 or rarely 2, hanging from top of compartment, cotyledons usually incumbent. (Isatis: classical name for a healing herb.)

A. Upper st.-lvs. with narrow auricles........................1. *I. tinctoria*
AA. Upper lvs. without auricles........................2. *I. glauca*

1. **I. tinctoria,** L. Dyers Woad. A plant once cult. for its blue dye and likely still to be found; bien., 1½–3 ft. or more, glabrous or somewhat hairy below: radical lvs. oblong or obovate, entire or toothed, glabrous and glaucous or hairy; st.-lvs. lanceolate to linear, sessile, with narrow auricles: fls. small, in early summer in panicled racemes: fr. ½–¾in. long and one-third as broad, tapering to base, truncate or notched at apex, glabrous or sometimes pubescent. Eu.

2. **I. glauca,** Auch. Strong very glaucous per., 2–4 ft. or more, grown for ornament: radical lvs. large, oblong, obtuse, tapering to base; st.-lvs. with no auricles: fls. numerous in a very large loose terminal panicle, in summer: fr. about ½in. long, narrow-oblong, obtuse or somewhat truncate-retuse, finely tomentose. Asia Minor, Iran.

9. **IBERIS,** L. Candytuft.* Species 30–40, ann. and per., often more or less woody, in the Medit. region, affording popular fl.-garden subjects.—Branching mostly glabrous plants, with entire or pinnatifid sometimes fleshy lvs.: fls. white to

purple, in corymbs or lengthening racemes, the outer ones in the cluster mostly radiate; 2 outer petals in the fl. larger than the others; filaments not appendaged nor connate: fr. an orbicular or ovate winged or margined pod often notched at top, the septum across the short diam.; seeds 1 in each compartment, ovate, usually not winged on margins, cotyledons accumbent. (Ibe-ris: Iberia, ancient name of Spain.)

A. Ann. fl.-bed candytufts (sometimes persisting throughout winter if sown late).
  B. Infl. lengthening in fr. so that it becomes a distinct raceme; fls. white........... 1. *I. amara*
  BB. Infl. remaining at least as broad as high in fr.; fls. usually colored.............. 2. *I. umbellata*
AA. Per. border or rock-garden candytufts, with persistent foliage.
  B. Fl.-sts. branched above, lateral infl. usually present in the axils of upper lvs.: lvs. usually dentate toward apex.. 3. *I. gibraltarica*
  BB. Fl.-sts. simple: lvs. usually entire.
    C. Main st. ending in an infl.: lvs. linear, mucronate......................... 4. *I. saxatilis*
    CC. Main st. ending in a leafy shoot, fl.-sts. lateral from below: lvs. linear-oblong to obovate, mostly obtuse.
      D. Infl. umbel-like in fr.: st. more or less pubescent..................... 5. *I. Tenoreana*
      DD. Infl. racemose in fr.: st. glabrous.. 6. *I. sempervirens*

1. **I. amara,** L. (*I. coronaria*, Hort.). ROCKET CANDYTUFT. Ann., erect, or lopping and with erect sts. 6–12 in. and more high, sparsely pubescent: lvs. oblanceolate to spatulate, 1–3 (4) in. long, obtuse, mostly with few or several large irregular obtuse teeth: fls. white, fragrant, in a close nearly globular terminal cluster that soon elongates until, in fr., it is 2–6 in. long: fr. nearly orbicular or slightly tapering at the winged emarginate top, the style evident or projecting, points of the pod short and erect. Eu.; often a weed of cult. grounds.—Common in fl.-gardens. There are many named races.

2. **I. umbellata,** L. GLOBE CANDYTUFT. Often taller, subglabrous: lvs. mostly elliptic-lanceolate, 1–3 in. long, acute, entire, or sometimes with very few small short teeth: fls. rose-colored, shades of red or purple, varying to nearly white, not fragrant, in clusters that remain, in fr., as broad as high: fr. obovate, with a deep wide sinus at top, very slender style, and apiculate spreading points. S. Eu.

3. **I. gibraltarica,** L. GIBRALTAR CANDYTUFT. Evergreen per., spreading, glabrous, to 16 in.: lvs. oblong-spatulate, 1–2 in. long, obtuse, with 2–4 blunt teeth on either side near apex, or sometimes entire, somewhat ciliate at base: infl. umbel-like, to 1½ in. across, not elongating in fr.; fls. reddish-lilac or white and becoming lilac-tinged, sometimes flesh-colored: fr. ovate, about ⅓in. long, deeply notched. Spain, Morocco.

4. **I. saxatilis,** L. Low-growing evergreen per. with finely hairy sts. woody at base, 2–4 in. high: lvs. linear, ½–¾in. long, abruptly mucronate, entire, somewhat fleshy, ciliate: infl. umbel-like, lengthening in fr.; fls. white: fr. about ¼in. long, notched, the wings obtuse. S. Eu.

5. **I. Tenoreana,** DC. Evergreen per. with finely hairy sts. woody at base, ascending or erect, 2–8 in. high: lvs. obovate below, oblong spatulate above, ¾–1½ in. long, obtuse, crenate-dentate or entire, fleshy, ciliate: infl. umbel-like, to 2 in. across, not elongating in fr.; fls. white to pinkish: fr. about ¼in. long, deeply notched. (Named for M. Tenore, page 52.) S. Eu.—Material cult. under this name is mostly *I. sempervirens*.

6. **I. sempervirens,** L. EDGING CANDYTUFT. Evergreen glabrous per., branching and woody at base, 6–12 in. high: lvs. linear-oblong, ½–1 in. or more long, obtusish, entire: infl. about 1 in. across, soon becoming racemose; fls. white, sometimes tinged lilac, not fragrant: fr. about ¼in. long, notched. S. Eu.

10. **ÆTHIONEMA,** R. Br. STONE-CRESS. Herbs and subshrubs in the Medit. region, 40–50 species, a few perennials grown in rock-gardens and borders for ornament.—Slender branched plants, mostly glabrous, more or less woody at base: lvs. usually sessile, glaucous, sometimes opposite, commonly entire: fls. white or rose-colored or seldom yellowish, in elongating terminal racemes, often rather showy; 4 longer filaments mostly dilated, sometimes toothed or connate; petals all equal: fr. a silicle, orbicular, boat-shaped or obovate, usually notched at top, winged, the septum or partition at right angles to the valves; seeds 1 to several, not winged, cotyledons incumbent. (Æthione-ma: Greek compound, probably alluding to appearance of stamens.)

A. Fls. white: sts. scabrous: locules of caps. each with 2 ovules.................. 1. *Æ. iberideum*
AA. Fls. pink to rose or lilac: sts. glabrous: locules of caps. each with 1 ovule (except in no. 7).
  B. Lvs. more than ⅔in. long: wings of pod crenate to irregularly toothed.
    C. Fl.-sts. usually simple: petals over ⅓in. long: pod orbicular, almost ½in. long.. 2. *Æ. grandiflorum*
    CC. Fl.-sts. branched: petals about ¼in. long: pod obovate, about ⅓in. long... 3. *Æ. pulchellum*
  BB. Lvs. not over ⅔in. long.
    C. Infl. paniculate: wings of pod irregularly toothed....................... 3. *Æ. pulchellum*
    CC. Infl. racemose.

D. Lvs. ¼–⅓in. long: wings of pod crenate............................4. *Æ. armenum*
DD. Lvs. ⅓–⅔in. long: wings of pod entire.
E. Sts. mostly 2–4 in. high: pods overlapping on dense imbricated racemes. 5. *Æ. schistosum*
EE. Sts. mostly 6–10 in. high: pods not imbricated, racemes open.
F. Lf. oblanceolate to spatulate, to ⅓in. long: each locule of pod 1-seeded...6. *Æ. coridifolium*
FF. Lf. narrowly elliptic, ⅕–⅝in. long: each locule of pod 2-seeded...... 7. *Æ. saxatile*

1. **Æ. iberideum,** Boiss. Cespitose, with short ascending scabrous sts.: lvs. oblong to linear-lanceolate, acute, alternate at base: fls. white, in short racemes: fr. obovate, obcordate, about ⅓in. long, style half as long as sinus, wings obtuse, entire, concave. Asia Minor.

2. **Æ. grandiflorum,** Boiss. & Hohen. PERSIAN STONE-CRESS. Erect, 12–18 in., the glabrous branches long and slender, procumbent and woody at base: lvs. long oblong-linear, ⅝–1½ in. long, nearly or quite obtuse: fls. large, rose-colored, in slender elongated racemes to 3 in. long and 1 in. wide, the petals three to four times as long as calyx; longer filaments dilated at base; stigma subsessile: fr. orbicular, almost ½in. across, with crenate wing more than double the width of the 2 1-seeded locules. Iran.

3. **Æ. pulchellum,** Boiss. & Huet (*Æ. coridifolium*, Hort. not DC.). Sts. erect or decumbent, shorter than in no. 2, much-branched above: lvs. linear-oblong, obtuse: fls. rosy-pink, in rather dense racemes, the petals about two and a half times as long as calyx: fr. obovate, about ⅓in. long, the style and stigma about one-fourth as long as the deeply closed sinus, wings irregularly toothed, more than double the width of the 2 locules. Asia Minor.

4. **Æ. armenum,** Boiss. Sts. erect, short, simple, 4–8 in. high: lvs. short-linear, ¼–⅓in. long, acute: fls. pink, less than ¼in. long: fr. obovate, less than ⅕in. long, style shorter than the broad obtuse sinus, wings crenate, broader than the locules. Asia Minor.

5. **Æ. schistosum,** Boiss. & Kotschy. Sts. 2–4 in. high, simple, erect, with lvs. dense to the tip: lvs. narrow-linear, about ½in. long, acutish: fls. rose, petals about ¼in. long: fr. imbricated resembling cone of hops, orbicular, ¼–⅓in. long, the style very short in the deep closed sinus, wings entire, broader than locules. Asia Minor.

6. **Æ. coridifolium,** DC. (*Iberis jucunda*, Schott & Kotschy). LEBANON STONE-CRESS. Sts. simple, rather thick, 4–10 in. high: lvs. oblong-linear or linear, ⅓–⅔in. long, obtuse or acutish: fls. pink to rosy-lilac, petals about ¼in. long, two and a half times as long as calyx: fr. narrowly obovate-oblong, scarcely ⅓in. long, the style much shorter than the narrow sinus, entire wings narrow and boat-shaped, locules each 1-seeded. Asia Minor.—Material cult. as *Æ. pulchellum* usually belongs here.

7. **Æ. saxatile,** R. Br. (*Thlaspi saxatile*, L.). Suffrutescent subshrub to 1 ft., sts. simple or branched: lvs. ⅕–⅝in. long and ⅙in. wide or less, very narrowly elliptic, acute, sessile: fls. pink, in dense but elongating racemes, to ⅛in. long, sepals half to three-fourths as long as petals, the infl. becoming 2–6 in. long in fr.: pod oblong to broadly obovate, ⅓–½in. long, broadly cuneate to obtuse basally, sinus U-shaped with wings closing it apically, stigma sessile, locules each 2- or more seeded. S. Eu.—Some of the material distributed under the hort. name of *Æ. persicum* belongs here. Var. **Thomasianum,** Thell. (*Æ. Thomasianum*, J. Gay), differs in being more dwarf and in having fr. with a longer style; France.

11. **IONOPSIDIUM,** Reichb. DIAMOND-FLOWER. One little ann. in Portugal, grown sometimes for its bloom.—Glabrous: fls. violet varying to white, on very long and slender pedicels, small but profusely produced and bright colored; filaments free and not toothed or appendaged: fr. a silicle, globular-oblong, truncate or slightly emarginate at apex, the septum at right angles to the valves, the valves not winged; seeds 2–5 in each compartment, slightly oblong, not winged or margined, minutely granular, the cotyledons incumbent. (Ionopsid-ium: Greek *violet-like*, from color of the fls.)

I. **acaule,** Reichb. (*Cochlearia acaulis*, Desf.). Nearly acaulescent, making runners, 3–4 in. high: lf.-blades nearly orbicular, entire, mostly less than ½in. across, abruptly narrowed into very long petiole: fls. very small, about ⅜in. across, fragrant, the rounded petals twice exceeding the calyx: fr. with pedicels eight to twelve times as long as pod.—In moist shady places it blooms summer to winter.

12. **HUTCHINSIA,** R. Br. Low-growing ann. or per. herbs, 8–10 species native mostly in Eu. and S. W. Asia, 1 in N. Amer. and Australia.—Plants more or less pubescent with forked hairs: lvs. entire or pinnately lobed: fls. white to reddish, small, in terminal racemes; sepals erect, not saccate; stamens free, simple; style lacking or short: fr. a silicle, oval, the septum at right angles to the valves, not winged; seeds numerous in each locule, cotyledons incumbent or accumbent. (Hutchin-sia: for Miss Ellen Hutchins, 1785–1815, an Irish botanist.)

H. alpina, R. Br. (*Lepidium alpinum,* L.). Per. 2–5 in. high, the woody root much-branched, bearing many usually simple and leafless sts., finely pubescent: lvs. in rosettes, 1 in. or less long, petioled, pinnatisect into 1–4 pairs of oval-oblong lobes: fls. white, in small dense racemes; petals about ⅕in. long; sepals shorter, green with white margin: fruiting raceme somewhat elongated, the pod erect, ⅛–⅜in. long; seeds 1 or 2 in each locule. Mts. of Eu.

13. **COCHLEARIA,** L. About 25 ann., bien., and perhaps per. herbs, one sometimes cult. for eating.—Mostly seaside more or less fleshy glabrous plants: lvs. simple, usually entire: fls. small, white, yellow, or purplish, in terminal racemes; stigma mostly capitate: fr. a small silicle, globose or very short-oblong, somewhat inflated but not bladdery, the valves very convex; seeds wingless, usually in 2 rows, cotyledons prevailingly accumbent. (Cochlea-ria: Greek *spoon,* alluding to shape of lvs.)

C. officinalis, L. Scurvy-Grass. Small bien. or per. but grown as an ann., 6–12 in. or more high when in bloom, much-branched and diffuse, making many long-petioled, oblong, reniform or cordate root-lvs., the blade ½–1 in. long, entire or dentate; st.-lvs. obovate to oblong, subsessile: fls. in spring, small, white, ¼in. or less broad, slender-pedicelled in a close cluster that becomes an elongating raceme: fr. ¼in. or less long. Northern boreal and arctic regions.—Formerly grown somewhat as a salad plant (with a tarry flavor), but the plant known mostly medicinally as an antiscorbutic.

14. **LUNARIA,** L. Moonwort. Satin-Flower. Herbs of Eu. and Asia, 2–3 species, grown for ornament.—Erect, branched, with sparse or scattered simple hairs: lvs. ovate-deltoid or ovate, simple, dentate, petioled, some of them opposite: fls. violet or purple, varying to white, in terminal racemes; sepals usually purplish apically, lateral ones saccate; petals prominent and long-clawed; stigmas minute, connate into an obtuse blunt apex; anthers obtuse: fr. a silicle, greatly enlarging flatwise, stipitate in the calyx, the valves parallel to septum and falling away at maturity leaving the persistent papery shiny septum; seeds few, flat and winged, cotyledons accumbent. (Luna-ria: *luna,* the moon, which the lustrous septum suggests.)

a. Pod nearly as broad as long, rounded or truncate at either end....................... 1. *L. annua*
aa. Pod twice or more longer than broad, tapering at either end........................ 2. *L. rediviva*

1. **L. annua,** L. (*L. biennis,* Moench). Honesty. Ann. or bien. 1½–3 ft. high: lvs. coarsely acutely toothed: fls. ¾–1 in. long and broad, mostly pink-purple (white in var. *alba*), fragrant: pod very thin and flat, 1 in. or more long, slightly oblong, the style-beak slender and ¼–⅜in. long; seeds nearly orbicular.—Grown for the fls., but chiefly for the thin lustrous septa that are held in the pod-margins, like spectacles in their rims, after the valves fall and persisting through the winter; often used in dry bouquets; plant also escaped.

2. **L. rediviva,** L. Per.: lvs. finely and sharply toothed: pod oblong-lanceolate, unequal-sided, 2–3 in. long and about 1 in. broad, tapering at both ends, style mostly shorter; seeds reniform.—Less grown than the last, the pods not so ornamental; perhaps escaped.

15. **RICOTIA,** L. About a half dozen annuals of the E. Medit. region, one infrequently grown in the fl.-garden for its bloom.—Weak herbs, glabrous, generally diffusely branching: lvs. more or less pinnatisect: fls. lilac, in terminal racemes; sepals green throughout, the lateral ones saccate at base; petals prominent, emarginate, clawed; stigma entire, acute or sharp-pointed; anthers apically acute: fr. a broad flat thin silique, not stipitate in calyx; seeds in 1 row, sometimes the compartment 1-seeded, flat, cotyledons accumbent. (Rico-tia: bears the name of Ricot, a little known French botanist.)

R. Lunaria, DC. (*Cardamine Lunaria,* L.). Very diffuse ann. 8–20 in. high, coming into bloom rapidly in May and June, the long-petioled obcordate large cotyledons usually persisting: lvs. pinnatisect, with 2 or 3 pairs of nearly opposite lobed lfts.: fls. ½in. or more across: fr. oblong, about 1 in. long, somewhat tapering either way, tipped with short style-beak, hanging. Syria, Egypt.

16. **PELTARIA,** Jacq. Shieldwort. Glabrous per. herbs, 4 or more species in the Medit. region, one sometimes grown for ornament.—Lvs. mostly entire, those on the st. usually sagittate-clasping: fls. white or rose-colored, small, in large terminal clusters; calyx with distinct sinus between the non-gibbous sepals; stamens free and without appendages or teeth; stigma usually sessile: fr. a silicle, orbicular or obovate,

much flattened and papery, valves parallel to septum, indehiscent, on spreading pedicels; seeds 1–4, wingless, hanging in the compartment, the cotyledons accumbent. (Pelta-ria: Greek *small shield*, the shape of the pod.)

P. alliacea, Jacq. Erect, 10–18 in., branched, with an onion-like odor: lvs. oblong, 2–3 in., tapering to a clasping base, obtuse, entire, the upper ones narrow: fls. white, slender-pedicelled, numerous in many short terminal clusters or racemes, in spring and early summer: fr. nearly orbicular, ¼–⅜in. across, with a seed in the center, shield-shaped. S. E. Eu.

17. **ALYSSUM,** L. MADWORT. Mostly in the Medit. region, ann. and per. herbs and subshrubs, probably more than 100 species, a few grown as rock-garden and border subjects.—Low, branching, stellate-pubescent, often cespitose or suffrutescent: lvs. small, undivided, entire or toothed: fls. usually yellow, small, in lengthening terminal racemes; petals entire or retuse; filaments toothed or appendaged by a single nectary gland at each side of base of short stamens: fr. a small silicle with septum flatwise, orbicular or short-oblong, with nerveless valves; seeds 1 or 2 in each locule, often narrowly winged, the cotyledons accumbent. (Alys-sum: the classical name, from Greek for *madness;* supposed to stop hydrophobia.)—Sweet Alyssum of gardens is Lobularia.

A. Plant a spiny low subshrub: fls. white to pinkish............................1. *A. spinosum*
AA. Plant without spines: fls. yellow.
  B. Locules 1-ovuled or 1-seeded: petals usually entire.
    C. Sts. more or less ascending, to 6 in. high: fls. in short racemes.................2. *A. alpestre*
    CC. Sts. erect, 10–24 in. high: fls. in rather broad corymbs.........................3. *A. murale*
  BB. Locules 2- (many-) ovuled or -seeded: petals usually emarginate.
    C. Basal lvs. 2–4 (5) in. long including the petiole; st.-lvs. smaller, subsessile .....4. *A. saxatile*
    CC. Basal and st.-lvs. similar, mostly less than 1 in. long.........................5. *A. montanum*

1. **A. spinosum,** L. Dense-growing spiny subshrub 4–16 in. high, silvery-scurfy and more or less stellate-hairy throughout: lvs. oblong to obovate, ½–2 in. long, obtusish, cuneate at base: fls. white to pinkish, fragrant, in short racemes: fr. orbicular, convex, rounded at tip, glabrous, each locule with 2 narrowly winged seeds. S. W. Eu., N. Afr. Var. **roseum,** Hort., has deep rose-colored fls.

2. **A. alpestre,** L. Tufted per. with a primary woody root and many more or less ascending sts. to 6 in. high: lvs. obovate to spatulate, ¼–½in. or more long, obtuse, cuneate, short-petioled or subsessile, grayish stellate-hairy on both sides: fls. small, yellow, in short dense racemes: fr. broadly elliptic, obtuse at ends, stellate-hairy, with 1 wingless seed in each locule. Mts. of Eu.—Much of the material cult. as *A. idæum* belongs here; *A. idæum,* Boiss. & Heldr., has glabrous frs. with more seeds to a locule. *A. serpyllifolium,* Desf., from S. W. Eu., differs in having smaller paler yellow fls. and elliptic-obovate frs. somewhat cuneate at base.

3. **A. murale,** Waldst. & Kit. YELLOW-TUFT. Per. dull or gray-green throughout, with erect branching sts. 10–24 in. high: basal lvs. not forming rosettes and usually having fallen by flowering time; st.-lvs. oblanceolate, ½–¾ (1½) in. long, acute to obtuse, cuneate, short-petioled, stellate hairs denser beneath: fls. yellow, small, numerous, in terminal corymbose infl. 2–6 in. across: fr. usually roundish, the stellate hairs on the mature fr. not forming a dense mat, the epidermis visible between the few (6–13) thick rays of the hairs, containing 1 winged seed in each locule. E. and S. E. Eu. to S. Russia and Syria.—Material cult. as *A. argenteum* belongs here; true *A. argenteum,* Vitm. (*Lunaria argentea,* All.), from the Italian Alps, is lower-growing with less stiff sts.; stellate hairs on mature frs. with many (14–30) thin rays and forming a dense mat through which the epidermis usually cannot be seen. Plants grown as *A. rostratum* are usually *A. murale; A. rostratum,* Steven, is an ann. not known to be cult.

4. **A. saxatile,** L. GOLDEN-TUFT. BASKET-OF-GOLD. Per. with grayish foliage, sts. erect, 8–12 in. high: basal lvs. many, oblanceolate to obovate-oblong, 2–5 in. long including the petiole, acute to obtuse, obscurely toothed or entire; st.-lvs. smaller, subsessile: fls. golden-yellow, in compact corymbose panicles that elongate in fr.: fr. suborbicular, compressed, glabrous. S. Eu. Var. **compactum,** Hort., is dwarf and dense-growing. Var. **luteum,** Hort. (*citrinum, sulphureum*), has pale yellow fls.

5. **A. montanum,** L. Per., woody at base, with many erect or ascending sts. 4–8 in. high: lvs. obovate to lanceolate, acute to obtusish, attenuate at base, stellate hairs usually denser on under side: fls. yellow, in dense short racemes that elongate in fr.: fr. orbicular to elliptic, stellate-pubescent, somewhat convex, apex subemarginate, with 2 narrowly winged seeds in each locule. Cent. and S. Eu., Caucasus.—Some of the material cult. as *A. idæum* belongs here. Three species closely related to *A. montanum* and sometimes cult. are: *A. Wulfenianum,* Bernh., from S. Eu., larger glabrous fr.; *A. Moellendorfianum,* Aschers, from Bosnia, pedicels of fr. silvery-lepidote; *A. repens,* Baumg., from S. E. Eu., orange fls. larger; hairs simple instead of forked hairs intermixed with stellate hairs on the pedicels.

18. **LOBULARIA,** Desv. About 5 Medit. species, differing from Alyssum in having forked and simple rather than stellate hairs, white entire petals, filaments not toothed but with 2 glands on each at base and 1 gland much longer than other. (Lobula-ria: Latin *lobulus*, a little lobe, probably in reference to the forked hairs.)

L. maritima, Desv. (*Clypeola maritima*, L. *Koniga maritima*, R. Br. *Alyssum maritimum*, Lam. *A. odoratum*, Hort.). SWEET ALYSSUM. Familiar little white-fld. (sometimes violet) fragrant half-hardy per. but usually grown as an ann., wide-spreading on the ground, branches rising 6–12 in.: lvs. lanceolate or linear, entire, tapering to base: fls. small but numerous, in lengthening racemes, slender-pedicelled: fr. small, nearly circular, tipped with short but evident beak. Sometimes escaped.—Cult. in large and small forms and with white-edged lvs. and sometimes with double fls.; blooms over a long season. The dwarf compact form is sometimes known as *Alyssum Benthamii* and *A. minimum*. Plants cult. as *Alyssum procumbens* may belong here.

19. **DRABA,** L. Little tufted annuals and perennials, largely of mts. and cold regions, about 270 species mostly in the northern hemisphere.—Pubescence simple, branched or stellate: lvs. simple, entire or dentate, mostly in basal rosettes: fls. small but usually profusely produced, in few-fld. racemes, white, yellow or purplish; filaments not toothed; stigma nearly or quite entire: fr. a silicle, short, linear to nearly globose, glabrous or pubescent; seeds in 2 rows, usually not margined, the cotyledons accumbent. (Dra-ba: old Greek name for a cress.)—Several species are good rock-garden subjects but are not much grown in N. Amer.

A. Lvs. narrowly oblong-linear, broadly sessile at base.
  B. Length of lvs. to ½in.: stamens subequal to petals........................1. *D. aizoides*
  BB. Length of lvs. to ¼in.: stamens half as long as petals........................2. *D. bruniifolia*
AA. Lvs. oblong-oblanceolate, cuneate at base.
  B. Plant with elongating prostrate sts.; fl.-sts. 2–10 in. high........................3. *D. sibirica*
  BB. Plant cespitose; fl.-sts. ½–2 in. high........................4. *D. fladnizensis*

1. **D. aizoides,** L. Densely cespitose per., the leafless fl.-sts. erect, 2–4 in. high: lvs. linear-oblong, to ½in. long, acute, broadly sessile at base, margins with long remote cilia, in dense basal rosettes: fls. yellow, 4–18 in corymbs elongating in fr.: fr. ellipsoid, somewhat compressed, three to four times as long as the curved style. Mts. of Eu.

2. **D. bruniifolia,** Steven. Densely cespitose per. with leafless fl.-sts. 2–4 in. high: lvs. narrowly linear-oblong, ¼in. long, acute, sessile, keeled, prominently ciliate, much crowded: fls. golden-yellow, 8–16 in corymbs elongating in fr.; petals twice as long as calyx: fr. ovoid, slightly longer than broad, hairy, with a short beak. Caucasus, Asia Minor.—Some of the plants cult. as *D. olympica* may belong here; true *D. olympica*, Sibth., has longer cilia on the lf.-margins and longer hair on the fr.; E. Medit. region. *D. rigida*, Willd., has stiff glossy broadly linear to elliptic lvs. and large clusters of yellow fls., and differs from *D. bruniifolia* in ovary with 32–36 rather than 4–10 ovules.

3. **D. sibirica,** Thell. (*Lepidium sibiricum*, Pall. *D. repens*, Bieb.). Soft green per. with more or less prostrate sts. sometimes elongating to 12 in.: lvs. oblong-oblanceolate, acute, attenuate at base, entire, somewhat hairy: fls. yellow, 8–20 on ascending sts. 2–10 in. long: fr. oblong-ellipsoid, often somewhat curved, style short. Caucasus, Siberia.

4. **D. fladnizensis,** Wulfen. Small cespitose per. forming tufts to 2 in. across, with ascending fl.-sts. ½–2½ in. high: lvs. oblong-oblanceolate, to ½in. long, obtusish, attenuate at base, mostly entire, ciliate or nearly glabrous: fls. whitish or yellowish-white, 2–12 in corymbs that scarcely elongate in fr.: fr. oblong-ellipsoid, compressed, glabrous, the style-beak not prominent. Arctic and alpine regions, Asia, Eu., N. Amer.

20. **ARMORACIA,** Gaertn., B. Mey. & Scherb. About 3 tall glabrous per. herbs in Eu. and Asia, the group not yet sufficiently defined; one is cult. for eating.—Roots deep and large: lvs. mostly dock-like, notched or some of them fimbriate: fls. white, many in naked panicled racemes, on slender pedicels; stigma capitate; ovules in 2 rows: fr. nearly orbicular, small, cotyledons accumbent. (Armora-cia: an old Latin substantive designating the horse-radish.)

A. lapathifolia, Gilib. (*A. rusticana*, Gaertn., B. Mey. & Scherb.). HORSE-RADISH. Strong long-lived per. with deep branching woody root used as a sauce and relish: lower lvs. large, oblong or oblong-ovate, long-petioled, crenate-dentate, some of the early ones much-lobed or even pectinate; st.-lvs. mostly sessile or tapering: fl.-st. 1½–3 ft., bearing many white fls., in spring, ⅛in. or more across: fr. ovoid to short-oblong, sometimes not forming and apparently not maturing viable seed. S. E. Eu., also run wild.—The plant is named in several genera, as *Cochlearia Armoracia*, L., *Nasturtium Armoracia*, Fries, *Rorippa Armoracia*, Hitchc., *Radicula Armoracia*, Rob.

21. **CARDAMINE,** L. Bitter-Cress. Species probably more than 100, ann. and per., of small size, one cult. for ornament and for salad, native in temp. regions, mostly in swamps and along streams.—Erect or ascending from rhizomes, mostly glabrous, lf.-bearing: lvs. simple, pinnate or lyrate: fls. white or purple, often showy for size of plant, mostly racemose; stigma simple: siliques linear and somewhat flattened, valves nerveless or nearly so and separating elastically from base; seeds in 1 row, usually wingless, cotyledons accumbent. (Cardam-ine: ancient name of a cress, from the Greek referring to supposed heart-healing qualities.)

C. pratensis, L. Cuckoo-Flower. Ladies-Smock. Slender erect glabrous per. 12–20 in. high, with attractive fls. in spring and early summer: lvs. pinnately divided, the pairs 3–7, segms. small, oblong or rounded, usually not exceeding ½in. long: fls. white or rose-purple, bright and pretty, ½in. long, in a terminal erect corymb-like raceme, sometimes double: fr. 1 in. or more long. Eu. and Amer., native in the northern parts.—The young lower lvs. are seldom eaten as cress.

22. **DENTARIA,** L. Toothwort. Pepper-Root. About 16 species of per. herbs native in the northern hemisphere.—Horizontal rhizomes nodulous, scaly or toothed, from which arise basal lvs. and erect usually simple fl.-sts. with 2–3 or more lvs. in their upper half: lvs. ternately divided or entire: fls. white to rose or purple, in racemose corymbs: fr. a linear silique, flattened, valves usually nerveless, separating elastically from the base; seeds in 1 row in each cell, wingless, cotyledons accumbent. (Denta-ria: Greek meaning *tooth,* from the tooth-like divisions of the rootstock.)

D. diphylla, Michx. Stout simple glabrous sts. 6–12 in. or more high, with usually 2 opposite lvs., from a long continuous rootstock: basal lvs. long-petioled; lvs. ternate, the lfts. ovate, dentate or lobed, about 2 in. or more long, glabrous: fls. white, ½in. or more across, in few-fld. short racemes: fr. 1 in. or more long, with slender style. N. S. to Minn. and S. C.—The related *D. laciniata,* Muhl., has moniliform rootstocks and oblong-linear lfts.

23. **BARBAREA,** Beckmann (*Campe,* Dulac). Winter-Cress. Upland-Cress. A half dozen or more species in temp. regions.—Erect and rather stiff usually glabrous branching herbs with angled sts. 2 ft. or less tall: lvs. pinnatifid or lyrate: fls. small, light or greenish-yellow, in elongating racemes; style short, stigma nearly entire, capitate: fr. linear, 4-sided or -angled, erect or spreading, valves keeled; seeds in 1 row, wingless, cotyledons accumbent. (Barbare-a: anciently dedicated to St. Barbara.)—The radical lvs. are sometimes used for seasoning and garnishing.

A. Pod obtusely angled, the pedicel slender although short: lateral lf.-segms. mostly less than 4 pairs....1. *B. vulgaris*
AA. Pod sharply angled, on a stout pedicel about as thick as itself: lateral segms. of main lower lvs. mostly more than 4 pairs....2. *B. verna*

1. **B. vulgaris,** R. Br. (*Erysimum Barbarea,* L.). Bien. or per. 1–2 ft. high, blooming in spring from over-winter rosettes: lvs. pinnatifid with mostly 1–3 pairs of lobes and a large rounded terminal lobe, petioled, the upper st.-lvs. sessile, clasping and only angled: pod spreading, about ¾–1 in. long, the short pedicels distinctly thinner than the pod. Eu.; widely nat. in N. Amer.—It has been offered as a salad or garnishing plant. An ornamental variegated-lvd. var. is known, also one that is double-fld. The plant is a common weed of crop lands, often known as Spring Mustard.

2. **B. verna,** Aschers. (*Erysimum vernum,* Mill. *B. præcox,* R. Br.). Early or Belle Isle Cress. Similar to *B. vulgaris* but lateral lobes of lvs. 4 or more pairs: pod longer, on pedicels of nearly equal thickness. Eu.; nat. in N. Amer.—The species usually grown as a cress, but it is not frequent.

24. **ARABIS,** L. Rock-Cress. Small ann., bien. and per. herbs, 100 and more species in temp. regions, very few grown for ornament in borders and rock-gardens.—Erect or spreading, mostly more or less hairy or pubescent with stellate or forked hairs: lvs. entire, lobed or pinnatifid: fls. white or purple, in terminal racemes or spikes, usually small but often profuse and appearing over a considerable period; stigma nearly or quite entire: fr. a silique, linear, flattened, the valves commonly 1-nerved; seeds in 1 or 2 rows, winged or wingless, cotyledons accumbent. (Arabis: Arabia.)

A. Fls. rose or pink to purple.
B. St.-lvs. oblong, not clasping at base, obtuse, with blunt teeth....1. *A. blepharophylla*
BB. St.-lvs. ovate-cordate, clasping at base, acute, with sharp teeth.

c. Petals ⅜–½in. or more long, 2 of the sepals saccate....................2. *A. aubrietioides*
cc. Petals ¼–⅜in. long, the 4 sepals nearly equal..............................3. *A. rosea*
AA. Fls. white.
B. Sts. usually not over 4 in. high; st.-lvs. few or almost lacking.............4. *A. Kellereri*
BB. Sts. 4–8 (16) in. high; st.-lvs. 2–8 or more.
c. Lvs. entire or with 1 tooth on each side; st.-lvs. not clasping............5. *A. procurrens*
cc. Lvs. dentate, sometimes only sparsely so; st.-lvs. clasping.
D. Petals ¼–⅜in. long: plant lightly hairy: lvs. sharply toothed...........6. *A. alpina*
DD. Petals ⅜–½in. long: plant whitish felty-tomentose: lvs. bluntly toothed..7. *A. caucasica*

1. **A. blepharophylla,** Hook. & Arn. Tufted per. with usually simple sts. 4–8 (12) in. high: basal lvs. obovate to elliptic, 1–2¾ in. long, obtuse, dentate or entire, pubescent or glabrous except for the margins; st.-lvs. few, oblong, sessile: fls. rose-purple, fragrant, in short dense racemes that elongate in fr.; petals about ½in. long: fr. suberect, 1–1½ in. long. Calif.

2. **A. aubrietioides,** Boiss. Densely cespitose per., more or less canescent-tomentose, sts. 4–8 in. high: basal lvs. obovate, obtuse, with few obtuse teeth; st.-lvs. ovate-cordate, clasping, acute, with acute teeth: fls. pink to purplish, in short dense racemes that elongate in fr.: fr. 1½–2 in. long. Asia Minor.

3. **A. rosea,** DC. (*A. muralis* var. *rosea*, Fiori). Tufted per. with erect or ascending sts. to 10 in. or more high, simple or branched below, glabrous at tip, pubescent beneath: basal lvs. obovate-oblong, attenuate at base to winged petiole, obtuse, dentate, sparsely pubescent; st.-lvs. oblong-ovate, cordate and somewhat clasping at base, acute, dentate: fls. rose-purple, in 12–15-fld. racemes that are nodding when young, erect and elongating in fr.; petals ¼–⅓in. long: fr. linear, compressed, erect, to 3 in. and more long. S. Eu., N. Afr.—Much material listed as *A. rosea* is *A. Arendsii*, see under no. 7.

4. **A. Kellereri,** Sünderm. (*A. brizoides* × *A. Ferdinandi-Coburgii*). Low densely cespitose per. with suberect sometimes branched sts. usually not over 4 in. high: lvs. mostly basal, lanceolate, sessile, about ¼–½in. long, ashy-gray, densely covered on both sides with long simple or stellate hairs: fls. white, ¼–⅜in. long, in terminal racemes. (Named for Johann Kellerer, page 46.) A sterile hybrid of garden origin.

5. **A. procurrens,** Waldst. & Kit. (*A. mollis*, Hort. not Steven). Per. with lvs. in basal tufts, spreading by underground stolons; sts. erect or ascending, usually simple, to 10 in. high, appressed-pubescent below: basal lvs. long-obovate, attenuate to winged petiole, acute, entire or with 1 tooth on each side, glabrous above, pubescent on margins and on veins beneath; st.-lvs. 2–8, narrowly ovate, sessile, broad but not clasping at base: fls. white, in many-fld. racemes; petals about ⅜in. long; sepals about half as long as petals, glabrous, membranous-margined: fr. linear, 1–1½ in. long, the valves with a distinct midnerve. S. E. Eu.—Some of the plants in the American trade as *A. Sturii* may belong here.

6. **A. alpina,** L. Mountain Rock-Cress. Low tufted per., rough-hairy, with simple stellate hairs and branched woody rootstock; sts. erect or ascending, simple or branched, 4–10 (16) in. high: basal lvs. oblong-obovate, cuneate, petioled, subacute, rather acutely toothed; st.-lvs. cordate-ovate, sessile, more or less clasping: fls. white, in dense short racemes; petals ¼–⅜in. long, the cuneate-obovate blade gradually narrowed to the claw: fr. 1–2½ in. long at maturity, in elongated racemes. Mts. of Eu., Siberia, boreal Amer.—Apparently not common in cult., much material so listed being *A. caucasica.* Listed varietal names include *grandiflora, nana, rosea, variegata.*

7. **A. caucasica,** Willd. (*A. albida*, Steven). Wall Rock-Cress. Similar to *A. alpina* but whitish-felty-tomentose, the hairs more distinctly stellate: lvs. obtusish, with duller teeth, the teeth often fewer or lacking toward the base: petals ⅜–½in. or more long, the blade abruptly narrowed to the claw. Medit. region to Iran. Var. **flore-pleno,** Hort., has double fls. Var. **variegata,** Hort., has lvs. conspicuously margined creamy-white.—**A. Arendsii,** Wehrhahn (*A. albida* var. *rosea*, Hort.), is a hybrid between *A. aubrietioides* and *A. caucasica*, with rose-colored fls.

25. **NASTURTIUM,** R. Br. Species probably more than 50, but the generic limitations are not agreed on, usually in wet and moist places in the temp. zone; one is everywhere known as a salad plant and for garnishing.—Mostly small glabrous plants, ann., bien., per.: lvs., some or all, variously pinnatifid or pinnate or sometimes entire: fls. small, white or yellow, in terminal racemes; stamens sometimes less than 6: fr. short, terete or nearly so, the valves convex and usually weakly nerved; seeds in 2 rows in most species, many and small, usually marginless, the cotyledons accumbent. (Nastur-tium: Latin *nasi tortium*, "distortion of the nose," in allusion to pungent qualities.)

N. officinale, R. Br. Water-Cress. Per., creeping or floating, rooting, thriving in clear cold water: lvs. odd-pinnate, with 1–4 pairs of small oblong or roundish lfts., the terminal lft. larger: fls. small, white, in elongating racemes, pedicelled: fr. a curved linear long-pedicelled somewhat turgid many-seeded silique with a short beak-like tip. Widespread in ditches and streams and often colonized for the supply of cress; nat. from Eu.—The plant has several names, as *Rorippa Nasturtium-aquaticum*, Hayek, *Sisymbrium Nasturtium-aquaticum*, L., *Radicula Nasturtium-aquaticum*, Britt. & Rendle, but the restoration and conservation of the name Nasturtium by the Third International Botanical Congress should simplify the practice.

26. **AUBRIETA,** Adans. About a dozen little perennials from the E. Medit. region to Iran, one frequent in rock-gardens and borders.—Cespitose or mat-forming plants of mts., pubescent with stellate or forked hairs: lvs. entire or angularly toothed: fls. few but large for size of plant, in short terminal racemes, violet or purple, rarely white; outer sepals saccate; shorter filaments toothed; style slender and stigma simple: fr. a short silique, in some species globose but in ours oblong; seeds in 2 rows, the cotyledons accumbent. (Aubrie-ta: Claude Aubriet, 1651–1743, French flower and animal painter.)

A. deltoidea, DC. (*Alyssum deltoideum*, L.). Attractive spring and summer bloomer, 2–6 (12) in. high, cespitose, spreading and often mat-forming, pubescence stellate at least in part: lvs. spatulate to rhomboidal, narrowed to a short petiole, with 1 or more teeth on each side: fls. few, bright rose-lilac to purple; petals to ¾in. long, long-clawed; calyx cylindrical, about half as long as petals: fr. long-ellipsoid, subcircular in cross-section, to ¾in. long including the ¼in. beak, with stellate and bristly hairs. Sicily, Greece to Asia Minor. Var. **græca,** Regel (*A. græca*, Griseb.), larger and taller; fls. ¾–1 in. long; beak of fr. one-half to three-fourths as long as ovary; Greece. Var. **rosea,** Hort., fls. pink.—Many hort. variants and intervarietal hybrids are in the trade under names, including: **Bougainvillei,** dwarf, compact, with light violet-purple fls.; **Eyrei,** free-branching, fls. large, rich violet-purple; **Hendersonii,** blue-violet fls.; **Leichtlinii,** pink to rose fls.; **Moerheimii,** large rose fls. These variants may be treated as derivatives of *A. cultorum*, Bergmans.

27. **MATTHIOLA,** R. Br. Stocks. Some 50 Old World species of ann. and per. herbs or subshrubs, one in common cult. in fl.-gardens and a commercial crop of florists.—Gray-stellate-pubescent plants with entire or pinnatifid lvs.: fls. purple to white or yellowish to maroon, the petals long-clawed; sepals erect, the inner saccate; style usually lacking; stigma clearly 2-lobed and the lobes either spreading or thickened on the sides and decurrent, a swollen gibbosity or horned projection usually present on back side: fr. a terete or compressed silique, the valves nerved; seeds in 1 row, often margined, cotyledons accumbent. (Matthi-ola: Peter Andrew Matthioli, 1500–1577, Italian physician and botanist.)

A. Pod terminating in 2 long horns: plant diffuse and slender........................1. *M. bicornis*
AA. Pod not horned: plant erect........................2. *M. incana*

1. **M. bicornis,** DC. (*Cheiranthus bicornis*, Sibth. & Smith). Evening Stock. Perfume-Plant. Diffuse much-branched ann. or bien., with long slender parts: lvs. linear-lanceolate to lanceolate, 1½–3½ in. long including the short petiole, acute, entire or remotely small-toothed: fls. sessile at intervals toward the end of the sts., about ¾in. long, broadly expanding at evening and closed by day, very fragrant when open, lilac or purplish: fr. 3–4 in. long, spreading and looking like branches, forked at the end. Greece.

2. **M. incana,** R. Br. (*Cheiranthus incanus*, L.). Stock. Brampton Stock. Gilliflower. Erect bien. or per., felty-pubescent, sts. stiff, 1–2 ft. high, more or less woody at base: lvs. long-oblong to oblanceolate, 2½–6 in. long including the narrow petiole-like base, very obtuse, entire: fls. in terminal racemes, on stout pedicels, about 1 in. long but becoming much broader in the double forms, purple or reddish but cult. in white, pink, scarlet, terra-cotta, and yellowish: fr. 1½–3 in. long, erect, thick and stout, suddenly terminated by the remains of the 2-lobed stigma. Eu. Var. **annua,** Voss (*Cheiranthus annuus*, L. *M. annua*, Sweet), Ten Weeks or Intermediate Stock, is ann., less woody, blooming earlier from seed.

28. **MALCOLMIA,** R. Br. Malcolm Stocks. Species about 25, of the Medit. region and eastward, one grown in the fl.-garden.—Mostly ann., differing from Hesperis technically in the 2 stigmas that are connate and form a tapering sharp-pointed cone-like beak; plants much-branching, often more or less prostrate, the pubescence of forked hairs or stellate: lvs. entire or pinnatifid: fls. white, reddish or purplish, in terminal racemes; petals either long-clawed or long and narrow: fr. a long and linear silique; seeds in 1 row (or side by side sometimes at base of pod), not winged or margined, the cotyledons incumbent. (Malcol-mia: for William Malcolm, 1769–1820, English nurseryman.)

M. maritima, R. Br. (*Cheiranthus maritimus,* L.). VIRGINIAN STOCK. Diffuse little ann. 8–15 in. high, the sts. erect or sometimes the main st. decumbent and erect branches rising from it, lightly pubescent with appressed forked hairs: lf.-blades to 1½ in. long, oblong, elliptic or linear-oblong, obtuse, entire or practically so, the lower ones narrowed into a petiole: fls. small, about ½in. long, bright, lilac, red, white, the petals strongly veined, borne in profusion and produced in long succession by means of repeated sowings; pedicels slender, mostly shorter than calyx: fr. very slender, about 2 in. long, sharp-pointed. Coasts of S. Eu.

29. **HESPERIS, L.** ROCKET. About two dozen species in the Medit. region and Cent. Asia, bien. or per., one known in cult. for its bloom.—Erect, glabrous, or with simple and forked hairs: lvs. mostly undivided, entire or toothed: fls. white or purple and showy in long terminal racemes, often fragrant; sepals erect, the inner saccate; lobes of stigma erect, blunt, and face to face: fr. long and linear, spreading, more or less torulose, remains of the 2-lobed stigma usually apparent; seeds in 1 row, wingless, cotyledons incumbent or almost accumbent. (Hes-peris: Greek *evening,* when the fragrance is most marked.)

H. matronalis, L. DAMES-VIOLET. Tall branching per. (or bien.), 1–3 ft., hirsute or sometimes glabrous: lvs. lanceolate to lance-ovate, 2–4 in. long, sharp-acuminate, sessile or with short base, denticulate: fls. about ¾in. long, in terminal racemes, lilac or light purple (white races, *alba,* and also double-fld. ones), sweet-scented: pod 2–4 in. long, very slender, the mature stigmas forming a sharp beak. Eu., Asia; nat. and frequent about old yards.—Blooms in spring and early summer.

30. **CHEIRANTHUS, L.** About 10 perennials, sometimes subshrubby, from the Madeira and Canary Isls. eastward to the Himalayas; one long well known in fl.-gardens.—Plant with appressed forked hairs: lvs. narrow, entire or nearly so: fls. prevailingly yellow and orange, often tinted brown or in cult. brown-purple, in terminal racemes or spikes; lateral sepals saccate at base; petals long-clawed; stigmas mostly with 2 short spreading lobes; stamens without median nectary glands: fr. a long 4-sided or -angled silique; seeds in almost 2 rows, usually not winged, cotyledons accumbent or incumbent. (Cheiran-thus: *cheiri* is said to be a modification of an Arabic name for a plant; here combined with the Greek *anthos,* flower.)

C. Cheiri, L. WALLFLOWER. Hardy per., erect, 1–2½ ft., thinly appressed-pubescent, with a grayish cast: lvs. lanceolate to narrow-lanceolate, acute, entire, 1½–3 in. long, usually bunched beneath the fls. and at the end of sterile shoots, the lower ones tapering to short broad petioles: fls. large, ¾–1 in. long, very fragrant, yellow or yellow-brown, in early spring; petals rounded, slender-clawed, much exceeding the calyx: fr. erect, 2–2½ in. long and rather thick, angled, with short style-tip. S. Eu.—An old garden favorite for early spring bloom, in many forms and colors, often much doubled. This diagnosis distinguishes the wallflower from the plant known amongst us as *C. Allionii,* for which see *Erysimum Perofskianum.* **C. kewensis,** Hort., is listed as a hybrid between *C. mutabilis* and a garden var. of *C. Cheiri;* fls. orange-yellow, fading to purplish, fragrant.

31. **ERYSIMUM, L.** BLISTER-CRESS. Some 80 species of ann., bien. and per. herbs, native in Eu., Asia and N. Amer.—Differs technically from Cheiranthus in having median as well as lateral nectaries at base of stamens, the seeds in 1 row, and the cotyledons incumbent: siliques usually more angular than in Cheiranthus: the cult. kinds are yellow-, orange- or lilac-fld. (Erys-imum: Greek name meaning to *draw blisters.*)

A. Fls. lilac .... 1. *E. linifolium*
AA. Fls. yellow or orange.
  B. Fl.-sts. usually not over 6 in. high.
    C. Style not as long as breadth of fr.: lvs. subentire .... 2. *E. silvestre* var.
    CC. Style two to three times longer than breadth of fr.: st.-lvs. dentate .... 3. *E. pulchellum* var.
  BB. Fl.-sts. 10 in.–3 ft. high.
    C. Pubescence on upper surface of lvs. 3-branched for the most part.
      D. Lvs. of fl.-sts. distinctly and sharply dentate .... 3. *E. pulchellum*
      DD. Lvs. subentire .... 4. *E. suffruticosum*
    CC. Pubescence of lvs. forked.
      D. Beak of fr. about ⅛in. long: claws of petals not exceeding calyx .... 5. *E. Perofskianum*
      DD. Beak of fr. less than 1/16in. long: claws of petals exceeding calyx .... 6. *E. asperum*

1. **E. linifolium,** J. Gay (*Cheiranthus linifolius,* Pers.). Low bien. or perhaps per., making a close clump of slender suberect fl.-sts. 6–12 in. high from the crown or from decumbent stolon-like sts.; pubescence appressed, simple or forked to the base and appearing

simple: lvs. entire or remotely toothed, 1–3 in. or more long, lower lvs. oblong, tapering to a long thin petiole, upper lvs. linear: fls. lilac or mauve, in dense terminal racemes; sepals purplish, erect, lateral ones saccate: fr. 2–2½ in. long, 4-sided, erect. Spain.

2. **E. silvestre,** Scop., var. **pumilum,** Beckmann (*Cheiranthus pumilus,* Murith. *E. pumilum,* Gaudin). Cespitose per. with sterile and fl.-sts. from a woody base; fl.-sts. simple, 2–6 in. high, with 3–5 lvs.; pubescence appressed, forked: lvs. linear-lanceolate, subentire, the lower ones petioled: fls. sulfur-yellow, slightly fragrant, in terminal racemes; sepals three to four times longer than pedicels, the lateral sepals saccate: fr. 4-angled, erect, on spreading pedicels. Mts. of Eu.

3. **E. pulchellum,** J. Gay (*Cheiranthus pulchellus,* Willd.). Per., cespitose or many-headed with simple or branched ascending sts. from a few in. to 2 ft. high; pubescence forked: lower lvs. oblong-spatulate, petioled, upper lvs. oblong-lanceolate, sessile; st.-lvs. distinctly and sharply dentate, lvs. of the sterile shoots subentire or with a few minute teeth: fls. deep yellow; sepals about twice as long as pedicels: fr. erect or somewhat spreading, style two to three times longer than breadth of silique. Greece to Asia Minor. Var. **microphyllum,** Boiss. (*Cheiranthus rupestris,* Sibth. & Smith. *E. rupestre,* DC.), dwarf, densely cespitose, with smaller more finely toothed lvs., fls. yellow; Greece.—Sometimes cult. as *Cheiranthus Allionii.*

4. **E. suffruticosum,** Spreng. (*E. murale,* Desf.). Bien. or per. but may be grown as an ann., woody at base, with many erect leafy usually branched sts. to about 20 in. high: lvs. oblong-lanceolate, acute, tapering at both ends, subentire, pubescence mostly 3-forked: fls. yellow, about ½in. long; sepals subequal to pedicels: fr. 1–1½ in. long, erect, on spreading pedicels, style not as long as width of the silique. Origin unknown; long cult. and possibly a hybrid.—The older name of *E. murale* is a *nomen nudum,* without description, and hence may not be employed. Some of the material cult. as *E. pulchellum* and *E. nanum* may belong here.

5. **E. Perofskianum,** Fisch. & Mey. Green-lvd. erect ann., perhaps persisting the winter if started in autumn, 10–20 in. or more high; st. simple or little branched; thin pubescence of appressed mostly 2-forked (sometimes 3–4-forked) hairs: lvs. oblong-lanceolate, rather thin, 2–3 in. long, tapering at both ends, lower lvs. petiolate, usually with a few prominent teeth: fls. orange or saffron-yellow, ½in. or more long, in terminal racemes: fr. 2–3 in. long, lightly pubescent, obscurely 4-angled, on short pedicels, ascending. (Bears the name of Velar de Perowski.) Afghanistan, Beluchistan.—**E. Allionii,** Hort. (*Cheiranthus Allionii,* Hort.), is apparently closely related but differs in being bien. and having slightly larger fls. with claws more or less exceeding the calyx; origin unknown and may be a garden hybrid; material so listed may also be *E. pulchellum.*

6. **E. asperum,** DC. (*Cheiranthus asper,* Nutt.). Bien. and per. with branched hard root and often with a woody stock, grayish-green, sometimes much-branched, 1–3 ft. high; pubescence of bifid (rarely trifid) hairs: lvs. rather firm, narrow-lanceolate to nearly linear, 2–4 in. long, tapering at both ends or the lower ones obtusish, more or less repand-dentate: fls. orange or dark yellow, ¾–1 in. long, in terminal racemes in summer: fr. 1–4 in. long, strongly 4-angled, on short spreading pedicels. Rocky Mts. and Great Plains.—Some of the material cult. as *E. Perofskianum* and *Cheiranthus Allionii* may belong here.

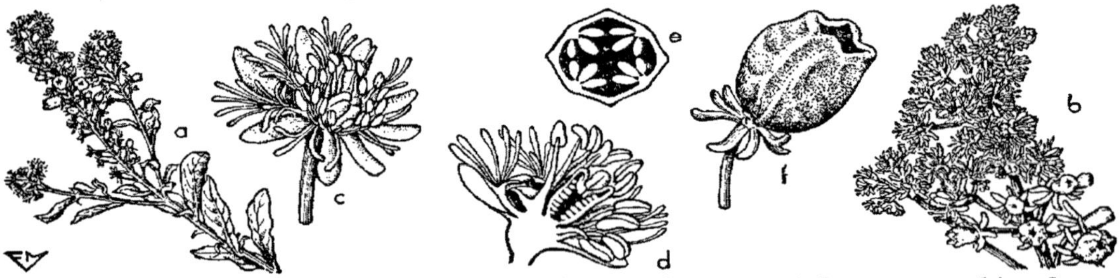

Fig. 84. Resedaceæ. *Reseda odorata:* a, flowering branch, × ⅛; b, inflorescence, × ½; c, flower, × 3; d, same, vertical section, × 3; e, ovary, cross-section, × 7; f, capsule, × 1.

84. RESEDACEÆ. MIGNONETTE FAMILY

Ann. and per. herbs or rarely shrubby, of 6 genera and about 65 species, native mostly in the Medit. region; 2 species are grown in fl.-gardens.—Lvs. alternate or fascicled, entire, 3-parted or pinnate, with gland-like stipules: fls. mostly bisexual, irregular, bracted, in terminal racemes or spikes; calyx persistent, 4–7-parted; petals usually 4–7, entire or cleft, hypogynous or perigynous; stamens 3–40, inserted on the irregular fleshy hypogynous disk; pistils 1–6, free or united into a 1-celled ovary which is usually open at top, placentation parietal, carpels 2–6, ovules many, the stigmas sessile: fr. usually an indehiscent 3–6-lobed gaping caps., sometimes a berry or composed of separate follicles.

RESEDA, L. About 50 species, native mostly in the vicinity of the Medit. and the Red Sea.—Erect or decumbent herbs, sometimes partially woody at base: lvs. simple or compound: fls. small, in terminal spikes or racemes; petals 4–7, greenish, toothed or cleft; stamens 8–40, attached on one side of fl.: caps. 3–6-horned or -angled, opening only at top at maturity. (Rese-da: from Latin name of a plant, from word *to heal* or *assuage*.)

A. Lvs. entire or notched.. 1. *R. odorata*
AA. Lvs. pinnate or deeply pinnatifid.. 2. *R. alba*

1. **R. odorata,** L. COMMON MIGNONETTE. Branching ann. 6–24 in. high, at first upright but becoming wide-spreading and more or less decumbent: lvs. spatulate or oblanceolate to elliptic-oblong, mostly obtuse, usually entire but sometimes notched or lobed: spicate racemes becoming loose and open with age, the fls. very fragrant, yellowish-white (varying to orange and red in cult.), petals finely cleft, anthers golden-yellow: caps. usually with 3 horns. N. Afr.—The mignonette has been greatly modified under cult. and there are many names representing stature, color and habit forms; also many named cultivars are in the trade. Grown for its fragrance.

2. **R. alba,** L. WHITE UPRIGHT MIGNONETTE. An erect rather coarse ann. or bien. 1–3 ft. high, glabrous, sometimes grown in the fl.-border: lvs. often crowded, pinnate or deeply pinnatifid, the segms. linear with entire or undulate margins: spicate racemes very long and slender, the fls. greenish-white, not sweet-scented, the 5 or 6 petals 3-cleft at top: caps. usually with 4 horns. S. Eu., adventive in N. Amer.

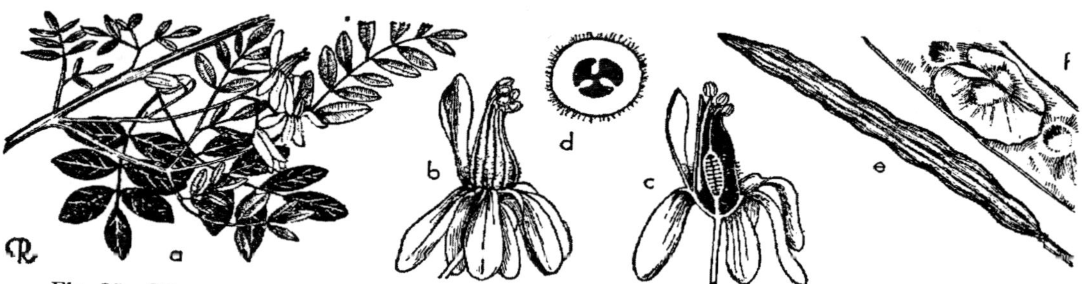

Fig. 85. MORINGACEÆ. *Moringa oleifera:* a, flowering branch, × ½; b, flower, × 1; c, same, vertical section, × 1; d, ovary, cross-section, × 5; e, fruit, × ⅙; f, seed on capsule-valve, × ½.

85. MORINGACEÆ. MORINGA FAMILY

A single genus of about 10 species native in N. Afr. and trop. Asia.—Deciduous trees with gummy bark: lvs. alternate, bi- or tri-odd-pinnate, the lfts. obovate, entire, caducous, stipules 0 or appearing as glands at base of the petioles and lfts.: fls. white or red, bisexual, irregular, perigynous, in axillary panicles; calyx of 5 imbricated sepals, reflexed in fl.; petals 5, unequal, the lower reflexed; stamens in 2 series, 5 perfect ones inserted on the margin of the disk and 5 staminodia, the filaments free; pistil 1, ovary superior and stipitate, 1-celled with 3 parietal placentæ, ovules numerous, style 1 with minute stigma: fr. an elongated beaked 3–12-angled caps. dehiscing the whole length by 3 valves.

MORINGA, Adans. (*Hyperanthera,* Forsk.). One species is grown in warm countries for ornament; the root, which has a pungent taste like the horse-radish, is sometimes eaten; the young frs. are also edible and ben oil, sparingly used in the arts, is extracted from the seeds. Technical characters as for the family. (Morin-ga: from native Malabar name.)

M. oleifera, Lam. (*M. pterygosperma,* Gaertn.). HORSE-RADISH-TREE. Small tree to 25 ft.: lvs. large, mostly 3-pinnate, all parts stalked: fls. white, fragrant, pedicelled, about 1 in. across: pods 1–1½ ft. long, the seeds large, 3-angled and winged. India; spontaneous and planted in W. Indies and N. S. Amer.; cult. in S. Fla.

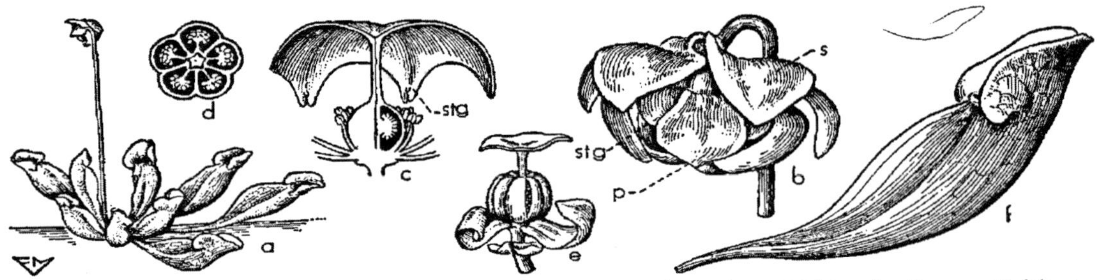

Fig. 86. SARRACENIACEÆ. *Sarracenia purpurea:* a, flowering plant, × ½; b, flower, × ¼; c, same, vertical section, less perianth, × ⅓; d, ovary, cross-section, × 1; e, capsule, × ¼; f, leaf, × ¼. (p petal, s sepal, stg stigma.)

86. SARRACENIACEÆ. SARRACENIA FAMILY

Three genera of about 14 species native in N. Amer. and N. S. Amer.—Specialized insectivorous low per. herbs from a horizontal round rhizome: lvs. basal, tubular and pitcher- or trumpet-like: fls. large, nodding, scapose, solitary or in few-fld. racemes, with 1–3 fl.-bracts; sepals 5 (4–6), persistent, imbricated; petals 5 (rarely 0), yellow or red to purple; stamens numerous; pistil 1, ovary 3–5-celled, superior, with many ovules on axile placentæ; style simple, often peltately dilated: fr. a round to ovoid loculicidal caps.

SARRACENIA, L. PITCHER-PLANT. About 9 species native in E. U. S. and Canada.—Lvs. hollow, with a terminal hood or lid: fls. solitary on an unbracted scape; fl.-bracts 3; sepals 5, greenish; petals 5, larger than the sepals, yellow to purple; stamens numerous; ovary 5-celled, style expanded into an umbrella-like structure, with the stigmas on the under side of the 5 rays or lobes: caps. round, 5-valved, surrounded by the calyx. (Sarrace-nia: named in honor of Dr. M. S. Sarrazin, 1659–1734, a medical doctor in Que. who sent *S. purpurea* to Tournefort.)—The species cross easily, and there are many named natural and hort. hybrids.

A. Pitchers (lvs.) decumbent, two to four times as long as broad . . . . 1. *S. purpurea*
AA. Pitchers erect, ten or more times as long as broad.
B. Fls. red: hood flat and green . . . . 2. *S. rubra*
BB. Fls. yellow: hood with reflexed sides, yellow . . . . 3. *S. flava*

1. **S. purpurea,** L. COMMON PITCHER-PLANT. Lvs. decumbent, curved, 4–12 in. long, much inflated, broadly winged, petiolate, usually purple-veined, pubescent inside with long stiff downward-pointing hairs; hood erect, often notched at tip: fls. purple, 2 in. or more across, on scapes 1–2 ft. high; petals obovate, incurved over the style; style-disk about 1½ in. across, with notched lobes: caps. ½–¾ in. across. Md. to Minn., Canada and Lab. Var. **venosa,** Fern. (*Sarazina venosa,* Raf.), has shorter broader pitchers; N. J. to Fla. and La.

2. **S. rubra,** Walt. SWEET PITCHER-PLANT. Lvs. erect, 4–16 in. tall, nearly tubular, narrowly winged, petiolate, faintly purple-veined, pubescent inside; hood finally erect: fls. red, 1¼–2 in. across, fragrant, on scapes usually exceeding the lvs.; style-disk about 1¼ in. across, with notched lobes: caps. ½–¾ in. across. N. C. to Fla.

3. **S. flava,** L. TRUMPETS. Lvs. erect, 1–3 ft. or more tall, trumpet-shaped, gradually expanding above, narrowly winged, petiolate; hood erect, 2–5 in. across, distinctly narrowed at base, usually yellow with reddish veins; winter lvs. of wing only, lacking tube and hood: fls. yellow, 4–5 in. across, on scapes about as tall as the lvs; expanded style-disk 3–3½ in. across, with 2-cleft lobes or rays: caps. about ¾ in. across. Va. to Fla. and Ala.

87. NEPENTHACEÆ. NEPENTHES FAMILY

"Pitcher-plants," sometimes grown in hothouses for curiosity; one genus of about 70 species native in E. Indies, Malay Peninsula, N. Australia, the Seychelle Isls. and Madagascar, and numerous artificial hybrids.—Semi-woody, prostrate, climbing or rarely erect, sometimes epiphytic: lvs. alternate, exstipulate, sessile or with petiole which is usually winged, the flat blade with 2–12 or more longitudinal veins which are often inconspicuous in fresh specimens, the midrib prolonged into a tendril of varying length which is greatly expanded and hollowed at end forming the "pitcher"; the pitcher usually has 2 fringed or ciliate longitudinal wings in front with a flat area between, copiously veined, rim thickened into collar or peristome that is corrugated or ridged and shining and bears on its serrated inner edge the openings of large sunken glands the excretions of which attract insects which slide off into the watery fluid of the pitcher; midrib ending in short spur just behind the lid or operculum which may be small and narrow or large and cordate, usually with many nectar glands on the under surface: plants diœcious: fls. not showy, often fetid, in simple or panicled racemes opposite a bract-lf. which is usually sessile and differs from the foliage lvs. in generally lacking a pitcher; sepals mostly 4, distinct or rarely connate at base, thick, the inner pair often smaller than the outer pair and bearing nectar-glands on inner surface; petals 0; stamens 4–24, usually 8–10, connate into a column, bearing the anthers in a rounded crowded mass; ovary 1, superior, commonly 4-celled with many ovules on axile placentæ, the style very short or none, with 4-lobed radiating stigma: fr. a caps. loculicidally dehiscent by 4 valves; seeds small, numerous.

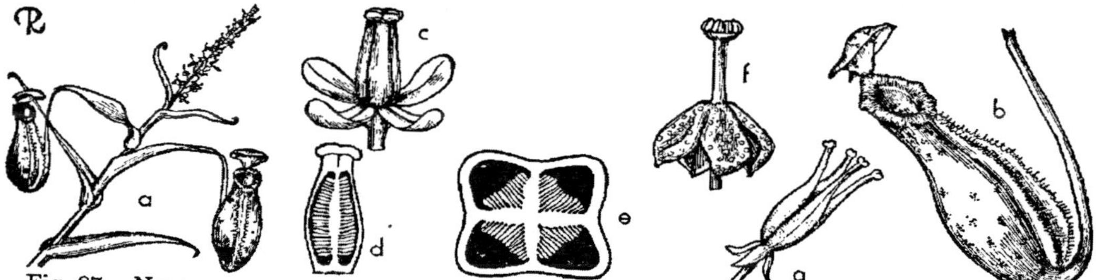

Fig. 87. NEPENTHACEÆ. Nepenthes: a, flowering branch, × 1/8; b, leaf-tip pitcher, × 1/6; c, pistillate flower, × 3; d, pistil, vertical section, × 4; e, ovary, cross-section, × 10; f, staminate flower, × 2; g, capsule, × 3.

NEPENTHES, L. PITCHER-PLANT. Characters as for the family. (Nepen-thes: from Greek *without care,* in allusion to the statement in the Odyssey where Helen so drugged the wine-cup that its contents freed men from grief and care.)

A. Wings of pitchers narrow, cord-like.......................................1. *N. mirabilis*
AA. Wings of lower pitchers broad, doubly fringed..........................2. *N. Hookeriana*

1. **N. mirabilis,** Druce (*Phyllamphora mirabilis,* Lour. *N. Phyllamphora,* Willd.). Prostrate or climbing: lvs. petioled, elliptic-oblong, 6–18 in. long, glabrous, herbaceous, margins dentate-ciliate when young, with 4–8 longitudinal veins on each side: pitchers nearly cylindric, the lower half slightly inflated, 3–6 in. long and 1–1½ in. across, pale green to reddish-green or red, the wings narrow and cord-like; peristome cylindrical, pale green to purple; lid ovate or orbicular. S. China, E. Indies, Australia.

2. **N. Hookeriana,** Lindl. Plants strong and high-climbing, young parts covered with dense tawny pubescence: lvs. petioled, elliptic-lanceolate, 10–24 in. long, somewhat leathery, with 5 longitudinal veins: pitchers 2–6 in. long and 1–3 in. across, dimorphic, the lower ovate or nearly globose, pale green with purple markings, the wings broad and doubly fringed; peristome with dentate margin, green or more or less striped with purple; lid oval or ovate, spur slender, recurved, densely tomentose; upper pitchers funnel-shaped with narrow unfringed wings. (Named for Wm. J. Hooker, page 45.) Malay Penins., Sumatra, Borneo.—Perhaps a natural hybrid between *N. ampullaria* and *N. Rafflesiana.*

The species of Nepenthes hybridize readily and many of the named hybrid forms may be found in choice hothouse collections. A few of them are as follows: **N. atrosanguinea,** Mast. (probably *N. distillatoria* × *N. Sedenii*). Pitchers reddish-purple mottled with pale green, wings fringed, wide below and narrow above. **N. Courtii,** Veitch (*N.?* × *N. Dominii*). Pitchers green mottled with purple, the wings fringed. **N. Dickinsoniana,** Lindsay (*N. Rafflesiana* × *N. Veitchii*). Pitchers cylindric-ventricose, somewhat villous, green with purple markings, the wings fringed, the lid oblong. **N. Dominii,** Veitch (*N. Rafflesiana* × ? a Bornean species probably *N. gracilis*). Pitchers ventricose below, contracted near mouth, mottled green and purple, wings fringed, broad below becoming narrower toward mouth, lid ovate. **N. edinensis,** Lindsay (*N. Rafflesiana* × *N. Chelsonii*). Pitchers ovate, yellow-green spotted with dark purple, wings broad and fringed, lid ovate. **N. Henryana,** Williams (*N. Hookeriana* × *N. Sedenii*). Pitchers cylindric-ventricose, red or greenish-red, mottled above, wings broad and ciliate, lid oval. **N. intermedia,** Veitch (*N. Rafflesiana* × a Bornean species). Pitchers ovate, green abundantly spotted with purple, wings fringed, peristome elevated into neck behind, lid ovate. **N. Mastersiana,** Veitch (*N. sanguinea* × *N. khasiana*). Pitchers dimorphic, crimson-green with purple spots to uniformly deep crimson, wings fringed or in upper pitchers rudimentary, lid ovate-orbicular. **N. Patersonii,** Mill. (parentage unknown; probably *N. mirabilis* × *N. Hookeriana*). Pitchers cylindric-ventricose, yellowish-green copiously mottled with red, wings narrow and ciliate, lid oval. **N. Sedenii,** Mast. (*N. khasiana* × ?). Pitchers cylindric, dilated at base and slightly contracted in middle, wings ciliate, the lid cordate-orbicular.

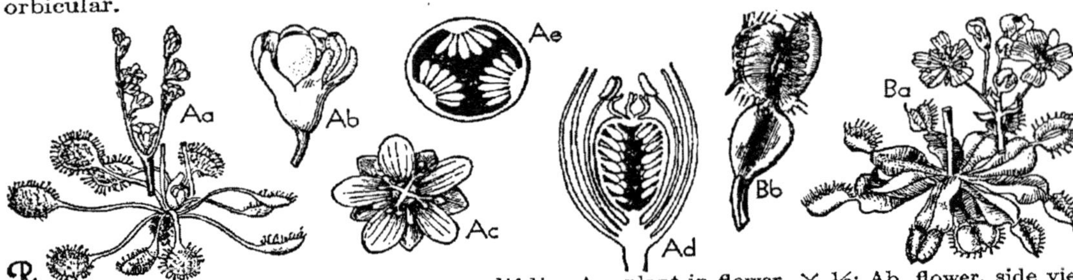

Fig. 88. DROSERACEÆ. A, *Drosera rotundifolia:* Aa, plant in flower, × ½; Ab, flower, side view, × 2; Ac, same, face view, × 2; Ad, same, vertical section, × 12; Ae, ovary, cross-section, × 15. B, *Dionæa muscipula:* Ba, plant in flower, × ¼; Bb, leaf, × ½. (Ab–Ae after Schnizlein.)

88. DROSERACEÆ. SUNDEW FAMILY

Four genera and about 88 species with wide geographic distribution.—Mostly per. low herbs of swampy places, with lvs. in basal rosettes which are glandular-hairy and insectivorous: fls. bisexual, solitary or in spikes or racemes which are sometimes coiled; fl.-bracts present or lacking; sepals usually 5, imbricated, persistent, more or less connate at base; petals usually 5, imbricated, free, membranous, withering without falling; stamens 4–20, the filaments free or slightly connate at the base; disk lacking; pistil 1, ovary 1-celled, of 3–5 carpels, superior, with parietal or basal placentation; styles 3–5, usually free and simple: caps. 3–5-celled, usually loculicidally dehiscent; seeds small, many.

A. Styles free; stamens 5 (4–8)..1. DROSERA
AA. Styles united; stamens 10–20..2. DIONÆA

1. **DROSERA,** L. SUNDEW. About 85 species of wide distribution.—Per. or rarely ann. herbs: lvs. basal, covered with glandular hairs which exude fluid that traps insects: fls. white to red; sepals, petals and stamens 5 (4–8); carpels 3–5: caps. loculicidally dehiscent. (Dros-era: from the Greek for dewy.)

D. rotundifolia, L. Lf.-blades suborbicular, ¼–½in. across, on pubescent flat petioles ½–2 in. long: fls. white, to ¼in. across, in simple or once-forked one-sided racemes, on scapes 2–12 in. high: caps. scarcely exceeding the sepals. N. Amer., Eu., Asia.

2. **DIONÆA,** Ellis. One insectivorous per. of restricted range in N. C. and S. C., sometimes grown as an oddity or for botanical demonstration.—Lvs. in a basal rosette, petioles winged, the round blades 2-lobed, with many long cilia on the margins and 3 sensitive cilia on the face of each lobe, the 2 lobes closing together when touched; digestion takes place by means of secretions from glands on the surface of the lf.: fls. in corymbs, on scapes; sepals 5, connate at base and somewhat grown to the ovary wall; petals 5; stamens 15 (10–20), connate at base; 5 styles united into a column with 5 fringed stigmas at the top; placentation basal: caps. irregularly dehiscent. (Dionæ-a: a surname of Venus, the daughter of Jupiter and Dione.)

D. muscipula, Ellis. VENUS FLY-TRAP. Lvs. 1½–6 in. long, with spatulate petioles and round or reniform 2-lobed blades: fls. white, 2–14 in corymbs on scapes 4–16 in. high; petals about ½in. long, irregularly notched at tip: caps. ovoid, less than ¼in. long.

89. CRASSULACEÆ. ORPINE FAMILY

Mostly fleshy herbs and subshrubs, included by gardeners among "succulents," of perhaps 900 species and about 25 genera, of wide dispersal; many are grown under glass as pot subjects and the hardy ones in rock-gardens and borders.—Lvs. alternate, opposite or whorled, mostly sessile, simple or rarely pinnate, without stipules, in many cult. kinds thick and fleshy: fls. mostly bisexual, usually cymose but sometimes racemose or even solitary, often in shades of yellow and red more or less combined with green, the parts typically free and distinct, known to botanists by their symmetry; sepals (or lobes of calyx) usually of same number (mostly 4 or 5) as petal-parts and pistils, the stamens of the same or double their number; receptacle without disk but bearing a little scale at the base of each pistil; pistils with ovary 1-celled, few- to many-ovuled, placentation parietal: fr. a usually ventrally dehiscent follicle, few- to many-seeded (seed rarely solitary).—Although the family presents in general much uniformity of structure and is readily recognized, there are marked departures; the petals are sometimes absent; corolla gamopetalous and lobed or comprised of separate petals; calyx mostly gamosepalous. Generic and specific names not here included are likely to be found in the special collections of amateurs and fanciers.

A. Stamens of same number as petals: lvs. opposite.
  B. Petals separate or connate only at base .... 1. CRASSULA
  BB. Petals joined to middle or higher .... 2. ROCHEA
AA. Stamens twice as many as petals, or if of same number lvs. not opposite.
  B. Corolla with parts free or essentially so (if joined, only slightly connate at base or not thick and fleshy).
    C. Fls. typically 4–5-merous, rarely 9-merous, petals usually not prominently hairy or fringed .... 3. SEDUM
    CC. Fls. typically more than 5-merous, usually 6–20-merous, if few-merous the petals fringed or prominently hairy.
      D. Plant a stemless or short-stemmed per. herb .... 4. SEMPERVIVUM
      DD. Plant an herb or subshrub with sts. .... 5. ÆONIUM
  BB. Corolla usually gamopetalous, with petals connate at least at base.
    C. Lobes of corolla 4 .... 6. KALANCHOË
    CC. Lobes of corolla 5.
      D. Infl. terminal .... 7. COTYLEDON
      DD. Infl. lateral, floral sts. arising in axils of lvs.
        E. Corolla-lobes spreading from near middle, banded or spotted .... 8. GRAPTOPETALUM
        EE. Corolla-lobes thick and fleshy, spreading only at tips, not banded or spotted.
          F. Petals not appendaged .... 9. ECHEVERIA
          FF. Petals with ventral appendages .... 10. PACHYPHYTUM

1. **CRASSULA**, L. Species probably 250 or more, mostly S. African, a few grown under glass and in windows or planted in the open far S. mostly for their foliage and interesting habit.—More or less succulent leafy shrubs and herbs, rarely ann.: lvs. fleshy, opposite and mostly sessile although frequently taper-based, often connate

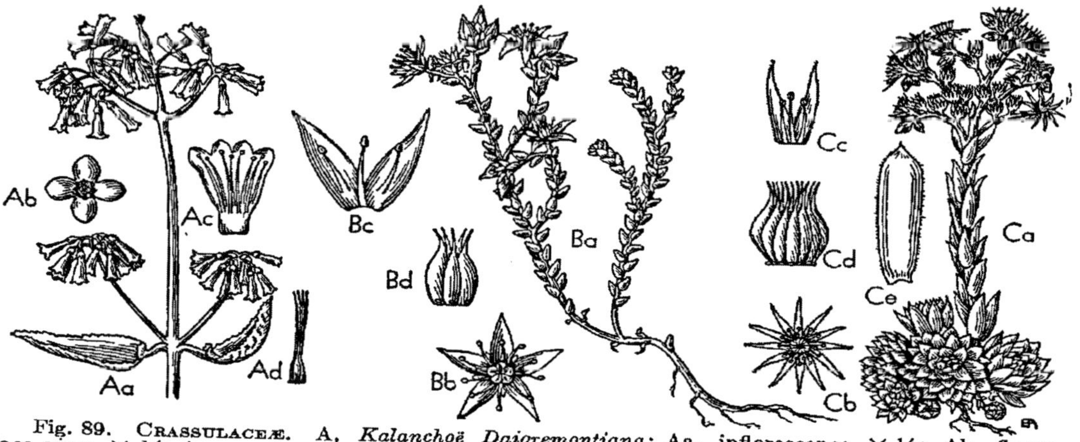

Fig. 89. CRASSULACEÆ. A, *Kalanchoë Daigremontiana:* Aa, inflorescence, × 1/6; Ab, flower, face view, × 1/2; Ac, corolla expanded with stamens, × 1/2; Ad, pistils, × 1/2. B, *Sedum acre:* Ba, habit in flower, × 1/2; Bb, flower, face view, × 1; Bc, two petals and stamens, × 2; Bd, pistils, × 2. C, *Sempervivum tectorum:* Ca, habit in flower, × 1/4; Cb, flower, face view, × 1/2; Cc, two petals with stamens, × 1; Cd, pistils, × 2; Ce, cauline bract, × 1.

by the bases, entire or nearly so, glabrous and shining or in some species pubescent or scaly: fls. mostly cymose or in compact clusters and thereby sometimes showy, white, rose or seldom yellow; sepals, petals, stamens and pistils of same number, usually 5 (sometimes as few as 4), the petals separate or connate only at base, the calyx parted or deeply cleft; pistils 4–5, ovary 1-celled and many-ovuled. (Crassula: Latin diminutive of *crassus*, thick.)

A. Fls. axillary, either solitary or in diminutive cymules: lvs. scale-like . . . . 1. *C. lycopodioides*
AA. Fls. in terminal cymes: lvs. not scale-like.
  B. Shape of lvs. obovate or spatulate, flat or essentially so.
    C. Margins of lvs. spotted with white dots . . . . 2. *C. lactea*
    CC. Margins of lvs. not spotted with white dots.
      D. Bases of lvs. narrowed into petioles which are connate across st. . . . . 3. *C. multicava*
      DD. Bases of lvs. narrowed but not connate.
        E. Lvs. gray, distinctly punctate, obtuse . . . . 4. *C. arborescens*
        EE. Lvs. shiny green, not distinctly punctate, acute or subacute . . . . 5. *C. argentea*
  BB. Shape of lvs. not obovate or spatulate, instead ovate, subterete, subtetragonous or falcate.
    C. Lvs. falcate, connate-perfoliate . . . . 8. *C. falcata*
    CC. Lvs. not falcate.
      D. Lf. ovate, connate-perfoliate, cartilaginous-ciliate on margins . . . . 7. *C. perforata*
      DD. Lf. neither ovate nor connate-perfoliate.
        E. The lvs. subtetragonous, glabrous . . . . 6. *C. tetragona*
        EE. The lvs. subterete, hairy . . . . 9. *C. trachysantha*

1. **C. lycopodioides,** Lam. Slender branched subshrub to 2 ft. high; sts. brittle, covered with numerous closely appressed scale-like lvs. in 4 ranks: fls. very small, 5-merous, greenish, solitary or in diminutive cymules in axils of upper lvs. S. Afr.—*C. pseudolycopodioides*, Dinter, said to have thicker sts. and more obtuse gray-green lvs., is a doubtful species.

2. **C. lactea,** Soland. Succulent shrub branched from base, with broad flattish obovate lvs., subacute or acuminate, spotted with white dots on margins: fls. white, in corymbose cymes. S. Afr.

3. **C. multicava,** Lem. (*C. quadrifida*, Baker). Rather low subshrub with more or less decumbent bases, moderately fleshy, glabrous: lvs. obovate with tapering bases, about 2½–3 in. long over all and 1½ in. broad, very obtuse, the petioles of the pairs joined: fls. panicled, about ¼in. across, 4-merous, petals white and very acute, carpels pink. S. Afr.

4. **C. arborescens,** Willd. Large glabrous much-branched shrub to 10 ft. high: lvs. roundish-obovate, gray, distinctly punctate, obtuse, 2–3 in. long, 2–2¾ in. broad: fls. white or rosy, in paniculate cymes. S. Afr.

5. **C. argentea,** Thunb. (*C. portulacea*, Lam.). Shrub to 10 ft., oppositely regularly branching and making a symmetrical erect comely jointed pot-plant with a fleshy woody structure: lvs. very thick, shining, oval or obovate or oblong-spatulate, narrowed at base but not petioled, the bases not connate: fls. in a close panicle, white or rosy-red, 5-merous, petals narrow and mucronate. S. Afr.—Sometimes grown in windows and conservatories under the misleading names "Japanese laurel" and "Japanese rubber-plant," often not blooming for years.

6. **C. tetragona,** L. Glabrous branched subshrub to 2 ft. high: lvs. subtetragonous, markedly upcurved, about 1 in. long: cymes corymbose, with small white fls. S. Afr.

7. **C. perforata,** Thunb. Subshrub with woody sts. and branches, to 4 ft. high: lvs. ovate, connate-perfoliate, retrorsely cartilaginous-ciliate on margins, to 1 in. long: fls. small, brownish-yellow, ⅛in. across, numerous, in paniculate cymes. S. Afr.

8. **C. falcata,** Wendl. (*Rochea falcata*, DC.). Succulent subshrub to 2½ ft. high, rarely branched, leafy throughout: lvs. oblong, obliquely falcate, connate-perfoliate, glaucous, about 4 in. long: fls. crimson, rarely white, in dense corymbose cymes. S. Afr.

9. **C. trachysantha,** Harvey. Sparingly branched subshrub to 1 ft. high: lvs. semi-terete, densely hairy, about ¾in. long: fls. in corymbose cymes, petals with a narrow fleshy apex. S. Afr.

2. **ROCHEA,** DC. (*Kalosanthes*, Haw.). S. African plants, 4 species, of which one or two are sometimes grown in greenhouses.—Erect, more or less shrubby: lvs. opposite, sessile and somewhat joined at base, simple: fls. rather large, white, yellow, or red, in dense terminal clusters, making a showy infl.; calyx 5-parted; corolla salver-shaped, with tube much exceeding calyx; stamens 5, joined to claws of corolla-lobes; pistils 5, ovaries many-ovuled: fr. a follicle. (Ro-chea: named after François Delaroche, French botanist, died 1813.)

R. coccinea, DC. Robust, 1–2 ft., with very closely imbricated ovate or ovate-oblong lvs. 1–1½ in. long, ciliate on margins: fls. bright scarlet, 1½–2 in. long, fragrant, in summer, phlox-form, with long slender tube. Cape Colony.—Several forms or hybrids are in cult.

3. **SEDUM,** L. STONECROP. ORPINE. The largest genus of the family, numbering about 350 species in the north temp. zone and in mts. in the tropics; favorite rock-garden subjects.—Herbs or subshrubs, usually glabrous: lvs. mostly alternate, in many species small and imbricated: fls. in terminal cymes, often with secund branches; calyx mostly 4–5-parted; petals mostly 4 or 5 and usually distinct, but sometimes united by their bases; stamens normally twice as many as the petals and in 2 whorls, but sometimes of the same number and in a single whorl; pistils mostly 4 or 5, usually distinct, but sometimes slightly connate at base, ovaries commonly many-ovuled. (Se-dum: Latin *to assuage*, from the healing properties of the house-leek, to which the name was applied, as well as to the stonecrops, by the Roman writers.)—Latin names are often much misapplied to the plants in cult.

A. Rootstocks stout: floral sts. arising in axils of scale-like lvs.: fls. often imperfect, mostly 4-merous .... 1. *S. Rosea*
AA. Rootstocks present or lacking: floral sts. not arising in axils of scale-like lvs.: fls. perfect, 4- or 5-merous.
B. Species of evergreen shrubs or subshrubs with floral sts. persisting for several or many years.
C. Lvs. flat, spatulate, broadly rounded .... 52. *S. dendroideum*
CC. Lvs. terete or subterete, not flat.
D. Lf. acute, ½–2 in. long, convex dorsally, flat ventrally, curved upwards: petals white .... 53. *S. Nussbaumerianum*
DD. Lf. obtuse or broadly rounded, rarely acute.
E. Shape of lf. ovate or ovate-lanceolate, obtuse or acute, ⅛in. long. 58. *S. moranense*
EE. Shape of lf. linear-oblong, oblong-ovate or suborbicular, as thick as broad, broadly rounded at apex.
F. Foliage almost flat on face, very glaucous .... 55. *S. Treleasei*
FF. Foliage truly terete, not flattened on any surface.
G. Sts. hairy: lvs. opposite, subglobular .... 57. *S. Stahlii*
GG. Sts. smooth: lvs. alternate, longer than broad.
H. Length of lvs. ½–1½ in., glaucous, slightly enlarged towards apex, curved upwards .... 54. *S. pachyphyllum*
HH. Length of lvs. ½–¾in., green, often suffused with red, scarcely enlarged upwards .... 56. *S. rubrotinctum*
BB. Species of per. or ann. herbs, rarely subshrubs, with floral sts. not persisting beyond a single growing season.
C. Petals erect at base for one-tenth or more their length, often connate or connivent.
D. Color of fls. pink or red, rarely white.
E. Lvs. opposite, coarsely crenate, prominently glandular at apex: plant per .... 42. *S. spurium*
EE. Lvs. alternate: plant bien.
F. Fls. purple or crimson: lvs. of rosettes oblong-spatulate, acute or apiculate, densely ciliate and papillose-pubescent on both surfaces .... 49. *S. sempervivoides*
FF. Fls. pink: lvs. of rosettes linear-spatulate, obtuse, incurved, densely pilose .... 50. *S. pilosum*
DD. Color of fls. yellow or white.
E. Fls. with petals free from the base or united for one-eighth of length, erect or widely spreading above.
F. The petals erect throughout, united at base for one-eighth of length: lvs. very fleshy, green suffused with red, never glaucous .... 44. *S. oreganum*
FF. The petals erect at base for about one-tenth of length, then spreading widely: lvs. green or gray, often glaucous.
G. Rosettes loose, not densely compressed, the lvs. loosely spreading, not closely compacted, minutely crenulate and papillose .... 45. *S. spathulifolium*
GG. Rosettes densely compressed with the lvs. closely compacted (pressed close together) and prominently papillate on margins .... 46. *S. Purdyi*
EE. Fls. with petals connivent or united for one-fourth or more of length, erect below, divergent above.
F. Lvs. densely glandular-hairy and glandular-ciliate .... 51. *S. chrysanthum*
FF. Lvs. glabrous.
G. Fl. yellow or pale yellow, sometimes fading to white or pink in age: lvs. of rosettes ¼–2 in. long .... 47. *S. obtusatum*
GG. Fl. white or creamy-white: lvs. of rosettes ⅜–1 in. long .... 48. *S. oregonense*
CC. Petals rotately spreading.
D. Plants with short stout rootstocks.
E. Fls. yellow; pistils gibbous ventrally, fused at base.
F. Lvs. ternately whorled.
G. Shape of lvs. broad-lanceolate: sts. prostrate .... 14. *S. sarmentosum*
GG. Shape of lvs. linear or linear-lanceolate: sts. decumbent .... 15. *S. lineare*
FF. Lvs. alternate.
G. Habit creeping, plants with many barren sts .... 11. *S. hybridum*

GG. Habit decumbent or erect, not creeping, many barren sts. not present at flowering time.
H. Sts. decumbent: infl. usually few-fld. (with 8–65 fls.): lvs. broadest above middle and toothed towards apex.. 12. *S. kamtschaticum*
HH. Sts. erect: infl. many-fld. (with 16–200 fls.): lvs. broadest at or below middle, toothed from below middle...... 13. *S. Aizoon*
EE. Fls. pink, purple, white or cream; pistils not gibbous ventrally.
F. Base of lvs. with petioles ⅛–1¼ in. long: sts. woody.......... 10. *S. populifolium*
FF. Base of lvs. sessile or subpetiolate: sts. herbaceous.
G. Sts. decumbent or creeping.
H. Lvs. in whorls of 3, mostly broadly obovate with margins usually toothed.............................. 7. *S. Sieboldii*
HH. Lvs. opposite or alternate, with entire margins.
I. Arrangement of lvs. opposite: sts. semi-trailing....... 8. *S. Ewersii*
II. Arrangement of lvs. alternate: sts. creeping.......... 9. *S. Anacampseros*
GG. Sts. erect, not decumbent or creeping.
H. Stamens prominent, much exceeding the pink petals.... 5. *S. spectabile*
HH. Stamens not conspicuous, equalling or only slightly exceeding petals.
I. Lvs. usually alternate.
J. Lf. oblong-ovate, mostly broadest towards base or at least below middle, markedly reduced in size upwards on sts.: petals usually deep pink, rarely white.................................. 2. *S. Telephium*
JJ. Lf. elliptic-spatulate, cuneate at base, not markedly reduced in size upwards on sts.: petals white...... 3. *S. telephioides*
II. Lvs. usually opposite, rarely whorled or alternate.
J. Diam. of fls. ⅛–⅜in.; pistils green or greenish-white: lvs. dark green....................... 4. *S. maximum*
JJ. Diam. of fls. ½in.; pistils pale pink: lvs. light green.. 6. *S. alboroseum*
DD. Plants without thickened rootstocks, mostly per. with creeping sts. forming mats, sometimes ann.
E. Duration ann. or bien., rarely perennating from vegetative shoots.
F. Color of petals blue with white bases; fls. 7–9-merous.......35. *S. cæruleum*
FF. Color of petals white or slightly pinkish; fls. 4–8-merous.
G. Infl. glandular-pubescent; fls. mostly 6-merous: lvs. glaucous, not sagittate-spurred..........................34. *S. hispanicum*
GG. Infl. glabrous; fls. mostly 4-merous: lvs. green or reddish, sagittate-spurred..................................39. *S. pulchellum*
EE. Duration per., usually perennating from vegetative shoots.
F. Lf. flat.
G. Color of fls. yellow; petals suberect.....................44. *S. oreganum*
GG. Color of fls. white, pink or red.
H. Fls. mostly 4-merous.
I. Lvs. in whorls of 3............................37. *S. ternatum*
II. Lvs. not in whorls of 3.
J. Foliage not sagittate-spurred, glaucous, papillose-crenulate.......................................38. *S. glaucophyllum*
JJ. Foliage sagittate-spurred, green, entire............39. *S. pulchellum*
HH. Fls. mostly 5-merous.
I. Lvs. in whorls or alternate: fls. white.
J. Cymes glandular-hairy: lvs. in whorls of 4.........40. *S. monregalense*
JJ. Cymes glabrous: lvs. alternate..................41. *S. magellense*
II. Lvs. opposite: fls. usually pink, rarely white.
J. The lvs. coarsely crenate, prominently glandular at apex: petals suberect..........................42. *S. spurium*
JJ. The lvs. obscurely crenate, not prominently glandular at apex: petals widely spreading............43. *S. stoloniferum*
FF. Lvs. terete or subterete.
G. Fls. yellow.
H. Lvs. opposite, suborbicular...........................27. *S. divergens*
HH. Lvs. alternate, ovate to linear, not suborbicular.
I. Surface of lf. papillose.
J. Habit bushy: lvs. broadly obtuse, persisting on sts., producing shaggy appearance..................26. *S. multiceps*
JJ. Habit tufted, not bushy: lvs. acute or obtuse, not broadly obtuse.
K. Pistils erect: lvs. not becoming scarious in age .... 24. *S. lanceolatum*
KK. Pistils widely spreading, ventricose ventrally: lvs. becoming scarious in age...................25. *S. stenopetalum*
II. Surface of lf. smooth, not papillose.
J. Shape of lvs. ovoid, closely imbricate.............16. *S. acre*
JJ. Shape of lvs. linear or linear-lanceolate.
K. Arrangement of lvs. in 6 spiral rows...........17. *S. sexangulare*
KK. Arrangement of lvs. not in 6 spiral rows.
L. Pistils spreading.
M. Sepals lanceolate, blunt; petals ⅙–¼in. long. 18. *S. Stribrnyi*
MM. Sepals ovate, acute or acuminate; petals 3/16–⅜in. long.......................... 25. *S. stenopetalum*
LL. Pistils erect; cymes usually compact.
M. Sepals lanceolate or ovate-lanceolate, acute, slightly concave dorsally, ⅛–¼in. long.

N. Lf. short-spurred, with the spurs not trilobate and scarious..................19. *S. anopetalum*
NN. Lf. with broad trilobate scarious spurs...20. *S. tenuifolium*
MM. Sepals ovoid, acute or obtuse, not concave dorsally, 1/16–1/8in. long.
N. Foliage terete........................21. *S. reflexum*
NN. Foliage plane ventrally.
O. Lf. linear or linear-lanceolate, acute or obtuse, not sharp-pointed..........22. *S. rupestre*
OO. Lf. elliptic-lanceolate, tapering to a sharp tip........................23. *S. sediforme*
GG. Fls. white.
H. Cymes paniculate; pedicels 1/24–1/8in. long.............28. *S. album*
HH. Cymes not paniculate; fls. sessile or pedicellate.
I. Foliage in 4 or 5 vertical rows, subglobular, white-mealy, sometimes reddish..........................29. *S. brevifolium*
II. Foliage alternate or opposite, not in 4 or 5 vertical rows.
J. Arrangement of lvs. opposite: infl. pubescent........30. *S. dasyphyllum*
JJ. Arrangement of lvs. alternate.
K. Shape of lf. elliptic: infl. of 2 or 3 branches........31. *S. anglicum*
KK. Shape of lf. linear, linear-lanceolate or oblong-lanceolate.
L. The cymes secund........................36. *S. diffusum*
LL. The cymes branched, not secund.
M. Lvs. 2-spurred........................39. *S. pulchellum*
MM. Lvs. not 2-spurred.
N. Infl. glandular-pubescent: lvs. glaucous...34. *S. hispanicum*
NN. Infl. glabrous: lvs. green or reddish.
O. Tip of lf. blunt: fls. 5-merous.
P. Cymes dense, flat-topped; sepals oblong, blunt....................32. *S. lydium*
PP. Cymes 2-branched (rarely 3-branched); sepals ovate, acute....33. *S. gracile*
OO. Tip of lf. spinulose: fls. 5–7-merous.
P. Sepals lanceolate, 1/8–1/4in. long: lvs. linear-lanceolate to linear-subterete........................19. *S. anopetalum*
PP. Sepals ovate, 1/16–1/8in. long: lvs. elliptic-lanceolate, flattened above..23. *S. sediforme*

1. **S. Rosea,** Scop. emend. Sprague (*Rhodiola Rosea,* L. *S. Rhodiola,* DC.). ROSE-ROOT. Glaucous, diœcious, variable, with thick scaly-topped stock that rises above the ground; sts. ann., 6–12 in. high: lvs. alternate and sometimes imbricated, sessile, strap-shaped to obovate, ¼–1½ in. long and half as broad, somewhat toothed at apex: fls. in spring and early summer, 4-parted, yellow, greenish-yellow, or purplish, about ¼in. across; stamens slightly exceeding the linear obtuse petals. (Rosea: an old generic name.) Circumpolar regions, south to N. C. and New Mex.

2. **S. Telephium,** L. Widespread and very variable species from W. Eu. to Japan, distinguished from no. 4 by the usually red-purple fls. in late summer and autumn and always alternate lvs.; sts. clustered, glabrous: lvs. strongly ascending, ¾–3 in. long and half as broad, oblong or ovate-oblong, toothed toward apex, markedly reduced in size upwards on sts.: stamens nearly equalling the lanceolate acute petals. (Telephium is an old name from Telephus, son of Hercules, of some obscure application; employed also as a generic name in Caryophyllaceæ.)—With this species *S. purpureum,* Link, and *S. Fabaria,* Koch, are to be associated as vars. or subspecies.

3. **S. telephioides,** Michx. Glabrous per. with stout rootstocks bearing a tuft of erect or slightly decumbent sts. 6–20 in. high: lvs. commonly alternate, rarely opposite or subopposite, usually elliptic-spatulate, rounded at apex, mostly cuneate at base, entire or remotely dentate, ⅜–1¾ in. long, ¼–1¼ in. wide: cymes many-fld., more or less flat-topped; stamens slightly shorter than the white petals. Md. to N. C., S. Ind. and Ill.

4. **S. maximum,** Suter. Variable species, one of the plants likely to be grown as *S. macrophyllum:* glabrous, roots thickened, fl.-sts. erect, 1–3 ft., ann., blooming late summer to autumn: lvs. prevailingly opposite or sometimes ternate or even alternate, broad-ovate, 2–3 in. long and half or two-thirds as broad, obtuse, irregularly and obscurely toothed: fls. green, less than ⅜in. across, in terminal and axillary corymbose cymes; stamens equalling or slightly exceeding the ovate-lanceolate somewhat acute petals: fr. erect and short-acuminate, green. Eu., S. W. Asia. Var. **atropurpureum,** Hort., lvs. and sts. deep purple.

5. **S. spectabile,** Boreau. Robust glaucous showy per., well known in cult., 12–22 in. high, from a clump of long tuberous roots, the sts. unbranched: lvs. opposite or ternate and widely spreading, about 3 in. long and two-thirds as broad, obovate, fleshy, somewhat toothed: fls. in autumn, very many in large dense corymbose cymes, ½in. across, pink; stamens prominent, part of them much longer than the lanceolate acute petals: fr. erect, attenuate. Possibly a cultigen, originally known from Japan.—Races with deeper colored fls. are known as Brilliant, or var. **atropurpureum,** Hort. Var. **variegatum,** Hort., has foliage variegated with yellow.

6. **S. alboroseum,** Baker (*S. japonicum,* Hort. not Sieb.). Hybrid between *S. spectabile* and *S. Tacquetii:* glaucous, glabrous, with tuberous roots, fl.-sts. 1–2 ft., unbranched, ann., blooming in early autumn: lvs. alternate or opposite, rarely ternate, ovate to obovate-cuneate, 2–4 in. long and half as broad, obtusely toothed: fls. greenish-white, ½in. across, in terminal and axillary corymbose cymes; stamens about equalling the oblong-lanceolate acute petals: pistils erect, acuminate, pinkish or rose.—The fls. are very irregular in number of parts and most of the pollen is abortive. One of the plants known in gardens as *S. macrophyllum;* see also no. 4. The true *S. japonicum* of Siebold is probably not in cult. in N. Amer.

7. **S. Sieboldii,** Sweet. Well-known decumbent hardy late autumn-blooming species with long unbranched sts. on the ground, blooming at the end, and a cluster of thick roots: lvs. ternate, glaucous-blue or sometimes red, broadly obovate or nearly orbicular but truncate or somewhat tapering at base, ¾–1 in. long, flat, sinuate or obscurely toothed above: fls. nearly ½in. across, in dense corymbose cymes, pink; stamens, part of them, slightly exceeding the broad-lanceolate acute petals: fr. erect, attenuate-pointed. (P. F. von Siebold, page 51.) Possibly Japan. Var. **variegatum, Hort.**, has variegated foliage.

8. **S. Ewersii, Ledeb.** Glabrous per. with numerous decumbent branched sts.: lvs. opposite, ovate-cordate, mostly entire, glaucous, ¼–1 in. long: fls. pink, about ½in. across, in corymbose cymes; stamens slightly shorter than petals: pistils erect, deep pink. (Named for J. Ph. G. Ewers, Russian official.) Cent. Asia.

9. **S. Anacampseros, L.** Nearly evergreen, glaucous, glabrous, procumbent, sometimes rooting, fl.-sts. about 6 in. high: lvs. alternate, sessile and flat, ½–1 in. long, obovate to orbicular, rather thin, rounded at end and sometimes slightly retuse or apiculate, margins entire: fls. in summer, not widely expanding, ¼in. across, in a very dense cluster, dull purple; stamens about equalling the ovate-lanceolate obtuse petals: fr. erect, with short tips. (Anacampseros: old Greek name, now applied also to a genus in Portulacaceæ.) S. Eu.

10. **S. populifolium,** Pall. Subshrub with short woody sts. from which arise many ann. fl.-sts. to 12 in. high: lvs. poplar-like, ovate or ovate-oblong, cordate or truncate at base, petiolate, coarsely dentate, 4–15 in. long: cymes corymbose; fls. pink or white, to ⅜in. across; stamens slightly shorter than the lanceolate petals: pistils erect. Cent. and N. Asia.

11. **S. hybridum,** L. Evergreen, glabrous, mat-forming, with prominent barren shoots, sts. creeping and branching, fl.-sts. 3–8 in. high, blooming in spring and again later: lvs. alternate, oblong-lanceolate to spatulate, about 1 in. long, coarsely toothed on upper half with teeth often tipped red: fls. yellow, ½–¾in. across, in much-branched terminal cymes; stamens about two-thirds as long as the lanceolate mucronate somewhat hooded petals: fr. slightly connate at base, green or red. Siberia, Mongolia.

12. **S. kamtschaticum,** Fisch. Glabrous, without barren shoots, not creeping, the fl.-sts. 6–12 in. high blooming in summer, having arisen the previous summer and remained green over winter, producing axillary fl.-branches: lvs. alternate, mostly spatulate, varying from broadly spatulate to linear-oblanceolate and linear, ½–2 in. long, toothed toward apex, margins minutely papillose: fls. yellow, ⅝–¾in. across, in dense or lax cymes; stamens nearly as long as the lanceolate acute petals: fr. reddish or brown, wide-spreading. E. Asia.—Plants with variegated foliage are listed as var. *variegatum.* Closely related are **S. Ellacombianum,** Praeger (*S. kamtschaticum* subsp. *Ellacombianum,* Clausen), of Japan, with light green spatulate crenate lvs. and fls. about ½in. across (named for Canon H. N. Ellacombe), and **S. Middendorffianum,** Maxim. (*S. kamtschaticum* subsp. *Middendorffianum,* Clausen), of north-cent. Asia, with linear or linear-oblanceolate lvs. crenate-dentate towards apex with 1–4 teeth on each margin (named for A. T. von Middendorff, page 208.)

13. **S. Aizoon,** L. (*S. Maximowiczii,* Regel). Glabrous, without barren shoots, leafless in winter, with a thick knotted rootstock from which fleshy and tuberous roots arise; sts. arise from the stock in spring and bloom in summer, 1–1½ ft. high, branched only above if at all: lvs. alternate, elliptic-lanceolate to oblong-lanceolate, 2–3 in. long, sharply toothed: fls. yellow, sessile, ½in. across, in crowded terminal cymes; stamens nearly as long as the linear-lanceolate apiculate petals: fr. yellow to red, spreading. (Aizoon: also a genus in Portulacaceæ, is Greek signifying *always alive.*) Siberia to Japan.—Common in cult.

14. **S. sarmentosum,** Bunge not Mast. Glabrous evergreen making long prostrate barren shoots that root at the tip: lvs. ternate, broad-lanceolate, acute, ½–1 in. long, flat and fleshy and entire, spurred at base: fls. in early summer, ⅝in. or less across, mostly sessile on 3 often forked branches, yellow; stamens shorter than the narrow acute petals: fr. exceeded by the persistent calyx. N. China and Japan; nat. in E. temp. N. Amer.

15. **S. lineare,** Thunb. Glabrous per. with decumbent sts. sometimes rooting below: lvs. ternate, linear or linear-lanceolate, obtuse, short-spurred, ¾–1 in. long: fls. in spring or early summer, ⅝in. across, in lax cymes; petals yellow, acute: pistils spreading. E. Asia. Var. **variegatum,** Hort., has variegated lvs.

16. **S. acre,** L. The common stonecrop of walls, rocky places, and yards, nat. from the Old World, and often colonized as a moss-like cover plant: small creeping glabrous mat-

forming evergreen, the shoots rising 1–3 or more in.: lvs. alternate and imbricated, ovoid-triangular and therefore broadest near base, 3⁄16in. or less long: fls. late spring or early summer, ½in. across or less, bright yellow, on 2 or 3 short branches; stamens shorter than the lanceolate acute petals: fr. wide-spreading. Var. **aureum,** Mast., has yellow foliage. Var. **majus,** Mast., is of large stature and var. **minus,** Hort., of small stature.

17. **S. sexangulare,** L. Small glabrous evergreen, forming a mat, sts. creeping; fl.-sts. 2½–5 in. high, barren shoots many: lvs. linear, terete, obtuse, ¼in. or less long, commonly in 6 spiral rows (hence the name), spurred at base: fls. in summer, ⅜in. across, on 3 short branches, yellow; stamens shorter than the acute spreading petals: fr. spreading, tapering. Eu. and S. W. Asia.

18. **S. Stribrnyi,** Velen. Glabrous per. with decumbent sts., prostrate below and forming a mat: lvs. alternate, linear-lanceolate, subterete, obtuse, spurred, ¼–⅜in. long, many-ranked: fls. yellow, ⅜in. across, appearing in early summer, in lax cymes: pistils widely divergent. (Named for Vaclav Stribrny, born 1853, Bulgarian botanist.) S. E. Eu.

19. **S. anopetalum,** DC. Glabrous per. with sterile shoots densely leafy towards their tips and fl.-sts. to 9 in. high: lvs. alternate, many-ranked, linear-lanceolate to linear, spinulose-tipped, subterete, ¼–½in. long: cymes flat-topped; fls. varying from white to yellow; sepals lanceolate or ovate-lanceolate, ⅛–¼in. long. S. and Cent. Eu.

20. **S. tenuifolium,** Strobl. Tufted per. with decumbent much-branched sts.: sterile shoots terminating in dense clusters of linear terete lvs. ¼–¾in. long, with broad scarious bases and 3-lobed spurs: cymes 2-branched with the yellow fls. ⅝in. across; sepals lanceolate, acute; stamens shorter than petals: pistils erect. Asia Minor, S. Eu., N. Afr. Var. *minus* refers to a variation of *S. rupestre.*

21. **S. reflexum,** L. Variable creeping glabrous evergreen, forming a mat, the fl.-sts. 6–13 in. high and unbranched: lvs. alternate and crowded, terete and acute, ½in. long, short-spurred at base: fls. in summer, 5–7-parted, ½in. across, on 3–5 forked branches (infl. drooping in bud), bright yellow; stamens shorter than the linear-lanceolate acute keeled petals: fr. tapering. Eu. Var. **cristatum,** Mast., is a crested variation.

22. **S. rupestre,** L. Recognized by its crowded linear lvs. flat on the upper surface, otherwise much like *S. reflexum;* evergreen, creeping, usually glaucous, the ascending branches shaggy at base with withered lvs., sts. much-branched: lvs. linear to linear-oblanceolate, ⅝in. or less long: fls. golden-yellow. Eu.—Small plants of this species may be listed as var. *minus* and others with green lvs. as *S. Forsterianum.* Plants available in cult. as *S. pruinatum* are mostly *S. rupestre.* True *S. pruinatum,* Brot., a native of Portugal, seems not to be cult. in Amer.; it has 2-branched cymes with straw-colored fls. and very glaucous lvs. at the ends of the sterile shoots which die in the autumn except at the rooting tips.

23. **S. sediforme,** C. Pau (*Sempervivum sediforme,* Jacq. *S. nicaeense,* All. *S. altissimum,* Lam.). Glabrous per. with prostrate sts. forming mats or tufts: lvs. alternate, spirally arranged; spreading, elliptic-lanceolate, flattened above and tapering to a sharp spine-like tip, ¼–¾in. long: fl.-sts. 6 in.–2 ft. high; fls. mostly 5–6-merous, white, rarely yellow; sepals ovate, acute or obtuse, ⅛in. long or less; petals oblanceolate: pistils erect, greenish. Asia Minor, S. Eu., N. Afr.

24. **S. lanceolatum,** Torr. (*S. stenopetalum,* Auth. not Pursh). Tufted per. with sterile shoots ascending, not creeping: lvs. alternate, linear-lanceolate, minutely papillose, ½–¾in. long: fls. ½in. across, yellow, in branched cymes: pistils erect. W. middle-temp. N. Amer.

25. **S. stenopetalum,** Pursh (*S. Douglasii,* Hook.). Per. with erect sterile shoots, leafy towards tips, clothed below with withered lvs.: lvs. linear-lanceolate or elliptic-oblong, short-spurred, glaucous, ¼–1¼ in. long; fl.-sts. to 16 in. high, decumbent, with lower lvs. becoming dry and scarious: fls. yellow, in 3-parted cymes; vegetative rosettes frequently developing in axils of lvs. of fl.-sts. and sometimes even in place of fls.; petals lanceolate, acute, 3⁄16–⅜in. long: pistils widely divaricate, ventricose ventrally. W. temp. N. Amer.

26. **S. multiceps,** Coss. & Dur. Bushy per. 3–4 in. high, with gray branched sts. shaggy below with withered remains of lvs.: lvs. linear-oblong, very blunt, finely papillose, closely crowded, ¼in. long: fls. ½in. across, yellow, in 3-parted cymes: pistils erect, becoming divergent in fruit. Algeria.

27. **S. divergens,** Wats. Glabrous per. with branched decumbent sts., rooting at nodes: lvs. opposite, almost globular, green or reddish-green, ⅛–⅜in. long: fl.-sts. to 7 in. high; fls. ⅜in. across, yellow, in small cymes: pistils erect, divergent below. W. temp. N. Amer.

28. **S. album,** L. (*S. balticum,* Hartm.). Commonly cult., variable: glabrous, creeping, evergreen, forming a large mat, fl.-sts. 3–8 in. high: lvs. alternate, linear-oblong to obovate or even globular, ⅛–⅝in. long, terete or flattened above, sessile: fls. in summer, ⅜in. across; petals obtuse, white, about equalling stamens: fr. erect, white streaked red. Eu., Asia, N. Afr.—Plants with purple foliage and pinkish fls. are var. **murale,** Hort. (forma *murale,* Praeger) and var. **purpureum,** Hort.

29. **S. brevifolium,** DC. Per. with procumbent or creeping sts.: lvs. opposite, arranged in 4 or 5 vertical rows, globular or almost so, chalky-gray, often suffused with red, 1/16–1/8in. long: fls. 5/16in. across, white, in few-fld. cymes. S. W. Eu., N. W. Afr.

30. **S. dasyphyllum,** L. Tufted evergreen 1–2 in. high, pinkish-gray: lvs. opposite, ovoid to obovoid, slightly flattened on one side but otherwise rounded, 1/8–3/16in. long, glandular-pubescent: fls. in early summer, 1/4in. across, 5–6-parted; petals white on front with yellowish base and pinkish on back, exceeding the stamens: fr. nearly erect, greenish. Eu., N. Afr. Var. **glanduliferum,** G. Moris (*S. corsicum,* DC. & Duby), is markedly glandular-pubescent.

31. **S. anglicum,** Huds. A little glabrous evergreen, with slender creeping sts. making mats, sts. 1–2 in. high: lvs. alternate, crowded, elliptic, sessile, terete, 3/16in. or less long: fls. 1/2in. across, in early summer, on 2, sometimes 3, simple branches; petals white, pinkish on back, equalling stamens: fr. white but turning red, erect. W. Eu. Var. **minus,** Praeger, is smaller in all its parts and with pinker fls.

32. **S. lydium,** Boiss. Very small evergreen 1–3 in. high, usually tinged red, the little sts. rooting and sending up branches bearing terete blunt linear sessile crowded lvs. about 1/4in. long: fls. 1/4in. across, in early summer; sepals oblong, blunt; petals white, about the length of the stamens: fr. white turning red. Asia Minor (Lydia being an ancient geographical name in that region).

33. **S. gracile,** Mey. Small per. with sts. procumbent but not creeping: lvs. linear or linear-lanceolate, blunt, subterete, minutely papillose, 1/8–3/16in. long: fl.-sts. to 2½ in. high, with 5-merous white fls. about 1/4in. across, in 2- (rarely 3-) branched cymes; sepals ovate, acute; petals slightly longer than stamens: pistils pale green, spreading in fr. Caucasus.—Plants differing in having creeping sts. and 3-branched cymes with branches forking have been listed as *Sedum* (or *Sempervivum*) *Albertii;* taxonomic status uncertain.

34. **S. hispanicum,** Jusl. (*S. glaucum,* Waldst. & Kit.). Glaucous bien. or sometimes per., with upper parts of sts. and infl. glandular-pubescent, to 7 in. high: lvs. oblong-linear, obtuse, terete or somewhat flattened above, 3/16–5/8in. long: fls. 4–8, mostly 6-merous, 1/4–1/2in. across; sepals ovate, pubescent; petals lanceolate, acuminate, white with pink or green median dorsal stripe: pistils erect to subdivergent, usually densely pubescent or glandular. Mts. of S. and W. Asia, S. E. Eu.—Plants in cult. as var. *minus,* Praeger, belong to another species, *S. bithynicum,* Boiss., characterized by the consistently per. habit, and very congested subglobose sterile shoots.

35. **S. cæruleum,** Vahl. Branching little ann. 3–4 in. high, smooth or somewhat hairy: lvs. alternate, ovoid or oblong, sessile, slightly flattened above but otherwise terete, 3/4in. or less long: fls. in summer, terminating all the branches, 7–9-parted, 1/4in. across; petals blue with white base, somewhat exceeding stamens: fr. becoming red. Medit. region.

36. **S. diffusum,** Wats. Glabrous per. with long creeping sts. rooting at the nodes: lvs. narrowly oblong-linear, blunt, subterete, papillose at apex, pale green, pink-tipped, 1/8–3/8in. long: cymes secund, with 5–12 white fls. 3/8–1/2in. across; anthers red: pistils divergent. Near Monterey, Mex.

37. **S. ternatum,** Michx. Glabrous or finely papillose per. with sts. prostrate below, eventually ascending: lvs. obovate or round-spatulate, mostly in whorls of 3: fls. usually 4-merous, white, 3/8–5/8in. across, chiefly in 3-parted cymes: pistils spreading in fr. E. temp. N. Amer.

38. **S. glaucophyllum,** Clausen. Glabrous per. with decumbent branched sts. terminating in dense rosettes and forming mats: lvs. spatulate or obovate, at least the central ones of the rosettes glaucous, papillose-crenulate at apex, up to 1 in. long and 1/16–3/8in. wide: fls. mostly 4-merous, white, 5/16–1/2in. across, in 3-parted or much-branched cymes: pistils divaricate. E. temp. N. Amer.—This passes in the American trade as *S. Nevii,* Gray, a rare species known only from Cent. Ala. and E. Tenn. The lvs. of *S. Nevii* are not glaucous, they are narrower, and the tips are smooth.

39. **S. pulchellum,** Michx. Ascending, 4–12 in., not creeping, bien. or sometimes per., glabrous: lvs. many and crowded, linear and terete, about 5/8in. long, obtuse, forked at base: fls. mostly 4-parted, nearly 1/2in. across, sessile on radiating recurved branches, rosy-purple and showy, in spring and early summer; stamens shorter than the acute petals: fr. tinted, long-tapering. E. U. S.

40. **S. monregalense,** Balbis. Slender per. with decumbent sts.: lvs. in whorls of 4, oblong-spatulate, light green, 1/8–3/8in. long: cymes paniculate, glandular-hairy; fls. white, 5-merous, on glandular pedicels, 1/16–1/4in. long. S. Eu.

41. **S. magellense,** Ten. Small per. with decumbent sts.: lvs. alternate, rarely opposite, obovate or oblong-elliptical, blunt or rounded, yellow-green, 1/16–1/4in. long: cymes racemose, glabrous; fls. white, 5-merous, 1/2in. across: pistils oblong, erect. S. Eu., Asia Minor.

42. **S. spurium,** Bieb. (*S. oppositifolium,* Sims). Nearly evergreen, with creeping sts. forming mats, the reddish fl.-sts. to 9 in. high: lvs. opposite, about 1 in. long, obovate with cuneate bases, prominently crenate-toothed on upper part, glandular-ciliate: fls. 1 in. long, pink varying to white, on about 4 forked branches, in summer; stamens shorter than petals: fr. reddish, with spreading beaks. Caucasus region.—Variable in color and common in

cult.; sometimes grown under the name *S. pallidum* and var. *roseum.* Plants with white fls. are designated by horticulturists as var. *album*, those with deep pink fls. as var. *splendens* or var. *coccineum.* Plants in the trade as *S. coccineum* are mostly this species, though the name is properly a synonym of *S. quadrifidum*, an Asiatic species not in cult. in Amer.

43. **S. stoloniferum,** Gmel. (*S. ibericum*, Bieb.). Nearly evergreen, creeping; fl.-sts. rising about 6 in., blooming in early summer: lvs. opposite, broadly or rhomboidly spatulate, about 1 in. long, entire or obscurely crenate toward top, pimpled on the margin: fls. ½in. across, nearly sessile, on 3 spreading forked branches; petals rose-colored, acute, considerably exceeding the stamens: fr. spreading and sepals persistent, giving a 10-rayed effect. S. W. Asia.—Often confused with *S. spurium.* Plants with deep bronze foliage are offered as var. *coccineum.*

44. **S. oreganum,** Nutt. Glabrous per. with creeping branched sts.; sterile shoots 1–6 in. high with the lvs. spirally arranged towards ends: lvs. spatulate, broadly rounded, very fleshy, shiny green often suffused with red, ½–¾in. long: fl.-sts. to 10 in. high; fls. 5-merous, about ½in. across, with the petals narrowly lanceolate, acuminate, erect, united at base for one-eighth of length, yellow. W. temp. N. Amer.

45. **S. spathulifolium,** Hook. Per. with procumbent or creeping sts., forming mats: lvs. spatulate, blunt, mostly glaucous or pruinose, crenulate on margins, to 1¼ in. long, mostly less, arranged in rosettes: fl.-sts. 2–12 in. high terminating in simple or compound cymes; fls. mostly 5-merous, usually yellow, to ⅝in. across; petals widely spreading. W. temp. N. Amer. Var. **purpureum,** Praeger, has purple foliage.

46. **S. Purdyi,** Jepson. Per. with procumbent or creeping sts., forming mats: lvs. spatulate, rounded or truncate, prominently papillose on margins, to ¾in. long, arranged in closely compacted rosettes with their apices pressed close together: fl.-sts. to 6 in. high terminating in 3-parted cymes; fls. usually 5-merous, bright yellow to white, ⅝in. across; petals widely spreading. (Carl Purdy, page 50.) N. Calif.

47. **S. obtusatum,** Gray. Per. with decumbent often long-creeping rootstocks, bearing rosettes of thick fleshy spatulate lvs., obtuse, rounded or retuse at apex, glaucous, ¼–2 in. long: fl.-sts. to 8 in. high; cymes paniculate, with fls. ¼–⅜in. across; petals erect below, connivent for two-fifths to three-fifths their length, somewhat spreading above, bright or pale yellow, becoming pink, buff or white with age. W. temp. N. Amer.

48. **S. oregonense,** Peck (*Cotyledon oregonense*, Wats. *Gormania Watsonii*, Britt. *S. Watsonii*, Tidestr.). Per. with much-branched spreading rootstocks bearing rosettes of fleshy spatulate lvs., rounded, truncate or slightly retuse at apex, glaucous, ⅜–1 in. long: fl.-sts. to 10 in. high; cymes paniculate, with white or creamy-white fls. in summer; petals erect below and connivent for one-sixth to two-thirds their length, somewhat spreading above. W. temp. N. Amer.

49. **S. sempervivoides,** Fisch. Pubescent bien. making first-year rosettes of very fleshy purplish oblong-spatulate acute lvs. nearly 1 in. long, and with similar lvs. alternate on the fl.-sts. that rise 6–12 in. the following year, blooming in summer: fl.-cluster 2–4 in. across, the purple or crimson 5-parted fls. about ½in. across; stamens nearly twice as long as sepals: fr. crimson. Asia Minor, Caucasus.

50. **S. pilosum,** Bieb. Densely hairy bien. making first-year subglobular rosettes of densely pilose incurved linear-spatulate obtuse lvs. about ½in. long: fl.-sts. to 4 in. high, with similar but larger lvs.; blooming in spring or early summer of second year; petals erect below, divergent above, pink. Asia Minor, Caucasus.

51. **S. chrysanthum,** Hamet (*Cotyledon chrysantha*, Bornm.). Glandular-hairy per. with short stout branched rootstocks, bearing numerous dense rosettes of oblong-spatulate blunt pale green lvs. ⅜–½in. long: fl.-sts. terminal, to 8 in. high; fls. 4–5-merous, with petals erect, united at base for 3⁄16in., slightly divergent above, ½in. long, white or greenish-white with pink dorsal keel: pistils erect, slightly united at base. Asia Minor.

52. **S. dendroideum,** DC. (*S. præaltum*, DC.). Glabrous subshrub to 2 ft. or more high, sts. branched: lvs. spatulate, broadly rounded, yellow-green, 1¾–2½ in. long: cymes paniculate, terminal, 2–6 in. long; fls. yellow, ½–¾in. across: pistils spreading in fr. Trop. Amer.

53. **S. Nussbaumerianum,** Bitter. Glabrous subshrub with stout spreading branches to 1 ft. high: lvs. thick, obtusely convex dorsally, plane on ventral surface, acute at apex, mostly curved upwards, yellow-green tinged with red, ½–2 in. long: fl.-sts. axillary, to 6 in. long; cymes umbel-like with the mostly 5-merous fls. on pedicels ¼–¾in. long; petals linear-lanceolate, white or pinkish: pistils erect. (Named for Ernst Nussbaumer, gardener at Bremen Bot. Gard.) Zacuapan, Mex.—Frequently listed as *S. Adolphii*, a related species rare in cult., which differs in having the cymes paniculate, petals ovate-lanceolate, pedicels shorter and lvs. acutely convex dorsally and green.

54. **S. pachyphyllum,** Rose. Glabrous subshrub attaining a height of 1 ft.; sts. branched, somewhat decumbent: lvs. thick, terete, enlarged towards apex, oblong-oblanceolate, rounded, somewhat upcurved, glaucous, ½–1½ in. long, about ⅜in. broad: fl.-sts. axillary, 4–5 in. long; fls. in Feb. and Mar., in small cymes; petals oblong-lanceolate, ¼in. long, yellow. Oaxaca, Mex.

55. **S. Treleasei,** Rose. Subshrub with sts. erect or procumbent, to 16 in. high: lvs. very fleshy and glaucous, oblong-obovate, blunt at apex, flattish ventrally, convex dorsally, widely divergent, but slightly upturned, 1–1½ in. long: fl.-sts. axillary; fls. in Jan., in corymbose cymes; petals lanceolate, bright yellow. (Wm. Trelease, page 53.) Tehuacan, Mex.

56. **S. rubrotinctum,** Clausen (*S. guatemalense,* Hort. not Hemsl.). Glabrous subshrub to 1 ft. high; sts. branched, decumbent: lvs. thick, terete, scarcely enlarged upwards, oblong, rounded at apex, almost straight, or slightly upcurved, lustrous green often suffused with red, ½–¾in. long, 3⁄16–¼in. broad: fls. yellow, in terminal cymes. Nativity unknown.

57. **S. Stahlii,** Solms. Evergreen, finely pubescent, with many decumbent slender sts. 4–8 in. high, woody at base: lvs. opposite, ovoid-oblong to globular, obtuse, ¼–½in. long, thick: fls. about ½in. across, summer to autumn, nearly sessile on 2 or 3 forked branches, yellow; stamens slightly shorter than the short-acuminate petals: fr. (or carpels) yellow. (Bears the name of Prof. Ernst Stahl, Jena, Germany.) Mex.

58. **S. moranense,** HBK. Glabrous subshrub with prostrate much-branched sts.; branches erect, 3–4 in. high, with lvs. closely crowded, ovate or ovate-lanceolate, obtuse or acute, turgid, light green, ⅛in. long: cymes elongate with fls. appearing in axils of uppermost lvs. on sts.; fls. 5-merous, white, sometimes pinkish, ⅜in. across: pistils erect or subdivergent. Mex.—Stouter, taller, much-branched plants of this species may be listed as *S. arboreum.*

4. **SEMPERVIVUM,** L. Houseleek. About 30 species in the Old World, planted sometimes for edgings, but mostly in rock-gardens.—Differs technically from Sedum in the parts of the fl. being usually 6 to many, the stamens usually twice as many as calyx-lobes, petals and pistils: petals distinct, acute or acuminate, mostly hairy or fringed: plants succulent and mostly condensed, the thick lvs. usually in dense rosettes and multiplying much by offsets: fls. pink, purple, yellow or white, in cymose panicles. (Sempervi-vum: Latin *live forever.*)

A. Petals 9–20 (mostly 11–12), wide-spreading, often ciliate, not fringed, whitish, yellow, pink, red or purple.
  B. Corolla pink, red or purple.
    C. Tips of lvs. of rosettes connected by arachnoid hairs.................. 1. *S. arachnoideum*
    CC. Tips of lvs. of rosettes not connected by arachnoid hairs.
      D. Rosettes with all or at least some lvs. hairy on both surfaces.
        E. Color of petals violet-purple or rose-red, not with white margins.
          F. Shape of petals long and narrow, ½ (⅜–¾in.) long, linear-lanceolate: glandular hairs on lvs. of uniform length.................. 2. *S. montanum*
          FF. Shape of petals broadly lanceolate, ⅜in. long: glandular hairs on lvs. of irregular length.................. 3. *S. dolomiticum*
        EE. Color of petals white on margins with broad crimson or rose-purple median bands.
          F. Lvs. red with green tips or green throughout: fls. 1 in. across..... 4. *S. Schlehanii*
          FF. Lvs. pale green, with or without red tips: fls. 1⅛–1½ in. across..... 5. *S. atlanticum*
      DD. Rosettes with young and old lvs. glabrous on faces.................. 6. *S. tectorum*
  BB. Corolla yellow or yellowish.
    C. Lvs. of rosettes pubescent on faces.
      D. Base of petals purple: lvs. mostly not purple at tip.................. 7. *S. ruthenicum*
      DD. Base of petals not purple: lvs. purple at tip.................. 8. *S. Pittonii*
    CC. Lvs. of rosettes glabrous on both faces.................. 9. *S. Wulfenii*
AA. Petals 6–7, erect or suberect, fringed, pale yellow or white.
  B. Rootstock thick, branched; slender-stemmed offsets absent.................. 10. *S. Heuffelii*
  BB. Rootstock none; slender-stemmed offsets numerous.
    C. Rosettes 1–2 in. across, usually open.................. 11. *S. hirtum*
    CC. Rosettes ⅜–¾in. across, rarely more, usually closed.
      D. Offsets produced high among lvs.................. 12. *S. soboliferum*
      DD. Offsets not produced high among lvs.................. 13. *S. arenarium*

1. **S. arachnoideum,** L. Cobweb Houseleek. Little plant with fl.-sts. 3–4 in. high: rosettes crowded at base, ½–¾in. diam., about 50-lvd., the lvs. oblong-cuneate and cuspidate, connected by cobwebby strands, outer ones about ⅜in. long, the new rosettes crowded and sessile: fl.-sts. leafy, hairy, bearing a forking cluster at top; fls. 9–12-merous, 1 in. across, bright red, the calyx-segms. linear and petals lanceolate. S. Eu. Var. **glabrescens,** Willk. (*S. Doellianum,* Lehm. *S. Moggridgei,* Hook. f.), has ovoid rosettes with sparse cobwebby hairs. Var. **tomentosum,** Hayek (*S. Laggeri,* Koch), has flattish rosettes with dense webs of cobwebby hairs.—Supposed hybrids are *S. Fauconnettii* (*S. arachnoideum* × *S. tectorum*), *S. fimbriatum* (*S. arachnoideum* × *S. montanum*), *S. Funckii* (*S. arachnoideum* × *S. montanum* × *S. Wulfenii*) and *S. Pomellii* (*S. arachnoideum* × *S. tectorum*).

2. **S. montanum,** L. (*S. flagelliforme,* Link). Rosettes 1–1½ in. diam., the new ones long-peduncled and not dense; lvs. 40–50 to a rosette, oblanceolate and only obscurely cuspidate, minutely downy, pale green, rarely red-tipped, margins ciliate, outer ones ¾in. long; sts. 3–4 in. high, with imbricated elliptic or lanceolate hairy lvs.: fls. 3–10 in a dense

cyme sessile or nearly so, about 12-merous, violet-purple, about 1½ in. across; calyx densely hairy, with lanceolate segms.; petals linear, glandular-pilose outside. Eu. Var. **Braunii,** Wettst. (forma *Braunii*, Praeger. *S. Braunii*, Koch), has petals white or yellowish-white.—A supposed hybrid of this species and *S. tectorum* is *S. Verlottii*, Lamotte.

3. **S. dolomiticum,** Facch. Tufted per. with dense rosettes 1–2 in. across: lvs. of rosettes broadly oblanceolate, ½–1 in. long, ciliate with glandular hairs of irregular length, tipped red-purple: fl.-sts. 3–4 in. high; fls. rose-red, ¾in. across; petals broadly lanceolate, ⅜in. long, with darker purple stripe and white dots. E. Alps.

4. **S. Schlehanii,** Schott (*S. assimile*, Schott. *S. blandum*, Schott. *S. rubicundum*, Schur. *S. Reginæ-Amaliæ*, Boiss.). Rosettes 2–4 in. diam., the new ones sessile, bearing 60–80 obovate-cuneate cuspidate pale glaucous lvs., red with a green tip or green and not red-tipped, minutely pubescent, margins short-ciliate, the outer lvs. 1 in. or less long: sts. rising about 6 in., bearing 12-merous pale rose fls. about 1 in. across, the calyx-segms. lanceolate and petals linear. (Named for Gustav Schlehan.) Transylvania.

5. **S. atlanticum,** Ball. Rosettes not widely open, 2–3 in. across, with lvs. often sub-erect; lvs. oblong-spatulate, pale green, finely pubescent on both faces, to 1½ in. long: fl.-sts. to 1 ft. high; fls. about 1¼ in. across; petals white with bright red-purple median bands. Morocco.

6. **S. tectorum,** L. (*S. arvernense*, Lecoq & Lamotte. *S. Metteniianum*, Schnittsp. & Lehm. *S. Lamottei*, Boreau. *S. pyrenaicum*, Lamotte. *S. juratense*, Jordan & Fourr. *S. pallidum*, Jordan & Fourr. *S. triste*, Baker. *S. royanum*, Correvon). COMMON HOUSE-LEEK. HEN-AND-CHICKENS. OLD-MAN-AND-WOMAN. Rosettes 3–4 in. across, with 50–60 cuneate-obovate cuspidate lvs. 1½–3 in. long, stoloniferous, with secondary sessile or stalked rosettes; st.-lvs. oblong-lanceolate and acute: stout plant, with densely hairy erect fl.-sts. 6–12 in. high: fls. mostly 12-merous, ¾–1 in. across, pink-red, on secund curving branches of a 10–12-branched panicle; calyx pilose, the segms. lanceolate; petals linear, with a deeper red keel. Eu., Asia; somewhat run wild in U. S. Var. **glaucum,** Praeger (*S. glaucum*, Ten. *S. acuminatum*, Schott. *S. Schottii*, Baker), has lvs. of rosettes glaucous, white at base. Var. **calcareum,** Cariot & St. Lager (*S. calcareum*, Jordan. *S. Greenei*, Baker), has lvs. very glaucous with conspicuous brown-purple tips.—Not to be confused with *Echeveria secunda*. Besides the many synonyms given above, *S. tectorum* may also be listed as *S. atroviolaceum*, *S. La Harpei*, *S. Pottsii*, or *S. tectorum* var. *violaceum*. A supposed hybrid is *S. Comollii*, Rota (*S. tectorum* × *S. Wulfenii*).

7. **S. ruthenicum,** Koch (*S. globiferum*, L. in part). Rosettes 1½–2½ in. across, rather dense, with spatulate pubescent lvs. to 1¼ in. long, green, rarely purple-tipped: fl.-sts. to 6 in. long; fls. to 1 in. across, pale yellow, purple at base. S. E. Eu., Asia Minor.

8. **S. Pittonii,** Schott, Nym. & Kotschy. Rosettes 1–2 in. across, flattish, with ob-lanceolate pubescent lvs., gray-green tipped with dark purple, about 1 in. long: fls. 1 in. across; petals linear-lanceolate, pale yellow throughout, not purple at base. (Named for its collector, Josef Claudius Pittoni.) Cent. Eu.

9. **S. Wulfenii,** Hoppe. Rosettes open, 2–3½ in. across; lvs. gray-green, rosy-purple at base, oblong-spatulate, smooth on both faces, ¾–1½ in. long: fl.-sts. to 1 ft. high; fls. about 1 in. across; petals pale yellow or greenish-yellow, purple at base. (Named for von Wulfen, page 54.) Cent. Eu.

10. **S. Heuffelii,** Schott. Rosettes open, flattish, 2–5 in. across, from stout rootstocks; new rosettes developing from division of the old, not as offsets; lvs. oblong-obovate, acute, finely pubescent: fl.-sts. to 8 in. high; fls. about ½in. across; petals 6–7, erect, ciliate, pale yellow. (J. Heuffel, page 45.) S. E. Eu.

11. **S. hirtum,** L. Rosettes 1–2 in. across, usually open; lvs. broadly lanceolate, broadest below middle, glabrous on faces, ciliate, ½–¾in. long: fl.-sts. to 6 in. high; fls. 6-merous; petals erect, fimbriate-ciliate, pale yellow, ⅝in. long. S. E. Eu.

12. **S. soboliferum,** Sims. HOUSELEEK. Fl.-sts. 4–8 in. high and finely pubescent: rosettes globose, ¾–1¼ in. diam., with 60–80 cuneate-obovate indifferently cuspidate light green red-tipped glabrous lvs. with margins minutely ciliate, the outer lvs. 1 in. or less long, the many new rosettes sessile and slenderly connected with the parent and easily detached: fls. 6–7-merous, pale yellow, in a short dense many-fld. cyme; calyx-segms. ciliate on margin; petals lanceolate, margins fimbriate, obscurely tricuspidate at apex. N. Eurasia.

13. **S. arenarium,** Koch. Rosettes globular, ⅛–¾in. across, bearing 60–80 lanceolate acute light green glabrous incurved lvs., of which the outer ones are ¾in. or less long and slightly red-brown on the back, the cauline ones ovate-lanceolate; offsets very small on slender horizontal sts.: fl.-sts. 3–5 in., leafy and pubescent, bearing many pale yellow 6-merous fls. in a dense cyme which is 1–2 in. through; calyx-segms. and petals lanceolate, the latter 3-cuspidate. Tyrol.—This species has been listed as *S. cornutum.*

5. **ÆONIUM,** Webb & Berth. Succulent herbs and subshrubs of Madeira, Canary Isls. and adjacent N. W. Afr.; about 36 species, cult. outdoors in warm-temp. regions, under glass in cooler climates.—Differs from Sempervivum primarily in having

sts.: lvs. usually spatulate or obovate, glabrous, in rosettes: cymes usually paniculate, with buds drooping; fls. mostly yellow, sometimes white or pink, 6–12-merous; stamens twice as many as petals. (Æo-nium: Dioscoridean synonym of *Æ. arboreum.*)

A. Fls. rotate, yellow.
  B. Diam. of fls. ⅝in.: lvs. 2–3 in. long........ 1. *Æ. arboreum*
  BB. Diam. of fls. ⅜in.: lvs. 1 in. or less long........ 2. *Æ. spathulatum*
AA. Fls. campanulate, yellow flushed with rose........ 3. *Æ. Haworthii*

1. **Æ. arboreum,** Webb & Berth. (*Sempervivum arboreum,* L.). Erect subshrub 2–3 ft. high, branches ending in dense rosettes: lvs. oblong-spatulate, green, 2–3 in. long: cymes paniculate, 4 in. long and broad; fls. bright yellow, ⅝in. across, with petals rotately spreading. Morocco.

2. **Æ. spathulatum,** Praeger (*Sempervivum spathulatum,* Hornem.). Shrubby plant with stout branched sts., the branches horizontal and then arching upward: rosettes flat and not dense, the lvs. oblong-spatulate and acute with papillose margins and red-brown linear markings on both surfaces, the st.-lvs. linear-lanceolate and acuminate: fls. 8–10-merous, ⅜in. across, in paniculate cymes; calyx-segms. deltoid; petals oblong-lanceolate, acute, golden. Canary Isls.

3. **Æ. Haworthii,** Webb & Berth. Much-branched subshrub 1–2 ft. high, branches with loose rosettes at tips, rough below: lvs. obovate, apiculate, thick, mostly glaucous and red-edged, 1–2 in. long: cymes lax, much-branched, 4–5 in. long and broad; fls. campanulate, pale yellow flushed with rose, ⅜in. across, with petals suberect. (For A. H. Haworth, page 44.) Canary Isls.

6. **KALANCHOË,** Adans. (*Bryophyllum,* Salisb.). Defined broadly, this genus has about 125 described species, mostly in Afr. and Madagascar, 1 in Brazil and a few in trop. Asia; several sometimes seen in greenhouses.—Erect branched succulents, sometimes slightly woody at base: lvs. mostly opposite, fleshy, simple but sometimes pinnatifid or pinnate: fls. medium to large, many in terminal panicled cymes, yellow, scarlet or purple, often showy; calyx and corolla 4-parted; corolla urn-shaped or salverform, exceeding the calyx; stamens mostly 8, attached on corolla-tube; pistils 4, distinct or somewhat connate, many-ovuled: fr. a follicle. (Kalan-choë: adapted from Chinese name.)

A. Calyx little or not at all inflated; sepals free or joined only to the middle.
  B. Color of fls. white; tube of corolla 2 in. or more long.
    C. Tube of corolla 4-angled........ 1. *K. marmorata*
    CC. Tube of corolla cylindric towards tips........ 2. *K. somaliensis*
  BB. Color of fls. yellow or red; tube of corolla not exceeding 1 in. long.
    C. Fls. ½in. or less across.
      D. Infl. dense: sts. to 1½ ft. high: plants glabrous: corollas red........ 3. *K. Blossfeldiana*
      DD. Infl. lax: sts. to 4 ft. high: plants glabrous or hairy: corollas yellow or reddish-orange........ 4. *K. laciniata*
    CC. Fls. ¾–1 in. across, yellow to orange or scarlet........ 5. *K. flammea*
AA. Calyx inflated; sepals usually joined for half or more of their length, the lobes generally short.
  B. Lvs. petiolate, opposite, flat.
    C. Corolla contracted at base.
      D. Length of calyx not more than ½in.: lvs. simple, obovate, bluish- or grayish-green........ 6. *K. Fedtschenkoi*
      DD. Length of calyx 1 in. or more: lvs. pinnate or simple with oblong blades, yellow-green margined with red........ 7. *K. pinnata*
    CC. Corolla not contracted at base.
      D. Petals reddish: lvs. crenate, usually auriculate........ 8. *K. laxiflora*
      DD. Petals purplish or lavender: lvs. dentate, never auriculate........ 9. *K. Daigremontiana*
  BB. Lvs. sessile, opposite or whorled, subcylindric........ 10. *K. verticillata*

1. **K. marmorata,** Baker. Erect or prostrate branched per.: lvs. ascending, obovate or oblong-obovate, coarsely crenate, glaucous, light green blotched with purple, 3–6 in. long: fls. erect, on pedicels 1–1½ in. long, in simple cymes; tube of corolla angular, 3 in. or more long, greenish below, white above. Abyssinia.

2. **K. somaliensis,** Hook. f. Similar to no. 1, but with larger paler lvs., less blotched and more shallowly toothed, tube of corolla cylindric rather than rectangular towards apex. Somaliland.

3. **K. Blossfeldiana,** v. Poellnitz. Glabrous branched per. to 1½ ft. high: lvs. oblong-spatulate or oblong-obovate, crenate or almost entire, green, to 3 in. long: fls. numerous, in dense cymes; petals scarlet. (Intro. to cult. by Robert Blossfeld of Potsdam.) Madagascar.—A favorite house-plant which blooms abundantly in early winter.

4. **K. laciniata,** DC. (*K. carnea,* Mast.). Sts. 1½–4 ft., simple up to infl., glabrous or hairy above: lvs. oblong, oval or obovate, short-petioled, 3–5 in. long, obtuse, margins entire, crenate-dentate or lobed: fls. yellow or reddish-orange and fragrant, nearly ½in.

across; calyx with linear pointed lobes separated to base; corolla-tube much exceeding calyx, swollen at base, the wide-spreading lobes broad and acute. S. Afr.

5. **K. flammea,** Stapf. Glabrous per. to 1½ ft. high: lvs. ovate-oblong, obtuse, entire or obscurely sinuate-crenate, light green, to 2 in. long, short-petiolate: cymes corymbiform, with fls. ¾–1 in. across, varying from yellow to orange or scarlet. Trop. E. Afr.

6. **K. Fedtschenkoi,** Hamet & Perrier. Glabrous branched per. 12–20 in. high: lvs. mostly obovate, broadly rounded, coarsely dentate, bluish- or grayish-green, 1–1½ in. long: cymes lax with fls. drooping; corolla constricted at base, salmon to orange. (For B. Fedtschenko, page 43.) Madagascar.

7. **K. pinnata,** Pers. (*Bryophyllum pinnatum,* Kurz. *B. calycinum,* Salisb.). AIR-PLANT. LIFE-PLANT. FLOPPERS. Stout plant 1–5 or 6 ft. tall, glabrous and more or less glaucous, the sts. terete and hollow: lvs. opposite, pinnate (the early ones simple), fleshy becoming leathery; lfts. 3–5, very short-stalked, oval, oblong or elliptic, 2–5 in. long, crenate and sometimes producing young plants from the crenatures even after removal from the plant: calyx paper-like and much inflated, 1–1½ in. long, greenish- or yellowish-white and often purple-tinted; corolla much thinner than calyx, more or less prominently projecting (sometimes nearly twice the length of calyx), reddish, the lobes acute. Nativity uncertain, but now established in trop. and subtrop. countries.—Grown under glass for students in botany to illustrate natural propagation by means of lvs.

8. **K. laxiflora,** Baker (*Bryophyllum crenatum,* Baker). Plant 8–10 in., glaucous-blue: lvs. simple, the blades ovate, 1–3 in. long, base rounded or cordate and sometimes auriculate on the petiole, coarsely crenate and glaucous: fls. small, the calyx ⅜in. long and red corolla ¾–1 in. long, the corolla-lobes with rounded segms. Madagascar.

9. **K. Daigremontiana,** Hamet & Perrier. Glabrous per. to 1½ ft. high or more: lvs. lanceolate-oblong, coarsely dentate, producing numerous plantlets from the serrations, green blotched with purple dorsally, 6–9 in. long, petiolate: fls. about 1 in. long, drooping, on slender pedicels in lax paniculate cymes. (Dedicated to Madame and Monsieur Daigremont.) Madagascar.—Of easy cult. and much grown as a curiosity because of the plantlets developing along the margins of the lvs.

10. **K. verticillata,** Elliot (*Bryophyllum tubiflorum,* Harvey). Glabrous per. with simple erect sts., to 3 ft. high or more: lvs. long-linear, subcylindric, mottled with violet-brown, 1–6 in. long, producing plantlets at the tips: fls. salmon to scarlet, pendulous, 1 in. long, in terminal cymes. S. Afr.—A desirable pot-plant for the showy fls. which develop in winter.

7. **COTYLEDON,** L. About 30 species of succulents, largely of S. Afr., little known in cult. in N. Amer., some adaptable to walls and rockeries in warm-temp. climates, others to growing under glass.—Shrubs or subshrubs: lvs. sessile, opposite or alternate, simple: fls. erect or drooping, yellow, red or greenish, in terminal cymes; calyx 5-parted; corolla gamopetalous, tubular, cylindrical, sometimes angled, usually much exceeding calyx; stamens 10, mostly included; pistils 5, free, with narrow scale at base of each: fr. of several-seeded follicles. (Cotyle-don: ancient Greek name, *a cavity,* from the cup-like lvs. of some kinds.)

C. orbiculata, L. Stout branching plant 2–4 ft. high: lvs. opposite, oblong to roundish-obovate or spatulate, 2–4 in. long, flat, entire, glaucous and powdery, often margined red or purple: fls. red, drooping in a paniculate cyme that has a peduncle 2 ft. long, the divisions of corolla reflexed, appearing in summer; corolla-tube ¾–1 in. long, four to five times as long as calyx and also much longer than its limb. S. Afr.—Sometimes seen in conservatories, variable, with several named forms. *C. simplicifolia,* a name without taxonomic status, has been applied to plants with tufts of rounded lvs., coarsely and irregularly toothed, and drooping branched racemes of small yellow fls.; it is said to be native in S. Eu. but its origin and identity are uncertain.

8. **GRAPTOPETALUM,** Rose. Succulent herbs and subshrubs; about 11 species in the Cordilleran area of warm-temp. N. Amer.—Somewhat intermediate between Sedum and Echeveria, distinguished by corollas with the petals united below and spreading from near the middle, marked with transverse bands of dots or spots: lvs. various, sometimes in rosettes, either relatively thin or thick and terete or subterete: fls. in axillary cymes; sepals equalling the tube of the corolla; stamens twice as many as the petals, becoming incurved; pistils erect. (Graptopet-alum: Greek *painted leaf* or *petal.*)

G. paraguayense, E. Walther (*Cotyledon paraguayense,* N. E. Br. *Echeveria Weinbergii,* T. B. Shepherd). Glabrous per. to 1 ft. high, with spreading branches terminated by lax rosettes of thick lvs.: lvs. oblong-spatulate, acuminate, carinate dorsally, concave ventrally, 2–3 in. long: fl.-sts. axillary, to 6 in. long, terminating in lax cymes; fls. 5-merous, about ½in. across; petals ovate, white speckled with transverse bands of red dots. Mex.

9. **ECHEVERIA,** DC. Per. succulents; species probably 100 in the mts. of warm-temp. and trop. Amer., a few grown under glass and sometimes planted out and used for flat carpet-bedding in warm climates.—Distinguished typically by the fls. with petals erect, spreading only at the tips, thick and fleshy, somewhat united at base, forming a short tube which does not exceed the calyx; corolla strongly angled and broad at base: lvs. commonly broad and flat, making dense rosettes: fls. in elongate often secund cymes, sometimes paniculate; fl.-sts. axillary. (Echeve-ria: Atanasio Echeverria, Mexican botanical draughtsman.)—A difficult genus to classify. Some names in use by horticulturists are of uncertain taxonomic status, as *E. Hoveyi,* Rose and *E. nobilis,* Hort.

A. Plants hairy.
  B. And stemless .... 1. *E. setosa*
  BB. And caulescent .... 2. *E. pulvinata*
AA. Plants glabrous.
  B. Sepals orbicular or ovate, $\frac{1}{8}$in. long or less.
    C. Corollas $\frac{1}{4}$in. long, pinkish; sepals ovate .... 3. *E. expatriata*
    CC. Corollas $\frac{3}{8}$in. long, coral-red; sepals orbicular, appressed .... 4. *E. amœna*
  BB. Sepals linear to acute, $\frac{1}{8}$–$\frac{1}{2}$in. long.
    C. Lvs. ovoid, thick, spine-tipped .... 5. *E. agavoides*
    CC. Lvs. spatulate to oblanceolate, rarely orbicular or ovate, mostly flat, sometimes mucronate but not spine-tipped.
      D. Cymes elongate, equilateral.
        E. Species caulescent .... 6. *E. multicaulis*
        EE. Species stemless .... 7. *E. carnicolor*
      DD. Cymes elongate, secund.
        E. The cymes mostly simple.
          F. Fls. sessile or almost so .... 8. *E. Peacockii*
          FF. Fls. pedicellate.
            G. Lf. very turgid.
              H. Fl. with sepals spreading .... 9. *E. elegans*
              HH. Fl. with sepals appressed .... 10. *E. simulans*
            GG. Lf. not turgid.
              H. Rosettes globular: fl.-sts. 3 in. high .... 11. *E. Derenbergii*
              HH. Rosettes flattish, not globular: fl.-sts. 1 ft. or more high.
                I. Foliage light green, only glaucous when young .... 12. *E. secunda*
                II. Foliage pruinose on both surfaces .... 13. *E. glauca*
        EE. The cymes compound.
          F. Foliage bright green, not glaucous .... 14. *E. stolonifera*
          FF. Foliage bluish-green, pale glaucous .... 15. *E. gibbiflora*

1. **E. setosa,** Rose & Purpus. Stemless per.: lvs. densely white-setose, spatulate to oblanceolate, acute, to 2 in. long, in nearly globular rosettes: fl.-sts. about 1 ft. high, with 6–12 fls. in elongate secund cymes; corolla red tipped with yellow. Mex.

2. **E. pulvinata,** Rose. Velvety-pubescent throughout, sts. to 10 in. high, somewhat branched: lvs. obovate, 1–2 in. long, pale green: fl.-sts. 1 ft. high, with fls. in one-sided cymes; corolla scarlet, $\frac{3}{4}$in. long. Mex.

3. **E. expatriata,** Rose. Sts. about 4 in. high, crowned by a rosette of glaucous oblanceolate lvs. 1 in. long: fl.-sts. ascending, weak; fls. on pedicels $\frac{1}{2}$in. long; sepals ovate; corolla pinkish, $\frac{1}{4}$in. long. Known only from cult.

4. **E. amœna,** Morr. Stemless or nearly so, with lvs. pinkish-pruinose, spatulate-oblanceolate, $\frac{3}{4}$in. long, in dense rosettes with numerous offsets: fl.-sts. 4–8 in. high, 1–8-fld.; corolla coral-red, $\frac{3}{8}$in. long. Mex.

5. **E. agavoides,** Lem. (*Cotyledon agavoides,* Baker. *Urbinia agavoides,* Britt. & Rose). Small and compact: lvs. thick and stiff, in dense rosettes, ovate, acute, spine-tipped, 2–2$\frac{1}{2}$ in. long, bright green: scapes from the rosette, 8–20 in. long, with yellow-red fls. 8 or less on long pedicels; calyx several times shorter than the cone-shaped corolla, the lobes of which are free three-quarters of the length. Mex.

6. **E. multicaulis,** Rose. Caulescent, with sts. bearing rosettes to 8 in. long, roughened below: lvs. obovate or spatulate, 1$\frac{1}{4}$–1$\frac{1}{2}$ in. long: fl.-sts. 2–3 ft. or more high; cymes equilateral, about 20-fld.; corolla reddish externally, yellow within. Mex.

7. **E. carnicolor,** Morr. Stemless, with dense rosettes of oblanceolate lvs. 1–3 in. long, glaucous tinged with red: fl.-sts. 6–8 in. high; cymes equilateral, of 6–20 fls.; corolla red. Mex.

8. **E. Peacockii,** Croucher (*E. Desmetiana,* Morr.). Acaulescent, with close rosettes of white-glaucous obovate-spatulate lvs. 2–3 in. long: fl.-sts. 1 ft. high, with the fls. sessile or subsessile in secund cymes; sepals linear; corolla bright red, $\frac{1}{2}$in. long. (Flowered in the collection of Mr. Peacock at Hammersmith, England.) Mex.

9. **E. elegans,** Rose. Stemless, with the lvs. numerous in compact rosettes, offsets on long sts.: lvs. obovate, very thick and turgid, glaucous, 1–2 in. long: fl.-sts. 4–10 in. high, with the 5–10 fls. in a secund cyme; sepals spreading; corolla $\frac{3}{8}$in. long, pinkish with yellow tips. Mex.

10. **E. simulans,** Rose. Similar to *E. elegans* but with flatter rosettes, narrower corolla and narrower appressed sepals. Mex.

11. **E. Derenbergii,** Purpus. Stemless or short-stemmed, with rosettes globular or almost so, 1–2½ in. across: lvs. broadly spatulate, glaucous, 1–2 in. long: fl.-sts. short, about 3 in. long; cymes secund, 1–5-fld.; corolla ½–⅝in. long, orange or almost yellow. (Named for Dr. Julius Derenberg of Hamburg, cactus fancier.) Mex.

12. **E. secunda,** Booth (*Cotyledon secunda,* Baker). Acaulescent, producing stolons that bear offsets: lvs. erect or nearly so in a sempervivum-like rosette, cuneate-obovate, narrowed to a short sharp point, glabrous, light green, red-tipped: fl.-sts. weak, 12–15 in. long, bracted, glaucous, bearing 8–24 pedicelled reddish fls. along one side; corolla about ½in. long, divided nearly to the base, the lance-acute lobes once or twice exceeding calyx, not spreading. Mex.—Common in cult., often planted out for edgings.

13. **E. glauca,** Baker (? *E. globosa,* Morr.). Stemless, with thick rosettes; lvs. obovate, almost orbicular, broadly rounded but mucronate-tipped, pale and glaucous, with the tips purple, about 2 in. long, ¾–1 in. broad: fl.-sts. 8–12 in. high, with 8–20 fls. in a simple secund racemose cyme; corolla ½in. long, pinkish or red externally, yellow within. Mex.

14. **E. stolonifera,** Otto. Stemless or very short-stemmed, with the lvs. in dense rosettes, broadly obovate or spatulate, bright green, not glaucous or only slightly so, 2–3 in. long: fl.-sts. 6–8 in. long, with 4–6 fls. in a dense umbel-like cyme; corolla ½in. long, yellowish. Mex.

15. **E. gibbiflora,** DC. (*Cotyledon gibbiflora,* Moc. & Sessé). Tall and branching, 1–2 ft. high, glabrous: lvs. obovate-spatulate or long-cuneate, 5–12 in. long, glaucous, in a rosette near the ground and also aggregate at ends of branches, becoming pinkish: fls. in spreading paniculate secund racemes, short-pedicelled, red, about ½–1 in. long, the corolla strongly angled; corolla-lobes lanceolate and long-acuminate, three or four times as long as the unequal calyx-lobes. Mex. Var. **metallica,** Baker (*E. metallica,* Lem.), probably the common form in cult., has glaucous purple foliage with metallic sheen.

10. **PACHYPHYTUM,** Link. Thick-lvd. succulents of about 10 species native in Mex., a few sometimes cult. in gardens in warm-temp. climates, or under glass in cooler regions.—Similar to Echeveria, differing in having appendages on the petals at the place of insertion of the epipetalous stamens: fls. solitary or few in secund racemose cymes: fl.-bracts characteristically large and rendering the cymes distinctive, also the sepals tending to be appressed, not spreading as in most species of Echeveria. (Pachyph-ytum: Latin *thick plant.*)—Some species hybridize with Echeveria.

P. compactum, Rose. Sterile sts. 4 in. or more high: lvs. very thick and fleshy, lanceolate-oblong, angulate, crowded, spreading, somewhat flattened ventrally, glaucous, ¾–1⅛ in. long: fl.-sts. to 16 in. high, with 7–10 reddish fls. in a secund cyme. Mex.

90. SAXIFRAGACEÆ. SAXIFRAGE FAMILY

Plants of various habit, inhabiting mostly temp. and subarctic regions; genera usually considered to be about 70, but by segregation the number may be 100; species 900–1,100; the family comprises ornamental herbs and shrubs and also pomological species.—The family is allied to Rosaceæ but differs in having fewer or more definite stamens, pistils mostly fewer than sepals and sometimes combined into a single compound pistil, lvs. usually without stipules and sometimes opposite: fls. bisexual or unisexual, usually regular; sepals prevailingly 4 or 5, and petals and stamens of same number or stamens twice as many (or more), the petals and stamens inserted at the edge of a disk; pistils free or united, ovary inferior or superior, placentation axile or parietal, usually 1–5-celled: fr. a caps. or berry with many seeds that contain abundant albumen.

A. Species woody, shrubs or small trees, sometimes climbers.
  B. Lvs. alternate or clustered: stamens 5 (4).
    C. Fr. a berry: lvs. usually palmately lobed. . . . . 1. RIBES
    CC. Fr. a caps.: lvs. entire to spiny-toothed.
      D. Ovary superior; petals white, not clawed, inflexed at tip. . . . . 2. ITEA
      DD. Ovary inferior; petals white to red, clawed, with a spreading limb. . . . . . 3. ESCALLONIA
  BB. Lvs. opposite: stamens 10 to numerous.
    C. Fls., some or all of them, sterile, with showy calyx, the fertile fls. smaller.
      D. Styles 2–5; sterile fls. 4–5-parted. . . . . 4. HYDRANGEA
      DD. Style 1; sterile fls. of 1 long-stalked unlobed sepal. . . . . 5. SCHIZOPHRAGMA
    CC. Fls. all fertile, petals showy.
      D. Stamens usually twice as many as petals: pubescence stellate. . . . . 6. DEUTZIA
      DD. Stamens more than twice as many as petals: pubescence simple.

E. Foliage persistent, entire: fls. 5–7-merous........................ 7. CARPENTERIA

EE. Foliage usually deciduous, often dentate: fls. 4-merous............ 8. PHILADELPHUS

AA. Species herbaceous, mostly per.

B. Fls. solitary, on scape-like fl.-sts.; staminodia present.................... 9. PARNASSIA

BB. Fls. not as above.

C. Lvs. pinnately parted, the terminal lobe largest: fls. 4-merous, ovary 4-celled.. 10. FRANCOA

CC. Lvs. not as above: fls. usually 5-merous, ovary of 2–3 distinct or united pistils.

D. Petals 3-cleft to pinnatifid.. 11. MITELLA

DD. Petals entire, sometimes lacking.

E. Stamens 3 (2); 3 upper sepals longer than the lower ones.............. 12. TOLMIEA

EE. Stamens 4–10; sepals subequal.

F. Lf. orbicular-peltate, to 16 in. or more across.................. 13. PELTIPHYLLUM

FF. Lf. not orbicular-peltate.

G. Number of stamens consistently 5; petals small, often shorter than sepals. (See also no. 15.) 14. HEUCHERA

GG. Number of stamens mostly 7–10, in ours; petals usually longer than sepals.

H. Caps. 1-celled, with 2 unequal valves and fls. with unequal carpels.

I. Fl. with 7–8 stamens (occasionally some fls. of infl. with 5).... 15. HEUCHERELLA

II. Fl. with 10 stamens.. 16. TIARELLA

HH. Caps. 2–3-celled, or the pistils distinct; pistils subequal.

I. Plant with thick fleshy rhizome above ground: lvs. orbicular to obovate, to 12 in. long, waxy...................... 17. BERGENIA

II. Plant with smaller or no rhizome: lvs. not as above.

J. The petals (in ours) distinctly long-clawed, reddish-purple.. 18. BOYKINIA

JJ. The petals (in ours) not distinctly clawed but often tapering toward base.

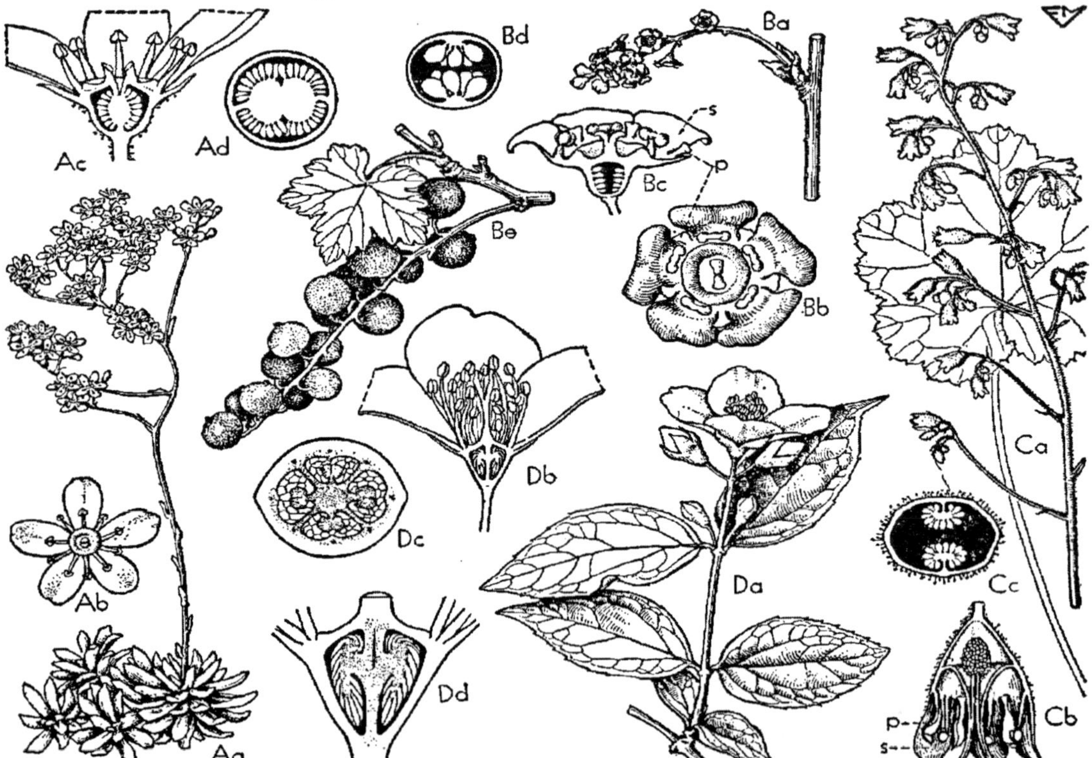

Fig. 90. SAXIFRAGACEÆ. A, *Saxifraga Macnabiana:* Aa, plant in flower, × ¼; Ab, flower, face view, × 1; Ac, same, vertical section, perianth excised, × 2; Ad, ovary, cross-section, × 3. B, *Ribes sativum:* Ba, inflorescence, × ½; Bb, flower, face view, × 3; Bc, same, vertical section, × 3; Bd, ovary, cross-section, × 8; Be, fruit, × ½. C, *Heuchera sanguinea:* Ca, inflorescence and basal leaf, × ½; Cb, flower, vertical section, × 2; Cc, ovary, cross-section, × 4. D, *Philadelphus inodorus:* Da, flowering branch, × ½; Db, flower, vertical section, petals excised, × 1; Dc, ovary, cross-section, × 3; Dd, ovary, vertical section, × 3. (p petal, s sepal.)

K. Lvs. commonly 2–4-ternate: fls. 300 or more, crowded in dense pyramidal panicles; petals narrow, 1/16–1/4in. long .... 19. ASTILBE
KK. Lvs. (in ours) entire to palmately parted: fls. usually less numerous, in looser infl., commonly larger .... 20. SAXIFRAGA

1. **RIBES,** L. CURRANTS and GOOSEBERRIES. Shrubs, about 150 species in temp. and cold regions in many parts of the world; some are cult. for the edible fr. and others for ornament.—Spiny or unarmed, deciduous or evergreen: lvs. alternate or fascicled, simple but usually palmately lobed, stipules none: fls. bisexual, or in some species the plants diœcious, 5- (4-) merous, solitary or in racemes, small but sometimes highly colored, the calyx being the showy part; hypanthium rotate to tubular, the lobes (sepals) erect or spreading; petals small or even minute (rarely absent), inserted on throat of calyx-tube; 5 (4) stamens alternate with petals; ovary inferior, 1-celled but with 2 parietal placentæ; styles 2, separate or united into 1: fr. a many-seeded berry, crowned with remains of calyx. (Ri-bes: the Arabic name.)

A. Infl. of 1–3 (4) fls.: branches more or less bristly, rarely almost unarmed—the gooseberries (GROSSULARIA).
B. Fls. red; stamens 4, two to four times as long as sepals .... 1. *R. speciosum*
BB. Fls. greenish to whitish; stamens 5, shorter than sepals or subequal to them.
C. Hypanthium and ovary pubescent .... 2. *R. Grossularia*
CC. Hypanthium and ovary glabrous or subglabrous.
D. Stamens longer than petals: spines usually lacking .... 3. *R. hirtellum*
DD. Stamens subequal to petals: spines present .... 4. *R. oxyacanthoides*
AA. Infl. a 4-to many-fld. raceme: branches unarmed—the currants.
B. Fls. unisexual, in upright racemes .... 5. *R. alpinum*
BB. Fls. bisexual, in usually spreading or drooping racemes.
C. Hypanthium saucer-shaped or rotate.
D. Base of lvs. more or less cordate: anther-cells separated by broad connective .... 6. *R. sativum*
DD. Base of lvs. usually truncate: anther-cells not separated .... 7. *R. rubrum*
CC. Hypanthium tubular to campanulate.
D. Color of fls. greenish- or yellowish-white: lvs. resin-dotted beneath.
E. Bracts usually shorter than pedicels; racemes few-fld .... 8. *R. nigrum*
EE. Bracts longer than pedicels; racemes many-fld .... 9. *R. americanum*
DD. Color of fls. red or yellow, showy: lvs. not resin-dotted beneath but sometimes glandular-sticky.
E. Fl. red .... 10. *R. sanguineum*
EE. Fl. yellow.
F. Sepals less than half the length of hypanthium .... 11. *R. odoratum*
FF. Sepals more than half the length of hypanthium .... 12. *R. aureum*

1. **R. speciosum,** Pursh (*Grossularia speciosa*, Cov. & Britt.). FUCHSIA-FLOWERED GOOSEBERRY. Attractive evergreen stout shrub to 10–12 ft., bristly and with long stout spines: lvs. thick, obovate, oblong to orbicular, 1½ in. or less long, rounded to subcuneate at base, few-toothed or sometimes 3–5-lobed, shining above, glabrous or only sparingly glandular-hairy: fls. bright red, 4-merous, 2–4, hanging on slender peduncles; hypanthium short, broadly campanulate, with upright sepals to ⅜in. long; petals equal to sepals; stamens two to four times as long as sepals: fr. ovoid, red, glandular-bristly. Calif.

2. **R. Grossularia,** L. (*R. reclinatum*, L. *Grossularia reclinata*, Mill.). ENGLISH GOOSEBERRY. Stockier stiffer plant than no. 3, about 3 ft., with ascending or reclining branches and stout spines mostly in 3's, sts. sometimes bristly: lvs. stiffish, nearly orbicular, 1–2½ in. broad, cordate or somewhat tapering at base, 3–5-lobed with lobes obtuse or indifferently acute, margins toothed and somewhat revolute, glabrous or pubescent: fls. 1 or 2 on nodding peduncles, greenish; hypanthium pubescent, about as long as the sepals; stamens shorter than the lobes; ovary pubescent and often glandular: fr. usually pubescent and glandular. Eu., N. Afr., S. W. Asia, sometimes escaped in N. Amer. Var. **Uva-crispa,** Smith (*R. Uva-crispa*, L.), has smaller pubescent lvs., pubescent usually not glandular ovary, and small yellowish pubescent fr.

3. **R. hirtellum,** Michx. (*R. oxyacanthoides* of most authors. *Grossularia hirtella*, Cov. & Britt.). Erect bush, 2–4 ft., the branches usually unarmed but often bristly: lvs. nearly orbicular to broad-ovate, 1–2 in. broad, 3–5-lobed, mostly narrowed or cuneate at base, very sharp-dentate, glabrous or nearly so, petioles often long-hairy, not glandular: fls. 1–3 together, small and greenish or purple-tinged, with bracts much shorter than pedicels, the peduncles not exceeding petioles; hypanthium glabrous or lightly hairy, about the length of the sepals; stamens subequal to the sepals and much longer than the petals: fr. usually glabrous, purple or black at maturity. Newf. to W. Va., S. D. and Man.—Supposed source of the American pomological gooseberries, either by direct amelioration or by hybridity with *R. Grossularia*, or both.

4. **R. oxyacanthoides,** L. (*Grossularia oxyacanthoides*, Cov. & Britt.). Low bush with slender often procumbent branches, bristly and armed with stout spines to ½in. long: lvs. suborbicular, 1–1½ in. broad, deeply 3–5-lobed, truncate to broadly cuneate at base, ob-

tusely dentate, subglabrous: fls. greenish-white, 1–2 on very short peduncles, pedicels short; sepals slightly longer than hypanthium; stamens and petals subequal, about two-thirds as long as sepals: fr. red to purplish, glabrous. Hudson Bay to B. C., Mont. and Mich.

5. **R. alpinum,** L. MOUNTAIN OR ALPINE CURRANT. Diœcious spreading dense shrub, 6–8 ft., growths whitish and glabrous: lvs. broad- or triangular-ovate, 1–2 in. across, mostly 3-lobed, base truncate or subcordate, glabrous, irregularly dentate: fls. small, greenish-yellow, borne profusely in upright racemes, the staminate 1–2½ in. long and 20–30-fld., the pistillate smaller; hypanthium nearly flat, the sepals ovate; petals minute: fr. scarlet, glabrous, persisting long. Eu.—An old garden ornamental, in several forms.

6. **R. sativum,** Syme (*R. rubrum*, Auth. not L. *R. rubrum* var. *sativum*, Reichb. *R. vulgare*, Jancz. not Lam.). COMMON OR GARDEN CURRANT. Familiar upright shrub, 4–6 ft., but kept lower in good cult., the young growth pubescent: lvs. triangular-ovate or sometimes broader than long, 3–5-lobed, 1–3 in. across, cordate or subcordate at base, dentate and cut, pubescent beneath at least on veins: fls. greenish-yellow, in many-fld. drooping racemes, the pedicels filiform; hypanthium saucer-shaped, with an elevated 5-angled ring inside between the stamens and style and this region purplish; anther-cells separated by a broad connective: fr. red ("red currants") or white ("white currants"), sometimes striped. W. Eu. Var. **macrocarpum,** Bailey (*R. vulgare* var. *macrocarpum*, Jancz.), CHERRY CURRANT, lvs. large, 3-lobed, prominently cordate: fr. large, red: plant usually less hardy.

7. **R. rubrum,** L. (*R. vulgare*, Lam.). NORTHERN RED CURRANT. Similar to *R. sativum* but the young growths, as also the lvs., quite or nearly glabrous: lvs. larger, truncate or rarely subcordate: racemes more spreading than drooping, the pedicels short; hypanthium almost cup-shaped, without the ring and the purplish color; anther-cells not separated: fr. small. Cent. and N. Eu. and N. Asia.—The currants grown in N. Amer. are probably all *R. sativum;* in N. Eu. some of them are apparently *R. rubrum;* perhaps some of our small-fruited very hardy kinds are hybrids of the two species.

8. **R. nigrum,** L. EUROPEAN BLACK CURRANT. Stout bush, 4–6 ft., with blackish old wood bearing large lenticels, the plant emitting strong odor: lvs. broad-triangular to nearly orbicular in outline, 2–4 in. across, 3–5-lobed, subcordate to cordate, irregularly serrate, nearly or quite glabrous, resin-dotted beneath: fls. greenish-white, in 4–10-fld. small-bracted pendulous racemes; hypanthium campanulate, pubescent and glandular, sepals longer than the hypanthium; petals about half length of sepals: fr. nearly globular, black. Eu., Asia.—Planted for its aromatic frs. which are used in cookery and conserves; there are green-fruited and yellow-fruited kinds and also cut-leaved and variegated forms grown for interest and ornament.

9. **R. americanum,** Mill. (*R. floridum*, L'Her.). AMERICAN BLACK CURRANT. Erect shrub to 5 ft., with spreading slender branches: lvs. suborbicular, 1–3½ in. across, 3–5-lobed, cordate to subtruncate, dentate, resin-dotted and pubescent on veins beneath: fls. yellowish-white, in many-fld. drooping racemes, with the bracts longer than the pedicels; sepals slightly longer than the tubular-campanulate hypanthium; petals and stamens about two-thirds as long as sepals: fr. black, glabrous. N. S. to Man., Va. and Colo.

10. **R. sanguineum,** Pursh. Shrub to 10 ft. or more, the young growth pubescent and usually somewhat glandular: lvs. triangular-ovate to reniform-orbicular, 1½–4 in. broad, cordate to truncate at base, obtusely 3–5-lobed, margins serrate to nearly entire, dull green and nearly or quite glabrous above, soft-pubescent beneath: fls. red or crimson, in several- to many-fld. racemes with prominent colored bracts, calyx and pedicels glandular-pubescent, in early spring; hypanthium about ⅙in. long and exceeded by lobes; petals white to reddish, about one-half as long as sepals: fr. blue-black, glaucous, mostly somewhat glandular. N. Calif. to B. C.—An old ornamental plant. Some of the plants in cult. under this name are **R. malvaceum,** Smith, which can be distinguished by the sepals shorter than the hypanthium; fls. rose to pink. **R. Gordonianum,** Lem., is a hybrid between *R. sanguineum* and *R. odoratum*, often planted: habit of *R. odoratum* but fls. yellow tinged red outside and somewhat glandular, sterile: lvs. glabrate, truncate, usually 3-lobed.

11. **R. odoratum,** Wendl. (*R. fragrans*, Lodd. *Chrysobotrya odorata*, Rydb.). MISSOURI OR BUFFALO CURRANT. Shrub, 5–7 ft., with pubescent young branches: lvs. ovate to orbicular-reniform in outline, 1–3 in. broad, deeply 3–5-lobed, cuneate or truncate at base, coarsely dentate, becoming glabrous: fls. yellow, fragrant, in 5–10-fld. pubescent racemes; hypanthium about ½in. long, the sepals reflexed or widely spreading and scarcely half as long as the hypanthium; petals nearly half as long as sepals, reddish: fr. black, nearly or quite globose, about ⅓in. diam. Great Plains, S. D. to Tex., east of the Rocky Mts; sometimes escaped from cult.—Planted for its fragrant yellow fls.; the Crandall currant, grown for its fr., belongs here.

12. **R. aureum,** Pursh (*R. tenuiflorum*, Lindl. *Chrysobotrya aurea*, Rydb.). GOLDEN CURRANT. Smaller and more slender bush than *R. odoratum*, young branches glabrous or puberulous: lvs. often subcordate at base and slightly crenate-dentate: fls. usually more numerous in the raceme and smaller, less fragrant; hypanthium somewhat shorter and more slender, the sepals more than half its length and the limb spreading but upright and closed in the faded fl.; petals shorter: fr. black to purplish, usually smaller. Rocky Mts. westward.—Some of the stock in cult. may represent this species.

2. **ITEA,** L. About 11 shrubs and small trees, one in E. U. S. and the others in trop. and temp. Asia.—Lvs. alternate, simple, exstipular: fls. white, bisexual, small but usually numerous in terminal or axillary racemes or panicles; calyx turbinate, with 5 persistent lobes; petals 5, very narrow, inflexed at tips; stamens 5, attached on disk; ovary superior, 2-celled, placentation axile, the style 2-grooved but becoming 2-parted, ovules many: fr. a narrow or conical septicidally 2-valved caps. (It-ea: Greek name of willow, applied probably from the resemblance of the lvs. of *I. virginica*, the original species.)

A. Lvs. serrulate, deciduous....................1. *I. virginica*
AA. Lvs. spiny-toothed, persistent....................2. *I. ilicifolia*

1. **I. virginica,** L. Sweet Spire. Virginia-Willow. Shrub, 3–10 ft., the young growth finely pubescent: lvs. deciduous, oval, oblong to oblanceolate, 1–4 in. long, short-pointed, narrowing into short petiole, minutely apiculate-serrate, glabrous above and lightly hairy on veins beneath: racemes terminal, erect, 2–6 in. long, of white fragrant fls., in early and midsummer; petals linear, nearly ¼in. long, somewhat exceeding the stamens: fr. ¼in. or more long including prominent style, standing upright on the raceme. Pa. and N. J. to Fla. and La.; hardy farther north.

2. **I. ilicifolia,** Oliv. Evergreen shrub to 10 ft.: lvs. elliptic, 2½–4½ in. long, obtuse, spiny and holly-like, subglabrous: fls. greenish-white, in dense terminal drooping racemes 6–14 in. long. Cent. China; not hardy north.

3. **ESCALLONIA,** Mutis. Fifty or more species, mostly evergreen shrubs and small trees, in the Andean region and S. Brazil to Argentina, some intro. into the southern states and Calif. for ornament.—Lvs. alternate or clustered, simple, glandular-serrate or entire, exstipulate although the small side lvs. may be taken for stipules, often resinous-dotted: fls. white, pink, or red, sometimes axillary but mostly in terminal racemes or panicles; calyx-lobes 5; petals 5, free but usually standing together as if forming a tube; stamens 5; style simple, the stigma 2–5-lobed and peltate or reniform; ovary inferior, 1-celled, placentation parietal: fr. a top-shaped septicidal many-seeded caps. bearing the calyx-lobes and style at the top. (Escallonia: named after Escallon, a Spanish traveller in S. Amer.)—The Latin names of Escallonia are much misplaced in cult.

A. Fls. white.
 B. Claws of petals spreading, not forming a tube; fls. in rounded panicles: lvs. often notched at tip....................1. *E. montevidensis*
 BB. Claws of petals forming a tube; fls. in pyramidal panicles: lvs. not notched.... 2. *E. Grahamiana*
AA. Fls. pink to rose or dark red.
 B. Length of lvs. mostly less than 1 in.: fls. in short racemes on lateral twigs...... 3. *E. langleyensis*
 BB. Length of lvs. mostly exceeding 1 in.: fls. in terminal panicles (sometimes racemose in *E. punctata*).
  C. Lvs. sharp-serrate, tapering to a narrow base: fls. dark red....................4. *E. punctata*
  CC. Lvs. bluntly serrate to crenulate, clearly short-petioled: fls. pink to rose-red or crimson.
   D. Lf. three to four times as long as broad....................5. *E. organensis*
   DD. Lf. once or twice as long as broad.
    E. Under surface of lf. only gland-dotted: axis of infl. pubescent with stalked glands intermixed; fls. rose-red to crimson, the tube of the corolla about as long as the limb is wide....................6. *E. macrantha*
    EE. Under and upper surfaces of lf. gland-dotted: axis of infl. viscid throughout as if varnished; fls. pink, the tube of the corolla much longer than the limb....................7. *E. franciscana*

1. **E. montevidensis,** DC. (*E. floribunda* var. *montevidensis*, Cham. & Schlecht.). Stout erect bush to 10 ft., with branches glabrous or bearing a few stalkless glands on the young parts: lvs. elliptic-obovate to spatulate, 1–2½ in. long, obtuse at apex and often with a small notch, gradually tapering to a short petiole, finely serrate, glabrous and shining, with small dots beneath: fls. white, in terminal large rounded panicles; petals more or less spreading and not overlapping to form tube; stigma large, angled, prominent after anthesis. S. Brazil, Uruguay.—Some of the plants cult. as *E. floribunda* belong here. *E. floribunda*, HBK., has acute minutely serrulate lvs. on petioles ⅜–¾in. long: fls. less than ¼in. long; calyx-teeth reduced to calluses: Venezuela and Colombia south in the Andes.

2. **E. Grahamiana,** Gill. Erect shrub with more or less spreading branchlets which bear sessile glands: lvs. elliptic-obovate to oblong, to 2 in. or more long, obtuse, narrowed to short petiole, finely serrate, glabrous and shining above, minutely gland-dotted beneath: fls. white, in terminal pyramidal panicles; calyx-teeth subulate; stamens and style not conspicuously exserted beyond the tube formed by the claws of the petals. Chile.—Cult. under various names, as *E. alba*, *E. floribunda*, *E. montevidensis*, and *E. virgata*.

3. **E. langleyensis,** Veitch (*E. virgata* × *E. punctata*). Somewhat glandular shrub with graceful arching branches: lvs. oval to obovate, ½–1 in. or more long, acute, long-tapering at base, finely serrulate: fls. rose-carmine, about ½in. across, in short racemes on lateral twigs; claws of petals broad and short.

4. **E. punctata,** DC. Bushy shrub, 3–10 ft., the young branches brown and sticky with stalked glands: lvs. oval, elliptic-ovate or somewhat obovate, 1–2 in. long, tapering both ways, acute at apex, the base long-narrow but without distinct petiole, sharp-serrate on upper two-thirds, glabrous and glossy above, lighter colored and resinous-dotted beneath: fls. dark red, mostly 2–4 together (sometimes 1) in a terminal infl. 1–3 in. long; calyx 5-angled, with spreading acute lobes, the base glandular; corolla cylindrical, ½in. or less long and three or four times exceeding calyx, the veined obtuse tips revolute; style about equalling petals, the stigma peltate. Chile.

5. **E. organensis,** Gardner. Shrub to 6 ft., with glabrous angled twigs: lvs. narrowly obovate to oblong, to 3 in. long, obtuse, long-tapering at base, bluntly serrate, glabrous, pale beneath: fls. rose-pink, in short dense terminal panicles; calyx-teeth subequal to hypanthium and about half as long as petals. Organ Mts., Brazil.

6. **E. macrantha,** Hook. & Arn. Dense shrub with stout twigs, the pubescence intermixed with stalked glands: lvs. thick, broad-oval to elliptic, 1½–3 (4) in. long, obtuse to acute, contracted to a short distinct petiole, bluntly serrate, green and shining above, gland-dotted beneath: fls. rose-red to crimson, in dense terminal panicles; corolla-tube as long as the limb is wide. Chile.—The largest fld. Escallonia, common in cult. Most of the material cult. as *E. rubra* belongs here. *E. rubra*, Pers. (*Stereoxylum rubrum*, Ruiz & Pav.), has smaller sharply serrate lvs., corolla-tube narrow, twice as long as the limb.

7. **E. franciscana,** Eastw. Tall glandular-viscid shrub with stout branches: lvs. thick, oblong to elliptic, obtuse to acute, tapering to a short petiole, margins crenulate becoming entire toward base, glandular on both sides but more so beneath: fls. pink, in a narrow viscid panicle; calyx subequal to ovary and with slender teeth, corolla-tube about ⅜in. long, with a spreading limb which is much shorter; stamens and pistil included in the tube. Probably a hybrid, origin unknown.—Some of the material grown as *E. organensis* may be *E. franciscana.* Most of the plants cult. as *E. rosea* belong here. *E. rosea*, Griseb., has small spatulate-lanceolate lvs. and fls. in leafy simple racemes.

4. **HYDRANGEA,** L. Species perhaps 80 in N. and S. Amer. and Asia, some of them much prized ornamentals.—Woody plants, mostly self-standing shrubs but sometimes root-climbers or even tree-like: lvs. opposite, simple, petioled, without stipules: fls. white, pink, or blue, in terminal panicles or cymes, some of the marginal fls. usually enlarged and sterile, the expanded parts being the calyx, and in certain cult. races all the fls. thus modified; calyx-lobes and petals 4–5, the calyx-tube joined to ovary; petals valvate (edge to edge) in bud; stamens 10 (8–20); ovary 2–5-celled, inferior or half-inferior, placentation axile, styles short, 2–5: fr. a 2–5-celled many-seeded caps. dehiscent from the top. (Hydran-gea: Greek *water-vessel*, from shape of the caps.)

A. Lvs. 3–7-lobed . . . . 1. *H. quercifolia*
AA. Lvs. not lobed.
  B. Under surface of lvs. tomentose: fls. white.
    C. Tomentum gray . . . . 2. *H. cinerea*
    CC. Tomentum white . . . . 3. *H. radiata*
  BB. Under surface of lvs. subglabrous or with scattered pubescence especially on veins.
    C. Infl. paniculate, 6–12 in. long . . . . 4. *H. paniculata*
    CC. Infl. rounded or globular.
      D. Length of lvs. 2–4 in.: plant climbing by aërial roots . . . . 5. *H. petiolaris*
      DD. Length of lvs. 3–8 in.: plant erect.
        E. Fls. creamy-white: lvs. rounded or subcordate at base: ovary inferior . . . 6. *H. arborescens*
        EE. Fls. pink or blue, rarely white: lvs. broad-cuneate at base, tapering into petiole: ovary partly superior . . . . 7. *H. macrophylla*

1. **H. quercifolia,** Bartram. Strong shrub, 4–6 ft., with brown-tomentose young parts: lvs. ovate to suborbicular, 4–8 in. long and nearly or quite as broad, strongly 3–7-lobed and the lobes serrate, glabrous or pubescent on veins above, tomentose beneath: fls. in a somewhat elongated panicle to 12 in. long, with many pink-white sterile fls. turning purple. Ga. and Fla. to Miss.

2. **H. cinerea,** Small (*H. arborescens* var. *Deamii*, St. John). Shrub to 6 ft., the young parts slightly pubescent: lvs. elliptic to oblong-ovate, 2–6 in. long, short-acuminate, rounded to subcordate at base, serrate, green above, gray-tomentose beneath: fls. in corymbs 2–8 in. across, with a few sterile fls. usually present. N. C. and Tenn. to Ala. Var. **sterilis,** Rehd., fls. white, all sterile, about ½in. across, in dense heads 3–6 in. across; sepals oval, obtuse.

3. **H. radiata,** Walt. (*H. nivea,* Michx.). Strong shrub, 3–8 ft.: lvs. rather thick and leathery, oval to ovate to ovate-lanceolate, 2–5 in. long, acuminate, rounded or somewhat cordate at base, prominently serrate, bright green and glabrous above, white-tomentose and reticulate beneath: infl. rounded, 2–6 in. across, always with sterile fls. ¾in. or more across about the margin. Mts., N. C. and S. C.

4. **H. paniculata,** Sieb. Shrub or tree-like, strong-growing, young parts lightly pubescent: lvs. elliptic to ovate, 2½–5 in. long, rather abruptly short-pointed, narrowed or rounded at base and short-petioled, serrate, sparsely setose above, somewhat pubescent on veins beneath: fls. whitish, in a panicle 6–10 in. long, the sterile ones few and long-pedicelled and changing to purplish; styles 2–3: caps. about half inferior. China, Japan; frequent in cult. Var. **grandiflora,** Sieb., PEEGEE HYDRANGEA, is the common outdoor hydrangea, with very large panicles to 12 in. long in which many or most of the fls. are sterile, large, persistent, and showy; cultigen.

5. **H. petiolaris,** Sieb. & Zucc. (*H. scandens,* Maxim. not Ser.). Tall root-climber, reaching to 50 ft. and more but making a straggling partly decumbent bush when not provided with support; young parts sparingly pubescent: lvs. long-petioled, the nearly orbicular blade about 2–4 in. long, very abruptly pointed, subcordate at base, serrate, quite or nearly glabrous: fls. in large nearly circular open clusters 6–10 in. across, the white sterile fls. few on very long pedicels; petals cohering and falling as a cap; stamens 15–20; styles usually 2; ovary inferior. Japan.

6. **H. arborescens,** L. Erect shrub, 3–10 ft., the young parts lightly pubescent: lvs. ovate to broad-ovate, 3–8 in. long, tapering to point or abrupt, rounded or subcordate at base, strongly serrate, mostly becoming glabrous on both surfaces except on veins beneath: fls. creamy-white, in rounded or globular clusters 2–6 in. across, the sterile ones usually few. N. Y. to Iowa, Fla. and La.—Frequently planted, particularly in var. **grandiflora,** Rehd., sometimes called "Hills of Snow"; fls. white, all sterile, in clusters 5–7 in. across, sepals ovate, acutish. Var. **sterilis,** Torr. & Gray, lvs. elliptic-ovate to oblong-ovate, rounded at base: fls. white, all sterile; sepals broad-oval, rounded or mucronate at tip.

7. **H. macrophylla,** Ser. (*Viburnum macrophyllum,* Thunb. *H. hortensis,* Smith. *H. Hortensia,* DC. *H. opuloides,* Koch). The greenhouse hydrangea and sometimes planted out; stout stiff shrub, 3–12 ft., glabrous except in infl.: lvs. elliptic to very broad-ovate or obovate, 3–6 in. long, acuminate, broad-cuneate at base and often decurrent on the petiole, coarsely toothed, light green, sometimes sparsely pubescent on veins beneath: fls. pink or blue, rarely white, in large dense bractless flat or roundish cymes; ovary partly superior. Japan.—Summer but grown to bloom under glass in winter. Var. **Otaksa,** Bailey (forma *Otaksa,* Wils. *H. Ctaksa,* Sieb. & Zucc.), dwarfer, with fls. pink or blue, sterile, in globose heads; lvs. obovate.

5. **SCHIZOPHRAGMA,** Sieb. & Zucc. Root-climbing shrubs, 3 or 4 species in E. Asia.—The genus differs from Hydrangea in the marginal sterile fls. comprising only 1 long-stalked unlobed sepal and style 1: fr. a small 10-ribbed caps.; valves with an inner layer divided into clustered fibers, whence the name Schizophrag-ma, Greek *cleft wall.*

S. hydrangeoides, Sieb. & Zucc. Tall climber to 25–30 ft.: lvs. broad-ovate to nearly orbicular, 2–4 in. long, long-petioled, short-acuminate, truncate or somewhat cordate at base, coarsely sharp-dentate, subglabrous, pale beneath: cymes 6–9 in. across, rather flat-topped; marginal calyx-lobe white, ovate, 1–1½ in. long, on a stalk of similar length; blooms in summer. Japan.—Often called Japanese Hydrangea-Vine. *Hydrangea petiolaris* is sometimes confused with Schizophragma.

6. **DEUTZIA,** Thunb. About 50 shrubs of E. Asia and the Himalayan region, 2 in Mex., some well known as planted subjects.—Lvs. opposite, usually deciduous, petiolate, serrate, commonly with stellate pubescence, bearing white, blush, or purplish fls. profusely, mostly in panicles or cymes: fls. bisexual, with 5-lobed calyx and 5 usually valvate petals; stamens 10 (12–15), the filaments usually winged and toothed; ovary inferior, 3–5-celled, placentation axile; styles 3–5, distinct: fr. a 3–5-celled and -lobed more or less dehiscent caps. crowned by the insertion of the floral parts. (Deu-tzia: Johann van der Deutz, about 1743–1784, patron of Thunberg.)

A. Fls. in 5–10-fld. corymbs.
  B. Calyx-lobes longer than tube; petals purplish on outside; corymbs mostly 4–7 in. across . . . . 1. *D. purpurascens*
  BB. Calyx-lobes shorter than tube; petals white on outside; corymbs to 3 in. across . 2. *D. parviflora*
AA. Fls. racemose or paniculate and usually more to a cluster.
  B. Lvs. subglabrous beneath or with scattered 4–6-rayed stellate hairs.
    C. Bark grayish, not peeling: calyx-teeth shorter than tube . . . . 3. *D. gracilis*
    CC. Bark brown, usually peeling.

D. Filaments strongly toothed; calyx-teeth much shorter than tube; styles shorter than stamens..4. *D. Lemoinei*
DD. Filaments weakly toothed; calyx-teeth longer than tube; styles usually longer than stamens..5. *D. rosea*
BB. Lvs. densely pubescent beneath with 10–15-rayed stellate hairs.
C. Calyx-teeth shorter than tube, usually deciduous in fr.; fls. white or blush to darker in the vars..6. *D. scabra*
CC. Calyx-teeth subequal to tube, usually persistent in fr.; fls. white............7. *D. magnifica*

1. **D. purpurascens,** Rehd. (*D. discolor* var. *purpurascens*, Henry). Shrub to 6 ft. with slender curving branches, the bark brown and exfoliating: lvs. ovate to ovate-lanceolate, 1½–2½ in. long, short-acuminate, mostly rounded at base, crenately unequally serrate, sparingly stellate-pubescent on both sides, the hairs beneath 5–7-rayed: fls. white inside and purplish outside, spreading, about ¾in. across, in 5–10-fld. corymbs; calyx-teeth exceeding the tube; outer stamens toothed, inner stamens with petaloid filaments bearing the anther below the apex. W. China.

2. **D. parviflora,** Bunge. Shrub to 6 ft., with many erect branches: lvs. ovate to oblong-ovate, 2–3 (4½) in. long, acuminate, mostly narrowed at base, finely serrate, bearing stellate hairs on both sides: fls. rather small but numerous, white, in many-fld. corymbs suggesting Aronia; calyx-teeth shorter than tube; petals roundish-obovate, widely spreading, overlapping rather than valvate in the bud; longer filaments without teeth, the shorter ones obscurely toothed. N. China.

3. **D. gracilis,** Sieb. & Zucc. Shrub, 3–6 ft., the branches slender and wide-spreading or arching, bark close and grayish: lvs. lanceolate to oblong-lanceolate, 1½–2½ in. long, long-acuminate, finely sharp-serrate, with few stellate hairs above, green and almost glabrous beneath: fls. pure white, in open simple or somewhat compound (paniculate) racemes; calyx-teeth shorter than the tube; petals ¼–⅜in. long, oblong, much exceeding stamens; filaments with wings and short teeth. Japan.—Common in cult.; there is a kind with yellowish and another with white-dotted lvs.

4. **D. Lemoinei,** Lemoine (*D. parviflora* × *D. gracilis*). Shrub to 7 ft., the branches with brown exfoliating bark: lvs. elliptic-lanceolate, 1–4 in. long, acuminate, cuneate at base, finely serrate, more or less stellate-pubescent on both surfaces: fls. white, in large broad clusters; calyx-teeth shorter than tube; petals partly valvate and partly overlapping in bud; filaments toothed; styles 3.

5. **D. rosea,** Rehd. (*D. gracilis* × *D. purpurascens. D. gracilis rosea*, Lemoine). Small shrub, the branches with brown bark usually peeling: lvs. ovate-oblong to ovate-lanceolate, 1–3 (4) in. long, acuminate, finely serrate, with scattered mostly 4–6-rayed stellate hairs: fls. pinkish outside, often fading white, in short paniculate clusters; calyx-teeth longer than the tube; filaments usually with short teeth. Var. **campanulata,** Rehd. (*D. gracilis campanulata*, Lemoine), fls. white with purplish sepals, filaments with long teeth. Var. **carminea,** Rehd. (*D. gracilis carminea*, Lemoine), fls. purplish outside with purplish sepals, filaments strongly toothed. Var. **eximia,** Rehd. (*D. gracilis eximia*, Lemoine), fls. slightly pinkish outside with purplish sepals, filaments short with broad wings and long teeth. Var. **venusta,** Rehd. (*D. gracilis venusta*, Lemoine), fls. white with green sepals, filaments toothed.—Some of the material cult. as *D. discolor* (not Hemsl.) belongs to *D. rosea*.

6. **D. scabra,** Thunb. (*D. crenata*, Sieb. & Zucc.). Strong shrub, 5–7 ft., with many erect or ascending branches and brownish bark more or less peeling: lvs. ovate-lanceolate to ovate, 1–3 (4) in. long, acute, broad or rounded at base, crenate-dentate, scabrid-pubescent on both sides with stellate hairs, the hairs beneath smaller and more (10–15)-rayed: fls. white or blush, in late spring and summer, in loose usually somewhat compound racemes; calyx-lobes shorter than the tube, prevailingly deciduous on mature fr.; petals ⅜–½in. long, slightly exceeding longest stamens; filaments toothed; styles usually 3. China, Japan.—The common deutzia of yards, known in many cultivars including: var. **candidissima,** Rehd. (*D. crenata candidissima plena*, Froebel), fls. pure white, double; var. **plena,** Rehd. (*D. crenata* var. *plena*, Maxim.), fls. rosy-purple outside, double; plants cult. as "Pride of Rochester" belong here; var. **Watereri,** Rehd. (*D. crenata Watereri*, Lemoine), fls. white tinted carmine outside, single.

7. **D. magnifica,** Rehd. (*D. scabra* × *D. Vilmorinæ. D. crenata magnifica*, Lemoine). Lvs. ovate-oblong, 1½–4 in. long, acute to short-acuminate, rounded at base, finely serrate, rough and with scattered stellate pubescence above, rather densely stellate-pubescent beneath with mostly 10–15-rayed hairs: fls. white, double, in short dense paniculate clusters; calyx-teeth subequal to tube and prevailingly persistent on fr.; filaments with larger teeth than in *D. scabra;* styles usually 4.

7. **CARPENTERIA,** Torr. One evergreen shrub, native on the southern parts of the Sierra Nevada Mts., Calif., and planted in that state and somewhat elsewhere.—Lvs. opposite: fls. showy, in few-fld. terminal cymes; hypanthium broad and shallow, adnate to base of ovary; sepals 5–7, persistent; petals 5–7, clawless;

stamens numerous; ovary superior, 5–7-celled; style short, persistent, with 5–7-lobed stigma: caps. conical, leathery, 5–7-valved; seeds numerous. (Carpente-ria: for William M. Carpenter, 1811–1848, botanist of La.)

C. californica, Torr. Erect, 6–10 ft., branchlets strongly 4-angled: lvs. thick, oblong to lanceolate, 2–4 in. long, margins entire and more or less revolute, narrowed to a short margined petiole, glaucous and finely pubescent beneath: fls. white, 2–3 in. across, fragrant, in 3–7-fld. cymes, the peduncles long; sepals becoming reflexed; petals orbicular-obovate; stamens with filiform filaments.

8. **PHILADELPHUS,** L. Mock-Orange. A confused genus horticulturally, of wide distribution, several in Asia, 1 species in Eu., 30 or more in U. S. and Mex., and many cultigens; popular in cult. for the showy white or somewhat colored bloom.—Erect shrubs with deciduous sometimes partially persistent foliage: lvs. opposite, simple: fls. white and often very fragrant, solitary or in few-fld. cymes, sometimes appearing racemose or paniculate; hypanthium joined to ovary, the sepals and petals 4 (5–6), the latter convolute in bud; stamens many (20–40); ovary 4- (3–5-) celled, inferior to half-superior, placentation axile, styles 4 (3–5): fr. a dehiscent many-seeded 4- (3–5-) valved caps. (Philadel-phus: King Ptolemy Philadelphus, in the 3rd century B. C.)—Sometimes called Syringa, but this name should be discontinued for Philadelphus. By variation and hybridizing the specific lines have become obscured. Some of the cult. Latin-named kinds may represent only asexual multiplication of a single plant (clone).

A. Calyx strongly pubescent outside.
  B. Vegetative shoots densely pubescent.
    C. Fls. 1–3 to a branchlet.......... 1. *P. mexicanus*
    CC. Fls. 5–7 to a branchlet.......... 2. *P. incanus*
  BB. Vegetative shoots subglabrous.
    C. Fls. usually double, 1–2 in. across.......... 7. *P. virginalis*
    CC. Fls. single, 1–1½ in. across.
      D. Second-year twigs with gray close bark.......... 3. *P. pubescens*
      DD. Second-year twigs with reddish-brown bark, usually somewhat peeling... 4. *P. verrucosus*
AA. Calyx glabrous or essentially so outside, but perhaps ciliate on margins, or rarely with few scattered hairs.
  B. Styles much exceeding stamens.......... 14. *P. Falconeri*
  BB. Styles subequal to or shorter than stamens.
    C. Fls. 1–3 to a branchlet.
      D. Flowering shoots with lvs. ½–1¼ in. long, tips acute: fls. fragrant.
        E. Lvs. mostly less than ¾ in. long, entire.......... 5. *P. microphyllus*
        EE. Lvs. mostly more than ¾ in. long, usually with 1–4 teeth on each side.. 6. *P. Lemoinei*
      DD. Flowering shoots with lvs. 1¼–4 in. long, tips more or less acuminate: fls. not or only slightly fragrant.
        E. Base of lf. prevailingly rounded.
          F. Margins of lf. subentire.......... 8. *P. inodorus*
          FF. Margins of lf. distinctly toothed.......... 15. *P. Zeyheri*
        EE. Base of lf. prevailingly cuneate, margins denticulate.
          F. Lvs. oblong-ovate, subglabrous or pubescent on veins beneath...... 9. *P. grandiflorus*
          FF. Lvs. ovate-lanceolate to lanceolate, with scattered pubescence beneath.......... 10. *P. laxus*
    CC. Fls. 5–11 or more to a branchlet.
      D. Bark of second-year twigs gray, not exfoliating: lvs. pubescent all over beneath.......... 11. *P. Gordonianus*
      DD. Bark of second-year twigs yellowish-brown to brown, exfoliating: lvs. with scattered pubescence beneath, mainly on veins or in their axils.
        E. Second-year twigs with tardily exfoliating bark: lvs. of flowering shoots commonly ¾–1½ in. long, entire to denticulate.
          F. Blossoms not fragrant: lvs. acute, villous in axils of veins.......... 12. *P. Lewisii*
          FF. Blossoms very fragrant: lvs. acuminate, pubescence scattered...... 6. *P. Lemoinei*
        EE. Second-year twigs with freely exfoliating bark: lvs. of flowering shoots commonly 2–3 in. or more long, dentate.
          F. Fl. creamy-white, very fragrant, 1–1½ in. across, 5–7 to a cluster.... 13. *P. coronarius*
          FF. Fl. white, almost scentless, 1½–2 in. across, 3–5 to a cluster.......... 15. *P. Zeyheri*

1. **P. mexicanus,** Schlecht. Shrub with slender drooping branches, the young twigs gray-hairy and with brownish-gray bark; bark of older branches not exfoliating: lvs. lanceolate to lance-ovate, 1–3 in. long, acuminate, acute at base, remotely toothed, with appressed stiff hairs on both surfaces or subglabrous above, on channelled petioles about ½ in. long: fls. fragrant, 1 in. or more across, solitary or in 2–3-fld. cymes; hypanthium and calyx gray-hairy, sepals acuminate; petals obovate, slightly pubescent on the middle outside; styles more or less united, stigmas usually free. Cent. Mex.

2. **P. incanus,** Koehne. Shrub 10–15 ft. high, the vegetative shoots densely pubescent; bark brown and exfoliating: lvs. ovate to oblong-ovate, 1–3½ in. long, acuminate, rounded

or somewhat narrowed at base, serrate, subglabrous above, densely pubescent beneath: fls. scentless, 1–1¼ in. across, in 5–7-fld. pubescent racemose clusters, calyx gray-tomentose. W. China.

3. **P. pubescens,** Loisel. (*P. latifolius*, Schrad.). Shrub to 10 ft., the bark of last year's branches gray and not exfoliating, the twigs glabrous: lvs. broadly ovate to elliptic to ovate-lanceolate, 2–4 in. long or larger on very vigorous shoots, acute to acuminate, dentate or sometimes almost entire, pubescent beneath: fls. creamy-white, somewhat fragrant, 1–1½ in. across, 5–10 in long somewhat leafy racemose clusters; pedicels and calyx pubescent outside. Tenn. and Ala. to Ark.—A hybrid between *P. pubescens* and *P. coronarius* is **P. nivalis,** Jacq.: shrub with brown bark usually exfoliating: lvs. ovate, less coarsely toothed and usually only scattered-pubescent beneath: fls. 1¼ in. or more across, in 5–9-fld. racemose clusters, pedicels and calyx villous.

4. **P. verrucosus,** Schrad. Shrub to 10 ft., bark brown or gray-brown and usually somewhat exfoliating: lvs. ovate to elliptic-ovate, 1½–5 in. long, acuminate, usually rounded at base, dentate, glabrous above, pubescent beneath: fls. often fragrant, 1–1¼ in. across, in 5–7-fld. racemose clusters; pedicels and calyx appressed-pubescent. Ill.

5. **P. microphyllus,** Gray. Erect, 3–5 ft., with brown exfoliating bark on last year's growth: lvs. ½–1 in. long, ovate-lanceolate to oblong-ovate, more or less acute at both ends, somewhat 3-ribbed from base, entire, glabrous or with short hairs: fls. fragrant, opening 1–1½ in., borne 1–3 at ends of branchlets that carry 2–4 pairs of lvs.; sepals ovate, mostly glabrous but sometimes scattered-hairy outside, woolly inside; petals obovate; styles united. S. Colo., New Mex., Ariz.

6. **P. Lemoinei,** Lemoine (*P. microphyllus* × *P. coronarius*). Spreading or upright handsome shrub, usually 4–6 ft.; young branchlets pubescent or glabrous; bark of two-year-old branches chestnut- or red-brown, tardily peeling off in small thin flakes: lvs. of flowering branchlets ovate to elliptic-oblong, ¾–1½ in. long, acute or acuminate, rounded to cuneate at base, those of shoots ovate or broad-ovate, up to 2 in. long, distinctly acuminate and rounded at base, entire or with 1–4 small teeth on each side, glabrous above, sparingly strigose beneath: fls. very fragrant, 1–1¾ in. across, in rather dense 3–7-fld. cymes; pedicels ⅛–⅕in. long, glabrous like the pale calyx; stamens about half as long as petals; styles shorter than stamens, connate nearly to the apex or divided to about the middle, stigmas narrow.—Here are placed the cultivars Avalanche, Boule d'Argent, Candelabre, Erectus, Mont Blanc.

7. **P. virginalis,** Rehd. (*P. Lemoinei* × *P. nivalis plenus*). Tall upright shrub; bark of last year's branches brown or grayish, usually exfoliating, the young branchlets subglabrous: lvs. ovate and acuminate, at base rounded or broad-cuneate, 1½–2½ in. long to more than 3 in. on strong shoots, dentate or denticulate, nearly glabrous above and villous-pubescent beneath: fls. double or semi-double, 1–2 in. across, in 3–7-fld. cymes or racemose clusters; calyx and pedicels pubescent; style divided to middle, shorter than stamens, stigmas small.—Cultivars Virginal, Glacier, Bouquet Blanc, Argentine are placed here.

8. **P. inodorus,** L. Vigorous upright shrub, 5–10 ft., with exfoliating bark on last year's growth: lvs. broad-ovate to elliptic-ovate, 1–4 in. long, acute or short-acuminate, rounded or somewhat narrowed at base, entire or remotely finely dentate, 3–5-ribbed at base, glabrous above and hairy in axils of veins beneath: fls. 1½–2 in. across, scentless, 1–3 cymosely placed on branchlets that bear 1–3 pairs of lvs.; calyx glabrous outside, sepals ovate and acute; petals orbicular; stigmas distinct. N. C. to Miss. and Ga.

9. **P. grandiflorus,** Willd. (*P. inodorus* var. *grandiflorus*, Gray). Upright shrub to 10 ft., with exfoliating brown bark: lvs. elliptic-obovate to oblong-ovate, 1½–5 in. long, acuminate, cuneate or rounded at base, more prominently toothed than no. 8, subglabrous above, sparingly pubescent on veins beneath: fls. somewhat fragrant, 2 in. across, 1–3 on branchlets; calyx glabrous outside, sepals acuminate; petals suborbicular to oval. N. C. and Tenn. to Fla.

10. **P. laxus,** Schrad. Shrub to 5 ft., with young twigs glabrous and bark exfoliating on older branches: lvs. often slightly recurved and sometimes pendulous, oblong-lanceolate to elliptic-ovate on young shoots, those on bearing shoots to 2 in. long and on young shoots 3–4 in., sharp-acuminate, cuneate at base, 2 side ribs prominent, slightly appressed-pubescent beneath, entire or sparingly denticulate: fls. solitary or cymose in 3's (or 2's), 1–1½ in. across, scentless; style as long as stamens. Ga.

11. **P. Gordonianus,** Lindl. Shrub with ascending branches, 9–12 ft., the bark of last year's growth gray and not exfoliating: lvs. ovate to elliptic, 1½–3 in. long or to 4 in. on strong shoots, more or less acuminate, at base narrow or rounded and scarcely toothed but on young shoots commonly many-toothed, 3–5-ribbed, pubescent both sides or subglabrous above: fls. fragrant, 1½–1¾ in. across, 7–11 in racemose clusters terminating short branchlets that bear 2–4 pairs of lvs.; sepals lance-ovate and abruptly slender-pointed, nearly or quite glabrous outside; petals oblong to oval, sometimes retuse; styles united more than half their length. (Dedicated to George Gordon, page 44.) Ida. to N. Calif. and B. C. Var. **columbianus,** Rehd. (*P. columbianus*, Koehne), has smaller lvs. and fls., the lvs. on shoots bearing usually 2–4 prominent coarse teeth.

12. **P. Lewisii,** Pursh. Shrub 3–8 ft. high, with reddish- or yellowish-brown bark eventually exfoliating: lvs. ovate to ovate-oblong, 1–3 in. long, acute, cuneate or rounded at base, entire or denticulate, pubescent in axils of veins beneath: fls. scentless, 1–1½ in. across, in 5–9-fld. dense racemose clusters; pedicels and calyx glabrous outside; styles united half their length or almost completely. (Named for Meriwether Lewis, page 365.) Mont. to Wash. and Ore.

13. **P. coronarius,** L. The prevailing mock-orange of yards, grown under many forms and names: strong upright shrub to 10 ft. and more; bark on last year's twigs light brown and peeling off: lvs. ovate to ovate-elliptic or oval, 1–4 in. long, acuminate, rounded or somewhat narrowed at base, denticulate or dentate, glabrous above and lightly pubescent in axils of and on veins beneath: fls. creamy-white, very fragrant, opening nearly or about 1½ in. across, borne 5–7 together in racemose clusters on flowering branches 2–6 in. long that bear 2 or 3 pairs of lvs.; sepals lance-ovate and acute; petals obovate, ½–¾in. long; styles distinct about half their length. Eu. and S. W. Asia; sometimes escaped in N. Amer. Var. **aureus,** Rehd., lvs. bright yellow when young, becoming greenish. Var. **pumilus,** West. (var. *nanus,* Schrad. *P. nanus,* Mill.), dwarf dense shrub with slightly pubescent branches and smaller lvs.

14. **P. Falconeri,** Sarg. (*P. coronarius* × *P. laxus*). Shrub to 8 ft., with brown exfoliating bark: lvs. ovate-lanceolate, 1–3 in. long, acuminate, cuneate at base, denticulate, glabrous except in axils of veins beneath: fls. fragrant, 1 in. or more across, cymose and 3–7 to a st.; petals oblong-acute; styles deeply divided and much exceeding stamens. (Named for William Falconer, 1850–1928, gardener at Kew and Harvard Univ.)

15. **P. Zeyheri,** Schrad. (*P. coronarius* × *P. inodorus* or *P. grandiflorus*). More spreading and lower shrub than *P. coronarius;* bark brown, exfoliating: lvs. ovate, 1–4 in. long, acuminate, rounded at base, denticulate, dentate on shoots, glabrous except on veins and in axils beneath: fls. scentless or nearly so, 1½–2 in. across, in 3–5-fld. cymes; pedicels and calyx glabrous except on margins of sepals; style subequal to stamens, divided one-third its length or nearly to base. (Named for J. M. Zeyher, 1770–1834, horticulturist.)

9. **PARNASSIA,** L. Grass-of-Parnassus. Over 25 species of glabrous per. herbs native in the north temp. and arctic regions.—Basal lvs. entire, usually thick, long-petioled; fl.-sts. scape-like, with 1 sessile lf. usually below the middle: fls. white to pale yellow, terminal, solitary, bisexual; sepals 5, somewhat united at base, more or less adnate to the ovary, persistent; petals 5, entire or fimbriate, longer than sepals, usually distinctly nerved, deciduous; stamens 5, alternate with the petals; staminodia in clusters at the base of each petal, often gland-tipped; ovary 1-celled, superior or partly inferior, with 3 or 4 parietal placentæ and as many stigmas on short styles: fr. a caps.; seeds numerous, winged. (Parnas-sia: plant called Grass of Parnassus by Dioscorides, from Mt. Parnassus.)

A. Petals fimbriate on the lateral margins, more or less distinctly clawed.......... 1. *P. fimbriata*
AA. Petals entire, sessile.
B. Staminodia usually 3 at the base of each petal.......................... 2. *P. caroliniana*
BB. Staminodia 9–15 at the base of each petal.......................... 3. *P. palustris*

1. **P. fimbriata,** Koenig. Fl.-st. 8–12 in. high, with 1 cordate clasping bract or small lf. at or above the middle: basal lvs. reniform to broadly cordate, to 1½ in. wide, thin, on petioles 2–6 in. long: fls. to 1 in. across, sepals about one-half as long as the veined clawed fimbriate petals; staminodia united into fleshy scales with 5–9 short lobes at the base of each petal: caps. about ½in. long, 4-valved. Colo. and Calif. to Alaska.

2. **P. caroliniana,** Michx. Fl.-st. 8–24 in. high, with 1 subsessile ovate clasping lf. below the middle: basal lvs. ovate to suborbicular, 1–2 in. long, tip obtuse, rounded to cordate at base, on petioles to 4 in. long: fls. white with greenish veins, 1 in. or more across; sepals obtuse, about one-third as long as the sessile petals; staminodia usually 3 to a cluster: caps. about ½in. long. N. B. to Va. and S. D.

3. **P. palustris,** L. Fl.-st. 4–12 in. high, with 1 sessile ovate clasping lf. below the middle: basal lvs. ovate, to 1½ in. long, obtuse, usually cordate at base, on petioles ½–2½ in. long: fls. ½–1 in. across; sepals about one-half as long as the veined sessile petals; staminodia 9–15 at the base of each petal: caps. about ½in. long, 4-valved. N. Amer. south to Mich. and Wyo.; Eu. and Asia.

10. **FRANCOA,** Cav. A small genus of herbaceous perennials from Chile.—Rhizome thick, many-headed: lvs. lyrate, alternate, mostly near the base of the erect simple or branched subscapose sts. which end in dense racemes of white or pink fls.: floral parts in 4's, rarely 5's, almost hypogynous; sepals lanceolate, persistent; petals alike, narrow-obovate, clawed; stamens mostly 8, alternating with linear outgrowths from the disk; filaments filiform, anthers elongate-cordate; ovary

elongate, 4-angled, 4-lobed above, 4-celled, with numerous horizontal ovules in 2 rows in each cell on axile placentæ; stigmas sessile: caps. leathery, septicidal; seeds small. (Franco-a: named for Francisco Franco, 16th century promoter of botany.)

F. ramosa, D. Don. Lvs. 6–12 in. long, broadly oblanceolate in outline, with few pairs of rounded-ovate lobes and large terminal one, glandular-dentate, more or less pubescent, with short winged petiole; sts. 2–4 ft. tall, usually branched, naked or with 1 or 2 reduced lvs.: racemes pubescent, 4–8 in. long; sepals about ⅛in. long; petals white or pink, about ½in. long: caps. ⅜in. long.—Sometimes made a var. of *F. sonchifolia*, Cav., which seems to differ in the more secund infl. and cuneate rather than obovate stigmas.

11. **MITELLA,** L. Bishops-Cap. Mitrewort. About 12 per. herbs native in N. Amer. and Japan.—Erect or ascending from a short rootstock: lvs. mostly basal, cordate, long-petioled, weakly lobed: fl.-sts. naked or with 1–2 lvs.; infl. a one-sided spicate raceme; hypanthium bowl-shaped, more or less adnate to the ovary, divided into 5 valvular sepals; petals 5, 3-cleft or pinnatifid; stamens 10 (5) with short filaments; ovary globose, 1-celled, placentæ 2, parietal; styles 2, short, with simple or 2-lobed stigma: caps. 2-valved at apex; seeds many. (Mitel-la: diminutive of *mitra*, a cap, referring to the shape of the young pod.)

M. diphylla, L. Fl.-st. 10–18 in. high, with 1 pair of subsessile lvs. about half way up: basal lvs. broadly ovate-cordate, 1–2 in. long, tip acute to acuminate, 3–5-lobed, dentate, hirsute, on petioles to 6 in. long; st.-lvs. similar: fls. white, in an erect spicate raceme 3–8 in. long, the fls. remote: caps. broad and flattish. Que. to Ky., Minn. and Mo.

12. **TOLMIEA,** Torr. & Gray. A monotypic genus native in W. N. Amer.—Glandular-pubescent per. herb from a scaly rootstock: lvs. cordate, long-petioled at the base, the st.-lvs. short-petioled: fls. in bracted racemes; hypanthium subcylindric, free from the ovary, split almost to the base on the lower side, divided into 3 long upper sepals and 2 short lower ones; petals 4 (5), filiform, entire; stamens 3 (2), inserted opposite the 3 larger sepals; ovary 1-celled, with 2 long equal beaks and 2 parietal placentæ; seeds many. (Tolmie-a: Dr. W. F. Tolmie, collector and surgeon of the Hudson Bay Co. at Fort Vancouver, died 1886.)

T. Menziesii, Torr. & Gray (*Tiarella Menziesii*, Pursh). Thousand Mothers. Youth-on-Age. Piggy-Back Plant. Sts. clustered, 1–2 ft. or more high: basal lvs. on petioles 2–9 in. long, the blades cordate, lobed, irregularly toothed, 1–5 in. across: fls. to ⅜in. long, the petals filiform, brown, about twice as long as the sepals. (For A. Menzies, page 399.) Alaska to Calif.—Adventitious buds usually occur in the sinuses of the lf.-blades.

13. **PELTIPHYLLUM,** Engler. A monotypic genus from Calif. and Ore.—Per. herb from a thick horizontal underground rootstock: lvs. appearing after the fls., orbicular-peltate, cupped in the center, petioles fleshy and stipular: fls. in corymbose cymes on scapes which sometimes have 1 small lf.; hypanthium flattish, shorter than the 5 reflexed sepals; petals 5, not clawed; stamens 10; pistils 2–3, somewhat united at the base; ovary of each pistil 1-celled with 1 parietal placenta or 2–3-celled basally by connation of pistils: fr. a caps. (Peltiphyl-lum: Greek, meaning *peltate leaf*.)

P. peltatum, Engler (*Saxifraga peltata*, Torr.). Umbrella-Plant. Lvs. 4–16 in. across, with serrate-dentate lobes, glabrous except on the veins beneath; petioles glandular-pubescent, shorter than the scapes: scapes 1–3 ft. or more high, erect, appearing before the lvs.; fls. white, aging pinkish, about ½in. across.

14. **HEUCHERA,** L. Alum-Root. About 50 N. American per. herbs, a few grown in the fl.-garden.—Erect or ascending from a stout erect often branching stock, with the general habit of the saxifrages: lvs. mostly basal and long-petioled, broad and variously toothed or lobed: infl. on bracted or somewhat leafy peduncles from the stock, narrowly paniculate or racemose; fls. not large, but often showy, campanulate, urn-shaped or saucer-shaped, greenish, white, red, or purplish, the conspicuous part being the 5-lobed calyx; petals small, often shorter than calyx-lobes, spatulate, inserted on calyx; stamens 5, attached on petals; styles 2, slender; ovary 1-celled, ovules many on 2 parietal placentæ: fr. a 2-valved dehiscent caps. (Heuche-ra: Johann Heinrich von Heucher, 1677–1747, German botanist.)

A. Fls. not over ⅛in. long; petals twice as long as sepals.......................1. *H. micrantha*
AA. Fls. ⅛–½in. long; petals shorter than sepals to one and a half times as long, or sometimes lacking.
B. Stamens at least twice as long as sepals and long-exserted.......................2. *H. americana*
BB. Stamens usually included (rarely somewhat exserted).
C. Petals subequal to sepals (also some hybrids of no. 4).......................3. *H. pubescens*
CC. Petals distinctly shorter than sepals or lacking.
D. Infl. paniculate; fls. red (white to pink in vars.).......................4. *H. sanguinea*
DD. Infl. spicate; fls. cream.......................5. *H. cylindrica*

1. **H. micrantha,** Dougl. Lvs. orbicular-cordate, 1–3 in. long, the margins toothed and obscurely lobed, with scattered stiff pubescence on both surfaces or sometimes glabrous, on shaggy petioles 2–6 (12) in. long: fls. whitish, or sometimes suffused with red, about ⅛in. long, in cymose panicles on somewhat leafy fl.-sts. 4 in. to 2 (3) ft. high; petals and stamens about twice as long as sepals; styles exserted. Wash., Ore., Ida.

2. **H. americana,** L. Lvs. orbicular-cordate, 1½–6 in. long, the margins toothed and lobed, with scattered stiff pubescence on both surfaces or subglabrous, upper surface sometimes mottled, on puberulent petioles 3–10 in. long: fls. to ¼in. long, in cymose panicles on scapose or 1–3-lvd. puberulent fl.-sts. 16–36 in. high; petals reddish-purple or paler, equal to or slightly longer than the greenish sepals; stamens and styles long-exserted. Pa. to N. C. and Tenn.

3. **H. pubescens,** Pursh. Lvs. round-cordate, 1½–4½ in. long, shallowly lobed, teeth broad and abruptly mucronate, upper surface becoming glabrous, lower surface puberulent, on glandular-puberulent petioles 4–8 in. long: fls. purplish-green (occasionally white), ¼–⅜in. long, in cymose panicles on 1–3-lvd. fl.-sts. 10–30 in. high; sepals about two-thirds as long as petals; stamens subequal to petals and clearly exserted. Pa. to Va. Var. **brachyandra,** Rosendahl, Butters & Lakela (*H. alba*, Rydb.), differs in having stamens subequal to the sepals and usually included; Md. to Ky. and N. C.; material in the trade as *H. alba* belongs here (as an albino) or is a var. or garden hybrid of *H. sanguinea*.

4. **H. sanguinea,** Engelm. Coral Bells. Lvs. reniform to ovate-orbicular, ¾–2 in. or more across, cordate at base, lobed and dentate, glandular-puberulent, on hairy petioles 1½–5 in. long: fls. (calyx) bright red, ¼–½in. long, bell-shaped, in cymose panicles on scapose or 2–3-lvd. glandular-puberulent fl.-sts. 10–20 in. high; petals and stamens shorter than sepals. Ariz., Mex.—Runs into many named vars. as: **alba,** Haage & Schmidt, white fls.; **gracillima,** Hort., slender form; **maxima,** Hort., fls. larger and deeper colored; **rosea,** Hort., fls. rosy-pink; **splendens,** Hort., fls. dark crimson. **H. Rosamundii,** Hort. (*H. micrantha rosea* × *H. sanguinea*), has terra-cotta fls. in slender spikes 2–3 ft. long. **H. brizoides,** Hort., is of hybrid origin, probably mostly *H. micrantha* × *H. sanguinea;* fls. pink, ⅛in. or more long, in narrow diffuse long panicles; much material so listed is probably *Heucherella tiarelloides* which has usually 7–8 stamens instead of 5.

5. **H. cylindrica,** Dougl. Lvs. ovate to suborbicular, 1½–2½ in. long, cordate to subtruncate at base, with 5–7 rather deep lobes, teeth broadly rounded and slightly mucronate, pubescence stiff and scattered, petioles hirsute and 1–6 in. long: fls. cream-colored to greenish, ¼–⅜in. long, in narrow spike-like cymose panicles on scapes 1–3 ft. high, the bracts of the infl. about ⅜in. long; petals often lacking, but one-half as long as sepals when present; stamens included. Ida., Wash. Var. **glabella,** Wheelock (*H. glabella*, Torr. & Gray), differs in having petioles subglabrous and bracts of infl. not exceeding ¼in.; B. C. and Mont. to Ore.

15. **HEUCHERELLA,** Wehrhahn. A genus containing a few bigeneric hybrids between species of Heuchera and Tiarella, one commonly cult. as a border and rockery per.—Characters intermediate between those of the two genera, the most conspicuous being fls. with tubular hypanthium, petals slightly larger than sepals, and stamens 5–10 in each infl. and often 7 or 8. (Heucherel-la: from heuchera and tiarella.)—Of hort. origin, first produced by Lemoine about 1912.

H. tiarelloides, Wehrhahn (*Heuchera tiarelloides*, Lemoine). A hybrid probably of *Heuchera brizoides* and *Tiarella cordifolia*, spreading by stolons: lvs. somewhat orbicular, to 5 in. long and broad, bristly-hairy above and beneath: infl. 15–18 in. high, paniculate; fls. with pale carmine hypanthium and petals, latter longer than sepals.—**H. alba,** Stearn (var. *alba*, Silva Tarouca & Schneid. *Heuchera tiarelloides alba*, Lemoine), has no stolons, lvs. longer than broad and white fls.—Probably most plants cult. and listed as *Heuchera brizoides* belong here.

16. **TIARELLA,** L. False Mitrewort. About 6 species in N. Amer. and Asia.—Per. erect herbs from a scaly rootstock: lvs. mostly basal, palmately lobed or 3-foliolate, on stipular long petioles: fls. small, in panicles or racemes, on erect 1- to few-lvd. fl.-sts.; hypanthium slightly united to the ovary at the base; sepals 5, more or less petaloid; petals 5 or sometimes lacking; stamens 10, conspicuously ex-

serted; pistil 1, ovary 1-celled with 2 parietal placentæ becoming basal in fr.: caps. 1-celled, 2-horned, with the 2 valves unequal; seeds few. (Tiarel-la: Greek diminutive for *tiara*, a high cap.)

T. cordifolia, L. Foam-Flower. Lvs. broadly ovate-cordate, 1–4 in. across, 3–7-lobed, toothed, with scattered pubescence on both surfaces, on hirsute petioles to 4 (6) in. long: fls. white, about ¼in. across, in glandular-puberulent simple racemes on sts. to 16 in. high; fl.-sts. scapose or with 1 lf. similar to but smaller than the basal lvs.; sepals and petals white, the sepals one-half to two-thirds as long as the clawed petals. N. S. to Minn. and Ga.

17. **BERGENIA,** Moench (*Megasea*, Haw.). Often named in Saxifraga but distinct in habit and certain other characters: about 8 Asian species, mostly in mts.—Rootstocks large and thick, whereby the plants produce large clumps or colonies: lvs. thick, heavy, large, simple, waxy, more or less persistent, entire, toothed or crenate, with gland-bearing pits and short broad petioles sheathed or vaginate at base: fls. large, pink or white, on scapes among the foliage; stamens 10; pistils 2, connate into 1, ovary 2-celled basally with 2 axile placentæ and 1-celled apically with 2 parietal placentæ, ovules many: fr. a caps. (Berge-nia: K. A. von Bergen, 1704–1760, German botanist.)—The species have been considerably hybridized. They are spring bloomers, the leafage rising 12–20 in.

A. Margins of lf. ciliate, subentire. . . . . 1. *B. ligulata*
AA. Margins of lf. lacking cilia, serrate or undulate.
  B. Lf. orbicular-cordate. . . . . 2. *B. cordifolia*
  BB. Lf. obovate to long-obovate. . . . . 3. *B. crassifolia*

1. **B. ligulata,** Engler (*Saxifraga ligulata*, Wall.). Lvs. obovate to suborbicular, to 12 in. long, obtuse, tapering at base, glabrous on both surfaces, margins subentire and ciliate, sheath at base of short petiole ciliate on margin: fls. white to rose or purplish, in suberect panicles; scapes, pedicels and calyx glabrous; petals suborbicular, clawed. Himalayas.

2. **B. cordifolia,** Sternb. (*Saxifraga cordifolia*, L.). Plant glabrous throughout: lvs. cordate-orbicular, fleshy, shining, margins undulate-serrate and not ciliate, petioles long and thick: fls. rose (purple and white vars.), nodding in panicles; petals roundish. Siberia.

3. **B. crassifolia,** Fritsch (*Saxifraga crassifolia*, L. *B. bifolia*, Moench). Plant glabrous throughout: lvs. obovate to long-obovate, the blades decurrent on petiole, margins more or less undulate-serrate and not ciliate: fls. rose, lilac or purple, nodding in dense panicles; petals elliptic-oblong. Siberia, Mongolia.

18. **BOYKINIA,** Nutt. About 9 species native in N. Amer. and E. Asia.—Glandular-pubescent per. herbs from creeping scaly rootstocks: lvs. mostly in basal tufts, reniform, variously lobed and dentate, stipules often present: fls. white to red or purple, in paniculate cymes; hypanthium cup-shaped and adnate to the lower half of the ovary; sepals 5, valvate; petals 5, spatulate or obovate, short-clawed; stamens 10 or 5, inserted on the rim of the hypanthium; ovary and caps. usually 2-celled, opening between the 2 divergent beaks, placentæ axile; seeds numerous. (Boykin-ia: named in honor of Dr. Boykin, a physician from Ga.)

B. Jamesii, Engler (*Saxifraga Jamesii*, Torr. *Telesonix Jamesii*, Raf.). Cespitose with thick rootstock: basal lvs. round-kidney-shaped, ¾–1½ in. across, long-petioled, doubly crenate; st.-lvs. becoming cuneate and subsessile: fls. reddish-purple, in paniculate cymes to 4 (8) in. high; petals about twice as long as sepals and long-clawed; stamens 10. (Named for Edwin James, page 45.) Mont. to Colo.

19. **ASTILBE,** Buch.-Ham. (*Hoteia*, Morr. & Decne.). Per. strong herbs, grown for the panicles of small white and pink fls.; species about 14, in Cent. and farther Asia, and 2 in E. U. S.—Lvs. simple to 2–4-ternately compound, with broad dentate or incised lfts.: fls. bisexual or unisexual, plants diœcious or polygamous; calyx small, usually 4–5-parted; petals 3–4 or more (sometimes absent), inserted at base of calyx; stamens of the same number or twice the number as the petals (mostly 8 or 10); pistils 2 or 3, distinct or variously united (when united, the fr. a 2–3-celled caps.): fr. of dehiscent follicles. (Astil-be: Greek *without sheen* or *not shining*, probably referring to lvs.)—Often confused with the herbaceous spirea group (Aruncus particularly), but those plants have many stamens and several to many separate pistils. The florists' astilbes are likely to be hybrids. The plants are sometimes forced under the name spirea.

A. Lvs. simple (1-ternate in a var.)..1. *A. simplicifolia*
AA. Lvs. 2–4-ternate.
B. Fls. on pedicels equalling or exceeding the bract........................2. *A. japonica*
BB. Fls. sessile or on very short pedicels.
C. Axis of infl. short-glandular-pubescent..................................3. *A. astilboides*
CC. Axis of infl. densely brown-tomentose...................................4. *A. chinensis*

1. **A. simplicifolia,** Makino. To 12 in. high, with scattered glandular pubescence, the axis of the infl. densely glandular-pubescent: lvs. simple, ovate-cordate, to 3 in. long, irregularly doubly serrate, palmately 3–5-lobed: fls. white, on pedicels, in loose arching panicles; petals subequal to sepals. Japan. Var. **rosea,** Arends (*A. simplicifolia* × *A. Arendsii*), lvs. 1-ternate, fls. rose.

2. **A. japonica,** Gray (*Hoteia japonica*, Morr. & Decne.). Erect, 1–3 ft., with scattered hairs on sts. and petioles, bearing many small white fls. in erect panicles: lvs. 2–3-ternate; lfts. narrow, lanceolate or lance-ovate, acute, tapering to base, sharp-serrate: fls. upright, on hairy pedicels equalling or exceeding the bract, thinly disposed as ascending branches; calyx ⅛in. or less long, closely subtended by narrow bracts, the lobes acute; petals about as long again as the calyx, spatulate, obtuse; stamens usually not prominent. Japan.—It runs into several cultivars, one with variegated and another with purple-tinted foliage; also with larger fls. and with more condensed panicle.

3. **A. astilboides,** Lemoine (*Spiræa astilboides*, Moore). Erect, 2–3 ft., scattered pubescence above, the under part of the st. subglabrous: lvs. 2-ternate, with the middle portion pinnate; lfts. ovate to ovate-oblong, broad at the base, subacute, sharply and doubly serrate: fls. white, sessile, in dense straight spreading spikes; petals narrowly spatulate, about two and a half times as long as the calyx. Japan.—Cult. and entering into garden hybrids.

4. **A. chinensis,** Franch. & Sav. (*Hoteia chinensis*, Maxim.). Erect, 1½–2 ft. or more, sts. and petioles with scattered shaggy pubescence, the axis of the infl. densely woolly: lvs. 2–3-ternate; lfts. ovate-oblong, doubly serrate: fls. white, sessile, in a rather narrow panicle; calyx yellowish; filaments lilac, anthers blue; petals about four times as long as calyx. China. Var. **pumila,** Hort., is offered as a dwarf. Var. **Davidii,** Franch. (*A. Davidii*, Henry), infl. narrower, petals violet and more acute, calyx pink; named for Armand David, page 230; Mongolia, Cent. China; this var. has entered into a race of hybrids, **A. Arendsii,** Arends, which has fls. ranging from purplish to nearly white.

20. **SAXIFRAGA,** L. Saxifrage. About 310 species mostly in temp. and subarctic regions if the genus is accepted in its customary sense; some authors prefer to separate it into several genera; many of the species are adapted to rock- and alpine-gardens and a few are planted in borders and one is common as a window- and basket-plant.—Herbs, a few ann. and bien., but mostly per. with caudices below ground or little emerged: lvs. commonly basal and clustered, those on the st. usually alternate, the petioles ordinarily without sheaths: infl. various, racemose, paniculate, cymose, or fls. sometimes solitary; fls. bisexual, white, pink, purple, or yellow; calyx 5-parted, the base either free or adhering to ovary; petals commonly 5, entire; stamens 10; ovary usually 2-celled, making a 2-beaked caps., or sometimes the 2 pistils nearly separate with ovules then on single parietal placentæ. (Saxif-raga: Latin *rock-breaking*, of disputed application.)—Aside from a few well-known species, saxifrages are fanciers' plants; many hybrids are recorded. The saxifrages are native mostly in mts. and in rocky places.

A. Petals unequal, 2 of them three to four times longer than the other 3: plant extensively stoloniferous..27. *S. sarmentosa*
AA. Petals equal.
B. Lvs. densely decussately opposite on the fl.-st............................26. *S. oppositifolia*
BB. Lvs. alternate or basal.
C. Lf. distinctly narrowed to a petiole, or if subsessile then some of them deeply lobed; pits lacking on the lvs.; lime not secreted.
D. Plant 4–36 in. high: lvs. entire to shallowly lobed or crenate.
E. Margin of lf. white: fls. often tinged pink with red dots.......... 4. *S. umbrosa*
EE. Margin of lf. not white: fls. white.
F. Shape of lf. broader than long or suborbicular.
G. Sepals reflexed; petals less than ¼in. long.................. 1. *S. Mertensiana*
GG. Sepals erect; petals ⅜–¾in. long........................ 5. *S. granulata*
FF. Shape of lf. longer than broad.
G. Sepals erect: lvs. ovate to oblong........................ 2. *S. virginiensis*
GG. Sepals reflexed in fr.: lvs. lanceolate to lance-ovate.......... 3. *S. pensylvanica*
DD. Plant to 8 in. high: lvs. (at least some of them) palmately 3–5-parted.
E. Fls. yellowish to rose or purple; petals scarcely exceeding sepals...... 10. *S. moschata*
EE. Fls. white (red in vars. of no. 9); petals two to three times as long as sepals.
F. Bulblets present in the lf.-axils on the sterile shoots: fls. ¼–½in. across.. 7. *S. hypnoides*

FF. Bulblets lacking: fls. to ¾in. across.
G. The lvs. 3-parted, the segms. 3-toothed or -lobed............ 6. *S. trifurcata*
GG. The lvs. 3–5-fid, the segms. entire.
H. Segms. obtuse.. 8. *S. cespitosa*
HH. Segms. acute.. 9. *S. rosacea*
CC. Lf. subsessile, entire to crenate or dentate; pits present on the lvs. (except in no. 11); lime often secreted.
D. Length of lvs. ¼–½in.: fl.-sts. 1–4 in. high (sometimes to 10 in. in no. 11).
E. Margins of lf. ciliate-dentate the entire length.
F. Stamens shorter than petals.................................11. *S. bronchialis*
FF. Stamens longer than petals.................................22. *S. sancta*
EE. Margins of basal lvs. ciliate only at base or not at all.
F. Tip of lf. abruptly expanding.................................16. *S. cochlearis* var.
FF. Tip of lf. not abruptly expanding.
G. Fl.-sts. 1-fld..24. *S. Burseriana*
GG. Fl.-sts. 2–12-fld.
H. Fls. white; stamens one-half as long as petals............. 23. *S. marginata*
HH. Fls. yellow; stamens slightly shorter than petals...........25. *S. Ferdinandi-Coburgii*
DD. Length of lvs. ½–4 in.: fl.-sts. 5–48 in. high.
E. Sepals two to three times longer than petals; infl. subspicate......... 21. *S. Grisebachii*
EE. Sepals shorter than petals; fls. on distinct pedicels.
F. Plant loosely cespitose: lf.-margins not lime-incrusted........... 12. *S. aizoides*
FF. Plant densely cespitose: lf.-margins lime-incrusted.
G. Panicle branched from the base.
H. Lf.-margins entire to crenate...............................13. *S. longifolia*
HH. Lf.-margins serrate...20. *S. Cotyledon*
GG. Panicle beginning one-third to half way up the fl.-st. or higher.
H. Shape of lf. linear at base, abruptly spreading above into a spoon-shaped blade...16. *S. cochlearis*
HH. Shape of lf. linear to spatulate or tongue-shaped.
I. Lf.-margins subentire.
J. Fl.-sts. glabrous or subglabrous: lvs. linear-spatulate.... 14. *S. lingulata*
JJ. Fl.-sts. densely glandular-pubescent: lvs. linear.........15. *S. crustata*
II. Lf.-margins crenate to serrate.
J. Branches of panicle mostly 3–10-fld.: plant to 16 in. high or more...19. *S. Hostii*
JJ. Branches of panicle mostly 1–3-fld.: plant to 12 in. high.
K. Tip of lf. obtuse...17. *S. Aizoon*
KK. Tip of lf. acuminate......................................18. *S. cartilaginea*

Section I. BORAPHILA (Micranthes). Per. from a subterranean rhizome which has secondary shoots permanently attached: lvs. without pits on upper surface, lime not secreted: fls. white, regular, 5-merous; ovary free: caps. somewhat inflated, splitting above the middle, or sometimes to the base; seeds fusiform or spindle-shaped.

1. **S. Mertensiana,** Bong. Lvs. mostly basal, orbicular to reniform, 1–3 in. across, cordate at base, shallowly palmately lobed, the lobes mostly 3-toothed, glabrous or with scattered pubescence, petioles 2–8 in. long with wing-like stipules at base: fls. white, in panicles on fl.-stalks to 12 in. or more high which are glandular-pubescent and have 1 or 2 lvs.; fls., except the terminal one, sometimes reduced to bulblets; calyx reflexed: beaks of mature frs. as long as the body and divergent. (Named for K. H. Mertens, page 116.) Alaska to Calif.

2. **S. virginiensis,** Michx. Lvs. in basal rosettes, ovate to oblong, 1–6 in. long including the usually short petiole, sinuate or dentate, pubescence scattered: fls. white, in bracted panicles on glandular-pubescent scapes 4–16 in. high; sepals erect: follicles united only at the base, beaks short and recurved. N. B. to Ga., Mo. and Minn.

3. **S. pensylvanica,** L. SWAMP SAXIFRAGE. Lvs. in basal rosettes, mostly erect, lanceolate to lance-ovate, 2–12 in. long, gradually tapering to a short clasping petiole, entire to remotely dentate, margins ciliate: fls. greenish-white, in 4–8-fld. cymes arranged in panicles on glandular-pubescent scapes to 3 ft. high; sepals reflexed in fr.; petals narrowly lanceolate, 1-nerved: beak of follicle stout and recurved. Me. to Minn., Va. and Mo.

Section II. ROBERTSONIA. Differs from Boraphila in the rhizome being above ground and fls. sometimes pink to carmine-red.

4. **S. umbrosa,** L. LONDON PRIDE. Lvs. fleshy, in basal rosettes, ovate to oblong-obovate, to 2½ in. long, tapering to a short usually pubescent petiole, margins obtusely crenate, with a narrow white border: fls. white to pink with red dots and a yellow spot on each petal, in 2–7-fld. loose cymes arranged in panicles on glandular-pubescent scapes to 12 (16) in. high; sepals reflexed. Eu. Var. **primuloides,** Hort., to 6 in. high, lvs. primrose-like, fls. rose-pink.

Section III. NEPHROPHYLLUM. Bien. or per., rarely ann., from a subterranean rhizome which has secondaries with shortened bulbous internodes separating from the st. with age: lvs. usually not persisting through winter; pits absent: fls. white, rarely yellow, regular, 5-merous; sepals never reflexed; ovary at least partly inferior.

5. **S. granulata,** L. MEADOW SAXIFRAGE. Sts. erect or ascending, 4–20 in. high, soft-hirsute, glandular-viscous above, usually somewhat leafy: basal lvs. kidney-shaped, to 1 in. long and 1½ in. wide, lobed, the lobes entire or crenate, more or less glandular-pubescent,

decurrent at base on the long petiole, with bulblets in the axils; st.-lvs. smaller, subsessile: fls. white, to about 1 in. across, somewhat drooping, in panicles; calyx-lobes longer than tube. Eu., N. Afr.

Section IV. DACTYLOIDES (Muscaria). Per., with the rhizome above ground, lacking bulblets: lvs. usually persisting through the winter, herbaceous or subcoriaceous, entire or lobed; pits absent: fls. white to red, rarely yellow, regular, 5-merous; ovary at least partly inferior.

6. **S. trifurcata,** Schrad. (*S. ceratophylla,* Dry.). Loosely cespitose, the rhizomes somewhat shrubby and covered with old reflexed lvs.; fl.-sts. erect, glabrous, 4–8 in. high: lvs. to ¾in. across, palmately 3-parted, the segms. 3-toothed or -lobed, on petioles two to three times longer than blades; st.-lvs. smaller, the segms. usually entire; bracts linear, acute: fls. milk-white, to about ¾in. across, in loose cymes; petals three times as long as the sepals. Pyrenees.

7. **S. hypnoides,** L. Loosely or densely cespitose, the sterile shoots usually bulbiferous in the axils; fl.-sts. to 8 in. high, glandular-pubescent: lvs. 3–5-fid (rarely more), the segms. acute to mucronate, pubescent, on short broad ciliate petioles; st.-lvs. few and bract-like: fls. white, ¼–½in. across, in 3–7-fld. cymes; petals about three times longer than the erect sepals. Eu.—Material cult. under this name is likely to be either *S. cespitosa* or *S. rosacea.*

8. **S. cespitosa,** L. Densely cespitose; fl.-sts. erect, to 6 in. high, few-lvd., glandular-pubescent: lvs. 3- (5) fid, the segms. mostly obtuse, with scattered pubescence, on broad ciliate petioles; st.-lvs. smaller, subsessile, bract-like above: fls. white, ½–¾in. or more across, in 1- to few-fld. cymes; petals two to three times longer than the erect sepals. Circumpolar in the northern hemisphere.

9. **S. rosacea,** Moench (*S. decipiens,* Ehrh. *S. petræa,* Roth not L.). Similar to *S. cespitosa* and sometimes made a subspecies of it; differs in having the lf.-segms. acute and sepals narrower and more acute. Eu. Var. **bathoniensis,** Hort. (*S. bathoniensis,* Hort.), somewhat taller with large scarlet-crimson fls. Var. **grandiflora,** Hort., has red fls. fading pink.—This species is commonly known as *S. decipiens,* but the name is a *nomen nudum.*

10. **S. moschata,** Wulfen. Densely or loosely cespitose, the rhizomes herbaceous or subwoody; fl.-sts. numerous, erect, to 5 in. high, with few lvs.: lvs. mostly basal, linear to narrowly spatulate, entire or 2–3- (5) lobed, obtuse: fls. yellowish to purple, rarely white, in 1–10-fld. racemose or paniculate cymes; petals slightly exceeding calyx. Eu. Var. **Rhei,** Hort. (*S. Rhei,* Schott), has many rather large rose-colored fls.; material cult. as *S. Rhei superba* has still larger deeper colored fls.; name refers to roots having odor of Rheum.

Section V. TRACHYPHYLLUM. Differs from Dactyloides in presence of bulblets: lvs. not herbaceous, margins usually very setose: fls. commonly yellow.

11. **S. bronchialis,** L. Densely cespitose; fl.-sts. ascending or erect, to 10 in. high, with few lvs., subglabrous or glandular-pubescent: lvs. mostly basal, usually linear-lanceolate, to ½in. or more long, stiffish, gray-green, margins ciliate: fls. yellowish-white, spotted reddish, to ½in. across, in few- to many-fld. cymose corymbs; petals about twice as long as sepals, scarcely clawed. Asia, Alaska.

Section VI. XANTHIZOON. Per., with the rhizome above ground, bulblets lacking: lvs. pitted but not lime-incrusted: fls. yellow to purple, regular, 5-merous; sepals spreading; ovary one-third to one-fourth inferior.

12. **S. aizoides,** L. Loosely cespitose, the sts. decumbent or ascending, to 1 ft. long: lvs. linear to linear-oblong, to 1 in. or more long, entire or toothed, sometimes ciliate, tip usually mucronate: fls. yellow, more or less orange-spotted, the infl. 1- to many-fld.; petals one and a half times as long as sepals. Eu., Asia, N. Amer. south to Vt. and N. Y.

Section VII. EUAIZOONIA. Mostly per., with the rhizome above ground, the secondary shoots with their rosettes soon separating: lvs. alternate, pits present, lime-incrusted: fls. white, spotted purple, rarely rose or yellow; sepals never reflexed; ovary more or less inferior.

13. **S. longifolia,** Lapeyr. Rosettes to 6–7 in. across, with erect densely glandular-pubescent fl.-sts. 1–2 ft. high: lvs. linear-lanceolate, to 3½ in. long, ciliate at base, acute or mucronate, margins entire or crenulate, silvery with incrusted lime: fls. white, sometimes spotted purple, to ½in. across, in a many-fld. pyramidal panicle branched from the base. Pyrenees.

14. **S. lingulata,** Bell. Lvs. in dense rosettes from which arise erect or ascending leafy fl.-sts. 6–14 in. high, glabrous or minutely glandular-pubescent, the panicle beginning about half way up the st.: basal lvs. linear-spatulate to linear-oblong, ½–3½ in. long, acute, glabrous, glaucous, margins subentire, ciliate at base, incrusted; st.-lvs. smaller, oblong, margins crenulate, not incrusted: fls. white, sometimes spotted reddish-purple, ½in. or more across, in panicles with the individual branches cymose and 3–6-fld. S. Eu. Var. **lantoscana,** Engler (*S. lantoscana,* Boiss. & Reut.), has short rather broad obtuse lvs.; Maritime Alps. Var. **Leichtlinii,** Hort., fls. rose-red; probably a hybrid.

15. **S. crustata,** Vest. Lvs. in dense rosettes; fl.-sts. erect ascending, sparingly leafy, to 16 in. high, densely glandular-pubescent, panicle beginning about half way up the st.: basal lvs. linear, to 1½ in. long, obtuse, dilated and pinkish at base, margins entire, in-

crusted, ciliate at the base: fls. white, rarely spotted purple at the base, about ½in. across, in panicles with the individual branches cymose and 1- to few-fld. Tyrol.

16. **S. cochlearis,** Reichb. Lvs. in dense rosettes; fl.-sts. suberect or ascending, to 18 in. high, glandular-pubescent becoming subglabrous in the upper half, panicle beginning less than half way up the st.: basal lvs. to 1 in. long, linear, abruptly expanding into a suborbicular tip, dilated and ciliate at base, margins subentire to obtusely crenulate, incrusted: fls. white, often spotted with purple below the middle, ½in. or more across, in thyrsoid panicles as in no. 15. Alps. Var. **minor,** Hort., rosettes minute and silvery, with fl.-sts. mostly 2 in. or less high.

17. **S. Aizoon,** Jacq. (*Chondrosea Aizoon,* Haw.). Lvs. more or less incurved, in dense rosettes; fl.-sts. erect, to 12 in. high, glandular-pubescent (rarely glabrous), panicle beginning half way up the st. or higher: basal lvs. obovate-oblong to narrow-spatulate, to 1½ in. long, obtuse or nearly so, serrate with incrusted white teeth: fls. white, sometimes spotted purple, to ½in. across, in thyrsoid panicles with the branches 1–3- (5) fld. Arctic N. Amer., Eu., Asia Minor. Var. **balcana,** Hort., fls. white with large red spots. Var. **baldensis,** Farrer, lvs. ash-gray, short and thick; young shoots glossy, red; fls. whitish; N. Italy. Var. **flavescens,** Hort., fls. clear lemon-yellow. Var. **lagaveana,** Hort., rosettes small and silvery, with fl.-sts. to 6 in. high bearing few creamy wax-like fls. Var. **lutea,** Hort., fls. yellow. Var. **rosea,** Hort., fls. bright pink.—**S. Andrewsii,** Harvey (*S. Aizoon* × *S. hirsuta*). Sts. 6–12 in. high, densely glandular-pubescent: basal lvs. cuneate-spatulate, to 2 in. long, margins serrate, white, scarcely if at all incrusted: fls. white spotted with red. (Named for its discoverer, William Andrews of Dublin.) **S. pectinata,** Schott, Nym. & Kotschy (*S. Aizoon* × *S. crustata*). Basal lvs. linear-spatulate, margins serrate, incrusted: fls. white, spotted with purple, branches of infl. mostly 3-fld. Alps.

18. **S. cartilaginea,** Willd. Very similar to *S. Aizoon;* differs in having basal lvs. acuminate; fl.-sts. glabrous or short-glandular-pubescent; fls. white, not spotted. Asia Minor.

19. **S. Hostii,** Tausch. Lvs. somewhat recurved, in dense rosettes to 6 in. across; fl.-sts. erect, to 16 in. high, glandular-pubescent, panicle beginning half way up the st. or higher: basal lvs. tongue-shaped to oblong, to 2 (3) in. long, obtuse at apex, ciliate at base, margins crenate, incrusted: fls. white, spotted with purple, about ½in. across, in thyrsoid panicles with the branches 2–10-fld. (Named for N. T. Host, page 45.) Mts. of Cent. Eu. Var. **altissima,** Engler & Irmsch. (*S. altissima,* Kerner), fl.-sts. to 24 in. high; lvs. 2–4 in. long, apex acutish, margins serrate; Tyrol.

20. **S. Cotyledon, L.** Fleshy lvs. in basal rosettes 2–6 in. (and more in cult.) across; fl.-sts. 6 in. to 2 ft. or more long, glandular-pubescent, often reddish, paniculate from the base: basal lvs. linear-tongue-shaped to broadly obovate-spatulate, to 3 in. long and ¾in. wide, obtuse or short-mucronate at tip, margins serrate, incrusted, ciliate at base; st.-lvs. and bracts smaller: fls. white, often tinged rose, rarely spotted with red, fragrant, to ¾in. across. Mts. of Eu. Var. **pyramidalis,** Ser. (*S. pyramidalis,* Lapeyr.), fl.-sts. to 4 ft., green; fls. very numerous; Pyrenees and Alps.—**S. Gaudinii,** Bruegg. (*S. Cotyledon* var. *pyramidalis* × *S. Aizoon*). Fl.-sts. to 12 in. high, branching near the base: lvs. to 1 in. long, narrower and more obtuse than in *S. Cotyledon* var. *pyramidalis.* Pyrenees and Alps. **S. Macnabiana,** Lindsay (*S. Cotyledon* × *?S. lingulata*). Similar in habit to *S. Cotyledon* but dwarfer: fls. white spotted with deep carmine.

Section VIII. Kabschia. Differs from Euaizoonia in secondary shoots remaining attached to the per. rhizome: fls. white, yellow, rose or purple.

21. **S. Grisebachii,** Degen & Doerfler. Cespitose, the short rhizomes densely leafy; fl.-sts. 5–8 in. high, erect or ascending, glandular-pubescent, leafy, floriferous in the upper third or fourth: basal lvs. spatulate-tongue-shaped, 1–1½ in. long, glabrous, tip rounded-acuminate, margins cartilaginous, ciliate near the base, pits present near the margin; st.-lvs. shorter, spreading, reddish, glandular-pubescent: fls. purple, subspicate, the pedicels shorter than the bracts; sepals reddish-purple, to ¼in. long, suberect, glandular-pubescent; petals purple, one-third to half as long as sepals. (Named for A. H. R. Grisebach, page 44.) E. Medit. region.

22. **S. sancta,** Griseb. Cespitose, with ascending branched rhizomes to 6 in. long; fl.-sts. erect, 1–1½ in. high, glabrous, leafy, 3–7-fld., reddish: basal lvs. rigid, lanceolate, to ½in. long, mucronate, margins cartilaginous, ciliate-dentate, 3–5 pits with a minute collar of lime near the apex: fls. yellow, ¼in. or more across; petals twice as long as sepals; stamens slightly longer than petals. Macedonia.—**S. apiculata,** Engler (*S. marginata* var. *Rocheliana* × *S. sancta*). Fl.-sts. 1½–3½ in. high, somewhat glandular-pubescent, 4–9-fld.: basal lvs. linear-oblong, ¼–⅜in. long, pits 5–9, otherwise similar to *S. sancta:* fls. yellow, to ½in. across; stamens slightly shorter than petals. Var. **alba,** Hort., has creamy-white petals.

23. **S. marginata,** Sternb. Cespitose, with rhizomes erect or ascending, woody and leafy; fl.-sts. erect, to 4 in. high, black-glandular-pubescent, 5–7-fld.: basal lvs. obovate-cuneate, to ½in. long, obtuse, glabrous, margins cartilaginous, ciliate at base, pits incrusted; st.-lvs. spatulate, glandular-pubescent: fls. white, ½–¾in. or more across; petals about three times as long as the obtuse sepals; stamens about one-half as long as petals.

Italy. Var. **Boryi,** Hayek (*S. Boryi,* Boiss. & Heldr.), lvs. oblong-spatulate, somewhat smaller; petals about twice as long as the acute sepals; S. E. Eu. Var. **Rocheliana,** Engler & Irmsch. (*S. Rocheliana,* Sternb.), lvs. linear-spatulate to spatulate, subobtuse; S. E. Eu.; named for Anton Rochel, 1770–1847.—**S. Petraschii,** Sünderm. (*S. tombeanensis* × *S. marginata* var. *Rocheliana*). Lvs. glaucous: fl.-sts. about 2 in. high, 1- to few-fld.: fls. white, to 1 in. across. Garden origin.

24. **S. Burseriana,** L. Densely cespitose, with woody rhizomes to 2 in. or more long, branched, ascending; fl.-sts. to 2½ in. high, 1-fld. or very rarely 2-fld., glandular-pubescent, somewhat leafy, purplish: basal lvs. stiff, linear-subulate, to ½in. long, apex long-mucronate and sharp, glabrous, glaucous, margins cartilaginous, short-ciliate at base, pits 5–7, lime-incrusted when young; st.-lvs. smaller, oblong-lanceolate, somewhat glandular-pubescent at the base: fls. white, solitary; petals about ⅜in. long, twice as long as sepals and stamens. (Named for J. Burser, 1583–1649.) Alps. Var. **major,** Jenkins (var. *magna,* Jenkins), lvs. to ⅝in. long, fls. to more than 1 in. across. Var. **sulphurea,** Hort., fls. yellow. —**S. Elizabethæ,** Sünderm. (*S. Burseriana* × *S. sancta*). Fl.-sts. to 2 in. high, 3-fld., otherwise similar in habit to *S. Burseriana:* fls. yellow, to more than ½in. across; petals two to three times as long as sepals; stamens three-fourths as long as petals. Garden origin. **S. Irvingii,** Hort. (*S. Burseriana* var. *macrantha* × *S. Friderici-Augustii*). Fl.-sts. about 1 in. high, 1-fld.: fls. blush-pink, about ½in. across. Spontaneous hybrid at Kew. **S. Obristii,** Sünderm. (*S. Burseriana* × *S. marginata*). Fl.-sts. 3–4 in. high, with 2–4 fls. to a st.: lvs. oblong-linear, to ⅜in. long, acute: fls. ivory-white, almost 1 in. across; petals broad, three to four times as long as sepals; stamens half to two-thirds as long as petals. Garden origin.

25. **S. Ferdinandi-Coburgii,** Kellerer & Sünderm. Densely cespitose, the rhizomes stiff, ascending, branched, columnar; fl.-sts. erect, to 2½ in. high, 2–12-fld., dark glandular-pubescent, leafy: basal lvs. ovate-oblong to oblong, ¼in. or rarely ½in. long, incurved-mucronate, glabrous, glaucous, margins cartilaginous, short-ciliate at base, pits 3–5; st.-lvs. linear, glandular-pubescent and sometimes purplish toward the base: fls. yellow, about ½in. across; petals abruptly narrowed to a short claw, about twice as long as sepals; stamens somewhat shorter than petals. (Named for Ferdinand of Saxe-Coburg, former King of Bulgaria.) Macedonia.—**S. Haagii,** Sünderm. (*S. Ferdinandi-Coburgii* × *S. sancta*). Fl.-sts. to 3½ in. high, 4–6-fld.: basal lvs. lanceolate-subulate, ¼in. long, acute, otherwise similar in habit to *S. Ferdinandi-Coburgii:* fls. yellow; stamens subequal to petals. Garden origin. **S. Paulinæ,** Sünderm. (*S. Ferdinandi-Coburgii* × *S. Burseriana* var. *minor*). Fl.-sts. to 2½ in. high, 1–3-fld.: similar to *S. Ferdinandi-Coburgii* but lvs. slightly shorter: fls. yellow, about ⅝in. across; petals to four times longer than sepals.

Section IX. PORPHYRION. Differs from Kabschia in lvs. decussately opposite: fls. rose or purple, sometimes white.

26. **S. oppositifolia,** L. Cespitose, with woody branched procumbent rhizomes to 8 in. long; fl.-sts. erect, rarely over 2 in. high, 1-fld., often glandular-pubescent above: lvs. decussately opposite, suborbicular to spatulate or oblong, ⅛–⅜in. long, margins ciliate, pits 1–5, sometimes distinctly lime-incrusted: fls. rose to purple, about ½in. across, solitary, subsessile; petals twice as long as sepals; stamens equal to or shorter than petals. N. Amer., Eu., Asia.

Section X. DIPTERA. Fls. irregular, having definitely unequal petals: plants generally pubescent and (in ours) stoloniferous.

27. **S. sarmentosa,** L. (*Sekika sarmentosa,* Moench). STRAWBERRY-GERANIUM. Per. with running habit like a strawberry plant, loosely hairy throughout: lvs. cordate-orbicular, to 4 in. across, repand and somewhat crenate-dentate, upper surface veined white, lower surface reddish, on long petioles from the crown: fls. white, on scapes in bracted panicles 6–24 in. high; 2 of the petals ½in. long, the others three to four times shorter and often spotted with purple or yellow. E. Asia.

91. PITTOSPORACEÆ. PITTOSPORUM FAMILY

Trees and shrubs, often climbing, of 9 genera and about 200 species, native mostly in Australia but Pittosporum distributed over the tropics of the Old World; the family yields ornamental subjects.—Lvs. alternate or seemingly whorled, simple, usually leathery, exstipulate: fls. bisexual or rarely unisexual, regular or slightly oblique, the infl. various; sepals 5, distinct or rarely united at base, imbricated; petals 5, hypogynous, the claws often connivent or coherent; stamens 5, hypogynous, free, alternating with petals; pistil 1, ovary superior, sessile or shortly stalked, composed of 2, rarely 3–5, carpels, with few or many ovules on parietal placentæ; style simple, with terminal stigma entire or minutely lobed: fr. a loculicidally dehiscent caps. or an indehiscent berry-like body.

A. Plant an erect tree or shrub: fls. not blue: fr. dehiscent.
  B. Petals rarely over ½in. long: seeds not winged.......................... 1. PITTOSPORUM
  BB. Petals, including claw, about 1½ in. long: seeds winged.................. 2. HYMENOSPORUM
AA. Plant a climbing subshrub: fls. bright blue: fr. indehiscent.................. 3. SOLLYA

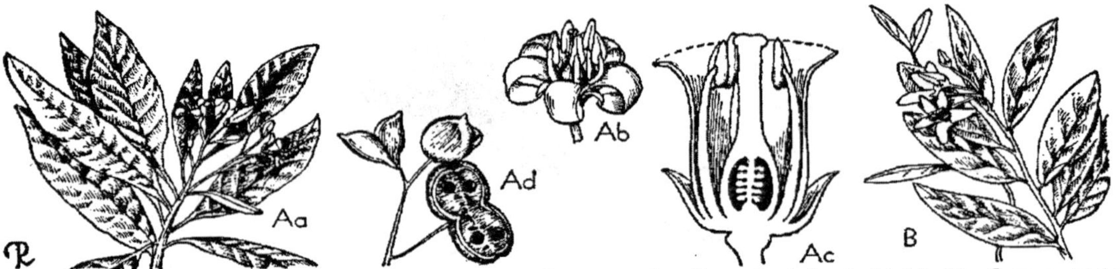

Fig. 91. PITTOSPORACEÆ. A, *Pittosporum undulatum:* Aa, flowering plant, × ¼; Ab, flower, × 1; Ac, same, vertical section, × 2 (after Schnizlein); Ad, fruiting branch, × ½. B, *Sollya fusiformis:* flowering branch, × ½.

1. **PITTOSPORUM,** Banks. Some 160 species of evergreen trees and shrubs widely distributed in trop. regions of the Old World, chiefly in the southern hemisphere, many grown for ornament in warm countries and sometimes under glass.—Lvs. entire or sinuate-dentate, often apparently whorled on the young growths: fls. in terminal panicles or corymbose clusters, or solitary and terminal or axillary; sepals, petals and stamens 5; petals coherent or connivent at base or to nearly the middle, rarely spreading from base; ovary incompletely 2-celled, rarely 3–5-celled, style short; ovules few to many, sometimes failing by abortion: fr. a globose, ovate, or obovate caps., often compressed laterally, with 2 to many smooth seeds, the 2–4 valves leathery or woody. (Pittos-porum: from Greek for *pitch* and *seed*, referring to the resinous coating of the seeds.)

A. Under surface of lvs. tomentose: fls. dark red or purple . . . . 1. *P. crassifolium*
AA. Under surface of lvs. glabrous: fls. white, greenish or yellow (except in no. 6).
  B. Lvs. ¼in. or less wide, to 4 in. long . . . . 2. *P. phillyræoides*
  BB. Lvs. ¾–2 in. wide.
    C. Lf. mostly obtuse, thick and leathery, margins revolute.
      D. Petals almost ½in. long, usually pure white . . . . 3. *P. Tobira*
      DD. Petals ¼in. or less long, greenish-yellow . . . . 4. *P. viridiflorum*
    CC. Lf. acute to acuminate, rather thin, margins often undulate.
      D. Margins of lf. coarsely toothed . . . . 5. *P. rhombifolium*
      DD. Margins of lf. entire, often undulate.
        E. Length of lf. 1–2 (3) in.: fls. dark purple, axillary . . . . 6. *P. tenuifolium*
        EE. Length of lf. 2–5 in.: fls. white to greenish-yellow, in terminal clusters.
          F. Petals about ½in. long, white . . . . 7. *P. undulatum*
          FF. Petals less than ¼in. long, greenish-yellow . . . . 8. *P. eugenioides*

1. **P. crassifolium,** Cunn. KARO. Tall shrub or small tree from 15–30 ft. high, useful for windbreaks near the sea; branchlets, under surface of lvs., petioles, and infl. densely white-tomentose: lvs. to 3 in. long, obovate or oblong, narrowed to short thick petiole, obtuse, leathery, dark green above and downy beneath, the margins revolute: fls. in terminal clusters; petals almost ½in. long, twice as long as sepals, dark red or purple: fr. large, ¾–1¼ in. long, subglobose, tomentose, dehiscing into 3 or 4 thick woody valves. New Zeal.

2. **P. phillyræoides,** DC. NARROW-LEAVED PITTOSPORUM. A graceful glabrous tree to 30 ft. or more, with pendent twigs: lvs. linear-lanceolate, 2–4 in. long, with a small hooked point, entire: fls. axillary, pedicelled, yellow, about ⅓in. long: fr. oval, about ½in. long, compressed, deep yellow. Deserts of Australia.

3. **P. Tobira,** Ait. (*Euonymus Tobira,* Thunb.). JAPANESE PITTOSPORUM. A winter-flowering shrub 10–20 ft. high, very attractive in shrubberies, and grown as a house-plant in the N.: lvs. very thick and leathery, obovate, very obtuse, 2–4 in. long, glabrous, margins revolute: fls. in terminal umbels, fragrant, white or greenish, nearly ½in. long: fr. ovoid, ¼–½in. long, angled, densely short-hairy. (Tobira: native Japanese name.) China, Japan. Var. **variegatum,** Hort., has lvs. variegated white.

4. **P. viridiflorum,** Sims. CAPE PITTOSPORUM. Closely resembling the above, but a tree-like shrub to 25 ft.: fls. smaller, ¼in. or less long, greenish or yellowish, in dense compound clusters: fr. subglobose, about ¼in. long. S. Afr.

5. **P. rhombifolium,** Cunn. QUEENSLAND PITTOSPORUM. Glabrous pyramidal tree to 80 ft. high, often planted for avenues: lvs. rhomboid-oval or rarely broadly oblong-lanceolate, 2–4 in. long, abruptly acuminate, narrowed into petiole ½–1 in. long, coarsely toothed from the middle upward: fls. white, numerous, in terminal compound corymbs, about ¼in. long: fr. nearly globose, about ¼in. long, becoming bright orange-yellow and persisting through the winter. Australia.

6. **P. tenuifolium,** Banks & Soland. (*P. nigricans,* Hort.). TAWHIWHI. KOHUHU. Shrub or tree from 20–40 ft. high, of symmetrical and compact growth, useful for hedges and mass planting: lvs. 1–3 in. long, oblong to elliptic-obovate, obtuse or acute, margins undulate, thin, dark green, glabrous and lustrous when mature: fls. solitary in the lf.-axils, rarely fascicled, ¼–½in. long, dark purple: fr. globose, ½in. diam., 3-valved. New Zeal.

7. **P. undulatum,** Vent. VICTORIAN-BOX. Tree to 40 ft. and more but often pruned as a shrub, suitable for hedges and avenues: lvs. oblong-lanceolate, 3–6 in. long, acuminate, petioles ½–¾in. long, deep green and shining, entire, margins usually undulate, often crowded near the ends of the branchlets: fls. white, very fragrant, almost ½in. long, in terminal few-fld. clusters: fr. nearly globose, smooth, nearly ½in. long. Australia.

8. **P. eugenioides,** Cunn. TARATA. Small round-headed tree to 40 ft., with pale bark, often planted for hedges and shrubberies: lvs. elliptic-oblong, acute, 2–4 in. long, the margins usually undulate: fls. greenish-yellow, numerous, in terminal compound umbels, less than ¼in. long, fragrant, sepals lanceolate, entire: fr. ovoid, acute, about ¼in. long. New Zeal.—Sometimes confused with *P. floribundum,* Wight & Arn., an Indian species with flat or weakly undulate lvs. and fls. with ovate calyces whose margins are erose-ciliate.

2. **HYMENOSPORUM,** R. Br. A monotypic genus from Australia, differing from Pittosporum in having the seeds winged and not embedded in a sticky substance. (Hymenos-porum: Greek *membrane* and *seed,* in reference to the seeds.)

H. flavum, F. Muell. (*Pittosporum flavum,* Hook. f.). Shrub or tree to 50 ft.: lvs. elliptic to obovate, 2–6 (9) in. long, abruptly acuminate or acute, cuneate at base, margins entire, glabrous: fls. yellow, marked with red at throat, very fragrant, 1 in. or more across, in loose terminal panicles; petals long-clawed, forming a tube; ovary cylindric with a short style, silky-pubescent: caps. about 1 in. long, stalked, with many winged seeds. Australia.

3. **SOLLYA,** Lindl. About 2 species of evergreen climbing subshrubs native in Australia, one grown in the S. as covering for banks, fences, and the like, and sometimes in greenhouses N.—Lvs. narrow, entire or rarely sinuate: fls. nodding, blue, in terminal loose few-fld. cymes, rarely solitary; sepals small, distinct; petals spreading from the base, obovate; anthers longer than the filaments, connivent in a cone around the ovary; ovary 2-celled, style short: fr. an oblong indehiscent many-seeded caps., becoming more or less baccate. (Sol-lya: after Richard Horsman Solly, 1778–1858, English botanist.)

S. fusiformis, Briq. (*Billardiera fusiformis,* Labill. *S. heterophylla,* Lindl.). AUSTRALIAN BLUEBELL CREEPER. Small shrub to 6 ft. high, with slender twining sts.: lvs. varying from ovate-lanceolate to oblong-linear, 1–2 in. long, obtuse or slightly acuminate, usually narrowed into a very short petiole: cymes mostly 4–8-fld., the fls. ⅓–½in. long: caps. ½–¾in. long, pubescent. W. Australia.

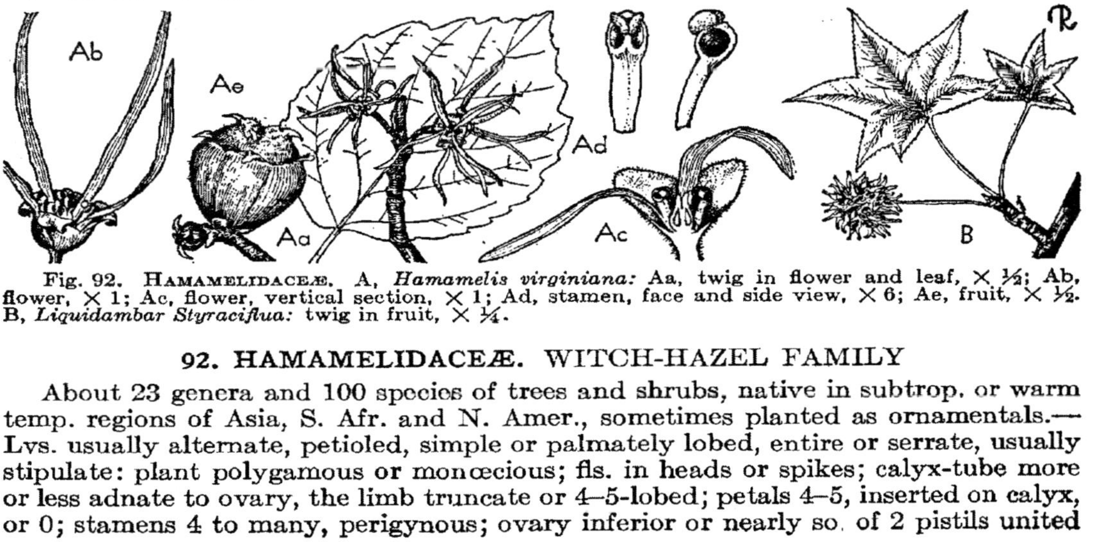

Fig. 92. HAMAMELIDACEÆ. A, *Hamamelis virginiana:* Aa, twig in flower and leaf, × ½; Ab, flower, × 1; Ac, flower, vertical section, × 1; Ad, stamen, face and side view, × 6; Ae, fruit, × ½. B, *Liquidambar Styraciflua:* twig in fruit, × ¼.

92. HAMAMELIDACEÆ. WITCH-HAZEL FAMILY

About 23 genera and 100 species of trees and shrubs, native in subtrop. or warm temp. regions of Asia, S. Afr. and N. Amer., sometimes planted as ornamentals.—Lvs. usually alternate, petioled, simple or palmately lobed, entire or serrate, usually stipulate: plant polygamous or monœcious; fls. in heads or spikes; calyx-tube more or less adnate to ovary, the limb truncate or 4–5-lobed; petals 4–5, inserted on calyx, or 0; stamens 4 to many, perigynous; ovary inferior or nearly so, of 2 pistils united below into one, ovules 1 or several in each cell on axile placentæ, styles 2: fr. a 2-celled 2-beaked woody caps. dehiscent at the summit, with usually only 1 or 2 fertile seeds in each cell.

A. Lvs. pinnately veined, entire to sinuate-dentate.
  B. Foliage deciduous, sinuate-dentate.
    C. Petals present; fls. yellow.
      D. Fls. 4-merous, in clusters .... 1. HAMAMELIS
      DD. Fls. 5-merous, in spikes or racemes .... 2. CORYLOPSIS
    CC. Petals lacking; fls. white .... 3. FOTHERGILLA
  BB. Foliage persistent, entire .... 4. LOROPETALUM
AA. Lvs. palmately veined and lobed: plant a large tree .... 5. LIQUIDAMBAR

1. **HAMAMELIS**, L. WITCH-HAZEL. Deciduous trees or shrubs, of about 6 species native in E. N. Amer. and China and Japan, grown for their yellow fls. which bloom in autumn to early spring.—Bark scaly; buds naked: lvs. straight-veined, unequal at base, sinuate-dentate, stipules deciduous: fls. bisexual, in short-peduncled, nodding, axillary, few-fld. clusters; calyx 4-parted; petals 4, strap-shaped, crumpled, yellow; stamens 4, very short, alternating with 4 scale-like staminodes; ovule solitary: fr. ripening the summer or autumn following the fls., usually 2 from each fl.-cluster, each with 2 shining black seeds which are forcibly discharged when ripe. (Hamame-lis: old Greek name, *together* and *apple*, the fls. and fr. being produced at the same time.)

A. Under surface of lvs. tomentose .... 1. *H. mollis*
AA. Under surface of lvs. glabrous or pubescent only on veins.
  B. Fls. in autumn; calyx brownish-yellow inside .... 2. *H. virginiana*
  BB. Fls. Dec.–Mar.; calyx dark red to purplish inside.
    C. Lvs. mostly obovate, with predominantly 5 pairs of veins: petals about ½in. long .... 3. *H. vernalis*
    CC. Lvs. mostly broad-ovate, with 6–7 pairs of veins: petals about ¾in. long .... 4. *H. japonica*

1. **H. mollis**, Oliv. Shrub or small tree to 30 ft., with densely tomentose young twigs: lvs. obovate to orbicular-obovate, 3–6 in. long, short-acuminate, rounded to cordate at base, shallowly sinuate-denticulate, pubescent above, densely tomentose beneath: fls. Jan.–Mar.; petals yellow, reddish at base, about ¾in. long; calyx purplish-red inside: caps. covered one-third to one-half by the calyx-tube. Cent. China.

2. **H. virginiana**, L. Spreading shrub or small tree to 15 ft.: lvs. elliptic to obovate, 3–6 in. long, short-acuminate to obtusish, narrowed to an unequal subcordate base, coarsely crenate-dentate, subglabrous or pubescent on the 5–7 pairs of veins beneath: fls. in autumn when lvs. fall; petals bright yellow, about ¾in. long; calyx brownish-yellow inside: caps. broad-obovoid, about ½in. long, covered one-half or slightly less by the calyx-tube. N. S. to Ga. and Neb.

3. **H. vernalis**, Sarg. Upright shrub to 6 ft., suckering: lvs. obovate to oblong-obovate, 2½–5 in. long, rounded to acute, usually cuneate to truncate at base, coarsely sinuate-dentate, often pubescent on the 4–6 pairs of veins beneath: fls. Dec.–Mar., fragrant; petals light yellow, reddish toward base, about ½in. long; calyx dark red inside: caps. broad-obovoid, about ½in. long, covered one-half or slightly less by the calyx-tube. Mo. to La. and Okla.

4. **H. japonica**, Sieb. & Zucc. Spreading shrub or small tree to 30 ft.: lvs. suborbicular to broad-ovate or rarely obovate, 2–4 in. long, acute to rounded at tip, base rounded to subcordate or rarely broad-cuneate, coarsely and unevenly sinuate-dentate, glabrous or sometimes pubescent on the 6–7 pairs of veins beneath: fls. Jan.–Mar.; petals bright yellow, ¾in. or more long; calyx purplish inside, the lobes revolute: caps. covered about one-fifth by the calyx-tube. Japan.

2. **CORYLOPSIS**, Sieb. & Zucc. WINTER HAZEL. About 12 species of deciduous shrubs or small trees, native in E. Asia and Himalayas.—Lvs. alternate, prominently veined, dentate, with linear-lanceolate to obovate deciduous stipules: fls. yellow, appearing before the lvs., in nodding racemes which have large bracts at the base; calyx-tube adnate to ovary or free, the limb short and 5-parted; petals usually 5, clawed; stamens 5, alternating with entire or 2–3-parted short staminodes; ovary usually half superior; styles 2: caps. with 2 shining black seeds.. (Corylop-sis: *corylus* and *opsis*, like; resembling the hazel in foliage.)

C. pauciflora, Sieb. & Zucc. Spreading shrub to 6 ft., the young branchlets glabrous: lvs. ovate to broad-ovate, 1–3 in. long, acute, unequally cordate to subcordate at base, sharply sinuate-dentate, somewhat glaucous and with scattered pubescence beneath: fls. yellow, about ⅜in. long, 2 or 3 in short spikes; petals longer than stamens. Japan.

3. **FOTHERGILLA,** Murr. Four species of deciduous shrubs in S. E. U. S.—Buds with 2 scales: lvs. alternate, petioled, coarsely toothed, stipulate: fls. white, in terminal spikes or heads, bisexual, apetalous; calyx campanulate, 4–7-lobed; stamens 15–24, with filaments thickened toward the end; ovary adnate to the receptacle at the base; styles 2: caps. dehiscent, 2-celled, 2-seeded. (Fothergil-la: after John Fothergill, 1712–1780, English physician, who intro. many new plants into cult.)

A. Lvs. glaucous beneath....................1. *F. major*
AA. Lvs. pale green beneath....................2. *F. monticola*

1. **F. major,** Lodd. (*F. alnifolia* var. *major*, Sims). Erect pyramidal shrub to 10 ft.: lvs. suborbicular to oval or obovate, 2–4 in. long, cordate to broad-cuneate at base, crenate-dentate becoming subentire in the lower half, green and glabrous above, glaucous beneath and stellate-pubescent at least on veins, turning reddish-purple in autumn: fls. white, with the lvs., in spikes 1–2 in. long: caps., including erect beak, about ½in. long, light brown inside with the inner suture red. Ga.

2. **F. monticola,** Ashe. Spreading shrub to 6 ft.: lvs. obovate to broad-oval, to 5 in. long, usually cordate, crenate-dentate, becoming subentire in the lowest third, light green beneath and with scattered stellate pubescence: fl.-spikes to 2½ in. long: beak of caps. spreading, the caps. darker brown inside and without the red markings. N. C. to Ala.

4. **LOROPETALUM,** R. Br. Monotypic genus from China and India.—Evergreen stellate-pubescent shrub, with alternate entire short-petioled lvs.: fls. sessile, fascicled in 4–8-fld. clusters at the ends of short branchlets; calyx short, 4-lobed; petals 4, strap-shaped; stamens 4, with very short filaments, the connective prolonged into a horn; ovary inferior, 2-celled; styles 2, short: caps. woody, dehiscent, 2-seeded. (Loropet-alum: from Greek *loros* strap and *petalum*.)

L. chinense, Oliv. (*Hamamelis chinensis*, R. Br.). Much-branched shrub to 12 ft., branchlets densely reddish-pubescent: lvs. ovate, to 2 in. long, short-acuminate, rounded and oblique at base, dull green, pubescent or ciliate: fls. in early spring, white to yellowish or greenish, feathery; petals ¾–1 in. long. China, India.

5. **LIQUIDAMBAR,** L. Four species of deciduous trees in N. and Cent. Amer. and Asia.—Buds ovoid, with 5 or 6 outer scales: lvs. alternate, slender-petioled, palmately 3–7-lobed, serrate, stipules small: plant usually monœcious; fls. apetalous, in globular heads; staminate fls. lacking calyx, intermixed with scales, in small heads clustered in terminal racemes; pistillate fls. in long-peduncled round heads composed of more or less cohering 2-beaked pistils subtended by small scales: fr.-heads round, spiny from the persisting styles, the caps. dehiscent and each with 1 or 2 winged seeds. (Liquidam-bar: Latin *liquidus*, fluid, and Arabic *ambar*, amber in reference to the fragrant resin from the bark of *L. orientalis*.)

L. Styraciflua, L. Sweet-Gum. Tree to 150 ft., with furrowed bark: branchlets reddish-brown, often with corky wings: lvs. suborbicular in outline, 4–7 in. long, on petioles of almost equal length, cordate to subtruncate at base, 5–7-lobed, the lobes acuminate and finely serrate, dark green and shining above, pale green beneath becoming glabrous except in axils of principal veins, turning deep crimson in autumn: fr.-heads 1 in. or more across, persisting during winter. Conn. to Fla., Mo. and Mex.

93. EUCOMMIACEÆ. EUCOMMIA FAMILY

A single monotypic genus; a deciduous diœcious tree resembling an elm, grown for its foliage and as a curiosity because of the rubber latex present beneath the bark of twigs and branches.—Branches with lamellate pith; buds ovoid, with 6 imbricate scales: lvs. alternate, petioled, serrate, exstipulate: fls. unisexual, without perianth, solitary in axils of bracts at base of twigs or adventitious; staminate fls. distinctly pedicelled, with 4–10 linear mucronate anthers on very short filaments; pistillate fls. short-pedicelled, with a 1-celled 2-carpelled 2-ovuled stipitate ovary bifid at apex, the apical ovary-lobes stigmatic on inside, placentation basal: fr. an oblong, pedicelled, compressed, winged, 1-seeded nutlet.

EUCOMMIA, Oliv. Characters as for the family. (Eucom-mia: Greek for *true gum*, alluding to the rubber content of the wood.)

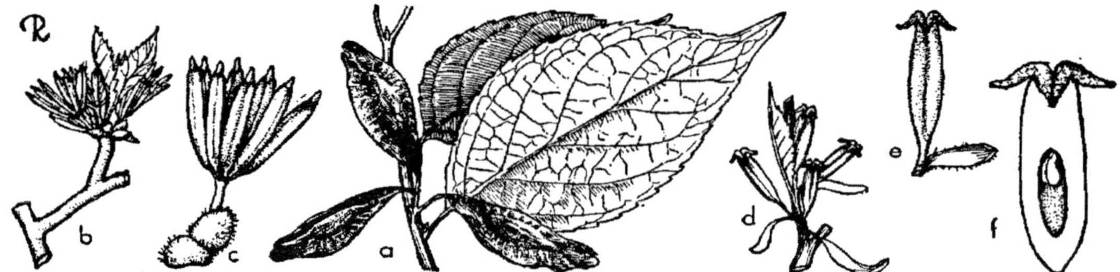

Fig. 93. EUCOMMIACEÆ. *Eucommia ulmoides:* a, habit in fruit, × ½; b, staminate inflorescence, × ½; c, staminate flower, × 1; d, pistillate inflorescence, × ½; e, pistillate flower, × 1; f, same; vertical section, × 2. (d–f after Hooker.)

E. ulmoides, Oliv. Tree to 60 ft. or more: lvs. 2½–4 in. long, elliptic, base broadly cuneate to obtuse and sometimes oblique, acuminate, serrate, glabrous to weakly hispidulous, the veins pubescent beneath when young, becoming somewhat rugose at maturity, dark green: staminate fls. reddish-brown, anthers nearly ½in. long: fr. 1–1¾ in. long, wings dark brown at maturity, pendent. China.

94. PLATANACEÆ. PLANE-TREE FAMILY

One genus of large monœcious trees, about a half dozen species in S. E. Eu. to India, and in N. Amer. south to Cent. Amer.—Bark of the branches exfoliating in plates rather than separating in ridges and furrows but at the base of old trunks becoming furrowed; young shoots and unfolding lvs. stellate-tomentose: lvs. large and broad, palmately ribbed and lobed, petiole enlarging at base and covering the bud, stipules conspicuous and joined into a tube with lf.-like margin: fls. unisexual, in dense globular peduncled separate heads; sepals, petals, stamens, and pistils 3–8, the floral envelopes not conspicuous; styles elongated beyond the head: the head in fr. is enlarged and hard but the frs. not coherent, each fr. an obconical 1-seeded nutlet surrounded at base by long hairs.

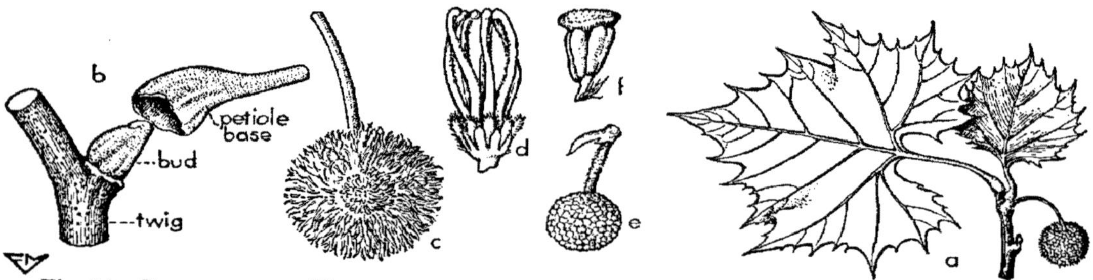

Fig. 94. PLATANACEÆ. *Platanus occidentalis:* a, twig with fruit, × ⅙; b, subpetiolar bud; c, pistillate inflorescence, × 2; d, pistillate flower, × 4; e, fruit, × ¼; f, staminate flower, × 4.

PLATANUS, L. PLANE-TREE. Characters of the family; forest and street trees in N. Amer., conspicuous because of the white branches more or less mottled with patches of gray, the wide-spreading arm-like branches and eventually the great flanging bole. The fr.-heads, on long peduncles, hang in winter; fls. in spring. (Platanus: ancient Greek name of the plane-tree.)—Sometimes called Sycamore, but this name belongs to *Ficus Sycomorus.*

A. Fr.-heads 3–7 to a peduncle: lvs. usually deeply lobed.
B. Mature lvs. glabrous beneath, lobes usually coarsely toothed .... 1. *P. orientalis*
BB. Mature lvs. tomentose beneath, lobes entire or minutely toothed .... 2. *P. racemosa*
AA. Fr.-heads 1–2 (3) to a peduncle: lvs. usually shallowly lobed.
B. Heads solitary, rarely 2: lobes of lf. broader than long .... 3. *P. occidentalis*
BB. Heads 2, sometimes more: middle lobe of lf. about as long as broad .... 4. *P. acerifolia*

1. **P. orientalis,** L. ORIENTAL PLANE. Tree to 100 ft., with spreading branches and rather short thick trunk; bark grayish to greenish-white: lvs. 4–8 in. across, broad-cuneate to truncate at base, lobes 5–7, longer than broad, extending about half way to base of the blade, coarsely toothed (rarely entire), becoming glabrous on both surfaces: fr.-heads 2–6,

about 1 in. diam., bristly. S. E. Eu. and W. Asia.—Little if at all planted in the U. S.; the name is frequent, being misapplied to *P. acerifolia*.

2. **P. racemosa,** Nutt. Tree to 90 ft., branching widely and irregularly; bark whitish on branches and young trunks: lvs. 4–10 in. across, truncate to cordate at base, deeply 3–5-lobed, the lobes usually longer than broad, entire or remotely dentate, tomentose on both surfaces when young, becoming glabrous above: fr.-heads 2–7, ¾–1 in. diam., bristly. Calif. and Lower Calif.—Not hardy N.

3. **P. occidentalis,** L. Buttonwood. American Plane. Tree to 140 (170) ft., with a broad open head; bark almost creamy-white, becoming dark brown at the base of old trunks: lvs. 4–10 in. across, cordate to truncate at base, sometimes decurrent on the petiole, shallowly 3–5-lobed, the lobes broader than long, sharply sinuate-dentate, becoming glabrous except on veins beneath: fr.-heads usually solitary, 1 in. diam., rather smooth at maturity. Me. to Minn., Fla. and Tex.—Infrequently planted as it is seriously attacked by leaf-blight.

4. **P. acerifolia,** Willd. (*P. orientalis* var. *acerifolia*, Ait. *P. occidentalis* × *P. orientalis*). London Plane. Tree to 120 ft., with erect trunk and pendulous lower branches; bark exfoliating in large flakes: lvs. 5–10 in. across, cordate to truncate at base, shallowly 3–5-lobed, the lobes usually about as broad as long and the sinuses wide and about one-third as long as the blade, usually irregularly toothed, becoming glabrous except on veins beneath: fr.-heads 2 (1–3), 1–1¼ in. diam., bristly. Origin unknown.—The common platanus of streets in N. Amer., little damaged by leaf-blight.

95. ROSACEÆ. ROSE FAMILY

As customarily accepted, perhaps 3,200 species and about 115 genera comprise the rose family, in which are some of the major ornamental and pomological plants; it is a somewhat heterogeneous family and yet it holds together by combinations of distinctive characters that fairly distinguish it from related families; the typical rose fl. looks like a typical buttercup fl. but it is perigynous (ovaries inferior or in the hypanthium), has a disk, and the stamens are in whorls or cycles; from the saxifrage family it is known by its numerous stamens in cycles, carpels usually more numerous, seeds mostly not albuminous.—Herbs, shrubs, small trees, spiny or unarmed, sometimes climbing, largely of temp. regions: lvs. usually alternate and stipular, but the stipules sometimes caducous: fls. mostly bisexual and regular, in many colors, but white, pink, and rose predominating, the envelopes borne on the edges (perigynous) of a hypanthium (calyx-tube) that is lined or rimmed with a glandular disk; sepals or calyx-lobes 4–5, and petals of same number or seldom wanting; stamens commonly numerous (but sometimes definite), in whorls or cycles of 5, perigynous; pistils 1 to many and when solitary the carpels 1–5 (or many), ovaries 1- to several-ovuled, placentation basal, axile or parietal, the styles as many as the carpels: fr. various, sometimes an achene, sometimes a follicle, hip, pome, or drupe; seeds usually exalbuminous.—The receptacle or hypanthium assumes various forms: in the rose it is hollow and bears the pistils (which become achenes) on the inside, forming a hip; in the strawberry it is much enlarged and fleshy, forming the "berry" on the outside of which the achenes or true frs. (usually called "seeds") are borne; in the raspberry it is the cone that remains on the bush when the cluster of drupelets is picked; in the blackberry it is the core to which the drupelets adhere; in the apple and pear (which are pomes) it is the fleshy part of the fr. outside the core. In the plum tribes the ovary is superior and forms a drupe without attachment of hypanthium. Many of the species in this family run into numberless cultivars.

A. Ovary or ovaries superior: fr. not a pome.
  B. Fls. apetalous.
    C. Plant a woody shrub: lvs. simple: stamens 15–30 or more .... 30. Neviusia
    CC. Plant herbaceous or suffrutescent: lvs. compound: stamens 1–12.
      D. Hypanthium covered with barbed prickles: pistil 1 .... 42. Acæna
      DD. Hypanthium not prickly: pistils 1–3 .... 41. Sanguisorba
  BB. Fls. with corolla of 4 or more petals.
    C. Pistils 1.
      D. Lvs. lobed or incised: branches slender and flexuous: fr. a follicle...... 4. Stephanandra
      DD. Lvs. not lobed: branches stout: fr. a drupe.......................... 44. Prunus
    CC. Pistils 2 to many (sometimes basally connate).
      D. Lvs. all simple.
        E. Plants herbaceous or suffrutescent.
          F. Number of pistils 5–10: fls. to ½in. across........................ 34. Dalibarda
          FF. Number of pistils many: fls. ¾–1½ in. across.................. 40. Dryas

Fig. 95. ROSACEÆ. A, *Spiræa Vanhouttei:* Aa, flowering branch, × ½; Ab, flower, face view, × 1; Ac, flower, vertical section, × 2; Ad, pistil, vertical section, × 6; Ae, follicles, × 2. B, *Geum bulgaricum:* Ba, flower, × ½; Bb, same, vertical section, × 1; Bc, achene, × 2. C, *Fragaria chiloensis:* Ca, fruit and basal leaf, × ¼; Cb, fruit, vertical section, × ½; Cc, nutlet with persistent style, × 5. D, *Rubus roribaccus:* Da, flower, × nearly 1; Db, same, vertical section, × 1; Dc, fruit, vertical section, × 1. E, *Rubus occidentalis:* Ea, flower, × 1; Eb, flower, vertical section, × 1; Ec, fruit separated from torus, × 1. F, *Malus sylvestris:* Fa, flower, vertical section, corolla excised, × 1; Fb, fruit, vertical section, × ⅓. G, *Rosa canina:* Ga, flowering branch, × ½; Gb, flower, vertical section, × 1; Gc, hip, × ½. H, *Chænomeles lagenaria:* Ha, flowering branch, × ½; Hb, flower, vertical section, × 1; Hc, ovary, cross-section, × 4.

EE. Plants woody trees or shrubs.
F. Fl. with 4 petals and 4 pistils.................................32. RHODOTYPOS
FF. Fl. with typically 5 petals, the pistils rarely 4.
G. Stipules absent: fls. with a disk on which the stamens are borne.
H. Lf. entire: pistils connate at least at base.
I. Diam. of fls. 1½–2 in.: fr. a caps......................11. EXOCHORDA
II. Diam. of fls. ¼in. or less: fr. a follicle.................. 6. SIBIRÆA
HH. Lf. usually serrulate to lobed or incised: pistils separate.
I. Infl. a pendent pyramidal panicle: fr. an achene..........12. HOLODISCUS
II. Infl. various, rarely as above: fr. a follicle............... 1. SPIRÆA
GG. Stipules present (sometimes early caducous): stamens not on a disk.
H. The pistils usually 15 or more, borne on a raised convex to subcylindrical torus, becoming drupelets and aggregated in fr....33. RUBUS
HH. The pistils 2–10, not on a torus, fr. not fleshy.
I. Infl. an umbellate raceme: fr. dehiscent by 2 sutures...... 2. PHYSOCARPUS
II. Infl. an elongated raceme, a panicle, or fls. solitary.
J. Number of pistils 2: fls. pink or whitish, in paniculate racemes.. 3. NEILLIA
JJ. Number of pistils 5–8: fls. orange-yellow, solitary........ 31. KERRIA
DD. Lvs., at least the basal ones, compound.
E. Plants woody trees or shrubs.
F. Number of pistils 5–8... 9. SORBARIA
FF. Number of pistils many (15 or more).
G. Fl. with pistils inclosed within an hypanthium................43. ROSA
GG. Fl. with pistils borne on a receptacle or torus.
H. Sts. usually prickly, not much-branched: pistils becoming drupelets in fr...33. RUBUS
HH. Sts. never prickly, forming much-branched shrubs: pistils becoming dry achenes..................................37. POTENTILLA
EE. Plants herbaceous or suffrutescent.
F. Number of pistils 2–10.
G. The fls. unisexual: plants diœcious.......................... 8. ARUNCUS
GG. The fls. bisexual.
H. Habit erect, 1–3 ft. high...............................10. GILLENIA
HH. Habit low, creeping.
I. Pistils 5, in an hypanthium: lvs. biternate: fls. white........ 7. LUETKEA
II. Pistils 2–5, on a receptacle: lvs. ternate: fls. yellow.........38. WALDSTEINIA
FF. Number of pistils many (15 or more).
G. Sts. usually prickly: fr. an aggregate of drupelets.............33. RUBUS
GG. Sts. never prickly: fr. an achene (sometimes imbedded in a fleshy receptacle).
H. Styles elongating after anthesis, becoming plumose or jointed.. 39. GEUM
HH. Styles not elongating after anthesis.
I. Receptacle much enlarged or fleshy in fr. (strawberry-like).
J. Color of fls. yellow: fr. receptacle not juicy.............. 36. DUCHESNEA
JJ. Color of fls. white or reddish: fr. receptacle juicy......... 35. FRAGARIA
II. Receptacle neither enlarged nor fleshy in fr.
J. Calyx bractless: pistils 2-ovuled, -seeded in fr. .... 5. FILIPENDULA
JJ. Calyx subtended by bractlets: pistils 1-ovuled...........37. POTENTILLA
AA. Ovary inferior: fr. a pome.
B. Lf. pinnately compound.
C. Lfts. entire, mostly ⅛–¼in. long..............................17. OSTEOMELES
CC. Lfts. toothed, mostly ½–2 in. long............................28. SORBUS
BB. Lf. simple (but may be lobed or dissected).
C. Margins of lvs. entire (in ours).
D. Fl. 1–2 in. across, solitary.
E. Styles glabrous: fr. carpels bony, with 1–5 nutlets.................15. MESPILUS
EE. Styles basally pubescent: fr. carpels with leathery or papery walls, no nutlets present...25. CYDONIA
DD. Fl. ¾in. across or less, usually not solitary.
E. Infl. a terminal raceme: lvs. persistent........................22. RHAPHIOLEPIS
EE. Infl. not as above: lvs. deciduous or persistent.
F. Styles 5, connate to the middle.............................20. STRANVAESIA
FF. Styles 2–5, separate..13. COTONEASTER
CC. Margins of lvs. toothed, lobed or dissected.
D. Lvs. persistent (plants evergreen), or if deciduous pedicels conspicuously warty.
E. Fls. in terminal racemes or panicles.
F. Infl. a raceme; fls. on glabrous thickened somewhat fleshy pedicels ¼–½in. long..22. RHAPHIOLEPIS
FF. Infl. a panicle; fls. on tawny woolly pedicels ⅛2–¼in. long..........21. ERIOBOTRYA
EE. Fls. in simple or compound corymbs.
F. Pistils 5, partially connate on ventral surface or adnate to calyx-tube; carpels bony at maturity: fr. of 5 2-seeded nutlets........14. PYRACANTHA
FF. Pistils distinctly 1; carpels with leathery or papery walls, not forming nutlets at maturity.
G. Stamens 10: styles separate..............................19. HETEROMELES
GG. Stamens 20 or more: styles basally connate...................18. PHOTINIA
DD. Lvs. deciduous: pedicels never warty.
E. Fls. in simple or compound corymbs (determinate infl.) or paniculate.
F. Diam. of fls. ½in. or more.

G. Cells of ovary many-ovuled..24. CHÆNOMELES
GG. Cells of ovary 1–2-ovuled.
H. The lvs. serrulate to serrate: fr. mostly 1½–4 in. across; carpels with leathery or papery walls........................26. PYRUS
HH. The lvs. crenate, dentate or lobed: fr. mostly ¼–1½ in. across; carpels bony at maturity........................16. CRATÆGUS
FF. Diam. of fls. ⅓in. or less: fr. small and berry-like.
G. Lf.-margins crenulate-serrulate, the midrib with glands above: styles united basally........................29. ARONIA
GG. Lf.-margins sharply serrate to doubly serrate or lobed, the midrib glandless above: styles separate........................28. SORBUS
EE. Fls. solitary, fascicled, racemose or umbellate (infl. indeterminate).
F. Infl. a raceme: ovary-cells incompletely 6–10, each 1-ovuled ....23. AMELANCHIER
FF. Infl. not racemose: ovary-cells mostly 5, each 2-ovuled.
G. Styles usually separate: fr. with grit-cells forming a ring beneath epidermis: lvs. involute in bud, pirostele evident.....26. PYRUS
GG. Styles usually connate at base: fr. without grit-cells: lvs. revolute or plicate in bud, pirostele lacking ....27. MALUS

1. **SPIRÆA**, L. SPIREA. As at present delimited, more than 80 species of deciduous shrubs in the northern hemisphere, many planted for ornament.—Habit various: lvs. alternate, simple, sometimes pinnately lobed, lacking stipules: fls. mostly bisexual, white, pink, or reddish, not large but conspicuous by being aggregated into umbel-like racemes, corymbs, or panicles; hypanthium bell-shaped or cup-shaped, bearing a disk; sepals (calyx-lobes) and petals usually 5, mostly broad; stamens many, distinct; pistils commonly 5, superior and distinct, 1-celled, 2- to many-ovuled, placenta 1, parietal: fr. a dehiscent uninflated follicle. (Spiræ-a: probably from the Greek *speira*, wreath.)—Some of the spireas in rather common cult. are hybrids, but their origins are for the most part clear. Plants of several other genera are often cult. under the same Spiræa; these include Aruncus, Astilbe, Filipendula, and others.

A. Infl. simple (pedicels arising from the axis, not borne on peduncles), racemose or umbel-like; fls. white.
B. Fls. in sessile leafless umbels on old wood (sometimes the lower clusters with lvs. at base).
C. Lvs. distinctly serrate or dentate: petals two to three times as long as stamens.
D. The lvs. pubescent, at least while young, elliptic to ovate............ 1. *S. prunifolia*
DD. The lvs. glabrous, linear-lanceolate........................ 2. *S. Thunbergii*
CC. Lvs. entire or small-toothed only at apex: petals subequal to stamens ..... 3. *S. hypericifolia*
BB. Fls. in umbel-like racemes on leafy shoots of the season.
C. Pedicels of infl. (the lower ones) with a leafy bract.................. 5. *S. nipponica*
CC. Pedicels not bracted.
D. Petals shorter than stamens.
E. Lvs. ¾–1½ in. long, margins entire or serrulate................. 4. *S. crenata*
EE. Lvs. 1½–3 in. long, margins irregularly often doubly toothed........ 7. *S. chamædryfolia*
DD. Petals subequal to or longer than stamens.
E. Lvs. lanceolate to rhombic-lanceolate, penninerved............... 8. *S. cantoniensis*
EE. Lvs. broad-ovate to suborbicular, often 3–5-nerved from base.
F. Apex of lf. rounded........................ 9. *S. trilobata*
FF. Apex of lf. short-acute........................10. *S. Vanhouttei*
AA. Infl. compound (fl.-stalks branched); fls. white or pink to purplish.
B. Fls. in corymbs or rounded clusters.
C. Corymbs on short lateral branchlets from the arching branches of the previous year; fls. white.
D. Lvs. villous beneath, especially on veins, coarsely dentate at apex....... 11. *S. Henryi*
DD. Lvs. glabrous beneath, or if slightly pubescent, then entire.
E. Follicles glabrous: lvs. entire, glaucous beneath..................12. *S. Veitchii*
EE. Follicles pubescent: lvs. usually with a few teeth at apex, pale beneath........................ 6. *S. trichocarpa*
CC. Corymbs predominantly terminal on erect shoots of the year; fls. white to carmine or rose.
D. Length of lvs. ½–1 in.
E. Shrub procumbent, branchlets glabrous: lvs. thin and flat......... 13. *S. decumbens*
EE. Shrub erect, branchlets villous while young: lvs. thickish and puckered........................18. *S. bullata*
DD. Length of lvs. 1–4 in.
E. Color of fls. white.
F. Lvs. elliptic, not more than twice as long as broad..............14. *S. japonica* var. *ovalifolia*
FF. Lvs. lanceolate to ovate-lanceolate, about three or more times as long as broad (see also no. 15)........................17. *S. albiflora*
EE. Color of fls. pink to rose or carmine, rarely whitish.
F. Shrub dwarf, rarely over 2 ft. high: fls. in hort. forms mostly crimson........................15. *S. Bumalda*
FF. Shrub to 5 ft. or more: fls. pink to rose.

G. Branchlets bright brown: ripe follicles diverging with ascending styles....14. *S. japonica*
GG. Branchlets purple-brown: ripe follicles parallel with upright styles....16. *S. Margaritæ*
BB. Fls. paniculate—in clusters at least as long as broad at maturity, sometimes nearly spicate.
C. Panicle short, about as broad as long: hybrid....22. *S. conspicua*
CC. Panicle elongate, much longer than broad.
D. Petals white; infl. broad, with the lower branchlets spreading and much exceeding the lvs.
E. Infl. tomentulose; stamens and disk white....20. *S. alba*
EE. Infl. glabrous; stamens and disk pink-purple....21. *S. latifolia*
DD. Petals pink to purple (rarely whitish); infl. narrow.
E. Mature lvs. densely felty-tomentose beneath (see also no. 25).
F. Lvs. 1–4 in. long, oblong, with a white tomentum: follicles glabrous....24. *S. Douglasii*
FF. Lvs. 1–2 in. long, ovate, with a tawny tomentum: follicles pubescent....26. *S. tomentosa*
EE. Mature lvs. glabrous or subglabrous beneath, sometimes somewhat pubescent in no. 25.
F. Lvs. obtuse, irregularly serrate above the middle....23. *S. Menziesii*
FF. Lvs. acute, sharply serrate almost to base.
G. Under surface of lvs. glabrous....19. *S. salicifolia*
GG. Under surface of lvs. pubescent, at least when young....25. *S. Billiardii*

1. **S. prunifolia,** Sieb. & Zucc. Bridal Wreath. Pleasing shrub, 4–6 ft. or more, erect, with very thin slightly pubescent young growth: lvs. elliptic to ovate, 1–2 in. long, finely serrate, shining above, pubescent beneath: fls. clear white, very early, ⅓–½in. across, on slender pedicels in few-fld. sessile umbels in advance of the lvs. and sometimes another small crop in autumn, mostly full double, the single form not common; petals exceeding stamens. China, Japan.

2. **S. Thunbergii,** Sieb. Characteristic narrow-lvd. shrub 3–5 ft. high, the tips usually dying back somewhat in winter so that the precocious profuse white bloom may not extend to the ends of the twigs, the plant of twiggy arching habit: lvs. linear-lanceolate, 1–1¾ in. long, sharp-serrate, glabrous: fls. white, ¼–⅓in. across, in 3–5-fld. sessile umbels in early spring, slender-pedicelled; petals obovate, longer than stamens. (Carl Peter Thunberg, page 52.) China, Japan.

3. **S. hypericifolia,** L. Small-lvd. vigorous shrub, 4–5 ft., with curving graceful branches that are glabrous or soon becoming so: lvs. short-obovate to lance-obovate, ¾–1½ in. long, prominently tapering to base, very short-petioled, acute and with few small teeth near apex or entire, with 3–5 lengthwise nerves, nearly glabrous: fls. pure white, about ¼in. across, in early spring in sessile umbels from last year's wood, just preceding the lvs. Eu., Siberia.—**S. multiflora,** Zabel (*S. crenata* × *S. hypericifolia*), lvs. obovate, 3–5-nerved at base, serrate in the upper half; fls. white, the lower umbels usually on short leafy stalks. **S. arguta,** Zabel (*S. Thunbergii* × *S. multiflora*), lvs. oblong-obovate to oblong-oblanceolate, to 1½ in. long, acute, sharply serrate; fls. white, about ⅓in. across, in many-fld. umbels with lvs. at the base; one of the most beautiful and free-flowering of the early spring spireas.

4. **S. crenata,** L. Bushy shrub to 3 ft., with slender striped somewhat angled nearly or quite glabrous sts.: lvs. firm in texture, obovate to oblanceolate, ¾–1½ in. long, acutish both ways, serrulate near the apex, 3-nerved, at first puberulent beneath: fls. white, small, on short leafy branches with the foliage, in mid-spring, in dense puberulous umbels; petals shorter than the stamens. S. E. Eu., Asia.

5. **S. nipponica,** Maxim. (*S. bracteata,* Zabel not Raf.). Somewhat stiff spreading shrub to 8 ft., with angled glabrous branches: lvs. obovate to oval, to 1½ in. long, cuneate at base, rounded and usually crenate at apex, bluish-green beneath, glabrous: fls. white, about ⅓in. across, in many-fld. umbel-like racemes on leafy stalks, lower pedicels often with a lf.-like bract; petals longer than stamens. Japan.

6. **S. trichocarpa,** Nakai. Compact shrub to 6 ft., with arching rigid branches: lvs. oblong to oblanceolate, 1–2 in. long, narrowed at base to a short petiole, acutish and usually with a few teeth at apex, green above, pale beneath, glabrous: fls. white, in pubescent rounded corymbose clusters about 2 in. across, on short lateral leafy shoots; lower branches of infl. 2–7-fld. and usually with a leafy bract; petals suborbicular, often emarginate: follicles pubescent. Korea.

7. **S. chamædryfolia,** L. Strong erect shrub to 5 ft., with angular zigzag glabrous branchlets: lvs. rather large, ovate to narrow-ovate, 1½–3 in. long, acute, irregularly often doubly toothed, bright green above, bluish-green and thinly pubescent on veins beneath: fls. white, about ⅓in. across, in several-fld. glabrous umbel-like racemes or corymbs on leafy shoots of the season; petals shorter than stamens. N. E. Asia.—Variable.

8. **S. cantoniensis,** Lour. (*S. Reevesiana,* Lindl.). Shrub, 4–5 ft., with curving branches, in some places partially evergreen, much-branched, young sts. glabrous: lvs. irregularly lanceolate to rhombic-lanceolate, 1–2½ in. long, acute or short-acute, irregularly double-serrate, bluish-green and glabrous beneath, penninerved with somewhat parallel veins:

fls. white, ⅓–½in. across, in rather dense glabrous umbel-like corymbs on leafy shoots of the season, appearing with and after the lvs.; petals longer than stamens. China, Japan.—Known mostly in the double-fld. lanceolate-lvd. var. **lanceata,** Zabel.

9. **S. trilobata,** L. (*S. triloba,* Murr.). Attractive twiggy broad shrub 3–5 ft. high, with slender glabrous often zigzag shoots: lvs. nearly or quite orbicular in outline, usually not more than 1 in. across, rounded on apex, cut-toothed and often obscurely or shallowly 3- or 5-lobed, bluish-green and glabrous beneath: fls. clear white, about ⅜in. across, many in leafy-peduncled umbels, appearing with the lvs.; petals exceeding the stamens. Turkestan to N. China.—One of the plants known in cult. as *S. cratægifolia* and *S. aquilegifolia.*

10. **S. Vanhouttei,** Zabel (*S. aquilegifolia* var. *Vanhouttei,* Briot). Hybrid between *S. trilobata* and *S. cantoniensis,* one of the finest of spring-blooming spireas, giving a fountain of bloom on long arching sts., the fls. larger and more showy than in no. 9: lvs. narrower and somewhat acute, rhombic-ovate to somewhat obovate in outline, often cuneate at base, to 1½ in. long. (Louis VanHoutte, page 53.)

11. **S. Henryi,** Hemsl. Wide-spreading shrub to 8 ft., with sparingly pubescent branchlets: lvs. obovate to oblong, 1–3 in. long, cuneate at base, acute or rounded and coarsely dentate at apex, slightly hairy above, villous beneath especially on veins: fls. white, about ¼in. across, in loose rounded pubescent corymbs to 2 in. across; petals longer than stamens. (A. Henry, page 45.) Cent. and W. China.

12. **S. Veitchii,** Hemsl. Shrub to 12 ft., with arching branches; branchlets reddish, puberulous when young: lvs. oblong to oval, ¾–1½ in. long, obtuse, cuneate at base, entire, subglabrous above, minutely pubescent and somewhat glaucous beneath: fls. white, less than ¼in. across, in dense pubescent corymbs to 2½ in. across; petals shorter than stamens. (Veitch, page 53.) Cent. and W. China.

13. **S. decumbens,** W. Koch. Dwarf procumbent shrub, with ascending glabrous branchlets to 10 in. high: lvs. elliptic to elliptic-oblong, ½–1 in. long, acute at both ends, serrate, glabrous; fls. white, in terminal corymbs 1–2 in. across, on leafy branches; imperfectly diœcious; petals subequal to stamens: follicles parallel. S. Eu.—Some of the material in cult. under this name may be *S. lancifolia,* Hoffmgg., which has narrower gray-pubescent lvs. serrate only toward apex; N. E. Italy.

14. **S. japonica,** L. f. (*S. callosa,* Thunb.). Shrub to 5 ft., with upright bright brown branches glabrous or becoming so: lvs. ovate to ovate-oblong, 1–3 in. long, acute, cuneate at base, doubly and sharply serrate, pale beneath and sometimes pubescent on veins: fls. pale to deep pink (rarely white), about ¼in. across, in terminal much-compounded puberulous corymbs; petals much shorter than stamens: follicles glabrous. Japan. Var. **Fortunei,** Rehd. (*S. Fortunei,* Planch. *S. callosa,* Lindl. not Thunb.), taller; lvs. oblong-lanceolate, to 4 in. long, glaucous and glabrous beneath; fls. pink; E. and Cent. China. Var. **ovalifolia,** Franch., lvs. elliptic, glabrous and somewhat glaucous beneath; fls. white, in corymbs to 5 in. across; W. China.

15. **S. Bumalda,** Burv. (*S. japonica* var. *Bumalda,* Bean). Hybrid of *S. japonica* and *S. albiflora:* plants dwarf, 2 ft. or less high: lvs. ovate-lanceolate, 2–3 in. long, glabrous: fls. deep pink to white, in large flat corymbs. (*Bumalda* is a personal name: see *Staphylea Bumalda,* page 635.)—Known in cult. mostly in the var. Anthony Waterer, a compact narrow-lvd. plant with brilliant carmine fls. Var. **Froebelii,** Rehd. (*S. Froebelii,* Hort.), is taller, with ovate-oblong lvs. and bright crimson fls.

16. **S. Margaritæ,** Zabel. Hybrid of *S. japonica* and *S. superba* (*S. albiflora* × *S. corymbosa*): shrub to 5 ft., with purplish-brown finely pubescent branchlets: lvs. elliptic-ovate to narrow-elliptic, 2–3 in. long, short-acuminate, cuneate to slightly rounded at base, doubly coarse-serrate, pale beneath and usually pubescent on the veins: fls. bright rose, about ⅓in. across, in leafy pubescent corymbs; petals one-half as long as stamens: follicles glabrous.

17. **S. albiflora,** Zabel (*S. callosa* var. *albiflora,* Miq.). Little bush, 1–2 ft., with upright branches bearing short lightly pubescent somewhat angled side branchlets: lvs. lanceolate, 1½–3 in. long, acuminate, coarsely simple or sometimes doubly serrate, glabrous: fls. in summer, white, about ¼in. across, with prominent central disk, many in dense terminal nearly flat-topped aggregated corymbs, the central one of which is largest. Japan.

18. **S. bullata,** Maxim. (*S. crispifolia,* Hort.). Shrub to 1½ ft., with branchlets brown and villous while young: lvs. roundish-ovate to ovate, ½–1 in. long, sharply serrate, subglabrous, thick and puckered (bullate), grayish beneath: fls. rose, in pubescent dense corymbs; petals slightly shorter than the reddish stamens. Japan.

19. **S. salicifolia,** L. Forming a dense shrub or clump 4–6 ft. high, with yellowish-brown branches that soon become glabrous: lvs. lanceolate to oblong-lanceolate, 1–3 in. long, short-acute, tapering to very short petiole, sharply somewhat doubly serrate, glabrous: fls. pink to rose, small, about ¼in. across, in many crowded clusters aggregate into a pyramidal terminal lightly tomentose panicle, late spring and summer; petals much shorter than stamens. Eu. to Japan.

20. **S. alba,** DuRoi (*S. salicifolia* var. *paniculata*, Ait.). MEADOWSWEET. Erect shrub to 6 ft., with reddish-brown branchlets soon becoming glabrous: lvs. narrowly oblanceolate to oblong, 1–2½ in. long, acute at both ends, sharply serrate, finely pubescent on veins beneath or subglabrous: fls. white, in broad-pyramidal tomentulose leafy panicles; stamens and disk white; petals shorter than stamens: follicles glabrous. N. Y. to Mo. and Ga.

21. **S. latifolia,** Borkh. (*S. salicifolia* var. *latifolia*, Ait.). MEADOWSWEET. Erect shrub to 5 ft., with reddish-brown glabrous branches: lvs. broad-elliptic to obovate, 1–3 in. long, acute at ends, coarsely serrate, glabrous: fls. white or slightly pinkish, in broad-pyramidal glabrous panicles; stamens and disk pinkish-purple; petals shorter than stamens: follicles glabrous. Newf. to N. C.

22. **S. conspicua,** Zabel. Hybrid of *S. albiflora* and ?*S. latifolia*, forming an upright shrub 3 ft. high, with branches dark brown and thinly pubescent but becoming nearly or entirely glabrous: lvs. elliptic or elliptic-oblong, 1½–2½ in. long, very short-petioled, acute, tapering both ways, rather coarsely simply or doubly serrate, strongly veined, glabrous except on veins beneath: fls. pinkish or nearly white, small, about ¼in. across, in many dense roundish or conical lightly pubescent clusters that are usually arranged at maturity in a panicle longer than broad but at first in a more or less expanded aggregate, summer to autumn; petals shorter than stamens.

23. **S. Menziesii,** Hook. Erect shrub to 5 ft., with brownish branchlets puberulous when young: lvs. oblong to oblong-obovate, 1–3 in. long, usually obtuse at both ends, irregularly serrate above the middle, subglabrous: fls. rose, in dense narrow pubescent panicles to 8 in. long; petals less than half as long as stamens: follicles glabrous. (A. Menzies, page 399.) Alaska to Ore.

24. **S. Douglasii,** Hook. Stout shrub to 6–8 ft., making dense patches, the branches reddish-brown and tomentose: lvs. thick, oblong to long-oblong, 1–4 in. long, obtuse or acutish at apex, abruptly contracted to very short petiole, unequally serrate on upper half, essentially glabrous above but densely white-tomentose beneath: fls. deep rose, in dense tomentose panicles that are usually narrow and elongated; petals one-half as long as stamens: follicles glabrous. (Discovered more than 100 years ago by David Douglas.) B. C. to Calif.

25. **S. Billiardii,** Hérincq. Hybrid of *S. Douglasii* and *S. salicifolia:* shrub to 6 ft., with erect brown-pubescent branchlets: lvs. oblong to lance-oblong, 2–3 in. long, acute at ends, sharply more or less doubly serrate except toward the base, grayish-tomentose beneath becoming subglabrous: fls. bright pink, in pubescent narrow dense panicles to 8 in. long; petals about one-half as long as stamens: follicles glabrous. Vars. *alba* and *rosea* are listed. —Some of the material cult. under the following names may belong here: *S. Lenneana, S. richmensis, S. triumphans.*

26. **S. tomentosa,** L. HARDHACK. STEEPLEBUSH. Shrub with erect mostly simple reddish-brown tomentose branches about 4 ft. high: lvs. mostly ovate, 1–3 in. long, acute, unequally usually doubly serrate, densely yellowish- or tawny-pubescent beneath: fls. pink or purple (a white var.), in narrow dense brownish-tomentose panicles; petals somewhat shorter than stamens: follicles pubescent. N. S. to Ga. and Kans.

2. **PHYSOCARPUS,** Maxim. (*Opulaster*, Raf.). NINEBARK. A dozen or more spirea-like shrubs of N. Amer. and N. E. Asia.—From Spiræa distinguished by the inflated little pods (Physocar-pus: *bladder-fruit*), glossy often elongated seeds, stipulate lvs.: bark peeling from the branches in strips: lvs. deciduous, alternate, simple but more or less lobed: fls. many, in umbel-like clusters, white or pinkish; stamens 20–40; pistils 1–5, more or less united at base, ovary 1-celled, placenta 1, parietal, ripening into 2-valved bladdery few-seeded follicles.

A. Pistils (also fr.) 3–5, glabrous.................................1. *P. opulifolius*
AA. Pistils (also fr.) usually 2, densely stellate-pubescent.................2. *P. monogynus*

1. **P. opulifolius,** Maxim. (*Spiræa opulifolia*, L.). COMMON NINEBARK. Strong wide-recurving shrub to 10 ft.: lvs. mostly ovate in outline, 1–3 in. long, usually more or less distinctly 3-lobed, margins dentate and serrate, glabrous or becoming so: fls. white to pinkish, in corymbs 1–2 in. across in summer on leafy shoots of the season: follicles 3–5 from each fl., about ⅜in. long and conspicuous, much exceeding the acute calyx-lobes. Que. to Va., Tenn. and Mich. Var. **luteus,** Zabel (var. *aureus*, Hort. *Spiræa opulifolia lutea*, Kirchn.), has bright yellow lvs. becoming bronzy. Var. **nanus,** Zabel (*Spiræa opulifolia nana*, Kirchn.), dwarf, with smaller less deeply lobed lvs.

2. **P. monogynus,** Coult. (*Spiræa monogyna*, Torr.). Shrub to 3½ ft.: lvs. broadly ovate to reniform, ½–1½ in. long, rounded to subcordate at base, mostly 3-lobed, the lobes serrate, glabrous or nearly so: fls. pinkish to white, to ½in. across, in few-fld. umbels; calyx and pedicels stellate-pubescent: follicles 2 (1–3), densely stellate-pubescent, with spreading beaks. Wyo. to S. D., Tex. and New Mex.

3. **NEILLIA,** D. Don. About 10 ornamental shrubs in China and the Himalayan region.—Something like Spiræa but differs in fls. lacking staminal disks, in the presence of stipules (though caducous), in shining crustaceous seeds which are commonly 5 in each of 2 ovaries, and usually in the more elongated calyx: lvs. alternate, deciduous, more or less lobed: fls. in true racemes which are separate or panicled; calyx prominent, sometimes long-tubular, the 5 lobes subequal to the petals; stamens 10–30; pistils usually 2 (sometimes 1), ovary 1-celled, placenta parietal, style terminal: fr. a dehiscent not inflated follicle. (Neil-lia: Patrick Neill, 1776–1851, secretary Caledonian Hort. Soc.)

N. sinensis, Oliv. Shrub to 5–6 ft., with brown shedding bark and very slender glabrous twigs: lvs. ovate to oblong-ovate, 2–3 in. long, sharp-pointed or acuminate, usually shallowly lobed, cut-serrate, becoming nearly or quite glabrous, with slender short petioles: fls. pink or whitish, in nodding racemes 1–2 in. long, in late spring to summer; calyx tubular and glabrous, becoming glandular-bristly at maturity, ⅜–½in. long on slender shorter pedicels; petals broad, usually shorter than the pointed calyx-lobes. Cent. China.

4. **STEPHANANDRA,** Sieb. & Zucc. Four or 5 graceful ornamental deciduous shrubs in Japan and China, distinguished from Neillia by the open or cup-shaped calyx-tube, stamens persistent, pistil 1 with lateral style, fr. 1- or 2-seeded and only partially dehiscent: fls. small, dull white or greenish, in corymbs or panicles. (Stephanan-dra: Greek compound, referring to the crown of stamens.)

S. incisa, Zabel (*S. flexuosa,* Sieb. & Zucc. *Spiræa incisa,* Thunb.). Shrub with long flexuose zigzag drooping glabrous or puberulent branches, 6–8 ft. high: lvs. triangular-ovate in outline, ¾–2 (3) in. long, long-acuminate, truncate or subcordate at base, many-lobed and often almost to the midrib and the margins doubly cut-serrate, glabrous except on veins beneath: fls. small, about ⅙in. across, few in open short more or less panicled racemes, the slender pedicels much exceeding the fls.; stamens 10. Japan, Korea.

5. **FILIPENDULA,** Adans. Meadowsweet. Tall hardy herbs grown for their showy fls.; 9–10 species in north temp. zone.—Lvs. alternate, interruptedly odd-pinnately divided, with a usually enlarged terminal lobe and stipules: fls. small but many, white, pink or purple, bisexual, in large terminal panicles or cymose corymbs; calyx-lobes and petals 5 (sometimes 4 or 6); stamens many; disk not evident; pistils 5–15, ovary 1-celled, 2-ovuled: fr. little achenes in a ring or twisted together. (Filipen-dula: Latin *hanging thread,* said to allude to the way in which the root-tubers of some species hang together by threads.)

A. Lfts. 12 or more pairs, 1 in. or less long, pinnatifid.............................1. *F. hexapetala*
AA. Lfts. few, the terminal one enlarged and palmately lobed.
  B. Mature achenes spirally twisted: fls. white.............................2. *F. Ulmaria*
  BB. Mature achenes straight: fls. pink to purple, rarely whitish.
    C. Lateral lfts. dentate, not lobed, sometimes lacking.............................3. *F. purpurea*
    CC. Lateral lfts. deeply palmately lobed.............................4. *F. rubra*

1. **F. hexapetala,** Gilib. (*Spiræa Filipendula,* L. *Ulmaria Filipendula,* Hill). Dropwort. Rootstock tuberous: lvs. mostly radical, fern-like, 6–18 in. long and 1–2 in. wide, with numerous sessile pinnatifid lfts., the terminal one not enlarged: sts. 1–3 ft., with few lvs., bearing a diffuse short cluster of white fls. ¼–⅜in. across, the petals usually 6: mature achenes erect, hispid. Eu., Asia.—Has been confused with *Achillea Filipendula.* A form has double fls.

2. **F. Ulmaria,** Maxim. (*Spiræa Ulmaria,* L.). Queen-of-the-Meadow. Stout, 3–6 ft., making large patches: lvs. nearly or quite glabrous above and whitish-tomentose beneath; terminal lft. large and 3–5-palmately lobed; side lfts. of radical lvs. several pairs with small ones interposed, ovate, doubly serrate: fls. white, in dense paniculate cymes, sometimes double. Eu., Asia; somewhat nat. in N. Amer.

3. **F. purpurea,** Maxim. (*Spiræa palmata,* Thunb. and Hort.). Glabrous, 2–4 ft.: lvs. glabrous except on veins beneath, margins double-serrate; terminal lobe large, cordate or on the upper lvs. cuneate, 5–7-palmately lobed; lateral lfts. few or none, oblong-ovate, not lobed: fls. pink or purplish, in a paniculate cyme in summer, stamens exserted but not specially prominent. Japan. Var. **elegans,** Voss, has white fls. with red stamens.—Most of the material in cult. as *Spiræa palmata* is referable here. *Filipendula palmata,* Maxim. (*Spiræa palmata,* Pall.), has the lateral lfts. lobed and lvs. usually whitish-tomentose beneath, and is rarely cult.; N. E. Asia.

4. **F. rubra,** Rob. (*Ulmaria rubra,* Hill. *Spiræa palmata,* L. *S. lobata,* Gronov.). Queen-of-the-Prairie. Tall and erect, 4–8 ft., glabrous: lvs. green both sides, pubescent

only on veins beneath, margins irregularly doubly serrate; terminal lfts. large and 7–9-parted into narrow lobes 2–4 in. long; lateral lfts. also lobed, but these lfts. absent on the upper st.-lvs.: fls. attractive peach-blossom pink, in a feathery paniculate cyme in summer, stamens conspicuous. Pa. to Iowa and Ga. Var. **venusta,** Voss, has deep pink fls.

6. **SIBIRÆA,** Maxim. Two spirea-like Asian shrubs, one more or less planted.—The genus differs from Spiræa in the 2-seeded follicles connate at base, also in being polygamo-diœcious, and lvs. narrow and entire. (Sibiræ-a: Siberia.)

S. lævigata, Maxim. (*Spiræa lævigata,* L.). Shrub to 5 ft., with stout erect glabrous branches: lvs. alternate, clustered on old shoots, oblanceolate to cuneate-oblong (varying to narrow-lanceolate in var. **angustata,** Rehd.), dull or bluish-green, 1½–3 in. long to 5 in. on young shoots, obtuse but apiculate, glabrous, base narrow but semi-clasping: fls. greenish-white, small, many in terminal glabrous panicles 2–5 in. long. Siberia.

7. **LUETKEA,** Bong. A monotypic genus of W. N. Amer.—Cespitose suffrutescent per. with creeping sts.: lvs. alternate, usually twice trifid, lacking stipules: fls. bisexual, racemose; hypanthium hemispheric, with 5 acute sepals; petals 5, longer than the 20 stamens; pistils 5, distinct, subequal to stamens, ovary 1-celled, placenta parietal: follicles dehiscent on both sutures, several-seeded. (Luet-kea: in honor of Count F. P. Luetke, 1797–1882, commander of a Russian exploring expedition.)

L. pectinata, Kuntze (*Saxifraga pectinata,* Pursh). Branches long and trailing, forming dense mats, with glabrous or sparsely hairy leafy fl.-shoots to 6 in. high: lvs. dissected into linear acute lobes, less than 1 in. long including the petiole: fls. white, about ⅓in. across, in terminal racemes to 2 in. long. Alaska to Calif.

8. **ARUNCUS,** Adans. GOATS-BEARD. Two or 3 tall per. herbs in the northern hemisphere, one sometimes planted for its ample open panicles of very numerous small white fls.—Diœcious: lvs. 2–3-pinnate, lacking stipules, cauline and basal, long-stalked: fls. nearly or quite sessile on long branches of the panicle; calyx 5-lobed; petals 5, small and narrow; stamens numerous; pistils commonly 3, ovary 1-celled, placenta parietal: follicles reflexed, usually with 2 very small dull seeds. (Arun-cus: a Greek word for *goat's-beard.*)—Usually grown under the name spirea.

A. sylvester, Kostel. (*Spiræa Aruncus,* L.). Attractive erect branching herb, 4–7 ft., glabrous or somewhat pubescent, with large much-divided lvs.: lfts. ovate to broad-lanceolate, 1–4 in. long, long-acuminate, doubly sharp-serrate: fls. about ⅛in. across, on dense spike-like branches arranged in panicles 4–16 in. long; calyx-lobes broad-lanceolate, rather thin, showing the midrib; stamens long-exserted: follicles brownish, the style one-tenth to one-fifth as long as the body. Eurasia, W. N. Amer.—*A. dioicus,* Fern. (*Actæa dioica,* Walt. *Aruncus allegheniensis,* Rydb.), occurring in E. N. Amer., is distinguished by having calyx-lobes broader and more deltoid, firmer and not showing midrib; follicles olive-brown, with the style one-fourth to one-half as long as the body; also the lvs. tend to have less long-acuminate tips. The older name, *A. vulgaris,* Raf., is sometimes used in place of *A. sylvester,* but the former is a *nomen nudum* and cannot be adopted.

9. **SORBARIA,** A. Br. Woody or semi-woody plants of about 8 species in Asia.—Lvs. deciduous, alternate, odd-pinnate, serrulate, stipulate: fls. bisexual, small and numerous in terminal panicles; petals 5; stamens 20–50; pistils 5, opposite the 5 calyx-lobes, somewhat connate, forming several-seeded dehiscent follicles. (Sorbaria: resembling Sorbus in foliage.)—Sometimes called False-Spirea.

A. Plant pubescent at least on young parts: lfts. usually more than ½in. wide.
 B. Panicle dense with erect branches: frs. erect .... 1. *S. sorbifolia*
 BB. Panicle loose with spreading branches: frs. on recurved pedicels .... 2. *S. arborea*
AA. Plant glabrous throughout: lfts. mostly less than ½in. wide .... 3. *S. Aitchisonii*

1. **S. sorbifolia,** A. Br. (*Spiræa sorbifolia,* L. *Schizonotus sorbifolia,* Lindl.). Erect soft-woody bush 3–6 ft. high, spreading freely by suckers, sts. usually pubescent above: lfts. 13–23, lanceolate to oblong-lanceolate, long-acuminate, doubly sharp-serrate, often stellate-pubescent beneath when young: fls. white with center reddish or yellowish, about ⅓in. across, in close or dense terminal panicles 4–10 in. long; hypanthium glabrous; petals rounded, clawed; stamens 40–50, twice as long as petals; pistils and frs. glabrous, on erect pedicels. Ural region to Japan; common in yards and often escaped. Var. **stellipila,** Maxim. (*S. stellipila,* Schneid.), is very similar but with lvs. more markedly stellate-pubescent beneath, pubescent calyx-tube, pistils and frs.; E. Asia.

2. **S. arborea,** Schneid. Spreading shrub to 18 ft., with sts. usually stellate-pubescent: lfts. 13–17, ovate-oblong to lanceolate, long-acuminate, doubly sharp-serrate, stellate-

pubescent to subglabrous beneath: fls. white, about ¼in. across, in loose panicles with spreading branches, to 12 in. long and 8 in. broad; stamens much longer than petals: frs. on recurved pedicels. China.

3. **S. Aitchisonii,** Hemsl. (*Spiræa Aitchisonii,* Hemsl.). Shrub to 10 ft., with glabrous branches which are usually purplish-red when young: lfts. 15–21, lanceolate to linear, acuminate, simply or somewhat doubly sharp-serrate, glabrous: fls. white, about ⅜in. across, in erect glabrous panicles to 10 in. long and 6 in. wide; stamens longer than petals. (Named for Dr. J. E. T. Aitchison, page 38.) W. Asia.

10. **GILLENIA,** Moench (*Porteranthus,* Britt.). Two erect per. herbs of E. N. Amer., adaptable for ornament.—Lvs. 3-foliolate or 3-parted, sessile or short-stalked, sharp-serrate or cut, stipulate: fls. bisexual, with showy white or pinkish narrow petals, borne on long pedicels in loose paniculate corymbs; hypanthium cylindric or deep cup-shaped, somewhat constricted at throat, persistent, with 5 sepals; petals 5, unequal; stamens 10–20, included; pistils 5, opposite the calyx-lobes, lightly connate but becoming distinct, ripening into 2–4-seeded follicles. (Gille-nia: Arnold Gille, Latinized Gillenius or Gilenius, German physician, who wrote on hort. in 1627.)

A. Stipules small and awl-shaped........1. *G. trifoliata*
AA. Stipules broad and lf.-like........2. *G. stipulata*

1. **G. trifoliata,** Moench (*Spiræa trifoliata,* L.). INDIAN PHYSIC. Erect, branching, 2–4 ft. high, glabrous or slightly pubescent, with slender reddish sts.: lfts. 3, ovate-oblong to lanceolate, 2–3 in. long, long-acuminate, serrate; stipules small and awl-shaped, entire or serrate: fls. nearly 1 in. across, with very narrow petals. Ont. to Ga. and Mo.

2. **G. stipulata,** Trel. (*Spiræa stipulata,* Muhl.). AMERICAN IPECAC. Similar to the preceding, but differs in being more pubescent: lfts. narrower and more deeply serrate, sometimes becoming pinnatifid; stipules lf.-like, ⅓–1 in. long and often as broad, sharply incised-serrate: fls. slightly smaller. N. Y. to Ga. and La.

11. **EXOCHORDA,** Lindl. PEARL-BUSH. Three or 4 shrubs in Asia.—Spirea-like, but individual fls. as large as apple-blossoms, fr. a 5-angled or -winged caps. that separates into 5 bony 1- or 2-seeded carpels, and the seeds wing-flattened: deciduous: lvs. alternate, simple, petioled: fls. white, more or less unisexual (polygamo-diœcious), in terminal racemes; hypanthium broadly top-shaped, with a large disk; sepals and petals 5; stamens 15–30, inserted at the margin of the disk; pistils 5, connate but the styles distinct. (Exoch-orda: Greek *external cord,* referring to an internal structure in the carpels.)

A. Stamens 15–25; petals broad, abruptly contracted to claw........1. *E. racemosa*
AA. Stamens 20–30; petals narrow, gradually tapering to claw........2. *E. Giraldii*

1. **E. racemosa,** Rehd. (*E. grandiflora,* Hook. *Amelanchier racemosa,* Lindl.). Slender glabrous shrub 8–10 ft. and more high, much-branched, bearing a profusion of clear white fls. in mid-spring: lvs. elliptic to oblong-obovate, blades 1½–2½ in. long and petioles about ½in. long, obtuse but apiculate at apex, shortly narrowed at base, those on flowering shoots usually entire but those on verdurous parts obscurely serrate on upper half: fls. 1½–2 in. across, 6–10 in a raceme, on pedicels ¼in. or less long; petals roundish to broad-obovate, rather abruptly short-clawed; stamens 15–25: fr. ⅜in. or less long and nearly or quite as broad, ovoid to broad top-shaped, scarcely pointed. China.

2. **E. Giraldii,** Hesse. Larger and more vigorous than no. 1, the fls. shorter-pedicelled, open in the center or more stellate because of the narrower and longer-clawed petals that do not meet or overlap, petals sometimes 2–4-toothed at apex; stamens 20–30: lvs. oval or elliptic, not serrate or only exceptionally so, petiole ½–1 in. long, slender and reddish: fr. ⅜–½in. long. China; intro. to Eu. by seeds collected by the missionary, Father Giraldi. Var. **Wilsonii,** Rehd. (*E. racemosa* var. *Wilsonii,* Rehd.), more upright and floriferous; petioles green; fls. 2 in. across, stamens 20–25; fr. to ⅝in. long; named for E. H. Wilson, page 54; China.

12. **HOLODISCUS,** Maxim. (*Sericotheca* and *Schizonotus,* Raf.). About 8 species of spirea-like shrubs of W. N. Amer., one sometimes planted for ornament.—Deciduous, usually pubescent: lvs. alternate, simple but often deeply lobed, stipules lacking: fls. many and small, white or whitish, in terminal panicles or racemes; hypanthium cup-shaped, with 5 sepals valvate in the bud; petals 5; stamens about 20, inserted on the entire disk; pistils 5, alternate with sepals: fr. of 5 pubescent or hairy achenes inclosed in the calyx. (Holodis-cus: Greek referring to the *entire disk* in the fl.)—Sometimes called Rock-Spirea.

H. discolor, Maxim. (*Spiræa discolor*, Pursh. *S. ariæfolia*, Smith). Spreading shrub to 20 ft., with young twigs pubescent and yellowish: lvs. ovate to ovate-oblong, 1¾–4 in. long, truncate or cuneate at base, doubly dentate with the first dentations deep and lobulate, green and subglabrous above, paler and villous to tomentose beneath: fls. creamy-white, many in dense villous panicles 3–10 in. long and as wide; stamens longer than sepals. B. C. to Mont. and Calif. Var. **franciscanus,** Jepson (*Sericotheca franciscana*, Rydb.), differs in having lvs. 1¼–1¾ in. long and smaller panicles; S. Ore. to Calif.

13. **COTONEASTER,** Medic. Old World temp.-region woody plants, grown for ornament; about 50 species.—Shrubs or seldom tree-like, evergreen or deciduous, not truly spiny, often with pubescent or tomentose parts: lvs. mostly small and numerous, alternate, short-petioled, simple and entire, stipulate: fls. white or pink, small but numerous, solitary or in cymose clusters terminating lateral spurs, appearing in late spring and summer after the lvs. are out; hypanthium adnate to ovary; sepals (calyx-lobes) 5, small, persistent on the fr.; petals 5; stamens about 20; pistil 1, ovary 2–5-celled, placentation axile, styles 2–5 and distinct: fr. a red or blackish pome, small, with 2–5 nutlets, mostly long-persistent and ornamental, appearing in summer and autumn and often attractive in winter. (Cotoneas-ter: Latin *quince-like*, from the lvs. of some species.)

A. Lvs. mostly ½in. or less long, sometimes to ¾in. (to 1 in. in a var. of no. 1): fls. 1–3 to a cluster (3–8 in a var. of no. 30).
B. Foliage evergreen: petals spreading, white (tinged pink in no. 32).
C. Length of lvs. ⅜in. or more: fls. 1–3 or more to a cluster .... 30. *C. rotundifolia*
CC. Length of lvs. (of the fl.-sts.) mostly less than ⅜in.: fls. usually solitary.
D. Fls. pure white: fr. ¼in. long .... 31. *C. microphylla*
DD. Fls. tinged pink in bud: fr. ⅜in. long .... 32. *C. conspicua*
BB. Foliage deciduous or half-evergreen: petals erect, pink (whitish in no. 3).
C. Fr. purple-black .... 7. *C. nitens*
CC. Fr. red.
D. Habit prostrate, height usually less than 2 ft.
E. Sts. appressed to ground, irregularly branched: nutlets usually 2 .... 1. *C. adpressa*
EE. Sts. spreading horizontally, distichously branched: nutlets usually 3 .... 2. *C. horizontalis*
DD. Habit erect, height 4–8 ft.
E. Lf. dull and pubescent above: fls. white with pink center .... 3. *C. disticha*
EE. Lf. shining and soon glabrous above: fls. pink.
F. Fls. usually solitary: frs. subsessile, subglobose .... 4. *C. apiculata*
FF. Fls. usually 3: frs. short-pedicelled, ellipsoid .... 6. *C. divaricata*
AA. Lvs. ¾–5 in. long: fls. 2 to many to a cluster (usually solitary in no. 29).
B. Fr. black.
C. Lf. 1½–4 in. long, more or less acuminate, usually puckered or with the veins impressed.
D. Calyx lightly pubescent: fls. many to a cluster .... 15. *C. moupinensis*
DD. Calyx densely pubescent: fls. 3–6 to a cluster .... 16. *C. foveolata*
CC. Lf. ¾–2 in. long, usually acute, flat.
D. Calyx pubescent: nutlets usually 2 .... 17. *C. acutifolia*
DD. Calyx subglabrous: nutlets 3–4 .... 18. *C. lucida*
BB. Fr. red.
C. Shrub prostrate with trailing often rooting branches .... 29. *C. Dammeri*
CC. Shrub erect or spreading to 6 ft. and more.
D. Lf. glabrous beneath or with scattered pubescence at maturity (thinly tomentulose in no. 20).
E. Fls. 2–7 to a cluster, rarely more.
F. Length of lvs. ¾–1½ in.: fls. white.
G. Shape of fr. obovoid: lvs. pubescent above while young .... 5. *C. Simonsii*
GG. Shape of fr. subglobose: lvs. glabrous above .... 20. *C. hupehensis*
FF. Length of lvs. 1½–3 in.: fls. pinkish.
G. Foliage flat: calyx pubescent: nutlets 2 .... 13. *C. acuminata*
GG. Foliage puckered: calyx glabrous: nutlets 4–5 .... 14. *C. bullata*
EE. Fls. many to a cluster (not setting numerous frs. in no. 19).
F. Length of lvs. ¾–2 in.
G. Pedicels and calyx glabrous .... 19. *C. multiflora*
GG. Pedicels and calyx villous .... 24. *C. Harroviana*
FF. Length of lvs. 2–5 in.
G. The lf. two to two and a half times as long as broad .... 22. *C. frigida*
GG. The lf. three to four times as long as broad .... 28. *C. Henryana*
DD. Lf. distinctly tomentose beneath at maturity (becoming subglabrous in vars. of nos. 21 and 27).
E. Calyx glabrous .... 8. *C. integerrima*
EE. Calyx pubescent or tomentose.
F. Length of lvs. 1¼–3¼ in.
G. Foliage deciduous: fls. pinkish, with erect petals .... 9. *C. tomentosa*
GG. Foliage evergreen or half-evergreen: fls. white, with spreading petals.
H. Shape of lvs. elliptic-oblong to lanceolate-ovate, acute or acuminate .... 27. *C. salicifolia*

HH. Shape of lvs. elliptic to broadly obovate, obtuse and mucronate.
I. Fr. subglobose, ⅜in. or more long........................ 25. *C. Parneyi*
II. Fr. ovoid, ¼in. long........................ 26. *C. lactea*
FF. Length of lvs. 1¼ in. or less.
G. Fls. white, with spreading petals: lvs. white- or gray-tomentose beneath.
H. Foliage deciduous, suborbicular to oval: fls. 3–12; anthers yellow........................ 21. *C. racemiflora*
HH. Foliage half-evergreen, elliptic to oval: fls. 6–20; anthers purple........................ 23. *C. pannosa*
GG. Fls. pinkish, with erect petals: lvs. yellow- or gray-tomentose beneath.
H. Foliage half-evergreen, acute to acuminate: fls. 5–15: fr. orange-red........................ 12. *C. Franchetii*
HH. Foliage deciduous, obtuse or acutish: fls. 3–9: fr. bright red.
I. Nutlets usually 2: fr. obovoid........................ 10. *C. Zabelii*
II. Nutlets 3–5: fr. subglobose........................ 11. *C. Dielsiana*

1. **C. adpressa,** Bois (*C. horizontalis* var. *adpressa*, Schneid.). Deciduous prostrate shrub with creeping irregularly branched sts.: lvs. broad-oval to obovate, ¼–½in. long, mucronulate, margins usually wavy, dull green above, with scattered pubescence beneath while young: fls. pinkish, 1–2 together, subsessile: fr. bright red, subglobose, about ¼in. long, usually with 2 nutlets. W. China. Var. **præcox,** Bois & Berthault (*C. præcox*, Vilm.), more vigorous, to 1½ ft. high; lvs. to 1 in. long; fr. ⅜–½in. thick.

2. **C. horizontalis,** Decne. Deciduous or half-evergreen shrub of squat habit and horizontal pubescent branches which are distichously branched: lvs. roundish to broad-oval, ½in. or less long, mucronate, glabrous and shining above, lightly hairy beneath: fls. pinkish, 1–2 together, subsessile: fr. globose or ovoid, about ⅕in. across, bright red, usually containing 3 nutlets. China. Var. **perpusilla,** Schneid., lower growing, with lvs. about ¼in. long. Var. **Wilsonii,** Wils., similar to the preceding var. but more vigorous; some of the material cult. as *C. Wilsonii* may belong here; *C. Wilsonii*, Nakai, grows to 4 ft. high and has white fls. in panicled clusters.

3. **C. disticha,** Lange (*C. rotundifolia*, Wall. not Lindl.). Deciduous or half-evergreen shrub to 8 ft., upright with the sts. often distichously branched: lvs. suborbicular to broad-obovate, ⅓–½in. long, rounded and mucronate at apex, broad-cuneate at base, dark green above, lighter beneath, scattered pubescence on both sides while young which is denser above: fls. white with a pink center, usually solitary, short-pedicelled; calyx glabrous: fr. bright red, broad-obovoid, about ⅜in. long. Himalayas, China.

4. **C. apiculata,** Rehd. & Wils. Deciduous shrub 4–6 ft. high, the young sts. yellow-strigose: lvs. suborbicular to orbicular-ovate, to ⅝in. long, apiculate, rounded or broad-cuneate at base, glabrous and shining above, paler and somewhat pubescent beneath at least while young: fls. pink, usually solitary: fr. red, subsessile, subglobose, ¼–⅜in. across. China.

5. **C. Simonsii,** Baker. Deciduous or half-evergreen erect shrub to 10 ft. or more, with young growth woolly: lvs. roundish-oval, ¾–1¼ in. long, acute or somewhat acuminate, broad-cuneate, dark green and glabrescent above, paler and pubescent beneath on veins: fls. white, in 2–4-fld. clusters; calyx appressed-pubescent: fr. bright red, mostly obovoid, about ⅜in. long. (Named for Mr. Simons, collector in Khasia Hills.) Himalayas.

6. **C. divaricata,** Rehd. & Wils. Deciduous upright shrub to 6 ft., with spreading branches: lvs. elliptic, ⅜–¾in. long, acute at both ends, shining dark green and glabrate above, lighter and usually pubescent beneath: fls. pink, 3 together, short-pedicelled; calyx pubescent: fr. red, ellipsoid, ⅓in. long; nutlets 2 (1–3). China.

7. **C. nitens,** Rehd. & Wils. Deciduous shrub 2–4 ft. high, with densely branched spreading branches, the young growth yellow-strigose: lvs. oval to suborbicular, ½ (⅜–¾) in. long, usually rounded at ends, rarely mucronate, green and shining above, paler beneath and glabrescent: fls. pink, usually 3 together; calyx somewhat pubescent: fr. purple-black, pendent on short pedicels, subglobose, about ⅓in. long; nutlets 1–2. China.

8. **C. integerrima,** Medic. (*C. vulgaris*, Lindl.). Erect deciduous shrub of bushy growth, 3–6 ft., with tomentose young growth: lvs. ovate to oval to almost orbicular, ¾–2 in. long, mucronulate and acute or rounded at apex, glabrous or nearly so above, whitish- or grayish-tomentose beneath: fls. white with rose tint, 2–4 together in nodding clusters, the calyx glabrous outside: fr. red, globular, ¼in. across; nutlets usually 2. Eu., Siberia.

9. **C. tomentosa,** Lindl. (*Mespilus tomentosa*, Ait.). Similar to *C. integerrima:* shrub to 10 ft.: lvs. broad-oval to elliptic, to 2½ in. long, usually obtuse at apex, pubescent above while young, whitish- or grayish-tomentose beneath: fls. pinkish, 3–12 together in nodding clusters; calyx tomentose: fr. brick-red, subglobose, about ⅓in. across; nutlets 3–5. S. E. Eu., W. Asia.

10. **C. Zabelii,** Schneid. Deciduous shrub to 6 ft., with slender spreading branches: lvs. oval to ovate, ¾–1½ in. long, usually obtuse, dull green with scattered pubescence above, grayish- or yellowish-tomentose beneath: fls. pinkish, in 3–9-fld. nodding clusters; calyx villous becoming more or less glabrous: fr. bright red, mostly obovoid, about ⅓in. long; nutlets usually 2. (For H. Zabel, page 54.) China.

11. **C. Dielsiana,** Pritz. (*C. applanata,* Duthie). Deciduous shrub, 6–8 ft., with very slender and long arching or pendulous branches, the growing parts at first tomentose: lvs. ovate or elliptic, 1 in. or less long, somewhat acute, the base rounded or broad-cuneate, veins prominent, at first hairy above, yellowish- or grayish-tomentose beneath: fls. pinkish, 3–7 on short lateral spurs, ripening 1–3 subglobose scarlet frs. about ¼in. long; nutlets 3–5. (Bears the name of Dr. L. Diels, page 42.) China. Var. **major,** Rehd., has broader and larger lvs.

12. **C. Franchetii,** Bois. Half-evergreen shrub, 8–10 ft., with spreading arching branches, the young growth tomentose: lvs. oval to ovate, 1¼ in. or less long, acute or acuminate, narrowed at base, somewhat hairy above when young but becoming glossy, lower surface yellowish-or grayish-tomentose: fls. pinkish, 5–15 in short close clusters on lateral branchlets to 1½ in. long; calyx villous: fr. orange-red, about ¼in. long, bearing mostly 3 nutlets. (Dedicated to Adrien Franchet, page 43.) W. China.

13. **C. acuminata,** Lindl. Erect deciduous shrub to 12 ft., the young shoots woolly: lvs. ovate-oblong, mostly 1½–2½ in. long, acute or acuminate, dark green and appressed-hairy above, paler and more pubescent beneath becoming subglabrous: fls. pinkish, in clusters of 2–5 on short leafy spurs; calyx pubescent: fr. scarlet, oblong to ellipsoid, ⅜in. long, bearing 2 nutlets. Himalayas.

14. **C. bullata,** Bois. Deciduous spreading shrub to 6 ft., with young branches pubescent: lvs. elliptic-ovate to ovate-oblong, 1½–3 in. long, acuminate, broad-cuneate at base, subglabrous above, usually pubescent beneath especially on the veins, wrinkled or somewhat puckered: fls. pinkish, 3–7; calyx glabrous: fr. red, subglobose to obovoid, ¼in. or more long; nutlets 4–5. China.

15. **C. moupinensis,** Franch. Deciduous spreading shrub to 15 ft.: lvs. elliptic-ovate to ovate-oblong, 1½–4 in. long, acuminate, usually broad-cuneate, dull green and puckered above, paler and more pubescent beneath: fls. pinkish, in many-fld. clusters; calyx somewhat pubescent: fr. black, subglobose to obovoid, ¼in. or more long; nutlets 4–5. China.

16. **C. foveolata,** Rehd. & Wils. Deciduous spreading shrub to 10 ft., the young growth densely pubescent: lvs. elliptic-ovate to ovate-oblong, 1½–3 in. long, acute to acuminate, broad-cuneate to rounded at base, becoming glabrous above, pubescent beneath, sometimes becoming subglabrous, veins impressed above: fls. pinkish, 3–6 together; calyx densely pubescent: fr. black, subglobose, ¼in. or more long; nutlets 3–4. China.

17. **C. acutifolia,** Turcz. (*C. pekinensis,* Zabel). Deciduous spreading shrub to 12 ft., the young branchlets pubescent: lvs. elliptic-ovate, ¾–2 in. long, usually acute, broad-cuneate, dull green and glabrescent above, paler and more pubescent beneath: fls. pinkish, in 2–5-fld. clusters; calyx-tube pubescent: fr. black, ellipsoidal, about ⅜in. long; nutlets usually 2. China. Var. **villosula,** Rehd. & Wils., lvs. larger, villous beneath; calyx-tube more densely villous; fr. slightly pubescent.

18. **C. lucida,** Schlecht. (*C. acutifolia,* Lindl. not Turcz.). Similar to the preceding: deciduous erect shrub to 10 ft.: lvs. glabrous and lustrous above: fls. pinkish, in 3–8-fld. clusters; calyx-tube glabrous or subglabrous: fr. black, subglobose to obovoid, about ⅜in. long; nutlets 3–4. Altai Mts.

19. **C. multiflora,** Bunge. Deciduous shrub to 6 ft., the branches arching; branchlets purplish, soon glabrous: lvs. broad-ovate to ovate, ¾–2 in. long, acute or obtuse, usually rounded at base, tomentose beneath becoming glabrous: fls. white, about ½in. across, in many-fld. loose rounded clusters; calyx glabrous: fr. red, subglobose to obovoid, about ⅓in. across; nutlets 1–2. China.

20. **C. hupehensis,** Rehd. & Wils. Deciduous spreading shrub to 6 ft., with arching branches; branchlets purple, soon glabrous: lvs. elliptic to ovate, ¾–1½ in. long, mucronulate, glabrous above, thinly gray-tomentose beneath: fls. white, about ⅜in. across, in 3–7(12)-fld. clusters; calyx villous: fr. bright red, lightly bloomy, subglobose, about ⅓in. across; nutlets 2. China.

21. **C. racemiflora,** Koch (*Mespilus racemiflora,* Desf. *C. nummularia,* Fisch. & Mey.). Deciduous usually spreading shrub to 8 ft., with the young growth gray-tomentose: lvs. suborbicular to oval, ¾–1¼ in. long, mucronulate, glabrous above, gray- or white-tomentose beneath: fls. white, in 3–12-fld. tomentose clusters: fr. red, subglobose, about ⅓in. across; nutlets 2. S. Eu., N. Afr., Asia. Var. **soongorica,** Schneid. (*C. nummularia* var. *soongorica,* Regel & Herd.), has oval mucronate lvs. which are less pubescent.

22. **C. frigida,** Lindl. Deciduous or half-evergreen tall shrub or small tree to 20 ft. or more, the branchlets soon glabrous: lvs. elliptic to oblong-obovate, 2½–5 in. long, obtuse or acute, cuneate, dull and glabrous above, paler beneath and tomentose usually becoming glabrous: fls. white, about ⅓in. across, in dense tomentose clusters to 2½ in. across: fr. bright red, subglobose, about ¼in. long; nutlets 2. Himalayas.—Not hardy N.

23. **C. pannosa,** Franch. Half-evergreen shrub, 6–10 ft., with arching branches, the young growth tomentose: lvs. elliptic to oval, 1 in. or less long, acute at both ends, dull and glabrous above, white-tomentose beneath: fls. white, about ⅓in. across, in 6–20-fld. pubescent clusters to 1½ in. across: fr. red, usually globose, about ¼in. long; nutlets 2. S. W. China.—Not hardy N. Var. **nana,** Hort., is listed as a dwarf.

24. **C. Harroviana,** Wils. Half-evergreen shrub to 6 ft., with curved branches, the young growth soon glabrous: lvs. elliptic to elliptic-oblong, 1–2 in. long, acute and mucronate, cuneate, green and shining above, densely villous beneath becoming more or less glabrous: fls. white, in dense villous clusters to 1½ in. across: fr. red. (Named for George Harrow, manager Veitch's Coombs Wood nursery, England.) China.

25. **C. Parneyi,** Hort. Evergreen shrub to 7 ft. or more, the young growth tomentose: lvs. elliptic to broadly obovate, 1¼–3 in. long, rounded and mucronulate, mostly cuneate at base, glabrous above, densely whitish-tomentose beneath: fls. white tinged pink in bud, in dense tomentose clusters to 2½ in. across: fr. red, subglobose, about ⅜in. long.

26. **C. lactea,** W. W. Smith. Evergreen shrub to 12 ft., with branchlets loosely white-tomentose the first season: lvs. broad-elliptic, 1½–3 in. long, usually obtuse and mucronulate at apex, rounded or cuneate at base, dull green above, white- to yellowish-tomentose beneath: fls. white, in tomentose clusters 1½–2½ in. across: fr. red, ovoid, about ¼in. long; nutlets 2. China.

27. **C. salicifolia,** Franch. More or less evergreen shrub to 15 ft., the young growth tomentose: lvs. elliptic-oblong to lance-ovate, 1–3 in. long, acute to acuminate, cuneate, glabrous and wrinkled above, tomentose beneath: fls. white, in woolly clusters to 2 in. across: fr. bright red, subglobose, about ¼in. across; nutlets 2–3. China. Var. **floccosa,** Rehd. & Wils., lvs. oblong to oblong-lanceolate, tomentose beneath becoming partly glabrous; nutlets usually 3.

28. **C. Henryana,** Rehd. & Wils. (*C. rugosa* var. *Henryana*, Schneid.). Semi-evergreen shrub to 12 ft., the branchlets arching: lvs. oblong to oblong-lanceolate, 2–5 in. long, acute both ways, glabrate above, grayish-tomentose beneath becoming more or less glabrous except on the veins: fls. white, in pubescent loose clusters to 1½ in. or more across: fr. dark red, ovoid, about ¼in. long; nutlets 2–3. (A. Henry, page 45.) China.—Not hardy N.

29. **C. Dammeri,** Schneid. (*C. humifusa*, Duthie). Evergreen prostrate shrub, the branches trailing and often rooting, twigs soon glabrous: lvs. elliptic to elliptic-oblong, ¾–1¼ in. long, acutish and mucronulate, cuneate, glabrous and shining above, paler and strigose beneath becoming somewhat glabrous: fls. white, about ⅜in. across, usually solitary; calyx commonly pubescent: fr. bright red, subglobose, about ¼in. across; nutlets usually 5. (Bears the name of Udo Dammer, 1860–1920, German botanist.) China.

30. **C. rotundifolia,** Lindl. (*C. prostrata*, Baker). Evergreen shrub to 12 ft., with long arching branches: lvs. mostly broad-oval, ⅜–¾in. long, somewhat rounded and mucronulate at apex, broad-cuneate at base, shining above, sparingly pubescent below: fls. white, almost ½in. across, 1–3 together; calyx sparingly pubescent: fr. red, subglobose, about ⅓in. across; nutlets 2. Himalayas.—Probably not hardy N. Some of the material cult. as *C. rotundifolia* is *C. disticha.* Var. **lanata,** Schneid. (*C. microphylla* var. *buxifolia* forma *lanata*, Dipp. *C. buxifolia*, Baker not Lindl.), lvs. elliptic to elliptic-oblong, tomentose beneath; fls. 3–8; *C. buxifolia*, Lindl., is a low compact shrub distinguished by having the lvs. tomentose but not papillose beneath; rarely cult.

31. **C. microphylla,** Lindl. Evergreen low spreading shrub 2–3 ft. high: lvs. obovate to cuneate-oblong, ⅓in. or less long, usually obtuse, cuneate, shining above, tomentose beneath: fls. white, about ⅜in. across, usually solitary; calyx pubescent: fr. red, globose, about ¼in. across. Himalayas. Var. **thymifolia,** Koehne (*C. thymæfolia*, Baker), lvs. narrower, fls. smaller, 2–4 in a cluster.—*C. congesta*, Baker (*C. microphylla* var. *glacialis*, Hook.), is sometimes cult. and is distinguished by its dull lvs. to ½in. long, becoming glabrous beneath; fls. pinkish-white, ¼in. across; Himalayas.

32. **C. conspicua,** Marquand. Evergreen spreading shrub to 6 ft., branchlets whitish-villous becoming subglabrous: lvs. elliptic-oblong, ¼–⅜ (¾) in. long, obtuse and usually mucronulate, pubescence scattered above, dense beneath: fls. white tinged pink in bud, about ⅜in. across, solitary: fr. scarlet, subglobose to obovoid, about ⅜in. long; nutlets 2. China. Var. **decora,** Russell (*C. decora*, Hort.), prostrate shrub with ascending branches.

14. **PYRACANTHA,** Roem. FIRETHORN. About a half dozen known hard-wooded evergreen shrubs of S. E. Eu. and Asia.—Closely allied to Cotoneaster and Cratægus: from the former distinguished by the presence of thorns, by usually serrate or crenate lvs., fls. in corymbs; pistil 1 (actually of 5 pistils ventrally connate or coherent along basal half and 5-celled basally, separating at maturity); fr. with 5 nutlets; from Cratægus it is separated by bearing 2 fertile ovules (rather than 1) in each cell, as also by the leafy thorns, unlobed lvs. which are persistent. (Pyracan-tha: Greek *fire* and *thorn*, from the red frs. and spiny branches.)

A. Calyx and under side of lvs. grayish-tomentose.......................... 1. *P. angustifolia*
AA. Calyx and under side of lvs. glabrous or lightly pubescent.
  B. Corymbs pubescent: lvs. mostly narrow-elliptic, acute.................. 2. *P. coccinea*
  BB. Corymbs subglabrous (except in var. of no. 3): lvs. oblong to obovate-oblong or oblanceolate, usually obtuse (except in no. 3).
    C. Lvs. acutish and mucronate, oblong to oblong-lanceolate.............. 3. *P. crenulata*

cc. Lvs. obtuse and often emarginate, generally obovate-oblong.
D. Lf.-margins entire....................4. *P. Koidzumii*
DD. Lf.-margins crenate-serrate (sometimes very slightly so)....................5. *P. crenato-serrata*

1. **P. angustifolia,** Schneid. (*Cotoneaster angustifolia*, Franch.). Stout somewhat thorny shrub to 12 ft., sometimes prostrate: lvs. narrow-oblong to oblanceolate-oblong, ¾–2 in. long, obtuse and mucronulate, margins revolute and entire or obscurely toothed toward apex, dark green and becoming glabrous above, grayish-tomentose beneath: fls. white, ⅓in. across, in rather dense tomentose corymbs to 1½ in. across: fr. orange to brick-red, subglobose, to ⅓in. across. China.

2. **P. coccinea,** Roem. (*Cotoneaster Pyracantha*, Spach. *Cratægus Pyracantha*, Borkh.). FIERY THORN. EVERLASTING THORN. Shrub to 6 ft., rarely to 20 ft., the young parts grayish-pubescent: lvs. mostly narrow-elliptic, ¾–2 in. long, acute, rarely obtusish, finely crenate-serrate, sometimes pubescent beneath when young: fls. white, ⅓in. across, in many-fld. corymbs to 1½ in. across, peduncle and pedicels pubescent: fr. bright red, subglobose, about ¼in. diam. S. Eu. to W. Asia; sometimes escaped in N. Amer. Var. **Lalandii,** Dipp., more vigorous and hardier, lvs. less deeply crenate, fr. larger and orange-red; originated with M. Lalande, Angers, France. —Used for hedges, and nearly evergreen as far north as N. Y.

3. **P. crenulata,** Roem. (*Cratægus crenulata*, Roxb. *Cotoneaster crenulata*, Wenz.). Shrub or small tree, with young twigs rusty-pubescent: lvs. oblong to oblanceolate, ¾–2 in. long, acute or obtusish and mucronate, crenate-serrulate, shining above, glabrous: fls. white, ⅓in. across, in glabrous corymbs to 1¼ in. across: fr. orange-red, subglobose, ¼–⅓in. across. Himalayas. Var. **kansuensis,** Rehd. (*P. kansuensis*, Hort.), lvs. narrow-oblong to oblanceolate, ⅜–1 in. long; corymbs pubescent; fr. smaller; N. W. China. Var. **Rogersiana,** A. B. Jackson (*P. Rogersiana*, Chittenden. *P. Rogersiana* forma *aurantiaca*, Bean), shrub to about 10 ft.; lvs. oblanceolate, ¾–1¾ in. long, unequally serrulate; fr. reddish-orange (yellow in a form), ⅓in. across.—Not as hardy as *P. coccinea*.

4. **P. Koidzumii,** Rehd. (*Cotoneaster Koizumii*, Hayata. *C. formosana*, Hayata. *P. formosana*, Kanehira). Shrub with grayish-pubescent branchlets which become glabrous: lvs. clustered at tips of short branchlets, oblong-obovate, 1–2 in. long, emarginate and rounded to truncate at apex, tapering at base to a short petiole, entire, becoming glabrous above, pale and more or less pubescent beneath: fls. white, ¼in. or more across, in bracteate nearly glabrous infl. 1 in. or more across; calyx lightly pubescent, with 5 triangular lobes: fr. red, depressed-globose, about ¼in. across. (For G. Koidzumi, page 46.) Formosa.

5. **P. crenato-serrata,** Rehd. (*Photinia crenato-serrata*, Hance. *Pyracantha yunnanensis*, Chittenden. *P. crenulata* var. *yunnanensis*, Mott. *P. Gibbsii*, Rehd. not A. B. Jackson). Shrub to 10 ft., the young branches rusty-pubescent: lvs. obovate or elliptic to obovate-oblong, 1–1½ in. long, rounded or acute at tip, crenate and serrate, shining and dark green above, paler beneath: fls. white, ⅜in. across, the infl. to 1½ in. across: fr. coral-red, subglobose, about ¼in. across. China.—*P. atalantioides*, Stapf (*Sportella atalantioides*, Hance. *P. Gibbsii*, A. B. Jackson. *P. discolor*, Rehd.), is sometimes cult.; distinguished by having the lvs. widest at or below the middle, acutish, and glaucescent beneath; fr. scarlet or bright crimson; China.

15. **MESPILUS,** L. MEDLAR. One deciduous small tree, grown for its edible fr., native of Eu. and Asia Minor.—Distinguished from Cratægus and Pyrus in bearing large solitary fls. on leafy shoots of the season, in the large leafy calyx-lobes and specially in the open-topped fr., the 5 carpels not being covered and the stones readily detached, the apex presenting a hairy disk or crater with the remains of the calyx-lobes about it. (Mes-pilus: old Greek name.)

M. germanica, L. (*Pyrus germanica*, Hook. f.). Crooked-growing tree or large shrub to 20 ft., often thorny, young growth hairy: lvs. simple, lance-oblong to oval-oblong, 3–5 in. long, very short-stalked, abruptly or somewhat gradually pointed, finely serrulate, pubescent, becoming nearly or quite glabrous above: fls. 1–1½ in. across, white, appearing after the foliage: fr. apple-shaped, 1–2 in. diam., without pedicel, eaten after frost and when incipient decay (bletting) has begun.

16. **CRATÆGUS,** L. HAWTHORN. Hardwooded usually thorny small trees and large shrubs sometimes planted for ornament and for hedges and one prized in the Orient for its edible frs. and somewhat intro. into N. Amer.; native in the north temp. zone, with the greatest extension in E. N. Amer.; about 1,000 species have been described, and any number are likely to be transferred to grounds, but very few are cult. plants.—Lvs. alternate, usually deciduous, simple, commonly lobed and rarely pinnatifid, stipulate: fls. white to red, mostly in cymose corymbs terminating short lateral leafy shoots; sepals and petals 5, inserted on a disk in the margin

of the hypanthium; stamens 5–25, in 1, 2, or 3 rows; pistil 1, ovary 1–5-celled, placentation typically axile, carpels 1–5, ovary enveloped by the hypanthium and adnate to it, fertile ovule 1 in each cell: fr. a small pome with 1–5 bony 1-seeded nutlets, red, yellow, or nearly black. (Cratæ-gus: Greek *strength*, from the strong wood.)

A. Lvs. distinctly lobed, with veins extending to the sinuses as well as to the points of the lobes.
  B. Base of lf. truncate to subcordate.
    C. Lf. mostly triangular-ovate, with the sinuses extending not more than half way to the midrib: spines to 3 in. long: fr. ⅓in. across.............. 9. *C. Phænopyrum*
    CC. Lf. mostly rhombic-ovate, with the sinuses of the lowest lobes extending almost to the midrib: spines short or lacking: fr. ⅝in. across............15. *C. pinnatifida*
  BB. Base of lf. cuneate.
    C. Nutlets 3–5, with plain or flat faces: lvs. mostly 2–4 in. long............15. *C. pinnatifida*
    CC. Nutlets 1–2, with cavities or grooves on the inner faces: lvs. mostly ⅝–2 in. long.
      D. Styles and nutlets usually 2: lvs. with 3–5 broad serrulate lobes.......13. *C. Oxyacantha*
      DD. Styles and nutlets usually 1: lvs. with 3–7 narrow subentire lobes.....14. *C. monogyna*
AA. Lvs. serrate or shallowly lobed, with veins extending only to teeth or points of lobes.
  B. Base of lf. truncate to subcordate.
    C. Stamens 10: nutlets 3–4.. 2. *C. Arnoldiana*
    CC. Stamens 20: nutlets 4–5.
      D. Fr. pubescent, calyx not enlarged in fr.: lvs. pubescent beneath, at least on veins.. 1. *C. mollis*
      DD. Fr. glabrous and shining, with enlarged calyx: lvs. becoming glabrous beneath.. 3. *C. coccinioides*
  BB. Base of lf. cuneate.
    C. Length of lvs. ¾–3 in., glabrous beneath: infl. glabrous, or if slightly villous then 3–7-fld.
      D. Lf. rounded at apex, sharp-serrate but not lobed: anthers rose........ 6. *C. Crus-galli*
      DD. Lf. acute to acuminate, doubly serrate and more or less lobed: anthers yellow.
        E. Stamens 10; calyx-lobes glandular-serrate: infl. 3–7-fld............. 4. *C. intricata*
        EE. Stamens 15–20; calyx-lobes subentire: infl. many-fld................ 5. *C. nitida*
    CC. Length of lvs. 2–5 in., pubescent beneath at least on veins while young: infl. pubescent, many-fld.
      D. Stamens about 10..12. *C. prunifolia*
      DD. Stamens 15–20.
        E. Nutlets without cavities on the inner surface.
          F. Upper surface of lvs. shining: sepals serrulate................. 7. *C. Lavallei*
          FF. Upper surface of lvs. dull: sepals subentire.................. 8. *C. punctata*
        EE. Nutlets with deep cavities on the inner surface.
          F. Fr. ellipsoid or pear-shaped, upright..........................10. *C. Calpodendron*
          FF. Fr. subglobose, nodding......................................11. *C. succulenta*

1. **C. mollis**, Scheele (*C. coccinea* var. *mollis*, Torr. & Gray). Tree to 30 ft. or more, with stout spines 1–2 in. long: lvs. broad-ovate, 2½–4 in. long, truncate to subcordate at base, doubly sharp-serrate, with 4–5 shallow acute lobes on each side, densely pubescent beneath becoming subglabrous except on veins: fls. white, 1 in. across, with red disk; stamens 20: fr. bright red, pubescent, usually pear-shaped, about ½in. across, flesh mealy and sweet; nutlets 4–5. Ont. to Va., S. D. and Kans.

2. **C. Arnoldiana**, Sarg. Tree to 20 ft., with zigzag branchlets armed with stout spines 2–3 in. long: lvs. broad-ovate to oval, 2–3 in. long, acute, often truncate at base, coarsely doubly serrate and shallowly lobed, pubescent at first on both surfaces, becoming shining and smooth above and slightly villous on veins beneath: fls. white, ¾in. across, in tomentose clusters, sepals glandular-serrate; stamens 10: fr. bright crimson, villous toward ends, subglobose, ¾in. long; nutlets 3–4. Mass. to Conn. and N. Y.

3. **C. coccinioides**, Ashe. Tree to 20 ft., with purplish shining spines to 2 in. long: lvs. broad-ovate, 2–3½ in. long, acute, rounded or truncate at base, doubly serrate, lobes broad, becoming nearly glabrous: fls. white, ¾in. across, in 5–7-fld. compact slightly villous clusters, sepals glandular-serrate; stamens 20: fr. dark crimson and shining, subglobose, to ¾in. across, calyx enlarged, flesh subacid; nutlets 4–5. Ind. to Kans.

4. **C. intricata**, Lange (*C. coccinea*, L. in part). Shrub to 10 ft., with long curved thorns: lvs. elliptic-ovate, ¾–3 in. long, acute, cuneate at base, doubly serrate with 3 or 4 acute short lobes on each side, glabrous above, nearly glabrous beneath: fls. white, in 3–7-fld. slightly villous clusters, sepals glandular-serrate; stamens 10, with yellow anthers: fr. subglobose to ellipsoid, reddish-brown; nutlets 3–4. Mass. to N. C.

5. **C. nitida**, Sarg. Tree to 30 ft., the branches spreading and unarmed or with straight thorns: lvs. elliptic to oblong-obovate, ¾–3 in. long, acuminate, cuneate at base, coarsely serrate and more or less lobed, glabrous, dark and shining above: fls. white, ¾in. across, in many-fld. glabrous clusters, sepals subentire; stamens 15–20, with pale yellow anthers: fr. dull red, subglobose, about ⅜in. long, flesh mealy; nutlets 2–5. Ill. to Ark.

6. **C. Crus-galli**, L. Cockspur Thorn. Large shrub or tree to 25 ft. or more, with numerous long slender spines: lvs. obovate to oblong-obovate, ¾–3 in. long, mostly rounded

at apex, cuneate, sharply serrate above, entire at base, glabrous: fls. white, ⅝in. across, in many-fld. glabrous clusters, sepals entire or with few teeth; stamens 10 (13), with rose-colored anthers: fr. red, subglobose, about ⅜in. across, with dry flesh; nutlets usually 2. Que. to N. C. and Kans.

7. **C. Lavallei,** Hérincq (*?C. Crus-galli* × *C. pubescens. C. Carrierei,* Vauv.). Tree to 20 ft. or more, with pubescent shoots and few strong spines: lvs. obovate-oblong to elliptic, 2–4 in. long, acute, cuneate, irregularly serrate becoming entire toward the base, finally subglabrous above, pubescent beneath: fls. white, about ¾in. across, with red disk, in many-fld. villous infl., sepals linear and serrulate; stamens 15–20, with red or yellow anthers: fr. brick- or orange-red, ellipsoid, about ⅝in. long. (For A. Lavallée, page 46.) Of garden origin.

8. **C. punctata,** Jacq. Tree to 30 ft., with horizontal branches, unarmed or with short stout spines, young growth pubescent: lvs. obovate, 2–4 in. long, obtuse or acute, base narrowed and entire, irregularly sharp-serrate above, sometimes lobed, villous beneath, veins impressed above: fls. white, ½–¾in. across, in many-fld. villous clusters; sepals subentire; stamens 20: fr. dull red, spotted, subglobose or pyriform, to ¾in. long; nutlets 5. Que. to Ill. and Ga.

9. **C. Phænopyrum,** Medic. (*Mespilus Phænopyrum,* L. f. *C. cordata,* Ait.). WASHINGTON THORN. Strong tree to 25 or 30 ft., with glabrous shoots and slender long spines: lvs. broad-ovate to triangular, 1¼–2¾ in. long, acute or acuminate, truncate to subcordate at base, 3–5-lobed, sharply or incisely serrate, becoming dark green and shining above, glabrous or nearly so beneath: fls. white, about ½in. across, in glabrous many-fld. corymbs; sepals glabrous, nearly triangular, entire; stamens 20: fr. shining scarlet, nearly globose, ⅓in. across, long-persisting. (The name Phænopyrum refers to the shining fr.: Greek *to shine.*) Va. to Ala. and Mo.; nat. northward and often cult. in the northern states.

10. **C. Calpodendron,** Medic. (*Mespilus Calpodendron,* Ehrh. *C. tomentosa,* Auth. not L.). PEAR or SUGAR HAWTHORN. Shrub or tree to 20 ft., the branches spreading and unarmed or with short stout spines: lvs. elliptic to obovate-oblong, 2–5 in. long, acute, cuneate at base, serrate and sometimes lobed, dull becoming glabrous above, pubescent beneath: fls. white, ½in. across, in many-fld. pubescent clusters to 5 in. across, sepals serrate; stamens 15–20, with pink anthers: fr. dull yellowish-red, ellipsoid or pyriform, about ⅜in. long, with pulpy flesh; nutlets 2–3. (Calpodendron: Greek for *urn* and *tree.*) Ont. to Ga. and Kans.

11. **C. succulenta,** Link. Tree to 15 ft., with stout branches and spines to 2 in. long: lvs. broad-elliptic to obovate, 2–3¼ in. long, acute or acuminate, cuneate, doubly coarse serrate, shining above, pubescent on veins beneath becoming glabrous: fls. white, ¾in. across, in many-fld. villous clusters, sepals glandular-serrate; stamens 15–20, with pink anthers: fr. bright red, globose, ⅝in. across, with pulpy flesh. Que. to Mass. and Ill.

12. **C. prunifolia,** Pers. (*Mespilus prunifolia,* Poir. not Marsh.). Tree to 30 ft., with spiny branches: lvs. obovate to broad-obovate, 2 in. or more long, doubly serrate, pubescent on veins beneath when young: fls. white, in pubescent clusters; stamens 10, with pink anthers: fr. dull crimson, subglobose, ⅜–⅝in. across; nutlets slightly furrowed on inner surface. Origin unknown, possibly a hybrid of *C. macracantha* and *C. Crus-galli.*

13. **C. Oxyacantha,** L. ENGLISH HAWTHORN. Shrub or small tree to 15 ft., with spreading branches and stout spines to 1 in. long: lvs. broad-ovate or obovate, ⅝–2 in. long, cuneate at base, with 3–5 usually serrate lobes, glabrous: fls. white, ⅝in. across, in glabrous 5–12-fld. clusters, sepals entire; stamens 20, with red anthers; styles 2–3: fr. scarlet, subglobose to broad-ellipsoid, ⅜–⅝in. long; nutlets 2, furrowed on the inner face. (Oxyacantha is a pre-Linnæan name; Greek *sharp thorn.*) Eu., N. Afr. Var. **Paulii,** Rehd. (var. *splendens,* Schneid.), fls. bright scarlet, double. Var. **rosea,** Willd., fls. rose.

14. **C. monogyna,** Jacq. Similar to the preceding species and hybridizing with it: shrub or tree to 30 ft.: lvs. more deeply 3–7-lobed, the lobes narrower and more acute and with only a few teeth toward the apex, calyx and pedicels sometimes pubescent; style 1, rarely 2: fr. ellipsoid; nutlet 1. Eu., N. Afr., W. Asia.

15. **C. pinnatifida,** Bunge. Shrub or small tree to 20 ft., with few small thorns and glabrous growth: lvs. broad- to rhombic-ovate, 2–4 in. long, truncate or broad-cuneate at base, pinnately 5–9-lobed, the lobes very sharp-serrate, glossy above, both surfaces with hairs along the veins: fls. white, ¾in. across, in villous clusters to 3 in. across; stamens 20, with pink anthers: fr. red, punctate-dotted, subglobose or pyriform, ⅝in. across; nutlets 3–5. N. E. Asia. Var. **major,** N. E. Br., has larger less deeply lobed lvs.; fr. shining deep red, about 1 in. across; cult. in China for its edible fr.

17. **OSTEOMELES,** Lindl. Three deciduous or evergreen odd-pinnate-lvd. shrubs of E. Asia and the Pacific isls., planted in Calif. and far S.—Lvs. alternate, with many pairs of small entire lfts., with linear caducous stipules: fls. white, in cymose open clusters on leafy shoots of the season; sepals and petals 5; stamens

15–20; pistil 1, ovary 5-celled, each cell 1-ovuled, placentation axile, styles 5 and distinct; ovary enveloped by the hypanthium and adnate with it (inferior): fr. small, pome-like, with calyx-lobes persistent on top and 5 nutlets. (Osteome-les: Greek *bone apple.*)

O. Schwerinæ, Schneid. (*O. anthyllidifolia,* Franch. not Lindl.). Deciduous or half-evergreen slender branching shrub to 10 ft., branchlets, petioles and under sides of lvs. grayish-pubescent: lvs. 1–2 (3) in. long, the rachis narrowly winged; lfts. 15–31, elliptic to obovate-oblong, ⅛–⅓in. long, mucronulate: fls. white, about ½in. across, in terminal clusters to 2½ in. across; sepals pubescent outside, glabrous inside, the hypanthium becoming glabrous: fr. blue-black, glabrous, subglobose, ¼–⅓in. long. (Named for Countess v. Schwerin.) China.—The material cult. as *O. anthyllidifolia* belongs here. *O. anthyllidifolia,* Lindl. (*Pyrus anthyllidifolia,* Smith), has lvs. 2–3 in. long with 13–19 lfts. ⅜–¾in. long; fr. pubescent, about ⅜in. long; Hawaii south.

18. **PHOTINIA,** Lindl. Small trees and shrubs sometimes planted for ornament, about 40 species native mostly in S. and E. Asia.—Deciduous or evergreen, thornless: lvs. alternate, short-petiolate, usually serrate, stipulate: fls. mostly white, rather small, in corymbs or close short terminal panicles; hypanthium mostly campanulate, sepals 5 and persistent on the fr.; petals 5, broad; stamens about 20; pistil 1, ovary usually 2–4-celled, placentæ axile, ovules mostly 1 in each cell; styles usually 2, connate at base: fr. a small berry-like 1–4-seeded pome hollow at the top. (Photin-ia: Greek *shining,* from the lvs.)

A. Foliage deciduous: infl. 1–2 in. across, terminating short lateral branches; pedicels with warty lenticels. . . . . 1. *P. villosa*
AA. Foliage persistent: infl. 2–6 in. across, terminal; pedicels smooth.
B. Lvs. 4–8 in. long: petals glabrous. . . . . 2. *P. serrrulata*
BB. Lvs. 2–3 rarely 4 in. long: petals villous at base . . . . 3. *P. glabra*

1. **P. villosa,** DC. (*Cratægus villosa,* Thunb.). Deciduous shrub or sometimes tree-like, to 15 ft., young parts pubescent: lvs. obovate to oblong-obovate, 1¼–3¼ in. long, acuminate, cuneate, finely sharp-serrate, glabrous above, villous beneath, with 5–7 pairs of veins: fls. white, about ½in. across, in villous compound infl. 1–2 in. across borne on short lateral branches: fr. bright red, ellipsoid, ⅓in. long. Japan, Korea, China. Var. **lævis,** Dipp. (*Cratægus lævis,* Thunb.), lvs. narrower and smaller, soon glabrous; infl. subsimple, glabrous; fr. ½in. long.—Hardy N.

2. **P. serrulata,** Lindl. Evergreen shrub or small tree to 30 ft. or more, with glabrous young growth: lvs. oblong to oblong-obovate, 4–8 in. long, with 40–50 pairs of veins, abruptly pointed or sometimes acuminate, cuneate at base, evenly serrulate, glossy above, glabrous, reddish when young, petioles about 1 in. long: fls. white, ¼–⅜in. across, in flattish terminal corymbose panicles 4–6 in. across, in late spring and summer, petals glabrous: fr. red, globose, about ¼in. across. China. Var. **aculeata,** Lawrence, has lvs. strongly aculeate to spinescent-serrate with subtruncate to obtuse base and 10–20 pairs of veins; Formosa.—Cult. in the southern parts of N. Amer.

3. **P. glabra,** Maxim. (*Cratægus glabra,* Thunb.). Evergreen shrub to 10 ft.: lvs. elliptic to oblong-obovate, 2–3 or rarely 4 in. long, mostly acute, cuneate, finely serrate, glabrous, pale beneath, red when young, petioles about ½in. long: fls. white, about ⅜in. across, in rather compact compound infl. 2–4 in. across, petals villous at base: fr. red, globose, about ¼in. across. Japan.—Not hardy N.

19. **HETEROMELES,** Roem. One evergreen shrub distinguished from Photinia by the 10 rather than 20 stamens in pairs opposite the sepals; filaments broadened at base and somewhat united; pistil 1, styles 2–3, distinct: fr. with persistent calyx-teeth inflexed over the carpels. (Heterome-les: Greek *different apple;* i.e., unlike related genera.)

H. arbutifolia, Roem. (*Cratægus arbutifolia,* Ait. *Photinia arbutifolia,* Lindl.). Tollon or Toyon. Christmas-Berry. Shrub or tree-like to 30 ft., with lightly pubescent young growth: lvs. thick, oblong to oblong-lanceolate, 2–4 in. long, acute or abruptly very short-pointed, short-petioled, sharp-serrate, shining above, usually glabrous: fls. white, about ¼in. across, in rather close panicles 2–3 in. high that spread in fr., in spring and summer: fr. broad-ovoid, ¼–⅓in. long, bright red varying to yellow, ripening late in season and persisting. Calif. and Lower Calif.—Much planted, not hardy N.

20. **STRANVAESIA,** Lindl. Four or 5 evergreen shrubs and trees in China and the Himalayas, sometimes planted in the middle country and S.—Thornless: lvs. alternate, entire or serrate, glandless, stipulate: fls. white, in terminal clusters; calyx-

teeth 5, persistent and incurved in fr.; petals 5, usually broad and clawed; stamens about 20; pistil 1, ovary 2-celled, the 5 styles joined half or more their length, cells 2-ovuled: fr. a little pome, usually 5-seeded. (Stranvae-sia: bears the name of Wm. T. H. Fox-Strangways, 1795–1865, English botanist.)

S. Davidiana, Decne. Spreading shrub or small tree to 20 ft. or more, the young parts hairy-pubescent: lvs. coriaceous, oblong to oblanceolate, 2–4 in. long, acute or acuminate, petiolate, entire, glabrous above and usually becoming so beneath: fls. ⅓in. across, in pubescent corymbs 2–3 in. across: fr. nearly globular, ⅓in. or less diam., scarlet. (Abbé David, page 230.) China. Var. **undulata,** Rehd. & Wils. (*S. undulata,* Decne.), is usually lower-growing; lvs. elliptic-oblong to oblong-lanceolate, 1¼–3¼ in. long, mostly with wavy margins; infl. sometimes subglabrous; fr. orange to coral, about ¼in. across.

21. **ERIOBOTRYA,** Lindl. Evergreen shrubs and small trees, about 10 species in E. Asia, one grown for ornament and for its edible frs.—Lvs. large, alternate, short-petiolate or nearly sessile, simple, with strong pinnate veins ending in teeth: fls. white or whitish, in terminal panicles; calyx-lobes 5, persistent on top of fr.; petals 5, broad, clawed; stamens about 20; pistil 1, ovary inferior, of 2–5 cells and an equal number of styles (usually 5), ovules 2 in each cell, placentation axile: fr. a pome with 1 or 2 or few large seeds. (Eriobot-rya: Greek *woolly cluster* from the tomentose infl.)

E. japonica, Lindl. (*Mespilus japonica,* Thunb. *Photinia japonica,* Gray). LOQUAT. Small round-headed tree 20 ft. or more high, with rusty-tomentose branchlets: lvs. stiff, obovate to elliptic-oblong, 5–10 in. long, acute or acuminate, the side nerves running to sharp teeth, glossy above but rusty-tomentose beneath: fls. white, almost ½in. across, in dry-bracted rusty-pubescent terminal panicles late in the year: fr. ripening following spring, pyriform, 1½ in. long, yellow, with a few large seeds, agreeably acid. China.—Planted far S., sometimes under the name "Japan plum."

22. **RHAPHIOLEPIS,** Lindl. Probably less than a half dozen species in Japan and China, evergreen shrubs grown for ornament in the S. and sometimes under glass.—Thornless: lvs. alternate, leathery, short-petioled, serrate or entire: fls. white or pinkish, of medium size, on thickened articulated pedicels in close racemes or panicles from scaly terminal buds; calyx-lobes 5, erect or reflexed, not persistent; petals 5, broad; stamens 15–20; pistils (and styles) 2 or 3, joined at the base, inferior: fr. a drupe-like little pome, purplish- or bluish-black, with 1 or 2 seeds. (Rhaphiol-epis: Greek *needle scale,* referring to the bracts in the infl.)—Commonly, but not originally, spelled Raphiolepis.

A. Lvs. rather sharp-serrate, acute or acuminate: fls. tinged pink.................... 1. *R. indica*
AA. Lvs. remotely dentate to entire, mostly obtuse: fls. white........................ 2. *R. umbellata*

1. **R. indica,** Lindl. (*Cratægus indica,* L.). INDIA-HAWTHORN. Variable, in several lf.-forms, a shrub 4–5 ft. high: lvs. oblong-lanceolate to obovate-lanceolate, 1½–3 in. long, pointed or acuminate, rather sharply serrate, not very thick or heavy or revolute, glabrous or at first somewhat pubescent: fls. about ½in. across, white tinged pink, in relatively loose mostly glabrous racemes; calyx-lobes usually red, lanceolate: fr. ¼–⅓in. across. S. China. —**R. Delacouri,** André (*R. indica* × *R. umbellata*), has serrate lvs. and pink fls.; grown in garden of M. Delacour at Cannes.

2. **R. umbellata,** Makino (*Laurus umbellata,* Thunb. *R. japonica,* Sieb. & Zucc.). YEDDO-HAWTHORN. Strong shrub to 10–12 ft.: lvs. very thick and leathery, 1–3 in. long, obovate or oval, obtuse or acute, margins revolute, remotely crenate-serrate, tomentose when young: fls. white, ¾in. across, fragrant, in dense pubescent dry-bracted racemes or panicles; calyx-lobes triangular-pointed, not red: fr. about ⅜in. across. Japan. Var. **integerrima,** Rehd. (*R. japonica* var. *integerrima,* Hook. f. *R. ovata,* Briot. *R. umbellata* forma *ovata,* Schneid.), lvs. broadly obovate, rounded at apex, entire or slightly toothed; Japan, Korea.

23. **AMELANCHIER,** Medic. SERVICE-BERRY. JUNEBERRY. SHADBUSH. Shrubs and small trees sometimes planted for the showy early white fls. and also for the edible frs.; species probably 25, in the north temp. zone, mostly in N. Amer.—Unarmed, deciduous: lvs. alternate, simple, on the ovate and oval order, serrate, petiolate, stipules deciduous: fls. racemose (seldom solitary or 2–3 together), appearing in advance of the foliage or with it; calyx 5-cleft, the tube campanulate, the lobes persistent and usually reflexed on the fr.; petals 5, narrow; stamens 10–20, short;

pistil 1, ovary inferior, 2–5-celled, the cells 2-ovuled, adnate in the hypanthium, the styles and carpels 2–5: fr. a fleshy little pome, dark blue or black, usually becoming 10-celled by the growth of 5 false partitions, each cell therefore 1-seeded when the ovules all mature. (Amelan-chier: name of doubtful origin, probably from a vernacular.)

A. Styles free, not exceeding the hypanthium .... 1. *A. ovalis*
AA. Styles more or less joined at the base, longer than the hypanthium.
B. Lvs. coarsely serrate toward the apex, usually entire in the lower half: summit of ovary woolly .... 2. *A. florida*
BB. Lvs. finely serrate becoming entire only toward the base: summit of ovary soon glabrous except in no. 4.
C. Lf. glabrous or nearly so from the first, usually purplish-bronze when young: racemes glabrous .... 3. *A. lævis*
CC. Lf. white-tomentose beneath when young: racemes tomentose when in fl.
D. Plant a stoloniferous shrub 1–4 ft. high: lvs. elliptic to elliptic-oblong: summit of ovary woolly .... 4. *A. stolonifera*
DD. Plant 6–30 ft. or more high: lvs. oblong to obovate: summit of ovary glabrous or nearly so.
E. Apex of lf. usually rounded: sepals erect or spreading: tall shrubs forming clumps .... 5. *A. canadensis*
EE. Apex of lf. usually short-acuminate: sepals reflexed: becoming small trees .... 6. *A. arborea*

1. **A. ovalis,** Medic. (*A. rotundifolia*, Dum.-Cours. *A. vulgaris*, Moench). Erect or spreading shrub to 8 ft., the young parts tomentose: lvs. oval to obovate, 1–2 in. long, mostly obtuse, rounded or subcordate at base, sharp-toothed from near the base, tomentose beneath when young but becoming glabrous: fls. white, 1–1½ in. across, in erect tomentose racemes; petals linear-oblanceolate, obtuse or emarginate; styles free, shorter than hypanthium: fr. size of black currant, glaucous-black, not palatable. Cent. and S. Eu.

2. **A. florida,** Lindl. Slender shrub 6–15 ft. high: lvs. oblong to elliptic-oblong, about 1½ in. long, mostly obtuse at ends, coarsely toothed toward the apex to subentire, usually subglabrous above, somewhat tomentose beneath: fls. white, in more or less tomentose racemes to 3 in. long; petals spatulate, to ⅝in. long; ovary woolly at summit: fr. dark purple, bloomy. Alaska to Calif. east to Ida.—Most of the material cult. as *A. alnifolia* belongs here. *A. alnifolia*, Nutt., a Great Plains plant, has broader usually shorter lvs., racemes to 1½ in. long, petals about ⅓in. long.

3. **A. lævis,** Wiegand. When full grown a tree 40 ft. high: lvs. ovate, oval or ovate-oblong or slightly obovate, 1–3 in. long, generally rounded at base, short-acuminate at apex, serrate with subulate teeth, glabrous from the first or very nearly so: fls. white, in slender nodding glabrous racemes appearing with the lvs.; sepals reflexed, lance-triangular; petals ½–¾in. long; top of ovary glabrous: fr. dark purple, bloomy, sweet and juicy. Newf. to Mich., Kans. and Ga.—Very ornamental because of contrast between large drooping or spreading fls. and the purplish-bronzy foliage.

4. **A. stolonifera,** Wiegand. Erect shrub to 4 ft., forming patches by underground stolons: lvs. elliptic to elliptic-oblong, 1–2 in. long, obtuse and mucronate at tip, usually rounded at base, finely serrate becoming entire toward base, white-tomentose beneath when young: fls. white, in erect glabrate racemes to 1½ in. high; petals to ⅜in. long: fr. purplish-black, bloomy, juicy, sweet. Newf. to Minn. and Va.—Cult. as Dwarf Juneberry; the strain "Success" has berries to ½in. diam.

5. **A. canadensis,** Medic. (*Mespilus canadensis*, L. *A. oblongifolia*, Roem. *A. canadensis* var. *oblongifolia*, Torr. & Gray). Shrub 6–20 ft. high, growing in clumps: lvs. oblong to narrowly obovate-oblong, 1–2½ in. long, rounded or subcordate at base and rounded or acute at apex, finely serrate, white-tomentose beneath when young, later glabrate: fls. white, in erect short dense tomentose racemes appearing with the lvs.; sepals erect or irregularly spreading; petals about ⅓in. long: fr. dark purple, ⅓in. diam., sweet and juicy. Swamps, Me. to S. C. along the coast.—Much planted in parks in the E. for the early white effect of fls. and foliage.

6. **A. arborea,** Fern. (*Mespilus arborea*, Michx. f. *M. canadensis* var. *cordata*, Michx. *A. canadensis*, Auth. not Medic.). Small irregular tree, or often shrub-like, 15–30 ft. or more high: lvs. generally obovate, rarely ovate, oval or oblong, 1–3 (4) in. long, subcordate, more acuminate than in other species, sharply serrate with broad-bodied teeth, densely white-tomentose when young, somewhat hairy beneath and on the petioles at maturity: fls. white, in dense nodding tomentose racemes appearing before (or with) the lvs.; hypanthium especially small, ⅒–⅕in. broad, sepals broadly ovate, reflexed; petals to ½in. long: fr. about ¼in. diam., maroon-purple, dry, tasteless, falling early. W. New England to Iowa, Ga. and La.—The white young foliage increases the pure white effect. Some of the material cult. as *A. Botryapium* may belong here.

24. **CHÆNOMELES,** Lindl. Flowering Quince. Species 3, usually thorny hardwooded shrubs, grown mostly for their brilliant very early fls.—Lvs. deciduous

or more or less persistent into winter, alternate, simple with serrate margins, stipules often very large: fls. solitary or in small clusters from lateral winter-buds, nearly or quite sessile, for the most part opening in advance of the foliage; sepals 5; stamens 20 or more; pistil 1, ovary inferior, mostly 5-celled, many-ovuled, placentæ axile, styles 5, joined at base: fr. a small or large pome with closed top, the sepals not persistent, pedicel or st. lacking. (Chænome-les: Greek compound, *to split* and *apple;* Thunberg supposed the fr. to split into 5 valves.)

A. Fls. solitary; sepals reflexed, serrulate: stipules small: fr. 4–6 in. long................1. *C. sinensis*
AA. Fls. in clusters; sepals erect, entire: stipules large: fr. 1–2 in. long.
B. Lvs. sharp-serrate, acute: branchlets glabrous................2. *C. lagenaria*
BB. Lvs. coarsely crenate-serrate, usually obtusish: branchlets scabrous................3. *C. japonica*

1. **C. sinensis,** Koehne (*Cydonia sinensis*, Thouin. (*Pseudocydonia sinensis*, Schneid.). CHINESE QUINCE. Small spineless tree, 10–20 ft., with half-evergreen foliage S. and hairy young growth: lvs. elliptic-ovate to somewhat obovate, 2–3½ in. long, very abruptly short-pointed, sharply callous-serrate, the short petiole with gland-tipped teeth, glabrous above, hairy beneath but becoming nearly glabrous: fls. solitary, 1–1½ in. across, light pink, on leafy shoots: fr. large, 4–6 in. long, oblong, yellow, with naked cavities at either end, gritty, the cells 2 in. or more long, pleasingly aromatic. China.—Not often hardy north of Philadelphia; sometimes recommended for its fr. for culinary purposes.

2. **C. lagenaria,** Koidz. (*Cydonia lagenaria*, Loisel. *Chænomeles japonica*, Hort. not Lindl. *Cydonia japonica*, Pers. *Pyrus japonica*, Sims not Thunb.). JAPANESE QUINCE. Stiff-branched thorny shrub with glabrous young growth, making a thick top, sometimes 10 ft. high: lvs. mostly oblong-ovate, 1½–3 in. long, acute or acuminate, finely sharp-serrate, glabrous, shining above: fls. 2–6, to 2 in. across, scarlet-red, the petals of a waxy consistency, appearing in advance of lvs.: fr. globular to ovoid, very hard, 1½–2 in. long, greenish-yellow with small dots, with cavity at either end, core very large. China.—Fr. sometimes used for preserves. Most of the material cult. as *Cydonia japonica* belongs here. There are many hort. vars. including: **nivalis,** fls. nearly white; **pygmæa,** listed as a dwarf; **rosea,** fls. rose; **rubra,** fls. deep crimson; **sanguinea,** fls. scarlet. Var. **cathayensis,** Rehd. (*C. cathayensis*, Schneid. *Cydonia cathayensis*, Hemsl.), is very thorny, to 15 ft. high; lvs. elliptic-lanceolate to lanceolate, to 4½ in. long, pubescent on midrib beneath when young, fr. sometimes oblately pyriform, to 5 in. long.

3. **C. japonica,** Lindl. (*C. Maulei*, Schneid. *Cydonia Maulei*, Moore. *Pyrus japonica*, Thunb.). DWARF JAPANESE QUINCE. Dwarf 3 ft. or less high, with warty pubescent young growth: lvs. nearly orbicular, roundish-oval to obovate, 1–2 in. long, obtuse or sometimes very short-acute, coarsely crenate-serrate, glabrous: fls. to 1½ in. across, orange-scarlet: fr. nearly globular, 1½ in. diam., yellow with red blush. Japan. Var. **alpina,** Maxim. (*C. Maulei* var. *alpina*, Schneid. *Cydonia Sargentii*, Lem.), is dwarf with procumbent sts. and ascending branches; lvs. roundish-oval, ½–1 in. long.—*C. superba*, Rehd. (*C. Maulei superba*, Frahm. *C. japonica* × *C. lagenaria*), has narrower more sharply serrate lvs. and larger blood-red fls.

25. **CYDONIA,** Mill. QUINCE. One species, a familiar small fr.-bearing tree, native from Iran to Turkestan.—Spineless: lvs. alternate, deciduous, simple and entire, stipulate: fls. large, white or light pink, solitary and terminating leafy shoots of the season; sepals 5, entire, reflexed; petals 5; stamens about 20; pistil 1, ovary inferior, mostly 5-celled, many-ovuled, placentæ axile, styles 5, free, indicating the 5 carpels: fr. a large 5-celled tomentose closed pome, with calyx-lobes persistent on top at least for a time, seeds many in each cell. (Cydo-nia: old geographical name, Cydon now Canea in Crete.)—For other names listed as Cydonia, see *Chænomeles*, the Japanese or Flowering Quince.

C. oblonga, Mill. (*C. vulgaris*, Pers. *Pyrus Cydonia*, L.). Round-headed tree 15–20 ft. or more high, with crooked branches and blackish bark: lvs. broad-ovate to oblong, 2–4 in. long, blunt or very short-pointed, often subcordate, short-petioled, becoming glabrous above, tomentose beneath: fls. appearing with the main foliage, 2–2½ in. across: fr. yellow, fragrant, fuzzy, pyriform, 3–4 in. diam. in improved vars., without true st. or pedicel.

26. **PYRUS,** L. PEAR. Something like 20 species of deciduous or half-evergreen small trees of Eurasia and N. Afr., grown in orchards.—Lvs. alternate, simple, serrate or entire, rarely lobed, involute in bud, petiolate, stipules small and sometimes early caducous: fls. white or rarely pinkish, normally bisexual, regular, in clusters appearing before or with the lvs.; sepals 5, connate into an urn-shaped calyx-tube or hypanthium, the lobes reflexed or spreading; petals 5, suborbicular to obovate,

clawed; pistil 1, ovary inferior, of as many 2-ovuled carpels (and cells) as styles, styles 2–5, separate but closely constricted basally by the staminal disk; stamens 20–30, anthers usually red: fr. a fleshy pome, with 2–5 axile carpels whose walls are of papery or cartilaginous cells, the flesh about them containing large quantities of grit-cells, a thin zone of grit-cells situated beneath the epidermis and observed as a ring when fr. is cut in cross-section. (Py-rus: classical name of the pear tree.)—Distinguished from the genus Malus by most of the lvs. glabrous, hard and glossy at maturity, lf.-margins with callous rather than acute serratures, winter-buds prevailingly glabrous or nearly so and acute, fl.-clusters compound with a central stout short column or pirostele from which some or all the pedicels arise and which persists for the single or few frs. that remain from the cluster, pome with abundant stone- or grit-cells.

A. Shoots and young lvs. white-tomentose, the lvs. usually remaining so beneath . . . . . . 1. *P. nivalis*
AA. Shoots and lvs. glabrous or soon becoming so.
 B. Margins of lf. setose-serrate. . . . . 2. *P. pyrifolia*
 BB. Margins of lf. crenate or crenate-serrate.
  C. Styles normally 5; calyx-lobes persistent on fr. . . . . 3. *P. communis*
  CC. Styles 2 or 3; calyx-lobes deciduous. . . . . 4. *P. Calleryana*

1. **P. nivalis,** Jacq. SNOW PEAR. Small tree with white-tomentose growth: lvs. oval to obovate, 2–3 in. long, entire or essentially so, white-tomentose on both sides at first and more or less remaining so beneath: fls. clear white, about 1 in. across: fr. globose, 1–2 in. diam. E. Eu., Asia Minor.—Cult. somewhat in Eu. for its white foliage, also sometimes for its frs. which are bletted or used for the making of perry (pear cider); probably not planted in N. Amer. outside experimental grounds and botanic gardens.

2. **P. pyrifolia,** Nakai, var. **culta,** Nakai (*P. serotina* var. *culta,* Rehd. *P. sinensis,* Hort. not Lindl.). JAPANESE and CHINESE PEAR. SAND PEAR. Tree 30–50 ft., young growth glabrous or soon becoming so: lvs. mostly ovate-oblong, 4–6 in. long and 3–4 in. broad, long and narrowly acuminate, conspicuously setose-serrate, glabrous or becoming so, glossy green: fls. white, 1½ in. across, about 6–9 to an umbel, with the foliage or just in advance of it; styles 5, rarely 4, glabrous: fr. very hard and usually rough, long-keeping, mostly apple-shaped with depression at st.-end, calyx-lobes falling before maturity, flesh very gritty.—The native form, *P. pyrifolia* (*Ficus pyrifolia,* Burm.), differing in its smaller lvs. and frs., is native in Cent. and W. China; var. *culta* is grown in N. Amer. to some extent for fr. and this or related species for stocks; LeConte, Kieffer, and others are hybrids with *P. communis.*

3. **P. communis,** L. PEAR. Large tree, attaining great age, in its wild and semi-wild state producing thorn-like leafy spurs, the young growth becoming glabrous: lvs. oval to oblong-ovate, 2–4 in. long, hard in texture, drying black, with prominent short point, serratures fine, crenate or appressed, or sometimes practically wanting, soon becoming glabrous: fls. white or rarely tinged pink, 1 in. or more across, 4–12 together on slender pedicels, appearing with the first foliage: fr. variable, mostly pyriform with tapering base but sometimes apple-shaped, calyx-lobes persisting, the flesh with gritty concretions unless ripened after removal from the tree. Eu. and W. Asia.—Cult. in many named pomological vars.; there are also ornamental forms, as cut-lvd., lobed-lvd., variegated.

4. **P. Calleryana,** Decne. Glabrous tree: lvs. ovate or broader, 1½–3 in. long, short-pointed, crenate, mostly glabrous: fls. white, 1 in. or less across, in a glabrous infl.; styles 2 or 3: fr. globular, about ½in. across, dotted brown; calyx deciduous. (Named for J. M. M. Callery, 1810–1862, Roman Catholic missionary and collector.) China.—Attracts attention as a pear stock.

27. **MALUS,** Mill. APPLE. About 25 species of small much-branched deciduous trees of the north temp. zone in both hemispheres, grown in orchards and as ornamentals.—Sometimes held as a subgenus of Pyrus, from which it is here distinguished by its soft more or less pubescent lf.-surfaces, acutely rather than callously serrate lf.-margins, broad pubescent or tomentose winter-buds, fl.-clusters prevailingly simple without a columnar central stalk or pirostele, pome lacking stone- or grit-cells: hypanthium open in anthesis and not closed about the styles which are more or less connate basally. (Ma-lus: classical name of the apple tree.)

A. Lvs. on elongated shoots not lobed or notched, acute to acuminate.
 B. Lobes of calyx distinctly longer than tube.
  C. Lf.-margins obtusely crenate-serrate. . . . . 1. *M. sylvestris*
  CC. Lf.-margins sharply serrulate to serrate.
   D. Styles predominately 5: lvs. folded face to face in bud. . . . . 7. *M. floribunda*
   DD. Styles predominately 4: lvs. rolled together in bud.
    E. Calyx persistent in fr. . . . . 2. *M. prunifolia*
    EE. Calyx deciduous. . . . . 4. *M. baccata*

BB. Lobes of calyx shorter than or as long as the tube.
C. Styles predominately 3 (4 in an occasional fl.); fls. white or pink.......... 5. *M. hupehensis*
CC. Styles predominately 4 or 5; fls. usually deep rose-red, sometimes fading to pink.
D. Fls. about 2 in. across; calyx persistent in fr.......................... 3. *M. spectabilis*
DD. Fls. about 1–1½ in. across; calyx deciduous........................ 6. *M. Halliana*
AA. Lvs. on elongated shoots lobed or strongly notched, or the apex obtuse.
B. Styles glabrous...10. *M. toringoides*
BB. Styles villous basally.
C. Pistil with 3 or 4 styles (occasional fls. with 5); calyx deciduous in fr.
D. Petals cuneate at base, pink or red.................................. 8. *M. Sieboldii*
DD. Petals obtuse at base, clawed, white................................ 9. *M. Sargentii*
CC. Pistil with 5 styles; calyx persistent in fr.
D. Lf. soft-pubescent or tomentose beneath at maturity..................13. *M. ioensis*
DD. Lf. glabrous or only puberulent beneath at maturity.
E. Apex of lf. acute or acuminate; lvs. ovate..........................11. *M. coronaria*
EE. Apex of lf. obtuse or bluntly acutish; lvs. lanceolate-oblong...........12. *M. angustifolia*

1. **M. sylvestris,** Mill. (*Pyrus Malus*, L. *M. communis*, DC.). APPLE. Familiar round-headed tree to 40 ft. or more, with tomentose or heavily pubescent young growth: lvs. oval or elliptic to broad-ovate, 2–4 in. long, thick and veiny, mostly abruptly short-pointed, broad at base, unequally mostly rather bluntly serrate, becoming glabrous and more or less glossy above, pubescent beneath: fls. white or light pink, 1½–2 in. across, appearing with the foliage or just in advance of it, on tomentose pedicels: fr. various in size, shape, color, and season, globular, oblate, conic, with depression at either end, calyx-lobes persisting, flesh without marked grit-cells. Probably original in Eu. and W. temp. Asia, now run wild in many neglected and unkempt places in N. Amer.—In its native or nat. state the small acerb frs. are known as crabs, although the term crab-apple is more definitely applied to *P. baccata*. Var. **aldenhamensis,** Bailey (*Pyrus Malus aldenhamensis*, Gibbs. *M. purpurea* var. *aldenhamensis*, Rehd.), small tree with ovate or ovate-oblong lvs. with purple rib and more or less pubescent underneath; fls. partially double, light red; fr. purple-red; offshoot of var. *Niedzwetzkyana*, perhaps hybrid with *M. atrosanguinea*. Var. **apetala,** Bailey (*Pyrus apetala*, Muenchh. *P. dioica*, Moench), the so-called Bloomless apple; fls. small, with greenish malformed petals, stamens lacking; styles 10–15 and ovary more than 5-celled; calyx-end of fr. not closed; an occasional monstrous state, the fr. probably produced by pollination from other apples. Var. **Eleyi,** Bailey (*Pyrus Eleyi*, Bean. *M. Eleyi*, Hesse. *M. purpurea* var. *Eleyi*, Rehd.), lvs. reddish when young, midrib purple, pubescent beneath; fls. and fr. purple-red, the fr. about 1 in. long; named for Chas. Eley of Suffolk, England. Var. **Niedzwetzkyana,** Bailey (*M. Niedzwetzkyana*, Dieck. *P. Niedzwetzkyana*, Hemsl.), bark and wood reddish; lvs. tinged red on nerves; fls. deep red; fr. purple-red inside and out; S. W. Siberia (first collected by Niedzwetzky) and Caucasus. Var. **paradisiaca,** Bailey (*M. pumila*, Mill. *M. pumila* var. *paradisiaca*, Schneid. *M. paradisiaca*, Medic.), the PARADISE APPLE, is a self-continuing race of very small stature. **M. purpurea,** Rehd. (*M. floribunda purpurea*, Barbier), hybrid between var. *Niedzwetzkyana* and *M. atrosanguinea;* lvs. smaller, shining, purple when young; fr. small, calyx sometimes deciduous.

2. **M. prunifolia,** Borkh. (*Pyrus prunifolia*, Willd.). Small tree with pubescent young branches: lvs. ovate to broad-oval, 2–4 in. long, short-pointed or acuminate, sharply serrate, pubescent beneath but finally glabrous: fls. white, about 1½ in. across, pedicels 1–1½ in. long, sometimes villous; calyx glabrous or sometimes villous, the lobes longer than tube: fr. globose or ovoid, about 1 in. across, yellow or red, with persistent calyx and cavity at base. Probably N. E. Asia, perhaps a range of hybrids. Var. **Rinkii,** Rehd. (*M. pumila* var. *Rinkii*, Koidz. *M. Ringo*. Carr.), RINGO CRAB-APPLE, lvs. pubescent beneath on shorter petioles; fls. pinkish, on pedicels about 1 in. long, calyx villous; fr. 1–1½ in. across, bitter-sweet, edible.

3. **M. spectabilis,** Borkh. (*Pyrus spectabilis*, Ait.). Erect tree to 25 ft.: lvs. oval to elliptic or oblong, 2–4 in. long, mostly much narrower than those of the apple, short-acuminate, mostly cuneate at base, finely crenate-serrate, glabrous and shining above, pubescent beneath while young, becoming subglabrous: fls. pink or rose, coral-red in bud, 1½–2 in. across, sometimes double; pedicels about 1 in. long, glabrous or slightly villous; sepals shorter than hypanthium, erect in anthesis: fr. subglobose, about ¾in. across, yellow, without cavity at base, calyx persistent, flesh bitter. China; apparently unknown wild.—**M. micromalus,** Makino (*Pyrus micromalus*, Bailey. *M. Kaido*, Pardé not Dipp.), probably a hybrid between *M. spectabilis* and ?*M. baccata;* from the former distinguished by the narrower lvs. attenuate into a slender petiole, deeper pink fls. about 1½ in. across, pubescent pedicels and calyx; fr. subglobose, red, with cavity at base, calyx sometimes deciduous.

4. **M. baccata,** Borkh. (*Pyrus baccata*, L. *P. baccata* var. *sibirica*, Maxim.). SIBERIAN CRAB-APPLE. Strong wide-topped tree to 30–40 ft., with glabrous wiry growths: lvs. oval or ovate to ovate-lanceolate, 1–3¼ in. long, acuminate, closely crenate-serrate with callous serratures, rather thin, glabrous or soon becoming so, the petioles long and slender: fls. white, about 1½ in. across, on slender green pedicels; calyx-lobes slender and glabrous: fr. about ⅜in. across in the wild, yellow or red, of a waxy look, on long slender pedicels,

the calyx-lobes falling away. Siberia to Manchuria and N. China. Var. **mandshurica,** Schneid. (*Pyrus baccata* var. *mandshurica*, Maxim. *P. cerasifera*, Tausch. *M. cerasifera*, Spach), lvs. mostly broad-elliptic, remotely serrulate, pubescent beneath when young; petioles, pedicels and calyx pubescent; fls. fragrant; frs. to ½in. across. **M. robusta,** Rehd. (*M. microcarpa robusta*, Carr. *M. cerasifera*, Schneid. not Spach. *Pyrus cerasifera*, Wenz. not Tausch), probably a hybrid of *M. baccata* and *M. prunifolia;* vigorous plant with large oblong or ovate-oblong lvs., glabrous or pubescent underneath; fls. white or pinkish, on slender pedicels, calyx mostly glabrous; fr. about ¾in. or less across, yellow and red, calyx sometimes deciduous; sometimes grown as Siberian crab-apple; the pomological var. "Red Siberian" belongs here. **M. adstringens,** Zabel, Major Crab-Apples, many forms of crab- and semi crab-apples, at least some of them hybrids of *M. sylvestris* and *M. baccata* or *M. robusta*, including Transcendent, Martha, Hyslop and the red-fld. Hopa (probably *M. baccata* × *M. sylvestris* var. *Niedzwetzkyana*)*;* lvs. pubescent beneath and mostly larger than those of *M. baccata;* fls. mostly pinkish, with villous calyx and short villous pedicels; fr. red, yellow or green, to 2 in. across, calyx usually persistent.

5. **M. hupehensis,** Rehd. (*Pyrus hupehensis*, Pampan. *P. theifera*, Bailey. *M. theifera*, Rehd.). Small stiff-branched spreading tree to 25 ft., with young growth soon glabrous: lvs. broad-ovate to ovate-oblong, 2–4 in. long, acuminate, finely sharp-serrate, more or less pubescent on veins beneath: fls. white or pink, fragrant, about 1½ in. across, 3–7 together on slender pedicels; hypanthium glabrous, calyx-lobes acute; styles 3 or rarely 4: fr. globose, about ⅜in. across, mostly greenish-yellow tinged red. Himalayas to China.

6. **M. Halliana,** Koehne (*Pyrus Halliana*, Voss). Hall Crab-Apple. Neat attractive bush or small tree, 15–18 ft., with purple branchlets soon becoming glabrous: lvs. long-ovate or oblong, 1½–3 in. long, firm in texture, acute or acuminate, very closely crenate-serrate or even entire, glabrous or sometimes pubescent on midrib above, glossy above, midrib usually purplish: fls. deep rose, 1–1½ in. across, on purple slender glabrous pedicels, 4–7 in each cluster with 1 or more fls. staminate; hypanthium purple, the calyx-lobes erect and nearly or wholly obtuse, short; styles 4–5: fr. about ⅓in. across, purplish, on pedicels 1½ in. long, the calyx falling early, ripening late in autumn. (Intro. into N. Amer. from Japan by Dr. Geo. R. Hall, 1820–1899.) Probably China.—The double-fld. form is var. **Parkmanii,** Rehd. (*P. Malus* var. *Parkmanii*, Temple), it having been early grown by Francis Parkman, the historian, near Boston. **M. atrosanguinea,** Schneid. (*Pyrus atrosanguinea*, Spaeth. *P. floribunda* var. *atropurpurea*, Bean), probably a hybrid, *M. Halliana* × *M. Sieboldii;* spreading shrub with subglabrous lvs.; fls. rose-purple, similar to the following species but not fading white and calyx-lobes shorter, acute.

7. **M. floribunda,** Sieb. (*Pyrus pulcherrima*, Aschers. & Graebn. *P. floribunda*, Kirchn. not Lindl.). Showy Crab-Apple. Profusely blooming bush or tree to 25 ft. or more, becoming glabrous: lvs. ovate to oblong-ovate, 1½–3 in. long, acuminate, sharp-serrate and sometimes notched on shoots, somewhat pubescent beneath, becoming subglabrous: fls. rose-red, usually fading white, 1–1¼ in. across, on pubescent purple pedicels 1 in. or more long; hypanthium pubescent, with acuminate calyx-lobes: fr. about ⅓in. across, red, with deciduous calyx. Probably Japan or China, or perhaps a race of hybrids.—From *M. Halliana* distinguished by the conduplicate vernation, general absence of purple, young parts pubescent, sharp-serrate lvs., longer acute calyx-lobes, lightly pubescent hypanthium and pedicels, absence of staminate fls., and usually rather smaller fls. From *M. baccata* it differs in smaller size of tree, vernation conduplicate, sharper-toothed lvs., shorter pubescent petioles, fls. darker colored, mostly smaller fr. **M. Arnoldiana,** Sarg. (*M. floribunda* var. *Arnoldiana*, Rehd. *Pyrus Arnoldiana*, Bean. *P. pulcherrima* var. *Arnoldiana*, Bailey), originated at Arnold Arboretum, Boston, as a seedling of *M. floribunda*, perhaps a hybrid with *M. baccata;* bushy plant, with larger ovate lvs.; fls. larger, pale rose; fr. larger, yellow. **M. Scheideckeri,** Zabel (*Pyrus Scheideckeri*, Spaeth. *P. pulcherrima* var. *Scheideckeri*, Bailey), originated at Scheidecker's nursery, Munich, as a seedling of *M. floribunda*, perhaps a hybrid with *M. prunifolia;* small erect tree, with pale pink usually semi-double fls. about 1½ in. across; fr. yellow, about ⅝in. across, calyx usually persistent. **M. brevipes,** Rehd. (*M. floribunda* var. *brevipes*, Rehd.), related to *M. floribunda* and perhaps a hybrid; of lower denser habit; lvs. smaller, very closely serrate; fls. whitish, on glabrous pedicels ½in. or less long; fr. about ½in. across, subglobose, on short stiff stalks.

8. **M. Sieboldii,** Rehd. (*Pyrus Sieboldii*, Regel. *P. Toringo*, Sieb. *M. Toringo*, Nakai). Toringo Crab-Apple. Shrub or small tree to 10–15 ft., with pubescent young growth: vernation conduplicate: lvs. ovate to oblong-ovate, 1–2½ in. long, short-acute or somewhat acuminate, strongly notched or lobed at or below the middle, the margins crenate-serrate or sharp-serrate on the shoots, pubescent on both surfaces but becoming glabrous above: fls. rather small, about ¾in. across, pink or rose in bud, fading white, on slender lightly pubescent pedicels; calyx-lobes triangular-ovate, about equalling the lightly pubescent or nearly glabrous hypanthium: fr. about ⅓in. across, yellow or red, shedding the calyx. (P. F. von Siebold, page 51.) Japan. Var. **arborescens,** Bailey, tree to 30 ft. with larger less deeply lobed less pubescent lvs.; fls. sometimes nearly white; Japan, Korea. **M. Zumi,** Rehd. (*Pyrus Zumi*, Matsum.), probably a hybrid, *M. baccata* var. *mandshurica* × *M. Sieboldii;* pyramidal much-branched tree to 20 ft. or more, with somewhat pubescent

young growth; lvs. oblong to ovate, 1½–3½ in. long, short-acuminate, crenate or entire, on shoots serrate and sometimes lobed, pubescent beneath becoming glabrous; fls. pink in bud but becoming white, about 1 in. across; sepals acuminate; styles 4–5; fr. red, about ½in. across, calyx deciduous; Zumi is a vernacular name in Japan. **M. Zumi var. calocarpa,** Rehd. (*M. Sieboldii* var. *calocarpa,* Rehd. *P. Sieboldii* var. *calocarpa,* Bailey), habit more spreading; lvs. on shoots more deeply lobed; fls. smaller with 3–4 styles.

9. **M. Sargentii,** Rehd. (*Pyrus Sargentii,* Bean). Bushy much-branched shrub, 3–6 ft., with pubescent young growths, the rigid branches often with thorn-like spurs: vernation conduplicate: lvs. ovate to elliptic-oblong, 2–3 in. long, very short-pointed, unequally sharp-serrate, slender-petioled, lightly pubescent on both surfaces when young but becoming glabrous above, dull green, those on vigorous young shoots broad-ovate and usually 3-lobed: fls. clear white, 1 in. across, 5 or 6 in a cluster on slender glabrous pedicels about 1 in. long; hypanthium glabrous outside, calyx-lobes acuminate; styles 4 (3–5): fr. nearly globose, ½in. or less diam., dark red with slight bloom, calyx deciduous. (Bears the name of C. S. Sargent, page 51.) Japan.

10. **M. toringoides,** Hughes (*M. transitoria* var. *toringoides,* Rehd. *P. transitoria* var. *toringoides,* Bailey). Shrub or tree to 25 ft., with young growths soon glabrous: lvs. ovate to oblong, 1¼–3¼ in. long, mostly with 2 pairs of lobes, margins crenate-serrate, becoming glabrous except on veins beneath: fls. creamy-white, 1 in. or less across, 3–6 or more together; styles mostly 4–5, glabrous; petals broad and overlapping, hairy above: fr. yellow becoming reddish in the sun, globular to somewhat pyriform, about ½in. across. China.

11. **M. coronaria,** Mill. (*Pyrus coronaria,* L.). Garland Crab-Apple. Wild Sweet Crab. Twiggy stiff-branched tree 20–30 ft. high, with thorn-like spurs and growths soon becoming glabrous: lvs. ovate to oval, 2–4 in. long, acute or acuminate, base mostly rounded, sharp-serrate and more or less notched, becoming glabrous; those on young shoots triangular-ovate and with 1–4 shallow lobes on either side: fls. bright rose as they open, then nearly white, fragrant, 1 in. or more across, on slender glabrous pedicels 1 in. or more long; hypanthium glabrous, the calyx-lobes erect and tomentose inside: fr. oblate (depressed at ends), 1 in. across, ridged about the depression at the apex, calyx persisting, yellow-green, hard and sour. N. Y. and Ont. to Ala. and Mo.—Attractive in cult.

12. **M. angustifolia,** Michx. (*Pyrus angustifolia,* Ait.). Southern Crab-Apple. Tree 20–25 ft. or more, partially evergreen, growth soon glabrous: lvs. lance-oblong to narrowly oblong-obovate, 1–3 in. long, obtuse or acutish, closely crenate-serrate or entire, soon glabrous above, sometimes retaining light pubescence on veins beneath; on vigorous shoots the lvs. may be ovate or elliptic and slightly lobed along the sides: fls. rose-colored and fragrant, about 1 in. across, on slender mostly glabrous pedicels about 1 in. long: fr. globose to somewhat pyriform, ¾–1 in. diam., yellow-green, with depressions on both ends. Va. to Fla. and Miss., in the coastal country.—Attractive in cult.

13. **M. ioensis,** Britt. (*Pyrus coronaria* var. *ioensis,* Wood. *P. ioensis,* Bailey). Prairie Crab-Apple. Tree to 20–30 ft., with young parts gray-tomentose: lvs. ovate-oblong to nearly ovate or somewhat obovate, 2–4 in. long, mostly acute at apex, irregularly and mostly bluntly serrate and notched, the larger ones often with shallow side lobes, becoming glabrous and somewhat glossy above, pubescent beneath: fls. white or rose-tinted, 1–2 in. across, mostly on pubescent pedicels 1 in. and more long: fr. short-oblong, sometimes angled, about 1 in. long, dull green with light dots and a greasy feel, calyx persistent, hardly edible. Ind. to Minn. and Kans.—Bechtel's crab is a double-fld. form. **M. Soulardii,** Britt. (*Pyrus Soulardii,* Bailey). Soulard Crab-Apple, is a series of natural hybrids of *M. ioensis* and *M. sylvestris,* represented by the Soulard crab intro. many years ago by James G. Soulard, Galen, Ill., and by other pomological vars.; aspect of *M. sylvestris* with tinted fls. in close tomentose clusters; lvs. much like those of *M. ioensis* but with less tendency to become lobed; fr. 2–3 in. across, apple-like, usually flattened endwise, yellow often with tinted cheek, more or less edible.

28. **SORBUS,** L. Mountain-Ash. Perhaps 85 species of deciduous trees or shrubs of the northern hemisphere, grown for ornament.—Lvs. alternate, stipulate, simple or pinnately compound, plicate or rarely convolute in bud: infl. a compound terminal corymb; fls. white or rarely pink, mostly bisexual; sepals and petals 5; stamens 15–20; pistils 1–5, each carpel 2-ovuled, ovaries either partially connate and half inferior or wholly connate and inferior, styles basally connate or wholly separate: fr. usually a small pome, of 2–5 locules, each 1–2-seeded, locule walls cartilaginous. (Sor-bus: ancient Latin name.)

A. Lvs. consistently odd-pinnate, with 9–21 subequal lfts.
  B. Fls. in flattened corymbs; styles 3–4: frs. ⅓in. or less across.
    C. Lf. becoming glabrous beneath: winter-buds sticky, subglabrous ....1. *S. americana*
    CC. Lf. pubescent beneath: winter-buds not sticky, densely pubescent ....2. *S. Aucuparia*
  BB. Fls. in broad-pyramidal pointed corymbs; styles 5: frs. ¾in. or more across......3. *S. domestica*
AA. Lvs. simple, serrate or lobed, sometimes basally pinnate.
  B. Lf. pinnate toward the base, the lowest sinuses reaching the midrib, tomentose beneath..........4. *S. hybrida*

BB. Lf. serrate or sinuses extending only half way to midrib.
 c. The lvs. distinctly lobed, becoming glabrous beneath....................5. *S. torminalis*
 cc. The lvs. serrate but not lobed, white-tomentose beneath..................6. *S. Aria*

1. **S. americana,** Marsh. (*Pyrus americana,* DC.). AMERICAN MOUNTAIN-ASH. Shrub or small tree to 30 ft., the young growths soon glabrous and terminal buds glutinous: lfts. 11–17, oblong-lanceolate to lanceolate, 1½–4 in. long, acuminate, sharp-serrate, bright green and glabrous above, paler and becoming glabrous beneath: fls. about ¼in. across, in dense flat-topped glabrous infl. 2½–6 in. across; stamens shorter than petals and subequal to the 3 styles: fr. bright red and shining, globose, about ¼in. across. Newf. to N. C. and Mich.

2. **S. Aucuparia,** L. (*Pyrus Aucuparia,* Gaertn.). EUROPEAN MOUNTAIN-ASH. ROWAN. Attractive round-headed tree to 50 ft., with pubescent young growth and pubescent but not sticky terminal buds, bark close and smooth: lfts. 9–15, oblong-lanceolate, ¾–2 in. long, short-pointed or blunt, sharp-serrate from near the base, mostly remaining pubescent beneath, sessile: fls. about ⅓in. across, in flat or somewhat rounded usually villous infl. 4–6 in. across; stamens subequal to petals; styles 3–4, shorter than stamens: fr. bright red, globular, about ⅓in. across, persisting and ornamental. (Aucuparia refers to the use of the fr. in catching birds: Latin *aucupatio,* fowling or bird-catching.) Eu. and Asia; now widely spread in cult. and sometimes spontaneous. Var. **pendula,** Rehd. (forma *pendula,* Kirchn.), has long drooping branches.

3. **S. domestica,** L. (*Pyrus domestica,* Smith not Medic. *P. Sorbus,* Gaertn.). SERVICE-TREE. Tree to 60 ft., branchlets soon glabrous and winter-buds glutinous: lfts. 11–21, narrow-oblong, 1¼–3¼ in. long, usually acute, sharp-serrate, glabrous above, tomentose beneath at least when young: fls. ⅝ in. across, in broad-pyramidal tomentose infl. to 4 in. across: fr. yellowish or brownish, tinged red, apple or pear-shaped, to 1 in. or more long. S. Eu., N. Afr., W. Asia.

4. **S. hybrida,** L. (*S. Aucuparia* × *S. intermedia. Pyrus pinnatifida,* Ehrh. *P. hybrida,* Smith not Moench). Tree to 40 ft., young growths floccose, winter-buds pubescent but not glutinous: lvs. oblong to oblong-ovate, 3–5 in. long, with 1–4 pairs of oblong serrate decurrent lfts. below, the upper part lobed, tomentose beneath: fls. ⅜in. across, in tomentose clusters to 4 in. across: fr. red, subglobose, ½in. across. Of European origin.—Material cult. as *Sorbus quercifolia* may belong here. *S. intermedia,* Pers. (*Pyrus intermedia,* Ehrh.), is sometimes confused with *S. hybrida,* but has no distinct lfts. and the sinuses do not reach the midrib.

5. **S. torminalis,** Crantz (*Cratægus torminalis,* L. *Pyrus torminalis,* Ehrh.). WILD SERVICE-TREE. Stout tree to 40–50 ft. or more, young parts floccose, winter-buds small and shining but not glutinous: lvs. broad-ovate, 2–4 or 5 in. long, cordate to broad-cuneate at base, with 3–5 angular pointed serrate lobes on either side, sinuses extending one-third to one-half the way to the midrib, usually becoming glabrous on both surfaces, shining above: fls. about ½in. across, in terminal tomentose clusters 3–5 in. across: fr. brown and dotted, ellipsoid, about ⅝in. long. (The name *torminalis* refers to *colic* or *gripes.*) Eu., N. Afr., Asia Minor.

6. **S. Aria,** Crantz (*Cratægus Aria,* L. *Pyrus Aria,* Ehrh.). WHITE BEAM-TREE. Stout tree to 50 ft., remaining a shrub on poor lands, with pubescent young parts and glutinous buds: lvs. elliptic to elliptic-oblong, 2–5 in. long, rather thick, rounded or short-acute, not lobed, the margin double-toothed, the straight side veins prominent, dark green above but white-tomentose beneath: fls. dull white, about ½in. across, with heavy scent, in tomentose clusters 2–3 in. across: fr. scarlet and speckled, nearly globular, ½in. or less across. (Aria is an old Greek name for the tree.) Eu.

29. **ARONIA,** Medic. CHOKEBERRY. Three little shrubs of swamps and low woods in E. N. Amer., planted for ornament.—Deciduous, thornless: lvs. alternate, simple, petiolate, serrate, glandular on the midrib above, stipules small and caducous: fls. white or sometimes tinted, in small compound terminal clusters appearing with the early lvs.; hypanthium urn-shaped with 5 sepals persistent on the top of fr.; petals 5, spreading; stamens many; pistil 1, ovary inferior, with usually 5 cells and as many carpels, the 5 styles joined at the base: fr. a little berry-like pome, with as many cells as styles, red, purplish or black. (Aro-nia: modified from Aria, a species of Sorbus.)

A. Lower surface of lvs. and infl. nearly or quite glabrous........................1. *A. melanocarpa*
AA. Lower surface of lvs. and infl. tomentose or pubescent.
 B. Fr. red..2. *A. arbutifolia*
 BB. Fr. purplish-black...3. *A. prunifolia*

1. **A. melanocarpa,** Ell. (*Mespilus arbutifolia* var. *melanocarpa,* Michx. *A. nigra,* Dipp. *Pyrus melanocarpa,* Willd. *P. nigra,* Sarg.). BLACK CHOKEBERRY. Low shrub 1½–4 ft. high: lvs. nearly or quite glabrous beneath: pedicels and hypanthium essentially glabrous, calyx-lobes somewhat glandular: fr. globose, about ⅓in. diam., black, usually not

long persisting. N. S. to Fla. and Mich. Var. **grandifolia**, Schneid. (*Pyrus grandifolia*, Lindl.), to 10 ft. high, with larger lvs., fls. and fr.

2. **A. arbutifolia**, Ell. (*Mespilus arbutifolia*, L. *Pyrus arbutifolia*, L. f.). RED CHOKEBERRY. Branching erect shrub to 10 ft.: lvs. obovate, oblong to elliptic, 1–3 in. long, abruptly short-pointed, narrowed to short petiole, sharply serrate, grayish-pubescent or -tomentose beneath: fls. white, often tinged red, ⅓–½in. across, in pubescent infl. terminating lateral branchlets; calyx-lobes with many glands: fr. subglobose or somewhat pear-shaped, about ¼in. diam., bright or dull red, long persistent. Mass. to Fla., Minn. and Tex. Var. **brilliantissima**, Hort., is offered.

3. **A. prunifolia**, Rehd. (*Mespilus prunifolia*, Marsh. *Pyrus floribunda*, Lindl. *P. arbutifolia* var. *atropurpurea*, Rob. *P. atropurpurea*, Bailey. *A. floribunda*, Spach. *A. atropurpurea*, Britt.). PURPLE CHOKEBERRY. Similar to the preceding species: shrub to 12 ft.: calyx-lobes little or not at all glandular: fr. larger, about ⅓in. diam., nearly globular, purple-black, long persistent. N. S. to Fla. and Ind.

30. **NEVIUSIA**, Gray. One shrub from Ala., but hardy to Mass.—Deciduous, with simple doubly serrate lvs.: fls. bisexual, apetalous, many, in open cymes; sepals 5, whitish, toothed, longer than the flattish hypanthium; stamens many, with conspicuous white filaments; pistils 2–4, the bodies pubescent, ovary 1-celled and 1-ovuled, styles slender, shorter than the stamens: achenes drupe-like. (Neviu-sia: discovered by R. D. Nevius, 1827–1913.)

N. alabamensis, Gray. SNOW-WREATH. Upright, pubescent, 2–6 ft. high: lvs. ovate to ovate-lanceolate, 1–3 in. long, stipules subulate: sepals elliptic to ovate, ⅓–½in. long.

31. **KERRIA**, DC. One shrub in Japan, commonly planted as an ornamental.—Spineless: lvs. alternate, simple, stipules awl-like and caducous: fls. solitary, terminating leafy shoots of the season, bisexual; sepals and petals 5, the former small and entire; disk annular in hypanthium; stamens many, filaments filiform; pistils 5–8, ovary 1-celled and 1-ovuled, the style slender: achene small and dry, seldom noted. (Ker-ria: William Kerr, Kew gardener and collector; died 1814.)

K. japonica, DC. (*Rubus japonicus*, L. *Corchorus japonicus*, Thunb.). Bramble-like bush but without prickles, 4–8 ft. high, the branches green and ridged: lvs. ovate to ovate-lanceolate, 2–4 in. long, long-acuminate, toothed and the teeth serrate, short-petioled, very lightly pubescent on both surfaces or becoming glabrous above: fls. golden-yellow, 1–2 in. across, in late spring to autumn, sometimes seen in the single state but usually double when it is sometimes known as Globe-flower (var. **pleniflora**, Witte): there are races with yellow-striped canes (var. **aureo-vittata**, Hartw. & Ruempl.) and white-margined lvs. (var. **picta**, Sieb.).

32. **RHODOTYPOS**, Sieb. & Zucc. One shrub in Japan, differing from Kerria in the opposite lvs., 4 sepals and petals, the former large and toothed, petals white, fr. a nearly black prominent 1-seeded dryish drupelet. (Rhodot-ypos: Greek *rose type* or *kind*, from the resemblance of the fls. to small single roses.)

R. tetrapetala, Makino (*Kerria tetrapetala*, Sieb. *R. scandens*, Makino. *R. kerrioides*, Sieb. & Zucc.). JETBEAD. Attractive hardy shrub 3–6 ft. and more high, spineless, with upright rather stiff habit, sts. becoming reddish: lvs. ovate to oblong-ovate, 2–4 in. long, acuminate, doubly sharp-serrate, short-petioled, rugose above, soft-pubescent beneath at least when young: fls. 1–1½ in. across, single, terminal on leafy shoots of the season, in late spring and early summer: drupelets about ¼in. across, shining, in the spreading persistent jagged sepals, persisting till late autumn or winter.

33. **RUBUS**, L. BRAMBLES, including blackberries, dewberries, raspberries, and certain species grown for ornament and ground-cover.—Mostly shrubs, many of them more or less erect, some prostrate and rooting at tips, a few with herbaceous top and per. woody root but only rarely if at all in cult.; some species more or less scandent, most of them prickly on canes, petioles and pedicels and frequently glandiferous; root durable, but the superstructure in many species bien., the first-year growth or primocane commonly not bearing fls., in the second year floricane producing a different set of lvs. with fls. and frs., floricane often dying at end of season although in a few intro. big woody species remaining alive and productive for two or more years: lvs. usually ample, alternate, simple in a few semi-herbaceous species but prevailingly pedate or pinnate, sometimes palmate, 3–5 lfts. being the rule ex-

cept some of them sometimes simple and bract-like in the infl.; stipules narrow but commonly prominent and more or less joined to petiole: fls. hermaphrodite, solitary, cymose, racemose, paniculate, prevailingly white but sometimes rose or pink, usually not noticeably fragrant, appearing in late spring and early summer; calyx 5-lobed or -parted, often subtended by an equal number of bracts; petals 5, separate, hypogynous, wide-spreading at maturity; stamens many and free; pistils few to many, simple, aggregated in center on an elongated receptacle or cone, each pistil becoming a sarcose drupelet and cohesively forming an edible "berry," a blackberry or dewberry when the core removes with the adhering drupelets, a hollow cone or raspberry when the core remains on the plant, style slender and nearly terminal, persistent, stigma not expanded. (Ru-bus: the classical name, associated with *ruber*, red.)—Very large and variable genus around the world, particularly abundant in the northern hemisphere; more than 400 species are known in N. Amer. The kinds have been much confused because of insufficient and inadequate herbarium specimens, whereby the species cannot be determined; as a result, the taxonomic custom has developed of calling the strange forms hybrids, yet hybridity can be nothing more than a blind guess until the species of the parents are known. It is only recently that the species in N. Amer. have begun to be understood. Both primocane and floricane material must always be present in botanical specimens for identification.

Many of the pomological varieties of blackberries and raspberries mentioned herein may not now be in cult. under those names, but the listing of them suggests the native species most likely to yield domestic forms and races, although varieties of other species may come into plantations at any time. In the N., at least, blackberry culture has not expanded in recent time. In some parts of the country great quantities of wild blackberries are picked and marketed, even though the species of them may not yet have been made out.

A. Grown for ground-cover or ornament, not primarily for edible fr. or as pomological varieties. (Nos. 20, 35, 36, also once known as fr. plants.)
  B. Plant mat-like and flat on the earth: lvs. persistent and glossy, obovate and nearly or quite obtuse, 3-lobed or 3-foliolate: grown for ground-cover. . . . . . 1. *R. hispidus*
  BB. Plant erect or at least ascending and mounding, bushy, grown for the showy bloom (nos. 3 and 20 intro. for fr.): lvs. palmate, pedate, pinnate or even simple.
    C. Lvs. of primocane palmate or palmatifid (general contour of maple lf.).
      D. Canes and other parts prominently glandular-hairy: fls. rose-purple . . . . 2. *R. odoratus*
      DD. Canes and other parts glandless: fls. white . . . . 3. *R. palmatus*
    CC. Lvs. of primocane not palmate.
      D. Lf. simple. 4. *R. deliciosus*
      DD. Lf. compound.
        E. Division of main lvs. on the 3-foliolate or perhaps 5-foliolate order, not pinnate, but more nearly pedate.
          F. Lfts. obtuse or nearly so, more or less obovate, the terminal or central one much the largest: canes and petioles reddish-hairy: fls. white . . . . 5. *R. ellipticus*
          FF. Lfts. long-acuminate: plant glandless: fls. reddish-purple. . . . . 6. *R. spectabilis*
        EE. Division of main lvs. pinnate, lfts. 5–9, opposite.
          F. Fls. full double, rose-like: prickles many and stout . . . . 7. *R. coronarius*
          FF. Fls. simple: prickles few or none, or very weak . . . . 8. *R. rosæfolius*
AA. Grown for the edible frs.: pomological or fruit-garden subjects. (No. 20 also mostly for ornament.)
  B. Fr. retaining the receptacle or core when it is picked: blackberries, dewberries. (Subgenus EUBATUS, the true blackberries.)
    C. Habit of plant trailing, or at least the mature primocanes procumbent and rooting at some or all the tips; floricanes mostly prostrate; sometimes the plant becomes mounding or tholiform, with prostrate but not trailing canes issuing from the clump.
      D. Floricane axes and usually also the mature primocanes pruinose (with a "bloom"); canes terete; extensive mounders and colonizers, with slender prickles, sometimes with a few glands: fls. commonly functionally unisexual. (Sect. URSINI, the Pacific berries.)
        E. The plant commonly devoid of stalked or pinhead glands, only the calyx and upper part of pedicel sometimes showing a few weak glands.
          F. Foliage light green, not felted-tomentose on under surface (unless on young ends); lfts. mostly long-pointed and acutely serrate to dentate. . . . . 9. *R. vitifolius*
          FF. Foliage dull green, felted-tomentose underneath; lfts. usually not long-pointed and serratures commonly not narrow and sharp. . . . 10. *R. ursinus*

EE. The plant heavily provided with glandular hairs at least on calyx and pedicels: foliage glabrescent. . . . . .11. *R. macropetalus*

DD. Floricane and primocane axes devoid of a glaucous or pruinose covering: fls. functionally perfect.

E. Foliage durable, mostly glossy, more or less perfectly evergreen in itself rather than because of mild climate; primocane lfts. conspicuously longer than broad and often narrow or long: bristles mostly abundant among the small prickles, glands often present. (Sect. VEROTRIVIALES, the Southern dewberries.)

F. Primocanes glandiferous, as well as frequently the petioles and calyx: slender flat trailer . . . . .12. *R. trivialis*

FF. Primocanes and other parts glandless: mounding trailer. . . . . .13. *R. mirus*

EE. Foliage not durable or evergreen and commonly not glossy, plant not bristly; primocane lfts. usually broad. (Sect. FLAGELLARES, the dewberries.)

F. Under surface of main lvs. glabrous or only slightly pubescent, not soft-pubescent or velvety to the finger.

G. Margins of floricane lfts. not deeply or unusually cut-toothed.

H. Lfts. on primocanes manifestly serrate (that is, finely indented).

I. Apex of primocane lfts. sharply or abruptly rather than gradually pointed, as if shouldered. . . . . .14. *R. flagellaris*

II. Apex of primocane lfts., or at least of the central lft., gradually tapered or narrowed to summit.

J. Shape of primocane lfts. broad-ovate and long-pointed: under surface of lvs. often distinctly pubescent but not velvety to finger. . . . . .15. *R. roribaccus*

JJ. Shape of primocane lfts. oblong to elliptic, apex acuminate, not distinctly pubescent underneath. . . . . .16. *R. velox*

HH. Lfts. on primocanes dentate or notched, the teeth or notches frequently serrate. . . . . .17. *R. geophilus*

GG. Margins of floricane lfts. deeply cut-toothed or even jagged. . . . .18. *R. almus*

FF. Under surface of main lvs. manifestly soft-pubescent or velvety to the finger. . . . . .19. *R. michiganensis*

CC. Habit of plant erect or upright, or if sometimes mounding or tholiform then only a branch now and then rooting at tip and plant not procumbent or trailing: the highbush blackberries.

D. Infl. paniculate at apex of stout woody sometimes per. and more or less lopping floricanes, other clusters perhaps on lateral shoots: European.

E. Lfts. deeply cut or laciniate, often dissected nearly or quite to the midrib. . . . . .20. *R. laciniatus*

EE. Lfts. not dissected, only serrate-dentate.

F. Margins of lfts. very closely finely and not very sharply serrate: primocane axis pruinose, often unarmed. 21. *R. ulmifolius*

FF. Margins of lfts. coarsely or at least conspicuously deeply and sharply dentate: primocane axis not pruinose.

G. Axis of primocane nearly or quite terete, thinly hairy or pubescent: lfts. finely serrate, usually narrow at base. . . . . .22. *R. bifrons*

GG. Axis of primocane strongly angled and furrowed, markedly hairy-pubescent: lfts. coarsely serrate-dentate, terminal or central one broad-based. . . . . .23. *R. procerus*

DD. Infl. not paniculate nor terminal on floricane: American.

E. Foliage commonly coriaceous or thick and very gray or white-tomentose beneath, sometimes glossy above; lfts. more or less cuneate, small. (Sect. CUNEIFOLII, the Sand blackberries.)

F. Leafage manifestly white-tomentose underneath, bush small and crabbed, mostly not 3 ft. tall: central lft. of primocane lvs. distinctly cuneate and entire at base and margins often revolute, subtruncate at apex; side-ribs prominent on lvs. . . . . .24. *R. cuneifolius*

FF. Leafage mostly gray-pubescent, bush larger and freer-growing; central lft. of primocane lvs. not cuneate-entire at base nor revolute; side-ribs usually not prominent.

G. Prickles very large and strong, prominently expanded or flattened at base.

H. Lfts. short-acute: clusters of fls. and frs. open. . . . . .25. *R. pascuus*

HH. Lfts. obtuse or nearly so: clusters of fls. and frs. compact, the pedicels short. . . . . .26. *R. serissimus*

GG. Prickles of ordinary or small size, not prominently expanded at base. . . . . .27. *R. acer*

EE. Foliage not white-tomentose underneath (in ours) nor glossy above; lfts. at least of primocanes large and soft and commonly narrowed to apex.

F. Infl., petioles and sometimes the canes conspicuously glandiferous: clusters prevailingly racemiform. (Sect. ALLEGHENIENSES, the Copsy highbush blackberries.)

G. Fl.-clusters usually long-racemiform and exceeding the associated foliage, the pedicels divaricate and rachis continuous: lfts. not conspicuously broad. . . . . .28. *R. allegheniensis*

GG. Fl.-clusters short and rachis not always continuous and pedicels more or less ascending, not exceeding associated foliage: lfts. large, broad and cordate. . . . . .29. *R. Rosa*

FF. Infl., petioles and canes devoid of glands (or only exceptionally and inconspicuously present now and then). (Sect. ARGUTI, the Field highbush blackberries.)
G. Lfts. of main mature primocane lvs. long and narrow-attenuate, length usually more than twice the width . . . . 30. *R. louisianus*
GG. Lfts. of main primocane lvs. ovate or elliptic, length less than twice the width.
H. Main fl.-clusters long or narrow and raceme-like with a continuing axis, even though the cluster may be leafy in its middle or lower part. . . . . 31. *R. bellobatus*
HH. Main fl.-clusters about as broad as long, without continuing axis, few-fld. and essentially cymiform and broad.
I. Clusters of fls. and frs. clearly exceeding the associated lvs., not covered by the lvs.
J. Floral lfts. and simple lvs. narrow and manifestly acute to attenuate. . . . . 32. *R. laudatus*
JJ. Floral lfts. and simple lvs. obtuse or only briefly acute . . . 33. *R. philadelphicus*
II. Clusters of fls. and frs. exceeded or equalled by the associated lvs. . . . . 34. *R. parcifrondifer*
BB. Fr. at maturity a hollow cone, the receptacle or core remaining on the plant. (Subgenus IDÆOBATUS, the raspberries.)
C. Infl. markedly paniculiform for the most part and terminating canes and strong branches: plant densely covered with purplish glandular hairs. . .35. *R. phœnicolasius*
CC. Infl. racemiform or cymiform or few-fld. and ascendate.
D. Lvs. strikingly pinnate, the opposite narrow lfts. 5 or more. . . . . .36. *R. illecebrosus*
DD. Lvs. pedate, sometimes simple, or only indifferently pinnate, lfts. mostly not long-narrow and many.
E. Clusters on the racemiform or open order, the few terminal fls. not aggregated at summit of shoot: fr. usually red.
F. Glandless: fr. a compact well-formed "berry" holding its shape when picked. . . . . 37. *R. idæus*
FF. Glandiferous on some or most of its axes and calyx: "berry" loose and crumbly when picked. . . . . .38. *R. strigosus*
EE. Clusters on the cymiform or umbelliform order, in a flat-topped more or less compact aggregation: "berry" firm when picked, usually black. . . . . 39. *R. occidentalis*

1. **R. hispidus,** L. GROUNDBERRY. Low flat-trailing glossy-lvd. evergreen trailer, primocanes at first somewhat ascending to 1 ft. or so but soon long-running; canes slender, hispid and often glandular: lvs. 3–5-foliolate, glabrous; lfts. broadly obovate, obtuse or nearly so, crenate-serrate, 2 in. or less long: fls. white, few, on upright shoots: fr. red becoming black, small, globular. E. Canada and U. S. to mts. of Tenn. west to Wis.—Grown as ground-cover in rock-gardens and on banks.

2. **R. odoratus,** L. FLOWERING RASPBERRY. THIMBLEBERRY. Vigorous unarmed very leafy bush 3–6 ft. high: lvs. broadly ovate, cordate, 4–10 in. across, with 3 or 5 acuminate lobes, soft-pubescent underneath: fls. in loose clusters, rose-purple (sometimes nearly white), about 1½ in. across: fr. red, small, crumbly. Woods and openings, N. S. to Ga.—Sometimes planted as an ornamental shrub.

3. **R. palmatus,** Thunb. Erect diffuse branching plant 4–7 ft. high, with few straight prickles on main canes: lvs. palmately 3–5-lobed, the middle longest, all acuminate and sharp-dentate, pubescent underneath: fls. white, single in the axils, 1 in. or less across: fr. yellow, drooping, ripening very early. China, Japan.—Ornamental shrub; once intro. by Luther Burbank for fr., as Mayberry.

4. **R. deliciosus,** Torr. Depressed or semi-scandent, glandless unless sometimes on calyx, unarmed, canes 3 ft. and more long: lvs. simple, broadly cordate-ovate, about 2 in. broad, serrate: fls. solitary on short leafy branchlets, about 2 in. across, white, petals rounded, like single roses: fr. dark purple, usually hardly edible. Colo., Wyo.—Long planted as an ornamental.

5. **R. ellipticus,** Smith. Stout, canes ascending or clambering, 5–15 ft. long, covered with long stiff reddish hairs and a few prickles: lvs. 3-foliolate, thick, more or less persistent, gray-tomentose underneath, becoming glabrous above; lfts. elliptic, 2–5 in. long, nearly or quite obtuse: fls. white, small, in terminal panicles: fr. yellow, raspberry-like. Hills and mts., India; nat. in American tropics.—Intro. as an ornamental.

6. **R. spectabilis,** Pursh. SALMONBERRY. Glandless branching bush with long erect or lopping canes that may be several ft. long and becoming glabrous or nearly so and unarmed, sometimes persisting more than two years: lvs. 3–5-foliolate, thin, nearly glabrous; lfts. ovate-pointed and often cordate, 4–5 in. long: fls. reddish-purple, about 1 in. across, 1–4 of them on long pedicels among the lvs.: fr. large, red to yellow, edible. Ida. to Calif. and Alaska.—Planted for ornament.

7. **R. coronarius,** Sweet. BRIER-ROSE. SALEM-ROSE. Erect, 3–4 ft., very leafy, with prickly canes, petioles and pedicels, glabrous, glandless: lvs. long-pinnate with 6–8 long narrow opposite lfts. and a terminal lft. of similar shape, serrate: fls. white, full double like a small rose, singly terminating short leafy branchlets, sterile. Probably Asian.—Grown for ornament; root-hardy in N. Y.

8. **R. rosæfolius,** Smith. Spreading or lopping much-branched bush 3 ft. or more tall, glandless, prickles very few and weak: lvs. long-pinnate, puberulent; lfts. opposite, 4–6 and an odd terminal one, narrow-acuminate, serrate: fls. white, simple (not double), few. on short leafy branchlets: fr. a many-seeded scarlet raspberry of indifferent quality, India to Java.—Planted far S. for ornament, widely nat. in tropics.

9. **R. vitifolius,** Cham. & Schlecht. Green-lvd. mounding and trailing tip-rooting glandless plant or partial low climber to 5 or 6 ft.; primocane axis soon glabrous, prickly: lvs. of primocanes 3-foliolate or sometimes trilobate, lightly pubescent to glabrous and not gray-tomentose (unless perhaps on tips); lfts. ovate, sometimes 4–6 in. long, acuminate, often subcordate, serrate: fls. few on prickly pedicels, white, mostly less than 1 in. across, not much if at all exceeding the foliage: fr. oblong, black. Cent. W. Calif. Var. **titanus,** Bailey (*R. titanus*, Bailey), MAMMOTH BLACKBERRY, CORY, strong runner, to 30 or 40 ft., large lvs., and cylindric frs. to 2 in. long; grown on wires and trellises; a form of it is the Mammoth Thornless blackberry, supposed to be of hybrid origin.

10. **R. ursinus,** Cham. & Schlecht. Gray-green-lvd. mounding and trailing usually glandless plant, primocanes pruinose, with weak prickles, often many ft. long: lvs. 3–5-foliolate, tomentose on both surfaces or becoming nearly glabrous underneath; lfts. not long-acuminate and often almost obtuse: fls. few on prickly pedicels about equalling foliage, white, usually small: fr. black varying to white and red. Lower Calif. to Ore. Var. **loganobaccus,** Bailey (*R. loganobaccus*, Bailey), LOGANBERRY, very strong grower and prickly, lfts. gray-felted underneath and very large, fr. 1 in. or more long and dark red; Boysenberry belongs with var. *loganobaccus*.—Youngberry is probably a derivative of *R. ursinus*, perhaps of hybrid origin.

11. **R. macropetalus,** Dougl. Long and vigorous runner and tip-rooter, canes to 12 or 20 ft. in length and prickly, pedicels and calyx glandular: lvs. of primocanes 3–5-foliolate, petioles prickly; lfts. narrowly ovate to lanceolate, acuminate, 4–5 in. long, more or less hairy-pubescent on both surfaces but not gray-tomentose (unless sometimes on tips): fls. few on ascending prickly glandular pedicels and about equalling the foliage, corolla sometimes 1 in. across: fr. ovoid to long-oblong, to 1 in. long. N. Calif. to B. C.—Source of such vars. as Skagit Chief, Zelinski, Washington Climbing.

12. **R. trivialis,** Michx. SOUTHERN DEWBERRY. Flat trailer, sometimes a mounder, with more or less persistent and essentially glabrous and often bronzy foliage; primocanes very slender, 3 ft. and more long, rooting, prickly and glandular-hairy: lvs. 3–5-foliolate, with prickly and glandular petioles; lfts. narrow to very narrow, 1–3 in. long, notched: fls. solitary or 2–3 on ascending prickly sometimes glandular pedicels: fr. oblong, mostly small, black (sometimes white), sweet at maturity. Va. south to Fla. and Tex.—Source of cult. dewberries, as Gregg, Houston, Manatee.

13. **R. mirus,** Bailey. MARVEL DEWBERRY. Prostrate and mounding glandless large-fld. strong dewberry, several ft. long, rooting at tips; primocanes stoutly prickly, without hairs: lvs. of primocanes mostly 5-foliolate, glabrous and shining above, more or less evergreen, lightly pubescent underneath; lfts. elliptic to nearly ovate, to 2 in. long, abruptly pointed, serrate: fls. on long prickly pedicels, more than 1 in. across, sometimes larger and polypetalous from double-blossom disease: fr. oblong, 1 in. long and nearly as thick, black, of high quality. Cult. in Fla., nativity not known.

14. **R. flagellaris,** Willd. (*R. procumbens*, Auth.). Strong glandless prickly nearly or quite glabrous dewberry, several ft. long and usually covering large area, rooting at tips, sometimes making low mounds: lvs. 3–5-foliolate, sometimes thinly pubescent on lower surface, sharply serrate-dentate; lfts. elliptic to ovate, abruptly pointed as if shouldered, 2 in. or more long: fls. 1–6 on long ascending sometimes prickly pedicels, corolla about 1 in. across: fr. prominent, about ½in. long and thick, of good quality. N. B. to Minn., Tenn., Okla.—A few cult. dewberries appear to belong to this eastern species.

15. **R. roribaccus,** Rydb. Very vigorous glandless trailer many ft. long, with large primocane lvs. soft-pubescent underneath; primocanes bearing scattered prickles, glabrous unless at the tips: lvs. of primocanes 3–5-foliolate; lfts. large, often 4 in. long, ovate and taper-pointed and often subcordate: fls. 2–5 to a lateral branchlet, on long separate aculeate pubescent pedicels, corolla perhaps 1½ in. across, calyx-lobes sometimes foliaceous: fr. large, broad and of good quality. W. Va., Ky.—Lucretia, Baker, and other dewberries are of this species.

16. **R. velox,** Bailey. Strong glandless trailer not freely rooting at tips, making mounds, canes and petioles prickly: lvs. large, 3–5-foliolate, glabrous above and pubescent underneath; lfts. oblong or elliptic, acuminate, 3–4 in. long, 1½–2 in. broad, closely sharply serrate: fls. about 3–5, on long ascending pedicels about equalling foliage, corolla about 1 in. across: fr. large, about 1 in. or more long, of good quality. Tex.—Pomological vars. McDonald, Haupt and others are referable here.

17. **R. geophilus,** Blanch. Glandless tip-rooting runner, 8–12 ft. long at full growth, with few scattered weak prickles: primocane lvs. 5-foliolate, nearly or quite glabrous on both surfaces, margins sharply doubly serrate-dentate: lfts. 3–4 in. long, ovate, rather abruptly short-acuminate, terminal lft. sometimes subcordate: fls. 1–5 on ascending

usually mildly armed pedicels ascending to top of foliage, corolla about 1 in. across: fr. short-oblong or nearly globular, perhaps 1 in. long, of good quality. Me., Mass., N. J., N. Y., Mich.—Once, and perhaps now, represented in garden dewberries.

18. **R. almus,** Bailey. Very vigorous glandless plant prostrate to 6–8 ft., prickles many but not stout or hooked, making dense low mounds and tip-rooting: lvs. 5–7-foliolate, soft-pubescent underneath, petioles prickly; lfts. 2–3 in. or more long, elliptic-ovate to broad-ovate, abruptly acuminate, sometimes subcordate, margins deeply cut-toothed: fls. few to several on each floral shoot, on stout ascending prickly pedicels mostly exceeding foliage, corolla about 1 in. or more across: fr. more than 1 in. long, firm, of good quality. N. E. Tex.—Mayes dewberry belongs here, often run wild.

19. **R. michiganensis,** Bailey. Strong trailer and tip-rooter, glandless, sparsely and weakly prickly, canes 3–4 ft. long: lvs. 3–5-foliolate, thinly pubescent on upper face, typically soft-pubescent to finger on lower face, margins deeply sharply toothed or incised; lfts. ovate or elliptic, 3–4 in. long, sometimes subcordate, rather abruptly acuminate: fls. 4–12 on ascending often aciculate pedicels about as high as foliage: fr. oblong-globular, of good quality when well mature. Mich., Ind., Wis., Minn.—Pomological vars. apparently belong to this species.

20. **R. laciniatus,** Willd. Cut-leaved Blackberry. Very stout much-branched cut-lvd. glandless shrub, erect or sprawling, the very prickly stiff angled canes 10–12 ft. long and usually more or less per.: lvs. of primocanes usually 5-foliolate and some of the lfts. again divided, glabrous on upper face, more or less soft-pubescent on lower face; lfts. mostly ovate-acuminate and perhaps divided into narrower parts, deeply laciniate and cut-toothed, margins dentate: fls. many in a long terminal projecting panicle, corolla about 1 in. across, rose-color: fr. large and globular, edible. Eu.; frequently escaped.—Grown for decoration and to cover rough spots; pomological vars. are Atlantic, Black Diamond, Pan American, Starr, Wonder.

21. **R. ulmifolius,** Schott. Stout stiff glandless strongly prickly shrub to 5 or 6 ft. tall and strong horizontal branches that sometimes root at tip: lvs. 5-foliolate, more or less persistent, gray-tomentose on lower face, nearly glabrous on upper face; lfts. 3–4 in. long, ovate to obscurely obovate, margins very finely serrate, petioles prickly: fls. many in long narrow terminal panicle, pink, corolla about 1 in. across: fr. conic, of edible quality. Eu.; nat. in some parts of the country.—Grown for fr., particularly the thornless race, var. **inermis,** Focke, origin of Burbank and Santa Rosa blackberries.

22. **R. bifrons,** Vest. Arching or low mounding strong glandless very prickly blackberry with nearly or quite terete thinly hairy or pubescent primocanes to 5 ft. long that sometimes lie on the ground and tip-root: lvs. of primocanes more or less persistent, 5-foliolate, glabrous above, canescent or tomentose underneath; lfts. oblong-elliptic to ovate-elliptic, 3–4 in. long, short-acuminate, usually not subcordate, margins finely and evenly serrate: fls. white or rose, in terminal more or less leafy panicles: fr. not large, black. Eu.; more or less escaped from stock grown for ornament and cover.

23. **R. procerus,** P. J. Muell. Sprawling somewhat evergreen rough very prickly briar with angled canes to 10 ft. high or long and prostrate parts rooting at tip: lvs. of primocanes large, 5-foliolate, becoming glabrous on upper face, canescent or tomentose on lower face; lfts. broad-ovate to nearly rounded, 4–5 in. long and often nearly as broad, often subcordate at base, very abruptly pointed, margins rather coarsely and unequally serrate-dentate: fls. in conspicuous projecting terminal panicles: fr. black, thick, large and succulent. Eu.—Cult. as Himalaya-berry and also spontaneous.

24. **R. cuneifolius,** Pursh. Sand Blackberry. Stiff erect short-branched glandless prickly briar 1–3 ft. high, growing more or less singly, with small stiff 3-foliolate lvs., hard and nearly glabrous on upper face, gray-tomentose on lower face; lfts. 1–2 in. long, cuneate or obovate, nearly or quite obtuse, petioles prickly: fls. 3–5 in little open clusters, white, often more than 1 in. across: fr. globular or short-oblong, about ½in. long. Dry hard lands, Conn. to S. C., in different natural vars.—Once intro. as a fr. plant.

25. **R. pascuus,** Bailey. Erect and very stiff, 3–5 ft. tall, strongly prickly, canes prominently angled, glandless, growing in clumps: lvs. 3-foliolate, thick, dull green above, gray-tomentose underneath, petioles stoutly armed; lfts. 2–3 in. long, ovate-oblong to nearly obovate, not cuneate, briefly pointed, margins double-serrate: fls. few terminating leafy prickly shoots, about ¾in. across: fr. nearly globular, almost 1 in. thick. Md.—Known in cult. as Tree, Topsy, Nanticoke blackberries.

26. **R. serissimus,** Bailey. Mounding and sprawling glandless very prickly blackberry with more or less lopping canes to 5 or 6 ft. long but not tip-rooting, very late-flowering: lvs. 3-foliolate, nearly or quite glabrous on upper face, tomentose underneath; lfts. about 2 in. long, elliptic to nearly orbicular, not cordate, apex obtuse or only very briefly pointed, margins closely serrate, petioles armed and hirsute: fls. few in close clusters terminal on the branches: fr. about 1 in. thick, of good quality. Everbearing blackberry cult. in Tex. and Okla.; native region unknown.

27. **R. acer,** Bailey. Dull gray but not tomentose densely prickly glandless bush 3–4 ft. tall, much-branched: lvs. 3–5-foliolate, rather thin in texture; lfts. ovate to obovate,

2–3 in. long, briefly pointed, sometimes subcordate at base, margins closely serrate: fls. 4–6 on short prickly pedicels at top of branchlets, often 1 in. across: fr. globose and seedy. N. Y. on Long Island. Var. **subacer,** Bailey, of Staten Isl., N. Y. and N. J., is a taller freer grower and less gray that has yielded the Robinson blackberry.

28. **R. allegheniensis,** Porter. Free-growing prickly shrub 5–10 ft. tall, abundantly glandular on petioles and pedicels as well as soft-pubescent: lvs. 5-foliolate, large and soft with prickly petioles; lfts. oblong-acuminate to ovate-acuminate, 3–5 in. long, sometimes subcordate, sharply and closely serrate: fls. many in racemiform clusters about equalling or exceeding the foliage and with continuing rachis: fr. distinctly oblong when well grown, 1 in. or more long, aromatic. N. S. to Minn., N. C., Mo., in several vars., a common species.—Taylor, once a popular pomological blackberry, is of this species.

29. **R. Rosa,** Bailey. Large erect leafy bush to 8 or 10 ft. high, strongly prickly on the angled canes that are sometimes glandiferous as are the petioles and pedicels: lvs. soft and cloth-like, large, petioles prickly; primocane lvs. mostly 5-foliolate, very soft-pubescent underneath; lfts. ovate to broad-ovate, 4–5 in. long, mostly cordate or subcordate, short-acuminate, margins unequally finely serrate: fls. many in rather short racemiform clusters that usually do not exceed the foliage: fr. large, short-conic, juicy. N. H. to Ind. and Mich.—Source of pomological blackberries, such as Agawam, Ancient Briton, Eldorado, Erie, Snyder.

30. **R. louisianus,** Berger. Large plant, 5–6 ft. tall, glandless, moderately prickly, furrowed canes: primocane lvs. 5-foliolate, dull green above, soft-pubescent underneath, sharply serrate; lfts. lanceolate to oblong-lanceolate, 4–5 in. long and less than one-half as broad, long-acuminate, narrowed to base, margins closely sharply serrate, petioles more or less prickly: fls. few in open leafy clusters among the leafage: fr. cylindric, often whitish, sweet. Md. to Ala., La.—Origin of Crystal White blackberry.

31. **R. bellobatus,** Bailey. Large strong glandless stoutly prickly showy bramble to 6 ft. and more tall, much-branched, making dense colonies: lvs. of primocanes 5-foliolate, nearly glabrous above, soft-pubescent beneath, petioles armed; lfts. broadly ovate to cordate-ovate, 3–4 in. long and one-half or more as broad, mostly gradually acuminate, margins coarsely double-serrate: fls. 8–10 in a more or less leafy raceme, often 2 in. across, somewhat overtopping foliage: fr. large, pulpy, good. N. W. N. J., also elsewhere perhaps escaped.—Source of the Kittatinny blackberry, once a major kind and still persisting about old places.

32. **R. laudatus,** Berger. Heavy upright glandless somewhat prickly bush, 5 or 6 ft. tall, canes furrowed: primocane lvs. 5-foliolate, becoming glabrous above, soft-pubescent underneath; lfts. to 5 in. long and one-half as broad, ovate to narrow-ovate, short-acuminate, often cordate or subcordate, margins closely double-serrate: fls. 7–9 on long slanting nearly or quite nude pedicels in more or less racemiform clusters somewhat exceeding the foliage: fr. oblong, early in ripening, good. Mo., Kans.—The Bundy blackberry, Kenoyer, and probably the true Erie are of this species.

33. **R. philadelphicus,** Blanch. Erect but recurving commonly glandless blackberry to 5 ft. tall, with short stout straight prickles: primocane lvs. 5-foliolate, nearly or quite glabrous above, soft-pubescent underneath; lfts. oblong-ovate to ovate, 5 in. or more long, tapering to apex from middle or below, base rounded or subcordate, margins unevenly and sharply serrate, petioles prickly: fls. 3–8 in short close clusters exceeding the foliage, corolla about 1 in. across: fr. short-oblong, good in quality. Mass. to Va.—Probable source of the Lawton, at one time the leading cult. blackberry.

34. **R. parcifrondifer,** Bailey. Diffuse open grower to about 4 ft. tall, sometimes with glandular pedicels, branches sometimes lopping and tip-rooting, prickles small and short, producing many fruiting parcifronds: primocane lvs. 3–5-foliolate, thinly hairy above, soft-pubescent underneath; lfts. ovate to broad-ovate, 3–4 in. long, short-pointed, mostly rounded at base, margins doubly serrate: fls. 6–8, on slender pedicels in lf.-axils, corolla often more than 1 in. across: fr. oblong, juicy, good. S. N. J.—Source of Wilson and Wilson Jr. blackberries, once popular, and probably of Rathbun.

35. **R. phœnicolasius,** Maxim. Upright and arching bush 4–6 ft. high, covered with bristly gland-tipped purplish hairs, the long branches tip-rooting: lvs. 3-foliolate, more or less pubescent on upper face and white-tomentose on lower face, terminal lft. much the largest and about 4 in. long, triangular-ovate, more or less subcordate at base, margins not acutely serrate-dentate: fls. usually many in extended terminal panicles, petals very small and white, calyx-lobes long-pointed: fr. at first inclosed in calyx, red. E. Asia.—Intro. as Wineberry, planted for ornament and run wild.

36. **R. illecebrosus,** Focke. Diffuse glandless raspberry propagating by suckers, glabrous or essentially so, prickly on canes, petioles and perhaps pedicels: lvs. conspicuously pinnate; lfts. 2–4 pairs, lanceolate, 3–4 in. long, sessile, acuminate: fls. in loose clusters not exceeding foliage, each one on a separate ascending nude or prickly petiole, petals large and white: fr. oblong, red, 1 in. or more long, of many drupelets. Japan.—Intro. as fr. plant under the names Strawberry-raspberry and Cardinal Balloonberry; now escaped.

37. **R. idæus,** L. RED and YELLOW GARDEN RASPBERRY. Upright and diffuse glandless shrub, not bristly, prickles none or few, short and wide-based, propagating by suckers, canes terete, 4–6 ft. high: primocane lvs. 3–5- or even 7-foliolate but not pinnate in appearance, nearly or quite glabrous on upper face, gray-tomentose on lower face; lfts. broad-ovate to oblong-ovate, 3–4 in. long, cordate at base, abruptly short-acuminate, margins sharply serrate, petioles unarmed: fls. 1–6 in upper axils terminating the shoots, petals small, narrow, white: fr. cone-shaped, the fleshy cohering drupelets falling together from the elongated persisting torus. Eu.—Extensively cult. as a pomological subject, sometimes escaped as a fugitive.

38. **R. strigosus,** Michx. WILD RED RASPBERRY. Much like no. 37 but glandiferous on primocanes or on lesser parts, bearing many bristles, lfts. mostly 3–5, narrow and long-acuminate, thin, not often white-tomentose underneath, mature fr. mostly flattened at ends, small, crumbly, torus short. Widespread in N. Amer. in several vars. and forms.—Not regularly cult. although perhaps a parent in garden hybrids and likely to introduce the element of hardiness.

39. **R. occidentalis,** L. BLACKCAP RASPBERRY. Robust erect glandless shrub to 6 ft. and more, primocanes pruinose with stout prickles, terete, recurving in autumn and rooting at tip: lvs. 3-foliolate, white-canescent underneath; lfts. broad-ovate to lance-ovate, 3–5 in. long, acuminate, central one often subcordate, margins sharply doubly serrate: fls. 3–7, close together among foliage terminating the branchlets, petals small, white: fr. firm, commonly black and glaucous, sometimes yellowish or amber, depressed-globular, aromatic and sweet at maturity. N. B. to Ga. and Colo.—Cult. in named pomological vars.

34. **DALIBARDA,** L. One low tufted creeping pubescent per.—Lvs. simple, rounded, long-petioled: peduncles scape-like, bearing 1–2 white fls.; sepals 5–6, unequal, the larger usually toothed; petals 5, white; stamens many; pistils 5–10, forming nearly dry drupelets inclosed in the connivent sepals. (Dalibar-da: T. F. Dalibard, a French botanist of the 18th century.)

D. repens, L. Lvs. 1–2 in. wide: peduncles slender, 1½–5 in. long; fls. to ½in. across. N. S. to Minn., N. J. and Ohio.

35. **FRAGARIA,** L. STRAWBERRY. Low per. herbs, in the north temp. zone and in the western hemisphere in high regions of the tropics; variable, and many species have been described, probably reducible to 20 or 30.—Plant making long runners but otherwise stemless, the fls. being borne on radical peduncles or scapes: lvs. pinnately 3-foliolate, stipules joined to base of petiole: fls. white or reddish, in small raceme-like clusters, sometimes nearly or quite unisexual, much as in Potentilla but receptacle enlarged and becoming very fleshy (forming the "berry") and holding the seed-like frs. on the surface. (Fraga-ria: Latin *fragrance*, from the odor of the fr.)

A. Fruiting scapes equal to or longer than lvs.: achenes superficial on the ripe fr.
  B. Hull (calyx and appendages) spreading in the ripe fr. .... 1. *F. vesca*
  BB. Hull strongly reflexed .... 2. *F. moschata*
AA. Fruiting scapes shorter than the lvs.: achenes sunken in pits.
  B. Lvs. thick, bluish-white beneath .... 3. *F. chiloensis*
  BB. Lvs. thin, green beneath .... 4. *F. virginiana*

1. **F. vesca,** L. Erect, 6–12 in. high, with spreading hairs on petioles and peduncles: lvs. thin and light green, glabrous or becoming so above, lighter colored and lightly silky-hairy beneath at least on the veins; lfts. cuneate-ovate to rhombic-ovate, coarsely sharp-toothed: fl.-cluster small, equalling or exceeding the lvs., forking; fls. about ½in. across, bisexual: fr. (receptacle) firm, small, hemispheric or somewhat elongated and with a short neck, achenes very prominent, hull widely spreading. Eu. Var. **americana,** Porter, has subappressed hairs on peduncles and pedicels, fr. red; E. N. Amer.—Source of the Alpine strawberries grown in Eu. and sometimes in N. Amer.; runs into white-fruited forms (var. **alba,** Bailey); it sometimes bears again in autumn, and some at least of the Ever-bearing strawberries are derivatives of it; there is an old group of Perpetual strawberries described in the books.

2. **F. moschata,** Duchesne (*F. elatior*, Ehrh.). HAUTBOIS STRAWBERRY. Taller plant, more pubescent, usually diœcious: fr. (receptacle) dull red, musky, the hull strongly reflexed. Eu.—Grown abroad but rarely known in N. Amer.

3. **F. chiloensis,** Duchesne. Low stocky plant, runners mostly forming after fruiting: lvs. thick, somewhat glossy above, bluish-white beneath and more or less hairy on veins; lfts. large, broadly cuneate-ovate, strongly toothed: fl.-clusters on short peduncle with long branches, scarcely erect or soon lopping; fls. ¾in. across: fr. (receptacle) large and firm, dark red, the very large hull spreading. Alaska to Calif., Chile. Var. **ananassa,** Bailey, represents most of the common cult. strawberries, with larger frs.; probably produced by hybridization.—Sometimes used as a ground-cover.

4. **F. virginiana,** Duchesne, the common wild strawberry of E. N. Amer. probably has entered into the evolution of the garden strawberries and is apparently discernible now and then in named vars.: more slender than no. 3, making runners early: lvs. thin, light green above and beneath: fl.-clusters small, on long peduncle which is usually erect: berry small, light scarlet, globular or oblong-conical, usually with a neck at base, the hull not very large and spreading.—Stout forms with more spreading hairs on pedicels are var. **illinoensis,** Gray.

36. **DUCHESNEA,** Smith. INDIA- or MOCK-STRAWBERRY. Two little running perennials like Fragaria but the fls. yellow, calyx-bractlets leafy and toothed, and the receptacle dry; both S. Asian, one widely nat. and also cult. (Duches-nea: A. N. Duchesne, monographer of Fragaria in 1766.)

D. indica, Focke (*Fragaria indica,* Andr.). Stemless except for the very long runners, more or less hairy: lvs. long-petioled; stipules free from petiole; lfts. 3, rhombic-ovate, very short-stalked, rather bluntly toothed, silky-hairy at least beneath: fls. solitary, the corolla yellow and about ½in. across: fr. (receptacle) small and dry, covered with the red achenes and surrounded by the large persistent calyx.—Sometimes used as ground-cover and in hanging-baskets and vases.

37. **POTENTILLA,** L. CINQUEFOIL. FIVE-FINGER. A widespread genus in the north temp. and frigid zones, with upward of 300 species, ann. and per. herbs and a few shrubs, a small number cult. for ornament.—Lvs. digitately or pinnately compound, the larger ones usually basal (exception in no. 1): fls. mostly bisexual, solitary or cymose; calyx wide open, 5-cleft and with 5 bractlets between; petals 5, usually broad, yellow, white, or in shades of red; stamens numerous; pistils many on a mostly pubescent or hairy receptacle, ovary 1-celled and 1-ovuled, the styles deciduous: achenes small, the receptacle dry in fr. (Potentil-la: Latin *potens,* powerful, from reputed medicinal qualities.)—There are named hybrids among the herbaceous kinds in cult.

A. Sts. distinctly woody, with shredding bark: lvs. pinnate, all cauline . . . . 1. *P. fruticosa*
AA. Sts. herbaceous or nearly so: lvs. partly basal.
B. Basal lvs. pinnately 5–7-foliolate: fls. white . . . . 5. *P. rupestris*
BB. Basal lvs. not as above.
C. The basal lvs. 3-foliolate.
D. Color of fls. yellow.
E. Fls. ½in. across, red at base: lfts. 1 in. long . . . . 8. *P. tormentillo-formosa*
EE. Fls. ¾–1 in. across, all yellow.
F. Lvs. white-tomentose beneath.
G. Lfts. 1½–2½ in. long, many-toothed along most of margin . . . . . 9. *P. argyrophylla*
GG. Lfts. 1–1¼ in. long, 5-toothed . . . . 11. *P. villosa*
FF. Lvs. more or less silky-villous beneath.
G. Bractlets between the sepals ovate, with rounded apex: lfts. as wide as long . . . . 4. *P. fragiformis*
GG. Bractlets lanceolate, sharp-pointed: lfts. usually not as wide as long. 14. *P. grandiflora*
DD. Color of fls. not yellow.
E. Fls. white, ¼in. across . . . . 2. *P. tridentata*
EE. Fls. rose to purple (rarely white), ¾–1 in. across.
F. Lfts. less than ½in. long: sts. 1–2 in. high . . . . 3. *P. nitida*
FF. Lfts. 1–3 in. long: sts. 8–20 in. high . . . . 10. *P. atrosanguinea*
CC. The basal lvs. palmately 5–7-foliolate.
D. Color of fls. rose to purple . . . . 7. *P. nepalensis*
DD. Color of fls. yellow.
E. Lvs. white-woolly or white-stellate-canescent beneath.
F. Caudex with numerous rooting stolons; sts. scarcely exceeding the basal lvs.: lvs. stellate-canescent . . . . 20. *P. cinerea*
FF. Caudex without stolons; sts. much surpassing lvs.: lvs. white-woolly beneath.
G. St. villous: lfts. oblanceolate, 1–2 in. long: fls. ¾in. across . . . . . 6. *P. gracilis*
GG. St. tomentose: lfts. obovate, ½–1¼ in. long: fls. ½in. across . . . . 12. *P. argentea*
EE. Lvs. green to silky beneath.
F. Length of lfts. 2–4 in.: sts. 1–2½ ft. high . . . . 13. *P. recta*
FF. Length of lfts. up to 1½ in.: sts. up to 1 ft. long.
G. Fls. 1 in. across: lvs. nearly glabrous beneath . . . . 15. *P. pyrenaica*
GG. Fls. ½–¾in. across: lvs. pilose beneath, at least on veins.
H. Lfts. silky-pilose on both surfaces, ¼–¾in. long: sts. almost prostrate . . . . 16. *P. nevadensis*
HH. Lfts. greenish: sts. decumbent to ascending.
I. Width of fls. ½–1 in.
J. Stipules of basal lvs. more or less ovate; lf.-margins with dull somewhat spreading hairs . . . . 17. *P. alpestris*
JJ. Stipules lanceolate; lf.-margins with shining silky appressed hairs . . . . 18. *P. aurea*
II. Width of fls. ¼–½in.: stipules linear . . . . 19. *P. verna*

1. **P. fruticosa,** L. (*Dasiphora fruticosa*, Rydb.). Widely variable very close-leafy little shrub 1–4 ft. high, with loosely shredding bark: lvs. all cauline, pinnate, more or less silky-pubescent above and prominently gray-silky beneath; lfts. 3–7, oblong to linear, ½ to frequently 1 in. long, entire, margins revolute: fls. bright yellow and showy, ¾–1¼ in. across, clustered in the top of the foliage or just above it, late spring to autumn. Around the world in the north temp. zone, in several forms that are sometimes recognized as species. Var. **Veitchii,** Bean (*P. Veitchii*, Wils.), has white fls., lvs. not silvery above, glaucous beneath; China. Var. **Vilmoriniana,** Kom., has ochroleucous fls., and lvs. silvery-green above.

2. **P. tridentata,** Soland. Tufted, woody at the base, with many erect branches 2–12 in. high, appressed-pubescent: lvs. 3-parted, mostly basal; lfts. oblanceolate, truncate, mostly 3-toothed at apex, coriaceous, dark green above, paler beneath, ½–1 in. long: fls. several in a nearly naked cyme, white, ¼in. across; petals oval: carpels villous. Greenland to Ga. and Minn.

3. **P. nitida,** L. Silky-hairy plant forming mats from a rather woody branched caudex, fl.-sts. 1–2 in. high, 1–2-fld.: basal lvs. mostly ternate, short-petioled, crowded; lfts. thick, sessile, oblong-obovate, usually with 3 apical teeth: fls. up to 1 in. across; sepals purple; petals obovate, rose or lilac, sometimes white; stamens purple: carpels pilose. Alps.

4. **P. fragiformis,** Willd. Herbaceous, from woody caudex, to about 8 in. high, soft-hairy: lvs. 3-parted into rounded lfts. ½–2 in. long and very coarsely toothed: fls. few, cymose, yellow, ¾–1 in. across, early summer. Siberia.

5. **P. rupestris,** L. Sts. 1–2 ft. high from thick woody caudex, few-lvd., branched, pilose and glandular-hairy: lvs. mostly basal, pinnate; lfts. 5–7 (9), round-elliptic or rhombic-ovate, toothed: fls. in open cymes, white, ½–1 in. across; sepals ¼in. long, somewhat red; petals ⅓–½in. long, obovate: carpels glabrous. Eurasia, mts. of W. N. Amer.

6. **P. gracilis,** Dougl. Sts. erect or ascending, 1–2 ft. high, villous: lower lvs. palmately 5–7-parted; lfts. oblanceolate, 1–2 in. long, greenish and silky-pubescent above, finely white-tomentose beneath, coarsely toothed half way to midrib: fls. many, cymose, yellow, about ¾in. across; sepals acuminate; petals obcordate: carpels glabrous. Alaska to Calif.

7. **P. nepalensis,** Hook. (*P. formosa*, Don). Plant stout, more or less purple, to 2 ft. high, with racemose or paniculate branches: basal lvs. 10–12 in. long, palmately 5-foliolate, long-petioled; lfts. oblong-obovate, 2–3 in. long, crenate-serrate at apex, green both sides, with few appressed hairs: fls. about 1 in. across, rose-red, summer; petals deeply emarginate. Himalayas.—Probably the leading parent in the garden mixtures. The purple-fld. potentillas with broad lfts. white-tomentose beneath are probably hybrids with no. 9; they are sometimes grown as *P. nepalensis*, *P. pyrenaica*, and *P. hybrida;* the fls. are frequently double. Var. **Willmottiæ,** Hort. (*P. Willmottiæ*, Hort.), is a dwarf free-flowering form or derivative with magenta-rose fls.

8. **P. tormentillo-formosa,** Maund (*P. Tonguei*, Hort.). Hybrid of *P. nemoralis*, Lehm. (*Tormentilla reptans*, Stokes) and *P. nepalensis:* sts. spreading to 1 ft. long: lvs. 3–5-foliolate, with obovate coarsely dentate lfts. about 1 in. long: fls. ½in. across, yellow, red at base.

9. **P. argyrophylla,** Wall. Herbaceous, 1–1½ ft., sts. nearly simple and leafy: lvs. large, long-petioled, mostly ternate; lfts. broad-obovate or -oblong, 1½–2½ in. long, coarsely sharp-serrate, silky above, densely white-tomentose beneath, sessile: fls. cymose, yellow, about 1 in. across, long-pedicelled, summer; petals broadly obcordate. Himalayas.

10. **P. atrosanguinea,** Wall. Like no. 9 but plant larger and more branched, lfts. silky rather than white-tomentose beneath, and usually petiolulate, fls. dark purple. Himalayas.

11. **P. villosa,** Pall. Sts. several, ascending 4–12 in. high, villous: lvs. few, ternate, silky above, white-tomentose beneath; lfts. 1–1¼ in. long, obovate, coarsely toothed toward apex: cymes few-fld.; sepals to ⅓in.; petals yellow, ¼–½in. long: carpels glabrous. Siberia, Alaska to Wash.

12. **P. argentea,** L. Sts. several, ascending, slender, 4–18 in. long, white-tomentose, loosely branched: basal lvs. palmately 5-parted into deeply lobed lfts., these cuneate-obovate, ½–1¼ in. long, coarsely incised-dentate, mostly greenish above, white-tomentose beneath: cymes open; fls. sulfur-yellow, ½in. across; sepals ⅛in. long; petals slightly longer: carpels glabrous. Eu., Asia, N. Amer.

13. **P. recta,** L. (*P. Warrensii*, Hort.). Sts. stout, 1–2½ ft. long, erect, leafy, freely branched, hirsute or pilose and pubescent, somewhat glandular: basal lvs. palmately 5–7-foliolate; lfts. 2–4 in. long, oblong, coarsely toothed, green on both sides, hairy: fls. yellow, to 1 in. across; sepals lance-ovate; petals obcordate: carpels glabrous, rugose. Eu.; nat. in E. N. Amer. as a weed.

14. **P. grandiflora,** L. Herbaceous above the thick caudex, 6–15 in. high: basal lvs. mostly ternate, long-petioled; lfts. 1 in. long more or less, obovate, cut-serrate, pubescent above, short-villous beneath: fls. cymose, golden-yellow, 1 in. or so across, summer; petals broadly obcordate. Alps

15. **P. pyrenaica,** Ramond. Herbaceous, 1 ft. or less high, arcuate-ascending: basal lvs. palmately 5-foliolate; lfts. ¾in. or less long, obovate with cuneate base, dentate toward apex, nearly glabrous beneath: fls. racemose, golden-yellow, about 1 in. across, summer; petals obovate and emarginate. Pyrenees.

16. **P. nevadensis,** Boiss. Sts. almost prostrate, silky-pilose, up to 8 in. long: basal lvs. silky-pilose on both surfaces, palmately 5-foliolate; lfts. broadly obovate, ¼–¾in. long, with few coarse teeth: fls. few, in open cymes, yellow, ½in. across; petals obcordate. Spain.

17. **P. alpestris,** Haller f. Sts. slender, arcuate-ascending, few-lvd., 2–8 in. long, loosely few-branched and pilose above: basal lvs. mostly palmately 5-foliolate; lfts. obovate, ½–1 in. long, deeply toothed, dull green, pilose on veins of under surface: fls. ½–1 in. across, yellow, sometimes with orange spots near center; petals obcordate: carpels glabrous. Eu.

18. **P. aurea,** L. Sts. few, ascending, mostly 2–8 in. long, slender, more or less strigose: basal lvs. palmately 5-foliolate; lfts. oblanceolate to obovate, ½–1 in. long, sharply toothed in terminal half, green on both surfaces, somewhat strigose on veins of lower surface: fls. few, yellow, ½–¾in. across; petals emarginate: carpels glabrous. Eu.

19. **P. verna,** L. Matted, sts. many, decumbent, 2–6 (12) in. long, slender, pilose: basal lvs. mostly palmately 5-foliolate; lfts. cuneate-obovate, ½–1½ in. long, few-toothed toward the tip, green and more or less pilose on both surfaces: fls. mostly 3–5, golden-yellow, ¼–½in. across; petals obcordate to obovate: carpels glabrous. Eu. Var. **nana,** Hort., to about 4 in., fls. ½–⅝in.

20. **P. cinerea,** Chaix. Matted, sts. 2–4 in. high: basal lvs. palmately 5-foliolate; lfts. cuneate-oblong-obovate, rounded and with few crenate teeth at apex, appressed-hirsute on both surfaces, also with stellate hairs: fls. pale yellow, about ½in. across; petals emarginate: carpels glabrous. Eu.

38. **WALDSTEINIA,** Willd. Small north temp. genus of creeping herbs with strawberry-like aspect.—Lvs. mainly basal, long-petioled, 3–5-foliolate or -lobed, with membranous stipules: fls. yellow, in corymbs borne on bracted scapes; hypanthium top-shaped, sepals 5, bractlets 5 and minute or lacking; petals 5, obovate; stamens many; pistils 2–6 with nearly terminal deciduous filiform styles, ovaries 1-celled and 1-ovuled: achenes pubescent. (Waldstei-nia: for F. A. Waldstein-Wartenburg, 1759–1823, German botanist.)

W. fragarioides, Tratt. (*Dalibarda fragarioides,* Michx.). BARREN-STRAWBERRY. Lfts. broadly wedge-shaped, dentate or crenate above and sometimes incised, 1–2 in. long: scapes 3–8-fld.; petals ¼–⅓in. long. Woods, N. B. to Ga. and Minn.

39. **GEUM,** L. AVENS. Species over 50, if the genus is broadly defined, per. herbs in temp. and cold regions, grown for ornament in the open.—Lvs. pinnate or lyrate with large terminal lobe, most of them radical or basal, those on the sts. smaller: fls. solitary or corymbose on simple or branching sts., bisexual, yellow, white or red; hypanthium bell-shaped or flattish, sepals 5 with usually 5 bractlets between; petals 5, broad and showy in the cult. species; stamens many; pistils many, on a conical or cylindrical receptacle, ripening into achenes with long persistent styles which in some species are jointed and sometimes plumose. (Ge-um: an ancient name, of no evident application.)

A. Bractlets exceeding sepals: terminal lft. not broad nor rounded. . . . . 1. *G. triflorum*
AA. Bractlets shorter than sepals: terminal lft. broad, rounded to reniform.
  B. Styles not shedding the upper portion, not hooked.
    C. Fls. erect, usually solitary. . . . . 2. *G. montanum*
    CC. Fls. nodding, usually several on a st. . . . . 3. *G. bulgaricum*
  BB. Styles shedding the upper part and becoming hooked in age: sts. usually with more than 1 fl.
    C. Fls. purplish, nodding; petals somewhat cuneate, with basal claw. . . . . 4. *G. rivale*
    CC. Fls. mostly orange-red to scarlet; petals almost round.
      D. Terminal lft. three to four times as long as the largest lateral lfts.; basal lvs. about twice as wide: filaments yellow. . . . . 5. *G. coccineum*
      DD. Terminal lft. about twice as long as largest lateral lfts.; basal lvs. three to five times as long as wide: filaments often red . . . . 6. *G. chiloense*

1. **G. triflorum,** Pursh (*Sieversia triflora,* Spreng. *Erythrocoma triflora,* Greene). Erect, from a stout rootstock, finely pilose and somewhat hirsute, 8–16 in. high, cymosely 3-fld.: basal lvs. pinnate; principal lfts. 7–15, cuneate-oblanceolate, ½–1½ in. long, at the apex 2–3-cleft less than half their length, pilose and glandular: hypanthium and sepals purplish, sepals ⅓in. long, bractlets ½–⅔in. long, narrow; petals yellowish or flesh-color, scarcely ½in. long; plumose styles 1½–2½ in. long in fr. Newf. to N. Y., Alta., Neb. Var. **ciliatum,** Fassett (*G. ciliatum,* Pursh), lfts. usually dissected at least half way into linear divisions; B. C. to Alta., Utah, New Mex.

2. **G. montanum,** L. (*Sieversia montana,* Spreng.). Sts. erect, up to 1 ft. high, pilose and puberulent, usually 1-fld.: basal lvs. 1–6 in. long, with large round terminal lobe and 3–6 pairs of smaller lateral ones, toothed; st.-lvs. much reduced: fls. erect, golden-yellow, ¾–1¼ in. across; sepals green; petals suborbicular; styles plumose, ¾in. long. S. Eu.

3. **G. bulgaricum,** Panc. Sts. pilose and glandular, to 2 ft. tall, commonly 3–7-fld.: basal lvs. soft-villous, up to 1 ft. long, pinnate, the terminal lft. very large, cordate-reniform, lateral numerous and small: fls. nodding; sepals lance-ovate, greenish, ⅜in. long; petals bright yellow or orange, rounded-truncate, about ¾in. long; styles villous, up to ½in. long, tips not deciduous. Balkans.—Garden material called *G. bulgaricum* and *G. sibiricum* has erect fls., deciduous style-tips and is nearer to *G. coccineum* and *G. Heldreichii*. **G. Borisii,** Kellerer (*G. bulgaricum* × *G. reptans*), has the lf. form of *G. bulgaricum,* with yellow hanging fls.; hort. material going under this name has orange-scarlet fls. and is nearer *G. coccineum.*

4. **G. rivale,** L. Sts. to 3 ft. long, glandular-pubescent, 3–5-fld.: basal lvs. pinnate, the 3 terminal lfts. very large, coarsely double-toothed, lower lfts. small, 1–2 pairs: fls. nodding; sepals purplish, ⅓–½in. long, exceeding bracteoles; petals purplish, emarginate, scarcely ½in. long, abruptly narrowed into a definite claw; styles about ½in. long, the tips deciduous. Eu., Asia, N. Amer.

5. **G. coccineum,** Sibth. & Smith. Sts. erect, to 1 ft. high, pubescent, 1–4-fld. and glandular above: lvs. commonly 4–6 in. long, soft-pubescent, pinnate, the terminal lft. large, subreniform, acutely lobed, the lateral small, few: fls. intense orange-red, erect, 1 in. across; sepals lanceolate, green, ⅓in. long, much exceeding bracteoles; petals almost round, up to ½in. long; stamens yellow; styles almost ½in. long, the upper part deciduous. S. Eu., Asia Minor.—Plants commonly cult. under this name belong to *G. chiloense.* **G. Heldreichii,** Hort., appears to be a yellow-fld. derivative of *G. coccineum.*

6. **G. chiloense,** Balbis (*G. coccineum,* Hort. not Sibth. & Smith. *G. atrosanguineum,* Hort.). Hardy per. with many erect radical hirsute lvs. 4–12 in. long bearing a large terminal lobe and many unequal smaller pairs and parts below, the margins unequally toothed: fls. erect, scarlet, single, about 1 in. across, or in full double races 1½ in., on slender pedicels in a determinate infl., the sts. bearing smaller lvs. passing into bracts above; filaments mostly red: achenes in a dense little head, hairy, with long hooked styles due to the falling of the upper joint. Chilean region.—One form is known in gardens as Mrs. Bradshaw.

40. **DRYAS,** L. Three species of northern hemisphere plants from high mts. or high altitudes.—Evergreen, creeping, subshrubby, with alternate simple lvs.: fls. white or yellowish, showy, solitary, on slender pedicels; hypanthium cup-shaped, sepals 8–10, persistent; petals 8–10, broad; stamens many; pistils many: achenes with persistent plumose styles. (Dry-as: Greek *wood-nymph.*)

A. Lvs. usually subcordate at base: fls. white; stamens not exceeding sepals.........1. *D. octopetala*
AA. Lvs. usually cuneate at base: fls. yellowish; stamens exceeding sepals............2. *D. Drummondii*

1. **D. octopetala,** L. Lvs. elliptic or oblong, crenate, ½–1 in. long, dark green above, white-tomentose beneath, petioles to ½in. long: pedicels 1–6 in. high; fls. erect, white, 1–1½ in. across: fruiting styles 1 in. long. Circumpolar, south in mts.

2. **D. Drummondii,** Hook. Lvs. oblong, to 1½ in. long, petioles to 1 in. long: fls. nodding, yellowish, about ¾in. across: fruiting styles to 1½ in. long. (Named for T. Drummond, page 255.) N. N. Amer. south to Que. and Mont. **D. Suendermannii,** Sünderm. (*D. octopetala* × *D. Drummondii*), fls. slightly nodding, yellowish in bud, white at anthesis.

41. **SANGUISORBA,** L. Defined broadly the genus comprises about 35 per. herbs in the north temp. zone.—Lvs. long, unequally odd-pinnate, alternate, stipules joined to petiole: fls. small, not showy, bisexual or unisexual, crowded in a dense head or spike terminating a long naked peduncle; petals 0; sepals 4, petal-like; stamens 4–12 or more, inserted on calyx-throat; pistils 1–3, styles slender, stigma fimbriate: fr. mostly a single achene inclosed in the persisting calyx-tube. (Sanguisorba: Latin *blood-stopping,* from reputed medicinal properties.)

A. Lfts. ¼–¾in. long: fls. greenish...............................1. *S. minor*
AA. Lfts. 1–3 in. long: fls. white or red.
B. Fls. white...............................2. *S. canadensis*
BB. Fls. red...............................3. *S. obtusa*

1. **S. minor,** Scop. (*Poterium Sanguisorba,* L.). BURNET. Per., forming an attractive basal clump of fine foliage, glabrous or only sparsely hairy: lvs. narrow, with 7–21 nearly orbicular to oblong little notched lfts.: sts. 12–30 in. tall, forking, bearing globular or short-oblong heads about ½in. broad; stamens and stigmas purplish and exserted, the lower fls. staminate and upper bisexual: achene 4-ribbed, muricate and wrinkled. Eu. and Asia; somewhat nat. in N. Amer.—Sparingly cult. for the young lvs. used as salad and mentioned as sheep forage.

2. **S. canadensis,** L. Sts. 1–6 ft. high: lfts. 7–17, oblong, to 3 in. long: fls. white, in elongated cylindrical spikes 1–6 in. long. Lab. to Ga. and Mich.

3. **S. obtusa,** Maxim. (*Poterium obtusum*, Franch. & Sav. *P. obtusatum*, Hort.). Sts. to 3 ft. high: lfts. mostly 7–13, oblong, toothed, 1–2½ in. long: fls. crimson, the spikes to 3½ in. long, 1 in. thick, nodding at tips. Japan.

42. **ACÆNA,** L. Shrubby or per. trailing herbs with more or less woody caudices; about 40 species mainly of southern hemisphere, but occurring in Mex., Calif., Hawaii; used as ground-cover in mild climates.—Lvs. unequally pinnate, with stipules adnate to petioles: fls. inconspicuous, in terminal heads or spikes; hypanthium ellipsoid, covered with barbed prickles, sepals 3–5, usually 4; petals 0; stamens 3–5; pistil usually 1, stigma many-cleft: achenes wholly inclosed in the hard spiny hypanthium. (Acæ-na: from Greek, meaning *thorn* and referring to hypanthium.)

A. Lvs. greenish, subglabrous: heads mostly peduncled.......................1. *A. microphylla*
AA. Lvs. pale whitish-glaucous, pilose: heads mostly sessile.......................2. *A. Buchananii*

1. **A. microphylla,** Hook. f. NEW ZEALAND BUR. Sts. prostrate, much-branched, fl.-branchlets to 3 in. high, erect, subglabrous: lvs. ¾–2 in. long, sparingly pilose or almost glabrous; lfts. 7–13, rounded, up to ¼in. long, crenate-dentate: heads globose, ⅓–¾in. thick when mature, with purplish-red unbarbed spines up to ½in. long. New Zeal.

2. **A. Buchananii,** Hook. f. Sts. prostrate, younger lvs. densely pilose: lvs. ½–¾in. long; lfts. 11–13, almost round, whitish-green on both surfaces: heads almost or quite sessile, spines greenish or yellowish, with reflexed flexuous hairs near tip. (Named for John Buchanan, New Zeal. botanist, died 1898.) New Zeal.—**A. cæsiglauca,** Bergmans (*A. Sanguisorbæ* subsp. *cæsiglauca*, Bitter. *A. glauca*, Hort.), has silky lvs. of a soft gray-blue, lfts. 7–9, round-oblong, coarsely toothed; origin uncertain but ascribed to New Zeal.

43. **ROSA,** L. ROSE. Prickly shrubs, sometimes climbing and trailing, more than 100 species (to which thousands of names have been given), mostly in the temp. parts of the northern hemisphere; many are prime favorites for ornament under glass and in the open.—Lvs. alternate, odd-pinnate (one species, not here described, with simple barberry-like lvs.), deciduous or persistent, with stipules adnate to petiole, often aromatic-glandular: fls. solitary or corymbose or paniculate; petals 5, broad and mostly rounded at end, these and the many whorled stamens inserted on a disk at the edge of the hypanthium; pistils many, borne on the inside of the deep hypanthium: fr. a fleshy hip (ripened hypanthium) containing the hairy achenes as if they were seeds. (Ro-sa: the ancient Latin name.)—The cult. roses may be ranged, for purposes of identification, under two groups: (1) The "species," those kinds grown as shrubbery or for general use in the landscape; here are comprised the native roses, some of which are more or less planted in grounds, and also such generalized exotic types as *R. rugosa*, *R. lævigata*, *R. Banksiæ*, *R. Wichuraiana*, *R. spinosissima*, and many others. (2) The highly developed specialized roses of the distinct hort. types, as the Teas, Hybrid Teas, Hybrid Perpetuals, Ramblers; here are included the forcing or florists' roses; they are the issue of several species, mostly of *R. odorata*, *R. chinensis*, *R. damascena*, *R. cathayensis*, *R. multiflora*, with other combinations in evidence and still others constantly appearing; these roses are mostly impossible of close identification with the original specific types, although the main lines of origin are usually fairly evident.

A. Styles manifestly exserted beyond the mouth of the hypanthium (or hip).
B. Stamens about as long as styles, the latter connate into a column.
C. Stipules deeply fringed or pectinate (no. 3 may be sought here).
D. Fls. white, many and small, in panicles.......................1. *R. multiflora*
DD. Fls. pink or rose, larger, 1½ in. or more across, few in short open clusters.......................2. *R. cathayensis*
CC. Stipules entire or only denticulate.
D. Plant prostrate or creeping.
E. Fls. commonly several together: lvs. more or less persistent and shining.
F. Lfts. usually 9, obtuse, broad.......................3. *R. Wichuraiana*
FF. Lfts. usually 5, acuminate or at least not obtuse, narrow.......................4. *R. sempervirens*
EE. Fls. commonly solitary: lvs. deciduous and dull; lfts. mostly 7.......................5. *R. arvensis*
DD. Plant erect or upright, with long arching branches, sometimes partially climbing.
E. Lfts. 3 or 5 on flowering branchlets, pubescent beneath.......................6. *R. setigera*
EE. Lfts. 5–9 on flowering branchlets.

F. Prickles nearly or quite straight: lfts. glabrous or clothed only on midrib beneath........ 7. *R. moschata*
FF. Prickles hooked: lfts. pubescent beneath........ 8. *R. Brunonii*
BB. Stamens about half as long as styles, the latter free.
C. Lvs. glabrous beneath: sts. with only prickles, not bristles.
D. Foliage persistent or essentially so.
E. Fls. very fragrant, white, light pink or yellowish; sepals entire........ 9. *R. odorata*
EE. Fls. little if at all fragrant, red or pink but only seldom whitish; sepals pinnate........10. *R. chinensis*
DD. Foliage deciduous: fls. many together........11. *R. Noisettiana*
CC. Lvs. somewhat pubescent beneath: sts. with bristles as well as prickles........12. *R. borboniana*
AA. Styles not exserted, forming a head-like stopper to the mouth of the hypanthium.
B. Plant commonly erect or at least not long-sarmentose, making a bush: stipules adnate to petiole more than half their length.
C. Lvs. of flowering branchlets large and firm, with 3 or 5 lfts.: hypanthium hispid (exception usually in no. 16).
D. Lfts. doubly glandular-serrate: sts. with very unequal prickles.
E. Fls. on upright pedicels, single or semi-double with spreading petals...13. *R. gallica*
EE. Fls. nodding or declined, commonly double, petals erect and imbricate.14. *R. centifolia*
DD. Lfts. simply serrate and not glandular: prickles uniform.
E. Shape of lfts. ovate-oblong: hypanthium glandular-hispid........15. *R. damascena*
EE. Shape broader: hypanthium commonly smooth........16. *R. alba*
CC. Lvs. of flowering branchlets not very large nor firm, mostly with 5–11 lfts.: hypanthium smooth.
D. Fls. clustered; or, if solitary, then the pedicel bearing 1 or more bracts.
E. Prickles of one kind, stout and hooked, but sts. sometimes also bearing glandular bristles: outer sepals usually pinnate.
F. Lfts. not glandular except sometimes on midrib, usually simply serrate.
G. Color of lfts. bluish-green tinged red, not shining........17. *R. rubrifolia*
GG. Color of lfts. bright or dark green, shining above........18. *R. canina*
FF. Lfts. glandular beneath or tomentose, doubly serrate.
G. The prickles slender, nearly straight: lfts. tomentose beneath, not aromatic........19. *R. pomifera*
GG. The prickles hooked: lfts. glabrous or pubescent beneath, glandular........20. *R. Eglanteria*
EE. Prickles of two kinds, usually straightish and slender at least toward base of plant and others more or less bristle-like: sepals usually entire.
F. Sepals after flowering spreading, deciduous: achenes only in the bottom of the more or less glandular-hispid hip.
G. Number of lfts. mostly 5; stipules narrow: sts. up to 3 ft. high...21. *R. carolina*
GG. Number of lfts. mostly 7–9.
H. Lfts. finely serrate; stipules involute........22. *R. palustris*
HH. Lfts. coarsely serrate; stipules flat.
I. The prickles usually curved: lfts. mostly 7, elliptic or broader, 1–2½ in. long: sts. to 7 ft........23. *R. virginiana*
II. The prickles straight: lfts. 7–9, narrow-oblong, ⅓–1⅓ in. long: sts. to 3 ft.
J. Sts. densely bristly: stipules dilated: pedicels ½–1 in. long........24. *R. nitida*
JJ. Sts. almost unarmed: stipules narrow: pedicels ⅙–⅓in. long........25. *R. foliolosa*
FF. Sepals after flowering upright, usually persistent: achenes on bottom and on walls of the usually smooth hip.
G. Infrastipular prickles not present.
H. Branchlets and prickles tomentose: lfts. thick, rugose above...26. *R. rugosa*
HH. Branchlets and prickles glabrous.
I. Sts. and branchlets bristly........27. *R. acicularis*
II. Sts. and branchlets unarmed, or the former with weak bristles when young........28. *R. blanda*
GG. Infrastipular prickles present.
H. Lfts. pubescent beneath: pedicels smooth: fr. red, ½in. long, almost round........29. *R. cinnamomea*
HH. Lfts. glabrous beneath except on pubescent midribs: pedicels with stalked glands: fr. orange-red, 2 in. long, with prominent neck........30. *R. Moyesii*
DD. Fls. usually solitary (rarely few), and the pedicels bractless, often yellow.
E. Sepals prevailingly pinnate: fls. yellow, with disagreeable odor......31. *R. fœtida*
EE. Sepals entire, sometimes ciliate.
F. Flowering branchlets bristly and prickly: fls. white or pink to yellowish........32. *R. spinosissima*
FF. Flowering branchlets usually not bristly: fls. yellow.
G. Lfts. simply serrate, eglandular.
H. Stipular wing scarcely evident on petiole: shoots bristly at least at base........33. *R. Hugonis*
HH. Stipular attachment along petiole making a prominent wing: shoots without bristles........34. *R. xanthina*
GG. Lfts. doubly glandular-serrate, glandular beneath........35. *R. Primula*
BB. Plant climbing or requiring high support: stipules small, free or adnate to petiole only at base: fls. white or yellowish.

C. Branches tomentose or pubescent: fls. with prominent bracts beneath.....36. *R. bracteata*
CC. Branches glabrous: fls. without evident bracts.
D. Fls. solitary, large, white (to blush).............................37. *R. lævigata*
DD. Fls. clustered, small, white or yellowish.............................38. *R. Banksiæ*

1. **R. multiflora,** Thunb. A vigorous prickly bush of attractive habit, the branches often long and somewhat climbing: stipules prominent, extending about half or more the length of the petiole, pectinate and with the terminal points slender and conspicuous; lfts. 5–11, but prevailingly 9 in full-formed lvs., mostly not exceeding 1½ in. long on flowering branchlets and often much less, broad-oval or slightly obovate and usually abruptly short-pointed: fls. many, 25 to more than 100, in a long or pointed panicle, white, very fragrant, ½–¾in. across; sepals pubescent, ovate-acuminate, becoming reflexed after flowering: fr. globular to ovoid or obovoid, ¼in. or less diam., brown-red. Japan.—There are double-fld. forms in cult.

2. **R. cathayensis,** Bailey (*R. multiflora* var. *cathayensis*, Rehd. & Wils.). Lfts. larger and more acuminate-pointed than in no. 1, usually 5–7; fls. larger, usually 1½ in. or more across, less fragrant, pink or rose-colored, 20 or less in an open corymb-like cluster on longer and often glandular pedicels: fr. usually larger. China.—From nos. 1 and 2, known as the Multiflora roses, have come many garden kinds, probably both by variation and by hybridization with other species, characterized in general by the clustered infl. and the pectinate stipules. No. 2 has probably entered more largely into them, carrying its color. *R. cathayensis* is represented in such vars. as Triomphe Orléanais, Erna Teschendorff, Wedding Bells, Queen Alexandra, Wartburg, Crimson Rambler. **R. Barbierana,** Rehd., is a series of hybrids between *R. cathayensis* and *R. Wichuraiana*, named in compliment to Barbier et fils, Orleans, France; here apparently belong Excelsa, Farquhar, Evangeline, Babette, Lady Godiva, Delight, Coquina, Paradise, and others. Hybrids between *R. multiflora* and *R. Wichuraiana* are represented in White Dorothy and other white ramblers. **R. polyantha,** Hort., represents hybrids of no. 1 or no. 2, or both, with *R. chinensis*, although the name is sometimes given a wider significance. There are many crosses of the Multifloras with *R. borboniana*, giving Abundant, Longwood, Dazzling Red, and others. There are also hybrids with *R. rugosa* and *R. dilecta*.

3. **R. Wichuraiana,** Crép. MEMORIAL ROSE. Evergreen or half-evergreen, prickly, with fine shining foliage and long sts. flat on the ground; sts. glabrous, but petioles, rachis, and pedicels usually glandular: lvs. small, 2–4 in. long; lfts. usually 9 but sometimes 7, short-oval or almost orbicular, ½–1 in. long, nearly sessile and the terminal one stalked, simply serrate; stipules conspicuous and glandular-denticulate: fls. few or rather many in a cluster, white, fragrant, 1¼–2 in. across: fr. ovoid, about ¼in. diam. (Bears the name of Max E. Wichura, botanist on the German expedition to China and Japan in 1859–61; died 1866.) Japan.—An attractive rose for ground-cover; it has entered into hybrids with the Multifloras and other species; Dorothy Perkins is one of the offshoots.

4. **R. sempervirens,** L. Evergreen with long lopping or decumbent branches and shining foliage; sts. prickly and glabrous: lfts. 5 but sometimes 7, lanceolate to ovate-lanceolate, ¾–2 in. long, abrupt or acuminate, simply serrulate, glabrous above but usually pubescent on ribs and rachis beneath: fls. few to several in corymbs, white, slightly fragrant, 1½–2 in. across, the pedicels more or less glandular-hispid: fr. globose or ovoid, ¼in. or less diam., orange-red. Medit. region.—Little planted in N. Amer.; there are double-fld. forms and apparent hybrids.

5. **R. arvensis,** Huds. Very thorny deciduous shrub with long more or less decumbent or creeping branches; sts. glabrous: lvs. 2–4 in. long; lfts. commonly 7, small, ½–1½ in. long, ovate to round-elliptic, acute but usually not acuminate but sometimes rounded at end and scarcely pointed, serrate, glabrous or slightly pubescent beneath: fls. few in umbel-like corymbs or sometimes nearly or quite solitary, white, not fragrant, 2 in. or less across: fr. ovoid. Eu.—Known in cult. mostly as the Ayrshire rose, double white or pink, which is probably a hybrid with *R. gallica*.

6. **R. setigera,** Michx. PRAIRIE ROSE. Strong bush with long branches that show a strong tendency to climb, with scattered nearly straight prickles but no bristles; sts. glabrous, but petioles, pedicels and calyx glandular: lfts. 3–5, ovate to oblong-ovate, 1–3 in. long, acute or short-acuminate, sharply serrate, glabrous or downy beneath (tomentose beneath in var. **tomentosa,** Gray): fls. few in corymbs, deep rose fading whitish, 2 in. across, nearly scentless: fr. globular, ⅓in. across. E. N. Amer.—Frequently planted and probably hybridized; Baltimore Belle is one of the old derivatives; American Pillar is a hybrid with *R. Wichuraiana*.

7. **R. moschata,** Herrm. MUSK ROSE. Shrub with curving or somewhat climbing branches, glabrous, with rather small straight or slightly hooked prickles: lfts. mostly 5 or 7, elliptic-ovate to oblong-ovate, 1–2 in. long, acute or acuminate, finely serrate, glabrous except on midrib beneath, petioles and rachis usually prickly but nearly or quite glabrous: fls. white, 1½–2 in. across, with the odor of musk, about 7 in a corymb; sepals lanceolate and much longer than the hypanthium, lobed, deciduous; pedicels slightly pubescent and glandular: fr. ovate, small. S. Eu. and N. Afr.—An old garden rose but now scarcely in cult. outside botanic gardens.

8. **R. Brunonii,** Lindl. HIMALAYAN MUSK ROSE. More tender than no. 7 and confused with it, apparently little cult.; differs in prickles short and hooked, in narrow lvs. that are soft-pubescent beneath and sometimes pubescent above, with petioles and rachis also pubescent and with scattered prickles: fls. in large many-fld. corymbs, white, 1½–2 in. across, fragrant. (Named in honor of the great botanist, Robert Brown.) Himalayas to W. China.—Usually cult. as *R. moschata.*

9. **R. odorata,** Sweet. TEA ROSE (from the odor). Evergreen or partially so, blooming on shoots of the year, with recurrent season of bloom; branches long and slender, more or less climbing; sts. glabrous, peduncles rather short and setose-glandular; prickles few, scattered and hooked: lfts. 5–7, elliptic to broad-ovate or oblong-ovate, 1½–3 in. long, acute or short-acuminate, strongly sharp-serrate, shining above, light colored and glabrous beneath; stipules glandular-ciliate only on upper part if at all: fls. 1–3, white, light pink or salmon-yellow, 2–3 in. and more across, very fragrant; sepals caudate-pointed and entire: fr. nearly or quite globose, red. W. China.—Widely cult. in many forms, many of them with double fls., others (var. **gigantea,** Rehd. & Wils.) with fls. 4–6 in. across; the tea roses of greenhouses and open gardens are variants and hybrids from this species. This and no. 10 are sometimes known as *R. indica.*

10. **R. chinensis,** Jacq. CHINA or BENGAL ROSE. Differs from no. 9 largely in the glandular-ciliate stipules, smaller usually red or sometimes pink (rarely varying to whitish) fls. that are odorless or nearly so, outer sepals pinnate or deeply lobed, fr. top-shaped. China.—Less grown than No. 9. The Fairy roses, var. **minima,** Voss (*R. Roulettii,* Correvon), are very dwarf compact bushes about 1 ft. high, much-branched, with small narrow acuminate lfts. and rose-red fls. 1–1½ in. across. The Green rose is var. **viridiflora,** Dipp., the petals being represented by narrow serrulate green lvs.

11. **R. Noisettiana,** Thory. NOISETTE or CHAMPNEY ROSE. Supposed hybrid of *R. chinensis* and *R. moschata,* raised by John Champney of Charleston, S. C., early last century, from which seedlings were obtained and distributed by the Noisette Brothers of Charleston and Paris: a summer and autumn bloomer with deciduous foliage, bearing uniform reddish hooked prickles: lfts. 5–7, narrowly or broadly oblong or oval, acute or short-acuminate: fls. usually many in a corymb, variously doubled, white, pink, red, yellow: known in many forms, not always clearly defined.—One of the offshoots is Maréchal Niel. Here belongs the Manetti rose (*R. Manettii,* Crivelli. *R. chinensis* var. *Manettii,* Dipp.), a vigorous upright shrub, fls. single or semi-double, pink; used for stocks on which to bud or graft other roses.

12. **R. borboniana,** Desp. (*R. borbonica,* Morr.). BOURBON ROSE. Supposed hybrid of *R. chinensis* and *R. damascena,* issuing from a rose intro. from the island of Bourbon about 1819: upright, the branches prickly and often glandular-hispid, pedicels usually glandular: lfts. mostly 7, ovate to ovate-lanceolate, 1–2 in. long, mostly acute, sometimes abruptly acuminate, shining above, slightly pubescent beneath; stipules glandular: fls. solitary, or few in a corymb, in summer and autumn, 1½–3 in. across, usually red or purple, double or semi-double; sepals entire or somewhat lobed.—An important parent stock for the breeding of roses; subsequent crossing of it with species of the *R. gallica* group (nos. 13 and 15) and forms of *R. chinensis* have given the Hybrid Bourbons; later arose the great class of Remontants or Hybrid Perpetuals known for their recurrent seasons of bloom, of which Général Jacqueminot is a representative kind. The Hybrid Teas are another class separated as **R. dilecta,** Rehd., derivatives of *R. odorata* and *R. borboniana;* this hybrid or group-species comprises slender-branched sometimes sarmentose roses, the sts. with scattered straight or hooked prickles: lvs. of firm texture, glabrous, often purplish when unfolding: fls. solitary or few in corymbs, white to red and yellow, fragrant; bud conical with recurving petals.

13. **R. gallica,** L. FRENCH ROSE. Small bush, 3–4 ft., with sharp unequal curved prickles, and beset with weak bristles and glands: lvs. thick and rugose, 3–6 in. long, the stipules prominent and glandular-serrate; lfts. mostly 5, sometimes 3, oblong-ovate to broad-oval, 1–2 in. long, obtuse or only short-pointed, rounded at base and lateral ones sessile, rather obtusely doubly serrate and glandular, very dull above, pubescent beneath, rachis glandular and often prickly: fls. solitary or 3–4 together, pink to crimson, 2–3 in. across, on erect glandular-hispid pedicels, the petals spreading; sepals often foliaceous and much cut or lobed: fr. nearly globular to pear-shaped, ⅜–½in. diam., dull red, with deciduous sepals. Eu., W. Asia.—An old and familiar garden rose and more or less escaped; occurs in many forms, double and semi-double. Var. **versicolor,** Thory, has petals striped white and red; an old favorite.

14. **R. centifolia,** L. CABBAGE ROSE. Very like no. 13, and often confused with it, but a larger bush: differs in bearing stouter prickles, lvs. sometimes pubescent above, the lfts. mostly larger and thin, the rachis not prickly, fls. very double and very fragrant and declined or nodding on long and slender pedicels and with the many petals erect and overlapping like lvs. in a cabbage-head, fr. globular or ovoid never pear-shaped, with persistent sepals. Caucasus.—One of the most ancient of cult. roses. Var. **muscosa,** Sér. (*R. muscosa,* Ait.), MOSS ROSE, calyx and pedicel very glandular and hispid, and sepals pectinate; sometimes the sepals are crested (var. *cristata,* Prév.).

15. **R. damascena,** Mill. Damask Rose. Differs from nos. 13 and 14 in having simply serrate not glandular lfts., prickles uniform or all alike, fr. long-pyriform (1 in. long): from *R. gallica* it is distinguished by the larger bush, thinner lfts., and large clusters of fls.: bush to 8 ft., the numerous stout hooked prickles often mixed with glandular bristles: lfts. smooth above and pubescent beneath: fls. 6–12 in a corymb, blush-white to red, sometimes striped, very fragrant, single or semi-double, on long upright pedicels which, with hypanthium, are glandular-hispid; blooms in summer and autumn. Origin unknown, probably a cultigen.—An important source of attar of roses; the leading parent in this group of the Hybrid Perpetual roses.

16. **R. alba,** L. Strong upright bush 6–8 ft., with scattered uniform more or less hooked prickles and sometimes with bristles: lfts. usually 5, sometimes 7, oblong to broad-elliptic to ovate, 1–2½ in. long, short-pointed, simply serrate, grayish and somewhat wrinkled, glabrous above and pubescent beneath; stipules and usually the pedicels glandular: fls. white or soft pink, single or often double, 2–3 in. across, very fragrant, usually few or several together; sepals large, mostly lobed and sometimes foliaceous; hypanthium bristly or smooth: fr. oblong or ovoid, ¾in. long, bright red, sepals deciduous. Eu., but apparently nowhere indigenous and supposed to be a hybrid between *R. gallica* and *R. canina* var. *dumetorum*.—Yields attractive garden roses, as Mme. Plantier; a source of attar of roses.

17. **R. rubrifolia,** Vill. (*R. glauca*, Pourr.). Upright, 6–7 ft., sts. purple-glaucous with few straight or hooked prickles: foliage prominently tinged red with a glaucous cast; lfts. 5–9, rather narrow, elliptic to ovate-lanceolate, 1–1½ in. long, mostly acute, simply serrate, glabrous: fls. single, pink to red, 1½ in. across, few to several in a cluster on mostly glandular-hispid short pedicels; sepals caudate, exceeding petals, usually a little expanded near the end: fr. globular or nearly so, about ½in. long, red, the sepals persisting for a time. Mts. in Cent. Eu.—Planted for its character as a shrub rather than specially for fls.

18. **R. canina,** L. Dog Rose. Strong variable species, 6–12 ft., with scattered uniform strongly hooked prickles and no bristles, sts. glabrous: lfts. 5 or 7, oval, elliptic or ovate, 1–1½ in. long, acute or acuminate, sharp-serrate, glabrous or thinly pubescent and often glandular beneath, not resinous-dotted; stipules broad, usually somewhat glandular: fls. single, white or pinkish, 1–2 in. across, solitary or 2–5 together on short glabrous or glandular pedicels; sepals prominent, reflexed, 2 of them pinnately lobed, 2 usually entire and 1 mostly lobed on one side: fr. globular to ovoid, nearly ½in. diam., red, smooth, the sepals finally deciduous. Eu. and W. Asia, a characteristic and common rose of lanes and waysides, somewhat escaped in N. Amer.—A frequent single rose in old gardens, sometimes coming up as the stock on which other roses are grafted. Var. **dumetorum,** Baker (*R. dumetorum*, Thuill. *R. corymbifera*, Borkh.), is distinguished by the dull gray foliage which is pubescent and not glandular beneath. There are many named vars.

19. **R. pomifera,** Herrm. Sturdy much-branched bush, 4–6 ft.; sts. glabrous or slightly hairy, with long straight scattered prickles: lfts. 5 or 7, oblong to ovate or oval, 1–2½ in. long, obtuse or acute, doubly glandular-serrate, grayish-pubescent above and tomentose beneath, seldom becoming almost glabrous: fls. single, rose-pink, 1½–2½ in. across, solitary or 2–6 together on bristly and glandular pedicels: fr. large, about 1 in. diam., pyriform to globular, scarlet. Cent. Eu.—Sometimes cult. for its ornamental fr.

20. **R. Eglanteria,** L. (*R. rubiginosa*, L.). Eglantine. Sweetbriar. Stiff erect branching bush, 5–8 ft., with many strong hooked prickles and sometimes with bristles, pedicels hispid and usually glandular: lfts. 5–9, mostly 7, small, oval to orbicular, ¼–¾in. long in flowering parts but to 1½ in. long on shoots, obtuse, doubly glandular-serrate, dull green and glabrous above, pale and often pubescent beneath, and sometimes above bearing many sweet-smelling glands: fls. single, pink, 1½–2 in. across, borne on short pedicels on leafy shoots singly or few or several together: fr. nearly globular or ovoid, about ½in. diam., orange-red to scarlet, crowned with the long glandular-serrate at length deciduous sepals. Eu., and widely nat. in N. Amer.—Much subject to the attacks of the gall-wasp, producing familiar hair-like galls. It is seldom grown as an ornamental but it is a parent in strong races of hybrids known as the Penzance Sweetbriar Hybrids, presumably crosses with *R. borboniana*. It also has been crossed with the Austrian Briar, *R. fœtida*, producing a race known as **R. Penzanceana,** Rehd., with the fragrant lvs. of Eglantine and pink fls. suffused yellow.

21. **R. carolina,** L. (*R. humilis*, Marsh.). Suckering shrub to 3 ft., blooming freely; sts. usually with slender weak straight prickles at or near the nodes and bristles on young shoots, the pedicels frequently glandular-hispid: lfts. commonly 5, rarely 7, oblong to narrow-oval or elliptic, ¾–1¼ in long, obtuse or short-acute, coarsely serrate, not shining above and usually pubescent beneath: fls. mostly solitary, sometimes 2 or 3 together, pink, single, 2 in. across; outer sepals lobed: fr. globose to ovoid, about ⅓in. diam. Me. to Fla. and Kans.—Now and then transferred to grounds and sometimes represented in double roses of apparent hybrid origin.

22. **R. palustris,** Marsh. Swamp Rose. Upright shrub to 7 ft., with usually more or less curved prickles: lfts. 7, rarely 9, elliptic to narrow-oblong, acute at both ends, finely serrate, usually pubescent beneath on veins: fls. commonly corymbose, pink, 2 in. across. N. S. to Fla., Minn. and Miss.

23. **R. virginiana,** Mill. (*R. lucida*, Ehrh.). Sts. to 7 ft., with few or no suckers, prickles stout and usually curved, bristles on young shoots only: lfts. mostly 7, elliptic or broader, 1–2½ in. long, dark green, thick, smooth and shining above, glabrous beneath or pubescent on veins: fls. usually few, sometimes solitary, 2–2½ in. across; pedicels glandular-hispid: fr. about ½in. diam. Newf. to Ala. and Mo.

24. **R. nitida,** Willd. Shrub to 2½ ft.; sts. densely bristly and with slender prickles: lfts. 7–9, usually narrow-oblong and narrowed at both ends, ⅓–1 in. long; stipules dilated: fls. mostly solitary, about 2 in. across; pedicels glandular-hispid; sepals entire: fr. ⅓in. diam. Newf. to Conn.

25. **R. foliolosa,** Nutt. Shrub to 3 ft.; sts. nearly unarmed or with short slightly reflexed prickles: lfts. mostly 9, sometimes 7, narrow-oblong, ⅓–1⅓ in. long, acute, glabrous and shining above, sharply serrate, glabrous or pubescent on veins beneath; stipules narrow: fls. 1 to few, rose, rarely white, 1–1½ in. across; pedicels sparingly glandular-hispid: fr. round, ⅓in. diam. Ark., Okla., Tex.

26. **R. rugosa,** Thunb. (*R. rugosa* var. *rubra*, Hort.). Sturdy hardy erect much-branching very leafy shrub, 4–6 ft., the stiff sts. densely covered with prickles and bristles of different sizes, young growth and pedicels pubescent: lvs. heavy, 3–6 or 7 in. long; lfts. 5–9, oblong to oval or somewhat obovate, 1–2 in. long, thick and rugose, obtuse to only short-acute, serrate, soft-pubescent and somewhat glaucous beneath; stipules broad and leafy: fls. few or solitary, fragrant, purple (or white in var. **alba,** W. Rob.), single or semi-double, 2½–4 in. across; sepals long and often leafy, the caudate ends often expanded: fr. large, long-persistent, showy, depressed-globose, 1 in. or more diam., red, crowned with the spreading sepals. China, Japan.—Common in yards and for hedges, sometimes escaped, making a characteristic and pleasing bush. Named double-fld. forms are in gardens. **R. Bruantii,** Rehd., is a hybrid group, represented by Mme. Georges Bruant, combining *R. rugosa* with one of the Tea roses (*R. odorata* or *R. dilecta*). **R. Arnoldiana,** Sarg., represents the hybrids between *R. rugosa* and *R. borboniana:* sts. stout and upright, with slender bristles and prickles: lfts. 5 or 7, elliptic-ovate: fls. purplish, semi-double, above 2 in. across, few in corymbs on densely glandular pedicels. Hybrids are also known with *R. rugosa* and *R. multiflora* (producing *R. Iwara*, Sieber), with *R. Wichuraiana* (yielding *R. Jacksonii*, Willm.), and with other species.

27. **R. acicularis,** Lindl. Low shrub, 1–3 ft. high; sts. densely covered with straight weak prickles, the branchlets sometimes unarmed: lfts. 3–7, mostly 5, elliptic to oblong, ½–2 in. long, sessile, simply serrate, dull and glabrous above, pubescent beneath; stipules dilated: fls. solitary, deep rose, about 2 in. across; pedicels mostly glabrous: fr. usually pear-shaped and with distinct neck, ⅔–⅘in. long. Alaska to Wyo. and N. Y.

28. **R. blanda,** Ait. Sts. to 7 ft., mostly unarmed: lfts. 5–7, rarely 9, elliptic to oblong-obovate, 1–2½ in. long, simply serrate, dull and glabrous above, paler and glabrous to pubescent beneath; stipules dilated: fls. solitary to few, pink, about 2 in. across; pedicels glabrous: fr. subglobose to ellipsoid, ½in. diam. Newf. to Pa., Mo. and Man.

29. **R. cinnamomea,** L. CINNAMON ROSE. Strong bush, 6 ft. or more but often blooming at 1 ft., with straight or slightly hooked prickles and others more or less bristle-like but not glandular, usually a pair of prickles at base of petioles: lfts. 5 or 7, oblong to obscurely obovate, 1–1½ in. long, simply sharp-serrate, obtuse or short-acute, glaucous-pubescent beneath: fls. often on unarmed branches, in shades of red, 2 in. across, single or variously double, fragrant, solitary or few-clustered; hypanthium and pedicels smooth: fr. mostly globular to oblong, ½in. diam., red, with erect sepals. Eu. to N. China; an old garden rose, running wild and persisting about old premises, along fences, in cemeteries, and by roadsides.

30. **R. Moyesii,** Hemsl. & Wils. Shrub to 10 ft.; sts. with scattered and paired short straight prickles: lfts. 7–13, ovate to elliptic, ½–1½ in. long, simply serrate, glabrous except for the pubescent midribs beneath; stipules wide, glandular-ciliate: fls. 1–2, deep red, 2–2½ in. across; pedicels with stalked glands: fr. oblong-ovoid, orange-red, 2 in. long, with prominent neck. (Named for Rev. J. Moyes, a missionary in China.) W. China.

31. **R. fœtida,** Herrm. (*R. lutea*, Mill.). AUSTRIAN BRIAR. Shrub 3–5 ft., but sometimes producing much longer semi-climbing shoots, with slender straight prickles and no bristles: lfts. 5–9, broad-ovate to oval or somewhat obovate, ½–2 in. long, doubly glandular-serrate, dark green above and glabrous or with only scattered hairs, pubescent and glandular beneath; stipules glandular-serrate: fls. deep yellow, with unpleasant odor, 2–3 in. across, single (also a double-fld. form), usually solitary, on glandular pedicels; sepals to 1 in. long, often coarsely toothed and expanded at tip: fr. globular, ½in. diam., red, not frequent. Asia. Var. **bicolor,** Willm. (*R. lutea* var. *punicea*, Aschers. & Graebn.), has coppery colored petals. **R. Harisonii,** Rivers (*R. fœtida* var. *Harisonii*, Rehd.), HARISONS YELLOW ROSE, common in American yards, is a free-flowering double pale yellow rose, a hybrid with *R. spinosissima;* originated about 1830 in New York City in the garden of Rev. Harison. The Pernetiana roses, starting with Jules Pernet-Ducher, a French hybridizer, are combinations of *R. fœtida* and Hybrid Teas.

32. **R. spinosissima,** L. SCOTCH ROSE. Low bush, 3–4 ft., very close-lvd., densely provided with slender nearly or quite straight spines and stout bristles; twigs glabrous,

pedicels sometimes glandular-hispid: lvs. small, 1–2 in. long; lfts. 5–11 but commonly 9, orbicular to oblong-ovate, very small, mostly ¼–½in. long, obtuse, serrate, glabrous but sometimes glandular beneath: fls. many along the branches but solitary, white, pale pink, or sometimes yellowish, 1½–2 in. across; sepals entire: fr. globose, becoming black, ¾in. or less diam. Eu. to China.—A widespread rose in cult. and running into many named forms. Var. **altaica,** Rehd. (*R. altaica*, Willd.), is larger in every way, with fewer bristles, pedicels smooth, fls. white.

33. **R. Hugonis,** Hemsl. Hugo Rose. Handsome hardy rose blooming very early in the season, making flexible drooping reddish canes 5–8 ft. long, bearing rather stout straight flattened prickles and with bristles also on the shoots: lvs. small, mostly 1–2½ in. long, glabrous, the stipular wings on the petiole very narrow; lfts. 5–11, obovate or oval, ¾in. or usually less long, obtuse, finely serrate: fls. solitary on short lateral shoots but very numerous, 2–2½ in. across, single, clear yellow, on glabrous pedicels; sepals pointed, much shorter than petals: fr. nearly globular, about ½in. diam., scarlet becoming blackish-red. W. China, where it was discovered by Father Hugo, a missionary.

34. **R. xanthina,** Lindl. Much like no. 33, but prickles stouter and more broadly flattened at base, bristles lacking, stipules prominent on the petiole, lfts. usually pubescent beneath at least on the midrib and mostly larger, fls. semi-double. N. China, Korea.—The single-fld. state (forma *normalis*, Rehd. & Wils.) has been intro.; long grown in China in the double-fld. form.

35. **R. Primula,** Boulenger (*R. Ecæ*, Hort. not Aitch.). Erect, to 6 ft.; branchlets slender, with many stout straight prickles having very broad bases: lfts. mostly 9–15, elliptic, ¼–¾in. long, doubly glandular-serrulate, glabrous, glandular beneath: fls. solitary, 1–1½ in. across, pale yellow; pedicels smooth: fr. subglobose, ⅓in. long. Turkestan to China.

36. **R. bracteata,** Wendl. (*R. Macartnea*, Dum.). Macartney Rose. Stout evergreen shrub making long lopping or half-climbing shoots to 10 or 20 ft.; sts. tomentose, armed with very stout flattened hooked prickles in pairs and many scattered bristles: lvs. stiff, 2–4 in. long; lfts. 5–11, stalked, oblong to obovate, ½–1 in. long and to 2 in. on vigorous parts, closely crenate-serrate, rounded but usually with a very short point, shining above, glabrous or nearly so beneath, stipules very short: fls. solitary or few together on very short stalks, white, single, 2–3 in. and more across, subtended by large toothed bracts; sepals densely silky-tomentose: fr. globular and woolly, 1½ in. diam., orange-red. S. China; planted and nat. far S.; intro. in England in 1793 by Lord Macartney.

37. **R. lævigata,** Michx. (*R. sinica*, Murr. *R. cherokeensis*, Donn). Cherokee Rose. Rampant evergreen, climbing over fences and trees, with very stout strongly hooked prickles: lvs. 3-foliolate, stiff, glossy green, glabrous; lfts. 3 (rarely 5), elliptic to ovate-lanceolate, 1½–3 in. or more long, sharp-serrate, acute: fls. solitary, pure white (varying sometimes to rose), 2–3½ in. across, very fragrant; sepals large, usually caudate: fr. obovoid with stipe-like base, ¾in. diam., bristly, with long upright sepals. China, Japan; planted in southern states and also extensively run wild as if native; first described from American plants.—**R. anemonoides,** Rehd., is a probable hybrid of this species with *R. odorata:* it is climbing, with 3 or 5 lfts., stipules adnate to petiole, and large single light pink fls.

38. **R. Banksiæ,** R. Br. Banksia Rose. High-climbing evergreen with few or no prickles, twigs slender and glabrous: lfts. 3 or 5, rarely 7, oblong to oblong-lanceolate, 1–2 in. long, sharp-serrulate, acute or obtuse, shining, glabrous above, hairy on midrib beneath; stipules free from petiole, subulate and caducous: fls. small, few to many on very slender pedicels in umbel-like clusters, about 1 in. across, white or yellow, somewhat fragrant, single or usually variously double: fr. pea-size, sepals caducous. (Described from plants from the garden of Sir Joseph Banks; named in compliment to Lady Banks.) China.—Much planted for trellises and arbors in southern states and Calif.

44. **PRUNUS,** L. Stone-Fruits. Trees and shrubs prevailingly of temp. climates mostly in the northern hemisphere, perhaps 150–175 species if the genus is defined broadly, of major importance in pomology and many prized for ornament; here are included the plums, cherries, peaches, apricots, and almonds.—Lvs. alternate and simple, deciduous or persistent, mostly serrate and sometimes bearing glands along the petiole or base of blade; stipules small, caducous: fls. bisexual, white or pink, sometimes solitary but mostly in umbel-like clusters or racemes, usually in spring and often preceding the foliage, the 5 calyx-lobes and 5 petals spreading; stamens many, inserted with the petals on the hypanthium; pistil normally 1, with undivided style and capitate stigma, superior in the bottom of the calyx-cup, 2-ovuled: fr. a drupe developed from a fleshy pericarp in which is embedded the hard stone formed of the endocarp inclosing usually a single seed, the other ovule having aborted. (Pru-nus: classical name of the plum.)—The edible

part of the fr. is usually the soft juicy outer flesh, but in the almonds the flesh is dry and often cracks at maturity and the kernel or seed is eaten; in many species the frs. are small, acerb and inedible. In N. Amer. 25–30 species are native, some of them of much importance horticulturally. As here defined, Prunus covers Amygdalus, Armeniaca, Cerasus, Laurocerasus, Padus, Persica.

A. Drupe furrowed on one side, usually bloomy, sometimes pubescent: lvs. convolute or conduplicate.
B. Axillary buds solitary; terminal bud wanting.
C. Fr. glabrous, usually with a slender pedicel that remains with it, the stone not prominently furrowed. (PRUNOPHORA, the Plums.)
D. Fls. mostly 1–2, sometimes 3: lvs. convolute: stone often sculptured.
E. Twigs pubescent: fr. ½in. diam.: fls. usually solitary.......... 1. *P. spinosa*
EE. Twigs glabrous or soon becoming so: fls. mostly 2.
F. Shape of fr. round to oblong: lvs. spreading or drooping.
G. Pedicels pubescent: lvs. pubescent beneath.............. 3. *P. domestica*
GG. Pedicels glabrous: lvs. glabrous beneath except on midrib.
H. Lvs. mostly not over 2 in. long: fr. to about 1 in. diam.... 2. *P. cerasifera*
HH. Lvs. 3–4 in. long: fr. 2–3 in. diam.................. 4. *P. salicina*
FF. Shape of fr. depressed-globose: lvs. upright, 3–4 in. long......... 5. *P. Simonii*
DD. Fls. 3 or more, rarely fewer: lvs. mostly conduplicate: stone usually smooth.
E. Lvs. round-ovate, subcordate, glabrous only when mature........ 6. *P. subcordata*
EE. Lvs. ovate to lanceolate.
F. Lf. sharply serrate, not shining above, usually pubescent beneath.
G. Diam. of fls. ½in.: lvs. acute: fr. purplish.............. 7. *P. maritima*
GG. Diam. of fls. 1 in.: lvs. acuminate: fr. yellow or red.......... 8. *P. americana*
FF. Lf. obtusely serrate.
G. Foliage not shining above, not narrower in upper half, coarsely serrate: fls. becoming pink in age...................... 9. *P. nigra*
GG. Foliage shining, narrowed in upper half, usually finely serrate: fls. white.
H. Length of lvs. 1–2 in., lanceolate: sepals not glandular......10. *P. angustifolia*
HH. Length of lvs. 2½–4 in., lanceolate to ovate: sepals glandular.
I. Shape of lvs. oblong-obovate or elliptic-oblong, irregularly serrate, with veins prominent beneath..............11. *P. hortulana*
II. Shape of lvs. oblong-lanceolate, finely glandular-serrate, with veins not conspicuous beneath..................12. *P. Munsoniana*
CC. Fr. pubescent, the pedicel short and separating at maturity, the stone usually furrowed on the margin: lvs. convolute. (ARMENIACA, the Apricots.)
D. Color of fr. red or yellow, almost or quite sessile.
E. Lvs. usually rounded at base, abruptly short-pointed at apex: fr. pulpy and soft.......................................13. *P. Armeniaca*
EE. Lvs. more or less cuneate at base, long-pointed: fr. hard and dry....14. *P. Mume*
DD. Color of fr. dark purple, with slender stalk....................15. *P. dasycarpa*
B. Axillary buds 3, the lateral ones fl.-buds; terminal bud present: fls. 1–2, mostly sessile: lvs. conduplicate. (AMYGDALUS, the Almonds and Peaches.)
C. Plants tree-form: lvs. 3–9 in. long.
D. Flesh of fr. hard, inedible, splitting to the stone at maturity: lvs. crenate-serrate, broadest below the middle....................16. *P. Amygdalus*
DD. Flesh of fr. soft, usually not splitting to the stone: young lvs. sharp-serrate.
E. Sepals villous without at least on margins: lvs. broad- to oblong-lanceolate: stone large and compressed.....................17. *P. Persica*
EE. Sepals glabrous: lvs. lanceolate, tapering from near base: stone small, almost round......................................18. *P. Davidiana*
CC. Plants bush-form: lvs. 1–3 in. long.
D. Lvs. obovate or broad-ovate, tending to be 3-lobed: hypanthium campanulate...19. *P. triloba*
DD. Lvs. elliptic-oblong: hypanthium tubular.......................20. *P. tenella*
AA. Drupe not furrowed nor bloomy, the stone turgid or almost round: lvs. conduplicate: terminal bud present.
B. Fls. 1 to few, usually with conspicuous bracts. (CERASUS, the Umbellate Cherries.)
C. Lvs. tomentose beneath, nearly as broad as long: fls. nearly sessile......21. *P. tomentosa*
CC. Lvs. otherwise: fls. distinctly pedicelled.
D. Plants bush-like: winter-buds in 3's: pedicels usually short. (See also no. 34, a bush.)
E. Lf. green beneath, serrate to the base: fr. red.
F. Shape of lvs. ovate to ovate-lanceolate, acuminate, 1–2 in. long...22. *P. japonica*
FF. Shape of lvs. oblong-obovate to -lanceolate, acute, 2–3½ in. long.23. *P. glandulosa*
EE. Lf. paler beneath, entire toward the base: fr. darker.
F. Shape of lvs. oblanceolate to obovate, ascending: fr. ⅓in. diam., astringent...24. *P. pumila*
FF. Shape of lvs. elliptic to elliptic-lanceolate, spreading: fr. ½in. diam., sweet..25. *P. Besseyi*
DD. Plants mostly tree-like: winter-buds single or on short spurs: pedicels often longer. (No. 34 is bushy.)

E. Sepals erect or slightly spreading, not reflexed.
F. Lf. incisely and doubly serrate or lobulate: fls. ¾in. across ......26. *P. incisa*
FF. Lf. simply or only slightly doubly serrate, not lobed.
G. Fruiting pedicels conspicuously thickened: fls. pendulous, deep rose, ½in. across ......28. *P. campanulata*
GG. Fruiting pedicels not thickened.
H. Infl. simple, the involucre (bud-scales) at base not conspicuous, fls. before the lvs.
I. Shape of lvs. ovate, 3–5 in. long: fls. white ......36. *P. Pseudocerasus*
II. Shape of lvs. largely lanceolate, mostly 1½–2 in. long: fls. pink ......27. *P. subhirtella*
HH. Infl. often branched, the involucre one-half or more as long, fls. with the lvs.
I. Hypanthium campanulate, glabrous: lvs. glabrous above and beneath ......29. *P. serrulata*
II. Hypanthium cylindric to turbinate, usually pubescent: lvs. pubescent at least on veins beneath.
J. Fl. double, pink; sepals entire: young lvs. bronzy ......30. *P. Sieboldii*
JJ. Fl. single, white or pink; sepals serrate: young lvs. pale green ......31. *P. yedoensis*
EE. Sepals reflexed.
F. Arrangement of fls. mostly in lateral clusters, with persistent involucre (bud-scales).
G. Habit tree-like: lvs. serrate, mostly 3–6 in. long.
H. Lf. pubescent beneath at least on veins, 4–6 in. long, abruptly short-pointed: infl. without leafy bracts: fr. sweet ......32. *P. avium*
HH. Lf. glabrous, 3–4 in. long, taper-pointed: infl. usually with leafy bracts at base: fr. sour ......33. *P. Cerasus*
GG. Habit bush-like: lvs. crenate, 1–2 in. long ......34. *P. fruticosa*
FF. Arrangement of fls. in terminal and lateral clusters, the involucre deciduous.
G. Lf. broad-ovate to round: fls. racemose ......35. *P. Mahaleb*
GG. Lf. oblong-lanceolate: fls. subumbellate ......37. *P. pensylvanica*
BB. Fls. 12 or more, in elongate racemes, bracts small.
C. Foliage deciduous: peduncles usually leafy. (PADUS, the Racemose Cherries.)
D. Sepals persistent at base of fr.: large trees with fls. appearing late, and with hard-glossy lvs ......38. *P. serotina*
DD. Sepals deciduous: small trees or bushes with very early fls. and soft not hard-glossy lvs.
E. Hypanthium pubescent within: fls. in wide-spreading or drooping racemes; petals twice as long as stamens ......39. *P. Padus*
EE. Hypanthium glabrous within: fls. in upright or ascending racemes (at first); petals scarcely exceeding stamens ......40. *P. virginiana*
CC. Foliage persistent: peduncles leafless. (LAUROCERASUS, the Laurel Cherries.)
D. Margins of lvs. crenate-dentate, 2–4 in. long: racemes exceeding lvs ......41. *P. lusitanica*
DD. Margins of lvs. not crenate-dentate: racemes usually not longer than lvs.
E. Lvs. strongly crisped, spinose-toothed, 1–2 in. long, ovate to almost round: fr. red ......44. *P. ilicifolia*
EE. Lvs. not as above, mostly 2–6 in. long.
F. Lf. 3–6 in. long, oblong, abruptly short-pointed, usually remotely serrate: sepals 3-toothed ......42. *P. Laurocerasus*
FF. Lf. 2–4 in. long, lance-ovate to oblong-lanceolate, acute to acuminate: sepals entire.
G. Base of lf. acute, lf. about one-third as wide as long: racemes about 1 in. long ......43. *P. caroliniana*
GG. Base of lf. rounded, lf. about one-half as wide as long: racemes 2–3 in. long ......45. *P. Lyonii*

1. **P. spinosa**, L. SLOE. BLACKTHORN. Thick-topped very thorny suckering hard-wooded tree or shrub, 10–15 ft. high, planted for ornament; young shoots pubescent: lvs. small and very numerous, mostly less than 2 in. long, obovate, oval, ovate or with oblong combinations of these forms, obtuse or nearly so, closely serrate, pubescent on veins beneath but becoming glabrous: fls. small, clear white, ½–¾in. across, borne singly or sometimes in pairs in early spring, the slender glabrous pedicels less than ¼in. long: fr. harsh, globular, about ½in. diam., blue becoming black, often persisting until winter. Eurasia.—Frequently planted for its profuse early bloom, its dense head of foliage, and abundant ornamental frs. There are purple-lvd. and double-fld. kinds.

2. **P. cerasifera**, Ehrh. CHERRY PLUM. MYROBALAN PLUM. Slender twiggy tree to 20 ft. or more, seldom thorny, sometimes grown for its edible fr. but known mostly as a stock for other plums and often forming thickets when the budded tops have failed or appearing in orchards; young shoots glabrous, or very soon becoming so: lvs. small and thin, light green, usually not exceeding 2 in. long, short-ovate to somewhat obovate, short-pointed, finely serrate, retaining light pubescence on veins beneath: fls. usually clear white, 1 in. or less across, borne singly or 2 or 3 together, often clustered on spurs, the slender glabrous pedicels seldom ½in. long: fr. small, mostly 1 in. or less diam., globular and cherry-like, red or yellow, the flesh soft, juicy and sweet. Probably native in

S. W. Asia. Var. **Pissardii**, Koehne (*P. Pissardii*, Carr. *P. cerasifera* var. *atropurpurea*, Dipp.), is a common purple-lvd. form with pink fls.; intro. to France by M. Pissard, gardener to the Shah of Persia. The Marianna plum is supposed to be a hybrid between *C. cerasifera* and one of the native plums. **P. Blireiana**, André, with broad purple ovate-acuminate lvs. and semi-double fls. is a hybrid of var. *Pissardii* and *P. Mume.*

3. **P. domestica,** L. COMMON OR EUROPEAN PLUM. Strong-growing small tree with thick twigs pubescent when young, not thorny except sometimes in run-wild forms, planted in orchards for the fr.: lvs. large, blade 2–4 in. long, ovate to obovate, thick and rugose, dull green, short-pointed to obtuse, coarsely and irregularly serrate, thin-hairy or scabrous above and pubescent beneath: fls. white or cream-color, 1 in. or less across, mostly clustered on spurs but sometimes single or 2–3 together, the mostly pubescent pedicels ½in. or less long: fr. very variable in size, color and texture, often blue-purple, representing the range of garden plums, usually ovoid to oblong. Probably from S. W. Asia, but known only as a cultigen and escape. Var. **insititia,** Bailey (*P. insititia*, L.), DAMSON, BULLACE, tree mostly smaller and head more compact; lvs. smaller and firmer in texture; fr. small, ovoid, borne usually in clusters. Var. **italica,** Schneid. (*P. italica*, Borkh.), GREEN-GAGE, branchlets thinly pubescent; fr. greenish, often large.—The PRUNE is a hort. var. or form of plum with a consistency and content that allow it to be dried for domestic use.

4. **P. salicina,** Lindl. (*P. triflora*, Roxb.). JAPANESE PLUM. Strong-growing small tree, grown for the edible frs., with glabrous parts, the reddish or brown twigs mostly shining: lvs. oblong-obovate to oblong-ovate, 3–4 in. long, not prominently rugose, usually shining above, abruptly but prominently pointed, closely blunt-serrate, dull and usually glabrous beneath: fls. white, ½–¾in. across, few (commonly 2 or 3) from each bud but appearing clustered on the spurs, the slender glabrous pedicels ½in. or less long: fr. various, yellow or light red, never blue-purple, tending to be pointed at apex. China.

5. **P. Simonii,** Carr. APRICOT PLUM. Straight-growing narrow-topped tree, planted for its frs., the glabrous branches erect: lvs. somewhat peach-like, long-oblanceolate to lance-obovate, 3–4 in. long, rather thick in texture, dull, very veiny but glabrous beneath, short-pointed, obtusely serrate, conduplicate or trough-like in position: fls. white, about ¾in. across, single or 2 or 3 together, on short glabrous pedicels: fr. 1–2 in. diam. crosswise, flattened lengthwise, very firm in texture and with strong aroma, smooth, maroon-red, deeply sutured, flesh yellow and clinging to the small rough nearly orbicular stone, pedicel usually not adhering. (Seeds sent to France before 1872 by Eugene Simon.) China, but not known wild.—The Wickson plum (*P. sultana*, Voss) is a hybrid with *P. salicina*.

6. **P. subcordata,** Benth. PACIFIC PLUM. Stout tree to 25 ft., or sometimes a bush, planted sometimes for ornament and also for the edible fr., the twigs glabrous or pubescent and sometimes spiny: lvs. broad-ovate to orbicular, usually subcordate at base, 1–3 in. long, sharply and often doubly serrate, rather thick in texture, pubescent beneath but becoming nearly or quite glabrous: fls. white fading to rose, ⅔ in. across, in advance of lvs., 2–4 together, on glabrous or pubescent pedicels ½in. or less long: fr. globular or short-oblong, dark red or yellow, often more than 1 in. diam., subacid flesh clinging to flat smooth or slightly rough stone. Calif. and Ore. Var. **Kelloggii,** Lemm., SISSON PLUM, a form or race with larger ovoid yellow or red fr. with soft and agreeable flesh; more slender in growth; lvs. usually not cordate and more glabrous.

7. **P. maritima,** Marsh. BEACH PLUM. Variable species, usually a straggling seldom thorny bush, but becoming tree-like when planted away from the coast, the young growth slightly pubescent, planted for ornament and rarely for the edible fr.: lvs. oval or obovate-oval, 1–2 in. long, short-acute to nearly obtuse, closely serrulate, dull green, more or less pubescent beneath: fls. numerous, white, about ½in. across, in few-fld. umbels preceding the foliage, pedicels ¼–½in. long and mostly pubescent: fr. depressed-globular, about ½in. or more diam., deep glaucous-purple, sweetish, the flesh free from the cherry-like stone. Beaches and near the coast, Me. to Va.—It has given rise to a tree-like var. with large and agreeable fr.; promising to the plant-breeder.

8. **P. americana,** Marsh. Twiggy usually thorny tree, 20–30 ft., or bush-like, with glabrous branchlets, yielding pomological vars.: lvs. obovate to oblong-ovate, 3–4 in. long, acuminate, thickish, not glossy, margins sharp-serrate or almost incised, strongly reticulated beneath and mostly pubescent on the veins, the petiole usually without glands: fls. rather large, about 1 in. across, in small umbel-like clusters in advance of foliage, the calyx-lobes entire and pubescent within, the pedicels glabrous and about ½in. long: fr. mostly small and hard, ¾in. diam. but sometimes much larger and excellent in flavor, yellow or red, glaucous, the stone turgid. S. New England south and west, a common plant in thickets.—It has given rise to many named vars., as Blackhawk, Forest Garden, De Soto, Rollingstone, Hawkeye. Var. **lanata,** Sudw. (*P. lanata*, Mack. & Bush), has lvs. and twigs soft-pubescent or even tomentose; it yields Wolf, Van Buren, Quaker, and other pomological vars.

9. **P. nigra,** Ait. (*P. americana* var. *nigra*, Waugh). The northern representative of no. 8, in Canada and southward to New England, N. Y., Ohio, and N. Ill. and north-

westward: lvs. mostly broader, with crenate-serrate margins and biglandular petiole: fls. larger, on dark red pedicels, white changing to pink, the calyx-lobes glandular-serrate and glabrous on the inside: fr. mostly oblong, orange-red, the stone large and flat.—It yields a few large-fruited vars., as Cheney, Itasca, Oxford.

10. **P. angustifolia,** Marsh. Chickasaw Plum. Twiggy tree to 20 ft., or a bush, with zigzag hard reddish glabrous branches, forming dense thickets in the wild, yielding a few pomological vars.: lvs. lanceolate to oblong-lanceolate, 1–2 in. long, conduplicate or trough-like, often clustered on spurs, shining, narrowed at both ends, finely close-serrate, glabrous or slightly pubescent on nerves beneath, petiole with or without 2 glands at top: fls. white, ⅓in. across, preceding foliage, 2–4 together, on glabrous pedicels ½in. or less long; calyx-lobes not glandular: fr. small and early, about ½in. diam., nearly globular, cherry-like (sometimes called "mountain cherry"), red or yellow and dotted, thinly glaucous, flesh soft and adhering to small rough stone. Del. south and west.—Caddo Chief is of this species. Var. **Watsonii,** Waugh (*P. Watsonii*, Sarg.), Sand Plum, bush 3–6 ft., with very zigzag twigs, lvs. smaller and less serrate, fls. smaller, fr. thicker-skinned; dry regions, Kans. south and southwest (named in compliment to Dr. Louis Watson, of Kans.); yields Strawberry, Red and Yellow Panhandle, and other pomological vars. Var. **varians,** Wight & Hedr., freer and larger grower than *P. angustifolia*, lvs. and pedicels longer, stone usually more pointed at apex; Okla. and Tex.; gives rise to Yellow Transparent, Coletta, and others. **P. orthosepala,** Koehne, hybrid of var. *Watsonii* and *P. americana;* spreading bush, 4–6 ft.; lvs. oblong-lanceolate to obovate-lanceolate, 1½–2½ in. long, not conduplicate, narrowed at both ends, rather sharply serrate; fls. ½in. broad; fr. globose, 1 in. thick; originally from Kans.

11. **P. hortulana,** Bailey. Hortulan Plum. Upright tree not sprouting from the root or forming thickets, becoming 20–30 ft. tall, yielding many pomological vars.: lvs. oblong-obovate to ovate-lanceolate, but mostly on the oblong order (sides parallel), blade 3–4 in. long, long-acuminate, rather broad or rounded at the base, yellowish-green, glabrous but dull or only little shining above, nearly or quite glabrous and prominently veined beneath, margins coarsely and unequally serrate or crenate-serrate, petiole with 1, 2, or more glands near top: fls. white, about ⅔in. across, mostly preceding foliage, 2–4 or more, the pedicels glabrous; calyx-lobes about as long as tube, margins glandular: fr. globose or short-oblong, 1 in. or less diam. (but larger in cult. vars.), red or yellow and usually white-dotted, with little if any bloom. Ky. and Tenn. to Kans.—Yields vars. Golden Beauty, Wayland, Kanawha. Var. **Mineri,** Bailey, well represented in the Miner plum, has darker duller thicker lvs. mostly obovate in outline, and a late very firm fr.; approaches *P. americana* in appearance.

12. **P. Munsoniana,** Wight & Hedr. Wild Goose Plum. Stout tree suckering and producing dense thickets: lvs. thinner than in no. 11, oblong-lanceolate to lanceolate to oval, often standing conduplicate or trough-shaped, 2½–4 in. long, glossy above and not prominently veined beneath, the margins finely and evenly serrate, petiole usually biglandular near top: fls. white, ½in. or more across, 2–4 together mostly preceding the lvs., the calyx-lobes glandular: fr. globular to oval, about ¾in. long, bright red or yellowish, slightly glaucous, with many pale dots. (Bears the name of T. V. Munson, page 48.) Ky. to Kans. and Tex.—Source of Wild Goose, Newman, Robinson, and other plums.

13. **P. Armeniaca,** L. (*Armeniaca vulgaris*, Lam.). Common Apricot. Small tree with reddish bark and glabrous twigs: lvs. ovate to round-ovate, sometimes subcordate, blade 2–3½ in. long, abruptly short-pointed, closely and mostly obtusely serrate, glabrous above, pubescent on veins beneath, petiole with conspicuous glands: fls. pinkish or nearly white, ¾–1 in. across, single and sessile or practically so, much in advance of foliage: fr. variable, pubescent but becoming nearly smooth at maturity, roundish but usually somewhat flattened, yellow overlaid with red, the flesh firm and sweet, mostly free from the flat ridged stone. China; once thought to have come from Armenia.—There are many races; the Russian apricots are very hardy mostly small-fruited kinds.

14. **P. Mume,** Sieb. & Zucc. Japanese Apricot; known as Plum in Japan and extensively planted for its very early bloom. Small tree; bark gray or greenish and lvs. grayish-green: lvs. smaller than in no. 13, narrow-ovate to roundish-ovate, long-pointed, rounded or tapering at base, finely and sharply serrate, more or less scabrous above, lighter colored and pubescent beneath (or essentially glabrous in the usual cult. forms, var. **tonsa,** Rehd.), petiole usually with glands: fls. sessile or nearly so, fragrant, white or pink, in many sizes and often full double, usually in advance of foliage: fr. mostly smaller than that of no. 13, yellow or greenish, the flesh dry and clinging to the pitted stone. Japan (Mume is a Japanese name).—Planted in N. Amer. mostly in a few fr.-bearing vars. as the Bungo or Bongoume apricots.

15. **P. dasycarpa,** Ehrh. Purple Apricot. Small apricot-like tree, 12–20 ft., with glabrous purplish branchlets: lvs. rather small and plum-like, the blade 2½ in. or less long, elliptic-ovate to oval, short-pointed, thin and dull green, closely serrate, more or less pubescent on veins beneath, the slender petiole 1 in. or less long and with or without glands: fls. 1 in. or more across, white, single or in 2's or 3's in advance of foliage, the pubescent slender pedicels about ¼in. long: fr. globular, plum-like, 1½ in. diam., pubescent

and dark purple, with soft sourish flesh; stone pubescent. Known only in cult.; by some thought to be native in N. E. Asia, by others supposed to be hybrid between apricot and *P. cerasifera*.

16. **P. Amygdalus,** Batsch (*Amygdalus communis*, L. *P. communis*, Arcang. not Huds.). ALMOND. Tree to 25 ft. with light colored glabrous branchlets, grown sometimes as an ornamental but chiefly (in Calif.) for the "almonds" (stones with the edible seed): lvs. firm, oblong-lanceolate, 3–4 in. long, acuminate, very closely crenate-serrate, glabrous, more or less shining above, lighter beneath, the petiole usually gland-bearing above: fls. large and showy, 1–1½ in. and more across, pink, solitary, sessile, appearing before or with the early foliage: fr. large, 1½ in. and more long, oblong-ovoid and compressed, pubescent, the flesh hard and splitting at maturity disclosing the shallow pitted stone. Probably Asian, perhaps indigenous in the Medit. region, now widely cult. and often escaped.—Bitter almonds, as distinguished from sweet almonds, are kinds in which the kernel is bitter; these kinds are employed mostly in the manufacture of prussic acid and extracts. The sweet or edible almonds may be either hard-shell or soft-shell; the tendency is to breed vars. with thinner walls in the stone, as the paper-shells. There are ornamental forms of the almond tree, as weeping, variegated, double-fld.

17. **P. Persica,** Batsch (*Amygdalus Persica*, L. *Persica vulgaris*, Mill.). PEACH. Small tree with glabrous twigs, grown extensively for the thick-fleshed fr., and there are many ornamental kinds: lvs. oblong-lanceolate to broad-lanceolate, 4–9 in. long, acuminate, finely sharp-serrate when small or young, otherwise variously coarsely crenate-serrate, glabrous, shining above and somewhat lighter beneath, the petiole and sometimes the lower margins usually gland-bearing: fls. solitary, sessile, in advance of foliage, pink, ½–2 in. across, the petals in some races only about ¼in. long and in others very large, much-expanded and showy: fr. widely variable in size and shape, 1–3 in. and more diam., pubescent, yellow or red, flesh white or yellow, stone very hard and deeply pitted. China, but once thought to be from Persia (whence the names Persica and peach).—There are purple-lvd., dwarf, double-fld., and other ornamental races; also hybrids with the almond. Var. **Nectarina,** Maxim. (var. *nucipersica*, Schneid. *Amygdalus Persica* var. *Nectarina*, Ait.), the NECTARINE, has fr. smooth at maturity, like a plum. Var. **compressa,** Bean (var. *platycarpa*, Bailey. *Persica vulgaris* var. *compressa*, Loud.), FLAT PEACH, has fr. much flattened endwise, often nearly as flat as a watch; the Peen-to peach belongs here.

18. **P. Davidiana,** Franch. (*Persica Davidiana*, Carr.). A very early-flowering willow-lvd. small tree grown for ornament where spring frosts do not destroy the bloom or the fl.-buds are not killed by winter, and sometimes used as a stock; branchlets glabrous: lvs. firm, 3–5 in. long, lanceolate, tapering from near the base into very long narrow points, finely very sharp-serrate, glabrous, much lighter colored beneath, the slender petiole often with undeveloped glands: fls. white, blush or light pink, 1 in. or more across, solitary, sessile: fr. nearly globular, about 1 in. diam., with prominent suture, grayish or yellowish, pubescent, the flesh whitish and dry and free from the small nearly spherical stone. (Abbé David, page 230.) China.

19. **P. triloba,** Lindl. FLOWERING ALMOND. Bush, sometimes becoming tree-like and 10 ft. or more tall, twigs nearly or quite glabrous, grown for its showy bloom which appears just in advance of the foliage: lvs. broadly ovate to obovate, 1–2 in. long and twice as large on verdurous shoots, tending to be trilobate, abruptly pointed, coarsely and sharply double-serrate, lightly hairy on both surfaces: fls. clear pink, sometimes white, 1–1½ in. across, in the cult. material mostly double or semi-double, solitary, short-pedicelled; calyx-tube hairy inside between the stamens: fr. small, red, hairy but becoming glabrous, seldom seen. China.—Common in cult., usually grafted on other stock. **P. Arnoldiana,** Rehd., is a hybrid of *P. triloba* by *P. cerasifera*, produced at the Arnold Arboretum: differs from *P. triloba* in white fls. appearing with lvs., lvs. less coarsely and scarcely doubly serrate, not trilobate, fr. larger, less hairy and more succulent.

20. **P. tenella,** Batsch (*Amygdalus nana*, L. *P. nana*, Stokes not Du Roi). RUSSIAN ALMOND. Hardy bush 3–5 ft. high, known in cult. mostly as an ornamental but intro. also as a fr. plant; branchlets glabrous: lvs. stiffish and narrow, 2–3 in. long, elliptic-lanceolate to oblanceolate, the bigger ones 1 in. broad but usually less than ½in., obtuse or scarcely pointed, gradually narrowed to a short petiole, sharp-serrate, glabrous, much lighter colored beneath: fls. solitary or paired, sessile or nearly so, appearing with the foliage, pink to white, about ¾in. across, the calyx-tube prominent and nearly ¼in. long: fr. ovoid, small and hard, bitter (but improved vars.), about ¾in. long, densely pubescent, with a wrinkled sharp-pointed somewhat cordate stone. S. Russia, E. Eu., Asia.

21. **P. tomentosa,** Thunb. Compact bushy-topped hardy small tree or very large shrub with heavily pubescent young growth, grown for ornament but likely to yield pomological forms: lvs. broad-oval to -obovate, 1–2½ in. long, thick and dull green, abruptly contracted to short point but the small ones on spurs often obtuse, unequally serrate, very short-petioled, rugose above and tomentose beneath: fls. mostly 1 or 2 or else clustered on spurs, nearly sessile, about ¾in. across, petals white or tinted, calyx red, appearing just before the lvs.; calyx-lobes erect or only slightly spreading: fr. size of cherry, globular, light red, slightly hairy. China, Manchuria, Japan.

22. **P. japonica,** Thunb. Dwarf Flowering Cherry. One of the three little plants grown for ornament under the name of "Flowering Almond," the others being nos. 23 and 19, the two former sometimes listed under the name *P. sinensis:* bush, 4–5 ft., growths glabrous: lvs. broad, 1–2 in. long, ovate, acuminate with acute apex, sharply and often doubly serrate, very short-petioled, dull green, glabrous or with a few hairs on veins beneath: fls. blush or pink, about 1 in. across, sometimes solitary but usually 2 or 3 together, short-pedicelled, appearing just before or with the foliage: fr. about globular, not appearing in cult. as the fls. are usually double, ½in. diam., light bright red. China.

23. **P. glandulosa,** Thunb. The second species of Dwarf Flowering Cherry or Flowering Almond and the common one in cult.: lvs. 2–3½ in. long, on the oblong order with sides nearly parallel for a distance or of nearly equal width, gradually tapering above but not acuminate, apex blunt, more crenate-serrate, firmer: fls. blush, pink, or white, usually double in cult. China.

24. **P. pumila,** L. Sand Cherry. Upright shrub to 8 ft., young branches glabrous, reddish: lvs. narrow-oblanceolate to spatulate, 1–2 in. long, acuminate or acute, closely serrate, glabrous, petiole ⅛–⅜in. long: fls. ⅓in. across, white, 2–4: fr. subglobose, ⅓in. diam., purple-black, shining. N. Y. to Ill. and Wis.—**P. cistena,** N. E. Hansen, is a hybrid with the Pissard plum; lvs. slightly pubescent on midrib beneath, reddish; fls. 1–2, white; fr. blackish-purple.

25. **P. Besseyi,** Bailey. Western Sand Cherry. Little bush with glabrous growths, 1–4 ft. high, diffuse or prostrate, ornamental and also yielding good edible fr.: lvs. elliptic to oval to somewhat oblanceolate, 1–3 in. long, spreading, thick, apex obtuse or only short-acute, tapering to slender petiole, finely appressed-serrate, glabrous, shining above and lighter colored beneath; stipules on strong shoots large and serrate: fls. few or several, profuse, about ½in. across, white, slender-pedicelled, appearing with the early foliage: fr. nearly globular, often with short point, about ½in. diam. and larger in some forms, black or mottled, bitter and astringent but often sweet and palatable. (Named in compliment to Chas. E. Bessey, 1845–1915, professor of botany in the Univ. of Neb., who had much to do with popularizing the large-fruited forms for food.) Plains, Man. south.—The species has been used as a dwarf stock and also in hybridizing.

26. **P. incisa,** Thunb. Shrub or tree to 30 ft., branchlets glabrous: lvs. at first purplish, 1–2 in. long, ovate to obovate, acuminate, incisely double-serrate, pubescent, petiole to ½in.: fls. nodding, white to pale pink, ¾–1 in. across, calyx red: fr. ovoid, purple-black, ⅓in. long. Japan.

27. **P. subhirtella,** Miq. Rosebud Cherry. Large shrub or small bushy tree to 25 ft., with brown glabrous or lightly hairy branches and gray bark, planted for its profuse handsome early bloom: lvs. lanceolate to ovate-lanceolate or ovate, 1½–2 in. long (to 3 in. on strong shoots), abruptly acuminate or short-pointed, narrowed to base, doubly sharp-serrate, dull, hairy on veins beneath, the short petioles and lower margins usually without developed glands: fls. pink, 1 in. across, 1, 2, or 3 normally from a winter-bud in advance of foliage and the bud-scales not enlarging, petals pink to nearly white and emarginate, calyx reddish and narrow, cylindric or somewhat enlarged at base, pedicels 1 in. or less long and hairy: fr. globular, about ⅓in. diam., shining black. Japan; not recognized wild.—A much larger tree, making massive wide-spreading branches and larger lvs., is var. **ascendens,** Wils. (*P. pendula* var. *ascendens*, Makino), native in Cent. China and probably elsewhere; apparently little planted in N. Amer. Var. **pendula,** Tanaka (*P. pendula*, Maxim.), Drooping Rosebud Cherry, small tree with crooked drooping branches; lvs. mostly larger, the basal glands usually large; Japan, not known wild. Var. **autumnalis,** Makino, fls. semi-double, appearing partly in autumn and partly in spring; Japan, not known wild.

28. **P. campanulata,** Maxim. Small tree to 25 ft., branchlets glabrous: lvs. ovate to oblong-ovate, 2–4 in. long, acuminate, closely often doubly serrate, glabrous: pedicels slender, to ½in. long, glandular: fls. pendulous, deep rose, campanulate, ½in. across, calyx rose, glabrous: fr. ovoid, ½in. long, red. S. Japan, Formosa.—Not very hardy.

29. **P. serrulata,** Lindl. Japanese Flowering Cherry. Tree of medium size, with smooth dark chestnut-brown bark and glabrous branchlets, sometimes planted for its showy fls.: lvs. unfolding greenish-brown, large, 3–6 in. long, ovate to narrow-ovate, abruptly long-acuminate, deep green, with prominent acute or short-aristate serratures, glabrous, glaucescent beneath, the glabrous petiole with 2–4 small glands or none: fls. white, double or semi-double, not fragrant, 1–1½ in. across, in 3–5-fld. clusters which are on long or short peduncles and which bear large fimbriate bracts, appearing with the foliage or just in advance of it; pedicels 1 in. or less long, glabrous; calyx-tube and style glabrous: fr. size of small pea, black. China, Japan, Korea.—It yields many kinds, some of them pink-fld. Var. **spontanea,** Wils., is the wild native form in Japan, with single small white or pink fls. Var. **sachalinensis,** Wils. (*P. Sargentii*, Rehd.), is hardier in cult.; a larger tree, with broader and more coarsely serrate lvs., the serratures less pointed although often gland-tipped; fls. ½–1¾ in. across, rose, pink or nearly white, not double; N. Japan, Korea. Var. **Lannesiana,** Rehd. (*Cerasus Lannesiana*, Carr. *P. Lannesiana*,

Wils.), parent apparently of the greater number of Japanese double-flowering cherries, distinguished by pale gray bark, lvs. unfolding green or only slightly reddish, long-aristate serratures of lvs. and its fragrant mostly pink fls.; it makes a large tree 30 ft. or more high; Japan; received in Eu. about 1870 by M. Lannes.

30. **P. Sieboldii,** Wittm. (*Cerasus Sieboldii,* Carr. *P. Pseudocerasus* var. *Sieboldii,* Maxim.). JAPANESE FLOWERING CHERRY. A double-fld. cherry much like no. 29 but the lvs. bronzy when young, densely soft-pilose beneath, caudate-acuminate, sharply and often obscurely double-serrate with small sharp teeth; petiole hairy, usually with 1 or 2 small glands: fls. double or at least semi-double, normally pink, the peduncle scarcely evident when they appear before the foliage but elongated when they come with the foliage; calyx-lobes entire; style hairy at base. (P. F. von Siebold, page 51.) Japan, not known in native state.

31. **P. yedoensis,** Matsum. Differs from no. 30 in pale green young lvs. and calyx-lobes sharp-serrate; from no. 29 in the hairy pedicels and style as also the veins and ribs on the under side of lvs. and also usually the outside of the calyx: fls. single (a double var.), white to pink, slightly fragrant, in clusters or sometimes only 2, mostly in advance of foliage but sometimes with it: lvs. obovate to broadly ovate-elliptic, 3–5 in. long, acuminate, doubly serrate with sharp gland-tipped serratures; bark smooth pale gray. Japan, but unknown native.—Much planted in parks and temple grounds, and to be expected in the living collections of Japanese cherries in N. Amer.

32. **P. avium,** L. SWEET CHERRY. Tall big tree with strong central leader, not suckering, with red-brown birch-like bark defoliating in transverse strips, with glabrous growth, planted extensively in orchards and, in the Mazzard, used as stock in nurseries: lvs. on the oblong-elongate order, usually oblong-ovate to oblong-obovate and gradually taper-pointed, blade 4–6 in. long, soft in texture and color, hanging limp on the young growths, margins doubly acute-glandular-serrate at first but becoming more or less obtuse-serrate, the petiole usually bearing 1 or more large glands near top: fls. white, about 1 in. across, appearing with the first lvs. from clusters of buds on lateral spurs, the inner glandular bud-scales large and persistent for a time, on glabrous pedicels about 1 in. long; calyx-tube constricted near top, the lobes entire: fr. globular or somewhat depressed or in some forms heart-shaped, yellow or red, with mostly sweet flesh or bitterish on run-wild trees. Eurasia.—There are ornamental forms, as weeping, cut-lvd., variegated, double-fld. Var. **Juliana,** W. Koch, HEART CHERRIES, fr. heart-shaped with soft flesh, as in Black Tartarian, Governor Wood, Black Eagle. Var. **duracina,** W. Koch, BIGARREAU CHERRIES, fr. firm breaking flesh and mostly of light color, as in Napoleon, Yellow Spanish, Windsor. The DUKE CHERRIES are **P. Gondouinii,** Rehd. (*P. effusa,* Schneid. *P. avium* var. *regalis,* Bailey. *Cerasus Gondouinii,* Poit. & Turpin); fr. acid; a race of hybrids between *P. avium* and *P. Cerasus.*

33. **P. Cerasus,** L. SOUR CHERRY. Small round-headed bushy-topped tree, with gray tight bark, glabrous growth, suckering from the root, planted mostly in orchards but with good ornamental forms: lvs. short-ovate to ovate-obovate, 3–4 in. long, abruptly short-pointed, stiff in texture, light or gray-green, doubly serrate, petiole or base of blade with more or less undeveloped glands, glabrous or with sparse hairs on veins beneath: fls. white, 1 in. or somewhat less across, appearing with the first foliage or slightly in advance of it, in small clusters from lateral buds of which the scales are small, on slender glabrous pedicels 1 in. or more long; calyx-tube little if any constricted at top, the lobes crenate: fr. globular or depressed, red, soft-fleshed, sour, the stone globular. Eurasia.—Here defined to include *P. acida,* Ehrh., and other botanical forms; these forms may represent either different original species or divergencies resulting from cult. The Morello, Amarelle, and other sour or pie cherries are here included. There are races of differing stature (some drooping), lf. forms, double-fld., and others. Var. **semperflorens,** W. Koch (*P. semperflorens,* Ehrh.), EVERBLOOMING or ALL-SAINTS CHERRY, with slender drooping habit and fls. in summer and autumn on leafy shoots of the season; lvs. small; often worked on upright stock.

34. **P. fruticosa,** Pall. (*P. Chamæcerasus,* Jacq.). EUROPEAN DWARF or GROUND CHERRY. Low spreading bush, 1–3 or 4 ft. high, with glabrous growths, planted for its mound-like shape and profuse fls., and often grafted on tall stocks to make a drooping compact head: lvs. oval to elliptic to oblanceolate or narrow-obovate, 1–2 in. long or somewhat longer on strong shoots, apex blunt or short-acute to acuminate on vigorous growth, closely crenate-serrate, shining above, at first somewhat hairy beneath, narrowed to petiole: fls. white, ¾in. across, in few-fld. somewhat branching clusters with the young foliage: fr. size of large pea, globular, deep reddish-purple, sour. Continental Eu., Siberia.

35. **P. Mahaleb,** L. MAHALEB or ST. LUCIE CHERRY. Small slender green-twigged small tree with thin hard glabrous branchlets (that may be pubescent when growing), cult. as a stock on which to bud other cherries and also somewhat for ornament: lvs. light green, 1½ to about 2½ in. long, broad-ovate to orbicular, abruptly very short-pointed or even blunt, often subcordate, closely crenate-serrate, the short petiole often bearing 1 or 2 glands: fls. small, ½–¾in. across, white, very fragrant, numerous, in small terminal and lateral umbel-like lengthening but short racemes with lvs. or bracts of the season at their

base, appearing with the early foliage and also later: fr. ovoid, about ¼in. long, black (sometimes yellow), with little flesh, on long pedicels. (Mahaleb is an Arabic name.) Cent. and S. Eu.; often escaped in N. Amer.—There are many forms or races differing in color of fr., shape and habit of top, modified foliage; also hybrids with no. 32 and probably others.

36. **P. Pseudocerasus,** Lindl. Small compact tree, with gray to purplish thinly hairy branchlets: lvs. ovate, 3–5 in. long, sharply double-serrate, sparsely hairy on veins: fls. white, ¾–1 in. across, 2–5 in a cluster; pedicels very hairy: fr. early, globose, red, sweet, ½–¾in. diam. (The name Pseudocerasus was long mistakenly applied to the oriental flowering cherries, nos. 29–31.) China.

37. **P. pensylvanica,** L. f. WILD RED or PIN CHERRY. Shrub or tree to 35 ft., with light red-brown bark; branchlets glabrous, reddish, slender: lvs. oblong-lanceolate, pointed, 2–4 in. long, finely and sharply serrulate, glabrous, petiole ⅓–⅔in. long: fls. white, 2–5 in a cluster, ½in. across, pedicels ½in. long, glabrous: fr. globose, red, ¼in. diam. Newf. to B. C. south to N. C. and Colo.

38. **P. serotina,** Ehrh. WILD BLACK CHERRY. Great tree, reaching 100 ft. in height and 4–5 ft. diam., with glabrous branchlets and bitter-aromatic qualities, sometimes planted for shade and ornament: lvs. oblong to oblong-lanceolate to oval, 2–6 in. long, stiff and firm at maturity, acuminate, mostly narrowed at base, serrate with appressed incurved callous teeth, shining above, lighter colored and nearly or quite glabrous beneath: fls. appearing when the lvs. are half or more grown, white, about ¼in. across, many in racemes 4–6 in. long on short lateral shoots of the season; calyx with remains of stamens, persistent: fr. nearly globose, ½in. or less diam., purple-black, with thin flesh, in late summer and autumn. N. S. to Fla. and westward.

39. **P. Padus,** L. EUROPEAN BIRD CHERRY. Small to medium-sized tree, becoming 30 ft. and more tall, with growing parts pubescent or glabrous, planted for ornament: lvs. elliptic or oval to oblong-ovate and sometimes somewhat obovate, 2–4 in. long, short-acuminate, rounded or subcordate at base, closely sharp-serrate, dull green above, glabrous beneath except on veins, the petiole usually biglandular at very apex: fls. white and fragrant, about ½in. across, on drooping or wide-spreading racemes 3–6 in. long that terminate short lateral growths of the season, appearing with the full foliage; petals large and expanding, twice exceeding the stamens: fr. globular, about ¼in. diam., black, bitter; stone corrugated with ridges and cross-ridges. (Padus is the ancient Greek name for this cherry.) Eu., Asia.—Known in cult. under several forms, as drooping, variegated, double-fld.

40. **P. virginiana,** L. (*P. nana,* DuRoi not Stokes). CHOKE CHERRY. Much like no. 39, but a bush or only occasionally a small tree, fls. earlier and smaller and less fragrant, racemes closer and less showy and at first ascending or upright, petals little if any exceeding stamens, fr. deep red (varying to yellow), stone not corrugated. Variable native species of wide distribution, not much planted.

41. **P. lusitanica,** L. (*Laurocerasus lusitanica,* Roem.). PORTUGAL-LAUREL. Evergreen large shrub or becoming tree-like, sometimes 40 ft. or more tall, with dark colored glabrous growth, planted S. for ornament and sometimes raised as tub specimens: lvs. thick and leathery, oblong-ovate to ovate-lanceolate, 2–4 in. long, acuminate, crenate-dentate, glabrous, glossy above, lighter colored or fulvous beneath: fls. white, about ⅓in. across, in racemes 5–10 in. long that much exceed the lvs., in late spring and early summer; calyx-lobes entire: fr. conic and pointed, ⅓in. long, not fleshy, dark purple. Spain, Portugal, and Canary Isls.—Cult. in many forms, and under various names as *P. azorica.*

42. **P. Laurocerasus,** L. (*Laurocerasus officinalis,* Roem.). COMMON CHERRY-LAUREL. Evergreen bush, seldom a small tree, widely variable but known by its lvs. usually remotely small-toothed, racemes slender but not exceeding the lvs., calyx-lobes very short and 3-toothed: the lvs. in usual forms are oblong, 3–6 in. long, short-stalked, abruptly short-pointed, obtuse or sometimes even retuse: fr. conic and pointed, about ½in. long, black-purple. S. E. Eu. to Iran.—In some cult. forms the lvs. are narrow and entire, in others short-oblong and blunt; the stature also is characteristic. The named cherry-laurels are mostly of this species, as *angustifolia, Bertinii, japonica, latifolia, parvifolia, rotundifolia, schipkaensis, versaillensis,* the names being used either as specific or varietal application.

43. **P. caroliniana,** Ait. (*Laurocerasus caroliniana,* Roem.). AMERICAN CHERRY-LAUREL. WILD-ORANGE and MOCK-ORANGE of the S. Evergreen tree 20–40 ft., often larger in cult.: lvs. oblong-lanceolate, acuminate, 2–4 in. long, narrowed to base, entire (only seldom with a few remote small teeth), margins slightly revolute, glossy: fls. very small, about ⅛in. across, with brownish calyx and minute cream-white petals, in dense axillary racemes about 1 in. long: fr. short-ovoid, pointed, ⅓–½in. long, dry with thin outer shell, black and shining. Stream valleys S. C. to Tex., mostly not far from the coast.—Planted for shade, ornament, and hedges in the Old South, and in S. Calif.

44. **P. ilicifolia,** Walp. HOLLY-LEAVED CHERRY. ISLAY. Evergreen bush or tree, to 20 ft., glabrous, planted in Calif. for its holly-like foliage: lvs. ovate to ovate-lanceolate, about 1–2 in. long, very stiff and glossy, acute to obtuse or even emarginate, broad or rounded at base, the margins spiny-toothed, strongly crisped: fls. small, white, about ⅓in.

Fig. 96. LEGUMINOSÆ. A, *Lathyrus latifolius:* Aa, flowering branch, × ½; Ab, perianth expanded, × ½; Ac, flower, less perianth, × 1; Ad, ovary, cross-section, × 8; Ae, fruit, × ½. B, *Trifolium pratense:* Ba, flowering branch, × ½; Bb, flower, × 3. C, *Amorpha fruticosa:* Ca, flowering branch, × ¼; Cb, flower, × 4; Cc, fruit with calyx, × 2. D, *Lupinus polyphyllus:* Da, flowering branch, × ¼; Db, flower, × 1. E, *Acacia decurrens:* Ea, flowering branch, × 1; Eb, inflorescence, × 4; Ec, flower, × 5; Ed, fruit, × ½. F, *Lotus corniculatus:* inflorescence, × 1. G, *Baptisia australis:* Ga, flowering branch, × ¼; Gb, flower, less perianth, × 1; Gc, fruit, × ½. H, *Bauhinia variegata:* Ha, flowering branches, × ⅓; Hb, fruit (dehisced), × ¼. (k keel, s standard, w wing.)

across, in erect or ascending racemes 1–3 in. long: fr. nearly globular, ½–⅔in. diam., red, with thin austere flesh. Lower Calif. north to San Francisco.

45. **P. Lyonii**, Sarg. (*Cerasus Lyonii*, Eastw. *P. integrifolia*, Sarg.). CATALINA CHERRY. Bushy tree on the islands of S. Calif., often planted: lvs. longer, lance-ovate, acute or acuminate, less crisped, with entire margins except sometimes remotely denticulate on young shoots: fr. larger, almost black, with thick flesh. (Bears the name of Wm. S. Lyon, California botanist.)

96. LEGUMINOSÆ. PEA or PULSE FAMILY

One of the major families, comprising herbs, shrubs, and trees, many of them climbing, inhabiting diverse situations in most parts of the world, widely varied in character but agreeing in the production of a true pod or legume; genera 450–500 and several thousand species, contributing many kinds for ornament and for food.—Lvs. prevailingly pinnate but sometimes simple and sometimes digitate, alternate or only rarely opposite, usually stipulate and often stipellate: fls. mostly bisexual, 1 to many on terminal or axillary peduncles; ovary superior, usually 1 and 1-celled with mostly several or many ovules, placentation parietal, 1-carpelled, style and stigma simple; sepals typically 5 and usually more or less united; petals 5 (reduced to 1 in Amorpha and sometimes lacking), but the floral parts various:—(1) corolla characteristically papilionaceous ("butterfly-like") in Leguminosæ proper or Lotoideæ, like a pea flower, with 1 upstanding dorsal petal (*standard, vexillum* or *banner*), 2 lateral horizontal petals (*wings*), 2 lower ventral petals more or less united (*keel*), stamens mostly 10, the upper one of which may be free and the other 9 united into a tube inclosing the long ovary (diadelphous), or all 10 may be separate, or sometimes 5 and monadelphous or separate, and sometimes only 9, petals imbricate with the upper one outside; (2) in the Cæsalpinoideæ the corolla is not papilionaceous or only imperfectly so but still irregular and the petals mostly imbricate with the upper one inside, stamens 10 or fewer and usually distinct; (3) in the Mimosoideæ the fls. are small and regular, petals valvate and mostly united below, stamens often numerous and distinct or variously united: fr. in the Leguminosæ is a 1-celled pod (legume) typically dehiscent by 1 or both sutures into 2 valves, but sometimes variously modified—as indehiscent, constricted between the seeds and breaking into joints (loments), reduced to 1 seed and resembling a follicle, more or less fleshy and filled with pulp, spiny and indehiscent.—Although incapable of clear brief definition, the Leguminosæ is a natural group readily recognized by general characters and similarities; apparently most of the kinds may bear root-tubercles containing nitrogen-fixing bacteria. The family is here defined to include the senna and mimosa subfamilies.

The lvs. afford good characters for use in keys. In some genera, as Genista, Ulex, and Chorizoma, the lvs. are strictly simple; in certain others, as sometimes in Hardenbergia and Kennedya, they are reduced to 1 lft., the fact of reduction being determined by the presence of more than 1 lft. in related species or sometimes even on one plant and by the articulation of the single lft. Some of the Leguminosæ have digitate lvs., as Trifolium and Lupinus, known by the fact that all the lfts. are sessile on the end of the petiole. Most of the genera, however, bear pinnate lvs.; in many cases the lfts. are only 3, as in all the beans, but these are distinguished from digitate lvs. by the fact that the rachis is somewhat extended beyond the lateral pair so that the terminal lft. is stalked and articulated with the rachis.

A. Fls. papilionaceous (pea-like); if petals wanting see AA.
B. Lvs. of 1 lft. or simple (rarely 3-foliolate on young shoots of no. 41).
C. Margins of lvs. prickly-toothed.................................61. CHORIZEMA
CC. Margins of lvs. entire.
D. Plant a twining vine.
E. Keel mostly acute, about as long as wings.....................46. KENNEDYA
EE. Keel obtuse, shorter than wings...............................47. HARDENBERGIA
DD. Plant erect or diffuse, not twining.
E. Venation of lvs. palmate, lvs. cordate at base.................68. CERCIS
EE. Venation of lvs. not palmate, lvs. not cordate at base.
F. Pod inflated or terete.
G. Petioles very short or lacking.................................35. CROTALARIA
GG. Petioles slender and distinct..................................14. ALYSICARPUS

FF. Pod flat.
G. Calyx 1-lipped.......40. Spartium
GG. Calyx 2-lipped.
H. The calyx divided to base.......41. Ulex
HH. The calyx divided to middle.
I. Petals free: seeds with appendage at base.......38. Cytisus
II. Petals, the lower ones, adnate at base to staminal tube: seeds without appendage.......39. Genista
BB. Lvs. of 2 or more lfts.
C. Foliage even-pinnate, the terminal lft. represented by a tendril or bristle or absent.
D. Plant a shrub or tree.
E. Pod 4-winged: lfts. 14–20.......15. Daubentonia
EE. Pod not winged.
F. Length of pod 1 ft. or more: lfts. 40–60.......16. Agati
FF. Length of pod 1–2 in.: lfts. 2–18.......17. Caragana
DD. Plant an herb or vine.
E. Pod constricted between seeds, ripening underground: fls. yellow.. 7. Arachis
EE. Pod not as above: fls. rarely pale yellow.
F. Stamens 9, the odd one obsolete: seeds (in ours) scarlet and black....... 5. Abrus
FF. Stamens 9 and 1: seeds green, brown or black.
G. Wings of corolla free, or essentially so, from keel....... 1. Lathyrus
GG. Wings of corolla adherent to keel half or more its length.
H. Style bearded in tuft or ring at apex....... 2. Vicia
HH. Style bearded down one side.
I. Calyx-lobes leafy: pod many-seeded....... 3. Pisum
II. Calyx-lobes long-subulate: pod 1–2-seeded....... 4. Lens
CC. Foliage odd-pinnate, trifoliolate or palmate.
D. Lfts. 5 or more.
E. Lf. digitate or palmate.
F. Pod swollen or inflated: lfts. 1–3.......35. Crotalaria
FF. Pod flat or nearly so: lfts. mostly 5–15.......36. Lupinus
EE. Lf. pinnate.
F. Margin of lfts. serrate....... 6. Cicer
FF. Margin of lfts. entire.
G. Habit twining.
H. Style bearded.......44. Clitoria
HH. Style beardless.
I. The fls. in articulated or knotted racemes: roots tuber-bearing.......45. Apios
II. The fls. not so: roots not tuber-bearing.
J. Number of lfts. 5.
K. Keel mostly acute, about as long as wings.......46. Kennedya
KK. Keel obtuse, shorter than wings.......47. Hardenbergia
JJ. Number of lfts. 7 or more.
K. Racemes simple: lvs. deciduous.......18. Wisteria
KK. Racemes usually panicled: lvs. persistent.......19. Milletia
GG. Habit erect, or at least not climbing.
H. Corolla of 1 petal (standard).......20. Amorpha
HH. Corolla of 5 petals.
I. Infl. umbellate.
J. Pod terete or 4-angled, separating into oblong joints: lfts. ½in. and more long....... 8. Coronilla
JJ. Pod flat, separating into horseshoe-shaped joints: lfts. less than ½in. long....... 9. Hippocrepis
II. Infl. not umbellate.
J. Fls. in dense clover-like heads subtended by bracts.......42. Anthyllis
JJ. Fls. in racemes, spikes or solitary.
K. Number of stamens 5.......21. Petalostemon
KK. Number of stamens 10.
L. Ovary with 1–2 ovules: herbs 1–2 ft. high.......10. Onobrychis
LL. Ovary with 3 to many ovules.
M. Pods flat.
N. Fr. separating into joints: herbs 2–4 ft. high.11. Hedysarum
NN. Fr. not separating into joints: trees or shrubs.
O. Infl. erect or ascending, not pendent.
P. Fls. in a panicle, white.......32. Maackia
PP. Fls. in a raceme, usually rose-colored...23. Gliricidia
OO. Infl. pendent.
P. Fls. in a panicle: lfts. alternate.......31. Cladrastis
PP. Fls. in a simple raceme: lfts. opposite...22. Robinia
MM. Pods terete or inflated.
N. Stamens separate or essentially so.
O. Lfts. 3–5 in. long: corolla deep yellow to orange-red, 1½in. long.......34. Castanospermum
OO. Lfts. ½–2 in. long: corolla ivory-white to bluish, ½–1 in. long.......33. Sophora
NN. Stamens distinctly diadelphous (9 and 1) or monadelphous (10).
O. Fl. with monadelphous stamens.......28. Galega
OO. Fl. with diadelphous stamens.

P. Keel long-acuminate and beak-like; fls. scarlet to crimson. . . . . .24. CLIANTHUS
PP. Keel not as above; fls. if red not of shades of scarlet or crimson.
Q. Wings with conspicuous lateral spur. .29. INDIGOFERA
QQ. Wings without spur.
R. Plants herbaceous: pods (ours) not inflated.
S. Foliage glandular-dotted or viscid: pods echinate or prickly . .27. GLYCYRRHIZA
SS. Foliage neither glandular-dotted nor viscid: pods not prickly. . .30. ASTRAGALUS
RR. Plants woody shrubs or subshrubs: pods inflated.
S. Fls. yellow to orange or brownish 25. COLUTEA
SS. Fls. red, purple or white. . . . . .26. SWAINSONA
DD. Lfts. 3.
E. Lf. palmate (terminal lft. neither stalked nor jointed).
F. Filaments of stamens separate, 10.
G. Ovary distinctly stalked, stalk one-fourth as long as ovary or longer: pod inflated. . . . . .59. BAPTISIA
GG. Ovary sessile or if stalked the stalk one-sixth as long as ovary or less: pod flat. . . . . .60. THERMOPSIS
FF. Filaments of stamens united.
G. Stamens diadelphous, 9 and 1.
H. Infl. a dense head or spike. . . . . .62. TRIFOLIUM
HH. Infl. umbellate or fls. solitary . . . . .43. LOTUS
GG. Stamens monadelphous, 10.
H. Pod inflated . . . . .35. CROTALARIA
HH. Pod not inflated.
I. Ovary and pod stalked in the calyx. . . . . .37. LABURNUM
II. Ovary and pod sessile or essentially so.
J. Petals free: seeds with white callous-like appendage at base. . . . . .38. CYTISUS
JJ. Petals, the lower ones, adnate at base to staminal tube: seeds without appendage . . . . .39. GENISTA
EE. Lf. pinnate (terminal lft. stalked or articulate).
F. Style bearded or pilose at or toward the top (stigmatic part).
G. Calyx-lobes shorter than tube. . . . . .44. CLITORIA
GG. Calyx-lobes as long or longer than tube.
H. Keel bent inwards at right angles, beaked . . . . .51. DOLICHOS
HH. Keel not as above.
I. Corolla with keel coiled or spiralled. . . . . .50. PHASEOLUS
II. Corolla with keel arched or curved but not coiled.
J. Stigma strongly oblique or introrse: roots not tuberous. 52. VIGNA
JJ. Stigma subglobose, strictly terminal or on inner face: roots tuber-bearing.
K. Pistil with stigma terminal: pods 4-winged . . . . .48. PSOPHOCARPUS
KK. Pistil with stigma on inner face: pods not winged. . . .49. PACHYRRHIZUS
FF. Style beardless on stigmatic part.
G. Plant a long-running or twining vine.
H. Racemes not articulated and knotted.
I. Keel mostly acute, about as long as wings . . . . .46. KENNEDYA
II. Keel obtuse, shorter than wings . . . . .47. HARDENBERGIA
HH. Racemes articulated and knotted, fls. falling as they dry.
I. Lower lip of calyx with equally prominent teeth: pod (in ours) hairy or pubescent.
J. Corolla two to three times as long as calyx. . . . . 53. STIZOLOBIUM
JJ. Corolla one and a half times as long as calyx. . . . . .54. PUERARIA
II. Lower lip of calyx much smaller than upper: pod glabrous. . . . . .55. CANAVALIA
GG. Plant not twining but erect or spreading.
H. Herbage glandular-viscid. . . . . .63. ONONIS
HH. Herbage not glandular-viscid.
I. Sts. or petioles prickly . . . . .56. ERYTHRINA
II. Sts. and petioles not prickly.
J. Margins of lfts. denticulate.
K. Stamens adherent to corolla; fls. in dense globose to oblong heads: pods straight. . . . . .62. TRIFOLIUM
KK. Stamens free from corolla; fls. various: pods not usually straight.
L. Infl. a laxly disposed elongated raceme. . . . . .66. MELILOTUS
LL. Infl. an umbel, head, or dense ovoid raceme.
M. Plant strongly scented of cumarin: fr. straight or somewhat curved. . . . . .65. TRIGONELLA
MM. Plant not scented as above: fr. falcately coiled . .64. MEDICAGO
JJ. Margins of lfts. entire.
K. Pod covered by calyx, of 1 joint. . . . . .12. LESPEDEZA
KK. Pod exceeding calyx, of several joints or elongated.
L. Fl. purple: fr. of several joints, flat. . . . . .13. DESMODIUM
LL. Fl. not purple (or if so the fr. 4-sided): fr. elongated, not jointed.

M. Length of lfts. 1 in. or less ....43. LOTUS
MM. Length of lfts. 2 in. or more.
N. Lfts. ovate: fls. white or purple ....57. GLYCINE
NN. Lfts. lanceolate-oblong: fls. yellow or orange.58. CAJANUS
AA. Fls. not papilionaceous.
B. Lvs. simple.
C. Number of stamens indefinite: fls. yellow ....80. ACACIA
CC. Number of stamens 10: fls. usually not yellow.
D. Lf.-blade 2-cleft or lobed ....67. BAUHINIA
DD. Lf.-blade entire ....68. CERCIS
BB. Lvs. 1–2-pinnate.
C. Petiole very short and rachis ending in spine; pinnæ 2 or 4, the rachilla long, flat and twig-like, bearing numerous small deciduous lfts ....72. PARKINSONIA
CC. Petiole not as above.
D. Petals wanting ....69. CERATONIA
DD. Petals present.
E. Number of petals 1 ....20. AMORPHA
EE. Number of petals 4–5.
F. Stamens indefinite, more than twice the number of floral envelopes.
G. Filaments of stamens free ....80. ACACIA
GG. Filaments of stamens united, at least at base.
H. Pod manifestly dehiscent.
I. Valves strongly elastically revolute from the apex; pod nearly or quite straight: lfts. 20–30 pairs ....81. CALLIANDRA
II. Valves splitting regularly: pod curled: lfts. (in ours) 1 pair ....82. PITHECELLOBIUM
HH. Pod indehiscent.
I. Interior of thick pod septate and pulpy ....83. SAMANEA
II. Interior of thin flat pod not so ....84. ALBIZIA
FF. Stamens 3–10.
G. Infl. a close head.
H. Floral envelopes in 4's: fr. breaking up into 1-seeded joints when ripe: ours thorny ....78. MIMOSA
HH. Floral envelopes in 5's: fr. not breaking up when ripe: ours unarmed ....79. LEUCÆNA
GG. Infl. not a head.
H. Seed (in ours) bright red: pod much coiled in dehiscence....77. ADENANTHERA
HH. Seed not red: pod not coiled.
I. Color of fls. greenish-white; fls. bisexual or unisexual, not showy.
J. Tree usually spiny: fls. in spike-like racemes: lfts. serrulate or crenate ....73. GLEDITSIA
JJ. Tree not spiny: fls. in loose panicles: lfts. entire ....74. GYMNOCLADUS
II. Color of fls. red, orange or yellow: fls. all bisexual, showy.
J. Lf. 1-pinnate.
K. Perfect stamens 3 ....71. TAMARINDUS
KK. Perfect stamens 5–10 ....70. CASSIA
JJ. Lf. 2-pinnate.
K. Calyx-lobes valvate: stamens included ....75. DELONIX
KK. Calyx-lobes strongly imbricate: stamens exserted ...76. POINCIANA

1. LATHYRUS, L. VETCHLING. More than 100 ann. and per. herbs in the northern hemisphere and S. Amer., yielding good ornamental subjects and some grown for food and forage.—Usually tendril-bearing vine-like or seldom erect plants with winged or mostly strongly angled sts. and even-pinnate lvs.: fls. commonly colored and showy, axillary, usually racemose; stamens 9 and 1, or sometimes all united at base, the sheath scarcely oblique at the opening: pod mostly flat, sometimes terete, dehiscent, not septate; seeds several to many; germination hypogeal: from Vicia the genus differs technically in the flattened style bearded down the inner face, and the wings in the corolla nearly or quite free from the keel. (Lathyrus: ancient Greek name for some leguminous plant.)

A. Plants usually erect, without tendrils.
B. Lfts. acuminate, not turning black on drying .... 1. *L. vernus*
BB. Lfts. obtuse, apiculate, turning black on drying .... 2. *L. niger*
AA. Plants vine-like, tendril-bearing.
B. Lfts. 2 or more pairs.
C. Stipules broadly ovate, leafy .... 3. *L. maritimus*
CC. Stipules narrow, not conspicuously leafy .... 4. *L. splendens*
BB. Lfts. 1 pair.
C. Sts. not winged: root tuberous .... 5. *L. tuberosus*
CC. Sts. winged: root not tuberous.
D. Fls. 1–3: plant ann.
E. Shape of lfts. oval or oblong: fls. very fragrant .... 6. *L. odoratus*
EE. Shape of lfts. linear or linear-lanceolate: fls. not fragrant.
F. Pod with upper margin 2-winged: calyx-teeth much longer than tube .. 7. *L. sativus*
FF. Pod not winged: calyx-teeth shorter than tube .... 8. *L. tingitanus*

DD. Fls. more than 3, racemose: plant per.
E. Stipules leafy, about as wide as winged sts. .... 9. *L. latifolius*
EE. Stipules not leafy, much narrower than winged sts.. .... 10. *L. sylvestris*

1. **L. vernus,** Bernh. (*Orobus vernus,* L.). SPRING VETCHLING. Low per. 1–2 ft., grown for ornament; sts. nearly or quite erect from a tough mass of fibrous roots, striate, glabrous, little-branched: lfts. 2–3 pairs, thin, ovate-acuminate, 1½–3 in. long, with 2 side veins from the base, stipules amplexicaul-ovate, tendril wanting: fls. 5–8, about ¾in. long, in a loose peduncled raceme, blue-violet, nodding and short-pedicelled: pod slender, about 1½ in. long, glabrous, with several brown globose angled seeds. Eu.

2. **L. niger,** Bernh. (*Orobus niger,* L.). BLACK VETCHLING. Low per., 1–2 ft., planted for ornament, the herbage turning black in drying; sts. erect or bushy, from hard rhizome-like roots, nearly glabrous, finely striate, branched: lfts. 5–8 pairs, oval, ¾–1½ in. long, apiculate and mostly obtuse, the stipules sharply lance-acuminate, tendril wanting: fls. 6–12, about ½in. long in a rather close slender-peduncled raceme, purple, horizontal or nodding, very short-pedicelled: pod slender, about 1½ in. long, glabrous, with black globose somewhat angled seeds. Eu.

3. **L. maritimus,** Bigel. (*Pisum maritimum,* L. *L. japonicus,* Willd.). BEACH PEA. Glabrous per. with decumbent wingless sts. 1–2 ft. long: lfts. 3–6 pairs, oblong or ovate, 1–2 in. long, obtuse and apiculate at apex, stipules broadly ovate, about equalling lvs., tendrils branched: fls. 6–10, ¾–1 in. long, on peduncles nearly as long as lvs., the purple standard longer than the paler wings and keel; calyx often ciliate: pod linear-oblong, 1½–2 in. long, veined, becoming brown and glabrous; seeds angled, black. Sea and lake shores, N. Amer., Eu., Asia.

4. **L. splendens,** Kellogg. PRIDE-OF-CALIFORNIA. Slender half-shrubby per. raised for its showy bloom; sts. angled, lightly pubescent, becoming several ft. long: lfts. 3–5 pairs, ovate-oblong or narrower, about 1 in. long, obtuse or retuse at apex but mostly also apiculate, stipules toothed, tendrils branched: fls. 6–12, 1 in. and more long, on stout peduncles that exceed the lvs., magenta-red; calyx pubescent, upper teeth short: pod 2–3 in. long, flat, glabrous, with prominent beak. S. Calif.

5. **L. tuberosus,** L. Glabrous per. with decumbent or climbing wingless sts. 2–3 ft. long, roots bearing tubers: lfts. 1 pair, oblong to broadly lanceolate, ½–1½ in. long, obtuse, short-mucronate, stipules lanceolate, tendrils branched: fls. 3–5, ½in. long, on peduncles much longer than lvs., red or rose: pod nearly terete, 1–1½ in. long; seeds usually angled, red-brown. Eu., W. Asia.

6. **L. odoratus,** L. SWEET PEA. Tall-climbing lightly pubescent ann. grown for the showy very fragrant fls.; sts. winged: lfts. 1 pair, oval or oblong, 1–2 in. long and usually ½in. or more broad, short-acute and mucronate, stipules small and not foliaceous, tendrils branched: fls. usually 1–3, sometimes 4, on stout peduncles exceeding the lvs., about 1 in. long, the standard now sometimes 2 in. across and not greatly exceeding the wings, purple with lighter wings but much modified in color, size, and conformation: pod about 2 in. long, pubescent; seeds several or many, nearly globular, gray-brown. Italy. Var. **nanellus,** Bailey, DWARF SWEET PEA, plant very condensed, not climbing; well represented in the kind known as Cupid.

7. **L. sativus,** L. GRASS PEA. Ann., mostly under 30 in., erect or nearly so, grown in some countries for food and also for forage; sts. winged, glabrous: lfts. 1 pair, linear and long-pointed, 2–3 in. long, stipules long and resembling lfts., tendrils branching: fls. solitary and long-pedicelled, about ½in. long, white tinged blue on the standard; calyx-teeth much longer than tube: pod 1–1½ in. long, broad and flat, the upper margin 2-winged, glabrous; seeds few, white, angled, usually wedge-shaped. S. Eu., Asia.

8. **L. tingitanus,** L. TANGIER PEA (as the Latin name signifies). Ann. climber infrequently grown for its brilliant fls. which are not sweet-scented; sts. winged, glabrous: lfts. 1 pair, linear-lanceolate and pointed, about 2 in. long: fls. usually 2, sometimes 3, on long peduncles, the purple standard about 1 in. across and much exceeding the scarlet wings and keel; calyx-teeth much shorter than tube: pod flat, 3–5 in. long, glabrous; seeds oblong and compressed, ¼in. or more long, light brown with darker marks. W. Medit.

9. **L. latifolius,** L. EVERLASTING PEA. Well-known climbing glabrous long-lived per., planted for its profuse bloom; sts. long, strongly winged: lfts. 1 pair, ovate-lanceolate, 2–4 in. long, acute and mucronate, prominently 3- or 5-nerved, stipules lanceolate and lf.-like and lobed at base, tendrils stout and branched: fls. several to many on peduncles exceeding the lvs., rose-color (varying to darker colors and to white), standard very large and 1 in. or more across: pod compressed, 3–5 in. long, containing several or many strongly angled brown seeds. Eu.

10. **L. sylvestris,** L. FLAT PEA. Long-lived glabrous per., somewhat grown for forage; sts. winged, 3–6 ft.: lfts. 1 pair, lanceolate or linear-lanceolate, with winged petiole, stipules small, tendrils branched: fls. about 4–10, and ½in. long, on peduncles equalling the lvs., the raceme loose, standard rose-colored with green spot on back, wings purple at top, keel greenish: pod 2–3 in. long, lanceolate; seeds globose and wrinkled, brown. Eu., S. W. Asia.

2. **VICIA**, L. VETCH. Ann. and per. mostly tendril-climbing herbs of wide distribution in temp. regions, a few grown for food, ornament, forage, and green-manuring; recognized species perhaps 150.—Much like Pisum, Lens, and Lathyrus, differing in technical characters: lvs. even-pinnate: fls. solitary or racemose; calyx-lobes short and broad; wings adherent to keel; style slender and not flattened, bearded at summit with tuft or ring of hairs; staminal tube oblique at its orifice, the stamens 9 and 1: fr. flat, mostly several- to many-seeded, the seeds globular or flattened; germination hypogeal. (Vic-ia: classical Latin name.)

A. Lvs. without tendrils.
  B. Lfts. 1–3 pairs: pod not constricted between seeds.
    C. Pod 1 in. or more broad; seeds very large .... 1. *V. Faba*
    CC. Pod linear; seeds ⅛in. diam. .... 2. *V. oroboides*
  BB. Lfts. 8–12 pairs: pod much constricted between seeds .... 3. *V. Ervilia*
AA. Lvs. tendril-bearing.
  B. Fls. few, usually 1 or 2 in an axil; infl. sessile or nearly so.
    C. Lfts. ¾in. or more broad; stipules leafy .... 4. *V. narbonensis*
    CC. Lfts. ¼in. or less broad; stipules not prominent.
      D. Main lfts. oblong, oval or obovate .... 5. *V. sativa*
      DD. Main lfts. linear or nearly so .... 6. *V. angustifolia*
  BB. Fls. several to many, 8 or more, the peduncle evident.
    C. Pod glabrous.
      D. Limb of standard equalling or exceeding its claw .... 7. *V. Cracca*
      DD. Limb of standard half or less as long as claw .... 8. *V. villosa*
    CC. Pod pubescent .... 9. *V. benghalensis*

1. **V. Faba**, L. (*Faba vulgaris*, Moench). BROAD BEAN. Hardy erect glabrous simple-stemmed ann., 2–6 ft. or in dwarf forms 1–1½ ft., very leafy: lfts. 1–3 pairs, mostly alternate, elliptic or oval to oblong, 2–4 in. long, commonly obtuse but apiculate, the terminal one wanting or represented by very rudimentary tendril: fls. 1 to several in the axils on a very short peduncle, 1–1½ in. long, dull white with large purplish blotch: pod large and thick, 2–4 in. and in certain vars. 1 ft. and more long; seeds strongly compressed and angled and 1 in. across, or in other races nearly globular and ¼in. diam., brown, green, purplish, or black. (Faba is the classical name for bean.) Probably native in N. Afr. and S. W. Asia.—The bean of history grown for man and animals, cult. somewhat in the cooler parts of N. Amer. or as a cool-season crop; Mazagan, Windsor, Horse bean, and English bean are frequent names.

2. **V. oroboides**, Wulfen (*Orobus lathyroides*, Sibth. & Smith not L.). Glabrous or somewhat pubescent per., grown for ornament; sts. mostly simple and erect, 1½ ft. or more: lfts. 2–3 pairs, ovate to oblong, 2–3 in. long, acute, tendril wanting: fls. 3–7, whitish to yellow, ¾in. or less long, short-pedicelled: pod linear-oblong, 1–1½ in. long; seeds ⅛in. diam., globular, brown. S. E. Eu.

3. **V. Ervilia**, Willd. (*Ervum Ervilia*, L.). ERVIL. BITTER VETCH. Pubescent erect ann., 12–30 in., without tendrils, anciently grown for forage and also useful as a winter cover-crop in mild climates: lfts. 8–12 pairs, linear or nearly so, ½in. or less long: fls. 2–4, rose-colored, ¼–⅜in. long, nodding on short pedicels: pod 1 in. or less long, usually 3–4-seeded, much constricted between the brown angular-globose seeds. (Ervilia is an ancient name, used by Pliny for a legume.) S. Eu.

4. **V. narbonensis**, L. NARBONNE VETCH. Ann., pubescent or glabrate, 2–4 ft., sometimes grown for forage: lfts. 2–3 pairs and a compound terminal tendril, oval to oblong, 2 in. or less long and ¾in. or more across, obtuse but mucronate, stipules large: fls. 1 or few, axillary, nearly or quite sessile, ¾in. or less long, purplish: pod linear or narrow, about 2 in. long; seeds dark gray, globular, ⅛–¼in. diam. S. Eu.

5. **V. sativa**, L. COMMON OR SPRING VETCH. TARE. Variable ann. or bien. not surviving winters in the N., grown for cover-crop and green-manuring, also for forage; sts. 2–3 ft., pubescent or glabrate: lfts. 4–8 pairs and a terminal tendril, oblong to oblanceolate, 1 in. or less long, truncate and apiculate: fls. usually 2 to an axil, short-pedicelled, 1 in. or less long, purplish: pod 2–3 in. long, pubescent at least when young, brown; seeds brownish, about ⅛in. diam. Eu., Asia; nat. in N. Amer.—Runs into white-fld. races (var. *alba*, Beck), large-fld. and large-seeded (var. *macrocarpa*, Moris), and scarlet-fld. (*V. fulgens*, Hort. not Batt.).

6. **V. angustifolia**, L. NARROW-LEAVED VETCH. Differs from *V. sativa* in the linear to linear-oblong and attenuate lfts., smaller fls., shorter and narrower black pod; matures earlier. Eu.; nat. in N. Amer. and sometimes used for forage.

7. **V. Cracca**, L. Per., usually lightly pubescent, sts. 2–4 ft. long and climbing or trailing, sometimes offered for ornament: lfts. 4–12 pairs, linear to linear-oblong, about ¾in. long, tendril prominent: racemes one-sided, densely many-fld.: fls. purplish (varying to white), about ½in. long, limb of standard as long or twice as long as claw: pod ¾–1 in. long, glabrous, 5–8-seeded. (Cracca: Latin for vetch.) Eu., Asia, N. Amer.

8. **V. villosa,** Roth. Hairy or Winter Vetch. Ann. or bien., much used for cover and green-manuring in orchards, surviving the winter at the N., villous, sts. reaching several ft.: lfts. 5–10 pairs, linear-oblong, 1 in. or less long, tendril prominent and branched: fls. many in long rather loose one-sided racemes, violet-blue (rarely white), about ¾in. long, limb of standard much shorter than claw: pod 1 in. or less long, pale, glabrous; seeds 2–8, small, globose, nearly black. Eu., Asia, sometimes escaped in N. Amer.

9. **V. benghalensis,** L. (*V. atropurpurea*, Desf.). Purple Vetch. Ann., softly white-hairy, sts. 3–6 ft. long, weak, grown for cover and green-manuring particularly on the Pacific Coast: lfts. 7–9 pairs, oval, 1 in. long more or less, blunt or truncate but mucronate, stipules toothed, tendril prominent and branched: fls. 10–24 in a rather close raceme, about ¾in. long, whitish at base and amaranth-purple at top, limb of standard much shorter than claw: pod broad, 1–1½ in. long, hairy-pubescent; seeds 4 or 5, velvety-black with prominent white scar. S. Eu.

3. **PISUM,** L. Pea. A half dozen soft ann. and per. herbs in the Medit. region and W. Asia, one widely grown for food and fodder.—Lvs. pinnate; pinnæ 1–3 pairs, rachis ending in a branched (pinnate) tendril; stipules large and lf.-like: fls. white or colored, solitary or few-racemose in the axils; calyx oblique or gibbous at base, the lobes more or less leafy; corolla papilionaceous, wings somewhat adherent to keel; stamens 9 and 1; style bearded down one side: fr. a flattened dehiscent many-seeded pod. (Pi-sum: the classical name.)—The origin of the cult. pea is yet in doubt. The garden races have been separated as *P. hortense*, Aschers. & Graebn., coordinate with *P. arvense;* and it has also been held that they are derivatives of the European *P. elatius*, Steven. Until further investigations have developed new evidence, it is here intended to treat all the cult. races as forms of *P. sativum*, understanding the species in a broad sense.

P. sativum, L. Garden Pea. Smooth glabrous glaucous ann., 3–6 ft., climbing: lfts. oval to oblong, 1–2 in. long, entire; stipules mostly larger than lfts., denticulate on lower part: fls. 1–3, mostly white: pod 2–4 in. long, nearly straight on the back, with a stiff paper-like lining; seeds 2–10, wrinkled or plane, hypogeal in germination. Eu. and Asia; grown for the edible seeds. Var. **humile,** Poir., Early Dwarf Pea, low, ½–2 ft., scarcely climbing; pod small. Var. **macrocarpon,** Ser., Edible-podded Pea, pod soft, lacking the stiff papery lining, not dehiscent, sometimes 5 to 6 in. long, eaten together with the seeds. Var. **arvense,** Poir. (*P. arvense*, L.), Field Pea, lvs. sometimes marked gray; peduncles short, little exceeding the stipules; fls. colored, standard usually pinkish, wings purple, keel greenish; pod and seeds small; grown for forage.

4. **LENS,** Moench. Small herbs, about a half dozen species in the Medit. region and W. Asia, one cult. for food.—Erect or partially climbing: lvs. pinnate; pinnæ 2 to many pairs, narrow and entire, the terminal wanting or represented by tendril or bristle: fls. small and inconspicuous, whitish, solitary or few-racemose, papilionaceous; calyx-lobes very narrow; wings adherent to keel; stamens 9 and 1; style bearded along inner face: pod short, 1–2-seeded, compressed, the seeds lenticular. (Lens: the classical name, whence comes the English word *lens*, from the shape of the lentil seed.)

L. culinaris, Medic. (*Ervum Lens*, L. *L. esculenta*, Moench). Lentil. Lightly pubescent short-season branchy ann. 10–18 in.: lfts. opposite or alternate, 4–7 pairs, about ½in. long, oblong-oval to linear-oblong, lf. usually ending in a short tendril: fls. 1–3 on a slender axillary peduncle, ¼in. or less long, corolla equalled or exceeded by calyx-lobes: pod ½–¾in. long and nearly as broad, containing 2 greenish-brown or dark colored seeds or lentils convex on both sides; germination hypogeal. S. Eu.—Much grown in Eu. for the edible seeds, but not often seen in N. Amer.

5. **ABRUS,** L. Slender more or less woody vines widely spread in the tropics, of 5 species, one sometimes grown under glass or in the open far S.—Lvs. even-pinnate, without tendrils but the rachis sometimes ending in a point, the lfts. many: fls. small, in short mostly dense axillary racemes, papilionaceous; standard broad, more or less joined at base to the staminal tube, the wings shorter and narrower than keel; stamens 9, monadelphous; ovary many-ovuled, the short incurved style glabrous: pod flat, commonly short and more or less septate between the seeds. (A-brus: Greek *delicate*, referring to the small lfts.)

A. precatorius, L. (*Glycine Abrus*, L. *Abrus Abrus*, W. F. Wight). ROSARY PEA. Woody twiner, 10 ft. or more, lightly appressed-hairy: lfts. 8–15 pairs, close together, oblong with broad ends, ½in. or less long, entire, minutely apiculate, easily falling: fls. red to purple, seldom white, about ⅜in. long, in peduncled racemes 1–3 in. long: pod flat and broad, 1½ in. or less long, close-pubescent, beaked; seeds ovoid, ¼in. or less long, shining brilliant scarlet with lower third black. Tropics.—Seeds used in bead work, and also for rosaries (whence *precatorius*, from Latin *precator*, one who prays).

6. **CICER,** L. A dozen or so W. Asian small annuals and perennials, one grown for its edible seeds.—Lvs. pinnate, the rachis ending in a spine or abortive tendril but in ours the terminal lft. foliaceous and normal, all dentate or serrate, stipules large and usually toothed: fls. small, white or purplish, solitary or few in the axils, papilionaceous; calyx deeply 5-toothed; standard broad, clawed; wings free; stamens 9 and 1; ovary sessile, 2-ovuled or more, the style incurved or inflexed and glabrous: pod short, turgid; seeds large; germination hypogeal. (Ci-cer: classical name.)

C. arietinum, L. CHICK PEA. GARBANZO. Ann., 1–2 ft., erect, branched, glandular-pubescent: lfts. 9–17, opposite or alternate, oval or oblong or somewhat obovate, ⅜–⅝in. long, obtuse, closely serrate: fls. solitary on peduncles shorter than lvs., white or tinted, ¼–⅜in. long: pod ¾–1 in. long and ½in. broad, pubescent; seeds 1 or 2, nearly or quite ⅜in. cross-diam., wrinkled, with a point on one end, bearing a fancied resemblance to a ram's head (whence the name *arietinum*), whitish, red or black. Probably W. Asia; long cult. in many countries.

7. **ARACHIS,** L. Low trop. herbs, mostly Brazilian, from 7–10 species, one widely planted for the edible seeds and the herbage used for forage.—Lvs. even-pinnate, mostly of 2 pairs of lfts. and no tendril, stipules prominent and adnate to base of petiole: fls. solitary or few in the axils, papilionaceous, at first sessile, with a very long tubular hypanthium resembling a pedicel; standard broad and large, wings free from the beaked keel; stamens 9 and 1, diadelphous or sometimes 9 and monadelphous: fr. maturing under ground, indehiscent, more or less constricted between the seeds. (Ar-achis: meaning and application obscure.)

A. hypogæa, L. PEANUT. GOOBER. GROUNDNUT. Ann., 10–20 in. high, lightly hairy, branched: lfts. 2 pairs, oval to oval-obovate, 1½–2½ in. long, obtuse or short-pointed, entire, long-peduncled, stipules linear-pointed and 1 in. or more long: showy fls. yellow, soon withering, then the true pedicel elongates greatly and soon enters the ground where the ovary ripens into the reticulated pod (or "nut") containing 1–3 edible seeds with constrictions; in germination the cotyledons come to the surface of the ground. Probably S. Amer.

8. **CORONILLA,** L. Shrubs and herbs, grown in the greenhouse or out-of-doors; species about 20, Canary Isls., Medit. region, W. Asia.—Ann. or per., often woody, glabrous or rarely silky-hairy: lvs. odd-pinnate, lfts. entire: fls. papilionaceous, yellow or sometimes purple or white and purple-veined, pendent, in long-stalked axillary umbels; calyx short-campanulate, almost equally 5-toothed; standard orbicular, keel incurved, wings obovate or oblong; stamens 9 and 1: pod slender, terete or 4-angled, separating into oblong 1-seeded joints; seeds oblong. (Coronil-la: Latin *a little crown*, from the arrangement of the fls.)

A. Fls. pinkish-white .... 1. *C. varia*
AA. Fls. yellow.
  B. Claw of petals much longer than calyx .... 2. *C. Emerus*
  BB. Claw of petals scarcely exceeding calyx.
    C. Plant glabrous .... 3. *C. glauca*
    CC. Plant minutely white-hairy .... 4. *C. cappadocica*

1. **C. varia,** L. CROWN VETCH. Glabrous herb, straggling or ascending, 1–2 ft. high: lvs. sessile or nearly so; lfts. 11–25, oblong or obovate, blunt and mucronate, ½–¾in. long: peduncles much longer than lvs., each bearing at the tip a dense umbel of pinkish-white fls. in summer and autumn; corolla about ½in. long, the claws of the petals scarcely longer than the calyx: pod 4-angled, erect or spreading, about 2 in. long. Eu.

2. **C. Emerus,** L. (*Emerus major*, Mill.). SCORPION SENNA. Dense symmetrical shrub, evergreen in southern states, glabrous or nearly so, 3–5 ft. or more high, the branches green and striate: lvs. deep glossy green; lfts. 7–9, obovate, ½–¾in. long: peduncles slender, shorter than lvs., bearing an umbellate cluster of 3–7 fls. in spring and summer; fls. ¾in. long, yellow tipped with red, the claw of the petals much longer than the calyx: pod terete, pendent, 2 in. long. (Emerus: ante-Linnæan name of no particular significance.) S. Eu.

3. **C. glauca,** L. Glabrous glaucous shrub 2–4 ft. high: stipules small, lanceolate; lfts. 5–7, obovate, ½–¾in. long, truncate or very obtuse: peduncles mostly longer than lvs., bearing umbels of about 7–8 fls.; fls. about ½in. long, yellow, the claw of petals scarcely exceeding the calyx: pod nearly terete, pendent, to ¾in. long. S. Eu.—Fls. all the year in S. Calif.

4. **C. cappadocica,** Willd. (*C. iberica,* Bieb.). Glaucous per. with sts. ascending to 1 ft., minutely white-hairy: stipules cuneate-obovate, toothed; lfts. 9–11, cuneate-obovate, retuse, ½–¾in. long: peduncles long, bearing umbels of 6–9 fls., fls. yellow, about ½in. long, the claw of petals about length of calyx: pod 4-angled, deflexed, ending in curved beak. Asia Minor.

9. **HIPPOCREPIS,** L. Horseshoe Vetch. Herbs or small shrubs native in the Medit. region, of about 12 species, one sometimes grown in the rock-garden.—Lvs. odd-pinnate, of many small entire lfts.; stipules small: fls. short-pedicelled, borne in axillary umbels, papilionaceous; calyx short-campanulate; corolla yellow, with rather long claw; keel beaked; wings bent; stamens 9 and 1; ovary sessile, with many ovules: pod flattened, separating into horseshoe-shaped joints; seeds bent. (Hippocre-pis: Greek for *horse* and *shoe,* referring to shape of pods.)

H. comosa, L. Per. with tufted or ascending sts. to 1 ft.: lfts. 7–15, oblong to linear, ¼–½in. long, obtuse, glabrous: fls. in 5–12-fld. umbels, about ½in. long: pod ¾–1 in. long. Eu.

10. **ONOBRYCHIS,** Gaertn. A genus contributing two cult. species, one known as sainfoin which is used as forage; species 80 or more, Eu., N. Afr., and W. Asia.—Per., herbaceous or sometimes shrubby and spiny: lvs. odd-pinnate, the lf.-stalks sometimes persisting and developing into thorns; lfts. entire, without stipels: fls. papilionaceous, purplish, rose-colored, whitish, or yellowish, in axillary peduncled spikes or racemes; calyx campanulate, with almost equal subulate teeth; standard obovate or obcordate, narrowed toward base; wings short; keel obtuse, equalling or longer than the standard; stamens 9 and 1; ovary sessile or shortly stalked, 1–2-ovuled: pod compressed, strongly veined or pitted, prickly, toothed, crested on the back, seldom 2-celled. (Onob-rychis: Greek *asses' food.*)

A. Pod about ¼in. long, toothed on the back: lfts. about 1 in. long................1. *O. viciæfolia*
AA. Pod nearly ¾in. long, with a deeply lobed crest on the back: lfts. not ½in. long.....2. *O. Crista-galli*

1. **O. viciæfolia,** Scop. (*O. sativa,* Lam. *Hedysarum Onobrychis,* Neck.). Sainfoin or Saintfoin. Holy Clover. Esparcet. Sts. ascending 1–1½ or rarely 2 ft.: stipules brown, thin, tapering to a fine point; lfts. 6–12 pairs, oblong, apiculate, about 1 in. long, slightly pubescent beneath: peduncle longer than lvs., the short spike lengthening in age; calyx-teeth very slender, longer than tube; corolla pale pink, standard and keel longer than wings: pod ¼in. long, almost semicircular, strongly reticulate and often toothed on the sides, margined and toothed on the back. Cent. and S. Eu., temp. Asia.—Seldom grown for forage in N. Amer., mostly far W.

2. **O. Crista-galli,** Lam. (*Hedysarum Crista-galli,* L.). More or less gray-hairy, st. prostrate or ascending: lfts. 5–8 pairs, oblong or obovate, cuneate, obtuse or retuse, mucronate, not ½in. long: fls. small; calyx-teeth lanceolate-subulate, four to five times as long as the tube; corolla flesh-colored, about as long as the calyx-teeth: pod nearly ¾in. long, coarsely pitted and spinose on the sides, crested dorsally, the crest deeply 3–4-lobed with toothed oblong lobes ¼in. long or more. Medit. region.—Grown for ornament or as a curiosity.

11. **HEDYSARUM,** L. Per. herbs or small shrubs, of about 70 species in the north temp. zone, one sometimes planted in the fl.-garden.—Lvs. odd-pinnate, the lfts. entire, stipules scarious: fls. white or purple, rarely yellow, in axillary racemes, papilionaceous; calyx campanulate with almost equal teeth; keel longer than wings; stamens 9 and 1; ovary sessile, with 4 to many ovules: pod flat, separating into nearly orbicular joints. (Hedys-arum: Greek for *sweet smell.*)

H. coronarium, L. French-Honeysuckle. Per. or bien. to 4 ft.: lfts. 3–7 pairs, elliptic, ¾–1½ in. long, pubescent beneath: fls. deep red, fragrant, ½–¾in. long, in crowded racemes on peduncles longer than lvs.: pod muricate. S. Eu.

12. **LESPEDEZA,** Michx. Bush Clover. Mostly upright per. herbs and sub-shrubs, rarely ann., 70 species or more in N. Amer., Asia, and Australia, a few of the

oriental kinds grown for ornament and two for forage.—Lfts. 3 (or rarely reduced to 1 but not in ours), entire, usually small, without stipels; stipules small: fls. small but often numerous and showy although prevailingly not conspicuous, often of 2 kinds, one bearing papilionaceous petals and mainly sterile and the other apetalous and fertile; calyx with 5 nearly equal lobes; standard obovate or oblong and clawed; keel incurved; stamens 9 and 1; ovary 1-ovuled, the style incurved and beardless, stigma small and terminal: pod more or less included in calyx, of only 1 fertile joint. (Lespede-za: Lespedez was Spanish governor of Fla. and patron of Michaux.)—Lespedeza and Desmodium (Meibomia) are closely related, and some of the species may be placed in either genus.

A. Fls. inconspicuous, in small heads or few in axils: grown for forage.
B. Plant an ann.: lfts. nearly glabrous beneath . . . . 1. *L. striata*
BB. Plant a per.: lfts. silky-pubescent beneath . . . . 2. *L. cuneata*
AA. Fls. conspicuous, in axillary racemes: grown for ornament.
B. Calyx-teeth shorter than tube . . . . 3. *L. bicolor*
BB. Calyx-teeth longer than tube, long-pointed.
C. Color of fls. purple . . . . 4. *L. Thunbergii*
CC. Color of fls. white . . . . 5. *L. japonica*

1. **L. striata**, Hook. & Arn. (*Hedysarum striatum*, Thunb.). JAPAN CLOVER. Ann., tufted and much-branched, somewhat pubescent, decumbent or ascending to 18 in. and sometimes more: lfts. ¾in. or less long, oblong or obovate, obtuse, nearly sessile: fls. small, 1–3 in an axil, pink or purple, not conspicuous: pod acute, slightly surpassing the calyx-lobes. China, Japan; nat. Pa. to Tex.—Grown in some of the southern states for hay and forage, as also the closely related *L. stipulacea*, Maxim.

2. **L. cuneata**, Don (*L. sericea*, Miq.). Per. to 3 ft., somewhat shrubby: lfts. to ¾in. long, cuneate, obtuse, silky-pubescent beneath: fls. small, in dense clusters shorter than lvs., whitish, not conspicuous: pod oval, 1/12in. long. Japan to Himalayas.—Grown for hay and as a soil-binder in the southern states.

3. **L. bicolor**, Turcz. Shrub, 4–10 ft.: lfts. oval or round-obovate, ¾–1½ in. long, obtuse or rounded at apex, apiculate, pale green beneath: fls. purple, ¼–⅜in. long, many but less numerous and showy than in *L. Thunbergii*, in shorter erect or ascending racemes, midsummer to autumn; calyx-lobes blunt or at least not long narrow-pointed, shorter than tube: pod ¼in. long, freely produced, lightly pubescent. Japan, N. China.

4. **L. Thunbergii**, Nakai (*Desmodium Thunbergii*, DC. *L. Sieboldii*, Miq. *D. penduliflorum*, Oudem.). Subshrub or in the N. an herb from per. root, 4–10 ft., lightly pubescent: lfts. elliptic or elliptic-oblong, 1–2 in. long, short-pointed and apiculate, light colored and appressed-hairy beneath: fls. rose-purple, in late summer and autumn, about ½in. long, numerous and showy, in drooping or flexuose long panicled racemes; calyx-lobes narrow and long-pointed, longer than tube: pod (not often produced, at least in the N.) about ½in. long, pubescent. Japan, China.—*L. formosa*, Koehne, has been confused with this species, but differs in the obovate more obtuse lfts.

5. **L. japonica**, Bailey (*Desmodium japonicum*, Hort. not Miq. *L. formosa* var. *albiflora*, Schindl.). Much like *L. Thunbergii* but a week or two later in blooming, sts. and herbage nearly glabrous and lighter colored, lfts. broader and less pointed, fls. pure white. Japan.—Infrequent in cult.

13. **DESMODIUM**, Desv. (*Meibomia*, Heister). TICK TREFOIL. Some 180 or more per. or sometimes ann. herbs, frequently woody at base, in temp. and trop. regions in the western hemisphere, and in Australia and S. Afr.; one species is grown far S. for hay, forage, and cover-cropping, and *D. canadense* often transplanted to the border.—Differs technically from Lespedeza in the lfts. being stipellate and the fr. consisting of several joints that soon break apart. (Desmo-dium: Greek for *a chain*, from the connected joints of the pod.)

A. Pod with constrictions about equal: fls. about ⅕in. long . . . . 1. *D. tortuosum*
AA. Pod with constrictions much deeper below than above: fls. about ¾in. long . . . . 2. *D. canadense*

1. **D. tortuosum**, DC. (*Hedysarum tortuosum*, Sw. *D. purpureum*, Fawcett & Rendle not Hook. & Arn. *Meibomia purpurea*, Vail). BEGGARWEED. Ann. or grown as such, erect, branched, hairy-pubescent, 6–8 ft.: lfts. ovate, oblong or elliptic, 3–4 in. long, obtuse but apiculate, more or less pubescent at least beneath, the stipels subulate: fls. blue to purple, about ⅕in. long, in simple or somewhat branched racemes 6–12 in. long; bracts narrow, two or three times longer than calyx, deciduous: pod 3–6-jointed, pubescent, equally undulate on both edges, twisted when young but becoming flat. W. Indies; somewhat nat. in S. U. S.

2. **D. canadense**, DC. (*Hedysarum canadense*, L. *Meibomia canadensis*, Kuntze). Per., 2–8 ft., pubescent: lfts. oblong or oblong-lanceolate, 2–4 in. long, obtuse, pubescent

beneath: fls. purple, to ¾in. long, in racemes forming dense panicles; bracts ovate-lanceolate, deciduous: pod 3–5-jointed, 1 in. long, pubescent, nearly straight on back. N. S. to N. C. and Okla.

14. **ALYSICARPUS,** Neck. ALYCE CLOVER. About 16 herbaceous species in Old World tropics, one grown in the S. as a forage plant.—Lvs. of 1 lft.: fls. small, purple or blue, papilionaceous, in few-fld. terminal racemes; calyx deeply lobed; standard clawed; wings adnate to keel; stamens 9 and 1; ovary nearly sessile, with many ovules: pod nearly terrete, of several joints. (Alysicar-pus: Greek *chain fruit.*)

A. vaginalis, DC. (*Hedysarum vaginale,* L.). Ann. with spreading or ascending sts. to 3 ft. long, glabrous or slightly pubescent: lft. varying from orbicular to lanceolate, ½–2 in. long, entire, on slender petioles ½in. or less long: fls. purple, about ¼in. long: pod about ¾in. long, reticulate. Nat. in W. Indies and Fla.

15. **DAUBENTONIA,** DC. Shrubs or trees, of about 5 American species, one planted in S. U. S.—Lvs. even-pinnate, of numerous lfts.: fls. yellow or rose, papilionaceous, in axillary racemes; calyx minutely lobed; standard orbicular; stamens 9 and 1; ovary usually stalked, many-ovuled: pod elongated, 4-angled or 4-winged. (Daubento-nia: named for Ludwig J. M. Daubenton, 1716–1799, physician and naturalist.)

D. punicea, DC. (*Piscidia punicea,* Cav. *Sesbania punicea,* Benth.). Shrub or small tree to 6 ft. or more: lfts. 12–40, oblong, ½–1 in. long, obtuse but apiculate: fls. red-purple, ¾in. long, in dense racemes about 4 in. long: pod reddish-brown, 3–4 in. long, 4-winged. S. Amer.; nat. Fla. to Miss.

16. **AGATI,** Adans. One large tree planted for ornament in warm regions.—Lvs. even-pinnate, of numerous entire lfts.: fls. large, papilionaceous, in axillary few-fld. racemes; calyx with short broad lobes; standard ovate to oblong; wings longer than standard; stamens 9 and 1; ovary stalked, many-seeded: pod long and narrow, nearly straight. (Aga-ti: Malabar name.)

A. grandiflora, Desv. (*Robinia grandiflora,* L. *Sesbania grandiflora,* Pers.). A short-lived soft-wooded tree 20–40 ft. high: lvs. 6–12 in. long; lfts. 40–60, linear-oblong, 1–2 in. long, pale green, glaucous: fls. 2–4 in short axillary racemes, rose-red, white, or rusty-red, 2½–4 in. long and showy; calyx campanulate, undulate-dentate, nearly ¾in. long: pod pendulous, 1 ft. long or more, compressed, slightly torulose, with swollen margins; seeds separated by ingrowths from the walls. Trop. Asia; nat. in W. Indies and S. Fla.

17. **CARAGANA,** Lam. PEA-TREE. Shrubs or sometimes small trees grown for ornament and hedges; more than 50 species from S. Russia to China, most of them in Cent. Asia.—Deciduous, spiny or unarmed: lvs. even-pinnate, mostly with a persistent spine or bristle at tip of rachis; lfts. small, entire; stipules deciduous or persistent and spinose: fls. papilionaceous, mostly yellow, solitary or clustered; standard upright, with long claws like the wings; keel obtuse and straight; stamens 9 and 1; ovary scarcely stipitate: pod linear, terete, straight, 2-valved, with several seeds. (Caraga-na: *Caragan,* its Mongolian name.)—In some species the rachis remains after the lfts. fall, developing into a slender woody spine which persists for years. The stipules, also, are often represented by a pair of spines. The spines of the wild state, however, often become mere bristles under cult.

A. Number of lfts. 2–4.
  B. Lfts. in remote pairs....................1. *C. sinica*
  BB. Lfts. close together, appearing digitate.
    C. Plant unarmed: pedicels about length of fls....................2. *C. frutex*
    CC. Plant with spiny stipules: pedicels about half length of fls....................3. *C. pygmæa*
AA. Number of lfts. 8–18.
  B. Lfts. 8–12, ½–1 in. long....................4. *C. arborescens*
  BB. Lfts. 12–18, to ⅓in. long....................5. *C. microphylla*

1. **C. sinica,** Rehd. (*Robinia sinica,* Buc'hoz. *C. Chamlagu,* Lam.). Rounded bushy shrub to 4 ft., with angular branches: lvs. with 2 unequal pairs of obovate lfts. variable in size, the terminal pair the larger, ½–1½ in. long, rachis spine-tipped, persisting after the lfts. have fallen, but not developing into a formidable thorn; stipules ¼–⅓in. long, becoming stiff thorns: fls. reddish-yellow, 1¼ in. long, solitary on a slender stalk ½–¾in. long, in spring; calyx bell-shaped, nearly ½in. long, with 5 short triangular teeth: pod 1½ in. long. N. China.—The bruised bark smells like licorice.

2. **C. frutex,** Koch (*Robinia frutex*, L. *C. frutescens*, DC.). Glabrous unarmed shrub to 10 ft., with long erect branches not much divided except near the ends: lvs. with 2 pairs of lfts., these stalkless and attached near the end of the common rachis, obovate, rounded at tip, ½–1 in. long or more, dull green: fls. bright yellow, ¾–1 in. long, 1–3 on pedicels about length of corolla, in spring; calyx ⅓in. long, bell-shaped: pod 1½ in. long. S. Russia to Japan.

3. **C. pygmæa,** DC. Shrub to 4 ft. or sometimes prostrate, glabrous: lvs. with 2 pairs of linear-lanceolate lfts. close together, ⅓–½in. long, spiny-pointed, rachis deciduous or persistent, stipules spiny: fls. yellow, ¾in. long, solitary on pedicels about half length of corolla, in spring; calyx narrow-bell-shaped: pod about 1 in. long. China, Siberia.

4. **C. arborescens,** Lam. Shrub or small tree to 20 ft., rather erect, sometimes of almost fastigiate habit; bark on young branchlets slightly winged: lvs. 1½–3 in. long, usually of 4–6 pairs of oval or obovate lfts. ½–1 in. long; rachis tipped with a bristle-like spine; stipules linear, spine-tipped, finally developing into a pair of stiff spines ¼in. long, or these lacking in cult.: fls. ⅝–⅞in. long, yellow, borne singly on slender downy pedicels ½–1½ in. long, several from each of the enlarged scaly buds on the previous year's wood, in spring and early summer; calyx ¼in. long, helmet-shaped, 5-toothed, with hairy margins; standard curled backward at the sides: pod 1½–2 in. long, on a slender stalk about as long. Siberia, Manchuria. Var. **Lorbergii,** Koehne, has linear lfts. about 1 in. long. Var. **pendula,** Carr., branches pendulous.

5. **C. microphylla,** Lam. (*C. Altagana*, Poir.). Shrub 6–10 ft. high, wider than high, with light gray young bark, the long slender branches little divided and ultimately more or less pendent: lvs. 1½–3 in. long, of 6–9 pairs of lfts.; rachis ending in a short spine but not persistent; stipules spiny, ⅙ in. long; lfts. ⅛–⅓in. long, oval or obovate, dull grayish-green, silky-hairy at first, becoming glabrate: fls. yellow, ¾in. long, solitary, the pedicels rather shorter, in spring and early summer; calyx ⅓in. long, cylindric, with short pointed teeth: pod about 1¼ in. long. Siberia, China.

18. **WISTERIA,** Nutt. (*Kraunhia*, Raf.). Woody twiners, planted for covering porches, arbors and buildings, 9 species in E. U. S. and E. Asia.—Vines often attaining great age and with woody trunks reaching several in. diam.: lvs. odd-pinnate, with 9–19 lfts.: fls. pea-like, blue, lilac, purplish, or white, in long drooping racemes in late spring and early summer; calyx 5-toothed, the upper 2 teeth often somewhat grown together, the lower often longer; standard large, reflexed, typically with 2 callosities or appendages at base above claw; wings falcate, auricled at base; keel obtuse, scythe-shaped; stamens 9 and 1: pod flattened, elongated, 2-valved, torulose. (Wiste-ria: named for Caspar Wistar, 1761–1818, professor of anatomy in the Univ. of Penn., but deliberately spelled Wisteria by Nuttall, author of the genus, the spelling Wistaria being a later adaptation.)

A. Pod velvety-pubescent.
  B. Mature lvs. nearly glabrous.
    C. Number of lfts. 15–19 . . . . 1. *W. floribunda*
    CC. Number of lfts. usually 11 . . . . 2. *W. sinensis*
  BB. Mature lvs. pubescent . . . . 3. *W. venusta*
AA. Pod glabrous.
  B. Racemes to 4 in. long . . . . 4. *W. frutescens*
  BB. Racemes 1 ft. or more long . . . . 5. *M. macrostachya*

1. **W. floribunda,** DC. (*Glycine floribunda*, Willd. *W. brachybotrys*, Sieb. & Zucc. *Kraunhia floribunda*, Taub.). Japanese Wisteria. Deciduous shrub with twining branches, at least when young: lfts. 15–19, ovate-elliptic, 1½–3 in. long, rather abruptly acuminate, rounded at base, appressed-downy when young, becoming glabrate: fls. violet or violet-blue, to ¾in. long, in racemes to 1½ ft. long (shorter toward end of season); standard oblong-orbicular, subcordate at base and auriculate, with a short stipe-like claw; calyx hairy, the 2 upper teeth very short and broad: pod velvety-pubescent, 4–6 in. long. Japan. Var. **macrobotrys,** Bailey (*W. macrobotrys*, Sieb. *W. multijuga*, VanHoutte), has racemes sometimes 2–3 ft. long and lfts. to 4 in. long. Var. **alba,** Bailey (*W. multijuga* var. *alba*, Carr.), fls. white. Var. **rosea,** Bailey (*W. multijuga* var. *rosea*, Bean), fls. pale pink with wing and tip of keel purple. Var. **violaceo-plena,** Bailey (*W. sinensis* var. *violaceo-plena*, Schneid.), fls. double, violet.

2. **W. sinensis,** Sweet (*Glycine sinensis*, Sims. *W. chinensis*, DC. *Kraunhia sinensis*, Makino). Chinese Wisteria. Lfts. 7–13, usually 11, ovate-acuminate or ovate-lanceolate, short-stalked, 2–3 in. long, silky with appressed hairs when young, glabrous or nearly so at maturity: fls. blue-violet, 1 in. long, in racemes 6–12 in. long terminating the branches; calyx villous: pod velvety-pubescent, 4–6 in. long. China. Var. **alba,** Bailey, fls. white.

3. **W. venusta,** Rehd. & Wils. Silky Wisteria. Reaching 30 ft. or more, the young parts pubescent: lfts. 9–13, velvety on both sides, oblong-lanceolate or elliptic- to ovate-oblong, 2–4 in. long, short-acuminate: racemes 6 in. or less long including the short pe-

duncle, the rachis densely appressed-villous; fls. 1 in. long, white, on nearly horizontal pedicels; upper calyx-teeth subulate; standard suborbicular, auricled at base: pod compressed, densely velvety, 6–8 in. long. China.

4. **W. frutescens,** Poir. (*Glycine frutescens,* L. *Kraunhia frutescens,* Greene). Stout climber 30–40 ft. in length, the trunk attaining several in. diam.: herbage somewhat pubescent; lfts. 9–15, ovate to ovate-lanceolate, 1–2 in. long, acuminate but blunt at apex: racemes dense, 3–4 in. long; fls. lilac-purple, ½–¾in. long; calyx finely pubescent, sometimes with club-shaped glands, the teeth shorter than the tube; auricles of the standard rather prominent: pod glabrous, 2–4 in. long. Va. to Fla. and Tex.

5. **W. macrostachya,** Nutt. (*W. frutescens* var. *macrostachya,* Torr. & Gray. *W. frutescens* var. *magnifica,* Hérincq. *Kraunhia macrostachya,* Small). Slender climber 25–30 ft.: lfts. usually 9, ovate, 1–3 in. long, acuminate, pubescent when young but becoming nearly glabrous: fls. lilac-purple or light blue, ¾in. long, in racemes 1 ft. or more long; calyx-teeth nearly as long as tube: pod glabrous, 3–5 in. long. Tenn. to Tex.

19. **MILLETTIA,** Wight & Arn. Trees, shrubs or vines, of over 50 species in trop. regions of Old World, one planted in S. U. S.—The genus differs from Wisteria in the pods being thicker and more leathery and splitting open later, and the racemes usually panicled. (Millet-tia: named for Dr. J. A. Millett, botanist, who wrote in China in 1726.)

M. reticulata, Benth. Twining woody evergreen vine: lfts. usually 7, elliptic-lanceolate to lanceolate, 2–3 in. long, acute, glabrous, paler beneath, somewhat leathery: fls. pinkish-blue, ½in. long, in dense racemes to 8 in. long forming large panicles: pod brown, 4–6 in. long. China.

20. **AMORPHA,** L. False Indigo. Ten to 15 closely related species in N. Amer. south to Mex., sometimes grown in the open for ornament.—Shrubs or subshrubs, glabrous or hairy, glandular-punctate: lvs. alternate, odd-pinnate, deciduous, with small entire lfts.: fls. small, papilionaceous, reduced to a single petal, dark to blue-violet or whitish, in dense terminal spikes which are often clustered; calyx campanulate, with 5 nearly equal teeth or the lower ones longer; corolla with wings and keel lacking, the standard folded around the stamens, these monadelphous at base, exserted; ovary sessile, 2-ovuled: pod short, indehiscent, slightly curved, usually with 1 seed. (Amor-pha: Greek *deformed,* the fls. destitute of wings and keel.)

A. Lowest pair of lfts. close to the st.: plant grayish- or whitish-pubescent . . . . 1. *A. canescens*
AA. Lowest pair of lfts. remote from the st.: plant glabrous or nearly so, rarely yellowish-pubescent . . . . 2. *A. fruticosa*

1. **A. canescens,** Nutt. Lead-Plant. Low shrub 1–4 ft. high, densely grayish- or whitish-pubescent: lvs. 2–4 in. long; lfts. 15–45, nearly sessile, oval or ovate-lanceolate, acutish or apiculate, ⅓–¾in. long: fls. blue, in dense spikes to 6 in. long crowded into terminal panicles: pod tomentose, ⅙in. long. Man. to La. and New Mex.—Used in rockeries and borders of shrubberies.

2. **A. fruticosa,** L. Bastard Indigo. Ornamental shrub 5–20 ft. high, with fine feathery foliage: lvs. 6–10 in. long; lfts. 11–25, oval or elliptic, ½–1½ in. long, mostly obtuse and mucronulate: spikes dense, 3–6 in. long, usually panicled; fls. dark purple-blue (varying to white): pod stout, glandular, ⅓in. long. Conn. to Fla. and Mex. Var. **angustifolia,** Pursh (*A. fragrans,* Sweet), has narrower pubescent lfts. and curved pod; Sask. to New Mex.

21. **PETALOSTEMON,** Michx. (originally spelled *Petalostemum*). Prairie-Clover. N. American per. herbs, of about 50 species, one sometimes planted in gardens.—Lvs. odd-pinnate: fls. papilionaceous, pink, purple or white, in dense spikes; calyx-lobes nearly equal; petals clawed, wings and keel attached to staminal tube; stamens 5, monadelphous; ovary sessile, 2-ovuled: pod included in calyx. (Petaloste-mon: Greek for *petal* and *stamen,* referring to the way in which they are joined; the spelling Petalostemon conserved by International Rules.)

P. purpureum, Rydb. (*Dalea purpurea,* Vent. *Kuhnistera purpurea,* MacM.). To 3 ft., nearly glabrous: lfts. 3–5, narrow-linear, ¼–¾in. long: fls. violet or purple, ⅙in. long, in dense oblong or cylindric spikes to 2 in. long; calyx silky-pubescent. Ind. to Sask. and Tex.

22. **ROBINIA,** L. Locust. American trees and shrubs, about 20 species, several planted for ornament.—Deciduous, usually spreading freely from underground parts, branches without terminal bud: lvs. alternate, odd-pinnate, with small often

spinose stipules; lfts. stalked, entire, stipellate: fls. papilionaceous, slender-pedicelled, in axillary usually pendulous or nodding racemes, in late spring and early summer; calyx campanulate, 5-toothed, slightly 2-lipped; petals short-clawed; standard large, rounded, scarcely longer than the wings and keel; stamens 9 and 1: pod oblong to linear, flat, several-seeded, dehiscent. (Robin-ia: after Jean and Vespasien Robin, herbalists to the king of France in the 16th and 17th centuries.)

A. Pod smooth: fls. usually white....................................1. *R. Pseudoacacia*
AA. Pod glandular-hispid: fls. rose or purple.
B. Branchlets glabrous....................................2. *R. Kelseyi*
BB. Branchlets hispid or viscid.
C. Peduncles and branchlets hispid: a shrub....................................3. *R. hispida*
CC. Peduncles and branchlets glandular-viscid: a tree....................................4. *R. viscosa*

1. **R. Pseudoacacia,** L. Black Locust. Nearly glabrous tree to 80 ft., with deeply furrowed dark brown bark and prickly branches: lfts. 7–19, oval or elliptic, 1–2 in. long, rounded or truncate and mucronate at apex: fls. white, very fragrant, about ¾in. long, in pendulous puberulous racemes 4–8 in. long: pod linear-oblong, reddish-brown, 3–4 in. long, smooth, remaining on the branches during the winter. Pa. to Ga. west to Ia., Mo. and Okla., often nat. elsewhere. Var. **Bessoniana,** Nichols., has slender unarmed branches. Var. **Decaisneana,** Carr., fls. light rose-colored.

2. **R. Kelseyi,** Hutchins. Shrub to 10 ft., with glabrous prickly branchlets: lfts. 9–11, oblong-lanceolate, 1–1½ in. long, acute, glabrous: fls. rose, 1 in. long, in 5–8-fld. racemes, pedicels and rachis somewhat glandular-hairy: pod oblong, 1½–2 in. long, bristly-hairy. (Named for its discoverer, Harlan P. Kelsey, Massachusetts nurseryman.) N. C.

3. **R. hispida,** L. Rose Acacia. Branching shrub 1–7 ft. high; sts., branchlets, peduncles and often the petioles glandular-bristly-hispid: lfts. 7–13, suborbicular to oval, ¾–1½ in. long, obtuse and mucronate, glabrous or nearly so: fls. rose-colored or pale purple, 1 in. long, in short 3–5-fld. racemes: pod densely hispid, 2–3 in. long, seldom developed. Va. to E. Tenn., Ga. and Ala. Var. **fertilis,** Clausen (*R. fertilis,* Ashe), differs in greater height, lfts. oblong to oblong-elliptic, acute, and fruiting freely; N. C., Ga. Var. **macrophylla,** DC., has larger fls. and lfts. and fewer bristles.

4. **R. viscosa,** Vent. Clammy Locust. Tree to 40 ft., the dark reddish-brown branchlets and usually the petioles and peduncles densely glandular-viscid; stipules sometimes spiny: lfts. 13–25, ovate to oblong, 1½–2 in. long, obtuse or acute, mostly rounded at base, pubescent beneath or sometimes glabrous: fls. ¾in. long, pink, in 6–15-fld. dense rather upright racemes 2–3 in. long; standard with a yellow blotch: pod linear-oblong, glandular-hispid, 2–3½ in. long. N. and S. C. to Ala.; nat. elsewhere.

23. **GLIRICIDIA,** HBK. Woody plants, differing from Robinia in having wingless or marginless pods and coriaceous valves; probably 6–8 species, Cuba and Mex. to S. Amer.—Lvs. odd-pinnate, the lfts. entire: fls. papilionaceous, rose-colored, racemose or fascicled; calyx campanulate, entire or obscurely toothed; standard large, reflexed; wings falcate-oblong; keel incurved, obtuse; ovary stipitate, many-ovuled, becoming a broad-linear 2-valved pod. (Gliricid-ia: Latin *rodent poison,* from the seeds.)

G. sepium, Steud. (*Robinia sepium,* Jacq. *G. maculata,* Steud.). Madre. Small tree 20–30 ft. high: lfts. 7–17, oblong-ovate, 1–3 in. long, acute or obtusish, somewhat appressed-pubescent: fls. pink and white, ½–¾in. long, in racemes 4–6 in. long, blooming profusely in spring often after the lvs. drop: pod linear, compressed, 4–6 in. long, with slightly thickened margin; seeds 3–6. Cent. Amer., Colombia.—Cult. in S. Fla.

24. **CLIANTHUS,** Soland. Half-trailing shrubs grown in the greenhouse or out-of-doors in the S.; 2–3 species from Australia and New Zeal.—Lvs. odd-pinnate, with many entire lfts.: fls. papilionaceous, very large, red, pendulous, in axillary racemes, the sharply acuminate curved and beak-like keel prolonged beyond the wings and standard; stamens 9 and 1: pod stalked, many-seeded, terete and turgid. (Clian-thus: Greek *glory-flower.*)

A. Plant hoary with long silky hairs: fls. 4–6 in a raceme....................................1. *C. Dampieri*
AA. Plant glabrous or nearly so: fls. 8 or more in a raceme....................................2. *C. puniceus*

1. **C. Dampieri,** Cunn. Glory Pea. Plant 2–4 ft. high, grayish-green, the st. clothed with long white hairs and slightly reddish-tinged: lfts. 15–21, sessile, oblong or elliptic, ½–1 in. long, usually acute: fl.-stalk upright, shorter than lvs., with 4–6 fls. clustered near the tip; fls. about 3 in. long, bright scarlet with a large velvety purple-black area on the lower half of the erect standard: pod oblong, to 2½ in. long, leathery, silky-hairy, glabrous within. (Named for its discoverer, W. Dampier, 1652–1715, English traveller and writer.) Australia.—Hort. vars. have petals differing in color.

2. **C. puniceus,** Banks & Soland. PARROTS-BILL. PARROT-BEAK. RED KOWHAI. Shrubby, much-branched, 3–6 ft. high, glabrous or nearly so: lfts. 17–29, short-stalked, linear-oblong, ½–1 in. long, blunt or slightly notched: fls. at least 3 in. long, in short axillary clusters of about 8 each, crimson fading in age, the standard slightly white-striped near center: pod 2–3 in. long, somewhat leathery, hairy within. New Zeal.—There are vars. with white or bright scarlet fls.

25. **COLUTEA,** L. BLADDER SENNA. About a dozen species of ornamental shrubs from the Medit. region to Abyssinia and the Himalayas.—Deciduous, with alternate odd-pinnate lvs.; lfts. many, rather small, entire, stipules small: fls. papilionaceous, yellow or brownish-red, rather large, in axillary long-peduncled few-fld. racemes; calyx campanulate, 5-toothed; standard suborbicular, with 2 folds or swellings above the claw; stamens 9 and 1; ovary stalked: pod inflated and bladder-like, many-seeded. (Colu-tea: ancient Greek name.)

A. Fls. bright yellow..1. *C. arborescens*
AA. Fls. deep orange or reddish..2. *C. media*

1. **C. arborescens,** L. To 15 ft.: lfts. 9–13, elliptic, obtuse and mucronulate or emarginate, ½–1 in. long, dull green, usually pubescent beneath: fls. bright yellow, about ¾ in. long, 3–8 in a raceme in summer and autumn; wings nearly as long as keel, flat: pod 2–3 in. long, tipped by the persistent style, greenish. S. Eu., N. Afr.—There are dwarf vars. with crisped or bullate lvs.

2. **C. media,** Willd. Hybrid between *C. arborescens* and *C. orientalis*, differing from the former in fls. deep orange or brownish-red, and pods purplish.

26. **SWAINSONA,** Salisb. An Australian genus of about 30 species of herbs or subshrubs, grown in greenhouses or in the extreme S. out-of-doors.—Plants glabrous or subappressed-pilose: lvs. odd-pinnate; lfts. many, small, entire, without stipels; stipules frequently herbaceous with broad base, rarely bristle-like: fls. papilionaceous, blue-violet, purple, red, rarely white or yellowish, in axillary usually peduncled many-fld. racemes; calyx of 5 subequal teeth, or the 2 upper grown together; standard orbicular or reniform, spreading or reflexed; wings oblong, falcate or somewhat twisted; keel broad, incurved, obtuse; stamens 9 and 1; ovary sessile or stipitate, many-ovuled: pod turgid or inflated. (Swainso-na: named for Isaac Swainson, English horticulturist, died 1806.)—Differs from Colutea chiefly in the smaller stature and large lateral stigma.

S. galegifolia, R. Br. (*Vicia galegifolia*, Andr. *Colutea galegifolia*, Sims). Glabrous erect branching shrub 3–4 ft. high, branches long, flexuous or half-climbing: lfts. 11–21, oblong, ¼–¾ in. long, obtuse or somewhat emarginate: racemes axillary, mostly exceeding lvs., bearing deep red fls. about ¾ in. long: pod 1–2 in. long, much inflated, stipitate. Var. **albiflora,** Lindl., has white fls.—An almost continuous bloomer.

27. **GLYCYRRHIZA,** L. About a dozen species in the Medit. region, trop. Asia, W. N. Amer. and S. Amer., one cult. for its roots from which the licorice of commerce is produced.—Per. often glandular-hairy herbs or half-shrubs with odd-pinnate lvs.: lfts. of indefinite number, seldom 3–5, entire or minutely glandular-toothed: fls. papilionaceous, white, yellow, blue or violet, in axillary racemes or spikes which are peduncled or sessile; stamens 9 and 1; ovary sessile, with 2 to many ovules: pod inflated, with leathery often prickly valves. (Glycyrrhi-za: Greek *sweet root.*)

G. glabra, L. LICORICE. LIQUORICE. From 2–3 ft. high: lfts. 9–17, ovate, 1–2 in. long, obtuse, glutinous beneath: spikes peduncled, shorter than lvs.; fls. pale blue, about ½ in. long, in many-fld. racemes 4–6 in. long, the calyx glandular-pubescent: pod red-brown, ½–1 in. long, glabrous, 3–4-seeded. Medit. region.—Extensively cult. in Eu. and Asia, whence the supply of licorice is derived; experimentally grown in the U. S.; it also has medicinal value.

28. **GALEGA,** L. Bushy perennials, one frequently cult.; 4 species in S. Eu. and W. Asia.—Glabrous erect herbs: lvs. odd-pinnate; lfts. numerous, entire: fls. papilionaceous, blue or white, in terminal and axillary racemes; bracts small, setaceous, mostly persistent; calyx with almost equal teeth; petals clawed; standard broad; wings somewhat joined to keel; stamens monadelphous; ovary sessile, with many ovules: pod linear, terete, tipped with the persistent style. (Gale-ga: Greek for *milk;* supposed to increase the flow of milk.)

G. officinalis, L. Goats-Rue. From 2–3 ft. high: lfts. 11–17, oblong or oblong-ovate, retuse or mucronate, sometimes nearly 2 in. long: fls. purplish-blue, about ½in. long, in racemes somewhat longer than lvs.: pod 1–1½ in. long, torulose, red-brown. Eu., W. Asia. Var. **albiflora,** Boiss., fls. white. Var. **Hartlandii,** Hort., fls. lilac, lvs. variegated when young.

29. **INDIGOFERA,** L. Indigo. Species probably 350, in trop. regions of the world and extending to the Cape region of S. Afr., several native to U. S.; some grown for ornament, and others cult. in various parts of the world for indigo.—Shrubs and per. herbs of various habit, more or less silky-hairy: lvs. odd-pinnate (rarely digitate), or sometimes simple (1-foliolate); lfts. entire: fls. papilionaceous, usually small, in axillary racemes or spikes, in color ranging from purple to rose and white; keel with a spur or swelling on either side; stamens 9 and 1; ovary nearly sessile, usually with many ovules: pod terete or angular, with thin partitions between the seeds. (Indigof-era: Latin *indigo bearing.*)

A. Pod strongly curved, about ½in. long . . . . 1. *I. suffruticosa*
AA. Pod not strongly curved, 1–2 in. long.
B. Lfts. glabrous above . . . . 2. *I. tinctoria*
BB. Lfts. pubescent above.
C. Number of lfts. 13–21 . . . . 3. *I. Gerardiana*
CC. Number of lfts. 5–11.
D. Fls. ½–¾in. long . . . . 4. *I. Kirilowii*
DD. Fls. about ¼in. long . . . . 5. *I. Potaninii*

1. **I. suffruticosa,** Mill. (*I. Anil,* L.). Shrub 3–6 ft. high, sts. erect, strigillose, angular, sparingly branched: lfts. 9–17, thin, oblong, oblanceolate or obovate, ½–1½ in. long, mucronate, acute at base, strigillose, often glabrous or glabrate above: racemes many-fld., shorter than the subtending lvs., in summer and autumn; corolla orange, about ⅙in. long: pod stout, ½–⅔in. long, curved, thickened at the sutures. W. Indies.—One of the sources from which the natural indigo of commerce is obtained.

2. **I. tinctoria,** L. Similar to *I. suffruticosa,* but with lfts. commonly smaller, and pods narrower and longer (1–1½ in.) and nearly straight. Cosmopolitan in the tropics.—Also a source of the indigo of commerce.

3. **I. Gerardiana,** Baker. Much-branched shrub 2–6 ft. high, with silvery-canescent branchlets: lfts. 13–21, ⅜–½in. long, obovate or oval, covered with gray appressed hairs, the apex notched or rounded and bristle-tipped: racemes 3–6 in. long, bearing numerous rose-purple fls. ½in. long, in summer: pod deflexed when ripe, 1½–2 in. long. (Named for John Gerarde, 1545–1607, perhaps the best known of the herbalists.) Himalayas.

4. **I. Kirilowii,** Maxim. Shrub to 4 ft.: lfts. 7–11, obovate or elliptic, ½–1½ in. long, slightly pubescent on both sides, obtuse and mucronate: racemes dense, to 5 in. long, on peduncles about twice length of petiole; fls. rose, ¾in. long, June: pod 1½–2 in. long. (Named for P. Kirilow.) N. China, Korea.

5. **I. Potaninii,** Craib. Shrub to 5 ft.: lfts. 5–9, oblong, ½–1¼ in. long, obtuse and mucronate, pubescent on both sides: racemes to 5 in. long, on peduncles about length of petiole; fls. lilac-pink, about ¼in. long, June–July: pod to 1½ in. long. (Named for Gr. N. Potanin, 1835–1920, naturalist and collector.) China.

30. **ASTRAGALUS,** L. Milk Vetch. Herbs or subshrubs, one sometimes planted in the rock-garden.—Lvs. usually odd-pinnate: fls. papilionaceous, white, yellow or purple, in axillary racemes or heads; calyx-teeth nearly equal; wings of corolla adhering to keel; stamens 9 and 1; ovary sessile or stalked, usually with many ovules: pod various, inflated or thin and bladder-like, 1–2-celled. (Astragalus: ancient Greek name.)—About 1,500 species in the northern hemisphere, by some authors separated into many genera.

A. monspessulanus, L. Per. to 10 in., sts. trailing: lfts. 12–20 pairs, ovate-oblong, to ⅓in. long, obtuse, hairy beneath, glabrate above: fls. purple, about 1 in. long, in short racemes on long ascending peduncles about length of lvs.: pod terete, 1–2 in. long, curved, long-beaked. Eu., N. Afr.

31. **CLADRASTIS,** Raf. Yellow-Wood. Four species of deciduous trees in N. Amer. and E. Asia, one planted for ornament.—Winter-buds naked, several superposed and concealed during the summer in the enlarged base of the petiole: lvs. odd-pinnate, with few rather large entire alternate short-stalked lfts.: fls. papilionaceous, white, in long usually panicled racemes; calyx campanulate, 5-toothed; stamens 10, distinct or nearly so: pod narrow-oblong, compressed, 3–6-seeded, with thin membranaceous valves. (Cladras-tis: Greek *brittle branch.*)

C. lutea, Koch (*C. tinctoria*, Raf. *Virgilia lutea*, Michx.). A beautiful flowering native tree with graceful head and short trunk and with yellow wood and smooth bark, sometimes 50 ft. high: lfts. 7–9, oval or ovate, 3–4 in. long, glabrous, bright green, turning bright yellow in autumn: panicles many-fld., loose, drooping, 10–20 in. long; fls. white, fragrant, over 1 in. long, in June: pod short-stalked, glabrous, 2–4 in. long. Ky., Tenn., N. C.

32. **MAACKIA,** Rupr. & Maxim. Deciduous trees, of 6 species in E. Asia, one planted.—Differs from Cladrastis in lfts. being opposite and the panicled racemes upright. (Maa-ckia: Richard Maack, 1825–1886, Russian naturalist.)

M. amurensis, Rupr. (*Cladrastis amurensis*, Koch). To 40 ft.: lfts. 7–11, ovate or elliptic, 2–3 in. long, short-acuminate, glabrous: racemes panicled, 6–8 in. long; fls. white, ⅓in. long, July–Aug.: pod flat, linear-oblong, 1½–2 in. long. Manchuria. Var. **Buergeri,** Schneid., lfts. pubescent beneath, more obtuse; Japan.

33. **SOPHORA,** L. About 20 species of ornamental woody or rarely herbaceous plants, native in the temp. and subtrop. regions of both hemispheres.—Deciduous or evergreen: lvs. odd-pinnate with opposite entire usually small lfts.: fls. pea-like, in terminal racemes or panicles; calyx with 5 short teeth; standard orbicular or broadly ovate; keel oblong, suberect; stamens 10, distinct or nearly so; ovary short-stalked: pod stalked, almost terete or 4-winged, rarely compressed, few- to many-seeded, moniliform, indehiscent, or tardily dehiscent. (Soph-ora: *sophera*, Arabian name of a tree with pea-shaped fls.)

A. Lfts. ½in. or less long: spinescent shrub . . . . 1. *S. viciifolia*
AA. Lfts. 1–2½ in. long: unarmed trees.
  B. Tree deciduous: fls. in panicles . . . . 2. *S. japonica*
  BB. Tree evergreen: fls. in racemes . . . . 3. *S. secundiflora*

1. **S. viciifolia,** Hance (*S. Davidii*, Kom.). Deciduous more or less spiny shrub to 6 ft., with slender spreading pubescent branchlets: lvs. 1–1½ in. long, short-petioled; lfts. 13–19, sessile, elliptic, ¼–½ in. long, obtuse and mucronulate, pubescent beneath: fls. bluish-violet or nearly white, about ½in. long, in short 6–12-fld. racemes terminating short branchlets, in summer; calyx violet, shortly 5-toothed; petals of nearly equal length; standard spatulate-obovate, reflexed: pod about 2 in. long, slender, long-beaked, glabrous. Cent. and W. China.

2. **S. japonica,** L. JAPANESE PAGODA-TREE. CHINESE SCHOLAR-TREE. Round-headed deciduous tree attaining 60 ft., with spreading branches: lvs. 7–9 in. long; lfts. 7–17, distinctly stalked, ovate to ovate-lanceolate, 1–2 in. long, acute, rounded at base, dark green and glossy above, more or less pubescent beneath: fls. yellowish-white, ½in. long, in loose panicles 15 in. long, in late summer and autumn: pod glabrous, 2–3 in. long, ⅓in. broad. China. Var. **pendula,** Loud., has long slender pendulous branches.

3. **S. sécundiflora,** Lag. (*Broussonetia secundiflora*, Ort.). MESCAL BEAN. Evergreen narrow-headed tree to 40 ft. or sometimes a shrub: lvs. 4–6 in. long, petioled; lfts. 7–9, nearly sessile, oblong-elliptic, 1–2½ in. long, shining above, silky beneath when young: fls. violet-blue, 1 in. long, very fragrant, in terminal one-sided racemes to 4 in. long: pod 1–8 in. long, woody, tomentose, seeds bright red, ½in. long. Tex. to N. Mex.

34. **CASTANOSPERMUM,** Cunn. Two large trees, one planted for ornament in warm regions.—Lvs. odd-pinnate, with large leathery lfts.: fls. large, yellow, in short racemes; calyx with very short broad lobes; standard obovate, recurved; wings and keel similar, shorter than standard; stamens 10, free; ovary long-stalked, with many ovules: pod leathery or woody, turgid, 2-valved. (Castanosper-mum: *chestnut seed*, referring to taste of seed.)

C. australe, Cunn. MORETON-BAY-CHESTNUT. BLACK BEAN. Evergreen tree to 60 ft., glabrous: lvs. to 1½ ft. long; lfts. 11–15, broadly oblong, 3–5 in. long: fls. yellow to orange and reddish, 1½ in. long, in sessile racemes to 6 in. long; stamens exserted: pod terete, to 9 in. long and 2 in. wide; seeds chestnut-like. Australia.

35. **CROTALARIA,** L. RATTLE-BOX. Large cosmopolitan genus, of probably 325 species, strongly developed in Asia, ann. and per. erect herbs and shrubs, a few cult. for ornament and cover-crops, mostly in Fla. and Calif.—Lvs. simple (unifoliolate) or digitate with 3, 5, or 7 lfts.: fls. yellow or brownish-yellow, sometimes blue or purplish, solitary or mostly racemose, papilionaceous, often showy; standard mostly prominent and larger than the wings, the keel beaked and curved; stamens 10,

connate; style strongly incurved or reflexed, somewhat bearded: fr. globose or oblong, inflated, not septate, the many seeds loose at maturity (whence Crotala-ria: Greek *a rattle;* from the same word comes *Crotalus*, the rattlesnake.)

A. Lvs. of 3 lfts.
  B. Lfts. to 1 in. long: fls. about 1 in. long.......1. *C. capensis*
  BB. Lfts. 2–4 in. long: fls. ½in. long.......2. *C. mucronata*
AA. Lvs. simple.
  B. Stipules and bracts broad-ovate.......3. *C. spectabilis*
  BB. Stipules and bracts lacking or linear.
    C. Pod glabrous: lfts. glabrous above.......4. *C. retusa*
    CC. Pod pubescent: lfts. pubescent on both sides.......5. *C. juncea*

1. **C. capensis,** Jacq. Branching shrub, 4–5 ft., with appressed-silky branches: lfts. 3, broadly obovate, obtuse but lightly mucronate, ¾–1 in. long, minutely pubescent both sides or glabrous: fls. more than 1 in. long, bright yellow, prominently veined and showy, many in loose racemes that are terminal or opposite the lvs.: pod pubescent, 1½ in. long. S. Afr.

2. **C. mucronata,** Desv. (*C. striata*, DC.). Woody per. to 8 ft.: lfts. 3, elliptic, 2–4 in. long, obtuse or emarginate: fls. yellow striped with brown, ½in. long, in many-fld. terminal racemes to 1 ft. long: pod linear-oblong, 1½ in. long, pubescent or glabrate. Tropics.—Planted in Fla. for green-manuring.

3. **C. spectabilis,** Roth (*C. Retzii*, Hitchc. *C. sericea*, Retz.). Subshrub to 4 ft., with stout branches: lvs. simple, oblanceolate, to 6 in. long, entire, glabrous above, pubescent beneath; stipules broad-ovate: fls. yellow, ¾in. long, in many-fld. terminal racemes to 1 ft. long; bracts broad-ovate: pod to 2 in. long and ¾in. wide, glabrous. India; escaped in S. Fla.

4. **C. retusa,** L. Ann., appressed-pubescent, 1½–3 ft.: lvs. simple, spatulate to oblanceolate, 2–3 in. long, very obtuse or even retuse, entire, gray-pubescent beneath, glabrous above; stipules minute or none: fls. yellow with variegated showy standard, ¾–1 in. long, in terminal peduncled racemes to 8 in. long; bracts small, linear: pod oblong, 1–1½ in. long, glabrous, short-beaked. Asia and Malaya; nat. in Fla. and trop. Amer. and elsewhere.

5. **C. juncea,** L. Sunn Hemp. Shrub to 8 ft., with slender silky branches: lvs. simple, linear to oblong, 2–4 in. long, brown-hairy on both sides; stipules minute or none: fls. bright yellow, ¾–1 in. long, in terminal racemes to 1 ft. long; bracts minute, linear: pod oblong, 1¼ in. long, pubescent. India; nat. in W. Indies.

36. **LUPINUS,** L. Lupine. Ann. and per. herbs, sometimes subshrubs, yielding good ornamental subjects, a few long used for soil renovation, fodder, and for human food; the genus is specially rich in N. Amer., but extends into Eu. and Afr.; upwards of 300 species have been described.—Lvs. digitate, of 5–15 narrow lfts. (rarely 1 or 3); stipules adnate to base of petiole: fls. mostly showy, in terminal racemes or sometimes whorled, white, yellow, blue, purplish, papilionaceous; calyx 2-lipped, deeply toothed; standard erect, broad, with reflexed edges; keel incurved with the beak included; stamens monadelphous; style incurved, the terminal stigma mostly somewhat bearded: pod flattened, mostly constricted or grooved crosswise between the seeds. (Lupi-nus: *lupus*, Latin for wolf, from some fancied ability of the plant to prey on the soil.)—Most of the lupines well known to cult. are annuals. There are two cultural groups—the large-seeded agricultural kinds and the small-seeded ornamental kinds. Aside from the lupines here treated, any of the showy native species may be transferred to grounds.

A. Color of fls. clear yellow.
  B. Calyx subtended by narrow reflexed persistent bracts: pod ¾in. long, 2-seeded. 1. *L. densiflorus*
  BB. Calyx with bracts deciduous: pod 2–3 in. long, several-seeded.
    C. Plant a shrub: fls. scattered in the raceme.......2. *L. arboreus*
    CC. Plant an ann.: fls. whorled in the raceme.......3. *L. luteus*
AA. Color of fls. white, blue or purple, sometimes spotted with yellow.
  B. Racemes interrupted, the fls. in whorls.
    C. Plant glabrous except the pod.......4. *L. mutabilis*
    CC. Plant pubescent.
      D. Bracts subtending pedicels persistent, narrow and reflexed.......1. *L. densiflorus*
      DD. Bracts in racemes deciduous.
        E. Sts. succulent, nearly glabrous.......5. *L. succulentus*
        EE. Sts. not succulent, manifestly pubescent.
          F. Height 6–15 in., plant forming compact clump, with linear lfts.......6. *L. nanus*
          FF. Height 1½–3 ft., plant not forming tuft or cushion, lfts. broader.......7. *L. pubescens*
  BB. Racemes continuous, the fls. scattered.
    C. Height to 6 in., alpine.......8. *L. Lyallii*
    CC. Height 1 ft. or more.

D. Plant per.
E. Lfts. usually 8, 1–1½ in. long .... 9. *L. perennis*
EE. Lfts. 9–16, 3–6 in. long .... 10. *L. polyphyllus*
DD. Plant ann.
E. Seeds large, ⅜in. or more across: agricultural species.
F. Corolla white, sometimes tinged bluish on margins.
G. Floral-bracts wanting .... 11. *L. albus*
GG. Floral-bracts present although deciduous .... 12. *L. Termis*
FF. Corolla normally blue, sometimes tinged white .... 13. *L. hirsutus*
EE. Seeds small, about ⅛in. across.
F. Stature 2 ft. and more: lfts. 7–10, very hairy .... 14. *L. Hartwegii*
FF. Stature 1 ft. or less: lfts. 5, pubescent beneath .... 15. *L. subcarnosus*

1. **L. densiflorus,** Benth. (*L. Menziesii,* Agardh. *L. microcarpus* var. *densiflorus,* Jepson). Hairy stout ann., 1½–2 ft., sts. branching mostly at the middle: lfts. 7–10, oblong-lanceolate, 1–2 in. long, acute and mucronate, hairy: fls. white, yellow, sometimes rose, ½–⅝in. long, in dense whorls on a long-peduncled raceme 6–10 in. long, calyx pubescent; bracts persistent, narrow and reflexed, little exceeding pedicels: pod ovoid, ¾in. or less long, hairy, 2-seeded; seeds about ¼in. across, compressed, whitish. Calif.—Plants grown as *L. sulphureus superbus* evidently belong here.

2. **L. arboreus,** Sims. TREE LUPINE. Shrub to 10 ft.: lfts. 5–11, oblanceolate, about 1 in. long, glabrous above, silky-pubescent beneath: fls. sulfur-yellow, ½–¾in. long, fragrant, in loose racemes to 10 in. long: pod 1½–3 in. long, pubescent, with 8–12 dark seeds. Calif.

3. **L. luteus,** L. YELLOW LUPINE. Ann., making many lvs. from the base, st. nearly simple, erect, hairy, 1–2 ft.: lfts. 7–11, linear-lanceolate, oblong to somewhat oblanceolate or the lower ones narrow-obovate, 1–1½ in. long, short-acute, hirsute: fls. yellow, fragrant, ¾in. long, whorled in long terminal racemes, usually standing well above the foliage, nearly sessile; upper lip of calyx 2-parted, lower 3-toothed: pod oblong, flat, 2 in. long, hairy; seeds 4–7, large, dull light gray with brown markings. S. Eu.—An old fodder plant and soil renovator; also useful for ornament.

4. **L. mutabilis,** Sweet. Stout glabrous showy ann., sts. becoming somewhat woody at base, 3–6 ft. high: lfts. 7–11, lanceolate to oblong to broad-oblanceolate, 2–3 in. long, obtuse, glabrous and gray-green; stipules very small, sometimes rudimentary: fls. white but with yellow and sometimes violet on the standard, about ¾in. long, prominently pedicelled in a long terminal raceme, the lower ones whorled and the upper ones often or usually alternate; calyx glabrous, the narrow long lips of similar length or the lower somewhat longer: pod 2–3 in. long and ¾in. broad, pubescent; seeds white (sometimes mottled brown), smooth and flat, ⅓in. long. Mts. in S. Amer., but apparently unknown native.—In cult. the colors are modified, becoming rose or purplish; these races are distinguished by the flat white rather large seeds and glabrous herbage.

5. **L. succulentus,** Dougl. (*L. affinis,* Brewer & Wats.). Stout and succulent ann., the sts. often markedly hollow, nearly glabrous, 1–2 ft., branching mostly at the middle: lfts. 7–9, oblong-oblanceolate to broadly wedge-obovate, 1–2 in. long, obtuse or retuse, equalling or shorter than petiole, sparsely pubescent underneath; stipules small and setaceous: fls. deep bluish-purple, about ½in. long, short-peduncled, whorled in racemes 5–7 in. long; upper lip of calyx 2-toothed, lower lip mostly entire: pod 1–2 in. long, pubescent; seeds 8–10. Calif.—A winter ann., blooming in spring.

6. **L. nanus,** Dougl. (*L. affinis,* Agardh). Slender ann. 6–15 in. high, branching from base, finely pubescent or somewhat hairy: lfts. 5–7, linear or narrowly oblanceolate, ¾–1¼ in. long, acute and mostly mucronate, pubescent at least beneath, margins ciliate; petioles exceeding lfts.; stipules very small: fls. blue, fragrant, standard with purple-dotted white spot, usually ½in. or less long, in more or less distinct whorls in terminal racemes to 5 in. long; calyx hairy, the lobes long: pod about 1 in. long, hairy; seeds 5–11, white, flat, ⅛in. or more long. Calif.—Running into color races in cult.

7. **L. pubescens,** Benth. Much-branched soft-pubescent ann., 1½–3 ft.: lfts. 7–9, oblanceolate, 1–2 in. long, mostly obtuse but mucronate (rarely retuse), pubescent on both sides, margins ciliate; petiole usually exceeding lfts.; stipules very small or nearly rudimentary: fls. violet-blue with white center, becoming purple-red, about ½in. long, whorled in long terminal racemes; calyx-lips entire: pod about 1 in. long, very hairy; seeds 4–6, oblong-reniform or angled, white but more or less marked or marbled, glossy, ⅛–³⁄₁₆in. long. Mex. and Guatemala.—Long in cult. and probably the source of most of the hairy ann. lupines of fl.-gardens, in many colors and combinations. These garden plants are sometimes known as **L. hybridus,** Voss, and very likely there is hybridity in them. To the group as a whole belong garden names *L. albococcineus, californicus, Dunnettii, elegans, guatemalensis, insignis, Moritzianus, speciosus, superbus, tricolor, venustus.* Distinguished from the *L. hirsutus* group by absence of brown-shaggy hairiness and small seeds.

8. **L. Lyallii,** Gray. Silky-pubescent alpine to 6 in.: lfts. 6–7, oblanceolate, about ⅓in. long, on long petioles: fls. deep blue with white or yellowish on standard, ½in. long, in short dense racemes on curved peduncles longer than lvs.: pod ½in. long, pubescent. (Named for Dr. David Lyall, 1817–1895, collector with the Oregon Boundary Commission.) Wash. to Calif.

9. **L. perennis,** L. Per. to 2 ft., pubescent: lfts. 7–11, usually 8, oblanceolate, 1–1½ in. long, obtuse and mucronate: fls. blue varying to pink and white, about ½in. long, in loose racemes to 10 in. long: pod 1½ in. long, pubescent; seeds 4–6. Me. to Fla and La.

10. **L. polyphyllus,** Lindl. Per., stout and erect, 3–5 ft., glabrate, or sparsely hairy-pubescent above: lvs. very long-stalked, the petioles 6–12 in. long or the upper ones shorter; lfts. 9–16, lanceolate to oblanceolate, 2–6 in. long, acute, glabrous above and sparsely hairy beneath; stipules pointed, adnate to petiole for one-third or one-half their length: fls. with purplish standard, blue wings and mostly dark-tipped point of keel, about ½in. long, many and alternate on slender pedicels in a rather dense terminal raceme 1–2 ft. long: pod 1–1½ in. long, woolly-hairy; seeds about 6, oblong, ⅛–³⁄₁₆in. long, brown-black and glossy. Calif. to B. C.—Hort. color races include var. **albiflorus,** Bergmans (var. *albus*, Bergmans), with white fls.; var. **bicolor,** Bergmans (var. *Foxii*, Hort.) fls. in shades of blue with white; var. **roseus,** Bergmans (forma *roseus*, Voss. var. *Moerheimii*, Hort.), a compact-growing race represented by many color forms, mostly in shades of rose-pink. **L. regalis,** Bergmans (*L. polyphyllus* var. *regalis*, Hort. *L. hybridus*, Hort. not Voss), is the name given to a group of hybrid per. lupines of mixed garden ancestry and includes the Russell lupines, Downer's hybrids, Harkness hybrids and others, represented by many fancy-named variants.

11. **L. albus,** L. White Lupine. Ann., erect, hairy, 1½–4 ft., branching: lfts. 5–7, obovate-oblong, 1–2 in. long, very short-acute, ciliate on margins, appressed-hairy beneath but becoming glabrous above: fls. white (or somewhat tinted), ½–¾in. long, alternate in short nearly sessile terminal racemes; calyx without bracts at base, upper lip entire: pod 2¼–4 in. long and ½–¾in. broad, stout-beaked, hairy; seeds whitish, nearly orbicular, compressed, ⅓in. across. Levant.—Anciently and still cult. for land improvement, fodder and human food, but little known in Amer.

12. **L. Termis,** Forsk. Egyptian Lupine. Very like *L. albus*, but calyx subtended with deciduous bracts: fls. white with usually bluish tint on apex of standard and bluish-green on apex of keel: silky-villous ann. to 4–5 ft. (Termis: the Arabic name.) Levant.—Cult. same as no. 11, and intro. into U. S. for dry regions.

13. **L. hirsutus,** L. Blue Lupine. Strongly brown-hairy ann., often very low but rising 2 ft. or more: lfts. 5–7, oblanceolate to oblong-obovate, 1–1½ in. long; stipules prominent, very narrow: fls. blue usually with white-tipped keel, ½–¾in. long, alternate or the upper ones more or less whorled in a terminal raceme, short-pedicelled; calyx silky-hairy, with short lobes: pod 1½–3 in. long and ¾in. broad, very hairy; seeds oblong-reniform, ½in. long, rough, gray or brownish. S. Eu.—An old agricultural large-seeded species; also grown for ornament, with races bearing white and reddish fls.

14. **L. Hartwegii,** Lindl. Stout erect shaggy-hairy ann., 2–3 ft., very leafy, little branched: lfts. 7–10, narrow-oblong to oblong-lanceolate, 2–3 in. long, obtuse but with a short mucro, very hairy; petioles commonly much exceeding lfts.; stipules with very long slender points: fls. blue in general but the parts of the corolla differently colored, the standard typically rose-colored in center, about ½in. long, mostly alternate (sometimes obscurely whorled) in a long terminal raceme in which the shaggy bracts are very long and prominent before the fls. open; calyx hairy, with long slender lobes: pod 1–1¼ in. long, hairy; seeds white and glossy, about ⅛in. long. (Theodor Hartweg, page 44.) Mex.

15. **L. subcarnosus,** Hook. (*L. texensis*, Hook.). Small ann., usually a foot or less high, silky-pubescent: lfts. 5, oblanceolate to narrowly oblong-obovate, ¾–1½ in. long, short-acute, obtuse or even retuse at apex, nearly or quite glabrous above and lightly hairy beneath; petiole exceeding the lfts.; stipules narrow and long-pointed: fls. blue with white or yellowish spot in center of standard, about ½in. long, scattered in a short terminal raceme; calyx hairy, with upper lip much shorter: pod about 1½ in. long, hairy; seeds ⅛–³⁄₁₆in. across, mottled. Tex.

37. **LABURNUM,** Medic. Ornamental deciduous trees or shrubs, of 3 species in S. Eu. and W. Asia, often included under Cytisus.—Lvs. alternate, petioled, 3-foliolate, without stipules: fls. papilionaceous, slender-pedicelled, in simple terminal mostly pendulous racemes; calyx 2-lipped, with short teeth; corolla yellow; keel shorter than wings; stamens monadelphous; ovary stalked: pod linear, compressed, several-seeded, both sutures thickened or the upper winged; seeds without appendage at base. (Labur-num: ancient Latin name.)—All parts of the plant are said to be poisonous, especially the young frs.

A. Pod with upper suture thickened and keeled but not winged: pubescent.........1. *L. anagyroides*
AA. Pod with upper suture winged: glabrous or nearly so.........................2. *L. alpinum*

1. **L. anagyroides,** Medic. (*L. vulgare*, Bercht. & Presl. *Cytisus Laburnum*, L.). Golden-Chain. Bean-Tree. Large shrub or small tree 20–30 ft. high, with erect or spreading branches often close to the ground; branchlets appressed-pubescent, grayish-green: lvs. on petioles 2–3 in. long; lfts. elliptic or elliptic-ovate, 1½–3 in. long, usually obtuse and mucronulate, downy beneath: racemes silky-pubescent, 4–12 in. long; fls. about ¾in. long, in late spring and early summer: pod 2–3 in. long, the upper suture thickened and keeled

but not winged, appressed-pubescent. S. Eu.—Vars. with curled or yellow lvs. and smaller fls. are often cult.

2. **L. alpinum,** Bercht. & Presl (*Cytisus alpinus,* Mill.). SCOTCH LABURNUM. Shrub or tree to 30 ft., similar to the foregoing but of stiffer and more upright growth and becoming glabrous: lvs. with a stalk 1–2 in. long; lfts. usually elliptic, acute, deep green, not so downy beneath as in no. 1: racemes slender, 10–16 in. long, in summer: pod flat, the upper suture flattened out into a thin edge or wing. S. Eu.—**L. Watereri,** Dipp. (*L. Vossii,* Hort.), is a hybrid between *L. anagyroides* and *L. alpinum:* the long slender racemes and under side of lvs. sparingly pubescent: pod slightly appressed-pubescent, narrowly winged and few-seeded.

38. **CYTISUS,** L. BROOM. Free-flowering woody plants widely grown in greenhouses and in the open in mild climates; about 80 species in S. Cent. Eu., Canary Isls., N. Afr. and W. Asia.—Low shrubs or rarely small trees, seldom with thorn-tipped branches: lvs. trifoliolate, sometimes unifoliolate, rather small, alternate, deciduous or persistent, sometimes few and minute and the branches almost leafless: fls. papilionaceous, axillary or in terminal heads or racemes, yellow, white or purple; calyx 2-lipped, teeth short; stamens monadelphous; style curved: pod flat, dehiscent, the few to many seeds with a callous appendage at base. (Cyt-isus: Greek name for a kind of clover.)

A. Calyx tubular, much longer than wide.
B. Arrangement of fls. in terminal heads with bracts at base.
C. Color of fls. white: pubescence of branchlets appressed .... 1. *C. albus*
CC. Color of fls. yellow: pubescence of branchlets spreading .... 2. *C. supinus*
BB. Arrangement of fls. axillary along the branches.
C. Branchlets glabrous or nearly so.
D. Fls. self-colored, purple varying to white .... 3. *C. purpureus*
DD. Fls. purple, white or yellowish in same bloom .... 4. *C. versicolor*
CC. Branchlets pubescent.
D. Color of fls. all white .... 5. *C. proliferus*
DD. Color of fls. not all white.
E. Fls. yellow marked with brown .... 6. *C. hirsutus*
EE. Fls. purple, white or yellowish .... 4. *C. versicolor*
AA. Calyx campanulate, as long or only slightly longer than wide.
B. Arrangement of fls. in terminal racemes.
C. Foliage deciduous: branchlets terete .... 7. *C. nigricans*
CC. Foliage persistent: branchlets grooved.
D. Lfts. less than ¾in. long.
E. Racemes dense and rather short .... 8. *C. canariensis*
EE. Racemes rather loose, 2–4 in. long .... 9. *C. racemosus*
DD. Lfts. ¾–2 in. long .... 10. *C. maderensis*
BB. Arrangement of fls. axillary along the branches.
C. Habit prostrate or decumbent.
D. Lvs. simple.
E. Shape of lvs. oblong-obovate: branches often rooting .... 11. *C. decumbens*
EE. Shape of lvs. linear: branches not rooting .... 12. *C. Beanii*
DD. Lvs. of 3 lfts.
E. Color of fls. golden-yellow .... 13. *C. Ardoinii*
EE. Color of fls. pale yellow or creamy-white .... 14. *C. kewensis*
CC. Habit upright.
D. Style longer than keel, becoming spirally incurved.
E. Standard of corolla pure yellow .... 15. *C. scoparius*
EE. Standard of corolla yellow suffused with pink .... 16. *C. Dallimorei*
DD. Style shorter than keel, slightly curved.
E. Lvs. sessile .... 17. *C. purgans*
EE. Lvs. short-petioled.
F. Lfts. always 3 .... 18. *C. fragrans*
FF. Lfts. seldom 3, usually 1.
G. Fls. white .... 19. *C. multiflorus*
GG. Fls. yellow or yellowish-white .... 20. *C. præcox*

1. **C. albus,** Hacq. (*C. leucanthus,* Waldst. & Kit. *C. leucanthus* var. *schipkaensis,* Dipp.). Deciduous shrub to 1 ft., with villous branches: petioles ¼–⅓in. long; lfts. oblong or elliptic, ⅓–1 in. long, obtuse or acutish, often mucronate, appressed-pubescent or above sometimes glabrous, ciliate: fls. in terminal bracted heads in summer, yellowish-white or pale yellow, ¾in. long; calyx and corolla appressed-villous outside: pod about 1 in. long, appressed-villous. S. E. Eu.

2. **C. supinus,** L. Deciduous shrub to 3 ft., sometimes procumbent, branchlets villous: petioles ½in. long; lfts. elliptic to oblong-obovate, ½–1 in. long, hairy on both sides: fls. in terminal bracted heads in summer, yellow fading brownish, 1 in. long; corolla silky outside: pod 1¼ in. long, villous. Eu.

3. **C. purpureus,** Scop. Glabrous deciduous shrub to 2 ft., procumbent or ascending: petioles ¼–1 in. long; lfts. oval or obovate, ½–1 in. long, dark green above: fls. 1–3,

axillary, in spring and early summer, purple, ¾in. long; calyx reddish: pod black, 1–1½ in. long. S. Austria.—There are vars. with white, pink or dark purple fls.

4. **C. versicolor,** Dipp. Hybrid between *C. purpureus* and *C. hirsutus:* to 3 ft., erect or spreading: lfts. slightly villous beneath: fls. with whitish standard, light purple keel and yellowish wings; calyx and pod villous.

5. **C. proliferus,** L. To 12 ft., the branches long, slender and pubescent: petioles ¼–½ in. long; lfts. oblanceolate, 1–1¾ in. long, silky-pubescent beneath, green and sparsely pubescent above: fls. axillary, 3–8 on rather long tomentose pedicels, in late spring and early summer, white, to ¾in. long; calyx tomentose; standard pubescent outside: pod densely tomentose-villous, 1½–2 in. long. Canary Isls.

6. **C. hirsutus,** L. Deciduous shrub to 2 ft., branchlets villous: petioles ½–¾in. long; lfts. obovate, ½–¾in. long, villous, or nearly glabrous above: fls. 2–4, axillary, in early summer, yellow with brown on standard; calyx villous: pod about 1 in. long, villous. S. E. Eu.

7. **C. nigricans,** L. Deciduous shrub 4–6 ft. high, with terete villous branchlets: petioles ¼–¾in. long; lfts. obovate, ½–1 in. long, slightly pubescent beneath: fls. in slender terminal racemes to 1 ft. long, in summer, yellow, ½in. long; calyx pubescent: pod 1 in. long, pubescent. Cent. and S. Eu.

8. **C. canariensis,** Kuntze (*Genista canariensis,* L.). Genista of florists. Evergreen much-branched shrub to 6 ft., with villous-pubescent branches: lvs. petioled; lfts. cuneate, obovate or oblong-obovate, ¼–½in. long, rounded at apex, pubescent on both sides: fls. in terminal many-fld. dense rather short racemes in spring and summer, fragrant, bright yellow, ½in. long: pod ½–¾in. long, pubescent. Canary Isls. Var. **ramosissimus,** Briq., lfts. very small, glabrous above; racemes short but numerous.

9. **C. racemosus,** Nichols. (*Genista racemosa,* Hort.). Evergreen shrub to 6 ft., with pubescent branches: lvs. rather long-petioled; lfts. oblong-obovate, ⅓–¾in. long, mucronulate, silky-pubescent on both sides: fls. in many-fld. secund rather loose racemes 2–4 in. long, yellow. Probably of garden origin and hybrid between *C. canariensis* and *C. maderensis* var. *magnifoliosus.*

10. **C. maderensis,** Masf. Evergreen shrub or small tree to 20 ft.: lvs. slender-petioled; lfts. oblong-obovate, ¾in. and more long, silky-pubescent: fls. in 6–12-fld. terminal racemes in spring, yellow, about ½in. long, slightly fragrant. Madeira. Var. **magnifoliosus,** Briq., has lvs. to 2 in. long and longer racemes.

11. **C. decumbens,** Spach (*Spartium decumbens,* Durande. *Genista prostrata,* Lam.). Prostrate deciduous shrub to 8 in., branches often rooting: lvs. simple, sessile, oblong-obovate, ½–¾in. long, pubescent on both sides: fls. 1–3, axillary, in spring and early summer, bright yellow, ½in. long; calyx hairy: pod 1 in. long, pubescent. S. Eu.

12. **C. Beanii,** Nichols. Hybrid between *C. Ardoinii* and *C. purgans:* to 16 in., partly prostrate: lvs. simple, linear, ½in. long, pubescent: fls. 1–3, golden-yellow. (Raised at Kew and named for W. J. Bean, page 39.)

13. **C. Ardoinii,** Fournier. Prostrate deciduous shrub to 8 in., branchlets villous: lvs. short-petioled; lfts. obovate or oblong, ⅓in. long, villous: fls. 1–3, axillary, in spring, golden-yellow, ½in. long; calyx villous: pod 1 in. long, villous. (Named for its discoverer, H. Ardoino, 1819–1874, botanist.) S. France.

14. **C. kewensis,** Bean. Hybrid between *C. Ardoinii* and *C. multiflorus:* to 1 ft. or less, procumbent: lvs. usually of 3 linear-oblong pubescent lfts.: fls. creamy-white or pale yellow, ½in. long, in spring.

15. **C. scoparius,** Link (*Spartium scoparium,* L. *Sarothamnus scoparia,* Wimm.). Scotch Broom. Deciduous shrub to 10 ft., with erect slender branches: lvs. short-petioled, 1–3-foliolate; lfts. obovate or oblanceolate, ¼–½in. long, slightly appressed-pubescent: fls. usually solitary in the axils, spring and summer, bright yellow or pale yellow, ¾in. long; calyx and pedicels nearly glabrous: pod 1½–2 in. long, brownish-black, villous only at margin, otherwise glabrous. Cent. and S. Eu.; nat. in N. Amer. Var. **Andreanus,** Dipp. (*Genista Andreana,* Puissant), has fls. yellow with dark crimson wings.

16. **C. Dallimorei,** Rolfe. Hybrid between *C. multiflorus* and *C. scoparius* var. *Andreanus:* to 8 ft.: lfts. mostly 3: fls. yellow suffused with pink, wings crimson, ½in. long. (Raised at Kew and named for W. Dallimore.)

17. **C. purgans,** Spach (*Genista purgans,* L.). Deciduous shrub to 3 ft., with many erect grooved branches, soon leafless: lvs. usually simple, sessile, oblanceolate, ¼–½in. long, silky-pubescent: fls. 1–2, axillary, in spring and early summer, yellow, ½in. long, fragrant: pod 1 in. long, pubescent. S. Eu., N. Afr.

18. **C. fragrans,** Lam. (*Genista fragrans,* Hort.). Shrub with erect branches to 6 ft.: lvs. short-petioled, early deciduous; lfts. lanceolate, densely pubescent: fls. axillary, in spring, white, fragrant; wings and standard somewhat longer than the keel: pod oblong, flat, short-stalked. Teneriffe.

19. **C. multiflorus,** Sweet (*Spartium multiflorum,* Ait.). WHITE SPANISH BROOM. Deciduous shrub to 10 ft., with erect grooved branchlets: lvs. short-petioled, usually simple, 3-foliolate on lower parts of sts., oblong-obovate, ½in. long, pubescent: fls. 1–3, axillary, in spring and early summer, white, ½in. long: pod 1 in. long, pubescent. Spain, N. Afr.

20. **C. præcox,** Bean. Hybrid between *C. multiflorus* and *C. purgans:* deciduous shrub to 10 ft., with slender erect or arching branches: lfts. usually 1, sometimes 3, short-petioled, oblanceolate or linear-spatulate, to ¾in. long: fls. 1–2, very numerous along the slender branches, in spring, yellowish-white or sulfur-yellow, odor unpleasant, nearly ½in. long: pod appressed-pubescent, about 1 in. long. Var. **albus,** Th. Smith, is dwarfer with white fls.

39. **GENISTA,** L. BROOM. Upwards of 140 species in Eu., Canary Isls., N. Afr. and W. Asia, a few planted in the hardy border.—Deciduous or evergreen shrubs, sometimes nearly leafless, unarmed or spiny; branches usually striped and green: lvs. alternate, rarely opposite, entire, simple or sometimes 3-foliolate: fls. papilionaceous, in terminal racemes or heads, rarely axillary, yellow or sometimes white; calyx 2-lipped, the upper lip deeply 2-parted; stamens 10, monadelphous; style incurved: pod almost globular to narrow-oblong, 1- to many-seeded, rarely indehiscent. (Genis-ta: ancient Latin name.)—Allied to Cytisus, but without callous appendage at base of seeds. The genista of florists is Cytisus.

A. Branchlets 2-winged........ 1. *G. sagittalis*
AA. Branchlets terete.
  B. Color of fls. white........ 2. *G. monosperma*
  BB. Color of fls. yellow.
    C. Plant with spiny branchlets.
      D. Lvs. 3-foliolate........ 3. *G. horrida*
      DD. Lvs. simple.
        E. Shrub tufted, to 6 in........ 4. *G. silvestris*
        EE. Shrub not tufted, 1–2 ft.
          F. Fls. in racemes........ 5. *G. germanica*
          FF. Fls. in heads........ 6. *G. hispanica*
    CC. Plant not spiny.
      D. Branches rush-like, leafless: fls. scattered........ 7. *G. æthnensis*
      DD. Branches not rush-like: fls. in racemes.
        E. Lvs. 3-foliolate........ 8. *G. radiata*
        EE. Lvs. simple.
          F. Shrub prostrate: lvs. pubescent beneath........ 9. *G. pilosa*
          FF. Shrub upright: lvs. nearly glabrous beneath........ 10. *G. tinctoria*

1. **G. sagittalis,** L. (*Cytisus sagittalis,* Koch. *Genistella sagittalis,* Gams). Dwarf procumbent shrub less than 1 ft. high, with ascending or erect mostly simple broadly 2-winged branchlets: lvs. ovate to oblong, ½–¾in. long, villous: fls. yellow, in terminal racemes 1–1½ in. long, in late spring and early summer; corolla glabrous: pod linear-oblong, ¾in. long, silky, 3–6-seeded. Eu.

2. **G. monosperma,** Lam. To 10 ft. or more high, with slender grayish branches, almost leafless: lvs. simple or rarely 3-foliolate, linear or linear-spatulate, ¼–¾in. long, silky: fls. about ⅓in. long, white, fragrant, in short lateral racemes in early spring; calyx purple; corolla silky: pod broadly oval, ½in. long, 1–2-seeded. Spain, N. Afr.

3. **G. horrida,** DC. To 1½ ft., densely branched, with stiff spiny branchlets: lvs. of 3 linear pubescent lfts. about ⅓in. long: fls. yellow, ¼in. long, in terminal heads in summer: pod oval-oblong, ½–¾in. long, pubescent, 1–4-seeded. France, Spain.

4. **G. silvestris,** Scop. Tufted subshrub to 6 in., the flowering branchlets spiny: lvs. linear, to ½in. long, pubescent beneath: fls. golden-yellow, ⅓in. long, in terminal racemes to 4 in. long, in summer: pod ovoid, ½in. long, usually 1-seeded. S. E. Eu. Var. **pungens,** Vis. (*G. dalmatica,* Bartling), is more spiny.

5. **G. germanica,** L. To 2 ft., with upright spiny pubescent branchlets: lvs. elliptic-oblong, ½–¾in. long, pubescent beneath: fls. yellow, ⅓in. long, in terminal racemes to 2 in. long, in summer: pod elliptic, ⅓in. long, pubescent, few-seeded. Eu.

6. **G. hispanica,** L. SPANISH BROOM. From 1–2 ft. high, densely branched, spiny: lvs. ovate-lanceolate, ½in. long, pubescent: fls. golden-yellow, ⅓in. long, in terminal heads 1 in. or more across, in spring: pod oval, ⅓in. long, pubescent, 1–2-seeded. S. W. Eu.

7. **G. æthnensis,** DC. To 20 ft., with many slender rush-like branches, nearly leafless: lvs. linear, ¼–½in. long: fls. yellow, fragrant, ⅓in. long, scattered near ends of branches, in summer: pod oval, ½in. long, glabrous, 2–3-seeded. Sicily, Sardinia.

8. **G. radiata,** Scop. (*Spartium radiatum,* L.). To 3 ft., much-branched: lvs. of 3 linear-lanceolate lfts. ½in. long, pubescent beneath, soon falling: fls. yellow, ½in. long, in few-fld. heads about 1 in. across, in spring and early summer: pod elliptic, ½in. long, pubescent, 1–2-seeded. S. Eu.

9. **G. pilosa,** L. Prostrate, sts. rooting: lvs. obovate to oblong, ¼–½in. long, pubescent beneath: fls. yellow, ½in. long, 1–3 in the axils forming racemes 2–6 in. long, in spring and early summer, pubescent outside: pod linear, 1 in. long, silky-pubescent, 5–8-seeded. Eu.

10. **G. tinctoria,** L. (*G. sibirica*, Hort. *G. polygalæfolia*, Hort. not DC.). Dyers-Greenweed. Branches striped, glabrous or slightly pubescent, flowering sts. to 3 ft. high: lvs. oblong-elliptic or oblong-lanceolate, ½–1 in. long, nearly glabrous, ciliate: racemes many-fld., 1–3 in. long, panicled at ends of branches, in summer; corolla yellow, ½in. long, glabrous: pod narrow-oblong, ½–¾in. long, glabrous or slightly pubescent, 6–10-seeded. Eu., W. Asia; nat. in N. Amer.

40. **SPARTIUM,** L. (*Spartianthus*, Link). One shrub native in the Medit. region and Canary Isls., hardy in the S. and Cent. U. S.—Allied to Genista and Cytisus but chiefly distinguished by the 1-lipped calyx: branches leafless or with few lvs.: lvs. alternate, simple, entire, small: fls. papilionaceous, in loose terminal racemes; calyx split above, hence 1-lipped, with 5 minute teeth; keel incurved, acuminate; stamens 10, monadelphous: pod linear, compressed, many-seeded; seeds with callous appendage at base as in Cytisus. (Spar-tium: ancient Greek name.)

S. junceum, L. (*Genista juncea*, Lam.). Spanish or Weavers Broom. To 10 ft., the long slender terete green branches rush-like and almost leafless: lvs. few, oblanceolate to linear, ½–1½ in. long, bluish-green and slightly appressed-pubescent: fls. fragrant, yellow, about 1 in. long, with showy standard; lower edge of keel hairy: pod pubescent, 2–4 in. long.—Blooms summer and autumn or almost the entire year in Calif. There is a double-fld. form and also a var. with whitish fls.

41. **ULEX,** L. Furze. Gorse. Whin. About 25 species of spiny shrubs, one grown as a cover-plant and for ornament, native in W. and S. Eu. and N. Afr.—Lvs. mostly reduced to scales or represented by the thorn-like lf.-stalk, only the young vigorous shoots near the ground bearing fully developed 3-foliolate lvs.: fls. papilionaceous, yellow, showy, axillary, often crowded toward the ends of the branchlets; calyx 2-lipped to base; petals clawed, of almost equal length; standard ovate, wings and keel obtuse; stamens monadelphous, alternately longer and shorter; style curved: pod small, few-seeded, seeds appendaged. (U-lex: ancient Latin name.)

U. europæus, L. Much-branched, bushy, 2–4 ft., very spiny; branchlets striate, villous when young: lvs. scale-like or narrow-lanceolate, pubescent: fls. about ¾in. long, 1–3 in the axils, crowded toward the ends of the branchlets; corolla bright yellow, fragrant; calyx yellow, hairy: pod oblong, over ½in. long, villous, dark brown. W. and S. Eu.; somewhat nat. in N. Amer.—Spring and early summer and often again in autumn; in Calif. blooms almost the entire year.

42. **ANTHYLLIS,** L. Per. herbs or sometimes subshrubs, one planted for forage; about 35 species in Eu., N. Afr. and Asia.—Lvs. usually odd-pinnate: heads axillary or 2–3 apparently terminal at the tips of the branches: fls. pea-like; calyx-tube inflated near base, the limb toothed or lobed; petals long-clawed, the 4 lower mostly united with the stamen-tube; stamens coalescent into a tube, the upper often becoming distinct at fruiting: pod inclosed in calyx, 1- or few-seeded. (Anthyl-lis: Greek meaning *downy fls.*)

A. Vulneraria, L. Kidney Vetch. Woundwort. Deep-rooted often tufted clover-like plant about 1 ft. high, somewhat appressed-pubescent, the st. rather sparsely leafy: lower lvs. with oblong terminal lft. 1 in. long or more, the lateral lfts. much smaller or sometimes lacking; upper lvs. with lfts. often numerous and not very unequal: heads 1–1½ in. across, single or in pairs at the ends of the branches, each subtended by 1 or more digitate leafy bracts; fls. numerous, closely sessile, small, varying from pale or bright yellow to deep red; calyx hairy, much inflated, contracted at the mouth. (Vulneraria: Latin *wound*, from its ancient use in healing wounds.) Eu. and W. Asia, where it is grown for forage, but little used in N. Amer.; sometimes planted for ornament.

43. **LOTUS,** L. Herbs or sometimes subshrubs, more than 150 species in W. N. Amer., the Medit. region and other parts of the Old World, a few cult. for ornament and food.—Plants erect: lvs. various and often puzzling—sometimes lfts. apparently 3 on an evident petiole but with 2 other lfts. (sometimes interpreted as stipules) at the base of the apparent petiole which is then considered to be rachis, at other times 3, 4, 5, or more narrow lfts. sessile on the st. as if separate small simple lvs.: fls. papilio-

naceous or sometimes modified, solitary, twin or umbellate, subtended, yellow, purple to white; calyx-teeth narrow-acute, nearly or quite equal; standard broad; keel pointed; stamens 9 and 1; style glabrous: pod cylindrical, mostly several-seeded, 2-valved. (Lo-tus: classical name applied to different plants.)—The genus is not homogeneous.

A. Pod 4-winged .... 1. *L. tetragonolobus*
AA. Pod not winged.
  B. Lfts. broad, ovate to obovate .... 2. *L. corniculatus*
  BB. Lfts. narrow, linear to linear-oblong
    C. Fls. papilionaceous, ½in. long .... 3. *L. jacobæus*
    CC. Fls. hardly papilionaceous, with beak-like keel, 1 in. long .... 4. *L. Berthelotii*

1. **L. tetragonolobus,** L. (*Tetragonolobus purpureus,* Moench). WINGED PEA. Ann., spreading on ground, hirsute, sts. 6–16 in. long: main lfts. 3, elliptic to somewhat obovate, about 1 in. long and nearly as broad, entire: fls. 1 or 2, purplish-red, about ¾in. long, the slender calyx-lobes one-half length of corolla: pod 2–3 in. long, 4-sided and 4-angled, containing spherical-oblong smooth brown seeds ⅛in. crosswise. (Tetragonolobus means *four-angled pod,* used also as a generic name for this plant.) S. Eu.—The seeds and young pods are eaten.

2. **L. corniculatus,** L. BIRDS-FOOT TREFOIL. Per. with many decumbent or ascending hirsute or glabrate sts. 6–24 in. high: lfts. 5, of which 2 are stipular, ovate to oblanceolate, ½in. long more or less: fls. 3–10, umbellate, yellow sometimes tinged red, about ½in. long: pod linear, about 1 in. long. Eu. and Asia, and adventive in N. Amer. and elsewhere.—Cult. for ornament, with a double-fld. form, and useful for forage.

3. **L. jacobæus,** L. ST. JAMES TREFOIL (as the name suggests, from the island of Santiago or St. James, of the Cape Verdes). Per., somewhat shrubby, 1–3 ft.: lfts. 3–5, practically sessile to the st., linear, ½–1 in. long, slightly hairy: fls. 3–6. sessile in an umbel, about ½in. long, black-purple varying to yellow on same plant: pod cylindrical, glabrous.

4. **L. Berthelotii,** Masf. (*L. peliorhynchus,* Hook. f.). Gray-pubescent much-branched bush, 2 ft.: lfts. 3–7, narrow-linear, about ½in. long, sessile to st., looking like small fascicled lvs.: fls. few together, about 1 in. long, scarlet fading orange, varying to dark crimson and spotted, standard narrow and recurved, keel long-pointed and exceeding the wings, making an odd bloom. (Named for Sabin Berthelot, page 39; sometimes mistakenly written Bertholetii.) Cape Verde and Canary Isls.—Grown under glass and in Calif.

44. **CLITORIA,** L. BUTTERFLY PEA. Twining per. herbs or shrubs, about 30 species in warm and temp. countries, 1 in N. Amer.; one species grown for ornament under glass in the N. and in the open far S.—Lvs. odd-pinnate, of 5–9 lfts.; stipules persistent, stipels always present: fls. axillary, large and showy, solitary or racemose, white, blue, reddish, violet; calyx tubular, with 5 teeth shorter than or not exceeding the tube; standard large and erect, not appendaged; wings somewhat adherent to the short keel; stamens 9 and 1, more or less imperfectly diadelphous; style long and incurved, hairy on the inner side: pod stipitate, long and narrow, compressed. (Clitoria: an old name of no significance.)

C. ternatea, L. Tall slender climber with pubescent sts.: lfts. 5–9, oval or oblong, obtuse, 1–2 in. long: fls. solitary and nearly sessile, 1–1½ in. long, the calyx subtended by orbicular bracts, corolla bright blue with lighter markings: pod 3–4½ in. long, ⅓in. broad, flat, beaked; seeds nearly black. Tropics, probably Asian but widely spread; name from the island of Ternate in the Moluccas.

45. **APIOS,** Medic. Five twining herbs with tuber-bearing roots, occasionally planted, 2 species in E. N. Amer. and 3 in Asia.—Lvs. odd-pinnate; lfts. 3–9, obscurely stipellate: fls. papilionaceous, in short dense often branching racemes; calyx somewhat 2-lipped, the 2 lateral teeth being nearly obsolete, the upper united and very short, the lower one longest; standard broad, reflexed; keel incurved, finally coiled; stamens 9 and 1: pod straight or slightly curved, linear, elongate, thickish, many-seeded. (A-pios: Greek *pear,* alluding to the shape of the tubers.)

A. americana, Medic. (*Glycine Apios,* L. *A. tuberosa,* Moench). GROUNDNUT. POTATO BEAN. WILD BEAN. Climbing 4–8 ft. high; root bearing strings of edible tubers 1–2 in. long: lfts. 5–7, ovate-lanceolate, 1–4 in. long: fls. chocolate-brown, to ½in. long, fragrant, in late summer; standard without appendages at summit: pod 2–4 in. long. N. B. to Minn. south to Fla. and Tex.

46. **KENNEDYA,** Vent. About a dozen more or less woody trailers and twiners, Australian, grown under glass and in the open in Calif. for ornament.—Sts. usually pubescent or hairy: lfts. commonly 3, sometimes 5 or even only 1, stipellate, entire or 3-lobed; stipules present, often prominent: fls. red to purple-black, large and usually showy, papilionaceous, often long and slender, axillary, sometimes solitary but usually in pairs, umbels or racemes; calyx somewhat 2-lipped, the 2 upper lobes united; standard broad, auriculate at base; wings about as long as the acute keel and jointed to it; stamens 9 and 1; style inflexed, beardless, the stigma terminal: pod narrow, flattened or terete, septate between seeds. (Kenned-ya: Lewis Kennedy, 1775–1818, of the English nursery firm of Kennedy & Lee.)

A. Fls. nearly black, slender .... 1. *K. nigricans*
AA. Fls. red, broad .... 2. *K. prostrata*

1. **K. nigricans,** Lindl. Robust pubescent twiner: lfts. mostly 3, sometimes 1, broad-ovate to rhomboid-ovate, 2–4 in. long, entire, obtuse and often emarginate: fls. secund-racemose, about 1 in. long, narrow, purple-black with green blotches on standard: pod flattened.

2. **K. prostrata,** R. Br. Sts. pubescent to nearly glabrous: lfts. 3, broad-obovate to orbicular, entire, not 1 in. long, stipules large and cordate: fls. scarlet, about ¾in. long, 2–4 terminating a long peduncle: pod nearly cylindrical, pubescent, 1½–2 in. long. Var. **major,** DC. (*K. Marryattæ,* Lindl.), a larger and more hairy plant, the lvs. strongly undulate and stipules sometimes as much as 1 in. across; fls. deep scarlet and larger.

47. **HARDENBERGIA,** Benth. Three woody Australian twining vines, grown as are the Kennedyas, differing in technical characters: fls. small, more numerous in the raceme, not running to very dark reds or purple-blacks, keel obtuse and shorter than the wings; lfts. in one species reduced to 1. (Hardenber-gia: named after Franziska, Countess of Hardenberg.)—The genus is sometimes united with Kennedya.

A. Lfts. 3 or 5 .... 1. *H. Comptoniana*
AA. Lft. 1 .... 2. *H. violacea*

1. **H. Comptoniana,** Benth. (*Kennedya Comptoniana,* Link). Lfts. 3, sometimes 5 and then the lateral ones 2 close together on either side, oval to narrow-lanceolate, 1½–3½ in. long, obtuse: fls. blue or violet-blue (a white var.), less than ½in. long, in 2's, 3's, or 4's along the raceme: pod flat or at least compressed, 1½–2 in. long. (Named in honor of Lady Northampton, the family name being Compton.)

2. **H. violacea,** Stearn (*Glycine violacea,* Schneevogt. *G. bimaculata,* Curt. *Kennedya monophylla,* Vent. *H. monophylla,* Benth. *H. bimaculata,* Domin. *H. ovata,* Benth.). Lft. commonly 1, 2–4 in. long, ovate, oblong-ovate, to narrow-lanceolate, obtuse: fls. less than ½in. long, white, rose, violet but not blue, in 2's or 3's in long prominent racemes: pod turgid, about 1½ in. long.

48. **PSOPHOCARPUS,** Neck. Five twining tuberous-rooted herbs in the tropics of Asia and Afr., one intro. as a food plant in trop. and subtrop. parts.—Lfts. 3, stipellate, and the stipules 2-parted: fls. prominent, few or several in a close nodulose raceme terminating an axillary peduncle, purplish; calyx slightly 2-lobed, the lower lobes blunt and equalling the upper; standard broad, auricled at base; keel incurved; stamens 9 and 1, the odd one sometimes free only at base; style prominent and incurved, stigma terminal with dense hairs around and below it: pod long, square in cross-section and 4-winged, filled between the seeds. (Psophocar-pus: Greek combination alluding to the sound the frs. make when they explode, being laid in the sun.)

P. tetragonolobus, DC. GOA BEAN. ASPARAGUS PEA. Ann., making an edible root tuber, and also prized for the edible young pods; st. glabrous: lfts. broad-ovate or deltoid-ovate, acuminate, 3–6 in. long: fls. bright blue, about 1¼ in. long: pod 6–9 in. long and 1 in. broad including the jagged wings; seeds nearly globular, ¼in. or somewhat more across, brown and shining, smooth, with very small hilum. India.

49. **PACHYRRHIZUS,** Rich. YAM BEAN. Five species of twining or erect perennials grown for their edible tuberous roots, little known in our territory; originally native in trop. Amer. but now widely nat. in the tropics of the Old World.—Sts. herbaceous or woody at base, hairy, pubescent or glabrate: lfts. 3, often lobed or strongly angled, stipellate: fls. violet or white, on fascicled pedicels in racemes

with swollen nodes, bracts setaceous and caducous; standard very broad, auriculate at base; keel obtuse and incurved; stamens 9 and 1; style compressed above and bearded along inner side; stigma more or less globose with tip involute: pod large, narrow, compressed or turgid, depressed or constricted between the ovate or very broad flattened seeds. (Pachyrrhi-zus: *thick root.*)

A. Terminal lft. lobed or dentate, rarely entire: seeds ¼–⅜in. long................1. *P. erosus*
AA. Terminal lft. entire: seeds ½in. long..2. *P. tuberosus*

1. **P. erosus,** Urban (*Dolichos erosus,* L. *P. angulatus,* Rich. *Cacara erosa,* Kuntze). Tubers simple or lobed, to 12 in. diam.: sts. trailing or climbing, to 18 ft. long: lfts. 1–6 in. long, the terminal rhomboidal or ovate-reniform, lateral ovate or rhomboidal, all dentate or palmately lobed, rarely entire: fls. violet or white, ⅝–⅞in. long; wings as long as standard and keel equalling or somewhat exceeding wings: pod 3–5½ in. long and ½–⅝in. broad, finely strigose; seeds almost square, ¼–⅜in. long and broad, poisonous. Mex. and Cent. Amer.—Much cult. in trop. regions for the edible tubers and widely nat. in tropics of Old World.

2. **P. tuberosus,** Spreng. (*Dolichos tuberosus,* Lam. *Cacara tuberosa,* Britt.). Tubers very large: sts. 10–25 ft. long: lfts. 3–10 in. long, the terminal rhomboid-acuminate, lateral unsymmetrical and more or less triangular, all entire: fls. violet or white, ¾–1 in. long; wings as long as standard and keel somewhat exceeding wings: pod 2½–12 in. long and ½–¾in. broad, beaked, reddish-hairy; seeds 6–8, large, about ½in. long and ⅓in. broad, red or black, poisonous. S. Amer. but widely spread in American tropics.—Roots and young pods eaten.

50. **PHASEOLUS,** L. Bean. A wide range of annuals and perennials, mostly in warm and trop. countries, usually herbs but a few woody at base, grown somewhat for ornament but mostly for the edible seeds and pods; the known species are probably 150–200, when the extensive synonymy shall have been reduced.—Mostly twining, some forms erect: lvs. pinnately 3-foliolate but sometimes reduced to 1 lft., stipulate and stipellate, the stipules persistent, lfts. entire: fls. few to many, racemose or fascicled on axillary peduncles, white, yellow, red, purple, papilionaceous, closely subtended by 2 bracts like an outer calyx which are sometimes deciduous; lobes of calyx equalling or exceeding its tube; keel coiled, being the distinctive mark of the genus; stamens 9 and 1; style bearded longitudinally: pod compressed or with convex sides, several- to many-seeded, dehiscent; germination hypogeal or epigeal. (Phase-olus: ancient name.)—The species of Phaseolus in general cult. are few, but the oriental kinds are in the country and should be understood.

A. Standard of fls. contorted; keel forming 4–5 spirals........................1. *P. Caracalla*
AA. Standard of fls. not contorted; keel forming 1–2 spirals.
B. Color of fls. white, cream-colored, violet or red.
C. Lfts. retuse or at least obtuse: plant with deep fleshy per. root: fls. reddish-purple..........2. *P. Metcalfei*
CC. Lfts. acute or pointed: ann. or grown as such.
D. Seeds (beans) on the small oblong or globular order, usually ⅝in. or less long, not broad or prominently flattened.
E. Calyx-bracts small and inconspicuous, much shorter than calyx itself...3. *P. acutifolius*
EE. Calyx-bracts broad and prominent, ovate, nearly equalling or exceeding calyx..........4. *P. vulgaris*
DD. Seeds on the large broad order, usually nearly or quite as wide as long, often very flat.
E. Fls. large and showy, mostly more than ½in. long, white or scarlet.....5. *P. coccineus*
EE. Fls. small, ⅜in. or less long, white or cream-color.
F. Calyx-bracts oval, strong-veined: pod thin-edged with sharp long beak..........6. *P. lunatus*
FF. Calyx-bracts linear, not strongly veined: pod thick-edged, large, with blunt or short tip..........7. *P. limensis*
BB. Color of fls. clear yellow: oriental beans.
C. Lfts. entire, or sometimes broadly 2- or 3-lobed.
D. Plant and pods very hairy or even shaggy: seeds usually dull.
E. Seeds (beans) oblong, blackish, with concave hilum or scar: pod long-hairy..........8. *P. Mungo*
EE. Seeds nearly or quite globular, green, brown, yellow, rarely blackish, the hilum not concave: pod short-hairy..........9. *P. aureus*
DD. Plant and pods glabrous or only thinly hairy: seeds glossy.
E. Pods constricted between seeds: hilum or scar not concave..........10. *P. angularis*
EE. Pods continuous: hilum concave..........11. *P. calcaratus*
CC. Lfts. parted to base into 3–5 narrow divisions..........12. *P. aconitifolius*

1. **P. Caracalla,** L. Snail-Flower. Corkscrew-Flower. Per., twining to 20 ft.: lfts. ovate, 3–5 in. long and 2–4 in. broad, acute or acuminate, slightly pubescent on both sides: fls. several on peduncles 4–8 in. long, white or yellow with pink or lilac wings, 2 in.

long, fragrant; calyx-bracts ovate, deciduous; standard contorted, reflexed; keel forming 4–5 spirals: pod linear, 6–7 in. long and ½in. broad; seeds nearly globose, ⅛in. long, brown. S. American tropics.

2. **P. Metcalfei,** Woot. & Standl. (*P. retusus*, Benth. not Moench). METCALFE BEAN, intro. as a forage plant in the S. W. by J. K. Metcalfe. Per., with a large fleshy deep root; sts. puberulent, trailing 10–12 ft. or more: lfts. thick, rhombic to oblong, 2–3 in. long and nearly as broad, obtuse and usually retuse, rough-puberulent on both sides, with prominent veins: fls. many on rigid peduncles scarcely exceeding the lvs., reddish-purple; calyx hairy; bracts subulate and short: pod flat, broad-oblong, 1¾–2½ in. long, somewhat curved; seeds circular, compressed, ⅝in. across, brown-black. New Mex., Ariz., Mex.

3. **P. acutifolius,** Gray, var. **latifolius,** Freem. TEPARY BEAN. Slender lightly pubescent or glabrate ann., bushy on poor land but otherwise making a twining vine several ft. long: lfts. ovate to broad-lanceolate, 2–3 in. long, pointed, entire, petioles 1–4 in. long: fls. 2–5 on peduncles mostly much shorter than lvs., white or light violet, about ⅓in. long; calyx-bracts very small and deciduous: pod 2–3 in. long and about ⅓in. broad, compressed, rimmed on the margins, prominently sharp-beaked, finely pubescent; seeds roundish to oblong, ¼–⅜in. long, convex or somewhat flattened, white, yellow, brown or bluish-black; germination epigeal. Ariz. and Mex.—Intro. as a drought-resistant food-plant for the dry beans.

4. **P. vulgaris,** L. KIDNEY BEAN. The common garden pole bean (Haricot of the French), grown for the dry or somewhat immature ("shell") seeds and some vars. for the edible pods ("string" beans). Ann., pubescent, tall-twining: lfts. broad-ovate to rhombic-ovate, 4–6 in. long, entire, long-acuminate: fls. few at or near the apex of peduncles shorter than lvs., white, ochroleucous, or violet-purple, ½–¾in. long; calyx-bracts broad, ovate-pointed, strongly several-nerved, mostly equalling the calyx: pod slender with convex or rounded sides, pubescent or glabrate, straight or somewhat curved, 4–8 in. long, with prominent beak; seeds globular to oblong, mostly not exceeding ⅝in. long and often much less, white, brown, blue-black or speckled in great variety; germination epigeal. Probably of American origin.—Cult. in such vars. as Horticultural Pole bean, Old Homestead, Dutch Case-Knife, Kentucky Wonder, Creaseback. Var. **humilis,** Alef. (*P. nanus*, Auth. not L.), is the common BUSH BEAN of gardens and farms, differing in its low stature and non-climbing habit.

5. **P. coccineus,** L. (*P. multiflorus*, Lam. *Lipusa multiflora*, Alef.). MULTIFLORA BEAN. SCARLET RUNNER. Per. but grown as an ann., tall-twining: lfts. broadly rhombic-ovate, 3–5 in. long, entire: fls. several to many, mostly ¾–1 in. long, on strong long peduncles nearly equalling the lvs. and sometimes exceeding them, bright scarlet; calyx-bracts lanceolate to linear-lanceolate and about equalling the calyx: pod 4–12 in. and more long, plump, lightly pubescent or glabrate, beak rather stout; seeds broad-oblong, ¾–1 in. long and two-thirds as broad, not tapering at ends, convex-flattened, nearly black with red markings; germination hypogeal. American tropics. Var. **rubronanus,** Bailey, bushy, not climbing; fls. red or scarlet; not often seen. Var. **albus,** Bailey (*Lipusa multiflora* var. *alba*, Alef.), WHITE DUTCH RUNNER, fls. and seeds white; grown mostly for the edible seeds. Var. **albonanus,** Bailey, plant bushy, not climbing; cult. for its white beans; it has been grown as a dwarf lima.

6. **P. lunatus,** L. SIEVA BEAN. Slender lightly pubescent or glabrate ann., with thin lvs.: lfts. not very large, broad-ovate, 2–3½ in. long, entire, sharp-pointed, side-veined: fls. many, small, ⅜in. or less long, white or ochroleucous, many in a long open peduncled raceme of variable length; calyx-bracts oval, nearly or quite equalling calyx, with strong central and usually 2 side nerves: pod 2–3½ in. long, flat, about ¾in. broad, thin-edged often broadening toward the apex, papery in texture and slightly pubescent, the beak very sharp and often strongly ascending, early dehiscing into twisting valves; seeds flat and thin, about ½in. long, rhomboidal in outline, with radiating lines, white, brown, red or speckled; germination epigeal. Trop. Amer.—Much cult., a heavy cropper; known also as Carolina, Civet, and Sewee bean. Var. **lunonanus,** Bailey, DWARF SIEVA BEAN, known also as dwarf lima; bush form, not climbing. Var. **salicis,** Bailey, WILLOW-LEAF BEAN, lfts. narrow-lanceolate to linear-lanceolate, 3–6 in. long, ½–¾in. broad.

7. **P. limensis,** Macf. LIMA BEAN. Per. but grown as ann., a much stouter stronger higher-climbing later-flowering plant than no. 6, pubescent, with thick heavy lvs.: lfts. long-angular-ovate or lance-ovate, 3–5 in. long, long-pointed but not sharp, thick in texture: fls. much as in *P. lunatus*, but calyx-bracts only one-third as long as calyx: pod large, thick and heavy, 3–5 in. long and often 1 in. broad, margins thick and sometimes double-ridged, the beak short, stout and blunt, tardily dehiscing; seeds larger than in no. 6, plump, white; germination epigeal. Probably trop. Amer. Var. **limenanus,** Bailey, (*P. lunatus* var. *limenanus*, Burkhart), BUSH or DWARF LIMA, plant bushy, not climbing.

8. **P. Mungo,** L. URD. BLACK GRAM. Plant spreading, 1–3 ft. high, prominently hairy, ann.: lfts. ovate to rhombic-ovate, 2–4 in. long, acuminate-pointed: fls. at the summit of a short peduncle that elongates in fr., yellow, ¼in. or less long; calyx-bracts linear and equalling or exceeding the keel: pod nearly terete, 1½–2 in. long, erect or spreading,

long-hairy, with a very short hooked beak; seeds oblong with square ends, ⅛in. or a little more long, mostly black, with white concave hilum; germination epigeal. Probably native in India.—There is a twining form.

9. **P. aureus,** Roxb. MUNG. GREEN or GOLDEN GRAM. Ann., a taller and more erect plant than no. 8, sometimes slightly twining at the tips: calyx-bracts ovate: pod 2½–4 in. long, slender, very short-hairy; seeds rather smaller, usually green, sometimes yellow and brown, the white hilum not concave; germination epigeal. (Mung and Mungo are native vernacular names.) Not known wild, but probably Indian.

10. **P. angularis,** Wight. ADZUKI BEAN. Bushy and erect ann., 1–2½ ft. high: lfts. ovate to rhombic-ovate, 2–3½ in. long, entire or shallowly 3-lobed, abruptly short-pointed: fls. bright yellow, 2–12 on axillary short peduncles; calyx-bracts ovate-lanceolate: pod cylindrical, 2½–5 in. long and ¼in. or less broad, glabrous, constricted between the seeds when mature, with short blunt beak; seeds 6–10, oblong, about ¼in. or less long, squared or slightly rounded at ends, not flattened, in many colors, as red-brown, blue-black, maroon, straw-colored to nearly white, with long white hilum not concave; germination hypogeal. Asia.—Much grown in Japan and China and best known of the oriental beans in this country.

11. **P. calcaratus,** Roxb. RICE BEAN. Half-climbing ann., from 12–30 in. high and making sts. 3–6 ft. long: lfts. ovate to broad-ovate, often somewhat rhombic, 2½–3½ in. long, short-acute to acuminate, entire or rarely 3-lobed: fls. bright yellow, several to many in axillary racemes; calyx-bracts subulate, much exceeding the calyx: pod slender, 3–5 in. long and about ¼in. broad, mostly curved or falcate, finely pubescent or glabrous, the beak prominent but not sharp; seeds 6–10, oblong, ¼–⅓in. long, rounded at ends, with a straight concave hilum, brown, maroon, black, straw-colored; germination hypogeal. Asia.

12. **P. aconitifolius,** Jacq. MOTH BEAN. Distinguished by the lfts. being divided into 3–5 narrow lobes ¼–⅓in. broad: trailing or diffuse lightly hairy ann. 1–2 ft. high: fls. yellow, very small, in close clusters on the ends of axillary peduncles, the bracts narrow and long-pointed: pod 1–2 in. long, nearly cylindrical, glabrous, with short blunt beak; seeds 5–7, very small, oblong, ⅛–3/16in. long, somewhat rounded at the ends, clay-colored or marbled with black, the hilum small; germination hypogeal. Probably native in India.

51. **DOLICHOS,** L. Trop. ann. and per. herbs and subshrubs, prostrate or partially erect but mostly long-twining, a few grown for ornament and the edible seeds; species probably upwards of 50, mostly in the eastern hemisphere.—Dolichos is technically distinguished by the narrow keel bent inward and upward at right angles rather than curved as in Vigna or coiled as in Phaseolus; the stigma is terminal, below which the style is bearded: lvs. pinnately 3-foliolate, stipellate, the stipules very small: fls. white, reddish to purple, solitary, or usually somewhat fascicled in nodulose racemes; standard very broad, auricled at base; wings adnate to the keel; stamens 9 and 1: pod large, flat, usually curved, beaked; seeds globose or flattened. (Dol-ichos: old Greek name of a bean.)

A. Pod ⅝in. or more broad at maturity and 2 in. or more long........................1. *D. Lablab*
AA. Pod linear, about 1 in. long..2. *D. lignosus*

1. **D. Lablab,** L. (*Lablab vulgaris*, Savi. *D. soudanensis*, Hort.). HYACINTH BEAN. BONAVIST. LABLAB (Egyptian name adopted by Linnæus). Potential per., but grown as an ann., immensely variable and therefore assuming many cultural forms; sts. twining, lightly hairy to glabrate, usually 5–10 ft. but sometimes reaching 30 ft. and some forms are dwarf or bush: lfts. very broad-ovate, the lateral ones lopsided, 3–6 in. long and sometimes equally broad, rather abruptly slender-acuminate: fls. purple or white, 2–4 at each node in an elongating raceme, ½ to nearly 1 in. long: pod flat, 1–2½ in. long, close-pubescent or smooth, papery, straight or somewhat curved on back but very convex in outline on front with a long upward curve toward the very prominent slender beak, sometimes truncate-retuse at end; seeds black or nearly so (white in the white-fld. forms), flat, oblong with rounded ends, ⅓in. or less long, the hilum and raphe long and prominent; germination epigeal. Probably Old World tropics but now widely cult. for food.—Prussic acid (poisonous) has been found in seeds of colored kinds; a "stringless" form, eaten as are string beans, has thick whitish retuse pods 3 in. and more long and 1 in. broad and borne 6–9 together, white fls., very large lvs. and heavy growth; the name "hyacinth bean" is more properly applied to the common ornamental form with showy violet-purple fls., purple-tinged sts., and black or purple-black seeds, known in the var. Darkness; the white-fld. forms, as in Daylight, are less known as ornamentals.

2. **D. lignosus,** L. AUSTRALIAN PEA. Evergreen somewhat woody per., slender, lightly pubescent: lfts. small, about 1½ in. or less long, triangular-ovate-acuminate and apiculate: fls. white or rose-purple, less than ½in. long, few in a close cluster on the end of an elongated peduncle: pod about 1 in. long, glabrous, containing black seeds. Probably Asian.

52. **VIGNA,** Savi. Herbs of warm and trop. countries, probably 60 species or more, a few grown for food and forage.—Vigna differs technically from Phaseolus in the fact that the keel is arched or curved inward rather than coiled and the fls. usually few and somewhat capitate (or close) rather than open-racemed: mostly twining, and ours ann.: lvs. pinnately 3-foliolate, stipulate: fls. whitish, yellowish, or purplish, mostly in alternate pairs on ends of very long peduncles, often falling soon after opening, the bracts caducous, and usually cushion-like nectaries between the fls.; standard broad and large, exceeding the wings, auricled at base; stamens 9 and 1; style bearded along inner side, the stigma lateral and oblique or introrse beyond which is a short beak: pod slender and often very long, nearly terete and sometimes slightly inflated; seeds various, small, not broad and flat. (Vig-na: Dominicus Vigna, Italian scientist of the 17th century.)—Most vignas are ann.; a few are per. and some are somewhat woody. Three species are in common cult., very likely all forms of one.

A. Pod more than 1–3 ft. long, pendent, more or less inflated and flabby when green . . 1. *V. sesquipedalis*
AA. Pod 12 in. or less, hard and firm, not at all inflated or flabby when green.
B. Seed mostly more than ¼in. long: pod 8–12 in. long, pendent . . . . 2. *V. sinensis*
BB. Seed mostly less than ¼in. long: pod 3–5 in. long, erect or ascending . . . . 3. *V. cylindrica*

1. **V. sesquipedalis,** Fruwirth (*Dolichos sesquipedalis*, L. *V. sinensis* var. *sesquipedalis*, Koern.). Asparagus Bean. Yard-long Bean. Strong long-running glabrous or glabrate ann.: lfts. rhomboid-ovate, 3–5 in. long, entire or seldom obscurely angled, the mature ones very short-pointed: fls. ochroleucous or violet, ¾–1 in. long, 2 or 3 on the end of a long peduncle, opening in early morning and closed flat by noon then soon falling; calyx-lobes lance-acuminate: pod at length hanging, often prone on the ground, upward of 1–3 ft. long and mostly less than ½in. broad, rather thick or fleshy, soft and somewhat inflated or flabby, shrinking when dry; seeds ⅜–½in. long and little more than half as broad, oblong or long-reniform, rounded at ends, not much if any compressed, mostly brown with a long white hilum; germination epigeal. Probably S. Asian, but now widely spread.—Grown for forage and human food: the long seeds and long soft shriveling pods distinguish the species; *sesquipedalis* is Latin for *a foot and a half*, but the pods do not always reach that length.

2. **V. sinensis,** Savi (*Dolichos sinensis*, L.). Cowpea. Like no. 1 in herbage: pod 8–12 in. long, pendent, not flabby or inflated when green; seeds about ¼–½in. long, usually smaller than in no. 1, globose to short-reniform, in many shades and markings, the solid colors being mostly brown, clay, white, maroon, purplish, and nearly black. Probably Asian.

3. **V. cylindrica,** Skeels (*Phaseolus cylindricus*, L. *V. Catjang*, Walp. *Dolichos Catjang*, Burm.). Catjang (an oriental vernacular name). Less developed in its pods, which are only 3–5 in. long and erect or only spreading, not flabby or inflated; seeds small, mostly not ¼in. long, oblong or cylindrical or slightly reniform, about as thick as broad. Probably Asian.—Little known in cult.

53. **STIZOLOBIUM,** P. Br. (*Mucuna*, Adans., in part). Velvet Bean. Ann. very strong twiners, about a dozen species from the Old World tropics, some planted far S. for forage and also for ornament.—Lfts. 3, broad, with bristle-like stipels; stipules small, lanceolate: fls. large and prominent, papilionaceous, mostly in 3's in long nodulose racemes, early shedding, 1¼–1¾ in. long, white or dark purple; calyx 2-lipped, lower teeth at least equalling the upper; standard much shorter than keel which is straight for part of its length and then curved upward; stamens 9 and 1; style filiform, usually pubescent nearly to tip but not bearded, the stigma terminal and small: pod turgid and thick or sometimes flattened, heavy, more or less ridged lengthwise, hairy or velvety; seeds large, subglobose to oblong; germination hypogeal. (Stizolo-bium: Greek compound *stinging pods*, from the hairs on the first described species.)—Several species have been intro. into the U. S. for test, but only two or three are yet prominent.

A. Pod with velvety-black pubescence . . . . 1. *S. Deeringianum*
AA. Pod with appressed white pubescence.
B. Fls. dark purple . . . . 2. *S. Hassjoo*
BB. Fls. white . . . . 3. *S. niveum*

1. **S. Deeringianum,** Bort (*Dolichos multiflorus*, Hort. not Torr. *Mucuna Deeringiana*, Small). Florida Velvet Bean. Running to great length, even 50 ft. and more, somewhat white-pubescent: lfts. ovate or rhomboid-ovate, 2–6 in. long, entire, acuminate and cuspidate, pubescent beneath and less so above: fls. 5–30 in a long pendent raceme or thyrse, solitary or mostly 2 or 3 together, purple, 1½ in. or more long: calyx large, white-pubescent, upper lip broad-triangular, middle lobe beneath longest; standard less than

half length of keel: pod 2–3 in. long, turgid, ridged, densely nearly black-pubescent; seeds 3–5, nearly globular, speckled, streaked, and marbled brown or black on a whitish ground, hilum less than half length of seed. Probably S. Asia or Malaya.—First described from plants growing in Fla., and dedicated to William Deering, patron of hort. in that state.

2. **S. Hassjoo,** Piper & Tracy. YOKOHAMA BEAN. Slender, to 20 ft., sparingly white-pubescent: lfts. ovate, somewhat acute and abruptly mucronate, 4–5 in. long, slightly white-pubescent above and beneath: fls. dark purple, 1½ in. long, in racemes 4–6 in. long; calyx saccate, densely pubescent, lower lobe half longer than lateral ones: pod 3–4½ in. long, with white appressed pubescence and prominent side ridge; seeds 3–6, oblong and flattened something like a plump lima bean, ash-colored, sometimes blackened at the ends. (Hassjoo: a vernacular name.) Probably Japanese.—An early-maturing species.

3. **S. niveum,** Kuntze. LYON BEAN. Known by its undulate lf. surfaces, very long fl.-clusters, white fls., white-pubescent strongly ridged pods 4–5 in. long, and flattish seeds. Probably S. Asia and Philippines.

54. **PUERARIA,** DC. About a dozen species of per. twining herbs and shrubs, in farther Asia and Pacific isls., one much planted for arbors and other ornament.—Lfts. 3, large, stipellate, sometimes lobed; stipules present, sometimes herbaceous: fls. blue or purple, in long axillary knotted racemes, papilionaceous, the narrow bracts early caducous; calyx more or less 2-lipped, half or more as long as petals; standard broad, auricled at base; wings somewhat adherent to keel; stamens 9 and 1; style incurved, beardless, the stigma apical and small: pod long and narrow, more or less flattened, many-seeded. (Puera-ria: bears the name of a European botanist, N. Puerari, 1765–1845.)

P. Thunbergiana, Benth. (*Pachyrrhizus Thunbergianus*, Sieb. & Zucc. *Pueraria hirsuta*, Schneid. not Kurz. *Dolichos japonicus*, Hort.). KUDZU-VINE. Very long-running hairy vine, somewhat woody, with tough thickened or tuberous roots: lfts. broad-ovate to rhombic-ovate or nearly orbicular, 3–6 in. long, entire or shallowly lobed, abruptly very sharp-pointed, hairy-pubescent: fls. purple, ½–¾in. long, in a long dense axillary raceme from which the narrow pointed bracts soon fall, appearing in late summer and fragrant: pod flat, oblong-linear, 2–4 in. long, hairy. China, Japan.

55. **CANAVALIA,** DC. Ann. and per. erect or strong twining and trailing herbs, one or two grown far S. for ornament and the edible beans; about two dozen or more species widely spread in the tropics.—Lfts. 3, mostly coriaceous: fls. rather large, papilionaceous, white, rose, bluish or violet, in tubercled axillary racemes; calyx 2-lipped, the upper lip much exceeding the lower; standard orbicular, the sides turned back; wings narrow and free; keel incurved; stamens 10, monadelphous or one partly free; style incurved with the keel, beardless, the small stigma terminal: pod large and woody, flat, with a strong rib on either side near upper margin; seeds large and flat. (Canava-lia: an aboriginal name.)

A. Plant erect: hilum half as long as seed. . . . . .1. *C. ensiformis*
AA. Plant twining: hilum nearly as long as seed. . . . . .2. *C. gladiata*

1. **C. ensiformis,** DC. (*Dolichos ensiformis*, L.). JACK BEAN. Erect or semi-erect, 2–4 ft., glabrate: lfts. ovate-oblong to elliptic, 3–5 in. long, acute or acuminate and mucronate: fls. purple, 1 in. or more long, in pendulous racemes 10–15 in. long: pod 8–14 in. long and about 1 in. broad, slightly curved, ridges moderately marked and sides usually plane; seeds 10–14, ¾in. long and about ½in. broad, compressed but plump, white, with brown hilum one-half their length; germination epigeal. W. Indies.

2. **C. gladiata,** DC. SWORD BEAN. Twining: pod 10–12 in. long, about 1½ in. broad, much curved, ridges very strong, often wrinkled on the sides or valves; seeds ¾–1 in. long, very flat, usually red, pink or brown, the narrow hilum running nearly their length. Old World tropics.

56. **ERYTHRINA,** L. CORAL-TREE. Mostly woody plants, but sometimes with herbaceous top, bearing showy fls., grown for ornament within our territory; species probably 50 or so in warm temp. and trop. regions around the world.—Plants mostly spiny: lvs. alternate, with 3 broad lfts., and glanduliform stipels: fls. usually large and bright colored, mostly scarlet, fascicled or in pairs in dense racemes, papilionaceous or nearly so, soon falling; calyx mostly oblique or 2-lipped, sometimes more or less equally 5-toothed, sometimes splitting to base; standard broad or narrow, sometimes on a long stalk-like base; wings frequently wanting; stamens either mona-

delphous or diadelphous (9 and 1); style incurved and beardless, the stigma small and terminal: fr. a long stipitate 2-valved pod constricted between the seeds, the latter often highly colored. (Erythri-na: Greek *red,* from the color of the fls.)—Some of the arboreous species are grown in coffee and cocoa plantations to provide the requisite shade, often under the name "immortelles"; the fls. appear mostly when the plant is not in lf. Within the U. S. the erythrinas are somewhat grown far S. for the brilliant fls., one species (no. 1) more or less under glass.

A. Fls. opening wide—the standard erect at full anthesis, usually very broad, standing at right angles to direction of wings and keel.
  B. Petioles strongly armed: calyx nearly truncate at full anthesis........... 1. *E. Crista-galli*
  BB. Petioles usually unarmed: calyx strongly oblique, splitting to base on back 2. *E. indica*
AA. Fls. closed in full anthesis—the standard in the same plane as wings and keel, covering them.
  B. Sts. ann. (herbaceous): fls. narrow, the standard when folded together usually $\frac{3}{16}$in. or less broad ....3. *E. herbacea*
  BB. Sts. persistent (woody): standard when folded ¼in. or more broad.
    C. Petioles glabrous, usually armed; stipels not prominent: calyx truncate, teeth not evident..4. *E. Corallodendrum*
    CC. Petioles more or less puberulous, unarmed; gland-form stipels large: calyx obliquely 2-labiate or splitting, the teeth usually evident...........5. *E. caffra*

1. E. **Crista-galli,** L. COCKSPUR CORAL-TREE. Shrub or small tree, the flowering branches dying back after blooming and strong ones arising from the root or stock; sts. with flat strong spines: petioles and sometimes the midribs stoutly armed; lfts. ovate-oblong to oblong-lanceolate, 4–6 in. long, or on the upper lvs. oval and smaller, firm in texture, entire, short-acute or muticous, glabrous: fls. brilliant crimson, about 2 in. long, the broad standard open and erect at full anthesis but at other times closed down over the shorter keel and still shorter rounded wings; calyx short and nearly truncate. Brazil.—Apparently the commonest species in cult. in the U. S., sometimes under glass and also planted out for the summer. Sometimes known erroneously as *E. speciosa.*

2. E. **indica,** Lam. Large tree, sometimes with small black prickles but usually unarmed: lfts. broad-ovate to rhombic-ovate, short-pointed or the terminal one cuspidate, 4–6 in. long and as broad, entire, rather thin, glabrous: fls. scarlet, large and showy, in dense racemes, 2–3 in. long; calyx spathe-like, oblique and not 2-lipped, splitting on the back down to the base; standard ovate or oval, standing erect or nearly so, the keel and wings shorter than calyx; stamens standing alone and prominent: pod 6–12 in. long, thick; seeds ⅝–¾in. long, turgid, bean-like. India, Malaya.—Planted in trop. Amer., but known in U. S. mostly in var. **picta,** Hort. (*E. picta,* L.), a kind with spotted or variegated lvs., known in the races *E. Parcellii* and *E. marmorata* of the trade; usually glasshouse subjects.

3. E. **herbacea,** L. Top herbaceous, the sts. 2–4 ft. high, slender, erect or spreading, the flowering ones with few lvs.: lvs. usually prickly on petiole and rachis; lfts. deltoid to hastate to angled-ovate, 2–3½ in. long, all of them or at least the middle one angle-lobed with a long point, thin, glabrous: fls. rather small, 2 in. or less long and narrow, nearly or quite closed, scarlet, few in each raceme which is 1–2 ft. long; calyx narrow, truncate, ciliate; standard infolding the much shorter remaining petals; wings slightly longer than calyx and exceeding the keel: pod 3–5 in. long, short-beaked; seeds bright scarlet with black spot. N. C. to Fla. and Tex. Var. **arborea,** Chapm. (*E. arborea,* Small), is a shrub or tree to 25–30 ft., with persistent sts. and racemes commonly only 4–8 in. long and few-fld.

4. E. **Corallodendrum,** L. Small tree, 15–20 ft., usually spiny or prickly but sometimes unarmed: lfts. broadly rhombic-ovate, 2–5 in. long, the middle one often angle-lobed and with a long point, rather thin, glabrous, sometimes with spines on the ribs as also on petioles: fls. brilliant deep crimson, 2 or 3 together in loose racemes, standing at right angles or deflexed, 1½–2½ in. long, but mostly under 2 in., narrow and nearly or quite closed; calyx open and truncate but with a sharp process or tooth on the under edge, little inflated and less than ½in. long; standard closed down over the keel which is only one-fourth as long; wings not much exceeding calyx and keel: pod about 4 in. long, beaked; seeds scarlet, usually with black spot. Trop. Amer.—A tree commonly confused with this in trop. Amer. has been separated as **E. pallida,** Britt. & Rose: fls. pale or salmon-red, 2½–3 in. long, calyx loose or inflated and much wider than the corolla and more than ½in. long.

5. E. **caffra,** Thunb. Good-sized tree, 30–40 or even 60 ft., with small prickles: lvs. with unarmed mostly puberulous petioles, clustered toward end of shoots; lfts. broad-ovate, obtusely acuminate, glabrous, 2–2½ in. long and 1½–2 in. broad, abruptly tapering to a blunt point-like apex, the glanduliform stipels conspicuous: fls. brilliant scarlet, many in dense racemes; calyx obliquely lipped or splitting, usually manifestly 5-toothed; standard 1½–2 in. long, folded downward over the wings and keel, which are very minute and concealed. S. Afr.

57. **GLYCINE,** L. Trop. and warm-temp. mostly twining plants of the Old World, one grown for human food and forage; species perhaps 40 or more.—Lfts. mostly (and in ours) 3, sometimes 5 or 7, stipellate; stipules small and free from the petiole: fls. small, white to purplish, in short axillary racemes, papilionaceous; calyx hairy, the 2 upper teeth more or less united; standard rather broad, somewhat auricled at base; wings lightly adherent to the short obtuse keel; stamens mostly monadelphous, the odd one sometimes partially free; style beardless, stigma small and terminal: pod narrow, flat or with somewhat convex sides, usually constricted between the seeds. (Glyci-ne: Greek *sweet*, probably from edible qualities of some plant.)

G. Max, Merr. (*Dolichos Soja*, L. *Phaseolus Max*, L. *G. hispida*, Maxim. *G. Soja*, Sieb. & Zucc. *Soja Max*, Piper). SOYBEAN. Erect brown-hairy bushy ann., 2–6 ft., some of the shoots vine-like: lfts. 3, ovate to narrow-ovate, 3–6 in. long, entire, obtuse or short-acute, apiculate: fls. inconspicuous, white or purple: pod hanging on very short stalk, 2–3 in. long and about ½in. broad, brown, hairy; seeds 2–4, globose, green, brown, yellow, or black, with small hilum; germination epigeal. China, Japan.—Much grown for forage, human food, and oil.

58. **CAJANUS,** DC. One erect small shrub, much grown in trop. and subtrop. countries for its edible seeds, probably native to the Old World.—Lfts. 3, entire, with minute resinous dots beneath: fls. in axillary racemes, papilionaceous; calyx with 2 upper lobes united; standard large and broad, auricled at base; keel obtuse and incurved; stamens 9 and 1; style thickened upward, beardless, the stigma terminal: pod compressed, with diagonal depressions, 4–7-seeded. (Caja-nus: from an aboriginal name.)

C. Cajan, Millsp. (*Cytisus Cajan*, L. *Cajanus bicolor*, DC. *C. indicus*, Spreng.). PIGEON PEA. CAJAN. Pubescent shrub 4–10 ft. or more, much-branched: lfts. lanceolate to narrow-elliptic, 2–4 in. long, acuminate, soft-pubescent on both surfaces: fls. yellow or orange, brownish on back, varying into other color combinations, ¾in. across: pod 2–3 in. long and ½in. broad more or less, long-beaked, hairy, abundantly produced; seeds orbicular with one edge flattened, compressed, about ¼in. across, usually brown with small white hilum.

59. **BAPTISIA,** Vent. FALSE OR WILD INDIGO. Some two dozen erect per. herbs in E. N. Amer., planted for ornament.—Branching, glabrous or pubescent, herbage usually turning black in drying: lvs. digitate (seldom simple); lfts. 3; stipules various, sometimes 0: fls. white, yellow, or blue, in lateral and terminal racemes, papilionaceous, often showy; standard with reflexed sides, not exceeding wings; keel straight, the petals nearly separate; stamens 10, distinct; style somewhat incurved, with very small terminal stigma: pod stalked in the calyx, short, oblong to nearly globose, inflated, many-seeded. (Baptis-ia: from Greek word *to dye;* some of the species yield an inferior indigo.)

A. Fls. blue....................1. *B. australis*
AA. Fls. white or yellow.
  B. Plant soft-pubescent....................2. *B. bracteata*
  BB. Plant glabrous.
    C. Color of fls. white....................3. *B. leucantha*
    CC. Color of fls. yellow....................4. *B. tinctoria*

1. **B. australis,** R. Br. (*Sophora australis*, L.). Glabrous, somewhat branched, stout, 3–6 ft.: lfts. obovate, 1½–3 in. long, short-pointed; stipules to ½in. long, persistent: fls. indigo-blue, in long terminal erect racemes, about 1 in. long: pod oblong, 1–1½ in. long. Vt. to N. C. and Tenn.

2. **B. bracteata,** Muhl. Soft-pubescent, branched, stout, 1–2 ft.: lfts. oblanceolate or obovate, 2–4 in. long, acute or obtuse; stipules ¾–1½ in. long, persistent: fls. cream-colored or yellow, ¾in. long, in axillary secund racemes: pod elliptic, 1½ in. long, with slender beak. N. C. to Ga. and Ala.

3. **B. leucantha,** Torr. & Gray. Glabrous, glaucous, branched, stout, 4–6 ft.: lfts. obovate to oblanceolate, 1–2½ in. long, obtuse, undulate; stipules ¼in. long, caducous: fls. white, 1 in. long, in racemes 8 in. and more long: pod ovoid or oblong, 1–1½ in. long. Ont. to N. Fla. and Tex., absent from Atlantic coastal plain.

4. **B. tinctoria,** Vent. (*Sophora tinctoria*, L.). Glabrous and somewhat glaucous, much-branched, 2–4 ft.: lfts. cuneate-obovate, about ½in. long, obtuse; stipules very small and caducous: fls. bright yellow, about ½in. long, few in numerous racemes: pod subglobose or ovoid, ½in. or less long, with slender beak. Mass. to Ga. west to Minn.

60. **THERMOPSIS,** R. Br. Per. herbs, of about 20 species in N. Amer. and Asia, sometimes planted in the garden.—Rhizomes woody: lfts. 3, digitate; stipules conspicuous: fls. papilionaceous, yellow, in racemes; calyx campanulate, 2-lipped; stamens 10, free: pod flat, usually linear, sessile or very short-stalked, many-seeded. (Thermop-sis: Greek *lupine-like.*)

A. Pod spreading....................1. *T. mollis*
AA. Pod erect, appressed to rachis.
B. Raceme dense: lfts. ovate or obovate....................2. *T. caroliniana*
BB. Raceme loose: lfts. obovate to linear-lanceolate....................3. *T. montana*

1. **T. mollis,** M. A. Curt. (*Podalyria mollis*, Michx.). Soft-pubescent, 2–3 ft. high, diffusely branched: lfts. elliptic, ¾–1½ in. long and ½–¾in. wide: racemes loose, to 6 in. long: pod 1–1½ in. long, spreading, pubescent. Va. to Ga.

2. **T. caroliniana,** M. A. Curt. From 2–4 ft., simply branched: lfts. ovate or obovate, 2–3 in. long and 1–1½ in. wide, pubescent and glaucous beneath: racemes dense and spike-like, to 10 in. long: pod 1½–2 in. long, densely villous, appressed to rachis. N. C. to Ga.

3. **T. montana,** Nutt. To 3 ft., sts. stout, somewhat branched: lfts. obovate to linear-lanceolate, 1–3 in. long, slightly pubescent beneath: racemes loose, 6–8 in. long: pod 2–3 in. long, villous, appressed to rachis. Rocky Mts. to Wash.

61. **CHORIZEMA,** Labill. Small evergreen shrubs grown in Calif. and sometimes in greenhouses; species 15, in Australia.—Diffuse plants with weak slender sts.: lvs. simple, thick and shining, often spiny-toothed: fls. pea-like, red, purple-red or orange, in terminal or axillary racemes in spring and summer; calyx-lobes 5, the 2 upper ones mostly broader; petals clawed; standard very broad, keel short; stamens 10, free: pod short, not constricted between the seeds. (Choriz-ema: fanciful Greek name.)

A. Full-open fls. usually spaced ½in. or more apart in slender long mostly terminal racemes: lvs. glabrous or essentially so, with shallow spiny small teeth....................1. *C. cordatum*
AA. Full-open fls. close together in short axillary as well as terminal racemes: lvs. strongly spiny-toothed or -lobed.
B. Lvs. pubescent at least beneath, teeth of moderate depth....................2. *C. varium*
BB. Lvs. glabrous, margins very deeply spiny-toothed or -lobed....................3. *C. ilicifolium*

1. **C. cordatum,** Lindl. Slender nearly or quite glabrous shrub to 10 ft., with weak branches: lvs. ovate-lanceolate, 2 in. long or less, small-toothed and prickly, the teeth ¼in. or less long, margins little if at all undulate: fls. many in long open terminal racemes; standard orange- or scarlet-red, wings and keel purplish.—Apparently the common species in cult., grown sometimes under the names *C. varium* and *C. ilicifolium.*

2. **C. varium,** Benth. (*C. elegans*, Hort.). Erect, 4–6 ft., pubescent on branches, infl. and under side of lvs.: lvs. broadly cordate-ovate, prickly-toothed and undulate, 2 in. long or less: fls. about ½in. long, in close axillary and terminal racemes; standard light orange, wings and keel purple-red.

3. **C. ilicifolium,** Labill. Low and diffuse, glabrous, with slender erect or drooping branches: lvs. ovate to lanceolate, 1 in. long, sometimes cordate at base, thick, coarsely veined, strongly undulate and with deep prickly teeth or lobes: fls. few, orange-red, close together in axillary and terminal racemes.

62. **TRIFOLIUM,** L. Clover. Probably well toward 300 species of temp. regions, ann. and per. herbs, some important forage and cover plants, and some are weeds.—Lvs. palmate (only rarely pinnate and not in ours) with commonly 3 non-articulated mostly sessile entire or denticulate lfts.; stipules adnate to petiole: fls. small, white, yellow, red or purplish, in dense heads or spikes, papilionaceous; calyx nearly equally toothed; petals withering rather than falling off, more or less adnate to stamen-tube; stamens 9 and 1, the odd one sometimes not wholly free; style filiform, beardless, the stigma more or less oblique: pod small, mostly indehiscent, usually 1–2-seeded, nearly or quite covered in the calyx. (Trifo-lium: Latin *three leaves.*)

A. Fl.-heads on long slender peduncles directly from the creeping rooting sts.: fls. white or pinkish.
B. Calyx not inflated in fr....................1. *T. repens*
BB. Calyx inflated in fr....................2. *T. fragiferum*
AA. Fl.-heads on long or short peduncles, or even sessile, from leafy erect or ascending branching sts.
B. Blossoms whitish or pink (see also var. of no. 6).

c. Fls. soon becoming reflexed in head..............................3. *T. hybridum*
cc. Fls. erect..............................4. *T. alexandrinum*
bb. Blossoms normally red or purplish.
c. Heads long-spicate.
d. Color bright crimson or scarlet: heads single..............................5. *T. incarnatum*
dd. Color purple-red: heads mostly in pairs..............................6. *T. rubens*
cc. Heads globular or nearly so.
d. Peduncle of head wanting or nearly so..............................7. *T. pratense*
dd. Peduncle prominent..............................8. *T. medium*

1. **T. repens,** L. White Clover. Glabrous or glabrate creeping per., the sts. 6–12 in., making a flat mat: lvs. long- and slender-petioled; lfts. obcordate, ¼–¾in. long, minutely denticulate: heads on slender peduncles (sometimes 12 in. or more high), from the horizontal sts.; fls. white, in rather loose globular heads to ¾in. across, pedicelled, reflexing with age: pod about 4-seeded. Eurasia, N. Amer.—Often sown in lawns and pastures as White Dutch clover; there are races with bronzy foliage and colored fls.; the lvs. are sometimes known as Shamrock. A giant form now widely grown in the northeastern states is the Ladino clover, intro. about 1900 from Lodi, Italy; it has heavy glossy foliage.

2. **T. fragiferum,** L. Strawberry Clover. Per. with creeping rooting sts. to 1 ft., glabrous or pubescent: lfts. cuneate-obovate, ¼–½in. long, strongly nerved: fls. pink to white, sessile, in dense globose heads about ½in. across on very long peduncles; calyx becoming inflated and vesciculose in fr. Medit. region.—Recently intro. for reclaiming wet and alkaline lands.

3. **T. hybridum,** L. Alsike Clover. Per.: much like no. 1 in general appearance when it becomes prostrate with age but very different: fls. pink or rose-tinted, in globose heads ¾–1 in. across, early becoming strongly reflexed, on mostly short peduncles 2–4 in. long (but sometimes longer) that arise from the axils of upright or lopping branching sts. 1–2 ft. high that do not root at joints: lfts. ovate, not emarginate, ½–1 in. long, denticulate: pod 2–3-seeded. Eu.; nat.—An important agricultural clover.

4. **T. alexandrinum,** L. Berseem. Egyptian Clover. Ann., lightly pubescent or glabrate, 1–2 ft., branched: lfts. oblong and obtuse, ¾–1 in. long, obscurely denticulate: fls. whitish or yellowish-white, in dense globular to oblong-ovate short-peduncled heads with bract-like involucre at base; calyx-teeth long-subulate, ciliate. Egypt, Syria.—Of much importance in the agriculture of Egypt, and somewhat grown in N. Amer. on dry alkaline lands.

5. **T. incarnatum,** L. Crimson Clover. Ann., persisting the winter if sown late, hairy, erect, forking, 1–3 ft.: lfts. broad-obovate to oblong-ovate, sometimes cuneate-obovate, ¾–1¼ in. long, obtuse or obscurely emarginate, denticulate: fls. crimson and showy, in an oblong pedunculate spicate head 1½–2½ in. long, without involucre; calyx hairy and strong-ribbed, the lobes long-subulate. Eu., and sparingly escaped.—Used as cover-crop and green-manure, particularly in orchards, and sometimes grown for ornament.

6. **T. rubens,** L. Per., erect, glabrous, forking, 18–24 in.: lfts. narrowly long-oblong, 1½–2½ in. long and ⅓in. broad; stipules 1½–3 in. long, very acute and prominent: fls. purplish-red and showy, in spicate usually twin heads 2–3 in. long and without involucre; calyx-lobes subulate and long-ciliate. Eu.—Sometimes grown for ornament; there is a white-fld. race.

7. **T. pratense,** L. Red Clover. Short-lived hairy or glabrate per., 1–2 ft.: lfts. oval to oblong-oval or obovate, 1½–2½ in. long, minutely denticulate, obtuse or somewhat emarginate, often white-blotched; stipules 1 in. or less long, scarious, veined, with hair-like points: fls. rose-purple or magenta (varying to nearly white), in dense ovoid sessile heads about 1 in. long (lf. subtending it); calyx hairy, the lobes very narrow and long. Eu.; extensively nat. and the common clover of meadows; becomes weak and tends to die out after the second year. Var. **perenne,** Host, Mammoth Clover, longer-lived, taller and stouter, the heads mostly darker colored and maturing later. Var. **foliosum,** Brand, Orel Clover, glabrous, very leafy, the basal lvs. long-persisting; a Russian race intro. as a hay plant.

8. **T. medium,** L. Zigzag or Cow Clover. Sts. zigzag or flexuose, nearly or quite glabrous: lfts. narrow, elliptic or oblong, entire except sometimes at base, not blotched: heads more or less stalked, the fls. deeper purple than in no. 7. Eu. and somewhat nat.—Doubtfully in cult., the agricultural plant passing under this name probably being *T. pratense* var. *perenne.*

63. **ONONIS,** L. Rest-Harrow. European herbs and shrubs, of over 70 species, planted in borders and rock-gardens.—Usually glandular-viscid: lvs. pinnate, of 3 toothed lfts.; stipules adnate to petiole: fls. papilionaceous, rose, white or yellow, 1–7 in the axils, often forming racemes; calyx deeply 5-parted; standard nearly orbicular; stamens united; ovary stalked, with 2 to many ovules: pod inflated or terete. (Ono-nis: ancient Greek name.)

A. Plant spiny: fls. solitary....................1. *O. spinosa*
AA. Plant not usually spiny: fls. 2–4.
B. Lfts. orbicular....................2. *O. rotundifolia*
BB. Lfts. obovate to oblong.
C. Racemes leafy, dense....................3. *O. hircina*
CC. Racemes not leafy, loose....................4. *O. fruticosa*

1. **O. spinosa,** L. Per. to 2 ft., woody at base, much-branched, spiny: lfts. oblong, to about ½in. long: fls. solitary, pink, ½–1 in. long, June–July: pod ovate, hairy. Eu.

2. **O. rotundifolia,** L. Subshrub to 1½ ft.: lfts. orbicular, ½–1½ in. long, the terminal one long-stalked: fls. bright rose, ¾in. long, 2–4 on long axillary peduncles, forming loose leafy terminal panicles, in summer: pod hanging, to 1¼ in. long and ¼in. wide, hairy. S. Eu.

3. **O. hircina,** Jacq. Subshrub to 2 ft.: lfts. oblong, ½–1 in. long: fls. rose and white, ½–¾in. long, usually 2 in the axils, forming a dense leafy raceme, in summer: pod ovate, glandular-hairy. Eu.

4. **O. fruticosa,** L. Shrub to 2 ft.: lfts. obovate, sessile, to 1 in. long, glabrous: fls. rose or whitish, ½–¾in. long, 2–3 in the axils, forming a loose raceme, June–Aug.: pod 1 in. long, hairy. S. Eu., N. Afr.

64. **MEDICAGO,** L. Medick. Species about 65 in Eu., Asia and Afr., mostly weedy plants, some of them grown or used for forage.—Mostly herbaceous, ann. and per., seldom woody, erect or wide-spreading: lvs. pinnate; lfts. 3, small, mostly denticulate, without apparent stipels; stipules adnate to petiole: fls. small, yellow or violet, in axillary short racemes or heads, papilionaceous; calyx-teeth nearly equal; standard oblong or obovate, not auricled; stamens 9 and 1; style subulate, beardless, stigma capitate: pod spiral or much curved, small, indehiscent, smooth or spiny, 1- to few-seeded. (Medica-go: indirectly from Medea, the country whence alfalfa was supposed to have been derived.)

A. Plant per.: fls. purplish....................1. *M. sativa*
AA. Plant ann.: fls. yellow.
B. Pod without spines: fls. in dense heads....................2. *M. lupulina*
BB. Pod spiny: fls. in loose clusters.
C. Spines of pod interlocking; seeds black....................3. *M. Echinus*
CC. Spines of pod erect; seeds yellowish.
D. Lfts. without spot in center: pod loosely coiled....................4. *M. hispida*
DD. Lfts. with red spot in center: pod densely coiled....................5. *M. arabica*

1. **M. sativa,** L. Alfalfa. Lucerne. Upright glabrous branched per., 1–3 ft., with very deep tap-root: lfts. obovate-oblong to linear-oblong, ¾–1 in. long, denticulate toward apex: fls. purplish, in close racemes ½–1 in. long: pod slightly pubescent, with 2 or 3 spirals, not spiny. Eu.; nat. in N. Amer.

2. **M. lupulina,** L. Black Medick. Hop Clover. Yellow Trefoil. Pubescent ann. with decumbent sts. to 2½ ft. long: lfts. oval or obovate, ¼–¾in. long, denticulate toward apex: fls. yellow, in dense oblong or cylindrical heads ¼–¾in. long: pod kidney-shaped, strongly veined, nearly glabrous, not spiny, with 1 yellow seed. Eu., Asia.; nat. in N. Amer.

3. **M. Echinus,** DC. Calvary Clover. Ann. with procumbent sts. to 3 ft. long: lfts. obovate, to 1 in. long and ½in. wide, denticulate, usually with reddish spot in center: fls. yellow, in small clusters: pod ovoid, with 7–9 spiral coils, to ¾in. long, glabrous, covered with stiff interlocking spines, seeds black. Medit. region. Var. **variegata,** Ricker (*M. intertexta Echinus variegata,* Urban), lfts. with large dark red triangular spot.

4. **M. hispida,** Gaertn. (*M. denticulata,* Willd.). Toothed Bur Clover. Ann. with decumbent sts. to 3 ft. or more: lfts. broad-obovate, to 1¼ in. long and ⅞in. wide, emarginate, denticulate: fls. yellow, in loose clusters: pod ¼in. across, with 2–3 loose coils, strongly veined, with 2 rows of spines, seeds yellow. Eu., Asia; nat. in N. Amer.

5. **M. arabica,** All. Spotted Bur Clover. Pubescent ann. with procumbent sts. to 3 ft. long: lfts. to 1 in. long and ⅞in. wide, denticulate toward apex, with dark red spot in center: fls. yellow, in small clusters: pod ⅛in. across, with 3–5 tight coils, veins inconspicuous, edges furrowed, with 2 rows of curved spines, seeds yellow. Eu.; nat. in N. Amer.

65. **TRIGONELLA,** L. Seventy or more species of ann. seldom per. herbs, mostly with strong odor, of the Old World, 1 in Australia, 1 in S. Afr., a few sometimes grown for forage and other uses, one for ornament.—Mostly low plants with pinnately 3-foliolate usually denticulate lvs., with stipules adnate to petiole: fls. yellow, white, or blue, solitary, capitate or short-racemose in the axils; stamens diadelphous: fr. a beaked long or short indehiscent pod, many-seeded. From Medicago it is distin-

guished by the straight rather than spiral pod; from Melilotus by the beaked pod, more capitate infl. and sometimes blue fls.; from Trifolium by the pinnate lvs. and exserted pod. (Trigonel-la: *a little triangle*, Latin, of obscure application.)

A. Fls. white: pod 3 in. or more long............1. *T. Fœnum-Græcum*
AA. Fls. blue: pod not much longer than calyx............2. *T. cærulea*

1. **T. Fœnum-Græcum,** L. FENUGREEK (i. e. *Greek hay*). Pubescent simple-stemmed heavy-scented ann., 1–2 ft., grown for forage and seeds used for medicinal purposes: lfts. obovate, ¾–1 in. long, obscurely denticulate toward apex: fls. whitish, 1 or 2 and practically sessile; calyx hairy, with subulate lobes: pod 3–6 in. long, very slender, curved, beak 1–2 in. long. S. Eu. and Asia.

2. **T. cærulea,** Ser. (*Trifolium Melilotus cærulea*, L. *Melilotus cærulea*, Desr.). Erect branching lightly pubescent or glabrate ann., 1–2 ft., grown for the blue-and-white fls. that are borne in long-peduncled heads to ½in. across: main lfts. oval, ¾–1 in. long, denticulate, lowest ones nearly orbicular, upper ones oblong: pod not much longer than calyx but the beak long-exserted. Cent. and S. Eu.

66. **MELILOTUS,** Mill. MELILOT. SWEET CLOVER. Some 20 species of Old World ann. and bien. sweet-smelling erect herbs, somewhat grown for forage, green-manuring, and rarely for ornament.—Lvs. pinnate; lfts. 3, small and mostly narrow, denticulate, without apparent stipels; stipules adnate to petiole: fls. small, white or yellow, in slender axillary racemes, papilionaceous; calyx-teeth nearly equal; standard oblong or obovate, not auricled; wings longer than the obtuse keel; stamens 9 and 1; style slender, incurved above, beardless, stigma small and terminal: pod very short, straight, mostly ovoid, 1–2-seeded, tardily or not at all dehiscent. (Melilotus: *honey lotus*, from the fragrance.)

A. Fls. white............1. *M. alba*
AA. Fls. yellow.
B. Pod turgid, coarsely reticulate............2. *M. indica*
BB. Pod not turgid, only slightly reticulate............3. *M. officinalis*

1. **M. alba,** Desr. WHITE SWEET CLOVER. Familiar roadside bien. weed, and also sown for forage, cover-crop, and green-manuring mostly under the name Bokhara clover; erect, glabrous or above finely pubescent, 3–10 ft.: lvs. fragrant when dried; lfts. narrowly or broadly oblong, ¾–1½ in. long, denticulate, obtuse or emarginate: fls. many, white, honey-sweet, ⅛ to less than ¼in. long, short-pedicelled, in long slender racemes: pod ⅛–⅙in. long, ovoid, tipped with style but not beaked, slightly reticulate. Eu., Asia; nat. in N. Amer. Var. **annua,** Coe, is a race maturing the same year from seed, known specially in the Hubam clover.

2. **M. indica,** All. (*Trifolium Melilotus indica*, L.). Used on the Pacific Coast as a cover-crop and also nat.: glabrous, 1½–3 ft.: lfts. cuneate-obovate, ½–1¼ in. long, truncate or retuse at apex, denticulate above the middle: fls. yellow, smaller than in no. 1, in racemes 1–2 in. long: pod small, 1/12in. long, nearly globose, turgid, irregularly reticulate or alveolate. Eurasia.

3. **M. officinalis,** Lam. (*Trifolium Melilotus officinalis*, L.). YELLOW SWEET CLOVER. To 4 ft. or more, glabrous or slightly pubescent above: lfts. obovate or oblanceolate, ½–1 in. long, rounded at apex, denticulate nearly all round: fls. yellow, ⅙–¼in. long: pod about ⅛in. long, slightly reticulate. Eurasia; nat. in N. Amer.

67. **BAUHINIA,** L. Trees and shrubs, sometimes tall-climbing, 150–200 species in the tropics of both hemispheres, planted Fla. to Calif.—Plant unarmed or with spines at nodes, sometimes tendril-bearing: lvs. broad, entire or in ours 2-cleft or -lobed, in some cases lfts. entirely distinct, the petiole (or midvein) usually prolonged into a short but characteristic awn or bristle between the lfts.: fls. white, rose, red, purple or yellow, in simple or panicled terminal or axillary racemes; calyx shortly or not at all toothed before flowering, variously lobed or cleft at flowering time, in some species the limb opening on one side and remaining as a single spathe-like organ; petals 5, somewhat unequal, usually narrowed into a claw; stamens 10, distinct or nearly so, or sometimes reduced even to 1 and perhaps bearing sterile filaments; ovary often stalked, many-ovuled: fr. a long flat pod, dehiscent or indehiscent. (Bauhin-ia: after John and Caspar Bauhin, 16th century herbalists, the twin lfts. suggesting two brothers.)

A. Color of fls. brick-red..1. *B. Galpinii*
AA. Color of fls. pink, purple, yellow or white.
B. Plant a woody climber..2. *B. Vahlii*
BB. Plant a shrub or tree.
C. Fls. small (about 1¼ in. or less across), yellow or white: not spiny.
D. Lvs. 1 in. or less long and very obtuse: fls. yellow, with blotch............3. *B. tomentosa*
DD. Lvs. 2–3 in. long, with acute divergent lobes: fls. white..................4. *B. mexicana*
CC. Fls. much larger, rose, red, purple or white: spines sometimes present.
D. Spines usually 2 at base of petiole: lf.-lobes narrow.
E. Lobes of lf. long-acuminate..5. *B. forficata*
EE. Lobes of lf. obtuse or essentially so...............................6. *B. corniculata*
DD. Spines wanting: lf.-lobes broad, very obtuse.
E. Fertile stamen (anther) 1..7. *B. monandra*
EE. Fertile stamens 3–10.
F. Petals 1 in. wide; calyx-limb spathaceous (remaining as 1 undivided conspicuous piece)..8. *B. variegata*
FF. Petals ⅓in. or less wide; calyx-limb long, splitting into 2 nearly equal reflexed parts..9. *B. purpurea*

1. **B. Galpinii,** N. E. Br. Half-climbing shrub 5–10 ft. high: lvs. ½–3 in. long, 2-lobed from one-fifth to one-half their length, 7-nerved, short-petioled: racemes few-fld., fls. borne continuously from spring to late autumn; calyx-tube slender, about 1 in. long, the limb spathaceous and usually a little shorter; petals practically all alike, 1–1½ in. long, the claw as long as the orbicular cuspidate brick-red limb; fertile stamens 3: pod 3–5 in. long, flat; seeds dark brown. (Bears the name of E. E. Galpin, an early collector of this species.) S. and trop. Afr.

2. **B. Vahlii,** Wight & Arn. MALU CREEPER. An extensive climber, with densely pubescent branchlets and circinate tendrils, pubescence gray or ferruginous: lvs. subcoriaceous, ¼–1½ ft. long and usually broader, 11–13-nerved, cleft one-fourth to one-third their length, with broadly rounded lobes, persistently pubescent on both surfaces: racemes or heads long-peduncled, terminal, with tomentose pedicels 1–1½ in. long with small linear bracts; calyx-tube ⅓in. long, the limb splitting into 2–3 lobes or parts; petals white fading yellowish, 1 in. long, obovate, with short claw, densely hairy without; fertile stamens 3: pod somewhat rusty-downy, ¾–1 ft. long, 8–12-seeded, finally dehiscent; seeds dark brown, shining. (Named for Martin Vahl, page 53.) Himalayas.—A striking big-lvd. plant.

3. **B. tomentosa,** L. (*Alvesia tomentosa*, Britt. & Rose). ST.-THOMAS-TREE. Erect branching shrub 1–15 ft. high, branchlets, lower surface of lvs. and pods somewhat tomentose to glabrate: lvs. mostly 1 in. or less long, broader than long, 7-nerved and veiny, split one-third to two-thirds to the base, the lobes very obtuse: fls. mostly in axillary pairs (sometimes 1 or 3) on pedicels bearing a pair of bractlets; calyx entire or with 2 small teeth at apex, tube short, limb spathaceous; corolla ¾–2 in. long, the petals obovate and much exceeding calyx, yellow with a red or chocolate blotch on upper petal; fertile stamens 10: pod stalked, 4–5 in. long and ½in. wide. Trop. Asia and Afr., escaped in W. Indies.

4. **B. mexicana,** Vog. PATA-VACA. Large bush or small tree to 15 ft., with rough bark: lvs. 2–3 in. long and nearly as broad, somewhat urn-shaped in outline, cordate at base, lobed one-third to one-half the length, lobes triangular, divergent, acute, lower surface lightly pubescent to glabrate: fls. small, white, in short crowded bracted clusters; petals narrow, ½–¾in. long, long-clawed, long-acuminate; stamens and style pilose, colored, long-protruding: pod falcate or straight, ½in. or more wide, beaked, puberulent or glabrate. Mex.—Planted along the Rio Grande.

5. **B. forficata,** Link. Bush or small tree with slender nearly or quite glabrous branches; spines at nodes small, nearly straight or hooked, sometimes almost obsolete: lvs. distinctly longer than broad, 7–9-nerved, puberulent beneath, ovate in outline and rounded to subcordate at base, 2–4 in. long, forficate (forked) to the middle or beyond into long narrow lobes which are usually acute at tip: fls. 1–3 in axils, white or cream-colored, long and narrow until fully expanded; calyx-tube long and cylindrical, usually exceeded by the spathaceous limb; petals narrow, 2–3 in. long, obtuse, tapering to base, equalled by the conspicuous stamens: pod 6–10 in. long and about 1 in. wide, stalked. Brazil.—Variable.

6. **B. corniculata,** Benth. Erect shrub, 8–15 ft., glabrous or puberulent: lvs. broad-ovate to oblong-ovate, lobed usually less than half the depth, lobes obtuse or essentially so, subcordate at base, with 2 main ribs on either side, pubescent beneath: fls. opposite the lvs. in a leafy raceme, mostly in 2's or 3's, white or greenish, 2½–3 in. long, petals 1 in. more or less broad at the end and long-clawed, the colored stamens and style long and prominent, buds densely pubescent: pod 6–8 in. long and about ½in. wide, short-stalked. Brazil, Paraguay.

7. **B. monandra,** Kurz (*B. Kappleri*, Sagot. *B. Krugii*, Urban. *Caspareopsis monandra*, Britt. & Rose). BUTTERFLY-FLOWER. JERUSALEM DATE. Shrub or small tree, 15–40 ft., without spines: lvs. ovate or orbicular, 3–8 in. long, truncate to cordate at base, 11–13-nerved, divided about one-third into rounded lobes, puberulent and lighter colored beneath: fls. few in terminal racemes, on pubescent pedicels; calyx with slender tube and

a shorter spathaceous limb, pubescent; petals whitish-rose with bright purplish markings, long-obovate, clawed, to 2 in. long and to ¾in. wide; fertile stamen 1, the others very small: pod 7–9 in. long and 1 in. wide, straightish; seeds black, shining. Probably native in Guiana, although it has been accredited to Asia; nat. in W. Indies.

8. **B. variegata,** L. ORCHID-TREE. MOUNTAIN EBONY. Tree of small to medium size, spineless, the twigs glabrous or nearly so: lvs. 2–5 in. long and usually broader, 11–13-nerved, puberulent on veins beneath, rather thick, nearly truncate to deeply cordate at base, the very obtuse broad lobes usually extending about one-third down the blade but sometimes deeper: fls. few together from the axils, showy and fragrant, 3–4 in. across, varying from lavender to purple, the lip often attractively marked or mottled purple; calyx-tube about 1 in. long and equalling or exceeding the limb which is prominently spathaceous and pubescent; petals obovate, narrowed to claw, the larger ones about 1 in. wide, sometimes apiculate; fertile stamens 5 or 6; stigma very small: pod 1 ft. or less long, long-stalked and sharp-beaked, flat. India, China. Var. **candida,** Buch.-Ham. (*B. candida,* Roxb. *B. alba,* Hort.), has clear white fls.—Much planted in Fla. and elsewhere, usually under the name *B. purpurea* and sometimes as *B. grandiflora.* It blooms freely Jan.–Apr., usually after the lvs. fall where the plant is freely deciduous.

9. **B. purpurea,** L. (*B. triandra,* Roxb.). Much less showy than *B. variegata,* the petals being narrowly oblanceolate, red but varying to white, ⅓in. or less broad; calyx-tube shorter than the limb which splits into 2 narrow nearly equal reflexed toothed parts; fertile stamens 3 or 4; stigma thicker than style. India, China.—Blooms usually in late autumn or early winter.

68. **CERCIS,** L. REDBUD. Ornamental deciduous trees or shrubs, of 7 species in N. Amer. and from S. Eu. to Japan.—Branches spreading, forming a broad irregular head when older: lvs. alternate, petioled, palmately nerved, entire: fls. imperfectly papilionaceous, pedicelled, pink or red, in clusters or racemes from the old wood; calyx 5-toothed, red; uppermost petals somewhat smaller than the others; stamens 10, distinct: pod compressed, narrow-oblong, narrow-winged on the ventral suture, many-seeded. (Cer-cis: ancient Greek name.)

A. Lvs. abruptly short-acuminate.
  B. Fls. ½in. long: lvs. with herbaceous margins. . . . . .1. *C. canadensis*
  BB. Fls. ¾in. long: lvs. with transparent cartilaginous margins. . . . . .2. *C. chinensis*
AA. Lvs. rounded or emarginate at apex.
  B. Width of lvs. 3–5 in. . . . . .3. *C. Siliquastrum*
  BB. Width of lvs. 2–3 in. . . . . .4. *C. occidentalis*

1. **C. canadensis,** L. Spreading shrub or tree to 40 ft.: lvs. roundish or broadly ovate, 3–6 in. long, broader than long, usually cordate, abruptly acuminate: fls. rosy-pink, ½in. long, before the lvs., 4–8 in a cluster: pod linear-oblong, 2½–3½ in. long, acute at each end. N. J. south, west to Mich., Mo. and Tex. Var. **alba,** Rehd., has white fls.

2. **C. chinensis,** Bunge (*C. japonica,* Planch.). In the wild a tree to 50 ft., but a shrub in cult.: lvs. deeply cordate, roundish, 3–5 in. long, abruptly acuminate, with a whitish transparent line at margin, rather thick, glabrous, shining above: fls. 5–8 in a cluster, purplish-pink, ¾in. long: pod 3–5 in. long, narrow, acuminate. China, Japan.

3. **C. Siliquastrum,** L. JUDAS-TREE. Shrub or tree to 40 ft.: lvs. roundish, 3–5 in. wide, deeply cordate, rounded or emarginate at apex, glabrous: fls. 3–6 in a cluster, purplish-rose or white in var. **alba,** West., ¾in. long: pod 3–4 in. long, flat and thin. (Siliquastrum: *siliqua,* in reference to the fr.) S. Eu., W. Asia.

4. **C. occidentalis,** Torr. Shrub or small tree to 18 ft.: lvs. orbicular, 2–3 in. wide, cordate, emarginate, glabrous: fls. 6–12 in a cluster, reddish-purple, ½in. long: pod to 3 in. long and ¾in. wide. Calif.

69. **CERATONIA,** L. A small or moderately large evergreen tree with thick crown, native to the E. Medit. region, now widely cult. for the edible pods.—Lvs. even-pinnate, with few pairs of broad leathery lfts.: fls. small, bisexual or unisexual, in short single or clustered racemes borne on the old wood; calyx-tube disk-bearing, the 5 short segms. deciduous; petals 0; stamens 5: pod elongate, compressed, leathery, indehiscent, filled with a pulpy substance between the seeds. (Cerato-nia: Greek *horn,* in reference to the large pod.)

C. Siliqua, L. CAROB. Known also as ALGAROBA, KAROUB, CAROUBIER, and ST. JOHNS-BREAD. Reaching a height of 40–50 ft.: lvs. with 2–3 pairs of obovate or rotund shining lfts., these obtuse or emarginate, 1½–4 in. long: racemes lateral; fls. red: pod 4–12 in. long. (Siliqua: name in reference to the silique-like fr.)

70. **CASSIA,** L. SENNA. Species nearly or quite 400 in trop. or cool temp. regions, the herbaceous and shrubby kinds cult. as border plants and under glass, the arboreous species out-of-doors in the S.; senna lvs. used in medicine as a cathartic are derived from various species.—Lvs. even-pinnate, sometimes much reduced: fls. nearly regular, solitary, racemose or paniculate; calyx-teeth nearly equal, mostly longer than tube; corolla of 5 nearly equal spreading clawed petals; stamens 5 or 10, frequently unequal and some of the anthers abortive, the good anthers commonly opening at the apex: pod sessile or stalked, terete or flattened, 4-angled or winged, containing numerous seeds and often partitioned crosswise. (Cas-sia: ancient Greek name.)—By some authors Cassia is broken up into several genera.

A. Under surface of lfts. densely tomentose.
B. Lfts. linear-terete .... 1. *C. artemisioides*
BB. Lfts. oblong, flat .... 2. *C. tomentosa*
AA. Under surface of lfts. glabrous or nearly so.
B. Plant an herb.
C. Lfts. sensitive, to ⅔in. long .... 3. *C. fasciculata*
CC. Lfts. not sensitive, 1–2 in. long .... 4. *C. marilandica*
BB. Plant a shrub or tree.
C. Edges of pod with broad crenulate wing .... 5. *C. alata*
CC. Edges of pod not winged.
D. Pod flat.
E. Infl. a narrow raceme .... 6. *C. nairobensis*
EE. Infl. a panicle or corymb.
F. Fertile stamens 7 .... 7. *C. siamea*
FF. Fertile stamens 10 .... 8. *C. planisiliqua*
DD. Pod cylindrical.
E. Length of pod 1–2 ft.
F. Raceme 1 ft. or more long; fls. pale yellow .... 9. *C. Fistula*
FF. Raceme shorter; fls. canary-yellow veined with red .... 10. *C. Beareana*
EE. Length of pod 3–6 in.
F. Apex of lfts. rounded .... 11. *C. bicapsularis*
FF. Apex of lfts. acute or acuminate.
G. Lfts. long-acuminate, ovate or ovate-lanceolate .... 12. *C. lævigata*
GG. Lfts. acute, oblong or oblong-lanceolate .... 13. *C. corymbosa*

1. **C. artemisioides,** Gaud. Bushy shrub, gray all over with silky appressed pubescence: lfts. 3–6 pairs, linear-terete, ¾–1 in. long, the lower pair with a gland at base: racemes axillary, 5–8-fld., the fls. sulfur-yellow, not over ¾in. across; fertile stamens 10: pod flat, 2–3 in. long, shining brown. Australia.

2. **C. tomentosa,** L. f. (*Adipera tomentosa*, Britt. & Rose). Shrub 10–12 ft. high; twigs and lower surface of lvs. tomentose: lfts. in 6–8 pairs, oblong, ¾–1½ in. long, rounded and apiculate at apex, each pair with a gland at base: fls. deep yellow, about 1 in. across; fertile stamens 7: pod compressed, pubescent, about 5 in. long. Mex., S. Amer.

3. **C. fasciculata,** Michx. (*C. Chamæcrista*, Walt. *Chamæcrista fasciculata*, Greene). PARTRIDGE PEA. Ann. to 3 ft., much-branched: lfts. 6–15 pairs, sensitive, linear-oblong, ½–¾in. long, with 1 petiolar gland: fls. yellow, clustered in axils, to ¾in. long; fertile stamens 10: pod flat, linear, 1½–2 in. long. Mass. to Fla. and Tex.

4. **C. marilandica,** L. (*Ditremexa marilandica*, Britt. & Rose). WILD SENNA. Per. 3–4 ft. high, glabrous or nearly so, with almost simple sts.: lvs. light green, far exceeding the racemes, petiole with a large raised gland on upper side near base; lfts. 5–10 pairs, oblong, 1–2 in. long, mucronate: fls. bright yellow, widely open, in axillary racemes near the ends of the sts. and often appearing panicled, to ¾in. across; fertile stamens 7: pod linear, flat, to 4 in. long. E. U. S.

5. **C. alata,** L. (*Herpetica alata*, Raf.). RINGWORM CASSIA. Shrub to 8 ft. or more: lvs. 1–3 ft. long, of 6–14 pairs of broad-oblong obtuse lfts. 2–7 in. long, glandless: fls. golden-yellow, 1 in. across, in large spike-like racemes; fertile stamens 7: pod flat, linear, 4–6 in. long, with 4 broad crenulate wings. Tropics.

6. **C. nairobensis,** Hort. Shrub to 10 ft.: lfts. 12–14 pairs, oblong, 1½–2 in. long, apiculate: fls. yellow, 1½ in. across, in narrow racemes: pod flat, 4 in. or more long, long-beaked. Afr.

7. **C. siamea,** Lam. (*Sciacassia siamea*, Britt.). KASSOD-TREE. Tree to 40 ft.: lvs. ½–1 ft. long, petiole and rachis without glands; lfts. 8–9 pairs, oblong, 2–3 in. long, obtuse and apiculate, subglabrous, glaucous, somewhat coriaceous: racemes corymbose, crowded, both axillary and in a terminal panicle ½–1 ft. long; fls. bright yellow, ½in. long; fertile stamens 7: pod nearly straight, flat, 6–9 in. long, ½in. wide, with thickened sutures. E. Indies and Malaya; somewhat nat. in W. Indies.

8. **C. planisiliqua,** L. (*C. glauca*, Lam. *Psilorhegma planisiliqua*, Britt. & Rose). Shrub or small tree: lfts. 4–10 pairs, oblong or elliptic, 1½–3 in. long, acute, glaucous beneath, the lower pairs with gland at base: fls. bright yellow, 1 in. long, in corymbose racemes; fertile stamens 10: pod flat, to 8 in. long and ½in. wide. Trop. Asia; nat. in Jamaica.

9. **C. Fistula,** L. GOLDEN-SHOWER. PUDDING-PIPE-TREE. Tree to 30 ft. or more: lvs. 1 ft. and more long, petiole and rachis without glands; lfts. 4–8 pairs, ovate, 3–8 in. long, subacuminate but blunt at apex: racemes loose, pendent, 1 ft. or more long, bearing pale yellow fls. 2 in. across, on pedicels 2 in. long, in spring before the lvs., without bracts; fertile stamens 10: pod cylindric, black, 1–2 ft. long, containing 1-seeded compartments. (Fistula: Latin for *tube*, for the long cylindrical pods.) India; intro. in W. Indies and other trop. countries.—Furnishes the cassia pods of commerce which are used in medicine.

10. **C. Beareana,** Holmes. Tree 20–30 ft. high: lvs. 8–10 in. long; lfts. 8–10 pairs, elliptic, 1½–2 in. long, obtuse, rounded or broadly cuneate at base, glabrous: racemes rather short and subcorymbose; pedicels straight, ascending, 2½ in. long; petals obovate-oblong, often 1 in. long, canary-yellow veined with dark red or chestnut; longer stamens exceeding the petals, filaments distinctly dilated near the middle: pod glabrous or nearly so, about 30 in. long, 1 in. broad and ½in. thick, the sutures not prominent, the dissepiments showing on the surface as transverse lines; seeds dark brown, shining, flat, nearly ½in. long. (Named for Dr. O'Sullivan Beare of Pemba, an island of E. Afr.) Trop. Afr.

11. **C. bicapsularis,** L. (*Adipera bicapsularis*, Britt. & Rose). Shrub to 10 ft.: lfts. 3–5 pairs, obovate to nearly orbicular, ½–1½ in. long, rounded at apex, lowest pair with gland at base: fls. yellow, ½in. long, in axillary racemes usually longer than lvs.; fertile stamens 7: pod cylindrical, 3–6 in. long; seeds brown, shining. Tropics.

12. **C. lævigata,** Willd. (*Adipera lævigata*, Britt. & Rose). Shrub 6–10 ft.: lfts. 3–4 pairs, ovate or ovate-lanceolate, 1–3 in. long, long-acuminate, usually with gland between each pair: fls. yellow, ½in. long, in racemes shorter than lvs.; fertile stamens 7: pod cylindrical, 2–3½ in. long; seeds shining. Tropics.

13. **C. corymbosa,** Lam. (*Adipera corymbosa*, Britt. & Rose). Glabrous free-flowering shrub 4–10 ft. high: lfts. 2–3 pairs, oblong or oblong-lanceolate, 1–2 in. long, acute or acutish, the lowermost with a gland between them: fls. yellow, ½in. long, in long-stalked small axillary corymbs usually longer than lvs.; fertile stamens 7: pod cylindrical, 2–3 in. long; seeds brown, shining. Argentina; nat. Ga. to La. Var. **plurijuga,** Benth. (*C. floribunda*, Hort.), has more and broader lfts. and larger fls.

71. **TAMARINDUS,** L. One species grown throughout the tropics as an ornamental and for its acid frs. which have many uses; probably indigenous to trop. Afr. and possibly to S. Asia.—Tree with alternate even-pinnate lvs., stipules minute, caducous: lfts. small, indefinite in number: fls. irregular, in racemes at the ends of the branches; bracts and bracteoles ovate-oblong, colored, caducous; calyx-tube narrow, the 4 segms. imbricate, membranaceous, colored; the 3 upper petals imbricate, the 2 lower reduced to bristles hidden at base of the staminal tube; fertile stamens 3, the filaments connate below into a sheath open on the upper side, the small staminodes at the tip of the sheath; ovary many-ovuled, on a stalk adnate to the calyx-tube: pod oblong or linear, somewhat compressed, indehiscent, thick and crustaceous without, pulpy within, septate between the seeds. (Tamarin-dus: from the Arabic *tamar-Hindi*, meaning "Indian date.")

T. indica, L. TAMARIND. TAMARINDO. Evergreen tree sometimes 80 ft. high and with a trunk 25 ft. in circumference; bark brownish-gray, somewhat shaggy: lfts. 20–40, oblong, opposite, ½–¾in. long: fls. about 1 in. broad, few in lax racemes, pale yellow, the petals veined red; calyx-teeth lanceolate, the 2 lowest connate: pod 3–8 in. long, cinnamon-brown, plump and slightly curved, with a thin brittle shell containing a soft brownish pulp transversed by a few strong branched fibers, inclosing 1–12 flattened glossy seeds ½in. across: fls. Apr.–May in the northern hemisphere, fr. ripening in late autumn and winter.

72. **PARKINSONIA,** L. Trop. and subtrop. trees or shrubs, of 5 species, 1 S. African, 1 S. American, 3 trop. and N. American.—Bark thin, smooth: lvs. alternate or fascicled, bipinnate, with 1–4 pairs of pinnæ, the common petiole short, the rachis ending in a spine; pinnæ 2–4, the rachilla (in ours) very long, flat and twig-like, bearing numerous small deciduous lfts.; stipules minute or none: fls. yellow or whitish, on slender pedicels in short loose axillary or terminal racemes; calyx 5-parted, produced at base and jointed upon the pedicel; petals 5, clawed, the upper one within and broader than the others, with claw pubescent and nectariferous on the inner side; stamens 10, distinct, hairy at base; ovary several-ovuled, short-stalked: pod compressed, leathery, linear to linear-oblong, tapering at each end. (Parkinso-nia: John Parkinson, 1567–1650, London apothecary, author of "Paradisus Terrestris" and "Theatrum Botanicum.")

P. aculeata, L. JERUSALEM-THORN. RATAMA. Tree to 30 ft., glabrous, the slender zigzag branches often pendulous: lvs. short-petioled, the rachis short and spine-tipped; lfts. 8–16 in. long, with flattened twig-like rachilla and numerous very small deciduous linear or oblong segms.: racemes loose, axillary, 3–6 in. long; fls. yellow, fragrant, pendulous on long slender pedicels; calyx glabrous or nearly so, with very short tube and oblong reflexed lobes: pod narrow, 2–6 in. long, constricted between the oblong seeds. Probably trop. Amer.

73. **GLEDITSIA,** L. HONEY LOCUST. About a dozen species in N. Amer., E. and Cent. Asia, trop. Afr., and S. Amer., planted as avenue or park trees and for hedges.—Large deciduous polygamous trees, with spreading branches forming a broad graceful rather loose head, the trunk and branches usually with large branched spines: lvs. alternate, without stipules, abruptly pinnate, some on the same tree partly bipinnate or even a single lf. partly bipinnate: fls. in racemes or rarely in panicles; calyx-lobes and petals 3–5, the petals nearly equal, not much longer than the calyx; stamens 6–10, distinct; style short, with large terminal stigma: pod compressed, mostly large and indehiscent, 1- to many-seeded. (Gledit-sia: after Johann Gottlieb Gleditsch, 1714–1786, director of the botanic garden at Berlin.)

G. triacanthos, L. HONEY OR SWEET LOCUST. THREE-THORNED ACACIA. Attaining 140 ft., usually with stout simple or branched spines 3–4 in. long: lvs. 6–8 in. long, pinnate or the same one often both pinnate and bipinnate; lfts. many, oblong-lanceolate, remotely crenulate-serrate, ¾–1½ in. long: fls. small, very short-pedicelled, in narrow racemes 1½–3 in. long in May–June: pod 12–18 in. long, slightly falcate and at length twisted. Pa. south to Miss., west to Neb. and Tex. Var. **inermis,** Willd., is unarmed.

74. **GYMNOCLADUS,** L. Two deciduous trees, native in N. Amer. and China, one often planted.—Lvs. bipinnate, with entire lfts.: fls. bisexual and unisexual, regular, in terminal panicles; calyx tubular, 5-lobed; petals 5, somewhat longer than sepals; stamens 10: pod flat, thick and pulpy. (Gymnoc-ladus: from Greek *naked branch,* referring to the few branchlets.)

G. dioica, Koch (*Guilandina dioica,* L. *Gymnocladus canadensis,* Lam.). KENTUCKY COFFEE-TREE. To 100 ft.: lfts. ovate, 2–3 in. long, acute, short-stalked: fls. greenish-white, ½in. long, long-stalked, pubescent, racemes of pistillate tree to 1 ft. long and of staminate to 4 in.: pod red-brown, oblong, 6–10 in. long; seeds to 1 in. long. N. Y. to Minn.

75. **DELONIX,** Raf. Unarmed trees with large very showy fls., one species much cult. in S. Fla. and the American tropics; species 2–3, natives of Afr.—Broad-topped trees with evenly bipinnate lvs.; stipules lacking; pinnæ with numerous small pinnules: fls. orange or scarlet, not papilionaceous, in terminal or axillary corymbose racemes; calyx deeply 5-lobed, the lobes valvate and nearly equal; petals 5, with long claw and rotund blade; stamens 10, distinct; ovary sessile, many-ovuled: pod broadly linear, flat, woody, nearly solid between the seeds. (Delo-nix: Greek, referring to the long-clawed petals.)

D. regia, Raf. (*Poinciana regia,* Bojer). ROYAL POINCIANA. PEACOCK-FLOWER. FLAMBOYANT. Widely branched rapid-growing tree reaching 20–40 ft. in height: lvs. 1–2 ft. long, with stout petiole and 10–20 pairs of pinnæ, each with 20–40 pairs of oblong lfts. to ⅓in. long: racemes of showy fls. 3–4 in. across, with bright scarlet petals, the yellow-striped upper petal more cuneate than the others: pod 16 in. to 2 ft. long and 2–3 in. wide, dark brown. Madagascar.—A most striking and gorgeous tree planted for shade and ornament in frostless countries as S. Fla., S. Calif., Bermuda, and in the tropics; blooms mostly in summer.

76. **POINCIANA,** L. Ornamental trees or shrubs, grown for their showy fls. and attractive finely divided foliage; a number of species native in trop. and subtrop. regions.—Unarmed or prickly: lvs. evenly bipinnate: fls. showy, orange, red, or yellow, in panicles or racemes, the bracts commonly early deciduous; calyx-tube short, the 5 lobes unequal, imbricated; petals 5, broad, more or less unequal; stamens 10, distinct, long-exserted; ovary sessile, with several ovules: pod linear to oblong, usually flat. (Poincia-na: M. de Poinci, governor of the Antilles in the 17th century.)

A. Branches prickly: infl. not at all glandular....................................1. *P. pulcherrima*
AA. Branches not prickly: infl. densely glandular....................................2. *P. Gilliesii*

1. **P. pulcherrima,** L. (*Cæsalpinia pulcherrima,* Sw.). BARBADOS PRIDE. BARBADOS FLOWER-FENCE. DWARF POINCIANA. Glabrous shrub, sometimes 10 ft. high, with prickly branches: lvs. delicate, persistent, mimosa-like, with 12–18 pinnæ, each with 20–24 oblique-oblong lfts. about ¾in. long and half as wide: fls. orange or yellow, about 2 in. wide, long-pedicelled in large loose terminal or axillary racemes or panicles; stamens and style red, 2½ in. long: pod thin, broadly linear, 4 in. or less long and ½–¾in. wide. Generally distributed in the tropics but its original place is unknown.

2. **P. Gilliesii,** Hook. (*Cæsalpinia Gilliesii,* Wall. *Erythrostemon Gilliesii,* Link, Klotzsch & Otto). Climbing or straggling shrub or small tree, not prickly: lvs. with many pinnæ, these more or less alternate above the lowest pair; ultimate lfts. narrowly oblong, ¼–½in. long and one-fourth to one-third as wide, black-punctate on the lower side near the margins: infl. densely glandular, racemose, terminal; fls. large, light yellow, with brilliant red stamens protruding 3–5 in.: pod to 4 in. long and ¾in. wide. (Named for its discoverer Gillies, page 43.) S. Amer.

77. **ADENANTHERA,** L. BEAD-TREE. Unarmed trees allied to Mimosa, one cult. in greenhouses and in warm countries, its bright red seeds being used somewhat for ornamental purposes and also as a food; 3–4 species of trop. Asia, Afr., and Australia.—Lvs. bipinnate or decompound, with many pairs of small lfts.: fls. small, racemose, usually golden-yellow or whitish; stamens 10, scarcely exserted; ovary sessile, many-ovuled: pod linear, compressed, mostly cross-walled within. (Adenanthe-ra: from the deciduous pedicellate gland on each anther.)

A. pavonina, L. RED SANDALWOOD-TREE. PEACOCK FLOWER-FENCE. Tree to 50 ft. in its native habitat: lfts. about 13, oblong or ovate, 1–1½ in. long, obtuse, glabrous: fls. about ⅙in. long, in an axillary spike-like raceme to 6 in. long, white and yellow in the same cluster; calyx cup-shaped and very shallowly lobed: pod about 9 in. long and ½in. wide, becoming much coiled in dehiscing; seeds red, shining, lens-shaped, "Circassian seeds," interesting as curiosities to travellers and used for necklaces and the like. Trop. Asia and Afr.—Planted in trop. Amer. and also within our limits; sometimes known as "Circassian bean."

78. **MIMOSA,** L. About 300 species, chiefly of trop. Amer., grown more or less in warm countries; the plants known to the florists as mimosas are acacias (chiefly *A. armata*).—Trees, shrubs, or herbs of varying habit (sometimes woody climbers), often thorny or prickly, with bipinnate often sensitive lvs.: fls. small, bisexual or unisexual, not papilionaceous, in close peduncled heads or spikes; calyx minute or obsolete; petals 4–5, more or less united; stamens 4–10, distinct, exserted; ovary sessile or short-stalked: pod flat, oblong or linear. (Mimo-sa: Greek *a mimic,* alluding to the fact that the lvs. of some species are sensitive.)

M. pudica, L. SENSITIVE-PLANT. HUMBLE-PLANT. Per. often cult. as an ann., somewhat shrubby, to 1½ ft., branching, hairy and spiny: lvs. sensitive, long-petioled, the 2–4 subdigitate pinnæ with numerous linear-oblong segms. about ¼in. long: fls. many, purplish, in globular-oblong heads on elongating axillary peduncles: pod ½in. long, of 3–4 flat rotund 1-seeded joints which separate and fall away leaving the spinose-bristly margins. Continental trop. Amer., but widely nat. in warm countries, and running wild in the Gulf states.

79. **LEUCÆNA,** Benth. Trees and shrubs with the habit and foliage of acacia, one species cult. in the S. and in Calif.; species 9–10, Mex., Guatemala, Peru, and Pacific isls.—Evergreen, usually unarmed: lvs. bipinnate; lfts. small and in many pairs or large and in few pairs: fls. white, in close heads, usually bisexual, not papilionaceous, the calyx 5-lobed, the 5 petals separate; stamens 10, exserted; ovary stalked, many-ovuled: pod stalked, broadly linear, flat, not cross-walled within. (Leucæ-na: probably from Greek *white,* referring to the fls.)

L. glauca, Benth. (*Mimosa glauca,* L.). WHITE POPINAC. Spineless tree reaching 30 ft. or more: pinnæ 4–8-paired; lfts. 10–20-paired, oblong-linear to lanceolate, to ½in. long, oblique, glaucous below: fls. white, in globose heads to 1¼ in. diam.; petals erect, very narrow, about one-third as long as the stamens: pod 4–6 in. long and ½in. wide. Trop. Amer. but occurring in Fla. and Tex.

80. **ACACIA,** Willd. A marked genus of about 450 species, dispersed throughout the tropics and to some extent in the temp. regions, largely Australian, some species grown out-of-doors in warmer parts of the U. S. and others in cool greenhouses.—Trees or shrubs, seldom herbs, thorny or unarmed: lvs. bipinnate and often with

many pairs of lfts. or reduced to lf.-like petioles (phyllodia): fls. small, numerous, bisexual or unisexual, mostly yellow or seldom whitish, in stalked globose heads or cylindric spikes, solitary or in pairs or clusters, or in axillary racemes; calyx toothed, lobed or seldom fringed or lacking; petals distinct or united, sometimes lacking; stamens many, distinct or shortly united at base; ovary sessile or stalked: pod ovate, oblong or linear, not partitioned within, commonly opening by 2 valves; funicle of seed filiform or ending in a club-shaped aril, either twice encircling the seed or bent back upon itself. (Aca-cia: from Greek meaning a *point* or *thorn*, referring to the parts often spinescent.)—The acacias are grown to some extent in greenhouses, particularly *A. armata*, as a florists' plant. In Calif. any number of species may be grown; but those here described are apparently the most common; for other species the student must consult special treatises.

A. Lvs. all bipinnate.
B. Plants unarmed.
C. Pinnæ few, 2–4 pairs, glaucous . . . . 1. *A. Baileyana*
CC. Pinnæ many, 8–25 pairs, not glaucous . . . . 2. *A. decurrens*
BB. Plants spinose.
C. Pod terete, pulpy inside . . . . 3. *A. Farnesiana*
CC. Pod flat, dry . . . . 4. *A. macracanthoides*
AA. Lvs. all or mostly reduced to phyllodia, i.e., the petiole flattened to resemble a simple lf.
B. Fls. in narrow spikes.
C. Phyllodia 1-nerved, linear-subulate . . . . 5. *A. verticillata*
CC. Phyllodia 3–5-nerved, broader.
D. Width of phyllodia ¼–½in. . . . . 6. *A. longifolia*
DD. Width of phyllodia 1½–2 in. . . . . 7. *A. latifolia*
BB. Fls. in globose heads.
C. Stipules reduced to spines, persistent . . . . 8. *A. armata*
CC. Stipules not as above.
D. Longitudinal veins of phyllodia 3–6 . . . . 9. *A. melanoxylon*
DD. Longitudinal veins of phyllodia 1 or very rarely 2.
E. Length of phyllodia 1½ in. or less.
F. Phyllodia pubescent . . . . 10. *A. podalyriæfolia*
FF. Phyllodia glabrous.
G. Shape of phyllodia obliquely ovate . . . . 11. *A. cultriformis*
GG. Shape of phyllodia linear to linear-lanceolate . . . . 12. *A. linearis*
EE. Length of phyllodia over 2 in.
F. Phyllodia sickle-shaped, blunt at apex . . . . 13. *A. pycnantha*
FF. Phyllodia not sickle-shaped, mostly sharp at apex.
G. Width of phyllodia about ¼in. . . . . 14. *A. neriifolia*
GG. Width of phyllodia ½–1¼ in. . . . . 15. *A. saligna*

1. **A. Baileyana**, F. Muell. An attractive shrub or small tree, glabrous, usually with gray glaucous foliage arranged spirally around the branchlets and nearly concealing them: lvs. bipinnate, 1–2 in. long, with gland at base of each pair of pinnæ; pinnæ 2–3 pairs (occasionally 4), 1 in. long; lfts. about 20 pairs, about ¼in. long: fls. 15 in a head, on peduncles ⅛–¼in. long, the heads globose, numerous, in simple axillary racemes longer than the lvs. or the racemes paniculately branched and terminal, in late winter: pod 1½–4 in. long, ½in. wide, flat, occasionally constricted between the seeds, glaucous; seeds transverse, ¼in. long, with club-shaped funicle one-half as long; ripe July–Aug. (Named after F. M. Bailey, 1827–1915, colonial botanist of Queensland.)

2. **A. decurrens**, Willd. GREEN WATTLE. Handsome tree, glabrous or more or less tomentose-pubescent, with branches usually prominently angled: lvs. bipinnate, the pinnæ 8–15 pairs or more (sometimes reduced to 5 or 6); lfts. 30–40 pairs or more, linear, ⅙–⅓in. long: heads 20–30-fld., the fls. yellow, mostly 5-merous: pod 3–4 in. long, more or less contracted between the seeds. Var. **mollis**, Lindl. (*A. mollissima*, Willd.). BLACK WATTLE. Tree 20–50 ft. high, with reddish bark showing under the fissures: pinnæ 8–20 pairs, 2–6 in. long, shining above; lfts. 30–60 pairs, crowded, not ⅛in. long; gland between each pair of pinnæ and often on the internodes between: heads globose, small, pale yellow, in panicled racemes mostly in June: pod dark, pubescent, 2–4 in. long, not ¼in. wide, constricted and contracted between the seeds; seeds longitudinal; ripe June–Oct. Var. **dealbata**, F. Muell. (*A. dealbata*, Link). Tree 50 ft. or more high, with smooth bark and gray pubescent branchlets: lvs. silvery-gray to light green, 3–6½ in. long, with 13–25 pairs of pinnæ; lfts. 30–40 pairs; 1 gland between each pair of pinnæ: heads of 30 deep yellow fls. in simple or often compound racemes in early spring: pod 1½–4½ in. long, ⅜–½in. wide, glabrous, rich brown; seeds longitudinal, funicle ending in a silvery club-shaped aril; ripe July–Aug.

3. **A. Farnesiana**, Willd. (*Mimosa Farnesiana*, L. *Vachelia Farnesiana*, Wight & Arn.). POPINAC. OPOPANAX. CASSIE. HUISACHE. SWEET ACACIA. Much-branching shrub 6–10 ft. high, with straight spines: stipules of some or all the lvs. persistent and spinescent; lvs. bipinnate, the pinnæ 2–6 pairs; lfts. mostly 10–25 pairs, linear, 1⁄12–⅙in. long, glabrous:

fls. deep yellow, very fragrant, in heads about ½in. across, these 2–3 in the older axils, on pubescent peduncles ½–¾in. long, in Feb.–Mar.: pod cylindric, 1½–3 in. long, scarcely dehiscent, filled with a pith which separates the seeds from each other. (Grown in early times in the Farnesian garden, Rome.) Tex., Mex., Asia, Afr., Australia; probably of American origin but now nat. in all trop. countries.

4. **A. macracanthoides,** Bert. (*Poponax macracanthoides*, Britt. & Rose). Shrub or tree to 40 ft. or more, with nearly cylindrical spines about 1½ in. long, branchlets pubescent: lvs. bipinnate, petiole with oblong sessile gland; pinnæ many pairs; lfts. many, about ¼in. long, obtuse: fls. yellow, in globose peduncled heads about ⅓in. across: pod flat, to 3 in. long and ½in. wide, pubescent. W. Indies, Venezuela.

5. **A. verticillata,** Willd. Star or Whorl-leaved Acacia. Spreading shrub or small tree of graceful habit; branches more or less pubescent: phyllodia in whorls or often scattered, linear-subulate, 1-nerved, about ½–⅝in. long or more, 1⁄12–⅛in. wide, ending in a pungent point; gland occasionally present near the middle: fls. yellow, in spikes ½–1 in. long, often concealing the phyllodia, Mar.–Apr.: pod flat, straight or slightly curved, 2–3 in. long, ⅛in. wide; seeds longitudinal, ¼in. long, with light colored funicle of about same length thickened at end of seed into a cup-shaped aril: ripe June and early July.

6. **A. longifolia,** Willd. Sydney Golden Wattle. Tall shrub or small tree, glabrous or the branchlets slightly pubescent: phyllodia oblong-lanceolate or oblanceolate, narrowed at base, acute or obtuse, 2–3 or even 4–6 in. long, ¼–½in. wide, with 3–4 longitudinal nerves; gland near base: fls. bright yellow, 4-merous, in axillary spikes ¾–2¼ in. long, in early spring: pod 1½–5 in. long, ¼in. broad, terete until fully ripe when the valves flatten and separate, becoming dark and curled and persisting on the tree; seeds longitudinal, plump, black and shining, funicle silvery, bent upon itself several times, dilated and fitted like a cap over one end of the seed; ripe Aug., Sept. Var. **floribunda,** F. Muell. Foliage all at ends of branches, giving the plant a thin delicate appearance; phyllodia linear-lanceolate, acuminate, tipped with an oblique point: fls. whitish-yellow: pod contracted and long-constricted between the seeds; ripe July, Aug.: differing greatly from type in its extreme form but all variations between the two exist.

7. **A. latifolia,** Benth. Glabrous and glaucous; branchlets with 2–3 raised acute or almost winged angles: phyllodia obliquely ovate-rhomboid or falcate, 3–6 in. long, 1½–2 in. broad, 3–5-nerved: spikes pedunculate, loose, 1–2 in. long; fls. mostly 4-merous: pod shortly stipitate, 2–4 in. long, nearly ¼in. broad; seeds oblong, longitudinal, funicle scarcely folded, thickened into an oblique lateral aril.

8. **A. armata,** R. Br. Kangaroo-Thorn. Spreading shrub 8–10 ft. wide, 7–11 ft. high, with pendent finger-like branchlets: phyllodia not over 1 in. long, half-ovate, the straight edge hugging the st., the outer edge more or less undulate; nerve excentric, ending in a short pungent point; stipules reduced to slender spines about ¼in. long: fl.-heads yellow, solitary, on peduncles ½–¾in. long; fls. blooming in early spring, 5-merous, the sepals more than one-half as long as corolla: pod hairy, straight or slightly curled, 1½–2 in. long, 3⁄16in. wide, in clusters of 2–5 or reduced to 1; funicle silvery, as long as the seed and enlarged to a cup-shaped aril; ripe Aug.

9. **A. melanoxylon,** R. Br. Blackwood Acacia. Evergreen tree to 20 ft. and more, of pyramidal form and with dense foliage: bipinnate lf.-blades sometimes present; phyllodia acute, oblanceolate to lanceolate, with one margin more strongly curved than the other, 2½–4½ in. long, ¾in. wide, with 3–6 longitudinal veins; gland near base of phyllodia: heads cream-color, 40–50-fld., in axillary racemes shorter than the phyllodia, in early spring: pod reddish-brown, more or less curved and twisted into shape of letter C or S, 3–5 in. long, ⅜in. wide; seeds longitudinal, ⅛in. long, encircled in double fold by the long red funicle which is very characteristic of the species; ripe July–Nov., the seed remaining on the tree for months.

10. **A. podalyriæfolia,** Cunn. Pearl Acacia. Tall shrub with conspicuous glaucous gray branchlets covered with soft pubescence: phyllodia penninerved, pubescent (rarely glabrous), very glaucous, ovate or oblong, 1–1½ in. long, ½–1¼ in. wide, with excentric midrib, obliquely apiculate; gland at or near the middle of the margin nearest the midrib: heads numerous, yellow, in simple racemes longer than the phyllodia; calyx not half as long as corolla; petals pubescent, with prominent midrib: pod flat, glabrous or pubescent, 1–3 or more in. long, ¾in. broad; seeds longitudinal, funicle not encircling seed but in short folds at hilum end, the last fold slightly thickened.

11. **A. cultriformis,** Cunn. Knife Acacia. Tall shrub with gray glaucous glabrous foliage thickly clothing the branches: phyllodia obliquely ovate to almost triangular, ½–1 in. long, ¼–½in. wide, mucronate-tipped; midvein excentric, curved; gland about one-third the distance from the base on the margin farthest from midrib: heads yellow, many in axillary racemes much longer than the phyllodia, in early spring: pod rich brown, 1½–3 in. long, ¼in. wide, flat, occasionally constricted between the seeds, the margins somewhat thickened; seeds oblong, longitudinal, funicle half as long as seed, silvery and enlarged into a cup-shaped aril almost from the beginning; ripe Sept.–Oct.—Often pruned and used as a hedge.

12. **A. linearis,** Macb. (*Mimosa linearis,* Wendl. *A. linifolia,* Willd.). A tall shrub, minutely pubescent on the branchlets and at base of the young phyllodia: phyllodia linear on young shoots to linear-lanceolate on more mature ones, ¾–1½ in. long, 1/16–⅛in. wide, 1-nerved, mucronate; gland small, below the middle of the lf.: heads 8–12-fld., in racemes mostly shorter than the phyllodia, in early spring: pod flat, 2½–4 in. long, ⅜in. wide; funicle half as long as seed, with club-shaped aril.—**A. prominens,** Cunn. (*A. linifolia* var. *prominens,* Moore), has wider phyllodia with prominent gland varying in position, and broader pod.

13. **A. pycnantha,** Benth. Golden Wattle. Broad-leaved Wattle. Small tree with more or less pendulous branchlets: phyllodia penninerved, falcate and oblong-lanceolate to lanceolate or even broadly obovate, blunt at apex, 2½–6 in. long, ¾–1½ in. wide (seedling lvs. sometimes 4 in. wide and 5 in. long), 1-nerved, the nerve more or less excentric; gland ½–¾in. from base: racemes simple or compound, fragrant and showy, often bending the tree with their weight of bloom, in early spring; heads yellow, 50–60-fld., the peduncles ⅛in. long; sepals 5, ciliate, almost as long as petals: pod 2–5 in. long, ¼in. wide, contracted and slightly constricted between the seeds; funicle whitish, club-shaped, half as long as seed, not folded or occasionally folded and transverse to the seed; ripe Aug.

14. **A. neriifolia,** Cunn. Small tree with slender angled branchlets: phyllodia oblanceolate, acute or apiculate, 1½–5¼ in. long, ¼–⅜in. wide, with a prominent central nerve; gland near base of upper margin: heads in simple or branching racemes shorter than the phyllodia; fls. 5-merous, about 40 in a head: pod contracted and often constricted between the seeds, 3–6 in. long, 5/16in. wide; seeds longitudinal, oval, with central depression, funicle white, short, not encircling seed, but thickened into a club-shaped aril.

15. **A. saligna,** Wendl. Low tree or tall shrub with angular rather drooping branches: phyllodia lanceolate to linear-lanceolate or even oblanceolate, acute to obtuse, narrowed to base, with or without gland at base, ½–1¼ or even 1¾ in. wide, 3–8½ in. or the lower lvs. 1 ft. long; longitudinal nerve 1, often excentric: heads globose, ½in. diam., in large terminal racemes or reduced to 4–5 axillary heads strung along for 2–3 ft., in spring; peduncles ¼–½in. long: pod 3–5 in. long, ¼in. wide, constricted between the seeds, flat with nerve-like margins; funicle club-shaped, three-fourths as long as seed; late summer.

81. **CALLIANDRA,** Benth. (*Anneslia,* Salisb.). Shrubs or trees planted out-of-doors in the far S. or in the greenhouse N.; about 120 species, widely distributed in the tropics.—Plants mostly unarmed: lvs. bipinnate, with numerous lfts.: fls. purplish-red or white, usually in globose heads or clusters; calyx toothed or deeply cleft; corolla small, obscured by the numerous long silky purple or white stamens; ovary with many ovules: pod straight or nearly so, usually compressed, with thickened margin (in this differing from Albizia), elastically dehiscen from the apex. (Calli-an-dra: Greek *beautiful stamens.*)

C. Tweedii, Benth. (*Inga pulcherrima,* Cerv.). Unarmed shrub, lightly hairy: stipules scale-like; pinnæ in 3–4 pairs; lfts. in 20–30 pairs, linear, ⅛–¼in. long, obtuse, shining: peduncles axillary, 1–2 in. long, from large scaly buds; calyx and corolla silky, the lobes erect; stamens 1–1½ in. long, numerous, purple. (Bears the name of James Tweedie, 1775–1862, English botanist who collected in Brazil.) Brazil.

82. **PITHECELLOBIUM,** Mart. (often but not originally spelled *Pithecolobium*). About 125 species of shrubs or trees especially numerous in trop. Amer. and Asia, a few in trop. Afr. and Australia, planted for ornament and shade far S.—Unarmed or with stipular or axillary spines: lvs. bipinnate; pinnæ with few to many pairs of lfts., rarely with only 1 lft.: peduncles solitary or clustered, axillary or the clusters at the ends of the branches; fls. commonly white, in globose heads or oblong or cylindric spikes, 5–6-merous, bisexual or rarely unisexual; calyx shortly toothed; stamens few or many, much-exserted, united into a tube; ovary sessile or stalked, many-ovuled: pod compressed, circinate or variously twisted or rarely nearly straight, dehiscent or indehiscent or separating into joints; seeds compressed, often fleshy, funicle filiform or expanded to form a fleshy aril. (Pithecello-bium: Greek *monkey* and *ear-ring,* alluding to the circular pods.)

A. Infl. a spike .... 1. *P. lanceolatum*
AA. Infl. a head.
  B. Fls. white-tomentose .... 2. *P. dulce*
  BB. Fls. glabrous .... 3. *P. Unguis-cati*

1. **P. lanceolatum,** Benth. (*Inga lanceolatum,* Humb. & Bonpl.). Tree to 40 ft., with stipular spines to ¾in. long: lvs. of 1 pair of pinnæ; lfts. 1 pair, oblique, 1½–3 in. long, glabrous: fls. white, pubescent, in dense spikes to 5 in. long: pod nearly straight or curved, to 5 in. long, glabrous. Mex. to Venezuela.

2. **P. dulce**, Benth. (*Mimosa dulcis*, Roxb.). GUAYMOCHIL. HUAMUCHIL. OPIUMA. MANILA TAMARIND. Large stately tree to 50 ft., stipules reduced to short spines: lvs. and lfts. 1-pinnate; lfts. obovate or oblong, 1–2 in. long, obtuse, very oblique, glabrous or slightly pubescent: heads short-peduncled, the upper paniculate-racemose; fls. white, finely pubescent, ¼in. long: pod spirally twisted, 5–6 in. long, ⅓–½in. broad, reddish; seeds shining black, flat and irregularly triangular, the funicle dilated at apex into a fleshy aril. Trop. Amer., Philippines, E. Indies.

3. **P. Unguis-cati**, Mart. (*Mimosa Unguis-cati*, L.). CATS-CLAW. BLACK-BEAD. Shrub or small tree to 15 ft., with stipular spines to ¾in. long: lvs. of 1 pair of pinnæ; lfts. 1 pair, obovate or oblong, oblique, 1–2 in. long, glabrous: fls. greenish-yellow, in slender-stalked heads, ⅓in. long: pod spirally twisted, 2–4 in. long, ⅓in. wide, red, glabrous. Fla., W. Indies, N. S. Amer.

83. **SAMANEA**, Merr. Trees or shrubs of the American tropics, where one or two are much planted for shade; about 30 species.—Spineless or rarely spiny: lvs. with several to many pairs of pinnæ; pinnæ with 1 to many pairs of lfts.: fls. in globose heads, these axillary or variously clustered at the ends of the branches: pod straight or nearly so, rigid, more or less constricted, flat or more or less thickened, usually indehiscent, septate between the seeds. (Samane-a: a corruption of its native Spanish name, *Zaman*.)

S. Saman, Merr. (*Mimosa Saman*, Jacq. *Pithecellobium Saman*, Benth.). RAIN-TREE. ZAMAN. SAMAN. MONKEY-POD. Flat-topped tree with a spread often of 100 ft. and 60–80 ft. high, the branchlets velvety-pubescent: lvs. 2–4-pinnate; lfts. 2–8-pinnate, oblique, ovate-oblong or suborbicular, to 1½ in. long, shining above, pubescent beneath; glands between the pinnæ and between the lfts.: peduncles 2–3½ in. long; fls. in short-pedicelled heads, more or less tomentose; calyx ¼in. long; corolla ½in. long, yellowish; stamens 20, light crimson, to 2 in. long: pod sessile, straight, thick-margined, indehiscent, 6–8 in. long, ½–1 in. wide; seeds to 25, surrounded by pulp. Cent. Amer. and W. Indies and now widely distributed through the tropics.

84. **ALBIZIA**, Durazz. About 50 species of unarmed trees or shrubs in trop. and subtrop. regions of Asia, Afr. and Australia, 1 in Mex., planted for ornament far S. and some also valuable timber trees.—Lvs. alternate, usually deciduous, bipinnate; lfts. mostly small and numerous, oblique: fls. yellowish, white or pink, mostly 5-merous, in globose heads or cylindric spikes which are axillary or paniculately arranged at the ends of the branches; calyx toothed or shortly lobed; corolla-segms. connate to above the middle; stamens numerous, connate at base, exserted: fr. a large strap-shaped non-septate pod without pulp. (Albiz-ia: after Albizzi, an Italian naturalist.)—Usually, but not originally, spelled Albizzia.

A. Fls. in cylindric axillary spikes: lvs. somewhat persistent.......................... 1. *A. distachya*
AA. Fls. in globose heads: lvs. deciduous.
  B. Lfts. 1–1½ in. long, ovate or oblong, obtuse.......................... 2. *A. Lebbeck*
  BB. Lfts. ¼in. long, falcate, with midrib close to the upper margin, acute............ 3. *A. Julibrissin*

1. **A. distachya**, Macb. (*Mimosa distachya*, Vent. *A. lophantha*, Benth. *Acacia lophantha*, Willd.). PLUME ALBIZIA. Shrub or small tree 6–20 ft. high: lvs. with 14–24 pinnæ; lfts. 40–60, linear-oblong, obtuse, about ⅓in. long: spikes mostly 2, about 2 in. long, yellowish; fls. distinctly pedicelled, in early spring: pod about 3 in. long and ½in. wide. S. W. Australia.

2. **A. Lebbeck**, Benth. (*Mimosa Lebbeck*, L. *Acacia Lebbeck*, Willd.). LEBBECK-TREE. SIRIS-TREE. WOMANS-TONGUE-TREE. Large tree to 50 ft.: lvs. large, with 4–8 pinnæ; lfts. 10–18, oblique, oblong or obovate, 1–1½ in. long, nearly sessile: fls. greenish-yellow, in short-peduncled axillary globose heads, 3–4 together; stamens exserted about 1 in.: pod ½–1 ft. long, about 1½ in. wide, glabrous, shining, rattling. (Lebbeck: Arabic name.) Trop. Asia, N. Australia; nat. in W. Indies.

3. **A. Julibrissin**, Durazz. (*Acacia Julibrissin*, Willd.). SILK-TREE. Tree attaining 40 ft.: rachis of lf. with a small gland near base; pinnæ 8–24, with numerous oblique falcate-oblong apiculate lfts. ¼in. long, these with midrib close to the upper edge: heads pink, slender-peduncled, crowded at the upper end of the branches; stamens exserted about 1 in.: pod 3–6 in. long, under 1 in. wide, glabrous. (Julibrissin: Persian name.) Warmer temp. Asia from Iran to Japan. Var. **rosea**, Mouillef., is smaller, with bright pink fls.

97. GERANIACEÆ. GERANIUM FAMILY

Herbs ann. and per., with a few kinds woody, of 11 genera and about 640 species, widely distributed in temp. and subtrop. regions; the cult. kinds are grown mostly for ornament.—Lvs. opposite or alternate, simple or compound, usually stipulate:

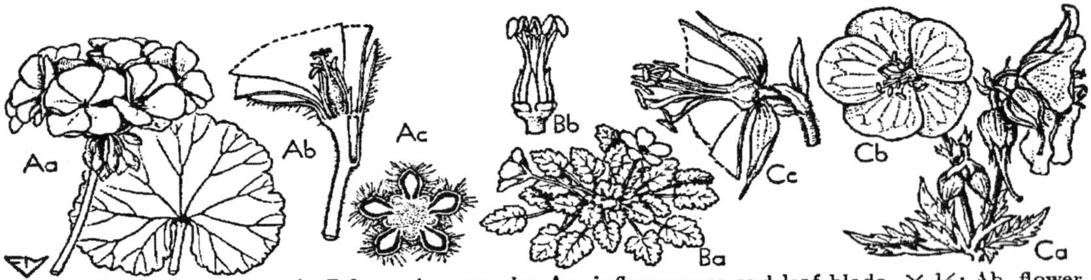

Fig. 97. Geraniaceæ. A, *Pelargonium zonale:* Aa, inflorescence and leaf-blade, × ¼; Ab, flower, perianth in vertical section, × 1; Ac, ovary, cross-section, × 5. B, *Erodium chamædryoides:* Ba, plant in flower, × ½; Bb, flower, less perianth, × 3. C, *Geranium pratense:* Ca, inflorescence, × ½; Cb, flower, face view, × ½; Cc, flower, perianth in vertical section, × 1.

fls. bisexual and mostly regular; sepals prevailingly 5 and distinct; petals also typically 5, hypogynous or nearly so, usually imbricate; stamens 5, or two to three times the number of the petals, some of them frequently sterile, filaments commonly more or less connate at base; pistil 1, 3–5-lobed and -celled, placentation axile, styles as many as ovary cells, ovules 1–2 in each cell: fr. dry, lobed, 1-seeded in each carpel, valves dehiscent from the base and joined by the styles.

A. Fls. without spur, having glands alternating with petals.
  B. Stamens all bearing anthers .... 1. Geranium
  BB. Stamens having outer filaments without anthers .... 2. Erodium
AA. Fls. with spur, which is adnate to pedicel (discovered when the pedicel is sectioned), without glands .... 3. Pelargonium

1. **GERANIUM,** L. Cranesbill. About 260 species, in temp. regions around the world, some of them ann. and weeds, a few of the perennials grown in the herbaceous garden.—Low usually diffuse plants with forking sts.: lvs. mostly orbicular to reniform, variously palmately lobed or dissected, the radical ones long-peduncled: fls. regular, without spur, the 5 petals imbricate and hypogynous; glands 5, alternating with petals; stamens 10, usually antheriferous: fr. comprised of turgid carpels mostly permanently attached to the styles. (Gera-nium: from the Greek word for *crane*, because of the beak-like fr.)

A. Plant alpine, 5–6 in. high.
  B. Peduncle 1-fld .... 5. *G. sanguineum* var. *prostratum*
  BB. Peduncle predominantly 2-fld.
    C. Foliage with dense silvery-silky pubescence .... 1. *G. argenteum*
    CC. Foliage slightly pubescent and glaucous, not silvery-silky .... 2. *G. cinereum*
AA. Plant not alpine, sts. 1–3 ft. long.
  B. Fls. ¼–½ in. across: plant ann. or bien .... 3. *G. Robertianum*
  BB. Fls. ¾–1½ in. across: plant per.
    C. Lvs. lobed to about the middle .... 4. *G. Traversii*
    CC. Lvs. lobed nearly or quite to base.
      D. Peduncle 1-fld .... 5. *G. sanguineum*
      DD. Peduncle 2- or more-fld.
        E. Hairs of pedicels glandular.
          F. Petals with dark spot at base .... 6. *G. psilostemon*
          FF. Petals without dark spot.
            G. Pedicels recurved in fr .... 7. *G. pratense*
            GG. Pedicels erect in fr.
              H. Sts. decumbent .... 8. *G. grandiflorum*
              HH. Sts. erect.
                I. Lobes of lvs. deeply toothed or cut, acute .... 9. *G. oreganum*
                II. Lobes of lvs. not deeply toothed, obtuse .... 10. *G. platypetalum*
        EE. Hairs of pedicels not glandular.
          F. Sts. erect.
            G. Lf.-blade 2–6 in. across: roots not bearing tubers.
              H. Petals retuse or somewhat 3-lobed .... 11. *G. ibericum*
              HH. Petals entire .... 12. *G. maculatum*
            GG. Lf.-blade to 1½ in. across: roots bearing little tubers .... 13. *G. Pylzowianum*
          FF. Sts. procumbent or ascending.
            G. Stipules broad-ovate: fls. purple .... 14. *G. Wallichianum*
            GG. Stipules lanceolate or linear: fls. violet .... 15. *G. Endressii*

1. **G. argenteum,** L. Per. 3–5 in. high, densely covered with silvery-silky pubescence: lvs. all basal, numerous, to 1 in. across, 5–7-parted nearly to base into lobed obtuse lobes, petioles 2–3 in. long: peduncles usually 2-fld.; pedicels often recurved in fr.; fls. pink with darker veins, 1–1¼ in. across, petals retuse. N. Italy.

2. **G. cinereum,** Cav. Per. 3–6 in. high, pubescent: lvs. mostly basal, numerous, about 1 in. across, 5–7-parted nearly to base into 3-lobed obtuse lobes, glaucous, petioles 2–4 in. long: peduncles 2-fld.; fls. violet with darker veins, 1–1½ in. across, petals emarginate. Pyrenees. Var. **subcaulescens,** Knuth (*G. subcaulescens,* L'Her.), differs in hairs of calyx spreading rather than appressed.

3. **G. Robertianum,** L. (*Robertiella Robertianum,* Hanks). Herb-Robert. Red Robin. Ann. or bien. with erect or decumbent sts. to 1½ ft., glandular-pubescent: lvs. 3–5-parted, the divisions deeply cut, long-petioled: peduncles 2-fld.; fls. red-purple, ¼–½in. across, petals entire. N. Amer., Eurasia, N. Afr.

4. **G. Traversii,** Hook. f. Per. with prostrate or decumbent sts. to 2 ft. long, gray-pubescent: lvs. 1–3 in. across, 5–7-lobed to the middle, lobes toothed at tips, petioles 4–9 in. long: peduncles 1-fld.; fls. pink or white, ¾–1 in. across, petals entire. (Named for W. T. L. Travers, 1819–1903, New Zealand botanist.) Chatham Isl.

5. **G. sanguineum,** L. Common per. border plant with cord-like roots, 15–20 in. high, much-branched and very leafy, with scattered spreading white glandless hairs: lvs. circular in outline, 1–2½ in. across, parted into 5–7 narrow nearly blunt lobed lobes, petioles 2–4 in. long: peduncles 1-fld.; fls. purple to bluish-purple or bright magenta, 1–1½ in. across, petals emarginate. Eurasia. Var. **prostratum,** Pers. (*G. lancastriense,* With.), is a dwarfer more compact form. Var. **album,** Hort., has white fls.

6. **G. psilostemon,** Ledeb. (*G. armenum,* Boiss.). Per., with few or solitary erect sts. 1–2 ft. high, much forked above, appressed-hairy: lvs. reniform-orbicular, deeply 5-parted, the acute or incised-dentate lobes more or less rhomboid, petioles 8–10 in. long: peduncles 2-fld.; pedicels with glandular hairs; fls. dark red, about 1½ in. across, the obovate retuse petals with dark spot at base. Armenia.

7. **G. pratense,** L. Erect per., 1–3 ft., hairy-pubescent, glandular above: lvs. 3–6 in. across, 7-divided into cut and dentate sharp lobes, petioles 6–12 in. long: peduncles 2-fld.; pedicels with glandular hairs, recurved in fr.; fls. purple, 1¼–1½ in. across, petals sometimes slightly notched, ciliate. Eurasia. Var. **album,** Hort., has white fls.

8. **G. grandiflorum,** Edgew. Per., with decumbent or ascending sts. to about 1 ft., glandular-hairy: lvs. 1¾ in. across, deeply 5-lobed, the lobes irregularly toothed, petioles to 6 in. long: peduncles several-fld.; pedicels with glandular hairs; fls. lilac with purple veins, 1½ in. across, petals rounded. Asia.

9. **G. oreganum,** Howell (*G. incisum,* Nutt.). Erect per. 1–2 ft. high, branched above: lvs. 2–6 in. across, loosely pubescent, 3–5-parted, the lobes deeply toothed or cut into acute divisions, petioles 8–16 in. long: peduncles 2- or more-fld.; pedicels with glandular hairs; fls. bright rose-purple, 1½ in. across. B. C. to N. Calif.

10. **G. platypetalum,** Fisch. & Mey. (*G. ibericum* var. *platypetalum,* Boiss.). Erect per. to 2 ft., glandular-hairy: lvs. deeply 5–7-lobed, the lobes obtuse and not deeply toothed: peduncles 2-fld.; fls. dark purple, 1 in. across. S. W. Asia.

11. **G. ibericum,** Cav. Per. from a strong rhizome; sts. several, stout, erect, branched above, 1½ ft.: basal lvs. few, long-petioled; blade angular-orbiculate, 2–6 in. across, lobed nearly to base, the lobes obovate or obovate-rhomboid and coarsely pinnatifid: fls. about 2 on a non-glandular peduncle, purple or purple-blue, without a dark center, about 1½ in. across, petals retuse or somewhat 3-lobed. S. W. Asia.

12. **G. maculatum,** L. Erect per. 1–2 ft. high, with usually solitary sts. and stout rhizome: lvs. 3–6 in. across, deeply 5–7-parted, the lobes coarsely toothed and acute, the basal long-petioled: peduncles 2–3 from the axils, 2- or more-fld.; fls. rose-purple, 1–1½ in. across, petals entire. N. Amer.

13. **G. Pylzowianum,** Maxim. Per., rhizome filiform, bearing little tubers; sts. erect, 1 ft. or more: lvs. to 1½ in. across, 5-parted into 3-lobed linear lobes: peduncles 2-fld.; fls. purple, 1¼ in. across. (Bears the name of Pylzow, Russian military officer.) China.

14. **G. Wallichianum,** D. Don. Per. with procumbent or ascending sts. 1–2 ft. long, many-lvd.: lvs. 2–3 in. wide, deeply 3–5-lobed, the lobes rhomboid and irregularly toothed, petioles 2–4 in. long; stipules broad-ovate, connate, ½–1 in. long: peduncles 2-fld.; fls. purple with darker veins, 1½–2 in. across, petals retuse. (Named for Nathaniel Wallich, page 53.) Himalayas.

15. **G. Endressii,** J. Gay. Per. with long stout rhizomes and procumbent or ascending sts. to 1½ ft. long: lvs. 2–3 in. across, deeply 5-lobed, the ovate acute lobes shallowly cut, hairy, petioles 4–12 in. long; stipules lanceolate, ⅓in. long: peduncles 2-fld.; fls. violet, about 1 in. across, petals entire. (Named for Ph. A. Chr. Endress, 1806–1831, collector in Pyrenees.) Pyrenees.

2. **ERODIUM,** L'Her. Heronsbill. About 60 widespread species in temp. and semitrop. regions.—Mostly low herbs, ann. or per., differing from Geranium in bearing only 5 antheriferous stamens, carpel-bodies or pistil-lobes slender or spindle-shaped, styles coiled at maturity. (Ero-dium: Greek *heron's bill.*)—Aside from two or three agricultural kinds, the species are grown in rock-gardens or borders.

A. Lvs. not compound, although sometimes pinnately lobed.
B. Plant ann. or bien.: lvs. pinnately lobed.............................. 1. *E. Botrys*
BB. Plant per.: lvs. shallowly toothed or lobed.
C. Peduncles usually 2-fld.: foliage gray-tomentose.................. 2. *E. corsicum*
CC. Peduncles 1-fld.: foliage sparsely hairy........................... 3. *E. chamædryoides*
AA. Lvs. pinnately compound.
B. Fls. yellow.. 4. *E. chrysanthum*
BB. Fls. pink to purple and white.
C. Foliage both basal and cauline.
D. Plant a per. to 8 in.. 5. *E. absinthioides*
DD. Plant an ann. or bien. to 1½ ft.
E. Sepals tipped with bristle-like hairs: stipules small and acute...... 6. *E. cicutarium*
EE. Sepals without terminal hairs: stipules large and obtuse......... 7. *E. moschatum*
CC. Foliage all basal.
D. Width of fls. to 1½ in.. 8. *E. Manescavii*
DD. Width of fls. ⅓–¾ in.
E. Petals with black spot at base.
F. Herbage gray-tomentose.. 9. *E. cheilanthifolium*
FF. Herbage green, pubescent or nearly glabrous...............10. *E. macradenum*
EE. Petals without black spot.
F. Pedicels and petioles densely glandular.....................11. *E. trichomanifolium*
FF. Pedicels and petioles not glandular.........................12. *E. romanum*

1. E. **Botrys**, Bert. (*Geranium Botrys*, Cav.). Prostrate white-pubescent ann. or bien., sometimes used for forage and nat. on the Pacific slope: lvs. 1–4 in. long, on long petioles, oblong-ovate, pinnatifid, with serrate acute lobes: peduncles 2–4-fld.; fls. violet; sepals tipped with 1 or 2 short bristles; petals rounded: beak of fr. 3–5 in. long. Medit. region.

2. E. **corsicum**, Leman. Per. to 6 in.: lvs. mostly basal, numerous, ovate, to ¾in. long, coarsely crenate-dentate, long-petioled, gray-tomentose: peduncles usually 2-fld.; fls. pink veined with rose, to ¾in. across; petals retuse: beak of fr. about ½in. long. Corsica, Sardinia.

3. E. **chamædryoides**, L'Her. (*Geranium chamædryoides*, Cav.). Stemless per. 2–3 in. high: lvs. mostly basal, numerous, ovate, ⅓in. long, wavy-toothed, long-petioled, sparsely hairy: peduncles 1-fld.; fls. white veined with rose, ¼–½in. across; petals retuse: beak of fr. ⅖in. long. Balearic Isls., Corsica. Var. **roseum**, Hort., has pink fls. with deeper rose veins.

4. E. **chrysanthum**, L'Her. Tufted per. to 5 in., densely silvery-tomentose: lvs. mostly basal, bipinnate into small lobes, to 3 in. long with petiole: peduncles 2–5-fld.; fls. yellow, ½in. across: petals retuse: beak of fr. 2 in. long. Greece.

5. E. **absinthioides**, Willd. Per. to 8 in., soft-pubescent: lvs. basal and cauline, bipinnate into linear-lanceolate small lobes, to 5 in. long with petiole: peduncles 2–8-fld.; fls. violet, rarely rose or white, ¾in. across; petals somewhat retuse: beak of fr. 1¾ in. long. Asia Minor. Var. **amanum**, Brumh. (*E. amanum*, Boiss. & Kotschy), is gray-pubescent with white fls.

6. E. **cicutarium**, L'Her. (*Geranium cicutarium*, L.). ALFILARIA. RED-STEM FILAREE. Ann. 6–18 in. and much-branched, soft-hairy and commonly red-stemmed, somewhat grown for hay W. and S. W. and utilized as wild pasture, it having been extensively nat. from Eu.: basal lvs. forming rosette 8–12 in. across where it grows as winter ann.; pinnæ 6–12 or more, sessile, small, oblong or ovate-oblong, pinnatifid into obtuse or acute narrow lobes: peduncles 5–10-fld.; fls. purple or pink, about ⅓in. across, the entire ciliate-clawed petals equalled or exceeded by the sharp sepals that are tipped by 1 or 2 bristle-like more or less deciduous white hairs: beak of fr. 1–1½ in. long. Medit. region.

7. E. **moschatum**, L'Her. (*Geranium moschatum*, L.). WHITE-STEM FILAREE. MUSK-CLOVER. Hirsute ann. known somewhat for forage and sometimes grown in the fl.-garden: differs from no. 6 in having mostly white sts., less deeply cut lfts., large membranaceous rather than small and acute stipules, sepals not tipped with bristle-like hairs. Medit. region and E.; extensively nat. in Calif.

8. E. **Manescavii**, Coss. Per. to 1½ ft., hairy: lvs. all basal, bipinnate into toothed lobes, to 1 ft. long: peduncles 5–12-fld., basal, to 1 ft. long; fls. rosy-purple, to 1½ in. across; petals obtuse: beak of fr. 1½ in. long. (Named in 1847 for its collector, Manescau.) Pyrenees.

9. E. **cheilanthifolium**, Boiss. Stemless per. to 4 in., gray-tomentose: lvs. all basal, 1–2 in. long, on long petioles, bipinnate into small oblong-ovate lobes: peduncles 2–4-fld.; fls. white veined with rose and with dark spot at base of 2 upper rounded petals, to ¾in. across: beak of fr. 1 in. long. Mts. of S. Spain and Morocco.

10. E. **macradenum**, L'Her. Stemless per. to 6 in.: lvs. all basal, 1–4 in. long, long-petioled, bipinnate into small linear-ovate lobes: peduncles 2–6-fld.; fls. veined with rose and 2 upper rounded petals with dark spot at base, about ½in. across: beak of fr. ¾in. long. Pyrenees.

11. E. **trichomanifolium**, L'Her. Stemless per. to 5 in.: lvs. all basal, 1–4 in. long, long-petioled, bipinnate into small linear lobes, densely pubescent and glandular: peduncles 2–7-fld.; fls. violet veined with rose, ⅓in. across; petals rounded: beak of fr. 1 in. long. Syria.

12. **E. romanum,** Ait. (*Geranium romanum*, Burm. f.). Stemless per. to 6 in.: lvs. all basal, 2–3 in. long, long-petioled, bipinnate into small ovate toothed lobes, gray-pubescent: peduncles 4–9-fld.; fls. rose, 1/2in. across; petals obtuse: beak of fr. to 2 in. long. Medit. region.

3. **PELARGONIUM,** L'Her. STORKSBILL. More than 230 per. herbs and subshrubs, mostly from S. Afr., a number much grown for ornament and yielding the "geraniums" of florists.—Plants often succulent: lvs. mostly opposite, either digitately or pinnately veined, lobed or dissected, often strong-smelling: fls. of many colors, the calyx with a nectar-spur that is joined to the pedicel for much of the length of the latter; sepals and petals usually 5, the 2 upper petals mostly larger and more prominently colored; stamens 10, somewhat connate at base, part of them without anthers: fr. of 5 valves which usually coil as they dehisce. (Pelargo-nium: Greek *stork's bill*, from the fr.)—The identity of garden races is still in need of new investigation; some of these races are undoubtedly the result of long hybridization and mutation; the cultivars are numerous.

A. Plant weak and trailing or climbing, smooth or nearly so . . . . 1. *P. peltatum*
AA. Plant erect, variously hairy or pubescent, more or less shrubby at base.
B. Sts. succulent, at least when young: lvs. scarcely if at all lobed, usually with a broad color zone inside the margin.
C. Height of the usually solitary st. 8–16 in.: petals 1/6–1/4 in. wide, 2/3–3/4 in. long . . . . 2. *P. zonale*
CC. Height of the usually several sts. much greater . . . . 3. *P. hortorum*
BB. Sts. not succulent: lvs. lobed or parted, without color zone inside margin.
C. Petals about 1/4in. long.
D. Stipules becoming spine-like, persistent on old sts . . . . 4. *P. echinatum*
DD. Stipules deltoid.
E. Lower part of pedicel about as long as spurred part: stipules usually connate . . . . 5. *P. odoratissimum*
EE. Lower part of pedicel shorter than spurred part: stipules usually separate . . . . 6. *P. fragrans*
CC. Petals mostly 1/2–1 1/2 in. long.
D. Lvs. angled or only obscurely lobed, sharp-toothed: petals 1 1/4–1 1/2 in. long . . . . 7. *P. domesticum*
DD. Lvs. variously lobed: petals to 1 in. long.
E. Color of petals white: lower part of pedicel much longer than spurred part . . . . 8. *P. tomentosum*
EE. Color of petals rose to purplish: lower part of pedicel not longer than spurred part.
F. Blades of lvs. pinnately lobed . . . . 9. *P. quercifolium*
FF. Blades of lvs. palmately lobed.
G. Lf. small, usually not over 1 in. long, 3-lobed . . . . 10. *P. crispum*
GG. Lf. larger, mostly over 2 in. long.
H. Lobes of lvs. about 1 in. broad, shallow and obtuse.
I. Habit diffuse or procumbent: lvs. lobed more than half way to midrib . . . . 11. *P. capitatum*
II. Habit erect: lvs. not lobed half way to midrib . . . . 12. *P. vitifolium*
HH. Lobes of lvs. pinnatifid into narrower divisions.
I. Upper petals bilobed . . . . 13. *P. denticulatum*
II. Upper petals entire.
J. Ultimate divisions of lf. sublinear, 1/8in. wide, with distant teeth . . . . 14. *P. Radula*
JJ. Ultimate divisions of lf. 1/4in. wide, with dentate margins. 15. *P. graveolens*

1. **P. peltatum,** Ait. (*Geranium peltatum*, L.). IVY GERANIUM. Plant weak, trailing, drooping or somewhat climbing; sts. 2–3 ft. or more long, glabrous or very nearly so: lvs. alternate, somewhat succulent, nearly orbicular, the petiole inserted within the margin (blade peltate), 2–3 in. across, shallowly 5-angle-lobed, the margin otherwise entire but ciliate, the stipules large and cordate-triangular: fls. few or several in an umbel terminating a peduncle 3–8 in. long, pedicels pubescent and 1–1 1/2 in. long including the spur; corolla rose-carmine, about 1 in. long, the upper petals blotched and striped, 3 lower petals separated from the others. S. Afr.—An old window-garden plant and also now much modified; often runs to white and lilac races.

2. **P. zonale,** Ait. (*Geranium zonale*, L.). ZONAL OR HORSESHOE GERANIUM. Sparsely branched, 8–16 in. high, more or less pilose: lvs. alternate, more or less pubescent, roundish-cordate, crenate-dentate, obscurely many-lobed, mostly with a dark horse-shoe mark above, blades 3–4 in. across, petioles 1–4 in. long; stipules cordate-oblong, 1/4–1 in. long: peduncles axillary, 4–8 in. long, 9–27-fld.; bracts ovate, abruptly acuminate, 1/4–2/3in. long; pedicels to about 1 1/4 in. long; sepals lanceolate, about 3/8in. long; petals 5/8–3/4 in. long, 3/16–1/4 in. wide, oblanceolate or spatulate, pink to deep red; pistil densely villous, to 1 1/2 in. long in fr. S. Afr.—It is doubtful whether the original wild form is in cult.

3. **P. hortorum,** Bailey. FISH GERANIUM. Stout plant with succulent sts. becoming woody when grown in the open (in mild regions) year by year, constituting the common geraniums for windows and bedding, often wintered-over in cellars: herbage with a strong

fishy odor, finely pubescent; lvs. mostly alternate, orbicular to reniform, 3–5 in. across, somewhat scalloped, more or less crenate-toothed, usually with a broad color zone inside the margin, on petioles 1–5 in. long: fls. many in an involucrate umbel terminating long peduncles from upper axils, the unopened ones deflexed, pedicels 1–1½ in. long including the very long spur; corolla red, pink, salmon, white, the 3 lower petals larger or all of them nearly equal, ½–1 in. long. Cultigen; probably derived from *P. inquinans* and *P. zonale*, and perhaps others, of S. Afr. Var. **marginatum**, Bailey, lvs. with white margins.

4. **P. echinatum,** Curt. (*Geranium echinatum*, Thunb.). St. fleshy, puberulent, 6–20 in. high, when old armed with persistent spine-like remains of the stipules ⅛–⅜in. long: lvs. opposite, cordate-ovate, pubescent above, white-tomentose beneath, somewhat 3–7-lobed, crenulate, 1–2½ in. across, on petioles 1–5 in. long: peduncles 3–8-fld., 1–6 in. long; pedicels including the spur about 1½ in. long; sepals white-hairy, oblong, ¼in. long; petals white to red-purple with darker blotches, obovate, slightly emarginate, ½in. long. S. Afr.

5. **P. odoratissimum,** Ait. (*Geranium odoratissimum*, L.). Apple or Nutmeg Geranium. Many-stemmed lax finely tomentose-pubescent plant with short woody caudex and many straggling slender branches 12–20 in. long, the herbage pleasantly scented: lvs. opposite, the slender petiole 1–10 in. long, the blade reniform-cordate or -truncate, 1–2 in. across, crenate, thin in texture; stipules deltoid, ⅛in. long, usually connate: fls. 5–10 in umbels on peduncles 2–3 in. long; pedicel about ½in. long, the lower part subequal to the spur; corolla about ¼in. long, not wide-spreading, white or whitish: fr. about ½–¾in. long, hairy. S. Afr.—Grown for its sweet-smelling herbage.

6. **P. fragrans,** Willd. Near to no. 5: strict rather stiff plant, sts. very leafy, with free stipules: spur much longer than lower part of pedicel; corolla whitish with pink veins. S. Afr.—Known for its fragrant herbage, but apparently not common in cult. (see no. 10).

7. **P. domesticum,** Bailey. Show or Fancy Geraniums or Pelargoniums. Erect soft-hairy forking plants, sts. not succulent, with long spreading soft hairs: lvs. broadly cordate-ovate to almost reniform, sometimes truncate at base, 2–4 in. across, more or less obscurely angled, margins with many unequal sharp teeth; stipules scarious, cordate-ovate, ¼–⅜in. long: fls. large and very showy, sometimes 2 in. across or more, few or several in an umbel terminating long or short peduncles, the pedicel various beneath the spur; sepals lanceolate to oblong, soft-hairy, about ½in. long; corolla white to pink, wine-red, and crimson, the 2 upper broad petals 1¼–1½ in. long, with brilliant blotches of darker color. Cultigen; apparently descended from several S. African species.—Grown as pot-plants, often as Lady Washington geraniums.

8. **P. tomentosum,** Jacq. Suffruticose, freely branched, soft white-hairy throughout, the sts. becoming several ft. long: lvs. opposite or alternate, hastate-cordate at base, 5–7-lobed, velvety, 3–5 in. across, on petioles 2–5 in. long; stipules deltoid-cordate, acuminate, to ½in. long: peduncles slender, 2–6 in. long, 4–20-fld.; pedicels ½–1 in. long, the lower part usually much longer than the spur; sepals about ¼in. long; petals white with red near center, the 3 lower narrow and longer than calyx, the 2 upper wider and often equalling calyx. S. Afr.—Peppermint-scented.

9. **P. quercifolium,** Ait. (*Geranium quercifolium*, L. f.). Oak-leaved Geranium. Strong plant to 3 ft., becoming shrubby, pubescent or at length nearly glabrous: lvs. triangular-oblong or -ovate, cordate at base, petioles 1–2 in. long; blade 2–4 in. long, pinnately 2–3-lobed on either side, the lobes serrate and more or less angled; stipules triangular-acute, bifid, ⅛–³⁄₁₆in. long: fls. few on peduncles usually not overtopping the foliage, the pedicel little if any below the spur and about ½in. long; sepals elliptical, about ⅜in. long; corolla about ¾in. long, blush to rose or violet with deeper veins and markings, petals narrow and upper 2 larger. S. Afr.—An old garden plant but apparently not now common.

10. **P. crispum,** L'Her. (*Geranium crispum*, L.). Stocky woody little strict-growing plant but becoming 2–3 ft. high with age, scabrous-pubescent, grayish, very leafy: lvs. alternate, small, usually not exceeding 1 in. long, often more or less 2-ranked, cordate-reniform to round-ovate, entire at base, the blade rounded and somewhat obtusely toothed and incised but not divided, the margin crisped; stipules cordate, acute, ⅛in. long: fls. 1–3 on short stout peduncles, the pedicels ½–¾in. long, the part below the spur usually very short; sepals oblong, ⅜in. long; corolla ¾–1 in. long, pink or rose with darker markings, the 2 upper petals larger and sometimes emarginate. S. Afr.—An old-time garden plant with lemon-scented foliage, sometimes grown as *P. fragrans* and *P. odoratum*. **P. Limoneum,** Sweet, Lemon Geranium, is a probable derivative from *P. crispum:* lvs. somewhat larger and not 2-ranked: fls. purple and lilac.

11. **P. capitatum,** Ait. (*Geranium capitatum*, L.). Sts. weak and trailing but suffruticose, densely and softly white-hairy, 3 or more ft. long: lvs. alternate, roundish-cordate, 1–3 in. across, dentate and with 3–5 rounded shallow obtuse lobes, petioles 1–2½ in. long; stipules broad-cordate, ¼in. or longer: peduncles slender, 1–4 in. long, densely 9–20-fld.; pedicels to ¼in. long, mostly of spurred part; sepals oblong, densely soft-hairy, ⅜in. long, mucronate; 2 upper petals rose veined deep purple, about ¾in. long, the 3 lower shorter and rose. S. Afr.—Rose-scented. Material cult. as *P. capitatum* seems largely to belong to no. 15.

12. **P. vitifolium,** Ait. (*Geranium vitifolium,* L.). Erect, becoming shrubby, to 3 ft., grayish-hirsute-pubescent: lvs. numerous, alternate, petioles stout, 1–2½ in. long; blades cordate-ovate to nearly reniform, 2–3 in. across and of equal or less length, with about 3 main shallow very obtuse lobes on the digitate order but which are not again manifestly lobed but variously angled, the margins crenate to somewhat acutely dentate; stipules broadly ovate-cordate, ¼–½in. long: fls. small, several to many in dense umbels on short peduncles, sessile or nearly so; sepals oblong, mucronate, ¼in. long; corolla about ½in. long or less, rose or pink with darker veins, 2 upper petals larger. S. Afr.—Long in cult. but not now often seen.

13. **P. denticulatum,** Jacq. A rather weak plant, suffruticose, 3 ft. or so high, glutinous and scabrous: lvs. alternate, petioles 2–5 in. long; blades triangular-ovate, palmately parted, 2–5 in. across, the lobes linear and long, margins of lobes and rachis cut down nearly to midrib with many teeth; stipules lance-ovate, 3/16–3/8in. long: peduncles short, hairy, 3–4-fld.; fls. subsessile; sepals ⅓in. long; petals ½in. long, lilac or rose-purple, the 2 upper lobed and with dark streaks. S. Afr.—Somewhat grown for its ornamental foliage as well as its balsamic odor, sometimes as *P. filicifolium* (fern-leaved).

14. **P. Radula,** L'Her. (*Geranium Radula,* Cav.). Much like no. 13 but rough-hairy, petioles mostly 1–2 in. long, lobes of blades less clammy and with very few and distant teeth: petals entire, ¾in. long. S. Afr.—Although long in cult., it is not often seen in the typical narrow-lobed form.

15. **P. graveolens,** L'Her. Fragrant-lvd. bushy plant, 2–3 ft., becoming woody, grayish-green, hairy-pubescent: lvs. long-petioled, broadly cordate-ovate to nearly circular, with 5–7 lobes close together extending nearly to the base, on a digitate order and the lobes again lobed into flat divisions something like ¼in. across, the margins variously dentate: fls. small, among the lvs. in dense little umbels on short peduncles, nearly or quite sessile; corolla about ½in. long, rose or pink and veined purple, petals entire, the 2 upper ones larger. S. Afr.—The commonest form of Rose geranium, and much grown in window-gardens for its sweet-scented herbage. Nos. 9, 13, 14 and 15 are all rose geraniums, but none so popular as this species. Many of the rose geraniums are apparently hybrids of different grades of complexity. *P. roseum* is a garden name applied in this group. **P. terebinthinaceum,** Small (*Geranium terebinthinaceum,* Cav.), is considered by the latest monographer to be *P. quercifolium* × *P. graveolens;* it has broad lobes, subsessile fls., petals purplish, ⅗in. long. **P. melissinum,** Sweet, is thought to be *P. crispum* × *P. graveolens:* lvs. deeply 5-lobed, 3–6 in. wide: pedicels unequal, 1–1½ in. long; petals white with purplish or deep red blotches.

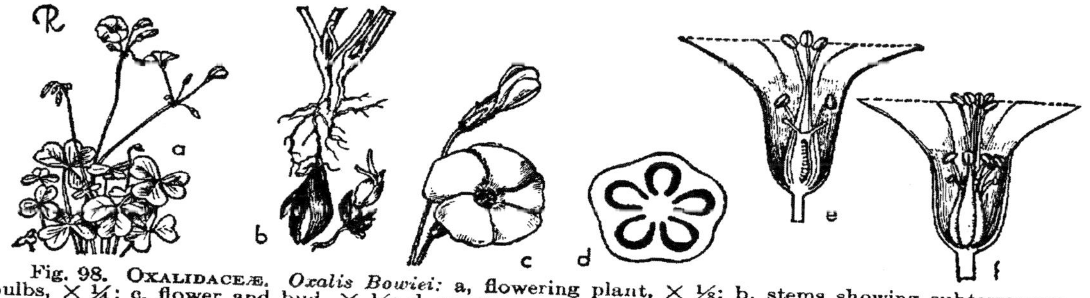

Fig. 98. OXALIDACEÆ. *Oxalis Bowiei:* a, flowering plant, × ⅛; b, stems showing subterranean bulbs, × ¼; c, flower and bud, × ½; d, ovary, cross-section, × 10; e, flower, vertical section, × 2; f, flower, perianth removed, × 2.

98. OXALIDACEÆ. OXALIS or WOOD-SORREL FAMILY

Species 500 and more, widely spread in temp. and trop. regions, ann. and per. herbs, sometimes shrubs and trees, several grown for ornament and very few for edible parts; probably 10 or more genera; juice usually sour.—Technically the family differs from Geraniaceæ in the carpels not splitting apart and stamens twice the number of petals: lvs. usually compound, either digitate or pinnate: fls. bisexual and regular, the sepals and petals 5 and sometimes more or less united at base; stamens 10 in at least 2 whorls, hypogynous, the outer set opposite the petals, filaments joined near base and some or all of them with glandular appendages at base; styles 5, separate; stigmas capitate or shortly 2-fid; ovary superior, 5-celled, 2- to many-ovuled, placentation axile: fr. a dry dehiscent caps. or fleshy and berry-like.

A. Lvs. digitate: herbs or subshrubs: fr. capsular........1. OXALIS
AA. Lvs. pinnate: trees: fr. baccate........2. AVERRHOA

1. **OXALIS,** L. Wood-Sorrel. As generally interpreted, a large genus of about 500 species of herbs and suffrutescent subshrubs.—Plant acaulescent or caulescent, ann. or per., often with tuberous or bulbous underground parts: lvs. alternate, digitate; lfts. 3 or 5 to 20 or more, sensitive to light (going to "sleep" at night): fls. 1 to several, terminating axillary peduncles, white, pink, red, yellow; stamens 10, monadelphous at base, 5 long and 5 short; styles 5: fr. a loculicidal caps. (Ox-alis: Greek for *sour*.)—Some of the species are grown in window-gardens and as hanging-basket subjects, also in the open border; a few are hothouse subjects; certain kinds are grown elsewhere for the edible bulbous roots; several species are common weeds. The fls. may be dimorphic or trimorphic (heterostyly being usual), and small inconspicuous cleistogamous fls. are produced by some species.

A. Color of fls. yellow.
  B. Lfts. 1½–2 in. long, fish-tailed at end … 1. *O. Ortgiesii*
  BB. Lfts. ½–¾in. long, not fish-tailed.
    C. Fls. 1–1½ in. across: plant producing bulbs … 2. *O. Pes-capræ*
    CC. Fls. ¼–½in. across: plant with fibrous roots.
      D. Sts. prostrate, often rooting … 3. *O. corniculata*
      DD. Sts. erect or ascending … 4. *O. valdiviensis*
AA. Color of fls. rose, purple or white.
  B. Number of lfts. 4 or more.
    C. Length of lfts. ¼–½in. … 5. *O. adenophylla*
    CC. Length of lfts. 1–3 in.
      D. Lfts. 4, obovate to orbicular … 6. *O. Deppei*
      DD. Lfts. 8–10, lingulate … 7. *O. lasiandra*
  BB. Number of lfts. 3.
    C. Fls. solitary.
      D. Lfts. glabrous, ⅕in. across … 8. *O. magellanica*
      DD. Lfts. hairy below and on margins, 1 in. across … 9. *O. oregana*
    CC. Fls. in cymes or umbels.
      D. Width of fls. 1½–2 in. … 10. *O. Bowiei*
      DD. Width of fls. ¼–¾in.
        E. Pedicels and under surface of lvs. pubescent … 11. *O. rubra*
        EE. Pedicels and under surface of lvs. glabrous.
          F. Plant having scaly bulbs: lvs. basal … 12. *O. violacea*
          FF. Plant not having scaly bulbs: lvs. cauline … 13. *O. rosea*

1. **O. Ortgiesii,** Regel. Per.; sts. strict and straight, purplish, 12–18 in., pubescent, leafy: lvs. long-petioled, 3-foliolate, purplish beneath; lfts. 1½–2 in. long, tapering to base, the terminal one broadly notched one-third its depth into nearly or quite acute lobes, the lateral ones with 1 lobe smaller than the other: fls. about ½in. long, yellow with darker veins, few in forking cymes on slender axillary peduncles. (Bears the name of E. Ortgies, 1829–1916, German horticulturist.) Andes of Peru.—A glasshouse plant.

2. **O. Pes-capræ,** L. (*O. cernua,* Thunb. *Bolboxalis cernua,* Small). Bermuda-Buttercup. Per. from a deep thickened or tuberous tap-root and scaly bulbs, acaulescent: lvs. 3-foliolate, very long-stalked; lfts. about 1 in. broad in well developed specimens and ¾in. long, deeply obcordate, thinly hairy beneath and ciliate, often spotted: fls. several on very long peduncles, nodding, 1–1½ in. across, bright yellow and showy. S. Afr.; nat. in Bermuda and Fla.

3. **O. corniculata,** L. (*Xanthoxalis corniculata,* Small). Small loosely pubescent or nearly glabrous plant with creeping sts., the shoots ascending 1–10 in.; per. but blooming first year: lvs. 3-foliolate; lfts. about ½in. long in large-lvd. races, broadly obcordate: fls. few, mostly not exceeding ¼in. long, light yellow, more or less reflexed. Old World, and a common weed in N. Amer. Frequent on the floor of greenhouses and on pots and tubs in the close-creeping form var. **repens,** Zucc. Var. **atropurpurea,** Planch. (*O. tropæoloides,* Schlecht.), is a purple-lvd. race sometimes used in bedding.

4. **O. valdiviensis,** Barn. Grown as an ann., probably per.; sts. ascending, 2–8 in. long and bearing many long-stalked erect lvs. and very long peduncles, glabrous: lvs. 3-foliolate; lfts. about ¾in. long, broadly obcordate: fls. in close umbellate cymes, ½in. long, bright yellow and striped brown inside, profusely produced. Chile.

5. **O. adenophylla,** Gill. Scapose per. to 6 in., with tuberous roots: lvs. basal, long-petioled, of about 12 obcordate glaucous lfts. ¼–½in. long: fls. solitary or few, pink with deeper veins, to 1½ in. across. Chile, Argentina.

6. **O. Deppei,** Lodd. (*Ionoxalis Deppei,* Small). Scapose per. to 1¼ ft., with simple scaly bulbs: lvs. basal, long-petioled, of 4 obovate to orbicular lfts. to 1½ in. long and wide: fls. in 5–12-fld. umbels, red, about ½–¾in. long. (Named for Mr. Deppe, German naturalist and collector of the 19th century.) Mex.

7. **O. lasiandra,** Zucc. (*Ionoxalis lasiandra,* Rose). Scapose per. to 1 ft., with simple scaly bulbs: lvs. basal, long-petioled, of 8–10 cuneate-lingulate lfts. 2–3 in. long: fls. in crowded umbels, crimson, to ¾in. long. Mex.

8. **O. magellanica,** Forst. Stoloniferous per. 1–2 in. high: lvs. mostly basal, long-petioled, of 3 obcordate glabrous lfts. ⅙in. long and wide: fls. solitary, white, about ⅓in. long. S. S. Amer., S. Australia, New Zeal.

9. **O. oregana,** Nutt. Scapose per. to 10 in., with horizontal rootstock: lvs. basal, long-petioled, of 3 broad-obcordate lfts. to 1 in. or more long and wide, pubescent beneath and ciliate on margins: fls. solitary, pale pink, ¾–1 in. long. Wash. to Calif.

10. **O. Bowiei,** Lindl. (*O. Bowieana*, Lodd. *O. purpurata* var. *Bowiei*, Sond. *Caudoxalis Bowieana*, Small). Per. from deep thickened roots and large separated scaly bulbs; parts finely pubescent: lvs. spreading, with rather short stout petioles, much overtopped by the long 3–12-fld. peduncles, 3-foliolate; lfts. 1–1½ in. across, orbicular-obovate and emarginate: fls. 1½–2 in. across, pink or rose-purple, very showy. (Named for James Bowie, 1789–1869, who collected for Kew.) S. Afr.

11. **O. rubra,** St. Hil. Per. from a woody crown and root-tubers, essentially acaulescent: lvs. very slender-petioled, upright, 3-foliolate; lfts. about ¾in. long and wide, very broadly obcordate, papillose or flecked, appressed-hairy both sides: fls. several to many in mostly compound umbellate cymes on peduncles surpassing the foliage, ½–¾in. long, pink or rose with deeper veins (varying to lilac and whitish). Brazil.—A frequent window plant, very floriferous; probably sometimes known as *O. rosea*.

12. **O. violacea,** L. (*Ionoxalis violacea*, Small). Scapose per. to 10 in., with scaly brown bulbs: lvs. basal, long-petioled, of 3 obreniform glabrous lfts. ¾–1 in. wide and not so long: fls. in simple umbels, violet, ½–¾in. long. Me. to Fla. west to Rocky Mts.

13. **O. rosea,** Jacq. Per. 4–14 in. high: lvs. cauline, on petioles about 1 in. long, of 3 obcordate glabrous lfts. about ½in. long and wide: fls. in loose cymes, rose with white throat and darker veins, ½in. long. Chile.

2. **AVERRHOA,** L. Two evergreen trees of trop. Asia., intro. into trop. Amer. and S. Fla. for the edible frs.—Lvs. alternate, odd-pinnate, somewhat sensitive; lfts. several to many, alternate or semi-opposite, entire: fls. very small, fragrant, borne in short clusters sometimes on naked branches or beneath the lvs.; sepals 5, the outer ones shorter; petals 5, white, red, or purple; stamens 10, alternate ones longer and shorter; styles 5 and distinct: fr. fleshy and large, drooping, longer than broad, lobed or furrowed lengthwise, with few or numerous seeds. (Averrho-a: bears the name of Averrhoes, 1149–1217, Arabian physician.)

A. Lfts. 25 or more .... 1. *A. Bilimbi*
AA. Lfts. 11 or less .... 2. *A. Carambola*

1. **A. Bilimbi,** L. Bilimbi (from the oriental vernacular name). Tree to 50 ft. or more, rusty-pubescent on young parts and petioles: lfts. numerous, 25–45, mostly oblong-lanceolate, acuminate, 2–3 in. long, pubescent: fls. on short branchlets or spurs below the lvs., on the trunk or branches; petals ½–¾in. long, red-purple; stamens all antheriferous: fr. 2–4 in. long, cylindrical, obscurely 5-angled, greenish-yellow becoming translucent, juicy, with few flattened seeds; very sour, and used as a relish or for making conserves. India or Malaya, known only as a cult. or nat. plant in trop. countries.

2. **A. Carambola,** L. Carambola (from oriental vernacular name). Tree to 30 ft., the young parts finely pubescent or glabrate: lfts. 5–11, ovate to elliptic, short-pointed, mostly 1–2 in. long, pubescent or nearly glabrous beneath: fls. in the lf.-axils; petals about ¼in. long, white marked purple; 5 stamens without anthers: fr. 3–5 in. long, ovoid or ellipsoid, with 3–5 deep ribs, yellow or yellow-brown, very pulpy, mildly acid or even sweet when ripe, fragrant, used as a vegetable or dessert. Malayan region, and widely spread in tropics.

99. TROPÆOLACEÆ. TROPÆOLUM FAMILY

Herbs ann. or per., often climbing by means of coiling petioles, only 1 genus of 50 species, Mex. to Chile, grown as fl.-garden subjects.—Roots sometimes tuberous; sts. soft, more or less succulent: lvs. alternate, digitately angled or peltate, sometimes lobed and dissected: fls. solitary on long axillary peduncles, very irregular, usually showy, yellow, orange, blue, or purple; sepals 5, one produced into a long slender nectar-spur; petals 5 or sometimes fewer by abortion, clawed, often cut or fringed, the 2 upper ones unlike the others and usually smaller and inserted in the opening of the spur; stamens 8, distinct, unequal; ovary 3-lobed and 3-celled, cells 1-oviled, placentation axile; style 1, apical, stigmas 3, linear: fr. of 3 1-seeded indehiscent connivent to connate carpels.

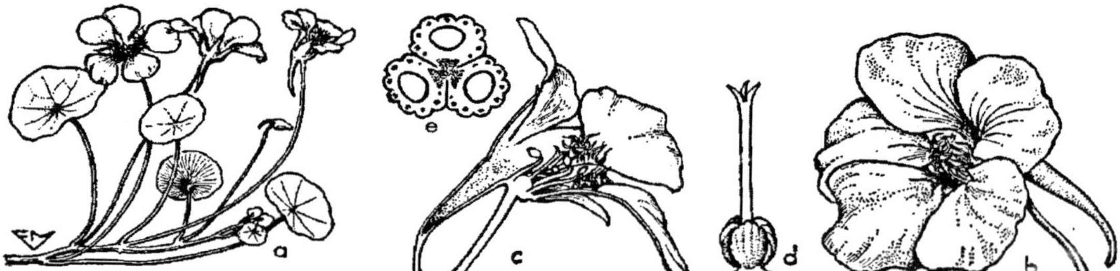

Fig. 99. TROPÆOLACEÆ. *Tropæolum majus:* a, flowering branch, × 1/6; b, flower, × 1/2; c, flower, vertical section, × 1/2; d, pistil, × 2; e, ovary, cross-section, × 5.

TROPÆOLUM, L. NASTURTIUM (of gardeners). Characters of the family. (Tropæ-olum: Greek *trophy,* from the peltate or shield-like lvs.)

A. Lvs. orbicular to reniform, not lobed, more or less angled.
  B. Plant glabrous.
    C. Petals blunt: nerves of lvs. not ending in point.......................... 1. *T. majus*
    CC. Petals mucronate: nerves of lvs. ending in point or mucro.............. 2. *T. minus*
  BB. Plant pubescent.. 3. *T. peltophorum*
AA. Lvs. divided to base or deeply lobed.
  B. Upper petals fimbriate: lvs. deeply lobed................................... 4. *T. peregrinum*
  BB. Upper petals not fimbriate: lvs. divided to base.
    C. Plant small, sts. prostrate: fls. yellow or orange.......................... 5. *T. polyphyllum*
    CC. Plant high-climbing: fls. vermilion-red.................................... 6. *T. speciosum*

1. **T. majus,** L. GARDEN NASTURTIUM. Common cult. tender ann. but probably per. or plur-ann., dwarf or climbing, glabrous or nearly so, more or less succulent: lvs. long-petioled, orbicular or somewhat reniform, 2–7 in. across, peltate and with about 9 main nerves radiating from the petiole, margins variously angled or sinuate but otherwise entire, under surface usually papillose: fls. yellow, red, scarlet, maroon, creamy-white, varicolored, 1–2½ in. across; spur 1–1½ in. long, straight or curved; petals mostly rounded but sometimes short-pointed or even toothed, the lower ones deeply fringed on the claw. S. Amer. Var. **nanum,** Vilm., TOM THUMB NASTURTIUM, is dwarf. Var. **Burpeei,** Eyster & Burpee, GOLDEN GLEAM NASTURTIUM, has double fls. (originated by W. Atlee Burpee Co.).—The common garden nasturtium is probably a cultigen, with *T. majus* contributing most of the character. The fl.-buds and young seeds of nasturtium are sometimes used in pickles for their piquancy, often under the name Indian Cress.

2. **T. minus,** L. Differs from *T. majus* in being smaller throughout, the nerves of the lvs. ending in a prominent point or mucro, petals mucronate, the 3 lower petals with dark central spot. Peru.

3. **T. peltophorum,** Benth. (*T. Lobbianum,* Veitch). Sts. climbing, hairy: lvs. long-petioled, orbicular, peltate, margins sinuate, nerves ending in a point, hairy beneath: fls. orange-red, with spur to 1 in. long, the 3 lower petals with long claws and deeply toothed blades. S. Amer.

4. **T. peregrinum,** L. (*T. canariense,* Hort.). CANARY-BIRD-FLOWER. Glabrous climbing ann.: lvs. long-petioled, peltate, 1–2 in. across, orbicular in outline deeply 5-lobed, the lobes mostly apiculate: fls. canary-yellow, ¾–1 in. across, with green curved spur about ¼in. long, the 2 upper petals large, erect and fimbriate, the 3 lower petals small and ciliate. Probably Peru and Ecuador.

5. **T. polyphyllum,** Cav. Small per. with prostrate many-lvd. sts., glabrous and glaucous: lvs. 5–7-parted into obovate entire or toothed lobes, on petioles longer than lvs.: fls. on peduncles exceeding the lvs., yellow or orange, spur ¾in. long, upper petals emarginate. Chile, Argentina.

6. **T. speciosum,** Poeppig & Endl. High-climbing per.: lvs. usually 6-parted into obovate emarginate lobes, hairy beneath, short-petioled: fls. on flexuous peduncles much exceeding lvs., vermilion-red, spur 1–1½ in. long, petals long-clawed and emarginate. Chile.

100. LINACEÆ. FLAX FAMILY

Herbs or shrubs, of about 14 genera and 150 species of wide geographical distribution, yielding a few cult. subjects.—Lvs. alternate or rarely opposite, simple; stipules small or none: fls. bisexual, regular; sepals 5, rarely 4, free or united at base, imbricated, persistent; petals of the same number and alternate with sepals, imbricated, convolute; stamens of same number and alternate with petals, the filaments monadelphous at the often glandular base, often with 5 or more staminodia;

ovary of 2–5 carpels, or seemingly 4–10-celled by the intrusion of false septa, with 1 or 2 ovules in each cell, placentation axile; styles as many as cells of ovary, filiform, usually distinct, stigmas subcapitate: fr. usually a septicidal caps., sometimes a drupe.

A. Plant an herb: styles 5. . . . . .1. LINUM
AA. Plant a subshrub: styles 3–4. . . . . .2. REINWARDTIA

1. **LINUM,** L. FLAX. Ninety or more species of ann. and per. herbs, in temp. and warm regions of the earth, several grown for ornament and *L. usitatissimum* for its fiber and its seeds which yield linseed oil.—Erect-growing, with tough cortex, glabrous or rarely pubescent: lvs. sessile, narrow, usually entire, with or without stipular glands, alternate in ours: fls. in terminal or axillary racemes or cymes, red, yellow, blue or white, opening in sunshine, the 5 petals fugacious; ovary 5-celled, or 10-celled by false partitions, with 2 ovules in each cell, the 5 styles free or united to the middle: caps. dehiscent or indehiscent. (Li-num: classical name of the flax.)

A. Fls. yellow.
B. Lvs. not forming basal rosettes. . . . . 1. *L. flavum*
BB. Lvs. forming basal rosettes.
C. Infl. subcapitate. . . . . 2. *L. capitatum*
CC. Infl. a loose cyme. . . . . 3. *L. campanulatum*
AA. Fls. blue, white or shades of red.
B. Plant glandular-hairy. . . . . 4. *L. viscosum*
BB. Plant glabrous or only slightly pubescent.
C. Sepals longer than caps.
D. Lvs. needle-like. . . . . 5. *L. salsoloides*
DD. Lvs. linear- to ovate-lanceolate.
E. Color of fls. pink to red. . . . . 6. *L. grandiflorum*
EE. Color of fls. blue or white. . . . . 7. *L. narbonense*
CC. Sepals equalling or shorter than caps.
D. Stigma clavate: plant ann. . . . . 8. *L. usitatissimum*
DD. Stigma capitate: plant per.
E. Pedicels deflexed or drooping in fr.
F. Lower third of st. leafless or nearly so. . . . . 9. *L. austriacum*
FF. Lower third of st. leafy. . . . . .10. *L. alpinum*
EE. Pedicels erect in fr.
F. Infl. usually many-fld. and much-branched. . . . . .11. *L. perenne*
FF. Infl. few-fld. and not much-branched. . . . . .12. *L. Lewisii*

1. **L. flavum,** L. Erect per. from a somewhat woody base, 1–2 ft. high, the branches grooved: lower lvs. spatulate and obtuse, upper lanceolate and acute, with gland on each side of base, 3-nerved: fls. in a much-branching cyme, the branches strongly ascending, golden-yellow, ¾–1 in. across; sepals glandular-ciliate, acuminate, about length of caps. Eu.

2. **L. capitatum,** Kit. Per. 6–18 in. high: rosette-lvs. obovate-lanceolate, obtuse or acute, cauline lanceolate, with gland on each side of base, 3-nerved: fls. in a many-fld. head, golden-yellow, to 1 in. across; sepals acuminate, glandular-fimbriate-ciliate, equalling the caps. Mts., S. Eu.

3. **L. campanulatum,** L. Glabrous per. 6–15 in. high, woody at base: lvs. both basal and cauline, spatulate to lanceolate, 1–3-nerved, with narrow transparent margins, minute glands on each side of base: fls. in loose cymes, pale yellow veined with orange, to 1¼ in. across; sepals acuminate, white-margined, about length of caps. S. Eu.

4. **L. viscosum,** L. Per. 1–2 ft. high, glandular-hairy: lvs. oblong-lanceolate, 3–5-nerved, margins densely glandular-ciliate: fls. in corymbs, pink veined with violet, to 1¼ in. across; sepals acuminate, margins glandular-ciliate, longer than caps. S. Eu.

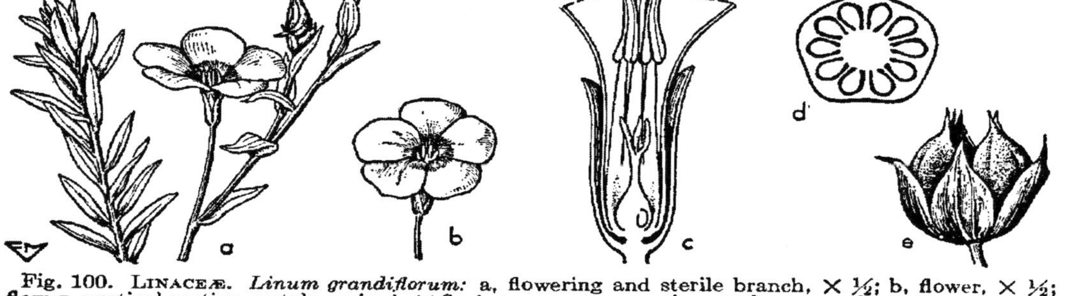

Fig. 100. LINACEÆ. *Linum grandiflorum:* a, flowering and sterile branch, × ½; b, flower, × ½; c, flower, vertical section, petals excised, × 3; d, ovary, cross-section, × 8; e, capsule, × 2.

5. L. **salsoloides,** Lam. Per. 6–16 in. high, sts. prostrate or ascending, evergreen, slightly pubescent: lvs. typically needle-like, 1-nerved, often clustered at apex: fls. in cymes, white veined with purple, to 1 in. across; sepals acuminate, glandular-ciliate, longer than caps. S. Eu. Var. **nanum,** Hort., is prostrate, forming a low clump to 1½ ft. across, with lvs. longer than type.

6. L. **grandiflorum,** Desf. FLOWERING FLAX. Erect branching leafy glabrous ann. 1–2 ft. high: lvs. linear- to ovate-lanceolate, acuminate, grayish-green: fls. 1–1½ in. across, red in different shades, terminating very slender pedicels which are 1–3 in. long, forming a lax panicle, the petals much exceeding the pointed scarious-margined ciliate sepals; sepals longer than caps. N. Afr. Var. **rubrum,** Vilm., has bright red fls.

7. L. **narbonense,** L. Per. 8 in.–2 ft. high, glabrous and glaucous: lvs. linear-lanceolate, 3-nerved, rough-margined: fls. in few-fld. cymes, azure-blue with white eye, to 1¾ in. across; sepals acuminate, white-margined, longer than caps.; stigma long and filiform. Medit. region.

8. L. **usitatissimum,** L. FLAX. Very slender-branching ann. 1–4 ft. high: lvs. small, linear or lanceolate, acute, 3-nerved: fls. about ½in. across, blue or white, in a terminal leafy many-fld. panicle; sepals acuminate, the interior ones scarious-margined and ciliate, about half as long as petals; stigma clavate: caps. slightly longer than calyx. Widely distributed, probably originally from Asia; escaped in waste places in N. Amer.—A plant of ancient and extensive cult.

9. L. **austriacum,** L. Glabrous per. 1–2 ft. high, leafless at lower part of st.: lvs. linear, 1-nerved: fls. in loose cymes, on pedicels which are drooping in fr., bluish-purple to pale wine-red, to ¾in. across; sepals scarious-margined, shorter than caps. S. Eu.

10. L. **alpinum,** L. Glabrous per. 6–20 in. high, with erect or ascending very leafy sts.: lvs. linear, 1-nerved: fls. in loose cymes, on pedicels deflexed in fr., deep chicory-blue, to ¾in. across; sepals scarious-margined, shorter than caps. Eu.

11. L. **perenne,** L. Glabrous per. seldom more than 2 ft. high, sts. usually leafless below: lvs. linear to lanceolate, 1–3-nerved: fls. in loose cymes, in a much-branched panicle, on erect pedicels, about 1 in. across, deep chicory-blue; sepals much shorter than caps. Eu. Var. **album,** Hort., has white fls.

12. L. **Lewisii,** Pursh (*L. perenne* var. *Lewisii,* A. Eaton & J. Wright). PRAIRIE FLAX. Similar to *L. perenne* and perhaps not distinct, differing in being somewhat larger throughout, and in the fewer-fld. not much-branched panicle. (Named for Capt. Meriwether Lewis, page 365.) W. N. Amer.

2. **REINWARDTIA,** Dum. YELLOW FLAX. Two Indian subshrubs, one grown in greenhouses.—Differing from Linum in habit, the larger lvs. with minute subulate caducous stipules, and the 3–4 styles: fls. yellow, in axillary or terminal cymose fascicles or rarely solitary, the 5 petals fugacious and much longer than the 5 entire sepals; ovary 3–4-celled with 2 ovules in each cell: caps. globose, dehiscing into 6–8 parts. (Reinwar-dtia: after K. G. K. Reinwardt, 1773–1822, scientist of Leyden.)

R. **indica,** Dum. (*R. trigyna,* Planch. *Linum trigynum,* Roxb.). Subshrub 2–4 ft. high: lvs. elliptic-obovate, 1–3 in. long, entire, mucronate: fls. yellow, 1–2 in. across, solitary or in few-fld. fascicles, the petals united below into tube; styles 3. Mts. of India.

101. RUTACEÆ. RUE FAMILY

Upwards of 100 genera and 1,000 or more species comprise the known members of the Rue family, in trop. and subtrop. countries with extensions into temp. regions, in many parts of the world; the family is rich in aromatic qualities, and it yields essential oils, edible frs., and ornamental or odorous subjects.—Mostly woody plants, often good-sized trees: lvs. alternate or opposite, commonly with pellucid dots, simple or pinnate (lft. only 1 in some cases), frequently persistent, exstipulate: fls. mostly bisexual but in some cases unisexual; sepals 3–5, often connate, sometimes wanting; petals also 3–5, imbricated or valvate; stamens same number or more often twice the number of the petals, rarely 15, inserted at the base of a thick annular disk; ovary single and with 2–5 cells and carpels or sometimes the unicellular pistils distinct and forming a 2–5-pistilled gynœcium; styles usually connate; cells with 1 to many ovules: fr. various, in some genera capsular and dehiscent, in others samara-like, in others fleshy and berry-like and often very large.—In Citrus and certain others, the apparently simple lvs. are really 1-foliolate as indicated by the joint at the apex of the rachis (petiole), the 2 lateral lfts. being absent (but sometimes present on young shoots).

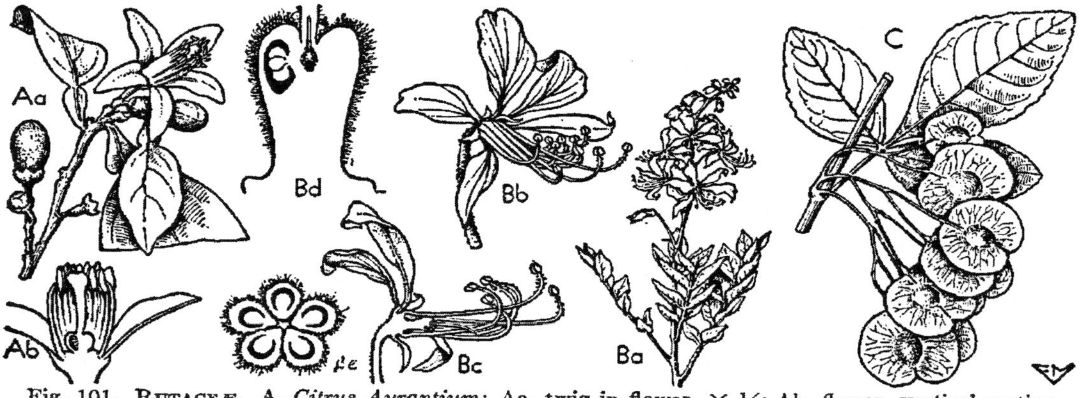

Fig. 101. RUTACEÆ. A, *Citrus Aurantium:* Aa, twig in flower, × ½; Ab, flower, vertical section, × 1. B, *Dictamnus albus:* Ba, flowering branch, × 1/10; Bb, flower, × ½; Bc, same, vertical section, × ½; Bd, ovary, vertical section, × 3; Be, same, cross-section, × 3. C, *Ptelea trifoliata:* fruiting branch, × ½.

A. Pistils distinct or the ovary deeply 2–5-lobed; styles ventral or basal or sometimes the stigmas connate: fr. capsular or follicular.
  B. Ovules 3 or more in each cell.
    C. Stamens straight and erect.
      D. Petals toothed or fimbriate: lvs. pinnate .... 1. RUTA
      DD. Petals entire: lvs. simple or 3-parted .... 2. HAPLOPHYLLUM
    CC. Stamens declined and usually curved .... 3. DICTAMNUS
  BB. Ovules 1 or 2 in each cell.
    C. Lvs. compound.
      D. Plant diœcious or polygamous: lvs. pinnate .... 4. ZANTHOXYLUM
      DD. Plant with perfect fls.: lvs. digitate, of 3 lfts .... 5. CHOISYA
    CC. Lvs. simple.
      D. Petals connivent or connate to form a tube, at least till expanded .... 6. CORREA
      DD. Petals distinct and more or less spreading.
        E. Plant a large tree with broad lvs .... 7. CALODENDRUM
        EE. Plant a heath-like shrub with narrow lvs.
          F. Stamens 5 .... 8. DIOSMA
          FF. Stamens 10, 5 of them sterile and inclosed in the channel of the petals .... 9. COLEONEMA
AA. Pistil 1, entire or only slightly lobed; style terminal: fr. baccate or drupaceous, sometimes dry.
  B. Fr. a dry samara .... 10. PTELEA
  BB. Fr. fleshy and often juicy, berry-like or orange-like.
    C. Lvs. of 3 or more lfts.
      D. Petiole and rachis not winged.
        E. Plant spiny .... 11. TRIPHASIA
        EE. Plant not spiny.
          F. Lf. digitate .... 12. CASIMIROA
          FF. Lf. pinnate.
            G. Lfts. acute or acuminate, lvs. mostly opposite .... 13. PHELLODENDRON
            GG. Lfts. obtuse, lvs. mostly alternate .... 14. MURRAYA
      DD. Petiole and rachis winged.
        E. Lfts. 3–7, persistent: ovules 1 in each cell .... 15. CITROPSIS
        EE. Lfts. 3, deciduous: ovules 2 or more in each cell .... 16. PONCIRUS
    CC. Lvs. apparently simple, of 1 lft.
      D. Fr. of the orange and lemon kind.
        E. Ovary 8–15-celled .... 17. CITRUS
        EE. Ovary 3–5-celled .... 18. FORTUNELLA
      DD. Fr. a small drupe .... 19. SKIMMIA

1. RUTA, L. RUE. Per. herbs and subshrubs of the Medit. region and eastward, one grown for aromatic and medicinal qualities.—Lvs. alternate, pinnate or multifid, glandular-punctate: fls. small and not showy, in terminal erect clusters; calyx small and persistent, with mostly 4 lobes or sepals; petals usually 4, toothed or fringed; stamens 8 or 10; ovary 4- or 5-celled with central style, the ovules several in each cell: fr. capsular, 4- or 5-lobed, dehiscent or indehiscent. (Ru-ta: the classical name of rue.)

R. graveolens, L. COMMON RUE. Strong-scented erect glaucous glabrous herb 1–3 ft. high: lvs. 2–3-pinnate or -divided, 2–4 in. long, margins nearly or quite entire, the segms. oblong to spatulate: fls. about ½in. across, with involute toothed margins and large obtuse carpels, yellowish. S. Eu.; often escaped, or persistent about old premises.

2. **HAPLOPHYLLUM,** Juss. Per. herbs of about 50 species in the Medit. region to Cent. Asia, one sometimes planted.—The genus is often included with Ruta but differs in the lvs. being entire or 3-parted and the 5 petals entire. (Haplophyl-lum: from Greek for *simple* and *leaf.*)

H. patavinum, Boiss. (*Ruta patavina,* L.). Low herb 4–8 in. high: lvs. oblong-spatulate, ½–¾in. long, glabrous, the upper 3-parted: fls. golden-yellow, in dense cymes. S. Eu.—Most of the material in gardens under the name *Ruta patavina* is *R. graveolens.*

3. **DICTAMNUS,** L. DITTANY. FRAXINELLA. Several forms but probably representing only 1 variable species, long grown in gardens for ornament.—Strong long-lived per., more or less woody at base: lvs. alternate, odd-pinnate, pellucid-punctate: fls. large and showy, in terminal racemes on bracted pedicels, white, pink, or rose-violet; sepals 5, lanceolate and not prominent; petals 5, narrow, acute, the lowest one declined; stamens 10, declined and usually upwardly curved, equalling or exceeding petals; ovary deeply 5-lobed, becoming a hard divided caps. (Dictam-nus: old Greek name.)

D. albus, L. (*D. Fraxinella,* Pers.). Stout strong-smelling plant, 2–3 ft., forming clumps: lfts. 9–11, ovate, 1–3 in. long, serrulate: fls. about 1 in. long. S. Eu. to N. China. Var. **caucasicus,** Bailey (*D. caucasicus,* Hort.), is a very large form. Var. **ruber,** Bailey, has rosy-purple fls.—Sometimes called Gas-Plant and Burning-Bush as it will often give a flash of light when a burning match is held under the fl.-cluster near the main st. on a still sultry evening.

4. **ZANTHOXYLUM,** L. (*Xanthoxylum,* Gmel.). Prickly aromatic trees and shrubs, of about 150 widely distributed species, sometimes planted for ornament.—Lvs. alternate, odd-pinnate, with pellucid dots: diœcious or polygamous: fls. small, in fascicles or panicles; sepals, petals and stamens 3–8, or sepals wanting: fr. of 1–5 carpels, each carpel 2-valved and containing 1 shiny black seed. (Zanthox-ylum: from Greek for *yellow* and *wood.*)

Z. americanum, Mill. PRICKLY-ASH. Shrub or tree to 25 ft., the branchlets with prickles to ½in. long: lfts. 5–11, ovate or elliptic, 1–2½ in. long, light green and pubescent beneath: fls. in axillary clusters before the lvs., yellowish-green, small: fr. about ⅙in. long, blackish. Que. to Va. and Neb.

5. **CHOISYA,** HBK. Shrubs, of 4–5 species from Ariz. to Mex., one planted in Calif. and Ore., also in Fla. and elsewhere, and sometimes under glass.—Lvs. opposite, persistent, digitately compound, of 3–13 lfts., with pellucid dots: fls. white, 5-merous; stamens 10; disk hairy; ovary 5-lobed, with 5-lobed stigma; ovules 2 in each cell: fr. a 5-valved caps. (Chois-ya: J. D. Choisy, 1799–1859, Swiss botanist and philosopher.)

C. ternata, HBK. MEXICAN-ORANGE, from the fragrance of the orange-like blossoms: 4–8 ft., pubescent on young parts: lfts. usually 3, thick, narrow-oblong, 1–3 in. long, obtuse, entire, with gland-dotted revolute margins: fls. about 1 in. across. Mex.

6. **CORREA,** Andr. About a half dozen Australian shrubs or small trees, sometimes raised under glass and planted in S. Calif. and elsewhere.—Stellate-pubescent: lvs. simple, thick, opposite, punctate: fls. showy and mostly large, more or less nodding, red, white, yellow, or greenish, 4-merous; calyx short and truncate, cup-shaped; corolla long and apparently tubular because of the connivent pubescent petals; stamens 8; disk 8-lobed; ovary 4-parted with single filiform style; ovules 2 in each cell: fr. of 4 nearly distinct carpels. (Corre-a: Jose Francesco Correa de Serra, 1750–1823, Portuguese botanist.)

A. Fl. short, the petals spreading on expansion....................................1. *C. alba*
AA. Fl. long, 1 in. or more, petals connivent or connate till fl. falls....................2. *C. speciosa*

1. **C. alba,** Andr. Branchy bush 3–4 ft.: lvs. orbicular, oval or broad-obovate, ½–1 in. long: fls. white or pink, about ½in. long, the petals soon spreading.

2. **C. speciosa,** Ait. (*C. pulchella,* Mackay. *C. bicolor,* Paxt.). Bush 2–3 ft.: lvs. various, orbicular, elliptic to oblong-lanceolate, ¾–2 in. long: fls. 1–1½ in. long, remaining tubular-campanulate, typically scarlet but varying to white and green; stamens exserted.—An old garden plant with a surprising range of color and form, as the species is usually defined.

7. **CALODENDRUM,** Thunb. One large tree from S. Afr., grown in warm regions for ornament.—Lvs. opposite or whorled, simple: fls. large, in terminal panicles; calyx 5-parted, deciduous; petals 5; stamens 10, 5 of them fertile and 5 petaloid staminodia; ovary 5-lobed, the lobes terminating in a glandular point, with 2 ovules in each cell: fr. a woody short-stalked caps. (Caloden-drum: Greek *beautiful tree.*)

C. capense, Thunb. CAPE-CHESTNUT. From 40–70 ft. high: lvs. ovate, 4–5 in. long, parallel-veined, short-petioled, with pellucid dots: fls. rose-lilac with purple glandular dots, 1½ in. long: fr. nearly spherical, covered with tubercles; seeds black and shining, to ¾in. long.

8. **DIOSMA,** L. About a dozen species of small heath-like shrubs in S. Afr., one frequently grown under glass for the small but bright bloom and in the open in Calif. and elsewhere.—Lvs. simple, small and numerous, lanceolate-acute or linear, alternate or opposite, glandular-punctate: fls. white or reddish, small but many, either nearly solitary or in axillary clusters, 5-merous; calyx deeply parted; disk sinuate and plaited; ovary prominently lobed: fr. a 5-carpelled caps., the cells 1-seeded. (Dios-ma: Greek *divine odor,* from the fragrance of bruised lvs.)

D. ericoides, L. BUCHU. Much-branched, 1–2 ft. high, glabrous: lvs. alternate, close together, nearly subulate, ⅙–¼in. long, keeled: fls. 2–3 together, short-pedicelled on short side shoots, about ⅕in. across, mostly reddish.

9. **COLEONEMA,** Bartling & Wendl. Heath-like shrubs of a few species in S. Afr., sometimes planted in warm climates or under glass.—Differs from Diosma in the solitary fls. having 10 stamens, 5 of them staminodia and inclosed in the channel of the petals. (Coleone-ma: Greek for *sheath* and *filament.*)

A. Fls. white..1. *C. album*
AA. Fls. red..2. *C. pulchrum*

1. **C. album,** Bartling & Wendl. (*Diosma alba,* Thunb.). Branches erect or ascending, 1 ft. or more high, nearly glabrous: lvs. linear or linear-lanceolate, ½in. long: fls. white, about ⅛in. across.

2. **C. pulchrum,** Hook. Differs from *C. album* in being larger throughout, and fls. red.

10. **PTELEA,** L. HOP-TREE. N. American spineless deciduous shrubs or small trees, of about 10 species; planted for ornament.—Foliage strong-smelling; lvs. mostly alternate and 3-foliolate, pellucid-punctate: fls. prevailingly unisexual, small, in short dense clusters that are exceeded by the lvs., usually 4- or 5-merous; petals exceeding the minute sepals; stamens 4 or 5, abortive in the pistillate fls.; ovary commonly 2-celled and compressed, ovules 2 in each cell: fr. dry, flat, circular, 2-celled and 2-seeded, samara winged all around. (Pte-lea: Greek name of another plant.)

P. trifoliata, L. Large rather coarse shrub or small tree to 25 ft.: lfts. ovate to elliptic-oblong, 2–5 in. long, nearly or quite sessile, tapering or acuminate, the terminal one narrowed at base, entire or finely crenulate, becoming glabrous: fls. ½in. or less across, greenish-white, in corymbs 2–3 in. wide: fr. oblong-orbicular, the thin broad wing very veiny, ¾–1 in. across. N. Y. to Fla. and west.

11. **TRIPHASIA,** Lour. Three species, one spiny evergreen shrub grown in warm countries, and sometimes under glass, for ornament.—Lvs. alternate, prevailingly 3-foliolate, strongly punctate: fls. solitary or several in axils, bisexual, white, 3–5-merous; calyx cup-like, 3–5-lobed; stamens 6–10, with flattened distinct filaments; ovary obovate, with a lobed stigma, ovules 1–2 in each cell: fr. an ovate 1–3-seeded (usually 1-seeded) berry with sweet sticky pulp. (Tripha-sia: Greek *triplex,* probably from the lvs.)

T. trifolia, P. Wils. (*Limonia trifolia,* Burm. f. *T. Aurantiola,* Lour.). LIME-BERRY. Shrub or sometimes tree-like, to 15 ft.: spines in pairs at the axils, small but sharp: lvs. dark green, on very short puberulent petioles; terminal lft. large, ovate and retuse, 1–2 in. long, crenate; lateral lfts. 2, much smaller: fls. very fragrant, ½–¾in. across: fr. dull red, ½in. diam. Probably Malayan; widely nat. in trop. countries.

12. **CASIMIROA,** Llave & Lex. Evergreen trees and shrubs of trop. Amer., one grown for its edible fr.—Lvs. alternate, digitate (rarely unifoliolate), coriaceous, usually with pellucid dots: fls. bisexual (ovary sometimes abortive), small, in short terminal or axillary panicles or corymbs, mostly 5-merous; calyx minute, deeply lobed; stamens as many as petals (commonly 5); ovary usually 5-lobed, with 5-lobed or entire stigma; ovule 1 in each cell: fr. a large more or less globose 2–5-seeded drupe. (Casimir-oa: bears the name of Casimiro Gomez de Ortega, Spanish botanist who published from 1763 onward.)

C. edulis, Llave & Lex. WHITE SAPOTE. Large tree with ash-gray warty bark: lfts. 3–7, ovate to obovate or lanceolate, 3–5 in. long, obtuse or retuse, entire or obscurely crenulate, stalked, shining above, lightly pubescent beneath: fls. greenish, ½in. or less across: fr. subglobose, 3–4 in. diam., greenish-yellow, with yellow soft edible flesh with somewhat bitter flavor. Highlands of Mex. and Cent. Amer.; intro. somewhat in southern parts of U. S.

13. **PHELLODENDRON,** Rupr. CORK-TREE. About 9 species of ornamental deciduous trees in E. Asia, closely related.—Lvs. opposite, odd-pinnate, aromatic when bruised: diœcious; fls. in terminal panicles or corymbs, small, greenish and not conspicuous; sepals and petals 5–8; stamens 5–6, exceeding the petals; ovary 5-celled, with single short stout style: fr. a small black berry-like drupe with 5 seeds. (Phelloden-dron: Greek *cork tree,* from the bark of the original species.)

A. Lvs. green or grayish-green, pubescent beneath.
  B. Infl. loose, as broad as high .... 1. *P. japonicum*
  BB. Infl. compact, higher than broad .... 2. *P. chinense*
AA. Lvs. more or less glaucous beneath, glabrous or with only a few hairs on midrib.
  B. Lfts. ciliate on margins: infl. puberulous .... 3. *P. amurense*
  BB. Lfts. not ciliate or only slightly so: infl. nearly or quite glabrous .... 4. *P. sachalinense*

1. **P. japonicum,** Maxim. Small or medium-sized tree to 30 ft., the bark not corky, branchlets reddish-brown: lfts. 9–13, ovate to ovate-oblong and acuminate, 3–4 in. long, very unequal and truncate at base, margins crenulate and ciliate, villous-pubescent beneath as well as the rachis: infl. tomentose, 2–3 in. across: fr. nearly ½in. diam. Cent. Japan.

2. **P. chinense,** Schneid. Differs from *P. japonicum* in somewhat narrower lfts. rounded at base and the compact infl. which is higher than broad. Cent. China.

3. **P. amurense,** Rupr. Strong tree to 50 ft., with deeply fissured corky bark, branchlets yellowish: lfts. 5–13, ovate to ovate-lanceolate, long-acuminate, 2–4 in. long, narrowed or rounded at base, crenulate and ciliate on margins, somewhat glaucous beneath and glabrous except perhaps for few hairs near base of midrib: infl. 2–3 in. high, puberulous: fr. ½in. or less diam., with turpentine odor when bruised. N. China, Amur, Japan.

4. **P. sachalinense,** Sarg. Differs from *P. amurense* in bark not being corky, branchlets reddish-brown: lfts. 7–11, ovate to ovate-oblong, acuminate, 3–5 in. long, sparingly or not at all ciliate: infl. nearly or quite glabrous, 2–3 in. high: fr. about ½in. diam. Saghalin, N. Japan, Korea, China; very hardy.

14. **MURRAYA,** L. (*Murræa,* Koenig, name rejected. *Chalcas,* L.). About 11 unarmed small trees or shrubs of the Indo-Malayan region, one planted for ornament and its fragrant fls. and as suggested stock for citrus frs.—Lvs. alternate, odd-pinnate: fls. in panicles, 5-merous, rather large; calyx very small, deeply toothed; stamens 10; ovary 2–5-celled, ovules 1 or 2 in each cell: fr. a small few- or several-seeded berry. (Murray-a: J. A. Murray, 1740–1791, editor of editions of Linnæus' "Systema Vegetabilium.")

M. paniculata, Jack (*Chalcas paniculata,* L. *M. exotica,* L.). ORANGE-JESSAMINE. Small attractive tree or large bush with abundant shining foliage, glabrous or the young parts puberulent: lfts. 3–9, ovate or somewhat rhombic, 1–2 in. long, obtuse or nearly so, sometimes emarginate, entire or crenulate: fls. white, campanulate, ¾in. or less long, the petals pointed: fr. ovoid, about ⅓–½in. long, pointed, red. India; frequently planted in trop. Amer. and also nat.

15. **CITROPSIS,** Swingle & Kellerm. CHERRY-ORANGE. About 11 small spiny African evergreen trees and shrubs differing from Citrus in having spines usually in pairs, large 3–7-foliolate lvs., 4- or 5-celled ovary with a single ovule in each cell, stamens only twice as many as petals, and somewhat different pulp vessels being sessile rather than stalked. (Citrop-sis: *citrus-like.*)—Possibly of use as stocks and as parents for hybridizing in citriculture, one of them at least a promising dooryard ornamental in Fla. and Calif.

C. Schweinfurthii, Swingle & Kellerm. (*Limonia Schweinfurthii*, Engler). Shrub or small tree: lvs. 3- or 5-foliolate; lfts. broad-lanceolate, 2–5 in. long, acute or subacute at tip, cuneate at base, prominently serrate; petiole broadly winged, with usually rounded top: fls. axillary in clusters of 4–10, white, about 1 in. across, mostly 4-parted; petals strap-shaped: stamens connate into a tube; ovary rounded, bearing a very short style: fr. lime-like, 1½ in. diam., sweet. Sudan, where it was early collected by G. A. Schweinfurth, the African explorer, also Uganda and Congo.

16. **PONCIRUS,** Raf. One very thorny small tree or large shrub from China, used as stock for citrus frs., for hedges, and entering into hybrids, as in the Citrange which is a cross with *Citrus sinensis* extending the range of citriculture much to the northward: differs from Citrus in ability to withstand cold; the 3-foliolate deciduous lvs.; fls. borne on old wood in early spring rather than on shoots of the season, stamens wholly distinct, ovary usually 7-celled (6–8), fr. densely pubescent with a different structure, the pulp vescicles containing oily drops and having hair-like appendages, and other minuter characters. (Ponci-rus: from *poncire*, French name for a kind of citron.)

P. trifoliata, Raf. (*Citrus trifoliata*, L.). Trifoliate-Orange. Branchlets stiff, angled and more or less flattened, with alternate very strong sharp flattened thorns: lvs. often borne on old wood; lfts. elliptic to obovate, ¾–1½ in. long, obtuse and perhaps emarginate but sometimes acutish, crenulate, the petiole slightly winged: fls. 1 or 2, usually in the axils of thorns in advance of the lvs., white, expanding wide, 1–2 in. across: fr. orange-like but small, 1½–2 in. diam., lemon-colored, very fragrant, downy, the pulp scant.

17. **CITRUS,** L. A dozen or more small glossy-lvd. evergreen often spiny trees and shrubs of trop. and subtrop. Asia and Malaysia, extensively grown for the edible frs. and also for ornament.—Lvs. unifoliolate (apparently simple), alternate, mostly with winged or margined petiole, glandular-dotted: spines, when present, single by the side of the buds: fls. solitary or mostly clustered in the axils or sometimes in lateral cymes or panicles, usually bisexual, white after expansion, commonly 5-merous; stamens 15 or more, arranged in a few bundles; ovary 8–15-celled, with large deciduous style, ovules usually several in each cell: fr. large (an hesperidium), globose or ovoid or oblate, the compartments containing pulp-vescicles and 1–8 large seeds. (Cit-rus: classical name, first applied to another tree.)—The Bergamot, *C. Bergamia*, Risso, cult. in S. Eu. for the essential oil made from the peel, is a small tree with oblong-oval lvs. and long winged petioles, fls. small, white, and very fragrant, fr. pear-shaped, pale yellow and thin-skinned, 3–4 in. diam.

A. Lf. without apparent articulation at top of the petiole, the latter wingless . . . . 1. *C. medica*
AA. Lf. manifestly articulated at top of petiole, the latter usually winged or margined.
B. Petioles margined (not winged): fl.-buds tinted outside . . . . 2. *C. Limon*
BB. Petioles more or less prominently winged: fl.-buds white.
C. Fls. small, usually 1 in. or less across: fr. 2½ in. or less diam., oval, exceedingly sour . . . . 3. *C. aurantifolia*
CC. Fls. larger: fr. usually much larger, mostly oblate or globose, mild, sweet or sour.
D. Fr. very large, 4 in. and more diam., smooth and pale yellow, sour.
E. Twigs and under side of lvs. sparingly pubescent . . . . 4. *C. grandis*
EE. Twigs and lvs. glabrous . . . . 5. *C. paradisi*
DD. Fr. medium in size, orange when ripe, the skin more or less rough.
E. Wing of petiole very broad: fr. sour . . . . 6. *C. Aurantium*
EE. Wing of petiole narrow.
F. Rind of fr. tight; pulp sweet . . . . 7. *C. sinensis*
FF. Rind loose . . . . 8. *C. reticulata*

1. **C. medica,** L. Citron. Small tree or large shrub with short stiff spines: lvs. large, 4–7 in. long, oblong, blunt or obtusely short-pointed, serrate, with a wingless petiole that is apparently not jointed at apex to the blade: fls. in panicles or axillary clusters, 1½ in. or more across, the petals blunt, white inside and purplish outside; stamens 30 or more; ovary tapering upward: fr. oval or oblong, 6–10 in. long, lemon-yellow at maturity, rough, thick skin very fragrant, the scant pulp acid. Asia (named for the ancient country Media). —Much grown in Medit. countries and somewhat in U. S., mostly for the rind which is candied. Var. **sarcodactylis,** Swingle (*C. sarcodactylis*, Noot.), has a fr. with finger-like parts (whence the name *sarcodactylis*, "fleshy-fingered"), each projection representing a carpel or segm.

2. **C. Limon,** Burm. f. (*C. medica* var. *Limon*, L. *C. Limonum*, Risso). Lemon. Small glabrous tree 10–20 ft. high, with stout stiff thorns: lvs. pale green, oblong to elliptic-

ovate, 2½–4 in. long, short-pointed or obtuse, crenate, the short petioles mostly with very narrow margins, the articulation with the blade prominent: fls. solitary or clustered in the axils, ⅓–⅔in. long, pinkish outside but white inside; stamens 20 or more; ovary tapering above: fr. oblong to ovoid, with a terminal nipple, 3–5 in. long, light yellow, shallowly roughened, segms. 8–10, very sour. Asia.—Otaheite orange, a little plant often grown by florists and seen in window-gardens, has been known as *C. taitensis*, Risso, but is probably a hybrid with *C. Limon* as one parent.

3. **C. aurantifolia,** Swingle (*Limonia aurantifolia*, Christm. *Citrus lima*, Lunan not Aitch. *C. limetta*, Auth. not Risso). LIME. Small glabrous tree with stiff sharp spines: lvs. elliptic-oblong, 2–3 in. long, blunt or sometimes rounded at apex, the short petiole manifestly but narrowly winged, articulation marked: fls. few in the axils, mostly not exceeding ½in. long, white throughout; stamens 20–25; ovary abrupt at apex: fr. round-oval to oval and small, 1½–2½ in. diam., sometimes with a small nipple, segms. 10, shallowly roughish, exceedingly acid. Asia.—Much planted in W. Indies and somewhat in S. Fla.

4. **C. grandis,** Osbeck (*C. Aurantium* var. *grandis*, L. *C. decumana*, L. *C. maxima*, Merr.). SHADDOCK. PUMMELO. POMPELMOUS. Tender tree 15–30 ft. high, the twigs pubescent: spines slender and not very sharp, or lacking: lvs. large, oval to broad-ovate, 4–8 in. long, rounded or even retuse, on young shoots tapering to blunt point, more or less sinuate-crenate, the petiole broadly winged and obcordate, sparingly pubescent beneath at least on veins: fls. solitary or usually in axillary clusters, ¾–1 in. long, the broad petals white; stamens 20–25; ovary rounded, bearing a columnar style and very large capitate stigma: fr. globular or oblate, 4–6 in. diam., borne singly, segms. about a dozen often separating readily, flesh coarse-grained, rind mostly smooth and pale yellow, sour. Asia.

5. **C. paradisi,** Macf. (*C. maxima* var. *uvacarpa*, Merr. & Lee). GRAPEFRUIT. POMELO. Differs from *C. grandis* in being a larger hardier tree, twigs and lvs. glabrous, frs. borne in clusters and having fine-grained flesh. Origin unknown.—Much grown in U. S.

6. **C. Aurantium,** L. (*C. Bigaradia*, Risso). SOUR or SEVILLE ORANGE. Glabrous tree of medium size, 20–30 ft., with long but not very sharp spines: lvs. of medium size, ovate-oblong, 3–4 in. long, shortly or bluntly acuminate, sinuate or crenate, the petiole broadly winged: fls. of medium size, single or several in the axils, white and very fragrant; stamens 20 or more; ovary globular: fr. globose and slightly flattened endwise, about 3 in. diam., roughish, pulp acid and membranes bitter, core hollow at maturity, segms. 10–12. (Aurantia is a pre-Linnæan name for the orange.) Asia, but nat. in Fla. and elsewhere.—Grown in S. Eu. for the making of marmalade, and for perfumery from the fls.; used also as stock for the sweet orange.

7. **C. sinensis,** Osbeck (*C. Aurantium* var. *sinensis*, L.). SWEET ORANGE. The common orange, extensively grown, not so hardy as no. 6 and also distinguished by spines few or wanting, petiole narrowly winged or only margined, frs. mostly smaller with pulp sweet and membranes not bitter and the core solid at maturity. Probably China.—The navel oranges also belong here, being known by the supernumerary carpels (or second fr.) interposed in the top of the fr.

8. **C. reticulata,** Blanco (*C. nobilis*, Andr. not Lour. *C. deliciosa*, Ten. *C. nobilis* var. *deliciosa*, Swingle). MANDARIN, TANGERINE, and SATSUMA ORANGES. Branches slender, spiny: lvs. lanceolate to ovate-lanceolate, 1½ in. long, entire or finely crenate-serrulate, the short thin petioles barely margined: fr. depressed or oblate, 2–3 in. diam., smooth and shining, orange or reddish-orange, with very loose skin, segms. easily separating, and small pointed seeds; sometimes known as "kid-glove orange" because the skin may be removed and the carpels separated without soiling the hands. S. E. Asia.—The Calamondin orange has been referred to *C. mitis*, Blanco, but is now considered to be a hybrid between *C. reticulata* and an unknown species of Fortunella with no Latin name assigned although it is known as "orangequat."

18. **FORTUNELLA,** Swingle. KUMQUAT. Differs from Citrus in the few cells (3–5 or 6) of the ovary, and the 2 ovules in each cell, hollowed stigma: lvs. of 1 lft., densely gland-dotted beneath, persistent: stamens four times as many as petals: fr. small, 1½ in. or less diam.; 4 or 5 species of E. Asia. (Fortunel-la: Robert Fortune, 1812–1880, English traveller, who introduced the first kumquat into Eu. in 1846.)

A. Fr. oval, retaining persistent base of style..1. *F. margarita*
AA. Fr. globular, without persisting style..2. *F. japonica*

1. **F. margarita,** Swingle (*Citrus margarita*, Lour.). OVAL and NAGAMI KUMQUAT. Shrub or small tree, 10–12 ft., nearly or quite thornless: lvs. lanceolate, tapering both ways, 1½–3 in. long, but sometimes to 6 in. long and 2 in. broad, blunt, usually obscurely crenate toward apex, pale green beneath, petiole slightly margined: fls. solitary or few in axils, ⅗ in. or less across on very short pedicels; style persistent, scarcely longer than

ovary which is 4- or 5-celled: fr. oval or oblong, 1–1½ in. long, yellow-orange, with imbedded oil-glands, the pulp acid, the skin biting.

2. **F. japonica,** Swingle (*Citrus japonica,* Thunb.). ROUND and MARUMI KUMQUAT. Dwarf: lvs. relatively broader, to 4 in. long, paler beneath: fr. globular, about 1 in. diam., without rudiment of style and segms. usually 5 or 6, bright orange, the skin less harsh.

19. **SKIMMIA,** Thunb. About 9 evergreen unarmed shrubs native Himalayas to Japan and China, long grown for the handsome foliage and red berries.—Lvs. alternate, simple and entire, short-petioled, punctate: fls. bisexual or unisexual, in panicles, small, the staminate fragrant, white or whitish, 4–5-merous; stamens 4 or 5; stigma 2–5-lobed; ovary 2–5-celled, each cell 1-ovuled: fr. a small drupe with 2–5 stones. (Skim-mia: *Skimmi* is a Japanese name.)

A. Plant polygamous or diœcious: fr. globose or compressed at ends................1. *S. japonica*
AA. Plant with bisexual fls.: fr. obovoid...2. *S. Reevesiana*

1. **S. japonica,** Thunb. Glabrous throughout except the infl., to 5 ft., well adapted to pot culture: lvs. contiguous at ends of branches, elliptic to oblong-obovate, 3–5 in. long, narrowed both ways, bright light green above and yellowish-green beneath: panicles 2–3 in. or more long; fls. mostly unisexual, 4-merous, yellowish-white: fr. globose or depressed-globose, ⅓in. diam., bright red. Japan.

2. **S. Reevesiana,** Fort. (*S. Fortunei,* Mast.). Differs from the above in dwarfer habit, bisexual 5-merous fls., longer and more acuminate-pointed lvs., dark green above and light green beneath: fr. obovoid, dull red. China.

Fig. 102. SIMARUBACEÆ. *Ailanthus altissima:* a, branch with staminate flowers, × ½; b, staminate flower, × 3; c, pistillate flower, vertical section, × 3; d, cluster of fruit, × ½.

102. SIMARUBACEÆ. QUASSIA FAMILY

About 30 genera and 150 species of trees and shrubs, of wide distribution in trop. and warm regions.—Bark bitter: lvs. alternate or rarely opposite, usually pinnate, not punctate, stipules minute or 0: fls. unisexual, regular, in panicles or racemes; calyx 3–5-lobed or -parted; petals 3–5, rarely 0; disk annular or elongated, entire or lobed, rarely 0; stamens as many or twice as many as petals, often with a scale at base of filament; ovary 2–5-lobed and 1–5-celled with axile placentation or of 2–5 distinct 1-celled pistils, the ovules usually solitary in the cells; styles 2–5, free or partially united: fr. a drupe, caps. or samara.

AILANTHUS, Desf. Deciduous trees of nearly 10 species in Asia and N. Australia, one commonly planted as a shade and street tree.—Polygamo-diœcious: lvs. odd-pinnate, the lfts. lanceolate and entire or toothed, of disagreeable odor when bruised: fls. small, greenish, in large terminal panicles; calyx short, 5-parted; petals 5–6, spreading; disk small, 10-lobed; staminate fls. with 10 stamens inserted at base of disk; pistillate fls. with deeply 2–5-parted ovary, the compressed lobes 1-celled with 1 ovule in each cell, the styles connate with divergent plumose stigmas: fr. of 1–6 distinct oblong samaras with the compressed seed in the middle. (Ailan-thus: from a vernacular name.)

A. altissima, Swingle (*Toxicodendron altissimum,* Mill. *A. glandulosa,* Desf. *A. japonica,* Hort.). TREE-OF-HEAVEN. Rapid-growing tree to 60 ft. or more: lvs. 1–3 ft. long, the 13–25 ovate-lanceolate lfts. stalked, usually truncate at base, acute or acuminate, 3–5 in. long, with 2–4 coarse teeth near base each with a large gland beneath: panicle 4–8 in. long; staminate fls. ill-scented: samaras nearly 2 in. long, twisted. China; nat. E. N. Amer.

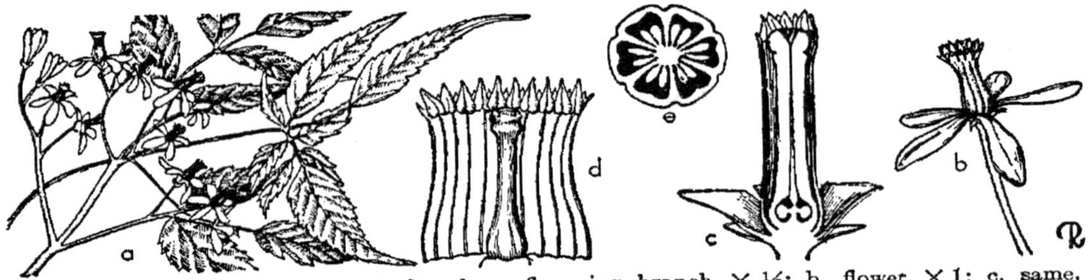

Fig. 103. MELIACEÆ. *Melia Azedarach:* a, flowering branch, × ½; b, flower, × 1; c, same, vertical section, × 3; d, pistil and expanded androecium, × 2; e, ovary, cross-section, × 6. (c–e adapted from Schnizlein.)

103. MELIACEÆ. MAHOGANY FAMILY

Trees and shrubs with hard scented wood, of over 40 genera and 600 species confined to trop. regions, one furnishing the mahogany of commerce and a few other genera planted for ornament.—Lvs. usually alternate, pinnate or rarely simple, exstipulate, not punctate: fls. commonly bisexual, regular, borne in panicles; calyx 4–5-cleft or -parted, imbricated; petals 4–5, rarely 3 or 10, free or united or adnate to stamens; stamens usually 8–10, the filaments commonly united into a tube which is entire or lacerate at top, rarely free; disk various; ovary superior, free or more or less united with the disk, 2–5-celled with axile placentation, rarely 1- or many-celled, with 1–2 or many ovules in each cell, style 1, stigma 1, often capitate or disciform, lobed or entire: fr. a caps., berry or drupe.—The Langsat, *Lansium domesticum,* Correa, native in Malaya, is grown for its edible frs., but does not thrive outside the tropics.

A. Lvs. pinnate.
  B. Fr. a small indehiscent drupe .... 1. MELIA
  BB. Fr. a septicidally dehiscent caps.
    C. Stamens free .... 2. CEDRELA
    CC. Stamens united into tube .... 3. SWIETENIA
AA. Lvs. simple .... 4. TURRÆA

1. **MELIA,** L. BEAD-TREE. About a score of species from trop. Asia and Australia have been described, one widely grown as a shade and ornamental tree.—Deciduous trees or shrubs: lvs. large, 1–3-pinnate, the lfts. entire or serrate: fls. in axillary branching many-fld. panicles, white or purple; sepals 5–6; petals 5–6, free, much exceeding the sepals; stamens united into tube which is divided at top into 10–12 entire or cleft lobes, the 10–12 anthers on the inside of the tube between the lobes; disk annular; ovary 5–8-celled with 2 ovules in each cell, the long style with 3–6-lobed capitate stigma: fr. a small indehiscent drupe; seeds wingless. (Me-lia: ancient Greek name.)

M. Azedarach, L. (*M. sempervirens,* Sw. *M. japonica,* Don). CHINA-BERRY. CHINA-TREE. PRIDE-OF-INDIA. Tree to 40 ft. and more, with thick trunk, spreading branches and furrowed bark: lvs. bipinnate, petioled, 1–3 ft. long, the numerous lfts. from ovate and elliptic to lanceolate, acute, sharply serrate or lobed, 1–2 in. long: fls. fragrant, purplish, in open long-peduncled panicles 4–8 in. long: drupe nearly globular, ½–¾ in. diam., yellow, smooth. (Azedarach: pre-Linnæan name of Arabic origin.) S. W. Asia; widely nat. in W. Indies and S. U. S. Var. **umbraculiformis,** Berckmans, the TEXAS UMBRELLA-TREE, has erect branches which radiate from the trunk, the drooping foliage giving the tree the appearance of a gigantic umbrella. Var. **floribunda,** Morr., is a precocious and very floriferous form, of bushy stature.

2. **CEDRELA,** L. Tall trees with attractive colored wood, of 9 species in trop. Amer. and 8 in E. India and Australia, a few grown as avenue trees and the wood of *C. odorata* much valued for making furniture and boxes.—Lvs. pinnate, the lfts. petioled, entire or slightly serrate: fls. small, whitish, in large pendulous terminal or axillary panicles; calyx short, 4–5-parted; petals 4–5, longer than calyx, keeled below and the keel adnate to the disk; stamens 4–6, inserted on disk, not united, sometimes

alternating with as many staminodia; ovary sessile on top of disk, 5-celled with 8–12 ovules in each cell, narrowed into style with disk-shaped stigma: fr. a leathery or woody caps. dehiscent at top by 5 valves, the seeds winged. (Ced-rela: from *cedrus*, the wood resembling that of Cedrus.)

A. Panicles much longer than lvs.: margins of lfts. more or less serrated..............1. *C. sinensis*
AA. Panicles shorter than lvs.: margins of lfts. entire.
B. Seeds winged at both ends: disk much shorter than the ovary..................2. *C. Toona*
BB. Seeds winged only below: disk much longer than ovary..........................3. *C. odorata*

1. **C. sinensis,** Juss. (*Toona sinensis*, Roem.). Shaggy-barked tree to 50 ft.: lvs. long-petioled, 10–20 in. long, the 10–20 lfts. oblong or oblong-lanceolate, acuminate, slightly and remotely serrate, light green beneath, 4–8 in. long: fls. white, in pendulous panicles much longer than the lvs.; disk much shorter than ovary; staminodes 5, subulate, alternating with stamens: fr. oblong or obovate, about 1 in. long, the seeds winged above. China.

2. **C. Toona,** Roxb. (*Toona ciliata*, Roem.). Nearly evergreen tree to 70 ft.: lfts. 10–20, lanceolate or ovate-lanceolate, acuminate, the margins entire or sometimes undulate, 3–6 in. long: fls. white, fragrant, in panicles shorter than the lvs.; disk much shorter than the hairy ovary: caps. ¾–1 in. long, the seeds winged at both ends. (Toona: E. Indian name.) Himalayas.

3. **C. odorata,** L. West-Indian- or Spanish-Cedar. Tree to 100 ft., with nearly smooth bark: lfts. 10–20, ovate-lanceolate, acuminate, entire, 4–6 in. long: fls. yellowish, in panicles shorter than the lvs.; disk much longer than ovary: caps. oblong, 1½ in. long, the seeds winged below. W. Indies.

3. **SWIETENIA,** Jacq. Large trees with hard red-brown wood, of several species in trop. Amer.—Lvs. pinnate, glabrous and shining, the petioled lfts. obliquely ovate or lanceolate, long-acuminate: fls. small, in axillary and terminal panicles; calyx small, 5-cleft; petals 5, spreading; stamens united into an urn-shaped tube which is 10-toothed at top, the 10 anthers affixed on the inside of the tube between the lobes; ovary sessile on top of annular disk, 5-celled with many ovules in each cell, the stigma discoid and 5-rayed: fr. a large woody caps., dehiscent from base to tip by 5 thick valves, the 5-winged axis persistent, the seeds winged above. (Swietenia: after Gerard von Swieten, 1700–1772.)

S. Mahogani, Jacq. Mahogany (an aboriginal American name). Evergreen tree to 75 ft., with large trunk and reddish scaly bark: lvs. even-pinnate, 4–8 in. long, with 4–8 entire leathery lfts. 1–3 in. long: fls. whitish, in panicles 2–6 in. long: caps. ovoid, to 5 in. long; seeds, including wings, 2 in. and more long. Trop. Amer., W. Indies, S. Fla.

4. **TURRÆA,** L. Trees or shrubs of more than 70 species in Afr., Madagascar and trop. Asia, one planted in S. Calif.—Lvs. alternate, simple: fls. axillary, usually in cymes; calyx 4–5-toothed; petals 4–5, free, much longer than calyx; stamens united into tube which is 10-toothed at top, anthers inserted between teeth; ovary sessile, 4–20-celled with 2 ovules in each cell: caps. loculicidally dehiscent by 4–20 valves. (Turræ-a: bears the name of Giorgio della Torre or Turra, 1607–1688, botanist of Padua, Italy.)

T. obtusifolia, Hochst. Compact shrub to 3 ft. or more: lvs. obovate, 1–2 in. long, sometimes 3-lobed near tip, margins revolute, glabrous: fls. on peduncles to 1 in. long, the narrow white petals 1½ in. long, stigma exserted. S. Afr.

104. MALPIGHIACEÆ. MALPIGHIA FAMILY

About 60 genera and 700 species of woody plants, of wide distribution in the tropics, particularly in trop. forests of S. Amer., but extending north to S. U. S. and south to S. Afr.—Trees, shrubs or woody vines: lvs. simple, usually opposite, with stipules at base of petiole or on it, often with glands on the blades or petioles: infl. various; fls. commonly bisexual, regular; sepals 5, free or united at base, persistent, some or all bearing glands; petals 5, usually unequal, fringed or toothed, slender-clawed; stamens mostly 10, often part of them staminodia, the filaments united at base or higher up, rarely free, the connectives of the anthers often large; ovary superior, of 3 united or distinct pistils, rarely 2, 4, or 5, each cell with 1 ovule; styles usually 3, free or rarely united: fr. commonly separating into 3 nut-like parts which are often winged, rarely a drupe or nut.

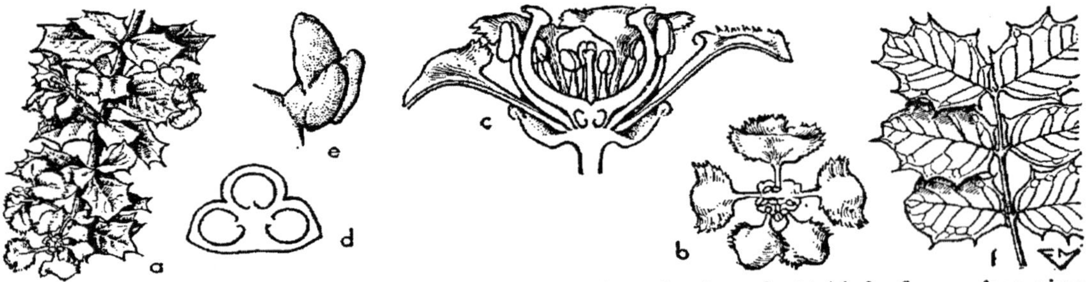

Fig. 104. MALPIGHIACEÆ. *Malpighia coccigera:* a, flowering branch, × ½; b, flower, face view, × 1; c, flower, vertical section, × 3; d, ovary, cross-section, × 10; e, sepal with basal glands, × 4; f, twig with leaves, × ½.

A. Plant an erect shrub.
B. Fr. a drupe: calyx glandular .... 1. MALPIGHIA
BB. Fr. a caps. dehiscing into 3 parts: calyx usually glandless .... 2 THRYALLIS
AA. Plant a woody vine .... 3. STIGMAPHYLLON

1. **MALPIGHIA,** L. Trees and shrubs of perhaps 40 species in trop. Amer., two grown in S. U. S. or as pot-plants.—Lvs. opposite, short-petioled, entire or spiny-toothed, glabrous or pubescent: fls. in axillary contracted cymes or rarely solitary; calyx with 6–10 large sessile glands; stamens 10, all anther-bearing, the filaments united below, glabrous: fr. a drupe, the 3 stones with 3–5 crests or wings on back. (Malpig-hia: for Marcello Malpighi, 1628–1693, Italian naturalist.)

A. Lvs. entire .... 1. *M. glabra*
AA. Lvs. spiny-toothed .... 2. *M. coccigera*

1. **M. glabra,** L. BARBADOS-CHERRY. Glabrous shrub to 10 ft.: lvs. ovate to elliptic-lanceolate, 1–3 in. long, mostly acute, entire, almost sessile, dark green above and paler beneath: fls. rose, about ½in. across, in 3–5-fld. peduncled cymes; petals erose or fringed: drupes red or scarlet, depressed-ovoid, about ⅓in. long, acid, the skin thin. N. S. Amer. to S. Tex.—Fr. used for the making of jams and preserves.

2. **M. coccigera,** L. Glabrous shrub 3 ft. high: lvs. oval or obovate, to ¾in. long, spiny-toothed and holly-like, sometimes entire lvs. with the others, shining above, dull beneath: fls. pink, ½in. across, solitary or few, peduncled: drupes red, nearly globose, ⅓in. across. W. Indies.

2. **THRYALLIS,** L. More than 15 species of shrubs, sometimes climbing, native from Tex. and Calif. south to Brazil.—Lvs. opposite, entire, sessile or petioled, bearing 2 glands at base or margin of blade or on tip of the petiole: fls. yellow or reddish, borne in simple or branched panicles, the bracts and bractlets mostly deciduous; calyx usually glandless; petals entire or toothed; stamens 10, all anther-bearing, the filaments united at base; ovary 3-lobed, the styles distinct: caps. 3-lobed, dehiscing into 3 parts. (Thryal-lis: old Greek name, transferred to this genus.)

T. glauca, Kuntze (*Galphimia glauca,* Cav. *G. gracilis,* Bartling). Slender shrub 4–5 ft. high: lvs. thin, oblong, slender-petioled, about 2 in. or less long, obtuse or abruptly pointed, glabrous and more or less glaucous: panicles many-fld., the rachis usually covered with dark red pubescence when young: fls. yellow, about ¾in. across, slender-pedicelled. Mex. to Panama, nat. in W. Indies.—Sometimes grown as *T. brasiliensis,* but the latter is a very different looking plant with small fls.

3. **STIGMAPHYLLON,** Juss. More than 50 species of trop. American woody vines, a few grown in greenhouses and over trellises.—Lvs. entire or toothed, rarely lobed, often glandular-ciliate, with 2 glands on upper part of petiole: fls. yellow, in axillary peduncled umbel-like corymbs; calyx with 8 glands; petals glabrous, unequal; stamens unequal, 6 anther-bearing, 4 opposite the gland-bearing sepals imperfect; ovary 3-lobed with 3 distinct unequal styles which are leafy or hook-like at apex: samaras 1–3 together, with a flat wing thickened along the ventral side. (Stigmaphyl-lon: from Greek for *stigma* and *leaf,* referring to the lf.-like appendages of the stigma.)—Sometimes but not originally written *Stigmatophyllon.*

S. ciliatum, Juss. (*Banisteria ciliata,* Lam.). A slender twiner: lvs. long-petioled, ovate to orbicular-ovate, 1½–3 in. long, deeply cordate at base, acuminate, the margins glandular-ciliate, bright green above, pale and glabrous beneath: fls. in clusters of 3–6, the petals to ¾in. long: samaras very broad, about 1 in. long. Brazil, N. S. Amer.

105. POLYGALACEÆ. MILKWORT FAMILY

Herbs, shrubs, or small trees, sometimes climbing, of about 10 genera and nearly 1,000 species widely distributed in trop. and temp. regions, a few cult. for ornament.—Lvs. alternate, opposite or verticillate, simple and entire, usually exstipulate: fls. bisexual, irregular, solitary or in racemes, spikes or panicles, the pedicels subtended by bracts; calyx of 5 imbricated free or more or less united sepals, the 2 inner large and often winged or petaloid; petals 3 or 5, at least the 2 upper ones united with each other or with the stamens, the lower petal concave and often with a fringed crest or keel; stamens 10 in 2 series, but mostly reduced to 8 or less, hypogynous, frequently united into a tube which is slit down and open behind, the anthers mostly opening by terminal pores or chinks; ovary superior, usually 2-celled with 1 ovule in each cell, placentation axile, the style simple with commonly 2-lobed stigma: fr. a caps., nut or drupe.

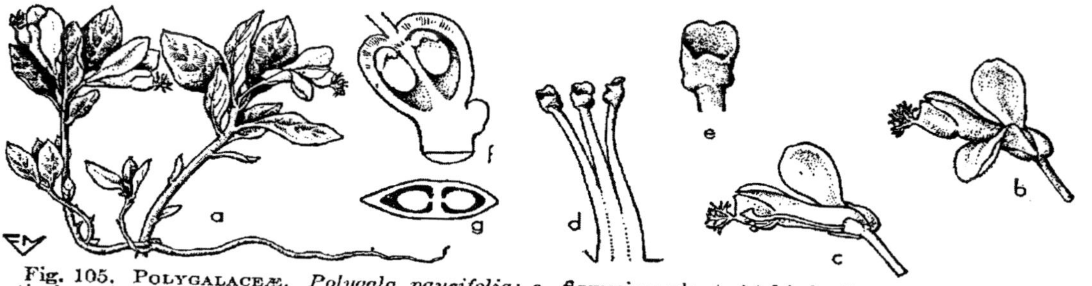

Fig. 105. Polygalaceæ. *Polygala paucifolia:* a, flowering plant, × ½; b, flower, × 1; c, same, vertical section, × 1; d, stamens, × 5; e, anther, × 15; f, ovary, vertical section, × 5; g, same, cross-section, × 8.

POLYGALA, L. Milkwort. Between 500 and 600 species around the world, a few grown out-of-doors and under glass.—Technical characters as for the family: stamens 8: fr. a loculicidally dehiscent caps., the seeds usually hairy or with an aril. (Polyg-ala: Greek *much milk;* some species reputed to increase the flow of milk.)

A. Plant creeping or trailing.
  B. Lvs. leathery: corolla not fringed .... 1. *P. Chamæbuxus*
  BB. Lvs. thin: corolla fringed .... 2. *P. paucifolia*
AA. Plant erect.
  B. Lvs. all alternate .... 3. *P. myrtifolia*
  BB. Lvs. both alternate and opposite on same plant .... 4. *P. Dalmaisiana*

1. **P. Chamæbuxus,** L. Creeping evergreen subshrub to 10 in.: lvs. alternate, lanceolate to obovate, ½–1 in. long, leathery: fls. 1–2 together, yellow with creamy-white wings, ½in. long. Eu. Var. **grandiflora,** Gaud. (var. *purpurea,* Neilr.), has purple or pink wings.

2. **P. paucifolia,** Willd. Fringed Polygala. Flowering Wintergreen. Trailing per. with ascending sts. to 6 or 7 in.: upper lvs. clustered, ovate to oblong, 1–1½ in. long, the lower lvs. distant and becoming scale-like: fls. 1–4 together, rose-purple or rarely white, to ¾in. long, corolla with conspicuous fringed crest. N. B. to Ga. and Minn.

3. **P. myrtifolia,** L. Densely branched shrub 4–8 ft. high, the young branches pubescent: lvs. alternate, flat, oblong or oblong-ovate, to 1 in. long, glabrous: fls. in short terminal racemes, the 3 outer sepals green, ovate, small, the 2 inner ones very large, broadly ovate, greenish-white veined with purple, the lower petal or keel large and bearing a conspicuous crest. S. Afr. Var. **grandiflora,** Hook., has fls. ½in. and more long, of a rich purple.

4. **P. Dalmaisiana,** Bailey (*P. myrtifolia* var. *Dalmaisiana,* Voss). A hybrid between *P. myrtifolia* var. *grandiflora* and *P. oppositifolia* var. *cordata,* Harvey; its lvs. resemble *P. myrtifolia* in shape but may be opposite and alternate on the same plant: fls. bright purplish- or rosy-red. (Named for M. Dalmais, French gardener who raised the plant from seed in 1839.)

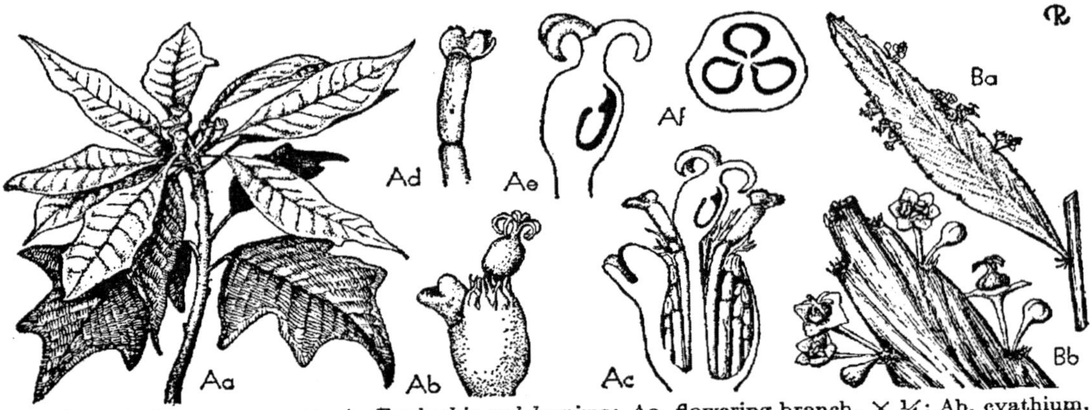

Fig. 106. EUPHORBIACEÆ. A, *Euphorbia pulcherrima:* Aa, flowering branch, × ¼; Ab, cyathium, × 1; Ac, same, vertical section, × 2; Ad, staminate flower, × 6; Ae, pistillate flower, vertical section, × 3; Af, ovary, cross-section, × 5. B, *Xylophylla angustifolia:* Ba, stem bearing flowering phyllodium, × ½; Bb, phyllodium tip with inflorescences, × 2.

106. EUPHORBIACEÆ. SPURGE FAMILY

Herbs, shrubs, or trees, of very diverse habit, some being fleshy and cactus-like; about 280 genera and over 8,000 species widely distributed around the world; many are cult. for ornament, others have valuable medicinal properties and some furnish edible parts.—Juice often milky: lvs. usually alternate and stipulate, sometimes with glands at base: monœcious or diœcious, the infl. various; fls. sometimes in a cyathium, i.e., the naked pistillate fl. is surrounded by several or numerous staminate fls., each consisting of a single stamen jointed at union of pedicel to peduncle, and all surrounded by an involucre; calyx and corolla present or absent, often different in staminate and pistillate fls., the parts free or rarely united; intrastaminal disk often present or reduced to glands; stamens as many or twice as many as sepals, or numerous, or reduced to 1, free or united; ovary superior, usually 3-celled, with 1 or 2 pendulous ovules in each cell, placentation axile, the styles free or united: fr. usually a 3-lobed caps. dehiscing elastically from a persistent axis, sometimes indehiscent and berry-like or drupaceous.

A. Fls. in cyathia.
B. Involucre regular .... 1. EUPHORBIA
BB. Involucre irregular, protuberant on one side of base .... 2. PEDILANTHUS
AA. Fls. not in cyathia.
B. Number of stamens 2–4.
C. Juice not milky: ovules 2 in each cell.
D. Branches not flattened into phyllodia: lvs. present.
E. Lvs. distichous on lateral branches, resembling pinnate lvs. .... 3. PHYLLANTHUS
EE. Lvs. alternate, broad .... 4. BREYNIA
DD. Branches flattened into phyllodia bearing fls. along margins: lvs. obsolete .... 5. XYLOPHYLLA
CC. Juice milky: ovules 1 in each cell .... 6. SAPIUM
BB. Number of stamens 5 to many.
C. Fr. an indehiscent drupe or indehiscent several-seeded nut.
D. Petals present .... 7. ALEURITES
DD. Petals absent .... 8. DAPHNIPHYLLUM
CC. Fr. a dehiscent caps.
D. Lvs. of 3 lfts .... 9. HEVEA
DD. Lvs. simple or lobed.
E. Lf. palmately lobed.
F. Juice not milky: lvs. peltate .... 10. RICINUS
FF. Juice milky: lvs. not peltate .... 11. MANIHOT
EE. Lf. simple.
F. Margin of lvs. dentate .... 12. ACALYPHA
FF. Margin of lvs. not dentate, entire or sometimes lobed or cut in hort. forms .... 13. CODIÆUM

1. **EUPHORBIA,** L. SPURGE. Upright or prostrate herbs or shrubs, often cactus-like, of very diverse appearance, some planted in the open, others under glass, one a popular florists' plant; probably over 1,000 species mostly in temp. regions, if the

genus is accepted broadly.—Juice milky and acrid: sts. fleshy and almost leafless or herbaceous or woody: lvs. alternate or opposite, simple, entire or dentate: fls. in cyathia borne in terminal cymes in the axils of the lvs. or in the axils of dichotomous twigs; involucre with 4–5 entire or laciniate lobes, regular or nearly so, resembling a calyx, with glands between the lobes sometimes bearing petal-like appendages; staminate fls. numerous in the involucre, each fl. consisting of a single stamen jointed on its pedicel, usually subtended by minute bracts; pistillate fl. solitary in the middle of the involucre, becoming exserted by lengthening of the pedicel, consisting of a 3-celled ovary sometimes subtended by 3 small scales, with solitary ovule in each cell, 3-parted style free or more or less united: caps. separating into 3 carpels, each splitting elastically into 2 valves. (Euphor-bia: old classical name.)

A. Spines present.
B. Branches woody and not strongly angled.......... 1. *E. Milii*
BB. Branches succulent and angled, cactus-like.
C. Angles 7–17.
D. Ribs with prominent cross-furrows.......... 2. *E. mammillaris*
DD. Ribs without prominent cross-furrows.......... 3. *E. Leviana*
CC. Angles 3–5.
D. Sides of branches marked with white or yellow.......... 4. *E. lactea*
DD. Sides of branches green.
E. Margins of wing-like angles horny and grayish.......... 5. *E. grandicornis*
EE. Margins of wingless angles not horny.......... 6. *E. canariensis*
AA. Spines absent.
B. Plant condensed and cactus-like.
C. St. unbranched, forming a globose body to 8 in. high.......... 7. *E. obesa*
CC. St. much-branched, the branches cylindric, 6–12 in. long, tuberculate.......... 8. *E. Caput-Medusæ*
BB. Plant not cactus-like.
C. Species a succulent tree with a brush-like crown of irregular leafless branches.......... 9. *E. Tirucalli*
CC. Species herbaceous or shrubby.
D. Glands of involucre with petal-like appendages.
E. Involucral appendages white: plant an herb.
F. Lvs. ovate, the upper margined with white.......... 10. *E. marginata*
FF. Lvs. oblong to linear, not white-margined.......... 11. *E. corollata*
EE. Involucral appendages bright scarlet: plant a shrub.......... 12. *E. fulgens*
DD. Glands of involucre without petal-like appendages.
E. Cyathia in cymes: upper lvs. red or white, at least at base.
F. Upper lvs. uniformly bright red (white or pink in some vars.): plant a shrub.......... 13. *E. pulcherrima*
FF. Upper lvs. blotched with red and white: plant an ann. herb.......... 14. *E. heterophylla*
EE. Cyathia in umbels: upper lvs. green or yellow.
F. Lvs. narrowly linear.......... 15. *E. Cyparissias*
FF. Lvs. lanceolate or broader.
G. Plant ann.: lvs. mostly opposite.......... 16. *E. Lathyrus*
GG. Plant per.: lvs. mostly alternate.
H. Habit erect, forming a hemispherical clump: glands of involucre oval, entire.......... 17. *E. epithymoides*
HH. Habit prostrate: glands of involucre 2-horned or crescent-shaped.......... 18. *E. Myrsinites*

1. **E. Milii,** Ch. des Moulins (*E. splendens,* Hook.). CROWN-OF-THORNS. Somewhat climbing, the thick woody sts. becoming 3–4 ft. long and armed with stout spines ½–1 in. long: lvs. few, mostly on the young growth, obovate to oblong-spatulate, 1–2½ in. long, mucronate, thin: fls. nearly all the year but mostly in winter, in long-peduncled dichotomous cymes, each cyathia closely subtended by 2 broadly ovate bright red bracts about ½in. across. (Named for Baron Milius, once governor of the island of Bourbon, who intro. the plant into cult. in France in 1821.) Madagascar.

2. **E. mammillaris,** L. Dwarf succulent to about 1 ft.; branches about 2 in. thick, 7–17-angled, the tubercles separated by prominent cross-furrows; spines gray, ¼–½in. long: cyathia clustered at tips of branches, peduncled, with small bracts and 5 glands. S. Afr.

3. **E. Leviana,** Croizat (*E. cereiformis,* Hort. not L.). Succulent branching shrub to 3 ft.; branches 1–2 in. thick, 9–15-angled, with small tubercles; spines reddish-brown, needle-like, ¼–½in. long: cyathia clustered at tips of branches, peduncled, with small purplish bracts and 5 glands. (Named for Irving B. Levi, Scarsdale, N. Y., connoisseur of succulents). S. Afr.

4. **E. lactea,** Haw. Much-branched succulent shrub 6–15 ft. or more high; branches 3–4-angled, each face 2–3 in. wide, dark green with marbled white or yellow band down center; spines brown, thick, to ¼in. long. E. Indies.—Widely planted in trop. Amer.

5. **E. grandicornis,** Goebel. Succulent shrub 3–6 ft. high, much-branched from base; branches 3-angled, constricted into wing-like segms. 2–4 in. long, margins grayish and horny; spines in pairs, stout, grayish, ½–3 in. long: cyathia yellowish, in very short-stalked cymes, with ovate bracts and 5 glands: fr. red. S. Afr.

6. **E. canariensis,** L. Succulent shrub or tree 15–20 ft. high, much-branched from base; branches 4–5-angled, nearly entire, each face about 1 in. wide; spines brown, about ⅛in. long: cyathia brownish-red, on upper part of branches, with 5–7 large glands. Canary Isls.

7. **E. obesa,** Hook. f. Spineless succulent with a globose body about 3½ in. diam., elongating in age to 8 in., gray-green marked with dull purple lines, with usually 8 tubercled ribs: cyathia small, green, near top of plant along the seams, with 5 glands. S. Afr.

8. **E. Caput-Medusæ,** L. MEDUSAS HEAD. Spineless succulent with a thick globose st. and many snake-like branches to 1 ft. long and 2 in. thick, often forming clumps 2–3 ft. across, remains of peduncles persistent on branches: cyathia in short-stalked clusters at tips of branches, with small bracts and 5 glands divided into linear white processes. S. Afr.

9. **E. Tirucalli,** L. MILK-BUSH. INDIAN TREE SPURGE. Succulent spineless tree 15–30 ft. high, with a brush-like crown of irregular leafless branches, the branchlets cylindric, about ¼in. thick: cyathia in sessile clusters at top of branchlets, with 5 glands. Afr., but described from cult. plants in Malabar, India, where Tirucalli is the native name.

10. **E. marginata,** Pursh (*E. variegata*, Sims. *Lepadenia marginata*, Nieuwl.). SNOW-ON-THE-MOUNTAIN. Ann. to 2 ft., the sts. usually pubescent: lvs. ovate to oblong, 1–3 in. long, entire, sessile, light green, the upper with conspicuous white petal-like margins: cyathia in umbels; involucres usually pubescent, the glands with white petal-like appendages: caps. depressed-globose, about ¼in. diam., commonly pubescent. Plains Minn. to Colo. and Tex.

11. **E. corollata,** L. (*Tithymalopsis corollata*, Small). FLOWERING SPURGE. Slender per. to 3 ft., diffusely branched above, usually glabrous: lvs. oblong or oblong-spatulate to linear, 1–2 in. long, entire, sessile or short-petioled, the lower alternate, the floral lvs. whorled: cyathia in umbels; involucral glands with white petal-like appendages: caps. subglobose, about ⅙in. diam., glabrous. Dry soil, Ont. to Fla. and Tex.

12. **E. fulgens,** Karw. (*E. jacquinæflora*, Hook.). SCARLET PLUME. Small glabrous shrub to about 4 ft., with slender recurved branches: lvs. lanceolate, 2–4 in. long, long-petioled: cyathia in small axillary cymes in winter, the involucral glands with bright scarlet petal-like appendages: caps. glabrous. Mex.—Often sold for cut-fls.

13. **E. pulcherrima,** Willd. (*Poinsettia pulcherrima*, R. Grah.). POINSETTIA. Popular greenhouse winter-flowering shrub 2–10 ft. or more high, or grown out-of-doors in the S.: lvs. ovate-elliptical to lanceolate, 3–6 in. long, entire or sinuate-toothed or lobed, long-petioled, pubescent beneath, the upper narrower, mostly entire, and bright vermilion-red: cyathia in cymes; involucres greenish, about ¼in. across, bearing a large yellow gland on one side. Trop. Mex., Cent. Amer.—There are forms in which the floral lvs. are white or pink.

14. **E. heterophylla,** L. (*Poinsettia heterophylla*, Small). MEXICAN FIRE-PLANT. Nearly glabrous ann. to 3 ft.: lvs. very variable, from ovate to linear, entire, sinuate-toothed or fiddle-shaped, slender-petioled, the upper red at base or blotched with red and white: cyathia in terminal cymes; involucres small, with 1 or 2 glands: caps. glabrous or slightly pubescent, about ¼in. diam. Ill. to Fla. and Tex., trop. Amer.

15. **E. Cyparissias,** L. (*Tithymalus Cyparissias*, Hill. *Galarhœus Cyparissias*, Small). CYPRESS SPURGE. Glabrous per. cult. in old gardens and cemeteries, with erect sts. leafy above, to 1 ft. high: lvs. linear, ½–1 in. long, entire, the floral lvs. whorled and ovate-cordate: cyathia in many-rayed umbels; involucre with 4 unappendaged crescent-shaped glands: caps. subglobose, ⅙in. or less across. Eu.; nat. from Mass. to Va. and Colo.

16. **E. Lathyrus,** L. (*Tithymalus Lathyrus*, Hill). CAPER SPURGE. MOLE-PLANT. Glabrous and glaucous ann. to 3 ft., sometimes planted to drive away moles or gophers: lvs. mainly opposite and decussate, those of the st. lanceolate, 1½–5 in. long, subcordate, sessile, entire, the floral lvs. ovate or ovate-lanceolate: cyathia in 3–4-rayed umbels; involucre with 4 unappendaged crescent-shaped glands which are prolonged into 2 short horns: caps. subglobose, about ½in. diam. (Lathyrus: ancient classical name.) Eu.; nat. in E. U. S. and Calif.

17. **E. epithymoides,** L. (*E. polychroma*, Kerner). Erect per., the many sts. forming a hemispherical clump about 1 ft. high: lvs. oblong, 2 in. long, the floral lvs. yellow at flowering time: cyathia in 5-rayed umbels; involucre with oval entire glands. E. Eu.

18. **E. Myrsinites,** L. Prostrate bien. or per. with fleshy sts. and fleshy, glaucous, concave, sessile lvs. arranged in close spirals: cyathia in 7–12-rayed umbels; involucre yellow with crescent-shaped or 2-horned glands. (Myrsinites: pre-Linnæan substantive name.) Medit. region.

2. **PEDILANTHUS,** Neck. About 30 species of cactus-like shrubs native in trop. Amer.—Technical characters as in Euphorbia, but differing in the irregular involucre which has a short spur at base on upper side containing the glands. (Pedi-lan-thus: Greek *slipper-flower*.)

P. tithymaloides, Poit. (*Euphorbia tithymaloides,* L.). REDBIRD-CACTUS. SLIPPER-FLOWER. JEW-BUSH. To 6 ft., the sts. often zigzag: lvs. ovate to ovate-lanceolate, 2–4 in. long, acute, the midrib keeled below and dentate: cyathia in dense terminal cymes, the bright red or purple involucres about ½in. long, glabrous except the terminal lobe slightly ciliate, stamens and style exserted: caps. about ¼in. long. Fla. to Venezuela.—There are vars. with lvs. bordered white.

3. **PHYLLANTHUS,** L. Shrubs, trees, or herbs, of over 50 species of wide distribution, two grown in warm regions for the frs. which are made into preserves.—Lvs. alternate, entire, often distichously arranged on the lateral branches and resembling pinnate lvs.: monœcious; fls. apetalous, in lateral panicles or solitary, often a pistillate and staminate fl. together in axils of lvs.; sepals 4–6, imbricated; intrastaminal disk present; stamens 3 or 4; ovary 3–4-celled with 2 ovules in each cell, each of the 3 styles usually 2-cleft: fr. a berry or caps. (Phyllan-thus: Greek *leaf-flower;* the fls. of some species apparently borne on the lvs.)

A. Sepals and stamens 4....................1. *P. acidus*
AA. Sepals 5–6; stamens 3....................2. *P. Emblica*

1. **P. acidus,** Skeels (*Averrhoa acida,* L. *P. distichus,* Muell. Arg. *Cicca disticha,* L. *C. acida,* Merr.). OTAHEITE-GOOSEBERRY. GOOSEBERRY-TREE. Tree to 20 ft., older branches with large scars where foliage-branches have fallen: lvs. distichous, ovate, 2–3 in. long, acute: fls. reddish, minute, in many-fld. panicles below the foliage or sometimes in the lf.-axils; sepals 4; stamens 4, free: berry depressed-globose, ½–¾in. across, angled. India, Madagascar; run wild in W. Indies and Fla.

2. **P. Emblica,** L. EMBLIC. MYROBALAN. Much-branched shrub or tree to 30 ft.: lvs. distichously arranged on the slender branchlets so as to resemble pinnate lvs., linear-oblong, ½–¾in. long, obtuse, nearly sessile: fls. yellow, small, short-pedicelled, in fascicles in the axils of the lower lvs.; sepals 5–6; stamens 3, the filaments connate: fr. fleshy, depressed-globose, ¾–1 in. diam., obscurely 6-lobed. (Emblica: from the Arabic name.) Trop. Asia.

4. **BREYNIA,** Forst. About 15 species of shrubs or trees native in trop. Asia, Afr., and Pacific isls., one planted for ornamental hedges in warm regions and under glass in the N.—Lvs. alternate, entire: monœcious; fls. apetalous, solitary in the lf.-axils or the staminate few together; calyx of staminate fls. turbinate and truncate, or pistillate with 6 broad imbricated lobes; stamens 3, the filaments united; ovary 3-celled with 2 ovules in each cell: fr. a berry. (Brey-nia: after J. P. Breyn, 1637–1697, German botanist.)

B. nivosa, Small (*Phyllanthus nivosus,* W. G. Smith). SNOW-BUSH. Shrub of loose habit, with dark red somewhat zigzag branches: lvs. oval or ovate, 1–2 in. long, green and white, or variegated with red and pink in a var.: fls. greenish, small, long-pedicelled: fr. depressed, ½in. or less across. S. Sea Isls.; run wild in W. Indies and Fla.

5. **XYLOPHYLLA,** L. About 10 species of shrubs native to the W. Indies and Brazil.—Branches lf.-like, flattened into phyllodia, the true lvs. obsolete or sometimes present in seedlings: monœcious; fls. apetalous, in clusters in the serratures of the phyllodia; sepals 5–6; stamens usually 3 and united into a column; ovules 2 in each cell: fr. a caps. (Xylophyl-la: Greek *woody-leaf.*)

A. Phyllodia broadly lanceolate, short-acute or obtuse, the fls. close together in indistinct notches....................1. *X. speciosa*
AA. Phyllodia lanceolate to linear-lanceolate, acuminate, the fls. rather far apart in truncate notches....................2. *X. angustifolia*

1. **X. speciosa,** Sweet (*Phyllanthus speciosus,* Jacq. *P. latifolius,* Hort.). Shrub or small tree to 20 ft.: flowering branches or phyllodia broadly lanceolate, 1½–3 in. long, ½–1 in. broad, obtuse or short-acute: fls. whitish, borne in indistinct notches which are close together near ends of branches. Jamaica.

2. **X. angustifolia,** Sw. (*Phyllanthus angustifolius,* Sw.). Shrub to 10 ft.: phyllodia lanceolate to linear-lanceolate, 2–4 in. long, ¼–½in. broad, acuminate: fls. reddish, borne in truncate distant notches. Jamaica.

6. **SAPIUM,** P. Br. Trees and shrubs native in the tropics of both hemispheres, of more than 100 species, several furnishing rubber and one grown for ornament and for the waxy seed-covering which is used for candles, soap and cloth-dressing.—Juice milky and poisonous: lvs. alternate, entire, glabrous, the petiole with 2 glands at

apex: monœcious; fls. apetalous, in terminal or lateral spikes, the staminate usually 3 under each bract and the pistillate solitary at the base of the spikes, the bracts with 2 glands; calyx 2–3-lobed; stamens 2–3, the filaments free; disk wanting; ovary 2–3-celled with 1 ovule in each cell, the 2–3 styles free or united at base: fr. a more or less fleshy caps., commonly loculicidally dehiscent. (Sa-pium: classical name used by Pliny.)

S. sebiferum, Roxb. (*Stillingia sebifera,* Michx.). CHINESE TALLOW-TREE. VEGETABLE TALLOW. Tree to 40 ft. or more: lvs. rhombic-ovate, 1–3 in. long, acuminate broadly cuneate or nearly truncate at base, on long slender petioles, turning red in age: fls. in continuous terminal spikes 2–4 in. long: caps. 3-lobed, about ½in. across, the large white seeds adhering to the central column. China, Japan; nat. S. U. S.

7. **ALEURITES,** Forst. Four species native in E. Asia and Pacific isls., yielding oil and sometimes grown as shade trees.—Juice milky: lvs. alternate, large, 5–7-veined from the base, entire or 3–5-lobed, the long petioles with 2 glands at apex: usually monœcious; fls. in lax terminal panicled cymes; calyx splitting into 2–3 valvate lobes at flowering time; petals 5, longer than the calyx; stamens 8–20, inserted on a conical receptacle, in 1–4 rows, the 5 outer opposite the petals and alternating with 5 glands of the disk; ovary 2–5-celled with 1 ovule in each cell, the style divided into 2 thick linear branches: fr. an indehiscent drupe or indehiscent 2–7-seeded nut. (Aleuri-tes: Greek for *farinose* or *floury.*)

A. Pubescence stellate: ovary 2-celled........1. *A. moluccana*
AA. Pubescence not stellate: ovary 3–5-celled........2. *A. Fordii*

1. **A. moluccana,** Willd. (*A. triloba,* Forst.). CANDLENUT. CANDLE-BERRY-TREE. VARNISH-TREE. Large tree to 60 ft., with long spreading or pendulous branches: lvs. ovate, to 8 in. long, acuminate, entire or repand-dentate, often with 3–5 short acuminate lobes, with rusty stellate pubescence beneath when young and persisting on the veins and petiole: fls. small, white, in rusty-pubescent panicled cymes 4–6 in. long; ovary 2-celled: fr. fleshy, glabrous, slightly 4-angled, about 2 in. across, with large rough seeds. Probably native in Malay region, but now widely distributed in the tropics.

2. **A. Fordii,** Hemsl. CHINA WOOD-OIL- or TUNG-OIL-TREE. Tree to 25 ft., with glabrous branches: lvs. ovate, 3–5 in. long, acuminate, truncate or cordate at base, sometimes 3-lobed, loosely pubescent beneath and becoming glabrate: fls. before the lvs., in panicled cymes, reddish-white; petals 1 in. or more long; ovary 3–5-celled: fr. subglobose or top-shaped, 2–3 in. diam., glabrous, the seeds rough. (Named for C. Ford, supt. botanic garden in Hongkong.) Cent. Asia.

8. **DAPHNIPHYLLUM,** Blume. Evergreen shrubs and trees, of about 25 species in S. Asia, one sometimes planted in warm regions.—Lvs. alternate or subverticillate, entire or revolute, long-petioled, exstipulate, leathery and smooth, glaucous below: diœcious; fls. apetalous, in axillary racemes which are somewhat umbellate at apex; calyx of 3–6 more or less united imbricate sepals or obsolete and ovary surrounded by 5–10 staminodia; stamens 6–12, the short filaments free; ovary imperfectly 2-celled with 2 ovules in each cell, the 1–2 styles very short or none, stigmas 2: fr. a 1-seeded drupe. (Daphniphyl-lum: Greek *laurel leaf,* from the similarity of the lvs.)—Sometimes separated as a monotypic family Daphniphyllaceæ.

D. macropodum, Miq. Shrub or small tree from 10–30 ft. or more high, with red smooth twigs: lvs. oblong, 3–8 in. long, apiculate, cuneate or rounded at base, usually bluish-white beneath, on petioles 1 in. or more long: racemes 1–4 in. long; calyx lacking; pistillate fls. with 10 staminodia; stamens 8–10: drupe oblong, ½in. long, black with a bloom, crowned by the persistent stigmas. China, Japan.

9. **HEVEA,** Aubl. Tall trees, of about 20 species in N. Brazil, particularly in the Amazon region, one sometimes planted for ornament in trop. countries and also an important source of Para rubber.—Juice milky: lvs. alternate or subopposite at ends of shoots, of 3 entire pinnate-veined lfts., the long petioles glandular at apex: monœcious; fls. apetalous, small, in panicled cymes; calyx 5-toothed or -lobed; disk of 5 free or united glands; stamens 5–10, the filaments united into a column and anthers sessile; ovary 3-celled with 1 ovule in each cell, the 2-lobed stigma nearly sessile: fr. a large caps. dehiscing into 2-valved cocci. (He-vea: from the Brazilian name.)

H. brasiliensis, Muell. Arg. (*Siphonia brasiliensis*, HBK.). PARA RUBBER or CAOUTCHOUC TREE. Tree to 60 ft.: lfts. elliptic to elliptic-lanceolate, 2 in. to 2 ft. long, acuminate, narrowed or cuneate at base, glabrous, reticulate: panicles pyramidal, shorter than lvs., the branches finely pubescent: fls. white-tomentose; stamens 10, in 2 series. Amazon region.—Now an important commercial tree in tropics of both hemispheres.

10. **RICINUS,** L. One variable species probably native in trop. Afr., but now widely distributed, planted for bold foliage effects and the seeds yielding oil.—Ann. herb or becoming a small tree in the tropics: lvs. alternate, large, peltate, palmately 5–11-lobed, the lobes serrate, the petioles with conspicuous glands: monœcious; fls. apetalous, in terminal panicles, staminate fls. below and pistillate above; calyx 3–5-parted, valvate; disk lacking; stamens very numerous, the filaments much-branched; ovary 3-celled with 1 ovule in each cell, the plumose styles deep red: fr. a spiny caps. dehiscing into 3 2-valved cocci; seeds glabrous, variously marked and colored. (Ricinus: classical Latin name.)

R. communis, L. CASTOR-BEAN. CASTOR-OIL-PLANT. PALMA CHRISTI. Tree to 40 ft., with an herbaceous st., or when grown as an ann. 3–15 ft.: lvs. to 3 ft. across, parted beyond middle into ovate-oblong or lanceolate acuminate glabrous lobes: panicles erect, 1–2 ft. or more long, flowering from base: caps. ½–1 in. long, covered with dark brown soft spines.—Runs into numbers of forms distinguished chiefly by the color of plant and lvs., glands of the petiole, size and processes of the caps., and markings of the seed. Some of the commonest vars. in cult. are the following: **borboniensis arboreus,** Nichols., sts. red, lvs. glaucous; **cambodgensis,** J.B.S. Norton, sts. and lvs. very dark; **Gibsonii,** Nichols., small form, lvs. dark red with metallic luster; **sanguineus,** J.B.S. Norton, lvs. red; **zanzibarensis,** Nichols., lvs. bright green with white veins.

11. **MANIHOT,** Adans. Herbs, shrubs or trees, of nearly 150 species in Amer., mostly in Brazil, some yielding rubber and one grown for the starch in the fleshy roots from which tapioca and other food products are manufactured.—Juice milky: lvs. alternate, entire or deeply 3–11-lobed, petioled or rarely sessile: monœcious; fls. apetalous, large, in terminal or axillary racemes or panicles; calyx campanulate, shortly or deeply 5-lobed, often colored; disk glandular; stamens 10 in 2 series, the filaments free; ovary 3-celled with 1 ovule in each cell, the styles united at base: fr. a caps. dehiscing into 2-valved cocci. (Man-ihot: native Brazilian name.)

A. Ovary and caps. 6-angled or -winged: lvs. 3–7-parted. . . . . 1. *M. esculenta*
AA. Ovary and caps. not winged: lvs. 3–13-parted . . . . 2. *M. dulcis*

1. **M. esculenta,** Crantz (*M. utilissima*, Pohl). BITTER CASSAVA. MANIOC. YUCA. TAPIOCA-PLANT. An herbaceous shrub to 9 ft., with fleshy elongated tuberous roots: lvs. usually deeply 3–7-parted into spatulate- or linear-lanceolate acuminate lobes 3–6 in. long, glabrous, glaucous beneath and minutely puberulent on veins: fls. less than ½in. long, in panicles: caps. globose, ½in. across, with 6 winged angles. Trop. Brazil.—Cult. in most trop. countries and under many forms.

2. **M. dulcis,** Pax (*Jatropha dulcis*, Gmel.). SWEET CASSAVA. AIPI. Similar to *M. esculenta*, the roots somewhat smaller: lvs. 3–13-parted, the lobes lanceolate to obovate: calyx ½–¾in. long: caps. not wing-angled. Brazil.

12. **ACALYPHA,** L. COPPER-LEAF. About 250 species of herbs or shrubs native in the tropics and subtropics of both hemispheres, grown as foliage plants in the greenhouse and for bedding and for hedges in the S.—Lvs. alternate, dentate, 3–5-nerved from the base or pinnately veined, long-petioled: monœcious or rarely diœcious; fls. apetalous, in axillary or terminal spikes or racemes; staminate fls. in axils of minute bracts, with 4-parted calyx and 8–16 free stamens; pistillate fls. subtended by foliaceous bracts, with 3–5 sepals and 3-celled ovary with 1 ovule in each cell and free often fringed styles: fr. a caps. dehiscing into 2-valved cocci. (Acaly-pha: old Greek name for nettle.)

A. Spikes ½–1 in. wide: lvs. green. . . . . 1. *A. hispida*
AA. Spikes ⅛–¼in. wide: lvs. mostly mottled with red and purple. . . . . 2. *A. Wilkesiana*

1. **A. hispida,** Burm. f. (*A. Sanderi*, N. E. Br.). CHENILLE-PLANT. REDHOT-CATTAIL. Diœcious shrub to 15 ft.: lvs. green, broadly ovate, 4–8 in. long, acute or acuminate, rounded at base, the long petiole and veins of lf. pubescent, coarsely toothed: pistillate spikes drooping, dense, cylindrical, up to 18 in. long and ½–1 in. wide, the long branched styles bright red or purple (or creamy-white in a var.); ovary densely villous. E. Indies.

2. **A. Wilkesiana,** Muell. Arg. (*A. tricolor,* Seem.). Monœcious shrub to about 15 ft.: lvs. elliptic or ovate, 4–8 in. long, shortly acuminate, rounded or shortly acute at base, glabrous except on the veins and petioles, dentate, bronzy-green variously mottled with shades of red and purple: spikes slender, 8 in. or less long and ⅛–¼in. wide, reddish, the pistillate bracts mostly broadly triangular and prominently toothed. (Bears the name of Admiral Chas. Wilkes, 1801–1877, American scientist and explorer.) S. Sea Isls.—Widely cult. both under glass and in warm countries in the open for the colored and variegated foliage; the bracts of the pistillate fls. are either extremely variable or else there are several species in cult. and passing under one name. Known to the trade under the following names: Var. **Macafeana,** W. Miller, with red lvs. marked with crimson and bronze; var. **marginata,** W. Miller, lvs. margined with crimson; var. **macrophylla,** N. Taylor, not *A. macrophylla,* HBK., with larger russet-brown lvs.; var. **musaica,** W. Miller, lvs. with orange and red markings. Perhaps not specifically distinct is **A. Godseffiana,** Mast., with green lvs. margined with cream-color, which in var. *heterophylla* are spatulate and ragged-looking, sometimes reduced to shreds, with variously sinuate-dentate margins.

13. **CODIÆUM,** Juss. Croton. Trees and shrubs of Malaya and Pacific isls., of 6 species, one widely cult. out-of-doors or under glass for the handsome variegated lvs.—Lvs. alternate, simple or rarely lobed, entire, leathery and rather thick, glabrous, pinnately-veined, petioled: mostly monœcious; fls. small, in elongated racemes solitary or 2 together in the axils of the upper lvs., the staminate clustered under the bracts, the pistillate solitary; calyx with 5 (rarely 3–6) imbricated lobes; petals 5–6, small, lacking in pistillate fls.; disk of 5–15 glands; stamens 15–30 or more, inserted on receptacle, the filaments free; ovary 3-celled with 1 ovule in each cell, the styles distinct or slightly united at base: fr. a globose caps. dehiscing into 2-valved cocci. (Codiæ-um: probably from Greek for *head,* the lvs. being used for wreaths.)—The genus Croton contains species not in cult.

C. variegatum, Blume, var. **pictum,** Muell. Arg. (*Croton variegatus,* L.). Glabrous shrub or small tree to 6 ft. or more: lvs. ovate-lanceolate to linear, marked with white, yellow, or red, entire or lobed: staminate racemes to 10 in. long: caps. white, about ⅓in. across.—The wild form, native from Java to Australia and S. Sea Isls., is rarely cult.; it has green obovate-oblong entire lvs. Codiæums are widely cult. under the name of "crotons"; they vary greatly and very many Latin- and English-named forms are in the trade. The lvs. vary from very broadly lanceolate to narrowly linear, from entire to cut almost to the midrib, sometimes with lf.-like apical appendage, margins of lvs. crisped or whole lf. spirally twisted, and with various forms and combinations of color variegation.

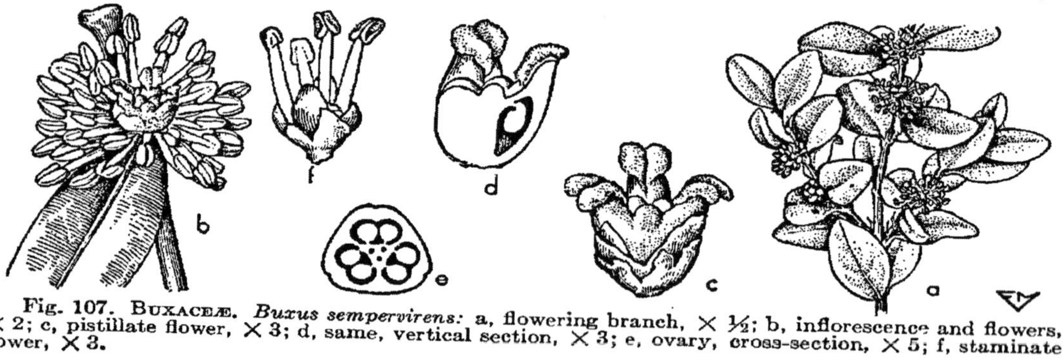

Fig. 107. Buxaceæ. *Buxus sempervirens:* a, flowering branch, × ½; b, inflorescence and flowers, × 2; c, pistillate flower, × 3; d, same, vertical section, × 3; e, ovary, cross-section, × 5; f, staminate flower, × 3.

107. BUXACEÆ. BOX FAMILY

About 6 genera and 40 species of herbs, shrubs and trees of wide distribution, mostly in warm regions, a few planted for ornament.—Often united with Euphorbiaceæ, but differing technically in the raphe of the pendulous ovules being directed away from rather than toward the axis of the ovary, or the ovules erect or ascending: also distinguished by the juice not being milky and hypogynous disk wanting: lvs. opposite or alternate, simple: monœcious; fls. apetalous; calyx 4–12-parted or none; stamens 4 or more, free; ovary superior, 2–4-, usually 3-celled with 1–2 ovules in each cell: fr. a caps. or drupe.

A. Plant an erect shrub: lvs. entire.
B. Lvs. opposite: fr. a caps .... 1. BUXUS
BB. Lvs. alternate: fr. drupe-like .... 2. SARCOCOCCA
AA. Plant a procumbent subshrub: lvs. dentate .... 3. PACHYSANDRA

1. **BUXUS,** L. Box. Evergreen much-branched shrubs, of about 30 species in both the Old and New World, two grown for ornament, hedges and edgings.—Lvs. opposite, leathery, entire, short-petioled, penninerved: fls. in axillary or terminal clusters; staminate fls. lateral in infl., of 4 imbricated sepals and 4 stamens opposite the sepals, the thick filaments free; pistillate fls. terminal, of 6 imbricated sepals and 3-celled ovary with 2 ovules in each cell and 3 short styles: fr. an ovoid loculicidally dehiscent caps., 3-pointed because of the persistent styles; seeds shining, black. (Bux-us: ancient Latin name.)

A. Branches minutely pubescent, angled or slightly winged: lvs. broadest below middle .... 1. *B. sempervirens*
AA. Branches glabrous, conspicuously winged: lvs. broadest above middle .... 2. *B. microphylla*

1. **B. sempervirens,** L. COMMON BOX. Wide-spreading shrub or small tree to 25 ft.; branches quadrangular or slightly winged, minutely pubescent: lvs. oval to oblong-lanceolate, broadest about or below the middle, ½–1½ in. long, obtuse or emarginate at apex, shining dark green above and pale beneath, the short petiole minutely pubescent: fls. pale green with yellow anthers, in early spring. Eu., N. Afr., W. Asia.—Runs into many forms, the commonest of which are: var. **arborescens,** L., which grows to a small tree; var. **Handsworthii,** Koch, bushy with large broad lvs.; var. **rotundifolia,** Baill., lvs. broad-oval; var. **suffruticosa,** L., dwarf with small lvs.

2. **B. microphylla,** Sieb. & Zucc. Compact shrub to 3 ft. or often prostrate; branches glabrous, quadrangular and conspicuously winged: lvs. obovate or rounded-obovate, broadest above middle, ⅓–1 in. long, obtuse or emarginate at apex, cuneate at base, light green, petiole glabrous: fls. mostly in terminal clusters, in early spring. China, Japan.—Cult. mostly in var. **japonica,** Rehd. & Wils. (*B. japonica,* Muell. Arg.), spreading shrub to 6 ft. with longer lvs. and axillary fl.-clusters; Japan. Var. **koreana,** Nakai, shrub to 2 ft. with lvs. ¼–½in. long; Korea.

2. **SARCOCOCCA,** Lindl. Ornamental evergreen Asian shrubs, planted in S. U. S.—Lvs. alternate, entire, leathery, petioled, usually penninerved: fls. in axillary racemes or heads, whitish, pistillate fls. at base; sepals 4–6; stamens 4–6; ovary 2–3-celled: fr. drupe-like, fleshy or leathery, 1–2-seeded. (Sarcococ-ca: from Greek for *fleshy* and *berry*.)

A. Lvs. ovate: fr. red .... 1. *S. ruscifolia*
AA. Lvs. lanceolate: fr. black .... 2. *S. Hookeriana*

1. **S. ruscifolia,** Stapf. To 6 ft.: lvs. ovate, 1–2 in. long, acuminate, dark green and shining above: fls. fragrant: fr. red, ¼in. across. China.

2. **S. Hookeriana,** Baill. To 6 ft.: lvs. lanceolate, 1–3 in. long, acuminate: fr. black, ¼in. across. (For J. D. Hooker, page 45.) Himalayas. Var. **humilis,** Rehd. & Wils. (*S. humilis,* Stapf), 1–4 ft. high, with shorter lvs. and stamens less exserted; W. China.

3. **PACHYSANDRA,** Michx. Procumbent herbs or subshrubs, of about 5 species in E. N. Amer. and E. Asia., grown as ground-cover.—Branches ascending, leafy above: lvs. alternate or clustered at ends of branches, petioled, usually coarsely toothed, 3-nerved from base, persistent or deciduous: fls. in axillary or terminal spikes, staminate fls. above, pistillate below; sepals 4, imbricated, or variable in pistillate fls.; stamens 4, opposite sepals, the thick filaments free and exserted; ovary usually 3-celled (sometimes 2–4-celled) with 2 ovules in each cell, with 2–3 spreading styles: fr. a dehiscent 2–3-pointed caps. or drupaceous. (Pachysan-dra: Greek *thick stamens*.)

A. Spikes terminal .... 1. *P. terminalis*
AA. Spikes axillary at base of st. .... 2. *P. procumbens*

1. **P. terminalis,** Sieb. & Zucc. JAPANESE PACHYSANDRA. Evergreen, to 8 or 10 in. high and forming a dense mass several ft. across: lvs. obovate, 2–4 in. long, coarsely and bluntly toothed above middle, entire and cuneate at base, glabrous: fls. white, in terminal spikes 1–2 in. long, in spring. Japan. Var. **variegata,** Manning, has lvs. variegated with white.

2. **P. procumbens,** Michx. ALLEGANY PACHYSANDRA. Differs in the lvs. being deciduous or semi-persistent, and the spikes of white or pinkish fls. to 5 in. long and axillary at base of st. W. Va. to Fla. and La.

Fig. 108. EMPETRACEÆ. *Empetrum nigrum:* a, fruiting branch, × ½; b, twig (*of Corema Conradii*), × 2; c, staminate flower, × 4; d, pistillate flower, × 8; e, same, vertical section, × 8.

108. EMPETRACEÆ. CROWBERRY FAMILY

Small evergreen pulvinate heather-like shrubs, sometimes diœcious, native in mountainous regions of N. and S. Amer.; 3 genera and 8 species.—Lvs. alternate, deeply grooved beneath, exstipulate, crowded: fls. usually bisexual, small, regular, apetalous, axillary or crowded into terminal heads; sepals 2–6, imbricate, sometimes absent or represented by minute bractlets and sometimes petaloid; stamens 2–4, alternate among the sepals, hypogynous, filaments free, anthers 2-celled, dehiscing by vertical splits; ovary superior, globose, 2–9-celled, placentation axile, ovule 1 in each cell, amphitropous; style very short, variously branched, the branches 2–9 and often fimbriate or toothed: fr. a berry, fleshy or dry, containing 2 or more pyrenes, each 1-seeded; seed albuminous with a straight embryo about as long as seed.

EMPETRUM, L. Five species, one occasionally grown in rock-gardens for the dark green foliage and attractive frs.—Plant diœcious or monœcious: fls. axillary, 1–3, nearly sessile, subtended by scale-like bracts; sepals 3, petaloid; stamens 3, exserted, filaments slender; ovary 6–9-celled with as many spreading toothed stigmas: fr. a succulent fleshy berry. (Em-petrum: Greek, meaning *growing on the rocks.*)

E. nigrum, L. CROWBERRY. Low procumbent shrub ascending to 10 in.; branchlets and margins of very young lvs. glandular: lvs. linear-oblong, to ¼in. long, spreading and soon reflexed, obtuse, glabrous at maturity: fls. purplish with pink anthers, Apr.–May: fr. about ⅛ in. diam., black, maturing Aug.–Sept. Arctic regions extending south into Calif. and the Adirondacks of N. Y. and to N. Mich.—Established colonies of cult. plants spread and form dense mass effects. The related **Corema Conradii,** Loud. (*Empetrum Conradii*, Torr.), is sometimes cult. in similar situations; recognized by its erect habit (lateral branches horizontal and often much elongated and appressed to ground, central axis erect and often very short), lvs. often whorled, and fls. in terminal heads.

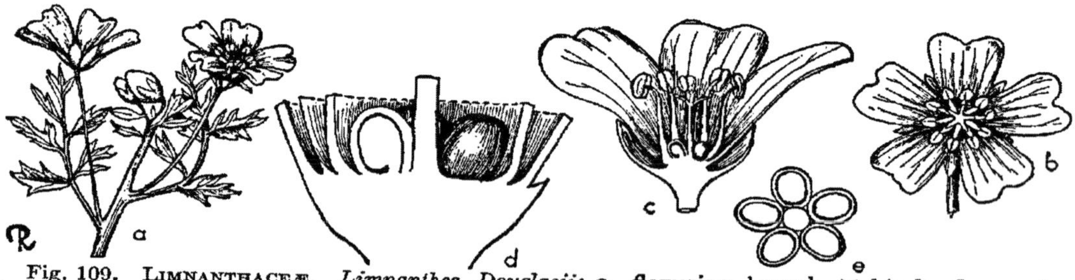

Fig. 109. LIMNANTHACEÆ. *Limnanthes Douglasii:* a, flowering branch, × ½; b, flower, face view, × 1; c, same, vertical section, × 2; d, pistils, × 5; e, gynœcium, cross-section, × 4. (c after Engler & Prantl, d–e from LeMaout & Decaisne.)

109. LIMNANTHACEÆ. LIMNANTHES FAMILY

Two genera and 8 species of herbs native in N. Amer., one sometimes grown as a garden ann.—Lvs. alternate, dissected or pinnate, exstipulate: fls. bisexual, regular, solitary on long axillary peduncles; sepals 3–5, valvate, persistent; petals 3–5, separate, alternating with as many small glands; stamens twice as many as petals, distinct; ovary of 3–5 nearly distinct 1-ovuled carpels, with single style arising in center and 3–5 stigmas: fr. at length separating from a very short axis into 3–5 indehiscent achenes.

LIMNANTHES, R. Br. About 7 species in W. N. Amer., with the technical characters of the family, the parts of the fl. being in 5's. (Limnan-thes: from Greek for *marsh flower*, referring to the habitat.)

L. Douglasii, R. Br. (*Floerkea Douglasii*, Baill.). MEADOW-FOAM. Spreading herb to 1 ft., branching from base: lvs. glabrous, yellowish-green, pinnate, the lfts. sharply lobed or parted: fls. fragrant, ¾–1 in. across, the white or sometimes roseate petals yellowish toward the base, notched at apex: fr. smooth or slightly corrugated. (After David Douglas, page 42.) Calif.

110. ANACARDIACEÆ. CASHEW FAMILY

Trees or shrubs with resinous bark, of about 60 genera and 400 species, most abundant in the tropics but a few extending into the temp. zone; in both eastern and western hemispheres.—Lvs. alternate, rarely opposite, simple or compound: fls. unisexual or bisexual, usually regular; calyx 3–5-cleft; petals 3–5, rarely 0; disk usually annular; stamens as many or twice as many as petals, rarely more, inserted at base of disk, filaments separate; ovary 1–5-celled with 1 ovule in each cell, placentation axile; styles 1–5: fr. usually a drupe, rarely dehiscent.

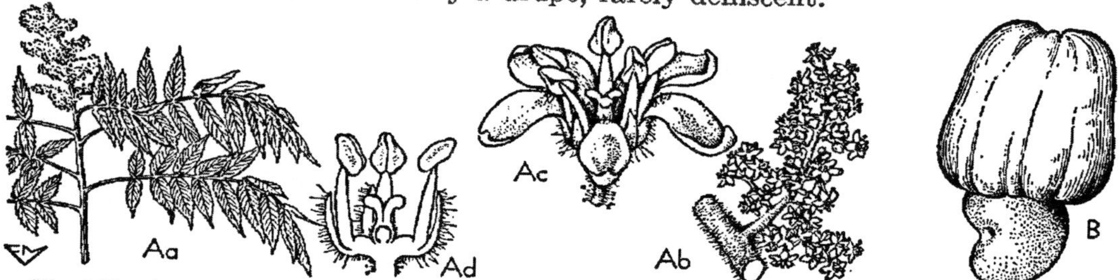

Fig. 110. ANACARDIACEÆ. *Rhus typhina:* Aa, flowering branch, × 1/16; Ab, segment of inflorescence, × ½; Ac, perfect flower, × 3; Ad, same, less petals, vertical section, × 4. B. *Anacardium occidentale:* fruit, × ½.

A. Lvs. simple.
  B. Stamens 8–10 .... 1. ANACARDIUM
  BB. Stamens 1–5.
    C. Fruiting panicles with plumose sterile pedicels .... 2. COTINUS
    CC. Fruiting panicles not plumose.
      D. Style lateral: fr. large and fleshy .... 3. MANGIFERA
      DD. Style terminal: fr. small and dry .... 8. RHUS
AA. Lvs. pinnate or composed of 3 lfts.
  B. Ovary 4–5-celled.
    C. Lf.-rachis not winged: petals valvate .... 4. SPONDIAS
    CC. Lf.-rachis slightly winged: petals imbricate .... 5. HARPEPHYLLUM
  BB. Ovary 1-celled.
    C. Petals 0 .... 6. PISTACIA
    CC. Petals 5.
      D. Stamens 10 .... 7. SCHINUS
      DD. Stamens 5 .... 8. RHUS

1. ANACARDIUM, L. Eight trop. American species of trees or shrubs, one widely cult. in the tropics for the nuts.—Plant polygamous: lvs. alternate, petioled, simple, entire, coriaceous: fls. in terminal branching panicles; calyx 5-parted, deciduous; petals 5, very narrow; stamens 8–10, all or only a few fertile; ovary 1-celled, sessile; style 1: fr. kidney-shaped, borne on a greatly enlarged receptacle. (Anacar-dium: from Greek for *like* and *heart*, referring to the heart-shaped nut.)

A. occidentale, L. CASHEW. Spreading evergreen tree to 40 ft., with milky juice: lvs. oblong-oval or obovate, rounded or sometimes emarginate at apex, 4–8 in. long, 2–4 in. wide: panicles 6–10 in. long; fls. yellowish-pink, about ⅓in. across: fr. kidney- or heart-shaped, about 1 in. long, with kernel edible when roasted; receptacle fleshy, 2–3½ in. long, bright yellow or red, edible (called the cashew-apple). Trop. Amer. but nat. in all trop. countries.

2. **COTINUS,** Adans. Two species of shrubs or small trees, grown for the feathery panicles and attractive foliage.—Plant polygamous or diœcious: lvs. alternate, entire, slender-petioled, without stipules: fls. in large loose terminal panicles, small, greenish or yellowish, the pedicels of sterile fls. elongating and clothed with spreading hairs; petals 5, twice as long as 5-parted calyx; stamens 5; ovary 1-celled with 3 lateral styles: drupe small, compressed, oblique-obovate. (Cot-inus: ancient Greek name of doubtful application.)

A. Lvs. prevailingly oval, 1–3 in. long: fruiting panicles very showy. . . . . .1. *C. Coggygria*
AA. Lvs. prevailingly obovate, 2½–5 in. long: fruiting panicles not showy. . . . . .2. *C. americanus*

1. **C. Coggygria,** Scop. (*Rhus Cotinus,* L.). SMOKE-TREE. Spreading dense shrub to 15 ft.: lvs. oval or obovate, 1½–3 in. long, abruptly contracted at base, glabrous: panicles to 8 in. long, densely plumose, usually purplish, blooming June–July: frs. few, about ⅛in. long. (Coggygria: ancient Greek name.) S. Eu. to Cent. China and Himalayas. Var. **purpureus,** Rehd. (var. *atropurpureus,* Dipp.), has dark purple panicles and purplish lvs. Var. **pendulus,** Dipp., has drooping branches.

2. **C. americanus,** Nutt. (*Rhus cotinoides,* Nutt.). Shrub or small tree to 30 ft.: lvs. obovate, 2½–5 in. long, cuneate at base, silky-pubescent beneath when young, turning red or orange in autumn: panicles 4–6 in. long, the sterile pedicels with purplish or brownish rather inconspicuous hairs: frs. few, ⅛in. across. Tenn., Ala. to Tex.

3. **MANGIFERA,** L. Large trees comprising about 30 species from trop. Asia, one widely grown throughout the tropics for its edible fr.—Plant polygamous: lvs. alternate, entire, petioled, coriaceous: fls. in branching terminal panicles, small, pedicelled; calyx 4–5-parted, deciduous; petals 4–5, free or adnate to the disk; stamens 1–5, usually only 1 or 2 fertile; ovary 1-celled with lateral style: drupe large and fleshy, with a compressed fibrous stone. (Mangif-era: from *mango,* vernacular name of one species, and Latin *to bear.*)

M. indica, L. MANGO. Large evergreen tree up to 90 ft. and sometimes with spread to 125 ft.: lvs. lanceolate, 6–16 in. long, rigid, deep green, almost glossy, on petioles 1–4 in. long swollen at base: panicles 1 ft. or more long; fls. pinkish-white; only 1 fertile stamen: fr. variable in shape, 2–6 in. long, greenish, yellowish or reddish, smooth. N. India, Burma, Malaya.—Numerous fancy-named clones are grown in S. U. S. for the aromatically flavored fr.

4. **SPONDIAS,** L. Trop. trees cult. for their edible frs., of about 12 species widely distributed.—Plant polygamous: lvs. usually clustered near the ends of the branchlets, alternate, odd-pinnate: fls. small, short-pedicelled, in racemes or panicles; calyx small, deciduous, 4–5-cleft; petals 4–5, spreading; stamens 8–10; ovary sessile, free, 4–5-celled; styles 4–5: fr. a fleshy drupe. (Spon-dias: Greek name used by Theophrastus for the plum, which its frs. resemble.)

A. Lfts. 1–1½ in. long: panicles axillary. . . . . .1. *S. purpurea*
AA. Lfts. 2½–4 in. long: panicles terminal.
  B. Rachis of lf. pubescent; veins branching at end. . . . . .2. *S. Mombin*
  BB. Rachis of lf. glabrous; veins not branching. . . . . .3. *S. cytherea*

1. **S. purpurea,** L. (*S. Mombin,* Auth.). RED MOMBIN. SPANISH-PLUM. Spreading tree to 30 ft.: lvs. 5–10 in. long; lfts. 7–23, obovate or oblong, 1–1½ in. long, acute or bluntish, entire or shallowly toothed: fls. in unbranched axillary panicles about ½in. long, small, greenish or purplish: fr. obovoid, 1–2 in. long, varying from yellow to deep red, the stone large and very hard. Trop. Amer.

2. **S. Mombin,** L. (*S. lutea,* L.). YELLOW MOMBIN. HOG-PLUM. Graceful tree to 60 ft.: lvs. 8–12 in. long, rachis pubescent; lfts. 7–17, ovate-lanceolate, 2½–4 in. long, acuminate, subentire, veins branching near edges of lfts.: fls. in large terminal panicles ½–1 ft. or more long, small, yellowish-white: fr. ovoid, 1–2 in. long, yellow, with large stone. (Mombin: a native American name.) Cosmopolitan in tropics.

3. **S. cytherea,** Sonn. (*S. dulcis,* Forst.). OTAHEITE-APPLE. VI. AMBARELLA. Spreading graceful tree to 60 ft.: lvs. 8–15 in. long; lfts. 11–23, oval-oblong, acuminate, 2½–3½ in. long, entire or slightly crenate, veins almost parallel, unbranching: fls. in terminal panicles 8–12 in. long, small, greenish-white: fr. oval or obovoid, golden-yellow, up to 3 in. long and 1–3 in. diam., with large stone. (Cytherea: one of the names of Venus.) Society Isls.

5. **HARPEPHYLLUM,** Bernh. Two S. African diœcious trees, one planted in S. U. S.—Lvs. clustered at ends of branches, odd-pinnate, leathery, the rachis

slightly winged: fls. small, in axillary compact panicles; sepals 4–5; petals 5, imbricate in bud; stamens 10: fr. 4-celled, 2 of the cells small and sterile. (Harpephyllum: Greek for *sickle* and *leaf*, referring to shape of lfts.)

H. caffrum, Bernh. KAFIR-PLUM. To 30 ft.: lvs. 6–10 in. long, shining, of 11–15 lanceolate lfts. to 2½ in. long, with prominent midrib: fls. white or greenish: fr. dark red, about 1 in. long and ½in. wide, edible.

6. **PISTACIA,** L. Perhaps 20 species of trees or shrubs from Medit. region to Asia, Mex. and Tex.; one species is grown for the nuts used in confectionery and others have been intro. as stock on which to graft *P. vera*.—Plant diœcious: lvs. alternate, persistent or deciduous, odd- or even-pinnate or of 3 lfts.: fls. without petals, small, in axillary racemes or panicles, pedicels bracted at base; staminate fls. with 1–2 sepals and 3–5 very short stamens with large anthers; pistillate fls. with 2–5 sepals, 1-celled sessile ovary and short 3-cleft style: fr. a dry drupe. (Pista-cia: derived indirectly from ancient Persian *pista*.)

A. Lvs. odd-pinnate; lfts. ovate .... 1. *P. vera*
AA. Lvs. even-pinnate; lfts. lanceolate .... 2. *P. chinensis*

1. **P. vera,** L. PISTACHIO. Spreading deciduous tree to 30 ft.: lvs. odd-pinnate, of usually 3–5 lfts.; lfts. ovate, 2–4 in. long, obtuse or mucronulate, slightly tapering to the base: drupe ovoid, oblong, pedicelled, up to 1 in. long, reddish and wrinkled, containing the green or yellow seed or kernel of commerce. Medit. region and Orient.

2. **P. chinensis,** Bunge. Deciduous tree to 60 ft. or more: lvs. even-pinnate, of 10–12 lfts., turning crimson in autumn; lfts. lanceolate, 2–4 in. long, acuminate, oblique: drupe obovoid, red turning purple, about ⅕in. across, in large panicles 6–10 in. long. China.

7. **SCHINUS,** L. Fifteen or more species of resinous trees mostly from S. Amer., two grown for ornament in Calif. and Fla.—Plant diœcious: lvs. alternate, odd-pinnate; lfts. sessile: fls. in axillary or terminal bracteate panicles, small, white; calyx short, 5-parted; petals 5, imbricated; stamens 10; ovary sessile, 1-celled; styles 3: drupe globose. (Schi-nus: Greek for the mastic-tree, *Pistacia Lentiscus*, which this genus resembles in its resinous juice.)

A. Lfts. numerous, linear-lanceolate .... 1. *S. Molle*
AA. Lfts. usually 7, oblong .... 2. *S. terebinthifolius*

1. **S. Molle,** L. CALIFORNIA PEPPER-TREE. PERUVIAN MASTIC-TREE. Evergreen tree to 20 ft. or more, with graceful pendulous branches: lvs. 10 in. and more long, of numerous linear-lanceolate lfts. 1½–2½ in. long and ¼–⅜in. wide, often serrate: fls. in much-branched panicles: fr. rose-color, ¼–⅜in. diam. (Molle: from *Mulli*, the Peruvian name.) American tropics.

2. **S. terebinthifolius,** Raddi. BRAZILIAN PEPPER-TREE. CHRISTMAS-BERRY-TREE. Differs from the above in its more rigid habit: lfts. usually 7, oblong, 1½–3 in. long, ¾–1½ in. wide, very dark green above, lighter below: fls. in denser panicles: fr. smaller, bright red. Brazil.

8. **RHUS,** L. SUMAC. Trees or shrubs with milky or resinous juice, native to temp. and subtrop. regions of both hemispheres, of about 150 species, grown for their ornamental foliage.—Plant polygamous or diœcious: lvs. alternate, usually odd-pinnate, sometimes simple or 3-foliolate, entire or serrate, without stipules: fls. small, in axillary or terminal panicles; calyx usually 5-parted, small; petals usually 5, imbricate, spreading; stamens 5; ovary sessile, 1-celled; styles 3, terminal: fr. small, dry, 1-seeded, smooth or hairy. (Rhus: ancient Greek name.)

A. Lvs. simple.
  B. Infl. glabrous: fr. whitish, glabrous .... 1. *R. laurina*
  BB. Infl. pubescent: fr. red, hairy.
    C. Lf. acuminate, folded upward .... 2. *R. ovata*
    CC. Lf. obtuse, flattened .... 3. *R. integrifolia*
AA. Lvs. compound.
  B. Number of lfts. 3.
    C. Lfts. 1–3 in. long, acute or acuminate .... 4. *R. aromatica*
    CC. Lfts. ½–1 in. long, obtuse .... 5. *R. trilobata*
  BB. Number of lfts. 7 or more.
    C. Rachis of lf. winged.
      D. Lfts. entire .... 6. *R. copallina*
      DD. Lfts. coarsely toothed .... 7. *R. chinensis*
    CC. Rachis of lf. terete.
      D. Branchlets glabrous .... 8. *R. glabra*
      DD. Branchlets densely pubescent .... 9. *R. typhina*

1. **R. laurina,** Nutt. LAUREL SUMAC. Evergreen glabrous shrub 8–12 ft. high, aromatic: lvs. oblong-lanceolate, 2–4 in. long, entire, light green beneath: fls. greenish-white, in dense panicles 2–4 in. long: fr. whitish. S. and Lower Calif.

2. **R. ovata,** Wats. SUGAR-BUSH. Evergreen shrub or small tree 10–20 ft. high: lvs. ovate, 2–4 in. long and 1–2 in. wide, entire, acuminate, folded upward, light green beneath: fls. yellowish tinged red, in dense spikes about 1 in. long: fr. deep red, glandular-hairy. S. Calif., Ariz.

3. **R. integrifolia,** Benth. & Hook. SOUR-BERRY. LEMONADE-BERRY. Evergreen shrub or small tree 25–30 ft. high: lvs. oblong-ovate, 1–2 in. long and about 1 in. wide, entire or somewhat toothed, obtuse, light green beneath: fls. white or pinkish, in dense panicles: fr. dark red, glandular-hairy. S. Calif.

4. **R. aromatica,** Ait. (*R. canadensis*, Marsh. not Mill. *Schmaltzia crenata*, Greene). FRAGRANT SUMAC. Diffuse shrub 3–8 ft. high, aromatic: lfts. 3, pubescent, ovate, 1–3 in. long, acute or acuminate, coarsely toothed: fls. yellowish, in spikes to ¾ in. long forming panicles, before the lvs.: fr. red, hairy. Ont. to Minn. south to Fla. and La.

5. **R. trilobata,** Nutt. (*Schmaltzia trilobata*, Small). ILL-SCENTED SUMAC. Shrub 3–6 ft. high, ill-scented: lfts. 3, pubescent when young, ovate or obovate, ½–1 in. long, obtuse, with few teeth at tips: fls. greenish, in clustered spikes before the lvs.: fr. red, hairy. Ill. to Calif.

6. **R. copallina,** L. (*Schmaltzia copallina*, Small). SHINING SUMAC. Shrub or small tree 20–30 ft. high: rachis winged, pubescent; lfts. 9–21, ovate-lanceolate, 2–4 in. long, entire or with only few teeth, shining above, pubescent beneath: fls. greenish, in dense terminal panicles in July and Aug.: fr. crimson, hairy. Me. to Minn. south to Fla. and Tex.

7. **R. chinensis,** Mill. (*R. javanica*, Thunb. not L. *R. Osbeckii*, Decne. *R. semialata*, Murr.). Shrub or flat-headed tree to 25 ft.: rachis winged, pubescent; lfts. 7–13, nearly sessile, ovate to ovate-oblong, 2–5 in. long, acute or short-acuminate, coarsely crenate-serrate, brownish-pubescent beneath: fls. creamy-white, in large broad panicles to 12 in. long, in Aug. and Sept.: fr. red, densely pubescent. Japan, China, S. Asia.

8. **R. glabra,** L. (*Schmaltzia glabra*, Small). SMOOTH SUMAC. Shrub or tree 10–20 ft. high, glabrous: lfts. 11–31, oblong-lanceolate, 2–5 in. long, acuminate, toothed, glaucous beneath, turning red in autumn: fls. greenish, in dense panicles 4–10 in. long, in July and Aug.: fr. scarlet, sticky-pubescent. N. Amer. Var. **laciniata,** Carr., has deeply cut lfts.

9. **R. typhina,** Torner (*R. hirta*, Sudw. *Schmaltzia hirta*, Small). STAGHORN SUMAC. Shrub or tree to 30 ft., with branchlets densely velvety-hairy: lfts. 11–31, 2–5 in. long, oblong-lanceolate, pointed, serrate, glaucescent beneath: fls. greenish, in dense hairy terminal panicles 4–8 in. long, in June and July: fr. crimson, hairy. Que. south to Ga. and Ia. Var. **dissecta,** Rehd., lfts. pinnately dissected. Var. **laciniata,** Wood, lfts. and bracts laciniately toothed.

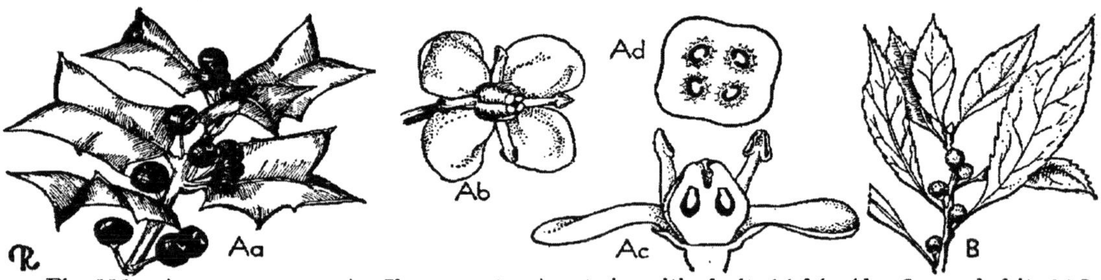

Fig. 111. AQUIFOLIACEÆ. A, *Ilex cornuta:* Aa, twig with fruit, × ½; Ab, flower habit, × 2; Ac, flower, vertical section, × 3; Ad, ovary, cross-section, × 6. B, *Ilex verticillata:* fruiting branch, × ⅜.

111. AQUIFOLIACEÆ. HOLLY FAMILY

A family of 3 genera and more than 300 species widely dispersed, the center of distribution being in Cent. and S. Amer.; several species of Ilex are cult. in Amer. for ornamental purposes, while other species have been used medicinally in various parts of the world.—Trees or shrubs, with alternate (or very rarely opposite), simple, often persistent lvs.: fls. unisexual, rarely bisexual, very small, axillary, solitary or fascicled or cymose; calyx 3–6-parted, usually persistent; petals 4–5, distinct or at base connate, imbricated; stamens as many as the petals or rarely more, free or slightly adhering to the petals; ovary superior, 3- to many-celled, each cell 1–2-

ovuled, placentation axile, the ovules pendulous from cell apex: fr. drupaceous with 3–18 1-seeded pyrenes.

A. Petals oblong or obovate, united at base; sepals persistent .... 1. ILEX
AA. Petals linear, distinct; sepals deciduous...2. NEMOPANTHUS

1. **ILEX**, L. HOLLY. About 300 species in N. and S. Amer., trop. and temp. Asia and few in Afr., Australia and Eu.; often planted for the handsome foliage and berries, sometimes made into hedges.—Evergreen or deciduous, usually diœcious: lvs. alternate, petioled, often shining, entire or toothed or spinose, with small caducous stipules: fls. small, inconspicuous, whitish, mostly in rather few-fld. axillary cymes; calyx-lobes, petals and stamens usually 4, sometimes more: fr. a globose berry-like drupe with 2–8 bony 1-seeded stones. (I-lex: ancient Latin name for *Quercus Ilex*.)

A. Foliage persistent.
B. Lvs. with coarse spiny teeth, rarely entire.
C. Fls. in axillary clusters on branches of the previous year.
D. Fr. and fls. stalked.
E. Shape of lvs. ovate or oblong-ovate.......................... 1. *I. Aquifolium*
EE. Shape of lvs. quadrangular-oblong, 3-pointed at apex............ 2. *I. cornuta*
DD. Fr. and fls. sessile.. 3. *I. Pernyi*
CC. Fls. in 1- to few-fld. axillary solitary cymes, on this year's growth......... 4. *I. opaca*
BB. Lvs. serrate, crenate or entire.
C. Fr. red or yellow; nutlets ribbed on back.
D. Margin of lvs. entire.
E. Peduncles of fr. 1–2 in. long .... 5. *I. pedunculosa*
EE. Peduncles of fr. ¼in. or less long.
F. Length of lvs. 2–4 in.
G. Fls. on branches of previous year: lvs. glabrous.............. 6. *I. integra*
GG. Fls. on this year's growth: young lvs. usually pubescent beneath. 7. *I. Cassine*
FF. Length of lvs. ½–1½ in.. 8. *I. myrtifolia*
DD. Margin of lvs. crenate or serrate.
E. Length of lvs. ½–1 in.. 9. *I. vomitoria*
EE. Length of lvs. 1½–7 in.
F. Apex of lvs. sharp; blades 3–7 in. long.........................10. *I. latifolia*
FF. Apex of lvs. blunt; blades mostly 1½–3 in. long...................11. *I. paraguariensis*
CC. Fr. black; nutlets smooth.
D. Fls. 4-merous: lvs. serrate...12. *I. crenata*
DD. Fls. 5–8-merous: lvs. toothed only at apex..................................13. *I. glabra*
AA. Foliage deciduous: fr. red.
B. Fr. not clustered; nutlets smooth on back.
C. Fls. 5–8-merous..14. *I. verticillata*
CC. Fls. 4–5-merous..15. *I. serrata*
BB. Fr. clustered; nutlets ribbed on back.
C. Lvs. broadest above middle, obtuse...16. *I. decidua*
CC. Lvs. broadest at or below middle, acute or acuminate.................17. *I. montana*

1. **I. Aquifolium**, L. ENGLISH HOLLY. Tree to 40 ft. or more, with many short spreading branches, forming an oblong or pyramidal head, in cult. often shrubby; branchlets glabrous or minutely downy: lvs. persistent, shining, 1½–3 in. long, short-petioled, usually ovate or oblong-ovate, waved and with strong spiny outstanding teeth often ¼in. long: fls. unisexual or bisexual, dull white, short-stalked, fragrant, produced in late spring and early summer, in axillary clusters on wood of the previous year: fr. globular, scarlet, shining, ¼in. diam., stalked. (Aquifolium: Latin *point* and *leaf*, referring to the spiny lvs.) Eu., W. Asia to China.—A very variable species, the lvs. of the numerous cultivars differing greatly in size, form, and spininess, and certain vars. having lvs. blotched or margined with white or yellow; many named forms are known in cult.

2. **I. cornuta**, Lindl. Evergreen shrub, glabrous, to 10 ft., bushy, dense and rounded, usually wider than high: lvs. dark glossy green, quadrangular-oblong, 1½–4 in. long, with 3 strong spines of nearly equal size at the dilated apex, the terminal one recurved, and with 1–2 strong spines on each side of the truncate base, but rounded and spineless at base on older plants: fls. produced in spring in axillary clusters on the branches of the previous year: fr. scarlet, ¼–½in. diam., stalked. China. Var. **Burfordii**, DeFrance, has obovate lvs. with few or no spines.

3. **I. Pernyi**, Franch. Compact evergreen shrub or tree to 30 ft.; branchlets slightly pubescent: lvs. shining, glabrous, rhombic-ovate, ¾–1 in. long, with 1–3 spines on each side: fls. pale yellow, in sessile clusters on wood of previous year, in May: fr. red, ¼in. long, nearly sessile. (Named for Paul Perny, a French missionary in China about 1850–1860.) China.

4. **I. opaca**, Ait. AMERICAN HOLLY. Evergreen tree sometimes to 50 ft., with short spreading branches forming a narrow pyramidal head, glabrous or the young shoots minutely downy: lvs. oval or elliptic-lanceolate, 2–4 in. long, pungently acuminate, with large remote spiny teeth, rarely entire, dull green above, yellowish-green beneath: fls.

borne in summer on the new year's growth; staminate fls. in 3–9-fld. slender-stalked cymes; pistillate fls. usually solitary; calyx-lobes ciliate: fr. dull scarlet, ¼in. diam. Mass. to Fla. west to Mo. and Tex. Var. **xanthocarpa,** Rehd., has yellow frs.—A variable species, shrubby or arborescent, with numerous selected clones identified by fancy names.

5. **I. pedunculosa,** Miq. (*I. fujisanensis,* Sakata). Evergreen shrub or tree to 30 ft., glabrous: lvs. ovate, 1–3 in. long, entire, acuminate, shining above: fls. in stalked cymes on season's growth, in June: fr. bright red, ¼in. across, on slender peduncles 1–2 in. long. Japan.

6. **I. integra,** Thunb. Evergreen shrub or tree to 40 ft., glabrous: lvs. dark glossy green, oval to elliptic-oblong or oblong-obovate, rarely oblanceolate, narrowed at base, at apex contracted into a short obtuse point, entire or very rarely few-toothed, indistinctly veined, 2–4 in. long: fls. in axillary fascicles on branches of the previous year, Feb.–Apr.: fr. red, ⅓–½in. diam., short-stalked. Japan.

7. **I. Cassine,** L. (*I. Dahoon,* Walt.). Dahoon. Evergreen shrub or small tree to 30 ft.; branchlets usually pubescent: lvs. obovate, 2–4 in. long, acute or obtuse, often mucronulate, entire or somewhat revolute, usually pubescent beneath when young: fertile cymes mostly 3-fld. and 3-fruited, on the season's growth, spring: fr. red or rarely yellow, ¼in. diam. (Cassine or Cassina is an Indian name.) N. C. to Fla. west to La. Var. **angustifolia,** Ait., has linear-oblong to linear lvs.

8. **I. myrtifolia,** Walt. Evergreen shrub or small tree, with stiff branches: lvs. oblong or linear, ½–1½ in. long, entire, somewhat revolute, apiculate, dark green above, pale beneath: fls. in spring, on season's growth: fr. red, rarely yellow, ¼in. diam., short-stalked. N. C. to Fla. and La.

9. **I. vomitoria,** Ait. (*I. Cassine,* Walt. not L.). Yaupon. Cassena. Much-branched shrub, rarely small tree, to 25 ft., with spreading branches: lvs. persistent, oval or oblong, ½–1 in., rarely to 2 in. long, obtuse, crenate-serrate, glabrous: fls. in spring, clustered on branches of the previous year, the sterile cymes 3–9-fld. and peduncled, the fertile 1–3-fld. and sessile: fr. scarlet, about ¼in. diam. Va. to Fla. and Tex.

10. **I. latifolia,** Thunb. Tarajo. Evergreen tree to 60 ft.: lvs. shining, oval to oblong-lanceolate, 3–7 in. long, toothed, acuminate: fr. red, ⅓in. across, in dense clusters. Japan.

11. **I. paraguariensis,** St. Hil. (*I. paraguayensis,* Hook.). Yerba Maté. Evergreen shrub or small tree to 20 ft.; branchlets glabrous to puberulous: lvs. elliptic-obovate, narrowed at base, obtuse to obtusely acuminate at apex, crenate-serrate, 1½–3 or more in. long, short-petioled: fls. axillary: fr. rounded, reddish, to ¼in. diam. Brazil to Argentina.—Important in cult. as source of maté; possibly other species are involved.

12. **I. crenata,** Thunb. (*I. Fortunei,* Hort.). Japanese Holly. Much-branched evergreen shrub, rarely small tree, to 20 ft.: lvs. crowded, oval, obovate or oblong-lanceolate, ½–1½ in. long, crenately serrate, sharp-pointed, glabrous, shining: fls. 4-merous, the pistillate usually solitary on this year's growth, May–June: fr. black, the nutlets smooth, ⅓in. across, short-stalked. Japan. Var. **convexa,** Makino (*I. crenata bullata,* Rehd.), has nearly round bullate lvs. convex above. Var. **Helleri,** Bailey, is dwarf with oval lvs. to ½in. long (named for Joseph Heller of Newport Nurseries, R. I.). Var. **latifolia,** Goldring, has oval or obovate lvs. Var. **microphylla,** Maxim., has oval to oblong lvs. to ½in. long. Var. **rotundifolia,** Hort., lvs. round.

13. **I. glabra,** Gray (*Prinos glaber,* L.). Inkberry. Winterberry. Much-branched evergreen shrub to 8 ft., with erect branches: lvs. obovate to oblanceolate, 1–2 in. long, obtuse, entire or with a few obtuse teeth toward the apex, glabrous: fls. in summer, 5–8-merous, the pistillate usually solitary on this year's growth: fr. black, about ¼in. diam., short-stalked. Mass. to Fla. west to Miss.

14. **I. verticillata,** Gray (*Prinos verticillatus,* L.). Black-Alder. Winterberry. Deciduous shrub to 10 ft., with spreading branches: lvs. obovate or oblanceolate to oval or lanceolate, 1½–3 in. long, acuminate or acute, serrate or doubly serrate, usually pubescent beneath: fls. 5–8-merous, short-stalked, produced in summer: fr. bright red, about ¼in. diam., maturing in autumn and remaining on the branches till midwinter, rarely eaten by birds. Canada to Fla. west to Wis. and Mo.

15. **I. serrata,** Thunb. (*I. Sieboldii,* Miq.). Slender deciduous shrub to 15 ft., similar to no. 14 but smaller in every part: lvs. elliptic or ovate, 1–2 in. long, acute or acuminate, finely serrate, pubescent beneath: fls. 4–5-merous, inconspicuous, in summer: fr. bright red, ⅙–⅕in. diam., in autumn. Japan.

16. **I. decidua,** Walt. Possum-Haw. Deciduous shrub or small tree to 30 ft., with spreading branches: lvs. obovate, 1½–3 in. long, serrate, obtuse, dark green and shining above, pubescent on midrib beneath: fls. in May: fr. red or orange, ⅓in. across, clustered. Va. to Fla. and Tex.

17. **I. montana,** Gray (*I. dubia,* Auth. not BSP. *I. monticola,* Gray). Deciduous shrub or tree to 30 ft.: lvs. ovate to oblong-lanceolate, 2–6 in. long, sharp-serrate, acute or acuminate, slightly pubescent on veins beneath: fls. in June: fr. orange-red, ½in. across, short-stalked, clustered. N. Y. to S. C. west to Ala.

2. **NEMOPANTHUS,** Raf. One species, sometimes planted for the attractive frs. and lvs. which turn yellow in autumn.—Deciduous diœcious shrub: lvs. alternate, slender-petioled, entire or slightly toothed: fls. small, whitish, the pistillate solitary, staminate 1–4 in the axils; sepals 4–5, deciduous; petals 4–5, linear: fr. a drupe with 4–5 bony nutlets. (Nemopan-thus: Greek for *thread* and *flower*, referring to pedicels.)

N. mucronatus, Trel. (*Vaccinium mucronatum,* L. *N. canadensis,* DC.). MOUNTAIN-HOLLY. To 10 ft., glabrous, young branchlets purplish: lvs. elliptic to oblong, 1–1½ in. long, mucronate: fls. May–June, on pedicels ½–1 in. long: fr. red, ¼–⅓in. diam. Mostly in bogs and swamps, Newf. to Wis. and Va.

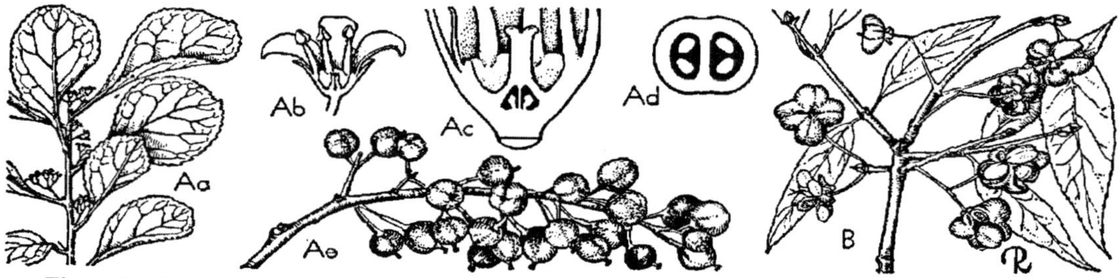

Fig. 112. CELASTRACEÆ. A, *Celastrus orbiculatus:* Aa, flowering branch, × ¼; Ab, staminate flower, vertical section, × 2; Ac, pistil of pistillate flower, vertical section, × 6; Ad, ovary, cross-section, × 20; Ae, fruiting inflorescence, × ½. B, *Euonymus Maackii:* fruiting branch, × ½.

112. CELASTRACEÆ. STAFF-TREE FAMILY

Trees and shrubs, often climbing, of about 40 genera and 400 species, widely distributed over the earth except in arctic regions.—Lvs. alternate or opposite, simple, stipules when present small and caducous: fls. usually bisexual, sometimes unisexual or functionally so, regular, small, in axillary or terminal cymes or racemes or solitary; calyx small, 4–5-lobed or -parted, imbricated, persistent; petals 4–5, imbricated; stamens 4–5, alternate with petals, inserted on the conspicuous disk; ovary 1–5-celled, free or imbedded in the disk, with short style and entire or 3–5-lobed stigma, ovules usually 2 in each cell, seldom 1 or many: fr. a caps., drupe or samara; seeds usually with a pulpy aril.

A. Lvs. alternate.
  B. Fr. a dehiscent caps.
    C. Plant climbing: ovary free........1. CELASTRUS
    CC. Plant erect: ovary imbedded in disk........2. MAYTENUS
  BB. Fr. a 3-winged samara........3. TRIPTERYGIUM
AA. Lvs. opposite or whorled.
  B. Fr. of 1 carpel........4. PACHISTIMA
  BB. Fr. of 3–5 carpels.
    C. Seed with white aril at base........5. CATHA
    CC. Seed inclosed in orange or red aril........6. EUONYMUS

1. **CELASTRUS,** L. More than 30 species of shrubs, usually climbing, native in S. and E. Asia, Australia, and Amer., useful as a wall or trellis cover and with bright colored fr. usually persistent throughout the winter.—Plant polygamo-diœcious: lvs. alternate, petioled, usually deciduous, glabrous: fls. usually unisexual or functionally so, small, greenish-white, in axillary or terminal panicles or racemes; calyx 5-parted; petals 5, inserted under the disk; stamens 5, with short filaments; disk entire or 5-lobed; ovary free, 3-lobed and -celled: caps. loculicidally dehiscent by 3 valves, each with 1–2 seeds inclosed in a crimson aril. (Celas-trus: ancient Greek name.)

A. Fls. in axillary few-fld. cymes along the branches........1. *C. orbiculatus*
AA. Fls. in terminal panicles or racemes........2. *C. scandens*

1. **C. orbiculatus,** Thunb. (*C. articulatus,* Thunb.). Vigorous, climbing to 40 ft.: lvs. suborbicular to oblong or obovate, acute or acuminate, crenate-serrate, 2–4 in. long: fls. 2–4 together in small axillary cymes along the branches: caps. globular, ⅓in. diam., the inner surface orange-yellow, aril crimson. Japan, China.

2. **C. scandens,** L. False or American Bitter-Sweet. Waxwork. Twining shrub to 25 ft., many plants often sterile: lvs. ovate to ovate-lanceolate, acuminate, crenate-serrate, 2–4 in. long: fls. in terminal many-fld. compound racemes 2–4 in. long, the pistillate nearly simple: caps. about ⅓in. diam., orange-yellow, when opening disclosing the crimson covering of the seeds. Que. to N. C. and New Mex.

2. **MAYTENUS,** Molina. Seventy or more species of evergreen trees and shrubs, native in trop. and temp. S. Amer. and W. Indies, one planted as a street and avenue tree in warm countries.—Plant polygamous: lvs. alternate, petioled, serrate, leathery: fls. small, in axillary clusters or solitary; calyx 5-lobed; petals 5, spreading; stamens 5; disk orbicular, margin undulate; ovary imbedded in disk, 2–4-celled, the style slender or 0, stigma 2–4-lobed: caps. leathery, 1–3-celled, loculicidally dehiscent by 2–3 valves. (Mayte-nus: from the Chilean name.)

M. Boaria, Molina. Mayten. Graceful evergreen to 25 ft. but said to attain 100 ft. in the wild, with pendulous branchlets: lvs. lanceolate or ovate-lanceolate, acute, 1–2 in. long: fls. minute, clustered, greenish: caps. about size of a pea, 2-valved, the seeds with scarlet aril. (Boaria: probably an aboriginal name.) Chile.

3. **TRIPTERYGIUM,** Hook. f. Asian deciduous polygamous shrubs of 3 species. —Lvs. large, alternate, petioled, glabrous: fls. small, white, in large terminal panicles; calyx 5-lobed; petals 5; stamens 5, inserted at edge of disk; ovary 3-angled and -celled, with 2 ovules in each cell: fr. a 1-seeded 3-winged samara. (Tripterygium: Greek for *three* and *wing.*)

T. Regelii, Sprague & Takeda. To 6 ft.; branches long and lithe, reddish-brown and warty: lvs. broad-elliptic to ovate, 2–6 in. long, crenate-serrate: panicles to 10 in. long: fr. nearly orbicular, ¾in. across, greenish-white. (Named for E. Regel, page 50.) Manchuria to Japan.

4. **PACHISTIMA,** Raf. Evergreen shrubs of 2 species in N. Amer.—Branches warty and 4-angled: lvs. small, opposite: fls. small, in axillary cymes; sepals and petals 4; stamens 4, short, inserted on edge of disk; ovary 2-celled, the stigma slightly 2-lobed: fr. a leathery loculicidally dehiscent caps., with 1–2 seeds having thin white aril at base. (Pachis-tima: Greek for *thick* and *stigma.*)

A. Sts. decumbent and rooting: pedicels about ⅓in. long........................1. *P. Canbyi*
AA. Sts. stiff and spreading: pedicels very short................................2. *P. Myrsinites*

1. **P. Canbyi,** Gray. Sts. decumbent and rooting, ascending to 1 ft.: lvs. narrow-oblong, to 1 in. long and less than ¼in. broad, the sides nearly parallel, revolute, toothed above the middle: fls. on slender pedicels to ⅓in. long. (Named for Wm. Marriott Canby, botanist of Wilmington, Del.) Mts. of Va. and W. Va.

2. **P. Myrsinites,** Raf. To 2 ft., sts. spreading and rather stiff: lvs. ovate to oblong-obovate, to 1¼ in. long, obtuse or acute, slightly toothed and revolute: fls. on very short pedicels. B. C. to Calif. and New Mex.

5. **CATHA,** Forsk. One evergreen shrub native from Abyssinia to S. Afr., sometimes planted in S. U. S.—Lvs. opposite, sometimes alternate on infertile shoots: fls. small, in axillary cymes; calyx 5-lobed; petals 5; stamens 5, inserted on edge of thin disk; ovary 3-celled with 3 styles and 2 ovules in each cell: fr. a 3-celled loculicidally dehiscent caps., seed with white aril at base. (Ca-tha: Arabian name, where the lvs. are used in the preparation of a drink.)

C. edulis, Forsk. Khat. Cafta. Arabian-Tea. To 10 ft.: lvs. oval, 2–4 in. long and ½–1½ in. wide, toothed: fls. white: caps. about ¼in. long.

6. **EUONYMUS,** L. Spindle-Tree. Upright trees and shrubs or rarely creeping or climbing by rootlets, of about 120 species in the north temp. zone, grown for the attractive foliage and frs.—Branches mostly 4-angled: winter-buds usually conspicuous, with imbricate scales: lvs. opposite, petioled, entire or serrate: fls. bisexual or functionally unisexual, small, greenish or purplish, in axillary peduncled cymes; sepals and petals 4–5; stamens 4–5, the filaments very short; disk flat, 4–5-lobed; ovary imbedded in the disk, 3–5-celled, the style short or 0, the stigma 3–5-lobed: caps. 3–5-lobed, loculicidally dehiscent into 3–5 valves, the white, red, or black seeds

inclosed in an orange-colored aril. (Euon-ymus: ancient Greek name.)—Sometimes spelled *Evonymus*.

A. Branches with broad corky wings .... 1. *E. alatus*
AA. Branches not winged.
  B. Lvs. linear to linear-oblong, usually whorled .... 2. *E. nanus*
  BB. Lvs. broader, all opposite.
    C. Foliage persistent.
      D. Tip of lf. abruptly long-acuminate .... 10. *E. Bungeanus* var.
      DD. Tip of lf. acute or obtuse.
        E. Fls. Aug.–Sept., in loose cymes: lvs. rather thin .... 3. *E. kiautschovicus*
        EE. Fls. June–July, in dense cymes: lvs. thick.
          F. Sts. procumbent or climbing, rooting .... 4. *E. Fortunei*
          FF. Sts. erect .... 5. *E. japonicus*
    CC. Foliage deciduous.
      D. Under surface of lvs. pubescent: fls. purple .... 6. *E. atropurpureus*
      DD. Under surface of lvs. glabrous, except perhaps on midrib: fls. yellowish or greenish.
        E. Caps. warty.
          F. Shrub upright .... 7. *E. americanus*
          FF. Shrub procumbent .... 8. *E. obovatus*
        EE. Caps. smooth.
          F. Fr. globose .... 3. *E. kiautschovicus*
          FF. Fr. 4–5-lobed.
            G. Lobes of caps. winged .... 9. *E. latifolius*
            GG. Lobes of caps. not winged.
              H. Petiole ½–1 in. long: lvs. abruptly long-acuminate .... 10. *E. Bungeanus*
              HH. Petiole ¼–⅓in. long: lvs. acute or acuminate.
                I. Lf. broadest above middle, 2½–5 in. long .... 11. *E. yedoensis*
                II. Lf. broadest at or below middle, 1½–3 in. long.
                  J. Seed red: anthers purple .... 12. *E. Maackii*
                  JJ. Seed white: anthers yellow .... 13. *E. europæus*

1. **E. alatus,** Sieb. (*Celastrus alatus,* Thunb.). Deciduous spreading shrub to 8 ft.; branches with 2–4 broad corky wings: lvs. elliptic or obovate, 1–2 in. long, tapering at both ends, short-petioled, finely and sharply serrate, turning bright crimson in autumn: fls. greenish-yellow, 1–3 in a cyme, May–June: caps. ¼–⅓in. long, purplish, divided to base into 4 or less ovoid lobes or pods; seeds brown with orange aril. China, Japan. Var. **compactus,** Bailey, is a compact dwarf form with narrow-winged branches.

2. **E. nanus,** Bieb. Deciduous shrub of spreading or procumbent habit, 2–3 ft. high, the young branches slender and often arching: lvs. usually whorled, sometimes alternate or opposite, linear or linear-oblong, 1–1½ in. long, obtuse or acute, the margins revolute and entire or remotely denticulate: fls. purplish, 1–3 together on slender pedicels, May–June: caps. deeply 4-lobed, pink; seeds brown with orange aril. W. Asia to China.

3. **E. kiautschovicus,** Loes. (*E. patens,* Rehd. *E. Sieboldianus,* Hort. not Blume). Partially evergreen spreading shrub to 10 ft., sometimes with prostrate rooting branches: lvs. oval or obovate, 2–3 in. long, acute or obtuse, short-petioled, crenate-serrate: fls. greenish-white, in loose cymes 2–2½ in. across, Aug.–Sept.: caps. globose, ½in. across, pink; seeds pinkish with orange aril. China.

4. **E. Fortunei,** Hand.-Mazz. (*E. radicans* var. *acutus,* Rehd.). Evergreen shrub, trailing or climbing to 20 ft. high by means of rootlets; branches densely covered with minute warts: lvs. roundish to elliptic-oval, 1–2 in. long, acute or acuminate, rounded or narrowed at base, crenately serrate, dark green above with whitish veins: fls. and fr. seldom produced except in the bush forms, the greenish 4-merous fls. in slender-peduncled clusters of 5 or more, June–July: caps. nearly globose, ⅓in. across, pinkish, aril orange. (Named for Robt. Fortune, page 43.) China.—A form of the typical element is **coloratus,** Rehd., with autumn lvs. dark purple above and paler beneath. Var. **radicans,** Rehd. (*E. radicans,* Miq.), differs in its smaller less pointed lvs. which are sharply serrate, of thicker texture and lateral veins obsolete; Japan, S. Korea. Forms of this var. are: **Carrierei,** Rehd., more shrubby and not climbing, lvs. glossy, sometimes white-margined; **gracilis,** Rehd. (*E. radicans* var. *argenteo-marginatus,* Rehd.), climbing, lvs. variegated with white, yellow or pink; **minimus,** Rehd. (*E. radicans* var. *minimus,* Simon-Louis. *E. radicans* var. *kewensis,* Bean), sterile creeping plant with lvs. ½in. or less long; **reticulatus,** Rehd., lvs. variegated white along veins. Var. **vegetus,** Rehd. (*E. radicans* var. *vegetus,* Rehd.), spreading shrub to 5 ft. or climbing when supported, differing from var. *radicans* in the orbicular-ovate coarsely toothed more leathery lvs. and larger infl.

5. **E. japonicus,** L. Upright densely leafy evergreen shrub to 15 ft., the smooth branches slightly quadrangular or striped: lvs. broadly oval, obovate to narrow-elliptic, 1–3 in. long, wedge-shaped at base, usually obtuse or rounded at apex, obtusely serrate, shining above: fls. greenish-white, 5 to many together in stout-peduncled cymes, June–July: caps. globose, ⅓in. across, pink, aril orange. Japan.—Runs into many hort. forms, a few of which are: var. **albo-marginatus,** Rehd., lvs. with narrow white border; var. **aureo-marginatus,** Rehd., lvs. edged with yellow; var. **aureo-variegatus,** Regel, lvs. blotched with yellow; var. **microphyllus,** Sieb. (*E. pulchellus,* Hort.), lvs. ½–1 in. long; var. **viridi-variegatus,** Rehd. (Duc d'Anjou), lvs. bright green variegated with yellow.

6. E. **atropurpureus,** Jacq. WAHOO. BURNING-BUSH. Deciduous shrub or tree to 25 ft.: lvs. elliptic, 2–5 in. long, acuminate, finely toothed, pubescent beneath: fls. purple, 7 or more in slender-peduncled cymes, May–June: fr. deeply 4-lobed, scarlet, ½in. across; seeds brown with scarlet aril. N. Y. to Fla. and Tex.

7. E. **americanus,** L. STRAWBERRY-BUSH. Deciduous glabrous shrub to 8 ft.: lvs. ovate-lanceolate to lanceolate, 1–3 in. long, acuminate, crenate-serrate: fls. reddish-green, 1–3 on slender stalks, June: fr. 3–5-lobed, pink, ½in. across, covered with warts, aril scarlet. N. Y. to Fla. and Tex.

8. E. **obovatus,** Nutt. RUNNING STRAWBERRY-BUSH. Deciduous procumbent shrub to 1 ft., the branches rooting: lvs. obovate, 1–2 in. long, acute or somewhat obtuse, crenate-serrate: fls. greenish-purple, 1–3 on slender stalks, May: fr. 3-lobed, crimson, ½in. across, warty, aril scarlet. Ont. to Ky.

9. E. **latifolius,** Scop. Deciduous shrub or small tree to 20 ft.: lvs. obovate-oblong, 2–5 in. long, acuminate, finely serrate: fls. yellowish-green, 7–15 together in slender-peduncled cymes, May–June: caps. about ¾in. across, pendulous, rosy-red, with usually 5 winged lobes; seeds white, aril orange. S. Eu., W. Asia.

10. E. **Bungeanus,** Maxim. Deciduous shrub to 15 ft., with slender graceful branches: lvs. ovate-elliptic or elliptic-lanceolate, 2–4 in. long, on petioles ½–1 in. long, abruptly long-acuminate, with fine incurved teeth: fls. yellowish-white, in few-fld. but numerous cymes, June, the anthers purple: caps. ½in. across, deeply 4-lobed and 4-angled, yellowish, the white or pinkish seeds with orange aril. (Named for Alex. von Bunge, page 40.) China, Manchuria. Var. **semipersistens,** Schneid., is a half-evergreen form.

11. E. **yedoensis,** Koehne. Deciduous shrub to 10 ft.: lvs. obovate, 2½–5 in. long and 1½–2 in. wide, acuminate, finely toothed: fls. yellowish with purple anthers, in many-fld. slender-stalked cymes, June: caps. deeply 4-lobed, pinkish, ½in. across, aril orange. Japan, Korea.

12. E. **Maackii,** Rupr. Deciduous shrub or small tree: lvs. oblong, 2–3 in. long, acuminate, finely toothed: fls. yellowish with purple anthers, in small cymes, June: caps. 4-lobed, pink, ⅓in. across; seeds red with orange aril. (Bears the name of Richard Maack, 1825–1886, Russian naturalist.) N. China to Korea.

13. E. **europæus,** L. Deciduous shrub or small tree to 20 ft., with spreading bushy head: lvs. ovate or oblong-lanceolate, 1–3 in. long, acuminate, crenately serrate: fls. yellowish-green, in 3–7-fld. slender-peduncled cymes, May: caps. deeply 4-lobed, red or pink, ½–¾in. across; seeds white with orange aril. Eu., W. Asia. Var. **albus,** West. (var. *leucocarpus,* DC.), has whitish fr.

113. STAPHYLEACEÆ. BLADDER-NUT FAMILY

Trees and shrubs, of about 5 genera and 25 species of wide distribution, only one genus being grown for ornament.—Lvs. opposite or alternate, pinnately compound, stipulate: fls. bisexual or sometimes unisexual, regular, in terminal or axillary clusters; sepals and petals 5, imbricated; stamens 5, alternate with petals, inserted outside the large cup-shaped disk; ovary superior, usually 3-celled with distinct or connate styles, ovules numerous, placentation axile: fr. a leathery or fleshy caps., sometimes indehiscent; seeds solitary or few in each cell (many ovules usually abortive prior to seed maturity).

STAPHYLEA, L. BLADDER-NUT. About 11 species of deciduous shrubs or small trees, native in temp. regions of the northern hemisphere.—Bark smooth, striped: lvs. opposite, 3–7-foliolate, the lfts. serrate and stipulate: fls. white, in terminal

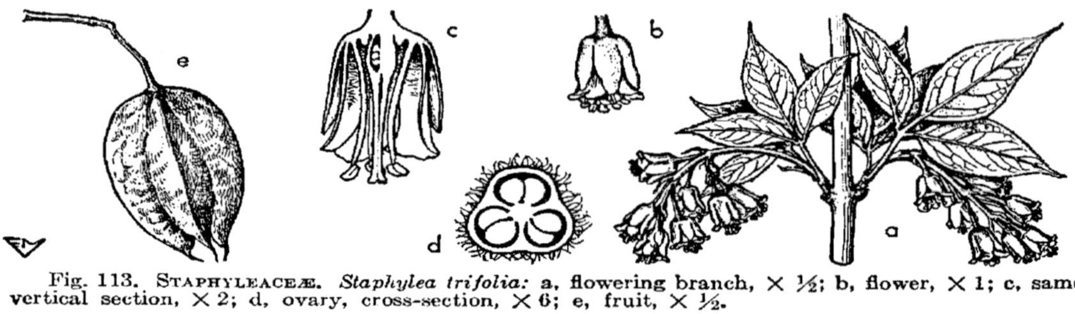

Fig. 113. STAPHYLEACEÆ. *Staphylea trifolia:* a, flowering branch, × ½; b, flower, × 1; c, same, vertical section, × 2; d, ovary, cross-section, × 6; e, fruit, × ½.

panicles; ovary 2–3-parted to base, the 2–3 styles free or connate above: caps. 2–3-lobed, inflated, membranaceous, dehiscent at summit along the inner side, the cells containing 1–4 large bony seeds. (Staphyle-a: Greek *cluster*, referring to the infl.)

A. Lfts. usually 5–7, glabrous beneath.
  B. Fr. 1½–3 in. long: panicles broad........1. *S. colchica*
  BB. Fr. 1–1½ in. long: panicles raceme-like........2. *S. pinnata*
AA. Lfts. 3, pubescent beneath at least on veins.
  B. Panicles erect: fr. 2-lobed........3. *S. Bumalda*
  BB. Panicles nodding: fr. 3-lobed........4. *S. trifolia*

1. **S. colchica,** Steven. Shrub to 12 ft.: lvs. usually 5-foliolate, sometimes 3, the lfts. oblong-ovate, 2–3½ in. long, acuminate, sharply serrate, glabrous and lustrous green beneath, the terminal lft. long-petioled, the lateral ones nearly sessile: fls. ½–¾in. long, in an upright or nodding panicle which is almost as broad as long; sepals yellowish-white, narrow-oblong, spreading; petals erect: caps. obovate, 2–3-lobed, much inflated, 1½–3 in. long, the styles persistent. Caucasus.

2. **S. pinnata,** L. European Bladder-Nut. Shrub to 15 ft.: lvs. 5–7-foliolate, the lfts. ovate-oblong, 2–4 in. long, acuminate, sharply and finely serrate, dull green above, pale and glaucescent beneath: fls. about ½in. long, in a raceme-like pendulous panicle; sepals oval, erect, greenish at base, reddish at apex: caps. subglobose, 2–3-lobed, much inflated, 1–1½ in. long. Eu.

3. **S. Bumalda,** DC. Shrub to 6 ft., with upright and spreading slender branches: lvs. 3-foliolate, the lfts. broadly oval to ovate, 1½–3 in. long, shortly acuminate, serrate with awned teeth, the middle lft. with petiole ½in. or less long, pubescent on veins beneath: fls. about ⅓in. long, in erect loose panicles; sepals yellowish-white, erect, little shorter than petals: caps. 2-lobed, compressed, ¾–1 in. long, the styles persistent. (Bumalda: name brought over from genus Bumalda which was named for Ovid Montalban, known as J. A. Bumalda, Italian botanical writer in 1657.) Japan.

4. **S. trifolia,** L. American Bladder-Nut. Shrub to 15 ft.: lvs. 3-foliolate, the lfts. oval or ovate, 1½–3 in. long, acuminate, sharply finely serrate, pubescent beneath at least when young: fls. about ⅓in. long, in nodding panicles; sepals greenish-white; petals white, longer than sepals: caps. 3-lobed, about 1½ in. long. Que. to Ga. and Mo.

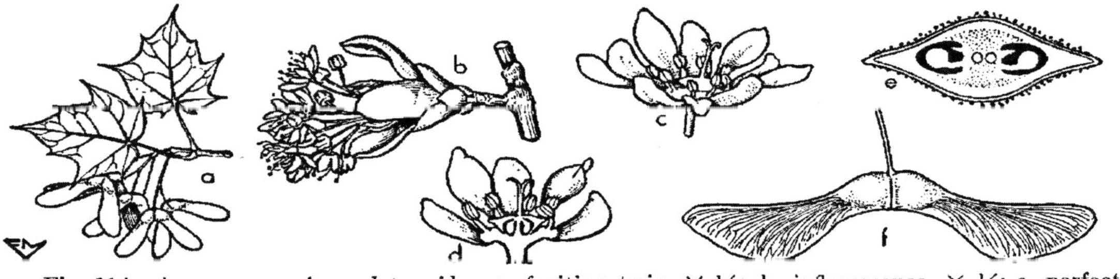

Fig. 114. Aceraceæ. *Acer platanoides:* a, fruiting twig, × ⅙; b, inflorescence, × ½; c, perfect flower, × ½; d, same, vertical section, × 1½; e, ovary, cross-section, × 8; f, fruit of two samaras, × ½.

114. ACERACEÆ. MAPLE FAMILY

Trees or shrubs with watery sap often saccharine, native in mountainous or upland countries of the northern hemisphere, of only 2 genera and more than 100 species.—Plants sometimes diœcious: lvs. opposite, petioled, exstipulate, simple or compound: fls. in axillary or terminal cymes or racemes, regular, bisexual or unisexual; sepals 4–5; petals 4–5, rarely 0; disk fleshy, annular, more or less lobed, rarely lacking; stamens 4–10, usually 8, inserted on summit or inside of disk, hypogynous, filaments filiform; ovary superior, 2-lobed, 2-celled with 2 ovules in each cell, much flattened contrary to the partition, placentation axile; styles 2, inserted between lobes of ovary, connate below: fr. splitting into 2 parts, each a samara.

ACER, L. Maple. Over 100 species in N. Amer., Cent. and E. Asia, Eu., N. Afr., many grown as shade trees and for their ornamental foliage.—Technical characters as for the family; nutlets with elongated wing on one side. (A-cer: classical Latin name.)

A. Lvs. 3–5-foliolate.
  B. Bark not flaky: fls. before lvs. .... 1. *A. Negundo*
  BB. Bark flaky: fls. after the lvs. .... 2. *A. griseum*
AA. Lvs. simple.
  B. Under surface of lvs. gray or white.
    C. Fls. appearing long before lvs.
      D. Petals present: fls. long-stalked .... 3. *A. rubrum*
      DD. Petals wanting: fls. short-stalked .... 4. *A. saccharinum*
    CC. Fls. appearing with or after lvs.
      D. Sepals united, petals wanting .... 5. *A. saccharum*
      DD. Sepals and petals distinct .... 6. *A. Pseudo-Platanus*
  BB. Under surface of lvs. green.
    C. Wings of frs. practically parallel.
      D. Lvs. not lobed .... 7. *A. tataricum*
      DD. Lvs. 3-lobed .... 8. *A. Ginnala*
    CC. Wings of frs. horizontally spreading, not parallel.
      D. Lvs. not lobed beyond middle.
        E. Lobes of lvs. obtuse .... 9. *A. campestre*
        EE. Lobes of lvs. acute.
          F. Margin of lobes entire .... 10. *A. Mono*
          FF. Margin of lobes toothed.
            G. Number of lobes 3–5.
              H. Bark green striped with white: infl. pendulous .... 11. *A. pensylvanicum*
              HH. Bark not so: infl. erect.
                I. Infl. a narrow spike: lvs. pubescent beneath .... 12. *A. spicatum*
                II. Infl. a corymb: lvs. pubescent beneath only in axils of veins .... 13. *A. platanoides*
            GG. Number of lobes 7–11.
              H. Branchlets, pedicels and peduncles pubescent, at least when young .... 14. *A. japonicum*
              HH. Branchlets, pedicels and peduncles glabrous .... 15. *A. circinatum*
      DD. Lvs. lobed beyond middle.
        E. Nutlet glabrous: lvs. 2–4 in. across .... 16. *A. palmatum*
        EE. Nutlet yellow-hairy: lvs. 8–12 in. across .... 17. *A. macrophyllum*

1. **A. Negundo,** L. (*Negundo fraxinifolium*, Nutt. *N. aceroides*, Moench. *Rulac Negundo*, Hitchc.). BOX-ELDER. Large tree to 70 ft.: lvs. pinnate; lfts. 3–5, rarely 7–9, ovate or oblong-lanceolate, coarsely serrate or terminal lft. 3-lobed, 2–5 in. long, acuminate, lighter green beneath and slightly pubescent: fls. appearing before lvs., yellowish-green, the staminate in pendulous corymbs, the pistillate in pendulous racemes; petals wanting: fr. glabrous, 1–1½ in. long, wings diverging at acute angle. (Negundo: name used by John Ray, 1688, without explanation.) Ont. to Fla. and Tex.—Runs into races with curled lfts., lvs. spotted or margined yellow, lvs. with broad white margins, or branches purplish with glaucous bloom.

2. **A. griseum,** Pax (*A. nikoense* var. *griseum*, Franch.). PAPERBARK MAPLE. Tree to 25 ft., with cinnamon-brown flaky bark: lfts. 3, elliptic to ovate-oblong, coarsely toothed, 1½–2½ in. long, acute, densely gray-pubescent beneath: fls. in pubescent short-stalked cymes: fr. pendulous, about 1 in. long, with tomentose nutlet and wings diverging at an acute angle. China.—The closely related **A. nikoense,** Maxim., differs in lfts. 2–6 in. long, nearly entire to remotely crenate-serrate, the bark not flaky, while **A. mandshuricum,** Maxim., differs from both in lfts. glabrous beneath except along midrib, bark not flaky.

3. **A. rubrum,** L. (*Rufacer rubrum*, Small). RED, SCARLET or SWAMP MAPLE. Large tree to 120 ft.: lvs. 2–4 in. long, subcordate, 3–5-lobed, lobes short-acuminate, crenate-serrate, shining above, glaucous beneath and pubescent on veins: fls. long before lvs., red, long-stalked: fr. on drooping pedicels, glabrous, ½–¾in. long, wings diverging at narrow angle, bright red when young. Newf. to Fla. and Tex.

4. **A. saccharinum,** L. (*A. dasycarpum*, Ehrh. *Argentacer saccharinum*, Small). SILVER or WHITE MAPLE. Large tree to 120 ft.: lvs. 3–6 in. across, very long-petioled, deeply 5-lobed, lobes acuminate, remotely dentate, green above, silvery-white beneath, pubescent when young: fls. appearing long before lvs., greenish-yellow, in nearly sessile lateral corymbs, apetalous: fr. on slender drooping pedicels, pubescent when young, 1½–2½ in. long, with large divergent wings. Que. to Fla. and Okla. Var. **laciniatum,** Pax (var. *Wieri*, Schwerin), WIERS WEEPING MAPLE, has pendulous branches and deeply cleft lvs. with dissected lobes.—Varies into many lf.-forms, as lvs. deeply cut and crimped, spotted with white or pink, yellow, 3-parted.

5. **A. saccharum,** Marsh. (*A. saccharophorum*, Koch. *Saccharodendron barbatum*, Nieuwl.). SUGAR or ROCK MAPLE. Large tree to 120 ft.: lvs. 3–6 in. across, cordate at base, 3–5-lobed, lobes acuminate, the sinuses rounded, green above, pale beneath: fls. appearing with lvs., in almost sessile lateral or terminal corymbs, on long hairy pedicels, greenish-yellow, apetalous: fr. glabrous, 1–1½ in. long, wings slightly diverging. Que. to Fla. and Tex.—The allied **A. nigrum,** Michx. f. (*A. saccharum* var. *nigrum*, Britt.), differs in lvs. usually pubescent and not glaucous beneath, stipules large inclosing the axillary bud when full grown.

6. **A. Pseudo-Platanus,** L. Sycamore Maple. To 100 ft.: lvs. 3–6 in. across, cordate at base, 5-lobed, lobes acute, coarsely crenate-serrate, dark green above, pale and glaucous beneath, usually glabrous: fls. yellowish-green, in pendulous racemes; stamens hairy, exserted: fr. glabrous, 1–2 in. long, wings widely diverging. Eu., W. Asia.—Runs into many vars. such as lvs. pubescent beneath, purplish or purplish-red beneath, lvs. yellow or with white or yellow spots or blotches, and one with bright red fr.

7. **A. tataricum,** L. Shrub or small round-headed tree to 20 ft.: lvs. 2–4 in. long, usually not lobed, roundish-oval or oblong, cordate at base, doubly serrate, pinnate-veined, pubescent on veins beneath when young: fls. white, in long-peduncled erect panicles: fr. glabrous, about 1 in. long, with nearly parallel wings, becoming bright red. S. E. Eu., W. Asia.

8. **A. Ginnala,** Maxim. (*A. tataricum* var. *aidzuense,* Franch.). Amur Maple. Graceful shrub or small tree to 20 ft.: lvs. 1–3 in. long, 3-lobed, the terminal lobe elongated, doubly serrate, glabrous, shining above: fls. yellowish, fragrant, in long-peduncled panicles: fr. glabrous, 1 in. long, with nearly parallel wings. (Ginnala: a vernacular name where the plant is native.) Manchuria, N. China, Japan.

9. **A. campestre,** L. Hedge Maple. Shrub or round-headed tree, seldom exceeding 20 ft., with corky fissured bark: lvs. 2–4 in. across, divided to about the middle into 3–5 obtuse lobes, entire or middle lobe slightly 3-lobed, glabrous above, pubescent beneath: fls. greenish, in loose erect pubescent corymbs: fr. pubescent, about 1 in. long, wings spreading horizontally forming a straight line. Eu., W. Asia.—Forms with lvs. blotched or sprinkled with white are sometimes seen.

10. **A. Mono,** Maxim. (*A. pictum,* Thunb.). Painted Maple. To 60 ft.: lvs. 3–6 in. across, with 5–7 entire acuminate lobes, sometimes very broad and short, glabrous except in axils of veins beneath: fls. yellow, in erect corymbs: fr. glabrous, about 1 in. long, wings horizontally spreading, hardly twice as long as nutlets. China, Japan.

11. **A. pensylvanicum,** L. (*A. striatum,* Lam.). Moosewood. Striped Maple. Small tree, rarely to 40 ft., bark green striped with white: lvs. 5–7 in. long, 3-lobed at apex, lobes acuminate, finely toothed, reddish-pubescent beneath when young: fls. yellow, in drooping glabrous racemes 4–6 in. long: fr. glabrous, about 1 in. long, wings diverging at wide angle. Que. to Ga.

12. **A. spicatum,** Lam. Mountain Maple. Shrub or small tree, rarely to 30 ft.: lvs. 2–5 in. long, 3- or slightly 5-lobed, lobes acuminate, coarsely toothed, pubescent beneath: fls. greenish-yellow, in erect pubescent spikes 3–6 in. long: fr. nearly glabrous, about ¾in. long, wings diverging at acute angle. E. N. Amer.

13. **A. platanoides,** L. Norway Maple. Large tree with round spreading head, to 100 ft.: lvs. 3–5 in. long and broad, 5-lobed, cordate at base, remotely sharp dentate, lobes acute, light green and lustrous beneath, pubescent in axils of veins: fls. yellowish-green, in erect glabrous corymbs: fr. glabrous, pendulous, 1½–2 in. long, with horizontally spreading wings. Eu., W. Asia. Var. **Schwedleri,** Nichols., has bright red lvs. when young, changing to dark green. Var. **palmatifidum,** Tausch, has lvs. divided nearly to base. Var. **globosum,** Nichols., has a dense globose head.

14. **A. japonicum,** Thunb. Fullmoon Maple. Small tree or shrub; branchlets, petioles and peduncles pubescent, at least when young: lvs. 2–5 in. long and broad, 7–11-lobed, not lobed to middle, cordate at base, lobes acuminate, doubly serrate, pubescent on veins beneath: fls. large, purple, in pendulous corymbs: fr. finally glabrous, about 1 in. long, with widely diverging wings. Japan. Var. **aconitifolium,** Meehan, Fernleaf Maple, has lvs. divided nearly to base into 9–11 pinnately cut lobes.

15. **A. circinatum,** Pursh. Vine Maple. Small round-headed tree, rarely to 40 ft.; branchlets, petioles and peduncles glabrous: lvs. almost circular in outline, 2–7 in. across, 7–9-lobed, lobes acute, doubly serrate, becoming glabrous beneath: fls. large, with purple sepals and smaller white petals, in pendulous corymbs: fr. 1½ in. long, with wings spreading almost at right angles, red, in early summer. W. N. Amer.

16. **A. palmatum,** Thunb. (*A. polymorphum,* Sieb. & Zucc.). Japanese Maple. Shrub or small tree to 20 ft.; branchlets, petioles and peduncles glabrous: lvs. 2–4 in. across, 5–9-lobed beyond middle or divided, lobes acuminate, doubly serrate or incised, glabrous: fls. small, purple, in glabrous erect corymbs: fr. less than 1 in. long, with widely spreading wings. Japan, Korea. Var. **atropurpureum,** VanHoutte, lvs. deep purple. Var. **dissectum,** Maxim. (var. *multifidum,* Koch), lvs. divided to base into pinnately cut lobes. Var. **heptalobum,** Rehd. (var. *septemlobum,* Koch), lvs. larger, usually 7-lobed.

17. **A. macrophyllum,** Pursh. Oregon Maple. Large tree to 100 ft.: lvs. 8–12 in. across, deeply 3–5-lobed or divided, cordate at base, long-petioled, shining above, pubescent beneath when young: fls. yellow, fragrant, in drooping racemes 4–5 in. long: fr. about 1½ in. long, with yellow-hairy nutlets and wings diverging at right angles. Alaska to Calif.

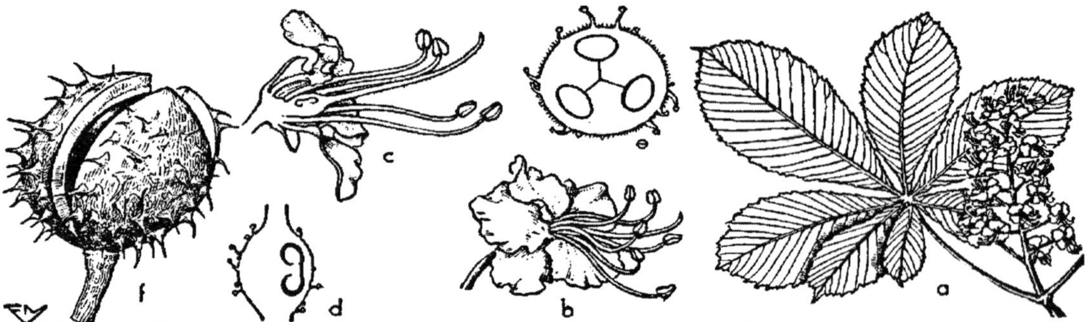

Fig. 115. HIPPOCASTANACEÆ. *Æsculus Hippocastanum:* a, twig with leaf and inflorescence, × 1/10; b, flower, × 1; c, same, vertical section, × 1; d, ovary, vertical section, × 2; e, ovary, cross-section, × 4; f, fruit, × ½.

115. HIPPOCASTANACEÆ. HORSE-CHESTNUT FAMILY

Trees or shrubs of 3 genera and over 25 species widely distributed in the north temp. zone.—Plant polygamous: lvs. opposite, exstipulate, digitately 3–9-foliolate: fls. irregular, in terminal panicles; calyx tubular or campanulate, 4–5-lobed; petals 4–5, clawed, unequal; stamens 5–9, inserted on disk, free, with filiform filaments; ovary superior, sessile, 3-celled, ovules 2 in each cell; style slender: fr. a leathery caps., smooth or spiny, 3-celled or by abortion 1-celled; seeds large, shining.

ÆSCULUS, L. HORSE-CHESTNUT. BUCKEYE. About 25 species, some grown for shade trees or for the conspicuous fls.—Technical characters as for the family: lvs. 5–9-foliolate, serrate, long-petioled. (Æs-culus: classical name of an oak tree.)

A. Winter-buds resinous: claw of petals shorter than calyx.
  B. Lfts. sessile or very short-stalked.
    C. Petals spreading, white spotted with red. . . . . .1. *Æ. Hippocastanum*
    CC. Petals erect, flesh-color to deep red. . . . . .2. *Æ. carnea*
  BB. Lfts. with stalks ½–1 in. long . . . . .3. *Æ. californica*
AA. Winter-buds not resinous: claw of petals equalling or exceeding calyx.
  B. Stamens exserted.
    C. Lfts. gray-pubescent beneath: fr. smooth. . . . . .4. *Æ. parviflora*
    CC. Lfts. glabrous beneath: fr. prickly . . . . .5. *Æ. glabra*
  BB. Stamens included.
    C. Calyx campanulate; petals hairy on margins.
      D. Fls. yellow, petals without glands on margins .6. *Æ. octandra*
      DD. Fls. red and yellow, petals with glands on margins. . . . . .7. *Æ. hybrida*
    CC. Calyx tubular; petals glandular, not hairy, on margins. . . . . .8. *Æ. Pavia*

1. **Æ. Hippocastanum**, L. COMMON HORSE-CHESTNUT. A large tree to 100 ft., with very resinous buds: lfts. 5–7, sessile, 4–10 in. long, cuneate-obovate, obtusely serrate, rusty-tomentose at base beneath when young: panicles very showy, up to 12 in. long; calyx ¼in. or less long, canescent; petals 5, spreading, white blotched with red and yellow; stamens exserted: fr. globose, prickly, about 2 in. across. Balkan Penins.—There are many cultivars, such as those with laciniate and incisely lobed lfts., round and pyramidal heads, dwarf habit, double fls., and lvs. variegated with yellow.

2. **Æ. carnea**, Hayne (*Æ. Hippocastanum × Æ. Pavia. Æ. rubicunda*, Loisel.). RED HORSE-CHESTNUT. Tree to 40 ft., with resinous winter-buds: lfts. usually 5, almost sessile, cuneate-obovate, 3–6 in. long, crenate-serrate, nearly glabrous beneath: panicles to 8 in. long; calyx ⅜in. or more long, canescent; petals 5, erect from calyx, not spreading, varying from flesh color to scarlet: fr. nearly globose, with small prickles, about 1½ in. across.—Varies into many garden forms according to shade in coloring and doubling of fls.

3. **Æ. californica**, Nutt. CALIFORNIA BUCKEYE. Round-headed tree to 40 ft., with resinous winter-buds: lfts. 5–7, with stalks ½–1 in. long, oblong, 3–6 in. long, fine-toothed, glabrous: panicles narrow, 3–8 in. long, pubescent; petals 5, equal, white or pale rose; stamens exserted: fr. obovoid, rough but not prickly, 2–3 in. long. Calif.

4. **Æ. parviflora**, Walt. BOTTLEBRUSH BUCKEYE. DWARF HORSE-CHESTNUT. Spreading shrub to 12 ft.: lfts. 5–7, nearly sessile, obovate, 3–10 in. long, crenate-serrate, gray-pubescent beneath: panicles narrow, 10–12 in. long; petals 4–5, white; stamens pinkish-white, long-exserted: fr. obovoid, smooth, 1–1½ in. long. S. C. to Fla. and Ala.—The latest of the cult. species to fl., fls. appearing July–Aug.

5. **Æ. glabra**, Willd. (*Æ. ohioensis*, DC.). OHIO BUCKEYE. Tree to 30 ft.: lfts. 5, short-stalked, elliptic to obovate, finely toothed, glabrous beneath at maturity: panicles

4–6 in. long; petals 4, nearly equal, greenish-yellow; stamens exserted: fr. obovoid, prickly, 1½–2 in. long. Pa. to Ala. and Neb.

6. **Æ. octandra,** Marsh. (*Æ. flava,* Ait.). YELLOW or SWEET BUCKEYE. Tree to 90 ft.: lfts. 5, short-stalked, cuneate-obovate, 4–6 in. long, fine-toothed, nearly glabrous at maturity: panicles 4–6 in. long; calyx campanulate; petals 4, very unequal, yellow, hairy on margins; stamens included: fr. nearly globose, smooth, 2–2½ in. across. Pa. to Ga. and Ill.

7. **Æ. hybrida,** DC. (*Æ. octandra* × *Æ. Pavia*). Tree, winter-buds not resinous: lfts. 5, short-stalked, oblong or obovate, 4–6 in. long, minutely crenulate-serrate, pubescent on veins beneath: panicles 4–6 in. long; calyx narrow-campanulate, red or yellowish-red; petals erect, not spreading, villous and glandular on margins, yellowish or reddish; stamens included: fr. nearly globose, smooth. Garden origin.

8. **Æ. Pavia,** L. RED BUCKEYE. Shrub or small tree to 20 ft.: lfts. 5, short-stalked, oblong-obovate, 3–6 in. long, irregularly toothed, slightly pubescent beneath: panicles loose, 4–6 in. long; calyx tubular, dark red; petals 4, very unequal, bright red, glandular on margins; stamens included: fr. obovoid or nearly globose, smooth, 1½–2 in. across. Va. to Fla. and La.

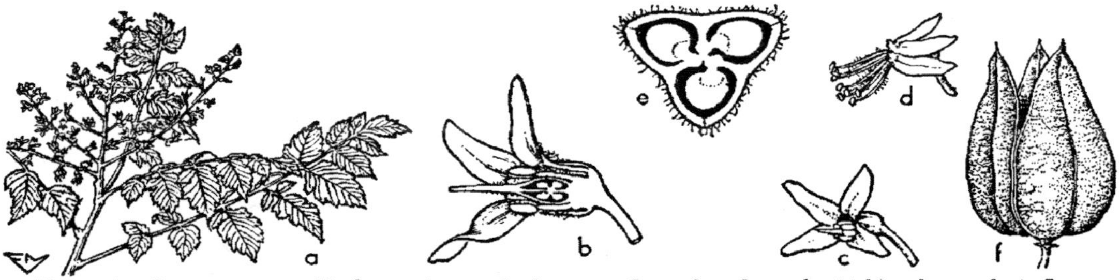

Fig. 116. SAPINDACEÆ. *Koelreuteria paniculata:* a, flowering branch, × ⅒; b, perfect flower, vertical section, × 2; c, same, habit, × 1; d, staminate flower, × 1; e, ovary, cross-section, × 10; f, capsule, × ½.

116. SAPINDACEÆ. SOAPBERRY FAMILY

About 125 genera and more than 1,000 species of trees and shrubs or rarely herbs, often climbing, of wide distribution in the tropics and warm regions.—Lvs. usually alternate, mostly pinnately or palmately compound, sometimes simple: fls. unisexual or bisexual, borne in racemes, panicles or corymbs, regular or irregular; calyx of 4–5 imbricated or valvate sepals; petals 4–5 or wanting, often with hairs or scales at the base inside; disk well developed, situated between petals and stamens; stamens usually 8–10, the filaments distinct or united at base; ovary superior, 2–4-celled (sometimes more), with 1 or more ovules in each cell, placentation axile or parietal, the style simple or divided: fr. very diverse.

A. Plant an erect tree or shrub.
  B. Fr. indehiscent, berry-like or drupe-like.
    C. Surface of fr. smooth.
      D. Diam. of fr. ½–¾ in., inedible; seed without aril .... 1. SAPINDUS
      DD. Diam. of fr. about 1 in. or more, edible; seed with pulpy aril .... 2. MELICOCCA
    CC. Surface of fr. tuberculate.
      D. Petals 0: fr. red to dull reddish-purple .... 3. LITCHI
      DD. Petals present: fr. yellow-brown .... 4. EUPHORIA
  BB. Fr. dehiscent, capsular.
    C. Caps. bladdery, with papery walls .... 5. KOELREUTERIA
    CC. Caps. with thick, hard or leathery walls.
      D. Lfts. serrate: fls. before the lvs.
        E. Fls. regular, white, in racemes .... 6. XANTHOCERAS
        EE. Fls. irregular, rose, in cymes .... 7. UNGNADIA
      DD. Lfts. entire: fls. with the mature foliage.
        E. Seeds with white fleshy aril at base .... 8. BLIGHIA
        EE. Seeds without white aril .... 9. HARPULLIA
AA. Plant a vine .... 10. CARDIOSPERMUM

1. **SAPINDUS,** L. SOAPBERRY. Trees and shrubs native in the tropics, of about 15 species, occasionally planted for ornament and sometimes grown for their frs. which are rich in saponin.—Plant polygamo-diœcious: lvs. usually odd-pinnate, exstipulate, the lfts. entire or serrate: fls. very small, regular, in axillary or terminal panicles or racemes; sepals 4–5, in 2 rows; petals 4–5, inserted under the annular

fleshy disk, naked or bearing a scale at summit of claw; stamens 8–10, inserted on disk, the filaments distinct; ovary 2–4-celled, with 1 ovule in each cell, the stigma 2–4-lobed: fr. a fleshy or leathery berry, the bony seeds black or nearly so, without aril. (Sapin-dus: Latin *soap* and *Indian,* from the soapy qualities of the berries.)

S. Saponaria, L. Small tree to 30 ft., with rough grayish bark: lvs. persistent, rachis usually broadly winged, but sometimes unwinged; lfts. usually 7–9, elliptic to oblong-lanceolate, 2–6 in. long, often falcate, obtuse or acute, entire or somewhat undulate, bright green and lustrous above, paler and tomentulose beneath: fls. in terminal panicles 7–10 in. long; sepals ciliate on margins; petals ovate, white, without scales, ciliate; filaments hairy: berry globose, ⅔–¾ in. diam., brown, shining, with orange-brown translucent flesh, ripening in spring or early summer. S. Fla., W. Indies, S. Amer.

2. **MELICOCCA,** L. Two species of trees native in trop. Amer., one grown in warm regions for its edible fr.—Plant polygamous or diœcious: lvs. even-pinnate, with 2–3 pairs of nearly sessile lfts., exstipulate: fls. small, regular, in elongated simple or branched racemes; calyx deeply 4–5-lobed; petals 4–5; disk flattened, 4–5-lobed; stamens 8, the filiform filaments distinct; ovary 2–3-celled with 1 or 2 ovules in each cell, the style short and stigma 2–3-lobed: fr. a drupe with fleshy pulp; seed with large fleshy aril. (Melicoc-ca: Greek *honey berry,* referring to taste of fr.) —Sometimes written *Melicoccus.*

M. bijuga, L. SPANISH-LIME. GENIP. MAMONCILLO. Slow-growing tree sometimes attaining 60 ft.: lvs. with rachis winged or wingless, with 2 pairs of elliptic or elliptic-lanceolate acute glabrous lfts. 2–4 in. long: racemes many-fld., to 4 in. long, in terminal panicles; fls. greenish-white, fragrant: drupe smooth, globose, green, about 1 in. or more in diam., the large round seed (which is sometimes roasted like a chestnut) surrounded by yellowish translucent juicy pulp. W. Indies, Cent. and S. Amer.

3. **LITCHI,** Sonn. Two species, one widely cult. in warm parts of the Orient for its fr. which is eaten either fresh or dried, in the latter form known as "litchi nuts."—Polygamous trees: lvs. even-pinnate: fls. regular, small, greenish-white or yellowish, in terminal panicles sometimes 1 ft. long; sepals small, valvate; petals wanting; disk fleshy; stamens usually 8, with hairy filaments; ovary on a short stalk, 2–3-lobed and -celled with 1 ovule in each cell, pubescent, the stigma 2-lobed: fr. a drupe, covered with angular prominent tubercles. (Lit-chi: Chinese name.)

L. chinensis, Sonn. (*Nephelium Litchi,* Cambess. *Dimocarpus Litchi,* Lour.). LITCHI. LEECHEE. LYCHEE. A round-topped tree 30–40 ft. high: lfts. 2–4 pairs, 3–6 in. long, coriaceous, elliptic-oblong to lanceolate, sharply acute, glabrous and shining above, glaucescent beneath: fr. 1–1½ in. diam., bright red when ripe, the outer covering hard, brittle and rough, the flesh or aril white, translucent and juicy, separating readily from the small seed. China.

4. **EUPHORIA,** Comm. Six or more species of trees native in trop. and subtrop. Asia, one grown in warm regions for its edible fr.—Very similar to Litchi but distinguished by its imbricate sepals, the presence of petals, and the fr. covered with flattened sometimes indistinct tubercles. (Eupho-ria: Greek *carries well,* alluding to the attractive frs.)

E. Longan, Steud. (*Dimocarpus Longan,* Lour. *E. Longana,* Lam. *Nephelium Longana,* Cambess.). LONGAN, LUNGAN (vernacular names). Tree 30–40 ft. high: lvs. of 2–5 pairs of elliptic to lanceolate rather obtuse lfts. with somewhat prominent veins, 3–12 in. long, glabrous and glossy: fls. small, yellowish-white, in axillary or terminal panicles: fr. globose, 1 in. or sometimes less in diam., yellow-brown, the outer covering thin and shell-like, with white juicy pulp surrounding the dark brown shining seed. India.

5. **KOELREUTERIA,** Laxm. Chinese and Japanese deciduous polygamous trees of 4 species, one planted for ornament.—Lvs. alternate, exstipulate, odd-pinnate or bipinnate, the lfts. serrate: fls. yellow, irregular, in large terminal panicles; calyx deeply divided into 5 unequal lobes; petals 4, or only 3 in many staminate fls., lanceolate, turned upward or strongly reflexed, clawed, with 2 upturned appendages at base of blade; disk crenate at upper margins; stamens 8 or less, with long distinct filaments; ovary 3-celled with 2 ovules in each cell, the style 3-cleft: fr. a bladdery caps., loculicidally dehiscent by 3 valves, the seeds roundish and black. (Koelreuteria: after Joseph G. Koelreuter, 1734–1806, professor of natural history at Karlsruhe.)

K. paniculata, Laxm. Goldenrain-Tree. Round-headed tree to 30 ft.: lvs. to 14 in. long, the 7–15 lfts. ovate to oblong-ovate, 1–3 in. long, coarsely and irregularly crenate-serrate or at base often incisely lobed and the central lfts. frequently pinnatisect, dark green and glabrous above, paler and usually pubescent on veins beneath: fls. pedicelled, about ½in. long, in many-fld. broad panicles to 18 in. long, in July and Aug.: caps. 1½–2 in. long, with papery walls, the ovate-oblong valves gradually narrowed into pointed apex. China, Korea, Japan.

6. **XANTHOCERAS**, Bunge. One species from N. China, a deciduous shrub planted for its attractive fls.—Plant polygamous: lvs. alternate, odd-pinnate, the lfts. serrate, exstipulate: fls. regular, in terminal or axillary racemes, appearing before or with the first lvs.; sepals 5; petals 5, about three times longer than sepals; disk produced into 5 suberect cylindric horns about half as long as stamens; stamens 8, with elongated distinct filaments; ovary 3-celled, with 7–8 ovules in each cell, stigma 3-lobed: fr. a hard thick-walled caps., loculicidally dehiscent by 3 valves. (Xanthoc-eras: Greek for *yellow* and *horn*, referring to the horn-like processes of the disk.)

X. sorbifolia, Bunge. Glabrous shrub or small tree to 15 ft.: lvs. 6–12 in. long, the 9–17 sessile lfts. narrow elliptic to lanceolate, 1–2 in. long, sharply serrate, dark green above, paler beneath: fls. white, slender-pedicelled, about ¾in. across, each petal with blotch at base changing from yellow to red, blooming in May: fr. green, 1–2½ in. long, with large dark brown seeds.

7. **UNGNADIA**, Endl. One polygamous shrub or small tree native in Tex. and Mex. and sometimes planted in S. U. S.—Lvs. alternate, odd-pinnate: fls. irregular, in cymes or fascicles before the lvs.; calyx 5-lobed; petals 4–5, clawed; disk tongue-shaped, unilateral; stamens 7–10, exserted: fr. a leathery caps. loculicidally dehiscent by 3–4 valves; seeds usually solitary in each cell. (Ungna-dia: named for Baron Ungnad, European botanist who published in 1757.)

U. speciosa, Endl. Mexican, Texan or Spanish Buckeye. To 30 ft.: lfts. 5–9, ovate-lanceolate, 3–5 in. long, acuminate, crenate-serrate, dark green and shining above: fls. rose, about 1 in. across: caps. 2 in. across, with black seeds ½in. diam.

8. **BLIGHIA**, Koenig. One species, native in W. Afr., grown in the tropics for its edible fr.—Polygamous tree: lvs. even-pinnate: fls. regular, borne in axillary racemes; calyx small, deeply 5-parted, valvate or slightly imbricated; petals 5, longer than the calyx, bearing scales on the inner side; disk annular, hairy; stamens 8–10, long-exserted in staminate fls., the filaments filiform; ovary short-stalked, 3-celled with 1 ovule in each cell, the stigma 3-toothed: fr. a caps., with thick hard walls, dehiscent from apex to base by 3 valves. (Bli-ghia: after W. Bligh, British mariner, commander of the "Bounty," who wrote on a journey in the South Seas, 1792.)

B. sapida, Koenig (*Cupania sapida*, Voigt). Akee. Stiff-branched tree to 40 ft.: lfts. 3–5 pairs, short-petioled, obovate-oblong, the upper ones 4–6 in. long, the lower ones much shorter, entire: fls. small, greenish-white: caps. about 3 in. long, roundish or triangular in general outline, straw-colored to magenta-red, each cell containing 1 round shining seed with a white fleshy aril at its base which is edible when cooked.

9. **HARPULLIA**, Roxb. Over 20 species in Asia, Australia and Afr., one planted in Fla. and Calif.—Trees, diœcious or polygamous: lvs. alternate, even-pinnate: fls. regular, in axillary racemes or panicles toward tops of branches; sepals 5, imbricate; petals 4–5, usually clawed; disk small; stamens 5–8, exserted in staminate fls.; ovary 2-celled with 2 ovules in each cell: fr. a leathery inflated caps., loculicidally dehiscent by 2 valves. (Harpul-lia: Indian name.)

H. arborea, Radlk. (*Ptelea arborea*, Blanco. *H. imbricata*, Thwaites. *H. cupanioides*, F. Vill. not Roxb.). To 35 ft. or more: lfts. 3–5 pairs, oblong-lanceolate, 3–7 in. long, acuminate, entire, shining: fls. greenish, about ½in. long, in loose drooping panicles: caps. bright orange, broader than long, about 1½ in. across, tipped with persistent style; seeds black, smooth, with small disk-like aril. India, Malaya, Philippines.

10. **CARDIOSPERMUM**, L. Heart-Seed. About 15 species of herbaceous vines, widely distributed in warm and temp. regions.—Extensively branching, the branches

grooved: polygamous or diœcious: lvs. alternate, biternate, the lfts. coarsely serrate, exstipulate: fls. slightly irregular, in axillary tendril-bearing corymbs; sepals 4, the 2 outer ones smaller; petals 4, unequal; disk one-sided, undulate; stamens 8, the unequal filaments distinct or united at base; ovary 3-celled with 1 ovule in each cell, the short style 3-cleft: fr. a membranaceous inflated veiny caps., loculicidally dehiscent by 3 valves. (Cardiosper-mum: Greek for *heart* and *seed*, from the white heart-shaped spot on the black seed.)

A. St. glabrous..1. *C. Halicacabum*
AA. St. densely hairy..2. *C. hirsutum*

1. **C. Halicacabum,** L. Balloon-Vine. Ann. or bien., climbing to 10 ft.: lvs. 2–4 in. long, the lfts. ovate or oblong, acute or acuminate: peduncles usually longer than lvs., bearing few-fld. corymbs; fls. white, 1¼ in. across: caps. much inflated, 3-angled, about 1 in. across and somewhat longer, pubescent, the black seeds about the size of a pea. (Halicacabum: pre-Linnæan substantive name, referring to the bladdery frs.) Trop. and subtrop. regions around the world; nat. S. U. S.

2. **C. hirsutum,** Willd. Per. creeping or ascending vine, the st. densely hairy: lvs. larger, less acuminate, and longer-stalked than in *C. Halicacabum,* usually pubescent below: fls. white: caps. much inflated, pointed, pubescent, 1½–2 in. long, much longer than broad. Afr.

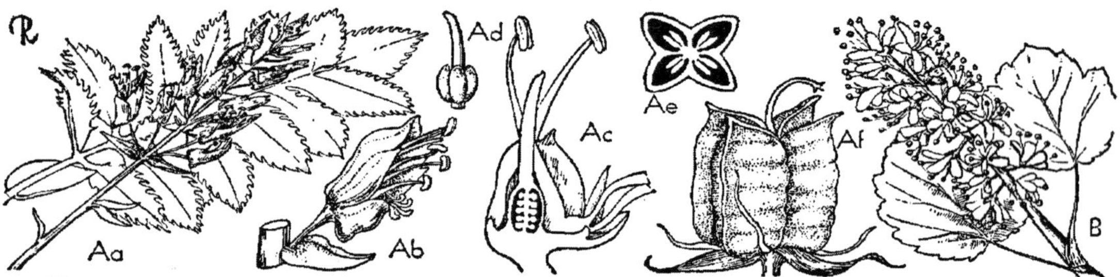

Fig. 117. Melianthaceæ. A, *Melianthus major:* Aa, inflorescence, × ¼ and leaf, × ⅛; Ab, flower, × 1; Ac, same, vertical section, × 2; Ad, pistil, × ½; Ae, ovary, cross-section, × 6; Af, fruit, × 1. B, *Greyia Sutherlandii:* flowering branch, × ¼. (Ab–Ae adapted from Schnizlein.)

117. MELIANTHACEÆ. MELIANTHUS FAMILY

African trees or shrubs, of 3 genera and about 20 species, grown for ornament in warm regions.—Lvs. alternate, simple or pinnate, the rachis often winged: fls. bisexual, inverted by the twisting of the pedicels, borne in racemes, irregular or regular; sepals 5 or 4, imbricate; petals 4 or 5; disk between petals and stamens crescent-shaped or annular with 10 projections; stamens 4, 5, or 10, the filaments distinct or connate at base; ovary superior, 4–5-celled with 1 or many ovules in each cell, placentation axile, the stigma 4–5-lobed: fr. a caps.

A. Lvs. pinnate: stamens 4..1. Melianthus
AA. Lvs. simple: stamens 10...2. Greyia

1. **MELIANTHUS,** L. A half dozen S. African strong-scented shrubs.—Lvs. odd-pinnate, stipulate, the lfts. unequal-sided: fls. in axillary or terminal racemes, very irregular; calyx laterally compressed, the 5 sepals united at base, unequal, often gibbous at base; petals 5, but the anterior one abortive, long-clawed; disk with nectar-bearing glands; stamens 4, didynamous; ovary 4-lobed and 4-celled with 2 or more ovules in each cell: caps. inflated, papery or woody, loculicidally dehiscent by 4 valves, usually with only 1 seed in each cell. (Melian-thus: Greek *honey flower.*)

A. Stipules connate into 1, 2 in. or more long; lfts. glabrous beneath..............1. *M. major*
AA. Stipules 2, free, ½in. long; lfts. white-tomentose beneath......................2. *M. comosus*

1. **M. major,** L. Glabrous shrub to 10 ft. or more, with widely creeping roots: lvs. 1 ft. or more long, dull green above, paler beneath; stipules connate into 1 intra-axillary piece, attached to lower part of petiole, 2 in. or more long; lfts. 9–11, deeply serrate, to 6 in. long, petiole with cuneate wings between lfts.: racemes densely fld., 1 ft. or more long; bracts ovate, acuminate; fls. red-brown, 1 in. long: caps. papery, 1–1¼ in. long, glabrous.

2. **M. comosus,** Vahl. Shrub with canescent or villous branches: lvs. 4–6 in. long; stipules 2, free, ½in. long; lfts. lanceolate, serrate, pubescent with stellate hairs above but

becoming glabrate, white-tomentose beneath, petiole winged between lfts.: racemes nodding, about 3 in. long, frequent between lvs. on branches; bracts cordate-acuminate; fls. alternate, orange inside, red-spotted outside and green at base: caps. 1 in. long, soft-pubescent.—Apparently sometimes grown as *M. minor*, L., which differs in the erect racemes with the fls. in whorls and lanceolate attenuate bracts.

2. **GREYIA,** Hook. & Harvey. Three species of small trees from S. Afr.—Lvs. simple, long-petioled, exstipulate: fls. showy, in dense many-fld. axillary racemes, regular; sepals 5, free, persistent; petals 5, perigynous, deciduous; stamens 10, inserted inside the disk and alternating with its 10 gland-bearing projections, with long slender filaments; ovary deeply 5-grooved, 5-celled, many-ovuled, with long style and small stigma: caps. membranaceous or leathery, septicidally dehiscent by 5 valves. (Gre-yia: after Sir George Grey, once governor of Cape Colony.)

G. Sutherlandii, Hook. & Harvey. Small tree with light colored bark: lvs. clustered at ends of branches, orbicular to oblong, 2–3 in. long, deeply cordate at base, irregularly toothed: fls. bright scarlet, 1½ in. long, in dense racemes to 10 in. long, the stamens and style long-exserted: caps. membranaceous, 5-lobed, the seeds minute. (Named for Dr. Sutherland.)

118. BALSAMINACEÆ. BALSAM FAMILY

Two genera and more than 600 species of soft or succulent herbs, of wide distribution around the world.—Lvs. simple, alternate, opposite or whorled, exstipulate, petioled: fls. bisexual, very irregular, solitary in the axils or somewhat clustered; sepals 3, rarely 5, the 2 lateral small and green, the posterior one large, petaloid, saccate, and gradually prolonged backward into a honey-spur; petals 5, or 3 by the union of 2 pair, unequal; stamens 5, alternate with petals, with short flat filaments and anthers coherent or connivent; ovary superior, 5-celled with 3 to many ovules in each cell, placentation axile, style short and stigma 5-lobed: fr. a caps. or berry.

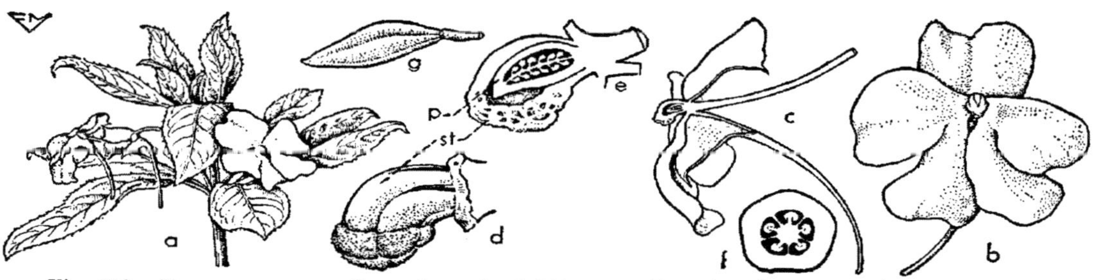

Fig. 118. Balsaminaceæ. *Impatiens glandulifera:* a, flowering branch, × ⅙; b, flower, × ½; c, same, vertical section, × ½; d, flower less perianth, × 2; e, same, vertical section, × 2; f, ovary, cross-section, × 5; g, undehisced capsule, × ½. (st stamen, p pistil.)

IMPATIENS, L. Snapweed. Probably 500 species, mostly in mountainous regions in warm temp. and trop. countries, one the balsam of fl. gardens and a few other species grown in the greenhouse or in the open.—Technical characters as above: fr. an oblong or linear caps., elastically dehiscent into 5 coiled valves, expelling the seeds. (Impa-tiens: from Latin, referring to the sudden bursting of the ripe pods when touched, "touch-me-not.")

A. Peduncles short, fls. borne close to main st. and branches, with leafy shoots at tip. . .1. *I. Balsamina*
AA. Peduncles long, fls. mostly toward ends of branches.
  B. Lvs. opposite or whorled: spur very short. . . . . .2. *I. glandulifera*
  BB. Lvs. mostly alternate: spur long.
    C. Fls. in short 6–8-fld. racemes . . . . .3. *I. Balfouri*
    CC. Fls. solitary or 2–3 together.
      D. Shape of lvs. prevailingly ovate-lanceolate, long-tapering at base. . . . . .4. *I. Sultanii*
      DD. Shape of lvs. prevailingly ovate, short- or not tapering at base . . . . .5. *I. Holstii*

1. **I. Balsamina,** L. Garden Balsam. Stout erect and branching ann. to 2½ ft., pubescent or nearly glabrous: lvs. all alternate, narrowly or broadly lanceolate, 1½–6 in. long, acuminate, deeply serrate, the petiole glandular: fls. large, short-peduncled, borne in the axils of the lvs. along the main st. and branches, overtopped by leafy shoots, in many colors from white to dark red, yellowish, and spotted; spur variable in length, in-

curved; standard orbicular and retuse; side petals or wings very broad, with the lateral lobes rounded and the terminal sessile and large: caps. ½–¾ in. long, hairy. Trop. and subtrop. India, Malaya, China.—Many forms, those in cult. mostly double-fld.

2. **I. glandulifera,** Royle (*I. Roylei,* Walp.). Rather coarse much-branched ann. to 1 ft.: lower lvs. opposite, upper usually in 3's and whorled, ovate or ovate-lanceolate, 2–6 in. long, sharply serrate: fls. 3 or more together in axillary long-peduncled clusters, very numerous toward top of plant, large, dark purple, the spur very short; standard 2-lobed; wings broad: caps. drooping, ½–¾ in. long, glabrous. Mts. of India; nat. in N. Amer.

3. **I. Balfouri,** Hook. f. Branching per. to 3 ft., glabrous: lvs. all alternate, ovate-lanceolate, 3–5 in. long, long-acuminate, with small recurved teeth, short-petioled: fls. large, in short 6–8-fld. racemes; pedicels very slender; standard orbicular, reflexed, light rose; keel red; wings yellow at base and rose at apex; spur horn-like, curved: caps. erect, 1–1½ in. long, glabrous. (Named for Isaac Baily Balfour, page 39.) W. Himalayas.

4. **I. Sultanii,** Hook. f. Erect branched glabrous per. to 2 ft.: lvs. alternate or upper whorled, prevailingly ovate-lanceolate, 1–3 in. long on petioles 1 in. or more long, long-tapering at base, crenate-serrate with a bristle in the angle of each serrature: fls. axillary, solitary or 2–3 together, 1–1½ in. across, originally rich scarlet but with pink and white vars.; lip less than half length of petals, suddenly narrowed into slender upward curved spur as long or twice as long as petals; standard obovate-orbicular, retuse; wings divided to base into 2 obovate-cuneate lobes: caps. apparently not forming in cult. (Named in compliment to the Sultan of Zanzibar.) Zanzibar.

5. **I. Holstii,** Engler & Warb. Very similar to *I. Sultanii* and largely taking its place in cult., of quicker and more vigorous growth: it differs in the broader lvs. which are prevailingly ovate, although the upper ones often ovate-lanceolate, short- or not tapering at base: fls. larger, to 1¾ in. across, brick red: branches striped with red. (Bears the name of Carl Holst, German collector in E. Afr.) E. trop. Afr.

119. RHAMNACEÆ. BUCKTHORN FAMILY

Erect or climbing trees or shrubs, rarely herbs, often spiny, of about 50 genera and 600 species of wide distribution.—Lvs. mostly alternate, simple, with minute deciduous stipules: fls. small, regular, bisexual or rarely unisexual, usually borne in cymes; calyx 4–5-lobed; petals 4–5 or 0; stamens 4–5, opposite petals and inserted with them at or below margins of fleshy disk which lines the calyx-tube, the filaments free, slender; ovary superior or inferior, free or partly immersed in disk, 2–4-celled, with 1 ovule axile or basal in each cell, stigma 2–4-lobed: fr. a drupe or caps.

A. Branchlets ordinary, not thickened or flattened.
  B. Peduncles not becoming fleshy and club-shaped in fr.
    C. Pubescence not of stellate hairs.
      D. Fr. more or less fleshy.
        E. Lvs. pinnate-veined .... 1. RHAMNUS
        EE. Lvs. strongly 3-nerved from base .... 2. ZIZIPHUS
      DD. Fr. dry.
        E. Wing of fr. broad and horizontal .... 3. PALIURUS
        EE. Wing lacking on fr. .... 4. CEANOTHUS
    CC. Pubescence of stellate hairs .... 5. POMADERRIS
  BB. Peduncles becoming fleshy and club-shaped in fr. .... 6. HOVENIA
AA. Branchlets thickened or flattened into short spine-tipped bodies: lvs. wanting .... 7. COLLETIA

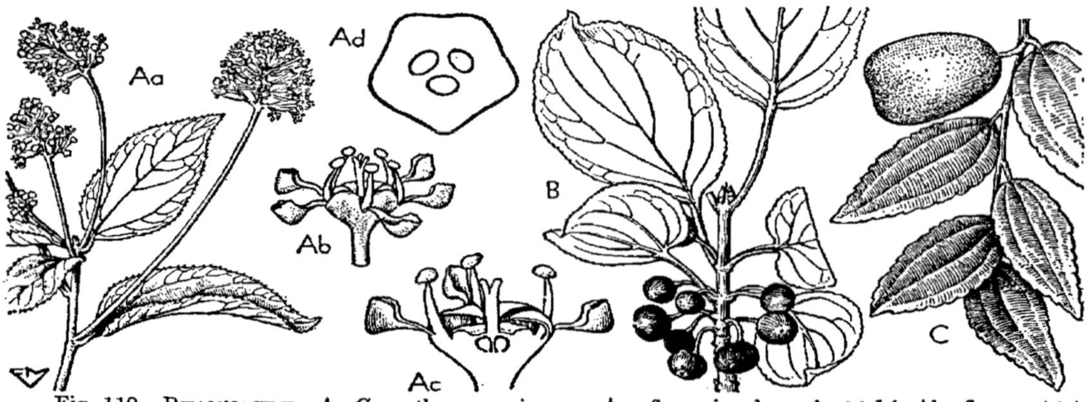

Fig. 119. RHAMNACEÆ. A, *Ceanothus americanus:* Aa, flowering branch, × ½; Ab, flower, × 4; Ac, same, vertical section, × 5; Ad, ovary, cross-section, × 10. B, *Rhamnus cathartica:* fruiting branch, × ½. *Ziziphus Jujuba:* twig with fruit, × ½.

1. **RHAMNUS,** L. BUCKTHORN. About 100 species of deciduous or evergreen trees or shrubs, native in temp. regions of the northern hemisphere, but a few extending into the tropics, planted for ornament.—Lvs. alternate or rarely nearly opposite, pinnate-veined, petioled, entire or dentate: fls. small, greenish or yellowish, bisexual or unisexual, in axillary clusters, umbels or racemes; sepals, petals, and stamens 4–5, or petals sometimes wanting; ovary 2–4-celled, free from the disk: fr. an oblong or globular drupe with succulent flesh, inclosing 2–4 separate nutlet-like stones. (Rham-nus: ancient Greek name.)

A. Foliage persistent.
  B. Petals lacking: fr. red....................1. *R. crocea*
  BB. Petals present: fr. black when mature.
    C. Fls. mostly unisexual: veins of lvs. 3–5 pairs....................2. *R. Alaternus*
    CC. Fls. bisexual: veins of lvs. 8–12 pairs....................3. *R. californica*
AA. Foliage deciduous.
  B. Veins of lvs. 3–6 pairs: branchlets usually spinescent.
    C. Lvs. dull above, ovate to elliptic....................4. *R. cathartica*
    CC. Lvs. shining above, obovate to oblong....................5. *R. davurica*
  BB. Veins of lvs. 8–15 pairs: branchlets not spinescent.
    C. Infl. glabrous....................6. *R. Frangula*
    CC. Infl. pubescent.
      D. Peduncles to 1 in. long: lvs. tufted at tips of branches....................7. *R. Purshiana*
      DD. Peduncles less than ½in. long: lvs. scattered along branches....................8. *R. caroliniana*

1. **R. crocea,** Nutt. RED-BERRIED BUCKTHORN. Typically a spreading shrub to 3 ft., evergreen, but varying to a tree to 30 ft.; branchlets often spinescent; winter-buds scaly: lvs. oval to nearly orbicular, ½–1½ in. long, obtuse, glandular-serrate, often reddish-brown beneath: fls. mostly unisexual, in short fascicles, without petals, 4-merous: fr. obovoid, ⅙in. long, red. Ariz., Calif., Mex.

2. **R. Alaternus,** L. Evergreen shrub 15–20 ft. high; winter-buds scaly: lvs. ovate to ovate-lanceolate, 1–2 in. long, acute, remotely spiny-toothed or nearly entire, with 3–5 pairs of veins, shining above: fls. mostly unisexual, in short racemes, 5-merous: fr. ¼in. across, black. S. Eu. Var. **argenteo-variegata,** West. (var. *variegata*, Bean), has lvs. margined with creamy-white.

3. **R. californica,** Esch. COFFEE-BERRY. Evergreen shrub 6–15 ft. high; winter-buds naked: lvs. oblong to oblong-lanceolate, 1–4 in. long, acute or obtuse, toothed or entire, with 8–12 pairs of veins: fls. bisexual, in peduncled pubescent umbels, usually 5-merous: fr. globose, ⅓–½in. across, red turning purple-black when mature. Ore. to Calif., Ariz. and Mex.

4. **R. cathartica,** L. COMMON BUCKTHORN. Deciduous shrub to 12 ft. or more, the branchlets usually tipped with stout spines; winter-buds scaly: lvs. opposite, ovate or elliptic, 1½–3 in. long, acute or obtuse, crenate-serrate, with 3–5 pairs of veins: fls. unisexual, in 2–5-fld. clusters, 4-merous: fr. globose, about ¼in. across, black. Eu., Asia; escaped in E. U. S.—Often planted for hedges; the bark and fr. have medicinal properties and also yield a dye.

5. **R. davurica,** Pall. (*R. Chadwickii*, Hort.). Very similar to *R. cathartica* but taller and more spreading, to 30 ft., lvs. larger, obovate to oblong, 2–4 in. long, shining above. Siberia to N. China and Korea.

6. **R. Frangula,** L. ALDER BUCKTHORN. Deciduous shrub or small tree to 18 ft.; winter-buds naked: lvs. broadly obovate to obovate-oblong, 1–2½ in. long, acute, entire or slightly undulate, with 8–9 pairs of veins, dark green and shining above: fls. bisexual, in 1–6-fld. sessile glabrous umbels, 5-merous: fr. globose, red changing to black, about ¼in. across. (Frangula: pre-Linnæan substantive name.) Eu., N. Afr., Cent. Asia; escaped in E. U. S. Var. **asplenifolia,** Dipp., has linear undulate lvs.

7. **R. Purshiana,** DC. CASCARA SAGRADA. Deciduous tree to 25 ft. or more; winter-buds naked: lvs. tufted at tips of branches, elliptic to ovate-oblong, 2–6 in. long, acute or obtuse, irregularly toothed or nearly entire, with 10–15 pairs of veins: fls. bisexual, in many-fld. pubescent umbels on peduncles to 1 in. long, 5-merous: fr. globose, ¼in. across, black. (Named for Frederick Pursh, page 50.) B. C. to Mont. and N. Calif.

8. **R. caroliniana,** Walt. INDIAN-CHERRY. Deciduous shrub or small tree to 30 ft.; winter-buds naked: lvs. scattered along branches, elliptic or oblong, 2–6 in. long, acute or acuminate, finely toothed or nearly entire, with 8–10 pairs of veins: fls. bisexual, in 4–10-fld. pubescent umbels on peduncles less than ½in. long, 5-merous: fr. globose, ⅓in. across, red changing to black. N. C. to Fla. and Tex.

2. **ZIZIPHUS,** Mill. JUJUBE. Deciduous or evergreen trees or shrubs, of about 40 species, distributed in trop. and subtrop. regions of both hemispheres, a few grown for ornament or their edible frs.—Lvs. alternate, petioled, entire or serrate, 3–5-nerved from base, the stipules often transformed into spines: fls. small, yellow,

in short axillary cymes; sepals, petals and stamens 5; ovary immersed in the disk and adnate to it at base, usually 2-celled and the style 2-parted: fr. a fleshy subglobose to oblong drupe. (Ziz-iphus: from Zizouf, the Arabian name of *Z. Lotus*, with which the name jujube is also connected.)—Commonly, but not originally, spelled Zizyphus.

A. Lvs. glabrous beneath........1. *Z. Jujuba*
AA. Lvs. densely tomentose beneath........2. *Z. mauritiana*

1. **Z. Jujuba**, Mill. (*Z. sativa*, Gaertn. *Z. vulgaris*, Lam.). COMMON JUJUBE. Glabrous shrub or small tree to 30 ft., spiny or unarmed; branchlets often fascicled, slender and having frequently the appearance of pinnate lvs.: lvs. oblong-ovate to ovate-lanceolate, 1–2 in. long, obtuse and sometimes emarginate, serrate: drupe dark red or brown, oblong or ovoid, ½–1 in. long, with whitish flesh and a hard 2-celled stone. S. Eu., S. and E. Asia.

2. **Z. mauritiana**, Lam. (*Z. Jujuba*, Lam. not Mill.). INDIAN or COTTONY JUJUBE. Differs from *Z. Jujuba* in being evergreen, and the twigs, infl. and under side of lvs. densely white- or rusty-tomentose. India; widely spread in warm countries.

3. **PALIURUS**, Mill. Six species of shrubs or small trees, native from S. Eu. to China and Japan, sometimes planted for ornament.—Lvs. alternate, petioled, entire or serrate, 3-nerved from base, the stipules usually changed into spines: fls. bisexual, in axillary or sometimes terminal cymes; sepals, petals and stamens 5; ovary partly immersed in the disk, 3-celled with 3 stigmas: fr. dry, depressed subglobose, with a broad orbicular horizontal wing, the whole fr. resembling a head with a broad-brimmed hat. (Paliu-rus: ancient Greek name.)

P. Spina-Christi, Mill. (*P. aculeatus*, Lam.). CHRIST-THORN (in Latin, *Spina Christi*). JERUSALEM-THORN. Spreading or sometimes procumbent shrub or small tree to 20 ft.: stipular spines 2, one straight, the other hooked and recurved: lvs. ovate, ¾–1½ in. long, obtuse, rounded and unequal at base, minutely serrulate, glabrous, dark green above, pale or grayish beneath: fls. greenish-yellow: fr. glabrous, brownish-yellow, ¾–1 in. across. S. Eu. to Himalayas and N. China.

4. **CEANOTHUS**, L. Deciduous and evergreen shrubs or small trees, of over 50 species in N. Amer., mostly in the Pacific Coast region, planted for their attractive fl.-clusters.—Lvs. alternate or sometimes opposite, petioled, entire or serrate, pinnate-veined or 3-nerved at base: fls. bisexual, in small umbels which are aggregated into dense axillary or terminal panicles or racemes; sepals, petals and stamens 5; ovary immersed in disk and adnate to it at base, 3-celled, the style 3-cleft: fr. 3-lobed, dry, separating longitudinally into 3 dehiscent nutlets. (Ceanothus: ancient Greek name.)

A. Lvs. opposite........1. *C. prostratus*
AA. Lvs. alternate.
  B. Foliage deciduous, membranous.
    C. Fls. white........2. *C. americanus*
    CC. Fls. blue or pink.
      D. Under side of lvs. pubescent, the tips acute........3. *C. Delilianus*
      DD. Under side of lvs. nearly glabrous or lightly pubescent on veins, the tips obtuse........4. *C. pallidus*
  BB. Foliage persistent, thick.
    C. Under side of lvs. densely white-tomentose........5. *C. arboreus*
    CC. Under side of lvs. glabrous or pubescent.
      D. Main veins from base of lf. 1.
        E. Plant usually spiny: lvs. glabrous beneath........6. *C. spinosus*
        EE. Plant not spiny: lvs. pubescent beneath........7. *C. Veitchianus*
      DD. Main veins from base 3.
        E. Branchlets not angled or ridged........8. *C. Lobbianus*
        EE. Branchlets angled or ridged.
          F. Veins on under surface of lvs. not raised: branchlets with glandular tubercles........9. *C. cyaneus*
          FF. Veins on under surface of lvs. raised: branchlets not rough........10. *C. thyrsiflorus*

1. **C. prostratus**, Benth. MAHALA MAT. SQUAW CARPET. Prostrate evergreen shrub with rooting branches, to 6 in. high and forming dense mats to 8 ft. across: lvs. opposite, obovate, ¼–1¼ in. long, coarsely spiny-toothed, 1-veined from base, dark green and glabrous above, pubescent beneath; petiole less than ⅛in. long: fls. lavender-blue, in flat short-stalked clusters, in spring. Mts., Wash. to Calif.

2. **C. americanus**, L. NEW-JERSEY-TEA. Deciduous shrub 2–3½ ft. high: lvs. alternate, ovate to ovate-oblong, 1½–4 in. long, acute or acuminate, finely toothed, 3-veined from base, dull green above, pubescent beneath; petiole ¼–½in. long: fls. white, in long-

stalked clusters 1–2 in. long forming large panicles at end of branches, in summer. Me. to Man. south to Fla. and Tex.

3. **C. Delilianus,** Spach (*C. americanus* × *C. cæruleus. C. Arnouldii,* Carr. *C. hybridus,* Hort. *C. versaillensis,* Schneid.). Upright deciduous shrub to 3 ft. or more; young branchlets finely pubescent: lvs. alternate, elliptic-ovate or ovate to oblong-ovate, 2–3 or sometimes 4 in. long, acute or short-acuminate, rarely obtusish, rounded at base, serrulate, dark green and slightly pubescent above, pubescent or sometimes nearly tomentose beneath; petiole ⅙–⅔in. long: fls. pale to deep blue, in slender-stalked lateral spikes forming terminal panicles, late summer. (Named for A. R. Delile, French botanist of the early 19th century.) Originated in Eu. about 1825.

4. **C. pallidus,** Lindl. (*C. Delilianus* × *C. ovatus*). Deciduous shrub similar to the preceding, but lower and less tender; young branchlets slightly pubescent or nearly glabrous, often purplish: lvs. elliptic- or ovate-oblong to oblong, 1½–2½ in. long, obtuse, rounded or broadly cuneate at base, serrulate, slightly pubescent chiefly on the veins beneath; petiole ⅛–¼in. long: fls. light blue, in rather short spikes on long leafy branchlets. Originated in Eu. probably between 1825 and 1830. Var. **roseus,** Rehd., has pink fls. and larger lvs. and var. **plenus,** Rehd., double nearly white fls. which are pink in bud.

5. **C. arboreus,** Greene. Catalina or Feltleaf Ceanothus. Small evergreen tree 15–25 ft. high: lvs. alternate, ovate or elliptic, 1–3 in. long, acute or obtuse, finely toothed, 3-veined from base, dark green above, densely white-tomentose beneath; petiole ⅓–¾in. long: fls. pale to deep blue, fragrant, in panicles 3–6 in. long, in early spring. Isls. off Calif. coast.

6. **C. spinosus,** Nutt. Greenbark or Redheart Ceanothus. Evergreen straggling shrub or small tree 8–20 ft. high, with yellow-green usually spiny branches: lvs. alternate, elliptic or oblong, ½–1 in. long, obtuse or emarginate, mostly entire, 1-veined from base, glabrous and shining on both sides; petiole ¼in. long: fls. pale blue to white, in panicles to 6 in. long, in early spring. Calif., Mex.

7. **C. Veitchianus,** Hook. (*C. griseus* × probably *C. rigidus*). Upright evergreen shrub to 10 ft. or more, with spreading branches: lvs. alternate, obovate, ½–¾in. long, obtuse, remotely denticulate with gland-tipped teeth, penninerved with about 3 pairs of veins, dark green and lustrous above, whitish and puberulous beneath; petiole ⅛in. long; fls. deep blue, in short-peduncled clusters 1–3 in. long forming dense panicles at end of branches, in early summer; pedicels slender, glabrous. (Named for Veitch, page 53.) Raised about 1850 in England from Calif. seeds.

8. **C. Lobbianus,** Hook. (probably *C. dentatus* × *C. griseus*). Upright evergreen shrub to 10 ft. or more: lvs. alternate, short-petioled, elliptic-oblong to oblong, ½–1 in. long, obtuse, remotely denticulate with gland-tipped teeth, 3-nerved at base, dark green above, whitish and finely pubescent beneath: fls. dark blue, in dense heads 1–2 in. long and borne on slender axillary peduncles; pedicels slightly pubescent. (Named for Wm. Lobb, 1809–1863, botanical traveller.) Raised in England from Calif. seed about 1850.

9. **C. cyaneus,** Eastw. San Diego Ceanothus. Evergreen shrub 4–10 ft. high; branchlets angled and covered with brown glandular tubercles: lvs. alternate, ovate-elliptic, 1–2 in. long, acute or obtuse, finely glandular-toothed to nearly entire, 3-nerved from base, glabrous above and nearly so beneath; petiole ⅛in. long: fls. dark blue, in long-stalked panicles 6–12 in. long, in spring. S. Calif.

10. **C. thyrsiflorus,** Esch. Blue-Blossom. Evergreen shrub or small tree 4–20 ft. high, with angled green branchlets: lvs. alternate, oblong-ovate, ¾–2 in. long, acute or obtuse, finely toothed, 3-nerved from base with veins beneath prominent and raised and hairy; petiole to ½in. long: fls. blue to nearly white, in panicles 1–3 in. long, in spring. Ore. to Calif.

5. **POMADERRIS,** Labill. Over 20 species of shrubs, native in Australia, New Zeal., and New Caledonia, sometimes planted for ornament in warm regions.—Plant more or less covered with hoary ferruginous stellate tomentum: lvs. alternate: fls. pedicelled, in small cymes, usually aggregated into many-fld. terminal or axillary corymbs or panicles; sepals, petals and stamens 5, or the petals wanting; disk inconspicuous; ovary partly inferior, usually 3-celled with 3-cleft style: fr. a small caps. which protrudes above the calyx-tube, 3-valved, separating into 3 nutlets. (Pomader-ris: from Greek for *lid* and *skin,* said to allude to the membranaceous covering of the caps.)

P. apetala, Labill. Shrub or small tree reaching 20 ft.: lvs. oblong-ovate or oblong-lanceolate, 2–4 in. long, petioled, irregularly crenulate, glabrous above, white-tomentose beneath or rusty on the prominent veins: panicles 3–7 in. long, the fls. greenish-white; calyx-tube stellate-tomentose; petals wanting: caps. obtuse, sparsely stellate-tomentose. Australia and New Zeal.

6. **HOVENIA,** Thunb. A monotypic genus comprising a deciduous shrub or small tree native in China, planted for ornament.—Lvs. alternate, long-petioled, serrate, pinnate-veined or 3-nerved from base: fls. greenish, in many-fld. axillary or terminal cymes; sepals, petals and stamens 5; ovary free, 3-celled, the style 3-cleft: fr. indehiscent, obscurely 3-lobed, the peduncles becoming fleshy and club-shaped in fr. and sometimes eaten. (Hove-nia: after David Hoven, 1724–1787, Dutch commissioner in Japan and of assistance to Thunberg in his researches.)

H. dulcis, Thunb. Japanese Raisin-Tree. Round-headed tree to 30 ft., with spicy smell: lvs. ovate or cordate-ovate, 3–7 in. long, acuminate, almost glabrous or pubescent on veins beneath: cymes 1½–2½ in. across: fr. about ¼in. across, the peduncles reddish.

7. **COLLETIA,** Comm. Odd spiny shrubs of about a dozen species in S. Amer., sometimes grown under glass or in the open in warm regions.—Branchlets short, arranged in opposite pairs, thickened and often flattened, spine-tipped: lvs. opposite, small and simple, usually wanting: fls. fascicled or solitary at base of spines, nodding on 1-fld. pedicels, yellowish or white, small; sepals, petals and stamens 4–6, or petals wanting; disk inconspicuous or margin rolled in; ovary immersed in disk at base, 3-celled, the stigma 3-lobed: fr. a dry leathery 3-lobed caps., separating into 3 nutlets. (Colle-tia: Philibert Collet, 1643–1718, French botanist.)

C. cruciata, Hook. (*C. horrida,* Hort.). Anchor-Plant. Shrub to 4 ft., with elliptic flattened very broad-spiny decurrent branches ½–1½ in. long: lvs. few, elliptic, entire: fls. borne profusely in autumn, yellowish-white, urn-shaped, ¼in. long. S. Brazil, Uruguay.

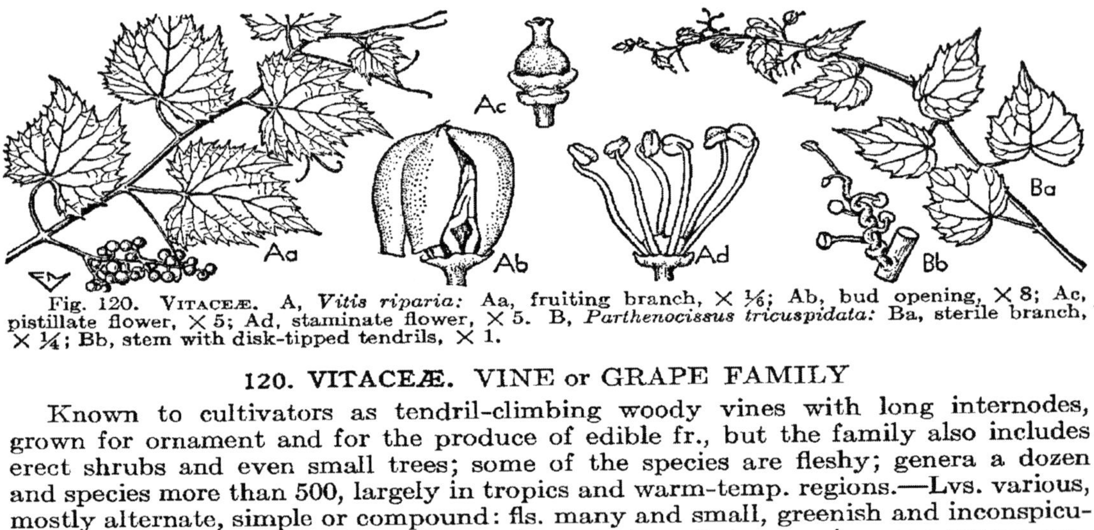

Fig. 120. Vitaceæ. A, *Vitis riparia:* Aa, fruiting branch, × ⅙; Ab, bud opening, × 8; Ac, pistillate flower, × 5; Ad, staminate flower, × 5. B, *Parthenocissus tricuspidata:* Ba, sterile branch, × ¼; Bb, stem with disk-tipped tendrils, × 1.

120. VITACEÆ. VINE or GRAPE FAMILY

Known to cultivators as tendril-climbing woody vines with long internodes, grown for ornament and for the produce of edible fr., but the family also includes erect shrubs and even small trees; some of the species are fleshy; genera a dozen and species more than 500, largely in tropics and warm-temp. regions.—Lvs. various, mostly alternate, simple or compound: fls. many and small, greenish and inconspicuous, variously clustered, bisexual or unisexual, 4- or 5-merous, in some genera provided with a prominent disk about the ovary; calyx entire or minutely toothed; petals either separately expanding or cohering and falling together as a "cap" (corolla gamopetalous in one genus not treated here); stamens prevailingly 4 or 5, opposite the petals; ovary superior, 2- or more-celled with mostly 2 axile ovules in each; style 1, or wanting: fr. a small berry.

A. Hypogynous disk prominent in the fl.: tendrils without expanding tips.
 B. Petals cohering into a cap, detaching at the base and falling together........1. Vitis
 BB. Petals separating and spreading.
  C. Fls. 5-merous: plant not fleshy........2. Ampelopsis
  CC. Fls. 4-merous: plant often fleshy........3. Cissus
AA. Hypogynous disk absent or not evident: tendrils usually with expanded tips.....4. Parthenocissus

1. **VITIS,** L. Vine. Grape. Variable vines, with indefinite specific limits, of probably 50 recognizable species in warm and temp. regions well around the world.—Lvs. simple, more or less palmately lobed: plant climbing by coiling tendrils (in

ours) which are simple or forked, and are either continuous (opposite every lf.) or intermittent (lacking at every third node): fls. mostly in thyrses that take the place of tendrils and sometimes bear a tendril-branch, mostly actually or functionally unisexual, 5-merous, the calyx minute; petals not expanding but cohering and separating at the base, falling together as a "cap"; disk glanduliferous and prominent: fr. a soft pulpy berry. (Vi-tis: the classical Latin name.)—The wine grape (*V. vinifera* of the Old World) produces the prevailing vineyard kinds of Calif. and also for cult. under glass; the vineyard grapes of other parts are derived from native species; many of them are hybrids. N. Amer. is rich in Vitis and species may be expected in botanic gardens and test-grounds. E. Asian species are similarly more or less in cult. The characteristic American vineyard grapes may be described here in terms of their supposed original species, which are of the Labrusca, Æstivalis, and Rotundifolia groups. Other species have yielded pomological vars. of very minor importance, perhaps not now cult., and need not be considered in this account.

A. Tendrils forked: bark on mature canes shredding and without lenticels: nodes with a diaphragm or cross-partition: seeds pyriform.
B. Fr. soft and edible: plants of the kind grown for the grapes although nos. 5 and 6 are planted mostly for arbors, porches or cover.
C. Placement of tendrils (or fl.-clusters) intermittent, every third joint vacant.
D. Skin and pulp of fr. closely adhering, so that the rind does not slip off ...... 1. *V. vinifera*
DD. Skin loose or separating from the flesh, so that the grape can be "pulped."
E. Young shoots and under surface of lvs. gray or whitish .... 2. *V. Girdiana*
EE. Young shoots and under surfaces rusty-tomentose or smooth and green.
F. Under color of lvs., as of young shoots, rusty or brown, associated with tomentum.
G. Berries small, ⅓in. or less in the native state .... 3. *V. æstivalis*
GG. Berries twice or more as large as in G .... 4. *V. Lincecumii*
FF. Under color green, the surface glabrous or practically so unless for tufts of hairs in axils of veins.
G. Lf.-blade cordate-ovate, mostly with gradually and regularly formed triangular apex, commonly not lobed, teeth not very acute .... 5. *V. vulpina*
GG. Lf.-blade broader than cordate-ovate and not triangularly acute, mostly 3-lobed in upper part, teeth large and acute .... 6. *V. riparia*
CC. Placement of tendrils continuous, at every joint on the tendriliferous shoots.
D. Berries few in short nearly simple often compact globular clusters: a wild plant .... 7. *V. Labrusca*
DD. Berries many in large usually pointed and shouldered clusters: vineyard plants .... 8. *V. Labruscana*
BB. Fr. small and hard: plant grown for ornament rather than for edible berries ..... 9. *V. Coignetiæ*
AA. Tendrils simple: bark tight, not peeling in shreds, bearing lenticels: nodes without diaphragm: seeds ovoid .... 10. *V. rotundifolia*

1. **V. vinifera,** L. The GRAPE of history. WINE GRAPE. Strong vine of medium altitude but often trained to a short stout trunk; young growth glabrous or somewhat floccose: tendrils (or clusters) intermittent: lvs. rather thin, circular or circular-ovate in outline, 4–9 in. broad, margins coarsely and more or less acutely toothed or jagged, basal sinus deep and the lobes often overlapping, those on young growths more or less lobed, glabrous or somewhat tomentose beneath at maturity: clusters large and long, the berries often oval or oblong, the skin not readily separating from the pulp. Probably native in S. E. Eu. to W. India, now widely dispersed and in many forms.—Widely grown in Calif. Var. **apiifolia,** Loud., has dissected lvs., sometimes grown for ornament.

2. **V. Girdiana,** Munson. Strong climbing vine in S. Calif. along streams in the foothills, hybridizing with *V. vinifera*, one of the supposed mixtures being the Mission grape: foliage light grayish-green, the young growth densely whitish-woolly: tendrils intermittent: lvs. broadly cordate-ovate to long-cordate, 4–7 in. broad, the teeth large, convex and acute, the basal sinus acute or rounded and the lobes sometimes overlapping: berries ⅓in. or less diam., black with little or no bloom, with tough skin, becoming sweet when very ripe. (Bears the name of H. H. Gird of S. Calif., who brought it to the attention of Munson.)

3. **V. æstivalis,** Michx. SUMMER OR PIGEON GRAPE. Tall climber with reddish-fuzzy young growth: tendrils intermittent: lvs. becoming rather thick, ovate-cordate to circular-cordate in outline, 4–7 in. broad, strongly dentate, 3–5-lobed or strongly angled, basal sinus various, apex broadly triangular, upper surface dull and becoming glabrous, the under surface rusty-tomentose or -pubescent with tufts in the axils of veins: clusters usually long-peduncled, not greatly branched: berries small, usually ⅓in. or less diam., glaucous-black, with tough skin and dry astringent flesh. New England to Fla., Wis., and Kans.—Represented in cult. by Norton (Norton's Virginia) either direct or as a hybrid, and supposed to enter into other races.

Var. **Bourquiniana,** Bailey (*V. Bourquiniana*, Munson). SOUTHERN ÆSTIVALIS. Apparently a cultural offshoot represented in such vars. as Herbemont, Lenoir, Rulander:

it has thinner lvs. and only slightly reddish tomentum, berries large and juicy, black or amber-colored. (Bears the name of Gougie Bourquin of Ga., associated with the history of the group.) Cultigen, perhaps of foreign origin and probably to be associated with *V. vinifera*.

4. **V. Lincecumii**, Buckl. POST-OAK GRAPE. The southwestern representative of *V. æstivalis*, but more stocky, lvs. larger and densely tomentose beneath and often not rust-colored; berries larger, ½–¾in. diam., most palatable in the wild state. (Named for Dr. Gideon Lincecum.) S. W. Mo. to E. La. and Tex., a few vars. for those regions having been somewhat intro. into cult.

5. **V. vulpina**, L. (*V. cordifolia*, Lam.). WINTER GRAPE. Tall, high-climbing, making thick trunks: lvs. cordate-ovate to obscurely triangular above the rather narrow basal sinus, firm and hard in texture, usually not lobed, but rounded on base, margins not deeply or very sharply lobed, lower surface clear bright green with tufts in axils of veins: clusters open and long with short side branches, fls. slender-pedicelled: berries nearly globular, about ⅓in. thick, usually not glaucous and black. Pa. to Fla., Kans., Okla., Tex.—Planted as an arbor or tree vine or cover.

6. **V. riparia**, Michx. (*V. vulpina*, Auth. not L.). FROST GRAPE. Vine of moderate height and size: lvs. broadly ovate, often as broad as long, basal sinus broad and open, apex more or less triangular and commonly with a short sharp lobe on either shoulder, teeth large, irregular, very acute: cluster small to medium, not elongated: berries globular, about ⅓in. thick, black with heavy bloom. N. B. to Tenn., Tex. and Colo.—Sometimes planted for cover and ornament.

7. **V. Labrusca**, L. FOX GRAPE. Strong high climber with tawny tomentum on young parts and continuous tendrils: lvs. large and heavy, broadly cordate-ovate to deltoid-ovate, 4–8 in. broad, margins somewhat scallop-toothed with mucros or nearly entire, obscurely 3-lobed toward apex except on strong shoots where the lobes may be one-half the width of blade, basal sinus mostly shallow and open, upper surface dull and becoming glabrous, lower surface with dull white or reddish tomentum: cluster short, nearly or quite simple and often as broad as long, developing few berries which are large and nearly globular, ½–¾in. diam., purple-black to red-brown, sweetish or astringent, with a strong musky or "foxy" flavor. (Labrusca is Latin for the wild vine.) New England to Ga. and S. Ind.—Rarely transferred to grounds for its abundant attractive foliage.

8. **V. Labruscana**, Bailey. The Labruscan vineyard grapes, of which *V. Labrusca* is the source, as Concord, Worden, Hartford, Vergennes, or the dominant parent as in Isabella, Iona, Niagara, Diana, Catawba, Brighton. The other parentage in most of the crosses is probably *V. vinifera*. The Labruscans are distinguished from the native *V. Labrusca* in the larger and usually shouldered and conic or thyrsoid cluster, larger berries of various colors and the more ameliorated pulp and less foxy flavor; lf. characters vary as between the different kinds, for the most part less tomentose than in Labrusca; tendrils often intermittent.

9. **V. Coignetiæ**, Pulliatt. Very strong vigorous hardy vine grown for ornament and sometimes called "Crimson Glory vine" from the bright autumn coloring of the heavy abundant foliage; young growth floccose-tomentose; tendrils intermittent: lvs. cordate-orbicular with 3 or 5 lobe-like points, 6–10 in. broad, shallowly apiculate-toothed, dull above and gray- or tawny-tomentose beneath: cluster long or short and branched: berries globular, about ⅓in. diam., scarcely edible. (Dedicated to Mme. Coignet, Lyons, France.) N. Japan.

10. **V. rotundifolia**, Michx. (*Muscadinia rotundifolia*, Small). MUSCADINE. Long-climbing nearly or quite glabrous hard-wooded vine with usually simple intermittent tendrils, often emitting aërial roots: lvs. medium, cordate-circular to cordate-ovate, 2–6 in. across, strongly angular-notched but not lobed, the basal sinus open, without tomentum: berries few to 20 in a nearly globular bunch, spherical or nearly so, ½–1 in. diam., dull purple and not glaucous, with thick tough skin and musk-tasting flesh. S. Del. to Fla., Kans., and Tex.—Several vineyard vars. are in cult., particularly the Scuppernong with silvery amber-green berries.

2. **AMPELOPSIS**, Michx. Some 25 species of mostly tendril-bearing ornamental vines of N. Amer. and Asia.—Technically the genus differs from Vitis in the absence of shredding bark, by cymose rather than paniculate infl., bisexual fls., and the spreading petals which fall separately: lvs. alternate, simple or compound: tendrils forking and not dilated at tips: fls. 5-merous for the most part; stamens short and as many as the petals; disk prominent, adnate to the 2-celled slender-styled ovary: fr. a small 1–4-seeded berry. (Ampelop-sis: Greek *vine-like*, ampelos being the vine, Vitis.)—The principal one in cult. is apparently *A. brevipedunculata* var. *elegans;* the distinctions are likely to be confused, and therefore descriptions are here given of several kinds that may be little planted.

A. Species with simple, entire or lobed lvs.
 B. Lvs. green beneath, thin..1. *A. brevipedunculata*
 BB. Lvs. whitish beneath, firm in texture.
  C. Fr. pale yellow or whitish or pale blue: lvs. bright lustrous-green above... 2. *A. humulifolia*
  CC. Fr. dark blue or violet: lvs. with a velvety sheen above when young...... 3. *A. Bodinieri*
AA. Species with most of the lvs. compound.
 B. Lvs. digitately 3–5-parted..4. *A. aconitifolia*
 BB. Lvs. pinnate or bipinnate.
  C. Lfts. obtusely or crenately serrate, 2–5 in. long.....................5. *A. megalophylla*
  CC. Lfts. coarsely toothed, mostly ⅓–1⅓ in. long.......................6. *A. arborea*

1. **A. brevipedunculata,** Trautv. (*Cissus brevipedunculata,* Maxim. *A. heterophylla* var. *amurensis,* Planch.). Tendril-climbing, the slender young parts and petioles hairy: lvs. cordate-ovate, 2–4 in. across, slightly 3-lobed or shouldered above the middle, short-acuminate, crenate-dentate with apiculate points, the basal sinus broad, hairy beneath at least on the prominent veins: cymes short and rather dense, not equalling the lvs.: fr. blue to lilac. Japan, Manchuria, N. China. Var. **Maximowiczii,** Rehd. (*Vitis heterophylla* var. *Maximowiczii,* Regel. *V. heterophylla,* Thunb. *A. heterophylla,* Sieb. & Zucc.), lvs. deeply 3-lobed, st. and foliage more glabrous. Var. **citrulloides,** Bailey (*A. citrulloides,* Lebas), lvs. still more deeply and narrowly lobed, with broad open sinuses, the middle lobe constricted at base and at or above the middle, the lateral lobes often again lobed so that the lf. appears to be primarily 5-lobed. Var. **elegans,** Bailey (*Vitis elegans,* Koch. *A. tricolor* and *A. variegata,* Hort.), the common cult. form with lvs. variegated white, greenish, or yellowish and sometimes pink.

2. **A. humulifolia,** Bunge. Differs from no. 1 by the firmer texture of the lvs. that are pale or whitish underneath, and in the small pale yellow or pale blue frs.: lvs. broad-ovate, 3–4 in. across, 3–5-lobed or sometimes the lobes little evident, acute or acuminate, base truncate or subcordate, lustrous-green above, glaucescent and either glabrous or hairy beneath: cymes slender-peduncled. N. China.

3. **A. Bodinieri,** Rehd. (*Vitis Bodinieri,* Lévl. & Vaniot. *A. micans,* Rehd.). Strong climbing grape-like vine, with purplish glabrous young growth: lvs. large and rather thick, cordate-ovate to triangular-ovate, 3–6 in. across, shouldered or shallowly lobed or not lobed, the point broad and nearly or quite obtuse, basal sinus shallow and open, margins crenate-toothed with apiculate points, velvety-lustrous above, somewhat glaucous and nearly or quite glabrous beneath: cymes rather dense, long-stalked: fr. dark blue. (Named for Emile Marie Bodinier, 1842–1901, missionary in China.) Cent. China.

4. **A. aconitifolia,** Bunge. Slender tendril-climber with glabrous young growth: lvs. broad-ovate to nearly circular in outline, 2–4 in. across, digitately 5-parted, the parts strongly toothed and sometimes more or less cut and divided, points acuminate, light green beneath, glabrous or somewhat hairy beneath on the veins: fr. small, orange, sometimes becoming bluish. N. China. Var. **glabra,** Diels, lvs. usually 3-parted and segms. toothed and lobed.

5. **A. megalophylla,** Diels & Gilg. Strong glabrous and more or less glaucous tendril-climber, making very large winter-buds: lvs. large, pinnate or bipinnate, 6–16 in. long, pale and somewhat glaucous beneath; lfts. or segms. several to many, ovate to ovate-oblong, 2–5 in. long, more or less acuminate, rounded or subcordate at base, crenate-serrate: cymes loose: fr. bluish-black. W. China.

6. **A. arborea,** Koehne (*Vitis arborea,* L. *V. bipinnata,* Torr. & Gray). PEPPER-VINE. Bushy, more or less climbing, tendrils sometimes small or wanting, young growth nearly or quite glabrous: lvs. bipinnate and finely divided, ornamental, 3–9 in. long; lfts. or segms. mostly ovate, ½–1½ in. long, deeply notched, hairy on veins and in axils beneath and also on rachis: fls. often 4-merous: fr. black-purple. Va. to Fla., Tex. and Mex.

3. **CISSUS,** L. Species 200 or more, widespread in trop. and warm-temp. regions, a few grown for ornament.—Erect or tendril-climbing (ours of the latter kind), distinguished from Vitis, with which it has been united, by the expanding separate petals, 4-merous fls., largely persistent foliage, and often fleshy or somewhat succulent lvs. and plant body: sts. often herbaceous: lvs. simple or compound: fls. bisexual or unisexual; disk 4-lobed: fr. a small 1–4-seeded inedible berry. (Cis-sus: Greek name of *ivy*.)

A. Lvs. simple, but sometimes lobed.
 B. Lf.-blade large, broad, and grape-like..1. *C. capensis*
 BB. Lf.-blade not grape-like, longer than broad.
  C. Branchlets pubescent: lvs. green..2. *C. antarctica*
  CC. Branchlets glabrous: lvs. colored..3. *C. discolor*
AA. Lvs. 3–5-foliolate.
 B. Lfts. rhombic, 1–4 in. long..4. *C. rhombifolia*
 BB. Lfts. cuneate-obovate, much smaller..5. *C. striata*

1. **C. capensis,** Willd. (*Vitis capensis,* Thunb.). Strong climbing evergreen grape-like vine, used in S. Calif. for arbors, producing globular ground tubers 6–8 in. diam.; young growths rusty-tomentose; tendrils very long, forked: lvs. simple, long-petioled, blade nearly

orbicular to reniform, with 3 strong nerves from base, 4–8 in. across, strongly repand-dentate, becoming glabrous above except perhaps along the ribs, rusty-tomentose beneath: fr. globular, in short clusters, about ½in. diam., red-black and glossy, said to be good for cooking. S. Afr.

2. **C. antarctica,** Vent. (*Vitis antarctica,* Benth.). Upright shrub with tendril-climbing branches, hairy-pubescent on young growths: lvs. ovate to oblong, 2–3½ in. long, short-acuminate, subcordate at base, shallowly upwardly toothed, glabrous and glossy above: fr. a globular few-seeded small berry. Australia.—Sometimes grown in cool greenhouses and also in the open in S. Calif.

3. **C. discolor,** Blume. Slender glabrous tendril-climber with red shoots: lvs. oblong-ovate to cordate-ovate, 4–6 in. long, gradually acuminate, basal sinus narrow, margins closely apiculate-serrate, highly colored—rich green above with white and pink and red-purple over-colors, purplish beneath: fr. globular, small, 1-seeded. Java.—A greenhouse foliage plant.

4. **C. rhombifolia,** Vahl (*Vitis rhombifolia,* Baker). Evergreen tendril-climber with loose-hairy wingless shoots: lfts. 3, stalked, rhombic-ovate, 1–4 in. long, pointed, sharp-toothed, reddish-hairy on veins beneath: peduncles glandulose-pubescent, the cymes 20–30-fld.: fr. small, globose, glabrous. N. S. Amer.

5. **C. striata,** Ruiz & Pav. (*Ampelopsis sempervirens,* Hort.). Low and shrubby small-lvd. somewhat pubescent evergreen with tendril-climbing branches: lvs. digitately 3–5-foliolate, coriaceous; lfts. mostly 1 in. or less long but on vigorous plants or shoots to 3 in. long, cuneate-obovate to spatulate, small-dentate toward apex, glabrous: fr. small, depressed-globose, 2–4-seeded. Peru, Chile to S. Brazil.—Grown in cool greenhouse and in the open in Calif.

4. **PARTHENOCISSUS,** Planch. (*Psedera,* Neck.). Ten to 12 woody tendril-climbers in N. Amer. and Asia, a few commonly grown for covering walls and arbors. —Distinguished from Vitis and closely related genera by disk-like tips of tendrils on some of the species, absence of prominent hypogynous disk in the fl., petals expanding and falling separately: lvs. alternate, digitate or lobed: fls. mostly bisexual, in compound cymes, usually 5-merous; ovary 2-celled, each cell 2-ovuled: fr. a small 1–4-seeded berry. (Parthenocis-sus: Greek *virgin ivy.*)

A. Lvs. 3-foliolate or -lobed..1. *P. tricuspidata*
AA. Lvs. 5-foliolate.
B. Branchlets 4-angled: lvs. usually with whitish marking and purple beneath .....2. *P. Henryana*
BB. Branchlets terete: lvs. green both sides.
C. Tendrils with 5–12 branches, with adhesive disks: cymes usually in panicles..3. *P. quinquefolia*
CC. Tendrils with 3–5 branches, without adhesive disks: cymes solitary..........4. *P. inserta*

1. **P. tricuspidata,** Planch. (*Ampelopsis tricuspidata,* Sieb. & Zucc.). Japanese or Boston Ivy. Glabrous high-climbing vine with lustrous foliage, clinging closely by means of short branched disciferous tendrils: lvs. variable, on young shoots or plants ovate to cordate-ovate or cordate-orbicular and few-toothed, more or less 3-lobed toward apex, 2–4 in. across, on older or established plants much larger and often 3-foliolate, becoming 8 in. across, the lfts. sessile: fr. bluish-black, more or less glaucous. Japan, China. Var. **Lowii,** Rehd. (*Ampelopsis Lowii,* Low), has very small lvs. 1½ in. or less long, purplish when young and brilliant red in autumn, the plant slender and smaller. Var. **Veitchii,** Rehd. (*P. Veitchii,* Graebn. *Ampelopsis Veitchii,* Hort.), lvs. small, crenate-serrate, purple when young, simple or 3-foliolate, lfts. with only 1–3 coarse teeth on each side.

2. **P. Henryana,** Diels & Gilg (*Vitis Henryana,* Hemsl.). Glabrous climber with 4-angled young growth, the tendrils slender-branched and with adhesive tips: lvs. purplish beneath and usually with whitish markings above; lfts. 5, elliptic-ovate to obovate, serrate above the base, 2½ in. or less long, stalked, glabrous both sides or somewhat pubescent on veins beneath: cymes narrow: fr. about 3-seeded, dark blue. (For A. Henry, page 45.) Cent. China.

3. **P. quinquefolia,** Planch. (*Hedera quinquefolia,* L. *Ampelopsis quinquefolia,* Michx.). Virginia Creeper. Woodbine. Very strong high-climbing vine, the 5–12-branched tendrils with expanded adhesive tips and the old sts. often emitting roots; young growth purplish: lfts. 5, rather thick, elliptic-ovate to more or less obovate, 3–6 in. long, pointed and coarsely toothed, prominently petiolulate, dull green above, much lighter and more or less glaucescent and light pubescent beneath: cymes not dichotomous, paniculate: fr. about ¼in. diam., bluish-black, more or less glaucous, 1–3-seeded. New England to Fla. and Mex. Var. **Engelmannii,** Rehd. (*P. Engelmannii,* Graebn.), is a form with smaller foliage. Var. **hirsuta,** Planch. (*Cissus hederacea* var. *hirsuta,* Pursh. *P. hirsuta,* Small), young parts and lvs. soft-pubescent.

4. **P. inserta,** Fritsch (*Vitis inserta,* Kerner. *P. vitacea,* Hitchc.). Virginia Creeper. Woodbine. Low and rambling over bushes and rocks; tendrils 3–5-branched, usually without adhesive disks; lfts. 2–4 in. long, glossy above, deep green beneath: cymes dichotomous, solitary: fr. bluish-black, ⅓in. diam., 3–4-seeded. New England to Rocky Mts.

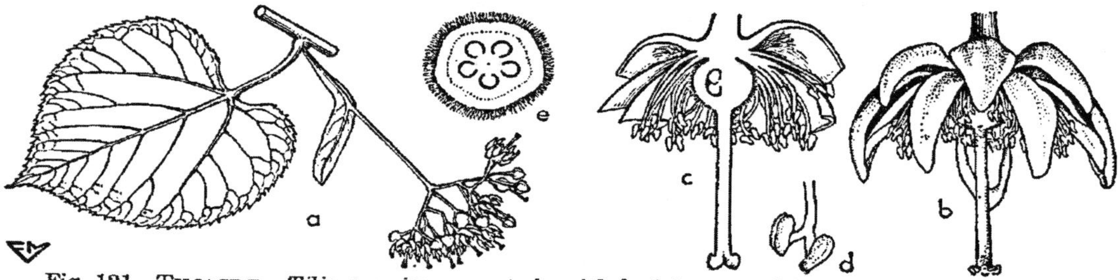

Fig. 121. TILIACEÆ. *Tilia americana:* a, twig with leaf, bract and inflorescence, × 1/4; b, flower, × 2; c, same, vertical section, × 2; d, anther, × 4; e, ovary, cross-section, × 4.

121. TILIACEÆ. LINDEN or BASSWOOD FAMILY

Trees, shrubs or rarely herbs, of about 35 genera and 370 species, widely distributed in warm and trop. regions, but a few in temp. zones, the lindens being among the best known ornamental trees.—Bark fibrous, with mucilaginous properties: lvs. usually alternate, simple, entire, dentate or lobed, stipules mostly small and deciduous: fls. regular, bisexual or rarely unisexual, usually in axillary or terminal cymes or panicles; sepals 5, rarely 3 or 4, free or connate, valvate, deciduous; petals 5 or fewer, or none, alternate with sepals, often glandular at base; stamens numerous, the filaments free or in fascicles of 5–10, some perhaps only staminodia; ovary superior, 2–10-celled with 1 to many ovules in each cell, placentation axile, the style entire or lobed: fr. a caps., drupe or berry, dehiscent or indehiscent, 1–10-celled.

A. Peduncles adnate for about half their length to membranaceous bract: fr. indehiscent, nut-like .... 1. TILIA
AA. Peduncles free: fr. a dehiscent caps.
B. Stamens all anther-bearing .... 2. CORCHORUS
BB. Stamens not all anther-bearing, the outer ones staminodia .... 3. SPARMANNIA

1. TILIA, L. LINDEN. BASSWOOD. LIME. About 30 species of deciduous trees native of the north temp. zone, planted for shade, ornament and avenues; some yield valuable timber and the tough inner bark is manufactured into mats, cords and the like.—Winter-buds axillary, large, with numerous imbricated scales: lvs. long-petioled, usually cordate, serrate: fls. small, fragrant, nectar-bearing, in long-peduncled drooping cymes, the peduncle adnate for about half its length to a membranaceous ligulate bract; sepals and petals 5, the latter often with a small scale at base; stamens numerous, free or in 5 clusters, sometimes with petaloid staminodia opposite the petals; ovary sessile, 5-celled, the stigma 5-lobed: fr. indehiscent, nut-like, globose or ovoid, 1–3-seeded. (Til-ia: classical Latin name.)

A. Lvs. glabrous beneath, except axillary tufts of hairs.
B. Fls. with staminodes: axillary tufts of hairs lacking at base of lvs. .... 1. *T. americana*
BB. Fls. without staminodes: axillary tufts of hairs present at base of lvs.
C. Under surface of lvs. glaucous: fr. thin-shelled .... 2. *T. cordata*
CC. Under surface of lvs. light green: fr. thick-shelled.
D. Upper surface of lvs. dull green, teeth short-pointed .... 3. *T. europæa*
DD. Upper surface of lvs. glossy, teeth with long slender points.
E. Fr. obtuse at ends .... 4. *T. dasystyla*
EE. Fr. narrowed at ends .... 5. *T. euchlora*
AA. Lvs. pubescent beneath.
B. Petioles glabrous .... 6. *T. Moltkei*
BB. Petioles pubescent.
C. Under side of lvs. lightly pubescent, also with axillary tufts of hairs .... 7. *T. platyphyllos*
CC. Under side of lvs. white-tomentose, without axillary tufts of hairs.
D. Branches upright .... 8. *T. tomentosa*
DD. Branches pendulous .... 9. *T. petiolaris*

1. **T. americana,** L. (*T. glabra*, Vent.). AMERICAN LINDEN or BASSWOOD. Tree to 120 ft., with deeply furrowed bark: lvs. broad-ovate, 4–6 in. or more long, abruptly acuminate, obliquely cordate or truncate at base, coarsely serrate with incurved long-pointed teeth, dark green above, light green and glabrous beneath except tufts of hairs in axils of lateral veins but wanting at base, turning yellow in autumn: fls. about 1/2 in. across, with staminodes: fr. ovoid or globose, 1/3–1/2 in. long, not ribbed, tomentose, thick-shelled. N. B. to Va. and Tex. Var. **macrophylla,** Rehd. (var. *mississippiensis*, Hort. *T. nigra* var. *macrophylla*, Bayer), is a large-lvd. form.

2. **T. cordata,** Mill. (*T. ulmifolia*, Scop. *T. parvifolia*, Ehrh. *T. europæa*, L. in part). SMALL-LEAVED LINDEN. To 100 ft.: lvs. nearly orbicular, often broader than long, 1½–2½ in. long, abruptly acuminate and cuspidate, cordate at base, finely serrate, dark green above, glaucous and glabrous beneath with axillary tufts of brown hairs: fls. about ⅓in. across, fragrant, in nearly upright cymes, without staminodes: fr. globose, about ¼in. diam., tomentose, faintly ribbed, with thin fragile shell. Eu.

3. **T. europæa,** L. (*T. vulgaris*, Hayne). EUROPEAN LINDEN. Hybrid between *T. cordata* and *T. platyphyllos:* to 120 ft.: lvs. broad-ovate, 2–4 in. long, abruptly acuminate, obliquely cordate or truncate at base, teeth short-pointed, dark green above, bright green beneath and glabrous except axillary tufts of hairs: fr. nearly globose, tomentose, faintly ribbed, thick-shelled.

4. **T. dasystyla,** Steven. To 100 ft.: lvs. broad-ovate, 3–6 in. long, abruptly acuminate, obliquely cordate at base, teeth aristate, shining above, bright green and glabrous beneath except axillary tufts of whitish hairs: fr. globose, ½in. long, slightly 5-ribbed, tomentose, obtuse at ends. S. E. Eu., W. Asia.

5. **T. euchlora,** Koch. CRIMEAN LINDEN. Hybrid between *T. dasystyla* and probably *T. cordata:* to 65 ft.; lvs. broad-ovate, 2–4 in. long, abruptly acuminate, obliquely cordate at base, teeth mucronate, shining above, pale green and glabrous beneath except axillary tufts of brown hairs: fr. elliptical, narrowed at ends, slightly 5-ribbed, tomentose, thick-shelled.

6. **T. Moltkei,** Spaeth (*T. spectabilis*, Dipp.). Hybrid between *T. americana* and *T. petiolaris:* to 40 ft. or more, branches somewhat pendulous: lvs. round-ovate, 4–7 in. long, grayish-tomentose beneath, without axillary tufts, petioles glabrous: fr. globose, faintly furrowed, tomentose. (Named for the field marshall who planted it in 1888.)

7. **T. platyphyllos,** Scop. (*T. grandifolia*, Ehrh. *T. europæa*, L. in part). LARGE-LEAVED LIME. To 120 ft.: lvs. orbicular-ovate, 3–4 in. long, obliquely cordate at base, abruptly acuminate, serrate, dull green above, light green and lightly pubescent beneath, with axillary tufts of hairs: fr. globose, ovoid or pyriform, tomentose, strongly 3–5-ribbed, apiculate, thick-shelled. Eu. Var. **fastigiata,** Bailey (forma *fastigiata*, Rehd. *T. grandifolia pyramidalis*, Beissn.), is of narrow pyramidal habit. Var. **laciniata,** Koch (var. *asplenifolia*, Kirchn.), has deeply cut lvs. Var. **vitifolia,** Simonk., has lvs. slightly 3-lobed.

8. **T. tomentosa,** Moench (*T. argentea*, DC. *T. alba*, Ait.). WHITE or SILVER LINDEN. Tree of upright dense habit, to 100 ft.; young branchlets stellate-tomentose: lvs. nearly orbicular, 3–5 in. long, truncate or cordate at base, abruptly acuminate, serrate or slightly lobed, white-tomentose beneath: infl. tomentose: fr. ovoid, ¼ to nearly ½in. long, tomentose, slightly 5-angled, shell woody. E. Eu., Asia Minor.

9. **T. petiolaris,** DC. WEEPING WHITE LINDEN. Very similar to *T. tomentosa*, differing in its pendulous branches, more finely serrate lvs., longer petioles, and 5-furrowed fr. Known only in cult.

2. **CORCHORUS,** L. Herbs or subshrubs, of about 40 species, widely dispersed in the tropics, a few grown for their fiber called "jute" and the young shoots used for pot-herbs.—Lvs. alternate, serrate: fls. small, yellow, solitary or in few-fld. cymes; sepals and petals 5, rarely 4; stamens 10 to many, free, all anther-bearing; ovary 2–5-celled: fr. a subglobose or elongated caps. loculicidally dehiscent by 2–5 valves, sometimes with transverse partitions between the seeds. (Cor-chorus: from Greek referring to some reputed medicinal quality, as an eye remedy, of one of the species.)—The corchorus of trade-lists is usually *Kerria japonica.*

A. Caps. globose, not beaked....................1. *C. capsularis*
AA. Caps. elongated, beaked....................2. *C. olitorius*

1. **C. capsularis,** L. JUTE. Ann., growing 15 ft. high, with straight st. branching only near top: lvs. oblong, 2–4 in. long, serrate, the 2 lower teeth prolonged into sharp points: caps. globose, wrinkled, dehiscing into 5 valves, without transverse partitions. India, but escaped from cult. in other trop. countries.

2. **C. olitorius,** L. NALTA JUTE. JEWS-MALLOW. Very similar to the above but differing in its almost cylindrical caps. about 2 in. long, dehiscing by 3–6 valves, with transverse partitions between the seeds. India; nat. widely in tropics.

3. **SPARMANNIA,** L. f. Five or more species of African shrubs or trees, one grown in greenhouses and out-of-doors in warm regions.—Pubescence soft, stellate: lvs. alternate, cordate, dentate or lobed: fls. white, in bracted terminal cymose umbels; sepals and petals 4; stamens numerous, free, the outer not anther-bearing; ovary 4-celled: fr. a globose spiny caps. loculicidally dehiscent by 4 valves. (Sparman-nia: after Andreas Sparmann, 1748–1820, Swedish naturalist.)

S. africana, L. f. Large shrub or tree to 20 ft., often forming many trunks: lvs. long-petioled, cordate-acuminate, from 3–9 in. long, unequally toothed, 5–7-angled: fls. long-pedicelled, 1–1½ in. diam., white with yellow stamens, in cymes sometimes 4 in. across. S. Afr.—There is a double-fld. form.

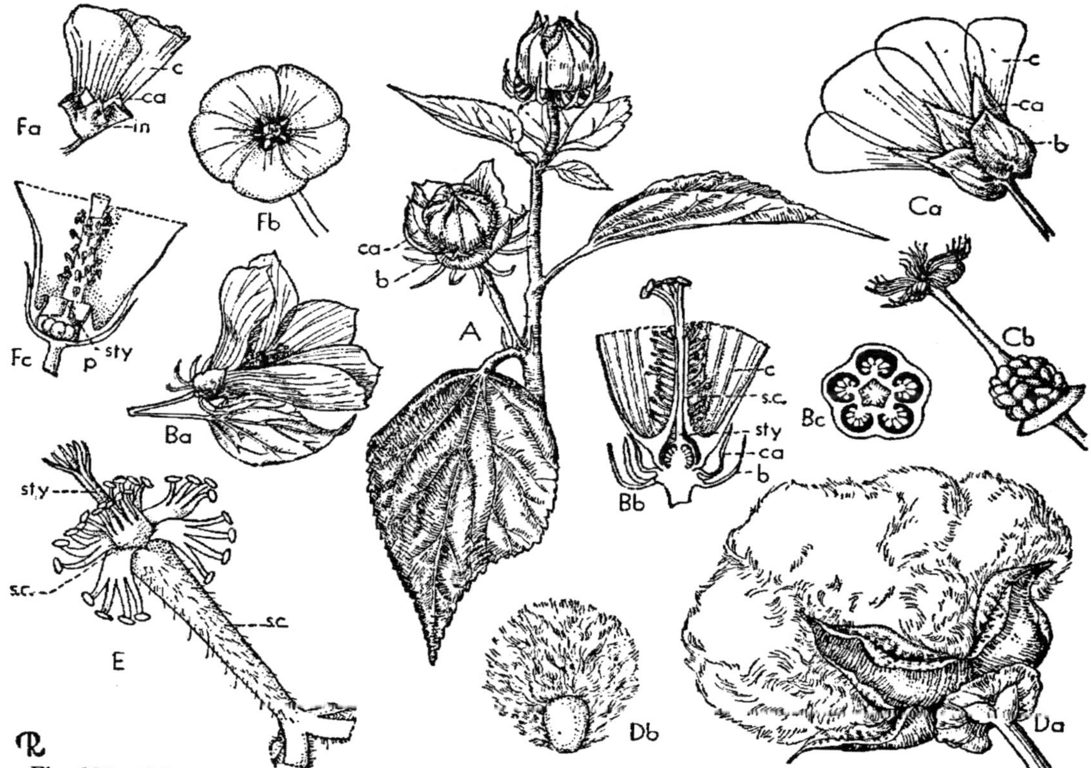

Fig. 122. MALVACEÆ. A, *Hibiscus palustris:* fruiting branch, × ⅜. B, *H. Moscheutos:* Ba, flower, × ¼; Bb, same, vertical section, perianth partially excised, × ½; Bc, ovary, cross-section, × 2. C, *Malope trifida:* Ca, flower habit, × ½; Cb, same, gynœcium, × 4. D, *Gossypium hirsutum:* Da, boll, × 1; Db, seed, × ½. E, *Sidalcea candida:* double staminal column enveloping style, × 2 (after Engler and Prantl). F, *Anoda cristata:* Fa, flower, side view, × ½; Fb, same, face view, × ½; Fc, partial vertical section, × 1. (b bract, c corolla, ca calyx, in involucre, p pistil, s. c. staminal column, sty style.)

122. MALVACEÆ. MALLOW FAMILY

A well-marked family of 40–50 genera and upwards of 1,000 species in temp. and trop. countries around the world, yielding fiber and ornamental and a few food plants.—Herbs, shrubs, and trees with alternate simple mostly palmately-veined and -lobed lvs. and small deciduous stipules: fls. regular and bisexual, only exceptionally unisexual, prevailingly 5-merous, white, yellow or various shades of red and purple, marked by the many stamens cohering into a tube about the pistil and which is often adnate to the 5 petals; sepals 5, often united and frequently subtended by calyx-like bracts or involucre; ovary superior, only rarely 1-celled, mostly 2- to many-celled, with 1 to several axile ovules in each cell; styles commonly as many as the carpels, mostly united below: fr. a caps. or separating into carpels (actually achenes or follicles) or sometimes berry-like.

A. Fr. separating into carpels: pistil consisting of several separate carpels.
  B. Carpels in a single ring, separating at maturity from the central axis.
    C. Column of stamens bearing anthers only at or very near the apex: stigmas as many as carpels.
      D. Ovule solitary in each cell.
        E. Stigma linear, on the inner side or face of the pointed style-branches.
          F. Staminal column simple, of one series of stamens.

G. Involucre of 1–3 distinct bracts, or wanting.
H. Petals obcordate: carpels without beaks or appendages .... 1. MALVA
HH. Petals usually truncate: carpels beaked and with transverse appendages inside and underneath the beak .... 2. CALLIRHOË
GG. Involucre of 3–9 connate bracts.
H. Axis of fr. surpassing the carpels, forming a cone or projection in the center .... 3. LAVATERA
HH. Axis not extending beyond the ring of carpels .... 4. ALTHÆA
FF. Staminal column of two series, the outer one in five parts or clusters .. 5. SIDALCEA
EE. Stigma capitate or club-shaped, occupying the end of the style-branch.
F. Fls. without involucre .... 6. ANODA
FF. Fls. with involucre .... 7. MALVASTRUM
DD. Ovules 2 or more in each cell.
E. Involucre usually of 3 bracts: carpels sharply differentiated into two parts .... 8. SPHÆRALCEA
EE. Involucre lacking: carpels not differentiated .... 9. ABUTILON
CC. Column of stamens bearing anthers below the top and more or less along the sides, the apex itself sterile and 5-toothed: stigmas twice as many as carpels.
D. Involucre of many bracts: carpels connate into a fleshy or berry-like body but later separating .... 10. MALVAVISCUS
DD. Involucre of 5–8 bracts: fr. dry .... 11. PAVONIA
BB. Carpels in a pile or cone (like a raspberry), connate about the axis .... 12. MALOPE
AA. Fr. a caps.: ovary of several carpels but all united in single pistil.
B. Styles united: seeds obovoid or angled.
C. Involucre of very small or narrow bracts.
D. Calyx persistent: seeds pubescent .... 13. THESPESIA
DD. Calyx deciduous: seeds glabrous .... 14. MONTEZUMA
CC. Involucre of large cordate bracts .... 15. GOSSYPIUM
BB. Styles distinct: seeds usually kidney-shaped.
C. Style-branches short and broad, making a capitate lobed radiating stigma .... 16. LAGUNARIA
CC. Style-branches slender and at maturity spreading .... 17. HIBISCUS

1. **MALVA**, L. MALLOW. Herbs, grown in the border and the fl.-garden; about 30 species in Eu., N. Afr., Asia, several nat. in N. Amer.—Ann., bien., or per., hirsute or nearly glabrous: lvs. angled, lobed or dissected: fls. solitary in the axils or clustered, sessile or peduncled, involucrate by 3 or rarely 2 distinct small bracts; calyx 5-cleft; petals 5, notched at the apex, rose-colored or white; staminal column bearing anthers at summit; stigmas as many as carpels, linear, on inner side of style-branches: fr. consisting of round-reniform, beakless, compressed 1-seeded carpels cohering in a depressed circle around the axis and at length separating from it and from each other. (Mal-va: old Latin name from Greek, referring to the emollient lvs.)

A. Fls. large and showy, 1–2 in. across.
B. Fr. not prominently wrinkled: lvs. deeply lobed.
C. St.-lvs. 5-parted and the parts 1–2-parted or -cleft: fr. downy .... 1. *M. moschata*
CC. St.-lvs. only once 5-parted or -cleft: fr. glabrous .... 2. *M. Alcea*
BB. Fr. prominently wrinkled-veiny: lvs. shallowly lobed .... 3. *M. sylvestris*
AA. Fls. small and inconspicuous, whitish .... 4. *M. crispa*

1. **M. moschata**, L. MUSK MALLOW. Per., 1–2 ft. high, with mostly simple pubescence: lower lvs. suborbicular, rather shallowly incised; st.-lvs. 5-parted, the divisions 1–2-parted or -cleft into linear segms.: fls. large and showy, 1½–2 in. across, rose, only from the upper axils, surpassing the subtending lvs.; calyx long-hairy: fr. downy, not wrinkled. Eu.; cult. and escaped. Var. **alba**, Bailey, has white fls.

2. **M. Alcea**, L. Much like *M. moschata*, but the pubescence stellate and the st.-lvs. 5-parted into toothed or barely incised divisions: fls. larger, 2 in. or more across, deep rose to white; calyx densely stellate-pubescent: fr. glabrous, minutely wrinkled or veiny. (Alcea: Greek, in reference to medicinal effect; an old name adopted by Linnæus.) Eu.; cult. and escaped.

3. **M. sylvestris**, L. Bien. perhaps sometimes per., or grown as ann., 2–3 ft. high, erect, branching, rough-hairy: lvs. round-cordate or reniform, with 5–7 obtuse crenate lobes: fls. purple-rose, 1–1½ in. across, borne in the axils of most of the lvs. and surpassed by the petioles; petals three times as long as the calyx: fr. prominently wrinkled-hairy. Eu., temp. Asia, waysides N. Amer. Var. **mauritiana**, Boiss. (*M. mauritiana*, L.), to 4 ft.: sts. and petioles more or less strigose-hairy: lvs. more shallowly and more obtusely lobed: fls. purple, the petals less deeply emarginate.

4. **M. crispa**, L. CURLED MALLOW. Unbranched ann. 4–8 ft. high, leafy throughout, the sts. sometimes 3 in. thick at base: lvs. rounded, 5–7-lobed or -angled, the margins attractively crisped and curled: fls. whitish, small and inconspicuous, about ¼in. across, in dense axillary clusters surpassed by the petioles of the subtending lvs.: fr. wrinkled. Old World; sparingly escaped from old gardens.

2. **CALLIRHOË,** Nutt. Poppy-Mallow. Herbs with showy fls., suitable for planting out-of-doors; 9 species native to N. Amer.—Perennials (mostly with thick root) or annuals: lvs. alternate, with lobed or cleft blades or more finely dissected: fls. mostly crimson-purple or flesh-colored, axillary or sometimes in terminal racemes, the petals irregularly cut or truncate at apex, in this differing from the notched petals of Malva; involucre of 1–3 bracts or wanting; staminal column bearing anthers at summit; stigmas as many as carpels, linear, on inner side of style-branches: carpels 10–20, more or less beaked or apiculate, 1-seeded. (Callir-hoë: Greek mythological name.)

C. involucrata, Gray (*Malva involucrata*, Nutt. *C. verticillata*, Groenl.). Per. 9–12 in. high, hirsute or even hispid; sts. procumbent: lvs. rounded in outline, palmately or pedately 5–7-parted or deeply cleft, the divisions mostly cuneate and with oblong or lanceolate lobes: bracts of involucre linear to oblong, half as long as the spreading calyx-lobes; fls. all summer, 1–2½ in. across, crimson-purple, cherry-red or paler, with broad erose-denticulate summit: carpels 18–25, beaked, often hairy. Minn. to Tex. Var. **lineariloba,** Gray (*C. lineariloba*, Gray), is less hirsute, with smaller lvs. dissected into linear lobes and lilac or pinkish fls.; Tex. and adjacent Mex.

3. **LAVATERA,** L. Tree-Mallow. About 25 species, mostly in the Medit. region but extending to the Canary Isls., Asia, Australia, and the isls. off S. and Lower Calif.; several grown in the fl.-garden.—Herbs, shrubs, or trees, tomentose or hairy: lvs. angled or lobed, sometimes maple-like: fls. variously colored, rarely yellow, in terminal racemes or 1–4 in the axils, sometimes 2–4 in. across; fl.-bracts 3–6 or 9, joined into an involucre; petals 5, reflexed after anthesis, emarginate or truncate, clawed; staminal column divided at summit into an indefinite number of filaments; ovaries few to many, united about an axis which is conical or umbrella-shaped at top and conspicuously surpasses the carpels; carpels beakless, 1-seeded. (Lavat-era: one of the Lavater family of Zurich at the time of Tournefort.)

A. Lvs. nearly round or the upper ones angled: plant ann. . . . . 1. *L. trimestris*
AA. Lvs. 3–9-lobed; plant bien. or per.
  B. Petals deeply 2-lobed . . . . 2. *L. thuringiaca*
  BB. Petals not deeply lobed.
    C. Pedicels 2–3 in. long . . . . 3. *L. assurgentiflora*
    CC. Pedicels very short or none.
      D. Fls. in clusters . . . . 4. *L. arborea*
      DD. Fls. solitary . . . . 5. *L. olbia*

1. **L. trimestris,** L. (*L. rosea*, Medic.). Branching ann. 3–6 ft. high: lvs. irregularly crenate-dentate, finely pubescent or nearly glabrous, the lower subrotund-cordate, the upper ones angled: fls. solitary, axillary, rose-pink or red, 4 in. across, blooming in summer and autumn, the pedicels mostly shorter than the subtending lvs.; involucre shorter than calyx: receptacle or axis of the fr. expanded at apex into a disk, inclosing the ovary. Medit. region. Var. **alba,** W. Miller, has white fls. Var. **splendens,** Bailey, is an improved garden strain.

2. **L. thuringiaca,** L. Per. 2–4 ft. high, stellate-pubescent: lower lvs. cordate-ovate, 5-angled, the upper 3-lobed, toothed: fls. solitary in the axils, forming a loose terminal raceme, pedicelled, rose-pink with darker veins, 2–3 in. across, petals deeply 2-lobed; involucre shorter than calyx. Eu.

3. **L. assurgentiflora,** Kellogg. Shrub 6–15 ft. high with simple sts., from seed reaching 6 ft. tall and blooming the first year: lvs. glabrous or finely stellate-pubescent, 3–6 in. broad, with 5–7 ovate-triangular lobes coarsely and irregularly toothed, pale beneath: fls. purple, with darker veins, 2–3 in. across, 1–4 in the axils, on slender commonly recurved-ascending pedicels 2–3 in. long; involucre shorter than the calyx-lobes; petals with long narrow glabrous claws and a pair of dense hairy tufts at base: fr. strongly winged below, the axis low-conical. S. Calif. isls.

4. **L. arborea,** L. Bien. with ann. flowering branches, forming a tree-like shrub 3–10 ft. high or less: lvs. long-stalked, 3–9 in. long and as broad, with 5–9 unequally round-toothed lobes, softly downy on both sides, rarely nearly glabrous: fls. pale purple-red with dark purple veins at base, about 2 in. across, borne very abundantly in short leafy racemes or in axillary clusters, short-pedicelled; involucre exceeding calyx: receptacle small, marked with little pits. Eu.—Cult. in the form of var. **variegata,** Bailey, which has mottled lvs.

5. **L. olbia,** L. Shrub 6 ft. high, branched from base: lvs. soft-tomentose, the lowest 5-lobed, the upper 3-lobed with elongate middle lobe, the uppermost oblong, scarcely divided: fls. reddish-purple, 1½–2 in. across, solitary, sessile; involucre nearly as long as calyx; petals emarginate. ("Habitat in Olbia insula Galloprovinciæ," according to Linnæus.) S. Eu.

4. **ALTHÆA,** L. Tall leafy-stemmed herbs, grown in the open garden for their abundant showy fls.; about 15 species in temp. regions of the Old World.—Ann., bien., or per., tomentose or pubescent: lvs. lobed or parted: fls. solitary or racemose, axillary, usually toward the summit of the st., with 6–9 bracts below the calyx which are connate at base; otherwise as in Malva. (Althæ-a: Greek *to cure.*)

A. Plant per.: fls. to 1½ in. across..1. *A. officinalis*
AA. Plant bien. or essentially so: fls. much larger, 3 in. or more across.
B. Lvs. wavy-angled or -lobed..2. *A. rosea*
BB. Lvs. deeply 7-lobed, toothed..3. *A. ficifolia*

1. **A. officinalis,** L. MARSH-MALLOW. Erect per. 3–4 ft. high, tomentose: lvs. ovate or heart-shaped, 3-lobed or undivided: fls. 1–1½ in. across, blush or rose, clustered in the lf.-axils. E. Eu. and occurring in N. Amer. as an escape in marshes near the coast.

2. **A. rosea,** Cav. (*Alcea rosea,* L.). HOLLYHOCK. Bien. to 9 ft.: st. strict and spire-like, hairy: lvs. large and rough, rugose, long-stalked, rounded-heart-shaped, 5–7-lobed or wavy-angled, crenate: fls. 3 in. and more across, nearly sessile, in a long wand-like raceme or spike, in many forms and colors, produced in late summer. China.—Many double forms occur.

3. **A. ficifolia,** Cav. (*Alcea ficifolia,* L.). FIGLEAF or ANTWERP HOLLYHOCK. Bien., 3–6 ft.: lvs. reniform-cordate in outline, somewhat pedately lobed or divided into 7 narrow obtuse irregularly toothed parts: fls. 3 in. and more across, showy, lemon-yellow or orange, single or double, in terminal spikes. Eu.—Not common in cult.

5. **SIDALCEA,** Gray. Annuals or those in cult. perennials, useful for the herbaceous border; about 20 species, natives of W. N. Amer.—Spring or mostly summer-flowering herbs with palmately cleft or parted stipular lvs.: fls. often showy, pink, purple, or white, in terminal racemes or spikes, mostly without bracts or involucre beneath, often unisexual by the abortion of the anthers, the female fls. being smaller; calyx 5-cleft or -parted; petals commonly emarginate or truncate; stamens united into groups in a double series, anthers borne near apex: carpels 5–9, beakless or apiculate, reniform, separating at maturity; stigmas as many as carpels and on inner side of style-branches. (Sidal-cea: compound of Sida and Alcea, related genera.)

A. Fls. white with bluish anthers..1. *S. candida*
AA. Fls. rose or purple.
B. Racemes loose: pubescence stellate and hirsute........................2. *S. malvæflora*
BB. Racemes spike-like: pubescence stellate, without long hairs..............3. *S. oregana*

1. **S. candida,** Gray. Erect per. from more or less creeping rootstocks, the sts. leafy, somewhat branched above, 2–3 ft. high, glabrous or nearly so: radical lvs. nearly orbicular, 2–6 in. across, cordate, obtusely lobed or deeply crenate; st.-lvs. 5–7-parted, the divisions narrow and often toothed or cleft: fls. 1 in. or more across, white, with blue anthers, in an erect spike-like raceme 3–4 in. long; petals ½in. or more long, emarginate. Rocky Mts.

2. **S. malvæflora,** Gray (*Sida malvæflora,* DC.). CHECKERBLOOM. Sts. simple or nearly so, erect or somewhat decumbent, 1–6 ft. high or more, with both stellate and hirsute pubescence: basal lvs. orbicular, 1–3 in. across, incised-crenate, upper ones 5-cleft or 5-divided, the segms. narrow and entire or broader and pinnately lobed: fls. rose or purple, to 2 in. across when fully expanded, in simple loosely fld. racemes; petals about 1 in. long, emarginate. Calif. Var. **Listeri,** Bailey (*S. Listeri,* Vilm.), known also as "Pink Beauty," has satiny pink fls.; it is of European origin.

3. **S. oregana,** Gray (*Sida oregana,* Nutt. *Sidalcea nervata,* A. Nels.). Per. with simple or branched sts. to 5 ft., stellate-pubescent to nearly glabrous: basal lvs. orbicular, to 4 in. across, on petioles to 1 ft. long, lobed and crenate, upper with 3–5 narrow nearly entire lobes: fls. rose-purple, 1–1½ in. across, in spike-like racemes to 1 ft. long; petals ½–¾in. long, emarginate. Mont. to Wash. and Calif.—The hort. form Rosy Gem belongs here.

6. **ANODA,** Cav. Ann. herbs of about 10 species, S. U. S. to S. Amer., sometimes grown in the garden.—Lvs. alternate, hastate or lobed at base: fls. solitary in the axils; involucre lacking; calyx 5-parted; ovary many-celled, with 1 hanging or horizontal seed in each cell, stigmas capitate: carpels forming a disk, the lateral walls becoming absorbed. (Ano-da: Greek *without nodes.*)

A. cristata, Schlecht. (*Sida cristata,* L. *A. lavaterioides,* Medic.?). Plant erect, branched, commonly 1–2 ft. high, with long scattered hairs: lvs. narrowly to broadly triangular in outline, coarsely crenate, often hastate, 1½–2 in. long, the lower sometimes digitately several-lobed; petioles 1–1½ in. long: pedicels slender, commonly 1–3 in. long; fls. lavender to pale blue or purple, 1–2 in. across: carpels 9–20, hispid, not reticulate, each having a projecting tip about 1/16in. long; seed dropped separately from the carpel wall. Tex. and Ariz. to S. Amer.—The plant in cult. as *A. hastata* apparently belongs here; the true *A. hastata*, Cav., is more procumbent, with the lateral walls of the carpels not entirely absorbed so that each seed remains within its carpel and drops with it.

7. **MALVASTRUM,** Gray. FALSE-MALLOW. Some 70–80 or more species in Amer. and S. Afr.; those grown in the fl.-garden are perennials, blooming in hot weather.—Herbs or undershrubs of various habit, sometimes low and diffuse, sometimes tall: lvs. ovate or orbicular, crenate or lobed: fls. scarlet, orange or yellow, short-peduncled or nearly sessile, axillary or in terminal spikes; calyx-like involucre of narrow bracts; calyx 5-cleft; petals emarginate or entire; styles 5 or more, stigmas capitate: carpels few, 1-ovuled, nearly or quite indehiscent and falling away from the axis at maturity. (Malvas-trum: name made from Malva.)

A. Fls. 1–2 in the axils, pedunculate....................1. *M. capense*
AA. Fls. in spikes on nearly naked branches, sessile or very short-peduncled..........2. *M. fasciculatum*

1. **M. capense,** Garke (*Malva capensis*, L.). Shrubby and branchy, 3–4 ft. high, slightly viscid and pubescent: lvs. ovate-oblong, somewhat 3-lobed and -angled, unequally toothed: fls. purple, 1–2 on axillary peduncles longer than petioles; involucre variable in size, the bracts lanceolate to ovate-lanceolate and shorter than the ciliate calyx-lobes: carpels glabrous. S. Afr.

2. **M. fasciculatum,** Greene (*M. Thurberi*, Gray. *Malva fasciculata*, Nutt. *Sphæralcea fasciculata*, Arthur). Sts. 3–15 ft. high, at base woody and often 1 in. or more thick, covered with short dense stellate pubescence: lvs. roundish, mostly subcordate, crenate, obscurely 3–5-lobed or some 3-cleft, 1–2 in. or more diam.: fls. in sessile or short-peduncled spikes or panicled clusters on nearly naked branches; calyx-lobes broad-ovate, twice as long as involucre; petals rose-purple, about ½in. long. Calif.

8. **SPHÆRALCEA,** St. Hil. GLOBE-MALLOW. About 65 species, 4 or 5 of which are S. African, the remainder from warmer regions of N. and S. Amer.; a few grown in greenhouses or in the open in the S.—Shrubs, subshrubs, or herbs of various habit: herbage often covered with gray stellate pubescence: lvs. usually angled or lobed: fls. violet, flesh-colored or red, solitary or in cymose clusters in the axils, or sometimes in terminal racemes or spikes; bracts 3, united at base or distinct; calyx 5-cleft; staminal column divided at top into many filaments; ovary many-celled; stigmas capitate: fr. subglobose, of many compressed 2-valved 2–3-seeded carpels united in a ring around a central axis from which they slowly separate; ovules sometimes 1, but genus distinguished from Malvastrum and Abutilon by carpels differentiated into a dehiscent smooth apical part and an indehiscent reticulate basal part. (Sphæral-cea: Greek for *globe* and *mallow*, the fr. commonly spherical.)

A. Lvs. pedately parted into narrow divisions....................1. *S. coccinea*
AA. Lvs. lobed but not divided.
B. Fls. 2 in. and more across....................2. *S. umbellata*
BB. Fls. 1–1¼ in. across....................3. *S. Munroana*

1. **S. coccinea,** Rydb. (*Cristaria coccinea*, Pursh. *Malvastrum coccineum*, Gray). Per., gray- or whitish-pubescent, with tap-root and usually decumbent sts. 8–20 in. long: lvs. prominently 3-veined from base, ½–2½ in. long and wider than long, pedately parted into narrow lobed or cut divisions: fls. brick-red, ½–¾in. long, short-pedicelled, in short terminal racemes; involucre usually lacking. Man. to Tex. and Ariz.

2. **S. umbellata,** Don (*Malva umbellata*, Cav.). Erect branched shrub or tree 3–20 ft. high, the sts., petioles and infl. densely stellate-tomentose: lvs. long-petioled, rotund-ovate, shortly somewhat 7-lobed, crenate-toothed, cordate, 3–8 in. long, more or less stellate-pubescent especially on the veins: peduncles axillary, usually 3-fld., rarely 2- or 5-fld.; calyx leathery, broad-campanulate, 5-lobed, the lobes semi-ovate, the bracts of the involucre shorter than calyx, distinct and abruptly narrowed into a claw; petals scarlet, white at base, obcordate, 1½ in. long; filaments forming a white column. Mex.—Grown mostly under the name *S. vitifolia*, but *S. vitifolia*, Hemsl., is a synonym of *S. rosea*, Standl., which is distinguished by the ovate bracts of the involucre united below the middle.

3. **S. Munroana,** Spach (*Malva Munroana*, Dougl.). Per. 1–3 ft. high, leafy to the top, minutely stellate-canescent, with large tap-root: lvs. broad at base, 1–2½ in. long and wider than long, obscurely 3–5-lobed, with broad blunt short lobes, crenate-toothed or sometimes incised: fls. scarlet or rose, 1 in. across and ½–¾in. long, short-pedicelled, in axillary or terminal clusters; calyx ¼in. long, not surpassing the depressed fr. (Named for Mr. Munro, gardener of the London Horticultural Society.) B. C. to Ida. and Calif.

9. **ABUTILON,** Mill. Flowering Maple. About 100 species of herbs and shrubs, in many warm countries, prized for ornament.—Lvs. alternate, long-petioled, cordate at base, sometimes lobed, often maple-like: fls. solitary and axillary, drooping, lacking involucres, the calyx 5-cleft and sometimes brightly colored; petals obovate, in some species erect and forming a trumpet-shaped or bell-shaped corolla, white, yellow, reddish, and often handsomely veined; staminal column anther-bearing at apex: fr. aggregate, of several to many 2-valved often beaked carpels in a ring around a central axis; carpels dehiscent nearly to base, with 2 or more ovules. (Abu-tilon: of Arabic origin.)

A. Lvs. not lobed although sometimes angled, mostly cordate (see also no. 7).
B. Corolla and calyx long and narrow . . . . 1. *A. megapotamicum*
BB. Corolla wide-spreading . . . . 2. *A. insigne*
AA. Lvs. prominently lobed, usually vitis-like or grape-like, cordate or truncate at base.
B. Fls. blue (sometimes varying to whitish), very large . . . . 3. *A. vitifolium*
BB. Fls. with yellow or orange ground color, of smaller size (2 in. or less long or across).
C. Lobes of lvs. 3, the side ones often short and small.
D. Middle lobe broadest at base: fls. usually single . . . . 4. *A. pictum*
DD. Middle lobe narrowed at its base: fls. double . . . . 5. *A. pleniflorum*
CC. Lobes of lvs. 5–7, middle one narrowed at base . . . . 6. *A. striatum*
BBB. Fls. of various colors, and lvs. either unlobed or more or less 3-lobed: mixed races . . . . 7. *A. hybridum*

1. **A. megapotamicum,** St. Hil. & Naud. (*A. vexillarium*, Morr.). Attractive species of drooping habit, the young growth slender and glabrous or nearly so: lvs. lance-ovate to narrow arrow-shaped, 1½–3 in. long, not lobed but sometimes obscurely shouldered near base, long-acuminate, shallowly cordate, irregularly crenate-serrate and somewhat jagged, glabrous or puberulent beneath, stipules sometimes large: fls. single in the axils, 1½ to above 2 in. long, including the protruding brush of stamens, hanging and fuchsia-like; calyx red and cylindrical, half or more as long as the yellow petals. S. Amer.; "megapotamicum" means "big river," signifying the Rio Grande of S. Brazil.—Favorite conservatory plant; lvs. often mottled.

2. **A. insigne,** Planch. Young parts stellate-hairy: lvs. ovate-acuminate, 3–4 in. long, cordate, not lobed, crenate-dentate, hairy beneath: fls. large, 2–2½ in. across, hanging, wide open, whitish or rose with rich dark veins, very showy. Colombia.

3. **A. vitifolium,** Presl. Strong large hardy shrub with white-tomentose parts: lvs. orbicular-ovate and cordate in outline, 4–5 in. across, 3–5–7-lobed, the lobes long-pointed, soft-velvety beneath: fls. clustered, open, cup-shaped or broad bell-shaped, 2–3½ in. across, light blue (white fls. are known), veined, the anthers yellow; petals very broad and rounded. Chile.

4. **A. pictum,** Walp. Lvs. 3-lobed, green or variegated, glabrous or pubescent beneath and perhaps on veins above, the middle lobe usually shorter than the main or undivided part of the blade but sometimes equalling it, broadest at the base, margins serrate: fls. about 1¼ in. long, orange or yellow and veined crimson; calyx 1 in. long, brown-velvety-pubescent, the lobes little longer than the tube. S. Brazil, Uruguay, Argentina.

5. **A. pleniflorum,** N. E. Br. Much like no. 4 but lvs. green, glabrous on both surfaces, middle lobe nearly half as long again as undivided part of blade and slightly narrowed or cut in at its base: fls. double (as the name implies). Cultigen; probably to be included with no. 7.

6. **A. striatum,** Dickson. Lvs. green, glabrous above and essentially so beneath, 5–7-lobed, middle lobe twice or more as long as main or undivided part of blade and more than twice as long as broad and also more or less narrowed at its base: fls. 1¾ in. or less long, orange veined dark crimson; calyx thickly brown-pubescent. Guatemala. Var. **Thompsonii,** Veitch, a race with not pubescent lvs. variegated and blotched with yellow; the plant commonly grown as *Thompsonii* is var. **spurium,** Lynch, which differs in pubescent lvs., fls. with less conspicuous veins, and calyx white-pubescent.

7. **A. hybridum,** Voss. The group of common conservatory and bedding abutilons that belong to none of the pure species, representing hybrids and perhaps mutations: lvs. various, unlobed or shallowly 3-lobed or shouldered, green, speckled or blotched, the margins serrate to crenate-dentate, glabrous or pubescent: fls. pink, red, purplish, yellow, white, open-bell-shaped or even more spreading, the prominent calyx mostly close-pubescent.—Here belong such garden vars. as Golden Fleece, Boule de Neige or Snowball, Fire Ball, Savitzii, Caprice.

10. **MALVAVISCUS,** Dill. (*Achania*, Sw.). Shrubs and stout herbs of trop. Amer., one of which reaches the U. S., grown for ornament under glass and in the open far S.—Plant hispid or grayish-pubescent: lvs. cordate or subcordate, shallowly

lobed or unlobed: fls. red and showy, on axillary peduncles, somewhat fuchsia-like as the petals do not spread but are held erect by an auricle toward the base; involucre of 7–12 narrow bracts; anthers exserted on the stipe-like column: fr. of fleshy carpels that are connate into a berry-like body, but that at length becomes dry and separate. (Malvavis-cus: *sticky mallow*, from the fr.)

M. arboreus, Cav. (*M. mollis,* DC.). Low shrub with grayish-pubescent-tomentose parts, the under side of lvs. velvety-tomentose with forked and stellate hairs: lvs. soft to the touch, broad-ovate to nearly orbicular-ovate, 2½–4½ in. across, short-pointed, mostly narrowly cordate, often shouldered or angled above, margins crenate-serrate to nearly entire: fls. 1–2 in. long, scarlet, with rather loose but usually not spreading-tipped very narrow bracts about equalling the calyx. Mex. to Peru and Brazil.—Planted on our southern borders and frequent in greenhouses. Var. **penduliflorus,** Schery (*M. penduliflorus,* DC. *M. grandiflorus,* Hort not HBK.), lvs. mostly ovate-lanceolate, stellate-pubescent above and beneath but not velvety; fls. more than 1½ in. long; Mex. to Colombia. Var. **mexicanus,** Schlecht., lvs. lanceolate to ovate, with the pubescence of the preceding var.; fls. 1–1½ in. long; Tex. to Panama, W. Indies. Var. **Drummondii,** Schery (*M. Drummondii,* Torr. & Gray), lvs. broad, obtusely lobed, mostly with straight hairs on upper surface; lobes of involucre broadest above the middle; fls. about 1 in. long; named for T. Drummond, page 255; Fla. to Tex., Mex.

11. **PAVONIA,** Cav. Herbs or shrubs, sometimes grown under glass or in the open in Calif.; species about 100, Cent. Amer. to Argentina, also in trop. Afr. and Asia to Australia and the Pacific.—Habit various: herbage stellate-tomentose, hispid or glabrescent: lvs. alternate, often angled or lobed: fls. of various colors, solitary or in axillary cymose clusters; involucre consisting of a whorl of 5 to many narrow bracts distinct or more or less connate and calyx-like, usually not clustered; calyx 5-cut or 5-toothed; petals spreading or convolute-connivent; staminal column truncate or 5-dentate; stigmas capitate, twice as many as carpels: carpels 5, 1-ovuled, unarmed or 1–3-awned. (Pavo-nia: J. Pavon, joint author of Ruiz and Pavon's "Floræ Peruviana et Chilensis"; died 1844.)

A. Fls. yellow: carpels spiny . . . . 1. *P. spinifex*
AA. Fls. red: carpels unarmed . . . . 2. *P. hastata*

1. **P. spinifex,** Cav. (*Hibiscus spinifex,* L.). Shrub to 15 ft., with slender st. and few wand-like branches: lvs. ovate, 2–4 in. long, acuminate, subcordate, doubly toothed or crenate, sometimes angled, pubescent on both surfaces: fls. yellow, 1 in. across, not fragrant, on axillary 1-fld. pedicels; bracts 5 or more, linear, somewhat hairy, about equalling calyx; calyx-lobes lanceolate or ovate; corolla open, 1 in. long, the petals obovate, equalled by the staminal column: carpels with 3 diverging barbed spines. (Spinifex: Latin *spiny-fruited.*) S. Amer.

2. **P. hastata,** Cav. Shrubby, 3–6 ft. high, much-branched, minutely grayish-pubescent: lvs. hastate, obtusely dentate, 1–2 in. long: fls. slender-peduncled, axillary; bracts of involucre 5–6, obovate to lanceolate, about equalling the calyx; fls. often cleistogamous; petals ½–1 in. long, pale red with dark maroon spot at base; staminal column short: carpels reticulated, unarmed. S. Amer.; nat. in S. U. S.

12. **MALOPE,** L. Herbs, of the Medit. region, one planted in the fl.-garden.—Ann., glabrous or pilose: lvs. alternate, entire or lobed: fls. violet, pink, or white, large, often showy, solitary, axillary, stalked, subtended by 3 large cordate distinct bracts; calyx 5-parted: carpels numerous, 1-seeded, congested into a head, indehiscent. (Mal-ope: name anciently used for some kind of mallow.)

M. trifida, Cav. Height 2–3 ft.: lvs. 3-nerved, 3-lobed, 1–3 in. long, long-petioled, dentate, glabrous, the lobes acuminate: peduncles axillary, 1-fld.; fls. rose and purple, with usually darker center, 2–3 in. across, blooming most of summer. Spain, N. Afr. Var. **grandiflora,** Paxt. (*M. grandiflora,* Dietr.), has large rose-red fls. veined darker inside.

13. **THESPESIA,** Soland. Trees or tall herbs, suitable for greenhouse cult. or in the open in warm regions; about 10 species in trop. Afr., Asia, and the isls. of the Pacific.—Distinguished from Hibiscus by the confluent stigmas, more woody caps., and obovoid compressed seeds: lvs. alternate, entire or angulate-lobed: fls. usually yellow, showy; bracts 3–5, small or deciduous; calyx truncate, minutely or bristle-toothed, rarely 5-cleft; ovary 5-celled, the cells with few ovules: caps. woody-coriaceous, loculicidally 5-valved or commonly indehiscent. (Thespe-sia: Greek *divine;* application doubtful.)

T. populnea, Soland. (*Hibiscus populneus,* L.). PORTIA-TREE. Small tree 30–40 or even 50 ft. high, with dense top; parts covered with peltate scales: lvs. long-petioled, ovate-cordate, acuminate, 2–5 in. long, somewhat poplar-like: fls. axillary, 2–3 in. across, varying from yellow to purple, blooming all the year in the tropics: caps. depressed-globose, 1–1½ in. across. Old World tropics; nat. S. Fla. and W. Indies.

14. **MONTEZUMA,** Sessé & Moc. Two trees from Cuba and Puerto Rico, one cult. in S. Fla.—The genus is distinguished from Thespesia by the deciduous circumscissile calyx, the 3–4-celled ovary, and glabrous seeds. (Montezu-ma: named for the Aztec ruler, Montezuma, about 1390–1464.)

M. speciosissima, Sessé & Moc. (*Thespesia grandiflora,* DC. *Maga grandiflora,* Urban). Tree to 50 ft., with deeply fissured gray bark: lvs. long-petioled, ovate-cordate, acuminate, 2–8 in. long, scaly beneath: fls. 5–6 in. across, glossy-red and very veiny with bright yellow anthers, on stout peduncles longer than petioles; calyx ¾in. long, scaly: caps. nearly globose, 1½–2 in. across. Puerto Rico.

15. **GOSSYPIUM,** L. COTTON. Over 20 species and many botanical vars., widely spread in trop. regions, several species cult. for the long hair on the seeds employed as fiber, a major field crop from S. E. U. S. west to Imperial Valley of Calif.—Stout ann. or per. shrubs, sometimes tree-like, with large palmately-ribbed or -lobed lvs., the parts often more or less glandular-dotted and also variously punctate; large glands on the under surface of lvs. and on involucres and peduncles often secrete freely: fls. axillary, bisexual, large, white, yellow, or purplish that often change color after opening; involucre of 3 or 5–7 large united or separate bracts that are usually more or less cut or fringed, giving character to the prominent bud or "square"; calyx entire or somewhat 5-lobed; petals large and broad, convolute; ovary single, superior, 3–4- or 5-celled, the ovules 2–7 or more in each cell: fr. a dehiscing caps. or "boll," from which the abundant cotton emerges in the fiber-producing species, comprising 3–5 cells or "locks"; seeds nearly globular, in most species bearing a close wool or fuzz in addition to the fleece, lint, or floss that is removable and forms the cotton of commerce; whether the seed is smooth or fuzzy (aside from the lint) is an important diagnostic character. (Gossyp-ium: an ancient name of the cotton plant.) —A few gossypiums have been grown for ornament, but they are little known in that capacity. The cotton-producing species are much modified by long domestication and hybridizing, and the original specific types are often difficult to make out. While the cottons of the U. S. are mostly of two species (nos. 3 and 4), other specific stocks have probably entered into them or are likely to be grown experimentally. The nativities are more or less conjectural. The following treatment is based on that of J. B. Hutchinson, R. A. Silow, and S. G. Stevens.

A. Involucral bracts entire or coarsely toothed or serrate toward apex, teeth (when present) usually one-half as broad as long or wider.
 B. Bracts of involucre close to the fl., longer than wide, entire or with 3–4 coarse teeth near apex: caps. tapering . . . . . 1. *G. arboreum*
 BB. Bracts flaring divergently from fl., usually wider than long, with usually 6–8 teeth near apex: caps. rounded or shouldered . . . . . 2. *G. herbaceum*
AA. Involucral bracts all coarsely toothed or serrate, the teeth one-third as broad as long or narrower.
 B. Staminal column long, anthers compactly arranged on uniformly short filaments . . 3. *G. barbadense*
 BB. Staminal column short, anthers loosely arranged on filaments of varying length (the upper usually longer than lower) . . . . . 4. *G. hirsutum*

1. **G. arboreum,** L. (*G. obtusifolium,* Roxb. *G. Nanking,* Meyen. *G. indicum,* Lam.). CEYLON COTTON. CHINESE COTTON. TREE COTTON of India. Plants variable in habit and duration, ann. or per. subshrubs or shrubs to 10 ft., herbaceous branches few or absent, twigs and young lvs. variously puberulent to stellate or becoming glabrous. lvs. (3-) 5–7-lobed, often with secondary lobes, broadly cuneate to subcordate or truncate, stipules caducous: involucral bracts triangular, usually longer than broad, close or appressed to the fl., teeth 3–4, apical and less than three times as long as wide: fls. solitary and axillary or in elongated infl., pale yellow with or without purplish blotches to purple-red with darker center, corolla two to three times as long as involucre; staminal column long, antheriferous throughout, filaments short: caps. tapering to apex, mostly 3-celled (rarely 4–5-celled); seeds fuzzy and linted or only linted. Japan, China, India, Arabia, Madagascar, Egypt to Angola.—Cult. in many botanical vars. and races in Asia and Afr., with six geographical races recognized nomenclatorially and having distinct cultural and regional affinities but lacking morphological stability.

2. **G. herbaceum,** L. LEVANT COTTON. Herbaceous ann. forming a subshrub to 4½ ft. with few herbaceous branches, sparsely hairy or rarely becoming glabrous: lvs. coriaceous and reticulate, strongly cordate, the 5–7 lobes extending less than half the depth of the blade, broad-ovate, short-acute, mostly narrowed at base: bracts rounded basally and broadly triangular, flaring widely from fl., mostly wider than long, cordate, margin with 6–8 teeth on each side: fls. medium in size, yellow with purple center: fr. to ¾in. long, rounded without prominent shoulders, beaked, 3–4-celled; seeds large, angled, with gray fuzz and grayish lint. Probably native in Arabia and Asia Minor.—Supposed to enter into some of the short-staple cottons of the U. S.

3. **G. barbadense,** L. (*G. peruvianum*, Cav. *G. vitifolium*, Lam.). SEA-ISLAND COTTON. Shrubby, tomentose or glabrous except on petioles and veins on under surface of mature lvs., the sts. dark colored and more or less angled, becoming woody and the plant attaining 5–8 ft. and more: lvs. as broad as long (sometimes broader), with 3 or 5 long-acuminate lobes extending half or more the depth of the blade, the lateral ones usually spreading and the central one longer or not much if any longer, the lf. base cordate or subcordate: peduncle usually shorter than petiole: bracts of involucre 5 or more, coarsely but not very deeply cut, distinct or only slightly united at base: fls. bright yellow with purplish tinge, short-tubed, commonly about two to three times length of involucre; calyx with large rounded teeth: fr. to 2 in. long, broadest at base, 3- or sometimes 4-valved or -celled and sharp-pointed; seeds ovate and beaked, about ⅓in. long, with gray-green fuzz or nearly or quite naked; lint very fine, from 1½–2 in. long. Trop. Amer., and now widespread.—Yields a very long-staple cotton in both the U. S. and Egypt; sometimes called "tree cotton," although other species equally merit that designation. Var. **brasiliense,** J. B. Hutchins., Silow & Stevens (*G. brasiliense*, Macf. *G. lapideum*, Tussac), is characterized by caps. usually more than 2¾ in. long and broadest at middle (tapering basally), seeds connate in pairs; in addition the strongly cordate lvs. are larger as are the fls.; E. trop. S. Amer., sporadic throughout trop. Amer., Afr. and India.

4. **G. hirsutum,** L. (*G. mexicanum*, Tod.). UPLAND COTTON of the U. S. of which there are short-staple and long-staple races, the latter perhaps hybrids with no. **3.** Mostly ann., shrubby, much-branched, with greenish-red hirsute or pubescent growth, 2–4 or 5 ft. tall: lvs. usually as broad as long and often broader, 3–6 in. across, 3-lobed of which the middle one is about one-half the depth of the blade, the lobes broad at base but abruptly acuminate-pointed, cordate or subcordate-truncate, more or less hirsute and as if dust-coated: fls. white or light yellow turning pink or purple, usually less than twice the length of the deeply lobed bracts: fr. larger than in no. 3, less tapering, 1½–2½ in. long, with usually 4–5 cells; seeds larger, densely covered with a persistent fuzz which is greenish when fresh; lint about ¾–1⅛ in. long in short-staple and 1¼–1⅝ in. long in the long-staples. Probably trop. Amer. Var. **punctatum,** J. B. Hutchins., Silow & Stevens (*G. religiosum*, L. *G. punctatum*, Schumacher & Thonn. *G. latifolium*, Murr. *G. nigrum* var. *punctatum*, Webb.), JAMAICA COTTON, differs primarily in woody per. habit, usually accompanied by many vegetative branches, forming a bushy much-branched shrub, sts. and petioles usually red or reddish-brown; caps. shouldered with usually black-punctate glands; Fla. to Cent. Amer., W. Indies, Bahama Isls.; nat. in W. and N. Afr. and Philippine Isls. to W. Australia where it is more or less cult. as also by the Indians of Ariz., but in Amer. known mostly as a wild or weedy plant.

16. **LAGUNARIA,** Don. Species considered to be only 1, from Australia and S. Pacific isls., planted for ornament in Calif.—Hibiscus-like, but differing in the radiating capitate stigma, usually 3 deciduous bracts in the involucre and the scurfy indumentum. (Laguna-ria: from its resemblance to Lagunæa, now merged in Hibiscus, which commemorates Andres de Laguna, Spanish botanist who died in 1560.)

L. Patersonii, Don. Attractive tree to 50 ft.: lvs. simple and entire, thick and margins somewhat revolute, ovate to oblong, 2–4 in. long, obtuse, rounded or subcuneate at base, gray-scurfy beneath: fls. solitary in axils on very stout pedicels, 2½ in. across, pale rose, the column of stamens not equalling the oblong-obovate scurfy petals; calyx with short triangular teeth: caps. splitting into 5 parts disclosing the bright brown kidney-shaped seeds about ¼in. long. (Seeds long ago sent to England from Norfolk Isl. by Colonel Paterson.)

17. **HIBISCUS,** L. ROSE-MALLOW. If defined broadly, as here intended, the genus has perhaps 200 species; they are herbs, shrubs, and trees, native in trop. and temp. regions around the world, a few yielding food and fiber products but in N. Amer. grown mostly for ornament.—Lvs. palmately veined, lobed, or parted: fls. bisexual, 5-merous, mostly bell-shaped, axillary and paniculate, often very large, scarlet, pink, white, yellow; involucre of few to several broad or narrow bracts; calyx 5-toothed or -parted; staminal column anther-bearing below the truncate or 5-toothed apex; style-branches 5, slender and spreading or becoming so: fr. a dry more or less dehiscent 5-valved caps. (Hibis-cus: ancient Greek and Latin name.)

A. Plant a low diffuse spreading hairy ann. . . . . . 1. *H. Trionum*
AA. Plant strong and erect.
B. Species of annuals and herbaceous perennials.
C. Calyx large and spathe-like, splitting down one side, usually early deciduous.
D. Bracts of involucre linear.
E. Pod 3 in. or less long . . . . . . 2. *H. Abelmoschus*
EE. Pod 4–5 in. or more long . . . . . . 3. *H. esculentus*
DD. Bracts ovate to oblong . . . . . . 4. *H. Manihot*
CC. Calyx regularly 5-lobed or -cleft, not spathe-like.
D. Involucre and calyx red, thick and fleshy, edible . . . . . . 5. *H. Sabdariffa*
DD. Involucre and calyx not so.
E. Sts. prickly . . . . . . 6. *H. cannabinus*
EE. Sts. not prickly.
F. Foliage nearly or quite glabrous.
G. Lvs. divided into narrow divisions . . . . . . 7. *H. coccineus*
GG. Lvs. hastate with short lobe on either side at base, or not lobed . . . 8. *H. militaris*
FF. Foliage prominently pubescent or tomentose, at least underneath.
G. Caps. hirsute . . . . . . 9. *H. grandiflorus*
GG. Caps. glabrous.
H. Branches of style pubescent . . . . . . 10. *H. palustris*
HH. Branches of style glabrous . . . . . . 11. *H. Moscheutos*
BB. Species of shrubs and small trees.
C. Involucre an 8–10-toothed cup . . . . . . 12. *H. tiliaceus*
CC. Involucre of separate bracts.
D. Fls. yellow . . . . . . 13. *H. calycinus*
DD. Fls. white, pink, red.
E. Lvs. linear or lanceolate, or parted into lobes of such shape . . . . . . 14. *H. heterophyllus*
EE. Lvs. broad.
F. Petals deeply cut and fringed . . . . . . 15. *H. schizopetalus*
FF. Petals not lobed or only shallowly emarginate.
G. Margins of lvs. entire or nearly so . . . . . . 16. *H. Arnottianus*
GG. Margins dentate or lobed, or both.
H. Staminal column long-exserted . . . . . . 17. *H. Rosa-sinensis*
HH. Staminal column not surpassing the corolla.
I. With pubescent lvs . . . . . . 18. *H. mutabilis*
II. With glabrous lvs . . . . . . 19. *H. syriacus*

1. H. Trionum, L. (*H. africanus*, Hort. *Trionum Trionum*, Woot. & Standl.). Flower-of-an-Hour. Depressed branching hairy ann. 1–2 ft. high, some of the branches becoming prostrate, sometimes grown in the fl.-garden for the solitary sulfur-yellow or white dark-centered fls. 2–3 in. across that close in shadow: lvs. 3-lobed or most of them 3–5-parted, middle one much the largest, all coarsely toothed: pedicel elongating in fr., the setose papery dark-striped calyx becoming inflated, bracts linear. (The name Trionum is derived from the 3-lobed lvs.) Cent. Afr.; now a weed in N. Amer.

2. **H. Abelmoschus,** L. (*Abelmoschus moschatus*, Medic.). Musk-Mallow. Hispid ann. or bien., 2–6 ft., grown in warm countries for the musk-fragrant seeds and the showy yellow crimson-centered axillary fls. which are about 4 in. across: lvs. various, usually with deep divaricate narrow strongly and irregularly toothed lobes, but some of them shallowly lobed and maple-like, all sparsely hairy on both surfaces: bracts linear, much shorter than the spathaceous many-toothed caducous calyx: fr. oblong-acuminate, hairy, 3 in. or less long. (Abelmoschus refers to the musky seeds, part at least of the word being Arabic.) India.

3. **H. esculentus,** L. (*Abelmoschus esculentus*, Moench). Okra. Gumbo. Stout nearly glabrous ann. 1½–6 ft. and more, grown as a garden vegetable for the soft immature edible pods: lvs. large, often 12 in. and more across, cordate-ovate or broader in outline, variously 3–9-lobed or -divided, lobes either narrow or broad, margins coarsely toothed: bracts subulate, ½–1 in. long, falling from the fr.: fls. solitary and axillary, yellow with a reddish center, 2–3 in. long: fr. a long ribbed beaked light-hairy or nearly glabrous pod with valves becoming revolute, 4–12 in. long and woody at maturity. Old World tropics.

4. **H. Manihot,** L. (*Abelmoschus Manihot*, Medic.). Tall rather coarse ann. or per., 3–9 ft., sparsely setose, grown often as an ann. for its showy pale yellow or whitish fls. 4–9 in. across with a dark brown center, clustered at the ends of branches: lvs. large, ovate to nearly orbicular in outline, 6–12 in. or more across, palmately divided into 5–9 long narrow lobes of variable widths and dentation, petioles long: bracts ovate to narrow-oblong, shorter than the spathaceous nearly entire calyx: fr. oblong, hispid, 2–3 in. long. (The name Manihot probably suggests the resemblance of the lvs. to those of the cassavas or manihots.) E. Asia.

5. **H. Sabdariffa,** L. Roselle. Jamaica Sorrel. Strong ann. 5–7 ft., making a broad clump with branches from the base, the sts. reddish and nearly or quite glabrous, grown far S. and in the tropics for the edible acid fleshy calyces and involucres taken before they or the pods develop woody matter: root-lvs. ovate and undivided; st.-lvs. 3–4 in. across, 3-lobed or -parted and the side lobes sometimes again lobed, the lobes 1 in. or more broad and crenate-serrate or -dentate: fls. axillary, solitary and nearly sessile; corolla yellow, twice as long as thick red calyx and involucre: fr. ovoid, pubescent, ½–¾in. long. (Sabdariffa: Turkish name.) Old World tropics.

6. **H. cannabinus,** L. Ann. or per. 1–6 ft. and more high, mostly with glabrous but prickly sts., a source of fiber in Asia, more or less mentioned in N. Amer.: lower lvs. cordate and not lobed, upper ones deeply digitately lobed into narrow serrate lobes or divisions: fls. large, yellow or red with crimson center, axillary; sepals lanceolate and bristly; bracts narrow, bristly: fr. nearly spherical and bristly, ½–¾in. long. Old World tropics.

7. **H. coccineus,** Walt. Glaucous and glabrous per. 3–10 ft. high, grown for its large rose-red or crimson fls. in the upper axils 5–6 in. across: lvs. digitately or somewhat pedately 3–5-parted, the divisions slender, acuminate, remotely toothed: bracts very narrow, almost setaceous, 1 in. long more or less, shorter than the large ovate-lanceolate pointed calyx-lobes; petals obovate and much narrowed toward base so that they stand well apart; column very long: fr. ovoid, about 1 in. long, acute. Swamps, Ga. and Fla.

8. **H. militaris,** Cav. Nearly or quite glabrous somewhat glaucous herbaceous per., 4–6 ft., sometimes planted for its white, blush, or pink purple-centered fls. 3–5 in. across, borne along the st. in the axils: lvs. hastate, with 2 short lobes at base and oblong-lanceolate or triangular-lanceolate long-acuminate serrate middle lobe 2–5 in. long; upper lvs. less lobed: bracts linear, ¾in. or less long, much shorter than the large triangular-pointed calyx-lobes: fr. 1 in. long more or less, inclosed in calyx. (The spear-shaped lvs. give the plant a military look.) Minn. to Fla. and La.

9. **H. grandiflorus,** Michx. Velvety-tomentose per. to 6 ft. or more: lvs. usually broader than long, hastately 3-lobed, lobes irregularly toothed: fls. pale pink with red base, to 6 in. long; bracts linear: caps. ovoid, 1–2 in. long, hirsute. Marshes, Ga., Fla. to Miss.

10. **H. palustris,** L. Per. 3–8 ft. high: lvs. broad-ovate, 3–7 in. long, usually 3-lobed, crenate-dentate, white-tomentose beneath: fls. pink, purple or white, mostly with crimson eye, 4–8 across; bracts linear; branches of style pubescent: caps. nearly globose, ¾–1 in. long, obtuse or abruptly tipped, glabrous. Swamps, Mass. to Va. west to Mich. and Ind.—The great-fld. garden mallows are forms or derivatives of this species.

11. **H. Moscheutos,** L. (*H. oculiroseus*, Britt.). This species has been confused with *H. palustris*, but differs in narrower usually unlobed lvs., peduncles often fused with petioles one-third or more their length, white or cream fls. with red or purple eye, branches of style glabrous, and larger tapering caps. (Moscheutos: an ancient name adopted by Linnæus; the herbalists thought this plant to be the Rosa Moscheutos of Pliny.) Swamps, Md. to Fla. west to Ind. and Ala.

12. **H. tiliaceus,** L. (*Paritium tiliaceum*, St. Hil. *H. elatus*, Sw. *P. elatum*, Don). Mahoe. Cuban Bast. Shrub or tree, 10–35 ft.: lvs. nearly orbicular, 3–8 in. across, abruptly acuminate, cordate, entire or obscurely crenate, very veiny and somewhat hairy or pubescent beneath: involucre tubular and deeply about 10-cleft; petals 2–3 in. long, yellow: fr. ovoid and tomentose, ½–¾in. long; seeds glabrous or pubescent. Tropics.

13. **H. calycinus,** Willd. (*H. chrysanthus*, Hort.). Pubescent small slender shrub, grown in Calif. for the lemon-yellow dark-centered axillary fls. 2–3 in. across: lvs. round-cordate, strongly 5–7-nerved, angled or shouldered, about 3–4 in. across, crenate, somewhat hairy: bracts 5, ovate and awl-pointed, about equalling the ovate-acute calyx-lobes: fr. tomentose. S. Afr.

14. **H. heterophyllus,** Vent. Tall shrub with frequently prickly branches, pubescent in infl. and on young growth, hairy on petals and stellate-tomentose on calyx, otherwise mostly glabrous, grown in S. Calif. for the white fls. 3–4 in. long with crimson or purple eye: lvs. variable, from simple to deeply parted, the simple ones and the lobes linear to long-lanceolate (lobes strongly ascending with narrow sinuses), more or less serrulate, light colored and perhaps scattered-hairy beneath: bracts very narrow, shorter than broad long-tapering calyx-lobes: fr. hairy. Australia.

15. **H. schizopetalus,** Hook. f. Large glabrous distinct shrub with many slender drooping branches, planted in warm countries for the red or orange-red fls. 2–3 in. across that have handsomely multisect recurved petals and that hang on very long jointed peduncles: lvs. ovate-elliptic, 2–3 in. long, acute or acuminate, dentate: calyx tubular, with short broad teeth; column long-exserted: fr. long. E. trop. Afr.

16. **H. Arnottianus,** Gray. A large shrub and sometimes a small tree native in Hawaii and to be expected under cult. in Calif. for its solitary axillary pure white fls., or white with pinkish veins, the petals 3–4 in. and more long: lvs. ovate, 4–6 in. long, entire, rather thick or stiff: bracts 5–7, triangular or lanceolate, ¼–⅓in. long, much shorter than the tubular shortly 5-toothed calyx: column long-exserted, the anthers on long spreading filaments: fr. as long as the calyx. (Dedicated to George A. W. Arnott, page 39.)

17. **H. Rosa-sinensis,** L. Rose-of-China (as the name means). Chinese Hibiscus. Becoming a large shrub or even tree-like and 25–30 ft. high, nearly glabrous, grown abundantly in subtrop. and trop. countries for its profuse large very showy fls. and in glasshouses for the summer bloom: lvs. broad-ovate to narrow-ovate, 3–4½ in. long, abruptly pointed or acuminate, not lobed, the margins variously toothed, notched, or almost entire except near apex, glabrous or with few scattered hairs on veins beneath: fls. in upper axils on short or long jointed spreading or declined peduncles; bracts linear, sepa-

rate and more or less loose, shorter than the ovate- or lance-pointed lobes of the half-cut calyx; corolla 4–6 in. across with flaring limb, rose-red but now varying into white, buff, and many other shades, sometimes double; column conspicuously exserted: fr. ovoid, beaked. Asia, probably China, but now conspicuous in all warm countries and grown under many varietal and Latin names.—Apparently hybridizes with *H. schizopetalus*, the forms being recognised by drooping long-peduncled fls. with more or less crisped corollas and short-toothed calyx. Some forms bear nearly entire lvs. and erect fls., perhaps hybrids. Var. **Cooperi**, Nichols. (*H. Cooperi*, Hort.), is a state with narrow more or less irregular lvs. splashed and blotched with white and crimson; fls. small, scarlet, usually distorted or imperfect; grown under glass for the foliage.

18. **H. mutabilis**, L. Cotton-Rose. Confederate-Rose. Pubescent to tomentose large shrub or tree-like, frequently planted in trop. and subtrop. regions for the fls. 3–4 in. across that open white or pink but change to deep red at night: lvs. large, broad-ovate to nearly round-ovate in outline, 4–8 in. across, 3–5-lobed to one-half or less depth of the blade, lobes triangular-acute or acuminate, cordate at base, shallowly crenate-dentate, lightly hairy above but pubescent or tawny-tomentose beneath: fls. axillary and clustered at tips, the corolla hairy outside, the broad-ovate calyx-lobes and very narrow bracts tomentose: fr. globose, about 1 in. long, hairy. China.

19. **H. syriacus**, L. Rose-of-Sharon. Shrubby Althea of gardens. Nearly or quite glabrous erect-growing shrub, sometimes almost tree-form, 10–20 ft., hardy in the northern states and much grown for its summer and autumn bloom of open-bell-shaped rose or purple axillary short-peduncled fls. 2–3 in. across that vary to cream-color, white, bluish, and otherwise, often double: lvs. rather small, triangular-ovate or rhombic, 2–3 in. long, strongly 3-ribbed, most of the lower ones 3-lobed (or with 2 side lobes), the margins variously toothed and notched: bracts linear, about the length of the triangular rather short calyx-lobes: fr. oblong-ovoid, about 1 in. long, abruptly short-beaked. E. Asia.—Cult. under hort. varietal names such as: **amplissimus**, purple-pink, double; **anemonæflorus**, pink, double; **ardens**, rose-violet, double; **cœlestis**, purplish-blue; **pæoniflorus**, pink marked with red, double; **pulcherrimus**, pink and white, double; **purpureus**, purple, semi-double; **ruber**, deep pink, single; **totus-albus**, pure white, single; **variegatus**, lvs. variegated, fls. purple, double.

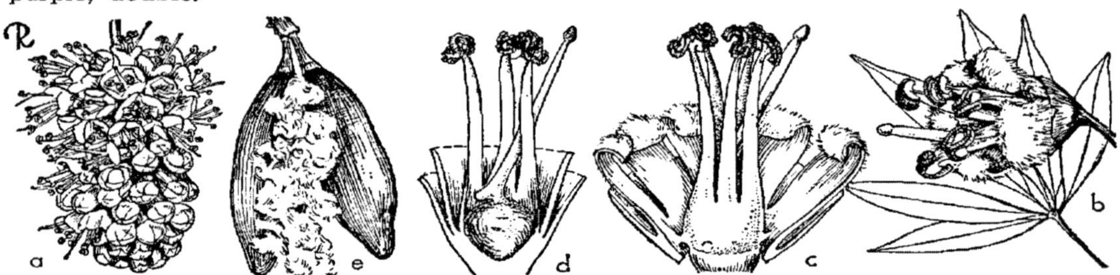

Fig. 123. Bombacaceæ. *Ceiba pentandra:* a, inflorescence, × ¼; b, flower, × 1 and leaf, × ¼; c, flower, perianth partially excised, × 1; d, same, stamens removed in part, × 1; e, fruit, × ½.

123. BOMBACACEÆ. BOMBAX FAMILY

About 20 genera and 150 species of trees in the tropics around the world.—Lvs. entire or digitate, the stipules deciduous: fls. bisexual, solitary or panicled, regular; calyx mostly 5-toothed, valvate; petals 5, sometimes adnate at base to stamen-tube; stamens 5 to many, separate or monadelphous, with long filaments and short anthers, the pollen smooth; ovary superior, 2–5-celled with 2 to many axile ovules in each cell, the simple style with 2–5 stigmas: fr. dry or fleshy, dehiscent or indehiscent.

A. Staminal column divided into 5 parts........1. Ceiba
AA. Staminal column divided into numerous filaments.
  B. Calyx 5-parted: fr. indehiscent........2. Adansonia
  BB. Calyx truncate: fr. dehiscent........3. Pachira

1. **CEIBA**, Adans. Large deciduous trees of about 12 species, mostly in trop. Amer. but extending to Asia and Afr.; one species planted as a shade tree in the tropics and the cotton-like material in the seed-pods furnishing the "kapok" of commerce.—Trunk buttressed at base, branches and young trunks spiny: lvs. alternate, petioled, digitately compound with 3–7 entire lfts.: fls. large, solitary or in axillary clusters; calyx irregularly 5-lobed; petals tomentose outside; stamens

monadelphous, the tube divided at apex into 5 parts, each bearing 2–3 twisting 1-celled anthers; ovary 5-celled: fr. a leathery caps. loculicidally dehiscent by 5 valves, the seeds embedded in the cotton-like fiber. (Cei-ba: aboriginal name.)

C. pentandra, Gaertn. (*Bombax pentandrum,* L. *C. Casearia,* Medic. *Eriodendron anfractuosum,* DC.). SILK-COTTON-TREE. To 100 ft. or more, having immense horizontal far-reaching branches and wide-flung thin buttresses or flanges sometimes prominent for 30 ft. or more: lfts. 6–9, arising from a nearly circular plate or disk at top of petiole, lanceolate or oblong, acuminate, 4–6 in. long, undulate, glabrous: fls. white or rose, solitary and sessile, fascicled, or in dense clusters to 8 in. long, often before the lvs.; petals densely white-woolly outside, about 1 in. long, the stamens slightly exserted: caps. oblong, 3–6 in. long, woody. Tropics of Amer., Asia, Afr.

2. **ADANSONIA,** L. Large trees of about 10 species in Afr. and Australia, one widely planted for shade in the tropics.—Lvs. digitately compound: fls. large, solitary in the axils, drooping on long peduncles; calyx 5-parted, leathery, silky-hairy within; petals 5; stamens monadelphous, the tube divided about half way into numerous filaments bearing 1 kidney-shaped anther; ovary 5–10-celled with many ovules in each cell: fr. woody, oblong, indehiscent; seeds kidney-shaped, surrounded by pithy substance. (Adanso-nia: named for Michel Adanson, 1727–1806, French naturalist.)

A. digitata, L. BAOBAB. MONKEY-BREAD TREE. To 60 ft., with relatively short trunk to 30 ft. diam. and spread of branches to 30 ft. or more: lvs. on petioles 4–5 in. long, of 3–7 oblong acuminate lfts. 3–5 in. long, pubescent beneath: fls. before the lvs., white with purplish stamens, 5–6 in. across, on peduncles twice as long as lvs.; petals becoming reflexed: fr. 4–12 in. long, densely tomentose. Trop. Afr.

3. **PACHIRA,** Aubl. Trees native in trop. Amer., of perhaps 20 species, grown in warm regions for the showy fls.—Lvs. digitately compound, the lfts. entire: fls. very large, solitary in the axils; calyx tubular, truncate; petals linear or linear-oblong; stamens monadelphous, with long tube which divides into 5 branches which are again divided into numerous long unequal filaments: fr. a woody caps. loculicidally dehiscent by 5 valves, each cell with several seeds coated in fleshy tissue. (Pachi-ra: native Guiana name.)

A. Caps. nearly globose: fls. to 9 in. long........................1. *P. macrocarpa*
AA. Caps. ovoid: fls. to 14 in. long........................2. *P. aquatica*

1. **P. macrocarpa,** Walp. (*Carolinea macrocarpa,* Schlecht. & Cham. *P. fastuosa,* Decne.). Lfts. 5–7, oblong to obovate, 3–8 in. long, glabrous: fls. to 9 in. long, with linear white or pink petals pubescent outside and purplish filaments, the staminal tube to 2 in. long: caps. nearly globose, to 9 in. long and 8 in. diam. Mex. to Costa Rica.

2. **P. aquatica,** Aubl. (*Carolinea princeps,* L. f.). Lfts. 5–7, oblong-lanceolate, 4–12 in. long, glabrous: fls. to 14 in. long, with linear pinkish or purplish petals pubescent outside and red stamens, the staminal tube $2\frac{1}{2}$–4 in. long: caps. ovoid, to 15 in. long and 5 in. diam. Trop. Amer.

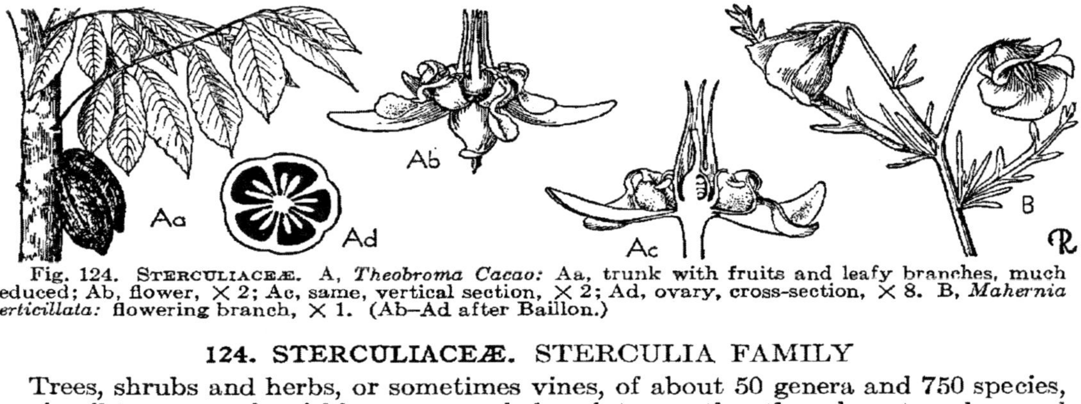

Fig. 124. STERCULIACEÆ. A, *Theobroma Cacao:* Aa, trunk with fruits and leafy branches, much reduced; Ab, flower, × 2; Ac, same, vertical section, × 2; Ad, ovary, cross-section, × 8. B, *Mahernia verticillata:* flowering branch, × 1. (Ab–Ad after Baillon.)

124. STERCULIACEÆ. STERCULIA FAMILY

Trees, shrubs and herbs, or sometimes vines, of about 50 genera and 750 species, nearly all trop., one furnishing cocoa and chocolate, another the cola nut, and several grown for ornament.—Lvs. alternate, simple or digitate, the stipules mostly deciduous: fls. bisexual or unisexual, usually regular, clustered or rarely solitary; calyx deeply 5-cleft, valvate; petals 5 or 0, hypogynous; stamens 5 or more, in 2 whorls, those opposite the sepals staminodia or lacking, those opposite petals anther-bearing and more or less connate into a tube; ovary superior, usually 5-celled with 2 to many axile ovules in each cell (sometimes 3–10-celled); styles 2–5, distinct or united: fr. dry, usually dehiscent. Differs from Malvaceæ in 2-celled rather than 1-celled anthers, and in other ways.

A. Anther-bearing stamens 2–5.
  B. Staminal tube with 5 petal-like staminodia; anthers 2–3: fr. indehiscent........1. THEOBROMA
  BB. Staminal tube without staminodia; anthers 5: fr. dehiscent.
    C. Lvs. (in ours) deeply cut: petals present..........2. MAHERNIA
    CC. Lvs. shallowly lobed: petals absent but calyx petal-like..........3. FREMONTIA
AA. Anther-bearing stamens 10–25.
  B. Petals present: fls. always bisexual..........4. DOMBEYA
  BB. Petals lacking: fls. unisexual or bisexual.
    C. Anthers crowded without order.
      D. Fr. woody, not dehiscing until ripe..........5. BRACHYCHITON
      DD. Fr. membranaceous, usually dehiscing long before maturity into lf.-like open carpels..........6. FIRMIANA
    CC. Anthers in a single ring..........7. COLA

1. **THEOBROMA,** L. Small trees native in trop. Amer., of about 20 species, extensively grown for the seed from which commercial chocolate and cocoa are produced.—Lvs. large, simple, entire, leathery and strongly veined: fls. bisexual, small, in few- or many-fld. axillary cymes or borne laterally on the branches or trunk; petals hooded at base; stamen-tube short, with 5 petaloid elongated staminodia and 2–3 sessile anthers; ovary sessile, 5-celled and each cell many-ovuled, the stigma 5-lobed: fr. a large woody drupe or pod, the numerous seeds imbedded in the pulp. (Theobro-ma: Greek *food of the gods*.)

T. Cacao, L. CACAO. Wide-branching evergreen tree to 25 ft. or more; twigs pubescent: lvs. oblong-oval or elliptic-oblong, to 1 ft. long, short-petioled, abruptly acuminate: fls. in fascicles directly on bark of trunk and main branches, on slender pedicels ½in. or more long, ½–¾in. across, calyx rose-colored, corolla yellowish: fr. elliptic-ovoid, 1 ft. or less long and about 4 in. diam., 5-ribbed, red, yellow, purplish or brown, the walls thick and hard, the flat seeds about 1 in. across imbedded in white or pinkish pulp. Cent. and S. Amer.

2. **MAHERNIA,** L. Per. herbs or subshrubs of more than 30 species in Afr., one often grown in greenhouses or hanging-baskets.—Lvs. usually deeply incised: fls. nodding, on usually 2-fld. peduncles, terminal or opposite the lvs.; calyx campanulate; petals 5, flat; stamens 5, opposite petals, the filaments dilated at middle, staminodia 0; ovary 5-celled with 5 styles more or less united at base, cells many-ovuled: fr. a caps. loculicidally dehiscent by 5 valves. (Maher-nia: anagram of *Hermannia*.)

M. verticillata, L. (*Hermannia verticillata*, Schum. *M. odorata*, Hort.). HONEY-BELL. A procumbent straggly subshrub with ascending or erect scabrous branches to 1 ft. high: lvs. small, to 1 in. long, pinnately cut into linear divisions, the stipules deep-cut and resembling the lvs.: peduncles 2-fld., subtended by linear distinct bracts; fls. about ½in. long, very fragrant, honey-yellow, blooming freely in winter and spring. S. Afr.

3. **FREMONTIA,** Torr. (*Fremontodendron*, Cov.). Evergreen shrubs of 3 species in Calif. and Mex., planted for ornament in the S.—Lvs. alternate, shallowly lobed or nearly entire, stellate-pubescent: fls. showy, solitary in the axils, short-peduncled; calyx deeply 5-parted and petal-like; petals lacking; stamens 5, united at base into short tube; ovary 5-celled with many ovules in each cell, style simple: fr. a hairy caps. loculicidally dehiscent by 4–5 valves. (Fremon-tia: named for General John Charles Fremont, 1813–1890, explorer of the West.)

A. Fls. yellow; gland near base of calyx-lobes hairy..........1. *F. californica*
AA. Fls. orange; gland near base of calyx-lobes hairless..........2. *F. mexicana*

1. **F. californica,** Torr. FLANNEL-BUSH. Spreading shrub to 15 ft.: lvs. orbicular-ovate, ½–1 in. long, obtuse, often shallowly 3-lobed, densely gray-tomentose beneath: fls. lemon-yellow, 2–2½ in. across, calyx-lobes with hairy gland near base: caps. ovate, about 1 in. long. Calif.

2. **F. mexicana,** Macb. (*Fremontodendron mexicanum,* Davidson). Differs from *F. californica* in straighter habit, orange-colored fls., and gland near base of calyx-lobes hairless. S. and Lower Calif.

4. **DOMBEYA,** Cav. Probably 100 species of African shrubs or small trees, sometimes grown out-of-doors in warm regions or a few occasionally cult. in the greenhouse.—Lvs. palmately-nerved, often cordate, angled or lobed: fls. rather showy, in axillary or terminal loose cymes or crowded into dense heads, with 3 small unilateral sometimes united bractlets; calyx-lobes at length reflexed, persistent; petals 5, flat; stamens united into a short or elongated tube bearing at apex 5 staminodia alternating with 10–25 anther-bearing stamens which are assembled into 2–5 bundles; ovary sessile, 2–5-celled and each cell 2- or more-ovuled, the 5 styles distinct or connate at base: fr. a caps. loculicidally dehiscent by 5 valves. (Dombey-a: after Joseph Dombey, 1742–1795, French botanist.)

A. Infl. on long pendulous peduncles; staminal tube half or more as long as petals.......1. *D. Wallichii*
AA. Infl. on erect peduncles; stamens united only at base.
B. Lvs. glabrous beneath, slightly pubescent above: fls. 1–3 to a cluster............2. *D. natalensis*
BB. Lvs. pubescent on both sides: fls. 5 to many to a cluster.
C. Ovary 5-celled: lvs. 3-lobed..........3. *D. calantha*
CC. Ovary 3-celled: lvs. entire..........4. *D. spectabilis*

1. **D. Wallichii,** Daydon Jackson (*Astrapæa Wallichii,* Lindl.). Tree to 30 ft.: lvs. broad-ovate, 6–10 in. and more across, acuminate, cordate, dentate, densely tomentose beneath with stellate hairs, 7–9-nerved from base, the stipules large and leafy: fls. scarlet or pink, in dense heads borne on hairy pendulous peduncles 6–14 in. long subtended by large ovate calyculate bracts; petals about 1 in. long; staminal tube nearly length of petals; ovary 5-celled with 2 ovules in each cell. (Named for Nathaniel Wallich, page 53.) Madagascar.—A hybrid between this species and *D. Mastersii* is **D. Cayeuxii,** André, with pendulous heads of pink fls., petals ½–⅔in. long.

2. **D. natalensis,** Sond. Small tree: lvs. orbicular, 1–2½ in. long, cordate, acuminate, irregularly toothed, palmately veined, minutely pubescent above, glabrous beneath: fls. white, fragrant, in small umbel-like clusters, the peduncles slender and pubescent, 1–2 in. long, the involucral bracts linear; petals about ⅔in. long; staminal tube short; ovary 3–5-celled with 2–4 ovules in each cell. Natal.

3. **D. calantha,** Schum. Shrub to 12 ft.: lvs. 3- or sometimes 5- lobed, the middle lobe largest, acuminate, to 1 ft. across, coarsely toothed, cordate, 7-nerved from base, pubescent on both sides: fls. rose, 1½ in. across, in corymbs borne on pubescent peduncles 6–8 in. long; petals obliquely obovate, 1 in. long; staminal tube short; ovary 5-celled with 6–8 ovules in each cell. Cent. Afr.

4. **D. spectabilis,** Bojer. Small tree to 10 ft. or more: lvs. orbicular, 4–5 in. long, cordate, unequally undulate but not dentate, rusty or white-tomentose beneath with stellate hairs, sparsely hairy above: fls. white, ¾in. across, the infl. much-branched and many-fld., on pubescent peduncles about 1½ in. long; involucral bracts lance-ovate; staminal tube short; ovary 3-celled with 2 ovules in each cell. Madagascar, trop. Afr.

5. **BRACHYCHITON,** Schott & Endl. BOTTLE-TREE. About 11 species of Australian trees, grown for ornament in warm climates.—Lvs. alternate, entire or palmately lobed: fls. unisexual or bisexual, in panicles or rarely racemes, mostly axillary; calyx usually campanulate; petals 0; stamens united into column which bears a head of 10–15 sessile anthers; ovary with 5 cells each 2- to many-ovuled, the style united under the peltate or lobed stigma: fr. a woody follicle, not dehiscing until ripe; seeds and inside of fr. usually hairy, often cohering; radicle next the hilum. (Brachych-iton: from Greek, referring to the short imbricated hairs and scales.)

A. Fls. bright scarlet..........1. *B. acerifolium*
AA. Fls. yellowish-white, sometimes spotted with red..........2. *B. populneum*

1. **B. acerifolium,** F. Muell. (*Sterculia acerifolia,* Cunn.). FLAME-TREE. Glabrous tree to 60 ft. or more: lvs. often 8–10 in. across, long-petioled, deeply 5- or 7-lobed, the lobes oblong-lanceolate to rhomboid, glabrous and shining: fls. brilliant scarlet, the glabrous calyx ¾in. long; ovary short-stalked, glabrous: fr. to 4 in. long, long-stalked, glabrous. New S. Wales.

2. **B. populneum,** R. Br. (*Sterculia diversifolia,* Don). KURRAJONG. Tree to 60 ft., glabrous except the fls.: lvs. various, ovate to ovate-lanceolate and entire or more or less deeply 3- or 5-lobed, 2–3 in. long, long-petioled, acuminate, glabrous and shining: fls. yellowish-white, often dark-spotted, reddish and glabrous inside, tomentose outside when young, ¾in. across; ovary slightly tomentose: fr. ½–3 in. long, glabrous, on stalks 1–2 in. long. Queensland to Victoria.

6. **FIRMIANA,** Marsili. About 10 species native in Asia, one planted S. for a lawn and shade tree.—Closely allied to Brachychiton but differing in its membranaceous fr. which usually dehisces long before maturity into lf.-like carpels, the seeds not cohering to the walls of the fr., and the lateral radicle. (Firmia-na: after Karl Joseph Graf v Firmian, 1718–1782, once governor-general of Lombardy.)

F. simplex, W. F. Wight (*Hibiscus simplex*, L. *F. platanifolia*, R. Br. *Sterculia platanifolia*, L. f.). CHINESE PARASOL-TREE. PHOENIX-TREE. Deciduous smooth-barked round-headed tree to 50 ft.: lvs. cordate-orbicular, palmately 3–5-lobed, the lobes sharp-pointed, glabrous or tomentose beneath, reaching 1 ft. or more in diam.: fls. in terminal panicles 1–1½ ft. long, small, greenish, the calyx-lobes reflexed: fr. 4–5 in. long, dehiscing into 4 lf.-like carpels which bear wrinkled globose seeds on their margins. China, Japan.

7. **COLA,** Schott. More than 100 species have been described from trop. Afr., one grown in the American tropics for the cola nut, the kernel being used in medicine and for stimulating drinks.—Lvs. entire or lobed: fls. unisexual or bisexual, in axillary fascicles or panicles; calyx campanulate; petals 0; stamens united into a short column, bearing at top a ring of 10–12 sessile anthers; ovary 3–10-celled with as many styles as carpels, the cells many-ovuled: fr. of 4–5 leathery or woody follicles. (Co-la: native name.)

C. acuminata, Schott & Endl. COLA or GOORA NUT. Evergreen tree to nearly 40 ft.: lvs. 6–8 in. long, leathery, obovate, acute, entire, the young lvs. often once or twice cut at base: fls. in corymbose panicles, ½in. across, yellow, the tube of calyx green: fr. 5–6 in. long; seeds 1½–2 in. long.

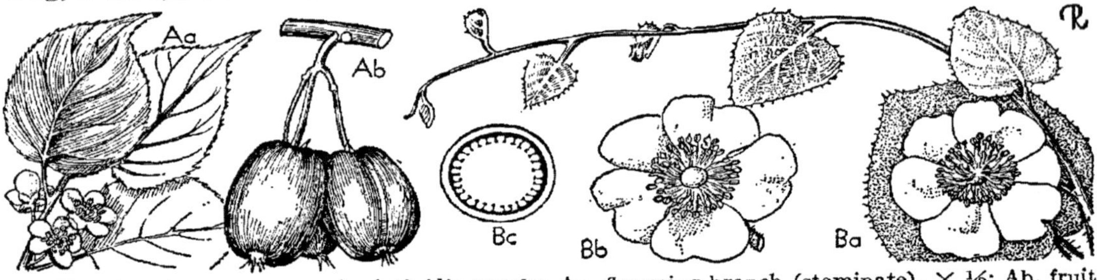

Fig. 125. ACTINIDIACEÆ. A, *Actinidia arguta:* Aa, flowering branch (staminate), × ½; Ab, fruit, × ½. B, *A. chinensis:* Ba, flowering branch, perfect flower, × ½; Bb, staminate flower, × ½; Bc, ovary, cross-section, × 3.

125. ACTINIDIACEÆ. ACTINIDIA FAMILY

About 300 species in 4 genera of trees and shrubs, often climbing, distributed throughout the tropics.—Lvs. alternate, entire or dentate: fls. bisexual, or plant sometimes polygamous or diœcious, the infl. various; sepals 5, imbricated, persistent and often enlarged after flowering; petals 5, imbricated, deciduous; stamens very numerous, seldom as few as 10, free or variously united at base; ovary of 1 to many carpels more or less united or the pistils distinct, the axile ovules 1 to many, with as many styles as carpels, usually free and spreading with simple terminal stigma, cells 5 or more or seemingly 1 by development of septæ: fr. a hard dehiscent caps., or fleshy and berry-like and indehiscent.—Formerly called Dilleniaceæ.

ACTINIDIA, Lindl. Climbing shrubs of over 20 species in E. Asia to the Himalayas, planted for the attractive foliage.—Lvs. alternate, entire or serrate, pinnately veined, the minute stipules caducous: plant polygamous or diœcious: fls. in axillary cymes or solitary; stamens many: fr. a many-celled berry, with numerous small seeds imbedded in pulp. (Actinid-ia: from Greek for *ray*, referring to the radiate styles.)

A. Branchlets and under surface of lvs. glabrous or pubescent only on the veins.
  B. Anthers dark purple: lvs. never variegated . . . . 1. *A. arguta*
  BB. Anthers yellow: lvs. often variegated.
    C. Pith of branches white, solid . . . . 2. *A. polygama*
    CC. Pith of branches brown, lamellate . . . . 3. *A. Kolomikta*
AA. Branchlets and under surface of lvs. tomentose . . . . 4. *A. chinensis*

1. **A. arguta,** Miq. (*Trochostigma arguta,* Sieb. & Zucc.). Bower Actinidia. Tara-Vine. High-climbing glabrous shrub; pith of branches brown, lamellate: lvs. long-petioled, broad-elliptic or broadly ovate, to 6 in. long, cuneate or truncate at base, abruptly acuminate, finely serrate: fls. white, ¾in. across, in many-fld. cymes; petals brownish at base; anthers dark purple: fr. nearly globose, greenish-yellow, about 1 in. long, sweet and sometimes eaten. Japan, Korea, Manchuria.

2. **A. polygama,** Maxim. (*Trochostigma polygama,* Sieb. & Zucc.). Silver-Vine. Glabrous climber to 25 ft.; pith of branches white, solid: lvs. long-petioled, broadly ovate to ovate-oblong, to 6 in. long, rounded or subcordate at base, obtuse or abruptly acuminate, serrate, often variegated with white or yellowish, the young lvs. of the staminate plant often silvery-white: fls. white, ¾in. across, solitary; anthers yellow; ovary bottle-shaped: fr. ovoid, yellow, about ¾–1 in. long. Japan, Korea, Manchuria to Cent. China.

3. **A. Kolomikta,** Maxim. (*Trochostigma Kolomikta,* Rupr.). Glabrous climber to 20 ft. and more; pith of branches brown, lamellate: lvs. long-petioled, ovate, to 5 in. long, rounded or cordate at base, acuminate, unequally and sharply serrate, often variegated with white or pink: fls. white, ¾in. across, solitary, fragrant; ovary cylindric: fr. oblong-ovoid, greenish or yellowish, ¾–1 in. long. (Kolomikta: native name.) Japan, Manchuria, Cent. and W. China.

4. **A. chinensis,** Planch. Yangtao. Climbing to 25 ft., the branchlets densely hairy; pith of branches lamellate: lvs. long-petioled, orbicular or oval, to 5 in. long, cordate or truncate at base, usually rounded or emarginate at apex but sometimes acute, ciliate-serrate, densely whitish-tomentose beneath with stellate hairs: fls. white changing to yellow, 1½–2 in. across, several: fr. ovoid or subglobose, 1–2 in. long, of gooseberry-like flavor and sometimes eaten. China.

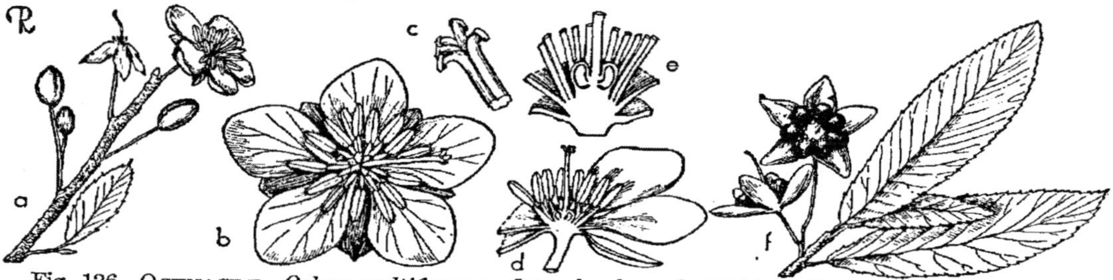

Fig. 126. Ochnaceæ. *Ochna multiflora:* a, flowering branch, × ½; b, flower, × 1; c, stigma, × 5; d, flower, vertical section, × 1; e, ovary, × 4; f, fruiting branch, × ½.

126. OCHNACEÆ. OCHNA FAMILY

Trees or shrubs, rarely herbs, of about 17 genera and 200 species widely distributed in the tropics.—Lvs. alternate, simple or pinnate, stipulate: fls. bisexual, regular, in terminal or axillary racemes or panicles; sepals 5, free or slightly united at base; petals 5, free; stamens as many or twice as many as petals or sometimes indefinite, often with staminodia, filaments free; ovary deeply 3–10-lobed, each lobe 1-celled and with 1 basal ovule, inserted on a thickened disk which enlarges in fr.: fr. a caps., drupe or ring of separate drupes or drupelets.

OCHNA, Schreber. Trees or shrubs of 25–30 species in trop. Asia and Afr., a few in trop. Amer., one grown under glass or in the open far south.—Lvs. toothed, glabrous, stipules deciduous: fls. yellow, with articulated pedicels; sepals colored, persistent; petals deciduous; stamens indefinite, with filiform filaments: fr. of 3–10 sessile drupes surrounding a central receptacle. (Och-na: old Greek name.)

O. multiflora, DC. Shrub to 5 ft. or more: lvs. oblong, 2–5 in. long, toothed, somewhat leathery: fls. in 10–15-fld. racemes 2–3 in. long, sepals turning red: fr. of black seed-like drupes surrounding a bright red receptacle. Trop. Afr.

127. THEACEÆ. TEA FAMILY

Trees or shrubs native in trop. and warm regions, of 18 genera and about 200 species, some planted for ornament and one furnishing the tea of commerce.—Lvs. alternate, simple, leathery, pinnate-veined, exstipulate: fls. solitary or few together, axillary or terminal, regular, usually bisexual; sepals 5–7, free or somewhat united at base, imbricated, the calyx often with 2 bracts at base; petals usually 5, rarely 4

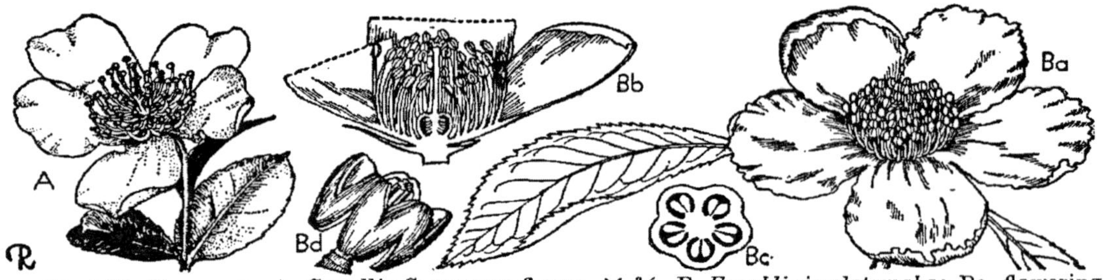

Fig. 127. Theaceæ. A, *Camellia Sasanqua:* flower, × 3/8. B, *Franklinia alatamaha:* Ba, flowering branch, × 1/2; Bb, flower, vertical section (petals excised), × 1/2; Bc, ovary, cross-section, × 1; Bd, capsule, × 1/2. (Ba–Bc redrawn from Sargent.)

to many, free or united at base, imbricated; stamens numerous, seldom as few as 5, free or more or less united at base with each other and with base of petals; ovary superior, 2–10-celled with 2 to many ovules axile in each cell, with 1 or several styles: fr. a dehiscent caps. or indehiscent, dry or drupaceous.—The family is often known as Ternstrœmiaceæ, which is the older name.

A. Fr. dehiscent: anthers versatile.
B. Foliage persistent.
C. Seeds not winged: stamens in 2 series.
D. Fls. pedicelled; sepals persistent....1. Thea
DD. Fls. sessile; sepals deciduous....2. Camellia
CC. Seeds winged; stamens in 1 series....3. Gordonia
BB. Foliage deciduous.
C. Fls. nearly sessile: fr. with persistent central axis....4. Franklinia
CC. Fls. stalked: fr. without persistent axis....5. Stewartia
AA. Fr. indehiscent: anthers basifixed.
B. Lvs. clustered or verticillate at ends of branches....6. Ternstrœmia
BB. Lvs. alternate.
C. Fls. bisexual; anthers hairy....7. Cleyera
CC. Fls. unisexual; anthers glabrous....8. Eurya

1. **THEA,** L. About 16 species of evergreen shrubs or small trees in trop. and subtrop. Asia, one species widely cult. for its lvs. which, when dried and cured, furnish tea.—Lvs. alternate, short-petioled, serrate: fls. pedicelled, nodding, solitary or 2–4 together; sepals persistent; petals united at base and with outer series of stamens; stamens numerous, in 2 series, the outer united into a short or long tube, the inner 5–15 and free, anthers versatile; ovary 3–5-celled with 4–6 ovules in each cell, the 3–5 filiform styles united below: fr. a woody caps., loculicidally dehiscent, with persistent axis, each cell with 1 large globose or ovoid unwinged seed. (The-a: the Latinized Chinese name of the tea plant.)

T. sinensis, L. (*Camellia Thea,* Link. *C. sinensis,* Kuntze). Tea. Shrub or sometimes tree to 30 ft., glabrous except the young lvs. beneath: lvs. elliptic- or obovate-lanceolate, 2–5 in. long, acute or obtuse, short-toothed: fls. white, fragrant, 1–1½ in. across; ovary villous: caps ½–¾ in. across. China, India.—Several vars. are cult., the most important being: Var. **Bohea,** Pierre (*T. Bohea,* L.), branches erect; lvs. elliptic-oblong, obtuse, dark green; fls. usually solitary, styles connate below. Var. **viridis,** Pierre (*T. viridis,* L.), branches spreading; lvs. oblong-lanceolate, acutish, light green; fls. 1–4 together, styles free. Var. **cantoniensis,** Pierre (*T. cantoniensis,* Lour.), lvs. oblong-lanceolate; fls. solitary, usually terminal, styles free only at apex. Var. **assamica,** Pierre (*T. assamica,* Mast.), lvs. oblong-lanceolate, acuminate; fls. 1–4 together, styles free only at apex.

2. **CAMELLIA,** L. Evergreen trees or shrubs grown for their showy fls. and handsome foliage, of about 10 species in trop. and subtrop. Asia.—Often united with Thea from which it differs in its sessile erect fls. and deciduous sepals. (Camel-lia: after George Joseph Camellus or Kamel, a Moravian Jesuit, who travelled in Asia in 17th century; in English, usually pronounced as if Came-lia.)

A. Fls. 3–7 in. across.
B. Lvs. very shining above....1. *C. japonica*
BB. Lvs. not shining above....2. *C. reticulata*
AA. Fls. 1½–2 in. across....3. *C. Sasanqua*

1. **C. japonica,** L. (*Thea japonica,* Nois.). Glabrous shrub or tree sometimes to 40 ft.: lvs. ovate or elliptic, 2–4 in. long, acuminate, very shining and dark green above: fls. red

in the type, 3–5 in. across; petals 5–7, roundish; ovary glabrous; seeds nearly globose, to ¾in. across. China, Japan.—Runs into white, pale rose, and variously double kinds. There are many named vars., a few of the commonest being: **Chandleri elegans,** cerise-red splashed with white, irregular double; **Mathotiana,** carmine-pink, regular double; **nobilissima,** white, irregular double; **tricolor Sieboldii,** white washed, striped and blotched madder-rose, semi-double.

2. **C. reticulata,** Lindl. (*Thea reticulata,* Pierre). Large glabrous shrub: lvs. elliptic-oblong, 3–5 in. long, acuminate, reticulate, dull green and not shining above: fls. purplish-rose, 5–7 in. across; petals 15–20, obovate, loosely arranged; ovary pubescent. China.

3. **C. Sasanqua,** Thunb. (*Thea Sasanqua,* Nois.). Loose straggling shrub, the young branches pubescent: lvs. elliptic to oblong-ovate, 1–3 in. long, bluntly pointed, shining dark green and hairy on the midrib above: fls. white, 1½–2 in. across; petals 5 or more, obovate or oblong; ovary pubescent. (Sasanqua: from a Japanese vernacular name.) China, Japan.—Runs into many forms, some with double fls.

3. **GORDONIA,** Ellis. Evergreen trees or shrubs sometimes planted for ornament; of about 16 species in S. U. S. and trop. and subtrop. Asia.—Lvs. alternate, petioled, entire or serrate: fls. solitary, axillary, long-pedicelled, the calyx subtended by 2–5 caducous bracts; sepals and petals 5; stamens numerous, united into a ring, anthers versatile; ovary sessile, 3–5-celled with 4–8 ovules in each cell, the single style with 3–5-lobed stigma: fr. a woody caps. loculicidally dehiscent by 5 valves, the axis persistent; seeds flat, winged. (Gordo-nia: after James Gordon, 1728–1791, English nurseryman.)

G. Lasianthus, Ellis (*Hypericum Lasianthus,* L.). LOBLOLLY BAY. To 60 ft., shrubby in cult.: lvs. obovate-lanceolate, 4–6 in. long, toothed, narrowed to short petiole, glabrous, dark green and shining above: fls. white, fragrant, 2–2½ in. across: caps. ovoid, ½–¾in. long. (Lasianthus: old generic name.) Va. to Fla. and La.

4. **FRANKLINIA,** Marsh. One species, a deciduous shrub or small tree, hardy as far north as Mass.—Often included in Gordonia but differing in fls. nearly sessile, stamens distinct and inserted on the petals, and seeds angled but not winged. (Franklin-ia: named for Benjamin Franklin, 1706–1790.)

F. alatamaha, Marsh. (*Gordonia alatamaha,* Sarg. *G. pubescens,* L'Her.). To 20 ft.: lvs. obovate-oblong, 5–6 in. long, remotely serrate usually above the middle only, bright green and shining above, pale and pubescent beneath, turning scarlet in autumn: fls. white, about 3 in. across, Sept.–Oct.; sepals silky-pubescent: caps. globose, ¾in. diam. Ga. near Ft. Barrington on the Altamaha (Alatamaha) River, but not found wild since 1790; now known only in cult.

5. **STEWARTIA,** L. About 8 species of deciduous trees or shrubs in E. N. Amer. and E. Asia, a few planted for their showy fls.—Bark smooth, flaky: lvs. alternate, short-petioled, serrate: fls. white, solitary, axillary, short-peduncled; sepals 5–6, subtended by 1 or 2 bracts; petals silky-pubescent outside, 5–6, connate below with each other and with the numerous stamens, anthers versatile; ovary 5-celled with 2 ovules in each cell, styles 5, free or united: fr. a woody caps. loculicidally dehiscent by 5 valves, the seeds usually narrowly winged. (Stewar-tia: sometimes but not originally written Stuartia: after John Stuart, Earl of Bute, 1713–1792, patron of botany.)

A. Styles distinct .... 1. *S. ovata*
AA. Styles united.
  B. Bracts longer than sepals .... 2. *S. monadelpha*
  BB. Bracts much shorter than sepals.
    C. Stamens purplish .... 3. *S. Malacodendron*
    CC. Stamens with white filaments and orange anthers .... 4. *S. Pseudo-Camellia*

1. **S. ovata,** Weatherby (*Malachodendron ovatum,* Cav. *M. pentagynum,* Dum.-Cours. *S. pentagyna,* L'Her.). Shrub to 15 ft.: lvs. ovate to ovate-oblong, 2–5 in. long, acuminate, remotely toothed, grayish-green and slightly pubescent beneath: fls. 2½–3 in. across; stamens with white filaments and orange anthers; styles distinct: caps. ovoid, ½–¾in. long, pubescent. N. C. and Tenn. to Fla. Var. **grandiflora,** Weatherby, has fls. 3–4 in. across with purple stamens.

2. **S. monadelpha,** Sieb. & Zucc. Tree to 80 ft.: lvs. elliptic, 1½–2½ in. long, acute, remotely toothed, pubescent beneath: fls. 1–1½ in. across; bracts lf.-like and longer than calyx; stamens with filaments united at base and violet anthers; styles united: caps. ovoid, ½in. long, pubescent. Japan.

3. **S. Malacodendron,** L. (*S. virginica*, Cav.). Shrub to 20 ft.: lvs. elliptic, 2–4 in. long, acute or short-acuminate, margins toothed and ciliate, pale green and pubescent beneath: fls. 3–4 in. across; stamens with purple filaments and bluish anthers; styles united: caps. depressed-globose, ½–¾in. across. Va. to Fla. and La.

4. **S. Pseudo-Camellia,** Maxim. Upright shrub or tree to 50 ft. or more; bark red, peeling off in thin flakes: lvs. elliptic to elliptic-lanceolate, 1–3 in. long, acuminate, remotely toothed, bright green and glabrous or nearly so: fls. 2–2½ in. across; stamens with white filaments and orange anthers; styles united: caps. ovoid, ¾in. long. Japan.

6. **TERNSTRŒMIA,** L. f. (*Taonabo*, Aubl.). A large genus native in the tropics of Asia and Amer., one planted in S. U. S.—Trees or shrubs, glabrous: lvs. spirally arranged, clustered or verticillate at ends of branches, entire or nearly so: fls. bisexual, solitary in the axils; sepals and petals 5, rarely 6; stamens numerous, usually in 2 series, filaments united; ovary commonly 2–3-celled with 2 or more ovules in each cell; style 1, usually entire: fr. an indehiscent caps. or rarely dehiscent at apex. (Ternstrœ-mia: named for Christopher Ternstrœm, Swedish naturalist, died 1745.)

T. gymnanthera, Sprague (*Cleyera gymnanthera*, Wight & Arn. *T. japonica*, Thunb.). To 20 ft., evergreen: lvs. obovate or oblong, 1½–3 in. long, tapered at both ends, short-petioled: fls. pale yellow, ¾in. across, nodding on stalks ¾–1 in. long: fr. globose, yellow, ¾in. long. Japan to India.

7. **CLEYERA,** Thunb. (*Sakakia*, Nakai). Trees or shrubs, of perhaps 20 species in both hemispheres, one planted in S. U. S.—Lvs. alternate, entire or serrate: fls. bisexual, solitary or clustered in axils, pedicelled; sepals 5, unequal; petals 5, slightly connate at base; stamens about 25, with setose anthers; ovary 2–3-celled with many ovules in each cell: fr. an indehiscent berry. (Cleye-ra: named for Andrew Cleyer, physician and botanist, Dutch Director of Commerce 1683–1688.)

C. japonica, Thunb. (*C. ochnacea*, DC. *Eurya ochnacea*, Szysz.). SAKAKI. Small evergreen tree or shrub: lvs. variable, elliptic or obovate, 2–6 in. long, usually entire, petioled: fls. white, fragrant, about ½in. across: fr. globose to ovoid, red. Japan to India. Var. **tricolor,** W. Miller (*C. Fortunei*, Hook. f.), has lvs. variegated with yellow and red.

8. **EURYA,** Thunb. Evergreen trees and shrubs, of more than 50 species in the eastern hemisphere, one adapted to S. U. S.—Differs from Cleyera in having unisexual fls., the petals united about one-third their length, glabrous anthers, and shorter curved pedicels. (Œu-rya: of uncertain derivation.)

E. japonica, Thunb. (*E. latifolia*, Koch). Glabrous shrub or small tree to 25 ft.: lvs. elliptic to oblong, 1–2½ in. long, serrate, short-petioled: fls. white, ¼in. across, in small clusters: fr. globose, black, ⅙in. across. Japan, Korea, Formosa.

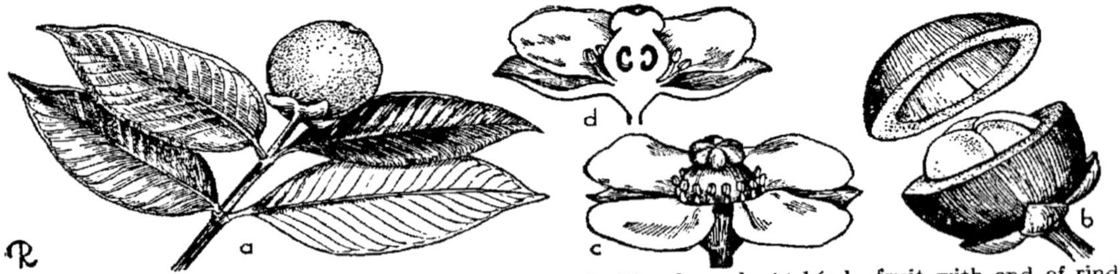

Fig. 128. GUTTIFERÆ. *Garcinia Mangostana:* a, fruiting branch, × ¼; b, fruit with end of rind removed, × ⅓; c, flower, × ½; d, same, vertical section, × ½. (d and c after Baillon.)

128. GUTTIFERÆ. GARCINIA FAMILY

About 35 genera and over 800 species in the tropics of both hemispheres; trees or shrubs, one yielding the mangosteen, another the mammee-apple.—Juice resinous, yellow or greenish: lvs. opposite, rarely verticillate, pinnate-veined, usually simple and entire, exstipulate: fls. regular, unisexual or bisexual, solitary or in cymes which may be united in a compound infl.; sepals and petals 2–6, rarely many, imbricated; stamens numerous, hypogynous, the filaments free or variously united, sometimes forming a globular mass; ovary 2- to many- rarely 1-celled, with 1 to many ovules in each cell, placentation axile or basal and rarely parietal, style long or short or none, free or united, the stigmatic lobes often thick and radiating: fr. fleshy or coriaceous, an indehiscent berry or drupe, or septicidally dehiscent. The following genera are sometimes separated in the family Clusiaceæ.

A. Sepals 4 .... 1. GARCINIA
AA. Sepals 2 .... 2. MAMMEA

1. **GARCINIA,** L. Trees native in the Old World tropics, of about 150 species, the mangosteen grown for its delicious fr.; the yellow resinous juice of many species yields commercial gamboge.—Plant polygamous: fls. axillary or terminal; sepals and petals 4; stamens free or united at base into 1–5 fascicles or united into an entire or 4-lobed mass; staminodia 8 to many in pistillate fls., free or variously united; ovary 2–12-celled with 1 ovule in each cell; stigma broadly peltate, entire or with radiating lobes: fr. a hard indehiscent berry, the seeds surrounded by a pulpy aril. (Garcin-ia: after Laurence Garcin, 1683–1751, French botanist and traveller.)

G. Mangostana, L. MANGOSTEEN. Slow-growing compact tree to 30 ft.: lvs. elliptic-oblong, 6–10 in. long, acuminate, thick and leathery, with numerous horizontal nerves: staminate fls. in 3–9-fld. terminal fascicles; bisexual fls. solitary or in pairs at ends of branches, 2 in. across; petals fleshy, rose-pink; stigma sessile, 4-lobed: fr. about 2½ in. diam., reddish-purple, the large leathery sepals persistent; rind thick and tough, inclosing 5–7 white segms. resembling an orange, the seeds thin and small or sometimes lacking. (Mangostana: adaptation of the Malayan name.) Malay region.

2. **MAMMEA,** L. Probably about a half dozen trees in the tropics of Amer., Afr., and Asia, although the genus is sometimes defined to include only the American species which is widely cult. for its edible fr.; a liqueur is also distilled from the fls.—Plant polygamous: fls. axillary, solitary or few together; calyx closed before flowering, then separating into 2 valvate sepals; petals 4–6; stamens free or united at base; ovary 2–4-celled, with 1–2 ovules in each cell; style short with peltate stigma entire or broadly 4-lobed: fr. a 1–4-seeded indehiscent drupe. (Mam-mea: from *mamey*, the aboriginal W. Indian name of *M. americana.*)

M. americana, L. MAMMEE-APPLE. MAMEY. Upright compact tree to 60 ft.: lvs. oblong-obovate, 4–8 in. long, rounded or blunt at apex, thick and glossy, with numerous fine transverse veins and pellucid dots: fls. white, fragrant, 1 in. across: fr. oblate to globose, 4–6 in. diam., the surface russet and slightly roughened, the 1–4 large seeds surrounded by bright yellow flesh. W. Indies, N. S. Amer.

129. HYPERICACEÆ. ST. JOHNSWORT FAMILY

Herbs or shrubs, of about 10 genera and over 300 species, widely distributed in temp. and warm regions.—Lvs. opposite or sometimes whorled, simple and usually entire, pellucid- or black-dotted, exstipulate: fls. bisexual, regular, solitary or in cymes; sepals and petals 4–5, imbricated; stamens numerous, hypogynous, commonly united into clusters; ovary 1–7-celled with as many distinct styles and numerous axile ovules: fr. usually capsular.

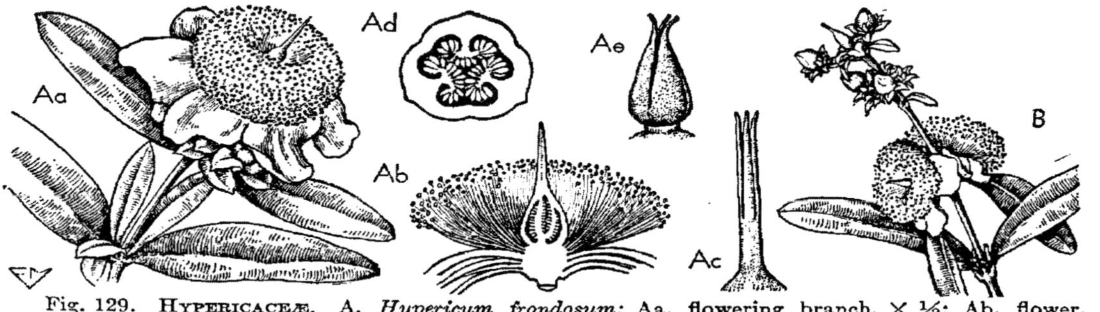

Fig. 129. HYPERICACEÆ. A, *Hypericum frondosum:* Aa, flowering branch, × ½; Ab, flower, vertical section, × 1; Ac, style and stigma, × 2; Ad, ovary, cross-section, × 3; Ae, capsule, × 1. B, *H. prolificum:* flowering branch, × ½.

HYPERICUM, L. St. Johnswort. About 200 species of herbs or shrubs, mostly in temp. and subtrop. regions of the northern hemisphere, grown out-of-doors for their attractive fls.—Fls. yellow, rarely pink or purplish; sepals 5, often unequal; petals 5, oblique, convolute in the bud; stamens numerous, free or usually connate at base into 3 or 5 bundles opposite the petals, sometimes with hypogynous glands alternating with petals; ovary superior, 1-celled with 3–5 parietal placentæ or 3–5-celled and axile placentation, ovules numerous, the 3–5 styles usually distinct at time of pollination but often tightly appressed and appearing as if 1 in early period of anthesis: fr. a septicidally dehiscent caps. or rarely a berry. (Hyperi-cum but by usage Hyper-icum: Greek name of obscure meaning.)

A. Margins of lvs. finely toothed and with conspicuous black glands.............. 1. *H. orientale*
AA. Margins of lvs. not so.
  B. Lvs. narrow-linear.. 2. *H. Coris*
  BB. Lvs. oblong to ovate.
    C. Sepals or tips of petals with black glands.
      D. Sts. and foliage densely tomentose.
        E. Calyx tomentose: stamens in distinct clusters.................. 3. *H. tomentosum*
        EE. Calyx glabrous or slightly pubescent: stamens nearly free........... 4. *H. rhodopæum*
      DD. Sts. and foliage glabrous or nearly so.
        E. Plant very glaucous: fls. 2 in. across..........................20. *H. polyphyllum*
        EE. Plant not glaucous: fls. about 1 in. across.
          F. Sepal margins entire.. 5. *H. perforatum*
          FF. Sepal margins toothed.
            G. Length of lvs. 1/6–1/4 in.............................. 6. *H. fragile*
            GG. Length of lvs. about 1 in.............................. 7. *H. elegans*
    CC. Sepals or tips of petals without black glands.
      D. Styles 5.
        E. Fls. 1/2–1 in. across... 8. *H. Kalmianum*
        EE. Fls. 1 1/2–3 in. across.
          F. Length of lvs. 1/2 in. or less.................................. 9. *H. reptans*
          FF. Length of lvs. 1 1/2 in. and more.
            G. Plant 1 ft. or less high, stoloniferous.......................10. *H. calycinum*
            GG. Plant 2 ft. or more high, not stoloniferous.
              H. Base of lf. clasping: plant herbaceous.....................11. *H. Ascyron*
              HH. Base of lf. cuneate: plant shrubby.
                I. Tip of lf. obtuse or acutish..........................12. *H. patulum*
                II. Tip of lf. mucronulate.............................13. *H. Moserianum*
      DD. Styles 3.
        E. Plant 2–6 ft. high, branches upright.
          F. Stamens in clusters, about length of petals.....................14. *H. Androsæmum*
          FF. Stamens distinct, shorter than petals.
            G. Fls. 1–2 in. across; sepals foliaceous.........................15. *H. frondosum*
            GG. Fls. 1/2–3/4 in. across; sepals not foliaceous.
              H. Lvs. acute, revolute: fls. in terminal cymes..................16. *H. densiflorum*
              HH. Lvs. obtuse: fls. in axillary cymes forming leafy panicles.....17. *H. prolificum*
        EE. Plant 16 in. or less high, branches procumbent to ascending.
          F. Tip of lf. obtuse...18. *H. Buckleii*
          FF. Tip of lf. acute.
            G. Sepals strongly acuminate.....................................19. *H. olympicum*
            GG. Sepals obtuse or acutish.
              H. Sts. ascending, plant very glaucous..........................20. *H. polyphyllum*
              HH. Sts. creeping, plant scarcely glaucous.......................21. *H. repens*

1. **H. orientale,** L. Per. with upright nearly simple sts. 6–12 in. high: lvs. obovate- to linear-oblong, 1/2–1 in. long, obtuse, margins finely toothed and with conspicuous black glands: fls. 1 in. across, in small terminal cymes; sepals with yellow-glandular toothed margins; stamens in 3 clusters; styles 3. Asia Minor.

2. **H. Coris,** L. Subshrub with upright or procumbent terete sts. 1–2 ft. high: lvs. in whorls of 4–6, narrow-linear, 1/2–1 in. long, revolute: fls. 3/4 in. across, in few-fld. loose cymes; sepals with toothed glandular margins; stamens in 3 clusters; styles 3. S. Eu.

3. **H. tomentosum,** L. Per. with ascending terete tomentose sts. 8–16 in. high: lvs. ovate, 1/3–3/4 in. long, obtuse, tomentose: fls. 1/2–3/4 in. across, in loose corymbs; sepals with ciliate glandular margins, tomentose; stamens in 3 clusters, as long as petals; styles 3. W. Medit. region.

4. **H. rhodopæum,** Friv. Tufted per. with prostrate tomentose sts. to 5 in. high: lvs. oblong, 1/2–3/4 in. long, obtuse, gray-tomentose: fls. about 1/2 in. across, in 1–3-fld. cymes; sepals with ciliate glandular margins, nearly glabrous; stamens distinct or slightly united at base, as long as petals; styles 3. Asia Minor.

5. **H. perforatum,** L. Per. with many upright sts. 1–2 ft. high: lvs. oblong or linear, 1/2–1 in. long, obtuse: fls. 3/4–1 in. across, in many-fld. cymes; sepals with few black glands; petals dotted with many black glands; stamens in 3 clusters; styles 3. Eu.; nat. in N. Amer.

6. **H. fragile,** Heldr. & Sart. Subshrub with 4-angled simple sts. to 3 in. high: lvs. ovate, 1/6–1/4in. long, glaucous and glabrous, margins black-dotted: fls. in 2–5-fld. cymes; sepals with black glandular teeth; stamens in 3 clusters; styles 3. Greece.

7. **H. elegans,** Steph. Per. with upright 2-angled sts. 6–16 in. high, glabrous: lvs. triangular or lanceolate, 3/4–1 1/2 in. long, revolute: fls. about 1 in. across, in narrow terminal panicles; sepals with few black glandular teeth; petals black-dotted on margins; stamens in 3 clusters; styles 3. Cent. Eu. to Altai Mts.

8. **H. Kalmianum,** L. Freely-branching evergreen shrub 2–3 ft. high, sts. 4-angled: lvs. oblong-linear to oblanceolate, 1–2 1/2 in. long, obtuse, glaucous below, often with smaller lvs. crowded in axils: fls. 1/2–1 in. across, in few-fld. cymes, in Aug.; sepals foliaceous, about half length of petals; stamens distinct; styles 5, united below into a beak. (Bears the name of Peter Kalm, page 46.) Que. to Ill.

9. **H. reptans,** Dyer. Shrub with prostrate 2-edged rooting sts.: lvs. elliptic-oblong, 1/4–1/2in. long, obtuse: fls. to 1 3/4 in. across, solitary; stamens in 5 clusters: styles 5. Himalayas.

10. **H. calycinum,** L. A stoloniferous evergreen subshrub 1 ft. or less high, the many procumbent or ascending 4-angled sts. occurring in thick tufts: lvs. ovate-oblong or oblong, 2–4 in. long, obtuse, glaucous beneath: fls. 3 in. across, solitary or 2–3 together, blooming from July to Sept.; sepals large and spreading, enlarging in fr.; stamens in 5 clusters, anthers red; styles 5, divergent. S. E. Eu., Asia Minor.

11. **H. Ascyron,** L. Per. with upright 4-angled sts. to 6 ft. high: lvs. ovate-oblong to ovate-lanceolate, clasping, 2–5 in. long, obtuse or acute: fls. 1–2 in. across, in few-fld. cymes; stamens in 5 clusters; styles 5. N. Asia, N. Eu., Que. to Kans.

12. **H. patulum,** Thunb. Evergreen spreading shrub to 3 ft., with purplish arching 2-edged sts.: lvs. ovate-lanceolate or ovate-oblong, 1 1/2–2 1/2 in. long, obtuse or somewhat acute, glaucous beneath: fls. 1 1/2–2 in. across, solitary or in cymes, blooming from July–Sept.; sepals suborbicular, nearly equal, longer than half the petals; stamens in 5 clusters; styles 5. Japan. Var. **Henryi,** Bean, is of hardy and vigorous growth, with obtuse lvs. 2–3 in. long and fls. 2–2 1/2 in. across; named for Augustine Henry, page 45; China. Var. **Forrestii,** Chittenden, is similar with larger fls.; named for George Forrest, page 43.

13. **H. Moserianum,** André (*H. patulum* × *H. calycinum*). GOLD-FLOWER. Erect subshrub to 2 ft., with arching reddish sts.: lvs. ovate, to 2 in. long, obtuse and mucronulate, glaucous beneath: fls. 2–2 1/2 in. across, in cymes of 1–5, blooming in July and Aug. (Named for Mr. Moser, who raised the hybrid in his nursery at Versailles in 1887.)

14. **H. Androsæmum,** L. TUTSAN. Semi-evergreen shrub with upright 2-edged sts. to 3 ft.: lvs. ovate to ovate-oblong, 2–4 in. long, obtuse, cordate at base, whitish beneath: fls. 1 in. across, in few-fld. cymes or solitary; sepals foliaceous, about as long as petals; stamens in 5 clusters, equalling the petals; styles 3. Eu., W. Asia.

15. **H. frondosum,** Michx. (*H. aureum,* Bartram). Deciduous shrub to 4 ft., of dense rounded habit, sts. 2-edged: lvs. ovate-oblong to oblong, 1–3 in. long, obtuse and mucronulate, bluish-green, pale beneath: fls. 1–2 in. across, sessile, solitary or few together, July–Aug.; sepals unequal, foliaceous, shorter than the somewhat deflexed petals; stamens distinct; styles 3. S. C. to Tenn. and Tex.

16. **H. densiflorum,** Pursh. Much-branched evergreen shrub to 6 ft., densely leafy, sts. 2-angled: lvs. linear-oblong to linear, 1–2 in. long, revolute, acute, with many small lvs. crowded in axils: fls. about 1/2in. across, in dense many-fld. terminal cymes, blooming from July–Sept.; stamens distinct; styles 3, more or less united. N. J. to Fla. and Tex.

17. **H. prolificum,** L. Dense erect evergreen shrub to 5 ft., the sts. 2-angled: lvs. narrowly oblong or oblanceolate, 1–3 in. long, obtuse, glossy dark green above, pale beneath, with tufts of small lvs. in the axils: fls. 1/2–3/4in. across, in several- to many-fld. axillary cymes forming leafy panicles, blooming from July–Sept.; stamens distinct; styles 3. Sandy and rocky soil, Ont. to Minn. and Ga.

18. **H. Buckleii,** M. A. Curt. Subshrub with decumbent or ascending 4-angled sts. to 1 ft.: lvs. obovate, 1/4–3/4in. long, obtuse: fls. 1 in. across, 1–3 together, June–July; stamens distinct; styles 3. (Named for S. B. Buckley, who collected the plant in 1842, page 40.) N. C. to Ga.

19. **H. olympicum,** L. Subshrub with procumbent 2-angled or terete sts. 6–12 in. high: lvs. elliptic-oblong, 1/2–1 in. long, acutish, grayish-green: fls. 2 in. across, in few-fld. cymes; sepals not glandular, strongly acuminate; stamens in 3 clusters; styles 3. S. E. Eu., Asia Minor.

20. **H. polyphyllum,** Boiss. & Bal. Similar to *H. olympicum,* differing in ascending or upright sts., smaller densely glaucous lvs., and acute sepals which are sparingly black-dotted. Asia Minor.

21. **H. repens,** L. Prostrate per. with creeping sts.: lvs. oblong or linear-oblong, 1/3in. long, revolute: fls. 1 in. across, in few-fld. cymes; sepals obtuse; stamens in 3 clusters; styles 3. S. E. Eu., Asia Minor.

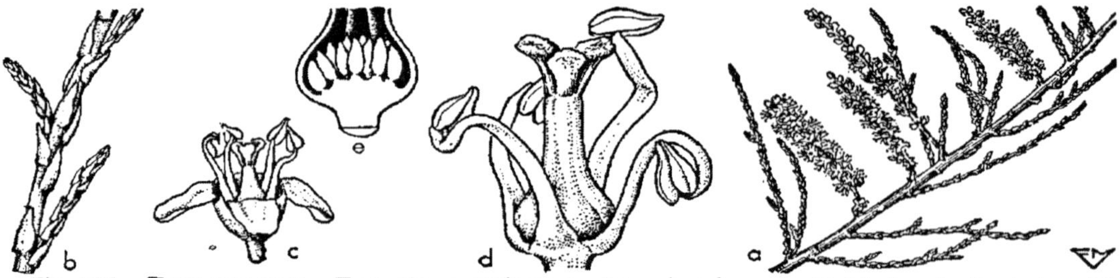

Fig. 130. TAMARICACEÆ. *Tamarix parviflora:* a, flowering branch, × ½; b, sterile twig with leaves, × 2; c, flower habit, × 4; d, flower, less perianth, × 10; e, ovary, vertical section, × 10.

130. TAMARICACEÆ. TAMARISK FAMILY

Shrubs or small trees from the Medit. region and Afr. to E. Asia, of 4 genera and about 100 species, several of the tamarisks planted for ornament.—Lvs. alternate, mostly small and sessile, scale-like, ericoid, exstipulate: fls. regular, bisexual, solitary or in racemes or panicles; sepals 4–5, free or more or less united; petals 4–5, imbricated, usually withering and persistent; stamens as many or twice as many as petals, free or united, inserted on a more or less evident disk; ovary superior, 1-celled, with 2 to many ovules attached at the base of the 3–5 parietal placentæ, the 3–5 styles free or united: fr. a caps. dehiscent to base, the seeds densely bearded or rarely winged.

TAMARIX, L. TAMARISK. About 75 species of deciduous or sometimes evergreen shrubs or trees from the Medit. region to E. Indies and Japan.—Technical characters as for the family. (Tam-arix: ancient Latin name.)—The species are very much alike and difficult to distinguish except by technical characters.

A. Fls. in terminal panicles, appearing in summer after the lvs.
B. Branchlets and lvs. finely pubescent.......... 1. *T. hispida*
BB. Branchlets and lvs. glabrous.
C. Lvs. and bracts sheathing: fls. sessile.......... 2. *T. aphylla*
CC. Lvs. and bracts not sheathing: fls. short-pedicelled.
D. Petals deciduous from half-ripe or mature frs., spreading; disk 5-angled or 5-lobed.
E. Stamens inserted between the shallow lobes of the disk: fl.-buds subglobose: bracts triangular-ovate.......... 3. *T. gallica*
EE. Stamens inserted on the corners of the 5-angled disk: fl.-buds ovoid: bracts lanceolate.......... 4. *T. anglica*
DD. Petals persistent; stamens deeply inserted between the lobes of the disk.
E. Bracts ovate-lanceolate: disk 10-lobed.......... 5. *T. pentandra*
EE. Bracts subulate.
F. Disk 5-lobed: panicles upright.......... 6. *T. odessana*
FF. Disk deeply 10-lobed: panicles usually pendulous.......... 7. *T. chinensis*
AA. Fls. in racemes on last year's branches, appearing in spring before or with the lvs.
B. Sepals, petals and stamens 5.
C. Racemes slender; fls. pedicelled.......... 8. *T. juniperina*
CC. Racemes thick; fls. nearly sessile.......... 9. *T. africana*
BB. Sepals, petals and stamens 4.
C. Petals persistent on fr.......... 10. *T. parviflora*
CC. Petals deciduous.......... 11. *T. tetrandra*

1. **T. hispida,** Willd. KASHGAR TAMARISK. Shrub to 4 ft., with slender upright branches downy when young: lvs. broad at base, bluish-green, finely pubescent: fls. pink, almost sessile, in dense racemes 2–3 in. long forming terminal panicles, in late summer; petals deciduous; disk 5-lobed. Caspian region.

2. **T. aphylla,** Karst. (*T. articulata,* Vahl). ATHEL TAMARISK. Shrub or small tree to 30 ft., with jointed branchlets and minute sheathing lvs. like a Casuarina, glaucous: fls. pink, sessile, in terminal panicles; bracts sheathing; disk 10-lobed. W. Asia, N. E. Afr.—Useful as a windbreak in desert regions.

3. **T. gallica,** L. FRENCH TAMARISK. Shrub or small tree to 12 or sometimes 30 ft., with slender spreading branches: lvs. rhombic-ovate, acute or acuminate, keeled, the margins scarious, glaucous: fls. white or pinkish, in slender panicled racemes 1–2 in. long, in early summer, the fl.-buds subglobose; bracts triangular-ovate, much longer than pedicels; petals deciduous; stamens 5, inserted between shallow lobes of disk. W. Eu. to Himalayas; escaped in Tex., Ariz. and New Mex. Var. **indica,** Ehrenb., has longer and slenderer racemes.

4. **T. anglica,** Webb. English Tamarisk. Closely allied to *T. gallica* and by some botanists united with it, differing in its ovoid fl.-buds and the stamens being inserted on the corners of the 5-angled disk. W. Eu.

5. **T. pentandra,** Pall. (*T. hispida æstivalis*, Hort. *T. amurensis*, Hort.). Shrub or small tree to 15 ft. or more, with purple plumose branches: lvs. lanceolate to ovate, acute, glaucous or pale green: fls. pink, in dense racemes forming large panicles sometimes 3 ft. long, in late summer; bracts ovate-lanceolate, as long or slightly longer than pedicels; petals 5, persistent; stamens deeply inserted between the lobes of the 10-lobed disk. S. E. Eu. to Cent. Asia.

6. **T. odessana,** Steven. Shrub to 6 ft., with slender upright branches: lvs. lanceolate, subulate, decurrent: fls. pink, in slender racemes about 1 in. long forming a large loose panicle, in summer; bracts subulate; pedicels about as long as lobes of the 5-lobed disk. Caspian region.

7. **T. chinensis,** Lour. Chinese Tamarisk. Shrub or small tree to 15 ft., with slender spreading or drooping branches: lvs. lanceolate, keeled, bluish-green: fls. pink, in racemes 1–2 in. long forming loose usually nodding panicles, in summer; bracts subulate, longer than pedicels; disk deeply 10-lobed. China.

8. **T. juniperina,** Bunge (*T. japonica* and *T. plumosa*, Hort.). Shrub or small tree to 15 ft., with slender spreading branches: lvs. oblong-lanceolate, acuminate: fls. pink, appearing in spring in lateral slender racemes 1–2 in. long on branches of the previous year; bracts linear-lanceolate, longer than pedicels; sepals, petals and stamens 5; petals persistent; disk 5-lobed. N. China, Japan.

9. **T. africana,** Poir. Shrub to 10 ft.: lvs. lanceolate, acuminate: fls. pinkish, nearly sessile, in thick dense racemes 2–3 in. long, borne in spring on branches of previous year; bracts oblong; sepals, petals and stamens 5. Medit. region.—Doubtfully in cult.

10. **T. parviflora,** DC. Shrub or small tree to 15 ft., with slender spreading branches and reddish-brown bark: lvs. ovate, acuminate: fls. pink, very short-pedicelled, appearing in spring in lateral racemes 1–1½ in. long on last year's branches; sepals, petals and stamens 4; petals persistent. S. Eu.

11. **T. tetrandra,** Pall. Shrub to 12 ft., with almost black branches: lvs. ovate-lanceolate, margins scarious: fls. pale pink, in lateral racemes on last year's branches; bracts triangular-lanceolate, longer than pedicels; petals, sepals and stamens 4; petals deciduous. Eu., Asia.

Fig. 131. Cistaceæ. *Helianthemum nummularium:* a, flowers, × ½; b, stem node, × 1; c, pistil, ovary in vertical section, × 4; d, ovary, cross-section; e, capsules, × 1; f, flower, vertical section, × 1.

131. CISTACEÆ. ROCK-ROSE FAMILY

Shrubs or woody herbs, about 8 genera and 160 species, native mostly in the northern hemisphere, a few planted for ornament.—Lvs. opposite or sometimes alternate, simple, entire, the stipules leafy, small or 0: fls. regular, usually bisexual, solitary or in racemes or panicles; sepals 5, the 2 outer smaller and bract-like or lacking, the 3 inner ones convolute, persistent at least until fruiting; petals 5, rarely 3 or 0, usually fugacious; stamens numerous, hypogynous, the filaments free and slender; ovary superior, sessile, 1-celled or falsely 5–10-celled by ingrowing partitions, with 2 to many ovules borne on parietal placentæ; style simple with entire or 3-lobed stigma: fr. a caps. dehiscent by 3–10 valves.

A. Valves of caps. and placentæ of ovary 5 or 10. . . . . 1. Cistus
AA. Valves of caps. and placentæ of ovary 3.
B. Style curved or bent, slender. . . . . 2. Helianthemum
BB. Style straight, very short. . . . . 3. Halimium

1. **CISTUS,** L. Rock-Rose. About 20 species in the Medit. region, low shrubs adapted to planting in rockeries.—Lvs. opposite, exstipulate: fls. showy, in terminal,

simple or compound cymes, rarely solitary; sepals 3 or 5; petals 5; stamens numerous; ovary with 5 placentæ bearing many ovules, the short or elongated style with a large 5–10-lobed stigma: caps. loculicidally dehiscent into 5, or seldom 10, valves, the fruiting pedicels erect. (Cis-tus: ancient Greek name.)—There are many garden and natural hybrids.

A. Color of fls. white.
  B. Sepals 5.
    C. Lvs. sessile, lanceolate to linear-lanceolate .... 1. *C. monspeliensis*
    CC. Lvs. petioled, oval to ovate.
      D. Margins of lvs. not undulate .... 2. *C. salvifolius*
      DD. Margins of lvs. undulate .... 3. *C. hybridus*
  BB. Sepals 3.
    C. Lvs. lanceolate, nearly sessile .... 4. *C. ladaniferus*
    CC. Lvs. ovate to ovate-lanceolate, petioled .... 5. *C. laurifolius*
AA. Color of fls. lilac, rose or purple.
  B. Fls. nearly sessile .... 6. *C. crispus*
  BB. Fls. stalked.
    C. Shape of lvs. oblong-lanceolate .... 7. *C. purpureus*
    CC. Shape of lvs. oval to ovate-oblong.
      D. Lvs. short-petioled, penninerved .... 8. *C. villosus*
      DD. Lvs. sessile, 3-nerved .... 9. *C. albidus*

1. **C. monspeliensis,** L. Erect shrub to 5 ft.: lvs. sessile, lanceolate to linear-lanceolate, ¾–2 in. long, obtuse or acutish, 3-nerved, rugose, the margins more or less revolute, pilose on nerves with long adpressed hairs: fls. white, about 1 in. across, in 3–10-fld. cymes; pedicels and 5 sepals hirsute: caps. globose, shining, the seeds blackish.

2. **C. salvifolius,** L. Erect or procumbent much-branched shrub to 2 ft.: lvs. petioled, oval or ovate-oblong, ½–1¾ in. long, rigid, very rugose above, tomentose on both sides: fls. white with yellow spot at base of petals, about 1½ in. across, solitary or several together; sepals 5, cordate-ovate, acuminate, densely tomentose outside: caps. ovate, 5-angled, pubescent, the seeds blackish.

3. **C. hybridus,** Pourr. (*C. corbariensis*, Pourr.). Hybrid between *C. salvifolius* and *C. populifolius:* to 4 ft.: lvs. petioled, ovate, 1–2 in. long, margins undulate and minutely toothed, tomentose on both sides: fls. white with yellow base, 1½ in. across.

4. **C. ladaniferus,** L. (*C. ladaniferus* var. *albiflorus*, Dunal). Erect glutinous shrub to 5 ft.: lvs. nearly sessile, lanceolate to linear-lanceolate, 1½–4 in. long, acute, dark green, glabrous and viscid above, whitish-tomentose beneath: fls. white with yellow spot at base of each petal, 3–3½ in. across, usually solitary at tips of axillary branches; bracts deciduous, the upper ones very broad, silky-haired on margins; sepals 3, orbicular, scaly, yellowish: caps. globose, 10-valved, the seeds tawny. Var. **maculatus,** Dunal, has crimson blotch at base of petals.

5. **C. laurifolius,** L. Stiff erect glutinous shrub 6–8 ft. high: lvs. petioled, ovate or ovate-lanceolate, 1–2½ in. long, acuminate, the margins undulate, 3-nerved, glabrous above, whitish or brownish-tomentose beneath: fls. white with yellow blotch at base of petals, 2–3 in. across, in several-fld. cymes at ends of axillary branches; bracts leathery, deciduous; sepals 3, oval, apiculate, silky-tomentose: caps, ovate, tawny, densely villous, 5-valved, the seeds tawny.

6. **C. crispus,** L. Spreading shrub to 2 ft., young branchlets white-hairy: lvs. sessile, lanceolate to ovate-lanceolate, ½–1½ in. long, acute, margins undulate, 3-nerved, rugose above, tomentose beneath: fls. deep rose, 1½–2 in. across, nearly sessile in dense terminal heads; bracts lf.-like, persistent; sepals 5, lanceolate, hairy: caps. ovate, glabrous, the seeds tawny.

7. **C. purpureus,** Lam. Hybrid between *C. villosus* and *C. ladaniferus:* to 4 ft., young branchlets hairy and resinous: lvs. nearly sessile, oblong-lanceolate, 1–2 in. long, 3-nerved at base, penninerved above, gray-tomentose beneath: fls. reddish-purple with dark red blotch at base of each petal, 2–3 in. across.

8. **C. villosus,** L. Erect shrub to 3 ft.: lvs. short-petioled, oval to ovate-oblong, 1–3 in. long, acuminate to obtuse, penninerved, rugose, tomentose beneath: fls. purple or rose, spotted yellow at base of petals, 2–2½ in. across, in 1–4-fld. terminal cymes on long peduncles; bracts lf.-like, persistent; sepals 5, ovate, hairy: caps. ovate, densely pubescent, the seeds tawny. Var. **incanus,** Freyn, densely white-hairy, not glandular, lvs. strongly vaginate. Var. **tauricus,** Grosser (*C. tauricus*, Presl), sparsely hairy, not glandular, lvs. loosely vaginate. Var. **undulatus,** Grosser (*C. creticus*, L.), glandular, lvs. undulate and crisped.

9. **C. albidus,** L. Erect shrub 4–6 ft. high, young parts densely white-tomentose: lvs. sessile, oval or ovate-oblong, ¾–2 in. long, obtuse, 3-nerved to apex, margins revolute, densely tomentose on both sides, reticulate beneath: fls. lilac or rosy, spotted yellow at base of petals, 2½ in. across, stalked, solitary or few together; bracts small, deciduous; sepals 5, ovate, acuminate: caps. ovoid, silky-hairy, the seeds tawny.

2. **HELIANTHEMUM,** Adans. Sun-Rose. A variable genus of about 120 species in the Medit. region, N. and S. Amer., a few grown in rockeries or borders.—Herbs or subshrubs: lvs. opposite or the upper ones alternate, entire, with or without stipules: fls. in simple or compound terminal racemes; sepals 5, the 2 outer smaller, enlarging in fr.; petals 5, sometimes very small or lacking; stamens numerous; ovary with 3 parietal placentæ bearing 2–12 ovules, the style slender and curved or bent: caps. dehiscent into 3 valves, the fruiting pedicels often recurved. (Helian-themum: Greek for *sunflower*.)

A. Stipules present, at least on upper lvs.
B. Style none....................1. *H. præcox*
BB. Style as long or longer than stamens.
C. Upper surface of lvs. not stellate-tomentose although usually hairy........2. *H. nummularium*
CC. Upper surface of lvs. stellate-tomentose.
D. Lvs. to 1¼ in. long; stipules linear-subulate....................3. *H. apenninum*
DD. Lvs. to ¾in. long; stipules linear-lanceolate....................4. *H. glaucum*
AA. Stipules lacking.
B. Lvs. green beneath, glabrescent or hairy....................5. *H. alpestre*
BB. Lvs. gray-tomentose beneath....................6. *H. Tuberaria*

1. **H. præcox,** Salzm. (*Tuberaria præcox,* Grosser). Gray-pubescent ann.: lvs. ovate-lanceolate, 1–1½ in. long; stipules on upper part of st. about length of lvs.: fls. yellow, small; pedicels and sepals with long white hairs; style none. Medit. region.

2. **H. nummularium,** Mill. (*Cistus nummularius,* L. *H. Chamæcistus,* Mill. *H. vulgare,* Gaertn.). Procumbent subshrub to about 1 ft., the young sts. erect or ascending: lvs. petioled, ovate to lanceolate, ½–1 in. long, flat, hairy or rarely glabrous above, gray-tomentose beneath; stipules linear-lanceolate, longer than petioles: fls. in many-fld. loose racemes, yellow but in cult. varying from white to purple and rose, about 1 in. across; outer sepals much shorter than broadly oval inner ones, loosely tomentose, the veins pilose; style as long as stamens. Medit. region.—A few of the many cult. forms are: Var. **aureum,** Hort., fls. deep yellow; var. **macranthum,** Schneid., fls. 1½–2 in. across, white with yellow blotch at base; var. **mutabile,** Rehd. (*H. mutabile,* Pers.), fls. rose to nearly white, sepals glabrous between veins; var. **roseum,** Schneid., fls. pale rose.

3. **H. apenninum,** Mill. (*Cistus apenninus,* L. *H. pulverulentum,* DC. *H. polifolium,* Pers.). Subshrub with erect or procumbent sts. to 15 in.: lvs. petioled, oblong, ½–1¼ in. long, usually revolute, gray-tomentose on both sides; stipules linear-subulate, about equalling petioles: fls. in 3–10-fld. loose racemes, white, 1–1¼ in. across; outer sepals much shorter than oval inner ones, white-pubescent; style as long as stamens. Eu., Asia Minor. Var. **roseum,** Grosser (var. *rhodanthum,* Bean), has reddish fls.

4. **H. glaucum,** Pers. (*Cistus glaucus,* Cav.). Tufted subshrub, with upright or procumbent sts.: lvs. petioled, nearly orbicular to oblanceolate, ⅙–¾in. long, only slightly revolute, tomentose on both sides, glaucous beneath; stipules linear-lanceolate, longer than petioles: fls. in 3–15-fld. racemes, yellow or white, ¾in. across; outer sepals linear-lanceolate, ciliate, inner ovate and tomentose between veins; style as long as stamens. S. Eu., N. Afr. Var. **croceum,** Boiss. (*H. croceum,* Pers.), has bright yellow fls.

5. **H. alpestre,** Dunal (*Cistus alpestris,* Crantz). Densely tufted subshrub about 6 in. high: lvs. ovate-lanceolate or lanceolate, ½–¾in. long, green and glabrous or slightly hairy on both sides: fls. in 2–7-fld. clusters, ½in. across, bright yellow; outer sepals linear-lanceolate, inner oval, tomentose; style shorter than stamens. Mts. of S. Eu.

6. **H. Tuberaria,** Mill. (*Cistus Tuberaria,* L. *Tuberaria vulgaris,* Willk. *T. melastomatifolia,* Grosser). Per. with ascending sts.: lvs. mostly basal, oval-lanceolate, 1–2 in. long, petioled, gray-tomentose beneath: fls. in 3–7-fld. clusters, yellow, 1½ in. across; outer sepals linear-lanceolate, inner oval, glabrous; style short. Medit. region.

3. **HALIMIUM,** Spach. Evergreen shrubs or herbs, of over 20 species in Medit. region and W. Asia.—Often included in Helianthemum, differing chiefly in the straight very short style. (Halim-ium: from Greek *halimos,* in reference to the salt plant.)

A. Sepals densely lepidote....................1. *H. halimifolium*
AA. Sepals not lepidote.
B. Fls. in loose long-stalked panicled clusters; sepals sparsely hairy....................2. *H. ocymoides*
BB. Fls. in 1–5-fld. clusters; sepals densely stellate-tomentose....................3. *H. lasianthum*

1. **H. halimifolium,** Willk. & Lange (*Helianthemum halimifolium,* Willd.). Much-branched shrub to 2 ft.: lvs. short-petioled, oblong to lanceolate, ½–1½ in. long, white-tomentose when young becoming grayish-green: fls. in 2–7-fld. clusters, yellow with dark spot at base of petals, 1½ in. across; sepals ovate, densely lepidote, somewhat hairy; style very short. Medit. region.

2. **H. ocymoides,** Willk. & Lange (*Cistus ocymoides,* Lam. *C. algarvensis,* Curt. *Helianthemum ocymoides,* Pers.). Shrub to 3 ft., sts. upright or procumbent: lvs. oblong or

lanceolate, those of sterile branches petioled and gray-tomentose, of flowering branches sessile and green: fls. in loose long-stalked panicled clusters, bright yellow with purple base, 1–1¼ in. across; pedicels and oval-lanceolate sepals glabrous or sparsely hairy; style very short. Spain, Portugal.

3. **H. lasianthum,** Koch (*Cistus lasianthus,* Lam. *H. formosum,* Dunal. *Helianthemum lasianthum,* Pers.). Shrub with many upright spreading branches to 3 ft.: lvs. short-petioled, oval to lanceolate, ½–1½ in. long, grayish-tomentose: fls. in 1–5-fld. clusters, yellow with purple base, 1½ in. across; pedicels and ovate sepals densely stellate-tomentose; style very short. Portugal.

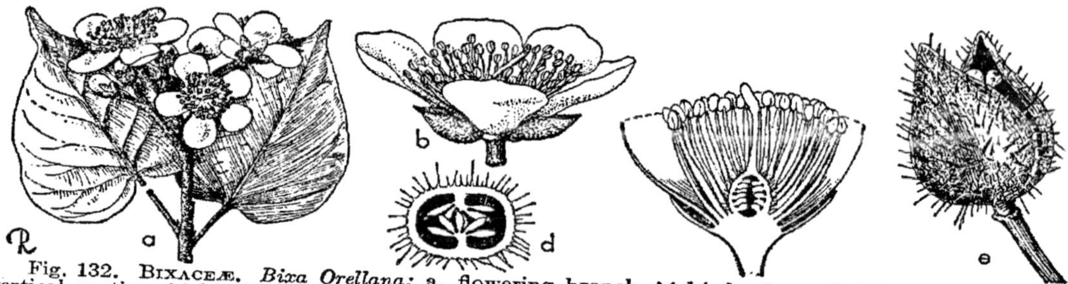

Fig. 132. Bixaceæ. *Bixa Orellana:* a, flowering branch, × ⅓; b, flower habit, × ½; c, same, vertical section, × ½; d, ovary, cross-section, × 2; e, fruit, × ½. (b after Schnizlein, c–d after LeMaout & Decaisne.)

132. BIXACEÆ. BIXA FAMILY

Trees or shrubs, of 2 genera; one species furnishes the "annatto" dye which is extracted and prepared from the pulp around the seeds.—Lvs. alternate, simple, entire, dentate or lobed, stipules usually soon deciduous: fls. bisexual, regular, paniculate; sepals 4–5, free, imbricated; petals 4–5, imbricated and twisted in the bud; stamens numerous, free or slightly connate at base; ovary superior, 1-celled or falsely more or less several-celled by the ingrowing of the parietal placentæ, the ovules many; style 1: fr. a caps. dehiscent by 2–5 valves.

BIXA, L. One tree native in trop. Amer. but widely distributed and run wild throughout the tropics.—Lvs. large, entire, palmately-veined: fls. showy, in terminal panicles; sepals 5, glandular at base, deciduous; petals 5: caps. ovoid, red-brown, 2-valved, soft-spiny. (Bix-a: S. American name.)

B. Orellana, L. Annatto. Arnotto. Shrub or small tree usually 10–12 ft. high, but growing to 30 ft.: lvs. slender-petioled, ovate, 3–7 in. long, cordate or truncate at base, acuminate: fls. pink or rose, about 2 in. across: caps. 1–2 in. long. (Orellana: pre-Linnæan name.)

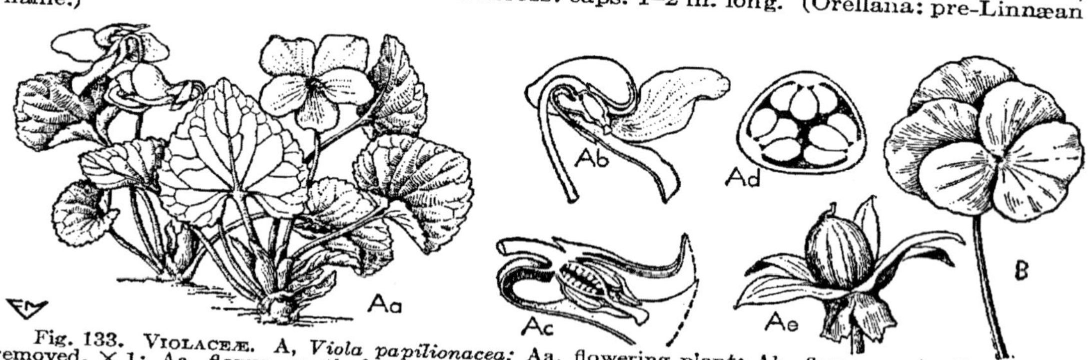

Fig. 133. Violaceæ. A, *Viola papilionacea:* Aa, flowering plant; Ab, flower, perianth partiall removed, × 1; Ac, flower, vertical section, × 2; Ad, ovary, cross-section, × 4; Ae, capsule, × 1. B, *V. tricolor* var. *hortensis:* flower, face view, × ½.

133. VIOLACEÆ. VIOLET FAMILY

Herbs, shrubs, or rarely trees, of 15 genera and about 400 species of wide distribution; the pansies and violets are among the best-known garden fls. and one is also forced in the greenhouse.—Lvs. alternate or basal, rarely opposite, simple, entire or sometimes laciniate, stipulate: fls. irregular or regular, bisexual, plant rarely polygamous or diœcious, solitary or in racemes, spikes, or fascicles, the peduncles usually 2-bracted; sepals 5, free or slightly connate, usually persistent; petals 5, hypogynous, the lower one usually larger than the others and saccate or spurred; stamens 5, alternate with petals, connate into ring around the ovary, often dissimilar and the 2 lower spurred or appendaged; ovary free, sessile, 1-celled, with 3, seldom 2–5, parietal placentæ bearing 1 to many ovules; style simple: fr. a caps. dehiscent by valves or rarely an indehiscent berry.

VIOLA, L. VIOLET. Probably 300 species of per. herbs, rarely subshrubs, stemless or leafy-stemmed, native in both the north and south temp. zones.—Stipules persistent, often leafy: peduncles axillary, 1- or rarely 2-fld.; fls. of two kinds, those in spring with showy petals and those in summer cleistogamous, apetalous, and bearing abundant seeds; petaliferous fls. nodding, the lower petal spurred and the other 4 in 2 unlike pairs; stamens 5, short, the 2 lower with nectar-bearing appendages projecting backward into the spur: caps. dehiscing into 3 boat-shaped valves with thick rigid keels, the drying and contracting of the thin sides causing the seeds to be forcibly discharged. (Vi-ola: classical name.)

A. Plant stemless, the peduncles arising directly from base or crown.
  B. Color of fls. yellow .... 1. *V. rotundifolia*
  BB. Color of fls. violet or white.
    C. Lvs. deeply palmately lobed or parted.
      D. Sepals not ciliate: fls. fragrant .... 2. *V. eizanensis*
      DD. Sepals ciliate: fls. not fragrant.
        E. Petals not bearded: cleistogamous fls. not produced .... 3. *V. pedata*
        EE. Petals, at least some of them, densely bearded: cleistogamous fls. produced.
          F. Petioles pubescent: spurred petal glabrous: peduncles of cleistogamous fls. prostrate .... 4. *V. palmata*
          FF. Petioles glabrous: spurred petal bearded: peduncles of cleistogamous fls. erect .... 5. *V. pedatifida*
    CC. Lvs. not palmately parted.
      D. Base of lf. tapering into margined petiole; blade lanceolate .... 6. *V. lanceolata*
      DD. Base of lf. cordate or truncate; blade oblong or ovate.
        E. Stolons produced.
          F. Upper petals reflexed or twisted .... 7. *V. blanda*
          FF. Upper petals not reflexed or twisted.
            G. Shape of lf. oblong to narrow-ovate, rounded at base .... 8. *V. primulifolia*
            GG. Shape of lf. broad-ovate to reniform, deeply cordate at base.
              H. Spur almost none .... 9. *V. hederacea*
              HH. Spur evident.
                I. Fls. very fragrant: lvs. finely pubescent .... 10. *V. odorata*
                II. Fls. not fragrant: lvs. glabrous .... 11. *V. palustris*
        EE. Stolons not produced.
          F. Sepals ciliate .... 12. *V. septentrionalis*
          FF. Sepals glabrous.
            G. Spurred as well as lateral petals bearded .... 13. *V. sagittata*
            GG. Spurred petal glabrous, lateral petals bearded.
              H. Beard of clavate hairs: cleistogamous fls. on erect peduncles .. 14. *V. cucullata*
              HH. Beard of fine hairs: cleistogamous fls. on prostrate peduncles.
                I. Rootstock slender .... 15. *V. Jooi*
                II. Rootstock stout.
                  J. Seeds dark brown: lvs. usually broader than long .... 16. *V. papilionacea*
                  JJ. Seeds buff: lvs. usually longer than broad .... 17. *V. missouriensis*
AA. Plant with evident sts., the peduncles arising some distance from ground.
  B. Lvs. deeply lobed or cut.
    C. Foliage pubescent, at least above.
      D. Sts. naked below, 6–15 in.: lvs. deeply lobed .... 18. *V. lobata*
      DD. Sts. not naked below, 2–6 in.: lvs. bipinnate .... 19. *V. Douglasii*
    CC. Foliage glabrous.
      D. Lower petals pale yellow .... 20. *V. Hallii*
      DD. Lower petals violet to white .... 21. *V. trinervata*
  BB. Lvs. not lobed or cut.
    C. Fls. very large, 1 in. or more across.
      D. Stipules pinnatifid or deeply toothed.
        E. Rootstock producing runners .... 22. *V. calcarata*
        EE. Rootstock not producing runners.
          F. Spur long and acute: plant tufted .... 23. *V. cornuta*
          FF. Spur short and obtuse: plant not tufted .... 24. *V. tricolor* var. *hortensis*
      DD. Stipules entire or only notched at base .... 28. *V. pedunculata*
    CC. Fls. small or medium-sized, less than 1 in. across.

D. Color of fls. yellow.
  E. Stipules pinnatifid . . . . 36. *V. saxatilis*
  EE. Stipules not pinnatifid.
    F. Sts. naked below.
      G. Herbage soft-pubescent . . . . 25. *V. pubescens*
      GG. Herbage glabrous or only slightly pubescent.
        H. Lf. halberd-shaped, tapering to point . . . . 26. *V. hastata*
        HH. Lf. orbicular to reniform, abruptly acute . . . . 27. *V. glabella*
    FF. Sts. leafy below.
      G. Peduncles much longer than lvs . . . . 28. *V. pedunculata*
      GG. Peduncles shorter than or about equalling lvs.
        H. Herbage pubescent only on lower side of lvs. and petioles . . . . 29. *V. Nuttallii*
        HH. Herbage pubescent throughout . . . . 30. *V. præmorsa*
DD. Color of fls. violet or white.
  E. Basic color of petals white, at least on the front.
    F. Base of petals without yellow spot . . . . 31. *V. striata*
    FF. Base of petals with yellow spot.
      G. Stipules with few filiform teeth . . . . 32. *V. ocellata*
      GG. Stipules entire.
        H. Under side of lvs. nearly glabrous: not producing runners . . . . 33. *V. canadensis*
        HH. Under side of lvs. pubescent: producing underground runners . . . . 34. *V. rugulosa*
  EE. Basic color of petals violet.
    F. Stipules entire . . . . 35. *V. Flettii*
    FF. Stipules toothed or pinnatifid.
      G. The stipules pinnatifid to middle or below.
        H. Spur about half length of corolla: terminal segm. of stipules broad and crenate . . . . 36. *V. saxatilis*
        HH. Spur nearly equalling corolla: terminal segm. of stipules narrow and not crenate.
          I. Herbage puberulous: stipules parted to base . . . . 37. *V. gracilis*
          II. Herbage nearly glabrous: stipules parted to middle . . . . . 38. *V. elegantula*
      GG. The stipules toothed or fimbriate but not pinnatifid.
        H. Lateral petals beardless; spur as long as corolla . . . . 39. *V. rostrata*
        HH. Lateral petals bearded; spur half or less as long as corolla.
          I. Margins of stipules with few spiny teeth.
            J. Spur ⅓in. or more long, often hooked . . . . 40. *V. adunca*
            JJ. Spur about ⅙in. long, not hooked . . . . 41. *V. conspersa*
          II. Margins of stipules ciliate.
            J. Spur violet, acute . . . . 42. *V. sylvestris*
            JJ. Spur yellowish-white, rounded . . . . 43. *V. Riviniana*

1. **V. rotundifolia,** Michx. Stemless, rootstock stout, late in season with purplish bracted raceme-like sts. bearing cleistogamous fls.: lvs. oval to orbicular, 1–4 in. wide, obtuse, cordate at base, crenate, pubescent when young but becoming nearly glabrous: fls. on peduncles 2–4 in. long, yellow, the 3 lower petals veined with brown, the lateral bearded: seeds nearly white. Me. to N. Ga.

2. **V. eizanensis,** Makino (*V. dissecta* var. *eizanensis,* Makino). Stemless from a thick rootstock: lvs. at flowering 3 in. long and 1½ in. wide, divided into lanceolate segms. which are again cleft, glabrous or slightly pubescent on nerves, on long petioles: fls. on peduncles 2–5 in. long, about 1 in. across, fragrant, pale rose or violet with deeper veins, petals rounded at apex, lateral slightly bearded at base, spur straight and rounded, about ¼in. long. Mts. of Japan.

3. **V. pedata,** L. (*V. pedata* var. *bicolor,* Pursh). Birds-foot Violet. Stemless from a short rootstock, not producing cleistogamous fls.: lvs. 3-cleft, the lateral divisions again cleft into linear toothed or cut segms., nearly glabrous: fls. on peduncles 2–6 in. long, ¾–1½ in. across, the upper petals dark violet, lower pale lilac with darker veins, all beardless: seeds copper-colored. Mass. to N. C. west to Minn. Var. **concolor,** Holm., has larger fls. of one shade of violet with white spot at base of lower petal; N. C. to Fla. and Tex.

4. **V. palmata,** L. Stemless from a stout rootstock, cleistogamous fls. borne on prostrate peduncles: lvs. palmately 5–11-lobed or parted into variously lobed or cut segms., pubescent beneath and on petioles: fls. on peduncles 3–5 in. long, to 1 in. across, violet, 3 lower petals veined with purple and with white base, lateral petals bearded: seeds brown. Mass. to Fla. and Miss.

5. **V. pedatifida,** Don. Stemless from a short vertical rootstock, the cleistogamous fls. on erect peduncles: lvs. palmately 3-parted into segms. which are again cut into linear lobed divisions, hairy on margins and veins below, on glabrous petioles 2–10 in. long: fls. on peduncles longer than lvs., to ¾in. across, reddish-violet, the 3 lower petals veined with purple and white-bearded at base: seeds buff or light brown. Prairies, Ohio to Sask. and New Mex.

6. **V. lanceolata,** L. Stemless from a creeping branching rootstock, the cleistogamous fls. on erect peduncles: lvs. elliptical or lanceolate, 2–6 in. long, tapering into margined reddish petioles, narrowed at tip, shallowly toothed, glabrous: fls. on peduncles 2–4 in. long, ¼–½in. across, white, the 3 lower petals veined with purple, lateral petals beardless or only slightly bearded: seeds dark brown. Moist soil, N. S. to Fla. and Tex.

7. **V. blanda,** Willd. Sweet White Violet. Stemless from a short rootstock, producing long runners and cleistogamous fls. on prostrate peduncles: lvs. ovate-cordate, 1–2 in. across, acute, crenate, petioles reddish, glabrous except for few hairs above: fls. on peduncles 2–4 in. long, fragrant, ¼–½in. across, white, 3 lower petals veined with purple, lateral petals usually beardless, upper petals narrow and reflexed or twisted: seeds dark brown. Que. to N. Ga. west to Minn.

8. **V. primulifolia,** L. Stemless from a vertical rootstock, producing leafy stolons and cleistogamous fls. on erect peduncles: lvs. oblong or narrow-ovate, rounded at base, apex rounded or acute, crenate, on reddish margined petioles, usually somewhat pubescent: fls. on scapes 2–10 in. long, ¼–⅓in. across, white, 3 lower petals veined with purple, lateral petals slightly bearded or beardless: seeds reddish-brown. Moist soil, N. B. to Fla. and Tex.

9. **V. hederacea,** Labill. (*Erpetion reniforme,* Sweet). Australian Violet. Stemless, densely tufted, producing creeping stolons: lvs. reniform, orbicular or spatulate, ½–1½ in. across, entire or irregularly toothed, glabrous or pubescent; stipules lanceolate-subulate: fls. on scapes longer than lvs., ¼–¾in. across, blue or rarely white, spur reduced to slight protuberance: seeds usually dark. Australia.

10. **V. odorata,** L. Sweet, Garden or Florists Violet. Tufted, stemless, producing long prostrate stolons flowering the second year, cleistogamous fls. on recurving peduncles: lvs. cordate-ovate to reniform, 1–2 in. across, obtuse, obtusely serrate, finely pubescent; stipules ovate-lanceolate, acuminate: peduncles arising directly from base or crown, bracted at about the middle; fls. deep violet, rarely rose or white, fragrant, about ¾in. across; spur short, obtuse, nearly straight; style terminating in a slender hooked beak: seeds cream-colored. Eu., Afr., Asia.—Runs into many forms varying in stature, size and color of fls.; there are double-fld. strains and everblooming (*semperflorens*).

11. **V. palustris,** L. Marsh Violet. Stemless, from a creeping underground rootstock: lvs. broad-cordate-ovate, 1–2½ in. across, crenate, glabrous; stipules ovate, reddish: fls. on peduncles 2–10 in. long, to ½in. across, lilac to nearly white, 3 lower petals with darker veins, lateral petals slightly bearded, spur short and obtuse: seeds dark brown. Moist soil, N. N. Amer., Eu., Asia.

12. **V. septentrionalis,** Greene. Northern Blue Violet. Stemless from a short stout rootstock, the cleistogamous fls. on ascending bristly peduncles: lvs. cordate-ovate to reniform, 2–3 in. across, acute, margins crenate and ciliate; petioles 3–5 in. long, pubescent: fls. on pubescent peduncles exceeding lvs., ½–¾in. across, violet to white veined with purple, 3 lower petals white at base and densely bearded; sepals ciliate: seeds dark brown. Newf. to B. C.

13. **V. sagittata,** Ait. Stemless from a short rootstock, the cleistogamous fls. on erect peduncles: lvs. oblong, 1½–4 in. long, cordate or truncate at base and hastately toothed, or sometimes triangular-ovate, pubescent or glabrous: fls. on peduncles as long as lvs., ½in. across, violet, 3 lower petals veined with purple and white and densely bearded at base: seeds dark brown. Moist places, Mass. to Ga. and Ark.

14. **V. cucullata,** Ait. Marsh Blue Violet. Stemless, from scaly rootstock, cleistogamous fls. on long erect peduncles: lvs. broad-cordate-ovate to reniform, 1–3½ in. across, acute, crenate, usually glabrous: fls. on peduncles 3–6 in. long, ½–1 in. across, violet, lower petal veined purple and white at base, lateral petals densely bearded with clavate hairs: seeds nearly black. Wet places, Newf. to Ga. and Ark.

15. **V. Jooi,** Janka. Stemless from a slender rootstock: lvs. ovate or oblong, cordate, ½–1½ in. long, acute or obtuse, finely crenate, glabrous, lateral veins extending to margins, on slender petioles to 2 in. long: fls. on bracted peduncles 2–3 in. long, about ¾in. across, pinkish-violet, lateral petals bearded: seeds purple-brown. (Named for Prof. Dr. Stephen Joo, authority on Hungarian flora in middle of 19th century.) Hungary.

16. **V. papilionacea,** Pursh. Stemless, from a stout rootstock, cleistogamous fls. on prostrate peduncles: lvs. cordate-ovate to reniform, to 5 in. across, acute, evenly serrate, glabrous except on petioles which become 4–8 in. long: fls. on peduncles about length of lvs., ½–¾in. across, violet to white, 3 lower petals veined with purple, lateral petals bearded, lower petal often boat-shaped: seeds dark brown. Me. to Ga. and Okla.—Closely related and perhaps a var. is **V. Priceana,** Pollard, Confederate Violet, fls. whitish heavily veined with violet-blue; Tenn. to Ark.

17. **V. missouriensis,** Greene. Differs from *V. papilionacea* in lvs. longer than broad, more attenuate at apex, glabrous, and seeds buff. Ill. to Tex.

18. **V. lobata,** Benth. Sts. erect, 6–15 in. high, naked below, from a thick rootstock: lvs. ovate, 1–4 in. across, palmately parted into 5–9 oblong lobes, pubescent; stipules lf.-like, toothed or cut: fls. on peduncles 1–2 in. long, about ½in. long, yellow veined with brown, the 2 upper reddish-brown on back, lateral petals yellow-bearded, spur very short and broad: seeds buff marked with brown. Ore. to Calif.

19. **V. Douglasii,** Steud. (*V. chrysantha,* Hook.). Sts. 2–6 in. above ground, from a deep rootstock: lvs. 1–1½ in. long, bipinnate into linear or oblong segms., pubescent above and on margins, long-petioled; stipules lanceolate, entire or cut: fls. on peduncles 2–3 in. long,

½–¾in. long, deep yellow veined with brown, the 2 upper purplish-brown on back, lateral petals yellow-bearded, spur very short: seeds buff. (Named for David Douglas, page 42.) Ore. to Calif.

20. **V. Hallii,** Gray. Sts. 4–6 in. above ground, from a deep rootstock: lvs. 1–1½ in. long, divided into linear or lanceolate apiculate segms., glabrous and somewhat glaucous; stipules entire or cut: fls. on peduncles 1–4 in. long, ½–¾in. long, upper petals dark violet, others pale yellow or cream-color veined with violet, lateral petals yellow-bearded, spur very short: seeds buff. (Named for its collector, Prof. Elihu Hall, of Willamette Univ., Salem, Ore.) Ore., Calif.

21. **V. trinervata,** Howell. Sts. 3–6 in. above ground, from a deep rootstock: lvs. thick, divided into 3–7 lanceolate segms. which are prominently 3-nerved, glabrous; stipules lanceolate, entire: fls. on peduncles longer than lvs., fragrant, ½in. long, upper petals purple, others violet to white veined with purple and yellow spot at base, lateral petals yellow-bearded, lower petal emarginate, spur short-saccate: seeds buff. Wash., Ore.

22. **V. calcarata,** L. Sts. to 4 in., with underground creeping runners: lvs. ovate to lanceolate, tapering into petiole, 1–1½ in. long, slightly crenate, nearly glabrous; stipules pinnatifid or toothed: fls. on erect peduncles 3–4 in. long, 1–1½ in. across, violet or sometimes yellow or white, petals broad, spur as long as corolla and straight or slightly curved. Mts. of S. Eu.

23. **V. cornuta,** L. Horned Violet. Tufted or Bedding Pansy. Tufted per. producing evident sts. 4–12 in. high: lvs. ovate, slightly cordate, 1–2 in. long, usually acuminate, crenately serrate, pubescent beneath on nerves and margins; stipules large, triangular, coarsely dentate, ciliate: fls. on peduncles 2–4 in. long, somewhat fragrant, 1–1½ in. across, violet, the obovate obtuse petals standing well apart, spur slender, acute, about as long as calyx; style enlarged upward. Spain and Pyrenees.—Hort. forms are: **alba,** fls. white; **atropurpurea,** fls. dark purple with yellow center; **lutea splendens,** fls. golden-yellow; **Papilio,** fls. violet with purple center, large. A hybrid between *V. cornuta* and a form of *V. tricolor* is **V. florariensis,** Correvon, blooming all year, fls. purple, lower petal yellow at base, spur short. The violet Jersey Gem belongs in *V. cornuta.*

24. **V. tricolor, L., var. hortensis, DC.** Pansy. Heartsease. Ann. or short-lived per., the sts. becoming long and much-branched: basal lvs. round-cordate; st.-lvs. ovate-oblong or lanceolate, crenate-dentate, petioled, the large stipules pinnately parted toward base: fls. large, 1–2 in. across, usually having three colors, mostly blue, whitish and yellow; petals nearly or quite orbicular, imbricated, spur short and obtuse; style enlarged upward. Eu.—The pansy is one of the oldest garden fls. and is usually considered an offshoot of *V. tricolor;* it is likely, however, that other wild species are involved in its parentage, and probably a separate designation should be given it. Typical *V. tricolor,* native in Eu. and adventive in N. Amer., with predominately purple fls. to ¾in. across, is common as a weed in many gardens where it is known as Wild and Field pansy; and its close relative, *V. arvensis,* Murr., with similar but predominately pale yellow fls., is infrequent in like situations.

25. **V. pubescens,** Ait. Sts. 8–12 in. high from a short rootstock, naked below: lvs. broad-ovate or reniform, cordate or truncate at base, apex acute or tapering, crenate, soft-pubescent; stipules large, ovate-lanceolate: fls. on short peduncles, ¼–½in. long, lemon-yellow, 3 lower petals veined with purple, lateral petals bearded, spur short: seeds brown. N. S. to N. C. and Mo.

26. **V. hastata,** Michx. Sts. 4–10 in. high from a white brittle rootstock, naked below: lvs. halberd-shaped with rounded basal lobes, tapering to a point, distantly toothed, slightly pubescent; stipules small, toothed: fls. on short peduncles, ¼–⅓in. long, lemon-yellow, lower veined with purple, 2 upper brownish-purple on back, lateral petals bearded, spur very short: seeds brown. Pa. to Fla.

27. **V. glabella,** Nutt. Sts. 3–12 in. high from a horizontal rootstock, naked below: lvs. orbicular to reniform, 1–3 in. across, abruptly acute, crenate, glabrous or slightly pubescent; stipules small, entire: fls. on short peduncles, ⅓–½in. long, lemon-yellow, 3 lower veined with purple, lateral petals bearded, spur very short: seeds brown. Alaska to Calif.

28. **V. pedunculata,** Torr. & Gray. Sts. 4–13 in. from a thick rootstock and branching at ground: lvs. broad-ovate, ½–2 in. long, truncate at base, crenate, pubescent; stipules narrow-lanceolate, slightly toothed: fls. on slender peduncles 4–7 in. long, ¾–1¼ in. across, golden-yellow, lower petals veined with brown, upper reddish-brown on back, lateral bearded, spur short: seeds dark brown. Calif., Lower Calif.

29. **V. Nuttallii,** Pursh. Sts. 2–7 in. from a tapering rootstock: lvs. oblong-lanceolate to lanceolate, ½in. across, tapering to petiole, slightly crenate, pubescent beneath and on petioles; stipules lanceolate, entire: fls. on peduncles shorter than lvs., ¼in. long, lemon-yellow, lower petals veined with brown, upper purple on back, lateral slightly bearded, spur short: seeds light brown. (Named for Thomas Nuttall, page 49.) Sask. to Kans. and Rocky Mts.

30. **V. præmorsa,** Dougl. (*V. Nuttallii* var. *præmorsa*, Wats.). Similar to *V. Nuttallii*, differing in being pubescent throughout, with broader lvs., longer petioles and larger fls. B C. to Calif.

31. **V. striata,** Ait. Sts. 6–12 in. from a woody rootstock, becoming decumbent and 2 ft. long: lvs. orbicular to ovate, cordate, 1–1½ in. across, finely toothed, nearly glabrous; stipules oblong-lanceolate, fimbriate: fls. on long peduncles, ½in. long, white or cream-colored, lower petals veined with purple, lateral densely bearded, spur blunt, ⅙in. long: seeds buff. N. Y. to Ga. and Mo.

32. **V. ocellata,** Torr. & Gray. Sts. 6–12 in. from a long rootstock: lvs. cordate- or triangular-ovate, 1–2½ in. long, acute, crenate, slightly pubescent; stipules with few filiform teeth, scarious: fls. on peduncles nearly equalling lvs., ½in. long, white with yellow at base of petals, veined with purple, upper violet on outside, lateral petals yellow-bearded, spur very short and broad: seeds brownish-purple. Ore. to Calif.

33. **V. canadensis,** L. Sts. 8–16 in. from thick rootstock: lvs. broad-ovate, cordate, tapering at tip, serrate, slightly pubescent above; stipules entire, scarious: fls. on short peduncles, ½in. long, white with yellow at base of petals, tinged violet on back, lower veined with purple, lateral petals bearded, spur very short: seeds brownish-purple. N. B. to Rocky Mts. and Ariz.

34. **V. rugulosa,** Greene. Similar to *V. canadensis* but a larger plant producing underground runners, lvs. to 4 in. across and pubescent beneath. Alaska to Colo.

35. **V. Flettii,** Piper. Sts. 4–6 in. from stout white rootstock: lvs. broad-ovate to reniform, 1–1¾ in. across, acute, shallowly serrate, glabrous or slightly pubescent, with conspicuous purplish veins; stipules lanceolate, entire, scarious: fls. on peduncles above the lvs., ½in. long, reddish-violet with yellow base, lower petals veined with purple, lateral with yellow clavate beards, spur yellow: seeds dark brown. (Named for J. B. Flett, who first collected it.) Olympic Mts., Wash.

36. **V. saxatilis,** F. W. Schmidt. Sts. several from a slender rootstock, about 6 in. high: lvs. nearly orbicular to ovate-lanceolate, narrowed into petiole, crenate, ciliate on margins and nerves beneath; stipules pinnatifid, terminal segm. broad and crenate: fls. on long peduncles, yellow or violet, ½–¾in. across, spur about half length of corolla, curved or straight. Cent. Eu.

37. **V. gracilis,** Sibth. & Smith. Sts. 2–4 in. or more high: lvs. oblong to linear-lanceolate, attenuate at base, slightly crenate, puberulous; stipules cut into 3–5 linear acute segms.: fls. violet, spur about as long as corolla and usually curved. Macedonia to Asia Minor.

38. **V. elegantula,** Schott (*V. bosniaca*, Form.). Sts. to 6 in., becoming straggling: lvs. orbicular to ovate-lanceolate, crenate, nearly glabrous; stipules pinnatifid to about the middle: fls. on long peduncles above the foliage, about ¾in. long, rose-purple with yellow striped spot at base of lower petal, spur about as long as corolla. S. E. Eu.

39. **V. rostrata,** Pursh. Long-spurred Violet. Sts. 4–8 in. from a slender rootstock: lvs. orbicular or broad-ovate, cordate, acute, serrate, nearly glabrous; stipules with spiny teeth: fls. on long peduncles above the foliage, violet with darker violet at base, lateral petals beardless, spur usually straight and about ½in. long, equalling the corolla: seeds brown. Que. to Mich. and Ga.

40. **V. adunca,** Smith. Sts. 4–10 in. from a stout rootstock: lvs. ovate, somewhat cordate, ½–1 in. across, obtuse, crenate, glabrous or somewhat pubescent; stipules with few spiny teeth: fls. on long peduncles, ½in. long, violet, lower petals with white base veined with purple, lateral petals white-bearded, spur about ⅓in. long, often hooked: seeds dark brown. N. Amer.

41. **V. conspersa,** Reichb. Sts. to 6 in. or more from a brown rootstock: lvs. orbicular to broad-ovate, cordate, crenate, glabrous; stipules with spiny teeth mostly on one side: fls. many on peduncles longer than lvs., pale violet, lower petals veined with purple, lateral petals densely bearded, spur slender, about ⅙in. long: seeds buff. Que. to Minn. and Ga.

42. **V. sylvestris,** Lam. (*V. silvatica*, Fries). Sts. to 8 or 12 in., ascending or reclining, from a creeping rootstock: lvs. ovate-cordate, 1–2 in. across, crenate, nearly glabrous; stipules linear-lanceolate, densely fimbriate: fls. on long peduncles, ½–¾in. long, violet, lower petals white at base veined with violet, spur straight, acute, ⅛–¼in. long. Eu.

43. **V. Riviniana,** Reichb. Differs from *V. sylvestris* in larger lvs. and fls., the latter with yellowish-white rounded spurs. Eu.

134. FLACOURTIACEÆ. FLACOURTIA FAMILY

Trees and shrubs of about 80 genera and 500 species in trop. regions, the governors-plum and the kei-apple planted for hedges in warm countries and the frs. also made into jams and preserves.—Lvs. mostly alternate (so in ours), simple, entire or dentate, the stipules usually deciduous: fls. regular, bisexual or unisexual, solitary

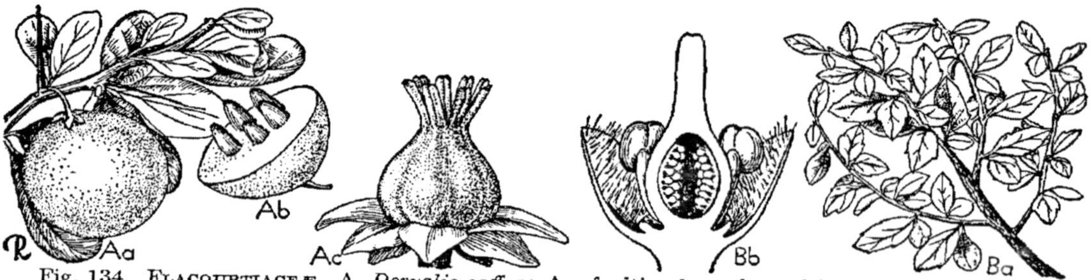

Fig. 134. FLACOURTIACEÆ. A, *Dovyalis caffra:* Aa, fruiting branch, × ¼; Ab, fruit, terminal half removed exposing seeds, × ¼; Ac, pistillate flower, × 3. B, *Azara microphylla:* Ba, vegetative branch, × ⅓; Bb, flower, vertical section, × 6.

in the axils or in axillary or terminal clusters or racemes; floral envelopes imbricated; sepals 2 or more, free or united; petals free, as many as sepals or rarely more, in ours wanting, often inserted on outer edge of a hypogynous or perigynous swollen disk, usually small; stamens numerous, seldom as few as petals and then alternate with sepals, in 1 or several series or in bundles opposite the petals, staminodia sometimes present; ovary superior or nearly so, often 1-celled, with few or many ovules borne on parietal placentæ, the styles as many as placentæ, free or united, or sometimes 2- or more-celled: fr. a caps., berry or drupe.

A. Infl. axillary: lvs. pinnately veined.
B. Styles 2 or more; ovary incompletely 2–8-celled.
C. Sepals imbricated: ovules many: seed inclosed in stone-like covering.........1. FLACOURTIA
CC. Sepals scarcely imbricated: ovules 1–6: seeds without stone-like covering.......2. DOVYALIS
BB. Styles 1; ovary 1-celled..3. AZARA
AA. Infl. terminal: lvs. palmately veined..4. IDESIA

1. **FLACOURTIA,** Comm. Fifteen or more species of shrubs or small trees, often spine-bearing, native in trop. Afr., Asia, and adjacent isls.—Lvs. short-petioled, usually dentate, pinnate-veined, without stipules: fls. small, bisexual or unisexual, usually in small axillary racemes or clusters, with small bracts; sepals 4–5, scale-like, slightly united at base, ciliate, imbricated, sometimes persistent; petals 0; stamens many, the filaments long and slender; ovary superior, incompletely 2–8-celled, surrounded by a lobed and glandular disk and sometimes by staminodia, ovules many on each placenta; styles 2–6 or many, free or slightly united at base: fr. an indehiscent berry-like drupe, each seed inclosed in a stone-like covering. (Flacourt-ia: after Etienne de Flacourt, 1607–1660, General Director French East India Co. and Governor of Madagascar.)

F. indica, Merr. (*Gmelina indica*, Burm. f. *F. Ramontchi*, L'Her.). RAMONTCHI. GOVERNORS-PLUM. BATOKO-PLUM. Glabrous commonly diœcious shrub or tree to 25 ft., with or without axillary spines: lvs. ovate to elliptic, 2–3 in. long, acuminate, crenate-dentate: fls. yellowish: fr. globose, ½–1 in. diam., deep maroon-colored, with juicy pulp surrounding the small thin seeds. S. Asia, Madagascar.

2. **DOVYALIS,** E. Mey. (sometimes but not originally spelled *Doryalis*). About 11 species of shrubs or small trees, with or without axillary spines, native in Afr. and Ceylon.—Lvs. short-petioled, pinnate-veined and usually 3-nerved at base, the stipules very small and deciduous: plant diœcious: staminate fls. many in the axils, with 4 seldom 5–7 hairy sepals, no petals, and numerous stamens on a fleshy disk alternating with large glands; pistillate fls. solitary or few together, with 5–9 hairy glandular sepals persistent until fruiting, no petals, sometimes staminodia; ovary completely or incompletely 2–8-celled with 1–6 ovules on each placenta and 2–8 styles: fr. an indehiscent berry. (Dovy-alis: name unexplained.)

A. Fr. yellow, nearly glabrous..1. *D. caffra*
AA. Fr. maroon-purple, velvety..2. *D. hebecarpa*

1. **D. caffra,** Warb. (*Aberia caffra*, Harvey & Sond.). KEI-APPLE. UMKOKOLO. To 20 ft., vigorous, armed with long stiff sharp thorns: lvs. oblong-obovate, about 2 in. long, often in small clusters at base of thorns, obtuse, entire: fls. greenish and inconspicuous: fr. oblate or nearly round, about 1 in. diam., bright yellow, the yellow juicy acid pulp surrounding the flattened seeds. S. Afr.

2. **D. hebecarpa**, Warb. (*Roumea hebecarpa*, Gardner. *Aberia Gardneri*, Clos). KITEMBILLA. CEYLON-GOOSEBERRY. To 15 or 20 ft., with long sharp spines: lvs. lanceolate to oval, 2–4 in. long, acute, entire or slightly toothed: fr. nearly round, 1 in. diam., maroon-purple with purplish edible sweet pulp. Ceylon and India.

3. **AZARA**, Ruiz & Pav. Evergreen shrubs or small trees with very bitter wood, of more than 20 species in S. Amer., mostly native to Chile, one species occasionally planted for a wall-cover in warm regions.—Lvs. alternate, leathery, short-petioled, with usually 1 of the stipules enlarged and lf.-like: fls. usually bisexual, small, fragrant, in axillary peduncled racemes or clusters, the bracts small; sepals 4–5, rarely 6, persistent; petals 0; stamens numerous, seldom 5 or 10, with 5 glands between stamens and sepals and opposite the latter; ovary superior, 1-celled with many ovules on 2–4 parietal placentæ, the style simple and elongated: fr. a berry which is sometimes dehiscent at apex. (Aza-ra: after J. N. Azara, 1731–1804, Spanish promoter of science, especially botany.)

A. microphylla, Hook. f. From 3–12 ft. high: lvs. obovate, ½–¾in. long, serrate or nearly entire, glabrous and shining, the stipules about half size of lf.: fls. in few-fld. clusters, greenish, with 5 stamens, blooming Feb.–Mar.: berries orange. Chile.

4. **IDESIA**, Maxim. One deciduous tree native in China and Japan, adapted to the southern states.—Lvs. alternate, long-petioled, stipules small: plant diœcious or polygamous: fls. in large terminal panicles; sepals usually 5, imbricated; petals 0; stamens numerous with filiform pubescent filaments; ovary superior, 1-celled with many ovules on each placenta; styles 5, spreading: fr. a fleshy many-seeded berry. (Ide-sia: named for Eberhard Ysbrant Ides, Dutch traveller in China 1691–1695.)

I. polycarpa, Maxim. To 50 ft.: lvs. ovate, 5–10 in. long, cordate, remotely toothed, palmately veined, glabrous except in axils of veins, glaucous beneath: fls. greenish-yellow, fragrant, in drooping panicles to 10 in. long: berries orange-red, ⅓in. across.

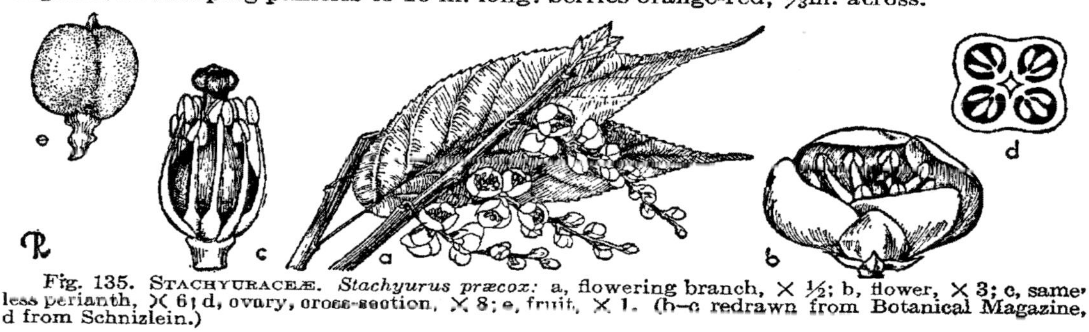

Fig. 135. STACHYURACEÆ. *Stachyurus præcox:* a, flowering branch, × ½; b, flower, × 3; c, same less perianth, × 6; d, ovary, cross-section, × 8; e, fruit, × 1. (b–c redrawn from Botanical Magazine, d from Schnizlein.)

135. STACHYURACEÆ. STACHYURUS FAMILY

A single genus of shrubs or small trees native in Asia, occasionally planted for ornament.—Lvs. alternate, toothed; stipules small, deciduous: fls. regular, bisexual or sometimes unisexual, borne in axillary racemes before the lvs.; sepals and petals 4, imbricated; stamens 8, distinct; ovary superior, 1-celled but appearing 4-celled by intrusion of parietal placentæ, style with 4-lobed stigma: fr. berry-like, with many small seeds surrounded by a soft aril.

STACHYURUS, Sieb. & Zucc. Species 5–6; technical characters of the family. (Stachyu-rus: Greek for *spike* and *tail*, referring to the infl.)

S. præcox, Sieb. & Zucc. Shrub to 12 ft.: lvs. ovate to ovate-lanceolate, 3–5½ in. long, acuminate, glabrous except on veins beneath: fls. yellow, campanulate, ⅓in. long, in short-stalked racemes 2–3 in. long: fr. globose, greenish-yellow, ⅓in. across. Japan.

136. PASSIFLORACEÆ. PASSION-FLOWER FAMILY

Herbaceous or woody plants, usually climbing by tendrils, of 12 genera and more than 500 species in warm and trop. regions, most abundant in S. Amer. and one

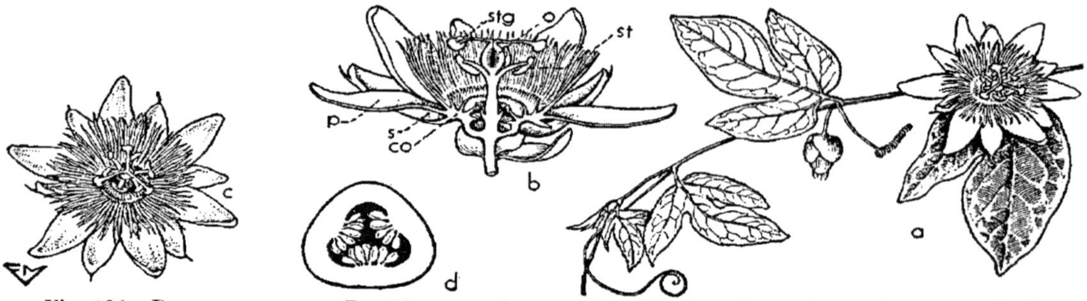

Fig. 136. Passifloraceæ. *Passiflora cærulea:* a, flowering branch, × 1/6; b, flower, vertical section, × 1/3 (co corona, o ovary, p petal, s sepal, st stamen, stg stigma); c, flower, face view, × 1/4; d, ovary, cross-section, × 2.

species extending north to Pa.; several passifloras are grown for their edible frs. and others as ornamental vines.—Lvs. alternate, usually petioled, simple or lobed, mostly stipulate; tendrils axillary, simple: fls. bisexual or unisexual, regular, solitary or clustered; sepals 3–5, imbricated, often petaloid; petals as many as sepals and alternating with them or sometimes wanting, inserted on throat of calyx, usually free, imbricated, sometimes fringed; corona, or outgrowth of receptacle, usually present, of 1 to several rows, composed of many filaments free or united at base, or tubular and often deeply fringed; stamens usually 5 and alternate with petals, seldom 3–10, the filaments free or monadelphous; ovary superior, often on a gynophore or stalk, 1-celled with 3–5 parietal placentæ bearing several to many ovules, the styles 1–5: fr. a caps. or berry, the seeds with a fleshy aril.

PASSIFLORA, L. Passion-Flower. About 400 species mostly native in Amer., a few in Asia and Australia and 1 in Madagascar.—Lvs. entire, digitately lobed or parted, the petioles usually gland-bearing: fls. bisexual, often large and showy, solitary or racemose, mostly axillary, on articulated and often 3-bracted peduncles; sepals 5; petals 5 or sometimes wanting; stamens 5, united in tube around stalk of ovary, the anthers versatile; styles 3: fr. a many-seeded berry. (Passiflo-ra: *passion-flower*, the parts of the fl. supposed to represent the implements of the crucifixion.)

A. Lvs. not lobed.
  B. Floral bracts free.
    C. Sts. and branches strongly 4-angled or -winged .... 1. *P. quadrangularis*
    CC. Sts. and branches terete, not winged .... 2. *P. laurifolia*
  BB. Floral bracts connate to about the middle .... 3. *P. ligularis*
AA. Lvs. lobed.
  B. Receptacle or tube short.
    C. Petals deep red .... 4. *P. racemosa*
    CC. Petals white or pink.
      D. Outer rays of corona about as long as petals: lvs. serrate.
        E. Fr. yellow when ripe: lvs. dull above .... 5. *P. incarnata*
        EE. Fr. deep purple when ripe: lvs. shining above .... 6. *P. edulis*
      DD. Outer rays of corona distinctly shorter than petals: lvs. entire.
        E. Lobes of lvs. 5–7 .... 7. *P. cærulea*
        EE. Lobes of lvs. 3 .... 8. *P. alato-cærulea*
  BB. Receptacle or tube elongated (1 1/2 in. or more long).
    C. Under surface of lvs. with pubescent veins .... 9. *P. antioquiensis*
    CC. Under surface of lvs. tomentose.
      D. Tube or receptacle of fl. about 1 1/2 in. long: fr. glabrous .... 10. *P. manicata*
      DD. Tube of fl. 4–5 in. long: fr. pubescent .... 11. *P. mollissima*

1. **P. quadrangularis,** L. Giant Granadilla. Strong glabrous climber with sts. sharply 4-angled and -winged: lvs. entire, ovate or round-ovate, 6–8 in. long, cordate, mucronate at apex, petiole with 6 glands; stipules ovate, acute, to 1 1/2 in. long: fls. 3–5 in. across, fragrant, the peduncles set in cavity at base of fl.; sepals green outside, rose-colored within, the crown of white and purple filaments, the outer series longer than the sepals and petals: fr. oblong, 8–12 in. long, greenish-yellow, with edible pulp. Trop. Amer.

2. **P. laurifolia,** L. Yellow Granadilla. Water-Lemon. Jamaica-Honeysuckle. Glabrous climber, sts. terete: lvs. entire, ovate-oblong or oblong, 3–5 in. long, acute or obtuse, petiole with 2 glands at apex; stipules linear, 1/8 in. long: fls. up to 4 in. across, white with red spots or blotches; sepals with a small horn on back; crown about length of petals, violet with white bands: fr. ovoid, about 3 in. long, yellow, edible. Trop. Amer.

3. **P. ligularis,** Juss. Sweet Granadilla. Vigorous glabrous climber, sts. terete: lvs. entire, broad-ovate, 5–6 in. long, cordate, acuminate, with 4–6 petiolar glands; stipules ovate-lanceolate, ½–1 in. long: fls. to 3 in. across, subtended by ovate-oblong bracts united to about the middle; sepals and petals greenish; crown about length of petals, white and red-purple: fr. ovoid, about 3 in. long, orange-brown or purplish, hard-shelled, with edible white pulp. Trop. Amer.

4. **P. racemosa,** Brot. (*P. princeps,* Lodd.). Glabrous climber, sts. terete and grooved: lvs. usually deeply 3-lobed, 3–5 in. long, thick, truncate or slightly cordate at base, the margins thick and entire, petiole with 2 small glands; stipules oblique, ovate, ½in. long: fls. 3–4 in. across, the cylindrical tube or receptacle swollen at base, with usually 2 peduncles from an axil, becoming racemose at ends of shoots; sepals keeled on back, ending in a sharp horn; petals shorter than sepals, deep red, wide-spreading; crown somewhat shorter than petals, white and purple: fr. oblong, 2–3 in. long, greenish-yellow, 3-grooved. Brazil.

5. **P. incarnata,** L. Wild Passion-Flower. Maypop. Strong per. vine climbing 20–30 ft., glabrous or nearly so: lvs. deeply 3-lobed, 3–6 in. long, somewhat cordate at base, serrate, petiole with 2 glands near summit; stipules setaceous, deciduous: fls. 1½–3 in. across, white; crown purple or pink, as long as or longer than petals: fr. ovoid, about 2 in. long, with 3 sutures, yellow, edible. Va. to Fla. and Tex., Bermuda.

6. **P. edulis,** Sims. Purple Granadilla. Woody climber with grooved branches: lvs. deeply 3-lobed, 2½–5 in. long, cuneate or cordate at base, serrate, shining above, petiole with 2 glands at apex: fls. 2–3 in. across; sepals white inside, horned on back; petals white; crown white, purple at base, about as long as petals: fr. oval, 2–3 in. long, deep purple when ripe, rind hard, edible. Brazil.

7. **P. cærulea,** L. Glabrous and somewhat glaucous slender vine with terete or slightly angled sts.: lvs. deeply divided into 5 lanceolate entire sharp-pointed lobes, the 2 lower ones sometimes again lobed, petiole with 2–4 glands; stipules ovate, ½–¾in. long: fls. 3–4 in. across, slightly fragrant; sepals white or pale pink within, with a short horn on back near apex; petals pale pink; crown white, purple at base and apex, distinctly shorter than petals: fr. ovate or subglobose, yellow, about 2 in. long. Brazil.—The commonest passion-flower grown in greenhouses, and there are many hybrids between this and related species.

8. **P. alato-cærulea,** Lindl. (*P. alata* × *P. cærulea. P. Pfordtii,* Hort.). Sts. 4-angled, climbing: lvs. with 3 ovate-lanceolate entire lobes, cordate, petiole with 2–4 glands: fls. fragrant, about 4 in. across; sepals white inside, revolute at margins; petals pink within, greenish-white outside; crown distinctly shorter than petals, dark purple at base, bluish in middle and white at tip. Raised at the nursery of Wm. Masters, Canterbury, England.

9. **P. antioquiensis,** Karst. (*P. Van-Volxemii,* Triana & Planch. *Tacsonia Van-Volxemii,* Lem.). Climber with terete brown-tomentose sts.: lvs. cordate-ovate in outline, about 4–5 in. long, deeply divided into 3 lanceolate acuminate serrate lobes, or sometimes entire, pubescent on veins beneath, petiole with many glands; stipules ⅛in. long: fls. 4–5 in. or more across, on long slender peduncles, bright red, the cylindrical tube or receptacle 1½ in. long and swollen at base; crown consisting of an inconspicuous toothed rim: fr. ellipsoid, edible. Colombia.

10. **P. manicata,** Pers. (*Tacsonia manicata,* Juss.). Sts. nearly terete: lvs. coriaceous, about 3 in. long, tomentose beneath, deeply divided into 3 ovate acute serrate lobes, petiole with 4–10 glands; stipules ½–¾in. long, coarsely toothed: fls. brilliant scarlet, about 4 in. across, the tube or receptacle about 1½ in. long and swollen at base; outer crown of many short blue filaments and the inner consisting of an inflexed membrane: fr. egg-shaped or subglobose, 1½–2 in. long, yellowish-green, thick-skinned, glabrous and shining. Venezuela, Colombia, Ecuador, Peru.

11. **P. mollissima,** Bailey (*Tacsonia mollissima,* HBK.). All parts of plant soft-pubescent except the tube of fl.; sts. terete or only slightly angled: lvs. cordate-ovate in outline, 4–5 in. long, deeply divided into 3 ovate-lanceolate serrate lobes, petiole with 8–12 glands; stipules ⅓in. long: fls. rose-colored, about 3 in. across, the cylindrical tube or receptacle about 4–5 in. long; crown consisting of a short rim: fr. ellipsoidal, 2½ in. long, yellow, pubescent. Andes.

137. CARICACEÆ. PAWPAW FAMILY

Small soft-wooded often diœcious or monœcious trees with milky juice, of 2 genera and about 30 species of trop. and subtrop. Amer. and 1 in Afr., the papaya widely grown for its edible melon-like fr.—Trunks straight and palm-like, rarely branched, with a terminal crown of large palmately-lobed lvs.: fls. may be one of four types: (1) *staminate,* sessile, on staminate plants in clusters on pendent racemes 1–3 ft. or more long, polypetalous corolla about 1 in. long, stamens 10 in 2 series, sessile, pistil rudimentary rarely functional; (2) *pistillate,* subsessile, on pistillate plants, solitary or in few-fld. corymbs, in lf.-axils, corolla gamopetalous, about 1½ in.

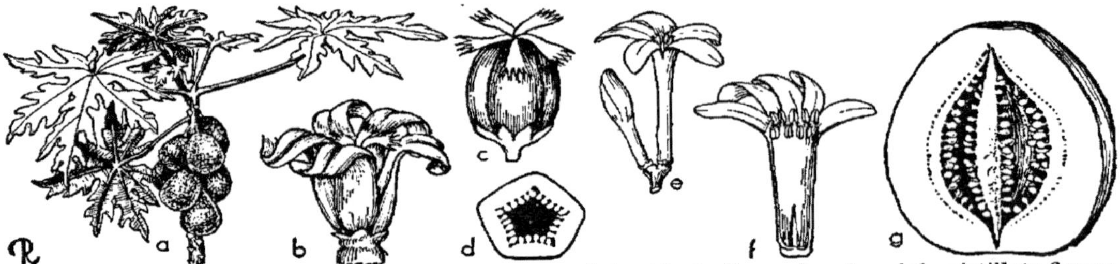

Fig. 137. CARICACEÆ. *Carica Papaya:* a, crown of plant in fruit, much reduced; b, pistillate flower, × 1/3; c, pistil, × 1; d, ovary, cross-section, × 1; e, staminate flower, × 1/2; f, same, expanded, × 1/2; g, fruit, vertical section, × 1/20. (b adapted from Engler & Prantl, c–d from Hutchinson.)

long, ovary large, globose, the 5 stigmas sessile and fimbriately fan-shaped, frs. globose to pyriform or ovoid; (3) *"long fruited"* type, similar to pistillate fls. but infl. multi-fld., about 3–5 in. long, comprised of 5–6-fld. corymbs, corolla gamopetalous, goblet-shaped, stamens 10, sessile, at base of petals, ovary usually functional and when so the fr. cucumber-shaped, mostly 12–18 in. long; (4) *polygamous*, fls. of two sorts, one with the 10 sessile stamens all at throat of corolla, petals connate into an elongated tube, the other with only 5 stamens, long-filamented, attached near base of ovary, corolla-tube very short or scarcely apparent; calyx very small in all types, gamosepalous; petals 5, connate or distinct as noted above; stamens usually 10 in 2 series but reduced to 5 in single series in one type; ovary superior, 1-celled, ovules many on 5 parietal placentæ, or falsely 5-celled by invagination of ovary wall; stigmas 5, sessile, fan-shaped, simple or fimbriate: fr. a large fleshy berry, maturing six to eight months after pollination, weighing 1–20 pounds.

CARICA, L. About 25 species native in trop. and subtrop. Amer., the papaya sometimes grown in greenhouses as a curiosity and extensively planted in the tropics and warm countries for the edible fr., from which also commercial papain is extracted.—Technical characters as for the family. (Ca-rica: named probably from certain resemblance to the fig, *Ficus carica*, which was erroneously supposed to come from Caria in S. W. Asia Minor.)

C. Papaya, L. (*Papaya Carica*, Gaertn.). PAPAYA. PAWPAW. Tree to 25 ft., the trunk with no lateral branches but sometimes dividing into several erect sts. bearing heads of lvs.: lvs. sometimes 2 ft. across, nearly orbicular in outline, usually palmately and deeply 7-lobed, each lobe pinnately lobed, pale or glaucous beneath; petioles hollow, 2 ft. or more long: staminate fls. sessile, in slender racemes often 3 ft. long, funnel-shaped, about 1 in. long, corolla yellow, the lanceolate lobes about half as long as tube; pistillate fls. nearly sessile, solitary or in few-fld. corymbs, about 1 in. long, corolla yellow, the 5 distinct petals lanceolate and twisted: fr. oblong or nearly spherical, yellow or orange, 3–20 in. long, the yellow thick flesh inclosing a 5-angled cavity and blackish seeds. Trop. Amer.

138. LOASACEÆ. LOASA FAMILY

Erect or climbing herbs or rarely shrubs and small trees, of about 20 genera and 250 species native in S. Amer. and a few in W. N. Amer., furnishing some fl.-garden subjects.—Plants with peculiar hairs, some stinging, some barbed: lvs. opposite or alternate, very diverse, usually exstipulate: fls. regular, bisexual, the infl. various; receptacle or calyx-tube adnate to the ovary, the sepals commonly 5, seldom 4 or 6–7, imbricated or contorted, persistent; petals of the same number and alternate with sepals, inserted inside the calyx on the receptacle, flat or hooded, usually free; stamens mostly many, seldom 5 or 10 or 2 by abortion, inserted with petals, sometimes in fascicles opposite the petals, staminodia often present which may be filiform or petaloid; ovary usually inferior and 1-celled, with 1 to many ovules borne on 3–5 parietal placentæ, the style entire or 2–3-parted: fr. a caps., dehiscent or indehiscent.

A. Petals hooded, alternating with as many hooded scales.
  B. Caps. dehiscent by 3–5 valves at apex, not twisted: plant not climbing . . . . .1. LOASA
  BB. Caps. spirally dehiscent by 3–5 valves, remaining closed at apex: plant climbing (in ours) . . . . .2. CAIOPHORA
AA. Petals not hooded, scales 0 . . . . .3. MENTZELIA

1. **LOASA,** Adans. Over 90 species of herbs or subshrubs, rarely climbing, armed with stinging hairs, native from Mex. to Patagonia.—Lvs. opposite or alternate, entire, lobed or decompound: fls. solitary in the axils, or in racemes or cymes; petals 5–7, hooded, spreading or nearly erect, alternating with 3 hooded nectar-scales bearing on the back 2–3 bristles and with 2 filiform staminodia opposite each scale; stamens numerous, the slender filaments in fascicles opposite the petals; ovary 1-celled with many ovules on the 3–5 parietal placentæ: caps. straight, club-shaped or obconic, dehiscent at apex by 3–5 valves between the persistent sepals. (Loa-sa: native S. American name.)

L. vulcanica, André (*L. Wallisii,* Regel). Erect bushy ann. 2–3 ft. high: lvs. palmately 3–5-lobed, 3–6 in. across, petioled, the ovate or ovate-lanceolate lobes serrate and long-petioled: fls. in 6–8-fld. leafy racemes, white, about 1½ in. across, the scales deep yellow barred with red and white: caps. about ¾ in. long. Ecuador, Colombia.

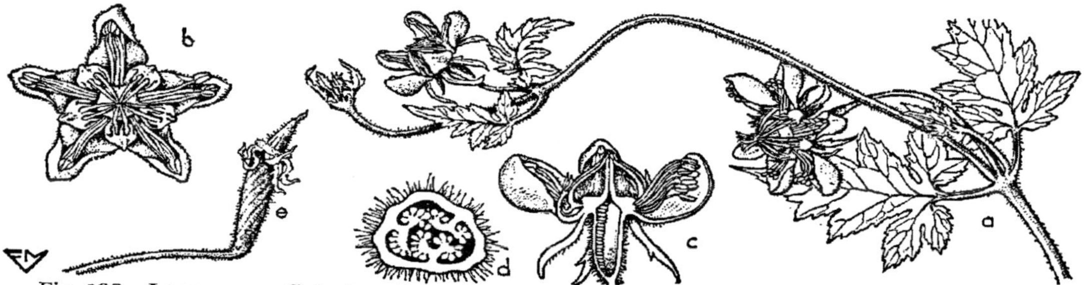

Fig. 138. LOASACEÆ. *Caiophora lateritia:* a, flowering branch, × ½; b, flower, face view, × 1; c, flower, vertical section, × 1; d, ovary, cross-section, × 4; e, capsule, × ½.

2. **CAIOPHORA,** Presl. Ann. or per. herbs, prostrate, erect or climbing, usually with stinging hairs; about 50 species in S. Amer.—Very similar to Loasa and differing principally in the caps. which is spirally twisted and dehisces longitudinally by 3–5 valves, rarely 6–10, but remains closed at apex: lvs. opposite. (Caioph-ora: from Greek for *burning* and *to bear,* referring to the stinging hairs.)

C. lateritia, Klotzsch (*Loasa lateritia,* Hook. *Blumenbachia lateritia,* Britt.). Slender climbing ann., the sts. 10–20 ft. long: lvs. long-petioled, 1–3 in. long, pinnate, the segms. toothed or lobed: fls. on very long peduncles, 1–2 in. across, orange-red; scales yellowish-green, their segms. meeting over top of stigma: caps. 2–3 in. long, cylindrical. S. Amer.

3. **MENTZELIA,** L. About 60 species distributed in trop. and subtrop. Amer. and W. U. S.; ann. or per. herbs, shrubs or trees, usually with barbed but not stinging hairs.—Lvs. alternate, rarely opposite, sessile or petioled, entire, lobed or pinnatifid: fls. solitary or in racemes or cymes, subtended by leafy bracts; sepals 5; petals 5, free or connate at base with each other and with the stamens; stamens numerous, free or in fascicles opposite the petals, sometimes the outer stamens sterile and petaloid; style simple or 4-cleft: caps. dehiscent at summit by 3–6 valves. (Mentze-lia: after Christian Mentzel, 1622–1701, German botanist.)

M. Lindleyi, Torr. & Gray (*Bartonia aurea,* Lindl.). Straggling ann. 1–4 ft. high, with simple or branched sts.: lvs. narrow-lanceolate to ovate, 2–5 in. or more long, coarsely toothed or pinnatifid: fls. 1½–2½ in. across, bright yellow, with orange base of petals, fragrant, opening in evening and remaining until following morning; petals rounded at apex but with an abrupt short point; anthers spiral: caps. club-shaped, 1–2 in. long. (Named for John Lindley, page 47.) Calif.—Much of the material offered in the trade as *Bartonia aurea* is **Eucnide bartonioides,** Zucc. (*Microsperma bartonioides,* Walp. *Mentzelia gronoviæfolia,* Fisch. & Mey.), a low-growing often decumbent and spreading ann. or bien. of W. Tex. and Mex., differing in its soft-hairy herbage not armed with stinging hairs, petals basally connate and opening only in full sun (not nocturnal), and ovary with 3 instead of 5 parietal placentæ.

139. BEGONIACEÆ. BEGONIA FAMILY

Five genera are recognized, but all except 5 or 6 of the more than 400 species are in the genus Begonia, and this genus is the only one interesting the general culti-

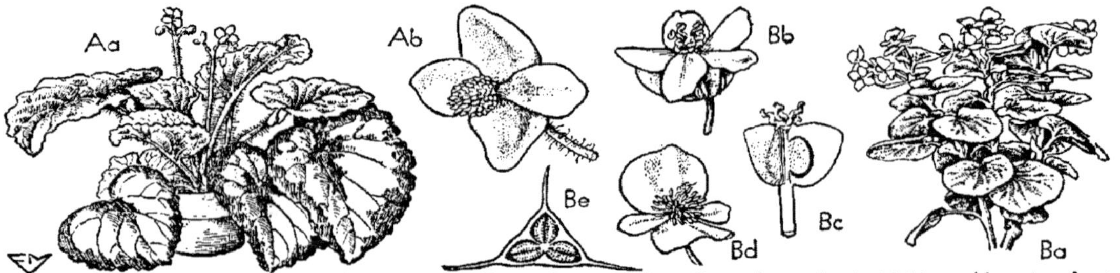

Fig. 139. BEGONIACEÆ. A, *Begonia Rex-cultorum:* Aa, flowering plant, × 1/10; Ab, staminate flower, × ½. B, *B. semperflorens:* Ba, flowering branch, × ⅛; Bb, pistillate flower, × ½; Bc, same, vertical section, × ½; Bd, staminate flower, × ½; Be, ovary, cross-section, × 1.

vator, yielding many kinds of glasshouse ornamentals and abounding in cultivars; native in many trop. countries.—Monœcious herbs or seldom shrubby, mostly per., usually somewhat succulent and with swollen nodes: roots rhizomatous, tuberous or fibrous: lvs. alternate and commonly oblique at base: fls. with parts mostly regular in each series except that one wing of the ovary may be strongly developed, disposed in clusters bearing staminate and pistillate blooms of which the former usually open first; perianth of staminate fls. commonly of 2 petals and 2 petal-like sepals, the 2 series often unlike; stamens many, with filaments distinct or connate; perianth of pistillate fls. of 2–5 or more parts; ovary inferior, 2–3-celled, angled or winged, styles 3 with prominent usually bent or twisted stigmas, ovules numerous: fr. usually a caps., with many fine seeds.

BEGONIA, L. Character of the family; distinguished from the other genera largely by the number, position, and distinctness of the perianth-parts and attachment of the ovary. (Bego-nia: Michel Bégon, 1638–1710, promoter of botany, supt. at St. Domingo.)—The genus yields many choice foliage pot-plants and also a good number with showy bloom in white, coral-red, rose, yellow, and other shades; the present tendency with gardeners is to restrict the number of species in cult., and to develop hort. races of the *B. Rex* foliage type, the hybridized tuberous kinds, and the very floriferous *B. semperflorens* group. Many of the plants in cult. cannot be referred to any clear specific type, and group names are needed. While the number of species in common cult. is now limited, many outlying kinds may be found in special collections. There is no vernacular name for the group, except Begonia itself, although the term Elephants-Ear is sometimes applied to those with large lopsided lvs., and Beefsteak-Geranium to the red-lvd. kinds with heavy hanging foliage of the Rex group.

A. Roots tuberous or bulbous.
  B. Lvs. centrally peltate: root bulbous .... 1. *B. socotrana*
  BB. Lvs. not so: roots tuberous.
    C. Sts. pubescent.
      D. Blossoms light yellow, single .... 2. *B. Pearcei*
      DD. Blossoms varicolored, mostly double .... 3. *B. tuberhybrida*
    CC. Sts. glabrous.
      D. Color of fls. white .... 4. *B. Dregei*
      DD. Color of fls. pink.
        E. Upper surface of lvs. spinulose, lower surface red .... 5. *B. Evansiana*
        EE. Upper surface of lvs. glabrous, lower surface green .... 6. *B. gracilis*
AA. Roots rhizomatous or fibrous.
  B. Begonias with roots fibrous or essentially so (or the rootstocks, if present, mostly subterranean and not prominent).
    C. Lvs. lobed or strongly angled.
      D. Sts. hairy or pubescent.
        E. Habit of plant proliferous—producing offsets on lvs., petioles and sts. .... 7. *B. phyllomaniaca*
        EE. Habit not proliferous.
          F. Height of plant 1 ft. or less .... 8. *B. Schmidtiana*
          FF. Height of plant 2–4 ft.
            G. Upper surface of lvs. purplish with broad midway band of green .... 9. *B. laciniata*
            GG. Upper surface of lvs. metallic green .... 10. *B. metallica*
      DD. Sts. glabrous.

E. Infl. practically sessile; fls. large, white or greenish.
F. Basal sinus margined by nerves destitute of lf.-tissue; lvs. not spotted .... 11. *B. palmaris*
FF. Basal sinus not so margined; lvs. spotted .... 12. *B. olbia*
EE. Infl. peduncled.
F. Fls. small, white .... 13. *B. dichotoma*
FF. Fls. showy, tinted or deeply colored.
G. Lf. thickly white-dotted .... 14. *B. argenteo-guttata*
GG. Lf. not spotted.
H. Wings of caps. unequal, one of them strongly developed .... 15. *B. incarnata*
HH. Wings 3 and practically equal .... 16. *B. nigricans*
CC. Lvs. toothed or entire, not lobed.
D. Length of lvs. about ½in. .... 17. *B. foliosa*
DD. Length of lvs. 1 in. and more.
E. Plant hairy or pubescent.
F. Lf. peltate: plant white-scurfy .... 18. *B. incana*
FF. Lf. not peltate: plant not white-scurfy.
G. Color of fls. rose-pink .... 19. *B. Haageana*
GG. Color of fls. white.
H. Under surface of lvs. green: fls. small .... 20. *B. ulmifolia*
HH. Under surface of lvs. red: fls. large.
I. Shape of lf. broad-ovate or broader, heavy .... 21. *B. Scharffiana*
II. Shape of lf. ovate-lanceolate, not thick or heavy .... 22. *B. Duchartrei*
EE. Plant glabrous.
F. Habit climbing, creeping or trailing .... 23. *B. glaucophylla*
FF. Habit erect or bushy.
G. Width of lvs. 1 in. or less.
H. Fls. white or greenish-white.
I. Lf. not spotted .... 24. *B. acutifolia*
II. Lf. spotted white .... 25. *B. albo-picta*
HH. Fls. pink or red.
I. Size of lvs. small, usually not exceeding 1½ in. long .... 26. *B. fuchsioides*
II. Size of lvs. larger and prominently double-serrate, 2–4 in. long .... 27. *B. Sandersonii*
GG. Width of lvs. more than 1 in.
H. Foliage white-dotted.
I. Margins of lvs. entire or undulate .... 28. *B. maculata*
II. Margins of lvs. serrate, often angled .... 14. *B. argenteo-guttata*
HH. Foliage not white-dotted.
I. Tip of lf. rounded or obtuse; petiole inserted at base of lf... 29. *B. semperflorens*
II. Tip of lf. acuminate; petiole inserted in sinus one-quarter or more distance from base of lf.
J. Color of fls. deep coral-red .... 30. *B. coccinea*
JJ. Color of fls. pink or white.
K. Lf. very thick, entire .... 31. *B. sanguinea*
KK. Lf. thin, serrate.
L. Margins of lvs. crenate-serrate: under surface green .... 32. *B. nitida*
LL. Margins of lvs. bristly-serrate: under surface red. . 16. *B. nigricans*
BB. Begonias with prominent horizontal or creeping shaggy sts. or rhizomes that frequently extend over the pot and from which the lvs. and peduncles arise: sometimes known as acaulescent species.
C. Lvs. lobed or divided.
D. Lobes to middle of blade or beyond .... 33. *B. heracleifolia*
DD. Lobes shallow, not to middle of blade.
E. Surface of lvs. bronzy-green, not spotted or speckled .... 34. *B. ricinifolia*
EE. Surface of lvs. spotted or speckled.
F. Blade speckled gray .... 35. *B. speculata*
FF. Blade with irregular dark brown spots .... 36. *B. rubellina*
CC. Lvs. not lobed or divided (crested in form of *B. Feastii*).
D. Lf. about centrally peltate .... 37. *B. nelumbiifolia*
DD. Lf. not peltate, although sometimes apparently so due to overlapping basal lobes.
E. Surface of lvs. not banded or blotched, although reddish beneath: peduncles nearly glabrous.
F. Shape of lf. obliquely cordate-ovate.
G. Margins entire, repand, or finely serrulate .... 38. *B. conchæfolia*
GG. Margins dentate .... 39. *B. manicata*
FF. Shape orbicular or nearly so, entire (unless crested), prominently ciliate on margin .... 40. *B. Feastii*
EE. Surface of lvs. banded or blotched: peduncles hairy.
F. Under surface of lvs. very hairy: infl. shorter than or about equalling foliage .... 41. *B. imperialis*
FF. Under surface of lvs. hairy only on veins: infl. surpassing foliage.
G. Blade metallic-green zoned with silvery-gray midway between margin and center .... 42. *B. Rex*
GG. Blade variously colored, blotched or marbled .... 43. *B. Rex-cultorum*

1. **B. socotrana,** Hook. f. Sts. ann., erect and succulent, to 1 ft., more or less hairy and somewhat branched, from a cluster of bulb-like bodies composed of scales: lvs. orbicular, centrally peltate, 4–7 in. across, with depressed center and rolled or recurved scalloped margins: fls. showy, rose-pink, in a forking small cluster on long bracted peduncles;

staminate 2 in. and more across, of 4 nearly equal parts; pistillate somewhat smaller, of 6 similar parts, the ovary with 1 narrow wing. Isl. of Socotra, south of Arabia.—Apparently not much cult. but entering into such types as Gloire de Sceaux, Gloire de Lorraine, Cincinnati.

2. **B. Pearcei,** Hook. f. About 1 ft. high, from a tuber, sts. lf.-bearing, branching, pubescent, and succulent: lvs. obliquely ovate-acuminate, 4–6 in. long, cordate, irregularly and doubly crenate-serrate, rich green and glabrous above, dull red beneath except the green veins, lightly hairy: peduncles about 2-fld. and standing above the foliage, with broad ciliate bracts at the forks; fls. yellow, 1–1¼ in. across; staminate with 2 pairs of unlike parts; pistillate with 5 parts: caps. prominently 3-winged. (Collected by Mr. Pearce for Messrs. Veitch of London.) Bolivia.—Source of the yellow fls. in the common tuberous begonias and also contributing the prevailing lf.-form, sometimes distinguishable in apparently its original character.

3. **B. tuberhybrida,** Voss. TUBEROUS BEGONIAS of gardens. A hort. race, resulting probably from the crossing of several species, some of them with only radical scapes: the cult. kinds have erect or diffuse more or less branching hairy succulent sts. about 1 ft. high, and fls. on axillary peduncles: lvs. mostly obliquely cordate-ovate, acuminate, with insertion of petiole in deep sinus about one-third distance from the basal end, margins angled, dentate and ciliate, hairy on veins beneath: fls. various, double or single, 2 in. or more across, yellow to red, purplish, and white.

4. **B. Dregei,** Otto & Dietr. Sts. soft and succulent, glabrous, red, 1–3 ft., ann. from a fleshy irregular tuber: lvs. ovate to rhombic-ovate, about 3 in. longest way, thin, long-petioled, truncate to cordate at base, mostly acuminate, angled and more or less indefinitely lobed, dentate, green, glabrous, digitately ribbed with veins reddish beneath: fls. white, few on rather short axillary peduncles; staminate 1 in. across, with commonly 2 large broad petals; pistillate smaller, with 5 unequal petals, the ovary bearing 3 broad unequal wings. (Collected near Port Natal by Drege.) S. Afr.—Apparently not frequent in cult. Var. **Macbethii,** Bailey (*B. Macbethii*, Hort.), mostly a smaller and more slender plant than *B. Dregei* itself and passing for it in cult., growing rapidly; glabrous, 1–1½ ft.: lvs. smaller, mostly not exceeding 2 in. longest way, deeply notched-lobed (sometimes to more than half the depth), the margins with few angle-teeth: fls. white, smaller, the staminate ¾in. or less across.

5. **B. Evansiana,** Andr. Tuberous, grown as an ann., sts. to 2 ft., branching, glabrous, producing axillary bulblets: lvs. ovate, 3–6 in. long, acute, unequally cordate at base, sharp-toothed, spinulose above, red beneath: fls. pink, large; staminate with 2 pairs of unequal parts; pistillate with 5 parts: caps. with 3 nearly equal wings. (Named for Thomas Evans for whom it was collected in Pulo-Penang in 1808.) Java, China, Japan.

6. **B. gracilis,** HBK. (*B. diversifolia*, R. Grah.). Tuberous, with glabrous mostly unbranched succulent sts.: root-lvs. reniform, broadly crenate, on very long petioles; st.-lvs. cordate-ovate, acuminate, somewhat lobed, unequally sharp-toothed, glabrous, pale green and somewhat glaucous beneath, bearing bulblets in axils: fls. pink; staminate with 2 pairs of unequal parts, the outer toothed, inner entire: caps. with 3 unequal wings. Mex.

7. **B. phyllomaniaca,** Mart. Stout, mostly hairy and shaggy, with erect branching thick sts., producing many buds and leafy growths (whence the name *phyllomaniaca*, "leaf-crazy") from sts., blades, and petioles: lvs. narrowly and obliquely cordate-ovate and very long-acuminate, 4–6 or 7 in. long, the sinus closed and blade semi-peltate, shallowly and acutely side-lobed and -toothed, the margins ciliate-serrate, green both sides: fls. pale pink, in hanging short-peduncled clusters; staminate about ¾in. across, with 2 large and 2 small parts; pistillate larger, with 4 parts and very large winged ovary. Brazil.

8. **B. Schmidtiana,** Regel. Low, 1 ft. or less, but often somewhat woody at base, sts. red-tinged, hairy: lvs. ovate-acuminate, about 2–3 in. long, angled and sometimes shallowly lobed, toothed, hairy on margins and underneath, reddish on under surface: fls. white and tinted rose, small but many. (Named for Mr. Schmidt, of Haage & Schmidt, Erfurt, Germany, seedsmen and nurserymen.) Brazil.

9. **B. laciniata,** Roxb. (*B. Bowringiana*, Champ.). More or less diffuse or straggling plant to 2 ft. high, with green pubescent branches: lvs. broadly cordate-ovate with oblique base, 5–7 or 8 in. long, nearly or quite glabrous but ciliate-serrulate on the margins, the outline somewhat angled or even continuous to sharp-lobed or even laciniate, purplish-black with broad green band midway: fls. white and few on a peduncle; staminate about 2 in. across, with 2 large and 2 medium-sized expanded parts; pistillate smaller, with 5 erect parts, ovary hairy. India to China.

10. **B. metallica,** G. Smith. Erect shaggy-hairy plant, 3–4 ft., branching: lvs. obliquely ovate, more or less cordate or subcordate at base, 3–6 in. long, lobed or deeply angled, with irregularly sinuate-serrate margins, the upper surface green but shaded and feathered with metallic tints and sparsely hairy, under surface lighter colored but shaded along the veins which are prominently hairy: fls. in peduncled clusters, blush-white or light rose, red-hairy; staminate 1½ in. across, with 2 very large nearly orbicular parts and very small oblong

ones. Brazil. **B. Thurstonii,** Hort., a reputed hybrid between *B. metallica* and *B. sanguinea,* has the habit of the former but with glabrous obliquely orbicular-acuminate lvs. red on under surface; originated with C. Thurston, Paterson, N. J.

11. **B. palmaris,** A. DC. Erect and glabrous but shaggy with dry deciduous stipules, 1–3 ft., more or less branched: lvs. obliquely reniform-ovate, 4–10 in. total length, with about 3 triangular-ovate acute main lobes extending to the middle or less of the blade, and intermediate acute lobes and teeth with serrulate margins between, more or less sparsely hairy, olive-green above and reddish beneath, not spotted but with darker palmate ribs; basal sinus broad, margined for a short distance above with lateral ribs that bear no lf.-tissue on the under side: fls. in sessile clusters but each fl. on a slender pedicel and covered or hidden by the foliage, white, the petals serrate; pistillate 1½ in. or more across, with very large 3-winged ovary. Brazil.—Sometimes confused with no. 12.

12. **B. olbia,** Kerchove. Sts. short, erect, more or less branched, succulent: lvs. on erect petioles, obliquely ovate in outline, 3–4 in. and more long, 5-nerved, somewhat bullate, shallowly angle-lobed and the margins irregularly dentate, pointed, the basal sinus rather narrow and not bordered with naked ribs, the under surface deep red, upper surface reddish-hairy and very dark bronzy green and sprinkled with small white spots (the illustration of the lvs. gives rise to the name "olbia," from Greek *olbios,* happy or rich): fls. white, drooping, in small axillary short clusters. Brazil.

13. **B. dichotoma,** Jacq. Strong quick-growing upright tall glabrous branching plant to 2–3 ft., with green thick sts. and very long-petioled lvs. that are thin and lively green: lvs. nearly orbicular in outline to obliquely ovate, 3–12 in. longest diam., shallowly cordate, with several very broad pointed angles and serrulate margins, palminerved, sometimes slightly hairy on veins beneath: fls. many, small and white, in long-peduncled dichotomous clusters, about ½in. across, with 2 large and 2 small parts. Venezuela.

14. **B. argenteo-guttata,** Lemoine. Of garden origin, common, said to be the issue of *B. albo-picta* and *B. olbia:* marked by the profusely white-speckled foliage: strong glabrous branching plant, 2–4 ft.: lvs. ovate-acuminate, 4–6 in. long, oblique but only subcordate at base, angle-notched or -toothed, the margins finely serrulate: fls. slender-pedicelled, in short-peduncled axillary clusters, white tinged pink, variable in size; staminate about 1 in. across, with 2 very broad and 2 narrow parts; ovary obovate, broad-winged.

15. **B. incarnata,** Link & Otto. Glabrous and erect branching plant, 2–3 ft.: lvs. oblong-ovate to ovate in outline, 4–10 in. long, oblique with narrow sinus, acuminate, variously notched, the margins with bristly or hairy serratures, reddish-green beneath, green above and more or less marked or feathered along veins: fls. many, in hanging long-peduncled clusters, rose-colored; staminate 1½ in. across, with 2 broad and 2 narrow parts; pistillate with 5 equal parts and large winged ovary. Mex.—Runs into forms in cult.

16. **B. nigricans,** Bailey (*B. subpeltata nigricans,* Hort. not *B. subpeltata,* Wight). Erect, glabrous, branching, 2–3 ft.: lvs. ovate in outline, acuminate, 4–9 in. long, with deep basal sinus that is sometimes closed by overlapping of the lobes as if the blade were peltate, irregularly angled-toothed all the way around, the margins bristly serrate, very red beneath, dark silvery-green and more or less dark-marked above and slightly hairy, the hairs sometimes dark red, sometimes becoming bronzy: fls. rose-tinted, in forking peduncled clusters; pistillate about 1 in. across, with 5 nearly equal parts and 3 similar wings. Of hort. origin.

17. **B. foliosa,** HBK. Small glabrous profusely small-lvd. begonia becoming shrubby at base, the sts. diffuse or drooping: lvs. about ½in. long, distichous, glossy-green, close together and numerous, oblong, serrulate, the scarious brown stipules prominent along the branchlets: fls. white or tinged rose, about ¼in. across, mostly solitary on slender hanging pedicels, the parts 4: caps. very unequally winged. Colombia.—Blossoms when small, a good basket and border species.

18. **B. incana,** Lindl. (*B. peltata,* Hort. not Hassk.). Soft rather succulent plant white scurfy-tomentose on sts. and foliage; sts. erect, mostly simple, 1–2 ft.: lvs. broad-ovate to orbicular-ovate, 4–9 in. long, oblique, peltate one-third or more from the margin, and strongly ribbed from the attachment, entire or somewhat repand: fls. in large forked clusters on long peduncles, white, petals and ovary white-pilose; staminate fls. 1 in. across with 2 large rounded parts and 2 narrow oblong parts; pistillate fls. with smaller petals, 2 large and 2 very small. Brazil.

19. **B. Haageana,** W. Wats. (*B. Scharffii,* Hook. f.). Tall and hairy shrubby branching plant: lvs. ovate-cordate and acuminate, oblique at base, 4–10 in. long, rather heavy, margins undulate and dentate, red-nerved above: fls. large, in very heavy drooping or hanging clusters that become 1 ft. broad, rose-pink; staminate perianth 2½ in. across, the parts 4, of which 2 are expanded and rounded and 2 narrow-spatulate; pistillate perianth smaller, of 5 nearly equal parts; ovary with long red hairs. (Named for Haage of the Erfurt nursery firm.) S. Brazil.

20. **B. ulmifolia,** Willd. Slender, branching, shaggy-hairy, becoming nearly or quite glabrous, sts. 1–2 ft., more or less angled, the large scarious stipules prominent: lvs. elm-like, ovate-oblong, 3–5 in. long, unequal at base, abruptly short-pointed, conspicuously

double-serrate, strongly pinnate-veined from the midrib, with scattered hairs above and below: fls. white and small but profusely borne in peduncled clusters; staminate of 2 or 4 similar parts, about 1 in. across. Colombia, Venezuela.

21. **B. Scharffiana,** Regel. Robust hairy herb, 1–3 ft., making heavy and handsome radical large hairy broad-ovate oblique abruptly strong-pointed lvs. 6–8 in. long, olive-green above and bright red beneath; stipules large and prominent: fls. large, in heavy long-peduncled clusters, waxy-white with prominent red hairs. (Named for the discoverer, Dr. Scharff.) Brazil.

22. **B. Duchartrei,** André. Hybrid from *B. Scharffiana* with branched hairy sts. 2–3 ft. and more high: lvs. ovate-lanceolate, long-acuminate, 5–8 in. long, rather thin, dentate, hairy, particularly on the violet-red nerves, green above and reddish beneath; stipules large, oval-lanceolate: fls. in rather compact long-peduncled clusters, large, waxy-white with a few red hairs; staminate 1½ in. across, with 4 suborbicular parts; pistillate somewhat larger, with 5 oval-oblong parts. (Dedicated about 1892 to Mons. Duchartre, secretary of the Nat. Hort. Soc. of France.)

23. **B. glaucophylla,** Hook. f. Glabrous rather slender begonia with pendulous or climbing white-spotted sts.: lvs. rather thick, oblong-lanceolate to narrowly oblong-ovate, acuminate, 3–5 in. long, pinnately-nerved, base regular, margins more or less sinuate, green both surfaces and glaucous: fls. rose-color, in ample mostly nodding short-peduncled clusters; staminate 1 in. or more across, with 2 large and 2 smaller parts; pistillate with 4 similar parts and a large ovary with 1 or 2 wings strongly developed. Probably Brazil.—The more scandent forms are often cult. as var. *scandens* as rafter plants in greenhouses. *B. scandens*, Sw., of the American tropics, with small white fls. and crenate-dentate lvs., is not to be expected in cult.

24. **B. acutifolia,** Jacq. (*B. acuminata*, Dry.). Slender, 3–4 ft., subshrubby but succulent, sts. glabrous, branching: lvs. narrowly oblong-acuminate to ovate-acuminate, 2–3 in. long, oblique at base, serrate and ciliate with fugacious hairs, glabrous or with sparse hairs on veins beneath; stipules prominent and dry: fls. small and white, about 1 in. across, 3–5 on a peduncle and slender-pedicelled: caps. truncate at top and rounded at base, the large wing triangular-ovate. Jamaica.

25. **B. albo-picta,** Hort. Much-branched shrubby compact begonia, grown for its numerously silvery-spotted glossy-green foliáge: lvs. elliptic-lanceolate, rather small: fls. rather small, greenish-white; staminate with 2 narrow and 2 broad parts, pistillate with 5 nearly equal parts. Brazil.

26. **B. fuchsioides,** Hook. Glabrous erect branching plant 2–3 ft. high, with short not prominent rootstock and tumid nodes: lvs. many, ovate, 1–1½ in. long, finely serrate, often tinged red; stipules scarious: fls. scarlet and drooping like fuchsias, ¾ in. or less long, on forking peduncles; staminate perianth of 4 parts, pistillate of 5; ovary prominent. Mex.

27. **B. Sandersonii,** Hort. Of garden origin, hybrid apparently from *B. fuchsioides*, probably with some form of the *B. semperflorens* group: glabrous, nearly or quite erect: lvs. ovate-acuminate, 1½–3 or 4 in. long, sharply double-serrate, dark green: fls. rose or rose-scarlet, drooping, 1 in. or less long, much like those of no. 26, freely produced.

28. **B. maculata,** Raddi (*B. argyrostigma*, Fisch.). Very smooth and glabrous, erect or straggling, 2–4 ft., and sometimes much more, branched: lvs. thick, obliquely oblong to oblong-ovate with a cordate sinus, 4–8 in. long, nearly or quite blunt, entire but margins undulate, red beneath, green with many circular white dots above: fls. pale rose or white, in short-peduncled hanging clusters; staminate about 1 in. across, with 2 large and 2 small parts; pistillate with 5 erect equal parts and large winged ovary. Brazil.—Cult. in several races varying in the abundance and size of lf.-spots, as well as in stature and habit.

29. **B. semperflorens,** Link & Otto. The prevailing type of florists' flowering begonias, now in many races and forms, some used for bedding: glabrous and somewhat succulent, sts. little branching except from base, 6–18 in. high, green or reddish: lvs. glossy, ovate or oval to broad-oval, 2–4 in. long, more or less oblique at base, rounded or obtuse at apex, finely serrulate and with ciliate margins, green but usually tinged red on ribs; stipules large and dry: fls. rose-red to whitish, on few-fld. axillary peduncles, the staminate with 4 parts an in. or less across and the pistillate smaller and with 5 parts: caps. green with prominent red-tinged wings. Brazil.—With this species belong such hort. kinds as Vernon, Triomphe de Lorraine, Chatelaine, Henry Martin, Gloire de Louveciennes, Carrierei, Erfordii, the two last being supposed hybrids with *B. Schmidtiana;* some races are white-fld. Gigantea rosea is a sterile semperflorens hybrid of large size, so distinct as usually not to be classed with this group by cultivators.

30. **B. coccinea,** Hook. (*B. rubra*, Hort.). Glabrous and tall branching plant to 3 or 4 ft. but often blooming freely when 1 ft. or less high: lvs. thick and stiff, very obliquely oblong to oblong-ovate, 4–6 in. long, the short petiole inserted in a sinus one-fourth or one-third the distance from the base, pointed, unlobed, margins undulate and sometimes obscurely toothed and red-bordered, glabrous, green above and reddish beneath: fls. brilliant coral-red, in drooping forking clusters on red peduncles, long-lasting; staminate fls. nearly

1 in. across, with 2 large and 2 smaller parts; pistillate more showy because of the brilliant 3-winged ovary which is ¾–1 in. and more long. Brazil.—Derivatives of this species, in whole or in part, are in cult. for the very showy hanging coral-red pistillate fls., and sometimes for white-spotted foliage. Among these are President Carnot and Lucerna.

31. **B. sanguinea,** Raddi. Very smooth and shining plant, the sts. several, more or less branched, red: lvs. thick, mostly near the base, obliquely cordate-ovate, 3–6 in. long, slightly peltate, very abruptly pointed, unlobed and entire, glabrous both sides, rich green above, brilliant blood-red beneath: fls. small, white, on long slender red peduncles; staminate about ¾in. across, of 2 large rounded and 2 small oblong parts. Brazil.—Prized for its mass of heavy persistent very red-bottomed foliage.

32. **B. nitida,** Dry. Glabrous erect branching plant 3–5 ft. high, with lively green glossy foliage: lvs. thick, reniform-ovate, 4–6 in. long, very oblique at base, prominently but rather abruptly pointed, irregularly crenate-dentate: fls. pale pink or rose, in large diffuse long-peduncled clusters; staminate 1½ in. across, with 2 large and 2 small parts; pistillate small, with 5 parts. Jamaica. Var. **odorata,** Hort., is a kind with smaller clear white very fragrant fls.

33. **B. heracleifolia,** Cham. & Schlecht. St. a short thick rhizome: long petioles and peduncles variously shaggy-hairy, the latter ascending 2–4 ft. and branching at the top and bearing large spreading bracts at the forks: lvs. orbicular in general outline, 6–12 in. or more across, with 5–9 narrow notched and dentate acute lobes that extend to the middle of the blade or beyond, ciliate on margins, dark green above and lighter beneath: fls. white or rose-tinted; staminate ½–1 in. across, with 2 rounded petals; pistillate of similar size, with 2 petals and a short ovary with mostly 1 developed wing. Mex.—Runs into several forms, varying in hairiness and in the color of foliage, sometimes with barred or maculate lvs.

34. **B. ricinifolia,** A. Dietr. Hybrid issue of *B. heracleifolia:* lvs. with short triangular lobes extending not nearly half the depth of the blade, bronzy-green with ciliate margins: fls. many, rose-pink, on tall peduncles.—There are variants of it.

35. **B. speculata,** Hort. Rhizome short and thick: lvs. broad-ovate to orbicular-ovate in outline, 4–8 in. longest way, cordate or subcordate, with an acuminate apex, lobes one-fourth to one-half depth of blade into sharp triangular lobes, on long slender hairy petioles, sparsely hairy and ciliate, dull green speckled gray, reddish beneath and with prominent ribs: peduncle long, bearing pink-white dipetalous fls., the staminate about 1 in. across: caps. with small red spots. Hort. hybrid.

36. **B. rubellina,** Bailey (*B. rubella,* Hort. not Don.) Much like no. 35, but large lvs. spattered with irregular dark brown spots. Garden origin.

37. **B. nelumbiifolia,** Cham. & Schlecht. (*B. macrophylla,* Hort.). A commanding plant with rhizome thick and short, parts more or less hairy but often becoming nearly glabrous: lvs. large, nearly orbicular to round-ovate, 8–18 in. long, peltate and with 7–9 main nerves, abruptly short-pointed, not lobed, margins ciliate-serrulate and with points at end of nerves, green both sides, hairy on the nerves beneath and sometimes sparsely so above, the petioles long and upstanding and loosely hairy or glabrous: fls. many and small, in a diffuse cyme on peduncles surpassing the lvs., white or pinkish, ½in. or less across; ovary small, with 1 wing developed. Mex.

38. **B. conchæfolia,** A. Dietr. (*B. Warscewiczii,* Hort.). Rhizome short, thick and creeping: lvs. ovate-cordate, 4–6 in. long, apparently peltate from the overlapping basal lobes, unlobed, margins more or less repand and somewhat serrulate and ciliate, green and smooth above, reddish and rusty-hairy beneath particularly along the veins: fls. pink to nearly white, fragrant, on peduncles 1 ft. or so long: 1 wing of caps. long. Cent. Amer.

39. **B. manicata,** Cels. Rhizome or st. short and succulent, and plant glabrous except on lvs. and top of petioles: lvs. fleshy, obliquely short-ovate, 4–8 in. long, abruptly short-pointed, the 5–7 ribs thick, sinuate-dentate and margins strongly ciliate, shining light green above and reddish beneath, the ribs and upper part of petiole bearing hair-like scales: fls. on peduncles 1 ft. or more high and overtopping the foliage, pink, small, the cymes open and forking; petals 2; staminate about ½in. across, with the parts narrow and divergent; ovary winged all around. Mex.

40. **B. Feastii,** Hort. Hybrid derivative from *B. manicata,* intro. by John Feast, Baltimore, before 1880 and still in cult.: lvs. nearly orbicular, fleshy, bases close or overlapping as if blade were peltate, short-petioled so that the foliage is close to the pot, 4–6 in. long, more or less ciliate on margins, green above with bronzy luster and reddish beneath, rounder and margins more continuous than in no. 39: fls. light pink, standing high above the foliage.—A form (*B. Bunchii,* **Hort.**) has crested or crinkled and frilled lvs.

41. **B. imperialis,** Lem. Low condensed green hairy plant, sometimes with a very short herbaceous st., but lvs. and peduncles essentially basal: lvs. cordate-ovate, 2–6 in. long, short-petioled, the base regular or oblique, point short and abrupt, unlobed, margins serrulate, alveolate and very hairy and brown-green beneath, rich green and pustulate above and velvety with many hairs, the regions along the veins light bright green: fls. small,

white, often appearing when the plant is very small and not equalling the lvs. but eventually often equalling the short foliage; staminate 2-petalled, about ½in. across, hairy; pistillate smaller, with 1 triangular wing of ovary most developed. Mex.—Commonly known in trade as Otto Foerster. Var. **smaragdina,** Lem., has lvs. all green, lacking the feathered veins.

42. **B. Rex,** Putz. Stock thick, mostly subterranean, from which rise the lvs. and peduncles in clusters as if from a crown: lf.-blade 8–12 in. long, hanging nearly perpendicular on a hairy petiole of similar length, ovate, abruptly pointed, oblique, with a closed or overlapped sinus about one-fourth distance from base, unlobed, margins sinuate-dentate and surface puckered or blistered (bullate), reddish beneath and hairy on veins, deep metallic-green above with an irregular zone of silvery-white about 1 in. wide all around and about midway between margin and center, outside of which the surface is tinged purple: fls. pale rose, few in dichotomous cymes surpassing the foliage; staminate about 2 in. across, of 2 cordate-ovate and 2 oblong somewhat smaller parts; pistillate much smaller, with 5 nearly equal parts, ovary with 1 extended wing. Assam.—Little known in cult.

43. **B. Rex-cultorum,** Bailey. The Rex begonias of cultivators, derivatives from no. 42 by hybridization with other species and perhaps by mutation, now representing an important class of plants with illustrated foliage, including many named vars.: distinguished by lvs. unlobed although in some vars. with angle-points and frequently sinuate, and with a wide variety of markings different from those of *B. Rex,* usually variously shaded, blotched and marbled in many tints; they have the Rex habit of a declined or hanging shield-like lf.-blade facing outward, the tip often nearly touching the ground.

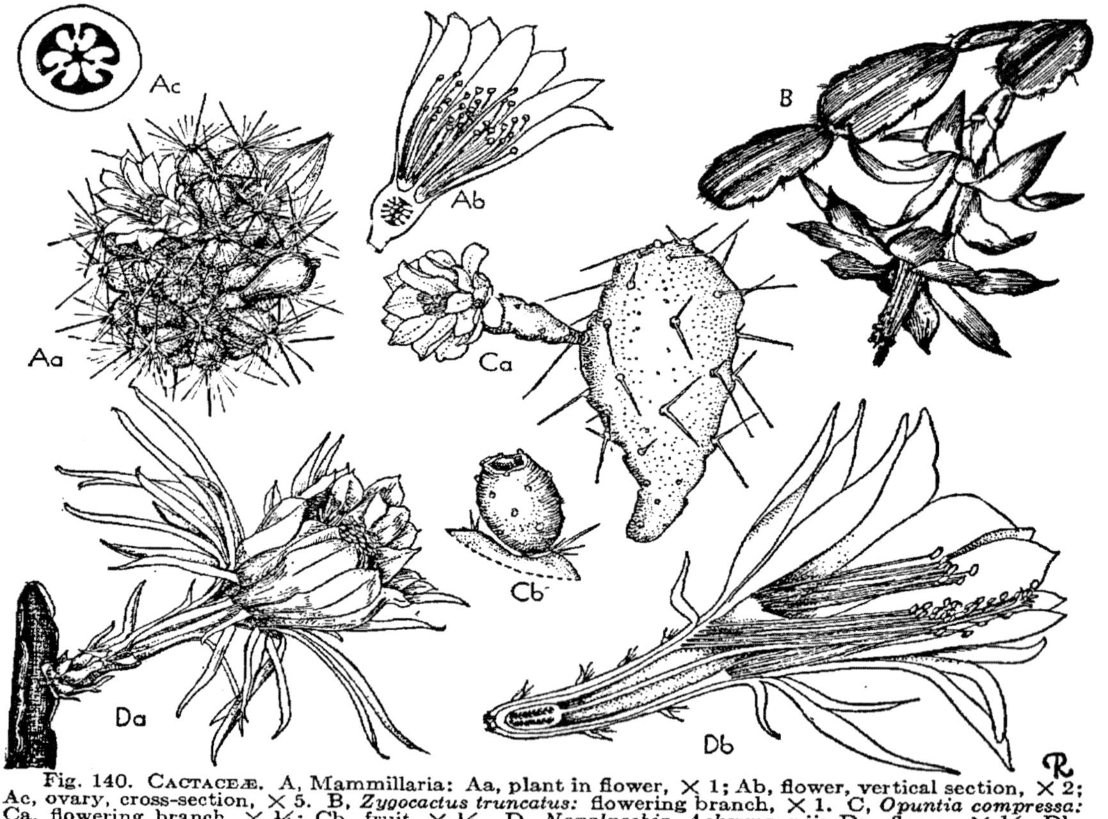

Fig. 140. CACTACEÆ. A, Mammillaria: Aa, plant in flower, × 1; Ab, flower, vertical section, × 2; Ac, ovary, cross-section, × 5. B, *Zygocactus truncatus:* flowering branch, × 1. C, *Opuntia compressa:* Ca, flowering branch, × ¼; Cb, fruit, × ¼. D, *Nopalxochia Ackermannii:* Da, flower, × ¼; Db, same, vertical section, × ⅖.

140. CACTACEÆ. CACTUS FAMILY

A singular family of American plants interesting because of the fleshy, condensed, usually spiny and leafless st. and the large often brilliant and showy fls., comprising, according to the most recent treatments, about 140 genera and not less than 1,700 species, practically confined to the dry regions of trop. and subtrop. Amer., Mex. being the center of distribution, one genus apparently native in Afr.; a few species are cult. for economic purposes, but mostly as odd plants for desert gardens and as greenhouse curiosities; any number of kinds may be found among fanciers' collections.—Per. plants of various habit, usually armed with spines and glochids (barbed spines or bristles), the sts. succulent and mostly spiny, cylindric, globular, flattened or fluted, and often constricted or jointed, mostly more or less branched: lvs. usually none, if present flat and commonly fleshy or much reduced and mostly caducous, with axillary areoles (oval or circular areas bearing branches, fls., spines, glochids, hairs or glands): fls. usually bisexual, regular or irregular, perigynous or epigynous, solitary or clustered, often large and showy; perianth with or without tube, sharply or not at all differentiated into sepals and petals, the petals few or numerous; stamens usually numerous, sometimes clustered; style 1; stigma 2- to many-lobed; ovary inferior, 1-celled, placentæ 3 or more and parietal, many-ovuled: fr. a berry, often spiny, glochidiate or bristly, juicy and often edible, or sometimes dry.

A. Lvs. broad, flat: glochids wanting: fls. stalked, often clustered............ 1. PERESKIA
AA. Lvs. terete or subterete or wanting: fls. sessile.
B. Areoles with glochids: vegetative parts bearing lvs. which are usually small and caducous: fls. rotate (petals erect in Nopalea).
C. Stamens much longer than petals............................ 2. NOPALEA
CC. Stamens shorter than petals................................ 3. OPUNTIA
BB. Areoles without glochids: vegetative parts usually without lvs.: fls. with definite tubes.
C. Joints many, long, flat: areoles mostly spineless.
D. Sts. divided into many short joints 2 in. or less long................ 4. ZYGOCACTUS
DD. Sts. with elongated joints, mostly 6–15 in. or more long.
E. Tube of fls. longer than limb.............................. 5. EPIPHYLLUM
EE. Tube of fls. shorter than limb............................ 6. NOPALXOCHIA
CC. Joints ribbed, angled or tubercled: areoles mostly spine-bearing.
D. Spines and fls. borne at different areoles.
E. Ovary and fr. scaly... 7. THELOCACTUS
EE. Ovary and fr. not scaly.
F. Fls. borne laterally, in axils of old tubercles.................. 8. MAMMILLARIA
FF. Fls. borne centrally, in axils of young tubercles.
G. Fr. greenish or yellowish, seeds light brown................ 9. CORYPHANTHA
GG. Fr. red, seeds dark brown or black.......................10. NEOBESSEYA
DD. Spines and fls. borne at same areoles.
E. Cacti of 1 or few usually short joints.
F. Fls. borne at lateral areoles.
G. Ovary and fl.-tube spiny...................................11. ECHINOCEREUS
GG. Ovary and fl.-tube not spiny, with hairs in axils of scales.
H. Plant very small, creeping.................................12. CHAMÆCEREUS
HH. Plant larger, not creeping.
I. Fl.-tube with papery scales and ring of wool inside above ovary..13. ACANTHOCALYCIUM
II. Fl.-tube with scales not papery and without ring of wool..14. ECHINOPSIS
FF. Fls. borne at central areoles.
G. Plant tuberculate, without distinct ribs...................15. ARIOCARPUS
GG. Plant with distinct ribs, often tuberculate.
H. Axils of scales on ovary and fr. naked.
I. Shape of fl. funnelform with narrow tube..............16. HAMATOCACTUS
II. Shape of fl. campanulate with short tube..............17. FEROCACTUS
HH. Axils of scales on ovary hairy, woolly or setose.
I. Ribs few, white-scaly, often spineless................18. ASTROPHYTUM
II. Ribs many, very spiny.
J. Plant-body depressed.................................19. HOMALOCEPHALA
JJ. Plant-body globose or cylindrical....................20. ECHINOCACTUS
EE. Cacti of several to many long joints.
F. Plants vine-like, with aërial roots.
G. Scales of ovary and fr. large and foliaceous, their axils not spiny, hairy or bristly.....................................21. HYLOCEREUS
GG. Scales of ovary and fr. not large nor foliaceous, their axils spiny, hairy or bristly.
H. Fls. elongate-funnelform, usually white...................22. SELENICEREUS
HH. Fls. short-funnelform or funnelform-campanulate, red.....23. APOROCACTUS
FF. Plants erect, bushy or diffuse.
G. Fls. 2 or more from an areole.
H. Flowering areoles with many long bristles................24. LOPHOCEREUS
HH. Flowering areoles similar to non-flowering ones..........25. MYRTILLOCACTUS
GG. Fls. 1 from an areole.
H. Ovary naked, or rarely bearing a few scales which sometimes subtend tufts of short hairs.
I. Perianth funnelform, elongate: flowering areoles similar to non-flowering ones..........................26. CEREUS

II. Perianth short-campanulate or short-funnelform to pyriform: flowering areoles differing from non-flowering ones....27. CEPHALOCEREUS
HH. Ovary with scales bearing wool, felt or spines in their axils.
I. Blooming at night.
J. Habit arching or clambering.
K. Branches regularly ribbed: scales of ovary with spines in their axils....28. NYCTOCEREUS
KK. Branches fluted or angled: scales of ovary with hair or felt in their axils.
L. Fr. yellow, indehiscent....29. HARRISIA
LL. Fr. red, splitting irregularly....30. ERIOCEREUS
JJ. Habit erect or columnar.
K. Scales on fl.-tube few, bearing small tufts of felt in their axils....31. CARNEGIEA
KK. Scales on fl.-tube numerous, bearing long hairs in their axils....32. TRICHOCEREUS
II. Blooming by day.
J. Areoles bearing long white hairs as well as spines.
K. Stamens and style exserted: fls. with nearly cylindrical tube....33. OREOCEREUS
KK. Stamens and style included: fls. short-campanulate.34. ESPOSTOA
JJ. Areoles bearing felt as well as spines.
K. Tube of fl. elongated; stamens exserted....35. CLEISTOCACTUS
KK. Tube of fl. short; stamens included.
L. Fr. dry and bur-like, very spiny....36. PACHYCEREUS
LL. Fr. fleshy, with few or deciduous spines.
M. Spines of flowering and non-flowering areoles different....31. CARNEGIEA
MM. Spines of flowering and non-flowering areoles similar....37. LEMAIREOCEREUS

1. **PERESKIA,** Mill. Trees, shrubs, or vines, some grown for ornament and also for the edible fr.; probably about 20 species native in Mex., W. Indies, Cent. and S. Amer.—Resembling other woody plants in having leafy branching sts.; spines in axillary pairs or clusters, neither sheathed nor barbed; glochids wanting: lvs. alternate, deciduous, broad and flat or somewhat fleshy: fls. rotate, solitary, stalked, corymbose or panicled, terminal or axillary; stamens numerous; style single; ovary naked or leafy: fr. juicy, sometimes edible; seeds black, thin-shelled. (Peres-kia: named for Nicolas Claude Fabry de Peiresc, 1580–1637.)

A. Plants of climbing habit: spines on young branches 2, short and recurved....1. *P. aculeata*
AA. Plants shrubby or tree-like: spines on young branches often solitary, straight... 2. *P. grandifolia*

1. **P. aculeata,** Mill. (*Cactus Pereskia*, L. *Pereskia Pereskia*, Karst.). BARBADOS-GOOSEBERRY. LEMON-VINE. Shrub erect at first, later forming a vine, the woody clambering sts. 10–30 ft. long: spines on lower part of st. slender and straight, solitary or in 2's or 3's, those of the young branches short and curved, usually in pairs: lvs. 2–3 in. long, lanceolate to oblong or ovate, short-acuminate, short-petioled: fls. showy and fragrant, white, pale yellow or pinkish, 1–1½ in. across, in panicles or corymbs; ovary leafy and often spiny: fr. light yellow, ¾in. diam., in age smooth. Widely spread in trop. Amer.

2. **P. grandifolia,** Haw. (*P. Bleo*, Auth., not *Cactus Bleo*, HBK. nor *P. Bleo*, DC.). Tree or shrub to 15 ft., mostly having a definite woody trunk up to 4 in. diam. which is very spiny and fleshy, elongated branches usually bearing 1–2 acicular spines at the areoles: lvs. oblong, 3–6 in. long, obtuse or acute, somewhat narrowed at base: fls. rose-colored or white, 1½–2 in. across, in small clusters; ovary lf.-bearing: fr. 2 in. long, pear-shaped, many-seeded. Brazil.—One of the most commonly cult. species appearing in many living collections and also in herbaria under the name *P. Bleo.*

2. **NOPALEA,** Salm-Dyck. Branching cacti, a few widely cult. in warmer parts of the world, either as ornamentals or for commercial purposes; species about 8, native to Mex., Guatemala, and perhaps also to Cuba; this genus is closely related to Opuntia from which it is distinguished by the erect petals and the elongated filaments and style.—Mostly arborescent with definite cylindric trunks and numerous fleshy flattened branches; areoles bearing white wool, glochids and often spines which are solitary or in clusters at the areoles, sheathless: lvs. small, soon deciduous: fls. borne in the areoles usually at or near the edges of the joints; sepals and petals erect, the latter red or pinkish, far exceeded by the numerous stamens and the style; ovary more or less tuberculate, naked or spiny, deeply umbilicate: fr. a juicy red berry, edible and commonly spineless, the numerous flat seeds covered by a hard bony aril. (Nopa-lea: from the Mexican name of the cochineal cactus.)

N. cochinellifera, Salm-Dyck (*Cactus cochenillifer*, L.). COCHINEAL CACTUS. To 12 ft., trunks 8 in. thick: branches of ascending or spreading oblong joints, spineless or the older ones with minute spines: glochids numerous, caducous: lvs. small, subulate, early caducous: fls. about 2½ in. long, usually abundant, borne on the upper parts of the joints; sepals and petals scarlet, the petals longer; stamens pinkish, exserted about ½in.; stigma with 6–7 greenish lobes, longer than the stamens; style with broad disk-like base; ovary subglobose, ¾in. long, tuberculate, its areoles with many glochids: fr. red, about 2 in. long, rarely maturing in cult. Original habitat unknown.—Widely grown in semi-trop. countries, but seldom found in the U. S. Interesting chiefly as being one of the important food-plants of the cochineal insect (whence the name, *cochinellifera*), yielding a scarlet dye.

3. **OPUNTIA,** Mill. PRICKLY-PEAR. Probably at least 300 species, growing naturally from Mass. to B. C. south to Magellan Strait; several have been nat. and have become abundant locally in the Old World; one species widely grown in warm regions for its edible fr., others used as hedges or as forage for stock; many species may be found in the collections of fanciers.—Very variable in size and habit, ranging from small prostrate plants a few in. high to widely spreading forms much-branched from base, or sometimes trees with definite trunks and spreading tops 20 or more ft. high; roots fibrous or sometimes thick and fleshy; sts. and branches of flat, cylindric or globose joints, usually very fleshy, sometimes woody; spines solitary or clustered, sometimes wanting, naked or sheathed; glochids commonly numerous, borne above the spines: lvs. mostly small, terete and soon deciduous: fls. borne singly toward the upper part of the joints; sepals green or colored, usually grading into the petals; corolla showy, green, red, or yellow, the petals spreading; stamens much shorter than the petals, sensitive; style single, thick, stigma shortly lobed: fr. a berry, often edible, spiny or naked, globose, ovoid or ellipsoid; seed white and flattened. (Opuntia: old Latin name used by Pliny, later employed for the Indian-fig, probably derived from Opus, a town in Greece.)

A. Branches cylindrical or terete. (CYLINDROPUNTIA.)
- B. Joints strongly tuberculate: fls. 2–3 in. across .... 1. *O. imbricata*
- BB. Joints only slightly tuberculate: fls. 1 in. or less across.
  - C. Color of fls. scarlet: joints 2 in. thick .... 2. *O. cylindrica*
  - CC. Color of fls. greenish or yellowish: joints ⅕in. thick .... 3. *O. leptocaulis*

AA. Branches flat. (PLATYOPUNTIA, except *O. brasiliensis.*)
- B. Areoles without spines.
  - C. Joints glabrous.
    - D. Habit bushy or tree-like: joints 20 in. or more long .... 4. *O. Ficus-indica*
    - DD. Habit low and spreading: joints about 5 in. long .... 14. *O. compressa*
  - CC. Joints pubescent.
    - D. Color of fls. rose or magenta varying to white .... 5. *O. basilaris*
    - DD. Color of fls. yellow or orange.
      - E. Glochids yellow: joints bright green .... 6. *O. microdasys*
      - EE. Glochids brown: joints grayish-green .... 7. *O. rufida*
- BB. Areoles with spines.
  - C. Plant with erect cylindrical unjointed trunk.
    - D. Fls. 1½ in. or less across .... 8. *O. brasiliensis*
    - DD. Fls. 3 in. across .... 9. *O. vulgaris*
  - CC. Plant usually branching near base, without definite cylindrical trunk.
    - D. Habit erect, often to 20 ft.: joints 12–20 in. long.
      - E. Spines yellowish to dark brown .... 9. *O. vulgaris*
      - EE. Spines, when present, white .... 4. *O. Ficus-indica*
    - DD. Habit spreading, 2 ft. or less high: joints 2–5 in. long.
      - E. Joints breaking off easily, 2 in. or less long .... 10. *O. fragilis*
      - EE. Joints not breaking easily, 3 and more in. long.
        - F. Surface of joint covered with spines which are many to an areole.
          - G. Spines appressed or deflexed .... 11. *O. polyacantha*
          - GG. Spines not appressed .... 12. *O. erinacea*
        - FF. Surface of joint spiny mostly near tip with few spines to an areole.
          - G. Fr. dry and spiny .... 13. *O. rhodantha*
          - GG. Fr. fleshy, bristly but not spiny.
            - H. Spines borne only on edges of joints, sometimes wanting .... 14. *O. compressa*
            - HH. Spines borne on upper half of joints .... 15. *O. Rafinesquei*

1. **O. imbricata,** DC. Tree-like, to 6 ft. and more, with cylindrical trunk 1–2 in. diam.; joints verticillate, cylindrical, 1–1½ in. long and 1 in. thick, covered with laterally compressed tubercles; spines 6–20, ½–1½ in. long, covered with papery sheaths: fls. purple or rose, about 2½ in. across, with white style and purple stamens: fr. dry, yellow, about 1 in. long, tuberculate. Colo. to Mex.—Has been known as *O. arborescens*, Engelm., but this name is not the oldest.

2. **O. cylindrica,** DC. (*Cactus cylindricus,* Lam.). Tree-like, to 12 ft., with trunk and few branches; joints cylindrical, 2 in. thick, with very flat tubercles; spines 2 or more, short, white: fls. scarlet, 1 in. across: fr. yellowish-green, 2 in. long, tuberculate. Ecuador, Peru.

3. **O. leptocaulis,** DC. Bush-like, branched at base, to 3 ft.; joints cylindrical, ⅛in. or less thick, only slightly tuberculate; spines 1 or few, 1–2 in. long, covered with papery sheaths: fls. bronze-yellow, about ¾in. long: fr. fleshy, scarlet, ½–¾in. long. S. W. U. S., Mex.

4. **O. Ficus-indica,** Mill. (*Cactus Ficus-indica,* L.). INDIAN-FIG. Bushy or sometimes tree-like with a woody trunk, 10–15 ft.; joints elliptic or oblong, thick, often 15–20 in. long, with a bluish bloom; spines usually lacking but when present solitary and white; glochids yellow, numerous, soon falling: fls. yellow, 3–4 in. across: fr. purple or red, edible, 2–3½ in. long, umbilicate. Nativity not known, but now widely cult. in the tropics and subtropics for its fr., and sometimes escaped.

5. **O. basilaris,** Engelm. & Bigel. BEAVERTAIL CACTUS. Forming clumps 1–3 ft. high; joints broad-obovate to orbicular, 3–8 in. long, velvety-pubescent, spineless; areoles deeply depressed, with brown glochids: fls. rose or magenta varying to white, 2–3 in. long: fr. dry and spineless. S. Utah to Mex.

6. **O. microdasys,** Pfeiffer (*Cactus microdasys,* Lehm.). BUNNY-EARS. Forming clumps 1–2 ft. high, often creeping; joints oblong to orbicular, 4–6 in. long, velvety-pubescent, bright green, spineless; areoles large and numerous, with yellow glochids: fls. yellow or tinged red, with white style and filaments, 2 in. long: fr. fleshy, dark red, globose. N. Mex.

7. **O. rufida,** Engelm. BLIND-PEAR. Similar to *O. microdasys* but with dark grayish-green joints and brown glochids. Tex., N. Mex.

8. **O. brasiliensis,** Haw. (*Cactus brasiliensis,* Willd. *Brasiliopuntia brasiliensis,* Berger). Tree-like, to 16 ft., with erect cylindrical unjointed trunk dividing into cylindrical branches; ultimate joints flat and lf.-like, deciduous; areoles white-woolly; spines usually solitary, ½–1 in. long: fls. yellow, about 1½ in. across: fr. fleshy, yellow, 1–2 in. long, with brown bristles. Brazil; nat. in S. Fla.

9. **O. vulgaris,** Mill. (O. *monacantha,* Haw.). Bushy, from 7–20 ft. high, or sometimes with cylindrical trunk 6 in. diam.; joints ovate to oblong, to 12 in. long, shining; spines usually 1 or 2, yellowish-brown to dark brown, ½–1½ in. long: fls. yellow, petals reddish at base, about 3 in. across: fr. fleshy, reddish-purple, 2–3 in. long, spineless. Brazil to Argentina.

10. **O. fragilis,** Haw. (*Cactus fragilis,* Nutt.). Low and spreading, sometimes forming mounds; joints globose or flattened, breaking off easily, about 1½ in. long; areoles close together, woolly; spines 3–5, brown, ½–1 in. long: fls. yellow with orange center, 2 in. across: fr. dry, ½–¾in. long, spiny. Wis. to B. C. south to Tex. and Ariz.

11. **O. polyacantha,** Haw. Spreading, usually forming clumps; joints obovate or nearly orbicular, about 4 in. across; areoles close together; spines numerous, about 1 in. long, appressed or deflexed, brown or variegated: fls. pale yellow, 2–3 in. across: fr. dry, ¾in. long, spiny and bristly. Alta. to Wash. south to Tex. and Ariz.

12. **O. erinacea,** Engelm. & Bigel. GRIZZLY-BEAR CACTUS. Forming low clumps with ascending or erect branches; joints ovate or nearly orbicular, 3–8 in. long; areoles close together; spines 4 or more, white or brownish, 1–2 in. long: fls. yellow or red, about 2½ in. long: fr. dry, about 1 in. long, spiny. Utah, Nev., Ariz., Calif.

13. **O. rhodantha,** Schum. (*O. erinacea* var. *rhodantha,* Benson). Spreading; joints obovate, 3–6 in. long; areoles distant; spines borne only in upper areoles, 1–4, white, yellow or brown, 1–2 in. long: fls. rose-purple, orange or yellow, 3 in. across: fr. dry, spiny. Neb. to Ariz.

14. **O. compressa,** Macb. (*Cactus Opuntia,* L. *C. compressus,* Salisb. *O. Opuntia,* Karst.). Low and spreading; joints obovate or nearly orbicular, 2–7 in. long, deep green; areoles distant; spines 1–2, brownish, about 2 in. long, borne only on edges, often lacking: fls. yellow or reddish in center, 2–3 in. across: fr. juicy, red, 1–2 in. long, bristly but not spiny. Mass to Ga.

15. **O. Rafinesquei,** Engelm. (*O. compressa* var. *microsperma,* Benson). Differs from *O. compressa* in being more spiny, the upper half of joints bearing spines. (Named for Rafinesque, page 50.) Wis. to Tex. and Ariz.

4. **ZYGOCACTUS,** Schum. Flat-stemmed short-jointed cacti often cult. for the bright showy fls. profusely borne in winter; a Brazilian genus, many of whose cult. forms have been produced through hybridization between the different species and with Epiphyllum and the allies of Cereus; typical plants are rarely seen.—Sts. much-branched, the many short joints flat or in age becoming rounded, bearing areoles only in the margins and more or less truncate ends, from which grow the new branches

and the conspicuously zygomorphic fls.: ovary bractless, the bracts of the tube rather large and colored as the petals. (Zygocac-tus: cactus with zygomorphic fls.)—Genus closely allied to Epiphyllum, the plants in their native surroundings growing as epiphytes on the trees.

Z. truncatus, Schum. (*Epiphyllum truncatum*, Haw.). CRAB CACTUS. CHRISTMAS CACTUS. Sts. much-branched and hanging in large bunches from the trees; joints obovate to oblong, 1¼–2 in. long, ¾–1 in. across, bright green, strongly truncate at apex, the margins coarsely serrate with 1–3 large acute teeth on each side, the 2 upper ones forming more or less incurved horns on either side of the truncation; areoles bearing a few short yellowish or dark colored bristles, or sometimes none: fls. horizontal, growing from the truncated end of the younger joints, strongly irregular, 2½–3½ in. long, in various shades of red: fr. pear-shaped, red, about ⅜in. diam. Brazil.

5. **EPIPHYLLUM,** Haw. Flat-stemmed unarmed branching cacti, with very large and showy fls., some popular as house-plants; natives of Mex., Cent. Amer. and trop. S. Amer., about 20 species.—Upright plants with flat 2-edged branches which are crenate or serrate on the margins, spineless: fls. usually large, mostly nocturnal, the tube longer than limb; petals white, red, or yellow; stamens elongated, numerous: fr. oblong, red, juicy, bearing a few bracts; seeds numerous, black. (Epi-phyl-lum: *on a leaf*, referring to the lf.-like branches on which the fls. grow.)

A. Tube of perianth seven to nine times longer than limb.......... 1. *E. Phyllanthus*
AA. Tube of perianth one to three times longer than limb.......... 2. *E. crenatum*

1. **E. Phyllanthus,** Haw. (*Cactus Phyllanthus*, L. *Phyllocactus Phyllanthus*, Link). Joints elongated, to 3 in. across, obtuse, shallowly crenate, margins reddish: fls. nocturnal, 10–12 in. long, with narrow tube seven to nine times longer than limb, tube green with few minute scales; petals white, narrow; style pink: fr. about 3 in. long. (Phyllanthus: Greek *leaf* and *flower*, young lvs. are borne in place of the old withered fls.) Panama to Brazil.

2. **E. crenatum,** Don (*Cereus crenatus*, Lindl. *Phyllocactus crenatus*, Lem.). Sts. about 3 ft. long; branches about 1 in. across, erect, thick, strongly crenate, somewhat glaucous, midrib very thick: fls. very fragrant, 6–10 in. long, 4 in. diam., day-blooming; perianth-tube 4–5 in. long, bearing leafy scales; petals white or cream-colored, drying yellow; style white. Guatemala.

6. **NOPALXOCHIA,** Britt. & Rose. Two Mexican species of branching cacti, grown as house and greenhouse subjects.—Closely allied to Epiphyllum, differing in perianth-tube being shorter than limb. (Nopalxo-chia: from the Aztec name.)

A. Fls. 6–8 in. long.......... 1. *N. Ackermannii*
AA. Fls. 3–4 in. long.......... 2. *N. phyllanthoides*

1. **N. Ackermannii,** Knuth (*Epiphyllum Ackermannii*, Haw. *Phyllocactus Ackermannii*, Salm-Dyck). Sts. numerous, sometimes 3 ft. long, somewhat recurved; branches mostly less than 1 ft. long, with evident middle and side ribs, crenate; areoles on the lower and younger shoots bearing short bristles: fls. day-blooming, scarlet-red outside, carmine-red within, the throat greenish-yellow, 6–8 in. long, tube very short, limb wide-spreading, 4–6 in. diam. (Bears the name of Geo. Ackermann, collector of this species in Mex.) Not known in the wild state.

2. **N. phyllanthoides,** Britt. & Rose (*Cactus phyllanthoides*, DC. *Epiphyllum phyllanthoides*, Sweet. *Phyllocactus phyllanthoides*, Link). Branches at length hanging, cylindric at base, lanceolate above, serratures obtuse, middle and side ribs evident; bristles few: fls. day-blooming, 3–4 in. long, rose or red, tube with spreading scales, limb often striate; style white. S. Mex.

7. **THELOCACTUS,** Britt. & Rose. Spiny globular or somewhat depressed cacti, of over 20 species in Tex. and Mex.—Plant with prominent tubercles arranged in indefinite or continuous ribs: fls. diurnal, borne in grooves on the young tubercles near center of plant, never from the spine-bearing areoles, campanulate; ovary scaly: fr. dry, scaly, dehiscing by basal pore; seeds black, with basal hilum. (Thelo-cac-tus: from Greek for *nipple* and *cactus*.)

A. Central spines 4, straight.......... 1. *T. bicolor*
AA. Central spine solitary, hooked at tip.......... 2. *T. uncinatus*

1. **T. bicolor,** Britt. & Rose (*Echinocactus bicolor*, Galeotti). Plant simple, 4–8 in. high and 3–4 in. diam., glaucous; ribs usually 8, tubercled; spines red or yellowish; radials 9–18, spreading or recurved, about 1 in. long; centrals mostly 4, straight, 1–2 in. long: fls. purplish-pink, about 2 in. long and wide: fr. ½in. long. S. Tex., Mex.

2. **T. uncinatus,** Marshall (*Echinocactus uncinatus*, Galeotti. *Ferocactus uncinatus*, Britt. & Rose. *Hamatocactus uncinatus*, Orcutt). Plant ovoid to short-cylindric, 4–8 in. high and 3 in. diam., blue-green, slightly glaucous; ribs 9–13, tubercled; spines red to creamy-white; radials 7–8, the lower hooked; central usually 1, to 5 in. long, hooked at tip: fls. dark reddish-brown, about 1 in. long: fr. green turning scarlet, ¾in. long. W. Tex., Mex.

8. **MAMMILLARIA,** Haw. (*Neomammillaria*, Britt. & Rose). Globose or condensed small spiny plants grown in greenhouses or some of the species out-of-doors in the far S.; about 215 species in Mex. and S. W. U. S.—Short 1-jointed cacti with sts. simple or clustered, commonly hemispheric or short-cylindric, the surface entirely broken up into tubercles: fls. usually short-funnelform, with naked or nearly naked tube and ovary, borne laterally in the more or less woolly axils between the old tubercles or at the upper extremity of a narrow groove on their upper surface, never from the spine-bearing areoles: fr. linear-clavate, nearly always smooth and berry-like; seeds brown or black, with minute hilum. (Mammilla-ria: Latin *mammila*, referring to the nipple-like tubercles.)

A. Radial spines represented by long white silky hairs.
  B. Juice watery: fls. white....................1. *M. bocasana*
  BB. Juice milky: fls. rose-carmine....................2. *M. Hahniana*
AA. Radial spines bristle-like.
  B. Tubercles with milky juice: fls. yellowish, surrounded by mass of wool....................3. *M. Parkinsonii*
  BB. Tubercles with watery juice: fls. red....................4. *M. elegans*

1. **M. bocasana,** Poselger. POWDER-PUFF CACTUS. Cespitose, forming mounds; individuals globose, 1½ in. diam., light green, with cylindrical tubercles hairy or bristly in axils; radial spines represented by many long silky white hairs; central spine 1, hooked, brown, to ⅓in. long: fls. yellowish-white, about ½in. across: fr. reddish; seeds brown. Mex.

2. **M. Hahniana,** Werd. OLD-WOMAN CACTUS. Cespitose, with milky juice; individuals globose, 4 in. diam., with cylindrical tubercles bearing in the woolly axils about 20 white bristles to 2 in. long which completely cover st.; radial spines represented by 20–30 soft white curly hairs to ½in. long; central spine usually 1, transparent white: fls. rose-carmine, small: fr. reddish; seeds brown. (Named for Mr. Hahn of Lichterfelde, Germany.) Mex.

3. **M. Parkinsonii,** Ehrenb. Cespitose, with milky juice; individuals cylindrical or depressed, to 6 in. high, glaucous, with conical tubercles woolly and bristly in the axils; radial spines 25–30, bristle-like, white; central spines 2 or 4, white, the lower about ¾in. long and recurved: fls. yellowish, small, surrounded by mass of wool: fr. scarlet, ½in. long; seeds brown. (Named for John Parkinson, once British official in Mex., died 1847.) Mex.

4. **M. elegans,** DC. Plant usually simple, globose or cylindrical, 2–4 in. high, glaucous, with closely set conical tubercles woolly or sometimes naked in axils; radial spines 25–30, bristle-like, white, about ¼in. long; central spines 1–3, white tipped brown, about ½in. long: fls. rose-carmine, ½in. long: fr. carmine, ¾in. long. Mex.

9. **CORYPHANTHA,** Lem. Small cacti native in the U. S., Mex. and Cuba, of about 65 species.—Differs from Mammillaria in tubercles grooved on upper surface and fls. borne centrally in axils of young tubercles near top of plant: fr. greenish or yellowish, ripening slowly; seeds light brown. (Coryphan-tha: from Greek for *top* and *flower*.)

A. Tubercles grooved to about middle: ovary with few scales....................1. *C. macromeris*
AA. Tubercles grooved to base: ovary naked.
  B. Fls. pale yellow: grooves of tubercles with large glands....................2. *C. erecta*
  BB. Fls. reddish or purple: grooves of tubercles without large glands....................3. *C. vivipara*

1. **C. macromeris,** Lem. (*Mammillaria macromeris*, Engelm.). Cespitose, grayish-green; plant-body to 8 in. high and 3 in. diam., tubercles grooved to about middle; radial spines 10–17, white; central spines 1–4, brown or black, 1–2 in. long: fls. purple, 2–3 in. across, with few fringed scales on ovary and tube: fr. green, ½–1 in. long, smooth. W. Tex. to Mex.

2. **C. erecta,** Lem. (*Mammillaria erecta*, Lem.). Solitary or clustered; plant-body cylindric, to 1 ft. high and 2–3 in. diam., yellowish-green, tubercles grooved to base, axils woolly, with yellow or brown gland; radial spines 8–14, yellow or brown; central spines 2, the lower curved, to ¾in. long: fls. pale yellow, 2–3 in. across. Mex.

3. **C. vivipara,** Britt. & Rose (*Cactus viviparus*, Nutt. *Mammillaria vivipara*, Haw.). Solitary or cespitose; plant-body globose, 1½ in. high and 2 in. diam., tubercles grooved to base, areoles woolly; radial spines about 16, white or brown; central spines 1–4, brown or variegated, ¾in. long: fls. purple or pink, 1½ in. across, sepals fringed: fr. greenish, ¾in. long, smooth. Man. to N. Tex.

10. **NEOBESSEYA,** Britt. & Rose. Six species of small cacti native in U. S. to Mex.—Closely allied to Coryphantha but differing in the bright red fr. which ripens rapidly, and the black or dark brown seeds with large white aril. (Neobesseya: named for Dr. C. E. Bessey, 1845–1915, American botanist.)

N. missouriensis, Britt. & Rose (*Mammillaria missouriensis*, Sweet. *Coryphantha missouriensis*, Britt. & Rose). Solitary or cespitose; plant-body depressed-globose, 2½ in. high and 3 in. diam., tubercles grooved on upper side, areoles woolly; spines usually about 14 and all radial, gray tipped with brown: fls. yellow with brown central stripe on sepals and petals, fragrant, 1 in. across: fr. ovoid, ½in. long. N. D. to Tex.

11. **ECHINOCEREUS,** Engelm. Low cacti, erect, prostrate or pendent, some cult. for their large attractive fls.; species about 60, confined to the arid regions of W. U. S. and Mex.—Sts. single or clustered, globose to cylindric, strongly ribbed, 1- to few-jointed; areoles borne on the ribs and usually spinose: fls. solitary, lateral, usually large, diurnal but in some species not closing at night; perianth campanulate to short funnel-shaped, red, purple, or rarely yellow, the tube and ovary spiny; lobes of stigma green: fr. colored, thin-skinned, often edible, with spines which are easily detached when mature and black tuberculate seeds. (Echinoce-reus: *spiny cereus.*)

A. Plant covered with long white curling hairs....1. *E. Delaetii*
AA. Plant spiny but not hairy.
B. Fls. greenish....2. *E. viridiflorus*
BB. Fls. red or purple.
C. Sts. prostrate....3. *E. Blanckii*
CC. Sts. erect or ascending.
D. Ribs 5–8: fls. scarlet....4. *E. triglochidiatus*
DD. Ribs 11–19: fls. purple.
E. Spines pectinate, to ⅓in. long....5. *E. Reichenbachii*
EE. Spines not pectinate, some of them 2 in. long....6. *E. Engelmannii*

1. **E. Delaetii,** Guerke. Old-Lady Cactus. Densely cespitose, to 8 in. high, covered with long white curling hairs; ribs indistinct; areoles with hairs 3–4 in. long and few reddish bristles: fls. pink, about 2 in. long. (Named for a Belgian cactus dealer, Frantz de Laet.) Mex.

2. **E. viridiflorus,** Engelm. Single or clustered, 1–3 in. high; ribs 14; spines white, brown or variegated, 13–15, centrals often lacking, ½in. or less long: fls. greenish, about 1 in. long: fr. greenish, about ½in. long. S. D. to Tex. and New Mex.

3. **E. Blanckii,** F. Palmer (*Cereus Blanckii*, Poselger. *C. Berlandieri*, Engelm. *E. Berlandieri*, Ruempl.). Prostrate, with joints 1–6 in. long and about 1 in. diam.; ribs 5–7, tubercled; radial spines 6–8, white, ⅓in. long; central 1, brown or black, ½–2 in. long: fls. purple, 2–3 in. long. (Named for P. A. Blanck, Berlin pharmacist.) Mex.

4. **E. triglochidiatus,** Engelm. (*Cereus triglochidiatus*, Engelm.). Claret-Cup Cactus. Cespitose, with erect or ascending sts.; joints 4–6 in. long and 2–2½ in. diam.; ribs 5–8; spines 3–8, spreading, about 1 in. long, gray, often all radial: fls. scarlet, 2–3 in. long: fr. bright red, 1 in. diam. Colo. to Tex. and New Mex.

5. **E. Reichenbachii,** Haage Jr. (*Echinocactus Reichenbachii*, Terscheck. *Cereus cæspitosus*, Engelm. *Echinocereus cæspitosus*, Engelm.). Cob Cactus. Lace Cactus. Somewhat cespitose, sts. 1–8 in. long and 2–3 in. diam.; ribs 12–19; radial spines 20–30, pectinate, spreading, ⅓in. long, of one color; centrals 1 or 2 or lacking: fls. purple, 2–3 in. long, fragrant: fr. ovoid, green, ½in. long. (H. G. L. Reichenbach, page 50.) Colo. to N. Mex.

6. **E. Engelmannii,** Ruempl. (*Cereus Engelmannii*, Parry). Forming large clumps, joints 4–12 in. long and 2 in. diam.; ribs 11–18; radial spines about 10, ½in. long; centrals 5–6, stout, curved or twisted, to 2 in. long, yellowish to brown: fls. purple, 2–3 in. long: fr. about 1 in. long. (Geo. Engelmann, page 42.) S. Utah to Mex.

12. **CHAMÆCEREUS,** Britt. & Rose. One small cactus native in Argentina.—Plants creeping and forming small clumps; ribs few and spiny: fls. solitary at lateral areoles, diurnal; tube cylindric, the scales hairy in axils: fr. globular, dry, woolly; seeds black, punctate. (Chamæce-reus: from Greek for *on the ground* and *cereus.*)

C. Silvestrii, Britt. & Rose (*Cereus Silvestrii*, Spegazzini). Peanut Cactus. Joints 2–3 in. high, pale green; ribs 6–9, low; spines 10–15, radiating, white, 1⁄12in. long, bristle-like: fls. scarlet, 2–3 in. long. (Named for Dr. Philip Silvestri.)

13. **ACANTHOCALYCIUM,** Backeberg. About 10 species of S. American globose to cylindrical cacti.—Ribs nearly spiral, prominently tubercled: fls. from lateral

areoles, the tube and ovary covered with stiff curved or erect papery scales woolly in axils, having a ring of wool inside tube above ovary: fr. scaly and woolly. (Acanthocalyc-ium: Greek for *spiny calyx.*)

A. formosum, Backeberg (*Echinocactus formosanus*, Pfeiffer. *Echinopsis formosa*, Jacobi). Sts. solitary, globular, 1–1½ ft. high and 6–8 in. diam., pale green; ribs 15–35, areoles woolly; radial spines 8–16, yellowish, to 1¾ in. long; centrals 2–4, brown, to 2¾ in. long: fls. golden-yellow, 3 in. long and broad. Argentina.

14. **ECHINOPSIS,** Zucc. HEDGEHOG CACTUS. More than 40 species of small cacti native in S. Amer.—Plant globular to cylindrical, ribs continuous or undulate, areoles felted or spiny: fls. night-blooming, borne in lateral areoles just above spines, with long funnelform tube which is scaly with long hairs in axils: fr. globose to ovoid, not spiny; seeds minute. (Echinop-sis: Greek for *hedgehog-like.*)

A. Spines very short, ⅕in. or less long........1. *E. Eyriesii*
AA. Spines ¾–2 in. long.
B. Central spine 1, curved upward........2. *E. campylacantha*
BB. Central spines 2–5, straight........3. *E. multiplex*

1. **E. Eyriesii,** Zucc. (*Echinocactus Eyriesii*, Turpin). Globular to columnar, 4–6 in. diam., dark green; ribs 11–18, areoles with yellowish-white felt; spines 14–18, ⅕ in. or less long: fls. white, 8–10 in. long. (Bears the name of Alexander Eyries of Havre, France.) S. Brazil to Argentina.

2. **E. campylacantha,** Pfeiffer. Globular to columnar, dark green; ribs 12–14; radial spines 7–8, yellowish or grayish; central spine 1, curved upward, about 2 in. long, dark brown: fls. white or pinkish, 6–7 in. long, slightly fragrant. Argentina.

3. **E. multiplex,** Zucc. (*Cereus multiplex*, Pfeiffer). Globular, 6 in. high, very proliferous; ribs 13–15, areoles with white wool; radial spines 8–10, spreading, to ¾in. long; centrals 2–5, to nearly 2 in. long: fls. pink or rose, 6–8 in. long, fragrant. S. Brazil.

15. **ARIOCARPUS,** Scheidweiler. Small spineless cacti of about 9 species in Tex. and Mex.—Plants low, with flat or rounded top and long tap-root, strongly tuberculate and without distinct ribs, the tubercles triangular and ending in a callus point; areoles in middle or toward tip of tubercle, often in a groove, woolly: fls. borne at center of plant, diurnal, rotate-campanulate: fr. oblong, smooth; seeds black, tuberculate. (Ariocar-pus: *aria-like fruit;* i.e. *Sorbus Aria.*)

A. fissuratus, Schum. (*Mammillaria fissurata*, Engelm. *Anhalonium fissuratum*, Engelm. *Roseocactus fissuratus*, Berger). LIVING ROCK. Plant-body mostly buried, 5–6 in. across; tubercles with central groove and one along each margin, surface warty: fls. white to shell-pink, to 1½ in. across: fr. pale green, ⅓in. long. W. Tex., Mex.

16. **HAMATOCACTUS,** Britt. & Rose. Two species of small cacti native in S. W. U. S. and Mex.—Plant globose or short-cylindric, distinctly ribbed and tubercled; areoles oval, woolly, with radial and central spines, one of them hooked at apex: fls. borne at central areoles, funnelform with narrow tube; ovary with few naked scales: fr. small, globular, red or green; seeds black, tuberculate. (Hamatocactus: *hooked* and *cactus.*)

A. Central spines 1–3: fr. red........1. *H. setispinus*
AA. Central spines 4: fr. green........2. *H. hamatocanthus*

1. **H. setispinus,** Britt. & Rose (*Echinocactus setispinus*, Engelm.). TWISTED RIB. To 6 in. high and 3–5 in. thick; ribs 13; radial spines 12–16, white or brownish, to 2 in. long; centrals 1–3, longer, hooked at tip: fls. yellow with red center, 2–3 in. long: fr. red, ⅓in. across. S. Tex., N. Mex.

2. **H. hamatocanthus,** Borg (*Echinocactus hamatocanthus*, Muehlenpfordt. *Ferocactus hamatocanthus*, Britt. & Rose). TURKS-HEAD. To 2 ft. high; ribs usually 13; radial spines 8–12, red, yellow or white, 2–3 in. long; centrals 4, half-round, the lower to 5 in. long and strongly hooked: fls. yellow, about 3 in. long and wide: fr. green, to 2 in. long. S. Tex., New Mex., Mex. Var. **Davisii,** Marshall (*Brittonia Davisii*, Houghton), has more pronounced tubercles.

17. **FEROCACTUS,** Britt. & Rose. BARREL CACTUS. About 30 species of globose or cylindric cacti of S. W. U. S. and Mex.—Sts. prominently ribbed, armed with well-developed straight or hooked spines; areoles mostly large, more or less felted when young: fls. commonly large, broadly funnelform to campanulate and with

short tube, borne only on the young areoles just above the spine-clusters; stamens very many, short, borne on the throat of the perianth; ovary and fl.-tube very scaly, the scales naked in the axils: fr. oblong, usually thick-walled and dry, opening by a large basal pore, with black, pitted, never tuberculate seeds. (Ferocac-tus: *ferus* and *cactus*, fierce cactus, referring to the very spiny character of the plants.)

A. Areoles with both bristles and spines: plants becoming 7 ft. or more high.
  B. Central spine strongly hooked, to 3 in. long........................1. *F. Wislizenii*
  BB. Central spine not hooked, to 5 in. long........................2. *F. acanthodes*
AA. Areoles with spines only: plants 2 ft. or less high.
  B. Spines all straight........................3. *F. melocactiformis*
  BB. Spines straight except one of the centrals which is strongly hooked.
    C. Central spine 1........................4. *F. nobilis*
    CC. Central spines 4 or more........................5. *F. latispinus*

1. **F. Wislizenii**, Britt. & Rose (*Echinocactus Wislizenii*, Engelm.). At first globose, finally cylindric and 7 ft. high or more, usually simple; ribs 15–25; areoles elliptic, sometimes 1 in. long, brown-felted, with many bristle-like radial spines, one of the stout central spines strongly hooked and to 3 in. long: fls. yellow or red, 2–2½ in. long: fr. yellow, 2 in. long. (Named for Dr. A. Wizlizenius, who collected in early days in W. U. S.) Tex. to Ariz. south into Mex.

2. **F. acanthodes**, Britt. & Rose (*Echinocactus acanthodes*, Lem.). Becoming cylindric and 8–9 ft. high, very spiny; ribs 13–27; areoles large, close together, brown-felted; radial spines weak; central spines 4, spreading and curved but not hooked, to 5 in. long: fls. yellow or orange, about 2 in. long: fr. about 1 in. long. S. Nev. to Lower Calif.

3. **F. melocactiformis**, Britt. & Rose (*Echinocactus melocactiformis*, DC. *E. electrocanthus*, Lem.). Cylindric, to 2 ft. high and 1 ft. thick, bluish-green; ribs about 24; areoles 1 in. apart; spines 10–12, with 3 or 4 of them more or less central and to 2 in. long: fls. bright yellow, reddish outside, 1–1½ in. long: fr. green, ¾in. long. Mex.

4. **F. nobilis**, Britt. & Rose (*Cactus nobilis*, L. *Echinocactus recurvus*, Link & Otto). Globular, to 10 in. high and 8 in. thick; ribs 10–14; areoles about 1 in. apart, gray-felted; radial spines several, stiff, 1 in. long; central solitary, strongly hooked at tip, 2 in. long: fls. pink, to 2 in. long: fr. ¾in. long. Mex.

5. **F. latispinus**, Britt. & Rose (*Cactus latispinus*, Haw. *Echinocactus cornigerus*, DC.). Globular or somewhat depressed, to 16 in. high; ribs 15–23; areoles 2 in. apart, gray-felted; radial spines 6–12, spreading, 1 in. long; centrals 4 or more, longer, one strongly hooked at tip: fls. reddish to purple, 1½ in. long: fr. to 1½ in. long. Mex.

18. **ASTROPHYTUM**, Lem. STAR CACTUS. Four small usually globular cacti native in Mex.—Ribs prominent but few, white-scaly; spines weak or wanting: fls. large, yellow or reddish, borne at top of plant; ovary and fl.-tube with scales woolly in axils: fr. globular, covered with scales which are woolly in axils; seeds dark brown, shining. (Astroph-ytum: Greek for *star* and *plant*.)

A. Spines present........................1. *A. ornatum*
AA. Spines absent.
  B. Plant much depressed, with flat ribs........................2. *A. Asterias*
  BB. Plant globose, with prominent ribs........................3. *A. myriostigma*

1. **A. ornatum**, Weber (*Echinocactus ornatus*, DC.). To 1 ft. high and 6 in. diam., white-woolly; ribs 8, angular, areoles woolly; spines several or many, radiating, yellow to brown, to 1 in. long, sharp: fls. lemon-yellow, 3 in. across.

2. **A. Asterias**, Lem. (*Echinocactus Asterias*, Zucc.). SEA-URCHIN CACTUS. Much depressed, about 1 in. high and 3 in. diam., spineless; ribs 8, flat, with row of small white woolly areoles: fls. yellow, 1 in. long.

3. **A. myriostigma**, Lem. BISHOPS-HOOD or BISHOPS-CAP. Globose, becoming cylindrical, to 2 ft. high and 4–8 in. diam., spineless; ribs usually 5, with row of brownish woolly areoles: fls. yellow tipped with brown, about 2 in. long.

19. **HOMALOCEPHALA**, Britt. & Rose. One very flat cactus native Tex. to N. Mex.—Separated from Echinocactus because of its juicier less woolly fr. which bursts irregularly. (Homaloceph-ala: from Greek for *level* and *head*.)

H. texensis, Britt. & Rose (*Echinocactus texensis*, Hopffer). HORSE CRIPPLER CACTUS. To 1 ft. diam. and 6 in. high, usually simple; ribs 13–27, very prominent, with few white-felted areoles; radial spines 6–7, reddish, ½–1½ in. long; central 1, 1–2½ in. long: fls. pink to reddish, about 2 in. long and broad, outer petals fringed: fr. scarlet, ½–1½ in. diam.

20. **ECHINOCACTUS**, Link & Otto. Large thick cylindric cacti, sometimes cult. as curiosities; a genus of 9 species as now understood, native to S. W. U. S.

and Mex.—Sts. several- to many-ribbed, the top clothed with a dense mass of wool or nearly naked; areoles very spiny, large, on old plants sometimes united: fls. usually yellow, rarely pink, medium-sized, borne on the crown of the plant and often partly obscured by the dense wool; outer perianth-segms. sometimes with pungent tips; scales of the fl.-tube numerous, persistent, those of the ovary narrow and with matted wool in the axils: fr. oblong, densely white-woolly, with blackish usually smooth and shining seeds. (Echinocac-tus: Greek *spine* and *cactus*.)

A. Spines bright yellow..1. *E. Grusonii*
AA. Spines brown..2. *E. ingens*

1. **E. Grusonii**, Hildmann. Golden Ball Cactus. Usually single, depressed-globose, becoming 4 ft. high and 2½ ft. diam.; ribs 21–37, acute and rather thin; spines numerous, golden-yellow when young, becoming pale, radials 8–10, about 1 in. long, centrals 4, to 2 in. long: fls. red and yellow, 1½–2½ in. long, opening in bright sunlight; stamens yellow, connivent into a cylinder: fr. oblong to globose, ½–¾in. long, white-woolly or naked below. (Named in honor of Herr Gruson of Buckow near Magdeburg.) Mex.

2. **E. ingens**, Zucc. Mexican Giant Barrel. Globular or oblong, to 5 ft. high and 4 ft. diam., transversely marked with purple when young; ribs 8–20, rounded, tuberculate; spines brown, stiff, radials 8, about 1 in. long, central 1: fls. yellow, 1 in. long and to 2 in. across: fr. ovoid, 1 in. long, woolly. Mex.

21. **HYLOCEREUS**, Britt. & Rose. Night-Blooming Cereus. About 18 species of climbing cacti, the sts. adhering to walls or other support by means of numerous aërial roots, native of the W. Indies, Mex., Cent. and N. S. Amer.—Sts. elongated, 3-angled or 3-winged; areoles felted and short-spinose or spineless, on young growths bristly: fls. white, rarely red, very large, nocturnal, funnelform, the limb very broad; ovary and tube with large scales, without spines, wool or hairs; stamens numerous, in 2 series, equalling or shorter than the style; stigma with many simple or branched lobes: fr. a fleshy berry, spineless but scaly, mostly large and edible; seeds small, black. (Hyloce-reus: *wood* and *cereus*, i.e., forest cereus.)

H. undatus, Britt. & Rose (*Cereus undatus*, Haw. *H. tricostatus*, Britt. & Rose. *C. triangularis*, Haw.). Long-clambering, the 3 broad thin ribs with margin undulate and in age more or less horny; areoles 1½ in. apart, with 1–3 small spines: fls. about 1 ft. long, the yellowish-green outer perianth-segms. turned back, the pure white inner ones erect; stamens and numerous stigma-lobes cream-colored: fr. oblong, 4½ in. diam., red, scaly or when mature nearly smooth, edible. Tropics and subtropics.—The best known of all night-blooming cereuses, widely cult. and in trop. countries making a beautiful hedge plant.

22. **SELENICEREUS**, Britt. & Rose. Moon Cereus. More or less epiphytic cacti with trailing or climbing sts.; 23 species, ranging from S. Tex. through E. Mex., Cent. Amer., the W. Indies, and along the northern coast of S. Amer., one in Argentina, several favorites in cult. because of the great size and beauty of their fls.—Sts. with ribbed or angled joints, with aërial roots; areoles small, sometimes elevated on small knobs, usually with small spines: fls. white, often very large, nocturnal, the scales of the ovary and long curved perianth-tube with axillary felt, hairs and bristles; outer perianth-segms. narrow, greenish, brownish or orange; stamens in 2 separate clusters; style elongate, often hollow, stigma with numerous lobes: fr. large, reddish, bearing deciduous spines, bristles and hairs in clusters. (Selenice-reus: *moon goddess* and *cereus*.)

A. Areoles borne on prominent knobs..1. *S. Macdonaldiæ*
AA. Areoles borne on angles or ribs.
B. Spines needle-like, about ½in. long..2. *S. grandiflorus*
BB. Spines conic, ⅛in. or less long..3. *S. pteranthus*

1. **S. Macdonaldiæ**, Britt. & Rose (*Cereus Macdonaldiæ*, Hook.). Sts. 5-angled, becoming terete, about ½in. thick; areoles borne on prominent knobs; spines about 1⁄12in. long: fls. 1 ft. or more long, tube with brown hairs and spines in axils of scales: fr. oblong, 3 in. long. (Named for Mrs. General MacDonald, who sent the plant from Honduras.) Uruguay, Argentina.

2. **S. grandiflorus**, Britt. & Rose (*Cactus grandiflorus*, L.). Sts. about 1 in. thick, with 7 or 8 low ribs; areoles with yellowish-white wool; spines needle-like, ¼–½in. long: fls. 7 in. or more long, tube with long brownish hairs: fr. ovoid, 3 in. long. Jamaica, Cuba.

3. **S. pteranthus,** Britt. & Rose (*Cereus pteranthus,* Link & Otto. *C. nycticallus* Link). Sts. 1½ in. diam., bluish-green to purple, with 4–6 strong angles; spines 1–4, conic, ⅛in. or less long: fls. very fragrant, often 1 ft. long; ovary covered with white silky hairs and bristles nearly ½in. long: fr. globose, 2½ in. diam. Mex.—One of the commonest night-blooming cacti, often found in conservatories.

23. **APOROCACTUS,** Lem. Vine-like plants, one common in cult. as a window-plant; species 5, mostly Mex.—Sts. creeping or clambering, sending out aërial roots: fls. pink or red, rather small, day-blooming, one at an areole, the funnelform tube straight or curved; outer perianth-segms. linear, scattered, the inner broad and more compact; stamens exserted, in a single one-sided cluster, the filaments attached along the throat: fr. globose, small, reddish, bristly, with few reddish-brown seeds. (Aporocac-tus: Greek *impenetrable* and *cactus.*)

A. flagelliformis, Lem. (*Cactus flagelliformis,* L. *Cereus flagelliformis,* Mill.). RAT-TAIL CACTUS. Sts. and branches slender and weak, ½–¾in. diam., at first ascending or erect, becoming prostrate and creeping or even pendent; ribs 10–12, low and inconspicuous, slightly tuberculate; areoles with many brownish spines: fls. crimson, 3 in. long, strongly bent just above ovary, opening for three to four days, the outer perianth-segms. more or less reflexed, the inner only slightly spreading: fr. ½in. diam., with yellowish pulp. Mex., Cent. and S. Amer.

24. **LOPHOCEREUS,** Britt. & Rose. Stout columnar cacti native S. Ariz. to Mex.; one variable species or by some authorities divided into 4.—Ribs few; areoles of flowering branches with many long bristles, other areoles with few stout spines: fls. several from an areole, nocturnal, funnelform; stamens short: fr. globular, red, bursting irregularly, glabrous or with few spines; seeds black, shining. (Lophocereus: *crested cereus.*)

L. Schottii, Britt. & Rose (*Cereus Schottii,* Engelm.). Branching at base, to 20 ft. high; ribs 5–7; bristles of flowering areoles gray, to 2½ in. long: fls. pink, greenish outside, 1–1½ in. long: fr. about 1 in. diam. (Named for Arthur Schott, collector with the Mex. Boundary Commission.)

25. **MYRTILLOCACTUS,** Console. MYRTLE CACTUS. Four species of tree-like cacti native in Mex. and Guatemala.—Trunks short, top with numerous erect branches; ribs few, all areoles with stout awl-shaped spines: fls. several at an areole, diurnal, with very short tube and spreading segms.; stamens exserted; ovary with few scales having wool in their axils: fr. globular, edible; seeds black, very small. (Myrtillocac-tus: *berry cactus.*)

M. geometrizans, Console (*Cereus geometrizans,* Mart.). GARAMBULLA. To 15 ft.; branches 2–4 in. thick, bluish-green, with 5–6 rounded ribs; radial spines usually 5, spreading, ½–⅓ in. long; central 1, sword-shaped, about 1 in. long: fls. white, about 1 in. across: fr. purplish or bluish, to ¾in. long.

26. **CEREUS,** Mill. Usually arborescent cacti with spiny ribs; about two dozen species, extending from the southern W. Indies through E. S. Amer. to Argentina.—With mostly tall and erect sts. but sometimes low and spreading or prostrate, usually much-branched; branches strongly angled or ribbed; areoles spiny, more or less short-woolly: fls. large, elongate, nocturnal, usually borne singly along the sides of the st.; perianth deciduous soon after anthesis, the outer segms. thick and greenish or dull-colored, the inner thin and white or in one species red; stamens numerous, not exserted; style often included, stigma lobed; ovary bearing a few scales which are naked in the axils: fr. fleshy, red, rarely yellow, naked, often edible, splitting down one side when mature; seeds black. (Ce-reus: from the Latin, but of uncertain application.)

A. Fls. 6 in. long: fr. orange . . . . 1. *C. peruvianus*
AA. Fls. 1 ft. long: fr. bright red . . . . 2. *C. Jamacaru*

1. **C. peruvianus,** Mill. (*Cactus peruvianus,* L.). HEDGE CACTUS. Tree-like with large much-branched top, 30–50 ft. high; branches usually green, sometimes glaucous, 4–8 in. diam., 6–9- (sometimes 4-) ribbed; spines 5–10, acicular, brown to black, ½–1¼ in. long: fls. white, red or brownish outside, about 6 in. long, with a thick tube: fr. almost globose, orange-yellow, somewhat glaucous, about 1½ in. diam. S. E. S. Amer.—Widely planted in trop. Amer.

2. **C. Jamacaru,** DC. Trunk short and woody, top with many erect branches, 30–40 ft. high, blue-green when young; ribs 4–6, very high and thin; spines numerous, yellowish, some of them to 5 in. or more long: fls. white, green outside, 1 ft. long: fr. bright red, to 5 in. long and 3 in. diam. (Jamacaru: native name.) Brazil.

27. **CEPHALOCEREUS,** Pfeiffer. Columnar cacti occasionally found in large collections; about 60 known species, from S. Fla. and N. Mex. to E. Brazil and Ecuador.—Mostly elongated and erect, but occasionally much-branched with a short trunk or rarely with spreading procumbent branches; areoles developing wool or long white hairs often forming a dense head-like mass at or near the top; armament of flowering areoles differing from that of non-flowering areoles: fls. nocturnal, small, short-campanulate or short-funnelform, the perianth usually persisting on the fr., ovary and tube naked or with few scales: fr. depressed-globose or oblong; seeds black. (Cephaloce-reus: Greek *head cereus.*)

A. Ribs 12–30 or more.......................................1. *C. senilis*
AA. Ribs 7–8.......................................2. *C. Palmeri*

1. **C. senilis,** Pfeiffer (*Cactus senilis,* Haw. *Cereus senilis,* DC. *Pilocereus senilis,* Lem.). OLD-MAN CACTUS. Columnar, simple or rarely branched, reaching a height of 35 ft. and a diam. of 1 ft., with numerous ribs and a head-like mass of gray bristles 2–5 in. long encircling the top or rarely confined to one side; spines 1–5, yellow, ½–2 in. long: fls. 2 in. long, rose-colored: fr. obovoid, 1–1¼ in. long, topped by the base of the fl., having a few minute scales with axillary hairs. Mex.

2. **C. Palmeri,** Rose (*Pilocereus Palmeri,* Knuth). Columnar, branched, to 18 ft. high, with 7–8 prominent rounded ribs; areoles with many grayish-white hairs 1–2 in. long covering upper part of plant; radial spines 7–12, yellow to brown, central 1 or 2, to 1 in. long: fls. 2–3 in. long, purplish or brownish: fr. globular, 2 in. across, naked. (Named for its collector, Dr. E. Palmer, page 350.) Mex.

28. **NYCTOCEREUS,** Britt. & Rose. Erect or clambering cacti sometimes grown for their showy night-blooming fls.; about 5 species, native to Mex. and Cent. Amer.—Slender, sparingly branched, the sts. and branches cylindric, with numerous low ribs; each areole with a tuft of short white wool and small bristles or weak spines: fls. large, white, nocturnal; perianth funnelform, the tube and ovary covered with small scales bearing axillary tufts of spines, the scales grading into the blunt outer perianth-segms.; inner perianth-segms. widely spreading; stamens numerous, shorter than the perianth; style about as long as the stamens: fr. fleshy, scaly, spiny or bristly, with large black seeds. (Nyctoce-reus: *night* and *cereus.*)

N. serpentinus, Britt. & Rose (*Cactus serpentinus,* Lag. & Rodriguez. *Cereus serpentinus,* DC.). SNAKE OR SERPENT CACTUS. Sts. clustered, at first erect, then clambering or hanging, often 9 ft. long and 1–2 in. diam., with 10–13 low rounded ribs; areoles close together, felted and with acicular or bristle-like spines, sometimes 1 in. long: fls. white, 6–7 in. long, 3 in. broad, terminal or at the upper areoles, the perianth-tube and ovary bristly: fr. red, 1½ in. long, bearing deciduous spines. Mex.; not recently reported in wild state, but is widely cult. in Mex. and now escaped.

29. **HARRISIA,** Britt. Slender arching cacti of about 10 species in W. Indies and Fla.—Sts. branched, with many very spiny ribs: fls. nocturnal, borne singly at areoles near top of branches, funnelform, the long tube with scales having hair in axils; stamens shorter than perianth: fr. yellow or orange, indehiscent. (Harris-ia: named for William Harris, formerly superintendent of Public Gardens and Plantations of Jamaica.)

H. fragrans, Small. To 15 ft., sts. erect or clambering, 10–12-ridged; spines 9–13, needle-like, ¾–1½ in. long: fls. white or pinkish, fragrant, 5–8 in. long; scales with long white hairs: fr. orange, about 2 in. diam. Fla.

30. **ERIOCEREUS,** Berger. About 11 species of slender cacti native Brazil to Argentina.—The genus is sometimes included in Harrisia but differs in more procumbent habit, fewer ribs and spines, and red frs. which split irregularly. (Erioce-reus: *woolly cereus.*)

A. Ribs 7, bright green: scales of ovary with white hairs.......................................1. *E. tortuosus*
AA. Ribs or angles 4–5, gray-green: scales of ovary with brown wool.
B. Spines brown with dark tip, 1 central and short radials.......................................2. *E. Martinii*
BB. Spines gray, 6–8.......................................3. *E. Bonplandii*

1. **E. tortuosus,** Riccobono (*Cereus tortuosus,* Forbes. *Harrisia tortuosa,* Britt. & Rose). Branches arching, to 1½ in. diam., with usually 7 low bright green ribs; spines 6–10, brown to grayish, central to 1½ in. long: fls. white to pink, 5–6 in. long; scales with white hairs: fr. 1½ in. diam., with few spines, tuberculate. Argentina.

2. **E. Martinii,** Riccobono (*Cereus Martinii,* Lab. *Harrisia Martinii,* Britt. & Rose). Clambering to 6 ft. or more, with many grayish-green 4–5-angled branches becoming nearly terete and spineless with age; spines a few short radials and 1 stout central about 1 in. long, brown with darker tip: fls. white or pinkish, 8 in. long; scales with brown felt: fr. 1½ in. long, scaly. Argentina.

3. **E. Bonplandii,** Riccobono (*Cereus Bonplandii,* Parmentier. *Harrisia Bonplandii,* Britt. & Rose). Arching or clambering to 10 ft. or more, with strongly 4-angled grayish-green branches 1–3 in. diam.; spines 6–8, needle-like, gray: fls. white, 6–9 in. long; scales with brown wool: fr. about 2 in. diam., scaly. (Bonpland, page 40.) Brazil, Paraguay, Argentina.

31. **CARNEGIEA,** Britt. & Rose. One giant columnar cactus native in the deserts of Ariz., S. Calif. and Sonora, Mex.—Ribs numerous, areoles with both spines and felt, spines of flowering and non-flowering areoles different: fls. white, borne singly in upper areoles, nocturnal but often persisting into the day; tube short, the few scales with tufts of felt in the axils; stamens numerous, shorter than perianth: fr. a berry with red pulp, splitting when ripe, spines few; seeds black and shining, very numerous. (Carne-giea: named for Andrew Carnegie.)

C. gigantea, Britt. & Rose (*Cereus giganteus,* Engelm.). SAHUARO or SAGUARO. GIANT CACTUS. Post-like, 20–60 ft. high and 2 ft. diam., sometimes with few akimbo branches; ribs 18–21; spines of flowering areoles needle-like, those of non-flowering areoles subulate and 2 in. and more long: fls. 4–5 in. long: fr. 2–3 in. long, edible.

32. **TRICHOCEREUS,** Riccobono. S. American columnar cacti, erect or procumbent, of about 28 species.—Ribs few or numerous, very spiny: fls. mostly white, nocturnal, funnelform; tube and ovary with many scales bearing long white hairs in their axils; stamens numerous, filiform: fr. dull colored, usually hairy but without bristles or spines. (Trichoce-reus: *thread cereus.*)

A. Ribs 4–8; spines 2–6 .... 1. *T. Bridgesii*
AA. Ribs 9 or more; spines 9 or more.
  B. Central spine solitary .... 2. *T. Spachianu*
  BB. Central spines 2 to several.
    C. Spines 2–4 in. long .... 3. *T. candicans*
    CC. Spines ½in. or less long .... 4. *T. Schickendantzii*

1. **T. Bridgesii,** Britt. & Rose (*Cereus Bridgesii,* Salm-Dyck). To 15 ft., branching from base, somewhat glaucous; branches 2–4 in. thick, 4–8-ribbed; spines 2–6, yellowish, unequal, 2–4 in. long: fls. 7 in. long: fr. 2 in. long, with long hairs. (Named for its collector, Thomas Bridges, 1807–1865.) Bolivia.

2. **T. Spachianus,** Riccobono (*Cereus Spachianus,* Lem.). To 6 ft., branching from base; branches about 2 in. thick, 10–15-ribbed; radial spines 8–10, spreading, yellow to brown, ¼–½in. long; central solitary, larger: fls. 8 in. long. (For Edouard Spach, page 52.) W. Argentina.

3. **T. candicans,** Britt. & Rose (*Cereus candicans,* Gill.). Forming large clumps to 10 ft. across, branches erect or spreading, to 2 ft. long and 6 in. diam., 9–11-ribbed; radial spines 10 or more, brownish-yellow, about 2 in. long; centrals several, to 4 in. long: fls. fragrant, 6 in. long. Argentina.

4. **T. Schickendantzii,** Britt. & Rose (*Echinopsis Schickendantzii,* Weber). Simple or cespitose, shining dark green, branches 10–18 in. high and 2–3 in. diam., 14–18-ribbed; radial spines 9–10, yellow or gray, ¼–½in. long; centrals 2–8: fls. 8–9 in. long. (Bears the name of Federico Schickendantz, 1837–1896, Argentinian botanist.) Argentina.

33. **OREOCEREUS,** Riccobono. OLD MAN OF THE ANDES. Attractive cacti forming large clumps; about 5 species native in the Andes.—Branches strongly ribbed and spined; areoles with long white hairs: fls. diurnal, with nearly cylindric somewhat curved tube and spreading oblique limb, tube and ovary with small scales having long hairs in axils; stamens numerous, exserted; style exserted: fr. dry, spineless, dehiscing by basal pore; seeds numerous, black. (Oreoce-reus: *mountain cereus.*)

A. Plant to 15 ft. high: hairs white and silky .... 1. *O. Celsianus*
AA. Plant to 2 ft. high: hairs becoming grayish and woolly .... 2. *O. Trollii*

1. **O. Celsianus,** Riccobono (*Pilocereus Celsianus,* Lem.). To 15 ft., with erect or ascending branches 6 in. or more diam., dark or grayish-green; ribs 10–17; areoles large, with white wool and white silky hairs; radial spines 9, yellowish-brown; centrals 1–4: fls. near top of plant, brownish-red, 4 in. long. (Named for Cels Brothers, French nurserymen of the middle of last century.) Bolivia.

2. **O. Trollii,** Backeberg (*Cereus Trollii,* Kupper). To 2 ft., simple or branched from base, light green; ribs 10–25; areoles large, with gray wool and creamy-white silky hairs which become woolly and grayish; radial spines 15, reddish-brown becoming waxy-white; centrals 1–3: fls. rose. (Named for its collector, Dr. C. Troll, German botanist.) Bolivia, Argentina.

34. **ESPOSTOA,** Britt. & Rose. Columnar cacti of Ecuador and Peru; by some authors considered a monotypic genus, by others to include 4 species.—Branching, with numerous low ribs; areoles with strong spines and long white hairs: fls. from a lateral pseudocephalium, diurnal, short-campanulate, tube and ovary with small scales bearing in their axils long silky deciduous hairs: fr. very juicy, white or reddish, smooth; seeds black. (Esposto-a: named for Nicolas E. Esposto, botanist at Lima, Peru.)

E. lanata, Britt. & Rose (*Cactus lanatus,* HBK. *Cereus lanatus,* DC.). COTTON BALL. To 4 ft. or more, branching at top; ribs up to 20; areoles whitish, bearing long silky white hairs covering the st.; radial spines about 12, yellowish or reddish; centrals 1–2, to 3 in. long: fls. white, to 2 in. long: fr. pink.

35. **CLEISTOCACTUS,** Lem. Erect or clambering cacti, of 12 species from Bolivia to Paraguay and Argentina.—Ribs numerous with many spines from close-set areoles: fls. diurnal, orange to scarlet, borne on sides of st. near top, tubular, the limb not expanding; tube and ovary with numerous scales having hair or wool in axils: fr. globular, red or orange, becoming smooth. (Cleistoçac-tus: *closed cactus.*)

A. Ribs 14, spines yellowish .... *1. C. Baumannii*
AA. Ribs 25, most of spines white .... *2. C. Strausii*

1. **C. Baumannii,** Lem. (*Cereus Baumannii,* Lem.). FIRECRACKER CACTUS. Sts. to 6 ft. high and 1½ in. diam.; ribs about 14; areoles yellowish, bearing numerous yellowish spines about ¼in. long, a few to 1½ in. long: fls. orange-scarlet, to 3 in. long, curved. (Named for Baumann Frères, French nurserymen.) Uruguay, Paraguay, Argentina.

2. **C. Strausii,** Backeberg (*Pilocereus Strausii,* Heese. *Cereus Strausii,* Vaupel). SILVER TORCH CACTUS. Sts. to 3½ ft., light green; ribs about 25; areoles with white wool and numerous hair-like white spines ½in. long; central spines 4, pale yellow, nearly 2 in. long: fls. red, 3–4 in. long, slightly curved. (Named for L. Straus, cactus lover, of Bruchsal, Germany.) Bolivia, Argentina.

36. **PACHYCEREUS,** Britt. & Rose. Tree-like cacti, branching from the trunk, of 10 or more species in Mex.—Branches ribbed, areoles with spines and wool: fls. diurnal, with short tube and short segms.; tube and ovary covered with scales having felt and bristles in their axils; stamens numerous, included: fr. dry and bur-like, very spiny; seeds black, large. (Pachyce-reus: *thick cereus.*)

A. Areoles of fl.-tube with long yellowish wool concealing the fls .... *1. P. chrysomallus*
AA. Areoles of fl.-tube felted but without long wool .... *2. P. Pringlei*

1. **P. chrysomallus,** Britt. & Rose (*Pilocereus chrysomallus,* Lem.). Much-branched with age, the erect branches making a compact top to 15 ft. through and 50 ft. or more high, glaucous; ribs 11–14; radial spines 8–10, stiff, to ⅜in. long; centrals 1–3, 2–5 in. long: fls. cream-colored, about 2½ in. long, concealed in a mass of yellowish-brown wool.

2. **P. Pringlei,** Britt. & Rose (*Cereus Pringlei,* Wats.). To 30 ft., with trunk to 6 ft. high and 2 ft. diam. and usually with erect branches; ribs 11–17; areoles with brown felt and numerous stiff spines about 1 in. long, often spineless when old: fls. white, reddish outside, 3 in. long. (Named for C. G. Pringle, who collected in Mex., 1838–1911.)

37. **LEMAIREOCEREUS,** Britt. & Rose. About 25 species native S. Ariz. to S. Amer., mostly large columnar cacti.—Ribs with large areoles having felt and numerous stout spines: fls. diurnal, funnelform or campanulate; stamens numerous, included; ovary slightly tuberculate, scales with felt in axils and few spines: fr. globular or oval, fleshy, bursting irregularly, the spines deciduous; seeds black, numerous. (Lemaireoce-reus: named for Charles Lemaire, 1800–1871, French horticulturist.)

A. Areoles close together, almost continuous....................1. *L. marginatus*
AA. Areoles ½–1 in. apart, borne on protuberances....................2. *L. pruinosus*

1. **L. marginatus**, Berger (*Cereus marginatus*, DC. *Pachycereus marginatus*, Britt. & Rose). ORGAN-PIPE CACTUS. Sts. branching from base, to 25 ft. high and 6 in. diam.; ribs 5–6, the areoles close together and almost continuous along edge of rib, with grayish or brown wool; radial spines 7, to ⅛in. long, centrals 1–2, to ⅝in. long: fls. greenish-white within and reddish outside, to 2 in. long. Mex.

2. **L. pruinosus**, Britt. & Rose (*Echinocactus pruinosus*, Otto. *Cereus pruinosus*, Otto). To 25 ft., with more or less definite trunk and branches 4–5 in. diam.; ribs 5–6, the areoles ½–1 in. or more apart and borne on protuberances; radial spines 7–9, about ½in. long; central 1, about 1 in. long: fls. white inside and greenish outside, 3½ in. long. Mex.

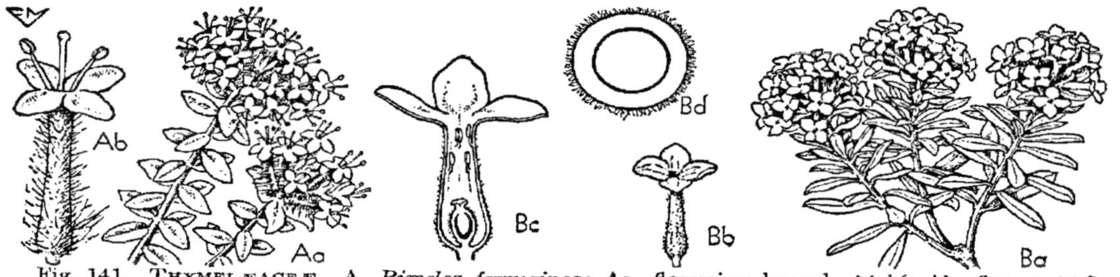

Fig. 141. THYMELÆACEÆ. A, *Pimelea ferruginea:* Aa, flowering branch, × ½; Ab, flower, × 2. B, *Daphne Cneorum:* Ba, flowering branch, × ½; Bb, flower, × 1; Bc, same, vertical section, × 2; Bd, ovary, cross-section, × 10.

141. THYMELÆACEÆ. MEZEREUM FAMILY

Trees or shrubs, rarely herbs, with tough acrid bark, of about 40 genera and 450 species widely distributed, a few grown for ornament.—Lvs. alternate or opposite, simple and entire, exstipulate: fls. regular, usually bisexual, in terminal or axillary heads, racemes or spikes or rarely solitary, the bracts various; receptacle or calyx-tube petaloid, the sepals 4–5 or rarely 6, petals lacking or represented by scales; stamens as many or twice as many as sepals or reduced to 2, usually inserted at mouth of tube; ovary 1-, rarely 2-celled, with 1 ovule in each cell; style short or long: fr. an indehiscent nut, berry or drupe, rarely a dehiscent caps.

A. Stamens not exserted: style short or wanting....................1. DAPHNE
AA. Stamens exserted: style as long as stamens.
B. Infl. axillary; stamens 8....................2. DIRCA
BB. Infl. terminal; stamens 2....................3. PIMELEA

1. **DAPHNE**, L. Erect or prostrate shrubs native in temp. and subtrop. Eu. and Asia; about 50 species, a few planted in borders or sometimes grown in the greenhouse.—Lvs. alternate or rarely opposite, persistent or deciduous, short-petioled: fls. fragrant, in clusters or short racemes, sometimes subtended by involucral bracts; receptacle or calyx-tube corolla-like, cylindrical, with a 4-lobed spreading limb; stamens 8, inserted in 2 rows on the tube, included or the upper sometimes slightly exserted, filaments very short; ovary 1-celled, the style very short or almost none with a large capitate stigma: fr. a fleshy or leathery drupe. (Daph-ne: Greek name of *Laurus nobilis.*)

A. Fls. in axillary clusters or racemes.
B. Foliage persistent....................1. *D. Laureola*
BB. Foliage deciduous, fls. before the lvs.
C. Lvs. alternate....................2. *D. Mezereum*
CC. Lvs. opposite....................3. *D. Genkwa*
AA. Fls. in terminal heads.
B. Tube of fl. densely pubescent outside: lvs. ½–1 in. long....................4. *D. Cneorum*
BB. Tube of fl. only slightly pubescent or glabrous outside: lvs. 1–3 in. long.
C. Habit upright, to 4 ft.: fls. glabrous outside....................5. *D. odora*
CC. Habit diffuse, to 1 ft.: fls. slightly pubescent outside....................6. *D. Blagayana*

1. **D. Laureola**, L. SPURGE-LAUREL. Glabrous evergreen shrub to 3 ft.: lvs. alternate or crowded, oblanceolate, 2–3 in. long, acute, dark green and shining above: fls. yellowish-green, ⅓in. long, in almost sessile axillary racemes in early spring, odorless or slightly fragrant: fr. ovoid, bluish-black. (Laureola: old substantive name.) S. Eu., W. Asia.

2. **D. Mezereum,** L. Erect deciduous shrub to 4 ft.: lvs. alternate, cuneate, oblong or oblanceolate, 2–3 in. long, obtuse or acute, thin and glabrous: fls. in sessile clusters of 2–5 along the branches of the previous year, appearing before the lvs. from Feb. to Apr., lilac-purple, fragrant, silky outside, ½in. or less long: fr. roundish-ovoid, scarlet, about ¼in. long. (Mezereum: native Persian name.) Eu., W. Asia. Var. **alba,** West., has white fls. and yellow fr.

3. **D. Genkwa,** Sieb. & Zucc. Deciduous shrub to 3 ft.: lvs. opposite, oblong-elliptic, 1–2 in. long, pubescent on veins beneath: fls. in short-stalked clusters of 3–7 along branches of the previous year, appearing in Mar. or Apr. before the lvs., lilac, not fragrant, about ½in. long, densely silky-villous outside: fr. white. (Genkwa: Japanese name.) China, Korea.

4. **D. Cneorum,** L. Low evergreen shrub to 1 ft., with trailing pubescent branches: lvs. alternate and crowded, cuneate, oblanceolate, ½–1 in. long, mucronulate, dark green and glossy above, glaucescent beneath: fls. in sessile many-fld. terminal heads without bracts, pink, fragrant, about ½in. long, densely pubescent outside: fr. yellowish-brown. (Cneorum: pre-Linnæan substantive name.) Mts. of Eu.—**D. Burkwoodii,** Burkwood ("Somerset"), is a hybrid between *D. caucasica* and *D. Cneorum:* upright, to 4 ft.: fls. blush-white, fragrant, freely produced.

5. **D. odora,** Thunb. Erect evergreen shrub to 4 ft., the branches glabrous: lvs. alternate or crowded, oblong-elliptic, 2–3 in. long, bluntly pointed, glabrous: fls. in dense terminal heads subtended by 6–10 persistent lanceolate bracts, white to purple, very fragrant, about ½in. long, blooming in early spring. China, Japan.—There are several color races having fls. white, purple, red, or white spotted with red; in one var. the lvs. are bordered with yellow.

6. **D. Blagayana,** Freyer. Evergreen diffusely branched glabrous shrub to 1 ft.: lvs. crowded, obovate, 1–2 in. long, cuneate, obtuse: fls. in terminal heads subtended by silky-pubescent bracts, creamy-white, fragrant, about ½in. across, slightly pubescent outside, blooming in early spring: fr. pinkish-white. (Named for its discoverer, Count Blagay, in 1837.) Mts. of S. E. Eu.

2. **DIRCA,** L. Leatherwood. Deciduous shrubs with tough flexible branches; 2 species in N. Amer.—Lvs. alternate, simple and entire, short-petioled: fls. in few-fld. axillary clusters before the lvs.; receptacle or calyx-tube corolla-like, narrow-funnelform, indistinctly 4-lobed; stamens 8, filiform, exserted; ovary 1-celled, the filiform style as long as stamens with small stigma: fr. a drupe. (Dir-ca: from a Greek mythological name.)

D. palustris, L. To 6 ft.: lvs. elliptic to obovate, 1–3 in. long, obtuse, cuneate at base, glaucescent beneath, pubescent when young: fls. pale yellow, ¼–⅓in. long, short-stalked: fr. somewhat spindle-shaped, to ½in. long, pale green with yellowish tinge. N. B. to Fla. and Mo.

3. **PIMELEA,** Banks & Soland. Rice-Flower. Evergreen shrubs of about 80 species in Australia and New Zeal., one grown in Calif.—Lvs. alternate or opposite, simple and entire, the upper often larger and forming an involucre beneath the terminal heads: fls. white, pink or reddish; receptacle or calyx-tube corolla-like, tubular, with spreading 4-lobed limb; stamens 2; ovary 1-celled, with long style and capitate stigma: fr. a small drupe. (Pime-lea: Greek *fat,* referring to the fleshy seeds.)

P. ferruginea, Labill. To 4 ft.: lvs. opposite or crowded, ovate or oblong, ¼–½in. long, revolute: heads globular, subtended by orbicular involucral lvs.; fls. rose-colored, hairy. W. Australia.

142. ELÆAGNACEÆ. OLEASTER FAMILY

Three genera of more than 45 species distributed mostly in temp. and subtrop. regions of the northern hemisphere, grown for ornament and a few for their edible frs.—Trees or shrubs covered with silvery or golden-brown peltate or stellate scales: lvs. alternate or opposite, entire, exstipulate: fls. bisexual or unisexual, in axillary clusters or racemes or at the nodes of last year's branches, rarely solitary, the bracts small and deciduous; receptacle of calyx-tube of bisexual and pistillate fls. long-tubular, 2–4-lobed, constricted above ovary and persistent, becoming fleshy in fr.; petals 0; stamens as many as sepals and alternate with them or twice as many, inserted in throat of receptacle, the filaments free; ovary sessile, 1-celled, 1-ovuled, with an elongated style: fr. an achene or nut inclosed by the fleshy receptacle.

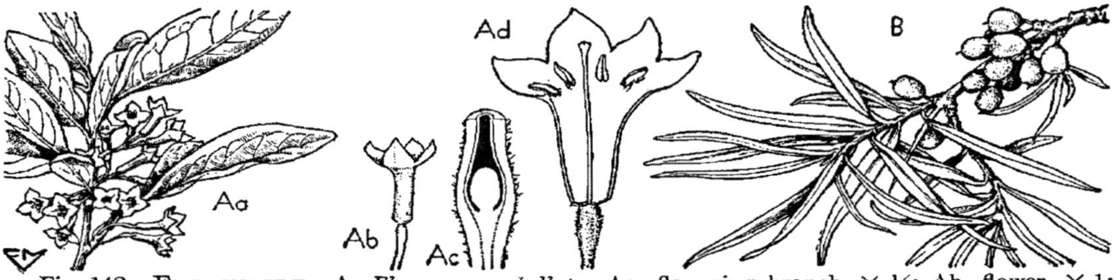

Fig. 142. ELÆAGNACEÆ. A, *Elæagnus umbellata:* Aa, flowering branch, × ½; Ab, flower, × 1; Ac, ovary, vertical section, × 5; Ad, flower, calyx expanded, × 2. B, *Hippophaë rhamnoides:* fruiting branch, × ⅓.

A. Lvs. alternate: stamens 4.
  B. Sepals 4: fls. bisexual........1. ELÆAGNUS
  BB. Sepals 2: fls. unisexual........2. HIPPOPHAË
AA. Lvs. opposite: stamens 8........3. SHEPHERDIA

1. **ELÆAGNUS,** L. Deciduous or evergreen sometimes spiny shrubs or small trees, of about 40 species in S. Eu., Asia and N. Amer.—Thickly covered with silvery or brownish peltate scales: lvs. alternate, short-petioled: fls. bisexual, usually solitary or clustered in the axils, often fragrant; perianth campanulate or tubular, the 4 lobes deciduous, white or yellow inside; stamens 4, the filaments very short: fr. drupe-like, the nut inclosed by the fleshy receptacle or perianth-tube. (Elæag-nus: ancient Greek name, applied to some other plant.)

A. Lvs. persistent: fls. in autumn.
  B. Branchlets brown-scaly, lvs. with both silvery and brown scales........1. *E. pungens*
  BB. Branchlets and lvs. with silvery scales only........2. *E. macrophylla*
AA. Lvs. deciduous: fls. in spring.
  B. Branchlets and lvs. with silvery scales only........3. *E. angustifolia*
  BB. Branchlets and lvs. with both brown and silvery scales.
    C. Stalks of fr. ¾–1 in. long: tube of fl. about length of limb........4. *E. multiflora*
    CC. Stalks of fr. short: tube of fl. much longer than limb.
      D. Fr. silvery: lvs. silvery on both sides........5. *E. commutata*
      DD. Fr. becoming red: lvs. silvery above only when young........6. *E. umbellata*

1. E. **pungens,** Thunb. Spreading evergreen shrub to 15 ft., mostly spiny; branchlets covered with brown scales: lvs. leathery, oval or oblong, 2–4 in. long, margins undulate, dark green and finally glabrous above, silvery beneath dotted with brown scales: fls. silvery, ½in. long, clustered in lf.-axils, pendulous, fragrant, blooming in autumn; cylindrical perianth-tube longer than limb and abruptly contracted at base: fr. about ¾in. long, short-stalked, covered with silvery and brown scales, red when ripe. Japan, China.—Runs into many forms, some of the most important of which are: Var. **Fredericii,** Bean, lvs. with yellow center and green margin; var. **maculata,** Rehd. (var. *aureo-maculata,* Hort.), lvs. with large yellow blotch in middle; var. **reflexa,** Servettaz (*E. reflexa,* Morr. & Decne.), branches elongated and flexile, lvs. very brown-scaly beneath, the margins not undulate; var. **Simonii,** Nichols. (*E. Simonii,* Carr.), lvs. with few or no brown scales beneath, sometimes variegated with yellowish- and pinkish-white; var. **variegata,** Rehd., lvs. margined with yellowish-white.

2. E. **macrophylla,** Thunb. Evergreen unarmed shrub to 12 ft.; branchlets silvery-white: lvs. broad-ovate, 2–5½ in. long, scaly above becoming glabrous, beneath densely silvery-scaly: fls. ½in. long, fragrant, pendulous, in autumn, with silvery and brownish scales outside; perianth-tube equalling limb, abruptly contracted at base: fr. ½in. long, red and scaly. Japan, Korea.—A supposed hybrid with this species as one parent is E. **Fruitlandii,** Berckmans, with large broad lvs., raised at Fruitland Nurseries, Augusta, Ga., about 1926.

3. E. **angustifolia,** L. (*E. hortensis,* Bieb.). OLEASTER. Deciduous shrub or small tree to 20 ft., sometimes spiny; branchlets silvery-white: lvs. lanceolate or oblong-lanceolate, 2–3 in. long, light green above, silvery beneath: fls. 1–3 in the axils of lvs., silvery outside, yellow within, fragrant, in June; perianth-tube campanulate, about as long as limb: fr. oval, about ½in. long, on very short stalks, yellow, covered with silvery scales. Eu., W. Asia. Var. **orientalis,** Kuntze (*E. orientalis,* L.), has oval to oblong lvs. and fr. to 1 in. long. Var. **spinosa,** Kuntze (*E. spinosa,* L.), is more spiny than type.—Also called Trebizonde-Date and Russian-Olive.

4. **E. multiflora,** Thunb. (*E. longipes,* Gray. *E. edulis,* Carr.). Deciduous shrub to 10 ft. or more, the branchlets covered with reddish-brown scales: lvs. elliptic, ovate or obovate-oblong, 1–2½ in. long, with stellate hairs above but becoming glabrous, silvery

beneath with scattered brown scales: fls. solitary or 2 together, with silvery and brown scales, fragrant, blooming in Apr. and May; perianth-tube about length of limb: fr. oblong, about ¾in. long, pendulous, on slender pedicels ¾–1 in. long, scarlet. Japan, China.—There are several lf.-forms, such as vars. *rotundifolia*, *ovata*, and *crispa*, Servettaz. Sometimes planted for its acid frs., as Gumi.

5. **E. commutata**, Bernh. (*E. argentea*, Pursh). SILVERBERRY. Deciduous stoloniferous unarmed shrub to 12 ft.; branchlets with reddish-brown scales: lvs. ovate to oblong, 1–4 in. long, silvery on both sides or sometimes with few brown scales beneath: fls. 1–3, silvery outside, yellow within, fragrant, May–June; perianth-tube much longer than limb: fr. roundish, ½in. long, on very short stalks, silvery. E. Canada to Minn. and Utah.

6. **E. umbellata**, Thunb. Spreading deciduous shrub to 12 ft. or more, often spiny; branchlets yellowish-brown, often partially silvery: lvs. elliptic to ovate-oblong, 1–3 in. long, with silvery scales above when young, shining and silvery beneath and usually with brown scales, often crisped at margin: fls. 1–3 or more together, yellowish-white, fragrant, in May or June; perianth-tube slender, much longer than limb: fr. globose or oval, ¼–⅓in. long, erect, on stalks about ¼in. long, scarlet, covered with silvery and brown scales when young. Japan, China, Korea.

2. **HIPPOPHAË**, L. SEA-BUCKTHORN. Two species of willow-like deciduous usually diœcious shrubs or small trees native in Eu. and W. and Cent. Asia.—Branches spiny; young growth covered with silvery scales or stellate hairs: lvs. alternate, narrow: fls. unisexual, in short racemes in axils of branches of previous year, the staminate sessile and deciduous, the pistillate short-stalked and the axis usually developing into a branchlet or thorn; staminate fls. with 2 large valvate sepals and 4 stamens with very short filaments; pistillate fls. with a long oblong receptacle or perianth-tube inclosing the ovary and bearing at tip 2 minute sepals: fr. drupe-like, the bony nut inclosed by the fleshy receptacle. (Hippoph-aë: ancient Greek name, referring to some other spiny plant.)

H. rhamnoides, L. To 30 ft., the twigs usually spine-tipped: lvs. linear-lanceolate, 1–3 in. long, short-petioled, covered on both sides with silvery scales but becoming glabrescent above: fls. very small, yellowish: fr. nearly globose or ovoid, about ¼in. long, bright orange-yellow, ripening in Sept. and persisting throughout the winter. Eu., W. and Cent. Asia. Var. **procera**, Rehd., is a taller race to 50 ft., from W. China. Var. **angustifolia**, Loud., has pendulous branches and narrow lvs.

3. **SHEPHERDIA**, Nutt. (*Lepargyrea*, Raf.). Diœcious shrubs or small trees with scurfy scales; 3 species in N. Amer., one grown for its frs. which are made into jelly.—Lvs. opposite, short-petioled: fls. small, in very short spikes or racemes, the staminate many-fld., pistillate 2-fld.; staminate fls. with 4 valvate sepals and 8 stamens alternating with as many lobes of disk, the filaments very short; pistillate fls. with urn-shaped perianth inclosing ovary and 4-lobed deciduous limb, the 8 lobes of the disk nearly closing the throat, style slightly exserted: fr. drupe-like, the nut inclosed by the fleshy receptacle. (Shepher-dia: after John Shepherd, 1764–1836, English botanist.)

S. argentea, Nutt. BUFFALO-BERRY. Upright thorny deciduous shrub to 18 ft., the young growth silvery-tomentose: lvs. oblong or oblong-lanceolate, 1–2 in. long, obtuse, silvery on both sides: fls. yellowish, in Apr. or May: fr. globular or ovoid, about ¼in. long, red or yellow. Man. to Minn. and Kans.

143. LYTHRACEÆ. LOOSESTRIFE FAMILY

More than 20 genera and 450 species of herbs, shrubs, or trees, widely distributed, but most abundant in trop. Amer., several grown for ornament.—Lvs. opposite or whorled (seldom alternate), entire, stipules 0 or small: fls. bisexual, regular or rarely irregular, mostly axillary, solitary or in cymes or panicles, the pedicels usually 2-bracted; calyx tubular or campanulate, persistent, free from ovary, with 4–6 (3–16) valvate lobes and often with accessory teeth between the lobes; petals as many as calyx-lobes and inserted at mouth of calyx, imbricated, or rarely 0; stamens few or many, inserted on the calyx; ovary superior, sessile or stalked, 2–6-, rarely 1-celled, with many or seldom few axile ovules in each cell, style simple: fr. a variously dehiscent caps. or indehiscent.

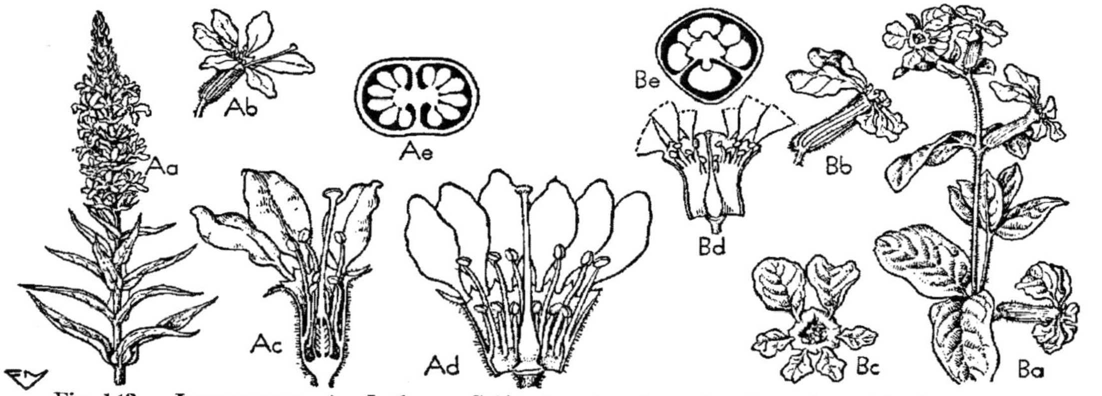

Fig. 143. LYTHRACEÆ. A, *Lythrum Salicaria:* Aa, flowering branch, × 1/4; Ab, flower, × 1; Ac, same, vertical section, × 2; Ad, flower, perianth expanded, × 2; Ae, ovary, cross-section, × 12. B, *Cuphea Hookeriana:* Ba, flowering branch, × 1/3; Bb, flower, side view, × 1/2; Bc, flower, face view, × 1/2; Bd, flower (less petals), hypanthium expanded, × 1/2; Be, ovary, cross-section, × 4.

A. Calyx-tube straight.
  B. Caps. completely inclosed by calyx: plant an herb ....1. LYTHRUM
  BB. Caps. not completely inclosed by calyx: plant a shrub or tree.
    C. Sepals and petals 4: fls. small ....2. LAWSONIA
    CC. Sepals and petals usually 6: fls. large and showy ....3. LAGERSTRŒMIA
AA. Calyx-tube gibbous or curved at base ....4. CUPHEA

1. LYTHRUM, L. Ann. or per. herbs widely scattered, of 24 species, a few grown in borders and bog-gardens.—Branches 4-angled: lvs. opposite, rarely whorled or alternate: fls. solitary in the axils or in spikes or racemes, often dimorphous or trimorphous; calyx-tube cylindrical, 8–12-ribbed, with 4–6 primary teeth or lobes and as many appendages in the sinuses; petals 4–6, rarely 0; stamens 4–12, included or exserted; ovary 2-celled, the style filiform: caps. completely inclosed by calyx, septicidally dehiscent by 2 valves or irregularly. (Lyth-rum: from Greek for *blood,* referring to color of fls. or perhaps to styptic properties of some species.)

A. Appendages of calyx twice or more longer than lobes: lvs. rounded or cordate at base . . 1. *L. Salicaria*
AA. Appendages of calyx about equalling the lobes: lvs. acute at base ....2. *L. virgatum*

1. **L. Salicaria,** L. SPIKED or PURPLE LOOSESTRIFE. Erect much-branched per. to 3 ft. and more, pubescent or sometimes glabrous: lvs. opposite or in whorls of 3, lanceolate, 2–4 in. long, rounded or cordate and clasping at base: fls. purple, to 3/4in. across, in almost sessile whorls aggregated into dense terminal interrupted leafy spikes, trimorphous as to lengths of stamens and style; appendages of calyx twice or more longer than lobes, often half as long as tube. Temp. regions of northern hemisphere and Australia. (Salicaria: resemblance to salix.) Var. **roseum superbum,** W. Miller, has larger rose-colored fls. Var. **tomentosum,** DC., whole plant, particularly the infl., white-tomentose.

2. **L. virgatum,** L. Differs from the above in its very twiggy or virgate glabrous growth, the linear or lanceolate lvs. acute at base: fls. purple, about 1/2in. across, distinctly pedicelled, 1–3 together in the axils of linear bracts, the growing flowering branch forming an open leafy raceme; appendages of calyx equalling or shorter than lobes. Eu., Asia; sparingly nat. in Mass.

2. LAWSONIA, L. One variable shrub from N. Afr., Asia, and Australia, but nat. in trop. Amer., planted for ornament in warm regions and furnishing the famous henna dye.—Glabrous, the branches often spinescent: lvs. opposite, short-petioled: fls. in few- to many-fld. corymbs forming a terminal panicle; calyx-tube very short or none, 4-angled, with 4 spreading lobes, without appendages; petals 4, with very short claw, wrinkled; stamens 8, sometimes 4 or 12, inserted at base of calyx-tube, exserted; ovary 2–4-celled, with long style: caps. not completely inclosed by calyx, irregularly dehiscent or indehiscent. (Lawso-nia: after John Lawson, Surveyor-General of N. C., burned by Indians in 1712.)

L. inermis, L. (*L. alba,* Lam.). HENNA. MIGNONETTE-TREE. To 20 ft.: lvs. elliptic or elliptic-lanceolate, 1/2–2 in. long: fls. very fragrant, white, rose, or cinnabar-red, 1/4in. or less across: caps. nearly 1/4in. diam.

3. **LAGERSTRŒMIA,** L. Shrubs or trees, one widely grown in the S. for its showy fls.; about 30 species in S. and E. Asia and adjacent isls. and Australia.—Lvs. opposite or the upper ones alternate: fls. in axillary or terminal panicles, the peduncles and pedicels with deciduous bracts; calyx top-shaped or hemispherical, often ridged or winged, with usually 5–8 lobes; petals 5–8, clawed, the limb often crinkled or fringed; stamens 15–200; ovary sessile, 3–6-celled, with long style: caps. woody, oblong, not completely inclosed by calyx, loculicidally dehiscent by 3–6 valves; seeds winged. (Lagerstrœ-mia: after Magnus v. Lagerstrœm, 1696–1759, Swedish friend of Linnæus.)

A. Lvs. 1–2 in. long: calyx smooth . . . . 1. *L. indica*
AA. Lvs. 4–12 in. long: calyx grooved . . . . 2. *L. speciosa*

1. **L. indica,** L. Crape-Myrtle. Deciduous glabrous shrub growing 10–20 ft. high, with smooth brown bark: lvs. very short-petioled or sessile, elliptic or oblong, 1–2 in. long, mostly acute, pubescent on veins beneath: fls. pink, white, or purple, 1–1½ in. across; calyx glabrous, not ribbed; petals 6, fringed, the claw very long and slender; stamens 36–42: caps. ⅓–½in. long. Asia, N. Australia; nat. in American tropics and in S. U. S.

2. **L. speciosa,** Pers. (*Munchausia speciosa,* L. *L. Flos-Reginæ,* Retz. *L. Reginæ,* Roxb.). Queen Crape-Myrtle. Large tree to about 80 ft., furnishing valuable timber: lvs. short-petioled, oblong- or ovate-elliptic, 4–12 in. long, leathery, obtuse or acuminate: fls. 2–3 in. across, in large terminal panicles, varying from mauve or pink to purple; calyx with 12 grooves or ridges, the lobes reflexed; petals 6, erose-wavy, with a short claw; stamens 130–200, in series: caps. globose or oblong, 1–2 in. long. India to S. China and E. Indies to Australia.

4. **CUPHEA,** Adans. Over 200 species of herbs or shrubs in N. and S. Amer., several grown in greenhouses and in the open S.—Lvs. opposite or whorled: fls. irregular, solitary or racemose, the pedicels between the petioles or rarely axillary; calyx-tube elongated and corolla-like, ribbed, spurred or gibbous at base, oblique at mouth, with 6 primary teeth or lobes and usually as many accessory teeth; petals 6, unequal or rarely 2 or 0; stamens 11, rarely 9, 6, or 4, the filaments short; ovary commonly superior, sessile, with gland at base, unequally 2-celled with few or many ovules in each cell, the slender style with capitate 2-lobed stigma: caps. oblong, inclosed by calyx, laterally dehiscent. (Cu-phea: Greek for *curved,* referring to protuberance at base of calyx-tube.)

A. Petals minute or lacking, but calyx showy.
B. Fls. solitary; calyx-tube slender . . . . 1. *C. ignea*
BB. Fls. in terminal leafy racemes; calyx-tube broad . . . . 2. *C. micropetala*
AA. Petals present, 2 or 6.
B. Lvs. about ½in. long: petals 6 and nearly alike . . . . 3. *C. hyssopifolia*
BB. Lvs. 1–5 in. long: petals 2, or when 6 then 4 of them minute.
C. Color of petals bright red . . . . 4. *C. Llavea*
CC. Color of petals purple.
D. Plant a shrub, branches only slightly pubescent . . . . 5. *C. Hookeriana*
DD. Plant an ann., branches sticky-pubescent . . . . 6. *C. lanceolata*

1. **C. ignea,** A. DC. (*C. platycentra,* Lem. not Benth. *Parsonsia ignea,* Standl.). Cigar-Flower. Common little plant in pots and bedded out, shrubby, much-branching and spreading, to 1 ft. or more, leafy, nearly or quite glabrous: lvs. lanceolate to ovate-lanceolate, 1–2½ in. long, sharply acuminate, narrowed to distinct petiole: fls. solitary in or near axils, slender-pedicelled, scattered among the lvs; calyx-tube about ¾in. long, slender, backward-spurred, 6-toothed, bright red but with dark ring at end and a white mouth (whence the name cigar-plant), ornamental; petals none. Mex.

2. **C. micropetala,** HBK. (*Parsonsia micropetala,* Hitchc.). Shrub 1–2 ft. high, more or less setose-hairy or almost glabrous, strongly erect, main shoots nearly or quite simple: lvs. lanceolate to oblong-lanceolate, short-petioled, 2–5 in. long, acute: fls. extra-axillary in a long terminal leafy raceme, about 1 in. long, yellowish with scarlet at base, the tube broad and hairy, constricted toward top and oblique at orifice; petals 6, shorter than the 12 small calyx-teeth; stamens red, exserted. Mex.

3. **C. hyssopifolia,** HBK. (*Parsonsia hyssopifolia,* Standl.). Little shrub 1–2 ft. high, much-branched, hairy: lvs. many and crowded, very small, usually ¼–½in. long but sometimes about 1 in., linear to lanceolate, sessile: fls. many, axillary, about ¼in. long, pedicelled; calyx straight, ribbed, gibbous at base above, flaring at top; petals 6, nearly equal, light violet to white; stamens included. Mex. and Guatemala.

4. **C. Llavea,** Llave & Lex. (*Parsonsia Llavea,* Standl.). St. shrubby and erect, with few strigose branches: lvs. ovate, 1–3 in. long, acute, short-petioled, the upper not quite opposite, hairy especially beneath: fls. solitary and nearly sessile, subaxillary, forming a leafy few-

fld. terminal raceme; calyx-tube about 1 in. long, ribbed and the opening 12-toothed, hispid, green at base and purplish above, only swollen or somewhat gibbous at base; petals 2, showy, wavy, bright red (varying to white). (Pablo de la Llave, page 47.) Mex. Var. **miniata,** Koehne (*C. miniata*, Brongn.), is the usual form in cult., with hirsute sts.

5. **C. Hookeriana,** Walp. (*C. Llavea*, Lindl. not Llave & Lex. *Parsonsia Hookeriana*, Standl.). Shrubby or subshrubby, 1–2½ ft., erect, scabrous: lvs. lanceolate or linear-lanceolate, 3–4 in. long, long-acuminate, nearly sessile, becoming linear in the infl.: fls. solitary near the axils, slender-pedicelled, forming open few-fld. terminal racemes; calyx ½–1 in. long, straight and rather slender, with an obtuse short spur at base on upper side, more or less red; petals mostly 6, of which 2 are large and prominent, oblong, wavy and deep purple, the other 4 very small or sometimes wanting. (Bears the name of Sir Wm. J. Hooker, page 45.) Mex.—Some of the large-fld. glasshouse and garden cupheas are apparently derived from this and perhaps no. 4, with possibly other admixtures.

6. **C. lanceolata,** Ait. Ann. to 4 ft. with sticky-pubescent sts.: lvs. oblong or lanceolate, 1–2 in. long, petioled, midrib prominent beneath: fls. solitary; calyx about ¾ in. long, purple, sticky-pubescent, gibbous at base; petals 6, 2 large and showy, purple, 4 much smaller; stamens slightly exserted. Mex. Var. **silenoides,** Regel (*C. silenoides*, Nees. *C. Zimpanii*, Morr.), smaller; lvs. without prominent midrib; 2 large purple petals white-margined.

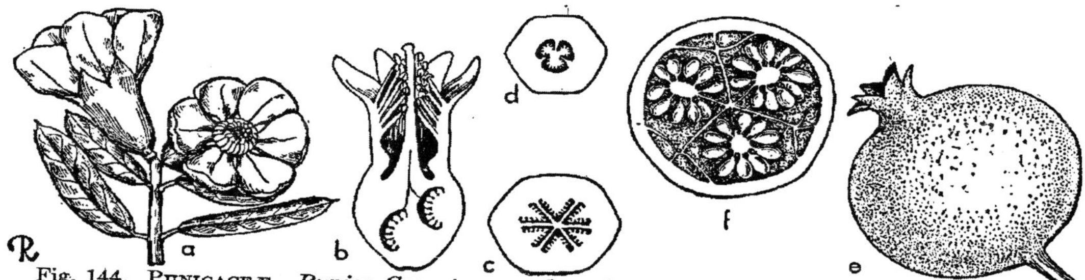

Fig. 144. PUNICACEÆ. *Punica Granatum:* a, flowering branch, × ½; b, flower, vertical section (less calyx), × 1; c, ovary, cross-section, upper part, × 1; d, same, lower part, × 1; e, fruit, × ½; f, fruit, cross-section, lower half, × ½. (b–f redrawn from Engler & Prantl.)

144. PUNICACEÆ. POMEGRANATE FAMILY

Small glabrous trees or shrubs, of 1 genus and 2 species native from Medit. region to Himalayas, but the pomegranate through long cult. widely distributed in trop. and subtrop. regions.—Branches often spiny-tipped: lvs. mostly opposite, exstipulate: fls. bisexual, 1–5 together on the tips of axillary shoots; receptacle or calyx-tube campanulate or tubular, leathery, the 5–7 thick sepals persistent on the fr.; petals 5–7, alternate with sepals and inserted on edge of receptacle, wrinkled; stamens many, clothing the inside of the receptacle, the filaments slender; ovary inferior, 3–7-celled, the cells superposed in 2 series, the lower with axile and upper with parietal placentation, ovules numerous on all placentæ; style and stigma 1: fr. a thick-skinned spherical several-celled berry, the seeds surrounded by juicy pulp.

PUNICA, L. The pomegranate is grown in the S. U. S. for ornament and for the edible frs. and also in the N. as a greenhouse subject.—Characters as for the family. (Pu-nica: *Malum punicum,* "apple of Carthage," an early name for pomegranate.)

P. Granatum, L. POMEGRANATE. Deciduous shrub or tree to 20 ft.: lvs. short-petioled, oblong or oval-lanceolate, 1–2 in. or more long, obtuse, glabrous and shining: fls. orange-red, 1–1½ in. across: fr. about size of an orange, bearing the persistent sepals, brownish-yellow to red, upper and lower portions divided by diaphragm and these separated into several cells, the numerous seeds surrounded by crimson or pink acid pulp. (Granatum: old substantive name.) S. Asia, but nat. in Medit. region, S. Amer., S. U. S.—There are many named vars., the double-fld. forms being most commonly grown. Var. **nana,** Pers., is a dwarf sort planted in greenhouses.

145. LECYTHIDACEÆ. LECYTHIS FAMILY

Trop. trees, of 18 genera and over 230 species native in S. Amer., W. Afr., Malay Peninsula, Mozambique to Samoan Isls.; often planted in the tropics for ornament

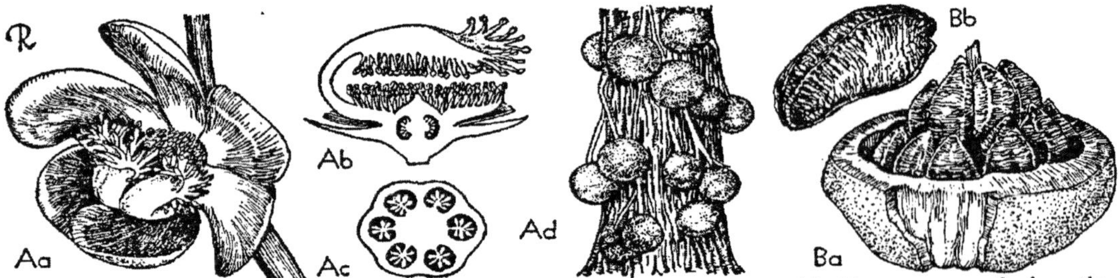

Fig. 145. LECYTHIDACEÆ. A, *Couroupita guianensis:* Aa, flower, × ½; Ab, same, vertical section, less perianth, × ½; Ac, ovary, cross-section, × 2; Ad, tree trunk with fruit. B, *Bertholletia excelsa:* Ba, fruit, × ¼; Bb, nut, × ½. (Ab adapted from Baillon, Ac from Engler & Prantl.)

or the edible nuts, but in N. Amer. known chiefly through the importation of the "nigger-toe" or Brazil-nut.—Lvs. usually large and striking, alternate, often crowded at ends of branches, exstipulate: fls. bisexual, regular, solitary or in racemes, axillary or terminal; sepals and petals usually 4–6 or sometimes petals lacking; stamens many in several series, more or less united at base, a part sometimes without anthers; intra-staminal disk often present; ovary inferior, 2–6- or more-celled with 1 to many ovules in each cell: fr. a leathery berry or drupe or a caps. dehiscent by a lid, in some species large and heavy, like a pot, and sometimes called "monkey pots."—**Bertholletia excelsa,** Humb. & Bonpl., supplies the BRAZIL- or PARA-NUTS of commerce, called in the trade "castanea"; it is a tree to 100 ft. or more high, native in N. Brazil: lvs. leathery, broadly oblong, 1–2 ft. or more long, 4–6 in. wide, undulate at margins: fls. in spike-like racemes, cream-colored, the sepals united but finally tearing into 2 deciduous sepals: fr. globose, dark brown, to 5–6 in. diam., with hard thick walls, inclosing 18–24 triangular nuts 2 in. or more long which have a single solid sweet kernel.—**Couroupita guianensis,** Aubl., CANNON-BALL TREE, is planted as a curiosity in S. Fla.; it is a tree to 50 ft., native in Trinidad and N. S. Amer.: lvs. oblong, 8 in. or more long: fls. borne on the trunk and larger branches, in racemes to 3 ft. long, yellow or red outside, crimson-lilac inside, 4 in. across: fr. nearly globose, to 8 in. diam., hard outside.

Fig. 146. NYSSACEÆ. *Nyssa sylvatica:* a, fruiting branch, × ½; b, staminate flower, × 6; c, same, vertical section, × 6; d, bisexual flower, × 4; e, same, vertical section, × 4. (b–e redrawn from Sargent.)

146. NYSSACEÆ. NYSSA FAMILY

Deciduous trees of 3 genera and about 8 species native in N. Amer. and Asia, planted for ornament.—Lvs. alternate, simple, entire or toothed, exstipulate: fls. unisexual or bisexual, in terminal or axillary heads; calyx very small; petals 5 or more or lacking; stamens usually in 2 series, twice as many as petals or fewer; ovary inferior, 1- or 6–10-celled, with 1 pendulous ovule in each cell: fr. a drupe.

A. Infl. without bracts: lvs. entire or nearly so.......................................1. NYSSA
AA. Infl. with 2 large bracts: lvs. toothed.......................................2. DAVIDIA

1. **NYSSA,** L. TUPELO. Deciduous trees with attractive autumn foliage; 6 species in N. Amer. and Asia.—Diœcious or polygamous: lvs. alternate, entire or

only remotely toothed: fls. minute, greenish-white, in axillary clusters; calyx 5-toothed; petals 5; stamens 5–12, exserted; ovary 1–2-celled: fr. a 1-seeded drupe. (Nys-sa: a water nymph, referring to the habitat in swampy places.)

A. Pistillate fls. in 2- to several-fld. clusters: fr. ¼–½in. long........................1. *N. sylvatica*
AA. Pistillate fls. solitary: fr. ¾–1 in. long........................2. *N. aquatica*

1. **N. sylvatica,** Marsh. PEPPERIDGE. SOUR or BLACK GUM. To 100 ft.: lvs. obovate or oval, 2–5 in. long, entire, shining above, pubescent on veins beneath when young: staminate fls. in many-fld. clusters, pistillate in 2- to several-fld. clusters on pubescent peduncles: fr. dark blue, ovoid, ¼–½in. long; stone slightly ribbed. Me. to Fla. and Tex.

2. **N. aquatica,** L. COTTON or TUPELO GUM. To 100 ft.: lvs. ovate to oval, 4–10 in. long, entire or with few angular teeth, shining above, pubescent beneath: staminate fls. in clusters, pistillate solitary on slender pubescent peduncles: fr. purple, oblong, ¾–1 in. long; stone with sharp ridges. Va. to Fla. and Tex.

2. **DAVIDIA,** Baill. One deciduous tree native in China, and hardy in the N.—Lvs. alternate, with acuminate teeth: fls. unisexual, apetalous, in dense nearly globose heads subtended by 2 large bracts; stamens 1–7, filaments slender; ovary 6–10-celled: fr. a drupe with a 3–5-seeded stone. (David-ia: named for Armand David, 1826–1900, French missionary who collected in China.)

D. involucrata, Baill. DOVE-TREE. To 60 ft.: lvs. broad-ovate, 3–6 in. long, acuminate, cordate at base, silky-pubescent beneath, strongly veined: heads ¾in. across, May–June; bracts unequal, to 6 in. long, creamy-white, drooping: fr. pyriform, about 1½ in. long, green with purple bloom. Var. **Vilmoriniana,** Wangerin, has lvs. glabrous beneath.

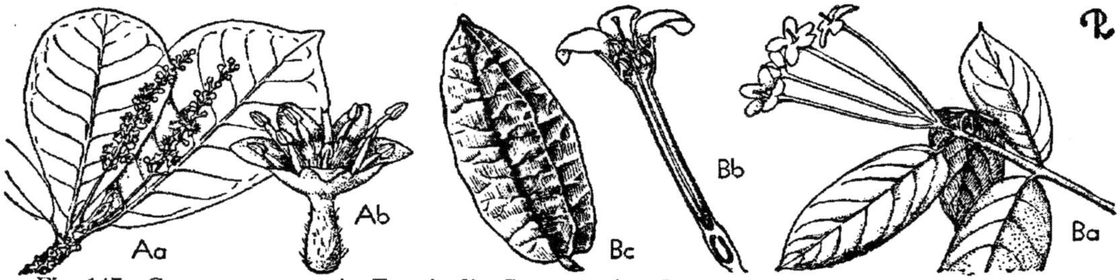

Fig. 147. COMBRETACEÆ. A, *Terminalia Catappa:* Aa, flowering branch, × ⅙; Ab, flower, × 5. B, *Quisqualis indica:* Ba, flowering branch, × ⅙; Bb, flower, vertical section, × ½; Bc, fruit, × ¾.

147. COMBRETACEÆ. COMBRETUM FAMILY

About 15 genera and 280 species of trees and shrubs rich in tannin, often climbing, mostly confined to the tropics; a few grown for ornament in warm regions and one for its edible nuts.—Lvs. alternate or rarely opposite, petioled, simple and entire, exstipulate: fls. bisexual or rarely unisexual, usually sessile in many-fld. spikes, panicles or heads, bracted at base; receptacle or calyx-tube adnate to ovary and often projecting into slender tube, the sepals 4–5; petals 4–5 or 0, commonly small; stamens inserted on calyx, usually twice as many as sepals and in 2 series; ovary inferior, 1-celled, mostly with as many angles as there are sepals and alternate with them, the ovules 2–5 or seldom more; style 1 and slender: fr. usually dry, 1-seeded, indehiscent or incompletely dehiscent, 2–5-angled, the angles often winged, sometimes crowned by the persistent calyx.

A. Plant erect: petals 0; receptacle or calyx-tube not produced beyond ovary...........1. TERMINALIA
AA. Plant climbing or sarmentose: petals 5; receptacle produced into long tube beyond ovary........................2. QUISQUALIS

1. **TERMINALIA,** L. Large hard-wooded trees, of over 100 species widely distributed in the tropics, one planted as a street and ornamental tree and for its edible fr.—Lvs. alternate, rarely opposite, often crowded toward ends of branchlets: fls. small, bisexual or sometimes unisexual, subtended by small deciduous bracts, mostly borne in loose spikes; receptacle or calyx-tube constricted above ovary, the limb 5-parted, campanulate, usually deciduous; petals 0; stamens 10, in 2 series; ovules

2 or rarely 3: fr. an angular drupe, compressed or 2–5-winged. (Termina-lia: from Latin *terminus*, alluding to the lvs. being borne on the tips of the shoots.)

T. Catappa, L. Tropical- or Indian-Almond. Myrobalan. Tall tree to 80 ft., with horizontal wide-spreading branches and smooth brownish-gray bark: lvs. obovate, 6–12 in. long, obtuse or abruptly acuminate, short-petioled, becoming rich red before they fall twice a year: fls. greenish-white, in slender spikes up to 6 in. long: fr. broadly oval, 2 in. or more long, flattened, the 2 angles winged, greenish or reddish; seed oblong-elliptical, often eaten in the tropics and furnishing valuable oil. (Catappa: native E. Indian name.) Madagascar, Malaya, E. Indies.

2. **QUISQUALIS,** L. Climbing or semi-climbing shrubs of about 4 species in trop. Asia and Afr., one widely grown for ornament in tropics and sometimes in the greenhouse N.—Lvs. opposite: fls. showy, in short axillary or terminal spikes, bisexual; receptacle or calyx-tube prolonged into a long slender tube above ovary, deciduous, with 5 small spreading or recurved sepals; petals 5; stamens 10; ovules 3 or 4: fr. dry and leathery, 5-angled or 5-winged, dehiscent at top along angles. (Quisqua-lis: Latin *who, what,* the application variously interpreted.)

Q. indica, L. Rangoon-Creeper. Rapid-growing scandent deciduous shrub, the young parts rusty-pubescent: lvs. oblong-lanceolate to elliptic, 3–5 in. long, acuminate, the lower part of the petiole persistent and becoming hard and thorn-like: fls. fragrant, in terminal drooping spikes, the green slender calyx-tube about 3 in. long with short triangular lobes; petals white, changing to red, ½–¾ in. long: fr. narrowly ellipsoid, about 1 in. long, 5-angled. Burma, Malaya, New Guinea, Philippines.—Now commonly planted in trop. and subtrop. countries, largely for ornament, although the bitter half-ripened fr. may be used medicinally as a vermifuge, and the coconut-flavored ripe seeds as a flavoring although they are poisonous when eaten in excess.

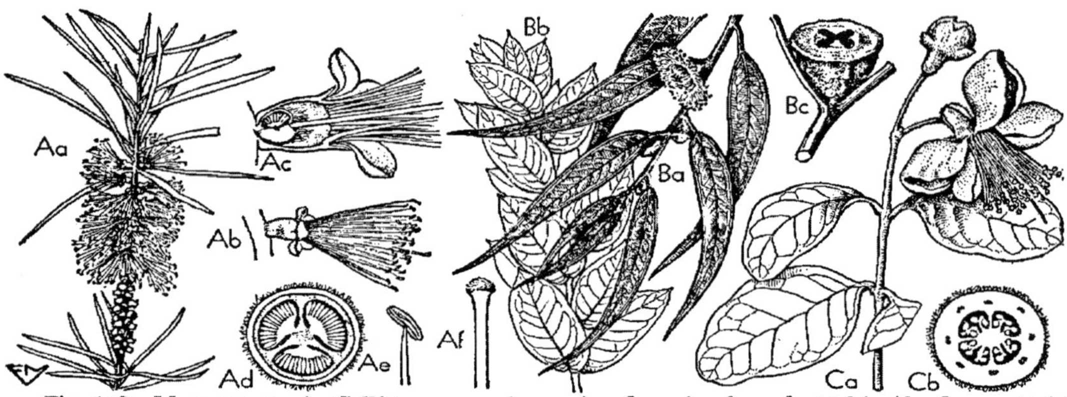

Fig. 148. Myrtaceæ. A, *Callistemon speciosus:* Aa, flowering branch, × ⅙; Ab, flower, × ½; Ac, flower, vertical section, stamens excised, × 1½; Ad, ovary, cross-section, × 4; Ae, anther, × 4; Af, end of style with stigma, × 4. B, *Eucalyptus Globulus:* Ba, flowering branch, × ⅙; Bb, branch with juvenile foliage, × ⅙; Bc, fruit, × ½. C, *Feijoa Sellowiana:* Ca, flowering branch, × ½; Cb, ovary, cross-section, × 3.

148. MYRTACEÆ. MYRTLE FAMILY

About 75 genera and probably 3,000 species of woody plants, as now defined, with aromatic fragrance, native in the tropics, particularly in trop. Amer. and Australia; many grown for ornament, park and avenue trees in warm regions, and some for edible frs.; one of the distinctive families.—Lvs. usually opposite, persistent, thick and mostly entire, short-petioled, exstipulate, more or less pellucid-punctate: fls. bisexual, regular, solitary in the axils or in corymbs or racemes, usually bracted; receptacle or calyx-tube more or less adnate to the ovary and often elongated, the 4–5 sepals usually free, persistent on fr.; petals 4–5, imbricated, or rarely lacking; stamens mostly numerous, often in fascicles opposite the petals, the filaments distinct or partially united; ovary inferior, 1- to many-celled, with 1 to many ovules in each cell, placentation mostly axile, rarely parietal, the style simple: fr. a berry, drupe, caps. or nut.

A. Infl. resembling a bottle-brush, the fls. in contiguous heads or spikes near ends of branches, each fl. sessile in axil of deciduous floral lf.
  B. Stamens free .... 1. CALLISTEMON
  BB. Stamens united into bundles opposite the petals .... 2. MELALEUCA
AA. Infl. various, but not resembling a bottle-brush.
  B. Stamens united into fascicles opposite the petals.
    C. Lvs. needle-like: anthers basifixed .... 3. CALOTHAMNUS
    CC. Lvs. not needle-like: anthers versatile .... 4. TRISTANIA
  BB. Stamens free or only slightly united at base.
    C. Fr. a dehiscent caps.
      D. Calyx-lobes and petals united to form a lid or cap which dehisces transversely .... 5. EUCALYPTUS
      DD. Calyx-lobes and petals distinct .... 6. LEPTOSPERMUM
    CC. Fr. an indehiscent berry or drupe.
      D. Plant heath-like, with linear-terete lvs.: ovary 1-celled .... 7. CHAMÆLAUCIUM
      DD. Plant not heath-like, lvs. broader: ovary 2–5-celled.
        E. Fls and frs. (in ours) borne along the trunk and branches .... 14. MYRCIARIA
        EE. Fls. and frs. not so borne.
          F. Ovary 4–5-celled.
            G. Lvs. white-tomentose below: stamens much longer than petals .... 8. FEIJOA
            GG. Lvs. not white-tomentose below: stamens about length of petals .... 9. PSIDIUM
          FF. Ovary 2–3-celled.
            G. The fls. solitary.
              H. Berry bluish-black or white: embryo curved or spiral .... 10. MYRTUS
              HH. Berry red, edible: embryo straight .... 12. EUGENIA
            GG. The fls. in cymes or panicles.
              H. Color of fr. dark brown or black: ovules pendulous from apex of cell; embryo spiral .... 11. PIMENTA
              HH. Color of fr. not black or brown: ovules not pendulous; embryo straight.
                I. Petals united to form a lid or cap, deciduous.
                  J. Anther-sacs divaricate, opening by a terminal slit or pore: lvs. 2–3 in. long .... 15. ACMENA
                  JJ. Anther-sacs parallel, opening longitudinally: lvs. usually more than 3 in. long .... 13. SYZYGIUM
                II. Petals free.
                  J. Seed-coat smooth, free from pericarp; embryo undivided .... 12. EUGENIA
                  JJ. Seed-coat roughish, adhering to pericarp; embryo divided (with distinct cotyledons) .... 13. SYZYGIUM

1. **CALLISTEMON**, R. Br. BOTTLE-BRUSH. About 25 Australian species of shrubs or small trees, planted for ornament in warm countries and sometimes in greenhouses.—Lvs. scattered, terete, linear or lanceolate: fls. in contiguous heads or spikes near ends of branches, each fl. sessile in axil of deciduous floral lf., in infl. resembling a bottle-brush; receptacle or calyx-tube ovoid or campanulate, the 5 lobes deciduous; petals 5, spreading, deciduous; stamens many in several series, free or rarely shortly united at base, much longer than petals, the anthers versatile; ovary 3–4-celled with many ovules in each cell: fr. a caps. inclosed in the calyx-tube, loculicidally dehiscent at top. (Calliste-mon: Greek for *beauty* and *stamen*.)—The species resemble each other very closely and are difficult of determination, particularly as there are apparent hybrids.

A. Anthers yellow .... 1. *C. speciosus*
AA. Anthers dark colored.
  B. Lvs. ¼in. or more across .... 2. *C. citrinus*
  BB. Lvs. ⅛in. across .... 3. *C. rigidus*

1. **C. speciosus**, DC. Shrub or small tree sometimes 40 ft. high: lvs. lanceolate, 3–4 in. long, about ¼in. wide, obtuse or acute, midvein prominent but lateral veins obscure: spikes very dense, to 5 in. long, the stamens rich red, about 1 in. long and shortly united at base into clusters opposite the petals, the anthers yellow: caps. globular, truncate at top and little contracted.

2. **C. citrinus**, Stapf (*Metrosideros citrina*, Curt. *M. semperflorens*, Lodd. *C. lanceolatus*, DC.). Shrub to 12 ft. (30 ft. in wild), with erect or spreading branches: lvs. lanceolate, 1–3 in. long and ¼in. or more wide, acute, rigid, the midvein and lateral nerves prominent: spikes not very dense, 2–4 in. long, the stamens bright red, about 1 in. long: caps. ovoid, contracted at summit.—Often known to the trade as *Metrosideros floribunda*.

3. **C. rigidus**, R. Br. (*C. linearifolius*, DC.). Lvs. linear, 2–5 in. long and about ⅛in. wide, rigid, sharp-pointed, the midvein and marginal veins prominent: spikes dense, the stamens 1 in. or more long, red.—**C. linearis**, DC., is closely related; its lvs. are very narrow and channelled above.

2. **MELALEUCA**, L. BOTTLE-BRUSH. Over 100 species of Australian trees and shrubs, many grown for ornament in warm regions, some furnishing timber, and

others used for fixing muddy shores.—Closely allied to Callistemon and differing chiefly in the stamens which are united in 5 bundles opposite the petals. (Melaleu-ca: from Greek for *black* and *white*, from the black trunk and white branches of one of the species.)

A. Lvs. 2 or more in long, ½–¾in. wide, flat. . . . . 1. *M. Leucadendra*
AA. Lvs. less than 2 in. long, ¼in. or less wide.
B. Fls. red. . . . . 2. *M. hypericifolia*
BB. Fls. white, lilac, or pink.
C. Length of lvs. usually more than ½in.
D. Width of lvs. about ¼in. . . . . 3. *M. nesophila*
DD. Width of lvs. 1/16in. or less. . . . . 4. *M. armillaris*
CC. Length of lvs. usually less than ½in.
D. Color of fls. lilac. . . . . 5. *M. decussata*
DD. Color of fls. yellowish-white. . . . . 6. *M. ericifolia*

1. **M. Leucadendra,** L. CAJEPUT-TREE. PUNK-TREE. Large tree with thick spongy bark, the branches often pendulous: lvs. elliptic or oblong, 2–4 in. or more long, ½–¾in. wide, tapering at both ends, with 3–7 parallel veins and numerous cross-veinlets: fls. creamy-white, in terminal spikes 2–6 in. long, the axis growing into a leafy shoot after flowering; staminal bundles nearly ½in. long, with 5–8 filaments at end: caps. nearly hemi-spherical, about ⅛in. across. (Leucadendra, Leucadendron: Greek combination meaning *white tree.*)

2. **M. hypericifolia,** Smith. Tall glabrous shrub: lvs. mostly opposite, lanceolate or oblong, ¾–1¾ in. long, obtuse or mucronate, the midrib prominent beneath: fls. rich red, in dense spikes about 2 in. long, the axis continuing as a leafy shoot; staminal bundles ¾–1 in. long, with 15–20 filaments at end: caps. sessile by broad base, to ¼in. diam.

3. **M. nesophila,** F. Muell. Glabrous shrub or small tree to 8 ft., with thick spongy bark: lvs. obovate-oblong, ½–1 in. long, about ¼in. wide, obtuse or sometimes mucronate, tapering at base, obscurely 3-nerved: fls. pink or rose, in dense terminal heads, the axis seldom growing out until after flowering; staminal bundles about ⅓in. long, with 10–15 filaments at end: caps. collected in globose mass. (Nesophila: from Greek for *island-loving.*)

4. **M. armillaris,** Smith. Tall glabrous shrub or small tree 15–30 ft. high, of graceful habit: lvs. crowded, narrowly linear, ½–¾in. long, 1/16in. or less wide, acute and often curved at tip: fls. white, in cylindrical spikes 2 in. or more long, the axis continued in a leafy shoot; staminal bundles about ¼in. long, with numerous filaments near upper end of claw: caps. with broad base partly embedded in st.

5. **M. decussata,** R. Br. Glabrous spreading shrub to 20 ft., the branches usually pendulous: lvs. opposite, lanceolate to oblong, ¼–½in. long, 1/16–⅛in. wide, narrowed at base, obtuse or acute: fls. lilac, in cylindrical spikes 1 in. or less long, the axis continuing as a leafy shoot, or the sterile fls. in globose lateral or terminal heads; staminal bundles about ¼in. long, with 10–15 filaments: caps. broad at base, partly embedded in st.

6. **M. ericifolia,** Smith. Large shrub or small tree to 20 ft.: lvs. narrowly linear or nearly cylindric, ½in. or less long, obtuse, often recurved from the middle: fls. yellowish-white, in cylindrical spikes ½–1 in. long, the axis soon growing out into a leafy shoot, or the sterile fls. in nearly globular terminal heads; staminal bundles ¼in. long, with 7 fila-ments at end: caps. with broad base partially embedded in st.

3. **CALOTHAMNUS,** Labill. Nearly 25 species of shrubs native in W. Australia, one sometimes grown for ornament in Calif.—Lvs. scattered, terete or flat, rigid, 1-nerved or nerveless: fls. showy, in clusters or often unilateral spikes, sometimes immersed in the rachis; receptacle or calyx-tube campanulate, the 4–5 lobes per-sistent or deciduous; petals 4–5, spreading, deciduous; stamens many, united into fascicles opposite the petals and much exceeding them, the anthers basifixed; ovary 3-, rarely 4-celled, with many ovules in each cell: fr. a caps. inclosed in the hardened and enlarged calyx-tube, loculicidally dehiscent by 3–4 valves. (Calotham-nus: Greek for *beautiful bush.*)

C. quadrifidus, R. Br. Erect shrub to 8 ft.: lvs. heath-like, terete or slightly flattened, ½–1 in. long: fls. sessile in clusters, calyx-lobes and petals 4; staminal bundles rich crimson, nearly equal, ¾–1 in. long: caps. with 2 connivent calyx-lobes.

4. **TRISTANIA,** R. Br. Trees or tall shrubs sometimes planted for ornament in warm countries, nearly 25 species in Australia, New Caledonia, and Malay Archi-pelago.—Lvs. alternate or whorled at ends of branches: fls. in peduncled axillary cymes; receptacle or calyx-tube turbinate-campanulate, the 5 lobes short; petals 5, spreading; stamens many, in fascicles opposite the petals, the anthers versatile;

ovary 3-celled with many ovules in each cell: fr. a caps. completely or partially inclosed in persistent calyx, loculicidally dehiscent by 3 valves. (Trista-nia: after Jules M. C. Tristan, 1776–1861, French botanist.)

T. conferta, R. Br. BRISBANE-BOX. Tree to 150 ft.: lvs. ovate-lanceolate, 3–6 in. long, glabrous, usually crowded at ends of branches: fls. white, about ¾in. across, in 3–7-fld. cymes, usually on young wood below clusters of lvs.; calyx pubescent: caps. nearly ½in. diam., scarcely exceeding the calyx-tube. Australia.

5. **EUCALYPTUS,** L'Her. GUM-TREE. About 300 or more species of trees in Australia and the Malayan region, furnishing valuable timber and a number grown for street and avenue trees in semitrop. and warm temp. regions.—Lvs. mostly alternate and vertical, rigid, pinnate-veined, entire, those on young shoots of many species opposite, horizontal, sessile and cordate: fls. 3 or more together or rarely solitary, in umbels or heads; receptacle or calyx-tube turbinate or campanulate, adnate to ovary at base, the free part entire or remotely 4-toothed; petals united with calyx-lobes to form a lid or cap which dehisces transversely; stamens many, in several series, usually free; ovary 3–6-celled with numerous ovules in each cell: fr. a caps. wholly or partially inclosed in the calyx-tube, loculicidally dehiscent at top by 3–6 valves. (Eucalyp-tus: from Greek for *well* and *calyptra* or lid, referring to the sepals and petals which are united to form a cap.)—Many species are offered in Calif., but only those sold in "flats" for large plantings are here described. To describe all the eucalypts likely to be grown in parks would be to make a monograph of the genus. The following species are Australian.

A. Infl. a many-fld. panicle.
  B. Fls. very large, 1–1½ in. long .... 1. *E. ficifolia*
  BB. Fls. smaller, ¼–½in. long.
    C. Lvs. prevailingly orbicular to ovate .... 2. *E. polyanthemos*
    CC. Lvs. lanceolate .... 3. *E. maculata*
AA. Infl. a stalked umbel, or sometimes fls. solitary and sessile in no. 4.
  B. Fl.-stalks flattened.
    C. Fr. ¾–1 in. across, angular: lid warty, shorter than calyx-tube .... 4. *E. Globulus*
    CC. Fr. to ½in. across, not angular: lid not warty, as long as or longer than calyx-tube .... 5. *E. robusta*
  BB. Fl.-stalks not flattened, although perhaps somewhat angular.
    C. Pedicels shorter than calyx-tube.
      D. Fr. contracted at mouth, caps. deeply sunk .... 6. *E. cladocalyx*
      DD. Fr. truncate, caps. not sunk .... 7. *E. viminalis*
    CC. Pedicels as long as or longer than calyx-tube.
      D. Fr.-valves plainly exserted.
        E. Lid two to four times longer than calyx-tube .... 8. *E. tereticornis*
        EE. Lid (without point or beak) about length of calyx-tube.
          F. Caps. not sunk: lid usually ending in abrupt point or beak .... 9. *E. camaldulensis*
          FF. Caps. somewhat sunk but convex in center: lid conical .... 10. *E. rudis*
      DD. Fr.-valves not exserted.
        E. Bark smooth, pale, deciduous .... 11. *E. leucoxylon*
        EE. Bark rough, dark red or black, persistent .... 12. *E. sideroxylon*

1. **E. ficifolia,** F. Muell. SCARLET-FLOWERING GUM. Ornamental tree to 30 ft. or more, with dark furrowed bark: lvs. thick, ovate to lanceolate, the veins almost transverse: fls. very large, 1–1½ in. long, long-pedicelled, usually bright scarlet but varying to pink and also a white var., borne in many-fld. panicles; lid thin and nearly flat: fr. very thick and woody, ovate-urn-shaped, 1–1½ in. across, the caps. deeply sunk.

2. **E. polyanthemos,** Schauer. RED-BOX. AUSTRALIAN-BEECH. Often irregular tree from 40–150 ft. high, with brown or gray persistent bark which becomes rough with age: lvs. prevailingly orbicular to ovate and obtuse, rarely ovate-lanceolate, dull grayish-green: fls. small, about ¼in. long, on pedicels about length of calyx-tube, white, borne in many-fld. close panicles; lid conical, obtuse: fr. goblet-shaped, not contracted at mouth, nearly ¼in. across, the caps. sunk. (Polyanthemos: Greek *many fls.*)

3. **E. maculata,** Hook. SPOTTED GUM. Tall tree to 150 ft. with column-like trunk, the whitish or reddish-gray bark deciduous in patches, giving the trunk a spotted appearance: lvs. lanceolate: fls. about ½in. long, on thick pedicels, usually in clusters of 3 in a many-fld. panicle; lid hemispherical, much shorter than calyx-tube: fr. globular-urn-shaped, nearly ½in. across, the caps. deeply sunk.—Cult. mostly in its var. **citriodora,** Bailey (*E. citriodora,* Hook.), LEMON-SCENTED SPOTTED GUM, in which the foliage is strongly lemon-scented.

4. **E. Globulus,** Labill. TASMANIAN BLUE GUM. Tall tree attaining 300 ft., widely grown for ornament and timber, the bark deciduous in long strips or sheets and leaving the trunk smooth grayish or bluish-white: lvs. lanceolate, those on the young shoots op-

posite, sessile, cordate and usually glaucous-white: fls. large, about 1½ in. across, solitary or 2–3 together, sessile or on short flattened peduncles; calyx-tube and lid hard and warty, covered with bluish-white wax, the lid conical in center, shorter than calyx-tube: fr. angular, ¾–1 in. across, the broad flat-topped rim projecting but the flat valves not exserted. (Globulus: old substantive name meaning *little globe*, here used in apposition.) Var. **compacta,** H. M. Hall, CALIFORNIAN BLUE GUM, is a densely branched dwarf form.

5. **E. robusta,** Smith (*E. multiflora*, Poir.). SWAMP-MAHOGANY. Slow-growing tree with rough dark brown persistent bark: lvs. ovate-lanceolate, long-pointed: fls. about ¾in. across, on thick pedicels, 4–12 together in an umbel having a stout flattened peduncle; lid acuminate, as long as or longer than calyx-tube: fr. goblet-shaped, about ½in. across, the caps. much sunk.

6. **E. cladocalyx,** F. Muell. (*E. corynocalyx*, F. Muell.). SUGAR GUM. Tree to 120 ft., with smooth bark deciduous in age: lvs. ovate-lanceolate to lanceolate: fls. about ½in. across, on pedicels shorter than calyx-tube, 6–12 or more together in a peduncled umbel; lid very short and nearly flat: fr. ovoid, about ½in. long and ¼in. across, often strongly ribbed, the caps. deeply sunk.

7. **E. viminalis,** Labill. RIBBON GUM. MANNA GUM. Tree to 300 ft., with pendulous branches, the bark rough, dark colored and persistent or smooth grayish-white and deciduous: lvs. lanceolate: fls. nearly ½in. across, on pedicels shorter than calyx-tube, 3–8 together in a stalked umbel; lid nearly conical, as long as or slightly longer than calyx-tube: fr. subglobose-truncate, ¼in. or more across, the rim flat but becoming rounded, caps. not sunk and valves sometimes protruding.

8. **E. tereticornis,** Smith (*E. umbellata*, Domin not Dum.-Cours.). FOREST RED GUM. GRAY OR SLATY GUM. To 150 ft., the gray bark smooth and deciduous in thin layers: lvs. lanceolate: fls. about ¾in. across, on pedicels about length of calyx-tube, 4–8 together in a stalked umbel; lid slenderly conical, acuminate, two to four times longer than calyx-tube: fr. obovoid or subglobose, ¼in. or more across, caps. not sunk, the valves exserted and rim prominent.

9. **E. camaldulensis,** Dehnhardt (*E. rostrata*, Schlecht. not Cav.). MURRAY RED GUM. Red-wooded tree to 200 ft., with smooth gray bark deciduous in thin layers; lvs. narrowly lanceolate: fls. ¼–½in. across, on pedicels as long as calyx-lobes, 4–8 together in a stalked umbel; lid usually with narrowed point or beak, about length of calyx-tube (without beak): fr. nearly globular, about ¼in. across, caps. not sunk, the valves exserted and rim broad and prominent.

10. **E. rudis,** Endl. DESERT GUM. MOITCH. To nearly 100 ft., with gray persistent bark rough but not deeply furrowed: lvs. ovate- to narrow-lanceolate: fls. about ½in. across, on pedicels about length of calyx-tube, 4–8 together in a stalked umbel; lid conical, not beaked, about as long as calyx-tube: fr. broadly turbinate, nearly ½in. across, the caps. somewhat sunk but convex in center and valves exserted.

11. **E. leucoxylon,** F. Muell. WHITE IRONBARK. Bark smooth, pale to dark gray, deciduous in strips: lvs. narrow-lanceolate, grayish or dull green, the young lvs. ovate and sessile: fls. about 1 in. across, on pedicels as long as or longer than calyx-tube, 3 or more together in stalked umbels, pale yellow varying to pink and bright purple; lid conical, about length of calyx-tube: fr. ovoid, truncate, nearly ½in. across, the rim thick and caps. slightly sunk. (Leucoxylon: Greek *white wood*.)

12. **E. sideroxylon,** Cunn. (*E. leucoxylon* var. *sideroxylon*, Auth.). RED IRONBARK. MUGGA. Closely resembling *E. leucoxylon*, but differing in the rough persistent dark red or black bark, the young lvs. linear-lanceolate. (Sideroxylon: Greek *iron wood*.)—Forms with rose-colored fls. are vars. **rosea,** Davy, and **pallens,** Davy, the latter also with silvery-gray foliage.

6. **LEPTOSPERMUM,** Forst. Shrubs or rarely small trees, of about 28 species in Australia, New Zeal., and Malay Archipelago, a few grown for ornament out-of-doors in warm regions or in greenhouses N.—Lvs. alternate, small and rigid, 1–3-nerved or nerveless: fls. solitary or 2–3 together in the axils or at the ends of short branchlets; receptacle or calyx-tube usually broadly campanulate, the lobes 5; petals 5, spreading; stamens many, free, in 1 series, about length of petals, the anthers versatile; ovary 5- to many-, rarely 3–4-celled, with few to many ovules in each cell: fr. a leathery caps. loculicidally dehiscent at top. (Leptosper-mum: Greek for *slender seed*.)

A. Lvs. obtuse, ½–1 in. long: caps. 8–10-celled . . . . 1. *L. lævigatum*
AA. Lvs. acute, ½in. or less long: caps. 5-celled . . . . 2. *L. scoparium*

1. **L. lævigatum,** F. Muell. AUSTRALIAN TEA-TREE. Glabrous and somewhat glaucous shrub to 30 ft.: lvs. obovate-oblong to narrow-oblong, ½–1 in. long and ¼–½in. wide, obtuse, 3-nerved: fls. white, ½–¾in. across, the calyx glabrous: caps. about ¼in. long, nearly flat above the insertion of calyx-lobes and dehiscent into 8–10 cells on top. Australia. —Extensively planted for the reclamation of moving sands.

2. **L. scoparium,** Forst. MANUKA TEA-TREE. Shrub to 6 ft. or more: lvs. linear or linear-lanceolate to oval, ½in. or less long, acute and pungent-tipped, silky beneath when young: fls. white, ¼–½in. across: caps. dehiscent at top into 5 cells. New Zeal., Australia. Var. **Chapmannii,** Dorrien Smith, has brownish lvs. and bright rose fls. Var. **Nichollsii,** Turrill, has bronzy lvs. and carmine fls. (name first published as *Nichollii* but subsequently corrected).

7. **CHAMÆLAUCIUM,** Desf. Heath-like shrubs of about 16 species in W. Australia, one planted in S. Calif.—Lvs. opposite, sessile: fls. in axils of upper lvs.; receptacle or calyx-tube campanulate or turbinate, with 5 spreading lobes; petals 5; stamens 10, alternating with 10 staminodia, in 1 series, slightly united at base; ovary 1-celled, with 6–10 ovules in 2 rows: fr. dry and indehiscent, inclosed in calyx. (Chamælau-cium: Greek for *dwarf* and *white.*)

C. uncinatum, Schauer. GERALDTON WAX-FLOWER. To 20 ft., glabrous: lvs. erect, linear-terete, ¾–1¼ in. long, apex with short recurved hook, white-glandular: fls. white, pink or lilac, about ⅜in. long, in 2–5-fld. cymes which often form large corymbs; calyx-lobes broad, entire; petals orbicular; stigma capitate and with fringe of purple hairs.—Often grown under the name *C. ciliatum,* but that species has obtuse lvs. ¼in. or less long, and very small fls. with fringed calyx-lobes.

8. **FEIJOA,** Berg (*Orthostemon,* Berg). Two species of shrubs or small trees native in S. Amer., one planted in warm countries for its edible fr. and also for ornament.—Lvs. opposite, pinnate-veined, white-tomentose beneath: fls. solitary, axillary, long-pedicelled; receptacle or calyx-tube elongated, lobes 4; petals 4, spreading; stamens many in several series, long-exserted, anthers versatile; ovary 4-celled with several ovules in each cell, the style as long as stamens: fr. an oblong berry, crowned by persistent calyx-lobes. (Feijo-a: after J. da Silva Feijo, Director Natural History Museum at San Sebastian, Spain.)

F. Sellowiana, Berg. To 18 ft.: lvs. oval-oblong to elliptic, 2–3 in. long, obtuse or acute, glossy-green above and silvery-gray beneath: fls. 1–1½ in. across, the petals white-tomentose outside and purplish within, the stamens and style dark red: fr. round, oval or oblong, 1–3 in. long, dull green sometimes tinged with red, with whitish bloom, the whitish flesh surrounding a jelly-like pulp in which the seeds are embedded. (Named after Fr. Sello, page 51.) S. Brazil, Paraguay, Uruguay, Argentina.

9. **PSIDIUM,** L. About 150 species of trees and shrubs native in trop. and subtrop. Amer., the guava widely cult. for its edible fr.—Lvs. opposite, glabrous or tomentose, pinnate-veined: fls. usually large, on axillary or lateral mostly 1–3-fld. peduncles; receptacle or calyx-tube campanulate or pyriform, the lobes 4–5, often closed before flowering and splitting irregularly; petals 4–5, spreading; stamens numerous, in many series, free, inserted on disk; ovary usually 4–5-celled, with many ovules in each cell: fr. a globose or pyriform berry, crowned with the persistent calyx-lobes. (Psid-ium: from *psidion,* Greek name of the pomegranate.)

A. Young branchlets 4-angled: veins of lvs. conspicuously impressed above and raised below..1. *P. Guajava*

AA. Young branchlets terete: veins of lvs. not prominent........................2. *P. Cattleianum*

1. **P. Guajava,** L. GUAVA. Shrub or small tree to 30 ft., the bark scaly and greenish-brown; young branchlets 4-angled: lvs. oblong-elliptic to oval, 3–6 in. long, acute or rounded at apex, finely pubescent below, the veins conspicuously impressed above and raised below: fls. white, about 1 in. across, solitary or 2–3 together on slender peduncles, the stamens about length of petals: fr. globose, ovoid or pyriform, 1–4 in. long, commonly yellow with white, yellow or deep pink flesh. (Guajava: from *guayaba,* the Spanish name in trop. Amer.) Trop. Amer.; nat. in Hawaii.

2. **P. Cattleianum,** Sabine (*P. littorale,* Raddi). STRAWBERRY GUAVA. Bushy shrub or small tree to 25 ft., with smooth gray-brown bark; young branchlets terete: lvs. elliptic to obovate, 2–4 in. long, acute, glabrous, thick and leathery, the veins not conspicuously impressed: fls. white, about 1 in. across, solitary: fr. obovate to globose, 1–1½ in. long, purplish-red (yellow in var. *lucidum*), the flesh white. (Named after William Cattley, died 1832, English horticulturist; page 304.) Brazil.

10. **MYRTUS,** L. MYRTLE. Perhaps 100 species of shrubs or rarely trees, of wide distribution, one grown out-of-doors in warm regions and as a greenhouse subject N.—Lvs. opposite, pinnately-veined, entire: fls. solitary in the axils or in

few-fld. cymes; receptacle or calyx-tube turbinate, with 4–5 sepals; petals 4–5, spreading; stamens numerous, in several series, free, longer than petals, anthers versatile; ovary 2–3-celled with many ovules in each cell: berry globose or ovoid, crowned by persistent calyx-lobes, the 1 to several seeds reniform, with a curved or spiral fleshy embryo. (Myr-tus: ancient Greek name.)

M. communis, L. The classic MYRTLE. Evergreen strong-scented shrub 3–10 ft. high: lvs. ovate to lanceolate, 1–2 in. long, acute, smooth and shining, very short-petioled: fls. white or tinged with rose, ½–¾in. across, on slender pedicels ¾–1 in. long: berry bluish-black (white in one var.), about ½in. long. W. Asia, Medit. region.—Runs into many forms differing chiefly in stature, shape and size of lvs., and there is also a var. with variegated lvs. Var. **microphylla,** Bailey, has small linear-lanceolate long-pointed lvs. close together, ascending, and more or less imbricated.

11. **PIMENTA,** Lindl. Very aromatic trees, of about 5 species in trop. Amer., one yielding allspice which is used in cookery and medicine.—Closely allied to Myrtus and Eugenia, differing chiefly in its 2-celled ovary with 1–6 ovules pendulous from the apex of cell, and from Eugenia in its spiral embryo: fls. small, in many-fld. cymes in the upper axils. (Pimen-ta: from Spanish name *pimento.*)

A. Calyx-lobes 4 .... 1. *P. dioica*
AA. Calyx-lobes 5 .... 2. *P. racemosa*

1. **P. dioica,** Merr. (*Myrtus dioica,* L. *M. Pimenta,* L. *P. officinalis,* Lindl. *Eugenia Pimenta,* DC.). ALLSPICE. PIMENTO. Tree to 40 ft.: lvs. leathery, oblong to oblong-lanceolate, to 6 in. long, the veins prominent beneath, petioles about ½in. long: fls. white, about ¼in. across, the calyx 4-lobed: fr. globose, about ¼in. across, dark brown. W. Indies, Cent. Amer., Mex.—Allspice is the unripe berry when dried.

2. **P. racemosa,** J. W. Moore (*Myrtus caryophyllata,* Jacq. not L. *Caryophyllus racemosus,* Mill. *P. acris,* Kostel. *Amomis caryophyllata,* Krug & Urban). BAY- or BAY-RUM-TREE. To 25 ft.: lvs. leathery, obovate or elliptic, to 5 in. long, obtuse, finely reticulate-veined, short-petioled: fls. white, the calyx 5-lobed: fr. ovoid, about ⅓in. long, black when ripe. W. Indies, Venezuela, Guiana.—Bay oil or oil of myrica is distilled from the lvs., which is used in the preparation of bay-rum.

12. **EUGENIA,** L. About 600 species in the tropics; evergreen trees or shrubs, often planted for ornament in warm regions, some yielding edible frs.—Fls. solitary or clustered in the axils; calyx with 4 or 5 lobes, the tube not produced beyond ovary; stamens numerous, the anther-sacs parallel and opening longitudinally; ovary 2–3-celled with 4 to many horizontal ovules in each cell: fr. a berry crowned by the calyx-lobes; embryo apparently undivided; seed-coats smooth, free from pericarp: very closely allied to Myrtus and separated by the seeds having a straight fleshy embryo. (Euge-nia: after Prince Eugene of Savoy, 1663–1736, patron of botany and hort.)

A. Peduncles 1-fld .... 1. *E. uniflora*
AA. Peduncles 3- or more-fld .... 2. *E. paniculata*

1. **E. uniflora,** L. PITANGA. SURINAM-CHERRY. Broad compact glabrous shrub or small tree to 25 ft.: lvs. nearly sessile, ovate to ovate-lanceolate, 1–2 in. long, acuminate, rounded at base, dark green and shining above: fls. solitary on the ends of long slender peduncles which are 1 or several together in the axils of lvs., about ½in. across, white, slightly fragrant: fr. oblate, ½–1 in. diam., conspicuously 8-ribbed, deep crimson when ripe, edible, having spicy flavor. Brazil.

2. **E. paniculata,** Banks (*Syzygium paniculatum,* Gaertn. *E. Hookeri* and *Hookeriana,* Hort.). AUSTRALIAN BRUSH-CHERRY. Glabrous tree to 40 ft. or more, often grown as hedge and kept clipped, not continuous-blooming: lvs. oblong-lanceolate, 1½–3 in. long, acuminate, cuneate at base, short-petioled, tinged with red when young: fls. white, ½–1 in. across, in branching axillary panicles or terminal on ends of short branchlets and showing beyond foliage, the peduncles 3–5- or more-fld.: fr. ovoid, rose-purple, about ¾in. diam., sometimes used in jelly. Australia. Var. **australis,** Bailey (*E. myrtifolia,* Sims. *E. australis,* Wendl. *Jambosa australis,* DC. *J. myrtifolia,* Niedz.), is smaller, blooming more continuously; lvs. on flowering shoots acute or obtuse; fls. not prominent beyond foliage; fr. smaller.

13. **SYZYGIUM,** Gaertn. A large genus of perhaps 75 species in the tropics of the Old World, two grown for the edible frs. and one the clove of commerce.—Separated from Eugenia by technical characters: embryo divided, with distinct

cotyledons; seed-coats roughish, adhering to the pericarp. (Syzyg-ium: from Greek *united*, referring to calyptrate petals of some species.)

A. Petals united into calyptra or cap. . . . . 1. *S. Cuminii*
AA. Petals free.
B. Fls. 2½–3 in. across. . . . . 2. *S. Jambos*
BB. Fls. ¼in. across. . . . . 3. *S. aromaticum*

1. **S. Cuminii,** Skeels (*Myrtus Cuminii*, L. *Eugenia Jambolana*, Lam. *E. Cuminii*, Druce. *S. Jambolanum*, DC.). JAMBOLAN or JAMBOLAN-PLUM. Glabrous tree 50–80 ft. high, the branchlets white: lvs. broadly oblong or oval, 2–5 in. or more long, bluntish-acuminate, on petioles ½–1 in. long, the lateral veins very close together: fls. white, about ⅓in. across, in branched cymes, the peduncles 3- or more-fid.; petals united into a calyptra or cap: berry oval, about ½in. long, purplish-red, edible. India to Malaysia.

2. **S. Jambos,** Alston (*Eugenia Jambos*, L. *Jambosa vulgaris*, DC. *J. Jambos*, Millsp. *Caryophyllus Jambos*, Stokes). ROSE-APPLE. Attractive glabrous tree to 30 ft.: lvs. oblong-lanceolate, 5–8 in. long, acuminate, thick and shining, short-petioled: fls. greenish-white, 2½–3 in. or more across, in short terminal corymbs, the numerous stamens much surpassing the petals: berry round or oval, 1–2 in. long, greenish or yellow, edible, used for preserves. (Jambos: native Malayan name.) E. Indies; nat. elsewhere.

3. **S. aromaticum,** Merr. & L. M. Perry (*Caryophyllus aromaticus*, L. *Eugenia aromatica*, Baill. not Berg. *E. caryophyllata*, Thunb. *Jambosa Caryophyllus*, Niedz.). CLOVE-TREE. Tree to 30 ft.: lvs. ovate-oblong, 2–5 in. long, acute, tapering at base: fls. pale purple, about ¼in. across, in terminal branching cymes. Moluccas.—The fl.-buds, when dried in the sun, furnish the cloves of commerce.

14. **MYRCIARIA,** Berg. Over 60 species native in S. Amer. and W. Indies, one grown for the edible fr.—Closely related to Eugenia and often included in that genus, differing in technical characters such as calyx-tube produced beyond the ovary and 2 erect ovules in each cell. (Myrcia-ria: *resembling myrcia.*)

M. cauliflora, Berg (*Eugenia cauliflora*, DC.). JABOTICABA. Tree to 40 ft., upward-branching from near the ground and bearing clusters of fls. and frs. along the trunk and branches: lvs. lanceolate to elliptic, 1–4 in. long, acuminate, glabrous: fls. white, small: fr. globular, purple, ¾–1½ in. diam. S. Brazil.

15. **ACMENA,** DC. About 11 species of trees native from S. E. China to Malaya and Australia, one planted for ornament.—Closely allied to Eugenia and Syzygium, differing in anther-sacs divaricate, opening by a terminal slit or pore; embryo apparently undivided; seed-coats adhering to the pericarp. (Acme-na: named for Acmene, a nymph.)

A. Smithii, Merr. & L. M. Perry (*Eugenia Smithii*, Poir. *Syzygium Smithii*, Niedz.). LILLY-PILLY. Tall tree 80–120 ft. in the wild, glabrous: lvs. ovate to ovate-lanceolate, 2–3 in. long: fls. white, small and numerous in terminal panicles; petals united to form a small lid or operculum, deciduous: fr. globular, white or purplish, ¼–½in. diam., edible. (Named for Sir James Edward Smith, page 51.) Australia.—Sometimes erroneously grown under the name *Syzygium operculatum*.

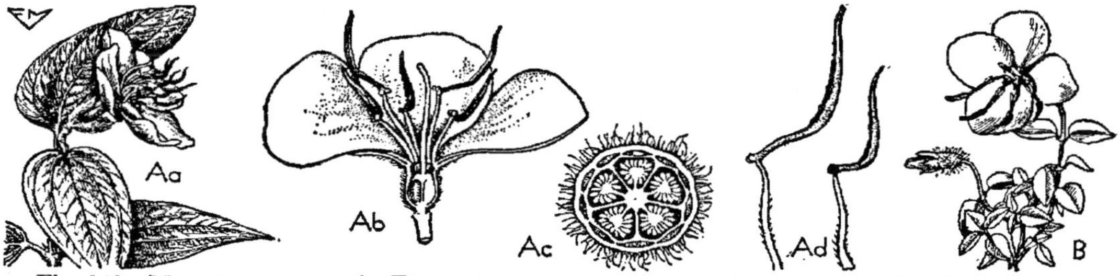

Fig. 149. MELASTOMACEÆ. A, *Tibouchina semidecandra:* Aa, flowering branch, × ¼; Ab, flower, vertical section, × 1; Ac, ovary, cross-section, × 2; Ad, dimorphic stamens, × 1. B, *Schizocentron elegans:* flowering branch, × ½.

149. MELASTOMACEÆ. MELASTOMA FAMILY

Herbs, shrubs or trees, of about 175 genera and 3,000 species mostly of trop. distribution, but the genus Rhexia native in E. U. S.; several genera may be grown in hothouses.—Lvs. opposite or rarely whorled, usually petioled, entire, serrulate or crenulate, commonly characteristically palmately 3–9-nerved, exstipulate: fls. bisexual, regular, often showy, the infl. various; calyx-tube free or adnate to ovary, usually 4–5-lobed; petals as many as calyx-lobes, inserted on mouth of calyx-tube, free or rarely slightly united; stamens as many or twice as many as petals and inserted with them, often inclined or declined, equal or alternate ones sometimes shorter, the anthers with very peculiar and diverse connective; ovary mostly inferior, 2- to several-celled with many ovules in each cell, with 1 style and stigma: fr. a berry or an irregularly or loculicidally dehiscent caps., usually inclosed in the calyx-tube.

A. Stamens equal or nearly so.......................................1. MEDINILLA
AA. Stamens very unequal (at least in ours).
B. Petals and calyx-lobes 5; stamens 10.......................................2. TIBOUCHINA
BB. Petals and calyx-lobes 4; stamens 8.
C. Branches 4-winged.......................................3. CENTRADENIA
CC. Branches not winged.
D. Fls. panicled.......................................4. HETEROCENTRON
DD. Fls. solitary.......................................5. SCHIZOCENTRON

1. **MEDINILLA,** Gaud. Erect or climbing branching shrubs of 125 or more species native in trop. E. Asia, Pacific isls., W. Afr., and Mascarene Isls.; furnishing a few attractive hothouse subjects.—Lvs. fleshy, opposite or verticillate, rarely solitary and alternate or the lvs. in each pair very unequal, 3–9-nerved or sometimes pinnate-veined: fls. white or rose, in lateral few- or many-fld. panicles or cymes, often with showy bracts; calyx-lobes usually 4–5, rarely irregularly cleft; petals 4–5, rarely 6; stamens 8 or 10, seldom 12, equal or nearly so, rarely strongly unequal, connective usually not produced at base, 2-lobed or -spurred in front, 1–2-lobed or 1-spurred at back; ovary 4–6-celled, adnate to calyx completely or by septa: fr. a berry crowned by the calyx-lobes. (Medinil-la: named after José de Medinilla of Pineda, Governor of the Ladrones.)

A. Panicles pendulous; bracts large and showy.......................................1. *M. magnifica*
AA. Panicles erect; bracts none.......................................2. *M. Teysmannii*

1. **M. magnifica,** Lindl. Evergreen shrub with 4-angled or -winged branches, having a dense ring of short fleshy processes at the joints between the lvs.: lvs. opposite, sessile, ovate or ovate-oblong, up to 1 ft. long: fls. coral-red, about 1 in. across, in pendulous pyramidal panicles sometimes 1 ft. long, having showy pinkish bracts 1–4 in. long; petals 5; anthers purple, the filaments yellow. Philippines.

2. **M. Teysmannii,** Miq. (*M. amabilis,* Dyer). Sts. 4-winged: lvs. opposite, sessile, obovate- or elliptic-oblong, to 1 ft. long: fls. rose-colored, 1½–2 in. diam., in an erect pyramidal panicle, without bracts; petals 5; stamens 10, with pale violet anthers. (J. E. Teysmann, page 52.) Celebes, New Guinea.

2. **TIBOUCHINA,** Aubl. (*Lasiandra,* DC.). GLORY-BUSH. Mostly hispid shrubs or subshrubs, rarely herbs, one grown in greenhouses and also out-of-doors far S.; about 215 species in trop. Amer., particularly Brazil.—Lvs. usually large and leathery, ovate or oblong, petioled, 3–7-nerved, entire: fls. large and showy, in terminal branched panicles or solitary; calyx hirsute or strigose, 5-lobed; petals 5, obovate, entire or retuse; stamens 10, equal or unequal, the connectives with 2 tubercles or lobes at base, often unappendaged; ovary 5-celled, free or adnate to ribs of calyx, hispid at apex: fr. a 5-valved caps. inclosed by the persistent calyx-tube. (Tibouchina: native name in Guiana.)

T. semidecandra, Cogn. (*Pleroma macranthum,* Hook. *P. splendens,* Hort.). Pubescent shrub 4–10 ft. high: lvs. ovate or oblong-ovate, 2–4 in. long, acuminate, densely villous on both sides, pale beneath: fls. violet to reddish-purple, 3–5 in. across, solitary or 3 together at ends of branchlets, subtended by 2 orbicular bracts; stamens purple, very unequal, the longest filaments glandular-pubescent. Brazil.

3. **CENTRADENIA,** Don. Perhaps 6 species of herbs and subshrubs native in Mex. and Cent. Amer., one sometimes grown in hothouses.—Branches 4-angled or 4-winged: lvs. lanceolate, those of each pair very unequal or one sometimes wanting: fls. rose, in cymes or corymbs; calyx-tube slightly 4-angled, the 4 lobes shorter than the tube; petals 4, rounded; stamens 8, unequal, connective produced at base,

curved, with a club-shaped or 2-lobed appendage; ovary 4-celled, free above, glabrous and toothed at top: fr. a 4-valved caps. as long as the calyx-tube. (Centradenia: Greek for *spur* and *gland*, referring to the anthers.)

C. grandifolia, Endl. To 2 ft. and more, the branches 4-winged: lvs. ovate-lanceolate to lanceolate, 2–6 in. long, acuminate and usually curving at end, bright red beneath: fls. rose-pink, ½in. across, in many-fld. cymes shorter than the lvs., stamens very unequal. Mex.

4. **HETEROCENTRON,** Hook. & Arn. Erect herbs or subshrubs native in the mts. of Mex. and Cent. Amer.; about 7 species, one sometimes grown under glass or in the open far S.—Lvs. lanceolate, pinnately-nerved, entire, membranaceous: fls. white, rose, or purple, in panicles; calyx-tube setose, the 4 triangular lobes about same length as tube; petals 4; stamens 8, very unequal, the connectives of the longer stamens produced at base, erect or curved, the club-shaped appendages 2-parted; ovary 4-celled, 8-ribbed, nearly free: fr. a 4-valved caps. about equalling calyx-tube. (Heterocen-tron: Greek *unlike spurs*, referring to the anthers.)

H. roseum, A. Br. & Bouché (*Heeria rosea*, Triana). To 2 ft. or more, the branches 4-angled: lvs. elliptic, about 1 in. long, setose: fls. bright rose (white in var. **album,** Hook.), about ½in. across, in terminal panicles, the pedicels pubescent. Mex.—Often cult. under the name *H. mexicanum*, but this species differs in its glandular calyx-tube, and the calyx-lobes are ciliate on margins.

5. **SCHIZOCENTRON,** Meissn. One creeping vine-like plant from Mex., sometimes grown in baskets and pots in the greenhouse.—Often united with Heterocentron but differing in its small lvs. 3-nerved from the base, the solitary long-pedicelled fls. and the persistent calyx-lobes. (Schizocen-tron: Greek *split spur*, referring to the anthers.)

S. elegans, Meissn. (*Heeria elegans*, Schlecht. *Heterocentron elegans*, Kuntze). Lvs. ovate, ½in. or less long, distinctly petioled, slightly pubescent: fls. purple, nearly 1 in. across; calyx-tube covered with glandular bristles, the lobes ciliate.

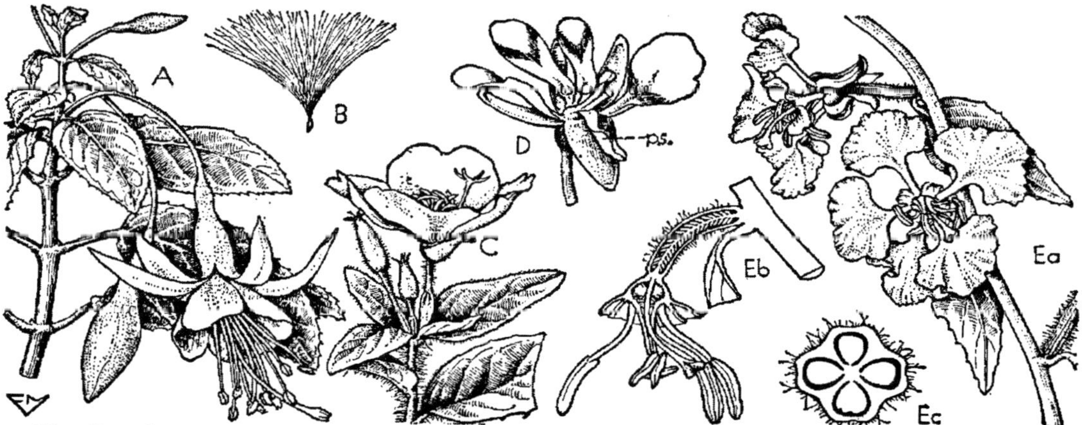

Fig. 150. ONAGRACEÆ. A, *Fuchsia hybrida:* flowering branch, × ½. B, *Epilobium angustifolium:* comose seed, × ¼. C, *Œnothera pilosella:* flowering branch, × 1. D, *Lopezia coronata:* flower, × 1 (p.s. petaloid staminodium). E, *Clarkia elegans:* Ea, flowering branch, × ½ (note doubling of corolla); Eb, flower, vertical section, less perianth, × 1; Ec, ovary, cross-section, × 4.

150. ONAGRACEÆ. EVENING-PRIMROSE FAMILY

A marked family consisting chiefly of herbaceous annuals or perennials (a few shrubs), many cult. for ornament, usually in the open, a few yielding products of commercial value; about 20 genera and 480 species, mostly natives of the temp. parts of the New World (W. U. S. and Mex.) but also abundant in S. Amer.—Lvs. alternate or opposite, simple, mostly exstipulate: fls. bisexual, regular or sometimes irregular, perigynous or epigynous, axillary, spicate or racemose; hypanthium (calyx-tube) adnate to the ovary and often produced beyond it, the limb 2–6-lobed (usually 4-lobed); petals 4, rarely more or fewer, often clawed, convolute in the bud; stamens as many or twice as many as petals, arising with them from the rim of the hypanthium or inserted on a disk, or sometimes 2; ovary inferior, 2–4-celled, placentation axile, style 1, stigmas 1–4: fr. a caps., rarely a berry or nut. Recognizable by the numerical plan (2–4) of the fls. and the inferior ovary with numerous ovules (with such exceptions as Trapa, which is often put into a separate family, Trapaceæ or Hydrocaryaceæ).

A. Habit truly aquatic in ours.
  B. Fr. horned, nut-like; ovary 2-celled with solitary ovules: lvs. in floating rosettes.. 1. TRAPA
  BB. Fr. a caps.; ovary 4-celled with many ovules: lvs. along st., floating or submerged.......... 2. LUDWIGIA
AA. Habit terrestrial.
  B. Stamens 2, one of them petal-like.......... 3. LOPEZIA
  BB. Stamens 4 or 8.
    C. Seeds with tuft of hairs (coma) at one end.
      D. Hypanthium less than ½in. long, without internal scales.......... 4. EPILOBIUM
      DD. Hypanthium about 1 in. long, with inner row of 8 scales.......... 5. ZAUSCHNERIA
    CC. Seeds without tuft of hairs.
      D. Fr. a dehiscent caps.
        E. Anthers innate, erect, attached near the base: fls. not yellow.
          F. Petals distinctly clawed, the claw at least one-sixth the blade.......... 6. CLARKIA
          FF. Petals not or scarcely clawed, the claw not more than one-tenth the blade.......... 7. GODETIA
        EE. Anthers versatile (attached near the middle): fls. often yellow.......... 8. ŒNOTHERA
      DD. Fr. indehiscent, a nut or berry.
        E. Hypanthium not showy: herbs with nut-like frs.......... 9. GAURA
        EE. Hypanthium colored and showy: shrubs with berries..........10. FUCHSIA

1. **TRAPA**, L. Floating plants adapted to the aquarium and one furnishing edible frs.; 3 species, native to the warmer parts of the eastern hemisphere.—Aquatic herbs with lvs. of two kinds, the submersed ones opposite, pinnatisect, the emersed ones rosulate, toothed, with spongy inflated petioles: fls. small, axillary, solitary, short-peduncled; hypanthium short, surrounding the base of the ovary, the 4-parted limb with persistent often spinescent segms.; petals and stamens 4, inserted at the base of an undulate epigynous disk; ovary 2-celled, ovules solitary, pendulous: fr. coriaceous or nut-like, 1-celled, 1-seeded. (Tra-pa: abbreviated from *calcitrapa*, which is the same as caltrops, an instrument of war; it has 4 spine-like projections, like the fr. of the common water caltrops.)

T. natans, L. WATER-CHESTNUT. WATER CALTROPS. JESUITS-NUT. An attractive aquatic, usually with mottled or variegated foliage; submersed lvs. long, slender, feathery; floating lvs. in a loose rosette, lf.-stalks swollen and spongy near the apex, the rhombic-orbicular blade dentate along the upper half, slightly villous along the nerves beneath: fls. white, small and inconspicuous: fr. 1–2 in. across, with 4 spinescent angles. Eu., Orient; sparingly nat. in E. U. S.—Fr. roasted and eaten in some parts of Eu. and Asia like the common chestnut. The water-chestnut of China is the tuber of an Eleocharis.

2. **LUDWIGIA**, L. (sometimes spelled *Ludvigia*). Mostly per. aquatic or semi-aquatic plants, one widely distributed amongst growers of aquarium subjects and prized for its graceful habit and persistent foliage; species about 30 widely spread in warm and temp. regions, mostly in N. Amer.—Small herbs often creeping, sometimes floating: lvs. opposite or alternate: fls. solitary and axillary or clustered in terminal spikes or heads, often inconspicuous, 4-parted, the stamens as many as the calyx-segms.; corolla small or lacking; ovary 4-celled with many ovules: caps. short, opening longitudinally or through pores at the apex. (Ludwig-ia: C. G. Ludwig, 1709–1773, botanist and botanical author at Leipzig.)

L. natans, Ell. (*L. Mulerttii*, Mulertt). Aquatic herb with weak sts. rooting at the nodes: lvs. opposite, oval to obovate, entire, narrowed to petioles about as long as the blade or shorter, glabrous, glossy dark green above and crimson-purple beneath when growing above water in the sun: fls. yellow, axillary: caps. oblong, truncate, ⅜in. long, crowned by the persistent calyx-lobes; seeds without hairs, retaining life six to eight years if left within the caps. N. C. to Fla. south to Mex.

3. **LOPEZIA**, Cav. Species a dozen or more, in Mex. and Cent. Amer.; little grown, but valuable for their interesting forms and gay colors.—Erect branching

subshrubs or herbs, glabrous or pubescent: lvs. alternate or the lower opposite, dentate to subentire: fls. usually small, slender-pedicelled, in leafy racemes or subcorymbose at the ends of the branches; hypanthium scarcely produced beyond the ovary, the limb 4-parted, unequal, deciduous, linear-lobed; petals 4, short- or long-clawed, unequal, the posterior ones narrower, the claws sometimes glandular at apex; stamens 2, attached to the pistil, 1 anther-bearing, the other petal-like; ovary 4-celled: caps. globose, coriaceous, many-seeded; seeds with a granulated coat. (Lope-zia: after the Spaniard, Thomas Lopez, who wrote on the natural history of the New World.)

A. Petals white, often pinkish-tinged..1. *L. albiflora*
AA. Petals not white.
  B. Plant shrubby: pedicels usually longer than the subtending lvs..................2. *L. lineata*
  BB. Plant ann.: pedicels usually shorter than the subtending lvs....................3. *L. coronata*

1. **L. albiflora,** Schlecht. Shrubby diffuse per. to 2 ft., young branches more or less villous: lvs. petioled, ovate-lanceolate to ovate, cuneate at base, irregularly serrate or remotely dentate to subentire, the largest 1½ in. long: pedicels horizontally spreading, equalling or longer than the subtending lvs.; petals white, often tinged slightly pinkish at base, the larger ones obliquely spatulate, obtuse or mostly notched, the smaller ones linear, obtuse, equalling or exceeding the calyx-lobes; late autumn and early winter. Mex.

2. **L. lineata,** Zucc. Shrubby, 3 ft. high, much-branched above, the sts. and petioles usually hairy: lvs. slender-petioled, ovate to lanceolate, acute or obtusish, crenate-serrate to subentire: fls. red, in racemes terminating the branchlets, the slender pedicels longer than the subtending lvs.; posterior petals bearing a single gland; late summer and winter. Mex.

3. **L. coronata,** Andr. Ann., 1½–3 ft. high, sts. subglabrous, angled: lvs. scattered or in whorls, petiolate, ovate to lanceolate, acute or acuminate, serrate or serrulate, glossy and glabrous: fls. rose-colored or lilac, solitary in the axils along at least the upper half of the st., the filiform pedicels commonly exceeded by the subtending lvs.; the 2 upper petals linear, the lateral ones broader and longer; summer to early autumn. Mex.

4. **EPILOBIUM,** L. Willow-Herb. Probably 200 species of wide distribution, mostly in temp. parts of the world, a few used as border-plants in moist places and in rock-gardens.—Herbs or subshrubs, sometimes ann., erect, sprawling or creeping: lvs. willow-like, opposite or alternate, toothed or entire: fls. solitary and axillary or in terminal spikes or racemes, rose-purple to white or flesh-colored, very rarely yellow; hypanthium little if at all produced beyond the ovary; petals 4, obovate or obcordate, erect or spreading; stamens 8, unequal; ovary 4-celled, stigma 4-lobed: caps. long and narrow, terete or 4-sided, 4-valved; seeds many, provided with a tuft of silky hairs. (Epilo-bium: Greek *upon the pod,* referring to the structure of the fl.)

A. Sts. erect: lvs. alternate.
  B. Racemes long, many-fld. and not leafy..............................1. *E. angustifolium*
  BB. Racemes short, few-fld., very leafy..................................2. *E. latifolium*
AA. Sts. procumbent: lvs. opposite.
  B. Fls. about 1 in. across, rose-purple.................................3. *E. obcordatum*
  BB. Fls. ¼in. or less across, white or pink.
    C. Lvs. orbicular..4. *E. nummularifolium*
    CC. Lvs. oblong or linear-oblong.....................................5. *E. Hectori*

1. **E. angustifolium,** L. (*Chamænerion angustifolium,* Scop.). Fireweed. Great Willow-Herb. Sts. erect, in cult. mostly branched and 3–5 ft. high, in the wild simple or branched, 2–8 ft. high: lvs. alternate, very short-petioled, lanceolate, 2–6 in. long, acute, entire or minutely toothed: fls. purple varying to white, ¾–1¼ in. across, in long terminal spike-like racemes: caps. terete, 2–3 in. long. Eu., Asia, N. Amer., abundant on newly burned-over areas.

2. **E. latifolium,** L. (*Chamænerion latifolium,* Sweet). Per. to 2 ft., sts. usually clustered: lvs. alternate, nearly sessile, lanceolate or ovate-lanceolate, 1–2 in. long, acute or obtuse, entire, thick, glaucous: fls. purple, 1–2 in. across, in short few-fld. very leafy racemes: caps. 2–3 in. long. N. N. Amer., Eu., Asia.

3. **E. obcordatum,** Gray. Sts. decumbent, 2–6 in. long: lvs. opposite or crowded, nearly sessile, ovate, ¼–¾in. long, obtuse or acutish, toothed, glabrous and glaucous: fls. rose-purple, about 1 in. across, in short few-fld. racemes in axils of upper lvs.: caps. about 1 in. long. Mts., Calif., Nev., Ida., Ore.

4. **E. nummularifolium,** R. Cunn. Densely tufted, with creeping sts. 3–8 in. long rooting at nodes: lvs. opposite, short-petioled, orbicular, ⅙–½in. long, obscurely toothed, glabrous: fls. pink or whitish, ⅙in. across, few in axils: caps. ¾–1½ in. long. New Zeal.

5. **E. Hectori,** Haussk. Sts. decumbent and rooting, ascending to 6 in.: lvs. opposite or crowded, oblong or linear-oblong, ¼–½in. long, obtuse, entire or obscurely toothed,

glabrous: fls. white, ¼in. across, in upper axils: caps. ½–1 in. long. (Named for Sir James Hector, 1834–1907, geologist and naturalist.) New Zeal.

5. **ZAUSCHNERIA,** Presl. Low perennials, with large brilliant scarlet fuchsia-like fls., sometimes grown in fl.-gardens; about 5 species.—Shrubby at base: lvs. alternate or the lowest opposite: fls. racemose; calyx scarlet, the hypanthium globose at base, funnelform above, bearing 8 small scales within, the limb 4-lobed; petals scarlet, inserted on throat of calyx, alternate with and little if any longer than its lobes; stamens 8, exserted: caps. slender-fusiform, obtusely 4-angled, 4-valved, with many seeds having tuft of hairs at apex. (Zauschne-ria: named for M. Zauschner, once professor of natural history at Prague.)

Z. californica, Presl. CALIFORNIA-FUCHSIA. About 1–2 ft. high, the sts. branched, decumbent or nearly erect: herbage tomentose to often somewhat villous; lvs. lanceolate to linear-lanceolate, ½–1½ in. long, entire or remotely serrate: fls. 1–2 in. long, in autumn. Calif.

6. **CLARKIA,** Pursh. Showy-fld. annuals, a few used for low masses and for edgings in fl.-gardens, also for vases and baskets; 7 species in W. N. Amer.; they have been much improved by domestication.—Virgately branching herbs, glabrous or pilose: lvs. alternate, entire or denticulate: fls. rose or purple, medium-sized, solitary in the axils or in terminal racemes; hypanthium short or elongated; petals 4, clawed, the limb dilated, entire or 3-lobed; stamens 4 or 8, inserted on throat of calyx, alternate ones short or rudimentary; ovary 4-celled, style filiform, stigma 4-lobed: caps. linear, straight or curved, somewhat 4-angled, 4-valved; seeds numerous. (Clar-kia: Capt. Wm. Clark, 1770–1838, companion of Lewis, explorer of the Rocky Mt. region and further west.)

A. Stamens 4; hypanthium elongated .... 1. *C. concinna*
AA. Stamens 8; hypanthium short.
  B. Petals entire, not toothed on the claws.......... 2. *C. elegans*
  BB. Petals 3-lobed, the claws toothed on each side.......... 3. *C. pulchella*

1. **C. concinna,** Greene (*Eucharidium concinnum*, Fisch. & Mey. *E. grandiflorum*, Fisch. & Mey. *C. grandiflora*, Greene). RED RIBBONS. Simple below or diffusely branched from base, 1–2 ft. high, glabrous or nearly so: lvs. oblong or oval, ¾–1½ in. long, petioled: fls. sessile, somewhat bilabiate because of the approximate 3 upper petals and distant lower one; hypanthium ¾in. long with crimson recurved lobes; petals often 1 in. long, rose-purple, long-clawed, 3-lobed: caps. sessile, about 1 in. long. Calif.

2. **C. elegans,** Dougl. Erect, 1–4 ft., glabrous except the frs. and calyces, the reddish glaucous sts. simple or sparingly branched: lvs. ovate to ovate-lanceolate, 1–1¾ in. long, remotely dentate: fls. purple or rose-colored, running into white vars., double forms in cult.; hypanthium very short; petals about ⅔in. long, often spreading laterally in pairs, the limb and claw of about equal length, the claw not toothed; anthers of long stamens often bright crimson, of short stamens whitish: caps. about 1 in. long, sessile, often long-hairy. Calif.

3. **C. pulchella,** Pursh. Twelve to 18 in. high, branching, often tufted and dwarf, the sts. mostly puberulent: lvs. linear to linear-lanceolate, 1–2 in. long, narrowed to a petiole, entire: fls. lilac running into white vars.; hypanthium very short; petals in wild plants ¾in. long, the blade with 3 wide-spreading lobes, the claw with a pair of recurved teeth: caps. stalked, ½–1 in. long, short-pubescent. B. C. to Ore. and S. D.—There are semi-double and dwarf forms and one with entire petals. Some of the garden clarkias are apparently hybrids between *C. elegans* and *C. pulchella.*

7. **GODETIA,** Spach. Erect annuals suitable for the fl.-garden; about 15 species in western parts of S. and N. Amer., especially Calif.—Lvs. alternate, narrow, short-petioled or sessile: fls. showy, in leafy racemes or spikes, opening during the day; calyx often colored, the hypanthium obconic or funnelform, long-produced beyond the ovary; petals 4, commonly broad and entire, rose, lilac-purple or white, often marked with a large deep crimson or purple spot; stamens 8, those opposite the petals shorter, anthers basifixed; ovary 4-celled, inferior: fr. a many-seeded 4-celled 4-valved caps. (Gode-tia: C. H. Godet, 1797–1879, Swiss botanist.)

G. amœna, Don (*Œnothera amœna*, Lehm. *G. grandiflora*, Lindl. *G. rubicunda*, Lindl.). FAREWELL-TO-SPRING. Slender, branching 1–3 ft. high: lvs. linear to lanceolate, ½–2½ in. long, often with smaller ones fascicled in the axils: buds erect, in early summer; calyx-lobes united and turned to one side on expansion of fl.; corolla lilac-crimson or red-pink, satiny, 1–2 in. broad, often with dark purple base or purple central spot: caps. teretish, not ribbed when mature, 1–1½ in. long, sessile or very short-pedicelled. Calif. to B. C.—Probably the plants in cult. as *G. Whitneyi* belong here. The true *G. Whitneyi*, Moore (*Œnothera Whitneyi*, Gray), is a rare local species in Calif., differing in sts. usually simple, larger fls. in a denser infl., and shorter 8-ribbed caps.

8. ŒNOTHERA, L. Evening-Primrose. A polymorphic genus concerning whose generic bounds there is much difference of opinion, regarded as one genus by some authorities and broken up into 10 or a dozen by others; the entire assemblage comprises perhaps 200 species, and is here treated as a single genus, since it is fairly homogeneous from the hort. point of view, and the names already in the trade are well established; the œnotheras are of wide distribution in the temp. zones of the New World, occurring more rarely in the tropics.—Ann., bien. and per. herbs, or sometimes shrubby at base: lvs. alternate, sessile or petiolate, entire, toothed, lobed or parted: fls. mostly showy, yellow, white, or rose-color, axillary and solitary or rarely in 2's or clusters; hypanthium 4-sided, produced beyond the ovary, the 4 usually strongly reflexed lobes commonly deciduous; petals 4, obovate or obcordate, sessile or nearly so; stamens 8, equal or alternating long or short; ovary 4-celled, stigma entire or 4-lobed or -parted: caps. loculicidal, 4-valved. (Œnothe-ra: said to be Greek for *wine-scenting*, a name given to some now unknown plant.)

A. Fls. yellow, often aging reddish or orange.
  B. Stigma capitate, not lobed .... 18. *Œ. bistorta*
  BB. Stigma with 4 linear lobes.
    C. Caps. club-shaped, the lower part usually sterile and narrow.
      D. Buds and tip of infl. nodding; petals ¼–⅓ in. long .... 7. *Œ. perennis*
      DD. Buds and infl. erect; petals ½–1 in. long.
        E. Body of caps. clavate when mature, with no gland-tipped hairs.
          F. Sepal-tips not free, or if so about 1/32 in. long: caps.-body ¼–⅓ in. long .... 8. *Œ. fruticosa*
          FF. Sepal-tips free, 1/16 in. long: caps.-body ½–¾ in. long .... 9. *Œ. pilosella*
        EE. Body of caps. oblong to ellipsoid, with gland-tipped hairs .... 10. *Œ. tetragona*
    CC. Caps. not club-shaped.
      D. Fr. broadly winged; seeds corky-tubercled .... 13. *Œ. missourensis*
      DD. Fr. not winged.
        E. Seeds sharply angled: caps. gradually narrowed upward.
          F. Width of fls. 1–2 in. .... 1. *Œ. biennis*
          FF. Width of fls. 3–5 in.
            G. Lf.-blades plane, not strongly crinkled, lanceolate: caps. ⅛ in. thick at base.
              H. St.-lvs. almost one-third as wide as long; rosette-lvs. deeply sinuate .... 2. *Œ. grandiflora*
              HH. St.-lvs. not more than one-fourth as wide as long; rosette-lvs. subentire .... 4. *Œ. Hookeri*
            GG. Lf.-blades strongly crinkled, oblong-ovate, at least one-third as wide as long: caps. ¼ in. thick .... 3. *Œ. erythrosepala*
        EE. Seeds not sharply angled: caps. somewhat enlarged in upper half.
          F. Sts. decumbent: cauline lvs. oblong-ovate, plane .... 5. *Œ. Drummondii*
          FF. Sts. erect: cauline lvs. lanceolate, conspicuously crisped .... 6. *Œ. odorata*
AA. Fls. white to red, not yellow.
  B. Caps. enlarged and winged in upper part.
    C. Sts. ascending to erect: base of caps. sterile and narrow.
      D. Buds nodding; petals 1–1⅙ in. long .... 11. *Œ. speciosa*
      DD. Buds erect; petals ⅕–½ in. long .... 12. *Œ. rosea*
    CC. Sts. lacking or prostrate: caps. not sterile and narrow at base .... 14. *Œ. acaulis*
  BB. Caps. not enlarged nor winged above.
    C. Sts. well-developed: caps. cylindric; seeds in 1 row in each cell.
      D. Plant a slender per.: basal lvs. oblanceolate, 1–3½ in. long: caps. not woody, 1/16 in. thick .... 15. *Œ. trichocalyx*
      DD. Plant a coarse ann.: basal lvs. rhombic, 2–6 in. long: caps. woody, ⅛ in. or more thick at base .... 16. *Œ. deltoides*
    CC. Sts. almost or quite lacking: caps. subovoid; seeds in 2 rows in each cell .... 17. *Œ. cæspitosa*

1. Œ. biennis, L. (*Onagra biennis*, Scop.). Common Evening-Primrose. Usually bien., but often flowering the first year, rosettes attaining 2 ft. diam.; roots large, fleshy, often 2 in. diam. at the crown; sts. about 3–4 ft. high, copiously branched, green to red: lower lvs. narrowly oblanceolate, the upper ovate: fls. yellow, opening at evening; hypanthium nearly 1½ in. long, enlarging at the throat; petals obcordate, 1 in. wide and not as long; stigma 4-cleft, surrounded by the anthers and self-pollinated in the bud: caps. 4-angled, 1 in. long, loosely aggregated in the lower part of the spike, more densely above, shorter than the mostly persistent leafy bracts; seeds angled, horizontal in the pod. Intro. into Eu. from Amer. and now a common weed in the Old World.—A number of obscure kinds pass in Amer. under the name *Œ. biennis*, most of them being more weedy than the European plant and the roots generally woody and tough.

2. **Œ. grandiflora,** Soland. (*Œ. biennis* var. *grandiflora*, Lindl.). Habit of preceding: basal lvs. deeply pinnately lobed; st.-lvs. lanceolate, distinctly petioled; papillæ at base of longer hairs on green portions of st. not red: infl. open, slender, bracts lanceolate, ⅛–¼ in. wide; hypanthium 1½–2½ in. long; fls. nocturnal, 2½–3½ in. wide; buds and ovary glabrous or nearly so. Ala.

3. **Œ. erythrosepala,** Borb. (*Œ. Lamarckiana*, DeVries not Ser. *Œ. Johnsonii*, Hort.). Differs from *Œ. grandiflora* in its more hairy red-tuberculate sts., sinuate-dentate basal lvs., broader crinkled almost sessile st.-lvs., denser spike with broader bracts: sepals and ovary strongly pilose and puberulent; fls. nocturnal. Apparently a garden plant originating in England in the middle of the 19th century, occasional as an escape.—**Œ. rubricalyx,** Gates, Afterglow, has calyx-tube and -segms. fine rich red.

4. **Œ. Hookeri,** Torr. & Gray (*Onagra Hookeri*, Small. *Œ. Clutei*, A. Nels.?). Canescent or somewhat hirsute throughout, 2–6 ft. high: lower lvs. oblanceolate, upper lanceolate, sessile to short-petioled, becoming lanceolate bracts in the elongate spicate infl.: hypanthium 1–2 in. long, often reddish; fls. nocturnal, 2½–3½ in. wide; buds and ovary pubescent to hirsute. (W. J. Hooker, page 45.) W. U. S.

5. **Œ. Drummondii,** Hook. (*Raimannia Drummondii*, Rose). Perhaps per. but grown as ann., 1–2 ft. high, from an oblique or decumbent base, densely soft-pubescent: lvs. lance-oblong to oblong-ovate, acute or obtuse, tapering gradually or abruptly to a short petiole, entire or slightly toothed: fls. 2–3 in. wide, nocturnal, bright yellow, showy; hypanthium 1–2 in. long and very narrow; stigma deeply 4-cleft: caps. narrow-cylindric, obtusely 4-angled, 1–2 in. long, with numerous fusiform seeds. (Thos. Drummond, page 255.) Tex. coast.

6. **Œ. odorata,** Jacq. (*Raimannia odorata*, Sprague & Riley. *Œ. undulata*, Ait.). Per., erect or ascending, ½–1 ft. high, strigose and pilose: lower lvs. linear-oblanceolate; cauline lvs. sessile, lanceolate, conspicuously crinkled: fls. solitary in upper axils, yellow, nocturnal, 1–2 in. wide: caps. 1 in. long, enlarged in upper half, subcylindric. Chile, Argentina.

7. **Œ. perennis,** L. (*Kneiffia perennis*, Pennell. *K. pumila*, Spach). Sundrops. Slender erect bien. or per. ½–2 ft. high, sts. simple or few-branched, strigulose-puberulent: lvs. linear-lanceolate to oblanceolate, entire or denticulate, 1–3 in. long, usually glabrous: fls. diurnal, yellow, ⅓–1 in. wide, in loose leafy-bracted spikes or racemes, nodding in bud: caps. clavate, short-stalked, ¼–½in. long, usually glandular-puberulent. Newf. to N. C., Minn., Mo.—*Œ. Pilgrimii*, Hort., with short spreading hairs, is *Œ. perennis* var. *rectifolia*, Blake.

8. **Œ. fruticosa,** L. (*Œ. linearis*, Michx. *Kneiffia linearis*, Spach). Sundrops. Slender bien. or per., sts. erect to spreading, ¼–2 ft. high, pubescent: basal lvs. ovate to spatulate, petioled; cauline lvs. mostly lanceolate, 1–2½ in. long, sessile or nearly so: fls. crowded, erect in bud, diurnal, yellow, 1–2 in. wide, petals usually shallowly toothed: caps. clavate, pubescent but not glandular, ¼–⅓in. long, sessile or pedicelled. Mass. to Fla. and Ala.—Many earlier references to this name apply to *Œ. tetragona*.

9. **Œ. pilosella,** Raf. (*Kneiffia pilosella*, Heller. *K. pratensis*, Small). Per., erect, simple or few-branched, spreading-hirsute, 6–24 in. high: basal lvs. obovate to oblanceolate, petioled; cauline gradually reduced up the st., lanceolate or wider, 1–4 in. long: fls. yellow, diurnal; hypanthium ½–1 in. long; sepals green, ⅖–¾in. long, hirsute, with divaricate tips; petals obcordate, to 1 in. long: caps. sessile, linear-clavate, hirsute, ½–¾in. long. Mo. and Iowa to Wis. and Ohio; intro. further east.

10. **Œ. tetragona,** Roth (*Kneiffia tetragona*, Pennell. *Œ. imperialis*, Hort. *Œ. Youngii*, Hort. *Œ. fruticosa* var. *Youngii*, Bailey). Sundrops. Per. or bien., erect, simple to branched, ⅔–3 ft. high, spreading-pubescent on sts. and infl.: basal lvs. spatulate to ovate, 1–8 in. long; cauline lvs. lance-linear to -ovate, ½–4 in. long, subentire to denticulate: infl. few-fld., dense, glandular-puberulent: fls. diurnal, yellow, 1–1½ in. wide: caps. clavate-oblong, ¼–¾in. long, glandular-puberulent, pedicelled. N. S. to Ga. and Tenn. Var. **longistipata,** Munz (*Kneiffia tetragona* var. *longistipata*, Pennell. *Œ. serotina*, Sweet), pubescence of sts. appressed; N. Y. to Ga., Mich., Tenn. Var. **Fraseri,** Munz (*Œ. Fraseri*, Pursh. *Kneiffia Fraseri*, Spach. *Œ. glauca*, Michx. *Kneiffia glauca*, Michx. *Œ. Fyrverkeri*, Hort. *Œ. fruticosa* var. *major*, Hort.), cauline lvs. lance-ovate to ovate, fls. 1½–2½ in. wide; S. Appalachian Mts.

11. **Œ. speciosa,** Nutt. (*Hartmannia speciosa*, Small). Canescent per. 2 ft. or less high, with a rootstock, branches erect or ascending: lvs. linear to lance-oblong, narrowed at base, 4 in. or less long, remotely or sinuately dentate, or the lower ones pinnatifid: fls. white or rose, diurnal, 1½–3½ in. wide, usually few, loosely spicate; hypanthium funnelform, as long as or longer than ovary; stamens unequal; stigma 4-lobed: caps. ½–¾in. long, 8-winged, acute at top, stalked. Mo. west and south. Var. **Childsii,** Munz (*Œ. tetraptera* var. *Childsii*, Bailey. *Œ. rosea* var. *mexicana*, Hort.), Mexican Evening-Primrose, branches very slender, prostrate or decumbent, ½–1 ft. long; lvs. 1–2 in. long; fls. rose, 1–1½ in. wide; coastal Tex. and adjacent Mex.; garden or conservatory plant, intro. from Tex. by John Lewis Childs in 1892.

12. **Œ. rosea,** Ait. (*Hartmannia rosea,* Don). Bien. or per., with erect or ascending sts. to 2 ft., branching from base: herbage finely hairy; lvs. lanceolate to narrow ovate-lanceolate, mostly acuminate, rather abruptly narrowed to a petiole, acuminate or acute, entire or remotely denticulate or the larger ones small-lobed at base: fls. small, fuchsia-like, purple or rose; hypanthium shorter than ovary: caps. much like that of *Œ. speciosa* but narrower at base. Tex. and New Mex. south.

13. **Œ. missourensis,** Sims (*Œ. macrocarpa,* Pursh. *Megapterium missouriense,* Spach). Low usually pubescent per. with a hard base, sts. ascending to about 1 ft.: lvs. thick, soft-pubescent, narrowly oval to lanceolate, 5 in. or less long, acuminate, narrowed to petiole, entire or remotely denticulate: fls. yellow, showy; hypanthium very long and slender, enlarging at top; petals 1–2½ in. long, very broad; stamens of unequal length; stigma 4-cleft: caps. 2–3 in. long and nearly as wide, broadly 4-winged; seeds crested. Mo. and Kans. to Tex.

14. **Œ. acaulis,** Cav. (*Œ. taraxacifolia,* Hort.). Glabrous or puberulent tufted per. or bien., at first stemless, later producing prostrate somewhat zigzag sts.: lvs. oblong in outline, 5–8 in. long, petioled, deeply parted into many narrow remote segms., often with 1–2 narrow salient teeth between the segms.: fls. axillary, usually opening white but changing to rose, 2–3 in. wide, the very slender tube 3–5 in. long; stamens unequal; stigma 4-lobed: caps. stalked, short-obovate, about ½in. long, the 4 broad triangular wings widest above the middle. Chile.

15. **Œ. trichocalyx,** Nutt. (*Anogra trichocalyx,* Small). Per., usually with rootstock, ½–1 ft. high, sts. few, strigulose, with additional spreading hairs in upper parts: lvs. more or less pinnatifid, ½–2½ in. long, the cauline sessile: fls. few, in upper axils, nocturnal, white, 1–1½ in. wide; hypanthium slender, tinged reddish, 1 in. long: caps. subcylindric, ½–1 in. long, 1/16in. thick, often contorted. Wyo. to Colo. and Utah.—Confused with *Œ. deltoides.*

16. **Œ. deltoides,** Torr. & Frem. Coarse ann., frequently branched from base, more or less hairy above, branches ½–2½ ft. long: lower lf.-blades rhombic-obovate to -lanceolate: fls. white, mostly 1½–3 in. wide, nocturnal but lasting well into next day: caps. woody, 1–3 in. long, ⅛in. thick at base, spreading to reflexed. Southwestern deserts.

17. **Œ. cæspitosa,** Nutt. (*Pachylophus cæspitosus,* Spach). Per. or bien. to 4 ft., stemless or essentially so: lvs. clustered, oblong to narrow-lanceolate or spatulate, sometimes 1 ft. long, attenuate, repand-toothed, pubescent: fls. nocturnal, white or pink, 1½–3 in. wide, petals obcordate; hypanthium very slender, enlarging upward, 2–6 in. long, longer than ovary; stamens unequal; stigma 4-cleft: caps. lance-ovoid, pointed, 1–2 in. long, with wrinkled or contorted angles. S. D., Neb. west and south.—A very variable species; rather fragrant.

18. **Œ. bistorta,** Nutt. (*Sphærostigma bistortum,* Walp.). Ann. 1–2 ft. high, decumbent at base, hairy: radical lvs. spatulate to lanceolate, petiolate, dentate; st.-lvs. mostly sessile, ovate to narrow-lanceolate, about 1 in. long, dentate: fls. yellow turning green; calyx hirsute, hypanthium ⅛in. long; petals about ½in. long, usually with a brown spot at base; ovary 4-celled; stigma capitate: caps. sessile, linear, 4-angled, contorted, about ½in. long, not beaked; seeds in 1 row in each cell. S. Calif. Var. **Veitchiana,** Hook. (*Sphærostigma Veitchianum,* Small), is more slender; caps. ¾–1½ in. long, less contorted and with long slender terminal beak.

9. **GAURA,** L. Ann., bien. or per. herbs sometimes grown in the hardy border; species 18, confined to the warmer regions of N. Amer.—Lvs. alternate, sessile or stalked, entire, dentate or sinuate: fls. usually white or rose, in spikes or racemes; hypanthium deciduous, obconic, much prolonged beyond the ovary, the 4 lobes reflexed; petals clawed, unequal; stamens mostly 8, with a small scale-like appendage before the base of each filament; stigma 4-lobed, surrounded by a ring or cup-like border; ovary becoming 1-celled with 1 pendulous ovule: fr. nut-like, 3–4-ribbed. (Gau-ra: Greek *superb.*)

G. Lindheimeri, Engelm. & Gray. Plant 3 ft. high, sts. hairy, more or less branched above: lvs. sessile, lanceolate or spatulate, 1½–3½ in. long, appressed-pubescent, margins recurved, sinuate and remotely toothed: fls. white, in a loose terminal simple spike or paniculate-spicate infl., only a few in bloom at the same time; petals spatulate, about ¾in. long: fr. oblong or elliptic-oblong, ¼–⅜in. long, with acute angles and 1-ribbed faces. (Named in honor of Ferdinand Lindheimer, discoverer of the plant.) La., Tex.

10. **FUCHSIA,** L. About 100 species of shrubs or small trees, seldom climbing, mostly in trop. Amer. but a few in New Zeal. and Tahiti.—Lvs. simple, opposite, alternate or whorled: fls. mostly showy, axillary or sometimes racemose or paniculate, usually pendulous, in shades of red and purplish and with some parts often white; hypanthium (calyx-tube) bell-shaped to tubular, prolonged beyond the ovary;

calyx-lobes (sepals) 4, spreading; petals 4 or in some species wanting; stamens 8, mostly unequal, often exserted; style long-exserted, the entire or 4-lobed stigma prominent: fr. a 4-celled soft berry. (Fu-chsia: Leonard Fuchs, 1501–1565, German professor of medicine, and botanical author.)

A. Petals none: sts. procumbent, slender .... 1. *F. procumbens*
AA. Petals present: sts. ascending, shrubby.
B. Fls. erect in terminal cymose panicles .... 2. *F. arborescens*
BB. Fls. drooping, not in cymes.
C. Fl. small, inconspicuous; stamens short, the epipetalous reflexed.
D. Hypanthium obconic: lvs. subentire .... 3. *F. thymifolia*
DD. Hypanthium subcylindric: lvs. serrulate .... 4. *F. microphylla*
CC. Fl. showy; stamens more or less exserted, erect.
D. Tube of calyx (hypanthium) usually not longer than the lobes; stamens long-exserted.
E. Hypanthium mostly less than ¼in. long: twigs puberulent to pilose .... 5. *F. coccinea*
EE. Hypanthium 3⁄16–¾in. long: twigs almost or quite glabrous.
F. Petioles mostly less than ⅝in. long: hypanthium up to ⅜in. long, lobes about ⅛in. wide .... 6. *F. magellanica*
FF. Petioles mostly ⅜–1 in. long: hypanthium ⅝–1 in. long, lobes about ⅜in. wide .... 7. *F. hybrida*
DD. Tube of calyx (hypanthium) several times as long as lobes; stamens usually not much exceeding calyx-lobes.
E. Hypanthium ½–1 in. long.
F. Stamens conspicuously exserted; petals green .... 8. *F. splendens*
FF. Stamens not exserted; petals red .... 9. *F. triphylla*
EE. Hypanthium 1–2 in. long.
F. Lobes of calyx red, spreading-reflexed .... 10. *F. boliviana*
FF. Lobes of calyx green, divergent .... 11. *F. fulgens*

1. **F. procumbens,** Cunn. TRAILING FUCHSIA. TRAILING QUEEN. Plant with slender trailing much-branched sts., useful for hanging-baskets: lvs. alternate, long-stalked, cordate-ovate, ⅓–½in. wide: fls. erect, solitary and axillary, apetalous, the short hypanthium orange-colored, the obtuse reflexed calyx-lobes dark purple; anthers blue: berry glaucous-red. New Zeal.

2. **F. arborescens,** Sims (*F. syringæflora*, Carr.). Winter-flowering shrub: lvs. opposite or ternate, lanceolate-oblong or oblanceolate, entire or nearly so, laurel-like: infl. a naked erect terminal panicle; fls. pink-red, small, lilac-scented; hypanthium short, calyx-lobes and petals about equal. Mex.

3. **F. thymifolia,** HBK. Shrub with slender puberulent twigs: lvs. opposite or alternate, oval, ½–1¼ in. long, subentire: fls. pendulous, solitary, axillary, white to pink; pedicels puberulent, filiform, ¼–½in. long; hypanthium obconic, 3⁄16–¼in. long, calyx-lobes 3⁄16in., white aging red, spreading-reflexed, petals as long: berry globose, ¼in. long. Mex.

4. **F. microphylla,** HBK. Densely branched shrub: lvs. crowded, opposite, oblong-ovate, ¼–1 in. long, serrulate: fls. axillary, perfect or pistillate, deep red; hypanthium ¼–⅜in. long, subcylindric; petals ⅛–¼in. long: berry subglobose, purple-black, ¼in. thick. Mex.

5. **F. coccinea,** Soland. (*F. montana*, Cambess. *F. pubescens*, Cambess.). Shrub, sometimes semi-scandent, the younger growth puberulent and sometimes pilose, more or less reddish: lvs. opposite or ternate, ovate, ⅔–3 in. long, serrulate, with petioles up to ⅛in.: fls. solitary in upper axils; pedicels filiform, 1–1½ in. long; hypanthium subfusiform, red, 3⁄16–¼in. long; calyx-lobes red, ½–¾in. long and about ⅛in. wide, connate at base for ⅛–¼in.; petals violet to purplish, ¼–⅜in. long; stamens long-exserted: berry oblong. Brazil.—Garden material referred to *F. globosa*, Lindl., and *F. magellanica* var. *globosa*, Bailey, seems nearest to *F. coccinea* in the lvs. and hypanthium, while much of *F. Riccartonii*, Hort., and *F. magellanica* var. *Riccartonii*, Bailey, has the fusiform hypanthium and broad calyx-lobes of *F. coccinea* but the narrower less pubescent lvs. of *F. magellanica*.

6. **F. magellanica,** Lam. (*F. conica*, Lindl. *F. magellanica* var. *conica*, Bailey. *F. pumila*, Hort. *F. tenella*, Hort. *F. corallina*, Hort.). Shrub glabrous or nearly so: lvs. opposite or ternate or even in 4's, lance-ovate, glabrous to puberulent beneath, usually serrulate, the blades mostly not exceeding 1 in., petioles ⅛–⅝in. long: fls. in upper axils; pedicels ¾–1½ in. long; hypanthium narrow, cylindrical, ¼–⅜in. long, red, the calyx-lobes ⅝–1 in. long and about ¼in. wide, red, scarcely connate at base; petals ⅜–¾in. long, purplish; stamens exserted, reddish. Chile, Argentina. Var. **macrostema,** Munz (*F. macrostema*, Ruiz & Pav. *F. gracilis*, Lindl. *F. magellanica* var. *gracilis*, Bailey), lf.-blades 1–2 in. long, pedicels about 2–2½ in. long; S. Chile.—Long cult.

7. **F. hybrida,** Voss (*F. speciosa*, Hort.). The common garden fuchsia of the present day, very variable in many of its characters, differing from *F. magellanica* in having stouter branches, longer and broader lvs. and larger fls.: plant shrubby, glabrous or somewhat pubescent: lvs. ovate, 1½–4 in. long, toothed, often exceeding the pedicels: calyx usually crimson, the hypanthium twice or more as long as the ovary; petals purple, rose or white, ⅝–1 in. long, shorter than the calyx-lobes; stamens and style usually well-exserted.—

Probably mostly hybrid derivatives of *F. magellanica* forms and the larger-lvd. larger-fld. Mexican species *F. fulgens.* The fls. show every gradation from fls. with short hypanthium to those with one 3 in. long.

8. **F. splendens,** Zucc. Much-branched shrub: lvs. ovate-cordate, pale green, serrate: fls. solitary on slender axillary pedicels, 1½ in. long, drooping, the calyx scarlet, tipped pale green, the scarlet hypanthium with swollen base and compressed tube; petals ovate, greenish, shorter than the calyx-lobes; stamens long-exserted, the anthers yellow. Mex.

9. **F. triphylla,** L. Bushy plant 1½ ft. high, pubescent: lvs. often in 3's, small, oblanceolate, petiolate, dentate, green above, purple and pubescent beneath: fls. 1½ in. long, in terminal racemes, cinnabar-red, the long hypanthium enlarging toward the top; petals very short; stamens 4, not exserted. Santo Domingo, Haiti.

10. **F. boliviana,** Carr., var. **luxurians,** Johnston (*F. corymbiflora,* Auth. not Lindl.). Bushy to open shrub, densely pubescent: lvs. mostly opposite, elliptic to oblong, soft-pubescent, 3–7 in. long: fls. in terminal drooping clusters; pedicels ½in. long; hypanthium dark red, 1–2 in. long, gradually widened; calyx-lobes dark red, lanceolate, ⅜–¾in. long, spreading-reflexed; petals oblong, almost ½in. long; stamens scarcely exserted. Jamaica, Guatemala to Venezuela.

11. **F. fulgens,** DC. Tall shrub, sparsely pubescent: lvs. opposite, ovate, 2–7 in. long, fine-pubescent, rounded to cordate at base, serrulate: fls. in terminal racemes; pedicels ½–1 in. long; hypanthium red, 2–2½ in. long; calyx-lobes greenish, ½in. long, divergent; petals red, ⅜in. long. Mex.

Fig. 151. Haloragaceæ. *Myriophyllum exalbescens:* a, flowering branch, × 1; b, staminate flower, × 5; c, pistillate flower, × 15; d, same, vertical section, × 10.

151. HALORAGACEÆ. WATER MILFOIL FAMILY

Aquatic or terrestrial herbs, of very diverse appearance, comprising 8 genera and about 100 species of wide distribution.—Lvs. opposite, alternate or verticillate, from linear or pectinate-pinnatifid to very large and kidney-shaped: fls. bisexual or unisexual, regular, often minute, solitary or in axillary clusters or spikes; calyx-tube adnate to ovary, the limb 2–4-lobed or entire; petals 2–4 and deciduous or 0; stamens 1–8, the filaments short; ovary inferior, 1–4-celled with usually 1 ovule axile in each cell, with 1–4 styles and papillose or plumose stigmas: fr. an indehiscent nutlet or drupe, angular or winged.

A. Plant aquatic: lvs. pectinate-pinnatifid, whorled or alternate.................1. Myriophyllum
AA. Plant terrestrial: lvs. ovate or orbicular, usually very large, all radical.........2. Gunnera

1. **MYRIOPHYLLUM,** L. About 20 species of fresh-water herbs, widely dispersed over the world, a few grown in aquaria and ponds.—Lvs. alternate or whorled, pinnatifid into hair-like segms. or the emersed lvs. entire or dentate: monœcious, diœcious, or polygamous, the upper fls. staminate, lower pistillate, and intermediate fls. often bisexual, solitary or spicate, often 2-bracted; calyx-limb 4-lobed or 0; petals 4, often 0 or reduced in pistillate fls.; stamens 4–8; ovary 4-celled with 1 ovule in each cell, the styles 4 and very short: fr. splitting into 4 indehiscent carpels, often tuberculate on back. (Myriophyl-lum: Greek *myriad-leaved.*)

M. brasiliense, Cambess. (*M. proserpinacoides,* Gill.). Parrots-Feather. Sts. weak, growing about 6 in. out of water: lvs. all alike, feathery, in whorls of 4–6, to 1 in. long, with 10–25 hair-like segms.: plant diœcious: fls. in axils of submersed lvs. S. Amer.—A common hardy E. American monœcious species, **M. exalbescens,** Fern., has its infl. borne above surface of water and fl.-bracts entire.

2. **GUNNERA,** L. Per. herbs, often gigantic, of about 25 species in the southern hemisphere, the following sometimes grown as lawn foliage plants.—Rhizomes

creeping: lvs. all radical, petioled, ovate or orbicular, entire, toothed, or variously lobed: monœcious or polygamous, the upper fls. staminate, lower pistillate, with bisexual fls. between, in spikes or panicles, sometimes the infl. very dense and spadix-like; calyx-lobes 2–3 or 0; petals 2, hooded, or 0; stamens 1 or 2; ovary 1-celled, 1-ovuled, with 2 papillose styles: fr. a drupe. (Gunne-ra: after J. Ernst Gunner, 1718–1773, Norwegian botanist and bishop.)

A. Lvs. palmately-lobed, not peltate....................1. *G. chilensis*
AA. Lvs. pedately-lobed, peltate....................2. *G. manicata*

1. **G. chilensis,** Lam. (*G. scabra,* Ruiz & Pav.). Rhizome short, sts. thick, ending in a lf.-bud which is surrounded by large laciniate bracts: petiole large and fleshy, green, cylindrical, to 6 ft. long, covered with stiff hairs; lf.-blade rounded, cordiform, attaining 6 ft. in diam., palmately-lobed and incised: infl. a large spike to 3 ft. high, bearing many small spikes with inconspicuous apetalous fls.: fr. red. Chile, Ecuador, Colombia.

2. **G. manicata,** Lind. Differs from *G. chilensis* in its larger stature, the widely spreading rhizome, the gigantic orbicular lvs. which are peltate and pedately-lobed, and the reddish spiny hairs on the petioles. S. Brazil.

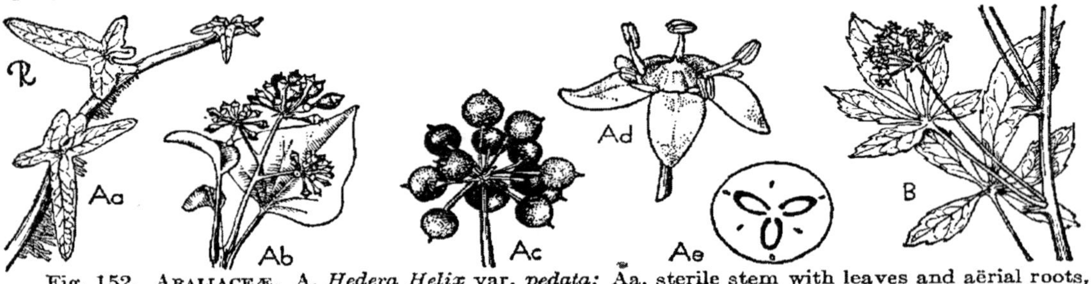

Fig. 152. Araliaceæ. A, *Hedera Helix* var. *pedata:* Aa, sterile stem with leaves and aërial roots, × ½; Ab, adult foliage with young fruiting inflorescence, × ¼; Ac, fruit, × ½; Ad, flower habit, × 2; Ae, ovary, cross-section, × 4. B, *Acanthopanax Sieboldianus:* flowering branch, × ½.

152. ARALIACEÆ. ARALIA or GINSENG FAMILY

Herbs, shrubs, and trees, sometimes climbing, upwards of 50 genera and probably 500 species, distributed around the world in both temp. and trop. regions, yielding a good number of subjects of ornamental foliage and habit and some medicinal products.—Sts. sometimes prickly: lvs. simple or in most genera compound or decompound, prevailingly alternate or verticillate: fls. small, greenish or whitish, not separately showy, commonly in umbels or umbellate heads, bisexual or unisexual, regular; calyx very small, adnate to ovary, the margin toothed or obsolete; petals mostly 5, valvate or imbricate, sometimes cohering at apex and falling as a cap; stamens usually as many as petals and alternate with them, attached on an epigynous disk; ovary 1, inferior, 1- to many-celled, ovule 1 in each cell and pendulous, styles as many as the cells or carpels: fr. a berry or drupe-like.—The family is much like Umbelliferæ, but the styles are usually more than 2, the fr. is mostly baccate and lacking in special internal structure, and the species run more into woody subjects.

A. Lvs. compound.
  B. Lf. odd-pinnate or multipinnate.
    C. Petals imbricate: herbs and deciduous woody plants....................1. Aralia
    CC. Petals valvate: evergrowing trop. woody plants....................2. Polyscias
  BB. Lf. palmate or multipalmate.
    C. Styles 10: evergrowing trop. woody plants....................3. Dizygotheca
    CC. Styles 5 or less.
      D. Petals valvate: woody deciduous plants....................4. Acanthopanax
      DD. Petals imbricate: little herbs....................5. Panax
AA. Lvs. simple, often deeply lobed.
  B. Plant erect (or not climbing).
    C. Fls. 5-merous or more.
      D. Styles connate: lvs. deciduous....................6. Kalopanax
      DD. Styles distinct: lvs. persistent....................7. Fatsia
    CC. Fls. 4-merous: lvs. persistent....................8. Tetrapanax
  BB. Plant normally climbing by aërial rootlets, at least at nodes....................9. Hedera

1. **ARALIA,** L. Aromatic herbs, shrubs, and small trees, about 20 species in Asia, Malaya, Australia, and N. Amer., some planted in the open; the greenhouse

aralias are species of Polyscias, Dizygotheca, and other genera.—Sts. spiny or unarmed: lvs. deciduous, alternate, 1- or more pinnate, lfts. serrate: fls. in panicled umbels, often very numerous and thereby showy, on articulated pedicels; calyx-lobes minute or wanting; petals imbricate; stamens 5; ovary usually 5-celled, the 5 styles distinct or connate only at base: fr. a few-seeded little berry or drupe-like body crowned by the styles, often becoming dry. (Ara-lia: etymology unexplained, perhaps from a vernacular name.)

A. Sts. unarmed: plant herbaceous.
  B. Plant stemless or nearly so: umbels few. . . . . 1. *A. nudicaulis*
  BB. Plant caulescent: umbels many in a panicle.
    C. Lvs. broad-ovate to nearly orbicular: fr. brown or purple . . . . 2. *A. racemosa*
    CC. Lvs. oblong-ovate: fr. black. . . . . 3. *A. cordata*
AA. Sts. armed with prickles or bristles: plant woody.
  B. Infl. of few umbels; pedicels glabrous: subshrub to 3 ft. . . . . 4. *A. hispida*
  BB. Infl. much compounded; pedicels pubescent: shrubs or trees to 30 ft. or more.
    C. Lfts. distinctly stalked. . . . . 5. *A. spinosa*
    CC. Lfts. nearly sessile.
      D. Main axis of infl. long. . . . . 6. *A. chinensis*
      DD. Main axis of infl. short, with spreading secondary axes . . . . 7. *A. elata*

1. **A. nudicaulis**, L. WILD SARSAPARILLA. Nearly stemless herb, with long rootstock and lf. and peduncle arising from the very short st. to about 1 ft. high: lvs. ternate, the parts pinnate into 3–5 ovate to ovate-lanceolate acuminate finely serrate lfts. 2–5 in. long: infl. usually of 3 simple umbels, the greenish fls. on slender glabrous pedicels: fr. purplish-black. Newf. to Ga. and Colo.

2. **A. racemosa**, L. AMERICAN SPIKENARD. Much-branched per. 3–6 ft. high, with large roots, glabrous or slightly pubescent: lvs. usually ternate, the parts pinnate into 3–5 ovate-cordate to nearly orbicular acuminate doubly serrate lfts. 2–6 in. long: umbels many, in panicles, the greenish fls. on pubescent pedicels: fr. purple or brown. N. B. to Ga. and Mo.

3. **A. cordata**, Thunb. (*A. edulis*, Sieb. & Zucc.). UDO. Stout spreading unarmed per. 4–10 ft. high, the young blanched shoots in spring eaten in Japan, and the plant now intro. in N. Amer. for similar purposes: lvs. 3–5-compound; lfts. long-ovate to oblong-ovate, 2–6 in. long, abruptly acuminate and short-stalked, cordate, rounded or oblique at base, coarsely serrate, glabrous above, light colored and more or less hairy on veins beneath: umbels many, in panicles to 1½ ft. long, pedicels slightly pubescent: fr. black. Japan, China.

4. **A. hispida**, Vent. BRISTLY SARSAPARILLA. Subshrub to 3 ft., with bristly sts. and petioles: lvs. bipinnate; lfts. ovate to oblong, 1–3 in. long, acute, sharply serrate, glabrous or pubescent on veins beneath: infl. of 3 to several simple umbels on slender peduncles, the white fls. on glabrous pedicels: fr. dark purple. Newf. to N. C. and Minn.

5. **A. spinosa**, L. DEVILS-WALKING-STICK. HERCULES CLUB. ANGELICA-TREE. Tree attaining 30 ft. or more, but usually known in gardens as a bush or tree-like shrub, with great lvs. clustered at the ends of the staff-like very spiny branches: lvs. 2-pinnate, 3–4 ft. long and half or more as broad, the clasping petiole and rachises usually bearing weak prickles; lfts. ovate, 2–3 in. long, acuminate, short-stalked, finely serrate, glaucous and glabrous or sometimes slightly pilose on veins beneath, veins curving before reaching margin: umbels assembled in great terminal clusters 3–4 ft. long, in midsummer, the whitish fls. on pubescent pedicels: fr. black. S. Pa. to Fla. and Tex.—Frequently planted for the oddity of its thick club-like branches.

6. **A. chinensis**, L. (*A. sinensis*, Hort.). CHINESE ANGELICA-TREE. Shrub or rarely tree to 30 ft., similar to *A. spinosa* but less prickly: lvs. bipinnate, 2–3 ft. long; lfts. ovate to broad-ovate, 2–6 in. long, acuminate, closely serrate, nearly or quite sessile, petiole and rachises unarmed, pubescent underneath, veins dividing before reaching margin and ending in teeth: umbels in a panicle 1–2 ft. long, the white fls. with pubescent pedicels. China.

7. **A. elata**, Seem. (*Dimorphanthus elatus*, Miq. *D. mandshuricus*, Rupr. & Maxim. *A. chinensis* var. *mandshurica*, Rehd. *A. japonica*, Hort.). JAPANESE ANGELICA-TREE. Differs from *A. chinensis* in the narrower lfts. remotely serrate and the infl. with short main axis and spreading secondary axes. N. E. Asia.

2. **POLYSCIAS**, Forst. Shrubs and trees with pungent-aromatic herbage, mostly glabrous, from Madagascar, the tropics of farther Asia and Polynesia, several ornamental glasshouse subjects and grown in yards and as hedges in Fla.; the genus is variously understood and the number of species uncertain, probably upwards of 75; some of the cult. kinds rarely bloom.—Lvs. variable, tending to be polymorphous, 1–5-pinnate, in cult. yielding cut-lvd. and other abnormal forms: fls. very small, in umbels or heads, sometimes in spikes, assembled in panicles or otherwise, on

articulated pedicels, 4-merous or 5-merous (usually the latter); calyx toothed or reduced to a truncate rim; petals valvate; ovary 5–8-celled, with styles usually of same number as cells. (Polys-cias: Greek *many* and *shade*, from the abundant foliage.)

A. Lvs. at least 3-pinnate; ultimate lfts. small........................1. *P. fruticosa*
AA. Lvs. 1-pinnate, or by monstrosity sometimes 2-pinnate.
  B. Lfts. elongated, entire or pinnatifid along the sides........................2. *P. filicifolia*
  BB. Lfts. nearly or quite as broad as long, apiculate-dentate.
    C. Base of lfts. tapering........................3. *P. Guilfoylei*
    CC. Base cordate, lfts. nearly orbicular........................4. *P. Balfouriana*

1. **P. fruticosa,** Harms (*Aralia fruticosa*, Hort. *Panax fruticosus*, *P. dissectus* and *P. excelsus*, Hort. *Nothopanax fruticosus*, Miq.). Erect glabrous shrub, 6–8 ft.: lvs. pinnately 3-compound or more finely divided in certain hort. forms, 1–2 ft. long, the petiole and rachis usually finely spotted; ultimate lfts. narrow-ovate to oblong or lanceolate, 1–4 in. long, stalked, variously serrate to laciniate, the regular serratures spinulose, apex very acute: infl. terminal and in the upper axils, the pedicels short making umbellate little heads; fls. very small, greenish: fr. about ⅓in. long. India to Polynesia.—Cult. in many forms, not often fruiting, some of them with dissected lvs. Var. **plumata,** Bailey, has small lvs., the blade 4–8 in. long, the ultimate segms. small and fine and very narrow; a prevailing series of forms.

2. **P. filicifolia,** Bailey (*Aralia filicifolia*, Moore). Stout glabrous shrub, 6–8 ft., the branchlets and petioles purplish: lvs. 1-pinnate, 1–2 ft. long, polymorphous on the same plant; lfts. all more or less stalked, what may be assumed to be the normal ones (even though less frequent) broad and wholly entire, long-lanceolate to oblong, 3–7 in. long and 2–3 in. broad, subcordate at base, short-pointed; other lvs. with all lfts. longer (often 1 ft.) or at least narrow, long-pointed, taper-based, pinnatifid and sharp-toothed: fls. small, on rather slender pedicels, in little umbels assembled in large diffuse panicles. Pacific isls., but widely spread in tropics, often under the name Angelica.

3. **P. Guilfoylei,** Bailey (*Aralia Guilfoylei*, Bull. *Nothopanax Guilfoylei*, Merr.). Strong erect glabrous shrub to 15–20 ft.: lvs. 1-pinnate, 12–18 in. long, with 2–4 pairs of well-separated stalked ovate, elliptic-ovate to nearly orbicular remotely tip-toothed lfts. 3–5 in. long, with short-pointed or obtusish apex and tapering or at least not cordate base, the petiole usually spotted or lined: fls. small, prominently pedicelled in long-peduncled umbels assembled in large open panicles. Polynesia; early collected by Guilfoyle.—Now much planted in American tropics, being known as Wild Coffee and Coffee-Tree. Usually the lfts. are variously edged and blotched white. It runs into many foliage forms, as var. **laciniata,** Bailey, with the white margins cut into narrow spreading very sharp unequal teeth or prongs, often with lfts. of different and odd sizes and shapes; var. **Victoriæ,** Bailey (*Aralia Victoriæ*, Hort.), a more compact form, with small much-divided and cut lfts., commonly grown in pots, the foliage more or less tufted or condensed.

4. **P. Balfouriana,** Bailey (*Aralia Balfouriana*, Hort.). A compact and bushy glabrous strict shrub as ordinarily grown under glass and in tubs, but in the tropics attaining 25 ft. and more, the young sts. usually bronzy-green speckled with gray: lvs. long-petioled; lfts. mostly 3, prominently stalked, usually white-margined-blotched, orbicular to somewhat reniform, 3–4 in. across, cordate or subcordate, not pointed, coarsely crenate or crenate-dentate, the teeth mostly apiculate: fls. slender-pedicelled in umbels clustered at the nodes on the long naked branches of a large infl. New Caledonia; now dispersed in the tropics.

3. **DIZYGOTHECA,** N. E. Br. FALSE ARALIA. A few unarmed woody araliads, probably from the Pacific isls.—Distinguished by digitate lvs., 10-celled ovary and 10 styles, and also by 4-celled rather than 2-celled anthers (whence the name Dizygothe-ca, *double receptacle*): certain greenhouse aralias are referred here provisionally until fls. and frs. are known; they are probably only juvenile forms of species, with slenderly divided foliage: in ours, the lfts. or digits are 7–11, narrowed to a petiolule-like base, attached at the apex of a long slender petiole; small shrubs as known in pot cult. Names of glasshouse stock are subject to revision.

A. Margins of lfts. undulate and serrate but not notched.
  B. Lfts. pendulous and filiform........................1. *D. elegantissima*
  BB. Lfts. scarcely pendulous, broader........................2. *D. Veitchii*
AA. Margins prominently notched........................3. *D. Kerchoveana*

1. **D. elegantissima,** Vig. & Guill. (*Aralia elegantissima*, Hort.). Petioles mottled white; lfts. 7–11, filiform, pendulous. Perhaps not in cult. in N. Amer.

2. **D. Veitchii,** N. Taylor (*Aralia Veitchii*, Hort.). Lfts. 9–11, about ¼in. broad, 5–6 in. long, undulate and more or less serrate, shining green above and reddish beneath. Runs into very narrow-lvd. forms, as var. **gracillima,** N. Taylor, with nearly filiform lfts. that have a narrow white rib.

3. **D. Kerchoveana,** N. Taylor (*Aralia Kerchoveana,* Hort.). Lfts. 7–11, mostly ½in. and more broad, prominently notched on both sides, the midrib pale; petioles handsomely mottled. (Kerchove de Denterghem, page 46.)

4. **ACANTHOPANAX,** Miq. A score or more of shrubs and trees of the E. Asian region, planted in the open for ornament.—Usually prickly: lvs. digitate, alternate, deciduous: fls. bisexual or unisexual, in umbels that often are arranged in large panicles; petals and stamens commonly 5, but sometimes 4, the former valvate; cells of ovary and styles 2–5: fr. a blackish 2–5-seeded little berry. (Acanthop-anax: *spiny panax.*)

A. Sieboldianus, Makino (*A. pentaphyllus,* March. *Aralia pentaphylla,* Sieb. & Zucc. not Thunb.). Large shrub or small tree to 10 ft., with arching branches and sharp rather weak spines below the petioles, diœcious: lvs. palmate, the ovate-oblong or oblong-obovate serrate glabrous rather thin lfts. 5 or 7 and 2½ in. or less long: umbels on last year's growth, about 1 in. across, solitary on peduncles 2–4 in. long; styles connate: fls. greenish-white: fr. black. Japan, China.—Planted for shrubbery, apparently only the pistillate plant cult. in N. Amer.; there is a form with white-edged lvs.

5. **PANAX,** L. As here accepted, a half dozen species of low per. herbs in N. Amer. and E. Asia, two cult. for the root that is used medicinally by Chinese and others.—Root erect or horizontal, elongated or tuber-like: st. simple, bearing a whorl of 3 or 5 palmate lvs., the lfts. usually 5 and serrate or dentate: fls. in terminal simple umbels, bisexual or unisexual, greenish; calyx obscurely 5-toothed; petals 5, imbricate; carpels and styles 2 or 3: fr. a small drupe-like berry. (Pa-nax: Greek, a panacea, *all healing.*)

A. Lfts more or less obovate, abruptly acuminate, coarsely serrate or toothed....... 1. *P quinquefolius*
AA. Lfts. not obovate, gradually acuminate, finely serrate........................ 2. *P. Schin-seng*

1. **P. quinquefolius,** L. American Ginseng. Glabrous, 6–18 in. high, from a deep spindle-shaped sometimes forked root; scales at base of st. thin and perishing: lfts. oblong-obovate, 3–5 in. long, thin, rather abruptly or boldly narrowed toward apex, the margins coarsely serrate or dentate, nerves on upper surface with few inconspicuous setæ: umbel solitary, with 6–20 pedicelled fls.: fr. nearly ½in. diam., bright red, on an elongated peduncle. Rich woods, Que., N. Y. to Mo.—Also cult. for the roots for export; often defined broadly to include the oriental species (no. 2).

2. **P. Schin-seng,** Nees (*P. Ginseng,* Mey.). Asiatic Ginseng. Root often divided at end; scales at base of st. fleshy and persistent: lvs. oblong-ovate, gradually tapering to point, finely double-serrate, the nerves above with conspicuous white setæ. Manchuria and Korea.—Little cult. in N. Amer.

6. **KALOPANAX,** Miq. One deciduous tree native in E. Asia, hardy in N. U. S.—Branches with short prickles: lvs. palmately lobed, long-stalked, toothed: fls. bisexual, in umbels forming large compound panicles; calyx minutely 5-toothed; petals 5, valvate; ovary 2-celled, styles connate: fr. a 2-seeded drupe. (Kalop-anax: Greek *handsome* and *panax.*)

K. pictus, Nakai (*Acer pictum,* Thunb. *Acanthopanax ricinifolius,* Seem. *A. septemlobus,* Koidz. *K. ricinifolius,* Miq.). To 80 ft. or more: lvs. nearly orbicular, 4–12 in. across, with 5–7 triangular-ovate acuminate toothed lobes, becoming glabrous, nerves prominent beneath: fls. white, the infl. 8–12 in. across: fr. bluish-black, crowned by style. Var. **Maximowiczii,** Hara (*Aralia Maximowiczii,* VanHoutte. *Acanthopanax ricinifolius* var. *Maximowiczii,* Schneid.), has lvs. lobed beyond the middle into oblong-lanceolate lobes pubescent beneath.

7. **FATSIA,** Decne. & Planch. One evergreen unarmed large bush or small tree, planted in mild regions for subtrop. effect.—Lvs. large, palmately lobed: fls. long-pedicelled, in many paniculate umbels, bisexual or unisexual; calyx with 5 or 6 teeth; petals 5, valvate; stamens 5; ovary 5-celled and with 5 distinct styles: fr. nearly globular, black, bearing the spreading styles. (Fat-sia: from a Japanese name.)

F. japonica, Decne. & Planch. (*Aralia japonica,* Thunb. *A. Sieboldii,* Hort.). Making a broad bushy subject, reaching 15 or 20 ft., glabrous or soon becoming so, little branched: lvs. stiff, shiny above, orbicular to reniform in outline, 8–16 in. across, cordate or truncate at base, cut below the middle into 5–9 ovate-oblong dentate and undulate lobes, with sinuses open at bottom; petiole 8–12 in. or more long; lvs. sometimes marked and bordered with golden-yellow: fls. whitish, in summer and autumn, in umbels more than 1 in. across: fr. ⅛in. across. Japan.

8. **TETRAPANAX,** Koch. One tomentose species, distinguished from Fatsia in the sepal-lobes, petals and stamens being 4; ovary 2-celled, styles 2. (Tetrap-anax: *four* and *panax*.)

T. papyriferus, Koch (*Aralia papyrifera*, Hook. *Fatsia papyrifera*, Benth. & Hook.). RICE-PAPER PLANT. Tall stout bush or small spineless tree 6–8 ft. high, the young growth covered heavily with stellate more or less deciduous tomentum: lvs. cordate-ovate in outline, 10–12 in. across, 7–12-lobed to middle or less, margins toothed, upper surface becoming nearly or quite glabrous, lower surface remaining felty: fls. yellowish-white, pedicelled, in many globular umbels in a large woolly panicle to 1½ ft. across: fr. small, globular. S. China, Formosa.—Planted in mild climates for its bold effect, and in the Orient for the making of rice-paper.

9. **HEDERA,** L. IVY. A half dozen or less species of evergreen shrubs native Eu. to Japan, one in common cult. to cover walls and as a house plant.—All species characterized by juvenile and adult habit and foliage; the more common sterile juvenile form climbing, sts. with aërial rootlets and lvs. lobed; the fertile adult form in nature branching from the juvenile, characterized by non-climbing sts. without aërial rootlets and lvs. unlobed; erect shrubs may be produced asexually from branches of adult form: lvs. alternate: fls. bisexual, greenish, in umbels assembled in terminal panicles or racemes; calyx 5-toothed; petals 5, valvate; stamens 5; ovary 5-celled, styles joined into 1: fr. a 3–5-seeded small berry. (Hed-era: classical name of ivy.)

A. Hairs of petiole and lower side of lf. all stellate. . . . . 1. *H. Helix*
AA. Hairs scale-like, or hairs of both scale-like and stellate types present.
B. Twigs and petioles usually burgundy-red: lvs. thin and glossy. . . . . 2. *H. canariensis*
BB. Twigs and petioles green: lvs. leathery, dull. . . . . 3. *H. colchica*

1. **H. Helix,** L. ENGLISH IVY. Polymorphous species represented by nearly 40 recognized foliage forms: juvenile lvs. widely various, stiffish, usually 3–5-lobed, sometimes cleft, margins nearly or quite entire, narrowly or broadly triangular-ovate to nearly reniform in outline, varying in size from ½–5 in. long and of similar width, bases usually cordate to truncate, veins often light colored; lvs. on fruiting branches usually narrowly ovate, unlobed, with truncate to cuneate base: fr. globose, usually black, about ¼in. across. (Helix: Latin name for a kind of ivy.) Eu., extensively nat. elsewhere.—There are many variegated-lvd. forms, the commonest being: Var. **Cavendishii,** Paul (*H. Helix* var. *marginata*, Hibb.), with marginal lf. areas variegated white or cream-colored; var. **discolor,** Lawrence (*H. Helix discolor*, Hibb.), with some or all lvs. showing variegation not forming a marginal band or zone. Of the non-variegated forms var. **hibernica,** Jaeg. (*H. Helix hibernica*, Kirchn.), IRISH IVY, is perhaps the commonest, characterized by large dark green lvs. whose terminal lobe is very broad with sinuses shallow, and distinguished further from the typical form by lf.-veins green above rather than whitish. Shrubby non-climbing asexual forms with no aërial rootlets include the typical adult stage (var. *arborescens*, Lodd. var. *arborea*, Hort.) and var. **poetica,** West., differing primarily in larger and orange fr., while a compact shrubby form with aërial rootlets is var. **conglomerata,** Rehd. (*H. conglomerata*, Haage & Schmidt), with small lvs. having rounded lobes; another similar to it but lvs. with sharply acute terminal lobes is var. **erecta,** Schulze, and a climbing element having 5-lobed lvs. with an elongated narrow terminal lobe broadest about one-third its length above the base is var. **pedata,** Rehd. (*H. Helix pedata*, Hibb. *H. Helix Caenwoodiana*, Nichols.). Many vernacular-named vars. are characterized by lateral branches produced abundantly and precociously in most lf.-axils and are often preferred for interior use.

2. **H. canariensis,** Willd. ALGERIAN IVY. Twigs slender, dull burgundy-red (green in one variegated form), becoming glabrous; aërial rootlets few and remote: juvenile lvs. glossy, pale green, mostly triangular, usually shallowly 3-lobed: fr. black. Azores, Canary Isls., N. W. Afr.—Not hardy under severe winter conditions. Several variegated-lvd. vars. are recognized, the commonest being var. **variegata,** Schulze (var. Gloire de Marengo. *H. algeriensis variegata*, Paul), lvs. cream-colored with blue- or gray-green zones in mid-section and along main veins. Var. **striata,** Lawrence, lvs. dark green marginally with mid-section of blade and lobes streaked pale green or ivory.

3. **H. colchica,** Koch (*H. amurensis*, Hort.). COLCHIS IVY. Twigs stout, pale green, densely scaly; aërial rootlets at most nodes: juvenile lvs. leathery, broadly ovate, 3-lobed, base cordate, usually 2–6 in. long, emitting celery-like odor when crushed: fr. blue-black. S. E. Eu., Asia Minor.—A denticulately-margined variant is known in both green and variegated-lvd. forms.

Fig. 153. UMBELLIFERÆ. A, *Apium graveolens:* Aa, inflorescence and leaf-blade, × ½; Ab, fruit, side and face view, × 10. B, *Eryngium planum:* Ba, flowering branch, × ½; Bb, flower, × 3. C, *Trachymene cærulea:* Ca, flowering branch, × ½; Cb, flower, × 3; Cc, same, vertical section, × 3; Cd, ovary, cross-section, × 10. D, *Fœniculum vulgare:* Da, fruit, × 3; Db, same, cross-section, × 6. E, *Levisticum officinale:* Ea, inflorescence and leaf-blade, × ½; Eb, fruit, face view, × 3; Ec, same, side view, × 3. F, *Daucus Carota:* Fa, inflorescence and leaf-blade, × ½; Fb, umbellet, × 4; Fc, fruit, side and face view, × 4.

153. UMBELLIFERÆ. PARSLEY FAMILY

A distinct or "natural" family of about 250 genera and 1,500–2,000 species widely dispersed throughout boreal, temp., and subtrop. regions but rare in the tropics except in the mts.; the name is derived from the prevailing umbellate infl.; many species are cult. for food, others for ornament and for medicinal products.—Herbs or rarely shrubs; sts. often hollow: lvs. alternate, mostly compound, the petioles expanded or sheathing at base: infl. consisting of a simple or compound umbel, the secondary being known as umbellets; general umbel often subtended by bracts which form an involucre, the umbellets subtended by bractlets forming the involucels; fls. small, usually bisexual, regular or the outer irregular, epigynous; sepals minute or wanting; petals 5, incurved in the bud; stamens 5, alternating with the petals, inserted around an epigynous disk; ovary inferior, 2-celled, each cell 1-seeded; styles 2: fr. (known to gardeners as "seeds") consisting of 2 dry, ribbed or winged, 1-seeded, indehiscent carpels (mericarps), which commonly separate at base, but remain attached at the top to a slender flexuous Y-shaped stalk (carpophore) from which they dangle; each carpel with 5 lengthwise primary ribs and often 4 intermediate secondary ones, the spaces between the ribs known as the intervals, and the plane of the contiguous faces the commissure; one or more oil-tubes or longitudinal canals (vittæ) carrying aromatic oil often occur in the intervals; the fr. is said to be dorsally compressed when flattened parallel to the plane of the commissural face, laterally compressed when flattened at right angles to the face (the technical structure of fr. is mostly omitted in this account of the horticultural kinds).

A. Fls. sessile, in involucrate heads or spikes: lvs. and bracts often spinose-tipped and more or less spinose-toothed .... 1. ERYNGIUM
AA. Fls. pedicelled, in umbels.
  B. Umbels simple; fls. blue or white .... 2. TRACHYMENE
  BB. Umbels compound.
    C. Lvs. palmately lobed or parted .... 3. ASTRANTIA
    CC. Lvs. ternate or pinnate.
      D. Ultimate lf.-segms. linear-filiform (in Coriandrum and Carum upper lf.-segms. may be filiform).
        E. Color of fls. white or pink: fr. bristly .... 4. CUMINUM
        EE. Color of fls. yellow: fr. not bristly.
          F. Rays equal or nearly so; umbels clustered at tip of st., the central umbel nearly sessile: fr. about ½in. long .... 5. FERULA
          FF. Rays unequal; umbels not as above: fr. not over ¼in. long.
            G. Fr. strongly flattened, the lateral ribs distinctly winged .... 6. ANETHUM
            GG. Fr. not strongly flattened, the ribs not winged .... 7. FŒNICULUM
      DD. Ultimate lf.-segms. not filiform, linear, lanceolate, or broader.
        E. Herbage or sts. hairy.
          F. Primary lf.-rachis ternate; lf.-segms. 3–6 in. across .... 8. HERACLEUM
          FF. Primary lf.-rachis pinnate (although ultimate divisions of lf. may be ternate); lf.-segms. much smaller.
            G. Lf. 1-pinnate or basal lf. simple .... 9. PIMPINELLA
            GG. Lf. 2- or more pinnate.
              H. Involucral bracts as long as rays of umbel .... 10. DAUCUS
              HH. Involucral bracts shorter than rays, or lacking.
                I. Bracts of involucre usually lacking: fr. beakless .... 11. CHÆROPHYLLUM
                II. Bracts present at flowering time: fr. abruptly narrowed into beak.
                  J. Primary and secondary divisions of lvs. acuminate: fr. ¾ to nearly 1 in. long .... 12. MYRRHIS
                  JJ. Primary and secondary divisions of lvs. acute: fr. about ⅜in. long .... 13. ANTHRISCUS
        EE. Herbage and sts. glabrous.
          F. Color of fls. yellow.
            G. Involucral bracts lacking .... 14. PASTINACA
            GG. Involucral bracts present.
              H. St. stout: bracts reflexed: fr. oblong .... 15. LEVISTICUM
              HH. St. slender: bracts not reflexed: fr. ovate .... 16. PETROSELINUM
          FF. Color of fls. white.
            G. Outer fls. of umbellets with petals enlarged and ray-like .... 17. CORIANDRUM
            GG. Outer fls. not as above.
              H. Lf. biternate.
                I. Plant 1½ ft. or less high: umbels 1½–3 in. across .... 18. ÆGOPODIUM
                II. Plant 6 ft. or more high: umbels 3–6 in. across .... 19. ANGELICA
              HH. Lf. pinnate.
                I. Involucral bracts lacking or minute.
                  J. Segms. of lf. linear .... 20. CARUM
                  JJ. Segms. of lf. lanceolate .... 21. CICUTA
                II. Involucral bracts conspicuous.
                  J. Sts. spotted with purple .... 22. CONIUM
                  JJ. Sts. not spotted.
                    K. The lf. 1-pinnate into lanceolate segms.: grown for the edible root .... 23. SIUM
                    KK. The lf. decompound into cuneate-obovate segms.: grown for the edible lf.-stalks .... 24. APIUM

1. **ERYNGIUM,** L. Eryngo. About 220 species, widely dispersed in warm and temp. regions, most abundant in the Medit. area; several are grown for their showy blue heads and often bluish upper lvs.—Glabrous ann. or per. herbs (or rarely shrubby): lvs. mostly rigid, coriaceous, simple, lobed or variously cut, the margins nearly always spiny: fls. small, white, greenish or blue, sessile or subsessile, bracteolate, in involucrate heads or spikes; calyx prominent, mostly rigid, sometimes spinose-tipped; petals erect; disk expanded; styles slender: fr. ovoid or obovoid or more or less globose, scaly or tuberculate, without ribs, the carpels nearly terete and with usually 5 oil-tubes. (Eryn-gium: Greek name for some sort of thistle.)

A. Lvs. sword-shaped, parallel-veined....................1. *E. yuccifolium*
AA. Lvs. broader, palmately-veined.
B. Heads subtended by bipinnate bracts....................2. *E. alpinum*
BB. Heads subtended by simple bracts.
C. Basal lvs. deeply lobed or divided.
D. Lf. pinnatifid....................3. *E. amethystinum*
DD. Lf. palmately 3–5-parted....................4. *E. Bourgatii*
CC. Basal lvs. entire or shallowly 3-lobed.
D. Plant to 6 ft. high: bracts 3–4 in. long....................5. *E. giganteum*
DD. Plant 1–3 ft. high: bracts 2 in. or less long.
E. Bracts ovate, with coarse spiny teeth....................6. *E. maritimum*
EE. Bracts linear, spinulose.
F. Length of head about ½in.: basal lvs. evenly dentate....................7. *E. planum*
FF. Length of head about 1½in.: basal lvs. irregularly laciniate-dentate.8. *E. Oliverianum*

1. **E. yuccifolium,** Michx. Button Snakeroot. Rattlesnake Master. St. 2–6 ft. high, branching above: lvs. sword-shaped or broadly linear, tapering to a point, rigid, mostly clasping, finely parallel-veined, bristly-margined, the lower sometimes 3 ft. long and 1½ in. wide: heads clustered, ovate-globose, ¾–1 in. diam., white or pale blue, with lanceolate cuspidate-tipped spreading or ascending bracts shorter than the head, the ovate bractlets similar, July–Sept. Conn. to Fla and Tex.—This species is often confused with *E. aquaticum,* L. (*E. virginianum,* Lam.), which differs in the reticulate-veined lvs. entire or remotely toothed, and the smaller heads with reflexed bracts equalling or exceeding the heads; N. J. to Ga.

2. **E. alpinum,** L. St. from a thick root, 2 ft. or more high, branching above: basal lvs. deeply cordate-triangular, about 10 in. long, acuminate, coarsely double-crenate, very long-petioled; st.-lvs. round-cordate, often 3-lobed at apex or palmatifid, the upper bluish-tinged: heads globose-cylindric, about 1¼ in. long, blue or white, July–Aug.; involucral bracts 12–18, lance-oblong, rigid, bipinnate, spinulose, equalling or surpassing the head; bractlets ¼in. long. Eu.

3. **E. amethystinum,** L. Plant stout, 1½ ft. or more high, blue or amethystine above, or sometimes whitish; root thick, long-cylindric; st. remotely leafy, branched, 4–6-forked at top: lvs. rigid, obovate or oblong-ovate, bipinnatifid, spinose-toothed, lower with long petioles; upper st.-lvs. clasping, pinnately parted, spinulose-toothed: heads ovoid-globose, ½in. or more long, blue, June–Sept.; involucral bracts 6–9, unequal, linear-subulate or lanceolate, sharp-pointed, entire or slightly spinulose; bractlets lanceolate-subulate, the lower 3-cuspidate, the upper entire. Eu.—Much of the material grown under this name is *E. planum.*

4. **E. Bourgatii,** Gouan. Low plant often to 1½ ft. high; root stout, turnip-shaped: basal lvs. nearly orbicular, about 2 in. long, palmately 3–5-parted nearly to base, long-petioled, segms. 3-lobed and spiny-toothed; st.-lvs. sessile: heads ovoid, about ¾in. long, blue; involucral bracts 9–15, unequal, entire or with few spiny teeth; bractlets entire. (Named for a French botanist, Bourgat.) Medit. region.

5. **E. giganteum,** Bieb. Plant stout, 6 ft. high, the root thick and turnip-shaped, the st. simple below and 4–5-forked above: lvs. leathery, spinulose-dentate or -serrate, to 6 in. long and 4 in. wide, petioled, the basal broadly cordate or cordate-triangular; st.-lvs. more or less 3-lobed: heads cylindric or ovoid-cylindric, 3–4 in. long, in an ample infl., blue or pale green; involucral bracts lanceolate or obovate, very rigid, much cut, 4 in. long; fls. very many. Caucasus, Asia Minor.

6. **E. maritimum,** L. Sea-Holly. Plant glaucous-bluish, stiff, much-branched, about 1 ft. high: lvs. fleshy, very stiff, strongly veined, broad-ovate, more or less 3-lobed, 2–4 in. long and wide, with coarse spinose teeth, the basal and lower st.-lvs. with long stout petioles, the upper sessile and clasping: heads nearly globular, to 1 in. long, pale blue; involucral bracts 5–8, ovate, spinose-toothed, much smaller than the lvs.; bractlets with 3 stout spines at tip. Eu.

7. **E. planum,** L. Plant 3 ft. high, the st. 3–5-forked at top; root thick, turnip-shaped, very long: basal lvs. cordate, oblong or oval or broadly obovate, obtuse, spinulose, usually palmately 7–9-nerved, about 6 in. long and 3 in. wide; lower st.-lvs. short-petioled, shaped like the basal lvs. or 3-lobed with lobes deeply serrate or cut; upper lvs. sessile, 3–5-parted: heads blue, ovoid or nearly globular, about ½in. long, July, Aug.; involucral bracts mostly

linear, rarely broader and subfoliaceous, rigid, somewhat spinulose-serrate, about 1 in. long; bractlets linear, the lower 3-cuspidate, the upper entire and spinose-tipped. Eu., Asia.

8. **E. Oliverianum,** Delar. (*E. alpinum* var. *Oliverianum,* Spreng.). Hybrid, of uncertain parentage: plant strong, 3 ft. high: lower lvs. long-petioled, broadly cordate-ovate, indistinctly 3-lobed at apex, unequally spinulose-serrate; younger and lower st.-lvs. 3-lobed or -parted, the lobes again more or less lobed or angled and the margins spinose-serrate; upper st.-lvs. palmately 4–5-parted: heads blue, cylindric-ovoid, many-fld., about 1½ in. long; involucral bracts 10–15, subulate or linear, somewhat spinulose, equalling the heads; bractlets 3-cuspidate or the upper entire. (Seeds sent from the East by Oliver.)

2. **TRACHYMENE,** Rudge. A dozen species or more, mostly Australian, but a few from Borneo, New Caledonia, and Celebes, one cult. for its showy fls.—Hirsute or rarely glabrous ann. or per. herbs or sometimes of woody growth: lvs. ternately dissected or rarely undivided, toothed: fls. white or blue, in simple umbels; involucral bracts linear, often connate: fr. often hirsute or tuberculate, laterally compressed. (Trachym-ene: Greek *rough membrane,* alluding to the fr.)

T. cærulea, R. Grah. (*Didiscus cærulea,* Hook.). Blue Lace-Flower. Erect ann. about 2 ft. high, somewhat hairy: lvs. 1–2-triparted with acute linear or cuneate entire or 3-fid lobes: fls. blue, very numerous, in umbels 2–3 in. across borne on long peduncles, July–Oct.; calyx-teeth obsolete; petals unequal, the external being longer: fr. broader than long, strongly compressed laterally, constricted at the commissure. Australia.

3. **ASTRANTIA,** L. Masterwort. Perhaps a half dozen species, native to Eu. and W. Asia, one in common cult. as a border-plant.—Erect glabrous herbs, with branching sts. and dark colored aromatic roots: lvs. palmately lobed or dissected, petioled, the st.-lvs. often sessile and more nearly simple: umbels irregularly compound or simple, the many bractlets often colored; polygamous, the sterile fls. long-pedicelled, fertile short-pedicelled: fr. ovoid to oblong, subterete or slightly compressed dorsally. (Astran-tia: name in allusion to the star-like appearance of the umbels.)

A. major, L. Per. with st. simple or nearly so, 1–3 ft. high: lvs. mostly in a basal tuft, long-petioled, deeply palmately 5-lobed or -parted, the acute lobes ovate-lanceolate and more or less toothed or cleft; st.-lvs. few, deeply 3–5-lobed, the petioles widely expanded and clasping: umbel compound, the rays unequal, often branching and bearing 2–3 umbellets, May, June; involucre resembling the st.-lvs. but sessile; rays often bracteolate midway or at the forks; involucel of 12–20 oblanceolate mucronate often purplish-tinged bractlets surpassing the fls.; umbellets mostly with long-pedicelled sterile fls. and short-pedicelled fertile fls., pinkish, rose or white; calyx-lobes lanceolate and spinulose-tipped, exceeding the petals: fr. obovate-cylindric, the ribs covered with bladdery scales. Eu.

4. **CUMINUM,** L. One little herb native to the Medit. region, occasionally cult., its aromatic fr. being used in flavoring.—Slender ann., glabrous except for its fr.: lvs. dissected into filiform divisions: fls. in compound few-rayed umbels with bracts and bractlets narrow and somewhat rigid: fr. narrowly oblong, slightly compressed laterally. (Cu-minum: ancient Greek word.)

C. Cyminum, L. (*C. odorum,* Salisb.). Cumin. About 6 in. or more high, the slender st. branched above: lvs. with few filiform acerose-tipped divisions ½–2 in. long: umbel few-fld., with short rays and raylets; involucral bracts simple or with 1–2 very narrow segms., ½–2 in. long; fls. white or rose-color, in late spring: fr. ¼in. long, bristly. (Cyminum: same as Cuminum.)

5. **FERULA,** L. Large plants of 50–60 species, native to S. Eu., N. Afr., and W. Asia, a few cult. as ornamentals for their finely cut lvs. and many umbels of yellow fls.—Glabrous, often glaucous per. herbs, with thick roots: lvs. pinnately decompound, the ultimate segms. commonly filiform or small: fls. small, in elevated compound many-rayed umbels; bracts and bractlets few to many or sometimes lacking: fr. orbicular or ovate, dorsally compressed, membranous-bordered. (Fer-ula: old Latin name, perhaps from the verb *to strike;* possibly the sts. were anciently used as ferules.)

F. communis, L. Common Giant Fennel. Plant robust, 8–12 ft. high: lvs. light green, very numerous, forming a mound or clump, the segms. linear-setaceous; lf.-sheaths very large: umbels clustered, the central umbel of a branch nearly sessile, the surrounding ones stalked and mostly of staminate fls.; rays equal or nearly so; fls. greenish-yellow, in spring: fr. strongly flattened dorsally, about ½in. long. S. Eu. to Syria.

6. **ANETHUM,** L. Two small herbs, native to the Old World, one widely grown for its frs. which are used as seasoning.—Ann. or bien., with branching st., glabrous: lvs. 3–4-pinnately divided into long narrowly linear or filiform segms.: umbels large, compound, with many long rays; involucres and involucels lacking; fls. yellow, on short pedicels: fr. elliptic, flattened dorsally, the lateral ribs winged. (Ane-thum: *anethon*, ancient Greek name of the dill.)

A. graveolens, L. Dill. St. very smooth, 2–3 ft. high: lvs. finely dissected, fennel-like, the ultimate divisions to ¾in. long: umbels to 6 in. across, rays somewhat unequal; fls. yellowish, the petals falling early, in late summer: fr. with dorsal ribs thin and sharp, lateral with distinct narrow wings, about ⅙in. long. Eu.; nat. in N. Amer. and W. Indies.—Seeds and sometimes foliage used for flavoring. Medicinal preparations are also made from the plant.

7. **FŒNICULUM,** Mill. Old World plants, about 4 species, one commonly cult. for its aromatic frs. and lvs.—Glabrous erect ann., bien., or per. herbs: lvs. pinnately decompound, the segms. linear or filiform: fls. yellow, in compound umbels; involucre and involucels none; calyx-teeth obsolete: fr. linear-oblong, glabrous, terete or nearly so, the carpels dorsally flattened and prominently ribbed; oil-tubes solitary in the intervals. (Fœnic-ulum: diminutive from the Latin for *hay*, because of its odor.)

F. vulgare, Mill. (*Anethum Fœniculum*, L. *F. officinale*, All. *F. Fœniculum*, Karst.). Fennel. Per. of short duration, cult. as an ann. or bien., more or less glaucous; st. erect, branching, 3–5 ft. high: lvs. 3–4-pinnately compound, the ultimate segms. very narrow and thread-like and to 1½ in. long, the petioles broad and clasping: umbels large, of 15–20 or more rays, summer and autumn. S. Eu. Var. **dulce,** Fiori (*F. dulce*, Mill.), Florence Fennel, Finocchio, base of lvs. much enlarged and thickened, an article of food when blanched. Var. **piperitum,** Ball (*F. piperitum*, DC.), Carosella, Italian Fennel, grown for the young sts. which are eaten.

8. **HERACLEUM,** L. Cow-Parsnip. About 60 species in the northern hemisphere, one sometimes planted for bold effects.—Per. herbs: lvs. large, ternately compound: umbels compound; involucre lacking or of few deciduous bracts; involucels of numerous linear bractlets; fls. white or pinkish, outer petals enlarged and ray-like: fr. oval to orbicular, flattened dorsally, lateral ribs broadly winged; oil-tubes conspicuous. (Heracle-um: dedicated to Hercules.)

H. maximum, Bartram (*H. lanatum*, Michx.). Stout, 4–8 ft. high: lvs. to 1½ ft. long, the petioles much inflated, ternate into cordate-ovate lobed and toothed segms. 3–6 in. across, tomentose beneath: umbels 6–20 in. across, on tomentose peduncles 2–8 in. long, the stout rays 2–4 in. long: fr. broad-oval, narrowed basally, to ½in. long, the ribs extending scarcely to middle. N. Amer., Siberia.—A coarser taller puberulent species is **H. Mantegazzianum,** Somm. & Levier, easily distinguished by the ribs of the frs. extending well beyond the middle and the frs. broadly obtuse basally; Italy (named for Paulo Mantegazza, 1831–1910, Italian physiologist and anthropologist).

9. **PIMPINELLA,** L. Herbaceous perennials or rarely annuals, numbering about 75 species, widely dispersed, one cult. for condimental and medicinal purposes.—Lvs. pinnately or ternately decompound or rarely only toothed: fls. white or yellow, in compound umbels; involucral bracts lacking or rarely 1–2; involucels commonly of few small bractlets: fr. ovate or broader than long, laterally compressed; oil-tubes various. (Pimpinel-la: possibly from the Latin *bipinnula*, bipinnate.)

P. Anisum, L. Anise. Ann. 2½ ft. high or less, pubescent: basal lvs. long-petiolate, 1–2 in. long, simple with coarse irregular teeth; st.-lvs. 1-pinnate or ternate, the lobes narrow, cuneate, entire or toothed: fls. small, yellowish-white, in large loose umbels, late summer and autumn: fr. ovate, slightly compressed laterally, constricted at the commissure, the ribs evident. (Anisum: *anysum*, old Arabic name.) Greece to Egypt; escaped in Mass.

10. **DAUCUS,** L. More or less weedy plants of about 60 species very widely distributed, one commonly cult. for its fleshy edible roots.—Bristly ann. or per. herbs: lvs. pinnately decompound with small narrow segms.: fls. small, white or yellowish, in compound involucrate umbels: fr. ovate or oblong, more or less dorsally

flattened, ribs bristly; oil-glands solitary under the secondary ribs. (Dau-cus: ancient Greek name.)

D. Carota, L., var. **sativa,** DC. CULTIVATED CARROT. Ann. or bien., more or less bristly, with erect much-branched st. 2–3 ft. high, from a thick fleshy tap-root: lvs. mostly on long petioles expanded at base, pinnately decompound, the many ultimate segms. nearly linear and acute: fls. white or yellowish, small and numerous, borne in showy compound many-rayed more or less globose umbels terminating long branches, in summer; involucral bracts lf.-like, cleft into linear divisions; umbellets numerous, globose, the outer fls. with larger and unequal petals, and usually on longer raylets than the inner, involucels linear or 3-parted: fr. oblong, ⅛in. long, bristly along the secondary ribs.—The wild carrot or Queen-Annes-Lace, *D. Carota,* is native to Eu., N. Afr., and Asia, and is widely spread as a weed in N. Amer.; it usually has a flatter umbel than the cult. carrot. (Carota: Latin for *carrot.*)

11. **CHÆROPHYLLUM,** L. Between 30 and 40 species of the northern hemisphere, one cult. for its fleshy edible root.—Ann., bien., or per. herbs, glabrous or hirsute, the root often tuberous or fusiform: lvs. pinnately or rarely ternately decompound, the segms. broad and pinnatifid or toothed, or narrow and fascicled: umbels compound, many-rayed; involucral bracts 1–2 or none; involucels of many small bractlets; fls. white or rarely yellow: fr. oblong or linear, compressed laterally or constricted at the commissure; carpels subterete or 5-angled; oil-tubes solitary in the intervals. (Chærophyl-lum: Greek-made name referring to the agreeably scented foliage.)

C. bulbosum, L. TURNIP-ROOTED CHERVIL. Erect branching bien., the hirsute st. 2–3 ft. high from an underground spindle-shaped tuber 2–4 in. long which is gray or blackish with yellowish-white flesh: lvs. decompound, the ultimate segms. lanceolate or linear, glabrous or hairy on nerves: fr. about ¼in. long, the carpels nearly linear, more or less curved, the broad ribs separated by dark colored furrows giving the fr. a striped appearance. Eu.

12. **MYRRHIS,** Scop. MYRRH. One species native to Eu. and an immigrant to other countries, sometimes grown for its pleasing odor.—Per. herb with the habit of Chærophyllum: lvs. pinnately decompound, the segms. pinnatifid and toothed: umbels compound, many-rayed; involucral bracts 1–2 or none; involucels membranaceous; fls. white: fr. oblong-linear, constricted at the commissure; oil-tubes numerous, very fine and obscure. (Myr-rhis: from the Greek word for *perfume.*)

M. odorata, Scop. SWEET CICELY of Eu. Hirsute-pubescent, erect, branching, 2–3 ft. high: lvs. thin and soft, 2–3-pinnately compound, with narrow-toothed or pinnatifid lanceolate segms.: polygamous; fls. small, whitish, in a strict compound umbel with unequal rays in summer; involucre present at flowering; involucels of about 6 lanceolate bractlets: fr. shining brown, ¾ to nearly 1 in. long, strongly ribbed and angled, the carpels beaked, the carpophore strongly cleft. Eu.

13. **ANTHRISCUS,** Hoffm. Small herbs; 10 or a dozen species indigenous to the regions of the Caucasus, S. Russia, and W. Asia, often found in vegetable-gardens, the lvs. being used like parsley.—Ann., bien., or rarely per., hirsute or sometimes glabrous: lvs. pinnately or subternately decompound, the segms. pinnatifid or toothed: fls. white, in compound umbels; involucral bracts 1–2 or none; involucels of several bractlets: fr. ovate or oblong, shortly attenuate at apex, laterally compressed or constricted at the commissure; oil-tubes very small, solitary in the intervals. (Anthris-cus: ancient name, probably Greek *flower* and *fence,* in reference to its usual station.)

A. Cerefolium, Hoffm. (*Scandix Cerefolium,* L. *Cerefolium Cerefolium,* Britt.). SALAD CHERVIL. More or less hairy fine-lvd. ann. with erect branching st. 1–2 ft. high: radical and main st.-lvs. decompound, the ultimate lfts. ⅛–¼in. long, ovate to oblong and deeply cut: fls. white, minute, in compound rather strict umbels in summer: fr. black, smooth, beaked, ¼–⅜in. long, the carpels linear, grooved on the inner face. (Cerefolium: from Chærophyllum which this species resembles, or named from the goddess Ceres.) Caucasus, S. Russia, W. Asia; nat. Que. to Pa.

14. **PASTINACA,** L. Strong herbs, probably a dozen, native of Eu. and Asia, one commonly cult. for its large edible root.—Tall bien. or per. herbs, with thick

roots and pinnately compound lvs.: fls. yellow or red, in compound umbels; involucre and involucels commonly none: fr. glabrous, oval or oblong, much flattened dorsally, broadly margined by the contiguous winged lateral ribs of the 2 carpels; oil-tubes solitary in the intervals and 2–4 on the commissural side. (Pastina-ca: Latin *pastus*, food.)

P. sativa, L. CULTIVATED PARSNIP. Robust bien. (rarely ann.), mostly glabrous with thickened tap-root which may become 18–20 in. long and 4 in. or more in diam. at the crown; st. grooved and becoming hollow, branching, 3–5 ft. high: lvs. odd-pinnate, with 3–4 pairs of sessile ovate or oblong toothed and more or less lobed lfts. 2–4 in. long: fls. greenish-yellow, in naked compound umbels with unequal rays, in summer: fr. thin and strongly flattened dorsally, oblong to rotund-oblong, wing-margined, strongly ribbed, 3/16–1/4 in. long. Eu. Var. **sylvestris,** DC., the wild parsnip, is extensively nat. in N. Amer.

15. **LEVISTICUM,** Koch. A single species in the mts. of S. Eu., grown for its aromatic frs.—Glabrous per. herb: lvs. ternately or pinnately decompound: umbels compound, many-rayed, with involucre and involucels: fr. ovate-oblong, slightly compressed dorsally. (Levis-ticum: origin of name obscure; thought to be a corruption of Ligusticum.)

L. officinale, Koch (*Ligusticum Levisticum,* L. *Hipposelinum Levisticum,* Britt. & Rose). LOVAGE. To 6 ft. high, st. stout: lvs. dark green, shining, 1–2-ternately compound, the segms. 2–4 in. long., ovate-cuneate, coarsely toothed toward the apex: umbels 2–3 in. across, with rays equal or nearly so, the conspicuous involucre of narrow reflexed bracts, the involucels with connate bractlets; fls. greenish-yellow, in summer: fr. oblong, about 1/4 in. long, the ribs more or less winged; oil-tubes solitary in the intervals; carpophore deeply cleft. S. Eu.; nat. in E. U. S.

16. **PETROSELINUM,** Hoffm. About 6 species of European herbs, one cult. for its herbage which is used in cooking and for garnishing.—Ann., bien. or per.: lvs. 1–3-pinnately compound, the segms. toothed and cut: fls. greenish-yellow or reddish, in compound umbels; involucre with few bracts; involucels with many small lanceolate bractlets: fr. ovate, laterally compressed, the carpels curving outward and apart so that they are contiguous only at base and apex. (Petroseli-num: Greek *rock parsley.*)

P. crispum, Nym. (*Apium Petroselinum,* L. *A. crispum,* Mill. *P. sativum,* Hoffm. *P. hortense,* Hoffm.). PARSLEY. Glabrous bien. or short-lived per., with much-branched st. 18–30 in. high: lvs. ternately decompound, the ultimate segms. cuneate-ovate, 1–2 in. long, stalked and deeply cut, curled and crisped: fls. small, greenish-yellow, in compound umbels with nearly equal rays, in summer; involucral bracts not reflexed: fr. about 1/8 in. long, conspicuously ribbed. N. and Cent. Eu.; escaped in N. Amer. and W. Indies. Var. **latifolium,** Airy-Shaw (*Apium latifolium,* Mill.), has lf.-segms. flat and not crisped, and fibrous roots. Var. **filicinum,** Bailey, has fern-like lvs. Var. **tuberosum,** Crovetto (var. *radicosum,* Bailey. *P. sativum* var. *tuberosum,* Bernh.), TURNIP-ROOTED PARSLEY, is grown for its thick parsnip-like tapering root, lf.-segms. not crisped.

17. **CORIANDRUM,** L. Two species, native to the E. Medit. region, one cult. for its frs. used as flavoring.—Glabrous ann. herbs, slender and branching: lvs. pinnately dissected, the segms. ovate and incised in the basal lvs., linear in the cauline: umbels compound, the rays commonly few; involucre lacking; involucels of few filiform bractlets; fls. white: fr. subglobose or ovoid; oil-tubes obscure. (Corian-drum: old Latin name, connected with Greek *bug.*)

C. sativum, L. CORIANDER. Strong-smelling plant 1–3 ft. high: lvs. pinnately or ternately decompound, the basal and lower st.-lvs. broadly ovate or cuneate and deeply cut, the upper more finely dissected into narrowly linear segms.: outer fls. of the umbellets with enlarged ray-like petals, in July: fr. subglobose, ribbed, less than 1/5 in. long. S. Eu.; escaped in N. Amer. and W. Indies.

18. **ÆGOPODIUM,** L. Two species, native to Eu. and Asia, a variegated form commonly planted as edging and mats against buildings and in shady places.—Coarse herbaceous perennials with creeping rootstocks: lvs. biternately compound, the ultimate segms. ovate or elliptic, serrate or toothed: fls. white or yellow, in compound umbels; bracts and bractlets commonly lacking: fr. ovate, laterally compressed, glabrous, with equal filiform ribs and no oil-tubes. (Ægopo-dium: Greek for *goat* and *little foot;* probably from the shape of its lfts.)

Æ. **Podograria**, L. Goutweed. Bishops-Weed. Glabrous, 12–14 in. high: basal and lower st.-lvs. long-petioled, the petiole expanded at base; upper lvs. with short broadly expanded petiole; segms. ½–3 in. long: umbels 1½–3 in. wide, rays 12–15, equal; fls. white, in June. (Podograria: Greek *foot* and *chain;* the plant an antidote for the gout.) Eu.; nat. in E. N. Amer. Var. **variegatum**, Bailey, with white-margined lvs., is the form commonly grown.

19. **ANGELICA,** L. Per. herbs sometimes planted for bold effects; about 50 species, native in the northern hemisphere and New Zeal.—Lvs. ternately compound: fls. white or greenish, in compound umbels; involucre lacking; involucels of small bractlets: fr. ovate to oval, dorsally compressed, lateral ribs with broad wings. (Angel-ica: supposed to have angelic healing virtues.)

A. **Archangelica**, L. (*Archangelica officinalis*, Hoffm.). Stout bien. or per. 6 ft. or more high, glabrous except in infl.: lvs. biternate, the lower lvs. sometimes 2–3 ft. long; segms. oval, 2–3 in. long, unevenly toothed or cut, terminal segm. usually 3-lobed: umbels 3–6 in. across, with 20–40 rays; umbellets subtended by many linear bractlets: fr. to ⅓in. long. Eu., Asia.

20. **CARUM,** L. Twenty-five or more species widely distributed in temp. regions, one cult. for its frs. which are used in flavoring.—Glabrous ann. or per. herbs with thick roots and lvs. pinnate or pinnately decompound: umbels compound, few- to many-rayed; involucral bracts few or none; involucels of several entire bractlets or none; fls. white or yellow: fr. ovate or oblong, laterally compressed, and often constricted at the commissure, the carpels 5-angled, with oil-tubes solitary (rarely 2) in the intervals. (Ca-rum: probably from Caria in Asia Minor.)

C. **Carvi**, L. Caraway. St. slender, erect, furrowed, 1–2 ft. high: lvs. pinnately decompound into narrowly linear segms.: rays and raylets unequal; involucral bracts very narrow; involucels often lacking; fls. white, June–July: fr. oblong, ⅛in. long, constricted at the commissure, strongly ribbed. (Carvi: derived from Carum.) Old World; much nat. in N. Amer.

21. **CICUTA,** L. Water-Hemlock. Per. glabrous herbs of about 8 species in the north temp. zone, one sometimes transplanted.—Roots tuberous, fleshy, poisonous: lvs. pinnately decompound: fls. white, in compound terminal umbels; involucre of few bracts or lacking; involucels of many bractlets: fr. ovoid or oblong, glabrous with somewhat corky ribs; oil-tubes solitary in the intervals, 2 in the commissures. (Cicu-ta: ancient Latin name.)

C. **maculata**, L. Musquash-Root. St. marked with purple lines, 3–6 ft. high: lvs. 2–3-pinnate into lanceolate toothed segms. 1–5 in. long: umbels many-fld., 1–3 in. across: fr. ⅙in. or less long. Wet ground, Que. to N. C. and Tex.

22. **CONIUM,** L. Two species widely distributed, one known for its medicinal qualities.—Tall glabrous bien. herbs: lvs. pinnately decompound, the segms. pinnatifid and toothed: fls. white, in compound many-rayed umbels with few bracts and bractlets: fr. broadly ovate, laterally compressed and at the commissure more or less constricted; carpels 5-ribbed, without oil-tubes. (Coni-um: Greek name.)

C. **maculatum**, L. Poison-Hemlock. A rank poisonous much-branched herb 2–4 ft. high, with sts. speckled reddish-purple, finely cut dark foliage and large umbels of small white fls.; rays equal or nearly so: fr. about ½in. long, with ribs somewhat tuberculate. Eu., and extensively run wild.—Sometimes known as "winter-fern."

23. **SIUM,** L. Ten species in the northern hemisphere and in S. Afr., one grown for its thickened edible root which is used in the same way as salsify.—Glabrous herbs: lvs. pinnate, the pinnæ dentate or entire: umbels compound, terminal or lateral, bracts of the involucres and involucels numerous; fls. white: fr. ovate or oblong, laterally compressed or constricted at the commissure; oil-tubes many. (Si-um: old Greek name for a marsh plant.)

S. **Sisarum**, L. Skirret. Tuberous-rooted plant 1–3 ft. high: lvs. odd-pinnate with 1–3 pairs of lanceolate toothed lfts. to 3 in. long: fls. small, in compound terminal umbels: fr. about ⅛in. long, ribbed, the carpels more or less curved, with usually 3 ribs on back and 1 on either edge. (Sisarum: from the Greek name for a plant with an esculent root.) E. Asia.

24. **APIUM,** L. A genus variously understood, but as mostly accepted comprising some 15–20 species widely distributed in temp. regions and in the mts. of the tropics; one species widely grown in vegetable-gardens.—Ann. or per. herbs, glabrous: lvs. pinnately or ternately decompound: fls. white, in compound umbels opposite the lvs. or terminal; involucral bracts few or none; involucels of several bractlets or none: fr. ovate or broader than long, laterally compressed, constricted at the commissure; carpels prominently 2-angled, with large oil-tubes solitary in the intervals. (A-pium: Latin for parsley.)

A. graveolens, L., var. **dulce,** Pers. (*A. dulce,* Mill. *A. Celleri,* Gaertn.) CELERY. Strong-smelling glabrous bien. (perhaps sometimes per.), the sts. erect, branching, 2–3 ft. high, many-grooved and conspicuously jointed: root-lvs. many and well developed, pinnate, ovate to oblong, with long petioles and rachises usually expanded; lfts. usually 2–3 pairs and a terminal one, each ternately compound and stalked, the lateral segms. often again divided, the ultimate divisions cuneate-obovate and coarsely toothed or cleft: fls. white, very small, June–Sept., the small compound umbels among the lvs., one sessile and several long-stemmed, naked or leafy-bracteate umbels springing from the same joint; rays somewhat unequal, raylets very short.—Cult. for its lf.-stalks which are blanched and eaten raw or cooked. Var. **rapaceum,** DC. (*A. rapaceum,* Mill.), CELERIAC, has a thickened and turnip-like edible root for which it is cult.; lf.-stalks not developed.

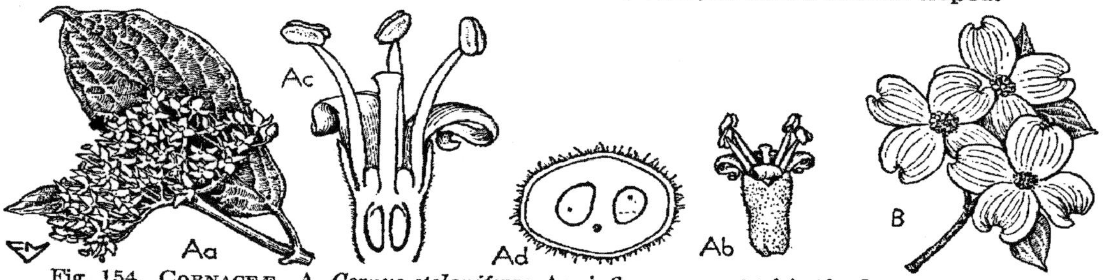

Fig. 154. CORNACEÆ. A, *Cornus stolonifera:* Aa, inflorescence, × ½; Ab, flower, × 2; Ac, flower, vertical section, × 4; Ad, ovary, cross-section, × 8. B, *C. florida:* inflorescences with bracts, × ¼.

154. CORNACEÆ. DOGWOOD FAMILY

About 10 genera and 90 species, most abundant in the northern hemisphere, several planted for ornament and cover.—Shrubs and trees, rarely herbs, with simple lvs. commonly opposite (or in a few important species alternate): fls. bisexual or unisexual, in terminal clusters; calyx-limb 4–5-toothed or none; petals 4–5 or 0; stamens equalling or outnumbering the petals, inserted with them at the base of a disk; ovary inferior, in ours 1–2-celled; style 1: fr. a 1–2-seeded drupe or berry.

A. Lvs. deciduous, entire: fls. usually white; ovary 2-celled........1. CORNUS
AA. Lvs. persistent, commonly toothed: fls. purple; ovary 1-celled........2. AUCUBA

1. **CORNUS,** L. DOGWOOD. About 40 species, natives of the north temp. zone, or a few in Mex., the Himalayas and Afr.—Mostly shrubs or trees, with simple entire opposite or rarely alternate deciduous lvs.: fls. (in ours) bisexual, 4-merous, small, white or greenish-white, in terminal cymes, panicles, umbels or heads, with or without involucre; stamens 4; ovary 2-celled; stigma truncate or capitate: fr. a 2-celled 2-seeded drupe. (Cor-nus: Latin *horn,* from the toughness of the wood.)

A. Plant a low herb........1. *C. canadensis*
AA. Plant a tall shrub or tree.
  B. Fls. in cymes or panicles without involucre.
    C. Lvs. alternate, often crowded at ends of branchlets........2. *C. alternifolia*
    CC. Lvs. opposite.
      D. Fr. black or green........3. *C. sanguinea*
      DD. Fr. white or blue.
        E. Under side of lvs. glabrous or with appressed hairs.
          F. Cymes round-topped, panicled........4. *C. racemosa*
          FF. Cymes flat-topped, not panicled.
            G. Sts. usually stoloniferous: lvs. acute or short-acuminate: disk commonly red: fr. with stone usually broader than high........5. *C. stolonifera*
            GG. Sts. not stoloniferous: lvs. gradually acuminate: disk yellow: fr. with stone usually higher than broad........6. *C. alba*

EE. Under side of lvs. woolly-pubescent, at least on veins
F. Color of fr. white . . . . 7. *C. Baileyi*
FF. Color of fr. blue.
G. Shape of lvs. broad-ovate to orbicular, gray-pubescent beneath . . . 8. *C. rugosa*
GG. Shape of lvs. oval or ovate-lanceolate, rusty-pubescent on veins beneath . . . . 9. *C. Amomum*
BB. Fls. in dense heads or umbels, with involucre.
C. Involucre yellowish, not exceeding fls. . . . . 10. *C. mas*
CC. Involucre showy and corolla-like, white or red, much exceeding fls.
D. Frs. connate into globular fleshy head.
E. Shape of lvs. ovate . . . . 11. *C. Kousa*
EE. Shape of lvs. oval-lanceolate: partially evergreen . . . . 12. *C. capitata*
DD. Frs. in dense clusters, but individually distinct.
E. Bracts 4, emarginate . . . . 13. *C. florida*
EE. Bracts 4–6, acuminate to obtuse . . . . 14. *C. Nuttallii*

1. **C. canadensis,** L. (*Chamæpericlymenum canadense,* Aschers. & Graebn.). BUNCHBERRY. Per. herb 3–9 in. high, woody at base, with creeping rootstock: lvs. whorled at top of st., oval to obovate, 1–3 in. long, acute, glabrous or slightly appressed-pubescent: fls. greenish, in dense peduncled heads subtended by an involucre of 4–6 white petal-like ovate bracts ½–¾in. long: fr. bright red, about ¼in. across. N. Amer., E. Asia.

2. **C. alternifolia,** L. f. (*Svida alternifolia,* Small). PAGODA DOGWOOD. Shrub or small tree to 25 ft., the branches in irregular whorls forming flat horizontal tiers: lvs. alternate, usually crowded at ends of branchlets, slender-petioled, elliptic or ovate, 2–5 in. long, usually cuneate at base, abruptly acuminate, nearly glabrous above, pale and appressed-pubescent beneath: cymes without involucre, 1½–2½ in. wide; fls. creamy-white, fragrant: fr. dark blue (rarely yellow), globular, ⅓in. across, on red peduncles. N. S. to Ga. and Mo.

3. **C. sanguinea,** L. BLOODTWIG DOGWOOD. Shrub to 12 ft., usually with purple or dark blood-red branches: lvs. broad-elliptic or ovate, 1½–3 in. long, rounded or narrowed at base, abruptly and shortly acuminate, usually pubescent on both sides, the hairs beneath somewhat woolly: fls. greenish-white, in dense cymes 2 in. across: fr. black or in one var. green, ¼in. across. Eu., Orient. Var. **variegata,** West., lvs. variegated with yellowish-white.

4. **C. racemosa,** Lam. (*C. paniculata,* L'Her.). PANICLED DOGWOOD. Shrub 6–15 ft. high, with gray branches: lvs. ovate-lanceolate to lanceolate, 1–4 in. long, cuneate at base, gradually acuminate, appressed-pubescent to nearly glabrous, glaucous beneath: fls. white on red peduncles in round-topped cymes 1–2 in. broad, forming loose panicles: fr. white, ⅙in. across. Me. to Fla. and Neb.

5. **C. stolonifera,** Michx. (*C. sericea* subsp. *stolonifera,* Fosberg). RED-OSIER DOGWOOD. Shrub to 10 ft., usually with dark blood-red branches and prostrate sts., stoloniferous: lvs. ovate or ovate-lanceolate, 2–4½ in. long, obtuse at base, acute or short-acuminate, appressed-pubescent above and beneath: cymes dense, 1–2 in. wide, flat-topped; disk commonly red: fr. globose, white to bluish, the stone usually broader than high. N. Amer. Var. **flaviramea,** Rehd. (vars. *aurea* and *lutea,* Hort.), GOLDENTWIG DOGWOOD, has yellow branchlets.

6. **C. alba,** L. TATARIAN DOGWOOD. Shrub to 10 ft., with usually erect st., the branches bright blood-red: lvs. ovate or elliptic, 2½–5 in. long. obtuse or cuneate at base, rather gradually acuminate, roughish appressed-pubescent above and below: cymes dense. 1–2 in. across, disk yellow: fr. ovoid, bluish-white or whitish, stone usually higher than broad, flat. Siberia, N. China. Var. **argenteo-marginata,** Rehd. (*elegantissima variegata,* Hort.), lvs. edged with white. Var. **sibirica,** Loud. (*C. sibirica,* Lodd.), branchlets bright coral-red. Var. **Spaethii,** Wittm., lvs. broadly edged with yellow.

7. **C. Baileyi,** Coult. & Evans (*C. stolonifera* var. *Baileyi,* Drescher. *C. sericea* forma *Baileyi,* Fosberg. *C. stolonifera* forma *Baileyi,* Rickett). Shrub to 10 ft., with reddish-brown branches: lvs. ovate to lanceolate, 2–5 in. long, rounded at base, acute or acuminate, glaucous and woolly-pubescent beneath: cymes dense, 1–2 in. across, pubescent: fr. white, ⅓in. across. (First collected by L. H. Bailey.) Ont. and Pa. to Minn., mostly on shores.

8. **C. rugosa,** Lam. (*C. circinata,* L'Her.). Shrub to 10 ft., with purplish branchlets: lvs. broad-ovate to orbicular, 2–6 in. long, acute or short-acuminate, pale and densely woolly-pubescent beneath: cymes dense, 2–2½ in. across: fr. light blue, ¼in. across. N. S. to Va. and N. D.

9. **C. Amomum,** Mill. (*C. sericea,* L. *Svida Amomum,* Small). SILKY DOGWOOD. Shrub to 10 ft., with purple branches: lvs. oval to ovate-lanceolate, 2–4 in. long, rounded or narrowed at base, acuminate, usually brownish woolly-pubescent beneath especially on the veins, glabrous or nearly so above: cymes flat, compact, 1½–2½ in. broad: fr. globose, blue or sometimes partly white, ¼in. across. (Amomum: old Greek name.) Newf. to Fla. and Tex.

10. **C. mas,** L. (*C. mascula,* Hort.). CORNELIAN-CHERRY. Shrub or small tree to 20 ft.: lvs. very short-petioled, ovate or elliptic, 1½–4 in. long, rounded or narrowed at base, acute or acuminate, appressed-pubescent, glossy-green: fls. yellow, in umbels terminating

short lateral branchlets, before the lvs.; involucre yellowish, about as long as the pedicels: fr. oblong, scarlet, ¾in. long, edible. S. Eu., Orient.

11. **C. Kousa,** Hance (*Benthamia japonica*, Sieb. & Zucc. *Benthamidia japonica*, Hara). Kousa. Shrub or small tree to 20 ft.: lvs. short-petioled, elliptic-ovate, 2–4 in. long, rounded or narrowed at base, abruptly long-acuminate, shortly appressed-pubescent: fls. greenish-yellow, sessile, with a creamy-white involucre 2½–3 in. wide; bracts ovate, acute: frs. pinkish, connate into a globular fleshy head ½–1 in. across. (Kousa: Japanese vernacular name.) Japan, Korea. Var. **chinensis.** Osborn, lvs. larger and more pubescent; bracts larger; China.

12. **C. capitata,** Wall. (*Benthamia fragifera*, Lindl. *Cynoxylon capitata*, Nakai. *Benthamidia capitata*, Hara). Tree to 40 ft., partially evergreen: lvs. oval-lanceolate, 2–4 in. long, narrowed at both ends, appressed-pubescent on both sides, whitish beneath: fls. sessile, with creamy-white involucre 2½–3 in. wide; bracts ovate, acute: frs. scarlet, connate into a globose head 1 in. or more across. Himalayas.

13. **C. florida,** L. (*Cynoxylum floridum*, Raf. *Benthamia florida*, Nakai. *Benthamidia florida*, Spach). Flowering Dogwood. Shrub or small tree 10–15 ft., rarely to 40 ft.: lvs. rather short-petioled, ovate or elliptic-ovate, 2–6 in. long, narrowed at base, acute or rather abruptly acuminate, appressed-pubescent or above glabrous: fls. greenish-yellow, sessile, with a white or pinkish involucre 3–4 in. wide; bracts 4, obovate, emarginate: fr. scarlet, ½in. long, in dense clusters but individually distinct. Mass. to Fla. and Mex. Var. **pendula,** Dipp., branches drooping. Var. **rubra,** West., bracts of involucre red or pink. Var. **Welchii,** Bailey, lvs. variegated with red and yellow.

14. **C. Nuttallii,** Audubon (*Cynoxylon Nuttallii*, Shafer. *Benthamia Nuttallii*, Nakai. *Benthamidia Nuttallii*, Moldenke). Tree to 75 ft.: lvs. ovate to obovate, 3–5 in. long, cuneate at base, short-acuminate, glaucous beneath and appressed-pubescent: heads very dense, to 1 in. across, with white or pinkish involucre; bracts 4–6, obovate to oblong, acuminate to obtuse, 2–3 in. long: fr. bright red or orange, ½in. long. (For T. Nuttall, page 49.) B.C. to Calif.

2. **AUCUBA,** Thunb. Species 3 (often considered as vars. of one polymorphous species), natives of E. and Cent. Asia, grown in tubs and out-of-doors for the ornamental foliage.—Diœcious evergreen shrubs with stout branches: lvs. opposite, coarsely and remotely dentate or serrate to entire, green or blotched with yellow or white, on short petioles: fls. small, purple, in terminal panicles, the pistillate with an inferior 1-celled ovary, short style and oblique stigma: fr. a 1-seeded berry-like drupe. (Aucu-ba: Latinized from its Japanese name.)

A. Lvs. ovate, oblong or oblong-lanceolate, obtusely acuminate: petals obtusely acuminate .... 1. *A. japonica*
AA. Lvs. narrower, sharply acuminate: petals long and slenderly acuminate .... 2. *A. himalaica*

1. **A. japonica,** Thunb. Stout shrub 4–15 ft. high: lvs. ovate or oblong or sometimes oblong-lanceolate, 3–7 in. long, coarsely toothed above the middle, obtusely acuminate or acute, dark green and shining: petals obtusely acuminate: berries scarlet, rarely white or yellow, usually oblong, in dense panicles to 3 in. long. Himalayas to Japan. Var. **variegata,** D'Ombrain, Gold-Dust Tree, lvs. spotted with yellow.

2. **A. himalaica,** Hook. f. & Thoms. Differs from *A. japonica* in lvs. narrower and sharply acuminate: petals long and finely acuminate: fr. orange to scarlet. E. Himalayas.

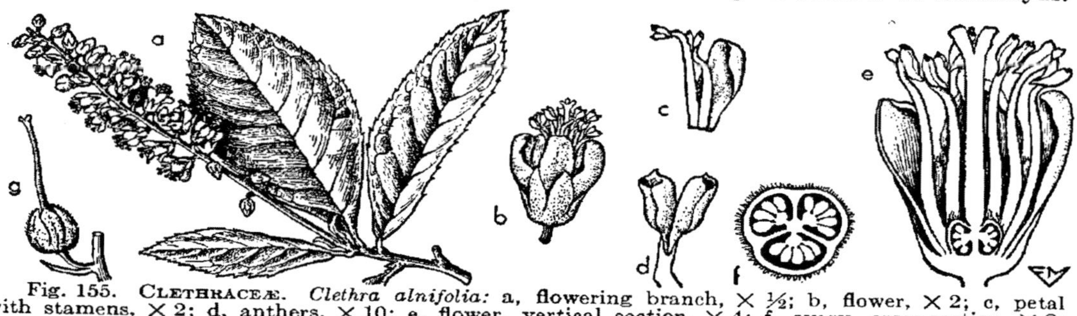

Fig. 155. Clethraceæ. *Clethra alnifolia:* a, flowering branch, × ½; b, flower, × 2; c, petal with stamens, × 2; d, anthers, × 10; e, flower, vertical section, × 4; f, ovary, cross-section, × 8; g, capsule, × 2.

155. CLETHRACEÆ. WHITE-ALDER FAMILY

Only 1 genus of about 30 species of shrubs or small trees distributed in trop. and subtrop. regions of both hemispheres, often planted for ornament.—Lvs. alternate, petioled, simple: fls. bisexual, regular, in terminal racemes or panicles, white or pinkish; calyx deeply 5-parted, imbricated, persistent; corolla of 5 nearly or wholly separate deciduous petals; stamens 10, hypogynous, the anthers at first inverted, later erect, opening by terminal pores; ovary superior, hairy, 3-celled with numerous ovules in each cell, placentation axile, style 1, stigma 3-lobed: fr. a caps. loculicidally dehiscent by 3 valves.

CLETHRA, L. WHITE-ALDER. Technical characters as for the family. (Clethra: ancient Greek name of the alder, probably applied here from the resemblance of the lvs.)

A. Lvs. glabrous or nearly so .... 1. *C. alnifolia*
AA. Lvs. pubescent, at least on veins beneath.
  B. Racemes usually simple; filaments hairy .... 2. *C. acuminata*
  BB. Racemes panicled; filaments glabrous .... 3. *C. barbinervis*

1. **C. alnifolia,** L. SWEET PEPPERBUSH. SUMMER SWEET. Deciduous shrub to 10 ft.: lvs. obovate, 2–4 in. long, acute, sharply serrate at least above middle, glabrous or nearly so: fls. fragrant, in erect usually panicled pubescent racemes in July–Sept., the pedicels subtended by narrow caducous bracts; filaments glabrous. Me. to Fla.

2. **C. acuminata,** Michx. Deciduous shrub or small tree to 18 ft.: lvs. ovate-elliptic to oblong, 3–8 in. long, acuminate, serrulate, pubescent beneath at least on veins: raceme usually solitary, 3–8 in. long, pubescent, nodding in fr.; filaments hairy. Va. to Ga. and Ala.

3. **C. barbinervis,** Sieb. & Zucc. Deciduous shrub or tree to 30 ft.: lvs. obovate, 2–5 in. long, acuminate, sharp-serrate, pubescent: racemes panicled, 4–6 in. long, pubescent; fls. fragrant; filaments glabrous. Japan.

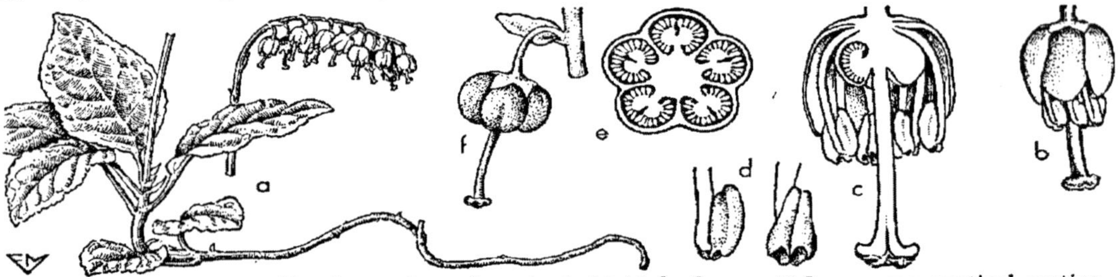

Fig. 156. PYROLACEÆ. Pyrola: a, flowering plant, × ½; b, flower, × 2; c, same, vertical section, × 3; d, anthers, side and ventral view, × 5; e, ovary, cross-section, × 5; f, capsule, × 2.

156. PYROLACEÆ. SHINLEAF FAMILY

Three genera and about 20 species comprise this family, if Monotropaceæ is kept distinct; native in the northern hemisphere.—Evergreen per. herbs, sometimes slightly woody at base: lvs. basal, opposite or whorled, petioled: fls. bisexual, nearly regular; calyx 5-parted; corolla of 5 separate petals; stamens twice as many as petals, anthers opening by pores or slits; ovary superior, 4–5-celled, with numerous axile ovules, style 1 and simple: fr. a caps. loculicidally dehiscent by 5 valves.

A. Fls. in racemes or umbels.
  B. Lvs. basal .... 1. PYROLA
  BB. Lvs. opposite or whorled .... 2. CHIMAPHILA
AA. Fls. solitary .... 3. MONESES

1. **PYROLA,** L. SHINLEAF. Small woods herbs sometimes transplanted; about 15 species in the northern hemisphere.—Stoloniferous, glabrous: lvs. basal: fls. white, greenish or purplish, in a raceme terminating a bracted scape; style filiform, straight or declined. (Pyr-ola: diminutive of *pyrus,* pear, from fancied resemblance of foliage.)

P. elliptica, Nutt. Lvs. oval or oblong-elliptic, 1½–3 in. long, obtuse, rounded at base, shallowly-toothed, thin and dark green: fls. white, fragrant, nodding, about ½ in. across, on scapes 5–10 in. high; calyx ovate-triangular; petals obtuse. N. Amer.

2. **CHIMAPHILA,** Pursh. PIPSISSEWA. Woods herbs of about 8 species in the northern hemisphere.—Sts. creeping: lvs. opposite or in whorls, short-petioled, toothed: fls. white or pinkish, nodding, in terminal long-stalked umbel-like racemes; style very short. (Chimaph-ila: Greek *winter-loving;* green in winter.)

A. Lvs. variegated with white .... 1. *C. maculata*
AA. Lvs. not variegated .... 2. *C. umbellata*

1. **C. maculata**, Pursh (*Pyrola maculata*, L.). To 10 in.: lvs. ovate-lanceolate to lanceolate, broadest below the middle, 1–3 in. long, acute or acuminate, variegated with white along the veins: fls. ½–¾ in. across. Me. to Ga. and Mex.

2. **C. umbellata**, Nutt. (*Pyrola umbellata*, L.). To 10 in.: lvs. oblong-obovate, broadest above the middle, 1–2 in. long, obtuse or acutish, bright green: fls. about ½ in. across. Eu., Asia. Var. **cisatlantica**, Blake, PRINCES-PINE, is the form native in E. N. Amer.

3. **MONESES**, Salisb. One low glabrous herb, sometimes transplanted.—Lvs. opposite or whorled, petioled, crenulate: fls. solitary, nodding at end of slender scape; style long and straight, club-shaped at top. (Mone-ses: Greek *single delight*, from the solitary fl.)

M. uniflora, Gray (*Pyrola uniflora*, L.). To 6 in.: lvs. toward base of st., orbicular or ovate, ⅓–1 in. long, obtuse, rounded at base: fls. white or pink, fragrant, ½–¾ in. across. Woods, N. Amer., Eu., Asia.

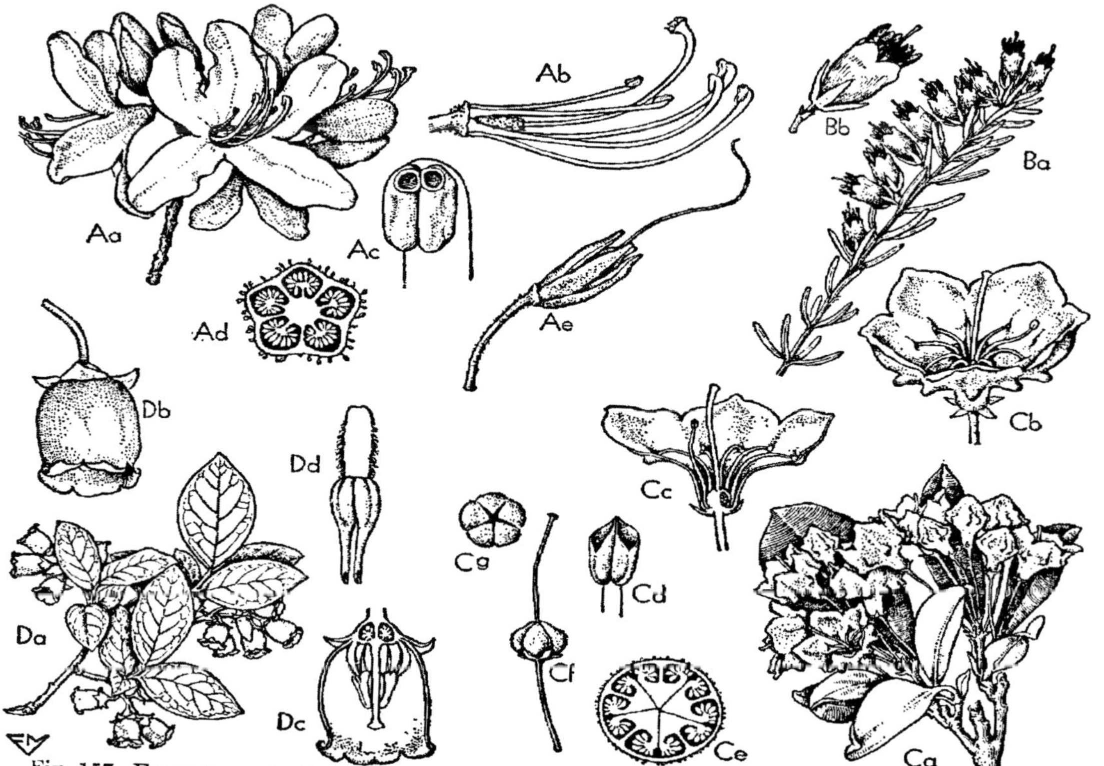

Fig. 157. ERICACEÆ. A, *Rhododendron Vaseyi*: Aa, inflorescence, × ½; Ab, flower, less perianth, × 1; Ac, anther, × 5; Ad, ovary, cross-section, × 5; Ae, capsule, × 1. B, *Erica mediterranea*: Ba, flowering branch, × 1; Bb, flower, × 2. C, *Kalmia latifolia*: Ca, flowering branch, × ½; Cb, flower, × 1; Cc, same, vertical section, × 1; Cd, anther, × 5; Ce, ovary, cross-section, × 6; Cf, capsule, side view, × 1; Cg, same, face view, × 1. D, *Vaccinium stamineum*: Da, flowering branch, × ½; Db, flower, × 2; Dc, same, vertical section, × 2; Dd, anther, × 5.

157. ERICACEÆ. HEATH FAMILY

Shrubs, subshrubs, or small trees of wide distribution, consisting of about 70 genera and 1,500 species; the family furnishes many highly ornamental subjects and several are grown for their edible frs.—Lvs. alternate, opposite or verticillate, simple, exstipulate, deciduous or persistent: fls. bisexual, regular or slightly irregular, solitary or in axillary or terminal racemes or panicles; calyx free or adnate to ovary,

4-5-cleft or -parted, usually persistent; corolla gamopetalous or rarely polypetalous, 4-5-lobed; stamens as many or twice as many as petals, inserted on outer edge of an epigynous or hypogynous disk, the 2-celled anthers opening by terminal pores or chinks or rarely longitudinally, sometimes awned, the pollen preponderantly of 4 united grains; ovary superior or inferior, usually 2-5- or 10-celled with 1 to many ovules in each cell, mostly many, the placentæ commonly axile; style and stigma 1: fr. a caps., berry or drupe.—Vaccinium and related genera are sometimes separated as family Vacciniaceæ.

A. Ovary superior.
B. Petals united (corolla gamopetalous).
C. Corolla persistent, inclosing the caps.
D. Calyx shorter than corolla.
E. Stamens inserted at base of prominent disk .... 1. ERICA
EE. Stamens inserted at base of corolla; disk minute .... 2. BRUCKENTHALIA
DD. Calyx longer than and concealing corolla .... 3. CALLUNA
CC. Corolla deciduous.
D. Lvs. scale-like and imbricated .... 4. CASSIOPE
DD. Lvs. not scale-like.
E. Fr. a berry or berry-like, or a drupe.
F. Calyx fleshy, surrounding the fr. .... 5. GAULTHERIA
FF. Calyx small, at base of fr.
G. Fls. usually solitary in the axils .... 6. PERNETTYA
GG. Fls. in terminal racemes or panicles.
H. Ovules many in each cell: fr. a granulose or warty berry .... 7. ARBUTUS
HH. Ovules 1 in each cell: fr. a smooth drupe .... 8. ARCTOSTAPHYLOS
EE. Fr. a caps.
F. Plant prostrate or decumbent.
G. Length of lvs. ⅓in. or less.
H. Stamens 5: lvs. opposite, oval .... 9. LOISELEURIA
HH. Stamens 8-12: lvs. alternate, linear .... 10. PHYLLODOCE
GG. Length of lvs. 1-3 in. .... 11. EPIGÆA
FF. Plant upright.
G. Pouches in the corolla 10, containing the anthers before anthesis. 12. KALMIA
GG. Pouches not present.
H. Lobes of calyx and corolla 4; stamens 8 .... 13. DABOËCIA
HH. Lobes of calyx and corolla 5; stamens usually 5 or 10.
I. Seeds 1 or few in ovary and caps. .... 14. ENKIANTHUS
II. Seeds many in ovary and caps.
J. Fls. open-campanulate to funnelform, not urceolate.
K. Anthers not awned: fls. large: caps. septicidally dehiscent .... 15. RHODODENDRON
KK. Anthers awned: fls. small: caps. loculicidally dehiscent .... 16. ZENOBIA
JJ. Fls. urceolate or cylindric with very short lobes.
K. Anther-sacs opening longitudinally: a deciduous tree. . 17. OXYDENDRUM
KK. Anther-sacs opening by terminal pore: evergreen or deciduous shrubs.
L. Foliage densely scaly beneath .... 18. CHAMÆDAPHNE
LL. Foliage not scaly beneath.
M. Caps. with thickened sutures separating from valves .... 19. LYONIA
MM. Caps. without thickened sutures.
N. Margins of lvs. entire .... 20. ANDROMEDA
NN. Margins of lvs. serrate or crenulate.
O. Anthers with 2 reflexed awns; calyx-lobes separate .... 21. PIERIS
OO. Anthers awnless or with 4 awns (in ours); calyx-lobes imbricated .... 22. LEUCOTHOË
BB. Petals distinct (corolla polypetalous).
C. Lvs. glabrous, ⅓in. or less long .... 23. LEIOPHYLLUM
CC. Lvs. tomentose beneath, 1-2 in. long .... 24. LEDUM
AA. Ovary inferior: fr. a berry or berry-like drupe crowned by the persistent calyx-lobes.
B. Fr. white .... 25. CHIOGENES
BB. Fr. colored.
C. Lvs. resinous-dotted beneath .... 26. GAYLUSSACIA
CC. Lvs. not resinous-dotted .... 27. VACCINIUM

1. ERICA, L. HEATH. Nearly 600 species of shrubs and subshrubs native in S. Afr. and the Medit. region, a few species grown in this country under glass and planted out-of-doors.—Lvs. usually in whorls of 3-6, small, needle-like: fls. solitary or in few- to many-fld. axillary or terminal umbels or spikes, usually nodding; calyx short, 4-parted; corolla withering-persistent, urceolate to long-cylindrical, with 4 small lobes; stamens usually 8, inserted at base of prominent disk; ovary 4- or rarely

8-celled with 2 to many ovules in each cell: fr. a loculicidally dehiscent caps. with many minute seeds. (Eri-ca: ante-Linnæan name of doubtful significance.)

A. Lvs. markedly ciliate.
  B. Whorls of 3 ovate lvs. .... 1. *E. ciliaris*
  BB. Whorls of 4 linear lvs.
    C. Length of fls. about ¼in. .... 2. *E. Tetralix*
    CC. Length of fls. ½–1 in.
      D. Fls. in dense umbels at ends of branchlets .... 3. *E. ventricosa*
      DD. Fls. borne all along branchlets, forming a leafy raceme .... 4. *E. hyemalis*
AA. Lvs. glabrous or essentially so.
  B. Stamens exserted.
    C. Whorls of 3 lvs. .... 5. *E. canaliculata*
    CC. Whorls of 4 or 5 lvs.
      D. Sepals narrow-oblong, half or more as long as corolla.
        E. Plant less than 1 ft. high, the branches becoming prostrate .... 6. *E. carnea*
        EE. Plant 4 ft. or more high, the branches upright .... 7. *E. mediterranea*
      DD. Sepals ovate, one-third or less as long as corolla .... 8. *E. vagans*
  BB. Stamens included.
    C. Blooming in summer, June–Sept.
      D. Whorls of 3 lvs. .... 9. *E. cinerea*
      DD. Whorls of 4 lvs. .... 10. *E. terminalis*
    CC. Blooming in winter or spring.
      D. Plant 8 ft. or more high.
        E. Hairs on st. short and slender, simple .... 11. *E. lusitanica*
        EE. Hairs stout and large, ciliate .... 12. *E. arborea*
      DD. Plant 1–2 ft. high .... 13. *E. subdivaricata*

1. **E. ciliaris,** L. FRINGED HEATH. Much-branched shrub 1 ft. or more high, with prostrate sts. pubescent when young: lvs. in whorls of 3, ovate, ciliate on margins with glandular hairs: fls. in whorls of 3 in terminal racemes 2–5 in. long, blooming from July–Oct., rosy-red, about ⅓in. long; sepals ciliate, one-third or more shorter than corolla which is contracted toward mouth: caps. glabrous. Eu.

2. **E. Tetralix,** L. From 6 in. to 2 ft. high, the branches becoming prostrate: lvs. in whorls of 4, whitish beneath, ciliate on margins with glandular hairs: fls. few to several in a terminal head, blooming from June to Oct., rose, about ¼in. long; sepals ciliate, about one-third length of the cylindrical corolla: caps. downy. (Tetralix: pre-Linnæan substantive signifying *cross-leaved.*) Eu.—**E. Mackaii,** Hook., is a hybrid between *E. Tetralix* and *E. ciliaris;* its fls. are of a deeper red and shorter and broader and ovary not so downy as in *E. Tetralix;* lvs. in whorls of 4, ovate-oblong. **E. Williamsii,** Druce, is a hybrid between *E. Tetralix* and *E. vagans;* lvs. slightly ciliate; fls. rose, urceolate, stamens included.

3. **E. ventricosa,** Thunb. Rigid shrub from 2–6 ft. high: lvs. in whorls of 4, margins ciliate and white: fls. in dense umbels at ends of branchlets, blooming in spring and summer, waxy-white, pink, or red, ½–⅔in. long; bracts ciliate; sepals glabrous, one-half or less as long as glabrous corolla which is ovoid-urceolate and constricted at throat. S. Afr.

4. **E. hyemalis,** Nichols. To about 2 ft. high: lvs. in whorls of 4, ciliate: fls. on the ends of short branchlets, forming a long dense leafy raceme, blooming from Nov.–Feb., pink with white at apex or white in var. *alba*, ¾–1 in. long; sepals ciliate, about one-third length of corolla. Of doubtful origin; probably a hybrid.

5. **E. canaliculata,** Andr. A profusely blooming compact shrub 3–5 ft. high or more: lvs. ¼in. long, erect or spreading, in whorls of 3, glabrous or sometimes hairy: fls. many, toward the ends of the branchlets, blooming in winter, pale pink to rose, about ⅛ in. long; corolla subcampanulate, lobes not spreading; sepals pink to rose, nearly or quite half as long as corolla, heart-shaped with central ridge scarcely or not at all apparent, calyx-tube very short or seemingly absent; stamens exserted and dark purplish-red, anthers bifid; ovary short depressed-globose. S. Afr.—Most of the material long cult. as *E. melanthera* belongs here; true *E. melanthera*, **L.**, differs in calyx having a distinct tube one-third as long as lobes or longer, sepals with a strong midrib or keel that is produced into an apiculate apex, corolla-lobes spreading and the tube narrow, anther-cells converged into a single attenuate apex, and ovary obovoid.

6. **E. carnea,** L. SPRING HEATH. Low tufted shrub 6–10 in. high, the branches becoming prostrate and spreading: lvs. in whorls of 4, glabrous and glossy: fls. solitary or in pairs in the axils of lvs., forming a raceme 1–2 in. long on branchlets of previous year, blooming Feb.–May, deep red, ¼in. or less long; sepals narrow-oblong, more than half as long as cylindrical corolla; anthers dark red, exserted. Eu. Var. **alba,** Bean, fls. white. Var. **Vivellii,** Bailey, fls. light carmine-red.—A hybrid between *E. carnea* and *E. mediterranea* is **E. darleyensis,** Bean, taller than *E. carnea* and blooming earlier, anthers less exserted (originated in nursery at Darley Dale, Derbyshire, England).

7. **E. mediterranea,** L. Bushy upright shrub 4–10 ft. high: lvs. in whorls of 4–5: fls. solitary or in pairs in axils of lvs., at ends of branchlets of previous year, forming short racemes, blooming in spring, deep red or white in var. **alba,** Bean, ¼in. or less long; sepals narrow-oblong, half as long as cylindrical corolla; anthers dark red, half-exserted. W. Eu.

8. **E. vagans,** L. Cornish Heath. Low spreading shrub to about 1 ft. high: lvs. in whorls of 4 or 5, glabrous: fls. usually in pairs in axils of lvs., forming a leafy cylindrical raceme 3–6 in. long, blooming from July–Oct., purplish-pink or white in var. **alba,** Bean, about ⅛in. long; sepals ovate, one-third or less as long as the almost globular corolla; anthers red or rarely yellow, exserted, split to base. W. Eu., Cornwall.

9. **E. cinerea,** L. Twisted Heath. Much-branched low shrub from 6–18 in. high: lvs. in whorls of 3, glabrous and shining above: fls. in whorls forming a short raceme or in terminal umbels to 3 in. long, blooming June–Sept., purple changing to blue, about ¼in. long; sepals about one-third as long as urceolate corolla. Eu.

10. **E. terminalis,** Salisb. (*E. stricta,* Andr. not Willd. *E. corsica,* DC.). Corsican Heath. Erect shrub to 4 ft., with strict rigid branches: lvs. in whorls of 4 or rarely 5–6, glabrescent: fls. in terminal umbels, blooming June–Sept., rosy-purple, about ¼in. long; sepals about one-third as long as cylindrical corolla which is narrowed at throat. S. Eu.

11. **E. lusitanica,** Rudolph (*E. codonodes,* Lindl.). Spanish Heath An erect dense shrub becoming 8–12 ft. high; sts. when young clothed with short slender simple hairs: lvs. irregularly arranged or from 3–5 in a whorl, glabrous: fls. produced in great profusion along entire length of branches, from Feb.–Apr., white or pink, about ⅙ in. long; sepals about one-fourth the length of the tubular-campanulate corolla. W. Eu.

12. **E. arborea,** L. Tree Heath. Shrub or sometimes tree with distinct trunk, to 20 ft. high: differs from *E. lusitanica* in the hairs of the st. being long, stout, and ciliate, the more globular almost white fls. about ⅛in. long which are very fragrant, and the much flattened white stigma. Medit. region.

13. **E. subdivaricata,** Bergius (*E. persoluta,* L.). Erect branching shrub 1–2 ft. high: lvs. in whorls of 4, glabrous: fls. in whorls of 4 or more at ends of short branchlets, forming a racemose infl., blooming in spring, white or rosy, about ⅙ in. long; sepals one-half or less as long as campanulate corolla which is widened at mouth. S. Afr.

2. **BRUCKENTHALIA,** Reichb. One evergreen heath-like shrub, useful for the rock-garden.—Closely allied to Erica, differing chiefly in stamens inserted at base of corolla, and disk minute. (Bruckentha-lia: named for Samuel von Bruckenthal, 1721–1803, Austrian nobleman.)

B. spiculifolia, Reichb. (*Erica spiculifolia,* Salisb.). Spike-Heath. To 10 in., branches erect and pubescent when young: lvs. crowded, linear, about ⅕ in. long, bristle-pointed, somewhat pubescent: fls. pink, campanulate, very small, in racemes about ¾in. long, in summer; style exserted. S. Eu., Asia Minor.

3. **CALLUNA,** Salisb. Heather. A monotypic genus native in Eu. and Asia Minor and adventive in E. N. Amer.; a low evergreen shrub blooming profusely in late summer.—Closely allied to Erica but differing in its deeply 4-parted colored calyx being longer than and concealing the corolla, subtended by 4 green bracts resembling a calyx: fr. a septicidally dehiscent few-seeded caps. (Callu-na: from Greek *to sweep;* the branches are sometimes used for making brooms.)

C. vulgaris, Hull (*Erica vulgaris,* L.). From 6 in. to 3 ft. high: lvs. imbricated in 4 rows, about 1/24in. long, sagittate at base, glabrous or pubescent: fls. pink, about ⅛in. long, in slender erect one-sided racemes.—There are many named forms, a few of which are: var. **alba,** Don, fls. white; var. **atrorubens,** Loud. (var. *Alportii,* Kirchn.), fls. crimson; var. **argentea,** Bean, lvs. pale; var. **aurea,** Don, lvs. golden, dwarf; var. **compacta,** Hort., of compact habit; var. **cuprea,** Bean, lvs. golden turning bronze; var. **hirsuta,** S. F. Gray (var. *tomentosa,* Don), lvs. gray-tomentose; var. **Hammondii,** Bean, tall, lvs. bright green, fls. white; var. **humilis,** Hort., low, fls. white; var. **hypnoides,** Bean, to 1 ft., fls. deep pink; var. **nana,** Kirchn. (var. *pygmæa,* Hort.), to 4 in., fls. purple; var. **plena,** Regel (var. *multiplex,* Sweet), fls. double, pink; var. **purpurea,** Don (var. *rubra,* Kirchn.), fls. dark purple; var. **rosea,** Hort., fls. pink; var. **Searlei,** Bean, fls. white, late-blooming.

4. **CASSIOPE,** D. Don. Low evergreen shrubs of about 12 species in polar regions and Himalayas.—Lvs. scale-like and imbricated or linear and spreading: fls. nodding, solitary, white or pinkish; calyx with 4–5 imbricated lobes; corolla 4–5-lobed, campanulate; stamens 8–10, anthers with recurved awns: fr. a 4–5-celled loculicidally dehiscent caps. with minute seeds. (Cassi-ope: Greek mythology, mother of Andromeda.)

C. Mertensiana, Don (*Andromeda Mertensiana,* Bong.). Tufted, to 1 ft. high, the sts. decumbent and branching, covered with thick imbricated ovate glabrous lvs. about ⅛in. long keeled on back: fls. white, ¼in. long, in upper axils; tips of corolla-lobes reflexed. (First collected by Mertens: see Mertensia, page 833.) Alaska to Calif.

5. **GAULTHERIA,** L. Evergreen shrubs of over 100 species in N. and S. Amer., Asia to Australia.—Erect or prostrate: lvs. usually alternate and serrate, short-petioled: fls. solitary or in racemes or panicles; calyx 5-parted; corolla urceolate or campanulate; stamens 10, anthers awned or obtuse: fr. a berry-like 5-valved caps. inclosed by the fleshy calyx, with many minute seeds. (Gaulthe-ria: named for Dr. Gaultier, physician in Quebec about 1750.)

G. procumbens, L. WINTERGREEN. CHECKERBERRY. Sts. creeping, the erect branches to 6 in. high and leafy at top: lvs. oval, 1–2 in. long, apiculate, teeth often bristly, glabrous and shining above: fls. solitary and nodding, white, to ¼in. long, May–Sept.: fr. scarlet, ⅓in. across. Newf. to Man. south to Ga.

6. **PERNETTYA,** Gaud. About 25 species of evergreen shrubs native from Mex. to antarctic S. Amer. and 1 species in Tasmania and New Zeal.—Lvs. alternate, small, serrate: fls. usually solitary, axillary, on slender nodding pedicels; calyx free from ovary, 5-parted, scarcely enlarged at maturity; corolla urceolate, with short 5-lobed limb; stamens 10, anthers 4-awned at apex: fr. a glabrous 5-celled many-seeded berry. (Pernet-tya: after A. J. Pernetty, 1716–1801, who accompanied Bougainville on his voyage around the world; originally spelled *Pernettia* but later corrected.)

P. mucronata, Gaud. (*Arbutus mucronata,* L. f.). Much-branched shrub to 2 ft. or more, the branches glabrous or slightly hairy: lvs. ovate to ovate-lanceolate, ⅓–¾in. long, short-petioled, serrate and spiny-pointed, glabrous: fls. solitary, blooming May–June, globose-ovoid, about ¼in. long, long-pedicelled, white or tinged with pink: berry globose, ⅓–½in. across, from white to red or dark purple, remaining on branches over winter. Magellan region to Chile.

7. **ARBUTUS,** L. About 14 species of evergreen trees or shrubs native in Medit. region, Canary Isls., and W. N. Amer., a few planted for ornament in warm regions.—Bark of sts. and branches smooth, red, peeling off in thin plates: lvs. alternate, petioled, entire or serrate: fls. in terminal panicles, the pedicels bracted; calyx free, 5-parted, persistent; corolla globular or urceolate, 5-toothed, deciduous; stamens 10, included, anthers with pair of reflexed awns on back; ovary 5- or rarely 4-celled with numerous ovules in each cell: fr. a globose berry, mostly granulose outside. (Ar-butus: ancient Latin name.)

A. Lvs. serrate: panicle nodding, about 2 in. long........................1. *A. Unedo*
AA. Lvs. entire: panicle erect, 5–6 in. long........................2. *A. Menziesii*

1. **A. Unedo,** L. STRAWBERRY-TREE. Tree to 30 ft. or more, but in cult. usually 15 ft. or less: lvs. oblong to obovate, 2–4 in. long, tapering at both ends, serrate, dark shining green: fls. white or rosy, about ¼in. long, in nodding panicles about 2 in. long in autumn: berry scarlet, warty, ¾in. across. (Unedo: ancient classical name.) S. Eu., Ireland.

2. **A. Menziesii,** Pursh. MADRONE. MADROÑO. Tree 50–120 ft. high: lvs. oval to oblong, 2–6 in. long, obtuse or acutish, entire or serrate on young shoots, shining dark green above, glaucous beneath: fls. white, ¼in. long, in erect panicles 5–6 in. long, May–June: berry orange-red, warty, ⅓in. across. (Named for Archibald Menzies, page 399.) B. C. to Calif.

8. **ARCTOSTAPHYLOS,** Adans. About 50 species from W. N. Amer. and 1 circumpolar in the northern hemisphere; evergreen shrubs or small trees, one often planted for ground-cover.—Closely related to Arbutus and differing chiefly in the ovules being solitary in the 4–10 cells of the ovary: fr. a mealy smooth berry or drupe with 4–10 coherent nutlets. (Arctostaph-ylos: Greek for *bear* and *grape.*)

A. Plant prostrate: lvs. ½–1 in. long........................1. *A. Uva-ursi*
AA. Plant tall and erect: lvs. 1–2 in. long........................2. *A. glauca*

1. **A. Uva-ursi,** Spreng. (*Arbutus Uva-ursi,* L.). BEAR-BERRY. Trailing or creeping shrub with sts. to 6 in. high: lvs. obovate, ½–1 in. long, tapering to base, obtuse, entire and revolute, glabrous, bright green: fls. white tinged with red, about ⅙in. long, in terminal clusters from May–June: drupe red, ¼–⅓in. diam., with reticulated nutlets. (Uva-ursi: Latin for *grape* and *bear.*) Cool regions of northern hemisphere.

2. **A. glauca,** Lindl. GREAT-BERRIED MANZANITA. Shrub to 20 ft. or more: lvs. oval or broad-ovate, 1–2 in. long, obtuse or acute, rounded at base, glabrous and glaucous: fls. white, ⅓in. long, in panicles broader than high: drupe light brown, ½–¾in. diam., glandular-viscid, with 1 smooth stone. S. Calif., Lower Calif.

9. **LOISELEURIA,** Desv. Evergreen prostrate shrub, circumpolar, suitable for the alpine-garden.—Lvs. opposite and crowded, small, entire, short-petioled: fls. in few-fld. terminal clusters, short-pedicelled; calyx 5-lobed; corolla campanulate, with lobes about length of tube; stamens 5, anthers opening lengthwise: fr. a 2–3-valved caps. surrounded by the persistent calyx, with many seeds. (Loiseleu-ria: named for J. L. A. Loiseleur-Deslongchamps, 1774–1849, French botanist and physician.)

L. procumbens, Desv. (*Azalea procumbens,* L.). ALPINE-AZALEA. Making mats 6–8 in. high, glabrous: lvs. oval or oblong, ⅙–⅓in. long, obtuse, revolute: fls. white or pink, ⅙ in. long, in summer: caps. ovoid, ⅛in. long. Eu., N. Asia, Alaska to N. H.

10. **PHYLLODOCE,** Salisb. Evergreen heath-like shrubs native in northern parts of Amer., Eu. and Asia.—Prostrate or ascending: lvs. alternate and crowded, linear, revolute: fls. nodding, in terminal umbels; calyx usually 5-parted; corolla campanulate or urceolate, 5-lobed; stamens 8–12, anthers opening by terminal pore: fr. a septicidally dehiscent 5-valved caps. with many seeds. (Phyllod-oce: name of a sea nymph.)

P. empetriformis, D. Don (*Menziesia empetriformis,* Smith). Sts. ascending to 6 in.: lvs. ¼–½in. long, glabrous: fls. rosy-purple, ¼in. long, campanulate, lobes much shorter than tube. Alaska to Calif. and Wyo.

11. **EPIGÆA,** L. Two species of prostrate evergreen branching shrubs native in E. N. Amer. and Japan, one sometimes planted.—Lvs. alternate, petioled, entire: sometimes diœcious, fls. sessile in the axil of green bracts as long as calyx, clustered at ends of branches, fragrant; sepals 5, green; corolla salverform, 5-lobed; stamens 10, attached to base of corolla-tube, the anthers dehiscent longitudinally by slits; ovary hirsute, 5-celled with numerous ovules in each cell: fr. a loculicidally dehiscent caps. (Epigæ-a: Greek for *upon earth,* referring to the trailing growth.)

E. repens, L. TRAILING ARBUTUS. MAYFLOWER. Spreading on ground in patches to 2 ft. diam.; sts. hirsute, rooting: lvs. oval to orbicular, 1–3 in. long, obtuse or broadly acute, cordate or rounded at base, sparingly hirsute: fls. pink or white, ½–⅔ in. long, blooming from Mar.–May: fr. whitish, ⅓in. across. Acid soils, E. N. Amer.

12. **KALMIA,** L. Evergreen or rarely deciduous shrubs furnishing a few ornamental subjects; about 8 species in N. Amer. and Cuba.—Lvs. alternate, opposite or in whorls of 3, entire: fls. in terminal or lateral corymbs or umbels, rarely solitary; calyx 5-parted; corolla broadly campanulate or somewhat salverform, 5-lobed, the tube with 10 pouches in which the anthers are held back and when touched spring up suddenly and discharge the pollen; stamens 10; ovary 5-celled with numerous ovules in each cell: fr. a septicidally dehiscent caps. (Kal-mia: after Peter Kalm, 1717–1779, Swedish botanist who travelled in N. Amer.)

A. Infl. lateral...1. *K. angustifolia*
AA. Infl. terminal.
  B. Lvs. to 1½ in. long, glaucous-white beneath..............................2. *K. polifolia*
  BB. Lvs. 2–5 in. long, green beneath..3. *K. latifolia*

1. **K. angustifolia,** L. SHEEP-LAUREL. LAMBKILL. From 6 in.–3 ft. high: lvs. mostly opposite or in whorls of 3, oblong or oblong-lanceolate, 1–2½ in. long, obtuse, glabrous, bright green above, pale beneath: fls. purple or crimson, ¼–½in. across, in simple or compound lateral corymbs in June–July, the leafy shoot produced beyond infl. E. N. Amer.

2. **K. polifolia,** Wangh. (*K. glauca,* Ait.). BOG KALMIA. To 2 ft., straggling: lvs. opposite or in 3's, oblong, ¾–1½ in. long, obtuse, nearly sessile, revolute, glaucous-white beneath, glabrous: fls. rose-purple, ½in. across, in terminal corymbs in May–June. N. N. Amer. Var. **microphylla,** Rehd. (*K. microphylla,* Heller), is 3–10 in. high with lvs. ¼–¾in. long; W. N. Amer.

3. **K. latifolia,** L. MOUNTAIN-LAUREL. CALICO-BUSH. Dense round-topped shrub to 10 ft. or rarely a tree to 30 ft.: lvs. alternate or irregularly whorled, oval to oblong or elliptic-lanceolate, 2–5 in. long, acute at both ends, glabrous, dark green above, yellowish-green below: fls. rose-colored to white, with purple markings within, about ¾in. across, in large terminal compound corymbs in May and June. E. N. Amer. Var. **myrtifolia,** Jaeg., is a dwarf form with lvs. 1–2 in. long.

13. **DABOËCIA,** D. Don. One low evergreen shrub native from N. Spain to Ireland, suitable for rockeries or borders.—Lvs. alternate, entire: fls. in long terminal racemes, drooping, short-pedicelled; calyx 4-parted; corolla ovoid, shortly 4-lobed; stamens 8, included, the anthers longer than filaments; ovary 4-celled with numerous ovules in each cell: fr. a septicidally dehiscent caps. (Daboë-cia: from its Irish name, St. Dabeoc's heath.)

D. cantabrica, Koch (*D. polifolia*, Don. *Menziesia polifolia*, Juss. *Boretta cantabrica*, Kuntze). IRISH-HEATH. To 2 ft., branches glandular-pubescent: lvs. elliptic, ¼–½in. long, revolute at margins, dark green and shining above, white-tomentose beneath: fls. purple, ⅓–½in. long, blooming from June–Oct.—Runs into several vars. with white, pink, dark purple, and white- and purple-striped fls., and a dwarf form with small narrow lvs.

14. **ENKIANTHUS,** Lour. Mostly deciduous shrubs with whorled branches, of about 10 species in China, Japan, and the Himalayas, a few planted for ornament.—Lvs. alternate, petioled, serrulate or entire, crowded toward end of branchlets: fls. in terminal drooping umbels or racemes; calyx with 5 small lobes; corolla campanulate or urceolate, shortly 5-lobed; stamens 10, the anthers opening by short slits, 2-awned at apex; ovary 5-celled with few ovules in each cell: fr. a loculicidally dehiscent caps., the 1 to few seeds winged or angled. (Enkian-thus: Greek for *enlarged* and *flower*, referring to the colored involucre of one species.)

A. Fls. urceolate, before the lvs. . . . . 1. *E. perulatus*
AA. Fls. campanulate, after the lvs.
  B. Limb of corolla of 5 broad lobes . . . . 2. *E. campanulatus*
  BB. Limb of corolla irregularly cut into sharp lanceolate lobes . . . . 3. *E. cernuus*

1. **E. perulatus,** Schneid. (*Andromeda perulata*, Miq. *E. japonicus*, Hook. f.). To 6 ft.: lvs. obovate to elliptic-ovate, 1–2 in. long, acute, serrulate, pubescent on veins below, turning yellow and scarlet in autumn: fls. urceolate, white, ⅓in. long, on slender glabrous pedicels in drooping umbels, in May, the corolla with 5 swellings or sacs at base: caps. oblong-ovoid, about ⅓in. long, on straight pedicels. Japan.

2. **E. campanulatus,** Nichols. (*Andromeda campanulata*, Miq.). To 6 or sometimes 30 ft.: lvs. elliptic, 1–3 in. long, acute or acuminate, serrulate, glabrous except on veins, turning scarlet in autumn: fls. campanulate, yellow or pale orange veined with dark red, ⅓–½in. long, slender-pedicelled, in 8–15-fld. puberulous racemes in May; corolla with 5 broad lobes: caps. ovoid, about ¼in. long, on drooping pedicels turned upward toward apex. Japan.

3. **E. cernuus,** Makino (*Meisteria cernua*, Sieb. & Zucc.). To 15 ft.: lvs. elliptic to oblong, 1–2 in. long, acute or somewhat obtuse, serrulate, pubescent on veins beneath: fls. campanulate, white, ¼–⅓in. long, slender-pedicelled, in 10–12-fld. pubescent racemes in May; corolla irregularly laciniate into sharp lanceolate lobes: caps. ellipsoid, ⅕in. long. Japan. Var. **rubens,** Makino, has deep red fls.

15. **RHODODENDRON,** L. ROSE BAY. Evergreen and deciduous shrubs or rarely trees, furnishing many highly ornamental subjects; about 600 species in the cool and temp. regions of the northern hemisphere and one extending to N. Australia. —Lvs. alternate, short-petioled, entire: fls. in terminal umbel-like racemes, rarely axillary or solitary; calyx 5-lobed or -parted, often minute; corolla rotate, campanulate or funnelform, 5-lobed or often 2-lipped; stamens usually 5 or 10, sometimes more, long-exserted or included, the anthers awnless, dorsifixed; ovary 5–10-celled with numerous ovules in each cell, the slender style with capitate stigma: fr. a caps. septicidally dehiscent from top. (Rhododen-dron: Greek for *rose-tree.*)—It has seemed best to key the azaleas separately from the true rhododendrons, as they are distinct to gardeners; but the botanical characters distinguishing Azalea are not constant; some of the azaleas are evergreen, and some of the rhododendrons are deciduous.

A. Foliage deciduous or sometimes persistent, pubescent but never lepidote: stamens 4–10: ovary setose, rarely glabrous.
  B. Fls. several or many from terminal buds: lvs. from lateral buds below.
    C. Corolla rotate-campanulate; stamens 5–10.
      D. Stamens 10; corolla divided to base . . . . 1. *R. canadense*
      DD. Stamens 5–7; corolla not divided to base . . . . 2. *R. Vaseyi*
    CC. Corolla funnelform; stamens 5.
      D. Tube of corolla much shorter than lobes.
        E. Lvs. gray-pubescent beneath . . . . 3. *R. molle*
        EE. Lvs. pubescent only on veins beneath . . . . 4. *R. japonicum*

DD. Tube of corolla as long as or longer than lobes.
E. Blooming before or with the young lvs.
F. Color of fls. yellow … 5. *R. flavum*
FF. Color of fls. white or pink.
G. Plant stoloniferous: corolla-tube glabrous inside: apex of fl.-buds with conspicuous stipitate glands … 6. *R. atlanticum*
GG. Plant not stoloniferous: corolla-tube pubescent inside: apex of fl.-buds without glands.
H. Lvs. soft-pubescent beneath … 7. *R. canescens*
HH. Lvs. strigose-pubescent beneath … 8. *R. nudiflorum*
EE. Blooming after the lvs.
F. Color of fls. orange to scarlet … 9. *R. calendulaceum*
FF. Color of fls. white or pink.
G. Upper lip of corolla with conspicuous yellow blotch … 10. *R. occidentale*
GG. Upper lip of corolla without yellow blotch.
H. Branchlets strigose-hairy: style pubescent … 11. *R. viscosum*
HH. Branchlets glabrous: style glabrous … 12. *R. arborescens*
BB. Fls. 1–3 from terminal buds: lvs. from same terminal bud.
C. Number of stamens 4–5.
D. Diam. of fls. ⅓–½in. … 13. *R. Tschonoskii*
DD. Diam. of fls. 1½–3 in.
E. Margins of lvs. crenulate: fls. 2–3 in. across … 14. *R. indicum*
EE. Margins of lvs. entire: fls. 1½ in. across … 15. *R. obtusum*
CC. Number of stamens 8–10.
D. Shape of lvs. elliptic to lanceolate: branchlets strigose-hairy.
E. Color of fls. white … 16. *R. mucronatum*
EE. Color of fls. rose, red, or purple.
F. Sepals minute: bud-scales not sticky … 17. *R. Simsii*
FF. Sepals ¼–½in. long: bud-scales sticky on inner surface.
G. Calyx-lobes glandular-ciliate: lvs. entire … 18. *R. pulchrum*
GG. Calyx-lobes not glandular: lvs. obscurely crenate-serrate … 19. *R. yedoense*
DD. Shape of lvs. broad-ovate to broad-obovate: branchlets becoming glabrous.
E. Blooming before the lvs., rose-purple … 20. *R. reticulatum*
EE. Blooming with the lvs., pink spotted with brown … 21. *R. Schlippenbachii*
AA. Foliage persistent, rarely deciduous, glabrous, lepidote or tomentose: stamens 5–20: ovary glabrous, lepidote or tomentose, not setose.
B. Lvs. not lepidote.
C. Under side of lvs. tomentose.
D. Fls. with 5 stamens.
E. Margins of lvs. crenulate: fls. 2–3 in. across … 14. *R. indicum*
EE. Margins of lvs. entire: fls. 1½ in. across … 15. *R. obtusum*
DD. Fls. with 8 or more stamens.
E. Stamens 14; corolla-lobes 7 … 22. *R. Metternichii*
EE. Stamens 8–10; corolla-lobes 5.
F. Corollas white.
G. Pedicels 1–2 in. long: lvs. 4–10 in. long … 25. *R. maximum*
GG. Pedicels ⅕–⅖in. long: lvs. 1–3 in. long … 16. *R. mucronatum*
FF. Corollas scarlet, rose-red to purple.
G. Filaments glabrous or papillose, not basally pubescent.
H. Infl. 2–3-fld.; calyx about ⅓in. long: shrub to 6 ft. … 19. *R. yedoense*
HH. Infl. 10–20-fld.; calyx ⅛in. long: tree 20–40 ft. … 23. *R. arboreum*
GG. Filaments hairy basally, often only puberulent.
H. Calyx ⅛in. long: pedicels 1½–2 in. long … 24. *R. Smirnowii*
HH. Calyx ¼in. long or more: pedicels ⅕–½in. long.
I. Inner bud-scales not sticky: style exserted: calyx 1/12–¼in. long … 17. *R. Simsii*
II. Inner bud-scales sticky: style not exserted: calyx about ⅓in. long … 18. *R. pulchrum*
CC. Under side of lvs. glabrous or with very few hairs.
D. Number of stamens 12–16.
E. Stamens pubescent at base; calyx small … 26. *R. decorum*
EE. Stamens glabrous; calyx minute … 27. *R. Fortunei*
DD. Number of stamens 10.
E. Ovary glabrous and glandular … 28. *R. ponticum*
EE. Ovary pubescent.
F. Pubescence rusty-tomentose: pedicels pubescent: lvs. obtuse … 29. *R. catawbiense*
FF. Pubescence white-silky: pedicels glabrous: lvs. acute … 30. *R. californicum*
BB. Lvs. lepidote.
C. Color of fls. yellow … 31. *R. Keiskei*
CC. Color of fls. purple, pink or white.
D. Scales on both sides of lf.
E. Length of lvs. ¼–½in.
F. Stamens included … 32. *R. intricatum*
FF. Stamens exserted.
G. Anthers brown: stigma lobed: lvs. dark green … 33. *R. impeditum*
GG. Anthers purple: stigma not lobed: lvs. hoary … 34. *R. fastigiatum*
EE. Length of lvs. ¾–3 in.
F. Tube of corolla about twice as long as lobes … 41. *R. ferrugineum*
FF. Tube of corolla much shorter than lobes.
G. Diam. of fls. ¾–1 in.: evergreen … 35. *R. hippophæoides*
GG. Diam. of fls. 1–2 in.: deciduous or semi-evergreen.

H. Tip of lf. obtuse....................36. *R. dauricum*
HH. Tip of lf. acute or acuminate....................37. *R. mucronulatum*
DD. Scales on lower surface of lf. only.
E. Diam. of fls. ½–¾ in.
F. Stamens exserted.
G. Fls. white: lvs. rusty beneath....................38. *R. micranthum*
GG. Fls. pink: lvs. glaucous beneath....................39. *R. racemosum*
FF. Stamens shorter than corolla.
G. Margins of lvs. ciliate....................40. *R. hirsutum*
GG. Margins of lvs. not ciliate....................41. *R. ferrugineum*
EE. Diam. of fls. 1–2½ in.
F. Lf. glabrous.
G. Style shorter than stamens.
H. Tube of corolla shorter than lobes, not lepidote....................42. *R. carolinianum*
HH. Tube of corolla longer than lobes, lepidote outside....................43. *R. minus*
GG. Style longer than stamens....................44. *R. oreotrephes*
FF. Lf. pubescent, at least on midrib.
G. Margin of lf. ciliate....................45. *R. ciliatum*
GG. Margin of lf. not ciliate....................46. *R. Augustinii*

1. **R. canadense,** Torr. (*Rhodora canadensis,* L. *Azalea canadensis,* Kuntze). RHODORA. Much-branched deciduous shrub to 3 ft.: lvs. elliptic to oblong, ¾–1½ in. long, obtuse or somewhat acute, margins revolute and ciliate, gray-tomentose beneath: fls. rose-purple, ½–¾ in. long, 2-lipped, the lower lip divided to base, in 3–7-fld. clusters in Apr.–May before the lvs.; stamens 10, equalling corolla, pubescent at base; style longer, glabrous. Newf. to Pa.

2. **R. Vaseyi,** Gray (*Azalea Vaseyi,* Rehd. *Biltia Vaseyi,* Small). Deciduous shrub to 15 ft.: lvs. elliptic or elliptic-oblong, 2–5 in. long, acuminate, ciliate, glabrous or slightly hairy on midrib: fls. pale rose-colored, spotted with orange or red-brown at base of upper lobes, 1½ in. across, in 5–8-fld. clusters in Apr.–May before lvs.; corolla rotate-campanulate, slightly 2-lipped, the tube very short, glabrous; stamens usually 7, unequal, the longer ones exserted, glabrous; style longer, glabrous. (For Geo. R. Vasey, page 53.) N. C.

3. **R. molle,** Don (*R. sinense,* Sweet. *Azalea sinensis,* Lodd. *A. mollis,* Blume). Deciduous shrub 3–5 ft. high: lvs. oblong to oblong-lanceolate, 2–6 in. long, obtuse and mucronate, ciliate, soft gray-pubescent beneath: fls. golden-yellow, 2 in. across, in many-fld. clusters in Apr.–May before the lvs.; corolla campanulate-funnelform, pubescent outside; stamens 5, as long as or longer than corolla. China.—A group of garden hybrids between this species and *R. japonicum* is known as **R. Kosterianum,** Schneid., Anthony Koster & Sons of Holland being the first to cross the two species; fls. white to red; lvs. slightly pubescent beneath.

4. **R. japonicum,** Suringar (*R. molle,* Sieb. & Zucc. not Don. *Azalea japonica,* Gray). Deciduous shrub to 6 ft.: lvs. obovate, 2–4 in. long, obtuse and mucronate, ciliate, glabrous except appressed bristles on veins and sparingly on upper surface: fls. orange-red to scarlet, 2–2½ in. across, in 6–12-fld. clusters from Apr.–June before the lvs.; corolla campanulate-funnelform, pubescent outside; stamens 5, shorter than corolla, pubescent at base. Japan.

5. **R. flavum,** Don (*Azalea flava,* Hoffmgg. *A. pontica,* L. *R. luteum,* Sweet not *A. lutea,* L.). Deciduous densely-branched shrub 6–12 ft. high: lvs. oblong-lanceolate, 2–5 in. long, acute or obtuse, ciliate, hairy on both sides when young: fls. yellow, very fragrant, about 2 in. across, in 10–12-fld. clusters in May before the lvs.; corolla-tube long and cylindrical, hairy; stamens 5, long-exserted; style longer. Caucasus.—The principal parent of the GHENT AZALEAS, **R. gandavense,** Rehd. (*Azalea gandavensis,* Koch), which has as the other parent *R. Mortieri,* Sweet, itself a hybrid between *R. calendulaceum, R. nudiflorum* and with some infusion of *R. speciosum.*

6. **R. atlanticum,** Rehd. (*Azalea atlantica,* Ashe). Stoloniferous deciduous shrub to 2 ft.: lvs. obovate, 1–2½ in. long, obtuse or somewhat acute, ciliate, glabrous except midrib beneath: fls. white tinged with pink, about 1 in. long, in 4–10-fld. clusters in Apr.–May before the lvs.; corolla funnelform with cylindrical tube, glandular-hairy outside, glabrous inside; stamens 5, much-exserted; style longer. Del. to S. C.

7. **R. canescens,** Sweet (*Azalea canescens,* Michx.). Deciduous shrub to 15 ft.: lvs. oblong-obovate, 2–4 in. long, acute, ciliate, soft-pubescent beneath: fls. pink or white, slightly fragrant, 1½ in. across, in 6–15-fld. clusters in Apr.–May before the lvs.; corolla funnelform, with cylindrical tube much longer than lobes, glandular-hairy outside, pubescent inside; stamens 5, much-exserted, pubescent at base; style about length of stamens. N. C. to Fla. and Tex.

8. **R. nudiflorum,** Torr. (*Azalea nudiflora,* L.). PINXTER-FLOWER. Deciduous shrub to 6 or rarely 9 ft.: lvs. oblong or obovate, 2–3 in. long, acute or acuminate, ciliate, bristly on midrib beneath: fls. pink to nearly white, about 1½ in. across, in 6–12-fld. clusters in Apr. or May before the lvs.; corolla funnelform, the tube longer than lobes, pubescent outside and inside; stamens 5, much-exserted, pubescent at base; style longer. Mass. to Fla. and La. Var. **roseum,** Wiegand (*R. roseum,* Rehd., *Azalea rosea,* Loisel. *A. prinophylla,* Small), is more pubescent, and the range is more inland.

9. **R. calendulaceum,** Torr. (*Azalea calendulacea,* Michx.). FLAME AZALEA. Deciduous shrub to 10 ft. or more: lvs. elliptic- to obovate-oblong, 2–3 in. long, acute, pubescent: fls. orange-yellow to scarlet with an orange blotch on upper lobe, about 2 in. across, in 5–7-fld. clusters in May and June with or shortly after lvs.; corolla funnelform, the tube cylindrical and as long as lobes, pubescent outside; stamens 5, long-exserted, pubescent at base; style longer. Pa. to N. Ga. and Ky.

10. **R. occidentale,** Gray (*Azalea occidentalis,* Torr. & Gray. *A. californica,* Torr. & Gray). Deciduous shrub to 9 ft.: lvs. elliptic to oblong-lanceolate, 1–4 in. long, acute or obtusish, ciliate, thinly pubescent on both surfaces when young: fls. white or pink with yellow blotch on upper lobe, fragrant, to 2 in. across, in 6–12-fld. clusters in June–July with or after lvs., rarely before lvs.; corolla funnelform, the pubescent tube as long as lobes; stamens 5, exserted, pubescent at base; style about length of stamens. Ore., Calif.

11. **R. viscosum,** Torr. (*Azalea viscosa,* L.). WHITE SWAMP HONEYSUCKLE. Deciduous shrub to 9 ft. or more, branchlets strigose-hairy: lvs. elliptic-obovate to oblong-lanceolate, 1–2½ in. long, acute or mucronulate, ciliate, bristly on midrib beneath: fls. white or tinged rose, fragrant, 1½–2 in. long, in 4–9-fld. clusters from June–July after the lvs.; corolla cylindrical, glandular-hairy outside; stamens 5, exserted, pubescent at base; style longer, pubescent. Swamps, Me. to S. C.

12. **R. arborescens,** Torr. (*Azalea arborescens,* Pursh). Deciduous shrub to 10 ft. or more, branchlets glabrous: lvs. obovate or elliptic, 1–3 in. long, acute or obtuse, ciliate, glabrous or slightly pubescent on midrib beneath, often glaucous beneath: fls. white or pinkish, fragrant, 2 in. long, in 3–6-fld. clusters in June–July after the lvs.; corolla funnelform, tube longer than lobes, pubescent; stamens 5, exserted, pubescent at base; style equalling or longer than stamens, usually glabrous. Pa. to Ga. and Ala.

13. **R. Tschonoskii,** Maxim. (*Azalea Tschonoskii,* Kuntze). Densely branched deciduous shrub to 8 ft. or less: lvs. narrow to broadly lanceolate, ¼–1½ in. long, acute, pubescent on both surfaces, turning shades of orange and crimson in autumn: fls. white, ¼–½in. across, in 2–6-fld. clusters in June; corolla funnelform, tube cylindrical, pubescent outside; stamens 4–5, exserted, pubescent at base. Korea, Japan, where it was collected by Tschonoski.

14. **R. indicum,** Sweet (*Azalea indica,* L. *R. macranthum,* Don). Much-branched evergreen or half-evergreen shrub to 6 ft.: lvs. elliptic to lanceolate, 1–1½ in. long, acute, crenulate and ciliate, pale beneath, with bristly hairs on both surfaces: fls. red to pink, 2–3 in. across, usually solitary, blooming June–July; corolla broad-funnelform; stamens 5, as long as or longer than corolla, anthers purple; style longer. Japan. Var. **balsaminæflorum,** Nichols. (var. *rosæflorum,* Rehd. *Azalea balsaminæflora,* Carr.), is a dwarf var. with salmon-red double fls.—With *R. mucronatum* and *R. Simsii* this species is the parent of most of the hybrid Indian azaleas.

15. **R. obtusum,** Planch. (*R. indicum* var. *obtusum,* Maxim. *Azalea obtusa,* Lindl.). Half-evergreen much-branched shrub to 3 ft.: lvs. dimorphic, the mature ones obovate, ½–1½ in. long, rounded and mucronate, the spring lvs. elliptic-lanceolate, acute, shining above, hairy on midrib beneath: fls. scarlet, slightly fragrant, 1–1½ in. across, in 2–3-fld. clusters in Apr.–May; corolla funnelform, glabrous outside; stamens 5, included or exserted, anthers yellow. Japan. Var. **amœnum,** Rehd. (*R. amœnum,* Planch. *Azalea amœna,* Lindl.), corolla usually double (hose-in-hose), purple, ½–1 in. across; there are many forms of this var. having white to deep crimson fls.; it is one of the "Kurume" azaleas, a group originating near the city of Kurume in Japan, common named forms being *Hinodegiri* with brilliant crimson fls., *Hinomoyo* with clear pink fls., *Benigiri* with deep red fls., *Yayegiri* with salmon-red fls. Var. **Arnoldianum,** Rehd., is a hybrid between vars. *amœnum* and *Kaempferi* with rose to red fls. Var. **Kaempferi,** Wils. (*R. Kaempferi,* Planch. *R. indicum* var. *Kaempferi,* Maxim.), deciduous or evergreen, fls. red to pink, 1½–2 in. across (named for E. Kaempfer, page 273).

16. **R. mucronatum,** Don (*R. ledifolium,* Don. *R. ledifolium* var. *album,* Rehd. *Azalea ledifolia,* Hook. *A. indica alba,* Lindl.). Evergreen or half-evergreen wide-spreading shrub from 1–6 ft. high, the branches, lvs. and pedicels densely clothed with gray or rusty hairs: lvs. elliptic or elliptic-lanceolate, 1–3 in. long, obtuse or acute, mucronate, both surfaces pubescent: fls. white or sometimes rosy, fragrant, 2–2½ in. across, in 1–3-fld. clusters in May; corolla wide-funnelform; stamens usually 10, about length of corolla. Japan.

17. **R. Simsii,** Planch. (*Azalea indica,* Sims not L.). Evergreen or half-evergreen shrub to 10 ft.: lvs. elliptic-ovate to lanceolate, 1–2 in. long, acute, hairy: fls. rose to red, 1½–2 in. across, in 2–6-fld. clusters in May–June; corolla wide-funnelform; stamens usually 10, as long as corolla; style ½–¼ in. long; sepals minute. (Named for John Sims, page 51.) China, Formosa. Var. **vittatum,** Wils. (*R. vittatum,* Planch.), has white fls. striped with lilac-purple.—This species has been involved in the parentage of the hybrid Indian azaleas, as *Vervæneanum,* having rose fls. bordered with white.

18. **R. pulchrum,** Sweet (*R. phœniceum* var. *Smithii,* Wils.). Evergreen shrub to 6 ft.: lvs. elliptic to oblong-lanceolate, to 2½ in. long, entire, somewhat hairy beneath: fls. rose-

purple, about 2½ in. across, the inner bud-scales sticky; stamens 10, shorter than corolla; style longer; sepals lanceolate, ¼–½in. long, glandular-ciliate. Cult. in China, perhaps a hybrid. Var. **Maxwellii,** Bowers, has bright rose-red fls. late in May.

19. **R. yedoense,** Maxim. (*R. poukhanense* var. *Yodogawa,* Rehd. *Azalea Yodogava,* Grignan). Deciduous or half-evergreen shrub to about 3 ft.: lvs. elliptic to lanceolate, 1–3 in. long, acute, obscurely crenate-serrate, hairy beneath at least on veins: fls. double, rosy-lilac spotted with purple, in 1–3-fld. clusters in May, the inner bud-scales sticky; stamens 10, shorter than corolla; style longer; sepals oval, ½in. long, ciliate. Japan, Korea. Var. **poukhanense,** Nakai (*R. poukhanense,* Lévl.), grows to 6 ft. and has fragrant fls. 2 in. across.

20. **R. reticulatum,** D. Don (*R. rhombicum,* Miq. *Azalea reticulata,* Koch). Much-branched deciduous shrub to 25 ft.: lvs. at ends of branchlets, broad-ovate or rhombic, 1–2½ in. long, acute and mucronate, becoming nearly glabrous except on veins beneath: fls. rose-purple, to 2 in. across, in 1–2-fld. clusters in Apr.–May before the lvs.; corolla rotate-campanulate, usually unspotted; stamens usually 10, about length of corolla; calyx minute. Japan.

21. **R. Schlippenbachii,** Maxim. (*Azalea Schlippenbachii,* Kuntze). Deciduous shrub from 3–15 ft. high, with glandular-pilose branchlets becoming glabrous: lvs. broad-obovate, 2–5 in. long, rounded and mucronate at apex, becoming glabrous beneath except on veins: fls. pale rose, the posterior lobes marked with brown, fragrant, 2–3 in. across, in 3–6-fld. clusters in May, the corolla-lobes longer than tube; stamens 10, of unequal length, as long as corolla. (Named for Baron A. von Schlippenbach, who collected it in 1854.) Korea, Manchuria, Japan.

22. **R. Metternichii,** Sieb. & Zucc. Evergreen shrub to 12 ft.: lvs. oblong, 3–6 in. long, obtuse, densely tomentose beneath: fls. rose, 2–3 in. across, on pedicels about 1 in. long, Apr.–May; corolla campanulate, 7-lobed; stamens 14. (Named for Prince Metternich, Austrian diplomat.) Japan.

23. **R. arboreum,** Smith. Evergreen shrub or small tree to 40 ft.: lvs. oblong to lanceolate, 4–7 in. long, tapering at both ends, white- or rusty-tomentose beneath: fls. blood-red, pink or white, usually spotted, 1–1½ in. across, in dense clusters from Mar.–May, pedicels very short; corolla campanulate, the tube much longer than lobes; stamens 10, shorter than corolla; calyx very small. Himalayas.

24. **R. Smirnowii,** Trautv. Evergreen shrub or small tree to 18 ft.: lvs. oblong, 3–6 in. long, obtuse or acute, woolly-tomentose beneath: fls. rose, 2–3 in. across, in May, on pedicels 1–2 in. long; corolla broad-funnelform, the frilled lobes longer than tube and with dark margins; stamens 10; calyx very short. (Named for Michael Smirnov, 1849–1889, Russian botanist.) Caucasus.

25. **R. maximum,** L. Evergreen shrub or small tree to 35 ft.: lvs. oblong to lanceolate-oblong, 4–10 in. long, acute at both ends, dark green above, whitish beneath and thinly tomentose: fls. rose-colored spotted within with greenish varying to white, about 1½ in. across, in many-fld. clusters in June–July; corolla campanulate, deeply lobed; stamens 10, usually included; sepals ovate, nearly ¼in. long. N. S. to Ga. and Ala.—Parent, with *R. catawbiense,* of many hardy hybrids.

26. **R. decorum,** Franch. Evergreen shrub to 18 ft.: lvs. oblong, 2–6 in. long, obtuse, glaucous beneath with few hairs: fls. white or pink usually spotted, 2 in. across, in 8–10-fld. clusters in May–June; corolla broad-funnelform, 6–8-lobed; stamens 12–16, pubescent at base. China.

27. **R. Fortunei,** Lindl. Evergreen shrub to 12 ft.: lvs. oblong, 4–8 in. long, abruptly acute, glabrous except for few hairs beneath: fls. lilac or pink, fragrant, 2–3 in. across, in racemes in June–July; corolla campanulate, 7-lobed; stamens 14–16, glabrous; calyx rim-like. (Robt. Fortune, page 43.) China.

28. **R. ponticum,** L. Evergreen shrub 10 ft. or more high: lvs. elliptic to oblong, 2–6 in. long, acute, pale beneath, glabrous: fls. purple, spotted brownish within, about 2 in. across, in many-fld. clusters in May–June; pedicels longer than corolla, pubescent; corolla funnelform-campanulate; stamens 10; ovary glandular and glabrous. Spain, Portugal, Asia Minor.—This species has entered into the "catawbiense hybrids."

29. **R. catawbiense,** Michx. Mountain Rose Bay. Evergreen shrub to 20 ft.: lvs. oval or oblong, 2–5 in. long, rounded or obtuse at both ends, mucronulate, pale beneath, glabrous: fls. lilac-purple spotted with green, 2–2½ in. across, in many-fld. clusters in May–June; corolla broad-campanulate; pedicels rusty-pubescent; stamens 10, mostly included; ovary rusty-tomenose. Mts., Va. to Ga. Var. **album,** Hort., has white fls. Var. **compactum,** Hort., is a dwarf form.—One of the most extensive group of garden hybrids has this species as one parent, the others being *R. maximum, R. ponticum, R. caucasicum, R. arboreum,* and perhaps others. The fls. vary in color from white to dark red. There are many forms named in Latin and English, some of the commonest being: **album elegans,** pale pink changing to white; **altaclarense,** crimson; **delicatissimum,** pale pink to white; **Morelianum** (*Everestianum*), lilac-violet; **purpureum elegans,** rich purple; **roseum elegans,** lilac; **roseum superbum,** rose-purple.

30. **R. californicum,** Hook. Evergreen shrub to 8 ft., rarely a small tree to 20 ft.: lvs. oblong or elliptic, 3–6 in. long, acute, pale beneath, glabrous: fls. rose or rose-purple spotted with brown, 2–2½ in. across, in many-fld. clusters in June–July; corolla broad-campanulate, lobes wavy; pedicels glabrous; stamens 10, pubescent at base; ovary white-silky. Wash. to Calif.

31. **R. Keiskei,** Miq. Evergreen shrub to 10 ft., sometimes procumbent: lvs. oblong to lanceolate, 1–2 in. long, mucronate, densely scaly beneath and somewhat above: fls. lemon-yellow, unspotted, about 1½ in. across, in 3–6-fld. clusters in May; corolla broad-campanulate, scaly outside; stamens 10, exserted; style longer. (Named for I. Keisk, Japanese botanist.) Japan.

32. **R. intricatum,** Franch. Small evergreen shrub to 1½ ft.: lvs. broad-ovate to elliptic, ¼–½in. long, densely scaly on both sides, pale beneath: fls. violet-purple, ½in. across, in 5–6-fld. clusters in June; corolla broad-funnelform, lobes short and rounded; stamens 10, included; style shorter. China.

33. **R. impeditum,** Balf. f. & W. W. Smith. Matted evergreen shrub from 6–20 in. high: lvs. elliptic to oblong, ⅓–½in. long, obtuse, densely scaly on both sides, red-brown beneath: fls. light purplish-blue, ½in. across, in 1–2-fld. clusters in June–July; corolla funnelform; stamens 10, long-exserted, anthers brown; style longer, with lobed stigma. China.

34. **R. fastigiatum,** Franch. Dwarf evergreen shrub: lvs. elliptic, ¼–⅓in. long, obtuse, densely scaly, hoary: fls. lilac-rose, ¾–1 in. across, in 4–5-fld. clusters; stamens 10, exserted, anthers purple; style longer, stigma not lobed. China.

35. **R. hippophæoides,** Balf. f. & W. W. Smith. Much-branched evergreen shrub 3–5 ft. high: lvs. oblong, ¾–1¼ in. long, obtuse and mucronate, densely scaly on both sides, pale beneath: fls. lavender-blue, ¾–1 in. across, in dense 4–8-fld. clusters in Apr.; corolla broad-campanulate; stamens 10, included. China.

36. **R. dauricum,** L. (*R. dahuricum*, DC. *Azalea dahurica*, Koch). Deciduous or semi-evergreen shrub to 6 ft.: lvs. elliptic to oblong-ovate, 1–2 in. long, obtuse, scaly above, paler and densely scaly beneath: fls. rosy-purple, 1–1½ in. across, solitary, in Mar.–Apr. before the lvs.; corolla rotate-campanulate, lobes longer than tube; stamens 10, about length of corolla; style longer. Siberia to Japan. **Var. sempervirens,** Sims (var. *atrovirens*, Ker.), has persistent lvs. and darker fls.

37. **R. mucronulatum,** Turcz. (*R. dauricum* var. *mucronulatum*, Maxim.). Deciduous shrub to 6 ft.: lvs. elliptic-lanceolate to lanceolate, 1–3 in. long, acute or acuminate, somewhat scaly on both sides: fls. pale rose-purple, 1½–2 in. across, in 3–6-fld. clusters in Mar.–Apr. before the lvs.; corolla campanulate; stamens 10, about length of corolla; style longer. China, Korea, Japan.

38. **R. micranthum,** Turcz. Evergreen densely-branched shrub to 8 ft.: lvs. oblong or oblanceolate, ¾–1½ in. long, acute, glabrous above, densely rusty-scaly beneath: fls. white, ⅓–½in. across, in dense many-fld. clusters in June–July; corolla campanulate, the oblong or oval lobes as long as tube, scaly outside; stamens 10, glabrous, longer than corolla. Manchuria, China, Korea.

39. **R. racemosum,** Franch. Evergreen shrub to 6 ft.: lvs. elliptic to obovate, ¾–1½ in. long, obtuse or acute, glabrous above, scaly and glaucous beneath: fls. pink, ¾in. across, in few-fld. clusters along the branchlets in Apr.–May; corolla broad-campanulate, the oblong lobes longer than tube; stamens 10, longer than corolla. China.

40. **R. hirsutum,** L. Evergreen shrub to 3 ft.: lvs. oblong to obovate, ½–1¼ in. long, obtuse or acutish, glabrous above, green and scaly beneath, margins with long hairs: fls. pink to carmine, ½in. across, in clusters in June; corolla funnelform with spreading lobes, slightly scaly outside; pedicels and calyx hairy; stamens 10, shorter than corolla. Mts. of Eu.—A hybrid between this species and *R. minus* is **R. myrtifolium,** Lodd., to 5 ft.; lvs. rusty-scaly beneath, ciliate near base when young; fls. rose, 1 in. across.

41. **R. ferrugineum,** L. Dense evergreen shrub to 3 ft.: lvs. oblong to oblong-lanceolate, 1–2 in. long, acute, shining and slightly scaly above, densely rusty-scaly beneath: fls. pink to carmine, ½in. across, in 6–12-fld. clusters in July–Aug.; corolla funnelform, tube twice as long as lobes, scaly outside; stamens 10, shorter than corolla. Mts. of Cent. Eu.—A hybrid between this species and *R. minus* is **R. arbutifolium,** Rehd. (*R. daphnoides*, Hort.), to 4 ft.; lvs. dull above, with dark and pale scales beneath; fls. rose, ½–¾in. across.

42. **R. carolinianum,** Rehd. Compact evergreen shrub to 6 ft.: lvs. elliptic, 2–3 in. long, acute or short-acuminate, glabrous above, rusty-scaly beneath: fls. pale rose-purple, about 1½ in. across, in 5–10-fld. clusters in May–June; corolla broad-funnelform, tube shorter than lobes, glabrous or rarely slightly scaly outside; stamens 10, shorter than corolla; style shorter. N. C. Var. **album,** Rehd., has white fls.—A hybrid between this species and *R. ferrugineum* is **R. lætevirens,** Rehd. (*R. Wilsonii*, Hort.), low and wide-spreading; fls. rose, 1¼ in. across.

43. **R. minus,** Michx. (*R. punctatum*, Andr.). Evergreen shrub to 10 ft.: lvs. elliptic to lanceolate, 1½–4 in. long, acute at both ends, glabrous above, scaly and sometimes

glaucous beneath: fls. pink, the upper lobe spotted with greenish, about 1 in. across, in 6–10-fld. clusters in June–July; corolla funnelform, tube longer than lobes, scaly outside; stamens 10, shorter than corolla; style shorter. S. C. to Ga. and Ala.

44. **R. oreotrephes,** W. W. Smith. Evergreen shrub to 8 ft. or small tree to 25 ft.: lvs. oval, 1½–3 in. long, obtuse to acute, dull green and glabrous above, densely scaly and glaucous beneath: fls. rose-lavender spotted with brownish, 2–2½ in. across, in 5–11-fld. clusters in Apr.–May; corolla broad-funnelform; stamens 10, equalling or slightly longer than corolla; style longer. (Oreotrephes: mountain dweller.) China.

45. **R. ciliatum,** Hook. f. Stiff evergreen shrub to 6 ft.: lvs. elliptic or obovate, 2–4 in. long, bristly-hairy above and on margins, scaly beneath: fls. white to reddish-purple, 1½–2½ in. across, in 3–5-fld. clusters in Mar.–Apr.; corolla broad-campanulate, the lobes notched; stamens 10. Himalayas.

46. **R. Augustinii,** Hemsl. Evergreen shrub to 20 ft.: lvs. oblong to oblong-lanceolate, 1–3 in. long, acute or acuminate, dark green and slightly pubescent above, scaly beneath and hairy on midrib: fls. pink spotted with yellow, 1½–2 in. across, in 3–4-fld. clusters in Apr.–May; corolla broad-campanulate, tube much shorter than lobes; stamens 10, about length of corolla; style longer. (Named for Dr. Augustine Henry, page 45.) China.

16. **ZENOBIA,** Don. One deciduous or half-evergreen shrub in E. N. Amer. (or by some authors separated into 2 species), planted out-of-doors or forced in the greenhouse.—Lvs. alternate, short-petioled, entire or crenulate: fls. long-pedicelled, bracted at base, in axillary clusters forming terminal racemes on the upper part of branches of the previous year; calyx with 5 short lobes; corolla campanulate, obtusely 5-lobed; stamens 10, the anthers with 4 slender awns; ovary 5-celled with numerous ovules in each cell: fr. a loculicidally dehiscent caps., the dorsal sutures somewhat thickened. (Zeno-bia: after Zenobia, queen of Palmyra, who lived in the 3rd century.)

Z. pulverulenta, Pollard (*Andromeda pulverulenta*, Bartram. *A. speciosa*, Michx. *Z. speciosa*, Don). To 6 ft., the branches upright or arching, glabrous: lvs. oval to oblong, 1–3 in. long, obtuse or acutish, tapering at base, crenulate, often covered with glaucous bloom: fls. white, ⅓–½in. across, nodding: caps. depressed-globose, about ¼in. across. N. C. to Fla. Var. **nuda,** Rehd. (*Z. cassinefolia*, Pollard. *Andromeda cassinefolia*, Vent.), lvs. green and without bloom.

17. **OXYDENDRUM,** DC. One deciduous tree in E. N. Amer., sometimes planted for ornament.—Lvs. alternate, petioled, serrate: fls. in terminal panicles composed of 6 or more one-sided racemes, the pedicels with 2 deciduous bractlets; sepals 5, persistent; corolla cylindric-ovoid with 5 minute lobes, puberulous; stamens 10, the anthers opening by chinks from apex to middle; ovary 5-celled with numerous ovules in each cell: fr. a loculicidally dehiscent caps. (Oxyden-drum: Greek for *sour tree*, from the acid taste of the foliage.)

O. arboreum, DC. (*Andromeda arborea*, L.). Sour-Wood. Sorrel-Tree. Tree to 60 ft., with deeply fissured bark: lvs. oblong-lanceolate, 4–8 in. long, acuminate, slender-petioled, glabrous except few hairs on midrib, turning scarlet in autumn: fls. white, ⅓in. long, in drooping panicles 7–10 in. long in July–Aug.: caps. ovoid-pyramidal, ⅓in. long, grayish-pubescent. Pa. to Fla. and La.

18. **CHAMÆDAPHNE,** Moench. One evergreen shrub circumpolar in bogs and sometimes planted in the rock-garden.—Lvs. alternate, short-petioled, nearly entire, scaly: fls. short-pedicelled, in terminal leafy racemes; calyx 5-lobed, subtended by 2 bractlets; corolla urceolate, with 5 short lobes; stamens 10, anther-sacs opening by a terminal pore: caps. loculicidally dehiscent, the wall of 2 layers, the outer splitting into 5 valves, the inner into 10; seeds many, small. (Chamædaph-ne: Greek for *dwarf* and *daphne*, laurel.)

C. calyculata, Moench (*Andromeda calyculata*, L.). Leather-Leaf. To 5 ft.: lvs. oblong, ½–2 in. long, obtuse or acute, revolute, densely scaly beneath: fls. white, ¼in. long, nodding, in racemes 2–5 in. long in Apr.–June: caps. depressed-globose, ⅙in. across. N. Amer., N. Eu., N. Asia.

19. **LYONIA,** Nutt. (*Xolisma*, Raf.). Evergreen or deciduous shrubs of N. Amer. and Asia, of about 30 species, sometimes transplanted.—Lvs. alternate, short-petioled: fls. white or pinkish, in axillary clusters or racemes or terminal panicles;

calyx usually 5-lobed; corolla urceolate or cylindrical with short lobes; stamens commonly 10, anther-sacs opening by terminal pores: caps. loculicidally dehiscent, with thickened sutures separating from valves; seeds many, small. (Lyo-nia: named for John Lyon, American botanist, died about 1818.)

A. Fls. in leafless racemes forming terminal panicles........................1. *L. ligustrina*
AA. Fls. in axillary clusters forming terminal leafy racemes.
B. Lvs. persistent: branchlets angled........................2. *L. lucida*
BB. Lvs. deciduous: branchlets terete........................3. *L. mariana*

1. **L. ligustrina,** DC. (*Vaccinium ligustrinum*, L. *Andromeda ligustrina*, Muhl. *Arsenococcus ligustrinus*, Small). MALE-BERRY. HE-HUCKLEBERRY. Deciduous shrub to 12 ft.: lvs. elliptic to oblong-lanceolate, 1–3 in. long, entire or serrulate: fls. whitish, ⅙in. long, in dense panicles 2–6 in. long in May–July. Me. to Fla. and Tex.

2. **L. lucida,** Koch (*Andromeda lucida*, Lam. *L. nitida*, Fern. *Pieris lucida*, Rehd. *P. nitida*, Benth. & Hook. *Neopieris nitida*, Britt. *Desmothamnus lucidus*, Small). FETTER-BUSH. Evergreen shrub to 6 ft., with smooth triangular branches: lvs. broadly elliptic to oblong, 1½–3 in. long, tapering at both ends, entire, the margins slightly revolute, glabrous: fls. white to pink, ¼–⅓in. long, in small axillary clusters forming a terminal leafy raceme from Mar.–May. Va. to Fla. and La.

3. **L. mariana,** D. Don (*Andromeda mariana*, L. *Pieris mariana*, Benth. & Hook. *Neopieris mariana*, Britt.). STAGGER-BUSH. Deciduous shrub to 6 ft.: lvs. elliptic to oblong, 1–2½ in. long, entire: fls. white or pinkish, nodding, about ½in. long, in axillary clusters forming a terminal leafy raceme in May–June. R. I. to Fla. and Ark.

20. **ANDROMEDA,** L. BOG-ROSEMARY. Two low evergreen shrubs of cold regions in the northern hemisphere.—Lvs. alternate, narrow, entire, short-petioled: fls. pinkish, in nodding terminal umbels; calyx 5-lobed; corolla urceolate, the 5 short lobes recurved; stamens 10, anther-sacs opening by terminal pores: caps. loculicidally dehiscent into 5 valves, with many seeds. (Androm-eda: Greek mythological name.)

A. polifolia, L. To 1 ft., with creeping rootstocks: lvs. oblong to linear, ½–1½ in. long, revolute, glabrous and glaucous beneath: fls. ¼in. long, May–July. Eu., N. Asia, N. N. Amer.

21. **PIERIS,** D. Don. Evergreen shrubs or rarely small trees, sometimes planted for ornament, of about 8 species in N. Amer. and E. Asia south to Himalayas.—Lvs. alternate, short-petioled, serrulate or crenulate: fls. short-pedicelled, bracted, in terminal panicles; calyx-lobes separate; corolla ovoid-urceolate, with 5 short recurved lobes; stamens 10, anthers with pair of awns near base; ovary 5-celled with numerous ovules in each cell: fr. a loculicidally dehiscent caps., the sutures not thickened. (Pie-ris: mythological name.)

A. Panicles upright: branches and petioles with strigose hairs........................1. *P. floribunda*
AA. Panicles drooping: branches and petioles glabrous........................2. *P. japonica*

1. **P. floribunda,** Benth. & Hook. (*Andromeda floribunda*, Pursh). Dense shrub to 6 ft., the branches and petioles with strigose brown hairs: lvs. ovate to oblong-lanceolate, 1½–3 in. long, acute, serrulate and setosely ciliate, otherwise glabrous: fls. white, ¼in. long, on slender racemes forming a dense terminal upright panicle 2–5 in. long in Apr. and May; corolla ovate, strongly 5-angled. Va. to Ga.

2. **P. japonica,** D. Don (*Andromeda japonica*, Thunb.). Shrub or sometimes small tree to 30 ft., the branches and petioles glabrous: lvs. obovate-lanceolate, 1½–3 in. long, acute, serrulate, glabrous: fls. white, ¼in. long, on slender racemes forming a terminal drooping panicle 3–6 in. long in Apr. and May; corolla ovate, not angled. Japan.

22. **LEUCOTHOË,** Don. About 35 species of evergreen or deciduous shrubs native in N. and S. Amer., Madagascar, Himalayas, and Japan.—Lvs. alternate, petioled, serrate: fls. in axillary or terminal racemes; calyx-lobes 5, imbricated; corolla ovoid, urceolate or cylindrical, with 5 imbricated teeth; stamens 10, the anthers obtuse or awned; ovary 5-celled with numerous ovules in each cell: fr. a loculicidally dehiscent caps., the sutures not thickened. (Leucoth-oë: named for the daughter of Orchamus, king of Babylonia.)

A. Foliage deciduous: anthers awned: calyx with 2 bractlets at base........................1. *L. racemosa*
AA. Foliage persistent: anthers not awned: calyx without bractlets.
B. Lvs. long-acuminate, conspicuously petioled........................2. *L. Catesbæi*
BB. Lvs. abruptly acuminate, very short-petioled........................3. *L. axillaris*

1. **L. racemosa,** Gray (*Andromeda racemosa*, L. *Eubotrys racemosa*, Nutt.). SWEET-BELLS. Deciduous shrub to 12 ft.: lvs. oblong or elliptic, 1–3 in. long, acute, pubescent at least on veins beneath: fls. white or pinkish, ⅓in. long, in racemes 1–3 in. long in May–June; calyx with 2 bractlets at base; anthers with 4 awns. Mass. to Fla. and La.

2. **L. Catesbæi,** Gray (*Andromeda Catesbæi*, Walt.). Evergreen shrub to 6 ft., with slender glabrous arching branches: lvs. ovate-lanceolate to lanceolate, 3–7 in. long, on petioles ⅓in. or more long, long-acuminate, closely serrulate, glossy green above and paler beneath, glabrous: fls. white, reddish in bud, about ¼in. long, in axillary racemes 1–2 in. long in Apr. and May; sepals ovate-oblong, acute. (Named for Mark Catesby, 1679–1749, English naturalist.) Va. to Ga. and Tenn.

3. **L. axillaris,** Don (*Andromeda axillaris*, Lam.). Very similar to the above but differing in its oval to oblong-lanceolate abruptly acuminate remotely serrulate lvs. with petioles ¼in. or less long, the fls. being greenish in bud, and the ovate sepals. Va. to Fla. and Ala.

23. **LEIOPHYLLUM,** Hedwig f. (*Dendrium*, Desv.). SAND-MYRTLE. Low evergreen shrubs of 3 species in E. N. Amer.—Lvs. alternate or opposite, entire, short-petioled: fls. white or pink, in terminal corymbs in spring; sepals 5; petals 5; stamens 10, exserted, anthers opening lengthwise: fr. a caps. septicidally dehiscent by 2–5 valves, many-seeded. (Leiophyl-lum: Greek *smooth leaf*.)

A. Plant upright: pedicels glabrous .... 1. *L. buxifolium*
AA. Plant prostrate: pedicels pubescent .... 2. *L. Lyonii*

1. **L. buxifolium,** Ell. (*Ledum buxifolium*, Bergius). To 2 ft., upright: lvs. mostly alternate, oblong, to ⅓in. long, shining above: fls. about ⅓in. across, on slender glabrous pedicels. N. J. to Fla.

2. **L. Lyonii,** Sweet (*L. buxifolium* var. *prostratum*, Gray). Prostrate: lvs. mostly opposite, oval or oblong, ¼in. long: fls. about ⅓in. across, on slender pubescent and glandular pedicels. (Named for John Lyon, page 772.) Mts., N. C. and Tenn.

24. **LEDUM,** L. Evergreen shrubs, of about 3 species in sphagnum bogs and damp places in colder parts of northern hemisphere.—Lvs. alternate, entire, short-petioled: fls. white, small, in terminal clusters in spring; calyx with 5 short lobes; petals 5; stamens 5–10, anthers opening by apical pores; ovary 5-celled with numerous ovules: fr. a septicidally dehiscent caps. (Le-dum: ancient Greek name.)

L. grœnlandicum, Oeder (*L. latifolium*, Ait.). LABRADOR-TEA. To 3 ft.: lvs. oblong, 1–2 in. long, obtuse, revolute, densely rusty-tomentose beneath: fls. ½in. across, on slender pubescent pedicels; stamens 5–8. N. N. Amer.

25. **CHIOGENES,** Salisb. Evergreen creeping plants, of 2 species in N. Amer. and E. Asia.—Sts. slightly woody: lvs. alternate, small, short-petioled: fls. solitary in the axils; calyx 4-parted, with 2 bractlets subtending it; corolla campanulate, deeply 4-parted; stamens 8; ovary inferior, 4-celled, with many ovules: fr. a white berry crowned by the persistent calyx-lobes. (Chiog-enes: Greek for *snow* and *offspring*.)

C. hispidula, Torr. & Gray (*Vaccinium hispidulum*, L.). CREEPING SNOWBERRY. Lvs. ovate, to ⅓in. long, narrowed at ends, revolute, glabrous and shining above, strigose and paler beneath: fls. white, ⅙in. long, May–June: berry nearly globose, ¼in. across. N. Amer.

26. **GAYLUSSACIA,** HBK. HUCKLEBERRY. About 50 American species of shrubs, having edible berries.—Lvs. alternate, usually entire, short-petioled: fls. white or reddish, in axillary racemes in spring; calyx 5-lobed; corolla urceolate or tubular-campanulate, 5-lobed; stamens 10; ovary inferior, 10-celled: fr. a blue or black berry-like drupe composed of 10 one-seeded nutlets, crowned by persistent calyx-lobes. (Gaylussa-cia: named for J. L. Gay-Lussac, 1778–1850, French chemist.)

G. baccata, Koch (*Andromeda baccata*, Wangh. *G. resinosa*, Torr. & Gray. *Decachæna baccata*, Small). BLACK HUCKLEBERRY. Deciduous shrub to 3 ft., branches sticky when young: lvs. elliptic to oblong-lanceolate, 1–2 in. long, pale and resinous-dotted beneath: fls. reddish, in dense drooping racemes ½–1 in. long: fr. black, shining, ⅓in. across. Newf. to Ga. west to Iowa.

27. **VACCINIUM,** L. About 130 species of erect or creeping shrubs of wide geographical distribution in the northern hemisphere, several grown for their edible fr. or for ornament.—Lvs. alternate, deciduous or persistent: fls. in axillary or ter-

minal racemes or solitary; calyx with 4–5 short lobes; corolla urceolate, cylindrical, campanulate or rotate, 4–5-lobed; stamens 8–10, the anthers sometimes 2-awned on back; ovary inferior, 4–5-celled or rarely 8–10-celled by intrusion of midrib of each carpel, with few or many ovules in each cell: fr. a berry crowned by the persistent calyx. (Vaccin-ium: ancient Latin name of the blueberry.)

A. Corolla deeply 4-lobed, the lobes reflexed.
B. Lvs. ovate, acute: fls. terminal....1. *V. Oxycoccus*
BB. Lvs. oblong, obtuse: fls. lateral....2. *V. macrocarpon*
AA. Corolla urceolate to campanulate, lobes not reflexed.
B. Foliage persistent.
C. Plant low and creeping: lvs. entire....3. *V. Vitis-idæa*
CC. Plant erect to 12 ft.: lvs. sharp-toothed....4. *V. ovatum*
BB. Foliage deciduous.
C. Fls. broad-campanulate, anthers exserted....5. *V. stamineum*
CC. Fls. cylindric or urceolate, anthers included.
D. Shrub to 15 ft. high....6. *V. corymbosum*
DD. Shrub 3 ft. or less high.
E. Lvs. entire....7. *V. pallidum*
EE. Lvs. finely toothed....8. *V. angustifolium*

1. **V. Oxycoccus,** L. (*Oxycoccus palustris*, Pers. *O. Oxycoccus*, MacM.). Small or European Cranberry. Sts. slender, creeping, rooting at nodes, to 1 ft. long: lvs. persistent, thick, ovate, ¼in. long, acute, the margins strongly revolute, dark green and glossy above, white-glaucous beneath: fls. pink, ¼in. long, in few-fld. terminal umbels, the corolla deeply 4-parted and the lobes revolute, anthers exserted: berry red, globose, ¼–⅓in. diam. Cold swamps in Eu., Asia, and N. Amer.

2. **V. macrocarpon,** Ait. (*Oxycoccus macrocarpus*, Pers.). Large or American Cranberry. Larger and stouter than preceding: lvs. oblong, ⅓–½in. long, obtuse, the margins less revolute: fls. in lateral clusters: berry red, oblong or subglobose, ⅓–¾in. diam. Newf. to N. C. and Minn.

3. **V. Vitis-idæa,** L. (*Vitis-idæa Vitis-idæa*, Britt.). Cowberry. Sts. 8–12 in. high, the rootstock creeping: lvs. persistent, oval or obovate, ½–1¼ in. long, obtuse, entire, shining above, paler and black-dotted beneath: fls. white or pink, ¼in. long, in nodding racemes, the corolla campanulate and 4-lobed: berry dark red, ⅓in. diam. Eu., N. Asia. Var. **minus,** Lodd., Mountain Cranberry, is dwarf, forming dense mats, lvs. to ¾in. long, fls. pink or red; N. N. Amer.

4. **V. ovatum,** Pursh. Stiff shrub to 12 ft.: lvs. persistent, ovate to oblong-ovate, ½–2 in. long, acute, sharp-toothed, pale beneath: fls. white to pink, ¼in. long, in short racemes, the corolla campanulate with 5 short lobes: berry black, ⅓in. diam. B. C. to Calif.—Branches sold as "Huckleberry" for use as greenery in floral displays and decorations.

5. **V. stamineum,** L. (*Polycodium stamineum*, Greene). Deerberry. Diffusely branched shrub 2–3 ft. high, with pubescent twigs: lvs. deciduous, oval to ovate-oblong, 1–4 in. long, acute, entire, pale, glaucous and pubescent beneath: fls. white or tinged purple, about ¼in. long, numerous in leafy-bracted racemes to 2½ in. long, jointed with the slender pedicels, open-campanulate, 5-parted, the anthers and style much-exserted; berry globose or pyriform, about ⅓in. diam., green or yellow, inedible. Mass. to Fla. and La.

6. **V. corymbosum,** L. (*Cyanococcus corymbosus*, Rydb.). Highbush or Swamp Blueberry. Bushy shrub to 15 ft., with yellowish-green warty branches: lvs. deciduous, ovate to ovate-lanceolate, 1½–3 in. long, acutish, entire, glabrous or slightly pubescent beneath: fls. white or pinkish, ¼–½in. long, in short racemes appearing with lvs., corolla cylindric-urceolate: berry blue-black with a bloom, about ⅓in. diam., edible. Me. to Fla. and La., in damp soil.

7. **V. pallidum,** Ait. (*V. vacillans*, Kalm. *Cyanococcus vacillans*, Rydb.). Dryland Blueberry. Shrub to 3 ft., with yellowish-green white-speckled branchlets: lvs. deciduous, oval to obovate, 1–2 in. long, acute or acuminate, entire, glaucous beneath: fls. white or tinged red, ¼–⅓in. long, in dense clusters, corolla short-cylindrical: berry blue with a bloom, ¼–⅓in. diam. Me. to Ga. and Mo., in dry soil.

8. **V. angustifolium,** Ait. (*V. pensylvanicum* var. *angustifolium*, Gray). Lowbush Blueberry. Low shrub to about 1 ft.: lvs. deciduous, lanceolate, ¼–¾in. long, acute, with bristle-tipped teeth, nearly glabrous and shining: fls. greenish-white, ¼in. long, in small clusters, corolla short-cylindrical: berry bluish-black with a bloom, ¼–½in. diam. Arctic Amer. south to mts. of N. H. and N. Y. Var. **lævifolium,** House (*V. pensylvanicum*, Lam. not Mill.), grows to 2 ft., lvs. to 1½ in. long; Newf. to Wis. and Va.

158. DIAPENSIACEÆ. DIAPENSIA FAMILY

Six genera and about 10 species, circumpolar, adapted to alpine and rock-gardens.—Evergreen per. herbs or little shrubs: lvs. simple, alternate or opposite, exstipulate: fls. bisexual, regular, solitary or in racemes; calyx 5-lobed; corolla 5-lobed or

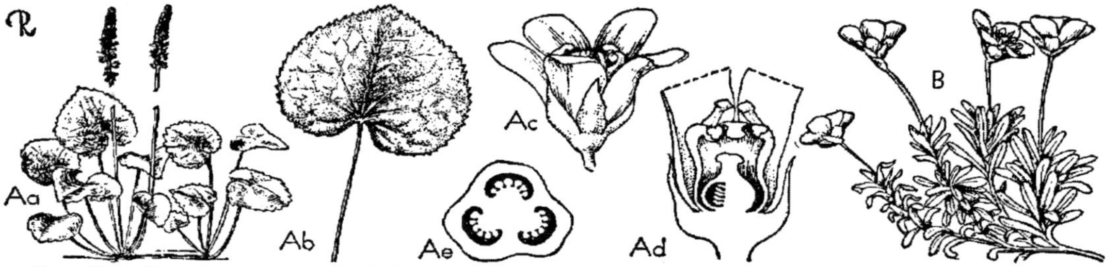

Fig. 158. DIAPENSIACEÆ. A, *Galax aphylla:* Aa, habit in flower, × 1/8; Ab, basal leaf, × 1/4; Ac, flower, × 2; Ad, same, vertical section, × 3; Ae, ovary, cross-section, × 8. B, *Diapensia lapponica:* flowering branch, × 1/2. (Ad adapted from Schnizlein.)

parted; stamens 5, dehiscing vertically, free or connate in a tube; ovary superior, 3-celled, with many ovules on axile placentæ; style with 3-lobed stigma: fr. a loculicidally dehiscent caps.

A. Fls. solitary or few in a loose infl.
  B. Lvs. imbricated, narrow........1. DIAPENSIA
  BB. Lvs. long-petioled, orbicular........2. SHORTIA
AA. Fls. in spike-like racemes........3. GALAX

1. **DIAPENSIA,** L. Tufted evergreen somewhat woody alpine plants; 4 species in N. Amer., N. Eu. and Asia.—Lvs. imbricated, narrow-spatulate, entire: fls. white or pink, solitary at end of terminal peduncle; calyx bracted at base; corolla campanulate, with 5 obtuse lobes: caps. inclosed in calyx. (Diapen-sia: ancient Greek name.)

D. lapponica, L. To 4 in., glabrous: lvs. 1/4–1/2in. long, obtuse: fls. white, 1/2–3/4in. across, June–July. Circumpolar, extending southward on mts. of N. Y. and New England.

2. **SHORTIA,** Torr. & Gray. Three evergreen stemless herbs native in N. Amer. and Japan, attractive in the rock-garden.—Rootstock creeping: lvs. basal, long-petioled, broad: fls. nodding, solitary at end of scape; calyx deeply 5-lobed; corolla campanulate, 5-lobed; stamens 5, alternating with 5 staminodia: fr. a globular caps. (Shor-tia: named for Dr. Chas. Wilkins Short, botanist of Kentucky.)

A. Corolla-lobes toothed but not fringed........1. *S. galacifolia*
AA. Corolla-lobes deeply fringed........2. *S. soldanelloides*

1. **S. galacifolia,** Torr. & Gray (*Sherwoodia galacifolia,* House). OCONEE-BELLS. Lvs. orbicular to oval, 1–3 in. long, crenate-dentate, teeth often spiny-tipped, glossy: fls. white, 1 in. across, on erect scape 2–8 in. high, corolla-lobes irregularly toothed. Mts. of N. C.

2. **S. soldanelloides,** Makino (*Schizocodon soldanelloides,* Sieb. & Zucc.). FRINGE-BELL. FRINGED GALAX. Lvs. orbicular to oblong, coarsely dentate, cordate at base, glossy: fls. deep rose, white or blush toward edge, 1 in. across, 3–6 in a loose raceme at tip of scape, 4–9 in. high, corolla-lobes deeply fringed. Japan.

3. **GALAX,** L. One evergreen stemless per. herb, useful for ground-cover and the foliage for floral decorations.—Lvs. in a basal tuft, long-petioled: fls. small, in spike-like racemes on long scapes; calyx and corolla 5-parted; stamens monadelphous, the tube with 5 petal-like lobes or staminodia and 5 anther-bearing: caps. somewhat longer than calyx. (Ga-lax: Greek for *milk,* application obscure.)

G. aphylla, L. Lvs. orbicular or broad-ovate, 1–5 in. across, deeply cordate at base, crenate-dentate, glossy, turning bronze color in autumn: fls. white, 1/6in. across, in narrow racemes 2–5 in. long on scapes 1 1/2–2 1/2 ft. high. Va. to Ga. and Ala.

159. MYRSINACEÆ. MYRSINE FAMILY

More than 30 woody genera and 550 species widely distributed in the tropics and subtropics, one a popular greenhouse plant.—Lvs. alternate, simple, exstipulate, leathery: fls. bisexual or unisexual, regular, in axillary or terminal many-fld. panicles or umbels, often glandular; calyx 4–5-parted, usually persistent; corolla gamopetalous, rarely polypetalous, 4–5-lobed; stamens 5, opposite the corolla-lobes, free

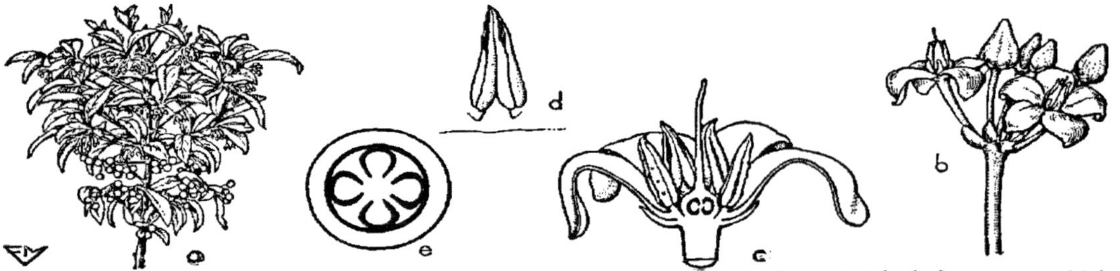

Fig. 159. MYRSINACEÆ. *Ardisia crenata:* a, plant in flower and fruit, × ⅛; b, inflorescence, × 1; c, flower, vertical section, × 3; d, stamen, × 3; e, ovary, cross-section, × 8.

or somewhat united, inserted on corolla, alternating staminodia sometimes present; ovary superior in ours, 1-celled with few or numerous ovules, placentation free-central, style and stigma 1: fr. a few-seeded drupe.

ARDISIA, Sw. Evergreen trees and shrubs native in hot and warm regions, of more than 200 species.—Lvs. entire or rarely dentate or crenate: fls. bisexual or unisexual; calyx usually 5-lobed; corolla rotate, 5-parted; stamens short, inserted on throat of corolla: fr. a globose 1-seeded drupe. (Ardis-ia: from Greek for *point*, referring to the stamens or corolla-lobes.)

A. crenata, Sims (*A. crenulata,* Lodd.). Shrub to 6 ft., glabrous: lvs. elliptic- or oblong-lanceolate, 2–8 in. long, acute or acuminate, with crisped-undulate glandular margins, usually raised-punctate beneath: fls. white or pink, about ¼in. long, in a terminal infl. on special lateral branches: fr. coral-red, ¼–⅓in. diam. Japan to S. Asia.—This species has been confused with *A. crispa*, A. DC. (*Bladhia crispa*, Thunb.), which differs in being slightly pubescent when young and lvs. not crisped-undulate.

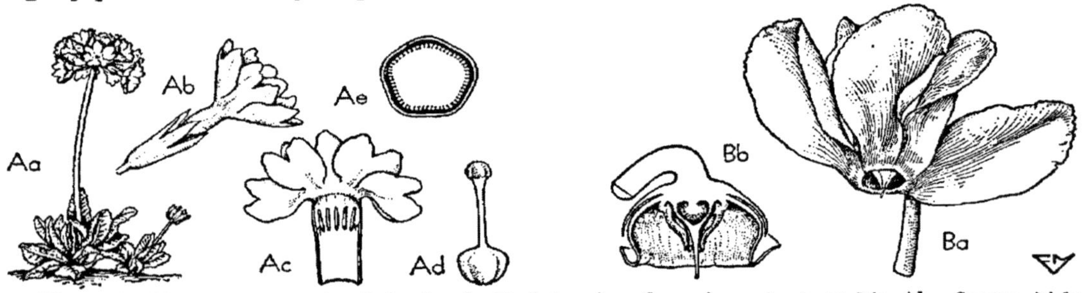

Fig. 160. PRIMULACEÆ. A, *Primula denticulata:* Aa, flowering plant, × ⅛; Ab, flower, × 1; Ac, corolla expanded, × 1; Ad, pistil, × 2; Ae, ovary, cross-section, × 5. B, *Cyclamen persicum:* Ba, flower, × ½; Bb, same, vertical section (corolla partially excised), × 1.

160. PRIMULACEÆ. PRIMROSE FAMILY

Ann. and per. herbs, rarely shrubby, of nearly 30 genera and 800 species widely distributed but most abundant in the northern hemisphere; many are showy-fld. and grown in rockeries, fl.-gardens and greenhouses.—Lvs. alternate, opposite or whorled, sometimes all basal, simple or lobed, exstipulate: fls. bisexual, regular, solitary or umbellate at end of a scape or in terminal or axillary racemes, panicles or spikes, or solitary in the axils; calyx usually 5-parted and persistent; corolla gamopetalous or rarely lacking, with long or short tube, usually 5-lobed; stamens 5, opposite corolla-lobes, epipetalous, sometimes staminodia present, the filaments distinct or united at base; ovary superior, rarely partly inferior, 1-celled with numerous ovules on free central placentæ, style and stigma 1: fr. a dehiscent caps.

A. Plant scapose with radical lvs. or densely cespitose.
  B. Corolla-lobes upright or spreading.
    C. Lobes of corolla entire or 2-lobed.
      D. Tube of corolla longer than calyx.
        E. Lvs. 1 in. or more long..1. PRIMULA
        EE. Lvs. small, ½in. or less long..............................2. DOUGLASIA

DD. Tube of corolla shorter than calyx.............3. ANDROSACE
CC. Lobes of corolla fimbriate.............4. SOLDANELLA
BB. Corolla-lobes reflexed.
C. Fls. single: root tuberous.............5. CYCLAMEN
CC. Fls. umbellate: root not tuberous.............6. DODECATHEON
AA. Plant with leafy sts.
B. Corolla funnelform or salverform.............3. ANDROSACE
BB. Corolla rotate or campanulate.
C. Caps. dehiscent by 2–5 valves: stamens usually glabrous.
D. Staminodia none.............7. LYSIMACHIA
DD. Staminodia 5, alternate with stamens.............8. STEIRONEMA
CC. Caps. circumscissile: stamens usually pubescent.............9. ANAGALLIS

1. **PRIMULA,** L. PRIMROSE. More than 400 species of per. scapose herbs in temp. regions of the northern hemisphere and a few in the southern hemisphere; many species are grown in borders and rockeries and several are amongst the most popular greenhouse and florists' plants.—Lvs. all basal, petioled or sessile, entire or lobed: fls. dimorphic, in umbels or heads or sometimes in involucrate superimposed whorls subtended by leafy or narrow involucral bracts; calyx tubular, campanulate or funnelform; corolla funnelform or salverform, exceeding the calyx, the lobes spreading or rarely erect, entire or 2-lobed; stamens inserted on tube or mouth of corolla, included, the filaments very short; ovules numerous: caps. globose or cylindrical, dehiscent by 5–10 valves. (Prim-ula: diminutive of *primus*, first, referring to its early blooming.)

A. Infl. a dense spike.............1. *P. Vialii*
AA. Infl. an umbel or head, or fls. sometimes solitary.
B. Umbels superimposed (one above the other).
C. Color of fls. yellow or orange.
D. Plant glandular-pubescent, not farinose.............2. *P. floribunda*
DD. Plant glabrous, slightly farinose.
E. Bracts subtending umbels minute.............3. *P. Cockburniana*
EE. Bracts subtending umbels ½in. or more long.
F. Shape of bracts lanceolate to ovate and toothed.............4. *P. verticillata*
FF. Shape of bracts linear.
G. Calyx lobed to middle, slightly farinose.............5. *P. Bulleyana*
GG. Calyx lobed one-third or less, densely yellow-farinose.............6. *P. helodoxa*
CC. Color of fls. purple, rose or white.
D. Base of lf. cordate, with distinct petiole.
E. Fls. ½in. or less across.
F. Petioles much longer than lf.-blades, the lobes incise-dentate.............7. *P. malacoides*
FF. Petioles as long as or shorter than blades, the shallow lobes minutely serrulate.............8. *P. Forbesii*
EE. Fls. 1 in. or more across.
F. Lvs. green beneath.............17. *P. sinensis* var. *stellata*
FF. Lvs. white-tomentose beneath.............16. *P. polyneura*
DD. Base of lf. attenuate into long winged petiole.
E. Lvs. fleshy, entire.............9. *P. chionantha*
EE. Lvs. membranous, toothed.
F. Fl.-clusters not farinose.............10. *P. anisodora*
FF. Fl.-clusters farinose.
G. Pedicels and calyx outside silvery-farinose.
H. Scape silvery-farinose.............11. *P. pulverulenta*
HH. Scape farinose only at top.............12. *P. Beesiana*
GG. Pedicels and calyx outside not white-farinose.
H. Diam. of fls. ½in.: lvs. to 1 ft. long.............13. *P. burmanica*
HH. Diam. of fls. 1 in. or more: lvs. 4–6 in. long.............14. *P. japonica*
BB. Umbels or heads single, or fls. solitary.
C. Base of lf. cordate or rounded, with distinct petiole.
D. Plant scapeless, to 3 in. high.............15. *P. Juliæ*
DD. Plant with scape, 8 in. or more high.
E. Lvs. lobed.
F. Under side of lvs. white-tomentose.............16. *P. polyneura*
FF. Under side of lvs. green.
G. Calyx inflated, truncate at base.............17. *P. sinensis*
GG. Calyx not inflated, attenuate at base.
H. Teeth of calyx very small, much shorter than tube.............18. *P. obconica*
HH. Teeth of calyx linear, about length of tube.
I. Fls. 1½–2 in. across.............19. *P. Sieboldii*
II. Fls. ½–¾in. across.
J. Pedicels about length of calyx, ½in. long.............20. *P. cortusoides*
JJ. Pedicels much longer than calyx, 1–2 in. long.............21. *P. saxatilis*
EE. Lvs. not lobed.
F. Width of lvs. nearly equalling length.
G. Teeth of calyx about one-third length of tube: plant glabrous.............22. *P. Florindæ*
GG. Teeth of calyx very small: plant pubescent.............18. *P. obconica*

FF. Width of lvs. much less than length.
G. Fl.-clusters farinose .... 23. *P. alpicola*
GG. Fl.-clusters not farinose.
H. Under surface of lf. pubescent.
I. Corolla with scale-like folds at the slightly contracted mouth: caps. one-half length of calyx .... 24. *P. veris*
II. Corolla without folds, not contracted at mouth: caps. as long or longer than calyx .... 25. *P. elatior*
HH. Under surface of lf. glabrous .... 26. *P. yargongensis*
CC. Base of lf. attenuate into winged petiole.
D. Fls. sessile, in heads.
E. Under surface of lf. silvery.
F. Upper surface of lf. somewhat white-farinose .... 27. *P. capitata*
FF. Upper surface of lf. green .... 28. *P. Mooreana*
EE. Under surface of lf. not silvery.
F. Plant glabrous: fls. erect .... 29. *P. denticulata*
FF. Plant pubescent: fls. nodding .... 30. *P. nutabilis*
DD. Fls. with distinct pedicels, in umbels or loose heads.
E. Lf. with conspicuous cartilaginous or farinose margins.
F. Calyx lobed to middle, ¼in. or less long: bracts broad-ovate: lvs. fleshy.
G. Margin of lf. cartilaginous, entire or toothed .... 31. *P. Auricula*
GG. Margin of lf. white-farinose, not cartilaginous, irregularly toothed .... 32. *P. marginata*
FF. Calyx not lobed to middle, ⅓–½in. long: bracts linear or lanceolate: lvs. leathery.
G. Lvs. pellucid-punctate .... 33. *P. spectabilis*
GG. Lvs. not pellucid-punctate .... 34. *P. Clusiana*
EE. Lf. without conspicuous margins.
F. Scape none or less than 2 in. high, fls. solitary.
G. Diam. of fls. ½in.: lvs. entire .... 35. *P. angustifolia*
GG. Diam. of fls. 1–1½ in.: lvs. crenulate .... 36. *P. vulgaris*
FF. Scape present, fls. several to many.
G. Under surface of lf. white-farinose.
H. Petiole indistinct: throat of corolla with distinct scales: calyx-lobes obtuse .... 37. *P. farinosa*
HH. Petiole apparent: throat of corolla with indistinct or no scales: calyx-lobes acute .... 38. *P. frondosa*
GG. Under surface of lf. green.
H. Color of fls. purple or rose.
I. Calyx glandular: lvs. to 8 in. long .... 39. *P. Parryi*
II. Calyx glabrous: lvs. to 2½ in. long .... 40. *P. rosea*
HH. Color of fls. yellow.
I. Calyx farinose .... 41. *P. sikkimensis*
II. Calyx pubescent but not farinose.
J. Corolla with scale-like folds at the slightly contracted mouth: caps. one-half length of calyx .... 24. *P. veris*
JJ. Corolla without folds, not contracted at mouth: caps. as long as or longer than calyx .... 25. *P. elatior*

1. **P. Vialii,** Delavay (*P. Littoniana*, Forrest). Lvs. broad-lanceolate, attenuate at base into winged petiole, to 8 in. long and 1½–2½ in. wide, obtuse, irregularly dentate, hairy: fls. violet-blue, fragrant, ¼–⅓in. across, in dense spikes 3–5 in. long on erect scape 1–2 ft. high which is farinose toward top; calyx deeply lobed, farinose at base; corolla-lobes entire and rounded. (Named for Père Vial, who brought the plant to France.) China.

2. **P. floribunda,** Wall. (*P. floribunda* var. *grandiflora*, Pax). Buttercup Primrose. Glandular-pubescent plant grown in the greenhouse for its winter bloom: lvs. elliptic or ovate, about 3 in. long and 1½ in. wide, acute or obtuse, narrowed into broad petiole, irregularly dentate: scape 4–8 in. high, bearing 3–5 many-fld. superimposed umbels subtended by ovate or lanceolate lf.-like bracts; fls. golden-yellow, fragrant, ¼–¾in. across; calyx divided to about middle; corolla-tube about twice as long as calyx; corolla-lobes rounded or somewhat emarginate. Himalayas.

3. **P. Cockburniana,** Hemsl. Lvs. obovate-oblong, 2–4 in. long, obtuse, attenuate at base, minutely denticulate, becoming glabrous: scape 4–12 in. high, bearing 2 3–6-fld. superimposed umbels subtended by minute bracts; fls. orange, 1 in. across; calyx farinose; lobes of corolla retuse. (Named in honor of H. Cockburn, British consul, and G. Cockburn, missionary in China.) China.

4. **P. verticillata,** Forsk. Glabrous slightly farinose herb, grown in the greenhouse: lvs. lanceolate or ovate-lanceolate, 4–8 in. long, acute or acuminate, narrowed into a short broad-winged petiole, irregularly serrate: scape to 2 ft. high, bearing several many-fld. superimposed umbels subtended by dentate lanceolate or linear-lanceolate bracts to 3 in. long, farinose below the umbels: fls. yellow, fragrant, ¾–1 in. across; calyx deeply divided; corolla-lobes slightly emarginate. S. Arabia.—A hybrid between *P. floribunda* and *P. verticillata* is **P. kewensis,** Hort., differing in the larger lf.-like ovate bracts.

5. **P. Bulleyana,** Forrest. Lvs. ovate-lanceolate, 5–7 in. long and 1½ in. wide, obtuse or acute, attenuate into a winged petiole, irregularly dentate, glabrous or sometimes slightly

pubescent beneath: scape 1½–2½ ft. high, bearing 5–7 many-fld. superimposed umbels subtended by linear bracts ½–1 in. long, farinose below the umbels; fls. deep reddish-orange, fragrant, ¾–1 in. across; calyx divided to middle; corolla-lobes rounded. (Named for A. K. Bulley for whom Forrest collected.) China.—A strain of hybrids between this species and *P. Beesiana* is **P. Bullesiana,** with fls. in shades of cream to orange, purple or lilac, pink to crimson.

6. **P. helodoxa,** Balf. f. Lvs. varying from 4–5 in. long and 1 in. wide to 14 in. long and 3 in. wide, oblanceolate, attenuate into winged petiole, obtuse, denticulate: scape to 2 ft. high, bearing 4–5 many-fld. superimposed umbels subtended by linear-lanceolate bracts ⅓in. or more long; fls. yellow, about ¾in. across; calyx lobed one-third or less, densely yellow-farinose; corolla-lobes entire or slightly retuse. China.

7. **P. malacoides,** Franch. Fairy Primrose. Popular greenhouse plant, glabrous above, pubescent below with white hairs: lvs. ovate or oblong-ovate, 1½–3 in. long, cordate at base, on petioles much exceeding the blades, sometimes 5–7 in. long, broadly 6–8-lobed, the lobes acutely incise-dentate, sparsely white-farinose beneath: scape 8–20 in. high, bearing 2–6 many-fld. superimposed umbels subtended by linear-lanceolate bracts which are white-farinose below; fls. rose and lilac, about ½in. across; calyx densely white-farinose, the lobes spreading; corolla-tube slightly longer than calyx. China. Var. **alba,** Hort., has white fls. and var. **rosea,** Hort., bright rose. **P. Erikssonii,** Hort., is an improved strain.

8. **P. Forbesii,** Franch. Baby Primrose. Smaller and less branched than the former, the cordate-ovate lvs. 1–2 in. long on petioles as long as or shorter than blades, slightly sinuate-lobed, the lobes denticulate, calyx not so farinose. (Named for Francis Blackwell Forbes, English botanist and co-author with W. B. Hemsley of "An Enumeration of Chinese Plants.") China, Burma.—Most of the "baby primrose" in cult. is *P. malacoides.*

9. **P. chionantha,** Balf. f. & Forrest. Lvs. broad-lanceolate to oblong-elliptic, to 10 in. long and 2 in. wide, acute or obtuse, attenuate into winged petiole, entire, fleshy, yellow-farinose beneath: scape to 1½ ft. high, bearing 2–3 many-fld. umbels subtended by yellow-farinose bracts ½in. long; fls. white, ¾in. across, on reflexed pedicels; calyx densely yellow-farinose; corolla-lobes entire and ciliate. China.

10. **P. anisodora,** Balf. f. & Forrest. Plant glabrous, not farinose, with anise-like odor: lvs. obovate, to 8 in. long and 3 in. wide, obtuse, attenuate into winged petiole, irregularly toothed: scape to 2 ft. high, bearing 3–5 8-fld. superimposed umbels subtended by linear bracts; fls. dark purple, almost black, with a 10-lobed yellow ring in throat; calyx lobed about one-third; corolla-lobes slightly emarginate. China.

11. **P. pulverulenta,** Duthie. Plant to 3 ft. high, with silvery farinose scape and infl., planted out-of-doors: lvs. obovate or oblanceolate, 6–16 in. long, obtuse, narrowed into long winged petiole, irregularly dentate: scape bearing several superimposed umbels subtended by linear bracts; fls. purple with orange-brown eye, about 1 in. across; calyx-lobes lanceolate and acuminate; corolla-lobes notched. China.

12. **P. Beesiana,** Forrest. Lvs. ovate-lanceolate, 5–10 in. long and 1–2 in. wide, obtuse or acute, narrowed at base into winged petiole, irregularly dentate, slightly pubescent beneath: scape 2–3 ft. high, farinose at top, bearing 5–8 12–16-fld. superimposed umbels subtended by linear bracts; fls. rose-carmine with yellow eye, ¾in. across, slightly fragrant; calyx divided to middle, white-farinose. (Named for the English nursery firm of Bees, Ltd.) China.

13. **P. burmanica,** Balf. f. & Ward. Lvs. oblanceolate, to 1 ft. long and 2 in wide, obtuse, attenuate into winged petiole, irregularly dentate, wrinkled, with farinose hairs: scape to 2 ft. high, farinose, bearing several about 16-fld. superimposed umbels subtended by linear-subulate bracts; fls. reddish-purple with orange eye, ½in. across; calyx glandular and green outside, white-farinose inside; corolla-lobes entire or emarginate. Burma.

14. **P. japonica,** Gray. Glabrous, only calyx farinose, grown out-of-doors and blooming in summer: lvs. obovate-oblong or spatulate, 4–6 in. long and about 2 in. wide, obtuse, narrowed into a winged petiole with a sheathing base, irregularly dentate: scape 8 in.–2 ft. high, bearing several many-fld. superimposed umbels subtended by linear-subulate bracts; fls. purple with yellow eye, rarely rose or white, 1 in. or more across; calyx farinose inside, the lobes broadly triangular and acuminate; corolla-tube about three times as long as calyx, lobes emarginate. Japan.—**P. Moerheimii** is a hybrid group in shades of yellow, pink and lilac, said to be a *japonica* form.

15. **P. Juliæ,** Kusn. Lvs. orbicular, ½–1 in. long, with petiole much longer than blade, cordate, coarsely dentate, glabrous: fls. solitary on pedicels 2–3 in. long, rose or red, with yellow throat, ¾–1 in. across; calyx-lobes lanceolate, acuminate, ciliate; corolla-tube twice as long as calyx, lobes deeply retuse. (Named for Julia L. Mlokossjewicz, who collected the plant in 1900.) Caucasus.—The plant grown as *P. Helenæ* probably belongs here; see also *P. angustifolia.*

16. **P. polyneura,** Franch. (*P. Veitchii,* Duthie. *P. lichiangensis,* Forrest). Lvs. orbicular, to 4 in. long and broad, lobed, the lobes dentate, with long petiole, white-tomen-

tose beneath: scape to 1 ft. high, bearing a many-fld. umbel or umbels superimposed, subtended by pubescent bracts much shorter than the pedicels; fls. rose or magenta, ¾–1 in. across; calyx divided to middle, pubescent; corolla-tube slightly exceeding calyx, lobes emarginate. China.

17. **P. sinensis,** Sabine (*P. chinensis,* Hort.). CHINESE PRIMROSE. Soft-hairy plant grown in the greenhouse for winter bloom: lvs. orbicular, 2–4 in. long, more or less cordate at base, the petioles longer than blades, several-lobed, the lobes unequally incise-dentate: scape 4–8 in. high, bearing a many-fld. umbel subtended by leafy bracts shorter than pedicels; fls. white, pink, red or purplish, about 1¼ in. across, long-pedicelled, salverform; calyx inflated, truncate at base, about length of corolla-tube, lobes emarginate. China. Var. **stellata,** Hort., STAR PRIMROSE, is taller and more free-flowering than type, fls. in superimposed umbels. Var. **fimbriata,** Hort., has fringed or crested fls.

18. **P. obconica,** Hance. Popular winter-blooming greenhouse plant, the soft hairs often poisonous and irritating: lvs. orbicular or oblong-ovate, 2–4 in. long, cordate at base, the petioles as long as or longer than blades, margins uneven, denticulate or somewhat lobed: scape 6–12 in. high, bearing a many-fld. umbel subtended by linear unequal bracts; fls. lilac or pink, ¾–1 in. across, long-pedicelled; calyx with very small triangular teeth much shorter than tube, pubescent. China. Var. **grandiflora,** Hort., has fls. 1½ in. diam. and var. **gigantea,** Hort., is a large form.

19. **P. Sieboldii,** Morr. Pubescent plant grown out-of-doors and blooming in late spring: lvs. ovate-oblong, 2–4 in. long, cordate at base, the petioles longer than blades, with numerous small unequally dentate lobes: scape 4–8 in. high, bearing a many-fld. umbel subtended by linear bracts; fls. white, rose, or purple, the throat usually striped, 1½–2 in. across; calyx glabrous, with linear teeth as long as tube; corolla-tube longer than calyx, lobes emarginate. (P. F. von Siebold, page 51.) Japan.

20. **P. cortusoides,** L. Pubescent, blooming in May out-of-doors: lvs. ovate-oblong, 2–4 in. long, cordate or subcordate at base, the petioles longer than blades, crenate-lobed, the lobes irregularly toothed: scape 6–12 in. high, bearing a many-fld. umbel subtended by linear bracts; fls. rose-colored, ½–¾in. across; pedicels short, about ½in. long; calyx-lobes lanceolate, about length of tube, slightly pubescent; corolla-lobes 2-lobed. W. Siberia.

21. **P. saxatilis,** Kom. Similar to *P. cortusoides,* differing chiefly in the slender pedicels 1–2 in. long. N. Asia.

22. **P. Florindæ,** Ward. Glabrous: lvs. ovate, to 8 in. long and 6 in. wide, obtuse, cordate at base with reddish grooved petiole to 1 ft. long, dentate: scape 1–4 ft. high, bearing a many-fld. farinose umbel subtended by lanceolate bracts about ½in. long; fls. sulfur-yellow, ½in. across, nodding; calyx-teeth triangular, about one-third length of tube; corolla funnelform, lobes rounded. (Named for Mrs. F. Kingdon Ward.) Tibet.

23. **P. alpicola,** Stapf (*P. microdonta* var. *alpicola,* W. W. Smith). Lvs. elliptic or oblong-elliptic, 3–6 in. long and 1–3 in. wide, obtuse, slightly cordate or suddenly contracted at base into petiole 2–4 in. long, crenulate, nearly glabrous: scape to 1½ ft. high, bearing a many-fld. farinose umbel subtended by oblong bracts ½in. long, rarely 2 superimposed umbels; fls. yellow, purple or violet, rarely white, ¾in. across; calyx lobed to about one-third, densely farinose; corolla-lobes emarginate or 2-lobed. Tibet.

24. **P. veris,** L. (*P. officinalis,* Hill). COWSLIP. Soft-pubescent plant well suited for borders and rockeries: lvs. ovate to ovate-oblong, 2–3 in. long, obtuse, contracted or attenuate at base into winged petiole as long as or shorter than blade, crenate: scape 4–8 in. high, bearing a many-fld. umbel subtended by small linear bracts; fls. bright yellow, rarely purplish, fragrant, ½–1 in. across; calyx about ½in. long, pubescent, with short ovate-acute lobes; limb of corolla concave, with scale-like folds at the slightly contracted mouth; corolla-lobes emarginate: caps oval, about one-half length and included in calyx. Eu. Var. **Kleynii,** Hort., has yellow fls. shading to apricot.—In N. Amer. the name Cowslip is applied to *Caltha palustris.*

25. **P. elatior,** Hill (*P. veris* var. *elatior,* L.). OXLIP. Closely resembling the above but differing in its usually flat corolla-limb without folds and not contracted at mouth, the narrowly lanceolate calyx-lobes, and the oblong caps. as long as or longer than calyx. Eu. to Iran.—A garden group including the common hardy spring-blooming primula is **P. polyantha,** Mill. (*P. variabilis,* Hort.), probably hybrid of *P. veris, P. elatior* and *P. vulgaris:* it grows from 6–12 in. high, the scapes usually exceeding the obovate obtuse lvs. which are narrowed into a winged petiole and bearing a many-fld. umbel or the fls. sometimes solitary and nearly scapeless; fls. of many colors, yellow, red and yellow, orange, bronze, maroon, or white, sometimes double.

26. **P. yargongensis,** Petitmengin (*P. Wardii,* Balf. f.). Glabrous, not farinose: lvs. ovate to lanceolate, oblong, 1–2 in. long, obtuse, suddenly contracted at base or somewhat attenuate into a petiole to 2 in. long, entire or finely denticulate: scape to 1 ft. high, bearing a few-fld. umbel subtended by lf.-like bracts ½in. long and spurred at base; fls. rose or violet with white eye, about 1 in. across, fragrant; calyx lobed to about one-third, ciliate; corolla salver-shaped, with ring of 10 yellowish scales in throat, lobes emarginate. (Named for Yar-gong in E. Tibet.) China.

27. **P. capitata,** Hook. Lvs. oblong-lanceolate, 4–5 in. long, obtuse or acute, attenuate into winged petiole, denticulate, densely silvery farinose beneath and less so above: scape 1–1½ ft. high, bearing a dense farinose head subtended by lanceolate bracts; fls. purplish-blue, ½in. across, outer developing before inner and reflexed or drooping; calyx lobed to middle; corolla-lobes emarginate. Himalayas.

28. **P. Mooreana,** Balf. f. & W. W. Smith (*P. capitata* subsp. *Mooreana*, W. W. Smith & Forrest). Similar to *P. capitata* but a larger plant with coarsely reticulate lvs. which are silvery farinose beneath and bright green above, more rounded at apex, and larger fls. Himalayas.

29. **P. denticulata,** Smith. Glabrous, often planted in rockeries: lvs. ovate-lanceolate, about 2 in. long but usually not full grown until after flowering, obtuse, narrowed into winged petiole, sharply denticulate, only slightly farinose, with fleshy leafy bracts at base: scape 4–8 in. high, bearing a many-fld. head subtended by lanceolate bracts; fls. lilac, ½in. or less across, very short-pedicelled; calyx deeply cut into narrow lobes; corolla-tube twice as long as calyx, lobes emarginate. Himalayas. Var. **cachemiriana,** Hook. f. (*P. cashmeriana*, Hort.), is more farinose than type, fls. rich purple with yellow center, blooming when the lvs. are nearly full grown. Var. **alba,** Hort., has white fls.

30. **P. nutabilis,** W. W. Smith (*P. nutans*, Delavay not Georgi). Lvs. oblong-ovate or oblong-lanceolate, 1–4 in. long, obtuse or acute, attenuate into winged petiole, dentate, pubescent: scape to 8 in. high, bearing a dense head subtended by small bracts; fls. violet, ¾in. across, sessile, nodding; calyx lobed to middle, farinose; corolla-lobes entire or 2-lobed. China.

31. **P. Auricula,** L. (*P. alpina*, Salisb. *Auricula lutea*, Opiz). Often densely farinose, grown in greenhouses and frames and also in rockeries: lvs. thick, obovate or oblong-lanceolate, 2–4 in. long, obtuse or acute, attenuate at base, margins cartilaginous, entire or dentate, sometimes ciliate: scape to 8 in. high, bearing a many-fld. umbel subtended by small ovate farinose bracts; fls. originally bright yellow but of many colors in cult., 1 in. across, often fragrant; calyx about ¼in. long, divided to middle; corolla-tube twice as long as calyx, lobes emarginate. (Auricula is an ante-Linnæan name, arising from frequently auricled lvs.) Alps of Eu.

32. **P. marginata,** Curt. Lvs. oblong or obovate, 1–4 in. long, obtuse, attenuate into short petiole, irregularly dentate, glandular-punctate, margins white-farinose: scape 1–5 in. high, bearing a 2–20-fld. umbel subtended by broad-ovate leafy farinose bracts; fls. violet-rose, ¾–1 in. across; calyx lobed to middle, farinose; corolla-tube much longer than calyx, lobes emarginate. Alps.

33. **P. spectabilis,** Tratt. Lvs. oblong, 1–4 in. long, acute, attenuate at base, stiff and glossy, entire with broad cartilaginous margins, pellucid-punctate: scape 4–6 in. high, bearing a 1–7-fld. umbel subtended by linear bracts to ½in. long; fls. rose, 1 in. across; calyx not lobed to middle; corolla-tube longer than calyx, lobes emarginate. Alps.

34. **P. Clusiana,** Tausch. Lvs. ovate or oblong, 1–3½ in. long, acute or obtuse, attenuate at base, stiff and glossy, entire with narrow cartilaginous margins which are glandular-ciliate: scape to 7 in. high, bearing a 1–6-fld. umbel subtended by lanceolate or linear bracts ½in. long; fls. rose or lilac; calyx not lobed to middle; corolla-tube about equalling calyx, lobes 2-lobed. (Named for Clusius, page 220.) Alps.

35. **P. angustifolia,** Torr. (*P. angustifolia* var. *Helenæ*, Pollard & Cockerell). Lvs. lanceolate or linear-lanceolate, ½–1 in. long, obtuse, attenuate into very short petiole, entire: fls. usually solitary, rarely 2, on scapes ½–2 in. high, rose pink, ½in. across; calyx-lobes shorter than tube; corolla-tube about equalling calyx, lobes emarginate. Colo. to New Mex.

36. **P. vulgaris,** Huds. (*P. veris* var. *acaulis*, L. *P. acaulis*, Hill). Lvs. oblong or obovate-oblong, about 2 in. long, obtuse, narrowed into petiole shorter than blades, crenulate, more or less pilose or glabrescent, wrinkled: scape none, the fls. solitary on pubescent pedicels to 6 in. long, pale yellow, purple or blue, becoming green in drying, 1–1½ in. across; calyx pubescent, the narrow lanceolate-acuminate lobes several times shorter than tube; throat of corolla slightly contracted and with scale-like folds. Eu.

37. **P. farinosa,** L. Birdseye Primrose. Lvs. obovate-lanceolate, ½–3 in. long, obtuse, attenuate into an indistinct petiole, denticulate or nearly entire, white-farinose beneath: scape 3–12 in. high, bearing a many-fld. umbel subtended by lanceolate bracts which are slightly saccate at base; fls. lilac-purple with yellow throat, about ½in. across; calyx-lobes short, obtuse; corolla-tube about equalling calyx, lobes deeply emarginate. Old World, in boreal or alpine regions.

38. **P. frondosa,** Janka. Lvs. oblong or obovate, 1 in. long and ½in. wide, obtuse, attenuate into distinct winged petiole, denticulate or crenate, white-farinose beneath: scape 2–4 in. high, bearing a many-fld. loose umbel subtended by small linear-lanceolate bracts; fls. rosy-lilac, ½in. across; calyx-lobes acute; corolla-tube slightly longer than calyx, lobes 2-lobed. Balkans.

39. **P. Parryi,** Gray. Lvs. fleshy, obovate-oblong, to 8 in. long and 1–2 in. wide, obtuse, attenuate into winged petiole, entire or denticulate, glabrous or slightly pubescent: scape 1–1½ ft. high, bearing a many-fld. umbel subtended by oblong-lanceolate bracts to ½in.

long; fls. purple with yellow eye, 1 in. across; calyx lobed to middle, glandular; corolla-tube about equalling calyx, lobes emarginate. (Named for C. C. Parry, page 49.) Rocky Mts.

40. **P. rosea,** Royle. Lvs. in a dense tuft, ovate-oblong or oblanceclate, 2–2½ in. long and ½–¾in. wide, obtuse or acute, narrowed into a very short petiole, denticulate or crenulate, glabrous, maturing a little after the fls.: scape 2–8 in. high, bearing a many-fld. umbel subtended by lanceolate bracts which are saccate at base; fls. bright rose, ¾in. across; calyx to ⅓in. long, glabrous; corolla-tube longer than calyx, deeply emarginate. Himalayas.

41. **P. sikkimensis,** Hook. Lvs. obovate, 4–5 in. long and 1½ in. wide, obtuse, attenuate into long winged petiole, sharp-serrate, wrinkled, glabrous: scape 10–14 in. high, bearing a many-fld. umbel subtended by narrow bracts; fls. yellow, 1 in. across, on slender pedicels about 1 in. long; calyx not lobed to middle, farinose; corolla-tube slightly longer than calyx, lobes emarginate. Himalayas.

2. **DOUGLASIA,** Lindl. Tufted per. herbs of 6 species in the mts. of N. Amer. and Eu., useful for the rock-garden.—Lvs. in rosettes, small: fls. solitary or in bracted umbels terminating the scape; calyx campanulate, 5-lobed; corolla 5-lobed, tube equalling or exceeding calyx, with 5 scales or crests beneath the sinuses; stamens 5, included; ovary with 5 ovules: fr. a turbinate caps. (Douglas-ia: named for David Douglas, 1799–1834, Scotch botanist and plant explorer.)

A. Fls. yellow . . . . 1. *D. Vitaliana*
AA. Fls. red or purple.
  B. Lvs. ciliate on margins . . . . 2. *D. montana*
  BB. Lvs. glabrous . . . . 3. *D. lævigata*

1. **D. Vitaliana,** Pax (*Primula Vitaliana,* L. *Aretia Vitaliana,* Lodd. *Gregoria Vitaliana,* Duby. *Androsace Vitaliana,* Reichb.). Sts. prostrate, bare at base, with imbricated linear entire pilose lvs. ¼–⅓in. long: fls. yellow, solitary or 2, rarely more, corolla-tube about twice length of calyx. (Named for Anton Vitalianus, 17th century botanist.) Alps, Pyrenees.

2. **D. montana,** Gray. Lvs. imbricated, linear-lingulate, to ⅓in. long, ciliate on margins: fls. purple or lilac, ⅓in. long, solitary or 2, corolla-tube about length of calyx. Mont., Wyo.

3. **D. lævigata,** Gray. Lvs. crowded at ends of sts., oblanceolate or linear-oblong, about ⅓in. long, glabrous: fls. rose, in 2–6-fld. umbels on slender scapes to 2½ in. high, corolla-tube longer than calyx. Wash., Ore.

3. **ANDROSACE,** L. ROCK-JASMINE. Ann. or per. herbs, planted in rock-gardens; about 85 species in Eu., Asia, N. Amer.—Distinguished from Primula only by the tube of the corolla being shorter than the calyx and the corolla constricted at the throat. (Andros-ace: old Greek name, of no significance here.)

A. Lvs. both basal and cauline . . . . 1. *A. lanuginosa*
AA. Lvs. all basal.
  B. Plant producing stolons.
    C. Lvs. ovate-spatulate, glabrous except the long-ciliate margins . . . . 2. *A. sempervivoides*
    CC. Lvs. ovate-lanceolate to linear, hairy, entire.
      D. Length of lvs. ¼–½in., of equal size . . . . 3. *A. villosa*
      DD. Length of lvs. ½–2 in., of unequal size.
        E. Bracts linear: fls. ¼in. across . . . . 4. *A. sarmentosa*
        EE. Bracts lanceolate: fls. ⅛–½in. across . . . . 5. *A. primuloides*
  BB. Plant not stoloniferous.
    C. Pedicels very short: scape 3 in. or less high . . . . 6. *A. carnea*
    CC. Pedicels 1–2 in. long: scape 8 in. or more high.
      D. Lvs. entire: plant per. . . . . 7. *A. lactea*
      DD. Lvs. unevenly toothed: plant ann. . . . . 8. *A. lactiflora*

1. **A. lanuginosa,** Wall. Whole plant densely white-pubescent, prostrate: lvs. rosulate and cauline, lanceolate-ovate, ½–¾in. long, acute, sessile: scapes axillary, about 2 in. long; fls. rose, about ⅓in. across, in umbels subtended by lanceolate or linear obtuse bracts. Himalayas. Var. **Leichtlinii,** Darnell, fls. white with yellow eye.

2. **A. sempervivoides,** Jacquem. Stoloniferous, the runners to 2 in. long, bearing rosettes about ½in. across: lvs. densely imbricated, fleshy, ovate-spatulate, about ¼in. long, glabrous except the margins which are long-ciliate: scapes 1–4 in. high; fls. rose, ¼in. across, in few-fld. umbels subtended by lanceolate obtuse bracts. Himalayas.

3. **A. villosa,** L. Densely white-hairy per. 2–3 in. high, producing stolons which bear rosettes ½–1 in. across: lvs. linear-lanceolate or ovate-lanceolate, ¼–½in. long, entire: fls. white or rose with yellowish-red throat, ⅓in. across, in umbels subtended by linear-lanceolate acute bracts. Eu., Asia.

4. **A. sarmentosa,** Wall. Stoloniferous, the runners to 5 in. long: lvs. in a basal rosette, lanceolate or ovate-lanceolate, ½–1½ in. long, acute, entire, sessile, white-pubescent when young: scape upright to 5 in. high, hairy; fls. rose, ⅙–¼ in. across, in many-fld. umbels subtended by linear-lanceolate ciliate bracts. Himalayas. Var. **Chumbyi,** Fitzherbert (*A. Chumbyi*, Hort.), rosette dense, plant very cespitose, lvs. densely woolly. Var. **Watkinsii,** Hook. f., lvs. crowded, small.

5. **A. primuloides,** Duby (*A. sarmentosa* var. *primuloides*, Hook. f.). Very similar to *A. sarmentosa*, differing in the lanceolate to linear obtuse lvs. to 2½ in. long, longer oblong-lanceolate bracts, and pink fls. ⅓–½in. across. Himalayas.

6. **A. carnea,** L. Tufted per. 1–3 in. high: lvs. in rosettes, linear or subulate, ¼–½in. long: fls. rose or white with yellow eye, ⅓in. across, very short-pedicelled, in 3–7-fld. umbels subtended by ovate-lanceolate small bracts. Alps, Pyrenees. Var. **brigantiaca,** Knuth (*A. brigantiaca*, Jordan & Fourr.), to 4 in. high, lvs. narrower, fls. soft pink. Var. **Laggeri,** Knuth (*A. Laggeri*, Huet), to 1 in., densely tufted, fls. bright pink.

7. **A. lactea,** L. Tufted glabrous per. 5–8 in. high: lvs. in rosettes, linear or linear-lanceolate, ½–¾in. long, obtuse, entire except slightly ciliate toward tip: fls. snow-white with small yellow eye, ⅓in. across, on pedicels 1–2 in. long, in umbels subtended by small lanceolate or subulate bracts. Mts. of Eu.

8. **A. lactiflora,** Pall. (*A. coronopifolia*, Andr.). Glabrous ann. 4–10 in. high: lvs. in rosettes, linear-lanceolate, ½–2 in. long, acute, irregularly toothed: fls. white, ½in. across, on pedicels 1–2 in. long, in many-fld. umbels subtended by small linear-lanceolate bracts. Siberia.

4. **SOLDANELLA,** L. Per. scapose herbs suitable for the rock-garden; about 6 species in the mts. of Eu.—Lvs. basal, petioled, entire: fls. blue or violet, rarely white, nodding, solitary or in umbels terminating the scape; calyx 5-parted; corolla 5-lobed to middle, the lobes fimbriate; ovary superior, with many ovules: fr. a caps. (Soldanel-la: Latin *a small coin*, referring to shape of lvs.)

S. alpina, L. Lvs. rounded-reniform, ½–1½ in. across, entire or slightly crenate: fls. blue, to ½in. long, in 2–3-fld. umbels on scapes 4–8 in. high. Alps, Pyrenees.

5. **CYCLAMEN,** L. About 20 species of tuberous scapose herbs in Medit. region and Cent. Eu., one a well-known florists' plant.—Lvs. cordate or reniform, long-petioled, entire or sinuate-dentate: scapes bearing a single nodding fl.; calyx 5-parted; corolla-lobes much longer than tube, strongly reflexed and contorted; stamens 5, inserted at base of corolla-tube, the nearly sessile anthers acuminate and included: caps. globose or ovoid, dehiscent from top to base by 5 valves, the valves becoming reflexed. (Cyc-lamen: classical Greek name.)

A. Lobes of corolla eared at base....1. *C. neapolitanum*
AA. Lobes of corolla not eared.
  B. Lvs. not marbled or variegated....2. *C. coum*
  BB. Lvs. usually marbled or variegated.
    C. Fls. ½in. long, very fragrant....3. *C. europæum*
    CC. Fls. 1 in. or more long, odorless....4. *C. persicum*

1. **C. neapolitanum,** Ten. (*C. hederæfolium*, Duby). Lvs. variable, usually obcordate, angled and irregularly toothed, dark green spotted with white above, green or brownish beneath: fls. rose or white, ½–¾in. long, slightly fragrant, in summer or autumn before the lvs.; corolla-lobes ovate, eared at base; pedicels coiling in fr. S. Eu.

2. **C. coum,** Mill. Lvs. orbicular or reniform, entire or slightly crenate: fls. purple with spotted throat, small, odorless, in winter or spring with or after the lvs.; corolla-lobes broad-ovate; pedicels coiling in fr. S. Eu. to Iran.

3. **C. europæum,** L. Lvs. cordate or reniform, slightly angled, marbled with white above, purplish beneath: fls. bright red, ½in. long, very fragrant, on scapes 4–5 in. high, in autumn or summer; corolla-lobes oblong or ovate; pedicels coiling in fr. Cent. and S. Eu.

4. **C. persicum,** Mill. (*C. indicum*, Auth. and Hort. not L. *C. hederæfolium*, Sibth. & Smith). FLORISTS CYCLAMEN. Tuber large and corky on outside, flattened endwise: lvs. cordate-ovate, acutish, crenate-dentate, usually marbled or variegated with white, appearing with the fls.: scape 6–8 in. high; fls. in spring or in winter under glass, white or rose, dark purple at the slightly contracted mouth, about 1½ in. long, odorless; corolla-lobes oblong-spatulate, not eared at base; pedicels not coiling in fr. Greece to Syria.—There are large-fld. strains (var. *giganteum*) in colors from white to red and purple, and also kinds having double, crested, or fimbriate fls.

6. **DODECATHEON,** L. SHOOTING-STAR. Per. scapose herbs of about 30 species in N. Amer.—Lvs. entire or repand, contracted into a more or less winged petiole:

scape bearing an involucrate several- to many-fld. umbel; fls. nodding; calyx 5-parted, the lobes reflexed at first; corolla-tube short, the 5 lobes reflexed, unequal, imbricated; stamens 5, attached at throat of corolla, the long slender anthers connivent into a cone and exserted: caps. oblong or cylindric, dehiscent by 5 valves. (Dodeca-theon: Greek *twelve gods*, old name of no application here.)

A. Anthers sessile, filaments not united into distinct tube.
B. Lvs. with distinct petiole, irregularly sharp-toothed........................1. *D. dentatum*
BB. Lvs. with winged petiole, entire or slightly crenate.
C. Connective deep purple, anthers reddish-yellow........................2. *D. Meadia*
CC. Connective and anthers both purple........................3. *D. Jeffreyi*
AA. Anthers borne at end of distinct tube.
B. Filament-tube yellow: lvs. entire........................4. *D. pulchellum*
BB. Filament-tube deep purple: lvs. somewhat toothed.
C. Connective of purple anthers yellow........................5. *D. Clevelandii*
CC. Connective and anthers purple........................6. *D. Hendersonii*

1. **D. dentatum,** Hook. Glabrous, 3–7 in. high: lvs. ovate, 1–2 in. long, cuneate at base with long distinct petiole, irregularly sharp-dentate: fls. white with purple at base of petals, about ½in. long, anthers reddish-purple. B. C. to Utah.

2. **D. Meadia,** L. Glabrous, to 2 ft.: lvs. ovate-oblong or oblong-linear, to 6 in. or more long, obtuse, narrowed into winged petiole, crenate or nearly entire: scape often purple-spotted, bearing a 10–20-fld. umbel subtended by lanceolate bracts; fls. in May–June, about 1 in. long, the linear-oblong corolla-lobes rose and white at base, anthers reddish-yellow and the broadly ovate connective body purple. (Named for Richard Mead, 1673–1754, English physician.) Pa. to Ga. and Tex.

3. **D. Jeffreyi,** VanHoutte. Glabrous or somewhat glandular-pubescent, 9–15 in. high: lvs. oblong-lanceolate, 6–12 in. long, narrowed to winged petiole, entire or slightly crenate-dentate: fls. rose-purple with base of petals yellow, ⅓–½in. long, anthers deep purple. (Named for John Jeffrey, page 45.) B. C. to Ida. and Calif.

4. **D. pulchellum,** Merr. (*Exinia pulchella*, Raf. *D. Meadia* var. *pauciflorum*, Durand. *D. pauciflorum*, Greene. *D. vulgare*, Piper). Glabrous or nearly so, 8–18 in. high: lvs. oblanceolate, 2–8 in. long, narrowed into winged petiole, entire or rarely slightly dentate: fls. rose-purple with yellow at base and dark purple wavy line in throat, ¾–1 in. long; stamens with yellow tube about half as long as purple anthers. Wash. to Sask. and New Mex.

5. **D. Clevelandii,** Greene. Glabrous, 1–1½ ft. high: lvs. obovate, 1½–2½ in. long, narrowed into petiole, irregularly toothed or sometimes entire: fls. purple or white with yellowish base, ½–¾in. long; stamens with deep purple tube and purple anthers having yellow much corrugated connective. (Named for the original collector, Mr. Cleveland, of San Diego.) S. Calif.

6. **D. Hendersonii,** Gray (*D. latifolium*, Piper. *D. integrifolium latifolium*, Hook.). Differs from *D. Clevelandii* in producing bulblets resembling rice-grains on the roots and the connective as well as anthers being purple. (Named for L. F. Henderson, page 44.) Wash. to Calif.

7. **LYSIMACHIA,** L. Loosestrife. About 100 species of mostly per. herbs of wide distribution in temp. and subtrop. regions, sometimes grown in open situations in the garden.—Lvs. alternate, opposite or whorled, entire, often glandular-punctate: fls. solitary in the axils, or in racemes, corymbs, or panicles; calyx 5–6-parted; corolla rotate or campanulate, 5–6-parted; stamens 5–6, inserted on corolla-tube, slightly monadelphous, staminodia none: caps. ovoid or globose, dehiscent by 5 valves, with few or many seeds. (Lysima-chia: probably after King Lysimachus.)

A. Of creeping habit........................1. *L. Nummularia*
AA. Of upright habit.
B. Color of fls. white........................2. *L. clethroides*
BB. Color of fls. yellow.
C. Fls. in axillary whorls; corolla-lobes glandular-ciliate........................3. *L. punctata*
CC. Fls. in leafy panicles; corolla-lobes glabrous........................4. *L. vulgaris*

1. **L. Nummularia, L.** Moneywort. Creeping Jenny or Charlie. Glabrous; sts. creeping, sometimes 2 ft. long, making a good ground-cover and also suitable for baskets: lvs. opposite, orbicular, to 1 in. long, obtuse, rounded or slightly cordate at base, short-petioled: fls. yellow, dark-dotted, ⅔–1 in. across, solitary in the axils, blooming June–Aug. (Nummularia: from *nummus*, coin, referring to the shape of the lvs.) Eu.; nat. in E. U. S.

2. **L. clethroides,** Duby. Puberulent or rarely glabrous, to 3 ft.: lvs. alternate, ovate-lanceolate, 3–6 in. long, tapering at both ends, the margins revolute: fls. white, nearly ½in. across, in a slender terminal spike, the bracts longer than the pedicels. China, Japan.

3. **L. punctata,** L. Usually densely pubescent; sts. erect, simple or branched, to 3 ft.: lvs. verticillate in 3's or 4's, ovate-lanceolate, 1–3 in. long, acute, nearly sessile: fls. yellow, about ¾in. across, in axillary whorls, blooming June–July; corolla-lobes glandular-ciliate; filaments minutely glandular-hairy. Eu.; nat. in E. U. S.

4. **L. vulgaris,** L. Densely pubescent herb to 3 ft., with erect branched sts.: lvs. verticillate in 3's or 4's or sometimes opposite, ovate-lanceolate, 2–4 in. long, acute, nearly sessile: fls. yellow, ½–¾in. across, in terminal leafy panicles or in the upper axils; calyx often dark-margined; corolla-lobes glabrous. Eu., Asia; nat. in E. U. S.

8. **STEIRONEMA,** Raf. Loosestrife. Per. herbs of about 5 species in N. Amer., one sometimes transplanted.—Lvs. opposite or whorled, entire: fls. yellow, solitary or clustered in the axils; calyx 5-parted; corolla rotate, 5-parted; stamens 5, distinct or slightly monadelphous, alternating with 5 staminodia: caps. dehiscent by 5 valves, several- to many-seeded. (Steirone-ma: Greek *sterile threads,* referring to the staminodia.)

S. ciliatum, Raf. (*Lysimachia ciliata,* L.). To 4 ft.: lvs. opposite, ovate-lanceolate, 2–6 in. long, acuminate, margins and petioles finely ciliate: fls. ½–1 in. across, on slender pedicels, corolla-lobes broad-ovate and denticulate. N. Amer.; nat. in Eu.

9. **ANAGALLIS,** L. Pimpernel. Creeping or erect herbs of about 25 species in many parts of the world, a few grown in gardens.—Lvs. opposite, alternate or verticillate, sessile or short-petioled, entire: fls. axillary, mostly solitary, pedicelled; calyx deeply 5-parted, the lanceolate or subulate lobes spreading; corolla deeply 5-parted, rotate or rotate-campanulate, the lobes obovate or linear; stamens 5, inserted at base of corolla, distinct or united at base, usually pubescent: caps. globose, circumscissile, many-seeded. (Anagal-lis: Greek *delightful.*)

A. Fls. ¼in. across: lvs. ovate .... 1. *A. arvensis*
AA. Fls. ¾in. across: lvs. linear or linear-lanceolate .... 2. *A. linifolia*

1. **A. arvensis,** L. Poor Mans Weatherglass (fls. close at approach of bad weather). Much-branched ann. with procumbent or ascending 4-angled sts.: lvs. opposite or in 3's, ovate, ¼–¾in. long, sessile, acutish, black-dotted beneath: fls. scarlet or white, about ¼in. across, on pedicels longer than lvs.; calyx slightly shorter than corolla; lobes of corolla finely toothed. Widely distributed. Var. **cærulea,** Gren. & Godr. (*A. cærulea,* Schreber), has blue fls.

2. **A. linifolia,** L. (*A. grandiflora,* Andr.). Per. or bien. with 4-angled sts. to 1½ ft., woody at base: lvs. opposite or verticillate, linear or linear-lanceolate, about 1 in. long, acute, sessile, the margins often revolute: fls. blue, reddish beneath, about ¾in. across, on pedicels two to four times longer than lvs.; calyx half as long as corolla; lobes of corolla entire. Medit. region. Var. **Monellii,** Knuth (*A. Monellii,* L.), lvs. ovate or oblong, often in 3's. Var. **collina,** Ball (*A. collina,* Schousb.), fls. rose or purplish.

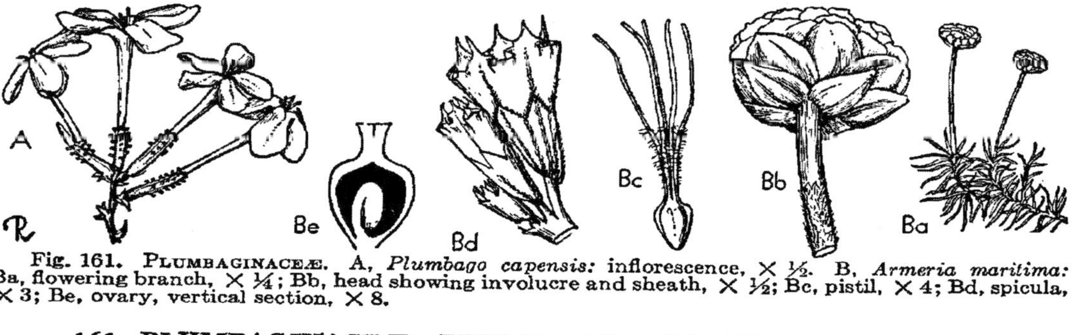

Fig. 161. Plumbaginaceæ. A, *Plumbago capensis:* inflorescence, × ½. B, *Armeria maritima:* Ba, flowering branch, × ¼; Bb, head showing involucre and sheath, × ½; Bc, pistil, × 4; Bd, spicula, × 3; Be, ovary, vertical section, × 8.

161. PLUMBAGINACEÆ. PLUMBAGO or LEADWORT FAMILY

About 10 genera and 300 species of herbs and shrubs of wide geographical distribution, usually in saline or limestone situations; many are grown in gardens and a few in the greenhouse.—Acaulescent with lvs. in a rosette or with elongated branched sts. and alternate lvs.: fls. bisexual, regular, in spikes, heads or panicles; calyx bracted at base, tubular or funnelform, 5-toothed or -lobed, 5–15-ribbed, plaited, often scarious and colored; corolla of 5 hypogynous petals united into tube or connate only at base; stamens 5, opposite petals, hypogynous or inserted on corolla; ovary superior, 1-celled with 1 ovule; styles 5, separate or united: fr. usually inclosed by calyx, dehiscent or indehiscent.

A. Plant with leafy sts.: calyx scarious only between the 5 ribs, lobes erect; corolla with long slender tube.
- B. Stamens free; calyx glandular.......................................1. PLUMBAGO
- BB. Stamens attached to corolla-tube; calyx not glandular.......................2. CERATOSTIGMA

AA. Plant usually with naked scapes: calyx scarious, colored, spreading, 10-ribbed; petals connate only at base.
- B. Fls. in racemes, cymes or panicles.......................................3. LIMONIUM
- BB. Fls. in dense heads.
  - C. Styles shortly fused at ovary apex; stigmas linear: lvs. usually flat.........4. ARMERIA
  - CC. Styles wholly free; stigmas subcapitate: lvs. mostly needle-like and pungent. 5. ACANTHOLIMON

1. **PLUMBAGO**, L. LEADWORT. Mostly per. herbs or subshrubs, sometimes climbing, in the tropics and subtropics; about 6 species, a few grown in greenhouses or out-of-doors in warm countries.—Lvs. auricled at base or clasping, entire: fls. in spikes at ends of branches, bracts shorter than calyx; calyx tubular, glandular, scarious only between the 5 ribs, the 5 short lobes erect; corolla salverform, with slender tube and 5 spreading lobes; stamens free from corolla: fr. a membranaceous circumscissile caps., the deciduous part often splitting into 5 valves from below. (Plumba-go: Latin for *lead*, of doubtful application.)

A. Fls. blue or white.......................................1. *P. capensis*
AA. Fls. red.......................................2. *P. indica*

1. **P. capensis**, Thunb. Semi-climbing subshrub or in the greenhouse upright and straggling, glabrous except in the infl.: lvs. oblong or oblong-spatulate, about 2 in. long, obtuse and shortly mucronate, tapering into short petiole: fls. in short spikes, azure-blue; corolla-tube about 1½ in. long; calyx pubescent, with stalked glands on upper part. S. Afr. Var. **alba**, Hort., fls. white.

2. **P. indica**, L. (*P. rosea*, L. *P. rosea* var. *coccinea*, Hook. *P. coccinea*, Salisb.). Glabrous, more or less climbing, the sts. striated: lvs. ovate-elliptic, to 4 in. long, tapering into a short somewhat clasping petiole: fls. in long racemes, purplish-red to scarlet; corolla-tube about 1 in. long; calyx pubescent with stalked glands. S. Asia.

2. **CERATOSTIGMA**, Bunge. About 8 per. herbs often woody at base or in 2 species shrubby, native in China, Himalayas, Abyssinia and Somaliland, grown as bedding and border plants.—Lvs. more or less ciliate: fls. in dense terminal bracted clusters or heads; calyx tubular, deeply 5-parted, not glandular, 10-nerved at base; corolla salverform, with slender tube and 5 spreading lobes; stamens attached to middle of corolla-tube: fr. a circumscissile caps. splitting into 5 valves. (Ceratostig-ma: Greek *horned stigma.*)

A. Plant a low suffrutescent per. to 1½ ft. high, foliage becoming bronzy in autumn; buds naked.......................................1. *C. plumbaginoides*
AA. Plant a shrub 3–5 ft. high, foliage remaining green in autumn; buds scaly.......2. *C. Willmottianum*

1. **C. plumbaginoides**, Bunge (*Plumbago Larpentæ*, Lindl.). To 1½ ft., suffrutescent; buds naked: lvs. broadly obovate, to 3 in. long, tapering at base, glabrous except for strongly hispidulous-ciliate margins, the dark green foliage becoming bronzy-red in autumn: fls. deep gentian-blue, about ½in. across, blooming Aug. to late autumn; sepals and bracts strongly ciliate. China.

2. **C. Willmottianum**, Stapf. Shrub 3–5 ft. high; buds scaly: lvs. oblanceolate or elliptic, to 2 in. long, tapering at base, hispid beneath, margins ciliate: fls. bright blue with rosy-red tube, about ½in. across, blooming through autumn; bracts rigidly ciliate. (Named for Miss E. A. Willmott, page 54.) W. China.

3. **LIMONIUM**, Mill. (*Statice*, Willd.). SEA-LAVENDER. Per. herbs, or sometimes ann. or shrubby, of about 180 species widely distributed, often grown in rockeries, greenhouses or for cut-fls.; some are useful for dry bouquets; those in cult. are summer-flowering.—Lvs. radical and tufted or alternate along st. in the shrubby species, entire or pinnatifid: fls. in branched cymose panicles or spikes, subtended by scale-like bracts; calyx tubular, scarious, often colored, spreading, 10-ribbed at base; petals free or connate only at base, clawed; stamens inserted at base of petals: fr. inclosed in calyx, indehiscent or dehiscent. (Limo-nium: ancient Greek name, probably from *meadow.*)—The application of the generic names Limonium and Statice was long transposed; see under Armeria.

A. Lvs. pinnatifid.
  B. Spikes dense, cylindrical .... 1. *L. spicatum*
  BB. Spikes loose and open, secund.
    C. Calyx blue, purple or white .... 2. *L. sinuatum*
    CC. Calyx yellow .... 3. *L. Bonduellii*
AA. Lvs. not pinnatifid.
  B. Fls. in dense cylindrical spikes .... 4. *L. Suworowii*
  BB. Fls. in one-sided spikelets, infl. a loose open corymbose panicle.
    C. Stigmas capitate; corolla red .... 5. *L. tataricum*
    CC. Stigmas cylindrical-filiform; corolla various.
      D. Corolla rose to purplish-lavender.
        E. Plants covered with short stellate hairs .... 6. *L. latifolium*
        EE. Plants glabrous or if hairy not stellately so.
          F. Height 3–10 in. when in flower .... 7. *L. bellidifolium*
          FF. Height 1 ft. or more in flower.
            G. Calyx white, lower bracts scarious-margined: lvs. oblong-lanceolate .... 8. *L. vulgare*
            GG. Calyx dark purplish-blue, lower bracts all membranaceous: lvs. broadly ovate or obovate .... 9. *L. Gmelinii*
      DD. Corolla yellow or yellowish-white.
        E. Calyx-limb obtusely lobed or erose: plant 4–10 in. high .... 10. *L. sinense*
        EE. Calyx-limb strongly folded, lobes mucronate to long-cuspidate.
          F. Floral branches winged.
            G. Lf. sessile .... 11. *L. macrophyllum*
            GG. Lf. petioled .... 12. *L. arborescens*
          FF. Floral branches not winged.
            G. Length of lf. ½–¾ in. .... 13. *L. puberulum*
            GG. Length of lf. 2½ in. or more.
              H. Blades about 2½ in. long, nearly as broad as long .... 14. *L. Preauxii*
              HH. Blades about 5–6 in. long and twice as long as broad .... 15. *L. Perezii*

1. **L. spicatum,** Kuntze (*Statice spicata,* Willd.). Ann. to 6 in.: lvs. oblong-lanceolate, obtuse, narrowed into short petiole, pinnately parted with obtuse lobes: scape bearing long dense cylindrical spikes often branched, the densely clustered spikelets 2–3-fld.; calyx hispid; corolla rose or white. Caucasus to Iran.

2. **L. sinuatum,** Mill. (*Statice sinuata,* L.). Rough-hairy per. or bien. to 2 ft.: lvs. lyrate-pinnatifid, about 8 in. long, the lobes and sinuses rounded, terminal lobe bearing a bristle: scape corymbosely-paniculate, the branches 3–5-winged, the wings below the forks produced into 3 linear-lanceolate appendages, spikelets 3–5-fld. in short one-sided spikes; calyx blue; corolla yellowish-white. Medit. region.—There are hybrid forms having yellow and white fls.

3. **L. Bonduellii,** Kuntze (*Statice Bonduellii,* Lest.). Ann. or bien. to 2 ft., the sts. hairy at base: lvs. lyrate-pinnatifid, to 6 in. long, hairy and ciliate, with rounded lobes and sinuses, the terminal lobe mucronate: scape corymbosely-paniculate, the branches winged, below the forks the wings produced into 2–3 linear appendages, spikelets 1–3-fld., in terminal corymbs; bracts with green spines; calyx yellow; corolla deeper yellow. (Named for M. Bonduelle, military surgeon in N. Afr.) Algeria.

4. **L. Suworowii,** Kuntze (*Statice Suworowii,* Regel). Glabrous ann. to 1½ ft.: lvs. all basal, oblong-lanceolate, 6–8 in. long, entire or coarsely toothed: scapes several, bearing a long terminal dense cylindrical spike and many sessile lateral ones 4–6 in. long; calyx green with lavender limb; corolla tubular, lavender. (Named for Iwan Petrowitsch Suworow, inspector of military hospitals in Turkestan forces.) W. Turkestan.—There is a white-fld. var.

5. **L. tataricum,** Mill. (*Statice tatarica,* L. *Goniolimon tataricum,* Boiss.). Glabrous slightly glaucous per. to 1 ft.: lvs. obovate or oblong-lanceolate, 4–6 in. long, acuminate and mucronate, narrowed to petiole: scape soon branching, the 1–2-fld. spikelets forming one-sided spikes in the corymbosely panicled infl., the branches of which are narrowly 3-winged; calyx white; corolla ruby-red: stigmas distinctly capitate. S. E. Eu. Var. **angustifolium,** Hubbard (*Statice incana,* Bieb.), has lanceolate narrower lvs.—There is also a dwarf form.

6. **L. latifolium,** Kuntze (*Statice latifolia,* Smith). Per. to 2 ft., covered with short stellate hairs: lvs. oblong-elliptic, to 10 in. long, obtuse, narrowed into long petiole: scape tall and very much-branched, the 1–2-fld. spikelets forming short one-sided spikes; calyx white; corolla blue (white or rose-colored vars.). Russia, Bulgaria, Caucasus.

7. **L. bellidifolium,** Dum. (*Statice bellidifolia,* Gouan. *L. reticulatum,* Mill. *S. reticulata,* Huds. not L. *S. caspia,* Willd.). Glabrous rough-granular per. to 8 in.: lvs. obovate or lanceolate, ½–1½ in. long, obtuse, narrowed into petiole: scape very much-branched, lower branches sterile, upper branches corymbose-paniculate, the 2–3-fld. spikelets on one-sided spikes at ends of branchlets; calyx white; corolla pale lilac. Eu., E. Asia.

8. **L. vulgare,** Mill. (*Statice Limonium,* L. *S. maritima,* Lam. in part). Glabrous per. to 1 ft. or more: lvs. elliptic-oblong, to 6 in. long, obtuse, mucronate, narrowed into long petiole: scape branched above into a corymbose-paniculate infl., the 1–3-fld. spikelets densely imbricated in one-sided spreading or recurved spikes; calyx white or bluish; corolla bluish-lilac. Eu., N. Afr., Asia Minor.

9. **L. Gmelinii,** Kuntze (*Statice Gmelinii,* Willd.). Per. to 2 ft.: lvs. ovate or obovate, obtuse, short-petioled or nearly sessile, glabrous: scape angled above, bearing a corymbose panicle, of 2-fld. spikelets densely imbricated in short one-sided spikes; calyx dark purplish-blue; corolla rose. (Named for Johann Georg Gmelin, 1709–1755, German botanist.) Caucasus and Siberia.

10. **L. sinense,** Kuntze (*Statice sinensis,* Girard). Glabrous per. 4–10 in. high: lvs. obovate-lanceolate, to 2 in. long, obtuse, base narrowly cuneate: fls. pale yellow to cream-colored, in compact corymbose panicle of 2-fld. spikelets; calyx-lobes rounded or erose; branches of infl. acutely angled. China.

11. **L. macrophyllum,** Kuntze (*Statice macrophylla,* Brouss. *S. Halfordii,* Hort.). Subshrub to 3 ft.: lvs. large, obovate-spatulate, obtuse, sessile and attenuate at base, glabrous: scape with very many broadly winged branches, corymbose-paniculate, spikelets 2-fld., borne 2 together on one-sided spikes; calyx blue or purple; corolla yellow or almost white. Teneriffe.

12. **L. arborescens,** Kuntze (*Statice arborescens,* Brouss.). Shrub to 2 ft.: lvs. ovate-oblong, to 10 in. long, obtuse, mucronate, attenuate into short petiole: scape with many narrowly winged branches, spikelets 2-fld. in short one-sided loose spikes; calyx blue; corolla yellow. Teneriffe.

13. **L. puberulum,** Kuntze (*Statice puberula,* Webb). Subshrub to 8 in., puberulous to white-pilose: lvs. ovate-rhomboid, to ¾in. long, apex sharply acute, margins long-ciliate: fls. showy with yellowish-white corolla and violet calyx; branches of infl. wingless but usually angled. Canary Isls.

14. **L. Preauxii,** Kuntze (*Statice Preauxii,* Webb). Glabrous subshrub to 2 ft.: lvs. rotundate-triangular, 2½–4 in. long, obtuse and mucronulate, truncate and short attenuate at base to petiole 4–5 in. or more long with a sheathing base: scape with many flattened but not winged branches, the spikelets in lax one-sided terminal spikes; calyx lavender; corolla pale yellow. (Named for Despréaux, who sent it from the Canaries.) Canary Isls.

15. **L. Perezii,** Hubbard (*Statice Perezii,* Stapf). Subshrub to about 2 ft.: lvs. rhomboid-ovate to triangular, base truncate or nearly so, long-petioled: fls. with pale yellow corolla and pubescent purplish-blue calyx, in 2-fld. spikelets; infl. much and diffusely branched. (Named for Dr. G. V. Perez of Orotava.) Canary Isls.

4. **ARMERIA,** Willd. (*Statice,* Mill. and of L. in part). THRIFT. SEA-PINK. Per. late spring- and summer-flowering herbs or subshrubs forming low evergreen tufts or colonies, useful for rock-gardens or borders; about 100 species have been described from the north temp. zone and S. S. Amer., but by recent studies these have been considered to represent about half that number, of which perhaps 15 are cult.—Differs from Limonium in narrow often linear lvs., and more especially in the fls. borne in condensed cymules in dense globular heads, the latter subtended by 2 or more whorls of usually scarious bracts forming a kind of involucre, subtended for a short distance by a sheath enveloping the distal end of the scape, this sheath formed by the 2 lowest involucral bracts reflexed and fused marginally. (Arme-ria: old Latin name.)—Armeria has been conserved as the valid name for this genus over the older one of Statice, the latter officially considered as an ambiguous name.

A. Outermost lvs. (close to the ground and few in number) about twice as wide and half as long as inner ones, the latter less than ⅛in. wide: fls. and involucral bracts white . . . . 1. *A. juncea*
AA. Outermost lvs. not distinguishable from inner and if shorter the inner ones ¼in. or more wide.
B. Lvs. oblanceolate, or at least much wider toward apex, mostly ¼–¾in. wide.
C. Fl.-heads 1–2 in. across: lvs., except youngest, limp and flaccid, lying on the ground . . . . 2. *A. pseud-armeria*
CC. Fl.-heads about ¾in. across: lvs. mostly erect or ascending . . . . 3. *A. plantaginea*
BB. Lvs. mostly linear to acicular, rarely more than ⅛in. wide.
C. Scapes 1–2½ in. long: lvs. rarely over ¾in. long, stiff and pungent . . . . . . 4. *A. juniperifolia*
CC. Scapes 4–20 in. long: lvs. 1–6 in. long, never (in ours) stiff or pungent . . . . . . 5. *A. maritima*

1. **A. juncea,** Girard (*Statice juncea,* Hubbard). Low tufted per. to 8 in.: lvs. dimorphic, the outermost ones few, about ³⁄₁₆in. wide and 1½–2 in. long, the abundant and conspicuous inner lvs. half as wide and twice as long, wire-like and filiform, usually glaucous: scapes slender; heads about ½in. across, nodding; corolla and involucre white. Pyrenees.—Much material so named in the American trade belongs to other species.

2. **A. pseud-armeria,** Mansfeld (*Statice pseud-armeria,* Murr. *S. cephalotes,* Ait. *S. pseudo-Armeria,* Paxt. *A. latifolia,* Willd. *A. grandiflora,* Hort. *A. formosa,* Hort. *A. gigantea,* Hort.). Glabrous and often glaucous, to 2½ ft.: lvs. broadly oblanceolate to oblong-lanceolate, mostly ½–¾in. wide, 5–7-veined, flaccid and only youngest ones erect

or strongly ascending: heads 1–2 in. across, on stout scapes, outermost involucral bracts lanceolate and typically longer than inner; corolla bright pink. Portugal.—A white-fld. form is known, with intermediates between it and the rose-red var. **rubra,** Hort. (*A. cephalotes* var. *rubra,* Hort.), being common. Some material distributed as this species belongs to *A. gaditana,* Boiss., distinguished by absence of membranous bracts subtending each fl. of the cymule.

3. **A. plantaginea,** Willd. (*Statice plantaginea,* All. *S. alliacea,* Cav.). Glabrous, to 2½ ft.: lvs. linear-lanceolate, mostly 3–6 in. long, usually 3–5-veined, erect, ascending or arching: heads about ¾in. across on erect scapes, outer involucral bracts lanceolate and in some forms exceeding the head. S. Cent. Eu. Var. **longibracteata,** Boiss. (*A. montana,* Wallr.), has smaller heads with outer involucral bracts much exceeding the head.—Two variants having involucral bracts shorter than head, producing larger more showy heads, and considered horticulturally more desirable are var. **bupleuroides,** Lawrence (*A. bupleuroides,* Godr.), with rose-pink to purplish-red corollas, and var. **leucantha,** Boiss., with white corollas and pale cream-colored involucre; these variants, while common in trade stocks listed under this and other species names, have not been so recognized nomenclatorially.

4. **A. juniperifolia,** Willd. (*Statice juniperifolia,* Vahl. *S. cæspitosa,* Cav. *A. cæspitosa,* Boiss.). Low very compact per., with lvs. in conspicuous rosettes: lvs. stiffly acicular, mucronate, 3-sided, typically not exceeding ½in. long but more in some hort. forms: heads about ⅜in. across, on short scapes to 1 in. long; corolla rose-pink. Sierra de Guadarrama Mts., Spain. Var. **splendens,** Lawrence (*Statice splendens,* Lag. & Rodr. *A. splendens,* Boiss. *A. cæspitosa* var. *splendens,* Vic. & Beltr.), has flat lvs. with scape much narrower than lvs. and usually three to four times as long, heads nodding.—A hybrid, **A. cæsalpina,** Hort. (*A. juniperifolia* × *A. maritima* var. *alpina. A. Sundermannii,* Hort.), differs from var. *splendens* in lvs. to 1 in. long, scape as wide as lvs. or wider, and larger not nodding heads. Unlike most other armerias *A. juniperifolia* is highly susceptible to a basal stem-rot, especially during the summer, and full surface drainage, such as is afforded by a rocky scree, is necessary for its cult.

5. **A. maritima,** Willd. (*Statice Armeria,* L. *S. maritima,* Mill. *A. vulgaris,* Willd. *A. vulgaris* var. *pubescens,* Bab. *S. maritima* var. *Laucheana,* Hubbard). To 1 ft. or more: lvs. linear, ⅛in. or less across, 1-nerved, acute or obtuse: scapes glabrous or pubescent, bearing heads ½–1 in. diam. subtended by scarious bracts, the outer ones shorter than head; calyx-base decurrent on the short pedicel, pubescent at least on the nerves; corolla pink, purple or white. Eurasia, N. Amer.—As now constituted, a large and polymorphic species embracing more than 20 botanical vars. representing the reduction of many entities previously treated as separate species but whose ill-defined and integrating characters preclude such recognition. Among the variants the following are cult.: var. **alpina,** Lawrence (*A. alpina,* Willd. *Statice alpina,* Poir. *A. montana,* Wallr. *S. montana,* Mill. *S. montana* var. *alpina,* Gams), lvs. 3⁄16in. across, heads about 1 in. across, outer involucral bracts acute and shorter than inner ones, scapes glabrous and stout, mts. of Eu.; var. **elongata,** Massart (*A. elongata,* Hoffm.), is a taller plant with scapes to 2 ft. high, outer involucral bracts longer than inner and often exceeding heads; var. *Laucheana,* cited above, represents typical material of *A. maritima* and is distinguishable only by its intense rose-colored fls.

5. **ACANTHOLIMON,** Boiss. Prickly-Thrift. Summer-flowering per. evergreen suffrutescent herbs or subshrubs, mostly from the E. Medit. region to Iran; about 100 species, a few cult. as rock-garden subjects, intolerant of severe winters and requiring good drainage in full sun exposure.—Plants tholiform or cespitose, sts. covered by persistent lvs. in greatly condensed spirals: lvs. linear, pungent, cylindrical or slightly 3-angled: infl. a head or briefly fastigiately branched spike or raceme, borne on a scape or elongated peduncle; fls. rose or white, usually subtended by closely appressed bracts; petals united at base, forming a ring about the 5 stamens; calyx tubular, funnelform, 10-ribbed and lobed; stigmas 5, capitate: fr. a utricle. (Acantholi-mon: from the Greek for *spiny sea-lavender.*)

A. venustum, Boiss. About 8 in. high: lvs. gray-green, very stiff, about ¾in. long: fls. rose, in long loose one-sided spikelets of 12–20 fls. each. Asia Minor.—A related species, **A. glumaceum,** Boiss., from Armenia, has a denser infl. of 6–9 smaller fls. and may be offered as *A. venustum.*

162. SAPOTACEÆ. SAPODILLA FAMILY

Shrubs or trees of wide distribution mostly in trop. regions; about 35 genera and 425 species, several grown for their edible frs. and one yielding gutta-percha.—Juice usually milky: lvs. alternate, simple and entire, pinnately veined, commonly leathery and exstipulate: fls. bisexual, regular, solitary or fascicled in the axils of lvs. or at the

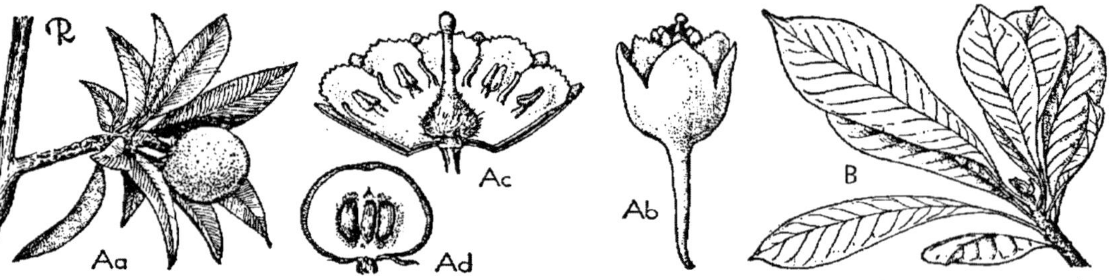

Fig. 162. SAPOTACEÆ. A, *Calocarpum Sapota:* Aa, fruiting branch, × 1/6; Ab, flower, × 1; Ac, same, perianth expanded, × 1; Ad, fruit, vertical section, × 1/4. B, *Achras Zapota:* vegetative branch, × 1/6.

lf.-scars on the naked branches; calyx usually of 4–6 separate sepals in 2 whorls, sometimes 5, imbricated; corolla gamopetalous, with as many or twice as many imbricated lobes as sepals in 1 or 2 whorls, often with entire or laciniate lobe-like appendages; stamens as many as corolla-lobes and opposite them, inserted on tube of corolla, often alternating with staminodia; ovary superior, 2- to many-celled, with 1 ovule in each cell; style and stigma 1: fr. a berry.

A. Fls. with staminodia.
  B. Staminodia petal-like, appearing as if additional corolla-lobes .... 1. ACHRAS
  BB. Staminodia filament-like.
    C. Sepals 10, densely imbricated in several series .... 2. CALOCARPUM
    CC. Sepals 4 or 5, in 1 or 2 series .... 3. LUCUMA
AA. Fls. without staminodia.
  B. Stamens 12; sepals 6 .... 4. PALAQUIUM
  BB. Stamens and sepals usually 5 .... 5. CHRYSOPHYLLUM

1. **ACHRAS,** L. (*Sapota*, Mill.). An evergreen tree native in trop. Amer. and extensively cult. in the tropics for its edible fr.—Lvs. petioled, crowded at ends of branchlets: fls. solitary in the axils, pedicelled; sepals 6, in 2 whorls, hairy outside; corolla urceolate, with 6 lobes half as long as tube; stamens 6, alternating with 6 petaloid staminodia; ovary villous, 10–12-celled: berry globose or conical, fleshy. (Ach-ras: from Greek for the pear-tree, referring to the resemblance of the frs.)

A. Zapota, L. (*A. Sapota*, L. *Sapota Achras*, Mill.). SAPODILLA. To 75 ft.: lvs. ovate-elliptic to elliptic-lanceolate, 2–5 in. long, entire or emarginate, glabrous and shining: fls. white, 1/4–1/2in. across: fr. 2–3 1/2 in. diam., with thin rusty-brown scurfy skin and yellow-brown translucent flesh surrounding the shining black obovate seeds.

2. **CALOCARPUM,** Pierre. Trees native in Cent. Amer. and widely grown in trop. Amer. for the edible fr.—Lvs. clustered toward ends of branchlets: fls. nearly sessile, 6–12 together in axils of fallen lvs.; sepals 10, densely imbricated in several series; corolla with 5 imbricated lobes longer than tube; stamens 5, alternating with 5 linear staminodia; ovary villous, 5-celled: berry oblong or ovoid. (Calocar-pum: Greek *beautiful fruit.*)

C. Sapota, Merr. (*Sideroxylon Sapota*, Jacq. *Achras Zapota*, Auth. not L. *A. mammosa*, L. *Sapota mammosa*, Mill. *Lucuma mammosa*, Gaertn. f. *Achradelpha mammosa*, O. F. Cook). SAPOTE. MARMALADE-PLUM. Tree to 65 ft., with thick trunk and stout branches: lvs. obovate to oblanceolate, to 16 in. long, obtuse or acute, attenuate at base, light green and glabrous: fls. white, about 1/2in. across: fr. russet-brown, 3–6 in. long, with thick skin and firm reddish flesh, 1-seeded by abortion. Cent. Amer.

3. **LUCUMA,** Molina. A large genus of trees and shrubs mostly native in trop. Amer., several furnishing edible frs. and one widely planted.—Differing from Calocarpum chiefly in the 4 or 5 sepals which are in 1 or 2 series. (Lucu-ma: Peruvian name of one species.)

L. nervosa, A. DC. (*L. Rivicoa* var. *angustifolia*, Miq.). CANISTEL. TI-ES. EGG-FRUIT. Small slender tree to 25 ft.: lvs. oblong-obovate to oblanceolate, 4–8 in. long, acute, bright green and glabrous: fls. greenish-white: fr. globose to ovoid, 2–4 in. long, orange-yellow, with soft orange flesh and 2–3 shining seeds. N. S. Amer.; nat. in S. Fla. and W. Indies.

4. **PALAQUIUM,** Blanco. More than 50 species of large trees native in E. Indies and Malaya, several yielding gutta-percha.—Lvs. leathery, stipulate: fls. in fascicles, pedicelled; sepals 6, in 2 whorls; corolla-tube as long as the 6 lanceolate acute lobes; stamens 12, in 2 series, staminodia 0; ovary villous, 6-celled: berry oblong or globose, fleshy. (Pala-quium: from native Philippine name.)

P. Gutta, Burck (*Isonandra Gutta,* Hook.). To 40 ft. or more: lvs. elliptic, 4 in. or more long, abruptly pointed, rusty-tomentose beneath, with numerous side veins: fls. small. Malaya.

5. **CHRYSOPHYLLUM,** L. Trees, of about 60 species in the tropics, particularly of Amer., one grown far S. for ornament and for the edible fr.—Lvs. leathery, often silky or tomentose beneath, with many parallel cross-veins: fls. small, fascicled, pedicelled or nearly sessile; sepals usually 5; corolla tubular-campanulate or somewhat rotate, with mostly 5 lobes; stamens 5, staminodia 0; ovary villous, 5–10-celled: berry globose to oblong, fleshy or leathery. (Chrysophyl-lum: Greek *golden leaf,* in reference to the color of the under side of lvs.)

C. Cainito, L. Star-Apple. Evergreen tree to 50 ft.: lvs. oval or oblong, 3–5 in. long, covered beneath with silky golden-brown tomentum: fls. purplish-white: fr. usually globose, 2–4 in. diam., with smooth purple or light green skin and translucent whitish pulp surrounding the 3–8 shining seeds. (Cainito is an early American, or aboriginal, name.) Trop. Amer.

Fig. 163. Ebenaceæ. *Diospyros virginiana:* a, flowering branch of pistillate plant, × ½; b, pistillate flower, × 1; c, same, vertical section, × 2; d, ovary, cross-section, × 4; e, staminate flower, × 1; f, same, vertical section, × 1.

163. EBENACEÆ. EBONY FAMILY

Trees or shrubs with very hard wood, of about 6 genera and 300 species mostly of trop. and subtrop. range, one widely cult. for its edible frs.—Lvs. alternate, entire, exstipulate, usually leathery: diœcious or polygamous; fls. regular, solitary or cymose in the axils; calyx 3–7-lobed, persistent, often enlarging in fr.; corolla gamopetalous, 3–7-lobed, deciduous; stamens of same or twice the number of corolla-lobes or rarely more, inserted on base of corolla-tube, the filaments short, free or united at base; ovary superior, 2–16-celled with 1 or 2 ovules in each cell; styles 2–8, free or united at base, with entire or 2-lobed stigma: fr. a leathery or fleshy indehiscent berry, or drupe-like, or rarely dehiscent.

DIOSPYROS, L. Persimmon. Ebony. Nearly 200 species of wide distribution.—Fls. in few- to many-fld. axillary cymes or the pistillate solitary; corolla campanulate, urceolate or tubular, the lobes 3–7, usually 4–5; stamens 4 to many, commonly 16, mostly with 4–8 staminodia in pistillate fls.; ovary 4–16-celled: fr. a large juicy 1–10-seeded berry. (Diospy-ros: Greek *grain of Jove,* referring to the edible frs.)

A. Lvs. glabrous beneath, or pubescent only when young........................1. *D. virginiana*
AA. Lvs. pubescent beneath, at least on veins.
B. Fr. 1–3 in. across........................2. *D. Kaki*
BB. Fr. about ½in. across........................3. *D. Lotus*

1. **D. virginiana,** L. Common Persimmon. Round-headed deciduous tree to 50 ft. and more, with spreading or pendulous branches: lvs. oval to ovate, 3–6 in. long, acuminate, cuneate, rounded or subcordate at base, glabrous or pubescent only when young, dark green and shining above, pale beneath: fls. greenish-yellow, the staminate ½in. long with

about 16 stamens, the pistillate to ¾in. long with 8 staminodia: fr. globose or obovate, 1–2 in. diam., on short thick st., pale orange, often with red cheek, with oblong flattened seeds. Conn. to Fla. and Tex.—There are several named vars., the frs. varying in size, shape, and flavor.

2. **D. Kaki,** L. f. (*D. chinensis*, Blume). KAKI. JAPANESE PERSIMMON. Round-headed deciduous tree to 40 ft., the branches with appressed brownish pubescence: lvs. ovate-elliptic to obovate, 3–7 in. long, acuminate, decurrent on petiole, the outer side veins strongly deflected toward base, pubescent beneath, glabrous and shining above: fls. yellowish-white, ¾in. long, the staminate with 16–24 stamens, the pistillate with 8 staminodia: fr. oblate to slender conical, usually ribbed at base, 1–3 in. diam., with thin orange-yellow to reddish skin and orange-colored pulp surrounding the elliptic flattened seeds. (Kaki: Japanese name.) Japan, China.

3. **D. Lotus,** L. DATE-PLUM. Round-headed deciduous tree to 45 ft., branches becoming glabrous: lvs. elliptic to oblong, 2–5 in. long, acuminate, rounded or cuneate at base, pubescent beneath at least on veins: fls. reddish or greenish, the staminate ⅙in. long with 16 stamens, the pistillate ⅓in. long: fr. globose, about ½in. diam., yellow turning black. Japan to W. Asia.

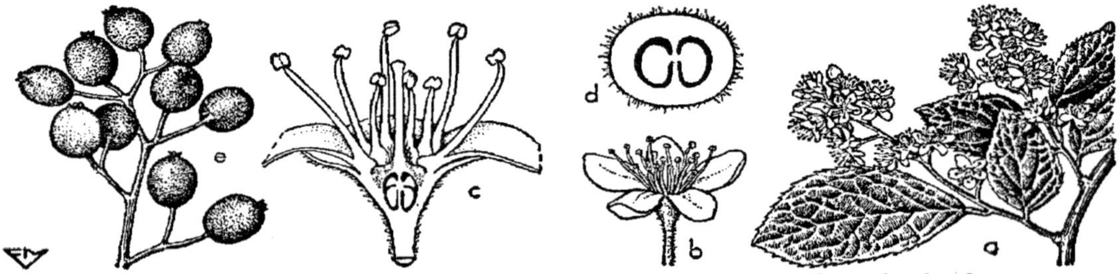

Fig. 164. SYMPLOCACEÆ. *Symplocos paniculata:* a, flowering branch, × ½; b, flower, × 2; c, same, vertical section (corolla partially excised), × 4; d, ovary, cross-section, × 10; e, fruit, × 1.

164. SYMPLOCACEÆ. SYMPLOCOS or SWEETLEAF FAMILY

Trees or shrubs, of only 1 genus, occasionally planted for ornament.—Lvs. alternate, simple, exstipulate: fls. bisexual or rarely unisexual, regular, in axillary clusters or panicles; calyx 5-lobed; corolla 5–10-lobed; stamens 15 or more, rarely fewer, distinct or united; ovary inferior, 2–5-celled with 2 ovules in each cell: fr. a drupe.

SYMPLOCOS, Jacq. SWEETLEAF. Nearly 300 species widely distributed in trop. and subtrop. regions.—Technical characters as for the family. (Sym-plocos: Greek for *connected*, referring to the stamens.)

S. paniculata, Wall. (*Prunus paniculata*, Thunb. *S. cratægoides*, Buch.-Ham. *Palura paniculata*, Nakai). SAPPHIRE-BERRY. To 40 ft., deciduous: lvs. obovate, 1–3 in. long, acute or acuminate, bright green and glabrous above, pubescent and conspicuously veined beneath: fls. white, fragrant, ⅓in. across, in panicles 2–3 in. long in May–June; stamens numerous, distinct: fr. bright blue, ⅓in. long. Japan, China to Himalayas.

165. STYRACACEÆ. STORAX FAMILY

Six genera and about 120 species of trees and shrubs in the warmer parts of N. and S. Amer., E. Asia, and Medit. region; a few planted for ornament.—Lvs. alternate, entire or dentate, exstipulate: fls. bisexual, regular, in axillary and terminal fascicles or racemes or rarely solitary; calyx campanulate or tubular, 4–5-lobed; corolla 4–5-lobed, the petals often united only at base; stamens twice as many as petals, rarely the same number, in 1 series, filaments united at base; ovary superior or inferior, 3–5-celled at base, 1-celled at top, with 1 or few ovules in each cell; stigma simple or 2–5-lobed: fr. a berry or drupe, or often dry and dehiscent by 3 valves, sometimes winged; seeds usually 1 in each cell of fr., some of the ovules failing.

A. Ovary superior or only slightly inferior: fr. not winged....................1. STYRAX
AA. Ovary inferior: fr. winged longitudinally....................2. HALESIA

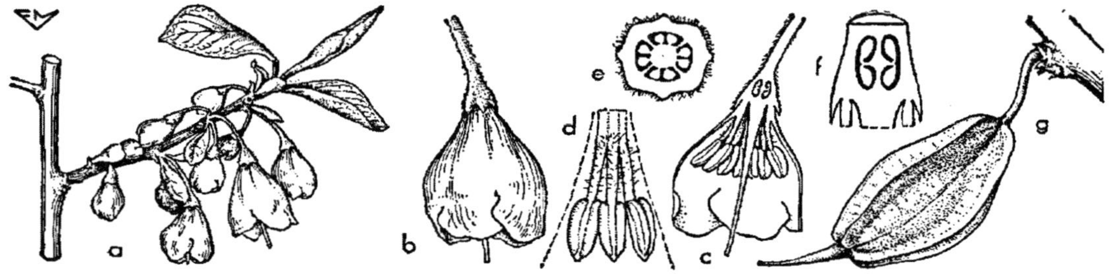

Fig. 165. STYRACACEÆ. *Halesia carolina:* a, flowering branch, × ½; b, flower, × 1; c, same, vertical section, × 1; d, stamens, × 2; e, ovary, cross-section, × 4; f, ovary, vertical section, × 3; g, fruit, × 1.

1. **STYRAX,** L. STORAX. SNOWBELL. Deciduous or evergreen shrubs or trees of about 100 species in trop. and subtrop. regions, grown for the attractive fls.—Lvs. petioled, entire or slightly serrate, more or less stellate-pubescent: fls. in axillary and terminal simple or branched racemes; calyx free or adnate to base of ovary, obscurely 5-toothed; corolla 5-parted; stamens 10, inserted on base of corolla, monadelphous below; ovary superior or only slightly inferior, 3-celled at base, with several ovules in each cell: fr. a globose or oblong drupe, fleshy or dry, often dehiscent. (Sty-rax: ancient Greek name for one of the species.)

A. Pedicels ¾–1½ in. long, glabrous....................1. *S. japonica*
AA. Pedicels ¼–½in. long, pubescent.
B. Racemes many-fld.: lvs. nearly orbicular to oval, 3–10 in. long..........2. *S. Obassia*
BB. Racemes few-fld.: lvs. oval to oblong, 1–3 in. long..........3. *S. americana*

1. **S. japonica,** Sieb. & Zucc. Deciduous shrub or small tree to 30 ft., young branchlets and lvs. pubescent but soon glabrous: lvs. oval or obovate, 1–3 in. long, tapering at both ends, crenately serrulate: fls. in June–July, white, fragrant, drooping, about ½in. long, in 3–6-fld. short glabrous racemes, pedicels 1–1½ in. long: fr. ovoid, about ½in. long, tomentose, dehiscent by 3 valves. Japan, China.

2. **S. Obassia,** Sieb. & Zucc. Deciduous shrub or small tree to 30 ft., the young branchlets pubescent: lvs. broadly oval to orbicular, 3–10 in. long, abruptly acuminate, usually rounded at base, remotely dentate above middle, glabrous above, pubescent beneath: fls. in May–June, white, fragrant, drooping, about ¾in. long, in racemes 4–8 in. long; calyx and pedicels tomentose: fr. ovoid, pointed, ¾in. long, tomentose, irregularly dehiscent. (Obassia: native Japanese name.) Japan.

3. **S. americana,** Lam. Deciduous shrub to 10 ft., the branchlets nearly glabrous: lvs. oval to oblong, 1–3 in. long, acute or acuminate, entire or serrulate, slightly pubescent: fls. in Apr.–June, white, nodding, about ½in. long, in 1–4-fld. racemes; calyx glandular-dotted; pedicels ¼–½in. long, pubescent: fr. obovoid, ⅓in. long, pubescent. Va. to Fla. and La.

2. **HALESIA,** Ellis. SILVER-BELL. SNOWDROP-TREE. Four or five species of deciduous trees or shrubs native in N. Amer. and China.—More or less stellate-pubescent: lvs. denticulate, petioled: fls. in axillary clusters or short racemes on branchlets of previous year; calyx adnate to ovary, shortly 4-toothed; corolla campanulate, 4-lobed or -parted; stamens 8–16, more or less monadelphous; ovary inferior, 2–4-celled with 4 ovules in each cell: fr. an oblong dry indehiscent drupe with 2–4 longitudinal wings and crowned by persistent style and calyx-teeth. (Hale-sia: named for Stephen Hales, 1677–1761, author of a famous work on "Vegetable Staticks.")

A. Fls. ½in. or less long: small tree or shrub..........1. *H. carolina*
AA. Fls. ¾–1 in. long: tall tree..........2. *H. monticola*

1. **H. carolina,** Ellis (*H. tetraptera*, Ellis. *Mohrodendron carolinum*, Britt.). To 40 ft.: lvs. ovate to ovate-oblong, 2–4 in. long, acuminate, cuneate or rounded at base, finely serrate, glabrous above, pubescent beneath: fls. white, drooping, to ½in. long, in 2–5-fld. clusters with the lvs. in Apr.–May, pedicels ½–1 in. long: fr. oblong, 1–1½ in. long, 4-winged. W. Va. to Fla. and Tex. Var. **Meehanii,** Perkins, has smaller fls., shorter pedicels and thicker rugose lvs. (named for Thos. Meehan, 1826–1901, American nurseryman).

2. **H. monticola,** Sarg. (*H. carolina* var. *monticola*, Rehd.). Very similar to above but larger throughout: to 100 ft.: lvs. 3–6 in. long, glabrous except on veins beneath: fls. ¾–1 in. long, in May: fr. about 2 in. long, 4-winged. N. C. to Ga. and Tenn.

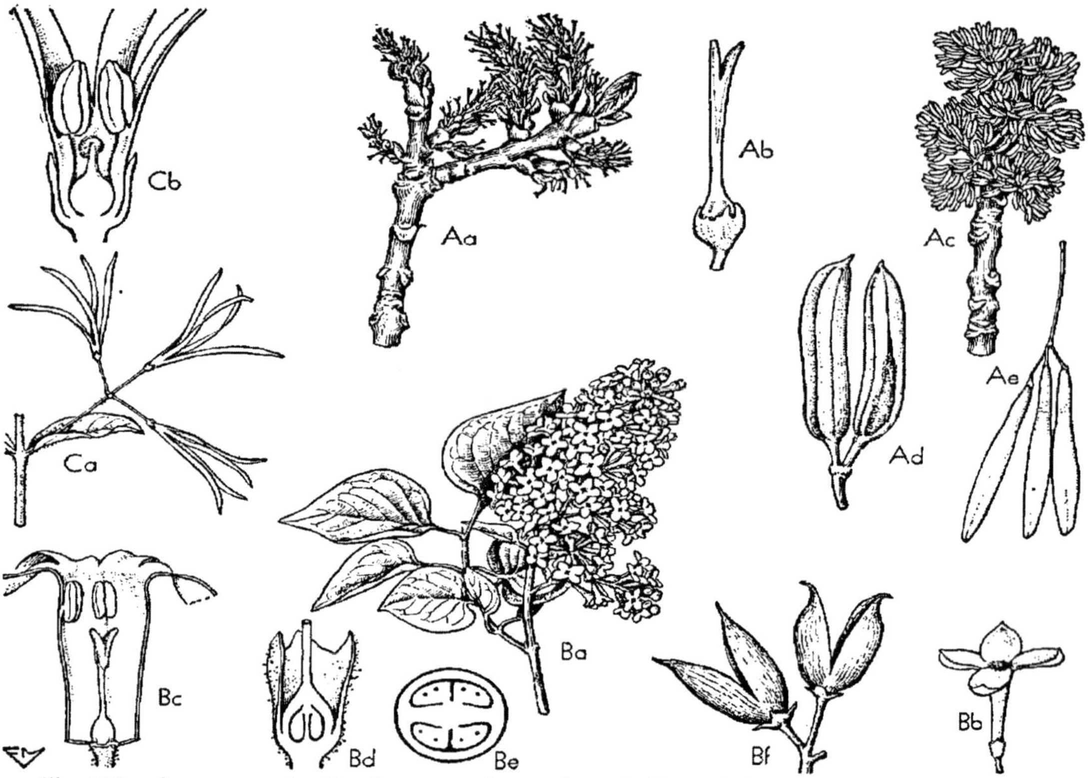

Fig. 166. OLEACEÆ. A, *Fraxinus americana:* Aa, pistillate inflorescence, × ½; Ab, pistillate flower, × 4; Ac, staminate inflorescence, × ½; Ad, staminate flower, × 4; Ae, samaras, × ½. B, *Syringa vulgaris:* Ba, flowering branch, × ¼; Bb, flower, × 1; Bc, same, perianth expanded, × 2; Bd, ovary, vertical section, × 5; Be, same, cross-section, × 10; Bf, capsules, × 1. C, *Chionanthus virginica:* Ca, flowers, × ½; Cb, flower, perianth partially excised, × 5.

166. OLEACEÆ. OLIVE FAMILY

Trees and shrubs of about 20 genera and over 500 species widely distributed in temp. and trop. regions, one furnishing the olive and several grown for ornament.—Lvs. opposite or rarely alternate or verticillate, simple or pinnate, entire or dentate, usually exstipulate: fls. regular, bisexual or unisexual, in terminal or axillary panicles, cymes or fascicles; calyx usually 4-lobed, often small or none; corolla of 4 or more free or united petals, rarely lacking; stamens 2, sometimes 3–5, hypogynous or epipetalous, the filaments commonly short; ovary superior, 2-celled with 2 (sometimes 4–10) ovules in each cell; style commonly short: fr. a drupe, berry, caps., or samara.

A. Foliage persistent.
  B. Lvs. simple: fr. a drupe or berry.
    C. Infl. commonly axillary.
      D. Corolla-lobes valvate: lvs. (in ours) silvery-lepidote beneath: grown for its edible fr. . . . . 1. OLEA
      DD. Corolla-lobes imbricate: lvs. green and glabrous beneath: grown for ornament.
        E. Tube of corolla shorter than or equalling lobes . . . . 2. OSMANTHUS
        EE. Tube of corolla much longer than lobes. . . . . 3. SIPHONOSMANTHUS
    CC. Infl. terminal . . . . 4. LIGUSTRUM
  BB. Lvs. pinnate (sometimes reduced to 1 lft. but the petiolule articulated): fr. a 2-lobed berry . . . . 5. JASMINUM
AA. Foliage deciduous.
  B. Lvs. pinnately compound (when reduced to 1 lft. petiolule articulated).
    C. Fls. with showy corolla, bisexual: shrubs: fr. a berry. . . . . 5. JASMINUM
    CC. Fls. mostly apetalous, usually unisexual and then the plants diœcious trees: fr. a samara . . . . 6. FRAXINUS

BB. Lvs. simple or sometimes ternate in no. 7.
  C. Fls. yellow, before the lvs. . . . . 7. FORSYTHIA
  CC. Fls. white to purple, not yellow, with or after the lvs.
    D. Corolla of 4 distinct petals or connate only at base.
      E. Stamens longer than petals: fr. a winged samara. . . . . 8. FONTANESIA
      EE. Stamens much shorter than petals: fr. a drupe. . . . . 9. CHIONANTHUS
    DD. Corolla gamopetalous, with distinct tube as long as limb or longer.
      E. Fr. a berry-like drupe: panicles mostly ½–5 in. long; fls. white or cream-colored. . . . . 4. LIGUSTRUM
      EE. Fr. a caps.: panicles mostly 4–12 in. long; fls. white, red, lavender to purple. . . . . 10. SYRINGA

1. **OLEA,** L. OLIVE. Nearly 40 species of evergreen trees and shrubs native in trop. and warm parts of the Old World to New Zeal., one extensively grown for its edible fr.—Lvs. opposite, usually entire: fls. white, bisexual or unisexual, in axillary branching panicles or fascicles; calyx short, 4-toothed; corolla with short tube and 4 valvate lobes or 0; stamens 2: fr. an oblong or ovoid drupe. (O-lea: classical Latin name.)

O. europæa, L. To 25 ft. or more, with thornless nearly terete branches: lvs. elliptic, oblong or lanceolate, 1–3 in. long, dark green above, densely silvery-lepidote beneath: panicles shorter than lvs., the fls. fragrant: drupe subglobose or oblong, black and shining when ripe, from ½–1½ in. long. Medit. region.—The wild form, var. **Oleaster,** DC., has 4-angled thorny branches, broader lvs. and smaller frs.

2. **OSMANTHUS,** Lour. Evergreen shrubs or small trees of about 15 species in Asia, Pacific isls., and N. Amer., a few grown out-of-doors in warm regions and one a favorite greenhouse subject.—Lvs. opposite, entire or serrate: fls. bisexual or unisexual, in axillary fascicles or short racemes; calyx short, 4-toothed; corolla with short tube and 4 imbricate lobes; stamens 2, rarely 4: fr. an ovoid drupe with hard somewhat woody endocarp and a 1-seeded stone. (Osman-thus: Greek *fragrant flower*.)

A. Lvs. entire or with small teeth.
  B. Corolla with tube about length of lobes. . . . . .1. *O. americanus*
  BB. Corolla divided nearly to base . . . . .2. *O. fragrans*
AA. Lvs. with a few coarse spiny teeth resembling holly, rarely entire.
  B. Length of lvs. 1–2½ in.; teeth about 4 on each side. . . . . .3. *O. ilicifolius*
  BB. Length of lvs. 3–4 in.; teeth 8 or more on each side. . . . . .4. *O. Fortunei*

1. **O. americanus,** Gray (*Olea americana,* L. *Amarolea americana,* Small). DEVIL-WOOD. To 45 ft.: lvs. lanceolate to obovate, 2–7 in. long, acute to obtuse, entire and slightly revolute, glossy above: fls. white, fragrant, in Apr., sessile or short-stalked, tube of corolla about equalling lobes: fr. about ½in. long, dark blue. N. C. to Fla. and Miss.

2. **O. fragrans,** Lour. (*Olea fragrans,* Thunb.). To 30 ft.: lvs. elliptic to oblong-lanceolate, 2–4 in. long, acute or acuminate, cuneate at base, entire or finely and sharply dentate: fls. white, very fragrant, on slender pedicels ⅓–½in. long, in early spring, corolla divided nearly to base: fr. about ½in. long, bluish. Himalayas, China, Japan.

3. **O. ilicifolius,** Mouillef. (*O. Aquifolium,* Benth. & Hook. *Olea Aquifolium,* Sieb. & Zucc. *Olea ilicifolia,* Hassk.). To 20 ft.: lvs. oval to elliptic-oblong, 1–2½ in. long, with 2–4 large spiny teeth on each side or rarely entire, dark green and very glossy above: fls. white, fragrant, on slender pedicels about ⅓in. long, in June–July, corolla divided nearly to base: fr. ½–¾in. long, bluish. Japan. Var. **myrtifolius,** Mouillef., has smaller entire lvs.

4. **O. Fortunei,** Carr. (*O. ilicifolius* × *O. fragrans*). Differs from the above in its larger broader lvs. having 8–10 teeth on each side and less glossy above. (For Robt. Fortune, page 43.)

3. **SIPHONOSMANTHUS,** Stapf. Evergreen shrubs of 2 species in Asia.—Separated from Osmanthus by the salverform corolla with cylindrical tube much longer than lobes, anthers dehiscing inwardly, and fr. with crustaceous endocarp. (Siphonosman-thus: Greek *tube* and *osmanthus*.)

S. Delavayi, Stapf (*Osmanthus Delavayi,* Franch.). To 6 ft.: lvs. ovate, ½–1 in. long, acute, toothed, glabrous, glandular-dotted beneath: fls. white, fragrant, about ½in. long, nearly sessile in few-fld. clusters in Apr.: fr. bluish-black, ½in. long. (Named for Abbé Delavay, page 42.) China.

4. **LIGUSTRUM,** L. PRIVET. Deciduous or evergreen shrubs or rarely small trees planted for ornament and several much used for hedges; about 50 species in

Asia, Australia and 1 in Medit. region.—Lvs. opposite, entire: fls. bisexual, white, in terminal panicles; calyx campanulate, with 4 small teeth; corolla funnelform, mostly with rather short tube and 4 spreading lobes; stamens 2, attached to corolla-tube; ovary 2-celled, with 2 ovules in each cell: fr. a drupe-like usually black berry, sometimes 1-seeded by abortion. (Ligu-strum: ancient Latin name.)

A. Foliage persistent.
  B. Corolla-tube two to three times longer than limb.
    C. Branchlets and panicles glabrous .... 5. *L. ovalifolium*
    CC. Branchlets and panicles pubescent.
      D. Lvs. ovate, persistent .... 1. *L. Henryi*
      DD. Lvs. oval to oblong, only semi-persistent .... 9. *L. amurense*
  BB. Corolla-tube equalling or shorter than limb.
    C. Under side of lvs. pubescent, at least on midrib .... 2. *L. indicum*
    CC. Under side of lvs. glabrous.
      D. Lvs. 4–6 in. long, acuminate: tube of corolla equalling lobes .... 3. *L. lucidum*
      DD. Lvs. 3–4 in. long, short-acuminate to nearly obtuse: tube of corolla slightly longer than lobes .... 4. *L. japonicum*
AA. Foliage deciduous.
  B. Corolla-tube two to three times longer than limb.
    C. Branchlets and lvs. glabrous .... 5. *L. ovalifolium*
    CC. Branchlets and midrib of lvs. beneath pubescent.
      D. Calyx pubescent .... 6. *L. obtusifolium*
      DD. Calyx glabrous.
        E. Anthers exserted to equal or exceed the corolla-lobes .... 7. *L. acuminatum*
        EE. Anthers only slightly exserted.
          F. Infl. to ½in. long, few-fld .... 8. *L. Ibota*
          FF. Infl. 1–2 in. long, many-fld .... 9. *L. amurense*
  BB. Corolla-tube as long as or shorter than limb.
    C. Fls. sessile .... 10. *L. Quihoui*
    CC. Fls. pedicelled.
      D. Stamens longer than limb: lvs. pubescent on midrib beneath .... 11. *L. sinense*
      DD. Stamens shorter than limb: lvs. glabrous .... 12. *L. vulgare*

1. **L. Henryi,** Hemsl. Evergreen shrub to 12 ft., with pubescent branchlets: lvs. ovate, ½–2 in. long, short-acuminate, glabrous, shining above: fls. in pubescent pyramidal panicles 2–5 in. long, in Aug.; tube of corolla about twice as long as lobes. (For Augustine Henry, page 45.) China.

2. **L. indicum,** Merr. (*Phillyrea indica,* Lour. *L. nepalense,* Wall.). Evergreen shrub or tree, with pubescent branchlets: lvs. oblong-ovate to ovate-lanceolate, 2–5 in. long, acuminate, pubescent beneath at least on midrib: fls. in large broad pubescent panicles interspersed with petioled bracts, to 5 in. long, in July and Aug.; corolla-tube as long as or shorter than limb. Himalayas, Indochina.

3. **L. lucidum,** Ait. Erect evergreen shrub or small tree to 30 ft., glabrous: lvs. ovate to ovate-lanceolate, 3–6 in. long, acute or acuminate, tapering at base, dark green and glossy above: fls. short-pedicelled, in erect panicles to 10 in. long, in Aug.–Sept.; corolla-tube about as long as limb. China, Korea, Japan.—There are variegated-lvd. vars.

4. **L. japonicum,** Thunb. Very similar to *L. lucidum* but smaller, rarely to 10 ft. high: lvs. shorter, 2–4 in. long, roundish-ovate to ovate-oblong, usually rounded at base, short-acuminate to obtuse, darker green: panicles looser, July–Sept.; tube of corolla slightly longer than lobes. Japan, Korea. Var. **rotundifolium,** Blume (*L. coriaceum,* Carr.), has nearly orbicular lvs. to 2½ in. long, obtuse or emarginate, glossy; fls. sessile.

5. **L. ovalifolium,** Hassk. (*L. californicum,* Hort.). CALIFORNIA PRIVET. Half-evergreen upright glabrous shrub to 15 ft., much planted for hedges: lvs. elliptic-ovate or -oblong, 1–2½ in. long, acute, cuneate at base, dark green and glossy above, yellowish-green beneath: fls. very short-pedicelled, in erect many-fld. panicles to 4 in. long, in July; corolla-tube two to three times as long as limb. Japan. Var. **aureum,** Bean (forma *aureum,* Rehd. var. **aureo-marginatum,** Rehd. *L. ovalifolium aureum,* Carr. *L. ovalifolium variegatum,* Bull), lvs. variegated with yellow.

6. **L. obtusifolium,** Sieb. & Zucc. (*L. Ibota,* Sieb.). Graceful deciduous shrub to 10 ft., with pubescent branchlets: lvs. elliptic to oblong-obovate, 1–2 in. long, acute or obtuse, pubescent beneath or only on midrib: fls. short-pedicelled, in nodding panicles to 1½ in. long borne on short branchlets in July; calyx pubescent; corolla-tube two to three times longer than limb. Japan. Var. **Regelianum,** Rehd. (*L. Regelianum,* Koehne), is a dwarfer denser shrub with horizontally spreading branches and more pubescent lvs. (Named for Eduard von Regel, page 50.)—A hybrid between this species and *L. ovalifolium* is **L. Ibolium,** E. F. Coe; it has pubescent branchlets and midrib of lf. beneath, and glabrous calyx.

7. **L. acuminatum,** Koehne (*L. ciliatum,* Rehd. not Blume or Sieb.). Deciduous shrub to 6 ft., with pubescent branchlets: lvs. ovate to ovate-lanceolate, 1–3 in. long, acute or acuminate, pubescent on midrib beneath: fls. nearly sessile, in pubescent panicles 1–2 in. long, in June; corolla-tube about three times longer than limb; anthers conspicuously exserted. Japan.

8. **L. Ibota,** Sieb. & Zucc. (*L. ciliatum*, Sieb.). Deciduous shrub to 6 ft., with spreading slightly pubescent branches: lvs. ovate to oblong, ½–2 in. long, acute, pubescent on midrib beneath: fls. very short-pedicelled, in few-fld. panicles to ½in. long, in June; corolla-tube about three times longer than limb. (Ibota: native Japanese name.) Japan.—The plant commonly grown as *L. Ibota* is *L. obtusifolium.*

9. **L. amurense,** Carr. Deciduous or almost half-evergreen shrub to 15 ft., with upright branches pubescent when young: lvs. oval or oblong, 1–2½ in. long, usually obtuse, glabrous except midrib of lf. beneath pubescent: fls. short-pedicelled, in erect many-fld. pubescent panicles to 2 in. long, in June–July; calyx glabrous or slightly pubescent near base; corolla-tube about three times longer than limb. China.

10. **L. Quihoui,** Carr. Deciduous shrub to 6 ft. or more, with spreading branches pubescent when young: lvs. elliptic- or narrow-oblong, 1–2 in. long, obtuse, glabrous: fls. sessile, in narrow spikes forming slender panicles to 8 in. long, in Aug.–Sept.; corolla-tube as long as limb; stamens exserted. (Named for M. Quihou, supt. of the Jardin d'Acclimatation at Paris.) China.

11. **L. sinense,** Lour. Deciduous shrub to 12 ft. or more, with slender spreading branches and pubescent branchlets: lvs. elliptic to oblong, 1–3 in. long, acute or obtusish, tapering at base, pubescent on midrib beneath: fls. pedicelled, in loose pubescent panicles to 4 in. long, in July; corolla-tube shorter than limb; stamens exserted. China.

12. **L. vulgare,** L. Common Privet. Deciduous shrub to 15 ft., with puberulous branchlets, much planted for hedges: lvs. oblong-ovate to lanceolate, 1–2½ in. long, obtuse or acute, glabrous: fls. pedicelled, in dense pyramidal panicles to 2½ in. long, in June–July; corolla-tube about length of limb; stamens included. Eu., N. Afr., W. Asia; nat. in E. U. S.—There are vars. with variegated lvs., yellow, white or greenish frs., and of various habit. The form known as *L. lodense* (forma *nanum*, Rehd.), is dwarf and compact.

5. **JASMINUM,** L. Jasmine. Jessamine. Climbing or erect shrubs grown out-of-doors in warm countries and in greenhouses N.; 200 or more species in trop. and subtrop. regions around the world.—Lvs. opposite or sometimes alternate, imparipinnate with 3–7 lfts. or reduced to 1 lft. but the petiolule articulated: fls. in simple or dichotomous terminal cymes or rarely solitary; calyx funnelform or campanulate, with 4–9 teeth of varying length; corolla salverform, with a cylindrical tube and 4–9-lobed or -parted imbricated limb; stamens 2, the short filaments included: fr. a 2-lobed berry, each carpel 1–2-seeded. (Jas-minum: ancient name of Arabic origin.)

A. Color of fls. yellow.
  B. Lvs. opposite.
    C. Limb of corolla ¾–1 in. across, shorter than tube: lvs. deciduous .... 1. *J. nudiflorum*
    CC. Limb of corolla 1½–2 in. across, longer than tube: lvs. persistent.......... 2. *J. Mesnyi*
  BB. Lvs. alternate.
    C. Lfts. to ¼in. long: fls. solitary .... 3. *J. Parkeri*
    CC. Lfts. ½–2 in. long: fls. in clusters.
      D. Calyx-teeth very short.......... 4. *J. humile*
      DD. Calyx-teeth subulate, as long as tube.......... 5. *J. floridum*
AA. Color of fls. white, pink or red.
  B. Lvs. of 3–7 lfts.
    C. Calyx-teeth very short.......... 6. *J. azoricum*
    CC. Calyx-teeth linear, ¼–½in. long.......... 7. *J. officinale*
  BB. Lvs. apparently simple.
    C. Fls. red or pink.......... 8. *J. Beesianum*
    CC. Fls. white.
      D. Calyx and branchlets glabrous.
        E. Teeth of calyx very short.......... 9. *J. gracile*
        EE. Teeth of calyx equalling or exceeding tube.
          F. Shape of lf. ovate-lanceolate, more than twice as long as broad ....10. *J. absimile*
          FF. Shape of lf. ovate, to 3 in. long and 2 in. wide ....11. *J. dichotomum*
      DD. Calyx and branchlets pubescent.
        E. Teeth of calyx about ⅙in. long..........12. *J. nitidum*
        EE. Teeth of calyx ¼–½in. long.
          F. Corolla double, lobes short and obtuse..........13. *J. Sambac*
          FF. Corolla not double, although lobes often more than 5 or 6.
            G. Lobes of corolla very narrow and long, three to four times longer than broad, strongly divaricate as are also the calyx-lobes.......... 14. *J. amplexicaule*
            GG. Lobes of corolla not prominently elongated, calyx-lobes not divaricate.
              H. Infl. a loose cluster; calyx-lobes densely yellow-pubescent..........15. *J. multiflorum*
              HH. Infl. a dense hanging head; calyx-lobes sparsely pubescent. ....16. *J. gracillimum*

1. **J. nudiflorum,** Lindl. Nearly erect deciduous shrub to 15 ft., with 4-angled glabrous stiff branchlets: lvs. opposite, of 3 ovate mucronate ciliate lfts. ½–1 in. long: fls. solitary, yellow, ¾–1 in. diam., borne in winter and spring on naked shoots, each fl. subtended by narrow green bracts; calyx-lobes leafy, spreading, as long as or longer than tube; corolla-lobes obovate, often wavy, about half as long as tube. China.—In one var. the lvs. are variegated with yellow.

2. **J. Mesnyi,** Hance (*J. primulinum*, Hemsl.). Evergreen floriferous rambling shrub to 10 ft., with glabrous 4-angled branchlets: lvs. opposite, of 3 oblong-lanceolate almost sessile lfts. 1–3 in. long: fls. solitary, bright yellow with darker eye, 1½–2 in. across, subtended by lf.-like bracts; calyx-lobes leafy, lanceolate, longer than tube; corolla-lobes obovate-spatulate, longer than tube, often semi-double. (Bears the name of its collector, W. Mesny.) W. China.

3. **J. Parkeri,** Dunn. Shrub to 1 ft., the branchlets slightly pubescent: lvs. alternate, of 3–5 ovate obtuse lfts. ⅛–¼in. long: fls. solitary, yellow, ½in. across; calyx-lobes subulate, half as long as tube; corolla-lobes 6, half as long as tube. (Named for R. N. Parker, who collected the plant in 1919.) Himalayas.

4. **J. humile,** L. Diffuse evergreen shrub 5–20 ft. high, requiring support, with glabrous angled branchlets: lvs. alternate, of 3–7 ovate to oblong obtuse or acute lfts. ¾–2 in. long, the terminal one long-petioled, more or less revolute on edges: fls. bright yellow, fragrant, ½in. across, in open clusters; calyx-teeth triangular, about one-third as long as tube; corolla-lobes obtuse and reflexed, much shorter than tube. Trop. Asia. Var. **revolutum,** Kobuski (*J. revolutum*, Sims), has 5–7 ovate to ovate-lanceolate acute or acuminate lfts., fls. to 1 in. across.

5. **J. floridum,** Bunge. Nearly evergreen glabrous shrub with erect flexuous angled branches: lvs. alternate, of 3, rarely 5, oval or ovate-oblong acute lfts. ½–1½ in. long: fls. golden-yellow, ½in. across, in open clusters; calyx-teeth as long as the angled tube; corolla-lobes ovate, acute, spreading, about half as long as tube. China.

6. **J. azoricum,** L. Evergreen climber, the terete branches tomentose when young but becoming glabrous: lvs. opposite, of 3 broadly ovate acute lfts. to 2 in. long, the terminal lft. long-stalked: fls. white, ½–1 in. across, in loose many-fld. cymes; calyx-teeth very short; corolla-lobes oblong, acute, half or more as long as tube. Canary Isls.

7. **J. officinale,** L. Poets Jessamine. Deciduous shrub with long weak sts. requiring support, glabrous or nearly so: lvs. opposite, of 5–7 elliptic or ovate acute or acuminate lfts. ½–2½ in. long, the terminal lft. longer and petioled: fls. white, fragrant, ¾–1 in. across, slender-pedicelled, in loose clusters; calyx-teeth linear, ¼–⅔in. long, half or fully as long as corolla-tube; corolla-lobes oblong, acute, about as long as tube. Iran to China. Var. **grandiflorum,** Bailey (*J. grandiflorum*, L.), has showy fls. to 1½ in. across.

8. **J. Beesianum,** Forrest & Diels. Climbing to 3 ft. or more, with slender grooved sts. somewhat pubescent at joints: lvs. simple, ovate-lanceolate or lanceolate, 1–2 in. long, acuminate, very short-petioled: fls. rose or pink, very fragrant, 1–3 together at ends of branchlets, ½–¾in. across; calyx-teeth linear, about ¼in. long; corolla-lobes broad-elliptic or suborbicular, about half as long as tube. (Named for Bees, Ltd., nurserymen, Liverpool, England.) W. China.—A hybrid between this species and *J. officinale* var. *grandiflorum* is **J. stephanense,** Lem., lvs. simple or of 3–5 lfts.; fls. pale pink, fragrant, about ½in. across.

9. **J. gracile,** Andr. Strong vine, sometimes bush-like, glabrous: lvs. simple, ovate, to 1½ in. long, blunt or apiculate, glossy above: fls. white, fragrant, ¾in. long, in upwardly branched panicles; calyx-teeth very short; corolla-lobes narrow, acute, about length of tube. Australia; nat. in Bermuda.—The plant grown as *J. simplicifolium* usually belongs here, the true species not being cult.

10. **J. absimile,** Bailey. Very floriferous evergreen glabrous climber: lvs. simple, ovate-lanceolate, 2–2½ in. long, more than twice as long as broad, blunt or apiculate: fls. white, about 1 in. long, in axillary and terminal panicles; calyx-teeth narrow and acute, about length of tube; corolla-lobes narrow, acute or obtuse, shorter than tube. Country unknown. —Usually grown under the name of *J. calcarium*, a species not known in cult. in N. Amer.

11. **J. dichotomum,** Vahl. Gold Coast Jasmine. Climbing evergreen, blooming continuously, glabrous: lvs. simple, ovate, to 3 in. long and 2 in. wide, acuminate, thick and glossy: fls. white, about 1 in. long, fragrant, opening at night; calyx-teeth about length of tube. W. Afr.

12. **J. nitidum,** Skan. Half-twining slender somewhat pubescent shrub: lvs. simple, elliptic-lanceolate, 2–3 in. long, short-acuminate, cuneate at base, pubescent on midrib beneath, petiole short and pubescent: fls. white, very fragrant, 1½ in. across; calyx pilose, the teeth linear and recurved, about ⅙in. long; corolla-lobes linear-lanceolate, spreading. Admiralty Isls.

13. **J. Sambac,** Ait. (*Nyctanthes Sambac*, L.). Arabian Jasmine. Climbing to 5 ft., with angular pubescent branchlets: lvs. simple, elliptic or broad-ovate, 1½–3 in. long, acute or obtuse, rounded or cuneate at base, nearly glabrous, prominently veined, the short pubescent petiole abruptly curved upward: fls. white, double, fragrant, ¾–1 in. across, in few- to many-fld. clusters; calyx-teeth linear, ¼in. long, hirsute on edges; corolla-lobes oblong to orbicular, obtuse, about length of tube. (Sambac: native Indian name.) India.

14. **J. amplexicaule,** Don (*J. undulatum*, Ker). Climbing, branchlets pubescent: lvs. simple, ovate-lanceolate or lanceolate on young shoots, 2–3 in. long, acuminate, pubescent on veins beneath: fls. 1 to several, white, to 1½ in. across, fragrant; calyx-teeth much

longer than tube, pubescent, strongly divaricate; corolla-lobes narrow and acute, three to four times longer than broad, divaricate. India.

15. **J. multiflorum,** Andr. (*Nyctanthes multiflorum*, Burm. f. *J. pubescens*, Willd.). Densely pubescent evergreen climber: lvs. simple, ovate, to 2 in. long, acute, rounded or cordate at base, short-petioled: fls. white, about 1 in. across, in few- to many-fld. clusters; calyx-teeth ½in. or more long, densely covered with spreading yellow hairs; corolla-lobes oblong, acute, one-half or more as long as tube. India.

16. **J. gracillimum,** Hook. f. Closely resembling the above but differing in its more graceful floriferous habit, the branches less pubescent, the somewhat larger fragrant fls. borne in dense hanging heads, calyx-teeth sparsely clothed with close not spreading pubescence. N. Borneo.

6. **FRAXINUS,** L. Ash. About 65 species of deciduous trees mostly native in the north temp. zone, valuable as street and park trees.—Lvs. opposite, impari-pinnate or rarely simple, usually serrate: fls. bisexual or unisexual, in panicles from terminal or lateral buds, before or with the lvs.; calyx small, 4-toothed or irregularly dissected, or 0; petals 2–6, united in pairs at base, or 0; stamens 2, inserted at base of corolla or hypogynous: fr. a 1-seeded winged samara. (Frax-inus: ancient Latin name.)

A. Fls. with the lvs.; corolla present .... 1. *F. Ornus*
AA. Fls. before the lvs.; corolla lacking.
  B. Calyx persistent on fr.
    C. Length of fr. ½–¾in.: lfts. 3–5 .... 2. *F. velutina*
    CC. Length of fr. 1–2 in.: lfts. 5–9.
      D. Wing of fr. terminal: lvs. glabrous .... 3. *F. americana*
      DD. Wing of fr. decurrent to below middle: lvs. pubescent beneath, at least on midrib .... 4. *F. pennsylvanica*
  BB. Calyx lacking or soon deciduous.
    C. Branchlets 4-angled and often winged .... 5. *F. quadrangulata*
    CC. Branchlets terete.
      D. Base of lfts. on rachis rusty-tomentose .... 6. *F. nigra*
      DD. Base of lfts. not tomentose .... 7. *F. excelsior*

1. **F. Ornus,** L. (*Ornus europæa*, Pers.). Flowering Ash. Round-headed tree to 60 ft., with gray or brownish somewhat downy winter-buds: lvs. 8–10 in. long, of 7–11 (usually 7) ovate or oblong lfts. 2–3 in. long, serrate, base of midrib beneath rusty-pubescent: fls. whitish, fragrant, in dense panicles 3–5 in. long, in May–June with the lvs.; calyx 4-parted; petals narrowly linear, acute: fr. linear or lanceolate, about 1 in. long, truncate or emarginate at apex. (Ornus is an ancient Greek and Latin name for a mountain ash.) S. Eu., W. Asia.

2. **F. velutina,** Torr. Diœcious tree to 50 ft., the branchlets pubescent: lfts. 3–5, elliptic to ovate, ¾–1½ in. long, acute, slightly serrate above middle, short-stalked or nearly sessile, pubescent beneath: fls. before the lvs., apetalous; calyx persistent on fr.: fr. oblong, ½–¾in. long, wing decurrent to about middle. Ariz. to Mex.

3. **F. americana,** L. White Ash. Tall diœcious tree to 120 ft., with glabrous branchlets and petioles: lvs. 8–15 in. long, of 5–9 ovate or ovate-lanceolate acuminate stalked lfts. 3–6 in. long, entire or serrate toward tip, dark green above, pale beneath and usually glabrous: fls. apetalous, produced in Apr.–June before the lvs.; calyx persistent on fr.: fr. linear-oblong, 1–2 in. long, obtuse or emarginate at apex, wing not decurrent. N. S. to Fla. and Tex.

4. **F. pennsylvanica,** Marsh. Red Ash. Diœcious tree to 60 ft., branchlets and petioles pubescent: lfts. 5–9, ovate to oblong-lanceolate, 3–6 in. long, acuminate, stalked, entire or serrate, pubescent beneath: fls. apetalous, before the lvs.; calyx persistent on fr.: fr. lanceolate, 1–2 in. long, wing decurrent nearly to base. N. S. to Ga. and Miss. Var. **lanceolata,** Sarg. (*F. lanceolata*, Borkh. *F. viridis*, Michx.), Green Ash, has narrower irregularly serrate lfts. pubescent only on midrib beneath.

5. **F. quadrangulata,** Michx. Blue Ash. To 80 ft. or more, the glabrous branchlets 4-angled and usually winged: lfts. 7–11, ovate to lanceolate, 2–5 in. long, short-stalked, serrate, glabrous except near base of midrib beneath: fls. bisexual, before the lvs., apetalous, with minute calyx soon deciduous: fr. oblong, 1–2 in. long, emarginate, winged to base. Mich. to Ark.

6. **F. nigra,** Marsh. (*F. sambucifolia*, Lam.). Black Ash. Diœcious tree to 75 ft., with glabrous branchlets: lfts. 7–11, oblong to oblong-lanceolate, 3–5 in. long, sessile, serrate, glabrous except midrib beneath and base of lfts. on rachis rusty-tomentose: fls. before lvs., without calyx or corolla: fr. oblong, 1–1½ in. long, winged to base. Low lands, Newf. to W. Va. and Ark.

7. **F. excelsior,** L. European Ash. Tall tree to 140 ft., with black buds, polygamous: lvs. 10–12 in. long; of 7–11 ovate, oblong or lanceolate acuminate sessile lfts. 2–5 in. long, serrate, dark green and glabrous above, paler and often pubescent on the veins beneath:

fls. in early spring before the lvs., without calyx or corolla: fr. oblong, about 1½ in. long, obtuse, emarginate or acute at apex. Eu., Asia Minor.—Runs into many forms such as: of dwarf or pendulous habit; yellow or striped branches; lvs. variegated or blotched with white; lvs. reduced to 1 lft. or with very narrow incisely serrate lfts.

7. **FORSYTHIA,** Vahl. GOLDEN-BELLS. About 8 species of deciduous shrubs native in China, Japan and S. E. Eu., very popular ornamental subjects.—Lvs. opposite, simple or ternate, entire or serrate, glabrous: fls. axillary, 1–3 or rarely 5, before the lvs., pedicelled, heterostylous; calyx deeply 4-parted; corolla campanulate, deeply 4-parted into oblong lobes; stamens 2, inserted at base of corolla-tube: fr. a woody septicidally dehiscent caps. with many winged seeds. (Forsyth-ia: after Wm. Forsyth, 1737–1800, English horticulturist.)

A. Branches hollow between the nodes . . . . 1. *F. suspensa*
AA. Branches usually with lamellate pith.
  B. Shape of lvs. ovate to broad-ovate . . . . 2. *F. ovata*
  BB. Shape of lvs. ovate-oblong to lanceolate.
    C. Lvs. always simple: branches upright . . . . 3. *F. viridissima*
    CC. Lvs. sometimes ternate: branches erect or arching: hybrid . . . . 4. *F. intermedia*

1. **F. suspensa,** Vahl (*Syringa suspensa,* Thunb.). To 10 ft., the hollow branches becoming pendulous and often taking root: lvs. ovate to ovate-oblong, to 4 in. long, irregularly serrate, simple or 3-parted, rounded or broadly cuneate at base or the lfts. tapering: fls. golden-yellow, the tube within striped with orange-yellow, about 1 in. long, in Apr. or May, opening wide; calyx about as long as corolla-tube: caps. narrowly ovoid, acuminate, about 1 in. long. China. Var. **Fortunei,** Rehd. (*F. Fortunei,* Lindl.), is of stiffer more upright growth, often with ternate lvs. Var. **Sieboldii,** Zabel (*F. Sieboldii,* Dipp.), has slender pendulous or trailing branches, lvs. mostly simple, and solitary fls.

2. **F. ovata,** Nakai. To 5 ft., the branches spreading: lvs. ovate to broad-ovate, 2–2½ in. long, serrate or nearly entire, abruptly acuminate, truncate or broadly cuneate at base: fls. solitary, amber-yellow, in Apr.–May, ½–¾in. long; calyx half as long as corolla-tube. Korea.

3. **F. viridissima,** Lindl. Erect shrub to 10 ft., with olive-green branchlets: lvs. always simple, oblong-lanceolate or lanceolate, to 6 in. long, tapering at both ends, entire or irregularly serrate above the middle: fls. bright greenish-yellow, ¾–1 in. long, in Apr. or May, not opening wide; calyx about half or less as long as corolla-tube: caps. broadly-ovoid, about 1 in. long. China.—Less showy species than no. 1, the fls. with much narrower segms., borne close to sts. from ground up.

4. **F. intermedia,** Zabel (*F. suspensa* × *F. viridissima*). Distinguished from *F. suspensa* by the branches with lamellate pith, the narrower oblong to ovate-lanceolate lvs. tapering at base, and from *F. viridissima* by its arching branches and the lvs. sometimes 3-parted. Var. **primulina,** Rehd., has pale yellow fls. crowded at base of branches. Var. **spectabilis,** Spaeth (*F. spectabilis,* Koehne), has bright yellow fls. more than 1 in. long.

8. **FONTANESIA,** Labill. Two Asian deciduous shrubs, one sometimes planted.—Lvs. opposite, simple and usually entire: fls. small, bisexual, white, in leafy panicles; calyx minute, 4-parted; corolla of 4 small distinct petals; stamens exserted; ovary superior, 2-celled: fr. a flat winged nutlet. (Fontane-sia: named for the French botanist, Réné Louiche Desfontaines, 1750–1833.)

F. Fortunei, Carr. Graceful shrub to 15 ft., with 4-angled glabrous erect branchlets: lvs. lanceolate or ovate-lanceolate, 1–4 in. long, entire, acuminate, shining: fls. about ⅛in. long, in panicles to 2 in. long, in May–June: fr. oval, ⅓in. long. (Named for Robt. Fortune, page 43.) China.

9. **CHIONANTHUS,** L. FRINGE-TREE. Deciduous shrubs or small trees, of 2 species in N. Amer. and China, one planted for ornament.—Lvs. opposite, entire: fls. white, bisexual or unisexual, in loose panicles from lateral buds at the ends of branches of previous year; calyx small, 4-lobed, persistent; corolla of 4 linear petals only slightly united at base; stamens 2, rarely 3, short, inserted on corolla: fr. a 1-seeded drupe. (Chionan-thus: Greek *snow flower.*)

C. virginica, L. Large shrub or slender tree to 30 ft.; lvs. oval or oblong, 3–8 in. long, acuminate, tapering at base, pubescent beneath when young: fls. about 1 in. long, in drooping panicles 4–8 in. or more long in early summer: drupe ovoid, ½–¾in. long, dark blue. Pa. to Fla. and Tex.

10. **SYRINGA,** L. LILAC. Deciduous shrubs or small trees, of nearly 30 species in Eu. and Asia; the lilacs are amongst the most popular ornamental flowering shrubs.

—Lvs. opposite, simple or rarely pinnate, entire: fls. in panicles from terminal or lateral buds; calyx campanulate, 4-toothed, persistent; corolla funnelform, with cylindrical tube and 4-lobed spreading limb; stamens 2, inserted on tube of corolla, included or exserted: fr. a leathery loculicidally dehiscent caps. with 2 winged seeds in each cell. (Syrin-ga: from Greek for *pipe;* of doubtful application.)

A. Tube of corolla scarcely longer than calyx; anthers on slender filaments, exserted.
B. Lvs. ovate to broad-ovate, rounded or subcordate at base, strongly veined ..... 1. *S. amurensis*
BB. Lvs. ovate to ovate-lanceolate, narrowed at base, not prominently veined ...... 2. *S. pekinensis*
AA. Tube of corolla much longer than calyx; anthers nearly sessile, usually included.
B. Mature shoots with 1 true terminal bud that continues the axis the following year or else gives rise to an infl. in the line of the main axis.
C. Infl. nodding or pendulous .... 3. *S. reflexa*
CC. Infl. upright.
D. Anthers exserted beyond the mouth, corolla-lobes becoming reflexed: lvs. papillose beneath .... 4. *S. emodi*
DD. Anthers below or reaching the mouth, corolla-lobes erect or spreading: lvs. not papillose.
E. Corolla-tube funnelform, the lobes nearly upright .... 5. *S. Josikæa*
EE. Corolla-tube cylindric, the lobes spreading.
F. Lvs. 2–7 in. long, acute at both ends .... 6. *S. villosa*
FF. Lvs. 2–4 in. long, abruptly acuminate, rounded or broad-cuneate at base .... 7. *S. Sweginzowii*
BB. Mature shoots ending in 2 lateral buds, the terminal one suppressed, giving rise the following spring to a lateral infl., the main axis not continuous.
C. Lvs. pubescent beneath, at least on veins.
D. Infl. glabrous .... 8. *S. pubescens*
DD. Infl. pubescent.
E. Length of lvs. ½–1½ in. .... 9. *S. microphylla*
EE. Length of lvs. 1½–4 in. .... 10. *S. velutina*
CC. Lvs. glabrous.
D. Base of lvs. truncate to cordate.
E. Width of lvs. equalling or exceeding length .... 11. *S. oblata*
EE. Width of lvs. less than length .... 12. *S. vulgaris*
DD. Base of lvs. attenuate.
E. Panicle 2–3 in. long: lvs. lanceolate.
F. Lf. simple .... 13. *S. persica*
FF. Lf. pinnate, lobed or cut .... 14. *S. laciniata*
EE. Panicle 3–6 in. long: lvs. ovate-lanceolate .... 15. *S. chinensis*

1. **S. amurensis,** Rupr. Spreading or upright shrub or tree to 20 ft.: lvs. ovate or broad-ovate, 2–5 in. long, acuminate, rounded or subcordate at base, glabrous, strongly veined beneath: panicles from lateral buds, usually 2 at the end of a shoot, 4–6 in. long, glabrous; fls. yellowish-white, ¼in. or less long, almost odorless, in June; corolla-tube very short; stamens long-exserted: caps. ½in. long, acute or obtuse. Manchuria, N. China. Var. **japonica,** Franch. & Sav. (*S. japonica,* Decne. *Ligustrina amurensis* var. *japonica,* Maxim.), an upright tree to 30 ft. with lvs. more or less pubescent beneath, the infl. to 12 in. long and sometimes pubescent; caps. to ¾in. long, warty; Japan.

2. **S. pekinensis,** Rupr. (*S. amurensis* var. *pekinensis,* Maxim.). Spreading shrub to 15 ft.: lvs. ovate to ovate-lanceolate, 2–4 in. long, acuminate, cuneate at base, glabrous, not strongly veined: fls. yellowish-white, in June in glabrous panicles 3–6 in. long; corolla-tube very short; stamens exserted: caps. ½–¾in. long, acute. N. China.

3. **S. reflexa,** Schneid. Shrub to 12 ft.: lvs. oblong, 3–6 in. long, acuminate, cuneate at base, pubescent beneath at least on veins: fls. pinkish, white inside, in terminal narrow nodding or pendulous panicles 4–10 in. long in June; corolla-tube ⅓in. long, lobes somewhat spreading; anthers reaching the mouth: caps. ¾in. long, obtuse. China.

4. **S. emodi,** Don. Himalayan Lilac. Upright shrub to 15 ft.: lvs. oval or oblong, 3–8 in. long, acute, attenuate at base, glabrous, glaucous and papillose beneath: fls. lilac or whitish, in dense terminal panicles 3–6 in. long; corolla-tube ⅓in. long, the lobes becoming reflexed; anthers exserted beyond mouth: caps. ½in. long, acuminate. W. Asia.

5. **S. Josikæa,** Jacq. Hungarian Lilac. Shrub to 12 ft.: lvs. oval or oblong, 2–5 in. long, acute or acuminate, rounded or broad-cuneate at base, shining above, glaucous and nearly glabrous beneath: fls. lilac, slightly fragrant, in terminal panicles 4–7 in. long; corolla-tube funnelform, gradually widening, ½in. long, the lobes nearly upright; anthers inserted below mouth: caps. ½in. long, acute. (Named after Baroness von Josika, who sent the plant to Jacquin in 1830.) Hungary.

6. **S. villosa,** Vahl. Shrub to 10 ft., the branches stout and upright: lvs. broadly elliptic to oblong, 2–7 in. long, acute, attenuate at base, dark green above, pale beneath, the nerves pubescent, margins finely ciliate: panicles from a terminal bud or often 3 at the end of a leafy shoot, many-fld., 4–12 in. long, in May or June; fls. lilac or pinkish-white, scarcely fragrant; corolla-tube cylindric, about ½in. long, the lobes spreading and obtuse; anthers inserted near mouth: caps. ½in. long, obtuse. China.

7. **S. Sweginzowii,** Koehne & Lingelsheim. Shrub to 10 ft.: lvs. oblong or ovate, 2–4 in. long, abruptly acuminate, rounded or broad-cuneate at base, pale beneath and

pubescent on veins: fls. lilac, fragrant, in terminal panicles 6–8 in. long in June; corolla-tube cylindric, ⅓in. long, the lobes spreading; anthers inserted near mouth: caps. about ½in. long, acute. (Named for Governor Sweginzov of the Russian province of Livonia, 19th century.) China.

8. **S. pubescens,** Turcz. Shrub to 6 ft.: lvs. broad-ovate to ovate, 1½–3 in. long, short-acuminate, broad-cuneate at base, pubescent beneath at least on veins: fls. pale lilac, fragrant, in dense lateral glabrous panicles 3–5 in. long in Apr.–May; corolla-tube ½in. long, the lobes spreading; anthers inserted below mouth: caps. about ½in. long, obtuse, warty. China.

9. **S. microphylla,** Diels. Small shrub: lvs. broad-ovate to ovate, ½–1½ in. long, abruptly acuminate or obtuse, rounded or broad-cuneate at base, pubescent beneath: fls. pale lilac, in loose lateral pubescent panicles 2–3 in. long in June; corolla-tube about ⅓in. long; anthers inserted below mouth: caps ½in. long, acuminate, warty. China.

10. **S. velutina,** Kom. (*S. Palibiniana,* Nakai). Shrub to 10 ft.: lvs. oval or ovate-oblong, 1½–4 in. long, acuminate, rounded or broad-cuneate at base, pubescent beneath: fls. lilac, in lateral pubescent panicles 2–10 in. long in May; corolla-tube ⅓in. long; anthers inserted near mouth: caps. ⅓in. long, acute, warty. China, Korea.

11. **S. oblata,** Lindl. Shrub or small tree to 12 ft.: lvs. reniform or orbicular, 2–4 in. wide and often exceeding length, abruptly acuminate, cordate at base, glabrous: fls. lilac, in dense lateral panicles 2–5 in. long in Apr.–May; corolla-tube ½in. long, the lobes spreading; anthers inserted below mouth: caps. ½–¾in. long, acuminate. China. Var. **dilatata,** Rehd. (*S. dilatata,* Nakai), has long-acuminate lvs. to 5 in. long.

12. **S. vulgaris,** L. Common Lilac. Upright glaucous shrub or small tree to 20 ft.: lvs. ovate, 2–5 in. long, acuminate, truncate or subcordate at base: panicles from lateral buds, usually 2 at end of a shoot, many-fld., 6–10 in. long; fls. lilac or white, fragrant, in Apr.–May; corolla-tube about ⅓in. long, the lobes spreading and obtuse; anthers inserted just below throat: caps. ½–¾in. long, acute. E. Eu. and sometimes escaped in E. U. S. Var. **alba,** West., has white fls.

13. **S. persica,** L. (*S. afghanica* × *S. laciniata*). Persian Lilac. Glabrous shrub to 6 ft., with slender arching branches: lvs. lanceolate, 1–2½ in. long, acuminate, attenuate at base: panicles from lateral buds, 2–3 in. long, many-fld.; fls. lilac or whitish, fragrant, in May; corolla-tube about ⅓in. long: caps. not produced. Originated in Persia. Var. **alba,** West., has white fls.

14. **S. laciniata,** Mill. (*S. persica* var. *laciniata,* West.). Formerly included in *S. persica* but fertile and differing in some or all the lvs. pinnately lobed or cut, and in producing a caps. about ½in. long. N. W. China.

15. **S. chinensis,** Willd. (*S. persica* × *S. vulgaris. S. rothomagensis,* Mord. de Laun.). Intermediate between the parents: to 15 ft.: lvs. ovate-lanceolate, 2–3 in. long, acuminate, attenuate at base: panicles large, many-fld., to 6 in. long. Var. **Saugeana,** Rehd. (*S. rothomagensis* var. *Saugeana,* Loud.), has lilac-red fls.

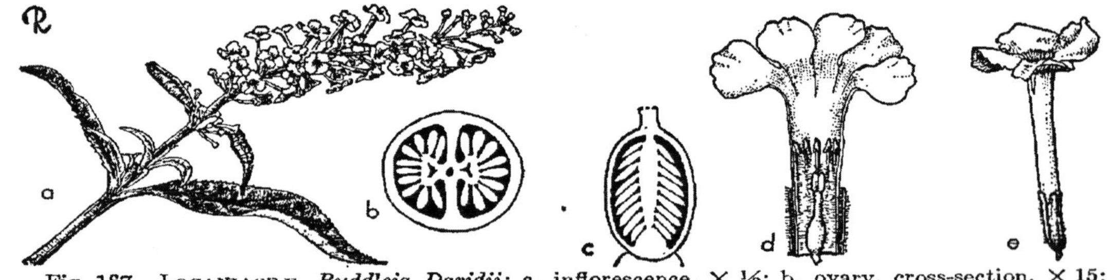

Fig. 167. Loganiaceæ. *Buddleja Davidii:* a, inflorescence, × ½; b, ovary, cross-section, × 15; c, ovary, vertical section, × 8; d, flower, perianth expanded, × 2; e, flower, × 2.

167. LOGANIACEÆ. LOGANIA FAMILY

Herbs, shrubs, or trees, of more than 30 genera and 400 species in trop. and warm regions of the world, a few cult. as ornamentals.—Lvs. commonly opposite, simple, entire or dentate, stipulate: fls. usually bisexual and regular, mostly in cymes or spikes; calyx with 4–5 imbricated lobes; corolla gamopetalous, with 4–5-parted limb; stamens as many as corolla-lobes and alternate with them, or rarely reduced to 1, inserted on tube or throat of corolla; ovary superior, usually 2-celled with many ovules in each cell, with simple 2-cleft or rarely 4-cleft style: fr. a dehiscent caps. or berry or drupe.

A. Habit climbing: style 4-cleft........................1. GELSEMIUM
AA. Habit not climbing: style simple.
B. Plant an herb........................2. SPIGELIA
BB. Plant a shrub or tree.
C. Fr. a caps.: lvs. not nerved from base........................3. BUDDLEJA
CC. Fr. a berry: lvs. 3–5-nerved from base........................4. STRYCHNOS

1. **GELSEMIUM,** Juss. Glabrous twining shrubs, of 2–3 species native in S. E. U. S. and E. Asia, one cult. as a porch or bank cover and sometimes in greenhouses.—Lvs. opposite or rarely verticillate, the bases connected by a stipular line: fls. showy, very fragrant, in axillary and terminal cymes, the pedicels scaly-bracted; corolla funnelform, 5-lobed; style slender, 4-cleft: fr. an ovoid or oblong caps. septicidally dehiscent by 2 valves at summit, the seeds flattened and winged. (Gelse-mium: from Italian *gelsomino*, name of the true jessamine.)

G. sempervirens, Ait. f. (*Bignonia sempervirens*, L.). CAROLINA YELLOW JESSAMINE. Evergreen vine sometimes climbing to 20 ft.: lvs. lanceolate to ovate-lanceolate, 1–4 in. long, entire, short-petioled, acute or acuminate, shining above: fls. dimorphous, in 1–6-fld. cymes, bright yellow, 1–1½ in. long, blooming throughout the season: caps. flat, ⅓–½in. long. Va. to Fla., Tex. and Guatemala.

2. **SPIGELIA,** L. American herbs of about 35 species, one sometimes transplanted.—Lvs. opposite, entire: fls. red, yellow or purplish, in one-sided cymes; calyx deeply parted into 5 narrow lobes; corolla funnelform, 5-lobed; stamens 5; style filiform: fr. a circumscissile caps. (Spige-lia: bears the name of Adrian van der Spigel, physician, born in Brussels in 1578 or 1579, died in Padua 1625.)

S. marilandica, L. (*Lonicera marilandica*, L.). PINK-ROOT. Per. 1–2 ft. high: lvs. ovate or ovate-lanceolate, 2–4 in. long, sessile, acute or acuminate, slightly pubescent on veins beneath: fls. red outside, yellow inside, 1–2 in. long, May–July; calyx-lobes subulate, about ½in. long. N. C. to Fla. and Tex.

3. **BUDDLEJA,** L. BUTTERFLY-BUSH. About 100 species of trees or shrubs or rarely herbs, in the tropics and subtropics of Amer., Asia and S. Afr., grown out-of-doors in the S. and in greenhouses.—Plants usually with stellate, glandular or scaly pubescence: lvs. opposite or rarely alternate, entire or dentate, the bases mostly connected by a stipular line: fls. in heads, racemes or panicles; calyx 4-lobed; corolla campanulate or funnelform, 4-lobed; style simple with 2-lobed stigma: fr. a caps. septicidally dehiscent by 2 valves. (Buddle-ja: after Adam Buddle, English botanist, 1660–1715.)—The generic name is usually written Buddleia, but it was not so spelled by Linnæus; pronunciation not affected.

A. Lvs. alternate........................1. *B. alternifolia*
AA. Lvs. opposite.
B. Fls. in globular heads........................2. *B. globosa*
BB. Fls. in racemes or panicles.
C. Foliage densely white- or yellowish-tomentose beneath.
D. Tomentum close: fls. lilac with orange eye........................3. *B. Davidii*
DD. Tomentum loose and fluffy: fls. white or orange.
E. Color of fls. white........................4. *B. asiatica*
EE. Color of fls. orange........................5. *B. madagascariensis*
CC. Foliage only slightly grayish-tomentose beneath.
D. Racemes erect; calyx-teeth short and broad; corolla granular-pubescent outside........................6. *B. Lindleyana*
DD. Racemes drooping; calyx-teeth longer than wide; corolla densely pubescent outside........................7. *B. japonica*

1. **B. alternifolia,** Maxim. To 12 ft., the branches arching: lvs. alternate, lanceolate, 1–4 in. long, grayish-tomentose beneath: fls. in dense short-stalked clusters to ¾in. long, borne along branches of previous year in June; corolla lilac-purple, ⅓in. long, glabrous or slightly pubescent outside. China.

2. **B. globosa,** Hope. To 15 ft. or more, half-evergreen, the branches and under side of lvs. densely yellowish-tomentose: lvs. lanceolate, 5–10 in. long, long-acuminate, tapering at base, round-toothed, dark green and wrinkled above: fls. fragrant, orange, in axillary dense long-peduncled globular heads ¾in. across, in late spring or early summer. Chile, Peru.

3. **B. Davidii,** Franch. (*B. variabilis*, Hemsl.). To 15 ft.: lvs. ovate-lanceolate or lanceolate, 4–10 in. long, acuminate, rounded or tapering at base, very short-petioled, fine-toothed, dark green above, densely clothed beneath with close white tomentum: fls. fragrant, lilac with orange-yellow mouth, in small clusters on slender cylindrical panicles 6–10 in. long, in late summer; corolla ⅓in. long, glabrous or only sparingly pubescent out-

side. (For Armand David, page 230.) China. Var. **magnifica,** Rehd. & Wils., has very dense panicles and larger rose-purple fls. with deep orange eye, the margins of petals reflexed. In var. **superba,** Rehd. & Wils., the petals are not reflexed and panicles larger than in var. *magnifica*. Var. **Veitchiana,** Rehd., is more robust than type, with gracefully arching branches, and denser and larger clusters of mauve-colored fls. with orange eye. Var. **Wilsonii,** Rehd. & Wils., has bright rosy-lilac fls. with orange eye in drooping spikes to 2 ft. long, blooming through Sept.—The plant known in the trade as *B. Hartwegii* belongs to this species, and many fancy-named color forms are available.

4. **B. asiatica,** Lour. Shrub or small tree, with branches densely tomentose when young: lvs. lanceolate, 4–8 in. long, entire or serrulate, dark green and glabrous above, densely clothed beneath with fluffy white or yellowish tomentum: fls. very fragrant, white, in slender drooping spikes 3–9 in. long, blooming in winter in the greenhouse; corolla villous outside. China to India.—Not hardy N. A hybrid between this species and *B. officinalis* is **B. Farquhari,** Farrington, with lvs. yellow-tomentose beneath and pale pink fls.

5. **B. madagascariensis,** Lam. Straggling shrub to 20 ft., with densely tomentose branchlets: lvs. ovate-oblong, to 5 in. or more long, acuminate, rounded or slightly cordate at base, entire, dark green and glabrous above, densely clothed beneath with fluffy white or yellow tomentum: fls. orange, in large terminal panicles in winter; corolla tomentose outside. Madagascar.—Grown in Calif.

6. **B. Lindleyana,** Fort. To 6 ft. or more, with angular or slightly winged branches pubescent when young: lvs. ovate or oblong-lanceolate, 2–4 in. long, acuminate, tapering at base, remotely denticulate, dark green above, pale and slightly pubescent beneath: fls. purplish-violet, in dense erect racemes from 3–12 in. and more long, July–Aug.; calyx-teeth short and broad; corolla granular-puberulent outside, slightly curved. (For John Lindley, page 47.) China.

7. **B. japonica,** Hemsl. Closely resembling the preceding but with more broadly-winged branches, the ovate-lanceolate lvs. to 8 in. long, racemes pendulous, the calyx-teeth longer than wide, and the lilac corolla densely hairy outside. Japan.

4. **STRYCHNOS,** L. About 100 woody species in tropics and subtropics, grown as drug plants and sometimes for ornament.—Trees and shrubs, sometimes climbing: lvs. opposite, entire, 3–5-nerved from base: fls. small, white or yellowish, in cymes; calyx deeply 4–5-parted; corolla 4–5-lobed; stamens 4–5, inserted in throat of corolla; ovary usually 2-celled with several to many ovules in each cell: fr. a globose berry with a hard shell. (Strych-nos: old Greek name.)

A. Lvs. 1½–2 in. long and about 1 in. wide . . . . 1. *S. spinosa*
AA. Lvs. 3–6 in. long and 2–3 in. wide . . . . 2. *S. Nux-vomica*

1. **S. spinosa,** Lam. NATAL-ORANGE. Shrub to 10 ft., with stiff spines ½in. long: lvs. obovate to nearly orbicular, 1½–2 in. long, dull and glabrous except for patch of hairs on veins beneath: fls. ⅙in. long, in terminal cymes: berry 3–4 in. across, green turning yellow, the seeds embedded in sweet edible pulp. Trop. and S. Afr.

2. **S. Nux-vomica,** L. STRYCHNINE. Tree 40 ft. and more, often with stiff spines: lvs. ovate, 3–6 in. long, glabrous and shining: fls. about ⅕in. long, in terminal compound cymes: berry 1–3 in. across, orange-red, slightly rough, shining, the seeds yielding the poison strychnina from which strychnine is prepared. India.

168. GENTIANACEÆ. GENTIAN FAMILY

Ann. and per. herbs or rarely shrubs, of about 70 genera and 750 species of cosmopolitan distribution, but most abundant in temp. regions, some species planted for ornament.—Lvs. opposite or rarely alternate or verticillate, entire, exstipulate: fls. regular, bisexual, mostly in axillary or terminal cymes; calyx 4–12-parted, persistent; corolla gamopetalous, the limb 4–5- or rarely 6–12-parted; stamens of same number as corolla-lobes and alternate with them, inserted on throat or tube of corolla, the filaments filiform or dilated at base; hypogynous disk inconspicuous or wanting; ovary superior, mostly 1-celled with 2 parietal placentæ and numerous ovules, or 2-celled; style simple with entire or 2-lobed stigma: fr. a caps., mostly septicidally dehiscent by 2 valves.

A. Lvs. opposite: plants of dry land.
  B. Ovary 1-celled: lvs. sessile or clasping.
    C. Corolla funnelform or campanulate, usually blue; style stout and short; anthers straight . . . . 1. GENTIANA
    CC. Corolla salverform, pink; style filiform; anthers twisting when old . . . . 2. CENTAURIUM
  BB. Ovary 2-celled: lvs. (in ours) petioled . . . . 3. EXACUM
AA. Lvs. alternate or basal (or opposite beneath the fls.): aquatic or swamp plants.
  B. Plant a floating aquatic: lvs. simple . . . . 4. NYMPHOIDES
  BB. Plant growing in swamps: lvs. 3-foliolate . . . . 5. MENYANTHES

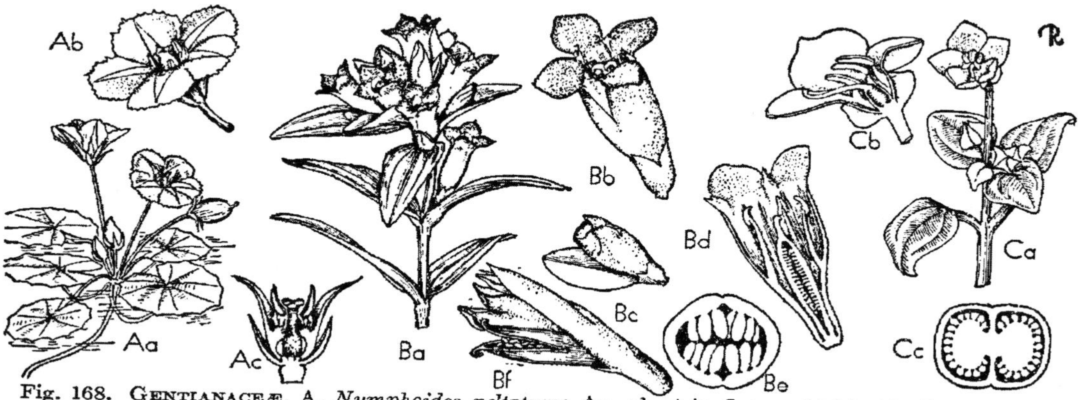

Fig. 168. GENTIANACEÆ. A, *Nymphoides peltatum:* Aa, plant in flower, × 1/4; Ab, flower, × 1/2; Ac, same, vertical section, × 1. B, *Gentiana cruciata:* Ba, flowering branch, × 1/2; Bb, flower, × 1; Bc, bud, × 1; Bd, flower, vertical section, × 3; Be, ovary, cross-section, × 5; Bf, capsule within calyx, × 1. C, *Exacum affine:* Ca, flowering branch, × 1/2; Cb, flower, vertical section, × 1; Cc, ovary, cross-section, × 5.

1. **GENTIANA**, L. GENTIAN. Per. or ann. herbs suitable for rock-gardens, of about 400 species widely distributed in temp. regions and in mts. in the tropics.—Lvs. usually opposite and sessile, entire: fls. commonly in shades of blue, but sometimes yellow or white, clustered or solitary; calyx usually 5-lobed; corolla funnelform or campanulate, commonly with 5 entire or fringed lobes and with plaits, teeth or appendages in the sinuses; stamens inserted on tube of corolla; stigmas 2, nearly sessile; ovary 1-celled. (Gentia-na: named for Gentius, King of Illyria.)

A. Corolla rotate, lobed nearly to base .... 1. *G. lutea*
AA. Corolla tubular.
  B. Lobes of corolla deeply fringed .... 2. *G. crinita*
  BB. Lobes of corolla not fringed.
    C. Calyx split down one side, resembling a spathe.
      D. Lvs. to 1 in. long .... 3. *G. Freyniana*
      DD. Lvs. 3–12 in. long.
        E. Fls. solitary on long pedicels .... 4. *G. gracilipes*
        EE. Fls. in clusters.
          F. Color of fls. blue .... 5. *G. macrophylla*
          FF. Color of fls. yellowish or greenish.
            G. Sts. spreading or ascending: upper lvs. not forming a close involucre below the pedicelled fls. .... 6. *G. straminea*
            GG. Sts. erect: upper lvs. forming a close involucre below the dense head .... 7. *G. tibetica*
    CC. Calyx not split down one side.
      D. Length of calyx 1½–2 in., the lobes much longer than tube.
        E. Lvs. and calyx-lobes linear and recurved: throat of corolla white .... 8. *G. Farreri*
        EE. Lvs. and calyx-lobes lanceolate and straight: throat of corolla blue .... 9. *G. sino-ornata*
      DD. Length of calyx 1 in. or less, the lobes equalling or shorter than tube.
        E. Anthers united into a tube.
          F. Plant about 4 in. high.
            G. Lvs. about twice as long as wide.
              H. Calyx-lobes contracted at base .... 10. *G. acaulis*
              HH. Calyx-lobes straight-sided, not contracted .... 11. *G. Clusii*
            GG. Lvs. three to five times as long as wide .... 12. *G. angustifolia*
          FF. Plant 1½–2 ft. high.
            G. Fls. closed .... 13. *G. Andrewsii*
            GG. Fls. open.
              H. Lvs. linear or linear-lanceolate: fls. mostly in terminal clusters .... 14. *G. linearis*
              HH. Lvs. ovate-lanceolate: fls. mostly solitary in the axils, resembling leafy racemes .... 15. *G. asclepiadea*
        EE. Anthers free.
          F. Shape of corolla salverform .... 16. *G. verna*
          FF. Shape of corolla campanulate.
            G. Color of fls. whitish .... 17. *G. Przewalskii*
            GG. Color of fls. blue.
              H. Plaits of corolla entire .... 18. *G. sceptrum*
              HH. Plaits of corolla 2- to many-cleft.
                I. Calyx-lobes broad-ovate .... 19. *G. calycosa*
                II. Calyx-lobes linear.
                  J. Lvs. to 5 in. long.
                    K. Lobes of calyx 1/16 in. long, tooth-like .... 20. *G. cruciata*
                    KK. Lobes of calyx 1/8–1/4 in. long, linear-oblong .... 21. *G. phlogifolia*

JJ. Lvs. 1½ in. or less long.
K. Divisions of the plaits many........................22. *G. septemfida*
KK. Divisions of the plaits 2–3.
L. Tube of calyx about ⅛in. long, the lobes much shorter.23. *G. Parryi*
LL. Tube of calyx about ¼in. long, the lobes about equalling it..................................24. *G. affinis*

1. **G. lutea,** L. Per. 3–6 ft. high, with simple erect sts.: lvs. oval, to 1 ft. long and 6 in. wide, 5–7-nerved, the lower short-petioled, upper sessile: fls. yellow, on long pedicels in 3–10-fld. axillary clusters, July–Aug.; calyx split down one side, ½in. long; corolla about 1 in. long, rotate, cut nearly to base into usually 5–6 oblong-linear acute lobes; anthers free. Eu., Asia Minor.

2. **G. crinita,** Froel. (*Anthopogon crinitum*, Raf.). FRINGED GENTIAN. Bien. to 3 ft., with erect branching sts.: basal lvs. obovate and obtuse, upper lvs. lanceolate, acute, 1–2 in. long, sessile: fls. bright blue, solitary on long pedicels, Sept.–Oct.; calyx about 1 in. long, with unequal acuminate lanceolate lobes; corolla 2 in. long, with usually 4 obovate rounded conspicuously fringed lobes; anthers free. Que. to Ga. and N. D.

3. **G. Freyniana,** Bornm. Small per. with erect leafy sts.: lvs. linear-lanceolate, acute, about 1 in. long, 3-nerved: fls. blue, sessile, solitary or few at top of sts., Aug.–Sept.; calyx split down one side, lobes linear with rough margins; corolla club-shaped, with ovate acute lobes; plaits 2-cleft, one-third length of corolla-lobes; anthers free. (Named for Joseph Freyn, page 43.) Asia Minor.—Material cult. under this name is often a dwarf form of *G. septemfida*.

4. **G. gracilipes,** Turrill. Per. with basal rosettes and ascending sts. to 6 in. or more: basal lvs. lanceolate, to 6 in. long and ¾in. wide, st.-lvs. smaller: fls. greenish outside, purplish-blue inside, solitary on long pedicels, Aug.; calyx split down one side, about one-third length of corolla; corolla narrow-campanulate, 1½ in. long, with 5 ovate-triangular lobes; plaits entire, about half length of corolla-lobes; anthers free. China.—Plants grown as *G. Purdomii* usually belong here, that species having fls. in terminal clusters and calyx not split, and apparently not in cult.

5. **G. macrophylla,** Pall. Per. to 1½ ft., with sts. nearly erect: lvs. lanceolate to oblong, to 1 ft. long, 3–5-nerved, st.-lvs. smaller: fls. pale blue, in terminal clusters and upper axils, Aug.–Sept.; calyx split down one side, ¼in. long; corolla about 1 in. long, with 4–5 ovate lobes; plaits entire or 2-cleft, one-third length of corolla-lobes; anthers free. Siberia, N. China.

6. **G. straminea,** Maxim. Per. with spreading or ascending sts. to about 1 ft. high: basal lvs. linear-lanceolate, to 8 in. long and ¾in. wide, acuminate, 5-nerved, st.-lvs. smaller: fls. pale yellow or greenish-white, several at top of sts., pedicelled, July–Sept.; calyx split down one side, whitish and papery, about ½in. long; corolla 1½ in. long, with 5 ovate acute lobes; plaits 2-cleft, one-third length of corolla-lobes; anthers free. China.—This plant is cult. under a variety of names.

7. **G. tibetica,** King. Per. with erect unbranched sts. to 2 ft.: lvs. lanceolate, to 1 ft. long and 3 in. wide, acute, 7-nerved: fls. greenish-white, in a dense terminal head and also in upper axils, Aug.; calyx split down one side, papery, ½in. long; corolla 1½ in. long, with 5 triangular lobes; plaits triangular, one-third length of corolla-lobes; anthers free. S. Tibet.

8. **G. Farreri,** Balf. f. Stoloniferous per. with basal rosette and ascending branching sts. to 8 in. long: lvs. linear, to 1½ in. long, recurved: fls. blue with white throat and yellowish-white band on petals, terminal and solitary on short pedicels, Aug.–Sept.; calyx nearly 2 in. long, with linear recurved lobes more than twice as long as tube; corolla to 2½ in. long, with 5 ovate recurved lobes; plaits entire or emarginate, much shorter than lobes; anthers free. (Named for its discoverer, Reginald Farrer.) China.

9. **G. sino-ornata,** Balf. f. Stoloniferous per. resembling *G. Farreri* but differing in the lvs. and calyx-lobes being lanceolate and straight and the fls. nearly sessile and with blue throat, Sept.–Oct. China.—A hybrid between this species and *G. Farreri* is **G. Macaulayi,** Hort. (raised by R. Macauley), which differs from the latter parent in the larger deeper blue fls. with spreading corolla-lobes.

10. **G. acaulis,** L. (*G. excisa*, Presl). Per. to 4 in., with basal rosettes: lvs. elliptic or lanceolate, 1 in. or more long and about half as wide, dark green and glossy: fls. dark blue and spotted, solitary and terminal, spring and early summer; calyx about ¾in. long, the ovate acute lobes half length of tube and contracted at base; corolla 2 in. long, with 5 ovate acute lobes; plaits irregular and triangular; anthers united into tube. Alps and Pyrenees.

11. **G. Clusii,** Perrier & Songeon. Often included in *G. acaulis* and perhaps only a form, differing in the straight-sided calyx-lobes not contracted at base and pressed close to corolla. (Named for Clusius.) Alps.

12. **G. angustifolia,** Vill. Similar to *G. acaulis* but with linear-lanceolate to lanceolate lvs. which are three to five times as long as wide, and calyx-lobes spreading and contracted at base. Alps.

13. **G. Andrewsii,** Griseb. (*Dasystephana Andrewsii*, Small). CLOSED GENTIAN. Per. 1–2 ft. high: lvs. ovate to lanceolate, 2–4 in. long, acuminate: fls. blue, in sessile termi-

nal clusters and in upper axils, Aug.–Oct.; calyx about ½in. long, the ovate lobes shorter than tube; corolla 1½ in. long, closed, the lobes inconspicuous and exceeded by the fimbriate-dentate plaits; anthers united into a tube. (Named for H. C. Andrews, page 39.) Que. to Ga.—Often confused with *G. clausa*, Raf., which has rounded corolla-lobes about ⅛in. long and plaits 2–5-cleft.

14. **G. linearis,** Froel. (*Dasystephana linearis*, Britt.). Per. 1–2 ft. high: lvs. linear or linear-lanceolate, 1½–3 in. long, 3-nerved: fls. blue, in terminal clusters and in upper axils, Aug.–Sept.; calyx with linear or lanceolate lobes shorter than tube; corolla 1–2 in. long, with erect rounded lobes slightly longer than the entire or 1–2-cleft plaits; anthers united into tube. N. B. to Md. and Minn.

15. **G. asclepiadea,** L. Per. 1½–2 ft. high: lvs. ovate-lanceolate, 2–3 in. long, long-acuminate, 5-nerved: fls. dark blue, usually solitary in the axils and resembling leafy racemes, July–Sept.; calyx about ½in. long, the lobes shorter than tube; corolla 1½ in. long, with 5 ovate long-acuminate lobes; plaits entire, much shorter than corolla-lobes; anthers united into tube. S. Eu. to Caucasus.

16. **G. verna,** L. Tufted per. to 4 in.: lvs. elliptic-lanceolate, to 1 in. long, acute, 3-nerved, broadest at middle: fls. blue, solitary and terminal, Apr.–June; calyx about ½in. long, with lanceolate acute lobes about half length of tube; corolla salverform, 1 in. long, with 5 ovate lobes; plaits 2-cleft, much shorter than corolla-lobes; anthers free. Eu., Asia.

17. **G. Przewalskii,** Maxim. Per. to 8 in.: lvs. linear-lanceolate to spatulate, 1–4 in. long: fls. white streaked with blue, nearly sessile in terminal 2–10-fld. clusters, July–Oct.; calyx about ½in. long, with linear unequal lobes about half length of tube; corolla about 2 in. long, with 5 triangular lobes; plaits triangular, about half length of corolla-lobes; anthers free. (Collected by Przewalski.) China.

18. **G. sceptrum,** Griseb. Stiff per. 2–4 ft. high: lvs. lanceolate or linear-oblong, 2–3 in. long, obtuse: fls. deep blue dotted inside with greenish, 2 to several, terminal and axillary, July–Aug.; calyx ¾in. long, with oblong unequal lobes about length of tube; corolla 1½ in. long, with 5 broad-ovate rounded lobes; plaits entire and very short; anthers free. B. C. to Calif.

• 19. **G. calycosa,** Griseb. (*Dasystephana calycosa*, Rydb.). Per. 6–12 in. high, with erect or ascending sts.: lvs. ovate, thick, 1 in. long, 3–5-nerved: fls. dark blue spotted with green, usually solitary and terminal, Aug.–Sept.; calyx about ½in. long, with ovate obtuse lobes equalling the tube; corolla 1½ in. long, with 5 ovate lobes; plaits many-cleft, about half length of corolla-lobes; anthers free. B. C. to Mont. and Calif.

20. **G. cruciata,** L. Per. 10–16 in. high: basal rosette lvs. ovate-lanceolate, 4–5 in. long, narrowed at both ends, 3-nerved, st.-lvs. placed crosswise in pairs: fls. dark blue, in terminal and axillary clusters, June–Aug.; calyx about ¼in. long, with linear teeth-like lobes ¹⁄₁₆in. long; corolla ¾–1 in. long, with 4 narrow pointed lobes; plaits 2-cleft, much shorter than corolla-lobes; anthers free. Eu., Asia.

21. **G. phlogifolia,** Schott & Kotschy. Similar to *G. cruciata*, but with narrower lvs., larger fls. with longer unequal calyx-lobes ⅛–¼in. long and broader rounded corolla-lobes. E. Eu.

22. **G. septemfida,** Pall. Per. 1–1½ ft. high: lvs. ovate-lanceolate, ½–1¼in. long, acute, 5–7-nerved: fls. dark blue, spotted inside, in terminal clusters, July–Aug.; calyx about ½in. long, with linear lobes equalling the tube; corolla 1½–2 in. long, with 5–7 spreading acute lobes; plaits much cut, nearly as long as corolla-lobes; anthers free. Asia. Var. **Lagodechiana,** Kusn., has prostrate sts. and solitary fls.—A hybrid between this var. and another form of *G. septemfida* is **G. hascombensis,** Hort., fls. 1½ in. across, bright blue spotted with white, in clusters.

23. **G. Parryi,** Engelm. (*Dasystephana Parryi*, Rydb.). Per. to 16 in.: lvs. lanceolate to ovate, ½–1½ in. long, thick and slightly glaucous: fls. bright blue, in terminal clusters of 1–6, July–Sept.; calyx about ½in. long, with linear or lanceolate lobes much shorter than tube; corolla 1½–2 in. long, with 5 obovate acute lobes; plaits 2-cleft, somewhat shorter than corolla-lobes; anthers free. (C. C. Parry, page 49.) Mts., Wyo. to Utah.

24. **G. affinis,** Griseb. (*Dasystephana affinis*, Rydb.). Per. to 1 ft.: lvs. oblong to lanceolate, ½–1½ in. long: fls. blue or purple, in few-fld. clusters, terminal and axillary, Aug.–Sept.; calyx about ½in. long, with oblong-linear lobes about length of tube; corolla 1 in. long, with 5 ovate acute lobes; plaits 2–3-cleft, shorter than corolla-lobes; anthers free. B. C. to Calif. and Colo.

2. **CENTAURIUM,** Hill (*Erythræa*, Neck.). CENTAURY. Herbs, mostly ann., about 25 Old World species and a few in W. N. and S. Amer., one grown in the rock-garden.—Lvs. opposite, sessile or clasping, entire: fls. usually pink, in cymes or spikes; calyx 4–5-lobed; corolla salverform, 4–5-lobed; stamens inserted on tube of corolla, anthers spirally twisting when old; style filiform, with 2-lobed stigma; ovary 1-celled. (Centau-rium: from Latin meaning 100 pieces of gold.)

C. scilloides, Druce (*Gentiana scilloides*, L. f. *Erythræa Massonii*, Sweet. *E. diffusa*, Woods. *E. scilloides*, Chaub.). Tufted, with ascending sts. to 4 in. or more high: lvs. orbicular to oblong-lanceolate, to ¾in. long: fls. bright rose or rarely white, ½–¾in. long, in loose 1–6-fld. cymes in summer. Azores, S. W. Eu. to S. Wales.

3. **EXACUM,** L. About 30 herbaceous species or rarely subshrubby, native in trop. and subtrop. Asia, Malaya, Madagascar, and trop. Afr., one sometimes grown under glass or out-of-doors in warm regions.—Lvs. sessile, clasping or short-petioled: fls. sessile or pedicelled, mostly in forking cymes or sometimes solitary at ends of sts.; calyx 4–5-parted, the lobes keeled, winged or flat and 3-nerved; corolla with short tube and 4 oblong twisted lobes; stamens 4 or 5, attached to mouth of corolla-tube, the filaments short; ovary 2-celled: caps. globose, 2-valved. (Ex-acum: classical name, of no application here.)

E. affine, Balf. Glabrous bien. 1–2 ft. high, much-branched from the base: lvs. elliptic-ovate, 1–1½ in. long, very broad and 3–5-nerved from base, on petioles ¼–½in. long: fls. bluish, about ½in. across; sepals with broad wing on back. Socotra. Var. **atrocæruleum,** Farrington, has dark lavender fls. with golden-yellow stamens.

4. **NYMPHOIDES,** Hill (*Limnanthemum*, Gmel.). FLOATING-HEART. Aquatic floating herbs rooting in the mud, of about 20 species of wide distribution in fresh water.—Lvs. alternate or nearly opposite beneath the fls., ovate or orbicular, deeply cordate or rarely peltate with a closed sinus, the margins entire or slightly wavy: fls. yellow or white, borne in the axils or on filiform sts. apparently from the petioles; calyx deeply 5-parted; corolla nearly rotate, deeply 5-parted, the lobes often fringed; stamens 5, attached at base of corolla; ovary 1-celled: caps. ovoid or oblong, indehiscent or irregularly dehiscent. (Nymphoi-des: *nymphæa-like.*)

A. Fl.-umbels in the axils of nearly opposite lvs.: margins of lvs. repand . . . . 1. *N. peltatum*
AA. Fl.-umbels borne on the petioles near the top: margins of lvs. entire . . . . 2. *N. indicum*

1. **N. peltatum,** Kuntze (*Menyanthes nymphoides*, L. *Limnanthemum peltatum*, Gmel. *L. nymphoides*, Hoffm. & Link. *N. nymphæoides*, Britt.). Stout branching plant producing runners and spreading rapidly: lvs. ovate-orbicular, 2–4 in. broad, often mottled, margins repand, on long stout petioles which on upper lvs. are dilated near base: fls. bright yellow, 1 in. or more across, on long stout pedicels, in umbels in the axils of nearly opposite lvs.; corolla-segms. short-fringed: seeds with fringe-like margins. Eu., Asia; nat. in E. U. S.

2. **N. indicum,** Kuntze (*Limnanthemum indicum*, Thwaites). WATER-SNOWFLAKE. Lvs. orbicular, 2–8 in. across, mostly entire, with a deep basal sinus and long petioles: fls. white, yellowish toward the base within, borne in sessile umbels on petioles near the top; corolla-lobes fimbriated and densely papillose: seeds not fringed. Tropics.

5. **MENYANTHES,** L. One per. herb native in swamps in cool parts of the northern hemisphere, useful for a bog-garden.—Rootstocks creeping: lvs. basal, long-petioled, of 3 lfts.: fls. in racemes borne on long scapes; calyx 5-parted; corolla with 5 spreading lobes which are bearded inside; stamens inserted on tube of corolla; ovary 1-celled: caps. oval, indehiscent or dehiscent with age. (Menyan-thes: old Greek name.)

M. trifoliata, L. BOGBEAN. BUCKBEAN. Glabrous: lfts. oblong or obovate, 1½–3 in. long, obtuse, entire, sessile, the lvs. on petioles to 10 in. long sheathing at base: fls. white or purplish with white beard, ½in. long, pedicelled: caps. ⅓in. long. N. Amer., Eu., Asia.

169. APOCYNACEÆ. DOGBANE FAMILY

About 300 genera and 1,300 or more species of herbs, shrubs or trees, often climbing, of wide range but most abundant in trop. regions, several grown for ornament and a few for the edible frs.—Juice milky: lvs. opposite, verticillate or alternate, simple and entire, mostly exstipulate: fls. bisexual, regular, in cymes or panicles or solitary; calyx deeply 5-parted, the lobes imbricated in the bud, persistent; corolla gamopetalous, the 5 lobes convolute and twisted in the bud, the tube often appendaged; stamens as many as corolla-lobes and alternate with them, inserted on tube or mouth of corolla, the filaments commonly free, the anthers usually sagittate and acute, pollen granular; hypogynous disk usually present, entire or lobed, some-

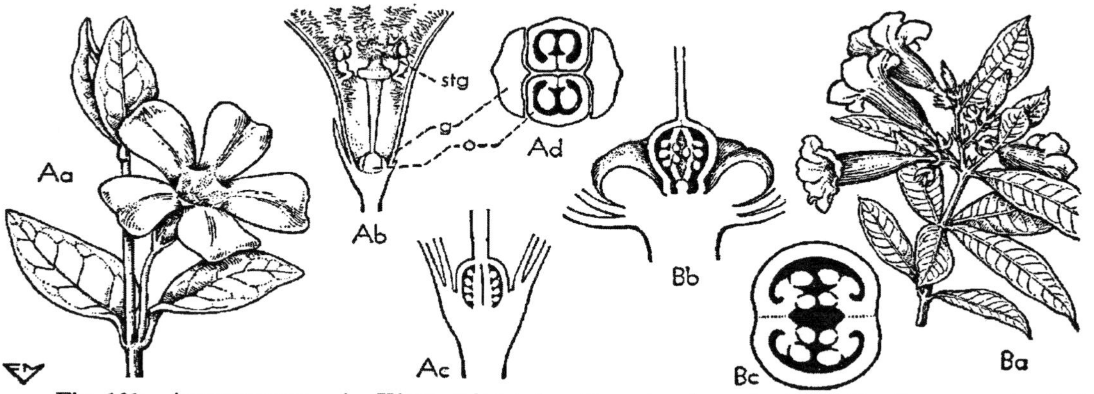

Fig. 169. Apocynaceæ. A, *Vinca minor:* Aa, flowering branch, × 1; Ab, flower, perianth in vertical section, × 2; Ac, ovaries, vertical section, × 4; Ad, same, cross-section, × 10. B, *Allamanda neriifolia:* Ba, flowering branch, × ¼; Bb, ovary, vertical section, × 3; Bc, same, cross-section, × 10. (g gland, o ovary, stg stigma.)

times of 2–5 scales; ovaries mostly 2, superior or partly inferior, or ovary 1- or 2-celled with few to many ovules; style 1, simple or divided: fr. mostly of 2 follicles, sometimes berry-like or drupe-like, the seeds often with a tuft of hairs.

A. Lvs. alternate.
  B. Ovules 2 in each cell: fr. a fleshy drupe .... 1. Thevetia
  BB. Ovules many in each cell: fr. of 2 follicles.
    C. Plant a shrub or tree with thick branches .... 2. Plumeria
    CC. Plant an herb .... 3. Amsonia
AA. Lvs. opposite or whorled.
  B. Habit climbing (at least in ours).
    C. Stamens not united .... 4. Allamanda
    CC. Stamens united around stigma and adherent to it.
      D. Calyx large and lf.-like; stamens with very long filaments .... 5. Beaumontia
      DD. Calyx small; stamens with short filaments.
        E. Fls. salverform, of medium size .... 6. Trachelospermum
        EE. Fls. funnelform, very large (in ours) .... 7. Mandevilla
  BB. Habit upright or trailing, not climbing.
    C. Anthers connivent around the stigma .... 8. Nerium
    CC. Anthers free.
      D. Fls. solitary in the axils .... 9. Vinca
      DD. Fls. in axillary or terminal cymes.
        E. Plant armed with spines .... 10. Carissa
        EE. Plant spineless.
          F. Ovaries 2.
            G. Fr. a drupe: ovules few .... 11. Ochrosia
            GG. Fr. of 2 follicles: ovules numerous.
              H. Calyx parted to base .... 12. Tabernæmontana
              HH. Calyx lobed to about middle .... 13. Ervatamia
          FF. Ovary 1.
            G. Fr. a berry: ovary 2-celled .... 14. Acokanthera
            GG. Fr. a 2-valved caps.: ovary 1-celled .... 4. Allamanda

1. **THEVETIA,** Adans. Glabrous shrubs or small trees, of about 10 species in trop. Amer., one grown under glass and out-of-doors in the S.—Lvs. alternate, more or less leathery, 1-nerved and pinnately veined: fls. large, yellow, in terminal peduncled cymes; calyx with many glands inside at base; corolla funnelform, with cylindrical tube and campanulate limb, with 5 hairy scales at throat; stamens borne at throat with the scales; disk 0; ovary 2-lobed and 2-celled with 2 ovules in each cell, the style filiform with 2-lobed stigma: fr. a drupe with thin flesh, broader than long. (Theve-tia: after André Thevet, 1502–1590, French monk who travelled in Brazil.)

T. peruviana, Schum. (*Cerbera Thevetia,* L. *C. peruviana,* Pers. *T. nereifolia,* Juss. *T. Thevetia,* Millsp.). Yellow Oleander. Densely leafy evergreen shrub or small tree to 30 ft.: lvs. linear, 3–6 in. long, ¼in. or less wide, tapering at both ends, nearly sessile, margins revolute, dark green and shining above: fls. yellow, fragrant, 2–3 in. long, the limb much longer than the tube: drupe compressed-triangular, 1 in. or more across, red turning black. Trop. Amer.

2. **PLUMERIA,** L. FRANGIPANI. Trees or shrubs, planted for ornament in warm regions; as now defined the genus contains about 7 species from the W. Indies to N. S. Amer.—Branches thick and fleshy, marked with scars from fallen lvs.: lvs. alternate, pinnate-veined, the primary veins joined to a nerve running parallel with the margin: fls. large, subtended by small deciduous bracts, in terminal peduncled cymes; calyx small, 5-parted, glandular at tips; corolla funnelform, without scales or hairs at throat; stamens inserted near base of corolla-tube, the anthers obtuse; disk 0; ovary of 2 distinct partly inferior carpels, with many ovules in each cell; style very short with 2-lobed stigma: fr. consisting of 2 leathery follicles; seeds winged at base. (Plume-ria: for Chas. Plumier, 1646–1706, French botanist who travelled in Amer.)

A. Lvs. 1½–6 in. wide, with conspicuous marginal vein .... 1. *P. rubra*
AA. Lvs. ½–3 in. wide, without marginal vein .... 2. *P. alba*

1. **P. rubra,** L. To 15 ft. and more: lvs. obovate, up to 18 in. long and 6 in. wide, obtuse or short-acuminate, glabrous or pubescent beneath, with conspicuous marginal vein: fls. pink to red or purple, very fragrant, 2 in. or more across, in terminal cymes which are shorter than lvs.; corolla-tube shorter than the broadly oval obtuse lobes: follicles to 1 ft. long and 1½ in. wide. Mex. to Venezuela, W. Indies. Var. **acutifolia,** Bailey (*P. acuminata*, Ait. *P. acutifolia*, Poir. *P. rubra* forma *acutifolia*, Woodson), has white fls. usually with yellow center and sometimes flushed rose.

2. **P. alba,** L. To 35 ft.: lvs. linear-oblong to oblong-lanceolate, to 12 in. long and ½–3 in. wide, long-acuminate, the margins revolute, usually densely white-pubescent beneath, without definite marginal vein: fls. white with yellow eye, fragrant, 1 in. and more across, the obovate corolla-lobes as long as or longer than tube: follicles to 6 in. long and ½in. wide. W. Indies.

3. **AMSONIA,** Walt. Per. herbs of 17 species in N. Amer. and Japan, one sometimes transplanted.—Lvs. alternate, entire: fls. blue to white, in terminal cymes; calyx 5-parted; corolla with cylindrical tube, with 5 spreading or erect lobes; stamens 5, inserted above middle of corolla-tube, anthers obtuse; disk 0; ovary of 2 carpels united at top by filiform style, with many ovules in each cell: fr. of 2 cylindrical follicles; seeds without appendages. (Amso-nia: named for Dr. Amson of Gloucester Co., Va.)

A. Tabernæmontana, Walt. (*Tabernæmontana Amsonia*, L. *A. Amsonia*, Britt.). To 3½ ft.: lvs. ovate to oblong, 2–6 in. long and 1–2 in. wide, acuminate, short-petioled, sometimes pubescent beneath: fls. blue, ½–¾in. long, in many-fld. cymes Apr.–July; corolla with oblong spreading lobes about equalling tube, pubescent outside: follicles 3–5 in. long. Pa. to S. C. and Kans. Var. **salicifolia,** Woodson (*A. salicifolia*, Pursh), has narrower glabrous lvs. ½–1 in. wide, and few-fld. loose cymes.

4. **ALLAMANDA,** L. About a dozen species of mostly climbing shrubs native in Brazil and 1 to Cent. Amer., grown under glass or in the open far S.—Lvs. whorled or opposite, pinnately veined: fls. large and showy, in lax few-fld. racemes at ends of branches; calyx deeply 5-parted, the outer lobes often larger, without glands at base within; corolla campanulate-funnelform, the lower tube cylindrical, with hairs or hairy scales at throat; stamens inserted at mouth of cylindrical tube, filaments very short, anthers not united with stigma; disk annular, entire or 5-lobed; ovary 1-celled with many ovules: fr. a prickly caps. dehiscent by 2 valves; seeds winged. (Allaman-da: after Dr. Fr. Allamand, professor of natural history in Leyden in the last part of the 18th century.)

A. Fls. swollen at base, 1½ in. across .... 1. *A. neriifolia*
AA. Fls. not swollen at base, 2–5 in. across .... 2. *A. cathartica*

1. **A. neriifolia,** Hook. Erect shrub to 3 ft., or half climbing: lvs. in whorls of 2–5, elliptic or oblong, 3–5 in. long, acuminate, short-petioled, pubescent on the veins beneath: fls. golden-yellow, 2–3 in. long and the limb 1½ in. across, striped inside with reddish-brown; tube swollen and greenish at base; corolla-lobes orbicular or oval, obtuse. Brazil.

2. **A. cathartica,** L. Tall-climbing: lvs. in whorls of 3 or 4 or sometimes opposite, obovate, 4–6 in. long, tapering at both ends, very short-petioled, thin, glabrous except on the veins beneath, wavy-margined: fls. golden-yellow marked with white in the throat, 2–3 in. across; corolla-lobes oval. Brazil.—Variable, running into many forms which do not seem sufficiently distinct to be given specific rank. Var. **Hendersonii,** Raffill (*A. Hendersonii*, Bull), is a glabrous free-flowering form with thick leathery lvs. and fls. 4–5

in. across (intro. by Henderson & Co. of England). Var. **Schottii,** Raffill (*A. Schottii*, Pohl), young shoots and petioles slightly pubescent, fls. very large, the throat darker yellow and striped (named for Heinrich Schott, Austrian botanist who travelled in Brazil in 1817). Var. **Williamsii,** Raffill, sts. pubescent, lvs. slightly pubescent on both sides, smaller than type, fls. 2–3 in. across, yellow, the throat deeper and stained with reddish-brown (grown at Williams' nursery, England). Var. **grandiflora,** Raffill (*A. grandiflora*, Hook.), of dwarf compact growth, with thin wiry sts., thin ovate-lanceolate lvs. and lemon- or primrose-yellow fls. 4–4½ in. across. Var. **nobilis,** Raffill (*A. nobilis*, T. Moore), pubescent form with purple twigs, fls. bright clear yellow with white spot at base of lobes, 4–5 in. across, with magnolia-like odor.

5. **BEAUMONTIA,** Wall. Four or 5 woody vines from E. India to Java, one grown in the greenhouse and out-of-doors in the S.—Lvs. opposite, pinnate-veined: fls. very large, subtended by lf.-like deciduous bracts, in terminal cymes; calyx large, with leafy acute lobes, with or without glands; corolla funnelform, without scales at throat; stamens inserted in upper part of tube, the filaments very long and dilated above, united around stigma and adherent to it; disk of 5 scales or 5-lobed; ovaries 2, superior, with many ovules in each cell, the style filiform: fr. long-cylindrical, woody, splitting into 2 follicles. (Beaumon-tia: after Lady Beaumont of Yorkshire, England.)

B. grandiflora, Wall. HERALDS-TRUMPET. Tall-growing: lvs. elliptic to obovate, 4–8 in. long, abruptly acuminate, short-petioled, glabrous above, slightly pubescent beneath: fls. white, fragrant, 5 in. long; sepals 1–1½ in. long; limb of corolla much shorter than tube. Himalayas.

6. **TRACHELOSPERMUM,** Lem. Woody vines of over 20 species from E. India to Japan, and 1 in S. U. S., one popular in greenhouses and out-of-doors in warm countries.—Lvs. opposite, the veins pinnate and distant: fls. in terminal or axillary loose cymes; calyx small, with 5–10 scales or glands inside at base; corolla salverform, with cylindrical tube and oblong lobes overlapping to the right, without scales in throat; stamens inserted above the middle of the tube, with short broad filaments, anthers united around stigma and adherent to it; disk annular, truncate or 5-lobed; ovaries 2, slightly inferior, with many ovules in each cell, the style filiform: fr. of 2 elongated terete follicles. (Trachelosper-mum: Greek for *neck* and *seed.*)

T. jasminoides, Lem. (*Rhynchospermum jasminoides*, Lindl.). STAR- or CONFEDERATE-JASMINE. Evergreen climbing shrub: lvs. elliptic or obovate, 2–4 in. long, acute or short-acuminate, short-petioled, glabrous or pubescent beneath: fls. white, fragrant, ¾–1 in. across, in axillary cymes, the peduncles longer than lvs.; calyx-lobes reflexed: follicles 4–7 in. long; seeds with tuft of white hairs to 1½ in. long. China.

7. **MANDEVILLA,** Lindl. Woody vines native from Mex. to Argentina, of more than 100 species, one sometimes grown in the greenhouse or out-of-doors in warm regions.—Lvs. opposite or verticillate: fls. funnelform, in axillary or terminal racemes; calyx 5-parted, with scales at base inside; corolla 5-parted; stamens with very short filaments and anthers united and adherent to stigma; disk of 2–5 lobes or scales; ovaries 2, with many ovules in each cell: fr. of 2 terete follicles; seeds with tuft of hairs at apex. (Mandevil-la: Henry John Mandeville, once British minister at Buenos Aires.)

M. laxa, Woodson (*Echites laxa*, Ruiz & Pav. *M. suaveolens*, Lindl.). CHILEAN-JASMINE. Tall climbing vine: lvs. ovate, 2–6 in. long and 1–2 in. wide, acuminate, cordate at base, petioled, glaucous beneath: fls. white or blush, fragrant, 2 in. long and nearly 2 in. across; corolla-lobes nearly as long as tube: follicles 10–16 in. long. Argentina, Bolivia.

8. **NERIUM,** L. Three upright shrubs or small trees native from Medit. region to Japan, the oleander commonly cult. in southern countries and as a house plant in the N.—Lvs. usually in whorls of 3, rarely in 4's or opposite, leathery: fls. showy, in terminal branching cymes; calyx with many glands inside near the base; corolla funnelform, tube cylindrical at base, campanulate throat with 5 broad or laciniate teeth, lobes spreading and twisted to right; stamens attached to throat of corolla, included, filaments very short, anthers with long appendages at apex, connivent

around the stigma and adherent to it, appendaged also at base; disk 0; ovaries 2, with many ovules in each cell; style filiform: fr. of 2 elongated follicles; seeds with tuft of hairs at apex. (Ne-rium: Greek name of the oleander.)

N. Oleander, L. OLEANDER. Evergreen shrub to 20 ft.: lvs. narrowly oblong-lanceolate, 4–12 in. long, acuminate, tapering at base into short petiole, dark green above, paler beneath with prominent midrib, glabrous: fls. white to red or purple, 1½–3 in. across, often double; appendages of corolla 3–4-toothed: pods drooping, 4–7 in. long. (Name refers to the resemblance of the lvs. to the olive.) Medit. region; nat. in S. U. S.—There are vars. in which the lvs. are variegated with white or yellow.

9. **VINCA,** L. PERIWINKLE. About 12 species of Old World trailing or erect herbs or subshrubs, planted as ground-cover, in window-boxes, or the fl.-garden.—Lvs. opposite: fls. rather large, solitary in axils; calyx small, the lobes narrow and acuminate, without glands; corolla salverform, with cylindrical tube and 5 lobes twisted to the left, hairy or thickened at throat; stamens inserted at about middle of tube, included; disk of 2 glands alternating with the 2 distinct ovaries which have 6 to many ovules; style filiform, stigma annular, its apex densely covered with clusters of hairs: fr. of 2 erect or spreading cylindrical follicles; seeds unappendaged. (Vin-ca: old Latin name.)

A. Plants erect: corolla-tube cylindrical, about 1 in. long....................1. *V. rosea*
AA. Plants trailing: corolla-tube funnelform, about ½in. long.
  B. Calyx-lobes ciliate: lvs. truncate or subcordate at base....................2. *V. major*
  BB. Calyx-lobes glabrous: lvs. narrowed at base....................3. *V. minor*

1. **V. rosea,** L. (*Catharanthus roseus,* Don. *Lochnera rosea,* Reichb. *Ammocallis rosea,* Small). MADAGASCAR PERIWINKLE. Erect everblooming pubescent herb or subshrub 1–2 ft. high, grown as an ann.: lvs. oblong, 1–3 in. long, rounded and mucronulate at apex, narrowed at base into short petiole: fls. rosy-purple, often with a reddish eye, 1–1½ in. across; calyx-lobes linear-subulate, pubescent; corolla-tube slender and cylindrical, about 1 in. long, finely pubescent: follicles about 1 in. long, pubescent. Cosmopolitan in the tropics. Var. **alba,** Sweet, fls. white.

2. **V. major,** L. Trailing evergreen herb, the short flowering sts. ascending: lvs. ovate, 1–2 in. long, obtuse or acutish, truncate or subcordate at base, rather long-petioled, ciliate on margins: fls. blue, 1–2 in. across; calyx-lobes narrowly linear, ciliate; corolla-tube funnelform, about ½in. long: follicles 2 in. long. Eu. Var. **variegata,** Loud., lvs. margined and spotted with yellowish-white.

3. **V. minor,** L. COMMON PERIWINKLE. Commonly called RUNNING-MYRTLE. Trailing evergreen per., with erect fl.-sts.: lvs. oblong to ovate, to 1½ in. long, obtuse or acutish, narrowed at base into short petiole, glabrous: fls. lilac-blue, ½–¾in. across; calyx-lobes lanceolate, glabrous; corolla-tube funnelform, ½in. or less long: follicles about 3 in. long. Eu.; run wild in E. U. S. Var. **alba,** West., fls. white. Var. **aureo-variegata,** West., lvs. spotted with yellow. Var. **multiplex,** Schneid. (var. *plena,* Hort.), has double fls. in several colors.

10. **CARISSA,** L. (*Arduina,* Mill.). Branching spiny shrubs of about 30 species in the tropics of Afr., Asia and Australia, a few grown in the S. as hedge plants and for the edible frs.—Lvs. opposite, leathery: fls. in few-fld. terminal branching peduncled cymes; calyx glandless or rarely with many glands at the base; corolla salverform, with cylindrical tube and lobes overlapping to right or left, without scales in throat; stamens inserted below top of tube; disk 0; ovary 2-celled with 1 to several ovules in each cell; style filiform with shortly 2-lobed stigma: fr. a globose or elliptical berry, sometimes abortively 1-celled. (Caris-sa: aboriginal name.)

A. Corolla-tube one-half or less as long as lobes....................1. *C. grandiflora*
AA. Corolla-tube about twice as long as lobes.
  B. Tube of corolla about ¼in. long, densely hairy at throat: berry scarlet, 1–2-seeded....................2. *C. Arduina*
  BB. Tube of corolla ¾in. long, glabrous or puberulous at throat: berry black, 4- or more-seeded....................3. *C. Carandas*

1. **C. grandiflora,** A. DC. (*Arduina grandiflora,* E. Mey.). NATAL-PLUM. AMATUNGULA. Spreading shrub to 18 ft., armed with stout bifurcate spines to 1½ in. long: lvs. ovate, 1–3 in. long, acute, mucronate, rounded at base: fls. white, fragrant, about 2 in. across; corolla-lobes overlapping to left, twice or more longer than tube: berry ovoid to elliptic, 1–2 in. long, scarlet, with firm reddish pulp surrounding the several circular papery seeds. S. Afr.—Fr. used for jelly and preserves.

2. **C. Arduina,** Lam. (*C. bispinosa,* Desf. *C. acuminata,* DC. *Arduina bispinosa,* L.). Distinguished from the above by its fls. only ½in. across, the lobes being much shorter

than the tube, the minutely ciliate sepals, and the frs. ½in. long with only 1–2 lanceolate seeds. (Arduina: old generic name commemorating A. P. Arduina, 1728–1805, prof. in Padua.) S. Afr.

3. **C. Carandas,** L. KARANDA. Large shrub or small tree, with spines 1–2 in. long: lvs. oblong to broadly ovate, 1½–3 in. long, obtuse, rounded at base: fls. white or pink, fragrant; sepals ciliate; corolla-tube ¾in. long, glabrous or puberulous, about twice as long as pubescent lobes: berry elliptic, ½–1 in. long, red but becoming black, with 4 or more seeds. (Carandas: native name.) India.

11. **OCHROSIA,** Juss. A small genus of trees native Australia and Pacific isls., one planted in S. Fla.—Lvs. opposite or whorled: fls. in terminal or axillary peduncled cymes; calyx glandless; corolla with cylindrical tube and spreading lobes; anthers free; disk 0 or of minute glands; ovaries 2 with few ovules in two rows in each cell: fr. a hard 1–2-seeded drupe. (Ochro-sia: from color of fls.)

O. elliptica, Labill. Glabrous tree to 20 ft.: lvs. obovate-oblong to elliptical, 3–6 in. long, obtuse or short-acuminate, short-petioled, leathery, with many transverse veins: fls. cream-colored, about ½in. long, sessile in dense corymbose cymes: fr. scarlet, usually in pairs, 1–2 in. long, ellipsoid with acuminate apex, with violet-like odor when crushed; seeds with narrow wing-like margins. Australia, New Caledonia, Pacific isls.

12. **TABERNÆMONTANA,** L. A large genus of trees or shrubs widely distributed throughout the tropics and sometimes planted for ornament.—Lvs. opposite: fls. in branching terminal cymes; calyx usually small, with many glands at the base inside, 5-parted to base; corolla salverform, with cylindrical or seldom dilated tube and lobes twisted to the left, without scales at throat; stamens inserted variously on corolla-tube; disk annular, lobed or 0; ovaries 2 with many ovules; style filiform: fr. of 2 follicles or berries, indehiscent or ventrally dehiscent; seeds imbedded in fleshy arils. (Tabernæmonta-na: after J. T. Tabernæmontanus, German physician and botanist, died 1590.)

T. citrifolia, L. Glabrous shrub or small tree 6–30 ft. high: lvs. oblong or obovate-lanceolate, 3–7 in. long, acuminate, attenuate at base into short petiole (*citrus-leaved*, as the name implies): fls. white, ¾–1 in. across, in terminal compound cymes much shorter than lvs., the corolla-lobes about as long as tube: follicles to 2 in. long and ½in. wide. W. Indies.

13. **ERVATAMIA,** Stapf. About 30 species in tropics of Old World, one widely grown in warm regions. Often included in Tabernæmontana, differing in calyx lobed to about middle, and the glands within few. (Ervata-mia: adapted from vernacular name.)

E. coronaria, Stapf (*Tabernæmontana coronaria*, Willd.). CRAPE-JASMINE. CLAVEL DE LA INDIA. Glabrous shrub to 8 ft. or more: lvs. oblong to lanceolate, 3–6 in. long, acuminate, short-petioled, thin, bright green above, paler below: fls. waxy-white with yellowish base, 1½–2 in. across, often double, fragrant; petals crimped on the margin: follicles to 2 in. long, oblong, with recurved beak. India and nat. in the tropics.

14. **ACOKANTHERA,** Don (*Toxicophlæa*, Harvey). Three African shrubs or small trees sometimes planted for ornament in warm countries.—Lvs. opposite, thick and leathery: fls. in nearly sessile axillary cymes; calyx without glands, the sepals nearly free; corolla salverform, with cylindrical tube and lobes overlapping to the left, without scales at throat; stamens inserted near mouth of corolla-tube; disk 0; ovary 2-celled with 1 ovule in each cell; style filiform and stigma minutely 2-lobed: fr. a globose or elliptical berry. (Acokanthe-ra: Greek, referring to the pointed anthers.)

A. Lvs. not more than twice as long as broad..1. *A. venenata*
AA. Lvs. about three times as long as broad..2. *A. spectabilis*

1. **A. venenata,** Don. BUSHMANS-POISON. Shrub or small tree to 14 ft.: lvs. mostly ovate or elliptic, to 4 in. long and 2 in. wide, acute and mucronulate or obtuse, narrowed at base into short thick petiole: fls. white to pink, fragrant, ½–¾in. long: berry globose, purplish-black, 1 in. diam.

2. **A. spectabilis,** Hook. f. (*Toxicophlæa spectabilis*, Dyer). WINTER-SWEET. Very similar to above but the lvs. longer in proportion to their width, from elliptic to oblong-lanceolate and longer-petioled, fls. longer and berries ellipsoid.

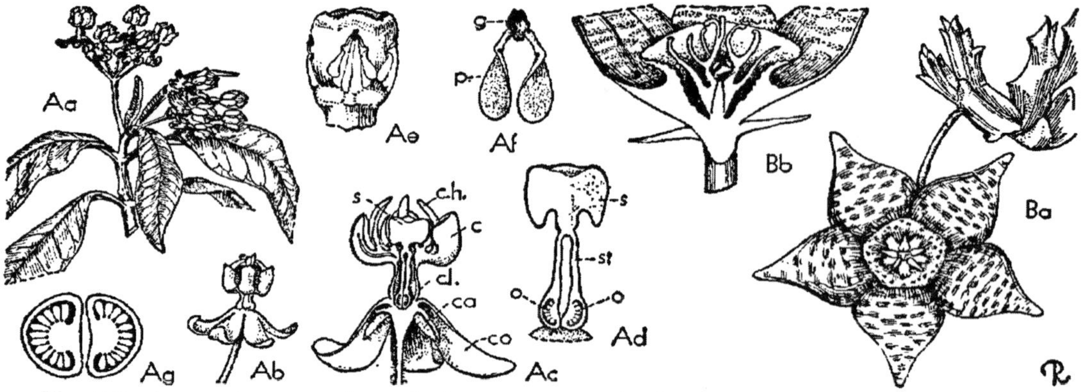

Fig. 170. Asclepiadaceæ. A, *Asclepias curassavica:* Aa, habit in flower, × ½; Ab, flower, × 1; Ac, same, vertical section, × 2; Ad, gynœcium, vertical section, × 4; Ae, stigma and anthers, × 4; Af, anther, × 10; Ag, ovaries, cross-section, × 10. B, *Stapelia variegata:* Ba, branch in flower, × ¼; Bb, flower, vertical section, perianth excised, × ½. (c corona, c.l. corona limb, c.h. corona horn, ca calyx, co corolla, g gland, o ovary, p pollinium, s stigma, st style.) (Ba–Bb redrawn from Pole-Evans.)

170. ASCLEPIADACEÆ. MILKWEED FAMILY

Herbs, vines, or shrubs, mostly with milky juice, of about 220 genera and 2,000 species of wide geographical range, but most abundant in trop. and subtrop. regions. —Lvs. opposite or sometimes verticillate or alternate, simple and mostly entire, exstipulate: fls. bisexual, regular, in terminal or axillary umbels, cymes or racemes; calyx of 5 nearly or completely free sepals; corolla gamopetalous, hypogynous, 5-lobed or -parted, the segms. usually reflexed; corona mostly present, consisting of a 5-lobed or -parted crown arising from the corolla or stamens; stamens 5, inserted usually near base of corolla and alternating with its lobes, the filaments commonly united into a staminal column, anthers adherent to stigma, the pollen coherent into waxy or granular masses (pollinia), 1 or 2 of these masses in each sac, attached in pairs of 4's to stigma either directly or by arm-like processes; disk 0; ovaries 2, superior, each 1-celled and many-ovuled, the short styles united into a usually discoid stigma: fr. of 2 follicles, the seeds usually appendaged by a long tuft of hairs.—The essential differences between this family and Apocynaceæ lie in the morphology of stamens and pollen. In Apocynaceæ the stamens are distinct or only lightly cohering, and the pollen is granular; in Asclepiadaceæ the filaments are united, anthers adherent to stigma, and pollen coherent into pollinia.

A. Plant-body not cactus-like, the sts. not thick and fleshy.
  B. Habit upright.
    C. Fls. yellow, red or purplish, to ½in. across .... 1. Asclepias
    CC. Fls. blue, about 1 in. across .... 5. Oxypetalum
  BB. Habit climbing (at least in ours).
    C. Cymes terminal (in our species); stamens free, the anthers connected at top.
      D. Corolla rotate .... 2. Periploca
      DD. Corolla funnelform .... 3. Cryptostegia
    CC. Cymes axillary (rarely 1-fld.); stamens united into column.
      D. Corolla rotate.
        E. Fls. white to pale pinkish, about ½in. across, in dense cymes: lvs. glabrous .... 4. Hoya
        EE. Fls. blue, about 1 in. across, in loose open cymes: lvs. tomentose .... 5. Oxypetalum
      DD. Corolla salverform or funnelform.
        E. Calyx small; anthers unappendaged .... 6. Ceropegia
        EE. Calyx large and leafy; anthers terminated by an erect or inflexed membrane.
          F. Scales of crown attached to corolla-tube: lvs. (in ours) white and mealy beneath .... 7. Araujia
          FF. Scales of crown attached to back of anthers, free at apex: lvs. green beneath .... 8. Stephanotis
AA. Plant-body thick and cactus-like.
  B. Outer crown of 5 distinct lobes free to base .... 9. Stapelia
  BB. Outer crown cup-shaped, lobes united at least at base .... 10. Caralluma

1. **ASCLEPIAS,** L. MILKWEED. SILKWEED. Per. herbs, of about 150 species mostly native in Afr. and N. and S. Amer., a few planted in wild-gardens or borders and one sometimes under glass.—Juice milky: lvs. opposite or verticillate, rarely alternate: fls. in terminal or axillary umbels; calyx usually small, often glandular within; corolla deeply 5-parted, the segms. strongly reflexed; crown of 5 erect or spreading hoods which are usually horned within; stamens inserted at base of corolla, filaments united into tube inclosing the stigma, anthers with membranaceous appendage at apex, pollen-masses solitary and pendulous in each anther-sac, attached in pairs to a handle or caudicle and attached to a gland which lies in a chink on the side of the stigma; stigma truncate, 5-angled or -lobed: follicles smooth or echinate. (Ascle-pias: ancient Greek name.)

A. Lvs. alternate....................1. *A. tuberosa*
AA. Lvs. opposite or verticillate.
B. Follicles echinate: fls. greenish or purplish-white....................2. *A. syriaca*
BB. Follicles smooth: fls. red- or rose-purple.
C. Corolla and hoods of same color, red-purple....................3. *A. incarnata*
CC. Corolla red-purple, hoods orange....................4. *A. curassavica*

1. **A. tuberosa,** L. BUTTERFLY-WEED. PLEURISY-ROOT. Rough-hairy leafy per. 2–3 ft. high, from long horizontal roots: lvs. alternate, lanceolate or oblong, 2–6 in. long and ¼–1 in. wide, acute or obtuse, sessile or very short-petioled: fls. about ¼in. across, in short-peduncled many-fld. umbels; corolla greenish-orange; hoods narrowly oblong, orange or yellow, slightly longer than the filiform horns: follicles finely pubescent, 4–5 in. long, erect on deflexed pedicels. Me. to Fla. and Ariz.

2. **A. syriaca,** L. (*A. Cornutii*, Decne.). COMMON MILKWEED. To 5 ft.: lvs. oblong to ovate, 4–9 in. long and 2–4½ in. wide, obtuse, petioled, densely pubescent beneath: fls. ¼in. across, in peduncled umbels; corolla greenish or purplish-white; hoods ovate-lanceolate, longer than incurved horns: follicles tomentose and echinate, 3–5 in. long, erect on deflexed pedicels. N. B. to Ga. and Kans.

3. **A. incarnata,** L. SWAMP MILKWEED. To 4 ft., nearly glabrous: lvs. lanceolate or oblong-lanceolate, 3–6 in. long and ½–1½ in. wide, acuminate, short-petioled: fls. ¼in. across, in many-fld. peduncled umbels; corolla red- or rose-purple, rarely white; hoods red-purple, shorter than incurved horns: follicles slightly pubescent, 2–3½ in. long, erect on erect pedicels. N. B. to La. and Colo. Var. **pulchra,** Pers. (*A. pulchra*, Ehrh.), is hairy with broader lvs.

4. **A. curassavica,** L. BLOOD-FLOWER. To 3 ft., glabrous or sts. only minutely pubescent above: lvs. oblong to oblong-lanceolate, 2–6 in. long, mostly acuminate, short-petioled: fls. about ¼in. across, in terminal or axillary umbels; corolla red-purple; hoods ovate, orange, shorter than the broad curved horns: follicles glabrous or minutely pubescent, 1½–4 in. long, erect on erect pedicels. (Named for the Dutch island of Curacao.) Trop. Amer.; nat. in S. U. S.

2. **PERIPLOCA,** L. SILK-VINE. About 12 species of woody twiners native in S. Eu., Asia, and trop. Afr., planted for ornament and hardy in the N.—Juice milky: lvs. opposite, entire: fls. in terminal or axillary cymes; calyx glandular within; corolla rotate; crown adnate to base of corolla, 5- or 10-lobed; stamens with very short free filaments, the anthers connected at apex and villous on back: follicles cylindrical, glabrous. (Perip-loca: Greek *around* and *twine*, referring to twining habit.)

P. græca, L. Deciduous twining glabrous shrub to 40 ft.: lvs. ovate to oblong-lanceolate, 2–5 in. long, acuminate, petioled, dark green and shining above, paler beneath: fls. 1 in. across, brownish-purple inside and greenish outside, in long-peduncled terminal cymes; corolla-lobes oblong, spreading, villous; crown with 5 slender thread-like appendages: follicles to 5 in. long, acuminate. S. Eu., W. Asia.

3. **CRYPTOSTEGIA,** R. Br. RUBBER-VINE. Climbing shrubs of probably 3 species in trop. Afr. and Madagascar, sometimes planted for ornament.—Juice milky, often furnishing caoutchouc: lvs. opposite: fls. large, in terminal trichotomous cymes; calyx large, with many glands at base; corolla funnelform, with short tube and campanulate limb; crown of 5 entire or 2-parted scales attached to corolla; stamens with short free filaments and sharply appendaged anthers connate around stigma: follicles angled or winged. (Cryptoste-gia: Greek for *conceal* and *cover*, referring to the crown.)

A. Scales of crown deeply divided: calyx ½in. long....................1. *C. grandiflora*
AA. Scales of crown entire: calyx about ¼in. long....................2. *C. madagascariensis*

1. **C. grandiflora,** R. Br. Woody strong-growing vine: lvs. oblong, 3–4 in. long and 1½–2 in. wide, glabrous and shining: fls. lilac-purple, 2–3 in. across; calyx leafy, ½in. long; scales of crown deeply bifurcate into filiform segms.: follicles to 4 in. long, sharply angled. Afr.; cult. in India.

2. **C. madagascariensis,** Bojer. Often confused with *C. grandiflora*, but differs in the reddish-purple fls. with smaller calyx about ¼in. long and scales of crown not divided. Madagascar.

4. **HOYA,** R. Br. Nearly 100 species of climbing shrubs native from E. Asia to Australia, one grown as a greenhouse or window-garden subject.—Lvs. opposite, thick: fls. large, in sessile or pedunculate axillary cymes; calyx small, glandular at base within; corolla rotate, fleshy, deeply 5-lobed, the lobes spreading or reflexed; crown of 5 fleshy scales affixed to corolla-tube and spreading into a horizontal star; stamens with filaments united into short tube and anthers connivent above stigma, terminated by an erect or inflexed membrane: follicles glabrous, acuminate. (Hoy-a: for Thomas Hoy, once gardener to the Duke of Northumberland, end of 18th century.)

H. carnosa, R. Br. Wax-Plant. Twining or climbing by means of roots to 8 ft. and more, glabrous: lvs. ovate-oblong, 2–4 in. long, acute, short-petioled, thick and fleshy: fls. white with pink center, about ½in. across, fragrant. China, Australia.

5. **OXYPETALUM,** R. Br. Per. herbs or suffrutescent subshrubs, of about 125 species native trop. and subtrop. Amer. from Panama to Buenos Aires, one subshrubby species treated as an ann. and of promise as a commercial fl.—Plants erect, decumbent, clambering or twining; juice milky: lvs. opposite: fls. in axillary and terminal open cymes; calyx 5-parted, lobes lanceolate, acute; corolla deeply lobed with very short campanulate tube and spreading lanceolate to ligulate lobes; scales of corona 5, adnate to base of corolla and staminal tube; stamens 5, pollinia pendulous in each anther-sac, attached by slender and horned connectives to a gland or caudicle that lies within a membranous envelope or fold in a depression on the side of the stigma, filaments united into a tube surrounding the 2 distinct styles; styles united by a single narrowly conical stigma: follicles usually fusiform or ovoid, smooth or briefly echinate; seeds comose. (Oxypet-alum: Greek *sharp* and *petal*, referring to the acute petals of some species.)

O. cæruleum, Decne. (*Tweedia cærulea*, Don). Tender suffrutescent weakly twining per. 3 ft. or more high; sts. woody at base, white-pubescent: lvs. oblong-lanceolate, mucronulate, cordate-hastate at base, densely and minutely tomentose, veins whitish and raised beneath: corolla 1 in. across, fleshy, rotate, pale blue tinged lavender beneath, pinkish in bud and purplish when faded, lobes ligulate, obtuse, tomentose beneath; crown of 5 erect scales about ⅙in. high, fleshy, strongly recurved, darker blue than corolla. Brazil, Uruguay.—Blossoms first season from early sown seed and may be treated as an ann.

6. **CEROPEGIA,** L. Upright or twining herbs or subshrubs, of more than 160 species in trop. Asia, Afr., and Malaya, one grown as a greenhouse vine.—Lvs. opposite or rarely lacking: fls. in axillary cymes (rarely 1-fld.); calyx small, glandular; corolla tubular, often inflated at base, the lobes free, erect or reflexed, or sometimes variously united at tips; crown attached to the staminal tube, double; stamens with filaments united into short column, the anthers unappendaged; stigma truncate or shortly conical: follicles lanceolate. (Cerope-gia: Greek for *wax* and *fountain*, the fls. having a waxy appearance.)

C. Woodii, Schlecht. Sts. glabrous, slender, prostrate or trailing, often bearing small tubers and rooting at nodes: lvs. fleshy, broadly ovate or orbicular, ¼–⅔in. long, acute or obtuse, cordate at base, glabrous, dark green with whitish veins: fls. ½–¾in. long, usually 2 together on long peduncles; corolla-tube slightly curved and inflated at base, pink or light purple; lobes connate at tips, dark purple, ciliate: follicles glabrous, 2–3 in. long. (Bears the name of J. M. Wood, who collected the plant in 1881.) Natal.

7. **ARAUJIA,** Brot. (*Physianthus*, Mart.). Probably about 5 glabrous or mealy climbing shrubs native in Brazil and Argentina, one grown out-of-doors in warm regions or under glass.—Lvs. opposite: fls. in few-fld. peduncled axillary cymes;

calyx large and leafy, without glands; corolla salverform or campanulate, the tube inflated at base; crown attached to corolla-tube, of 5 ovate or ligulate scales appressed to the staminal tube; stamens with filaments united in short tube, the anthers terminated by a small inflexed membrane; stigma umbonate: follicles leathery, sometimes inflated. (Arau-jia: native S. American name.)

A. sericofera, Brot. (*Physianthus albens,* Mart.). Lvs. oblong, 2–4 in. long, acuminate, wide and square at base, petioled, dark green above and pale and mealy beneath: fls. white or pale pink, ¾–1 in. across, not fragrant. S. Brazil.

8. **STEPHANOTIS,** Thouars. Climbing glabrous shrubs of about 16 species native in Madagascar and Malaya, one a popular greenhouse vine and also grown out-of-doors in warm countries.—Lvs. opposite, leathery: fls. large, in short-peduncled axillary cymes; calyx large and leafy, without glands; corolla funnelform or salverform, the tube enlarged at base; crown of 5 scales adnate to anthers on back, free at apex; stamens united into a very short tube, the anthers terminated by an erect or inflexed membrane; stigma conical or shortly beaked: follicles thick, obtuse or acuminate. (Stephano-tis: Greek for *crown* and *ear,* alluding to the 5 ear-like appendages of the crown.)

S. floribunda, Brongn. Madagascar-Jasmine. Twining to 15 ft.: lvs. elliptic, 2–4 in. long, with short abrupt point, petioled, thick and shining: fls. white and waxy, fragrant, 1–2 in. long: follicles fleshy, 3–4 in. long. Madagascar.

9. **STAPELIA,** L. Carrion-Flower. Probably about 85 species of African fleshy cactus-like leafless herbs, a number grown in collections of succulents.—Sts. thick and fleshy, coarsely 4-angled, the angles usually toothed and rarely bearing small lvs.: fls. often large, pedicellate, borne 1 to several together along the sts., usually fetid and barred and mottled with dark or dull colors; corolla rotate or broadly campanulate; crown double, arising from staminal column, the outer usually of 5 entire or divided free lobes, the inner of 5 lobes adnate to base of anthers; stamens with filaments united into very short tube, the unappendaged anthers inflexed on top of style: follicles spindle-shaped, smooth. (Stape-lia: for J. B. Van Stapel, Dutch physician, died 1636.)

A. Fls. 11–16 in. across: plant pubescent. . . . . 1. *S. gigantea*
AA. Fls. 2–3 in. across: plant glabrous. . . . . 2. *S. variegata*

1. **S. gigantea,** N. E. Br. Pubescent, sts. erect from a decumbent base, 4–8 in. long and to 1¼ in. across, angles compressed: fls. buff with transverse lines of brown and covered with purple hairs, 11–16 in. across, borne 1–2 together at base or middle of sts.; corolla-lobes 4–6 in. long, spreading or recurved; inner lobes of crown 1-horned: follicles 5–6½ in. long, pubescent. Trop. and S. Afr.

2. **S. variegata,** L. Glabrous, sts. erect from a decumbent base, 2–6 in. long and to ½ in. across, very obtusely 4-angled, often mottled all over or tinted with purple at the tips: fls. pale greenish-yellow with dark purple-brown spots, 2–3 in. across, borne 1–5 together at base of young sts.; annulus or ring around the crown very prominent; inner lobes of crown distinctly 2-horned; inner surface of corolla rugose. S. Afr.—**S. hirsuta,** L., has softly puberulous green sts. 5–8 (12) in. high and fls. 4–5 in. across, the lobes basally cream-colored with distal half dark purplish-brown and banded with transverse yellow or whitish lines; S. Afr.

10. **CARALLUMA,** R. Br. More than 100 species of succulent leafless herbs native in Afr. and from Spain to India.—Sts. thick and fleshy, 4–6-angled, the angles with or without teeth: fls. usually in clusters; corolla with 5 spreading or ascending lobes and mostly with distinct tube; crown double, the outer cup-shaped with lobes united at least at base, the 5 inner lobes often adnate to the outer crown; stamens with filaments united into tube adnate to the style, anthers free. (Carallu-ma: adapted from aboriginal Indian name.)

C. lutea, N. E. Br. Sts. to 4 in. long and ¾ in. thick, with 4 sharp-toothed angles, glabrous, mottled with purple: fls. in clusters at middle or lower part of st., 1½–2½ in. across, yellow, glabrous outside, rugose within; corolla-tube short, lobes to 1¼ in. long, attenuate, ciliate with purple hairs; outer crown cup-shaped, margins recurved: follicles about 3½ in. long. S. Afr.

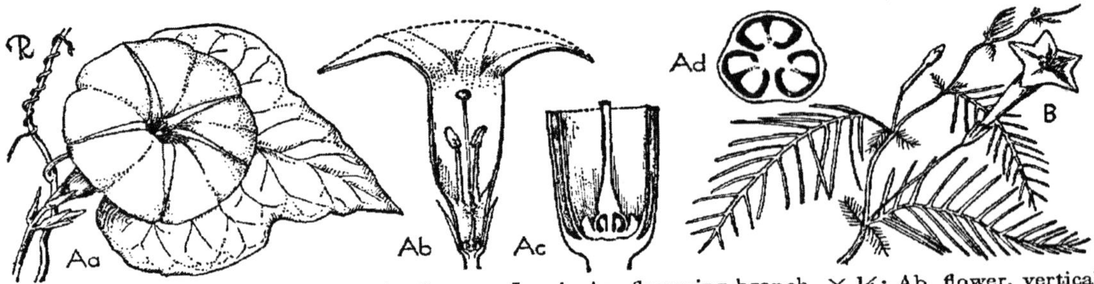

Fig. 171. CONVOLVULACEÆ. A, *Ipomœa Leari:* Aa, flowering branch, × ¼; Ab, flower, vertical section, × ½; Ac, ovary, vertical section, × 4; Ad, ovary, cross-section, × 20. B, *Quamoclit pennata:* flowering branch, × ½.

171. CONVOLVULACEÆ. MORNING-GLORY FAMILY

As known to cultivators, mostly twining ann. and per. herbs, but the family comprises many erect herbs as well as shrubs and even trees; the species are probably 1,000, widely spread around the world, particularly in the tropics, in 40–50 genera.—Juice sometimes milky: lvs. alternate, exstipulate, simple or rarely compound, in certain parasitic kinds (the Cuscutas, sometimes placed in a separate family) reduced to scales: fls. regular and usually bisexual, gamopetalous; calyx 5-parted and persistent; corolla mostly funnelform with a flaring limb which is often angled or lobed, usually convolute or twisted in the bud; stamens 5, inserted deep in the tube, alternating with the lobes; ovary superior, 2-celled for the most part and prevailingly with 2 ovules in each cell; styles 1, 2, or 3: fr. mostly capsular, sometimes baccate, often separating into 2–4 carpels.

A. Fls. large, solitary or in clusters.
  B. Corolla funnelform or campanulate; stamens and style not exserted beyond throat.
    C. Stigmas 2, oblong or linear....................1. CONVOLVULUS
    CC. Stigmas 1–2, globose.
      D. Foliage not silky although perhaps pubescent: fr. a dehiscent caps.......2. IPOMŒA
      DD. Foliage silky-pubescent: fr. indehiscent....................3. ARGYREIA
  BB. Corolla salverform; stamens and style conspicuously exserted beyond throat.
    C. Color of fls. white or purple: night-bloomers....................4. CALONYCTION
    CC. Color of fls. red or yellow: fls. opening by day....................5. QUAMOCLIT
AA. Fls. small, ⅓in. or less across, in racemes or panicles....................6. PORANA

1. **CONVOLVULUS,** L. BINDWEED. Annuals or perennials grown mostly in the open for their showy fls. or some for their trailing or twining habit; about 200 species, widely distributed in temp. and trop. regions.—Herbs or sometimes suffruticose, mostly silky-pubescent, twining, trailing, erect, or ascending: lvs. petiolate, entire or seldom lobed or cleft, usually cordate or sagittate: fls. solitary or loosely cymose, mostly opening only in early morning; corolla campanulate or funnelform, the limb plicate, 5-angled or rarely 5-lobed; stamens inserted near the base of the corolla, included, equal or unequal, the filaments often dilated at base; ovary 2-celled, with 4 ovules; stigmas 2, oblong or linear: caps. globose, opening by 4 valves or bursting irregularly; seeds glabrous. (Convol-vulus: Latin *to entwine.*)

A. Plant a shrub: fls. terminal....................1. *C. Cneorum*
AA. Plant an herb: fls. axillary.
  B. Calyx with 2 large membranaceous bracts at base; peduncles usually 1-fld.
    C. Lvs. lanceolate, hastate....................2. *C. japonicus*
    CC. Lvs. round-cordate to deltoid-hastate....................3. *C. sepium*
  BB. Calyx without bracts; peduncles 1–6-fld.
    C. Lvs. round-ovate: st. white-villous....................4. *C. mauritanicus*
    CC. Lvs. linear-oblong or subspatulate: st. brownish-hairy....................5. *C. tricolor*

1. **C. Cneorum,** L. Evergreen shrub 2–4 ft. high: lvs. oblanceolate, to 2½ in. long and ½in. wide, acute or obtuse, tapering at base, densely covered with silvery silky pubescence: fls. in terminal clusters, white tinged with pink and with yellow throat, about 1¼in. long and 1½–2 in. across, blooming throughout the summer; calyx densely hairy. S. Eu.

2. **C. japonicus,** Thunb. (*Calystegia pubescens,* Lindl.). CALIFORNIA-ROSE. Herbaceous per. twiner of vigorous growth, often 20 ft. long, more or less densely and minutely pubescent throughout: lvs. hastate, lanceolate, 2–4 in. long, obtuse or broadly acute, with

angular or rounded lobes at base or occasionally without lobes, rarely sharp lanceolate: fl.-stalks 1-fld.; fls. bright pink, 1–2 in. broad, produced freely during the summer months, remaining open for several days; calyx with 2 bracts at base. Japan and E. Asia.—A completely sterile double form with narrow wavy petals irregularly arranged is now nat. from S. E. N. Y. to D. C. and Mo.

3. **C. sepium,** L. (*Calystegia sepium*, R. Br.). RUTLAND BEAUTY. Per. trailer 3–10 ft. long, glabrous or minutely pubescent: lvs. round-cordate to deltoid-hastate, 2–5 in. long, the basal lobes divaricate, entire or angulate: peduncle 1-fld., exceeding the petioles; fls. white, rose or pink, with white stripes, 2 in. long and across; calyx with 2 bracts at base. A very variable species cosmopolitan in temp. regions.

4. **C. mauritanicus,** Boiss. Herb with strong per. roots, sts. slender, prostrate, rarely branched: herbage more or less villous with white hairs; lvs. round-ovate, ½–1½ in. long, obtuse, short-petioled: peduncle 1–6-fld.; fls. blue to violet-purple, with a lighter throat, ½–1 in. across, freely produced throughout the summer; calyx without bracts. N. Afr.

5. **C. tricolor,** L. (*C. minor*, Hort.). DWARF MORNING-GLORY. Ann. often branching from base and covering a ground space 2 ft. across, sts. trailing, ascending, 6–12 in., angulate, brownish-villous: lvs. narrow-oblong or subspatulate, obtuse or rounded at apex, pubescent or sometimes glabrous, ciliate toward base: peduncles 3-fld., usually exceeding the lvs.; calyx without bracts, the sepals ovate, acute, villous; corolla about 1½ in. across, with azure-blue limb and yellow throat margined with white; blooming continuously throughout the summer, the fls. remaining open all day during pleasant weather. S. Eu.—There are vars. with variously striped or spotted fls. and one with white blossoms.

2. **IPOMŒA,** L. IPOMEA. MORNING-GLORY. A genus of various habit but fairly distinct in technical characters of fls. and fr., of 400 or more species as it is here understood, native in many parts of the world and mostly in trop. countries, many of the climbing kinds grown for the very showy fls. and one for its edible tuberous roots; some kinds yield medicinal roots.—Ann. and per. herbaceous twiners, erect herbs, and even shrubs and trees: juice sometimes milky: lvs. alternate, entire, lobed, palmate or pinnate: fls. solitary in the axils or in clusters, in the cult. species large and brilliantly colored; calyx deeply lobed or parted, outer lobes often larger, without bracts; corolla mostly funnelform to bell-shaped, the limb with 5 points or angles; stamens 5, included; ovary 2–4-celled; stigma capitate, sometimes indented or slightly 2-lobed: fr. a dehiscent globose or ovoid caps.; seeds glabrous or bearded. (Ipomœ-a: Greek combination, *worm-bindweed*, of no particular significance.)

A. Plant with glabrous sts.
B. Sts. long-trailing and rooting: grown for the edible tuberous roots........... 1. *I. Batatas*
BB. Sts. twining, not rooting: grown for ornament.
C. Lvs. entire or sometimes fiddle-shaped.
D. Limb of corolla blue changing to purplish-red........................ 2. *I. tricolor*
DD. Limb of corolla white.. 3. *I. pandurata*
CC. Lvs. digitately 5–7-lobed or -parted.
D. Fls. yellow.. 4. *I. tuberosa*
DD. Fls. pink or purple.
E. Lf. not lobed to base.. 5. *I. paniculata*
EE. Lf. parted to base.
F. Lfts. broad, mostly not exceeding 2 in. long, retuse or apiculate..... 6. *I. cairica*
FF. Lfts. rather narrow, 3 in. or more long, sharp-acuminate............ 7. *I. Horsfalliæ*
AA. Plant with villous or pubescent sts.
B. Calyx glabrous.
C. Lvs. digitately 5–7-parted.. 8. *I. dissecta*
CC. Lvs. deeply 3-lobed.. 9. *I. setosa*
BB. Calyx villous.
C. Lvs. glabrous beneath.. 10. *I. melanotricha*
CC. Lvs. pubescent or villous beneath.
D. Sepals acute, about ½in. long.. 11. *I. purpurea*
DD. Sepals long-acuminate, ¾–1 in. long.
E. Fls. 1–1½ in. long; tips of sepals spreading or recurved............. 12. *I. hederacea*
EE. Fls. 1½–3½ in. long; tips of sepals erect.
F. Under surface of lf. not silvery-pubescent.
G. Peduncles bearing 1–3 fls.. 13. *I. Nil*
GG. Peduncles bearing 5 or more fls..................................... 14. *I. Leari*
FF. Under surface of lvs. silvery-pubescent.............................. 15. *I. mutabilis*

1. **I. Batatas,** Lam. (*Convolvulus Batatas*, L.). SWEET-POTATO. Long-trailing per. from deep tuberous roots, the sts. mostly glabrous, rooting, juice milky: lvs. various even on the same plant, mostly ovate to orbicular-ovate in outline, 2–6 in. long, cordate or truncate at base, entire or angled and notched, or digitately lobed: fls. few or several on stout axillary peduncles, funnelform, 1½–2 in. long, rose-violet or blush with a darker center; sepals about ½in. long, cuspidate and sometimes ciliate: seeds angular, glabrous. (Batatas

or batata is the aboriginal American word from which "potato" is derived.) Cultigen; world tropics, where it flowers abundantly and often fruits, and cult. in temp. regions; it sometimes blooms in the S. U. S.

2. **I. tricolor,** Cav. (*I. rubro-cærulea,* Hook.). Tall glabrous twiner, probably per., the st. tinged purple: lvs. rather thin and showing prominent veins, broadly cordate-ovate, 3–5 in. long and often broader than long, entire, acuminate, glabrous both surfaces: fls. few to several on thick pedicels and peduncles, about 2 in. long and 3–4 in. across, blue fading to purplish-red with white tube, the limb red before opening; sepals ¼in. long, hyaline-edged, blunt: seeds glabrous. Trop. Amer.—Showy in cult., running into cultivars, the fls. sometimes dashed and blotched with white; Heavenly Blue morning-glory belongs here.

3. **I. pandurata,** G. F. W. Mey. (*Convolvulus panduratus,* L.). Wild Sweet-Potato Vine. Sts. glabrous, trailing or somewhat climbing from a great tuberous persistent root: lvs. broad-ovate, 2–6 in. long, cordate, acuminate, entire or sometimes pandurate (fiddle-shaped) or angled, glabrous both surfaces: fls. 1–5 on elongating peduncles, 2–3 in. long and 2–4 in. across, white with dark purple throat; sepals about ½in. long, obtuse or acute: seeds woolly. Conn. to Fla. and Tex.

4. **I. tuberosa,** L. (*Operculina tuberosa,* Meissn.). Glabrous per. vine: lvs. 3–8 in. across, digitately parted nearly to base into 5–7 elliptic-lanceolate acuminate entire lobes: fls. 1 to several on stout peduncles, yellow, 2 in. long; sepals about 1 in. long, ovate, obtuse, enlarging in fr.: seeds angular, glabrous. Tropics.—Sometimes known as Wooden-Rose.

5. **I. paniculata,** R. Br. (*Convolvulus paniculatus,* L. *I. digitata,* L.). Stout long-twining or -trailing glabrous per.: lvs. orbicular or reniform in outline, 3–7 in. across, deeply digitately 5–7-parted, sometimes more or less pedate, the sinuses narrow but often somewhat rounded at bottom, lobes narrow and nearly or quite entire and pinnate-veined from the rib: fls. 2 to several, short-pedicelled on a mostly long peduncle; corolla with a rather narrow tube, limb 2–3 in. across, lilac or pinkish; sepals about ⅓in. long, broad and rounded: seeds woolly. Tropics of both hemispheres.

6. **I. cairica,** Sweet (*Convolvulus cairicus,* L.). Slender glabrous per. twiner, the sts. more or less warty: lvs. 5-palmate, about as broad as long, usually 2–3 in. across; lfts. elliptic to broad-ovate, abruptly tapering to base, retuse or apiculate at apex, margins entire, pinnate-veined: fls. 1 to few, pedicelled, on very short peduncles, about 2–2½ in. long, rose-lilac, slightly 5-lobed, with prominent plaits; sepals ¼–⅓in. long, broad and very obtuse: seeds with silky hairs. (Cairica: presumably refers to Cairo, as the plant was early accredited to Egypt.) Tropics, and sometimes running wild in subtrop. regions.

7. **I. Horsfalliæ,** Hook. More or less woody per. tall glabrous twiner: lvs. of a more or less circular or orbicular-ovate outline, palmate, with 5 or 7 lfts. that are obovate to oblanceolate to elliptic, 3–4 in. long, acuminate, entire, rather thick in texture: fls. many in a forking cluster, pedicelled; corolla narrow-funnelform, 2–2½ in. long, shining rose or light purple, the limb with prominent plaits and becoming revolute, the stamens short-exserted; sepals reddish, nearly ½in. long, very broad: seeds with long hairs. (Dedicated to Mrs. Charles Horsfall, at whose place it was first raised in England.) American tropics, and perhaps Old-World tropics.

8. **I. dissecta,** Pursh (*Convolvulus dissectus,* Jacq. *Operculina dissecta,* House). Tall per. twiner, usually long-villous on sts. and petioles: lvs. digitately 5–7-parted, 2–4 in. across and about the same length, the parts lobed and coarsely toothed and acuminate: fls. 1 or 2 on long axillary peduncles, open-funnelform, 1½–2 in. across, nearly white with reddish center; calyx glabrous, 1 in. or less long, enlarging and containing the big-seeded caps.: seeds glabrous. Tropics; Ga. and Fla to Tex.—Sometimes called Alamo-Vine.

9. **I. setosa,** Ker. Brazilian Morning-Glory. Very vigorous per. twiner, known by the stiff purplish hairs of sts., petioles and peduncles: lvs. orbicular-ovate in outline and large, 5–10 in. across, vitis-like, deeply cordate, angular or 3-lobed, the middle lobe narrowed at base, margins strongly sinuate-toothed, points all attenuate: fls. 3–9 on fleshy pedicels and peduncles, somewhat salverform, 2–3 in. long, rose-purple; sepals oblong and obtuse, about ½in. long: seeds hairy, angular. Brazil; nat. Fla. to La.

10. **I. melanotricha,** Brandegee. Vigorous long twiner with blackish retrorsely hirsute sts.: lvs. orbicular-cordate, about 5 in. across, glabrous, deeply 5–7-lobed into acuminate entire lobes, the sinuses broad and rounded: fls. purple, 3–4 in. long and broad, pedicels and peduncles hirsute; sepals oblong and obtuse, ¾in. long, densely hirsute. Mex.

11. **I. purpurea,** Lam. (*Convolvulus purpureus,* L. *C. major,* Hort. *Pharbitis purpurea,* Voigt). Common Morning-Glory. Tall twining ann., with hairy sts.: lvs. broadly cordate-ovate, 3–5 in. long, entire, short-pointed, pubescent: fls. 1–5 on axillary peduncles, the pedicels evident, funnelform, 2–3 in. long, purplish and related colors, with lighter tube; calyx-lobes less than half length of tube, about ½in. long, acute but not elongated, not spreading, somewhat exceeding caps. in fr.: seeds glabrous. Trop. Amer., and somewhat spontaneous in our territory.—Runs into many races in cult., varying in color of fls., with color-marked foliage, and sometimes with double fls.

12. **I. hederacea,** Jacq. (*Convolvulus hederaceus*, L. *Pharbitis hederacea*, Choisy). Slender twining hairy ann.: lvs. cordate-ovate in outline, rather small, 2–3½ in. long, sometimes entire but prevailingly 3-lobed to the middle or beyond (the larger basal lobes sometimes again lobed), the sinuses narrow but broadened and rounded at the bottom: fls. 1–3 and practically sessile on short axillary peduncles, rather small (usually under 2 in. long), funnelform, limb blue or light purple, tube lighter; sepals hairy at base, contracted into a linear projection, spreading or recurving, half or more length of corolla-tube (about ¾in. long), much exceeding the caps. in fr.: seeds glabrous. Trop. Amer., and run wild in N. Amer.

13. **I. Nil,** Roth (*Convolvulus Nil*, L. *Pharbitis Nil*, Choisy). Often referred to *I. hederacea*, but a stronger and much more showy plant: lvs. larger, commonly shallowly 3-lobed with broad open sinuses (lobes not constricted at base), the apices acuminate: fls. much larger, pedicelled; sepals gradually narrowed, 1 in. or more long, erect or little spreading, nor recurved, in fr. much exceeding the caps. (Nil is an Arabic name of the plant.) Old World tropics; also in the western hemisphere, perhaps intro.—A showy species, with fls. violet, purple, rose, blue, and in many rich markings; some forms have fringed, frilled, fluted, and double fls.; lvs. sometimes spotted and variegated; there are many named hort. forms, as Scarlett O'Hara. The Imperial Japanese morning-glories (*I. imperialis*, Hort.), often highly developed, belong here. Var. **limbata,** Bailey (*I. limbata*, Hort.), has violet-purple corollas margined white.

14. **I. Leari,** Paxt. (*Pharbitis Leari*, Hook.). Blue Dawn-Flower. Rapid and tall per. twiner, sometimes woody at base, the sts. finely pubescent: lvs. broad-ovate, 3–8 in. long, acuminate, base cordate or subcordate, entire or sometimes 3-lobed with acute or angular not rounded sinuses, glabrous above, finely pubescent beneath: fls. in capitate clusters of 5 (rarely 3) to many, 3–5 in. broad, bright blue with lighter ribs and plaits but turning rose with age, the tube white below; sepals lance-linear, hairy-pubescent, about 1 in. long: seeds glabrous. (Bears the name of Mr. Lear, collector in Ceylon, from whom seeds were supposed to have been received in England, but the plant is not known in the Old World and the seeds probably came from Amer.) Trop. and subtrop. Amer.—A handsome and prolific species.

15. **I. mutabilis,** Lindl. (*Pharbitis mutabilis*, Bojer). Distinguished by its soft grayish-canescent under face of the foliage, the sts. also densely and softly pubescent, tall-twining and rapid-growing from a per. woody root: lvs. orbicular-ovate, 4–6 in. long, cordate at base, acuminate, entire or angled or 3-lobed: fls. mostly several in a rather close cluster, 2–3½ in. long, blue or purplish with a white tube; sepals lance-linear, hairy-pubescent, about ¾in. long: seeds glabrous. Trop. Amer.

3. **ARGYREIA,** Lour. Twining shrubs of 25–30 species in Asia and Afr., grown for ornament in warm regions.—Lvs. simple, silky-pubescent: fls. showy, purple or rose, in sessile or peduncled cymes; sepals 5, leathery; corolla funnelform, the limb plicate and short-lobed; stamens 5, included; ovary 4-celled, with 4 ovules; stigmas 2, globose: fr. indehiscent, a berry or nearly dry; seeds embedded in mealy pulp. (Argyre-ia: *silvery*, referring to under sides of lvs.)

A. speciosa, Sweet. Woolly Morning-Glory. Large climber with white-tomentose sts.: lvs. ovate-cordate, 3–12 in. across, glabrous above, densely white-silky-tomentose beneath, on white-tomentose pedicels 2–6 in. long: fls. rose-purple, 2–3 in. long, in cymes on white-tomentose peduncles 3–6 in. long; calyx ¾in. long, white-tomentose; corolla glabrous inside, pubescent outside: fr. globose, ¾in. across. India, Java, China.

4. **CALONYCTION,** Choisy. Moonflower. Twining per. herbs widely cult. for their large night-blooming fls.; 3 or 4 species in trop. Amer.—Lvs. simple, broad, cordate, subreniform, or hastate: fls. white or purple, large and showy, fragrant; sepals 5, the outer ones with horn-like tips; corolla salverform, the limb broad and more or less flat, the tube very long and slender and not dilated at the throat; stamens 5, exserted; style exserted, with capitate obscurely 2-lobed stigma: fr. a dehiscent caps.; seeds glabrous. (Calonyc-tion: Greek, referring to the beauty of the fls. and their night-blooming habit.)

A. Fls. white, sometimes with greenish plaits. . . . . 1. *C. aculeatum*
AA. Fls. purple. . . . . 2. *C. muricatum*

1. **C. aculeatum,** House (*C. speciosum*, Choisy. *Convolvulus aculeatus*, L. *Ipomœa Bona-Nox*, L. *I. noctiflora*, Griff. *I. grandiflora*, Roxb. and Hort.). Glabrous or nearly so, with milky juice, sts. 10–20 ft. long: lvs. cordate to subreniform or hastate, 3–8 in. long, angular or 3-lobed, acute, long-petioled: peduncles 2–6 in. long, 1–7-fld.; fls. fragrant, usually closing in the morning, sometimes remaining open till noon; sepals about ½in. long, the outer with subulate appendages; corolla white, sometimes with greenish plaits,

the tube 3–6 in. long, the limb 3–6 in. wide: caps. ovoid, ¾in. long. Tropics, running wild in S. Fla.—Most of the large-fld. and very fragrant kinds in cult. may be referred here.

2. **C. muricatum,** Don (*Convolvulus muricatus,* L. *Calonyction speciosum* var. *muricatum,* Choisy). Fls. purple, smaller than in the preceding, the tube very slender, the expanded portion not over 3 in. broad. Trop. regions.

5. **QUAMOCLIT,** Moench. Twining vines grown for their attractive foliage as well as for the profusion of small bright fls.; about 10 species in the tropics.—Ann. or in trop. regions per.: lvs. simple or more or less lobed or divided: fls. red or yellow, in long-stalked axillary clusters; sepals 5, equal or nearly so, often very abruptly tipped with long awl-like points; corolla small or medium-sized, the tube somewhat widened above, often slightly contracted below the spreading or cup-shaped limb; stamens exserted and often declined; style exserted, with capitate stigma: fr. a caps. with false partitions between the seeds. (Quam-oclit: Greek *a dwarf kidney bean.*)

A. Sepals without awn-like tips: lvs. regularly pinnately divided into nearly thread-like parts .... 1. *Q. pennata*
AA. Sepals (at least outer ones) with awn-like tips: lvs. entire or variously lobed.
B. Corolla salverform or somewhat funnelform, with a broadly expanding limb.
C. Lvs. deeply parted into 7 or more narrow divisions .... 2. *Q. Sloteri*
CC. Lvs. entire, angled, or sometimes broadly 3-lobed .... 3. *Q. coccinea*
BB. Corolla curved and with small scarcely spreading lobes; stamens long-exserted .... 4. *Q. lobata*

1. **Q. pennata,** Bojer (*Ipomœa Quamoclit,* L. *Convolvulus pennatus,* Desr. *Q. vulgaris.* Choisy. *Q. Quamoclit,* Britt.). CYPRESS-VINE. Glabrous slender ann. 10–20 ft. high: lvs. short-petioled or sessile, 2–7 in. long, pinnately divided into long almost filiform segms.: peduncles few-fld., commonly much longer than the lvs.; pedicels thickened; sepals appressed to the corolla-tube, obtuse or slightly mucronate, not long-pointed; corolla 1–1½ in. long, scarlet, the narrowly funnelform tube inflated above, the limb nearly flat, shortly 5-lobed; July–Oct. Nat. from trop. Amer., Va. to Fla., west to Kans. and Tex.; sparingly escaped from cult. farther north.—There is a white-fld. var.

2. **Q. Sloteri,** Nieuwl. (*Ipomœa Sloteri,* House. *I. cardinalis,* Hort.). CARDINAL-CLIMBER. Hybrid of *Q. pennata* and *Q. coccinea:* free-flowering ann. glabrous tall twiner: lvs. broadly deltoid-ovate, 2–4½ in. across, lobed nearly to base and in a semi-palmate way into 7–15 long-acuminate segms. ⅛–½in. broad: fls. salverform, crimson or cardinal. with white eye, 1½–2 in. long; outer and sometimes the inner calyx-lobes short-awned. Originated by Logan Sloter, Ohio; intro. by Dreer in 1912.

3. **Q. coccinea,** Moench (*Ipomœa coccinea,* L.). STAR IPOMŒA. Glabrous ann., sts. freely twining for 10 ft., branching: lvs. slender-petioled, ovate, 2–6 in. long, entire, dentate, or angular, cordate, acute or acuminate: peduncles about equalling the lvs. or longer, 2- to several-fld.; sepals appressed to the corolla-tube, terminating in a long awn-like point; corolla salverform, the tube ¾–1½ in. long, the cup-like limb ½–⅔ in. broad, obscurely lobed, scarlet with yellow throat; Aug.–Oct. Trop. Amer; nat. in N. Amer. Var. **hederifolia,** House (*Mina sanguinea,* Hort.), has 3-lobed or 3–5-parted lvs. and usually larger fls.

4. **Q. lobata,** House (*Q. Mina,* Don. *Ipomœa versicolor,* Meissn. *Mina lobata,* Llave & Lex.). Per. climber 15–20 ft. high: lvs. 2–3 in. across, cordate with a broad sinus, 3-lobed, the lobes acuminate, the middle one narrowed below: infl. somewhat secund; peduncles stout below, dichotomously several-fld.; sepals tipped with short awn-like points; corolla rich crimson, soon fading to pale yellow, short and tubular below, abruptly widening into a cylindric or bag-shaped limb about ¾in. long with 5 small acute lobes; stamens well-exserted; July–Sept. Mex.

6. **PORANA,** Burm. About 15 species of climbing herbs in Old World tropics and N. Australia, one intro. in trop. Amer. and planted in Fla. and perhaps other parts.—Lvs. usually cordate-ovate, entire, alternate, stalked: fls. small, white, blue, or purple, cymose, racemose or paniculate, 5-merous; calyx of similar lobes or sepals, enlarging in fr., much shorter than the campanulate or funnelform corolla; stamens 5, included; ovary 2-celled, 2–4-ovuled; style 1, capitate or 2-lobed: fr. a small indehiscent or 2-valved oblong caps.; seeds glabrous. (Pora-na: native name.)

P. paniculata, Roxb. CHRISTMAS-VINE. Profuse, white-pubescent, twining and clambering to 20 and 30 ft.: lvs. cordate-ovate, 3–6 in. long, entire, acuminate, very veiny: fls. many in numerous axillary panicles, ⅓in. or less across, white: caps. globose, about ⅙in. across, hairy. India.—Sometimes inappropriately called "White Corallita" (see Antigonon, page 351).

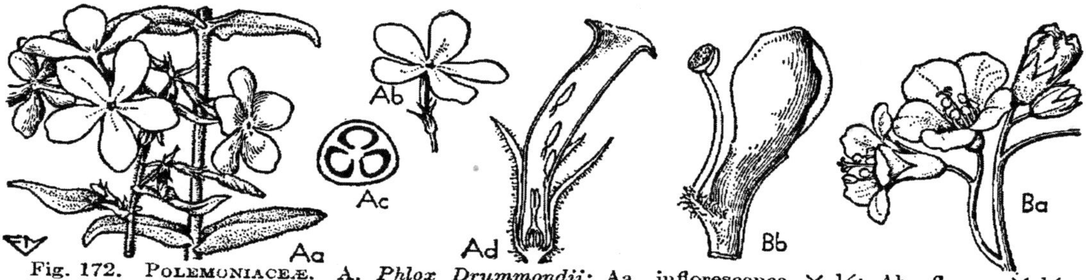

Fig. 172. POLEMONIACEÆ. A, *Phlox Drummondii:* Aa, inflorescence, × ½; Ab, flower, × ½; Ac, ovary, cross-section, × 10; Ad, flower, vertical section, corolla partially excised, × 2. B, *Polemonium reptans:* Ba, flowers, × 1; Bb, segment of corolla with stamen, × 3.

172. POLEMONIACEÆ. PHLOX FAMILY

About 13 genera of ann. and per. herbs with a few woody plants, in Eu., Asia, and Amer., mostly in N. Amer., in about 300 species; the family yields many species with ornamental fls.—Lvs. alternate or opposite, simple, pinnate or palmate, exstipulate: fls. bisexual, regular or nearly so, 5-merous as to envelopes and stamens, the latter attached on the corolla and alternate with its lobes, bearing an hypogynous disk; ovary superior, usually 3-celled, with axile placentæ, ovules commonly many in each cell; style 1, mostly 3-fid: fr. a loculicidal or exceptionally septicidal small caps., with few or many seeds.

A. Species herbaceous or essentially so.
B. Plant erect, or not tendril-climbing.
C. Attachment of stamens at same height, or practically so, on throat or tube of corolla.
D. Stamens declined in the corolla: caps. not rupturing calyx . . . . 1. POLEMONIUM
DD. Stamens not declined (or curved downward) in corolla: caps. rupturing calyx when mature . . . . 2. GILIA
CC. Attachment of stamens unequal (at different heights) in corolla-tube.
D. Lvs. alternate, often incised or pinnatifid . . . . 3. COLLOMIA
DD. Lvs. (at least lower ones) opposite, entire . . . . 4. PHLOX
BB. Plant tendril-climbing . . . . 5. COBÆA
AA. Species branching shrubs . . . . 6. CANTUA

1. POLEMONIUM, L. Herbs, with attractive blue, purplish, white, or yellowish fls.; 25–50 species, mostly W. N. American, extending into Mex. but also in Eu., Asia and S. Amer.—Per., rarely ann. or bien., tall or dwarf, often from a creeping rhizome: herbage often viscid; lvs. alternate, pinnatisect or odd-pinnate, lfts. sessile: infl. terminal, loosely corymbose or subcapitate; calyx campanulate, 5-cleft, enlarging after anthesis; corolla tubular, funnel-shaped, broadly bell-shaped or subrotate, with obovate lobes; stamens 5, equally inserted, declinate, bearded at base; disk crenate; ovary with 2–12 seeds in each cell: caps. ovoid, 3-valved. (Polemonium: ancient name.)

A. Tube of corolla longer than lobes: lfts. verticillate . . . . 1. *P. confertum*
AA. Tube of corolla shorter than lobes: lfts. not verticillate.
B. Stamens much-exserted . . . . 2. *P. VanBruntiæ*
BB. Stamens shorter than or equalling corolla.
C. Plant glabrous or nearly so . . . . 3. *P. reptans*
CC. Plant glandular-pubescent, at least in infl.
D. Lfts. less than ½in. long, usually about ¼in . . . . 4. *P. Richardsonii*
DD. Lfts. ½in. or more long.
E. Fls. ⅓in. and less long . . . . 5. *P. pulcherrimum*
EE. Fls. ½–1 in. long.
F. Color of fls. blue; style slightly exserted . . . . 6. *P. cæruleum*
FF. Color of fls. pink fading to purplish; style included . . . . 7. *P. carneum*

1. **P. confertum,** Gray. Tufted glandular-pubescent ill-scented per. to 8 in. high: lvs. 3–7 in. long, of numerous verticillate oblong to obovate lfts. to ⅓in. long: fls. blue or violet, about 1 in. long, in dense head-like clusters; tube of corolla much longer than lobes; stamens and style included. Rocky Mts., Wyo. to New Mex.

2. **P. VanBruntiæ,** Britt. To 2½ ft., with stout horizontal roots and sts. glandular-pubescent above and leafy to top: lfts. numerous, ovate to lanceolate, acute, ½–1½ in. long: fls. bluish-purple, ¾in. across, in few-fld. clusters which are usually panicled; stamens and style much-exserted. (Named for Mrs. VanBrunt, who collected the plant in Ulster Co., N. Y.) Vt. to Va.

3. **P. reptans,** L. Not over 1 ft. high, slender, weak and diffuse but not creeping, glabrous or nearly so, sts. leafy: lvs. to 8 in. long, of 5–15 ovate to lanceolate-oblong lfts. ½–1½ in. long: fls. light blue, ½–¾in. long, loosely paniculate-corymbose on the branches; stamens included; style exserted. N. Y. to Ala. and Kans.

4. **P. Richardsonii,** R. Grah. (*P. humile,* Roem. & Schult. not Salisb.). About 9 in. high, from thickened somewhat creeping rootstocks, viscid-pubescent: lfts. 15–21, round-oval to oblong, to ½in. long but usually about ¼in.: flowering sts. only 1–2-lvd., with rather few fls. in the clusters; corolla blue or purplish, ½in. across, the tube not surpassing the calyx, and much shorter than the rounded lobes; stamens slightly shorter than corolla; style somewhat exserted. Arctic regions.—Cult. material may be **P. Jacobæ,** Bergmans (*P. cæruleum* × *P. pulcherrimum*), lfts. lanceolate, ¾–1 in. long, fls. to 1¼ in. across.

5. **P. pulcherrimum,** Hook. Per. with erect or ascending sts. to 10 in. high and mostly basal lvs., glandular-pubescent: lvs. 2–6 in. long, of 13–21 oblong or elliptic lfts. about ½in. long: fls. blue or violet with white or yellow throat, to ⅓in. long, in dense cymes; stamens included; style exserted. Wash. to Calif. and Rocky Mts.

6. **P. cæruleum,** L. Jacobs-Ladder. Greek Valerian. Charity. Glandular-pubescent at least in infl., sts. erect, leafy, 1–3 ft. high: basal lvs. forming dense tufts, long-petiolate, 3–5 in. long, the lfts. 11–21, lanceolate, mostly acuminate, ½–¾in. long; st.-lvs. smaller, very short-petioled or the upper sessile: fls. blue, many, panicled, drooping, 1 in. or less diam.; calyx campanulate; stamens about length of corolla; style slightly exserted. Eu. Var. **lacteum,** Benth. (var. *album,* Hort.), fls. white. Var. **himalayanum,** Baker (var. *grandiflorum,* Manning), fls. 1½ in. across, lilac-blue.

7. **P. carneum,** Gray. Sts. 1–2 ft. high, weak, erect or ascending, glabrous or pubescent: lvs. 3–8 in. long, of 11–19 lanceolate to ovate acute lfts. ½–1½ in. long: fls. pink fading to purplish, in loose glandular-pubescent cymes; corolla with short tube and spreading limb; stamens and style included. Calif., Ore.

2. **GILIA,** Ruiz & Pav. Herbs or rarely slightly shrubby, several cult. in fl.-gardens; a polymorphic genus of more than 100 species, often separated into several genera, mostly native to W. N. Amer., a few to S. Amer.—Ann., bien., or per.: habit, infl. and color of fls. various: lvs. alternate or opposite, entire, toothed, lobed or divided: calyx-teeth of equal length; corolla regular, campanulate to funnelform or salverform; stamens equally inserted on the tube or throat of the corolla, the filaments naked, not declined: caps. 3-celled and 3-valved, 1- to many-seeded, rupturing the calyx when mature. (Gil-ia: Felipe Luis Gil, Spanish botanist of the latter half of the 18th century.)

A. Lvs. palmately divided to base, looking as if whorled.
  B. Fls. on slender pedicels, in panicled cymes .... 1. *G. liniflora*
  BB. Fls. sessile, in dense clusters or heads.
    C. Tube of corolla filiform, ¾–1½ in. long, much longer than lobes .... 2. *G. lutea*
    CC. Tube of corolla about equalling lobes, ½in. long .... 3. *G. grandiflora*
AA. Lvs. pinnately cut or divided.
  B. Infl. a dense head borne at end of naked peduncle .... 4. *G. capitata*
  BB. Infl. not as above.
    C. Fls. purple and white, in loose clusters: plant ann. .... 5. *G. tricolor*
    CC. Fls. scarlet, in a long panicle or thyrse: plant per.
      D. Plant glabrous: corolla-lobes ovate and spreading .... 6. *G. rubra*
      DD. Plant usually pubescent: corolla-lobes lanceolate or linear, reflexed .... 7. *G. aggregata*

1. **G. liniflora,** Benth. (*Linanthus liniflorus,* Greene). Ann. ½–1½ ft. high, erect or at length diffuse, nearly glabrous: lower lvs. mostly opposite, the upper alternate, all palmately divided into 3–7 needle-like or spurry-like segms. ¼–½in. long; fls. panicled, on slender pedicels; corolla ½in. long, white or blush, nearly rotate, with obtuse lobes. Calif.

2. **G. lutea,** Steud. (*G. micrantha,* Steud. *Leptosiphon luteus* and *parviflorus,* Benth. *Linanthus parviflorus,* Greene). Slender somewhat hairy ann. not over 8 in. high, the sts. most leafy near the top: lvs. opposite, palmately divided into 3–7 oblanceolate to linear segms. ¼–½in. long: fls. in a leafy-bracteate cluster, the color range very wide, from purple to lilac, red, yellow, and white; corolla-tube filiform, ¾–1½ in. long, projecting prominently above the upper fascicles of lvs.; corolla-lobes much shorter, spreading and obtuse. Calif.

3. **G. grandiflora,** Steud. (*G. densiflora,* Benth. *Leptosiphon grandiflorus* and *densiflorus,* Benth. *Linanthus grandiflorus,* Greene). Hairy ann. 1–2 ft. high, often strict: lvs. opposite, palmately parted into numerous filiform somewhat rigid segms. ¾–1 in. long: fls. crowded into a leafy-bracteate cluster; calyx-divisions very narrow, little exceeded by the corolla-tube; corolla lilac or nearly white, the tube ½in. long, the limb about as long, the lobes spreading, obtuse, often dentate. Calif.

4. **G. capitata,** Dougl. Erect ann., simple or branching above, 1½–3 ft. high, glabrous or nearly so: lvs. alternate, 2–3-pinnately divided into very unequal linear segms.: fls.

light blue, about ½in. long, in dense globose heads ½–¾in. across at the ends of long naked peduncles; calyx glabrous or nearly so, with lanceolate teeth; stamens exserted. Calif. to Wash.

5. **G. tricolor,** Benth. BIRDS-EYES. Erect garden ann. usually branching and at length diffuse, 1–2½ ft. high, more or less glandular-pubescent: lvs. alternate, bipinnately dissected into narrowly linear segms.: fls. few or several in loosely corymbose clusters; corolla about ½in. long, two to three times as long as calyx, fragrant, with yellowish tube, purple-marked throat and lilac or violet roundish lobes. Calif.

6. **G. rubra,** Heller (*Polemonium rubrum,* L. *G. coronopifolia,* Pers. *Ipomopsis aurantiaca, I. elegans* and *I. sanguinea,* Hort.). STANDING-CYPRESS. Leafy-stemmed per. 2–6 ft. high, glabrous or nearly so, unbranched: lvs. alternate, pinnately parted into needle-like divisions about 1 in. long: fls. many, showy, inodorous, 1½ in. long, borne in a long narrow terminal thyrsus or panicle, the calyces inconspicuous among the segms. of the subtending bracts; corolla bright scarlet, within yellowish dotted with red, the ovate lobes somewhat spreading. S. C. to Fla. and Tex.—An old garden plant, best treated as a bien.

7. **G. aggregata,** Spreng. (*Cantua aggregata,* Pursh). SCARLET or SKYROCKET GILIA. Per. or bien. 1–3 ft. high, simple or slightly branched, pubescent: lvs. alternate, 1–2-pinnately dissected into linear segms.: fls. scarlet varying to pink or white, 1–1½ in. long, nearly sessile, in small clusters forming a long thyrse; corolla salverform, with cylindrical tube and lanceolate or linear acuminate lobes which become reflexed. B. C. to Mex., east to Colo. and Tex.

3. **COLLOMIA,** Nutt. About 18 species of herbs sometimes referred to Gilia, but the stamens are unequally inserted and usually protruded, the sinuses of the calyx become distended into a revolute lobe and the mature caps. does not rupture the calyx; infl. often subtended by involucre-like bracts; lvs. prevailingly alternate. (Collo-mia: Greek *glue* or *gluten,* the seeds becoming mucilaginous when wet.)

A. Lvs. entire .... 1. *C. grandiflora*
AA. Lvs. mostly toothed or cut at the ends .... 2. *C. Cavanillesii*

1. **C. grandiflora,** Dougl. (*Gilia grandiflora,* Gray). Erect ann. 1–3 ft. high, puberulous: lvs. linear to oblong-lanceolate, 1–3 in. long, entire: fls. about 1 in. long, in close leafy-bracted heads, the corolla buff or salmon-color, narrow funnelform, much projecting beyond the broad and obtuse calyx-lobes. Rocky Mts. to Calif.

2. **C. Cavanillesii,** Hook & Arn. (*C. biflora,* Brand. *C. coccinea,* Lehm.). Very like *C. grandiflora,* but lvs. mostly narrower and some or all of them toothed or cut near the end, sometimes subopposite near base of st.; calyx-lobes acute and ciliate; corolla scarlet, more or less buff outside. (Named for Cavanilles, page 41.) Bolivia, Chile, Argentina.

4. **PHLOX,** L. About 50 ann. and per. temp.-region herbs, sometimes woody at base, with showy fls. of the blue, purple, pink, and crimson series, frequently white, of which one is Siberian and the others N. American.—Sometimes cespitose: lvs. opposite or the upper ones infrequently alternate, entire: fls. cymose, paniculate or thyrsoid; calyx narrow, prominently toothed or lobed, becoming distended and at length burst by the maturing fr.; corolla prominent, strongly convolute, salverform, the tube slender and constricted at the throat, the lobes obovate or orbicular and often retuse or lobed; stamens unequally placed, with short filaments and the anthers mostly included; style commonly filiform: caps. ovoid, 3-valved. (Phlox: Greek *flame,* anciently applied to Lychnis.)

A. The ann. phloxes: upper lvs. usually alternate .... 1. *P. Drummondii*
AA. The per. phloxes: lvs. all opposite.
  B. Shape of lvs. subulate to linear, ⅛in. or less across.
    C. Fls. pedicelled, in few-fld. cymes.
      D. Corolla-lobes usually deeply notched.
        E. Lvs. crowded, ¾in. or less long .... 2. *P. subulata*
        EE. Lvs. well separated, lower to 2 in. long .... 3. *P. bifida*
      DD. Corolla-lobes entire or only erose .... 4. *P. nivalis*
    CC. Fls. sessile or nearly so, solitary.
      D. Corolla-tube much longer than calyx: pubescence glandular.
        E. Margins of lvs. revolute .... 5. *P. cæspitosa*
        EE. Margins of lvs. not revolute .... 6. *P. Douglasii*
      DD. Corolla-tube equalling or only slightly longer than calyx: pubescence not glandular.
        E. Branches usually only slightly pubescent .... 7. *P. diffusa*
        EE. Branches usually densely woolly .... 8. *P. Hoodii*
  BB. Shape of lvs. linear to ovate, ¼in. and more across.
    C. Style and stamens much shorter than corolla-tube.
      D. Sterile shoots rooting at nodes .... 9. *P. divaricata*
      DD. Sterile shoots not rooting.

E. Hairs of calyx glandular: bracts scattered through cyme..........10. *P. pilosa*
EE. Hairs of calyx not glandular: bracts closely subtending the cyme......11. *P. amœna*
CC. Style and stamens about equalling corolla-tube, visible at throat.
D. Plant stoloniferous.
E. Lower lvs. obovate, pubescent..........12. *P. stolonifera*
EE. Lower lvs. elliptic, glabrous..........13. *P. adsurgens*
DD. Plant not stoloniferous.
E. Margins of lvs. minutely bristly-ciliate..........14. *P. paniculata*
EE. Margins of lvs. not bristly-ciliate.
F. Flowering sts. arising from cluster of lvs. of sterile shoots..........15. *P. ovata*
FF. Flowering sts. arising from leafless rootstocks, sterile shoots lacking or inconspicuous.
G. Panicles narrow: sts. usually purple-spotted..........16. *P. maculata*
GG. Panicles or corymbs broad: sts. usually not spotted..........17. *P. carolina*

1. **P. Drummondii,** Hook. Annual or Drummond Phlox. Much-branched erect villous-glandular ann. 6–18 in. tall: lowermost lvs. opposite, others alternate, broad-ovate to oblong and lanceolate, 1–3 in. long, acute and mucronate, narrowed to base or clasping: fls. showy, rose-red, about 1 in. across, in copious close cymose clusters; calyx-lobes long and narrow, spreading or recurving in fr.; style and stamens much shorter than corolla. Tex., whence seeds were received in England in 1835 from Thos. Drummond.—The common ann. phlox of seedsmen, now known in many forms and colors, white, buff, pink, red, purple. The cultivars bear many Latin names. There are dwarf, compact and semi-double strains. Var. **rotundata,** Voss, is a race with petals large and broad, giving the fl. a circular outline. Var. **stellaris,** Voss (*P. cuspidata,* Hort.), Star Phlox, is a group with narrow cuspidate often cut and fringed petals. Var. **grandiflora,** Regel, has purple fls. which are white below. A large-fld. strain with wide range of colors is known as *P. Drummondii gigantea.*

2. **P. subulata,** L. (*P. setacea,* L.). Ground- or Moss-Pink. Tufted spring-blooming per. forming mats, at first pubescent: lvs. many and crowded, subulate, mostly ½in. or less long but longer on vigorous shoots: fls. many, standing just above the foliage, pedicelled, ¾in. or more across, pink, purplish, white, the lobes usually obcordate and deeply notched; stamens slightly exserted. N. Y. and Mich. to N. C. Var. **Moerheimii,** Ruys, has deep pink fls. Var. **Nelsonii,** Hort., is a compact form with white rose-centered fls. A race with large deep pink fls. raised at Camla Gardens, East Grinstead, England, is known as *P. camlaensis* or *P. subulata* var. *Camla.* Plants grown in gardens as *P. lilacina* or *P. Stellaria* (not *P. Stellaria* of Gray which is a form of *P. bifida*) are apparently hybrids between *P. subulata* and *P. bifida.*—Common in cemeteries and gardens, running into named vars. mostly representing color races as *rosea, atropurpurea, alba.*

3. **P. bifida,** Beck. Sand Phlox. Resembling *P. subulata* but with fewer nodes, the lvs. being well separated and the lower ones 1–2 in. long, the lavender to white corolla-lobes more deeply notched. Tenn. and S. W. Mich. to Okla.

4. **P. nivalis,** Lodd. (*P. Hentzii,* Nutt.). Trailing Phlox. Similar to *P. subulata* in habit and foliage, but differing in the much shorter stamens and style and the larger fls. which have entire or only erose corolla-lobes: varies in color from white to pink and pale purple: lvs. to 1 in. long. Va. to Fla. and Ala. Var. **sylvestris,** Hort., is listed as having large rose-pink fls.

5. **P. cæspitosa,** Nutt. (*P. Douglasii* var. *cæspitosa,* Mason). Moss-like densely tufted per. with branches 1–5 in. high, pubescent with both glandular and glandless hairs: lvs. imbricated. linear-oblong, ¼–⅓in. long, stiff, margins revolute giving lf. a 3-ribbed appearance, ciliate: fls. lilac, about ½in. across, solitary; corolla-tube about twice as long as calyx; stamens and style short. Mont. and Ore. to New Mex.

6. **P. Douglasii,** Hook. Loosely tufted per. 2–8 in. high, densely glandular-pubescent: lvs. linear or subulate, ⅓–½in. long, stiff: fls. lilac, pink or white, to ½in. across, solitary; corolla-tube much longer than calyx; stamens and style short. (Named for David Douglas, page 42.) Wash. to W. Mont.

7. **P. diffusa,** Benth. (*P. Douglasii* var. *diffusa,* Gray). Distinguished from *P. Douglasii* by the scant pubescence not being glandular, thinner obtuse to bluntly acute longer lvs., and the shorter corolla-tube. B. C. to Calif.

8. **P. Hoodii,** Richardson. Tufted gray-green per. about 2 in. high, branches usually densely woolly: lvs. subulate, stiff, ¼–⅓in. long, pubescent to arachnoid, rarely nearly glabrous: fls. white, ⅓in. across, solitary; corolla-tube about equalling the arachnoid calyx, lobes entire; stamens and style short. (Named for Lieut. Robt. Hood, who accompanied the expedition of Capt. John Franklin to the shores of the Polar Sea, 1819–1822.) W. N. Amer.

9. **P. divaricata,** L. Wild Sweet William. Diffuse spreading per. with many sterile decumbent and creeping shoots rooting at nodes and variable foliage; sts. erect, 10–18 in. high, viscid-pubescent: lvs. of sterile shoots ovate and sessile; of the flowering sts. oblong to lance-ovate, 1–2 in. long and ¾in. wide, acute or nearly obtuse, sessile: fls. bluish or pinkish-blue varying to white, ¾–1½ in. across, pedicelled, in rather open clusters, somewhat fragrant, the lobes entire or obcordate and rather narrow so that they stand well

apart; calyx-teeth narrow-subulate, longer than the calyx-tube; stamens and style shorter than corolla. Woodlands, Que. and Man. to La. and Fla. Var. **canadensis,** Wherry (*P. canadensis,* Sweet), is the eastern form with notched corolla-lobes. Var. **Laphamii,** Wood (*P. Laphamii,* Clute), is the western form with obtuse entire petals (named after Dr. I. A. Lapham, botanist in Wis., died 1875).—**P. Arendsii** represents a strain of hybrids between *P. divaricata* and *P. paniculata;* exhibited in England in 1912 by Georg Arends, Ronsdorf, Germany, and now grown in this country in such kinds as Elizabeth, Amanda, Katha, Louise, very floriferous.

10. **P. pilosa,** L. Villous, sometimes glandular, per. usually 1–1½ ft. high, the sts. erect or ascending from a more or less tufted base: lvs. linear to lanceolate, 1–3 in. long, divaricate, long-pointed, sessile: fls. in a rather small corymb, pink, purple or rose varying to white, ½–¾in. across, the corolla-lobes entire or erose; calyx-teeth awn-like, equalling or exceeding the calyx-tube; stamens and style shorter than corolla. Dry places, Conn. to Fla. and Tex. Var. **argillacea,** Wherry (*P. argillacea,* Clute & Ferriss), Silver Phlox, has pale lilac fls. and a long blooming season.

11. **P. amœna,** Sims. Pilose per., the slender sts. 6–12 in. high from a decumbent base: lvs. oblong-lanceolate, 1–2 in. long, narrowed at base but sessile, mostly rather blunt, the upper ones forming a ciliate rosette or involucre for the compact infl.: fls. nearly sessile, purplish, pink or white, ¾–1 in. across, the corolla-lobes usually entire; calyx bristly-hairy, the teeth sharp-acute but not aristate and equalling or exceeding the calyx-tube; stamens and style shorter than corolla. Dry lands, N. C. to Fla. and Miss.—The plant commonly grown under this name is **P. procumbens,** Lehm. (*P. verna,* Hort.), a hybrid between *P. subulata* and *P. stolonifera,* having bright purple fls. with long stamens and style, and gland-tipped hairs.

12. **P. stolonifera,** Sims (*P. reptans,* Michx.). Creeping Phlox. Low and weak glandular-hairy per. 5–12 in. high, the sterile shoots long and rooting at nodes: lvs. on sterile sts. obovate and obtuse, 1–3 in. long and much narrowed at base; those on the erect fl.-sts. 3 or 4 pairs, oval, oblong or lanceolate, about 1 in. or less long, obtuse or only short-acute, the lowest more or less obovate: fls. few in a simple not involucrate cyme, purple or violet, about ¾in. across, the corolla-lobes rounded and usually entire and about one-half length of the tube; calyx-teeth linear-subulate, equalling or exceeding the calyx-tube; stamens and style about as long as corolla. Woods, Pa. to Ga. and Ohio.

13. **P. adsurgens,** Torr. Decumbent per., the sterile shoots rooting at nodes, flowering sts. to 1 ft. high, slightly pubescent above: lvs. elliptic, ½–1¼ in. long, glabrous, shining: fls. rose with paler center, to nearly white, about 1 in. across, in loose cymes, the corolla-lobes entire and about half length of tube; calyx-teeth subulate, longer than tube; stamens and style equalling corolla. Ore., N. Calif.

14. **P. paniculata,** L. Summer Perennial Phlox. Stout and erect, puberulous or glabrous, 2–4 ft. or more high: lvs. thin, veiny, oblong-lanceolate to ovate-lanceolate or sometimes oval-acuminate, 3–5 in. long, pointed, tapering to base, the upper ones sometimes partially clasping, the margins minutely bristly-ciliate: fls. in a large usually pyramidal panicle, in summer and early autumn, pink-purple, 1 in. or more across, the tube to 1½ in. long and often pubescent; calyx-lobes setaceous or aristate, prominent; stamens and style equalling or longer than corolla. N. Y. to Ga. and Ark.—The common per. phlox of gardens, now developed into many colors, white, buff, salmon, rose, scarlet, lilac, magenta, purple. Wild roots transferred to the garden soon bear large panicles and are practically indistinguishable from some of the cult. kinds. Hybrid races are designated as *P. hortorum,* Bergmans, and *P. pyramidalis,* Smith (*P. decussata,* Lyon).

15. **P. ovata,** L. Mountain Phlox. Glabrous or only exceptionally with scattered hairs, sts. 10–20 in. high from a decumbent base, per.: lvs. firm, rather narrowly ovate to oblong-lanceolate, 1–4 in. long, the lower ones on the st. likely to be narrower and tapering into a short petiole, those on the sterile shoots larger, broad-ovate and long-petioled: fls. distinctly pedicelled, in small rather close clusters, bright pink or light red, about 1 in. across, the corolla-lobes rounded; calyx-teeth long-acute but not aristate, one-third to one-half the length of the calyx-tube; stamens and style about as long as corolla. Pa. to Ga. and Ala., mostly in the mts.

16. **P. maculata,** L. Meadow Phlox. Per. to 5 ft., from a slender horizontal rootstock, sterile shoots lacking, the sts. usually purple-spotted: lvs. linear to ovate, to 5 in. long and 1 in. wide, nearly sessile: fls. purple to white, ½in. across, in a cylindrical panicle to 1 ft. long; teeth of calyx about one-third length of tube; stamens and style about length of corolla. Conn. to N. C. and Mo.

17. **P. carolina,** L. Thick-leaf Phlox. Per. to 4 ft., glabrous or pubescent, the sts. sometimes streaked with purple, sterile shoots poorly developed: lvs. linear to ovate, to 5 in. long and 1½ in. wide, the lower lvs. petioled: fls. purple, rarely white, about ¾in. across, in corymbs or broad panicles; stamens and style about length of corolla. Ohio to Fla. and Miss.—Crosses of this species are known as *P. suffruticosa,* Hort., represented by Miss Lingard and other early-blooming kinds. The *P. suffruticosa,* Vent. (*P. glaberrima* var. *suffruticosa,* Gray), is a late-blooming form properly referable to var. **altissima,**

Wherry (*P. altissima*, Moench). Most of the plants in cult. as *P. glaberrima* belong to *P. carolina;* the true *P. glaberrima*, L., differs in its more numerous nodes, narrower lvs. and shorter calyx.

5. **COBÆA,** Cav. About 10 species of strong tendril-climbers, one grown in the open and under glass for the large bell-shaped fls.; natives of trop. Amer.—Shrubby plants climbing by lf.-tendrils, but known in cult. as herbs: lvs. alternate, pinnatisect, mostly terminating in a branched tendril: fls. violet to bright green, solitary on long peduncles in the axils; calyx large, 5-parted, the segms. broad and lf.-like; corolla campanulate or broadly cylindric, with 5-lobed limb; stamens exserted, woolly at the place of insertion: caps. leathery, 3-valved, septicidal, the seeds broadly winged. (Cobæ-a: after Father Cobo, Spanish Jesuit of the 17th century, naturalist and resident of Amer. for many years.)

C. scandens, Cav. (*Rosenbergia scandens*, House). Grown commonly as an ann., height 10–25 ft., glabrous, climbing by means of lft.-tendrils: lfts. oval or oblong, to 4 in. long and 2 in. wide, in 2 or 3 pairs, the lowest close to the st. and more or less hastate or auriculate, placed like stipules: fls. single on peduncles 6–10 in. long, bearing a great leafy calyx; calyx-segms. elliptic or oblong, mucronate; corolla about 2 in. long, 1½ in. or more across, light violet or greenish-purple; filaments recurving above the middle: caps. 1¾ in. long; seeds about ⅓in. broad, thin and flat. Mex.—There is a white-fld. kind and one with variegated lvs.

6. **CANTUA,** Juss. A half dozen shrubs or small trees in S. Amer., one planted in Calif. and sometimes grown under glass for its very showy fls.—Lvs. alternate or crowded and simple, often entire, short-stalked or sessile: fls. usually many in rather close terminal clusters, red, violet, or white, the corolla long-tubular with short lobes and much exceeding the calyx; stamens 5, equally inserted at the base of the corolla, included or exserted, the filaments naked; style very slender, often exserted, stigma 3-lobed: caps. loculicidal, 3-valved, many-seeded. (Can-tua: a Peruvian name.)

C. buxifolia, Lam. (*C. dependens*, Pers.). Shrub 4–10 ft., the young parts hirsute: lvs. crowded, elliptic or lanceolate, mostly less than 1 in. long, entire, sometimes with few teeth on sterile shoots: fls. in terminal clusters more or less pendent by the bending of the twigs, pinkish-red with yellow-striped tube; corolla 2½–3 in. long, the stamens about equalling the long tube. Peru, Bolivia, N. Chile.

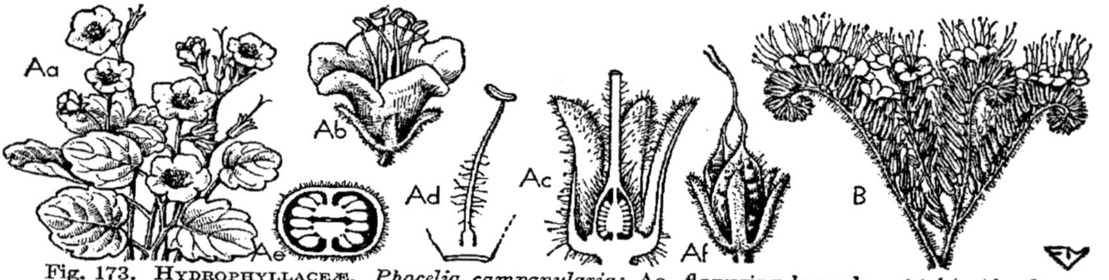

Fig. 173. HYDROPHYLLACEÆ. *Phacelia campanularia:* Aa, flowering branches, × ½; Ab, flower, × 1; Ac, same, vertical section, × 3; Ad, stamen, × 1½; Ae, ovary, cross-section, × 6; Af, capsule, × 1. B, *Phacelia tanacetifolia:* inflorescence, × ½.

173. HYDROPHYLLACEÆ. WATER-LEAF FAMILY

Herbs, or rarely shrubs, of 18 genera and about 250 species of wide distribution about the world but most abundant in N. Amer., many grown for ornament.—Lvs. alternate or opposite, simple or compound: fls. bisexual, regular, mostly in terminal or axillary scorpioid cymes, rarely solitary; calyx deeply 5-parted (seldom 10–12-parted); corolla gamopetalous, 5- (rarely 6–10-) lobed; stamens 5 (seldom 6–10), inserted on corolla and alternate with its lobes, the filaments free and filiform; ovary superior, usually 1-celled with 2 placentæ and 2 to many ovules, or sometimes 2-celled; styles 1 or 2: fr. a caps. loculicidally dehiscent by 2 valves, rarely septicidally or irregularly dehiscent.

A. Calyx with reflexed or spreading appendage in each sinus.......................1. NEMOPHILA
AA. Calyx unappendaged.
B. Number of styles 2...2. WIGANDIA
BB. Number of styles 1.
C. Style entire: lvs. mostly basal.......................................3. ROMANZOFFIA
CC. Style 2-parted to middle or less: lvs. cauline............................4. PHACELIA

1. **NEMOPHILA,** Nutt. Diffuse ann. herbs of 11 species in N. Amer., often planted in the fl.-garden and blooming from early spring to late summer.—Lvs. opposite or alternate, usually pinnatifid: fls. solitary and peduncled, rarely racemose; calyx 5-parted nearly to base, with a spreading or reflexed appendage in each sinus; corolla campanulate, tubular or rotate, usually longer than calyx, mostly with 10 small appendages at base within; stamens glabrous, included; ovary 1-celled with 2–10 ovules, the style 2-cleft: caps. globose, hairy, loculicidally dehiscent. (Nemoph-ila: Greek *grove-loving.*)

A. Corolla white, with deep purple spot at tip of each lobe.......................1. *N. maculata*
AA. Corolla blue or white, dotted or veined, but without purple spot at tip of lobes.......2. *N. Menziesii*

1. **N. maculata,** Benth. FIVE-SPOT. From 3–12 in. high: lvs. opposite, oblong, 1–2 in. long, pubescent, lyrate-pinnatifid into 5–9 ovate often toothed segms., the upper 3–5-lobed and cuneate at base, or rarely oblanceolate and entire: fls. solitary on long axillary peduncles, about 1 in. across; corolla almost rotate, white with light purple veins and deep purple spot at tip of each broad lobe, with broad ciliate nearly free scales: seeds light brown, smooth or pitted. Calif. in Sierra Nevadas.

2. **N. Menziesii,** Hook. & Arn. (*N. insignis,* Dougl.). BABY BLUE-EYES. Procumbent ann. with straggling succulent sts. 4–12 in. long: lvs. opposite, oblong to oval, 1–2 in. long, pubescent, pinnatifid into 3–11 entire or toothed segms.: fls. solitary on axillary peduncles longer than lvs., ½–1½ in. across; corolla bright blue with white center, with narrow scales adherent on one edge, the free edge densely ciliate: seeds dark brown or black, tuberculate. (Bears the name of Archibald Menzies, page 399.) Calif. to Ore. Var. **atomaria,** Chandler (*N. atomaria,* Fisch. & Mey.), has white or pale blue fls. dotted with black. There are many garden forms differing in color markings, the best known being var. **discoidalis,** Voss, in which the spots of corolla are confluent into a large brownish-purple eye and only the edges of the lobes are white; and var. **crambeoides,** Hort., with light blue fls. to 1 in. across, veined not spotted with purple.

2. **WIGANDIA,** HBK. Large per. herbs or subshrubs of 5 species native in trop. Amer., planted for bold foliage effects.—Lvs. very large, simple and dentate, covered with stinging glistening hairs: fls. sessile, in terminal scorpioid cymes; calyx deeply 5-parted; corolla broadly campanulate, without scales inside, the limb large, spreading, 5-lobed; stamens usually exserted and barbed; ovary 1-celled or falsely 2-celled, with very many ovules, the 2 filiform styles with club-shaped capitate stigmas: caps. usually loculicidally dehiscent by 2 valves. (Wigan-dia: after Johannes Wigand, 1523–1587, Prussian bishop and writer on plants.)

W. caracasana, HBK. Erect robust subshrub to 10 ft., pubescence yellow or silky: lvs. ovate, to 1½ ft. long and 1 ft. wide, obtuse, subcordate at base, long-petioled, coarsely and doubly crenate: fls. violet with white tube, ½–¾in. long and about 1 in. across. S. Mex. to Venezuela and Colombia (described from the Caracas region, as the name indicates). Var. **macrophylla,** Brand (*W. macrophylla,* Cham. & Schlecht.), has larger lvs. and white-pubescent infl.

3. **ROMANZOFFIA,** Cham. Low per. herbs of 5 species in W. N. Amer. and Asia.—Lvs. mostly basal, simple, the few cauline lvs. alternate: fls. white, in loose racemes on scape-like sts.; calyx deeply 5-parted; corolla broad-funnelform; stamens 5, unequal, inserted at base of corolla; style filiform with small stigma: caps. 2-celled by intrusion of placentæ, with numerous seeds. (Romanzof-fia: named in honor of Count Nikolai von Romanzoff, patron of science.)

R. sitchensis, Bong. To 10 in.: lvs. round-cordate, ½–1½ in. across, crenate-lobed, glabrous; petioles 1–4 in. long, those of basal lvs. bulbous-dilated: fls. about ½in. long, on long pedicels. Alaska to Calif.

4. **PHACELIA,** Juss. More than 100 American species of ann. or per. herbs grown in the fl.-garden for the attractive spring and summer bloom.—Lvs. alternate or the lower opposite, simple or compound: fls. in scorpioid cymes or racemes; calyx

5-parted nearly to base, often enlarged in fr.; corolla nearly rotate, campanulate or tubular, soon deciduous, the tube usually with appendages within which are free or united with the stamens; ovary 1-celled or falsely 2-celled by the intrusion of the placentæ, with 2 to many ovules, the style 2-cleft: caps. 2-valved. (Phace-lia: Greek *cluster,* referring to the crowded fl.-clusters of some species.)

A. Lvs. pinnately dissected.
  B. Plant per.: racemes in spike-like panicle, not scorpioid.........1. *P. sericea*
  BB. Plant ann.: racemes scorpioid.
    C. Pubescence bristly: corolla-lobes about half as long as tube; appendages entirely adnate.........2. *P. tanacetifolia*
    CC. Pubescence soft: corolla-lobes about length of tube; appendages free at apex.........3. *P. congesta*
AA. Lvs. simple, dentate.
  B. Stamens without appendages at base: lower lvs. short-petioled.........4. *P. viscida*
  BB. Stamens with a small appendage attached to base of each filament: lower lvs. long-petioled.
    C. Lobes of corolla equalling or exceeding tube.........5. *P. Parryi*
    CC. Lobes of corolla one-half or less as long as tube.
      D. Corolla-tube inflated, three times as long as lobes; appendages hairy.....6. *P. minor*
      DD. Corolla-tube not inflated, twice as long as lobes; appendages glabrous....7. *P. campanularia*

1. **P. sericea,** Gray. Per. from 4–18 in. high, silvery-pubescent: lvs. 1–3 in. long, pinnatifid into toothed or entire linear or oblong lobes: fls. violet-blue to white, in short racemes borne in spike-like panicles 1–6 in. long; corolla ¼in. long, lobed to middle; stamens long-exserted, with the appendage free: seeds reticulated and pitted. Alta. to Calif. and Ariz.

2. **P. tanacetifolia,** Benth. Erect ann. 1–4 ft. high, sparsely covered with bristly hairs: lvs. 6–9 in. long, pinnatifid into 9–17 linear-oblong divisions which are 1- or 2-pinnately parted: fls. blue or lavender, in dense terminal cymosely clustered scorpioid racemes 2–4 in. long; sepals linear, hirsute with rigid white bristles; corolla ¼in. long, the tube about twice as long as lobes; stamens usually long-exserted, with the appendage at its base entirely adnate: seeds reticulated and tuberculate, with an elevated keel on one side. Calif.

3. **P. congesta,** Hook. Very similar to *P. tanacetifolia* but with softer not bristly pubescence, less divided lvs., corolla-tube about length of lobes, stamens not so long-exserted and with the appendage free at apex, and the seeds reticulated. Tex. to Ariz.

4. **P. viscida,** Torr. (*Eutoca viscida,* Benth.). Ann. 1–2 ft. high, hirsute below and very glandular above: lvs. ovate, 1–3 in. long, doubly or incisely and irregularly dentate, cuneate or truncate at base, short-petioled or upper lvs. nearly sessile: fls. deep blue with purple or whitish center, ½–¾in. across, in terminal cymes; sepals linear; corolla rotate-campanulate, without scales; stamens included, slightly hairy: seeds small, reticulated. S. Calif.

5. **P. Parryi,** Torr. Ann. ½–1½ ft. high, glandular and hirsute: lvs. ovate, 1–2 in. long, singly or doubly irregularly toothed, often subcordate at base, the lower long-petioled, upper nearly sessile: fls. deep violet with paler center, ¾–1 in. across, in loose racemes; sepals linear; corolla open-campanulate, the lobes equalling or exceeding tube; stamens slightly exserted, hairy, with appendages at base: seeds reticulated. (Named for C. C. Parry, page 49.) S. to Lower Calif.

6. **P. minor,** Thell. (*Whitlavia minor,* Harvey. *W. grandiflora,* Harvey. *P. Whitlavia,* Gray. *P. minor* var. *Whitlavia,* Macb.). California Bluebell. Loosely branching ann. 1–2 ft. high, hirsute and glandular: lvs. ovate, 1–2 in. long, incisely toothed, truncate or cordate at base, the upper lvs. short-stalked, the lower ones with long petioles: fls. purple, about ¾in. across, with linear sepals and ventricose tube about three times as long as lobes; stamens slightly exserted, with hairy appendages at base: seeds reticulated. S. Calif.—A strain with white corolla-tube is known as *gloxinoides* (*Whitlavia gloxinoides,* Vilm.).

7. **P. campanularia,** Gray. Very similar to *P. minor* but lvs. less deeply dentate, corolla deep blue, truly campanulate with scarcely dilated tube about twice as long as lobes, and glabrous appendages. S. Calif.

174. BORAGINACEÆ. BORAGE FAMILY

Mostly herbs, but sometimes woody, yielding a number of ornamentals, of about 100 genera and some 1,700 species in the temp. regions and tropics of many parts of the world.—In temp. regions the species are herbs or subshrubs, largely rough-hairy and with blue or white fls. in scorpioid racemes or reduced cymes; in the tropics and subtropics they are bushes and small trees, as in Cordia: lvs. prevailingly alternate (so in ours), sometimes opposite or verticillate, simple and mostly entire, without stipules: fls. bisexual, usually regular, the calyx and corolla for the most part 5-cleft (sometimes 4-cleft); calyx persistent; corolla often appendaged in the throat; stamens 5, alternate with the corolla-lobes and inserted on the throat or tube; disk

Fig. 174. BORAGINACEÆ. A, *Symphytum asperum:* Aa, flowering branch, × ¼; Ab, cymule, × 1; Ac, flower, × 1; Ad, same, vertical section, × 2; Ae, corolla expanded, × 1; Af, ovary, habit, × 4; Ag, same, vertical section, × 4. B, *Anchusa azurea:* Ba, portion of flowering branch, × ½; Bb, flower, × 1; Bc, nutlet, × 5. C, *Echium plantagineum:* flowers, × ½. D, *Heliotropium arborescens:* Da, flowering branch, × ½; Db, flower, × 1; Dc, pistil, × 3; Dd, same, vertical section, × 3.

usually present; ovary of 2 superior 2-ovuled carpels, often 4-lobed as if of 4 single-ovuled carpels: fr. usually 4 nutlets, each 1-seeded, sometimes 2 nutlets each 2-seeded, sometimes more or less fleshy and berry-like, the nutlets attached to the enlarged or elongated torus (gynobase) by the base or the side; the method of attachment is important in distinguishing genera; the scars show plainly on the dry nutlets or "seeds."

A. Ovary divided into 4 parts that become nutlets in fr., with the simple or seldom 2-lobed style standing in the center between them.
  B. Fls. regular; stamens equal.
    C. Corolla rotate; anthers connivent into a cone . . . . 1. BORAGO
    CC. Corolla tubular, funnelform or salverform; anthers not forming a cone.
      D. Nutlets covered with prickles . . . . 2. CYNOGLOSSUM
      DD. Nutlets not prickly.
        E. Infl. without bracts (except sometimes at very base).
          F. The fls. borne in dense corymbose cymes . . . . 3. MYOSOTIDIUM
          FF. The fls. borne in loose racemes or few-fld. cymes.
            G. Base of nutlet surrounded by a tumid annular rim: basal lvs. cordate . . . . 14. BRUNNERA
            GG. Base of nutlet without rim: basal lvs. not cordate.
              H. Shape of corolla tubular or campanulate . . . . 4. MERTENSIA
              HH. Shape of corolla salverform.
                I. Nutlets attached basally, smooth and shining . . . . 5. MYOSOTIS
                II. Nutlets attached near apex, not smooth and shining . . . . 6. OMPHALODES
        EE. Infl. with bracts.
          F. Stamens exserted beyond throat . . . . 7. MOLTKIA
          FF. Stamens included.
            G. Anthers deeply sagittate . . . . 8. ONOSMA
            GG. Anthers not conspicuously sagittate.

H. Base of nutlet not surrounded by a tumid annular rim........ 9. LITHOSPERMUM
HH. Base of nutlet surrounded by a tumid annular rim.
I. Throat of corolla with tufts of hair but without scales.......10. PULMONARIA
II. Throat of corolla with scales.
J. Scales or appendages in throat of corolla linear and acute..11. SYMPHYTUM
JJ. Scales or appendages broad and blunt.
K. Lvs. oblong or lanceolate, obscurely veined..........12. ANCHUSA
KK. Lvs. ovate, netted-veined..........................13. PENTAGLOTTIS
BB. Fls. irregular; stamens unequal..............................15. ECHIUM
AA. Ovary undivided or only lobed, the style terminal.
B. Style entire.
BB. Style 4-lobed or -parted.................................16. HELIOTROPIUM
....17. CORDIA

1. **BORAGO,** L. BORAGE. Ann. or per. herbs, 3 species native to the Medit. region, one intro. into other countries and cult. for its fls. or used as a pot-herb and sometimes with salads.—Erect strigose-hispid plants with alternate lvs. and loose leafy cymes of blue fls. on long pedicels: calyx 5-parted into linear segms.; corolla rotate or campanulate, with short tube and 5 acute lobes, the throat with scales or hairy crests; stamens 5, attached near the base of the corolla, exserted or included, anthers linear, erect and connivent into a cone; ovary distinctly 4-lobed; style filiform, stigma subentire: nutlets 4, ovoid or oblong, erect, smooth or muricate, attached by the base. (Bora-go: Late Latin *burra*, rough hair, alluding to the foliage.)

B. officinalis, L Coarse hairy ann. 1½–2 ft. high: lvs. oblong or ovate, narrowed to a margined or broadly winged petiole or sessile, the larger often 4–6 in. long: corolla rotate, about ¾in. across: stamens exserted, together forming a cone ¼in. high: nutlets verrucose. Eu., N. Afr.—Mostly known as a bee-plant and for its blue or purplish fls. which bloom throughout the season.

2. **CYNOGLOSSUM,** L. HOUNDS-TONGUE. Herbs of 80–90 species widely distributed in temp. regions, a few grown for ornament.—Usually stiff-hairy: lvs. alternate, entire: fls. blue, purple or white, in one-sided somewhat scorpioid bractless racemes; calyx 5-parted, enlarged in fr.; corolla funnelform or salverform, with conspicuous crests or scales in throat; stamens included, with short filaments and ovate or oblong anthers; ovary deeply 4-lobed, style filiform: nutlets 4, attached laterally to the receptacle, covered with prickles, forming a bur or "stick-tight." (Cynoglos-sum: Greek *dog's tongue*.)

A. Lvs. ovate, mostly basal, all long-petioled.................................1. *C. grande*
AA. Lvs. lanceolate or oblong, mostly cauline, the upper lvs. sessile or short-petioled.
B. Plant hoary-tomentose: nutlets adherent to style at apex.....................2. *C. amabile*
BB. Plant hairy but not hoary: nutlets free from style.........................3. *C. nervosum*

1. **C. grande,** Dougl. Per. with glabrous sts. 1–3 ft. high: lvs. mostly basal, ovate, 3–8 in. long, long-petioled, rounded or truncate at base, hairy below and slightly so above: fls. blue, ⅓–½in. long; calyx densely hairy; corolla-tube about equalling lobes, with thick crests: nutlets depressed, free from style. Wash to Calif.

2. **C. amabile,** Stapf & Drummond. CHINESE FORGET-ME-NOT. Bien. with tomentose sts. 1–2 ft. high: lower lvs. lanceolate or oblong-lanceolate, 2–8 in. long, attenuate into a winged petiole, the upper lvs. smaller and sessile, hoary-tomentose: fls. blue, ¼in. long; calyx densely hairy; corolla-tube shorter than lobes: nutlets ovoid, adherent to style at apex until maturity. E. Asia.

3. **C. nervosum,** Benth. Bien. or per. with hairy sts. to 3 ft. high: lower lvs. lanceolate, to 8 in. long, short-petioled, upper lvs. oblong and nearly sessile, to 4 in. long, sparsely hairy on both sides: fls. blue, ⅔in. across; calyx hairy; corolla with very short tube: nutlets ovoid, free from style. Himalayas.

3. **MYOSOTIDIUM,** Hook. A per. herb, 1 species in the Chatham Isls., New Zeal., sometimes planted.—Lvs. both basal and cauline: fls. blue, in dense terminal bractless corymbose cymes; calyx deeply 4-parted; corolla with short tube and spreading lobes and with 5 appendages in throat; stamens included, with very short filaments and oblong anthers; ovary 4-lobed; style short and thick, stigma indistinctly 2-lobed: nutlets 4, broad-ovate, winged. (Myosotid-ium: *like myosotis*.)

M. Hortensia, Baill. (*Myosotis Hortensia*, Dcne. *Cynoglossum nobile*, Hook. f. *Myosotidium nobile*, Hook.). Sts. 1–2 ft. high, pubescent: basal lvs. numerous, ovate-cordate, to 1 ft. long and 5 in. wide, petioled, glabrous, thick and fleshy; st.-lvs. few and smaller, sessile: cymes 6 in. across; corolla blue, paler toward outside, ½in. across, appendages yellow: fr. ½–¾in. across. (Hortensia: for Hortense von Nassau.)

4. **MERTENSIA,** Roth. Bluebells. Per. herbs with showy clusters of fls., used in borders; species probably 40, in cooler parts of the northern hemisphere, a good part in N. Amer.—Plants glabrous or hairy: lvs. alternate, entire, often with pellucid dots: fls. blue or purplish, rarely white, more or less drooping, pedicelled and without bracts, the terminal racemes or loosely branching few-fld. cymes unilateral and often panicled; calyx 5-cleft or -parted, with ovate-lanceolate or linear lobes, unchanging in fr.; corolla-tube cylindric below, expanded and more or less campanulate above, the 5 lobes short and broad, the throat naked or with folds or scales; stamens included or exserted, attached at or above the middle of the corolla-tube; ovary 2-lobed, stigma entire or slightly lobed: nutlets 4, erect and more or less wrinkled, attached laterally to the receptacle. (Merten-sia: after Franz Karl Mertens, 1764–1831, German botanist.)

A. Under surface of lvs. pubescent.
B. Corolla-lobes erect; scales in throat lacking: pubescence soft. . . . . 1. *M. echioides*
BB. Corolla-lobes spreading; scales in throat conspicuous: pubescence rough. . . . . . . 2. *M. paniculata*
AA. Under surface of lvs. glabrous.
B. Calyx-lobes not ciliate; scales in throat inconspicuous . . . . 3. *M. virginica*
BB. Calyx-lobes ciliate; scales in throat prominent.
C. Tube of corolla twice or more as long as limb: lower lvs. with winged petioles . 4. *M. longiflora*
CC. Tube of corolla equalling or slightly longer than limb: lower lvs. with distinct petioles.
D. Lobes of calyx obtuse, about ⅛in. long. . . . . 5. *M. ciliata*
DD. Lobes of calyx acute, about ¼in. long. . . . . 6. *M. oblongifolia*

1. **M. echioides,** Benth. Soft-hairy, 6–15 in. high: lvs. oblong or spatulate, 1½ in. long and ½in. wide, long-petioled: fls. deep blue, in dense racemes 1–3 in. long; corolla ⅓in. long, the erect lobes slightly shorter than tube, without scales in throat; stamens longer than corolla-tube: nutlets white and shining. Himalayas.

2. **M. paniculata,** Don (*Pulmonaria paniculata*, Ait.). Sts. 1–3 ft. high: lvs. ovate to lanceolate, basal 2–8 in. long and 1–5 in. wide, long-petioled, rough-pubescent on both surfaces: fls. blue or pinkish when young, sometimes white, in late spring or early summer; calyx-lobes acute, ciliate; corolla about ½in. long, the spreading lobes longer than the tube, the glabrous scales conspicuous in throat: nutlets rugose. Que. to Alaska south to Mich. and Wash.

3. **M. virginica,** Pers. (*Pulmonaria virginica*, L.). Virginia Bluebells or Cowslip. Smooth and glabrous, 1–2 ft. high, with erect sts.: basal lvs. elliptic or rotund, 2–8 in. long and 1–5 in. wide, long-stalked, st.-lvs. smaller and nearly sessile: fls. in more or less nodding clusters in early spring; corolla trumpet-shaped, about 1 in. long, with purple tube and blue bell, the lobes not prominent, scales in throat inconspicuous; filaments much longer than the anthers: nutlets rugose. N. Y. to Tenn. and Ala.

4. **M. longiflora,** Greene (*M. pulchella*, Piper). Sts. 4–12 in. high, from a short tuberous root: st.-lvs. oblong-lanceolate to ovate, 1–3 in. long and ½–1½ in. wide, glabrous or hairy above, glabrous beneath: fls. bright blue, in early spring, the infl. short and congested; calyx-lobes acute, ciliate, to ⅙in. long; corolla ½–¾in. long, the tube twice or more as long as limb, the glabrous scales conspicuous in throat: nutlets rugose. Mont. to B. C. and N. Calif.

5. **M. ciliata,** Don (*Pulmonaria ciliata*, James). Sts. usually many, 1–4 ft. high: basal lvs. ovate to lanceolate, 2–6 in. long and 1½–4 in. wide, ciliate on margins, glabrous beneath and sometimes papillate above, often glaucous, long-petioled, the upper lvs. nearly sessile: fls. bright blue, in late spring or summer; calyx-lobes obtuse, ciliate, ⅛in. or less long; corolla ½–¾in. long, the tube about length of limb, the glabrous or pubescent scales conspicuous in throat: nutlets rugose. Mont. to Ore. and New Mex.

6. **M. oblongifolia,** Don (*Pulmonaria oblongifolia*, Nutt.). Sts. 4–12 in. high: basal lvs. oblong, 1–3 in. long and ¼–¾in. wide, petioled, hairy above, glabrous beneath, the st.-lvs. sessile: fls. blue, in spring; calyx-lobes acute, ciliate, about ¼in. long; corolla ½–¾in. long, the tube equalling or slightly longer than limb, the usually glabrous scales conspicuous in throat: nutlets rugose. Mont. to Wash. and N. Calif. Var. **nevadensis,** L. O. Williams (*M. nevadensis*, A. Nels. *M. nutans*, Howell), has lvs. glabrous above.

5. **MYOSOTIS,** L. Forget-me-not. Low ann. or per. herbs widely grown for their clusters of dainty fls.; about 50 species inhabiting both the north and south temp. zones, the cult. forms coming mainly from Eu.—Plants branching, diffuse or erect, more or less hairy: lvs. alternate, entire: fls. blue, rose, or white, in simple or branched terminal racemes, without bracts; calyx small, 5-cleft; corolla salverform, the 5 lobes convolute in the bud, the throat usually crested; stamens 5, included;

ovary of 4 almost separate lobes, in fr. forming 4 smooth shining nutlets attached by their bases. (Myoso-tis: Greek signifying *mouse-ear,* from the lvs.)

A. Lobes of calyx broad and short, much less than half the length of calyx-tube; calyx with appressed hairs..1. *M. scorpioides*
AA. Lobes of calyx sharp and narrow, half or more the length of tube; calyx with prominently divergent hairs.
B. Lvs. large, often 3–4 in. long, lower ones broadly oblanceolate and distinctly petioled..2. *M. azorica*
BB. Lvs. smaller, mostly lanceolate to oblong and not or scarcely petioled..........3. *M. sylvatica*

1. **M. scorpioides,** L. (*M. palustris,* Lam.). TRUE FORGET-ME-NOT of Eu. Sts. from slender stolon-like rootstocks, decumbent and rooting below, pubescent or nearly glabrous, 6–18 in. long: lvs. oblong-lanceolate or oblanceolate, 1–2 in. long, nearly sessile: racemes loosely fld., pedicels in fr. much longer than the calyx, spreading; calyx with hairs all straight and appressed, the lobes deltoid, acutish, much shorter than the tube; corolla ¼in. or more across with flat limb, bright blue with yellow eye or pink or white: nutlets sessile, margined. Eu., Asia; nat. in N. Amer. Var. **semperflorens,** Bergmans (*M. palustris* var. *semperflorens,* Hort.), dwarf, to 8 in., flowering all summer.

2. **M. azorica,** H. C. Wats. Coarse per. with decumbent base, 12–18 in. high, the lower part of the st. with prominent retrorse white hairs: lvs. large, the lower ones 3–4 in. long, broadly oblanceolate and rounded at apex, narrowed into petiole, the upper st.-lvs. oblong and sessile but usually ½in. or more broad: racemes dense in anthesis and more or less secund; calyx usually unequally lobed, and covered with strong setose hairs much like a little bur; corolla blue, about ¼in. across, with whitish eye. Azores, Canaries, Algeria.

3. **M. sylvatica,** Hoffm. Erect ann. or bien., 1–2 ft. high, hirsute-pubescent, green or cinereous, profusely branched from base: lvs. oblong-linear or oblanceolate, ½–2 in. long, nearly sessile, obtuse or acutish: racemes long and loose; pedicels ascending, usually much longer than calyx; calyx deeply cleft, hirsute, lower hairs spreading and hooked, upper erect and straight; corolla ¼–⅓in. broad, blue with a yellow eye, or in some vars. pink or white: nutlets more or less margined and carinate ventrally, sessile. Eu., N. Asia; sparingly nat. in N. Amer.—Grown under many names, as Distinction, Oblongata Perfecta, Perfection, Robusta Grandiflora, Victoria, White Gem, and others. Known in cult. frequently as *M. alpestris* and *M. dissitiflora;* the true **M. alpestris,** F. W. Schmidt (*M. rupicola,* Smith), is a densely tufted per. having loose papery sheaths at base of sts., native in arctic regions of Eu. and N. Amer.; **M. dissitiflora,** Baker, differs mainly in having stalked nutlets, native of Switzerland.

6. **OMPHALODES,** Moench. NAVELWORT. NAVEL-SEED. Low-growing herbs, resembling the forget-me-not, a few sometimes grown in fl.-gardens; about 24 species native to the Medit. region, Cent. Asia, and Japan, also in Mex.—Ann. or per. herbs, glabrous or minutely hairy: basal lvs. long-petiolate, the st.-lvs. few and alternate: racemes loose, without bracts or at base leafy-bracteate; fls. white or blue, usually long-stalked; calyx 5-parted, enlarging in fr.; corolla-tube very short, with blunt scales in throat, the 5 broad obtuse lobes imbricated; stamens 5, inserted on the corolla-tube, included; ovary 4-lobed: nutlets with smooth or toothed and inturned border, depressed, with nearly horizontal seeds, in this differing from Myosotis. (Omphalo-des: Greek *navel-shaped,* referring to the seeds.)

A. Plant ann., glabrous: st.-lvs. linear or lanceolate..1. *O. linifolia*
AA. Plant per., pubescent: st.-lvs. elliptic to ovate.
B. Racemes short: plant stoloniferous..2. *O. verna*
BB. Racemes elongated: plant not stoloniferous..3. *O. cappadocica*

1. **O. linifolia,** Moench (*Cynoglossum linifolium,* L.). Erect ann. 1 ft. high, glabrous and slightly glaucous: basal lvs. spatulate or oblong-spatulate, slender-petioled; st.-lvs. linear-lanceolate, remotely ciliate, 1–2½ in. long, sessile: fls. white or rarely bluish, to ½in. across, long-pedicelled, in elongated racemes in summer and autumn: nutlets with toothed inflexed margin. Spain and Portugal.

2. **O. verna,** Moench. CREEPING FORGET-ME-NOT. Stoloniferous per., the slender ascending fl.-sts. 4–8 in. high: lvs. ovate to ovate-lanceolate, the basal long-petioled, 1–3 in. long, the st.-lvs. few and short-petioled, all with acuminate callous-tipped apex, sparsely hairy: fls. blue, varying to white, ½in. across, borne on long pedicels in a few-fld. short raceme in spring: nutlets hairy, with narrow entire margin. Eu.

3. **O. cappadocica,** DC. (*Cynoglossum cappadocicum,* Willd. *O. cornifolia,* Lehm.). Per. from a creeping rhizome, with erect or ascending sts. to 10 in. high: basal lvs. cordate-ovate, to 4 in. long, acute, long-petioled, densely hairy, with prominent lateral nerves; st.-lvs. smaller and nearly sessile: fls. bright blue, ⅓in. across, borne on long pedicels in elongated racemes in spring: nutlets with an entire hairy margin. Asia Minor.

7. **MOLTKIA,** Lehm. Herbs or subshrubs, 6 species native in Medit. region and Asia, one sometimes planted in the rock-garden.—Lvs. alternate, entire: fls. blue or yellow, in terminal scorpioid bracted cymes or racemes; calyx with 5 linear lobes; corolla funnelform, with 5 erect lobes and sometimes pubescent throat; stamens exserted, with slender filaments and oblong anthers; style filiform, the stigma small: nutlets 4 or sometimes only 1 or 2, smooth or wrinkled. (Molt-kia: named for Count Joachim Gadske Moltke, founder of the natural history museum at Copenhagen, 1746–1818.)

M. suffruticosa, Brand (*Pulmonaria suffruticosa,* L. *Lithospermum graminifolium,* Viv. *M. graminifolia,* Benth. & Hook.). Pubescent subshrub to 1½ ft.: lvs. linear, 1–5 in. long, revolute, white-tomentose beneath: fls. purple-blue, ½in. long: nutlets rugose. Italy.

8. **ONOSMA,** L. Hairy herbs or subshrubs, nearly 90 species in Medit. region to Himalayas, a few planted for ornament.—Lvs. alternate, entire, with prominent midnerve: fls. yellow, blue or white, borne in bracted one-sided racemes; calyx with linear or lanceolate lobes, enlarged in fr.; corolla tubular or ventricose, with very short lobes and throat without scales; stamens usually included, the linear anthers deeply sagittate at base; style filiform, with small stigma: nutlets 4, usually smooth and shining. (Onos-ma: from *ass* and *smell.*)

A. Corolla yellow.
  B. Fls. short-pedicelled; bracts shorter than calyx.......................1. *O. stellulatum*
  BB. Fls. sessile; lower bracts longer than calyx.......................2. *O. tauricum*
AA. Corolla white or rose.......................3. *O. albo-roseum*

1. **O. stellulatum,** Waldst. & Kit. Per. from a woody base; sts. numerous, herbaceous, to about 8 in. or more, pendent to ascending, the stiff appressed hairs from a stellate-hispid tubercle: lvs. linear-oblong, also stellate-hispid, plane, mostly 1–2 in. long: cymes forking; pedicels ¼–⅓in. long; bracts shorter than calyx; calyx-lobes about ¼in. long; corolla pale yellow, glabrous, tubular, about ¾in. long. S. E. Eu.

2. **O. tauricum,** Pall. Very near to *O. stellulatum* but fls. sessile and longer, lower bracts exceeding calyx. S. E. Eu.—*O. tauricum,* Willd., a later homonym, is probably a synonym of no. 1.

3. **O. albo-roseum,** Fisch. & Mey. (*O. album,* Hort.). Habit and pubescence much as in *O. stellulatum:* lvs. spatulate-oblong, rounded at apex: fls. short-pedicelled; calyx ½in. or longer; corolla white, later red, finally bluish, almost 1 in. long, puberulent. Asia Minor.

9. **LITHOSPERMUM,** L. Cromwell. Ann. or per., herbaceous or fruticose, 60–70 species in N. and S. Amer. and Eurasia.—Lvs. alternate, entire: fls. white, yellow or violet, in bracted racemes or spikes; calyx usually divided; corolla tubular or salverform, the tube cylindrical, lobes spreading, imbricate; throat with intruded appendages or with pubescent or glandular areas; stamens affixed in tube, included; style filiform; stigmas geminate; ovules 4: nutlets usually 4, smooth or verrucose. (Lithosper-mum: Greek *stone seed,* the seeds being like small stones.)

A. Fls. yellow or orange.
  B. Corolla-tube ⅝–1 in. long, lobes more or less fimbriate, throat with well-developed crests.......................1. *L. incisum*
  BB. Corolla-tube ¼in. long, lobes entire, throat without crests.......................2. *L. canescens*
AA. Fls. blue or purple.
  B. Lvs. 1–3 in. long: corolla-tube ¼in. long.......................3. *L. purpureo-cæruleum*
  BB. Lvs. ¼–1 in. long: corolla-tube ½in. long.......................4. *L. diffusum*

1. **L. incisum,** Lehm. (*L. angustifolium,* Michx.). Puccoon. Per. by a deep root, strigose and scabrous, ½–2 ft. tall, with erect or ascending sts.: lvs. linear, sessile, acutish, ½–2 in. long, about ⅛in. wide: fls. of two kinds, in terminal leafy racemes; corolla of the earlier ones salverform, about 1 in. long, bright yellow, the tube three to five times as long as the lance-linear calyx-segms., lobes erose or fimbriate, throat crested, tube not bearded within; later fls. smaller and pale yellow, cleistogamous: nutlets white, shining, more or less pitted. Ont. to Ill., B. C. to Mex.

2. **L. canescens,** Lehm. (*Batschia canescens,* Michx.). Puccoon. Per. ½–1½ ft., silky-strigose at least on younger growth: lvs. oblong or linear-oblong, subsessile, ½–1½ in. long, ⅙–½in. wide: fls. about ½in. long, dimorphous; calyx-segms. linear-lanceolate, shorter than corolla-tube; corolla orange-yellow, the tube somewhat funnel-shaped, about ¼in. long, not bearded nor crested within, lobes entire: nutlets white, smooth, shining. Pa. to Sask., Kans., Ala.

3. **L. purpureo-cæruleum,** L. Per. with sterile prostrate sts. rooting at the tips and 1–3 suberect fertile sts. 1–2 ft. high and forking above, more or less hispid: lvs. lanceolate, 1–3

in. long, ¼–½in. wide, strigose: fls. in dense clusters; calyx-lobes linear, ¼in. long; corolla first purple then blue, the tube enlarged upward, ¼in. long, bearded and with 5 folds within, lobes ⅛in. long: nutlets white, shining. Eu.

4. **L. diffusum,** Lag. (*L. prostratum,* Loisel.). Dwarf or prostrate evergreen subshrub, freely branched, 2–8 in. high: lvs. linear to linear-lanceolate, sessile, revolute, ¼–1 in. long, hairy on both surfaces: fls. purplish or blue; calyx-lobes linear, hairy, 3⁄16in. long; corolla-tube enlarged upward, about ½in. long, pubescent without and within, lobes ⅛in. long: nutlets yellowish, shining. W. Medit.—Several hort. vars. and color forms are cult.

10. **PULMONARIA,** L. Lungwort. Per. herbs of about 12 species in Eu. and Asia, a few grown in fl.-gardens.—Rootstock creeping: basal lvs. long-stalked and often broad; cauline lvs. few and alternate: fls. rather large, blue or purplish, in terminal forked cymes, the lower or almost all bracteate; calyx tubular-campanulate, 5-toothed or -cleft to the middle, enlarging in fr.; corolla with cylindric tube and 5 obtuse lobes, the throat with 5 tufts of hair instead of scales; stamens included in the corolla-tube: nutlets 4, smooth, base surrounded by a tubular annular rim. (Pulmona-ria: Latin *lung;* one species having been regarded as a remedy for diseases of the lungs.)

A. Cauline lvs. broadly ovate, sessile, the base auriculate-cordate: plant sparsely glandular.......1. *P. officinalis*
AA. Cauline lvs. linear-lanceolate to narrowly ovate-elliptic in outline, the base subsessile to petioled, somewhat cuneate: plant glandular.
B. Lvs. white-spotted, ovate-elliptic.......2. *P. saccharata*
BB. Lvs. entirely green, linear- to oblong-lanceolate.......3. *P. angustifolia*

1. **P. officinalis,** L. Blue Lungwort. Jerusalem-Sage. Plant 6–12 in. high, rough-hairy but only sparsely or not at all glandular: lvs. white-spotted, basal 2–4 in. long, ovate-cordate, distinctly petioled; cauline lvs. sessile, broadly ovate, base auriculate-cordate, apex acute: fls. ½–¾in. long, rose-violet to blue, seldom remaining reddish, in spring. Eu. Var. **immaculata,** Opiz (*P. obscura,* Dum.), has lvs. entirely green.

2. **P. saccharata,** Mill. Bethlehem-Sage. Plant 6–18 in. high, with setose-hairy sts. having few articulate glands: lvs. white-spotted, basal oval, acuminate at both ends, slightly decurrent into petiole; cauline lvs. ovate-oblong, petioled or subsessile: fls. whitish or reddish-violet, in spring. Eu.—Material so listed may be *P. picta,* Rouy.

3. **P. angustifolia,** L. (*P. azurea,* Bess.). Sts. setose-hairy with few glands, 6–12 in. high: lvs. green, basal linear- to oblong-lanceolate, gradually tapering to and decurrent on petiole; cauline lvs. few, linear-lanceolate to lanceolate-elliptic, semi-amplexicaul to cuneate: fls. blue, in spring. Eu.

11. **SYMPHYTUM,** L. Comfrey. About 25 species of erect often hispid herbs, sometimes grown for the variegated foliage in certain vars., native in Eu., N. Afr., and W. Asia.—Roots sometimes tuberous: lvs. basal or alternate or the upper occasionally nearly opposite; st.-lvs. often decurrent: fls. in bracted scorpioid often branching racemes or in terminal cymes; calyx 5-cleft or 5-parted into linear segms.; corolla broadly tubular, almost campanulate above the insertion of the stamens, the throat with 5 lanceolate or linear scales, the 5 lobes very short; ovary 4-lobed: nutlets 4, obliquely ovoid, erect, rugose, the base surrounded by a tumid annular rim. (Sym-phytum: Greek *to grow together,* in reference to the supposed healing virtues.)

A. Lvs. decurrent on the st.: hairs not recurved: tips of corolla-lobes recurved.......1. *S. officinale*
AA. Lvs. not decurrent on the st.: hairs recurved and prickle-like: tips of corolla-lobes erect.......2. *S. asperum*

1. **S. officinale,** L. Common Comfrey. Hispid branching per. about 3 ft. high, with thick root: lvs. 3–6 in. long, basal and lower cauline oblong-ovate, upper oblong-lanceolate, all decurrent at base and acuminate: fls. white, yellowish, purple, or rose, long-pedicelled, about ½in. long, in drooping scorpioid racemes, the tips of corolla-lobes recurved. Eu., Asia; nat. in N. Amer.

2. **S. asperum,** Lepech. (*S. asperrimum,* Donn). Prickly Comfrey. Branching per. 2½–5 ft. high or more, with thick root; sts. rough with retrorse prickles: lvs. hispid-prickly on both surfaces, petioled, ovate or elliptic, acuminate, the lower cordate or rounded at base and to 8 in. long: fls. at first rose then blue, smaller than those of *S. officinale,* the tips of corolla-lobes erect. Russia to Iran; nat. in N. Amer.

12. **ANCHUSA,** L. Alkanet. Bugloss. Ann. or per. herbs of the Old World, a few cult. for their showy fls.; 30 or 40 species.—Hispid or villous plants with al-

ternate lvs. and panicled leafy-bracteate scorpioid cymes or racemes with elongate branches: fls. blue, violet or white, seldom yellow; calyx 5-cleft or -parted into narrow lobes; corolla trumpet-shaped, the throat closed by scales, the 5 lobes obtuse; stamens inserted at the middle of the corolla-tube, included, the filaments short: nutlets attached at base and surrounded by a tumid annular rim, rugose. (Anchusa: Greek *anchousa*, a paint for the skin.)

A. Fls. large, ½–¾in. across; calyx ⅓–½in. long, the lobes linear.................1. *A. azurea*
AA. Fls. small, ⅛–¼in. across; calyx ¼in. or less long, the lobes triangular to lanceolate.
  B. Tube of corolla much shorter than limb: nutlets erect........................2. *A. Barrelieri*
  BB. Tube of corolla longer than limb: nutlets horizontal.
    C. Lobes of calyx about equalling tube: lvs. ⅓–1 in. across..................3. *A. officinalis*
    CC. Lobes of calyx shorter than tube: lvs. ⅓in. or less across..................4. *A. capensis*

1. **A. azurea,** Mill. (*A. italica*, Retz.). Hispid per. 3–5 ft. high: lvs. oblong or lanceolate, 2–6 in. and more long, with broad sessile or somewhat clasping base narrowed to a winged petiole: fls. bright blue, ½–¾in. across, blooming in summer and autumn; scales in throat densely covered with tufted hairs; calyx ⅓–½in. long, cut nearly to base into linear acuminate segms.: nutlets oblong, erect. Medit. region.—Known in such hort. forms as Dropmore, Opal, Perrys, Picotee, Pride of Dover.

2. **A. Barrelieri,** Vitm. (*Buglossum Barrelieri*, All.). Hispid per. to 2 ft.: lvs. spatulate or oblong-lanceolate, to 6 in. long, lower attenuate into long petiole, the upper sessile, sometimes with denticulate or wavy margins: fls. deep blue, to ¼in. across, in panicled racemes in spring; corolla with short tube and white scales in throat having very short papillæ at apex; calyx about ⅛in. long, cut to middle or below into obtuse broad lobes: nutlets erect, cylindrical. (Named for Jacques Barrelier, 1634–1673, French botanical collector.) Eu., Asia Minor.

3. **A. officinalis,** L. Hairy bien. or per. 1–2 ft. high: lvs. lanceolate, sessile, 3–6 in. long and to 1 in. wide, the basal ones clustered and attenuate into petiole: fls. bright blue or purple, ⅛–¼in. across, sometimes flesh-colored, in loose one-sided racemes becoming 5 in. long, opening in pairs, blooming in summer and autumn; corolla-tube longer than limb, scales in throat densely pubescent; calyx ¼in. long, cut to middle or below into lanceolate or triangular lobes: nutlets horizontal, ovoid. Eu., Asia Minor.

4. **A. capensis,** Thunb. Hairy bien. 1½ ft. high: lvs. narrow-lanceolate or linear, to 5 in. long and ⅓in. wide, the lower attenuate at base: fls. blue margined with red and with white throat, varying to white, ¼in. across, in summer and autumn in racemes to 2 in. long; calyx about ⅙in. long, with triangular lobes shorter than tube: nutlets horizontal, ovoid. S. Afr.

13. **PENTAGLOTTIS,** Tausch (*Caryolopha*, Fisch. & Trautv.). One per. herb native in Eu.—Differs from Anchusa in the ovate netted-veined lvs. and nutlets with a small stalked attachment rather than sessile and broad. (Pentaglot-tis: Greek *five-tongued*.)

P. sempervirens, Tausch (*Anchusa sempervirens*, L.). Hairy, 1–3 ft. high: lvs. ovate, acuminate, conspicuously veined, the lower attenuate into a long petiole: fls. rich blue, about ¼in. long, nearly sessile in long-peduncled bracted cymes in spring and summer; tube of corolla shorter than calyx; scales in throat ciliate.

14. **BRUNNERA,** Steven. Three species of herbs native in Eu., one planted for ornament.—Distinguished from Anchusa by the ovate conspicuously veined lvs. and the infl. without bracts. (Brunne-ra: named for S. Brunner, 1790–1844, Swiss botanist.)

B. macrophylla, Johnston (*Myosotis macrophylla*, Bieb. *Anchusa myosotidiflora*, Lehm.). Somewhat hispid per. branched from base, 1½ ft. high, the sts. slender and leafy: basal lvs. long-petioled, ovate, sometimes to 8 in. across, cordate or reniform at base, short-acuminate; lower st.-lvs. similar but smaller and with shorter petioles; upper st.-lvs. narrower, tapering to a short petiole or sessile base: fls. small, ⅛–¼in. across, blue, long-pedicelled, in panicled racemes in summer. Siberia, Caucasus.

15. **ECHIUM,** L. Vipers Bugloss. Some 30–40 herbaceous or shrubby species from the Canaries and Madeira to W. Asia, a few grown out-of-doors in Calif. or in the greenhouse.—Plants usually scabrous, hispid or canescent: lvs. alternate: fls. in scorpioid simple or forked spikes, with bracts small or foliaceous; calyx with 5 narrow lobes; corolla tubular-trumpet-shaped, the throat oblique and dilated, without appendages; corolla-lobes 5, roundish, unequal, somewhat spreading or erect; stamens 5, inserted below the middle of the corolla-tube, unequal and exserted;

ovary deeply 4-lobed: fr. of 4 nutlets, erect, wrinkled. (Ech-ium: from the Greek for a viper.)—The hort. species are not well understood botanically.

A. Plant herbaceous, more or less hispid with stiffish white hairs: infl. a loose panicle of coiled racemes.
  B. Stamens little exserted, not exceeding the longer corolla-lobes .... 1. *E. plantagineum*
  BB. Stamens far-exserted from corolla .... 2. *E. vulgare*
AA. Plant more or less shrubby, not at all hispid: infl. a long narrow spike or thyrse composed of coiled racemes or spikelets.
  B. Fls. deep blue or purple: plant more or less hirsute .... 3. *E. fastuosum*
  BB. Fls. white or blue with white lines: plant with short appressed often silky pubescence.
    C. Corolla exserted at least half its length: fls. pedicelled .... 4. *E. giganteum*
    CC. Corolla exserted barely half its length: fls. sessile or nearly so .... 5. *E. candicans*

1. **E. plantagineum,** L. Erect or somewhat diffuse ann. or bien. to 3 ft. high, subsimple and hispid-villous with long white hairs: lvs. obtuse, appressed-hairy, the basal oval and attenuate to a petiole, the cauline oblong-lanceolate: fls. in elongate paniculately disposed one-sided racemes; bracts linear-lanceolate, dilated at base, about equalling the calyx; calyx-lobes elongate, linear-lanceolate; corolla violet and blue, ⅞in. long, nearly twice as long as the calyx, the lobes unequal; stamens about equalling the longer corolla-lobes. S. Eu.

2. **E. vulgare,** L. BLUE-WEED. BLUE-DEVIL. Bristly-hairy bien., with erect much-branched sts. 1–2½ ft. high: lvs. oblong to linear-lanceolate, 2–6 in. long, obtuse or acute, sessile, or the lower and basal ones attenuate into petioles: fl.-buds pink; fls. bright blue to violet-purple, ⅞in. long, many on short one-sided racemes forming a narrow thyrse; segms. of calyx much shorter than corolla; limb of corolla oblique, the lobes very unequal; stamens long-exserted. Eu., Asia.

3. **E. fastuosum,** Jacq. Shrubby branching plant 3–6 ft. high, grayish-hirsute with soft hairs: lvs. lanceolate, acuminate, nervose: infl. cylindric and spike-like, about 6 in. long and 2 in. wide, consisting of numerous densely-fld. coiled one-sided spikelets; buds pink; fls. purple or dark blue, about ½in. long; stamens red, long-exserted. Eu. coast, Canaries.

4. **E. giganteum,** L. Shrubby and branching, 6–10 ft. high, whitish with short fine hairs: lvs. lanceolate, acuminate, subattenuate at base into a petiole, whitish with silky appressed hairs, the basal lvs. becoming 1½ ft. long: fls. in forked one-sided scorpioid racemes aggregated in a dense thyrsoid panicle; corolla white, somewhat irregular, about twice as long as the calyx; stamens strongly exserted. Teneriffe.

5. **E. candicans,** L. f. Shrubby and branching, 4–6 ft. high, grayish with closely appressed hairs and also with more or less fine tomentum: lvs. lanceolate, acuminate, nervose: infl. a long spike, dense or somewhat lax, composed of very many one-sided densely-fld. scorpioid spikelets; corolla white or blue with white lines, exserted barely half its length; stamens well-exserted. Madeira, Canaries.

16. **HELIOTROPIUM,** L. Herbs or sometimes shrubs, widely grown in borders and greenhouses for the fragrant fls.; upwards of 250 species in warm regions.—More or less villous or scabrous, seldom glabrous: lvs. alternate or rarely nearly opposite: fls. small, borne in terminal forking often scorpioid clusters or sometimes axillary; calyx 5-parted or -lobed, with linear or lanceolate segms.; corolla-tube cylindric, with naked throat; stamens included, the filaments very short; ovary 4-celled, with entire terminal style: fr. of 4 nutlets, splitting apart or cohering in pairs. (Heliotropium: *heliotropic*, turning to the sun.)

H. arborescens, L. (*H. peruvianum*, L. *H. corymbosum*, Ruiz & Pav.). COMMON HELIOTROPE. Per. to 4 ft. high: lvs. oval or oblong-lanceolate, 1–3 in. long, very veiny: fls. ⅛–¼in. long, violet or purple varying to white, fragrant, in a close cyme, the corolla-tube longer than calyx. Peru.

17. **CORDIA,** L. Trees or shrubs (some of them vines or above the base herbaceous) occasionally planted for their showy fls.; species about 250 in trop. and subtrop. regions, mostly in the western hemisphere.—Lvs. mostly alternate, petioled, entire or dentate: fls. bisexual or unisexual, in dense head-like clusters or scorpioid cymes; calyx tubular or campanulate, 3–5-toothed or -lobed; corolla usually white or orange, tubular, funnelform or salverform, with 4 or more lobes; stamens as many as the corolla-lobes, exserted or included; style 4-lobed or -parted: fr. a 4-celled usually 4-seeded drupe, subtended or more or less inclosed by the persistent calyx. (Cor-dia: a German botanist, Valerius Cordus, 1515–1544.)

A. Fls. orange or scarlet, 1–2 in. long .... 1. *C. Sebestena*
AA. Fls. white, ½in. or less long .... 2. *C. Myxa*

1. **C. Sebestena,** L. (*Sebesten Sebestena*, Britt.). GEIGER-TREE. Evergreen shrub or small tree to 30 ft.: lvs. rough-hairy, ovate, 4–8 in. long, entire or undulate: fls. 1–2 in. long, orange or scarlet, pedicelled, in large open terminal clusters, the crumpled corolla-lobes and stamens 5–12; tube of corolla twice as long as calyx: drupe about ¾in. long, white, inclosed in the hazel-like husk formed by the persistent calyx. (Sebestena: Arabic name originally applied to a different plant.) Keys of Fla. and S.

2. **C. Myxa,** L. Deciduous polygamous tree to 40 ft.: lvs. broad-ovate, 3–5 in. long, entire or undulate, glabrous, rough above: fls. ½in. or less long, white, in large clusters; tube of corolla about length of calyx; corolla-lobes 5, oblong, recurved, equalling tube: drupe ovoid, about ¾in. across, tan-colored to nearly black, shining, with sweetish mucilaginous pulp. (Myxa: from Greek for pulp, referring to the fruits.) India to Australia.

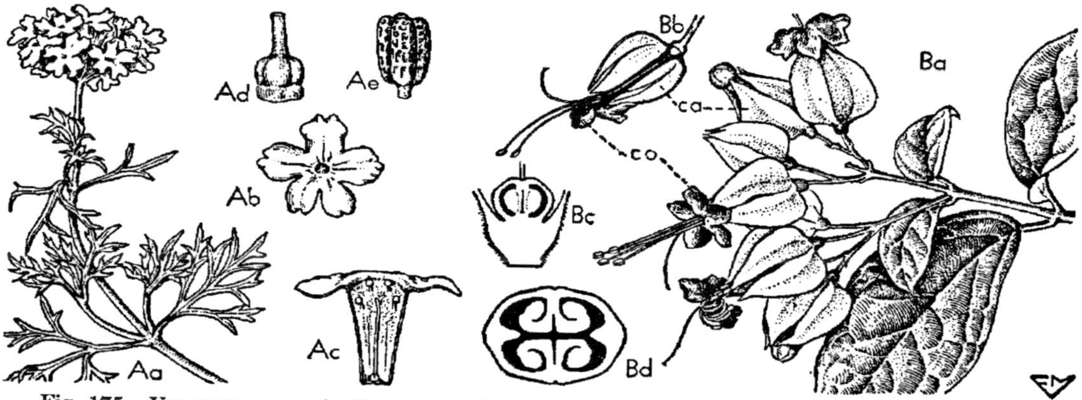

Fig. 175. VERBENACEÆ. A, *Verbena bipinnatifida:* Aa, flowering branch, × ½; Ab, flower, face view, × ¾; Ac, flower, corolla expanded, × 1; Ad, ovary, × 8; Ae, nutlets, × 3. B, *Clerodendrum Thomsoniæ:* Ba, flowering branch, × ½; Bb, flower, vertical section, × ½; Bc, ovary, vertical section, × 3; Bd, same, cross-section, × 6. (ca calyx, co corolla.)

175. VERBENACEÆ. VERVAIN FAMILY

Herbs, shrubs, or trees, of trop. and subtrop. distribution, about a score of the genera being in cult. in N. Amer., either as ornamentals or for medicinal or other economic purposes; in all 75 genera and about 1,300 species; the family is closely related to the Labiatæ and not clearly distinct.—Lvs. opposite, rarely whorled or alternate, simple or compound: fls. bisexual, rarely regular, usually oblique or 2-lipped; calyx 4–5-, rarely 6–8-toothed; corolla gamopetalous, 4–5-lobed, the lobes imbricated; stamens 4 and didynamous or rarely 5 or 2, epipetalous; disk present; ovary superior, of 2 or rarely 4 or 5 carpels, entire or 2–4-lobed, 2–5-celled, but by false partitions 4–10-celled, each cell with a solitary ovule, or sometimes 1-celled; style 1, stigma usually 1: fr. a drupe or berry, often separating into drupelets.

A. Fls. sessile in spikes which are simple or clustered.
B. Ovary 4-celled, the fr. separating into 4 nutlets. . . . . 1. VERBENA
BB. Ovary 2-celled, the fr. separating into 2 nutlets.
C. Fls. in long slender spikes . . . . 2. ALOYSIA
CC. Fls. in dense spikes or heads.
D. Spikes globose or cylindrical: fr. dry . . . . 3. PHYLA
DD. Spikes flat-topped: fr. drupaceous . . . . 4. LANTANA
AA. Fls. pedicelled.
B. Calyx spreading broadly and uniformly from base upward, the margin entire or very obscurely sinuate-lobed, large . . . . 5. HOLMSKIOLDIA
BB. Calyx not as above.
C. Infl. a simple raceme.
D. Lobes of calyx shorter than tube . . . . 6. DURANTA
DD. Lobes of calyx longer than tube . . . . 7. PETREA
CC. Infl. of cymose or head-like clusters which are variously arranged.
D. Lvs. palmately compound . . . . 8. VITEX
DD. Lvs. not compound.
E. Corolla regular . . . . 9. CALLICARPA
EE. Corolla irregular.
F. Fr. drupe-like: fls. (in ours) large . . . . 10. CLERODENDRUM
FF. Fr. dry, subcapsular: fls. ½in. or less long . . . . 11. CARYOPTERIS

1. **VERBENA,** L. Ann. or per. herbs or subshrubs, some of them common fl.-garden or greenhouse subjects grown for their clusters of showy and often fragrant fls. which bloom in constant succession from June till frost; about 125 species, chiefly natives of trop. and extra-trop. Amer.; some are weedy plants in fields and waste grounds of the U. S. and Canada.—Diffuse or sometimes creeping, glabrous or more or less hairy: lvs. opposite, seldom whorled or alternate, toothed or incised or dissected, rarely entire: spikes terminal, seldom axillary, compact or elongate and remotely fld., sometimes broadly corymbose or paniculate on an erect st.; fls. small or medium-sized, sessile; calyx tubular, 5-ribbed, 5-toothed; corolla-tube straight or incurved, the limb spreading, somewhat 2-lipped, the 5 lobes oblong or broad, obtuse or retuse; stamens 4, in pairs; ovary entire or very shortly 4-lobed at apex, 4-celled, the cells 1-ovuled: fr. dry, inclosed in the calyx, separating into 4 narrow pyrenes or nutlets. (Verbe-na: ancient Latin name of the common European vervain, *V. officinalis.*)

A. Plant upright, stiff: spikes or heads borne in panicles or cymes.
  B. Lvs. petioled .... 1. *V. hastata*
  BB. Lvs. sessile or partially clasping.
    C. Bracts much longer than calyx .... 2. *V. rigida*
    CC. Bracts about equalling calyx .... 3. *V. bonariensis*
AA. Plant decumbent or ascending: spikes or heads solitary.
  B. Calyx-lobes very slender and setaceous.
    C. Lvs. cut into linear divisions .... 4. *V. bipinnatifida*
    CC. Lvs. not cut into linear divisions .... 5. *V. canadensis*
  BB. Calyx-lobes short, not setaceous.
    C. Spikes compact and not much elongated in fr.
      D. Lvs. toothed .... 6. *V. peruviana*
      DD. Lvs. lobed or cut .... 7. *V. elegans*
    CC. Spikes elongated in fr.
      D. Foliage lobed or cleft, but divisions not linear.
        E. Length of lvs. 2 in. or more .... 8. *V. hybrida*
        EE. Length of lvs. less than 2 in .... 9. *V. Teasii*
      DD. Foliage cut into linear divisions.
        E. Length of calyx ⅓–½in .... 9. *V. Teasii*
        EE. Length of calyx ¼–⅓in.
          F. Hairs of calyx sordid, slightly spreading .... 10. *V. tenera*
          FF. Hairs of calyx white, closely appressed .... 11. *V. tenuisecta*

1. **V. hastata,** L. Erect per. to 5 ft., roughish-pubescent: lvs. lanceolate or oblong-lanceolate, to 6 in. long, serrate or dentate, sometimes hastately 3-lobed at base, petioled, acute or acuminate: spikes narrow, peduncled, 2 in. or more long, forming a panicle; bracts ovate, shorter than calyx; corolla blue, about ⅛in. across. N. S. to B. C. south to Fla. and Ariz. Var. **alba,** Bergmans, has white fls.

2. **V. rigida,** Spreng. (*V. venosa,* Gill. & Hook.). Herbaceous per. 1–2 ft. high, with tuberous roots; sts. simple, creeping at base, ascending, 4-angled, hispid: lvs. rigid, hispid, prominently nerved, oblong to oblong-lanceolate, 2–4 in. long, unequally subincisely and often saliently dentate or serrate, acute at apex, entire and half-clasping at base: spikes in a close terminal panicle, subternate, fastigiate and finally cylindric, at least the lateral pedunculate; bracts subulate, ciliate, often purplish, exceeding the hairy calyx; corolla lilac or bluish-purple to nearly sky-blue, ¼in. across, very thinly villous without, the slender tube three times as long as calyx. S. Brazil and Argentina; nat. N. C. to Fla. and Tex. Var. **lilacina,** Hort., has lilac fls.

3. **V. bonariensis,** L. Ann. or per. 2–4 ft. high, rough-pubescent: lvs. elliptic to elliptic-lanceolate, to 4 in. long, toothed, clasping at base: spikes dense, to 1½ in. long, borne in clusters which are often panicled; bracts shorter than or equalling calyx; corolla lilac, about 1/12in. across, tube less than twice as long as calyx. S. Amer.; nat. S. C. to Tex.

4. **V. bipinnatifida,** Nutt. More or less prostrate per. with ascending sts. to 15 in., hirsute-pubescent: lvs. divided into oblong or linear divisions, 1–2 in. long, long-petioled: heads dense, about 1 in. long but elongating in fr.; bracts about length of calyx which has setaceous lobes; corolla lilac-purple, about ¼in. across, tube slightly longer than calyx. S. D. to Calif. and Mex.

5. **V. canadensis,** Britt. (*Buchnera canadensis,* L. *V. Aubletia,* Jacq. *V. Drummondii,* Hort. *Glandularia canadensis,* Small). CLUMP VERBENA. Per. 6–18 in. high but often grown as ann., branching and ascending from a creeping or rooting base, slender, soft-pubescent, hirsute or glabrate: lvs. 1–4 in. long, ovate or ovate-oblong, with truncate or broadly cuneate base tapering into a margined petiole, incisely lobed and toothed, often more deeply 3-cleft: spikes pedunculate, elongated in fr.; bracts subulate or linear-attenuate, shorter than or equalling the similar slender and unequal teeth of the narrow calyx; corolla reddish-purple or lilac, rarely white, the limb ½–⅔in. broad; tube bearded within and at the orifice, slightly longer than calyx. Colo. and Mex. eastward across the continent.

6. **V. peruviana,** Britt. (*Erinus peruvianus,* L. *V. chamædryfolia,* Juss. *Glandularia peruviana,* Small). Per. but grown as ann.; sts. slender, forking, creeping at base, rather stiffly pubescent, branches somewhat ascending: lvs. oblong-lanceolate or ovate, ½–2 in. long, more or less attenuate at base into a short petiole, crenate or subincisely and often unequally serrate, appressed-hispid: fls. in flattish capitate spikes which are solitary on long ascending peduncles; bracts lanceolate-subulate, ciliate; calyx sparingly glandular, more than twice as long as bracts, with short teeth; corolla-limb irregular, rich scarlet; tube white, to ¾in. long, nearly twice as long as calyx; stamens included. Argentina, S. Brazil; escaped in Fla.

7. **V. elegans,** HBK. Per. with prostrate rooting sts.: lvs. lanceolate-ovate, 1–2 in. long, tapering into margined petioles, incisely pinnatifid, hirsute, lighter green beneath: spikes pedunculate, few-fld.; bracts lanceolate, ciliate, shorter than the short-toothed calyx; corolla rose or purple, ⅖in. across, tube nearly twice as long as calyx. S. Mex. Var. **asperata,** L. M. Perry, has ascending sts. and many-fld. spikes; this var. is in cult. under many erroneous names.

8. **V. hybrida,** Voss (*V. hortensis,* Vilm.). COMMON GARDEN VERBENA. Per. but grown as ann.; sts. stoutish, 1–1¾ ft. long, decumbent and commonly creeping at base; entire plant grayish with long stiffish more or less spreading hairs or these less pronounced on upper surface of lvs.: lvs. petioled, oblong or oblong-ovate, 2–4 in. long, obtuse, margins with broad unequal rounded teeth or near the base somewhat lobed: peduncles and infl. glandular; heads flattish or convex but elongating in fr. to 3 in., mostly long-peduncled, fls. red, pink, white, blue, purple, or variegated; bracts longer than short-toothed calyx; corolla-tube often twice as long as calyx, hairy within and often glandular-pubescent without, the limb about ¾in. across, with broad obovate deeply notched lobes and white or yellowish eye at center; stamens included.—A race running into many color forms and resulting probably from the fusion of *V. peruviana* with other species. From *V. peruviana* it differs mainly in its stouter sts., its grayish hue due to longer and more dense spreading stiffish hairs, in the more uniformly rounded teeth and lobes of the usually obtuse lvs., in the larger size of heads and fls. and in the proportionally broader corolla-lobes.

9. **V. Teasii,** Moldenke. Hybrid between *V. hybrida* and *V. tenuisecta,* first raised by Edward Teas of Houston, Tex.; sts. decumbent or ascending, hairy: lvs. variable, less than 2 in. long, 3-parted, pinnatifid or bipinnatifid into linear divisions, hairy: heads dense, many-fld., elongating in fr. to 6 in. or more, long-peduncled; bracts much shorter than white-hairy short-toothed calyx; corolla blue, purple, red, pink or white, limb to ⅓in. across, tube longer than calyx.

10. **V. tenera,** Spreng. Somewhat shrubby per.; sts. cespitose, decumbent, rooting; branches slender, 4-angled, ascending, sparsely hairy: lvs. 3-parted and again pinnately cut into linear acute entire subrevolute divisions, narrowed at base to a short petiole, strigose-hispidulous: spikes pedunculate; calyx elongated, twice as long as bracts, with short more or less spreading hairs, sprinkled at angles with short stipitate patellaform glands; corolla rose-violet, ¾in. long; anther-appendages barely exserted, claviculate, subrecurved. S. Brazil and La Plata region. Var. **Maonettii,** Regel (*V. pulchella* var. *Maonettii,* Regel), has white-margined corolla-lobes; Italy.

11. **V. tenuisecta,** Briq. (*V. erinoides,* Chodat not Lam. *Glandularia tenuisecta,* Small). MOSS VERBENA. Per. to 1 ft., with decumbent ascending sts.: lvs. 1–1½ in. long, 3-pinnatifid into linear entire or dentate divisions, becoming glabrescent: spikes pedunculate, dense and short but elongating to 1½ in.; calyx with long tube and short setaceous teeth, strigose-pubescent, four times as long as bracts, with black glands; corolla blue, ¼–⅓in. across, tube longer than calyx. S. Amer.; nat. Ga. to La. Var. **alba,** Moldenke, has white fls.

2. **ALOYSIA,** Ort. About 20 species of aromatic shrubs native in warm parts of the Americas, one widely grown in the tropics and in the greenhouse N.—Lvs. opposite or whorled: fls. small, in long spikes which are axillary or panicled, bracts deciduous; calyx 4-toothed, inclosing the dry fr. which becomes 2 separate nutlets; corolla of 2 nearly equal lips; stamens 4, didynamous; ovary 2-celled. (Aloy-sia: Latinized form of Louisa, for Maria Louisa, wife of King Charles IV of Spain, died 1819.)

A. triphylla, Britt. (*Verbena triphylla,* L'Her. *A. citriodora,* Ort. *Lippia citriodora,* HBK.). LEMON VERBENA. Small shrub to about 10 ft., with striate and more or less scabrous branches: lvs. in whorls of 3 or 4, lanceolate, 2–3 in. long, short-petioled, entire or toothed at the middle, glabrous, densely covered beneath with glandular dots, lemon-scented: spikes whorled and axillary or collected in terminal panicles often 3 in. across; fls. white, about $^3/_{16}$in. long, blooming in summer and autumn; calyx densely puberulent; corolla-tube longer than calyx. Argentina, Chile.

3. **PHYLA,** Lour. Creeping or procumbent per. herbs, of about 15 trop. species, one cult. in warm regions for ground-cover.—Lvs. opposite, toothed or lobed: fls.

in dense cylindrical axillary spikes, bracts cuneate to flabellate; calyx short, 2-lobed, inclosing the dry fr. which becomes 2 separate nutlets; corolla of 2 unequal lips, tube longer than calyx; stamens 4, didynamous; ovary 2-celled. (Phy-la: from Greek, referring to dense fl.-heads.)

P. nodiflora, Greene (*Lippia repens,* Spreng.). Rooting and widely spreading, sts. somewhat woody at base: lvs. small, to about ¾in. long on creeping flowering shoots, spatulate to oblong or lanceolate, attenuate to petiole, obtuse or subacute, dentate toward apex, glabrous or pubescent: heads ovoid or subcylindric, ¼ to nearly ½in. across, on long peduncles; bracts herbaceous with narrow membranaceous villous margins, acuminate, imbricated, shorter than corolla-tube; corolla purple or white, 1/12in. long. Tropics. Var. **canescens,** Moldenke (*Lippia canescens,* HBK.), is canescent. Var. **rosea,** Moldenke, has lilac fls. with yellow throat.

4. **LANTANA,** L. Shrubs or herbs sometimes half-climbing, one a popular florists' plant; probably 75 species mostly in trop. and subtrop. Amer. but also in the Old World.—Scabrous-hirsute, pubescent or tomentose: lvs. opposite, dentate, often rugose: fls. small, sessile in the axils of the bracts, borne in dense spikes or heads which are terminal or axillary and stalked; calyx very small; corolla somewhat irregularly 4–5-parted but not bilabiate, the tube slender; stamens 4, didynamous, attached midway in the tube, included; ovary 2-celled, becoming a fleshy or juicy drupe with 2 bony nutlets. (Lanta-na: old name, also applied to a Viburnum.)

A. Fls. orange or yellow changing to red: sts. erect, more or less prickly.
B. Plant short-pubescent to puberulent, unless spreading-hirsute on young peduncles........1. *L. Camara*
BB. Plant coarsely and harshly spreading-hirsute on sts., branches, peduncles, petioles and lf.-surfaces........2. *L. tiliæfolia*
AA. Fls. rosy-lilac: sts. trailing, not prickly........3. *L. montevidensis*

1. **L. Camara,** L. Hairy shrub to 6 ft. or more, unarmed or slightly prickly: lvs. ovate or oblong-ovate, 1–5 in. long, mostly short-acuminate, crenate-dentate, short-petioled, rather thick, rugose, scabrous above, pubescent beneath: heads dense, 1–2 in. across, flat-topped, on stout axillary peduncles often longer than lvs.; bracts narrow, about half as long as corolla; fls. ¼–½in. long, usually opening yellow or orange but changing to red or scarlet. (Camara: S. American name.) Trop. Amer. north to Tex. and S. Ga. Var. **aculeata,** Moldenke (*L. aculeata,* L.), is armed with stout recurved prickles. Var. **flava,** Moldenke (var. *crocea,* Bailey. *L. flava,* Medic.), has sulfur-yellow fls. changing to saffron. Var. **hybrida,** Moldenke (*L. hybrida,* Neubert), is the dwarf garden form with yellow fls. Var. **mista,** Bailey, has outer fls. yellowish changing to saffron and brick-red, and yellow inner fls. becoming orange. Var. **nivea,** Bailey, fls. white.

2. **L. tiliæfolia,** Cham. Unarmed or slightly prickly, coarsely and harshly spreading-hirsute almost throughout: lvs. round or oval, cordate at base, 1–4 in. long, crenate-dentate, petioled: heads hemispherical, 1–2 in. across, on peduncles equalling lvs.; fls. orange becoming brick-red, ⅓in. long; outer bracts strigose-hairy and about length of white-hairy corolla-tube. Brazil.—Often cult. under the name *L. Camara.*

3. **L. montevidensis,** Briq. (*Lippia montevidensis,* Spreng. *Lantana Sellowiana,* Link & Otto. *L. delicatissima,* Hort.). WEEPING OR TRAILING LANTANA. Free-flowering shrub with lopping or trailing pubescent branches to 3 ft. long: lvs. ovate, about 1 in. long, abruptly narrowed at base, coarsely toothed: fls. about ½in. long, in long-peduncled heads 1 in. or more across, rosy-lilac, the outer bracts or scales of the involucre broad-ovate and hairy and not more than half as long as the slender pubescent corolla-tube. S. Amer. and an escape in Fla.

5. **HOLMSKIOLDIA,** Retz. Shrubs sometimes grown under glass or in the open far S.; probably 3 species, African and Asian.—Glabrous or white-hairy: lvs. opposite, entire or dentate: fls. racemose or cymose; calyx spreading from base, membranaceous, colored, the border entire or broadly and indistinctly 5-lobed; corolla-tube curved, the oblique limb with 5 short lobes; stamens 4, didynamous, exserted together with the style: fr. an obovoid drupe, 4-lobed, included in the enlarged calyx. (Holmskiol-dia: Theodor Holmskiold, 1732–1794, Danish nobleman and scientist.)

H. sanguinea, Retz. CHINESE-HAT-PLANT. A straggling evergreen shrub 10–30 ft. high: lvs. ovate, 2–4 in. long, petioled, entire or serrate, acuminate: calyx brick-red to orange, spreading broadly and uniformly from base upward, the margin entire or very obscurely sinuate-lobed, becoming 1 in. diam.; corolla darker colored, 1 in. long, the up-curved tube widening upward: drupe ⅓in. or less long. Subtrop. Himalayan region.

6. **DURANTA,** L. Shrubs and trees of 8–10 species in Mex., W. Indies, S. Amer., one reaching Key West, cult. in the open S. and sometimes in the greenhouse.—Glabrous or woolly, often armed with axillary spines: lvs. opposite or whorled, entire or toothed: racemes long or short, terminal or rarely axillary; fls. small, in the axils of small bracts; calyx inclosing the fr. at maturity but not attached to it, with short teeth; corolla-limb of 5 spreading oblique or equal lobes, the tube usually curved; stamens 4, didynamous; stigma unequally 4-lobed: fr. an 8-seeded juicy drupe inclosed by the enlarged calyx. (Duran-ta: after Castor Durantes, physician in Rome and botanist, died about 1590.)

A. Length of lvs. 2 in. or less .... 1. *D. repens*
AA. Length of lvs. 3–8 in. .... 2. *D. stenostachya*

1. **D. repens,** L. (*D. Plumieri,* Jacq.). GOLDEN DEWDROP. PIGEON-BERRY. SKY-FLOWER. Shrub or small tree to 18 ft., branches unarmed or spiny, often drooping or trailing: lvs. ovate-elliptic, oval or obovate, ½–2 in. long, attenuate into short petiole, entire or coarsely serrate above middle, obtuse or acute, finely pubescent or glabrous at length: fls. in loose panicled racemes to 6 in. long; calyx with acute lobes shorter than tube; corolla lilac, tube longer than calyx, limb less than ½in. across: fr. yellow, globose, ¼ to nearly or quite ½in. diam., covered by calyx which is closed into a curved beak. Key West, W. Indies, Mex. to Brazil. Var. **alba,** Bailey, fls. white. Var. **canescens,** Moldenke, fls. purple with white center, calyx densely white-hairy. Var. **grandiflora,** Moldenke, fls. to ¾in. across. Var. **variegata,** Bailey, foliage variegated.

2. **D. stenostachya,** Tod. Shrub to 15 ft., spineless: lvs. oblong-lanceolate, 3–8 in. long, serrate or entire, acuminate, pubescent on veins beneath: fls. in slender racemes; corolla lilac, limb less than ½in. across: fr. yellow, ⅓in. across. Brazil.—Some of the material grown as *D. repens* belongs here.

7. **PETREA,** L. PURPLE WREATH. Species about 30 in Mex., W. Indies to Brazil; twining or arborescent shrubs, planted in warm regions.—Lvs. opposite or whorled, leathery, pinnately veined: fls. violet, purple, bluish or white, in long terminal racemes; calyx with 5 scales in throat, the colored lobes often becoming green and rigid in fr.; corolla usually a little more intensely colored, the oblique limb 5-cut, tube short-cylindric; stamens 4, didynamous; ovary imperfectly 2-celled, cells 1-ovuled: fr. a drupe included in the calyx, indehiscent, 2-celled and 2-seeded or by abortion 1-seeded. (Petre-a: Robt. James, Baron Petre, 1713–1743, an English patron of botany.)

P. volubilis, Jacq. QUEENS WREATH. Woody vine or subshrub to 35 ft.: lvs. rough on both sides, elliptic, 2–8 in. long, entire or undulate, acute or short-acuminate, petioles to ½in. long: fls. pale blue to purple, in axillary racemes 3–12 in. long in early spring; calyx-tube densely pubescent outside, one-quarter to one-half as long as pedicel, the 5 oblong obtuse lobes three to four times longer than tube in fr., exceeding the funnelform deciduous corolla. Cuba to Brazil. Var. **albiflora,** Moldenke, fls. white.

8. **VITEX,** L. Trees or shrubs yielding a few ornamental subjects; about 100 species, distributed throughout trop. and subtrop. regions of both hemispheres, few in temp. regions.—Lvs. deciduous or persistent, opposite, digitate, with 3–7 (rarely 1) lft.: fls. white, blue, or yellowish, in few to many-fld. cymes which are often panicled; calyx campanulate, usually 5-toothed; corolla tubular-funnelform, with 5-lobed oblique and slightly 2-lipped limb; stamens 4, didynamous, often exserted: fr. a small drupe, with a 4-celled stone. (Vi-tex: ancient Latin name for this or a similar shrub.)

A. Lfts. 5–7, stalked.
B. Fl.-clusters dense, arranged in a single spike-like infl. or these in groups of several: lfts. lanceolate .... 1. *V. Agnus-castus*
BB. Fl.-clusters loose, in a widely spreading panicle: lfts. mostly broader .... 2. *V. Negundo*
AA. Lfts. 3, sessile .... 3. *V. trifolia*

1. **V. Agnus-castus,** L. CHASTE-TREE. HEMP-TREE. MONKS PEPPER-TREE. Grayish-tomentose shrub or small tree to 10 ft., with strong aromatic odor: lvs. long-petioled, velvety; lfts. 5–7, lanceolate, 3–4 in. long, ¼–¾in. wide, acuminate, narrowed at base to short stalk, entire or with few coarse teeth, very dark green above, grayish-tomentose beneath: fls. in late summer and autumn, the dense clusters arranged in spikes 5–7 in. long, these terminal or in upper axils, often forming groups of several; corolla usually pale or lilac, grayish outside, ⅓in. long; stamens and style exserted. (Agnus-castus: ancient classi-

cal name.) S. Eu. Var. **alba,** West., fls. white. Var. **latifolia,** Loud. (*V. latifolia,* Mill. *V. macrophylla,* Hort.), has lfts. mostly oblong-lanceolate and ¾–1¼ in. wide.

2. **V. Negundo,** L. Shrub or small tree to 15 ft., with quadrangular branchlets: lvs. long-petioled; lfts. usually 5, occasionally 3, stalked, elliptic-ovate to lanceolate, 1½–4 in. long, acuminate, serrate or entire, dark green above, grayish-tomentulose beneath: fls. lilac or lavender, scarcely ¼in. long, stalked, in rather loose clusters arranged in a loose widely spreading terminal panicle 5–8 in. long; stamens and style slightly exserted. (Negundo: Malabar name.) China, India. Var. **heterophylla,** Rehd. (var. *incisa,* Clarke. *V. incisa* var. *heterophylla,* Franch. *V. laciniata,* Hort.), has lfts. incisely serrate, or in extreme forms deeply pinnatifid, and less showy fls. in late summer; N. China, Mongolia.

3. **V. trifolia,** L. Shrub to 12 ft., sometimes prostrate: lfts. 3 or sometimes 1, sessile, oblong or oblong-elliptic, 2–3 in. long, acute, glabrous above, gray-pubescent beneath: fls. in terminal panicles to 4 in. long; corolla lavender or blue with white spot at base of lip, ½in. across. Asia to Australia. Var. **variegata,** Moldenke, lvs. variegated with white.

9. **CALLICARPA,** L. BEAUTY-BERRY. Over 40 species in trop. and subtrop. regions of Asia, Australia, N. and Cent. Amer.; planted for ornament.—Shrubs or trees, often with stellate or scurfy pubescence: lvs. opposite, usually serrate, deciduous: fls. small, pink, bluish, or whitish, in axillary clusters; calyx short-campanulate, truncate or slightly 4-toothed, rarely 4-parted; corolla with short tube, 4-lobed; stamens 4, equal, exserted; ovary 4-celled, the cells 1-ovuled: fr. a subglobose berry-like drupe with 2–4 stones. (Callicar-pa: Greek *beauty* and *fruit.*)

A. Lvs. tomentose or pubescent beneath.
  B. Cymes nearly sessile . . . . 1. *C. americana*
  BB. Cymes with peduncles to ½in. long . . . . 2. *C. Bodinieri*
AA. Lvs. glabrous or only slightly pubescent beneath.
  B. Branchlets scurfy-pubescent . . . . 3. *C. dichotoma*
  BB. Branchlets glabrous . . . . 4. *C. japonica*

1. **C. americana,** L. FRENCH-MULBERRY. Shrub to 6 ft., with scurfy-stellate down and glandular-dotted: lvs. ovate-oblong, 2–6 in. long, acuminate, obtusely serrate, acute or cuneate at base, greenish above, whitish or rusty beneath: cymes nearly sessile, many-fld.; corolla bluish, hardly ⅙in. long: fr. violet. Va. to Tex. and W. Indies. Var. **lactea,** F. G. Muller (var. *alba,* Rehd.), has white fr. very conspicuous in autumn and early winter.

2. **C. Bodinieri,** Lévl. (*C. Giraldiana* var. *subcanescens,* Rehd.). Shrub to 10 ft., branchlets scurfy-pubescent: lvs. elliptic to oblong-elliptic, 2–5 in. long, acuminate, dentate, pubescent beneath: cymes many-fld., 1 in. across, on peduncles to ½in. long; corolla lilac: fr. violet. (Named for E. M. Bodinier, page 651.) China. Var. **Giraldii,** Rehd. (*C. Giraldiana,* Hesse), has lvs. and cymes less pubescent (named for Giuseppe Giraldi, Italian missionary in China about 1890).

3. **C. dichotoma,** Koch (*C. purpurea,* Juss.). Shrub to 4 ft., branchlets scurfy-pubescent: lvs. elliptic or obovate, 1½–3 in. long, acuminate, crenately serrate above the middle, entire toward the cuneate base, glandular beneath: cymes few- to many-fld., about ½in. across, on peduncles ¼in. or more long; fls. pink, about ⅛in. long: fr. lilac-violet. Japan, China.

4. **C. japonica,** Thunb. Shrub to 5 ft., branchlets soon becoming glabrous: lvs. elliptic or ovate-lanceolate, 2½–5 in. long, long-acuminate, serrulate, cuneate at base: cymes many-fld., ½–1 in. across, on peduncles ¼in. or more long; fls. pink or whitish, about ¼in. long: fr. violet or white in var. **leucocarpa,** Sieb. Japan. Var. **angustata,** Rehd., has narrower lvs.

10. **CLERODENDRUM,** L. GLORYBOWER. Shrubs or trees, often scandent, cult. in the greenhouse and out-of-doors; perhaps 100 species in the tropics, mostly of the eastern hemisphere.—Lvs. opposite or verticillate, mostly entire, sometimes toothed or lobed, not compound: fls. usually in terminal cymes or panicles, white, violet or red; calyx campanulate or rarely tubular, shallowly 5-toothed or 5-lobed; corolla-tube usually slender and cylindric, the limb somewhat unequally 5-lobed and spreading; stamens 4, inserted on the corolla-tube, long-exserted and curved; style exserted, shortly 2-cleft; ovary imperfectly 4-celled, the cells 1-ovuled: fr. a drupe often inclosed in the calyx. (Cleroden-drum: Greek *chance* and *tree;* of no significance.)

A. Plant of twining habit.
  B. Calyx white . . . . 1. *C. Thomsoniæ*
  BB. Calyx pale red . . . . 2. *C. speciosum*
AA. Plant of erect or self-supporting habit.
  B. Corolla-tube 1 in. or less long.
    C. Calyx large and spreading, ⅜–½in. long.

D. Lvs. truncate or cordate at base, coarsely toothed, acute: infl. dense. . . . 3. *C. fragrans*
DD. Lvs. narrowed at base, very closely serrate or entire, long-acuminate: infl. loose . . . . 4. *C. trichotomum*
CC. Calyx small, less than ¼in. long.
D. Fls. 1½–2 in. diam.: lvs. densely pubescent above . . . . 5. *C. speciosissimum*
DD. Fls. ½–¾in. diam.: lvs. glabrous or sparsely pubescent above.
E. Color of fls. rose-red: lvs. toothed . . . . 6. *C. Bungei*
EE. Color of fls. white or pinkish: lvs. entire . . . . 7. *C. glabrum*
BB. Corolla-tube to 4 in. long . . . . 8. *C. indicum*

1. **C. Thomsoniæ,** Balf. (*C. Balfouri*, Hort.). Tall twining glabrous evergreen shrub: lvs. opposite, oblong-ovate or ovate, often 4–6 in. long, acuminate, entire, petiolate, prominently veined: fls. in lax forking axillary or terminal racemes; calyx about ¾in. long, strongly 5-angled, narrowed at apex, white, the 5 segms. ovate and acute; corolla with slender tube about 1 in. long, and spreading crimson rotund-lobed limb; stamens and style long and well-exserted. (Named for the wife of W. C. Thomson, missionary at Old Calabar on the west coast of trop. Afr., who in 1861 sent specimens of this plant to Balfour at Edinburgh.) W. Afr.

2. **C. speciosum,** D'Ombrain. A garden hybrid between *C. Thomsoniæ* and *C. splendens*, Don., the latter being a climber with slender woody sts. producing on leafy growths dense many-fld. cymes of fls. 1 or more in. diam., bright scarlet passing into bright yellow: the hybrid is intermediate between the parents in habit and foliage, producing continuously throughout the summer a profusion of dull red fls. whose old calyces are more or less persistent and ornamental after the fls. are past.

3. **C. fragans,** R. Br. Subshrub to 8 ft., with angled branches, pubescent: lvs. broadly ovate, 3–10 in. or more long, truncate or cordate at base, on long stout petioles, acute, coarsely toothed: fls. in terminal compact hydrangea-like corymbs to 3 in. across, single-fld. in the wild form, usually double in cult. (var. **pleniflorum,** Schauer), very fragrant; calyx about ½in. long, purple or red, the 5 segms. lanceolate and acuminate; corolla white or pink, 1 in. across, tube about length of calyx. China, Japan.

4. **C. trichotomum,** Thunb. Erect graceful subshrub to 10 ft. or more: lvs. mostly opposite, soft and flaccid, ovate, to 5 in. long, somewhat narrowed at base, entire or closely serrate, long-acuminate, pubescent with short stiffish hairs: fls. on slender forking reddish peduncles, the white corolla with slender tube sometimes twice as long as the reddish-brown (½in. long) calyx; segms. of calyx ovate, acute: fr. bright blue. Japan.

5. **C. speciosissimum,** VanGeert (*C. fallax*, Lindl.). Erect shrub to 12 ft., branching after flowering, sts. bluntly 4-angled: lvs. opposite, cordate-ovate, often 1 ft. long on stout hairy petioles, entire or toothed, acute or acuminate, densely pubescent: infl. in erect panicles often 18 in. or more long; fls. numerous, bright scarlet, 1½–2 in. diam., the narrow tube 1 in. long, much exceeding the short-toothed calyx, the rounded lobes reflexed: fr. scarlet. Java.

6. **C. Bungei,** Steud. (*C. fœtidum*, Bunge). Shrub to 6 ft., of spreading habit, sparsely branched: lvs. opposite, very broadly ovate, often 1 ft. long, long-petioled, coarsely toothed, acuminate, dark green above, pubescent and reddish beneath, strong-scented: fls. rosy-red, ¾in. diam., in a dense capitate corymb 4–8 in. across; calyx short, toothed, slender corolla-tube three to four times longer, to 1 in. long. (Named for A. von Bunge, page 40.) China.

7. **C. glabrum,** E. Mey. Shrub or small tree to 15 ft.: lvs. opposite or whorled, oblong-ovate, to 5 in. long, entire, glossy above, glabrous or slightly pubescent on veins beneath: fls. small, in dense cymes 3 in. or more across, white or pinkish; corolla-tube about ¼in. long, exceeding the small calyx: fr. white. S. Afr.

8. **C. indicum,** Kuntze (*Siphonanthus indica*, L. *C. Siphonanthus*, R. Br.). TUBE-FLOWER. TURKS-TURBAN. Shrub or woody herb to 8 ft.: lvs. usually whorled, lanceolate-oblong, to 6 in. long, entire, glabrous: fls. in axillary cymes or forming a panicle, closing in morning; calyx about ½in. long, lobes ovate; corolla white, tube to 4 in. or more long: fr. red or purple. E. India; escaped in S. U. S.

11. **CARYOPTERIS,** Bunge. BLUEBEARD. About a half dozen species of deciduous shrubs in E. Asia, planted for ornament.—Glabrous, pubescent or tomentose: lvs. opposite, short-petioled, serrate or entire: cymes many-fld., axillary or panicled and terminal; calyx campanulate, deeply 5-lobed with lanceolate teeth, spreading and somewhat enlarged in fr.; corolla 5-lobed, with short cylindric tube and spreading limb, 1 segm. larger and fringed; stamens 4, exserted, 2 of them longer; style slender, 2-parted at apex: fr. dry, capsular, shorter than the calyx, 4-valved, separating into 4 somewhat winged nutlets. (Caryop-teris: Greek for *nut* and *wing*.)

A. Lvs. ovate or oblong-ovate, serrate . . . . 1. *C. incana*
AA. Lvs. linear-lanceolate, nearly entire . . . . 2. *C. mongholica*

1. **C. incana,** Miq. (*C. Mastacanthus*, Schauer. *C. tangutica*, Maxim.). Small shrub to 5 ft. but often dying back and treated essentially as a per. herb: lvs. ovate or oblong-ovate,

1½–3 in. long, petioled, coarsely serrate, very dark green above, grayish-tomentose beneath: cymes in pedunculate clusters, densely-fld.; fls. violet-blue or lavender-blue, in autumn; corolla about ¼in. long; stamens exserted about ¼in. China, Japan. Var. **candida,** Schneid., has white fls.—Known to the nursery trade as "blue spirea."

2. **C. mongholica,** Bunge. Shrub to 4 ft.: lvs. linear-lanceolate to linear, to 2 in. long, petioled, nearly entire, dull green above, whitish-pubescent beneath: cymes few-fld., with slender peduncles; fls. blue, about ½in. long. China, Mongolia.

Fig. 176. LABIATÆ. A, *Salvia splendens:* Aa, inflorescence, × ½; Ab, flower, vertical section, × 1; Ac, ovary, × 3; Ad, same, vertical section, × 3; Ae, nutlets, × 2. B, *Stachys grandiflora:* Ba, inflorescence, × ¼; Bb, flower, × ½; Bc, same, corolla expanded, × 1. C, *Molucella lævis:* whorl of flowers, × ½. D, *Teucrium lucidum:* Da, inflorescence, × 1; Db, flower, × 2. E, *Monarda didyma:* Ea, inflorescence, × ½; Eb, flower, × 1. F, *Mentha spicata:* Fa, inflorescence, × ½; Fb, flower, × 3. G, *Nepeta Faassenii:* Ga, inflorescence, × ½; Gb, flower, × 2.

176. LABIATÆ. MINT FAMILY

A family of more than usual economic importance owing to the volatile oil and bitter principles, comprising 160 genera and about 3,000 species distributed over the whole earth, but especially abundant in the Medit. region, the Orient and the mts. of the subtropics; about 60 genera are in cult. in N. Amer., most of them being garden annuals or perennials cult. for the flavor or odor, for ornamental purposes or for medicine; the name refers to the 2-lipped (bilabiate) character of the corolla of most species.—Herbs or shrubs, commonly with 4-angled sts., and usually containing a fragrant oil: lvs. opposite or whorled: infl. capitate or more usually the fls. in verticillate spikes or racemes; fls. bisexual, very rarely unisexual, irregular, seldom regular, usually bilabiate; calyx regular or 2-lipped, commonly 5-toothed or -cleft; corolla hypogynous, gamopetalous, 5-lobed or rarely 4-lobed, 1 lip sometimes obsolete, the lobes imbricated; stamens 4, didynamous, or only 2, epipetalous; hypogynous disk well developed, thick, entire or lobed; ovary superior, of 2 carpels, deeply 4-lobed, 4-celled, each cell 1-ovuled; style 1, basal or sub-basal, stigmas 2: fr. of 4 1-seeded nutlets ("seeds"), the exocarp rarely fleshy and persisting with the seed.

A. Fls. unisexual, the plants diœcious: winter-flowering per. grown in warm regions .... 34. IBOZA
AA. Fls. bisexual, both stamens and pistil present in each fl.
B. Perfect stamens 2, the other 2 rudimentary or obsolete.
C. Limb of calyx 5-toothed, the teeth equal or nearly so.
D. Fls. (in ours) 1–2 in. long, in dense head-like clusters .... 20. MONARDA
DD. Fls. (in ours) ¼in. long, in loose cymose clusters .... 29. CUNILA
CC. Limb of calyx bilabiate (the 2 lips may or may not be toothed).
D. Lf.-margins revolute; lvs. persistent .... 3. ROSMARINUS
DD. Lf.-margins not revolute; lvs. deciduous.
E. Upper lip of corolla entire or bifid; fertile anther-cells usually 1 .... 18. SALVIA
EE. Upper lip of corolla 4-lobed; fertile anther-cells 2 .... 19. PEROVSKIA
BB. Perfect stamens 4.
C. Corolla regular or nearly so, mostly 4-lobed, the upper lobe sometimes slightly larger than others.
D. Plant herbaceous: stamens of about equal length .... 30. MENTHA
DD. Plant woody or strongly suffrutescent: 2 stamens much longer than others and much-exserted .... 32. ELSHOLTZIA
CC. Corolla bilabiate, the upper lip often 2-lobed and lower lip 3-lobed.
D. Filaments connate along basal third or more, forming a sheath about the style .... 33. COLEUS
DD. Filaments not basally connate.
E. Back of calyx bearing conspicuous erect crest or flap-like fold; calyx with 2 entire lips .... 4. SCUTELLARIA
EE. Back of calyx without crest; calyx normally with 3, 5 or 10 teeth.
F. The fls. in verticels (false whorls) arranged compactly along axis in dense uninterrupted head or spike (verticels not separated by open internodes except sometimes at base), heads or spikes may be solitary, racemose or paniculate.
G. Infl. (in ours) paniculate; calyx split down one side, flaring and bract-like .... 26. MAJORANA
GG. Infl. spicate or racemose; calyx not split and bract-like.
H. Calyx bilabiate, lips entire or toothed.
I. Calyces subtended by large entire and reniform bracts, closed when in fr. .... 10. PRUNELLA
II. Calyces subtended by small bracts, never reniform, open in fr.
J. Plants erect, 1–2½ ft. high .... 7. AGASTACHE
JJ. Plants prostrate, or sts. decumbent, mostly less than 1 ft. high .... 28. THYMUS
HH. Calyx of 5 teeth, equal or nearly so.
I. Plants woody shrubs, at least basally so.
J. Fls. scarlet-orange: herbage white-woolly .... 17. COLQUHOUNIA
JJ. Fls. lavender-purple to white: herbage tomentose to puberulent .... 5. LAVANDULA
II. Plants ann. or per. herbs, not basally woody.
J. Upper lip of corolla obsolete, very short and reduced to 3 minute lobes: ovary shallowly 4-lobed .... 1. AJUGA
JJ. Upper lip of corolla well developed, usually longer than lower lip: ovary deeply 4-parted.
K. Nerves of calyx mostly 15: upper pair of stamens (closest to upper lip and middle of the 2 pair) longer than lower pair .... 8. NEPETA
KK. Nerves of calyx 5–10: upper (posterior) pair of stamens shorter than lower (anterior) pair.
L. Stamens long-exserted: fl.-bracts large, obtuse, often orbicular and imbricated .... 27. AMARACUS

LL. Stamens included or scarcely exserted: fl.-bracts small, never imbricated.
M. Lvs. sharply serrate to serrulate: calyx inflated in fr.: plants glabrous or nearly so, mostly 3–5 ft. high .... 11 PHYSOSTEGIA
MM. Lvs. entire or crenate-dentate: calyx not inflated in fr.: plants hairy, often densely so, usually 1–2½ ft. high .... 16. STACHYS
FF. The fls. axillary, or in verticels that are spaced apart along axis, separated by open internodes (sometimes the very uppermost verticels confluent and slightly spicate at apex), infl. spicate, racemose, or paniculate.
G. Length of calyx about equalling corolla and always longer than corolla-tube.
H. Limb of calyx broadly dilated (not split), weakly and mucronulately 5-toothed, reticulately veined .... 15. MOLUCELLA
HH. Limb of corolla not dilated, teeth strongly prominent, venation not conspicuously reticulate.
I. Lf.-blade broad-ovate, 2½–4½ in. long: each floral lf. subtending 1 fl. .... 31. PERILLA
II. Lf.-blade ovate, mostly less than 2 in. long: each floral lf. subtending 3 fls. .... 35. OCIMUM
GG. Length of calyx much less than corolla, rarely ever as long as corolla-tube.
H. Calyx bilabiate, lips entire or comprised of two or more teeth.
I. Upper (posterior) pair of stamens longer than lower (anterior) pair: calyx 15-nerved .... 9. DRACOCEPHALUM
II. Upper pair of stamens shorter than lower pair: calyx 5–13-nerved.
J. Anthers parallel or divergent, never appressed together and coherent: sts. low, mostly prostrate or decumbent. 28. THYMUS
JJ. Anthers of each pair of stamens appressed together and coherent, under upper lip of corolla.
K. Infl. a leafless spike: lvs. mostly basal .... 21. HORMINUM
KK. Infl. branched: lvs. cauline.
L. Corolla-tube somewhat arched and ascending, being weakly S-shaped .... 22. MELISSA
LL. Corolla-tube erect and essentially straight .... 23. SATUREJA
HH. Calyx with 3, 5 or 10 teeth or lobes that are more or less uniform in size, not bilabiate.
I. Upper lip of corolla none, lower lip 5-lobed (4 of the lobes minute) .... 2. TEUCRIUM
II. Upper lip of corolla very apparent, entire or 2–3-lobed.
J. Style and stamens included within tube of corolla .... 6. MARRUBIUM
JJ. Style and stamens much exceeding tube of corolla.
K. Anthers coherent and close-appressed in pairs under upper lip of corolla .... 23. SATUREJA
KK. Anthers divergent or parallel, not coherent nor appressed.
L. Stamens divergent, anthers of each pair turned or spreading outwards.
M. Plant suffrutescent: lvs. lanceolate: fls. blue or lilac .... 24. HYSSOPUS
MM. Plant a per. herb: lvs. ovate: fls. purple or white .... 25. ORIGANUM
LL. Stamens parallel under the lower lip or only the lower 2 occasionally turned outwards.
M. Posterior or upper stamens longer than the lower or anterior pair .... 8. NEPETA
MM. Posterior or upper stamens shorter than the lower or anterior pair.
N. Floral lvs. subtending verticels shorter than fls. .... 16. STACHYS
NN. Floral lvs. subtending verticels as large as st.-lvs. or nearly so, conspicuous in infl. and exceeding fls.
O. Bracts subtending fls. nearly or quite as long as calyx-tube; corollas conspicuously hairy outside.
P. Upper lip of corolla much longer than lower; fls. deep orange or white, 1½–2 in. long .... 12. LEONOTIS
PP. Upper lip of corolla not longer than lower; fls. yellow or purple, not over 1¼ in. long .... 13. PHLOMIS
OO. Bracts not over half as long as calyx-tube; corollas not conspicuously hairy.
P. Calyx-teeth mostly subulate; fls. red-purple to white .... 14. LAMIUM
PP. Calyx-teeth acute; fls. orange-scarlet .... 17. COLQUHOUNIA

1. **AJUGA,** L. BUGLE-WEED. Ann. or per. herbs, a few used in rock-gardens and for border planting; 40–50 species widely distributed.—Herbaceous or occasionally with somewhat woody base, often decumbent or stoloniferous: lvs. coarsely toothed or incised or rarely entire, the floral similar or reduced to bracts: spikes terminal, consisting of 2- to many-fld. whorls, dense or interrupted below; fls. blue, white, or rose, 2 to many sessile in the axils of the floral lvs., the corolla withering and often persisting in fr.; upper lip obsolete and reduced to 3 minute usually tooth-like lobes; stamens 4. (Aju-ga: *not yoked,* the calyx not bilabiate.)

A. Plant stoloniferous; sts. prostrate, glabrous or nearly so........................1. *A. reptans*
AA. Plant not stoloniferous; sts. erect, grayish with long jointed hairs.
  B. Lvs. definitely toothed, the upper ones scarcely longer than fls..............2. *A. genevensis*
  BB. Lvs. scarcely or not toothed, the upper ones two to four times as long as fls......3. *A. pyramidalis*

1. **A. reptans,** L. Four to 12 in. high, stoloniferous, the sts. more or less prostrate, glabrous or nearly so: lvs. entire or repand, the basal and cauline oblong-elliptic or obovate, narrowed to a margined petiole, rounded at apex, the upper and floral ones elliptic or ovate, sessile: lower whorls of spike distant, the upper close; fls. usually violet-blue, sometimes red, white or purplish, blooming in early summer; corolla exserted. Eu. Var. **purpurea,** Hort., has dark purple lvs. Var. **variegata,** Hort., lvs. splashed and edged creamy-yellow.

2. **A. genevensis,** L. (*A. rugosa,* Hort. *A. alpina,* Hort.). Five to 14 in. high, not stoloniferous, the erect sts. grayish with long jointed hairs: lvs. mostly crenate-dentate, the lower oblong-elliptic or obovate, to 3 in. long, petioled or narrowed to a subsessile base, rounded at apex, the upper and floral ones ovate or cuneate, sessile, all sparsely hairy: fls. in spiked whorls, the lower whorls distant, the upper close; fls. blue, in early summer; corolla exserted; stamens pubescent, well-exserted. Eu. to Caucasus. Var. **rosea,** Hort., fls. red.—**A. Brockbankii,** Hort., a blue-fld. vigorous plant with some hair on sts. and with short stolons, is intermediate with *A. reptans.*

3. **A. pyramidalis,** L. Two to 10 in. high, not stoloniferous, the erect sts. thick, more or less hairy: lower lvs. obovate, 1½–4 in. long, gradually narrowed into a shorter petiole, the cauline mostly bearing fls. in the axils, broad-elliptic, almost entire, two to four times as long as the bright violet-blue fls. which bloom in early summer: stamens glabrous, scarcely exserted. Eu. Var. **metallica-crispa,** Hort., lvs. brownish-red, of metallic sheen.

2. **TEUCRIUM,** L. GERMANDER. Herbs, subshrubs, or shrubs with leafy branches of rather showy fls., a few cult.; over 100 species widely distributed through warm and temp. regions.—Lvs. entire, dentate or incised; floral lvs. similar or reduced to bracts: floral whorls 2- to rarely many-fld., in racemose spikes or heads; calyx tubular or campanulate, seldom inflated, 5-toothed; corolla-tube included or rarely exserted, limb seemingly 1-lipped, with lower lip large and upper lip small and deeply cleft; stamens 4, strongly exserted between the lobes of the upper corolla-lip: nutlets obovoid, reticulate, rugose. (Teu-crium: Teucer was the first king of Troy.)

A. Lvs. pinnate with linear segms..1. *T. orientale*
AA. Lvs. entire to toothed.
  B. Fls. about 1 in. long: lvs. mostly entire..................................2. *T. fruticans*
  BB. Fls. about ½in. long: lvs. toothed.
    C. Length of lvs. 2–5 in.: fls. not in regular whorls..........................3. *T. canadense*
    CC. Length of lvs. mostly 1 in. or less: fls. in regular whorls.
      D. St.-hairs recurved or matted; sts. ascending, often mat-forming: whorls dense, usually many-fld..4. *T. Chamædrys*
      DD. St.-hairs straight, erect; sts. erect, not mat-forming: whorls mostly 2–4-fld...5. *T. lucidum*

1. **T. orientale,** L. Shrub or subshrub to 1½ ft., spreading-hairy: lvs. to 2 in. long, green or grayish, 1- or 2-pinnate into linear segms.: fls. blue-violet, on 1–3-fld. peduncles in panicle-like infl., corolla three to four times length of calyx. S. W. Asia.

2. **T. fruticans,** L. Shrub to 3 ft., divaricately branched, covered with dense white or yellowish tomentum which is more or less deciduous from the older lvs.: lvs. petioled, ovate, obtuse, 1¼ in. long, with entire revolute margins; floral lvs. similar but smaller: fls. in racemes terminating the sts. or on short lateral branches; pedicels shorter than calyx; calyx broad-campanulate, the tube and the 5 broad lobes of about equal length; corolla blue, with long declined lower lip; stamens of about the same length, erect or strongly recurved. Eu.—Has a long blooming season.

3. **T. canadense,** L. Per. to 3 ft., appressed-pubescent: lvs. lanceolate to ovate, serrate, 1–2 in. wide, hoary beneath, green above: whorls about 6-fld., rather crowded in spike-like racemes; calyx canescent, about ⅜in. long; corolla purplish to pink or cream-color. Me. to Neb., Fla. and Tex.

4. **T. Chamædrys,** L. Per., often shrubby, 1–2 ft. high, decumbent or ascending at base, branching: lvs. short-petioled, ovate or oblong, ½–¾in. long, often rather deeply

serrate- or crenate-toothed, cuneate at base; floral lvs. smaller, often subentire: floral whorls usually 6–10-fld., the upper racemose; fls. red-purple or bright rose with red and white spots, ¾in. long, rather showy; calyx tubular-campanulate, with lanceolate acuminate teeth. Eu.—Blooming in late summer and used as a border plant.

5. **T. lucidum,** L. Shrub similar to *T. Chamædrys* and often offered as that species, distinguished by sts. always erect, pubescent with the hairs straight and erect from the st., usually densely so, and whorls of the infl. mostly 2–4-fld. Eu.—Used extensively as an edging plant or for very low formal hedges.

3. **ROSMARINUS,** L. Rosemary. A single species native to the Medit. region, well known as a garden plant, its aromatic lvs. being used as a seasoning and furnishing a volatile oil common in drug-stores.—Evergreen shrub: lvs. narrow, entire, with revolute margins: fls. subsessile, in short axillary racemes, with minute bracts; calyx ovoid-campanulate, the limb 2-lipped, the upper lip very shortly 3-toothed, the lower 2-toothed; corolla bilabiate, the upper lip emarginate or 2-cleft, the lower strongly 3-lobed, with large middle lobe strongly concave and declined; perfect stamens 2: nutlets smooth, ovoid-subglobose. (Rosmari-nus: Latin *sea-dew,* the plant common on the chalk hills of the south of France and near the seacoast.)

R. officinalis, L. Shrub 2–4 ft. high, a var. prostrate: lvs. numerous, linear, to 1¼ in. long, obtuse, thick, punctate, tomentose beneath, with strongly revolute margins: fls. light blue, about ½in. long, in short axillary more or less tomentose racemes, borne in early spring; stamens exserted.

4. **SCUTELLARIA,** L. Skullcap. Herbs or subshrubs with often showy fls., sometimes used for outdoor planting; a large genus of 150 or more species, widely distributed, mostly in temp. and mountainous regions.—Ann. or per., of various habit: lvs. often dentate, sometimes pinnatifid or entire; floral lvs. similar or bract-like: fls. blue, violet, scarlet, or yellow, opposite in pairs, sometimes in all or in the lower axils, sometimes in terminal racemes or spikes; calyx campanulate, 2-lipped, with short broad entire lips, closed after the corolla falls, finally splitting open to the base; upper lip of calyx with a crest-like projection on the back, often falling away at maturity of fr.; corolla with long-exserted tube, naked within; stamens 4, the anthers hairy: nutlets subglobose or depressed, seldom smooth. (Scutella-ria: Latin *dish,* referring to the form of the persistent calyx.)

A. Lvs. about five times as long as wide, entire. . . . . .1. *S. baicalensis*
AA. Lvs. not more than twice as long as wide, toothed.
  B. Fls. ½–¾in long: lvs. cordate at base. . . . . .2. *S. indica*
  BB. Fls. about 1 in. long: lvs. not cordate. . . . . .3. *S. alpina*

1. **S. baicalensis,** Georgi. Half-erect per. ½–1 ft. high, nearly glabrous: lvs. lanceolate, entire, obtuse, ciliate; floral lvs. similar, longer than calyx: fls. blue, in many simple racemes; calyx-hood incurved. E. Asia. Var. **cœlestina,** Hort. (*S. cœlestina,* Hort.), has large spikes of bright blue fls. nearly 1 in. long, in summer.

2. **S. indica,** L. Per., sts. procumbent at base, to 1¼ ft. long, densely pilose, slender: lvs. shorter than internodes, round-cordate, ½–1¼ in. long, round-toothed, petioled: fls. bluish, in dense terminal racemes to 4 in. long. China, Japan. Var. **japonica,** Franch. & Sav. (*S. japonica,* Morr. & Decne.), to 6 in. high, fls. lilac to blue-purple; Japan.

3. **S. alpina,** L. Per. to half-shrubby, spreading, sts. to almost 1 ft. high, more or less pubescent: lvs. lance-ovate to ovate, to 1 in. long, serrate with few blunt teeth: fls. blue-violet, sometimes white to yellowish, in dense terminal racemes to about 3 in. long. Eu.

5. **LAVANDULA,** L. Lavender. Several cult. in fl.-gardens; species upward of 25, Canary Isls. to India.—Per. herbs, subshrubs or shrubs: lvs. entire, pinnately toothed or dissected: whorls 2–10-fld., crowded into long-peduncled cylindric spikes unbranched or branched from base; fls. blue, violet, or lilac; calyx tubular, 13–15-nerved, 5-toothed; corolla-lobes nearly equal or the upper lip 2-cleft and the lower lip 3-cleft; stamens 4, declined, included; style shortly 2-cleft. (Lavan-dula: Latin *lavo,* to wash, referring to the use of lavender in the bath.)

A. Lvs. pinnately dentate: peduncles 3–8 in. long. . . . . .1. *L. dentata*
AA. Lvs. entire.
  B. Spike with a terminal tuft of enlarged bracts.
    C. Peduncle to 1 in. long: lvs. linear. . . . . .2. *L. Stœchas*
    CC. Peduncle to 2 in. long: lvs. lanceolate. . . . . .3. *L. pedunculata*

BB. Spike lacking terminal tuft of enlarged bracts.
  C. Lf.-blades about eight times as long as wide: floral bracts ovate. . . . . .4. *L. officinalis*
  CC. Lf.-blades four to six times as long as wide: floral bracts linear . . . . .5. *L. latifolia*

1. **L. dentata,** L. Somewhat shrubby: lvs. pubescent, linear, pinnately dentate, 1–1½ in. long, the teeth truncate: spikes long-peduncled; fls. deep purple, ¼–½in. long. Medit. region.

2. **L. Stœchas,** L. Shrub to 3 ft., gray-tomentose: lvs. linear, ½in. long, entire, sessile, with somewhat revolute margins: fls. dark purple, about ⅛in. long, in dense short-peduncled (1 in.) spikes with terminal tuft of large purple bracts. (Stœchas: an old generic name.) Medit. region.

3. **L. pedunculata,** Cav. Similar to *L. Stœchas* but lvs. lanceolate, peduncles longer, 1–2 in., fls. smaller. W. Medit. region.

4. **L. officinalis,** Chaix (*L. Spica*, L. *L. vera*, DC.). Subshrub to 3 ft.: lvs. oblong-linear or lanceolate, to 2 in. long, entire: younger lvs. often clustered in the axils, white-tomentose, the margins revolute; floral lvs. or bracts rhomboid-ovate, acuminate, short: fls. lavender, ¼–½in. long, in 6–10-fld. whorls forming interrupted spikes. Medit. region. Var. **atropurpurea,** Hort., fls. dark lavender-purple. Var. **compacta,** Hort., low and compact, early bloomer.

5. **L. latifolia,** Vill. (*L. Spica*, Auth.). SPIKE. Lvs. broader than in *L. officinalis* and flat; bracts subtending the whorls linear and more herbaceous, usually equalling the calyces. Medit. region.

6. **MARRUBIUM,** L. HOARHOUND. HOREHOUND. One of the 30–40 species of Eu., N. Afr., and extra-trop. Asia, is widely nat. in the U. S. where it is used in large quantities in confections and medicines.—Per., branched from base, mostly silky or woolly: lvs. wrinkled, crenate or cut: fls. small, white or purplish, in many-fld. axillary whorls; calyx tubular, 5–10-nerved and with 5 or 10 awl-shaped teeth; corolla 2-lipped, the upper lip erect and notched or entire, the lower spreading and 3-cleft with a broad middle lobe; stamens 4, not exserted; ovary deeply 4-lobed, the style 2-lobed: nutlets smooth. (Marru-bium: ancient name, referring to the bitter qualities.)

M. vulgare, L. COMMON HOARHOUND. Aromatic herb 1–3 ft. high, with branched ascending white-woolly sts.: lvs. ovate to round-ovate, ½–2 in. long, narrowed to a petiole, tomentose or becoming glabrate above: calyx with 10 short teeth, each terminating in a hooked spine, the alternating ones shorter; fls. whitish, summer-blooming.

7. **AGASTACHE,** Clayton. GIANT HYSSOP. About 20 species, 1 from E. Asia, the others N. Amer.—Per. herbs: lvs. usually ovate, sometimes narrower: fls. in dense or loose whorls borne in spikes or narrow panicles, frequently with conspicuous subtending bracts; calyx turbinate or tubular in fl., 15-veined or more, 5-toothed with equal teeth or the 3 posterior ones more or less united; corolla rose, violet or white, with oblique opening; perfect stamens 4, usually exserted beyond the upper lip. (Agas-tache: from Greek *many-spiked.*)

A. cana, Woot. & Standl. (*Cedronella cana*, HOOK. *Brittonastrum canum*, Briq.). Sts. to 1 ft., puberulent: lower lvs. deltoid, to 1 in. long, coarsely crenate-serrate, petioled, upper lvs. ovate-lanceolate, subentire, subsessile, all puberulent, green, glandular pitted: spikes to 1 ft. long; calyx about ⅓in. long; corolla rose, tubular, slightly over ½in. long. Tex., New Mex.

8. **NEPETA,** L. A large genus comprising 150 species mostly in the northern hemisphere outside the Old World tropics; a few rather commonly cult., some for medicinal purposes, others as ground-cover in shady places.—Per. or ann. herbs: lvs. dentate or incised, the floral ones like the others or reduced to bracts: whorls of fls. crowded in a dense spike or in a loose cyme, rarely few-fld. and axillary; fls. mostly blue or white; calyx tubular, 15-nerved, 5-toothed; corolla somewhat 2-lipped, the upper lip straight or erect, the lower spreading and 3-lobed, with the large middle lobe concave; perfect stamens 4, in pairs, the 2 shorter ones in front; ovary 4-parted. (Nep-eta: Latin, perhaps from *Nepete*, an Etrurian city.)

A. Plant creeping: lvs. broader than long, round or reniform. .1. *N. hederacea*
AA. Plant erect: lvs. longer than broad, ovate to linear-lanceolate.
  B. Fls. ¾–1½ in. long. . . . . .2. *N. grandiflora*
  BB. Fls. ¼–⅝in. long.
    C. Lvs. mostly 2–4 in. long, linear-lanceolate: corolla almost tubular, ½in. long. . .3. *N. nervosa*

cc. Lvs. ½–2½ in. long, more or less ovate.
D. Length of lvs. ½–¾in.: corolla blue, ⅜in. long........................4. *N. Mussinii*
DD. Length of lvs. 1–2½ in.
E. Corolla whitish, ¼in. long: lvs. petioled........................5. *N. Cataria*
EE. Corolla violet or pale with purple spots, ⅝in. long: lvs. subsessile........6. *N. nuda*

1. **N. hederacea**, Trev. (*N. Glechoma*, Benth. *Glecoma hederacea*, L.). GROUND-IVY. GILL-OVER-THE-GROUND. FIELD-BALM. Somewhat pubescent per., the leafy sts. creeping and making a dense mat: lvs. long-petioled, rotund or reniform, to 1½ in. across, coarsely crenate, deeply cordate at base: fls. 2–3 together in the lf.-axils, opening in late spring and summer; bracts and calyx-teeth setaceous; corolla light blue, 1 in. long or less; pairs of stamens very unequal. Nat. from Eu., Asia.—A variegated form is sometimes cult.

2. **N. grandiflora**, Bieb. Per. to 5 ft., sts. glabrescent: lvs. ovate, 1¼–2 in. long, obtuse or infrequently acute, cordate becoming subcordate apically, crenate, paler and glabrescent beneath: verticels few-fld., pedicelled, on peduncles ½–1½ in. long, interrupted along axis, racemose; fls. ¾–1½ in. long, with bluish-purple corollas and often steel-blue glabrescent calyces and peduncles. Caucasus.—Material so named in cult. may be *M. betonicæfolia*, Mey., which differs in sts. and calyces densely and softly pubescent to tomentulose as are the lvs. beneath, or it may be *Dracocephalum sibiricum*.

3. **N. nervosa**, Royle. Per. to 2 ft., glabrous below, pubescent above, branched: lvs. linear-lanceolate, to 4 in. long, shallowly serrate, puberulent beneath: fls. light blue, in short-peduncled spikes 3–6 in. long; floral bracts nerved, ovate, sharp-acuminate, ciliate; calyx-lobes linear, long-acuminate, ciliate; corolla ½in. long, almost tubular. India.

4. **N. Mussinii**, Spreng. Diffusely branched per., whitish with soft pubescence or the lvs. green above: lvs. oblong-ovate, not exceeding ¾in. long, crenate, cordate or narrowed at base: calyx-teeth sharply acute, white-woolly or sometimes blue-woolly; corolla blue with darker spots, about ⅜in. long, the tube well-exserted from the calyx; summer and autumn. (Bears the name of Count A. Mussin-Puschkin, who in 1800–1805 visited the Caucasus in the interests of botany.) Caucasus, Iran.—Much of the material cult., as this species is of hybrid origin: **N. Faassenii**, Bergmans (*N. pseudomussinii*, Floto. *N. Mussinii*, Hort. not Spreng.), a garden hybrid of *N. Mussinii* and *N. nepetella*, cult. extensively as *N. Mussinii* but differing in its low habit, ascending sts. 12–15 in. high, smaller more oblong-lanceolate lvs. with coarser crenate-serrate margins, blue-violet fls. with shrivelled non-viable pollen and produced over a much longer blossoming period, no seed produced (named for Johannes Hubertus Faassen, 1892–, Dutch nurseryman); the plant distributed as *N. Mussinii* var. DROPMORE is presumed to be a hybrid of *N. Mussinii* and *N. grandiflora*, and differs from the former in being more strict, with narrower lvs. on longer petioles and longer corollas.

5. **N. Cataria**, L. CATNIP or CATNEP. CATMINT. Erect branching per. to 3 ft., pale green and densely downy: lvs. ovate or oblong-ovate, the larger 1½–2½ in. long, cordate at base, coarsely crenate, petioled, green above, whitish below: fls. in summer and autumn, the many-fld. clusters spicate-crowded at the ends of the branches, subtended by small floral lvs.; bracts and calyx-teeth slender-subulate, soft; corolla whitish or pale purple, dark-dotted, about ¼in. long, the tube scarcely exserted. (Cataria: from Latin for *cat*, because of the fondness of cats for this plant.) Eu., Orient.

6. **N. nuda**, L. Branching per. to 3 ft., green, subglabrous to somewhat puberulent: lvs. oblong-ovate, subsessile, crenulate, to 2 in. long: infl. paniculate, grayish-pubescent, with many whorls of 10–20 fls.; bracts subulate, about as long as pedicels; calyx ⅜in. long; corolla violet to white with purple spots, about ⅝in. long, gaping. S. Eu.

9. **DRACOCEPHALUM**, L. DRAGONHEAD. Forty species in Eu. and Asia, about 4 in N. Amer., sometimes found in fl.-gardens.—Ann. or per. herbs or sometimes woody at base, mostly erect: lvs. entire, toothed or deeply cut, the floral lvs. similar or reduced to bracts: floral whorls axillary or in terminal spikes; calyx tubular, 2-lipped, 5-toothed; corolla purple, blue or rarely white, the upper lip notched and arched, the lower 3-cleft with the middle lobe notched or cleft; stamens 4, the 2 anther-cells divaricate: nutlets smooth. (Dracoceph-alum: Greek *dragon's head*, from shape of corolla.)—As here considered, the genus includes *Moldavica*, Adans.

A. Lvs. entire.
B. Fls. ⅜–½in. long........................1. *D. Ruprechtii*
BB. Fls. ⅝–1 in. long or more........................2. *D. Ruyschiana*
AA. Lvs. toothed.
B. Fls. ½in. long........................3. *D. nutans*
BB. Fls. 1–2 in. long.
C. Calyx-tube only as long as lower lobes or shorter: lvs. incised-crenate........4. *D. Moldavica*
CC. Calyx-tube twice as long as lower lobes: lvs. serrate........................5. *D. sibiricum*

1. **D. Ruprechtii**, Regel. Per. to 2 ft., suffrutescent, sts. glabrous: lvs. narrowly elliptic to linear-lanceolate, to 1½ in. long, entire, glabrous, acute; bracts elliptic-lanceolate, ciliate, resinous-dotted, apiculate: calyx puberulent, resinous-dotted, teeth sharply acuminate and

setaceous; corolla blue to bluish-lavender, about ⅜in. long, minutely and sparsely puberulous without, glabrous within, tube not exceeding calyx; anthers glabrous; July–Aug. (Named for Franz J. Ruprecht, page 50.) Turkestan.

2. **D. Ruyschiana,** L. Per. 2 ft. high, with slightly pubescent sts.: lvs. linear-lanceolate, to 2 in. long, entire, glabrous; bracts ovate-lanceolate, ciliate, cuspidate-tipped: calyx finely pubescent, resinous-dotted, the teeth cuspidate-tipped; corolla 1 in. long, blue or bluish or in one var. white shaded with blue, hairy, the tube not exceeding the calyx, the throat funnelform; anthers villous. (Named for Frederik Ruysch, 1638–1731, Dutch anatomist and botanist.) Eu., Asia. Var. **japonicum,** Mast. (*D. argunense,* Fisch.), corolla paler, to 1½ in. long; Japan.

3. **D. nutans,** L. Per., sts. to 1 ft. high, appressed-pubescent: lvs. ovate or oblong, ¾–2 in. long, coarsely crenate-serrate, subglabrous except for ciliate margins, petioled: fl.-whorls in leafy spikes commonly 2–6 in. long; corolla bright blue, ½in. long, puberulent. Cent. Asia.

4. **D. Moldavica,** L. (*Moldavica suaveolens,* Gilib.). Fragrant ann. 1–2 ft. high, erect and branching, branches glabrous or finely pubescent: lvs. lanceolate, to 1½ in. long, blunt, incised-crenate, the lower long-petioled, the upper and floral lvs. short-petioled and toward base bristly-toothed: fls. few in a whorl, the whorls in a long raceme, July–Aug.; corolla blue or white, two to three times as long as the calyx. (First described under the old genus Moldavica, named from Moldavia, formerly a province along the Danube.) Eu., N. Asia.

5. **D. sibiricum,** L. (*D. Stewartianum,* Hort. not Dunn. *Nepeta macrantha,* Fisch.). Per. to 4½ ft., branched, subglabrous below, puberulent above: lvs. short-petioled, ovate-lanceolate, to 4 in. long, serrate, truncate or cordate at base: infl. subpaniculate, with few-fld. clusters, bracts not conspicuous; fls. blue, 1½ in. long, funnelform, conspicuously bilabiate; calyx-tube twice as long as lower lobes. Siberia.

10. **PRUNELLA,** L. Low per. herbs, about 5 species widely dispersed in temp. climates.—Sts. ascending, usually simple, with few pairs of petioled lvs.: fls. mostly in 3's in axils of leafy ovate bracts and compacted into terminal head-like spikes; calyx tubular-campanulate, irregularly 10-nerved, with broad 3-toothed upper lip and 2-cleft lower lip; corolla ascending, slightly contracted at throat, 2-lipped, upper lip arched, lower 3-lobed; stamens 4, filaments glabrous, 2-toothed at apex, the lower tooth bearing the anther; style glabrous, stigmas 2, short: nutlets ovoid, smooth, angled. (Prunel-la: name said to be from the German *Braune,* a disease of the throat, for which the plant was a remedy; genus sometimes spelled Brunella.)

A. Upper foliage lvs. ½–3 in. below the floral spike: calyx-teeth of upper lip at least as long as broad.
 B. Lvs. cuneate or rounded at base, scarcely if at all toothed .... 1. *P. grandiflora*
 BB. Lvs. truncate-cordate at base, strongly toothed .... 2. *P. hastæfolia*
AA. Upper foliage lvs. adjacent to spike: middle upper calyx-tooth not more than half as long as broad .... 3. *P. vulgaris*

1. **P. grandiflora,** Jacq. (*P. vulgaris* var. *grandiflora,* L.). Sts. to 1½ ft. high, somewhat pilose: lvs. lance-ovate, 1–3 in. long, entire or slightly toothed, scattered-pilose, petioled: spikes 1½–2 in. long; calyx ½in. long, ciliate; corolla almost glabrous, purple, 1 in. long. Eu.

2. **P. hastæfolia,** Brot. Like *P. grandiflora* but lvs. ovate-hastate with truncate-cordate base and well-developed broad rounded teeth especially near base: corolla slightly longer, more inflated at throat. Spain and Portugal.—*P. Webbiana,* Hort., is near this species.

3. **P. vulgaris,** L. Heal-All. Self-Heal. Sts. to 2 ft., often procumbent, more or less pubescent: lvs. ovate-oblong, entire or toothed, 1–3 in. long, petioled: spikes to 1½ in. long; calyx about ¼in. long; corolla purple or violet, ½in. long. Eu., Asia, N. Amer.—White-fld. forms are var. **leucantha,** Schur, pink-fld. ones var. **rubrifolia,** Beckhaus.

11. **PHYSOSTEGIA,** Benth. False Dragonhead. Per. herbs native to N. Amer., grown in borders and in wild-gardens for their showy fls.; about 5 species.—Erect plants almost glabrous, with slender wand-like sts.: lvs. lanceolate to oblong, toothed or serrate, the upper sessile, the lowest tapering into a petiole; floral lvs. small and bract-like, mostly shorter than the calyx: floral whorls 2-fld.; calyx nearly regular and equally 5-toothed; corolla purple, rose or white, the tube gradually inflated upward, the lips short; stamens 4; style 2-cleft: nutlets 3-angled, smooth. (Physoste-gia: Greek *bladder* and *covering,* referring to the inflated fruiting calyx.)

P. virginiana, Benth. (*P. virginica,* Hort. *Dracocephalum virginianum,* L.). Sts. leafy, simple, terminated by a single virgate or sometimes several panicled spikes, to 4 ft. high, forming large clumps in cult.: lvs. oblong to lanceolate, 3–5 in. long, serrate, acuminate; floral lvs. bract-like, lanceolate: infl. finely puberulent; calyx-teeth acuminate; corolla

¾–1 in. long, purplish-red to rose-pink or lilac; flowering in summer. Que. west and south. Var. **alba,** Hort., fls. white. Var. **grandiflora,** Hort., fls. bright pink, on longer infl.

12. **LEONOTIS,** R. Br. LIONS-EAR. About 12 species in trop. and S. Afr., one planted for ornament in the S.—Ann. or per. herbs or shrubs: lvs. ovate to lanceolate, petioled or subsessile: fls. white to orange, in very dense axillary whorls; calyx 8–10-ribbed, the tube arched and funnel-shaped, the teeth often acerose-tipped; corolla-tube as long as calyx or longer, upper lip long and concave, hairy outside, lower lip deflexed, shorter, the 3 lobes nearly equal; stamens 4, arched; style 2-lobed. (Leono-tis: Greek *lion's ear*, which the fls. are supposed to resemble.)

L. Leonurus, R. Br. Shrubby branched per. 3–6 ft. high, with hairy sts. (a dwarf form not over 2½ ft. high): lvs. lanceolate or oblong-lanceolate, 2–5 in. long, acute to nearly obtuse, coarsely serrate, narrowed at base, pubescent; bracts nearly as long as calyx-tube: corolla 1½–2 in. long, more than three times the length of calyx, red-yellow or orange-red (in one form white), the upper lip large and elongate, densely hirsute, the lower small; stamens not exserted. (Leonurus: Linnæan name for the genus under which this species was formerly included: Greek *lion's tail.*) S. Afr.

13. **PHLOMIS,** L. A few of the 70 species are cult. in wild-gardens, native Medit. region to China.—Shrubs or per. herbs, often more or less woolly: lvs. all similar or the upper bract-like: whorls few- to many-fld., the fls. sessile; calyx regular, truncate or 5-toothed; upper lip of corolla densely hairy, erect or curving over the lower lip, lower lip spreading, with 3 rounded lobes; corolla-tube often with a hairy ring inside; stamens 4, one pair of filaments often appendaged at base; style 2-lobed: nutlets 4, ovoid and 3-angled, glabrous or pubescent. (Phlo-mis: old Greek name.)

A. Fls. yellow: a shrub .... 1. *P. fruticosa*
AA. Fls. purple: an herb .... 2. *P. tuberosa*

1. **P. fruticosa,** L. JERUSALEM-SAGE. Divaricately branched shrub 2–4 ft. high, branches floccose-woolly: lvs. ovate or oblong, entire or crenate, rounded or cuneate at base, rugose, white-tomentose beneath; floral lvs. subsessile, scarcely longer than the dense many-fld. floral whorls which are borne singly or in 2's at the ends of the branches; bracts ovate to ovate-lanceolate, mostly surpassed by the calyx; corolla yellow, conspicuous; blooming in summer in the E., in winter in warm climates. S. Eu.

2. **P. tuberosa,** L. Subglabrous herb 3–6 ft. high, with thickened tuber-like roots: lvs. broad-ovate, obtuse, crenate, deeply cordate at base, lower long-petioled and 8 in. or more long; floral lvs. oblong-lanceolate, coarsely serrate-toothed, at base often hastate-dilated and subincised, 2–3 in. long: floral whorls remote, 30–40-fld., bracts subulate; calyx-teeth emarginate, tipped with a rigid spine; corolla purple, upper lip suberect, densely pilose within. S. Eu., E. and N. Asia.

14. **LAMIUM,** L. DEAD NETTLE. Low ann. or per. herbs, one or two sometimes cult. as border plants, the 40 species being native to the Old World.—Commonly diffuse or decumbent at base: lvs. mostly crenate-dentate and petiolate: fls. often rather showy, in axillary or terminal whorls; bracts short; calyx awl-toothed; corolla 2-lipped, the tube somewhat longer than calyx, upper lip ascending and concave, lower one 3-lobed; stamens 4, in 2 pairs, ascending under the upper lip. (La-mium: Greek for *throat*, referring to the shape of the corolla.)

L. maculatum, L. (*L. variegatum*, Hort.). Straggling or half-trailing per., slightly hairy, tips of the branches ascending: lvs. long-petioled (except the uppermost), cordate-ovate, 1–2 in. long, obtuse, crenate-dentate, in one var. whitish-blotched along the midrib: fls. appearing in spring and summer, usually purple-red, sometimes varying to white, 1 in. long, ascending in the clusters; corolla-tube two to three times as long as calyx, hairy within, upper lip strongly arched or hooded. Eu.

15. **MOLUCELLA,** L. Two species of the Medit. region, sometimes found in old-fashioned gardens.—Ann. herbs with petiolate lvs. toothed or cut: fls. axillary, borne in whorls of 6–10; bracts subulate, spinose; calyx campanulate, the limb broadly dilated; corolla white, tipped pink, scarcely if at all thrust out of the calyx, the tube with oblique hairy ring within, the upper lip erect, the lower trilobed with broad notched middle lobe; stamens 4, ascending under the hood, the anthers attached by lateral pedicels to the tip of the filament, the cells divergent; style bifid: nutlets 4, convex on one side, angular on the other, broader upward, truncate. (Molucel-la: diminutive of Molucca.)

M. lævis, L. Shell-Flower (so-called because of the shell-like calyx in which the seeds nestle like eggs). Molucca-Balm. Sts. simple or branching below, 2–3 ft. high, fl.-bearing almost from base: lvs. long-petioled, rounded-subcordate, ¾–1¼ in. long, with coarse rounded teeth: fls. fragrant, in 6-fld. whorls; bracts shorter than calyx-tube; calyx with large spreading membranaceous border, inconspicuously 5-angled, with 5 small thorns; corolla white, shorter than calyx. W. Asia.—Sometimes called "Bells of Ireland."

16. **STACHYS**, L. Betony. Woundwort. Probably 200 species or more, in temp. regions but a few in the trop. and colder parts, a few sometimes cult. for economic or ornamental purposes.—Herbs or rarely shrubs: lvs. entire, crenate or dentate, the floral lvs. similar or reduced to bracts: floral whorls 2- to many-fld., axillary or in terminal spikes; fls. sessile or shortly pedicelled, purplish, scarlet, yellow, or white; calyx tubular-campanulate, 5–10-nerved, 5-toothed, very seldom 2-lipped; corolla-tube cylindric, included or exserted, bilabiate, the expanded lower lip 3-lobed; stamens 4: nutlets ovoid or oblong. (Sta-chys: old Greek name.)

A. Corolla short, included in calyx or very slightly exserted: lvs. densely silky-woolly....1. *S. olympica*
AA. Corolla longer, the tube exserted.
B. Plant ann., procumbent: fls. pinkish-white..........2. *S. corsica*
BB. Plant per., erect: fls. purple to violet.
C. Lowest floral lvs. lanceolate: fls. ½in. long..........3. *S. officinalis*
CC. Lowest floral lvs. cordate-ovate: fls. 1 in. long..........4. *S. grandiflora*

1. **S. olympica**, Poir. (*S. lanata*, Jacq. not Crantz nor Moench). Lambs-Ears. Per. 1–1½ ft. high, very densely silky-woolly throughout: lvs. petiolate, oblong-elliptic, narrowed at both ends, minutely crenate, rugose; floral lvs. smaller, sessile or nearly so, the uppermost scarcely longer than the fls.: floral whorls many-fld., the uppermost close together, the lower distant; bracts linear-lanceolate, about equalling the calyx; calyx with slightly unequal teeth; corolla purple, about ½in. long, lanate without, the tube not exserted from the calyx. Caucasus to Iran.

2. **S. corsica**, Pers. Dwarf prostrate ann. forming a dense carpet, pubescent: lvs. bright green, ovate, ½in. long, very obtuse, crenate: fls. pinkish-white, ½in. long, very numerous, lips large. Corsica, Sardinia.

3. **S. officinalis**, Franch. (*S. Betonica*, Benth. *Betonica officinalis*, L.). Per. 1–3 ft. high, somewhat pilose: lower lvs. long-petioled, ovate-oblong, obtuse, crenate, cordate at base, the upper remote; lower floral lvs. sessile, oblong-lanceolate, toothed, acute, the upper linear, entire, equalling the calyx: floral whorls arranged in an oblong spike, somewhat interrupted or the lower distinct; bracts ovate, mucronate; corolla purple, ½in. long, twice the calyx, the tube naked within; summer. Eu., Asia Minor.—There are vars. with white and rose-colored fls.

4. **S. grandiflora**, Benth. (*S. rosea*, Hort. *Betonica grandiflora*, Willd. *B. rosea*, Hort. *B. spicata*, Hort.). Villous per. about 1 ft. high: lvs. long-petioled, broadly ovate, obtuse, crenate, broadly cordate at base; floral lvs. similar, sessile, amplexicaul, successively smaller, the uppermost bract-like: floral whorls few, 10–20-fld., distinct, the lower remote; outer bracts similar to the floral lvs., the inner narrower, entire; calyx purplish, with rigid subulate subspinose teeth; corolla violet, glabrous, the curving tube about 1 in. long and three to four times surpassing the calyx. Asia Minor.—Vars. occur with rose-pink or purple-violet fls.

17. **COLQUHOUNIA**, Wall. Shrubs cult. to some extent in the S., the entire genus comprising only 2–4 species native to S. Asia.—Erect or loosely twining, at least the younger parts tomentose: lvs. large, crenate, the floral ones similar or above reduced and bract-like: fls. scarlet, borne in loose few-fld. whorls, these axillary or in a dense terminal spike or raceme; bracts small; corolla-tube exserted, incurved; stamens 4, the anther-cells confluent: nutlets produced at the apex into wings. (Colquhou-nia: after Sir Robt. Colquhoun; lived 100 years ago.)

C. vestita, Wall. Erect plant to about 4 ft., permanently white-woolly: lvs. elliptic or elliptic-ovate, 1½–2½ in. long: orange-scarlet fls. appearing in autumn and winter; calyx-teeth acute; corolla ¾in. long.

18. **SALVIA**, L. Sage. A vast genus with upward of 700 species, widely distributed in the temp. and warmer regions of both hemispheres, furnishing many ornamental subjects and a few grown for culinary or medicinal purposes.—Ann., bien., or per. herbs, subshrubs, and shrubs: lvs. entire, variously toothed, incised or pinnatisect; floral lvs. frequently small and bract-like, rarely similar to the cauline: fls. variously colored, rarely yellow, of various sizes, in 2- to many-fld. verticels or

whorls, spicate, racemose, paniculate or rarely all axillary; calyx commonly 2-lipped, the upper lip entire or 3-toothed, the lower 2-cleft; corolla-tube included or exserted, the limb 2-lipped; stamens inserted on the throat of the corolla, only the lower pair fertile, the upper pair rudimentary or lacking; anther-cells widely separated on a long slender connective articulated with the filament, the upper end of the connective bearing a perfect anther-cell, the lower end usually with an imperfect one or none: nutlets ovoid, 3-edged or somewhat compressed, smooth. (Sal-via: Latin name, used by Pliny, meaning *safe, unharmed*, referring to the medicinal properties of some of the species.)

A. Fls. 1½–2 in. long.
  B. Sts. densely pubescent: fls. blue....13. *S. patens*
  BB. Sts. glabrous except in infl.: fls. usually red....20. *S. splendens*
AA. Fls. not over 1 in. long.
  B. Lf.-blades usually ½–1 in. long: fls. red, 1 in. long.
    C. Lvs. mostly obovate, entire: branches with recurved hairs....15. *S. Greggii*
    CC. Lvs. ovate to elliptic, crenulate-serrate: branches with erect hairs....18. *S. microphylla*
  BB. Lf.-blades longer.
    C. Lvs. more or less white-woolly.
      D. Plants thistle-like, with spiny teeth: fls. lavender, with vermilion anthers.. 1. *S. carduacea*
      DD. Plants not thistle-like.
        E. Length of lf. 1–2½ in.
          F. Height 1–2 ft.: calyx definitely 2-lipped.... 4. *S. officinalis*
          FF. Height 3–4 ft.: calyx spathe-like, the teeth wholly united into a single cucullate lip.... 2. *S. leucophylla*
        EE. Length of lf. 2½–7 in.
          F. Corolla ½in. long; racemes nodding....11. *S. nutans*
          FF. Corolla ¾in. long; racemes erect.
            G. Lf. sinuate-lobed, broadly ovate.... 7. *S. argentea*
            GG. Lf. crenate, lance-linear....19. *S. leucantha*
    CC. Lvs. not at all white-woolly.
      D. Foliage pinnatisect into linear segms....12. *S. Jurisicii*
      DD. Foliage not pinnatisect.
        E. Upper st.-lvs. sessile.
          F. Lower st.-lvs. largely sessile; lf.-blades 1–3 in. long.... 9. *S. superba*
          FF. Lower st.-lvs. petioled; lf.-blades 2–6 in. long.
            G. Infl. glandular; fls. 1 in. long.... 8. *S. pratensis*
            GG. Infl. not glandular; fls. ½in. long....10. *S. Tenorii*
        EE. Upper st.-lvs. petioled.
          F. Floral lvs. large, persistent, the uppermost purple, red, or white.
            G. Blades of lvs. 1–1½ in. long, obtuse or cuneate at base: calyx tubular.... 5. *S. Horminum*
            GG. Blades of lvs. 4–9 in. long, cordate at base: calyx campanulate... 6. *S. Sclarea*
          FF. Floral lvs. small, often early deciduous, rarely colored.
            G. Corolla red, ¾–1 in. long; fls. in verticels of mostly 3–6....14. *S. coccinea*
            GG. Corolla bluish to white, ⅜–¾in. long; fls. more numerous.
              H. Lf. sinuate-crenate to lyrate-pinnatifid: floral whorls remote.... 3. *S. verticillata*
              HH. Lf. entire to serrate: floral whorls crowded at least during anthesis.
                I. Calyx white to purplish with dense tomentum: floral lvs. mostly deciduous....16. *S. farinacea*
                II. Calyx grayish-green, finely puberulent: floral lvs. persistent.. 17. *S. azurea*

1. **S. carduacea**, Benth. Thistle Sage. Loosely tomentose thistle-like ann. 1–2 ft. high; sts. scape-like, erect: lvs. oblong, sinuate-pinnatifid, spinulose-toothed, 3–6 in. long, in a basal cluster: whorls densely many-fld., head-like, 1–1½ in. diam., single or few and remote, subtended and commonly surpassed by a cluster of lanceolate or ovate-lanceolate spinose-toothed bracts giving it a carduus-like or thistle-like appearance; calyx white with long wool, the throat villous, the upper lip 3-toothed and much surpassing the lower, the teeth all spinose-tipped; corolla lavender or bluish-purple, 1 in. long, with a hairy ring inside and with 2-lobed upper and 3-lobed lower lip, the lowest lobe elongate and deeply fringed; connectives directed forward, the anterior portions remote and bearing fertile anther-cells. Calif., where it blooms in spring as a winter ann., especially southward.

2. **S. leucophylla**, Greene (*Audibertia nivea*, Benth.). Hoary throughout with close tomentum, 3–4 ft. high, shrubby below, leafy: lvs. oblong-lanceolate or the lowest ovate, obtuse, 1–2½ in. long, the upper very short-petioled with truncate base; bracts oval or oblong, obtuse: calyx splitting down the front, finally emarginate on the back; corolla light purple, over ½in. long, the tube only slightly surpassing the calyx; stamens and style long-exserted; connective of stamens almost continuous with filament. Calif.

3. **S. verticillata**, L. Erect per. 2–3 ft. high, more or less pilose-hispid throughout: lvs. petioled, broadly ovate, at base cordate or lyrate-pinnatifid, sinuate-crenate, barely acute, 2–6 in. long: whorls few to many, densely many-fld., remote, subtended by small bract-like deflexed floral lvs.; calyx with short setaceous-acuminate teeth; corolla lilac-blue, about ⅜in. long, with a hairy ring inside; connectives very short, deflexed and subulate but remote anteriorly; summer and autumn. Eu., Asia Minor and Caucasus region.

4. **S. officinalis,** L. SAGE. Subshrub ½–2 ft. high, more or less white-woolly: lvs. petioled, oblong, 1–2 in. long, entire or finely crenate, acute or obtuse, rugose; floral lvs. sessile, ovate to ovate-lanceolate, often acuminate: racemes nearly simple, the fl.-whorls rather few, interrupted, many-fld.; calyx membranaceous, purplish-tinged, campanulate, the 2 lower teeth longer than the 3 upper, all subulate-acuminate; corolla ½–¾in. long, purple, blue or white, with a hairy ring inside; in summer. Medit. region.—Vars. are offered with lvs. variegated with yellow, white or red.

5. **S. Horminum,** L. Erect ann., about 1½ ft. high, more or less villous throughout: lvs. shortly petiolate, oblong to ovate, crenulate, obtuse or cuneate at base, 1–2½ in. long; floral lvs. very broadly ovate, sessile and acute, nearly as long as fls., the upper colored or sometimes white: racemes simple, the whorls distant and about 6-fld.; calyx tubular, shortly bilabiate, the upper lip with 3 small unequal teeth, the lower 2-cleft; corolla light lilac or pale violet to reddish-violet or purple, about ½in. long, without a hairy ring inside; anterior portion of connectives deflexed, abruptly dilated, connected at the extremity; summer. (Horminum: old Greek name, adopted by Linnæus.) S.Eu.

6. **S. Sclarea,** L. CLARY. Erect bien. 2–3 ft. high, with stout villous sts. glandular above: lvs. hairy, 4–9 in. long, broadly ovate, mostly cordate at base, petiolate, crenate or toothed; floral lvs. very broad, abruptly acuminate, surpassing the glandular calyx, colored, their bases white, tips rose: racemes panicled, the fl.-whorls distant, about 6-fld.; calyx broadly campanulate, upper lip 3-toothed, lower 2-cleft, teeth somewhat spiny-acuminate; corolla whitish-blue varying to rose and purplish, to 1 in. long, without a hairy ring inside, tube not exserted from calyx; anterior portion of connectives deflexed, abruptly dilated, connected at the extremity; late summer. (Sclarea: Latin for *clear, bright*, in reference to the color of the fls., an ante-Linnæan name.) S. Eu. Var. **turkestaniana,** Mott. (*S. turkestanica*, Hort.), involucral bracts to twice as long as calyces or more; fls. white tinged pink; Turkestan.

7. **S. argentea,** L. Bien. 2–4 ft. high, with erect villous herbaceous sts.: basal and lower st.-lvs. white-woolly, 2–6 in. long, broad-ovate, sinuate-lobed, the lobes erose-crenate; floral lvs. very broad: panicles divaricate-branched; fl.-whorls remote, 6–10-fld., the uppermost fls. abortive; calyx campanulate, the teeth all subspinose; corolla showy, rose-white, whitish, purplish, or yellowish, about ¾in. long, without a hairy ring inside, the upper lip much longer than the lower; anterior portion of connectives deflexed, abruptly dilated, connected at extremity; summer. Medit. region.

8. **S. pratensis,** L. Herbaceous per. 1–3 ft. high, with root sometimes tuberous and sts. erect, pubescent: lvs. more or less blood-red spotted; basal lvs. petiolate, oblong-ovate, 2–6 in. long, obtuse, crenate or incised, cordate at base, rugose, glabrous above, pubescent beneath along the petiole and nerves, only upper sessile; floral lvs. cordate-ovate, green: racemes nearly simple, viscid, the whorls distant and 6-fld., pedicels shorter than calyx; calyx almost sessile, campanulate, viscid-villous; corolla bright blue, rarely reddish or white, 1 in. long, without a hairy ring inside; anterior portion of connectives deflexed, abruptly dilated, connected at the extremity; summer. Eu.—Numerous vars. are offered whose fls. range from violet to purple, red, light blue, or white, or sometimes variegated. *S. silvestris*, L., also with lower st.-lvs. petioled, has fls. about ½in. long and floral bracts purple-red.

9. **S. superba,** Stapf (*S. nemorosa*, Mott. not L. *S. virgata*, Hort. not Ait. *S. virgata* var. *nemorosa*, Hort.). Much-branched per. 2–3 ft. high, sts. roughish-pubescent: lvs. lanceolate to oblong, crenate, obtuse or acute, glabrous and rugose above, somewhat pubescent beneath, the basal short-petioled, cauline sessile and often clasping; floral lvs. ovate, acuminate, shorter than or about equalling the calyx: racemes long, slender, terminating the branches, the many whorls 6-fld., distinct; calyx purplish, hairy, resinous-dotted, 2-lipped, upper lip shortly and sharply 3-toothed, lower with 2 longer acerose-tipped teeth; corolla bright violet or purple, ⅜–½in. long, without a hairy ring inside, swollen at the throat, tube little or not at all exserted, limb more or less profusely resinous-dotted; anterior portion of connectives deflexed, abruptly dilated, connected at the extremity; summer and autumn. Hybrid of *S. silvestris* and *S. villicaulis*.

10. **S. Tenorii,** Spreng. (*S. pratensis* var. *Tenorii*, Hort.). Per. with erect sts. paniculate-racemose above, short pilose-hispid, not glandular in infl.: lvs. short-pilose beneath, ovate, double-crenate, cordate or obtuse at base, 3–6 in. long; upper st.-lvs. half-clasping; floral lvs. cordate-ovate, acuminate, less than one-fourth the pilose calyx; corolla dark blue, ⅜–½in. long. (M. Tenore, page 52.) N. E. Medit. region.—By some treated as conspecific with the older *S. hæmatodes*, L.

11. **S. nutans,** L. Per., sts. puberulent, to 3 ft., paniculate-branched above: lvs. crowded toward base of sts., long-petioled, cordate-ovate, rugose, doubly crenate, appressed white-woolly beneath, 4–7 in. long: racemes slender, nodding in bud, with crowded whorls; floral bracts minute; calyx hirsute; corolla bright blue to violet, ⅓in. long, with straight upper lip. S. E. Eu.

12. **S. Jurisicii,** Kosanin. Per., sts. bristly, pilose, simple or branched, to 1½ ft.: lvs. to 4 in. long, glabrous except for ciliate margins, 1–2-pinnatisect into linear-oblong segms.; uppermost lvs. entire, linear-lanceolate: whorls 2–4-fld.; calyx pilose; corolla deep blue, pilose, ¼in. long. (Named for Jurisici, who sent the plant to Kosanin.) Serbia.

13. **S. patens,** Cav. Per. 1–2½ ft. high, rather densely clothed with stiffish often viscid hairs: lvs. ovate or oblong-ovate, 2–5 in. long, hastate or rounded and subcordate at base, crenulate, obtuse, the lower long-petioled, the upper subsessile; floral lvs. surpassing the calyx: whorls 2- to few-fld.; calyx campanulate, with setaceous-acuminate teeth, the upper lip often 3-cuspidate; corolla blue, 1½–2 in. long, without hairy ring inside; anterior portion of connectives deflexed, linear; early autumn. Mts. of Mex.

14. **S. coccinea,** Juss. (*S. rosea,* Vahl). Ann. or sometimes per. and subshrubby, 1–2 ft. high, more or less pubescent or towards the base hirsute with long spreading hairs: lvs. ovate or deltoid, 1–2 in. long, mostly acute, crenate, on long slender petioles; floral lvs. ovate, acuminate-setaceous, seldom equalling the calyx: racemes virgate, clusters few- to several-fld. and rather distant; calyx tubular-campanulate, upper lip entire, often purplish, lower 2-parted, all the teeth acute; corolla deep scarlet, ¾–1 in. long, without a hairy ring inside, the narrow tube moderately enlarging above, the lower lip twice as long as upper; anterior portion of connectives deflexed, linear; summer. S. C. to Fla. and Tex., Mex., W. Indies, and trop. Amer.—Not to be confused with *S. splendens.* Fls. varying to white.

15. **S. Greggii,** Gray. Half-shrub to 3 ft., with slender branches, glabrous or the sts. obscurely mealy-puberulent: lvs. petiolate, ½–1 in. long, oblong or spatulate, entire, obtuse or mucronate, fascicled, 1-nerved: racemes loosely few-fld., the ovate floral lvs. falling before the fls. open; calyx narrow-campanulate, upper lip entire, lower 2-parted, all the teeth acute; corolla red or purplish-red, 1 in. long, without a hairy ring inside, the exserted portion of tube strongly swollen, lower lip large and showy; anterior portion of connectives deflexed, linear; autumn. (Named for Dr. Josiah Gregg, who collected this species in Saltillo, Mex.) Tex. and Mex.

16. **S. farinacea,** Benth. Minutely puberulent per. 2–3 ft. high, with numerous clustered sts.: lvs. often somewhat fascicled, 1½–3 in. long, the lower ovate-lanceolate to ovate, coarsely and irregularly serrate, obtuse or acute at apex, at base obtuse or narrowed to slender petiole; upper lvs. lanceolate or linear-lanceolate; floral lvs. mostly caducous: whorls numerous, many-fld., rather close or the lower remote; calyx oblong-campanulate, white or purplish-tinged with soft dense tomentum, the 3 teeth broad and very short; corolla violet-blue, ½–⅝in. long, without a hairy ring inside; anterior portion of connectives deflexed, linear. Tex.—Probably including some of the material offered as *S. azurea* var. *grandiflora.*

17. **S. azurea,** Lam. Glabrous or puberulent per. with hairs appressed upward, branching, 1–6 ft. high: lvs. lanceolate to oblong or linear, obtuse or acute, tapering to a very short petiole, 2–4 in. long, serrate or the upper entire; floral lvs. subulate, small, persistent: infl. elongate, spike-like, composed of numerous many-fld. whorls rather close or the lower remote; calyx oblong-campanulate, ¼in. long, short-bilabiate, the upper lip very broad and obtuse, the lobes all similar; corolla deep blue varying to white, ⅝–¾in. long, without a hairy ring inside; anterior portion of connectives deflexed, linear; summer. S. C. to Fla. and La. Var. **grandiflora,** Benth. (*S. Pitcheri,* Torr.), sts. densely retrorse-pubescent; Mo. and Neb. to Tex.

18. **S. microphylla,** HBK. (*S. Grahamii,* Benth.). Shrub to 3 ft., diffusely branched, sts. rounded, short-pubescent: lvs. deltoid-ovate to elliptic, ½–1 in. long, mostly crenulate-serrate, petioled: fls. in open racemes, red; calyx ½in. long; corolla almost 1 in. long, glandular-puberulent toward tip. Mex.

19. **S. leucantha,** Cav. Shrub about 1½–2 ft. high, branches subterete and white with finally deciduous wool: lvs. short-petioled, 2–6 in. long, lanceolate-linear, acute, crenate, rugose, pubescent above, tomentose beneath; floral bracts ovate, acuminate, shorter than calyx, deciduous: racemes 6–10 in. long, whorls many-fld., the lower rather remote; calyx funnel-shaped, with about equal lobes, densely violet to lavender-lanate; corolla white, ⅝–¾in. long, swollen at throat, without a hairy ring inside, limb lanate with upper lip much exceeding lower; anterior portion of connectives deflexed, linear; summer. Mex.

20. **S. splendens,** Sello (*S. colorans,* Hort.). SCARLET SAGE. Herb or subshrub, 3 ft. high, glabrous or the infl. villous with colored hairs, cult. as an ann. for its masses of brilliant scarlet fls. which bloom in autumn: lvs. petioled, ovate, 2–3½ in. long, acuminate, dentate; floral lvs. and bracts ovate, acuminate, colored: racemes terminal, simple or panicled, the whorls 2–6-fld.; calyx campanulate, scarlet, with 3 broad-ovate acute teeth; corolla scarlet, glabrous or villous, 1½ in. long, without a hairy ring inside; anterior portion of connectives deflexed, linear. Brazil.—There are many vars. common in cult., the fls. varying in color from scarlet to purple, crimson, or even to white.

19. **PEROVSKIA,** Karel. Herbs or subshrubs valued chiefly for their late blue fls.; 4 species of W. and Cent. Asia.—Upright, aromatic when bruised: lvs. serrate to pinnatifid: fls. in distant whorls forming terminal spikes; bracts minute; calyx 2-lipped, tubular-campanulate, upper lip entire to tridentate, lower lip bidentate; corolla with short funnelform tube, upper lip 4-lobed, lower lip entire, deflexed;

fertile stamens 2. (Perov-skia: named for V. A. Perovski, 1794–1857, once governor of Russian province Orenburg.)

P. atriplicifolia, Benth. Subshrub to 5 ft., with stellate-hoary sts.: lvs. narrow-ovate to lanceolate, 1–2½ in. long, serrate, glabrescent, short-petioled: fls. blue, 2–6 to a whorl, in paniculate infl.; calyx hoary or purplish, ³⁄₁₆in. long; corolla ⅜in. long. W. Himalayas.

20. **MONARDA,** L. Horse-Mint. N. American genus, several of the 17–18 species occasionally grown for their showy fls.—Erect aromatic ann. or per. herbs, usually tall: lvs. dentate or serrate: fls. rather large, white, red, purplish, yellowish or mottled, in dense capitate clusters, terminal or sometimes axillary, mostly bracteate, the bracts often highly colored; calyx tubular, narrow, 15-nerved, almost equally 5-toothed, more or less villous or hirsute at the mouth; corolla glabrous within, tube slightly dilated above, upper lip erect or arched, lower lip spreading, 3-lobed with middle lobe largest; perfect stamens 2, usually exserted, the posterior pair rudimentary or wanting, anthers linear; ovary 4-parted. (Monar-da: after Nicholas de Monardes, Spanish physician and botanist, 1512–1588, who in 1571 published a book containing accounts of American products.)

A. Calyx slightly hairy at throat: sts. acutely angled....................1. *M. didyma*
AA. Calyx densely bearded at throat: sts. mostly obtusely angled....................2. *M. fistulosa*

1. **M. didyma,** L. (*M. coccinea*, Hort.). Oswego-Tea. Bee Balm. Fragrant Balm. Villous-hirsute becoming glabrous, sts. acutely 4-angled: lvs. thin, ovate to ovate-lanceolate, to 6 in. long, acuminate: bracts tinged with red: calyx slightly hirsute in the throat, the teeth narrowly subulate; corolla nearly glabrous, scarlet-red, 1½–2 in. long; late summer or early autumn. Que. to Mich. south to Ga.—Many color variants occur, such as vars. **rosea, salmonea, violacea,** Hort.

2. **M. fistulosa,** L. Wild Bergamot. Soft-pubescent to glabrate, sts. mostly obtusely angled: lvs. to 4 in. long, firmer than in *M. didyma:* bracts whitish or rarely purplish, the inner mostly hirsute-ciliate: calyx conspicuously and densely bearded at throat; corolla pubescent, at least on the upper lip, purple or purplish dotted, 1 in. or more long; late summer and early autumn. Ont. and Que. to Fla. and Tex. west to B. C. and Ariz. Var. **alba,** Hort., has white fls.—Crimson, lilac, or deep-purple-fld. forms occur.

21. **HORMINUM,** L. A per. herb from S. Eu., adapted to the rock-garden.—Lvs. mostly in basal rosettes, ovate to broadly elliptical, obtusely dentate, petioled: fls. in whorls of 2–6, arranged in leafless spikes; calyx 13-nerved, deeply 2-lipped, the upper lip with 3 sharp-pointed lobes, lower 2-lobed; corolla bluish-purple, tube broad and exceeding the calyx, upper lip almost flat, scarcely toothed, lower 3-lobed; stamens 4. (Hormi-num: ancient Greek name for some sage.)

H. pyrenaicum, L. Lf.-blades 1–2½ in. long: spikes 3–12 in. high, glandular-pubescent and strigose; fls. about ⅝in. long.

22. **MELISSA,** L. Known in cult. from a single species with lvs. having a lemon-like flavor and used in seasoning, particularly in liqueurs, and also as a medicine; 3–4 species of the Medit. region and Cent. Asia.—Erect per. herbs, with leafy branched sts.: lvs. broad, toothed: fls. white or yellowish, in axillary clusters; corolla exserted from the long-campanulate calyx, curved, enlarged above and naked within, 2-lipped, the upper lip erect and notched, the lower spreading and 3-lobed; stamens 4, ascending and approximate under the upper lip; style cleft at apex: nutlets smooth. (Melis-sa: Greek *bee.*)

M. officinalis, L. Lemon Balm. Bee Balm. Aromatic herb loosely branched, somewhat hairy, 1–2 ft. high: lvs. ovate, to 3 in. long, petioled, narrowed or cordate at base, coarsely crenate-dentate: fls. yellowish or whitish, appearing in late summer; calyx 2-lipped, the upper lip shortly and broadly 3-toothed, the lower with 2 longer acuminate-spinose teeth; corolla ½in. long.

23. **SATUREJA,** L. Savory. Aromatic herbs and subshrubs grown in borders and also as pot-herbs; about 180 species in the warmer regions of both hemispheres.—Lvs. narrow and entire or broader and toothed; floral lvs. similar or sometimes smaller: fls. in few- to many-fld. whorl-like cymes, the infl. simple and subspicate, more or less racemose-paniculate; calyx tubular-campanulate or tubular, 5-toothed or sometimes 2-lipped; corolla-tube short or long, exserted or scarcely so, upper lip

flat and entire or emarginate, lower lip expanded, 3-cleft; stamens 4: nutlets ovoid, smooth. (Sature-ja: old Latin name for savory; letter *j* pronounced as *i*.)

A. Lvs. suborbicular or ovate, subserrate, not more than twice as long as wide, distinctly petioled.
B. Calyx-lobes linear-lanceolate: sts. 4–8 in. high . . . . 1. *S. alpina*
BB. Calyx-lobes short-deltoid: sts. 8–18 in. high . . . . 2. *S. thymifolia*
AA. Lvs. mostly lanceolate to linear, entire, sessile or nearly so.
B. Sts. glabrous or pubescent only in lines, distinctly 4-angled: corolla purple . . . . . . 3. *S. subspicata*
BB. Sts. pubescent, subterete: corolla usually paler.
C. Plant a subshrub with minutely pubescent branches: opposite lf.-bases joined by a ridge . . . . 4. *S. montana*
CC. Plant an ann. with densely white-pubescent branches: opposite lf.-bases not joined by a ridge . . . . 5. *S. hortensis*

1. **S. alpina,** Scheele (*Calamintha alpina,* Lam.). Diffuse per., pubescent or villous, much-branched and somewhat woody at base, about 6 in. high: lvs. petioled, subrotund or ovate, not over ½in. long, subserrate; floral lvs. sometimes narrower: floral whorls 4–6-fld., pedicels short; calyx ribbed, hairy in the throat, narrowed below the sharp rigid-tipped teeth; corolla purple, ½in. long, with strongly dilated throat. Medit. region.

2. **S. thymifolia,** Scop. (*S. rupestris,* Wulfen. *Micromeria rupestris,* Benth.). Aromatic subshrub to 1½ ft.; branches slender, glabrous to minutely puberulent: lvs. ovate, ¼–¾in. long, subentire to crenate-dentate, glabrous, petioled, glandular-punctate: fls. in several-fld. short cymes arranged in long racemes; calyx tubular, 13-nerved, glabrous to puberulent, lobes short-triangular; corolla white to violet, ¼in. long. S. E. Eu.

3. **S. subspicata,** Bartling (*S. montana* var. *subspicata,* Vis. *S. pygmæa,* Sieber). Subshrub, mostly 3–8 in. high; branches sharply quadrangular, glabrous or with 2 bands of hair: lvs. crowded, linear-lanceolate to oblanceolate, ½–1 in. long, glandular-punctate beneath, sometimes ciliate, entire, subsessile: cymes 2–5-fld., in leafy crowded spikes; calyx tubular-campanulate, mostly purplish, 10-nerved, lobes about as long as tube, sharp-pointed; corolla purple-violet, ⅜–½in. long. S. E. Eu.—Some of the material cult. as *S. pygmæa* belongs to *S. montana.*

4. **S. montana,** L. (*Calamintha montana,* Lam.). WINTER SAVORY. Glabrous or finely hispid subshrub, woody at base, 6–15 in. high, with minutely pubescent branches erect or ascending: lvs. hispid-ciliate, sessile, oblong-linear or oblanceolate, ½–1 in. long, entire, acute or the lower obtuse, pellucid-punctate; upper and floral lvs. narrower: floral whorls few- to many-fld., loosely racemose-paniculate; calyx and corolla resinous-dotted; throat of calyx bristly, teeth long-acuminate, shorter than tube; corolla white or lilac, ⅜in. long, tube little or not at all exserted. Eu., N. Afr.—Widely cult.

5. **S. hortensis,** L. (*Calamintha hortensis,* Hort.). SUMMER SAVORY. Ann. herb about ½–1½ ft. high, with rather densely pubescent erect branching sts.: lvs. oblong-linear, ½–1½ in. long, entire, acute, narrowed to a subsessile base or a short petiole; floral lvs. similar: floral whorls about 6-fld., in subspicate infl. which is dense above, interrupted and somewhat branched below; calyx resinous-dotted, teeth acuminate, hispid-ciliate, about as long as tube; corolla rose, ⅓in. long. Eu.; widely escaped from cult.

24. **HYSSOPUS,** L. HYSSOP. A single species of Eu. and temp. Asia, grown for ornament in borders; also used for medicinal purposes and occasionally as a pot-herb.—Per. subshrub: lvs. entire: floral whorls in leafy-bracteate spikes; calyx tubular, 15-nerved; upper corolla-lip 2-lobed, the lower 3-lobed; stamens 4: nutlets ovoid and somewhat 3-sided, smooth. (Hysso-pus: ancient name; but precisely what plant was the sacred hyssop of the Jews is uncertain.)

H. officinalis, L. Sts. herbaceous from a woody base, slender, 1½ ft. high, simple or branching: lvs. linear to oblong, 1½–2 in. long, sessile or nearly so, acute at both ends or the lower obtuse at the apex: floral whorls secund, in terminal spikes; fls. blue or in some vars. red, rose or white; corolla exserted, ⅓–½in. long; stamens and pistil well-exserted.

25. **ORIGANUM,** L. MARJORAM. About 6 species of per. herbs, one cult. for the aromatic herbage and purple-pinkish spikes of fls.; 5–7 species in the Medit. region.—Lvs. entire or toothed: fls. in small erect spikes with ovate or lanceolate green or colored bracts, the spikes more or less corymbosely or paniculately clustered; calyx ovate-campanulate, equally 5-toothed, with bearded throat; corolla with more or less exserted limb, upper lip erect, lower outspread and 3-lobed; stamens 4, exserted; style unequally 2-lobed: nutlets ovate, smooth. (Orig-anum: ancient Greek name, said to mean *delight of the mountains.*)—For the plant cult. as *O. Dictamnus* see *Amaracus Dictamnus.*

O. vulgare, L. WILD MARJORAM. Erect aromatic herb 1–2½ ft. high, sts. more or less hairy, rootstocks nearly horizontal: lvs. petiolate, broadly ovate, to 1½ in. long, subserrate or entire, broadly rounded or subcordate at base, acute or blunt at apex: fls. in summer, purplish (varying to pink or nearly white), in corymbed clusters or short spikes; bracts purplish, glabrous, about the length of the calyx; corolla ¼in. long; stamens all or only 2 exserted. Eu.—A var. has golden or yellow foliage.

26. **MAJORANA,** Moench. Per. herbs or undershrubs, chiefly of the Orient, with aromatic herbage; about 6 species, two in cult.—Mostly tomentose: lvs. entire or toothed: floral whorls in thick clustered spikes; bracts not colored, densely white-hairy; calyx-limb oblique, the lower lip small or poorly developed; corolla with short limb, the upper lip erect, the lower outspread, 3-lobed; stamens 4, exserted or included; style somewhat unequally 2-lobed: nutlets ovoid, smooth. (Majora-na: derivation uncertain.)

A. Lvs. petioled .... 1. *M. hortensis*
AA. Lvs. sessile .... 2. *M. Onites*

1. **M. hortensis,** Moench (*Origanum Majorana,* L.). SWEET MARJORAM. ANNUAL MARJORAM. Per. 1–2 ft. high, cult. as an ann.: lvs. petiolate, elliptic, ¼–1 in. long, entire, broadly obtuse, tomentose: spikelets oblong, 3–5 in a cluster; bracts not prominently colored; calyx oblique; corolla white to pink or pale lilac, ⅙in. long. Eu.

2. **M. Onites,** Benth. (*Origanum Onites,* L.). Per., sts. erect, nearly simple, hirsute: lvs. sessile, ovate, slightly serrate, villous or tomentose, mostly cordate at base: fls. as in *M. hortensis* but a little larger; spikelets ovoid, very numerous in a dense cluster. (Onites: ante-Linnæan substantive name.) S. E. Eu., Asia Minor, Syria.

27. **AMARACUS,** Gleditsch. A small genus of about 15 Medit. species of per. herbs, two cult. for their aromatic herbage and showy bracted infl.—By some authors combined with Origanum, but now quite universally retained by botanists as a distinct genus; separated from Origanum by the long-exserted stamens with widely divaricate anther-cells, the corolla gibbous to ventricose, and the calyx oblique and edentate. (Amarac-us: Greek *amaros,* meaning bitter.)

A. Dictamnus, Benth. (*Origanum Dictamnus,* L. *A. tomentosus,* Moench). CRETE DITTANY. Procumbent, white-woolly, sts. often ascending, to 1 ft. long: lvs. broadly ovate to orbicular, entire, thick, to ¾in. long, somewhat mottled: fls. pink to purplish, ½in. long, subtended by large loosely imbricated bracts that become rose-purple in fr., arranged in hop-like heads. (Dictamnus: a genus of Rutaceæ.) Mts. of Greece.—A related plant of hybrid origin is **A. hybridus,** A. K. Jackson (*Origanum hybridum,* Mill.), presumably *A. Dictamnus* × *A. sipyleus,* long known in cult.; stellate-hairy to pilose, much branched, lvs. orbicular to ovate-elliptic, to 1¼ in. long and nearly 1 in. broad. By some authors this hybrid has been treated as a synonym of *A. sipyleus,* Briq. (*Origanum sipyleum,* L.), but this is a taller more slender mostly glabrous plant to 2 ft., lvs. narrowly ovate and those of the flowering sts. glabrous at flowering time.

28. **THYMUS,** L. THYME. Small shrubs or subshrubs used for edgings or for rockeries, or the shoots and lvs. sometimes employed for seasoning; species 50, more or less, widely dispersed in temp. climates, the greatest number native to the Medit. region.—Erect or prostrate, with strong mint-like odor: lvs. small, entire; floral lvs. similar or bract-like: floral whorls mostly few-fld., axillary and distant or gathered in short loose head-like terminal clusters; bracts minute; calyx ovoid or cylindric, 2-lipped, the broad upper lip 3-cleft or -toothed, the lower lip deeply cut into 2 small or subulate ciliate segms.; corolla-tube included or exserted, the limb somewhat 2-lipped; stamens 4: nutlets ovoid or oblong, smooth. (Thy-mus: old Greek name used by Theophrastus either for this plant or for savory.)

A. Lvs. sessile, with revolute margins .... 1. *T. vulgaris*
AA. Lvs. short-petioled, not revolute.
  B. Shape of lvs. narrow-spatulate: calyx-tube not hairy .... 2. *T. azoricus*
  BB. Shape of lvs. elliptic to ovate or lanceolate: calyx hairy.
    C. Sts. covered with long white spreading hairs (as long as st. is thick).
      D. Upper and lower surfaces of lf. hairy, ⅙in. long .... 3. *T. lanuginosus*
      DD. Upper surface of lf. not hairy, ⅓–½in. long .... 4. *T. lanicaulis*
    CC. Sts. with very short mostly retrorse hairs.
      D. Blade of lf. scarcely longer than wide: lower calyx-lobes lance-linear .... 5. *T. nummularius*
      DD. Blade of lf. more than twice as long as wide.
        E. Lf. not resin-dotted above .... 6. *T. nitidus*
        EE. Lf. resin-dotted on both surfaces.
          F. Apex of lf. acute .... 7. *T. Herba-barona*
          FF. Apex of lf. obtuse.

G. Length of lvs. ½–¾in.: upper middle calyx-lobe longer than wide........8. *T. Marschallianus*
GG. Length of lvs. ¼–⅓in.: upper middle calyx-lobe about as long as wide........9. *T. Serpyllum*

1. **T. vulgaris,** L. COMMON THYME. Suberect, 6–8 in. high, the slender branches stiff and woody, usually white-pubescent: lvs. sessile, linear to ovate, about ¼in. long, fascicled; floral lvs. lanceolate to ovate: floral whorls loosely several- to many-fld., in rather dense head-like clusters on the branchlets or interrupted-racemose-clustered at the ends of the sts.; pedicels slender, about as long as calyx-tube; fls. resinous-dotted; calyx hairy in the throat, teeth of the upper lip lanceolate, of the lower lip subulate and ciliate; corolla lilac or purplish, tube little or not at all exserted. S. Eu.

2. **T. azoricus,** Lodd. (*T. micans,* Lowe). Compact, the flowering branches 1–2 in. high, retrorse-pubescent: lvs. narrow-spatulate, about ¼in. long, resinous-punctate, glabrous except for the stiff-ciliate basal half: fls. in head-like clusters; calyx ⅛in. long, punctate, with subglabrous tube and ciliate lance-deltoid lower lobes; corolla 3/16in. long, resin-dotted and somewhat pubescent. Azores.

3. **T. lanuginosus,** Mill. (*T. Serpyllum* var. *lanuginosus,* Briq.). Flowering sts. 2–3 in. high, hairy all the way around: lvs. thickish, stiff, ⅙in. long, narrowly to broadly elliptic, covered with long stiff white hairs: fls. in heads; calyx thick-hairy, ⅙in. long, upper middle lobe as wide as long. N. Eu.—Much of the material cult. under this name has longitudinal bands of hair on the sts. and belongs to *T. brittanicus,* Ronn., or other species.

4. **T. lanicaulis,** Ronn. Flowering branches 4–5 in. high, with spreading hairs at least as long as diam. of st.: lvs. elliptic, ⅓–½in. long, glandular-punctate on both sides, glabrous above, hairy on midrib beneath, ciliate at least on basal half: fls. rose-pink, in globose heads; calyx villous, ⅙in. long, lower lobes almost subulate, ciliate, middle upper lobe longer than wide; corolla ¼in. long, resin-dotted and stiff-pubescent. S. E. Eu.

5. **T. nummularius,** Bieb. (*T. Serpyllum* var. *nummularius,* Koch). Branches 4–5 in. high, stiff-pubescent: lvs. ovate to orbicular, with round or subcordate base, ¼–⅜in. long: fls. rose, in globose heads; calyx stiff-hairy, lower lobes lance-linear, stiff-ciliate, middle upper lobe slightly longer than wide; corolla 3/16in. long. S. W. Asia.

6. **T. nitidus,** Guss. Subshrub with ascending pubescent branches 2–3 in. long: lvs. ovate to oblong-ovate, ⅙in. long, obtuse, subglabrous, short-petioled, shining above, glandular-punctate and nerved beneath: fl.-whorls in a dense spike; calyx purplish toward apex, short-hairy, lower lobes strongly ciliate. Sicily.

7. **T. Herba-barona,** Loisel. Subshrub, procumbent, flowering branches retrorse-pubescent or becoming glabrescent, 2–4 in. long: lvs. rhomboid or ovate-lanceolate, ⅛–¼in. long, acute, resin-dotted, glabrous or ciliate at base: fls. rose to white, in globose heads; calyx white-hairy especially at throat, lobes ciliate, lower 3 lance-linear; corolla rose, 3/16in. long. Corsica, Sardinia.

8. **T. Marschallianus,** Willd. (*T. Serpyllum* var. *Marschallianus,* Boiss.). Suberect from somewhat woody procumbent base, branches 8–16 in. high, retrorse-pubescent in upper half: lvs. narrowly to broadly lanceolate, ½–¾in. long, punctate on both sides, glabrous except for ciliate base: infl. subcapitate; calyx ⅛in. long, pilose, lower lobes linear-lanceolate, upper deltoid-lanceolate; corolla pale red, pilose, punctate, to ¼in. long. (For F. A. Marschall von Bieberstein, page 40.) S. E. Eu.

9. **T. Serpyllum,** L. MOTHER-OF-THYME. Subshrubby, with creeping pubescent sts. rooting below, erect branches 2–3 in. high, retrorse-pubescent: lvs. elliptic to oblong, ¼–⅓in. long, resin-dotted, glabrous except ciliate at least near base, very short-petioled, entire: infl. capitate; calyx ⅙in. long, tubular-campanulate, 10-nerved, pubescent at base, long-ciliate on the linear-lanceolate lower lobes, upper lobes as wide as long; corolla purplish, to ¼in. long. (Serpyllum: Greek *creeping,* a pre-Linnæan name.) N. Eu.; nat. in N. Amer. Var. **albus,** Hort., fls. white. Var. **argenteus,** Hort., lvs. variegated with silver. Var. **aureus,** Hort., lvs. variegated with yellow. Var. **coccineus,** Hort., to 3 ft., fls. crimson. Var. **roseus,** Hort., fls. rose. Var. **splendens,** Hort., fls. brilliant red. Var. **vulgaris,** Benth. (*T. citriodorus,* Hort. not Schreber), lemon-scented.—Exceedingly variable and often made to include many of those here treated as species.

29. **CUNILA,** L. Known in cult. as a profusely blooming plant used for borders; of the 16 species constituting the genus, 2 are N. American, 2 Mexican, and the others S. American.—Low-growing tufted per. herbs or shrubs: lvs. usually small: fl.-whorls in loosely corymbed cymes or dense spikes or heads, axillary or terminal; fls. small; calyx 10–13-nerved, equally 5-toothed; corolla white or purplish, 2-lipped; perfect stamens 2. (Cuni-la: Latin name for a mint plant.)

C. origanoides, Britt. (*Satureja origanoides,* L. *C. mariana,* L.). MARYLAND DITTANY. STONE-MINT. Plant 1 ft. high: lvs. ovate, about 1 in. long, serrate, rounded or cordate at base, nearly sessile, punctate: fls. purplish-pink, about ¼in. long, in a loose cymose cluster terminating the st. or branchlets, blooming in early autumn; calyx densely bearded in the throat; corolla ⅜in. long. S. N. Y. to Ind. south to Fla.

30. **MENTHA,** L. MINT. Cult. more or less for the production of the aromatic essential oil present in all parts of the herb; sparingly used for ornamental purposes; species 25–30, all natives of the temp. zone, about half of them being native or nat. in N. Amer.—Erect branching herbs. often per. by leafy runners, stolons or underground rootstocks: lvs. opposite, sessile or petioled: fls. small, in axillary clusters or in terminal spikes or heads, the floral lvs. reduced to small bracts; calyx equally 5-toothed or somewhat bilabiate, the throat naked or hairy within; corolla-limb almost equally 4-lobed, or the upper lobe broader and entire or notched; stamens 4; ovary 4-parted: nutlets ovoid and smooth. (Men-tha: from the Greek name of a nymph, Minte.)

A. Plant a miniature creeper..1. *M. Requienii*
AA. Plant larger, erect or ascending.
  B. Whorls of fls. all axillary.
    C. Fls. nearly sessile; calyx villous in throat........................2. *M. Pulegium*
    CC. Fls. distinctly pedicelled; calyx glabrous within....................3. *M. arvensis*
  BB. Whorls of fls. in terminal spikes or some in the upper axils.
    C. Lvs. petioled: spikes thick.
      D. Shape of lvs. lanceolate or ovate-lanceolate, acute....................4. *M. piperita*
      DD. Shape of lvs. mostly ovate or elliptic, obtuse.........................5. *M. citrata*
    CC. Lvs. sessile or nearly so: spikes slender (except in *M. longifolia*).
      D. Blades of lvs. crinkled and irregularly toothed or laciniate.............6. *M. aquatica* var. *crispa*
      DD. Blades of lvs. not crinkled, regularly serrate.
        E. Species glabrous: lvs. lanceolate......................................7. *M. spicata*
        EE. Species pubescent or tomentose.
          F. Lf.-blades elliptic or ovate-oblong, with rounded apex..............8. *M. rotundifolia*
          FF. Lf.-blades lanceolate or oblong-lanceolate, acute to subacuminate...9. *M. longifolia*

1. **M. Requienii,** Benth. Minute creeping herb with filiform minutely pubescent sts.: lvs. round, 1⁄16–⅛in. across, petioled, slightly pubescent: fls. mauve or pale purple, in loose few-fld. whorls; calyx 1⁄16in. long; corolla slightly longer. (Named for E. Requien, page 50.) Corsica, Sardinia.

2. **M. Pulegium,** L. PENNYROYAL. Much-branched, sts. mostly ascending, 4–18 in. long: lvs. petioled, about ½in. or less long, round-oval, entire or slightly crenate, pubescent, in one var. sometimes variegated: fls. small, bluish-lilac, nearly sessile, in dense axillary whorls in late summer and early autumn; mouth of calyx closed by hairs; upper lobe of corolla notched. (Pulegium: an herbalist name, Latin *flea-bane*, supposed to drive away the fleas.) Eu., W. Asia.

3. **M. arvensis,** L. Per. by running rootstocks; sts. mostly ascending or prostrate, 8–24 in. long, variously pubescent: lvs. mostly short-petioled, ovate to broadly lanceolate, 1–2½ in. long, rather weakly toothed: cymes rather dense, axillary; calyx short-campanulate, to ⅛in. long, pubescent, resin-dotted; corolla mostly lilac, about 3⁄16in. long. Widely spread in the northern hemisphere. Var. **villosa,** S. R. Stewart (*M. canadensis,* L. *M. canadensis* var. *villosa,* Benth.), lvs. of infl. lanceolate and with cuneate base; N. Amer. Var. **piperascens,** Malinvaud, JAPANESE MINT, plant to 3 ft., lvs. larger; Japan; cult. for the menthol-containing oil.

4. **M. piperita,** L. PEPPERMINT. Per. by runners and rootstocks, with strong essential pungent or pepper-like oil (whence the name *piperita*); sts. erect or ascending, 1–3 ft. high, branched, glabrous: lvs. petioled, lanceolate or ovate-lanceolate, 1–3 in. long, sharply serrate, acute, glabrous or pubescent on veins beneath, punctate with minute oil-globules: fls. in thick terminal spikes 1–3 in. long, in fr. the central spike often finally exceeded by the lateral; calyx resinous-dotted, glabrous below, its sharp teeth usually ciliate; corolla purple, rarely white, about ⅛in. long, glabrous. Eu.

5. **M. citrata,** Ehrh. BERGAMOT MINT. Per. by leafy stolons, glabrous throughout or nearly so; sts. decumbent, 1–2 ft. long, branched: lvs. thin, petioled, broadly ovate or elliptic and obtuse or the uppermost lanceolate and acute, ½–2 in. long: fls. in the uppermost axils and in short dense terminal spikes; calyx glabrous, with subulate teeth; corolla glabrous, lavender, ¼in. long. Eu.; nat. in Amer.

6. **M. aquatica,** L., var. **crispa,** Benth. (*M. crispa,* L.). Per. by stolons, much-branched; sts. weak, glabrous to somewhat puberulent, to 3 ft. long: lvs. ovate, ½–2 in. long, crisped, laciniate-serrate, obtuse to acute, short-petioled: fls. lilac, in terminal spikes to 1½ in. long; calyx puberulent, 1⁄8in. long; corolla ⅛in. long. Eu.; nat. in E. U. S.

7. **M. spicata,** L. (*M. viridis,* L.). SPEARMINT. Per. by leafy stolons, glabrous or nearly so; sts. erect, with ascending branches, 1–2 ft. high: lvs. sessile or nearly so, lanceolate or ovate-lanceolate, 2½ in. or less long, sharply serrate: whorls of fls. in narrow interrupted

spikes 2–4 in. long, the central spike exceeding the lateral ones, in summer and autumn; calyx-teeth hirsute or glabrate; corolla about ⅛in. long. Eu., Amer.; widely nat. about old gardens.

8. **M. rotundifolia,** Huds. (*M. spicata* var. *rotundifolia*, L.). APPLE OR ROUND-LEAVED MINT. Per. by leafy stolons, pubescent, somewhat viscid; sts. slender, erect or ascending, simple or branched, 20–30 in. high: lvs. sessile, elliptic or ovate-oblong, 1–4 in. long, subcordate at base, mostly obtuse, crenate-serrate, reticulated beneath: fls. in dense or interrupted spikes 2–4 in. long; calyx pubescent; corolla puberulent, white to reddish, 1⁄16–⅛in. long. Eu.; nat. from Me. to New Mex. Var. **variegata,** Hort., lvs. variegated.

9. **M. longifolia,** Huds. (*M. spicata* var. *longifolia*, L. *M. silvestris*, L.). Stoloniferous; sts. erect, simple or branched, puberulent to tomentose, 1½–4 ft. high: lvs. nearly or quite sessile, lanceolate to lance-ovate, 2–5 in. long, sharply serrate, acute, pubescent to tomentose above, white-tomentose beneath: spikes thickish, dense or interrupted at base; calyx villous-tomentose; corolla purplish, pubescent, ⅛in. long. Eu., Asia.

31. **PERILLA,** L. Two or 3 herbs in the Himalayas to China and Japan, one sometimes grown for its colored foliage.—Lvs. opposite: fls. small, in axillary or terminal, simple or panicled racemes, each floral lf. subtending a single fl.; calyx campanulate, 5-toothed, in fr. bilabiate and much enlarged and swollen; corolla with short tube not exceeding calyx, the limb oblique and somewhat unequally 5-lobed; stamens 4, erect and distinct; disk represented by a large gland; style 2-parted. (Peril-la: said to be a native name in India.)

P. frutescens, Britt., var. **crispa,** Deane (var. *nankinensis*, Bailey). Slightly hairy or rarely glabrous ann.: lvs. long-petioled, broad-ovate, acute or short-acuminate, coarsely dentate, narrowed or rounded at base, 2½–4½ in. long, dark purple-brown with a bronzy luster; floral lvs. ovate, shorter than calyx: fls. inconspicuous, borne in racemes and blooming in autumn, the calyx shaggy with long hairs, the white or reddish corolla about ¼in. long. Himalayas, Burma, China, Japan.—Other vars. of the same species have lvs. wrinkled or crisped and fringed or cut, sometimes variegated.

32. **ELSHOLTZIA,** Willd. Twenty species in E. and Cent. Asia, south to Java, in Eu. and Abyssinia, a few grown in the fl.-garden.—Herbs or undershrubs, usually aromatic: lvs. short-petioled, serrate, often glandular-punctate: fls. small, often minute, in usually one-sided terminal spikes; calyx tubular or campanulate, 5-toothed; corolla 4-lobed, scarcely bilabiate, upper lobe emarginate and slightly concave, others flat and obtuse; stamens 4, the longer pair much-exserted, anther-cells diverging: nutlets ovoid or ovoid-oblong. (Elsholt-zia: John Sigismund Elsholtz, 1623–1688, German physician and botanist.)

E. Stauntonii, Benth. Undershrub reaching 5 ft., with terete pubescent branchlets: lvs. ovate-oblong to oblong-lanceolate, 3–5 in. long, acuminate, crenate-serrate, bright green and glabrous above, densely glandular-punctate below, floral lvs. minute and bracteiform: fls. lilac-purple, in dense one-sided spikes 4–8 in. long, usually panicled at the ends of the branches, Sept., Oct.; stamens and style long-exserted. (Named for G. L. Staunton, 1737–1801, born in Ireland, physician in London and the E. Indies, later an ambassador to China.) N. China.

33. **COLEUS,** Lour. Herbs or small shrubs, several forms widely cult. in window-gardens and greenhouses because of their variously colored and showy foliage; 90 or more species in the trop. and subtrop. parts of Asia, Afr., Australia and the Pacific isls.—Ann. or per., of upright growth: lvs. crenate, dentate or serrate, petioled or sessile: fls. small or medium-sized, mostly blue or lilac, in terminal spike-like racemes which are often branched; calyx 5-toothed, often deflexed in fr.; corolla with tube exserted and bilabiate limb, the lower lip longer than the upper and often inclosing the stamens and pistil; stamens 4, didynamous and declinate, filaments at base united into a short tube free from the corolla, anthers confluent: nutlets smooth. (Co-leus: Greek for *sheath*, referring to the monadelphous stamens.)

A. Peduncles short or nearly none; whorls close .... 1. *C. Blumei*
AA. Peduncles slender, bearing 3 to several fls., making loose panicled whorls........ 2. *C. thyrsoideus*

1. **C. Blumei,** Benth. Probably to be regarded as an assemblage of forms: soft per. herb or subshrub, little branched, 2–3 ft. high: lvs. ovate, narrowed or broad at base, sharply and nearly regularly toothed, in some forms laciniate, long-acuminate, variously colored with yellow, dull red and purplish: fls. dark blue or whitish. (Bears the name of K. L.

Blume, page 40.) Java. Var. **Verschaffeltii,** Lem., more robust and branchy; lvs. more brilliantly colored, acute, truncate or cordate at base, irregularly cut-dentate with rounded teeth giving the margin a crispy effect; the commoner form.

2. **C. thrysoideus,** Baker. Shrub 2–3 ft. high, with pubescent sts.: lvs. cordate, acuminate, coarsely crenate, the lower 7 in. long: fls. bright blue, in racemes which contain many forking cymes of 3–10 fls. each, corolla ⅝in. long. Cent. Afr.

34. **IBOZA,** N. E. Br. Represented in the trade by a single showy-fld. small shrub or tall herb blooming in winter; more than a dozen species in S. and trop. Afr.—Plant diœcious: bracts and fls. very small, the staminate fls. larger and bearing an abortive ovary or style; calyx minute, 3-lobed; corolla very small, with funnelform tube and more or less unequally 4–5-lobed limb; stamens 4, free and separate; ovary 4-lobed: nutlets erect, oblong or ovoid, dorsally compressed. (Ibo-za: Kafir name.)

I. riparia, N. E. Br. (*Moschosma riparium*, Hochst.). Stout per. 2–5 ft. high, with branching and obtusely 4-angled st.: lvs. broadly ovate, 1–2 in. long, mostly notched at base and coarsely toothed: fls. creamy-white with dark anthers, very numerous, in erect panicles above the foliage; corolla ⅛in. or more long, two to three times longer than calyx, the tube exserted.

35. **OCIMUM,** L. Little known in cult. except the basil which is used in seasoning and also grown for its pleasing fragrance; species 50–60 in the warmer parts of the world.—Ann. or per. herbs or small shrubs of variable habit: fls. mostly small, the whorls usually 6-fld. and in terminal or paniculate racemes; calyx deflexed in fr., the teeth unequal, the margin of the broad upper teeth decurrent into the tube; corolla-tube usually not exceeding the calyx, 2-lipped, the upper lip 4-lobed; stamens 4, declined; style shortly 2-cleft: nutlets ovoid or subglobose, smooth or punctate. (O-cimum: an old Greek name.)

O. Basilicum, L. Basil. Glabrous or slightly pubescent ann., much-branched, 1–2 ft. high, often with purplish foliage: lvs. petioled, ovate, 1–2 in. long, entire or toothed: fls. white or more or less tinged purple, in moderately dense racemes; calyx becoming ¼in. long; corolla ⅓–½in. long; stamens slightly exserted. (Basilicum: old name, Greek *kingly*, because of its healing properties.) Trop. Asia, Afr., and Pacific isls.—**O. minimum,** L., Bush Basil, is probably a small cult. form of the foregoing, with sts. to 1 ft. high and lvs. subentire and ½–¾in. long.

Fig. 177. Nolanaceæ. *Nolana paradoxa:* a, flowering branch, × ½; b, flower, vertical section, × 1; c, ovary, vertical section, × 5; d, stamen, on section of corolla-tube, × 3; e, pistil, × 5; f, fruit, × 1.

177. NOLANACEÆ. NOLANA FAMILY

Herbs or small shrubs of 2 genera and over 60 species native in Chile and Peru, many of them maritime.—Lvs. alternate or in pairs: fls. solitary, bisexual, regular; calyx 5-cleft; corolla gamopetalous, hypogynous, 5-lobed, plicate in the bud; stamens 5, unequal, alternating with lobes of corolla and inserted in the base of it; disk present, often lobed; ovary superior, usually of 5 carpels which are radially or transversely lobed and split into 3 to many distinct nutlets or follicles which are 1–8-seeded.

NOLANA, L. About 57 species of prostrate herbs, suitable for planting in borders, rocky hillsides, and baskets.—Technical characters as for the family. (Nola-na: *nola*, a little bell, referring to the shape of the corolla.)

A. Lvs. with distinct petioles and broad blades . . . . 1. *N. paradoxa*
AA. Lvs. strap-shaped, without distinct petioles . . . . 2. *N. acuminata*

1. **N. paradoxa,** Lindl. (*N. atriplicifolia,* D. Don. *N. grandiflora,* Lehm.). Succulent per. with fleshy tap-root; sts. spotted and streaked with purple above, to 1 ft. or more long: lvs. 2–3 in. long, with distinct petioles which are abruptly expanded into broad blades: fls. blue with white throat which is yellow within, 1–2 in. across, on long slightly hairy peduncles; corolla-lobes angular, each with 3 straight branched ribs; stamens villous at base; ovaries numerous, 1-seeded, surrounded at base by an annular nectary.

2. **N. acuminata,** Miers (*Sorema acuminata,* Miers. *N. lanceolata,* Miers). Succulent hairy somewhat glandular ann., distinguished from *N. paradoxa* by the strap-shaped lvs. decurrent at base and without distinct petioles, and the smaller nutlets.

Fig. 178. Solanaceæ. A, *Nierembergia hippomanica* var. *violacea:* Aa, flowering branch, × ½; Ab, flower, × ½; Ac, same, perianth partly excised, × 2; Ad, flower, face view, × ½. B, *Lycopersicon esculentum:* Ba, flowering branch, × ½; Bb, flower, × 1; Bc, flower, vertical section, corolla partly excised, × 2; Bd, ovary, cross-section, × 5. C, *Schizanthus pinnatus:* Ca, flower, × 1; Cb, same, perianth expanded, × 1. D, *Browallia viscosa:* Da, flower, face view, × ½; Db, flower, perianth excised in vertical section, × 1. E, *Nicotiana alata* var. *grandiflora:* Ea, flower, vertical section, × ½; Eb, bud, partially expanded, × ½; Ec, capsule, × ½.

178. SOLANACEÆ. NIGHTSHADE FAMILY

A great family abounding in the tropics but well represented also in temp. regions, of 75 or more genera and more than 2,000 species, yielding many subjects for ornament as also for food and drugs.—Erect or climbing herbs, shrubs, or small trees, with mostly alternate entire or variously dissected or pinnate exstipulate lvs.: fls. mostly bisexual and regular, with valvate or plicate æstivation, 5-lobed, the gamopetalous corolla prevailingly rotate but varying greatly in its shape and structure, sometimes very irregular; calyx 5-lobed; stamens typically as many as lobes of corolla and alternate with them, often connivent by their anthers, sometimes 1 or more of them sterile; hypogynous disk usually present; family marked by superior normally 2-celled ovary with axile placentæ together with usually plicate or valvate corolla-lobes, ovules mostly many, style 1 and stigma simple or lobed: fr. a berry or caps.—The family has many poisonous members.

A. Stamens all fertile and not didymous (twin), usually 5.
 B. Fr. a berry (sometimes very large) or at least not capsular and not dehiscent.
  C. Anthers connivent around the style.
   D. Two cells of anthers close together and parallel, not separated by a broadened filament or connective.
    E. Opening of anthers mostly by a pore or slit at or near the apex .... 1. SOLANUM
    EE. Opening from base to top, the apex extended into an empty extremity.. 2. LYCOPERSICON
   DD. Two cells separated by a prominently broadened or thickened filament or connective .... 3. CYPHOMANDRA
  CC. Anthers not connivent around style, dehiscing longitudinally.
   D. Calyx enlarging in fr.
    E. Plants herbaceous: fls. rotate or at most funnelform.
     F. Fruiting calyx spreading, about as long as fr. .... 4. ATROPA
     FF. Fruiting calyx bladdery-inflated, permanently inclosing the berry.
      G. Ovary 2-celled: fruiting calyx 5-toothed .... 5. PHYSALIS
      GG. Ovary 3–5- elled: fruiting calyx 5-parted .... 6. NICANDRA
    EE. Plants woody: calyx appressing or inclosing the berry: fls. long-tubular, with narrow limb .... 7. IOCHROMA
   DD. Calyx not so: mostly woody plants.
    E. Nodes bearing spines .... 8. LYCIUM
    EE. Nodes not spiniferous.
     F. Fls. 2 in. or less long: not true climbers.
      G. Corolla rotate or bell-shaped.
       H. Foliage radical: root very large .... 9. MANDRAGORA
       HH. Foliage cauline and root fibrous .... 10. CAPSICUM
      GG. Corolla distinctly tubular or cylindrical or urn-shaped.
       H. Ovules (and seeds) 3–6 in each cell, some of them usually abortive in fr. .... 11. CESTRUM
       HH. Ovules many in each cell .... 12. SALPICHROA
     FF. Fls. very large, corolla 4 in. or more long: tall climber .... 13. SOLANDRA
 BB. Fr. capsular, mostly dehiscent or at length splitting.
  C. Foliage heath-like .... 14. FABIANA
  CC. Foliage wholly otherwise.
   D. Caps. opening by a lid (circumscissile) .... 15. HYOSCYAMUS
   DD. Caps. splitting lengthwise or bursting irregularly.
    E. Calyx nearly or quite covering the fr. .... 16. NICOTIANA
    EE. Calyx much shorter than fr., mostly reflexing .... 17. DATURA
AA. Stamens paired, one or more of them often smaller or abortive.
 B. Perfect stamens 2 .... 18. SCHIZANTHUS
 BB. Perfect stamens 4 or 5.
  C. Number of perfect stamens 5.
   D. And affixed at top of tube .... 19. NIEREMBERGIA
   DD. And affixed at middle of tube or lower .... 20. PETUNIA
  CC. Number of perfect stamens 4.
   D. Anthers with all cells developed.
    E. Fr. a dry caps.: herb viscid-pubescent .... 21. SALPIGLOSSIS
    EE. Fr. fleshy, more or less berry-like: plant woody, not viscid .... 22. BRUNFELSIA
   DD. Anthers with 1 cell in each of shorter pair not developed.
    E. Tube of corolla straight and cylindrical .... 23. BROWALLIA
    EE. Tube twisted, broadened at throat .... 24. STREPTOSOLEN

1. SOLANUM, L. NIGHTSHADE. One of the largest genera of plants, of which about 1,500 species are described, in temp. and trop. climates around the world, yielding a number to hort. and agriculture.—Herbs, shrubs, sometimes trees, many of them climbing, some species strongly spiny, often with stellate pubescence: lvs. alternate, simple or compound: infl. mostly super-axillary or opposite the lvs., the buds before anthesis commonly drooping: fls. gamosepalous and gamopetalous, corolla mostly rotate or shallowly bell-shaped and plaited in the bud, white, blue, purple, yellow, often showy; stamens typically 5, inserted on throat of corolla, the anthers connivent in a cone about the pistil and mostly opening at the apex; ovary prevailingly 2-celled, many-ovuled; stigma small: fr. a berry. (Sola-num: said to be from Latin *solamen*, quieting, alluding to sedative qualities.)—Some of the coarse species are grown in the open for their bold foliage effect, others for their showy fls. and frs.; others for edible parts.

A. Species not climbing.
 B. Kinds grown for subterranean tubers .... 1. *S. tuberosum*
 BB. Kinds grown for the edible fr. or for ornament.
  C. Plant without spines.
   D. Fls. violet or purple, 1 in. or more across.
    E. Fr. 2–12 in. long, maturing singly .... 10. *S. Melongena*
    EE. Fr. ½–1 in. long, in clusters .... 2. *S. Rantonnettii*

DD. Fls. white, ½in. or less across.
E. Lvs. ovate: fr. black, in clusters.............................. 3. *S. nigrum*
EE. Lvs. oblong: fr. scarlet or yellow, often solitary.
F. Twigs glabrous.............................. 4. *S. Pseudo-Capsicum*
FF. Twigs stellate-pubescent.............................. 5. *S. Capsicastrum*
CC. Plant spiny.
D. Young parts and under surface of lvs. rusty-tomentose.
E. Sts. strongly winged.............................. 6. *S. robustum*
EE. Sts. not winged.............................. 7. *S. Warscewiczii*
DD. Young parts and lvs. with gray or whitish pubescence.
E. Fls. white.............................. 8. *S. integrifolium*
EE. Fls. blue or violet.
F. Lvs. narrow, finely pubescent or silky.............................. 9. *S. muricatum*
FF. Lvs. broad-ovate or broader, mostly scurfy or coarsely pubescent.............................. 10. *S. Melongena*
AA. Species of climbing plants.
B. With prickles on lvs. and sts.............................. 11. *S. Wendlandii*
BB. Without prickles.
C. Sts. and lvs. glabrous.
D. Lvs. 1–3 in. long, upper ones entire.............................. 12. *S. jasminoides*
DD. Lvs. 4 in. or more long, mostly pinnate or pinnatifid.............................. 13. *S. Seaforthianum*
CC. Sts. and lvs. usually pubescent.............................. 14. *S. Dulcamara*

1. **S. tuberosum,** L. POTATO. Herbaceous from underground st.-tubers, the weak pubescent or glabrate sts. 1–3 ft. long: lvs. odd-pinnate, 4–10 in. long, with 3 or 4 pairs of ovate pointed entire lfts. with smaller ones between: fls. few in long-peduncled forking clusters, white to bluish, 1–1¼ in. across, the corolla rotate; calyx-lobes linear-lanceolate, about one-third length of corolla: fr. (infrequently produced) a 2-celled or 3-celled globular berry ¾in. or less diam., yellowish or green. Temp. Andes.

2. **S. Rantonnettii,** Carr. Erect puberulent or glabrate shrub, 3–6 ft., with ridge-lines on the sts.: lvs. simple and entire but margins more or less undulate, ovate, lance-ovate to elliptic, 1–4 in. long, acute or obtuse, narrowed to slender petiole, mostly puberulent at least on veins: fls. few, slender-pedicelled, in axillary nearly or quite sessile clusters, about 1 in. across, potato-like, dark blue or violet and usually with a lighter center: berries drooping, ½–1 in. long, heart-formed, red. (Grown as a novelty the middle of last century in France by Mons. Rantonnet.) Paraguay, Argentina.

3. **S. nigrum,** L. A prostrate, ascending or erect glabrous or somewhat pubescent variable branchy weed of world-wide distribution, but certain forms cult. for the large edible berries and then known as Morelle, Garden Huckleberry, Wonderberry, Sunberry; the lvs. are eaten as greens in some countries: lvs. simple, usually ovate or lance-ovate, 2–5 in. long or often longer in the cult. plant, pointed, entire or variously angled, petioled: fls. ¼in. or less across, white, in pendulous lateral little clusters: berries black, about ¼in. diam. or perhaps twice as large in the cult. kinds: ann. or perhaps of longer duration in warm climates, 1–2½ ft. high: perhaps more than one species is involved in the multitude of forms.—Unripe frs. and lvs. may be poisonous.

4. **S. Pseudo-Capsicum,** L. JERUSALEM-CHERRY. Widely distributed small branching erect shrub, 2–4 ft., glabrous: lvs. narrow-oblong to oblanceolate, 2–4 in. long, obtuse or only short-acute, narrowed to a short petiole, entire but more or less undulate, glabrous both sides, upper surface shining: fls. white, ⅓–½in. across, solitary or few, lateral: fr. globular, size of cherry, scarlet or yellow, long-persistent and therefore giving the plant a highly ornamental character, poisonous when eaten. (Pseudo-Capsicum: *false capsicum*, an ante-Linnæan name for the plant.) Probably of Old World origin.

5. **S. Capsicastrum,** Link. FALSE JERUSALEM-CHERRY. Much like no. 4 but differing in the stellate pubescence or light tomentum on the young parts, pedicels, and under surfaces of lvs., giving the plant a grayish not shining appearance: lvs. often 2 together, one large and one small, the larger ones 2–3 in. long, sometimes variegated: fr. usually ovoid and somewhat pointed, scarlet or orange-red, relatively not long-persistent. (Capsicastrum: *capsicum-like*.) Brazil.

6. **S. robustum,** Wendl. (*S. alatum*, Seem. & J. Schmidt). Strong shrub, 3–5 ft. or more, with strongly winged sts. and strong spines, the growing parts and under surfaces of lvs. rusty-tomentose: lvs. simple, sinuately lobed or angled, ovate-elliptic in outline, 10–12 in. and more long, the ribs and long winged petiole spiny, puberulent above with forked and stellate hairs: fls. few to several in rather close rusty-tomentose lateral peduncled clusters, white, 1 in. or more across, corolla-lobes narrow and acute: fr. globose, about ½in. diam., with rusty tomentum. Brazil.

7. **S. Warscewiczii,** Weick. Strong shrub, 4–6 ft., much like *S. robustum* but without winged sts., and lvs. with several narrow lobes on either side sometimes extending half or more the width of the blade: corolla white, 1½ in. across: fr. pale yellow, glabrous, shining. (Von Warscewicz, page 291.) Probably from S. Amer.

8. **S. integrifolium,** Poir. (*S. coccineum*, Hort.). SCARLET or TOMATO EGGPLANT. Ann. coarse herb, branched, 3 ft., the growing parts pubescent and scurfy, with strong hooked spines: lvs. ovate to oblong-ovate, simple, sinuate-lobed to one-third or less width of blade,

4–8 in. long, more or less spiny on ribs and petiole, becoming glabrate above, stellate-pubescent or tomentose beneath: fls. white, in short-peduncled clusters of 2–6, about ¾in. across, calyx prickly: fr. globular but usually flattened on the ends, 1–2 in. across, the sides prominently furrowed, scarlet or yellow, smooth and bright. Probably African, but widely spread.—Sometimes grown for its ornamental frs. *S. texanum*, Hort., appears to be a spineless race of this species.

9. **S. muricatum,** Ait. PEPINO. Erect spiny per. herb or subshrub, 2–3 ft., finely pubescent to glabrate: lvs. simple, entire or margins undulate, oblong-lanceolate to lance-ovate, 3–6 in. long, tapering to obtuse or acutish apex, long-petioled: fls. in a long-peduncled cluster, about ½–¾in. across, bright blue, the corolla deeply 5-lobed and puberulent outside: fr. ovoid and usually with a point, 4–6 in. long and hanging on a long peduncle, yellow with splashes and streaks of violet-purple, flesh yellow and seedless in cult., acid, aromatic, long-keeping, edible, with a melon-like quality (plant sometimes called Melon Shrub). Probably Peru.—Now and then cult. in the U. S., largely as a curiosity.

10. **S. Melongena,** L. Erect and much-branched stout herb or subshrub, probably native in S. Asia, only the vars. much cult. in this country. (Melongena: a pre-Linnæan name, perhaps associated with the Greek word for apple.) Var. **esculentum,** Nees. COMMON EGGPLANT. Bushy erect per. grown commonly as an ann., 2–3 ft., gray-tomentose and more or less scurfy, sometimes with a few spines: lvs. simple, oblong, oval or ovate, 6–15 in. long, thick and heavy, unequal at base, acute or obtuse at apex, obscurely angled or lobed: fls. mostly solitary, opposite the lvs. or subopposite, inclined or nodding, 1¾–2 in. across, violet, rotate, the calyx usually prickly: fr. a large pendent ovoid, oblong or obovoid berry, 2–12 in. long, shining, purple, white, yellowish, or striped. Var. **serpentinum,** Bailey. SNAKE EGGPLANT. Differs in its fr., which is a curiosity, to 12 in. long and only 1 in. or less thick, curled at the end. Var. **depressum,** Bailey. DWARF EGGPLANT. Small and straggling plant nearly or quite glabrous and the young parts usually purplish, mostly spineless: lvs. only 2–6 in. long, thin, scarcely lobed: fls. small and long-peduncled: fr. pyriform to obovoid, 4–5 in. long, purple.

11. **S. Wendlandii,** Hook. f. Very strong large glabrous shrubby climber: lvs. 6–10 in. long, pinnatifid with 2–3 pairs of rather small segms., the terminal part large and mostly 3-lobed, usually the midrib, petiole and young sts. prickly; some of the upper lvs. simple and oval to oblong-acuminate: fls. lilac-blue, 2–2½ in. across, in large forking clusters: fr. globose. (Received at Kew from Dr. Wendland of the Botanic Garden in Hanover.) Costa Rica.—A showy arbor and porch climber in S. Fla., S. Calif., and S.

12. **S. jasminoides,** Paxt. Climbing slender-stemmed glabrous spineless shrub grown under glass and in the open in mild climates, 10 ft. and more: lvs. 1–3 in. long, the upper ones simple and entire, lance-ovate to lanceolate, long-pointed, many of the lower ones irregularly pinnatifid or pinnate with small side or basal segm.: fls. slender-pedicelled, in forking terminal and lateral clusters, about 1 in. across, white tinged blue, the corolla star-shaped and attractive. Brazil.

13. **S. Seaforthianum,** Andr. Slender climbing glabrous spineless shrub, 10 ft. and more: lvs. 4–8 in. long, all essentially odd-pinnate or those on flowering twigs sometimes simple, petiolate; pinnæ (or segms.) 2–4 pairs and often smaller ones between, narrow-ovate to lanceolate, acuminate, narrowed to base and often petiolulate, margins entire, often undulate: fls. many in small cymes, divaricately arranged on the sides of a rachis, 1 in. or less across, star-shaped, blue or purple: fr. ovoid to globose, scarlet, ⅓in. across. (Intro. into England from the W. Indies in 1804 by Lord Seaforth.) Probably Brazil.

14. **S. Dulcamara,** L. EUROPEAN BITTER-SWEET. Shrubby climber to 8 ft., usually pubescent but becoming glabrate: lvs. ovate, 2–4 in. long, entire or 3-lobed at base: fls. in long-stalked cymes, violet spotted with green, rotate, ½in. across, corolla-lobes acuminate and reflexed: fr. ovoid, scarlet, ½in. long, poisonous when eaten in quantity. (Dulcamara: Latin bitter-sweet.) Eu., Asia; nat. in N. Amer.

2. **LYCOPERSICON,** Mill. TOMATO. About a half dozen S. American soft herbs, per. and perhaps ann., two of them grown for the edible fr.; sometimes united with Solanum but differing in being always unarmed, lvs. always pinnate or pinnatifid, and particularly in the anthers which are projected into sharp or narrow sterile tips and which dehisce from top to bottom: fls. yellow: fr. a pulpy berry; cells 2 or few, multiplying under domestication. (Lycoper-sicon: Greek *wolf peach,* probably in reference to supposed poisonous qualities.)

A. Plant hairy, with strong odor..1. *L. esculentum*
AA. Plant not hairy, very slender, with little or indifferent odor................2. *L. pimpinellifolium*

1. **L. esculentum,** Mill. (*Solanum Lycopersicum,* L. *Lycopersicon Lycopersicon,* Karst.). Spreading hairy-pubescent and more or less glandular strong-smelling plur-ann. or per., 3–6 ft. or more, the young growth on mature plants erect: lvs. odd-pinnate with small lfts. interposed, 6–18 in. long; main lfts. 5–9, stalked, ovate to oblong, 2–3 in. long,

acuminate, irregularly toothed, margins tending to roll inward: fls. 3–7, nodding, ¾in. or more across, on jointed pedicels: fr. red or yellow, usually flattened at the ends, 2–3 in. across, the sides furrowed or angled. W. S. Amer. Var. **cerasiforme,** Alef. (*L. cerasiforme,* Dunal). CHERRY TOMATO. Lvs. thinner and mostly smaller and usually less acuminate: fls. prevailingly in longer clusters: fr. globular and regular, about ¾in. diam., red or yellow, few-celled; forms with oblong fr. are the Plum tomatoes. Var. **pyriforme,** Alef. (*L. pyriforme,* Dunal). PEAR TOMATO. Differs in bearing pear-shaped frs., which are usually about 1½ in. long. Var. **commune,** Bailey (var. *vulgare,* Bailey not Alef.). COMMON TOMATO. Lfts. little if at all conduplicate or curled, the plants heavier and more lopping: fr. mostly globular or only moderately oblate, 3 in. and more across, not furrowed or lobed on the sides; parts of the fl. often multiplied, the cells becoming many. Cultigen. Var. **grandifolium,** Bailey. LARGE-LEAVED or POTATO-LEAVED TOMATO. Lvs. large and plane; lfts. usually not more than 5, large, with entire margins, the secondary lfts. few or none. Cultigen. Var. **validum,** Bailey. UPRIGHT TOMATO. Plant stout and erect, very compact, the lvs. crowded and curled. Cultigen; little grown in this country.—The tomato species is yet under taxonomic study.

2. **L. pimpinellifolium,** Mill. (*Solanum pimpinellifolium,* Jusl. *L. racemiforme* and *L. racemigerum,* Lange). CURRANT TOMATO. Weak, slender-stemmed, not hairy but finely puberulent, the odor not pronounced: lfts. 5–7 with smaller ones interposed, long-stalked, ovate, ¾–1½ in. long, pointed or obtuse, base sometimes cordate: fls. 10–25 in an elongating 2-sided raceme, the pedicels prominently geniculate: fr. red, currant-like, about ½in. diam., 2-celled. Peru.

3. **CYPHOMANDRA,** Sendt. Thirty or more S. American herbs, shrubs, and small trees, technically separated from Solanum in the fact that the 2 anther-cells are separated by a thickened connective which appears as a column on the back of the anther: erect spineless plants, with large, entire, 3-lobed or pinnatisect lvs.: fls. pedicellate in racemes or scorpioid cymes, calyx and rotate or bell-shaped corolla 5-lobed; anthers opening at apex or on side: fr. a 2-celled many-seeded berry, sometimes large, in one species prized as a cult. esculent. (Cyphoman-dra: Greek, referring to the peculiar anthers.)

C. betacea, Sendt. (*Solanum betaceum,* Cav.). TREE-TOMATO. Tree-like somewhat woody shrub 6–10 ft., mostly pubescent or puberulent: lvs. simple and entire, cordate-ovate, 8–12 in. long, short-pointed, prominently pinnate-veined, soft-pubescent: fls. about ½in. across, pinkish, fragrant, the corolla-lobes long and narrow: fr. egg-shaped, 2–3 in. long, smooth, long-peduncled, dull red, with a slightly acid tomato-like flavor. S. Amer. —Grown in the open in subtrop. parts and sometimes under glass in the N.

4. **ATROPA,** L. Two to 4 species of Old World herbs, one of economic importance as a source of atropine and other powerful drugs.—Erect: lvs. entire: calyx bell-shaped, with 5 ovate leafy divisions, enlarging in fr.; corolla bell-shaped or funnel-form: fr. a berry, subtended by enlarged calyx-lobes, poisonous. (At-ropa: after Atropos, the Fate who severs the thread of life.)

A. Belladonna, L. BELLADONNA. Branching leafy per., 2–3 ft., sparsely pubescent to glabrate: lvs. entire, ovate or oblong-ovate, 3–6 in. long, acuminate, narrowed to a petiole: fls. solitary or in pairs, nodding, on axillary pedicels; corolla blue-purple or dull red, about 1 in. long: berry nearly globular, slightly 2-lobed, about ½in. across,seedful, shining black. (Belladonna: Italian *beautiful woman,* the red sap used as a cosmetic in Italy.) Eu. and Asia.

5. **PHYSALIS,** L. HUSK-TOMATO. GROUND-CHERRY. Low herbs of warm and temp. countries, largely America, a few grown for the edible frs. and also for the ornamental fruiting calyx of some species; probably 100 or more species.—Ann. and per. summer-flowering herbs or sometimes slightly woody at base, straggling, diffuse or creeping, glabrous or pubescent: lvs. alternate, often 2 together, simple, mostly angled and distinctly petioled, commonly soft in texture: fls. usually on axillary or extra-axillary pedicels, mostly blue or yellowish or whitish and not showy; calyx 5-toothed, becoming large and bladder-like and inclosing the 2-celled globular yellow or greenish often more or less viscid berry; corolla rotate or short-campanulate, usually with purplish spots in the center, plicate, short-tubed and mostly 5-toothed; stamens 5; style slender, the stigma somewhat 2-lobed. (Phys-alis: Greek *bladder,* referring to the fruiting calyx.)—Species of Physalis are yet confused and in need of further study.

A. Plants with large red calyces in fr. . . . . 1. *P. Alkekengi*
AA. Plants with green or yellow or at most only red-veined calyces: mostly grown for the edible berry.
B. Sts. glabrous or very nearly so . . . . 2. *P. ixocarpa*
BB. Sts. pubescent or hairy.
C. Base of lf. conspicuously uneven or oblique. . . . . 3. *P. pruinosa*
CC. Base of lf. usually evenly cordate or truncate. . . . . 4. *P. peruviana*

1. **P. Alkekengi,** L. (*P. Franchetii*, Hort. *P. Alkekengi* var. *Franchetii*, Makino. *P. Bunyardii*, Hort.). ALKEKENGI. WINTER-CHERRY. CHINESE LANTERN-PLANT. Diffuse per. but sometimes grown as an ann. with long creeping underground sts., 1–2 ft. high, usually with zigzag mostly simple angl d pubescent or glabrous sts.: lvs. ovate with broad base, 2–3 in. long, short-acuminate, often angular, ciliate, the petiole widening at top: fls. ¾in. across, whitish, the anthers yellow: fr. red, the large ripened calyx blood-red, about 2 in. long, and very showy. (Alkekengi: Arabian name.) Apparently native from S. E. Eu. to Japan, but now adventive or nat. in many parts of the world.—An old garden plant, grown for its highly colored bladders.

2. **P. ixocarpa,** Brot. (*P. edulis*, Hort.). TOMATILLO. Erect branching ann. 3–4 ft. high, glabrous or very nearly so: lvs. thin, ovate to lance-ovate, 2–3 in. long, variously toothed or notched, long-petioled: fls. large and open, ¾in. or more across, the border bright yellow and throat bearing 5 black-brown spots; anthers purplish: husk or enlarged calyx purple-veined, entirely filled by the large round purplish sticky berry, and sometimes torn by it. Mex., intro. northward.—Sometimes cult. for the fr.

3. **P. pruinosa,** L. STRAWBERRY-TOMATO. DWARF CAPE-GOOSEBERRY. Low gray-pubescent ann., with stout sts. more or less erect but becoming diffuse: lvs. ovate, 2–4 in. long, mostly acuminate, very oblique or semi-cordate at base, obtusely dentate or angled to the base: fls. ⅜in. or less long, bell-shaped, the limb or border erect and whitish-yellow, the throat marked with 5 brown spots inside; anthers yellow or tinged purple; calyx much shorter than corolla but enlarging in fr. and inclosing the globular yellow berry which is ¾in. diam., sweetish and not glutinous. Mass. to Fla and Ala.—Frs. eaten raw or cooked, or used for preserves or pickles. Often confused with *P. pubescens*, L., which is more slender, less pubescent, lvs. often entire and not toothed to base; Pa. to Calif. and tropics.

4. **P. peruviana,** L. (*P. edulis*, Sims). CAPE-GOOSEBERRY. Stronger grower than *P. pruinosa*, attaining a height of 1½–3 ft., maturing later: lvs. thicker, soft-pubescent, broad, often not toothed, evenly cordate or truncate at base: fls. ½–⅝in. long, open-campanulate, the limb or border widely spreading and light yellow, the inside of the throat purple-blotched and veined; anthers blue-purple: husk thicker and larger, somewhat hairy, and longer-pointed; berry yellow, not glutinous, much like that of *P. pruinosa* but usually less sweet. Tropics.

6. **NICANDRA,** Adans. Ann. herbs from Peru, one an old-fashioned fl.-garden plant.—Differs from Physalis in the 3–5-celled ovary and the fruiting calyx deeply 5-parted. (Nican-dra: named for Nicander, poet of Colophon, who wrote on plants about 100 B. C.)

N. Physalodes, Gaertn. (*Atropa Physalodes*, L. *Physalodes peruvianum*, Kuntze. *P. Physalodes*, Britt.). APPLE-OF-PERU. SHOO-FLY PLANT. To 4 ft., much-branched: lvs. ovate to oblong, 2–6 in. long, narrowed at base, sinuate-toothed: fls. blue, 1–1½ in. long and broad, solitary and nodding in axils on slender pedicels; limb of corolla nearly entire: berry inclosed in the enlarged green calyx 1–1½ in. long, the lobes auricled at base. Escaped in E. N. Amer. and tropics.

7. **IOCHROMA,** Benth. Shrubs and small trees, sometimes grown under glass and in the open in subtrop. parts; species about 20, mostly in W. trop. S. Amer.—Spineless, glabrous or stellate-tomentose: lvs. entire, often large: fls. purple, blue, scarlet, yellow or white, in pairs, or sometimes clustered; calyx tubular or campanulate, 5-toothed, enlarging in fr. and appressing or inclosing the berry; corolla long-tubular or narrow-trumpet-shaped, with 5 short or very small lobes, the throat more or less closed by appendages or folds; stamens inserted below the middle of the corolla-tube; disk present or absent; ovary 2-celled: fr. a pulpy globose or ovoid berry. (Iochro-ma: Greek *violet-colored.*)

A. Fls. blue: lvs. acute, long-petioled. . . . . 1. *I. lanceolatum*
AA. Fls. orange-scarlet (varying to white): lvs. very obtuse, short-petioled. . . . . 2. *I. fuchsioides*

1. **I. lanceolatum,** Miers. Shrub 4–8 ft. high, more or less downy: lvs. alternate, ovate or elliptic-lanceolate, acute, entire, tapering to a long petiole: umbels supra-axillary and terminal; fls. rich deep purple-blue; calyx abrupt at base, shallowly blunt-toothed, puberulent or glabrate; corolla pubescent, the tube slightly curved, the margin shortly and unequally 5-lobed or -toothed. Ecuador.—*I. tubulosum*, Benth., is to be looked for; it is a

shrub 6–8 ft., with ovate ciliate lvs. and deep blue fls. on hairy pedicels; calyx subinflated, hairy, tapering, sharp-toothed; Colombia.

2. **I. fuchsioides,** Miers. Shrub, glabrous or nearly so: lvs. often clustered, obovate to oval or oblong, very obtuse, tapering to a short petiole: fls. more or less clustered, orange-scarlet (a white-fld. form is also offered), drooping; calyx broad or abrupt at base, shallowly blunt-toothed, puberulent; corolla thrice exceeding the 5-toothed bursting calyx, the tube long-cylindric and nearly straight, the limb 5-angled and with intermediate teeth. Peru.

8. **LYCIUM,** L. Box-Thorn. Matrimony-Vine. Woody plants, often climbing, grown for their fls. and attractive frs.; about 100 species in temp. and subtrop. parts of both hemispheres, often in dry regions.—Deciduous or evergreen shrubs, thorny or unarmed: lvs. alternate, often fascicled, short-petioled, small and commonly narrow, usually grayish-green, entire, without stipules: fls. greenish, whitish, purplish, or violet, axillary, solitary or clustered, not large but often numerous on the long branches; calyx campanulate, 3–5-toothed, not enlarging in fr.; corolla funnelform, with usually 5-lobed limb; stamens mostly 5, often with a bearded ring near the base of the filament: fr. a berry with few to many seeds, usually scarlet. (Lyc-ium: Greek name from the country Lycia given to a Rhamnus, transferred later to this genus.)

A. Corolla-tube longer than limb, much narrower below the middle: lvs. lanceolate.
  B. Base of filaments pubescent........1. *L. halimifolium*
  BB. Base of filaments glabrous........2. *L. barbarum*
AA. Corolla-tube shorter than limb, rather wide: lvs. rhombic-ovate to ovate-lanceolate........3. *L. chinense*

1. **L. halimifolium,** Mill. Upright or spreading shrub with arching or recurving branches, usually spiny, to 10 ft.; branchlets light gray, angled: lvs. oblong-lanceolate to lanceolate or oblanceolate, rarely elliptic-lanceolate, 1–2½ in. long, acute or obtusish, gradually narrowed at base into a slender petiole to ¾in. long, grayish-green, thickish: fls. 1–4, on slender pedicels ⅓–¾in. long; calyx usually 1–3-lobed, divided about one-half, with obtusish lobes; corolla dull lilac-purple, the tube longer than the lobes and much narrowed below the middle; stamens hairy at base: fr. subglobose to ovoid or short-oblong, ½–¾in. long, scarlet to orange-red. S. E. Eu. and W. Asia.

2. **L. barbarum,** L. Distinguished from *L. halimifolium* by the smaller narrower lvs. and glabrous filaments: branchlets canescent, spines to ⅓in. long: lvs. linear to linear-oblong, to 1 in. long: corolla pale rose often fading to whitish. N. Afr. to Iraq.—Not hardy N. and grown mostly in S. W. U. S. The *L. barbarum* of most European authors is *L. halimifolium.*

3. **L. chinense,** Mill. Rambling shrub with arching and often prostrate branches, usually unarmed, to 12 ft. long: branchlets light yellowish-gray, angled: lvs. rhombic-ovate or ovate to ovate-lanceolate, 1½–3½ in. long, acute or obtusish, broad- to narrow-cuneate at base, bright green and remaining green until late in autumn; petiole usually not exceeding ½in.: fls. 1–4, on pedicels ⅛–⅓in. rarely to ½in. long; calyx 3–5-toothed, usually divided less than one-half, with acute lobes; corolla purple, the lobes slightly longer than the rather wide tube; stamens hairy at base: fr. ovoid to oblong, ⅔–1 in. long, scarlet to orange-red. E. Asia.

9. **MANDRAGORA,** L. Mandrake. Three or 4 species of practically stemless per. herbs with thick or tuberous roots and undivided lvs., native in the Medit. country and the Himalayan region, interesting for medicinal qualities and also for connection with old superstitions; these are the true mandrakes, but in N. Amer. the name is applied to the may-apple (*Podophyllum peltatum*).—Lvs. all basal or semi-basal, broad, undulate: fls. rather large, solitary or fascicled among the foliage, whitish, blue-violet or purple, the 5-parted calyx somewhat enlarging in fr.; corolla bell-shaped, 5-lobed, bearing the 5 stamens on the tube below the middle; ovary 2-celled, with long style and expanded stigma: fr. a fleshy many-seeded globose berry. (Mandrag-ora: ancient name of doubtful application.)—Seldom cult. Plants yield powerful extracts; the thick root sometimes has a human-like form of branching, and was formerly ascribed magical values.

M. officinarum, L. A ft. or so high, with spindle-shaped often branching root: lvs. ovate, to 1 ft. long, obtusish, undulate: fls. greenish-yellow, the corolla to 1 in. long, usually scarcely longer than the calyx. Medit. region and E.—*M. autumnalis,* Spreng., has violet fls., the corolla exceeding the calyx; Medit. countries.

10. CAPSICUM, L. Red Pepper. Per. woody plants but known in northern vegetable-gardens as herbaceous annuals, probably native in Cent. and S. Amer., and 1 anomalous species in Japan; American species 1 or many, depending on the definition.—Erect much-branching essentially glabrous plants: lvs. ovate, elliptic to narrow-lanceolate, simple and entire: fls. white or greenish-white sometimes tinged violet, pedicelled, solitary or in 2's or 3's, erect or declined; calyx short, nearly truncate but usually with very short points, somewhat enlarging about the base of the fr.; corolla rotate or nearly so, usually 5-lobed; stamens commonly 5, not closely connivent, mostly bluish, anthers opening longitudinally; ovary 2–3-celled, but the cells often multiplying under domestication, style simple, stigma capitate: fr. a pod-like indehiscent many-seeded berry with thick integument, widely various in size, shape and color, pungent to the taste. (Cap-sicum: name not satisfactorily explained.)

C. frutescens, L. (*C. annuum* and *C. baccatum*, L.). Shrub to 6–8 ft., trunk becoming 3 in. through, the wood very hard, but plants capable of fruiting the first year from seed and, in the N., not developing woody tissue before frost: lvs. various, often less than 1 in. long, in cult. forms sometimes 5 in. long, narrowed to petiole, usually acuminate: fls. ⅜–⅝in. across, in developed and monstrous forms sometimes larger: fr. various in the wild or spontaneous shrubby trop. forms, strangely diverse in the cult. kinds, sometimes remaining erect, sometimes declined or drooping.—The capsicums may be variously and almost endlessly ranged into vars. The most practical classification is on the frs., as to position, size and shape. The biological type of *C. frutescens* may well be considered to be the little Bird Pepper, with undeveloped frs. (*C. microcarpum*, DC.): twiggy shrub with short internodes: lvs. ovate, 1–2 in. long: fr. erect, spherical or oblong, ¾in. or less long and ¼in. or less broad, mostly red: a prevailing wild or spontaneous form in warm countries. The races with developed frs. may be conveniently ranged in about four main groups: Var. **cerasiforme,** Bailey, Cherry Pepper, lvs. of intermediate size, ovate or oblong, 2–3 in. long; fr. erect or declined, spherical, subcordate or oblate, ½–1 in. diam., red, yellow, or purplish, very pungent. Var. **conoides,** Bailey, Cone Pepper, like the last, but frs. conical or oblong-cylindrical, 1–2 in. long, usually erect. Var. **fasciculatum,** Bailey, Red Cluster Pepper, plant compact, with narrow clustered lvs.; fr. erect, fascicled, very slender, 3 in. long and ¼in. thick, red, very pungent. Var. **longum,** Bailey, Long Pepper, lvs. medium to large; fr. mostly drooping, elongated, 3–12 in. long and mostly tapering to apex, often curved, sometimes 2 in. thick at base; includes Long Red, Long Yellow, Chilli, Cayenne, and others. Var. **grossum,** Bailey, Bell or Sweet Pepper, plant stout and tall; lvs. oblong-ovate, 4–5 in. long, fls. 1 in. or more across; fr. large and puffy with depression at base, the sides usually furrowed, either oblong, bell-shaped or apple-shaped and tomato-like, red or yellow, mild in flavor.

11. CESTRUM, L. Shrubs and small trees of the American tropics, planted in warm countries and grown under glass for the attractive and often very fragrant fls.; species about 150.—Lvs. simple and entire, mostly narrow rather than broad: fls. in axillary or terminal clusters, tubular, not large but numerous or bright-colored, greenish, white, yellow, or red, the limb salver-like or trumpet-like, the long tube either enlarged or contracted at the throat, the 5-toothed calyx relatively short; stamens attached in the tube, included; ovary 2-celled, with 3–6 ovules in each cell, usually on a short stipe; style slender, stigma expanded and sometimes 2-lobed: fr. a small berry, often scarcely succulent. (Ces-trum: old Greek name of some plant.)

A. Fls. conspicuously contracted at mouth; corolla red or rose. (Habrothamnus.)
  B. Infl. rather loose or elongated: corolla glabrous .... 1. *C. purpureum*
  BB. Infl. globular-compact, commonly closely subtended by lvs.: corolla pubescent outside .... 2. *C. fasciculatum*
AA. Fls. not contracted at throat, but usually expanded: corolla white or yellow. (Cestrum proper, sometimes known as Jessamines.)
  B. Lobes of corolla becoming distinctly reflexed.
    C. Corolla orange-yellow .... 3. *C. aurantiacum*
    CC. Corolla white .... 4. *C. diurnum*
  BB. Lobes erect or spreading.
    C. Lvs. oblong-ovate or elliptic, short-acuminate .... 5. *C. nocturnum*
    CC. Lvs. on the lanceolate order, very long-tapering .... 6. *C. Parqui*

1. **C. purpureum,** Standl. (*Habrothamnus purpureus*, Lindl. *H. elegans*, Brongn. *C. elegans*, Schlecht.). Slender bush to 10 ft. or more, with flexuose hairy-pubescent branches with a somewhat scandent habit: lvs. narrow-ovate to ovate-lanceolate, 2½–5 in. long and 1–1½ in. broad, gradually acuminate, short-petioled, pubescent beneath and light-pubescent to glabrate above: fls. in rather loose terminal clusters that are more or less

nodding; corolla ¾–1 in. long, red-purple, glabrous, upwardly swollen but constricted at the throat, very slender at the base, several times longer than the calyx, the acute lobes becoming reflexed: berries globular, about ⅓in. across, red. Mex. Var. **Smithii,** Bailey (*C. Smithii,* Hort.), has blush-rose fls.—An old greenhouse plant, of continuous bloom.

2. **C. fasciculatum,** Miers (*Meyenia fasciculata,* Schlecht.). Fls. purplish-red, larger than those of no. 1, mostly in spring, in compact globular clusters that are usually attended by small lvs. like an involucre; corolla pubescent outside: lvs. ovate, 2–2½ in. broad. Mex. Var. **Newellii,** Bailey (*C. Newellii,* Nichols.), has large bright crimson fls., andis a free bloomer.

3. **C. aurantiacum,** Lindl. Half-climbing nearly or quite glabrous shrub: lvs. ovate or oval, 3–4 in. long and 1¾–2½ in. broad, short-pointed and not very acute, often somewhat undulate: fls. 2–5 together, sessile, combined in a terminal panicle; corolla orange-yellow, ¾–1 in. long, the large acutish lobes strongly reflexed. Guatemala.

4. **C. diurnum,** L. Day Jessamine. Large shrub to 15 ft., with wiry and puberulent growth: lvs. thick, persistent, oblong or elliptic, 2–3½ in. long, about 1 in. broad, obtuse or only indifferently acute, glabrous and glossy above, lighter colored and puberulent on veins beneath or becoming glabrate: fls. white, sweet-scented by day, sessile in short clusters on long axillary peduncles; corolla ⅓–½in. long, the short bluntish lobes reflexed at full anthesis. W. Indies.

5. **C. nocturnum,** L. Night Jessamine. Shrub to 12 ft., with glabrous angled branchlets: lvs. thin, mostly oblong-ovate to elliptic and rather short-acuminate, 4–8 in. long, mostly about 1½ in. broad, glabrous and more or less shining both sides, usually broad-based, petiole distinct: fls. greenish-white to cream-colored, very fragrant at night, nearly or quite sessile on axillary elongating but not long-peduncled clusters; corolla very slender, about ¾in. long, the acute lobes erect or only spreading. W. Indies.

6. **C. Parqui,** L'Her. Willow-leaved Jessamine. Nearly glabrous shrub to 6 ft., distinguished by short-petioled narrow lvs. that are lanceolate and long-tapering at apex and base, 3–6 in. long, usually not much exceeding 1 in. broad: fls. greenish-white to greenish-yellow, fragrant at night, sessile in profuse axillary and terminal clusters; corolla ¾–1 in. long, the acute lobes wide-spreading and the edges sometimes revolute. (Parqui is the name of the plant in Chile, once proposed as a generic name.) Chile.—In certain broad-lvd. forms difficult to separate from *C. nocturnum.*

12. **SALPICHROA,** Miers. About a dozen shrubs, subshrubs, or herbs of extra-trop. S. Amer. and 1 in Ariz., one sometimes used for cover-planting in S. Calif.—Lvs. entire, often hairy, narrowing to a long petiole: fls. white or yellow, solitary; calyx tubular, 5-cleft, in fr. hardly enlarged; corolla tubular or urn-shaped, with or without a woolly ring inside; stamens inserted at about the middle of the corolla-tube or even higher: berry ovoid or oblong, 2-celled, with numerous compressed seeds. (Salpichro-a: Greek *tube* or *trumpet,* and *skin* or *complexion,* in reference to the form and texture of the fl.)

S. rhomboidea, Miers (*Atropa rhomboidea,* Gill.). Cocks-Eggs. A weedy climber, per. from a fleshy root, somewhat woody, with green flexuous branches and strong odor: lvs. subopposite, ovate-rhomboid, ½–¾in. long, narrowed to a petiole: fls. white, solitary or rarely in pairs, nodding, on filiform pedicels scarcely shorter than the petioles; corolla short, urceolate, constricted below the middle and at the throat, about ⅓in. long, the inside of the tube with a woolly ring: berry ovate-oblong, yellow or white, many-seeded, said to be edible but of poor flavor. Argentina.—Thrives in dry and alkaline places; mentioned as a forage plant for bees.

13. **SOLANDRA,** Sw. Chalice-Vine. About a half dozen tall glabrous woody plants with branches climbing, bearing very showy fls., suitable for the warmhouse and grown in the open in the warmest parts of the U. S.—Lvs. entire, leathery, shining: fls. solitary, very large, white or yellow; calyx long-tubular, sleeve-like, 2–3-toothed at the apex; corolla funnelform, with long cylindric tube and oblique broad-campanulate throat, the limb with broad lobes; stamens 5, inserted near the base of the corolla; ovary 2-celled, with many ovules: berry globose or elongated, pulpy, more or less included in the calyx, with large smooth seeds. (Solan-dra: named for Daniel C. Solander, 1736–1786, Swedish naturalist and traveller.)

S. guttata, Don (*Swartzia guttata,* Standl.). Strong branching climbing shrub: lvs. elliptic-oblong, acute or very short-acuminate or sometimes blunt at apex, 2–6 in. long: fls. terminal, solitary, fragrant; calyx tubular, about 3 in. long, with 3-lobed limb; corolla ochre-yellow, funnelform, 9 in. long, the slender part much exceeding calyx, the limb with

5 crenate and undulate lobes, the throat with 5 purple-brown ridges; stamens subequal, scarcely protruding beyond the throat; pistil prominent. Mex.—Sometimes grown as *S. grandiflora*, Sw., in which, however, the slender part of the tube is not longer than calyx.

14. **FABIANA,** Ruiz & Pav. A score or so of small heath-like shrubs, one sometimes grown for ornament in cool greenhouses and in mild climates; Bolivia and Brazil to Patagonia.—Erect branching plants, sometimes viscid: lvs. small and crowded: fls. small, white, usually many, terminal or opposite the lvs.; calyx tubular-campanulate, shortly 5-toothed; corolla-tube elongate, dilated or ventricose above, the short limb 5-lobed or scarcely lobed; stamens 5, unequal, inserted at or below the middle of the corolla-tube, included; disk fleshy, annular or lobed; ovary 2-celled: caps. oblong, 2-valved. (Fabia-na: after Francisco Fabiano, 1719–1801, Spanish Archbishop and amateur botanist.)

F. imbricata, Ruiz & Pav. Height 3–8 ft.; branchlets many, erect, puberulous: lvs. numerous, ovate, scale-like, imbricated: fls. sessile or nearly so, borne singly but profusely on the ends of short branchlets; corolla about ½in. long, much constricted at the base, the lobes short, rounded and reflexed. Peru.

15. **HYOSCYAMUS,** L. Henbane. Erect or prostrate coarse herbs of the Medit. region; about 15 species, one nat. in Amer. and sometimes grown for medicinal uses.—Plant usually hairy, ann., bien., per.: lvs. alternate, coarsely toothed or pinnatifid, rarely entire: fls. axillary, the uppermost forming a leafy cluster or spike; calyx 5-toothed, enlarging in fr.; corolla pallid or lurid and reticulate, funnel-shaped, 5-lobed and sometimes unequally so, often splitting down one side; stamens usually exserted; disk inconspicuous or lacking: caps. more or less 2-celled, circumscissile or sometimes opening by valves. (Hyoscy-amus: Greek *hog bean*, supposed to poison swine.)

H. niger, L. Ann. or usually bien., 1–2½ ft. high, with fusiform root: lvs. oblong, 3–8 in. long, irregularly sinuate-toothed or pinnatifid, the lower petiolate, the others more or less clasping and decurrent: fls. 1–2 in. across, subsessile, erect, in simple one-sided terminal spikes; corolla greenish-yellow, purple-veined: caps. about ½in. long, inclosed in the enlarging calyx: lvs. and flowering tops medicinal.

16. **NICOTIANA,** L. Over 100 species and many subspecies of herbaceous or rarely shrubby or arborescent plants, certain of them valued for their stately habit, rapid growth, and large lvs., others for showy fls.; one is the tobacco; native mostly in N., Cent., and S. Amer., especially in the western trop. part, a few species in the Pacific isls. and Australia.—Annuals or perennials, often viscid-pubescent, strongly scented, possessing narcotic-poisonous properties: lvs. alternate, simple, entire or rarely sinuate, mostly sessile or nearly so by a tapering base: fls. white, yellow, greenish, or purple, usually opening at night and then most fragrant, arranged in a terminal panicle or in elongate one-sided racemes, or the lower solitary in the axils; calyx tubular-campanulate, 5-lobed; corolla with long tube and 5-lobed often oblique limb; stamens 5, included or exserted: caps. 2- or seldom 4-valved, the valves 2-toothed or -cleft; seeds numerous, minute. (Nicotia-na: named for Jean Nicot, 1530–1600, French consul to Portugal, who is said to have first presented tobacco to the courts of Portugal and France.)

A. Shape of fls. funnelform .... 1. *N. Tabacum*
AA. Shape of fls. salverform.
 B. Lobes of corolla rounded or obtuse .... 2. *N. suaveolens*
 BB. Lobes of corolla acute or acuminate.
  C. Teeth of calyx ovate, acute; corolla entirely white .... 3. *N. sylvestris*
  CC. Teeth of calyx linear-acuminate to subulate; corolla colored.
   D. Color of fls. greenish-yellow and violet .... 4. *N. alata*
   DD. Color of fls. rose .... 5. *N. Sanderæ*

1. **N. Tabacum,** L. Tobacco. Ann. and herbaceous or sometimes of longer duration and somewhat shrubby at base, viscid-pubescent, erect, branching above: lvs. large, often 1 ft. or more long, oblong-lanceolate, acuminate, sessile, the lower decurrent and half-clasping: fls. diurnal, 1½–2 in. long, pedicelled, bracteate, in short many-fld. panicled racemes; calyx oblong, with lanceolate acute unequal segms.; corolla woolly without, funnel-form, the throat somewhat swollen, the rose-colored or red limb with acute lobes: caps. ovoid, ¾in. long, about equalling the calyx. (Tabacum: Latinization of an aboriginal

American name from which comes also the word *tobacco.*) Trop. Amer.—Cult. by the Indians from earliest times and often running wild. A striking garden plant and also important commercially as the source of tobacco; there are many cultivars.

2. **N. suaveolens,** Lehm. Ann. or bien., usually viscid, 1–2 ft., the subsimple sts. villous below, glabrous above: basal lvs. subpetiolate, spatulate, obtuse, the cauline ovate-lanceolate, undulate, acute, decurrent on the petiole, the uppermost subsessile: fls. 1–2 in. long, nodding, distant, in terminal bracteate racemes; calyx deeply 5-cleft, pubescent, with narrow unequal acute lobes; corolla greenish-purple, opening at night, fragrant, the limb somewhat 2-lipped and 1–1½ in. across with upper lobes very small, all subrotund, obtuse, or emarginate: caps. ovate, obtuse, included. Australia.

3. **N. sylvestris,** Spegazzini & Comes. Tall per., glandular-hairy throughout, the sts. leafy below, branching above: lvs. rugose, sessile, broadly oblong-spatulate, the lower dilated at base, half-clasping and auricled, somewhat decurrent, rotund or obtuse at apex, the upper acute: fls. in short head-like panicles, drooping, on pedicels nearly equalling the calyx, not closing in the morning on cloudy days; calyx 5-angled, somewhat swollen, with short unequal ovate acute teeth; corolla entirely white, fragrant, salverform, the tube about 3½ in. long, above somewhat inflated, the ovate-triangular often emarginate lobes nearly equal, becoming reflexed. Argentina.

4. **N. alata,** Link & Otto. Per., 3–5 ft., glandular-hairy, with erect branching sts.: lvs. lanceolate or oblong, 3–4 in. or more long, decurrent in narrow wings, more or less repand-dentate or undulate, acute or obtuse, the upper narrower: fls. in a loose terminal raceme; calyx hirsute, tubular, the 5 lobes subulate and nearly equal; corolla villous, fragrant, opening at night, and closing in cloudy weather, the slender tube yellowish-green, swollen above, four to five times longer than calyx, the limb oblique, nearly 2 in. across, pale violet beneath, white within, with ovate acute or often emarginate lobes; stamens unequal, not exserted: caps. oblong, shorter than the calyx. Brazil, Uruguay, Paraguay.—Perhaps not in cult., the garden form being var. **grandiflora,** Comes (*N. affinis*, Moore), with very large fragrant fls., the corolla-tube much dilated, the limb yellowish without; known only in cult.

5. **N. Sanderæ,** Sander (*N. alata* × *N. Forgetiana*). The red-fld. garden nicotiana: viscid-pubescent ann. 2–3 ft. high, of bushy habit: basal lvs. 6–12 in. long, spatulate, undulate; st.-lvs. oblong-lanceolate, short-petioled, acuminate, undulate: fls. bracteolate, in large loose panicles; corolla salverform, the cylindric tube three times as long as the calyx, swollen above, greenish-yellow tinted with rose, the limb oblique, with carmine-rose lobes elliptic, acute, obtuse or often emarginate. Originated in 1903 by Sander & Sons, St. Albans, England.—**N. Forgetiana,** Sander, is an ann. rose-fld. species from Brazil with oblong-lanceolate obtuse wing-petioled lvs. about 1 ft. long, and narrow corolla 1–1¼ in. long, with broad mostly obtuse lobes; probably not in cult. here; procured in Brazil for Messrs. Sander by their collector, Mr. Forget.

17. **DATURA,** L. Large coarse erect plants, several cult. for their great trumpet-like odorous fls.; a dozen to 15 species, mostly with strong-smelling herbage, in the warmer parts of the globe, but some widespread weeds.—Forking bushy annuals, shrubs, or trees, with narcotic principles: lvs. large, simple, entire or coarsely sinuate-dentate: fls. large, axillary and solitary, erect or pendulous, white, red, violet, or yellow; calyx long-tubular, 5-toothed or spathe-like, splitting lengthwise or circumscissile with the base left as a cup on the fr.; corolla trumpet-shaped with spreading plicate limb shortly and broadly lobed, the lobes often acuminate; stamens inserted near the base of the corolla-tube, included or only slightly exserted; style long-filiform, 2-lobed: fr. a large 2-celled (falsely 4-celled) caps. mostly prickly or spiny, usually dry and 4-valved at top but sometimes fleshy and bursting irregularly or indehiscent; seeds large. (Datu-ra: vernacular E. Indian name.)

A. Fls. erect; calyx circumscissile, the upper part falling off: caps. dehiscent, usually prickly.
  B. Caps. erect, regularly dehiscent . . . . 1. *D. Stramonium*
  BB. Caps. pendulous, irregularly dehiscent.
    C. Plant glabrous . . . . 2. *D. Metel*
    CC. Plant puberulent and somewhat glaucous . . . . 3. *D. meteloides*
AA. Fls. pendulous; calyx not circumscissile: caps. indehiscent, not prickly. (BRUGMANSIA, Angels-Trumpet.)
  B. Calyx spathe-like, running to a single point . . . . 4. *D. arborea*
  BB. Calyx toothed at the apex.
    C. Corolla red; anthers separate . . . . 5. *D. sanguinea*
    CC. Corolla white; anthers joined around the style . . . . 6. *D. suaveolens*

1. **D. Stramonium,** L. JIMSON- or JAMESTOWN-WEED. Ann. 1–5 ft. high, glabrous or slightly pubescent: lvs. ovate, 3–8 in long, with irregular acute lobes: fls. erect; calyx angular, 2 in. long; corolla white or violet, 4 in. long and limb 1½–2 in. across: caps. erect, ovoid, 2 in. long, very prickly, regularly dehiscent into 4 valves. (Stramonium: a pre-Linnæan name.) Tropics; nat. in N. Amer.

2. **D. Metel,** L. (*D. fastuosa*, L. *D. cornucopia*, Hort.). Ann. glabrous herb 4–5 ft. high: lvs. ovate-lanceolate, acuminate or acute, unequal at base, sinuate-toothed or repand, glabrous on both sides, solitary or the upper in pairs with one larger than the other, the larger 7–8 in. long: fls. erect, 6½–7 in. long; calyx purple, tubular-angulate, 2 in. long, 5-toothed, the teeth triangular-lanceolate, acuminate; corolla white, often violet outside, to yellowish, the limb typically with 5 but sometimes with 6 long-cuspidate acute angles, in cult. often double, the inner corollas 5–10-lobed; stamens 5–6: caps. nodding, subglobose, short-spiny, 1¼ in. diam., irregularly dehiscent. (Metel is an Arabic or E. Indian vernacular name.) India; nat. in the tropics of both hemispheres.—The most frequent garden datura. The color is variable; the plant known as *D. chlorantha*, Hook., has greenish-yellow fls.

3. **D. meteloides,** Dunal (*D. Wrightii*, Hort.). Handsome herbaceous per., 1–3 ft., cult. as an ann., glaucescent and puberulent, grayish, the slender branches forked: lvs. unequally ovate, repand or subentire, acuminate, the upper often in unequal pairs, the larger 2–2¼ in. long: fls. erect, 5½–9 in. long; calyx tubular, 3 in. long, with long acute unequal teeth; corolla white tinged with rose or violet, sweet-scented, about twice as long as calyx, with 5 or 10 slender-subulate teeth: caps. nodding, subglobose, 2 in. diam., with long sharp spines, bursting irregularly; seeds narrowly margined. Tex. to Calif. and N. Mex.—Used medicinally and ceremonially by certain Indian tribes.

4. **D. arborea,** L. Small tree: lvs. ovate-lanceolate, oblong or ovate, entire or nearly so, pubescent, in pairs, one a third shorter than the other; petioles 1 in. or more long: fls. with a musk-like odor, nodding, on solitary axillary pedicels; calyx tubular, spathe-like, entire; corolla 6–9 in. long, white with greenish nerves, the limb with very long acuminate lobes; anthers distinct: caps. broad-ovoid, 2½in. long, unarmed. Peruvian Andes.

5. **D. sanguinea,** Ruiz & Pav. Tree-like shrub 4–12 ft. high; branches fragile, leafy at apex: lvs. clustered, 5–7 from the same point, narrow-oblong, acute or acuminate, 7 in. long, pubescent on both sides, shining green above, paler beneath, the lower sinuate-angled, the upper entire; petioles 2½ in. long, channeled, pubescent: fls. 8–10 in. long, terminal, peduncled, pendulous, brilliant orange-red with yellow nerves, inodorous; calyx ovate, 5-angled, variegated, one-third as long as corolla; anthers separate: caps. turbinate, 3½ in. long, unarmed, at maturity yellow; seeds with narcotic properties. Peru.

6. **D. suaveolens,** Humb. & Bonpl. (*D. Gardneri*, Hook.). Tree-like shrub 10–15 ft. high: lvs. ovate-oblong, petioled, often unequal at base, entire, acute, glabrous, 6–12 in. long: fls. white, 9–12 in. long, nodding, on pedicels ¾–1½ in. long; calyx inflated, angled, obscurely 5-toothed; corolla-tube plicate, the limb with 5 short segms.; anthers connate about the style: caps. unarmed, spindle-shaped, about 5 in. long, destitute of calyx. Brazil. —Usually cult. as *D. arborea.*

18. **SCHIZANTHUS,** Ruiz & Pav. Butterfly-Flower. Ann. or bien. herbs grown out-of-doors and also in pots for the profusion of showy bloom; about a score of species in Chile.—Erect, branching, more or less glandular-viscid: lvs. frequently pinnatisect or even pinnate, the segms incised or dentate: fls. variously colored, in terminal cymes or panicles; calyx tubular, deeply 5-cleft, with narrow lobes; corolla with long or short tube and spreading almost bilabiate limb, the lobes deeply cut; perfect stamens 2 and exserted, accompanied by 3 staminodia, one of them minute; ovary oblong, 2-celled: caps. with 2-cleft valves; seeds numerous. (Schizan-thus: Greek *cut flower*, from the incised corolla.)

A. Corolla-tube shorter than calyx.
  B. Stamens prominently exserted from the throat....................1. *S. pinnatus*
  BB. Stamens little if at all projecting from the throat....................2. *S. wisetonensis*
AA. Corolla-tube equalling or exceeding the calyx.
  B. Middle segm. of anterior corolla-lip notched at apex....................3. *S. retusus*
  BB. Middle segm. not so notched....................4. *S. Grahamii*

1. **S. pinnatus,** Ruiz & Pav. (*S. papilionaceus* and *S. grandiflorus*, Hort.). Thinly hairy and somewhat glandular, 1½–4 ft. or more, slender-branching: lvs. 1–2-pinnatisect, the segms. entire, toothed or incisely pinnatifid: infl. elongate, of numerous fls. in panicled racemes; fls. ¾–1¼ in. across, varying in depth of color and markings, the lower lip usually violet or lilac, the upper paler, its middle segm. with a yellow blotch toward base, spotted with purple or violet; corolla-tube shorter than calyx; stamens prominently showing at the throat.—The common and most variable species, with many hort. forms and vars. distinguished by height of st. and color markings of the fls.; sometimes the fls. are blush or lilac and without spots or streaks.

2. **S. wisetonensis,** Low (*S. pinnatus* × *S. Grahamii*). Mostly intermediate between the parents, the fls. resembling *S. Grahamii* in outline, varying in color from white through bluish and pink to carmine-brown, the mid-lobe of the upper lip often suffused with yellow; corolla-tube seemingly shorter than calyx; stamens usually rather short-exserted: foliage and habit like *S. pinnatus.*

3. **S. retusus,** Hook. Branching but rather stocky, 2–2½ ft. high, the sts. finely hairy or nearly glabrous: lvs. petioled, 5 in. or more long, unequally pinnatisect, the segms. incised or dentate: fls. solitary in the axils on long glandular-hairy pedicels or forming a large loose terminal panicle; calyx glandular-hairy; corolla 1–1¾ in. across, the tube as long as the calyx or longer, the large middle segm. of the upper lip orange except at the emarginate tip, the lateral segms. of the posterior lip falcate, acute, linear, longer than the middle segm.; stamens short-exserted.—There are several vars. differing in color, sometimes almost clear white.

4. **S. Grahamii,** Gill. Glabrous, 1½–5 ft. high: lvs. 1–2-pinnatisect, the segms. entire or toothed-pinnatifid: fls. typically lilac or rose; corolla-tube as long as the calyx; middle segm. of anterior lip not notched at apex, its central portion yellow or orange; lateral segms. of posterior lip falcate, linear, acute, shorter than the middle segm.; stamens short-exserted. (Presumably named for Robt. Graham, page 44.)—There are vars. with white, flesh-colored, lilac, rose, or carmine fls.; apparently not common.

19. **NIEREMBERGIA,** Ruiz & Pav. CUP-FLOWER. Subshrubs and low per. herbs with showy white or pale fls., grown in the open border and as pot-plants, ordinarily treated as annuals; about 30 species from trop. and subtrop. Amer., allied to Petunia and characterized by the long and very slender corolla-tube.—Decumbent or creeping, sometimes erect, mostly glabrous, diffusely branched, the branches slender: lvs. alternate, scattered, simple and entire: fls. white to deep violet, often with purple center, borne singly at or near the tips of the branchlets; calyx tubular or campanulate, 5-parted; corolla with slender elongate tube abruptly expanded above, the limb with 5 broad lobes; stamens inserted on the upper part of the corolla-tube, more or less exserted, 4 of them paired, the fifth smaller: caps. 2-valved, the valves mostly 2-cleft. (Nierember-gia: for Juan Eusebio Nieremberg, 1595–1658, a Spanish Jesuit and first professor of natural history at Madrid.)

A. Lvs. oblong or spatulate, ¼–1 in. wide: sts. creeping and rooting at nodes . . . . .1. *N. repens*
AA. Lvs. linear, less than ¼in. wide: sts. erect or ascending, not rooting at nodes.
B. Pedicels at anthesis about 1/16in. long: plant suffruticose . . . . .2. *N. frutescens*
BB. Pedicels at anthesis about ⅛–½in. long: plant herbaceous.
C. Stamens ¼–5/16in. long; corolla-limb ½–⅗in. long, bright blue . . . . .3. *N. hippomanica* var. *violacea*
CC. Stamens about ⅛–3/16in. long; corolla-limb ⅗in. long, white tinged with pink or purple.
D. Lf. less than 1/16in. wide, ⅙–⅔in. long. . . . . .3. *N. hippomanica*
DD. Lf. 1/16–⅙in. wide, ½–1 in. long. . . . . .4. *N. gracilis*

1. **N. repens,** Ruiz & Pav. (*N. spathulata*, HBK. *N. rivularis*, Miers). WHITE-CUP. Glabrous throughout, the slender creeping sts. rooting freely at the nodes and forming a dense mat, branches seldom rising over 6 in. high: lvs. membranaceous, oblong to oblong-spatulate, ¾–1½ in. long, ¼–½in. wide, with long slender petioles: fls. sessile or short-pedicelled, creamy-white sometimes tinged rose or blue; calyx cylindric, lobes oblong-lanceolate, slightly spreading; corolla-limb broadly bell-shaped, 1–2 in. broad, with golden-yellow throat, the tube 1–2 in. long. Argentina, Chile, Uruguay.

2. **N. frutescens,** Dur. (*N. fruticosa*, Hort.). TALL CUP-FLOWER. Puberulent or nearly glabrous, 1–3 ft. high, shrubby, much-branched: lvs. scattered, linear, ½–1½ in. long, 1/16–⅛in. wide: fls. about 1 in. across, the saucer-shaped limb white tinted with lilac or blue, throat yellow, tube scarcely or somewhat longer than calyx. Chile.—Valuable in the greenhouse or for the border, or as a pot-plant blooming almost continuously. There are vars. with white or purple fls., also with larger ones.

3. **N. hippomanica,** Miers. Small pubescent herb 3–6 in. high: lvs. linear-spatulate, ⅙–⅔in. long, to 1/16in. wide: pedicels about 1/10in. long; calyx about ¼in. long; corolla-tube ⅜in. long, limb slightly longer, white tinged rose; stamens unequal, about 3/16in. long. Argentina.—The plant common in cult. is var. **violacea,** Millan (var. *cærulea*, Millan. *N. cærulea*, Sealy not Miers). Plant 4–12 in. high, scabrous-pubescent, with suberect branches: lvs. solitary and fascicled, lanceolate-spatulate, ½–1 in. long, less than 1/16in. wide: pedicels at anthesis about ⅙in. long; calyx about ¼in. long; corolla bright blue; stamens subequal, ¼–5/16in. long.

4. **N. gracilis,** Hook. (*N. filicaulis*, Hort. *N. calycina*, Hort. not Hook.). Branches very slender, ascending 6–15 in., slightly downy: lvs. scarcely ½in. long, linear or only sub-spatulate, those on the younger branches somewhat hairy: pedicels ⅛–⅜in. long at anthesis; corolla-limb spreading, convex, about 1 in. across, white tinged and veined with purple toward the center and throat yellow, tube ⅜–⅝in. long. Argentina.

20. **PETUNIA,** Juss. Fl.-garden annuals, or grown as such for their showy bloom; over 25 species, mostly natives of the southern part of S. Amer., some with small not attractive fls.—Branching viscid-pubescent annuals or perennials, of weak or

straggling growth: lvs. soft, simple and entire, alternate or the upper opposite: fls. white or in shades of pink to purple, on solitary, terminal or axillary peduncles; calyx deeply 5-cleft, the lobes oblong or linear, obtuse; corolla funnelform or salverform, the long tube straight or nearly so and fitting loosely in the calyx, limb broad and normally 5-lobed, equal or oblique or obscurely 2-lipped; stamens 5, inserted on or below the middle of corolla-tube, 4 in pairs, the fifth much smaller or rudimentary: caps. 2-celled, the 2 valves undivided; seeds small, many. (Petu-nia: from a S. American aboriginal name.)

A. Fls. dull white, the tube long and narrow....................1. *P. axillaris*
AA. Fls. usually colored, the tube short and broad.
B. Sts. very slender: fls. rose-red or violet, about 1 in. long....................2. *P. violacea*
BB. Sts. stocky: fls. of various colors, larger....................3. *P. hybrida*

1. **P. axillaris**, BSP. (*P. nyctaginiflora*, Juss.). LARGE WHITE PETUNIA. Tall and relatively stout, usually erect, 1–2 ft.: lvs. large and rather thick, oval-oblong, the upper sessile or nearly so, the lower narrowed into a distinct petiole: fls. dull white, 2–2½ in. long, fragrant at evening, the cylindric tube three to four times as long as calyx. Argentina.—Frequently seen in old gardens and also escaped.

2. **P. violacea**, Lindl. VIOLET-FLOWERED PETUNIA. Glandular-hairy, viscid, sts. 6–10 in. long, slender, branching, prostrate or the tips erect: lvs. ovate, shortly petioled, acute, the upper ovate-lanceolate, the floral in pairs: fls. 1–1½ in. long, rose-red or violet, the tube lighter; calyx deeply 5-parted into linear segms. about half or more as long as the funnel-shaped corolla-tube; corolla with subequal limb, the lobes ovate and acute. Argentina.—This species and its garden derivatives sometimes persist for a time as escapes.

3. **P. hybrida**, Vilm. COMMON GARDEN PETUNIA. Cultigen; apparently a series of hybrids from the two preceding, remarkably variable but differing from either parent, although varying toward either one: fls. 2–3½ in. long, with funnel-shaped tube and mostly very broad limb; tube broader than in *P. axillaris*, longer with broader limb than in *P. violacea;* from both it differs in the much larger and multiform fls. in various colors and more stocky growth. The various strains have fls. varying in size, form and color, sometimes measuring 4–5 in. across, often deeply fringed or full double, ranging from white to deep red-purple, variously striped and barred or with star-like markings radiating from the throat; the group comprises all the highly developed garden petunias.

21. **SALPIGLOSSIS**, Ruiz & Pav. A tall erect fl.-garden ann. and 7 or 8 other species, native of Chile.—Ann., bien. or per., glandular-hairy, with sts. erect: lvs. alternate, simple, entire, sinuate dentate or pinnatifid: fls. few, mostly large, long-pedicelled; calyx tubular, 5-lobed; corolla funnelform with wide throat, the limb with 5 emarginate lobes; stamens 4, didynamous, included, the fifth wanting or represented by a staminode: caps. oblong or ovoid, the valves 2-cleft; seeds small. (Salpiglos-sis: Greek *tube* and *tongue*, alluding to the form of the corolla and the appearance of the style.)

S. sinuata, Ruiz & Pav. (*S. variabilis, S. hybrida, S. grandiflora, S. gloxiniæflora* and *S. superbissima*, Hort.). PAINTED-TONGUE. Branching ann. 1–2½ ft. high: lower lvs. petiolate, elliptic, sinuately toothed or pinnatifid; upper lvs. lanceolate or linear, entire or nearly so, subsessile, passing into the bracts of the infl.: fls. 2–2½ in. long and as wide, ranging from straw-color, primrose and yellow through scarlet nearly to blue, with great variation in venation and rich markings.—Several hort. vars. are offered, differing in color of fls.; perhaps other species have entered into some of these forms.

22. **BRUNFELSIA**, L. (*Franciscea*, Pohl). Woody plants, a few grown for the showy or fragrant bloom in warm glasshouses and out-of-doors in the far S.; species about 30 in Cent. and S. Amer. and W. Indies.—Shrubs or small trees: lvs. alternate, simple and entire, often thick and glossy: fls. in loose or dense terminal cymes or solitary, mostly large or at least showy, often fragrant, commonly blooming under glass in winter; calyx tubular or campanulate, 5-toothed or -cleft; corolla funnelform, the tube long, the limb with 5 broad obtuse lobes; stamens 4, inserted on the corolla-tube, included, didymous, all with anther-cells alike; ovary sessile, 2-celled, many-ovuled: fr. capsular or berry-like, with undivided valves. (Brunfel-sia: Otto Brunfels, physician and first German botanist, died 1534.)—Originally spelled Brunsfelsia by Linnæus but subsequently corrected by him to Brunfelsia.

A. Corolla violet, purple, or blue, at least on tube (or fading lighter), nearly or quite inodorous.
B. Calyx long-tubular, half or more the length of the corolla-tube................1. *B. calycina*
BB. Calyx short, split nearly or quite to the base................................2. *B. latifolia*
AA. Corolla white or yellowish, very fragrant at night................................3. *B. americana*

1. **B. calycina,** Benth. Erect or spreading, branching: lvs. short-petioled, ovate-oblong or elliptic, 3–4 in. long, acute, glabrous or nearly so, dark green above, pale green below: fls. rich dark purple, mostly inodorous, in few-fld. usually terminal cymes; calyx tubular, inflated, light green, ¾–1 in. long, rather bluntly short-lobed; corolla-limb 2 in. diam., the broadly 5-lobed limb with slightly wavy margins. Brazil. Var. **eximia,** Raffill, free-flowering, slightly downy throughout, intermediate in size between the type and var. *macrantha:* branches mostly short and spur-like: lvs. elliptic, acutish or obtuse: fls. rich purple on first opening, soon fading to almost pure white, about 1½in. diam., in 2–5-fld. clusters; calyx slender, slightly curved, hairy, about 1¼ in. long. Var. **floribunda,** Raffill (*B. floribunda,* Hort.), dwarf floriferous free-branching shrub, glabrous throughout: lvs. 2–4 in. long, elliptic, rich dark green, prominently veined beneath: fls. rich violet with small white eye, produced rather early in the year, on stout pedicels ½in. long; calyx ⅝in. long, elliptic in outline; corolla-limb flat or nearly so. Var. **macrantha,** Raffill (*B. macrantha,* Lem. *B. grandiflora,* Don), floriferous shrub for a warm greenhouse or subtrop. country, of strong vigorous growth, glabrous or nearly so: lvs. rich dark green, often 8 in. long and 2½ in. broad: cymes dense, terminal or in the axils of all the upper lvs.; calyx 1 in. long, bright green; corolla 2½–3 in. diam., rich deep purple, with prominent lavender-blue ring surrounding the white eye at mouth of tube; Peru.

2. **B. latifolia,** Benth. Rather dwarf, with slender branches: lvs. elliptic, much as in no. 1: fls. nearly white to lavender and purple with lighter center, solitary or few in a cluster, the corolla-limb 1½ in. across and the lobes obtuse; calyx not inflated, about ⅓in. long, cleft nearly or quite to the base, the lobes acute and reaching only one-third length of corolla-tube. Trop. Amer.

3. **B. americana,** L. Lady-of-the-Night. Shrub 4–8 ft., twigs puberulent or glabrous: lvs. mostly elliptic to elliptic-ovate or -obovate, 1½–4 in. long, entire, tapering to short petiole, apex acute, obtuse or even emarginate: fls. mostly solitary, terminal and axillary, very slender tube 2½–4 in. long, limb 1½–2 in. across, opening yellowish and becoming white, powerfully sweet-fragrant; calyx short and nearly truncate: fr. a yellowish berry ¾in. diam. W. Indies.

23. **BROWALLIA,** L. About a half dozen mostly blue-fld. trop. American herbs, some cult. for the profuse bloom.—Annuals, glabrous or glandular: lvs. nearly or quite simple: fls. blue, violet, or sometimes white, solitary and axillary or in more or less one-sided racemes; calyx mostly 5-toothed; corolla with long straight slender 15-nerved tube and spreading 5-lobed more or less irregular limb; stamens 4, didymous, inserted above the middle of the corolla-tube, the anthers of the shorter pair with 1 cell undeveloped, fifth stamen sometimes represented by a rudiment: caps. with 2-lobed valves, included in calyx. (Browal-lia: after Johan Browallius, 1707–1755, Bishop of Abo, and botanist, Sweden.)

A. Corolla-segms. long, not notched, some of them acute or acuminate; tube 1 in. long. 1. *B. speciosa*
AA. Corolla-segms. short, 2-lobed or -notched; tube ¾in. long or less.
B. Calyx hairy................................2. *B. americana*
BB. Calyx sticky or clammy................................3. *B. viscosa*

1. **B. speciosa,** Hook. (*B. major,* Hort.). Glabrous or nearly so, half-shrubby, 2–5 ft. high: lvs. ovate, acute, opposite or alternate: fls. solitary, axillary, on pedicels shorter than lvs.; corolla-tube at least 1 in. long, two to three times as long as calyx, abruptly swollen at the top beneath the limb; limb outspreading, of 5 ovate striate dark purple entire segms., pale lilac beneath, 1½–2 in. across up and down. Colombia.—There are blue-, violet-, and white-fld. vars.

2. **B. americana,** L. (*B. demissa,* L. *B. elata,* L.). Branching, 1–2 ft. high; sts. and lvs. pubescent or glabrous: lvs. ovate, rotund, cuneate or rarely cordate, petioled: fls. solitary and axillary below, racemose above; calyx hairy, the teeth unequal, acute and much shorter than the corolla-tube; corolla about ½in. long and broad, blue, violet, or, in some forms, white, the short segms. bifid. Trop. Amer.

3. **B. viscosa,** HBK. (*B. pulchella,* Hort.). Viscous and glandular-hairy, about 1 ft. high, stiffer in habit than *B. americana* and fls. more numerous: lvs. short-petioled, ovate, rough-hairy on both sides: lower fls. solitary in the axils, the upper racemose; pedicels a little shorter than the calyx; calyx-teeth very clammy, oblong, shorter than the corolla-tube; corolla dark blue with a white eye (varying to white), not over ¾in. long, the short segms. bifid. S. Amer.

24. **STREPTOSOLEN,** Miers. One evergreen shrub, native in Colombia and Ecuador, with large clusters of orange-red fls., suitable for greenhouse culture and

for out-of-doors in mild climates.—Lvs. alternate, simple, entire, not large, rugose and veiny: fls. in a terminal corymbose panicle; calyx tubular-campanulate, shortly 5-cleft; corolla-tube elongated, somewhat twisted as shown by the spiral direction of the nerves at the base of the corolla, inside the calyx and upward, widening above, the spreading limb with 5 broad obtuse lobes; perfect stamens 4, didymous, the anthers of the shorter pair with 1 cell not developed; ovary stipitate, 2-celled: caps. somewhat leathery, the 2 valves 2-cleft. (Streptoso-len: Greek *twisted* and *tube*, with reference to the form of the corolla-tube.)

S. Jamesonii, Miers. Scabrous-pubescent plant, 4–6 ft., with long flexuose branches on the ends of which the clusters of fls. are borne: lvs. petioled, oval, 1½ in. long or less, obtuse or acute: corolla 1–1¼ in. long, the limb darker colored. (Named for Dr. Wm. Jameson, who sent specimens of this plant to Kew.)

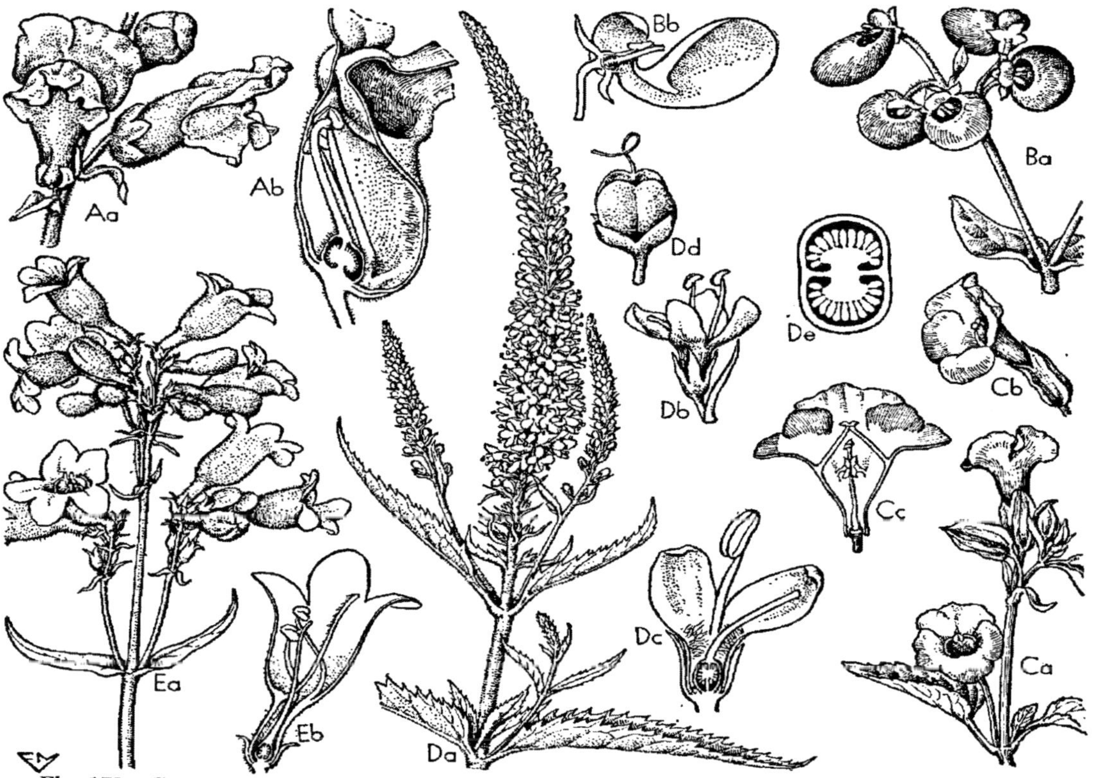

Fig. 179. SCROPHULARIACEÆ. A, *Antirrhinum majus:* Aa, flowers, × ½; Ab, flower, vertical section, perianth partially excised, × 1. B, *Calceolaria crenatiflora:* Ba, portion of inflorescence, × ½; Bb, flower, vertical section, × 1. C, *Torenia Fournieri:* Ca, flowering branch × ½; Cb, flower, side view, × ½; Cc, flower, perianth expanded and partially excised, × ½. D, *Veronica longifolia:* Da, inflorescence, × ½; Db, flower, × 2; Dc, same, vertical section, × 3; Dd, capsule, × 2; De, ovary, cross-section, × 10. E, *Penstemon lævigatus:* Ea, inflorescence, × ½; Eb, flower, vertical section, × 1.

179. SCROPHULARIACEÆ. FIGWORT FAMILY

Herbs, shrubs, or trees, of about 190 genera and 3,000 or more species widely distributed over the earth, many grown for ornament.—Lvs. alternate, opposite, or verticillate, exstipulate: fls. bisexual, usually irregular, the infl. various; calyx 4–5-toothed or divided, persistent; corolla gamopetalous, rotate or broadly campanulate or with cylindrical tube, the limb 4–5-lobed, equally spreading or bilabiate; stamens usually 4, didynamous, inserted on corolla-tube and alternate with its lobes, or sometimes 2 or 5 or the fifth stamen sterile or reduced to a gland; hypogynous disk present or obsolete; ovary superior, perfectly or imperfectly 2-celled, usually with many ovules in each cell, style entire or 2-lobed: fr. a caps. or berry.

A. Number of stamens 2.
  B. Corolla 2-lipped, the lower lip inflated and slipper-like .... 1. CALCEOLARIA
  BB. Corolla with spreading 4–5-lobed limb.
    C. Calyx 2-lipped or -parted .... 24. ZALUZIANSKYA
    CC. Calyx 4–5-parted.
      D. Lvs. basal.
        E. Lobes of calyx 5 .... 2. WULFENIA
        EE. Lobes of calyx 4 .... 3. SYNTHYRIS
      DD. Lvs. cauline.
        E. Foliage persistent; plant woody .... 4. HEBE
        EE. Foliage deciduous: plant (ours) herbaceous.
          F. Tube of corolla shorter than lobes: lvs. mostly opposite .... 5. VERONICA
          FF. Tube of corolla much longer than lobes: lvs. in whorls of 3–5 .... 6. VERONICASTRUM
AA. Number of stamens 4–5.
  B. Anther-bearing stamens 5 .... 7. VERBASCUM
  BB. Anther-bearing stamens 4 (rarely 8).
    C. Habit climbing .... 19. MAURANDYA
    CC. Habit not climbing.
      D. Sterile stamen evident.
        E. Staminode as long as fertile stamens: seeds wingless .... 8. PENSTEMON
        EE. Staminode shorter than fertile stamens: seeds winged .... 9. CHELONE
      DD. Sterile stamen lacking or gland-like.
        E. Calyx spathe-like.
          F. Lvs. entire or toothed .... 10. HEBENSTRETIA
          FF. Lvs. pinnatisect .... 13. PEDICULARIS
        EE. Calyx not spathe-like.
          F. Lvs. all alternate.
            G. Corolla-tube none .... 11. CELSIA
            GG. Corolla with tube.
              H. Throat closed by prominent palate: plant creeping .... 21. CYMBALARIA
              HH. Throat not closed by palate: plant usually erect.
                I. Lobes of calyx not more than half its length.
                  J. Length of corolla 2 in. or more .... 12. REHMANNIA
                  JJ. Length of corolla 1 in. or less .... 13. PEDICULARIS
                II. Lobes of calyx extending nearly to base.
                  J. Corolla-lobes 5.
                    K. Plant a low herb .... 14. ERINUS
                    KK. Plant a shrub .... 15. LEUCOPHYLLUM
                  JJ. Corolla-lobes 2.
                    K. Length of corolla 1 in. or more.
                      L. Upper lip of corolla shorter than under lip .... 16. DIGITALIS
                      LL. Upper lip of corolla as long as or longer than under lip. 17. ISOPLEXIS
                    KK. Length of corolla about ⅛in. .... 18. ANARRHINUM
          FF. Lvs. opposite or verticillate or sometimes upper lvs. alternate.
            G. Plant an herb or shrub.
              H. Corolla-tube long.
                I. Throat with a prominent palate.
                  J. Fls. neither saccate nor spurred at base .... 26. MIMULUS
                  JJ. Fls. saccate or spurred at base.
                    K. Corolla saccate or gibbous at base .... 20. ANTIRRHINUM
                    KK. Corolla spurred at base.
                      L. Veining of lvs. palmate: fls. solitary .... 21. CYMBALARIA
                      LL. Veining of lvs. pinnate: fls. in racemes or spikes.
                        M. The plant glabrous or nearly so: throat nearly closed by palate .... 22. LINARIA
                        MM. The plant glandular-pubescent: throat not closed by palate .... 23. CHÆNORRHINUM
                II. Throat without palate.
                  J. Calyx 2-lipped or 2-parted .... 24. ZALUZIANSKYA
                  JJ. Calyx 5-lobed or -parted.
                    K. Lobes of calyx shallow; calyx tubular.
                      L. Ribs of calyx winged .... 25. TORENIA
                      LL. Ribs of calyx wingless .... 26. MIMULUS
                    KK. Lobes of calyx to middle or below; calyx not tubular.
                      L. Sts. creeping .... 27. MAZUS
                      LL. Sts. erect.
                        M. Stamens exserted .... 28. PHYGELIUS
                        MM. Stamens included .... 29. RUSSELIA
              HH. Corolla-tube very short or none.
                I. Tube of corolla none.
                  J. Under lip 2-spurred .... 30. DIASCIA
                  JJ. Under lip not 2-spurred.
                    K. Corolla turned upside down by torsion of pedicel .... 31. ALONSOA
                    KK. Corolla not turned upside down .... 32. ANGELONIA
                II. Tube of corolla short.
                  J. Calyx parted to base: sterile stamen lacking .... 33. NEMESIA
                  JJ. Calyx not parted to base: sterile stamen gland-like .... 34. COLLINSIA
            GG. Plant a tree, with large ovate pubescent lvs. .... 35. PAULOWNIA

1. **CALCEOLARIA,** L. (*Fagelia,* Schwencke). SLIPPERWORT. Some 300 herbs and shrubby plants, a few cult. for the odd and showy saccate fls.; nearly all are native from Mex. to the Andes of Peru and Chile.—Lvs. opposite or verticillate, simple or pinnate: fls. bisexual, in irregular cymes, mostly yellow, sometimes purple, often oddly spotted; calyx 4-parted; corolla strongly irregular, 2-parted, the upper lip small and ascending and usually more or less saccate, under which are borne the essential organs, the lower lip in the cult. kinds very large and inflated and more or less slipper-like (whence the name *calceolus,* Latin "slipper"); stamens 2; style short, the stigma entire or only obscurely 2-lobed: fr. a septicidal caps. splitting at the top; seeds many and minute.

A. Lvs. pinnatisect or pinnate .... 1. *C. scabiosæfolia*
AA. Lvs. not lobed.
  B. Height of plant 2–6 ft.
    C. Plant herbaceous: lvs. very large and soft, ovate .... 2. *C. crenatiflora*
    CC. Plant woody: lvs. small, mostly on the oblong or lanceolate order .... 3. *C. integrifolia*
  BB. Height of plant 2–8 in.
    C. Shape of lvs. lanceolate .... 4. *C. polyrrhiza*
    CC. Shape of lvs. broad-ovate .... 5. *C. tenella*

1. **C. scabiosæfolia,** Roem. & Schult. Ann. pilose herb, 1–2 ft., branching: lvs. variously pinnatisect or pinnate, 5–8 in. long, the bases of petioles connate across the st. by membrane or projecting ridge; lfts. or segms. 2–3 pairs, ovate to broad-lanceolate, dentate or pinnatifid: fls. many, small, ½in. across more or less, pale yellow, the slipper usually obovate; summer. Ecuador to Chile.—Infrequently grown. *C. chelidonioides,* HBK., with which this species may be confused and which is to be looked for in cult., is sparsely hairy only above, and the petioles not connate, fls. larger.

2. **C. crenatiflora,** Cav. Stout branchy herbaceous plant 1–2½ ft. high, soft-hairy: lvs. simple, large and soft, ovate to broad-ovate, obtuse or with only a short bluntish point, sinuate or dentate, basal ones petioled and 4–8 in. long, cauline becoming sessile and successively smaller: fls. hanging on slender pedicels, in corymbs, ¾in. or more long, yellow and with orange-brown spots on the large much-inflated crenate or fluted lower lip; upper lip not exceeding the broad-ovate green calyx-lobes. Chile.—Source of the common florists' herbaceous calceolarias in different races; probably some of the current cult. strains are the result of hybridization (*C. herbeohybrida,* Voss), the parentage now being a matter of conjecture. The material grown as *C. multiflora nana* belongs here.

3. **C. integrifolia,** Murr. (*C. rugosa,* Ruiz & Pav.). Sts. woody, the plant becoming a subshrub 2–6 ft., more or less branched, the young parts viscid-scurfy or -pubescent, dark brown: lvs. simple, rather firm, oblong or sometimes oval, 1–3 in. long and 1 in. or more broad, rugose, acute or obtuse, narrowed to short petiole, margins crenate-serrate: fls. short-pedicelled, in rather close peduncled clusters, yellow to red-brown, not spotted, the globular or short-oblong lip about ½in. across. Chile. Var. **angustifolia,** Lindl. (*C. angustifolia,* Sweet), lvs. lanceolate and more acute, about ½in. or less broad.—Common under glass and planted out; there are named cultivars, as *C. Lymanii* and *C. Stewartii.* Some cult. forms are probably hybrids (*C. fruticohybrida,* Voss) of obscure derivation.

4. **C. polyrrhiza,** Cav. Dwarf tufted per. to 2 in., sparsely hairy: lvs. crowded at base of st., lanceolate, to 2½ in. long; narrowed into long petiole, entire: fls. solitary on scapes to 4 in. long, yellow spotted purple, 1 in. long and ½in. wide. Chile.—Hardy, with protection, to N. Y.

5. **C. tenella,** Poeppig & Endl. Low creeping subshrub to 8 in. high, sparsely hairy: lvs. broad-ovate, to ½in. long, very short-petioled or sessile, obtuse, remotely toothed: fls. usually 2–3 on peduncles to 6 in. long, yellow, spotted within, to ½in. long. Chile.—Hardy on Pacific Coast, if protected.

2. **WULFENIA,** Jacq. Per. herbs hardy in rock-gardens or borders; about 8 species in Eu. and Asia.—Lvs. basal, petioled, crenate: fls. in spikes or racemes at top of simple scape-like peduncles, nodding, blue; calyx 5-parted; corolla with cylindrical tube and 4-lobed limb; stamens 2: caps. septicidally and loculicidally dehiscent, 4-valved; seeds many. (Wulfe-nia: F. X. Wulfen, 1728–1805, botanist.)

W. carinthiaca, Jacq. Basal lvs. oblong, to 8 in. long, short-petioled, obtuse, double-crenate, glabrous or sparsely hairy on veins beneath, dark green, shining; st.-lvs. few, small, scale-like: fls. in dense spike-like racemes on scapes 1–2 ft. high; pedicels very short; corolla deep blue-violet, to ⅓in. long, with long tube and short lobes. Mts. of Carinthia.

3. **SYNTHYRIS,** Benth. W. N. American per. herbs of 14 species, one grown in the border.—Rootstock thick; lvs. basal, petioled, toothed or pinnatisect: fls. blue or purple, in racemes on simple scape-like peduncles bearing few bract-like lvs.;

calyx 4-parted; corolla campanulate, with very short tube and deeply 4-lobed limb; stamens 2, exserted: caps. compressed, loculicidal; seeds many or few. (Syn-thyris: Greek *together* and *little door*, referring to the valves of the caps. adhering to the placentæ.)

S. reniformis, Benth. (*S. rotundifolia*, Gray). Lvs. orbicular-cordate to reniform, 2–3 in. long, on petioles to 4 in. long, doubly crenate, glabrous or slightly pubescent: fls. blue to white, in racemes on scapes 5–9 in. high; corolla about ¼in. long. Wash. to Calif. Var. **cordata,** Gray (*S. rotundifolia* var. *Sweetseri*, L. F. Henderson), has more deeply lobed ovate-cordate lvs. and deeper blue fls.

4. **HEBE,** Comm. About 140 species of shrubs or small trees native mostly in New Zeal., often planted in temp. climates.—Lvs. persistent and leathery, leaving conspicuous scars, opposite: fls. white or pink, in axillary racemes or small heads; calyx usually 4-parted; corolla with short tube and commonly 4-lobed spreading limb; stamens 2, exserted; ovary (and caps.) elliptic in cross-section with septum extending lengthwise, not crosswise: caps. septicidally dehiscent; seeds few or many. (He-be: Greek for *small*.)

A. Margin of lvs. coarsely serrate .... 1. *H. Hulkeana*
AA. Margin of lvs. entire.
  B. Lvs. strictly scale-like .... 2. *H. cupressoides*
  BB. Lvs. not scale-like.
    C. Length of lvs. 2 in. or more.
      D. Racemes broad and dense, not much longer than lvs.: lvs. obovate, obtuse .... 3. *H. speciosa*
      DD. Racemes slender, longer than lvs.: lvs. lanceolate, acute .... 4. *H. salicifolia*
    CC. Length of lvs. rarely more than 1 in.
      D. Fls. spicate: lvs. imbricate.
        E. Lf. very short-petioled, keeled by prominent midrib .... 5. *H. buxifolia*
        EE. Lf. sessile and somewhat amplexicaul, not keeled, nerveless .... 6. *H. amplexicaulis*
      DD. Fls. racemose: lvs. not imbricate.
        E. Diam. of fls. ½in. or more .... 7. *H. elliptica*
        EE. Diam. of fls. ¼in. .... 8. *H. Traversii*

1. **H. Hulkeana,** Andersen (*Veronica Hulkeana*, F. Muell.). Laxly branched shrub 1–3 ft. high: lvs. in distant pairs, ovate or oblong-ovate, 1–2 in. long, coarsely serrate, dark green and glossy, petioles to ½in. long: panicle terminal, much-branched, 6–12 in. long; fls. numerous, small, about ¼in. across, sessile, pale lilac: caps. twice as long as calyx.

2. **H. cupressoides,** Cockayne & Allan (*Veronica cupressoides*, Hook. f.). Globose closely branched shrub 3–6 ft. high; branches very slender, clothed with decussate scale-like lvs. resembling cypress: lvs. in distant pairs, ovate-oblong, 1/15in. or less long, rather fleshy: fls. in small terminal heads, small, ⅙in. or less diam., bluish-purple or rarely white, sessile: caps. 1/12in. long, about twice as long as calyx, obovoid, narrow.

3. **H. speciosa,** Cockayne & Allan (*Veronica speciosa*, R. Cunn.). Stout glabrous shrub 2–5 ft. high, with spreading leafy branches: lvs. obovate or obovate-oblong, 2–4 in. long, almost sessile, rounded at apex, entire, thick, dark green and glossy: racemes axillary, near tips of branches, broad and dense, to 1½ in. across, not much longer than lvs.; fls. ⅓in. diam., reddish-purple: caps. more than twice as long as calyx.—A variable species running into color and variegated forms. It hybridizes freely; the best known garden hybrid is **H. Andersonii,** Cockayne (*Veronica Andersonii*, Lindl. & Paxt. *H. salicifolia* × *H. speciosa*), intermediate between the parents, lvs. narrower and thinner than in *H. speciosa* but broader than in *H. salicifolia;* infl. with fls. white at bottom and rich violet at top; raised by Mr. Anderson near Edinburgh. **H. imperalis,** Cockayne, is probably a product of the same cross.

4. **H. salicifolia,** Pennell (*Veronica salicifolia*, Forst.). Much-branched shrub 2–10 ft. high: lvs. almost sessile, lanceolate, 2–6 in. long, acute, entire, glabrous, rather thin: racemes slender, longer than lvs., many-fld.; fls. ⅙in. or less diam., white tinged with lilac or blue: caps. about twice as long as calyx.—Very variable, appearing in many vars. It hybridizes freely with related species.

5. **H. buxifolia,** Cockayne & Allan (*Veronica buxifolia*, Benth.). Stout glabrous shrub to 5 ft.: lvs. closely imbricate, broadly oblong-obovate, to ⅓in. long, truncate at base with very short petiole, keeled by the prominent midrib, entire, very thick, dark green and glossy above, paler and usually minutely dotted beneath: fls. white, ¼–⅓in. diam., sessile, in spikes in the axils of the upper lvs. forming a corymbose head: caps. almost twice as long as calyx.

6. **H. amplexicaulis,** Cockayne & Allan (*Veronica amplexicaulis*, Armstr.). Erect or decumbent shrub to 3 ft., with spreading branches: lvs. imbricate, oblong or elliptic-oblong, ½–1 in. long, obtuse, sessile and somewhat amplexicaul at base, nerveless and not keeled, very thick and glaucous: fls. white, ¼in. diam., sessile, in stout dense-fld. spikes 1–1½ in. long in axils of upper lvs.: caps. longer than calyx.

7. **H. elliptica,** Pennell (*Veronica elliptica,* Forst. *V. decussata,* Ait.). Much-branched shrub or small tree 5–20 ft. high, glabrous: lvs. elliptic-oblong, ½–1 in. long, apiculate, petiolate, close-set, truncate at base, midrib prominent beneath, entire, margins edged with white pubescence, thick, pale green: racemes near tips of branches, 4–12-fld., to 1½ in. long; fls. ⅓–⅔in. diam., white with purple lines, sweet-scented: caps. twice as long as calyx. New Zeal., subantarctic S. Amer.

8. **H. Traversii,** Cockayne & Allan (*Veronica Traversii,* Hook. f.). Dense glabrous shrub forming round bush 3–5 ft. diam.: lvs. elliptic- to linear-oblong, ½–1 in. long, acute, petiolate or nearly sessile, entire, thick: racemes near tips of branches, 1–3 in. long, many-fld.; fls. ¼in. diam., white: caps. twice as long as calyx. (Named for W. T. L. Travers, page 595.)

5. **VERONICA,** L. Speedwell. About 150 species of herbs or subshrubs, distributed over temp. and cold regions, but rare in the tropics.—Lvs. opposite or rarely the cauline alternate or whorled, floral lvs. always alternate: fls. in bracteate terminal or axillary racemes or spikes or sometimes solitary; calyx 4–5-parted, rarely 3-parted; corolla mostly with very short tube and spreading 4–5-lobed limb; stamens 2; ovary superior, 2-celled with axillary placentation: caps. compressed or turgid, 2-grooved, loculicidally dehiscent. (Veron-ica: named for St. Veronica.)

A. Foliage pinnatisect or predominantly so.
  B. Plant 8–24 in. high .... 1. *V. austriaca*
  BB. Plant mostly 6 in. or less, sts. usually prostrate.
    C. Herbage white-pubescent .... 2. *V. pectinata*
    CC. Herbage not white-pubescent.
      D. Fls. white .... 3. *V. peduncularis*
      DD. Fls. blue .... 4. *V. armena*
AA. Foliage entire or toothed.
  B. Infl. axillary, main st. continuing as leafy shoot.
    C. Pedicels filiform, four to five times longer than calyx.
      D. Fls. white: lvs. coarsely toothed or pinnatisect .... 3. *V. peduncularis*
      DD. Fls. blue: lvs. slightly crenate.
        E. Plant prostrate, mat-forming: lvs. to ¼in. long .... 5. *V. filiformis*
        EE. Plant erect or nearly so: lvs. mostly ⅝–1 in. long .... 10. *V. Chamædrys*
    CC. Pedicels not much exceeding or shorter than calyx.
      D. Calyx-lobes 5.
        E. Plant tufted, sterile sts. prostrate .... 6. *V. prostrata*
        EE. Plant not tufted, sterile sts. erect or ascending .... 7. *V. latifolia*
      DD. Calyx-lobes 4.
        E. Lvs. glabrous or nearly so .... 8. *V. Allionii*
        EE. Lvs. pubescent.
          F. Racemes loose and spreading, often compounded into panicles .... 10. *V. Chamædrys*
          FF. Racemes spike-like, often densely so.
            G. Lf. to ½in. long, usually white-pubescent .... 2. *V. pectinata*
            GG. Lf. 1 in. long or more, not white-pubescent .... 9. *V. officinalis*
  BB. Infl. terminal.
    C. Plant white-woolly .... 11. *V. incana*
    CC. Plant not white-woolly, although often pubescent.
      D. Habit erect.
        E. Pedicels three to four times longer than calyx .... 12. *V. gentianoides*
        EE. Pedicels equalling or shorter than calyx.
          F. Lvs. all opposite.
            G. Racemes rather loose: margins of lvs. toothed to base .... 13. *V. Bachofenii*
            GG. Racemes dense: margins of lvs. entire at base and tip .... 14. *V. spicata*
          FF. Lvs. often in whorls of 3–4, at least on some of the sts. of a clump.
            G. Racemes panicled, loose: pedicels as long as calyx .... 15. *V. spuria*
            GG. Racemes solitary or few, dense: pedicels shorter than calyx .... 16. *V. longifolia*
      DD. Habit prostrate.
        E. Calyx-lobes 5 .... 17. *V. satureioides*
        EE. Calyx-lobes 4.
          F. Sts. rooting, herbaceous .... 18. *V. repens*
          FF. Sts. not rooting, woody at base.
            G. Lvs. ovate-orbicular, clustered near top of st. .... 19. *V. Nummularia*
            GG. Lvs. oblong, evenly distributed .... 20. *V. fruticans*

1. **V. austriaca,** L. (*V. prenja,* G. Beck). Per. to 2 ft., with many erect or ascending sts., pubescent: lvs. sessile, pinnatisect into oblong or linear entire or incised segms.: racemes elongated, many-fld., 2–4 from upper axils; fls. deep blue, to ½in. across; calyx of 5 unequal lobes: caps. obcordate-ovate, about equalling calyx, glabrous or hairy. Eu., Asia Minor.

2. **V. pectinata,** L. Plant prostrate, rooting at nodes, densely white-pubescent: lvs. obovate or elliptic-lanceolate, crenate or often pinnatifid, to ½in. long, cuneate at base and nearly sessile: racemes elongated, many-fld., solitary in axils; fls. blue with white center, about ¼in. across; pedicels about equalling calyx: caps. triangular-ovate, truncate or notched, exceeding calyx, pubescent. Asia Minor. Var. **rosea,** Hort., has rose fls.

3. **V. peduncularis,** Bieb. Per. with prostrate or ascending sts. 6–12 in. high: lvs. ovate or oblong, coarsely toothed or pinnatisect, very short-petioled or sessile, glabrous or hirsute: racemes loosely-fld., in upper axils; fls. white veined with pink, ⅓in. across; pedicels four to five times longer than calyx, to ½in. long: caps. compressed, equalling calyx, pubescent. Asia Minor.

4. **V. armena,** Boiss. & Huet. Tufted per. with many decumbent or ascending sts. to 4 in. high, hairy: lvs. sessile, pinnate into narrowly linear revolute segms. ¼in. long: racemes few-fld., in upper axils; fls. deep blue, ¼in. across; pedicels two to three times longer than calyx; calyx of 5 unequal lobes: caps. obcordate, much exceeding calyx, glabrous. Armenia.

5. **V. filiformis,** Smith (*V. Tournefortii*, Gmel.). Ann. or per. with filiform prostrate rooting sts., somewhat pubescent: lvs. orbicular or ovate, to ⅓in. across, obtuse, subcordate and short-petioled, slightly crenate: fls. blue, to ⅓in. across, solitary on filiform axillary pedicels four to five times longer than calyx: caps. orbicular, 2-lobed to middle, ciliate. Asia Minor.

6. **V. prostrata,** L. (*V. rupestris*, Hort.). Tufted per. with gray-hairy sts., the sterile prostrate, the flowering ascending to 8 in.: lvs. oblong to linear, ½–¾in. long, short-petioled, crenate or dentate, margins sometimes revolute: fls. pale blue, ⅓in. across, in short dense axillary racemes; pedicels about equalling bracts and 5-parted calyx: caps. obcordate, length of calyx, glabrous. Eu.—*V. Trehanii* of hort. belongs here.

7. **V. latifolia,** L. (*V. Teucrium*, L.). Pubescent per., sterile sts. ascending or erect, to 2 ft.: lvs. sessile or the lower ones short-petioled, oblong- or linear-lanceolate, to 1½ in. long, obtusely crenate or remotely toothed: racemes 2–4 from the upper axils, elongated; fls. large, ½in. across, blue, rarely rose or white; pedicels equalling bracts; calyx 5-parted: caps. obcordate, pubescent, about length of calyx. Eu., Cent. Asia.

8. **V. Allionii,** Vill. Per. with prostrate rooting sts. to 1 ft. long: lvs. oval to oblong, very short-petioled, entire or serrulate, glabrous or nearly so: fls. violet, in spike-like axillary racemes; corolla four times as long as calyx; pedicels very short: caps. obcordate, about length of calyx, slightly pubescent. (Named for C. Allioni, page 38.) S. Eu.

9. **V. officinalis,** L. Pubescent prostrate per. with rooting ascending sts. 6–18 in. long: lvs. oblong, 1–2 in. long, obtuse, narrowed into petiole, serrate: racemes spike-like, dense, axillary, much longer than lvs.; fls. blue, ¼in. across; pedicels much shorter than calyx: caps. obovate, compressed, exceeding calyx, hairy. Eu., Asia, N. Amer.

10. **V. Chamædrys,** L. (*V. pulchella*, Salisb.). Germander Speedwell. Per. to 1½ ft., with sts. ascending from a creeping base: lvs. ovate, mostly ⅝–1½ in. long, rounded at base but sessile, crenately dentate, pubescent: racemes axillary, loose, to 6 in. long; fls. blue, to ½in. across; pedicels slender, usually one to three times as long as calyx: caps. obcordate, pubescent, shorter than calyx. Eu.; nat. N. S. to Ohio.

11. **V. incana,** L. (*V. candida*, Hort.). Upright or ascending white-woolly plant 1–2 ft. high, with many sterile matted branches: lvs. petioled, oblong or lanceolate, 1–3 in. long, narrowed at base, obtusely crenate: racemes solitary or many, terminal, to 6 in. long; fls. many, blue, ¼in. across, short-pedicelled: caps. nearly orbicular, exceeding the woolly calyx. N. Asia, Russia.

12. **V. gentianoides,** Vahl. Sts. tufted, erect, simple, 6 in.–2 ft. high: lvs. thickish, glabrous or glandular-pilose, entire or small crenate, the lower forming rosettes, oblong-lanceolate, to 3 in. long, the upper lvs. remote, linear-lanceolate: racemes terminal, elongated, laxly many-fld., hairy; fls. to ½in. across, pale blue with darker streaks; pedicels three to four times longer than calyx: caps. orbicular, twice as long as calyx, glandular. S. E. Eu.

13. **V. Bachofenii,** Heuff. Per. with erect or ascending sts. to 2 ft.: lvs. triangular-lanceolate, to 2 in. long, subcordate at base with rather long petioles, doubly serrate, nearly glabrous or pubescent on veins beneath: racemes terminal, many, elongated, rather loose; fls. blue; pedicels about length of calyx: caps. obcordate, about equalling calyx. (Named for D. Bachofen.) Hungary.

14. **V. spicata,** L. Sts. erect or ascending, to 1½ ft.: lvs. ovate or oblong, to 2 in. long, attenuate at base, crenate, but entire at base and tip, pubescent: racemes terminal, solitary or few, densely many-fld.; fls. blue, about ¼in. across; pedicels shorter than bracts and calyx: caps. orbicular, exceeding calyx, pubescent. Eu., Asia. Var. **orchidea,** Fiori (*V. orchidea*, Crantz), fls. pale blue or pinkish, corolla revolute in bud. Var. **Erica,** Hort., heather-like, fls. pink. Smaller hort. forms are **corymbosa** and **nana,** and color forms **alba** and **rosea.**

15. **V. spuria,** L. (*V. amethystina*, Willd.). Sts. erect to 2 ft., densely pubescent: lvs. opposite or in whorls of 3, oblong-lanceolate, 1 in. long, acute, attenuate into short petiole, toothed: racemes in terminal panicles, rather loose; fls. blue, to ½in. across; pedicels as long as calyx: caps. nearly orbicular, exceeding calyx. S. E. Eu. Var. **elegans,** Voss, is more branched and pubescent.

16. **V. longifolia,** L. (*V. maritima,* L.). Sts. upright, glabrous or slightly pubescent, to 2 ft. high: lvs. opposite or ternately whorled, lanceolate or oblong, acute, short-petioled, sharply serrate entire length of lf.: racemes solitary or few, terminal, densely-fld.; fls. lilac, ¼in. across; pedicels shorter than calyx and bracts: caps. obcordate, about length of calyx. N. Eu., N. Asia.—A useful border plant running into many vars., the most frequent of which is var. **subsessilis,** Miq. (*V. subsessilis,* Hort.), with very short-petioled lvs. and larger deep blue fls.

17. **V. satureioides,** Vis. Densely tufted per. with many creeping sts. somewhat woody at base: lvs. densely imbricated, obovate, ⅓in. long, entire or slightly toothed at tip, glabrous or nearly so: fls. blue, in terminal racemes, ½in. long; pedicels very short; calyx 5-parted: caps. orbicular, ciliate. Dalmatia.

18. **V. repens,** Loisel. A low delicate moss-like creeper good for ground-cover: lvs. to ½in. long, ovate, slightly crenate, shining green, glabrous, very short-petioled: racemes terminal, slender, few-fld.; fls. ¼in. across, rose or nearly white, with a trace of blue, in spring; pedicels about equalling calyx and bracts: caps. broader than long, deeply notched, exceeding the sepals, ciliate-glandulose. Corsica, Spain.

19. **V. Nummularia,** Pourr. Glabrous per. to 6 in., with many prostrate sts. somewhat woody at base: lvs. thickly clustered above, scale-like below, ovate-orbicular, ⅙in. long, obtuse, entire, very short-petioled: fls. blue or pink, in small terminal heads; pedicels very short: caps. orbicular, slightly notched, exceeding the sepals, ciliate. (Nummularia: old genus name meaning *coin,* because of shape of lvs.) Pyrenees.

20. **V. fruticans,** Jacq. (*V. saxatilis,* Scop.). Per. with prostrate sts. woody at base, ascending to 8 in. high: lvs. elliptic to oblong, ¼–½in. long, entire or slightly crenate, sessile or lower very short-petioled, glabrous: fls. blue, ½in. across, in few-fld. terminal racemes; pedicels short: caps. ovoid, scarcely emarginate. Eu.

6. **VERONICASTRUM,** Heister. Two species of per. herbs native in E. N. Amer. and E. Asia, one often transplanted.—Lvs. in whorls of 3–5: fls. in spike-like racemes, terminal and usually several together; calyx 4-parted; corolla with tube more than twice length of 4 lobes; stamens 2, exserted: caps. ovoid, dehiscing by septicidal and loculicidal slits at apex. (Veronicas-trum: from *veronica* and *astrum,* star.)

V. virginicum, Farwell (*Veronica virginica,* L. *Leptandra virginica,* Nutt.). Culvers-Root. To 7 ft.: lvs. lanceolate or oblong-lanceolate, to 6 in. long, toothed, short-petioled, long-acuminate: fls. white or pinkish, ¼in. long, in dense racemes to 9 in. long; pedicels very short. Mass. to Man. south to Fla. and Tex.

7. **VERBASCUM,** L. Mullein. Bien. herbs of 250 and more species, rarely per. or subshrubs, native to the Medit. region, several escaped in N. Amer., a few species sometimes grown in the border.—Lvs. all alternate, entire, crenulate, dentate or pinnatifid: fls. in terminal spikes or racemes; calyx usually deeply 5-parted; corolla rotate, the tube almost none, with 5 broad slightly unequal lobes; stamens 5, the 3 posterior or all bearded: caps. globose or ovoid, septicidally dehiscent by 2 valves; seeds numerous. (Verbas-cum: classical Latin name.)

A. Color of fls. purple, red or white .... 1. *V. phœniceum*
AA. Color of fls. yellow.
  B. Fls. with pedicels as long as or longer than calyx.
    C. Anthers all alike, kidney-shaped .... 2. *V. olympicum*
    CC. Anthers of lower and longer stamens almost parallel with filament and attached to it .... 3. *V. longifolium*
  BB. Fls. nearly sessile.
    C. Corolla 1½–2 in. across .... 4. *V. thapsiforme*
    CC. Corolla ½–¾in. across .... 5. *V. Thapsus*

1. **V. phœniceum,** L. Purple Mullein. To 5 ft.: lvs. glabrous above, pubescent beneath; radical lvs. petiolate, ovate or oblong-rhomboid, to 6 in. long, obtusely crenate or repand; cauline lvs. few, small, oblong or lanceolate, sessile: fls. solitary on long pedicels, about 1 in. across, borne in a simple slender nearly glabrous raceme, purple or red (white in a var.); calyx glandular, obtuse segms. elliptical; filaments purple-woolly. S. Eu., E. Asia.

2. **V. olympicum,** Boiss. To 5 ft., densely white-tomentose: lower lvs. oblong or lanceolate, entire, attenuate at base, 2 ft. and more long: fls. about 1 in. across, bright yellow, in many-fld. fascicles subtended by white-tomentose bracts, in loose racemes forming large panicles; pedicels two to three times longer than the white-tomentose calyx; filaments white-bearded, anthers kidney-shaped, all alike. Greece.

3. **V. longifolium,** Ten. To 4 ft., white- or yellowish-tomentose: lvs. numerous, densely superimposed, undulate, lower to 2 ft. long, oblong; upper oblong-lanceolate, base amplexicaul: racemes about 1 ft. long, densely-fld.; fls. golden-yellow, 1 in. across, in fascicles

of 4–10, with pedicels as long as or longer than densely tomentose calyx; anthers of lower stamens adnate-decurrent, filaments glabrous, short filaments white- or violet-bearded. S. Eu. Var. **pannosum,** Murbeck (*V. pannosum,* Vis. & Panc.), is more densely tomentose and all the filaments bearded.

4. **V. thapsiforme,** Schrad. (*V. densiflorum,* Vis.). To 5 ft., densely yellowish-tomentose: lower lvs. oblong-elliptic or elliptic-lanceolate, attenuate at base into petiole, to 16 in. long, coarsely crenate; cauline lvs. narrowly decurrent: fls. yellow, nearly sessile, 1½–2 in. across, in usually 4-fld. fascicles forming a dense spike; corolla flat; calyx with lanceolate tomentose segms.; filaments of 2 anterior stamens glabrous with adnate long-decurrent anthers, posterior stamens densely bearded. Eu.

5. **V. Thapsus,** L. COMMON MULLEIN. To 7 ft., densely yellowish-tomentose: lower lvs. oblong, to 1 ft. long, short-petioled, crenate or nearly entire; cauline lvs. long-decurrent: fls. yellow, sessile, ½–¾ in. across, in 1–7-fld. fascicles forming long dense spikes; corolla concave at throat; calyx-segms. lanceolate, densely tomentose; filaments of 2 anterior stamens glabrous or slightly hairy with adnate short-decurrent anthers, posterior stamens densely bearded. (Thapsus: from the Greek *yellow.*) Eu., Asia; nat. in N. Amer.

8. **PENSTEMON,** Mitch. About 250 species of per. herbs or shrubs, native in N. Amer., Mex., and 1 species in N. E. Asia, furnishing many ornamental subjects.—Sparingly branched: lvs. opposite or whorled, lower ones petioled, upper sessile: fls. in terminal racemes or panicles, showy; calyx 5-parted, segms. imbricated; corolla-tube elongated, usually dilated at throat, more or less bilabiate, upper lip 2-lobed, lower lip 3-lobed; fertile stamens 4, the fifth sterile stamen about as long as others, naked or bearded; style filiform, stigma capitate: caps. septicidally dehiscent; seeds numerous, wingless. (Penste-mon: Greek *five stamens,* the fifth stamen being present, although sterile; often written Pentstemon.)

A. Margins of lvs. entire.	
B. Fls. scarlet.	
C. Lower lip bearded	1. *P. barbatus*
CC. Lower lip not bearded.	
D. Length of corolla 1¼ in. or less.	
E. Sterile stamen glabrous.	
F. Lvs. linear	2. *P. Torreyi*
FF. Lvs. ovate-lanceolate	3. *P. centranthifolius*
EE. Sterile stamen bearded	4. *P. corymbosus*
DD. Length of corolla 2 in.	5. *P. Hartwegii*
BB. Fls. blue, purple, white or yellow.	
C. Sts. erect, 1 ft. or more high.	
D. Color of fls. yellow.	
E. Length of lvs. ½ in.	6. *P. antirrhinoides*
EE. Length of lvs. 1–2 in.	7. *P. confertus*
DD. Color of fls. blue, purple, lilac or white.	
E. Infl. glandular-pubescent.	
F. Sterile stamen glabrous	8. *P. Roezlii*
FF. Sterile stamen bearded.	
G. Corolla bearded within.	
H. Length of fls. 1 in.	33. *P. fruticosus*
HH. Length of fls. about ½ in.	9. *P. humilis*
GG. Corolla not bearded within	10. *P. tubiflorus*
EE. Infl. glabrous.	
F. Calyx-lobes erose, broadly scarious-margined.	
G. Corolla bearded within	11. *P. procerus*
GG. Corolla not bearded within.	
H. Radical lvs. small or none: infl. short and dense	12. *P. alpinus*
HH. Radical lvs. oblanceolate: infl. long and narrow.	
I. Sterile stamen bearded at tip	13. *P. glaber*
II. Sterile stamen glabrous	15. *P. speciosus*
FF. Calyx-lobes not erose, margins, if scarious, narrow.	
G. Sterile stamen glabrous.	
H. Length of fls. to ¾ in.: infl. secund	16. *P. unilateralis*
HH. Length of fls. 1¼–1½ in.: infl. not secund.	
I. Herbage green	17. *P. heterophyllus*
II. Herbage glaucous	18. *P. azureus*
GG. Sterile stamen bearded.	
H. Lvs. ovate.	
I. Length of fls. ¾–1 in.	
J. Racemes interrupted	19. *P. acuminatus*
JJ. Racemes dense and compact	14. *P. cyananthus*
II. Length of fls. 1½–2 in.	20. *P. grandiflorus*
HH. Lvs. linear or lanceolate.	
I. Racemes interrupted	21. *P. secundiflorus*
II. Racemes dense and compact	22. *P. angustifolius*
CC. Sts. prostrate, 2–8 in. high.	

D. Lvs. ovate........32. *P. Davidsonii*
DD. Lvs. linear-lanceolate........28. *P. Crandallii*
AA. Margins of lvs. serrate.
B. Color of fls. red.
C. Habit climbing........23. *P. cordifolius*
CC. Habit not climbing.
D. Infl. open and leafy: lvs. deeply lobed or pinnatifid........24. *P. Richardsonii*
DD. Infl. compact: lvs. shallowly toothed.
E. Anthers densely woolly.
F. Lvs. ¼–½in. long........35. *P. rupicola*
FF. Lvs. ¾–1¼ in. long........36. *P. Newberryi*
EE. Anthers not woolly........4. *P. corymbosus*
BB. Color of fls. blue, purple or white.
C. Infl. glabrous.
D. Length of corolla ¼–½in........25. *P. deustus*
DD. Length of corolla 1–1½ in.
E. Anthers glabrous........26. *P. spectabilis*
EE. Anthers hairy or woolly.
F. Lobes of corolla ciliate........27. *P. venustus*
FF. Lobes of corolla not ciliate........29. *P. Barrettæ*
CC. Infl. glandular-pubescent.
D. Sterile stamen glabrous........30. *P. Scouleri*
DD. Sterile stamen bearded.
E. Anthers densely woolly.
F. Length of lvs. ½in. or less........31. *P. Menziesii*
FF. Length of lvs. ¾–1 in.
G. Lvs. acute........33. *P. fruticosus*
GG. Lvs. obtuse........34. *P. Cardwellii*
EE. Anthers not densely woolly.
F. Fls. very broad, to 1 in. across at mouth........37. *P. Cobæa*
FF. Fls. not more than ½in. across.
G. Sts. glabrous below the infl.
H. Lvs. very long-acuminate........38. *P. campanulatus*
HH. Lvs. acute or short-acuminate.
I. Calyx-lobes linear-subulate, to ⅜in. long........39. *P. calycosus*
II. Calyx-lobes lanceolate, less than ⅜in. long.
J. Corolla bearded within.
K. St.-lvs. ovate-lanceolate........40. *P. Rattanii*
KK. St.-lvs. linear-lanceolate........41. *P. gracilis*
JJ. Corolla not bearded within.
K. Corolla-tube gradually enlarged, purplish........42. *P. lævigatus*
KK. Corolla-tube abruptly enlarged, white or pinkish........43. *P. Digitalis*
GG. Sts. pubescent below the infl.
H. Throat bearded.
I. St.-lvs. lanceolate........44. *P. hirsutus*
II. St.-lvs. ovate.
J. Corolla abruptly constricted at base; color pink-purple........45. *P. Smallii*
JJ. Corolla not abruptly constricted; color blue-purple........46. *P. ovatus*
HH. Throat not bearded.
I. Corolla white........47. *P. albidus*
II. Corolla blue or purple........48. *P. diffusus*

1. **P. barbatus,** Nutt. (*Chelone barbata,* Cav.). To 6 ft., glabrous: lvs. 2–6 in. long, lower oblong or ovate, upper lanceolate or linear, entire: infl. long and open; fls. about 1 in. long, red, strongly 2-lipped, the lower lip bearded with yellow hairs; sterile stamen glabrous. Mts., Utah to Mex.

2. **P. Torreyi,** Benth. (*P. barbatus* var. *Torreyi,* Gray). Differs from *P. barbatus* in its larger scarlet fls. and the lower lip not being bearded. (For John Torrey, page 53.) Utah to Mex.

3. **P. centranthifolius,** Benth. SCARLET BUGLER. From 1–3 ft., glaucous: lvs. thick, entire, from ovate- to oblong-lanceolate, 1½–2½ in. long, the upper with subcordate clasping base: infl. long and narrow; fls. about 1 in. long, scarlet, tubular, the lobes very short; sterile stamen glabrous. Calif. to Ariz.

4. **P. corymbosus,** Benth. Subshrub to 16 in., tufted: lvs. oblong or obovate, ¼–1¼ in. long, toothed or entire: infl. short, glandular-pubescent; fls. scarlet, 1–1¼ in. long; sterile stamen bearded. Calif.

5. **P. Hartwegii,** Benth. (*P. gentianoides,* Lindl.). From 3–4 ft., glabrous except infl.: lvs. lanceolate to ovate-lanceolate, 2–4 in. long, entire: infl. long and open; fls. to 2 in. long, scarlet, slightly curved; sterile stamen glabrous. (Hartweg, page 44.) Cool regions in Mex.—**P. gloxinoides,** Hort., is a race of hybrids between *P. Hartwegii* and *P. Cobæa,* many colors.

6. **P. antirrhinoides,** Benth. Shrub to 6 ft., branched and leafy, slightly pubescent: lvs. very small, to ½in. long, linear or oblong, entire: infl. a leafy panicle; sepals broadly ovate; corolla very broad, ¾in. long, ventricose, yellow; sterile stamen densely bearded on one side. S. Calif.

7. **P. confertus,** Dougl. To 2 ft., glabrous: lvs. oblong or lanceolate, 2 in. and more long, entire: infl. interupted, of whorled clusters; fls. pale yellow, about ½in. long, lower lip yellow-hairy within; sterile stamen bearded. Alta. to Calif.

8. **P. Roezlii,** Regel (*P. lætus* var. *Roezlii,* Jepson). To 1 ft., sts. erect or ascending: lvs. linear to oblanceolate, 1–3 in. long, entire: infl. an open glandular-pubescent panicle; fls. pale blue or violet, ½–¾in. long; sterile stamen glabrous. (Named for B. Roezl, page 50.) Mts., Ore. to Calif.

9. **P. humilis,** Nutt. To 1 ft., pubescent: lvs. ovate to lanceolate, about 1 in. long, entire: infl. interrupted, glandular-pubescent; fls. deep blue, to ½in. long, throat bearded within; sterile stamen bearded at apex. Wyo., Ida., Utah.

10. **P. tubiflorus,** Nutt. To 3 ft.: lvs. ovate to lanceolate, to 4 in. long, entire: infl. interrupted, glandular-pubescent; fls. white or purplish, ¾in. long; sterile stamen bearded. Mo. to Ark. and Okla.

11. **P. procerus,** Dougl. To 1 ft., glabrous: lvs. oblanceolate, to 3in. long: infl. compact; fls. purplish-blue, ¼–½in. long, bearded within; calyx-lobes erose and scarious-margined; sterile stamen bearded. Sask. to Calif.

12. **P. alpinus,** Torr. (*P. glaber* var. *alpinus,* Gray). Usually not more than 1 ft. high: st.-lvs. lanceolate, 2–4 in. long, entire: infl. short and dense; fls. bluish-purple, 1 in. long; calyx-lobes erose, with broad scarious margins; sterile stamen yellow-bearded at apex. Rocky Mts.

13. **P. glaber,** Pursh. From 1–2 ft., glabrous and somewhat glaucous: lvs. oblanceolate to lanceolate, to 6 in. long, entire: infl. densely many-fld., long and narrow; fls. 1 in. or more long, blue or purple; calyx-lobes erose, with broad scarious margins; sterile stamen bearded at tip. N. D. to Wyo.

14. **P. cyananthus,** Hook. (*P. glaber* var. *cyananthus,* Gray). From 1–3 ft., glabrous and glaucous: st.-lvs. ovate or subcordate, ¾–3 in. wide: infl. dense; fls. about 1 in. long, bright blue; sterile stamen bearded. Mts., Utah, Ida., Wyo.

15. **P. speciosus,** Dougl. To 2 ft., glabrous: lvs. oblanceolate to linear-lanceolate, to 4 in. long, entire: infl. long and narrow; fls. bluish-purple, 1 in. long, ventricose; calyx-lobes erose with broad scarious margins; sterile stamen glabrous. Wash. to Calif.

16. **P. unilateralis,** Rydb. To 2 ft., glabrous: lvs. oblanceolate to linear-lanceolate, to 4 in. long, entire: infl. narrow and secund; fls. blue, ¾in. long, abruptly ventricose; calyx-lobes with slightly scarious entire margins; sterile stamen glabrous. Wyo. to New Mex.

17. **P. heterophyllus,** Lindl. To 5 ft., base woody, glabrous: lvs. lanceolate or linear, to 2½ in. long and ⅛in. or less wide, entire: infl. loose and open, narrow; fls. 1¼–1½ in. long, purple or pinkish-blue, slender at base but dilated above; sterile stamen glabrous. Calif.

18. **P. azureus,** Benth. (*P. heterophyllus* var. *azureus,* Jepson). Differs from *P. heterophyllus* in being somewhat pubescent and glaucous and with slightly broader lvs. Calif.

19. **P. acuminatus,** Dougl. To 1½ ft., glabrous and glaucous: lvs. thick and leathery, entire, lower oblanceolate, to 3 in. long, upper ovate-cordate: infl. interrupted; fls. blue, ¾in. long, funnelform; sterile stamen densely bearded. Wash. to Tex.

20. **P. grandiflorus,** Nutt. From 2–6 ft., glabrous: lvs. obovate to broadly ovate, to 2½ in. long, obtuse, entire: infl. loose; fls. about 2 in. long, lavender-blue, tube abruptly dilated above calyx; sterile stamen minutely pubescent at tip. Prairies, Ill. to Wyo.

21. **P. secundiflorus,** Benth. To 2 ft., glabrous and glaucous: lvs. oblanceolate to lanceolate, to 3 in. long, entire: infl. interrupted, secund; fls. bluish-purple, ¾in. long, funnelform; sterile stamen densely bearded. Wyo. to New Mex.

22. **P. angustifolius,** Pursh (*P. cæruleus,* Nutt.). To 1 ft., glabrous and glaucous: lvs. linear or linear-lanceolate, to 4 in. long, entire: infl. dense; fls. blue, lilac or white, to ¾in. long, funnelform; calyx-lobes lanceolate, with narrow scarious margins; sterile stamen bearded. Plains, S. D. to New Mex.

23. **P. cordifolius,** Benth. Somewhat pubescent very leafy plant half climbing over shrubs, to 10 ft.: lvs. ovate, ½–1½ in. long, truncate or subcordate at base, serrate: infl. short and leafy, glandular-pubescent; fls. 1¼–1½ in. long, scarlet, tubular with short lobes; sterile stamen bearded. S. Calif.

24. **P. Richardsonii,** Dougl. To 2 ft., loosely branched: lvs. ovate to lanceolate, 1–2 in. long, deeply toothed or pinnatifid: infl. open and leafy, glandular-pubescent; fls. red, 1–1¼ in. long, lower lip bearded within; sterile stamen exserted, bearded at apex. (Named for J. Richardson, page 50.) B. C. to Ida.

25. **P. deustus,** Dougl. To 1 ft., woody at base, nearly glabrous: lvs. ovate to oblanceolate, ½–1¼ in. long, toothed: infl. of small clusters in upper axils; fls. whitish, ¼–½in. long; sterile stamen usually bearded. B. C. to Calif.

26. **P. spectabilis,** Thurber. From 2–6 ft., glabrous and glaucous: lvs. ovate to ovate-lanceolate, 3–4 in. long, the upper ones connate at base, sharply dentate: infl. a narrow panicle 1 ft. or more long; fls. 1 in. or more long, rose-purple or lilac, the narrow part of tube about twice length of calyx, upper part dilated; sterile stamen glabrous. New Mex. to S. Calif.

27. **P. venustus,** Dougl. To 2 ft., glabrous and glaucous: lvs. lanceolate or oblanceolate, 1–2 in. long, toothed: infl. narrow; fls. blue or light purple, 1 in. long; calyx with erose scarious margins; corolla with ciliate lobes and lower lip often hairy within; sterile stamen bearded, anthers hairy. Wash., Ore., Ida.

28. **P. Crandallii,** A. Nels. Slightly glandular-pubescent, sts. densely tufted, prostrate or ascending, to 8 in. high: lvs. linear-oblanceolate, to 1 in. long, entire: fls. solitary or in small clusters, blue, ¾–1 in. long; sterile stamen bearded. (Named for C. S. Crandall, 1852–1929.) Mts., Colo.

29. **P. Barrettæ,** Gray. To 1 ft., glabrous and glaucous: lvs. ovate to lanceolate, to 3 in. long, toothed: infl. narrow; fls. lilac-purple, 1–1½ in. long, lower lip bearded within; sterile stamen slightly hairy, anthers densely woolly. (Named for the original collector, Mrs. Barrett.) Ore.

30. **P. Scouleri,** Dougl. Shrub to 1½ ft.: lvs. lanceolate, to 2 in. long, toothed: infl. few-fld., slightly glandular-pubescent; fls. lilac-purple, to 2 in. long; sterile stamen glabrous, anthers densely woolly. (Named for John Scouler, 1804–1871, who collected in N. W. U. S. in 1825.) Mts., B. C. to Ida.

31. **P. Menziesii,** Hook. To 6 in., densely tufted: lvs. thick, obovate, ¼–½in. long, toothed: infl. glandular-pubescent; fls. purple, 1 in. long; sterile stamen bearded, anthers densely woolly. (Named for Archibald Menzies, page 399.) Alta. to B. C. and Wash.

32. **P. Davidsonii,** Greene (*P. Menziesii* var. *Davidsonii*, Piper). Prostrate, with matted sts. to 3 in. high: lvs. ovate, ⅓in. long, entire: infl. few-fld., glandular-pubescent; fls. lilac-purple, 1–1¼ in. long; sterile stamen bearded. (Named for its collector, Dr. Geo. Davidson.) B. C. to Calif.

33. **P. fruticosus,** Green (*Gerardia fruticosa*, Pursh). Shrubby, with erect sts. 8 in.–3 ft. high: lvs. oblanceolate, ¾–1 in. long, serrulate or entire: infl. simple, glandular-pubescent; fls. purplish-blue, 1 in. long, throat bearded within; sterile stamen bearded at apex. Alta. to Ore.

34. **P. Cardwellii,** Howell (*P. fruticosus* var. *Cardwellii*, Piper). To 10 in., loosely tufted: lvs. thick, oblong-elliptic to oval, 1–1¼ in. long, obtuse, toothed: infl. slightly glandular-pubescent; fls. purple, 1¼ in. long, bearded within; sterile stamen bearded, anthers densely woolly. Wash., Ore.

35. **P. rupicola,** Howell. Much-branched decumbent pubescent shrub to 4 in. high: lvs. thick, ovate or orbicular, ¼–½in. long, toothed, glaucous: infl. of few fls., glandular-pubescent; fls. bright rose-crimson, 1–1½ in. long, ventricose; sterile stamen usually bearded, shorter than fertile ones, anthers densely woolly. Wash., Ore.

36. **P. Newberryi,** Gray. MOUNTAIN PRIDE. To 20 in., woody at base: lvs. leathery, ovate or orbicular, ¾–1¼ in. long, toothed: infl. short, glandular-pubescent; fls. red, about 1 in. long; sterile stamen bearded at apex, anthers densely woolly and exserted. (Named for Dr. J. S. Newberry, 1822–1892, collector on railroad surveys.) Mts., Calif.

37. **P. Cobæa,** Nutt. To 2 ft., stout: lvs. oblong to ovate, 3–5 in. long, dentate: infl. open, glandular-pubescent; fls. about 2 in. long, purple, tube abruptly dilated above calyx, the limb scarcely 2-lipped; sterile stamen bearded. (Cobæa: fls. cobæa-like.) Mo. and Kans. to Tex.

38. **P. campanulatus,** Willd. (*Gerardia hybrida*, Hort.). To 2 ft., glabrous below infl.: lvs. lanceolate, long-acuminate, to 4 in. long, strongly serrate: infl. long and narrow, slightly glandular-pubescent; fls. about 1 in. long, rose-purple or violet, sometimes white, dilated at middle; sterile stamen bearded. Mex., Guatemala.

39. **P. calycosus,** Small. From 1–4 ft. high, sts. glabrous below the sparingly pubescent infl.: lvs. spatulate to lanceolate, to 6 in. long, sharply serrate or nearly entire: fls. about 1 in. long, purple; corolla-tube abruptly dilated at middle; calyx-lobes linear-subulate, becoming fully ⅖in. long; sterile stamen bearded. Ind. to Ala.

40. **P. Rattanii,** Gray. Sts. 1–2 ft., glabrous: lower lvs. lanceolate, to 6 in. long, petioled, toothed, st.-lvs. ovate-lanceolate and clasping, to 2½ in. long: infl. glandular-pubescent; fls. lavender, 1 in. long, tube abruptly expanded, lower lip bearded within; sterile stamen bearded, exserted. (Named for Volney Rattan, Calif., botanist of the last century.) Ore., Calif.

41. **P. gracilis,** Nutt. To 1½ ft., sts. glabrous or nearly so: lower lvs. oblanceolate, to 3 in. long, toothed or entire, st.-lvs. linear-lanceolate, toothed: infl. glandular-pubescent, open; fls. lilac or whitish, ¾–1 in. long, slightly bearded within, tube gradually enlarged; sterile stamen bearded. Man. to Sask. and New Mex.

42. **P. lævigatus,** Soland. (*Chelone Pentstemon*, L.). To 3 ft., sts. glabrous: lvs. oblong or lanceolate, to 6 in. long, toothed: infl. open, many-fld., glandular-pubescent; fls. purplish, ¾–1 in. long, tube gradually enlarged; sterile stamen bearded. Pa. to Fla. and Ala.

43. **P. Digitalis,** Nutt. (*P. lævigatus* var. *Digitalis*, Gray). To 5 ft., sts. glabrous: lvs. oblong, lanceolate or ovate-lanceolate, to 7 in. long, sharply toothed: infl. open, many-fld., glandular-pubescent; fls. white or pinkish, about 1 in. long, tube abruptly dilated at middle; sterile stamen bearded. (Digitalis: a genus of Scrophulariaceæ.) Me. to S. D. and Tex.

44. **P. hirsutus,** Willd. (*P. pubescens,* Soland. *Chelone hirsuta,* L.). To 3 ft., usually viscid-pubescent: lvs. oblong to lanceolate, to 4½ in. long, toothed: infl. loose and open; fls. purplish or violet, about 1 in. long, densely bearded in throat; sterile stamen densely bearded above middle. Me. to Tenn. and Wis.

45. **P. Smallii,** Heller. To 4 ft., sts. puberulent: lvs. lanceolate to ovate-lanceolate, 3–6 in. long, sharply toothed: infl. loose and panicle-like, glandular-pubescent; fls. pink-purple striped with white within, 1–1½ in. long, tube abruptly dilated near middle, with long yellow hairs in throat; sterile stamen bearded to base. (Named after J. K. Small, page 51.) N. C., Tenn.

46. **P. ovatus,** Dougl. To 4 ft., sts. pubescent: lvs. broad-ovate, 2–3 in. long, toothed: infl. loose, glandular-pubescent; fls. less than 1 in. long, blue changing to purple; lower lip bearded in throat; sterile stamen bearded. B. C. to Ore. and Mont.

47. **P. albidus,** Nutt. To 1 ft., glandular-pubescent: lvs. oblong or lanceolate, to 2½ in. long, toothed: infl. narrow, racemose; fls. white, sometimes with purple lines, ¾in. long, funnelform; sterile stamen slightly bearded. Man to Tex.

48. **P. diffusus,** Dougl. To 2 ft., diffuse, sts. somewhat puberulent: lvs. ovate or lanceolate, upper subcordate, 2 in. or more long, unevenly and deeply toothed: infl. leafy, pedicels very short, glandular-pubescent; fls. funnelform, ¾in. long, blue or purple; sterile stamen bearded above. B. C. to Ore.

9. **CHELONE,** L. Turtle-Head. About 8 species of per. herbs native in N. Amer., grown in the hardy border.—Lvs. opposite, serrate: fls. sessile in dense axillary or terminal spikes; calyx 5-parted; corolla with elongated ventricose tube and 2-lipped limb, the upper lip concave and notched, the lower 3-lobed; stamens 4, the fifth sterile stamen shorter than others, filaments woolly; stigma capitate: caps. ovoid, septicidally dehiscent; seeds winged. (Chelo-ne: Greek *tortoise;* the corolla resembling a turtle's head.)

A. Lvs. ovate, long-petioled: bracts ciliolate........1. *C. Lyonii*
AA. Lvs. narrow- to broad-lanceolate: bracts not ciliolate........2. *C. glabra*

1. **C. Lyonii,** Pursh. To 3 ft.: lvs. ovate, 3–7 in. long, acuminate, long-petioled: fls. rose-purple, about 1 in. long, in July–Sept.; anterior lip yellow-bearded; bracts ciliolate and puberulent. (John Lyon, page 772.) Mts., N. C., S. C., Tenn.

2. **C. glabra,** L. To 3 ft.: lvs. narrow- to broad-lanceolate, 2½–6 in. long, acuminate, short-petioled: fls. white or rose-tinged, about 1 in. long, in July–Sept.; anterior lip white-bearded; bracts glabrous, not ciliolate. Wet grounds, Newf. to Ga. and Minn.

10. **HEBENSTRETIA,** L. Ann. herbs, subshrubs, or shrubs, of about 30 species mostly from S. Afr., one sometimes grown in the fl.-garden.—Lvs. alternate or lower ones opposite, entire or dentate: fls. sessile in dense terminal spikes, yellow or white; calyx spathe-like, split down the front; corolla with slender tube, deeply cut in front, with 4-lobed posterior limb; stamens 4, inserted on corolla-tube; style entire: fr. indehiscent. (Hebenstre-tia: after John Ernst Hebenstreit, 1703–1757, professor of medicine in the Univ. of Leipzig.)

H. comosa, Hochst. To 4 ft.: lvs. numerous, lanceolate, ½–2 in. long, remotely sharp-toothed, glabrous: fls. yellow or white with orange-red blotch on limb, very fragrant at night, about ½in. long, in dense slender long-tapering spikes 2–10 in. long. Natal.

11. **CELSIA,** L. About 40 species of bien. or per. herbs, mostly from the Medit. region and Asia, 1 from S. Afr.—Differs from Verbascum only in having 4 stamens instead of 5. (Cel-sia: Olaus Celsius, 1670–1756, Swedish theologian and naturalist, teacher of Linnæus.)

A. Fls. almost sessile........1. *C. cretica*
AA. Fls. long-pedicelled........2. *C. Arcturus*

1. **C. cretica,** L. f. Cretan Mullein. To 6 ft., hairy: lvs. ovate or oblong, dentate, the lower petioled, lyrate-pinnatifid or undivided: bracts lanceolate, serrate or entire, longer than calyx: fls. in lax racemes, almost sessile, yellow marked with purple; shorter filaments violet-bearded, longer glabrous: caps. glabrous, shorter than calyx. Medit. region.

2. **C. Arcturus,** Jacq. Cretan Bears-Tail. Differs from *C. cretica* in the long-pedicelled fls., the triangular denticulate bracts being much shorter than the pedicels, the filaments all violet-bearded, and the caps. almost three times length of calyx. (Arcturus: *bear* and *tail,* a genus of Scrophulariaceæ.) Crete and Asia Minor.

12. **REHMANNIA,** Libosch. (*Sparmannia,* Buc'hoz, not L.f.). Five or more species of per. sticky-hairy herbs from China and Japan, grown in a cool greenhouse or out-of-doors in the S.—Sts. branching from the base, in cult. tall and few-lvd.: lvs. alternate, obovate or oblong, coarsely toothed: fls. large, borne in the axils of the lvs. or in terminal racemes, short-pedicelled; calyx ovoid, campanulate, 5-cleft at top; corolla slightly incurved, tube ventricose, limb oblique, lobes spreading, the rear or inner one 2-cleft, the front lobe 3-cleft; stamens 4, included: caps. broad, almost inclosed by calyx, loculicidally dehiscent; seeds numerous. (Rehman-nia: Jos. Rehmann, 1779–1831, physician in Leningrad.)

R. angulata, Hemsl. From 1–3 ft. high: lvs. either having many marginal teeth, or the few lobes or large teeth being again toothed: bracts with very broad and rather abruptly cuneate bases wider than any other part of blade: corolla about 2 in. long, red with band of scarlet at margin of upper lip and orange dots inside lower lip. China.—Garden forms are var. **tigrina,** Hort., with fls. marked, and var. **tricolor,** Hort., with fls. at first bright purple, later almost violet-rose, upper lip shaded with vermilion and throat whitish, spotted with purple.

13. **PEDICULARIS,** L. Wood-Betony. Lousewort. A large genus in the northern hemisphere, about 350 herbaceous species, suitable for the rock-garden.—Lvs. alternate, opposite or rarely whorled, usually pinnatisect: fls. in terminal bracted spikes; calyx tubular, 2–5-toothed; corolla with cylindrical tube, 2-lipped, the lower lip 3-lobed; stamens 4, included: caps. oblique, loculicidally dehiscent; seeds numerous. (Pedicula-ris: from Latin for *louse,* supposed to cause lice on stock feeding on these plants.)

P. canadensis, L. Pubescent per. 1–1½ ft. high: lvs. mostly alternate, oblong-lanceolate, to 5 in. long, divided nearly to midrib into toothed lobes: fls. yellow or reddish, rarely white, ¾in. long, in spring, borne in pubescent spikes becoming 8 in. long in fr.: caps. twice as long as calyx. Que. to Fla. and Mex.

14. **ERINUS,** L. One alpine species native in the mts. of W. and Cent. Eu.—Root-lvs. crowded, st.-lvs. alternate: fls. in simple racemes; corolla-lobes 5; calyx 5-parted nearly to base; stamens 4, included; style very short, 2-lobed at apex: caps. ovate, dehiscent; seeds numerous. (Eri-nus: Greek name used by Dioscorides.)

E. alpinus, L. Tufted per. to 4 in.: lvs. spatulate, ¼–½in. long, toothed: fls. purple, ½in. across, in racemes 1–2½ in. long, in spring. Var. **albus,** Hort., fls. white. Vars. **carmineus** and **roseus,** Hort., fls. rose.

15. **LEUCOPHYLLUM,** Humb. & Bonpl. Pubescent shrubs of about a dozen species from Tex. to Mex., one popular as a hedge plant in its region.—Lvs. alternate, entire: fls. solitary in the axils; calyx 5-parted nearly to base; corolla funnelform-campanulate with 5 lobes; stamens 4, included: caps. 2-valved; seeds numerous. (Leucophyl-lum: Greek for *white leaf.*)

L. frutescens, Johnston (*Teramia frutescens,* Berl. *L. texanum,* Benth.). Cenizo. White-tomentose, 4–8 ft. high: lvs. obovate, ½–1 in. long, obtuse, narrowed at base, nearly sessile: fls. violet-purple, 1 in. long and across, hairy within.

16. **DIGITALIS,** L. Foxglove. About 25 species from Eu. and W. and Cent. Asia, useful for the herbaceous border.—Herbs, rarely woody at base, glabrous, tomentose or villous, usually simple: lvs. alternate, lower often crowded and elongated, entire or dentate: fls. in long terminal racemes often one-sided, showy, purple, yellowish, or white; calyx 5-parted; corolla declined, tube inflated or campanulate, often constricted above the ovary, the limb erect-spreading and somewhat 2-lipped, the upper lip shorter than lower; stamens 4, usually included: caps. ovate, septicidally dehiscent; seeds numerous. (Digita-lis: Latin, finger of a glove, referring to the shape of the fls.)

A. Middle lobe of lower lip markedly longer than others and equalling or exceeding corolla-tube.
B. Rachis of racemes glandular-pubescent.
C. Bracts much longer than calyx: racemes dense .... 1. *D. lanata*
CC. Bracts about length of calyx: racemes loose .... 2. *D. orientalis*
BB. Rachis of racemes glabrous.

c. Lobes of calyx ovate, obtuse, scarious-margined........................3. *D. ferruginea*
cc. Lobes of calyx lanceolate, acute, not scarious-margined....................4. *D. lævigata*
AA. Middle lobe of lower lip not markedly longer than others and much shorter than corolla-tube.
B. Under surface of lvs. and pedicels glabrous..5. *D. lutea*
BB. Under surface of lvs. and pedicels hairy.
c. Lobes of calyx linear...6. *D. grandiflora*
cc. Lobes of calyx ovate...7. *D. purpurea*

1. **D. lanata,** Ehrh. GRECIAN FOXGLOVE. Per. or bien., 2–3 ft., sts. strict and unbranched, white-pubescent above: lvs. many, long-lanceolate, somewhat ciliate or smooth, sessile: racemes closely many-fld., downy with many long soft hairs; calyx-lobes linear, downy, shorter than corolla; corolla about 1 in. long, half of which is an urn-shaped closely brown-reticulated body with very short upper and lateral teeth; middle lower lobe about as long as body and projecting, pointed, nearly white with fine veins; bracts much longer than calyx, equalling or exceeding corolla. Danube region and Greece.

2. **D. orientalis,** Lam. Per. to 3 ft., sts. white-glandular-pubescent above: lvs. lanceolate, glabrous, sessile: racemes loose and interrupted; calyx-lobes elliptic, obtuse, downy; corolla 1 in. long, white finely striped with red except the long lower lip; bracts about length of calyx. Levant.

3. **D. ferruginea,** L. RUSTY FOXGLOVE. Bien. or per. to 6 ft., with simple very leafy sts.: lvs. long-lanceolate, deeply veined, sessile, glabrous or ciliate: racemes long and dense; calyx-lobes ovate, obtuse, glabrous, scarious-margined; corolla ¾–1½ in. long, yellowish marked with rusty-red, pubescent, middle lobe longer than others. S. Eu., W. Asia.

4. **D. lævigata,** Waldst. & Kit. Per. 2–3 ft. high, glabrous: lvs. obovate- to linear-lanceolate, sessile: racemes long and loose; calyx-lobes lanceolate, acute; corolla ¾–1¼ in. long, yellow marked with brown-purple, middle lobe as long as corolla-tube. S. Eu.

5. **D. lutea,** L. STRAW FOXGLOVE. Per. or bien. 2–3 ft. high, glabrous: lvs. oblong or lanceolate: racemes many-fld., one-sided; calyx-lobes lanceolate, acute; corolla ¾in. long, yellow to white, upper lip 2-parted. Eu.

6. **D. grandiflora,** Mill. (*D. ambigua,* Murr.). YELLOW FOXGLOVE. Per. or bien. 2–3 ft. high, hairy: lvs. ovate-lanceolate, toothed, sessile or clasping: fls. large, 2 in. long, yellowish marked with brown; calyx-lobes linear; middle lobe of lower lip shorter than the corolla-tube; lower bracts about as long as fl. Eu., W. Asia.

7. **D. purpurea,** L. COMMON FOXGLOVE. Bien., sometimes per., 2–4 ft. high: lvs. rugose, somewhat downy, the radical ones long-stalked and ovate to ovate-lanceolate, the st.-lvs. short-stalked or sessile, becoming small toward top of st.: fls. large, 2–3 in. long, pendulous, borne in a one-sided raceme 1–2 ft. long, purple more or less spotted, lobes ciliate; calyx-lobes broadly ovate: caps. ovoid, exceeding calyx. W. Eu.—Variable, running into many garden forms as: var. **gloxiniæflora,** Vilm. (*D. gloxinioides,* Carr.), of more robust habit, having longer racemes and more wide open fls. strongly spotted; var. **campanulata,** Vilm., with upper fls. united into a bell-shaped large bloom; var. **alba,** Hort., fls. white; var. **maculata,** Voss, fls. spotted; var. **monstrosa,** Hort., a double peloric form. **D. Isabellina,** Hort., has yellow fls. **D. Lutzii,** Hort., represents a hybrid group with fls. in shades of crimson.

17. **ISOPLEXIS,** Lindl. Two species of subshrubs from the Canary Isls., grown in the open in Calif.—Lvs. alternate: fls. in dense terminal racemes, yellow; calyx 5-parted; corolla incurved, tube ventricose, upper lip as long as or longer than under lip; stamens 4, shorter than corolla and slightly exserted; style 2-lobed at top: caps. ovate, septicidally dehiscent; seeds numerous. (Isoplex-is: Greek *equal* and *cut,* referring to the lips of the corolla being equal.)

I. canariensis, Steud. (*Digitalis canariensis,* L.). Undershrub with stiff erect sts., 3–4 ft., lightly pilose: lvs. thick, persistent, usually crowded, lanceolate to oblanceolate or somewhat broader, pointed, narrowed to partly clasping base, sharp-serrate, shining above and lighter beneath: fls. yellow-brown, in a dense terminal bracted spike, strongly bilabiate with long acute or obtuse lobes; stamens included under upper lip, the corolla about 1 in. long when fully expanded; calyx-lobes lanceolate: caps. conic, tipped with style.—**I. Sceptrum,** Steud. (*Digitalis Sceptrum,* L.), differs in fls. not bilabiate, the lobes obtuse.

18. **ANARRHINUM,** Desf. Bien. or per. herbs of about 12 species in the Medit. region, one grown in the fl.-garden.—Basal lvs. in rosettes, st.-lvs. alternate: fls. in long slender racemes; calyx 5-parted to base; corolla 2-lipped, with or without spur, throat open; stamens 4: caps. globose, dehiscent at apex; seeds numerous. (Anarrhi-num: Greek *without nose.*)

A. bellidifolium, Desf. To 2 ft. high, glabrous, sts. simple or branched above middle: basal lvs. spatulate, deeply toothed, to 3 in. long, st.-lvs. 3–7-parted into linear segms.: fls. blue, limb edged with white, about ⅛in. long, spur short and recurved.

19. **MAURANDYA,** Ort. Herbs climbing by coiling petioles and pedicels, with showy fls., comprising about 10 species mostly from Mex.—Lvs. alternate or the lower ones opposite, triangular or halberd-shaped, angular-lobed or coarsely toothed: fls. axillary; calyx 5-parted; corolla-tube slightly gibbous at base, throat open (with palate in *M. antirrhiniflora*), marked with bearded lines; stamens 4: caps. opening by oblique or irregular valves; seeds many. (Mauran-dya: after Maurandy, promoter of botany at Cartagena, Spain.)—Sometimes spelled Maurandia.

A. Lvs. entire.
  B. Calyx glabrous....................1. *M. antirrhiniflora*
  BB. Calyx glandular-hairy....................2. *M. Barclaiana*
AA. Lvs. serrate.
  B. Corolla-tube ventricose, glandular-hairy....................3. *M. erubescens*
  BB. Corolla-tube straight, glabrous....................4. *M. Lophospermum*

1. **M. antirrhiniflora,** Humb. & Bonpl. (*Antirrhinum maurandioides*, Gray). Plant glabrous: lvs. arrow- or halberd-shaped, about 1 in. long, entire, long-petioled: fls. purple or rose, solitary on filiform pedicels, 1 in. long; sepals lanceolate. Tex. to Calif. and Mex.

2. **M. Barclaiana,** Lindl. Lvs. hastate, cordate, 1–1½ in. long, entire, the petioles long and twining: fls. about 1½ in. long, on long pedicels, purple, downy outside; sepals glandular-pilose, long-attenuate. (Bears the name of Robt. Barclay, who collected in Mex.) Mex.—Runs into many color forms.

3. **M. erubescens,** Gray (*Lophospermum erubescens*, D. Don). Plant glandular-hairy: lvs. triangular, to 3 in. long, with petioles as long as blades, serrate: fls. rose-red, 3 in. long, tube somewhat ventricose; sepals ovate and leafy, to 1 in. long. Mex.—Commonly cult. under the name *M. scandens*.

4. **M. Lophospermum,** Bailey (*M. scandens*, Gray not Pers. *M. erubescens* var. *glabrata*, Johnston. *M. glabrata*, Johnston. *Lophospermum scandens*, D. Don). Branches glandular-pubescent: lvs. triangular-ovate, cordate, unequally serrate, petioles twining: fls. about 3 in. long, on long pedicels, rose-purple, obscurely dotted outside, tube white and straight and glabrous outside; sepals oblong and leafy, 1 in. long. Mex.

20. **ANTIRRHINUM,** L. SNAPDRAGON. About 50 herbaceous species, native in the northern hemisphere, abundant in N. Amer., popular in fl.-gardens and under glass.—Lvs. opposite or upper ones alternate: fls. in terminal racemes or solitary in the axils of lvs.; calyx 5-parted; corolla saccate or gibbous at base, not spurred, upper lip erect and 2-lobed, lower 3-lobed and spreading, throat almost closed by palate; stamens 4: caps. ovoid or globose, opening by pores below the summit. (Antirrhi-num: Greek for *like* and *nose*, referring to shape of fls.)

A. Plant erect: lvs. lanceolate....................1. *A. majus*
AA. Plant procumbent: lvs. ovate....................2. *A. Asarina*

1. **A. majus,** L. COMMON OR LARGE SNAPDRAGON. Per. 1–3 ft. high but grown as ann., not downy except in fl.-cluster: lvs. lanceolate or oblong-lanceolate, to 3 in. long, entire: fls. to 1½ in. long, in elongated terminal spikes or racemes, in many colors from red and purple to white. Medit. region, escaped in Atlantic states.—Many named forms are in the trade.

2. **A. Asarina,** L. Procumbent sticky-pubescent per. with sts. to 2 ft. long: lvs. cordate-ovate, 1½–2 in. across, crenate-lobed, long-petioled: fls. solitary, white or pinkish, 1–1½ in. long. (Asarina: a folk name for Antirrhinum.) S. W. Eu.

21. **CYMBALARIA,** Hill. Nine Old World species of creeping per. herbs, a few grown as ground-cover in greenhouses and the open.—Often united with Linaria but differing in the axillary solitary fls. and the palmately-veined lvs. (Cymbala-ria: from the Greek for *cymbal*.)

A. Sts. and lvs. glabrous.
  B. Lvs. mostly alternate, prominently lobed....................1. *C. muralis*
  BB. Lvs. mostly opposite, shortly or indistinctly lobed....................2. *C. hepaticifolia*
AA. Sts. and lvs. hairy.
  B. Peduncles equalling or shorter than lvs.; spur ⅙–¼in. long....................3. *C. pallida*
  BB. Peduncles longer than lvs.; spur ⅛in. long....................4. *C. æquitriloba*

1. **C. muralis,** Gaertn., Mey. & Scherb. (*Antirrhinum Cymbalaria*, L. *Linaria Cymbalaria*, Mill. *C. Cymbalaria*, Wettst.). KENILWORTH-IVY. Glabrous: sts. trailing and rooting at nodes: lvs. mostly alternate, cordate-orbicular or reniform, irregularly 3–7-lobed, on petioles usually longer than blades: fls. about ⅓in. long, lilac-blue with yellowish throat: caps. longer than linear-lanceolate sepals. Eu.; nat. Ont. to Pa.—Runs into color variants.

2. **C. hepaticifolia,** Wettst. (*Antirrhinum hepaticifolium*, Poir. *Linaria hepaticæfolia*, Steud.). Distinguished from *C. muralis* by the lvs. being mostly opposite and with 3–5 short or indistinct lobes, larger fls. and caps. shorter than linear sepals. Corsica.

3. **C. pallida,** Wettst. (*Antirrhinum pallidum,* Ten.). Sts. trailing or at first erect to 4 in.: lvs. opposite, entire or shallowly 3–5-lobed, short-hairy beneath and on petioles: fls. blue-violet with yellow palate, ½in. long, on peduncles about length of lvs.: caps. equalling or shorter than sepals. Italy.—Material in cult. as *C. pilosa* usually belongs here; *C. pilosa,* Bailey (*Antirrhinum pilosum,* Jacq.), differs in being more hairy, lvs. 5–11-lobed, fls. smaller with shorter spur.

4. **C. æquitriloba,** Cheval. (*Antirrhinum æquitrilobum,* Viv. *Linaria æquitriloba,* Spreng.). Differs from *C. pallida* in peduncles longer than lvs., pale mauve fls. with shorter spur, and caps. longer than sepals. S. Eu.

22. **LINARIA,** Mill. Toadflax. Mostly ann. or per. herbs suitable for the fl.-garden; over 150 species widely distributed in temp. parts of the northern hemisphere.—Lvs. opposite or verticillate or the upper ones alternate, pinnate-veined, entire, dentate or lobed: fls. in terminal racemes or spikes, of many colors; calyx 5-parted; corolla with long tube, long-spurred at base, the palate often nearly closing the throat; stamens 4, filaments and style filiform: caps. dehiscent by 1 or more mostly 3-toothed pores or slits below the summit. (Lina-ria: Latin *linum,* flax, which the lvs. of some species resemble.)

A. Fls. yellow.
  B. Lvs. linear .... 1. *L. vulgaris*
  BB. Lvs. lanceolate to ovate.
    C. Length of fls. ½–¾in. .... 2. *L. genistifolia*
    CC. Length of fls. 1–2 in. .... 3. *L. dalmatica*
AA. Fls. not yellow.
  B. Plant a tufted per. to 6 in. high .... 4. *L. alpina*
  BB. Plant an ann. 1–1½ ft. high.
    C. Spur slightly shorter than remainder of corolla .... 5. *L. bipartita*
    CC. Spur half as long again as corolla .... 6. *L. maroccana*

1. **L. vulgaris,** Mill. Butter-and-Eggs. Per. to 3 ft., slightly glaucous: lvs. linear, to 1½ in. long, sessile, entire: fls. light yellow with orange-bearded palate, 1¼ in. long, spur about length of corolla, pedicels longer than calyx. Eu., Asia; nat. in N. Amer.

2. **L. genistifolia,** Mill. (*Antirrhinum genistifolium,* L.). Per. 1–4 ft. high, glabrous: lvs. lanceolate, to 1½ in. long, sessile, entire, glaucous: fls. yellow with orange palate, ½–¾in. long, spur about length of corolla, pedicels longer than calyx. Eu.

3. **L. dalmatica,** Mill. (*Antirrhinum dalmaticum,* L.). Robust branching per. to 4 ft., grayish-green and glabrous: lvs. ovate-lanceolate, nearly sessile, entire, somewhat cordate at base: fls. bright yellow with orange-bearded palate, 1–2 in. long, spur about length of corolla. S. E. Eu. Var. **grandiflora,** Boiss., has large very short-pedicelled fls. Var. **macedonica,** Fenzl (*L. macedonica,* Griseb.), differs in the smaller longer-pedicelled fls. and sepals shorter than corolla-tube; Macedonia.

4. **L. alpina,** Mill. Tufted per. with procumbent or ascending sts. to 6 in. high, glabrous, glaucous: lvs. linear or lanceolate, sessile, entire: fls. blue or violet with orange palate, ½–¾in. long, spur as long as corolla, pedicels slightly longer than calyx. Mts. of Eu.

5. **L. bipartita,** Willd. Ann., about 1 ft. high, glabrous, glaucous: lvs. linear, 1–2 in. long: fls. violet-purple, ¾in. long, in lax racemes, palate orange-colored, whitish at base, upper lip deeply 2-parted, spur curved, not quite as long as corolla, standing oblique or horizontal, pedicels about three times longer than calyx. Portugal, N. Afr.—Vars. with white and deep purple fls. are cult.

6. **L. maroccana,** Hook. f. Ann. to 1½ ft., glabrous below, viscid-pubescent above: lvs. to 1½ in. long, narrowly linear: racemes many-fld., elongating in fr.; corolla bright violet-purple with small yellow patch on center of palate, spur often half as long again as fl. or pedicel, pointed, nearly parallel to axis of raceme, pedicels longer than calyx. Morocco.

23. **CHÆNORRHINUM,** Lange. Ann. or per. herbs of about 20 species in the Medit. region and Asia, one grown in the rock-garden.—Plants glandular-pubescent: lvs. opposite or the upper alternate, entire: fls. solitary in axils of upper lvs. but forming racemes; calyx 5-parted; corolla 2-lipped, spurred at base, throat with palate but not closed; stamens 4: caps. dehiscing by narrow distal openings. (Chænorrhi-num: Greek for *gaping* and *nose.*)

C. origanifolium, Willk. & Lange (*Linaria origanifolia,* DC. *C. glareosum,* Lange). Per. to 10 in.: lvs. oblong to obovate, ¼–½in. long, short-petioled: fls. pale purple with yellow palate, sometimes white, ½in. long, spur shorter than corolla. S. Eu.

24. **ZALUZIANSKYA,** F. W. Schmidt (*Nycterinia,* Don). Night-Phlox. Nearly 40 species of herbs or subshrubs native in S. Afr., a few sometimes grown in the fl.-

garden.—Lower lvs. opposite, upper alternate, few-toothed, the floral lvs. very small and entire: fls. sessile in terminal spikes, fragrant toward evening; calyx 2-lipped or 2-parted, 5-toothed; corolla with long tube and 5 spreading entire or bifid lobes; stamens 4 (rarely 2 by abortion), 2 inserted on corolla-tube and 2 on throat: caps. oblong, septicidally dehiscent. (Zaluzian-skya: after Adam Zaluziansky von Zaluzian, Polish physician in late 16th century.)

A. Lvs. linear or lower ones lanceolate: outside of corolla-tube short-pubescent..........1. *Z. capensis*
AA. Lvs. obovate or spatulate: outside of corolla-tube glabrous or nearly so..........2. *Z. villosa*

1. **Z. capensis,** Walp. (*Nycterinia capensis*, Benth.). Erect or ascending ann. to 1½ ft.: lvs. linear or lower lanceolate, ½–2 in. long, obtuse, entire or sparingly toothed: fls. 1–1¾ in. long, white inside, purple-black and short-pubescent outside.

2. **Z. villosa,** F. W. Schmidt (*Z. selaginoides*, Walp. *Nycterinia selaginoides*, Benth.). Pubescent ann. to 1 ft.: lvs. obovate or spatulate, ¼–1 in. long, obtuse, attenuate at base, nearly entire: fls. ½–1 in. long, white or lilac inside, purple and nearly glabrous outside; stamens 2.

25. **TORENIA,** L. Over 30 species of per. or ann. herbs from trop. Asia and Afr., mostly grown as garden annuals.—Plants glabrous, pubescent or hirsute, branching and somewhat decumbent: lvs. opposite, entire, crenate or serrate: fls. in short few-fld. racemes or axillary; calyx tubular, plicate or 3–5-winged; corolla-tube cylindrical or often broadened above, 2-lipped, the lower lip 3-lobed; stamens 4, perfect, in 2 pairs of unequal length: caps. oblong, septicidally dehiscent. (Tore-nia: Olaf Toren, Swedish clergyman, discovered *T. asiatica* in China, 1750–1752.)

T. Fournieri, Lind. Much-branched, to 1 ft., glabrous, sts. 4-angled: lvs. ovate or ovate-cordate, serrate, 1½–2 in. long; petiole more than half as long as blade: fls. in upper axils or forming terminal racemes, on stout pedicels; calyx rather inflated, broadly 5-winged, obscurely ciliate; corolla-tube pale violet, yellow on back; upper lip pale blue, obscurely 2-lobed, lower lip of 3 purplish-blue rounded lobes the central one with yellow blotch at base. (Named for Eug. Fournier, page 43.) Cochin-China.—There are white-fld. vars. and also forms of compact habit. Other species of Torenia occasionally met with in cult. are **T. asiatica,** L., with the corolla-tube dark purple and a pale purple limb with a dark blotch on 3 of the 4 lobes, and **T. flava,** Buch.-Ham. (*T. Baillonii*, Godefroy), with yellow tube red-purple above and yellow limb with purple eye.

26. **MIMULUS,** L. MONKEY-FLOWER. About 150 species of decumbent or erect herbs or sometimes shrubs, native in N. and S. Amer., Asia, Australia, S. Afr., particularly numerous in W. N. Amer., a few grown in the fl.-garden.—Plants glabrous or pilose, often viscid or glandular-pubescent: lvs. opposite, entire or dentate: fls. solitary, axillary or in terminal racemes, usually showy; calyx tubular, 5-angled, 5-toothed; corolla-tube cylindrical; upper lip 2-lobed, reflexed or erect; lower 3-lobed, spreading; stamens 4, inserted on corolla-tube; style filiform with 2-lobed sensitive stigma: caps. oblong or linear, loculicidally dehiscent. (Mim-ulus: Latin diminutive of *mimus*, mimic actor, referring to the grinning fls.)

A. Plant woody or shrubby.
  B. Calyx and upper part of st. white-woolly or villous..........1. *M. longiflorus*
  BB. Calyx and upper part of st. glabrous or only pubescent.
    C. Color of fls. yellow: lvs. densely pubescent beneath..........2. *M. aurantiacus*
    CC. Color of fls. red: lvs. sparsely pubescent beneath..........3. *M. puniceus*
AA. Plant herbaceous.
  B. Foliage viscid-pubescent.
    C. Fls. yellow..........4. *M. moschatus*
    CC. Fls. red.
      D. Stamens exserted; corolla strongly bilabiate..........5. *M. cardinalis*
      DD. Stamens included; corolla with nearly equal lobes..........6. *M. Lewisii*
  BB. Foliage not sticky.
    C. Corolla with open throat.
      D. Mature fls. yellow, often spotted with red or purple..........7. *M. luteus*
      DD. Mature fls. copper-colored..........8. *M. cupreus*
    CC. Corolla bilabiate, with throat closed or nearly so.
      D. Fls. yellow..........9. *M. guttatus*
      DD. Fls. blue..........10. *M. ringens*

1. **M. longiflorus,** Grant (*Diplacus longiflorus*, Nutt. *M. glutinosus* var. *brachypus*, Gray). Low shrub to 3 ft., much-branched, sts. glandular-pubescent: lvs. lanceolate, to 3 in. long, entire or denticulate, sessile, pubescent beneath: fls. cream-color to salmon-yellow, 2–3 in. long, lobes irregularly cut, short-pedicelled; calyx and pedicels villous, the calyx-throat much expanded; stamens included. S. Calif.

2. **M. aurantiacus,** Curt. (*M. glutinosus*, Wendl. *Diplacus glutinosus*, Nutt.). Shrub 2–6 ft. high: lvs. mostly narrow-oblong, to 2 in. long, entire or denticulate, sessile, the margins becoming revolute, densely pubescent beneath: fls. deep yellow, 1–1½ in. long, short-pedicelled, the spreading lobes toothed or notched; calyx glabrous or only slightly pubescent; stamens somewhat exserted. S. Ore. to S. Calif.

3. **M. puniceus,** Steud. (*M. glutinosus* var. *puniceus*, Gray. *Diplacus puniceus*, Nutt.). Very similar to the above but with narrower lvs. which are only sparsely pubescent beneath, and red fls. S. Calif.

4. **M. moschatus,** Dougl. MUSK-PLANT. Per. by spreading and creeping stolons, slimy viscid-villous, with a musky odor: lvs. oblong-ovate, to 1½ in. long, entire or denticulate, short-petioled: fls. pale yellow, lightly dotted with brown, about ⅔in. long, long-pedicelled: corolla-lobes nearly equal; stamens included, anthers pubescent. Rocky Mt. and Pacific Coast states.

5. **M. cardinalis,** Dougl. Per. with erect or weak sts. to 1 ft. long, villous and viscid: lvs. obovate, 1–4½ in. long, sharply toothed, sessile: fls. scarlet, rarely yellow, 1½–2 in. long, on elongated pedicels, the tube longer than the limb which is markedly bilabiate; stamens exserted, anthers bearded. Utah to Ore. and Lower Calif.

6. **M. Lewisii,** Pursh. Per. to 2½ ft., viscid-pubescent: lvs. oblong, 1–3 in. long, irregularly toothed, sessile: fls. rose-red or pink with lines in throat, varying to white, to 2 in. long, on long pedicels, corolla-lobes nearly equal; stamens included, anthers somewhat hairy. (Type collected by Meriwether Lewis on Lewis & Clark Expedition.) Alta. to Calif.

7. **M. luteus,** L. Glabrous per. with prostrate or decumbent sts. to 1 ft. long, rooting at nodes: lvs. broad-ovate, 1 in. long, sharply toothed, 5–7-nerved from base, lower short-petioled, upper sessile: fls. yellow, often with red or purple spots, in loose few-fld. racemes, long-pedicelled, 1–2 in. long. Chile.—There are several color forms, as var. **rivularis,** Lindl., in which one lobe has a large brown spot, and var. **Youngeanus,** Hook., each lobe with a spot, and var. **variegatus,** Hook., with pale yellow throat and the margins of the lobes pinkish-purple. Under the name **M. tigrinus** are offered the large-fld. bright colored crosses of *M. luteus* and its vars. and *M. guttatus*.

8. **M. cupreus,** D'Ombrain. Of more compact growth than *M. luteus*, the lvs. 3–5-nerved, the fls. becoming brilliant copper-color and with more expanded throat. Chile.

9. **M. guttatus,** DC. (*M. Langsdorfii*, Donn). Glabrous or pubescent ann. or per. to 1½ ft. high, sts. rooting at nodes: lvs. ovate to oblong-lanceolate, ½–6 in. long, irregularly toothed, lower long-petioled, upper sessile: fls. yellow, generally with purple or brown dots in throat, about 1 in. long, in many-fld. close racemes, pedicels usually shorter than fls.; corolla bilabiate, with closed throat; calyx much inflated in fr. Alaska to Mex.

10. **M. ringens,** L. ALLEGHENY MONKEY-FLOWER. Glabrous per. with 4-angled sts. to 4 ft. high: lvs. oblong, 1–4 in. long, toothed, usually sessile: fls. blue varying to pink or white, 1–1½ in. long, short-pedicelled; corolla bilabiate with throat nearly closed; stamens slightly exserted. Ont. to Fla. and Tex.

27. **MAZUS,** Lour. Low herbs, sometimes grown in rock-gardens or as ground-cover, of about 6 species in Asia, Australia and Malay Archipelago.—Lower lvs. opposite or radical, upper mostly alternate, toothed or incised: fls. blue or white, in terminal subsecund racemes; calyx campanulate, 5-lobed; corolla 2-lipped, the upper erect and 2-lobed, the lower much larger, spreading, 3-lobed, with 2 prominent ridges in throat, the tube short or exceeding the calyx; stamens 4, inserted on corolla-tube; style 2-lobed: caps. globose or compressed, loculicidally dehiscent. (Ma-zus: Greek for *teat*, referring to the ridges of corolla.)

A. Fls. blue, with large lower lip.
B. Sts. rooting at nodes.......................................1. *M. reptans*
BB. Sts. not rooting.......................................2. *M. japonicus*
AA. Fls. white, lower lip not large.......................................3. *M. Pumilio*

1. **M. reptans,** N. E. Br. Tufted per. 1–2 in. high, the sts. rooting at nodes: lvs. lanceolate to elliptic, to 1 in. long, with few coarse teeth: fls. ¾in. long, purplish-blue, large lower lip spotted with white, yellow and purple. Probably Himalayas.—Much of the material grown as *M. rugosus* belongs here.

2. **M. japonicus,** Kuntze (*M. rugosus*, Lour.). Low trailing per., the flowering sts. sometimes to 1 ft. high: lvs. obovate-spatulate, to 2½ in. long, coarsely crenate-dentate: fls. ½–¾in. long, blue, the ridges of the lower lip brown-spotted and bearded with club-shaped hairs. E. Asia.

3. **M. Pumilio,** R. Br. Per. with creeping underground sts.: lvs. obovate-spatulate, tufted, ¾–3 in. long, entire or coarsely toothed: fls. ¼–½in. long, white or bluish-white with yellow center. (Pumilio: a dwarf.) New Zeal., Australia.

28. **PHYGELIUS,** E. Mey. Two species of small shrubs from S. Afr., one grown in greenhouses or planted out-of-doors.—Lvs. glabrous, opposite or sometimes upper ones alternate, petioled, crenate: fls. in terminal panicles, scarlet, drooping; calyx 5-parted; corolla-tube elongated, curved or almost straight, with 5 nearly equal rounded lobes; stamens 4, exserted; style filiform, exserted: caps. septicidally dehiscent. (Phyge-lius: Greek *sun flight*, referring to its supposed shade-loving habit.)

P. capensis, E. Mey. CAPE-FUCHSIA. To about 3 ft., sts. 4-angled or narrowly winged: lvs. ovate or ovate-lanceolate, 1–5 in. long, bluntly small-toothed: fls. showy, 2 in. long, on ends of straight-spreading peduncles forming a loose infl., corolla-tube somewhat incurved, slender. Cape of Good Hope.—Not hardy N.

29. **RUSSELIA,** Jacq. CORAL-BLOW. Twenty species of shrubs in trop. Amer., grown in greenhouses and in the open far S.—Lvs. opposite or verticillate, often reduced to scales on the branches: fls. in bracteate dichotomous cymes, many-fld. or sometimes only 1, red; calyx deeply 5-cleft or 5-parted; corolla-tube cylindrical, somewhat 2-lipped, 5-cleft, the lobes rounded; stamens 4, included: caps. subglobose, septicidally dehiscent. (Russe-lia: Alexander Russell, English physician and traveller, died 1768.)

R. equisetiformis, Schlecht. & Cham. (*R. juncea*, Zucc.). CORAL-PLANT. FOUNTAIN-PLANT. Much-branched shrub 1–4 ft. high, glabrous, branches rush-like, nodding or pendulous at top, sts. striate: lvs. ovate or linear-lanceolate, mostly reduced to minute bracts on the branches: fls. about 1 in. long, peduncles elongated, 1–3-fld. Mex.; nat. in Fla. and W. Indies.—**R. sarmentosa,** Jacq., may be distinguished by its many-fld. short peduncles and the lvs. never reduced to scales. Reputed hybrids between *R. equisetiformis* and *R. sarmentosa* are known under the garden names of *R. Lemoinei* and *R. elegantissima;* these are more floriferous forms.

30. **DIASCIA,** Link & Otto. About 50 species of herbs from S. Afr., one grown in fl.-gardens.—Ann. or rarely per. tender herbs, diffuse or erect: lvs. usually opposite: fls. violet or rose, borne in axillary or fascicled racemes at ends of branches, racemes leafy or bracted; calyx 5-parted; corolla-tube almost none, limb flat or concave, 2-lipped, upper lip 2-lobed, lower 3-lobed, all lobes flat and broad, lower lip 2-spurred; stamens 4; style filiform: caps. subglobose or elongated, septicidally dehiscent; seeds numerous. (Dias-cia: from Greek for *two* and *pouch,* referring to the two-spurred corolla.)

D. Barberæ, Hook. f. TWINSPUR. Ann., erect, about 1 ft. high: lvs. ovate, to 1½ in. long, toothed, petioled or upper ones sessile: fls. in terminal racemes to 6 in. long, slender-pedicelled, rosy-pink with yellow spot on throat, ½in. across, lower lobe of corolla much larger than others, the spurs about as long as lower lobe; anthers yellow. (Bears the name of Mrs. Barber, who sent seeds from S. Afr.)

31. **ALONSOA,** Ruiz & Pav. MASK-FLOWER. Herbs or shrubs from trop. Amer., of 10 or more species, grown in fl.-gardens.—Glabrous except infl., sts. 4-sided: lvs. opposite or whorled in 3's, entire or serrate: fls. red, in terminal racemes; calyx 5-parted; corolla turned upside down by torsion of pedicel, bringing the lower lobe uppermost, flat-rotate, tube almost none; stamens 4, with short filaments: caps. ovate or oblong, obtuse, septicidally 2-valved; seeds numerous, small. (Alonso-a: for Alonso Zanoni, Spanish official at Bogota about 1798.)

A. Warscewiczii, Regel (*A. grandiflora*, Hort. *A. compacta*, Hort.). To 3 ft., very bushy, erect: lvs. ovate-lanceolate, somewhat cordate at base, simple- or double-toothed, bright green above, paler beneath: fls. cinnabar- or scarlet-red, in loose racemes at ends of branches; upper lip four to five times longer than calyx; anthers three to four times shorter than curved filaments; style (with stigma) about as long as filaments. (Named for J. von Warscewicz, page 291.) Peru.—Runs into cultivars. Probably *A. Mutisii* of the trade belongs here.

32. **ANGELONIA,** Humb. & Bonpl. About 25 species of herbs or subshrubs native in trop. Amer., especially Brazil, grown in greenhouses in the N. or out-of-doors in warm climates.—Lvs. opposite or upper ones alternate: fls. blue, solitary in the axils or in terminal racemes; calyx 5-parted or 5-toothed; corolla-tube almost

none, upper lip 2-lobed, lower 3-lobed; throat ventricose, with a 2-toothed protuberance at lower end; stamens 4, with short filaments: caps. globose or elliptical, 2-valved, loculicidally dehiscent, rarely indehiscent. (Angelo-nia: from *angelon*, Venezuelan name of one of the species.)

A. Plant sticky-pubescent........1. *A. salicariæfolia*
AA. Plant glabrous........2. *A. angustifolia*

1. **A. salicariæfolia,** Humb. & Bonpl. Sticky-pubescent per. to 2 ft.: lvs. lanceolate to linear-oblong, to 3 in. long, toothed, nearly sessile: fls. blue, ¾in. across, on slender pedicels in long leafy-bracted racemes, lower corolla-lobes oblong. N. S. Amer., W. Indies.—This is the *A. grandiflora* of gardens.

2. **A. angustifolia,** Benth. Differs from the above in being glabrous, lvs. narrower, and lower corolla-lobes obovate. W. Indies, Mex.

33. **NEMESIA,** Vent. Tender herbs or subshrubs of about 50 species from S. Afr., a few from trop. Afr., attractive for the fl.-garden.—Lvs. opposite: fls. variable in color, in terminal racemes or rarely solitary in the axils; calyx 5-parted; corolla-tube short with spur or sac in front; lower lip entire or emarginate with palate at base, upper 4-cleft; stamens 4, the 1-celled anthers often cohering about the stigma: caps. septicidally dehiscent, with boat-shaped valves. (Nemes-ia: old name used by Dioscorides for some sort of snapdragon.)

A. Fls. with sac or pouch at base........1. *N. strumosa*
AA. Fls. with spur at base........2. *N. versicolor*

1. **N. strumosa,** Benth. Ann. 1–2 ft. high: st.-lvs. lanceolate or linear, dentate, sessile, lower to 3 in. long: fls. ¾–1 in. across, in terminal racemes to 4 in. long, white or in shades of yellow and purple, often purple marked on the outside, the bearded throat spotted on a yellow ground, with pouch at base. S. Afr.—Runs into many vars., var. **Suttonii,** Hort., being a series of improved forms.

2. **N. versicolor,** E. Mey. Ann. to about 1 ft.: st.-lvs. few, oblong, lanceolate or linear, to 1½ in. long, entire or toothed, sessile: fls. about ½in. long, in terminal racemes to 3 in. long, variable in color, throat with 2 callosities, pubescent; spur incurved or nearly straight, about as long as lower lip. S. Afr.—There is a free-flowering compact race, var. **compacta,** Hort., 8 in. to 1 ft. high. Hybrids between the spurred and saccate forms occur in cult.

34. **COLLINSIA,** Nutt. Hardy ann. herbs, of more than 20 species, native mostly in W. N. Amer.—Lvs. opposite or verticillate in 3's: fls. in axils of lvs., solitary or in umbel-like clusters; calyx campanulate, 5-cleft; corolla with short tube, bilabiate, upper lip 2-lobed, recurved, lower lip 3-lobed, the side lobes drooping or spreading, inclosing the 4 stamens; fifth stamen reduced to a gland at base of corolla-tube; style filiform, capitate: caps. septicidally dehiscent; seeds few. (Collin-sia: after Zaccheus Collins, 1764–1831, Philadelphia botanist.)

A. Pedicels very short, almost none........1. *C. heterophylla*
AA. Pedicels about as long as fls........2. *C. grandiflora*

1. **C. heterophylla,** R. Grah. (*C. bicolor,* Benth.). From 1–2 ft. high, glabrous, hairy or viscid: lvs. oblong or lanceolate, to 2 in. long, dentate or entire, upper sessile: fls. in 2–7-fld. whorls, ½–¾in. long; pedicels shorter than calyx-lobes; lower lip of corolla violet or rose-purple, upper lip white; upper filaments with basal appendage, bearded half their length. Calif.—Several vars. are in cult. with variegated and white fls.

2. **C. grandiflora,** Dougl. BLUE-LIPS. To 15 in., glabrous or pubescent: lvs. oblong to linear, to 1¾ in. long, finely toothed or entire, sessile: fls. in 3–7-fld. whorls, ⅓–½in. long; pedicels about length of fls.; lower lip deep blue or violet, upper lip white to purple, reflexed; filaments not appendaged, slightly bearded at base. B. C. to Calif.

35. **PAULOWNIA,** Sieb. & Zucc. About 10 species of deciduous Chinese trees, one planted for ornament.—Lvs. opposite, entire or 3-lobed: fls. in terminal panicles; calyx deeply 5-cleft; corolla-tube elongated, enlarged above, lobes 5, spreading obliquely, somewhat unequal; stamens 4: caps. loculicidally dehiscent by 2 valves; seeds numerous, small, winged. (Paulow-nia: Anna Paulowna, 1795–1865, princess of the Netherlands.)—The genus has strong affinities with Bignoniaceæ.

P. tomentosa, Steud. (*P. imperialis,* Sieb. & Zucc.). Tree to 40 ft., with the habit of catalpa: lvs. broadly cordate-ovate, 5–10 in. or more long, entire or 3-lobed, acuminate, long-petioled, pubescent above, tomentose beneath: fls. 2 in. or more long, showy, pale violet darker spotted inside, fragrant, in many-fld. terminal panicles to 1 ft. long, appearing before the lvs.; pedicels and calyx densely rusty-tomentose; calyx-lobes short, rounded: caps. woody, ovoid, 1½–2 in. long, beaked. China; cult. in Japan; escaped in U. S. from S. N. Y. to Ga.—There are vars. with whitish fls. and with lvs. more densely yellow-tomentose beneath.

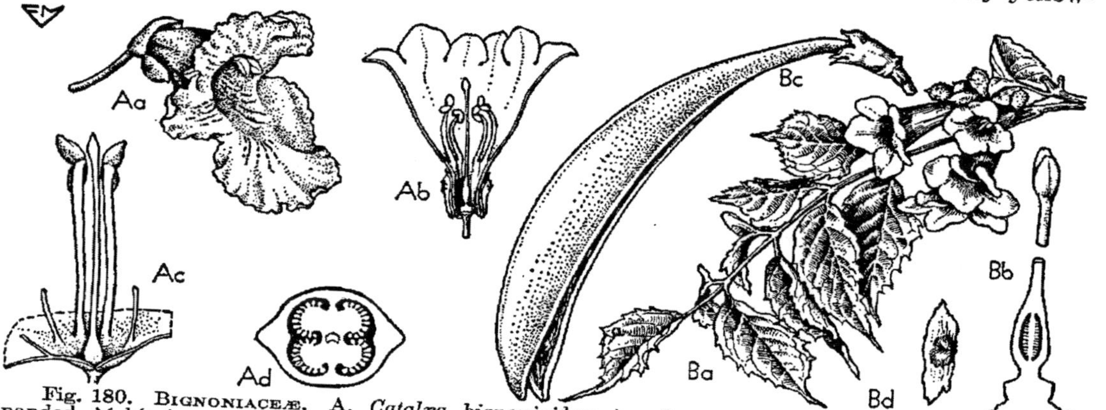

Fig. 180. BIGNONIACEÆ. A, *Catalpa bignonioides:* Aa, flower, × ½; Ab, flower, perianth expanded, × ¼; Ac, pistil with two stamens, × 1; Ad, ovary, cross-section, × 4. B, *Campsis radicans;* Ba, flowering branch, × ⅛; Bb, pistil with ovary in vertical section, × 1; Bc, capsule, × ⅓; Bd, seed, × ½.

180. BIGNONIACEÆ. BIGNONIA FAMILY

Trees, shrubs, and woody vines, or rarely herbs, of about 100 genera and 600 or more species distributed in trop. regions, a few extending into the temp. zone.—Lvs. opposite or rarely alternate, simple or compound, exstipulate: fls. bisexual, more or less irregular, mostly showy, in terminal or axillary panicles or racemes; calyx tubular, truncate or 5-toothed, sometimes spathe-like; corolla gamopetalous, campanulate, funnelform or tubular, 5-lobed, seldom somewhat 2-lipped; fertile stamens commonly 4, inserted on corolla-tube and alternate with its lobes, sometimes 2 or the fifth stamen anther-bearing; hypogynous disk present; ovary superior, 1- or 2-celled, with numerous ovules on parietal placentæ; style slender, with 2-lobed stigma: fr. a loculicidally or septifragally (valves breaking away from partition) dehiscent caps., rarely indehiscent; seeds compressed, usually winged.

A. Habit climbing.
  B. Ovary 2-celled.
    C. Climbing by tendrils.
      D. Plant with 3-parted tendrils.
        E. Caps. not prickly.
          F. Stamens included: corolla-lobes without white margins.
            G. Corolla to 2 in. long.
              H. Tendrils not claw-like but climbing by small disks .... 1. BIGNONIA
              HH. Tendrils claw-like or hooked .... 2. DOXANTHA
            GG. Corolla to 4 in. long .... 3. PHÆDRANTHUS
          FF. Stamens slightly exserted: corolla-lobes (in ours) with prominent white velutinous margins .... 4. PYROSTEGIA
        EE. Caps. densely covered with prickles: tendrils filiform .... 5. PITHECOCTENIUM
      DD. Plant with simple tendrils .... 6. CLYTOSTOMA
    CC. Climbing but not by tendrils.
      D. Stamens exserted .... 20. TECOMARIA
      DD. Stamens included.
        E. Fls. scarlet or orange: climbing by aërial rootlets .... 7. CAMPSIS
        EE. Fls. white or pink: climbing without rootlets.
          F. Fr. short-oblong: calyx not inflated .... 8. PANDOREA
          FF. Fr. long-linear: calyx inflated .... 9. PODRANEA
  BB. Ovary 1-celled .... 10. ECCREMOCARPUS
AA. Habit upright.
  B. Ovary 1-celled: fr. indehiscent.
    C. Lvs. simple .... 11. CRESCENTIA
    CC. Lvs. pinnate .... 12. KIGELIA
  BB. Ovary 2-celled: fr. dehiscent.
    C. Plant an herb: caps. opening only or more deeply along ventral suture .... 13. INCARVILLEA
    CC. Plant a shrub or tree: caps. separating into 2 valves.
      D. Lvs. simple or digitately compound.
        E. Fertile stamens 2
        EE. Fertile stamens 4 .... 14. CATALPA

F. Seeds not winged, long-hairy: lvs. simple . . . . 15. CHILOPSIS
FF. Seeds winged: lvs. (in ours) compound . . . . 16. TABEBUIA
DD. Lvs. pinnately compound.
E. Calyx spathe-like, splitting down one side . . . . 17. SPATHODEA
EE. Calyx campanulate.
F. Staminodia about as long as fertile stamens: fls. blue or violet . . . . . 18. JACARANDA
FF. Staminodia short: fls. yellow or scarlet.
G. Stamens included . . . . 19. STENOLOBIUM
GG. Stamens exserted . . . . 20. TECOMARIA

1. **BIGNONIA,** L. (*Doxantha*, Schum. not Miers. *Anisostichus*, Bur.). Woody tendril-climber, desirable because of the profusion and beauty of the fls., grown in the open in warmer parts of the country and also under glass; a single species native to S. E. U. S.—Vines with opposite 2-foliolate lvs., the terminal lft. reduced to a tendril: fls. large, in axillary cymes; calyx campanulate, the limb undulate, truncate or slightly 5-toothed; corolla-tube abruptly much-expanded above the calyx, the limb somewhat 2-lipped, with 5 rounded lobes; stamens 4, paired, included, inserted near base of corolla, the sterile rudiment of a fifth sometimes present: fr. a 2-celled septifragal caps. flattened parallel to the partition, the valves thickened; seeds winged. (Bigno-nia: the Abbé Jean Paul Bignon, 1662–1743, court librarian to Louis XIV.)

B. capreolata, L. (*B. crucigera*, L. in part. *Anisostichus capreolata*, Bur. *Doxantha capreolata*, Miers). TRUMPET-FLOWER. CROSS-VINE. QUARTER-VINE. Evergreen climber to 50 ft. or more, glabrous: lvs. petioled, ending in a branched tendril that clings by small disks, the 2 lfts. stalked, oblong or ovate, 2–6 in. long, entire, acute or acuminate: cymes many, 2–5-fld., short-peduncled; corolla yellow-red and lighter within, tubular, 2 in. long, with a stout limb: caps. very flat, 4–7 in. long; seeds broadly winged laterally, narrowly winged above and below. Va. to Fla. and La.

2. **DOXANTHA,** Miers (*Bignonia*, Auth. not L.). Shrubby climbers grown out-of-doors in the S. for their large showy fls., in greenhouses farther N.; 2 species from the W. Indies and Mex. to S. Brazil and Argentina.—Lvs. opposite, 2-foliolate, with a terminal 3-cleft claw-like tendril, or 3–1-foliolate; lfts. oblong, sometimes toothed: fls. conspicuous, solitary or in short panicles; calyx campanulate, truncate, with irregular or lobed border; corolla campanulate-funnelform, the limb with 5 often unequal lobes; stamens paired, included; ovary almost 4-angled, with numerous seeds in each cell: caps. elongate-linear, with leathery valves; seeds elliptic with membranaceous wings. (Doxan-tha: Greek *glory-flower* in allusion to its beauty.)

D. Unguis-cati, Rehd. (*D. Unguis*, Miers. *Bignonia Unguis-cati*, L. *B. Tweediana*, Lindl. *Batocydia Unguis*, Mart.). CATS-CLAW (in Latin *Unguis-cati*). Lvs. persistent, terminated by a 3-parted claw-like tendril; lfts. 1 pair, lanceolate and pointed, cordate, 3 in. or less long: fls. trumpet-shaped, 2 in. long, allamanda-like; corolla-tube clear bright yellow, the throat with orange lines; limb 2–4 in. across, the lobes spreading, the upper surface orange-yellow: fr. 1 ft. or more long and about ½in. wide. W. Indies to Argentina.—The plant grown under the name *Bignonia Chamberlaynii* belongs here. The true *Bignonia Chamberlaynii* of Sims is properly **Anemopægma Chamberlaynii,** Bur. & Schum. (*A. racemosum*, Mart.), and is not cult.; it has simple tendrils, oblong or ovate lfts. to 7 in. long, fls. to 3 in. long, and oval fr. to 6 in. long; Brazil.

3. **PHÆDRANTHUS,** Miers. One evergreen climbing shrub from Mex., grown in warm countries.—Lvs. compound, of 2 entire lfts. and a 3-parted filiform tendril: fls. in terminal racemes; calyx leathery and tomentose, campanulate, with 5 unequal short teeth; corolla tubular-funnelform, curved, the lobes imbricate in bud; stamens 4, included; disk fleshy; ovary tomentose, with many ovules in several rows. (Phæ-dran-thus: Greek for *gay* and *flower*.)

P. buccinatorius, Miers (*Pithecoctenium buccinatorium*, DC. *Bignonia Cherere*, Lindl. *B. buccinatoria*, Mairet). Branches 4-angled: lfts. elliptic to ovate-oblong, 2–4 in. long, cuspidate or obtuse, glabrous above, tomentose beneath when young, petioles pubescent: fls. blood- or purple-red, yellow at base, 4 in. long, pendulous, with spreading emarginate lobes. Mex.

4. **PYROSTEGIA,** Presl. Four species of evergreen climbing shrubs native in S. Amer., cult. in greenhouses and out-of-doors S.—Lvs. of 2–3 lfts. and filiform 3-parted tendrils: fls. in terminal panicles; calyx campanulate or tubular, truncate

or toothed; corolla tubular-funnelform, curved, the lobes valvate in bud; stamens exserted; disk annular; ovary linear, the many seeds arranged in 2 rows or zigzag: caps. long-linear, with leathery valves. (Pyroste-gia: Greek for *fire* and *roof*, referring to color of fls. and shape of upper lip.)

P. ignea, Presl (*Bignonia ignea*, Vell. *B. venusta*, Ker. *P. venusta*, Baill.). Branchlets striate or somewhat angled: lfts. ovate to ovate-oblong, 2–3 in. long, short or abruptly acuminate, broadly cuneate at base, petioles pubescent: fls. crimson-orange, 2–3 in. long, in many-fld. pendulous panicles; calyx glandular, ciliate; corolla-lobes oblong, obtuse, reflexed, with prominent white velutinous margins: fr. to 1 ft. long. Brazil.

5. **PITHECOCTENIUM,** Mart. Evergreen tendril-climbing shrubs, of about 20 species from Mex. to Argentina.—Lvs. opposite, 3-foliolate or the terminal lft. replaced by a filiform 3-parted tendril: fls. in terminal racemes or panicles; calyx leathery and tomentose, campanulate, truncate or with small teeth; corolla campanulate, curved, leathery, the lobes imbricate in bud; stamens included; disk large; ovary warty, with many ovules in several rows: caps. large and broad, densely covered with prickly warts, the persistent septum with enlarged margin. (Pithecocte-nium: Greek *monkey's comb*, referring to the spiny fr.)

P. cynanchoides, DC. (*P. clematideum*, Griseb.). Branchlets slightly hairy: lfts. ovate, 1–2 in. long, long-acuminate, subcordate and ciliate at base, glabrous above: fls. white, 1½–2 in. long, pubescent outside, in few-fld. racemes, with funnelform tube and spreading limb: fr. covered with yellowish spines, 2½ in. long. Argentina, Uruguay.

6. **CLYTOSTOMA,** Bur. Climbing evergreen shrubs, of about 8 species in S. Amer.—Lvs. of 2 entire lfts., the terminal lft. usually represented by a simple slender tendril: fls. in axillary or terminal panicles; calyx campanulate, with 5 subulate teeth; corolla funnelform-campanulate, the rounded lobes imbricated in the bud; stamens included; disk short; ovary warty, the many ovules in 2 rows: caps. broad and prickly. (Clytos-toma: Greek for *splendid* and *mouth*, alluding to the beautiful fls.)

C. callistegioides, Bur. (*Bignonia callistegioides*, Cham. *B. speciosa*, R. Grah.). Lfts. elliptic-oblong, 2–4 in. long, acuminate, glabrous and lustrous, undulate: fls. lavender, streaked, 3 in. long; calyx-lobes produced into long linear points; limb of corolla 2–3 in. across, the spreading lobes broadly oval and wavy: fr. 3–5 in. long, prickly, with many flat winged seeds. S. Brazil, Argentina.—The plant known to hort. as *Bignonia violacea* belongs to this species.

7. **CAMPSIS,** Lour. TRUMPET-CREEPER. Deciduous woody vines; 1 species in N. Amer. and 1 in China and Japan.—Climbing by aërial rootlets: lvs. opposite, odd-pinnate, the lfts. toothed: fls. large, orange or scarlet, in terminal clusters or panicles in summer or early autumn; calyx tubular-campanulate, leathery, unequally 5-toothed; corolla funnelform-campanulate, enlarged above the calyx, slightly 2-lipped, with 5 spreading lobes; stamens 4, 2 longer and 2 shorter; ovary 2-celled, surrounded at base by a large disk: fr. an elongated caps. loculicidally dehiscent, the 2 valves separating from the septum to which the seeds are attached; seeds numerous, compressed, with 2 large translucent wings. (Camp-sis: Greek *curve*, referring to the curved stamens.)

A. Lfts. 9–11, pubescent beneath at least along the midrib: calyx-teeth short . . . . . . 1. *C. radicans*
AA. Lfts. 7–9, glabrous beneath: calyx 5-lobed to the middle . . . . 2. *C. grandiflora*

1. **C. radicans,** Seem. (*Bignonia radicans*, L. *Tecoma radicans*, Juss.). TRUMPET-VINE. Climbing to 30 ft. or more: lfts. 9–11, oval to ovate-oblong, 1½–2½ in. long, acuminate, serrate, dark green above, pale and pubescent beneath (at least along the midrib): fls. usually orange with scarlet limb, about 3 in. long; corolla-tube almost three times as long as the short-toothed calyx: caps. cylindric-oblong, 3–5 in. long, keeled along the sutures, stalked, beaked at apex. Pa. to Fla. and Tex.

2. **C. grandiflora,** Loisel. (*Bignonia grandiflora*, Thunb. *B. chinensis*, Lam. *C. chinensis*, Voss. *Tecoma grandiflora*, Loisel. *T. chinensis*, Koch). CHINESE TRUMPET-CREEPER. Aërial rootlets few or none: lfts. usually 7–9, ovate to ovate-lanceolate, 1½–2½ in. long, serrate, glabrous beneath: fls. scarlet, the corolla shorter and broader than in the preceding species, about 2 in. across; calyx 5-lobed to the middle, one-half to about as long as the corolla-tube: caps. obtuse at apex. China, Japan.

8. **PANDOREA,** Spach. Seven species of ornamental woody vines from Australia to Malay Archipelago.—Climbing without tendrils or roots: lvs. persistent, opposite, odd-pinnate; lfts. entire or serrate: fls. white or pink, in terminal few- or many-fld. panicles; calyx small, campanulate, 5-toothed; corolla funnelform-campanulate, with imbricate lobes; stamens 4, didynamous, included; disk thick, ring-like; ovary ovoid, the seeds in many series: pod oblong, with woody valves which dehisce into 2 longitudinal segms.; seeds broadly elliptic, winged. (Pando-rea: Pandora, Greek mythological name.)

A. Panicles many-fld.; corolla ¾in. long .... 1. *P. pandorana*
AA. Panicles rather few-fld.; corolla 1½–2 in. long .... 2. *P. jasminoides*

1. **P. pandorana,** VanSteenis (*Bignonia pandorana*, Andr. *B. australis*, Ait. *Tecoma australis*, R. Br. *P. australis*, Spach). WONGA-WONGA VINE. High climbing: lfts. 3–9 or more, ovate to lanceolate, 1–3 in. long, acuminate but bluntly pointed, entire or sometimes coarsely crenate, glabrous, shining above: fls. ¾in. long, yellowish-white, the throat spotted violet, in many-fld. panicles; corolla-limb spreading, 5-lobed: fr. 1–3 in. long, pointed. Australia, Malaysia.

2. **P. jasminoides,** Schum. (*Tecoma jasminoides*, Lindl. *Bignonia jasminoides*, Hort.). BOWER-PLANT of Australia. Lfts. 5–9, almost sessile, ovate to lanceolate, 1–2 in. long, acuminate but bluntly pointed, entire, glabrous: fls. white, sometimes suffused with pink, usually rosy-pink in the throat, 1½–2 in. long, in few-fld. panicles; corolla-limb large and spreading, with crenate lobes: fr. 2–4 in. long, pointed. Australia.

9. **PODRANEA,** Sprague. Two African climbing shrubs, sometimes planted in warm regions.—Distinguished from Pandorea by the inflated calyx, oblong ovary and the long-linear caps. with flexible leathery entire valves. (Podra-nea: anagram of Pandorea.)

P. Ricasoliana, Sprague (*Tecoma Ricasoliana*, Tanfani. *T. Mackenii*, W. Wats. *Pandorea Ricasoliana*, Baill.). Lfts. 7–9, short-petioled, ovate, 1–2 in. long, acute or acuminate, serrate, glabrous, dark green above and pale beneath: fls. 2 in. long, light pink striped with red, in loose terminal panicles; corolla with spreading 5-lobed limb, glabrous: fr. linear, terete, 10–12 in. long. (Presumably named from the gardens of Baron Ricasoli, Italy.) S. Afr.

10. **ECCREMOCARPUS,** Ruiz & Pav. Tendril-climbers grown for their showy fls.; 3 or 4 species from Peru and Chile.—Tall-climbing shrubs grown as annuals in the N.: lvs. opposite, 2-parted or -pinnate, terminated by a branching tendril: fls. more or less irregular, yellow, scarlet, or orange, mostly racemose; calyx campanulate, 5-parted; corolla-tube elongate, the limb more or less 2-lipped or small and nearly entire; stamens 4, didynamous, included; disk annular: fr. an ovate or elliptic loculicidal 1-celled caps. (Eccremocar-pus: Greek *pendent fruit.*)

E. scaber, Ruiz & Pav. Per. about 10 ft. high, blooming from seed the first year, glabrous: lvs. bipinnate; lfts. ovate, ⅓–1¼ in. long, obliquely cordate, entire or serrate, obtuse or acute: fls. 1 in. long, orange, in racemes 4–6 in. long; corolla-tube narrow at base, the upper half gibbous and constricted just below the narrow limb which has 5 short rounded lobes: caps. 1½ in. long. Chile.

11. **CRESCENTIA,** L. About 5 species in trop. Amer., one yielding the calabash fr. which is used for water-gourds.—High or low trees, glabrous: lvs. alternate, solitary or clustered at the nodes, simple: fls. yellowish with red or purple veins, large; calyx 2-parted or deeply 5-cut; corolla tubular, with a fluted 5-cut limb; stamens 4, didynamous, usually included; disk annular; ovary 1-celled with many ovules: fr. a hard-rinded berry with many wingless seeds surrounded by a pulp. (Crescen-tia: after Pietro de Crescenzi, 1230–1321, Italian agricultural writer.)

C. Cujete, L. CALABASH-TREE. Tree 20–40 ft. high, readily distinguished by its peculiar habit of growth, as it bears large wide-spreading horizontal scarcely divided branches with clusters of lvs. at intervals: lvs. broadly oblanceolate, 4–6 in. long, tapering to base: fls. solitary, pendulous; calyx 2-parted; corolla yellowish-purple, about 2 in. long, constricted below the middle, swollen above, the lobes cut, malodorous when decaying: fr. frequently 18–20 in. through, smooth, nearly globular. (Cujete: Brazilian name.) Trop. Amer., especially familiar in the W. Indies.

12. **KIGELIA,** DC. African trees of 10 species, one planted in warm regions.—Lvs. odd-pinnate: fls. orange or red, in loose long-stalked drooping panicles; calyx

campanulate, leathery, irregularly lobed; corolla with cylindric tube and 2-lipped limb, the lower lip deflexed and 3-lobed; stamens 4, didynamous; disk annular; ovary 1-celled, with numerous ovules: fr. hard, cylindrical, indehiscent. (Kige-lia: from a native name.)

K. pinnata, DC. SAUSAGE-TREE. To 50 ft.: lvs. ternate, of 7–9 oblong or obovate lfts. 3–6 in. long, toothed or entire, glabrous or somewhat pubescent beneath: fls. claret-colored, 3 in. and more long: fr. somewhat gourd-like, 1–1½ ft. long, hanging on cord-like stalks to several ft. long.

13. **INCARVILLEA,** Juss. Herbs suitable for border planting; species about a dozen in Turkestan, Tibet, China.—Sts. simple or somewhat branched, glabrous: lvs. alternate, simple or 2–3-pinnate, with narrow segms.: fls. large, red or yellow, in terminal clusters; calyx campanulate, 5-lobed; corolla-tube elongate, enlarging outward, limb somewhat 2-lipped, the 5 lobes broad and spreading; stamens 4, didynamous, included; disk ring-like; ovary 2-celled: fr. a caps. with many winged seeds. (Incarvil-lea: after Incarville, 1706–1757, French Jesuit missionary to China, correspondent of Jussieu.)

A. Foliage cauline.
B. Lvs. 2–3-pinnate . . . . 1. *I. variabilis*
BB. Lvs. 1-pinnate . . . . 2. *I. Olgæ*
AA. Foliage basal.
B. Lfts. many, toothed . . . . 3. *I. Delavayi*
BB. Lfts. few, often entire, the terminal one much larger . . . . 4. *I. compacta*

1. **I. variabilis,** Batalin. Shrubby per. 1–2 ft. high, with leafy sts.: lvs. 2–4 in. long, 2–3-pinnate into small segms. which are entire or toothed: fls. rose-purple or pink, about 1½ in. long and 1 in. or more across, short-pedicelled, in loose racemes; calyx-lobes setiform, as long as tube: caps. 1 in. long. China.

2. **I. Olgæ,** Regel. Shrubby per. to 3 ft. or more high, with leafy sts.: lvs. 1-pinnate into linear-oblong lfts. which are entire or coarsely toothed toward apex: fls. rose-purple to pale pink, 1–1½ in. long and ½–1 in. across, pedicelled, in panicles; calyx shortly 5-toothed, the lobes broader than long: caps. linear. (Named for Olga Fedtschenko, page 43.) Cent. Asia.

3. **I. Delavayi,** Bur. & Franch. Per.: lvs. few, radical, 1 ft. long, pinnately compound; lfts. 15–20, dentate, 4–5 in. long, not quite opposite: peduncle 1–2 ft. high, bearing 2–12 large trumpet-shaped fls. 2–3 in. long and as wide: corolla rose-purple with yellow tube, the 2 upper lobes of the limb smaller than the 3 lower; calyx-lobes triangular, much shorter than tube: caps. 2–3 in. long. (Named for the Abbé Delavay, who collected in China.) China.

4. **I. compacta,** Maxim. Per.: lvs. radical, pinnate into decurrent entire or somewhat toothed lfts., the terminal one nearly orbicular and much larger than lateral lfts.: peduncle 1 ft. high, bearing 1 to many rose-purple fls. 2–3 in. long and 2 in. wide; calyx-lobes triangular, shorter than tube. China. Var. **grandiflora,** Wehrhahn (*I. grandiflora,* Bur. & Franch.), has solitary long-stalked fls. Var. **brevipes,** Wehrhahn (*I. grandiflora* var. *brevipes,* Sprague), has short-stalked brilliant crimson fls.

14. **CATALPA,** Scop. Trees, frequently planted for ornament and also in timber plantations; about 10 species in N. Amer. and E. Asia.—Deciduous or rarely evergreen: lvs. opposite or sometimes whorled, long-petioled, large and simple, entire or coarsely lobed, emitting in most species a disagreeable odor when bruised: fls. white, pinkish, or yellowish, in large showy terminal panicles; calyx splitting irregularly or 2-lipped; corolla campanulate, 2-lipped, with 2 smaller upper and 3 larger lower lobes; fertile stamens 2, curved, with diverging anther-sacs, not exserted; style 2-lobed at apex, slightly longer than the stamens: fr. a very long cylindric caps. separating into 2 valves, with numerous small oblong compressed seeds bearing a tuft of white hairs at each end. (Catal-pa: Indian name for *C. bignonioides.*)

A. Fls. yellow, inside striped orange and spotted dark violet, less than 1 in. long . . . . . 1. *C. ovata*
AA. Fls. white, with 2 yellow stripes inside, and spotted purplish-brown, 1½–2 in. long.
B. Lvs. pubescent beneath.
C. Apex of lvs. abruptly acuminate: panicles many-fld.
D. Diam. of fls. about 2 in. . . . . 2. *C. bignonioides*
DD. Diam. of fls. less than 2 in. . . . . 3. *C. hybrida*
CC. Apex of lvs. long-acuminate: panicles few-fld. . . . . 4. *C. speciosa*
BB. Lvs. glabrous beneath . . . . 5. *C. Bungei*

1. **C. ovata,** Don (*C. Kaempferi*, Sieb. *C. Henryi*, Dode). Tree to 20–30 ft., with spreading head: lvs. broadly cordate-ovate, 5–10 in. long, abruptly acuminate, often 3–5-lobed and each lobe slender-pointed, finely pubescent with simple hairs or at length nearly glabrous, with reddish spots in the axils of the veins beneath: panicles many-fld., 4–10 in. long, fragrant; fls. yellow, not 1 in. long, inside striped orange and spotted dark violet: pod 12 in. long, ⅓in. diam. China; much cult. in Japan.

2. **C. bignonioides,** Walt. (*C. Catalpa*, Karst. *C. syringæfolia*, Sims). COMMON CATALPA. INDIAN-BEAN. Tree 20–60 ft., with round spreading head: lvs. often whorled, broadly cordate-ovate, 5–8 in. long, abruptly acuminate, sometimes with 2 small lateral lobes, pubescent beneath, with an unpleasant odor: panicles broadly pyramidal, 8–10 in. long, many-fld.; fls. about 2 in. diam., white with 2 yellow stripes inside and thickly spotted purplish-brown: pod 6–15 in. long, ¼in. diam. Ga. to Fla. and Miss.; nat. farther north. Var. **nana,** Bur. (*C. Bungei*, Hort.), is dwarf, usually grafted on upright boles forming standards with dense umbrella-like heads.—Pods, seeds, and bark said to possess medicinal properties.

3. **C. hybrida,** Spaeth (*C. bignonioides* × *C. ovata*. *C. Teasii*, Penhall. *C. Teasiana*, Dode). HYBRID CATALPA. Large tree intermediate between the parents: lvs. resembling more those of *C. ovata* but much larger, pubescent beneath, purplish when unfolding: fls. resembling those of *C. bignonioides* but smaller and the infl. often twice as long. Originated at J. C. Teas nursery at Baysville, Ind.

4. **C. speciosa,** Warder. WESTERN CATALPA. To 100 ft.: lvs. inodorous, cordate-ovate, 6–12 in. long, long-acuminate, downy beneath: panicles comparatively few-fld., about 6 in. long and rather wider; fls. white, 2–2½ in. diam., inconspicuously spotted inside, the lobes spreading and frilled at the margin: pod 8–18 in. long, ½–¾in. thick. S. Ill. to Ark.

5. **C. Bungei,** Mey. Small pyramidal tree: lvs. triangular-ovate, 3–6 in. long, long-acuminate, sometimes toothed or angled near base, glabrous: fls. white, 1½ in. long, spotted with purple inside: caps. 10–14 in. long. (Named for Alexander von Bunge, page 40.) N. China.—The plant usually cult. under this name is *C. bignonioides* var. *nana*.

15. **CHILOPSIS,** Don. A single deciduous shrub or low tree native to S. W. U. S. and Mex., planted for its attractive bloom.—Lvs. narrow, often not opposite: corolla more trumpet-shaped than in Catalpa, the lobes jagged; anther-bearing stamens 4, a fifth rudimentary; ovary 2-celled: fr. cylindric, 2-valved, with many long-hairy seeds. (Chilop-sis: Greek *lip-like*.)

C. linearis, Sweet (*Bignonia linearis*, Cav. *C. saligna*, Don). DESERT-WILLOW. FLOWERING-WILLOW. Height 10–20 ft.; branches slender, leafy: lvs. narrow-lanceolate or linear, 6–12 in. long: fls. bignonia-like, in a short terminal raceme; corolla 1–2 in. long, 5-lobed and crimped, the tube and throat lilac, with 2 yellow stripes inside: pod 6–12 in. long and ¼in. thick. Dry districts from S. Tex. to Calif. and in Mex.

16. **TABEBUIA,** Gomez. About 100 species of evergreen trees or shrubs native in trop. Amer., planted in warm regions.—Lvs. opposite, simple or digitately compound: fls. showy, in terminal panicles or racemes; calyx tubular, irregularly lobed; corolla funnelform, with spreading irregular limb; stamens 4, didynamous, included: fr. a linear loculicidally dehiscent caps. with many winged seeds. (Tabebuia: Brazilian name.)

A. Fls. yellow . . . . 1. *T. argentea*
AA. Fls. white or pink . . . . 2. *T. pentaphylla*

1. **T. argentea,** Britt. (*Tecoma argentea*, Bur. & Schum.). Tree to 25 ft.: lvs. of 5–7 oblong lfts. 2–6 in. long, densely silvery-scaly on both sides: fls. yellow, 2½ in. long: caps. to 4 in. long, gray lined with black. Paraguay.

2. **T. pentaphylla,** Hemsl. (*Bignonia pentaphylla*, L. *Tecoma pentaphylla*, Juss. *Tabebuia pallida*, Miers). ROBLE BLANCO. Tree 20–60 ft. or more, somewhat scaly: lvs. of 3–5 long-petioled oblong or elliptic entire lfts. 3–6 in. long: fls. rose, pink or white, 2–4 in. long: caps. 8–10in. long and ¼–½in. thick. W. Indies, Mex. to Venezuela.

17. **SPATHODEA,** Beauv. Handsome evergreen trees with large showy fls., grown out-of-doors in trop. and subtrop. regions or rarely in greenhouses; 2 or 3 species native of trop. Afr.—Lvs. large, opposite, odd-pinnate or sometimes ternate, with entire lfts.: fls. orange-red or scarlet, in terminal panicles or racemes; calyx split on one side and recurved, exposing the corolla to base; corolla broadly campanulate and ventricose; stamens 4, exserted, with spreading pendulous anther-cells; disk large, cup-shaped; ovary oblong, 2-celled, the ovules in several rows: caps.

oblong-lanceolate, acuminate at both ends, loculicidal with woody valves; seeds elliptic, broadly winged. (Spatho-dea: Greek *spathe-like*, referring to the shape of the calyx.)

S. campanulata, Beauv. To 70 ft.: lvs. 1–1½ ft. long; lfts. 9–19, short-stalked, ovate-lanceolate or elliptic, 2–4 in. long, abruptly short-acuminate, with 2–3 fleshy glands at base, glabrous or somewhat pubescent beneath when young: fls. scarlet, about 4 in. long, in many-fld. racemes or panicles; calyx leathery, boat-shaped, 2½ in. long; corolla-lobes ovate, plicate, somewhat undulate: caps. flattened, 8 in. long, 2 in. through, glabrous. Trop. Afr.—A showy tree in the American tropics (where it is sometimes called "Santo Domingo Mahogany"), and somewhat planted within our limits.

18. **JACARANDA,** Juss. Trees and shrubs grown out-of-doors far S. and also under glass for the attractive finely cut foliage and showy tubular fls.; species about 50 in the American tropics.—Lvs. opposite, 2- or rarely 1-pinnate; lfts. usually numerous, small, entire or dentate: fls. blue or violet, mostly in terminal or axillary panicles; calyx small, truncate or 5-toothed; corolla-tube straight or curved, the limb somewhat 2-lipped, with 5 rounded spreading nearly equal lobes; disk thick and cushion-like; perfect stamens 4, didynamous, staminode about as long as the stamens, club-shaped and often bearded at the top; ovary 2-celled: fr. an oblong, ovate or broad dehiscent caps. with many winged seeds. (Jacaran-da: Brazilian name.)

A. Lvs. pubescent: fls. 2 in. long........................1. *J. acutifolia*
AA. Lvs. glabrous: fls. 1½ in. long........................2. *J. cuspidifolia*

1. **J. acutifolia,** Humb. & Bonpl. (*J. ovalifolia,* R. Br. *J. mimosifolia,* D. Don). Tree 50 ft. or more high, deciduous only in early spring, with foliage finely cut and fern-like: lvs. distant, each with 16 or more pairs of pinnæ, each pinna having 14–24 pairs of oblong cuspidate pubescent pinnules, the terminal one long-acuminate: fls. blue, more or less horizontal, 2 in. long, 1½ in. wide, many, in loose pyramidal panicles 8 in. high; corolla-tube long, bent, swollen above, the 2 lobes of one lip smaller than the 3 other lobes: caps. orbicular, 2 in. across. Brazil.

2. **J. cuspidifolia,** Mart. Lvs. glabrous, with 8–10 pairs of lfts., these again divided into 10–15 lanceolate cuspidate pinnules, the secondary rachis winged: fls. in a large terminal thyrse, blue-violet, the corolla nearly 1½ in. long. Brazil, Argentina.

19. **STENOLOBIUM,** D. Don. A few species of erect shrubs native Fla. to Mex. and S. Amer., one commonly planted in the S.—Lvs. odd-pinnate or simple, the lfts. toothed: fls. showy, in terminal racemes or panicles; calyx campanulate, 5-lobed; corolla funnelform or campanulate, tube contracted at base and hairy inside toward bottom; stamens 4, didynamous, included; ovary 2-celled with many ovules: fr. a linear caps. with thin-winged seeds. (Stenolo-bium: Greek for *small fruit.*)

A. Fls. pure yellow, funnelform-campanulate, abruptly contracted toward base: lfts. 5–13, acuminate........................1. *S. stans*
AA. Fls. yellow and red, tubular-funnelform, gradually narrowed toward base: lfts. 11–17, obtuse or acutish........................2. *S. alatum*

1. **S. stans,** Seem. (*Bignonia stans,* L. *Tecoma stans,* HBK.). Yellow-Bells. Shrub or small tree to 20 ft.: foliage glabrous or minutely pubescent; lvs. 4–8 in. long; lfts. 5–13, oblong-ovate to lanceolate, 1½–4 in. long, acuminate, sharply serrate, sessile or nearly so· fls. bright yellow, 1½–2 in. long, abruptly contracted toward base, the limb with undulate lobes; anthers pubescent: caps. 5–8 in. long and ¼in. wide. S. Fla. to W. Indies and S. Amer.

2. **S. alatum,** Sprague (*Tecoma alata,* DC. *T. Smithii,* W. Wats.). Shrub or small tree: lfts. 11–17, oblong, 1–2 in. long, obtuse or acutish, serrate: fls. in large compound panicles sometimes 8 in. long and as broad; corolla bright yellow tinged with orange, 1½–2 in. long, tubular-funnelform, with 5 reflexed rounded lobes. Peru.

20. **TECOMARIA,** Spach. Three species in Afr., grown out-of-doors in warm regions for their showy fls.—Half-climbing or nearly upright evergreen shrubs with slender often sarmentose branches: lvs. opposite, odd-pinnate; lfts. serrate: fls. yellow, orange or scarlet, in dense terminal panicles or racemes; calyx campanulate, regularly 5-toothed; corolla funnelform, slightly curved, 2-lipped; stamens exserted, with pendulous diverging cells; disk cupulate; ovules 4 rows in each cell: caps. linear, compressed. (Tecoma-ria: name derived from Tecoma, alluding to its affinity.)

T. capensis, Spach (*Bignonia capensis,* Thunb. *Tecoma capensis,* Lindl.). CAPE-HONEYSUCKLE. Half-climbing shrub with branches 6 ft. or more long: lvs. petioled, 4–6 in. long; lfts. 5–9, broadly oval to ovate, ½–2 in. long, acute or acuminate, serrate, glabrous or woolly underneath in the axils of the veins: fls. in peduncled terminal racemes; corolla orange-red to scarlet, about 2 in. long, with 4-parted spreading limb, the upper lip emarginate: caps. 1–2 and more in. long and about ⅓in. wide. S. Afr.

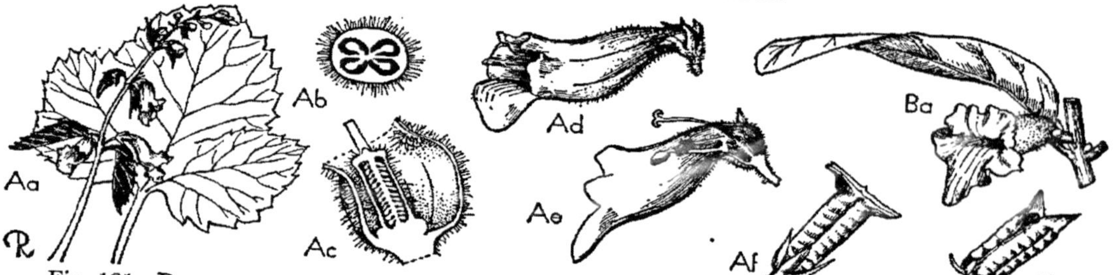

Fig. 181. PEDALIACEÆ. A, *Ceratotheca triloba:* Aa, inflorescence, × ⅛, and leaf, × ¼; Ab, ovary, cross-section, × 5; Ac, ovary and calyx, vertical section, × 2; Ad, flower, × ½; Ae, flower, vertical section, × ½; Af, capsule, × ½. B, *Sesamum indicum:* Ba, flower, × ½; Bb, capsule, × ½.

181. PEDALIACEÆ. PEDALIUM FAMILY

Herbs or rarely shrubs of trop. and subtrop. regions of Afr., Asia, Australia and E. Indies; genera 16 and species about 60.—Herbage covered with peculiar slime-secreting glands: lvs. opposite or the upper alternate: fls. bisexual, irregular; calyx 5-cleft; corolla gamopetalous, the tube more or less curved, the limb 5-lobed, markedly to indistinctly 2-lipped; stamens 4, didynamous, often with an entire staminode, subepipetalous; disk present, irregular; ovary superior or rarely inferior, 2–4-celled or falsely 1-celled: fr. a caps. or a hard indehiscent structure often covered with stiff hooked spines or wings.—Closely related to the Scrophulariaceæ and Martyniaceæ.

A. Caps. acuminate or obtuse at apex: fls. (ours) ¾–1½ in. long....................1. SESAMUM
AA. Caps. truncate at apex, the angles divaricately awned or horned: fls. (ours) 2½–3 in. long....................2. CERATOTHECA

1. **SESAMUM,** L. Erect or prostrate herbs, suitable for the warmhouse or in the S. growing in the open; about 20 species of trop. and S. Afr. and E. Asia, one cult. for its seeds, sold under the name "bene" and yielding an oil which has various commercial uses.—Herbage scabrous or rarely glabrous: lowest lvs. opposite, the others alternate to subopposite, all petioled and entire or toothed or incised: fls. pale or violet, solitary in the axils; corolla-limb 2-lipped and 5-lobed; stamens included; ovary 2-celled, the nearly complete invagination of ovary wall causing it to appear as if 4-celled: caps. oblong or ovoid, acuminate or obtuse at apex. (Sesamum: Greek name taken by Hippocrates from the Arabic.)

S. indicum, L. (*S. orientale,* L.). SESAME. Height 1–3 ft.: lvs. variable, ovate to lanceolate, 3–5 in. long, the lower often 3-lobed or -parted: corolla pale rose or white, 1 in. long, the 2 lobes of the upper lip shorter than the 3 lobes of the lower: caps. about 1 in. long and ⅓in. wide, grooved, with short beak. Tropics.

2. **CERATOTHECA,** Endl. A trop. and S. African genus of about 5 species, closely allied to Sesamum, grown as a garden ann. or as a conservatory plant.—Per. or ann. hairy herbs, often viscid: lvs. petioled, simple or 3-lobed: fls. pink to lavender, in pairs in the axils; corolla-tube about thrice as long as limb, the latter 2-lipped and 5-lobed; stamens included; ovary 4-celled: caps. oblong, truncate at apex with awns or horns extending outward divaricately. (Ceratothe-ca: Greek for *horned caps.*)

C. triloba, E. Mey. Ann. to 5 ft., densely soft-pubescent to tomentose: lower lvs. broadly ovate to suborbicular, upper lvs. 3-lobed, coarsely crenate-dentate, to 5 in. long: fls. to 3 in. long, rose-lavender to pale violet, pubescent, pendent and in pairs, the lower lip much prolonged: caps. about 1 in. long. S. Afr.—Plant becoming bushy, grown readily from seed and should be sown early.

182. MARTYNIACEÆ. MARTYNIA FAMILY

Glandular-hairy herbs inhabiting trop. and subtrop. Amer., one species reaching S. Ind.; about 5 genera and 16 species.—Ann. or per., with lvs. opposite or alternate: fls. bisexual, irregular; calyx 5-cleft; corolla gamopetalous, 5-lobed; stamens 4, didynamous, or rarely 2 and the others staminodial, inserted on the corolla and alternating with its lobes; disk present, regular; ovary superior, of 2 carpels but 1-celled, placentation parietal, ovules several: fr. a more or less long curved beaked caps. with fleshy pericarp, becoming falsely 4-celled.—Closely related to the Pedaliaceæ but distinguished by the horned fr., 1-celled ovary, parietal placentæ, and less slimy pubescence.

A. Calyx of more or less connate sepals: infl. open, of 4–8 fls.: fr. viscid-tomentose.....1. PROBOSCIDEA
AA. Calyx of 5 free sepals: infl. dense, of few to many fls.: fr. echinate.................2. IBICELLA

Fig. 182. MARTYNIACEÆ. *Proboscidea Jussieui:* a, flowering branch, × ½; b, flower, side view, × ½; c, same, vertical section, × ½; d, anthers, face view, × 1½; e, ovary, cross-section, × 6; f, fruit, × ¼.

1. **PROBOSCIDEA,** Keller. UNICORN-PLANT. Rank branchy plants sometimes grown for their odd showy fls., abundant foliage and peculiar pods; the young tender pods are used for pickles the same as cucumbers; 9 species, U. S. to S. Amer.—Coarse annuals or perennials, viscid-pubescent, mostly partially prostrate: lvs. large, hairy, long-petioled: fls. large, yellowish-purple, in axillary few-fld. racemes; calyx-lobes 5, more or less unequal; corolla campanulate to broad-funnelform, obscurely 2-lipped; stamens 4: fr. a curved beaked caps. becoming hard and woody, the beak splitting and forming 2 large opposed hook-like appendages when dry; seeds irregularly angled or flattened. (Proboscid-ea: Greek *snout,* in allusion to the long-horned fr.)

P. Jussieui, Keller (*Martynia louisiana,* Mill. *M. Probiscidea,* Glox. *P. louisiana,* Woot. & Standl.). COMMON UNICORN-PLANT. PROBOSCIS-FLOWER. Densely clammy-pubescent ann., low and wide-spreading, with thick opposite divaricate branches to 3 ft. long: lvs. alternate or subopposite, soft and thick, round-ovate to oblong-ovate, 4–12 in. across, cordate and often unequal at base, wavy-margined, obtuse: racemes becoming central in the forks; fls. square-ended in bud; calyx bracteolate, unequally 5-lobed, slit to base on lower side; corolla creamy-white to light red or violet, 2 in. long, the limb unequally 5-lobed; stamens 4, in 2 pairs joined by their 2-celled anthers: fr. hanging, the thick body 4 in. long, the curved beak of equal or greater length. (Bears the name of de Jussieu, a French family with two brothers, Antoine and Bernard, 18th century botanists.) Ind. to N. Mex.—The trade names under Proboscidea and Martynia usually refer to this species. **P. fragrans,** Dcne. (*M. fragrans,* Lindl.), differs in the mature lvs. being 5-lobed and fls. deep purplish.

2. **IBICELLA,** VanEseltine. Coarse viscid-pubescent ann. or per. herbs; 2 species in S. Amer.—Lvs. broad-ovate to suborbicular, entire, on rather stout semi-succulent sts.: fls. yellow, showy, in dense terminal infl.; calyx of 5 free sepals, the upper 3 linear-lanceolate to obovate, the lower 2 much broader; corolla obliquely campanulate, 5-lobed; fertile stamens 4 with staminodium usually present: fr. a long-beaked woody caps., the body cylindric-ovoid, echinate, slightly shorter than the slender horns. (Ibicel-la: Latin *little goat* or chamois, probably in allusion to horns of fr.)

I. lutea, VanEseltine (*Martynia lutea,* Lindl. *Proboscidea lutea,* Stapf). To 1½ ft., coarsely bushy: lvs. to 1 ft. across, on petioles 4–8 in. long: fls. about 1 in. long, bright yellow, sometimes dotted red within, in dense usually many-fld. racemes: fr. 6–8 in. long. Brazil to Argentina.

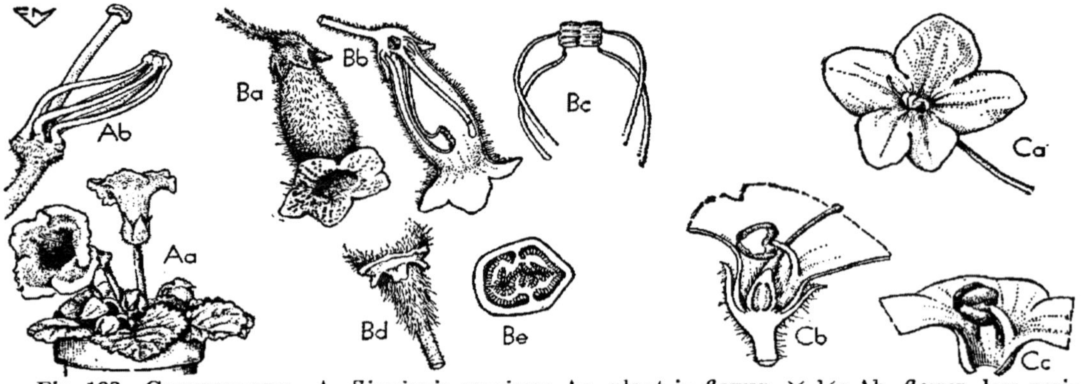

Fig. 183. GESNERIACEÆ. A, *Sinningia speciosa:* Aa, plant in flower, × 1/6; Ab, flower, less perianth, × 1/2. B, *Kohleria hirsuta:* Ba, flower, × 1/2; Bb, same, vertical section, × 1/2; Bc, stamens, × 1; Bd, glandular disk at top of ovary, × 1 1/2; Be, ovary, cross-section, × 3. C, *Saintpaulia ionantha:* Ca, flower, × 1/2; Cb, same, vertical section, corolla partially excised, × 1 1/2; Cc, stamens, × 1 1/2.

183. GESNERIACEÆ. GESNERIA FAMILY

Herbs or rarely shrubs or small trees, widely distributed in the tropics of both hemispheres; about 100 genera and 800 species, a number cult. in N. Amer. for their showy fls.—Herbaceous forms with sts. rhizomatous, tuberous, or prostrate, the woody forms erect or climbing: lvs. opposite or sometimes alternate or whorled, simple: fls. bisexual; calyx tubular, 5-toothed or -parted; corolla commonly 5-merous, the tube mostly elongate, the limb of usually unequal segms., often 2-lipped; stamens epipetalous, usually 4 and didynamous, rarely 5, or 2 and the sterile present as staminodes; hypogynous disk present; ovary superior or inferior, of 2 carpels, 1-celled or falsely 2–4-celled, placentation parietal, ovules numerous; style 1; stigmas 1–2: fr. fleshy with pulpy placentæ, or capsular or silique-like with twisted valves.

A. Perfect stamens 2.
  B. Corolla with tube much shorter than lobes.......... 1. SAINTPAULIA
  BB. Corolla with cylindrical tube much longer than lobes.......... 2. STREPTOCARPUS
AA. Perfect stamens 4–5.
  B. Plant stemless, the fls. on naked scapes.
    C. Corolla rotate, with very short tube.......... 3. RAMONDA
    CC. Corolla with long tube.
      D. Fls. about 1 in. long.......... 4. HABERLEA
      DD. Fls. 3 in. or more long.......... 10. SINNINGIA
  BB. Plant with evident sts.
    C. Foliage leathery and glabrous (in ours).......... 5. ÆSCHYNANTHUS
    CC. Foliage soft and hairy.
      D. Anther-cells distinct.
        E. Disk of 5 distinct glands; ovary partly inferior.......... 6. KOHLERIA
        EE. Disk of 1 large posterior gland; ovary wholly superior.......... 7. EPISCIA
      DD. Anther-cells confluent.
        E. Fls. in a terminal leafless raceme.......... 8. SMITHIANTHA
        EE. Fls. solitary or clustered in axils.
          F. Corolla salverform; disk annular.......... 9. ACHIMENES
          FF. Corolla campanulate; disk of 5 glands.......... 10. SINNINGIA

1. SAINTPAULIA, Wendl. Four herbaceous species grown in the greenhouse, native in trop. Afr.—Mostly acaulescent hairy perennials with long-petioled fleshy lvs. in a basal cluster and violet fls. in a loose few-fld. rather long-peduncled cyme: fls. 5-merous, zygomorphic; calyx deeply 5-parted; corolla-tube short, the limb 2-lipped, spreading, with elliptic lobes; stamens 2, the large yellow orbicular anther-cells confluent at apex, not parallel; staminodes 2; disk annular; ovary hairy: caps. oblong, loculicidally 2-valved. (Saintpau-lia: from the discoverer of the plant, Baron Walter von Saint Paul-Illaire, 1860–1910.)

A. Hairs of lf. of uniform length: caps. short, subglobose.......... 1. *S. ionantha*
AA. Hairs of lf. of two types, uniformly long ones intermixed with uniformly short dense ones: caps. cylindrical.......... 2. *S. diplotricha*

1. S. ionantha, Wendl. (*S. kewensis,* Clarke). AFRICAN-VIOLET. Lvs. many, basal, orbicular to oblong-ovate, 1 1/2–3 in. long, shallowly crenate to nearly entire, often purplish beneath, densely and uniformly pilose: peduncles 1–4 in. long, 1–6-fld.; corolla to 1 in. across, lobes somewhat unequal: caps. short and subglobose, nearly ⅓in. long. Coastal region, E. Afr.—Many fancy-named color forms of this and the following are cult.

2. **S. diplotricha,** B. L. Burtt (*S. kewensis,* Hort. not Clarke). USAMBARA-VIOLET. Differs in lvs. densely short-pilose with longer hairs intermixed throughout: caps. cylindrical, about ½in. long. Usambara Mts., E. Afr.—A closely related species also cult. is **S. tongwensis,** B. L. Burtt, with elliptic bluntly acutish lvs. and very hairy cylindrical frs.; N. E. Tanganyika, E. Afr.

2. **STREPTOCARPUS,** Lindl. CAPE-PRIMROSE. Choice greenhouse herbs, grown for the showy bloom; about 60 species, natives of S. Afr. and Madagascar and 1 in Asia.—Plant stemless, with 1 or more spreading radical lvs. or rarely with a st. and opposite lvs.: fls. pale purple or blue, 1 or 2 or several, sometimes cymose, on scape-like or axillary peduncles; calyx small, divided into 5 linear segms.; corolla with long cylindric tube and 2-lipped limb, the 5 lobes somewhat unlike, rounded; perfect stamens 2, inserted high on the corolla-tube, the anther-cells confluent at apex, not parallel; disk short-annular; ovary superior, imperfectly 4-celled: caps. linear, splitting into 2, rarely 4 valves. (Streptocar-pus: Greek *twisted fruit.*)

S. kewensis, Hort. (*S. Rexii* × *S. Dunnii*). Garden hybrid, acaulescent, with 2–3 large oblong or elongate-ovate bright green lvs.: fl.-sts. numerous, forming a rather compact mass, each stalk 6–8-fld.; corolla about 2 in. long, 1¼–1½ in. across, bright mauve-purple, the throat striped with dark brownish-purple. The parent species S. African.

3. **RAMONDA,** Rich. (usually, but not originally, spelled *Ramondia*). Four species of small herbs native in the mts. of S. Eu. and adapted to the rock-garden.—Foliage in a basal rosette, hairy: fls. in few-fld. clusters at top of leafless scape; calyx deeply 4–5-parted; corolla rotate, with very short tube, 4–5-parted into obtuse nearly equal lobes; stamens 4–5, with very short filaments; ovary superior, with filiform style: caps. septicidally dehiscent into 2 valves, much exceeding the calyx. (Ramon-da: L. F. E. von Ramond de Carbonnières, 1753–1827, French botanist.)

A. Fls. 4-parted..1. *R. Nathaliæ*
AA. Fls. 5-parted..2. *R. Myconi*

1. **R. Nathaliæ,** Panc. & Petrov. (*R. serbica* var. *Nathaliæ,* Hort.). Lvs. oval, densely rusty-hairy particularly beneath, wavy-toothed, the petiole about equalling blade: fls. 4-parted, lavender-blue with golden center, ¾in. across. (Named for Natalia Keijko, born 1859, daughter of a Russian officer.) Serbia, Bulgaria.

2. **R. Myconi,** F. Schultz (*Verbascum Myconi,* L. *R. pyrenaica,* Rich.). Lvs. ovate, 2–3 in. long, densely rusty-hairy, deeply toothed, the petiole short: fls. on scapes 3–6 in. high, 5-parted, purple or violet varying to white, with orange eye, 1–1½ in. across. Pyrenees.

4. **HABERLEA,** Friv. Small per. herbs of a few species in the Balkans, grown in rock-gardens.—Lvs. forming a basal rosette, hairy: fls. nodding, in few-fld. clusters terminating the leafless scape; calyx deeply 5-parted; corolla with long tube and irregularly 5-lobed limb; stamens 4; ovary superior: caps. septicidally dehiscent into 2 valves, scarcely exceeding the calyx. (Haber-lea: named for K. K. Haberle, 1764–1832, botanist at Pesth.)

A. Lvs. hairy on both sides..1. *H. rhodopensis*
AA. Lvs. glabrous above..2. *H. Ferdinandi-Coburgii*

1. **H. rhodopensis,** Friv. Lvs. obovate- or ovate-oblong, 2–3 in. long, obtuse, long-attenuate at base, coarsely wavy-toothed, thick, hairy on both sides: fls. on somewhat hairy scapes 3–6 in. high, pale lilac, about 1 in. long and broad. From the Rhodope Mts. in the Balkans.

2. **H. Ferdinandi-Coburgii,** Urum. Differs from *H. rhodopensis* in lvs. glabrous above but hairy beneath, and the somewhat smaller fls. with shorter tube. (Named for Ferdinand of Saxe-Coburg, former king of Bulgaria.)

5. **ÆSCHYNANTHUS,** Jack (*Trichosporum,* D. Don, the older name but rejected by the International Rules). Woody plants often climbing on trees, cult. in the warmhouse for the attractive fls.; about 55 species, India, Malaya, and E. trop. Asia.—Free-flowering shrubs or subshrubs, glabrous or villous: lvs. opposite or occasionally in 3's or 4's, fleshy or leathery: fls. showy, solitary or clustered, axillary or at the tips of the shoots; calyx-tube long, the limb 5-toothed or -parted, usually

deciduous; corolla mostly with elongate somewhat curved tube and 2-lipped usually oblique limb; stamens 4, commonly exserted, the anther-cells parallel and distinct or nearly so; disk annular, often weakly 5-lobed; ovary superior, oblong or linear: caps. long-linear, 2-valved. (Æschynan-thus: Greek for *ashamed* and *flower*.)

A. Corolla glabrous, three times longer than calyx........................1. *Æ. pulchra*
AA. Corolla downy, not over twice as long as calyx........................2. *Æ. Lobbiana*

1. **Æ. pulchra,** Don (*T. pulchrum,* Blume). Plant trailing: lvs. short-petioled, broadly ovate, about 1 in. long, distantly small-toothed, fleshy, with sunken veins: fls. clustered, terminal, the fl.-stalk 2-fid., with 2 bracts; corolla glabrous, brilliant scarlet with yellow throat, 2½ in. long, three times longer than the glabrous greenish calyx, the tube with globose base and slightly curved, the limb scarcely 2-lipped; stamens about equalling the upper corolla-lip. Java.

2. **Æ. Lobbiana,** Hook. (*T. Lobbianum,* Kuntze). Differs from the preceding in having narrower nearly entire lvs.; corolla downy, twice or less as long as the purple downy calyx. (Named for Thos. Lobb, a collector of this species.) Java.

6. **KOHLERIA,** Regel (*Isoloma,* Decne.). Species perhaps 50, in trop. Amer., suitable for greenhouse cult.—Herbs with creeping roots or rhizome or sometimes more or less woody: lvs. opposite, often villous: fls. scarlet, orange, or vari-colored, solitary or clustered in the axils or in a leafy terminal raceme; calyx obtusely 5-lobed; corolla-tube cylindric, ventricose or enlarged above, erect or more or less declined or incurved; corolla-limb short, with 5 subequal lobes; disk of 5 distinct glands; stamens inserted near the base of the corolla-tube, the anthers with distinct cells: caps. inferior to above the middle. (Kohle-ria: for Michael Kohler, lecturer at Zurich, 1834–1872.)—Most of the forms in cult. are probably of hybrid origin, the two species here described most nearly representing them, although other species may be grown.

A. Calyx-segms. triangular; corolla more than three times as long as calyx..........1. *K. amabilis*
AA. Calyx-segms. linear-lanceolate; corolla three times as long as calyx..............2. *K. hirsuta*

1. **K. amabilis,** Fritsch (*I. amabile,* Mott. *Tydæa amabilis,* Planch. & Lind.). Hairy, 1–2 or more ft. high, with erect sts.: lvs. petioled, ovate, 2–5 in. long, bluntly dentate-serrate, acute or acuminate, dull green blotched and reticulated with purple along the main veins: fls. pendent, to 2 in. long; calyx green, the limb oblique, of 5 spreading triangular segms.; corolla-tube long, slightly curved, swollen, pale within and purple-blotched, the limb dark rose dotted with purple; fifth stamen rudimentary. Colombia.

2. **K. hirsuta,** Regel (*I. hirsutum,* Regel not Hort., which is probably a hybrid). Erect branching shrub, hairy, 4 ft. high: lvs. short-petioled, oblong-ovate, acuminate, rounded at base, crenate-serrate: fls. nodding, nearly 1 in. long, solitary, on axillary paired lf.-stalks; calyx 5-cleft into equal linear-lanceolate segms.; corolla three times as long as the calyx, the tube incurved, ventricose above, hairy outside, purple with spotted 5-cleft limb; stamens 4, inserted at the base of the corolla, included. Trinidad, Venezuela.

7. **EPISCIA,** Mart. Perhaps 30 species of trop. American plants, one much prized for hanging-baskets in the warmhouse.—Pubescent, villous or rarely glabrous herbs; sts. simple or branching, from a creeping root: lvs. opposite, of equal or unequal size: fls. scarlet or rarely whitish or purplish, solitary or fascicled, on axillary pedicels, or several on a common peduncle; calyx-limb 5-lobed or -parted; corolla-tube straight or curved, often spurred or swollen at base, the limb oblique or subequal, with 5 rounded lobes; stamens 4, distinct, inserted near the base of the corolla tube, the anther-cells distinct and parallel, a staminode representing the fifth stamen; disk with a large posterior gland, otherwise small or wanting; ovary superior: fr. dehiscing by 2 coriaceous valves. (Epis-cia: Greek *shady,* growing wild in shady places.)

E. cupreata, Hanst. (*Achimenes cupreata,* Hook.). Sts. slender, branched, rooting at the nodes, drooping, the main branch rising erect for a few in., and bearing the fls. and the largest lvs.: lvs. elliptic, oval or rotund-oval, about 2–3 in. long, blunt, crenate, rough-hairy, rugose above, often reddish-tinged or copper-colored: fls. scarlet, solitary, ¾in. wide, the tube with a small sac, the limb denticulate. Nicaragua.—Growing throughout the year. A var. has green foliage and fls. 1 in. across.

8. **SMITHIANTHA,** Kuntze (*Nægelia,* Regel). Herbs grown in the warmhouse for their showy panicled fls., in cult. often called Gesnerias; species about a half

dozen in trop. Amer.—Usually rhizomatous or propagating by stolons or offsets and not by tubers; sts. subsimple: lvs. opposite, long-petioled, often cordate, soft: fls. showy, mostly red, sometimes yellowish-white or suffused, alternate in a terminal leafless cluster, the pedicels subtended by small bracts; calyx-tube adnate to the ovary, the limb with 5 subequal lobes; corolla-tube declined, narrow at base, broadening outward, the short limb with 5 rounded slightly unequal lobes; stamens inserted at the base of the corolla-tube, included; disk annular, entire or 5-lobed; ovary half inferior: caps. equally or obliquely 2-valved. (Smithian-tha: named for Matilda Smith, 1854–1926, botanical artist at Kew.)

A. Fls. scarlet or brick-red with white or yellow markings
  B. Calyx-lobes spreading: fls. with white markings..........1. *S. cinnabarina*
  BB. Calyx-lobes appressed: fls. with yellow markings..........2. *S. zebrina*
AA. Fls. white or cream-color..........3. *S. multiflora*

1. **S. cinnabarina,** Kuntze (*N. cinnabarina*, Lind. *Gesneria cinnabarina*, Lind.). Winter-blooming, 1½–2 ft. high, soft-hairy: lvs. rotund-ovate, crenate-dentate, thickish, green, with red or purplish hairs: fls. about 1½ in. long, pendent from the ends of the spreading pedicels; calyx-lobes acuminate, spreading; corolla cinnabar-red or nearly scarlet on the upper side, paler and spotted beneath, the tube gibbous to the narrow base. Mex.

2. **S. zebrina,** Kuntze (*N. zebrina*, Regel. *Gesneria zebrina*, Paxt.). To 2 ft. high, densely pubescent, much resembling the preceding: lvs. ovate-subrotund, cordate or reniform, dark purple-red or dark brownish along the nerves on the upper surface: fls. red on the upper side, yellow with dark or red dots within and on the under side; calyx-lobes short and appressed; corolla 1½ in. long, contracted toward base. Brazil.—The commonest species. Names belonging here are *Gesneria regalis* and *G. splendens*.

3. **S. multiflora,** Fritsch (*Gloxinia multiflora*, Mart. & Galeotti. *N. multiflora*, Hook. *N. amabilis*, Decne. *S. amabilis*, Kuntze. *Gesneria amabilis*, Hort.). Erect, 1–1½ ft. high: lower lvs. broadly heart-shaped, petioled, crenate; st.-lvs. ovate-cordate, coarsely toothed, lightly hairy and glandular: fls. white or cream-color, pendulous, the corolla-tube curved and little swollen. Mex.—Much like *S. zebrina*.

9. **ACHIMENES,** P. Br. About 40 herbaceous species, native to trop. Amer., grown under glass.—Simple or branching, mostly villous, with scaly underground rhizomes: lvs. opposite or occasionally whorled, serrate or toothed, sometimes with scaly catkin-like vegetative growths in the axils: fls. solitary or fascicled in the axils; calyx-tube adnate to the ovary, the 5 lobes mostly small, subequal; corolla ranging from red to violet, seldom white, with cylindric declined tube and spreading 5-lobed limb; stamens 4, inserted at the lower part of the corolla-tube, included, the anthers connivent, a staminode representing the fifth stamen; disk annular, sometimes 5-angled or -lobed; ovary inferior; stigma dilated or 2-lobed: caps. 2-valved. (Achimenes: Greek to *suffer from cold*.)—The garden kinds are much confused by hybridization and it is doubtful whether any of the pure species are in general cult. in this country. The species here described are some of those that have contributed most largely to garden forms.

A. Limb of corolla spreading, throat narrow.
  B. Fls. solitary in the axils; corolla-tube not swollen or spurred at base..........1. *A. longiflora*
  BB. Fls. usually more than 1 in the axils; corolla-tube swollen or spurred at base...2. *A. grandiflora*
AA. Limb of corolla recurved, throat wide open..........3. *A. magnifica*

1. **A. longiflora,** DC. With root-like filiform rhizomes, producing pear-shaped tubers at their ends; sts. 1–2 ft. high, hairy: lvs. opposite or 3–4 in a whorl, oval or ovate-oblong, 1½–3 in. long, serrate, narrowed at base, acute or short-acuminate, hairy, pale or somewhat tinted beneath: fls. solitary in the axils; corolla salver-shaped, with long cylindric tube and large widely spreading limb violet-blue above and whitish beneath, the lowest segm. sometimes divided. Guatemala.—A var. has white fls.

2. **A. grandiflora,** DC. Stiffly hairy: lvs. ovate, pointed, unequal at base, irregularly toothed, often reddish beneath: fls. large, numerous, often more than 1 in the axils, bright red-purple; corolla-tube swollen or spurred at base. Mex.

3. **A. magnifica,** Voss. Lvs. oblong, pointed, toothed, soft-hairy on both sides, reddish on veins beneath: fls. solitary, 2 in. across, dark scarlet-red marked with dark purple; corolla with recurved limb and wide open throat. Colombia.

10. **SINNINGIA,** Nees. Trop. herbs suitable for glasshouse cult., including the florists' gloxinia; species 20–25, Brazil.—Low herbs or sometimes almost woody,

pubescent or villous, with simple or branching sts. from a tuberous rhizome, or sometimes almost stemless: lvs. opposite, usually large, long-petioled, the upper floral ones reduced to bracts: fls. mostly large, solitary or fascicled in the axils, on short or long pedicels; calyx-tube shortly and broadly turbinate, 5-angled or 5-winged, the limb 5-cleft or -parted; corolla-tube subequal at base, gibbous posteriorly, elongate, broadly cylindric, or widened above or campanulate; corolla-limb with 5 broad subequal lobes; stamens inserted at the base of the corolla, included, the anther-cells confluent at apex; glands of the disk 5, distinct or the 2 posterior more crowded together or connate; ovary half inferior: caps. 2-valved above. (Sinnin-gia: for Wilhelm Sinning, gardener at the University of Bonn.)

S. speciosa, Benth. & Hook. (*Gloxinia speciosa*, Lodd.). Gloxinia. Sts. short or not evident: lvs. petiolate, oblong or oblong-ovate, 6 in. or more long, crenate, obtuse or acutish, villous-hairy: peduncles with fls. about the length of the lvs.; fls. 3 in. or more long, showy, usually violet or purplish; calyx-lobes ovate-lanceolate, longer than the tube, somewhat villous; corolla broadly campanulate, the limb with 5 short rounded lobes.—This is the cult. gloxinia, other species being little known horticulturally. Variable, giving rise to forms with thick elongated sts. and larger lvs., or with white-nerved lvs. or with white or red fls.

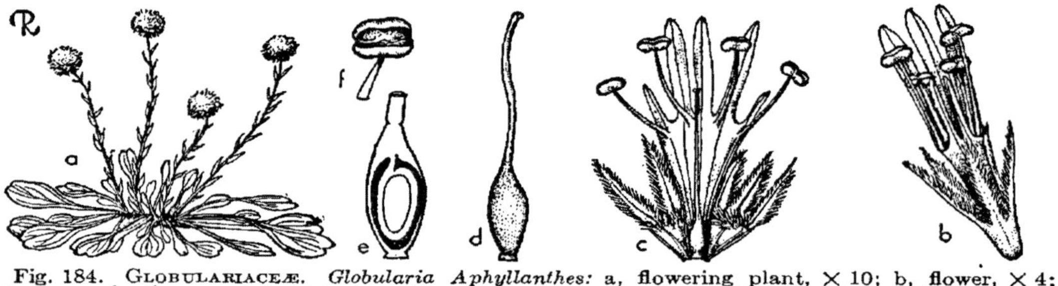

Fig. 184. Globulariaceæ. *Globularia Aphyllanthes:* a, flowering plant, × 10; b, flower, × 4; c, flower, perianth expanded, × 4; d, pistil, × 6; e, ovary, vertical section, × 10; f, anther, × 10.

184. GLOBULARIACEÆ. GLOBULARIA FAMILY

About two dozen herbs and shrubs in 3 genera, from the Cape Verde Isls. to Socotra, known chiefly in the Medit. region, yielding plants for ornament.—The shrubs are usually heath-like, the herbs low and mostly cespitose or repent: fls. small, in Globularia in dense globular bracted or involucrate heads; corolla 2-lipped, the upper lip short and 2-lobed, the lower 3-lobed; calyx 5-toothed or -lobed; stamens 2 or 4, attached in the tube, exserted; ovary 1, superior, 2-celled or 1-celled by abortion, with a single terminal style, and 1 hanging ovule in each cell: fr. a little indehiscent nutlet included in the calyx.

GLOBULARIA, L. Globe-Daisy. About 22 herbs or little subshrubs in S. Eu. and S. W. Asia, mostly in mountainous regions, with characters of the family; adapted to rock-gardens, fls. usually blue. (Globula-ria: fls. in globular heads.)

A. Plant not stoloniferous.
B. Scapes with conspicuous leafy bracts.
C. Lvs. obtuse: bracts short-pointed .... 1. *G. Aphyllanthes*
CC. Lvs. acute: bracts long-aristate .... 2. *G. vulgaris*
BB. Scapes with inconspicuous or no bracts .... 3. *G. nudicaulis*
AA. Plant producing stolons.
B. Scape with leafy bracts .... 4. *G. trichosantha*
BB. Scape with very small or no bracts.
C. Lvs. obovate to nearly orbicular, retuse .... 5. *G. cordifolia*
CC. Lvs. lanceolate to obovate-lanceolate, short-acuminate, rarely retuse.
D. Heads long-peduncled: lvs. 1–4 in. long .... 6. *G. meridionalis*
DD. Heads nearly sessile: lvs. to ¾ in. long .... 7. *G. repens*

1. **G. Aphyllanthes**, Crantz (*G. vulgaris*, Lam. *G. Willkommii*, Nym.). Lvs. in a rosette, spatulate to ovate, 2–5 in. and more long, long-petioled, obtuse, entire or emarginate, sometimes 3-toothed at apex but middle tooth much shorter than side teeth: heads on scapes 10–12 in. high, with leafy short-pointed bracts. (Aphyllanthes: st. with few small upper lvs.) S. Eu.

2. **G. vulgaris,** L. Probably not in cult., the plant grown under this name being *G. Aphyllanthes:* differs from that species in more woody base, acute lvs. with sharp teeth of equal size, long-aristate bracts and involucral lvs., and shorter calyx-lobes. S. E. Eu.

3. **G. nudicaulis,** L. Lvs. in a rosette, oblong, to 8 in. long, long-attenuate into petiole, obtuse or somewhat acute: heads ¾–1 in. across, on scapes longer than the lvs. which are naked or with 1 or 2 very small bracts. S. Eu.

4. **G. trichosantha,** Fisch. & Mey. Stoloniferous, densely tufted: lvs. in rosettes, spatulate-oval, the blade 1 in. or less long, attenuate into short petiole, apex usually 3-toothed, the middle tooth shorter than side teeth: heads about ½in. across, on scapes to 8 in. high, with linear-lanceolate long-acuminate bracts. Asia Minor.

5. **G. cordifolia,** L. Small procumbent subshrub about 4 in. high, stoloniferous: lvs. in rosettes, obovate to nearly orbicular, to 1 in. long, attenuate at base, retuse, emarginate or somewhat 3-toothed at apex: heads about ½in. across, on naked scapes. S. Eu.

6. **G. meridionalis,** Schwarz (*G. bellidifolia,* Ten.). Distinguished from *G. cordifolia* by the narrower lanceolate to obovate-lanceolate short-acuminate lvs. 1–4 in. long: heads long-peduncled. S. Eu.

7. **G. repens,** Lam. (*G. nana,* Lam.). Small prostrate densely tufted per. with woody sts., stoloniferous: lvs. lanceolate or obovate-lanceolate, ⅙–¾in. long, short-acuminate: heads to ½in. across, usually nearly sessile. Mts. of Spain and S. France.

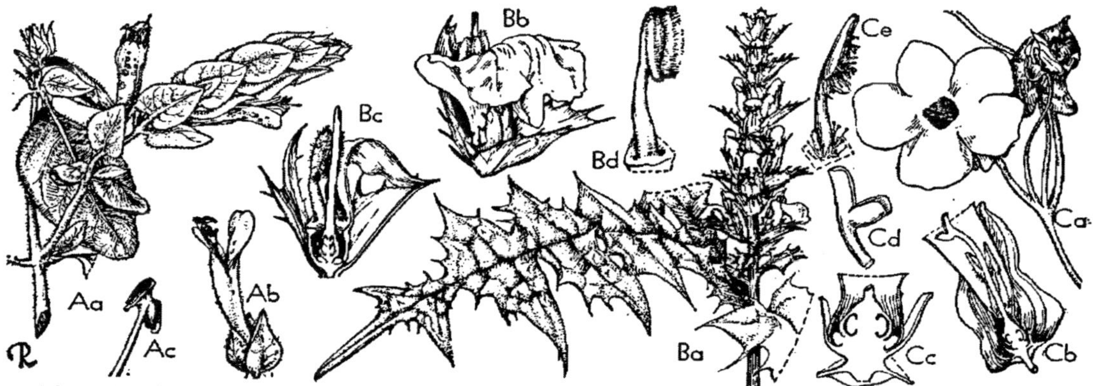

Fig. 185. ACANTHACEÆ. A, *Beloperone guttata:* Aa, flowering branch, × ½; Ab, flower, × ½; Ac, anther, × 2. B, *Acanthus montanus:* Ba, inflorescence with leaf, × ⅛; Bb, flower with bract, × 1; Bc, same, vertical section, × 1; Bd, stamen, × 2. C, *Thunbergia alata:* Ca, flower, × ½; Cb, same, vertical section (corolla-limb excised), × 1; Cc, ovary, vertical section, × 3; Cd, stigma, × 4; Ce, stamen, × 3.

185. ACANTHACEÆ. ACANTHUS FAMILY

Over 2,000 species, in 200 genera, mostly in the tropics around the world, but some extending into temp. regions; they yield many plants for ornament, particularly under glass.—A difficult family for the beginner, as the characters of separation are technical, some of the best of them residing in the anthers and the pollen-grains: it is known specially by the convolute or imbricate æstivation of the corolla which is usually irregular or 2-lipped, stamens 2 or else 4 in 2 pairs, ovary superior, fr. capsular and 2-celled and usually dehiscing elastically, lvs. opposite, simple and exstipular: herbs or shrubs bearing bisexual fls., often with a tube and limb 5-lobed or -toothed, infl. prevailingly spicate or glomerate and prominently bracted; style 1 and mostly long and very slender (often long-exserted) and commonly remaining after the corolla has fallen, stigmas 1 or 2, ovules 1 to many in a cell, placentation axile; stamens inserted on the corolla, and sometimes a staminode present; seeds borne on little hooks with the exception of the Thunbergia tribe (amongst ours).

A. Perfect stamens 4.
  B. Limb of corolla split to make a single 3–5-lobed lip.
    C. Tube of corolla very short; calyx 4-parted........................ 1. ACANTHUS
    CC. Tube of corolla long; calyx 5-parted........................ 2. CROSSANDRA
  BB. Limb of corolla 2-lipped or nearly regular.
    C. Corolla strongly 2-lipped........................ 3. APHELANDRA
    CC. Corolla 5-lobed, not distinctly 2-lipped.

D. Ovules 3–10 in each cell.......... 4. RUELLIA
DD. Ovules 2 in each cell.
E. Bracts (at least in ours) shorter than calyx.
F. Plant (ours) herbaceous or only suffrutescent.
G. Sts. procumbent or clambering.......... 5. ASYSTASIA
GG. Sts. erect.......... 4. RUELLIA
FF. Plant (ours) an upright shrub 2–4 ft. high .... 6. STROBILANTHES
EE. Bracts longer than calyx.
F. Calyx truncate or with many small teeth.......... 7. THUNBERGIA
FF. Calyx 4-parted to base.......... 8. BARLERIA
AA. Perfect stamens 2.
B. Corolla not 2-lipped although perhaps not regular, lobes expanding flat or nearly so.
C. Bracts large and conspicuous.
D. Limb of corolla (in ours) small, forming a revolute rim; stamens long-exserted.......... 9. SANCHEZIA
DD. Limb of corolla large and spreading; stamens not or only slightly exserted..........10. ERANTHEMUM
CC. Bracts small and inconspicuous.
D. Lobes of corolla small, ¼in. or less long.
E. Fls. bright red (in ours), cylindrical..........11. ODONTONEMA
EE. Fls. blue, violet or white, campanulate.......... 6. STROBILANTHES
DD. Lobes of corolla prominent, ½in. or more long.
E. Tube of corolla abruptly enlarged from slender base..........12. MACKAYA
EE. Tube of corolla not abruptly enlarged..........13. PSEUDERANTHEMUM
BB. Corolla strongly 2-lipped, lobes very unequal.
C. Anther-cells alike and equal.
D. Staminodes 2, small: bracts shorter than calyx..........14. GRAPTOPHYLLUM
DD. Staminodes 0: bracts covering the calyx..........15. FITTONIA
CC. Anther-cells unlike in shape, size or position, one often above the other.
D. Stamens attached at base of corolla-tube..........16. PACHYSTACHYS
DD. Stamens attached in throat of corolla or near middle of tube.
E. Anthers blunt.
F. Attachment of stamens in throat of corolla..........17. PERISTROPHE
FF. Attachment of stamens near middle of corolla-tube..........18. JACOBINIA
EE. Anthers pointed or spurred.
F. Connective (separating the anther-cells) narrow and little noticeable: floral bracts, in ours, not conspicuous..........19. JUSTICIA
FF. Connective broad, so that anther-cells are much separated: bracts, in ours, broad and showy..........20. BELOPERONE

1. **ACANTHUS**, L. BEARS-BREECH. A score or more of per. herbs or small shrubs in the Medit. region, Asia and Afr., a few planted for ornament.—The cult. kinds are thistle-like, with stately simple sts. and mostly radical lvs., the showy fls. in long heavy erect spikes: lvs. mostly sinuate-dentate to pinnatifid, the teeth often ending in spines: fls. subtended by a large foliaceous more or less colored spiny bract, and by 2 narrow often spine-tipped lateral bractlets; calyx 4-parted, 2 lobes very large and 1 of them often spine-toothed, the 2 interior ones very small and scale-like; corolla with a very short tube from one side of which extends a single large 3–5-lobed expanded lip; stamens 4, attached at throat of tube, the filaments very thick and prominent, the anthers yoked and white-woolly on dehiscence; ovules 2 in each cell, the style shortly 2-lobed: caps. oblong or ovoid, scarcely contracted at base, 4-seeded. (Acan-thus: Greek *thorn.*)

A. Lvs. spiny-toothed..........1. *A. montanus*
AA. Lvs. not spiny, sinuate-lobed..........2. *A. mollis*

1. **A. montanus**, T. Anders. Subshrubby, sts. nearly or quite glabrous, to 3 ft.: lvs. long-oblong, 1 ft. or more long, pinnatifid, those on the st. more or less ovate and 4–8 in. long and dentate, all of them spinose on the margins, scabrous and more or less hairy on veins beneath: fls. rose-tinted and prominently veined, about 2 in. long, in a terminal spike to 10 in. long on a leafy st. W. Afr.

2. **A. mollis**, L. Sts. strict and straight, to 2 ft., pubescent above: lvs. oblong to oblong-ovate, more or less cordate, 1–2 ft. long and half as broad on mature plants, sinuate-lobed or -pinnatifid, sometimes with lobes separate at base of blade, without spines: fls. whitish, rose or lilac, in spikes 1½ ft. long. S. Eu. Var. **latifolius**, Vilm. (*A. latifolius*, Goeze), is a larger-lvd., bigger and more robust form.

2. **CROSSANDRA**, Salisb. Shrubs and herbs with showy fls. in thick four-sided spikes; species probably 20 and more, in the Old World tropics; choice plants under glass.—Glabrous for the most part, erect: lvs. sometimes whorled, entire or toothed: fls. white, yellow, orange-red, sessile in dense axillary and terminal bracted spikes with imbricate bracts and linear bractlets; calyx 5-lobed, strongly irregular; corolla

slender-tubed, the limb usually split to the throat so as to make a single 5-lobed lip; perfect stamens 4, didynamous, inserted in upper part of tube; ovules 2 in each cell; style shortly 2-lobed: caps. oblong, more or less 4-angled, seeds normally 4. (Crossan-dra: Greek *fringed anthers.*)

C. infundibuliformis, Nees (*Justicia infundibuliformis*, L. *C. undulæfolia*, Salisb.). Shrub, 1–3 ft., pubescent toward the top: lvs. narrow-ovate to lanceolate, 3–5 in. long, narrowed to petiole, acuminate, more or less undulate, puberulent or glabrous: fls. scarlet-orange, in dense pubescent sessile or stalked spikes, the slender tube ¾ in. long, the one-sided limb about 1 in. across; bract about as long as the caps.; seeds bearing feather-like scales. India.

3. **APHELANDRA,** R. Br. Herbs and shrubs of trop. Amer., producing spikes of showy bloom for which they are grown under glass; species 70 or 80.—Lvs. usually many and ample, often showy, entire or toothed: fls. sessile in dense simple or branched axillary and terminal spikes, with large often colored imbricating bracts; corolla yellow, orange, red, strongly 2-lipped, upper lip ascending and lower one usually outspreading or declined or rolled; perfect stamens 4, attached in base of the mostly cylindrical corolla-tube, the 1-celled anthers equal and pointed; ovules usually 4 in each cell; style entire: caps. oblong, little if at all contracted at base, the seeds normally 4. (Aphelan-dra: Greek *simple anther.*)

A. Side lobes of lower lip similar to central lobe.
  B. Fls. pale yellow: lvs. white-veined .... 1. *A. squarrosa*
  BB. Fls. orange: lvs. green .... 2. *A. aurantiaca*
AA. Side lobes very small: fls. scarlet .... 3. *A. tetragona*

1. **A. squarrosa,** Nees, var. **Leopoldii,** Van Houtte. Robust glabrous more or less succulent plant: lvs. crowded, ovate to ovate-elliptic, 8–12 in. long, acuminate, entire, pale green beneath but dark green above and in the cult. plant with white rib and veins: fls. pale yellow, 1½ in. long, somewhat exserted, lobes of lip oblong, the densely imbricated bracts orange-yellow; spikes terminal, solitary or in 3's. Brazil.

2. **A. aurantiaca,** Lindl. (*Hemisandra aurantiaca*, Scheidweiler). Plant of medium size and stature, glabrous: lvs. ovate-elliptic or oblong, 4–6 in. long, acuminate, entire, more or less undulate, strongly veined, light green beneath and deep green above: fls. orange sometimes tinged scarlet, the lower lip with large oval-pointed declined lobes; bracts serrate. Mex. to S. Amer.

3. **A. tetragona,** Nees (*Justicia tetragona*, Vahl). Shrub with nearly or quite glabrous branches: lvs. large, elliptic to elliptic-ovate, 4–9 in. long, tapering to petiole, acuminate, entire, green, lightly hairy beneath: fls. long and narrow, the tube 2 in. long, scarlet, upper lip hooded, lower with 1 long narrow lobe and 2 very small lateral lobes, in clustered four-sided spikes; bracts obtuse, pubescent. W. Indies, N. S. Amer.

4. **RUELLIA,** L. Herbs and small shrubs of wide distribution in trop. countries and some in temp. regions, a few grown under glass and in the open in mild climates for the showy bloom and sometimes ornamental foliage; species upwards of 200, largely American.—Plants usually pubescent, the lvs. prevailingly entire and the pairs equal: fls. white to rose, violet, purple, yellow, variously disposed in clusters or panicles or sometimes solitary; calyx deeply cleft or parted, with the parts linear or narrow; corolla with a short or long tube but narrow and slender and the upper part more or less enlarging, the 5 lobes spreading and nearly or quite equal; perfect stamens 4, the filaments dilated and more or less paired or connected at base; ovules 2–10 in each cell; style slender, mostly recurved at apex and simple or 2-lobed: caps. oblong or clavate, mostly stipitate, 6–20-seeded. (Ruel-lia: Jean de la Ruelle, 1474–1537, French physician and botanist.)

A. Foliage purple, often veined with white.
  B. Fls. white marked with lilac .... 1. *R. Devosiana*
  BB. Fls. bright carmine .... 2. *R. Makoyana*
AA. Foliage green.
  B. Fls. 3 in. and more long and broad .... 3. *R. macrantha*
  BB. Fls. 1–2 in. long.
    C. Corolla red, gibbous at base .... 4. *R. græcizans*
    CC. Corolla blue or lavender, with slender tube, not gibbous.
      D. Lvs. linear or linear-lanceolate, long-attenuate, nearly glabrous .... 5. *R. Brittoniana*
      DD. Lvs. oblong or obovate, obtuse, hairy .... 6. *R. ciliosa*

1. **R. Devosiana,** Morr. Shrubby with more or less decumbent base and erect branches, 1–1½ ft., sts. pubescent: lvs. elliptic, 1½–2 in. long, short-acute, slender-petioled, entire,

velvety, purple beneath, white-ribbed and -veined above: fls. solitary and sessile, about 1¾ in. long, white with lilac throat and lines, tube slender but widening above, lobe nearly ½in. long and emarginate. (Dedicated to A. Devos of the Univ. of Liege.) Brazil.—Grown for foliage.

2. **R. Makoyana,** Hort. Differs from *R. Devosiana* in the bright crimson fls. (Intro. to cult. by Jacob-Makoy et Cie of Liege.) Brazil.

3. **R. macrantha,** Mart. Shrub to 6 ft., with nearly glabrous angular branches constricted above the ciliate nodes: lvs. ovate-lanceolate, 4–6 in. long, tapering both ways, essentially entire, with small scattered hairs: fls. axillary and contiguous, rosy-purple with prominent veins, 3 in. or more long and about the same in breadth, the lower half of corolla-tube slender and cylindrical but the upper part much expanded, the 5 lobes rounded and spreading. Brazil.

4. **R. græcizans,** Backer (*R. amœna,* Nees. *R. longifolia,* Griseb. not Rich. *Stephanophysum longifolium,* Pohl). Subshrub, 1–2 ft., usually herbaceous as grown in pots, twigs glabrous or puberulent: lvs. ovate to oblong-lanceolate, 2–5 in. long, somewhat narrowed into short petiole, acuminate, serrate to repand, more or less finely puberulent: fls. several on long axillary peduncles that branch as they grow, bright red, about 1 in. long, gibbous, the corolla-tube suddenly expanding just above the linear-lobed calyx, the 5-lobed limb short. S. Amer.

5. **R. Brittoniana,** Leonard. Somewhat woody, 1–3 ft. high, nearly glabrous: lvs. linear-oblong to linear, 3–12 in. long and ¼–¾in. wide, long-attenuate, entire or slightly undulate: fls. in a leafy corymbiform infl., blue-violet, 1–1½ in. long, lower part of tube cylindrical, expanded above, the limb with broad rounded lobes. (Named for N. L. Britton, page 40.) Mex.; escaped Tex. to Fla.—Usually grown under the name *R. malacosperma,* Greenman, which differs in being somewhat hairy when young, lvs. oblong or elliptic-lanceolate and shorter and mostly toothed and undulate, and calyx-segms. about twice longer. Mex.

6. **R. ciliosa,** Pursh. Very hairy, often rosulate, main sts. 2–12 in. long: lvs. oblong or obovate, 1–4 in. long and ½–1 in. wide, obtuse, sometimes undulate: fls. usually solitary and axillary, bluish to lavender, 1–2 in. long, with long slender tube and expanded limb. S. C. to Fla. and La.

5. **ASYSTASIA,** Blume. Herbs or shrubs of over 30 species in tropics of Old World, one grown as a ground-cover.—Lvs. entire or somewhat toothed: fls. in terminal racemes or panicles; bracts and bracteoles small; calyx parted to base; corolla with cylindrical tube enlarged in upper half and 5 nearly equal lobes; stamens 4, inserted below the throat, anther-cells oblong, parallel; ovules 2 in each cell: caps. oblong, 4-seeded above. (Asysta-sia: name of doubtful application.)

A. gangetica, T. Anders. (*Justicia gangetica,* L. *A. coromandeliana,* Nees). Per. with procumbent or clambering branches 1–4 ft. long, somewhat pubescent: lvs. ovate, 1–4 in. long, acute: fls. purple to yellowish or white, in one-sided racemes 4–6 in. long; corolla to 1½ in. long and 1 in. across the limb: caps. 1 in. long, pubescent. Malaya to Afr.; nat. in W. Indies.

6. **STROBILANTHES,** Blume. Species probably 200, herbs and small shrubs, mostly in the warm parts of Asia, cult. for ornamental bloom or foliage, under glass in the N. and in the open in warm regions.—Lvs. of the pairs sometimes much unlike, entire or toothed: fls. blue, violet, white, less frequently yellowish, solitary in axils or in spikes and panicles; calyx deeply cleft or parted, with narrow segms.; corolla with a narrow or constricted base but much broader above, the 5-lobed limb spreading and more or less unequal but not bilabiate; perfect stamens 4 and didynamous, or sometimes 2 and others represented by staminodes, the filaments more or less connected at base; ovules 2 in each cell; style slender and recurved, mostly evidently 2-lobed at apex: caps. bearing 4 seeds (or fewer by abortion), oblong or linear, scarcely contracted at base. (Strobilan-thes: Greek *cone-flower,* from the infl. of some species.)

A. Grown for the bloom: lvs. small and narrow, taper-based, green.................1. *S. isophyllus*
AA. Grown for foliage: lvs. large, cordate, iridescent...............................2. *S. Dyerianus*

1. **S. isophyllus,** T. Anders. (*Goldfussia isophylla,* Nees). Nearly glabrous branchy shrub, 2–3 ft., with angled twigs: lvs. of the pairs equal (as the name indicates), narrow-lanceolate, willow-like, 2–4 in. long, contracted to short petiole, very long-acuminate, bluntly serrulate, veiny: fls. several on axillary peduncles shorter than the lvs., about 1 in. long, bluish-pink or blue and white, the short blunt corolla-lobes emarginate. India.

2. **S. Dyerianus,** Mast. Branching shrub grown in hothouses for the foliage which is rose-purple beneath and variegated above in iridescent tints of blue and lilac: lvs. elliptic-

lanceolate or lance-ovate, 6–8 in. long, contracted or fiddle-shaped toward base, sessile, cordate at attachment, serrulate: fls. 1½ in. long, in erect spikes, pale violet, the corolla-tube curved, the 5 short broad lobes revolute. (W. T. Thiselton-Dyer, page 42.) Burma.

7. **THUNBERGIA,** Retz. CLOCK-VINE. Trop. plants, most of them climbers, woody or herbaceous, several grown under glass or in the open in S. U. S. for the showy fls.; about 75 species, mostly African and Asian.—Lvs. opposite, simple, prevailingly hastate at base: fls. solitary in the axils or racemose, yellow, white, blue, purple, subtended by 2 large more or less foliaceous bracts; calyx various, either truncate or 10–15-toothed; corolla large, funnelform or somewhat bell-shaped, the tube curved or straight, limb 5-lobed and nearly regular or at least not distinctly bilabiate: stamens 4, didynamous, attached near base of the tube; ovules 2 in each cell: caps. seed-bearing at base, produced into a beak. (Thunber-gia: Carl Peter, or Carl Pehr, Thunberg, Swede, 1743–1822, was a student of Linnæus and a successor, traveller in Japan and S. Afr., of which he wrote floras; sometimes written Karl Peter.)

A. Plant an erect shrub: fls. solitary, blue with yellow center . . . . 1. *T. erecta*
AA. Plant twining.
  B. Petiole winged.
    C. Corolla-lobes strongly emarginate . . . . 2. *T. Gibsonii*
    CC. Corolla-lobes essentially truncate or obtuse . . . . 3. *T. alata*
  BB. Petiole not winged.
    C. Lvs. large and thick, 5–8 in. long, coarsely notched, cordate or subcordate . . . . 4. *T. grandiflora*
    CC. Lvs. medium or small, nearly or quite entire, not cordate.
      D. Fls. in terminal or axillary racemes.
        E. Corolla blue, limb expanded . . . . 5. *T. laurifolia*
        EE. Corolla scarlet, limb short and reflexed . . . . 6. *T. coccinea*
      DD. Fls. solitary in axils . . . . 7. *T. fragrans*

1. **T. erecta,** T. Anders. (*Mayenia erecta,* Benth.). Much-branched glabrous erect shrub, 2–8 ft., the branches flexuose: lvs. ovate, 1–3 in. long, short-petioled, acute, margins entire or obscurely repand-toothed or -angled: fls. solitary on axillary pedicels, 1½–2¾ in. long, limb blue-purple, the curved tube yellowish-white; calyx very short, with 10 or more small teeth, hidden by the bracts: caps. 1 in. long, with large flat beak. Trop. Afr.—In cult. varies to white and blue fls.

2. **T. Gibsonii,** S. Moore. Per. herb but readily grown as an ann., twining 4–5 ft., the sts. hairy: lvs. short-ovate or nearly triangular-ovate, 2–3 in. long, subcordate or cordate-sagittate at base, obtuse or only very short-acute at apex, sinuate-toothed, pubescent both surfaces, the petiole 1½–2 in. long with the wing, expanding upward: fls. solitary on very long axillary hairy peduncles, the corolla orange, 1½ in. or more across, the lobes broad and emarginate; calyx small, many-lobed; bracts ovate, half or more as long as the corolla-tube, strongly veined and rust-colored. Trop. Afr., at high elevations; first collected at the equator in 1892 by Mr. Gibson.

3. **T. alata,** Bojer. BLACK-EYED SUSAN. Herbaceous per. twiner but often grown as an ann. with slender hairy sts.: lvs. ovate to triangular-ovate, 1–3 in. long, the base cordate and more or less hastate, obtuse or acutish and usually apiculate, margins repand-toothed, pubescent both surfaces, the long petiole winged: fls. solitary on long axillary pedicels, about 1½ in. long, limb buff or cream-color and throat dark purple, the 5 segms. rounded; calyx very small, beneath the 2 green bracts that nearly equal the corolla-tube: caps. about 1 in. long, with a globular base and flat beak. Trop. Afr., but now nat. widely in tropics.—Runs into races without the dark eye, also white and other colors.

4. **T. grandiflora,** Roxb. Extensive woody twiner with sts. nearly or quite glabrous: lvs. thick, large, 5–8 in. long, ovate to broad-ovate, 3-nerved from base, cordate or subcordate, acuminate-pointed, angle-toothed or slightly lobed or some of them entire, scabrous or pubescent both surfaces, petiole not winged: fls. in stout dense hanging racemes or sometimes solitary, large and showy, about 3 in. across, light or dark blue or white, the expanded limb almost 2-lipped with 3 lobes beneath and 2 above; calyx reduced to a rim; bracts large, nearly equalling broad corolla-tube. Bengal; now widespread in trop. countries.

5. **T. laurifolia,** Lindl. (*T. Harrisii,* Hook. f.). Sometimes confused with no. 4, but separated by its narrow not lobed or toothed lvs., which are lanceolate to lance-ovate, 3–5 in. long, rounded or tapering at base, mostly long-acuminate, margins sometimes obscurely repand but not dentate, not scabrous and scarcely pubescent beneath: fls. light blue with whitish or yellowish throat, 3 in. across, in racemes, the large rounded lobes not very unequal. India.

6. **T. coccinea,** Wall. (*Hexacentris coccinea,* Nees). Tall glabrous woody twiner with 4-angled branchlets: lvs. lance-ovate to broad-ovate, 3–5 in. long, subcordate or hastate at base, acuminate-pointed, 3–5-nerved from base, upper margins entire or somewhat sinuate-

dentate: fls. in pendulous mostly large terminal and axillary racemes, the corolla with a scarlet lobed reflexed limb and yellow throat, ¾–½in. across; calyx very small and indistinctly toothed, this and corolla-tube covered by the large spathe-like bracts. India.

7. **T. fragrans,** Roxb. Slender somewhat woody glabrous twiner: lvs. lanceolate to triangular-ovate, 2–3 in. long, broadened or subcordate and with 1 or 2 angle-teeth at base, apex acute, margins entire or somewhat repand, slender-petioled, lightly scabrous: fls. solitary and axillary, white, fragrant, the spreading limb 1½–2 in. across, the lobes toothed at apex; calyx small, many-toothed; bracts acute, shorter than the cylindrical tube: caps. about ¾in. long, with flat beak. India.

8. **BARLERIA,** L. Shrubs and herbs of more than 100 species, nearly all in the Old World tropics, a few sometimes grown under glass for the showy fls. and planted out in warm countries.—Glabrous or pubescent, erect, sometimes spiny: lvs. entire: fls. showy (in the cult. kinds), white, blue or yellow, solitary or fascicled in the axils, sometimes in terminal spikes, accompanied by large often spinose bracts; calyx 4-parted, the 2 outer ones large, the lateral interior ones small and narrow; corolla-tube mostly long, the lower part slender and upper part broad, the 5 spreading broad lobes mostly subequal; perfect stamens 4 and didynamous, attached near base of corolla; ovules 2 in each cell, the style mostly entire: caps. ovoid or oblong, bearing normally 4 seeds. (Barle-ria: Jacques Barrelier, 1606–1673, French botanical collector and author.)

B. cristata, L. Little shrub, 2–3 ft., branches yellowish-pubescent, sts. not spiny: lvs. elliptic, 1–3½ in. long, tapering to short petiole, short-acute, scabrous-puberulent: fls. blue, nearly or quite sessile in the axils, corolla about 2 in. long; bracts elliptic, ¾in. long, strongly nerved and light green or whitish, with long spiny teeth; corolla-lobes obtuse. India.

9. **SANCHEZIA,** Ruiz & Pav. About a dozen strong erect large herbs and shrubs of S. Amer., one grown in the warmhouse in the N. for the ornamental foliage and showy spikes.—Lvs. large, strongly pinnate-veined, entire or somewhat toothed: fls. large and showy, orange, red, or purple, with large calyx-like bracts, in terminal and axillary spikes or in some species solitary; corolla-tube long, cylindrical below and enlarging upward, the 5 lobes short and broad; perfect stamens 2, attached below middle of tube, with 2 staminodia between them, the 2 anther-cells mucronate; ovules 4 in each cell; style very slender, obscurely 2-lobed at apex: caps. scarcely contracted at base, the seeds normally 8. (Sanche-zia: Jos. Sanchez, early professor of botany at Cadiz.)

S. nobilis, Hook. f. Shrub 3–4 ft., with strong upright branches, sts. glabrous except perhaps in infl.: lvs. oblong-ovate, 4–12 in. long, short-petioled, tapering at base, abruptly acuminate, sinuate-dentate to nearly entire: fls. 2 in. long, the corolla yellow, with revolute rim; bracts 1–1½ in. long, red. Ecuador.—There are named cultivars with variegated lvs.

10. **ERANTHEMUM,** L. (*Dædalacanthus*, T. Anders.). About a score of shrubs and herbs, native in trop. Asia, one a common ornamental under glass and in the open in warm countries.—Lvs. entire or perhaps somewhat dentate: fls. blue or rose-colored, in close bracted often panicled spikes; calyx 5-lobed or -parted, covered by the bracts; corolla with long very slender often curved tube, the limb spreading and 5-lobed, not 2-lipped; perfect stamens 2, attached in throat of corolla: caps. ovoid or oblong, with 4 seeds or perhaps fewer by abortion. (Eran-themum: Greek *lovely flower*.)

E. nervosum, R. Br. (*Justicia nervosa*, Vahl). Shrub 2–4 ft., nearly or quite glabrous: lvs. ovate to elliptic, 4–8 in. long, rather thick, prominently pinnate-veined, tapering to mostly long petiole, acuminate, margins obscurely crenate-dentate: fls. in axillary and terminal spikes, with appressed very acute prominently nervose bracts; corolla blue, the tube ¾–1 in. long and curved, limb about ¾in. across. India.—Early known as *Eranthemum pulchellum*, and yet sometimes cult. under that name.

11. **ODONTONEMA,** Nees (*Thyrsacanthus*, Nees). About 20 shrubs and herbs in trop. Amer., several more or less grown for ornament, one apparently now frequent on our southern borders and southward.—Lvs. usually large and entire: fls. commonly many in terminal spicate racemes in the axils of small and inconspicuous

bracts; corolla with slender straight or slightly curved tube that much exceeds the narrow-lobed calyx, the tube somewhat widened toward the top; corolla-limb essentially regular (in ours) or somewhat 2-lipped, the upper lip entire or 2-toothed and the lower 3-lobed; stamens 2, attached in upper part of tube, with dorsifixed anthers of which the 2 cells are equal or nearly so and not spurred; staminodia 2 and small; ovules 2 in each cell. (Odontone-ma: Greek combination referring to toothed filaments.)

O. strictum, Kuntze (*T. strictus*, Nees). Nearly or quite glabrous erect shrub, 5–6 ft.: lvs. oblong-ovate to oblong-lanceolate, 3–6 in. long, acuminate, very short-petioled, entire but often undulate, more or less short-hairy on veins beneath: fls. bright crimson, ¾–1 in. long, straight, in erect simple close racemes, the limb regular or practically so and the little obtuse lobes about ⅛in. long. Forests of Cent. Amer.—Sometimes grown as *Jacobinia coccinea.*

12. **MACKAYA,** Harvey. As now accepted, a genus of 4 shrubs, 1 in Afr. and 3 in India, the former in frequent cult. under glass and in the open in S. Calif. and elsewhere.—Corolla somewhat curved, much broadened in the upper half, the 5 prominent lobes subequal; perfect stamens 2, and 2 long filiform staminodes, the anthers muticous and equal; ovules 2 in each cell; stigma 2-lobed; floral bracts very small: caps. stipitate. (Macka-ya: James T. Mackay, about 1775–1862, Irish botanist.)

M. bella, Harvey (*Asystasia bella*, Benth. & Hook.). Nearly or quite glabrous, 3–4 ft.: lvs. oblong to ovate-oblong, 3–5 in. long, tapering below to short petiole, gradually or abruptly pointed, the margins variously sinuate-dentate: fls. several in terminal racemes, 1½–2½ in. long and as much across, lavender and veined; calyx small, with linear-subulate lobes. S. Afr.

13. **PSEUDERANTHEMUM,** Radlk. (*Eranthemum*, Auth. not L.). Species 60–70 or more in many trop. countries, a few small shrubs grown under glass for the attractive bloom and often colored foliage.—Herbaceous or woody, erect, glabrous: lvs. entire or coarsely toothed: fls. white, blue, purple, red, often more or less marked with yellow, 1–3 in the axils of linear bracts and arranged in spikes, cymes or racemes; calyx with 5 narrow lobes; corolla with long or short tube, the 5 spreading lobes nearly equal or the 2 posterior ones smaller; perfect stamens 2, attached in the tube, staminodes 2; ovules 2 in each cell; style filiform, apex entire or 2-toothed: caps. oblong, stipitate, seeds 4 unless aborted. (Pseuderan-themum: *false eranthemum.*)

A. Tube of corolla very slender, about 1 in. or more long........................1. *P. bicolor*
AA. Tube not slender, ½in. or less long.
B. Lvs. broad-ovate, usually marked wine-red........................2. *P. atropurpureum*
BB. Lvs. ovate-lanceolate to lanceolate, usually veined yellow................3. *P. reticulatum*

1. **P. bicolor,** Radlk. (*Eranthemum bicolor*, Schrank). Shrub, 2–3 ft., sts. glabrous: lvs. narrow- or long-ovate, 4–8 in. long, tapering to short petiole, very long-acuminate, dark green, entire, glabrous: fls. sessile in clusters on elongating axillary and terminal unbranched spikes, salverform, white with lower lobes spotted purple, corolla-tube cylindrical and very slender, 1– about 1½ in. long, the 5 spreading lobes oval and obtuse, the expanded corolla 1 in. or somewhat more across; calyx-lobes acute but not subulate. Probably Polynesia.

2. **P. atropurpureum,** Radlk. (*Eranthemum atropurpureum*, Bull not Hook. f.). Glabrous shrub, 3–4 ft.: lvs. broad-ovate to oval, 3–6 in. long and usually about two-thirds as broad, rounded or slightly tapering at base and short-petioled, apex broad and obtuse but usually with a little point, entire, wine-purple or pink-purple and variously blotched (but sometimes green and sometimes spotted yellow): fls. short-pedicelled and clustered on axillary and terminal spikes, white with rose-purple center and spots but sometimes entirely purplish, the tube rather stout and about ⅓in. long, the 5 obtuse lobes spreading to ¾–1 in. across. Probably Polynesia; frequent in American tropics as a cult. and spontaneous plant.

3. **P. reticulatum,** Radlk. (*Eranthemum reticulatum*, Bull). Shrub, 2–3 ft., with angled glabrous branchlets: lvs. ovate-lanceolate, 5–10 in. long, mostly abrupt or rounded at base, the petiole short, long-tapering but apex obtuse, entire but undulate, dark green with golden veins: fls. short-pedicelled in axillary and terminal panicles, white with wine-purple throat and spots on one lobe, the rather thick tube about ½in. long, the 5 oblong obtuse spreading lobes about 1½ in. across; calyx-lobes linear-subulate. Probably Polynesia.

14. **GRAPTOPHYLLUM,** Nees. Trop. shrubs of Australia and Polynesia, 4 or 5 species, one widely grown in warm regions for the handsome foliage.—Glabrous, with entire or dentate lvs. which are often colored and variegated: fls. pedicelled, red or purple, in short nearly sessile cymes or panicles, the bracts and bractlets very small and not covering the linear-lobed calyx; corolla with curved tube, 2-lipped, the upper lip 2-lobed and lower 3-lobed; perfect stamens 2, staminodia 2 and small, anthers 2-celled and sharp-pointed below; ovules 2 in each cell; style somewhat 2-toothed: caps. contracted into stalk. (Graptophyl-lum: Greek *to write, leaf,* from the pictured foliage.)

G. pictum, Griff. (*Justicia picta,* L. *G. hortense,* Nees). Erect, to 8 ft.: lvs. elliptic, 4–6 in. long, more or less tapering to short petiole, acuminate or short-acute, entire, purplish or green, variously marked and splotched yellow: fls. dark purple or crimson, about 1½ in. long, some of them yawning and strongly 2-lipped with side lobes of lower lip turned down; stamens ascending and prominent. Probably New Guinea.

15. **FITTONIA,** Coem. Low or creeping herbs, 2 or 3 reputed species, probably forms of one, grown under cover for the handsome foliage, native in S. Amer., probably in Peru.—Sts. very hairy: lvs. broad, entire, with colored veins on upper surface: fls. pale or yellowish, small and not ornamental, underneath broad obtuse or short-acute scales in long slender spikes; calyx deeply cut, the lobes equal or one of them larger; corolla with a slender tube, deeply 2-lipped; stamens inserted at middle of tube, the anthers not pointed; ovules 2 in each cell; style filiform, with 2-notched stigma: caps. ovate, long-stipitate. (Fitto-nia: dedicated to Elizabeth and Sarah Mary Fitton, authors of "Conversations on Botany," which appeared in London in the early part of 19th century.)

A. Sts. creeping and rooting, herbaceous: lvs. obtuse........................1. *F. Verschaffeltii*
AA. Sts. erect or ascending, becoming somewhat woody: lvs. with very short point....2. *F. gigantea*

1. **F. Verschaffeltii,** Coem. Low creeping and rooting herb with shaggy-hairy sts.: lvs. oval to nearly ovate, 3–4 in. long, rounded or subcordate at base, mostly rounded at apex, dark green with deep red veins and midrib. (Bears the name of Ambroise Verschaffelt, 1825–1886, Belgian horticulturist.) Var. **Pearcei,** Nichols., has veins and midrib bright carmine and under surface somewhat glaucous. Var. **argyroneura,** Nichols. (*F. argyroneura,* Coem.), has lvs. bright light green with veins and rib white.

2. **F. gigantea,** Lind. Erect and branching, 12–18 in., becoming somewhat shrubby: lvs. with a very short point, veins and rib carmine.

16. **PACHYSTACHYS,** Nees. About a half dozen trop. American plants, sometimes referred to Jacobinia, but differing in technical characters of pollen, and otherwise distinguished by the attachment of the stamens in the base of the corolla-tube: fls. yellow or purple, 1–3 in the axil of large bracts in thick head-like thyrses (whence the name Pachys-tachys: Greek *thick spike.*)

P. coccinea, Nees (*Justicia coccinea,* Aubl. *Jacobinia coccinea,* Hiern.). CARDINALS GUARD. Strong glabrous shrub, 5–7 ft., the thick sts. constricted above the joints: lvs. ovate or elliptic, to ovate-lanceolate in the small ones, 5–8 in. long, rather short-acuminate, entire, strongly pinnate-veined: fls. scarlet, in dense terminal heads; corolla about 2 in. long, lipped nearly or quite to the middle, upper lip somewhat arched, the lower one reflexed; bracts large, ovate-pointed, entire. Trinidad, N. S. Amer.

17. **PERISTROPHE,** Nees. Old World trop. herbs and subshrubs, grown under glass for the free showy bloom; species about 15.—Erect or partially creeping: lvs. entire: fls. solitary or in clusters surrounded by involucre-like bracts mostly longer than the deeply 5-lobed calyx; corolla rose or purple, with slender tube slightly enlarged above, the limb in 2 nearly equal parts and widely expanded, upper lip nearly entire and lower one 3-toothed or -lobed; stamens 2, attached in throat of corolla, the anthers blunt; calyx 5-lobed into equal segms., subtended by calyculate bractlets: caps. ellipsoid, stalked, 4-seeded. (Peris-trophe: Greek *belted around,* referring to the involucre.)

A. Lvs. lanceolate: ann..1. *P. salicifolia*
AA. Lvs. essentially ovate: woody per..........................2. *P. speciosa*

1. **P. salicifolia,** Miq. (*Justicia salicifolia,* Blume. *P. angustifolia,* Nees). Perhaps ann., grown as such, low, diffuse but erect, much-branched, glabrous except near tips: lvs. lanceo-

late, 2–3 in. long, tapering both ways: fls. few in terminal cymes, light red; involucre of 2 ovate-oblong unequal ciliate bracts. Java.—Grown for the yellow-variegated foliage of the cult. race.

2. **P. speciosa,** Nees. Erect spreading glabrous plant becoming woody at base, 2–3 ft., sts. constricted above the nodes: lvs. ovate, lance-ovate or elliptic, 4–5 in. long, acuminate, entire: fls. violet-purple, 2 or 3 together on slender branches or peduncles, subtended by 2 bract-like lvs.; corolla 1¾–2 in. across and nearly or quite as long, the 2 stamens exserted over the lower lip; bractlets narrow, widening upward. India.

18. **JACOBINIA,** Moric. (incl. *Cyrtanthera,* Nees). Herbs and shrubs of the American tropics, 20–40 species, distinguished from Justicia by the absence of spur-like points on anthers: stamens usually attached about the middle of corolla-tube, staminodia often represented by 2 hairy elevations, and dissimilarities in pollen-grains. (Jacobin-ia: probably a personal name.)

A. Infl. a dense head-like thyrse or spike, often with broad floral bracts.
 B. Floral bracts acute.
  C. Color of fls. yellow .... 1. *J. umbrosa*
  CC. Color of fls. purplish or red.
   D. Fls. rose-purple or flesh-colored .... 2. *J. carnea*
   DD. Fls. crimson .... 3. *J. Pohliana*
 BB. Floral bracts (at least above the base) obtuse.
  C. Plant glabrous .... 4. *J. obtusior*
  CC. Plant velutinous .... 5. *J. velutina*
AA. Infl. open, racemose, paniculate, or fls. solitary, bracts not prominent. (LIBONIA, Koch. SERICOGRAPHIS, Nees.)
 B. Corolla deeply bilabiate, the lower lip coiled or deflexed.
  C. Calyx-lobes triangular- or ovate-acute .... 6. *J. Ghiesbreghtiana*
  CC. Calyx-lobes linear and long-acute .... 7. *J. spicigera*
 BB. Corolla shortly bilabiate, lower lip not reflexed or coiled.
  C. Length of corolla about 1 in. or less: lvs. essentially obtuse .... 8. *J. pauciflora*
  CC. Length of corolla 1¼ in. or more: lvs. acute .... 9. *J. penrhosiensis*

1. **J. umbrosa,** Blake (*Justicia aurea,* Schlecht. *Justicia umbrosa,* Benth. *Jacobinia aurea,* Hemsl. not Hiern). Shrub, 4–12 ft., with thick more or less angled puberulent sts.: lvs. lanceolate-oblong or ovate, 6–12 in. long, rounded or very broad at base, acuminate, entire or sinuate, mostly puberulent beneath: fls. yellow, in dense terminal spike-like thyrses to 1 ft. long; corolla pubescent, about 2 in. long, lipped to the middle; bracts narrow and acute, ½–¾in. long. Mex., Cent. Amer.

2. **J. carnea,** Nichols. (*Justicia carnea,* Hook. *Cyrtanthera magnifica,* Pohl. *Jacobinia magnifica,* Lindau). Stout forking pubescent shrub, 2–5 ft., with short internodes: lvs. ovate or oblong, 6–7 in. long, tapering at base, acuminate, entire or crenulate: fls. rose-purple or flesh-colored, in dense terminal heads about 4 in. long with oblong acuminate bracts ¾in. long; corolla about 2 in. long, viscid-pubescent, lipped to the middle or below, the lower lip broad. Brazil.—Confused in cult. with *J. obtusior.*

3. **J. Pohliana,** Lindau (*Cyrtanthera Pohliana,* Nees). More robust and leafy than no. 2 and less pubescent, even nearly glabrous: lvs. ovate-oblong or ovate, acuminate, often purple-tinged: fls. bright crimson, in a long or oblong spike; bracts ovate-acute. Brazil (where it was early collected by J. E. Pohl).

4. **J. obtusior,** Bailey (*Cyrtanthera Pohliana* var. *obtusior,* Nees). Plant glabrous: lvs. lanceolate to lance-ovate, long-acuminate: infl. short and compact, the floral bracts very obtuse or perhaps the outer involucral ones somewhat acute; fls. pink to crimson. Brazil.

5. **J. velutina,** Voss (*Cyrtanthera Pohliana* var. *velutina,* Nees). Similar to *J. obtusior* but lvs. velutinous on both sides: fls. rose, hairy. Brazil.

6. **J. Ghiesbreghtiana,** Hemsl. (*Justicia Ghiesbreghtiana,* Lem.). Glabrous or lightly pubescent shrub to 5 ft., nodes somewhat enlarged, much-branched: lvs. lance-ovate to narrow-elliptic, 3–6 in. long, tapering both ways, short-petioled, entire, arching: fls. mostly 2 together and sessile in forking axillary peduncled open little panicles with small bracts not larger than the calyx; corolla orange to crimson, mostly upwards of 1½ in. long, lipped about one-third distance from apex, about ¼in. broad at widest part, the rather broad lower lip deflexed and becoming coiled; calyx with broad but acute lobes about ⅛in. long. Mex., intro. from the collections of Ghiesbreght.

7. **J. spicigera,** Bailey (*Justicia spicigera,* Schlecht. *Justicia atramentaria,* Benth. *Justicia Mohintlii,* Moc. & Sessé). Fls. more slender than in no. 6, orange-yellow to purplish, lvs. smaller and narrower; calyx-lobes longer, linear-acute to nearly subulate: shrub to 10 ft. Mex.

8. **J. pauciflora,** Lindau (*Sericographis pauciflora,* Nees. *Libonia floribunda,* Koch). Little shrub, 1–2 ft., with terete pubescent sts.: lvs. small, unequal in the pairs, oblong to oval to obovate, ¾in. or less long or the upper ones larger, obtuse, entire, very short-petioled: fls. solitary on short axillary peduncles, mostly nodding, about ¾in. long, scarlet with the upper one-fourth yellow, the lips less than ¼in. deep. Brazil.

9. **J. penrhosiensis,** Bailey (*Libonia penrhosiensis,* Lav. *Sericobonia ignea,* Lind. & André). Recorded as a hybrid between *J. pauciflora* and *J. Ghiesbreghtiana:* in character much like the former but lvs. mostly larger and in equal pairs, tapering-acute at apex: fls. 1¼ in. or somewhat more long, bright carmine-red with yellow only about the opening, the lips ¼in. or more deep.—Some of the plants passing as *J. pauciflora* belong here.

19. **JUSTICIA,** L. Herbs and shrubs of widespread trop. distribution, 250–300 species if the genus is defined broadly, 100 or more species if taken in a restricted sense; few are cult., the ornamental plants grown under this name being mostly Jacobinias.—Calyx deeply 5-parted (only seldom 4-parted), the lobes usually about equal: fls. small or large, white, violet or red, solitary, racemose, spicate or fascicled, sometimes with prominent imbricated bracts; corolla straight or curved, 2-lipped, tube short and mostly dilated above, upper lip erect or ascending and entire or 2-toothed, lower one spreading and 3-lobed; stamens 2 and staminodia none, attached in the throat and exserted or prominent, the anthers unequal in height and one of them produced below into a spur or evident point; stigma capitate or 2-toothed: caps. ovate or oblong, with 2 or 4 seeds. (Justic-ia: James Justice, Scotch gardener, author of "British Gardener's Director," 1754.)

J. secunda, Vahl. Red Justicia. Shrub to 8 ft., puberulous above: lvs. ovate-oblong to lance-ovate, to 6 in. long, somewhat tapering to petiole, very long-acuminate, entire or obscurely crenate: fls. in a terminal narrow elongating panicle, red, 1½ in. long, narrow, lips longer than tube; calyx-lobes sharp, much shorter than corolla-tube; bracts smaller than calyx. N. S. Amer.

20. **BELOPERONE,** Nees. Trop. American shrubs or subshrubs of some 30 species, one planted in the open and also an attractive pot-plant under glass.—From Justicia the genus is distinguished by the broad connective or upper part of filament, whereby the 2 anther-cells are considerably separated so that the edges are not at all contiguous; anther-cells mostly unlike, one standing higher than the other, one or both of them sharp-pointed or spurred on the lower end: fls. 2-lipped, and much as in Jacobinia, the lower lip 3-lobed: caps. long-stalked, the floral bracts often large and imbricate. (Beloper-one: Greek, from the arrow-shaped anthers.)

B. guttata, Brandegee. Shrimp-Plant. Much-branched from base, 12–20 in., the terete sts. short-hirsute: lvs. ovate, 1–2½ in. long, short-acuminate, abruptly tapering to slender petiole, entire, short-hirsute both surfaces: fls. in curving-erect strobile-like spikes 2½–3½ in. long borne beneath ornamental overlapping reddish-brown broad-ovate pubescent bracts ½–¾in. long; corolla slender and exserted beyond the bracts, 1¼ in. long, divided nearly to the middle into narrow lips, white and pubescent but lower lip with 3 rows of purplish spots in throat; upper lip entire; lower lip somewhat declined but not recurved, a little longer and broader than the upper and with 3 shallow close obtuse lobes; calyx about one-fourth as long as corolla-tube, whitish, 5-cleft and regular; stamens 2, ascending under the upper lip but not exserted, the lower anther-cell more pointed at base; style filiform and slightly exserted, the stigma small and entire; ovules 2 in each cell. Mex.

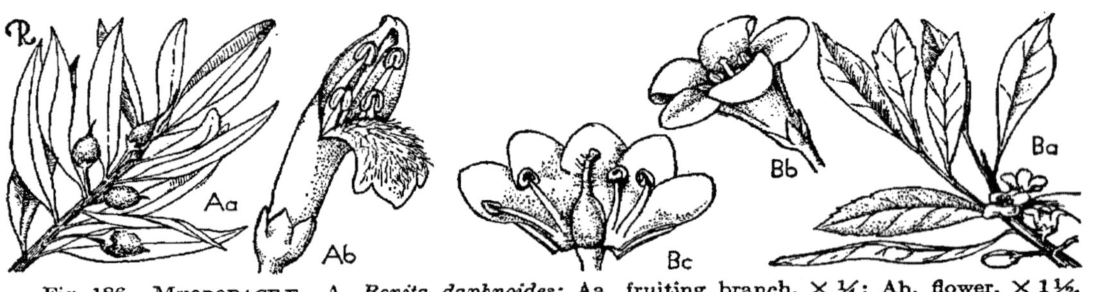

Fig. 186. Myoporaceæ. A, *Bonita daphnoides:* Aa, fruiting branch, × ¼; Ab, flower, × 1½. B, *Myoporum lætum:* Ba, flowering branch, × ¼; Bb, flower, × 3; Bc, same, perianth expanded, × 3. (Ab redrawn from Engler and Prantl, Bb–Bc adapted from Skottsberg.)

186. MYOPORACEÆ. MYOPORUM FAMILY

Woody plants, mainly natives of Australia but also represented by scattered species in the W. Indies, Japan, China, Hawaiian Isls. and elsewhere; genera 5 and species about 90.—Shrubs or trees, glandular or woolly: lvs. alternate or rarely opposite, simple, entire or rarely toothed: fls. bisexual, regular or irregular, axillary, solitary or fascicled, subsessile or pedicillate; calyx 5-parted or -cleft, persistent; corolla gamopetalous, the limb 5–6-lobed, sometimes bilabiate; stamens 4, didynamous, the fifth represented by a staminode, epipetalous; ovary superior, 2-celled or falsely 3–10-celled; ovules usually 1–2, rarely 8 in a cell; style 1, stigmas 1–2: fr. drupaceous.—Related to the Scrophulariaceæ and the Verbenaceæ, the distinctive characters being the presence of oil-glands, the few ovules and the pendulous seeds.

A. Corolla regular or obscurely irregular, predominatingly white....................1. MYOPORUM
AA. Corolla deeply 2-lipped, prevailingly yellow....................2. BONTIA

1. **MYOPORUM,** Banks. More or less heath-like shrubs (or sometimes trees), a few grown in a cool greenhouse; species 25–30, Australia, New Zeal., China, Japan, Pacific isls.—Lvs. alternate, rarely opposite, entire or toothed, with pellucid glands: fls. axillary, usually clustered, small or medium-sized, mostly white; calyx 5-toothed or -parted; corolla regular or nearly so, the tube short and campanulate or longer and funnelform; stamens 4, didynamous, seldom 5; ovary 2–10-celled, each cell 1–2-seeded: fr. a small more or less succulent drupe. (Myop-orum: Greek, referring to the translucent resinous dots on the lvs.)

A. Corolla white or deep pink....................1. *M. acuminatum*
AA. Corolla white spotted purple....................2. *M. lætum*

1. **M. acuminatum,** R. Br. Variable shrub, erect and glabrous: lvs. alternate, elliptic-oblong to lanceolate or linear, to 3 in. long, entire or very few-toothed, somewhat acuminate: fls. in small clusters or solitary, white, the corolla subcampanulate, about ⅓in. long, bearded within, the lobes shorter than the tube: drupe almost globular, ¼in. or less in diam. Australia.

2. **M. lætum,** Forst. f. Shrub or small tree to 25 ft.: lvs. lanceolate or obovate-lanceolate, 2–4 in. long, finely serrate above the middle, acute or acuminate, bright green, shining, almost fleshy: fls. 2–6 in a fascicle, white spotted purple, ⅓–⅔in. wide, the rounded lobes hairy inside: drupe oblong, about ⅓in. long, reddish-purple. New Zeal.

2. **BONTIA,** L. Woody plants with persistent lvs.; a single species in the W. Indies infrequently cult.—Glabrous tree or shrub: lvs. small, scattered, entire: fls. axillary, solitary or clustered; calyx 5-parted; corolla 2-lipped, pilose within, the lower lip reflexed; stamens didynamous, the lower exserted; ovary 2-celled, 4-ovuled: drupe usually 4-seeded. (Bon-tia: named for Jacob Bontius, physician, born at Leiden, 1592–1631.)

B. daphnoides, L. Ten to 30 ft. high: lvs. lanceolate or oblong, 2–4 in. long, acuminate, olive-like: pedicels as long as the fls.; calyx-segms. subulate, ciliate; corolla yellow, variegated with purple, almost 1 in. long: drupe ovate, pointed, about ½in. long, yellow.

187. RUBIACEÆ. MADDER FAMILY

A marked family of about 425 genera and 5,000 species, mainly trop., many of them important economically, yielding dyes and various medicinal and edible products; many genera and species in cult. in N. Amer., mostly in the greenhouse and in the S. for ornament.—Trees, shrubs or herbs: lvs. opposite or whorled, simple, usually entire: fls. bisexual or rarely unisexual, regular or sometimes slightly irregular; calyx 2–6-cleft or lacking; corolla gamopetalous, 4–6-lobed, mostly valvate; stamens 4–6, epipetalous; ovary inferior, 1- to many-, commonly 2-celled; ovules 1 to many in each cell; style 1, stigma 1, capitate or several-branched: fr. a caps., berry or drupe.—Closely related to the Caprifoliaceæ, but usually having stipules or whorled lvs., or a stipular line connecting the opposite lvs. The genus **Cinchona,** L., is scarcely a hort. subject and is not included here; the bark of several species is collected in Peru and furnishes commercial quinine; in Java it is grown on the *Ledgeriana* stock.

A. Number of ovules in each cell 1.
  B. Plants herbaceous or sometimes shrubby at base.
    C. Lvs. mostly in whorls of 3 or more.
      D. Corolla rotate or rotate-campanulate.

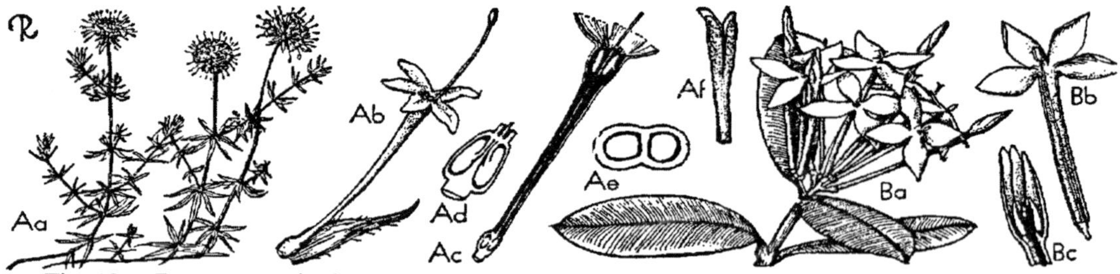

Fig. 187. RUBIACEÆ. A, *Crucianella stylosa:* Aa, flowering stems, × ⅛; Ab, flower with subtending bract, × 1½; Ac, same, vertical section (corolla-lobes excised), × 2; Ad, ovary, vertical section, × 5; Ae, ovary, cross-section, × 8; Af, stigma, × 4. B, *Ixora coccinea:* Ba, flowering twig, × ½; Bb, flower, perianth expanded, × ½; Bc, opening bud tip, vertical section, showing stamens, × 1.

E. Fls. 5-merous: fr. fleshy.......... 1. RUBIA
EE. Fls. 4-merous: fr. dry.......... 2. GALIUM
DD. Corolla funnelform.
E. Fls. 4-merous, with or without bracts and without bractlets; style-branches subequal.......... 3. ASPERULA
EE. Fls. (in ours) 5-merous, bracted and with bractlets; style-branches unequal.......... 4. CRUCIANELLA
CC. Lvs. opposite.
D. Infl. a dense involucrate head.......... 5. RICHARDIA
DD. Infl. of solitary or twin fls.
E. Fls. solitary.......... 6. NERTERA
EE. Fls. in pairs.......... 7. MITCHELLA
BB. Plants woody, growing to shrubs or small trees.
C. Fls. borne in dense globose pedunculate heads.......... 8. CEPHALANTHUS
CC. Fls. not borne as above.
D. Tube of corolla two to three times longer than limb, very slender...... 9. IXORA
DD. Tube of corolla not as above.
E. Corolla salverform: fr. a berry..........10. COFFEA
EE. Corolla funnelform or campanulate: fr. a drupe.
F. Lobes of corolla-limb entire or notched, revolute..........11. COPROSMA
FF. Lobes of corolla-limb obtusely 3-lobed..........12. SERISSA
AA. Number of ovules in each cell more than 1.
B. Habit twining..........13. MANETTIA
BB. Habit not twining.
C. Fr. a caps.
D. Plant a tufted herb..........14. HOUSTONIA
DD. Plant a shrub.
E. Seeds winged or appendaged..........15. BOUVARDIA
EE. Seeds not winged or appendaged.
F. Stipules multifid or multi-setose..........16. PENTAS
FF. Stipules triangular.
G. Fls. (in ours) white, about 3 in. across..........17. PORTLANDIA
GG. Fls. (in ours) not white, not over 1 in. across..........18. RONDELETIA
CC. Fr. not a caps.
D. Stamens mostly 4; corolla-lobes 4 (rarely 5)..........19. HOFFMANNIA
DD. Stamens 5–11; corolla-lobes 5–11.
E. Lvs. (in ours) usually in whorls of 3: stamens inserted near base of corolla-tube..........20. HAMELIA
EE. Lvs. (in ours) usually opposite: stamens inserted at throat or mouth of corolla-tube.
F. Infl. axillary (very rarely terminal).
G. Throat of corolla usually glabrous: fr. sessile..........21. GARDENIA
GG. Throat of corolla hairy: fr. shortly pedicelled..........22. GENIPA
FF. Infl. terminal..........23. POSOQUERIA

1. **RUBIA,** L. About 40 species in Medit. region, trop. and S. Afr., temp. Asia, trop. and temp. S. Amer., one of economic value.—Per. herbs, sometimes shrubby at base, frequently rather stiff, hispid or prickly: lvs. in whorls of 4–8 or very rarely opposite: fls. small, in axillary or terminal cymes, 5-merous; involucre none; calyx-tube ovoid or globose, the limb lacking; corolla rotate or slightly campanulate; ovary 2-celled with 1 ovule in each cell, or through abortion 1-celled: fr. fleshy. (Ru-bia: Latin *red,* referring to the color of the dye extracted from the root.)

R. tinctorum, L. MADDER. Climbing herbaceous per., the long fleshy roots furnishing a dye: lvs. mostly lanceolate, 2–4 in. long, sessile or very short-petioled, not cordate, in whorls of 4–6, prickly-scabrous on the margins and midrib: cymes terminal, panicled, spreading, leafy; fls. greenish-yellow, 1/12in. across: fr. red turning black, ⅛–¼in. across. S. Eu., Asia.

2. **GALIUM,** L. Bedstraw. Slender herbs, the profuse-flowering species often used in rockeries and fl.-beds for their soft and filmy effect, also in bouquets; about 300 species in various parts of the world.—Sts. mostly square, often barbed: lvs. whorled, sessile, without stipules: fls. very small, usually bisexual, epigynous, 4-(rarely 3-) merous, mostly in axillary or terminal panicles; calyx almost or quite obsolete; corolla rotate, deeply 4-parted, the divisions in our species acute or acuminate; stamens 4; ovary 2-celled, with 1 ovule in each cell, forming a 2-lobed, 2-seeded, dry, indehiscent fr., the lobes nearly globular. (Ga-lium: Galion was the name of a plant mentioned by Dioscorides as used in curdling milk.)—The vernacular name is derived from the old practice of using the plants in the making of beds; Ladies Bedstraw, so-called because of the legend that one of these plants was in the hay on which the Mother of Christ rested.

A. Fls. yellow........1. *G. verum*
AA. Fls. white.
  B. Lvs. in 4's, several-nerved, not bristle-tipped........2. *G. boreale*
  BB. Lvs. in 8's or 6's, 1-nerved, bristle-tipped.
    C. Length of lvs. ½–1 in., not glaucous........3. *G. Mollugo*
    CC. Length of lvs. to 1½ in., somewhat glaucous........4. *G. aristatum*

1. **G. verum,** L. Yellow Bedstraw. Per. from a somewhat woody base, glabrous and smooth, or the edges of the lvs. roughish; sts. decumbent or ascending, tufted, 1–3 ft. long: lvs. in 8's or 6's, linear, ½–1 in. long, bristle-tipped: panicle ample, its lower branches exceeding the lvs.; fls. yellow, blooming all summer: fr. small, smooth. Eu., now also a weed in fields in E. U. S.

2. **G. boreale,** L. Northern Bedstraw. Stoloniferous per. forming patches; sts. smooth, 1–3 ft. high, erect, strict: lvs. lanceolate, ¾–1½ in. long, not bristle-tipped, mostly in 4's and often with fascicles of smaller ones in the axils, 3-nerved: panicle ample; fls. white: fr. usually minutely bristly or becoming glabrous. Que. to Alaska south to Pa. and Colo.

3. **G. Mollugo,** L. White Bedstraw. False Babys-Breath. Per., smooth; sts. erect or diffuse, 1–3 ft. long, mostly in clumps: lvs. oblanceolate to linear, ½–1 in. long, bristle-tipped, 1-nerved, in whorls of 8 or on the branchlets 6: fls. very numerous in ample almost leafless panicles, white: fr. smooth or nearly so. (Mollugo: Latin *mollis*, soft, in reference to the delicate lvs.; an herbalist name, employed also in a genus of the Aizoaceæ.) Eu., but a weed in fields in the eastern states.

4. **G. aristatum,** L. False Babys-Breath. Confused with *G. Mollugo* and the plant commonly grown under that name: differs in the longer lanceolate lvs. gradually acuminate at both ends, to 1½ in. long, often glaucous beneath, and the hair-like pedicels making a looser panicle. Eu.

3. **ASPERULA,** L. Woodruff. Ann. and per. herbs, a few planted in borders and rock-gardens; 90 species, Eu., Asia and Australia.—Sts. square: lvs. whorled (some of the lf.-like organs are really stipules): fls. many, small, mostly 4-merous, produced freely from May to July, without bractlets; calyx inconspicuous; corolla funnelform; style-branches subequal; ovules 1 in each cell: fr. leathery, seldom fleshy. (Asper-ula: *roughish*, referring to the lvs.)

A. Plant ann.: fls. blue........1. *A. orientalis*
AA. Plant per.: fls. white or pink.
  B. Lvs. lanceolate, ¼–½in. across........2. *A. odorata*
  BB. Lvs. linear, ⅛in. or less across.
    C. Corolla-tube two to three times longer than lobes........3. *A. hexaphylla*
    CC. Corolla-tube only slightly longer than lobes.
      D. Sts. erect: fls. white, often 3-lobed........4. *A. tinctoria*
      DD. Sts. diffuse or ascending: fls. pink, 4-lobed........5. *A. cynanchica*

1. **A. orientalis,** Boiss. & Hohen. (*A. azurea-setosa*, Hort.). Branching ann. to 1 ft. high: lvs. in whorls of 8, lanceolate, to ¾ or 1 in. long, rough on edges: fls. blue, ⅜in. long, in terminal head-like clusters subtended by leafy bristly bracts half as long as fls.; corolla-tube about four times length of lobes: fr. with small lines. Asia Minor, Caucasus.

2. **A. odorata,** L. Sweet Woodruff. Rootstock slender and creeping; sts. erect or ascending, 6–12 in. high, glabrous: lvs. in whorls of 6–8, lanceolate, 1–1½ in. long and ¼–½ in. across, bristle-tipped, roughish at the margin, with a hay-like fragrance when dried: fls. white, ⅛–¼in. long, in loose branching cymes; corolla-tube about equalling lobes: fr. very hispid. Eu., Asia, N. Afr.

3. **A. hexaphylla,** All. Per.; sts. glabrous, ascending, slender, 1–2 ft. or more high: lvs. in whorls of 6, linear, ¼–½in. long, acute, rough on edges: fls. pink, in small loose heads subtended by bracts shorter than fls.; corolla-tube two to three times longer than lobes: fr. smooth. S. Eu.

4. **A. tinctoria,** L. Dyers Woodruff. Per., with reddish creeping rootstock; sts. erect, 1–2 ft. high, glabrous, branching: lvs. in whorls of 4–6, linear, of unequal length, slightly rough on edges: fls. white, about ⅛in. long, usually 3-lobed, in branching cymes; corolla-tube slightly longer than lobes: fr. smooth. Eu.—*A. ciliata*, Rochel, is similar, but differs in the finely setose-ciliate lf.-margins and corolla-lobes as long as tube.

5. **A. cynanchica,** L. Per.; sts. decumbent or ascending, much-branched, 10–16 in. high, glabrous: lvs. in whorls of 4, linear, to ⅔in. long, of unequal length: fls. pink or lilac, ⅛–¼in. long, in few-fld. branching cymes; corolla-tube slightly longer than lobes: fr. thickly tuberculate. Eu. to Caucasus.

4. **CRUCIANELLA,** L. Crosswort. About 30 species, native of the Medit. region and W. Asia, one sometimes grown in rock-gardens.—Herbs or half-shrubs; branches usually long, slender, 4-angled: upper lvs. opposite, without stipules; lower lvs. in whorls of 3 or more: fls. small, white, rosy or blue, bracteolate; calyx indistinct; corolla funnelform, 4–5-lobed; style-branches distinctly unequal; ovules 1 in each cell: fr. dry. (Crucianel-la: Latin *a little cross*, from the arrangement of the lvs.)

C. stylosa, Trin. (*Phuopsis stylosa*, Benth. & Hook. f.). Prostrate ann. (sometimes grown as a per.), 6–9 in. high: lvs. in whorls of 8 or 9, lanceolate, ½–¾in. long, hispid: fls. small, 5-merous, crimson-pink, in round terminal heads ½in. diam., June–Aug.; style club-shaped, long-exserted, very shortly 2-cleft at apex. Iran.

5. **RICHARDIA,** L. (*Richardsonia*, Kunth). Pubescent or hairy herbs of about 8 American species, one grown in S. U. S. as a forage and cover-crop.—Lvs. opposite, stipules and petioles united into a sheath: fls. in terminal dense involucrate heads; calyx 4–6-parted; corolla funnelform, 4–6-lobed; ovules 1 in each cell: fr. separating into 3–4 carpels. (Richar-dia: named for R. Richardson, 1663–1741, English physician.)

R. scabra, L. Mexican Clover. Hairy ann. with prostrate or ascending sts. to 4 ft. long: lvs. oblong to lanceolate, 1–3 in. long, acute, rough: fls. white, to ¼in. long; corolla-tube over three times longer than lobes. S. C. to S. Amer.

6. **NERTERA,** Banks & Soland. Low creeping herbs, one grown in the greenhouse or the open in Calif.; about 8 species widespread in the southern hemisphere.—Slender perennials: lvs. small, opposite, stalked or sessile, glabrous or somewhat pilose; stipules small: fls. solitary, axillary or terminal, bisexual, inconspicuous, sessile; corolla 4–5-lobed, the tube funnelform-orbicular; stamens 4–5, inserted at the base of the corolla-tube, the anthers exserted; ovary 2-celled, ovules 1 in each cell: drupe fleshy, 2-seeded. (Nerte-ra: Greek *lowly*, referring to the habit.)—Gomozia, Mutis, is the older generic name but Nertera has been conserved.

N. granadensis, Druce (*Gomozia granadensis*, L. *N. depressa*, Banks & Soland.). Bead-Plant. Glabrous, variable in size, often forming dense mats; sts. 6–10 in. long, 4-angled: lvs. broadly ovate, ⅙in. long, acute or obtuse, leathery or almost fleshy, the petioles about as long as the blades: fls. greenish: fr. orange-colored, berry-like, about ¼in. across, lasting from midsummer well into the winter. Cent. to S. Amer., New Zeal., Tasmania.

7. **MITCHELLA,** L. One evergreen trailing herb, scarcely woody, native in N. Amer., and suitable for the rock-garden.—Lvs. opposite, short-petioled: fls. twin, short-peduncled; calyx 4-toothed; corolla funnelform, with 4 spreading lobes; stamens inserted on throat of corolla; ovary 4-celled, ovules 1 in each cell, stigma 4-lobed: fr. a berry-like drupe crowned by persistent calyx. (Mitchel-la: named for John Mitchell, early American botanist, died 1772.)

M. repens, L. Partridge-Berry. Twin-Berry. Squaw-Berry. Sts. to 1 ft. long, rooting: lvs. orbicular-ovate, ¼–¾in. long, dark green and shining above and often with white lines: fls. white, fragrant, ½in. long, the lobes bearded within: fr. scarlet, to ⅓in. across. N. S. to Fla. and Tex.

8. **CEPHALANTHUS,** L. Button-Bush. Ornamental woody plants of 6 species in Amer. and Asia, of which only 1 N. American species is cult.—Shrubs or small trees with opposite or whorled, entire, stipulate lvs.: fls. small, tubular, white or yellowish, 4-merous, in dense globose pedunculate heads; calyx with short obtuse

lobes; stamens included, the filaments inserted on the corolla-throat; style long-exserted; ovary 2-celled, each cell 1-ovuled: fr. dry, separating into 2 nutlets. (Cephalan-thus: Greek *head* and *flower;* fls. in heads.)

C. occidentalis, L. Shrub 3–20 ft. high, glabrous or pubescent, deciduous: lvs. ovate to oval-lanceolate, 3–6 in. long, acuminate, shining above, with triangular stipules between the petioles: heads about 1 in. diam., long-peduncled, 3 or more at the ends of the branches, in summer; fls. with setiform bractlets between them; calyx often slightly hairy at base. N. Amer., E. Asia.

9. **IXORA,** L. Evergreen shrubs or small trees; upwards of 150 species (or split into many more by some authorities) in trop. regions well around the globe, desirable for warmhouse cult.—Lvs. opposite or whorled: fls. showy, in terminal or axillary usually dense corymbs, white, rose or scarlet; pedicels bracteate; corolla with very long and slender tube, the throat sometimes barbed, the limb 4–5-lobed and wide-spreading; stamens 4–5, inserted on the throat, the filaments short or none; style filiform, exserted, 2-branched; ovary on a fleshy disk, 2-celled, ovules solitary: fr. a hard or fleshy 2-pyrenous berry. (Ixo-ra: a Malabar deity.)—There are many garden forms of Ixora under Latin names, these complicating a botanical account of the genus; these forms need special study.

A. Color of fls. white.
  B. Fls. about ⅓in. long....................1. *I. parviflora*
  BB. Fls. 1–1½ in. long....................2. *I. acuminata*
AA. Color of fls. red or yellow.
  B. Lvs. 6–12 in. long: infl. of about 100 fls....................3. *I. macrothyrsa*
  BB. Lvs. to 4 in. long: infl. of fewer fls.
    C. Corolla-lobes obtuse....................4. *I. chinensis*
    CC. Corolla-lobes acute....................5. *I. coccinea*

1. **I. parviflora,** Vahl. Small evergreen tree, much-branched: lvs. oblong or oval, 3–6 in. long, obtuse, glabrous and shining, very short-petioled: fls. white, fragrant, about ⅓in. long, in nearly globose clusters: fr. ¼in. across. India, Ceylon.

2. **I. acuminata,** Roxb. Tall glabrous shrub: lvs. leathery, variable, oval to linear-oblong, to 9 in. and more long, acuminate: fls. white, fragrant, 1–1½ in. long and nearly 1 in. across, in many-fld. corymbs 2–4 in. across: fr. ¼–¾in. long. India.—Often grown as *I. alba* but this Linnæan species was never typified and is unidentifiable, being founded on old pictures.

3. **I. macrothyrsa,** Moore (*Pavetta macrothyrsa,* Teys. & Binn.). Shrub 3–10 ft. high: lvs. lanceolate to oblong, 6–12 in. long and 1½–2½ in. wide, acuminate, somewhat leathery: fls. deep red, to 2 in. long and nearly 1 in. across, in loose puberulent corymbs of about 100 fls. to 8 in. across. Celebes.

4. **I. chinensis,** Lam. Glabrous shrub: lvs. oval-lanceolate to obovate, 2–3 in. long, subsessile, gradually narrowed to rounded base: fls. yellow turning brick-red, about 1½ in. long, in dense corymbs 2–4 in. across having red branches; petals obtuse. Malaya, China.

5. **I. coccinea,** L. Shrub to 15 ft.: lvs. oval with mostly cordate amplexicaul base, 1–4 in. long: fls. red, 1–1½ in. long, in corymbs 2–4 in. across having puberulous green branches; petals acute. India, China. Var. **Bandhuca,** Corner (*I. Bandhuca,* Roxb.), has broader petals and fuller fls. Var. **lutea,** Corner (*I. lutea,* Hutchins.), has yellow fls. with broader petals.

10. **COFFEA,** L. Evergreen shrubs or small trees, producing the coffee of commerce, sometimes cult. for ornament; from 25–40 species in trop. Afr. and Asia, the species not yet clearly defined nor well understood horticulturally.—Lvs. mostly opposite, rarely in 3's: fls. in axillary clusters, cream-colored or white; calyx-limb 5- rarely 4-parted; corolla salverform, the throat sometimes villous; stamens inserted in or below the corolla-throat: fr. a berry; seeds 2, horny, the well-known coffee of commerce. (Coffe-a: from the Arabian name for the drink, itself conjecturally derived from Caffa, a district in S. Abyssinia.)

C. arabica, L. COMMON or ARABIAN COFFEE. Shrub 10–15 ft. high, at first with one main trunk, later with others developing from this; lateral branches horizontal, opposite or very rarely in whorls of 3: lvs. dark glossy green, opposite, rather thin, elliptic, 3–6 in. long, nearly three times as long as broad, more or less abruptly acuminate, the point about ½in. long: fls. pure white, star-like, delicately fragrant; corolla-segms. about ¾in. long, longer than the tube; stigma 2-branched: fr. a 2-seeded deep crimson berry, about ½in. long, the seeds known commercially as "berries" or "beans." Trop. Afr., early intro. into Arabia.—Extensively grown in American tropics and subtropics. A form with variegated lvs. is more showy.

11. **COPROSMA,** Forst. Evergreen shrubs or small trees, sometimes planted for their attractive fr. and shining green or variegated lvs.; about 60 species, Australia and New Zeal., extending to Borneo, Hawaii and Juan Fernandez.—Usually diœcious; low-spreading or upright, with commonly opposite lvs. stalked or nearly sessile: fls. small, solitary or fascicled, white or greenish; corolla funnelform or campanulate, lobes 4–5, revolute; stamens 4–5: fr. an ovoid or globose usually 2-celled drupe. (Copros-ma: Greek name, referring to the fetid odor of the plants.)

C. Baueri, Endl. Shrub or small tree attaining a height of 20–25 ft.: lvs. thick, shining green, broad-ovate or oblong, 1–3 in. long, obtuse or notched at apex, the margins often revolute: staminate fls. in dense heads on short axillary peduncles; pistillate fls. 3–6, in heads with shorter peduncles, calyx very small, corolla tubular, 4-lobed: fr. orange-yellow, ovoid, ⅓in. long. (Named after the collector, F. Bauer, 1760–1826, who was in New Zeal. in 1804–1805.) New Zeal.—Forms with yellow or yellowish-green blotches on the lvs. are in cult. Useful for hedges as it withstands clipping.

12. **SERISSA,** Comm. Greenhouse shrub or grown in the open in warm regions; 1 or more species in S. E. Asia.—Glabrous or the branches puberulent, fetid when bruised: lvs. rather small, opposite, subsessile; stipules persistent: fls. small, axillary or terminal, solitary or fascicled, white; calyx-tube obconic, limb 4–6-parted, lobes subulate-lanceolate; corolla funnelform, tube and throat pilose inside, limb 4–6-lobed, the lobes obtusely 3-lobed; stamens 4–6; ovary 2-celled with 1 ovule in each cell, style shorter than stamens, stigma of 2 linear lobes: fr. a subglobose drupe. (Seris-sa: from the Indian name.)

S. fœtida, Lam. (*S. japonica,* Thunb.). About 2 ft. high: lvs. rather leathery, ovate, ¼–½in. long, acuminate (in a var. yellow-margined): fls. rose-pink in bud, becoming white when expanded, ¼– nearly ½in. long. Japan.

13. **MANETTIA,** Mutis (*Lygistum,* P. Br.). Graceful twining plants, sometimes grown for their ornamental fls. either under glass or in warmer parts of the country out-of-doors as roof-plants or on trellises, blooming more or less the year round; perhaps 40 species in warmer parts of Amer.—Evergreen herbs or shrubs, glabrous or villous, weak and climbing: lvs. petioled, opposite or rarely whorled: fls. axillary, solitary or in short corymbs or panicles, white, yellow or red; calyx-lobes 4 or 8, sometimes lf.-like; corolla-limb 4–5-lobed, the lobes usually shorter than the tube, erect or recurved; stamens 4–5, inserted at the mouth or in the throat of the corolla: fr. an obovoid or turbinate 2-celled dehiscent many-seeded caps. (Manet-tia: Xavier Manetti, of the botanic garden at Florence, born 1723.)

A. Fls. 1½ in. long, red .... 1. *M. glabra*
AA. Fls. ¾in. long, red tipped with yellow.
B. Calyx-lobes erect or spreading; style exserted .... 2. *M. bicolor*
BB. Calyx-lobes reflexed; style about as long as corolla-tube .... 3. *M. inflata*

1. **M. glabra,** Cham. & Schlecht. Lvs. cordate-ovate, 1–2 in. long. acuminate, glabrous: fls solitary, red, 1½ in. long; calyx-lobes erect or spreading; corolla-lobes small, revolute; stamens exserted. S. S. Amer.

2. **M. bicolor,** Paxt. Glabrous: lvs. nearly sessile, lanceolate, acuminate, slightly glaucous: fls. solitary, on short axillary pedicels; calyx-lobes erect or spreading; corolla ¾in. long, somewhat swollen at base, red below and yellow toward the tip, the short lobes spreading-reflexed; style exserted. Brazil.

3. **M. inflata,** Sprague. Differs from the foregoing in the sts. slightly pubescent, lvs. tomentulose on veins beneath, petioled, the leafy reflexed calyx-lobes, corolla more swollen at base and more coarsely hairy, the yellow part much smaller, style (in long-styled plant) about as long as corolla-tube. Paraguay, Uruguay.—Most of the material grown as *M. bicolor* belongs to this species.

14. **HOUSTONIA,** L. Herbs, usually tufted, sometimes planted in rock-gardens; about 25 N. American species.—Lvs. opposite, entire: fls. small, white, blue or purple, solitary or cymose; calyx 4-lobed; corolla funnelform or salverform, 4-lobed; stamens 4, inserted on corolla-tube or throat; ovary 2-celled with numerous ovules in each cell: fr. a caps. free from calyx at top. (Housto-nia: named for Dr. William Houstoun, 1695–1733, physician and botanical collector.)

A. Fls. in cymes: plant to 1½ ft. high .... 1. *H. purpurea*
AA. Fls. solitary: plant to 7 in. high.
B. Lvs. orbicular: sts. prostrate .... 2. *H. serpyllifolia*
BB. Lvs. oblanceolate: sts. erect .... 3. *H. cærulea*

1. **H. purpurea,** L. Erect tufted per. 8–18 in. high: lvs. ovate to ovate-lanceolate, ½–2½ in. long, sessile or the lower ones short-petioled: fls. purple or lilac, ⅓in. long, in terminal cymes; corolla-tube twice as long as lobes. Md. to Ga. and Miss.

2. **H. serpyllifolia,** Michx. CREEPING BLUETS. Per. with prostrate matted sts. to 10 in. long: lvs. orbicular to oval, to ⅓in. long, abruptly petioled: fls. deep blue, ⅓–½in. across, solitary on filiform pedicels; corolla-tube slightly shorter than lobes. Pa. to Ga. and Tenn.

3. **H. cærulea,** L. BLUETS. Tufted per. with erect sts. 1–7 in. high: lvs. oblanceolate or spatulate, ⅛–½in. long, narrowed into petiole: fls. violet, blue or white with yellow eye, ⅓–½in. across, solitary on filiform pedicels; corolla-tube about length of lobes. N. S. to Ga. and Mo.—Sometimes perennating and mat-forming in shaded situations and there useful as a ground-cover.

15. **BOUVARDIA,** Salisb. Attractive greenhouse plants, once popular as florists' subjects; about 30 species from Tex. and Ariz. to Colombia and southward, chiefly in Mex. and Cent. Amer.—Small shrubs, rarely per. herbs: lvs. opposite or whorled, stipules subulate: fls. red, yellow or white, showy, in terminal cymes; calyx with 4 persistent lobes; corolla long-tubular or salverform, with 4 spreading or erect lobes; stamens 4, alternate with the corolla-lobes and attached in the tube or throat; styles included or exserted; stigmas 2; ovary 2-celled, many-ovuled: fr. a loculicidal caps.; seeds winged. (Bouvar-dia: Chas. Bouvard, 1572–1658, physician to Louis XIII and superintendent of Royal Gardens in Paris.)—The bouvardias of florists are evergreen derivatives perhaps not represented by any of the type species.

A. Fls. in shades of red: lvs. normally in 3's except perhaps on the branchlets.
B. Corolla pubescent outside .... 1. *B. ternifolia*
BB. Corolla glabrous outside .... 2. *B. leiantha*
AA. Fls. white: lvs. opposite .... 3. *B. longiflora*

1. **B. ternifolia,** Schlecht. (*Ixora ternifolia*, Cav. *B. triphylla*, Salisb. *B. hirtella*, HBK. *B. Jacquinii*, HBK.). Shrub 2–6 ft. high, sts. hairy when young: lvs. in 3's or 4's, or opposite on the branchlets, lanceolate to ovate, 1½–2½ in. long, scabrous or glabrate: infl. few-fld., terminal; fls. red, the tube to 1 in. long, pubescent outside, lobes erect or ascending, stamens included. Mex. to W. Tex.

2. **B. leiantha,** Benth. Shrub, sts. hairy: lvs. in 3's or 4's or opposite on branchlets, ovate, 1–3 in. long, pubescent: infl. many-fld., terminal; fls. deep red, tube ½in. long and glabrous outside, lobes erect or ascending, stamens included or exserted. Mex. to Costa Rica.

3. **B. longiflora,** HBK. (*Æginetia longiflora*, Cav. *B. Humboldtii*, Hort.). Glabrous shrub 3–5 ft. high: lvs. opposite, ovate to lanceolate, 1–2 in. long: infl. loose; fls. white, very fragrant, the slender tube 1½–3 in. long, glabrous, lobes spreading and 1 in. or more across, stamens included. Mex.

16. **PENTAS,** Benth. Herbs or subshrubs grown under glass; 30 species in trop. and S. Afr. and Madagascar.—Erect or prostrate, hispid or tomentose: lvs. opposite, petioled, stipules multifid or bristly: fls. usually in corymbs; calyx-lobes 4–6, unequal; corolla pilose, the long tube dilated and villous in the throat, the lobes valvate; stamens 4–6, inserted below the throat; style exserted; disk often produced into a cone after anthesis: caps. membranaceous or leathery, 2-celled, loculicidal; seeds many, minute. (Pen-tas: Greek *five*, referring to the floral parts)

P. lanceolata, Schum. (*Ophiorrhiza lanceolata*, Forsk. *P. carnea*, Benth., under which name it is known to gardeners). Erect or decumbent, shrubby at base, 1–2 ft. high, hairy: lvs. ovate, elliptic or lance-oblong, 1–6 in. long, ⅓–2 in. wide, more or less acute, narrowed at base into a short petiole: fls. dimorphic, pale purple, to 1 in. long, nearly sessile, in cymose clusters; corolla very hairy at throat, limb spreading, about ½in. across. Trop. Afr., Arabia.—There are several hort. vars. with fls. white, rosy or carmine-rose.

17. **PORTLANDIA,** P. Br. Woody plants with showy fls. grown in the open far S.; 8–10 species in Mex., W. Indies.—Glabrous shrubs or small trees: lvs. opposite, coriaceous, petiolate, the stipules between the petioles connate with them and forming a sheath: fls. large, white or purple, on axillary peduncles; calyx 4–5-lobed, persistent; corolla large, nearly campanulate or funnelform, 5-lobed; stamens 5; ovary 2-celled with many ovules: fr. a leathery obovoid-oblong caps. (Portlan-dia: named in honor of the Duchess of Portland, 1715–1785.)

P. platantha, Hook. Evergreen shrub 1½–3 ft. high: lvs. nearly sessile, elliptic-ovate, acute; stipules broadly triangular, obtuse: calyx-lobes 4, lanceolate, leafy, spreading; corolla white, about 3 in. across and 6 in. long, broadly funnelform approaching campanulate, with 5 ovate spreading lobes. (Platantha: Greek *broad-fld.*) Probably trop. Amer., but source unknown; a doubtful species botanically.

18. **RONDELETIA,** L. Evergreen shrubs and trees with clusters of large often fragrant fls., a few species grown under glass or out-of-doors in the extreme S.; more than 100 species in trop. Amer.—Lvs. opposite, rarely in 3's, coriaceous or membranaceous; stipules broad, usually persistent: fls. red, yellow or white, in axillary corymbed or panicled or rarely terminal cymes; calyx-lobes 4–5; corolla-tube usually slender, sometimes swollen, the throat glabrous or bearded; limb 5-lobed or in some species 4-lobed; stamens 4–5; ovary 2-celled, many-ovuled: caps. loculicidal, usually globose. (Rondele-tia: named in memory of G. Rondelet, 1507–1566, French physician and naturalist.)

A. Corolla densely yellow-bearded in throat, pink or dull red.
B. Lvs. densely pubescent beneath . . . . 1. *R. amœna*
BB. Lvs. glabrous or nearly so . . . . 2. *R. cordata*
AA. Corolla not yellow-bearded in throat, bright orange-red . . . . 3. *R. odorata*

1. **R. amœna,** Hemsl. (*Rogiera amœna,* Planch.). Shrub or small tree: lvs. ovate, 3–6 in. long, short-acuminate, short-petioled, densely pubescent beneath, with oblong reflexed stipules: fls. pink, pubescent, the stout tube to ½in. long, throat densely yellow-bearded. Mex. to Panama.

2. **R. cordata,** Benth. Shrub 3–7 ft. high: lvs. sessile or nearly so, ovate-oblong to ovate, 3–5 in. long, acute or acuminate, glabrous or nearly so, with oblong-triangular obtuse reflexed stipules: fls. pink or dull red, ¼in. or less across, short-pedicelled, in dense terminal and axillary corymbose cymes; corolla ⅜in. long, strigillose without, the stout tube with densely yellow-hairy throat. Guatemala.

3. **R. odorata,** Jacq. (*R. speciosa,* Lodd.). Shrub to 6 ft.: lvs. ovate to elliptic or oblong, about 2 in. long, often with revolute margins, shortly petioled, hairy along veins beneath, often rugose, stipules triangular, erect: fls. bright orange-red with yellow throat, about ½in. across, in few- to many-fld. terminal cymes; corolla-tube slender, about ½in. long, the 5 lobes rounded. Cuba, Panama.

19. **HOFFMANNIA,** Sw. Herbs or woody plants cult. for their very showy foliage; species above 50 in Cent. and S. Amer.—Branches terete or 4-angled: lvs. opposite or whorled, conspicuously veined, very showy: fls. small, white, yellow or red; calyx with 4 short lobes; corolla tubular, with 4 (rarely 5) oblong or linear obtuse lobes; stamens mostly 4; disk ring-like or cushion-like; ovary 2–3-celled: fr. an oblong or narrow many-seeded berry. (Hoffman-nia: Georg Franz Hoffmann, 1761–1826, professor of botany at Goettingen.)

A. Fl.-clusters on long stalks. . . . . 1. *H. discolor*
AA. Fl.-clusters not on long stalks.
B. Lvs. oblong-lanceolate . . . . 2. *H. Ghiesbreghtii*
BB. Lvs. round-ovate . . . . 3. *H. regalis*

1. **H. discolor,** Hemsl. (*Campylobotrys discolor,* Lem.). Slightly hairy plant about 6 in. high but drooping over the side of the pot or pan and forming a mat, sts. terete: lvs. short-petioled, oblong-obovate, to 6 in. long and 2½ in. wide, satiny green above and rich light purple to green beneath: fls. ½in. long, red, in long-stalked recurving racemes, on red pedicels. Mex.

2. **H. Ghiesbreghtii,** Hemsl. (*Campylobotrys Ghiesbreghtii,* Lem.). Subshrub to 4 ft., nearly glabrous, sts. 4-angled and narrowly winged: lvs. oblong-lanceolate, usually 1 ft. or less long and 2½–3½ in. wide, acuminate, very strongly veined, purple-red beneath and dark velvety green above, the short winged petiole somewhat decurrent: fl.-clusters crowded in the axils; fls. yellow, with a red spot in the center, ¼in. long. Mex., Guatemala, collected by Ghiesbreght.—A hort. form has handsomely mottled lvs.

3. **H. regalis,** Hemsl. (*Higginsia regalis,* Hook.). Strong-growing glabrous subshrub, the branches obtusely 4-angled and somewhat fleshy: lvs. large, round-ovate, abruptly acuminate, plicate with arched nerves, purple-red beneath and dark rich green above: fl.-clusters crowded in the axils; fls. yellow, sessile. Mex.

20. **HAMELIA,** Jacq. About 25 species, in trop. and subtrop. Amer.; one grown in the greenhouse or out-of-doors in the extreme S.—Evergreen upright shrubs with herbaceous shoots: lvs. membranaceous, entire, opposite or sometimes in whorls,

petioled, with interpetiolar stipules: fls. short-stalked or sessile, in terminal forking cymes; calyx with 5 short erect persistent lobes; corolla tubular or subcampanulate, contracted at base, the limb with 5 short lobes; stamens 5, the filaments connate below and inserted near base of corolla-tube; ovary 5-celled: fr. a small ovoid or globose berry with numerous minute seeds. (Hame-lia: Henri Louis Duhamel du Monceau, 1700–1781, prominent French botanical author.)

H. patens, Jacq. (*H. erecta*, Jacq.). SCARLET-BUSH. To 12 ft., cinereous-pubescent on all young parts: lvs. usually in whorls of 3, elliptic-ovate to oblong, 3–8 in. long, acute or acuminate, petiolate: fls. scarlet-orange, almost sessile along the branches of the 3–5-rayed cyme: calyx-segms. short, triangular; corolla with narrowly cylindric tube about ¾in. long; stamens exceeding the very short corolla-lobes: fr. ovoid, ¼in. long, dark red or purple. Fla. to Paraguay.

21. **GARDENIA,** Ellis. Two species planted in the open in the S. and one a florists' plant N.; species about 60 in subtrop. regions of the eastern hemisphere.—Glabrous, pubescent or even tomentose shrubs or rarely small trees: lvs. opposite or in 3's, with interpetiolar stipules: fls. large, yellow or white, axillary and solitary or sometimes corymbose; calyx-tube ovoid or obconic, the limb lobed or parted, persistent; corolla salverform or tubular, the limb with 5–11 spreading or recurved contorted lobes; stamens 5–9, inserted on the corolla-throat: fr. leathery or fleshy, sessile, sometimes breaking open irregularly. (Garde-nia: after Alexander Garden, 1730–1791, physician of Charleston, S. C., a correspondent of Linnæus.)

A. Calyx with 5 long teeth, about length of corolla-tube........................1. *G. jasminoides*
AA. Calyx spathe-like, two to three times shorter than corolla-tube................2. *G. Thunbergia*

1. **G. jasminoides,** Ellis (*Varneria augusta*, L. *G. florida*, L. *G. radicans*, Thunb. *G. augusta*, Merr.). CAPE-JASMINE. Variable evergreen shrub, 2–6 ft. high, the st. sometimes rooting: lvs. lanceolate to obovate, to 4 in. long, short-acuminate, thick, sometimes variegated: fls. to 3 in. across, often double, waxy, camellia-like, fragrant; calyx ribbed, with 5 long teeth; corolla-tube cylindric, 1–1½ in. long: fr. fleshy, orange-colored, ribbed, 1½ in. long. China. Var. **Fortuniana,** Lindl. (*G. Fortunei*, Hort.), larger-fld. form; presumably the *G. Veitchii* of gardens belongs here.

2. **G. Thunbergia,** L. f. To 10 ft.: lvs. elliptic, 4–6 in. long, acuminate: fls. white, waxy, very fragrant, 3–4 in. across; calyx split down one side; corolla-tube 2½–3 in. long: fr. very hard, white, smooth, 2–2½ in. long. (Thunbergia: a genus in Acanthaceæ, named for C. P. Thunberg, page 52.) S. Afr.

22. **GENIPA,** L. A W. Indian genus of 3–4 species, one furnishing edible fr.—Trees: lvs. opposite, shortly petioled or sessile, large, leathery, shining; stipules interpetiolar, deciduous: cymes axillary or terminal, few-fld.; fls. white to yellowish, large; calyx campanulate, truncate or 5–6-toothed, persistent; corolla salverform, the limb twisted to the left, 5–6-parted; stamens 5–6, inserted at the top of the corolla-tube; ovary 1–2-celled: fr. a large subglobose edible berry with numerous seeds. (Geni-pa: Brazilian name.)

G. americana, L. Tree to 50 ft.: lvs. obovate to oblong, to 1 ft. long: pedicels shorter than the calyx; calyx truncate or shallowly crenate; corolla silky, white or light yellow, about 1 in. across, the tube 1 in. long, the 5–6 lobes obtuse, the throat villous: berry russet-brown, about 2½ in. diam., smooth or sparsely tuberculate, glabrous or short-pilose; seeds irregular, thick, nearly ½in. long, dark brown.—The fr. is largely used in trop. Amer., as a preserve under the name "Genipap"; sometimes called "Marmalade-Box."

23. **POSOQUERIA,** Aubl. Shrubs or small trees, sometimes grown under glass or in the far S. out-of-doors, for their glossy foliage and fragrant fls.; about 15 species in trop. Amer.—Branches terete, glabrous: lvs. opposite, short-petioled, coriaceous, entire; stipules interpetiolar, rather large, deciduous: fls. fragrant, white, rose or scarlet, in many-fld. terminal corymbs; calyx-limb 5-toothed, persistent; corolla with long slender tube, scarcely dilated at throat, the limb with 5 obtuse subequal lobes, somewhat contorted; stamens 5, inserted at mouth of the corolla; ovary 1–2-celled: berry ovoid, fleshy, rather large, few- to many-seeded. (Posoque-ria: from a native name in Guiana.)

P. latifolia, Roem. & Schult. (*Tocoyena latifolia*, Lam. *Oxyanthus isthmia*, Hort.). Large shrub or tree to 20 ft.: lvs. oval to oblong, 4–10 in. long, shortly acuminate, obtuse or rounded at base; calyx-teeth acute or obtuse; corolla white, the tube 4–6 in. long and about ⅛in. diam., the limb abruptly spreading and about 1 in. across: fr. yellow, 2 in. across; seeds black, nearly ½in. long. W. Indies, Mex. to S. Amer.

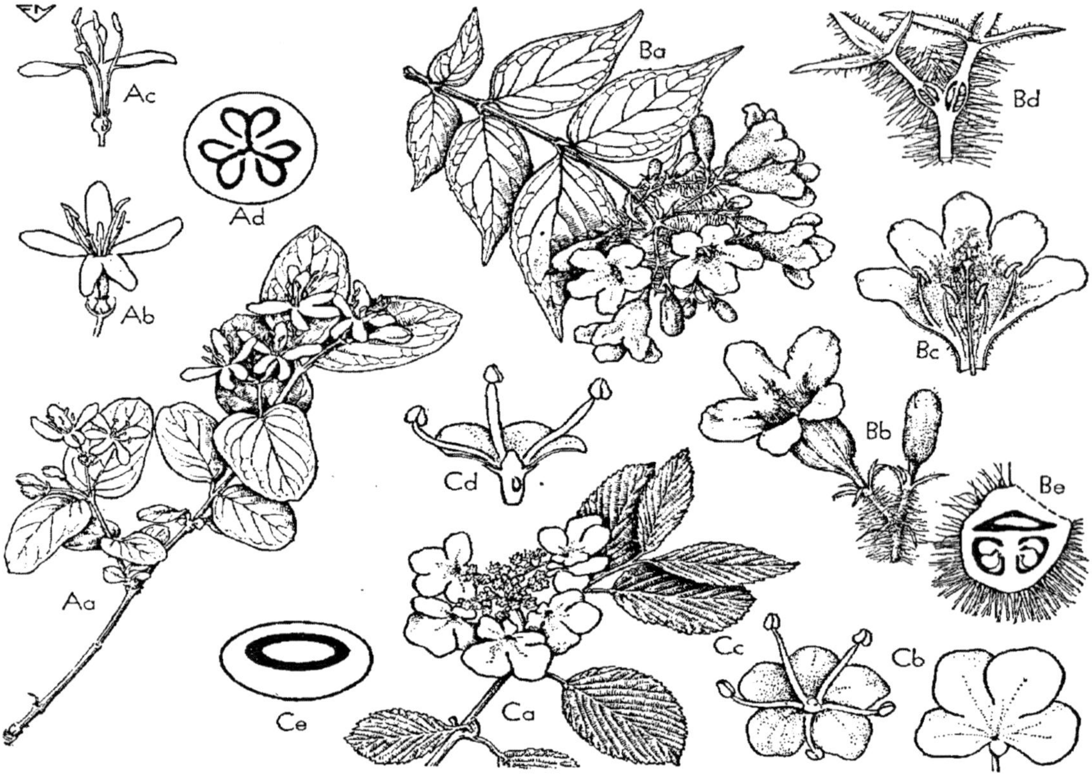

Fig. 188. Caprifoliaceæ. A, *Lonicera tatarica:* Aa, flowering branch, × ½; Ab, flower, × 1; Ac, same, vertical section, × 1; Ad, ovary, cross-section, × 10. B, *Kolkwitzia amabilis:* Ba, flowering branch, × ½; Bb, flower and bud, × 1; Bc, corolla expanded, × 1; Bd, ovaries, vertical section, × 2; Be, same, cross-section, × 10. C, *Viburnum tomentosum:* Ca, flowering branch, × ¼; Cb, sterile flower, × ½; Cc, perfect flower, × 3; Cd, same, vertical section, × 3; Ce, ovary, cross-section, × 15.

188. CAPRIFOLIACEÆ. HONEYSUCKLE FAMILY

A family consisting largely of woody plants, many cult. in N. Amer. for ornamental purposes, a few for their medicinal properties; genera 14 and species about 400, distributed principally in the north temp. zone, a few in the mts. of the tropics.—Shrubs or very rarely herbs: lvs. opposite, simple or pinnate, mostly without stipules: fls. bisexual, regular or irregular; calyx 4–5-toothed or 4–5-fid, the tube adnate to the ovary; corolla gamopetalous, 4–5-lobed, tubular or rotate; stamens as many as lobes of corolla and alternate with them, epipetalous; ovary inferior, 1–5-celled, each cell 1- to many-ovuled, placentation axile, style 1 or obsolete, stigmas 1–5: fr. a berry, caps. or achene.

A. Corolla rotate or nearly so (except in a few species of Viburnum), the limb regular; style short, 3–5-lobed.
 B. Lvs. pinnately cut . . . . 1. Sambucus
 BB. Lvs. simple . . . . 2. Viburnum
AA. Corolla tubular or bell-shaped, the limb usually irregular; style long, mostly with capitate stigma.
 B. Fr. a berry.
  C. Ovary 5–8-celled . . . . 3. Leycesteria
  CC. Ovary 2–4- (rarely 5-) celled.
   D. Shape of corolla regular; ovary 4-celled, 2 of the cells sterile: fr. a berry-like drupe with 2 nutlets . . . . 4. Symphoricarpos

DD. Shape of corolla commonly more or less irregular; ovary 2–3-celled: fr. a few- to several-seeded berry.......... 5. LONICERA
BB. Fr. an achene or caps.
C. Plant trailing.......... 6. LINNÆA
CC. Plant upright.
D. Stamens 4: fr. a 1-seeded achene.
E. Achene ovoid, bristly.......... 7. KOLKWITZIA
EE. Achene narrow and long, leathery, not bristly.......... 8. ABELIA
DD. Stamens 5: fr. a 2-valved caps. with numerous seeds.
E. Fls. yellow, 2-lipped.......... 9. DIERVILLA
EE. Fls. white, pink or crimson, not 2-lipped.......... 10. WEIGELA

1. **SAMBUCUS,** L. ELDER. About 20 species in the temp. and subtrop. regions of both hemispheres, furnishing ornamental subjects.—Large and rather coarse shrubs or small trees, rarely per. herbs, some spreading by suckers, the vigorous shoots with large pith: lvs. opposite, odd-pinnate, the lfts. serrate, with or without stipules and stipels: fls. small, usually bisexual and 5-merous, in terminal compound cymes or panicles; calyx-lobes minute; corolla rotate or nearly so; stamens as many as the corolla-lobes, the filaments short: ovary 3–5-celled, style short, 3–5-lobed: fr. a small drupe with 3–5 cartilaginous nutlets. (Sambu-cus: old Latin name for the elder.)

A. Cymes flat: pith white: fr. black or dark purple.
B. Fr. glaucous.......... 1. *S. cærulea*
BB. Fr. not glaucous.
C. Branches strongly lenticellate: lfts. usually 5.......... 2. *S. nigra*
CC. Branches slightly lenticellate: lfts. usually 7.......... 3. *S. canadensis*
AA. Cymes paniculate: pith brown: fr. red, varying to yellow or white.
B. Plant glabrous.......... 4. *S. racemosa*
BB. Plant pubescent, at least when young.......... 5. *S. pubens*

1. **S. cærulea,** Raf. (*S. glauca*, Nutt.). BLUE ELDER. Shrub or tree to 50 ft., with slender branches glaucous when young: lvs. bright green; lfts. 5–7, oblong or oblong-lanceolate, 2½–6 in. long, coarsely serrate, glabrous: fls. yellowish-white, produced in June–July in 5-rayed cymes 4–6 in. across: fr. blue-black, about ⅙in. across, glaucous, Aug.–Sept. B. C. to Calif. and Utah.

2. **S. nigra,** L. EUROPEAN ELDER. Shrub or tree to 30 ft., with deeply furrowed bark and gray strongly lenticellate branches: lvs. dark green; lfts. 3–7, usually 5, elliptic or ovate, 2–6 in. long, acute or acuminate, serrate, with a short petiolule, usually pubescent beneath while young: fls. yellowish or dull white, with a heavy odor, produced in late spring and early summer in flat 5-rayed cymes 5–8 in. across: fr. globose, shining black, 3-celled, ¼–⅙in. diam., ripe in Sept. Eu., W. Asia, N. Afr. Var. **aurea,** Sweet, foliage golden-yellow. Var. **aureo-variegata,** West., lvs. variegated with yellow. Var. **laciniata,** L., lfts. deeply dissected.

3. **S. canadensis,** L. AMERICAN or SWEET ELDER. Stoloniferous shrub to 12 ft., with white pith and pale yellowish-gray slightly lenticellate branches: lvs. bright green; lfts. usually 7, elliptic to lanceolate, 2–6 in. long, acuminate, sharply toothed, on short petiolules, the lowest pair frequently 2–3-lobed, the lower surface smooth or slightly downy: fls. white, produced in June–July in 5-rayed cymes to 10 in. across: fr. purplish-black, usually 4-celled, about ¼in. diam., in Sept. N. S. to Fla and Tex. Var. **acutiloba,** Ellwanger & Barry (var. *laciniata*, Cowell), lfts. much dissected. Var. **aurea,** Cowell, foliage golden-yellow, fr. red.—Sometimes grown for the edible fr. and there are pomological vars.

4. **S. racemosa,** L. EUROPEAN RED ELDER. Shrub to 12 ft., with branches and pith light brown and young branchlets glabrous: lfts. 5–7, oval or ovate, 2–3 in. long, acuminate, sharply and regularly toothed, glabrous: infl. a dense terminal pyramidal panicle 1½–3 in. high and scarcely as wide in which lower branches are usually reflexed; fls. yellowish-white, blooming in spring: fr. scarlet, 3-seeded, ¼in. across, in summer. Eu., W. Asia.

5. **S. pubens,** Michx. (*S. racemosa* var. *pubens*, Wats.). AMERICAN RED ELDER. Shrub to 15 ft., with brownish-red pith and branches pubescent when young: lfts. 5–7, oblong, 2–4 in. long, toothed, pubescent beneath at least when young: infl. a loose pyramidal panicle to 4 in. long in which lower branches are spreading; fls. yellowish-white, in spring: fr. scarlet, about ¼in. across, in summer. N. B. to Ga. and Colo.

2. **VIBURNUM,** L. Attractive and popular ornamental shrubs; about 120 species in N. and Cent. Amer. and in the Old World from Eu. and N. Afr. to E. Asia, distributed as far south as Java.—Upright mostly rather large shrubs or rarely small trees, the foliage mostly deciduous and assuming a bright fall coloring, or sometimes persistent: lvs. opposite, simple, medium-sized, with or without stipules: fls. small, in terminal paniculate or mostly umbel-like cymes, the marginal fls. sterile and

radiate in several species; calyx with 5 minute teeth; corolla rotate or campanulate, rarely tubular; stamens 5; ovary usually 1-celled, ovule 1 or more and pendulous, style very short, 3-lobed: fr. a drupe with a 1-seeded commonly compressed stone. (Vibur-num: ancient Latin name.)

A. Lvs. habitually lobed.
B. Cymes with uniform fls. . . . . 1. *V. acerifolium*
BB. Cymes with marginal fls. sterile and enlarged.
C. Petioles with small glands . . . . 2. *V. trilobum*
CC. Petioles with few large disk-like glands.
D. Bark thin: lvs. all lobed . . . . 3. *V. Opulus*
DD. Bark thick and somewhat corky: lvs. sometimes narrow and unlobed . . 4. *V. Sargentii*
AA. Lvs. not lobed.
B. Marginal fls. of cymes sterile and enlarged, sometimes occupying whole head.
C. Lf. 4–8 in. long, cordate at base . . . . 5. *V. alnifolium*
CC. Lf. 2–4 in. long, rounded at base.
D. Veins of lvs. anastomosing before reaching margin: winter-buds naked. 6. *V. macrocephalum*
DD. Veins of lvs. straight, ending in points of teeth: winter-buds scaly . . . . . 7. *V. plicatum*
BB. Marginal fls. of cymes similar to others.
C. Foliage persistent.
D. Under surface of lvs. gray- or yellow-tomentose . . . . 8. *V. rhytidophyllum*
DD. Under surface of lvs. glabrous or nearly so.
E. Corolla with tube twice as long as limb . . . . 9. *V. suspensum*
EE. Corolla rotate or with tube shorter than limb.
F. Veins of lvs. straight, ending in the teeth . . . . 10. *V. japonicum*
FF. Veins of lvs. anastomosing before reaching margin.
G. Margins of lvs. usually revolute: cymes umbel-like, flat-topped . . . . 11. *V. Tinus*
GG. Margins of lvs. not revolute: cymes paniculate . . . . 12. *V. odoratissimum*
CC. Foliage deciduous.
D. Corolla with cylindrical tube.
E. Blooming before the lvs., the infl. nearly glabrous . . . . 13. *V. fragrans*
EE. Blooming with the lvs., the infl. tomentose . . . . 14. *V. Carlesii*
DD. Corolla rotate-campanulate.
E. Cymes sessile (no common peduncle).
F. Lf. acuminate; petioles usually with broad wavy margin . . . . 15. *V. Lentago*
FF. Lf. obtuse or acute; petioles with narrow not wavy margin . . . . 16. *V. prunifolium*
EE. Cymes (whole cluster) peduncled.
F. Margins of lvs. nearly entire or finely serrate.
G. Under surface of lvs. tomentose: winter-buds naked . . . . 17. *V. Lantana*
GG. Under surface of lvs. only slightly pubescent: winter-buds scaly.
H. Fr. red at maturity . . . . 18. *V. setigerum*
HH. Fr. black at maturity.
I. Peduncle as long as or longer than cyme: lvs. usually entire . . . . 19. *V. nudum*
II. Peduncle shorter than cyme: lvs. usually denticulate . . . . . 20. *V. cassinoides*
FF. Margins of lvs. coarsely dentate.
G. Fr. red at maturity.
H. Axes of infl. pubescent: lvs. pubescent on both sides . . . . 21. *V. dilatatum*
HH. Axes of infl. nearly glabrous: lvs. glabrous except veins beneath . . . . 22. *V. Wrightii*
GG. Fr. blue-black at maturity.
H. Lf. obovate, narrowed at base . . . . 23. *V. Sieboldii*
HH. Lf. ovate to orbicular, rounded or cordate at base.
I. Axes of infl. glabrous . . . . 24. *V. dentatum*
II. Axes of infl. pubescent.
J. Branchlets light gray, bark flaky: stipules present . . . . . . 25. *V. molle*
JJ. Branchlets grayish-brown, bark not flaky: stipules absent . . . . 26. *V. pubescens*

1. **V. acerifolium,** L. DOCKMACKIE. Deciduous shrub to 6 ft., the slender upright branches downy at first becoming glabrate; winter-buds scaly: lvs. maple-like, 3-lobed, 2–5 in. long, coarsely dentate, with acuminate lobes, pubescent or at length almost glabrous, turning dark purple in autumn: fls. white, ⅙in. diam., uniform and bisexual, produced during early summer in long-stalked cymes 2–3 in. across: fr. oval, ⅓in. long, red changing to purple-black. N. B. to Minn. south to N. C.

2. **V. trilobum,** Marsh. (*V. americanum*, Auth. not Mill. *V. Oxycoccus*, Pursh). CRANBERRY-BUSH. Deciduous shrub to 12 ft., with gray glabrous branches; winter-buds scaly: lvs. broad-ovate, 2–5 in. long, lobes coarsely toothed or nearly entire, pubescent on the veins beneath or nearly glabrous; petioles with shallow groove and small usually stalked glands: cymes 3–4 in. across, short-peduncled, with marginal showy sterile fls. produced in early summer; stamens exserted: fr. bright scarlet, beginning to color by the end of July and keeping their color till the following spring, ⅓in. long. N. B. to B. C. south to N. J. to Ore.

3. **V. Opulus,** L. EUROPEAN CRANBERRY-BUSH. Deciduous shrub to 12 ft., with smooth light gray branches; winter-buds scaly: lvs. maple-like, 2–4 in. long, with 3 (sometimes 4–5) acuminate lobes, coarsely and irregularly toothed, pubescent beneath; petioles ½–1 in.

long, with 2 narrow stipules near base and few large disk-like glands near lf.-blade: cymes 3–4 in. across, peduncled, with a border of sterile showy white fls. ¾in. diam., the center composed of small fertile fls., in early summer; stamens exserted, the anthers yellow: fr. subglobose, scarlet, ⅓in. diam. (Opulus: same as Populus.) Eu., N. Afr., N. Asia. Var. **roseum,** L. (var. *sterile,* DC.), SNOWBALL, GUELDER-ROSE, all fls. sterile, forming large globose heads. Var. **nanum,** Jacq., is a very dwarf form with small lvs.—There are also variegated strains, and one yellow-fruited var.

4. **V. Sargentii,** Koehne. Deciduous shrub to 12 ft., with dark gray fissured somewhat corky bark; winter-buds scaly: lvs. 3–6 in. long, with 3 toothed lobes or the middle lobe often elongated and entire, or sometimes lvs. oblong-lanceolate and unlobed; petioles ¾–1½ in. long, with large disk-like glands: cymes to 4 in. across, long-peduncled, with border of sterile white fls. 1 in. diam., in early summer; stamens exserted, anthers purple: fr. subglobose, scarlet, ⅓in. long. (C. S. Sargent, page 51.) N. E. Asia.

5. **V. alnifolium,** Marsh. (*V. lantanoides,* Michx.). HOBBLE-BUSH. AMERICAN WAYFARING-TREE. Deciduous bushy shrub to 10 ft., the wide-spreading often procumbent branches scurfy-pubescent when young; winter-buds naked: lvs. orbicular or broadly ovate, 3–8 in. broad, acute or short-acuminate, cordate at base, irregularly serrate, nearly glabrous above, scurfy and stellate-pubescent beneath especially on the veins, turning deep claret-red in autumn; petioles 1–2 in. long, scurfy: cymes sessile, 3–5 in. broad; fls. white, the marginal ones enlarged (often 1 in. across) and sterile, on long pedicels, late spring and early summer: fr. ovoid-oblong, dark purple, ⅓in. long. N. B. and Mich. to N. C.

6. **V. macrocephalum,** Fort. Deciduous or semi-evergreen shrub to 12 ft. or more, with spreading branches, the young shoots densely stellate-pubescent; winter-buds naked: lvs. oval to ovate-oblong, 2–4 in. long, denticulate, rounded at base, short-petioled, acute or rounded at apex, dark green and sparsely stellate-pubescent above, densely stellate-pubescent beneath: cymes peduncled, 3–5 in. across; fls. pure white, the marginal ones sterile and radiate, ¾–1 in. across, late spring and early summer. China. Var. **sterile,** Rehd. (*V. Fortunei,* Hort.), CHINESE SNOWBALL, has all the fls. sterile and radiate, forming a subglobose ball sometimes 7–8 in. across.

7. **V. plicatum,** Thunb. (*V. tomentosum* var. *sterile,* Koch. *V. tomentosum* var. *plenum,* Rehd.). JAPANESE SNOWBALL. Bushy shrub to 10 ft., deciduous, the spreading branches tomentose when young; winter-buds scaly: lvs. broadly ovate to oblong-ovate, sometimes obovate, 1½–4 in. long, acute or abruptly acuminate, rounded or cuneate at base, dentate-serrate, dark green and nearly glabrous above, stellate-pubescent beneath, at least on the veins: infl. a globose head, with all the fls. sterile. Var. **tomentosum,** Miq. (forma *tomentosum,* Rehd. *V. tomentosum,* Thunb.), is the wild form in China and Japan: infl. a flat umbel-like pubescent cyme, long-peduncled, 2½–4 in. across; marginal fls. white, sterile, long-pedicelled, 1–1½ in. across, more or less irregular, May–June: fr. ovoid, red, changing to bluish-black.

8. **V. rhytidophyllum,** Hemsl. Shrub, with stout upright branches and persistent lvs., to 10 ft., branchlets densely stellate-tomentose; winter-buds naked: lvs. ovate-oblong to oblong-lanceolate, 3–7½ in. long, entire or slightly denticulate, acute or obtuse, rounded or subcordate at base, stout-petioled, the upper surface dark green and glabrous, lustrous, deeply wrinkled, the lower surface reticulate and covered with thick gray or yellowish stellate tomentum: cymes 4–8 in. across, stellate-tomentose, peduncled; fls. yellowish-white, about ¼in. diam., the buds forming in autumn and remaining exposed all winter and expanding the following May and June: fr. ovoid, ⅓in. long, red changing to black, in Sept.–Oct. Cent. and W. China.

9. **V. suspensum,** Lindl. Evergreen shrub reaching 6 ft., the slender branches appearing warty due to the conspicuous lenticels; branches and infl. stellate-pubescent: lvs. oval or oval-oblong, 2–4 in. long, acute or somewhat obtuse, usually crenate-serrate toward the apex, shining and dark green above, paler beneath, glabrous: fls. white, tinged pink, summer-blooming, the dense semi-globose panicles becoming 1½ in. across; corolla ⅜–½in. long, with cylindric tube twice as long as limb: fr. red, subglobose. Liu-kiu Isl.

10. **V. japonicum,** Spreng. (*V. macrophyllum,* Blume). Upright evergreen glabrous shrub to 6 ft. high; winter-buds scaly: lvs. leathery, ovate, 3–6 in. long, acute or short-acuminate, rounded or broadly cuneate at base, remotely dentate except at base, lustrous above: cymes short-peduncled, glabrous, 2–4 in. broad; fls. white, very fragrant, bisexual, uniform, produced in summer: fr. globose, red, ⅓in. long. Japan.

11. **V. Tinus,** L. LAURESTINUS. Much-branched evergreen shrub to 10 ft., often cult. as a pot-plant N., the branches glabrous or somewhat hairy: lvs. ovate-oblong or oblong, 2–3 in. long, entire and usually revolute at margins, acute, glossy dark green and glabrous above, commonly pubescent only on the veins beneath: cymes somewhat convex, 2–3 in. broad; fls. white or pinkish-white, slightly fragrant, ¼–⅜in. across, the corolla-limb longer than the tube, in summer or in the greenhouse in winter and early spring: fr. ovoid, black, rather dry. (Tinus: pre-Linnæan name for the plant.) Medit. region.

12. **V. odoratissimum,** Ker. Glabrous evergreen shrub to 10 ft., with stout warty branches: lvs. elliptic to elliptic-oblong, 3–6 in. long, acute, remotely serrate toward the

apex or entire, bright glossy green above, paler beneath: fls. pure white, fragrant, produced in late spring and early summer, in broadly pyramidal panicles 4 in. high; corolla rotate-campanulate: fr. red, changing to black. India to Japan.

13. **V. fragrans,** Bunge. Deciduous shrub to 10 ft., with brown slightly pubescent branches: lvs. oval, 1½–3 in. long, acute, cuneate at base, serrate, slightly pubescent, short-petioled: fls. white or pinkish, in nearly glabrous panicles 1–2 in. long, in Apr.–May before the lvs.; corolla with cylindrical tube and spreading limb ¼–½in. across: fr. black or purple. China.

14. **V. Carlesii,** Hemsl. Deciduous much-branched spreading shrub reaching 4 ft., young branchlets stellate-tomentose; winter-buds naked: lvs. broadly ovate or oval, 1–4 in. long, acute, commonly rounded at base, short-petioled, irregularly toothed, dull green above, pale beneath, stellate-pubescent on both surfaces: fls. salverform, about ½in. long and with limb as wide, fragrant, changing from pinkish to white, in dense subglobose cymes 2–3 in. across, appearing in spring with the lvs.: fr. blue-black, ⅓in. long. (Named after W. R. Carles, the collector of this species.) Korea.—A hybrid between *V. Carlesii* and *V. utile* is **V. Burkwoodii,** Burkwood, semi-evergreen, lvs. shining above and gray-tomentose beneath veined with brown, corolla-tube about equalling lobes.

15. **V. Lentago,** L. Sheep-Berry. Nanny-Berry. Slender-branched deciduous shrub or small tree to 30 ft., with long-pointed scaly winter-buds: lvs. ovate, 2–4 in. long, acuminate, finely and sharply serrate, glabrous or scurfy on the veins beneath; petioles ½–1 in. long, usually winged with wavy margin: cymes sessile, many-fld., 2–5 in. broad; fls. white, in late spring and early summer: fr. oval, ½in. long, bluish-black, bloomy, remaining until spring. (Lentago: same as Lantana, an old name once applied to Viburnum.) Hudson Bay to Ga. and Miss.

16. **V. prunifolium,** L. Black-Haw. Spreading deciduous shrub or small tree to 15 ft., with short-pointed glabrous or reddish-pubescent scaly winter-buds: lvs. roundish to ovate or oval, 1–3 in. long, finely and sharply serrate, acute or obtuse, glabrous or nearly so; petioles ⅓–½in. long, often with narrow entire margins, glabrous or rusty-tomentose: cymes sessile, 2–4 in. broad; fls. pure white, ¼in. across, produced in spring and early summer: fr. oval to subglobose, bluish-black, glaucous, about ½in. long. Conn. to Fla. and Tex.

17. **V. Lantana,** L. Wayfaring-Tree. Deciduous shrub to 15 ft., or sometimes tree-like, with young branches scurfy-pubescent; winter-buds naked: lvs. ovate to ovate-oblong, 2–5 in. long, acute or obtuse, cordate or rounded at base, minutely toothed, slightly stellate-pubescent and wrinkled above, stellate-tomentose beneath; petioles ½–1 in. long, tomentose: fls. white, ¼in. across, produced in May–June, in peduncled pubescent cymes 2–4 in. broad: fr. ovoid-oblong, ⅓in. long, bright red changing to almost black. (Lantana: old name once applied to Viburnum.) Eu., W. Asia.

18. **V. setigerum,** Hance (*V. theiferum,* Rehd.). Deciduous shrub to 12 ft., branchlets glabrous; winter-buds scaly: lvs. ovate-oblong, 3–5 in. long, acuminate, slightly denticulate, dark green above, glabrous except on veins beneath; petioles about ½in. long, glabrous: cymes short-peduncled, 1–2 in. across; fls. May–June: fr. ovoid, red, ⅓in. long. China.

19. **V. nudum,** L. Smooth Withe-Rod. Deciduous shrub to 15 ft.; winter-buds scaly: lvs. oval to obovate or oval-lanceolate, 2–5 in. long, acute or obtuse, mostly entire and somewhat revolute or obscurely crenulate, scurfy on both sides when young, becoming glabrous above: cymes long-peduncled, 3–5 in. broad; fls. white or yellowish-white, in summer: fr. globose, ⅓in. long, blue-black. L. I. to Fla. and La.

20. **V. cassinoides, L.** (*V. nudum* var. *cassinoides,* Torr. & Gray). Withe-Rod. Deciduous shrub attaining 12 ft.; winter-buds scaly: lvs. oval to ovate, 1–4 in. long, acute or bluntly acuminate, cuneate or rounded at base, usually obscurely dentate, nearly glabrous, rather thick, dull green above: fls. and fr. similar to those of the preceding species but the peduncles usually shorter than the cyme. Newf. to N. C. and Minn.

21. **V. dilatatum,** Thunb. Deciduous shrub to 10 ft., with erect sts. and branches pubescent when young; winter-buds scaly: lvs. roundish or broadly ovate or obovate, 2–5 in. long, usually abruptly short-acuminate, rounded or subcordate at base, saliently toothed, somewhat hairy on either side: cymes stalked, pubescent, 3–5 in. across; fls. May–June, white, corolla pubescent outside: fr. ovate, scarlet, ⅓in. long, numerous, remaining a long time on the branches. China, Japan.

22. **V. Wrightii,** Miq. Deciduous shrub to 10 ft., branchlets nearly glabrous; winter-buds scaly: lvs. broad-ovate, 3–6 in. long, abruptly acuminate, rounded at base, coarsely dentate, glabrous except on veins beneath, turning red in autumn: cymes short-peduncled, nearly glabrous, 2–4 in. across; fls. white, May–June: fr. ovoid, red, ⅓in. long. (Named for Chas. Wright, 1811–1886, American botanist.) Japan.

23. **V. Sieboldii,** Miq. Stout shrub to 10 ft., with young branches pubescent and deciduous foliage exhaling disagreeable odor when bruised: lvs. oval or oblong-obovate, 3–6 in. long, coarsely crenate-serrate except toward the base, acute or rounded at apex, narrowed at base, glossy dark green above, paler and stellate-pubescent beneath: fls. creamy-

white, rotate-campanulate, in panicles 2½–4 in. broad, May–June: fr. oblong, changing from pink to bluish-black, dropping soon after ripening. (P. F. von Siebold, page 51.) Japan.

24. **V. dentatum,** L. Arrow-Wood. Nearly glabrous deciduous shrub to 15 ft.; winter-buds scaly: lvs. broadly ovate or rotund, 1½–3 in. long, acute or short-acuminate, rounded or cordate at base, coarsely toothed, pubescent only in the axils of the veins beneath; petioles ½–1 in. long, glabrous: cymes umbel-like, long-peduncled, glabrous, 2–3 in. broad; fls. white, ⅕in. across, May–June: fr. subglobose, ¼in. long, bluish-black, glaucous. N. B. to Minn. south to Ga.

25. **V. molle,** Michx. Deciduous bushy shrub to 12 ft., older bark separating in thin flakes and peeling off: lvs. broadly ovate to rotund, 3–5 in. long, short-acuminate, cordate at base, long-petioled, stipulate, coarsely dentate, glabrous above, more or less pubescent beneath: cymes long-peduncled, finely pubescent, about 2½ in. broad; fls. white, ¼in. across, in June: fr. oval, bluish-black, scarcely ½in. long. Ind. to Ky. and Mo.

26. **V. pubescens,** Pursh (*V. venosum*, Britt. *V. nepalense*, Hort.). Deciduous shrub to 12 ft., young branches and petioles stellate-pubescent: lvs. ovate to rotund, 2–4 in. long, acute or acuminate, rounded or cordate at base, coarsely and sharply toothed, glabrous or nearly so above, stellate-pubescent beneath particularly on the veins and in their axils: cymes long-stalked, 2½–4 in. across, stellate-pubescent; fls. white, ⅙in. across, June–July: fr. globose or roundish-oval, ¼–⅓in. long, blue-black. Mass. to Va.

3. **LEYCESTERIA,** Wall. Deciduous shrubs cult. in warm regions; species 3, Himalayan and Chinese.—Lvs. opposite, simple, with very small or no stipules: fls. in erect or drooping verticillate leafy-bracted spikes; calyx persistent, unequally 5-lobed; corolla funnelform, nearly equally 5-lobed and swollen at base; stamens 5, inserted on the corolla-tube; ovary 5–8-celled, the stigma capitate: fr. a many-seeded berry. (Leyceste-ria: Wm. Leycester, judge in Bengal.)

L. formosa, Wall. Himalaya-Honeysuckle. Vigorous shrub attaining 6 ft., branches hollow: lvs. broadly ovate to ovate-lanceolate, 2–7 in. long, long-acuminate, cordate at base, entire or finely toothed, glabrous or finely puberulent beneath: spikes drooping, 1–4 in. long; fls. purplish, ½–¾in. long, each whorl subtended by claret-colored leafy bracts which persist until the fr. is ripe: fr. dark red, glandular-pubescent, subglobose, about ½in. long, in autumn. Himalayas, 5,000–10,000 ft., to W. China.

4. **SYMPHORICARPOS,** Duham. About 15 species of deciduous ornamental shrubs, native in N. Amer. south to Mex. and 1 in W. China; many of the American species are very closely related and difficult to distinguish.—Lvs. opposite, simple, entire or sometimes sinuately toothed or lobed, exstipulate: fls. short-pedicelled, in terminal or axillary clusters or spikes or sometimes solitary; calyx 4–5-toothed; corolla campanulate or salverform, 4–5-lobed, nearly regular; stamens as many as the corolla-lobes, included or somewhat exserted; style slender, stigma capitate; ovary with 2 fertile and 2 sterile cells: fr. a berry-like drupe with 2 nutlets. (Symphoricar-pos: Greek to *bear together* and *fruit*, referring to the clustered frs.)

A. Fr. red .... 1. *S. orbiculatus*
AA. Fr. white or pinkish.
  B. Style and stamens exserted .... 2. *S. occidentalis*
  BB. Style and stamens included.
    C. Plant upright .... 3. *S. albus*
    CC. Plant diffuse or procumbent.
      D. Lvs. and young twigs soft-pubescent .... 4. *S. acutus*
      DD. Lvs. and young twigs sparsely hairy to glabrous .... 5. *S. hesperius*

1. **S. orbiculatus,** Moench (*Lonicera Symphoricarpos*, L. *S. vulgaris*, Michx.). Indian-Currant. Coral-Berry. Bushy shrub 3–7 ft. high; branchlets slender, upright, densely leafy, downy: lvs. broadly oval or ovate, ¾–1½ in. long, obtuse or acute, somewhat glaucous and usually pubescent beneath, very shortly petioled: fls. produced in summer, in dense short axillary clusters or spikes from the lower sides of the twigs; corolla campanulate, ⅛–⅙in. long, dull white; style hairy: fr. purplish-red, subglobose, ⅙–¼in. across, in late autumn. N. J. to Ga. and Tex.; sometimes escaped.—A hybrid between *S. orbiculatus* and *S. microphyllus* is **S. Chenaultii,** Rehd., with small lvs. pubescent beneath and red frs. spotted with white.

2. **S. occidentalis,** Hook. Wolfberry. Shrub to 4 ft., with upright rather stiff branches: lvs. oval or ovate, 1–3 in. long, entire or undulate-crenate, apiculate, grayish-green and pubescent beneath: fls. in summer, in dense axillary or terminal spikes or racemes ½–1 in. long; corolla pinkish-white, campanulate, ¼in. long, deeply 5-lobed; style and stamens exserted: fr. subglobose, white, about ½in. long, produced in early autumn. Mich. to B. C. south to Colo. and Kans.

3. **S. albus,** Blake (*Vaccinium album,* L. *S. racemosus,* Michx.). SNOWBERRY. WAXBERRY. Shrub to 3 ft., with upright slender branches: lvs. round-oval to oblong, 1–2 in. long, obtuse, often apiculate, pubescent beneath, those on the young shoots often sinuately lobed: fls. in terminal or axillary spikes or clusters, all summer; corolla campanulate, pinkish, about ¼in. long; style and stamens included: fr. globose or ovoid, snow-white, ¼–½in. long, maturing in autumn and persisting through the winter. N. S. to Minn. and Va. Var. **lævigatus,** Blake (*S. racemosus* var. *lævigatus,* Fern. *S. rivularis,* Suks.), to 6 ft.; lvs. glabrous, usually larger; fr.-clusters larger; Alaska to Calif. and Colo.; this var. is the snowberry generally cult. as *S. racemosus.*

4. **S. acutus,** Dieck (*S. mollis* var. *acutus,* Gray). Low diffuse or procumbent soft-pubescent shrub: lvs. oval to ovate, ½–1 in. long, acute at both ends, grayish or whitish beneath, often irregularly dentate: fls. in summer, solitary or in 2's in the axils of upper lvs.; corolla campanulate, pink, about ⅛in. long: fr. subglobose, white, ¼in. long. Ore., Calif., Nev.

5. **S. hesperius,** G. N. Jones (*S. mollis,* Macoun and Hort. not Nutt.). Distinguished from *S. acutus* by being less pubescent, the hairs short and curved rather than straight and spreading, lvs. nearly glabrous except on veins beneath. B. C. to Calif. and Ida.

5. **LONICERA,** L. HONEYSUCKLE. Shrubs widely planted for ornament; about 180 species throughout the northern hemisphere in Amer. south to Mex. and in Asia south to Java.—Deciduous or rarely half-evergreen or evergreen, erect or climbing: lvs. opposite, simple, entire or rarely sinuately lobed, usually short-petioled, sometimes with distinct stipules: fls. more or less irregular, in axillary peduncled pairs subtended by 2 bracts and 4 bractlets, the latter often more or less connate or sometimes wanting, or fls. in sessile whorls at the ends of the branches; calyx 5-toothed; corolla with short or slender often gibbous tube, 2-lipped or almost equally 5-lobed; stamens 5; style slender, stigma capitate; ovary usually 2–3- rarely 5-celled: fr. a few- to many-seeded berry. (Lonic-era: after Adam Lonicer or Lonitzer, 1528–1586, German physician and naturalist.)

A. Fls. in usually 6-fld. whorls at ends of branchlets, or sometimes axillary, but not paired.

B. Limb of corolla very short, the lobes nearly regular . . . . 1. *L. sempervirens*

BB. Limb of corolla as long or half as long as tube, 2-lipped.

C. Corolla about 1 in. long.

D. Style and inside of corolla-tube pubescent: disk formed by connate upper lvs. very glaucous above . . . . 2. *L. prolifera*

DD. Style and inside of corolla-tube glabrous: disk of connate upper lvs. bright green above . . . . 3. *L. flava*

CC. Corolla 1½–3 in. long.

D. Upper lvs. distinct . . . . 4. *L. Periclymenum*

DD. Upper lvs. connate.

E. Tube of corolla slightly longer than limb: whorls usually sessile in axils of connate lvs . . . . 5. *L. Caprifolium*

EE. Tube of corolla one and a half times longer than limb: whorls usually in long-peduncled heads . . . . 6. *L. etrusca*

AA. Fls. in axillary pairs.

B. Habit climbing.

C. Length of fls. 4–7 in . . . . 7. *L. Hildebrandiana*

CC. Length of fls. ½–1½ in.

D. Bracts subtending fls. ovate, leafy . . . . 8. *L. japonica*

DD. Bracts subtending fls. subulate, small . . . . 9. *L. Henryi*

BB. Habit not climbing, branches erect or spreading, rarely prostrate.

C. Corolla with regular or nearly regular 5-lobed limb.

D. Bracts ovate.

E. Stamens as long as corolla-limb: lvs. nearly glabrous beneath . . . . . . 10. *L. involucrata*

EE. Stamens not exceeding corolla-tube: lvs. pubescent beneath . . . . . . 11. *L. Ledebouri*

DD. Bracts linear or subulate.

E. Base of corolla not gibbous.

F. Stamens and style exserted: fr. bluish or whitish . . . . . . 12. *L. spinosa*

FF. Stamens and style included: fr. red.

G. Lvs. white-tomentose beneath . . . . . . 13. *L. thibetica*

GG. Lvs. glabrous beneath . . . . . . 14. *L. syringantha*

EE. Base of corolla gibbous or saccate.

F. Lvs. deciduous: frs. seemingly connate . . . . . . 15. *L. cærulea*

FF. Lvs. persistent or semi-persistent, shining above: frs. distinct.

G. Branches upright: lvs. ¼–½in. long . . . . . . 16. *L. nitida*

GG. Branches spreading or prostrate: lvs. ¼–1½ in. long . . . . . . 17. *L. pileata*

CC. Corolla 2-lipped.

D. Branches with solid white pith.

E. Lvs. not apiculate: branchlets hispid with recurved bristles . . . . . . 18. *L. Standishii*

EE. Lvs. apiculate: branchlets glabrous . . . . . . 19. *L. fragrantissima*

DD. Branches hollow, with brown pith.

E. Fr. white and translucent.................................20. *L. quinquelocularis*
EE. Fr. red or rarely yellow.
F. Peduncles shorter than petioles.............................21. *L. Maackii*
FF. Peduncles much longer than petioles.
G. Outside of corolla glabrous.
H. Color of fls. pale pink to crimson, or if white not fading to yellow: lvs. ½–2 in. long.
I. Lvs. mostly 1–2 in. long, dark green above: lateral lobes of upper lip divided to base of limb or nearly so........22. *L. tatarica*
II. Lvs. ½–1 in. long, distinctly pale blue-green above: lateral lobes of upper lip divided to middle or less....23. *L. Korolkowii*
HH. Color of fls. white fading to yellow after anthesis: lvs. 2–4 in. long.................................24. *L. Ruprechtiana*
GG. Outside of corolla pubescent.
H. Stamens glabrous: bractlets about as long as ovaries.......25. *L. Morrowii*
HH. Stamens pubescent below middle: bractlets half or less as long as ovaries.
I. Lvs. acuminate.................................26. *L. chrysantha*
II. Lvs. acute or obtuse.............................27. *L. Xylosteum*

1. **L. sempervirens,** L. TRUMPET HONEYSUCKLE. Glabrous high-climbing shrub, evergreen southward: lvs. oval or oblong, 1½–3 in. long, obtuse or rounded and often apiculate at apex, glaucous beneath, the uppermost 1–2 pairs connate at base: fls. in a peduncled interrupted terminal spike consisting of several usually 6-fld. whorls, not fragrant, late spring to early autumn; corolla orange-scarlet outside, yellow within, 1½–2 in. long, the short limb with nearly equal lobes, the slender tube slightly swollen at base; stamens and style slightly exserted: fr. scarlet, ¼in. diam. Conn. to Fla. and Tex.; farther north sometimes escaped from cult.—There are several vars. with fls. yellow, orange-red or more brilliant scarlet, and a late-flowering improved variant known as **magnifica.** A hybrid between *L. sempervirens* and *L. hirsuta* is **L. Brownii,** Carr. (*L. etrusca* var. *Brownii,* Regel), differing in the limb somewhat 2-lipped, and lvs. sparingly pubescent beneath. **L. Tellmanniana,** Spaeth, is a hybrid between *L. sempervirens* and *L. tragophylla,* with larger lvs. and deep yellow 2-lipped fls. 2 in. long, the corolla-tube about twice as long as limb. A hybrid probably between *L. americana* and *L. sempervirens* is **L. Heckrottii,** Rehd., with 2-lipped fls. to 2 in. long, purplish outside and yellow inside.

2. **L. prolifera,** Rehd. (*Caprifolium proliferum,* Kirchn. *L. Sullivantii,* Gray). Climbing, very glaucous: lvs. oval, obovate or oblong, 2–4 in. long, often finely pubescent beneath, sessile or connate, the uppermost into an orbicular disk very glaucous above: fls. in short-stalked spikes of several whorls each, June–July; corolla 2-lipped, about 1 in. long, pale yellow, often purplish-marked outside, the slender tube slightly swollen on one side and only a little longer than limb, pubescent within; stamens exserted; style hairy: fr. scarlet, ¼–½in. diam. Ohio to Tenn. and Mo.

3. **L. flava,** Sims. Climbing: lvs. broadly oval to elliptic, 1½–3 in. long, glaucous beneath, glabrous, the upper connate into a broad disk bright green above: fls. bright or orange-yellow, fragrant, 1–1¼ in. long, in a peduncled head, May–June; corolla-tube slender, not swollen, longer than the limb, glabrous inside; style glabrous; stamens exserted: fr. red, ¼in. diam. N. C. to Okla.—Rare in cult. and *L. prolifera is* often grown under this name.

4. **L. Periclymenum,** L. WOODBINE. Twining shrub, the sts. often over 20 ft. long: lvs. all distinct, ovate to oblong-ovate, 1½–3 in. long, mostly acute, dark green above, pale or glaucous beneath and sometimes sparingly pubescent: fls. very fragrant, in a dense peduncled terminal head, summer to early autumn; corolla 2-lipped, yellowish-white, usually carmine or purple outside, 1½–2 in. long, the tube slender, tapering, glandular-pubescent outside; stamens and style exserted: fr. red. (Periclymenum, herbalist name: Greek *around* and *surround,* referring to the twining habit.) Eu., N. Afr., W. Asia.—There are several vars., one with lvs. sinuately lobed. Var. **belgica,** Ait., DUTCH WOODBINE, has glabrous lvs. whitish beneath and fls. pale purple outside. Var. **aurea,** Lind. & André, has yellow or yellowish lvs.

5. **L. Caprifolium,** L. (*L. pallida,* Host). Deciduous climber to 20 ft., glabrous or nearly so: lvs. oval, 2–4 in. long, rounded at apex, the 2–3 uppermost pairs connate forming a cup: fls. fragrant, 1½–2 in. long, in whorls of usually 2–3, produced in the axils of the connate lvs., May–June; corolla 2-lipped, yellowish-white, often slightly purplish and hairy outside, the tube slender: fr. orange-colored, the bractlets very small or none. (Caprifolium, herbalist name: Latin *goat* and *leaf,* i. e., a plant which climbs like a goat.) Cent. Eu. to W. Asia; sometimes escaped from cult.—A hybrid sometimes grown as *L. Caprifolium* and with *L. etrusca* as the other parent is **L. americana,** Koch, fls. yellowish, usually purplish and glandular-pubescent outside, June–July.

6. **L. etrusca,** Santi. Vigorous climber, partially evergreen: lvs. broadly oval to obovate, 1–3 in. long, usually obtuse, glabrous above, pubescent and glaucous beneath, the upper ones connate into an oval obtuse disk: fls. fragrant, in dense usually long-peduncled heads borne in terminal or axillary groups of 3, June–July; corolla yellowish-white, usually reddish tinged, 2-lipped, 1½–2 in. long, with very slender tube sometimes glan-

dular: fr. red, bractlets nearly as long as ovary. Distributed through the whole Medit. region in many different forms.

7. **L. Hildebrandiana,** Coll. & Hemsl. GIANT HONEYSUCKLE. Evergreen glabrous climber: lvs. ovate, 3–6 in. long and 1½–4 in. wide, abruptly acuminate, rounded at base: fls. in axillary short-peduncled pairs, fragrant, creamy-white changing to orange, 4–7 in. long, 2-lipped, with slender tube and limb 2–3 in. across; stamens included: fr. ovoid, 1–1¼ in. long. (Named about 1890 for Mr. Hildebrand, supt. of the Southern Shan States.) Burma.—Not hardy N.

8. **L. japonica,** Thunb. Half-evergreen climber to 20 or even 30 ft., with hollow twining sts., branchlets usually hairy when young: lvs. ovate or oblong, 1½–3½ in. long, acute or obtuse and apiculate, pubescent, becoming glabrous above: fls. white, often purplish outside, changing to yellow, fragrant, produced all summer, in axillary pairs on young shoots, often much crowded toward the ends; peduncles short, bearing 2 ovate bracts ⅛–¾in. long; bractlets half to as long as the ovary; corolla 1¼–1½ in. long, pubescent, the tube slender, the limb 2-lipped: fr. black, distinct. E. Asia; nat. in some places from N. Y. to N. C. Var. **aureo-reticulata,** Nichols. (*L. aureo-reticulata,* Moore), lvs. smaller, veined with yellow. Var. **chinensis,** Baker (*L. chinensis,* Wats.), fls. carmine outside, young lvs. tinged with purple. Var. **Halliana,** Nichols. (*L. flexuosa* var. *Halliana,* Dipp.), fls. pure white changing to yellow. Var. **repens,** Rehd. (var. *flexuosa,* Nichols. *L. brachypoda* var. *repens,* Sieb.), lower lvs. often veined with purple.

9. **L. Henryi,** Hemsl. Twining or prostrate, partially evergreen, branchlets hairy: lvs. oblong-lanceolate, 2–3 in. long, acute or acuminate, ciliate, pubescent on midrib beneath: fls. in peduncled pairs, often congested near ends of branches, in summer; corolla ½–¾in. long, yellowish- or purple-red, tube and limb nearly equal: fr. black. (Named for Augustine Henry, page 45.) China.

10. **L. involucrata,** Banks (*Xylosteon involucratum,* Richardson. *Distegia involucrata,* Cockerell). Upright shrub 3–9 ft. high, glabrous or somewhat pubescent: lvs. elliptic-ovate to oblong-lanceolate, 2–5 in. long, acutish to acuminate, bright green, glabrous or slightly hairy beneath, short-petioled: fls. yellow or tinged with red, about ½in. long, borne in pairs on long erect axillary peduncles, subtended by broad bracts which are often reddish or purple, May–June; corolla-tube saccate on one side at base, the limb with nearly equal spreading lobes, glandular-pubescent outside; stamens as long as limb: fr. black, shining, globose, almost inclosed by the enlarged purple bractlets. Que. to Alaska south to Mex.

11. **L. Ledebouri,** Esch. (*Distegia Ledebouri,* Greene). Erect shrub to 8–9 ft.: lvs. ovate-oblong, 2–4 in. long, dull dark green above, downy beneath, short-petioled: fls. in summer, deep orange-yellow tinged with red, in axillary pairs on a downy erect stalk 1–1¾ in. long, subtended by 2 reddish bracts and bractlets, these enlarged in fr.; corolla tubular, to ¾in. long, saccate at base, the lobes rounded and erect; stamens not longer than tube: fr. black, almost enveloped by the bractlets, ripening in late summer and autumn. (C. F. v. Ledebour, page 47.) Calif.

12. **L. spinosa,** Walp. Stiff shrub to 4 ft., the spinescent branches with solid white pith: lvs. linear-oblong, ½–1 in. long, glabrous: fls. ¾in. long, in axillary pairs; corolla with slender cylindric tube and spreading limb; stamens and style exserted; bracts linear: fr. pale bluish-red or whitish, bloom-covered, ⅓in. diam. Himalayas. Var. **Albertii,** Rehd. (*L. Albertii,* Regel), graceful shrub with slender arching or procumbent unarmed branches; lvs. linear or linear-lanceolate, ½–1¼ in. long, sometimes with 2–4 teeth at base, glaucous or bluish-green; fls. rosy-pink, fragrant, June; Turkestan.

13. **L. thibetica,** Bur. & Franch. Shrub to 5 ft., with spreading sometimes prostrate branches: lvs. often in 3's, oblong-lanceolate, ½–1¼ in. long, acute, shining dark green above, white-tomentose beneath: fls. in axillary peduncled pairs in May–June, pale purple, ½in. long; corolla-tube two to three times longer than limb, pubescent outside: fr. red, ¼in. long. China.

14. **L. syringantha,** Maxim. Glabrous shrub 8–10 ft. high, with slender upright branches: lvs. often in 3's, oval or oblong, ½–1 in. long, acute or obtuse: fls. in axillary pairs in May–June, pinkish or lilac, ½in. long, fragrant; corolla-tube three to four times longer than limb: fr. red, ¼in. long. China. Var. **Wolfii,** Rehd., branches partially prostrate, lvs. longer and narrower, fls. carmine.

15. **L. cærulea,** L. Variable branching erect or spreading shrub to 5 ft., branchlets glabrous or pubescent when young: lvs. oval, obovate or oblong, ½–3 in. long, rounded at apex, pale or glaucous-green, pubescent or nearly glabrous, often stipulate: fls. twin, yellowish or greenish-white, ⅓–½in. long, axillary, short-peduncled, produced in spring; corolla-tube gibbous at base, the limb nearly regular; ovaries united, commonly exceeded by the subulate or linear bracts: fr. blue, bloom-covered, consisting of the 2 berries connate at base and wholly covered by the connate bractlets, hence seemingly connate throughout. N. Eu., N. Asia; nat. in N. Amer.

16. **L. nitida,** Wils. Evergreen shrub to 6 ft., with upright densely leafy branches; young shoots slender, purplish, sparsely bristly: lvs. ovate to oblong-ovate, ¼–½ in. long,

obtuse, subcordate to broadly cuneate at base, glossy above, glabrous or nearly so: fls. creamy-white, fragrant, produced in axillary short-stalked pairs: fr. globular, blue-purple, transparent, about ¼in. across, the berries distinct but surrounded by the connate bractlets. W. China.

17. **L. pileata,** Oliv. Evergreen or semi-evergreen spreading shrub, sometimes prostrate: lvs. oval to oblong-lanceolate, ¼–1½ in. long, obtusish, glabrous or pubescent on midrib beneath, dark green and glossy above, tapering at base, very short-stalked: fls. whitish, fragrant, opening in spring, erect, in pairs on short axillary peduncles; corolla funnelform, ⅓in. long, the tube gibbous at base, limb nearly regular; stamens exserted: fr. a translucent purple color, ⅙in. wide, surrounded by a cupule formed by the connate bractlets and invested at top by a curious outgrowth of the calyx. China.

18. **L. Standishii,** Jacques. Semi-evergreen shrub to 8 ft., the spreading branches with reflexed bristly hairs: lvs. oblong-ovate to ovate-lanceolate, 3–4 in. long, acute or acuminate, sparsely hispid: fls. creamy-white or slightly blushed, very fragrant, ¼–½in. long, borne in pairs on rather short curved bristly peduncles, often 2 pairs at each joint, Mar.–Apr.; corolla bilabiate, usually bristly outside: fr. red, the 2 ovaries united nearly to the top and forming a berry, early June. (Named for the nurseryman who grew many of Fortune's collections.) China.

19. **L. fragrantissima,** Lind. & Paxt. Shrub to 8 ft., deciduous or evergreen, glabrous except for the lf.-margins and midrib: lvs. rather stiff and leathery, broadly oval, 1–3 in. long, short-stalked, strongly apiculate, dull dark green above, rather glaucous beneath: fls. creamy-white, very fragrant, ⅝in. long, several pairs in an axil, on short glabrous peduncles, Mar.-Apr.; corolla 2-lipped, glabrous outside: fr. as in *L. Standishii.* China.

20. **L. quinquelocularis,** Hardw. Shrub to 15 ft., young shoots very downy: lvs. ovate or oval, 1–3 in. long, mostly acuminate, rounded or tapered at base, short-petioled, slightly pubescent: fls. creamy-white becoming yellow, borne in axillary pairs on peduncles about equalling the petioles; corolla 2-lipped, ¾in. long, the tube somewhat swollen; stamens about as long as the upper lip, pubescent at base: fr. translucent white, globose to ovoid. W. Asia.

21. **L. Maackii,** Maxim. Spreading upright shrub to 15 ft., the branchlets short-pubescent: lvs. elliptic-ovate to ovate-lanceolate, 1½–3 in. long, acuminate, narrowed at base, dark green, pubescent on veins, short-petioled: fls. fragrant, pure white becoming yellowish with age, in axillary pairs on peduncles shorter than the petioles, in June; corolla ¾in. long, bilabiate, the upper lip erect with outer clefts deeper than the middle, the tube short and not gibbous, usually glabrous outside; stamens about twice as long as corolla-tube, downy at base; style hairy: fr. dark red, the berries distinct. (Named for Richard Maack, page 563.) Asia. Var. **podocarpa,** Franch., of more spreading habit, lvs. more pubescent, corolla smaller and pubescent outside.

22. **L. tatarica,** L. Tatarian Honeysuckle. Deciduous bushy glabrous shrub reaching 10 ft.: lvs. ovate to oblong-ovate, 1–2½ in. long, pale green beneath: fls. pink, crimson or white, ¾–1 in. long, in pairs on slender axillary peduncles, May–June; corolla bilabiate, glabrous without, hairy within, the upper lip with outer lobes distinct, the tube gibbous at base, much shorter than the spreading or reflexed oblong lobes; ovaries distinct, subtended by the small bractlets, these distinct or connate at base: fr. red, rarely yellow. Russia to Turkestan. Var. **alba,** Loisel., fls. pure white. Var. **grandiflora,** Rehd., fls. larger, white. Var. **latifolia,** Loud., lvs. to 4 in. long and 2 in. across, fls. pink. Var. **rosea,** Regel, fls. rose outside, pink inside. Var. **sibirica,** Pers. (var. *rubra,* Sweet), fls. deep pink.—**L. bella,** Zabel, is a hybrid between *L. Morrowii* and *L. tatarica,* lvs. nearly glabrous, corolla glabrous on outside, pink or white fading to yellowish; color variants are known as *L. bella albida, candida* and *rosea.*

23. **L. Korolkowii,** Stapf. Deciduous shrub to 12 ft., with spreading branches pubescent when young: lvs. ovate or oval, ½–1½ in. long, acute, pubescent on both sides, short-petioled: fls. rose or rarely white, ½in. long, in axillary long-peduncled pairs in May–June; corolla 2-lipped, glabrous outside, tube slightly gibbous at base: fr. bright red. (Named for Colonel Korolkow of Moscow.) Turkestan. Var. **floribunda,** Nichols., lvs. broad-ovate. Var. **Zabelii,** Rehd. (*L. Zabelii,* Rehd.), lvs. glabrous, broad-ovate.—A hybrid between this species and *L. tatarica* is **L. amœna,** Zabel, with ovate slightly pubescent lvs. and pink or white fls. ¾in. long.

24. **L. Ruprechtiana,** Regel. To 12 ft.: lvs. ovate-lanceolate to lanceolate, 2–4 in. long, acuminate, commonly dark green above, grayish-pubescent beneath: fls. twin, on peduncles longer than the petioles, May–June; corolla 2-lipped, pure white changing to yellowish, about ½in. long, tube gibbous, glabrous outside: fr. red or sometimes yellow. (F. J. Ruprecht, page 50.) Manchuria, N. China.—A hybrid between this species and *L. tatarica* is **L. notha,** Zabel, nearly glabrous, fls. pinkish fading to yellowish.

25. **L. Morrowii,** Gray. Deciduous shrub to 8 ft., with wide-spreading branches: lvs. oval or oblong-ovate, 1–2½ in. long, acute or obtusish, grayish-tomentose beneath: fls. ½in. long, twin, on slender axillary peduncles exceeding the petioles in May–June; bractlets distinct, about as long as the ovary; corolla 2-lipped, downy, creamy-white, becoming

yellow in age, the slender tube slightly swollen at base, the spreading spatulate lobes twice as long as tube; stamens glabrous: fr. blood-red, berries distinct. (Named for a famous traveller in Japan; page 163.) Japan.

26. **L. chrysantha,** Turcz. Erect shrub to 12 ft., with pilose rarely glabrous branchlets: lvs. rhombic-ovate to rhombic-lanceolate, 2–5 in. long, acuminate, pilose or above nearly glabrous: fls. yellowish-white changing to yellow, in pairs on hairy axillary peduncles longer than the petioles in May–June; bractlets distinct, ovate, one-third to one-half as long as the ovary; corolla ½–¾in. long, slightly pubescent outside, the upper lip cleft about one-half, the short tube strongly gibbous; stamens pubescent below middle: fr. coral-red, the berries distinct. N. E. Asia to Cent. Japan.

27. **L. Xylosteum,** L. EUROPEAN FLY HONEYSUCKLE. Deciduous shrub to 10 ft., very bushy, young shoots downy: lvs. ovate to obovate, 1–2½ in. long, acute or obtuse, glabrous or sparsely pubescent above, more densely pubescent beneath: fls. yellowish-white or reddish-tinged, in pairs on axillary peduncles longer than the petioles in May–June; bractlets pubescent, suborbicular, about half as high as the ovary; corolla very downy, conspicuously 2-lipped, the tube short and gibbous; stamens well-exserted, pubescent at base: fr. dark red, berries distinct. (Xylosteum: Greek *wood* and *bone*, in allusion to the hardness of the wood, an herbalist name.) Eu., Asia, sometimes escaped from cult.—A hybrid with *L. tatarica*, known as **L. xylosteoides,** Tausch. (*L. nepalensis*, Kirchn.), has rhombic-ovate bluish-green lvs. and small pinkish fls.

6. **LINNÆA,** L. One evergreen trailing subshrub useful for the rock-garden.—Lvs. opposite, petioled, without stipules: fls. in pairs at ends of long terminal peduncles; calyx 5-parted; corolla 5-lobed, campanulate or funnelform; stamens 4, inserted near base of corolla-tube; ovary 3-celled, but only 1 cell fertile and 1-ovuled; stigma slender: fr. an ovoid achene. (Linnæ-a: named for Linnæus by Gronovius.)

L. borealis, L. TWIN-FLOWER. Lvs. roundish, ¼–1 in. long, with few teeth, usually ciliate and slightly hairy above: fls. white or rose, fragrant, ¼–⅓in. long, on peduncles 2–3 in. long, in summer: fr. yellow, ⅛in. long. N. Eu., N. Asia, Alaska. Var. **americana,** Rehd. (*L. americana*, Forbes), lvs. usually glabrous, fls. more tubular and to ½in. long; N. Amer.

7. **KOLKWITZIA,** Graebn. Handsome deciduous shrub, 1 Chinese species.—Lvs. opposite, short-petioled, without stipules: fls. in axillary pairs forming terminal corymbs; calyx 5-parted; corolla 5-lobed, campanulate; stamens 4; ovaries 2, each 3-celled but only 1 cell fertile and 1-ovuled: fr. a bristly achene. (Kolkwit-zia: named for Richard Kolkwitz, born 1873, professor of botany in Berlin.)

K. amabilis, Graebn. BEAUTY-BUSH. To 8 ft.: lvs. ovate, 1–3 in. long, acuminate, slightly toothed, ciliate and hairy at least on veins: fls. pink with yellow throat, ½in. long, in corymbs 2–3 in. across in May–June; pedicels and sepals bristly: fr. ovoid, ¼in. long, covered with bristles.

8. **ABELIA,** R. Br. Over 25 species in E. and Cent. Asia, 1 in the Himalayas and 2 in Mex., several planted for ornament.—Small or medium-sized bushy shrubs with deciduous or persistent foliage: lvs. opposite, short-petioled, entire or dentate: fls. rather small but numerous, varying from white to pink or purple, in 1- to several-fld. cymes, axillary or terminal on short branchlets, sometimes forming panicles at the ends of the branches; calyx with 5 (rarely 2–4) elongate segms. usually purplish and conspicuous, persistent after the corolla has fallen; corolla tubular, campanulate or salverform, the limb equally 5-lobed; stamens 4, paired, inserted on the base of the corolla-tube; ovary 3-celled, only 1 cell fertile: fr. a 1-seeded leathery achene, crowned by the persistent calyx. (Abe-lia: bears the name of Dr. Clarke Abel, 1780–1826, physician and author on China.)

A. Fls. axillary, 1½–2 in. long . . . . 1. *A. floribunda*
AA. Fls. in terminal panicles, ½–1 in. long.
  B. Corolla salverform . . . . 2. *A. triflora*
  BB. Corolla campanulate or funnelform.
    C. Sepals 2 . . . . 3. *A. Schumannii*
    CC. Sepals 5 . . . . 4. *A. chinensis*

1. **A. floribunda,** Decne. (*Vesalea floribunda*, Martens & Galeotti). Evergreen shrub 6–10 ft. high, young branches downy: lvs. oval or ovate, ¾–1½ in. long, acute or obtusish, shallowly toothed, glossy-green, hairy only on the margin: fls. pendulous, 1–3 at or near the ends of short twigs, in summer; sepals 5, green; corolla carmine-purple, tubular narrowing toward base, 1½–2 in. long, with 5 rounded spreading lobes; stamens hairy. Mex.

2. **A. triflora,** R. Br. Deciduous upright shrub to 12 ft.: lvs. lanceolate or ovate-

lanceolate, 1–3 in. long, long-acuminate, entire or with few large teeth, somewhat hairy: fls. rosy-white, fragrant, in terminal clusters 2 in. across in June; sepals 4–5; corolla salverform, with slender pubescent tube ½in. long and spreading lobes about ½in. across. Himalayas.

3. **A. Schumannii,** Rehd. (*Linnæa Schumannii*, Graebn.). Slender deciduous shrub 5 ft. or more high: lvs. ovate or oval, ½–1 in. long, obtuse and mucronate, entire or slightly toothed, pubescent on midrib beneath: fls. pink, several borne at ends of short side growths, in summer; sepals 2; corolla campanulate, about ¾in. long, somewhat glandular-pubescent outside. (Named for K. M. Schumann, page 51.) China.

4. **A. chinensis,** R. Br. (*A. rupestris*, Lindl.). Deciduous shrub 3–6 ft. high, of spreading habit, young branches minutely reddish-downy: lvs. ovate, ¾–1½ in. long, acute or short-acuminate, rounded at base, serrate, more or less hairy above and on the midrib beneath: fls. white, fragrant, in dense terminal panicles in summer; sepals 5, rosy-tinted; corolla funnelform, ½in. long; stamens exserted. China.—The most commonly cult. abelia is **A. grandiflora,** Rehd. (*A. rupestris* var. *grandiflora*, André), a hybrid between *A. chinensis* and *A. uniflora;* half-evergreen; lvs. shining; panicles dense, sepals 2–5 and more or less connate, stamens not exserted.

9. **DIERVILLA,** Adans. Bush-Honeysuckle. Deciduous stoloniferous shrubs; 3 species in N. Amer.—Lvs. opposite, mostly petioled, serrate: fls. in small leafless axillary clusters that are sometimes aggregated into terminal cymes, in summer, yellow or greenish-yellow; calyx 5-parted, mostly persistent; corolla 2-lipped, the tube funnelform; stamens 5, exserted; ovary 2-celled, style exserted, stigma capitate: fr. a slender 2-valved caps. with numerous minute seeds. (Diervil-la: after N. Dierville, a French surgeon who took *D. Lonicera* to Eu. early in the 18th century.)

A. Branchlets and lvs. pubescent . . . . 1. *D. rivularis*
AA. Branchlets and lvs. glabrous.
  B. Lvs. distinctly petioled . . . . 2. *D. Lonicera*
  BB. Lvs. sessile . . . . 3. *D. sessilifolia*

1. **D. rivularis,** Gatt. To 6 ft., branches terete and densely pubescent: lvs. ovate to oblong-lanceolate, 2–3 in. long, acuminate, nearly sessile, pubescent on both sides: cymes several-fld., crowded into terminal panicles; corolla lemon-yellow, limb about equalling tube: caps. ¼in. long. N. C., Tenn., Ga., Ala.

2. **D. Lonicera,** Mill. (*D. trifida*, Moench. *D. canadensis*, Willd.). Spreading, 2–4 ft. high, branchlets nearly terete, glabrous: lvs. ovate or ovate-oblong, 1½–4 in. long, acuminate, distinctly petioled, nearly glabrous, finely ciliate: axillary cymes commonly 3-fld., terminal ones 3–5-fld.; corolla yellow or in age darker, tube ½in. long, limb nearly as long and sometimes irregular, 3 of the lobes more united, the middle one deeper yellow and villous on the face; style and stamens hairy below: caps. about ⅓in. long, oblong, with a slender beak, crowned with the calyx-lobes. Newf. to Sask. south to N. C.

3. **D. sessilifolia,** Buckl. To 5 ft., branchlets quadrangular and glabrous: lvs. ovate-lanceolate, 2–6 in. long, gradually acuminate, sessile, nearly glabrous, of firmer texture: cymes 3–7-fld., often crowded into dense terminal panicles; corolla sulfur-yellow, the limb shorter than tube, lobes nearly equal, one of them obscurely pilose: caps. ⅓–½in. long, short-oblong, short-necked, crowned with short lanceolate-subulate calyx-lobes. N. C., Tenn., Ga., Ala.

10. **WEIGELA,** Thunb. Showy shrubs frequently planted in many forms, of 10–12 species in E. Asia.—Formerly included in Diervilla but quite distinct: not stoloniferous: fls. on short leafy shoots of the season, large, pink, purplish to carmine or white, not 2-lipped although corolla-lobes often unequal: caps. long and narrow, woody, dehiscing by 2 valves from the top, leaving a central column. (Named for C. E. Weigel, 1748–1831, German professor.)

A. Calyx divided about to middle into lanceolate lobes: seeds not winged.
  B. Lvs. pubescent on both sides . . . . 1. *W. præcox*
  BB. Lvs. glabrous above, pubescent only on veins beneath.
    C. Corolla abruptly contracted below middle . . . . 2. *W. florida*
    CC. Corolla gradually contracted into slender tube . . . . 3. *W. venusta*
AA. Calyx divided to base into linear lobes: seeds winged.
  B. Lvs. and branchlets glabrous . . . . 4. *W. coræensis*
  BB. Lvs. and branchlets pubescent.
    C. Caps. pubescent: style much-exserted . . . . 5. *W. floribunda*
    CC. Caps. glabrous: style not or slightly exserted.
      D. Corolla gradually widening upwards: lvs. pubescent mostly on veins beneath . . . . 6. *W. japonica*
      DD. Corolla abruptly expanded above middle: lvs. densely pubescent beneath . . . 7. *W. hortensis*

1. **W. præcox,** Bailey (*Diervilla præcox,* Lemoine). To 6 ft., with glabrous or hairy branchlets: lvs. elliptic or elliptic-ovate, 2–3½ in. long, acuminate, short-petioled, serrate, hairy above, soft-pubescent beneath: fls. in clusters of 3–5, nodding, in early spring; calyx with subulate lobes about as long as tube, very hairy; corolla 1½ in. long, abruptly narrowed below the middle, purplish-pink or rose-carmine, pubescent outside: caps. glabrous. Korea.—The earliest of all species to bloom; has given rise to a race of early-blooming hybrids.

2. **W. florida,** A. DC. (*Diervilla florida,* Sieb. & Zucc. *D. pauciflora,* Carr. *W. rosea,* Lindl. *W. amabilis,* Hort.). Spreading shrub to 6 ft., branchlets with 2 hairy stripes: lvs. elliptic or ovate-oblong to obovate, 2–4 in. long, long-pointed, short-petioled or nearly sessile, serrate except toward base, glabrous above except at the midrib, tomentose on the veins beneath: fls. often in terminal 3's or 4's on short lateral twigs, May–June; calyx nearly glabrous, with 5 lanceolate lobes nearly as long as the tube; corolla funnel-shaped, 1¼ in. long, downy and deep rose outside, paler within, the limb 1 in. across, with 5 spreading rounded lobes; stigma 2-lobed: caps. glabrous. N. China, Korea. Var. **variegata,** Bailey (*Diervilla florida* var. *variegata,* Bean), lvs. margined with yellowish-white.—Names associated with this species and allegedly hybrids between it and *W. hortensis* or *W. coræensis* include *Steltzneri, Vanhouttei,* Eva Rathke and Mont Blanc. The plant known as *W. candida* is probably a white-fld. form of *W. florida* (forma *alba,* Rehd. *W. rosea alba,* Moore).

3. **W. venusta,** Bailey (*W. florida* var. *venusta,* Nakai. *Diervilla venusta,* Stapf). Differs from *W. florida* in the smaller nearly glabrous lvs., rose-purple fls. which are gradually contracted into a slender tube and small lobes, calyx small and 2-lipped. Korea.

4. **W. coræensis,** Thunb. (*Diervilla coræensis,* DC. *D. grandiflora,* Sieb. & Zucc. *D. amabilis,* Carr.). Vigorous shrub 5–15 ft. high, nearly glabrous: lvs. broadly ovate to elliptic, 3–4 in. long, abruptly acuminate, crenate-serrate, glabrous or sparingly hairy on veins beneath and on petioles: fls. in 1–3-fld. peduncled cymes in May–June; calyx divided to base into linear lobes; corolla 1¼ in. long, broadly funnelform abruptly narrowed below the middle, changing from whitish or pale pink to carmine, glabrous; stigma capitate: caps. glabrous. Japan.

5. **W. floribunda,** Mey. (*Diervilla floribunda,* Sieb. & Zucc.). To 10 ft., branches slender, soft-hairy: lvs. ovate or oval, 3–4 in. long, acuminate, short-petioled, narrowed at base, serrate, pubescent on both surfaces especially the lower: fls. mostly sessile, usually crowded at ends of short branchlets, in May–June; calyx divided to base into linear lobes; corolla 1 in. long, funnelform, rather gradually narrowed toward base, with 5 spreading lobes about one-fifth as long as tube, pubescent outside, dark almost blood-red; style well-exserted, stigma capitate: caps. pubescent. Japan.—Names belonging to this group are *Desboisii, Hendersonii,* Abel Carrière, the two latter probably hybrids with *W. florida.*

6. **W. japonica,** Thunb. (*Diervilla japonica,* DC.). To 10 ft., branchlets nearly glabrous: lvs. oblong-obovate or elliptic, 2–4 in. long, acuminate, serrate, sparingly pubescent above, pubescent on veins beneath: fls. usually in 3-fld. short-peduncled cymes, often crowded at ends of short branchlets, May–June; calyx divided to base, hairy; corolla 1–1¼ in. long, broadly funnelform, gradually narrowed below the middle, whitish at first changing to carmine, slightly pubescent or nearly glabrous outside; style somewhat exserted: caps. glabrous. Japan.

7. **W. hortensis,** Mey. (*Diervilla hortensis,* Sieb. & Zucc. *D. japonica* var. *hortensis,* Rehd.). Differs from *W. japonica* in more pubescent branchlets, lvs. densely tomentose beneath, longer-peduncled cymes, corolla abruptly expanded above middle and pubescent outside. Japan.

189. VALERIANACEÆ. VALERIAN FAMILY

Herbs and sometimes shrubs of wide distribution, most abundant in the northern hemisphere; about 9 genera and 300 species, some grown for ornament and for food.—Lvs. opposite, without stipules: fls. small, bisexual or unisexual, in cymose or capitate clusters; corolla usually 5-merous as to envelopes, gamopetalous and epigynous, somewhat irregular, often spurred or swollen at base, bearing 1–3 rarely 4 stamens on its tube and alternate with lobes; ovary inferior, invested by the calyx-tube, 1–3-celled, one of the cells with a single ovule, the others empty: fr. a kind of achene, indehiscent.

A. Lvs. (in ours) pinnatisect. . . . . 1. VALERIANA
AA. Lvs. not pinnatisect.
  B. Fr. 1-celled: stamen 1. . . . . 2. CENTRANTHUS
  BB. Fr. 3-celled: stamens 2–3.
    C. Stamens 3: fr. about $\frac{1}{16}$ in. long . . . . 3. VALERIANELLA
    CC. Stamens 2: fr. $\frac{1}{5}$–$\frac{3}{16}$ in. long . . . . 4. FEDIA

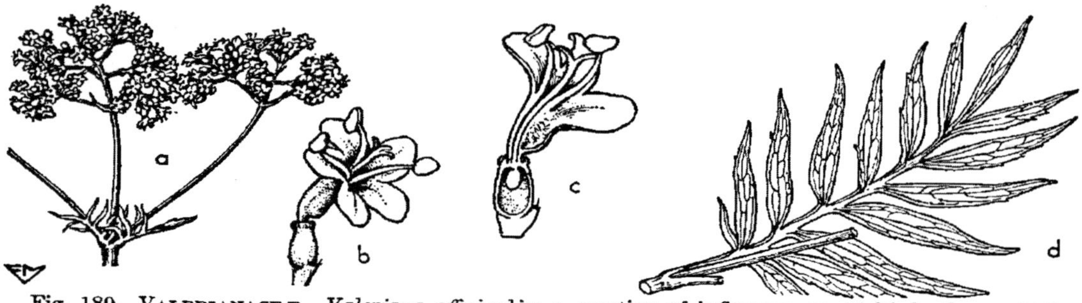

Fig. 189. VALERIANACEÆ. *Valeriana officinalis:* a, portion of inflorescence, × ½; b, flower, × 3; c, same, vertical section, × 4; d, leaf, × ¼.

1. **VALERIANA,** L. VALERIAN. Genus of some 175 species, mostly in the temp. and colder regions of the northern hemisphere, one planted in fl.-gardens and borders.—Commonly glabrous herbs, subshrubs or shrubs, erect or scandent, with strong-smelling roots and often with very fragrant fls.: lvs. entire or dentate or 1–3-pinnatisect: cymes few-fld. and terminal or in dense or interrupted spikes or variously panicled; fls. small, white or rose, in ours bisexual; calyx-limb of 5–15 lobes inconspicuous before fruiting, then unrolling and forming a kind of plumose pappus; corolla-tube attenuate at base, limb 5-cleft; stamens 3, rarely 1 or 2: fr. a compressed achene, the rear face 1-nerved, the front face 3-nerved. (Valeria-na: Latin *to be strong,* in allusion to medicinal uses.)

V. officinalis, L. COMMON VALERIAN. GARDEN-HELIOTROPE. Per. to 5 ft., glabrous or below pubescent; rhizome truncate, sometimes stoloniferous; sts. erect, simple or above somewhat branched, grooved: lvs. all pinnatisect into 7–10-paired, entire or dentate-serrate, ovate-oblong or lanceolate segms., those of the upper lvs. acuminate: corymb broadly paniculate, long-branched; fls. small, numerous, very fragrant, whitish, pinkish or lavender, in the vars. white or red. Eu., N. Asia; frequent in old gardens and also escaped.

2. **CENTRANTHUS,** DC. (or *Kentranthus*). CENTRANTH. About a dozen species in the Medit. region, grown for ornament.—Ann. or per. herbs or sometimes half shrubby: lvs. entire, dentate or pinnatisect: fls. small, red or white, in dense terminal clusters; calyx cut into 5–15 narrow divisions, enlarging after flowering; corolla slender-tubed, 5-parted, spurred at base; stamen 1: fr. 1-celled, crowned with a pappus-like crest. (Centran-thus: Greek *spurred flower.*)

A. Plant per.: lvs. mostly entire.......................1. *C. ruber*
AA. Plant ann.: lvs. toothed or lobed.......................2. *C. macrosiphon*

1. **C. ruber,** DC. (*Valeriana rubra,* L. *V. coccinea,* Hort.). RED VALERIAN. JUPITERS-BEARD. Smooth and glaucous per., 1–3 ft. high, somewhat woody at base, forming a compact floriferous bushy plant: lvs. ovate to lanceolate, to 4 in. long, sessile and very broad at base or tapering to petiole, entire or sometimes toothed at base: fls. numerous, fragrant, deep crimson to pale red (or white in var. **albus**), about ½in. long, the spur slender. Eu. to S. W. Asia.

2. **C. macrosiphon,** Boiss. Ann. cult. in rockeries and borders, 1–2 ft. high: lvs. ovate, 1½–3 in. long, some sessile, others very long-petioled, toothed or lobed, glaucous: fls. deep rose, about ½in. long. Spain.—There are white-fld. and dwarf forms.

3. **VALERIANELLA,** Mill. Some 50 or more species of the northern hemisphere, mostly in the Medit. region, two grown in the vegetable-garden.—Ann. dichotomously branched herbs, glabrous or nearly so except the fr. and lf.-bases: lvs. of basal rosette entire; st.-lvs. entire, dentate or rarely incise-pinnatifid: fls. whitish, pale bluish or rose, in cymes which are sometimes corymbosely paniculate-fastigiate, or sometimes densely globose at the ends of the branches; corolla-tube short or rarely elongate, with or without sac or spur, limb 5-cleft and spreading; stamens 3, rarely 2: fr. 3-celled, 2 cells empty. (Valerianel-la: diminutive of Valeriana.)

A. Fr. with empty cells as large as fertile one and its corky back: basal lvs. (including petiole) 2–3 in. long.......................1. *V. olitoria*
AA. Fr. with empty cells much narrower than fertile one: basal lvs. (including petiole) 3–5 in. long.......................2. *V. eriocarpa*

1. **V. olitoria,** Poll. (*V. Locusta* var. *olitoria,* L. *V. Locusta,* Betcke). Corn-Salad. Small nearly glabrous branching ann. to 1 ft., in Eu. growing among the corn (grain), whence the name "corn-salad": basal lvs. abundant and tufted, spatulate or oblong, toothed or entire, obtuse, 2–3 in. long including petiole; st.-lvs. similar, successively smaller, sometimes toothed: fls. very small, light blue, 5-lobed, in dense heads terminating forking branches: fr. ("seed") nearly orbicular, but with a short 2-pointed beak, flattened sidewise, $\frac{1}{16}$in. long, the 2 empty cells as large as the fertile one and its corky back. Eu.; nat. in N. Amer.

2. **V. eriocarpa,** Desv. Italian Corn-Salad. Distinguished from the preceding by having lvs. 3–5 in. long (including petiole): seed flattened, convex on one side, hollowed on the other, surmounted by the obliquely truncate corolla-like calyx-limb, the empty cells very much narrower than the fertile one. S. Eu.

4. **FEDIA,** Moench. A single species of the Medit. region, grown as an ornamental and also somewhat as a salad plant.—Glabrous branching ann.: lvs. entire or dentate: fls. small, red, in more or less dense terminal cymes; peduncles thick and hollow; corolla-tube elongate, limb 2-lipped, the 5 lobes unequal; stamens 2; style entire or 2–3-fid: fr. with the 2 empty cells narrower than the fertile one. (Fe-dia: application doubtful.)

F. Cornucopiæ, DC. (*Valeriana Cornucopiæ,* L. *F. scorpioides,* Dufr. *Mitrophora Cornucopiæ,* Kuntze). African Valerian. Sts. stout, densely leafy, usually purplish, 10–16 in. long: lvs. ovate-spatulate, 1½–4 in. long, shining green: fr. ⅛–$\frac{3}{16}$in. long, in shape somewhat resembling a grain of wheat. (Cornucopiæ: cornucopia-like.)

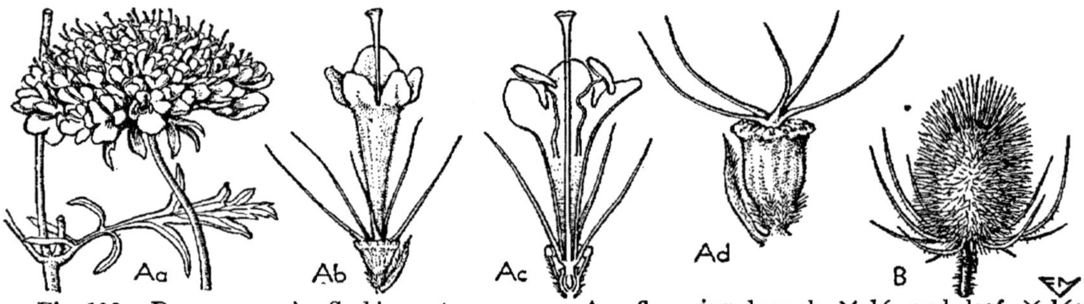

Fig. 190. Dipsaceæ. A, *Scabiosa atropurpurea:* Aa, flowering branch, × ½, and leaf, × ¼; Ab, flower, × 2; Ac, same, vertical section, × 2; Ad, fruit, × 2. B, *Dipsacus sylvestris;* fruiting inflorescence, × ¼.

190. DIPSACEÆ. TEASEL FAMILY

Per., bien. or ann. herbs of the Old World, a few cult. for commercial or ornamental purposes; about 11 genera and 160 species.—Lvs. opposite or rarely whorled, entire, toothed or pinnatifid: fls. small, in dense bracted and involucrate heads or in interrupted spikes; calyx-tube adnate to the 1-celled simple ovary; stamens inserted on corolla-tube and alternate with its lobes, of the same number or fewer, distinct; ovary inferior, 1-celled, style filiform, stigma simple, ovule 1: fr. an achene.

A. Plant spiny and thistle-like.
  B. Fls. in dense heads .... 1. Dipsacus
  BB. Fls. in interrupted spikes .... 2. Morina
AA. Plant not spiny.
  B. Involucral bracts rigid, in several series and overlapping .... 3. Cephalaria
  BB. Involucral bracts herbaceous, in 1–2 series.
    C. Calyx of 5 setæ, persistent .... 4. Scabiosa
    CC. Calyx of 10 or more setæ, often deciduous .... 5. Pterocephalus

1. **DIPSACUS,** L. Teasel. About 15 species in Eu., N. Afr. to Abyssinia and Asia, one of commercial value.—Prickly or rough-hairy stout biennials: cauline lvs. mostly connate and cup-like at base: fls. in a terminal head or short spike with involucral bracts and those of the receptacle sharp or spine-tipped; calyx-limb cup-like, 4-toothed or -lobed; corolla 4-lobed, nearly regular; stamens 4; stigma lateral: fr. an achene adnate to and inclosed by the calyx-like involucel. (Dip-sacus: Greek *thirst,* because the connate lf.-bases in some species hold water.)

D. fullonum, L. (*D. sativus*, Honckeny). FULLERS TEASEL (fullonum, of the fullers). To 6 ft. high, sts. prickly: lvs. lanceolate or oblong, to 1 ft. long, entire or toothed, prickly on midrib beneath: fls. pale lilac, in cylindric heads 2–4 in. long, on long prickly peduncles; bracts of involucre usually shorter than head, at length reflexed; bracts of receptacle with recurved spine-tipped apex. An escape from Eu. about wool mills in the eastern and middle states.—Cult. for the "teasels" or ripe heads which are used by machinery for fulling (raising the nap) on woolen cloth. *D. sylvestris*, Huds., differs in bracts of receptacle tipped with a straight barbed awn; nat. in E. U. S. from Eu. and Asia.

2. **MORINA,** L. Thistle-like perennials, one sometimes raised for ornament; about 10 species native to Asia.—Lvs. mostly spinose-toothed: fls. whorled in spikes, with wide spinose-toothed lf.-like bracts and with spinose bracteoles among the fls., the lower whorls distant; calyx 2-lipped, the lips entire or 2-lobed; corolla 5-lobed, somewhat 2-lipped, the tube curved, in ours long; stamens 2 or 4, with sometimes a sterile one. (Mori-na: after Louis Morin, 1636–1715, a French botanist.

M. longifolia, Wall. WHORL-FLOWER. Per. with stout sts. pubescent above, 3–4 ft. high: foliage thistle-like; lvs. narrowly oblong or linear, 6 in. and more long, 1 in. wide: fls. showy, deepening from white in the bud to pink and finally crimson, the uppermost whorls densely crowded; calyx-lobes unequal, 2-lobed with obtuse not spinose lobes; corolla-tube 1¼ in. long; fertile stamens 2, the filaments much shorter than the corolla-lobes. Himalayas, 9,000–14,000 ft.

3. **CEPHALARIA,** Schrad. Plants of the Medit. region, N. and S. Afr. and W. Asia, also in Abyssinia; about 30 species, somewhat planted for ornament.—Coarse ann. or per. herbs: lvs. entire or pinnate: bloom somewhat like that of Scabiosa; heads terminating long peduncles, ovoid or globular, bearing many 4-parted yellowish, whitish, or bluish florets; involucre of several series of overlapping stiff bracts: stamens 4, perfect: fr. a 4–8-ribbed achene, the calyx-border often remaining on its summit. (Cephala-ria: Greek *head*, alluding to the capitate fl.-clusters.)

A. Marginal fls. enlarged and radiating .... 1. *C. tatarica*
AA. Marginal fls. not so .... 2. *C. alpina*

1. **C. tatarica,** Schrad. Per. to 6 ft. or more, the sts. retrorse-hairy below and nearly naked above: lvs. pinnatisect into oblong or oval-lanceolate toothed segms. decurrent on petiole, nearly glabrous above, hairy beneath as also the petiole: fls. cream or yellow, in rather flat heads to 2 in. across, the marginal fls. enlarged and radiating; involucral bracts ovate, obtuse or acute, hairy. Russia, W. Asia.

2. **C. alpina,** Schrad. Evidently not in cult., the plant grown under this name being *C. tatarica;* differs in sts. velutinous, lf.-segms. lanceolate, marginal fls. not conspicuously enlarged, involucral bracts acuminate and silky-hairy. Mts. of S. Eu.

4. **SCABIOSA,** L. SCABIOUS. MOURNING BRIDE. PINCUSHION-FLOWER. Herbs, of about 80 species in Eu., Asia and Afr., rare in the tropics; a few popular fl.-garden plants.—Ann. or per., more or less woody at base: lvs. entire, dentate, lobed or dissected: heads depressed subglobose or ovoid-conical, terminating long peduncles or rarely dichotomously sessile; bracts of the involucre 1–2-rowed, herbaceous; fls. blue, rose, yellowish or white, the marginal fls. usually larger and radiating; calyx bristly, of 5 setæ united at base; outer calyx or involucel adnate to achene, with free cup-like limb; corolla-limb 4–5-cleft, subequal or oblique or 2-lipped; stamens 4, rarely 2; ovary inferior, crowned with persistent calyx. (Scabio-sa: Latin *itch*, referring to medicinal use.)

A. Lvs. all linear and entire .... 1. *S. graminifolia*
AA. Lvs. not linear, some of them lobed or cut.
  B. Limb of involucel crenate and inflexed: plant ann. .... 2. *S. atropurpurea*
  BB. Limb of involucel erect and cup-like: plant per.
    C. Involucels terete, with 5 deep pits below the limb .... 3. *S. caucasica*
    CC. Involucels 8-grooved the entire length, without deep pits.
      D. Fls. yellowish-white .... 4. *S. ochroleuca*
      DD. Fls. lilac or blue.
        E. Basal lvs. toothed or lyrate-pinnatifid.
          F. Sts. and lvs. usually glabrous: calyx-setæ distinctly keeled .... 5. *S. lucida*
          FF. Sts. and lvs. usually hairy: calyx-setæ not keeled .... 6. *S. Columbaria*
        EE. Basal lvs. pinnatisect.
          F. Corolla 4-lobed .... 7. *S. japonica*
          FF. Corolla 5-lobed .... 8. *S. Fischeri*

1. **S. graminifolia,** L. Per. to 1½ ft., with creeping rootstock and ascending pubescent sts. leafy to about middle: lvs. linear, grass-like, entire, hoary-pubescent: fls. lilac or blue, hairy, in heads 1½–2 in. across; involucre hairy; calyx-setæ slightly longer than the many-nerved limb of the involucels. Eu.

2. **S. atropurpurea,** L. SWEET SCABIOUS. Branching ann. about 2 ft. high, the sts. nearly glabrous: basal lvs. oblong-spatulate, undivided or lyrate, coarsely dentate; st.-lvs. pinnately parted, the oblong lobes dentate or cut: fls. dark purple, rose or white, in long-peduncled heads to 2 in. across, becoming ovate or oblong in fr.; involucels with ribs dilated toward apex, the limb crenate and inflexed, much exceeded by the calyx-setæ. S. Eu.—Very variable in size, habit and color of fls., the different forms being among the most popular fl.-garden annuals.

3. **S. caucasica,** Bieb. Hardy per. 1½–2½ ft. high, the sts. glabrous or slightly pubescent: basal lvs. oblong, attenuate into long petiole, entire or sometimes pinnatisect, the upper cut and divided into linear segms.: fls. light blue, in flattish heads to 3 in. across; basal portion of involucre clothed with long dense matted gray hairs; involucels with 5 deep pits below the many-nerved limb, the calyx-setæ about twice as long as limb. Caucasus. Var. **alba,** Hort., fls. white. Var. **goldingensis,** Hort., fls. deep lavender, large. Var. **perfecta,** Hort., fls. large and fringed.

4. **S. ochroleuca,** L. Per. or bien. 1–2½ ft. high, the sts. pubescent and branched: basal lvs. lyrate or sometimes undivided, the upper 1–2-pinnate into linear-lanceolate segms., grayish-pubescent: fls. yellowish-white, in heads ¾–1½ in. across, the involucre densely pubescent; calyx-setæ two to three times longer than erect limb of involucel. Eu., W. Asia.

5. **S. lucida,** Vill. Per. 1–2 ft. high, sts. glabrous, leafy below: basal lvs. ovate or rhombic, undivided and coarsely toothed or somewhat lyrate, upper 1–2-pinnate into lanceolate or linear segms., glabrous or ciliate: fls. rose-lilac, pubescent outside, 1–1½ in. across, involucre glabrous; calyx-setæ distinctly keeled, shining dark purple, four to five times longer than limb of involucel. Eu.

6. **S. Columbaria,** L. Per. or bien. 1–2½ ft. high, sts. white-hairy to nearly glabrous: basal lvs. lyrate and crenate, upper 1–2-pinnate into lanceolate or linear segms., usually pubescent: fls. lilac, in heads ¾–1½ in. across, involucre pubescent; calyx-setæ two to four times as long as limb of involucel or lacking, not keeled. (Columbaria: from *columba*, dove; fls. dove-like, bluish.) Eu., W. Asia, Afr.

7. **S. japonica,** Miq. Per. to 2 ft., sts. branched and pubescent: basal lvs. pinnatisect, upper pinnate into linear entire or toothed segms., somewhat pubescent: fls. violet-blue, in heads about 2 in. across, involucre densely pubescent; corolla 4-lobed; calyx-setæ three to four times as long as limb of involucel. Japan.

8. **S. Fischeri,** DC. Per. to 2½ ft., sts. much-branched and nearly glabrous: lvs. all pinnatisect into linear entire segms., nearly glabrous: fls. bluish-purple, in heads 2–2½ in. across; corolla 5-lobed; calyx-setæ twice as long as limb of involucel. (Named for E. L. Fischer, who collected the seeds.) Dahuria.

5. **PTEROCEPHALUS,** Vaill. Herbs or subshrubs of about 20 species in Eu. and Asia, one planted in rock-gardens.—Differs from Scabiosa chiefly in the calyx-setæ being 10 or more, and often deciduous. (Pteroceph-alus: Greek for *wing* and *head.*)

P. parnassii, Spreng. (*Scabiosa Pterocephala,* L.). Per. 3–4 in. high, spreading and making broad patches, densely silky-tomentose: lvs. undivided or lyrate-pinnatifid, crenate, to 1½ in. long: fls. purplish-pink, in heads about 1 in. across standing above foliage; calyx-setæ plumose, three to four times longer than involucels. Mts. of Greece.

191. CUCURBITACEÆ. GOURD FAMILY

As known in cult., tendril-climbing (except in Ecballium and a few cultivars of *Cucurbita Pepo*) ann. and per. rapid-growing frost-tender herbs, grown for the edible frs. and for ornament; genera about 90 and species about 700, mostly in trop. regions around the world, some extending into temp. zones.—Sts. mostly soft, glabrous, hairy or prickly: lvs. alternate, broad, usually simple but often deeply cut, sometimes compound: tendrils lateral, simple or branched: fls. unisexual (plants monœcious, sometimes diœcious), regular; calyx adnate to ovary, 5-lobed; petals 5 or corolla gamopetalous and 5-lobed; stamens apparently 3 but really 5 with 2 pairs united, mostly monadelphous by contorted anthers, filaments connate or free; ovary inferior, placentation parietal, ovules many, carpels commonly 3: fr. mostly indehiscent, sometimes a papery bladdery pod, more typically a fleshy berry-like structure (pepo) with a rind and spongy seedy interior.

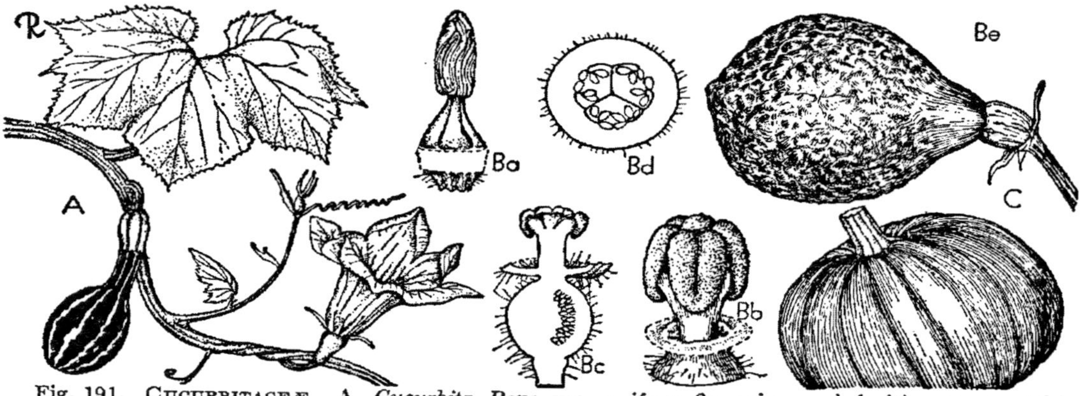

Fig. 191. CUCURBITACEÆ. A, *Cucurbita Pepo* var. *ovifera:* flowering and fruiting stem, × 1/8. B, *Cucurbita maxima:* Ba, staminate flower, perianth removed, × 1/2; Bb, style and stigma, × 1; Bc, pistillate flower, vertical section, perianth removed, × 1/2; Bd, ovary, cross-section, × 1; Be, fruit, much reduced. C, *Cucurbita Pepo:* fruit, much reduced.

A. Fr. fleshy, with hard or firm rind, indehiscent, mostly edible.
  B. Pepo many-seeded, with 3 evident cells or compartments.
    C. Corolla bell-shaped and distinctly gamopetalous, 5-lobed to middle or a little more.
      D. Anthers coherent .... 1. CUCURBITA
      DD. Anthers free .... 2. SICANA
    CC. Corolla of 5 petals or parted to base, rotate or open-bell-shaped.
      D. Staminate fls. in racemes .... 3. LUFFA
      DD. Staminate fls. solitary (although perhaps more than 1 in an axil).
        E. Sepals leafy, serrate, reflexed .... 4. BENINCASA
        EE. Sepals small, entire, erect or only spreading.
          F. Tendrils branched.
            G. Lvs. not lobed .... 5. LAGENARIA
            GG. Lvs. pinnatifid .... 6. CITRULLUS
          FF. Tendrils simple .... 7. CUCUMIS
  BB. Pepo with 1 great seed .... 8. SECHIUM
AA. Fr. quite otherwise, several- to many-seeded, small berry, pod-like, bladdery, dryish or fleshy, mostly inedible: for the most part ornamental plants.
  B. Corolla bell-shaped, gamopetalous, lobed to middle .... 9. COCCINIA
  BB. Corolla rotate or cup-shaped, lobed to base or of separate petals.
    C. Petals fimbriate .... 10. TRICHOSANTHES
    CC. Petals or corolla not fimbriate.
      D. Peduncle, particularly of staminate fls., bearing a shield-shaped bract (in our species) .... 11. MOMORDICA
      DD. Peduncle of staminate fls. naked.
        E. Staminate fls. solitary .... 12. ABOBRA
        EE. Staminate fls. in racemes or corymbs.
          F. Lvs. compound or parted to base (in ours) .... 13. CYCLANTHERA
          FF. Lvs. simple.
            G. Ovules erect: filaments connate .... 14. ECHINOCYSTIS
            GG. Ovules horizontal: filaments free (separate), but anthers free or coherent.
              H. Tendrils present.
                I. Plant (in ours) diœcious: ovary globular .... 15. BRYONIA
                II. Plant monœcious: ovary elongated .... 16. MELOTHRIA
              HH. Tendrils 0 .... 17. ECBALLIUM

1. CUCURBITA, L. (*Pepo,* Mill.). PUMPKINS. SQUASHES. About 25 species, ann. and per. (ours ann. or cult. as such), all supposed to be American; grown for the frs., either as esculents or ornaments.—Long-running coarse rough-hairy scabrous monœcious plants with branched tendrils and simple mostly lobed lvs.: fls. solitary in axils in our species, the staminate long-peduncled, large, yellow, the corolla gamopetalous and lobed about half way down; anthers united; ovary 1-celled, with 3–5 placentæ, stigmas 2-lobed, 3–5 in number: fr. a large pepo. (Cucur-bita: the Latin name for gourd.)

A. Seeds white or tan-white at dry maturity.
  B. Plant harsh, rough or scratchy to the feel, more or less setiferous: lvs. mostly strongly lobed and triangular-pointed, dentate or serrate: peduncle angled, expanded at junction with fr. but seldom flared: seeds thick-edged: tips of floral segms. connivent (bud pointed) in evening preceding anthesis; calyx-lobes of st. fl. seldom if ever foliaceous .... 1. *C. Pepo*

BB. Plant soft or at least not harsh to the feel, not setiferous but variously pilose: lvs. only shallowly if at all lobed, rounded or triangulate, mostly not or only obscurely serrate.
  C. Margin of thin seed at fresh maturity very thin, the hyaline ragged edge often wearing away in seed-packet: lf.-blade broad-ovate to somewhat triangular in outline: tips of floral segms. connivent in bud at evening before anthesis: calyx-lobes of st. fl. often prolonged and foliaceous: peduncle long and furrowed, flared at junction with fr. . . . . 2. *C. moschata*
  CC. Margin of plump seed obtuse and more or less elevated: lf.-blade circular to reniform in outline: tips of floral segms. open or spreading in bud at evening preceding anthesis: calyx-lobes of st. fl. not foliaceous: peduncle short and spongy, nearly cylindric, not flared at attachment to fr. . . . . 3. *C. maxima*
AA. Seeds black or brown-black, or with a wide blue-black or cyaneous marginal band.
  B. Mature lvs. deeply lobed with rounded sinuses: seeds uniformly black or brown-black . . . . 4. *C. ficifolia*
  BB. Mature lvs. nearly entire: seeds banded in color . . . . 5. *C. argyrosperma*

1. **C. Pepo,** L. (*C. verrucosa*, L. *C. polymorpha*, Duchesne). FIELD PUMPKIN. Plant with sharp stiff translucent harsh hairs, making it rough or scratchy to the hands, sts. long-running: lvs. stiff and somewhat rigid, erect, triangular or ovate-triangular in outline, 6–12 in. long, pointed, usually prominently lobed and apiculate, margins irregularly sharp-serrate: corolla mostly with erect or spreading pointed lobes, the tube commonly narrow at base and flaring upward; calyx-lobes short and narrow: peduncle strongly angled or cornered and expanding at attachment: fr. large, orange, furrowed, perishable; seeds white, elliptic, with raised obtuse margin, ¾–1 in. long, less than ½in. broad. (Pepo: ante-Linnæan name for the plant.)—The common field, pie and cattle pumpkin.

Var. **ovifera,** Alef. (*C. ovifera*, L. *C. texana*, Gray). YELLOW-FLOWERED GOURDS. Slender long-running and climbing plant with abundant tendrils: lf.-blades 8 in. or less long, broad-ovate in outline, angled to lobed: fr. small and hard-shelled, bitter and inedible, in many shapes and sizes, used for curiosity and ornament, mostly under 4 or 5 in. thick or long, unicolored or striped.—Here belong Apple, Bell, Bicolor, Egg, Orange, Pear gourds, and many others.

Var. **Melopepo,** Alef. (*C. Melopepo*, L. *C. Pepo* var. *condensa*, Bailey). BUSH SQUASHES and PUMPKINS. SUMMER SQUASHES. Plant covering small space, compact, not running or tendril-bearing: fr. various; seeds usually not much exceeding ½in. long and often less. Known mostly in two historic fr. forms or subraces: *Melopepo clypeiformis*, Bailey, the flat shield-shaped or scalloped or pattypan squashes; *Melopepo torticollis*, Bailey (*C. Pepo* var. *torticollis*, Alef.), the summer crookneck usually warty squashes, elongated and club-shaped, crooked or hooked at the basal end but sometimes straight (Straightneck).

Var. **medullosa,** Alef. VEGETABLE MARROW. Fr. elongate, 16–18 in. or more and perhaps 6–8 in. thick and of nearly equal thickness throughout, not warted, longitudinal ridges few and low or none, yellowish-green to irregularly striped or cream-color, peduncle angled and somewhat expanded at attachment to pepo, flesh often nearly solid: usually a long runner, but in some races plant condensed and tendrils abortive as in Zuccini: seeds about ½in. or a little more long.

2. **C. moschata,** Duchesne. CUSHAW and WINTER CROOKNECK SQUASHES. Plant long-running, soft to the hand: lvs. limpish and velvety, not stoutly upright, usually broad-ovate to nearly circular-ovate in outline and not lobed, but sometimes lobed and much like *C. Pepo* in shape, often with whitish marks and blotches: corolla with wide-spreading crinkly lobes, the tube broad at base and usually not bulging above; calyx-lobes often long and frequently expanded and lf.-like at the end: peduncle angled, widely expanded at fr.: seeds thin, ¾in. or less long, margin usually hyaline when fresh.—The frs. are known both as pumpkins and squashes; they are autumn and winter products, including the Sweet Potato, Quaker Pie and Japanese Pie pumpkins. Var. **melonæformis,** Bailey, lvs. more rounded; peduncle long, angled, expanded at apex; fr. furrowed.

3. **C. maxima,** Duchesne. AUTUMN and WINTER SQUASHES. Plant long-running, tendrils many, rather soft to the hand: lvs. not rigid, moderately upright, orbicular or nearly so, not lobed, base cordate with very deep sinus, margins shallow-serrate with soft points: corolla with broad usually reflexed lobes, the tube with parallel sides or bulging toward the base; calyx-lobes short and narrow: peduncle short and cylindrical or enlarged at middle, often somewhat spongy, not expanded at attachment: fr. often glaucous or bluish; seeds plump, ½– about 1 in. long, margin obtuse.—The Hubbard and Boston Marrow are of this species; also the Mammoth Chile and other immense frs.

Var. **turbaniformis,** Alef. (*C. turbaniformis*, Roem.). TURBAN SQUASHES. Fr. turban-shaped, the central part or ovary enlarged and protruding and holding remains of the corolla, the outer pericarp wall also developing fully so that it results in "a squash within a squash": vines long and vigorous, tendriliferous.

4. **C. ficifolia,** Bouché (*C. melanosperma*, Gaspar.). FIGLEAF and MALABAR GOURD. Extensively running, the sts. setose and harsh to the hand: lvs. circular-ovate to nearly reniform, 7–10 in. across, sinuate to lobed and with obtuse sinuses, the basal sinus broad

and margined by the lateral ribs, margins apiculate-serrate to practically entire: corolla with spreading large lobes, the tube broad and expanding upward; calyx-lobes very narrow and short: peduncle angled, expanded at attachment: fr. oblong or nearly globular, 6–12 in. long, green with white stripes, flesh white, rind hard and gourd-like; seeds black or nearly so, about ⅝in. long, with a raised margin.—Grown for its abundant foliage and ornamental frs.

5. **C. argyrosperma,** Hort. Silverseed Gourd. Vigorous grower and runner, main sts. glabrous: lvs. broad-ovate to nearly reniform, about 9 in. across either way at maturity, outline nearly regular or indifferently wavy or sublobed, margins serrate, petiole sparsely apiculate: fls. deep yellow and usually green-striped, limb and tube broad and flaring: fr. short-oblong to somewhat pyriform, 7–9 in. long and thick, striped green and white, peduncle angled and expanded at attachment; seeds large and flat, more than 1 in. long and to ¾in. broad, center white, border banded broadly with bluish.

2. **SICANA,** Naud. Glabrous monœcious long-running vine sometimes cult. in U. S. and frequent in tropics; 1 or 2 other species from trop. Amer.—Differs from Cucurbita in anthers being free although connivent; lobes of calyx and corolla short and reflexed. (Sica-na: name in Peru.)

S. odorifera, Naud. Curuba. Cassabanana. Per., sts. angled, tendrils branched: lvs. large, nearly orbicular to reniform in outline, 5–12 in. across, strongly lobed, cordate at base, margins angled or repand-toothed: fls. solitary, yellowish, staminate about ¾in. long, pistillate about 2 in. long with the slender ovary; stigmas 3, each 2-lobed: fr. long-oblong, 1–2 ft., nearly cylindrical, black-purple to orange-crimson, sometimes with strong aroma; seeds small and thin, about ½in. long, with prominent brown border, otherwise white or tawny. Probably Brazil, but spread elsewhere.—Grown mostly for its ornamental fragrant fr., which is also sometimes eaten.

3. **LUFFA,** L. Annuals, or grown as such; species few, in Old World tropics.—Monœcious, nearly or quite glabrous: tendrils branched: lvs. 5–7-lobed: fls. yellow or whitish, showy; staminate racemose, pistillate solitary and short- or long-peduncled; corolla of 5 deep lobes; anthers free; ovary with 3 placentæ, the stigmas 3 and 2-lobed, ovules many: fr. long and cylindrical or short and clavate, the rind becoming dry and papery, not hairy, the interior fibrous; seeds small, black. (Luf-fa: from *luff*, the Arabic name.)—The dried fibrous interior of the frs. is used as a sponge, whence the names Vegetable-Sponge, Dishcloth gourd, Rag gourd; young fr. sometimes eaten.

A. Ovary not ribbed and cornered, usually cylindrical and tomentose: lvs. mostly deeply lobed....................1. *L. cylindrica*
AA. Ovary ribbed and angled, mostly rather short and club-shaped and not tomentose: lvs. not deeply lobed....................2. *L. acutangula*

1. **L. cylindrica,** Roem. Strong vine, sts. slender and angled: lvs. deltoid to nearly circular in outline but pointed, 5–12 in. long, mostly 3–7-lobed, with close or open base, margins dentate, scabrous but not pubescent: fls. 2–4 in. across, light yellow: fr. nearly or quite cylindrical, 1–2 ft. or more long, straight or curved, usually with light furrows and stripes but not ribbed or angled; seeds flat, about ½in. long, black or nearly so, smooth, margined.—The common species in cult. in N. Amer., and escaped in American tropics.

2. **L. acutangula,** Roxb. Lvs. usually not so large, very scabrous, angled but not deeply lobed: fr. clavate, 6–12 in. long, strongly ridged; seeds thicker than in *L. cylindrica*, flattish, about ½in. long, black, reticulate or sculptured, not margined.

4. **BENINCASA,** Savi. Two ann. vines of trop. Asia, one sometimes grown for the fr. which is eaten, mostly as conserves and pickles.—Monœcious: tendrils branched: fls. solitary, yellow, large and showy, the staminate long-peduncled and pistillate short-stalked or nearly sessile; corolla rotate, 5-parted to base; anthers free; ovary with 3 placentæ, stigmas 3, ovules many: fr. fleshy and without durable rind. (Beninca-sa: name of an Italian nobleman, patron of botany.)

B. hispida, Cogn. (*B. cerifera,* Savi). White Gourd. Chinese Preserving Melon. Long-running, with brown-hairy sts.: lvs. broad-ovate to reniform-ovate, 6–10 in. across, angled but not lobed, cordate at base with sinus bordered at top by the lateral ribs, margins dentate, hairy or becoming nearly glabrous: fls. 3–4 in. across: fr. nearly spherical to long-oblong, often 10–16 in. long, hairy and white-waxy, becoming glabrous; seeds about ⅓in. long, smooth, white.—Sometimes sold as Cassabanana.

5. **LAGENARIA,** Ser. Bottle Gourd. One variable long-running ann., probably native in Old World tropics but now widespread in warm countries and cult. for ornament and for the astonishing variety of thin-shelled frs. that are used for receptacles, utensils, bird-houses and decoration.—Monœcious, or only rarely diœcious: tendrils branched: fls. solitary, white, showy, perishing toward midday, 5-petalled; staminate on very long peduncles, often surpassing the foliage; anthers lightly cohering, but not connate; ovary long or short, with 3 placentæ, ovules numerous and horizontal: fr. of many sizes and shapes, with hard durable shell; seeds oblong to nearly square, ¾in. or less long, ridged on margins and cornered, tan to brown. (Lagena-ria: Latin *lagena*, a bottle, from the fr.)

L. siceraria, Standl. (*Cucurbita siceraria*, Molina. *C. leucantha*, Duchesne. *L. vulgaris*, Ser. *L. leucantha*, Rusby). White-flowered Gourd. Musky-scented soft viscid-pubescent vine with branched tendrils: lvs. cordate-ovate to reniform-ovate, 6–12 in. across, not lobed or sometimes only indifferently so, broad-cordate at base, margins apiculate-dentate: fls. 2–4 in. across: fr. 3 in. to 3 ft. and more long, from disk-like to nearly globular and bottle-shaped, dumbbell-shaped, club-shaped, crooknecked and coiled, sometimes striped or mottled but prevailingly greenish or tan, in some cases knobby or ridged. (Siceraria: from *sicera*, a drinking vessel.)—Here are included the Dipper, Sugar-trough, Hercules Club and other gourds; also the Calabash gourd, although the name calabash belongs with Crescentia.

6. **CITRULLUS,** Neck. Four recognized species, all in trop. Afr. and 1 probably native also in Asia; one species widely grown for its edible fr.—Monœcious annuals or perennials, long-running, more or less hairy, with branched tendrils: lvs. deeply pinnatifid, the lobes again lobed: fls. of medium size, light yellow, solitary in the axils; corolla 5-parted nearly to base; anthers free; ovary with 3 placentæ and many ovules, the stigmas 3. (Citrul-lus: diminutive of *citrus*, in some allusion to the frs.)

C. vulgaris, Schrad. Watermelon. Hairy ann.: lvs. ovate to ovate-oblong in outline, 4–7 in. long, cordate at base, pinnately divided into 3 or 4 pairs of lobes and these again lobed and toothed, the segms. broad at the apex: peduncles much shorter than the lvs.: corolla about 1½ in. across, rotate, the 5 lobes obovate and obtuse: fr. globular or oblong, sometimes 2 ft. or more long, mostly glabrous, with a hard but not durable rind, striped green, and sweet red, green or yellow flesh; seeds white, black or reddish, flat, smooth, ¼–½in. long. Trop. and S. Afr., spontaneous in warm countries. Var. **citroides,** Bailey, Citron, Preserving Melon, fr. hard, white-fleshed, not edible from the hand, surface often mottled, lf.-lobes broad and obtuse, seeds greenish or tan.

7. **CUCUMIS,** L. Some 30 species of annuals and perennials, trailing or climbing, in warm countries, mostly African, a few grown for the edible and interesting frs.—Monœcious or rarely diœcious, mostly hairy: tendrils simple: lvs. entire or dissected: fls. yellow, not large, solitary but the staminate sometimes more than 1 in an axil, usually short-stalked and underneath the foliage; corolla open-bell-shaped to rotate, deeply 5-parted; anthers free; ovary with 3–5 placentæ and stigmas, many-ovuled, the style short: fr. fleshy and usually indehiscent, globular to elongated, glabrous, pubescent or echinate. (Cu-cumis: Latin name of a plant with cucumber-like odor.)

A. Fr. spiny, muricate or echinate.
  B. Lvs. deeply lobed, with rounded sinuses....1. *C. Anguria*
  BB. Lvs. not lobed or only shallowly so and with acute or very narrow sinuses or angulate.
    C. Mature fr. bur-like, beset with hairs, not edible....2. *C. dipsaceus*
    CC. Mature fr. prickly or muricate, edible....3. *C. sativus*
AA. Fr. glabrous or only pubescent (sometimes somewhat warty)....4. *C. Melo*

1. **C. Anguria,** L. (*C. grossulariæformis*, Hort.). West India or Bur Gherkin. Slender rough-hairy trailing vine with angled sts. and small tendrils: lvs. 1½–3½ in. long, with 3 prominent main lobes divided by sinuses with enlarged rounded bottoms, the lateral lobes usually again lobed, lobes broad and obtuse, margins apiculate, sinuate-serrate, very scabrous: fls. ⅛–½in. across, or the staminate sometimes broader, on slender peduncles: fr. oval or oblong, about 2 in. long, on crooked peduncles, furrowed, prickly, with very many small white smooth seeds less than ¼in. long. (Anguria: a Greek name for some cucurbitous fr.) Fla. and Tex. to S. Amer.—Grown for curiosity and for use in pickles; the "gherkins" of mixed pickles, however, are usually young cucumbers.

2. **C. dipsaceus,** Ehrh. Hedgehog or Teasel Gourd. Slender trailer with strongly setose angled sts.: lvs. much like those of *C. Melo*, broad-ovate to nearly reniform-ovate, 3–4½ in. across, not lobed, cordate at base, sinuate-serrate, setose and scabrous: fls. small, the staminate ½–¾in. across, on long peduncles: fr. a hard dry bristly oblong bur 1–2 in. long; seeds flat, white, little more than ⅛in. long. Arabia.—Grown for ornament and curiosity.

3. **C. sativus,** L. Cucumber. Trailing or climbing, rough-hairy, with strong angled sts.: lvs. triangular-ovate, 3–6 in. long, angled or somewhat 3-lobed and with acute or not rounded sinuses, the middle lobe pointed, very scabrous: fls. 1–1½ in. across, very short-pedicelled, the staminate often several in one axil, the corolla-lobes acute: fr. from nearly globular to oblong and elongated, prickly with sharp elevations; seeds flat, white, a little more than ¼in. long. S. Asia. Var. **anglicus,** Bailey, English Forcing Cucumber, a group of cultivars with very strong and vigorous sts.: lvs. large and broad, rather short in proportion to breadth, sometimes 1 ft. long: fls. very large: fr. slender, sometimes 3 ft. long, little furrowed and nearly or quite spineless, producing few seeds.

4. **C. Melo,** L. Melon. Muskmelon. Trailing or somewhat climbing soft-hairy vine with striate or angled sts.: lvs. orbicular-ovate to nearly reniform, 3–5 in. across, angled but usually not distinctly lobed, rounded at apex, margins sinuate-dentate, hairy and somewhat scabrous: fls. about 1 in. across, the staminate sometimes more than 1 in an axil, the corolla-lobes essentially obtuse: fr. various, in the usual forms globular or oblong, more or less furrowed, not spiny or echinate, pubescent but usually becoming glabrous, with a pronounced musky odor, usually with yellow or green flesh; seeds white, slender, nearly ½in. long. (Melo: old Latin name for a form of melon.) Probably Cent. Asia.—It has given rise to many races and cultivars. Var. **reticulatus,** Naud., Netted or Nutmeg Melons, fr. small with the surface net-ribbed. Var. **cantalupensis,** Naud., Cantaloupe Melons (from Cantaluppi, near Rome, where these melons were early grown from S. W. Asian stock), fr. with hard rinds, often furrowed, scaly, warty or rough; in N. Amer. the name cantaloupe is commonly improperly applied to muskmelons in general.

Var. **inodorus,** Naud. Winter or Cassaba Melon (the latter a geographical name in S. W. Asia). Strong and long-tendrilled vines: lvs. large, often 8 in. and more long, sparsely hairy, sometimes deeply lobed: fls. often 2 in. across: fr. large, maturing late and keeping in winter, squash-like in shape and often striped and splashed, usually white-fleshed, with little musky odor and flavor.

Var. **flexuosus,** Naud. (*C. flexuosus*, L.). Snake or Serpent Melon. Plant like *C. Melo* itself: fls. often larger, the ovary very long: fr. 18–40 in. long and 1–3 in. thick, furrowed, often crooknecked or coiled, slightly pubescent, the flesh white and cucumber-like, slightly acid.—Fr. sometimes used in preserving, but raised mostly as a curiosity.

Var. **Conomon,** Makino (*C. Conomon*, Thunb.). Oriental Pickling Melon. Vine the stature of *C. Melo*, with setose-prickly sts.: lvs. on the ovate-oblong order, shallowly side-lobed and the middle lobe large and rounded, petioles setose: fls. large: fr. various in shape, smooth and glabrous, with longitudinal lines and perhaps somewhat furrowed, pale green, flesh white or green, not musky and not sweet, sometimes oblong-cylindrical and slightly clavate, to 24 in. long and 6 in. thick, in other forms much shorter, again turban-shaped or constricted midway. (Conomon: from the Japanese *konomono*, a food used with rice but principally prepared from the radish.)

Var. **Chito,** Naud. (*C. Chito*, Morr.). Mango Melon. Stature of *C. Melo*, with setose-hairy sts.: lvs. as in *C. Melo*, except mostly smaller: fr. size and shape of orange or lemon, or sometimes oblong, yellow or greenish-yellow, not variegated nor fragrant, the flesh white and cucumber-like. (Chito is probably a geographical name.)—Frs. used in the making of preserves and pickles, under the names Mango, Orange Melon, Vegetable-Orange, Lemon-Cucumber, Melon-Apple, Vine-Peach.

Var. **Dudaim,** Naud. (*C. Dudaim*, L. *C. odoratissimus*, Moench). Dudaim Melon. Small plant with hairy-setose slender angled sts.: lvs. ovate-oblong and unlobed, usually about 2 in. long but becoming 6 in. long: fls. relatively large: fr. size of a medium orange, somewhat oblate, longitudinally marbled with rich brown, very fragrant. (Dudaim: a Hebrew name, said to be scriptural.)—Grown for the ornamental perfumed fr.

8. **SECHIUM,** P. Br. (*Chayota*, Jacq.). One slender glabrous or sparsely hairy per. vine of trop. Amer., cult. for its edible fr. and tubers.—Monœcious: tendrils large, branched: fls. small, the staminate in small peduncled clusters, pistillate shorter-stalked in the same axils; corolla cup-shaped to nearly rotate, deeply 5-lobed; anthers free, but the filaments, as well as the styles, connate: fr. fleshy, with 1 large seed. (Se-chium: name obscure.)

S. edule, Sw. Chayote. Christophine. Roots tuberous: sts. ann., trailing and climbing: lvs. broad-ovate to triangular-ovate, 4–8 in. long, angled but scarcely or shallowly lobed, the points apiculate, margins entire: fr. mostly pyriform, 3–8 in. long, furrowed and wrinkled, green or whitish, at the end nearly closing over the single large flat seed which is 1–2 in. long.—Fr. and root-tubers much prized in trop. and subtrop. regions as vegetables.

9. **COCCINIA,** Wight & Arn. (*Cephalandra*, Schrad.). Per. trop. vines of Asia and Afr., usually with tuberous roots, one more or less grown for ornament and as an arbor vine.—Mostly diœcious: tendrils branched in ours: lvs. angled or lobed, sometimes glandular: fls. large, white or yellowish, solitary or clustered; corolla bell-shaped, lobed to middle; stamens connate; ovary with many ovules: fr. small, berry-like, oblong or cylindrical, often highly colored. (Coccin-ia: Latin *scarlet.*)

C. cordifolia, Cogn. (*C. indica*, Wight & Arn.). Ivy Gourd. Sts. slender, long-running and -climbing, furrowed, glabrous; tendrils simple: lvs. triangular-ovate, 2–3 in. across, angle-lobed but not deeply so, cordate at base, sinuate-serrulate or entire on margins: fls. white, slender-peduncled, about 1½ in. long, with acute flaring corolla-lobes: fr. 1–2 in. long, scarlet; seeds white, about ¼in. long. S. E. Asia.

10. **TRICHOSANTHES,** L. Ann. and per. herbs, perhaps woody at base, sometimes with tuberous roots, in the tropics of Asia, Polynesia and Australia, one frequently grown for ornament and food.—Monœcious or diœcious: tendrils mostly branched: lvs. entire or lobed: fls. white, the staminate racemose; corolla rotate or cup-shaped, the petals or lobes 5 and laciniate; stamens 3; ovary 1-celled, with many ovules: fr. fleshy, short or elongated. (Trichosan-thes: Greek *hair-flower*, from the fimbriate corolla.)

T. Anguina, L. (*T. colubrina*, Jacq.). Serpent or Snake Gourd. Long-running or -climbing ann., with slender angled short hairy sts.; tendrils branched: lvs. broad-ovate to triangular-ovate, 4–9 in. long, shallowly 3-lobed or unlobed, deeply and broadly cordate at base, margins sinuately apiculate-dentate, nearly or quite glabrous: fls. long-peduncled and showy, 2 in. or more across: fr. 1–6 ft. long, very slender, long-tapering to the point, variously curved or coiled, glabrous, greenish-white; seeds about ½in. long, thick, scalloped on the edges, brownish. (Anguina: Latin *anguis*, serpent.) India.—Grown for the curious fr., which is also sometimes eaten. The name "snake gourd" is sometimes applied to forms of Lagenaria.

11. **MOMORDICA,** L. Ann. and per. climbing herbs of 35–40 species in trop. Afr. and Asia, 2 commonly cult. for ornament and somewhat for food.—Monœcious or diœcious: tendrils simple or forked: lvs. simple or compound: pistillate fls. solitary, yellow or sometimes white, the staminate solitary or panicled (solitary in ours), peduncle in ours bearing a prominent broad bract; corolla rotate or open-bell-shaped, mostly parted nearly to the base; anthers free; ovary with 3 placentæ, the stigmas 3 and sometimes 2-lobed: fr. oblong or nearly spherical, small or large, often spiny-tuberculate, usually indehiscent but sometimes splitting at maturity into 3 valves. (Momor-dica: Latin *mordeo*, to bite, the seeds sometimes jagged as if bitten.)—Ours are porch vines and run wild in warm countries.

A. Bract serrate, on the sterile peduncle placed on the upper part................1. *M. Balsamina*
AA. Bract entire, at the middle or base of peduncle...............................2. *M. Charantia*

1. **M. Balsamina,** L. Balsam-Apple. Very slender but high-climbing glabrous monœcious ann. with simple tendrils: lvs. thin and glabrous, cordate-orbicular to broadly triangular-ovate in outline, 2–4 in. across, 3–5-lobed with broad or rounded sinuses and pointed-toothed: fls. yellowish and usually with darker center, the staminate 1–1¼ in. across and on slender peduncles, the pistillate smaller and usually on shorter stalks; bract shield-like, serrate, well toward the top of the staminate peduncle: fr. ovoid or ellipsoid, 1½–3 in. long, narrowed to both ends, with points or prominences (sometimes nearly smooth), orange; seeds elliptic, about ½in. long, thick but flat, gray or brown, somewhat scalloped on edges and pattern-veined. (Balsamina: herbalist name adopted by Linnæus.) Old World tropics.

2. **M. Charantia,** L. Balsam-Pear. Mostly a longer vine than no. 1, ann., with larger more deeply lobed lvs., the margins sinuate and with apiculate points: bracts entire, at the base or not above the middle of the peduncle: fr. oblong or oval and narrowed both ways, 4–8 in. long, orange-yellow, covered with blunt warts, bursting at maturity and showing the scarlet arils; seeds about ½in. long, cornered at the ends, thick but flat, light gray or brown, with prominent patterns. (Charantia: herbalist name, used by Dodonæus.) Old World tropics.—An ingredient of curries with some peoples, and used medicinally.

12. **ABOBRA,** Naud. A single species in extra-trop. S. Amer., sometimes grown under glass for its ornamental frs. and finely cut foliage.—Diœcious, with small green axillary solitary fragrant fls. and mostly forked tendrils: corolla rotate, 5-parted, woolly within; anthers free; ovary 3–4-celled, with 2 erect ovules in each cell: fr. ovoid and berry-like. (Abo-bra: Brazilian name.)

A. tenuifolia, Cogn. (*A. viridiflora,* Naud.). Per. with fleshy root and herbaceous sts., 10–30 ft.: lvs. broad-ovate in outline, 2–5 in. long and about as broad, cut into linear divisions, more or less white-punctate: fr. smooth, about ⅓–½in. long, becoming carmine, glabrous.

13. **CYCLANTHERA,** Schrad. Thirty and more species in warm and trop. Amer., ann. and per.; one sometimes grown as an arbor or veranda vine.—Monœcious ann. and per. herbs with simple or branched tendrils, mostly glabrous: lvs. usually lobed or palmate: fls. small, white or greenish, the pistillate solitary and staminate racemose or paniculate; corolla rotate, 5-parted; ovary commonly 3-celled, with 2 or more ovules in each cell; style short, stigma large and circular: fr. ovoid and oblique, usually spiny, beaked, elastically dehiscent. (Cyclanthe-ra: Greek *circle anther.*)

C. pedata, Schrad. Ann. strong-smelling vigorous glabrous vine with branched tendrils: lvs. pedately parted to the base, with 5–7 lance-oblong dentate parts or lfts. and the lateral ones again lobed or parted: fls. small and inconspicuous: fr. elliptic-oblong, about 2 in. long, soft-prickly, yellowish-white, short-stalked; seeds ¼–⅓in. long, flat, cornered, blackish. Mex., Cent. Amer.—Quickly covers fences and screens.

14. **ECHINOCYSTIS,** Torr. & Gray (*Micrampelis,* Raf.). About 25 ann. and per. species in N. and S. Amer., one offered by seedsmen as a screen and veranda vine.—Monœcious, with branched tendrils and lobed or angled lvs.: fls. white or whitish, mostly small but often profuse, the staminate racemose or paniculate and the pistillate usually solitary; corolla rotate, deeply 6-parted or of 6 petals; filaments connate, anthers variously coherent; ovary mostly 2-celled or 1-celled with 2 placentæ, ovules erect and 2 in each cell: fr. fleshy or dry, sometimes bladdery, not large, opening at the top. (Echinocys-tis: Greek *hedgehog* and *bladder.*)

E. lobata, Torr. & Gray. Wild-Cucumber. Ann.; sts. slender, angled, glabrous or hairy at nodes, reaching 20 ft. or more: lvs. cordate-ovate, 3–5 in. long, 3–7-lobed less than to middle, lobes apiculate, margins entire or sparsely serrate: staminate fls. numerous in long compound axillary racemes: fr. short-oblong, 1½–2 in. long, puffy, with slender weak spines; seeds ½–⅝in. long, brownish, nearly plain. Thickets N. B. to Man. and Tex.

15. **BRYONIA,** L. Bryony. Per. herbs, 10–12 species, mostly in Eu., one sometimes sold by seedsmen as a cover vine.—Mostly diœcious, with simple or forked tendrils, and angled or lobed lvs.: fls. rather small, the staminate in peduncled racemes or cymes, the pistillate solitary or in short axillary clusters; corolla rotate or open-bell-shaped, 5-parted; anthers free; ovary with 3 placentæ, the 3-parted style slender, stigmas simple or 2-lobed; ovules horizontal: fr. a spherical berry. (Bryo-nia: Greek *to sprout,* referring to the shoots that come annually from the tuber.)

B. dioica, L. Strong-climbing from tuberous roots, with simple tendrils: lvs. scabrous, cordate-ovate or broader, 3–5 in. across, 3–5-lobed, lobes sharp-pointed or apiculate, margins sinuate or obscurely toothed: corolla greenish, ¾in. or less across: fr. ¼–⅓in. diam., red, with few small plump brownish seeds. Eu. and W. Asia.

16. **MELOTHRIA,** L. If defined broadly, probably 70 species, native in the warmer parts of both hemispheres; annuals and perennials; seed of one is offered as an ornamental vine.—Monœcious, at least in ours which also has simple tendrils: lvs. entire or lobed: fls. small, the staminate racemose or corymbose, pistillate solitary or clustered; corolla rotate or short-bell-shaped, deeply 5-parted; filaments free, anthers free or barely coherent; ovary contracted beneath the corolla, with 3 placentæ, and many horizontal ovules; style short, stigmas mostly 3: fr. small and berry-like, glabrous or warty. (Melo-thria: old name, not satisfactorily explained.)

M. scabra, Naud. Slender climber, with lightly hairy angled or grooved sts.: lvs. triangular-ovate, 2–4 in. long, shallowly 3–5-lobed, rather deeply cordate, margins remotely apiculate, scabrous above, light-hairy on veins beneath: fls. very small, slender-peduncled, the staminate 3–7: fr. ovoid to short-oblong, ¾–1 in. long, glabrous, more or less green-spotted; seeds dull white, very small and smooth. Mex.

17. **ECBALLIUM,** A. Rich. Squirting-Cucumber. One trailing per. in the Medit. region, without tendrils, grown for its odd frs.—Monœcious: fls. yellow, pedunculate, pistillate solitary and often in the same axil with the staminate raceme; corolla rotate or open-bell-shaped, deeply 5-parted with acute lobes; anthers free; ovary long, with 3 placentæ and many ovules, the style very short and bearing 3 bifurcate stigmas. (Ecbal-lium: Greek *to eject*, from the fr.)

E. Elaterium, A. Rich. (*Momordica Elaterium*, L.). Hairy-pubescent: lvs. triangular-ovate, 3–4 in. long, broadly cordate, angled or somewhat obscurely lobed, margins sinuate, gray-tomentose beneath: fls. 1 in. across: fr. oblong, 1½–2 in. long, rough-hairy, greenish, at maturity detaching from the peduncle and squirting the brownish seeds from the point of attachment. (Elaterium: old substantive, associated with Greek *to drive.*)

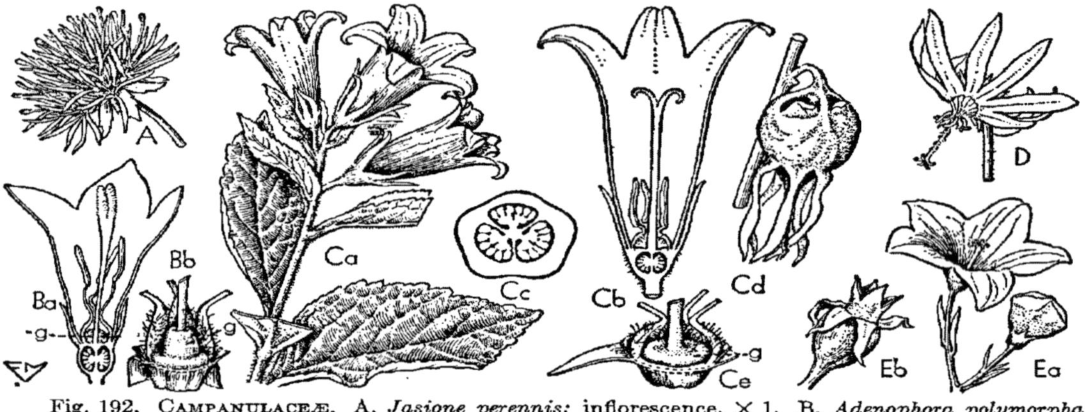

Fig. 192. Campanulaceæ. A, *Jasione perennis:* inflorescence, × 1. B, *Adenophora polymorpha:* Ba, flower, vertical section, × ½; Bb, detail of gland above ovary, × 2. C, *Campanula latifolia:* Ca, flowering branch, × ½; Cb, flower, vertical section, × 1; Cc, ovary, cross-section, × 3; Cd, capsule, × about 1; Ce, detail of gland above ovary. D, *Michauxia campanuloides;* flower, × ½. E, *Platycodon grandiflorum:* Ea, flower and bud, × ½; Eb, capsule, × ½. (g gland.)

192. CAMPANULACEÆ. BELLFLOWER FAMILY

Herbs as usually known to cultivators, but sometimes shrubs and even trees, about 1,000 species in some 40 genera, of wide distribution in trop. and temp. regions; the family yields many choice ornamentals.—Cult. species erect but others climbing, mostly with milky juice: lvs. usually alternate, exstipulate, simple and only rarely much lobed or divided: fls. bisexual and regular or nearly so, solitary, spicate, racemose or paniculate, prevailingly blue but sometimes white, the gamopetalous corolla 5-lobed or -divided; calyx-tube adnate to ovary, the limb 5-lobed, usually persistent on the fr.; stamens 5, inserted on calyx-rim or slightly on corolla base, the filaments separate or united, sometimes dilated at base; ovary inferior in the genera here included, mostly 2–5-celled and with axile placentæ, or 1-celled with 2 parietal placentæ, the ovules many; style 1, stigmas sometimes several: fr. in ours a dehiscent caps.—The bellflowers add an interesting note to gardens because so many of them provide fls. in the blue series, although prevailingly the greater number of these colors are lilac or shades of purple.

a. Lvs. alternate on st., or in some cases clustered at base of plant.
  b. Fls. separate from each other rather than aggregate in dense involucrate or bracted terminal heads.
    c. Corolla open-bell-shaped.
      d. Caps. or seed-pod opening at maturity on its sides or base by slits or pores, its apex closed.
        e. Ovary hemispheric or top-shaped or conical.
          f. Anthers distinct or separate from each other.
            g. Style not surrounded by a cup-like disk.................... 1. Campanula

GG. Style surrounded by or immersed in a deep cup-like disk or gland. 2. ADENOPHORA
FF. Anthers connate into a tube .... 3. SYMPHYANDRA
EE. Ovary linear or narrowly oblong .... 4. SPECULARIA
DD. Caps. opening at apex, by valves between the calyx-lobes.
E. Plant weak, vine-like or decumbent, mostly soon lying on the ground.. 5. CODONOPSIS
EE. Plant erect or arching, even if sometimes small and low.
F. Stature of plant tall; leafy, bearing very large open-bell-shaped fls. blue to white, mostly solitary .... 6. PLATYCODON
FF. Stature low, often tufted and lvs. clustered at base: fls. small.
G. Apex of caps. opening regularly by compartments .... 7. WAHLENBERGIA
GG. Apex of caps. opening irregularly .... 8. EDRAIANTHUS
CC. Corolla divided nearly to base, lobes reflexed .... 9. MICHAUXIA
BB. Fls. in compact terminal involucrate or bracted heads or short spikes or close corymbiform clusters, mostly not bell-shaped.
C. Form of corolla bell-shaped, even if narrowly so .... 8. EDRAIANTHUS
CC. Form of corolla not bell-shaped, very narrow, often closed at apex.
D. Caps. closed at apex.
E. Corolla narrow-tubular, 5-fid, not prolonged at apex .... 10. TRACHELIUM
EE. Corolla long-tubular at apex, not parted, curved, split at base .... 11. PHYTEUMA
DD. Caps. opening at apex: corolla narrow, 5-fid to base .... 12. JASIONE
AA. Lvs. long, whorled on st.: large plant with white or tinted fls.: caps. opening by many long valves on side .... 13. OSTROWSKIA

1. **CAMPANULA,** L. BELLFLOWER. Sometimes ann. and bien., but mostly per. herbs, of some 250 species largely in the northern hemisphere, chiefly in Eu.; many are choice garden plants.—Often tufted: root-lvs. frequently unlike the st.-lvs., the latter sometimes few: genus specially known by the pod ovoid or turbinate and dehiscing below the persistent calyx-rim by pores or separate valves, the clavate style not surrounded by a fleshy disk, corolla bell-shaped to rotate and 5-toothed or -lobed and not split at base or otherwise, fls. solitary, spicate, racemose, paniculate, not in compact composite-like heads; stamens usually dilated at base; stigmas 3 in ours except *C. Medium,* and caps. 3-celled: caps. opening near the base in some species, near the top in others. (Campan-ula: Latin *little bell.*)—Species greatly confused in cult. and many of the garden names are unreliable. Such persistent and variable species as *C. rapunculoides, C. rotundifolia, C. carpatica, C. persicifolia* are likely to be grown under different names, and so explained in the following text. Canterbury bells, *C. Medium,* is an old easily grown garden favorite.

A. Species fl.-garden annuals, grown from seeds each year.
B. Plant erect to 2 ft.: style large and long-protruded .... 1. *C. macrostyla*
BB. Plant small, diffuse and weak, more or less decumbent: style not prolonged.
C. Corolla bell-shaped .... 2. *C. drabifolia*
CC. Corolla wide open, nearly or quite rotate .... 3. *C. ramosissima*
AA. Species per. (bien. in no. 21), being border and plantation subjects.
B. Plant very low, tufted: small rock-garden and alpine subjects. (Dwarf hort. forms of *C. carpatica,* no. 28, with cordate-ovate dentate lvs., not to be sought here.)
C. Lvs. on st. and usually also at base long and narrow, often sharp-pointed, sometimes nearly grass-like, not bearing a distinct petiole.
D. Fls. in nature single or solitary on each leafy st. or shoot (sometimes more than 1 on developed hort. subjects).
E. Corolla large and tubular .... 4. *C. Allionii*
EE. Corolla small and bell-shaped .... 5. *C. excisa*
DD. Fls. in nature prevailingly few or several on each leafy st., although an occasional shoot or plant may be 1-fld.
E. Narrow lvs. condensed at base of plant, few if any on st. .... 6. *C. cæspitosa*
EE. Narrow lvs. scattered on st. .... 7. *C. Scheuchzeri*
CC. Lvs. on st. and at base of plant expanded or broad, often dentate or notched.
D. Fls. single or solitary on each leafy st.
E. Calyx-lobes with prominent auricles at base .... 8. *C. Saxifraga*
EE. Calyx-lobes lacking auricles at base.
F. Lobes of calyx sharply notched, very long and spreading .... 9. *C. lasiocarpa*
FF. Lobes of calyx not notched.
G. Blossom closely subtended by foliage .... 10. *C. Raineri*
GG. Blossom long-pedicelled .... 11. *C. pulla*
DD. Fls. prevailingly more than 1 on each leafy st., only exceptionally with a single blossom.
E. Sts. simple (not branched), from base of plant.
F. Calyx-lobes very slender, ¾in. or less long, about equalling corolla .... 12. *C. Piperi*
FF. Calyx-lobes much shorter than corolla.
G. These lobes with linear short point: st.-lvs. very narrow and finely dentate .... 13. *C. cochlearifolia*
GG. These lobes flat and not much narrowed to end: st.-lvs. broadened and closely obtusely serrate .... 14. *C. collina*

EE. Sts. usually prominently branched; plant weak and diffuse, often droopy or vine-like; sometimes grown in pots.
F. Corolla very large and open, mostly 1 in. or more across at full expansion.
G. Main cauline lvs. rounded in apical outline: corolla-lobes obtuse or only very broadly tapered to apex.
H. These lvs. mostly less than 1 in. broad, reniform: calyx-lobes short, usually less than corolla-tube ....15. *C. fragilis*
HH. These lvs. mostly more than 1 in. broad, reniform-ovate: calyx-lobes equalling or exceeding corolla-tube..........16. *C. isophylla*
GG. Main cauline lvs. triangularly narrowed to evident point or apex: corolla-lobes long-narrowed and conspicuously acute ..17. *C. Poscharskyana*
FF. Corolla small, ¾in. or less across, or else tubular and not open.
G. Main cauline lvs. ovate or broader, toothed....................18. *C. Elatines*
GG. Main cauline lvs. lanceolate, nearly or quite entire.
H. Shape of corolla tubular, very shortly lobed: lower lvs. acute..19. *C. Tommasiniana*
HH. Shape of corolla nearly rotate at expansion, cut about half way down: lower lvs. broad and obtuse................20. *C. Waldsteiniana*
BB. Plant tall (unless in dwarf hort. forms), commonly much-branched, often coarse: not rock-garden subjects.
C. Duration bien., blooming and podding second year from seed and plant then dying: corolla large, in many colors, tubular: old garden favorite, tall and erect..21. *C. Medium*
CC. Duration per.; long-enduring plants of hardy borders, tall and either erect or diffuse, mostly freely branching.
D. Position of fls., or of most of them, erect or strongly ascending on the plant even though the plant itself may be diffuse or drooping.
E. St.-lvs. linear or at most lance-linear.
F. Lobes of calyx filiform.
G. These lobes much shorter than corolla....................22. *C. abietina*
GG. These lobes equalling or exceeding corolla..................23. *C. Rapunculus*
FF. Lobes of calyx ⅛in. or more broad, flat.......................24. *C. persicifolia*
EE. St.-lvs. ovate or on that order (narrower in no. 26).
F. Lobes of corolla bearded inside...........................25. *C. Trachelium*
FF. Lobes of corolla not bearded.
G. Shape of corolla broadly or openly bell-form to almost saucer-form.
H. Cauline lvs. sessile or essentially so.........................26. *C. latiloba*
HH. Cauline lvs. long-petioled.
I. Fls. in elongated racemes..........................27. *C. pyramidalis*
II. Fls. terminating long peduncles.....................28. *C. carpatica*
GG. Shape of corolla narrowly bell-form to tubular.
H. Bloom in dense globular terminal and axillary subtended heads...29. *C. glomerata*
HH. Bloom racemose or long-spicate.
I. Lower lvs. cordate or subcordate: fls. large, 1¼ in. or more long, normally rich blue.......................30. *C. latifolia*
II. Lower lvs. not cordate or subcordate: fls. 1 in. long, normally white or pale blue.........................31. *C. lactiflora*
DD. Position of fls. habitually nodding, deflexed or declined.
E. Calyx with prominent appendage at base of each sinus.
F. St. and under surface of lvs. tomentose or soft-pubescent: fls. white...32. *C. alliariæfolia*
FF. St. and lvs. glabrous or only hairy or lightly pubescent or roughish: fls. violet or blue.
G. Basal lvs. broadly cordate-ovate to reniform.
H. Fls. sessile or practically so, in axils....................33. *C. Grossekii*
HH. Fls. distinctly pedicelled.
I. Corolla 1½–2 in. long: coarse plant..................34. *C. punctata*
II. Corolla 1 in. or less long: small slender plant...........35. *C. Raddeana*
GG. Basal lvs. narrow, lance-oval or much longer than broad.
H. Style long-projected at full anthesis.....................36. *C. longestyla*
HH. Style not projected.......................................37. *C. sarmatica*
EE. Calyx lacking appendages in sinuses or at base.
F. Foliage fleshy and viscid.....................................38. *C. Vidalii*
FF. Foliage not fleshy or viscid.
G. Fl.-sts. mostly devoid of developed lvs., bearing bracts, lvs. basal...39. *C. barbata*
GG. Fl.-sts. leafy.
H. St.-lvs. of the ovate pattern.
I. Fls. secund, in a long one-sided raceme................40. *C. rapunculoides*
II. Fls. not secund...41. *C. rhomboidalis*
HH. St.-lvs. linear or grass-like: calyx-lobes linear and short.....42. *C. rotundifolia*

1. **C. macrostyla,** Boiss. & Heldr. Hispid branching ann., 1–2 ft.: lvs. ovate-oblong, 1–2 in. long, the upper ones ovate-lanceolate, all sessile and more or less clasping, margins entire or remotely denticulate: fls. solitary and erect on stout peduncles, 2–2½ in. across, the corolla broad and open, dull purple and violet-marked within, pale purple without; calyx strongly appendaged, the lobes long-pointed and nearly or quite equalling the corolla; stigmas long-protruded, about 1 in. long. Taurus Mts., Asia Minor.

2. **C. drabifolia,** Sibth. & Smith (*C. attica,* Boiss.). Ann., somewhat erect, much-branched, 3–6 in. high, hispid: lvs. hairy, elliptic-oblong and dentate toward apex, somewhat lobed, most of them less than ½in. long, lower ones tapering to base: fls. pedicellate; corolla open-bell-shaped, ½in. or less long, with a white glabrous tube and blue pilose limb; calyx-lobes narrow, erect. Greece, Asia Minor.

3. **C. ramosissima,** Sibth. & Smith (*C. Loreyi,* Poll.). Ann., erect, 6–12 in., glabrous or somewhat hairy, branched above: lower lvs. obovate to ovate-lanceolate, crenate, nearly glabrous, obtuse; upper lvs. ¾–2 in. long, lanceolate or narrower, acute: fls. solitary on long erect peduncles, violet with lighter base (a white var.), 1 in. or more across; calyx hairy at base, the lobes narrow and long-acuminate and about equalling or even exceeding the nearly rotate or saucer-shaped corolla. S. E. Eu.

4. **C. Allionii,** Vill. Compact tufted hirsute-pubescent per. 2 or 3 in. high in nature: lvs. narrow-oblong to nearly linear, 2 in. or less long, entire: fls. usually single on each leafy st., about 1¾ in. long, hanging or declined, tubular with flaring pointed lobes, bright violet-blue varying to white; corolla much exceeding the pointed calyx-lobes; calyx with lobes in sinuses: caps. opening by 3 basal pores. (For C. Allioni, page 38.) Alps of Italy and S. France.

5. **C. excisa,** Schleich. Very slender per., glabrous, erect, 3–6 in. high in tufts: lvs. linear, spreading: fls. upright but becoming deflexed, bell-shaped, about ¾in. long, blue, without reflexed lobes in sinuses; calyx-lobes short, spreading: caps. declined, opening with 3 basal pores. Alps of S. Eu.

6. **C. cæspitosa,** Scop. Low densely tufted per., erect but very slender, glabrous, 3–6 in. high: lvs. small, linear, mostly crowded near base, tapering to petiole: fls. few, spreading to nodding, about ¾in. long, blue, said to vary to white; corolla-lobes very short; calyx-lobes very narrow and short: caps. with 3 pores at base. Mts., S. Eu.—*C. Bellardii* is a species of doubtful validity, but the plant in cult. under that name is usually *C. cæspitosa: C. Bellardii-Miranda* of gardens is a dwarf form of *C. carpatica.* See *C. cochlearifolia,* no. 13.

7. **C. Scheuchzeri,** Vill. Erect slender per. about 1 ft. or less, glabrous or essentially so, little if at all branched, sts. leafy: lvs. linear or the basal ones to ¼in. broad, narrowed to long point: fls. mostly 1 but sometimes 2–4, blue, 1 in. or less long, mostly erect at first, bell-shaped; calyx-lobes filiform, almost or quite equalling the corolla: caps. with 3 basal pores. (Bears the name of Johann Jakab Scheuchzer, 1672–1733, Swiss botanist.) Mts., Cent. Eu.—Stock grown in N. Amer. under this name is likely to be *C. rotundifolia,* which is told by its taller diffuse much-branched stature, cordate radical lvs., shorter calyx-lobes.

8. **C. Saxifraga,** Bieb. Little glabrous per. 3–6 in. high, sts. simple, leafy, bearing a solitary violet-purple erect fl.: lvs. mostly broadened toward end to ¼in. wide with long petiole-like base, margins somewhat dentate: fls. ¾–1 in. long, bell-shaped, lobes short; calyx-lobes about one-fourth length of corolla, not pointed, with reflexed appendages: caps. with 3 basal pores, nodding. Mts., Caucasus.

9. **C. lasiocarpa,** Cham. Very low per. 1–6 in. high, glabrous, short sts. leafy, erect, simple: lvs. all notched on margins, upper ones almost linear, lower ones distinctly broadened: fls. 1 in. and more long and broad, blue, fragrant, open-bell-shaped, lobed to nearly middle; calyx-lobes prominent and spreading, about one-half length of corolla, notched: caps. opening near top, somewhat hairy. W. Canada, Wash., Alaska, Siberia, Japan.—In cult. becoming taller, somewhat branched and 3–4-fld.

10. **C. Raineri,** Perp. Tufted little lightly pubescent per. 2–4 in. high: lvs. crowded on the short st., oblong-spatulate, blunt, tapered to petiole, 1 in. long, ½in. broad, bluntly toothed: fls. very large, usually solitary, sessile in the foliage, broadly bell-shaped, lilac, about 1 in. long, lobes shallow and blunt; calyx-lobes long and prominent, acute, not equalling corolla, appendages none: caps. with 3 pores. (Dedicated to Archduke Rainer von Österreich, 1783–1864.) Alps of N. Italy, Switzerland.—The name is confused in cult., often employed for dwarf forms of *C. carpatica;* sometimes the stock is *C. Raddeana* and dwarf races of *C. rotundifolia.* The plant called *C. pseudo-Raineri* is a small *C. carpatica.*

11. **C. pulla,** L. Low glabrous per. making many slender erect sts. 2–6 in. high, bearing a solitary dark purple nodding fl. on a slender pedicel: upper lvs. nearly linear, others oblong to oval and briefly acute and narrowed to short petiole, margins obscurely indented: fls. bell-shaped, about 1 in. long, shallowly lobed; calyx-lobes short and very narrow: caps. opening by lateral pores. Alps in Austro-Hungarian region.—*C. pulloides,* a name for a garden variant, is suggestive of *C. carpatica.*

12. **C. Piperi,** Howell. Tufted glabrous per. 1–4 in. high, with leafy sts.: lvs. cuneate to spatulate, ½in. or more long, narrowed to petiole, sharply serrate: fls. several (seldom only 1), blue, open-bell-shaped, about ¾in. long; calyx-lobes very narrow, about equalling corolla: caps. nearly globular. (For C. V. Piper, page 49.) Olympic Mts., Wash.

13. **C. cochlearifolia,** Lam. Small floriferous nearly or quite glabrous per. 2–8 in. high, not compactly tufted: st.-lvs. narrow, nearly lanceolate, becoming broader toward the ground and somewhat notched; basal lvs. broad, cordate or truncate at base, blade distinct from petiole and not tapered into it: fls. few, sometimes solitary in the wild, blue-violet

(to white in var. **alba**), spreading or nodding, ¾in. or less long; corolla bell-shaped, shallowly lobed; calyx-lobes narrow, short and spreading: caps. opening at apex. Mts. of Eu.—Good garden subject; often called *C. cæspitosa* but that is a more compact plant with narrow basal lvs. tapering into the petiole; sometimes grown as *C. pusilla* which is apparently a synonym; some of the stock is dwarf races of *C. carpatica* and sometimes *C. rotundifolia*.

14. **C. collina,** Bieb. Somewhat pubescent clump-forming per. with simple sts. 1 ft. or less high, blooming most freely when two or three years old: lvs. few and very small on st. but many of them at base, thick, blades 1–2 in. long, oblong or narrower, blunt or short-pointed, margins crenate, petiole distinct: fls. few, divaricate or nodding at top of st., deep purple, about 1 in. long, bell-shaped with large recurving lobes; calyx-lobes short and broad: caps. opening at base. Caucasus.

15. **C. fragilis,** Cyr. Graceful glossy-lvd. diffuse or vine-like per., making lopping branches 12–16 in. long: lvs. cauline and basal, ovate to broad-ovate, often 1 in. across, cordate or truncate at base, notched: fls. axillary mostly toward end of branches, blue with light center, bell-shaped but opening widely; corolla lobes usually less than half way down, about 1 in. long before expansion; calyx-lobes very short, flaring; style prominent. S. Italy.

16. **C. isophylla,** Moretti. Per. with glabrous or somewhat hairy but green diffuse sts. a few in. high, the many weak long flowering branches drooping: lvs. shortly cordate-ovate, 1½ in. long and broad, long-petioled below, point very short, margins dentate, the upper ones becoming narrower and smaller: fls. solitary on bracted branchlets, profusely borne toward the end of the sts., pale blue (but a white var.), 1 in. or more across; calyx-lobes lanceolate and prominent, wide-spreading or reflexed, equalling or exceeding corolla-tube; corolla saucer-shaped, the lobes broad, style long-exserted. Italy.—A floriferous and attractive plant; sometimes grown in pots and greenhouses.

17. **C. Poscharskyana,** Degen. Diffuse or lopping very leafy and floriferous nearly glabrous per. with many sts. and branches: lvs. long-petioled, cauline ones ovate-pointed, basal ones cordate-ovate and 1½ in. across, margins mostly bluntly toothed to almost crenate: fls. scattered on ends of st., bright blue-lilac, broad-bell-shaped, very deeply lobed, becoming almost rotate and ½ to almost 1 in. across; calyx spreading, the acute lobes equalling or exceeding tube of corolla. (Bears the name of G. A. Poscharsky, horticulturist and botanist in the Balkan region.) Dalmatia.

18. **C. Elatines,** L. ADRIA BELLFLOWERS in cult. Somewhat tufted much-branched floriferous per., ascending or decumbent, sts. 3–8 in. long, glabrous to pubescent: lvs. ovate or the basal ones cordate-ovate and long-petioled, large blades nearly or about 1 in. broad, margins sharply toothed: fls. many, small, ¾in. or less across, solitary or 2–3 together in axils, making an indefinite raceme-like infl., style conspicuously exserted; corolla blue-violet to nearly azure, bell-shaped, wide open at maturity, the long lobes narrow and acute; calyx about equalling or exceeding corolla, lobes very narrow: caps. opening midway on side or near base. Italy and the Balkan region.—Geographically variable, cult. under many names; Elatines is an old Greek-Latin name for a kind or group of plants, now appearing in different forms in botanical nomenclature. For the group as a whole in cult. there is the recent useful name *C. Adria*, van Melle, on the assumption that hybridity occurs among the races when grown in gardens. To the Elatines group belong the names *C. Portenschlagiana*, Roem. & Schult., *C. muralis*, Portens., and the following: Var. **Barbeyi,** Fiori (*C. Barbeyi*, Feer), very green plant, glabrous, fls. violet-blue, lobed nearly to bottom, calyx-lobes one-half or more length of corolla, named for its cultivator William Barbey; var. **elatinoides,** Fiori (*C. elatinoides*, Moretti), white-tomentose plant of compact growth and thickish lvs.; var. **fenestrellata,** Bailey (*C. fenestrellata*, Feer), glabrous and glossy plant, fls. violet-blue, lobes very deep and recurving; var. **garganica,** Fiori (*C. garganica*, Ten.), gray-pubescent plant, light violet-blue fls. with long corolla-lobes, style not much exserted, calyx-lobes one-half or less as long as corolla; var. **istriaca,** Fiori (*C. istriaca*, Feer), tomentose plant, corolla lobed nearly to base, lobes widely spreading, style long-exserted. *C. Erinus* has been listed as an associate with *C. Elatines*, perhaps from confusion of names; true *C. Erinus*, L., is a little not showy ann. in the Medit. region, probably not in cult.

19. **C. Tommasiniana,** Reut. Floriferous glabrous very slender per. with only short side branchlets or none, 6–18 in. tall: lvs. many on sts., narrow-lanceolate, 2 in. or less long, all acute, margins not quite entire, radical lvs. none: fls. several or many toward end of sts. and slender-pedicelled, mostly nodding, pale blue; corolla tubular or subcylindric, ¾in. or less long, lobes very short, blunt and little spreading; calyx very short, lobes divaricate. (For M. Tomasini, page 266.) Istria, in N. Adriatic.

20. **C. Waldsteiniana,** Roem. & Schult. Small usually condensed plant 3–9 in. high: lvs. many, the main ones lanceolate-acute and about 1 in. or less long, lower lvs. broad and nearly or quite obtuse: fls. relatively few, on slender pedicels, lavender-blue, small, somewhat rotate or star-shaped at expansion and the lobing deep; calyx-lobes about one-half as long as corolla-tube. (F. A. Waldstein, page 53.) Croatia, Dalmatia.

21. **C. Medium,** L. CANTERBURY BELLS. Stout erect hispid-hairy bien., 1½–3 or 4 ft.:

root-lvs. oblanceolate or somewhat broader, long-tapering to base, 6–10 in. long, crenate; st.-lvs. lance-oblong, 3–5 in. long, sessile and more or less clasping, crenulate and undulate: fls. erect or ascending, 1 or 2 together on stout peduncles in a long open terminal raceme, violet-blue but now in many shades; calyx with broad-lanceolate lobes one-fourth or one-third length of corolla and bearing large reflexed broad-cordate appendages; corolla inflated bell-shaped or urn-shaped, the tube in cult. plants 1 in. diam., the lobes short and flaring or somewhat reflexed; stigmas 5: caps. normally 5-celled and opening at base. (Medium: *middle-size;* a Tournefortian substantive adopted by Linnæus in apposition.) S. Eu.—The most popular of the bellflowers and now represented in many cultivars, with fls. white, pink, and various shades, and also double. Var. **calycanthema,** Nichols. (i. e. *calyx-fld.*), has the calyx developed into an outer corolla-like organ, of the same color as corolla, the appendages disappearing; of this there are two forms, each in different colors, one with outer corolla flaring or rotate, the Cup-and-Saucer race, one with the outer corolla bell-shaped, nearly or quite as long as the regular corolla and duplicating it, the Hose-in-Hose or Duplex race.

22. **C. abietina,** Griseb. & Schenk. Upright diffuse glabrous per. with slender sts. to 2½ ft. high: st.-lvs. few and scattered, linear to lanceolate and acute, 1–2 in. long, nearly entire; basal or rosette lvs. narrow-elliptic with prominent petiole, nearly or quite obtuse, blade about 1 in. long and ½in. broad: fls. light blue, on end of long peduncles and therefor scattered, erect or ascending, long-bell-shaped with deep lobes, 1½ in. across at expansion; calyx-lobes filiform and flaring, not equalling corolla. Balkan region.—Stock grown under this name is likely to be *C. rotundifolia.*

23. **C. Rapunculus,** L. Rampion. Per., sometimes bien., slender, erect, glabrous, 2–3 ft., the many branches strongly ascending, making a thick tap-root the first year which is sometimes used in autumn and winter, together with lvs., as salad: radical lvs. many, 4–8 in. long, the blade oval or elliptic and tapering into long petiole, margins crenulate; main st.-lvs. linear-lanceolate, long-pointed, sessile, nearly or quite entire: fls. erect or ascending, lilac, about ½in. long, in long erect narrow racemes; calyx-lobes subulate, nearly as long as the open-bell-shaped acute-lobed corolla. (Rapunculus: herbalists' name, diminutive from *rapum,* turnip.) Eu.—Seldom grown as a garden vegetable; good roots are unbranched above, 2–3 in. long and ⅓in. thick at top.

24. **C. persicifolia,** L. Strong erect per., making many basal lvs., glabrous; sts. 2–3 ft., sometimes branching toward the top: radical lvs. narrowly oblanceolate, 4–8 in. long, long-tapering below, nearly or quite obtuse, crenulate, glabrous; st.-lvs. not numerous, linear-lanceolate to linear, 2–4 in. long, the lower more or less spatulate, sessile, mostly acuminate, finely crenulate: fls. erect, short-stalked and more or less remote, in an elongated terminal raceme, blue to blue-violet, 1–1½ in. long and often broader; calyx glabrous or hairy, the lobes linear-lanceolate, one-half or less the length of the broad open corolla which has broad mostly acute lobes: caps. opening on side or near top. (Persicifolia; *peach-lvd.,* not a very appropriate name.) Eu., Asia.—An old favorite, in several colors and forms, sometimes under Latin names; basal tufts of long lvs. conspicuous in autumn. Var. **alba,** Hort., fls. white. Var. **dasycarpa,** Hegi (*C. dasycarpa,* Kit.), caps. hairy or setigerous. Var. **minor,** G. Beck, small, fls. only 1 in. or less long. Var. **Moerheimei,** Bailey, fls. white and double, showy. This distinct and separate species has been grown under several other specific names, probably because its roots have persisted while the others have died out and the labels remained.

25. **C. Trachelium,** L. Variable erect per., 2–3 ft., more or less rough-hairy; sts. usually simple, hairs mostly retrorse: lvs. ovate-lanceolate, 2–3 in. long, the lower ones long-stalked, cordate to truncate, acuminate, margins coarsely serrate, hispid-hairy at least on the veins: fls. blue-purple but running to other shades and to white, about 1 in. long, more or less inclined or drooping when fully open, 1–3 on a peduncle combined in a terminal loose raceme or panicle; corolla broad-campanulate, the lobes acute and not much spreading and more or less bearded; calyx-tube usually hispid, the lobes ovate-lanceolate, much shorter than corolla. (Trachelium: Greek *the neck,* supposed to cure diseases of the trachea; an old generic name.) Eu., Asia, and escaped in N. Amer.—Double-fld. forms (*flore-pleno*) are known. It often appears in gardens erroneously under other specific names.

26. **C. latiloba,** A. DC. (*C. grandis,* Fisch. & Mey.). Per., 1½–4 ft., with glabrous terete but furrowed simple sts.: st.-lvs. lanceolate, 3–5 in. long and ½in. or less broad, narrowed both ways, crenate-serrate: fls. blue (a white var.), often 2 in. across, sessile, solitary or somewhat fascicled, erect, in a terminal panicle; calyx-lobes ovate-acute, less than half as long as the open-bell-shaped broad-lobed corolla; 3 styles very long. Caucasus, Asia Minor.

27. **C. pyramidalis,** L. Chimney Bellflower. Strict strong glabrous per., 4–5 ft. (there is a dwarf compact form), nearly or quite simple but with many short flowering branchlets; main st. thick, pithy or hollow: radical lvs. very long-petioled, cordate-ovate, about 2 in. long, glandular-dentate; lower st.-lvs. much like the radical, upper ones narrowly ovate-acute: fls. numerous in a long narrow racemose terminal panicle, erect, pale blue and varying to white, producing a rocket-like effect; calyx-lobes nearly or quite linear, much spreading, usually not equalling the corolla-tube; corolla open and saucer-shaped, the acute lobes reaching to middle or below. S. Eu.

28. **C. carpatica,** Jacq. TUSSOCK BELLFLOWER. Variable and well known glabrous and smooth per. forming a clump, with sts. more or less decumbent or spreading at base and rising 9–18 in.: basal and cauline lvs. similar but the lower ones longer-petioled, ovate, 1–1½ in. long, subcordate to truncate at base, short-pointed, crenate-dentate: fls. solitary and erect on long sts. or peduncles, bright blue (and a white var. and shades of blue to mauve), 1–nearly 2 in. across; calyx-lobes linear-acute, reflexed, short; corolla open-bell-shaped, broadly lobed to one-third or one-half the depth, the lobes acute. Carpathian region, E. Eu. Var. **turbinata,** Nichols. (*C. turbinata,* Schott), has fls. more deeply bell-shaped or top-shaped, and decumbent habit.—*C. carpatica* is one of the commonest garden bellflowers, long in cult. and variable. Old hort. names of color forms are vars. **alba, cærulea, cœlestina, pallida,** and there are vernacular names such as Blue Star, Isabel, Mauve Cup, Moonlight, White Star. Dwarf forms are vars. **compacta, nana;** some of these forms are grown erroneously as *C. Raineri* (no. 10) and as *C. pseudo-Raineri*, a name without botanical standing. *C. Stansfieldii* is a hort. name for a form of *C. carpatica,* said to be a hybrid with *C. Waldsteiniana.*

29. **C. glomerata,** L. Strict hairy or glabrous per. with erect side branches, 1–2 ft.: lvs. rather thick, scabrous and rugose and more or less hairy, the radical ones very long-petioled, narrowly cordate-ovate, 4–5 in. long, obtuse, crenate; st.-lvs. ovate to ovate-oblong, 3–4 in. long, mostly sessile and more or less clasping, obtuse or short-acute, irregularly crenate-serrate: fls. many in dense clusters in the axils and terminating main st. and side branches, blue but varying to white and sometimes double in the cultivars; calyx-lobes linear, erect, shorter than corolla-tube; corolla 1 in. or less long, rather narrow-bell-shaped, with acute flaring lobes about one-half its length. Eurasia, and somewhat escaped in N. Amer. Var. **acaulis,** Rehnelt (*nana*), little tufts 3–6 in. high, lvs. narrow, fls. blue-violet; of garden origin. Var. **dahurica,** Fisch. (*speciosa, superba*), stout, terminal clusters 3 in. or more across, lateral clusters small; fls. pink-violet to purple; probably of garden origin.

30. **C. latifolia,** L. Strong early-blooming, very leafy per., 3–4 ft., sts. nearly simple and usually with scattered hairs: lvs. oblong-ovate to lance-ovate, the lower ones long-petioled and subcordate and 5–6 in. long, upper ones shorter-petioled and becoming narrower, all acuminate, dentate, rugose and hairy: fls. erect or ascending in a rather short leafy terminal raceme, about 1¼–1⅜ in. long, purplish-blue (and a white var.); calyx-lobes broad-linear and acute, ascending, about ½in. long; corolla narrow-bell-shaped, the lobes about one-third its length: caps. opening at base. Eurasia. Var. **macrantha,** Sims, is a large-fld. form, the corolla 2–2¼ in. long; plant usually taller. Var. **eriocarpa,** Fisch. (*C. eriocarpa,* Bieb.), the BRANTWOOD BELLFLOWER, has caps. tomentose.

31. **C. lactiflora,** Bieb. (*C. celtidifolia,* Boiss.). Per., 2–4 ft. and more, the sts. with a few declined hairs and branching above: lvs. oval-oblong to ovate-lanceolate, st.-lvs. 2–3 in. long, sessile, short-acute, serrate: fls. in a terminal panicle 3–4 in. long, milk-white but varying to pale blue, about 1 in. long and somewhat broader; calyx-lobes ovate, veined, more or less hispid; corolla open-bell-shaped to nearly saucer-shaped: caps. opening at base. Caucasus region.

32. **C. alliariæfolia,** Willd. Gray-pubescent per. branching at top, 1½–3 ft. high: basal lvs. large, ovate-cordate to reniform, long-petioled, crenate; st.-lvs. ovate and smaller, becoming sessile: fls. white, nodding on short stalks in the upper axils; calyx-lobes ovate and leafy, appendaged; corolla rather broad-campanulate, ciliate on margins, with a projection at the bottom of each sinus. Caucasus, Asia Minor.

33. **C. Grossekii,** Heuff. Rough coarse erect per. to 2½ ft., with very broad radical lvs. and many hanging or divaricate violet fls. along the leafy st.: lvs. of st. ovate-lanceolate; radical lvs. reniform-ovate, 2–5 in. across, cordate, dentate: fls. 1 or more at a node and subtended by bracts or lvs., about 1 in. long, cut one-third way down, lobes acute; calyx short, bristly-hairy, with large appendages in sinuses: caps. opening at base. (Named for Rev. Caspar Grossek, student of the flora of Banat, S. Hungary.) Hungary.

34. **C. punctata,** Lam. (*C. nobilis,* Lindl.). Stout hairy erect per., 1–2 ft., with angled sts. and many slender erect branches: basal lvs. broadly cordate-ovate, 3–5 in. long and long-petioled, sinus narrow, margins crenate- or blunt-dentate; st.-lvs. ovate to lance-ovate, sessile near the top: fls. declined from the tops of branches or stout peduncles, about 2 in. long, white to light clear lilac and mostly spotted within; corolla long-bell-shaped, lobed to about one-third the depth, ciliate with long soft hairs; calyx with an ovate appendage reflexed from each sinus or the appendage wholly wanting in some forms or departures. Siberia, China, Japan.—Now frequent in cult., particularly in the lilac-blue unspotted form or derivative Marian Gehring.

35. **C. Raddeana,** Trautv. Graceful and attractive thinly pubescent erect per. to 16 in. or less: radical lvs. cordate-ovate, slenderly petiolate, blades 1 in. and less long, obtusely dentate; st.-lvs. much smaller, ovate to lanceolate: fls. more or less secund in disposition near top of plant, nodding, amethyst-blue, bell-shaped with flaring lobes and nearly 1 in. long, style long-exserted; calyx-lobes prominent and about half length of corolla, with reflexed long appendages. (G. Radde, page 50.) Caucasus.

36. **C. longestyla,** Fomin. More or less hairy branching per., 18–30 in.: basal **lvs.**

lance-oval and lobed, with long winged petiole; st.-lvs. oblong and sessile: fls. hanging, amethyst-violet; calyx-lobes lanceolate-pointed and divaricate, appendages reflexed on the peduncle; corolla nearly urn-shaped, constricted below the limb or in one form bell-shaped. Caucasus.

37. **C. sarmatica,** Ker. Gray soft-pubescent per. with erect simple sts. 1–2 ft. high, lower lvs. making a radical tuft: basal lvs. arrow-shaped and acute, 3–5 in. long, with broad basal sinus and dentate margins; st.-lvs. smaller and narrower, either acute or obtuse: fls. several, well separated in terminal raceme, declined or nodding, 1½ in. or less long, lilac; corolla narrow-bell-shaped, acutely lobed one-third the length; calyx tomentose, lobes above one-half length of corolla, with caducous appendages: caps. opening by basal pores. Caucasus (part of the ancient Sarmatia).

38. **C. Vidalii,** H. C. Wats. Odd clammy glabrous glossy-stemmed per., 1–2 ft., branching from base: lvs. oblong to oblong-spatulate, 3–4 in. long, fleshy and viscid, coarsely serrate: fls. nodding, 2 in. long, in a short terminal raceme, white with yellow at the very base; calyx-lobes thick, triangular; corolla tubular and constricted above the base. Azores, where it was discovered the middle of last century by Capt. Vidal, R. N.

39. **C. barbata,** L. Hairy erect small per. 4–18 in. high, with clump of long basal foliage and nodding lilac-blue fls.: st.-lvs. 1–3, oblong or narrower; bottom lvs. linear- to oblong-lanceolate or oblanceolate, 2–5 in. long, nearly or quite obtuse: fls. 1–6 near top of plant, about 1 in. long, short-stalked or sessile, bell-shaped, lobes one-third length of corolla which is bearded within, style not protruding; calyx-lobes broad and not elongated: caps. opening at base. Alps, S. Eu.

40. **C. rapunculoides,** L. Rover Bellflower. The commonest intro. campanula, making large patches by means of its slender rootstocks and thick tap-roots, persisting about houses and along roadsides, the colonies sometimes producing few fls., but seldom really cult.; sts. slender but erect, 2–3 ft. and more, glabrous or pubescent: root-lvs. long-petioled, cordate-ovate, 1–3 in. long; st.-lvs. lance-ovate, 3–4 in. long, short-petioled to sessile, long-acuminate, irregularly serrate: fls. blue, 1 in. long or a little more, nodding on short pedicels in a long one-sided terminal raceme; calyx-lobes turning back; lobes less than one-half depth of corolla, acute: caps. opening at base. Eu., Asia.—Becomes a weedy persistent spreading plant taking the place of other species and carrying their names with it.

41. **C. rhomboidalis,** L. Per. with erect slender angled glabrous or slightly hairy sts., 1–2 ft.: lvs. ovate and acute, 1–2 in. long, sessile or very short-petioled, dentate or serrate, with a few scattered hairs: fls. purplish-blue or lilac (a white var.), ¾–1 in. long, usually drooping, in a slender terminal raceme of 8–10; calyx strongly ribbed, with subulate lobes nearly or quite half as long as the bell-shaped rather shallow-lobed corolla: caps. opening by basal pores. Mts. of Eu.

42. **C. rotundifolia,** L. Bluebell. Harebell. Very slender variable per. 6–20 in. and more high, glabrous but with pubescent forms, often diffuse at base: root-lvs. broadly ovate to nearly orbicular, about 1 in. across, long-petioled, often disappearing by flowering time; st.-lvs. linear and grass-like, 2–3 in. long, or the lower ones lanceolate: fls. few to several (or even solitary), in an open terminal raceme with the lower filiform pedicels elongated, hanging, bright blue (a white var. known in cult.), ½–1 in. long; calyx-lobes awl-shaped, one-half as long more or less as the broad-bell-shaped rather shallow-lobed corolla: caps. opening at base, Eurasia, N. Amer. Var. **soldanellæflora,** Nichols, is semi-double with the corolla split to the base into many narrow shreds.—*C. rotundifolia* is a persistent species in cult. and it passes under many specific names that do not belong to it. Variation within the species apparently depends greatly on the habitat.

2. **ADENOPHORA,** Fisch. Ladybell. Upwards of 50 per. herbs with milky juice, in Eu. and Asia.—Differs from Campanula in the cup-like or cushion-like disk or gland surrounding the base of the style, the stamens free from the corolla and filaments dilated and usually ciliate toward base; stigmas and cells of caps. 3. (Adenoph-ora: Greek *gland-bearing.*)—The ladybells are much like the bellflowers or Campanulas in general appearance but more slender in growth, often much-branched, with declined or hanging corollas in shades of lilac-blue. They are largely inhabitants of cool northern regions, yet easy of cult. They have fleshy roots. Species and names in gardens are confused.

A. Calyx-lobes distinctly cut or lobed lengthwise . . . . 1. *A. Potaninii*
AA. Calyx-lobes not cut or denticulate.
B. Cauline lvs. very narrow and long, 3–4 in., margins entire or remotely denticulate . . . . 2. *A. coronopifolia*
BB. Cauline lvs. short and relatively broad, lanceolate to ovate, margins various.
C. Margins of cauline lvs. with small close mostly obtuse serratures . . . . 3. *A. confusa*
CC. Margins of cauline lvs. with large acute irregular teeth . . . . 4. *A. polymorpha*

1. **A. Potaninii,** Korsh. Root thickened; sts. many, perhaps oblique at base then upright to 2 ft. and more: st.-lvs. ovate-lanceolate to lanceolate, 1–2 in. long, nearly entire to few-toothed: infl. racemiform and simple; fls. 1–3 at a node on very short pedicels, spreading or nodding, blue or lilac, narrow-bell-shaped, about ¾in. long and somewhat broader at expansion and lobed one-third to base; calyx-lobes lanceolate, toothed or cut, about one-third to one-fourth as long as corolla. (Collected in 1885 by G. N. Potanin.) W. China.

2. **A. coronopifolia,** Fisch. Diffuse slender branching per. 2–3 ft. high, with ascending branches from a more or less horizontal st.: lvs. long and narrow, 3–4 in. long and ¼in. or less broad, mostly narrowed to short petiole, margins nearly entire to remotely small-toothed: fls. many in racemiform clusters on main st. and laterals, lilac-blue, declined or nodding, nearly or quite 1 in. long, bell-shaped, lobed about one-third way down; calyx-lobes about one-fourth length of corolla. Manchuria.

3. **A. confusa,** Nannf. (*A. Farreri,* Nannf.). Root fleshy; sts. simple or branched at top, 18 in. or less high: root-lvs. reniform and dentate; st.-lvs. narrow-ovate to oval, 1½ in. or less long and 1 in. broad, short-acute, margins closely serrate: fls. hanging, lilac-blue, in racemose formation, ¾in. or less long, broadly bell-shaped, lobed about one-third to base; calyx-lobes very narrow and short. China.

4. **A. polymorpha,** Ledeb. Root thick and fleshy; sts. stout, erect or arching, to 3 ft., branching: st.-lvs. lanceolate to broad-lanceolate, about 2 in. long and ½in. broad, acute, margins sharply coarsely dentate: fls. nodding in racemiform order on main st. and branches, lilac-blue, bell-shaped, very shallowly lobed; calyx-lobes very narrow, spreading, short. Russia, E. Asia.

3. **SYMPHYANDRA,** A. DC. Ring Bellflower. About 8 per. and bien. herbs from the E. Medit. region and 1 from Asia.—Differs from Campanula in having the anthers united in a tube around the style (whence Symphyan-dra, *anthers grown together*); stigmas and cells of caps. 3.

A. Cauline lvs. gradually narrowed into winged petiole . . . . 1. *S. Hofmannii*
AA. Cauline lvs. not tapered at base, petiole slender and not winged to base . . . . 2. *S. pendula*

1. **S. Hofmannii,** Pant. Sts. branched, 1–2 ft., hispid-hairy, per. said sometimes to be bien.: lvs. oblanceolate to obovate, 4–7 in. long on the lower part and tapering to long winged base, shorter and becoming sessile on the upper part, toothed, hairy: fls. in terminal leafy panicles, white, drooping, 1–1½ in. long and of similar breadth; calyx-lobes auricled at base, leafy, half or more length of corolla-tube; corolla open-bell-shaped, shallowly broad-lobed, somewhat hairy inside; stigmas 3, exserted. (Dedicated to Florence Hofmann.) Bosnia.

2. **S. pendula,** A. DC. Small per. usually of many sts., 1 ft. or less high: radical lvs. ovate to truncate-reniform, 1½ in. or less across, irregularly serrate-dentate; cauline lvs. mostly ovate, blade about 1 in. long, broad or not long-tapered at base, coarsely serrate: fls. large, white, bell-shaped, about 1 in. or more long, broadly lobed to nearly one-half its depth; calyx-lobes long and broad, one-half or more length of corolla. Caucasus.

4. **SPECULARIA,** Heister. About 10 or 12 ann. herbs in the northern hemisphere, one grown in fl.-gardens.—Differs from Campanula primarily in the elongated cylindric or prismatic ovary with calyx-lobes prominent at its apex as well as in the prevailingly rotate corolla; stigmas and cells of ovary 3. (Specula-ria: derived from Latin *speculum,* a mirror.)

S. Speculum, A. DC. (*Campanula Speculum,* L. *S. Speculum-Veneris,* Caruel). Venus Looking-Glass. Nearly or quite glabrous branching ann. 9–15 in. high: lvs. alternate, oblong to spatulate, 1½ in. or less long, narrowed below or upper ones sessile, mostly obtuse, crenulate: fls. 1–3 on peduncles in all the upper axils, bright violet-blue varying to white and double, the rotate corolla about ¾in. across; calyx-lobes narrow and prominent, reaching or surpassing the corolla-sinuses; often bracts at base of long ovary much like corolla-lobes. Cent. Eu. and Medit. region.

5. **CODONOPSIS,** Wall. Asian small herbs, often with strong smell; species 40–50.—Low perennials with milky juice and often tuberous roots, the cult. species vine-like in growth: fls. bell-shaped, in blue, purple, white, yellowish, commonly nodding; corolla 5-lobed, glandular disk lacking; stamens 5, free from corolla: fr. a caps., opening at top between the large calyx-lobes, with conspicuous beak. (Co-donop-sis: Greek *bell-like.*)

C. clematidea, Clarke (*C. ovata,* Hort. not Benth.). Sprawling decumbent thinly pubescent slender plant, upright when young, mature sts. to 2 ft. or more long becoming much-branched: lvs. alternate or subopposite, ¾in. or less long, ovate to lance-ovate, cordate to subcordate at base, apex blunt or nearly so: fls. borne singly from axils and apices, broad-bell-shaped, 1 in. long, light lilac and purple markings inside; calyx prominent with flaring broad lobes. Cent. W. Asia.

6. **PLATYCODON,** A. DC. One showy per. in E. Asia, common in cult.—Distinguished from Campanula by caps. opening at the top by means of valves rather than on the sides or at base by means of lids or other separate openings; stamens much dilated at base, the anthers not united; stigmas 5 and caps. 5-celled. (Platycodon: Greek *broad bell*, from the shape of the fls.)

P. grandiflorum, A. DC. (*Campanula grandiflora*, Jacq.). Balloon-Flower (from the inflated buds). Sts. erect, branched above, glabrous, 1½–2½ ft.: lvs. ovate to ovate-lanceolate, 1–3 in. long, short-petioled, usually acute, sharp-dentate, glabrous, glaucous-blue beneath: fls. mostly solitary terminating long branches or peduncles, 2–3 in. across, dark rich blue to pale blue or lilac to white; calyx-lobes narrow, ¼–⅝in. long; corolla open-bell-shaped or deep-saucer-shaped, with 5 or sometimes more broad acute lobes. Var. **Mariesii,** Nichols., is a dwarf form 12–18 in. high, compact, the fls. large; sent from Japan to England by Maries. Var. **japonicum,** Dreer, is a strong bushy tall form with about 10 lobes to corolla, giving a stellate effect.

7. **WAHLENBERGIA,** Schrad. Tufty Bells. Small plants of wide distribution about the earth but mostly of southern hemisphere.—Per. herbs (sometimes grown as annuals) with the general appearance of Campanula but pod or caps. opening by valves at apex between adhering calyx-lobes rather than by slits or pores on side or at base, ovary being partially or wholly inferior: lvs. varying from broad to linear, in cult. kinds more or less clustered at base: fls. bell-shaped to rotate, violet-blue to purplish, erect or nodding, usually borne singly and not in involucrate heads. (Wahlenber-gia: George Wahlenberg, 1780–1851, Swedish botanist.)

A. Corolla bell-shaped: fl.-st. simple and scape-like from a tuft of radical lvs., fls. solitary, lvs. on st. none....1. *W. albomarginata*
AA. Corolla rotate or nearly so: fl.-st. forking or branched, sometimes leafy.
B. St.-lvs. many and conspicuous, at least on lower half....2. *W. vincæflora*
BB. St.-lvs. none or only a few bracts....3. *W. annularis*

1. **W. albomarginata,** Hook. f. Lvs. in a basal tuft, lanceolate to spatulate, about 1 in. long, obscurely denticulate: scape 1–10 in. high, erect, very slender, leafless; fl. at top of scape, nearly or quite erect, ¾in. or more long and usually 1 in. or more across, white to violet-blue, bell-shaped; corolla-lobes broad, to nearly one-half the depth. New Zeal.—The plant sometimes cult. as *W. tasmanica* is probably *W. saxicola*, Hook. f., a lower subject with fls. ½in. or less across.

2. **W. vincæflora,** Decne. Slender, erect, 9–20 in. high, making an open or diffuse tuft, sts. branched at least toward base: lvs. oblong to spatulate, 1–2 in. long, basal and cauline, often undulate: fls. 1 or more to a st., erect or nodding, white to light blue, open to nearly rotate, about 1 in. across; corolla lobed one-half or more the way down. Australia, New Zeal.

3. **W. annularis,** A. DC. Branching, diffuse, 8–24 in. high: lvs. in basal tufts, linear-lanceolate or narrower, 1–2 in. long, more or less denticulate, represented on the st. if at all by linear bracts: fls. several to each st., deeply lobed and nearly rotate, about 1 in. across, opening white changing to light violet, spots on inside. S. Afr.

8. **EDRAIANTHUS,** A. DC. Grassy Bells. Group of tufted perennials of perhaps a dozen species; useful compact rock-garden plants.—Often included in Wahlenbergia but technically distinguished by the caps. that opens irregularly rather than by compartments and for the most part with grass-like tufted lvs., and fls. prevailingly in close involucrate heads or subtended by bracts; they also inhabit a different part of the world, all European chiefly Balkan, probably with a different line of evolution: fls. bell-shaped to trumpet-shaped, purplish or violet. (Edraian-thus: *sessile flowers.*)—Sometimes but not originally written Hedraianthus.

A. Bloom borne singly at end of short branches.
B. Fl. sessile in upper lvs....1. *E. Pumilio*
BB. Fl. stalked above bracts or involucre.
C. Lvs. hairy on upper face: lobes of corolla acute....2. *E. dinaricus*
CC. Lvs. glabrous on both faces: lobes of corolla nearly or quite blunt....3. *E. serpyllifolius*
AA. Bloom compacted into involucrate heads.
B. Calyx bearing a minute auricle or lobe in each sinus....4. *E. Kitaibelii*
BB. Calyx without auricles.
C. Lobes of calyx as broad as long....5. *E. dalmaticus*
CC. Lobes of calyx long and narrow....6. *E. tenuifolius*

1. **E. Pumilio,** A. DC. (*Wahlenbergia Pumilio,* A. DC.). Somewhat hairy-pubescent condensed low plant 2–4 in. high: lvs. close together, narrow-linear, 1½ in. or less long: fls. erect just above the foliage, amethyst-violet, narrow-bell-shaped, 1 in. long or less, flaring lobes acute; calyx-lobes one-third to one-half as long as corolla, acute, spreading. (Pumilio: Latin *a dwarf.*) Dalmatia, upper Adriatic region.

2. **E. dinaricus,** Wettst. Low open grower a few in. high: lvs. grass-like, both basal and cauline, 1–2 in. long, hirsute on upper face: fls. above the foliage, placed singly but subtended by calyx-like bracts, nearly 1 in. long, erect, violet-blue, lobes acute and not reflexed, twice or more length of broad hairy calyx-lobes. Dinaric Alps, Dalmatia.

3. **E. serpyllifolius,** A. DC. (*Wahlenbergia serpyllifolia,* G. Beck). Compact and mat-forming, spreading, very low: lvs. linear-spatulate, glabrous: fls. open-bell-shaped, large, violet, broad lobes more or less obtuse; calyx-lobes about one-fourth length of corolla. Dalmatia and adjacent regions.

4. **E. Kitaibelii,** A. DC. (*Wahlenbergia Kitaibelii,* A. DC.). Low, tufted, few in. high: lvs. fascicled, narrow-linear, nearly or completely glabrous: fls. blue-violet, in compact heads above the foliage, tubular-bell-shaped with broad short erect lobes; calyx-lobes pointed, with small auricle in each sinus. (P. Kitaibel, page 46.) Transylvania.

5. **E. dalmaticus,** A. DC. (*Wahlenbergia dalmatica,* A. DC.). Tufted, 4–6 in. high: lvs. linear-spatulate, more or less ciliate on margins: fls. violet-blue, tubular-bell-shaped, short broad lobes nearly or fully obtuse, 6–10 of them compacted in a terminal head subtended by long involucral lvs.; calyx-lobes short, broad and obtuse. Dalmatia and Croatia.

6. **E. tenuifolius,** A. DC. (*Wahlenbergia tenuifolia,* A. DC.). Compact and mat-forming, 4–6 in.: lvs. long-linear, glabrous: fls. violet-blue, large, 6–15 of them in dense head subtended by narrow lvs. exceeding it, lobes short and nearly obtuse; calyx-lobes slender, about equalling corolla-tube. Montenegro and adjacent regions east of the Adriatic Sea.

9. **MICHAUXIA,** L'Her. Few odd plants of W. Asia, ours per. but reputedly bien.—Erect, tall: lvs. narrow, scattered on st., toothed or lobed: fls. with 8–10-parted corolla, the narrow lobes recurved, borne singly on end of branches and on short laterals; calyx with 8–10 short flaring acute lobes; stamens 8–10, short, anthers linear and recurved; ovary inferior, 8–10-celled; styles united into long projecting tube bearing stigmas in a head-like end: caps. hemispheric, crowned with dead floral parts, opening near base. (Michau-xia: André Michaux, page 48.)

M. campanuloides, L'Her. Rough-hairy plant with stout straight side-branched sts. to 4 or 6 ft., and tap-root: lvs. lyrate, clasping, 5–8 in. long: fls. scattered but abundant on nearly leafless branches, white more or less tinged purplish on back, 2 in. or more long from tip of reflexed corolla-lobes to end of prominent exserted style.

10. **TRACHELIUM,** L. Throatwort. Per. erect often more or less woody herbs, of few species in Medit. region.—St.-lvs. alternate: fls. small, tubular, in terminal branched corymbiform clusters; corolla 5-lobed; stamens 5, free from tube: caps. subglobose and angled, opening near base. (Trache-lium: Greek name for *neck,* from supposed remedial value for throat diseases; see *Campanula Trachelium,* page 963.)

T. cæruleum, L. Leafy glabrous plant 3–4 ft. high, widely branching toward top: lvs. ovate to elliptic, to 3 in. long, petiolate, margins bluntly toothed: fls. many, deep blue, in clusters 2–4 in. across; corolla about ¼in. long, lobes obtuse; style conspicuously long-exserted. S. Eu.

11. **PHYTEUMA,** L. Horned Rampion. Per. mostly erect herbs, sometimes decumbent; several species in Eu. and temp. Asia.—Sts. usually simple: radical and cauline lvs. different: fls. (in ours) in close subtended terminal heads or spikes, shape obscure because of crowding; corolla blue, purplish or white, relatively small, 5-parted at bottom (like basal slits or pores) but tubular and commonly curved in upper part, each with a single long-exserted 2–3-lobed style: caps. inferior, closed at apex, opening on side between ribs. (Phyteu-ma: classical name of no special significance.)—In the following species the fls. are in compact globose heads or umbels rather than in elongated spikes.

A. Plant very low and decumbent: lvs. broad and deeply toothed............1. *P. comosum*
AA. Plant erect even though low: cauline lvs. narrow, entire or nearly so.
  B. Lvs. very narrow, grass-like, entire: plant very low....................2. *P. hemisphæricum*
  BB. Lvs. lanceolate or broader, usually more or less dentate: plant 1 ft. or more high.

C. Apex of lvs. produced into long narrow point........................3. *P. Scheuchzeri*
CC. Apex of lvs. not so produced.
D. Blade of cauline lvs. tapered to base..............................4. *P. orbiculare*
DD. Blade of lower cauline and radical lvs. truncate or cordate at base........5. *P. Vagneri*

1. **P. comosum,** L. Glabrous, decumbent, diffuse, 3–6 in. high: radical lvs. orbicular to reniform, notched; st.-lvs. ovate to elliptic, sometimes cordate, deeply notched, about 1 in. long, upper ones nearly lanceolate: fls. lilac to dark purple, in a close head or umbel among the foliage, slender style long-exserted. Alps.

2. **P. hemisphæricum,** L. Little condensed plant, 4–6 in., erect, with upright linear entire pointed lvs. nearly or quite as high as the st.: fls. blue varying to whitish, in dense globular or oval short-bracted heads. Alps.

3. **P. Scheuchzeri,** All. Loose-growing, to 1½ ft.: basal lf.-blades short and broad and sometimes cordate; st.-lvs. 2–4 in. long and with well-developed petiole, long-attenuate to slender point, mostly obscurely toothed: fls. violet-blue, in dense heads subtended by lf.-like bracts. (J. J. Scheuchzer, page 961.) Mts., S. E. Eu.

4. **P. orbiculare,** L. Tall stout glabrous plant to 2 ft. high: radical lf.-blades broad-oval to elliptic and ½in. broad, not very acute, margins obscurely and bluntly serrate; st.-lvs. 2–4 in. long with petiole, blade perhaps ¼in. broad, hardly acute: fls. purple, in dense global short-bracted heads. Alps.

5. **P. Vagneri,** Kerner. Upright: radical or lower lvs. long-petioled and cordate, toothed; st.-lvs. sessile and lanceolate to linear: fls. dark violet, in dense globose but elongating heads. (Named for its collector, L. Vagner.) Hungary.—Plants grown under this name may not be true.

12. **JASIONE,** L. Little or medium herbs, of several species in Cent. and S. Eu.—Bien. or ann., erect, diffuse or prostrate: lvs. simple, small, alternate, entire, with rosette at base: fls. in dense briefly involucrate terminal heads, blue varying to white; corolla and calyx cut into 5 very narrow lobes; anthers more or less united at base: caps. inferior, open by short valves at apex. (Jasio-ne: classical name with suggestion of healing qualities.)

A. Lvs. ½in. or less long: plant 9 in. or less high..................................1. *J. humilis*
AA. Lvs. more than 1 in. long and abundant: plant 1 ft. and more high..................2. *J. perennis*

1. **J. humilis,** Loisel. Per. 6–9 in. high, congested at base, sts. simple: lvs. crowded on lower parts, linear to somewhat oblong-linear, entire, about ½in. or less long: fls. blue, in small compact heads above the foliage on a peduncle. Pyrenees.

2. **J. perennis,** Lam. Per., often branching, 1–1½ ft. high: lvs. many scattered on st., broad-linear to oblong-linear on the sts., blunt or nearly so, often obscurely serrate: fls. blue, in long peduncled terminal and lateral heads: basal lvs. and offsets usually prominent. S. Eu.

13. **OSTROWSKIA,** Regel. GIANT BELLFLOWER. Great Asian per., 1 species in Bokhara, Turkestan.—Known by its broad long lvs., its terminal cluster of very large upstanding fls., many-parted calyx, open-bell-shaped corolla with 8 flaring broad lobes, caps. woody, bearing the long calyx-lobes and opening by several lateral slits. (Ostrow-skia: bears the name of N. ab Ostrowsky, patron of science.)

O. magnifica, Regel. Erect to 5 or 8 ft., from tuberous roots, glabrous, stout, branching at top, juice milky: lvs. 4–5 at each node passing into bracts toward the top, blades oblong-acute or broader, 4–6 in. long, narrowed to base, dentate: fls. pale lilac, 4–6 in. across; calyx-lobes narrow, one-half or more as long as corolla.—Apparently an uncertain plant in cult. in many parts of N. Amer.; seeds often not available and sometimes not true to name. It is a good summer bloomer in B. C. to Ore.

193. LOBELIACEÆ. LOBELIA FAMILY

Herbs or in trop. regions rarely shrubs or trees, often with acrid milky juice; about 20 genera and 600 species widely distributed, some grown for their bright showy fls.—Lvs. alternate or basal, simple, entire, toothed or pinnately parted: fls. solitary, spicate, racemose or paniculate; calyx-limb 5-lobed or -parted, the lobes equal or unequal; corolla gamopetalous, irregular, often bilabiate, its tube often open on one side nearly or quite to base, its limb 5-lobed; stamens 5, inserted with the corolla; filaments sometimes forming a tube; anthers united around the style; ovary inferior, 2–5-celled, stigma fringed: fr. a caps. or berry, with numerous seeds.—Often united with Campanulaceæ; separated primarily by the ring or tube formed by the union of the anthers and by the very irregular corolla.

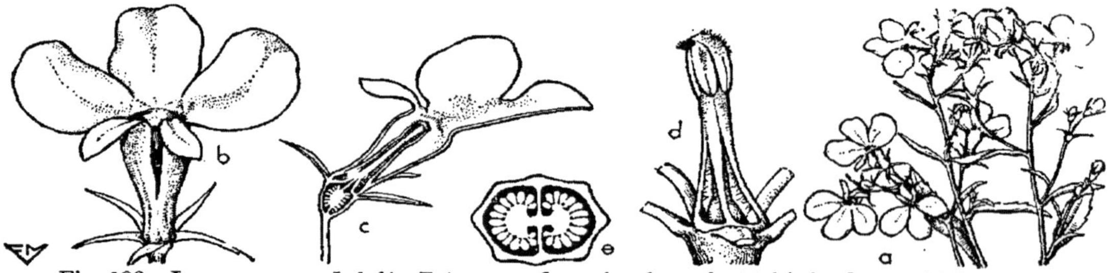

Fig. 193. LOBELIACEÆ. *Lobelia Erinus:* a, flowering branch, × ½; b, flower, × 2; c, same, vertical section, × 2; d, flower, less perianth, × 4; e, ovary, cross-section, × 8.

A. Corolla-tube split to base on one side.
 B. Fr. a dehiscent caps.: fls. (in ours) in racemes or spikes ....1. LOBELIA
 BB. Fr. an indehiscent berry: fls. solitary..............................2. PRATIA
AA. Corolla-tube not split..............................3. DOWNINGIA

1. **LOBELIA,** L. Ann. or per. fl.-garden and border plants; species 250 or more, in many parts of the world, well represented in E. U. S.—Mostly herbs, some trop. species somewhat woody: lvs. alternate, the cauline sometimes reduced to bracts: fls. blue, red, yellowish or white, in terminal racemes, spikes or panicles, or solitary; calyx with short or globular tube and short teeth; corolla-tube split to the base on one side, the limb with 5 lobes, the 3 on the lower side forming a lip, the other 2 (1 on either side of the cleft) erect or turned back; anthers united into a tube or ring around the style, 2 or all hairy at tips; ovary 2-celled, many-ovuled: fr. a 2-valved caps. (Lobe-lia: Matthias de Lobel or L'Obel, 1538–1616, a Flemish botanist and author.)

A. Lower lvs. cut or divided.
 B. Plant glabrous..............................1. *L. gracilis*
 BB. Plant pubescent..............................2. *L. tenuior*
AA. Lower lvs. not cut or divided.
 B. Plant diffuse and half-trailing, 1 ft. or less high..............................3. *L. Erinus*
 BB. Plant erect, to 2 ft. and more.
  C. Color of fls. blue or purplish (sometimes varying to white).
   D. Fls. to ¼ in. long..............................4. *L. inflata*
   DD. Fls. ¾–1 in. long..............................5. *L. siphilitica*
  CC. Color of fls. red (rarely white).
   D. Lobes of corolla united at tips..............................6. *L. Tupa*
   DD. Lobes of corolla not so.
    E. Lower lip notched, corolla cylindrical..............................7. *L. laxiflora*
    EE. Lower lip deeply 3-lobed and deflexed.
     F. Bracts mostly very narrow, the upper little exceeding the pedicels: plants glabrous or nearly so..............................8. *L. cardinalis*
     FF. Bracts more leafy: plant mostly pubescent..............................9. *L. fulgens*

1. **L. gracilis,** Andr. Slender glabrous ann. decumbent at base, 1 ft. or less high: lower lvs. ovate, deeply cut, the upper narrower and pinnatifid, becoming linear and entire at top of st.: fl.-cluster long and open, more or less one-sided; fls. ½–¾ in. across, blue with a whitish eye, the middle lower corolla-lobe strongly obovate, the 2 upper lobes small and curved and usually hairy; anthers all bearded. New S. Wales.

2. **L. tenuior,** R. Br. Erect or ascending ann., with slender sparsely leafy branches, 12–18 in. high, pubescent: lower lvs. small, mostly ternately parted or divided; upper lvs. linear or lanceolate, mostly entire: fls. about 1 in. long, bright blue, borne far apart on long slender pedicels; middle corolla-lobe obovate, much larger than the others; anthers all bearded. W. Australia.

3. **L. Erinus,** L. Diffuse and half-trailing ann., 6–12 in. high, glabrous or slightly hairy below, the slender branching sts. leafy throughout: lower lvs. obovate or spatulate, crenate-toothed, very obtuse; upper lvs. oblanceolate or oblong (becoming linear and acute near the top of the st.), mostly sharp-angled: fls. ½–¾ in. across, on slender pedicels; calyx-segms. awl-like, spreading, as long as the corolla-tube; corolla light blue or violet with white or yellowish throat, the 3 lower lobes large and spreading; the 2 lower anthers bearded. (Erinus: ancient name of a plant of this habit, used also as a generic name in Scrophulariaceæ.) S. Afr.—One of the commonest ann. edging plants. Exceedingly variable in habit, in color of foliage and color and size of fls. The dense low-growing forms are used for low close edgings, as vars. *compacta* and *pumila;* the forms with long slender sts., as vars. *gracilis* and *pendula*, are suitable for vases or baskets. Other strains have yellowish or bronzy foliage. Still other kinds have fls. white, crimson, rose, blue or purplish, one being double-fld. Var. *speciosa* has large azure-blue fls. with a white eye.

4. **L. inflata,** L. INDIAN TOBACCO. Hairy ann. 1–3 ft. high: lvs. oval or ovate-lanceolate, obtuse or the upper acute, toothed: fls. light blue, 1/6–1/4 in. long, rather far apart in loose spike-like racemes; calyx inflated in fr., with linear lobes as long as corolla; lower lip of corolla shorter than tube. Lab. to Ga. and Ark.

5. **L. siphilitica,** L. Strong weedy per. 2–3 ft. high, glabrous or with scattered hairs, sts. mostly simple, leafy throughout: lvs. thin, oblong-oval to lanceolate, tapering to both ends, wing-petioled or sessile, bluntish at apex, crenate-denticulate or irregularly toothed, the longest 5–6 in. long: fls. deep blue or purplish (a var. has nearly white fls.), in a long wand-like narrow-bracted racemose spike; calyx hairy, enlarging in fr., the lance-acuminate lobes conspicuous, the sinuses with an auriculate appendage; corolla about 1 in. long, the tube half as long, the lower lip 3-lobed and deflexed, the upper lip very small; larger anthers naked at tip. Me. to La.

6. **L. Tupa,** L. Erect per. or subshrub 4–7 ft. high: lvs. oblong-oval, acuminate, finely toothed, tomentose and wrinkled: fls. blood-red, 2 in. long, on long pedicels in large terminal racemes; calyx-lobes shorter than tube; lip curving downward and lobes united at tip; column of stamens ascending. (Tupa: vernacular name for this plant.) Chile.

7. **L. laxiflora,** HBK. Branching per. or subshrub 2–5 ft. high, grown mostly under glass, with thinly hairy sts.: lvs. nearly sessile, lanceolate or ovate-lanceolate, acuminate, sharp-denticulate: fls. red and yellow, pubescent, cylindric, 1½ in. long, on long axillary pedicels, the stamens projecting from one side; lower lip notched, upper lip 2-parted. Mex. Var. **angustifolia,** DC. (*L. Cavanillesii*, Hort.), lvs. long and narrow, sometimes even linear; corolla 1–1¼ in. long, scarlet with yellow lip.

8. **L. cardinalis,** L. CARDINAL-FLOWER. INDIAN-PINK. Straight-growing per. 2–4 ft. high, usually unbranched and glabrous: lvs. short-petiolate or sessile, oblong-ovate to oblong-lanceolate, acute or acuminate, irregularly serrate or serrulate: fls. intensely bright cardinal (rarely varying to white), in a long narrow-bracted racemose spike; calyx-tube hemispherical, much shorter than the subulate-linear lobes; corolla-tube 1 in. long, the 3 lower lobes very narrow and deflexed; larger anthers naked at tip. N. B. to Fla. and Tex.

9. **L. fulgens,** Willd. Per. 2–3 ft. high, grown under glass and planted out, usually pubescent, variously tinged with brown or bronze, sts. sending out short offsets at base: lvs. sessile, lanceolate, pointed, somewhat toothed, the lower 3–4 in. long: bracts of infl. leafy, often three to four times as long as the pedicels: fls. about 1½ in. long, deep red, showy; calyx-segms. linear, pointed, about as long as corolla-tube; corolla with 3 broad deflexed lobes. Mex.

2. **PRATIA,** Gaud. Prostrate or creeping herbs, of nearly 20 species native Asia to Australia and S. Amer.—Differs from Lobelia primarily in the fr. which is an indehiscent berry crowned by the persistent calyx-lobes: fls. solitary in the axils. (Pra-tia: named for Prat-Bernon, who made a journey with Freycinet in 1817–1820.)

P. angulata, Hook. f. Per., sts. creeping and rooting, to 1 ft. long, glabrous or nearly so: lvs. ovate-oblong to orbicular, to ½in. long, short-petioled: fls. white streaked with purple, 1/3–2/3in. long, on long erect peduncles; corolla with short tube, 2-lipped, the 3 lower lobes spreading: berry reddish-purple, ½in. across. New Zeal.

3. **DOWNINGIA,** Torr. Low annuals with showy fls., interesting as pot-plants or for edgings; species about 13, mostly in Ore. and Calif., 1 in Chile.—Lvs. alternate, entire, passing above into bracts: fls. blue, violet, yellow or white, sessile in the axils of the lvs. or bracts; corolla-tube short, not split, the bilabiate limb with the upper lobes much narrower than the 3 lower ones; stamens free from corolla; ovary 2-celled or by the disappearance of the thin division wall 1-celled: caps. linear, dehiscent lengthwise by 1–3 valves or fissures, bearing at its apex the leafy linear calyx-lobes; seeds smooth, small, numerous. (Downing-ia: after Andrew Jackson Downing, 1815–1852, American horticulturist.)

A. Lower corolla-lip concave; stamen-column much-exserted, the anther-tube nearly hook-shaped . . . . 1. *D. elegans*
AA. Lower corolla-lip plane; stamen-column little or not at all exserted, the anther-tube straight or only slightly curved . . . . 2. *D. pulchella*

1. **D. elegans,** Torr. (*Clintonia elegans*, Dougl.). Sts. usually simple, 4–7 in. or more high: lvs. oblong to oblong-lanceolate, 1/5–1 in. long: corolla light blue with darker veinlets, the palate of the lower lip white with 2 green or yellowish spots and yellow lines; upper lip cut two-thirds of the way down, the lower with 3 parallel lobes at apex; stamen-column long-exserted, the down-curved anther-column almost hook-shaped and with 2 bristles on the lower side. Calif. to Wash.

2. **D. pulchella,** Torr. (*Clintonia pulchella*, Lindl.). Erect or ascending, 2–10 in. high: lvs. oblong-ovate or narrower, ½in. long: calyx-limb rotate, the 5 lobes blunt; corolla deep

blue; center of lower lip white with 2 yellow and 3 purple spots; corolla-tube short, the upper lip deeply 2-cleft into oblanceolate lobes, the lower lip wide-spreading, deeply cleft into 3 broad lobes; stamen-column little or not at all exserted, the anther-tube nearly straight, with 2 short bristles at apex. Calif. and Ore.

Fig. 194. Compositæ. A, *Aster tanacetifolius:* Aa, flowering branch, × ½; Ab, disk-flower, × 2. B, *Chrysanthemum rubellum:* Ba, flowering branch, × ½; Bb, ray-flower, × 1; Bc, same, corolla partially excised, × 2; Bd, disk-flower, × 3; Be, same, corolla expanded to show syngenesious stamens, × 3. C, *Cichorium Intybus:* Ca, flowering branch, × ½; Cb, ray-flower, corolla partially excised, × 2. D, *Gerbera Jamesonii:* Da, head, × ½; Db, ray-flower, corolla partially excised, × 2; Dc, disk-flower, × 2. E, *Helianthus annuus:* Ea, flowering branch, × ¼; Eb, segment of receptacle bearing disk-flowers, ray-flowers and interfloral bracts, × 2; Ec, disk-flower, × 2.

Fig. 195. COMPOSITÆ. A, flowering branch *Tagetes patula*, × ½. B, *Calendula officinalis:* Ba, flowering branch, × ½; Bb, anthers, × 8; Bc, ray-flower, × 1; Bd, disk-flower, corolla expanded, × 2; Be, seeds, × 2. C, *Ageratum Houstonianum:* Ca, flowering branch, × ½; Cb, anthers, × 8; Cc, disk-flower, × 3; Cd, same, corolla expanded, filaments excised, × 3. D, *Centaurea montana:* Da, flowering branch, × ½; Db, ray-flower, × 1; Dc, disk-flower, × 1; Dd, style and syngenesious stamens of disk-flower, × 2. E, *Echinops exaltatus:* Ea, flowering branch, × ½; Eb, 1-flowered inflorescence, × 1; Ec, flower, × 1.

194. COMPOSITÆ. COMPOSITE FAMILY

A vast family represented in all parts of the world, deriving its name from the many blossoms (or florets) combined into an involucrate head, as if they were inclosed in a single calyx and constituted a compound or composite fl.; mostly ann. and per. herbs, but a few are woody but not usually true trees; many genera are prized among ornamentals, mostly in the open garden, and several others yield kitchen-garden vegetables; the genera are upwards of 800, and the known species are probably 20,000.—Plants erect or twining or drooping, sometimes with milky juice, often with strong aromatic qualities: lvs. very various, alternate, opposite or whorled, without stipules: fls. bisexual or unisexual, aggregated into small or large compact heads (known to gardeners as "flowers"); corolla gamopetalous, 4–5-lobed or -toothed, either all regular or all ligulate (produced into a long limb on one side) or the interior ones regular and the marginal ones ligulate and constituting rays to the head; in some cases the corolla is 2-lipped; stamens 4 or 5, alternating with the corolla-lobes, joined by their anthers to form a ring around the style (syngenesious), the 2 long stigmas projecting; ovary 1, inferior, 1-celled: fr. an achene ("seed" of gardeners), usually crowned by a pappus (representing the calyx-limb) comprised of scales, barbs, hairs or plumes: the fls. are borne on a variously modified and enlarged receptacle, each one subtended by a scale or bract or in many cases the receptacle naked.—The Compositæ represent a generalized group, only few of the species being highly specialized. For the most part they have not been greatly modified and confused by cult., the marked exceptions being Chrysanthemum, Dahlia, Callistephus, Zinnia and Lactuca. They constitute a "natural" family. Keys 1 and 2 comprise a guide to the tribes and to their accounted genera and are based on the more fundamental but often technical and minute characters. Key 3 is provided as a more artificial guide based on more obvious characters by which the genera, as delimited by the species here treated, may be determined.

1. KEY TO THE TRIBES (leads to Key 2).

A. Juice milky: disk-corollas ligulate.................................... 1. CICHORIUM TRIBE
AA. Juice not milky: disk-corollas not ligulate (except in "double" hort. forms).
B. Heads with true rays.
C. Fls. of disk all or some of them bilabiate: lvs. pinnately lobed or parted. 2. MUTISIA TRIBE
CC. Fls. of disk not bilabiate (except sometimes in Ligularia).
D. Involucral bracts wholly or partly dry and scarious, imbricated: lvs. in ours commonly lobed or dissected: strongly scented or bitter-aromatic plants.. 3. ANTHEMIS TRIBE
DD. Involucral bracts in ours not as above, or if so the plants not strongly scented.
E. Receptacle with chaffy bracts or bristles subtending at least the outer disk-fls.; anthers not tailed at base (produced into long points below pollen-sacs).
F. Pappus never of capillary bristles (sometimes of rigid bristles): lvs. all or some of them opposite (alternate in a few genera)... 4. HELIANTHUS TRIBE
FF. Pappus wholly or only the inner series of slender bristles: lvs. commonly alternate.
G. Disk commonly yellow; rays seldom yellow, not with a dark spot at base.. 5. ASTER TRIBE
GG. Disk not yellow or if so the rays yellow with a dark spot at base.. 6. ARCTOTIS TRIBE
EE. Receptacle naked.
F. Herbage in ours punctate or glandular- or resinous-dotted: anthers not tailed at base.. 7. HELENIUM TRIBE
FF. Herbage not as above.
G. Bracts of involucre in 1–3 series, equal or nearly so and not imbricated.
H. Pappus in ours none; rays yellow, orange or whitish; anthers tailed at base.. 8. CALENDULA TRIBE
HH. Pappus of numerous soft capillary bristles; anthers not tailed at base.
I. Rays commonly yellow or orange.................. 9. SENECIO TRIBE
II. Rays seldom yellow.. 5. ASTER TRIBE
GG. Bracts of involucre commonly in several to many series, unequal and imbricated.
H. Rays seldom yellow, not dark colored at base; disk-fls. commonly yellow (sometimes turning purple); anthers not tailed at base.. 5. ASTER TRIBE
HH. Rays commonly yellow, or if otherwise the anthers tailed at base.
I. Disk-fls. not yellow or if so the rays with a dark spot at base; anthers not tailed at base.................. 6. ARCTOTIS TRIBE
II. Disk-fls. commonly yellow, the rays without a dark spot at base; anthers tailed at base...............10. INULA TRIBE

BB. Heads without true rays (marginal disk-corollas or inner involucral bracts sometimes enlarged and ray-like).
C. Marginal disk-corollas enlarged, resembling ray-fls.; involucral bracts in many series: tips and margins of lvs. and of involucral bracts often spinose.
D. Receptacle bristly or chaffy; fls. sometimes yellow; anthers tailed at base .... 12. CYNARA TRIBE
DD. Receptacle naked; fls. never yellow; anthers not tailed .... 13. VERNONIA TRIBE
CC. Marginal disk-corollas not enlarged nor resembling true rays.
D. Lvs. opposite, never spinose: fls. regular, all alike; anthers not tailed at base.
E. Plants with heads clustered; disk-fls. never yellow nor elongated .. 11. EUPATORIUM TRIBE
EE. Plants with heads solitary; disk-fls. greenish-yellow, elongated and ovoid or conic .... 4. HELIANTHUS TRIBE (*Spilanthes*)
DD. Lvs. alternate or basal.
E. Inner involucral bracts enlarged and petal-like, white or colored; anthers tailed at base.
F. Pappus of long-acuminate scales; receptacle chaffy .... 12. CYNARA TRIBE (*Xeranthemum*)
FF. Pappus consisting of bristles or of short scales; receptacle naked or sometimes chaffy .... 10. INULA TRIBE
EE. Inner involucral bracts not enlarged nor petal-like.
F. Tips and margins of lvs. or of involucral bracts spinose ...... 12. CYNARA TRIBE
FF. Tips and margins of lvs. or of involucral bracts not spinose.
G. Plants with lobed or dissected lvs.
H. Receptacle bristly; involucre ovoid or globose .... 12. CYNARA TRIBE
HH. Receptacle never bristly; involucre neither ovoid nor globose.
I. Involucral bracts imbricated, wholly or partly dry and scarious .... 3. ANTHEMIS TRIBE
II. Involucral bracts not as above .... 9. SENECIO TRIBE
GG. Plants with lvs. not lobed nor dissected.
H. Fl.-heads in dense clusters surrounded by a whorl of woolly floral lvs.; anthers tailed at base .... 10. INULA TRIBE (*Leontopodium*)
HH. Fl.-heads not as above; anthers not tailed at base.
I. Lf. linear, not fleshy: disk-fls. yellow .... 5. ASTER TRIBE
II. Lf. broader or fleshy.
J. Involucral bracts imbricated: fls. never yellow .... 11. EUPATORIUM TRIBE
JJ. Involucral bracts not imbricated: fls. sometimes yellow .... 9. SENECIO TRIBE

2. KEY TO THE GENERA (sequence from Key 1).

1. CICHORIUM TRIBE. Herbs (seldom shrubs or trees) with milky juice: fls. all bisexual, with ligulate corolla 5-toothed; anthers sagittate-eared, not tailed at base; style-branches filiform, not appendaged.

A. Fls. purple, blue or white (in ours).
B. Heads sessile .... 1. CICHORIUM
BB. Heads long-peduncled.
C. Bracts of involucre in many series .... 2. CATANANCHE
CC. Bracts of involucre in 1 series .... 3. TRAGOPOGON
AA. Fls. yellow or red (in ours).
B. Plant thistle-like, with spiny-toothed lvs.: heads sessile .... 4. SCOLYMUS
BB. Plant not thistle-like: heads peduncled.
C. Pappus-bristles plumose .... 5. SCORZONERA
CC. Pappus-bristles simple.
D. Foliage all basal.
E. Lvs. mostly pinnatifid .... 6. TARAXACUM
EE. Lvs. not pinnatifid .... 8. HIERACIUM
DD. Foliage basal and cauline.
E. Achenes flattened, beaked: grown for the edible lvs. or sts. .... 7. LACTUCA
EE. Achenes cylindrical, usually not beaked: not edible.
F. Lvs. in ours long-hairy: pappus-bristles rather rigid, usually dirty or neutral-colored .... 8. HIERACIUM
FF. Lvs. in ours nearly glabrous: pappus-bristles usually soft, white .. 9. CREPIS

2. MUTISIA TRIBE. Heads with or without rays; involucral bracts usually in many series, imbricated; fls. commonly with corollas bilabiate or deeply 5-cleft or the ray-fls. ligulate; anthers with long tails at base; style-branches not appendaged. 10. GERBERA

3. ANTHEMIS TRIBE. Commonly strong-scented or bitter-aromatic: lvs. mostly alternate and more or less dissected: heads radiate or discoid; involucral bracts imbricated in 2 to many series, wholly or in part dry and scarious; disk-corollas regular, tubular; anthers not tailed at base; style-branches of the bisexual fls. commonly truncate.

A. Rays usually present.
B. Receptacle naked.
C. Involucral bracts in many series: receptacle flat or convex .... 11. CHRYSANTHEMUM
CC. Involucral bracts in few series: receptacle conic or ovoid .... 12. MATRICARIA
BB. Receptacle with chaffy bracts.
C. Heads solitary on long peduncles: achenes angled or only slightly compressed .... 13. ANTHEMIS
CC. Heads usually in dense clusters: achenes strongly compressed .... 14. ACHILLEA

AA. Rays lacking or inconspicuous.
  B. Heads in panicles or corymbs.
    C. Pappus a short crown: heads in corymbs.
      D. Receptacle naked.
        E. Lvs. pinnately divided .... 15. TANACETUM
        E. Lvs. simple .... 11. CHRYSANTHEMUM
      DD. Receptacle with chaffy bracts .... 16. LONAS
    CC. Pappus none: heads in panicles .... 17. ARTEMISIA
  BB. Heads solitary on long peduncles.
    C. Plant a subshrub: receptacle with chaffy bracts .... 18. SANTOLINA
    CC. Plant a small herb: receptacle without chaffy bracts .... 19. COTULA

4. HELIANTHUS TRIBE. Lvs. commonly opposite (at least the lower ones): heads mostly radiate; involucral bracts usually herbaceous, in 1 to many series; receptacle (in ours) with chaffy bracts subtending at least the outer disk-fls.; anthers not tailed at base; style-branches truncate or appendaged: pappus never of capillary bristles.

A. Plants (ours) with all or some of the lvs. alternate.
  B. Bracts of involucre enfolding the ray-achenes: plant glandular-viscid .... 20. LAYIA
  BB. Bracts of involucre not enfolding the ray-achenes: not glandular or viscid.
    C. Ray-fls. short and inconspicuous, head appearing discoid .... 21. PARTHENIUM
    CC. Ray-fls. conspicuous.
      D. Disk hemispheric or globose to columnar.
        E. Rays rose-purple or rose .... 22. ECHINACEA
        EE. Rays yellow or white.
          F. Achenes 4-angled, wingless .... 23. RUDBECKIA
          FF. Achenes flattened, margined or winged .... 24. RATIBIDA
      DD. Disk flat or convex.
        E. Involucral bracts in 2 distinct series, the outer narrower than inner .. 37. COREOPSIS
        EE. Involucral bracts imbricated in several series, nearly equal.
          F. Achenes winged, strongly flattened: disk-fls. sterile .... 25. SILPHIUM
          FF. Achenes angled, slightly flattened: disk-fls. fertile.
            G. Peduncle fistulose and enlarged below head: pappus persistent. 26. TITHONIA
            GG. Peduncle not fistulose or enlarged: pappus soon deciduous ..... 27. HELIANTHUS
AA. Plants with opposite lvs.
  B. Heads (in ours) without rays .... 28. SPILANTHES
  BB. Heads with rays.
    C. Pappus of 2–4 retrorsely barbed awns.
      D. Achenes not beaked: rays yellow, white or none .... 29. BIDENS
      DD. Achenes beaked: rays commonly not yellow .... 30. COSMOS
    CC. Pappus of scales, teeth or awns, but awns not retrorsely barbed.
      D. Roots tuberous.
        E. Lvs. pinnate .... 31. DAHLIA
        EE. Lvs. simple .... 27. HELIANTHUS
      DD. Roots not tuberous.
        E. Disk-fls. sterile.
          F. Achenes winged: ray-fls. in 2–3 series .... 25. SILPHIUM
          FF. Achenes not winged: ray-fls. in 1 series .... 32. CHRYSOGONUM
        EE. Disk-fls. fertile.
          F. Ray-fls. persisting on the achene and falling with it.
            G. Margins of lvs. coarsely toothed: plant per .... 33. HELIOPSIS
            GG. Margins of lvs. entire: plant ann. (ours).
              H. Lvs. sessile .... 34. ZINNIA
              HH. Lvs. petioled .... 35. SANVITALIA
          FF. Ray-fls. withering and falling before the achenes.
            G. Bracts of involucre in more than 2 series .... 27. HELIANTHUS
            GG. Bracts of involucre in 2 series.
              H. Inner involucral bracts connate to or above the middle .... 36. THELESPERMA
              HH. Inner involucral bracts connate at base .... 37. COREOPSIS

5. ASTER TRIBE. Lvs. alternate or rarely opposite: heads radiate or discoid; involucral bracts usually unequal and in many series; receptacle seldom chaffy; disk-fls. chiefly yellow; anthers not tailed at base; style-branches of the bisexual fls. flattened, appendaged: pappus various, or none.

A. Heads of disk-fls. only: plant (ours) a tall shrub .... 38. BACCHARIS
AA. Heads of both disk- and ray-fls.: plant herbaceous.
  B. Size of heads 2–5 in. across (1–1½ in. in the pompon vars.); outer involucral bracts commonly leafy, longer than the others and reflexed .... 39. CALLISTEPHUS
  BB. Size of heads smaller; outer involucral bracts not leafy nor reflexed.
    C. Foliage (in ours) all basal.
      D. Pappus none: heads 1–2 in. across .... 40. BELLIS
      DD. Pappus of bristles and scales: heads ½in. or less across .... 41. BELLIUM
    CC. Foliage cauline as well as basal.
      D. Rays yellow.
        E. Infl. of few-fld. small heads, in ours forming large panicles or dense racemes .... 42. SOLIDAGO
        EE. Infl. of many-fld. heads usually 1 in. or more across, solitary or in loose corymbs.
          F. Fl.-heads several in corymbs .... 43. CHRYSOPSIS
          FF. Fl.-heads solitary or sometimes 2.
            G. Pappus rigid: plant an ann. 1–4 ft. high .... 44. XANTHISMA
            GG. Pappus fragile: plant (ours) a per. 1 ft. or less high .... 50. ERIGERON

DD. Rays blue, purple, rose or white.
E. Lvs. pinnately divided into narrow segms.
F. Pappus of short scale-like bristles or wanting: bracts of involucre with scarious margins....45. BRACHYCOME
FF. Pappus of conspicuous bristles: bracts of involucre not scarious-margined....51. ASTER
EE. Lvs. (at least the upper) entire or only toothed.
F. Plant an evergreen shrub with lvs. white-tomentose beneath....46. OLEARIA
FF. Plant an herb or if shrubby lvs. not as above.
G. Bristles of pappus plumose....47. CHARIEIS
GG. Bristles of pappus, when present, not plumose.
H. Pappus not uniform in all fls.
I. Bracts of involucre in few series: pappus of scales with few stiff bristles....48. BOLTONIA
II. Bracts of involucre in many series: pappus of short and long chaffy bristles....49. HETEROPAPPUS
HH. Pappus of uniform bristles.
I. Involucral bracts in 1–2 series: rays in 2 or more series..50. ERIGERON
II. Involucral bracts in 2 to many series: rays in 1–2 series.
J. Bracts of involucre without scarious margins....51. ASTER
JJ. Bracts of involucre with scarious margins.
K. Color of rays purple or lilac (in ours): lvs. incised-dentate....52. CALIMERIS
KK. Color of rays bright blue: lvs. entire or denticulate...53. FELICIA

6. ARCTOTIS TRIBE. Lvs. mostly alternate or basal: heads commonly radiate; involucral bracts imbricated in several rows, separate or united at base; fls. of the disk tubular and regular; anthers not tailed at base; style-branches not appendaged.

A. Herbage tomentose: receptacle naked or bristly.
B. Involucral bracts separate from each other.
C. Achenes usually villous, crowned by hyaline, often convolute scales....54. ARCTOTIS
CC. Achenes glabrous, with or without crown of minute scales....55. VENIDIUM
BB. Involucral bracts grown together at base....56. GAZANIA
AA. Herbage glabrous or pubescent: involucral bracts not grown together; receptacle chaffy....57. URSINIA

7. HELENIUM TRIBE. Lvs. not rarely glandular-punctate or glandular- or resinous-dotted: heads radiate or rarely discoid; involucral bracts in 1 to several series; receptacle naked; fls. commonly yellow; anthers not tailed at base; style-branches truncate or appendaged.

A. Involucral bracts united nearly throughout: herbage glabrous....58. TAGETES
AA. Involucral bracts separate or united only at base: herbage seldom glabrous.
B. Plant white-woolly (in ours).
C. Rays persistent on achene and becoming papery....59. BAILEYA
CC. Rays deciduous....60. ERIOPHYLLUM
BB. Plant not white-woolly.
C. Receptacle with small bristle-like fringe among the fls.: base of lf. not decurrent on st....61. GAILLARDIA
CC. Receptacle not as above: base of lf. often decurrent on st.
D. Bracts of involucre erect: low herbs, ours with basal lvs....62. ACTINEA
DD. Bracts of involucre spreading or reflexed: tall leafy-stemmed herbs....63. HELENIUM

8. CALENDULA TRIBE. Herbs or shrubs: lvs. commonly alternate: heads radiate; involucral bracts subequal, in 1–3 series, often with dry-scarious border; receptacle naked, or very seldom with a few bristles; disk-fls. regular, tubular, 5-toothed, mostly infertile; ray-fls. pistillate and fertile, commonly ligulate; anthers with base sagittate or sometimes eared or tailed; style-branches bifid or entire: achenes usually large; pappus commonly none, sometimes of a few deciduous hairs.

A. Disk-fls. fertile.
B. Ray-fls. fertile; style divided into 2 branches....64. DIMORPHOTHECA
BB. Ray-fls. sterile; style none or undivided....65. CASTALIS
AA. Disk-fls. sterile.
B. Achenes straight....66. OSTEOSPERMUM
BB. Achenes, at least the inner ones, incurved....67. CALENDULA

9. SENECIO TRIBE. Lvs. mostly alternate or basal: heads commonly radiate; involucral bracts mostly equal and in 1 or 2 series, with or without short accessory bracts at base; receptacle naked; anthers not tailed at base; style-branches truncate or obtuse, with or without appendages.

A. Bracts of involucre united one-third or one-half their length: pappus none.....68. GAMOLEPIS
AA. Bracts of involucre distinct or united only at base: pappus of bristles.
B. Ray-fls. lacking.
C. Habit (in ours) climbing....76. SENECIO
CC. Habit not climbing.
D. Plant densely pubescent, the st. with violet or purple hairs....69. GYNURA
DD. Plant glabrous or only slightly pubescent.
E. Lvs. clasping at base, flat: plant not succulent....70. EMILIA
EE. Lvs. not clasping, often cylindrical: plant succulent....71. KLEINIA
BB. Ray-fls. present.
C. Disk-fls. sterile; style undivided: lvs. (in ours) fleshy and cylindrical.....72. OTHONNA
CC. Disk-fls. fertile; style branched: lvs. not fleshy and cylindrical.
D. St.-lvs. opposite....73. ARNICA

DD. St.-lvs. alternate.
E. Involucral bracts in 2–3 nearly equal series ....74. DORONICUM
EE. Involucral bracts in 1 series, often with short bracts at base.
F. Margins of involucral bracts overlapping ....75. LIGULARIA
FF. Margins of involucral bracts not overlapping....................76. SENECIO

10. INULA TRIBE. Often woolly: lvs. commonly alternate or basal, entire or nearly so: heads radiate or discoid; involucral bracts commonly dry and scarious and in several series, sometimes foliaceous or petaloid; receptacle naked or scaly; anthers tailed at base.

A. Heads surrounded by a whorl of white-woolly floral lvs....................77. LEONTOPODIUM
AA. Heads not surrounded by a whorl of floral lvs.
B. Involucral bracts not white or colored and petal-like: heads with both ray- and disk-fls., the rays yellow.
C. Pappus of bristles: receptacle not chaffy....................78. INULA
CC. Pappus of scales united into a crown: receptacle chaffy....................79. BUPHTHALMUM
BB. Involucral bracts commonly white or colored and petal-like: heads with disk-fls. only.
C. St. and branches (in ours) conspicuously winged: pappus crown- or cup-shaped....................80. AMMOBIUM
CC. St. and branches not winged: pappus bristly.
D. Herbage not white-woolly.
E. Pappus-bristles plumose throughout....................81. HELIPTERUM
EE. Pappus-bristles plumose only at tip....................82. HELICHRYSUM
DD. Herbage white-woolly.
E. Plant stoloniferous or trailing (in ours).
F. Fl.-heads (in ours) solitary....................82. HELICHRYSUM
FF. Fl.-heads clustered....................83. ANTENNARIA
EE. Plant not stoloniferous or trailing.
F. Pappus-bristles plumose....................81. HELIPTERUM
FF. Pappus-bristles not plumose or only so at tip.
G. Lvs. ovate (in ours): branches vine-like....................82. HELICHRYSUM
GG. Lvs. linear-lanceolate: branches erect....................84. ANAPHALIS

11. EUPATORIUM TRIBE. Lvs. simple: heads discoid; involucral bracts imbricate in several series or in 1–2 series and only slightly unequal; corollas tubular, regular, never pure yellow; anthers not tailed at base; style-branches commonly elongate, more or less thickened above: pappus commonly setose.

A. Habit climbing: involucre of 4 bracts....................85. MIKANIA
AA. Habit not climbing: involucre of more than 4 bracts.
B. Heads in spikes or racemes: achenes 10-ribbed....................86. LIATRIS
BB. Heads in clusters or corymbs, often panicled: achenes 4–5-angled.
C. Pappus of capillary bristles....................87. EUPATORIUM
CC. Pappus none or of scales.
D. Anthers appendaged at apex: heads many-fld....................88. AGERATUM
DD. Anthers truncate at apex, not appendaged: heads 3–5-fld....................89. PIQUERIA

12. CYNARA TRIBE. Lvs. alternate, often spinose-toothed or -lobed: involucral bracts imbricated in many series, often spinose or scarious or foliaceous at tip; fls. bisexual, the corollas tubular with 5 long narrow lobes, or the marginal enlarged ray-like and usually neutral; anthers tailed at base; style-branches short, distinct or united.

A. Plants not thistle-like or spiny.
B. Lvs. roundish and mostly cordate: involucral bracts with hooked tips....90. ARCTIUM
BB. Lvs. elongate, not cordate, sometimes pinnatifid: involucral bracts usually without hooked tips.
C. Inner bracts of involucre petal-like....................91. XERANTHEMUM
CC. Inner bracts of involucre not petal-like....................92. CENTAUREA
AA. Plant thistle-like, often spiny.
B. Pappus of scales or none.
C. Fls. (in ours) orange-yellow: lvs. green and glabrous....................93. CARTHAMUS
CC. Fls. blue or white: lvs. white-tomentose beneath....................94. ECHINOPS
BB. Pappus of bristles.
C. Fls. yellow....................95. CNICUS
CC. Fls. purple to white.
D. Achenes hairy: plant stemless (in ours)....................96. CARLINA
DD. Achenes not hairy: plant with sts.
E. Sts. winged by the decurrent lf.-bases: receptacle not bristly......97. ONOPORDUM
EE. Sts. seldom winged by the decurrent lf.-bases: receptacle bristly.
F. Lvs. glabrous, white-spotted above....................98. SILYBUM
FF. Lvs. tomentose beneath, not white-spotted above....................99. CYNARA

13. VERNONIA TRIBE. Lvs. commonly alternate and simple: heads discoid; fls. never yellow; involucral bracts imbricated in several series or rarely few in 1–2 series; corollas tubular and regular except in Stokesia which has its outer corollas enlarged and with palmately cleft limb simulating a ligule; anthers not tailed at base; style-branches slender, filiform or attenuate.

A. Outer row of disk-fls. resembling inner ones, not enlarged or slit; heads (in ours) ½in. across....................100. VERNONIA
AA. Outer row of disk-fls. slit down one side, enlarged and ray-like; heads 3–4 in. across....................101. STOKESIA

COMPOSITÆ

3. ARTIFICIAL KEY TO GENERA AND SPECIES HEREIN TREATED.

A. Plant thistle-like, usually lvs. and involucral bracts spiny.

B. Heads of ligulate or ray-fls. only .... 4. SCOLYMUS

BB. Heads of tubular or disk-fls. only.

C. Pappus of scales or none.

D. Fls. (in ours) orange-yellow: lvs. green and glabrous.................93. CARTHAMUS

DD. Fls. blue or white: lvs. white-tomentose beneath..................94. ECHINOPS

CC. Pappus of bristles.

D. Fls. yellow..95. CNICUS

DD. Fls. purple to white.

E. Achenes hairy: plant stemless (in ours)........................96. CARLINA

EE. Achenes not hairy: plant with sts.

F. Sts. winged by the decurrent lf.-bases: receptacle not bristly .....97. ONOPORDUM

FF. Sts. seldom winged by decurrent lf.-bases: receptacle bristly.

G. Lvs. glabrous, white-spotted above........................98. SILYBUM

GG. Lvs. tomentose beneath, not white-spotted above............99. CYNARA

AA. Plant not thistle-like.

B. Pappus (at least one series) of bristles or bristle-like hairs (not widened at base).

C. Ray- or ligulate fls. lacking.

D. Lvs. opposite or whorled.

E. Habit climbing: involucre of 4 bracts ....85. MIKANIA

EE. Habit not climbing: involucre of more than 4 bracts..............87. EUPATORIUM

DD. Lvs. alternate or basal.

E. Heads surrounded by a whorl of white-woolly floral lvs...........77. LEONTOPODIUM

EE. Heads not surrounded by whorl of floral lvs.

F. Habit (in ours) climbing...................................76. SENECIO

FF. Habit not climbing.

G. Inner involucral bracts white or colored, often petal-like (known as "Everlastings").

H. Bristles of pappus plumose throughout....................81. HELIPTERUM

HH. Bristles of pappus simple or plumose only at tip.

I. Height of plant mostly 1 ft. or less, stoloniferous or trailing.

J. Fl.-heads solitary (in ours) ....82. HELICHRYSUM

JJ. Fl.-heads clustered ....83. ANTENNARIA

II. Height of plant 1–3 ft., not stoloniferous.

J. Shape of lvs. linear-lanceolate........................84. ANAPHALIS

JJ. Shape of lvs. oblong to ovate ....82. HELICHRYSUM

GG. Inner involucral bracts green, not petal-like.

H. Fl.-heads in narrow spikes or racemes...................86. LIATRIS

HH. Fl.-heads in clusters, panicles or solitary.

I. Involucral bracts imbricated in several series.

J. Receptacle densely bristly: involucral bracts usually with fringed or spine-tipped appendages............92. CENTAUREA

JJ. Receptacle naked: involucral bracts not as above.

K. Color of heads white or yellowish: plant a shrub .....38. BACCHARIS

KK. Color of heads deep purple: plant an herb ....100. VERNONIA

II. Involucral bracts in 1 series, sometimes with spreading bracts at base.

J. Pubescence dense, the st. with violet or purple hairs.....69. GYNURA

JJ. Pubescence slight or none.

K. Base of lvs. clasping: plant not succulent..........70. EMILIA

KK. Base of lvs. not clasping: plant succulent..........71. KLEINIA

CC. Ray- or ligulate fls. present.

D. Heads of ligulate fls. only.

E. Bristles of pappus plumose.

F. Bracts of involucre in 1 row .... 3. TRAGOPOGON

FF. Bracts of involucre in several series...................... 5. SCORZONERA

EE. Bristles of pappus not plumose.

F. Infl. a panicle.. 7. LACTUCA

FF. Infl. a long-peduncled cluster or fls. solitary.

G. Foliage all basal.

H. Lvs., at least some of them, pinnatifid.................. 6. TARAXACUM

HH. Lvs. not pinnatifid...................................... 8. HIERACIUM

GG. Foliage cauline as well as basal.

H. Fl.-heads usually 2–5 in. across: basal tuft of lvs. lacking....39. CALLISTEPHUS

HH. Fl.-heads ½–2 in. across: basal lvs. forming tuft.

I. Lvs. long-hairy (in ours): pappus neutral-colored and stiff .... 8. HIERACIUM

II. Lvs. nearly glabrous (in ours): pappus white and soft..... 9. CREPIS

DD. Heads of both ray- and disk-fls.

E. Color of heads yellow or orange.

F. Fl.-heads in corymbs, panicles or racemes.

G. Pappus in 2 series, the outer of scales or smaller bristles........43. CHRYSOPSIS

GG. Pappus of equal bristles.

H. Involucral bracts unequal, imbricated in several series.

I. Size of heads ½in. or less ....42. SOLIDAGO

II. Size of heads 1 in. or more ....78. INULA

HH. Involucral bracts nearly equal, in 1–3 series, sometimes with calyx-like bracts at base.

I. St.-lvs. clasping: bracts of involucre in 2–3 series, without short bracts at base . . . . . 74. DORONICUM
II. St.-lvs. not clasping: bracts of involucre in 1 series, often with short bracts at base.
J. Margins of involucral bracts overlapping . . . . . 75. LIGULARIA
JJ. Margins of involucral bracts not overlapping . . . . . 76. SENECIO
FF. Fl.-heads solitary.
G. Sts. trailing or drooping: lvs. succulent . . . . . 72. OTHONNA
GG. Sts. upright: lvs. not succulent.
H. Corolla of disk-fls. bilabiate . . . . . 10. GERBERA
HH. Corolla of disk-fls. not bilabiate.
I. Bracts of involucre enfolding the ray-achenes . . . . . 20. LAYIA
II. Bracts of involucre not enfolding the ray-achenes.
J. Involucral bracts nearly equal, in 1–3 series.
K. St.-lvs. opposite . . . . . 73. ARNICA
KK. St.-lvs. alternate.
L. Height of plant less than 1 ft.: heads 1 in. across . . . 50. ERIGERON
LL. Height of plant 1–5 ft.: heads 1½–4 in. across . . . . . 74. DORONICUM
JJ. Involucral bracts unequal, imbricated in several series.
K. Receptacle densely bristly . . . . . 92. CENTAUREA
KK. Receptacle not bristly.
L. Margins of involucral bracts whitish: plant ann. . . . 44. XANTHISMA
LL. Margins of involucral bracts not whitish: plant per . . . . . 78. INULA
EE. Color of heads pink, purple or white, never yellow.
F. Bristles of pappus plumose . . . . . 47. CHARIEIS
FF. Bristles of pappus not plumose.
G. Corolla of disk-fls. bilabiate . . . . . 10. GERBERA
GG. Corolla of disk-fls. not bilabiate.
H. Fl.-heads in corymbs or panicles.
I. An evergreen shrub with lvs. white-tomentose beneath . . . . 46. OLEARIA
II. An herb, or if shrubby lvs. not as above.
J. Pappus not uniform in all fls.
K. Rays blue; margins of involucral bracts not scarious . . 49. HETEROPAPPUS
KK. Rays white to purple; margins of involucral bracts scarious . . . . . 48. BOLTONIA
JJ. Pappus uniform in all fls.
K. Bracts of involucre imbricated in 2 to many series . . . . 51. ASTER
KK. Bracts of involucre in 1–2 series.
L. Involucre of 1–2 series of nearly equal bracts . . . . . 50. ERIGERON
LL. Involucre of 1 series of equal bracts, subtended by small bracts resembling a calyx . . . . . 76. SENECIO
HH. Fl.-heads solitary.
I. Foliage all basal . . . . . 41. BELLIUM
II. Foliage cauline as well as basal.
J. Receptacle densely bristly; involucral bracts usually with fringed or spine-tipped appendages . . . . . 92. CENTAUREA
JJ. Receptacle not bristly; involucral bracts not as above.
K. Outer involucral bracts commonly leafy, longer than others and reflexed: heads usually 2–5 in. across . . . 39. CALLISTEPHUS
KK. Outer involucral bracts not leafy or reflexed: heads smaller.
L. Rays in 2 or more series; involucral bracts in 1–2 series . . . . . 50. ERIGERON
LL. Rays in 1–2 series; involucral bracts in 2 to many series.
M. Bracts of involucre without scarious margins . . . . 51. ASTER
MM. Bracts of involucre with scarious margins.
N. Lvs. incised-dentate: rays purple or lilac . . . . 52. CALIMERIS
NN. Lvs. entire or denticulate: rays bright blue . . . 53. FELICIA
BB. Pappus of scales or awns, or lacking.
C. Bracts of involucre papery, white or colored and ray-like (known as "Everlastings").
D. Branches conspicuously winged: bracts white . . . . . 80. AMMOBIUM
DD. Branches not winged: bracts purple or rose . . . . . 91. XERANTHEMUM
CC. Bracts of involucre not papery and ray-like.
D. Rays lacking or inconspicuous.
E. Fl.-heads solitary.
F. Lvs. opposite . . . . . 28. SPILANTHES
FF. Lvs. alternate.
G. Receptacle densely bristly: involucral bracts commonly with fringed or spine-tipped appendages . . . . . 92. CENTAUREA
GG. Receptacle not bristly; involucral bracts not as above.
H. A creeping herb: receptacle without chaffy bracts . . . . . 19. COTULA
HH. A subshrub 1–2 ft. high: receptacle with chaffy bracts . . . . . 18. SANTOLINA
EE. Fl.-heads in clusters, corymbs or panicles.
F. Lf. pinnately or palmately divided.
G. Heads in corymbs: pappus a short crown.
H. Receptacle naked . . . . . 15. TANACETUM
HH. Receptacle with chaffy bracts . . . . . 16. LONAS
GG. Heads in panicles or racemes: pappus none . . . . . 17. ARTEMISIA
FF. Lf. simple.

G. Involucral bracts with hooked tips, the head becoming a bur . 90. ARCTIUM
GG. Involucral bracts not hooked, head not bur-like.
H. Lvs. opposite.
I. Heads few-fld.: lvs. oblong-lanceolate .... 89. PIQUERIA
II. Heads many-fld. and dense: lvs. ovate .... 88. AGERATUM
HH. Lvs. alternate.
I. Heads in racemes forming a panicle: pappus none .... 17. ARTEMISIA
II. Heads in a long-peduncled corymb: pappus a crown or of scales or awns.
J. Herbage silvery-pubescent .... 21. PARTHENIUM
JJ. Herbage green .... 11. CHRYSANTHEMUM
DD. Rays present and conspicuous.
E. Outer involucral bracts united to form a cup or tube.
F. Lvs. white-tomentose beneath, mostly basal .... 56. GAZANIA
FF. Lvs. glabrous, not basal.
G. Pappus lacking: lvs. alternate .... 68. GAMOLEPIS
GG. Pappus of scales: lvs. opposite .... 58. TAGETES
EE. Outer involucral bracts free or united only at base.
F. St.-lvs. lacking, heads on naked scapes.
G. Heads of ligulate fls. only .... 2. CATANANCHE
GG. Heads of both ray- and disk-fls.
H. Ray-fls. white, rose or blue, never yellow.
I. Diam. of heads 1–2 in.: pappus none .... 40. BELLIS
II. Diam. of heads to ½in.: pappus present .... 41. BELLIUM
HH. Ray-fls. yellow.
I. Lvs. entire .... 62. ACTINEA
II. Lvs. pinnatifid or lyrate.
J. Whole plant white-woolly: involucral bracts nearly equal and erect .... 59. BAILEYA
JJ. Whole plant not white-woolly, only lvs. underneath: outer involucral bracts smaller and reflexed or spreading .... 54. ARCTOTIS
FF. St.-lvs. present.
G. Lvs. opposite.
H. Lf. compound.
I. Awns of pappus retrorsely barbed.
J. Achenes beaked .... 30. COSMOS
JJ. Achenes not beaked .... 29. BIDENS
II. Awns of pappus not retrorsely barbed.
J. Roots tuberous .... 31. DAHLIA
JJ. Roots not tuberous.
K. Herbage rough-hispid: involucral bracts in several nearly equal series .... 25. SILPHIUM
KK. Herbage not rough: involucral bracts in 2 unequal series.
L. Inner involucral bracts connate to or above the middle .... 36. THELESPERMA
LL. Inner involucral bracts connate only at base .... 37. COREOPSIS
HH. Lf. simple.
I. Awns of pappus retrorsely barbed .... 30. COSMOS
II. Awns of pappus not retrorsely barbed.
J. Disk-fls. sterile.
K. Achenes winged: ray-fls. in 2–3 series .... 25. SILPHIUM
KK. Achenes not winged: ray-fls. in 1 series .... 32. CHRYSOGONUM
JJ. Disk-fls. fertile.
K. Ray-fls. withering and falling before the achenes.
L. Involucral bracts in 2 series, the inner connate at base .... 37. COREOPSIS
LL. Involucral bracts in more than 2 series, the inner not connate .... 27. HELIANTHUS
KK. Ray-fls. persisting on the achene and falling with it.
L. Margins of lvs. coarsely toothed .... 33. HELIOPSIS
LL. Margins of lvs. entire.
M. Base of lf. sessile .... 34. ZINNIA
MM. Base of lf. petioled .... 35. SANVITALIA
GG. Lvs. alternate.
H. Color of rays blue, purple, red or white, but not yellow.
I. Heads sessile along the branches .... 1. CICHORIUM
II. Heads not as above.
J. Involucral bracts herbaceous, not dry and scarious.
K. Disk flat.
L. Receptacle bristly .... 92. CENTAUREA
LL. Receptacle naked .... 101. STOKESIA
KK. Disk convex to globose or conical.
L. Receptacle naked .... 63. HELENIUM
LL. Receptacle with bristles or chaffy bracts.
M. Apex of rays shallowly 2-toothed .... 22. ECHINACEA
MM. Apex of rays deeply 3-toothed or -parted ...... 61. GAILLARDIA
JJ. Involucral bracts with dry and scarious margins or tips.
K. Heads of ligulate fls. only.
L. Receptacle bristly: lvs. simple .... 2. CATANANCHE
LL. Receptacle naked: lvs. divided .... 11. CHRYSANTHEMUM

KK. Heads of both ligulate and disk-fls.
L. Lf. simple, although sometimes lobed.
M. Base of achenes with tuft of silky hairs........54. ARCTOTIS
MM. Base of achenes without tuft of hairs.
N. Pappus of conspicuous scales and bristles...48. BOLTONIA
NN. Pappus a cup-like rim or lacking.
O. Achenes of disk-fls. broadly winged: involucral bracts in 1–2 series.
P. Ray-fls. fertile; style divided into 2 branches.
Q. Disk-fls. fertile: ours an ann. to 16 in. high..........................64. DIMORPHOTHECA
QQ. Disk-fls. sterile: ours a shrubby per. 2 ft. or more high..............66. OSTEOSPERMUM
PP. Ray-fls. sterile; style none or undivided..65. CASTALIS
OO. Achenes not winged: involucral bracts in several to many series.
P. Receptacle naked...................11. CHRYSANTHEMUM
PP. Receptacle with chaffy bracts.........14. ACHILLEA
LL. Lf. compound.
M. Receptacle with chaffy bracts.
N. Achenes strongly compressed: heads usually small and in dense clusters..............14. ACHILLEA
NN. Achenes angled or only slightly compressed: heads solitary on long peduncles.........13. ANTHEMIS
MM. Receptacle naked.
N. Fl.-heads with blue rays..................45. BRACHYCOME
NN. Fl.-heads with white, pink or purple rays.
O. Disk flat or convex; involucral bracts in many series.......................11. CHRYSANTHEMUM
OO. Disk conical or ovoid; involucral bracts in few series.........................12. MATRICARIA
HH. Color of rays yellow, sometimes with red or purple at base.
I. Margins or tips of involucral bracts, at least the inner ones, dry and scarious.
J. Involucral bracts in 1–2 series.
K. Achenes of ray-fls. straight: lvs. toothed or lobed....64. DIMORPHOTHECA
KK. Achenes of ray-fls. incurved: lvs. entire or only slightly toothed..............................67. CALENDULA
JJ. Involucral bracts imbricated in several to many series.
K. Scales of pappus enlarged and white on mature achene......................................57. URSINIA
KK. Scales not as above, or lacking.
L. Receptacle honeycombed......................55. VENIDIUM
LL. Receptacle not honeycombed.
M. Chaffy scales lacking on receptacle...........11. CHRYSANTHEMUM
MM. Chaffy scales present on receptacle.
N. Lf. pinnately compound.
O. Achenes strongly compressed: heads usually small and in dense clusters.........14. ACHILLEA
OO. Achenes angled or only slightly compressed: heads solitary on long peduncles. 13. ANTHEMIS
NN. Lf. simple.
O. Heads ¼ in. or less across................14. ACHILLEA
OO. Heads 1–2½ in. across..................79. BUPHTHALMUM
II. Margins or tips of involucral bracts herbaceous, not dry and scarious.
J. Disk hemispheric or globose to columnar.
K. Receptacle naked...........................63. HELENIUM
KK. Receptacle with chaffy bracts or bristles.
L. Apex of rays deeply 3-toothed or -parted........61. GAILLARDIA
LL. Apex of rays shallowly toothed or entire.
M. Achenes 4-angled, wingless...................23. RUDBECKIA
MM. Achenes flattened, margined or winged........24. RATIBIDA
JJ. Disk flat.
K. Receptacle naked.
L. Ray-fls.persistent on achene and becoming papery.59. BAILEYA
LL. Ray-fls. deciduous..........................60. ERIOPHYLLUM
KK. Receptacle with bristles or chaffy bracts.
L. The receptacle densely bristly.................92. CENTAUREA
LL. The receptacle with chaffy bracts.
M. Peduncle fistulose and enlarged below the head..26. TITHONIA
MM. Peduncle not as above.
N. Achenes winged, strongly flattened: disk-fls. sterile..............................25. SILPHIUM
NN. Achenes angled, slightly flattened: disk-fls. fertile..............................27. HELIANTHUS

1. **CICHORIUM,** L. Species about 9, mostly in the Medit. region and to Abyssinia, two yielding food products.—Per., bien. or ann. herbs, branching and diffuse

when in bloom, mostly with deep hard roots: lvs. alternate, usually towards base of plant: heads mostly axillary and sessile, some terminal; involucral bracts in 2 series, at least the apical one-half herbaceous; fls. all ligulate, blue, purple or white, several to many in a head; rays truncate, 5-toothed at apex: achenes long-beaked, crowned by a pappus of blunt paleæ or scales. (Cicho-rium: from an old Arabic name.)

A. Bracts subtending heads commonly shorter than heads: fls. blue, white or pink........1. *C. Intybus*
AA. Bracts subtending heads leafy, commonly longer than heads: fls. purple............2. *C. Endivia*

1. **C. Intybus,** L. Chicory. Succory. Stout deep-rooted per., 3–6 ft.; upper branches practically leafless: lvs. broadly oblong, oblanceolate or lanceolate, more or less clasping, the lower ones nearly entire to runcinate, the upper passing into bracts commonly shorter than the heads; lower lvs. bristly-hairy beneath, at least on midrib: fls. bright azure-blue, in heads 1½ in. or more across, closing about noon: pappus about one-eighth to one-tenth as long as achene. (Intybus: Latin for chicory.) Eu.—Fls. in some races pink or white. Cult. for the root (substitute for coffee) and for the salad-lvs. (Witloof, Barbe).

2. **C. Endivia,** L. Endive. Ann. or bien., the branching leafy sts. 2–3 ft., glabrous: lvs. many at base, brittle, oblong, lobed or cut, the upper passing into leafy bracts commonly much exceeding the heads: fls. purple, in heads about 1½ in. across: pappus about one-sixth to one-fourth as long as achene. (Endivia: probably derived from same root as Intybus.) Probably India.—Cult. as a salad plant.

2. **CATANANCHE,** L. Cupids-Dart. About 5 species native to the Medit. region, one cult. for the showy bloom.—Ann. or per. herbs: lvs. linear or lanceolate, crowded toward the base of the st.: fls. all ligulate, blue or yellow, in long-peduncled heads; involucral bracts in many series, the apical two-thirds scarious; receptacle bristly: achenes oblong, usually villose or setose, crowned with bristles or lanceolate long-acuminate scales. (Catanan-che: Greek name, referring to ancient custom of using the plant in making love-philters.)

C. cærulea, L. Per. to 2 ft., but blooming first year from seed: lvs. tomentose, lanceolate or oblanceolate, 8–12 in. long, entire or few-toothed: fl.-heads 2 in. across, on long slender peduncles, the wide flat-toothed rays blue: pappus of 5–8 aristate scales. S. Eu. Var. **alba,** Hort., has all white rays and var. **bicolor,** Hort., white rays blue at base.

3. **TRAGOPOGON,** L. Goats-Beard. About 45 species native to S. Eu., N. Afr. and Cent. and S. Asia, one cult. in the vegetable-garden.—Erect glabrous bien. or per. herbs with a tap-root and narrow grass-like lvs.: fls. all ligulate, purple or yellow, in large long-peduncled heads; rays 5-toothed at apex; involucre cylindric or nearly so, with approximately equal-length bracts in a single row; anthers sagittate; style-branches slender: pappus composed of plumose bristles in a single series. (Tragopo-gon: Greek for *goat's beard.*)

T. porrifolius, L. Salsify. Vegetable-Oyster. Oyster-Plant. Strict bien. to 4 ft., with edible roots to 1 ft. long: lvs. keeled, tapering from a broad often clasping base: peduncle thickened and hollow beneath head; fls. purple, showy, opening in the morning and closing by noon, the outer rays exceeded by the involucral bracts; receptacle naked: achenes ("seeds") stick-like, long-beaked; pappus yellowish. S. Eu.; nat. in N. Amer.

4. **SCOLYMUS,** L. Erect thistle-like herbs, native of the Medit. region, one somewhat cult. for its edible tap-root; 3 or 4 species.—Lvs. alternate, pinnately spinose-toothed or -lobed, with bases decurrent in spinose wings: fls. all ligulate, yellow, in sessile heads; involucral bracts spinescent-tipped, in few rows; receptacle chaffy: achenes beakless; pappus a ring or few bristles. (Scol-ymus: old Greek name, used by Hesiod.)

S. hispanicus, L. Golden Thistle. Spanish Oyster-Plant. Much-branched bien. 2–2½ ft. high, usually pubescent: basal lvs. spiny, oblong, pinnatifid, dark green with paler ribs and veins: heads few-fld., about 1 in. long: achenes chaff-like, wing-margined; pappus consisting of scarious unequal paleæ. S. Eu.

5. **SCORZONERA,** L. About 100 species of the Old World, one yielding a root-vegetable.—Per. herbs or rarely ann.: lvs. commonly entire and grass-like or wider, sometimes more or less pinnately lobed or dissected: fls. all ligulate, yellow, rose or lilac, in long-peduncled heads; involucral bracts in several series, the outer much

shorter than the inner: achenes many-ribbed, beakless; pappus-bristles plumose with soft hairs, often naked at tip. (Scorzone-ra: old French *scorzon*, serpent; *S. hispanica* was used against snake-bite.)

S. hispanica, L. Black Salsify. Much-branched per., woolly-pubescent to nearly glabrous, 2–3 ft., with a long fleshy tap-root like that of salsify, but having a black skin: lvs. oblong to lanceolate or in some forms linear, undulate, tapering below into a long winged petiole: fls. yellow, in long-peduncled heads to 2 in. long: achenes nearly white, many-ribbed, the ribs of the outer ones papillate. Cent. and S. Eu.—Cult. for its fleshy edible root and for its lvs. which are sometimes used for salads.

6. **TARAXACUM,** Haller. Dandelion. Per. herbs mostly of the northern hemisphere, by recent authorities separated into many species.—Lvs. basal, runcinate-pinnatifid or lyrate or sometimes nearly entire: fls. all ligulate, yellow, in many-fld. heads terminating a naked hollow scape; involucral bracts in 2 series, the inner erect and narrow, the outer smaller and spreading or reflexed; receptacle naked: achenes angled, fusiform, attenuated into a slender beak; pappus simple and capillary. (Tarax-acum: from a native Arabian name.)

A. Involucral bracts without appendages. . . . . 1. *T. officinale*
AA. Involucral bracts with horn-like appendages. . . . . 2. *T. kok-saghyz*

1. **T. officinale,** Weber (*Leontodon Taraxacum,* L.). Common Dandelion. Lvs. obovate-lanceolate to linear, to 10 in. long, sinuate-dentate or pinnatifid, rarely nearly entire: heads 1–2 in. across, on scapes to 1½ ft. high; outer involucral bracts narrower than inner, reflexed, without appendages: achenes greenish-brown, with copious white pappus. Eu. but widely nat.—Grown and collected for greens.

2. **T. kok-saghyz,** Rodin. Differs in lvs. not so deeply lobed, often nearly entire, smaller heads, involucral bracts not reflexed and with well-developed horn-like appendages. Turkestan.—One of the plants yielding rubber.

7. **LACTUCA,** L. Tall ann. and per. herbs, mostly of the northern hemisphere, about 100 species, many weedy, one widely cult. as a garden vegetable.—Lvs. alternate, variable, often pinnatifid: heads small, in long irregular panicles, the rays white, yellow, pink or blue; involucre cylindric, with several series of imbricated bracts of which the outermost are short; receptacle flat and naked; rays few or many, truncate but 5-toothed at the apex: achenes oval to linear, flat, plainly 3–5-ribbed on either side, the soft thin white or brown pappus elevated on a long or short beak. (Lactu-ca: from *lac,* Latin for milk, in allusion to the milky juice.)

L. sativa, L. Lettuce. Ann. erect smooth herb grown for its crisp edible highly developed radical lvs. which appear before the fl.-stalk; sts. 3–4 ft., leafy, branching above: radical lvs. 5–10 in. long, thin, nearly orbicular, oblong, obovate or lingulate, plane, bullate or curled; st.-lvs. auriculate-clasping, apiculate-serrate: fl.-heads erect, 12–16-fld., with yellow rays, open in forenoon: achenes ("seeds") lenticular-oblong, broadest toward apex, straw-colored or black. Cultigen.—The plant known as Celtuce belongs here; the sts. are edible until the fl.-buds appear, and the young lvs. may be used for salad. Var. **asparagina,** Bailey (*L. angustana,* Vilm. not All. *L. sativa* var. *angustana,* Irish), Asparagus Lettuce, grown for its thick edible st., not forming a head; lower lvs. narrow-lanceolate and long-attenuate, 8–12 in. long. Var. **capitata,** L., Head Lettuce, rosette very dense and cabbage-like. Var. **crispa,** L., Curled Lettuce, loose rosette of cut, fringed or crisped lvs. Var. **longifolia,** Lam. (*L. romana,* Gars.), Cos and Romaine Lettuce, head upright and narrow or columnar, its lvs. obovate to oblong, obtuse, 8–12 in. long, midrib very broad.

8. **HIERACIUM,** L. Hawkweed. More than 700 species mostly native to Eu. and S. Amer., variable, a few sometimes grown for ornament.—Per. herbs, often hirsute, with commonly leafy sts. and rosulate tuft of basal lvs.: lvs. often toothed but never deeply lobed: heads variously panicled or rarely solitary; receptacle flat, usually naked; fls. all ligulate, rays truncate and 5-toothed at apex; involucre of 1–3 series of unequal bracts: achenes oblong or columnar, crowned with stiff usually brownish pappus-bristles. (Hiera-cium: Greek *hawk;* it is said that the ancients thought that hawks sharpened their eyesight by using the sap of these plants.)

A. Heads ½–1 in. across: lvs. mostly basal, obtuse and often apiculate. . . . . 1. *H. aurantiacum*
AA. Heads 1½–2 in. across: lvs. cauline as well as basal, acute . . . . 2. *H. villosum*

1. **H. aurantiacum,** L. Orange Hawkweed. Devils-Paintbrush. Somewhat stoloniferous from tufted rootstocks, hirsute with long spreading hairs, the involucre dark with

black glandular hairs: lvs. mostly in a basal tuft, oblong to spatulate-oblong, 2–6 in. long, obtuse, often apiculate; st.-lvs. few, becoming bract-like: heads ½–1 in. across, in a naked cymose cluster at the tip of a long simple peduncle; fls. deep orange to flame color. Eu.; now extensively intro. as a bad weed in grass lands in some parts of the country, and probably no longer cult.

2. **H. villosum,** L. Shaggy Hawkweed. Leafy-stemmed per., silky-villous throughout: lvs. acute, the basal oblanceolate, 2–4 in. long, the cauline ovate, sessile or clasping: heads 1½–2 in. across, often solitary at the end of the st.; involucre without black glandular hairs; fls. bright golden. Eu.

9. **CREPIS,** L. About 200 species, mostly natives of the northern hemisphere, one a showy fl.-garden subject.—Ann., bien. or per. herbs with mostly runcinate-pinnatifid or -toothed lvs.: heads solitary or paniculate, on long peduncles; fls. all ligulate, yellow, orange or red; involucre of 2 or more series of unequal bracts; rays truncate and 5-toothed at apex: achenes columnar to fusiform crowned with soft white pappus. (Cre-pis: Greek for *sandal;* application obscure.)

C. rubra, L. Branching ann. ½–1½ ft. high, with leafy sts. many from the base: lvs. runcinately toothed or lobed, glabrous or nearly so, the basal tapering to a narrow winged petiole, the cauline sessile: heads solitary on long peduncles; involucre hispid; fls. red varying to flesh-colored or whitish, summer. Italy, Greece.

10. **GERBERA,** Cass. (*Perdicium,* L.). Per. herbs of S. Afr. and Asia, about 32 species, one planted for ornament.—Lvs. in a basal tuft, petiolate, entire or lobed: peduncles naked or with a few small bracts, bearing solitary heads of yellow, pink or orange fls.; rays conspicuous, in 1 or 2 rows, those of the inner row, when present, very short and sometimes tubular and 2-lipped as are the disk-fls.: achenes beaked; pappus of bristles in 2 or more series. (Ger-bera: named in honor of Traug. Gerber, a German naturalist who travelled in Russia.)—Originally spelled Gerberia, but the spelling Gerbera conserved.

G. Jamesonii, Bolus. Transvaal Daisy. Barberton Daisy. To 1½ ft., hairy throughout, the mature lvs. very woolly beneath: lvs. numerous, the petiole 6–8 in. long, the blade 5–10 in. long, pinnately lobed or parted: heads to 4 in. across, with showy orange-flame-colored strap-shaped rays, May. (Named after Jameson, one of the discoverers of the species.) Transvaal.—Improved and garden forms have fls. white, pink, orange, salmon, violet.

11. **CHRYSANTHEMUM,** L. (incl. *Pyrethrum,* Haller. *Leucanthemum,* Mill. *Balsamita,* Desf.). Ann. and per. herbs, sometimes more or less woody at base, mostly native in the Old World, probably 160 species, yielding major ornamental subjects to hort.—Plants mostly of erect growth and the greater number much-branched, glabrous, pubescent or rarely viscid, often strong-scented, bearing usually many fl.-heads in white, pink, red, purple, yellow and intermediate colors: lvs. alternate, very various, from practically entire to lobed and multifid: heads terminating long peduncles or in corymbose clusters, many-fld., typically radiate; disk-fls. bisexual and usually fertile; ray-fls. pistillate and also mostly fertile, the rays entire or toothed; receptacle flat or convex, naked; bracts of involucre usually in several series, imbricated and appressed, the margins commonly scarious: achenes of disk- and ray-fls. much alike or those of the rays more 3-angled, all of them usually more or less striate, angled or ribbed; pappus a scale-like cup or border, or wanting. (Chrysan-themum: Greek compound *golden flower.*)—The genus is variously understood and defined, and it has been divided into genera by different authors.

A. Herbage with pronounced sweet fragrance: lvs. not lobed, serrate: heads clustered, on short peduncles, small and usually rayless, the disk mostly not exceeding about ¼in. across . . . . 1. *C. Balsamita*
AA. Herbage not sweet-smelling, often with strong pungent odor: lvs. various: rays prominent even if small.
B. The annuals, grown from seeds each year, being common summer or fl.-garden chrysanthemums.
C. Rays of fl.-head clear white: plant small . . . . 2. *C. Nivellei*
CC. Rays yellow or yellow-tinged, or ringed with yellow or red: plant robust.
D. Achene ("seed") flat, winged: outer involucral bracts keeled . . . . 3. *C. carinatum*
DD. Achene angled and prismatic, not winged: bracts usually not keeled.

E. Lvs. linear-lobed and incised, the main lower part narrowed almost to a petiole-like base: achene strongly angled but without prominent intermediate ribs .... 4. *C. coronarium*

EE. Lvs. not reduced to linear lobes, the main part usually about ¼ in. broad: achene with many deep ribs .... 5. *C. segetum*

BB. The perennials, ordinarily living over winter, commonly propagated by cuttings and division, of various sizes and habits, one of them (the usual florists' chrysanthemum) usually bloomed in autumn under glass or other protection.

C. Plants commonly known as pyrethrum or feverfew, with finely divided fern-like foliage.

D. Sts. terminated by 1 large head, colors various in white, pink, crimson, red, but not true yellow: achenes similar in both ray- and disk-fls. ... 6. *C. coccineum*

DD. Sts. branched: heads small, the disk mostly less than ½in. across, aggregated in more or less definite clusters at top of plant, sometimes in close corymbs.

E. Lf.-blades short, not exceeding 3 in. (except perhaps some of the radical lvs.), the main side lobes 2 or 3 pairs .... 7. *C. Parthenium*

EE. Lf.-blades much longer, the main side lobes 4 or more pairs and deep.

F. Rays showy, more than ¼ in. long: lvs. finely cut and pyrethrum-like, divided to midrib .... 8. *C. corymbosum*

FF. Rays very small: lvs. pinnatifid, main divisions ½in. broad ... 9. *C. macrophyllum*

CC. Plants known to cultivators as chrysanthemums, marguerites, Paris daisies, including outdoor subjects and the florists' cut-fl. chrysanthemums.

D. Radical and lower cauline lvs. about as broad as long, more or less palmate in dentation or lobing from the apex rather than from the sides: plant small, glabrous and green: heads not clustered, white tinged rose .... 10. *C. arcticum*

DD. Radical and cauline lvs. much longer than broad or else deeply lobed and divided.

E. Texture of cauline lf.-blade thick and succulent, shape oblanceolate and obtuse, lightly toothed toward apex .... 11. *C. nipponicum*

EE. Texture of cauline lf.-blade not manifestly thick or succulent, dentation or lobing lateral, blade or main lobes ordinarily not obtuse.

F. Blade of cauline lvs. dentate or simply lobed, not divided or multiplied as if compound.

G. Apex of cauline lvs. long-acute, the deep teeth sharp and pointed forward: plant much-branched .... 12. *C. uliginosum*

GG. Apex of cauline lvs. obtuse or only indifferently acute, not deeply toothed: plant little branched or simple.

H. Fl.-heads small, 1½ in. and often much less across: lvs. narrow, remotely (separately) toothed or notched .... 13. *C. Leucanthemum*

HH. Fl.-heads large and showy, 2 in. and more across, often doubled: lvs. sometimes as much as 1½ in. broad, shallowly and closely toothed.

I. Branched toward top so that the st. has 3 or more heads, plant tall: st.-lvs. not much narrowed to base, broadly clasping .... 14. *C. lacustre*

II. Branched at base or below middle, or not at all, so that the sts. appear to be single-headed, plant low: st.-lvs. usually tapered to long base .... 15. *C. maximum*

FF. Blade of cauline and basal lvs. much cut and divided into narrow lobes and segms., as if compound.

G. Leafage at base of plant, the short low sts. naked or bearing only small bracts: fl.-head solitary .... 16. *C. alpinum*

GG. Leafage borne along the tall sts. as well as at base: fl.-heads usually several to a st. or plant.

H. Herbage manifestly glaucous, or with a "bloom."

I. Lf.-divisions linear, strongly ascending .... 17. *C. anethifolium*

II. Lf.-divisions short, in several lateral pairs, spreading ..... 18. *C. cinerariæfolium*

HH. Herbage green (in no. 19 sometimes lightly bluish, as if hybrids).

I. Foliage glabrous, or at least not gray-pubescent or tomentose.

J. Lobes and teeth of lvs. many, projected forward, commonly very acute at apex: involucral scales broadly hyaline-margined: plant woody at base .... 19. *C. frutescens*

JJ. Lobes and teeth of lvs. relatively few, mostly divaricate and not markedly acute: involucral scales not very broad-margined: plant hardly woody at base.

K. Ultimate lf.-segms. very narrow, ⅛in. or less broad.

L. Segms. linear, strongly ascending .... 20. *C. Mawii*

LL. Segms. broader and mostly very obtuse, divaricate. 21. *C. Zawadskii*

KK. Ultimate segms. ⅓–½in. broad.

L. Length of lf.-blade ordinarily 3–5 or 6 in., lower blades with more or less acute outline, width of primary lobes often more than ½in. and apex not distinctly rounded but subacute: heads usually about 3 in. across .... 22. *C. rubellum*

LL. Length of lf.-blade usually 3 in. or less, apex rounded, lobes ½in. or less broad and teeth mostly obtuse: heads usually about 2 in. across .23. *C. sibiricum*

II. Foliage and sts. gray-pubescent or tomentose, with strong odor: lvs. heavy, of the ovate type, lobed one-third to two-thirds to the midrib.

J. Rays yellow: heads many, clustered, disk usually not exceeding ½in. across: lvs. parted, the teeth very sharp or mucronate: undeveloped plants ....24. *C. indicum*

JJ. Rays of many colors, sometimes much modified, and heads usually large: lvs. lobed but usually not deeply, teeth bluntish or short-acute: highly developed hort. plants, source of common cut-fl. chrysanthemums ....25. *C. morifolium*

1. **C. Balsamita,** L. COSTMARY. MINT-GERANIUM. Persistent per., kept in old yards for the sweet odor of its foliage, sometimes erroneously called "lavender"; sts. stiff, 2–4 ft., finely pubescent, much-branched along the sides, bearing many little heads on very short peduncles: lvs. oblong or oval, 2–6 in. long or the radical ones longer, obtuse, finely and obtusely serrate, often with a pair of small narrow lobes at base: heads about ½in. broad, usually yellowish with a few white rays; involucral bracts oblong, narrow, hyaline, obtuse: pappus a small crown. (Balsamita: an old substantive, from the balsamic odor.) W. Asia; more or less escaped in N. Amer. Var. **tanacetoides,** Hayek (*Balsamita major*, Desf. *C. major*, Auth.), heads rayless and usually smaller, about ¼–⅓in. across.

2. **C. Nivellei,** Br.-Blanq. & Maire. Ann.; sts. erect, about 1 ft. tall, simple, very leafy: lvs. thickish, light green or purplish, sparsely hairy to nearly tomentose, obovate, pinnately parted, blade 1½ in. or less long, lobes cut-toothed with acute or mucronate teeth: fl.-heads solitary, 1 in. or more across, involucre whitish-hairy, rays white and retuse or dentate at apex. (Named for its collector, Commander Nivelle.) Mts., Morocco.

3. **C. carinatum,** L. (*C. tricolor*, Andr.). TRICOLOR CHRYSANTHEMUM. Glabrous simple or moderately forked ann., 2–3 ft.: lvs. somewhat succulent, remotely 2-pinnatifid into linear lobes that are obtuse or nearly so, little or not at all auricled on the st.: heads solitary and mostly long-peduncled, 1½–2½ in. across, the rays differently colored at base so as to make a ring in the fl.-head, the disk purple, giving the heads a tricolor effect; the rays are white with ring yellow, or red with yellow ring, or brownish-purple with yellow ring, or pink with purple ring, and other combinations as also double fls.; involucral bracts broad and hyaline-margined, the outer ones keeled: achenes flat, winged or margined on either edge, not ribbed. Morocco.—Several garden races are in cult., known as *C. Burridgeanum* and otherwise.

4. **C. coronarium,** L. GARLAND CHRYSANTHEMUM. CROWN DAISY. Often taller than no. 3, stiff: lvs. not succulent, with broader and sharper-toothed divisions more closely placed, the main rachis about ⅛in. broad, manifestly auricled on st.: heads usually smaller and more likely to be full double and globular, yellow or yellowish-white; involucral bracts not keeled: achenes somewhat prismatic, strongly angled but not winged, with minor ribs between. Medit. region.—**C. spatiosum,** Bailey (var. *spatiosum*, Bailey), is a robust very leafy plant with lvs. much less divided and more simply pinnatifid, cult. in China for the young edible lvs.; to be looked for among Chinese.

5. **C. segetum,** L. CORN CHRYSANTHEMUM or CORN-MARIGOLD. Rather sparsely foliaged ann., 1–1½ ft., much-branched: lvs. notched, or when pinnatifid not deeply so, the main part ¼in. or more broad, the lobes broad-linear and more or less obtuse, base usually clasping, lowest ones narrowed to a petiole-like part: involucral bracts broad and obtuse, hyaline-margined: heads mostly long-peduncled, 1–2 in. across, golden-yellow, varying to white: achenes prismatic but not sharply angled, the ribs all prominent. A grain and field weed in Eu., N. Afr. and W. Asia, and adventive in N. Amer.—Known also as a fl.-garden ann.

6. **C. coccineum,** Willd. (*C. roseum*, Adam. *Pyrethrum roseum*, Bieb. *P. hybridum* and *P. carneum*, Hort.). COMMON PYRETHRUM. Popular per. producing a clump of finely cut very green foliage and sending up simple or sparingly forked nearly or quite glabrous sts. usually 16–30 in. tall, bearing bright heads in late spring and summer: lvs. thin, long and narrow, the lower ones 5–15 in. long with the long petiole and 3 or 4 in. broad, pinnate and the pinnæ pinnatifid and segms. cut, upper st.-lvs. simply pinnatifid and sessile: heads solitary, large, 1½–3 in. across, the long rays white, pink, lilac, crimson, dark red (as *Pyrethrum atrosanguineum*), but not true yellow, sometimes full and double, sometimes with developed tubular fls. on the disk producing anemone forms; involucral bracts rather narrow, brown-margined. S. W. Asia.—A good florists' and cut-fl. plant.

7. **C. Parthenium,** Pers. (*Matricaria Parthenium*, L. *M. parthenoides, capensis, eximia*, Hort. *Pyrethrum Parthenium*, Smith). FEVERFEW. Bushy much-branched per., leafy, nearly glabrous, strong-scented, 1–3 ft., some of the forms very dwarf and compact and sometimes curl-lvd. and yellow-foliaged (GOLDEN FEATHER, var. **aureum,** Hort.), suitable for edgings: lvs. broad-ovate to oblong-ovate in outline, blades usually not exceeding 3 in. long and often much less on the st., the lower ones pinnate and then pinnatisect, the upper ones deeply pinnately parted, segms. only 2 or 3 pairs, ¼in. or so broad and variously

toothed, obtuse or nearly so: heads many and aggregated, ⅜–¾in. across, disk yellow and rays white; in some forms the heads are discoid and in others double (all fls. rayed); involucre mostly lightly pubescent, outer bracts green-centered. (Parthenium: ancient name suggesting reputed medicinal merits.) Eu. to Caucasus; more or less spontaneous in U. S.—An old garden favorite.

8. **C. corymbosum,** L. (*Pyrethrum corymbosum*, Scop. *Matricaria corymbosa*, Desr.). Stout per. 1–4 ft., much-branched toward top, nearly or quite glabrous: lvs. tansy-like, 4–6 in. long, 2-pinnatisect into linear acute and sharp-toothed lobes, lower ones petiolate, the segms. 4 or more pairs: heads many and small in a flat-topped cluster, about ¾in. across including the rays, slender-peduncled the showy rays white; bracts oblong, green-centered and brown-margined. Medit. region.

9. **C. macrophyllum,** Waldst. & Kit. (*Pyrethrum macrophyllum*, Willd.). Tansy Chrysanthemum. Stout per., with erect puberulent angled sts. to 3 ft.: lvs. large, nearly or quite sessile, divided well toward midrib into 4 or more pairs of long toothed segms. ½in. or so broad: heads many in close yarrow-like clusters, ¼in. or less across the disk, the white or yellowish little rays not equalling the disk; involucral bracts of nearly equal length, keeled, hirsute. Hungary.

10. **C. arcticum,** L. (*Leucanthemum arcticum*, DC.). Autumn-blooming per., forming a clump, pubescent at least above, the sts. simple or branched near base, 6–12 or sometimes 18 in.: lvs. spatulate in outline, 1–3 in. long, long-narrowed to base, primarily 3-lobed or -cleft with secondary lobing, the uppermost becoming linear bracts: heads solitary, 1–2 in. across, white tinged rose or lilac, numerous and attractive; involucre with tomentum that covers the top of the peduncle, bracts brown-margined and green-centered. High north and arctic regions, western and eastern hemispheres.

11. **C. nipponicum,** Matsum. (*Leucanthemum nipponicum*, Franch.). Nippon Daisy. Subshrub, the foliage soon falling from the lower part of the woody sts. which are 1½–2 ft. tall, stiff, angled, nearly or quite glabrous: lvs. crowded on upper part of st., thick and stiffish, 2–3½ in. long, spatulate and obtuse, bluntly serrate-dentate toward apex: heads single, terminating the sts., white-rayed and 2–3½ in. across; involucral bracts obtuse, scarious-margined. Japan.—Blooms very late.

12. **C. uliginosum,** Pers. High Daisy. Very tall handsome per., 4–7 ft., much-branched and finely pubescent above, with aspect of a big aster: lvs. long-lanceolate, 3–4 in. long at middle of st., very sharp-pointed and sharply upward-toothed, st.-lvs. mainly sessile: heads many, on rather short leafy peduncle or sts. in autumn, 1½–3 in. across, the narrow obtuse rays white; involucral bracts long-oblong, hyaline-tipped and green-centered. Eu.

13. **C. Leucanthemum,** L. Ox-eye Daisy. Whiteweed. Weedy per., nearly or quite glabrous; sts. 1–3 ft., simple or sparingly branched, bearing terminal heads 1–2 in. across with white rays: lvs. largely basal and radical, the blades mostly 1–2 in. long and spatulate or obovate with rounded end, strongly toothed or toward base incised-pinnatifid, the st.-lvs. incised-toothed, sessile and clasping. (Leucanthemum: ante-Linnæan name meaning *white flower*.) A common weed eastward, nat. from Eu. and Asia.—Probably not regularly cult., although perhaps appearing in gardens; stock sometimes known under this name is likely to be *C. maximum.*

14. **C. lacustre,** Brot. (*C. latifolium*, DC.). Portuguese Daisy. A taller plant than *C. maximum*, 3–6 ft., branched toward top so that the fl.-sts. are relatively shorter: lvs. mostly broader and less narrowed at base: pappus of ray-fls. 2–3-eared. Portugal.

15. **C. maximum,** Ramond. Max Daisy. Short-lived per., sometimes treated as a bien.; sts. 12–30 in., erect, simple or sparingly long-forked, somewhat pubescent becoming glabrous: lvs. long-oblanceolate, the radical ones often 1 ft. long, upper successively shorter and becoming lanceolate, coarsely and bluntly toothed, obtuse at end, the st.-lvs. usually 1 in. or less broad: heads appearing in summer and autumn, terminating the long sts., 2–3 in. across, with broad and obtuse white rays; involucral bracts broad-oblong, obtuse, hyaline-margined, more or less brown- or green-centered: pappus none. Pyrenees.—Now known in several large-headed forms, 4 in. or more across, including the Shasta Daisy; some of the forms have serrate, fringed or drooping rays. Here belong the hort. forms known as *C. Robinsonii*, King Edward VII, Glory of the Wayside, Chrysanthemum Daisy.

16. **C. alpinum,** L. Rock-garden per. 2–6 in. tall, sometimes a little more, with dissected foliage clustered at the base: lvs. green, mostly not much if any exceeding 1½ in. long (a tomentose var.), in a cluster or rosette, divided nearly or quite to the base into very narrow small acute segms.: heads white, terminating a st. that much exceeds the basal tuft of lvs., 1½ in. or less across, fragrant, the rays many and entire or only obscurely dentate at apex, white. High Alps.

17. **C. anethifolium,** Brouss. Differs from *C. frutescens* in the glaucous finer foliage: lvs. shorter-petioled, the segms. narrow-linear and usually more deeply cut as well as more separated or distant: fls. white but recorded as sometimes lemon-yellow. Canaries.—Now seldom seen in cult.

18. **C. cinerariæfolium,** Vis. Dalmatian Pyrethrum. Slender glaucous grayish-pubescent per. interesting as a source of insect powder and sometimes cult. for ornament;

sts. 12–30 in. tall, simple, overtopping the fine foliage: lvs. 6–12 in. long, including petiole, oblong or oval in outline, pinnate and then pinnatifid into linear acute segms.: heads about 1½ in. across, on long slender peduncles or sts., solitary, the oblanceolate obtuse veined rays white and showy; involucral bracts oblong, very obtuse, hyaline-tipped and darker-centered, pubescent. Dalmatia.

19. **C. frutescens,** L. Marguerite or Paris Daisy. Much-branched bush, woody at base, glabrous, 2–3 ft., producing heads freely on slender peduncles well above the foliage: lvs. thickish, oblong to ovate in outline, 2–4 in. long, petioled, 2-pinnatifid, the segms. all very sharp: heads solitary, 1½–2 in. across, with long narrow white or sometimes lemon-yellow rays; involucral bracts very broad and widely hyaline-margined. Canaries.—Apparently not all the stock passing as Marguerite is of this species.

20. **C. Mawii,** Hook. f. Erect slender per. to 18 in. or less, the finely cut foliage sparsely bearing lax hairs: lvs. about 1 in. long or more, narrowly pinnatifid to base into 3 almost or quite linear lobes, most of them again divided into acute linear lobelets: heads solitary on long naked upper part of sts., about 1½ in. across, the peduncle slightly thickened at its top, rays white with rose-color on back, linear-oblong and more or less toothed at apex: achenes of ray and disk similar, cylindric-oblong and prominently ribbed. (Grown in the garden of Mr. Maw, Broseley, England.) Mts., Morocco.

21. **C. Zawadskii,** Herbich (*C. sibiricum,* Turcz.). Smaller and more slender plant than *C. rubellum* with which it has been confused, and apparently not so much grown with us: about 1½ ft. tall, with spare simple branching or fls. single and terminal: lvs. green and glabrous, thin in texture, 1½ in. or less long, 5-parted nearly to rib into very narrow or linear segms. which are again toothed or lobed, the lobelets either obtuse or acute, uppermost lvs. slightly hairy: heads small, 2 in. or less across, pink, rays ¾in. or less long. (Alexander Zawadski, 1798–1868, writer of botanical, zoological and geological works.) Galacia in Cent. Eu., Siberia.

22. **C. rubellum,** Sealy (*C. erubescens,* Hort. *Chrysoboltonia pulcherrima,* Hort.). Per. 2–3 ft. tall, more or less branched, making a compact very floriferous leafy clump, with green foliage lightly pubescent underneath: lvs. 3–5 in. long, pinnately about 5-parted nearly three-fourths to the midrib, segms. well separated and coarsely toothed or lobed, the lobes subacute and often ½in. or more broad: heads many, single or few to a st. but not closely clustered, 2½–3¼ in. across, pink or rose-red, rays narrow and well separated, not notched, about 1 in. or less long: achenes thin-margined, ridged in center. Nativity not determined.—It has been grown erroneously as *C. Zawadskii.* Satisfactory hardy plant, one of the forms being known as Clara Curtis, deep pink. The *C. erubescens* of Stapf is probably not in cult. outside botanic gardens; its lvs. are relatively broader and more rounded, cut only half way or less to midrib, mostly 2 in. or less long; heads about 1 in. across, rays pink; plant about 1 ft. tall; Chinese; this plant is apparently *C. naktongense,* Nakai, of Japan.

23. **C. sibiricum,** Forbes & Hemsl. (*C. Zawadskii* var. *sibiricum,* Sealy. *C. coreanum,* Hort.). Upstanding glabrous or only slightly pubescent plant 2–3 ft. tall with abundant green foliage: lvs. 2–3 in. long, main ones with rounded or obtuse outline, irregularly pinnately divided two-thirds or more to the midrib into segms. ¼–½in. wide broadening to apex, shallowly dentate into obtuse or indifferently acute or obtuse teeth: heads single terminating the sts. and frequently on short lateral erect branches, 2–2½ in. across, rays white with faint tinge of rose or fading to rose, late-blooming. Siberia.

24. **C. indicum,** L. (*C. japonicum,* Thunb.). Per. with branching slender more or less lopping sts. 2–3 ft. long, herbage gray-pubescent: lvs. thin, ovate in outline, most of those on the sts. not exceeding 3 in. long, parted nearly to midrib, the small teeth acute or mucronate: heads many in small clusters, on short peduncles, the disk usually not exceeding ½in. across and often much less, the yellow rays not equalling the disk; outer involucral bracts broadly scarious, the midnerve being green and herbaceous. China, Japan.—Hardy undeveloped border plant, little known in cult.

25. **C. morifolium,** Ramat. (*C. sinense,* Sabine. *C. hortorum,* Bailey). Florists Chrysanthemum. Stout branching per., erect or spreading, 2–5 ft., herbage gray-pubescent or tomentose: lvs. large, usually thick and heavy, lobed one-third to one-half depth of the blade, teeth short-acute or nearly blunt: heads naturally somewhat clustered, on peduncles 2–3 or more in. long, large, rays usually much exceeding disk; outer involucral scales herbaceous, with only narrow scarious margins. Cultigen, from E. Asian sources.—There is speculation on origin in hybridization with other species and subsequent selection by cultivators. Perhaps it is derivable from *C. indicum.* Known in many cult. races, some of them grown in the permanent border, others raised by florists for autumn and early winter bloom under glass; heads vary from 1 in. across in the pompons to 1 ft. in the great-fid. kinds; colors yellow, pink, lilac, shades of red, white; the fls. are sometimes quilled, and many developed forms are known. This is "the chrysanthemum" of commerce.

12. **MATRICARIA,** L. (incl. *Chamomilla,* Gilib.). Matricary. About 50 species, natives of S. Afr., the Medit. region, and the Orient, some grown as ornamentals.—Ann., bien. or per. herbs, often strongly scented: lvs. 1–3 times finely dissected:

heads peduncled, the disk-fls. yellow, those of the ray white or sometimes wanting; involucral bracts in few series; receptacle conical or ovoid, naked: achenes 3–5-ribbed on the face or sides, rounded on the back. (Matrica-ria: *mater*, mother, from its medicinal use.)

A. Plant a mat-forming per. with creeping sts., spring-blooming. . . . . 1. *M. Tchihatchewii*
AA. Plant an ann. with erect sts., summer and autumn-blooming.
B. Ray-fls. ½–¾in. long, spreading: achenes with 2–3 conspicuous ribs with oil glands at top. . . . . 2. *M. inodora*
BB. Ray-fls. about ¼in. long, becoming reflexed: achenes with 3–5 faint ribs, without oil glands . . . . 3. *M. Chamomilla*

1. **M. Tchihatchewii**, Voss (*Chamæmelum Tchihatchewii*, Boiss. *Chrysanthemum* and *Pyrethrum Tchihatchewii*, Hort.). TURFING DAISY. Mat-forming glabrous per. with creeping rooting sts., nearly scentless: lvs. 1–2-pinnate into small segms.: heads solitary at ends of naked sts. 6–12 in. high, about 1 in. across, rays white: achenes conspicuously 2–3-ribbed; pappus short, white. (Named for P. A. Tchihatchew, 1808–1890, Russian collector in Asia Minor.) Asia Minor.

2. **M. inodora**, L. (*Chrysanthemum inodorum*, L.). SCENTLESS FALSE CHAMOMILE. Diffuse branching ann., 1–2 ft. high, glabrous or nearly so, little or not at all scented: lvs. many, sessile, 2–3-pinnately divided into short narrowly linear segms.: heads 1½ in. across, on peduncles terminating the branchlets, the 15–25 white rays acute and spreading: achenes inversely pyramidal with 2–3 conspicuous ribs; pappus a minute entire or 4-toothed border. Eu.; somewhat nat. in E. N. Amer. Var. **plenissima**, Hort. (*M. grandiflora*, Hort.), has large very double heads; known as Bridal-Rose.

3. **M. Chamomilla**, L. SWEET FALSE CHAMOMILE. Glabrous erect much-branched ann. to 2 ft. high: lvs. 2–3-pinnately dissected into short very narrowly linear segms.: heads nearly 1 in. across, on short terminal peduncles, with 10–20 truncate or emarginate white rays becoming strongly reflexed; involucral bracts about equal, the edges scarious; receptacle without scales, elongating and becoming hollow as anthesis advances: achenes with 3–5 faint ribs; pappus wanting. (Chamomilla: Greek *earth apple*, because of the small round heads which are said to smell like apples.) Eu., N. Asia; nat. in N. Amer.

13. **ANTHEMIS**, L. Species about 100, native to Eu. and the Medit. region, a few planted for ornament.—Ann., bien. or per. herbs, with strongly scented herbage: lvs. 1–3-pinnately dissected: heads on slender peduncles terminating the branches, many-fld., the disk yellow, the rays white or yellow and (in ours) pistillate; involucral bracts imbricated in several series, with scarious margins; receptacle conical, chaffy: achenes angled or ribbed; pappus a short crown or lacking. (An-themis: Greek name of the chamomile.)

A. Lvs. with ultimate segms. linear-setaceous to filiform . . . . 1. *A. nobilis*
AA. Lvs. with ultimate segms. broader, linear to oblong.
B. Ray-fls. white . . . . 2. *A. montana*
BB. Ray-fls. yellow.
C. Involucral bracts margined with dark brown: pappus a persistent irregularly toothed crown. . . . . 3. *A. Sancti-Johannis*
CC. Involucral bracts not margined with brown: pappus scarcely visible. . . . . . 4. *A. tinctoria*

1. **A. nobilis**, L. (*Ormenis nobilis*, Gray). CHAMOMILE. Half-spreading much-branched per. 6–12 in. high, downy and pleasantly aromatic, cult. for medicinal purposes and as a border plant: lvs. 2-pinnate into linear-setaceous or filiform segms.: heads ¾–1 in. across, rays white; bracts of involucre obtuse, with broad scarious margins: achenes turbinate, obtusely 3-angled; pappus wanting. Eu.; escaped in N. Amer.

2. **A. montana**, L. Per. 4–10 in. high: lvs. 2–3-pinnate into linear or lanceolate segms., pubescent: heads 1–1½ in. across, rays white; bracts of involucre lanceolate, acute or obtuse, with narrow brownish margins: achenes slightly 4-angled; pappus scarcely visible. S. Eu.

3. **A. Sancti-Johannis**, Stoy., Steff. & Turrill. Per. with erect sts. 2½–3 ft. high, soft-pubescent: lvs. 2–3-pinnate into oblong segms. with hard white points: heads 1½–2 in. across, rays deep orange; involucral bracts lanceolate, acute, with dark brown margins: achenes 4-angled and slightly compressed, striate; pappus a persistent irregularly toothed crown. (Named for the patron saint of the Rila Monastery, near where the plant was collected.) Bulgaria.

4. **A. tinctoria**, L. GOLDEN MARGUERITE. Bushy per. 2–3 ft. high, pubescent, with angular erect or ascending sts., used as a border plant and for cut fls.: lvs. pinnately divided, the segms. pinnatifid into ovate or oblong toothed mucronate lobes: heads 1–1½ in. across, golden-yellow; bracts of involucre lanceolate, acute, inner obtuse and with scarious margins: achenes quadrangular, striate; pappus very short. Eu., Asia; somewhat escaped in N. Amer. Var. **Kelwayi**, Hort. (*A. Kelwayi*, Hort.), has more finely cut foliage and deeper yellow fls.

14. **ACHILLEA,** L. Yarrow. About 100 species in the north temp. zone, a few cult. for their ornamental fls. and foliage.—Per. herbs or seldom subshrubs: lvs. mostly 1–3-pinnately parted, sometimes only toothed: heads commonly small and in dense clusters; involucral bracts imbricated, in several series; receptacle chaffy, convex or nearly flat; ray-fls. pistillate, fertile, yellow, white or pink; disk-fls. bisexual, fertile, commonly yellow: achenes strongly compressed, truncate; pappus none. (Achille-a: virtues for healing wounds said to have been utilized by Achilles.)

A. Ray-fls. yellow.
B. Lvs. toothed but not pinnate.................1. *A. Ageratum*
BB. Lvs. 1–2-pinnately parted.
C. Plant 3–5 ft. high, pubescent.................2. *A. filipendulina*
CC. Plant 8–12 in. high, woolly.................3. *A. tomentosa*
AA. Ray-fls. white, pink or reddish.
B. Height of plant 1–3 ft.
C. Lvs. finely dissected: rays 4–5.................4. *A. Millefolium*
CC. Lvs. undivided or coarsely pinnatifid: rays 6–15.
D. Lf. undivided but serrate.................5. *A. Ptarmica*
DD. Lf. pinnatifid.................6. *A. sibirica*
BB. Height of plant 5–12 in.
C. Heads solitary.................7. *A. ageratifolia*
CC. Heads several to many.
D. Lvs. undivided.
E. Involucral bracts hairy; ray-fls. 12–13.................7. *A. ageratifolia* var. *serbica*
EE. Involucral bracts nearly glabrous; ray-fls. 7–9.................8. *A. rupestris*
DD. Lvs. pinnatifid.
E. Plant stoloniferous.................9. *A. nana*
EE. Plant not stoloniferous.
F. Involucral bracts nearly glabrous: lvs. pectinate, the segms. narrow and close together.................10. *A. umbellata*
FF. Involucral bracts tomentose: lvs. with ultimate segms. few and separated.................11. *A. Clavennæ*

1. **A. Ageratum,** L. Sweet Yarrow. Leafy-stemmed branching plant 1–1½ ft. high, glabrous or somewhat pubescent: lvs. fascicled, oblong, 1–2 in. long, obtuse, tapering to a slender petiole or the st.-lvs. sessile, toothed and the teeth serrulate: heads about ⅛in. across, in dense convex-topped clusters; ray-fls. few, yellow. (Ageratum: from the Greek *not growing old;* herbalist and generic name.) S. Eu.

2. **A. filipendulina,** Lam. (*A. Eupatorium,* Bieb.). Fernleaf Yarrow. Stiffly erect, more or less hairy, 4–5 ft. high, the leafy sts. furrowed and glandular-spotted: lvs. 1–2-pinnatifid into linear-lanceolate toothed segms.: heads small, in dense convex compound corymbs which are often 5 in. across; ray-fls. about 5, yellow. Orient.

3. **A. tomentosa,** L. Woolly Yarrow. Plants 8–12 in. high, forming mats, clothed with long wool: lvs. 1–3-pinnatifid into small closely spaced segms.: heads in rather small convex clusters; ray-fls. about 5, yellow. Eu., Orient.

4. **A. Millefolium,** L. Milfoil. Common Yarrow. Sts. simple, leafy, 1–3 ft. high: lvs. sessile, long and narrow, 1–2-pinnately parted into linear toothed segms., pubescent or nearly glabrous: heads about ¼in. across, in flat-topped corymbs; ray-fls. about 5, white. (Millefolium: the lvs. cut into innumerable parts; an herbalist name.) Eu., Asia, Amer. Var. **rosea,** Desf., has pink rays, and var. **rubra,** Hort., dark pink rays.

5. **A. Ptarmica,** L. Sneezewort. Sts. simple or branched above, 1–2 ft. high: lvs. linear-lanceolate, 1–3 in. long, finely toothed, sessile, nearly glabrous: heads ½–¾in. across, in loose corymbs; ray-fls. 6–15, white. (Ptarmica: Greek *sneeze-producing,* in reference to the use of the root for snuff; herbalist name.) North temp. regions.—The most commonly cult. form is The Pearl, in which all the fls. are ligulate; other named kinds are Boule de Neige, Perry White and Globe.

6. **A. sibirica,** Ledeb. Sts. simple or branched, 1–5 ft. high: lvs. pinnatifid into lanceolate or oblong triangular-toothed segms., pubescent or nearly glabrous: heads ⅛–½in. across, in many-fld. corymbs; ray-fls. 6–8, white. N. Asia.

7. **A. ageratifolia,** Boiss. (*Anthemis ageratifolia,* Sibth. & Smith). Tufted, the erect or ascending sts. 4–10 in. high: lvs. linear or linear-lanceolate, nearly entire to pinnatifid, silvery-pubescent: heads solitary, ½–1 in. across; ray-fls. 12–20, white. Balkan region. Var. **Aizoon,** Boiss. (*Ptarmica* and *Anthemis Aizoon,* Griseb.), lvs. entire or slightly toothed, heads solitary. Var. **serbica,** Hayek (*Anthemis serbica,* Nym.), lvs. entire or toothed, heads smaller, in corymbs of 2–5.

8. **A. rupestris,** Huter. Loosely tufted, the ascending or erect sts. 3–8 in. high: lvs. spatulate, mucronate, rarely deeply toothed, somewhat pubescent, densely glandular: heads about ½in. across, in corymbs of 4–8; ray-fls. 7–9, white. S. Italy.

9. **A. nana,** L. Plant stoloniferous, sts. creeping at base, the erect flowering sts. 2–8 in. high: lvs. 1–2-pinnatifid into short acute segms., densely woolly, glandular: heads about ⅓in. across, in dense corymbs; ray-fls. 6–9, white. S. Eu.

10. **A. umbellata,** Sibth. & Smith. Sts. erect, 2–6 in. high: lvs. pectinate-pinnatifid, with many narrow entire or toothed segms. close together, white-tomentose: heads about ½in. across, in dense corymbs; ray-fls. 7–9, white. Greece.

11. **A. Clavennæ,** L. (*A. sericea,* Vis. not Janka). Sts. erect, 4–10 in. high: lvs. pinnatifid into few well-separated entire or toothed segms., white-silky-tomentose: heads ½–¾in. across, in simple or compound corymbs; ray-fls. 5–9, white. (Named for N. Clavena von Belluno, author of an essay on related groups about 1610.) S. Eu. Var. **argentea,** Reichb. (*A. argentea,* Vis.), has densely silvery-silky foliage and simple corymbs.

15. **TANACETUM,** L. Tansy. Odorous ann. or per. herbs, of the northern hemisphere, about 35 species, with 7 native to N. Amer., yielding one old garden plant.—Lvs. alternate, dissected or entire: heads yellow, small to medium-sized, disk-shaped, corymbosely clustered or rarely solitary; involucral bracts in many series; pistillate fls. with 3–5-toothed tubular corollas; receptacle naked: achenes 5-ribbed or 3–5-angular, with broad truncate summit, bearing a coroniform pappus or none. (Tanace-tum: name of doubtful derivation.)

T. vulgare, L. (*Chrysanthemum vulgare,* Bernh.). Common Tansy. Robust erect per., 2–3 ft. high: lvs. pinnately divided into oblong or lanceolate segms. which are sharply serrate or pinnately cut: heads ¼–½in. across, numerous, in a dense flat-topped cyme; ray-corollas inconspicuous, with oblique 3-toothed limb. Eu.; escaped in N. Amer.—Formerly grown for medicinal purposes and for its use as a seasoning.

16. **LONAS,** Adans. One ann. herb native in the Medit. region, planted in the fl.-garden.—Lvs. alternate, pinnatifid into linear entire segms.: heads of disk-fls. only, borne in dense corymbs; involucral bracts imbricated in many series; receptacle chaffy: achenes prominently 5-angled, with toothed coroniform pappus. (Lonas: of uncertain derivation.)

L. annua, Vines & Druce (*Athanasia annua,* L. *L. inodora,* Gaertn.). To 1 ft., branching, glabrous: heads yellow, about ⅜in. across, in corymbs to 2 in. across. Italy, Sicily, N. W. Afr.—Sometimes called African Daisy.

17. **ARTEMISIA,** L. About 200 species, mostly in the northern hemisphere and most abundant in arid regions, several grown for ornament and also for medicinal and aromatic qualities.—Herbs or low shrubs, bitter-aromatic: lvs. alternate, often dissected: heads wholly discoid, small and inconspicuous, numerous, paniculately disposed and generally nodding; fls. yellow or whitish, bisexual, marginal pistillate fls. fertile or lacking; involucre imbricated in several rows; receptacle glabrous or pubescent, not chaffy: achenes without pappus. (Artemis-ia: in mythology, Artemisia, wife of Mausolus.)

A. St.-lvs. entire or somewhat lobed.
  B. Plant green and glabrous .... 1. *A. Dracunculus*
  BB. Plant silvery-pubescent to white-tomentose.
    C. Marginal pistillate fls. lacking: plant a shrub .... 2. *A. tridentata*
    CC. Marginal pistillate fls. present: plant an herb.
      D. Upper st.-lvs. ovate-lanceolate .... 3. *A. Purshiana*
      DD. Upper st.-lvs. linear or nearly so .... 4. *A. albula*
AA. St.-lvs. pinnatisect to 2–3 pinnate, or palmatisect.
  B. Foliage green and glabrous or nearly so.
    C. Lvs. coarsely divided .... 5. *A. lactiflora*
    CC. Lvs. finely dissected.
      D. Plant a subshrub: ultimate lf.-segms. filiform .... 6. *A. Abrotanum*
      DD. Plant an ann.: ultimate lf.-segms. not filiform .... 7. *A. annua*
  BB. Foliage silvery-pubescent, at least beneath.
    C. Lf. palmately divided.
      D. Infl. a simple raceme or corymb.
        E. Heads in loose rather leafy racemes .... 8. *A. laxa*
        EE. Heads in small dense corymbs .... 9. *A. glacialis*
      DD. Infl. of panicled racemes .... 10. *A. frigida*
    CC. Lf. pinnately divided.
      D. Lvs. finely dissected, the ultimate segms. linear.
        E. Involucre white-tomentose: plant gray-pubescent .... 11. *A. pontica*
        EE. Involucre somewhat hairy but not white-tomentose: plant green in var. *viridis* .... 12. *A. sacrorum*
      DD. Lvs. coarsely lobed or divided.
        E. Upper surface of lvs. green and glabrous .... 13. *A. vulgaris*
        EE. Upper surface of lvs. white-pubescent.
          F. Pubescence silky: heads ⅛in. across; receptacle pubescent .... 14. *A. Absinthium*
          FF. Pubescence woolly: heads ¼in. across; receptacle glabrous .... 15. *A. Stelleriana*

1. **A. Dracunculus,** L. TARRAGON. ESTRAGON. Green glabrous per. 2 ft. high, with erect branched sts.: basal lvs. 3-parted at tip; st.-lvs. linear or lanceolate, 1–4 in. long, entire or small-toothed: heads whitish-green, nearly globular, 1/16–1/8 in. across, in a spreading panicle; fls. of two kinds, pistillate and bisexual, the latter sterile; receptacle glabrous. (Dracunculus: *little dragon*, the root coiled serpent-like; an herbalist name.) Eu.—Cult. for its lvs. which are used for seasoning.

2. **A. tridentata,** Nutt. SAGE-BRUSH. Shrub to 12 ft., much-branched, silvery-pubescent: lvs. wedge-shaped, ½–1½ in. long, obtusely 3–7-toothed at apex or upper ones entire: heads numerous, about 1/8 in. across, in dense panicles; fls. all bisexual and fertile; receptacle glabrous. B. C. to Calif. and Neb.

3. **A. Purshiana,** Bess. Per. 1–2 ft. high, sts. and lvs. white-woolly on both sides: lvs. entire or lower coarsely toothed, oblanceolate to ovate-lanceolate, 1–2 in. long: heads white, about 1/8 in. across, in spike-like panicles; receptacle glabrous; bisexual fls. fertile, marginal fls. pistillate. (Named for F. T. Pursh, page 50.) B. C. to Calif. and Neb.

4. **A. albula,** Woot. SILVER KING ARTEMISIA. Per. with slender spreading branches 1–3½ ft. high, sts. and lvs. white-woolly on both sides: lower lvs. ovate or obovate, ½–2 in. long, usually with 3–5 lanceolate lobes; upper lvs. linear or nearly so, entire or toothed: heads about 1/12 in. across, in racemes often forming panicles; receptacle glabrous; bisexual fls. fertile, marginal fls. pistillate. Colo. to Tex. and Mex.

5. **A. lactiflora,** Wall. WHITE MUGWORT. Erect per. to 4 ft., the sts. and main veins of lvs. somewhat hispidulous-roughened, otherwise glabrous: st.-lvs. pinnatifid or pinnately parted into large broad-lanceolate toothed or incised segms., pale beneath: heads white, slightly more than 1/16 in. across, loosely panicled; receptacle glabrous; bisexual fls. fertile, marginal fls. pistillate. China.—Resembling *A. vulgaris*.

6. **A. Abrotanum,** L. SOUTHERNWOOD. OLD MAN. Green subshrub to 5 ft., sts. much-branched and rather strict: lvs. 1½–2½ in. long, 1–3-pinnately divided, the divisions fine-filiform, glabrous or slightly pubescent: heads yellowish-white, 1/6 in. across, in a loose panicle; receptacle glabrous; involucre pubescent; bisexual fls. fertile, marginal fls. pistillate. (Abrotanum: from the Greek *elegant*, in reference to the form of the lvs. and their aromatic odor; herbalist name.) Eu.; somewhat nat. in N. Amer.

7. **A. annua,** L. SWEET WORMWOOD. Sweet-scented glabrous ann. 1–5 ft. high: lvs. 1–2½ in. long, 1–2-pinnately divided into lanceolate-oblong deeply cut segms.: heads yellow, about 1/12 in. across, in loose panicles; receptacle glabrous; involucre glabrous; bisexual fls. fertile, marginal fls. pistillate. Asia; nat. in N. Amer.

8. **A. laxa,** Fritsch (*A. mutellina*, Vill. *Absinthium laxum*, Lam.). Tufted per. with erect or ascending sts. 4–8 in. high, silvery-pubescent: lvs. long-petioled, the blade palmatisect into linear-lanceolate acute entire or toothed segms.: heads yellow, about 1/6 in. across, in loose rather leafy racemes; receptacle pubescent; bisexual fls. fertile, marginal fls. pistillate. Alps.

9. **A. glacialis,** L. Tufted per. with erect or ascending sts. 2–6 in. high, silky-silvery-pubescent: lvs. petioled, 1–3-palmatisect into linear-lanceolate short segms.: heads yellow, about ¼in. across, in small dense corymbs; receptacle pubescent; bisexual fls. fertile, marginal fls. pistillate. Alps.

10. **A. frigida,** Willd. Per. with woody decumbent or ascending sts. 1–1½ ft. high, silky-silvery-pubescent: lvs. ½–1½ in. long, ternately or quinately palmatisect into short linear entire segms., upper lvs. sessile: heads yellow, about 1/6 in. across, in racemes forming narrow leafy panicles; receptacle pubescent; bisexual fls. fertile, marginal fls. pistillate. Alaska to Minn. and Tex., Siberia.

11. **A. pontica,** L. ROMAN WORMWOOD. Erect, shrubby, 1–4 ft. high: lvs. ½–2 in. long, 2-pinnatisect into linear lobes gray-pubescent on both sides, denser beneath: heads whitish-yellow, globular, about 1/8 in. across, nodding, borne in a long open panicle; receptacle glabrous; involucre white-tomentose; bisexual fls. fertile, marginal fls. pistillate. Eu.; escaped in E. N. Amer.

12. **A. sacrorum,** Ledeb. RUSSIAN WORMWOOD. Subshrub to 5 ft., gray-pubescent: lvs. 2–3 in. long, long-petioled, pinnatisect and the segms. again pectinate, the rachis winged: heads 15–20-fld., about 1/8 in. across, nodding, in slender racemes forming large terminal panicles; receptacle glabrous; involucre somewhat hairy; bisexual fls. fertile, marginal fls. pistillate. Russia, Siberia. Var. **viridis,** N. Taylor, SUMMER-FIR, is of pyramidal habit to 10 ft., grown as an ann., with rich green much dissected foliage.

13. **A. vulgaris,** L. MUGWORT. Erect paniculately branched per. 2–4 ft. high, sts. often purplish: lvs. 2–4 in. long, fragrant, white-tomentose beneath, soon green above, 2-pinnately cleft into lanceolate lobes; upper lvs. sometimes linear: heads many, oblong, yellowish, 1/16–1/8 in. across, spicate-paniculate; receptacle glabrous; involucre tomentose; bisexual fls. fertile, marginal fls. pistillate. Eu., Asia; nat. in N. Amer.

14. **A. Absinthium,** L. COMMON WORMWOOD. ABSINTHIUM. Spreading and branchy almost shrubby per. 2–4 ft. high, white-silky: lvs. 2–5 in. long, 2–3-pinnately parted into oblong obtuse lobes: heads 1/8 in. across, numerous, in leafy panicles; receptacle hairy;

bisexual fls. fertile, marginal fls. pistillate. (Absinthium: Latin name of wormwood, associated with its bitter taste; also herbalist name.) Eu.; escaped in N. Amer.

15. **A. Stelleriana,** Bess. BEACH WORMWOOD. OLD WOMAN. DUSTY MILLER. Densely white-tomentose per. 2 ft. high, from a creeping woody base: lvs. 1–4 in. long, pinnatifid, the lobes oblong and obtuse: heads yellow, ¼in. across, many-fld., in a narrow spike-like panicle; receptacle glabrous; bisexual fls. fertile, marginal fls. pistillate. (Bears name of G. W. Steller, 1709–1745, German collector in Russia.) Coasts, N. E. Asia, Que. to N. J.

18. **SANTOLINA,** L. Shrubs or rarely herbs of about 8 species, mostly from the Medit. region, useful as low border or edging plants.—Herbage aromatic; lvs. alternate, pinnately toothed or lobed or finely divided: heads many-fld., of disk-fls. only, yellow or rarely white, solitary on long peduncles; involucre mostly campanulate, the bracts imbricated, appressed; receptacle with chaffy bracts: achenes angled, without pappus. (Santoli-na: derivation of name doubtful.)

A. Plant gray-tomentose....................1. *S. Chamæcyparissus*
AA. Plant green and glabrous....................2. *S. virens*

1. **S. Chamæcyparissus,** L. (*S. incana*, Lam.). LAVENDER-COTTON. Much-branched evergreen subshrub 1½–2 ft. high, silvery-gray and tomentose: lvs. ½–1½ in. long, pinnately divided into minute ovate-oblong segms.: heads yellow, globular, ½–¾in. diam., summer. (Chamæcyparissus: Greek *dwarf* and *cypress*, the lvs. resembling those of the cypress.) Medit. region.

2. **S. virens,** Mill. (*S. viridis*, Willd.). Spreading per. to 15 in., green and glabrous: lvs. 1–2 in. long, narrow-linear, with very short acute teeth: heads yellow, to ⅝in. across. Medit. region.

19. **COTULA,** L. Ann. or per. creeping or tufted herbs, one grown in the rock-garden; 50–60 species of wide distribution in the southern hemisphere.—Lvs. alternate, pinnatifid or rarely entire: heads small, yellow, solitary on long peduncles, of disk-fls. only; involucral bracts in 2 or more series; receptacle without scales: achenes compressed, without pappus. (Cot-ula: Greek for *small cup*.)

C. squalida, Hook. f. (*Leptinella squalida*, Hook. f.). Per., branches creeping 1 ft. or more, soft-hairy: lvs. linear-obovate, 1–2 in. long, deeply pinnatifid into cut segms.: heads unisexual, the pistillate to ⅓in. across, on peduncles 1–3 in. high; involucral bracts purplish, often incurved and concealing the florets. New Zeal.

20. **LAYIA,** Hook. & Arn. Low ann. herbs of about 14 species in W. N. Amer., one cult. for the showy fls.—Simple or branching, stipitate-glandular, flowering in spring or early summer: lvs. chiefly alternate, all entire or some, particularly the lower, pinnately toothed or lobed: heads showy, solitary, on peduncles terminating the sts. or branches; rays 8–20, yellow or white, with 3-toothed ligules; disk-fls. with 5-toothed tubular corolla; receptacle bearing a series of chaffy bracts between the ray- and disk-fls., sometimes additional ones among the disk-fls.: ray-achenes without pappus, inclosed by the involucral bracts; disk-achenes with pappus of bristles or awns. (La-yia: Geo. Tradescant Lay, flourished about 1825–1843, naturalist in Beechey's voyage.)

L. elegans, Torr. & Gray (*Madaroglossa elegans*, Nutt.). Diffuse branching ann. to 2 ft., more or less hirsute-pubescent throughout: lvs. oblong or linear, to 3 in. long, toothed or pinnatifid: heads large and showy, on naked peduncles; involucral bracts very unequal, the longer alternating with the shorter; rays 10–12, ½–¾in. long, yellow or sometimes white-tipped; disk yellow: pappus of stiff bristles and shorter soft interlaced hairs. Calif.

21. **PARTHENIUM,** L. Shrubs or herbs of perhaps a dozen species in Amer., one grown as a source of rubber.—Lvs. alternate: heads small, in corymbs or panicles; ray-fls. few and short, pistillate and fertile, white or yellow; disk-fls. bisexual and sterile, corolla 5-toothed, style undivided; involucre with nearly equal bracts imbricated in 2 or 3 series; receptacle chaffy: achenes flattened, adnate to scales of receptacle, bearing persistent rays on summit; pappus of scales or awns. (Parthenium: ancient name.)

P. argentatum, Gray. GUAYULE. Much-branched shrub to 3 ft.: lvs. lanceolate to ovate-lanceolate, entire or with few lobes, ½–2 in. long, silvery-pubescent on both sides: heads ¼in. across, in long-peduncled cymes. Mex., Tex.

22. **ECHINACEA,** Moench (*Brauneria,* Neck.). PURPLE CONEFLOWER. Five species in N. Amer., more or less grown in the border or wild-garden.—Coarse per. herbs with thick black roots of pungent taste and stout erect sts.: lvs. alternate, simple, the lower long-petioled: heads large, solitary, on long peduncles terminating the sts. and few branches; involucral bracts lanceolate, herbaceous, imbricated in 2 or more series, finally reflexed; disk convex becoming ovoid or conic; bracts of the receptacle persistent, narrowed to a rigid cusp surpassing the disk-fls.; rays rose-purple or rose-color, withering-persistent, sterile: achenes quadrangular; pappus a thick crown, toothed at the angles. (Echina-cea: Greek for *hedgehog,* alluding to the sharp-pointed bracts of the receptacle.)

A. Lvs. ovate to ovate-lanceolate, commonly denticulate or serrate................1. *E. purpurea*
AA. Lvs. broadly lanceolate to nearly linear, entire..............................2. *E. angustifolia*

1. **E. purpurea,** Moench (*Rudbeckia purpurea,* L. *Brauneria purpurea,* Britt.). Stout coarse per. 2–5 ft. high, smooth and glabrous or rough with short hispid hairs: lvs. ovate-lanceolate or the lower broadly ovate, 3–8 in. long, commonly denticulate or serrate, with short winged petiole, or the lower with elongate barely margined petiole: heads solitary on stout terminal naked peduncles; rays purple (rarely almost white), broadish, at first 1 in. long, becoming 3 in. long, 2-toothed at apex, spreading or drooping; disk purplish. Pa. to Ga. and La.

2. **E. angustifolia,** DC. (*Brauneria angustifolia,* Heller). Mostly simple, 1–2 ft. high, sparsely or densely hispid: lvs. lanceolate to nearly linear, 3–8 in. long, entire, all attenuate at base, the lower into slender petioles; heads and fls. nearly of *E. purpurea,* but spreading rays about 1 in. long; fruiting disk often 1 in. high. Sask. to Tex.

23. **RUDBECKIA,** L. CONEFLOWER. Coarse summer-flowering herbs, native in N. Amer., a number cult. for their showy fls.; about 30 species.—Mostly per., sometimes ann. or bien.: lvs. alternate, simple or compound: heads pedunculate, commonly showy, terminating the sts. and branches; involucre often foliaceous, loose; rays yellow, sometimes with brownish base, often becoming reflexed; disk hemispheric to columnar, greenish or yellowish to purplish-black: achenes 4-angled; pappus crown-like, cup-shaped or none. (Rudbeck-ia: in honor of Olof Rudbeck, 1660–1740, Swedish botanist and counsellor of Linnæus.)

A. Base of upper lvs. cordate- or subcordate-clasping..........................1. *R. maxima*
AA. Base of upper lvs. not cordate-clasping.
  B. Disk greenish or yellowish.
    C. Margin of lvs. entire or barely dentate.....................................2. *R. nitida*
    CC. Margin of lvs. (upper st.-lvs.) 3-cleft....................................3. *R. laciniata*
  BB. Disk brown or dark purple.
    C. Lower lvs. deeply 3-cut.
      D. Plant bien.: st.-lvs. subsessile: disk black-purple......................4. *R. triloba*
      DD. Plant per.: st.-lvs. distinctly petiolate: disk dull brownish............5. *R. subtomentosa*
    CC. Lower lvs. not deeply 3-cut.
      D. Style-branches subulate: pappus none: plant densely hispid.
        E. Rays 1–2 in. long: lvs. 2–5 in. long, the lower petioled..............6. *R. serotina*
        EE. Rays ½–1 in. long: lvs. 1–2 in. long, all sessile.......................7. *R. bicolor*
      DD. Style-branches short and obtuse: pappus a short crown: plant pubescent.
        E. Rays ¾–1 in. long: lvs. mostly entire......................................8. *R. fulgida*
        EE. Rays to 1½ in. long: lvs. irregularly serrate...........................9. *R. speciosa*

1. **R. maxima,** Nutt. Glabrous glaucous per. 4–9 ft. high: lvs. broadly ovate to oblong, mostly obtuse, minutely toothed or entire, the larger to 1 ft. long; upper st.-lvs. cordate-clasping: heads solitary or few, long-peduncled; rays yellow, 1–2 in. long, drooping; disk brownish, conic or columnar, 1–2 in. long; style-branches short and obtuse: pappus conspicuous. Mo. to Tex.

2. **R. nitida,** Nutt. Per. with sts. simple or nearly so, 2–4 ft. high, glabrous: lvs. bright green, entire or minutely toothed, the basal and lower cauline ovate-spatulate to lanceolate-oblong, petioled, the upper oblong to lanceolate, mostly acute, sessile, 3–6 in. long: heads solitary or few, long-peduncled; rays several or numerous, pure yellow, drooping; disk finally columnar, 1–2 in. long; style-branches short and obtuse: pappus conspicuous. Ga. to Fla. and Tex.

3. **R. laciniata,** L. Branching per. 2–12 ft. high, smooth and glabrous or more or less roughened with short stiff hairs: lvs. broad, the basal pinnately divided into 5–7 often 2–3-cleft segms.; st.-lvs. 3–5-parted or -cleft, those of the branches few-toothed or entire: heads solitary or few, long-peduncled; involucral bracts loose and irregular, foliaceous; rays yellow, few or several, oblanceolate, 1–1½ in. long, soon drooping; disk greenish-yellow; style-branches short and obtuse: pappus a short crown. Que. to Fla. and Ariz. Var. **hortensia,** Bailey, GOLDEN-GLOW, a full double form common in cult.

4. **R. triloba,** L. BROWN-EYED SUSAN. Bright green glabrous or sparsely short-hispid bien. blooming the first year, 2–5 ft. high: basal lvs. petiolate, the st.-lvs. ovate-lanceolate to broader, with cuneate subsessile base, coarsely serrate, or the upper lanceolate and nearly entire, the lower 3-lobed or -parted: heads short-peduncled; involucral bracts foliaceous, mostly linear, unequal, in 1–2 series, soon reflexed; rays 8–10, ½–1 in. long, deep yellow or with orange or brown-purple base; disk black-purple, ½in. across; style-branches short and obtuse: pappus a minute crown. N. J. to Ga. and La.

5. **R. subtomentosa,** Pursh. SWEET CONEFLOWER. Leafy gray-pubescent per., 2–5 ft. high, branching above: lvs. nearly all petioled, serrate, ovate or 3-lobed and the terminal lobe ovate, 3–5 in. long: involucral bracts foliaceous, soon reflexed; rays numerous, 1–1½ in. long, yellow, sometimes with dark base; disk dull brownish, ½in. broad; style-branches short and obtuse: pappus a short crown. Ill. to Tex.

6. **R. serotina,** Nutt. BLACK-EYED SUSAN. YELLOW DAISY. Rough-hairy bien. or sometimes ann., 1–3 ft. high: lvs. oblong to lanceolate, subentire, 2–5 in. long, the lower with margined petioles: rays golden-yellow or sometimes deeper colored toward base, 1–2 in. long; disk nearly black becoming dull brown; style-branches subulate: pappus none. E. Rocky Mts. to Newf.—Known mostly as *R. hirta* but this Linnæan species differs in broader coarsely toothed lvs., and ranges from W. Mass. to Ga. and Ala.

7. **R. bicolor,** Nutt. Bristly ann. simple or branching, 1–2 ft. high: lvs. lanceolate to oblong or obovate, mostly sessile and nearly entire, 1–2 in. long: rays ½ to barely 1 in. long, wholly yellow or with lower half or base dark-colored; disk black, ¾in. high; style-branches subulate: pappus none. Ark. and Tex. to Ga.—A hort. var., **superba,** ERFURT CONEFLOWER, has heads 2 in. across, rays yellow above, purplish-brown below; it is uncertain whether this var. belongs here or to *R. serotina.*

8. **R. fulgida,** Ait. Hairy per. 1–2 ft. high: lvs. mostly entire, narrowly to oblong-lanceolate, the lowest and basal spatulate-lanceolate, petiolate, 2–4 in. long: foliaceous bracts of involucre often wide, ½–1 in. long; rays 12–14, golden-yellow or with orange base, as long as the bracts; disk black-purple, over ½in. diam.; style-branches short and obtuse: pappus a minute crown. Pa. to Mo., and Tex.

9. **R. speciosa,** Wenderoth (*R. Newmanii,* Loud.). Per. 1–3 ft. high, sparsely hairy, the spreading branches ending in long naked peduncles: basal and lower st.-lvs. oblong or ovate, petiolate, the upper ovate-lanceolate to lanceolate, irregularly serrate, 2–5 in. long: rays 12–20, yellow, often orange at base, at length 1½ in. long; disk brown-purple, ⅔–¾in. high at maturity; style-branches short and obtuse: pappus a short crown. Pa. to Mich., Ark. and Ala.

24. **RATIBIDA,** Raf. (*Lepachys,* Raf.). CONEFLOWER. Per. herbs, of 5 species in N. Amer., sometimes planted.—Lvs. alternate, pinnately divided: heads terminal and solitary on long peduncles; involucre of 2 series, the outer longer and reflexed or spreading; receptacle narrow-columnar, with chaffy pubescent bracts; ray-fls. yellow to purplish, neutral, spreading or reflexed, toothed; disk-fls. bisexual and fertile: achenes flattened, margined or winged; pappus none or of few teeth. (Ratibida: name of uncertain meaning.)

A. Ray-fls. ½–¾in. long..1. *R. columnifera*
AA. Ray-fls. 1–2½ in. long..2. *R. pinnata*

1. **R. columnifera,** Woot. & Standl. (*R. columnaris,* D. Don. *Rudbeckia columnifera,* Nutt. *Lepachys columnaris,* Torr. & Gray. *L. columnifera,* Macb.). Rough-hairy, 1–2½ ft. high: segms. of lf. linear to lanceolate, entire or 3-parted: ray-fls. 3–7, yellow, broad-oval, ½–¾in. long; disk 1–2 in. long. Ill. to Mont. and Mex. Var. **pulcherrima,** Woot. & Standl. (*Obeliscaria pulcherrima,* DC.), has rays partly or wholly brown-purple.

2. **R. pinnata,** Barnhart (*Rudbeckia pinnata,* Vent. *Lepachys pinnata,* Torr. & Gray). Rough-hairy, 3–5 ft. high: segms. of lf. linear to lanceolate, serrate or entire, 3-nerved: ray-fls. 5–10, yellow, oblong-lanceolate, 1–2½ in. long; disk ½–1 in. long. Ont. to Fla. and La.

25. **SILPHIUM,** L. ROSINWEED. Per. herbs of over 30 species in N. Amer., a few planted in the border.—Lvs. alternate or opposite, entire, toothed or pinnate: heads yellow, sunflower-like, in peduncled corymbs or panicles; involucral bracts imbricated in few series; receptacle flat, with chaffy bracts; ray-fls. in 2–3 series, fertile; disk-fls. bisexual but sterile: achenes conspicuously flattened, winged; pappus of awns or none. (Sil-phium: ancient name, referring to the resinous juice.)

A. Lvs. coarsely toothed, the upper connate-perfoliate..1. *S. perfoliatum*
AA. Lvs. pinnatifid, not connate-perfoliate..2. *S. laciniatum*

1. **S. perfoliatum,** L. CUP-PLANT. INDIAN CUP. Sts. square, glabrous, 4–8 ft. high: lvs. opposite, ovate, 6–12 in. long, coarsely toothed, the upper connate-perfoliate, the lower narrowed to margined petioles, rough-pubescent: heads 2–3 in. across. Ont. to Ga. and La.

2. **S. laciniatum,** L. COMPASS-PLANT. Sts. terete, rough-hispid, 6–12 ft. high: basal lvs. 1 ft. or more long, pinnate into lanceolate or linear entire or pinnatifid segms., long-petioled; st.-lvs. alternate, sessile or clasping, smaller and less divided: heads 2–5 in. across. Ohio to Tex.

26. **TITHONIA,** Desf. Tall herbs, woody at base, of about 10 species in Mex. to Cent. Amer., grown as annuals in the N. or out-of-doors in mild climates.—Lvs. mostly alternate, petioled, 3-nerved: heads yellow, sunflower-like, borne on long fistulose peduncles enlarged above; involucral bracts in 2–5 series, nearly equal or graduated; receptacle convex, with stiff striate scales; ray-fls. showy, neutral; disk-fls. bisexual and fertile: achenes slightly flattened or 4-sided; pappus of awns or scales, persistent. (Titho-nia: named for Tithon, consort of Aurora.)

A. Heads 2–3 in. across; involucral bracts acute or acuminate .... 1. *T. rotundifolia*
AA. Heads 2½–6 in. across; involucral bracts rounded .... 2. *T. diversifolia*

1. **T. rotundifolia,** Blake (*Tagetes rotundifolia*, Mill. *Tithonia speciosa*, Hook.). To 6 or 8 ft.: lvs. broad-ovate, 3–10 in. long, acuminate, crenate or the lower 3-lobed, pubescent at least on veins: heads 2–3 in. across; involucre 2 series of nearly equal acute or acuminate bracts. Mex., Cent. Amer.; nat. in W. Indies.

2. **T. diversifolia,** Gray (*Mirasolia diversifolia*, Hemsl.). To 15 ft. or more: lvs. ovate or triangular-ovate, 3–8 in. long, acuminate, usually 3–5-lobed, pubescent, paler beneath: heads 2½–6 in. across; involucre 4 series of graduated broadly rounded bracts or the outer somewhat acute. Mex., Cent. Amer.

27. **HELIANTHUS,** L. SUNFLOWER. Mostly a N. American genus of about 100 species, a number grown as ornamentals and one for its edible tubers.—Rather coarse ann. or per. herbs: lvs. simple, usually opposite below and alternate above: heads solitary or corymbed, on peduncles terminating the sts. and branches: summer and autumn bloomers; involucral bracts in 2 to several series, the outer often leafy at tips; ray-fls. neutral, yellow, usually conspicuous; disk-fls. bisexual and fertile, yellow, brown or purplish; receptacle flat or convex, with chaffy bracts: achenes obovate, slightly flattened; pappus of 2 scale-like awns, deciduous. (Helian-thus: Greek *helios*, the sun, and *anthos*, a flower.)

A. Disk brown or purple.
B. Shape of lvs. linear, entire.
C. Sts. glabrous .... 1. *H. salicifolius*
CC. Sts. hispid .... 2. *H. angustifolius*
BB. Shape of lvs. broad-lanceolate to ovate, toothed.
C. Plant per.: lvs. opposite.
D. Lvs. abruptly contracted into winged petioles: heads about 2 in. across. 3. *H. atrorubens*
DD. Lvs. gradually narrowed into petioles: heads 2½–4 in. across .... 4. *H. rigidus*
CC. Plant ann.: lvs. alternate.
D. Pubescence white-silky .... 5. *H. argophyllus*
DD. Pubescence scabrous-hispid.
E. Involucral bracts ovate or ovate-lanceolate, strongly ciliate .... 6. *H. annuus*
EE. Involucral bracts narrow-lanceolate, scarcely ciliate .... 7. *H cucumerifolius*
AA. Disk yellowish.
B. Lower lvs. cordate-clasping .... 8. *H. mollis*
BB. Lower lvs. petioled or attenuate at base.
C. Lvs. prevailingly lanceolate.
D. Rays pale yellow: lvs. rough above, only slightly so beneath .... 9. *H. giganteus*
DD. Rays deep yellow: lvs. very rough on both sides .... 10. *H. Maximilianii*
CC. Lvs. prevailingly ovate or ovate-lanceolate.
D. Sts. glabrous .... 11. *H. decapetalus*
DD. Sts. rough or hairy.
E. Roots tuberous: lvs. abruptly contracted into winged petioles .... 12. *H. tuberosus*
EE. Roots not tuberous: lvs. gradually narrowed to petioles .... 13. *H. lætiflorus*

1. **H. salicifolius,** A. Dietr. (*H. orgyalis*, DC.). Per. 8–10 ft. high, the strict sts. glabrous, very leafy to the top: lvs. mostly alternate, linear or lanceolate to almost filiform, 8–16 in. long, slightly scabrous, drooping, the lower petiolate: heads numerous, 2 in. across; involucral bracts linear-subulate, acuminate-aristate, slightly ciliate; rays lemon-yellow; disk brown or purplish. Mo. to Colo. and Tex.

2. **H. angustifolius,** L. SWAMP SUNFLOWER. Per. 2–7 ft. high, sts. hispid: lvs. mostly alternate, linear, 2–7 in. long, entire, margins becoming revolute, sessile, slightly scabrous and pubescent: heads few or solitary, 2–3 in. across; involucral bracts linear-lanceolate, acute or acuminate, pubescent; rays bright yellow; disk purple. Swamps, N. Y. to Fla. and Tex.

3. **H. atrorubens,** L. (*H. sparsifolius*, Hort.). DARKEYE SUNFLOWER. Rough-hairy per. 2–5 ft. high, the hispid sts. forking above: lvs. thin, ovate to ovate-lanceolate, 3–10 in.

long, serrate, abruptly contracted into winged petioles, scabrous-hispid, opposite, the few st.-lvs. alternate: heads about 2 in. across, corymbed; involucral bracts oblong, mucronate, slightly ciliate; rays deep yellow; disk dark red. Va. to Fla. and La.

4. **H. rigidus,** Desf. (*Harpalium rigidum*, Cass. *Helianthus scaberrimus*, Ell.). STIFF SUNFLOWER. Per. 1–8 ft. high, sts. strict, sparingly branched, rough or hairy: lvs. opposite, firm, thick, oblong- to ovate-lanceolate, 6–12 in. long, entire or slightly toothed, gradually narrowed into petioles, scabrous on both sides: heads showy, 2½–4 in. across, long-stalked, solitary or few; involucral bracts ovate, obtuse or acute, ciliate; disk purple or brown. Ill. to Ga. and Tex.—Varies under cult. in doubling (multiplication of rays).

5. **H. argophyllus,** Torr. & Gray. SILVERLEAF SUNFLOWER. Ann., the usually solitary sts. 4–6 ft. high, soft gray with dense silky pubescence especially on the upper branches: lvs. alternate, ovate, 4–8 in. long, petioled, slightly toothed, densely pubescent: heads 3 in. or more across; involucre densely silky, the bracts ovate, acuminate; disk brownish-purple. Tex.

6. **H. annuus,** L. COMMON SUNFLOWER. Robust rough-hairy ann. 3–12 ft. high, sts. often mottled: lvs. mostly alternate, long-petioled, ovate, acute or acuminate, 4–12 in. long, serrate, the lower cordate: heads 3–6 in. across in wild specimens, sometimes 14 in. in cult.; involucral bracts ovate or ovate-lanceolate, acuminate-caudate at tip, strongly ciliate; disk brownish-purple. Minn. to Wash. and Calif.—Grown for economic and ornamental purposes. Several hort. forms occur, differing in size of heads, color of rays and in the extent of multiplication of rays in so-called double heads.

7. **H. cucumerifolius,** Torr. & Gray. CUCUMBER-LEAF SUNFLOWER. Ann. with erect mottled sts. 3–6 ft. high, rough above: lvs. alternate, long-petioled, triangular-ovate, 2–4 in. long, acute, serrate, cordate, rough-hairy: heads 2–3 in. across; involucral bracts narrow-lanceolate, acuminate-caudate at tip, scarcely ciliate; disk brownish-purple. Fla. to Tex.—Often included in *H. debilis*, Nutt., but that species is a weaker plant with decumbent not mottled sts. and smaller heads.

8. **H. mollis,** Lam. ASHY SUNFLOWER. Per. 2–5 ft. high, the stout leafy sts. hoary-villous at least when young: lvs. mostly opposite, ovate, 3–5 in. long, cordate and usually clasping, finely toothed, white-pubescent or the upper side scabrous: heads solitary or few, 2–3 in. across; involucral bracts lanceolate, densely pubescent; disk yellowish. Mass. to Ga. and Tex.

9. **H. giganteus,** L. GIANT SUNFLOWER. Stout per. 3–12 ft. high, the rough-hispid sts. branched above: lvs. lanceolate, 3–7 in. long, serrate to nearly entire, rough above and slightly so beneath: heads usually several, somewhat corymbed, mostly long-peduncled, 1½–3 in. broad; involucral bracts linear or linear-lanceolate, acuminate, ciliate; rays pale yellow; disk yellowish. Wet places, Ont. to N. C. and Colo.

10. **H. Maximilianii,** Schrad. Gray-green per. 3–12 ft. high, with several rough sts.: lvs. lanceolate, 3–7 in. long, conduplicate, serrate or entire, very rough on both sides: heads few together, short-peduncled, 2–3 in. across; involucral bracts linear-lanceolate; ray-fls. deep yellow; disk yellow. (Named after Maximilian Alexander Philip, Prince of Neuwied, traveller in Brazil and N. Amer. early in the 19th century in the interests of natural science.) Minn. to Tex.

11. **H. decapetalus,** L. THINLEAF SUNFLOWER. Per. 2–5 ft. high, the glabrous sts. branched above: lvs. thin, ovate to ovate-lanceolate, 3–8 in. long, serrate, with narrowly margined petioles, roughish above, pubescent beneath: heads numerous, 2–3 in. across; involucral bracts linear-lanceolate, ciliate; rays light yellow; disk yellow. Que. to Ga. and Tenn.

12. **H. tuberosus,** L. GIRASOLE. Per. cult. for the tubers produced on the ends and branches of underground sts. or rootstocks as well as midway on the rootstocks; sts. erect, 5–10 ft. high, rough-hispid: lvs. opposite or the upper alternate, long-ovate to ovate-oblong, 4–8 in. long, serrate-dentate, abruptly contracted into winged petioles, rough above, pubescent beneath: heads 2–3½ in. across, few or many, terminating the branches; involucral bracts lanceolate or linear-lanceolate, spreading; ray-fls. light yellow; disk yellow. N. S. to Fla. and Tex.—Cult. under the meaningless name "Jerusalem artichoke." In improved strains the terminal tubers are club-shaped, 4 in. long, 2–3 in. diam. at the end, and weigh 3–4 ozs.; they constitute an excellent and neglected source of food.

13. **H. lætiflorus,** Pers. SHOWY SUNFLOWER. Per. 4–8 ft. high, sts. leafy and rough but shining: lvs. ovate-lanceolate, 4–10 in. long, slightly serrate, gradually narrowed and decurrent on petioles, rough on both sides, shining: heads several, 2–4 in. across, short-peduncled; ray-fls. deep yellow; disk yellow. Ill. to Ga. and Mo.

28. **SPILANTHES,** Jacq. Usually spreading or creeping herbs, about 60 species, widely distributed in warm parts of both hemispheres.—Lvs. opposite, serrate: heads on peduncles terminating the st. and branches; involucral bracts in about 2 series, loosely appressed; receptacle convex or elongated, with chaffy bracts; ray-

fls. pistillate, yellow or whitish or none; disk-fls. yellow, bisexual and fertile: pappus of awns. (Spilan-thes: Greek for *spot-flower*, in reference to the markings on the disk in some species.)

S. oleracea, L. Sparsely pubescent, diffusely branched: lvs. petiolate, blade broadly ovate, 1½–3 in. long, repand-subdentate: heads discoid, solitary, Aug.–Oct.; involucral bracts oblong, equal; disk greenish-yellow, ovoid or conical, becoming nearly 1 in. long. Tropics; cultigen.—Rarely cult. for its pungent flavor in salads, also to a slight extent as an ornamental on account of its odd cylinder-like heads.

29. **BIDENS,** L. BUR-MARIGOLD. STICK-TIGHTS. TICKSEED. Weedy plants, more than 200 species widely distributed but mostly American, little known in cult.—Ann. or per. herbs: lvs. opposite, serrate or incised, or often pinnately or ternately divided: heads solitary or clustered, with or without rays; involucral bracts in 2 series, the outer green and more or less foliaceous, the inner thinner and differing in texture; rays yellow or white, neutral; disk-fls. bisexual and fertile, yellow: achenes flat or angled; pappus of 2–4 stiff bristles or awns, usually retrorsely barbed. (Bidens: Latin *two teeth*, in reference to the pappus awns.)

A. Habit erect: heads in corymbs .... 1. *B. ferulæfolia*
AA. Habit procumbent: heads solitary .... 2. *B. triplinervia* var. *macrantha*

1. **B. ferulæfolia,** DC. (*Coreopsis ferulæfolia*, Jacq.). Ann. or bien. with nearly erect branches 1–3 ft. high, glabrous or slightly pubescent: lvs. bipinnately dissected into small narrow divisions: heads loosely corymbose, slender-peduncled, ¾–1½ in. across; rays and disk bright yellow: achenes linear, flattened; pappus of 2 short awns with a few minute retrorse prickles. S. Ariz. to Guatemala.

2. **B. triplinervia,** HBK., var. **macrantha,** Sherff (*B. humilis*, HBK. *B. humilis* var. *macrantha*, Wedd.). Diffuse per. with procumbent or ascending sts. to 1 ft. long: lvs. irregularly bipinnate into linear divisions: heads solitary on long peduncles, 1–2 in. across; rays and disk yellow: achenes linear, 4-angled; pappus of 2–3 awns with retrorse prickles. S. Mex. to Ecuador.

30. **COSMOS,** Cav. Showy herbs, some cult. for ornament; over 25 species, all trop. American, mostly Mexican.—Late-flowering annuals or perennials, often tall: lvs. opposite, entire or lobed or mostly pinnately cut: heads long-peduncled, solitary or in loose corymbose panicles; involucral bracts in 2 series, connate at base; receptacle flat, chaffy; rays showy, variously colored, neutral; disk-fls. bisexual and fertile: achenes linear, commonly beaked, the beak terminating in 2–4 retrorsely barbed awns. (Cos-mos: from a Greek word with a root idea of orderliness; hence an ornament or beautiful thing.)

A. Division of lvs. linear to filiform .... 1. *C. bipinnatus*
AA. Division of lvs. lanceolate or broader.
B. Color of fls. yellow .... 2. *C. sulphureus*
BB. Color of fls. rose or red.
C. Rays rose or lilac, disk yellow .... 3. *C. diversifolius*
CC. Rays and disk deep red .... 4. *C. atrosanguineus*

1. **C. bipinnatus,** Cav. Glabrous or somewhat pubescent ann. 7–10 ft. high: lvs. 2–4 in. long, bipinnately cut into remote linear to filiform entire lobes: heads 2–3 in. across; rays white, pink or crimson, truncate or somewhat toothed; disk yellow: achenes glabrous, ⅓–½in. long, with an abrupt beak much shorter than body. Mex.—Double- or anemone-fld. forms have disk replaced by petal-like parts.

2. **C. sulphureus,** Cav. YELLOW COSMOS. Pubescent ann. 4–7 ft. high, much-branched: lvs. often 1 ft. or more long, 2–3-pinnately cut into lanceolate to elliptic mucronate lobes, shortly ciliate: heads 2–3 in. across; rays strongly 3-toothed at apex, pale pure or golden-yellow; disk yellow, anthers exserted, black with orange tips: achenes hispid, ¾–1 in. long, including the slender beak. Mex. to Brazil.

3. **C. diversifolius,** Otto (*Bidens dahlioides*, Wats.). Per. with tuberous roots but grown as an ann., 1–3 ft. high, usually glabrous: lvs. simple and spatulate or pinnatisect into 5–7 lanceolate to ovate segms., the terminal largest: heads 2–3 in. across; rays rose or lilac, entire or obscurely toothed; disk yellow: achenes glabrous or rough, ½–1 in. long, with slender beak. Mex.

4. **C. atrosanguineus,** Ort. (*C. diversifolius* var. *atrosanguineus*, Hook. *Bidens atrosanguinea*, Ort. *Dahlia Zimpanii*, Roezl). BLACK COSMOS. Differs from *C. diversifolius* in the somewhat smaller heads, with red disk-fls. and dark velvety-red rays. Mex.

31. **DAHLIA,** Cav. (*Georgina*, Willd.). Some dozen or 15 species are now known from the mts. of Mex. and Guatemala (ours Mexican), strong erect branching plants with tuberous roots, some well known for their large showy heads.—Perennials, but sometimes blooming the first year from seed and treated as annuals although the resulting tubers may be carried over: lvs. opposite, 1–3-odd-pinnate, the pinnæ or segms. usually variously ovate and toothed: heads long-peduncled, with yellow disk and red, purple, pink or white rays; disk-fls. bisexual and fertile; ray-fls. neutral or pistillate; involucre with double series of bracts, the inner thin and scale-like and slightly united at base, the outer smaller and somewhat leafy; receptacle flat or curved, chaffy: achenes oblong or obovate, compressed, the pappus lacking or of 2 obscure teeth. (Dah-lia: Andreas Dahl, a Swedish botanist, pupil of Linnæus, 1751–1789.)—The botany of Dahlia is not yet well understood, and the specific names are tentative. Descriptions of the original species were from domesticated and modified plants, and their application is open to doubt; and the native forms have not been sufficiently collected. The lower lvs. and roots, as well as the fls., are essential to a careful understanding of the species.

A. The tree dahlias,—the plants tall and tree-form with one or more trunks, somewhat woody.
  B. Heads bell-shaped from the position of the rays, nodding....................1. *D. imperialis*
  BB. Heads flat from the expanding rays, erect....................2. *D. excelsa*
AA. The bush dahlias,—plants producing many sts., not woody, usually not more than 6 ft.
  B. Lf.-segms. 1–2 in. long, blunt but apiculate....................3. *D. Merckii*
  BB. Lf.-segms. 2 in. or more long, acuminate.
    C. Rays flat (at least in single or prominently rayed forms).
      D. Lfts. rather bluntly or at least coarsely toothed....................4. *D. pinnata*
      DD. Lfts. sharp-serrate....................5. *D. coccinea*
    CC. Rays with margins strongly recurved....................6. *D. Juarezii*

1. **D. imperialis,** Roezl. BELL TREE DAHLIA. CANDELABRA DAHLIA. Sts. few or several, 6–18 ft. tall and trunk-like, mostly not branched, angled: lvs. large, openly 3-pinnate like an aralia, finely pubescent; ultimate lfts. ovate, 1–2 in. long, sharp-pointed, sessile or short-stalked, incurved-serrate: heads standing high above the foliage, nodding, 4–7 in. across, white and more or less tinged red, the rays about 8, thin, long and narrow, prominently pointed and not toothed at apex.

2. **D. excelsa,** Benth. (*D. arborea*, Hort. *D. arborea*, Regel is a *nomen nudum*). FLAT TREE DAHLIA. Sts. usually several, to 20 ft. or more, mostly not branched, woody, glaucous: lvs. very large, often 2½ ft. long and nearly as broad, 2-pinnate; ultimate lfts. many, ovate, acuminate, more or less contracted at base, coarsely-few-toothed, nearly or quite glabrous: heads erect, 4–5 in. across; rays about 8, flat-expanding, purplish or crimson-pink; disk of the anemone type.

3. **D. Merckii,** Lehm. (*D. glabrata*, Lindl. *D. scapigera* var. *typica* forma *Merckii*, Sherff). BEDDING DAHLIA. Diffuse slender wholly glabrous plant, 2–3 ft., with slender tubers: lvs. pinnate and the pinnæ pinnatifid into decurrent segms. 1–2 in. long and nearly as broad, which are nearly blunt but apiculate and only few-toothed or obscurely serrate, making an attractive foliage plant: heads on long wiry sts., 1–2 in. across, the flat short rays nearly blunt and obscurely apiculate, lilac; involucral bracts linear. (Named in compliment to H. J. Merck, Senator in Hamburg.)

4. **D. pinnata,** Cav. COMMON or GARDEN DAHLIA. Sts. glabrous or essentially so, branched, 4 ft.: lvs. 2-pinnate or the upper ones pinnate, the expanded petioles nearly connate, the ultimate pinnæ ovate, crenate-dentate, very green above and grayish beneath, the rachis more or less winged: heads horizontal or somewhat nodding, 2–3 in. across but much larger in developed and double forms; rays 8, fertile, rose-colored (other colors now common), ovate, obscurely 3-toothed at apex; outer involucral bracts 6 or 7 and leafy.—The name *D. rosea* (1794 or 1795) is sometimes used for the common hort. dahlias, now much doubled and modified; but *D. pinnata*, Cav., 1791, the type of the genus, undoubtedly must be employed; Cavanilles made both names and considered that he had two good species; and he says that in *D. pinnata* the lvs. are pinnate while in *D. rosea* they are bipinnate. It has been customary to use the name *D. variabilis* for this group; this name starts as *Georgina variabilis*, Willd., 1806, transferred to Dahlia by Desfontaines in 1829; Willdenow states that the lvs. are pinnate, although the lower pinnæ of the radical lvs. are ternate; but these characters probably have minor significance in the old descriptions since both lf.-forms may occur freely on the same plant. Further investigation with these plants in cult. and in the wild may make considerable change in diagnosis of the group; *D. pinnata* was based on cult. subjects, with many (double) rays.

5. **D. coccinea,** Cav. Very like no. 4 and perhaps not possible to distinguish in cult. plants: more slender; sts. glaucous: lvs. 2-pinnate, the ultimate pinnæ narrower, ovate-

acuminate and sharply serrate, the foliage not so heavy, rachis little or not at all winged: rays 8 (although originally figured with 9), usually not fertile, scarlet on upper surface and lighter colored beneath; outer involucral bracts 5 and reflexed.

6. **D. Juarezii,** Hort. CACTUS DAHLIA. Like no. 4 in stature and growth: most or all of the many rays with recurved margins and mostly brilliant scarlet; rays irregular in length and overlapping, giving a characteristic appearance to the head. Probably a hybrid, the nearest ancestral form being the 8-rayed *D. Popenovii*, Safford, of Guatemala; the first stock is said to have come from Mex.; the specific name is in compliment to Benito Juarez, Mexican president and patriot.

32. **CHRYSOGONUM,** L. One or two per. herbs in E. N. Amer., sometimes transferred to gardens.—Stoloniferous: lvs. opposite and basal, simple: heads long-peduncled, yellow; involucral bracts in 2 series, the outer large and leafy; receptacle with chaffy bracts; ray-fls. pistillate and fertile; disk-fls. bisexual but sterile: achenes flattened, not winged; pappus a short crown. (Chrysog-onum: Greek *golden-knee.*)

C. virginianum, L. GOLDEN-STAR. Pubescent, 3–12 in. high, light green: lvs. triangular-ovate, 1–2 in. long, long-petioled, toothed, truncate or abruptly cuneate at base: heads 1–1½ in. across, Apr.–July. Pa. to Fla. and La.

33. **HELIOPSIS,** Pers. Sunflower-like plants, about 7 species native to N. Amer., several cult. for their showy fls.—Per. herbs or one ann., sts. loosely branched: lvs. opposite, petioled, 3-ribbed, coarsely toothed: heads pedunculate, showy; involucral bracts imbricated in 2 or 3 series; rays with large yellow oblong or linear-oblong ligules, persistent on the achenes; disk-fls. partly inclosed in chaffy bracts of the receptacle, bisexual and fertile: achenes without pappus or with a toothed border. (Heliop-sis: Greek *like the sun.*)

A. Plant smooth and glabrous throughout or the lvs. roughish above............1. *H. helianthoides*
AA. Plant rough throughout with hispid-scabrous hairs........................2. *H. scabra*

1. **H. helianthoides,** Sweet (*Buphthalmum helianthoides*, L. *H. lævis*, Pers.). Coarse per. 3–5 ft. high (dwarfed forms 2–3 ft.), smooth and glabrous throughout or nearly so: lvs. thinnish, oblong-ovate or ovate-lanceolate, 3–6 in. long, sometimes roughish above: heads numerous, somewhat corymbed, 1½–2½ in. across; rays broadly linear, 1 in. long: achenes smooth and glabrous, truncate or obscurely 2–4-toothed at summit. Ont. to Fla. and Miss. Var. **Pitcheriana,** Hort. (*H. Pitcheriana*, Hort.), has deeper yellow fls.

2. **H. scabra,** Dunal. Differs from *H. helianthoides* chiefly in being rough throughout with hispid-scabrous hairs: upper lvs. sometimes entire: heads few, often solitary: achenes pubescent on the angles when young; pappus a chaffy crown or sometimes of 2–3 teeth. Me. to N. J. and Ark.—Hort. vars. are: **excelsa,** nearly double chrome-yellow heads; **gratissima,** pale yellow; **incomparabilis,** heads double, 3 in. across, golden-yellow; **zinniæflora,** double.

34. **ZINNIA,** L. Ann. or per. herbs or subshrubs of N. and S. Amer., chiefly Mex., cult. for their showy fls.; about 15 species.—Lvs. opposite, mostly sessile and entire: heads solitary, showy, terminating the branches, the bright-colored rays long-enduring; the disk in cult. forms nearly or wholly lacking; ray-fls. pistillate and fertile; disk-fls. bisexual and fertile; involucral bracts obtuse, imbricated in several to many series; receptacle becoming conical to cylindric, with chaffy scales, enveloping the fls.: achenes flattened, wingless or nearly so, the pappus when present of erect awns or chaffy teeth. (Zin-nia: Johann Gottfried Zinn, 1727–1759, professor of medicine at Goettingen.)

A. Scales of receptacle pectinate-fimbriate at tip: heads 2–4½ in. across............1. *Z. elegans*
AA. Scales of receptacle entire: heads 1–2 in. across.
B. Lvs. linear-lanceolate...2. *Z. linearis*
BB. Lvs. oblong to ovate-lanceolate.....................................3. *Z. angustifolia*

1. **Z. elegans,** Jacq. YOUTH-AND-OLD-AGE. Erect ann. 1–3 ft. high, sts. short-hairy: lvs. sessile, more or less clasping, cordate-ovate to elliptic, 1½–4 in. long and 1–2 in. wide, shortly rough-hispid: heads 2–4½ in. across; chaffy bracts of the receptacle pectinate-fimbriate at tip; rays broad and showy, becoming reflexed, originally purple or lilac but now of nearly every color except blue and green; disk originally yellow or orange but in common double forms nearly or quite absent. Mex.—The plant in cult. as *Z. pumila* is a dwarf form of *Z. elegans;* the true *Z. pumila*, Gray, is a tufted grayish per. with linear lvs. ½in. or less long and pale yellow or white heads ½in. across.

2. **Z. linearis,** Benth. Branching ann. to 1 ft.: lvs. linear-lanceolate, 2–3 in. long and

1/8–1/4 in. wide: heads 1½–2 in. across, orange, the rays brighter orange on margins; chaffy bracts of receptacle entire and acute at tip. Mex.

3. **Z. angustifolia,** HBK. (*Z. mexicana,* Vilm. *Z. Haageana,* Regel). Branching ann. 1–1½ ft. high, sts. short-hairy: lvs. sessile, oblong to ovate-lanceolate, 1½–2½ in. long and ½–¾ in. wide at base: heads 1–1½ in. across, orange, the disk-fls. darkening with age; chaffy bracts of receptacle entire and acute at tip. Mex.

35. **SANVITALIA,** Lam. American ann. herbs, about 7–8 species, chiefly from Ariz. to Cent. Amer.—Mostly low and branching: lvs. opposite, more or less petioled, commonly entire: heads rather small, solitary, terminating the branchlets; involucral bracts imbricated in about 3 rows, the outer foliaceous-tipped; ray-fls. white or yellow; disk-fls. brown or purple: disk-achenes more or less compressed, the pappus of 1–2 awns or teeth or none; ray-achenes commonly 3-sided, 3-awned. (Sanvita-lia: *Sanvitali,* name of a noble Italian family.)

S. procumbens, Lam. Hairy low-growing ann. with trailing sts. branching and leafy: lvs. ovate, ½–1 in. long, petiolate: heads summer to late autumn, solitary, about ¾ in. across, closely subtended by a pair of leafy bracts; rays yellow; disk-fls. dark purple. Mex.

36. **THELESPERMA,** Less. Glabrous herbs or subshrubs of W. N. Amer. and extra-trop. S. Amer., cult. for the fls.; about 10 species.—Lvs. opposite or the upper alternate, 1–2-pinnately parted into linear or filiform segms., or the uppermost simple and linear: heads medium-sized, solitary on long peduncles; involucral bracts in 2 rows, the inner row campanulate and connate to the middle or higher and with whitish or yellowish margins; rays 8–10, neutral, yellow or brownish, in 1 row; disk-fls. purplish, fertile: achenes glabrous, smooth or tuberculate; pappus of 2 awns or scales. (Thelesper-ma: Greek *wart* and *seed,* the achenes often papillose.)

T. Burridgeanum, Blake (*Cosmidium Burridgeanum,* Regel. *C. Burridgeanum atropurpureum,* VanHoutte. *T. hybridum,* Voss. Probably *Coreopsis atrosanguinea,* Hort.). Branching ann., 1½ ft. high: lvs. 1–2-pinnately divided into filiform lobes: heads 1¼–1½ in. across, on long slender peduncles, Aug.–Sept.; rays broad, brown-purple with yellow margin; outer involucral bracts densely hairy.

37. **COREOPSIS,** L. (incl. *Calliopsis* and *Leptosyne*). TICKSEED. An attractive genus of over 100 species native to Amer., trop. Afr. and the Hawaiian Isls., a number cult. in the open garden for their showy fls. blooming in summer and autumn.—Ann. or per. herbs or seldom shrubs: lvs. commonly opposite, entire or variously lobed or dissected: heads usually showy, pedunculate, solitary or loosely panicled; involucral bracts in 2 distinct series of 8 each, the outer herbaceous and narrower than the inner, all commonly united at base; receptacle flat or convex, chaffy; rays in 1 series, neutral or rarely fertile, yellow, parti-colored or sometimes rose-color; disk-fls. bisexual and usually fertile: achenes flat or becoming incurved, winged or wingless; pappus of 2–4 awns, scales or teeth, or entirely lacking. (Coreop-sis: Greek, signifying *bug-like,* from the fr.)

A. Lf.-blades palmately divided.
B. Lvs. petioled: segms. oblong-lanceolate.................... 1. *C. tripteris*
BB. Lvs. sessile: segms. linear.
C. Disk-fls. yellow.................... 2. *C. verticillata*
CC. Disk-fls. purple-brown.................... 3. *C. delphinifolia*
AA. Lf.-blades pinnately divided or simple.
B. Disk-fls. dark or purplish-red.
C. Segms. of lvs. usually oblong to ovate: outer involucral bracts about as long as inner.................... 4. *C. basalis*
CC. Segms. of lvs. linear to linear-lanceolate: outer involucral bracts much shorter than inner.
D. Achenes wingless.................... 5. *C. tinctoria*
DD. Achenes narrowly winged.................... 6. *C. Atkinsoniana*
BB. Disk-fls. yellow.
C. Color of rays rose.................... 7. *C. rosea*
CC. Color of rays yellow.
D. Lvs. pinnate into narrow-linear divisions: ray-fls. fertile.
E. Heads 2–3 in. across: plant per.................... 8. *C. maritima*
EE. Heads ¾–1¼ in. across: plant ann.................... 9. *C. Stillmanii*
DD. Lvs. or lf.-segms. lanceolate or broader: ray-fls. sterile.
E. Achenes with thick incurved narrow wings.................... 10. *C. auriculata*
EE. Achenes with thin spreading wings.
F. Sts. leafy only toward base: lvs. mostly simple.................... 11. *C. lanceolata*
FF. Sts. leafy throughout: lvs. mostly divided.................... 12. *C. grandiflora*

1. **C. tripteris,** L. Per. 3–10 ft. high, usually glabrous: lvs. petioled, 2–5 in. long, palmately 3-parted into oblong-lanceolate somewhat revolute segms., upper lvs. commonly simple: heads 1½–2 in. across, in corymbs, long-peduncled; outer involucral bracts about half as long as inner; rays 7–8, yellow, nearly entire or toothed; disk yellow becoming brown or purplish: achenes oblong-obovate, narrowly winged. Ont. to Ga. and La.

2. **C. verticillata,** L. Thread-leaf Coreopsis. Slender glabrous per. 1–3 ft. high, sparingly branched: lvs. appearing verticillate, sessile, 2–3 in. long, palmately 3-parted, the divisions dissected into linear or filiform segms.: heads 1–2 in. across, few in corymbs, slender-peduncled; outer involucral bracts about as long as inner; rays about 8, deep yellow, entire or minutely toothed; disk yellow: achenes oblong-obovate, narrowly winged. Md. to Fla. and Ala.

3. **C. delphinifolia,** Lam. Larkspur Coreopsis. Nearly glabrous very leafy per. 2–5 ft. high: lvs. sessile, 2–3 in. long, palmately 3-parted into linear segms., the middle segms. again 3–5-divided: heads 1–2 in. across, in corymbs, slender-peduncled; outer involucral bracts about as long as inner; rays about 8, yellow, entire or slightly toothed; disk purple-brown: achenes oblong-obovate, narrowly winged. Va. to Ga. and Ala.

4. **C. basalis,** Blake (*Calliopsis basalis*, Dietr. *Coreopsis Drummondii*, Torr. & Gray. *C. picta*, Hort.). Golden-Wave. Ann. 1–2 ft. high, pubescent or glabrous: lvs. petioled, pinnately divided, the lobes round-ovate to oblong or in the upper lvs. sometimes linear: heads 1–2 in. across, on long peduncles; outer involucral bracts nearly equalling the inner; rays about 8, yellow, brownish-purple at base, toothed or lobed at apex; disk dark purple: achenes obovate, much incurved, with a thick cartilaginous margin. Tex.

5. **C. tinctoria,** Nutt. (*Calliopsis bicolor*, Reichb. *Calliopsis marmorata*, Hort. *Coreopsis elegans*, Hort.). Glabrous ann. 1–3 ft. high, branching above, rather strict: basal and lower cauline lvs. long-petioled, 2-pinnately divided into linear or linear-lanceolate lobes 2–4 in. long, the upper sessile or wing-petioled and with linear lobes: heads ¾–2 in. across, loosely panicled, on slender peduncles; outer involucral bracts much shorter than inner; rays 7–8, yellow with reddish-brown base, the apex toothed or lobed; disk brownish-purple: achenes linear-oblong, somewhat incurved, wingless. Minn. to La. and Calif. Var. **atropurpurea,** Hook. (*C. nigra*, Hort.), has rays brownish-red throughout.

6. **C. Atkinsoniana,** Dougl. (*Calliopsis Atkinsoniana*, Hook.). Ann. or per. 2–4 ft. high, glabrous: lvs. 1–2-pinnately divided into linear lobes: heads ¾–2 in. across, on slender elongated peduncles; outer involucral bracts much shorter than inner; rays 8, yellow with brown-purple base and 3–4-toothed or -lobed apex; disk purple or brownish: achenes flattened, oblong, narrowly winged. (Named for Wm. Atkinson of Grove End, English hort. architect.) Sask. to Ore. and Ariz.

7. **C. rosea,** Nutt. Glabrous per. ¾–2 ft. high, leafy, from slender creeping rootstocks: lvs. 1–2 in. long, entire and linear, or the lower 2–3-parted and the lobes linear: heads ¾–1 in. across, on short peduncles; outer involucral bracts much shorter than inner; rays about 8, rose-color, coarsely 3-toothed or -lobed; disk yellow: achenes oblong, wingless. N. S. to Ga. Var. **nana,** Hort., is smaller with lilac-rose rays.

8. **C. maritima,** Hook. f. (*Tuckermannia maritima*, Nutt. *Leptosyne maritima*, Gray). Sea-Dahlia. Per. 1–3 ft. high, with fleshy sts. and roots: lvs. bipinnately divided into narrowly linear lobes: heads 2½ in. or more across, solitary, on peduncles 9–12 in. long terminating the branches, in spring; outer involucral bracts only slightly shorter than inner; rays 14–20, yellow, obscurely toothed, fertile; disk yellow: achenes oblong obovate, narrowly winged. Coasts, S. Calif.

9. **C. Stillmanii,** Blake (*Leptosyne Stillmanii*, Gray). Glabrous ann. 6–18 in. high, sts. leafy below: lvs. pinnately 3–7-parted into narrow-linear segms.: heads ¾–1¼ in. across, solitary on long peduncles; outer involucral bracts about equalling inner; rays about 8, yellow, coarsely toothed; disk yellow: achenes orbicular or obovate, with corky somewhat roughened wings. (First collected by Dr. J. D. B. Stillman.) Calif.

10. **C. auriculata,** L. Per. to 1½ ft., leafy at base, with erect or ascending sts., usually pubescent, stoloniferous: lvs. long-petioled, 2–5 in. long, orbicular or ovate, often with 1 or 2 small lobes at base of blade: heads 1½–2 in. across, solitary on long peduncles; outer and inner involucral bracts about equal; rays about 8, yellow, 3-lobed at apex; disk yellow: achenes oblanceolate or obovate, with thick incurved narrow wings. Va. to Fla. and La.—Often confused with *C. pubescens*, Ell., which differs chiefly in the nearly orbicular achenes with thin spreading wings; plant to 3 ft., erect, more leafy to the top.

11. **C. lanceolata,** L. Glabrous or somewhat hirsute-pubescent per. 1–2 ft. high: lvs. usually in a few pairs or mostly in a tuft near the base, oblong-spatulate or lanceolate or nearly linear, 2–6 in. long, obtuse, entire or rarely with 1–2 small lateral lobes: heads 1½–2½ in. across, on very long peduncles; outer involucral bracts commonly shorter than inner; rays about 8, yellow, 2–3-toothed; disk yellow: achenes orbicular, with thin scarious wings. Mich. to Fla. and New Mex.

12. **C. grandiflora,** Hogg (*C. floribunda*, Hort.). Usually somewhat hairy per. 1–2 ft. high, sts. branching and leafy: basal and some of the lower st.-lvs. lanceolate or spatu-

late, entire; upper or sometimes all the st.-lvs. 3–5-parted into lanceolate or linear obtuse lobes, terminal lobes three to five times as long as wide: heads 1½–2½ in. across, long-peduncled; outer involucral bracts nearly equalling inner; rays usually 8, yellow, 3-lobed at apex; disk yellow: achenes orbicular, with broad thin scarious wings. Mo. to Fla. and New Mex.

38. **BACCHARIS,** L. Shrubs or herbs of more than 250 species in the Americas.—Lvs. alternate: heads diœcious, small, in panicles or corymbs, of many white or yellowish disk-fls.; involucral bracts imbricated in several series; receptacle flat, naked; corolla of staminate fls. tubular and 5-lobed, of pistillate fls. filiform: achenes somewhat flattened, ribbed; pappus of long white bristly hairs. (Bac-charis: from ancient Greek name.)

B. halimifolia, L. GROUNDSEL-BUSH. Deciduous much-branched shrub to 12 ft.: lvs. obovate or oblong, 1–3 in. long, acute, short-petioled, coarsely toothed, the upper entire: heads in peduncled clusters forming large panicles in late summer: pappus ⅓in. long. Coastal and marsh lands, Mass. to Fla. and Tex.

39. **CALLISTEPHUS,** Cass. (name conserved as against the earlier *Callistemma*, Cass.). A single species, native to Asia, yielding many races of well-known annuals for the fl.-garden.—Erect stiffish herb with alternate lvs. coarsely toothed or incised: heads large, radiate, solitary at the ends of the branches; ray-corollas of various colors, often violet; involucral bracts in many series, the outer herbaceous, the inner membranaceous-scarious: pappus-bristles in 2 rows. (Callis-tephus: Greek for *beautiful crown*, said to be in allusion to character of achene.)

C. chinensis, Nees (*Aster chinensis*, L. *C. hortensis*, Cass.). CHINA ASTER. Erect, hispid-hairy, branching, ½–2½ ft. high: lvs. broadly ovate or triangular-ovate, deeply and irregularly toothed, the blade decurrent into a petiole, the upper lvs. becoming spatulate and narrower: heads showy, 1–5 in. and more across, in late summer and fall, terminal, in the wild plant with 1–2 series of pistillate ray-fls. and numerous tubular yellow disk-fls. which are bisexual and fertile; involucre hemispherical, the large outer bracts green and often reflexed: achene compressed. China and Japan.—Under cult. the rays become greatly multiplied and show a wide range of variation in size, shape and color,—violet, purple, blue, rose and white, never a true yellow.

40. **BELLIS,** L. DAISY. Small plants, 10 species in Eu. and the Medit. region, one long cult.—Ann. or per. herbs, cespitose or with branching sts.: lvs. alternate or all basal, entire or sinuate, toothed: heads radiate, solitary, on naked peduncles; involucral bracts herbaceous, in 1–2 series; receptacle naked, conical; rays white or rose-color, in 1 series, pistillate; disk-fls. yellow, bisexual and fertile: achenes flattened, margined; pappus lacking. (Bel-lis: Latin *bellus*, pretty.)

A. Lvs. obovate .... 1. *B. perennis*
AA. Lvs. ovate or orbicular .... 2. *B. rotundifolia*

1. **B. perennis,** L. TRUE OR ENGLISH DAISY. Per. 3–6 in. high: lvs. forming a basal tuft, spatulate or obovate, 1–2 in. long, narrowed into margined petioles, slightly toothed, pubescent: heads solitary, 1–2 in. across, on hairy peduncles; involucral bracts oblong, obtuse, hairy; rays numerous, linear, white or rose, in vars. wholly or partly red ("monstrosa") and often incurved or reflexed or quilled. W. Eu.—Grown in fl.-gardens and often escaping to lawns.

2. **B. rotundifolia,** Boiss. & Reut. Differs from *B. perennis* in the ovate to orbicular lvs. ¾–1¼ in. long, on slender petioles 1–3 in. long, sinuate-toothed: heads ¾–1¼ in. across, with fewer broader white rays. Morocco, Algeria. Var. **cærulescens,** Hook., has blue rays.

41. **BELLIUM,** L. A few species of small herbs in the Medit. region, grown in the rock-garden.—Lvs. in basal tufts: heads solitary on long peduncles; involucral bracts in about 2 series; receptacle naked; rays-fls. pistillate, white; disk-fls. yellow, bisexual and fertile: achenes somewhat flattened; pappus in 2 series, of bristles and scales. (Bel-lium: *resembling bellis.*)

A. Plant per., stoloniferous .... 1. *B. bellidioides*
AA. Plant ann. .... 2. *B. minutum*

1. **B. bellidioides,** L. Stoloniferous per. 2–5 in. high: lvs. spatulate or rhombic, the blade ⅛–¼in. across, entire, with long pubescent petioles: heads ½in. or less across, rays white or pinkish.

2. **B. minutum,** L. Ann. 1–3 in. high: lvs. ovate-spatulate, obtuse, entire, long-petioled, glabrous or somewhat hairy: heads about ¼in. across, rays white tipped purplish.

42. **SOLIDAGO,** L. GOLDENROD. Per. herbs blooming in late summer and autumn and sometimes transferred to gardens; over 125 species, mostly in N. Amer.—Lvs. alternate, simple: heads small and few-fld., borne in panicles, thyrses, corymbs or racemes; involucral bracts imbricated in several series; receptacle not chaffy, usually pitted; ray-fls. yellow, in 1 series, pistillate; disk-fls. yellow, bisexual: achenes terete or angled; pappus of bristles in 1 or 2 series. (Solida-go: from Greek, to make solid or whole.)

A. Heads not in one-sided racemes, in clusters forming a corymb or thyrse.
  B. Plant rough-pubescent, 1–5 ft. high . . . . . 1. *S. rigida*
  BB. Plant glabrous or nearly so, 3–12 in. high . . . . . 2. *S. Cutleri*
AA. Heads in one-sided racemes forming large panicles.
  B Lvs. pinnately veined, entire.
    C. Basal lvs. to 1 ft. long, thick and fleshy . . . . . 3. *S. sempervirens*
    CC. Basal lvs. to 6 in. long, not fleshy . . . . . 4. *S. odora*
  BB. Lvs. 3-nerved (the 2 lateral nerves prominent), toothed.
    C. Plant with long horizontal stolons: lvs. linear-lanceolate, deep green above . . . 5. *S. canadensis*
    CC. Plant without horizontal stolons: lvs. oblanceolate or spatulate, gray-pubescent . . . . . 6. *S. nemoralis*

1. **S. rigida,** L. Rough-pubescent, 1–5 ft. high: lvs. ovate or oblong, stiff, the upper sessile and clasping and 1–2 in. long, the basal long-petioled and to 1 ft. long, entire or finely toothed, pinnately veined: heads about ⅓in. long, in clusters forming dense compound corymbs. Me. to Ga. and Mo.

2. **S. Cutleri,** Fern. (*S. Virgaurea* var. *alpina*, Bigel.). Alpine 3–12 in. high, glabrous or slightly pubescent: lvs. obovate or spatulate, 2–4 in. long, toothed, narrowed into petioles, pinnately veined, st.-lvs. few and sessile: heads ¼–⅓in. long, in short racemes or thyrses. (Named for Manasseh Cutler, 1742–1823, botanist and early explorer of White Mts.) Mts., Me. to N. N. Y.

3. **S. sempervirens,** L. Sts. leafy, 2–8 ft. high, glabrous below the infl.: lvs. thick and fleshy, oblong or lanceolate, the lower long-petioled and to 1 ft. long, entire, with several pairs of lateral veins, upper lvs. sessile: heads ¼–⅓in. long, in one-sided racemes forming large narrow often leafy panicles. N. S. to Fla. and Mex., along coast.

4. **S. odora,** Ait. Sts. simple, 2–4 ft. high, pubescent in lines: lvs. lanceolate or linear-lanceolate, 2–6 in. long, entire, pinnately veined, sessile or the lower petioled, often anise-scented: heads about ⅙in. long, in one-sided spreading racemes forming large panicles. Me. to Fla. and Tex.

5. **S. canadensis,** L. Plant with long horizontal stolons, 1–5 ft. high, glabrous or pubescent: lvs. linear-lanceolate, 2–5 in. long, 3-nerved, with remote sharp teeth, narrowed at base, sessile or lower lvs. petioled, deep green above: heads 1⁄12–⅛in. long, in one-sided spreading or recurved racemes forming large panicles. Newf. to S. C. and Tex.

6. **S. nemoralis,** Ait. Grayish-green pubescent plant 1–2 ft. high: lvs. thick, oblanceolate or spatulate, 3–6 in. long, 3-nerved, crenate-dentate or upper entire, petioled: heads ⅙–¼in. long, in one-sided spreading or recurved racemes forming usually one-sided panicles. N. S. to Fla. and Tex.

43. **CHRYSOPSIS,** Nutt. GOLDEN ASTER. Herbs of about 20 N. American species, sometimes transferred to gardens.—Lvs. alternate, entire, sessile or lower petioled: heads many-fld., in loose corymbs or sometimes solitary; involucral bracts imbricated in several series; receptacle flat, not chaffy, usually pitted; ray-fls. yellow, pistillate; disk-fls. yellow, mostly bisexual: achenes flattened, pubescent; pappus of 2 series, the inner of bristles, the outer of smaller bristles or scales. (Chrysop-sis: Greek *resembling gold.*)

A. Lvs. linear: heads ¼–⅓in. across . . . . . 1. *C. falcata*
AA. Lvs. oblong or lanceolate: heads ¾–1 in. across.
  B. Bracts of involucre glandular: peduncles long . . . . . 2. *C. mariana*
  BB. Bracts of involucre not glandular: peduncles short . . . . . 3. *C. villosa*

1. **C. falcata,** Ell. (*Inula falcata*, Pursh). Very leafy per. to 1 ft., woolly-pubescent when young: lvs. stiff, linear, 1–4 in. long: heads ¼–⅓in. across, few on slender pedicels, in corymbs; involucral bracts slightly pubescent. Mass. to N. J.

2. **C. mariana,** Ell. (*Inula mariana*, L.). Per. 1–2½ ft. high, loosely pubescent or becoming nearly glabrous: lvs. oblong or spatulate to lanceolate, 1–5 in. long: heads ¾–1 in. across, many on long glandular peduncles, in corymbose panicles; involucral bracts glandular, sticky-pubescent. S. N. Y. to Fla. and La.

3. **C. villosa,** Nutt. (*Amellus villosus*, Pursh). Per. 1–2 ft. high, pubescent: lvs. oblong or lanceolate, 1–2 in. long, the pubescence appressed: heads about 1 in. across, few on short peduncles, in corymbs; involucral bracts pubescent and sometimes ciliate. Minn. to B. C. and New Mex.

44. **XANTHISMA,** DC. One ann. or bien. herb in Tex., planted in the fl.-garden.—Lvs. alternate: heads solitary at end of branches; involucral bracts imbricated in many series; receptacle flat, pitted and somewhat fimbriate; rays yellow, in 1 series; disk-fls. yellow, bisexual and fertile: achenes angled; pappus of stiff bristles. (Xan-this-ma: Greek *dyed yellow.*)

X. texanum, DC. (*Centauridium Drummondii,* Torr. & Gray). STAR-OF-TEXAS. Branching, nearly glabrous, 1–4 ft. high: lvs. oblong to lanceolate, to 2½ in. long, entire or toothed, the lower sometimes pinnatifid: heads 1–2 in. across; involucral bracts with whitish margins.

45. **BRACHYCOME,** Cass. About 50 species, mostly natives of Australia, one grown in the fl.-garden.—Ann. or per. herbs with simple or branching sts.: lvs. basal or alternate, entire to pinnatifid: heads solitary and pedunculate or loosely corymbose at the ends of the branches; receptacle without scales; involucre broad, the bracts in about 2 series and with dry scarious margins; rays in 1–2 series, white, blue or lilac, pistillate; disk-fls. yellow, bisexual: achenes flattened, angled or winged; pappus of bristles or scales or lacking. (Brachyc-ome: Greek *short hair,* alluding to the pappus.)

B. iberidifolia, Benth. SWAN RIVER DAISY. Branching ann. 6–18 in. high: lvs. alternate, small, pinnately divided into narrow segms.: heads 1 in. across, on slender peduncles, the rays blue, rose-color or white. Australia.

46. **OLEARIA,** Moench. TREE ASTER. DAISY-BUSH. Small evergreen trees or shrubs sometimes planted in Calif.; over 125 species, mostly in New Zeal. and Australia.—Lvs. usually alternate, white or yellowish-tomentose beneath: heads solitary or in corymbs or panicles; involucral bracts imbricated in several series, margins dry or scarious; receptacle flat or convex, pitted; ray-fls. white, blue or purple, in 1 series, pistillate; disk-fls. bisexual: achenes terete or slightly flattened; pappus of several rows of bristles. (Olea-ria: believed to refer to the resemblance to Olea.)

O. Haastii, Hook. f. Shrub 4–10 ft. high, much-branched: lvs. crowded, oblong or ovate, ½–1¼ in. long, entire, obtuse, short-petioled, shining dark green above, white-tomentose beneath: heads about ⅓in. across, in long-peduncled corymbs 2–3 in. across; rays 3–5, white; disk yellow. (Named for Sir Johann Franz Julius von Haast, 1824–1887, geologist and explorer.) New Zeal.

47. **CHARIEIS,** Cass. One species, in the western Cape region of S. Afr., occasionally cult. in gardens.—Ann. herb, diffuse or branched at base, hairy: lower lvs. opposite, the upper alternate, all entire or nearly so: heads solitary; involucre broad, the bracts in 1 series; receptacle flat, naked; ray-fls. pistillate; disk-fls. bisexual: achenes flattened, margined; pappus of plumose bristles. (Char-ieis: Greek *elegant,* from the pleasing fls.)

C. heterophylla, Cass. (*C. Neesii,* Hort. *Kaulfussia amelloides,* Nees). Small branchy hairy plant 6–12 in. high: lvs. oblong-spatulate or oblong-lanceolate, to 2½ in. long: heads about ¾in. across, long-pedunculate; rays blue (violet or red-violet in vars.); disk yellow or blue.

48. **BOLTONIA,** L'Her. Tall per. herbs, 4 or 5 species native to the U. S. and E. Asia, sometimes planted in borders and wild gardens, flowering in late summer and fall.—Glabrous, erect, leafy-stemmed, branching above: lvs. alternate, entire or minutely toothed, sessile and commonly becoming vertical by a twist at base, rarely decurrent: heads usually in panicles, short-peduncled, rather showy, the numerous rays white, purplish or violet; involucral bracts imbricated in few series, scarious-margined; disk-fls. bisexual: achenes flattened, with thick or winged margins; pappus of scales with a few stiff bristles. (Bolto-nia: James Bolton, English botanist, who wrote 1775–1795.)

A. Involucral bracts lanceolate, acute: heads ¾in. across........................1. *B. asteroides*
AA. Involucral bracts oblong to ovate, obtuse or mucronate: heads 1 in. across..........2. *B. latisquama*

1. **B. asteroides,** L'Her. (*Matricaria asteroides,* L. *B. glastifolia,* L'Her.). Sts. 2–8 ft. high: lvs. broadly lanceolate or the upper narrower, 2–5 in. long, minutely serrulate: heads ¾in. across; involucral bracts lanceolate, acute; rays white to violet and purple: pappus-scales numerous, conspicuous, the bristles sometimes lacking. Conn. to Fla. and La.

2. **B. latisquama,** Gray. Heads larger, 1 in. or more across; involucral bracts oblong to ovate, obtuse or mucronate; rays blue-violet: pappus-scales small, the bristles present and conspicuous. Mo. to Okla. Var. **nana,** Hort., is 2–3 ft. tall with pinkish rays.

49. **HETEROPAPPUS,** Less. Per. herbs, about 4 Asiatic species, one planted in the fl.-garden.—Lvs. alternate, entire or coarsely toothed: heads solitary or loosely panicled; involucral bracts imbricated in many series; receptacle flat or convex, naked or pitted; ray-fls. blue or white, pistillate, in 1 series; disk-fls. bisexual and fertile: achenes flattened; pappus of short and long chaffy bristles. (Heteropap-pus: Greek *two kinds of pappus.*)

H. hispidus, Less. (*Aster hispidus*, Thunb.). Sts. rough, 2 ft. and more high: basal lvs. broadly spatulate to lanceolate, often coarsely toothed; st.-lvs. linear, acute: heads to 1¾ in. across; rays blue; disk-fls. yellow. Japan, Mongolia.

50. **ERIGERON,** L. FLEABANE. About 150 species scattered over the world, particularly in temp. and mountainous regions, a number cult. as border plants.—Annuals or perennials, acaulescent, or with erect loosely or corymbosely branched sts.: lvs. entire, toothed, or rarely dissected, those of the st. alternate: heads radiate (in ours), solitary or clustered; involucre campanulate or hemispheric, the bracts narrow, nearly equal, in 1–2 series; rays in 2 or more series, mostly rose, violet or purple, rarely cream-colored or white and in one species orange: achenes flattened; pappus of soft bristles. (Erig-eron: Greek *old man in spring;* some of the early kinds are somewhat hoary.)

A. Color of ray-fls. orange-yellow.......... 1. *E. aurantiacus*
AA. Color of ray-fls. white, violet or purple.
  B. Lvs. ternately divided.......... 2. *E. compositus*
  BB. Lvs. not divided, entire or only toothed.
    C. Branches decumbent and trailing: lvs. 1 in. or less long.......... 3. *E. Karvinskianus*
    CC. Branches erect or ascending: at least the basal lvs. more than 1 in. long.
      D. Rayless pistillate fls. present between disk- and ray-fls.......... 4. *E. alpinus*
      DD. Rayless pistillate fls. lacking.
        E. Heads 2–3 in. across.......... 5. *E. multiradiatus*
        EE. Heads ¾–1½ in. across.
          F. Plant producing stolons and offsets.......... 6. *E. pulchellus*
          FF. Plant not producing stolons.
            G. Pubescence dense throughout: plant ann. or bien.......... 7. *E. divergens*
            GG. Pubescence sparse below the infl.: plant per.
              H. Number of heads several to many, forming a leafy corymb... 8. *E. speciosus*
              HH. Number of heads few, usually solitary.
                I. Involucre glandular but not hirsute.......... 9. *E. callianthemus*
                II. Involucre hirsute or woolly.
                  J. Pappus double: lower lvs. much larger than st.-lvs.
                    K. Foliage thick and fleshy..........10. *E. glaucus*
                    KK. Foliage thin..........11. *E. glabellus*
                  JJ. Pappus simple: lower lvs. not much larger than st.-lvs.
                    K. Rays lilac or purple; involucre densely woolly: lvs. entire..........12. *E. elatior*
                    KK. Rays usually white; involucre hirsute: lvs. often dentate..........13. *E. Coulteri*

1. **E. aurantiacus,** Regel. DOUBLE ORANGE DAISY. More or less velvety; sts. leafy, 6–10 in. high, usually several from a tuft of basal lvs., these and the lower st.-lvs. spatulate-oblong or elliptic-oblong, more or less twisted; upper st.-lvs. ovate and sessile or clasping: heads usually solitary, about 1 in. across; involucral bracts loose, reflexed, pubescent; rays orange-yellow, linear, in 5–6 rows with series of tubular pistillate fls. between ray- and disk-fls.: pappus simple. Turkestan.

2. **E. compositus,** Pursh. Per. with scape-like sts. 2–8 in. high: lvs. crowded at base of st., 2–3-ternate into linear or spatulate segms., long-petioled, ½–3 in. long, hirsute: heads solitary, about ¾in. across; involucre hirsute and glandular; rays 40–60, white or purplish, to ⅓in. long: pappus simple. Alaska to Calif. and Rocky Mts. Var. **discoideus,** Gray (var. *trifidus*, Gray. *E. trifidus*, Hook.), is smaller, with heads about ½in. across, lvs. prevailingly 1-ternate.

3. **E. Karvinskianus,** DC. (*E. mucronatus*, DC. *Vittadinia triloba*, Hort. not DC.). Much-branched per. but blooming first year from seed, to 18 in., some or all the branches decumbent and more or less trailing: lower st.-lvs. obovate-cuneate, to 1 in. long, ciliate at base, otherwise glabrous, often 3–5-toothed at apex, the teeth coarse, obtuse and mucronate; upper lvs. oblong, subentire: heads on solitary peduncles, to ¾in. across; rays numerous, twice as long as the disk-fls., in 2 series, white with purple back; involucre slightly hirsute: pappus double. (Named for Baron v. Karwinski, page 46.) Mex. to Panama.

4. **E. alpinus,** L. (*Trimorpha alpina,* Vierhapper). Per. 1–12 in. high: basal lvs. obovate or spatulate, ½–5 in. long, hairy on both sides and ciliate, st.-lvs. lanceolate to linear: heads solitary or several, ¾–1 in. across; involucre hirsute; rays 60–150, rose or purple, to ¼in. long, with rayless narrow-tubular pistillate fls. between ray- and disk-fls., the latter yellow with purple tips. N. Eu., N. Asia.

5. **E. multiradiatus,** Benth. Himalayan Fleabane. Per. 1–2 ft. high, hairy: lvs. obovate or lanceolate, 1½–3 in. long, entire or with few coarse teeth: heads solitary or few on long peduncles, 2–3 in. across; involucre densely hirsute; rays very numerous, purple, to ¾in. long: pappus double, red. Himalayas.

6. **E. pulchellus,** Michx. Poor Robins Plantain. Per. 1–2 ft. high, producing stolons and offsets, hairy: basal lvs. tufted, spatulate, 1–6 in. long, short-petioled, toothed, st.-lvs. sessile and usually entire: heads 1–6 on slender peduncles, 1–1½ in. across; involucre pubescent; rays 50–65, violet or bluish-purple, ⅓–½in. long: pappus simple. N. S. to Ga. and Tex.

7. **E. divergens,** Torr. & Gray. Diffuse ann. or bien. 6–12 in. high, densely gray-pubescent throughout: lower lvs. spatulate or oblanceolate, 1–2 in. long, entire or cut-toothed, upper lvs. smaller: heads usually numerous, solitary or in corymbs, ¾–1 in. across; rays to 100, filiform, violet to nearly white, to ⅓in. long: pappus double. B. C. to Mex. and Neb.

8. **E. speciosus,** DC. (*Stenactis speciosa,* Lindl.). Erect per. 1½–2 ft. high, sts. more or less woody below, leafy, branching and sparsely hairy above: lvs. entire, short-ciliate, glabrous, those of the st. lanceolate, acuminate, somewhat clasping, the basal ones spatulate, 3–6 in. long, petioled: heads 1–1½ in. across, borne at the tips of the corymbosely clustered branchlets; involucre hirsute and slightly glandular; rays very numerous, dark violet or lavender, about ½in. long: pappus double. B. C. to W. Ore. and Lower Calif. Var. **macranthus,** Cronquist (*E. macranthus,* Nutt.), has glandular but not hirsute involucre.—The plant grown as *E. caucasicus* seems to belong here; the true *E. caucasicus,* Steven, has cordate-ovate clasping st.-lvs., hairy sts. with few heads; Caucasus.

9. **E. callianthemus,** Greene (*E. salsuginosus,* Gray not *Aster salsuginosus,* Richardson). Per. 6–18 in. high, slightly pubescent: lower lvs. oblanceolate, petioled, 2–5 in. long, glabrous except the ciliate margins, upper lvs. smaller and sessile: involucre glandular; rays 35–65, purple or violet, broad-linear, to ½in. long: pappus simple. B. C. to Calif. and New Mex.

10. **E. glaucus,** Ker. Beach Aster. Seaside Daisy. More or less pubescent per. 9–12 in. high, the rather fleshy crown bearing a tuft of basal lvs. and several leafy simple 1-headed or occasionally branching sts.: lvs. commonly entire, slightly glaucous or often green in cult., spatulate or the upper oblong: heads 1¼–1½ in. across; involucre hirsute; rays 70–90, bright violet, ¼–½in. long: pappus double. Ore. to Calif., along coasts.

11. **E. glabellus,** Nutt. (*E. asper,* Nutt.). More or less pubescent per. 6–20 in. high, the leafy sts. usually bearing 1–3 heads: upper lvs. lanceolate, becoming small and bract-like in the flowering branches; lower lvs. oblanceolate or spatulate, 2–4 in. long: heads 1–2 in. across; involucre bristly or pubescent; rays 100–150, violet, purple or rarely white, ⅓–½in. long: pappus double. Alaska to Wis.

12. **E. elatior,** Greene (*E. grandiflorus* var. *elatior,* Gray). Per. 1–2 ft. high, hairy: lvs. ovate-lanceolate to lanceolate, 1–2 in. long, entire: heads 1–3, 1–1½ in. across; involucre densely woolly; rays numerous, lilac or purple, about ½in. long: pappus simple. Colo. to Utah.

13. **E. Coulteri,** Porter. Slender equally leafy per. 10–20 in. high: lvs. more or less pubescent, the lower obovate to oblong, 2–6 in. long, entire or serrate; upper lvs. ovate to lanceolate: heads solitary (rarely 2 or 3), the 50–70 rays ½in. or more long, white varying to purplish; involucre hirsute: pappus simple. (For Thos. Coulter, page 110.) Rocky Mts. to Calif. and Wash.

51. **ASTER,** L. Aster. Starwort. Michaelmas Daisy. A large temp. zone genus of more than 600 species particularly abundant in N. Amer., a number in cult. as border plants for autumn or summer bloom.—Leafy-stemmed herbs, mostly per. and occasionally somewhat woody at base, very rarely ann.: lvs. always alternate: heads usually clustered, sometimes solitary, seldom small; involucral bracts commonly unequal and in part herbaceous, imbricated in several or few series, sometimes subequal and little imbricated; receptacle flat or convex, pitted; rays numerous in 1–2 series, flattish, white, blue, red or purple; disk-fls. yellow, in several species changing to purple or rose-color: achenes nerved, mostly compressed, the pappus-bristles copious in 1–2 series. (As-ter: Latin *star.*)—For the aster of fl.-gardens, see Callistephus.

A. Lvs. pinnatifid . . . 1. *A. tanacetifolius*
AA. Lvs. simple.
B. Sts. simple and scape-like, 1-headed.
C. Plant stoloniferous: pappus-bristles much shorter than florets . . . 2. *A. tongolensis*
CC. Plant not stoloniferous: pappus-bristles about length of florets.
D. Pappus simple: plant less than 1 ft. high . . . 3. *A. alpinus*
DD. Pappus of 2 series, the outer very short: plant 1½–3 ft. high.
E. Disk-fls. reddish-orange with purple tip . . . 4. *A. diplostephioides*
EE. Disk-fls. yellow.
F. Shape of lvs. linear to linear-lanceolate . . . 5. *A. Farreri*
FF. Shape of lvs. lanceolate to obovate . . . 6. *A. yunnanensis*
BB. Sts. usually branched and several- to many-headed.
C. Plant a shrub with wand-like branches bearing many short lateral twigs with a solitary head . . . 7. *A. fruticosus*
CC. Plant an herb with spreading branches.
D. Shape of lvs. cordate-ovate . . . 8. *A. cordifolius*
DD. Shape of lvs. not cordate-ovate.
E. Base of upper lvs. clasping.
F. Foliage smooth and glabrous.
G. Bracts of involucre closely appressed: st. glabrous . . . 9. *A. lævis*
GG. Bracts of involucre somewhat spreading: st. slightly pubescent . . . 10. *A. novi-belgii*
FF. Foliage pubescent or rough.
G. Bracts of involucre pubescent and viscid . . . 11. *A. novæ-angliæ*
GG. Bracts of involucre glabrous or ciliate . . . 12. *A. puniceus*
EE. Base of lvs. not clasping.
F. Width of lvs., at least some of them, ½in. or more, lanceolate to oblong or oval.
G. Heads ½–¾in. across, rays white . . . 13. *A. umbellatus*
GG. Heads 1–2 in. across, rays violet or blue.
H. Basal lvs. to 2 ft. long, coarsely toothed . . . 14. *A. tataricus*
HH. Basal lvs. to 5 in. long, entire or slightly toothed.
I. Bracts of involucre glandular-viscid . . . 15. *A. spectabilis*
II. Bracts of involucre hairy but not glandular . . . 16. *A. Amellus*
FF. Width of lvs. ¼in. or less, linear or linear-lanceolate.
G. Foliage strongly punctate-dotted . . . 17. *A. sedifolius*
GG. Foliage not punctate.
H. Ray-fls. 1 in. long . . . 18. *A. grandiflorus*
HH. Ray-fls. ⅓in. or less long.
I. Under surface of lvs. glabrous.
J. Rays violet . . . 19. *A. linariifolius*
JJ. Rays white . . . 20. *A. ptarmicoides*
II. Under surface of lvs. pubescent.
J. Bracts of involucre with obtuse or mucronate spreading tips: lvs. ½–1 in. long . . . 21. *A. ericoides*
JJ. Bracts of involucre with acuminate appressed tips: lvs. 1–3 in. long . . . 22. *A. pilosus*

1. **A. tanacetifolius,** HBK. (*Machæranthera tanacetifolia,* Nees). TAHOKA DAISY. Bien. or ann. 1–2 ft. high, branched from base, glandular-pubescent: lvs. 1–2 in. long, 2–3-pinnatifid into linear-oblong bristle-tipped segms.: heads numerous, 1–2 in. across; involucral bracts with whitish base and linear-subulate spreading green tips; rays blue-violet, ½–¾in. long; disk yellow. S. D. to Tex. and Mex.

2. **A. tongolensis,** Franch. (*A. subcæruleus,* S. Moore). Erect hairy stoloniferous per. 4–12 in. high, from a tuft of oblong-spatulate entire petioled lvs. 2–5 in. long; st.-lvs. oblong-lanceolate, sessile: heads terminating the main st. 1½–2 in. across, in June; involucral bracts oblong, obtuse, hairy; rays pale blue, ½–¾in. long; disk yellow: pappus much shorter than florets. W. China to India.

3. **A. alpinus,** L. Appressed-pubescent per., the simple leafy sts. 6–12 in. high, several from base: lvs. entire, the basal and lower cauline spatulate or oblong-spatulate, tapering to a winged petiole and 2–3 in. long, the upper cauline linear-lanceolate, sessile: heads solitary at the ends of the st., 1½ in. across, May–June; involucral bracts nearly equal, lanceolate, ciliate; rays blue or violet (white in var. **albus** and rosy-purple in **ruber**), about ¾in. long; disk-fls. yellow, becoming almost purple: pappus simple, about length of florets. Rocky Mts. and mts. of Eu.

4. **A. diplostephioides,** Clarke (*Heterochæta diplostephioides,* DC.). Erect hairy glandular per. to 3 ft.: lvs. lanceolate, to 4 in. long and 1 in. wide, entire or few-toothed, the lower petioled, st.-lvs. sessile: heads solitary, to 3 in. across; involucral bracts triangular, acute; rays violet or blue, 1 in. or more long; disk-fls. reddish-orange with purple tips: pappus of 2 series, the outer very short. Himalayas.

5. **A. Farreri,** W. W. Smith & Jeffrey. Similar to *A. diplostephioides* but lvs. narrower, linear to linear-lanceolate, the lower 4–6 in. long and about ⅓in. wide; disk-fls. yellow. (Collected by R. J. Farrer.) China.

6. **A. yunnanensis,** Franch. (*A. diplostephioides* var. *yunnanensis,* Onno). Distinguished from *A. Farreri* by the broader obovate lvs., the basal deciduous. W. China.

7. **A. fruticosus,** L. (*Diplopappus fruticulosus,* Less.). Shrub 2–4 ft. high, with wand-like branches bearing many short lateral twigs with a solitary head on peduncles 1–3 in. long:

lvs. linear, ½–¾in. long, margins entire and recurved, punctate, 1-nerved, attenuate at base, glabrous and glandular: heads 1 in. across; involucral bracts glabrous, tipped with an oblong gland; rays purple. S. Afr.

8. **A. cordifolius,** L. BLUE WOOD ASTER. Much-branched per. 1–5 ft. high, sts. usually glabrous: lvs. ovate-cordate, the lower long-petioled and 2–5 in. long, toothed, slightly pubescent: heads numerous, ½–¾in. across; involucral bracts appressed, linear, glabrous; rays violet or blue, ¼in. long. N. B. to Ga. and Miss.

9. **A. lævis,** L. Stoutish per. 2–3 ft. high, branching above, glabrous below the infl., often glaucous: lvs. ovate or oblong to lanceolate, ciliate-serrulate and often toothed, the basal and lowest cauline 4–5 in. long, narrowed at base to a winged petiole, the upper with auriculate or subcordate and partly clasping base: heads about 1 in. across, panicled, numerous, crowded, on rather stout leafy-bracteate peduncles; involucral bracts herbaceous-tipped, closely appressed; rays blue or violet. Me. to Ga. and La.—Source of cultivars; grown also in gardens in the tropics.

10. **A. novi-belgii,** L. NEW YORK ASTER. Per. 1–3 ft. high, smooth and glabrous or slightly pubescent above: lvs. oblong to linear-lanceolate, 2–6 in. long, entire or serrate, the upper sessile and partly clasping: heads crowded, panicled, about 1 in. across; involucral bracts linear, acute, with herbaceous tips, somewhat spreading; rays bright blue-violet, ½in. long. Newf. to Ga.—Runs into many named cultivars, largely of European origin.

11. **A. novæ-angliæ,** L. NEW ENGLAND ASTER. Per. with stout strict sts. 3–5 ft. high, branching above and very leafy to the top, coarsely hirsute or hispid with jointed hairs, also with glandular pubescence: lvs. lanceolate to broadly linear, 2–5 in. long, entire, half-clasping by a strongly auriculate-cordate base, pubescent: heads crowded, 1–2 in. across; involucral bracts linear-subulate, glandular-viscid and pubescent; rays deep purple, ½–¾in. long. Que. to S. C. and Colo. Var. **roseus,** DC., has rose-colored rays.

12. **A. puniceus,** L. Per. 3–8 ft. high, with reddish hairy sts.: lvs. lanceolate or oblong-lanceolate, 3–6 in. long, toothed or entire, base broad or narrow and clasping, rough above, pubescent on midrib beneath: heads numerous, 1–1½ in. across; involucral bracts linear or oblong, glabrous or ciliate; rays violet-purple or rarely white, about ½in. long. Swamps, Newf. to Ga. and Ala.

13. **A. umbellatus,** Mill. (*Doellingeria umbellata,* Nees). Per. 1–8 ft. high, branched at top: lvs. lanceolate or oblong-lanceolate, 5–6 in. long and ½–1 in. wide, entire, short-petioled or upper sessile, glabrous above and slightly pubescent beneath: heads ½–¾in. across, the infl. flat-topped; involucral bracts lanceolate, pubescent or ciliate; rays white, about ⅓in. long. Newf. to Ga. and Iowa.

14. **A. tataricus,** L. f. Per. to 7 ft., sts. erect and hispid, corymbose at summit: lvs. large, the basal 2 ft. long and 6 in. wide, lanceolate or ovate-lanceolate, attenuate at base, coarsely toothed; st.-lvs. sessile, to 6 in. long and 1 in. wide: heads 1 in. or more across; involucral bracts purplish at tip; rays blue or purple, ¾in. long; disk yellow. Siberia, Japan, China.

15. **A. spectabilis,** Ait. Per. 1–2 ft. high, sts. simple or branched above, pubescent and somewhat glandular: lower lvs. oval, 3–5 in. long and 1–1½ in. wide, petioled, slightly toothed; upper st.-lvs. linear-oblong, sessile, nearly entire: heads about 1½ in. across, in corymbs; involucral bracts linear-oblong, glandular-viscid, tips spreading; rays bright violet, ½–¾in. long. Mass. to N. C.

16. **A. Amellus,** L. ITALIAN ASTER. Roughish short-hispid per. 1–2 ft. high, sts. commonly corymbosely branched above: lvs. oblong to oblong-lanceolate, obtuse and apiculate or acute, entire or nearly so, narrowed to a sessile base, the lower to 5 in. long and 1 in. wide: heads 1–1¾ in. across; involucral bracts oblong, obtuse, hairy; rays broad, purple, ¾in. long; disk yellow. (Amellus: from the river Mella in Mantua where this plant occurs.) Eu., Asia. Var. **elegans,** Hort., is lower and free-flowering.—A popular hybrid between this species and *A. Thomsonii* is **A. Frikartii,** raised by Carl Frikart, nurseryman at Stafa, Switzerland; to 2 ft., heads solitary, to 3 in. across, fragrant, rays violet-blue.

17. **A. sedifolius,** L. (*A. acris,* L.). Roughish-hispid per., slender-branched, 2–3 ft. high (a var. dwarf): lvs. linear or lanceolate-linear, 1–1½ in. long, entire, attenuate at both ends, strongly punctate: heads corymbosely clustered, 1–1¼ in. across, the slender peduncles often bracteate; involucral bracts lanceolate, appressed; rays blue, ½–⅝in. long, spreading or somewhat reflexed; disk yellow. S. Eu.

18. **A. grandiflorus,** L. Much-branched per. to 2½ ft., hispid: lvs. linear to oblong, ¼–2 in. long, entire, sessile: heads solitary at ends of branchlets, 2 in. across; involucral bracts linear or linear-oblong, glandular, leafy, tips spreading; rays deep violet, to 1 in. long. Va. to Fla.—Grown under the name *A. mesa-grande speciosus.*

19. **A. linariifolius,** L. (*Ionactis linariifolius,* Greene). Stiff tufted very leafy per. 1–2 ft. high, branched above: lvs. linear, 1–1½ in. long and to ⅙in. wide, entire, sessile, rough, glabrous: heads several, 1 in. across; involucral bracts linear-lanceolate, appressed, ciliate; rays violet, ⅓in. long. Me. to Fla. and Tex.

20. **A. ptarmicoides,** Torr. & Gray (*Doellingeria ptarmicoides,* Nees. *Unamia alba,*

Rydb.). WHITE UPLAND ASTER. Per. 1–2 ft. high, with tufted stiff sts. branched near the top: lvs. linear-lanceolate, the lower 3–6 in. long and ⅙–¼in. wide, entire, petioled or sessile, shining, rough on margins: heads ¾–1 in. across, in corymbs; involucral bracts linear-oblong, nearly glabrous; rays white, ¼in. long. Mass. to Ga. and Colo.—A bigeneric hybrid between this species and a Solidago is **Solidaster luteus,** M. L. Green (*Solidaster hybridus*, Wehrhahn. *Asterago lutea*, Everett. *Aster hybridus luteus*, Hort.), ray-fls. canary-yellow, disk-fls. golden-yellow.

21. **A. ericoides,** L. (*A. multiflorus*, Ait.). HEATH ASTER. Pubescent much-branched per. 1–7 ft. high: lvs. stiff, linear, ½–1 in. long, entire, sessile: heads ¼–⅓in. across, densely crowded; involucral bracts with obtuse or mucronate spreading tips, pubescent; rays white, ⅛–⅙in. long. Me. to Ga. and Tex.

22. **A. pilosus,** Willd. (*A. ericoides*, Auth. not L. *A. villosus*, Michx. not Thunb. *A. ericoides* var. *villosus*, Torr. & Gray). Differs from *A. ericoides* in longer lvs., somewhat larger heads, and involucral bracts with acuminate appressed tips. Pa. to Ga. and Miss.

52. **CALIMERIS,** Nees. Aster-like plants, about 10 species native to Asia, one cult. in the border.—Low per. herbs differing from Aster in the hemispherical involucre of more nearly equal scarious-margined bracts in few rows, and broad convex receptacle: achenes flat and hairy. (Calim-eris: Greek *beautiful arrangement.*)

C. incisa, DC. (*C. incisæfolia*, Hort. *Aster incisus*, Fisch.). Erect, leafy-stemmed, 1–2 ft. high, corymbose at summit, finely appressed-hispid: lvs. oblong-lanceolate, remotely incise-dentate, those of the branchlets narrowly oblanceolate and entire or nearly so: heads solitary at the tips of the branchlets, 1 in. across; involucral bracts reddish-tipped, obtuse; rays purple or almost white; disk yellow: pappus much shorter than florets. Siberia.

53. **FELICIA,** Cass. African subshrubs or rarely ann. herbs, of about 50 species, yielding a fine winter blue.—Lvs. alternate or opposite, entire or dentate: heads radiate, usually long-peduncled; involucral bracts imbricated in 2 to many series, with narrow scarious margins; receptacle flat, usually pitted; rays blue or white, in 1–2 series, usually fertile; disk yellow: achenes flattened; pappus-bristles in 1 series. (Felic-ia: for Herr Felix, a German official, died 1846.)

A. Plant a sparsely hairy subshrub 1–3 ft. high ....1. *F. amelloides*
AA. Plant a very hairy ann. 3–8 in. high ....2. *F. Bergeriana*

1. **F. amelloides,** Voss (*Agathæa cœlestis*, Cass.). BLUE DAISY. BLUE MARGUERITE. Bushy subshrub 1–3 ft. high, sparsely hairy: lvs. opposite, elliptic or oblong-obovate, about 1 in. long, entire or nearly so, tapering to a short winged petiole: heads solitary, 1–1¼ in. across, on long naked peduncles; involucral bracts in 2 series, the outer with herbaceous tips; rays numerous, sky-blue. S. Afr.

2. **F. Bergeriana,** O. Hoffm. (*Cineraria Bergeriana*, Spreng. *Aster Bergerianus*, Harvey). KINGFISHER DAISY. Ann. 3–8 in. high, densely hairy with long spreading hairs: lvs. opposite or alternate, obovate-oblong, 1–1½ in. long, toothed: heads solitary on long pubescent peduncles; involucral bracts in 1 series, with hairy keel; rays bright blue; disk-fls. sterile. S. Afr.

54. **ARCTOTIS,** L. Herbs, of 30 or more species, mostly native to S. Afr., a few grown in fl.-gardens.—Herbage more or less white-woolly: lvs. alternate: heads of large or medium size, solitary, long-peduncled, radiate; involucral bracts imbricated in several series, the inner scarious; receptacle honeycombed, mostly bristly: achenes grooved, usually villous, ours with tuft of silky hairs at base; pappus crown-like or composed of scales. (Arcto-tis: Greek for *bear's ear*, alluding to the pappus-scales.)

A. Plant with leafy sts.: ray-fls. white or violet ....1. *A. stœchadifolia*
AA. Plant stemless, with scape-like peduncles: ray-fls. yellow or orange.
B. Rays purplish outside: root per. ....2. *A. acaulis*
BB. Rays coppery outside: root ann. ....3. *A. breviscapa*

1. **A. stœchadifolia,** Berg. AFRICAN DAISY. Bushy per. to 2½ ft., with leafy sts.: lvs. oblong or obovate, 1–4 in. long, usually lyrate and lobed and slightly toothed, white-tomentose when young: heads to 3 in. across, on peduncles much longer than lvs.; outer involucral bracts tomentose; rays white, violet outside; disk violet. Var. **grandis,** Less. (*A. grandis*, Thunb.), is grown as an ann., lvs. to 6 in. long, peduncles 6–12 in. long, fls. Aug.–Sept.

2. **A. acaulis,** L. (*A. scapigera*, Thunb.). Stemless or nearly so, with a thick woody per. root: lvs. oblong, 6–8 in. long, pinnately cut, lobed or lyrate, white-tomentose beneath, green and rough or hairy above: heads 2 in. and more across, on long scape-like hairy

peduncles, blooming spring to autumn; bracts of involucre nearly glabrous, the outer with a recurved tomentose point; rays yellow, purplish outside; disk purple-black.

3. **A. breviscapa,** Thunb. (*A. leptorhiza* var. *breviscapa,* DC.). Stemless, with a slender ann. root: lvs. oblong-lanceolate, to 6 in. long, pinnately cut or lyrate, white-tomentose beneath, green and hairy above: heads to 2 in. across, on hairy scapes 6–18 in. high; outer involucral bracts tomentose, spreading and reflexed, inner glabrous; rays orange-yellow, sometimes with brown or bluish area at base, coppery outside; disk dark brown.

55. **VENIDIUM,** Less. Namaqualand Daisy. S. African plants of about 20 species, grown in the fl.-garden.—Ann. or per. herbs, more or less tomentose: lvs. alternate: heads solitary, long-peduncled, radiate; involucral bracts in several rows, the outer narrower and herbaceous, the inner scarious; receptacle honeycombed, mostly naked; ray-fls. in 1 or few series, usually yellow: achenes glabrous, dorsally 3–5-winged or -ridged, the lateral ridges inflexed, the median straight, narrower; pappus lacking or of 4 minute scales. (Venid-ium: name of obscure application.)

A. Rays with paler zone at base....................1. *V. decurrens*
AA. Rays with purple-brown zone at base....................2. *V. fastuosum*

1. **V. decurrens,** Less. (*V. calendulaceum,* Less.). Diffuse tomentose per., or grown as ann., sts. 1–2 ft. long: lvs. mostly lyrate, white-tomentose, later becoming glabrate above, on petioles 2 in. and more long; terminal lobe ovate or roundish, sinuate-lobed or repand, to 1½ in. long: heads 1–2½ in. across; rays golden-yellow with paler zone at base; disk yellowish-brown.

2. **V. fastuosum,** Stapf. Monarch-of-the-Veld. Ann. 1–3 ft. high, branched from base, cobwebby when young: lvs. oblanceolate or obovate, to 3½ in. long, irregularly lobed or nearly lyrate, lower on petioles to 2 in. long: heads to 4 in. across; rays bright orange with dark purple-brown zone at base; disk yellowish-brown.

56. **GAZANIA,** Gaertn. (*Meridiana,* Hill, an earlier but rejected name). About 25 herbaceous species native to S. Afr., a few grown in warm sunny climates.—Per. or rarely ann., with short leafy sts. or with lvs. crowded in a basal tuft: lvs. entire or pinnatifid: heads radiate, medium-sized to large, solitary on long peduncles; involucral bracts in 2 to several rows, united and cup-like at base; rays ranging widely in color, white, yellow, orange, scarlet, closing at night; receptacle pitted: achenes villous; pappus of 2 series of delicate scarious toothed scales, often hidden in the wool of the achene. (Gaza-nia: after Theodore of Gaza, 1398–1478, translator of Aristotle and Theophrastus.)

A. Teeth of involucre much shorter than tube, linear and acute....................1. *G. rigens*
AA. Teeth of involucre as long as or longer than tube, linear-subulate and very finely pointed....................2. *G. longiscapa*

1. **G. rigens,** R. Br. (*G. splendens,* Moore. *Gorteria rigens,* L.). Sts. short and densely leafy or diffuse and laxly leafy, 6–12 in. long, with ascending branches: lvs. densely white-tomentose below, green and glabrous above, simple, linear-lanceolate, 4–5 in. long, tapering to a long winged petiole, or some with 1–2 large lateral lobes: heads large and showy, 2½–3 in. across, blooming throughout the year in warm climates, on glabrous peduncles longer than lvs.; rays orange with a black white-eyed spot at base or the basal markings containing brown; involucre glabrous, the teeth short, linear and acute.

2. **G. longiscapa,** DC. Stemless or nearly so: lvs. variable, lanceolate and entire or pinnately cut, white-tomentose beneath, glabrous or nearly so above, margins somewhat revolute and ciliate: heads 1½–3 in. across, on glabrous peduncles longer than lvs.; rays yellow, often with black spot at base; involucre glabrous, the teeth linear-subulate and very finely pointed and as long as or longer than tube, outer bracts ciliate.

57. **URSINIA,** Gaertn. Species about 60, native to S. Afr., a few grown in the fl.-garden.—Glabrous or pubescent ann. or per. herbs or subshrubs, strongly scented: lvs. alternate, mostly pinnatisect: heads radiate, solitary or loosely clustered; involucral bracts in many series, with membranous tips; disk-fls. more or less inclosed in the chaffy bracts of the receptacle: achenes 10-ribbed; pappus (in ours) of 5–6 scales which are enlarged and white in fr. (Ursin-ia: Johann Ursinus of Regensburg, 1608–1666, author of Arboretum Biblicum.)

A. Ray-fls. of one color, yellow: plant per....................1. *U. anethoides*
AA. Ray-fls. yellow marked with purple or brown: plant ann.
B. Under side of rays purple....................2. *U. anthemoides*
BB. Under side of rays yellow....................3. *U. pulchra*

1. **U. anethoides,** N. E. Br. (*Sphenogyne anethoides,* DC.). Shrubby per. 1–2 ft. high, glabrous or thinly webby-pubescent: lvs. crowded, 1–1½ in. long, pinnatisect into semi-terete segms.: heads to 1 in. across, solitary on peduncles 6–8 in. long; rays bright golden-yellow.

2. **U. anthemoides,** Poir. (*Sphenogyne anthemoides,* R. Br.). Ann. to 1 ft., glabrous or slightly pubescent: lvs. pinnate into flat linear to filiform segms.: heads about 1 in. across, solitary on long nodding peduncles; rays yellow or orange, purple beneath.

3. **U. pulchra,** N. E. Br. (*Sphenogyne speciosa,* Knowles & Westc.). Leafy-stemmed branching ann. 1–2 ft. high: lvs. bipinnately dissected into linear lobes: heads 1½–2 in. across, solitary on rather long peduncles terminating the branchlets; involucre 4-rowed, the outer rows with a brown scarious border, the inner longer and with a white scarious border; rays bright yellow with purple-brown spot at base; disk darker.

58. **TAGETES,** L. MARIGOLD. Scented herbs of more than 30 species, New Mex. and Ariz. to Argentina, a few popular as fl.-garden plants.—Mostly ann., branching, erect or diffuse, glabrous, with oil-glands on lvs. and involucres: lvs. usually opposite, pinnately dissected or rarely only serrulate: heads radiate, solitary or clustered, small to large; involucral bracts in 1 series, united nearly throughout into a long tube or cup: achenes with pappus of 3–10 unequal scales or bristles. (Tage-tes: Tages, an Etruscan god, or perhaps of other derivation.)

A. Lvs. simple: heads clustered .... 1. *T. lucida*
AA. Lvs. compound: heads solitary.
B. Rays few, usually about 5; heads about 1 in. across .... 2. *T. tenuifolia*
BB. Rays numerous; heads 1½–4 in. across.
C. Fls. usually marked with red; heads about 1½ in. across .... 3. *T. patula*
CC. Fls. not marked with red; heads 2–4 in. across .... 4. *T. erecta*

1. **T. lucida,** Cav. SWEET-SCENTED MARIGOLD. Per. (cult. as an ann.), 1–1½ ft. high, commonly branching: lvs. sessile, oblong-lanceolate or oblanceolate, 2–4 in. long, sharply serrulate, glandular-punctate: heads ½in. across, 2–3-rayed, golden or orange-yellow, in a dense terminal cluster; involucre narrow-cylindric, glandular-punctate, the short teeth often sharply pointed: achenes with 2 or 3 blunt scales and 2 longer awn-like ones. Mex.

2. **T. tenuifolia,** Cav. (*T. signata,* Bartling). Branching ann., 1–2 ft. high: lvs. pinnately divided into about 12 linear or oblong sharply serrate segms. ¼–¾in. long, each segm. with 2 rows of large glandular dots: heads solitary, about 1 in. across, yellow, the rays rather few; involucre oblong-cylindric with acutish teeth and large glandular dots: pappus of several scales, 1 or 2 sharp-pointed or awned. Mex. Var. **pumila,** Hort., is dwarf, less than 1 ft. high.

3. **T. patula,** L. FRENCH MARIGOLD. Bushy ann., branched from near base, 1–1½ ft. high: lvs. pinnately divided into about 12 lanceolate or oblong serrate segms. ½–1 in. long, these or their teeth tipped with a long weak awn, each tooth usually with a large gland at base: heads solitary, about 1½ in. across, long-pedunculate, the thick oblong involucre with acute teeth, glandular-dotted; rays numerous, yellow with red markings: pappus of 1–2 long awned scales and 2–3 shorter blunt ones. Mex.

4. **T. erecta,** L. BIG or AZTEC MARIGOLD. AFRICAN MARIGOLD (once supposed to be native in Afr.). Stout erect branching ann. about 2 ft. high: lvs. pinnately divided into oblong or lanceolate serrate segms. ½–2 in. long, all with a few large glands near the margin and some (or their teeth) tipped with a long weak awn: heads solitary, yellow to orange, 2–4 in. across, the many rays long-clawed, in vars. 2-lipped or quilled, the stout peduncle swollen just below the head; involucre campanulate, the teeth elongate and often dentate: pappus with 1 or 2 long awned scales and 2 or 3 shorter blunt ones. Mex.

59. **BAILEYA,** Harvey & Gray. DESERT-MARIGOLD. White-woolly herbs of about 3 species in W. N. Amer.—Lvs. alternate, upper entire, lower pinnatifid: heads solitary on long peduncles; involucre of 2–3 series of distinct nearly equal woolly bracts; ray-fls. 5–50, yellow, persistent on achene and becoming papery and reflexed: achenes striate and glabrous: pappus none. (Ba-ileya: named for Jacob Whitman Bailey, 1811–1857, West Point, American chemist and microscopist.)

B. multiradiata, Harvey & Gray. Bien. or per. to 1½ ft.: lvs. mostly basal, pinnatifid, upper few and entire: heads 1½–2 in. across, on naked peduncles 6–12 in. long; rays 20–50, toothed. Utah to Calif. and Mex.

60. **ERIOPHYLLUM,** Lag. About 11 herbaceous species, white-woolly at least when young, native in W. N. Amer.—Lvs. alternate, entire or pinnatisect: heads solitary or in corymbs at ends of branches; involucral bracts in 1 series, usually distinct, stiff and erect; receptacle convex or flat, naked, pitted; ray-fls. yellow,

pistillate and fertile, in 1 series; disk-fls. yellow, bisexual: achenes 4-angled; pappus of scales or rarely lacking. (Eriophyl-lum: Greek *wool* and *leaf*.)

E. lanatum, Forbes (*Actinella lanata*, Pursh. *Bahia lanata*, DC. *E. cæspitosum*, Dougl.). Per. to 2 ft.: lvs. variable, 1–2½ in. long, the st.-lvs. pinnatifid into oblong entire, toothed or lobed segms., becoming glabrous and green above, margins revolute: heads ¾–1½ in. across, solitary or in loose corymbs; rays 8–12, ½–¾in. long, toothed at apex. B. C. to Ore. and Mont.

61. **GAILLARDIA,** Foug. About 20 American species, mostly from the far West, several cult. in borders and fl.-gardens.—Ann. or per. herbs with leafy sts., erect or branching or reduced to a short caudex: lvs. alternate or basal, more or less toothed, punctate-dotted: heads radiate, showy, solitary on long peduncles; rays yellow or yellow and red, neutral, 3-toothed or -cleft giving the head a fringed appearance; disk-fls. purple, fertile; involucre broad, the bracts in 2–3 series; receptacle convex or globose, with small bristle-like fringe among the fls.: achenes densely villous or with villous hairs only at base; pappus of 5–10 mostly awned scales. (Gaillar-dia: named for M. Gaillard, patron of botany in France.)

A. Plant ann.: fls. normally red.
B. Rays red throughout; lobes of disk-fls. obtuse: lvs. sessile and auriculate........ 1. *G. Amblyodon*
BB. Rays red tipped with yellow; lobes of disk-fls. acute or awned: lvs. nearly sessile..2. *G. pulchella*
AA. Plant per.: fls. normally yellow..3. *G. aristata*

1. **G. Amblyodon,** J. Gay. Ann. 1–2 ft. high, leafy to the top, mostly hirsute: lvs. oblong or the lower spatulate, 1–3 in. long, auriculate and sessile, entire or nearly so: heads 2 in. across; rays numerous, brown-red throughout; lobes (or teeth) of the disk-corollas short and obtuse: achenes with villous hairs only at base. (Amblyodon: a genus of mosses with blunt peristome-teeth.) Tex.

2. **G. pulchella,** Foug. Erect branching ann. 12–20 in. high, soft-pubescent: lvs. oblong, lanceolate or spatulate, 2–4 in. long, nearly sessile, entire or the lower lyrate-pinnatifid: heads 2 in. across; rays flat, yellow at tip and rose-purple at base; lobes of disk-fls. acute or awned: achenes hairy all over. Va. to Fla. and New Mex. Var. **picta,** Gray (*G. picta*, Sweet), is the usual cult. form, with somewhat succulent lvs. and large heads in different shades, in **Lorenziana** the ray-fls. and sometimes disk-fls. enlarged and tubular.

3. **G. aristata,** Pursh (*G. grandiflora, lutea, maxima* and *perennis*, Hort.). Erect per. 2–3 ft. high, more or less hirsute: lvs. lanceolate or oblong or lower spatulate, 2–8 in. long, entire to sinuate-pinnatifid: heads 3–4 in. across, the flat rays yellow or with purple base; lobes of disk-corollas acuminate: achenes densely hairy all over. Colo. to B. C. and Ore.

62. **ACTINEA,** Juss. American ann. or per. herbs, one grown in the rock-garden.—Lvs. alternate, entire or pinnatisect, resinous-dotted: heads solitary, of yellow ray- and disk-fls.; involucral bracts in 2 or more series, distinct or somewhat united at base, stiff and erect: pappus of 5–12 scales. (Actine-a: from Greek for *ray*.)

A. herbacea, Rob. (*Actinella scaposa* var. *glabra*, Gray. *Tetraneuris herbacea*, Greene). Tufted per.: lvs. basal, linear-spatulate, 2–3 in. long, hairy but becoming nearly glabrous: heads 2–2½ in. across, on hairy scapes 4–8 in. high; involucre hairy; rays about ½in. long, toothed. Ont. to Ill.

63. **HELENIUM,** L. Sneezeweed. Coarse erect ann. or per. herbs of over 30 species, N. Amer., Mex.—Lvs. alternate, often decurrent on the st., entire or toothed, punctate with dark dots: heads mostly radiate, solitary or corymbose, yellow or brownish; involucral bracts in 2 or 3 series, spreading or soon reflexed, mostly herbaceous; receptacle convex to oblong, naked; rays wedge-shaped, 3–5-lobed, commonly drooping: pappus of usually 5–6 thin scales. (Hele-nium: possibly from Helenus, the son of Priam.)

A. Lvs. not decurrent on the st. and branches: sts. tomentose when young..........1. *H. Hoopesii*
AA. Lvs. decurrent on the st. and branches: sts. not tomentose.
B. Heads solitary or few on long peduncles..................................2. *H. Bigelovii*
BB Heads numerous, in corymbs.
C. Disk brownish or purplish, globose: upper lvs. entire..................3. *H. nudiflorum*
CC. Disk yellow or reddish, subglobose or hemispheric: lvs. mostly serrate or dentate..4. *H. autumnale*

1. **H. Hoopesii,** Gray (*Dugaldia Hoopesii*, Rydb.). Stout per. 1–3 ft. high, sts. tomentose when young, becoming glabrate, leafy, bearing 1 to several large long-pedunculate heads: lvs. entire, oblong-lanceolate, or the lower spatulate, not decurrent at base, 4–10 in. long, yellowish-green: heads yellow, commonly 3 in. across, the rays only slightly drooping. (First collected by Thos. Hoopes.) Rocky Mts. to Ore. and Calif.

2. **H. Bigelovii,** Gray. Per. with simple sts. 2–4 ft. high, slightly pubescent or glabrous: lvs. lanceolate, 4–10 in. long, entire, decurrent at base, strongly glandular-punctate: heads to 2½ in. across, solitary or 2–3 on long peduncles; rays yellow, pistillate; disk brown or brownish-yellow. (Named for its discoverer, Dr. John M. Bigelow, 1804–1878.) Ore. to Calif.

3. **H. nudiflorum,** Nutt. Per. 1–3 ft. high, sts. roughish, leafy: lvs. narrowly lanceolate to oblong, 2–6 in. long, entire, or the basal spatulate and toothed: heads 1–2 in. across, corymbose, short-peduncled, the drooping wedge-shaped neutral rays yellow, brown-purple or striped with both colors; disk globose, brownish or purplish. Conn. to Fla. and Tex.

4. **H. autumnale,** L. (*H. grandiflorum,* Nutt.). Leafy-stemmed nearly glabrous per. 2–6 ft. high: lvs. lanceolate to ovate-lanceolate, 2–5 in. long, decurrent at base, mostly toothed: heads 1–2 in. across, corymbose at the ends of the st. and branches; rays pistillate, drooping, 3-cleft, yellow; disk hemispheric or subglobose, yellow. Que. to Fla. and Ariz.—Some of the hort. vars. are: **gaillardiæflorum,** rays bronzy-red tipped with golden-yellow; **peregrinum,** rays mahogany-red faintly edged with yellow; **pumilum,** 1–2 ft. high, free-blooming; **rubrum,** fls. deep red; **superbum,** fls. large.

64. **DIMORPHOTHECA,** Vaill. Cape-Marigold. Herbs or subshrubs of 7 species in S. Afr., two grown in the fl.-garden.—Lvs. alternate, entire to pinnatifid: heads solitary on terminal peduncles; involucre broadly campanulate, bracts in 1 series, with scarious margins; receptacle naked; ray-fls. pistillate and fertile, in 1 row, style divided into 2 long stigmatic branches; disk-fls. bisexual and fertile, style divided into 2 very short branches: achenes of ray-fls. 3-angled or nearly terete, usually wrinkled or tuberculate, of disk-fls. smooth and with thickened margins. (Dimorphothe-ca: Greek *two-formed achenes.*)

A. Rays orange-yellow....................1. *D. sinuata*
AA. Rays white above, violet or purple beneath....................2. *D. pluvialis*

1. **D. sinuata,** DC. (*D. calendulacea,* Harvey. *D. aurantiaca,* Hort. not DC.). Ann. 4–12 in. high, loosely branching from base, sts. ascending, glandular-pubescent throughout: lvs. oblong-lanceolate, to 3½ in. long and 1 in. wide, narrowed at base, coarsely sinuate-dentate, upper lvs. smaller and sessile: heads 1½ in. across; rays orange-yellow, sometimes deep violet at base, style-branches violet; disk yellow.—Hybrids occur between this species and *D. pluvialis,* known as *D. aurantiaca hybrida,* with rays yellow above mixed with violet or purple below.

2. **D. pluvialis,** Moench (*Calendula pluvialis,* L. *D. annua,* Less.). Ann. 4–16 in. high, usually branched with ascending sts., densely glandular-pubescent: lvs. obovate to oblanceolate, to 3½ in. long and 1 in. wide, narrowed at base, coarsely sinuate-dentate, upper linear and sessile: heads 1–2 in. across; rays white above, violet or purple beneath or mixed with copper or other colors, style-branches deep violet; disk yellow, corolla-lobes often violet at tips. Var. **ringens,** Hort., has pure white fls. with a blue ring around the center.

65. **CASTALIS,** Cass. Per. herbs, 3 species native in S. Afr.—Lvs. alternate, entire or pinnatifid: heads solitary at ends of branchlets, peduncled; involucre broadly campanulate, bracts in 1–2 series, with scarious margins; receptacle naked; ray-fls. pistillate and sterile, in 1 row, yellow or violet, style none or undivided; disk-fls. bisexual and fertile, style divided into 2 very short branches: achenes with thickened margins, smooth. (Casta-lis: for the nymph Castalia.)

C. spectabilis, Norl. (*Dimorphotheca spectabilis,* Schlechter). To 16 in. from a woody rootstock, sts. single or few, glandular-pubescent: lvs. lanceolate or narrowly elliptic, 1–2½ in. long and to ½in. wide, sessile, entire or rarely 1–3-toothed: heads to 2½ in. across; rays lilac-purple on both sides; disk yellow with violet corolla-lobes. Transvaal.—This plant does not appear to be in cult., although the name *Dimorphotheca spectabilis* is frequently listed.

66. **OSTEOSPERMUM,** L. Nearly 70 species, native S. Afr. to Arabia, one grown for ornament.—Herbs, subshrubs or shrubs: lvs. alternate or rarely opposite, entire to pinnatifid: involucral bracts in 1–3 series, with scarious margins; receptacle naked; ray-fls. pistillate and fertile, in 1 row, yellow or violet, style filiform and divided into 2 stigmatic branches; disk-fls. sterile, style shortly 2-lobed: achenes terete or 3-angled, smooth or tuberculate. (Osteosper-mum: Greek for *bone* and *seed,* referring to the hard achenes.)

O. Ecklonis, Norl. (*Dimorphotheca Ecklonis,* DC.). Shrub or subshrub 3–4 ft. high, branching: lvs. obovate or oblanceolate, narrowed into petiole, 2–4 in. long and ¼–¾in.

wide, remotely toothed, glandular-pubescent: heads solitary and long-peduncled at ends of branches or in loose corymbs, 2–3 in. across; rays white above, violet or blue beneath often with a white border; disk azure-blue. (Named for C. F. Ecklon, page 42.) S. Afr.

67. **CALENDULA, L.** Species about 15, from Medit. region, Canary Isls. to Iran; yields an old herb grown in several races for ornament.—Ann. or per. herbs with simple alternate lvs. and mostly large heads with yellow or orange rays: involucre broad, the usually scarious-margined bracts in 1 or 2 rows; receptacle naked, plane: ray-achenes glabrous, incurved; disk-fls. infertile; pappus none. (Calen-dula: Latin *calendæ* or *calends*, throughout the months.)

C. officinalis, L. Pot-Marigold. More or less hairy ann. 1–2 ft. high: lvs. thickish, oblong to oblong-obovate, 2–6 in. or more long, entire or minutely and remotely denticulate, more or less clasping: heads solitary, on stout stalks, showy, 1½–2 or 4 in. across, the flat spreading rays white-yellow to deep orange, closing at night, blooming the whole season; sometimes the plant is proliferous from the involucre, bearing several peduncled heads in a circle. S. Eu. Var. **chrysantha,** Hort. (*C. chrysantha*, Hort.), is a strain with chrysanthemum-like double buttercup-yellow fls.—A common fl.-garden ann.; also grown under glass for winter bloom. The heads are said to have been used sometimes for flavoring in cookery.

68. **GAMOLEPIS,** Less. Herbs or mostly small shrubs, of about a dozen species native to S. Afr., one cult. for edgings and for fls.—Lvs. alternate and mostly pinnatisect: heads solitary, pedunculate; involucre of 1 series of bracts united one-third or one-half their length or more; ray-fls. yellow, pistillate, in 1 series; disk-fls. fertile: achenes without pappus, wingless and glabrous. (Gamol-epis: Greek *united scales*, referring to the involucre.)

G. Tagetes, DC. (*Othonna Tagetes*, L. *G. annua*, Less.). Glabrous wiry ann. 1 ft. or less high, much-branched and very floriferous: lvs. 1–1½ in. long, pinnately parted into linear segms., these often saliently toothed or pinnatifid: heads bright yellow or orange, ¾in. across; involucre nearly or quite urn-shaped, the bracts united for more than half their length. (Tagetes: a genus of Compositæ.)

69. **GYNURA,** Cass. (*Crassocephalum*, Moench). About 24 species in the warmer parts of Asia and Afr., grown under glass as foliage plants.—Herbs or rarely subshrubs: lvs. alternate, entire or lobed, numerous: heads discoid, not very showy; involucre cylindric or bell-shaped, of numerous bracts in 1 series with several very narrow spreading accessory bracts at base: achenes 5–10-striate, with copious slender white pappus-bristles. (Gynu-ra: name referring to the tailed stigmas.)

G. aurantiaca, DC. Velvet-Plant. Stout and branching, 2–3 ft. high; sts. almost succulent, densely pubescent with violet or purple hairs: lvs. soft, ovate, 3–6 in. and more long, jagged-toothed, hairy, with short often narrowly winged petioles, the wings with few remote salient teeth; uppermost lvs. sessile, clasping: heads to ¾in. across, in loose terminal clusters, yellow or orange. Java.

70. **EMILIA,** Cass. Slender plants, about a dozen species, in warm parts of Afr., Asia to China, Polynesia and Amer., one species cult. for its fls.—Ann. or per. herbs with alternate lvs.: heads rayless, rather small, solitary or clustered; involucre in 1 series, cup-shaped, with no small outer bracts; florets all bisexual: achenes with 5 acute ciliate angles; pappus of soft white bristles. (Emil-ia: perhaps a personal name.)

E. sagittata, DC. (*Cacalia sagittata*, Vahl. *C. coccinea*, Sims. *E. flammea*, Cass.). Tassel-Flower. Floras-Paintbrush. Erect ann. 1–2 ft. high, glabrous or sparsely hairy: basal lvs. and lowest st.-lvs. narrowly wing-petioled, rotund or elliptic; middle st.-lvs. oblong or elliptic, broadly wing-petioled or narrowed below to a sessile auriculate-clasping base; upper st.-lvs. oblong-lanceolate or ovate-lanceolate, acute or acuminate, with broad sagittate-clasping base: heads scarlet, loosely corymbed, about ½in. across, from June till frost. Tropics. Var. **lutea,** Hort. (*Cacalia aurea*, Hort.), heads golden-yellow.

71. **KLEINIA, L.** Succulent herbs or shrubs, of perhaps 20 species in S. Afr.—Often united with Senecio, differing mainly in the style-branches minutely cone-tipped: heads of disk-fls. only. (Named for J. Th. Klein, 1685–1759, German naturalist.)

A. Heads orange or red..1. *K. fulgens*
AA. Heads white or pale yellow.
B. Sts. prostrate and rooting..2. *K. radicans*
BB. Sts. erect.
C. Lvs. flat, deeply lobed..3. *K. articulata*
CC. Lvs. cylindrical or semi-cylindrical, entire.
D. Tip of lf. blunt: heads 2–3..4. *K. repens*
DD. Tip of lf. sharp: heads 10–13..5. *K. Mandraliscæ*

1. **K. fulgens,** Hook. f. (*Senecio fulgens*, Nichols.). Herb or subshrub 2–3 ft. high, pale green and glaucous: lvs. spatulate, to 3½ in. long and 1¼ in. wide, obtuse, narrowed at base into winged petiole, with 2–3 teeth on either side: heads 1–2, red or orange, 1 in. across, on bracted peduncles 4–8 in. long.

2. **K. radicans,** Haw. (*Cacalia radicans*, L. f. *Senecio radicans*, Sch. Bip.). Sts. prostrate and rooting, 1–2 ft. long, bearing lvs. on one side only: lvs. cylindrical, 1–1½ in. long and about ⅓in. thick, pointed at both ends, gray-green: heads 1–2, white, ½–¾in. across, on long naked peduncles.

3. **K. articulata,** Haw. (*Cacalia articulata*, L. f. *Senecio articulatus*, Sch. Bip.). CANDLE-PLANT. Sts. 1–2 ft. high, branches swollen and jointed: lvs. 1–2 in. long, deeply lobed, the end lobe largest and acute, on petioles as long as or longer than blade: heads white, about ½in. across, in corymbs on naked peduncles 4–10 in. long.

4. **K. repens,** Haw. (*Cacalia repens*, L. *Senecio succulentus*, Sch. Bip.). Subshrub to 1 ft., from a creeping rootstock: lvs. clustered at tips of branches, cylindrical or flattened above, 2–3 in. long and ⅓in. wide, blunt, glaucous: heads 2–3, white, about ½in. across, on naked peduncles about twice as long as lvs.

5. **K. Mandraliscæ,** Tineo. Subshrub 10–12 in. high: lvs. semi-cylindrical, flattened above, 3–4 in. long and ⅓in. wide, sharp-pointed, glaucous: heads 10–13, whitish, on naked peduncles much longer than lvs. (Collected by Count Mandralisca on the island of Vulcano in the Medit. where it is adventive.)

72. **OTHONNA,** L. Species about 80, native to S. Afr., one sometimes grown in hanging baskets and on greenhouse benches.—Shrubs or herbs, the latter often with thickened roots: lvs. often fleshy, basal or cauline, the st.-lvs. alternate or clustered at the ends of the branches: heads solitary or clustered, commonly yellow; involucral bracts in 1 series, more or less united at base; rays fertile; disk-fls. sterile, tubular, style not divided: pappus of copious bristles. (Othon-na: ancient Greek name of no particular application here.)

O. capensis, Bailey (*O. crassifolia*, Harvey not L.). Nearly glabrous per. with slender trailing or drooping sts., becoming shrubby at base: lvs. scattered or in clusters, fleshy and cylindric-obovoid, sharp pointed, 1 in. or less long, woolly at base: heads nearly or quite ½in. across, solitary or few on slender ascending peduncles 2–6 in. long; rays bright yellow, narrow, wide-spreading.—Blooming in nearly all seasons, the fls. opening only in sun.

73. **ARNICA,** L. Per. herbs of the northern hemisphere, about 50 species, one sometimes grown in the rock-garden.—Lvs. opposite or the basal lvs. clustered: heads long-peduncled, yellow; involucre of 1–2 series of nearly equal bracts; receptacle not chaffy; ray-fls. pistillate and fertile; disk-fls. bisexual and fertile; style with slender branches: achenes ribbed; pappus of stiff slender bristles. (Ar-nica: derivation uncertain.)

A. montana, L. Sts. erect, 1–2 ft. high, simple or slightly branched, hairy: basal lvs. forming a rosette, oblong, 2–5 in. long, sessile, entire, short-hairy, st.-lvs. few and smaller: heads deep yellow, solitary or few, 2–3 in. across; involucre hairy and glandular: pappus yellowish. Eu.

74. **DORONICUM,** L. LEOPARDS-BANE. Per. herbs; 30 or more species, native to Eu. and temp. Asia, several cult. for their fls.—Sts. simple or somewhat branched: basal lvs. long-petioled; st.-lvs. alternate, often clasping: heads yellow, long-peduncled, 1 to several at the end of st.; involucral bracts in 2–3 nearly equal series; receptacle convex, not chaffy, often hairy; ray-fls. pistillate, in 1 series; disk-fls. bisexual: achenes 10-ribbed; pappus 1–2 series of simple hairs, often lacking in ray-fls. (Doron-icum: Latinized Arabic name.)

A. Basal lvs. not cordate at base.
B. Ray-fls. without pappus..1. *D. plantagineum*
BB. Ray-fls. with pappus..2. *D. Clusii*
AA. Basal lvs. cordate at base.
B. Heads solitary, on nearly naked peduncles..3. *D. caucasicum*

BB. Heads usually several, the sts. leafy to top.
 c. Plant not stoloniferous, without cluster of basal lvs. at flowering time . . . . . . 4. *D. austriacum*
 cc. Plant stoloniferous, with cluster of basal lvs. at flowering time . . . . 5. *D. Pardalianches*

1. **D. plantagineum,** L. (*D. excelsum,* Hort.). Rhizome tuberous, roundish or creeping obliquely, stoloniferous; sts. stout, 2–5 ft. high, pubescent and glandular above: basal lvs. ovate or oblong-ovate, wavy-margined, long-petioled; lower st.-lvs. entire or toothed, ovate, abruptly narrowed into a broad-winged clasping petiole; upper st.-lvs. sessile, oblong or oblong-ovate, more or less toothed: heads 1½–4 in. across, solitary or rarely 2–3 on peduncles terminating the sts. and branches; ray-fls. without pappus. S. Eu.

2. **D. Clusii,** Tausch (*Arnica Clusii,* All.). About 2 ft. high, with creeping rhizome; sts. hairy and glandular above: basal and lower st.-lvs. oblong to oval, narrowed to short winged petiole, toothed, hairy on edges; upper st.-lvs. partially clasping: heads solitary, 1½–2 in. across; ray- as well as disk-fls. with pappus. (Named for Chas. de l'Escluse, page 220.) Swiss and Austrian Alps.

3. **D. caucasicum,** Bieb. Stoloniferous, sts. 1–1½ ft. high, somewhat pubescent: lvs. coarsely dentate, the basal subrotund, deeply cordate, petiolate; lower st.-lvs. petiolate, subcordate; upper st.-lvs. ovate, cordate-clasping, those near the head linear-lanceolate: heads solitary on nearly naked peduncles, 1½–2 in. across; ray-fls. without pappus. Sicily to Asia Minor. Var. **magnificum,** Hort., is more robust with larger heads.

4. **D. austriacum,** Jacq. Hairy per. with stout rootstock; sts. somewhat branched, 2–4 ft. high: lvs. dentate, the basal petioled, ovate-rhombic, cordate at base, not present at flowering time; lower st.-lvs. ovate, cordate, the petiole with a broad wing which is cordate-clasping at base; upper st.-lvs. sessile, cordate-clasping at base: heads usually several, on leafy sts., about 2 in. across; ray-fls. without pappus. Eu.

5. **D. Pardalianches,** L. Stoloniferous, with basal rosettes at flowering time; sts. 1–4 ft. high, hairy and glandular above: basal lvs. deeply cordate, with long winged petiole, entire or slightly toothed, hairy and ciliate; st.-lvs. oblong-lanceolate, cordate and clasping, toothed or entire: heads several on sts. with scattered lvs., 1½–2½ in. across; ray-fls. without pappus. (Pardalianches: from Greek for *panther* and *choke.*) Eu.

75. **LIGULARIA,** Cass. Per. herbs from W. Eu. to Siberia, Himalayas and China-Japan, about 30 species, grown in the open or indoors.—Lvs. alternate or sometimes all basal, mostly long-petioled, broad or orbicular or reniform, sometimes palmate, those of the st. smaller and bearing large sheaths: heads large, reflexed or nodding, in corymbs or racemes; involucral bracts in 1 series at the insertion, but of two forms, so that the narrow outer ones overlap the edges of the broader inner ones; rays mostly long and narrow, usually yellow: achenes glabrous, bearing soft pappus. (Ligula-ria: name refers to the strap-shaped or more or less bilabiate fls.)

A. Margin of lvs. sharply toothed: rays orange-yellow . . . . 1. *L. clivorum*
AA. Margin of lvs. repand-angulate: rays light yellow . . . . 2. *L. Kaempferi*

1. **L. clivorum,** Maxim. (*Senecio clivorum,* Maxim.). Robust per. 4 ft. high, at first tawny-pubescent, glabrate: basal lvs. long-petiolate, reniform or subrotund, sometimes 20 in. diam., sharply mucronate-dentate: fl.-sts. branched: heads to 4 in. across, many-fld., with orange-yellow rays; disk-fls. dark brown. (Clivorum: of the hills.) Japan, China.

2. **L. Kaempferi,** Sieb. & Zucc. (*L. Farfugium,* Koch. *Farfugium Kaempferi,* Benth. *Senecio Kaempferi,* DC.). Rhizomatous per. sending up many lvs. on slender flocculent-woolly petioles: lvs. often 6–10 in. across, orbicular to nearly reniform, cordate at base, angular-toothed, green: fl.-sts. 1–2 ft. tall, flocculent-woolly, branched, with only small bract-like lvs.: heads with light yellow rays spreading 1½–2 in. across: pappus white and copious. (Engelbert Kaempfer, page 273.) Japan. Var. **aureo-maculata,** Hook. (*Farfugium grande,* Lindl. *F. maculatum,* Hort.), LEOPARD-PLANT, is commonly cult. for its lvs. which are blotched with yellow or white or sometimes with light rose, seen in window-gardens.

76. **SENECIO,** L. GROUNDSEL. One of the largest genera of plants, about 1,200 species when broadly interpreted, in all parts of the world, a number cult. for their fls. or foliage, or for their climbing habit.—Herbs, shrubs or even trees, with alternate lvs. or sometimes the lvs. all basal: heads solitary or clustered, variously colored, usually radiate, the rays fertile; disk-fls. tubular, 5-toothed; involucral bracts in 1 series usually reinforced at base by shorter bracts or bracteoles having a calyx-like appearance: achenes mostly terete and ribbed; pappus of soft whitish often copious bristles. (Sene-cio: Latin name for plants of this genus, ultimately from *senex,* "old man," said to be in allusion to the hoary pappus.)

A. Habit climbing.
 B. Ray-fls. lacking . . . . 1. *S. mikanioides*

BB. Ray-fls. present.
 C. Heads yellow, ½in. across: lvs. finely pubescent........................ 2. *S. scandens*
 CC. Heads orange or orange-red, ¾–1 in. or more across: lvs. glabrous......... 3. *S. confusus*
AA. Habit not climbing.
 B. Lvs. not pinnatifid, although toothed or shallowly lobed.
 C. Rays yellow.
 D. Plant shrubby, hairy.. 4. *S. Petasitis*
 DD. Plant herbaceous, glabrous.................................. 5. *S. aureus*
 CC. Rays red, purple or white.
 D. Shape of lvs. cordate-ovate.................................. 6. *S. cruentus*
 DD. Shape of lvs. oblong-lanceolate, attenuate at base................ 7. *S. pulcher*
 BB. Lvs. pinnatifid.
 C. Plant white-woolly.
 D. Segms. of lvs. oblong, becoming green above...................... 8. *S. Cineraria*
 DD. Segms. of lvs. linear, white on both surfaces.................... 9. *S. leucostachys*
 CC. Plant not white-woolly.
 D. Rays purple.. 10. *S. elegans*
 DD. Rays yellow or orange.
 E. Basal lvs. bipinnate.. 11. *S. abrotanifolius*
 EE. Basal lvs. cordate-ovate..................................... 5. *S. aureus*

1. **S. mikanioides,** Otto (*S. scandens,* DC.). GERMAN-IVY. Slender and glabrous, tall-twining: lvs. ovate or deltoid-ovate, mostly with a deep basal sinus, sharply 5–7-angled or angle-lobed: heads about ⅓in. across, of 8–10 disk-fls., yellow, in close clusters on axillary and terminal branches. S. Afr.

2. **S. scandens,** Buch.-Ham. not DC. Sts. woody, climbing, reaching a height of several ft., branches slightly hirsute: lvs. short-petiolate, ovate- or elliptic-lanceolate, undivided or with 2 or more divisions at base of blade, triangular-dentate, grayish-green and finely pubescent on both surfaces: infl. a terminal panicle; heads about ½in. across; rays commonly 8, yellow. China.

3. **S. confusus,** Britten. Glabrous woody climber, sts. to 15 ft. or more: lvs. ovate or ovate-lanceolate, 1–4 in. long and ½–2 in. wide, coarsely toothed: heads ¾–1 in. or more across, in terminal clusters; rays about 15, orange or orange-red; disk-fls. 60 or more. Mex.

4. **S. Petasitis,** DC. (*Cineraria Petasitis,* Sims). VELVET GROUNDSEL. CALIFORNIA-GERANIUM. Robust shrubby per. 3–8 ft. high, somewhat velvety-hirsute on the younger parts: lvs. petiolate, broadly ovate or suborbicular, 1½–8 in. wide, cordate to subtruncate at base, sinuately 9–13-lobed, callous-denticulate, somewhat hairy above, grayish-tomentose beneath: infl. a terminal many-headed panicle; heads about ½in. across; rays usually 5, yellow; disk-fls. about 15. (Petasitis: Greek *broad-brimmed* or *sun-hat,* in reference to the large rounded lvs.) S. Mex.

5. **S. aureus,** L. GOLDEN RAGWORT. Per. 1–2½ ft. high, glabrous or nearly so: basal lvs. cordate-ovate or reniform, 1–6 in. long, obtuse, long-petioled, coarsely toothed, sometimes purplish beneath; st.-lvs. lanceolate or oblong, pinnatifid or lyrate: heads ½–¾in. across, in corymbs; rays 8–12, yellow. Newf. to Fla. and Tex.

6. **S. cruentus,** DC. (*Cineraria cruenta,* Masson). FLORISTS CINERARIA. Short-stemmed floccose-woolly per.: lvs. large, cordate-ovate to cordate-triangular, angled or undulate and sinuate-toothed, rather long-stalked, dark green above, white-tomentose beneath: heads ½–1 in. across in the wild; rays purple-red. Canary Isls.—*S. cruentus* is the supposed parent of the florists' cineraria now modified by cult., its large double fls., to 3 in. across, running in white and in shades of blue, pink and purple-red. The plant sold under the name *Cineraria stellata* (Star Cineraria) is an open grower, 2 ft. high, whose heads are single, mostly smaller and not borne in the solid masses of the florists' cineraria; its rays are separated as in the wild aster.

7. **S. pulcher,** Hook. & Arn. Robust erect per. 2–4 ft. high, white-cobwebby, sts. simple or nearly so, scarcely leafy: lvs. oblong-lanceolate, 4–10 in. and more long, thick, shallow-lobed and crenate-toothed, basal lvs. attenuate at base into broad petiole, upper lvs. clasping: heads 2–3 in. across, in corymbs, with many long red-purple rays and a yellow disk. Uruguay, Argentina.

8. **S. Cineraria,** DC. (*Cineraria maritima,* L. *Senecio acanthifolius,* Hort.). DUSTY MILLER. Stiff per. 2½ ft. or less tall, branching from base, very white-woolly: lvs. pinnatifid, with oblong obtuse segms., becoming green above: heads usually radiate, ¼–½in. across, in small compact cymes, yellow or cream-color. (Cineraria: Latin *ash,* from the ashy color of foliage.) Medit. region.

9. **S. leucostachys,** Baker (*S. Cineraria* var. *candidissimus,* Hort.). Often confused with *S. Cineraria* but habit not so stiff. lvs. white on both surfaces, the segms. linear and acute, heads somewhat larger. Argentina.

10. **S. elegans,** L. (*S. purpureus,* Hort. *Jacobæa elegans,* Moench). PURPLE RAGWORT. Viscid-pubescent ann., erect or diffuse, 1–2 ft. high: lvs. various, mostly oblong, 1–3 in. long, pinnate, lobed or toothed with sinuses chiefly broad and rounded, clasping at base: heads ¾–1 in. across, in loose corymbs; rays purple or reddish varying to white; disk-fls. yellow. S. Afr.—Fls. sometimes double.

11. **S. abrotanifolius,** L. Per. 6–18 in. high, with creeping rootstock, sts. ascending, glabrous or slightly pubescent: lower lvs. bipinnate, upper pinnate into linear-lanceolate acute segms.: heads 1–2 in. across, in corymbs; rays 10–13, orange-yellow. Eu. Var. **tiroliensis,** Hegi (*S. tiroliensis*, Kerner), is very similar, with orange-red rays.

77. **LEONTOPODIUM,** R. Br. EDELWEISS. Low plants of over 30 species, native to the mts. of Eu., Asia and S. Amer., sometimes grown in rock-gardens for ornament and interest.—Per. herbs, tufted and woolly; sts. ascending or erect, simple or branched at the very top: lvs. entire, basal or those of the st. alternate: heads discoid, small, crowded into dense cymes at the top of the st., surrounded by a tuft of floral lvs.; bisexual fls. sterile: pappus of bristles. (Leontopo-dium: Greek *lion's foot*.)

A. Lvs. oblong to lanceolate........1. *L. alpinum*
AA. Lvs. linear to linear-lanceolate........2. *L. leontopodioides*

1. **L. alpinum,** Cass. (*Gnaphalium Leontopodium*, L.). ALPINE EDELWEISS. White-woolly plant 4–12 in. high, creeping by rootstocks: lvs. oblong-oblanceolate, in age shedding the wool from their upper surface: heads 7–9, about ¼in. across, closely crowded together, surrounded by a tuft of densely and persistently white-woolly oblong or lanceolate floral lvs. which far surpass the heads; involucral bracts densely woolly, with blackish tips. High mts., Eu., Asia.

2. **L. leontopodioides,** Beauverd (*Gnaphalium leontopodioides*, Willd. *L. sibiricum*, Cass.). SIBERIAN EDELWEISS. Differs from *L. alpinum* chiefly in the narrower linear to linear-lanceolate lvs. and the larger heads. Russia to Korea.

78. **INULA,** L. Species over 100 in Eu., Asia and Afr., affording showy perennials for borders and fl.-gardens.—Usually per. herbs, more or less glandular and hairy: lvs. alternate or basal, entire or serrate: heads radiate, solitary or clustered; rays pistillate, 3-toothed, yellow, rarely white; disk-fls. bisexual, with tubular corollas 5-toothed; receptacle pitted, not chaffy; involucral bracts imbricated in several series: achenes 4–5-ribbed; pappus consisting of bristles. (In-ula: ancient name.)

A. Foliage glabrous except for ciliate margins and nerves beneath.
  B. Lvs. linear-lanceolate, parallel-veined, base attenuate and sessile........1. *I. ensifolia*
  BB. Lvs. oblong-lanceolate, netted-veined, base cordate and clasping........2. *I. salicina*
AA. Foliage villous or tomentose.
  B. Outer involucral bracts lanceolate to linear-subulate.
    C. Margins of lvs. entire or nearly so........3. *I. glandulosa*
    CC. Margins of lvs. toothed........4. *I. grandiflora*
  BB. Outer involucral bracts ovate.
    C. Heads in corymbs or racemes.
      D. Peduncles long and stout........5. *I. Helenium*
      DD. Peduncles very short or none........6. *I. racemosa*
    CC. Heads solitary.
      D. Base of upper lvs. cordate or auriculate........7. *I. Royleana*
      DD. Base of upper lvs. attenuate........8. *I. macrocephala*

1. **I. ensifolia,** L. Sts. simple, about 2 ft. high, villous beneath the heads: lvs. narrowly linear-lanceolate, with several somewhat parallel nerves, the margins ciliate-serrulate, otherwise glabrous, attenuate to a sessile base: heads 1–2 in. across, yellow, solitary or in small clusters; outer involucral bracts ovate-lanceolate, ciliate, parallel-nerved. Eu., Asia.

2. **I. salicina,** L. Sts. simple or branched above, 1–2½ ft. high, glabrous or slightly hairy below: lvs. oblong-lanceolate, netted-veined, glabrous except nerves beneath and ciliate margins, cordate and clasping at base: heads 1–1½ in. across, golden-yellow, in loose terminal corymbs or sometimes solitary; outer involucral bracts lanceolate, ciliate. Eu., Asia.

3. **I. glandulosa,** Willd. Erect, hairy, the simple sts. leafy to the top, 2½–4 ft. high: lower lvs. oblong-spatulate, long-attenuate at base, the uppermost oblong with subcordate-decurrent base, all entire or very obscurely denticulate and with remote glands at the margin: heads solitary, 3 in. or more across, yellow; involucral bracts lanceolate-subulate, hairy. Caucasus. Var. **laciniata,** Hort., has fringed half-drooping golden-yellow rays.

4. **I. grandiflora,** Willd. Sts. simple, villous, 3–4 ft. high, leafy to top: lvs. elliptic-oblong, serrulate, all sessile, finely villous and with numerous glands, the lower 2–4 in. long: heads solitary, orange-yellow, 3¼–4 in. across; involucral bracts lanceolate to linear-subulate, hairy. Himalayas, Caucasus.

5. **I. Helenium,** L. ELECAMPANE. Sts. 2–6 ft. high, hairy, from thick per. root: lvs. large, unequally dentate-serrate, velvety beneath, hispid-roughened above, the basal elliptic-oblong, to 2 ft. long, narrowed to petiole, st.-lvs. oblong-ovate, cordate-clasping: heads 2–4 in. across, in loose terminal corymbs or sometimes solitary; outer involucral bracts leafy, ovate, pubescent; rays yellow, very many, long and slender. (Helenium: of doubtful significance; page 1014; herbalist name.) Eu., N. Asia; nat. N. S. to N. C. and Mo.

6. **I. racemosa,** Hook. f. Sts. 2–5 ft. high, grooved and hairy: basal lvs. to 1½ ft. long, narrowed into petiole; upper lvs. oblong, sessile and clasping, rough above, white-tomentose beneath: heads 2–3 in. across, sessile or very short-peduncled, in the axils of the upper lvs. and forming a raceme; outer involucral bracts ovate, tomentose, recurved at tips; rays very narrow, yellow. Himalayas.

7. **I. Royleana,** DC. Sts. 1–2 ft. high, grooved: lvs. toothed, hairy, often densely tomentose beneath, obtuse, basal ovate or oblong with winged petiole, to 10 in. long, upper lvs. cordate or auriculate at base: heads 3–4 in. across, orange-yellow, solitary on stout hairy peduncles; outer involucral bracts ovate. (J. F. Royle, page 50.) Himalayas.

8. **I. macrocephala,** Kotschy & Boiss. Sometimes included in *I. Royleana,* but differing in upper lvs. attenuate at base. Caucasus.

79. **BUPHTHALMUM,** L. Ox-Eye. Per. herbs, of about 4 species in Eu. and W. Asia, grown for the showy yellow heads.—Lvs. alternate, entire or toothed: heads solitary or few and terminal, radiate; involucral bracts imbricated in several series; receptacle chaffy; ray-fls. in 1–2 rows, pistillate, fertile; disk-fls. bisexual and fertile: achenes 3-angled to nearly terete; pappus of scales united into a short crown. (Buphthal-mum: Greek for *ox* and *eye.*)

A. Lvs. lanceolate, attenuate at base............1. *B. salicifolium*
AA. Lvs. cordate-ovate............2. *B. speciosum*

1. **B. salicifolium,** L. Sts. erect, 1–2 ft. high, pubescent: lvs. oblong-lanceolate to lanceolate, attenuate at base, entire or slightly toothed, hairy: heads 1–2 in. across, solitary; involucre silky-hairy, long-pointed. S. Eu.

2. **B. speciosum,** Schreber (*Telekia speciosa,* Baumg. *B. cordifolium,* Waldst. & Kit.). Sts. erect, 3–6 ft. high, hairy: lvs. toothed, nearly glabrous above, hairy beneath, the lower triangular-cordate and petioled, upper oval or oblong and sessile: heads 2–2½ in. across, usually 2–8 in a corymb; involucral bracts with recurved tips. S. Eu.

80. **AMMOBIUM,** R. Br. Two or 3 Australian species, one grown as an "everlasting."—Per. herbs (ours grown as an ann.), more or less white-tomentose: lvs. alternate or basal: heads solitary at the ends of the branchlets, consisting of disk-fls. only, these yellow, bisexual and fertile, surrounded by an involucre of dry silvery-white bracts and subtended by chaffy scales: achenes 4-angled; pappus of 2–4 teeth, or shortly cristate. (Ammo-bium: Greek *living in sand.*)

A. alatum, R. Br. Winged Everlasting. Erect, branching, to 3 ft. high, white-woolly, the wool more or less deciduous in age; sts. and branches conspicuously winged (sometimes merely angled): basal lvs. ovate at the ends and long-tapering below (javelin-shaped); st.-lvs. lanceolate, small and distant, entire or nearly so: heads about 1 in. across; involucral bracts ovate, pearly white and petal-like, thickened and greenish at base, fluted and erose at tips. Var. **grandiflorum,** Hort., has fls. to 2 in. across.

81. **HELIPTERUM,** DC. About 48 species, native to S. Afr. and Australia, a few grown as "everlastings" or immortelles.—Mostly herbs, ann. or per., more or less white-tomentose to glabrate: lvs. commonly alternate, entire: heads discoid, of few to many fls., solitary or clustered; fls. bisexual, yellow; involucral bracts in many series, the outer rows scarious or membranaceous, imbricated, the inner (in ours) mostly expanded and petal-like, white, yellow or rose-color, with thickened greenish or brownish basal portion: achenes in ours densely silky-hairy; pappus-bristles plumose. (Helip-terum: Greek for *sun* and *wing;* said to refer to the light-plumed pappus.)

A. Heads 1–2 in. across, solitary or in loose clusters of 2 or 3: plant glabrous.
B. Lvs. broad: peduncles with scarious bracts............1. *H. Manglesii*
BB. Lvs. linear or spatulate-linear: peduncles without scarious bracts............2. *H. roseum*
AA. Heads about ½ in. across, in rather close clusters of several to many: plant somewhat woolly............3. *H. Humboldtianum*

1. **H. Manglesii,** Muell. (*Rhodanthe Manglesii,* Lindl.). Glabrous glaucous ann. 1–1½ ft. high, with slender somewhat tortuous branches: lvs. thin, elliptic or ovate, entire, strongly clasping at base: heads showy, 1–1½ in. across, solitary or loosely clustered, nodding, on slender stalks, these bracteate, the bracts passing into those of the involucre; involucre consisting of several outer series of loosely imbricated ovate bracts which are silvery-scarious except at base, and of 2–3 series of inner bracts resembling ray-fls., clear pink varying to white or to dark red. (Named after James Mangles, an English naturalist, died 1867.) Australia. Var. **maculatum,** Hort. (*Rhodanthe maculata,* Drumm.), has bracts flecked with red.

2. **H. roseum,** Benth. (*Acroclinium roseum,* Hook. *Roccardia rosea,* Voss). Glabrous ann., 1–2 ft. high, with many strict simple branches from near the base: lvs. numerous, linear, spatulate-linear or the upper lanceolate: heads 1–2 in. across, on short naked (or nearly so) peduncles, terminating the branches; involucral bracts of the outer rows ovate to oblong with brownish scarious tips, those of the inner rows much enlarged and petal-like, pink or white with thickened brownish or greenish basal portion. Australia.

3. **H. Humboldtianum,** DC. (*H. Sandfordii,* Hook.). Ann. (or cult. as such), 1–1½ ft. high, erect, or with a decumbent base, white-tomentose at least when young: lvs. linear or oblanceolate-linear, somewhat clasping: heads about ⅛in. across, obconic, in a dense terminal corymb; outer involucral bracts in many series, brownish-scarious, imbricated, the inner 1–2 series with short spreading yellowish-green tips. (Named after Alex. von Humboldt, page 45.) Australia.

82. **HELICHRYSUM,** Gaertn. Species about 350 in Eu., Asia, Afr. and Australia, a few grown for ornament.—Herbs or shrubs, commonly somewhat tomentose: lvs. alternate or the lower rarely opposite, entire: heads discoid, solitary or clustered at the ends of the branches; involucral bracts in many rows, imbricated and scarious or membranaceous, the inner often enlarged and white or gaily colored, petaloid, with thickened brownish bases; fls. yellow: pappus of bristles simple or plumose only at tip. (Helichry-sum: Greek for *sun* and *gold,* referring to the fl.-heads.)

A. Heads solitary.
B. Lvs. 2–5 in. long, green and glabrous .... 1. *H. bracteatum*
BB. Lvs. ¼–½in. long, white-woolly beneath .... 2. *H. bellidioides*
AA. Heads in corymbs .... 3. *H. petiolatum*

1. **H. bracteatum,** Andr. STRAWFLOWER. Stout ann., 1½–3 ft. high, somewhat branched, minutely scabrous-roughened: lvs. rather numerous, oblong-lanceolate, 2–5 in. long, tapering to short petiole, glabrous or nearly so: heads solitary, 1–2½ in. across; outer involucral bracts short and obtuse, imbricated, those of the inner rows elongated and petaloid, yellow, orange, red or white, with thickened greenish basal portion. Australia. Var. **monstrosum,** Hort. (*H. monstrosum,* Hort.), has larger heads with more numerous petaloid bracts.—Frequently grown as an "everlasting."

2. **H. bellidioides,** Willd. Per. with trailing sts. 6–18 in. long and erect or ascending leafy branches: lvs. obovate, ¼–½in. long, white-woolly beneath, green above: heads ½–¾in. across, solitary on bracteate tomentose peduncles 1–5 in. long; involucral bracts tomentose at base, the long tips silvery-white and radiating. New Zeal.

3. **H. petiolatum,** DC. (*Gnaphalium petiolatum,* L. *G. lanatum,* Hort.). Somewhat shrubby at base, the sts. woolly, to 2 ft. or more: lvs. ovate, to 1 in. long, abruptly petiolate, very woolly: heads about ⅛in. across, in corymbs 1–2 in. across; involucral bracts oblong, obtuse, cream-white. S. Afr.—Grown under glass and in the open for its vine-like shoots that cover rocks or hang from baskets.

83. **ANTENNARIA,** Gaertn. EVERLASTING. PUSSYS-TOES. Woolly per. diœcious herbs, of about 50 widely distributed species, a few grown in rock-gardens.—Lvs. mostly basal, or alternate on the st.: heads small, in clusters or corymbs, of disk-fls. only; involucral bracts imbricated in several series, the inner membranous and white or colored; receptacle not chaffy: pappus of staminate fls. thickened above, of pistillate fls. of capillary bristles slightly united at base. (Antenna-ria: from the resemblance of pappus to antennæ.)

A. Lvs. permanently white-tomentose above .... 1. *A. rosea*
AA. Lvs. becoming green and glabrous or nearly so above.
B. Involucral bracts usually rose, obtuse: achenes glabrous .... 2. *A. dioica*
BB. Involucral bracts white, acute or acuminate: achenes papillose .... 3. *A. neodioica*

1. **A. rosea,** Greene (*A. dioica* var. *rosea,* A. Eaton). Stoloniferous, 8–16 in. high: lvs. oblanceolate, ½–¾in. long, permanently white-tomentose on both sides: heads about ¼in. long, short-peduncled, in rounded compound clusters; involucre woolly at base, tips of bracts pink to rose: achenes glabrous. Alaska to Calif. and Colo.

2. **A. dioica,** Gaertn. (*Gnaphalium dioicum,* L. *A. insularis,* Greene). Stoloniferous, 3–12 in. high: lvs. spatulate, to 1 in. long, white-tomentose beneath, becoming green and nearly glabrous above: heads about ¼in. long, peduncled, in compound clusters; involucre woolly at base, tips of bracts white or pink: achenes glabrous. Eu., Asia, Aleutian Isls.

3. **A. neodioica,** Greene (*A. neglecta* var. *attenuata,* Cronquist in part). Differs from *A. dioica* in the broader roundish lvs. abruptly narrowed at base, and the narrower prevailingly acute or acuminate white involucral bracts: achenes papillose. Newf. to Va. and S. D.

84. **ANAPHALIS,** DC. White-woolly per. diœcious herbs, of about 35 species in the north temp. zone, useful for the rock-garden.—Sts. leafy, erect: lvs. alternate,

entire, sessile: heads in small corymbs, of disk-fls. only; involucral bracts imbricated in several series, usually white; receptacle not chaffy: pappus of slender bristles. (Anaph-alis: from old Greek name.)

A. margaritacea, Gray (*Gnaphalium margaritaceum,* L. *Antennaria margaritacea,* Hook.). PEARL EVERLASTING. Sts. 1–3 ft. high, woolly, branched above: lvs. linear-lanceolate, 3–5 in. long, revolute, green and pubescent above, white-tomentose beneath: heads about ¼in. across, short-peduncled or sessile; involucral bracts white, usually glabrous. N. Amer., Eu., N. Asia.

85. **MIKANIA,** Willd. American herbaceous or shrubby climbers, of about 150 species.—Lvs. opposite, petioled: heads small, usually of 4 disk-fls., borne in panicled cymes; involucre of 4 nearly equal narrow bracts; receptacle naked: achenes 5-angled; pappus of capillary bristles. (Mika-nia: named for Joseph Gottfried Mikan, 1743–1814, professor at Prague.)

M. scandens, Willd. (*Eupatorium scandens,* L.). CLIMBING HEMPWEED. Glabrous herbaceous twiner to 15 ft.: lvs. ovate or hastate, 2–4 in. long, deeply cordate at base, long-acuminate, slightly dentate, slender-petioled: heads about ¼in. long, white or pink, in terminal compound clusters. Me. to Fla. and Tex.

86. **LIATRIS,** Schreber (*Laciniaria,* Hill, an older but rejected name). BLAZING STAR. GAYFEATHER. BUTTON SNAKEROOT. Per. herbs of strict habit, of about 40 N. American species.—Roots thick, often tuberous: lvs. alternate, entire, narrow: heads in spikes or racemes in late summer and autumn, rose-purple or white, of disk-fls. only; involucral bracts imbricated in several series; receptacle naked: achenes 10-ribbed; pappus of bristles. (Lia-tris: name of unknown derivation.)—A difficult group, complicated by the hybridizing of some of the species.

A. Pappus-bristles very plumose to the naked eye.
  B. Inner bracts much longer than fls., with petal-like tips........1. *L. elegans*
  BB. Inner bracts shorter than fls., not petal-like........2. *L. punctata*
AA. Pappus-bristles barbellate (sometimes plumose as viewed under a lens).
  B. Heads oblong, ¼–⅓in. across, in dense spikes.
    C. Rachis of spike pubescent: involucral bracts acuminate........3. *L. pycnostachya*
    CC. Rachis of spike glabrous: involucral bracts prevailingly obtuse........4. *L. spicata*
  BB. Heads hemispherical, ½–1 in. across, in interrupted racemes.
    C. Involucral bracts with narrow entire scarious borders........5. *L. scàriosa*
    CC. Involucral bracts with broad lacerate scarious borders........6. *L. ligulistylis*

1. **L. elegans,** Willd. (*Stoepelina elegans,* Walt. *Laciniaria elegans,* Kuntze). Pubescent, 2–3 ft. high: lvs. linear, 1–6 in. long and 1/12–¼in. wide, very punctate: heads about ½in. long, of 4–5 purple fls., in spikes or racemes to 1½ ft. long; involucral bracts pubescent, the inner with petal-like acuminate rose-colored tips much longer than fls.: pappus very plumose. Va. to Fla. and Tex.

2. **L. punctata,** Hook. (*Laciniaria punctata,* Kuntze). Nearly glabrous, 1–2½ ft. high: lvs. linear, 2–6 in. long and 1/12–⅙in. wide, stiff, very punctate, ciliate on margins: heads ½–¾in. long, of 3–6 purple fls., sessile in dense spikes 4–8 in. long which are leafy below; involucral bracts ciliate, acuminate or cuspidate: pappus very plumose. Man. to New Mex.

3. **L. pycnostachya,** Michx. (*Laciniaria pycnostachya,* Kuntze). Very leafy, 2–5 ft. high, pubescent above: lvs. linear-lanceolate, the lower to 1 ft. long and ½in. wide, upper smaller, punctate: heads about ½in. long, of 3–6 purple fls., in dense spikes 6–18 in. long having a pubescent rachis; involucral bracts pubescent, with acuminate purplish tips: pappus barbellate. Wis. to La. and Tex.

4. **L. spicata,** Willd. (*Serratula spicata,* L. *Laciniaria spicata,* Kuntze). Glabrous or nearly so, 1–6 ft. high: lvs. linear, the lower to 1 ft. long and ⅓in. wide, somewhat punctate: heads ⅙–⅓in. across, of 5–13 blue-purple fls. (or white in var. **alba**), in dense spikes to 15 in. long; involucral bracts mostly obtuse, glabrous: pappus barbellate. Mass. to Fla. and La.—The plant known to cult. as *L. callilepis* belongs here.

5. **L. scariosa,** Willd. (*Serratula scariosa,* L. *Laciniaria scariosa,* Hill). Glabrous or pubescent, 1–3 ft. high: lower lvs. broad-lanceolate, to 5 in. long and 1 in. wide, with petioles to 4 in. long, the upper much smaller, punctate: heads hemispherical, ½–1 in. across, of 28–40 bluish-purple fls. (a white var. **alba** listed), peduncled, in interrupted racemes; involucral bracts glabrous or slightly pubescent, obtuse, with narrow entire scarious borders: pappus barbellate. S. Pa. to Ga.

6. **L. ligulistylis,** Schum. (*Laciniaria ligulistylis,* A. Nels.). Differs from *L. scariosa* in the somewhat larger heads of 30–106 fls., the glabrous involucral bracts with broad lacerate scarious borders. Wis. to Wyo. and New Mex.

87. **EUPATORIUM,** L. THOROUGHWORT. BONESET. At least 600 species, chiefly of Mex., the W. Indies and trop. S. Amer., yielding good greenhouse plants and also subjects for the hardy border.—Per. herbs, a few species ann., many of the trop. ones shrubby or even arborescent: lvs. mostly opposite: heads rayless, mostly in dense flat-topped or rounded clusters, less frequently in open panicles; involucre cylindric to hemispherical, its bracts in 2 to many overlapping ranks; fls. bisexual, 5 or more (rarely 1–4) in each head, purple, rose-colored or white, more rarely lilac or bluish-violet, never yellow; style-branches long, thread-like or club-shaped, protruding far out of the corolla-tube: achenes 5-angled, crowned with a well-developed pappus of hair-like bristles. (Eupato-rium: named for an ancient king of Pontus, said by Pliny to have employed one of this group of plants in medicine.)

A. Base of lvs. connate around st. . . . . 1. *E. perfoliatum*
AA. Base of lvs. petioled.
B. Lvs. in whorls of 3–6.
C. Sts. usually not mottled, glaucous, hollow: heads 6–7-fld. . . . . 2. *E. purpureum*
CC. Sts. mottled, solid, not glaucous: heads 9–15-fld. . . . . 3. *E. maculatum*
BB. Lvs. in pairs or rarely alternate.
C. Fls. pink, blue or lilac.
D. Sts. glabrous . . . . 4. *E. glabratum*
DD. Sts. pubescent.
E. Plant a shrub; sts. with reddish pubescence . . . . 5. *E. sordidum*
EE. Plant herbaceous; pubescence not reddish.
F. Shape of lvs. oblong-lanceolate, narrowed at base . . . . 6. *E. Lasseauxii*
FF. Shape of lvs. triangular-ovate, truncate or broad at base . . . . 7. *E. cœlestinum*
CC. Fls. white (pappus sometimes colored).
D. Shape of lvs. ovate, truncate or broad at base.
E. Margins of lvs. with large sharp teeth . . . . 8. *E. rugosum*
EE. Margins of lvs. with shallow blunt teeth.
F. Pubescence glandular . . . . 9. *E. glandulosum*
FF. Pubescence not glandular . . . . 10. *E. vernale*
DD. Shape of lvs. oblong to lanceolate, cuneate at base.
E. Margins of lvs. entire or with few teeth.
F. Heads 4–8-fld. . . . . 11. *E. ligustrinum*
FF. Heads 15–18-fld. . . . . 4. *E. glabratum*
EE. Margins of lvs. conspicuously toothed.
F. Pubescence dense and glandular . . . . 6. *E. Lasseauxii*
FF. Pubescence sparse and not glandular . . . . 12. *E. riparium*

1. **E. perfoliatum,** L. Pubescent per. 2–5 ft. high, branched above: lvs. lanceolate, 4–8 in. long, the pairs united at base around the st., long-acuminate, fine-toothed, rugose: heads of 10–16 white or rarely blue fls., in crowded corymbs. N. B. to Fla. and Tex.

2. **E. purpureum,** L. JOE-PYE WEED. Per. 3–10 ft. high, the sts. hollow, glaucous and glabrous, uniformly purplish or rarely mottled: lvs. 4–6 in a whorl, elliptic-lanceolate, 4–12 in. long, acuminate, tapering at base, coarsely toothed, glabrous except on veins beneath: heads of 6–7 purple fls. in a loose convex infl. Me. to Fla. and Tex.

3. **E. maculatum,** L. JOE-PYE WEED. Differs from *E. purpureum* in the solid not glaucous sts. which are mottled with purple, lvs. usually 4–5 in a whorl, elliptic-ovate or -lanceolate, infl. dense and flat-topped, heads 9–15-fld. Newf. to Pa. west to B. C. and New Mex.

4. **E. glabratum,** HBK. Shrub 3–8 ft. high, erect, with slender hard glabrous brown sts.: lvs. lance-oblong or ovate-oblong, 1–2½ in. long, tapering into a strong petiole, blunt or pointed, entire or small-toothed: heads of 15–18 pale pink fls. in ascending cymose clusters, together forming a long terminal leafy panicle. Mex.

5. **E. sordidum,** Less. (*E. ianthinum*, Hemsl.). Shrub to 6 ft. or more, the sts., at least when young, densely reddish-tomentose: lvs. ovate or ovate-oblong, 3–4 in. long and 2–3 in. wide, short-acuminate, toothed, on petioles 1–2 in. long: heads of many fragrant violet fls. in dense convex corymbs. Mex.

6. **E. Lasseauxii,** Carr. (*Ageratum Lasseauxii*, Carr.). Per. 1–2 ft. high, densely covered with short glandular hairs: lvs. alternate above, oblong-lanceolate, narrowed at each end, bluntly toothed: heads in small compact unequally stalked clusters; fls. very numerous, at first white, at maturity vivid rose-color. (Named after M. Lasseaux, who first sent the seeds to France.) Temp. S. Amer.

7. **E. cœlestinum,** L. (*Conoclinium cœlestinum*, DC.). MIST-FLOWER. Per. 1–3 ft. high, branching and somewhat pubescent: lvs. triangular-ovate, 1½–3 in. long, obtuse or acute, truncate or abruptly contracted at base, coarsely toothed: heads in compact clusters, many-fld., light blue to violet, Aug.–Oct. N. J. to Fla. and Tex.

8. **E. rugosum,** Houtt. (*E. urticæfolium*, Reichard. *E. ageratoides*, L. f.). WHITE SNAKEROOT. Smoothish branching herb 2–4 ft. high, glabrous or pubescent: lvs. ovate, 3–6 in. long, acuminate, truncate or broad at base, coarsely and sharply serrate, green on both sides: heads in loose but ample clusters, of 5–8 bright white fls., July–Sept. Que. to Fla. and La.—Sometimes in the trade as *E.* and *Ageratum Fraseri.*

9. **E. glandulosum,** HBK. Diffuse and often decumbent herb, the slender round branches, petioles, and pedicels finely glandular-puberulent: lvs. triangular-ovate or rhombic-ovate, slender-petioled, taper-pointed, coarsely and sometimes unevenly crenate-dentate, sparingly puberulent beneath: heads pure white, ageratum-like, in close clusters, late autumn and early winter. Mex.

10. **E. vernale,** Vatke & Kurtz. Strong herb, slightly woody in the wild, with hairy sts.: lvs. oblong-ovate, 3–5 in. long, long-petioled, taper-pointed, serrate, finely hairy above, paler and grayish velvety beneath, veiny: heads in an ample terminal corymb, fls. bright white, Sept. Mex.

11. **E. ligustrinum,** DC. (*E. micranthum,* Lag. *E. Weinmannianum,* Regel & Koern.). Upright shrub 4–15 ft. high: lvs. oblong, 2–3½ in. long, acuminate, the blade somewhat toothed and slightly decurrent in narrow crisped wings on the short petiole, glandular beneath: heads of 4–8 white fls., very numerous in a large round-topped terminal corymb; pappus pink-tinged to deep rose. Mex.

12. **E. riparium,** Regel. Diffuse, becoming woody at base, 2 ft. high, sts. slender, puberulent and usually reddish: lvs. long lance-shaped, 2–4 in. long, taper-pointed and at base narrowed to a petiole, prominently 3-ribbed, serrate: heads of 20 or more white fls., in rather compact long-stalked clusters. Mex.

88. **AGERATUM,** L. Mostly trop. American herbs, of about 30 species, two frequently cult. in fl.-gardens and blooming all summer.—Herbs or shrubs, ours ann., mostly loose-growing, 1–2 ft. high, with compact dwarf and variegated forms: lvs. mostly opposite, ovate, crenate-serrate, petiolate: heads tassel-like, clustered; involucral bracts narrow, subequal, in 2–3 series; receptacle naked or with scales; fls. all tubular, blue (rarely pink) or white; anthers appendaged: achenes 5-angled; pappus of separate or united scales. (Ager-atum: Greek *not growing old,* first applied to some everlasting.)

A. Involucral bracts sparingly if at all hairy on back: lvs. commonly blunt or rounded at base . . . . 1. *A. conyzoides*
AA. Involucral bracts densely and somewhat viscidly hairy on back: lvs. commonly heart-shaped at base . . . . 2. *A. Houstonianum*

1. **A. conyzoides,** L. Lvs. blunt or rounded at base, rarely heart-shaped: heads seldom ¼in. across; fls. blue or white; involucral bracts oblong, abruptly acuminate, sparingly if at all hairy on the back, erose and ciliate. Tropics.

2. **A. Houstonianum,** Mill. (*A. mexicanum,* Sims). Lvs. usually heart-shaped at base: heads commonly a little more than ¼in. across; fls. blue; involucral bracts lance-linear, attenuate, entire, ciliate, the back finely, densely, and somewhat viscidly hairy. (Named after Wm. Houston, American physician who collected plants in the Antilles and Mex., died 1733.) Mex.

89. **PIQUERIA,** Cav. Trop. American shrubs or seldom herbs, of about 20 species, one common under glass.—Lvs. opposite, entire or toothed: heads small, thickly clustered; involucre campanulate, the bracts in 2 series; anthers not appendaged at apex: achenes 4–5-angled; pappus none or very short. (Pique-ria: A. Piquerio, Spanish physician of 18th century.)

P. trinervia, Cav. (*Stevia serrata,* Hort. not Cav.). Per. to about 3 ft. high: lvs. lanceolate to oblong-lanceolate, 1–3 in. long, serrate-dentate, in one var. broadly white-edged: heads small, 3–5-fld., borne in small panicled corymbs, each cluster terminating a slender axillary branch or peduncle; fls. tubular, whitish, fragrant, flowering till frost or in greenhouses winter-blooming. Mex., Cent. Amer., Haiti.

90. **ARCTIUM,** L. (*Lappa,* Juss.). BURDOCK. About a half dozen species of very coarse rank-smelling large-lvd. bur-bearing biennials or short-lived perennials, scarcely known as ornamentals but of medicinal reputation and one sometimes grown for its edible roots; native in Eu. and Asia, some widely distributed as rank weeds of yards and neglected places.—Lvs. alternate, tomentose or soft-pubescent at least beneath, cordate and undivided: heads many and clustered, the fls. all tubular and little projecting from the tight globose or urceolate involucre, the bracts of which are produced into long hooked tips so that the whole head becomes a bur; fls. bisexual, purple to nearly white; receptacle setose: achenes oblong and somewhat compressed, more or less 3-angled; pappus of short serrulate deciduous scales. (Arctium: Greek *bear,* probably from the bur-like involucre.)

A. Bracts of involucre flat, straight and spreading, all equalling the fls.: heads usually exceeding 1 in. diam. . . . . 1. *A. Lappa*
AA. Bracts angled or very narrow, curving and less spreading, at least the inner ones shorter than the fls.: heads usually less than 1 in. diam. . . . . 2. *A. minus*

1. **A. Lappa,** L. (*Lappa major*, Gaertn. *L. edulis*, Sieb.). Great Burdock. Gobo of the Japanese. Very stout, much-branched, to 8 ft., a frequent weed, but to be looked for as a cult. plant with the Japanese, the straight young roots esteemed as a vegetable when the plant is a few months old and the roots 10–15 in. long and ½in. or less thick or in larger sizes 2 ft. long and 1 in. thick at top: lower lvs. broadly cordate-ovate and obtuse, the blade sometimes 20 in. and more long, canescent or floccose-tomentose beneath: heads about 1½ in. broad with the spread of the bracts, aggregate into flat-topped or corymb-like clusters. (Lappa: an ante-Linnæan name, signifying the clinging nature of the burs.)—The plant is handled essentially as an ann. in Japan, seed of early vars. sown in May and roots taken in autumn, of late vars. sown in Aug. and roots taken in spring.

2. **A. minus,** Schk. (*Lappa minor*, DC.). Common Burdock. Smaller than no. 1, 3–4 ft. or to 6 ft. in cult.: lvs. similar but smaller: heads usually about ¾in. broad with the less spreading or not reflexed curved narrow bracts, placed along the branches in a racemose order. A common weed and sometimes grown for medicinal purposes.

91. **XERANTHEMUM,** L. Ann. herbs of the Medit. region, about 6 species, one grown in the fl.-garden.—Densely pubescent or tomentose, with branching leafy sts.: lvs. alternate, narrow, entire, not spinose: heads solitary on long naked peduncles; outer involucral bracts well-imbricated, the inner elongate, petal-like, papery and persistent; receptacle chaffy; outer fls. few and sterile, inner ones fertile: achenes silky-hairy; pappus a single row of pointed scales. (Xeran-themum: Greek *dry flower;* one of the everlastings.)

X. annuum, L. Common Immortelle. Erect, branching, 2–3 ft. high, white-tomentose: lvs. oblong to oblong-lanceolate, sharply acute, ½–2 in. long: heads 1–1½ in. across, the purple or rose shining inner involucral bracts twice as long as disk, Aug. S. Eu.—One of the oldest and best-known of the "everlastings." Runs into many vars. differing in size and color of heads.

92. **CENTAUREA,** L. A prominent genus of some 500 species mostly in the Old World, many cult. for the fls.—Ann. or per. herbs, rarely somewhat shrubby, with alternate entire or pinnately lobed or divided lvs.: heads rather small to very large, solitary or panicled; involucre ovoid or globose, the bracts often appendaged and fringed, sometimes prickly; receptacle bristly; fls. purple, blue, yellow or white, the marginal ones sometimes sterile and elongated, making the head look as if rayed: pappus of bristles or scales or none. (Centaure-a: a *centaur*, famous for healing.)

A. Bracts of involucre and their appendages entire.
B. Plant tomentose: involucral bracts with recurved spiny tips . . . . 1. *C. babylonica*
BB. Plant glabrous: involucral bracts not spine-tipped.
C. Pappus uniform, equalling the hairy achene: plant ann. . . . . 2. *C. moschata*
CC. Pappus unequal, about one-third length of glabrous achene: plant per. . . . . . . 3. *C. ruthenica*
AA. Bracts of involucre or their appendages fringed or ciliate.
B. Lvs. entire or merely toothed.
C. Fls. yellow, the marginal ones similar to interior fls. . . . . 4. *C. macrocephala*
CC. Fls. rose, blue or purple to white, never yellow, the marginal ones enlarged and ray-like.
D. Heads 3–5 in. across: plant rough but nearly glabrous . . . . 5. *C. americana*
DD. Heads 1¼–2¼ in. across: plant pubescent, at least when young.
E. Plant ann.: lvs. linear . . . . 6. *C. Cyanus*
EE. Plant per.: lvs. broad-lanceolate . . . . 7. *C. montana*
BB. Lvs. pinnatifid.
C. Foliage white-tomentose throughout.
D. Fls. yellow . . . . 8. *C. ragusina*
DD. Fls. pink to purple.
E. Pappus about length of achene . . . . 9. *C. Cineraria*
EE. Pappus none . . . . 10. *C. gymnocarpa*
CC. Foliage white-tomentose only beneath if at all.
D. Under surface of lvs. green . . . . 11. *C. Scabiosa*
DD. Under surface of lvs. white- or gray-tomentose.
E. Pappus short and caducous, not plumose: flowering sts. branching. . . . 12. *C. dealbata*
EE. Pappus longer than achene, persistent, somewhat plumose: flowering sts. not branching . . . . 13. *C. pulcherrima*

1. **C. babylonica,** L. Stiff per. 4–12 ft. high, covered with white webby tomentum: basal lvs. lyrate, to 2 ft. long and 10 in. wide, petioled; st.-lvs. long-decurrent, oblong to lanceolate, acuminate, entire or wavy: heads yellow, 1½ in. long, nearly sessile, in a long narrow panicle; bracts of involucre entire, with recurved spiny tips: pappus white, equalling the achenes. Asia Minor.

2. **C. moschata,** L. (*C. suaveolens,* L. *C. odorata,* Hort. *Amberboa moschata,* Boiss.). SWEET SULTAN. Green glabrous ann., erect, branching below, to 2 ft.: lvs. toothed or pinnatifid and the lobes dentate: fls. white, yellow or purple, fragrant, in long-peduncled solitary heads 2 in. across, the marginal fls. enlarged; bracts of involucre entire, the innermost with scarious margins: pappus equalling the hairy achene. Orient.—**C. imperialis,** Hort., is a variant or hybrid of this species.

3. **C. ruthenica,** Lam. Glabrous erect branching per. 3 ft. high: lvs. pinnatisect into linear-toothed lobes, sharply narrowed at both ends, the base often somewhat decurrent: heads usually solitary, 2 in. across, long-peduncled, the pale yellow marginal fls. about ¾in. long; bracts of involucre entire: pappus reddish, about one-third length of glabrous achene. Eu., W. Asia.

4. **C. macrocephala,** Puschk. Erect per. 2½–3 ft. high, the simple leafy sts. swollen below the fl.-head: lvs. ovate-lanceolate, slightly decurrent, the basal short-petioled, acute, somewhat serrate, scabrous, gradually diminishing upward to the base of the single terminal head: heads subglobose, often 3–4 in. diam.; fls. yellow, all alike; involucre of 8–12 rows of appressed scarious-margined fringed rusty bracts: pappus shorter than achene. Armenia.

5. **C. americana,** Nutt. BASKET-FLOWER. Nearly glabrous roughish ann., sts. stout, simple or nearly so, 2–6 ft., thickened under the naked solitary head: lvs. mostly entire, oblong-lanceolate, 2–5 in. long, sessile or lower petioled, mucronate: heads 3–5 in. across; fls. rose- or flesh-colored, sometimes purplish (white in var. **alba,** Hort.), the bisexual ones forming a disk 1–3 in. diam., the neutral enlarged outer ones with narrow lobes often 1 in. long; bracts of involucre with fringed scarious appendages: pappus longer than achene. Mo. to La. and Mex.

6. **C. Cyanus,** L. CORNFLOWER. BACHELORS-BUTTON. BLUE-BOTTLE. Slender branching ann. 1–2 ft. high, woolly-white at least when young: lvs. linear, 3–6 in. long, entire or the lower toothed, sometimes pinnatifid: heads naked on slender peduncles, 1–1½ in. across; fls. blue, purple, pink or white, the marginal ones enlarged and ray-like; involucral bracts rather narrow, fringed with short scarious or blackish teeth: pappus about equalling achene. (Cyanus: Greek *blue;* herbalist name.) S. E. Eu., escaped in N. Amer.

7. **C. montana,** L. MOUNTAIN BLUET. Per. 12–16, rarely 20 in. high, sts. usually unbranched, often stoloniferous: lvs. broad-lanceolate or obovate-oblanceolate, toothed, decurrent, the younger ones silvery-white: heads solitary on short peduncles, 1–2½ in. across; fls. blue (white in var. **alba,** Hort.), the marginal ones to 1 in. long; involucral bracts with black fringed margins: pappus short. Eu.

8. **C. ragusina,** L. White-tomentose per. 1–3 ft. high, sts. usually simple and naked above: lvs. pinnatifid or lyrate-pinnatifid into ovate obtuse entire or pinnately lobed segms., the lower long-petioled: heads solitary or rarely 2–3, 1–1½ in. across; fls. bright yellow, the marginal ones not spreading; involucre with small reddish or black ciliate appendages with a short terminal spine: pappus white, about length of achene. (Named for Ragusa.) Dalmatia.—Grown in Calif.

9. **C. Cineraria,** L. (*C. candidissima,* Lam.). DUSTY MILLER. Erect branching per. 1 ft. or more high, the entire plant white-tomentose: lvs. pinnately parted into broad very obtuse lobes, the lower petioled, all the lobes linear-lanceolate, obtuse: heads rather large; fls. purple, the marginal slightly enlarged; bracts of involucre with a membranaceous black margin, long-ciliate, the apical bristle thicker than the others: pappus about equalling achene. (Cineraria: Latin *ashy,* referring to the color of the foliage; adopted from herbalist sources.) S. Eu.—The plant usually grown as *C. candidissima* is *Senecio leucostachys.*

10. **C. gymnocarpa,** Moris & de Not. DUSTY MILLER. Erect per. 1–3 ft. high, covered throughout with felt-like white tomentum: lvs. pinnately or usually bipinnately cut into linear or oblong obtuse entire segms., the lower petioled: heads solitary or few at tips of branches; fls. rose-violet or purple; bracts of involucre reddish, at tips short-ciliate: achene puberulous, without pappus, the scales of the receptacle capillary and longer than achene. Capri.—Most of the material passing as *C. gymnocarpa* is referable to *C. Cineraria.*

11. **C. Scabiosa,** L. Pubescent per. to 2 ft.: lvs. pinnatisect, to 6 in. long, petioled, the upper smaller and sessile: heads about 2 in. across, solitary on bracted peduncles; fls. purple, the marginal ones enlarged; involucral bracts fringed and black-margined: pappus equalling achene. (Scabiosa: genus in Dipsaceæ.) Eu.; nat. in N. Amer.

12. **C. dealbata,** Willd. (*Psephellus dealbatus,* Boiss.). Suberect per. 8–24 in. high: lvs. white-tomentose beneath, glabrous above, the lower ones 1–1½ ft. long, petioled, pinnate, the obovate lobes coarsely cut-toothed or auricled at base; st.-lvs. mostly sessile, pinnately divided, with oblong-lanceolate decurrent lobes: heads solitary, just above the uppermost lf., 2 in. or more across; inner fls. red, marginal ones rosy or white; involucral bracts deeply fringed and ciliate: pappus short and caducous. Asia Minor, Iran.

13. **C. pulcherrima,** Willd. (*Ætheopappus pulcherrimus,* Boiss.). Per. to 2½ ft.: lvs. pinnatisect or toothed, to 7 in. long, glabrous above, gray-tomentose beneath, petioled: heads solitary, about 2 in. across; fls. purple, marginal ones enlarged; involucral bracts papery, fringed, brown, the lower white: pappus reddish, somewhat plumose, longer than achene. Caucasus.

93. **CARTHAMUS,** L. Species about 20, from the Canary Isls. to Cent. Asia, one cult. for the fls. which have various economic uses, as the yielding of dye; also ornamental.—Annuals with alternate spiny lvs.: heads terminal, solitary or corymbose; involucre with spreading leafy outer bracts and more or less spiny inner ones; receptacle chaffy; corolla 5-fid, nearly regular, expanded above the tube: achenes glabrous, mostly 4-ribbed, the pappus none or scale-like. (Car-thamus: Arabic name, alluding to a color yielded by the fls.)

C. tinctorius, L. SAFFLOWER. FALSE SAFFRON. One to 3 ft. high, glabrous, branched above: lvs. oblong or ovate-lanceolate, the upper clasping, minutely spinose-toothed: heads 1–1½ in. across, surrounded by a cluster of leafy bracts which pass over gradually into the bracts of the involucre; inner bracts of involucre spine-tipped; fls. orange-yellow: achenes white and shining, ¼in. long. Eu., Asia.

94. **ECHINOPS,** L. GLOBE THISTLE. Nearly 100 species from Spain and Portugal to Cent. Asia and Afr., grown for their foliage and large prickly heads.—Coarse thistle-like herbs, ours per., with sts. and lower surfaces of lvs. more or less white-woolly: lvs. alternate, usually pinnately toothed or 2–3-pinnatisect, the teeth and lobes prickly: fls. solitary, each with a little involucre of its own consisting of bristle-like outer bracts and linear or lanceolate inner bracts which are free or united, all aggregated into a dense spherical head subtended by a small reflexed involucre: achenes elongate, 4-angled or nearly terete, usually villous, crowned by an inconspicuous pappus of many short scales. (Echi-nops: Greek *like a hedge-hog*, alluding to the spiny involucral bracts.)

A. Plant glandular: inner involucral bracts pubescent on back . . . . . 1. *E. sphærocephalus*
AA. Plant not glandular: inner involucral bracts glabrous on back.
  B. Lvs. cobwebby-pubescent above . . . . . 2. *E. humilis*
  BB. Lvs. not cobwebby-pubescent above.
    C. Upper surface of lvs. glabrous and not setulose: sts. 1–2 ft. high . . . . . 3. *E. Ritro*
    CC. Upper surface of lvs. rough and setulose: sts. 3–12 ft. high . . . . . 4. *E. exaltatus*

1. **E. sphærocephalus,** L. Bushy per. 3–8 ft. high, the forked sts. and fl.-stalks gray-woolly and glandular-sticky: lvs. sinuate-pinnatifid into oblong-triangular spinose-dentate lobes, the upper surface green and roughish with glandular pubescence, the lower surface white-tomentose or arachnoid: heads about 2 in. across, blue or whitish; outer bristle-like bracts of individual fls. about one-half as long as the inner which are fimbriate at the middle, oblong contracted to a point, and with the back pubescent: achenes gray-silky-hairy; pappus of ciliate scales united to middle. Eu. to Siberia.—Apparently not in cult.; see *E. exaltatus*.

2. E. **humilis,** Bieb. Per. 3–4 ft. high, with simple one-headed sts.: lvs. cobwebby-pubescent above, white-tomentose beneath, the lower sinuate-lyrate and nearly spineless, the upper oblong and spiny-toothed and pinnatifid: outer bristle-like bracts of fls. half as long as the inner ciliate bracts which are glabrous on back: pappus of scarcely ciliate scales united at base. Siberia.

3 **E. Ritro,** L. Per. 1–2 ft. high, without glands, sts. usually unbranched, white-tomentose: lvs. 1–2-pinnatifid into lanceolate spinose-toothed segms., the upper surface nearly glabrous, the lower densely gray-tomentose: outer bristle-like bracts of the fls. one-third to one-fourth as long as the broad keeled bristly-ciliate and spinose-tipped bluish inner ones in which the back is glabrous: pappus of ciliate scales united only at base. (Ritro: name of this plant in S. Eu.) S. Eu. to Siberia.—The plant grown under this name is *E. exaltatus*.

4. **E. exaltatus,** Schrad. Per. 3–12 ft. high, sts. simple or branched, white-tomentose: lvs. pinnatifid into lanceolate acuminate spinose-toothed segms., the upper surface rough and setulose and deep green, the lower white-tomentose, radical lvs. much larger and petioled: heads 1½–2 in. across, bluish, on tomentose peduncles; outer bristle-like bracts about half as long as the acuminate fimbriate inner bracts which are glabrous on back: achenes hairy; pappus-scales toothed. Siberia.—Apparently this is the commonly cult. species, grown under many names, usually erroneously as *E. sphærocephalus* and *E. Ritro*.

95. **CNICUS,** L. BLESSED THISTLE. One species, native to the Medit. region and the Caucasus.—Thistle-like branching ann.: heads sessile, rayless, surrounded by a cluster of large bristly leafy bracts; involucral bracts in few rows, the outer tipped with a long simple spine, the inner terminating in a long spinose-pinnatifid thorn: pappus-bristles in 2 series, the inner longer than the outer. (Cni-cus: Latin name of safflower, early applied to thistles; pronounced *ni-kus*.)

C. benedictus, L. (*Carduus benedictus,* Auth.). To 2 ft. high, sts. hairy: lvs. oblong, 2–6 in. long, sinuate-pinnatifid and toothed, the lobes and teeth spiny: heads 1 in. wide, terminating the branches; fls. yellow. Nat. in N. Amer.—Sometimes cult. for curiosity or ornament.

96. **CARLINA,** L. Thistle-like herbs, of about 20 species in Eu. and Asia, one sometimes planted.—Lvs. pinnatifid, with spiny teeth: heads large, solitary or in corymbs, many-fld.; involucral bracts imbricated in many series, the outer lf.-like and spiny-toothed, the inner colored and ray-like and much longer than fls.; receptacle bristly; fls. bisexual, all alike: achenes cylindrical, hairy; pappus deciduous, of 1 row of plumose bristles. (Carli-na: name of uncertain derivation.)

C. acaulis, L. Per., stemless or nearly so, with thick woody root: lvs. in rosettes, oblong, to 1 ft. long and 2½ in. wide, pinnate into spiny segms., glabrous or somewhat pubescent beneath: heads solitary, 2–6 in. across; inner involucral bracts linear and pointed, shining white or somewhat yellowish on back; fls. white or reddish: pappus two to three times as long as achene. S. Eu.

97. **ONOPORDUM,** L. Coarse woolly thistle-like annuals or biennials of the Old World, over 20 species, one not infrequent in gardens for ornament.—Sts. stout (sometimes acaulescent), winged by the decurrent lf.-bases: lvs. large, alternate, prickly dentate or pinnately cut: heads large, solitary or clustered, of disk-fls. only; involucre globose, the bracts sometimes spiny; receptacle flat, fleshy, honeycombed, not bristly: pappus of bristles in several series. (Onopor-dum: old Greek name.)

O. Acanthium, L. SCOTCH THISTLE. White-cottony-tomentose bien., vigorous, much-branched, 3–9 ft. high: lvs. oblong, prickly, sinuate-lobed and toothed, acute, the lower often 1 ft. long: heads 1½–2 in. across, usually borne singly on the branches; fls. pale purple, in a var. white: bristles of pappus brownish, longer than achene. (Acanthium: Greek *thorn;* herbalist name.) Eu., Asia; nat. in E. N. Amer.

98. **SILYBUM,** Adans. MILK THISTLE. Two species, Eu., Afr. and Asia, one rarely grown for ornament.—Glabrous erect thistle-like herbs: lvs. with spinose-toothed lobes, conspicuously white-spotted above: heads large, solitary, terminal, nodding; involucre broadly subglobose, the bracts in many rows, stiff, spiny-margined and spine-tipped; receptacle fleshy, bristly; fls. purplish, all bisexual; corolla-tube slender, the limb 5-cleft to middle or base: pappus-bristles minutely barbellate, in several series, united at base, deciduous. (Sil-ybum: an old Greek name applied by Dioscorides to some thistle-like plants.)

S. Marianum, Gaertn. (*Carduus Marianus,* L.). ST. MARYS, BLESSED or HOLY THISTLE. Glossy-leaved ann. or bien. 1–4 ft. high: lvs. clasping, 1½–2½ ft. long and 6–12 in. across, undulate: heads 1½–2½ in. across; involucral bracts leathery, with a spine ½–¾in. long, or the outer mucronate; fls. rose-purple: achenes glabrous, ¼in. long, spotted brown; pappus shining white. (Marianum: Mary, Mother of Christ, of early usage.) S. Eu., N. Afr. and Asia; nat. in Calif. and elsewhere in U. S.

99. **CYNARA,** L. Ten or 12 species in the Medit. region and Canary Isls., two grown as garden vegetables.—Thistle-like per. herbs, mostly coarse and sometimes prickly: lvs. commonly large, variously lobed or pinnatisect: heads large, terminating important branches, the corollas violet, blue or white; involucre broad or nearly globular, with bracts in many series and more or less enlarged at base; receptacle fleshy and plane, bristly; corolla slender-tubed, 5-parted: fr. a thick glabrous compressed or 4-angled achene with truncate apex; pappus of many series of plumose bristles. (Cyn-ara: involucre-spines likened to a dog's tooth.)

A. Lvs. prominently spiny: involucral bracts spinose-tipped....................1. *C. Cardunculus*
AA. Lvs. hardly at all spiny: involucral bracts unarmed..........................2. *C. Scolymus*

1. **C. Cardunculus,** L. CARDOON. Robust plant to 6 ft. high or more, cult. for its edible root and thickened lf.-stalks, also sometimes for ornament: lvs. very large, deeply pinnatifid, grayish-green above, whitish beneath with dense tomentum, prominently spiny: heads purple-fld. with spine-tipped involucral bracts. (Cardunculus: diminutive of Carduus. S. Eu.

2. **C. Scolymus,** L. ARTICHOKE. Less stout than the cardoon, usually 3–5 ft.: lvs. less pinnatifid, hardly at all spiny: heads larger, the receptacle enlarged and fleshy; involucral

bracts broad, thickened at base, unarmed. (Scolymus: a genus of thistles, the word meaning spine or thorn.) Probably a derivative of the last.—Cult. for the soft fleshy receptacle of the fl.-head and the thickened base of the involucral bracts which are edible.

100. **VERNONIA,** Schreber. IRONWEED. A large widely distributed genus of over 500 species, one often transferred to the garden.—Herbs, vines or shrubs: lvs. usually alternate: heads of disk-fls. only, purple, pink or white, borne in terminal clusters in late summer and autumn; involucre of bracts imbricated in several series; receptacle naked; corolla tubular, 5-parted: achenes ribbed; pappus in 2 series, the inner of bristles, the outer of short bristles or scales. (Verno-nia: named for William Vernon, English botanist of late 17th century.)

V. noveboracensis, Willd. (*Serratula noveboracensis*, L.). Per. 3–9 ft. high: lvs. oblong to lanceolate, 3–10 in. long and ½–1½ in. wide, acuminate, finely toothed: heads deep purple, ½in. across, peduncled; involucral bracts with filiform tips: pappus purplish. Mass. to N. C. and Miss.

101. **STOKESIA,** L'Her. STOKES ASTER. One species, native to N. Amer., cult. for its fls.—Coarse per. herb: lvs. alternate, spinose-toothed toward base or entire, the lower petiolate, upper sessile: heads large, many-fld., terminating the branches; involucral bracts in many series, the outer leafy, inner with foliaceous pinnately spinose-toothed appendages; receptacle fleshy, flat, naked; marginal fls. much larger than inner, deeply 5-lobed: achenes angled; pappus of 4–5 slender deciduous scales. (Stoke-sia: Jonathan Stokes, M. D., 1755–1831, English botanist.)

S. lævis, Greene (*Carthamus lævis*, Hill. *S. cyanea*, L'Her.). One to 2 ft. high, much-branched, sts. tomentose above: lvs. broad-lanceolate, acute, 2–8 in. long: heads solitary, blue or purplish-blue, 3–4 in. across. S. C. to Fla. and La.—Color variations are **alba,** white, **cærulea,** blue, **lilacina,** lilac.

INDEX

The entries in usual roman type are the names of genera and species printed in blackface in the book, and of English names. The entries in italic type are those of synonyms and incidental references.

INDEX

INDEX

INDEX

INDEX

INDEX

INDEX

INDEX

INDEX

INDEX

INDEX

INDEX

INDEX

INDEX

INDEX

INDEX

INDEX

INDEX

INDEX

INDEX

INDEX

INDEX

INDEX

INDEX

INDEX

INDEX

INDEX

INDEX

INDEX

INDEX

*Bartram's *Heracleum maximum* is not considered to be validly published, and the name **H. lanatum** must be reinstated.

INDEX

INDEX

INDEX

INDEX

*The correct name of the Japanese walnut is **Juglans ailantifolia**, Carr., and that of the Heartnut J. **ailantifolia** var. **cordiformis**, Rehd. *J. cordiformis*, Maxim., is antedated by *J. cordiformis*, Wangh., a basonym of *Carya cordiformis*.

INDEX

INDEX

INDEX

INDEX

INDEX

*The correct name of the Canistel is **Pouteria campechiana**, Baehni (*Lucuma campechiana*, HBK.). By some authors *L. nervosa* has been segregated as *P. campechiana* var. *nervosa*, Baehni.

INDEX

INDEX

INDEX

INDEX

INDEX

INDEX

INDEX

INDEX

INDEX

INDEX

INDEX

*The name of the Longleaf pine should be **Pinus australis,** Michx. f., with *P. palustris*, Auth. not Mill., as a synonym; the *P. palustris* of Miller is a synonym of *P. Taeda*.

INDEX

INDEX

INDEX

*The name *Pteris serrulata*, L.f., is a later homonym of *P. serrulata*, Forst., and as such is illegitimate. The correct name for this fern is **Pteris multifida**, Poir.

INDEX

INDEX

INDEX

INDEX

INDEX

INDEX

INDEX

INDEX

INDEX

INDEX

INDEX

INDEX